Good News Bible

With Deuterocanonical Books/Apocrypha

Good News
Bible

With Deuterocanonical Books /Apocrypha

Today's English Version

THE SEED IS THE WORD

CANADIAN BIBLE SOCIETY

British usage edition of the Bible first published 1976
British usage edition Deuterocanonical Books/Apocrypha
first published 1979

Permission to use any part of the British Edition
should be requested from:
The British & Foreign Bible Society
Stonehill Green, Westlea, Swindon SN5 7DG

English TEV DC053P
BFBS/1986/60M

Text set by computer by C. R. Barber and Partners, Wrotham, Kent
Printed in Great Britain by William Collins Sons & Co. Ltd, Glasgow

IMPRIMATUR:
authorized by the
Canadian Conference of Catholic Bishops
May 1986

ISBN 0-88834-024-9 Flexcover
ISBN 0-88834-025-7 Casebound

TEV60P-D/A Flexcover 11150   CBS-1986-30M
TEV63P D/A Casebound 11151   CBS-1986-20M

Printed in Great Britain

The *United Bible Societies* is a worldwide fellowship of National Bible Societies working in more than 150 countries. Their aim is to reach every person with the Bible or some part of it in a language he can understand and at a price he can afford. Between them they distribute more than 300 million Scriptures every year. You are invited to share in this work by your prayers and gifts.
The Bible Society in your country will be very happy to provide details of its activity.

Foreword

The Bible in Today's English Version is a new translation which seeks to state clearly and accurately the meaning of the original texts in words and forms that are widely accepted by people who use English as a means of communication. This translation does not follow the traditional vocabulary and style found in the historic English Bible versions. Instead it attempts to present the Biblical content and message in standard, everyday, natural English.

The aim of this Bible is to give today's readers maximum understanding of the content of the original texts. The Preface explains the nature of special aids for readers which are included in the volume. It also sets out the basic principles which the translators followed in their work.

The Bible in Today's English Version has been translated and published by the United Bible Societies for use throughout the world. The Bible Societies trust that people everywhere will not only find increased understanding through the reading and study of this translation, but will also find a saving hope through faith in God who made possible this message of Good News for all people.

Preface

In September 1966 the American Bible Society published *The New Testament in Today's English Version,* a translation intended for people everywhere for whom English is either their mother tongue or a language they learn. Shortly afterwards the United Bible Societies requested the American Bible Society to undertake on its behalf a translation of the Old Testament following the same principles. Accordingly the American Bible Society appointed a group of translators to prepare the translation. In 1971 this group added a British consultant representing the British and Foreign Bible Society and the National Bible Society of Scotland. The translation of the Old Testament now appears together with the fourth edition of the New Testament.

In a section immediately before the New Testament this Bible contains two series of books: (1) Tobit, Judith, Esther (Greek text), Wisdom of Solomon, Sirach, Baruch, Letter of Jeremiah, Song of the Three Young Men, Susanna, Bel and the Dragon, 1 Maccabees, and 2 Maccabees, and (2) 1 Esdras, 2 Esdras, and the Prayer of Manasseh. With the exception of 2 Esdras, these books circulated widely in Greek at the time of Christ. The first series of books is accepted by Roman Catholics as part of the canon of the Old Testament; and both series are regarded by many (including especially Anglicans and Lutherans) as worthy of at least private reading, though they are not regarded as a basis for doctrine. For further information about these books, see the Introductions to the respective series.

The basic text for the Old Testament is the Masoretic Text printed in *Biblia Hebraica* (3rd edition, 1937), edited by Rudolf Kittel. In some instances the words of the printed consonantal text have been divided differently or have been read with a different set of vowels; at times a variant reading (*qere*) in the margin of the Hebrew text has been followed instead of the reading in the text *(kethiv)*; and in other instances a variant reading supported by one or more Hebrew manuscripts has been adopted. Where no Hebrew source yields a satisfactory meaning in the context, the translation has either followed one or more of the ancient versions (*e.g.* Greek, Syriac, Latin) or has adopted a reconstructed text (technically referred to as a conjectural emendation) based on scholarly agreement; such departures from the Hebrew are indicated in footnotes.

With the exception of 2 Esdras, the basic text for the two sections of books occurring before the New Testament is the Greek text printed in the Septuagint (3rd edition, 1949), edited by Alfred Rahlfs. For 2 Esdras the text is the Latin text printed in *Biblia Sacra* (1st edition, 1969), edited by Robert Weber.

The basic text for the New Testament is *The Greek New Testament* published by the United Bible Societies (3rd edition, 1975), but in a few instances the translation is based on a variant reading supported by one or more Greek manuscripts.

Drafts of the translation in its early stages were sent for comments and suggestions to a Review Panel consisting of prominent theologians and Biblical scholars appointed by the American Bible Society Board of Managers in its capacity as trustee for this text. In addition, drafts were sent to major English-speaking Bible Societies. Final approval of the text on behalf of the United Bible Societies was given by the American Bible Society's Board of Managers upon the recommendation of its Translations Department Commitee.

The primary concern of the translators has been to provide a faithful translation of the meaning of the Hebrew, Aramaic, and Greek texts. Their first task was to understand correctly the meaning of the original. At times the original meaning cannot be precisely known, not only because the meaning of some words and phrases cannot be determined with a great degree of assurance but also because the underlying cultural and historical context is sometimes beyond recovery. All aids available were used in this task, including the ancient versions and the modern translations in English and other languages. After ascertaining as accurately as possible the meaning of the original, the translators' next task was to express that meaning in a manner and form easily understood by the readers. Since this translation is intended for all who use English as a means of communication, the translators have tried to avoid words and forms not in current or widespread use; but no artificial limit has been set to the range of the vocabulary employed. Every effort has been made to use language that is natural, clear, simple, and unambiguous. Consequently there has been no attempt to reproduce in English the parts of speech, sentence-structure, word-order, and grammatical devices of the original languages. Faithfulness in translation also includes a faithful representation of the cultural and historical features of the original, without any attempt to modernize the text. Certain features, however, such as the hours of the day and the measures of weight, capacity, distance, and area, are given their modern equivalents, since the information contained in those terms is of greater importance to the reader than the biblical form of those terms. The metric system of weights and measures has been adopted in the British edition.

In cases where a person or place is called by two or more different names in the original, this translation has normally used only the more familiar name in all places; e.g., King Jehoiachin of Judah (Jeremiah 52.31), also called Jeconiah (Jeremiah 24.1) and Coniah (Jeremiah 37.1). Where a proper name is spelt in two or more different ways in the original text, this translation has used only one spelling; e.g., Nebuchadnezzar, also spelt Nebuchadrezzar (compare Jeremiah 29.3 and 29.21), and Priscilla, also spelt Prisca (compare Acts 18.26 and Romans 16.3).

In view of the differences in vocabulary and form which exist between the American and the British use of the English language, this British edition is being published, incorporating such changes as are in keeping with British usage. Final approval of this text was given by the General Committee of the British and Foreign Bible Society.

Following an ancient tradition, begun by the first translation of the Hebrew Scriptures (the Septuagint) and followed by the vast majority of English translations, the distinctive Hebrew name for God (usually transliterated

Jehovah or *Yahweh*) is in this translation represented by "The LORD." When the Hebrew word *Adonai*, normally translated "Lord," is followed by *Yahweh*, the combination is rendered by the phrase "Sovereign LORD."

In order to make the text easier to understand, various kinds of readers' helps are supplied. The text itself has been divided into sections, and headings are provided which indicate clearly the contents of the section. Where there are parallel accounts elsewhere in the Bible, a reference to such a passage appears in brackets below the heading. There are, in addition, several kinds of notes which appear at the bottom of the page. (1) *Cultural or Historical Notes.* These provide information required to enable the reader to understand the meaning of the text in terms of its original setting (*e.g.* the explanation of *Rahab* in Psalm 89.10; the explanation of *Day of Atonement* in Acts 27.9). (2) *Textual Notes.* In the Old Testament these indicate primarily those places where the translators were compelled for a variety of reasons to base the translation on some text other than the Hebrew. Where one or more of the ancient versions were followed, the note indicates this by *One ancient translation* (*e.g.* Genesis 1.26) or *Some ancient translations* (*e.g.* Genesis 4.8); where a conjectural emendation was adopted, the note reads *Probable text* (*e.g.* Genesis 10.14). In the New Testament, as well as in the Deuterocanonical Books and other books of the Apocrypha, there are textual notes indicating some of the places where there are significant differences among the Greek manuscripts. These differences may consist of additions to the text (*e.g.* Matthew 21.43), deletions (*e.g.* Matthew 24.36), or substitutions (*e.g.* Mark 1.41). (3) *Alternative Renderings.* In many places the precise meaning of the original text is in dispute, and there are two or more different ways in which the text may be understood. In some of the more important of such instances an alternative rendering is given (*e.g.* Genesis 2.9; Matthew 6.11). (4) *References to Other Passages.* In addition to the notes there are references, by book, chapter, and verse, to other places in the Bible where identical or similar matters or ideas are dealt with.

There are several appendices at the end of the volume. A Word List identifies many objects or cultural features whose meaning may not be known to all readers. A Chronological Chart gives the approximate dates of the major events recorded in the Bible. An *Index* locates some of the more important subjects, persons, places, and events in the Bible. A List of Passages from the ancient Greek translation (the Septuagint) of the Old Testament, which are quoted or paraphrased in the New Testament and which differ significantly in meaning from the Hebrew Masoretic Text, will help the reader to understand some otherwise puzzling differences in quotations. The maps are designed to help the reader to visualize the geographical setting of countries and localities mentioned in the Bible.

The line drawings which accompany the text were especially prepared for this edition by the Swiss artist Annie Vallotton.

The numbering of chapters and verses in this translation follows the traditional system of major English translations of the Bible. In some instances, however, where the order of thought or events in two or more verses is more clearly represented by a rearrangement of the material, two or more verse numbers are joined (*e.g.* Exodus 2.15-16; Acts 1.21-22).

No one knows better than the translators how difficult has been their task. But they have performed it gladly, conscious always of the presence of the Holy Spirit and of the tremendous debt which they owe to the dedication and scholarship of those who have preceded them. The Bible is not simply great literature to be admired and revered; it is Good News for all people everywhere—a message both to be understood and to be applied in daily life. It is with the prayer that the Lord of the Scriptures will be pleased to use this translation for his sovereign purpose that the United Bible Societies now publish *The Bible in Today's English*. And to Christ be the glory for ever and ever!

Contents

THE BOOKS OF THE OLD TESTAMENT

	Abbreviation	Page		Abbreviation	Page
Genesis	Gen	3	Ecclesiastes	Ecc	648
Exodus	Ex	59	Song of Songs	Song	659
Leviticus	Lev	102	Isaiah	Is	665
Numbers	Num	131	Jeremiah	Jer	729
Deuteronomy	Deut	170	Lamentations	Lam	791
Joshua	Josh	208	Ezekiel	Ezek	798
Judges	Judg	233	Daniel	Dan	852
Ruth	Ruth	259	Hosea	Hos	869
1 Samuel	1 Sam	264	Joel	Joel	879
2 Samuel	2 Sam	300	Amos	Amos	884
1 Kings	1 Kgs	331	Obadiah	Obad	893
2 Kings	2 Kgs	366	Jonah	Jon	895
1 Chronicles	1 Chr	400	Micah	Mic	899
2 Chronicles	2 Chr	431	Nahum	Nah	906
Ezra	Ezra	467	Habakkuk	Hab	909
Nehemiah	Neh	479	Zephaniah	Zeph	912
Esther	Esth	496	Haggai	Hag	916
Job	Job	504	Zechariah	Zech	918
Psalms	Ps	538	Malachi	Mal	928
Proverbs	Prov	622			

THE DEUTEROCANONICAL BOOKS/APOCRYPHA

	Abbreviation	Page		Abbreviation	Page
Tobit	Tob	1			
Judith	Jdt	16	Susanna	Sus	119
Esther - Greek	Gk Est	31	Bel and the Dragon	Bel	122
Wisdom of Solomon	Wis	43	1 Maccabees	1 Macc	124
Sirach			2 Maccabees	2 Macc	156
(Ecclesiasticus)	Sir	60			
Baruch	Bar	107	*Some Additional Books*		
Letter of Jeremiah	Let Jer	113	1 Esdras	1 Esd	185
Prayer of Azariah			2 Esdras	2 Esd	202
and the Song of the			Prayer of Manasseh	Man	232
Three Young Men	S of 3Y	116			

THE BOOKS OF THE NEW TESTAMENT

	Abbreviation	Page		Abbreviation	Page
Matthew	Mt	3	1 Timothy	1 Tim	259
Mark	Mk	44	2 Timothy	2 Tim	264
Luke	Lk	73	Titus	Tit	268
John	Jn	117	Philemon	Phlm	270
Acts	Acts	148	Hebrews	Heb	272
Romans	Rom	189	James	Jas	284
1 Corinthians	1 Cor	205	1 Peter	1 Pet	289
2 Corinthians	2 Cor	221	2 Peter	2 Pet	294
Galatians	Gal	231	1 John	1 Jn	297
Ephesians	Eph	238	2 John	2 Jn	302
Philippians	Phil	244	3 John	3 Jn	303
Colossians	Col	249	Jude	Jude	304
1 Thessalonians	1 Thes	253	Revelation	Rev	306
2 Thessalonians	2 Thes	257			

Word List	325
Index	333
Septuagint Readings	355
Outline Chart of Bible History	359

The above abbreviations are used for the books of the Bible
in the reference system. In addition OT = Old Testament,
D/A = Deuterocanonical Books/Apocrypha, NT = New Testament.

Contents

ALPHABETICAL LIST OF BOOKS

	Page		Page
Acts	NT 148	Letter of	
Amos	OT 884	Jeremiah	D/A 113
Baruch	D/A 107	Leviticus	OT 102
Bel and the		Luke	NT 73
Dragon	D/A 122	1 Maccabees	D/A 124
1 Chronicles	OT 400	2 Maccabees	D/A 156
2 Chronicles	OT 431	Malachi	OT 928
Colossians	NT 249	Mark	NT 44
1 Corinthians	NT 205	Matthew	NT 3
2 Corinthians	NT 221	Micah	OT 899
Daniel	OT 852	Nahum	OT 906
Deuteronomy	OT 170	Nehemiah	OT 479
Ecclesiastes	OT 648	Numbers	OT 131
Ephesians	NT 238	Obadiah	OT 893
1 Esdras	D/A 185	1 Peter	NT 289
2 Esdras	D/A 202	2 Peter	NT 294
Esther	OT 496	Philemon	NT 270
Esther – Greek	D/A 31	Philippians	NT 244
Exodus	OT 59	Prayer of	
Ezekiel	OT 798	Manasseh	D/A 232
Ezra	OT 467	Proverbs	OT 622
Galatians	NT 231	Psalms	OT 538
Genesis	OT 3	Revelation	NT 306
Habakkuk	OT 909	Romans	NT 189
Haggai	OT 916	Ruth	OT 259
Hebrews	NT 272	1 Samuel	OT 264
Hosea	OT 369	2 Samuel	OT 300
Isaiah	OT 665	Sirach	
James	NT 284	(Ecclesiasticus)	D/A 60
Jeremiah	OT 729	Song of Songs	OT 659
Job	OT 504	Song of Three	
Joel	OT 879	Young Men	D/A 116
John	NT 117	Susanna	D/A 119
1 John	NT 297	1 Thessalonians	NT 253
2 John	NT 302	2 Thessalonians	NT 257
3 John	NT 303	1 Timothy	NT 259
Jonah	OT 895	2 Timothy	NT 264
Joshua	OT 208	Titus	NT 268
Jude	NT 304	Tobit	D/A 1
Judges	OT 233	Wisdom of	
Judith	D/A 16	Solomon	D/A 43
1 Kings	OT 331	Zechariah	OT 918
2 Kings	OT 366	Zephaniah	OT 912
Lamentations	OT 791		

List of Maps

Old Testament   Page

The World of Genesis   14
The Route of the Exodus   58
The Division of Canaan   220
The United Israelite Kingdom   278
Jerusalem in Old Testament Times   332
The Divided Israelite Kingdoms   350

Deuterocanonical Books/Apocrypha

Palestine in the Time of the Maccabees   iv
Judaea in the Time of the Maccabees   v

New Testament

Jerusalem in New Testament Times   2
Palestine in the Time of Jesus   78
Palestine and Syria in Acts   150
Paul's First Missionary Journey   166
Paul's Second and Third Missionary Journeys   170
Paul's Journey to Rome   184

THE
OLD TESTAMENT

GENESIS

INTRODUCTION

The name *Genesis* means 'origin.' The book tells about the creation of the universe, the origin of mankind, the beginning of sin and suffering in the world, and about God's way of dealing with mankind. Genesis can be divided into two main parts:

1. *Chapters 1-11* The creation of the world and the early history of the human race. Here are the accounts of Adam and Eve, Cain and Abel, Noah and the flood, and the Tower of Babylon.

2. *Chapters 12-50* The history of the early ancestors of the Israelites. The first is Abraham, who was notable for his faith and his obedience to God. Then follow the stories of his son Isaac, and grandson Jacob (also called Israel), and of Jacob's twelve sons, who were the founders of the twelve tribes of Israel. Special attention is given to one of the sons, Joseph, and the events that brought Jacob and his other sons with their families to live in Egypt.

While this book tells stories about people, it is first and foremost an account of what God has done. It begins with the affirmation that God created the universe, and it ends with a promise that God will continue to show his concern for his people. Throughout the book the main character is God, who judges and punishes those who do wrong, leads and helps his people, and shapes their history. This ancient book was written to record the story of a people's faith and to help keep that faith alive.

Outline of Contents

Creation of the universe and of mankind   1.1—2.25
The beginning of sin and suffering 3.1-24
From Adam to Noah   4.1—5.32
Noah and the flood   6.1—10.32
The tower of Babylon   11.1-9
From Shem to Abram   11.10-32
The patriarchs: Abraham, Isaac, Jacob   12.1—35.29
The descendants of Esau   36.1-43
Joseph and his brothers   37.1—45.28
The Israelites in Egypt   46.1—50.26

Let the earth produce all kinds of plants (1.11)

Lights in the sky...to rule over the day and the night (1.17, 18)

Creatures that live in the water and all kinds of birds (1.21)

The Story of Creation

1 In the beginning, when God created the universe,[a] 2 the earth was formless and desolate. The raging ocean that covered everything was engulfed in total darkness, and the power of God[b] was moving over the water. 3 Then God commanded, "Let there be light"—and light appeared. 4 God was pleased with what he saw. Then he separated the light from the darkness, 5 and he named the light "Day" and the darkness "Night". Evening passed and morning came—that was the first day.

6-7 Then God commanded, "Let there be a dome to divide the water and to keep it in two separate places"—and it was done. So God made a dome, and it separated the water under it from the water above it. 8 He named the dome "Sky." Evening passed and morning came—that was the second day.

9 Then God commanded, "Let the water below the sky come together in one place, so that the land will appear"—and it was done. 10 He named the land "Earth," and the water which had come together he named "Sea." And God was pleased with what he saw. 11 Then he commanded, "Let the earth produce all kinds of plants, those that bear grain and those that bear fruit"—and it was done. 12 So the earth produced all kinds of plants, and God was pleased with what he saw. 13 Evening passed and morning came—that was the third day.

14 Then God commanded, "Let lights appear in the sky to separate day from night and to show the time when days, years, and religious festivals[c] begin; 15 they will shine in the sky to give light to the earth"—and it was done. 16 So God made the two larger lights, the sun to rule over the day and the moon to rule over the night; he also made the stars. 17 He placed the lights in the sky to shine on the earth, 18 to rule over the day and the night, and to separate light from darkness. And God was pleased with what he saw. 19 Evening passed and morning came—that was the fourth day.

20 Then God commanded, "Let the water be filled with many kinds of living beings, and let the air be filled with birds." 21 So God created the great sea-monsters, all kinds of creatures that live in the water, and all kinds of birds. And God was

[a] In the beginning...the universe; *or* In the beginning God created the universe; *or* When God began to create the universe.
[b] the power of God; *or* the spirit of God; *or* a wind from God; *or* an awesome wind.
[c] religious festivals; *or* seasons.
1.3: 2 Cor 4.6   **1.6–8:** 2 Pet 3.5

pleased with what he saw. 22 He blessed them all and told the creatures that live in the water to reproduce, and to fill the sea, and he told the birds to increase in number. 23 Evening passed and morning came—that was the fifth day.

24 Then God commanded, "Let the earth produce all kinds of animal life: domestic and wild, large and small"—and it was done. 25 So God made them all, and he was pleased with what he saw.

26 Then God said, "And now we will make human beings; they will be like us and resemble us. They will have power over the fish, the birds, and all animals, domestic and wild, d large and small." 27 So God created human beings, making them to be like himself. He created them male and female, 28 blessed them, and said, "Have many children, so that your descendants will live all over the earth and bring it under their control. I am putting you in charge of the fish, the birds, and all the wild animals. 29 I have provided all kinds of grain and all kinds of fruit for you to eat; 30 but for all the wild animals and for all the birds I have provided grass and leafy plants for food"—and it was done. 31 God looked at everything he had made, and he was very pleased. Evening passed and morning came—that was the sixth day.

2 And so the whole universe was completed. 2 By the seventh day God finished what he had been doing and stopped working. 3 He blessed the seventh day and set it apart as a special day, because by that day he had completed his creation e and stopped working. 4 And that is how the universe was created.

The Garden of Eden

When the LORD x God made the universe, 5 there were no plants on the earth and no seeds had sprouted, because he had not sent any rain, and there was no one to cultivate the land; 6 but water would come up from beneath the surface and water the ground.

7 Then the LORD God took some soil from the ground f and formed a man f out of it; he breathed life-giving breath into his nostrils and the man began to live.

8 Then the LORD God planted a garden in Eden, in the East, and there he put the man he had formed. 9 He made all kinds of beautiful trees grow there and produce good fruit. In the middle of the garden stood the tree that gives life and the tree that gives knowledge of what is good and what is bad. g

10 A stream flowed in Eden and watered the garden; beyond Eden it divided into four rivers. 11 The first river is the Pishon; it flows round the country of Havilah. (12 Pure gold is found there and also rare perfume and precious stones.) 13 The second river is the Gihon; it flows round the country of Cush. h 14 The third river is the Tigris, which flows east of Assyria, and the fourth river is the Euphrates.

15 Then the LORD God placed the man in the Garden of Eden to cultivate it and guard it. 16 He said to him, "You may eat the fruit of any tree in the garden, 17 except the tree that gives knowledge of what is good and what is bad. g You must not eat the fruit of that tree; if you do, you will die the same day."

18 Then the LORD God said, "It is not good for the man to live alone. I will make a suitable companion to help him." 19 So he took some soil from the ground and formed all the animals and all the birds. Then he brought them to the man to see what he would name them; and that is how they all got their names. 20 So the man named all the birds and all the animals; but not one of them was a suitable companion to help him.

21 Then the LORD God made the man fall into a deep sleep, and while he was sleeping, he took out one of the man's ribs and closed up the flesh. 22 He formed a woman out of the rib and brought her to him. 23 Then the man said,

"At last, here is one of my own kind—
Bone taken from my bone, and flesh
    from my flesh.
'Woman' is her name because she was
    taken out of man." i

d One ancient translation animals, domestic and wild; Hebrew domestic animals and all the earth.
e by that day he had completed his creation; or on that day he completed his creation.
x THE LORD: See LORD in Word List.
f GROUND...MAN: The Hebrew words for "man" and "ground" have similar sounds.
g knowledge of what is good and what is bad; or knowledge of everything.
h Cush (of Mesopotamia); or Sudan.
i WOMAN...MAN: The Hebrew words for "woman" and "man" have rather similar sounds.
1.26: 1 Cor 11.7   **1.27:** Mt 19.4; Mk 10.6   **1.27-28:** Gen 5.1-2   **2.2:** Heb 4.4,10
2.2-3: Ex 20.11   **2.7:** 1 Cor 15.45   **2.9:** Rev 2.7, 22.2,14

How wonderful it would be to become wise (3.6)

²⁴That is why a man leaves his father and mother and is united with his wife, and they become one.

25 The man and the woman were both naked, but they were not embarrassed.

The Disobedience of Man

3 Now the snake was the most cunning animal that the LORD God had made. The snake asked the woman, "Did God really tell you not to eat fruit from any tree in the garden?"

2 "We may eat the fruit of any tree in the garden," the woman answered, ³"except the tree in the middle of it. God told us not to eat the fruit of that tree or even touch it; if we do, we will die."

4 The snake replied, "That's not true: you will not die. ⁵God said that, because he knows that when you eat it you will be like God*ʲ* and know what is good and what is bad."*ᵏ*

6 The woman saw how beautiful the tree was and how good its fruit would be to eat, and she thought how wonderful it would be to become wise. So she took some of the fruit and ate it. Then she gave some to her husband, and he also ate it. ⁷As soon as they had eaten it, they were given understanding and realized that they were naked; so they sewed fig leaves together and covered themselves.

8 That evening they heard the LORD God walking in the garden, and they hid from him among the trees. ⁹But the LORD God called out to the man, "Where are you?"

10 He answered, "I heard you in the garden; I was afraid and hid from you, because I was naked."

11 "Who told you that you were naked?" God asked. "Did you eat the fruit that I told you not to eat?"

12 The man answered, "The woman you put here with me gave me the fruit, and I ate it."

13 The LORD God asked the woman, "Why did you do this?"

She replied, "The snake tricked me into eating it."

God Pronounces Judgement

14 Then the LORD God said to the snake, "You will be punished for this; you alone of all the animals must bear this curse: From now on you will crawl on your belly, and you will have to eat dust as long as you live. ¹⁵I will make you and the woman hate each other; her offspring and yours will always be enemies. Her offspring will crush your head, and you will bite their*ˣ* heel."

16 And he said to the woman, "I will increase your trouble in pregnancy and your pain in giving birth. In spite of this, you will still have desire for your husband, yet you will be subject to him."

17 And he said to the man, "You listened to your wife and ate the fruit which I told you not to eat. Because of what you have done, the ground will be under a curse. You will have to work hard all your life to make it produce enough food for you. ¹⁸It will produce weeds and thorns, and you will have to eat wild

---

*ʲ*God; *or* the gods.
*ᵏ*know what is good and what is bad; *or* know everything.
*ˣ*their; *or* his.
2.24: Mt 19.5; Mk 10.7–8; 1 Cor 6.16; Eph 5.31   **3.1:** Rev 12.9. 20.2
3.13: 2 Cor 11.3; 1 Tim 2.14   **3.15:** Rev 12.17   **18.** Heb 6. 8.

plants. [19] You will have to work hard and sweat to make the soil produce anything, until you go back to the soil from which you were formed. You were made from soil, and you will become soil again."

20 Adam [l] named his wife Eve, [m] because she was the mother of all human beings. [21] And the LORD God made clothes out of animal skins for Adam and his wife, and he clothed them.

Adam and Eve Are Sent Out of the Garden

22 Then the LORD God said, "Now the man has become like one of us and has knowledge of what is good and what is bad. [n] He must not be allowed to take fruit from the tree that gives life, eat it, and live for ever." [23] So the LORD God sent him out of the Garden of Eden and made him cultivate the soil from which he had been formed. [24] Then at the east side of the garden he put living creatures [o] and a flaming sword which turned in all directions. This was to keep anyone from coming near the tree that gives life.

Cain and Abel

4 Then Adam had intercourse with his wife, and she became pregnant. She bore a son and said, "By the LORD's help I have acquired a son." So she named him Cain. [p] [2] Later she gave birth to another son, Abel. Abel became a shepherd, but Cain was a farmer. [3] After some time, Cain brought some of his harvest and gave it as an offering to the LORD. [4] Then Abel brought the first lamb born to one of his sheep, killed it, and gave the best parts of it as an offering. The LORD was pleased with Abel and his offering, [5] but he rejected Cain and his offering. Cain became furious, and he scowled in anger. [6] Then the LORD said to Cain, "Why are you angry? Why that scowl on your face? [7] If you had done the right thing, you would be smiling; [q] but because you have done evil, sin is crouching at your door. It wants to rule you, but you must overcome it."

8 Then Cain said to his brother Abel, "Let's go out in the fields." [r] When they were out in the fields, Cain turned on his brother and killed him.

9 The LORD asked Cain, "Where is your brother Abel?"

He answered, "I don't know. Am I supposed to take care of my brother?"

10 Then the LORD said, "Why have you done this terrible thing? Your brother's blood is crying out to me from the ground, like a voice calling for revenge. [11] You are placed under a curse and can no longer farm the soil. It has soaked up your brother's blood as if it had opened its mouth to receive it when you killed him. [12] If you try to grow crops, the soil will not produce anything; you will be a homeless wanderer on the earth."

13 And Cain said to the LORD, "This punishment is too hard for me to bear. [14] You are driving me off the land and away from your presence. I will be a homeless wanderer on the earth, and anyone who finds me will kill me."

15 But the LORD answered, "No. If anyone kills you, seven lives will be taken in revenge." So the LORD put a mark on Cain to warn anyone who met him not to kill him. [16] And Cain went away from the LORD's presence and lived in a land called "Wandering," which is east of Eden.

The Descendants of Cain

17 Cain and his wife had a son and named him Enoch. Then Cain built a city and named it after his son. [18] Enoch had a son named Irad, who was the father of Mehujael, and Mehujael had a son named Methushael, who was the father of Lamech. [19] Lamech had two wives, Adah and Zillah. [20] Adah gave birth to Jabal, who was the ancestor of those who raise livestock and live in tents. [21] His brother was Jubal, the ancestor of all musicians who play the harp and the flute. [22] Zillah gave birth to Tubal Cain, who made all kinds of tools [s] out of bronze

[l] ADAM: *This name in Hebrew means "mankind."*
[m] EVE: *This name sounds similar to the Hebrew word for "living," which is rendered in this context as "human beings."*
[n] knowledge of what is good and what is bad; *or* knowledge of everything.
[o] LIVING CREATURES: *See Word List.*
[p] CAIN: *This name sounds like the Hebrew for "acquired."*
[q] you would be smiling; *or* I would have accepted your offering.
[r] *Some ancient translations* Let's go out in the fields; *Hebrew does not have these words.*
[s] who made all kinds of tools; *one ancient translation* ancestor of all metal-workers.
3.22: Rev 22.14   **4.4:** Heb 11.4   **4.8:** Mt 23.35; Lk 11.51; 1 Jn 3.12   **4.10:** Heb 12.24

Why that scowl on your face? (4.6)

and iron. The sister of Tubal Cain was Naamah.

23 Lamech said to his wives,

"Adah and Zillah, listen to me: I have
    killed a young man because he
    struck me.
²⁴ If seven lives are taken to pay for
    killing Cain,
Seventy-seven will be taken if anyone
    kills me."

Seth and Enosh

25 Adam and his wife had another son. She said, "God has given me a son to replace Abel, whom Cain killed." So she named him Seth.^t ²⁶ Seth had a son whom he named Enosh. It was then that people began using the LORD's holy name in worship.

The Descendants of Adam
(1 Chr 1.1–4)

5 This is the list of the descendants of Adam. (When God created human beings, he made them like himself. ² He created them male and female, blessed them, and named them "Mankind.") ³ When Adam was 130 years old, he had a son who was like him, and he named him Seth. ⁴ After that, Adam lived another 800 years. He had other children ⁵ and died at the age of 930.

6 When Seth was 105, he had a son, Enosh, ⁷ and then lived another 807 years. He had other children ⁸ and died at the age of 912.

9 When Enosh was 90, he had a son, Kenan, ¹⁰ and then lived another 815

---

^t SETH: *This name sounds like the Hebrew for "has given."*
4.24: Mt 18.22   **5.1–2:** Gen 1.27–28   **5.2:** Mt 19.4; Mk 10.6

years. He had other children [11] and died at the age of 905.

12 When Kenan was 70, he had a son, Mahalalel, [13] and then lived another 840 years. He had other children [14] and died at the age of 910.

15 When Mahalalel was 65, he had a son, Jared, [16] and then lived another 830 years. He had other children [17] and died at the age of 895.

18 When Jared was 162, he had a son, Enoch, [19] and then lived another 800 years. He had other children [20] and died at the age of 962.

21 When Enoch was 65, he had a son, Methuselah. [22] After that, Enoch lived in fellowship with God for 300 years and had other children. [23] He lived to be 365 years old. [24] He spent his life in fellowship with God, and then he disappeared, because God took him away.

25 When Methuselah was 187, he had a son, Lamech, [26] and then lived another 782 years. He had other children [27] and died at the age of 969.

28 When Lamech was 182, he had a son, [29] and said, "From the very ground on which the LORD put a curse, this child will bring us relief from all our hard work"; so he named him Noah. [u] [30] Lamech lived another 595 years. He had other children [31] and died at the age of 777.

32 After Noah was 500 years old, he had three sons, Shem, Ham, and Japheth.

The Wickedness of Mankind

6 When mankind had spread all over the world, and girls were being born, [2] some of the heavenly beings [v] saw that these girls were beautiful, so they took the ones they liked. [3] Then the LORD said, "I will not allow people to live for ever; they are mortal. From now on they will live no longer than a hundred and twenty years." [4] In those days, and even later, there were giants on the earth who were descendants of human women and the heavenly beings. [v] They were the great heroes and famous men of long ago.

5 When the LORD saw how wicked everyone on earth was and how evil their thoughts were all the time, [6] he was sorry that he had ever made them and put them on the earth. He was so filled with regret

[7] that he said, "I will wipe out these people I have created, and also the animals and the birds, because I am sorry that I made any of them." [8] But the LORD was pleased with Noah.

Noah

9-10 This is the story of Noah. He had three sons, Shem, Ham, and Japheth. Noah had no faults and was the only good man of his time. He lived in fellowship with God, [11] but everyone else was evil in God's sight, and violence had spread everywhere. [12] God looked at the world and saw that it was evil, for the people were all living evil lives.

13 God said to Noah, "I have decided to put an end to all mankind. I will destroy them completely, because the world is full of their violent deeds. [14] Build a boat for yourself out of good timber; make rooms in it and cover it with tar inside and out. [15] Make it 133 metres long, 22 metres wide, and 13 metres high. [16] Make a roof [w] for the boat and leave a space of 44 centimetres between the roof [w] and the sides. Build it with three decks and put a door in the side. [17] I am going to send a flood on the earth to destroy every living being. Everything on the earth will die, [18] but I will make a covenant with you. Go into the boat with your wife, your sons, and their wives. [19-20] Take into the boat with you a male and a female of every kind of animal and of every kind of bird, in order to keep them alive. [21] Take along all kinds of food for you and for them." [22] Noah did everything that God commanded.

The Flood

7 The LORD said to Noah, "Go into the boat with your whole family; I have found that you are the only one in all the world who does what is right. [2] Take with you seven pairs of each kind of ritually clean animal, but only one pair of each kind of unclean animal. [3] Take also seven pairs of each kind of bird. Do this so that every kind of animal and bird will be kept alive to reproduce again on the earth. [4] Seven days from now I am going to send rain that will fall for forty days and nights, in order to destroy all the living beings that I have made." [5] And

[u] NOAH: *This name sounds like the Hebrew for "relief."*
[v] heavenly beings; *or* sons of the gods; *or* sons of God.
[w] roof; *or* window.

5.24: Heb 11.5; Jude 14   **6.1–4:** Job 1.6, 2.1   **6.4:** Num 13.33
6.5–8: Mat 24.37; Lk 17.26; 1 Pet 3.20   **6.9:** 2 Pet 2.5   **6.22:** Heb 11.7

Noah did everything that the LORD commanded.

6 Noah was six hundred years old when the flood came on the earth. 7 He and his wife, and his sons and their wives, went into the boat to escape the flood. 8 A male and a female of every kind of animal and bird, whether ritually clean or unclean, 9 went into the boat with Noah, as God had commanded. 10 Seven days later the flood came.

11 When Noah was six hundred years old, on the seventeenth day of the second month all the outlets of the vast body of water beneath the earth burst open, all the floodgates of the sky were opened, 12 and rain fell on the earth for forty days and nights. 13 On that same day Noah and his wife went into the boat with their three sons, Shem, Ham, and Japheth, and

their wives. 14 With them went every kind of animal, domestic and wild, large and small, and every kind of bird. 15 A male and a female of each kind of living being went into the boat with Noah, 16 as God had commanded. Then the LORD shut the door behind Noah.

17 The flood continued for forty days, and the water became deep enough for the boat to float. 18 The water became deeper, and the boat drifted on the surface. 19 It became so deep that it covered the highest mountains; 20 it went on rising until it was about seven metres above the tops of the mountains. 21 Every living being on the earth died—every bird, every animal, and every person. 22 Everything on earth that breathed died. 23 The LORD destroyed all living beings on the earth—human beings, animals, and birds. The only ones left were Noah and those who were with him in the boat. 24 The water did not start going down for a hundred and fifty days.

The End of the Flood

8 God had not forgotten Noah and all the animals with him in the boat; he caused a wind to blow, and the water started going down. 2 The outlets of the water beneath the earth and the floodgates of the sky were closed. The rain stopped, 3 and the water gradually went down for a hundred and fifty days. 4 On

Every kind of animal and bird...went into the boat (7.8,9)

7.7: Mt 24.38-39; Lk 17.27 **7.11:** 2 Pet 3.6

Everything on earth that breathed died (7.22)

the seventeenth day of the seventh month the boat came to rest on a mountain in the Ararat range. 5 The water kept going down, and on the first day of the tenth month the tops of the mountains appeared.

6 After forty days Noah opened a window 7 and sent out a raven. It did not come back, but kept flying around until the water was completely gone. 8 Meanwhile, Noah sent out a dove to see if the water had gone down, 9 but since the water still covered all the land, the dove did not find a place to alight. It flew back to the boat, and Noah reached out and took it in. 10 He waited another seven days and sent out the dove again. 11 It returned to him in the evening with a fresh olive leaf in its beak. So Noah knew that the water had gone down. 12 Then he waited another seven days and sent out the dove once more; this time it did not come back. 13 When Noah was 601 years old, on the first day of the first month, the water was gone. Noah removed the covering of the boat, looked round, and saw that the ground was getting dry. 14 By the twenty-seventh day of the second month the earth was completely dry.

15 God said to Noah, 16 "Go out of the boat with your wife, your sons, and their wives. 17 Take all the birds and animals out with you, so that they may reproduce and spread over all the earth." 18 So Noah went out of the boat with his wife, his sons, and their wives. 19 All the animals and birds went out of the boat in groups of their own kind.

Noah Offers a Sacrifice

20 Noah built an altar to the LORD; he took one of each kind of ritually clean animal and bird, and burnt them whole as a sacrifice on the altar. 21 The odour of the sacrifice pleased the LORD, and he said to himself, "Never again will I put the earth under a curse because of what man does; I know that from the time he is young his thoughts are evil. Never again will I destroy all living beings, as I have done this time. 22 As long as the world exists, there will be a time for planting and a time for harvest. There will always be cold and heat, summer and winter, day and night."

God's Covenant with Noah

9 God blessed Noah and his sons and said, "Have many children, so that your descendants will live all over the earth. 2 All the animals, birds, and fish will live in fear of you. They are all placed under your power. 3 Now you can eat them, as well as green plants; I give them all to you for food. 4 The one thing you must not eat is meat with blood still in it; I forbid this because the life is in the blood. 5 If anyone takes human life, he will be punished. I will punish with death any animal that takes a human life. 6 Man was made like God, so whoever murders

9.1: Gen 1.28   **9.4:** Gen 7.26–27, 17.10–14; Lev 19.26; Deut 12.16,23, 15.23
9.6: Gen 1.26; Ex 20.13

So Noah knew that the water had gone down (8.11)

a man will himself be killed by his fellow-man.

7 "You must have many children, so that your descendants will live all over the earth."

8 God said to Noah and his sons, 9 "I am now making my covenant with you and with your descendants, 10 and with all living beings—all birds and all animals—everything that came out of the boat with you. 11 With these words I make my covenant with you: I promise that never again will all living beings be destroyed by a flood; never again will a flood destroy the earth. 12 As a sign of this everlasting covenant which I am making with you and with all living beings, 13 I am putting my bow in the clouds. It will be the sign of my covenant with the world. 14 Whenever I cover the sky with clouds and the rainbow appears, 15 I will remember my promise to you and to all the animals that a flood will never again destroy all living beings. 16 When the rainbow appears in the clouds, I will see it and remember the everlasting covenant between me and all living beings on earth. 17 That is the sign of the promise which I am making to all living beings."

Noah and His Sons

18 The sons of Noah who went out of the boat were Shem, Ham, and Japheth. (Ham was the father of Canaan.) 19 These three sons of Noah were the ancestors of all the people on earth.

20 Noah, who was a farmer, was the first man to plant a vineyard. 21 After he drank some of the wine, he became drunk, took off his clothes, and lay naked in his tent. 22 When Ham, the father of Canaan, saw that his father was naked, he went out and told his two brothers. 23 Then Shem and Japheth took a robe and held it behind them on their shoulders. They walked backwards into the tent and covered their father, keeping their faces turned away so as not to see him naked. 24 When Noah was sober again and learnt what his youngest son had done to him, 25 he said,

"A curse on Canaan!
He will be a slave to his brothers.
26 Give praise to the LORD, the God of
        Shem!
Canaan will be the slave of Shem.
27 May God cause Japheth[x] to increase!
May his descendants live with the
        people of Shem!
Canaan will be the slave of Japheth."

28 After the flood Noah lived for 350 years 29 and died at the age of 950.

The Descendants of Noah's Sons
(1 Chr 1.5-23)

10 These are the descendants of Noah's sons, Shem, Ham, and Japheth. These three had sons after the flood.

2 The sons of Japheth—Gomer, Magog, Madai, Javan, Tubal, Meshech, and Tiras—were the ancestors of the peoples who bear their names. 3 The descendants of Gomer were the people of Ashkenaz,

[x] JAPHETH: *This name sounds like the Hebrew for "increase."*
9.7: Gen 1.28

The sign of my covenant with the world (9.13)

Riphath, and Togarmah. ⁴The descendants of Javan were the people of Elishah, Spain, Cyprus, and Rhodes; ⁵they were the ancestors of the people who live along the coast and on the islands. These are the descendants of Japheth, living in their different tribes and countries, each group speaking its own language.

6 The sons of Ham—Cush, Egypt, Libya and Canaan—were the ancestors of the peoples who bear their names. ⁷The descendants of Cush were the people of Seba, Havilah, Sabtah, Raamah, and Sabteca. The descendants of Raamah were the people of Sheba and Dedan. ⁸Cush had a son named Nimrod, who became the world's first great conqueror. ⁹By the LORD's help he was a great hunter, and that is why people say, "May the LORD make you as great a hunter as Nimrod!" ¹⁰At first his kingdom included

Babylon, Erech, and Accad, all three of them in Babylonia. ¹¹From that land he went to Assyria and built the cities of Nineveh, Rehoboth Ir, Calah, ¹²and Resen, which is between Nineveh and the great city of Calah.

13 The descendants of Egypt were the people of Lydia, Anam, Lehab, Naphtuh, ¹⁴Pathrus, Casluh, and of Crete, from whom the Philistines are descended.ʸ

15 Canaan's sons—Sidon, the eldest, and Heth—were the ancestors of the peoples who bear their names. ¹⁶Canaan was also the ancestor of the Jebusites, the Amorites, the Girgashites, ¹⁷the Hivites, the Arkites, the Sinites, ¹⁸the Arvadites, the Zemarites, and the Hamathites. The different tribes of the Canaanites spread out, ¹⁹until the Canaanite borders reached from Sidon southwards to Gerar near Gaza, and eastwards to

ʸ *Probable text* and of Crete...descended; *Hebrew* from whom the Philistines are descended, and Crete.

THE WORLD OF GENESIS

0 100 200 300 400 500
Kilometres

Sodom, Gomorrah, Admah, and Zeboiim near Lasha. 20 These are the descendants of Ham, living in their different tribes and countries, each group speaking its own language.

21 Shem, the elder brother of Japheth, was the ancestor of all the Hebrews. 22 Shem's sons—Elam, Asshur, Arpachshad, Lud, and Aram—were the ancestors of the peoples who bear their names. 23 The descendants of Aram were the people of Uz, Hul, Gether, and Meshek. 24 Arpachshad was the father of Shelah, who was the father of Eber. 25 Eber had two sons: one was named Peleg, z because during his time the people of the world were divided; and the other was named Joktan. 26 The descendants of Joktan were the people of Almodad, Sheleph, Hazarmaveth, Jerah, 27 Hadoram, Uzal, Diklah, 28 Obal, Abimael, Sheba, 29 Ophir, Havilah, and Jobab. All of them were descended from Joktan. 30 The land in which they lived extended from Mesha to Sephar in the eastern hill country. 31 These are the descendants of Shem, living in their different tribes and countries, each group speaking its own language.

32 All these peoples are the descendants of Noah, nation by nation, according to their different lines of descent. After the flood all the nations of the earth were descended from the sons of Noah.

The Tower of Babylon

11 At first, the people of the whole world had only one language and used the same words. 2 As they wandered about in the East, they came to a plain in Babylonia and settled there. 3 They said to one another, "Come on! Let's make bricks and bake them hard." So they had bricks to build with and tar to hold them together. 4 They said, "Now let's build a city with a tower that reaches the sky, so that we can make a name for ourselves and not be scattered all over the earth."

5 Then the LORD came down to see the city and the tower which those men had built, 6 and he said, "Now then, these are all one people and they speak one language; this is just the beginning of what they are going to do. Soon they will be able to do anything they want! 7 Let us go down and mix up their language so that they will not understand one

another." 8 So the LORD scattered them all over the earth, and they stopped building the city. 9 The city was called Babylon, a because there the LORD mixed up the language of all the people, and from there he scattered them all over the earth.

The Descendants of Shem
(1 Chr 1.24–27)

10 These are the descendants of Shem. Two years after the flood, when Shem was 100 years old, he had a son, Arpachshad. 11 After that, he lived another 500 years and had other children.

12 When Arpachshad was 35 years old, he had a son, Shelah; 13 after that, he lived another 403 years and had other children.

14 When Shelah was 30 years old, he had a son, Eber; 15 after that, he lived another 403 years and had other children.

16 When Eber was 34 years old, he had a son, Peleg; 17 after that, he lived another 430 years and had other children.

18 When Peleg was 30 years old, he had a son, Reu; 19 after that, he lived another 209 years and had other children.

20 When Reu was 32 years old, he had a son, Serug; 21 after that, he lived another 207 years and had other children.

22 When Serug was 30 years old, he had a son, Nahor; 23 after that, he lived another 200 years and had other children.

24 When Nahor was 29 years old, he had a son, Terah; 25 after that, he lived another 119 years and had other children.

26 After Terah was 70 years old, he became the father of Abram, Nahor, and Haran.

The Descendants of Terah

27 These are the descendants of Terah, who was the father of Abram, Nahor, and Haran. Haran was the father of Lot, 28 and Haran died in his native city, Ur in Babylonia, while his father was still living. 29 Abram married Sarai, and Nahor married Milcah, the daughter of Haran, who was also the father of Iscah. 30 Sarai was not able to have children.

31 Terah took his son Abram, his grandson Lot, who was the son of Haran, and his daughter-in-law Sarai, Abram's wife, and with them he left the city of Ur in Babylonia to go to the land of Canaan. They went as far as Haran and

---

z PELEG: *This name sounds like the Hebrew for "divide."*
a BABYLON: *This name sounds like the Hebrew for "mixed up."*

settled there. ³²Terah died there at the age of two hundred and five.

God's Call to Abram

12 The LORD said to Abram, "Leave your country, your relatives, and your father's home, and go to a land that I am going to show you. ²I will give you many descendants, and they will become a great nation. I will bless you and make your name famous, so that you will be a blessing.

³ I will bless those who bless you,
But I will curse those who curse you.
And through you I will bless all the
    nations."*b*

4 When Abram was seventy-five years old, he started out from Haran, as the LORD had told him to do; and Lot went with him. ⁵Abram took his wife Sarai, his nephew Lot, and all the wealth and all the slaves they had acquired in Haran, and they started out for the land of Canaan.

When they arrived in Canaan, ⁶Abram travelled through the land until he came to the sacred tree of Moreh, the holy place at Shechem. (At that time the Canaanites were still living in the land.) ⁷The LORD appeared to Abram and said to him, "This is the country that I am going to give to your descendants." Then Abram built an altar there to the LORD, who had appeared to him. ⁸After that, he moved on south to the hill-country east of the city of Bethel and set up his camp between Bethel on the west and Ai on the east. There also he built an altar and worshipped the LORD. ⁹Then he moved on from place to place, going towards the southern part of Canaan.

Abram in Egypt

10 But there was a famine in Canaan, and it was so bad that Abram went farther south to Egypt, to live there for a while. ¹¹When he was about to cross the border into Egypt, he said to his wife Sarai, "You are a beautiful woman. ¹²When the Egyptians see you, they will assume that you are my wife, and so they will kill me and let you live. ¹³Tell them that you are my sister; then because of you they will let me live and treat me well." ¹⁴When he crossed the border into Egypt, the Egyptians did see that his wife was

beautiful. ¹⁵Some of the court officials saw her and told the king how beautiful she was; so she was taken to his palace. ¹⁶Because of her the king treated Abram well and gave him flocks of sheep and goats, cattle, donkeys, slaves, and camels.

17 But because the king had taken Sarai, the LORD sent terrible diseases on him and on the people of his palace. ¹⁸Then the king sent for Abram and asked him, "What have you done to me? Why didn't you tell me that she was your wife? ¹⁹Why did you say that she was your sister, and let me take her as my wife? Here is your wife; take her and get out!" ²⁰The king gave orders to his men, so they took Abram and put him out of the country, together with his wife and everything he owned.

Abram and Lot Separate

13 Abram went north out of Egypt to the southern part of Canaan with his wife and everything he owned, and Lot went with him. ²Abram was a very rich man, with sheep, goats, and cattle, as well as silver and gold. ³Then he left there and moved from place to place, going towards Bethel. He reached the place between Bethel and Ai where he had camped before ⁴and had built an altar. There he worshipped the LORD.

5 Lot also had sheep, goats, and cattle, as well as his own family and servants. ⁶And so there was not enough pasture land for the two of them to stay together, because they had too many animals. ⁷So quarrels broke out between the men who took care of Abram's animals and those who took care of Lot's animals. (At that time the Canaanites and the Perizzites were still living in the land.)

8 Then Abram said to Lot, "We are relatives, and your men and my men shouldn't be quarrelling. ⁹So let's separate. Choose any part of the land you want. You go one way, and I'll go the other."

10 Lot looked round and saw that the whole Jordan Valley, all the way to Zoar, had plenty of water, like the Garden of the LORD*c* or like the land of Egypt. (This was before the LORD had destroyed the cities of Sodom and Gomorrah.) ¹¹So Lot chose the whole Jordan Valley for himself and moved away towards the east. That

---

b And through...nations; *or* All the nations will ask me to bless them as I have blessed you.
c GARDEN OF THE LORD: *a reference to the Garden of Eden.*
12.1: Acts 7.2–3; Heb 11.8   **12.3:** Gal 3.8   **12.7:** Acts 7.5; Gal 3.16   **12.13:** Gen 20.2, 26.7
13.10: Gen 2.10

is how the two men parted. 12 Abram stayed in the land of Canaan, and Lot settled among the cities in the valley and camped near Sodom, 13 whose people were wicked and sinned against the LORD.

Abram Moves to Hebron

14 After Lot had left, the LORD said to Abram, "From where you are, look carefully in all directions. 15 I am going to give you and your descendants all the land that you see, and it will be yours for ever. 16 I am going to give you so many descendants that no one will be able to count them all; it would be as easy to count all the specks of dust on earth! 17 Now, go and look over the whole land, because I am going to give it all to you." 18 So Abram moved his camp and settled near the sacred trees of Mamre at Hebron, and there he built an altar to the LORD.

Abram Rescues Lot

14 Four kings, Amraphel of Babylonia, Arioch of Ellasar, Chedorlaomer of Elam, and Tidal of Goiim, 2 went to war against five other kings: Bera of Sodom, Birsha of Gomorrah, Shinab of Admah, Shemeber of Zeboiim, and the king of Bela (or Zoar). 3 These five kings had formed an alliance and joined forces in the Valley of Siddim, which is now the Dead Sea. 4 They had been under the control of Chedorlaomer for twelve years, but in the thirteenth year they rebelled against him. 5 In the fourteenth year Chedorlaomer and his allies came with their armies and defeated the Rephaim in Ashteroth Karnaim, the Zuzim in Ham, the Emim in the plain of Kiriathaim, 6 and the Horites in the mountains of Edom, pursuing them as far as Elparan on the edge of the desert. 7 Then they turned round and came back to Kadesh (then known as Enmishpat). They conquered all the land of the Amalekites and defeated the Amorites who lived in Hazazon Tamar.

8 Then the kings of Sodom, Gomorrah, Admah, Zeboiim, and Bela drew up their armies for battle in the Valley of Siddim and fought 9 against the kings of Elam, Goiim, Babylonia, and Ellasar, five kings against four. 10 The valley was full of tar pits, and when the kings of Sodom and Gomorrah tried to run away from the battle, they fell into the pits; but the other three kings escaped to the mountains.

11 The four kings took everything in Sodom and Gomorrah, including the food, and went away. 12 Lot, Abram's nephew, was living in Sodom, so they took him and all his possessions.

13 But a man escaped and reported all this to Abram, the Hebrew, who was living near the sacred trees belonging to Mamre the Amorite. Mamre and his brothers Eshcol and Aner were Abram's allies. 14 When Abram heard that his nephew had been captured, he called together all the fighting men in his camp, 318 in all, and pursued the four kings all the way to Dan. 15 There he divided his men into groups, attacked the enemy by night, and defeated them. He chased them as far as Hobah, north of Damascus, 16 and recovered the loot that had been taken. He also brought back his nephew Lot and his possessions, together with the women and the other prisoners.

Melchizedek Blesses Abram

17 When Abram came back from his victory over Chedorlaomer and the other kings, the king of Sodom went out to meet him in the Valley of Shaveh (also called the King's Valley). 18 And Melchizedek, who was king of Salem and also a priest of the Most High God, brought bread and wine to Abram, 19 blessed him, and said, "May the Most High God, who made heaven and earth, bless Abram! 20 May the Most High God, who gave you victory over your enemies, be praised!" And Abram gave Melchizedek a tenth of all the loot he had recovered.

21 The king of Sodom said to Abram, "Keep the loot, but give me back all my people."

22 Abram answered, "I solemnly swear before the LORD, the Most High God, Maker of heaven and earth, 23 that I will not keep anything of yours, not even a thread or a sandal strap. Then you can never say, 'I am the one who made Abram rich.' 24 I will take nothing for myself. I will accept only what my men have used. But let my allies, Aner, Eshcol, and Mamre, take their share."

God's Covenant with Abram

15 After this, Abram had a vision and heard the LORD say to him, "Do not be afraid, Abram. I will shield you from danger and give you a great reward."

13.15: Acts 7.5   **14.18-20:** Heb 7.1-10

2 But Abram answered, "Sovereign LORD, what good will your reward do me, since I have no children? My only heir is Eliezer of Damascus.[x] 3 You have given me no children, and one of my slaves will inherit my property."

4 Then he heard the LORD speaking to him again: "This slave Eliezer will not inherit your property; your own son will be your heir." 5 The LORD took him outside and said, "Look at the sky and try to count the stars; you will have as many descendants as that."

6 Abram put his trust in the LORD, and because of this the LORD was pleased with him and accepted him.

7 Then the LORD said to him, "I am the LORD, who led you out of Ur in Babylonia, to give you this land as your own."

8 But Abram asked, "Sovereign LORD, how can I know that it will be mine?"

9 He answered, "Bring me a cow, a goat, and a ram, each of them three years old, and a dove and a pigeon." 10 Abram brought the animals to God, cut them in half, and placed the halves opposite each other in two rows; but he did not cut up the birds. 11 Vultures came down on the bodies, but Abram drove them off.

12 When the sun was going down, Abram fell into a deep sleep, and fear and terror came over him. 13 The LORD said to him, "Your descendants will be strangers in a foreign land; they will be slaves there and will be treated cruelly for four hundred years. 14 But I will punish the nation that enslaves them, and when they leave that foreign land, they will take great wealth with them. 15 You yourself will live to a ripe old age, die in peace, and be buried. 16 It will be four generations before your descendants come back here, because I will not drive out the Amorites until they become so wicked that they must be punished."

17 When the sun had set and it was dark, a smoking fire-pot and a flaming torch suddenly appeared and passed between the pieces of the animals. 18 Then and there the LORD made a covenant with Abram. He said, "I promise to give your descendants all this land from the border of Egypt to the River Euphrates, 19 including the lands of the Kenites, the Keniz-

zites, the Kadmonites, 20 the Hittites, the Perizzites, the Rephaim, 21 the Amorites, the Canaanites, the Girgashites, and the Jebusites."

Hagar and Ishmael

16 Abram's wife Sarai had not borne him any children. But she had an Egyptian slave-girl named Hagar, 2 and so she said to Abram, "The LORD has kept me from having children. Why don't you sleep with my slave-girl? Perhaps she can have a child for me." Abram agreed with what Sarai said. 3 So she gave Hagar to' him to be his concubine. (This happened after Abram had lived in Canaan for ten years.) 4 Abram had intercourse with Hagar, and she became pregnant. When she found out that she was pregnant, she became proud and despised Sarai.

5 Then Sarai said to Abram, "It's your fault that Hagar despises me.[d] I myself gave her to you, and ever since she found out that she was pregnant, she has despised me. May the LORD judge which of us is right, you or me!"

6 Abram answered, "Very well, she is your slave and under your control; do whatever you want with her." Then Sarai treated Hagar so cruelly that she ran away.

7 The angel of the LORD met Hagar at a spring in the desert on the road to Shur 8 and said, "Hagar, slave of Sarai, where have you come from and where are you going?"

She answered, "I am running away from my mistress."

9 He said, "Go back to her and be her slave." 10 Then he said, "I will give you so many descendants that no one will be able to count them. 11 You are going to have a son, and you will name him Ishmael,[e] because the LORD has heard your cry of distress. 12 But your son will live like a wild donkey; he will be against everyone, and everyone will be against him. He will live apart from all his relatives."

13 Hagar asked herself, "Have I really seen God and lived to tell about it?"[f] So she called the LORD who had spoken to her "A God Who Sees." 14 That is why people call the well between Kadesh and

[x] My...Damascus; Hebrew unclear
[d] It's your fault...me; or May you suffer for this wrong done against me.
[e] ISHMAEL: This name in Hebrew means "God hears."
[f] Probable text lived to tell about it?; Hebrew unclear.
15.5: Rom 4.18; Heb 11.12　　**15.6:** Rom 4.3; Gal 3.6; Jas 2.23　　**15.12:** Job 4.13,14
15.13: Ex 1.1–14; Acts 7.6　　**15.14:** Ex 12.40–41; Acts 7.7　　**15.18:** Acts 7.5

Bered "The Well of the Living One Who Sees Me."

15 Hagar bore Abram a son, and he named him Ishmael. 16 Abram was eighty-six years old at the time.

Circumcision, the Sign of the Covenant

17 When Abram was ninety-nine years old, the LORD appeared to him and said, "I am the Almighty God. Obey me and always do what is right. 2 I will make my covenant with you and give you many descendants." 3 Abram bowed down with his face touching the ground, and God said, 4 "I make this covenant with you: I promise that you will be the ancestor of many nations. 5 Your name will no longer be Abram, but Abraham,*g* because I am making you the ancestor of many nations. 6 I will give you many descendants, and some of them will be kings. You will have so many descendants that they will become nations.

7 "I will keep my promise to you and to your descendants in future generations as an everlasting covenant. I will be your God and the God of your descendants. 8 I will give to you and to your descendants this land in which you are now a foreigner. The whole land of Canaan will belong to your descendants for ever, and I will be their God."

9 God said to Abraham, "You also must agree to keep the covenant with me, both you and your descendants in future generations. 10 You and your descendants must all agree to circumcise every male among you. 11-12 From now on you must circumcise every baby boy when he is eight days old, including slaves born in your homes and slaves bought from foreigners. This will show that there is a covenant between you and me. 13 Each one must be circumcised, and this will be a physical sign to show that my covenant with you is everlasting. 14 Any male who has not been circumcised will no longer be considered one of my people, because he has not kept the covenant with me."

15 God said to Abraham, "You must no longer call your wife Sarai; from now on her name is Sarah.*x* 16 I will bless her, and I will give you a son by her. I will bless her, and she will become the mother

of nations, and there will be kings among her descendants."

17 Abraham bowed down with his face touching the ground, but he began to laugh when he thought, "Can a man have a child when he is a hundred years old? Can Sarah have a child at ninety?" 18 He asked God, "Why not let Ishmael be my heir?"

19 But God said, "No. Your wife Sarah will bear you a son and you will name him Isaac.*h* I will keep my covenant with him and with his descendants for ever. It is an everlasting covenant. 20 I have heard your request about Ishmael, so I will bless him and give him many children and many descendants. He will be the father of twelve princes, and I will make a great nation of his descendants. 21 But I will keep my covenant with your son Isaac, who will be born to Sarah about this time next year." 22 When God finished speaking to Abraham, he left him.

23 On that same day Abraham obeyed God and circumcised his son Ishmael and all the other males in his household, including the slaves born in his home and those he had bought. 24 Abraham was ninety-nine years old when he was circumcised, 25 and his son Ishmael was thirteen. 26 They were both circumcised on the same day, 27 together with all Abraham's slaves.

A Son Is Promised to Abraham

18 The LORD appeared to Abraham at the sacred trees of Mamre. As Abraham was sitting at the entrance of his tent during the hottest part of the day, 2 he looked up and saw three men standing there. As soon as he saw them, he ran out to meet them. Bowing down with his face touching the ground, 3 he said, "Sirs, please do not pass by my home without stopping; I am here to serve you. 4 Let me bring some water for you to wash your feet; you can rest here beneath this tree. 5 I will also bring a bit of food; it will give you strength to continue your journey. You have honoured me by coming to my home, so let me serve you."

They replied, "Thank you; we accept."

6 Abraham hurried into the tent and said to Sarah, "Quick, take a sack of your best flour, and bake some bread." 7 Then he ran to the herd and picked out a calf

---

g ABRAHAM: *This name sounds like the Hebrew for "ancestor of many nations."*
x SARAH: *This name in Hebrew means "princess."*
h ISAAC: *This name in Hebrew means "he laughs."*
16.15: Gal 4.22   **17.5:** Rom 4.17   **17.7:** Lk 1.55   **17.8:** Acts 7.5
17.10: Acts 7.8; Rom 4.11   **18.2a:** Heb 13.2

that was tender and fat, and gave it to a servant, who hurried to get it ready. 8 He took some cream, some milk, and the meat, and set the food before the men. There under the tree he served them himself, and they ate.

9 Then they asked him, "Where is your wife Sarah?"

"She is there in the tent," he answered.

10 One of them said, "Nine months from now[i] I will come back, and your wife Sarah will have a son."

Sarah was behind him, at the door of the tent, listening. 11 Abraham and Sarah were very old, and Sarah had stopped having her monthly periods. 12 So Sarah laughed to herself and said, "Now that I am old and worn out, can I still enjoy sex? And besides, my husband is old too."

13 Then the LORD asked Abraham, "Why did Sarah laugh and say, 'Can I really have a child when I am so old?' 14 Is anything too hard for the LORD? As I said, nine months from now I will return, and Sarah will have a son."

15 Because Sarah was afraid, she denied it. "I didn't laugh," she said.

"Yes, you did," he replied. "You laughed."

Abraham Pleads for Sodom

16 Then the men left and went to a place where they could look down at Sodom, and Abraham went with them to send them on their way. 17 And the LORD said to himself, "I will not hide from Abraham what I am going to do. 18 His descendants will become a great and mighty nation, and through him I will bless all the nations.[j] 19 I have chosen him in order that he may command his sons and his descendants to obey me and to do what is right and just. If they do, I will do everything for him that I have promised."

20 Then the LORD said to Abraham, "There are terrible accusations against Sodom and Gomorrah, and their sin is very great. 21 I must go down to find out whether or not the accusations which I have heard are true."

22 Then the two men left and went on towards Sodom, but the LORD remained with Abraham. 23 Abraham approached the LORD and asked, "Are you really going to destroy the innocent with the guilty? 24 If there are fifty innocent people in the city, will you destroy the whole city? Won't you spare it in order to save the fifty? 25 Surely you won't kill the innocent with the guilty. That's impossible! You can't do that. If you did, the innocent would be punished along with the guilty. That is impossible. The judge of all the earth has to act justly."

26 The LORD answered, "If I find fifty innocent people in Sodom, I will spare the whole city for their sake."

27 Abraham spoke again: "Please forgive my boldness in continuing to speak to you, Lord. I am only a man and have no right to say anything. 28 But perhaps there will be only forty-five innocent people instead of fifty. Will you destroy the whole city because there are five too few?"

The LORD answered, "I will not destroy the city if I find forty-five innocent people."

29 Abraham spoke again: "Perhaps there will be only forty."

He replied, "I will not destroy it if there are forty."

30 Abraham said, "Please don't be angry, Lord, but I must speak again. What if there are only thirty?"

He said, "I will not do it if I find thirty."

31 Abraham said, "Please forgive my boldness in continuing to speak to you, Lord. Suppose that only twenty are found?"

He said, "I will not destroy the city if I find twenty."

32 Abraham said, "Please don't be angry, Lord, and I will speak just once more. What if only ten are found?"

He said, "I will not destroy it if there are ten." 33 After he had finished speaking with Abraham, the LORD went away, and Abraham returned home.

The Sinfulness of Sodom

19 When the two angels came to Sodom that evening, Lot was sitting at the city gate. As soon as he saw them, he got up and went to meet them. He bowed down before them 2 and said, "Sirs, I am here to serve you. Please come to my house. You can wash your feet and stay the night. In the morning you can get up early and go on your way."

But they answered, "No, we will spend the night here in the city square."

---

[i] Nine months from now; *or* This time next year.
[j] through...nations; *or* all the nations will ask me to bless them as I have blessed him.
18.10: Rom 9.9   **18.12:** 1 Pet 3.6   **18.14:** Lk 1.37

3 He kept on urging them, and finally they went with him to his house. Lot ordered his servants to bake some bread and prepare a fine meal for the guests. When it was ready, they ate it.

4 Before the guests went to bed, the men of Sodom surrounded the house. All the men of the city, both young and old, were there. 5 They called out to Lot and asked, "Where are the men who came to stay with you tonight? Bring them out to us!" The men of Sodom wanted to have sex with them.

6 Lot went outside and closed the door behind him. 7 He said to them, "Friends, I beg you, don't do such a wicked thing! 8 Look, I have two daughters who are still virgins. Let me bring them out to you, and you can do whatever you want with them. But don't do anything to these men; they are guests in my house, and I must protect them."

9 But they said, "Get out of our way, you foreigner! Who are you to tell us what to do? Out of our way, or we will treat you worse than them." They pushed Lot back and moved up to break down the door. 10 But the two men inside reached out, pulled Lot back into the house, and shut the door. 11 Then they struck all the men outside with blindness, so that they couldn't find the door.

Lot Leaves Sodom

12 The two men said to Lot, "If you have anyone else here—sons, daughters, sons-in-law, or any other relatives living in the city—get them out of here, 13 because we are going to destroy this place. The LORD has heard the terrible accusations against these people and has sent us to destroy Sodom."

14 Then Lot went to the men that his daughters were going to marry, and said, "Hurry up and get out of here; the LORD is going to destroy this place." But they thought he was joking.

15 At dawn the angels tried to make Lot hurry. "Quick!" they said. "Take your wife and your two daughters and get out, so that you will not lose your lives when the city is destroyed." 16 Lot hesitated. The LORD, however, had pity on him; so the men took him, his wife, and his two daughters by the hand and led them out of the city. 17 Then one of the angels said,

"Run for your lives! Don't look back and don't stop in the valley. Run to the hills, so that you won't be killed."

18 But Lot answered, "No, please don't make us do that, sir. 19 You have done me a great favour and saved my life. But the hills are too far away; the disaster will overtake me, and I will die before I get there. 20 Do you see that little town? It is near enough. Let me go over there— you can see it is just a small place—and I will be safe."

21 He answered, "All right, I agree. I won't destroy that town. 22 Hurry! Run! I can't do anything until you get there."

Because Lot called it small, the town was named Zoar. [k]

The Destruction of Sodom and Gomorrah

23 The sun was rising when Lot reached Zoar. 24 Suddenly the LORD rained burning sulphur on the cities of Sodom and Gomorrah 25 and destroyed them and the whole valley, along with all the people there and everything that grew on the land. 26 But Lot's wife looked back and was turned into a pillar of salt.

27 Early the next morning Abraham hurried to the place where he had stood in the presence of the LORD. 28 He looked down at Sodom and Gomorrah and the whole valley and saw smoke rising from the land, like smoke from a huge furnace. 29 But when God destroyed the cities of the valley where Lot was living, he kept Abraham in mind and allowed Lot to escape to safety.

The Origin of the Moabites and Ammonites

30 Because Lot was afraid to stay in Zoar, he and his two daughters moved up into the hills and lived in a cave. 31 The elder daughter said to her sister, "Our father is getting old, and there are no men in the whole world [l] to marry us so that we can have children. 32 Come on, let's make our father drunk, so that we can sleep with him and have children by him." 33 That night they gave him wine to drink, and the elder daughter had intercourse with him. But he was so drunk that he didn't know it.

34 The next day the elder daughter said to her sister, "I slept with him last night; now let's make him drunk again tonight, and you sleep with him. Then each of

---

[k]ZOAR: *This name sounds like the Hebrew for "small."*　　　[l]the whole world; *or* this land.

19.5–8: Judg 19.22–24　　**19.11:** 2 Kgs 6.18　　**19.16:** 2 Pet 2.7
19.24–25: Mt 10.15, 11.23–24; Lk 10.12, 17.29; 2 Pet 2.6; Jude 7　　**19.26:** Lk 17.32

Lot's wife looked back (19.26)

us will have a child by our father." ³⁵ So that night they made him drunk, and the younger daughter had intercourse with him. Again he was so drunk that he didn't know it. ³⁶ In this way both of Lot's daughters became pregnant by their own father. ³⁷ The elder daughter had a son, whom she named Moab.ᵐ He was the ancestor of the present-day Moabites. ³⁸ The younger daughter also had a son, whom she named Benammi.ⁿ He was the ancestor of the present-day Ammonites.

Abraham and Abimelech

20 Abraham moved from Mamre to the southern part of Canaan and lived between Kadesh and Shur. Later, while he was living in Gerar, ² he said that his wife Sarah was his sister. So King Abimelech of Gerar had Sarah brought to him. ³ One night God appeared to him in a dream and said: "You are going to die, because you have taken this woman; she is already married."

⁴ But Abimelech had not come near her, and he said, "Lord, I am innocent! Would you destroy me and my people? ⁵ Abraham himself said that she was his sister,

and she said the same thing. I did this with a clear conscience, and I have done no wrong."

⁶ God replied in the dream, "Yes, I know that you did it with a clear conscience; so I kept you from sinning against me and did not let you touch her. ⁷ But now, give the woman back to her husband. He is a prophet, and he will pray for you, so that you will not die. But if you do not give her back, I warn you that you are going to die, you and all your people."

⁸ Early the next morning Abimelech called all his officials and told them what had happened, and they were terrified. ⁹ Then Abimelech called Abraham and asked, "What have you done to us? What wrong have I done to you to make you bring this disaster on me and my kingdom? No one should ever do what you have done to me. ¹⁰ Why did you do it?"

11 Abraham answered, "I thought that there would be no one here who has reverence for God and that they would kill me to get my wife. ¹² She really is my sister. She is the daughter of my father,

ᵐ MOAB: *This name sounds like the Hebrew for "from my father."*
ⁿ BENAMMI: *This name in Hebrew means "son of my relative" and sounds like the Hebrew for "Ammonite."*
20.2: Gen 12.13, 26.7

but not of my mother, and I married her. [13] So when God sent me from my father's house into foreign lands, I said to her, 'You can show how loyal you are to me by telling everyone that I am your brother.' "

14 Then Abimelech gave Sarah back to Abraham, and at the same time he gave him sheep, cattle, and slaves. [15] He said to Abraham, "Here is my whole land; live anywhere you like." [16] He said to Sarah, "I am giving your brother a thousand pieces of silver as proof to all who are with you that you are innocent; everyone will know that you have done no wrong."

17-18 Because of what had happened to Sarah, Abraham's wife, the LORD had made it impossible for any woman in Abimelech's palace to have children. So Abraham prayed for Abimelech, and God healed him. He also healed his wife and his slave-girls, so that they could have children.

The Birth of Isaac

21 The LORD blessed Sarah, as he had promised, [2] and she became pregnant and bore a son to Abraham when he was old. The boy was born at the time God had said he would be born. [3] Abraham named him Isaac, [4] and when Isaac was eight days old, Abraham circumcised him, as God had commanded. [5] Abraham was a hundred years old when Isaac was born. [6] Sarah said, "God has brought me joy and laughter.[m] Everyone who hears about it will laugh with me." [7] Then she added, "Who would have said to Abraham that Sarah would nurse children? Yet I have borne him a son in his old age."

8 The child grew, and on the day that he was weaned, Abraham gave a great feast.

Hagar and Ishmael Are Sent Away

9 One day Ishmael, whom Hagar the Egyptian had borne to Abraham, was playing with[n] Sarah's son Isaac.[o] [10] Sarah saw them and said to Abraham, "Send this slave-girl and her son away. The son of this slave woman must not get any part of your wealth, which my son Isaac should inherit." [11] This troubled Abraham very much, because Ishmael was also his son.

[12] But God said to Abraham, "Don't be worried about the boy and your slave Hagar. Do whatever Sarah tells you, because it is through Isaac that you will have the descendants I have promised. [13] I will also give many children to the son of the slave-girl, so that they will become a nation. He too is your son."

14 Early the next morning Abraham gave Hagar some food and a leather bag full of water. He put the child on her back and sent her away. She left and wandered about in the wilderness of Beersheba. [15] When the water was all gone, she left the child under a bush [16] and sat down about a hundred metres away. She said to herself, "I can't bear to see my child die." While she was sitting there, she[p] began to cry.

17 God heard the boy crying, and from heaven the angel of God spoke to Hagar, "What are you troubled about, Hagar? Don't be afraid. God has heard the boy crying. [18] Get up, go and pick him up, and comfort him. I will make a great nation out of his descendants." [19] Then God opened her eyes, and she saw a well. She went and filled the leather bag with water and gave some to the boy. [20] God was with the boy as he grew up; he lived in the wilderness of Paran and became a skilful hunter. [21] His mother found an Egyptian wife for him.

The Agreement between Abraham and Abimelech

22 At that time Abimelech went with Phicol, the commander of his army, and said to Abraham, "God is with you in everything you do. [23] So make a vow here in the presence of God that you will not deceive me, my children, or my descendants. I have been loyal to you, so promise that you will also be loyal to me and to this country in which you are living."

24 Abraham said, "I promise."

25 Abraham complained to Abimelech about a well which the servants of Abimelech had seized. [26] Abimelech said, "I don't know who did this. You didn't tell me about it, and this is the first I have heard of it." [27] Then Abraham gave some sheep and cattle to Abimelech, and

---

[m] LAUGHTER: *The name Isaac in Hebrew means "he laughs" (see also 17.17–19).*
[n] playing with; *or making fun of.*
[o] *Some ancient translations* with Sarah's son Isaac; *Hebrew does not have these words.*
[p] she; *one ancient translation* the child.

21.2: Heb 11.11   **21.4:** Gen 17.12; Acts 7.8   **21.10:** Gal 4.29–30   **21.12:** Rom 9.7; Heb 11.18
21.22: Gen 26.26

the two of them made an agreement.
[28] Abraham separated seven lambs from his flock, [29] and Abimelech asked him, "Why did you do that?"

30 Abraham answered, "Accept these seven lambs. By doing this, you admit that I am the one who dug this well." [31] And so the place was called Beersheba, [q] because it was there that the two of them made a vow.

32 After they had made this agreement at Beersheba, Abimelech and Phicol went back to Philistia. [33] Then Abraham planted a tamarisk-tree in Beersheba and worshipped the LORD, the Everlasting God. [34] Abraham lived in Philistia for a long time.

God Commands Abraham to Offer Isaac

22 Some time later God tested Abraham; he called to him, "Abraham!" And Abraham answered, "Yes, here I am!"

2 "Take your son," God said, "your only son, Isaac, whom you love so much, and go to the land of Moriah. There on a mountain that I will show you, offer him as a sacrifice to me."

3 Early the next morning Abraham cut some wood for the sacrifice, loaded his donkey, and took Isaac and two servants with him. They started out for the place that God had told him about. [4] On the third day Abraham saw the place in the distance. [5] Then he said to the servants, "Stay here with the donkey. The boy and I will go over there and worship, and then we will come back to you."

6 Abraham made Isaac carry the wood for the sacrifice, and he himself carried a knife and live coals for starting the fire. As they walked along together, [7] Isaac said, "Father!"

He answered, "Yes, my son?"

Isaac asked, "I see that you have the coals and the wood, but where is the lamb for the sacrifice?"

8 Abraham answered, "God himself will provide one." And the two of them walked on together.

9 When they came to the place which God had told him about, Abraham built an altar and arranged the wood on it. He tied up his son and placed him on the altar, on top of the wood. [10] Then he picked up the knife to kill him. [11] But the angel of the LORD called to him from heaven, "Abraham, Abraham!"

He answered, "Yes, here I am."

12 "Don't hurt the boy or do anything

Now I know that you honour and obey God (22.12)

to him," he said. "Now I know that you honour and obey God, because you have not kept back your only son from me."

13 Abraham looked round and saw a ram caught in a bush by its horns. He went and got it and offered it as a burnt-offering instead of his son. [14] Abraham named that place "The LORD Provides." [r] And even today people say, "On the LORD's mountain he provides." [s]

15 The angel of the LORD called to Abraham from heaven a second time, [16] "I make a vow by my own name—the LORD is speaking—that I will richly bless you. Because you did this and did not keep back your only son from me, [17] I promise that I will give you as many descendants as there are stars in the sky or grains of sand along the seashore. Your descendants will conquer their enemies. [18] All the nations will ask me to bless them as I have blessed your descendants—all

---

[q] BEERSHEBA: *This name in Hebrew means "Well of the Vow" or "Well of Seven" (see also 26.33).*
[r] Provides; *or* Sees.   [s] provides; *or* is seen.
22.1-13: Heb 11.17-19   **22.2:** 2 Chr 3.1   **22.9:** Jas 2.21   **22.16-17:** Heb 6.13-14
22.17: Heb 11.12   **22.18:** Acts 3.25

because you obeyed my command."
19 Abraham went back to his servants, and they went together to Beersheba, where Abraham settled.

The Descendants of Nahor

20 Some time later Abraham learnt that Milcah had borne eight children to his brother Nahor: 21 Uz the first-born, Buz his brother, Kemuel the father of Aram, 22 Chesed, Hazo, Pildash, Jidlaph, and Bethuel, 23 Rebecca's father. Milcah bore these eight sons to Nahor, Abraham's brother. 24 Reumah, Nahor's concubine, bore Tebah, Gaham, Tahash, and Maacah.

Sarah Dies and Abraham Buys a Burial-Ground

23 Sarah lived to be a hundred and twenty-seven years old. 2 She died in Hebron in the land of Canaan, and Abraham mourned her death.

3 He left the place where his wife's body was lying, went to the Hittites, and said, 4 "I am a foreigner living here among you; sell me some land, so that I can bury my wife."

5 They answered, 6 "Listen to us, sir. We look upon you as a mighty leader; bury your wife in the best grave that we have. Any of us would be glad to give you a grave, so that you can bury her."

7 Then Abraham bowed before them 8 and said, "If you are willing to let me bury my wife here, please ask Ephron son of Zohar 9 to sell me Machpelah Cave, which is near the edge of his field. Ask him to sell it to me for its full price, here in your presence, so that I can own it as a burial-ground."

10 Ephron himself was sitting with the other Hittites at the meeting-place at the city gate; he answered in the hearing of everyone there, 11 "Listen, sir; I will give you the whole field and the cave that is in it. Here in the presence of my own people, I will give it to you, so that you can bury your wife."

12 But Abraham bowed before the Hittites 13 and said to Ephron, so that everyone could hear, "May I ask you, please, to listen. I will buy the whole field. Accept my payment, and I will bury my wife there."

14 Ephron answered, 15 "Sir, land worth only four hundred pieces of silver—what is that between us? Bury your wife in

it." 16 Abraham agreed and weighed out the amount that Ephron had mentioned in the hearing of the people—four hundred pieces of silver, according to the standard weights used by the merchants.

17 That is how the property which had belonged to Ephron at Machpelah, east of Mamre, became Abraham's. It included the field, the cave which was in it, and all the trees in the field up to the edge of the property. 18 It was recognized as Abraham's property by all the Hittites who were there at the meeting.

19 Then Abraham buried his wife Sarah in that cave in the land of Canaan. 20 So the field which had belonged to the Hittites, and the cave in it, became the property of Abraham for a burial-ground.

A Wife for Isaac

24 Abraham was now very old, and the LORD had blessed him in everything he did. 2 He said to his oldest servant, who was in charge of all that he had, "Place your hand between my thighs [t] and make a vow. 3 I want you to make a vow in the name of the LORD, the God of heaven and earth, that you will not choose a wife for my son from the people here in Canaan. 4 You must go back to the country where I was born and get a wife for my son Isaac from among my relatives."

5 But the servant asked, "What if the girl will not leave home to come with me to this land? Shall I send your son back to the land you came from?"

6 Abraham answered, "Make sure that you don't send my son back there! 7 The LORD, the God of heaven, brought me from the home of my father and from the land of my relatives, and he solemnly promised me that he would give this land to my descendants. He will send his angel before you, so that you can get a wife there for my son. 8 If the girl is not willing to come with you, you will be free from this promise. But you must not under any circumstances take my son back there." 9 So the servant put his hand between the thighs of Abraham, his master, and made a vow to do what Abraham had asked.

10 The servant, who was in charge of Abraham's property, took ten of his master's camels and went to the city where Nahor had lived in northern Mesopotamia. 11 When he arrived, he

---

[t] PLACE...THIGHS: *This was the way in which a vow was made absolutely unchangeable.*
23.4: Heb 11.9,13; Acts 7.16

Rebecca arrived (24.15)

made the camels kneel down at the well outside the city. It was late afternoon, the time when women came out to get water. 12 He prayed, "LORD, God of my master Abraham, give me success today and keep your promise to my master. 13 Here I am at the well where the young women of the city will be coming to get water. 14 I will say to one of them, 'Please, lower your jar and let me have a drink.' If she says, 'Drink, and I will also bring water for your camels,' may she be the one that you have chosen for your servant Isaac. If this happens, I will know that you have kept your promise to my master."

15 Before he had finished praying, Rebecca arrived with a water-jar on her shoulder. She was the daughter of Bethuel, who was the son of Abraham's brother Nahor and his wife Milcah. 16 She was a very beautiful young girl and still a virgin. She went down to the well, filled her jar, and came back. 17 The servant ran to meet her and said, "Please give me a drink of water from your jar."

18 She said, "Drink, sir," and quickly lowered her jar from her shoulder and held it while he drank. 19 When he had finished, she said, "I will also bring water for your camels and let them have all

they want." 20 She quickly emptied her jar into the animals' drinking-trough and ran to the well to get more water, until she had watered all his camels. 21 The man kept watching her in silence, to see if the LORD had given him success.

22 When she had finished, the man took an expensive gold ring and put it in her nose and put two large gold bracelets on her arms. 23 He said, "Please tell me who your father is. Is there room in his house for my men and me to spend the night?"

24 "My father is Bethuel son of Nahor and Milcah," she answered. 25 "There is plenty of straw and fodder at our house, and there is a place for you to stay."

26 Then the man knelt down and worshipped the LORD. 27 He said, "Praise the LORD, the God of my master Abraham, who has faithfully kept his promise to my master. The LORD has led me straight to my master's relatives."

28 The girl ran to her mother's house and told the whole story. 29 Now Rebecca had a brother named Laban, and he ran outside to go to the well where Abraham's servant was. 30 Laban had seen the nose-ring and the bracelets on his sister's arms and had heard her say what the man had told her. He went to Abraham's servant, who was standing by his camels at the

well, 31 and said, "Come home with me. You are a man whom the LORD has blessed. Why are you standing out here? I have a room ready for you in my house, and there is a place for your camels."

32 So the man went into the house, and Laban unloaded the camels and gave them straw and fodder. Then he brought water for Abraham's servant and his men to wash their feet. 33 When food was brought, the man said, "I will not eat until I have said what I have to say."

Laban said, "Go on and speak."

34 "I am the servant of Abraham," he began. 35 "The LORD has greatly blessed my master and made him a rich man. He has given him flocks of sheep and goats, cattle, silver, gold, male and female slaves, camels, and donkeys. 36 Sarah, my master's wife, bore him a son when she was old, and my master has given everything he owns to him. 37 My master made me promise with a vow to obey his command. He said, 'Do not choose a wife for my son from the girls in the land of Canaan. 38 Instead, go to my father's people, to my relatives, and choose a wife for him.' 39 And I asked my master, 'What if the girl will not come with me?' 40 He answered, 'The LORD, whom I have always obeyed, will send his angel with you and give you success. You will get for my son a wife from my own people, from my father's family. 41 There is only one way for you to be free from your vow: if you go to my relatives and they refuse you, then you will be free.'

42 "When I came to the well today, I prayed, 'LORD, God of my master Abraham, please give me success in what I am doing. 43 Here I am at the well. When a young woman comes out to get water, I will ask her to give me a drink of water from her jar. 44 If she agrees and also offers to bring water for my camels, may she be the one that you have chosen as the wife for my master's son.' 45 Before I had finished my silent prayer, Rebecca came with a water-jar on her shoulder and went down to the well to get water. I said to her, 'Please give me a drink.' 46 She quickly lowered her jar from her shoulder and said, 'Drink, and I will also water your camels.' So I drank, and she watered the camels. 47 I asked her, 'Who is your father?' And she answered, 'My father is Bethuel son of Nahor and Milcah.' Then I put the ring in her nose

and the bracelets on her arms. 48 I knelt down and worshipped the LORD. I praised the LORD, the God of my master Abraham, who had led me straight to my master's relative, where I found his daughter for my master's son. 49 Now, if you intend to fulfil your responsibility towards my master and treat him fairly, please tell me; if not, say so, and I will decide what to do."

50 Laban and Bethuel answered, "Since this matter comes from the LORD, it is not for us to make a decision. 51 Here is Rebecca; take her and go. Let her become the wife of your master's son, as the LORD himself has said." 52 When the servant of Abraham heard this, he bowed down and worshipped the LORD. 53 Then he brought out clothing and silver and gold jewellery, and gave them to Rebecca. He also gave expensive gifts to her brother and to her mother.

54 Then Abraham's servant and the men with him ate and drank, and spent the night there. When they got up in the morning, he said, "Let me go back to my master."

55 But Rebecca's brother and her mother said, "Let the girl stay with us a week or ten days, and then she may go."

56 But he said, "Don't make us stay. The LORD has made my journey a success; let me go back to my master."

57 They answered, "Let's call the girl and find out what she has to say." 58 So they called Rebecca and asked, "Do you want to go with this man?"

"Yes," she answered.

59 So they let Rebecca and her old family servant go with Abraham's servant and his men. 60 And they gave Rebecca their blessing in these words:

"May you, sister, become the mother
    of millions!
May your descendants conquer the
    cities of their enemies!"

61 Then Rebecca and her young women got ready and mounted the camels to go with Abraham's servant, and they all started out.

62 Isaac had come into the wilderness of v "The Well of the Living One Who Sees Me" and was staying in the southern part of Canaan. 63 He went out in the early evening to take a walk in the fields and saw camels coming. 64 When Rebecca saw Isaac, she got down from her camel 65 and

v Some ancient translations into the wilderness of; Hebrew from coming.

asked Abraham's servant, "Who is that man walking towards us in the field?"

"He is my master," the servant answered. So she took her scarf and covered her face.

66 The servant told Isaac everything he had done. 67 Then Isaac brought Rebecca into the tent that his mother Sarah had lived in, and she became his wife. Isaac loved Rebecca, and so he was comforted for the loss of his mother.

Other Descendants of Abraham
(1 Chr 1.32-33)

25 Abraham married another wife, whose name was Keturah. 2 She bore him Zimran, Jokshan, Medan, Midian, Ishbak, and Shuah. 3 Jokshan was the father of Sheba and Dedan, and the descendants of Dedan were the Asshurim, the Letushim, and the Leummim. 4 The sons of Midian were Ephah, Epher, Hanoch, Abida, and Eldaah. All these were Keturah's descendants.

5 Abraham left everything he owned to Isaac; 6 but while he was still alive, he gave presents to the sons his other wives had borne him. Then he sent these sons to the land of the East, away from his son Isaac.

The Death and Burial of Abraham

7-8 Abraham died at the ripe old age of a hundred and seventy-five. 9 His sons Isaac and Ishmael buried him in Machpelah Cave, in the field east of Mamre that had belonged to Ephron son of Zohar the Hittite. 10 It was the field that Abraham had bought from the Hittites; both Abraham and his wife Sarah were buried there. 11 After the death of Abraham, God blessed his son Isaac, who lived near "The Well of the Living One Who Sees Me."

The Descendants of Ishmael
(1 Chr 1.28-31)

12 Ishmael, whom Hagar, the Egyptian slave of Sarah, bore to Abraham, 13 had the following sons, listed in the order of their birth: Nebaioth, Kedar, Adbeel, Mibsam, 14 Mishma, Dumah, Massa, 15 Hadad, Tema, Jetur, Naphish, and Kedemah. 16 They were the ancestors of twelve tribes, and their names were given to their villages and camping-places.

17 Ishmael was a hundred and thirty-seven years old when he died. 18 The descendants of Ishmael lived in the territory between Havilah and Shur, to the east of Egypt on the way to Assyria. They lived apart from the other descendants of Abraham.

The Birth of Esau and Jacob

19 This is the story of Abraham's son Isaac. 20 Isaac was forty years old when he married Rebecca, the daughter of Bethuel (an Aramean from Mesopotamia) and sister of Laban. 21 Because Rebecca had no children, Isaac prayed to the LORD for her. The LORD answered his prayer, and Rebecca became pregnant. 22 She was going to have twins, and before they were born, they struggled against each other in her womb. She said, "Why should something like this happen to me?" So she went to ask the LORD for an answer.

23 The LORD said to her,

"Two nations are within you;
You will give birth to two rival peoples.
One will be stronger than the other;
The older will serve the younger."

24 The time came for her to give birth, and she had twin sons. 25 The first one was reddish, and his skin was like a hairy robe, so he was named Esau. w 26 The second one was born holding on tightly to the heel of Esau, so he was named Jacob. x Isaac was sixty years old when they were born.

Esau Sells His Rights as the First-Born Son

27 The boys grew up, and Esau became a skilled hunter, a man who loved the outdoor life, but Jacob was a quiet man who stayed at home. 28 Isaac preferred Esau, because he enjoyed eating the animals Esau killed, but Rebecca preferred Jacob.

29 One day while Jacob was cooking some bean soup, Esau came in from hunting. He was hungry 30 and said to Jacob, "I'm starving; give me some of that red stuff." (That is why he was called Edom.) y

31 Jacob answered, "I will give it to you if you give me your rights as the first-born son."

32 Esau said, "All right! I am about

---

w ESAU: *This name is taken to refer to Seir, the territory later inhabited by Esau's descendants; Seir sounds like the Hebrew for "hairy."*
x JACOB: *This name sounds like the Hebrew for "heel."*
y EDOM: *This name sounds like the Hebrew for "red."*
25.10: Gen 23.3-16   **25.23:** Rom 9.12

Then Jacob gave him...some of the soup (25.34)

and kept all my laws and commands."

6 So Isaac lived at Gerar. [7] When the men there asked about his wife, he said that she was his sister. He would not admit that she was his wife, because he was afraid that the men there would kill him to get Rebecca, who was very beautiful. [8] When Isaac had been there for some time, King Abimelech looked down from his window and saw Isaac and Rebecca making love. [9] Abimelech sent for Isaac and said, "So she is your wife! Why did you say she was your sister?"

He answered, "I thought I would be killed if I said she was my wife."

10 "What have you done to us?" Abimelech said. "One of my men might easily have slept with your wife, and you would have been responsible for our guilt." [11] Abimelech warned all the people: "Anyone who ill-treats this man or his wife will be put to death."

12 Isaac sowed seed in that land, and that year he harvested a hundred times as much as he had sown, because the LORD blessed him. [13] He continued to prosper and became a very rich man. [14] Because he had many herds of sheep and cattle and many servants, the Philistines were jealous of him. [15] So they filled in all the wells which the servants of his father Abraham had dug while Abraham was alive.

16 Then Abimelech said to Isaac, "Leave our country. You have become more powerful than we are." [17] So Isaac left and set up his camp in the Valley of Gerar, where he stayed for some time. [18] He dug once again the wells which had been dug during the time of Abraham and which the Philistines had stopped up after Abraham's death. Isaac gave the wells the same names that his father had given them.

19 Isaac's servants dug a well in the valley and found water. [20] The shepherds of Gerar quarrelled with Isaac's shepherds and said, "This water belongs to us." So Isaac named the well "Quarrel."

21 Isaac's servants dug another well, and there was a quarrel about that one also, so he named it "Enmity." [22] He moved away from there and dug another well. There was no dispute about this one, so he named it "Freedom." He said, "Now the LORD has given us freedom to live in the land, and we will be prosperous here."

to die; what good will my rights do me then?"

33 Jacob answered, "First make a vow that you will give me your rights."

Esau made the vow and gave his rights to Jacob. [34] Then Jacob gave him some bread and some of the soup. He ate and drank and then got up and left. That was all Esau cared about his rights as the first-born son.

Isaac Lives at Gerar

26 There was another famine in the land besides the earlier one during the time of Abraham. Isaac went to Abimelech, king of the Philistines, at Gerar. [2] The LORD had appeared to Isaac and had said, "Do not go to Egypt; stay in this land, where I tell you to stay. [3] Live here, and I will be with you and bless you. I am going to give all this territory to you and to your descendants. I will keep the promise I made to your father Abraham. [4] I will give you as many descendants as there are stars in the sky, and I will give them all this territory. All the nations will ask me to bless them as I have blessed your descendants. [5] I will bless you, because Abraham obeyed me

25.33: Heb 12.16   **26.3-4:** Gen 22.16-18   **26.7:** Gen 12.13, 20.2

23 Isaac left and went to Beersheba.
24 That night the LORD appeared to him
and said, "I am the God of your father
Abraham. Do not be afraid; I am with
you. I will bless you and give you many
descendants because of my promise to my
servant Abraham." 25 Isaac built an altar
there and worshipped the LORD. Then he
set up his camp there, and his servants
dug another well.

The Agreement between Isaac and Abimelech

26 Abimelech came from Gerar with
Ahuzzath his adviser and Phicol the
commander of his army to see Isaac. 27 So
Isaac asked, "Why have you now come
to see me, when you were so unfriendly
to me before and made me leave your
country?"

28 They answered, "Now we know that
the LORD is with you, and we think that
there should be a solemn agreement
between us. We want you to promise
29 that you will not harm us, just as we
did not harm you. We were kind to you
and let you leave peacefully. Now it is
clear that the LORD has blessed you."
30 Isaac prepared a feast for them, and
they ate and drank. 31 Early next morning
each man made his promise and sealed
it with a vow. Isaac said good-bye to them,
and they parted as friends.

32 On that day Isaac's servants came
and told him about the well which they
had dug. They said, "We have found
water." 33 He named the well "Vow." That
is how the city of Beersheba z got its name.

Esau's Foreign Wives

34 When Esau was forty years old, he
married two Hittite girls, Judith the
daughter of Beeri, and Basemath the
daughter of Elon. 35 They made life
miserable for Isaac and Rebecca.

Isaac Blesses Jacob

27 Isaac was now old and had become
blind. He sent for his elder son
Esau and said to him, "My son!"

"Yes," he answered.

2 Isaac said, "You see that I am old
and may die soon. 3 Take your bow and
arrows, go out into the country, and kill
an animal for me. 4 Cook me some of that
tasty food that I like, and bring it to me.

After I have eaten it, I will give you my
final blessing before I die."

5 While Isaac was talking to Esau,
Rebecca was listening. So when Esau
went out to hunt, 6 she said to Jacob, "I
have just heard your father say to Esau,
7 'Bring me an animal and cook it for me.
After I have eaten it, I will give you my
blessing in the presence of the LORD before
I die.' 8 Now, my son," Rebecca continued,
"listen to me and do what I say. 9 Go
to the flock and pick out two fat young
goats, so that I can cook them and make
some of that food your father likes so
much. 10 You can take it to him to eat,
and he will give you his blessing before
he dies."

11 But Jacob said to his mother, "You
know that Esau is a hairy man, but I
have smooth skin. 12 Perhaps my father
will touch me and find out that I am
deceiving him; in this way I will bring
a curse on myself instead of a blessing."

13 His mother answered, "Let any curse
against you fall on me, my son; just do
as I say, and go and get the goats for
me." 14 So he went to get them and
brought them to her, and she cooked the
kind of food that his father liked. 15 Then
she took Esau's best clothes, which she
kept in the house, and put them on Jacob.
16 She put the skins of the goats on his
arms and on the hairless part of his neck.
17 She handed him the tasty food, together
with the bread she had baked.

18 Then Jacob went to his father and
said, "Father!"

"Yes," he answered. "Which of my sons
are you?"

19 Jacob answered, "I am your elder
son Esau; I have done as you told me.
Please sit up and eat some of the meat
that I have brought you, so that you can
give me your blessing."

20 Isaac said, "How did you find it so
quickly, my son?"

Jacob answered, "The LORD your God
helped me to find it."

21 Isaac said to Jacob, "Please come
closer so that I can touch you. Are you
really Esau?" 22 Jacob moved closer to his
father, who felt him and said, "Your voice
sounds like Jacob's voice, but your arms
feel like Esau's arms." 23 He did not
recognize Jacob, because his arms were
hairy like Esau's. He was about to give

---

z BEERSHEBA: *This name in Hebrew means "Well of the Vow" or "Well of Seven" (see also 21.31).*
26.26: Gen 21.22

He gave him his blessing (27.27)

him his blessing, 24 but asked again, "Are you really Esau?"

"I am," he answered.

25 Isaac said, "Bring me some of the meat. After I have eaten it, I will give you my blessing." Jacob brought it to him, and he also brought him some wine to drink. 26 Then his father said to him, "Come closer and kiss me, my son." 27 As he came up to kiss him, Isaac smelt his clothes—so he gave him his blessing. He said, "The pleasant smell of my son is like the smell of a field which the LORD has blessed. 28 May God give you dew from heaven and make your fields fertile! May he give you plenty of corn and wine! 29 May nations be your servants, and may peoples bow down before you. May you rule over all your relatives, and may your mother's descendants bow down before you. May those who curse you be cursed, and may those who bless you be blessed."

Esau Begs for Isaac's Blessing

30 Isaac finished giving his blessing, and as soon as Jacob left, his brother Esau came in from hunting. 31 He also cooked some tasty food and took it to his father. He said, "Please, father, sit up and eat some of the meat that I have brought you, so that you can give me your blessing."

32 "Who are you?" Isaac asked.

"Your elder son Esau," he answered.

33 Isaac began to tremble and shake all over, and he asked, "Who was it, then, who killed an animal and brought it to me? I ate it just before you came. I gave him my final blessing, and so it is his for ever."

34 When Esau heard this, he cried out loudly and bitterly and said, "Give me your blessing also, father!"

35 Isaac answered, "Your brother came and deceived me. He has taken away your blessing."

36 Esau said, "This is the second time that he has cheated me. No wonder his name is Jacob.[a] He took my rights as the first-born son, and now he has taken away my blessing. Haven't you saved a blessing for me?"

[a] JACOB: *This name sounds like the Hebrew for "cheat."*
27.27-29: Heb 11.20   **27.29:** Gen 12.3   **27.36:** Gen 25.29-34

37 Isaac answered, "I have already made him master over you, and I have made all his relatives his slaves. I have given him corn and wine. Now there is nothing that I can do for you, my son!"

38 Esau continued to plead with his father: "Have you only one blessing, father? Bless me too, father!" He began to cry.

39 Then Isaac said to him,

"No dew from heaven for you,
No fertile fields for you.
40 You will live by your sword,
But be your brother's slave.
Yet when you rebel,*b*
You will break away from his control."

41 Esau hated Jacob, because his father had given Jacob the blessing. He thought, "The time to mourn my father's death is near; then I will kill Jacob."

42 But when Rebecca heard about Esau's plan, she sent for Jacob and said, "Listen, your brother Esau is planning to get even with you and kill you. 43 Now, my son, do what I say. Go at once to my brother Laban in Haran, 44 and stay with him for a while, until your brother's anger cools down 45 and he forgets what you have done to him. Then I will send someone to bring you back. Why should I lose both my sons on the same day?"

Isaac Sends Jacob to Laban

46 Rebecca said to Isaac, "I am sick and tired of Esau's foreign wives. If Jacob also marries one of these Hittite girls, I might as well die."

28 Isaac called Jacob, greeted him, and said to him, "Don't marry a Canaanite girl. 2 Go instead to Mesopotamia, to the home of your grandfather Bethuel, and marry one of the girls there, one of your uncle Laban's daughters. 3 May Almighty God bless your marriage and give you many children, so that you will become the father of many nations! 4 May he bless you and your descendants as he blessed Abraham, and may you take possession of this land, in which you have lived and which God gave to Abraham!" 5 Isaac sent Jacob away to Mesopotamia, to Laban, who was the son of Bethuel the Aramean and the brother of Rebecca, the mother of Jacob and Esau.

Esau Takes Another Wife

6 Esau learnt that Isaac had blessed Jacob and sent him away to Mesopotamia to find a wife. He also learnt that when Isaac blessed him, he commanded him not to marry a Canaanite woman. 7 He found out that Jacob had obeyed his father and mother and had gone to Mesopotamia. 8 Esau then understood that his father Isaac did not approve of Canaanite women. 9 So he went to Ishmael son of Abraham and married his daughter Mahalath, who was the sister of Nebaioth.

Jacob's Dream at Bethel

10 Jacob left Beersheba and started towards Haran. 11 At sunset he came to a holy place*c* and camped there. He lay down to sleep, resting his head on a stone. 12 He dreamt that he saw a stairway reaching from earth to heaven, with angels going up and coming down on it. 13 And there was the LORD standing beside him.*d* "I am the LORD, the God of Abraham and Isaac," he said. "I will give to you and to your descendants this land on which you are lying. 14 They will be as numerous as the specks of dust on the earth. They will extend their territory in all directions, and through you and your descendants I will bless all the nations.*e* 15 Remember, I will be with you and protect you wherever you go, and I will bring you back to this land. I will not leave you until I have done all that I have promised you."

16 Jacob woke up and said, "The LORD is here! He is in this place, and I didn't know it!" 17 He was afraid and said, "What a terrifying place this is! It must be the house of God; it must be the gate that opens into heaven."

18 Jacob got up early next morning, took the stone that was under his head, and set it up as a memorial. Then he poured olive-oil on it to dedicate it to God. 19 He named the place Bethel.*f* (The town there was once known as Luz.) 20 Then Jacob made a vow to the LORD: "If you will be with me and protect me on the journey I am making and give me food and clothing, 21 and if I return safely to my father's home, then you will be my God. 22 This memorial stone which I have

---

*b*rebel; *or* grow restless.   *c*a holy place; *or* a place.   *d*beside him; *or* on it.
*e*through you...nations; *or* all the nations will ask me to bless them as I have blessed you and your descendants.   *f*BETHEL: *This name in Hebrew means "house of God."*
27.38: Heb 12.17   **27.39–40:** Heb 11.20   **27.40:** Gen 36.8; 2 Kgs 8.20   **28.4:** Gen 17.4–8
28.12: Jn 1.51   **28.13:** Gen 13.14–15   **28.14:** Gen 12.3, 22.18

A stairway...from earth to heaven (28.12)

they would put the stone back in place.

4 Jacob asked the shepherds, "My friends, where are you from?"

"From Haran," they answered.

5 He asked, "Do you know Laban son of Nahor?"

"Yes, we do," they answered.

6 "Is he well?" he asked.

"He is well," they answered. "Look, here comes his daughter Rachel with his flock."

7 Jacob said, "Since it is still broad daylight and not yet time to bring the flocks in, why don't you water them and take them back to pasture?"

8 They answered, "We can't do that until all the flocks are here and the stone has been rolled back; then we will water the flocks."

9 While Jacob was still talking to them, Rachel arrived with the flock. 10 When Jacob saw Rachel with his uncle Laban's flock, he went to the well, rolled the stone back, and watered the sheep. 11 Then he kissed her and began to cry for joy. 12 He told her, "I am your father's relative, the son of Rebecca."

She ran to tell her father; 13 and when he heard the news about his nephew Jacob, he ran to meet him, hugged him and kissed him, and brought him into the house. When Jacob told Laban everything that had happened, 14 Laban said, "Yes, indeed, you are my own flesh and blood." Jacob stayed there a whole month.

Jacob Serves Laban for Rachel and Leah

15 Laban said to Jacob, "You shouldn't work for me for nothing just because you are my relative. How much pay do you want?" 16 Laban had two daughters; the elder was named Leah, and the younger Rachel. 17 Leah had lovely[g] eyes, but Rachel was shapely and beautiful.

18 Jacob was in love with Rachel, so he said, "I will work seven years for you, if you will let me marry Rachel."

19 Laban answered, "I would rather give her to you than to anyone else; stay here with me." 20 Jacob worked seven years so that he could have Rachel, and the time seemed like only a few days to him, because he loved her.

21 Then Jacob said to Laban, "The time is up; let me marry your daughter." 22 So Laban gave a wedding-feast and invited everyone. 23 But that night, instead of Rachel, he took Leah to Jacob, and Jacob

set up will be the place where you are worshipped, and I will give you a tenth of everything you give me."

Jacob Arrives at Laban's Home

29 Jacob continued on his way and went towards the land of the East. 2 Suddenly he came upon a well out in the fields with three flocks of sheep lying round it. The flocks were watered from this well, which had a large stone over the opening. 3 Whenever all the flocks came together there, the shepherds would roll the stone back and water them. Then

[g] lovely; *or* weak.

had intercourse with her. (24 Laban gave his slave-girl Zilpah to his daughter Leah as her maid.) 25 Not until the next morning did Jacob discover that it was Leah. He went to Laban and said, "Why did you do this to me? I worked to get Rachel. Why have you tricked me?"

26 Laban answered, "It is not the custom here to give the younger daughter in marriage before the elder. 27 Wait until the week's marriage celebrations are over, and I will give you Rachel, if you will work for me another seven years."

28 Jacob agreed, and when the week of marriage celebrations was over, Laban gave him his daughter Rachel as his wife. (29 Laban gave his slave-girl Bilhah to his daughter Rachel as her maid.) 30 Jacob had intercourse with Rachel also, and he loved her more than Leah. Then he worked for Laban another seven years.

The Children Born to Jacob

31 When the LORD saw that Leah was loved less than Rachel, he made it possible for her to have children, but Rachel remained childless. 32 Leah became pregnant and gave birth to a son. She said, "The LORD has seen my trouble, and now my husband will love me"; so she named him Reuben. g 33 She became pregnant again and gave birth to another son. She said, "The LORD has given me this son also, because he heard that I was not loved"; so she named him Simeon. h 34 Once again she became pregnant and gave birth to another son. She said, "Now my husband will be bound more tightly to me, because I have borne him three sons"; so she named him Levi. i 35 Then she became pregnant again and gave birth to another son. She said, "This time I will praise the LORD"; so she named him Judah. j Then she stopped having children.

30 But Rachel had not borne Jacob any children, and so she became jealous of her sister and said to Jacob, "Give me children, or I will die."

2 Jacob became angry with Rachel and said, "I can't take the place of God. He is the one who keeps you from having children."

3 She said, "Here is my slave-girl Bilhah; sleep with her, so that she can have a child for me. In this way I can become a mother through her." 4 So she gave Bilhah to her husband, and he had intercourse with her. 5 Bilhah became pregnant and bore Jacob a son. 6 Rachel said, "God has judged in my favour. He has heard my prayer and has given me a son"; so she named him Dan. k 7 Bilhah became pregnant again and bore Jacob a second son. 8 Rachel said, "I have fought a hard fight with my sister, but I have won"; so she named him Naphtali. l

9 When Leah realized that she had stopped having children, she gave her slave-girl Zilpah to Jacob as his wife. 10 Then Zilpah bore Jacob a son. 11 Leah said, "I have been lucky"; so she named him Gad. m 12 Zilpah bore Jacob another son, 13 and Leah said, "How happy I am! Now women will call me happy"; so she named him Asher. n

14 During the wheat-harvest Reuben went into the fields and found mandrakes, o which he brought to his mother Leah. Rachel said to Leah, "Please give me some of your son's mandrakes."

15 Leah answered, "Isn't it enough that you have taken away my husband? Now you are even trying to take away my son's mandrakes."

Rachel said, "If you will give me your son's mandrakes, you can sleep with Jacob tonight."

16 When Jacob came in from the fields in the evening, Leah went out to meet him and said, "You are going to sleep with me tonight, because I have paid for you with my son's mandrakes." So he had intercourse with her that night.

17 God answered Leah's prayer, and she became pregnant and bore Jacob a fifth son. 18 Leah said, "God has given me my reward, because I gave my slave to my husband"; so she named her son Issachar. p 19 Leah became pregnant again and bore Jacob a sixth son. 20 She said,

---

g REUBEN: This name sounds like the Hebrew for "see, a son" and "has seen my trouble."
h SIMEON: This name sounds like the Hebrew for "hear."
i LEVI: This name sounds like the Hebrew for "bound."
j JUDAH: This name sounds like the Hebrew for "praise."
k DAN: This name sounds like the Hebrew for "judge in favour."
l NAPHTALI: This name sounds like the Hebrew for "fight."
m GAD: This name in Hebrew means "luck."   n ASHER: This name in Hebrew means "happy."
o MANDRAKES: Plants which were believed to produce fertility and were used as love-charms.
p ISSACHAR: This name sounds like the Hebrew for "a man is hired" and "there is reward."

"God has given me a fine gift. Now my husband will accept me, because I have borne him six sons"; so she named him Zebulun. *q* ²¹ Later she bore a daughter, whom she named Dinah.

22 Then God remembered Rachel; he answered her prayer and made it possible for her to have children. ²³ She became pregnant and gave birth to a son. She said, "God has taken away my disgrace by giving me a son. ²⁴ May the LORD give me another son"; so she named him Joseph. *r*

Jacob's Bargain with Laban

25 After the birth of Joseph, Jacob said to Laban, "Let me go, so that I can return home. ²⁶ Give me my wives and children that I have earned by working for you, and I will leave. You know how well I have served you."

27 Laban said to him, "Let me say this: I have learnt by divination that the LORD has blessed me because of you. ²⁸ Name your wages, and I will pay them."

29 Jacob answered, "You know how I have worked for you and how your flocks have prospered under my care. ³⁰ The little you had before I came has grown enormously, and the LORD has blessed you wherever I went. *s* Now it is time for me to look out for my own interests."

31 "What shall I pay you?" Laban asked.

Jacob answered, "I don't want any wages. I will continue to take care of your flocks if you agree to this suggestion: ³² Let me go through all your flocks today and take every black lamb *t* and every spotted or speckled young goat. That is all the wages I want. ³³ In the future you can easily find out if I have been honest. When you come to check up on my wages, if I have any goat that isn't speckled or spotted or any sheep that isn't black, you will know that it has been stolen."

34 Laban answered, "Agreed. We will do as you suggest." ³⁵ But that day Laban removed the male goats that had stripes or spots and all the females that were speckled and spotted or which had white on them; he also removed all the black sheep. He put his sons in charge of them, ³⁶ and then went away from Jacob with this flock as far as he could travel in three days. Jacob took care of the rest of Laban's flocks.

37 Jacob got green branches of poplar, almond, and plane trees and stripped off some of the bark so that the branches had white stripes on them. ³⁸ He placed these branches in front of the flocks at their drinking-troughs. He put them there, because the animals mated when they came to drink. ³⁹ So when the goats bred in front of the branches, they produced young that were streaked, speckled, and spotted.

40 Jacob kept the sheep separate from the goats and made them face in the direction of the streaked and black animals of Laban's flock. In this way he built up his own flock and kept it apart from Laban's.

41 When the healthy animals were mating, Jacob put the branches in front of them at the drinking-troughs, so that they would breed among the branches. ⁴² But he did not put the branches in front of the weak animals. Soon Laban had all the weak animals, and Jacob all the healthy ones. ⁴³ In this way Jacob became very wealthy. He had many flocks, slaves, camels, and donkeys.

Jacob Flees from Laban

31 Jacob heard that Laban's sons were saying, "Jacob has taken everything that belonged to our father. All his wealth has come from what our father owned." ² He also saw that Laban was no longer as friendly as he had been earlier. ³ Then the LORD said to him, "Go back to the land of your fathers and to your relatives. I will be with you."

4 So Jacob sent word to Rachel and Leah to meet him in the field where his flocks were. ⁵ He said to them, "I have noticed that your father is not as friendly towards me as he used to be; but my father's God has been with me. ⁶ You both know that I have worked for your father with all my strength. ⁷ Yet he has cheated me and changed my wages ten times. But God did not let him harm me. ⁸ Whenever Laban said, 'The speckled goats shall be your wages,' all the flocks produced speckled young. When he said, 'The striped goats shall be your wages,' all the flocks produced striped young. ⁹ God has

---

q ZEBULUN: *This name sounds like the Hebrew for "accept" and "gift."*
r JOSEPH: *This name sounds like the Hebrew for "may he give another" and "he has taken away."*
s wherever I went; *or* because of me.
t *One ancient translation* every black lamb; *Hebrew* every spotted and speckled lamb, and every black lamb.

Jacob...drove all his flocks ahead of him (31.18)

taken flocks away from your father and given them to me.

10 "During the breeding season I had a dream, and I saw that the male goats that were mating were striped, spotted, and speckled. ¹¹The angel of God spoke to me in the dream and said, 'Jacob!' 'Yes,' I answered. ¹²'Look,' he continued, 'all the male goats that are mating are striped, spotted, and speckled. I am making this happen because I have seen all that Laban is doing to you. ¹³I am the God who appeared to you at Bethel, where you dedicated a stone as a memorial by pouring olive-oil on it and where you made a vow to me. Now get ready to go back to the land where you were born.'"

14 Rachel and Leah answered Jacob, "There is nothing left for us to inherit from our father. ¹⁵He treats us like foreigners. He sold us, and now he has spent all the money he was paid for us. ¹⁶All this wealth which God has taken from our father belongs to us and to our children. Do whatever God has told you."

17–18 So Jacob got ready to go back to his father in the land of Canaan. He put his children and his wives on the camels, and drove all his flocks ahead of him, with everything that he had acquired in Mesopotamia. ¹⁹Laban had gone to

31.13: Gen 28.18–22

shear his sheep, and during his absence Rachel stole the household gods that belonged to her father. ²⁰Jacob deceived Laban by not letting him know that he was leaving. ²¹He took everything he owned and left in a hurry. He crossed the River Euphrates and started for the hill-country of Gilead.

Laban Pursues Jacob

22 Three days later Laban was told that Jacob had fled. ²³He took his men with him and pursued Jacob for seven days until he caught up with him in the hill-country of Gilead. ²⁴In a dream that night God came to Laban and said to him, "Be careful not to threaten Jacob in any way." ²⁵Jacob had set up his camp on a mountain, and Laban set up his camp with his kinsmen in the hill-country of Gilead.

26 Laban said to Jacob, "Why did you deceive me and carry off my daughters like women captured in war? ²⁷Why did you deceive me and slip away without telling me? If you had told me, I would have sent you on your way with rejoicing and singing to the music of tambourines and harps. ²⁸You did not even let me kiss my grandchildren and my daughters goodbye. That was a foolish thing to do! ²⁹I have the power to do you harm, but last night the God of your father warned me

not to threaten you in any way. ³⁰ I know that you left because you were so anxious to get back home, but why did you steal my household gods?"

31 Jacob answered, "I was afraid, because I thought that you might take your daughters away from me. ³² But if you find that anyone here has your gods, he will be put to death. Here, with our men as witnesses, look for anything that belongs to you and take what is yours." Jacob did not know that Rachel had stolen Laban's gods.

33 Laban went and searched Jacob's tent; then he went into Leah's tent, and the tent of the two slave-women, but he did not find his gods. Then he went into Rachel's tent. ³⁴ Rachel had taken the household gods and put them in a camel's saddlebag and was sitting on them. Laban searched through the whole tent, but did not find them. ³⁵ Rachel said to her father, "Do not be angry with me, sir, but I am not able to stand up in your presence; I am having my monthly period." Laban searched but did not find his household gods.

36 Then Jacob lost his temper. "What crime have I committed?" he asked angrily. "What law have I broken that gives you the right to hunt me down? ³⁷ Now that you have searched through all my belongings, what household article have you found that belongs to you? Put it out here where your men and mine can see it, and let them decide which one of us is right. ³⁸ I have been with you now for twenty years; your sheep and your goats have not failed to reproduce, and I have not eaten any rams from your flocks. ³⁹ Whenever a sheep was killed by wild animals, I always bore the loss myself. I didn't take it to you to show that it was not my fault. You demanded that I make good anything that was stolen during the day or during the night. ⁴⁰ Many times I suffered from the heat during the day and from the cold at night. I was not able to sleep. ⁴¹ It was like that for the whole twenty years I was with you. For fourteen years I worked to win your two daughters—and six years for your flocks. And even then, you changed my wages ten times. ⁴² If the God of my fathers, the God of Abraham and Isaac, had not been

with me, you would have already sent me away empty-handed. But God has seen my trouble and the work I have done, and last night he gave his judgement."

The Agreement between Jacob and Laban

43 Laban answered Jacob, "These girls are my daughters; their children belong to me, and these flocks are mine. In fact, everything you see here belongs to me. But since I can do nothing to keep my daughters and their children, ⁴⁴ I am ready to make an agreement with you. Let us make a pile of stones to remind us of our agreement."

45 So Jacob took a stone and set it up as a memorial. ⁴⁶ He told his men to gather some rocks and pile them up. Then they ate a meal beside the pile of rocks. ⁴⁷ Laban named it Jegar Sahadutha,ᵘ while Jacob named it Galeed.ᵛ ⁴⁸ Laban said to Jacob, "This pile of rocks will be a reminder for both of us." That is why that place was named Galeed. ⁴⁹ Laban also said, "May the LORD keep an eye on us while we are separated from each other." So the place was also named Mizpah.ʷ ⁵⁰ Laban went on, "If you ill-treat my daughters or if you marry other women, even though I don't know about it, remember that God is watching us. ⁵¹ Here are the rocks that I have piled up between us, and here is the memorial stone. ⁵² Both this pile and this memorial stone are reminders. I will never go beyond this pile to attack you, and you must never go beyond it or beyond this memorial stone to attack me. ⁵³ The God of Abraham and the God of Nahorˣ will judge between us." Then, in the name of the God whom his father Isaac worshipped, Jacob solemnly vowed to keep this promise. ⁵⁴ He killed an animal, which he offered as a sacrifice on the mountain, and he invited his men to the meal. After they had eaten, they spent the night on the mountain. ⁵⁵ Early the next morning Laban kissed his grandchildren and his daughters good-bye, and left to go back home.

Jacob Prepares to Meet Esau

32 As Jacob went on his way, some angels met him. ² When he saw them, he said, "This is God's camp"; so

---

ᵘ JEGAR SAHADUTHA: *This name in Aramaic means "a pile to remind us."*
ᵛ GALEED: *This name in Hebrew means "a pile to remind us."*
ʷ MIZPAH: *This name sounds like the Hebrew for "place from which to watch."*
ˣ ABRAHAM...NAHOR: *Abraham was Jacob's grandfather and Nahor was Laban's father.*

he called the place Mahanaim.*y*

3 Jacob sent messengers ahead of him to his brother Esau in the country of Edom. 4He instructed them to say: "I, Jacob, your obedient servant, report to my master Esau that I have been staying with Laban and that I have delayed my return until now. 5I own cattle, donkeys, sheep, goats, and slaves. I am sending you word, sir, in the hope of gaining your favour."

6 When the messengers came back to Jacob, they said, "We went to your brother Esau, and he is already on his way to meet you. He has four hundred men with him." 7Jacob was frightened and worried. He divided into two groups the people who were with him, and also his sheep, goats, cattle, and camels. 8He thought, "If Esau comes and attacks the first group, the other may be able to escape."

9 Then Jacob prayed, "God of my grandfather Abraham and God of my father Isaac, hear me! You told me, LORD, to go back to my land and to my relatives, and you would make everything go well for me. 10I am not worth all the kindness and faithfulness that you have shown me, your servant. I crossed the Jordan with nothing but a walking-stick, and now I have come back with these two groups. 11Save me, I pray, from my brother Esau. I am afraid—afraid that he is coming to attack us and destroy us all, even the women and children. 12Remember that you promised to make everything go well for me and to give me more descendants than anyone could count, as many as the grains of sand along the seashore."

13-15 After spending the night there, Jacob chose from his livestock as a present for his brother Esau: two hundred female goats and twenty males, two hundred female sheep and twenty males, thirty milk camels with their young, forty cows and ten bulls, twenty female donkeys and ten males. 16He divided them into herds and put one of his servants in charge of each herd. He said to them, "Go ahead of me, and leave a space between each herd and the one behind it." 17He ordered the first servant, "When my brother Esau meets you and asks, 'Who is your master? Where are you going? Who owns these animals in front

of you?' 18you must answer, 'They belong to your servant Jacob. He sends them as a present to his master Esau. Jacob himself is just behind us.'" 19He gave the same order to the second, the third, and to all the others who were in charge of the herds: "This is what you must say to Esau when you meet him. 20You must say, 'Yes, your servant Jacob is just behind us.'" Jacob was thinking, "I will win him over with the gifts, and when I meet him, perhaps he will forgive me." 21He sent the gifts on ahead of him and spent that night in camp.

Jacob Wrestles at Peniel

22 That same night Jacob got up, took his two wives, his two concubines, and his eleven children, and crossed the River Jabbok. 23After he had sent them across, he also sent across all that he owned, 24but he stayed behind, alone.

A man came and wrestled with him (32.24)

Then a man came and wrestled with him until just before daybreak. 25When the man saw that he was not winning the struggle, he struck Jacob on the hip, and it was thrown out of joint. 26The man said, "Let me go; daylight is coming."

"I won't, unless you bless me," Jacob answered.

27 "What is your name?" the man asked.

"Jacob," he answered.

28 The man said, "Your name will no

*y*MAHANAIM: *This name in Hebrew means "two camps."*
32.12: Gen 22.17   **32.24-26:** Hos 12.3-4   **32.28:** Gen 35.10

longer be Jacob. You have struggled with God and with men, and you have won; so your name will be Israel." [z]

29 Jacob said, "Now tell me your name."

But he answered, "Why do you want to know my name?" Then he blessed Jacob.

30 Jacob said, "I have seen God face to face, and I am still alive"; so he named the place Peniel. [a] 31 The sun rose as Jacob was leaving Peniel, and he was limping because of his hip. 32 Even today the descendants of Israel do not eat the muscle which is on the hip-joint, because it was on this muscle that Jacob was struck.

Jacob Meets Esau

33 Jacob saw Esau coming with his four hundred men, so he divided the children among Leah, Rachel, and the two concubines. 2 He put the concubines and their children first, then Leah and her children, and finally Rachel and Joseph at the rear. 3 Jacob went ahead of them and bowed down to the ground seven times as he approached his brother. 4 But Esau ran to meet him, threw his arms round him, and kissed him. They were both crying. 5 When Esau looked round and saw the women and the children, he asked, "Who are these people with you?"

"These, sir, are the children whom God has been good enough to give me," Jacob answered. 6 Then the concubines came up with their children and bowed down; 7 then Leah and her children came, and last of all Joseph and Rachel came and bowed down.

8 Esau asked, "What about that other group I met? What did that mean?"

Jacob answered, "It was to gain your favour."

9 But Esau said, "I have enough, my brother; keep what you have."

10 Jacob said, "No, please, if I have gained your favour, accept my gift. To see your face is for me like seeing the face of God, now that you have been so friendly to me. 11 Please accept this gift which I have brought for you; God has been kind to me and given me everything I need." Jacob kept on urging him until he accepted.

12 Esau said, "Let's prepare to leave. I will go ahead of you."

13 Jacob answered, "You know that the children are weak, and I must think of the sheep and livestock with their young. If they are driven hard for even one day, the whole herd will die. 14 Please go on ahead of me, and I will follow slowly, going as fast as I can with the livestock and the children until I catch up with you in Edom."

15 Esau said, "Then let me leave some of my men with you."

But Jacob answered, "There is no need for that for I only want to gain your favour." [b] 16 So that day Esau started on his way back to Edom. 17 But Jacob went to Sukkoth, where he built a house for himself and shelters for his livestock. That is why the place was named Sukkoth. [c]

18 On his return from Mesopotamia Jacob arrived safely at the city of Shechem in the land of Canaan and set up his camp in a field near the city. 19 He bought that part of the field from the descendants of Hamor father of Shechem for a hundred pieces of silver. 20 He put up an altar there and named it after El, the God of Israel.

The Rape of Dinah

34 One day Dinah, the daughter of Jacob and Leah, went to visit some of the Canaanite women. 2 When Shechem son of Hamor the Hivite, who was chief of that region, saw her, he took her and raped her. 3 But he found the girl so attractive that he fell in love with her and tried to win her affection. [d] 4 He said to his father, "I want you to get this girl for me as my wife."

5 Jacob learnt that his daughter had been disgraced, but because his sons were out in the fields with his livestock, he did nothing until they came back. 6 Shechem's father Hamor went out to talk with Jacob, 7 just as Jacob's sons were coming in from the fields. When they heard about it, they were shocked and furious that Shechem had done such a thing and had insulted the people of Israel by raping Jacob's daughter. 8 Hamor said to him, "My son Shechem has fallen in love with your daughter; please let him marry her. 9 Let us make an agreement

---

[z] ISRAEL: *This name sounds like the Hebrew for "he struggles with God" or "God struggles."*
[a] PENIEL: *This name sounds like the Hebrew for "the face of God."*
[b] for I only want to gain your favour; *or if it's all right with you.*
[c] SUKKOTH: *This name in Hebrew means "shelters."* [d] tried to win her affection; *or comforted her.*
32.29: Judg 13.17-18   **33.19:** Josh 24.32; Jn 4.5

Esau...threw his arms round him (33.4)

that there will be intermarriage between our people and yours. ¹⁰Then you may stay here in our country with us; you may live anywhere you wish, trade freely, and own property."

11 Then Shechem said to Dinah's father and brothers, "Do me this favour, and I will give you whatever you want. ¹²Tell me what presents you want, and set the payment for the bride as high as you wish; I will give you whatever you ask, if you will only let me marry her."

13 Because Shechem had disgraced their sister Dinah, Jacob's sons answered Shechem and his father Hamor in a deceitful way. ¹⁴They said to him, "We cannot let our sister marry a man who is not circumcised; that would be a disgrace for us. ¹⁵We can agree only on the condition that you become like us by circumcising all your males. ¹⁶Then we will agree to intermarriage. We will settle among you and become one people with you. ¹⁷But if you will not accept our terms and be circumcised, we will take her and leave."

18 These terms seemed fair to Hamor and his son Shechem, ¹⁹and the young man lost no time in doing what was suggested, because he was in love with Jacob's daughter. He was the most important member of his family.

20 Hamor and his son Shechem went to the meeting-place at the city gate and spoke to their fellow-townsmen: ²¹"These

men are friendly; let them live in the land with us and travel freely. The land is large enough for them also. Let us marry their daughters and give them ours in marriage. 22 But these men will agree to live among us and be one people with us only on condition that we circumcise all our males, as they are circumcised. 23 Won't all their livestock and everything else they own be ours? So let us agree that they can live among us." 24 All the citizens of the city agreed with what Hamor and Shechem proposed, and all the males were circumcised.

25 Three days later, when the men were still sore from their circumcision, two of Jacob's sons, Simeon and Levi, the brothers of Dinah, took their swords, went into the city without arousing suspicion, and killed all the men, 26 including Hamor and his son Shechem. Then they took Dinah from Shechem's house and left. 27 After the slaughter Jacob's other sons looted the town to take revenge for their sister's disgrace. 28 They took the flocks, the cattle, the donkeys, and everything else in the city and in the fields. 29 They took everything of value, captured all the women and children, and carried off everything in the houses.

30 Jacob said to Simeon and Levi, "You have brought trouble on me; now the Canaanites, the Perizzites, and everybody else in the land will hate me. I haven't many men; if they all band together against me and attack me, our whole family will be destroyed."

31 But they answered, "We cannot let our sister be treated like a common whore."

God Blesses Jacob at Bethel

35 God said to Jacob, "Go to Bethel at once, and live there. Build an altar there to me, the God who appeared to you when you were running away from your brother Esau."

2 So Jacob said to his family and to all who were with him, "Get rid of the foreign gods that you have; purify yourselves and put on clean clothes. 3 We are going to leave here and go to Bethel, where I will build an altar to the God who helped me in the time of my trouble and who has been with me everywhere

I have gone." 4 So they gave Jacob all the foreign gods that they had and also the ear-rings that they were wearing. He buried them beneath the oak-tree near Shechem.

5 When Jacob and his sons started to leave, great fear fell on the people of the nearby towns, and they did not pursue them. 6 Jacob came with all his people to Luz, which is now known as Bethel, in the land of Canaan. 7 He built an altar there and named the place after the God of Bethel, because God had revealed himself to him there when he was running away from his brother. 8 Rebecca's nurse Deborah died and was buried beneath the oak south of Bethel. So it was named "Oak of Weeping."

9 When Jacob returned from Mesopotamia, God appeared to him again and blessed him. 10 God said to him, "Your name is Jacob, but from now on it will be Israel." So God named him Israel. 11 And God said to him, "I am Almighty God. Have many children. Nations will be descended from you, and you will be the ancestor of kings. 12 I will give you the land which I gave to Abraham and to Isaac, and I will also give it to your descendants after you." 13 Then God left him. 14 There, where God had spoken to him, Jacob set up a memorial stone and consecrated it by pouring wine and olive-oil on it. 15 He named the place Bethel.

The Death of Rachel

16 Jacob and his family left Bethel, and when they were still some distance from Ephrath, the time came for Rachel to have her baby, and she was having difficult labour. 17 When her labour pains were at their worst, the midwife said to her, "Don't be afraid, Rachel; it's another boy." 18 But she was dying, and as she breathed her last, she named her son Benoni,e but his father named him Benjamin.f

19 When Rachel died, she was buried beside the road to Ephrath, now known as Bethlehem. 20 Jacob set up a memorial stone there, and it still marks Rachel's grave to this day. 21 Jacob moved on and set up his camp on the other side of the tower of Eder.

---

eBENONI: *This name in Hebrew means "son of my sorrow."*
fBENJAMIN: *This name in Hebrew means "son who will be fortunate."*
35.1: Gen 28.11-17   **35.10:** Gen 32.28   **35.11-12:** Gen 17.4-8   **35.14-15:** Gen 28.18-19

The Sons of Jacob
(1 Chron 2.1-2)

22 While Jacob was living in that land, Reuben had sexual intercourse with Bilhah, one of his father's concubines; Jacob heard about it and was furious. *g*

Jacob had twelve sons. 23 The sons of Leah were Reuben (Jacob's eldest son), Simeon, Levi, Judah, Issachar, and Zebulun. 24 The sons of Rachel were Joseph and Benjamin. 25 The sons of Rachel's slave Bilhah were Dan and Naphtali. 26 The sons of Leah's slave Zilpah were Gad and Asher. These sons were born in Mesopotamia.

The Death of Isaac

27 Jacob went to his father Isaac at Mamre, near Hebron, where Abraham and Isaac had lived. 28 Isaac lived to be a hundred and eighty years old 29 and died at a ripe old age; and his sons Esau and Jacob buried him.

The Descendants of Esau
(1 Chr 1.34-37)

36 These are the descendants of Esau, also called Edom. 2 Esau married Canaanite women: Adah, the daughter of Elon the Hittite; Oholibamah, the daughter of Anah son *h* of Zibeon the Hivite; 3 and Basemath, the daughter of Ishmael and sister of Nebaioth. 4 Adah bore Eliphaz; Basemath bore Reuel; 5 and Oholibamah bore Jeush, Jalam, and Korah. All these sons were born to Esau in the land of Canaan.

6 Then Esau took his wives, his sons, his daughters, and all the people of his house, together with all his livestock and all the possessions he had acquired in the land of Canaan, and went away from his brother Jacob to another land. 7 He left because the land where he and Jacob were living was not able to support them; they had too much livestock and could no longer stay together. 8 So Esau lived in the hill-country of Edom.

9 These are the descendants of Esau, the ancestor of the Edomites. 10-13 Esau's wife Adah bore him one son, Eliphaz, and Eliphaz had five sons: Teman, Omar, Zepho, Gatam, and Kenaz. And by another wife, Timna, he had one more son, Amalek.

Esau's wife Basemath bore him one son, Reuel, and Reuel had four sons: Nahath, Zerah, Shammah, and Mizzah.

14 Esau's wife Oholibamah, the daughter of Anah son *h* of Zibeon, bore him three sons: Jeush, Jalam, and Korah.

15 These are the tribes descended from Esau. Esau's first son Eliphaz was the ancestor of the following tribes: Teman, Omar, Zepho, Kenaz, 16 Korah, Gatam, and Amalek. These were all descendants of Esau's wife Adah.

17 Esau's son Reuel was the ancestor of the following tribes: Nahath, Zerah, Shammah, and Mizzah. These were all descendants of Esau's wife Basemath.

18 The following tribes were descended from Esau by his wife Oholibamah, the daughter of Anah: Jeush, Jalam, and Korah. 19 All these tribes were descended from Esau.

The Descendants of Seir
(1 Chr 1.38-42)

20-21 The original inhabitants of the land of Edom were divided into tribes which traced their ancestry to the following descendants of Seir, a Horite: Lotan, Shobal, Zibeon, Anah, Dishon, Ezer, and Dishan.

22 Lotan was the ancestor of the clans of Hori and Heman. (Lotan had a sister named Timna.)

23 Shobal was the ancestor of the clans of Alvan, Manahath, Ebal, Shepho, and Onam.

24 Zibeon had two sons, Aiah and Anah. (This is the Anah who found the hot springs in the wilderness when he was taking care of his father's donkeys.) 25-26 Anah was the father of Dishon, who was the ancestor of the clans of Hemdan, Eshban, Ithran, and Cheran. Anah also had a daughter named Oholibamah.

27 Ezer was the ancestor of the clans of Bilhan, Zaavan, and Akan.

28 Dishan was the ancestor of the clans of Uz and Aran.

29-30 These are the Horite tribes in the land of Edom: Lotan, Shobal, Zibeon, Anah, Dishon, Ezer, and Dishan.

The Kings of Edom
(1 Chr 1.43-54)

31-39 Before there were any kings in Israel, the following kings ruled over the

---

g One ancient translation and was furious; *Hebrew does not have these words.*
h Some ancient translations son; *Hebrew* daughter; *or* granddaughter.
35.22: Gen 49.4   **35.27:** Gen 13.18   **36.2:** Gen 26.34   **36.3:** Gen 28.9

land of Edom in succession:

Bela son of Beor from Dinhabah

Jobab son of Zerah from Bozrah

Husham from the region of Teman

Hadad son of Bedad from Avith (he
    defeated the Midianites in a
    battle in the country of Moab)

Samlah from Masrekah

Shaul from Rehoboth-on-the-River

Baal Hanan son of Achbor

Hadad from Pau (his wife was
    Mehetabel, the daughter of
    Matred and granddaughter of
    Mezahab)

40–43 Esau was the ancestor of the following Edomite tribes: Timna, Alvah, Jetheth, Oholibamah, Elah, Pinon, Kenaz, Teman, Mibzar, Magdiel, and Iram. The area where each of these tribes lived was known by the name of the tribe.

Joseph and His Brothers

37 Jacob continued to live in the land of Canaan, where his father had lived, ²and this is the story of Jacob's family.

Joseph, a young man of seventeen, took care of the sheep and goats with his brothers, the sons of Bilhah and Zilpah, his father's concubines. He brought bad reports to his father about what his brothers were doing.

3 Jacob loved Joseph more than all his other sons, because he had been born to him when he was old. He made a long robe with full sleeves*j* for him. ⁴When his brothers saw that their father loved Joseph more than he loved them, they hated their brother so much that they would not speak to him in a friendly manner.

5 One night Joseph had a dream, and when he told his brothers about it, they hated him even more. ⁶He said, "Listen to the dream I had. ⁷We were all in the field tying up sheaves of wheat, when my sheaf got up and stood up straight. Yours formed a circle round mine and bowed down to it."

8 "Do you think you are going to be a king and rule over us?" his brothers asked. So they hated him even more because of his dreams and because of what he said about them.

9 Then Joseph had another dream and said to his brothers, "I had another dream, in which I saw the sun, the moon, and eleven stars bowing down to me."

10 He also told the dream to his father, and his father scolded him: "What kind of a dream is that? Do you think that your mother, your brothers, and I are going to come and bow down to you?" ¹¹Joseph's brothers were jealous of him, but his father kept thinking about the whole matter.

Joseph Is Sold and Taken to Egypt

12 One day when Joseph's brothers had gone to Shechem to take care of their father's flock, ¹³Jacob said to Joseph, "I want you to go to Shechem, where your brothers are taking care of the flock."

Joseph answered, "I am ready."

14 His father said, "Go and see if your brothers are safe and if the flock is all right; then come back and tell me." So his father sent him on his way from the Valley of Hebron.

Joseph arrived at Shechem ¹⁵and was wandering about in the country when a man saw him and asked him, "What are you looking for?"

16 "I am looking for my brothers, who are taking care of their flock," he answered. "Can you tell me where they are?"

17 The man said, "They have already left. I heard them say that they were going to Dothan." So Joseph went after his brothers and found them at Dothan.

18 They saw him in the distance, and before he reached them, they plotted against him and decided to kill him. ¹⁹They said to one another, "Here comes that dreamer. ²⁰Come on now, let's kill him and throw his body into one of the dry wells. We can say that a wild animal killed him. Then we will see what becomes of his dreams."

21 Reuben heard them and tried to save Joseph. "Let's not kill him," he said. ²²"Just throw him into this well in the wilderness, but don't hurt him." He said this, planning to save him from them and send him back to his father. ²³When Joseph came up to his brothers, they ripped off his long robe with full sleeves.*k* ²⁴Then they took him and threw him into the well, which was dry.

25 While they were eating, they sud-

---

j robe with full sleeves; *or* decorated robe.   *k* robe with full sleeves; *or* decorated robe.

37.11: Acts 7.9

HIGHLIGHTS IN JOSEPH'S LIFE

denly saw a group of Ishmaelites travelling from Gilead to Egypt. Their camels were loaded with spices and resins. 26 Judah said to his brothers, "What will we gain by killing our brother and covering up the murder? 27 Let's sell him to these Ishmaelites. Then we won't have to hurt him; after all, he is our brother, our own flesh and blood." His brothers agreed, 28 and when some Midianite traders came by, the brothers¹ pulled Joseph out of the well and sold him for twenty pieces of silver to the Ishmaelites, who took him to Egypt.

29 When Reuben came back to the well and found that Joseph was not there, he tore his clothes in sorrow. 30 He returned to his brothers and said, "The boy is not there! What am I going to do?"

31 Then they killed a goat and dipped Joseph's robe in its blood. 32 They took the robe to their father and said, "We found this. Does it belong to your son?"

33 He recognized it and said, "Yes, it is his! Some wild animal has killed him. My son Joseph has been torn to pieces!" 34 Jacob tore his clothes in sorrow and put on sackcloth. He mourned for his son a long time. 35 All his sons and daughters came to comfort him, but he refused to be comforted and said, "I will go down to the world of the dead still mourning for my son." So he continued to mourn for his son Joseph.

36 Meanwhile, in Egypt, the Midianites had sold Joseph to Potiphar, one of the king's officers, who was the captain of the palace guard.

Judah and Tamar

38 About that time Judah left his brothers and went to stay with a man named Hirah, who was from the town of Adullam. ²There Judah met a Canaanite girl whose father was named Shua. He married her, ³ and she bore him a son, whom he named Er. ⁴ She became pregnant again and bore another son and named him Onan. ⁵ Again she had a son and named him Shelah. Judah was at Achzib when the boy was born.

6 For his first son Er, Judah got a wife whose name was Tamar. ⁷ Er's conduct was evil, and it displeased the LORD, so the LORD killed him. ⁸ Then Judah said to Er's brother Onan, "Go and sleep with your brother's widow. Fulfil your obli-

gation to her as her husband's brother, so that your brother may have descendants." ⁹ But Onan knew that the children would not belong to him, so whenever he had intercourse with his brother's widow, he let the semen spill on the ground, so that there would be no children for his brother. ¹⁰ What he did displeased the LORD, and the LORD killed him also. ¹¹ Then Judah said to his daughter-in-law Tamar, "Return to your father's house and remain a widow until my son Shelah grows up." He said this because he was afraid that Shelah would be killed, as his brothers had been. So Tamar went back home.

12 After some time Judah's wife died. When he had finished the time of mourning, he and his friend Hirah of Adullam went to Timnah, where his sheep were being sheared. ¹³ Someone told Tamar that her father-in-law was going to Timnah to shear his sheep. ¹⁴ So she changed from the widow's clothes she had been wearing, covered her face with a veil, and sat down at the entrance to Enaim, a town on the road to Timnah. As she well knew, Judah's youngest son Shelah had now grown up, and yet she had not been given to him in marriage.

15 When Judah saw her, he thought that she was a prostitute, because she had her face covered. ¹⁶ He went over to her at the side of the road and said, "All right, how much do you charge?" (He did not know that she was his daughter-in-law.)

She said, "What will you give me?"

17 He answered, "I will send you a young goat from my flock."

She said, "All right, if you will give me something to keep as a pledge until you send the goat."

18 "What shall I give you as a pledge?" he asked.

She answered, "Your seal with its cord and the stick you are carrying." He gave them to her. Then they had intercourse, and she became pregnant. ¹⁹ Tamar went home, took off her veil, and put her widow's clothes back on.

20 Judah sent his friend Hirah to take the goat and get back from the woman the articles he had pledged, but Hirah could not find her. ²¹ He asked some men at Enaim, "Where is the prostitute who was here by the road?"

¹ the brothers; Hebrew they.
37.28: Acts 7.9

"There has never been a prostitute here," they answered.

22 He returned to Judah and said, "I couldn't find her. The men of the place said that there had never been a prostitute there."

23 Judah said, "Let her keep the things. We don't want people to laugh at us. I did try to pay her, but you couldn't find her."

24 About three months later someone said to Judah, "Your daughter-in-law Tamar has been acting like a whore, and now she is pregnant."

Judah ordered, "Take her out and burn her to death."

25 As she was being taken out, she sent word to her father-in-law: "I am pregnant by the man who owns these things. Look at them and see whose they are—this seal with its cord and this stick."

26 Judah recognized them and said, "She is in the right. I have failed in my obligation to her—I should have given her to my son Shelah in marriage." And Judah never had intercourse with her again.

27 When the time came for her to give birth, it was discovered that she was going to have twins. 28 While she was in labour, one of them put out an arm; the midwife caught it, tied a red thread round it, and said, "This one was born first." 29 But he pulled his arm back, and his brother was born first. Then the midwife said, "So this is how you break your way out!" So he was named Perez. *m* 30 Then his brother was born with the red thread on his arm, and he was named Zerah. *x*

Joseph and Potiphar's Wife

39 Now the Ishmaelites had taken Joseph to Egypt and sold him to Potiphar, one of the king's officers, who was the captain of the palace guard. 2 The LORD was with Joseph and made him successful. He lived in the house of his Egyptian master, 3 who saw that the LORD was with Joseph and had made him successful in everything he did. 4 Potiphar was pleased with him and made him his personal servant; so he put him in charge of his house and everything he owned. 5 From then on, because of Joseph the LORD blessed the household of the Egyptian and everything that he had in his house and in his fields. 6 Potiphar handed over everything he had to the care

of Joseph and did not concern himself with anything except the food he ate.

Joseph was well-built and good-looking, 7 and after a while his master's wife began to desire Joseph and asked him to go to bed with her. 8 He refused and said to her, "Look, my master does not have to concern himself with anything in the house, because I am here. He has put me in charge of everything he has. 9 I have as much authority in this house as he has, and he has not kept back anything from me except you. How then could I do such an immoral thing and sin against God?" 10 Although she asked Joseph day after day, he would not go to bed with her.

11 But one day when Joseph went into the house to do his work, none of the house servants was there. 12 She caught him by his robe and said, "Come to bed with me." But he escaped and ran outside, leaving his robe in her hand. 13 When she saw that he had left his robe and had run out of the house, 14 she called to her house servants and said, "Look at this! This Hebrew that my husband brought to the house is insulting us. He came into my room and tried to rape me, but I screamed as loud as I could. 15 When he heard me scream, he ran outside, leaving his robe beside me."

16 She kept his robe with her until Joseph's master came home. 17 Then she told him the same story: "That Hebrew slave that you brought here came into my room and insulted me. 18 But when I screamed, he ran outside, leaving his robe beside me."

19 Joseph's master was furious 20 and had Joseph arrested and put in the prison where the king's prisoners were kept, and there he stayed. 21 But the LORD was with Joseph and blessed him, so that the jailer was pleased with him. 22 He put Joseph in charge of all the other prisoners and made him responsible for everything that was done in the prison. 23 The jailer did not have to look after anything for which Joseph was responsible, because the LORD was with Joseph and made him succeed in everything he did.

Joseph Interprets the Prisoners' Dreams

40 Some time later the king of Egypt's wine steward and his chief baker offended the king. 2 He was angry with

m PEREZ: This name in Hebrew means "breaking out."
x ZERAH: This name sounds like a Hebrew word for the red brightness of dawn.
39.2: Acts 7.9   **39.21:** Acts 7.9

these two officials ³and put them in prison in the house of the captain of the guard, in the same place where Joseph was being kept. ⁴They spent a long time in prison, and the captain assigned Joseph as their servant.

5 One night there in prison the wine steward and the chief baker each had a dream, and the dreams had different meanings. ⁶When Joseph came to them in the morning, he saw that they were upset. ⁷He asked them, "Why do you look so worried today?"

8 They answered, "Each of us had a dream, and there is no one here to explain what the dreams mean."

"It is God who gives the ability to interpret dreams," Joseph said. "Tell me your dreams."

9 So the wine steward said, "In my dream there was a grapevine in front of me ¹⁰with three branches on it. As soon as the leaves came out, the blossoms appeared, and the grapes ripened. ¹¹I was holding the king's cup; so I took the grapes and squeezed them into the cup and gave it to him."

12 Joseph said, "This is what it means: the three branches are three days. ¹³In three days the king will release you, pardon you, and restore you to your position. You will give him his cup as you did before when you were his wine steward. ¹⁴But please remember me when everything is going well for you, and please be kind enough to mention me to the king and help me to get out of this prison. ¹⁵After all, I was kidnapped from the land of the Hebrews, and even here in Egypt I didn't do anything to deserve being put in prison."

16 When the chief baker saw that the interpretation of the wine steward's dream was favourable, he said to Joseph, "I had a dream too; I was carrying three bread-baskets on my head. ¹⁷In the top basket there were all kinds of pastries for the king, and the birds were eating them."

18 Joseph answered, "This is what it means: the three baskets are three days. ¹⁹In three days the king will release you— and have your head cut off! Then he will hang your body on a pole, and the birds will eat your flesh."

20 On his birthday three days later the king gave a banquet for all his officials; he released his wine steward and his chief baker and brought them before his officials. ²¹He restored the wine steward to his former position, ²²but he executed the chief baker. It all happened just as Joseph had said. ²³But the wine steward never gave Joseph another thought—he forgot all about him.

Joseph Interprets the King's Dreams

41 After two years had passed, the king of Egypt dreamt that he was standing by the River Nile, ²when seven cows, fat and sleek, came up out of the river and began to feed on the grass. ³Then seven other cows came up; they were thin and bony. They came and stood by the other cows on the river-bank, ⁴and the thin cows ate up the fat cows. Then the king woke up. ⁵He fell asleep again and had another dream. Seven ears of corn, full and ripe, were growing on one stalk. ⁶Then seven other ears of corn sprouted, thin and scorched by the desert wind, ⁷and the thin ears of corn swallowed the full ones. The king woke up and realized that he had been dreaming. ⁸In the morning he was worried, so he sent for all the magicians and wise men of Egypt. He told them his dreams, but no one could explain them to him.

9 Then the wine steward said to the king, "I must confess today that I have done wrong. ¹⁰You were angry with the chief baker and me, and you put us in prison in the house of the captain of the guard. ¹¹One night each of us had a dream, and the dreams had different meanings. ¹²A young Hebrew was there with us, a slave of the captain of the guard. We told him our dreams, and he interpreted them for us. ¹³Things turned out just as he said: you restored me to my position, but you executed the baker."

14 The king sent for Joseph, and he was immediately brought from the prison. After he had shaved and changed his clothes, he came into the king's presence. ¹⁵The king said to him, "I have had a dream, and no one can explain it. I have been told that you can interpret dreams."

16 Joseph answered, "I cannot, Your Majesty, but God will give a favourable interpretation."

17 The king said, "I dreamt that I was standing on the bank of the Nile, ¹⁸when seven cows, fat and sleek, came up out of the river and began feeding on the grass. ¹⁹Then seven other cows came up

41.8: Dan 2.2

which were thin and bony. They were the poorest cows I have ever seen anywhere in Egypt. 20 The thin cows ate up the fat ones, 21 but no one would have known it, because they looked just as bad as before. Then I woke up. 22 I also dreamt that I saw seven ears of corn which were full and ripe, growing on one stalk. 23 Then seven ears of corn sprouted, thin and scorched by the desert wind, 24 and the thin ears of corn swallowed the full ones. I told the dreams to the magicians, but none of them could explain them to me."

25 Joseph said to the king, "The two dreams mean the same thing; God has told you what he is going to do. 26 The seven fat cows are seven years, and the seven full ears of corn are also seven years; they have the same meaning. 27 The seven thin cows which came up later and the seven thin ears of corn scorched by the desert wind are seven years of famine. 28 It is just as I told you—God has shown you what he is going to do. 29 There will be seven years of great plenty in all the land of Egypt. 30 After that, there will be seven years of famine, and all the good years will be forgotten, because the famine will ruin the country. 31 The time of plenty will be entirely forgotten, because the famine which follows will be so terrible. 32 The repetition of your dream means that the matter is fixed by God and that he will make it happen in the near future.

33 "Now you should choose some man with wisdom and insight and put him in charge of the country. 34 You must also appoint other officials and take a fifth of the crops during the seven years of plenty. 35 Order them to collect all the food during the good years that are coming, and give them authority to store up corn in the cities and guard it. 36 The food will be a reserve supply for the country during the seven years of famine which are going to come on Egypt. In this way the people will not starve."

Joseph Is Made Governor over Egypt

37 The king and his officials approved this plan, 38 and he said to them, "We will never find a better man than Joseph, a man who has God's spirit in him." 39 The king said to Joseph, "God has shown you all this, so it is obvious that you have greater wisdom and insight than anyone else. 40 I will put you in charge of my country, and all my people will obey your orders. Your authority will be second only to mine. 41 I now appoint you governor over all Egypt." 42 The king removed from his finger the ring engraved with the royal seal and put it on Joseph's finger. He put a fine linen robe on him, and placed a gold chain round his neck. 43 He gave him the second royal chariot to ride in, and his guard of honour went ahead of him and cried out, "Make way! Make way!" And so Joseph was appointed governor over all Egypt. 44 The king said to him, "I am the king—and no one in all Egypt shall so much as lift a hand or a foot without your permission." 45-46 He gave Joseph the Egyptian name Zaphenath Paneah, and he gave him a wife, Asenath, the daughter of Potiphera, a priest in the city of Heliopolis.

Joseph was thirty years old when he began to serve the king of Egypt. He left the king's court and travelled all over the land. 47 During the seven years of plenty the land produced abundant crops, 48 all of which Joseph collected and stored in the cities. In each city he stored the food from the fields around it. 49 There was so much corn that Joseph stopped measuring it—it was like the sand of the sea.

50 Before the years of famine came, Joseph had two sons by Asenath. 51 He said, "God has made me forget all my sufferings and all my father's family"; so he named his first son Manasseh. o 52 He also said, "God has given me children in the land of my trouble"; so he named his second son Ephraim. p

53 The seven years of plenty that the land of Egypt had enjoyed came to an end, 54 and the seven years of famine began, just as Joseph had said. There was famine in every other country, but there was food throughout Egypt. 55 When the Egyptians began to be hungry, they cried out to the king for food. So he ordered them to go to Joseph and do what he told them. 56 The famine grew worse and spread over the whole country, so Joseph opened all the storehouses and sold corn to the Egyptians. 57 People came to Egypt from all over the world to buy corn from Joseph, because the famine was severe everywhere.

o MANASSEH: This name sounds like the Hebrew for "cause to forget."
p EPHRAIM: This name sounds like the Hebrew for "give children."
41.40: Acts 7.10   41.42: Dan 5.29   41.54: Acts 7.11   41.55: Jn 2.5

Joseph's Brothers Go to Egypt to Buy Corn

42 When Jacob learnt that there was corn in Egypt, he said to his sons, "Why don't you do something? ²I hear that there is corn in Egypt; go there and buy some to keep us from starving to death." ³So Joseph's ten half-brothers went to buy corn in Egypt, ⁴but Jacob did not send Joseph's full-brother Benjamin with them, because he was afraid that something might happen to him.

5 The sons of Jacob came with others to buy corn, because there was famine in the land of Canaan. ⁶Joseph, as governor of the land of Egypt, was selling corn to people from all over the world. So Joseph's brothers came and bowed down before him with their faces to the ground. ⁷When Joseph saw his brothers, he recognized them, but he acted as if he did not know them. He asked them harshly, "Where do you come from?"

"We have come from Canaan to buy food," they answered.

8 Although Joseph recognized his brothers, they did not recognize him. ⁹He remembered the dreams he had dreamt about them and said, "You are spies; you have come to find out where our country is weak."

10 "No, sir," they answered. "We have come as your slaves, to buy food. ¹¹We are all brothers. We are not spies, sir, we are honest men."

12 Joseph said to them, "No! You have come to find out where our country is weak."

13 They said, "We were twelve brothers in all, sir, sons of the same man in the land of Canaan. One brother is dead, and the youngest is now with our father."

14 "It is just as I said," Joseph answered. "You are spies. ¹⁵This is how you will be tested: I swear by the name of the king that you will never leave unless your youngest brother comes here. ¹⁶One of you must go and get him. The rest of you will be kept under guard until the truth of what you say can be tested. Otherwise, as sure as the king lives, you are spies." ¹⁷Then he put them in prison for three days.

18 On the third day Joseph said to them, "I am a God-fearing man, and I will spare your lives on one condition. ¹⁹To prove

that you are honest, one of you will stay in the prison where you have been kept; the rest of you may go and take back to your starving families the corn that you have bought. ²⁰Then you must bring your youngest brother to me. This will prove that you have been telling the truth, and I will not put you to death."

They agreed to this ²¹and said to one another, "Yes, now we are suffering the consequences of what we did to our brother; we saw the great trouble he was in when he begged for help, but we would not listen. That is why we are in this trouble now."

22 Reuben said, "I told you not to harm the boy, but you wouldn't listen. And now we are being paid back for his death." ²³Joseph understood what they said, but they did not know it, because they had been speaking to him through an interpreter. ²⁴Joseph left them and began to cry. When he was able to speak again, he came back, picked out Simeon, and had him tied up in front of them.

Joseph's Brothers Return to Canaan

25 Joseph gave orders to fill his brothers' packs with corn, to put each man's money back in his sack, and to give them food for the journey. This was done. ²⁶The brothers loaded their donkeys with the corn they had bought, and then they left. ²⁷At the place where they spent the night, one of them opened his sack to feed his donkey and found his money at the top of the sack. ²⁸"My money has been returned to me," he called to his brothers. "Here it is in my sack!" Their hearts sank, and in fear they asked one another, "What has God done to us?"

29 When they came to their father Jacob in Canaan, they told him all that had happened to them: ³⁰"The governor of Egypt spoke harshly to us and accused us of spying against his country. ³¹'We are not spies,' we answered, 'we are honest men. ³²We were twelve brothers in all, sons of the same father. One brother is dead, and the youngest is still in Canaan with our father.' ³³The man answered, 'This is how I will find out if you are honest men: One of you will stay with me; the rest will take corn for your starving families and leave. ³⁴Bring your youngest brother to me. Then I will know that you are not spies, but honest men; I will give

42.2: Acts 7.12   42.9: Gen 37.5–10   42.22: Gen 37.21–22

your brother back to you, and you can stay here and trade.'"

35 Then when they emptied out their sacks, every one of them found his bag of money; and when they saw the money, they and their father Jacob were afraid. 36 Their father said to them, "Do you want to make me lose all my children? Joseph is gone; Simeon is gone; and now you want to take away Benjamin. I am the one who suffers!"

37 Reuben said to his father, "If I do not bring Benjamin back to you, you can kill my two sons. Put him in my care, and I will bring him back."

38 But Jacob said, "My son cannot go with you; his brother is dead, and he is the only one left. Something might happen to him on the way. I am an old man, and the sorrow you would cause me would kill me."

Joseph's Brothers Return to Egypt with Benjamin

43 The famine in Canaan got worse, 2 and when the family of Jacob had eaten all the corn which had been brought from Egypt, Jacob said to his sons, "Go back and buy a little food for us."

3 Judah said to him, "The man sternly warned us that we would not be admitted to his presence unless we had our brother with us. 4 If you are willing to send our brother with us, we will go and buy food for you. 5 If you are not willing, we will not go, because the man told us we would not be admitted to his presence unless our brother was with us."

6 Jacob said, "Why did you cause me so much trouble by telling the man that you had another brother?"

7 They answered, "The man kept asking about us and our family, 'Is your father still living? Have you got another brother?' We had to answer his questions. How could we know that he would tell us to bring our brother with us?"

8 Judah said to his father, "Send the boy with me, and we will leave at once. Then none of us will starve to death. 9 I will pledge my own life, and you can hold me responsible for him. If I do not bring him back to you safe and sound, I will always bear the blame. 10 If we had not waited so long, we could have been there and back twice by now."

11 Their father said to them, "If that is how it has to be, then take the best products of the land in your packs as a present for the governor: a little resin,

a little honey, spices, pistachio nuts, and almonds. 12 Take with you also twice as much money, because you must take back the money that was returned in the top of your sacks. Maybe it was a mistake. 13 Take your brother and return at once. 14 May Almighty God cause the man to have pity on you, so that he will give Benjamin and your other brother back to you. As for me, if I must lose my children, I must lose them."

15 So the brothers took the gifts and twice as much money, and set out for Egypt with Benjamin. There they presented themselves to Joseph. 16 When Joseph saw Benjamin with them, he said to the servant in charge of his house, "Take these men to my house. They are going to eat with me at noon, so kill an animal and prepare it." 17 The servant did as he was commanded and took the brothers to Joseph's house.

18 As they were being brought to the house, they were afraid and thought, "We are being brought here because of the money that was returned in our sacks the first time. They will suddenly attack us, take our donkeys, and make us his slaves." 19 So at the door of the house, they said to the servant in charge, 20 "If you please, sir, we came here once before to buy food. 21 When we set up camp on the way home, we opened our sacks, and each man found his money in the top of his sack—every bit of it. We have brought it back to you. 22 We have also brought some more money with us to buy more food. We do not know who put our money back in our sacks."

23 The servant said, "Don't worry. Don't be afraid. Your God, the God of your father, must have put the money in your sacks for you. I received your payment." Then he brought Simeon to them.

24 The servant took the brothers into the house. He gave them water so that they could wash their feet, and he fed their donkeys. 25 They got their gifts ready to present to Joseph when he arrived at noon, because they had been told that they were to eat with him. 26 When Joseph got home, they took the gifts into the house to him and bowed down to the ground before him. 27 He asked about their health and then said, "You told me about your old father—how is he? Is he still alive and well?"

28 They answered, "Your humble servant, our father, is still alive and well."

And they knelt and bowed down before him.

29 When Joseph saw his brother Benjamin, he said, "So this is your youngest brother, the one you told me about. God bless you, my son." 30 Then Joseph left suddenly, because his heart was full of tender feelings for his brother. He was about to break down, so he went to his room and cried. 31 After he had washed his face, he came out, and controlling himself, he ordered the meal to be served. 32 Joseph was served at one table and his brothers at another. The Egyptians who were eating there were served separately, because they considered it beneath their dignity to eat with Hebrews. 33 The brothers had been seated at table, facing Joseph, in the order of their age from the eldest to the youngest. When they saw how they had been seated, they looked at one another in amazement. 34 Food was served to them from Joseph's table, and Benjamin was served five times as much as the rest of them. So they ate and drank with Joseph until they were drunk.

The Missing Cup

44 Joseph commanded the servant in charge of his house, "Fill the men's sacks with as much food as they can carry, and put each man's money in the top of his sack. 2 Put my silver cup in the top of the youngest brother's sack, together with the money for his corn." He did as he was told. 3 Early in the morning the brothers were sent on their way with their donkeys. 4 When they had gone only a short distance from the city, Joseph said to the servant in charge of his house, "Hurry after those men. When you catch up with them, ask them, 'Why have you paid back evil for good? 5 Why did you steal my master's silver cup?q It is the one he drinks from, the one he uses for divination. You have committed a serious crime!'"

6 When the servant caught up with them, he repeated these words. 7 They answered him, "What do you mean, sir, by talking like this? We swear that we have done no such thing. 8 You know that we brought back to you from the land of Canaan the money we found in the top of our sacks. Why then should we steal silver or gold from your master's house? 9 Sir, if any one of us is found to have it, he will be put to death, and the rest of us will become your slaves."

10 He said, "I agree; but only the one who has taken the cup will become my slave, and the rest of you can go free." 11 So they quickly lowered their sacks to the ground, and each man opened his sack. 12 Joseph's servant searched carefully, beginning with the eldest and ending with the youngest, and the cup was found in Benjamin's sack. 13 The brothers tore their clothes in sorrow, loaded their donkeys, and returned to the city.

14 When Judah and his brothers came to Joseph's house, he was still there. They bowed down before him, 15 and Joseph said, "What have you done? Didn't you know that a man in my position could find you out by practising divination?"

16 "What can we say to you, sir?" Judah answered. "How can we argue? How can we clear ourselves? God has uncovered our guilt. All of us are now your slaves and not just the one with whom the cup was found."

17 Joseph said, "Oh, no! I would never do that! Only the one who had the cup will be my slave. The rest of you may go back safe and sound to your father."

Judah Pleads for Benjamin

18 Judah went up to Joseph and said, "Please, sir, allow me to speak with you freely. Don't be angry with me; you are like the king himself. 19 Sir, you asked us, 'Have you got a father or another brother?' 20 We answered, 'We have a father who is old and a younger brother, born to him in his old age. The boy's brother is dead, and he is the only one of his mother's children still alive; his father loves him very much.' 21 Sir, you told us to bring him here, so that you could see him, 22 and we answered that the boy could not leave his father; if he did, his father would die. 23 Then you said, 'You will not be admitted to my presence again unless your youngest brother comes with you.'

24 "When we went back to our father, we told him what you had said. 25 Then he told us to return and buy a little food. 26 We answered, 'We cannot go; we will not be admitted to the man's presence unless our youngest brother is with us. We can go only if our youngest brother

q One ancient translation Why did you steal my master's silver cup?; Hebrew does not have these words.

goes also.' ²⁷Our father said to us, 'You know that my wife Rachel bore me only two sons. ²⁸One of them has already left me. He must have been torn to pieces by wild animals, because I have not seen him since he left. ²⁹If you take this one from me now and something happens to him, the sorrow you would cause me would kill me, old as I am.'

30-31 "And now, sir," Judah continued, "if I go back to my father without the boy, as soon as he sees that the boy is not with me, he will die. His life is wrapped up with the life of the boy, and he is so old that the sorrow we would cause him would kill him. ³²What is more, I pledged my life to my father for the boy. I told him that if I did not bring the boy back to him, I would bear the blame all my life. ³³And now, sir, I will stay here as your slave in place of the boy; let him go back with his brothers. ³⁴How can I go back to my father if the boy is not with me? I cannot bear to see this disaster come upon my father."

Joseph Tells His Brothers Who He Is

45 Joseph was no longer able to control his feelings in front of his servants, so he ordered them all to leave the room. No one else was with him when Joseph told his brothers who he was. ²He cried with such loud sobs that the Egyptians heard it, and the news was taken to the king's palace. ³Joseph said to his brothers, "I am Joseph. Is my father still alive?" But when his brothers heard this, they were so terrified that they could not answer. ⁴Then Joseph said to them, "Please come closer." They did, and he said, "I am your brother Joseph, whom you sold into Egypt. ⁵Now do not be upset or blame yourselves because you sold me here. It was really God who sent me ahead of you to save people's lives. ⁶This is only the second year of famine in the land; there will be five more years in which there will be neither ploughing nor reaping. ⁷God sent me ahead of you to rescue you in this amazing way and to make sure that you and your descendants survive. ⁸So it was not really you who sent me here, but God. He has made me the king's highest official. I am in charge of his whole country; I am the ruler of all Egypt.

⁹"Now hurry back to my father and tell him that this is what his son Joseph

says: 'God has made me ruler of all Egypt; come to me without delay. ¹⁰You can live in the region of Goshen, where you can be near me—you, your children, your grandchildren, your sheep, your goats, your cattle, and everything else that you have. ¹¹If you are in Goshen, I can take care of you. There will still be five years of famine; and I do not want you, your family, and your livestock to starve.' "

12 Joseph continued, "Now all of you, and you too, Benjamin, can see that I am really Joseph. ¹³Tell my father how powerful I am here in Egypt and tell him about everything that you have seen. Then hurry and bring him here."

14 He threw his arms round his brother Benjamin and began to cry; Benjamin also cried as he hugged him. ¹⁵Then, still weeping, he embraced each of his brothers and kissed them. After that, his brothers began to talk with him.

16 When the news reached the palace that Joseph's brothers had come, the king and his officials were pleased. ¹⁷He said to Joseph, "Tell your brothers to load their animals and to return to the land of Canaan. ¹⁸Let them get their father and their families and come back here. I will give them the best land in Egypt, and they will have more than enough to live on. ¹⁹Tell them also to take wagons with them from Egypt for their wives and small children and to bring their father with them. ²⁰They are not to worry about leaving their possessions behind; the best in the whole land of Egypt will be theirs."

21 Jacob's sons did as they were told. Joseph gave them wagons, as the king had ordered, and food for the journey. ²²He also gave each of them a change of clothes, but he gave Benjamin three hundred pieces of silver and five changes of clothes. ²³He sent his father ten donkeys loaded with the best Egyptian goods and ten donkeys loaded with corn, bread, and other food for the journey. ²⁴He sent his brothers off and as they left, he said to them, "Don't quarrel on the way."

25 They left Egypt and went back home to their father Jacob in Canaan. ²⁶"Joseph is still alive!" they told him. "He is the ruler of all Egypt!" Jacob was stunned and could not believe them.

27 But when they told him all that Joseph had said to them, and when he saw the wagons which Joseph had sent

45.1: Acts 7.13   **45.9-11:** Acts 7.14

to take him to Egypt, he recovered from the shock. ²⁸ "My son Joseph is still alive!" he said. "This is all I could ask for! I must go and see him before I die."

Jacob and His Family Go to Egypt

46 Jacob packed up all he had and went to Beersheba, where he offered sacrifices to the God of his father Isaac. ² God spoke to him in a vision at night and called, "Jacob, Jacob!"

"Yes, here I am," he answered.

3 "I am God, the God of your father," he said. "Do not be afraid to go to Egypt; I will make your descendants a great nation there. ⁴ I will go with you to Egypt, and I will bring your descendants back to this land. Joseph will be with you when you die."

5 Jacob set out from Beersheba. His sons put him, their small children, and their wives in the wagons which the king of Egypt had sent. ⁶ They took their livestock and the possessions they had acquired in Canaan and went to Egypt. Jacob took all his descendants with him: ⁷ his sons, his grandsons, his daughters, and his granddaughters.

8 The members of Jacob's family who went to Egypt with him were his eldest son Reuben ⁹ and Reuben's sons: Hanoch, Pallu, Hezron, and Carmi. ¹⁰ Simeon and his sons: Jemuel, Jamin, Ohad, Jachin, Zohar, and Shaul, the son of a Canaanite woman. ¹¹ Levi and his sons: Gershon, Kohath, and Merari. ¹² Judah and his sons: Shelah, Perez, and Zerah. (Judah's other sons, Er and Onan, had died in Canaan.) Perez' sons were Hezron and Hamul. ¹³ Issachar and his sons: Tola, Puah, Jashub, and Shimron. ¹⁴ Zebulun and his sons: Sered, Elon, and Jahleel. ¹⁵ These are the sons that Leah had borne to Jacob in Mesopotamia, besides his daughter Dinah. In all, his descendants by Leah numbered thirty-three.

16 Gad and his sons: Zephon, Haggi, Shuni, Ezbon, Eri, Arod, and Areli. ¹⁷ Asher and his sons: Imnah, Ishvah, Ishvi, Beriah, and their sister Serah. Beriah's sons were Heber and Malchiel. ¹⁸ These sixteen are the descendants of Jacob by Zilpah, the slave-girl whom Laban gave to his daughter Leah.

19 Jacob's wife Rachel bore him two sons: Joseph and Benjamin. ²⁰ In Egypt Joseph had two sons, Manasseh and Ephraim, by Asenath, the daughter of Potiphera, a priest in Heliopolis. ²¹ Benjamin's sons were Bela, Becher, Ashbel, Gera, Naaman, Ehi, Rosh, Muppim, Huppim, and Ard. ²² These fourteen are the descendants of Jacob by Rachel.

23 Dan and his son Hushim. ²⁴ Naphtali and his sons: Jahzeel, Guni, Jezer, and Shillem. ²⁵ These seven are the descendants of Jacob by Bilhah, the slave-girl whom Laban gave to his daughter Rachel.

26 The total number of the direct descendants of Jacob who went to Egypt was sixty-six, not including his sons' wives. ²⁷ Two sons were born to Joseph in Egypt, bringing to seventy the total number of Jacob's family who went there.

Jacob and His Family in Egypt

28 Jacob sent Judah ahead to ask Joseph to meet them in Goshen. When they arrived, ²⁹ Joseph got in his chariot and went to Goshen to meet his father. When they met, Joseph threw his arms round his father's neck and cried for a long time. ³⁰ Jacob said to Joseph, "I am ready to die, now that I have seen you and know that you are still alive."

31 Then Joseph said to his brothers and the rest of his father's family, "I must go and tell the king that my brothers and all my father's family, who were living in Canaan, have come to me. ³² I will tell him that you are shepherds and take care of livestock and that you have brought your flocks and herds and everything else that belongs to you. ³³ When the king calls for you and asks what your occupation is, ³⁴ be sure to tell him that you have taken care of livestock all your lives, just as your ancestors did. In this way he will let you live in the region of Goshen." Joseph said this because Egyptians will have nothing to do with shepherds.

47 So Joseph took five of his brothers and went to the king. He said, "My father and my brothers have come from Canaan with their flocks, their herds, and all that they own. They are now in the region of Goshen." ² He then presented his brothers to the king. ³ The king asked them, "What is your occupation?"

"We are shepherds, sir, just as our ancestors were," they answered. ⁴ "We have come to live in this country, because in the land of Canaan the famine is so severe that there is no pasture for our flocks. Please give us permission to live

46.6: Acts 7.15   **46.20:** Gen 41.50–52   **46.27:** Acts 7.14

in the region of Goshen." 5 The king said to Joseph, "Now that your father and your brothers have arrived, 6 the land of Egypt is theirs. Let them settle in the region of Goshen, the best part of the land. And if there are any capable men among them, put them in charge of my own livestock."

7 Then Joseph brought his father Jacob and presented him to the king. Jacob gave the king his blessing, 8 and the king asked him, "How old are you?"

9 Jacob answered, "My life of wandering has lasted a hundred and thirty years. Those years have been few and difficult, unlike the long years of my ancestors in their wanderings." 10 Jacob gave the king a farewell blessing and left. 11 Then Joseph settled his father and his brothers in Egypt, giving them property in the best of the land near the city of Rameses, as the king had commanded. 12 Joseph provided food for his father, his brothers, and all the rest of his father's family, including the very youngest.

The Famine

13 The famine was so severe that there was no food anywhere, and the people of Egypt and Canaan became weak with hunger. 14 As they bought corn, Joseph collected all the money and took it to the palace. 15 When all the money in Egypt and Canaan was spent, the Egyptians came to Joseph and said, "Give us food! Don't let us die. Do something! Our money is all gone."

16 Joseph answered, "Bring your livestock; I will give you food in exchange for it if your money is all gone." 17 So they brought their livestock to Joseph, and he gave them food in exchange for their horses, sheep, goats, cattle, and donkeys. That year he supplied them with food in exchange for all their livestock.

18 The following year they came to him and said, "We will not hide the fact from you, sir, that our money is all gone and our livestock belongs to you. There is nothing left to give you except our bodies and our lands. 19 Don't let us die. Do something! Don't let our fields be deserted. Buy us and our land in exchange for food. We will be the king's slaves, and he will own our land. Give us corn to keep us alive and seed to sow in our fields."

20 Joseph bought all the land in Egypt for the king. Every Egyptian was forced to sell his land, because the famine was so severe; and all the land became the king's property. 21 Joseph made slaves of the people from one end of Egypt to the other. 22 The only land he did not buy was the land that belonged to the priests. They did not have to sell their lands, because the king gave them an allowance to live on. 23 Joseph said to the people, "You see, I have now bought you and your lands for the king. Here is seed for you to sow in your fields. 24 At the time of harvest you must give one-fifth to the king. You can use the rest for seed and for food for yourselves and your families."

25 They answered, "You have saved our lives; you have been good to us, sir, and we will be the king's slaves." 26 So Joseph made it a law for the land of Egypt that one-fifth of the harvest should belong to the king. This law still remains in force today. Only the lands of the priests did not become the king's property.

Jacob's Last Request

27 The Israelites lived in Egypt in the region of Goshen, where they became rich and had many children. 28 Jacob lived in Egypt for seventeen years, until he was a hundred and forty-seven years old. 29 When the time drew near for him to die, he called for his son Joseph and said to him, "Place your hand between my thighs[r] and make a solemn vow that you will not bury me in Egypt. 30 I want to be buried where my fathers are; carry me out of Egypt and bury me where they are buried."

Joseph answered, "I will do as you say."

31 Jacob said, "Make a vow that you will." Joseph made the vow, and Jacob gave thanks there on his bed.

Jacob Blesses Ephraim and Manasseh

48 Some time later Joseph was told that his father was ill. So he took his two sons, Manasseh and Ephraim, and went to see Jacob. 2 When Jacob was told that his son Joseph had come to see him, he gathered his strength and sat up in bed. 3 Jacob said to Joseph, "Almighty God appeared to me at Luz in the land of Canaan and blessed me. 4 He said to me, 'I will give you many children, so that your descendants will become many nations; I will give this land to your

[r]PLACE...THIGHS: *See 24.2.*
47.29-30: Gen 49.29-32, 50.6   **48.3-4:** Gen 28.13-14

descendants as their possession for ever.'"

5 Jacob continued, "Joseph, your two sons, who were born to you in Egypt before I came here, belong to me; Ephraim and Manasseh are just as much my sons as Reuben and Simeon. 6 If you have any more sons, they will not be considered mine; the inheritance they get will come through Ephraim and Manasseh. 7 I am doing this because of your mother Rachel. To my great sorrow she died in the land of Canaan, not far from Ephrath, as I was returning from Mesopotamia. I buried her there beside the road to Ephrath." (Ephrath is now known as Bethlehem.)

8 When Jacob saw Joseph's sons, he asked, "Who are these boys?"

9 Joseph answered, "These are my sons, whom God has given me here in Egypt."

Jacob said, "Bring them to me so that I may bless them." 10 Jacob's eyesight was failing because of his age, and he could not see very well. Joseph brought the boys to him, and he hugged them and kissed them. 11 Jacob said to Joseph, "I never expected to see you again, and now God has even let me see your children." 12 Then Joseph took them from Jacob's lap and bowed down before him with his face to the ground.

13 Joseph put Ephraim at Jacob's left and Manasseh at his right. 14 But Jacob crossed his hands, and put his right hand on the head of Ephraim, even though he was the younger, and his left hand on the head of Manasseh, who was the elder. 15 Then he blessed Joseph: s

"May the God whom my fathers
   Abraham and Isaac served bless
   these boys!
May God, who has led me to this very
   day, bless them!
16 May the angel, who has rescued me
   from all harm, bless them!
May my name and the name of my
   fathers Abraham and Isaac live
   on through these boys!
May they have many children, many
   descendants!"

17 Joseph was upset when he saw that his father had put his right hand on Ephraim's head; so he took his father's hand to move it from Ephraim's head to the head of Manasseh. 18 He said to his father, "Not that way, father. This is the elder boy; put your right hand on his head."

May God...bless these boys! (48.15)

19 His father refused, saying, "I know, my son, I know. Manasseh's descendants will also become a great people. But his younger brother will be greater than he, and his descendants will become great nations."

20 So he blessed them that day, saying, "The Israelites will use your names when they pronounce blessings. They will say, 'May God make you like Ephraim and Manasseh.'" In this way Jacob put Ephraim before Manasseh.

21 Then Jacob said to Joseph, "As you see, I am about to die, but God will be with you and will take you back to the land of your ancestors. 22 It is to you and not to your brothers that I am giving Shechem, that fertile region which I took from the Amorites with my sword and my bow."

The Last Words of Jacob

49 Jacob called for his sons and said, "Gather round, and I will tell you what will happen to you in the future:
2 "Come together and listen, sons of
   Jacob.
Listen to your father Israel.

3 "Reuben, my first-born, you are my
   strength
And the first child of my manhood,
The proudest and strongest of all my
   sons.

s JOSEPH: *In blessing Ephraim and Manasseh, Jacob was in fact blessing Joseph.*
48.7: Gen 35.16–19   **48.20:** Heb 11.21

⁴ You are like a raging flood,
But you will not be the most important,
For you slept with my concubine
And dishonoured your father's bed.

⁵ "Simeon and Levi are brothers.
They use their weapons to commit
violence.
⁶ I will not join in their secret talks,
Nor will I take part in their meetings,
For they killed men in anger
And they crippled bulls for sport.
⁷ A curse be on their anger, because it
is so fierce,
And on their fury, because it is so cruel.
I will scatter them throughout the land
of Israel.
I will disperse them among its people.

⁸ "Judah, your brothers will praise you.
You hold your enemies by the neck.
Your brothers will bow down before
you.
⁹ Judah is like a lion,
Killing his victim and returning to his
den,
Stretching out and lying down.
No one dares disturb him.
¹⁰ Judah will hold the royal sceptre,
And his descendants will always rule.
Nations will bring him tribute ˢ
And bow in obedience before him.
¹¹ He ties his young donkey to a
grapevine,
To the very best of the vines.
He washes his clothes in blood-red wine.
¹² His eyes are bloodshot from drinking
wine,
His teeth white from drinking milk. ᵗ

¹³ "Zebulun will live beside the sea.
His shore will be a haven for ships.
His territory will reach as far as Sidon.

¹⁴ "Issachar is no better than a donkey
That lies stretched out between its
saddlebags.
¹⁵ But he sees that the resting-place is
good
And that the land is delightful.
So he bends his back to carry the load
And is forced to work as a slave.

¹⁶ "Dan will be a ruler for his people.
They will be like the other tribes of
Israel.
¹⁷ Dan will be a snake at the side of
the road,
A poisonous snake beside the path,
That strikes at the horse's heel,
So that the rider is thrown off
backwards.

¹⁸ "I wait for your deliverance, LORD.

¹⁹ "Gad will be attacked by a band of
robbers,
But he will turn and pursue them.

²⁰ "Asher's land will produce rich food.
He will provide food fit for a king.

²¹ "Naphtali is a deer that runs free,
Who bears lovely fawns. ᵘ

²² "Joseph is like a wild donkey by a
spring,
A wild colt on a hillside. ᵛ
²³ His enemies attack him fiercely
And pursue him with their bows and
arrows.
²⁴ But his bow remains steady,
And his arms are made strong ʷ
By the power of the Mighty God of
Jacob,
By the Shepherd, the Protector of Israel.
²⁵ It is your father's God who helps you,
The Almighty God who blesses you
With blessings of rain from above
And of deep waters from beneath the
ground,
Blessings of many cattle and children,
²⁶ Blessings of corn and flowers, ˣ
Blessings of ancient mountains, ʸ
Delightful things from everlasting hills.
May these blessings rest on the head
of Joseph,
On the brow of the one set apart from
his brothers.

²⁷ "Benjamin is like a vicious wolf.
Morning and evening he kills and
devours."

28 These are the twelve tribes of Israel,

ˢ Probable text Nations...tribute; Hebrew unclear.
ᵗ His eyes...milk; or His eyes are darker than wine, his teeth are whiter than milk.
ᵘ Naphtali...fawns; or Naphtali is a spreading tree that puts out lovely branches.
ᵛ Joseph...hillside; or Joseph is like a tree by a spring, a fruitful tree that spreads over a wall.
ʷ But...strong; or But their bows were broken and splintered, the muscles of their arms torn apart.
ˣ Probable text corn and flowers; Hebrew your fathers are mightier than.
ʸ One ancient translation ancient mountains; Hebrew my ancestors to.
49.9: Num 24.9; Rev 5.5

and this is what their father said as he spoke a suitable word of farewell to each son.

The Death and Burial of Jacob

29 Then Jacob commanded his sons, "Now that I am going to join my people in death, bury me with my fathers in the cave that is in the field of Ephron the Hittite, 30 at Machpelah, east of Mamre, in the land of Canaan. Abraham bought this cave and field from Ephron for a burial-ground. 31 That is where they buried Abraham and his wife Sarah; that is where they buried Isaac and his wife Rebecca; and that is where I buried Leah. 32 The field and the cave in it were bought from the Hittites. Bury me there." 33 When Jacob had finished giving instructions to his sons, he lay down again and died.

50 Joseph threw himself on his father, crying and kissing his face. 2 Then Joseph gave orders to embalm his father's body. 3 It took forty days, the normal time for embalming. The Egyptians mourned for him seventy days.

4 When the time of mourning was over, Joseph said to the king's officials, "Please take this message to the king: 5 'When my father was about to die, he made me promise him that I would bury him in the tomb which he had prepared in the land of Canaan. So please let me go and bury my father, and then I will come back.' "

6 The king answered, "Go and bury your father, as you promised you would."

7 So Joseph went to bury his father. All the king's officials, the senior men of his court, and all the leading men of Egypt went with Joseph. 8 His family, his brothers, and the rest of his father's family all went with him. Only their small children and their sheep, goats, and cattle stayed in the region of Goshen. 9 Men in chariots and men on horseback also went with him; it was a huge group.

10 When they came to the threshing-place at Atad east of the Jordan, they mourned loudly for a long time, and Joseph performed mourning ceremonies for seven days. 11 When the citizens of Canaan saw those people mourning at Atad, they said, "What a solemn ceremony of mourning the Egyptians are holding!" That is why the place was named Abel Mizraim. z

12 So Jacob's sons did as he had commanded them; 13 they carried his body to Canaan and buried it in the cave at Machpelah, east of Mamre, in the field which Abraham had bought from Ephron the Hittite for a burial-ground. 14 After Joseph had buried his father, he returned to Egypt with his brothers and all who had gone with him for the funeral.

Joseph Reassures His Brothers

15 After the death of their father, Joseph's brothers said, "What if Joseph still hates us and plans to pay us back for all the harm we did to him?" 16 So they sent a message to Joseph: "Before our father died, 17 he told us to ask you, 'Please forgive the crime your brothers committed when they wronged you.' Now please forgive us the wrong that we, the servants of your father's God, have done." Joseph cried when he received this message.

18 Then his brothers themselves came and bowed down before him. "Here we are before you as your slaves," they said.

19 But Joseph said to them, "Don't be afraid; I can't put myself in the place of God. 20 You plotted evil against me, but God turned it into good, in order to preserve the lives of many people who are alive today because of what happened. 21 You have nothing to fear. I will take care of you and your children." So he reassured them with kind words that touched their hearts.

The Death of Joseph

22 Joseph continued to live in Egypt with his father's family; he was a hundred and ten years old when he died. 23 He lived to see Ephraim's children and grand-children. He also lived to receive the children of Machir son of Manasseh into the family. 24 He said to his brothers, "I am about to die, but God will certainly take care of you and lead you out of this land to the land he solemnly promised to Abraham, Isaac, and Jacob." 25 Then Joseph asked his people to make a vow. "Promise me," he said, "that when God leads you to that land, you will take my body with you." 26 So Joseph died in Egypt at the age of a hundred and ten. They embalmed his body and put it in a coffin.

THE ROUTE OF THE EXODUS

EXODUS

INTRODUCTION

The name *Exodus* means 'departure,' and refers to the most important event in Israel's history, which is described in this book—the departure of the people of Israel from Egypt, where they had been slaves. The book has four main parts: (1) the freeing of the Hebrews from slavery; (2) their journey to Mount Sinai; (3) God's covenant with his people at Sinai, which gave them moral, civil, and religious laws to live by; (4) the building and furnishing of a place of worship for Israel, and laws regarding the priests and the worship of God.

Above all, this book describes what God did, as he liberated his enslaved people and formed them into a nation with hope for the future.

The central human figure in the book is Moses, the man whom God chose to lead his people from Egypt. The most widely known part of the book is the list of the Ten Commandments in chapter 20.

Outline of Contents

The Israelites set free from Egypt   1.1—15.21
  a. Slaves in Egypt   1.1–22
  b. Moses' birth and early life   2.1—4.31
  c. Moses and Aaron confront the king of Egypt   5.1—11.10
  d. The Passover and the departure from Egypt   12.1—15.21
From the Red Sea to Mount Sinai   15.22—18.27
The Law and the covenant   19.1—24.18
The Covenant Tent and instructions for worship   25.1—40.38

The Israelites Are Treated Cruelly in Egypt

1 The sons of Jacob who went to Egypt with him, each with his family, were ²Reuben, Simeon, Levi, Judah, ³Issachar, Zebulun, Benjamin, ⁴Dan, Naphtali, Gad, and Asher. ⁵The total number of these people directly descended from Jacob was seventy.ˣ His son Joseph was already in Egypt. ⁶In the course of time Joseph, his brothers, and all the rest of that generation died, ⁷but their descendants, the Israelites, had many children and became so numerous and strong that Egypt was filled with them.

8 Then, a new king, who knew nothing about Joseph, came to power in Egypt. ⁹He said to his people, "These Israelites are so numerous and strong that they are a threat to us. ¹⁰In case of war they might join our enemies in order to fight against us, and might escape fromᵃ the country. We must find some way to keep them from becoming even more numerous." ¹¹So the Egyptians put slave-drivers over them to crush their spirits with hard labour. The Israelites built the cities of Pithom and Rameses to serve as supply centres for the king. ¹²But the more the Egyptians oppressed the Israelites, the more they increased in number and the

ˣ *One ancient translation* seventy-five (*see Acts 7.14*).
ᵃ escape from; *or* take control of.
1.1-4: Gen 46.8–27   **1.7:** Acts 7.17   **1.8:** Acts 7.18   **1.10:** Acts 7.19

further they spread through the land. The
Egyptians came to fear the Israelites
13-14 and made their lives miserable by
forcing them into cruel slavery. They
made them work on their building
projects and in their fields, and they had
no mercy on them.

15 Then the king of Egypt spoke to
Shiphrah and Puah, the two midwives
who helped the Hebrew women. 16 "When
you help the Hebrew women give birth,"
he said to them, "kill the baby if it is
a boy; but if it is a girl, let it live." 17 But
the midwives feared God and so did not
obey the king; instead, they let the boys
live. 18 So the king sent for the midwives
and asked them, "Why are you doing
this? Why are you letting the boys live?"

19 They   answered,   "The   Hebrew
women are not like Egyptian women; they
give birth easily, and their babies are born
before either of us gets there." 20-21 Because the midwives feared God, he was
good to them and gave them families of
their own. And the Israelites continued to
increase and become strong. 22 Finally the
king issued a command to all his people:
"Take every new-born Hebrew boy and
throw him into the Nile, but let all the
girls live."

The Birth of Moses

2 During this time a man from the tribe
of Levi married a woman of his own
tribe, 2 and she bore him a son. When
she saw what a fine baby he was, she
hid him for three months. 3 But when she
could not hide him any longer, she took
a basket made of reeds and covered it
with tar to make it watertight. She put
the baby in it and then placed it in the tall
grass at the edge of the river. 4 The baby's
sister stood some distance away to see
what would happen to him.

5 The king's daughter came down to the
river to bathe, while her servants walked
along the bank. Suddenly she noticed the
basket in the tall grass and sent a slave-
girl to get it. 6 The princess opened it and
saw a baby boy. He was crying, and she
felt sorry for him. "This is one of the
Hebrew babies," she said.

7 Then his sister asked her, "Shall I go
and call a Hebrew woman to act as a
wet-nurse?"

8 "Please do," she answered. So the girl

*The king's daughter...noticed the basket
(2.5)*

went and brought the baby's own mother.
9 The princess told the woman, "Take this
baby and nurse him for me, and I will
pay you." So she took the baby and nursed
him. 10 Later, when the child was old
enough, she took him to the king's
daughter, who adopted him as her own
son. She said to herself, "I pulled him
out of the water, and so I name him
Moses." *b*

Moses Escapes to Midian

11 When Moses had grown up, he went
out to visit his people, the Hebrews, and
he saw how they were forced to do hard
labour. He even saw an Egyptian kill a
Hebrew, one of Moses' own people.
12 Moses looked all round, and when he
saw that no one was watching, he killed
the Egyptian and hid his body in the sand.
13 The next day he went back and saw
two Hebrew men fighting. He said to the
one who was in the wrong, "Why are
you beating up a fellow-Hebrew?"

14 The man answered, "Who made you
our ruler and judge? Are you going to
kill me just as you killed that Egyptian?"
Then Moses was afraid and said to
himself, "People have found out what I
have done." 15-16 When the king heard
about what had happened, he tried to have
Moses killed, but Moses fled and went
to live in the land of Midian.

One day, when Moses was sitting by
a well, seven daughters of Jethro, the
priest of Midian, came to draw water and
fill the troughs for their father's sheep

b MOSES: *This name sounds like the Hebrew for "pull out."*
1.22: Acts 7.19   **2.2:** Acts 7.20; Heb 11.23   **2.10:** Acts 7.21   **2.11:** Heb 11.24
2.11-14: Acts 7.23-28   **2.15:** Acts 7.29; Heb 11.27

and goats. 17 But some shepherds drove Jethro's daughters away. Then Moses went to their rescue and watered their animals for them. 18 When they returned to their father, he asked, "Why have you come back so early today?"

19 "An Egyptian rescued us from the shepherds," they answered, "and he even drew water for us and watered our animals."

20 "Where is he?" he asked his daughters. "Why did you leave the man out there? Go and invite him to eat with us."

21 So Moses agreed to live there, and Jethro gave him his daughter Zipporah in marriage, 22 who bore him a son. Moses said to himself, "I am a foreigner in this land, and so I name him Gershom." c

23 Years later the king of Egypt died, but the Israelites were still groaning under their slavery and cried out for help. Their cry went up to God, 24 who heard their groaning and remembered his covenant with Abraham, Isaac, and Jacob. 25 He saw the slavery of the Israelites and was concerned for them. d

God Calls Moses

3 One day while Moses was taking care of the sheep and goats of his father-in-law Jethro, the priest of Midian, he led the flock across the desert and came to Sinai, the holy mountain. 2 There the angel of the LORD appeared to him as a flame coming from the middle of a bush. Moses saw that the bush was on fire but that it was not burning up. 3 "This is strange," he thought. "Why isn't the bush burning up? I will go closer and see."

4 When the LORD saw that Moses was coming closer, he called to him from the middle of the bush and said, "Moses! Moses!"

He answered, "Yes, here I am."

5 God said, "Do not come any closer. Take off your sandals, because you are standing on holy ground. 6 I am the God of your ancestors, the God of Abraham, Isaac, and Jacob." So Moses covered his face, because he was afraid to look at God.

7 Then the LORD said, "I have seen how cruelly my people are being treated in Egypt; I have heard them cry out to be rescued from their slave-drivers. I know all about their sufferings, 8 and so I have come down to rescue them from the Egyptians and to bring them out of Egypt to a spacious land, one which is rich and fertile and in which the Canaanites, the Hittites, the Amorites, the Perizzites, the Hivites, and the Jebusites now live. 9 I have indeed heard the cry of my people, and I see how the Egyptians are oppressing them. 10 Now I am sending you to the king of Egypt so that you can lead my people out of his country."

11 But Moses said to God, "I am nobody. How can I go to the king and bring the Israelites out of Egypt?"

12 God answered, "I will be with you, and when you bring the people out of Egypt, you will worship me on this mountain. That will be the proof that I have sent you."

13 But Moses replied, "When I go to the Israelites and say to them, 'The God of your ancestors sent me to you,' they will ask me, 'What is his name?' So what can I tell them?"

14 God said, "I am who I am. This is what you must say to them: 'The one who is called I AM e has sent me to you.' 15 Tell the Israelites that I, the LORD, the God of their ancestors, the God of Abraham, Isaac, and Jacob, have sent you to them. This is my name for ever; this is what all future generations are to call me. 16 Go and gather the leaders of Israel together and tell them that I, the LORD, the God of their ancestors, the God of Abraham, Isaac, and Jacob, appeared to you. Tell them that I have come to them and have seen what the Egyptians are doing to them. 17 I have decided that I will bring them out of Egypt, where they are being treated cruelly, and will take them to a rich and fertile land—the land of the Canaanites, the Hittites, the Amorites, the Perizzites, the Hivites, and the Jebusites.

18 "My people will listen to what you say to them. Then you must go with the leaders of Israel to the king of Egypt and say to him, 'The LORD, the God of the

---

c GERSHOM: *This name sounds like the Hebrew for "foreigner."*
d was concerned for them; *one ancient translation* revealed himself to them.
e I am who I am...I AM: *or* I will be who I will be...I WILL BE. *"I am" sounds like the Hebrew name Yahweh, traditionally transliterated as Jehovah. This name is represented in this translation by "the LORD" in capital letters, following a usage which is widespread in English versions.*
2.24: Gen 15.13-14   **3.2-10:** Acts 7.30-34   **3.13:** Ex 6.2-3   **3.14:** Rev 1.4,8

To prove...that the LORD...*has appeared to you (4.5)*

Hebrews, has revealed himself to us. Now allow us to travel for three days into the desert to offer sacrifices to the LORD, our God.' ¹⁹I know that the king of Egypt will not let you go unless he is forced to do so. ²⁰But I will use my power and will punish Egypt by doing terrifying things there. After that he will let you go.

21 "I will make the Egyptians respect you so that when my people leave, they will not go empty-handed. ²²Every Israelite woman will go to her Egyptian neighbours and to any Egyptian woman living in her house and will ask for clothing and for gold and silver jewellery.

I AM...This is my name for ever (3.14-15)

The Israelites will put these things on their sons and daughters and carry away the wealth of the Egyptians."

3.21-22: Ex 12.35-36

God Gives Moses Miraculous Power

4 Then Moses answered the LORD, "But suppose the Israelites do not believe me and will not listen to what I say. What shall I do if they say that you did not appear to me?"

2 So the LORD asked him, "What are you holding?"

"A stick," he answered.

3 The LORD said, "Throw it on the ground." When Moses threw it down, it turned into a snake, and he ran away from it. ⁴Then the LORD said to Moses, "Bend down and pick it up by the tail." So Moses bent down and caught it, and it became a stick again. ⁵The LORD said, "Do this to prove to the Israelites that the LORD, the God of their ancestors, the God of Abraham, Isaac, and Jacob, has appeared to you."

6 The LORD spoke to Moses again, "Put your hand inside your robe." Moses obeyed; and when he took his hand out, it was diseased, covered with white spots, like snow. ⁷Then the LORD said, "Put your hand inside your robe again." He did so, and when he took it out this time, it was healthy, just like the rest of his body. ⁸The LORD said, "If they will not believe you or be convinced by the first miracle, then this one will convince them. ⁹If in spite of these two miracles they still will not believe you, and if they refuse to listen to what you say, take some water from the Nile and pour it on the ground. The water will turn into blood."

10 But Moses said, "No, LORD, don't send me. I have never been a good speaker, and I haven't become one since you began to speak to me. I am a poor speaker, slow and hesitant."

11 The LORD said to him, "Who gives man his mouth? Who makes him deaf or dumb? Who gives him sight or makes him blind? It is I, the LORD. ¹²Now, go!

I will help you to speak, and I will tell you what to say."

13 But Moses answered, "No, Lord, please send someone else."

14 At this the LORD became angry with Moses and said, "What about your brother Aaron, the Levite? I know that he can speak well. In fact, he is now coming to meet you and will be glad to see you. 15 You can speak to him and tell him what to say. I will help both of you to speak, and I will tell you both what to do. 16 He will be your spokesman and speak to the people for you. Then you will be like God, telling him what to say. 17 Take this stick with you; for with it you will perform miracles."

Moses Returns to Egypt

18 Then Moses went back to Jethro, his father-in-law, and said to him, "Please let me go back to my relatives in Egypt to see if they are still alive." Jethro agreed and said good-bye to him.

19 While Moses was still in Midian, the LORD said to him, "Go back to Egypt, for all those who wanted to kill you are dead." 20 So Moses took his wife and his sons, put them on a donkey, and set out with them for Egypt, carrying the stick that God had told him to take.

21 Again the LORD said to Moses, "Now that you are going back to Egypt, be sure to perform before the king all the miracles which I have given you the power to do. But I will make the king stubborn, and he will not let the people go. 22 Then you must tell him that I, the LORD, say, 'Israel is my first-born son. 23 I told you to let my son go, so that he might worship me, but you refused. Now I am going to kill your first-born son.'"

24 At a camping place on the way to Egypt, the LORD met Moses and tried to kill him. 25-26 Then Zipporah, his wife, took a sharp stone, cut off the foreskin of her son, and touched Moses' feet[f] with it. Because of the rite of circumcision she said to Moses, "You are a husband of blood to me." And so the LORD spared Moses' life.

27 Meanwhile the LORD had said to Aaron, "Go into the desert to meet Moses." So he went to meet him at the holy mountain; and when he met him, he kissed him. 28 Then Moses told Aaron everything that the LORD had said when he told him to return to Egypt; he also told him about the miracles which the LORD had ordered him to perform. 29 So Moses and Aaron went to Egypt and gathered all the Israelite leaders together. 30 Aaron told them everything that the LORD had said to Moses, and then Moses performed all the miracles in front of the people. 31 They believed, and when they heard that the LORD had come to them and had seen how they were being treated cruelly, they bowed down and worshipped.

Moses and Aaron before the King of Egypt

5 Then Moses and Aaron went to the king of Egypt and said, "The LORD, the God of Israel, says, 'Let my people go, so that they can hold a festival in the desert to honour me.'"

2 "Who is the LORD?" the king demanded. "Why should I listen to him and let Israel go? I do not know the LORD; and I will not let Israel go."

3 Moses and Aaron replied, "The God of the Hebrews has revealed himself to us. Allow us to travel for three days into the desert to offer sacrifices to the LORD our God. If we don't do so, he will kill us with disease or by war."

4 The king said to Moses and Aaron, "What do you mean by making the people neglect their work? Get those slaves back to work! 5 You people have become more numerous than the Egyptians. And now you want to stop working!"

6 That same day the king commanded the Egyptian slave-drivers and the Israelite foremen: 7 "Stop giving the people straw for making bricks. Make them go and find it for themselves. 8 But still require them to make the same number of bricks as before, not one brick less. They haven't enough work to do, and that is why they keep asking me to let them go and offer sacrifices to their God! 9 Make these men work harder and keep them busy, so that they won't have time to listen to a pack of lies."

10 The slave-drivers and the Israelite foremen went out and said to the Israelites, "The king has said that he will not supply you with any more straw. 11 He says that you must go and get it for yourselves wherever you can find it, but you must still make the same number of bricks." 12 So the people went all over

---

[f] FEET: *This reference to "feet" is thought by some to be a euphemism for the genitals.*
4.23: Ex 12.29

Egypt looking for straw. 13 The slave-drivers kept trying to force them to make the same number of bricks every day as they had made when they were given straw. 14 The Egyptian slave-drivers beat the Israelite foremen, whom they had put in charge of the work. They demanded, "Why aren't you people making the same number of bricks as you made before?"

15 Then the foremen went to the king and complained, "Why do you do this to us, Your Majesty? 16 We are given no straw, but we are still ordered to make bricks! And now we are being beaten. It is your people that are at fault."

17 The king answered, "You are lazy and don't want to work, and that is why you ask me to let you go and offer sacrifices to the LORD. 18 Now get back to work! You will not be given any straw, but you must still make the same number of bricks." 19 The foremen realized that they were in trouble when they were told that they had to make the same number of bricks every day as they had made before.

20 As they were leaving, they met Moses and Aaron, who were waiting for them. 21 They said to Moses and Aaron, "The LORD has seen what you have done and will punish you for making the king and his officers hate us. You have given them an excuse to kill us."

Moses Complains to the LORD

22 Then Moses turned to the LORD again and said, "Lord, why do you ill-treat your people? Why did you send me here? 23 Ever since I went to the king to speak for you, he has treated them cruelly. And you have done nothing to help them!"

6 Then the LORD said to Moses, "Now you are going to see what I will do to the king. I will force him to let my people go. In fact, I will force him to drive them out of his land."

God Calls Moses

2 God spoke to Moses and said, "I am the LORD. 3 I appeared to Abraham, to Isaac, and to Jacob as Almighty God, but I did not make myself known to them by my holy name, the LORD.*g* 4 I also made my covenant with them, promising to give them the land of Canaan, the land in which they had lived as foreigners. 5 Now I have heard the groaning of the Israelites, whom

the Egyptians have enslaved, and I have remembered my covenant. 6 So tell the Israelites that I say to them, 'I am the LORD; I will rescue you and set you free from your slavery to the Egyptians. I will raise my mighty arm to bring terrible punishment upon them, and I will save you. 7 I will make you my own people, and I will be your God. You will know that I am the LORD your God when I set you free from slavery in Egypt. 8 I will bring you to the land that I solemnly promised to give to Abraham, Isaac, and Jacob; and I will give it to you as your own possession. I am the LORD.'" 9 Moses told this to the Israelites, but they would not listen to him, because their spirit had been broken by their cruel slavery.

10 Then the LORD said to Moses, 11 "Go and tell the king of Egypt that he must let the Israelites leave his land."

12 But Moses replied, "Even the Israelites will not listen to me, so why should the king? I am such a poor speaker."

13 The LORD commanded Moses and Aaron: "Tell the Israelites and the king of Egypt that I have ordered you to lead the Israelites out of Egypt."

The Family Record of Moses and Aaron

14 Reuben, Jacob's first-born, had four sons: Hanoch, Pallu, Hezron, and Carmi; they were the ancestors of the clans that bear their names. 15 Simeon had six sons: Jemuel, Jamin, Ohad, Jachin, Zohar, and Shaul, the son of a Canaanite woman; they were the ancestors of the clans that bear their names. 16 Levi had three sons: Gershon, Kohath, and Merari; they were the ancestors of the clans that bear their names. Levi lived 137 years. 17 Gershon had two sons: Libni and Shimei, and they had many descendants. 18 Kohath had four sons: Amram, Izhar, Hebron, and Uzziel. Kohath lived 133 years. 19 Merari had two sons: Mahli and Mushi. These are the clans of Levi with their descendants.

20 Amram married his father's sister Jochebed, who bore him Aaron and Moses. Amram lived 137 years. 21 Izhar had three sons: Korah, Nepheg, and Zichri. 22 Uzziel also had three sons: Mishael, Elzaphan, and Sithri.

23 Aaron married Elisheba, the daughter of Amminadab and sister of Nahshon; she bore him Nadab, Abihu,

g THE LORD: *See 3.14.*

6.2–3: Gen 17.1, 28.3, 35.11; Ex 3.13–15   **6.16–19:** Num 3.17–20, 26.57–58; 1 Chr 6.16–19

Eleazar, and Ithamar. 24 Korah had three sons: Assir, Elkanah, and Abiasaph; they were the ancestors of the divisions of the clan of Korah. 25 Eleazar, Aaron's son, married one of Putiel's daughters, who bore him Phinehas. These were the heads of the families and the clans of the tribe of Levi.

26 Aaron and Moses were the ones to whom the LORD said, "Lead the tribes of Israel out of Egypt." 27 They were the men who told the king of Egypt to free the Israelites.

The LORD's Command to Moses and Aaron

28 When the LORD spoke to Moses in the land of Egypt, 29 he said, "I am the LORD. Tell the king of Egypt everything I tell you."

30 But Moses answered, "You know that I am such a poor speaker; why should the king listen to me?"

7 The LORD said, "I am going to make you like God to the king, and your brother Aaron will speak to him as your prophet. 2 Tell Aaron everything I command you, and he will tell the king to let the Israelites leave his country. 3-4 But I will make the king stubborn, and he will not listen to you, no matter how many terrifying things I do in Egypt. Then I will bring severe punishment on Egypt and lead the tribes of my people out of the land. 5 The Egyptians will then know that I am the LORD, when I raise my hand against them and bring the Israelites out of their country." 6 Moses and Aaron did what the LORD commanded. 7 At the time when they spoke to the king, Moses was eighty years old, and Aaron was eighty-three.

Aaron's Stick

8 The LORD said to Moses and Aaron, 9 "If the king demands that you prove yourselves by performing a miracle, tell Aaron to take his stick and throw it down in front of the king, and it will turn into a snake." 10 So Moses and Aaron went to the king and did as the LORD had commanded. Aaron threw his stick down in front of the king and his officers, and it turned into a snake. 11 Then the king called for his wise men and magicians, and by their magic they did the same thing. 12 They threw down their sticks, and the sticks turned into snakes. But Aaron's stick swallowed theirs. 13 The king, however, remained stubborn and, just as the LORD had said, the king would not listen to Moses and Aaron.

Disasters Strike Egypt

Blood

14 Then the LORD said to Moses, "The king is very stubborn and refuses to let the people go. 15 So go and meet him in the morning when he goes down to the Nile. Take with you the stick that was turned into a snake, and wait for him on the bank of the river. 16 Then say to the king, 'The LORD, the God of the Hebrews, sent me to tell you to let his people go, so that they can worship him in the desert. But until now you have not listened. 17 Now, Your Majesty, the LORD says that you will find out who he is by what he is going to do. Look, I am going to strike the surface of the river with this stick, and the water will be turned into blood. 18 The fish will die, and the river will stink so much that the Egyptians will not be able to drink from it.'"

19 The LORD said to Moses, "Tell Aaron to take his stick and hold it out over all the rivers, canals, and pools in Egypt. The water will become blood, and all over the land there will be blood, even in the wooden tubs and stone jars."

20 Then Moses and Aaron did as the LORD commanded. In the presence of the king and his officers, Aaron raised his stick and struck the surface of the river, and all the water in it was turned into blood. 21 The fish in the river died, and it smelt so bad that the Egyptians could not drink from it. There was blood everywhere in Egypt. 22 Then the king's magicians did the same thing by means of their magic, and the king was as stubborn as ever. Just as the LORD had said, the king refused to listen to Moses and Aaron. 23 Instead, he turned and went back to his palace without paying any attention even to this. 24 All the Egyptians dug along the bank of the river for drinking water, because they were not able to drink water from the river.

25 Seven days passed after the LORD struck the river.

7.3: Acts 7.36   **7.17:** Rev 16.4

They will jump up on you (8.4)

Frogs

8 Then the LORD said to Moses, "Go to the king and tell him that the LORD says, 'Let my people go, so that they can worship me. ²If you refuse, I will punish your country by covering it with frogs. ³The Nile will be so full of frogs that they will leave it and go into your palace, your bedroom, your bed, the houses of your officials and your people, and even into your ovens and baking-pans. ⁴They will jump up on you, your people, and all your officials.' "

5 The LORD said to Moses, "Tell Aaron to hold out his stick over the rivers, the canals, and the pools, and make frogs come up and cover the land of Egypt." ⁶So Aaron held it out over all the water, and the frogs came out and covered the land. ⁷But the magicians used magic, and they too made frogs come up on the land.

8 The king called for Moses and Aaron and said, "Pray to the LORD to take away these frogs, and I will let your people go, so that they can offer sacrifices to the LORD."

9 Moses replied, "I will be glad to pray for you. Just set the time when I am to pray for you, your officers, and your people. Then you will be rid of the frogs, and there will be none left except in the Nile."

8.19: Lk 11.20

10 The king answered, "Pray for me tomorrow."

Moses said, "I will do as you ask, and then you will know that there is no other god like the LORD, our God. ¹¹You, your officials, and your people will be rid of the frogs, and there will be none left except in the Nile." ¹²Then Moses and Aaron left the king, and Moses prayed to the LORD to take away the frogs which he had brought on the king. ¹³The LORD did as Moses asked, and the frogs in the houses, the courtyards, and the fields died. ¹⁴The Egyptians piled them up in great heaps, until the land stank with them. ¹⁵When the king saw that the frogs were dead, he became stubborn again and, just as the LORD had said, the king would not listen to Moses and Aaron.

Gnats

16 The LORD said to Moses, "Tell Aaron to strike the ground with his stick, and all over the land of Egypt the dust will change into gnats." ¹⁷So Aaron struck the ground with his stick, and all the dust in Egypt was turned into gnats, which covered the people and the animals. ¹⁸The magicians tried to use their magic to make gnats appear, but they failed. There were gnats everywhere, ¹⁹and the magicians

said to the king, "God has done this!" But the king was stubborn and, just as the LORD had said, the king would not listen to Moses and Aaron.

Flies

20 The LORD said to Moses, "Early tomorrow morning go and meet the king as he goes to the river, and tell him that the LORD says, 'Let my people go, so that they can worship me. 21 I warn you that if you refuse, I will punish you by sending flies on you, your officials, and your people. The houses of the Egyptians will be full of flies, and the ground will be covered with them. 22 But I will spare the region of Goshen, where my people live, so that there will be no flies there. I will do this so that you will know that I, the LORD, am at work in this land. 23 I will make a distinction[h] between my people and your people. This miracle will take place tomorrow.'" 24 The LORD sent great swarms of flies into the king's palace and the houses of his officials. The whole land of Egypt was brought to ruin by the flies.

25 Then the king called for Moses and Aaron and said, "Go and offer sacrifices to your God here in this country."

26 "It would not be right to do that," Moses answered, "because the Egyptians would be offended by our sacrificing the animals that we offer to the LORD our God. If we use these animals and offend the Egyptians by sacrificing them where they can see us, they will stone us to death. 27 We must travel three days into the desert to offer sacrifices to the LORD our God, just as he commanded us."

28 The king said, "I will let you go to sacrifice to the LORD, your God, in the desert, if you do not go very far. Pray for me."

29 Moses answered, "As soon as I leave, I will pray to the LORD that tomorrow the flies will leave you, your officials, and your people. But you must not deceive us again and prevent the people from going to sacrifice to the LORD."

30 Moses left the king and prayed to the LORD, 31 and the LORD did as Moses asked. The flies left the king, his officials, and his people; not one fly remained. 32 But even this time the king became stubborn, and again he would not let the people go.

Death of the Animals

9 The LORD said to Moses, "Go to the king and tell him that the LORD, the God of the Hebrews, says, 'Let my people go, so that they may worship me. 2 If you again refuse to let them go, 3 I will punish you by sending a terrible disease on all your animals—your horses, donkeys, camels, cattle, sheep, and goats. 4 I will make a distinction between the animals of the Israelites and those of the Egyptians, and no animal that belongs to the Israelites will die. 5 I, the LORD, have set tomorrow as the time when I will do this.'"

6 The next day the LORD did as he had said, and all the animals of the Egyptians died, but not one of the animals of the Israelites died. 7 The king asked what had happened and was told that none of the animals of the Israelites had died. But he was stubborn and would not let the people go.

Boils

8 Then the LORD said to Moses and Aaron, "Take a few handfuls of ashes from a furnace; Moses shall throw them into the air in front of the king. 9 They will spread out like fine dust over all the land of Egypt, and everywhere they will produce boils that become open sores on the people and the animals." 10 So they got some ashes and stood before the king; Moses threw them into the air, and they produced boils that became open sores on the people and the animals. 11 The magicians were not able to appear before Moses, because they were covered with boils, like all the other Egyptians. 12 But the LORD made the king stubborn and, just as the LORD had said, the king would not listen to Moses and Aaron.

Hail

13 The LORD then said to Moses, "Early tomorrow morning meet with the king and tell him that the LORD, the God of the Hebrews, says, 'Let my people go, so that they may worship me. 14 This time I will punish not only your officials and your people, but I will punish you as well, so that you may know that there is no one like me in all the world. 15 If I had raised my hand to strike you and your people with disease, you would have been completely destroyed. 16 But to show you

---

[h] *Some ancient translations* a distinction; *Hebrew* redemption.
9.10: Rev 16.2   **9.16:** Rom 9.17

my power I have let you live so that my fame might spread over the whole world. 17 Yet you are still arrogant and refuse to let my people go. 18 This time tomorrow I will cause a heavy hailstorm, such as Egypt has never known in all its history. 19 Now give orders for your livestock and everything else you have in the open to be put under shelter. Hail will fall on the people and animals left outside unprotected, and they will all die.' " 20 Some of the king's officials were afraid because of what the LORD had said, and they brought their slaves and animals indoors for shelter. 21 Others, however, paid no attention to the LORD's warning and left their slaves and animals out in the open.

22 Then the LORD said to Moses, "Raise your hand towards the sky, and hail will fall over the whole land of Egypt—on the people, the animals, and all the plants in the fields." 23 So Moses raised his stick towards the sky, and the LORD sent thunder and hail, and lightning struck the ground. The LORD sent 24 a heavy hailstorm, with lightning flashing to and fro. It was the worst storm that Egypt had ever known in all its history. 25 All over Egypt the hail struck down everything in the open, including all the people and all the animals. It beat down all the plants in the fields and broke all the trees. 26 The region of Goshen, where the Israelites lived, was the only place where there was no hail.

27 The king sent for Moses and Aaron and said, "This time I have sinned; the LORD is in the right, and my people and I are in the wrong. 28 Pray to the LORD! We have had enough of this thunder and hail! I promise to let you go; you don't have to stay here any longer."

29 Moses said to him, "As soon as I go out of the city, I will lift up my hands in prayer to the LORD. The thunder will stop, and there will be no more hail, so that you may know that the earth belongs to the LORD. 30 But I know that you and your officials do not yet fear the LORD God."

31 The flax and the barley were ruined, because the barley was ripe, and the flax was budding. 32 But none of the wheat was ruined, because it ripens later.

33 Moses left the king, went out of the city, and lifted up his hands in prayer to the LORD. The thunder, the hail, and the rain all stopped. 34 When the king saw

what had happened, he sinned again. He and his officials remained as stubborn as ever 35 and, just as the LORD had foretold through Moses, the king would not let the Israelites go.

Locusts

10 Then the LORD said to Moses, "Go and see the king. I have made him and his officials stubborn, in order that I may perform these miracles among them 2 and in order that you may be able to tell your children and grandchildren how I made fools of the Egyptians when I performed the miracles. All of you will know that I am the LORD."

3 So Moses and Aaron went to the king and said to him, "The LORD, the God of the Hebrews, says 'How much longer will you refuse to submit to me? Let my people go, so that they may worship me. 4 If you keep on refusing, then I will bring locusts into your country tomorrow. 5 There will be so many that they will completely cover the ground. They will eat everything that the hail did not destroy, even the trees that are left. 6 They will fill your palaces and the houses of all your officials and all your people. They will be worse than anything your ancestors ever saw.' " Then Moses turned and left.

7 The king's officials said to him, "How long is this man going to give us trouble? Let the Israelite men go, so that they can worship the LORD their God. Don't you realize that Egypt is ruined?"

8 So Moses and Aaron were brought back to the king, and he said to them, "You may go and worship the LORD your God. But exactly who will go?"

9 Moses answered, "We will all go, including our children and our old people. We will take our sons and daughters, our sheep and goats, and our cattle, because we must hold a festival to honour the LORD."

10 The king said, "I swear by the LORD that I will never let you take your women and children! It is clear that you are plotting to revolt. 11 No! Only the men may go and worship the LORD if that is what you want." With that, Moses and Aaron were driven out of the king's presence.

12 Then the LORD said to Moses, "Raise your hand over the land of Egypt to bring the locusts. They will come and eat everything that grows, everything that

9.24: Rev 8.7, 16.21

has survived the hail." ¹³ So Moses raised his stick, and the LORD caused a wind from the east to blow on the land all that day and all that night. By morning it had brought the locusts. ¹⁴ They came in swarms and settled over the whole country. It was the largest swarm of locusts that had ever been seen or that ever would be seen again. ¹⁵ They covered the ground until it was black with them; they ate everything that the hail had left, including all the fruit on the trees. Not a green thing was left on any tree or plant in all the land of Egypt.

16 Then the king hurriedly called Moses and Aaron and said, "I have sinned against the LORD your God and against you. ¹⁷ Now forgive my sin this once and pray to the LORD your God to take away this fatal punishment from me." ¹⁸ Moses left the king and prayed to the LORD. ¹⁹ And the LORD changed the east wind into a very strong west wind, which picked up the locusts and blew them into the Gulf of Suez.[i] Not one locust was left in all Egypt. ²⁰ But the LORD made the king stubborn, and he did not let the Israelites go.

Darkness

21 The LORD then said to Moses, "Raise your hand towards the sky, and a darkness thick enough to be felt will cover the land of Egypt." ²² Moses raised his hand towards the sky, and there was total darkness throughout Egypt for three days. ²³ The Egyptians could not see each other, and no one left his house during that time. But the Israelites had light where they were living.

24 The king called Moses and said, "You may go and worship the LORD; even your women and children may go with you. But your sheep, goats, and cattle must stay here."

25 Moses answered, "Then you would have to provide us with animals for sacrifices and burnt-offerings to offer to the LORD our God. ²⁶ No, we will take our animals with us; not one will be left behind. We ourselves must select the animals with which to worship the LORD our God. And until we get there, we will not know what animals to sacrifice to him."

27 The LORD made the king stubborn, and he would not let them go. ²⁸ He said

to Moses, "Get out of my sight! Don't let me ever see you again! On the day I do, you will die!"

29 "You are right," Moses answered. "You will never see me again."

Moses Announces the Death of the First-Born

11 Then the LORD said to Moses, "I will send only one more punishment on the king of Egypt and his people. After that he will let you leave. In fact, he will drive all of you out of here. ² Now speak to the people of Israel and tell all of them to ask their neighbours for gold and silver jewellery." ³ The LORD made the Egyptians respect the Israelites. Indeed, the officials and all the people considered Moses to be a very great man.

4 Moses then said to the king, "The LORD says, 'At about midnight I will go through Egypt, ⁵ and every first-born son in Egypt will die, from the king's son, who is heir to the throne, to the son of the slave-woman who grinds corn. The first-born of all the cattle will die also. ⁶ There will be loud crying all over Egypt, such as there has never been before or ever will be again. ⁷ But not even a dog will bark at the Israelites or their animals. Then you will know that I, the LORD, make a distinction between the Egyptians and the Israelites.' " ⁸ Moses concluded by saying, "All your officials will come to me and bow down before me, and they will beg me to take all my people and go away. After that, I will leave." Then in great anger Moses left the king.

9 The LORD had said to Moses, "The king will continue to refuse to listen to you, in order that I may do more of my miracles in Egypt." ¹⁰ Moses and Aaron performed all these miracles before the king, but the LORD made him stubborn, and he would not let the Israelites leave his country.

The Passover

12 The LORD spoke to Moses and Aaron in Egypt: ² "This month is to be the first month of the year for you. ³ Give these instructions to the whole community of Israel: On the tenth day of this month each man must choose either a lamb or a young goat for his household. ⁴ If his family is too small to eat a whole animal, he and his next-door

[i] GULF OF SUEZ: *See Red Sea in 13.18.*
10.14-15: Rev 9.2-3   **10.22:** Ps 105.28; Rev 16.10

neighbour may share an animal, in proportion to the number of people and the amount that each person can eat. 5 You may choose either a sheep or a goat, but it must be a one-year-old male without any defects. 6 Then, on the evening of the fourteenth day of the month, the whole community of Israel will kill the animals. 7 The people are to take some of the blood and put it on the door-posts and above the doors of the houses in which the animals are to be eaten. 8 That night the meat is to be roasted, and eaten with bitter herbs and with bread made without yeast. 9 Do not eat any of it raw or boiled, but eat it roasted whole, including the head, the legs, and the internal organs. 10 You must not leave any of it until morning; if any is left over, it must be burnt. 11 You are to eat it quickly, for you are to be dressed for travel, with your sandals on your feet and your stick in your hand. It is the Passover Festival to honour me, the LORD.

12 "On that night I will go through the land of Egypt, killing every first-born male, both human and animal, and punishing all the gods of Egypt. I am the LORD. 13 The blood on the door-posts will be a sign to mark the houses in which you live. When I see the blood, I will pass over you and will not harm you when I punish the Egyptians. 14 You must celebrate this day as a religious festival to remind you of what I, the LORD, have done. Celebrate it for all time to come."

The Festival of Unleavened Bread

15 The LORD said, "For seven days you must not eat any bread made with yeast—eat only unleavened bread. On the first day you are to get rid of all the yeast in your houses, for if anyone during those seven days eats bread made with yeast, he shall no longer be considered one of my people. 16 On the first day and again on the seventh day you are to meet for worship. No work is to be done on those days, but you may prepare food. 17 Keep this festival, because it was on this day that I brought your tribes out of Egypt. For all time to come you must celebrate this day as a festival. 18 From the evening of the fourteenth day of the first month to the evening of the twenty-first day, you must not eat any bread made with yeast.

19-20 For seven days no yeast must be found in your houses, for if anyone, native-born or foreign, eats bread made with yeast, he shall no longer be considered one of my people."

The First Passover

21 Moses called for all the leaders of Israel and said to them, "Each of you is to choose a lamb or a young goat and kill it, so that your families can celebrate Passover. 22 Take a sprig of hyssop, dip it in the bowl containing[j] the animal's blood, and wipe the blood on the door-posts and the beam above the door of your house. Not one of you is to leave the house until morning. 23 When the LORD goes through Egypt to kill the Egyptians, he will see the blood on the beams and the door-posts and will not let the Angel of Death enter your houses and kill you. 24 You and your children must obey these rules for ever. 25 When you enter the land that the LORD has promised to give you, you must perform this ritual. 26 When your children ask you, 'What does this ritual mean?' 27 you will answer, 'It is the sacrifice of Passover to honour the LORD, because he passed over the houses of the Israelites in Egypt. He killed the Egyptians, but spared us.'"

The Israelites knelt down and worshipped. 28 Then they went and did what the LORD had commanded Moses and Aaron.

The Death of the First-Born

29 At midnight the LORD killed all the first-born sons in Egypt, from the king's son, who was heir to the throne, to the son of the prisoner in the dungeon; all the first-born of the animals were also killed. 30 That night, the king, his officials, and all the other Egyptians were awakened. There was loud crying throughout Egypt, because there was not one home in which there was not a dead son. 31 That same night the king sent for Moses and Aaron and said, "Get out, you and your Israelites! Leave my country; go and worship the LORD, as you asked. 32 Take your sheep, goats, and cattle, and leave. Also pray for a blessing on me."

33 The Egyptians urged the people to hurry and leave the country; they said, "We will all be dead if you don't leave."

---

j dip it in the bowl containing; or put it on the threshold covered with.
12.1-13: Lev 23.5; Num 9.1-5, 28.16; Deut 16.1-2
12.14-20: Ex 23.15, 34.18; Lev 23.6-8; Num 28.17-25; Deut 16.3-8   **12.23:** Heb 11.28
12.29: Ex 4.22-32

The people filled their baking-pans with unleavened dough (12.34)

34 So the people filled their baking-pans with unleavened dough, wrapped them in clothing, and carried them on their shoulders. 35 The Israelites had done as Moses had said, and had asked the Egyptians for gold and silver jewellery and for clothing. 36 The LORD made the Egyptians respect the people and give them what they asked for. In this way the Israelites carried away the wealth of the Egyptians.

The Israelites Leave Egypt

37 The Israelites set out on foot from Rameses for Sukkoth. There were about six hundred thousand men, not counting women and children. 38 A large number of other people and many sheep, goats, and cattle also went with them. 39 They baked unleavened bread from the dough that they had brought out of Egypt, for they had been driven out of Egypt so suddenly that they did not have time to get their food ready or to prepare leavened dough.

40 The Israelites had lived in Egypt for 430 years. 41 On the day the 430 years ended, all the tribes of the LORD's people left Egypt. 42 It was a night when the LORD kept watch to bring them out of Egypt; this same night is dedicated to the LORD for all time to come as a night when the Israelites must keep watch.

Regulations about Passover

43 The LORD said to Moses and Aaron, "These are the Passover regulations: No foreigner shall eat the Passover meal, 44 but any slave that you have bought may eat it if you circumcise him first. 45 No temporary resident or hired worker may eat it. 46 The whole meal must be eaten in the house in which it was prepared; it must not be taken outside. And do not break any of the animal's bones. 47 The whole community of Israel must celebrate this festival, 48 but no uncircumcised man may eat it. If a foreigner has settled among you and wants to celebrate Passover to honour the LORD, you must first circumcise all the males of his household. He is then to be treated like a native-born Israelite and may join in the festival. 49 The same regulations apply to native-born Israelites and to foreigners who settle among you." 50 All the Israelites obeyed and did what the LORD had commanded Moses and Aaron. 51 On that day the LORD brought the Israelite tribes out of Egypt.

Dedication of the First-Born

13 The LORD said to Moses, 2 "Dedicate all the first-born males to me, for every first-born male Israelite and every first-born male animal belongs to me."

The Festival of Unleavened Bread

3 Moses said to the people, "Remember this day—the day on which you left Egypt, the place where you were slaves. This is the day the LORD brought you out by his great power. No leavened bread is to be eaten. 4 You are leaving Egypt on this

12.35–36: Ex 3.21-22   **12.40:** Gen 15.13; Gal 3.17   **12.46:** Num 9.12; Jn 19.36
13.2: Num 3.13; Lk 2.23

day in the first month, the month of Abib.
5 The LORD solemnly promised your ancestors to give you the land of the Canaanites, the Hittites, the Amorites, the Hivites, and the Jebusites. When he brings you into that rich and fertile land, you must celebrate this festival in the first month of every year. 6 For seven days you must eat unleavened bread and on the seventh day there is to be a festival to honour the LORD. 7 For seven days you must not eat any bread made with yeast; there must be no yeast or leavened bread anywhere in your land. 8 When the festival begins, explain to your sons that you do all this because of what the LORD did for you when you left Egypt. 9 This observance will be a reminder, like something tied on your hand or on your forehead; it will remind you to continue to recite and study the Law of the LORD, because the LORD brought you out of Egypt by his great power. 10 Celebrate this festival at the appointed time each year.

The First-Born

11 "The LORD will bring you into the land of the Canaanites, which he solemnly promised to you and your ancestors. When he gives it to you, 12 you must offer every first-born male to the LORD. Every first-born male of your animals belongs to the LORD, 13 but you must buy back from him every first-born male donkey by offering a lamb in its place. If you do not want to buy back the donkey, break its neck. You must buy back every first-born male child of yours. 14 In the future, when your son asks what this observance means, you will answer him, 'By using great power the LORD brought us out of Egypt, the place where we were slaves. 15 When the king of Egypt was stubborn and refused to let us go, the LORD killed every first-born male in the land of Egypt, both human and animal. That is why we sacrifice every first-born male animal to the LORD, but buy back our first-born sons. 16 This observance will be a reminder, like something tied on our hands or on our foreheads; it will remind us that the LORD brought us out of Egypt by his great power.'"

The Pillar of Cloud and the Pillar of Fire

17 When the king of Egypt let the people go, God did not take them by the road that goes up the coast to Philistia, although it was the shortest way. God thought, "I do not want the people to change their minds and return to Egypt when they see that they are going to have to fight." 18 Instead, he led them in a roundabout way through the desert towards the Red Sea. k The Israelites were armed for battle.

19 Moses took the body of Joseph with him, as Joseph had made the Israelites solemnly promise to do. Joseph had said, "When God rescues you, you must carry my body with you from this place."

20 The Israelites left Sukkoth and camped at Etham on the edge of the desert. 21 During the day the LORD went in front of them in a pillar of cloud to show them the way, and during the night he went in front of them in a pillar of fire to give them light, so that they could travel night and day. 22 The pillar of cloud was always in front of the people during the day, and the pillar of fire at night.

Crossing the Red Sea

14 Then the LORD said to Moses, 2 "Tell the Israelites to turn back and camp in front of Pi Hahiroth, between Migdol and the Red Sea, near Baal Zephon. 3 The king will think that the Israelites are wandering about in the country and are closed in by the desert. 4 I will make him stubborn, and he will pursue you, and my victory over the king and his army will bring me honour. Then the Egyptians will know that I am the LORD." The Israelites did as they were told.

5 When the king of Egypt was told that the people had escaped, he and his officials changed their minds and said, "What have we done? We have let the Israelites escape, and we have lost them as our slaves!" 6 The king got his war chariot and his army ready. 7 He set out with all his chariots, including the six hundred finest, commanded by their officers. 8 The LORD made the king stubborn, and he pursued the Israelites,

k RED SEA: (in Hebrew literally "Sea of Reeds") evidently referred to (1) a series of lakes and marshes between the head of the Gulf of Suez and the Mediterranean, the region generally regarded as the site of the events descibed in Exodus 13, and was also used to designate (2) the Gulf of Suez, and (3) the Gulf of Aqaba.
13.12: Ex 34.19–20; Lk 2.23   **13.19:** Gen 50.25; Josh 24.32

The LORD went in front of them (13.21)

who were leaving triumphantly.[l] 9 The Egyptian army, with all the horses, chariots, and drivers, pursued them and caught up with them where they were camped by the Red Sea near Pi Hahiroth and Baal Zephon.

10 When the Israelites saw the king and his army marching against them, they were terrified and cried out to the LORD for help. 11 They said to Moses, "Weren't there any graves in Egypt? Did you have to bring us out here in the desert to die? Look what you have done by bringing us out of Egypt! 12 Didn't we tell you before we left that this would happen? We told you to leave us alone and let us go on being slaves of the Egyptians. It would be better to be slaves there than to die here in the desert."

13 Moses answered, "Don't be afraid! Stand your ground, and you will see what the LORD will do to save you today; you will never see these Egyptians again. 14 The LORD will fight for you, and there is no need for you to do anything."

15 The LORD said to Moses, "Why are you crying out for help? Tell the people to move forward. 16 Lift up your stick and hold it out over the sea. The water will divide, and the Israelites will be able to walk through the sea on dry ground. 17 I will make the Egyptians so stubborn that they will go in after them, and I will gain honour by my victory over the king, his army, his chariots, and his drivers. 18 When I defeat them, the Egyptians will know that I am the LORD."

19 The angel of God, who had been in front of the army of Israel, moved and went to the rear. The pillar of cloud also moved until it was 20 between the Egyptians and the Israelites. The cloud made it dark for the Egyptians, but gave light to the people of Israel,[n] and so the

[l] triumphantly; *or* under the protection of the LORD.
[n] *Probable text* The cloud...Israel; *Hebrew unclear.*

The Egyptians will know that I am the LORD (14.18)

armies could not come near each other all night.

21 Moses held out his hand over the sea, and the LORD drove the sea back with a strong east wind. It blew all night and turned the sea into dry land. The water was divided, 22 and the Israelites went through the sea on dry ground, with walls of water on both sides. 23 The Egyptians pursued them and went after them into the sea with all their horses, chariots, and drivers. 24 Just before dawn the LORD looked down from the pillar of fire and cloud at the Egyptian army and threw them into a panic. 25 He made the wheels of their chariots get stuck, so that they

14.22: 1 Cor 10.1–2; Heb 11.29

moved with great difficulty. The Egyptians said, "The LORD is fighting for the Israelites against us. Let's get out of here!"

26 The LORD said to Moses, "Hold out your hand over the sea, and the water will come back over the Egyptians and their chariots and drivers." 27 So Moses held out his hand over the sea, and at daybreak the water returned to its normal level. The Egyptians tried to escape from the water, but the LORD threw them into the sea. 28 The water returned and covered the chariots, the drivers, and all the Egyptian army that had followed the Israelites into the sea; not one of them was left. 29 But the Israelites walked through the sea on dry ground, with walls of water on both sides.

30 On that day the LORD saved the people of Israel from the Egyptians, and the Israelites saw them lying dead on the seashore. 31 When the Israelites saw the great power with which the LORD had defeated the Egyptians, they stood in awe of the LORD; and they had faith in the LORD and in his servant Moses.

The Song of Moses

15 Then Moses and the Israelites sang this song to the LORD:

"I will sing to the LORD, because he
    has won a glorious victory;
he has thrown the horses and their
    riders into the sea.
2 The LORD is my strong defender;
    he is the one who has saved me.
He is my God, and I will praise him,
    my father's God, and I will sing about
    his greatness.
3 The LORD is a warrior;
    the LORD is his name.

4 "He threw Egypt's army and its chariots
    into the sea;
the best of its officers were drowned
    in the Red Sea.
5 The deep sea covered them;
    they sank to the bottom like a stone.

6 "Your right hand, LORD, is awesome in
    power;
it breaks the enemy in pieces.
7 In majestic triumph you overthrow your
    foes;
your anger blazes out and burns them
    up like straw.

8 You blew on the sea and the water piled
    up high;
it stood up straight like a wall;
the deepest part of the sea became
    solid.
9 The enemy said, 'I will pursue them and
    catch them;
I will divide their wealth and take all
    I want;
I will draw my sword and take all
    they have.'
10 But one breath from you, LORD, and
    the Egyptians were drowned;
they sank like lead in the terrible
    water.

11 "LORD, who among the gods is like
    you?
Who is like you, wonderful in
    holiness?
Who can work miracles and mighty
    acts like yours?
12 You stretched out your right hand,
    and the earth swallowed our enemies.
13 Faithful to your promise, you led the
    people you had rescued;
by your strength you guided them to
    your sacred land.
14 The nations have heard, and they
    tremble with fear;
the Philistines are seized with terror.
15 The leaders of Edom are terrified;
    Moab's mighty men are trembling;
the people of Canaan lose their
    courage.
16 Terror and dread fall upon them.
They see your strength, O LORD,
    and stand helpless with fear
until your people have marched
    past—
the people you set free from slavery.
17 You bring them in and plant them on
    your mountain,
the place that you, LORD, have chosen
    for your home,
the Temple that you yourself have
    built.
18 You, LORD, will be king for ever and
    ever."

The Song of Miriam

19 The Israelites walked through the sea on dry ground. But when the Egyptian chariots with their horses and drivers went into the sea, the LORD brought the water back, and it covered them.

20 The prophet Miriam, Aaron's sister, took her tambourine, and all the women

15.1: Rev 15.3   **15.2:** Ps 118.14; Is 12.2

followed her, playing tambourines and dancing. 21 Miriam sang for them:

"Sing to the LORD, because he has won
   a glorious victory;
he has thrown the horses and their
   riders into the sea."

Bitter Water

22 Then Moses led the people of Israel away from the Red Sea into the desert of Shur. For three days they walked through the desert, but found no water. 23 Then they came to a place called Marah, but the water there was so bitter that they could not drink it. That is why it was named Marah.*o* 24 The people complained to Moses and asked, "What are we going to drink?" 25 Moses prayed earnestly to the LORD, and the LORD showed him a piece of wood, which he threw into the water; and the water became fit to drink.

There the LORD gave them laws to live by, and there he also tested them. 26 He said, "If you will obey me completely by doing what I consider right and by keeping my commands, I will not punish you with any of the diseases that I brought on the Egyptians. I am the LORD, the one who heals you."

27 Next they came to Elim, where there were twelve springs and seventy palmtrees; there they camped by the water.

The Manna and the Quails

16 The whole Israelite community set out from Elim, and on the fifteenth day of the second month after they had left Egypt, they came to the desert of Sin, which is between Elim and Sinai. 2 There in the desert they all complained to Moses and Aaron 3 and said to them, "We wish that the LORD had killed us in Egypt. There we could at least sit down and eat meat and as much other food as we wanted. But you have brought us out into this desert to starve us all to death."

4 The LORD said to Moses, "Now I am going to make food rain down from the sky for all of you. The people must go out every day and gather enough for that day. In this way I can test them to find out if they will follow my instructions. 5 On the sixth day they are to bring in twice as much as usual and prepare it."

6 So Moses and Aaron said to all the Israelites, "This evening you will know that it was the LORD who brought you out of Egypt. 7 In the morning you will see the dazzling light of the LORD's presence. He has heard your complaints against him—yes, against him, because we are only carrying out his instructions." 8 Then Moses said, "It is the LORD who will give you meat to eat in the evening and as much bread as you want in the morning, because he has heard how much you have complained against him. When you complain against us, you are really complaining against the LORD."

9 Moses said to Aaron, "Tell the whole community to come and stand before the LORD, because he has heard their complaints." 10 As Aaron spoke to the whole community, they turned towards the desert, and suddenly the dazzling light of the LORD appeared in a cloud. 11 The LORD said to Moses, 12 "I have heard the complaints of the Israelites. Tell them that at twilight they will have meat to eat, and in the morning they will have all the bread they want. Then they will know that I, the LORD, am their God."

13 In the evening a large flock of quails flew in, enough to cover the camp, and in the morning there was dew all round the camp. 14 When the dew evaporated, there was something thin and flaky on the surface of the desert. It was as delicate as frost. 15 When the Israelites saw it, they didn't know what it was and asked each other, "What is it?"

Moses said to them, "This is the food that the LORD has given you to eat. 16 The LORD has commanded that each of you is to gather as much of it as he needs, two litres for each member of his household."

17 The Israelites did this, some gathering more, others less. 18 When they measured it, those who gathered much did not have too much, and those who gathered less did not have too little. Each had gathered just what he needed. 19 Moses said to them, "No one is to keep any of it for tomorrow." 20 But some of them did not listen to Moses and saved part of it. The next morning it was full of worms and smelt rotten, and Moses was angry with them. 21 Every morning each one gathered as much as he needed; and when the sun grew hot, what was left on the ground melted.

22 On the sixth day they gathered twice

---

*o*MARAH: This name in Hebrew means "bitter."
16.4: Jn 6.31   **16.15:** 1 Cor 10.3   **16.18:** 2 Cor 8.15

The food that the LORD has given you to eat (16.15)

as much food, four litres for each person. All the leaders of the community came and told Moses about it, 23 and he said to them, "The LORD has commanded that tomorrow is a holy day of rest, dedicated to him. Bake today what you want to bake and boil what you want to boil. Whatever is left should be put aside and kept for tomorrow." 24 As Moses had commanded, they kept what was left until the next day; it did not spoil or get worms in it. 25 Moses said, "Eat this today, because today is the Sabbath, a day of rest dedicated to the LORD, and you will not find any food outside the camp. 26 You must gather food for six days, but on the seventh day, the day of rest, there will be none."

27 On the seventh day some of the people went out to gather food, but they did not find any. 28 Then the LORD said to Moses, "How much longer will you people refuse to obey my commands? 29 Remember that I, the LORD, have given you a day of rest, and that is why on the sixth day I will always give you enough food for two days. Everyone is to stay where he is on the seventh day and not leave his home." 30 So the people did no work on the seventh day.

31 The people of Israel called the food manna.P It was like a small white seed,

P MANNA: *This word sounds like the Hebrew for* "what is it?" *(see verse 15).*
16.23: Ex 20.8-11   **16.31:** Num 11.7-8

They held his arms steady until the sun went down (17.12)

and tasted like biscuits made with honey. ³²Moses said, "The LORD has commanded us to save some manna, to be kept for our descendants, so that they can see the food which he gave us to eat in the desert when he brought us out of Egypt." ³³Moses said to Aaron, "Take a jar, put two litres of manna in it, and place it in the LORD's presence to be kept for our descendants." ³⁴As the LORD had commanded Moses, Aaron put it in front of the Covenant Box, so that it could be kept. ³⁵The Israelites ate manna for the next forty years, until they reached the land of Canaan, where they settled. ³⁶(The standard dry measure then in use equalled twenty litres.)

Water from the Rock
(Num 20.1–13)

17 The whole Israelite community left the desert of Sin, moving from one place to another at the command of the LORD. They made camp at Rephidim, but there was no water there to drink. ²They complained to Moses and said, "Give us water to drink."

Moses answered, "Why are you complaining? Why are you putting the LORD to the test?"

3 But the people were very thirsty and continued to complain to Moses. They said, "Why did you bring us out of Egypt? To kill us and our children and our livestock with thirst?"

4 Moses prayed earnestly to the LORD and said, "What can I do with these people? They are almost ready to stone me."

5 The LORD said to Moses, "Take some of the leaders of Israel with you, and go on ahead of the people. Take along the stick with which you struck the Nile. ⁶I will stand before you on a rock at Mount Sinai. Strike the rock, and water will come out of it for the people to drink." Moses did so in the presence of the leaders of Israel.

7 The place was named Massah and Meribah,�q because the Israelites complained and put the LORD to the test when they asked, "Is the LORD with us or not?"

War with the Amalekites

8 The Amalekites came and attacked the Israelites at Rephidim. ⁹Moses said to Joshua, "Pick out some men to go and fight the Amalekites tomorrow. I will stand on top of the hill holding the stick that God told me to carry." ¹⁰Joshua did as Moses commanded him and went out to fight the Amalekites, while Moses, Aaron, and Hur went up to the top of the hill. ¹¹As long as Moses held up his arms, the Israelites won but when he put his arms down, the Amalekites started winning. ¹²When Moses' arms grew tired, Aaron and Hur brought a stone for him to sit on, while they stood beside him and held up his arms, holding them steady until the sun went down. ¹³In this way Joshua totally defeated the Amalekites.

q MASSAH...MERIBAH: *These names in Hebrew mean "testing" and "complaining."*
16.33: Heb 9.4   **16.35:** Josh 5.12

14 Then the LORD said to Moses, "Write an account of this victory, so that it will be remembered. Tell Joshua that I will completely destroy the Amalekites." 15 Moses built an altar and named it "The LORD is my Banner." 16 He said, "Hold high the banner of the LORD!r The LORD will continue to fight against the Amalekites for ever!"

Jethro Visits Moses

18 Moses' father-in-law Jethro, the priest of Midian, heard about everything that God had done for Moses and the people of Israel when he led them out of Egypt. 2 So he came to Moses, bringing with him Moses' wife Zipporah, who had been left behind, 3 and Gershom and Eliezer, her two sons. (Moses had said, "I have been a foreigner in a strange land"; so he had named one son Gershom.s 4 He had also said, "The God of my father helped me and saved me from being killed by the king of Egypt"; so he had named the other son Eliezer.)t 5 Jethro came with Moses' wife and her two sons into the desert where Moses was camped at the holy mountain. 6 He had sent word to Moses that they were coming, 7 so Moses went out to meet him, bowed before him, and kissed him. They asked about each other's health and then went into Moses' tent. 8 Moses told Jethro everything that the LORD had done to the king and the people of Egypt in order to rescue the Israelites. He also told him about the hardships the people had faced on the way and how the LORD had saved them. 9 When Jethro heard all this, he was happy 10 and said, "Praise the LORD, who saved you from the king and the people of Egypt! Praise the LORD,.who saved his people from slavery! 11 Now I know that the LORD is greater than all the gods, because he did this when the Egyptians treated the Israelites with such contempt." 12 Then Jethro brought an offering to be burnt whole and other sacrifices to be offered to God; and Aaron and all the leaders of Israel went with him to eat the sacred meal as an act of worship.

The Appointment of Judges
(Deut 1.9-18)

13 The next day Moses was settling disputes among the people, and he was kept busy from morning till night. 14 When Jethro saw everything that Moses had to do, he asked, "What is all this that you are doing for the people? Why are you doing this all alone, with people standing here from morning till night to consult you?"

15 Moses answered, "I must do this because the people come to me to learn God's will. 16 When two people have a dispute, they come to me, and I decide which one of them is right, and I tell them God's commands and laws."

17 Then Jethro said, "You are not doing it the right way. 18 You will wear yourself out and these people as well. This is too much for you to do alone. 19 Now let me give you some good advice, and God will be with you. It is right for you to represent the people before God and bring their disputes to him. 20 You should teach them God's commands and explain to them how they should live and what they should do. 21 But in addition, you should choose some capable men and appoint them as leaders of the people: leaders of thousands, hundreds, fifties, and tens. They must be God-fearing men who can be trusted and who cannot be bribed. 22 Let them serve as judges for the people on a permanent basis. They can bring all the difficult cases to you, but they themselves can decide all the smaller disputes. That will make it easier for you, as they share your burden. 23 If you do this, as God commands, you will not wear yourself out, and all these people can go home with their disputes settled."

24 Moses took Jethro's advice 25 and chose capable men from among all the Israelites. He appointed them as leaders of thousands, hundreds, fifties, and tens. 26 They served as judges for the people on a permanent basis, bringing the difficult cases to Moses but deciding the smaller disputes themselves.

27 Then Moses said good-bye to Jethro, and Jethro went back home.

The Israelites at Mount Sinai

19 1-2 The people of Israel left Rephidim, and on the first day of the third month after they had left Egypt they came to the desert of Sinai. There

---

r Probable text Hold...LORD; Hebrew unclear.
s GERSHOM: This name sounds like the Hebrew for "foreigner."
t ELIEZER: This name sounds like the Hebrew for "God helps me."
17.14: Deut 25.17-19; 1 Sam 15.2-9 **18.2-3:** Ex 2.21-22 **18.3:** Acts 7.29

they set up camp at the foot of Mount Sinai, 3 and Moses went up the mountain to meet with God.

The LORD called to him from the mountain and told him to say to the Israelites, Jacob's descendants: 4 "You saw what I, the LORD, did to the Egyptians and how I carried you as an eagle carries her young on her wings, and brought you here to me. 5 Now, if you will obey me and keep my covenant, you will be my own people. The whole earth is mine, but you will be my chosen people, 6 a people dedicated to me alone, and you will serve me as priests." 7 So Moses went down and called the leaders of the people together and told them everything that the LORD had commanded him. 8 Then all the people answered together, "We will do everything that the LORD has said," and Moses reported this to the LORD.

9 The LORD said to Moses, "I will come to you in a thick cloud, so that the people will hear me speaking with you and will believe you from now on."

Moses told the LORD what the people had answered, 10 and the LORD said to him, "Go to the people and tell them to spend today and tomorrow purifying themselves for worship. They must wash their clothes 11 and be ready the day after tomorrow. On that day I will come down on Mount Sinai, where all the people can see me. 12 Mark a boundary round the mountain that the people must not cross, and tell them not to go up the mountain or even get near it. If anyone sets foot on it, he is to be put to death; 13 he must either be stoned or shot with arrows, without anyone touching him. This applies to both men and animals; they must be put to death. But when the trumpet is blown, then the people are to go up to the mountain."

14 Then Moses came down the mountain and told the people to get ready for worship. So they washed their clothes, 15 and Moses said to them, "Be ready by the day after tomorrow and don't have sexual intercourse in the meantime."

16 On the morning of the third day there was thunder and lightning, a thick cloud appeared on the mountain, and a very loud trumpet blast was heard. All the people in the camp trembled with fear. 17 Moses led them out of the camp to meet God, and they stood at the foot of the mountain. 18 The whole of Mount Sinai was covered with smoke, because the LORD had come down on it in fire. The smoke went up like the smoke of a furnace, and all the people trembled violently. 19 The sound of the trumpet became louder and louder. Moses spoke, and God answered him with thunder. 20 The LORD came down on the top of Mount Sinai and called Moses to the top of the mountain. Moses went up 21 and the LORD said to him, "Go down and warn the people not to cross the boundary to come and look at me; if they do, many of them will die. 22 Even the priests who come near me must purify themselves, or I will punish them."

23 Moses said to the LORD, "The people cannot come up, because you commanded us to consider the mountain sacred and to mark a boundary round it."

24 The LORD replied, "Go down and bring Aaron back with you. But the priests and the people must not cross the boundary to come up to me, or I will punish them." 25 Moses then went down to the people and told them what the LORD had said.

The Ten Commandments
(Deut 5.1–21)

20 God spoke, and these were his words: 2 "I am the LORD your God who brought you out of Egypt, where you were slaves.

3 "Worship no god but me.

4 "Do not make for yourselves images of anything in heaven or on earth or in the water under the earth. 5 Do not bow down to any idol or worship it, because I am the LORD your God and I tolerate no rivals. I bring punishment on those who hate me and on their descendants down to the third and fourth generation. 6 But I show my love to thousands of generations u of those who love me and obey my laws.

7 "Do not use my name for evil purposes, for I, the LORD your God, will punish anyone who misuses my name.

8 "Observe the Sabbath and keep it

---

u thousands of generations; or thousands.
19.5: Deut 4.20, 7.6, 14.2, 26.18; Tit 2.14   **19.5–6:** 1 Pet 2.9   **19.6:** Rev 1.6, 5.10
19.12–13: Heb 12.18–20   **19.16:** Rev 4.5   **19.16–18:** Deut 4.11–12
20.4–5: Ex 34.17; Lev 19.4, 26.1; Deut 4.15–18, 27.15
20.5–6: Ex 34.6–7; Num 14.18; Deut 7.9–10   **20.7:** Lev 19.12   **20.8:** Ex 16.23–30, 31.12–14

God answered him with thunder (19.19)

holy. ⁹You have six days in which to do your work, ¹⁰but the seventh day is a day of rest dedicated to me. On that day no one is to work—neither you, your children, your slaves, your animals, nor the foreigners who live in your country. ¹¹In six days I, the LORD, made the earth, the sky, the sea, and everything in them, but on the seventh day I rested. That is why I, the LORD, blessed the Sabbath and made it holy.

12 "Respect your father and your mother, so that you may live a long time in the land that I am giving you.

13 "Do not commit murder.

14 "Do not commit adultery.

15 "Do not steal.

16 "Do not accuse anyone falsely.

17 "Do not desire another man's house; do not desire his wife, his slaves, his cattle, his donkeys, or anything else that he owns."

The People's Fear
(Deut 5.22-33)

18 When the people heard the thunder and the trumpet blast and saw the lightning and the smoking mountain, they trembled with fear and stood a long way off. ¹⁹They said to Moses, "If you speak to us, we will listen; but we are afraid that if God speaks to us, we will die."

20 Moses replied, "Don't be afraid; God has only come to test you and make you keep on obeying him, so that you will not sin." ²¹But the people continued to stand a long way off, and only Moses went near the dark cloud where God was.

Laws about Altars

22 The LORD commanded Moses to say to the Israelites: "You have seen how I, the LORD, have spoken to you from heaven. ²³Do not make for yourselves gods of silver or gold to be worshipped in addition to me. ²⁴Make an altar of earth for me, and on it sacrifice your sheep and your cattle as offerings to be completely burnt and as fellowship-offerings. In every place that I set aside for you to worship me, I will come to you and bless you. ²⁵If you make an altar of stone for me, do not build it out of cut stones, because when you use a chisel on stones, you make them unfit for my use. ²⁶Do not build an altar for me with steps leading up to

20.9-10: Ex 23.12, 31.15, 34.21, 35.2; Lev 23.3   **20.11:** Gen 2.1-3; Ex 31.17
20.12: Deut 27.16; Mt 15.4, 19.19; Mk 7.10, 10.19; Lk 18.20; Eph 6.2,3
20.13: Gen 9.6; Lev 24.17; Mt 5.21, 19.18; Mk 10.19; Lk 18.20; Rom13.9; Jas 2.11
20.14: Lev 20.10; Mt 5.27, 19.18; Mk 10.19; Lk 18.20; Rom 13.9; Jas 2.11
20.15: Lev 19.11; Mt 19.18; Mk 10.19; Lk 18.20; Rom 13.9
20.16: Ex 23.1; Mt 19.18; Mk 10.19; Lk 18.20   **20.17:** Rom 7.7, 13.9   **20.18-19:** Heb 12.18-19
20.25: Deut 27.5-7; Josh 8.31

it; if you do, you will expose yourselves as you go up the steps.

The Treatment of Slaves
(Deut 15.12–18)

21 "Give the Israelites the following laws: ²If you buy a Hebrew slave, he shall serve you for six years. In the seventh year he is to be set free without having to pay anything. ³If he was unmarried when he became your slave, he is not to take a wife with him when he leaves; but if he was married when he became your slave, he may take his wife with him. ⁴If his master gave him a wife and she bore him sons or daughters, the woman and her children belong to the master, and the man shall leave by himself. ⁵But if the slave declares that he loves his master, his wife, and his children and does not want to be set free, ⁶then his master shall take him to the place of worship. There he is to make him stand against the door or the doorpost and pierce his ear. Then he will be his slave for life.

7 "If a man sells his daughter as a slave, she is not to be set free, as male slaves are. ⁸If she is sold to someone who intends to make her his wife, but he doesn't like her, then she is to be sold back to her father; her master cannot sell her to foreigners, because he has treated her unfairly. ⁹If a man buys a female slave to give to his son, he is to treat her like a daughter. ¹⁰If a man takes a second wife, he must continue to give his first wife the same amount of food and clothing and the same rights that she had before. ¹¹If he does not fulfil these duties to her, he must set her free and not receive any payment.

Laws about Violent Acts

12 "Whoever hits a man and kills him is to be put to death. ¹³But if it was an accident and he did not mean to kill the man, he can escape to a place which I will choose for you, and there he will be safe. ¹⁴But when a man gets angry and deliberately kills another man, he is to be put to death, even if he has run to my altar for safety.

15 "Whoever hits his father or his mother is to be put to death.

16 "Whoever kidnaps a man, either to sell him or to keep him as a slave, is to be put to death.

17 "Whoever curses his father or his mother is to be put to death.

18–19 "If there is a fight and one man hits another with a stone or with his fist, but does not kill him, he is not to be punished. If the man who was hit has to stay in bed, but later is able to get up and walk outside with the help of a stick, the man who hit him is to pay for his lost time and take care of him until he gets well.

20 "If a man takes a stick and beats his slave, whether male or female, and the slave dies on the spot, the man is to be punished. ²¹But if the slave does not die for a day or two, the master is not to be punished. The loss of his property is punishment enough.

22 "If some men are fighting and hurt a pregnant woman so that she loses her child, but she is not injured in any other way, the one who hurt her is to be fined whatever amount the woman's husband demands, subject to the approval of the judges. ²³But if the woman herself is injured, the punishment shall be life for life, ²⁴eye for eye, tooth for tooth, hand for hand, foot for foot, ²⁵burn for burn, wound for wound, bruise for bruise.

26 "If a man hits his male or female slave in the eye so that he loses the use of it, he is to free the slave as payment for the eye. ²⁷If he knocks out a tooth, he is to free the slave as payment for the tooth.

The Responsibility of Owners

28 "If a bull gores someone to death, it is to be stoned, and its flesh shall not be eaten; but its owner is not to be punished. ²⁹But if the bull had been in the habit of attacking people and its owner had been warned, but did not keep it penned up—then if it gores someone to death, it is to be stoned, and its owner is to be put to death also. ³⁰However, if the owner is allowed to pay a fine to save his life, he must pay the full amount required. ³¹If the bull kills a boy or a girl, the same rule applies. ³²If the bull kills a male or female slave, its owner shall pay the owner of the slave thirty pieces of silver, and the bull shall be stoned to death.

33 "If a man takes the cover off a pit

21.2–6: Lev 25.39–46   **21.12:** Lev 24.17   **21.13:** Num 35.10–34; Deut 19.1–13; Josh 20.1–9
21.16: Deut 24.7   **21.17:** Lev 20.9; Mt 15.4; Mk 7.10
21.24: Lev 24.19–20; Deut 19.21; Mt 5.38

They...eat up the crops growing in another man's field (22.5)

or if he digs one and does not cover it, and a bull or a donkey falls into it, [34] he must pay for the animal. He is to pay the money to the owner and may keep the dead animal. [35] If one man's bull kills another man's bull, the two men shall sell the live bull and divide the money; they shall also divide up the meat from the dead animal. [36] But if it was known that the bull had been in the habit of attacking and its owner did not keep it penned up, he must make good the loss by giving the other man a live bull, but he may keep the dead animal.

Laws about Repayment

22 "If a man steals a cow or a sheep and kills it or sells it, he must pay five cows for one cow and four sheep for one sheep. [2-4] He must pay for what he stole. If he owns nothing, he shall be sold as a slave to pay for what he has stolen. If the stolen animal, whether a cow, a donkey, or a sheep, is found alive in his possession, he shall pay two for one.

"If a thief is caught breaking into a house at night and is killed, the one who killed him is not guilty of murder. But if it happens during the day, he is guilty of murder.

5 "If a man lets his animals graze in a field or a vineyard and they stray away and eat up the crops[v] growing in another man's field, he must make good the loss with the crops from his own fields or vineyards.

6 "If a man starts a fire in his field and it spreads through the weeds to another man's field and burns up corn that is growing or that has been cut and stacked, the one who started the fire is to pay for the damage.

7 "If a man agrees to keep another man's money or other valuables for him and they are stolen from his house, the thief, if he is found, shall repay double. [8] But if the thief is not found, the man who was keeping the valuables is to be brought to the place of worship and there he must take an oath that he has not stolen the other man's property.

9 "In every case of a dispute about property, whether it involves cattle, donkeys, sheep, clothing, or any other lost object, the two men claiming the property shall be taken to the place of worship. The one whom God declares to be guilty shall pay double to the other man.

10 "If a man agrees to keep another man's donkey, cow, sheep, or other animal for him, and the animal dies or is injured or is carried off in a raid, and if there was no witness, [11] the man must go to the place of worship and take an oath that he has not stolen the other man's animal. If the animal was not stolen, the owner shall accept the loss, and the other man need not repay him; [12] but if the animal was stolen, the man must repay the owner. [13] If it was killed by wild animals, the man is to bring the remains as evidence; he need not pay for what has been killed by wild animals.

14 "If a man borrows an animal from another man and it is injured or dies when its owner is not present, the man must pay for it. [15] But if that happens when the owner is present, the man need not

---

[v] If...crops; *or* If a man burns off a field or a vineyard, and lets the fire get out of control and burn up the crops.

repay. If it is a hired animal, the loss is covered by the hiring charge.

Moral and Religious Laws

16 "If a man seduces a virgin who is not engaged, he must pay the bride-price for her and marry her. 17 But if her father refuses to let him marry her, he must pay the father a sum of money equal to the bride-price for a virgin.

18 "Put to death any woman who practises magic.

19 "Put to death any man who has sexual relations with an animal.

20 "Condemn to death anyone who offers sacrifices to any god except to me, the Lord.

21 "Do not ill-treat or oppress a foreigner; remember that you were foreigners in Egypt. 22 Do not ill-treat any widow or orphan. 23 If you do, I, the Lord, will answer them when they cry out to me for help, 24 and I will be angry and kill you in war. Your wives will become widows, and your children will be fatherless.

25 "If you lend money to any of my people who are poor, do not act like a money-lender and require him to pay interest. 26 If you take someone's cloak as a pledge that he will pay you, you must give it back to him before the sun sets, 27 because it is the only covering he has to keep him warm. What else can he sleep in? When he cries out to me for help, I will answer him because I am merciful.

28 "Do not speak evil of God, w and do not curse a leader of your people.

29 "Give me the offerings from your corn, your wine, and your olive-oil when they are due.

"Give me your first-born sons. 30 Give me the first-born of your cattle and your sheep. Let the first-born male stay with its mother for seven days, and on the eighth day offer it to me.

31 "You are my people, so you must not eat the meat of any animal that has been killed by wild animals; instead, give it to the dogs.

Justice and Fairness

23 "Do not spread false rumours, and do not help a guilty man by giving false evidence. 2 Do not follow the majority when they do wrong or when they give evidence that perverts justice. 3 Do not show partiality to a poor man at his trial.

4 "If you happen to see your enemy's cow or donkey running loose, take it back to him. 5 If his donkey has fallen under its load, help him get the donkey to its feet again; don't just walk off.

6 "Do not deny justice to a poor man when he appears in court. 7 Do not make false accusations, and do not put an innocent person to death, for I will condemn anyone who does such an evil thing. 8 Do not accept a bribe, for a bribe makes people blind to what is right and ruins the cause of those who are innocent.

9 "Do not ill-treat a foreigner; you know how it feels to be a foreigner, because you were foreigners in Egypt.

The Seventh Year and the Seventh Day

10 "For six years sow your field and gather in what it produces. 11 But in the seventh year let it rest, and do not harvest anything that grows on it. The poor may eat what grows there, and the wild animals can have what is left. Do the same with your vineyards and your olive-trees.

12 "Work six days a week, but do no work on the seventh day, so that your slaves and the foreigners who work for you and even your animals can rest.

13 "Listen to everything that I, the Lord, have said to you. Do not pray to other gods; do not even mention their names.

The Three Great Festivals
(Ex 34.18-26; Deut 16.1-17)

14 "Celebrate three festivals a year to honour me. 15 In the month of Abib, the month in which you left Egypt, celebrate the Festival of Unleavened Bread in the way that I commanded you. Do not eat any bread made with yeast during the seven days of this festival. Never come

w God; or the judges.
22.16–17: Deut 22.28-29   **22.18:** Deut 18.10,11   **22.19:** Lev 18.23, 20.15-16; Deut 27.21
22.20: Deut 17.2-7   **22.21–22:** Ex 23.9; Lev 19.33-34; Deut 24.17-18, 27.19
22.25: Lev 25.35-38; Deut 15.7-11, 23.19-20   **22.26–27:** Deut 24.10-13   **22.28:** Acts 23.5
22.31: Lev 17.15   **23.1:** Ex 20.16; Lev 19.11-12; Deut 5.20   **23.3:** Lev 19.15
23.4–5: Deut 22.1-4   **23.6–8:** Lev 19.15; Deut 16.19
23.9: Ex 22.21; Lev 19.33-34; Deut 24.17-18, 27.19   **23.10–11:** Lev 25.1-7
23.12: Ex 20.9-11, 31.15, 34.21, 35.2; Lev 23.3; Deut 5.13-14
23.15: Ex 12.14-20; Lev 23.6-8; Num 28.17-25

to worship me without bringing an offering.

16 "Celebrate the Harvest Festival when you begin to harvest your crops.

"Celebrate the Festival of Shelters in the autumn, when you gather the fruit from your vineyards and orchards. 17 Every year at these three festivals all your men must come to worship me, the Lord your GOD.

18 "Do not offer bread made with yeast when you sacrifice an animal to me. The fat of animals sacrificed to me during these festivals is not to be left until the following morning.

19 "Each year bring to the house of the LORD your God the first corn that you harvest.

"Do not cook a young sheep or goat in its mother's milk.

Promises and Instructions

20 "I will send an angel ahead of you to protect you as you travel and to bring you to the place which I have prepared. 21 Pay attention to him and obey him. Do not rebel against him, for I have sent him, and he will not pardon such rebellion. 22 But if you obey him and do everything I command, I will fight against all your enemies. 23 My angel will go ahead of you and take you into the land of the Amorites, the Hittites, the Perizzites, the Canaanites, the Hivites, and the Jebusites, and I will destroy them. 24 Do not bow down to their gods or worship them, and do not adopt their religious practices. Destroy their gods and break down their sacred stone pillars. 25 If you worship me, the LORD your God, I will bless you with food and water and take away all your illnesses. 26 In your land no woman will have a miscarriage or be without children. I will give you long lives.

27 "I will make the people who oppose you afraid of me; I will bring confusion among the people against whom you fight, and I will make all your enemies turn and run from you. 28 I will throw your enemies into a panic;x I will drive out the Hivites, the Canaanites, and the Hittites as you advance. 29 I will not drive them out within one year; if I did, the land would become deserted, and the wild animals would be too many for you. 30 Instead, I will drive them out little by little, until there are enough of you to take possession of the land. 31 I will make the borders of your land extend from the Gulf of Aqaba to the Mediterranean Sea and from the desert to the Euphrates River. I will give you power over the inhabitants of the land, and you will drive them out as you advance. 32 Do not make any agreement with them or with their gods. 33 Do not let those people live in your country; if you do, they will make you sin against me. If you worship their gods, it will be a fatal trap for you."

The Covenant Is Sealed

24 The LORD said to Moses, "Come up the mountain to me, you and Aaron, Nadab, Abihu, and seventy of the leaders of Israel; and while you are still some distance away, bow down in worship. 2 You alone, and none of the others, are to come near me. The people are not even to come up the mountain."

3 Moses went and told the people all the LORD's commands and all the ordinances, and all the people answered together, "We will do everything that the LORD has said." 4 Moses wrote down all the LORD's commands. Early the next morning he built an altar at the foot of the mountain and set up twelve stones, one for each of the twelve tribes of Israel. 5 Then he sent young men, and they burnt sacrifices to the LORD and sacrificed some cattle as fellowship-offerings. 6 Moses took half the blood of the animals and put it in bowls; and the other half he threw against the altar. 7 Then he took the book of the covenant, in which the LORD's commands were written, and read it aloud to the people. They said, "We will obey the LORD and do everything that he has commanded."

8 Then Moses took the blood in the bowls and threw it on the people. He said, "This is the blood that seals the covenant which the LORD made with you when he gave all these commands."

9 Moses, Aaron, Nadab, Abihu, and seventy of the leaders of Israel went up the mountain 10 and they saw the God of Israel. Beneath his feet was what looked like a pavement of sapphire, as blue as the sky. 11 God did not harm these leading men of Israel; they saw God, and then they ate and drank together.

---

x I will...panic; or I will send hornets among your enemies.
23.16: Lev 23.15-21,39-43; Num 28.26-31   **23.19:** Ex 34.26; Deut 14.21, 26.2
24.8: Mt 26.28; Mk 14.24; Lk 22.20; 1 Cor 11.25; Heb 9.19-20, 10.29

Moses on Mount Sinai

12 The LORD said to Moses, "Come up the mountain to me, and while you are here, I will give you two stone tablets which contain all the laws that I have written for the instruction of the people." [13] Moses and his helper Joshua got ready, and Moses began[y] to go up the holy mountain. [14] Moses said to the leaders, "Wait here in the camp for us until we come back. Aaron and Hur are here with you; and so whoever has a dispute to settle can go to them."

15 Moses went up Mount Sinai, and a cloud covered it. [16-17] The dazzling light of the LORD's presence came down on the mountain. To the Israelites the light looked like a fire burning on top of the mountain. The cloud covered the mountain for six days, and on the seventh day the LORD called to Moses from the cloud. [18] Moses went on up the mountain into the cloud. There he stayed for forty days and nights.

Offerings for the Sacred Tent
(Ex 35.4-9)

25 The Lord said to Moses, [2] "Tell the Israelites to make an offering to me. Receive whatever offerings any man wishes to give. [3] These offerings are to be: gold, silver, and bronze; [4] fine linen; blue, purple, and red wool; cloth made of goats' hair; [5] rams' skin dyed red; fine leather; acacia-wood; [6] oil for the lamps; spices for the anointing oil and for the sweet-smelling incense; [7] carnelians and other jewels to be set in the ephod[m] of the High Priest and in his breast-piece. [8] The people must make a sacred tent for me, so that I may live among them. [9] Make it and all its furnishings according to the plan that I will show you.

The Covenant Box
(Ex 37.1-9)

10 "Make a box out of acacia-wood, 110 centimetres long, 66 centimetres wide, and 66 centimetres high. [11] Cover it with pure gold inside and out and put a gold border all round it. [12] Make four carrying-rings of gold for it and attach them to its four legs, with two rings on each side.

[13] Make carrying-poles of acacia-wood and cover them with gold [14] and put them through the rings on each side of the box. [15] The poles are to be left in the rings and must not be taken out. [16] Then put in the box the two stone tablets that I will give you, on which the commandments are written.

17 "Make a lid of pure gold, 110 centimetres long and 66 centimetres wide. [18] Make two winged creatures[z] of hammered gold, [19] one for each end of the lid. Make them so that they form one piece with the lid. [20] The winged creatures are to face each other across the lid, and their outspread wings are to cover it. [21] Put the two stone tablets inside the box and put the lid on top of it. [22] I will meet you there, and from above the lid between the two winged creatures I will give you all my laws for the people of Israel.

The Table for the Bread Offered to God
(Ex 37.10-16)

23 "Make a table out of acacia-wood, 88 centimetres long, 44 centimetres wide, and 66 centimetres high. [24] Cover it with pure gold and put a gold border round it. [25] Make a rim 75 millimetres wide round it and a gold border round the rim. [26] Make four carrying-rings of gold for it and put them at the four corners, where the legs are. [27] The rings to hold the poles for carrying the table are to be placed near the rim. [28] Make the poles of acacia-wood and cover them with gold. [29] Make plates, cups, jars, and bowls to be used for the wine-offerings. All of these are to be made of pure gold. [30] The table is to be placed in front of the Covenant Box, and on the table there is always to be the sacred bread offered to me.

The Lamp-stand
(Ex 37.17-24)

31 "Make a lamp-stand of pure gold. Make its base and its shaft of hammered gold; its decorative flowers, including buds and petals, are to form one piece with it. [32] Six branches shall extend from its sides, three from each side. [33] Each of the six branches is to have three decorative flowers shaped like almond blossoms with buds and petals. [34] The

---

[y] Moses began; *one ancient translation* they began.
[m] EPHOD: *In most contexts the term ephod refers to a type of garment, in certain respects resembling a waistcoat. It was made of costly and colourful cloth and to it was attached a kind of pouch containing the Urim and Thummim, two objects used in determining God's will.*
[z] WINGED CREATURES: *See Word List.*
24.18: Deut 9.9　　**25.17:** Heb 9.5　　**25.30:** Lev 24.5-8

shaft of the lamp-stand is to have four decorative flowers shaped like almond blossoms with buds and petals. 35 There is to be one bud below each of the three pairs of branches. 36 The buds, the branches, and the lamp-stand are to be a single piece of pure hammered gold. 37 Make seven lamps for the lamp-stand and set them up so that they shine towards the front. 38 Make its tongs and trays of pure gold. 39 Use thirty-five kilogrammes of pure gold to make the lamp-stand and all this equipment. 40 Take care to make them according to the plan that I showed you on the mountain.

The Tent of the LORD's Presence [a]
(Ex 36.8-38)

26 "Make the interior of the sacred Tent, the Tent of my presence, out of ten pieces of fine linen woven with blue, purple, and red wool. Embroider them with figures of winged creatures. 2 Make each piece the same size, twelve metres long and two metres wide. 3 Sew five of them together in one set, and do the same with the other five. 4 Make loops of blue cloth on the edge of the outside piece in each set. 5 Put fifty loops on the first piece of the first set and fifty loops matching them on the last piece of the second set. 6 Make fifty gold hooks with which to join the two sets into one piece.

7 "Make a cover for the Tent out of eleven pieces of cloth made of goats' hair. 8 Make them all the same size, thirteen metres long and two metres wide. 9 Sew five of them together in one set, and the other six in another set. Fold the sixth piece double over the front of the Tent. 10 Put fifty loops on the edge of the last piece of one set, and fifty loops on the edge of the other set. 11 Make fifty bronze hooks and put them in the loops to join the two sets so as to form one cover. 12 Hang the extra half-piece over the back of the Tent. 13 The extra fifty centimetres on each side of the length is to hang over the sides of the Tent to cover it.

14 "Make two more coverings, one of rams' skin dyed red and the other of fine leather, to serve as the outer cover.

15 "Make upright frames for the Tent out of acacia-wood. 16 Each frame is to be four metres long and 66 centimetres wide, 17 with two matching projections, so that the frames can be joined together.

All the frames are to have these projections. 18 Make twenty frames for the south side 19 and forty silver bases to go under them, two bases under each frame to hold its two projections. 20 Make twenty frames for the north side of the Tent 21 and forty silver bases, two under each frame. 22 For the back of the Tent on the west, make six frames, 23 and two frames for the corners. 24 These corner frames are to be joined at the bottom and connected all the way to the top. The two frames that form the two corners are to be made in this way. 25 So there will be eight frames with their sixteen silver bases, two under each frame.

26 "Make fifteen cross-bars of acacia-wood, five for the frames on one side of the Tent, 27 five for the frames on the other side, and five for the frames on the west end, at the back. 28 The middle cross-bar, set half-way up the frames, is to extend from one end of the Tent to the other. 29 Cover the frames with gold and fit them with gold rings to hold the cross-bars, which are also to be covered with gold. 30 Set up the Tent according to the plan that I showed you on the mountain.

31 "Make a curtain of fine linen woven with blue, purple, and red wool. Embroider it with figures of winged creatures. 32 Hang it on four posts of acacia-wood covered with gold, fitted with hooks, and set in four silver bases. 33 Place the curtain under the row of hooks in the roof of the Tent, and behind the curtain put the Covenant Box containing the two stone tablets. The curtain will separate the Holy Place from the Most Holy Place. 34 Put the lid on the Covenant Box. 35 Outside the Most Holy Place put the table against the north side of the Tent and the lamp-stand against the south side.

36 "For the entrance of the Tent make a curtain of fine linen woven with blue, purple, and red wool and decorated with embroidery. 37 For this curtain make five posts of acacia-wood covered with gold and fitted with gold hooks; make five bronze bases for these posts.

The Altar
(Ex 38.1-7)

27 "Make an altar out of acacia-wood. It is to be square, 2.2 metres long and 2.2 metres wide, and it is to be 1.3

---

[a] TENT OF THE LORD'S PRESENCE: *See Word List.*
25.40: Acts 7.44; Heb 8.5   **26.33:** Heb 6.19, 9.3-5

metres high. ² Make projections at the top of the four corners. They are to form one piece with the altar, and the whole is to be covered with bronze. ³ Make pans for the greasy ashes, and make shovels, bowls, hooks, and firepans. All this equipment is to be made of bronze. ⁴ Make a bronze grating and put four bronze carrying-rings on its corners. ⁵ Put the grating under the rim of the altar, so that it reaches half-way up the altar. ⁶ Make carrying-poles of acacia-wood, cover them with bronze, ⁷ and put them in the rings on each side of the altar when it is carried. ⁸ Make the altar out of boards and leave it hollow, according to the plan that I showed you on the mountain.

The Enclosure for the Tent of the Lord's Presence
(Ex 38.9-20)

9 "For the Tent of my presence make an enclosure out of fine linen curtains. On the south side the curtains are to be 44 metres long, ¹⁰ supported by twenty bronze posts in twenty bronze bases, with hooks and rods made of silver. ¹¹ The same is to be done on the north side of the enclosure. ¹² On the west side there are to be curtains 22 metres long, with ten posts and ten bases. ¹³ On the east side, where the entrance is, the enclosure is also to be 22 metres wide. ¹⁴⁻¹⁵ On each side of the entrance there are to be 6.6 metres of curtains, with three posts and three bases. ¹⁶ For the entrance itself there is to be a curtain 9 metres long made of fine linen woven with blue, purple, and red wool, and decorated with embroidery. It is to be supported by four posts in four bases. ¹⁷ All the posts round the enclosure are to be connected with silver rods, and their hooks are to be made of silver and their bases of bronze. ¹⁸ The enclosure is to be 44 metres long, 22 metres wide, and 2.2 metres high. The curtains are to be made of fine linen and the bases of bronze. ¹⁹ All the equipment that is used in the Tent and all the pegs for the Tent and for the enclosure are to be made of bronze.

Taking Care of the Lamp
(Lev 24.1-4)

20 "Command the people of Israel to bring you the best olive-oil for the lamp, so that it can be lit each evening. ²¹ Aaron and his sons are to set up the lamp in the Tent of my presence outside the curtain which is in front of the Covenant Box. There in my presence it is to burn from evening until morning. This command is to be kept for ever by the Israelites and their descendants.

Garments for the Priests
(Ex 39.1-7)

28 "Summon your brother Aaron and his sons, Nadab, Abihu, Eleazar, and Ithamar. Separate them from the people of Israel, so that they may serve me as priests. ² Make priestly garments for your brother Aaron, to provide him with dignity and beauty. ³ Call all the craftsmen to whom I have given ability, and tell them to make Aaron's clothes, so that he may be dedicated as a priest in my service. ⁴ Tell them to make a breast-piece, an ephod, a robe, an embroidered shirt, a turban, and a sash. They are to make these priestly garments for your brother Aaron and his sons, so that they can serve me as priests. ⁵ The craftsmen are to use blue, purple, and red wool, gold thread, and fine linen.

6 "They are to make the ephod of blue, purple, and red wool, gold thread, and fine linen, decorated with embroidery. ⁷ Two shoulder-straps, by which it can be fastened, are to be attached to the sides. ⁸ A finely woven belt made of the same materials is to be attached to the ephod so as to form one piece with it. ⁹ Take two carnelian stones and engrave on them the names of the twelve sons of Jacob, ¹⁰ in the order of their birth, with six on one stone and six on the other. ¹¹ Get a skilful jeweller to engrave on the two stones the names of the sons of Jacob, and mount the stones in gold settings. ¹² Put them on the shoulder-straps of the ephod to represent the twelve tribes of Israel. In this way Aaron will carry their names on his shoulders, so that I, the Lord, will always remember my people. ¹³ Make two gold settings ¹⁴ and two chains of pure gold twisted like cords, and attach them to the settings.

The Breast-piece
(Ex 39.8-21)

15 "Make a breast-piece for the High Priest to use in determining God's will. It is to be made of the same materials as the ephod and with similar embroidery. ¹⁶ It is to be square and folded double, 22 centimetres long and 22 centimetres wide. ¹⁷ Mount four rows of precious stones on it; in the first row mount a ruby, a topaz, and a garnet; ¹⁸ in the

second row, an emerald, a sapphire, and a diamond; 19 in the third row, a turquoise, an agate, and an amethyst; 20 and in the fourth row, a beryl, a carnelian, and a jasper. These are to be mounted in gold settings. 21 Each of these twelve stones is to have engraved on it the name of one of the sons of Jacob, to represent the tribes of Israel. 22 For the breast-piece make chains of pure gold, twisted like cords. 23 Make two gold rings and attach them to the upper corners of the breast-piece, 24 and fasten the two gold cords to the two rings. 25 Fasten the other two ends of the cords to the two settings, and in this way attach them in front to the shoulder-straps of the ephod. 26 Then make two rings of gold and attach them to the lower corners of the breast-piece on the inside edge next to the ephod. 27 Make two more gold rings and attach them to the lower part of the front of the two shoulder-straps of the ephod near the seam and above the finely woven belt. 28 Tie the rings of the breast-piece to the rings of the ephod with a blue cord, so that the breast-piece rests above the belt and does not come loose.

29 "When Aaron enters the Holy Place, he will wear this breast-piece engraved with the names of the tribes of Israel, so that I, the LORD, will always remember my people. 30 Put the Urim and Thummim[b] in the breast-piece, so that Aaron will carry them when he comes into my holy presence. At such times he must always wear this breast-piece, so that he can determine my will for the people of Israel.

The Other Priestly Garments
(Ex 39.22–31)

31 "The robe that goes under the ephod is to be made entirely of blue wool. 32 It is to have a hole for the head, and this hole is to be reinforced with a woven binding to keep it from tearing. 33-34 All round its lower hem put pomegranates of blue, purple, and red wool, alternating with gold bells. 35 Aaron is to wear this robe when he serves as priest. When he comes into my presence in the Holy Place or when he leaves it, the sound of the bells will be heard, and he will not be killed.

36 "Make an ornament of pure gold and engrave on it 'Dedicated to the LORD.' 37 Tie it to the front of the turban with a blue cord. 38 Aaron is to wear it on his forehead, so that I, the LORD, will accept all the offerings that the Israelites dedicate to me, even if the people commit some error in offering them.

39 "Weave Aaron's shirt of fine linen and make a turban of fine linen and also a sash decorated with embroidery.

40 "Make shirts, sashes, and caps for Aaron's sons, to provide them with dignity and beauty. 41 Put these clothes on your brother Aaron and his sons. Then ordain them and dedicate them by anointing them with olive-oil, so that they may serve me as priests. 42 Make linen shorts for them, reaching from the waist to the thighs, so that they will not expose themselves. 43 Aaron and his sons must always wear them when they go into the Tent of my presence or approach the altar to serve as priests in the Holy Place, so that they will not be killed for exposing themselves. This is a permanent rule for Aaron and his descendants.

Instructions for Ordaining Aaron and His Sons as Priests
(Lev 8.1–36)

29 "This is what you are to do to Aaron and his sons to dedicate them as priests in my service. Take one young bull and two rams without any defects. 2 Use the best wheat flour, but no yeast, and make some bread with olive-oil, some without it, and some in the form of biscuits brushed with oil. 3 Put them in a basket and offer them to me when you sacrifice the bull and the two rams.

4 "Bring Aaron and his sons to the entrance of the Tent of my presence, and tell them to take a ritual bath. 5 Then dress Aaron in the priestly garments—the shirt, the robe that goes under the ephod, the ephod, the breast-piece, and the belt. 6 Put the turban on him and tie on it the sacred sign of dedication engraved 'Dedicated to the LORD.' 7 Then take the anointing oil, pour it on his head, and anoint him.

8 "Bring his sons and put shirts on them; 9 put sashes round their waists and tie caps on their heads. That is how you are to ordain Aaron and his sons. They and their descendants are to serve me as priests for ever.

---

[b] URIM AND THUMMIM: *Two objects used by the priest to determine God's will; it is not known precisely how they were used.*
28.30: Num 27.21; Deut 33.8; Ezra 2.63; Neh 7.65

10 "Bring the bull to the front of the Tent of my presence and tell Aaron and his sons to put their hands on its head. ¹¹Kill the bull there in my holy presence at the entrance of the Tent. ¹²Take some of the bull's blood and with your finger put it on the projections of the altar. Then pour out the rest of the blood at the base of the altar. ¹³Next, take all the fat which covers the internal organs, the best part of the liver, and the two kidneys with the fat on them and burn them on the altar as an offering to me. ¹⁴But burn the bull's flesh, its skin, and its intestines outside the camp. This is an offering to take away the sins of the priests.

15 "Take one of the rams and tell Aaron and his sons to put their hands on its head. ¹⁶Kill it, and take its blood and throw it against all four sides of the altar. ¹⁷Cut the ram in pieces; wash its internal organs and its hind legs, and put them on top of the head and the other pieces. ¹⁸Burn the whole ram on the altar as a food offering. The odour of this offering pleases me.

19 "Take the other ram—the ram used for dedication—and tell Aaron and his sons to put their hands on its head. ²⁰Kill it, and take some of its blood and put it on the lobes of the right ears of Aaron and his sons, on the thumbs of their right hands and on the big toes of their right feet. Throw the rest of the blood against all four sides of the altar. ²¹Take some of the blood that is on the altar and some of the anointing oil, and sprinkle it on Aaron and his clothes and on his sons and their clothes. He, his sons, and their clothes will then be dedicated to me.

22 "Cut away the ram's fat, the fat tail, the fat covering the internal organs, the best part of the liver, the two kidneys with the fat on them, and the right thigh. ²³From the basket of bread which has been offered to me, take one loaf of each kind: one loaf made with olive-oil and one made without it and one biscuit. ²⁴Put all this food in the hands of Aaron and his sons and tell them to dedicate it to me as a special gift. ²⁵Then take it from them and burn it on the altar, on top of the burnt-offering, as a food-offering to me. The odour of this offering pleases me.

26 "Take the breast of this ram and dedicate it to me as a special gift. This part of the animal will be yours,

27 "When a priest is ordained, the breast and the thigh of the ram being used for the ordination are to be dedicated to me as a special gift and set aside for the priests. ²⁸It is my unchanging decision that when my people make their fellowship-offerings, the breast and the thigh of the animal belong to the priests. This is the people's gift to me, the LORD.

29 "Aaron's priestly garments are to be handed on to his sons after his death, for them to wear when they are ordained. ³⁰The son of Aaron who succeeds him as priest and who goes into the Tent of my presence to serve in the Holy Place is to wear these garments for seven days.

31 "Take the meat of the ram used for the ordination of Aaron and his sons and boil it in a holy place. ³²At the entrance of the Tent of my presence they are to eat it along with the bread left in the basket. ³³They shall eat what was used in the ritual of forgiveness at their ordination. Only priests may eat this food, because it is sacred. ³⁴If some of the meat or some of the bread is not eaten by morning, it is to be burnt; it is not to be eaten, for it is sacred.

35 "Perform the rites of ordination for Aaron and his sons for seven days exactly as I have commanded you. ³⁶Each day you must offer a bull as a sacrifice, so that sin may be forgiven. This will purify the altar. Then anoint it with olive-oil to make it holy. ³⁷Do this every day for seven days. Then the altar will be completely holy, and anyone or anything that touches it will be harmed by the power of its holiness. ᶜ

The Daily Offerings
(Num 28.1–8)

38 "Every day for all time to come, sacrifice on the altar two one-year-old lambs. ³⁹Sacrifice one of the lambs in the morning and the other in the evening. ⁴⁰With the first lamb offer one kilogramme of fine wheat flour mixed with one litre of pure olive-oil. Pour out one litre of wine as an offering. ⁴¹Sacrifice the second lamb in the evening, and offer with it the same amounts of flour, olive-oil, and wine as in the morning. This is a food offering to me, the LORD, and its

---

ᶜBE HARMED BY THE POWER OF ITS HOLINESS: *It was believed that ordinary people or things would be harmed by touching something holy.*
29.18: Eph 5.2; Phil 4.18

odour pleases me. ⁴²For all time to come, this burnt-offering is to be offered in my presence at the entrance of the Tent of my presence. That is where I will meet my people and speak to you. ⁴³There I will meet the people of Israel, and the dazzling light of my presence will make the place holy. ⁴⁴I will make the Tent and the altar holy, and I will set Aaron and his sons apart to serve me as priests. ⁴⁵I will live among the people of Israel, and I will be their God. ⁴⁶They will know that I am the LORD their God who brought them out of Egypt so that I could live among them. I am the LORD their God.

The Altar for Burning Incense
(Ex 37.25–28)

30 "Make an altar out of acacia-wood, for burning incense. ²It is to be square, 45 centimetres long and 45 centimetres wide, and it is to be 90 centimetres high. Its projections at the four corners are to form one piece with it. ³Cover its top, all four sides, and its projections with pure gold, and put a gold border round it. ⁴Make two gold carrying-rings for it and attach them below the border on two sides to hold the poles with which it is to be carried. ⁵Make these poles of acacia-wood and cover them with gold. ⁶Put this altar outside the curtain which hangs in front of the Covenant Box. That is the place where I will meet you. ⁷Every morning when Aaron comes to get the lamps ready, he is to burn sweet-smelling incense on it. ⁸He must do the same when he lights the lamps in the evening. This offering of incense is to continue without interruption for all time to come. ⁹Do not offer on this altar any forbidden incense, any animal-offering, or any grain-offering, and do not pour out any wine-offering on it. ¹⁰Once a year Aaron is to perform the ritual for purifying the altar by putting on its four projections the blood of the animal sacrificed for sin. This is to be done every year for all time to come. This altar is to be completely holy, dedicated to me, the LORD."

The Tax for the Tent of the LORD's Presence

11 The LORD said to Moses, ¹²"When you take a census of the people of Israel, each man is to pay me a price for his life, so that no disaster will come on him

while the census is being taken. ¹³Everyone included in the census must pay the required amount of money, weighed according to the official standard. Everyone must pay this as an offering to me. ¹⁴Everyone being counted in the census, that is, every man twenty years old or older, is to pay me this amount. ¹⁵The rich man is not to pay more, nor the poor man less, when they pay this amount for their lives. ¹⁶Collect this money from the people of Israel and spend it for the upkeep of the Tent of my presence. This tax will be the payment for their lives, and I will remember to protect them."

The Bronze Basin

17 The LORD said to Moses, ¹⁸"Make a bronze basin with a bronze base. Place it between the Tent and the altar, and put water in it. ¹⁹Aaron and his sons are to use the water to wash their hands and feet ²⁰before they go into the Tent or approach the altar to offer the food offering. Then they will not be killed. ²¹They must wash their hands and feet, so that they will not die. This is a rule which they and their descendants are to observe for ever."

The Anointing Oil

22 The LORD said to Moses, ²³"Take the finest spices—six kilogrammes of liquid myrrh, three kilogrammes of sweet-smelling cinnamon, three kilogrammes of sweet-smelling cane, ²⁴and six kilogrammes of cassia (all weighed according to the official standard). Add four litres of olive-oil, ²⁵and make a sacred anointing oil, mixed like perfume. ²⁶Use it to anoint the Tent of my presence, the Covenant Box, ²⁷the table and all its equipment, the lamp-stand and its equipment, the altar for burning incense, ²⁸the altar for burning offerings, together with all its equipment, and the wash-basin with its base. ²⁹Dedicate these things in this way, and they will be completely holy, and anyone or anything that touches them will be harmed by the power of its holiness.ᵈ ³⁰Then anoint Aaron and his sons, and ordain them as priests in my service. ³¹Say to the people of Israel, 'This holy anointing oil is to be used in my service for all time to come. ³²It must not be poured on ordinary men, and you must not use the same formula to make any

---

ᵈHARMED BY THE POWER OF ITS HOLINESS: *See 29.37.*
30.13: Ex 38.25–26; Mt 17.24   **30.18:** Ex 38.8   **30.22–38:** Ex 37.29

mixture like it. It is holy, and you must treat it as holy. 33 Whoever makes any like it or uses any of it on anyone who is not a priest will no longer be considered one of my people.' "

The Incense

34 The LORD said to Moses, "Take an equal part of each of the following sweet spices—stacte, onycha, galbanum, and pure frankincense. 35 Use them to make incense, mixed like perfume. Add salt to keep it pure and holy. 36 Beat part of it into a fine powder, take it into the Tent of my presence, and sprinkle it in front of the Covenant Box. Treat this incense as completely holy. 37 Do not use the same formula to make any incense like it for yourselves. Treat it as a holy thing dedicated to me. 38 If anyone makes any like it for use as perfume, he will no longer be considered one of my people."

Craftsmen for the Tent of the LORD's Presence
(Ex 35.30–36.1)

31 The LORD said to Moses, 2 "I have chosen Bezalel, the son of Uri and grandson of Hur, from the tribe of Judah, 3 and I have filled him with my power.e I have given him understanding, skill, and ability for every kind of artistic work— 4 for planning skilful designs and working them in gold, silver, and bronze; 5 for cutting jewels to be set; for carving wood; and for every other kind of artistic work. 6 I have also selected Oholiab son of Ahisamach, from the tribe of Dan, to work with him. I have also given great ability to all the other skilful craftsmen, so that they can make everything I have commanded to be made: 7 the Tent of my presence, the Covenant Box and its lid, all the furnishings of the Tent, 8 the table and its equipment, the lamp-stand of pure gold and all its equipment, the altar for burning incense, 9 the altar for burnt-offerings and all its equipment, the wash-basin and its base, 10 the magnificent priestly garments for Aaron and his sons to use when they serve as priests, 11 the anointing oil, and the sweet-smelling incense for the Holy Place. In making all these things, they are to do exactly as I have commanded you."

Sabbath, the Day of Rest

12 The LORD commanded Moses 13 to say to the people of Israel, "Keep the Sabbath, my day of rest, because it is a sign between you and me for all time to come, to show that I, the LORD, have made you my own people. 14 You must keep the day of rest, because it is sacred. Whoever does not keep it, but works on that day, is to be put to death. 15 You have six days in which to do your work, but the seventh day is a solemn day of rest dedicated to me. Whoever does any work on that day is to be put to death. 16 The people of Israel are to keep this day as a sign of the covenant. 17 It is a permanent sign between the people of Israel and me, because I, the LORD, made heaven and earth in six days, and on the seventh day I stopped working and rested."

18 When God had finished speaking to Moses on Mount Sinai, he gave him the two stone tablets on which God himself had written the commandments.

The Gold Bull-Calf
(Deut 9.6–29)

32 When the people saw that Moses had not come down from the mountain but was staying there a long time, they gathered round Aaron and said to him, "We do not know what has happened to this man Moses, who led us out of Egypt; so make us a godf to lead us."

2 Aaron said to them, "Take off the gold earrings which your wives, your sons, and your daughters are wearing, and bring them to me." 3 So all the people took off their gold earrings and brought them to Aaron. 4 He took the earrings, melted them, poured the gold into a mould, and made a gold bull-calf.

The people said, "Israel, this is our god, who led us out of Egypt!"

5 Then Aaron built an altar in front of the gold bull and announced, "Tomorrow there will be a festival to honour the LORD." 6 Early the next morning they brought some animals to burn as sacrifices and others to eat as fellowship-offerings. The people sat down to a feast, which turned into an orgy of drinking and sex.

epower; or spirit.　　fa god; or some gods.
31.15: Ex 20.8–11, 23.12, 34.21, 35.2; Lev 23.3; Deut 5.12–14
31.17: Ex 20.11　　**32.1:** Acts 7.40　　**32.4:** 1 Kgs 12.28; Acts 7.41　　**32.6:** 1 Cor 10.7

7 The LORD said to Moses, "Go back down at once, because your people, whom you led out of Egypt, have sinned and rejected me. 8 They have already left the way that I commanded them to follow; they have made a bull-calf out of melted gold and have worshipped it and offered sacrifices to it. They are saying that this is their god, who led them out of Egypt. 9 I know how stubborn these people are. 10 Now, don't try to stop me. I am angry with them, and I am going to destroy them. Then I will make you and your descendants into a great nation."

11 But Moses pleaded with the LORD his God and said, "LORD, why should you be so angry with your people, whom you rescued from Egypt with great might and power? 12 Why should the Egyptians be able to say that you led your people out of Egypt, planning to kill them in the mountains and destroy them completely? Stop being angry; change your mind and do not bring this disaster on your people. 13 Remember your servants Abraham, Isaac, and Jacob. Remember the solemn promise you made to them to give them as many descendants as there are stars in the sky and to give their descendants all that land you promised would be their possession for ever." 14 So the LORD changed his mind and did not bring on his people the disaster he had threatened.

15 Moses went back down the mountain, carrying the two stone tablets with the commandments written on both sides. 16 God himself had made the tablets and had engraved the commandments on them.

17 Joshua heard the people shouting and said to Moses, "I hear the sound of battle in the camp."

18 Moses said, "That doesn't sound like a shout of victory or a cry of defeat; it's the sound of singing."

19 When Moses came close enough to the camp to see the bull-calf and to see the people dancing, he was furious. There at the foot of the mountain, he threw down the tablets he was carrying and broke them. 20 He took the bull-calf which they had made, melted it, ground it into fine powder, and mixed it with water. Then he made the people of Israel drink it. 21 He said to Aaron, "What did these people do to you, that you have made them commit such a terrible sin?"

22 Aaron answered, "Don't be angry with me; you know how determined these people are to do evil. 23 They said to me, 'We don't know what has happened to this man Moses, who brought us out of Egypt; so make us a god to lead us.' 24 I asked them to bring me their gold ornaments, and those who had any took them off and gave them to me. I threw the ornaments into the fire and out came this bull-calf!"

25 Moses saw that Aaron had let the people get out of control and make fools of themselves in front of their enemies. 26 So he stood at the gate of the camp and shouted, "Everyone who is on the LORD's side come over here!" So all the Levites gathered round him, 27 and he said to them, "The LORD God of Israel commands every one of you to put on his sword and go through the camp from this gate to the other and kill his brothers, his friends, and his neighbours." 28 The Levites obeyed, and killed about three thousand men that day. 29 Moses said to the Levites, "Today you have consecrated yourselves h as priests in the service of the LORD by killing your sons and brothers, so the LORD has given you his blessing."

30 The next day Moses said to the people, "You have committed a terrible sin. But now I will again go up the mountain to the LORD; perhaps I can obtain forgiveness for your sin." 31 Moses then returned to the LORD and said, "These people have committed a terrible sin. They have made a god out of gold and worshipped it. 32 Please forgive their sin; but if you won't, then remove my name from the book in which you have written the names of your people."

33 The LORD answered, "It is those who have sinned against me whose names I will remove from my book. 34 Now go, lead the people to the place I told you about. Remember that my angel will guide you, but the time is coming when I will punish these people for their sin."

35 So the LORD sent a disease on the people, because they had caused Aaron to make the gold bull-calf.

h Some ancient translations Today you have consecrated yourselves; Hebrew consecrate yourselves today; or you have been consecrated today.
32.11-14: Num 14.13-19   32.13: Gen 22.16-17, 17.8   32.32: Ps 69.28; Rev 3.5

They would bow down (33.10)

The LORD Orders Israel to Leave Mount Sinai

33 The LORD said to Moses, "Leave this place, you and the people you brought out of Egypt, and go to the land that I promised to give to Abraham, Isaac, and Jacob and to their descendants. ²I will send an angel to guide you, and I will drive out the Canaanites, the Amorites, the Hittites, the Perizzites, the Hivites, and the Jebusites. ³You are going to a rich and fertile land. But I will not go with you myself, because you are a stubborn people, and I might destroy you on the way."

4 When the people heard this, they began to mourn and did not wear jewellery any more. ⁵For the LORD had commanded Moses to say to them, "You are a stubborn people. If I were to go with you even for a moment, I would completely destroy you. Now take off your jewellery, and I will decide what to do with you." ⁶So after they left Mount Sinai, the people of Israel no longer wore jewellery.

33.1: Gen 12.7, 26.3, 28.13

The Tent of the LORD's Presence

7 Whenever the people of Israel set up camp, Moses would take the sacred Tent and put it up some distance away from the camp. It was called the Tent of the LORD's presence, and anyone who wanted to consult the LORD would go out to it. ⁸Whenever Moses went out there, the people would stand at the door of their tents and watch Moses until he entered it. ⁹After Moses had gone in, the pillar of cloud would come down and stay at the door of the Tent, and the LORD would speak to Moses from the cloud. ¹⁰As soon as the people saw the pillar of cloud at the door of the Tent, they would bow down. ¹¹The LORD would speak with Moses face to face, just as a man speaks with a friend. Then Moses would return to the camp. But the young man who was his helper, Joshua son of Nun, stayed in the Tent.

The LORD Promises to Be with His People

12 Moses said to the LORD, "It is true that you have told me to lead these people to that land, but you did not tell me whom

you would send with me. You have said that you know me well and are pleased with me. [13] Now if you are, tell me your plans, so that I may serve you and continue to please you. Remember also that you have chosen this nation to be your own."

14 The LORD said, "I will go with you, and I will give you victory."

15 Moses replied, "If you do not go with us, don't make us leave this place. [16] How will anyone know that you are pleased with your people and with me if you do not go with us? Your presence with us will distinguish us from any other people on earth."

17 The LORD said to Moses, "I will do just as you have asked, because I know you very well and I am pleased with you."

18 Then Moses requested, "Please, let me see the dazzling light of your presence."

19 The LORD answered, "I will make all my splendour pass before you and in your presence I will pronounce my sacred name. I am the LORD, and I show compassion and pity on those I choose. [20] I will not let you see my face, because no one can see me and stay alive, [21] but here is a place beside me where you can stand on a rock. [22] When the dazzling light of my presence passes by, I will put you in an opening in the rock and cover you with my hand until I have passed by. [23] Then I will take my hand away, and you will see my back but not my face."

The Second Set of Stone Tablets
(Deut 10.1-5)

34 The LORD said to Moses, "Cut two stone tablets like the first ones, and I will write on them the words that were on the first tablets, which you broke. [2] Be ready tomorrow morning, and come up Mount Sinai to meet me there at the top. [3] No one is to come up with you; no one is to be seen on any part of the mountain; and no sheep or cattle are to graze at the foot of the mountain." [4] So Moses cut two more stone tablets, and early the next morning he carried them up Mount Sinai, just as the LORD had commanded.

5 The LORD came down in a cloud, stood with him there, and pronounced his holy name, the LORD.[j] [6] The LORD then passed in front of him and called out, "I, the LORD, am a God who is full of compassion and pity, who is not easily angered and who shows great love and faithfulness. [7] I keep my promise for thousands of generations[k] and forgive evil and sin; but I will not fail to punish children and grandchildren to the third and fourth generation for the sins of their parents."

8 Moses quickly bowed down to the ground and worshipped. [9] He said, "Lord, if you really are pleased with me, I ask you to go with us. These people are stubborn, but forgive our evil and our sin, and accept us as your own people."

The Covenant Is Renewed
(Ex 23.14-19; Deut 7.1-5; 16.1-17)

10 The LORD said to Moses, "I now make a covenant with the people of Israel. In their presence I will do great things such as have never been done anywhere on earth among any of the nations. All the people will see what great things I, the LORD, can do, because I am going to do an awesome thing for you. [11] Obey the laws that I am giving you today. I will drive out the Amorites, the Canaanites, the Hittites, the Perizzites, the Hivites, and the Jebusites, as you advance. [12] Do not make any treaties with the people of the country into which you are going, because this could be a fatal trap for you. [13] Instead, tear down their altars, destroy their sacred pillars, and cut down the symbols of their goddess Asherah.

14 "Do not worship any other god, because I, the LORD, tolerate no rivals. [15] Do not make any treaties with the people of the country, because when they worship their pagan gods and sacrifice to them, they will invite you to join them, and you will be tempted to eat the food they offer to their gods. [16] Your sons might marry those foreign women, who would lead them to be unfaithful to me and to worship their pagan gods.

17 "Do not make and worship gods of metal.

18 "Keep the Festival of Unleavened Bread. As I have commanded you, eat unleavened bread for seven days in the month of Abib, because it was in that month that you left Egypt.

---

[j] THE LORD: See 3.14.　　[k] thousands of generations; or thousands.
33.19: Rom 9.15　　**34.6-7:** Ex 20.5-6; Num 14.18; Deut 5.9-10, 7.9-10　　**34.13:** Deut 16.21
34.17: Ex 20.4; Lev 19.4; Deut 5.8, 27.15　　**34.18:** Ex 12.14-20; Lev 23.6-8; Num 28.16-25

19 "Every first-born son and first-born male domestic animal belongs to me, 20 but you are to buy back every first-born donkey by offering a lamb in its place. If you do not buy it back, break its neck. Buy back every first-born son.

"No one is to appear before me without an offering.

21 "You have six days in which to do your work, but do not work on the seventh day, not even during ploughing time or harvest.

22 "Keep the Harvest Festival when you begin to harvest the first crop of your wheat, and keep the Festival of Shelters in the autumn when you gather your fruit.

23 "Three times a year all your men must come to worship me, the LORD, the God of Israel. 24 After I have driven out the nations before you and extended your territory, no one will try to conquer your country during the three festivals.

25 "Do not offer bread made with yeast when you sacrifice an animal to me. Do not keep until the following morning any part of the animal killed at the Passover Festival.

26 "Each year bring to the house of the LORD the first corn that you harvest.

"Do not cook a young sheep or goat in its mother's milk."

27 The LORD said to Moses, "Write these words down, because it is on the basis of these words that I am making a covenant with you and with Israel." 28 Moses stayed there with the LORD forty days and nights, eating and drinking nothing. He wrote on the tablets the words of the covenant—the Ten Commandments.

Moses Goes Down from Mount Sinai

29 When Moses went down from Mount Sinai carrying the Ten Commandments, his face was shining because he had been speaking with the LORD; but he did not know it. 30 Aaron and all the people looked at Moses and saw that his face was shining, and they were afraid to go near him. 31 But Moses called them, and Aaron and all the leaders of the community went to him, and Moses spoke to them. 32 After that, all the people of Israel gathered round him, and Moses gave them all the laws that the LORD had given him on Mount Sinai. 33 When Moses had finished speaking to them, he covered his face with a veil. 34 Whenever Moses went into the Tent of the LORD's presence to speak to the LORD, he took the veil off. When he came out, he would tell the people of Israel everything that he had been commanded to say, 35 and they would see that his face was shining. Then he would put the veil back on until the next time he went to speak to the LORD.

Regulations for the Sabbath

35 Moses called together the whole community of the people of Israel and said to them, "This is what the LORD has commanded you to do: 2 You have six days in which to do your work, but the seventh day is to be sacred, a solemn day of rest dedicated to me, the LORD. Anyone who does any work on that day is to be put to death. 3 Do not even light a fire in your homes on the Sabbath."

Offerings for the Sacred Tent
(Ex 25.1–9)

4 Moses said to all the people of Israel, "This is what the LORD has commanded: 5 Make an offering to the LORD. Everyone who wishes to do so is to bring an offering of gold, silver, or bronze; 6 fine linen; blue, purple, and red wool; cloth made of goats' hair; 7 rams' skin dyed red; fine leather; acacia-wood; 8 oil for the lamps; spices for the anointing oil and for the sweet-smelling incense; 9 carnelians and other jewels to be set in the High Priest's ephod and in his breast-piece.

Articles for the Tent of the LORD's Presence
(Ex 39.32–43)

10 "All the skilled workmen among you are to come and make everything that the LORD commanded: 11 the Tent, its covering and its outer covering, its hooks and its frames, its cross-bars, its posts, and its bases; 12 the Covenant Box, its poles, its lid, and the curtain to screen it off; 13 the table, its poles, and all its equipment; the bread offered to God; 14 the lamp-stand for the light and its equipment; the lamps with their oil; 15 the altar for burning incense and its poles; the anointing oil; the sweet-smelling incense; the curtain for the entrance of the Tent; 16 the altar on which to burn offerings, with its bronze grating

34.19: Ex 13.2   **34.20:** Ex 13.13
34.21: Ex 20.9–10, 23.12, 31.15, 35.2; Lev 23.3; Deut 5.13–14
34.22: Lev 23.15–21, 39.43; Num 28.26–31   **34.25:** Ex 12.10   **34.26:** Deut 24.21, 26.2
34.29–35: 2 Cor 3.7–16   **35.2:** Ex 20.8–11, 23.12, 31.15, 34.21; Lev 23.3; Deut 5.12–14

attached, its poles, and all its equipment; the wash-basin and its base; ¹⁷the curtains for the enclosure, its posts and bases; the curtain for the entrance of the enclosure; ¹⁸the pegs and ropes for the Tent and the enclosure; ¹⁹and the magnificent garments the priests are to wear when they serve in the Holy Place—the sacred clothes for Aaron the priest and for his sons."

The People Bring Their Offerings

20 All the people of Israel left, ²¹and everyone who wished to do so brought an offering to the LORD for making the Tent of the LORD's presence. They brought everything needed for use in worship and for making the priestly garments. ²²All who wanted to, both men and women, brought decorative pins, earrings, rings, necklaces, and all kinds of gold jewellery and dedicated them to the LORD. ²³Everyone who had fine linen; blue, purple, or red wool; cloth of goats' hair; rams' skin dyed red; or fine leather, brought it. ²⁴All who were able to contribute silver or bronze brought their offering for the LORD, and all who had acacia-wood which could be used for any of the work brought it. ²⁵All the skilled women brought fine linen thread and thread of blue, purple, and red wool, which they had made. ²⁶They also made thread of goats' hair. ²⁷The leaders brought carnelians and other jewels to be set in the ephod and the breast-piece ²⁸and spices and oil for the lamps, for the anointing oil, and for the sweet-smelling incense. ²⁹All the people of Israel who wanted to brought their offering to the LORD for the work which he had commanded Moses to do.

Craftsmen for the Tent of the LORD's Presence
(Ex 31.1-11)

30 Moses said to the Israelites, "The LORD has chosen Bezalel, the son of Uri and grandson of Hur, from the tribe of Judah. ³¹God has filled him with his power[1] and given him skill, ability, and understanding for every kind of artistic work, ³²for planning skilful designs and working them in gold, silver and bronze; ³³for cutting jewels to be set; for carving wood; and for every other kind of artistic work. ³⁴The LORD has given to him and to Oholiab son of Ahisamach, from the tribe of Dan, the ability to teach their

crafts to others. ³⁵He has given them skill in all kinds of work done by engravers, designers, and weavers of fine linen; blue, purple, and red wool; and other cloth. They are able to do all kinds of work and are skilful designers.

36 "Bezalel, Oholiab, and all the other craftsmen to whom the LORD has given skill and understanding, who know how to make everything needed to build the sacred Tent, are to make everything just as the LORD has commanded."

The People Bring Many Gifts

2 Moses called Bezalel, Oholiab, and all the other skilled men to whom the LORD had given ability and who were willing to help, and Moses told them to start working. ³They received from him all the offerings which the Israelites had brought for constructing the sacred Tent. But the people of Israel continued to bring Moses their offerings every morning. ⁴Then the skilled men who were doing the work went ⁵and reported to Moses, "The people are bringing more than is needed for the work which the LORD commanded to be done."

6 So Moses sent a command throughout the camp that no one was to make any further contribution for the sacred Tent; so the people did not bring any more. ⁷What had already been brought was more than enough to finish all the work.

Making the Tent of the LORD's Presence
(Ex 26.1-37)

8 The most skilled men among those doing the work made the Tent of the LORD's presence. They made it out of ten pieces of fine linen woven with blue, purple, and red wool and embroidered with figures of winged creatures. ⁹Each piece was the same size, twelve metres long and two metres wide. ¹⁰They sewed five of them together in one set and did the same with the other five. ¹¹They made loops of blue cloth on the edge of the outside piece in each set. ¹²They put fifty loops on the first piece of the first set and fifty loops matching them on the last piece of the second set. ¹³They made fifty gold hooks, with which to join the two sets into one piece.

14 Then they made a cover for the Tent out of eleven pieces of cloth made of goats' hair. ¹⁵They made them all the same size, thirteen metres long and two

[1] power; or spirit.

metres wide. [16] They sewed five of them together in one set and the other six in another set. [17] They put fifty loops on the edge of the last piece of one set and fifty loops on the edge of the other set. [18] They made fifty bronze hooks to join the two sets, so as to form one cover. [19] They made two more coverings, one of rams' skin dyed red and the other of fine leather, to serve as an outer cover.

20 They made upright frames of acacia-wood for the Tent. [21] Each frame was four metres tall and sixty-six centimetres wide, [22] with two matching projections, so that the frames could be joined together. All the frames had these projections. [23] They made twenty frames for the south side [24] and forty silver bases to go under them, two bases under each frame to hold its two projections. [25] They made twenty frames for the north side of the Tent [26] and forty silver bases, two under each frame. [27] For the back of the Tent, on the west, they made six frames [28] and two frames for the corners. [29] These corner frames were joined at the bottom and connected all the way to the top. The two frames that formed the two corners were made in this way. [30] So there were eight frames and sixteen silver bases, two under each frame.

31 They made fifteen cross-bars of acacia-wood, five for the frames on one side of the Tent, [32] five for the frames on the other side, and five for the frames on the west end, at the back. [33] The middle cross-bar, set half-way up the frames, extended from one end of the Tent to the other. [34] They covered the frames with gold and fitted them with gold rings to hold the cross-bars, which were also covered with gold.

35 They made a curtain of fine linen, woven with blue, purple, and red wool and embroidered it with figures of winged creatures. [36] They made four posts of acacia-wood to hold the curtain, covered them with gold, and fitted them with gold hooks. Then they made four silver bases to hold the posts. [37] For the entrance of the Tent they made a curtain of fine linen woven with blue, purple, and red wool and decorated with embroidery. [38] For this curtain they made five posts fitted with hooks, covered their tops and their rods with gold, and made five bronze bases for the posts.

Making the Covenant Box
(Ex 25.10-22)

37 Bezalel made the Covenant Box out of acacia-wood, 110 centimetres long, 66 centimetres wide, and 66 centimetres high. [2] He covered it with pure gold inside and out and put a gold border all round it. [3] He made four carrying-rings of gold for it and attached them to its four feet, with two rings on each side. [4] He made carrying-poles of acacia-wood, covered them with gold, [5] and put them through the rings on each side of the box. [6] He made a lid of pure gold, 110 centimetres long and 66 centimetres wide. [7] He made two winged creatures of hammered gold, [8] one for each end of the lid. He made them so that they formed one piece with the lid. [9] The winged creatures faced each other across the lid, and their outspread wings covered it.

Making the Table for the Bread Offered to God
(Ex 25.23-30)

10 He made the table out of acacia-wood, 88 centimetres long, 44 centimetres wide, and 66 centimetres high. [11] He covered it with pure gold and put a gold border round it. [12] He made a rim 75 millimetres wide round it and put a gold border round the rim. [13] He made four carrying-rings of gold for it and put them at the four corners, where the legs were. [14] The rings to hold the poles for carrying the table were placed near the rim. [15] He made the poles of acacia-wood and covered them with gold. [16] He made the dishes of pure gold for the table: the plates, the cups, the jars, and the bowls to be used for the wine offering.

Making the Lamp-stand
(Ex 25.31-40)

17 He made the lamp-stand of pure gold. He made its base and its shaft of hammered gold; its decorative flowers, including buds and petals, formed one piece with it.

18 Six branches extended from its sides, three from each side. [19] Each of the six branches had three decorative flowers shaped like almond blossoms with buds and petals. [20] The shaft of the lamp-stand had four decorative flowers shaped like almond blossoms with buds and petals. [21] There was one bud below each of the three pairs of branches. [22] The buds, the branches, and the lamp-stand were a

single piece of pure hammered gold. [23] He made seven lamps for the lamp-stand, and he made its tongs and trays of pure gold. [24] He used 35 kilogrammes of pure gold to make the lamp-stand and all its equipment.

Making the Altar for Burning Incense
(Ex 30.1-5)

25 He made an altar out of acacia-wood, for burning incense. It was square, 45 centimetres long and 45 centimetres wide, and it was 90 centimetres high. Its projections at the four corners formed one piece with it. [26] He covered its top, all four sides, and its projections with pure gold and put a gold border round it. [27] He made two gold carrying-rings for it and attached them below the border on the two sides, to hold the poles with which it was to be carried. [28] He made the poles of acacia-wood and covered them with gold.

Making the Anointing Oil and the Incense
(Ex 30.22-38)

29 He also made the sacred anointing oil and the pure sweet-smelling incense, mixed like perfume.

Making the Altar for Burning Offerings
(Ex 27.1-8)

38 For burning offerings, he made an altar out of acacia-wood. It was square, 2.2 metres long and 2.2 metres wide, and it was 1.3 metres high. [2] He made the projections at the top of the four corners, so that they formed one piece with the altar. He covered it all with bronze. [3] He also made all the equipment for the altar: the pans, the shovels, the bowls, the hooks, and the firepans. All this equipment was made of bronze. [4] He made a bronze grating and put it under the rim of the altar, so that it reached half-way up the altar. [5] He made four carrying-rings and put them on the four corners. [6] He made carrying-poles of acacia-wood, covered them with bronze, [7] and put them in the rings on each side of the altar. The altar was made of boards and was hollow.

Making the Bronze Basin
(Ex 30.18)

8 He made the bronze basin and its bronze base out of the mirrors belonging to the women who served at the entrance of the Tent of the LORD's presence.

The Enclosure for the Tent of the LORD's Presence
(Ex 27.9-19)

9 For the Tent of the LORD's presence he made the enclosure out of fine linen curtains. On the south side the curtains were 44 metres long, [10] supported by twenty bronze posts in twenty bronze bases, with hooks and rods made of silver. [11] The enclosure was the same on the north side. [12] On the west side there were curtains 22 metres long, with ten posts and ten bases and with hooks and rods made of silver. [13] On the east side, where the entrance was, the enclosure was also 22 metres wide. [14-15] On each side of the entrance there were 6.6 metres of curtains, with three posts and three bases. [16] All the curtains round the enclosure were made of fine linen. [17] The bases for the posts were made of bronze, and the hooks, the rods, and the covering of the tops of the posts were made of silver. All the posts round the enclosure were connected with silver rods. [18] The curtain for the entrance of the enclosure was made of fine linen woven with blue, purple, and red wool and decorated with embroidery. It was 9 metres long and 2 metres high, like the curtains of the enclosure. [19] It was supported by four posts in four bronze bases. Their hooks, the covering of their tops, and their rods were made of silver. [20] All the pegs for the Tent and for the surrounding enclosure were made of bronze.

Metals Used in the Tent of the LORD's Presence

21 Here is a list of the amounts of the metals used in the Tent of the LORD's presence, where the two stone tablets were kept on which the Ten Commandments were written. The list was ordered by Moses and made by the Levites who worked under the direction of Ithamar son of Aaron the priest. 22 Bezalel, the son of Uri and grandson of Hur, from the tribe of Judah, made everything that the LORD had commanded. [23] His helper, Oholiab son of Ahisamach, from the tribe of Dan, was an engraver, a designer, and a weaver of fine linen and of blue, purple, and red wool. 24 All the gold that had been dedicated to the LORD for the sacred Tent weighed

a thousand kilogrammes, weighed according to the official standard. 25 The silver from the census of the community weighed 3,430 kilogrammes, weighed according to the official standard. 26 This amount equalled the total paid by all persons enrolled in the census, each one paying the required amount, weighed according to the official standard. There were 603,550 men twenty years old or older enrolled in the census. 27 Of the silver, 3,400 kilogrammes were used to make the hundred bases for the sacred Tent and for the curtain, 34 kilogrammes for each base. 28 With the remaining 30 kilogrammes of silver Bezalel made the rods, the hooks for the posts, and the covering for their tops. 29 The bronze which was dedicated to the LORD amounted to 2,425 kilogrammes. 30 With it he made the bases for the entrance of the Tent of the LORD's presence, the bronze altar with its bronze grating, all the equipment for the altar, 31 the bases for the surrounding enclosure and for the entrance of the enclosure, and all the pegs for the Tent and the surrounding enclosure.

Making the Garments for the Priests
(Ex 28.1-14)

39 With the blue, purple, and red wool they made the magnificent garments which the priests were to wear when they served in the Holy Place. They made the priestly garments for Aaron, as the LORD had commanded Moses.

2 They made the ephod of fine linen; blue, purple, and red wool; and gold thread. 3 They hammered out sheets of gold and cut them into thin strips to be worked into the fine linen and into the blue, purple, and red wool. 4 They made two shoulder-straps for the ephod and attached them to its sides, so that it could be fastened. 5 The finely woven belt, made of the same materials, was attached to the ephod so as to form one piece with it, as the LORD had commanded Moses. 6 They prepared the carnelians and mounted them in gold settings; they were skilfully engraved with the names of the twelve sons of Jacob. 7 They put them on the shoulder-straps of the ephod to represent the twelve tribes of Israel, just as the LORD had commanded Moses.

Making the Breast-piece
(Ex 28.15-30)

8 They made the breast-piece of the same materials as the ephod and with similar embroidery. 9 It was square and folded double, 22 centimetres long and 22 centimetres wide. 10 They mounted four rows of precious stones on it: in the first row they mounted a ruby, a topaz, and a garnet; 11 in the second row, an emerald, a sapphire, and a diamond; 12 in the third row, a turquoise, an agate, and an amethyst; 13 and in the fourth row, a beryl, a carnelian, and a jasper. These were mounted in gold settings. 14 Each of the twelve stones had engraved on it the name of one of the sons of Jacob, in order to represent the twelve tribes of Israel. 15 For the breast-piece they made chains of pure gold, twisted like cords. 16 They made two gold settings and two gold rings and attached the two rings to the upper corners of the breast-piece. 17 They fastened the two gold cords to the two rings 18 and fastened the other two ends of the cords to the two settings and in this way attached them in front to the shoulder-straps of the ephod. 19 They made two rings of gold and attached them to the lower corners of the breast-piece, on the inside edge next to the ephod. 20 They made two more gold rings and attached them to the lower part of the front of the two shoulder-straps of the ephod, near the seam and above the finely woven belt. 21 Just as the LORD had commanded Moses, they tied the rings of the breast-piece to the rings of the ephod with a blue cord, so that the breast-piece rested above the belt and did not come loose.

Making the Other Priestly Garments
(Ex 28.31-43)

22 The robe that goes under the ephod was made entirely of blue wool. 23 The hole for the head was reinforced with a woven binding to keep it from tearing. 24-26 All round its lower hem they put pomegranates of fine linen and of blue, purple, and red wool, alternating with bells of pure gold, just as the LORD had commanded Moses.

27 They made the shirts for Aaron and his sons, 28 and the turban, the caps, the linen shorts, 29 and the sash of fine linen and of blue, purple, and red wool, decorated with embroidery, as the LORD

38.25-26: Ex 30.11-16   **38.26:** Mt 17.24

had commanded Moses. [30] They made the ornament, the sacred sign of dedication, out of pure gold, and they engraved on it "Dedicated to the LORD." [31] They tied it to the front of the turban with a blue cord, just as the LORD had commanded Moses.

The Completion of the Work
(Ex 35.10–19)

32 All the work on the Tent of the LORD's presence was finally completed. The Israelites made everything just as the LORD had commanded Moses. [33] They brought to Moses the Tent and all its equipment, its hooks, its frames, its cross-bars, its posts, and its bases; [34] the covering of rams' skin dyed red; the covering of fine leather; the curtain; [35] the Covenant Box containing the stone tablets, its poles, and its lid; [36] the table and all its equipment, and the bread offered to God; [37] the lamp-stand of pure gold, its lamps, all its equipment, and the oil for the lamps; [38] the gold altar; the anointing oil; the sweet-smelling incense; the curtain for the entrance of the Tent; [39] the bronze altar with its bronze grating, its poles, and all its equipment; the wash-basin and its base; [40] the curtains for the enclosure and its posts and bases; the curtain for the entrance of the enclosure and its ropes; the pegs for the Tent; all the equipment to be used in the Tent; [41] and the magnificent garments the priests were to wear in the Holy Place— the sacred clothes for Aaron the priest and for his sons. [42] The Israelites had done all the work just as the LORD had commanded Moses. [43] Moses examined everything and saw that they had made it all just as the LORD had commanded. So Moses blessed them.

Setting Up and Dedicating the Tent of the LORD's Presence

40 The LORD said to Moses, [2] "On the first day of the first month set up the Tent of the LORD's presence. [3] Place in it the Covenant Box containing the Ten Commandments and put the curtain in front of it. [4] Bring in the table and place the equipment on it. Also bring in the lamp-stand and set up the lamps on it. [5] Put the gold altar for burning incense in front of the Covenant Box and hang the curtain at the entrance of the Tent. [6] Put in front of the Tent the altar for burning offerings. [7] Put the wash-basin between the Tent and the altar and fill

it with water. [8] Put up the surrounding enclosure and hang the curtain at its entrance.

9 "Then dedicate the Tent and all its equipment by anointing it with the sacred oil, and it will be holy. [10] Next, dedicate the altar and all its equipment by anointing it, and it will be completely holy. [11] Also dedicate the wash-basin and its base in the same way.

12 "Bring Aaron and his sons to the entrance of the Tent, and tell them to take a ritual bath. [13] Dress Aaron in the priestly garments, anoint him, and in this way consecrate him, so that he can serve me as priest. [14] Bring his sons and put the shirts on them. [15] Then anoint them, just as you anointed their father, so that they can serve me as priests. This anointing will make them priests for all time to come."

16 Moses did everything just as the LORD had commanded. [17] So on the first day of the first month of the second year after they left Egypt, the Tent of the LORD's presence was set up. [18] Moses put down its bases, set up its frames, attached its cross-bars, and put up its posts. [19] He spread out the covering over the Tent and put the outer covering over it, just as the LORD had commanded. [20] Then he took the two stone tablets and put them in the Covenant Box. He put the poles in the rings of the box and put the lid on it. [21] Then he put the box in the Tent and hung up the curtain. In this way he screened off the Covenant Box, just as the LORD had commanded.

22 He put the table in the Tent, on the north side outside the curtain, [23] and placed on it the bread offered to the LORD, just as the LORD had commanded. [24] He put the lamp-stand in the Tent, on the south side, opposite the table, [25] and there in the LORD's presence he lit the lamps, just as the LORD had commanded. [26] He put the gold altar in the Tent, in front of the curtain, [27] and burnt the sweet-smelling incense, just as the LORD had commanded. [28] He hung the curtain at the entrance of the Tent, [29] and there in front of the curtain he placed the altar for burning offerings. On it he sacrificed the burnt-offering and the grain-offering, just as the LORD had commanded. [30] He put the wash-basin between the Tent and the altar and filled it with water. [31] Moses, Aaron, and his sons washed their hands and their feet there [32] whenever they went into the Tent or to the altar, just as the

LORD had commanded. ³³ Moses set up the enclosure round the Tent and the altar and hung the curtain at the entrance of the enclosure. So he finished all the work.

The Cloud over the Tent of the LORD's Presence
(Num 9.15–23)

34 Then the cloud covered the Tent and the dazzling light of the LORD's presence filled it. ³⁵ Because of this, Moses could not go into the Tent. ³⁶ The Israelites moved their camp to another place only when the cloud lifted from the Tent. ³⁷ As long as the cloud stayed there, they did not move their camp. ³⁸ During all their wanderings they could see the cloud of the LORD's presence over the Tent during the day and a fire burning above it during the night.

40.34: 1 Kgs 8.10–11; Is 6.4; Ezek 43.4–5; Rev 15.8

LEVITICUS

INTRODUCTION

Leviticus contains regulations for worship and religious ceremonies in ancient Israel, and for the priests who were responsible for carrying out these instructions.

The main theme of the book is the holiness of God and the ways in which his people were to worship and live so as to maintain their relationship with him, "the holy God of Israel."

The best known words from the book, found in 19.18, are those which Jesus called the second great commandment: "Love your neighbour as you love yourself."

Outline of Contents

Laws about offerings and sacrifices   1.1—7.38
The ordination of Aaron and his sons as priests   8.1—10.20
Laws about ritual cleanness and uncleanness   11.1—15.33
The Day of Atonement   16.1-34
Laws about holiness in life and worship   17.1—27.34

Sacrifices Burnt Whole

1 The LORD called to Moses from the Tent of the LORD's presence and gave him the following rules ² for the Israelites to observe when they offer their sacrifices.

When anyone offers an animal sacrifice, it may be one of his cattle or one of his sheep or goats. ³ If he is offering one of his cattle as a burnt-offering, he must bring a bull without any defects. He must present it at the entrance of the Tent of the LORD's presence so that the LORD will accept him. ⁴ The man shall put his hand on its head, and it will be accepted as a sacrifice to take away his sins. ⁵ He shall kill the bull there, and the Aaronite priests shall present the blood to the LORD and then throw it against all four sides of the altar which is at the entrance of the Tent. 6 Then he shall skin the animal and cut it up, 7 and the priests shall arrange firewood on the altar and light it. 8 They shall put on the fire the pieces of the animal, including the head and the fat. 9 The man must wash the internal organs and the hind legs, and the officiating priest will burn the whole sacrifice on the altar. The smell of this food-offering is pleasing to the LORD.

10 If the man is offering one of his sheep or goats, it must be a male without any defects. 11 He shall kill it on the north side of the altar, and the priests shall throw its blood on all four sides of the altar. 12 After the man cuts it up, the officiating priest shall put on the fire all the parts, including the head and the fat. 13 The man must wash the internal organs and the hind legs, and the priest will present the sacrifice to the LORD and burn all of it on the altar. The smell of this food-offering is pleasing to the LORD.

14 If the man is offering a bird as a burnt-offering, it must be a dove or a pigeon. 15 The priest shall present it at the altar, wring its neck, and burn its head on the altar. Its blood shall be drained out against the side of the altar. 16 He shall remove the crop and its contents and throw them away on the east side of the altar where the ashes are put. 17 He shall take hold of its wings and tear its body open, without tearing the wings off, and then burn it whole on the altar. The smell of this food-offering is pleasing to the LORD.

Grain-Offerings

2 When anyone presents an offering of grain to the LORD, he must first grind it into flour. He must put olive-oil and incense on it 2 and bring it to the Aaronite priests. The officiating priest shall take a handful of the flour and oil and all of the incense and burn it on the altar as a token that it has all been offered to the LORD. The smell of this food-offering is pleasing to the LORD. 3 The rest of the grain-offering belongs to the priests; it is very holy, since it is taken from the food offered to the LORD.

4 If the offering is bread baked in an oven, it must be made without yeast. It may be thick loaves made of flour mixed with olive-oil or biscuits brushed with olive-oil.

5 If the offering is bread cooked on a griddle, it is to be made of flour mixed with olive-oil but without yeast. 6 Crumble it up and pour the oil on it when you present it as an offering.

7 If the offering is bread cooked in a pan, it is to be made of flour and olive-oil. 8 Bring it as an offering to the LORD and present it to the priest, who will take it to the altar. 9 The priest will take part of it as a token that it has all been offered to the LORD, and he will burn it on the altar. The smell of this food-offering is pleasing to the LORD. 10 The rest of the offering belongs to the priests; it is very holy, since it is taken from the food offered to the LORD.

11 None of the grain-offerings which you present to the LORD may be made with yeast; you must never use yeast or honey in food offered to the LORD. 12 An offering of the first corn that you harvest each year shall be brought to the LORD, but it is not to be burnt on the altar. 13 Put salt on every grain-offering, because salt represents the covenant between you and God. (You must put salt on all your offerings.) 14 When you bring to the LORD an offering of the first corn harvested, offer roasted grain or ground meal. 15 Add olive-oil and put incense on it. 16 The priest will burn that part of the meal and oil that is to serve as a token, and also all the incense, as a food-offering to the LORD.

Fellowship-Offerings

3 When anyone offers one of his cattle as a fellowship-offering, it is to be a bull or a cow without any defects. 2 The man shall put his hand on the head of the animal and kill it at the entrance of the Tent of the LORD's presence. The Aaronite priests shall throw the blood against all four sides of the altar 3 and present the following parts of the animal as a food-offering to the LORD: all the fat on the internal organs, 4 the kidneys and the fat on them, and the best part of the liver. 5 The priests shall burn all this on the altar along with the burnt-offerings. The smell of this food-offering is pleasing to the LORD.

6 If a sheep or goat is used as a fellowship-offering, it may be male or female, but it must be without any defects. 7 If a man offers a sheep, 8 he shall put his hand on its head and kill it in front of the Tent. The priests shall throw its blood against all four sides of the altar 9 and present the following parts of the

animal as a food-offering to the LORD: the fat, the entire fat tail cut off near the backbone, all the fat covering the internal organs, ¹⁰the kidneys and the fat on them, and the best part of the liver. ¹¹The officiating priest shall burn all this on the altar as a food-offering to the LORD.

12 If a man offers a goat, ¹³he shall put his hand on its head and kill it in front of the Tent. The priests shall throw its blood against all four sides of the altar ¹⁴and present the following parts as a food-offering to the LORD: all the fat on the internal organs, ¹⁵the kidneys and the fat on them, and the best part of the liver. ¹⁶The priest shall burn all this on the altar as a food-offering pleasing to the LORD. All the fat belongs to the LORD. ¹⁷No Israelite may eat any fat or any blood; this is a rule to be kept for ever by all Israelites wherever they live.

Offerings for Unintentional Sins

4 The LORD commanded Moses ²to tell the people of Israel that anyone who sinned and broke any of the LORD's commands without intending to, would have to observe the following rules.

3 If it is the High Priest who sins and so brings guilt on the people, he shall present a young bull without any defects and sacrifice it to the LORD for his sin. ⁴He shall bring the bull to the entrance of the Tent, put his hand on its head, and kill it there in the LORD's presence. ⁵ Then the High Priest shall take some of the bull's blood and carry it into the Tent. ⁶He shall dip his finger in the blood and sprinkle it in front of the sacred curtain seven times. ⁷Then he shall put some of the blood on the projections at the corners of the incense-altar in the Tent. He shall pour out the rest of the blood at the base of the altar used for burning sacrifices, which is at the entrance of the Tent. ⁸From this bull he shall take all the fat, the fat on the internal organs, ⁹the kidneys and the fat on them, and the best part of the liver. ¹⁰The priest shall take this fat and burn it on the altar used for the burnt-offerings, just as he does with the fat from the animal killed for the fellowship-offering. ¹¹But he shall take its skin, all its flesh, its head, its legs, and its internal organs including the intestines, ¹²carry it all outside the camp to the ritually clean place where the ashes are poured out, and there he shall burn it on a wood fire.

13 If it is the whole community of Israel

He shall bring the bull (4.4)

that sins and becomes guilty of breaking one of the LORD's commands without intending to, ¹⁴then as soon as the sin becomes known, the community shall bring a young bull as a sin-offering. They shall bring it to the Tent of the LORD's presence; ¹⁵the leaders of the community shall put their hands on its head, and it shall be killed there. ¹⁶The High Priest shall take some of the bull's blood into the Tent, ¹⁷dip his finger in it, and sprinkle it in front of the curtain seven times. ¹⁸He shall put some of the blood on the projections at the corners of the incense-altar inside the Tent and pour out the rest of it at the base of the altar used for burning sacrifices, which is at the entrance of the Tent. ¹⁹Then he shall take all its fat and burn it on the altar. ²⁰He shall do the same thing with this bull as he does with the bull for the sin-offering, and in this way he shall make the sacrifice for the people's sin, and they will be forgiven. ²¹Then he shall take the bull outside the camp and burn it, just as he burns the bull offered for his own sin. This is an offering to take away the sin of the community.

22 If it is a ruler who sins and becomes guilty of breaking one of the LORD's

commands without intending to, 23 then as soon as his attention is called to the sin, he shall bring as his offering a male goat without any defects. 24 He shall put his hand on its head and kill it on the north side of the altar, where the animals for the burnt-offerings are killed. This is an offering to take away sin. 25 The priest shall dip his finger in the blood of the animal, put it on the projections at the corners of the altar, and pour out the rest of it at the base of the altar. 26 Then he shall burn all its fat on the altar, just as he burns the fat of the animals killed for the fellowship-offerings. In this way the priest shall offer the sacrifice for the sin of the ruler, and he will be forgiven.

27 If it is one of the common people who sins and becomes guilty of breaking one of the LORD's commands without intending to, 28 then as soon as his attention is called to the sin, he shall bring as his offering a female goat without any defects. 29 He shall put his hand on its head and kill it on the north side of the altar, where the animals for the burnt-offerings are killed. 30 The priest shall dip his finger in the blood of the animal, put it on the projections at the corners of the altar, and pour out the rest of it at the base of the altar. 31 Then he shall remove all its fat, just as the fat is removed from the animals killed for the fellowship-offerings, and he shall burn it on the altar so that the smell pleases the LORD. In this way the priest shall offer the sacrifice for the man's sin, and he will be forgiven.

32 If a man brings a sheep as a sin-offering, it must be a female without any defects. 33 He shall put his hand on its head and kill it on the north side of the altar, where the animals for the burnt-offerings are killed. 34 The priest shall dip his finger in the blood of the animal, put it on the projections at the corners of the altar, and pour out the rest of it at the base of the altar. 35 Then he shall remove all its fat, just as the fat is removed from the sheep killed for the fellowship-offerings, and he shall burn it on the altar along with the food-offerings given to the LORD. In this way the priest shall offer the sacrifice for the man's sin, and he will be forgiven.

Cases Requiring Sin-Offerings

5 Sin-offerings are required in the following cases.

If someone is officially summoned to give evidence in court and does not give information about something he has seen or heard, he must suffer the consequences. 2 If someone unintentionally touches anything ritually unclean, such as a dead animal, he is unclean and guilty as soon as he realizes what he has done. 3 If someone unintentionally touches anything of human origin that is unclean, whatever it may be, he is guilty as soon as he realizes what he has done. 4 If someone makes a careless vow, no matter what it is about, he is guilty as soon as he realizes what he has done. 5 When a person is guilty, he must confess the sin, 6 and as the penalty for his sin he must bring to the LORD a female sheep or goat as an offering. The priest shall offer the sacrifice for the man's sin.

7 If a man cannot afford a sheep or a goat, he shall bring to the LORD as the payment for his sin two doves or two pigeons, one for a sin-offering and the other for a burnt-offering. 8 He shall bring them to the priest, who will first offer the bird for the sin-offering. He will break its neck without pulling off its head 9 and sprinkle some of its blood against the side of the altar. The rest of the blood will be drained out at the base of the altar. This is an offering to take away sin. 10 Then he shall offer the second bird as a burnt-offering, according to the regulations. In this way the priest shall offer the sacrifice for the man's sin, and he will be forgiven.

11 If a man cannot afford two doves or two pigeons, he shall bring one kilogramme of flour as a sin-offering. He shall not put any olive-oil or any incense on it, because it is a sin-offering, not a grain-offering. 12 He shall bring it to the priest, who will take a handful of it as a token that it has all been offered to the LORD, and he will burn it on the altar as a food-offering. It is an offering to take away sin. 13 In this way the priest shall offer the sacrifice for the man's sin, and he will be forgiven. The rest of the flour belongs to the priest, just as in the case of a grain-offering.

Repayment-Offerings

14 The LORD gave the following regulations to Moses. 15 If anyone sins unintentionally by failing to hand over the payments that are sacred to the LORD, he shall bring as his repayment-offering to

4.27-31: Num 15.27-28

the LORD a male sheep or goat without any defects. Its value is to be determined according to the official standard. ¹⁶He must make the payments he has failed to hand over and must pay an additional twenty per cent. He shall give it to the priest, and the priest shall offer the animal as a sacrifice for the man's sin, and he will be forgiven.

17 If anyone sins unintentionally by breaking any of the LORD's commands, he is guilty and must pay the penalty. ¹⁸He must bring to the priest as a repayment-offering a male sheep or goat without any defects. Its value is to be determined according to the official standard. The priest shall offer the sacrifice for the sin which the man committed unintentionally, and he will be forgiven. ¹⁹It is a repayment-offering for the sin he committed against the LORD.

6 The LORD gave the following regulations to Moses. ²An offering is to be made if any one sins against the LORD by refusing to return what a fellow-Israelite has left as a deposit or by stealing something from him or by cheating him ³or by lying about something that has been lost and swearing that he did not find it. ⁴⁻⁵When a man sins in any of these ways, he must repay whatever he got by dishonest means. On the day he is found guilty, he must repay the owner in full, plus an additional twenty per cent. ⁶He shall bring to the priest as his repayment-offering to the LORD a male sheep or goat without any defects. Its value is to be determined according to the official standard. ⁷The priest shall offer the sacrifice for the man's sin, and he will be forgiven.

Sacrifices Burnt Whole

8 The LORD commanded Moses ⁹to give Aaron and his sons the following regulations for burnt-offerings. A burnt-offering is to be left on the altar all night long, and the fire is to be kept burning. ¹⁰Then the priest, wearing his linen robe and linen shorts, shall remove the greasy ashes left on the altar and put them at the side of the altar. ¹¹Then he shall change his clothes and take the ashes outside the camp to a ritually clean place. ¹²The fire on the altar must be kept burning and never allowed to go out. Every morning the priest shall put firewood on it, arrange the burnt-offering on it, and burn the fat of the fellowship-offering. ¹³The fire must

always be kept burning on the altar and never allowed to go out.

Grain-Offerings

14 The following are the regulations for grain-offerings. An Aaronite priest shall present the grain-offering to the LORD in front of the altar. ¹⁵Then he shall take a handful of the flour and oil, and the incense on it, and burn it on the altar as a token that all of it has been offered to the LORD. The smell of this offering is pleasing to the LORD. ¹⁶⁻¹⁷The priests shall eat the rest of it. It shall be made into bread baked without yeast and eaten in a holy place, the courtyard of the Tent of the LORD's presence. The LORD has given it to the priests as their part of the food-offerings. It is very holy, like the sin-offerings and the repayment-offerings. ¹⁸For all time to come any of the male descendants of Aaron may eat it as their continuing share of the food offered to the LORD. Anyone else who touches a food-offering will be harmed by the power of its holiness.

19 The LORD gave Moses the following regulations ²⁰for the ordination of an Aaronite priest. On the day he is ordained, he shall present as an offering to the LORD one kilogramme of flour (the same amount as the daily grain-offering), half in the morning and half in the evening. ²¹It is to be mixed with oil and cooked on a griddle and then crumbled and presented as a grain-offering, a smell pleasing to the LORD. ²²For all time to come this offering is to be made by every descendant of Aaron who is serving as High Priest. It shall be completely burnt as a sacrifice to the LORD. ²³No part of a grain-offering that a priest makes may be eaten; all of it must be burnt.

Sin-Offerings

24 The LORD commanded Moses ²⁵to give Aaron and his sons the following regulations for sin-offerings. The animal for a sin-offering shall be killed on the north side of the altar, where the animals for the burnt offerings are killed. This is a very holy offering. ²⁶The priest who sacrifices the animal shall eat it in a holy place, the courtyard of the Tent of the LORD's presence. ²⁷Anyone or anything that touches the flesh of the animal will be harmed by the power of its holiness. If any article of clothing is spattered with the animal's blood, it must be washed in

6.1–7: Num 5.5–8

a holy place. 28 Any clay pot in which the meat is boiled must be broken, and if a metal pot is used, it must be scrubbed and rinsed with water. 29 Any male of the priestly families may eat this offering; it is very holy. 30 But if any of the blood is brought into the Tent and used in the ritual to take away sin, the animal must not be eaten; it must be burnt.

Repayment-Offerings

7 The following are the regulations for repayment-offerings, which are very holy. 2 The animal for this offering is to be killed on the north side of the altar, where the animals for the burnt-offerings are killed, and its blood is to be thrown against all four sides of the altar. 3 All its fat shall be removed and offered on the altar: the fat tail, the fat covering the internal organs, 4 the kidneys and the fat on them, and the best part of the liver. 5 The priest shall burn all the fat on the altar as a food-offering to the LORD. It is a repayment-offering. 6 Any male of the priestly families may eat it, but it must be eaten in a holy place, because it is very holy.

7 There is one regulation that applies to both the sin-offering and the repayment-offering: the meat belongs to the priest who offers the sacrifice. 8 The skin of an animal offered as a burnt-offering belongs to the priest who offers the sacrifice. 9 Every grain-offering that has been baked in an oven or prepared in a pan or on a griddle belongs to the priest who has offered it to God. 10 But all uncooked grain-offerings, whether mixed with oil or dry, belong to all the Aaronite priests and must be shared equally among them.

Fellowship-Offerings

11 The following are the regulations for the fellowship-offerings presented to the LORD. 12 If a man makes this offering as a thank-offering to God, he shall present, together with the animal to be sacrificed, an offering of bread made without yeast: either thick loaves made of flour mixed with olive-oil or biscuits brushed with olive-oil or cakes made of flour mixed with olive-oil. 13 In addition, he shall offer loaves of bread baked with yeast. 14 He shall present one part of each kind of bread as a special contribution to the LORD; it belongs to the priest who takes the blood of the animal and throws it against the altar. 15 The flesh of the animal

must be eaten on the day it is sacrificed; none of it may be left until the next morning.

16 If a man brings a fellowship-offering in fulfilment of a vow or as his own freewill offering, not all of it has to be eaten on the day it is offered, but any that is left over may be eaten on the following day. 17 Any meat that still remains on the third day must be burnt. 18 If any of it is eaten on the third day, God will not accept the man's offering. The offering will not be counted to his credit but will be considered unclean, and whoever eats it will suffer the consequences. 19 If the meat comes into contact with anything ritually unclean, it must not be eaten, but must be burned.

Anyone who is ritually clean may eat the meat, 20 but if anyone who is not clean eats it, he shall no longer be considered one of God's people. 21 Also, if anyone eats the meat of this offering after he has touched anything ritually unclean, whether from a man or an animal, he shall no longer be considered one of God's people.

22 The LORD gave Moses the following regulations 23 for the people of Israel. No fat of cattle, sheep, or goats shall be eaten. 24 The fat of an animal that has died a natural death or has been killed by a wild animal must not be eaten, but it may be used for any other purpose. 25 Anyone who eats the fat of an animal that may be offered as a food-offering to the LORD will no longer be considered one of God's people. 26 No matter where the Israelites live, they must never use the blood of birds or animals for food. 27 Anyone who breaks this law will no longer be considered one of God's people.

28 The LORD gave Moses the following regulations 29 for the people of Israel. Whoever offers a fellowship-offering must bring part of it as a special gift to the LORD, 30 bringing it with his own hands as a food-offering. He shall bring the fat of the animal with its breast and present it as a special gift to the LORD. 31 The priest shall burn the fat on the altar, but the breast shall belong to the priests. 32 The right hind leg of the animal shall be given as a special contribution 33 to the priest who offers the blood and the fat of the fellowship-offering. 34 The breast of the animal is a special gift, and the right hind leg is a special contribution that the LORD has taken from the people of Israel and

7.26–27: Gen 9.4; Lev 17.10–14, 19.26; Deut 12.16,23, 15.23

given to the priests. This is what the people of Israel must give to the priests for all time to come. ³⁵This is the part of the food offered to the LORD that was given to Aaron and his sons on the day they were ordained as priests. ³⁶On that day the LORD commanded the people of Israel to give them this part of the offering. It is a regulation that the people of Israel must obey for all time to come.

³⁷ These, then, are the regulations for the burnt-offerings, the grain-offerings, the sin-offerings, the repayment-offerings, the ordination-offerings, and the fellowship-offerings. ³⁸There on Mount Sinai in the desert, the LORD gave these commands to Moses on the day he told the people of Israel to make their offerings.

The Ordination of Aaron and His Sons
(Ex 29.1-37)

8 The LORD said to Moses, ²"Take Aaron and his sons to the entrance of the Tent of my presence and bring the priestly garments, the anointing oil, the young bull for the sin-offering, the two rams, and the basket of unleavened bread. ³Then call the whole community together there."

⁴ Moses did as the LORD had commanded, and when the community had assembled, ⁵he said to them, "What I am now about to do is what the LORD has commanded."

⁶ Moses brought Aaron and his sons forward and told them to take a ritual bath. ⁷He put the shirt and the robe on Aaron and the sash round his waist. He put the ephod^a on him and fastened it by putting its finely woven belt round his waist. ⁸He put the breast-piece on him and put the Urim and Thummim^b in it. ⁹He placed the turban on his head, and on the front of it he put the gold ornament, the sacred sign of dedication, just as the LORD had commanded him.

¹⁰ Then Moses took the anointing oil and put it on the Tent of the LORD's presence and everything that was in it, and in this way he dedicated it all to the LORD. ¹¹He took some of the oil and sprinkled it seven times on the altar and its equipment and on the basin and its base, in order to dedicate them to the LORD. ¹²He ordained Aaron by pouring some of the anointing oil on his head. ¹³Next, Moses brought the sons of Aaron

forward and put shirts on them, put sashes round their waists, and tied caps on their heads, just as the LORD had commanded.

¹⁴ Then Moses brought the young bull for the sin-offering, and Aaron and his sons put their hands on its head. ¹⁵Moses killed it and took some of the blood, and with his finger put it on the projections at the corners of the altar, in order to dedicate it. He then poured out the rest of the blood at the base of the altar. In this way he dedicated it and purified it. ¹⁶Moses took all the fat on the internal organs, the best part of the liver, and the kidneys with the fat on them, and burnt it all on the altar. ¹⁷He took the rest of the bull, including its skin, flesh, and intestines, and burnt it outside the camp, just as the LORD had commanded.

¹⁸ Next, Moses brought the ram for the burnt-offering, and Aaron and his sons put their hands on its head. ¹⁹Moses killed it and threw the blood on all four sides of the altar. ^{20–21}He cut the ram in pieces, washed the internal organs and the hind legs with water, and burnt the head, the fat, and all the rest of the ram on the altar, just as the LORD had commanded. This burnt-offering was a food-offering, and the smell was pleasing to the LORD.

²² Then Moses brought the second ram, which was for the ordination of priests, and Aaron and his sons put their hands on its head. ²³Moses killed it and took some of the blood and put it on the lobe of Aaron's right ear, on the thumb of his right hand, and on the big toe of his right foot. ²⁴Then he brought Aaron's sons forward and put some of the blood on the lobes of their right ears, on the thumbs of their right hands, and on the big toes of their right feet. Moses then threw the rest of the blood on all four sides of the altar. ²⁵He took the fat, the fat tail, all the fat covering the internal organs, the best part of the liver, the kidneys with the fat on them, and the right hind leg. ²⁶Then he took one loaf of bread from the basket of unleavened bread dedicated to the LORD, one loaf made with oil, and one biscuit, and he put them on top of the fat and the right hind leg. ²⁷He put all this food in the hands of Aaron and his sons, and they presented it as a special gift to the LORD. ²⁸Then Moses took the food from them and burnt it on the altar,

---

^aEPHOD: *See Word List.*
^bURIM AND THUMMIM: *Two objects used by the priest to determine God's will; it is not known precisely how they were used.*

on top of the burnt-offering, as an ordination offering. This was a food-offering, and the smell was pleasing to the LORD. 29 Then Moses took the breast and presented it as a special gift to the LORD. It was Moses' part of the ordination ram. Moses did everything just as the LORD had commanded.

30 Moses took some of the anointing oil and some of the blood that was on the altar and sprinkled them on Aaron and his sons and on their clothes. In this way he consecrated them and their clothes to the LORD.

In this way he consecrated them (8.30)

31 Moses said to Aaron and his sons, "Take the meat to the entrance of the Tent of the LORD's presence, boil it, and eat it there with the bread that is in the basket of ordination offerings, just as the LORD commanded. 32 Burn up any meat or bread that is left over. 33 You shall not leave the entrance of the Tent for seven days, until your ordination rites are completed. 34 The LORD commanded us to do what we have done today, in order to take away your sin. 35 You must stay at the entrance of the Tent day and night for seven days, doing what the LORD has commanded. If you don't, you will die. This is what the LORD has commanded me." 36 So Aaron and his sons did everything that the LORD had commanded through Moses.

9.7: Heb 7.27

Aaron Offers Sacrifices

9 The day after the ordination rites were completed, Moses called Aaron and his sons and the leaders of Israel. 2 He said to Aaron, "Take a young bull and a ram without any defects and offer them to the LORD, the bull for a sin-offering and the ram for a burnt-offering. 3 Then tell the people of Israel to take a male goat for a sin-offering, a one-year-old calf, and a one-year-old lamb without any defects for a burnt-offering, 4 and a bull and a ram for a fellowship-offering. They are to sacrifice them to the LORD with the grain-offering mixed with oil. They must do this because the LORD will appear to them today."

5 They brought to the front of the Tent everything that Moses had commanded, and the whole community assembled there to worship the LORD. 6 Moses said, "The LORD has commanded you to do all this, so that the dazzling light of his presence can appear to you." 7 Then he said to Aaron, "Go to the altar and offer the sin-offering and the burnt-offering to take away your sins and the sins of the people. Present this offering to take away the sins of the people, just as the LORD commanded."

8 Aaron went to the altar and killed the young bull which was for his own sin-offering. 9 His sons brought him the blood, and he dipped his finger in it, put some of it on the projections at the corners of the altar, and poured out the rest of it at the base of the altar. 10 Then he burnt on the altar the fat, the kidneys, and the best part of the liver, just as the LORD had commanded Moses. 11 But he burnt the meat and the skin outside the camp.

12 He killed the animal which was for his own burnt-offering. His sons brought him the blood, and he threw it on all four sides of the altar. 13 They handed him the head and the other pieces of the animal, and he burnt them on the altar. 14 Then he washed the internal organs and the hind legs and burnt them on the altar on top of the rest of the burnt-offering.

15 After that, he presented the people's offerings. He took the goat that was to be offered for the people's sins, killed it, and offered it, as he had done with his own sin-offering. 16 He also brought the animal for the burnt-offering and offered it according to the regulations. 17 He presented the grain-offering and took a

handful of flour and burnt it on the altar. (This was in addition to the daily burnt-offering.) [18] He killed the bull and the ram as a fellowship-offering for the people. His sons brought him the blood, and he threw it on all four sides of the altar. [19] Aaron put the fat parts of the bull and the ram [20] on top of the breasts of the animals and carried it all to the altar. He burnt the fat on the altar [21] and presented the breasts and the right hind legs as the special gift to the LORD for the priests, as Moses had commanded.

22 When Aaron had finished all the sacrifices, he raised his hands over the people and blessed them, and then stepped down. [23] Moses and Aaron went into the Tent of the LORD's presence, and when they came out, they blessed the people, and the dazzling light of the LORD's presence appeared to all the people. [24] Suddenly the LORD sent a fire, and it consumed the burnt-offering and the fat parts on the altar. When the people saw it, they all shouted and bowed down with their faces to the ground.

The Sin of Nadab and Abihu

10 Aaron's sons Nadab and Abihu, each took his fire-pan, put live coals in it, added incense, and presented it to the LORD. But this fire was not holy, because the LORD had not commanded them to present it. [2] Suddenly the LORD sent fire, and it burnt them to death there in the presence of the LORD. [3] Then Moses said to Aaron, "This is what the LORD was speaking about when he said, 'All who serve me must respect my holiness; I will reveal my glory to my people.'"[c] But Aaron remained silent.

4 Moses called Mishael and Elzaphan, the sons of Uzziel, Aaron's uncle, and said to them, "Come here and carry your cousins' bodies away from the sacred Tent and put them outside the camp." [5] So they came and took hold of the clothing on the corpses and carried them outside the camp, just as Moses had commanded.

6 Then Moses said to Aaron and to his sons Eleazar and Ithamar, "Do not leave your hair uncombed or tear your clothes to show that you are in mourning. If you do, you will die, and the LORD will be angry with the whole community. But all your fellow-Israelites are allowed to mourn this death caused by the fire which

the LORD sent. [7] Do not leave the entrance of the Tent or you will die, because you have been consecrated by the anointing oil of the LORD." So they did as Moses said.

Rules for Priests

8 The LORD said to Aaron, [9] "You and your sons are not to enter the Tent of my presence after drinking wine or beer; if you do, you will die. This is a law to be kept by all your descendants. [10] You must distinguish between what belongs to God and what is for general use, between what is ritually clean and what is unclean. [11] You must teach the people of Israel all the laws which I have given to you through Moses."

12 Moses said to Aaron and his two remaining sons, Eleazar and Ithamar, "Take the grain-offering that is left over from the food offered to the LORD, make unleavened bread with it and eat it beside the altar, because this offering is very holy. [13] Eat it in a holy place; it is the part that belongs to you and your sons from the food offered to the LORD. That is what the LORD commanded me. [14] But you and your families may eat the breast and the hind leg that are presented as the special gift and the special contribution to the LORD for the priests. You may eat them in any ritually clean place. These offerings have been given to you and your children as the part that belongs to you from the fellowship-offerings of the people of Israel. [15] They shall bring the hind leg and the breast at the time the fat is presented as a food-offering to the LORD. These parts belong to you and your children for ever, just as the LORD commanded."

16 Moses asked about the goat for the sin-offering and learnt that it had already been burnt. This made him angry with Eleazar and Ithamar, and he demanded, [17] "Why didn't you eat the sin-offering in a sacred place? It is very holy, and the LORD has given it to you in order to take away the sin of the community. [18] Since its blood was not brought into the sacred tent, you should have eaten the sacrifice there, as I commanded."

19 Aaron answered, "If I had eaten the sin-offering today, would the LORD have approved? The people presented their sin-offering to the LORD today, and they brought their burnt-offering, but still

---

[c] I will reveal my glory to my people; *or* my people must honour me.
9.18: Lev 3.1–11   **9.22:** Num 6.22–26   **10.12–13:** Lev 6.14–18   **10.14–15:** Lev 7.30–34
10.17: Lev 6.24–26

Unclean animals (chapter 11)

these terrible things have happened to me." ²⁰When Moses heard this, he was satisfied.

Animals That May Be Eaten
(Deut 14.3-21)

11 The Lord gave Moses and Aaron the following regulations ²for the people of Israel. You may eat any land animal ³that has divided hoofs and that also chews the cud, ⁴⁻⁶but you must not eat camels, rock-badgers, or rabbits. They must be considered unclean; they chew the cud, but do not have divided hoofs. ⁷Do not eat pigs. They must be considered unclean; they have divided hoofs, but do not chew the cud. ⁸Do not eat these animals or even touch their dead bodies; they are unclean.

⁹You may eat any kind of fish that has fins and scales, ¹⁰but anything living in the water that does not have fins and scales must not be eaten. ¹¹Such creatures must be considered unclean. You must not eat them or even touch their dead bodies. ¹²You must not eat anything that lives in the water and does not have fins and scales.

¹³⁻¹⁹You must not eat any of the following birds: eagles, owls, hawks, falcons; buzzards, vultures, crows; ostriches; seagulls, storks, herons, pelicans, cormorants;ˣ hoopoes; or bats.

20 All winged insects are unclean, ²¹except those that hop. ²²You may eat locusts, crickets, or grasshoppers. ²³But

all other small things that have wings and also crawl must be considered unclean.

24-28 Whoever touches the dead bodies of the following animals will be unclean until evening: all animals with hoofs, unless their hoofs are divided and they chew the cud, and all four-footed animals with paws. Whoever carries their dead bodies must wash his clothes, but he will still be unclean until evening.

29-30 Moles, rats, mice, and lizards must be considered unclean. ³¹Whoever touches them or their dead bodies will be unclean until evening. ³²And if their dead bodies fall on anything, it will be unclean. This applies to any article of wood, cloth, leather, or sacking, no matter what it is used for. It shall be dipped in water, but it will remain unclean until evening. ³³And if their bodies fall into a clay pot, everything that is in it shall be unclean, and you must break the pot. ³⁴Any food which could normally be eaten, but on which water from such a pot has been poured, will be unclean, and anything drinkable in such a pot is unclean. ³⁵Anything on which the dead bodies fall is unclean; a clay stove or oven shall be broken, ³⁶but a spring or a cistern remains clean, although anything else that touches their dead bodies is unclean. ³⁷If one of them falls on seed that is going to be sown, the seed remains clean. ³⁸But if the seed is soaking in water and one of them falls on it, the seed is unclean.

39 If any animal that may be eaten dies,

ˣ *The identification of some of the birds in verses 13-19 is uncertain.*

anyone who touches it will be unclean until evening. 40 And if anyone eats any part of the animal, he must wash his clothes, but he will still be unclean until evening; anyone who carries the dead body must wash his clothes, but he will still be unclean until evening.

41 You must not eat any of the small animals that move on the ground, 42 whether they crawl, or walk on four legs, or have many legs. 43 Do not make yourselves unclean by eating any of these. 44 I am the LORD your God, and you must keep yourselves holy, because I am holy. 45 I am the LORD who brought you out of Egypt so that I could be your God. You must be holy, because I am holy.

46 This, then, is the law about animals and birds, about everything that lives in the water, and everything that moves on the ground. 47 You must be careful to distinguish between what is ritually clean and unclean, between animals that may be eaten and those that may not.

The Purification of Women after Childbirth

12 The LORD gave Moses the following regulations 2 for the people of Israel. For seven days after a woman gives birth to a son, she is ritually unclean, as she is during her monthly period. 3 On the eighth day, the child shall be circumcised. 4 Then it will be thirty-three more days before she is ritually clean from her loss of blood; she must not touch anything that is holy or enter the sacred Tent until the time of her purification is completed.

5 For fourteen days after a woman gives birth to a daughter, she is ritually unclean, as she is during her monthly period. Then it will be sixty-six more days before she is ritually clean from her loss of blood.

6 When the time of her purification is completed, whether for a son or daughter, she shall bring to the priest at the entrance of the Tent of the LORD's presence a one-year-old lamb for a burnt-offering and a pigeon or a dove for a sin-offering. 7 The priest shall present her offering to the Lord and perform the ritual to take away her impurity, and she will be ritually clean. This, then, is what a woman must do after giving birth.

8 If the woman cannot afford a lamb, she shall bring two doves or two pigeons, one for a burnt-offering and the other for a sin-offering, and the priest shall perform the ritual to take away her impurity, and she will be ritually clean.

Laws Concerning Skin-Diseases

13 The LORD gave Moses and Aaron these regulations. 2 If anyone has a sore on his skin or a boil or an inflammation which could develop into a dreaded skin-disease, he shall be brought to the Aaronite priest. 3 The priest shall examine the sore, and if the hairs in it have turned white and the sore appears to be deeper than the surrounding skin, it is a dreaded skin-disease, and the priest shall pronounce the person unclean. 4 But if the sore is white and does not appear to be deeper than the skin round it and the hairs have not turned white, the priest shall isolate the person for seven days. 5 The priest shall examine him again on the seventh day, and if in his opinion the sore looks the same and has not spread, he shall isolate him for another seven days. 6 The priest shall examine him again on the seventh day, and if the sore has faded and has not spread, he shall pronounce him ritually clean; it is only a sore. The person shall wash his clothes and be ritually clean. 7 But if the sore spreads after the priest has examined him and pronounced him clean, he must appear before the priest again. 8 The priest will examine him again, and if it has spread, he shall pronounce him unclean; it is a dreaded skin-disease.

9 If anyone has a dreaded skin-disease, he shall be brought to the priest, 10 who will examine him. If there is a white sore on his skin which turns the hairs white and is full of pus, 11 it is a chronic skin-disease. The priest shall pronounce him unclean; there is no need to isolate him, because he is obviously unclean. 12 If the skin-disease spreads and covers the person from head to foot, 13 the priest shall examine him again. If he finds that it actually has covered the whole body, he shall pronounce the person ritually clean. If his whole skin has turned white, he is ritually clean. 14 But from the moment an open sore appears, he is unclean. 15 The priest shall examine him again, and if he sees an open sore, he shall pronounce him unclean. An open sore means a dreaded skin-disease, and the person is unclean. 16 But when the sore heals and becomes white again, the person shall go to the priest, 17 who will examine him again. If the sore has turned white, he is ritually clean, and the priest shall pronounce him clean.

11.44: Lev 19.2; 1 Pet 1.16   **12.3:** Gen 17.12; Lk 2.21   **12.8:** Lk 2.24

18 If anyone has a boil that has healed ¹⁹and if afterwards a white swelling or a reddish-white spot appears where the boil was, he shall go to the priest. ²⁰The priest shall examine him, and if the spot seems to be deeper than the surrounding skin and the hairs in it have turned white, he shall pronounce him unclean. It is a dreaded skin-disease that has started in

The priest shall examine him (13.20)

the boil. ²¹But if the priest examines it and finds that the hairs in it have not turned white and that it is not deeper than the surrounding skin, but is light in colour, the priest shall isolate him for seven days. ²²If the spot spreads, the priest shall pronounce him unclean; he is diseased. ²³But if it remains unchanged and does not spread, it is only the scar left from the boil, and the priest shall pronounce him ritually clean.

24 In the case of a person who has been burnt, if the raw flesh becomes white or reddish-white, ²⁵the priest shall examine him. If the hairs in the spot have turned white and it appears deeper than the surrounding skin, it is a dreaded skin-disease that has started in the burn, and the priest shall pronounce him unclean. ²⁶But if the hairs in it have not turned white and it is not deeper than the surrounding skin, but is light in colour, the priest shall isolate him for seven days. ²⁷The priest shall examine him again on the seventh day, and if it is spreading, it is a dreaded skin-disease, and the priest shall pronounce him unclean. ²⁸But if the spot remains unchanged and does not spread and is light in colour, it is not a dreaded skin-disease. The priest shall pronounce him ritually clean, because it is only a scar from the burn.

29 When a man or a woman has a sore on the head or the chin, ³⁰the priest shall examine it. If it seems to be deeper than the surrounding skin and the hairs in it are yellowish and thin, it is a dreaded skin-disease, and he shall pronounce the person unclean. ³¹If, when the priest examines him, the sore does not appear to be deeper than the surrounding skin, but there are still no healthy hairs in it, he shall isolate him for seven days. ³²The priest shall examine the sore again on the seventh day, and if it has not spread and there are no yellowish hairs in it and it does not seem to be deeper than the surrounding skin, ³³the person shall shave the head except the area round the sore. The priest shall then isolate him for another seven days. ³⁴On the seventh day the priest shall again examine the sore, and if it has not spread and does not seem to be deeper than the surrounding skin, he shall pronounce him ritually clean. The person shall wash his clothes, and he will be clean. ³⁵But if the sore spreads after he has been pronounced clean, ³⁶the priest shall examine him again. If the sore has spread, he need not look for yellowish hairs; the person is obviously unclean. ³⁷But if in the priest's opinion the sore has not spread and healthy hairs are growing in it, the sore has healed, and the priest shall pronounce him ritually clean.

38 When a man or a woman has white spots on the skin, ³⁹the priest shall examine that person. If the spots are dull white, it is only a blemish that has broken out on the skin; the person is ritually clean.

40–41 If a man loses his hair at the back or the front of his head, this does not make him unclean. ⁴²But if a reddish-white sore appears on the bald spot, it is a dreaded skin-disease. 43 The priest shall examine him, and if there is a reddish-white sore, 44 the priest shall pronounce him unclean, because of the dreaded skin-disease on his head.

45 A person who has a dreaded skin-disease must wear torn clothes, leave his hair uncombed, cover the lower part of his face, and call out, "Unclean, unclean!" 46 He remains unclean as long as he has the disease, and he must live outside the camp, away from others.

Laws Concerning Mildew

47 When there is mildew d on clothing, whether wool or linen, 48 or on any piece of linen or wool cloth or on leather or anything made of leather, 49 if it is greenish or reddish, it is a spreading mildew and must be shown to the priest. 50 The priest shall examine it and put the object away for seven days. 51 He shall examine it again on the seventh day, and if the mildew has spread, the object is unclean. 52 The priest shall burn it, because it is a spreading mildew which must be destroyed by fire.

53 But if, when he examines it, the priest finds that the mildew has not spread on the object, 54 he shall order it to be washed and put away for another seven days. 55 Then he shall examine it, and if the mildew has not changed colour, even though it has not spread, it is still unclean; you must burn the object, whether the rot is on the front or the back. 56 But if, when the priest examines it again, the mildew has faded, he shall tear it out of the clothing or leather. 57 Then, if the mildew reappears, it is spreading again, and the owner shall burn the object. 58 If he washes the object and the spot disappears, he shall wash it again, and it will be ritually clean.

59 This, then, is the law about mildew on clothing, whether it is wool or linen, or on linen or wool cloth or on anything made of leather; this is how the decision is made as to whether it is ritually clean or unclean.

Purification after Having Skin-Diseases

14 The LORD gave Moses 2 the following regulations about the ritual purification of a person cured of a dreaded skin-disease. On the day he is to be pronounced clean, he shall be brought to the priest, 3 and the priest shall take him outside the camp and examine him. If the disease is healed, 4 the priest shall order two ritually clean birds to be brought, together with a piece of cedar-wood, a red cord, and a sprig of hyssop. 5 Then the priest shall order one of the birds to be killed over a clay bowl containing fresh spring water. 6 He shall take the other bird and dip it, together with the cedar-wood, the red cord, and the hyssop, in the blood of the bird that was killed. 7 He shall sprinkle the blood seven times on the person who is to be purified from his skin-disease, and then he shall pronounce him clean. He shall let the live bird fly away over the open fields. 8 The person shall wash his clothes, shave off all his hair, and have a bath; he will then be ritually clean. He may enter the camp, but he must live outside his tent for seven days. 9 On the seventh day he shall again shave his head, his beard, his eyebrows, and all the rest of the hair on his body; he shall wash his clothes and have a bath, and then he will be ritually clean.

10 On the eighth day he shall bring two male lambs and one female lamb a year old that are without any defects, three kilogrammes of flour mixed with olive-oil, and a third of a litre of olive-oil. 11 The priest shall take the man and these offerings to the entrance of the Tent of the LORD's presence. 12 Then the priest shall take one of the male lambs and together with the one-third of a litre of oil he shall offer it as a repayment-offering. He shall present them as a special gift to the LORD for the priest. 13 He shall kill the lamb in the holy place where the animals for the sin-offerings and the burnt-offerings are killed. He must do this because the repayment-offering, like the sin-offering, belongs to the priest and is very holy. 14 The priest shall take some of the blood of the lamb and put it on the lobe of the right ear, on the thumb of the right hand, and on the big toe of the right foot of the man who is to be declared ritually clean. 15 The priest shall take some of the olive-oil and pour it in the palm of his own left hand, 16 dip a finger of his right hand in it, and sprinkle some of it seven times there in the LORD's presence. 17 He shall take some of the oil that is in the palm of his hand and some of the blood of the lamb and put them on the lobe of the right ear, on the thumb of the right hand, and on the big toe of the right foot of the man who is to be declared ritually clean. 18 He shall put the

d MILDEW: *The Hebrew word for "dreaded skin-disease" and "mildew" is the same.*
14.2: Mt 8.4; Mk 1.44; Lk 5.14, 17.14

The stones...shall be removed (14.40)

rest of the oil that is in the palm of his hand on the man's head. In this way he shall perform the ritual of purification.

19 Then the priest shall offer the sin-offering and perform the ritual of purification. After that, he shall kill the animal for the burnt-offering 20 and offer it with the grain-offering on the altar. In this way the priest shall perform the ritual of purification, and the man will be ritually clean.

21 If the man is poor and cannot afford any more, he shall bring for his purification only one male lamb as his repayment-offering, a special gift to the LORD for the priest. He shall bring only one kilogramme of flour mixed with olive-oil for a grain-offering and a third of a litre of olive-oil. 22 He shall also bring two doves or two pigeons, one for the sin-offering and one for the burnt-offering. 23 On the eighth day of his purification he shall bring them to the priest at the entrance of the Tent. 24 The priest shall take the lamb and the olive-oil and present them as a special gift to the LORD for the priest. 25 He shall kill the lamb and take some of the blood and put it on the lobe of the man's right ear, on the thumb of his right hand, and on the big toe of his right foot. 26 The priest shall pour some of the oil into the palm of his own left hand 27 and with a finger of his right hand sprinkle some of it seven times there in the LORD's presence. 28 He shall put some of the oil on the same places as he put the blood: on the lobe of the man's right ear, on the thumb of his right hand, and on the big toe of his right foot. 29 The rest of the oil that is in his palm he shall put on the man's head and in this way

perform the ritual of purification. 30 Then he shall offer one of the doves or pigeons 31 as the sin-offering and the other as the burnt-offering with the grain-offering. In this way the priest shall perform the ritual of purification. 32 This is the law for the man who has a dreaded skin-disease but who cannot afford the normal offerings required for his purification.

Mildew in Houses

33 The LORD gave Moses and Aaron 34-35 the following regulations about houses affected by spreading mildew. (These were to apply after the people of Israel entered the land of Canaan, which the LORD was going to give them as their possession.) If someone finds that the LORD has sent mildew on his house, then he must go and tell the priest about it. 36 The priest shall order everything to be moved out of the house before he goes to examine the mildew; otherwise everything in the house will be declared unclean. Then he shall go to the house 37 and examine the mildew. If there are greenish or reddish spots that appear to be eating into the wall, 38 he shall leave the house and lock it up for seven days. 39 On the seventh day he shall return and examine it again. If the mildew has spread, 40 he shall order the stones on which the mildew is found to be removed and thrown into some unclean place outside the city. 41 After that he must have all the interior walls scraped and the plaster dumped in an unclean place outside the city. 42 Then other stones are to be used to replace the stones that were removed, and new plaster will be used to cover the walls.

43 If the mildew breaks out again in the house after the stones have been removed and the house has been scraped and plastered, 44 the priest shall go and look. If it has spread, the house is unclean. 45 It must be torn down, and its stones, its wood, and all its plaster must be carried out of the city to an unclean place. 46 Anyone who enters the house while it is locked up will be unclean until evening. 47 Anyone who lies down or eats in the house must wash his clothes.

48 If, when the priest comes to look, the mildew has not reappeared after the house has been replastered, he shall pronounce the house ritually clean, because the mildew has been completely removed. 49 To purify the house, he shall take two birds, some cedar-wood, a red cord, and a sprig of hyssop. 50 He shall kill one of the birds over a clay bowl containing fresh spring water. 51 Then he shall take the cedar-wood, the hyssop, the red cord, and the live bird and shall dip them in the blood of the bird that was killed and in the fresh water. And he shall sprinkle the house seven times. 52 In this way he shall purify the house with the bird's blood, the fresh water, the live bird, the cedar-wood, the hyssop, and the red cord. 53 Then he shall let the live bird fly away outside the city over the open fields. In this way he shall perform the ritual of purification for the house, and it will be ritually clean.

54 These are the laws about dreaded skin-diseases; 55-56 sores, boils, or inflammations; and about mildew in clothes or houses. 57 These laws determine when something is unclean and when it is clean.

Unclean Bodily Discharges

15 The LORD gave Moses and Aaron the following regulations 2 for the people of Israel. When any man has a discharge from his penis, the discharge is unclean, 3 whether the penis runs with it or is stopped up by it. 4 Any bed on which he sits or lies is unclean. 5 Anyone who touches his bed 6 or sits on anything the man has sat on must wash his clothes and have a bath, and he remains unclean until evening. 7 Anyone who touches the man with the discharge must wash his clothes and have a bath, and he remains unclean until evening. 8 If the man with the discharge spits on anyone who is ritually clean, that person must wash his clothes and have a bath, and he remains

unclean until evening. 9 Any saddle or seat on which the man with the discharge sits is unclean. 10 Anyone who touches anything on which the man sat is unclean until evening. Anyone who carries anything on which the man sat must wash his clothes and have a bath, and he remains unclean until evening. 11 If a man who has a discharge touches someone without first having washed his hands, that person must wash his clothes and have a bath, and he remains unclean until evening. 12 Any clay pot that the man touches must be broken, and any wooden bowl that he touches must be washed.

13 After the man is cured of his discharge, he must wait seven days and then wash his clothes and bathe in fresh spring water, and he will be ritually clean. 14 On the eighth day he shall take two doves or two pigeons to the entrance of the Tent of the LORD's presence and give them to the priest. 15 The priest shall offer one of them as a sin-offering and the other as a burnt-offering. In this way he will perform the ritual of purification for the man.

16 When a man has an emission of semen, he must bathe his whole body, and he remains unclean until evening. 17 Anything made of cloth or leather on which the semen falls must be washed, and it remains unclean until evening. 18 After sexual intercourse both the man and the woman must have a bath, and they remain unclean until evening.

19 When a woman has her monthly period, she remains unclean for seven days. Anyone who touches her is unclean until evening. 20 Anything on which she sits or lies during her monthly period is unclean. 21-23 Anyone who touches her bed or anything on which she has sat must wash his clothes and have a bath, and he remains unclean until evening. 24 If a man has sexual intercourse with her during her period, he is contaminated by her impurity and remains unclean for seven days, and any bed on which he lies is unclean.

25 If a woman has a flow of blood for several days outside her monthly period or if her flow continues beyond her regular period, she remains unclean as long as the flow continues, just as she is during her monthly period. 26 Any bed on which she lies and anything on which she sits during this time is unclean. 27 Anyone who touches them is unclean and must wash his clothes and have a bath; he remains

unclean until evening. ²⁸ After her flow stops, she must wait seven days, and then she will be ritually clean. ²⁹ On the eighth day she shall take two doves or two pigeons to the priest at the entrance of the Tent of the LORD's presence. ³⁰ The priest shall offer one of them as a sin-offering and the other as a burnt-offering, and in this way he will perform the ritual of purification for her.

31 The LORD told Moses to warn the people of Israel about their uncleanness, so that they would not defile the Tent of his presence, which was in the middle of the camp. If they did, they would be killed.

32 These are the regulations about a man who has a discharge or an emission of semen, ³³ a woman during her monthly period, or a man who has sexual intercourse with a woman who is ritually unclean.

The Day of Atonement

16 The LORD spoke to Moses after the death of the two sons of Aaron who were killed when they offered unholy fire to the LORD. ² He said, "Tell your brother Aaron that only at the proper time is he to go behind the curtain into the Most Holy Place, because that is where I appear in a cloud above the lid on the Covenant Box. If he disobeys, he will be killed. ³ He may enter the Most Holy Place only after he has brought a young bull for a sin-offering and a ram for a burnt-offering."

4 Then the LORD gave the following instructions. Before Aaron goes into the Most Holy Place, he must have a bath and put on the priestly garments: the linen robe and shorts, the belt, and the turban.

5 The community of Israel shall give Aaron two male goats for a sin-offering and a ram for a burnt-offering. ⁶ He shall offer a bull as a sacrifice to take away his own sins and those of his family. ⁷ Then he shall take the two goats to the entrance of the Tent of the LORD's presence. ⁸ There he shall draw lots, using two stones, one marked "for the LORD" and the other "for Azazel." ᵉ ⁹ Aaron shall sacrifice the goat chosen by lot for the LORD and offer it as a sin-offering. ¹⁰ The goat chosen for Azazel shall be presented alive to the LORD and sent off into the desert to Azazel,

in order to take away the sins of the people.

11 When Aaron sacrifices the bull as the sin-offering for himself and his family, ¹² he shall take a fire-pan full of burning coals from the altar and two handfuls of fine incense and bring them into the Most Holy Place. ¹³ There in the LORD's presence he shall put the incense on the fire, and the smoke of the incense will hide the lid of the Covenant Box so that he will not see it and die. ¹⁴ He shall take some of the bull's blood and with his finger sprinkle it on the front of the lid and then sprinkle some of it seven times in front of the Covenant Box.

15 After that, he shall kill the goat for the sin-offering for the people, bring its blood into the Most Holy Place, and sprinkle it on the lid and then in front of the Covenant Box, as he did with the bull's blood. ¹⁶ In this way he will perform the ritual to purify the Most Holy Place from the uncleanness of the people of Israel and from all their sins. He must do this to the Tent, because it stands in the middle of the camp, which is ritually unclean. ¹⁷ From the time Aaron enters the Most Holy Place to perform the ritual of purification until he comes out, there must be no one in the Tent. When he has performed the ritual for himself, his family, and the whole community, ¹⁸ he must then go out to the altar for burnt-offerings and purify it. He must take some of the bull's blood and some of the goat's blood and put it all over the projections at the corners of the altar. ¹⁹ With his finger he must sprinkle some of the blood on the altar seven times. In this way he is to purify it from the sins of the people of Israel and make it holy.

The Scapegoat

20 When Aaron has finished performing the ritual to purify the Most Holy Place, the rest of the Tent of the LORD's presence, and the altar, he shall present to the LORD the live goat chosen for Azazel. ᶠ ²¹ He shall put both his hands on the goat's head and confess over it all the evils, sins, and rebellions of the people of Israel, and so transfer them to the goat's head. Then the goat is to be driven off into the desert by a man appointed to do it. ²² The goat will carry all their sins away with him into some uninhabited land.

ᵉ AZAZEL: *The meaning of this Hebrew word is unknown; it may be the name of a desert demon.* ᶠ AZAZEL: *See 16.8.*
16.2: Heb 6.19   **16.3:** Heb 9.7   **16.15:** Heb 9.12

The goat will carry all their sins away (16.22)

23 Then Aaron shall go into the Tent, take off the priestly garments that he had put on before entering the Most Holy Place, and leave them there. 24 He must bathe in a holy place and put on his own clothes. After that, he shall go out and offer the burnt-offering to remove his own sins and those of the people. 25 He shall burn on the altar the fat of the animal for the sin-offering. 26 The man who drove the goat into the desert to Azazel must wash his clothes and have a bath before he comes back into camp. 27 The bull and the goat used for the sin-offering, whose blood was brought into the Most Holy Place to take away sin, shall be carried outside the camp and burnt. Skin, meat, and intestines shall all be burnt. 28 The one who burns them must wash his clothes and have a bath before he returns to camp.

Observing the Day of Atonement

29 The following regulations are to be observed for all time to come. On the tenth day of the seventh month the Israelites and the foreigners living among them must fast and must not do any work. 30 On that day the ritual is to be performed to purify them from all their sins, so that they will be ritually clean. 31 That day is to be a very holy day, one on which they fast and do no work at all. These regulations are to be observed for all time to come. 32 The High Priest, properly ordained and consecrated to succeed his father, is to perform the ritual of purification. He shall put on the priestly garments 33 and perform the ritual to purify the Most Holy Place, the rest of the Tent of the LORD's presence, the altar, the priests, and all the people of the community. 34 These regulations are to be observed for all time to come. This ritual must be performed once a year to purify the people of Israel from all their sins.

So Moses*g* did as the Lord had commanded.

The Sacredness of Blood

17 The Lord commanded Moses 2 to give Aaron and his sons and all the people of Israel the following regulations. 3-4 An Israelite who kills a cow or a sheep or a goat as an offering to the LORD anywhere except at the entrance of the Tent of the LORD's presence has broken the Law. He has shed blood and shall no longer be considered one of God's people. 5 The meaning of this command is that the people of Israel shall now bring to the LORD the animals which they used to kill in the open country. They shall now bring them to the priest at the entrance of the Tent and kill them as fellowship-offerings. 6 The priest shall throw the blood against the sides of the altar at the entrance of the Tent and burn the fat to produce a smell that is pleasing to the LORD. 7 The people of Israel must

g Moses; *or* Aaron.
16.23: Ezek 44.19　　**16.27:** Heb 13.11　　**16.29–34:** Lev 23.26–32; Num 29.7–11

no longer be unfaithful to the LORD by killing their animals in the fields as sacrifices to the goat-demons. The people of Israel must keep this regulation for all time to come.

8 Any Israelite or any foreigner living in the community who offers a burnt-offering or any other sacrifice 9 as an offering to the LORD anywhere except at the entrance of the Tent shall no longer be considered one of God's people.

10 If any Israelite or any foreigner living in the community eats meat with blood still in it, the LORD will turn against him and no longer consider him one of his people. 11 The life of every living thing is in the blood, and that is why the LORD has commanded that all blood be poured out on the altar to take away the people's sins. Blood, which is life, takes away sins. 12 That is why the LORD has told the people of Israel that neither they nor any foreigner living among them shall eat any meat with blood still in it.

13 If any Israelite or any foreigner living in the community hunts an animal or a bird which is ritually clean, he must pour out its blood on the ground and cover it with earth. 14 The life of every living thing is in the blood, and that is why the LORD has told the people of Israel that they shall not eat any meat with blood still in it and that anyone who does so will no longer be considered one of his people.

15 Any person, Israelite or foreigner, who eats meat from an animal that has died a natural death or has been killed by wild animals must wash his clothes, have a bath, and wait until evening before he is ritually clean. 16 If he does not, he must suffer the consequences.

Forbidden Sexual Practices

18 The LORD told Moses 2 to say to the people of Israel, "I am the LORD your God. 3 Do not follow the practices of the people of Egypt, where you once lived, or of the people in the land of Canaan, where I am now taking you. 4 Obey my laws and do what I command. I am the LORD your God. 5 Follow the practices and the laws that I give you; you will save your life by doing so. I am the LORD."

6 The LORD gave the following regulations. Do not have sexual intercourse with any of your relatives. 7 Do not disgrace your father by having intercourse with your mother. You must not disgrace your own mother. 8 Do not disgrace your father by having intercourse with any of his other wives. 9 Do not have intercourse with your sister or your stepsister, whether or not she was brought up in the same house with you. 10 Do not have intercourse with your granddaughter; that would be a disgrace to you. 11 Do not have intercourse with a half-sister; she, too, is your sister. 12-13 Do not have intercourse with an aunt, whether she is your father's sister or your mother's sister. 14 Do not have intercourse with your uncle's wife; she, too, is your aunt. 15 Do not have intercourse with your daughter-in-law 16 or with your brother's wife. 17 Do not have intercourse with the daughter or granddaughter of a woman with whom you have had intercourse; they may be related to you, and that would be incest. 18 Do not take your wife's sister as one of your wives, as long as your wife is living.

19 Do not have intercourse with a woman during her monthly period, because she is ritually unclean. 20 Do not have intercourse with another man's wife; that would make you ritually unclean. 21 Do not hand over any of your children to be used in the worship of the god Molech, because that would bring disgrace on the name of God, the LORD. 22 No man is to have sexual relations with another man; God hates that. 23 No man or woman is to have sexual relations with an animal; that perversion makes you ritually unclean.

24 Do not make yourselves unclean by any of these acts, for that is how the pagans made themselves unclean, those pagans who lived in the land before you and whom the LORD is driving out so that you can go in. 25 Their actions made the land unclean, and so the LORD is punishing the land and making it reject the people who lived there. 26-27 They did all these disgusting things and made the land unclean, but you must not do them. All of you, whether Israelites or foreigners living with you, must keep the LORD's laws

17.10: Gen 9.4; Lev 7.26-27, 19.26; Deut 12.16,23, 15.23   17.11: Heb 9.22
18.5: Neh 9.29; Ezek 18.9, 20.11-13; Lk 10.28; Rom 10.5; Gal 3.12
18.8: Lev 20.11; Deut 22.30, 27.20   18.9: Lev 20.17; Deut 27.22   18.12-14: Lev 20.19-20
18.15: Lev 20.12   18.16: Lev 20.21   18.17: Lev 20.14; Deut 27.23   18.19: Lev 20.18
18.20: Lev 20.10   18.21: Lev 20.1-5   18.22: Lev 20.13
18.23: Ex 22.19; Lev 20.15-16; Deut 27.21

and commands, 28 and then the land will not reject you, as it rejected the pagans who lived there before you. 29 You know that whoever does any of these disgusting things will no longer be considered one of God's people.

30 And the LORD said, "Obey the commands I give and do not follow the practices of the people who lived in the land before you, and do not make yourselves unclean by doing any of these things. I am the LORD your God."

Laws of Holiness and Justice

19 The LORD told Moses 2 to say to the community of Israel, "Be holy, because I, the LORD your God, am holy. 3 Each of you must respect his mother and his father, and must keep the Sabbath, as I have commanded. I am the LORD your God.

4 "Do not abandon me and worship idols; do not make gods of metal and worship them. I am the LORD your God.

5 "When you kill an animal for a fellowship-offering, keep the regulations that I have given you, and I will accept the offering. 6 The meat must be eaten on the day the animal is killed or on the next day. Any meat left on the third day must be burnt, 7 because it is ritually unclean, and if anyone eats it, I will not accept the offering. 8 Anyone who eats it will be guilty of treating as ordinary what is dedicated to me, and he will no longer be considered one of my people.

9 "When you harvest your fields, do not cut the corn at the edges of the fields, and do not go back to cut the ears of corn that were left. 10 Do not go back through your vineyard to gather the grapes that were missed or to pick up the grapes that have fallen; leave them for poor people and foreigners. I am the LORD your God.

11 "Do not steal or cheat or lie. 12 Do not make a promise in my name if you do not intend to keep it; that brings disgrace on my name. I am the LORD your

God.

13 "Do not take advantage of anyone or rob him. Do not hold back the wages of someone you have hired, not even for one night. 14 Do not curse a deaf man or put something in front of a blind man so as to make him stumble over it. Fear me; I am the LORD your God.

15 "Be honest and just when you make decisions in legal cases; do not show favouritism to the poor or fear the rich. 16 Do not spread lies about anyone, and when someone is on trial for his life, speak out if your testimony can help him. I am the LORD.

17 "Do not bear a grudge against anyone, but settle your differences with him, so that you will not commit a sin because of him. h 18 Do not take revenge on anyone or continue to hate him, but love your neighbour as you love yourself. I am the LORD.

19 "Obey my commands. Do not cross-breed domestic animals. Do not plant two kinds of seed in the same field. Do not wear clothes made of two kinds of material.

20 "If a slave-girl is the recognized concubine of a man and she has not been paid for and freed, then if another man has sexual relations with her, they will be punished but not i put to death, since she is a slave. 21 The man shall bring a ram to the entrance of the Tent of my presence as his repayment-offering, 22 and with it the priest shall perform the ritual of purification to remove the man's sin, and God will forgive him.

23 "When you come into the land of Canaan and plant any kind of fruit tree, consider the fruit ritually unclean for the first three years. During that time you must not eat it. 24 In the fourth year all the fruit shall be dedicated as an offering to show your gratitude to me, j the LORD. 25 But in the fifth year you may eat the fruit. If you do all this, your trees will bear more fruit. I am the LORD your God.

26 "Do not eat any meat with blood still in it. Do not practise any kind of

---

h so...him; or so that you do not commit this sin against him.
i they...not; or but an investigation will be made but they will not be.
j to show your gratitude to me; or in praise of me.
19.2: Lev 11.44–45; 1 Pet 1.16   **19.3:** Ex 20.8,12; Deut 5.12,16
19.4: Lev 26.1; Ex 20.23, 34.17; Deut 27.15   **19.9–10:** Lev 23.22; Deut 24.19–22
19.11: Ex 20.15,16; Deut 5.19,20   **19.12:** Ex 20.7; Deut 5.11; Mt 5.33   **19.13:** Deut 24.14–15
19.14: Deut 27.18   **19.15:** Ex 23.6–8; Deut 16.19   **19.17:** Mt 18.15
19.18: Mt 5.43, 19.19, 22.39; Mk 12.31; Lk 10.27; Rom 13.9; Gal 5.14; Jas 2.8
19.19: Deut 22.9–11   **19.26:** Gen 9.4; Lev 7.26–27, 17.10–14; Deut 12.16, 23, 15.23, 18.10

magic. ²⁷ Do not cut the hair on the sides of your head or trim your beard ²⁸ or tattoo yourselves or cut gashes in your body to mourn for the dead. I am the LORD.

29 "Do not disgrace your daughters by making them temple prostitutes;ᵏ if you do, you will turn to other gods and the land will be full of immorality. ³⁰ Keep the Sabbath, and honour the place where I am worshipped. I am the LORD.

31 "Do not go for advice to people who consult the spirits of the dead. If you do, you will be ritually unclean. I am the LORD your God.

32 "Show respect for old people and

Show respect for old people (19.32)

honour them. Reverently obey me; I am the LORD.

33 "Do not ill-treat foreigners who are living in your land. ³⁴ Treat them as you would a fellow-Israelite, and love them as you love yourselves. Remember that you were once foreigners in the land of Egypt. I am the LORD your God.

35 "Do not cheat anyone by using false measures of length, weight, or quantity. ³⁶ Use honest scales, honest weights, and honest measures. I am the LORD your God, and I brought you out of Egypt. ³⁷ Obey

Love them as you love yourselves (19.34)

all my laws and commands. I am the LORD."

Penalties for Disobedience

20 The LORD told Moses ²to say to the people of Israel, "Any of you or any foreigner living among you who gives any of his children to be used in the worship of the god Molech shall be stoned to death by the whole community. ³ If anyone gives one of his children to Molech and makes my sacred Tent unclean and disgraces my holy name, I will turn against him and will no longer consider him one of my people. ⁴ But if the community ignores what he has done and does not put him to death, ⁵ I myself will turn against the man and his whole family and against all who join him in being unfaithful to me and worshipping Molech. I will no longer consider them my people.

6 "If anyone goes for advice to people who consult the spirits of the dead, I will turn against him and will no longer consider him one of my people. ⁷ Keep yourselves holy, because I am the LORD

ᵏ TEMPLE PROSTITUTES: *These women were found in Canaanite temples, where fertility gods were worshipped. It was believed that intercourse with these prostitutes assured fertile fields and herds.*
19.27–28: Lev 2.5; Deut 14.1   **19.29:** Deut 23.17   **19.30:** Lev 26.2
19.31: Deut 18.11; 1 Sam 28.3; 2 Kgs 23.4; Is 8.19   **19.33–34:** Ex 22.21; Deut 24.17–18, 27.19
19.35–36: Deut 25.13–16; Prov 20.10; Ezek 45.10

your God. ⁸Obey my laws, because I am the LORD and I make you holy."

9 The LORD gave the following regulations. Anyone who curses his father or his mother shall be put to death; he is responsible for his own death.

10 If a man commits adultery with the wife of a fellow-Israelite, both he and the woman shall be put to death. ¹¹A man who has intercourse with one of his father's wives disgraces his father, and both he and the woman shall be put to death. They are responsible for their own death. ¹²If a man has intercourse with his daughter-in-law, they shall both be put to death. They have committed incest and are responsible for their own death. ¹³If a man has sexual relations with another man, they have done a disgusting thing, and both shall be put to death. They are responsible for their own death. ¹⁴If a man marries a woman and her mother, all three shall be burnt to death because of the disgraceful thing they have done; such a thing must not be permitted among you. ¹⁵If a man has sexual relations with an animal, he and the animal shall be put to death. ¹⁶If a woman tries to have sexual relations with an animal, she and the animal shall be put to death. They are responsible for their own death.

17 If a man marries his sister or half-sister, they shall be publicly disgraced and driven out of the community. He has had intercourse with his sister and must suffer the consequences. ¹⁸If a man has intercourse with a woman during her monthly period, both of them are to be driven out of the community, because they have broken the regulations about ritual uncleanness.

19 If a man has intercourse with his aunt, both of them must suffer the consequences for incest. ²⁰If a man has intercourse with his uncle's wife, he disgraces his uncle, and he and the woman will pay the penalty; neither of them will have children. ²¹If a man marries his brother's wife, they will die childless. He has done a ritually unclean thing and has disgraced his brother.

22 The LORD said, "Keep all my laws and commands, so that you will not be rejected by the land of Canaan, into which I am bringing you. ²³Do not adopt the customs of people who live there; I am driving out those pagans so that you can enter the land. They have disgusted me with all their evil practices. ²⁴But I have promised you this rich and fertile land as your possession, and I will give it to you. I am the LORD your God, and I have set you apart from the other nations. ²⁵So then, you must make a clear distinction between animals and birds that are ritually clean and those that are not. Do not eat unclean animals or birds. I have declared them unclean, and eating them would make you unclean. ²⁶You shall be holy and belong only to me, because I am the LORD and I am holy. I have set you apart from the other nations so that you would belong to me alone.

27 "Any man or woman who consults the spirits of the dead shall be stoned to death; any person who does this is responsible for his own death."

The Holiness of the Priests

21 The LORD commanded Moses to say to the Aaronite priests, "No priest is to make himself ritually unclean by taking part in the funeral ceremonies when a relative dies, ²unless it is his mother, father, son, daughter, brother, ³or unmarried sister living in his house. ⁴He shall not make himself unclean at the death of those related to him by marriage.^l

5 "No priest shall shave any part of his head or trim his beard or cut gashes on his body to show that he is in mourning. ⁶He must be holy and must not disgrace my name. He offers food-offerings to me, and he must be holy. ⁷A priest shall not marry a woman who has been a prostitute or a woman who is not a virgin or who is divorced; he is holy. ⁸The people must consider the priest holy, because he presents the food-offerings to me. I am the LORD; I am holy and I make my people holy. ⁹If a priest's daughter becomes a prostitute, she disgraces her father; she shall be burnt to death.

10 "The High Priest has had the anointing oil poured on his head and has been consecrated to wear the priestly garments, so he must not leave his hair uncombed or tear his clothes to show that he is in mourning. ¹¹⁻¹²He has been dedicated to me and is not to make himself

---

^lVerse 4 in Hebrew is unclear.

20.9: Ex 21.17; Mt 15.4; Mk 7.10　　**20.10:** Ex 20.14; Lev 18.20; Deut 5.18
20.11: Lev 18.8; Deut 22.30, 27.20　　**20.12:** Lev 18.15　　**20.13:** Lev 18.22
20.14: Lev 18.17; Deut 27.23　　**20.15–16:** Ex 22.19; Lev 18.23; Deut 27.21
20.17: Lev 18.9; Deut 27.22　　**20.18:** Lev 18.19　　**20.19–20:** Lev 18.12–14　　**20.21:** Lev 18.16
21.5: Lev 19.27–28; Deut 14.1

ritually unclean nor is he to defile my sacred Tent by leaving it and entering a house where there is a dead person, even if it is his own father or mother. 13 He shall marry a virgin, 14 not a widow or a divorced woman or a woman who has been a prostitute. He shall marry only a virgin from his own clan. 15 Otherwise, his children, who ought to be holy, will be ritually unclean. I am the LORD and I have set him apart as the High Priest."

16 The LORD commanded Moses 17 to say to Aaron, "None of your descendants who has any physical defect may present the food-offering to me. This applies for all time to come. 18 No man with any physical defect may make the offering: no one who is blind, lame, disfigured, or deformed; 19 no one with a crippled hand or foot; 20 no one who is a hunchback or a dwarf; no one with any eye or skin disease; and no eunuch. 21 No descendant of Aaron the priest who has any physical defect may present the food-offering to me. 22 Such a man may eat the food offered to me, both the holy food-offering and the very holy food-offering, 23 but because he has a physical defect, he shall not come near the sacred curtain or approach the altar. He must not profane these holy things, because I am the LORD and I make them holy."

24 This, then, is what Moses said to Aaron, the sons of Aaron, and to all the people of Israel.

The Holiness of the Offerings

22 The LORD commanded Moses 2 to say to Aaron and his sons, "You must not bring disgrace on my holy name, so treat with respect the sacred offerings that the people of Israel dedicate to me. I am the LORD. 3 If any of your descendants, while he is ritually unclean, comes near the sacred offerings which the people of Israel have dedicated to me, he can never again serve at the altar. This applies for all time to come. I am the LORD.

4 "None of the descendants of Aaron who has a dreaded skin-disease or a discharge may eat any of the sacred offerings until he is ritually clean. Any priest is unclean if he touches anything which is unclean through contact with a corpse or if he has an emission of semen 5 or if he has touched an unclean animal or person. 6 Any priest who becomes unclean remains unclean until evening,

and even then he may not eat any of the sacred offerings until he has had a bath. 7 After the sun sets he is clean, and then he may eat the sacred offerings, which are his food. 8 He shall not eat the meat of any animal that has died a natural death or has been killed by wild animals; it will make him unclean. I am the LORD.

9 "All priests shall observe the regulations that I have given. Otherwise, they will be guilty and die, because they have disobeyed the sacred regulations. I am the LORD and I make them holy.

10 "Only a member of a priestly family may eat any of the sacred offerings; no one else may eat them—not even someone staying with a priest or hired by him. 11 But a priest's slaves, bought with his own money or born in his home, may eat the food the priest receives. 12 A priest's daughter who marries someone who is not a priest may not eat any of the sacred offerings. 13 But a widowed or divorced daughter who has no children and who has returned to live in her father's house as a dependant may eat the food her father receives as a priest. Only a member of a priestly family may eat any of it.

14 "If any person who is not a member of a priestly family eats any of the sacred offerings without intending to, he must repay the priest its full value plus an additional twenty per cent. 15 The priests shall not profane the sacred offerings 16 by letting any unauthorized person eat them; this would bring guilt and punishment on such a person. I am the LORD and I make the offerings holy."

17 The LORD commanded Moses 18 to give Aaron and his sons and all the people of Israel the following regulations. When any Israelite or any foreigner living in Israel presents a burnt-offering, whether in fulfilment of a vow or as a freewill offering, the animal must not have any defects. 19 To be accepted, it must be a male without any defects. 20 If you offer any animal that has any defect, the LORD will not accept it. 21 When anyone presents a fellowship-offering to the LORD, whether in fulfilment of a vow or as a freewill offering, the animal must be without any defect if it is to be accepted. 22 Do not offer to the LORD any animal that is blind or crippled or mutilated, or that has a running sore or a skin eruption or scabs. Do not offer any such animals on the altar as a food-offering. 23 As a freewill offering

22.20: Deut 17.1

you may offer an animal that is stunted or not perfectly formed, but it is not acceptable in fulfilment of a vow. 24 Do not offer to the LORD any animal whose testicles have been crushed, cut, bruised, or torn off. This is not permitted in your land.

25 Do not offer as a food-offering any animal obtained from a foreigner. Such animals are considered defective and are not acceptable.

26-27 When a calf or a lamb or a kid is born, it must not be taken from its mother for seven days, but after that it is acceptable as a food-offering. 28 Do not sacrifice a cow and its calf or a sheep and its lamb or a goat and its kid on the same day. 29 When you offer a sacrifice of thanksgiving to the LORD, follow the rules so that you will be accepted; 30 eat it the same day and leave none of it until the next morning.

31 The LORD said, "Obey my commands; I am the LORD. 32 Do not bring disgrace on my holy name; all the people of Israel must acknowledge me to be holy. I am the LORD and I make you holy; 33 and I brought you out of Egypt to become your God. I am the LORD."

The Religious Festivals

23 The LORD gave Moses 2 the following regulations for the religious festivals, when the people of Israel are to gather for worship. 3 You have six days in which to do your work, but remember that the seventh day, the Sabbath, is a day of rest. On that day do not work, but gather for worship. The Sabbath belongs to the LORD, no matter where you live. 4 Proclaim the following festivals at the appointed times.

Passover and Unleavened Bread
(Num 28.16–25)

5 The Passover, celebrated to honour the LORD, begins at sunset on the fourteenth day of the first month. 6 On the fifteenth day the Festival of Unleavened Bread begins, and for seven days you must not eat any bread made with yeast. 7 On the first of these days you shall gather for worship and do none of your daily work. 8 Offer your food-offerings to the LORD for seven days. On the seventh day you shall again gather for worship, but you shall do none of your daily work.

9-10 When you come into the land that the LORD is giving you and you harvest your corn, take the first sheaf to the priest. 11 He shall present it as a special offering to the LORD, so that you may be accepted. The priest shall present it the day after the Sabbath. 12 On the day you present the offering of corn, also sacrifice as a burnt-offering a one-year-old male lamb that has no defects. 13 With it you shall present two kilogrammes of flour mixed with olive-oil as a food-offering. The smell of this offering is pleasing to the LORD. You shall also present with it an offering of one litre of wine. 14 Do not eat any of the new corn, whether raw, roasted, or baked into bread, until you have brought this offering to God. This regulation is to be observed by all your descendants for all time to come.

The Harvest Festival
(Num 28.26–31)

15 Count seven full weeks from the day after the Sabbath on which you bring your sheaf of corn to present to the LORD. 16 On the fiftieth day, the day after the seventh Sabbath, present to the LORD another new offering of corn. 17 Each family is to bring two loaves of bread and present them to the LORD as a special gift. Each loaf shall be made of two kilogrammes of flour baked with yeast and shall be presented to the Lord as an offering of the first corn to be harvested. 18 And with the bread the community is to present seven one-year-old lambs, one bull, and two rams, none of which may have any defects. They shall be offered as a burnt-offering to the LORD, together with a grain-offering and a wine-offering. The smell of this offering is pleasing to the LORD. 19 Also offer one male goat as a sin-offering and two one-year-old male lambs as a fellowship-offering. 20 The priest shall present the bread with the two lambs as a special gift to the LORD for the priests. These offerings are holy. 21 On that day do none of your daily work, but gather for worship. Your descendants are to observe this regulation for all time to come, no matter where they live.

22 When you harvest your fields, do not cut the corn at the edges of the fields, and do not go back to cut the ears of corn that were left; leave them for poor

23.3: Ex 20.8–10, 23.12, 31.15, 34.21, 35.2; Deut 5.12–14   **23.5:** Ex 12.1–13; Deut 16.1–2
23.6–8: Ex 12.14–20, 23.15, 34.18; Deut 16.3–8   **23.15–21:** Ex 23.16, 34.22; Deut 16.9–12
23.22: Lev 19.9–10; Deut 24.19–22

Leave them for poor people (23.22)

people and foreigners. The LORD is your God.

The New Year Festival
(Num 29.1-6)

23-24 On the first day of the seventh month observe a special day of rest, and come together for worship when the trumpets sound. 25 Present a food-offering to the LORD and do none of your daily work.

The Day of Atonement
(Num 29.7-11)

26-27 The tenth day of the seventh month is the day when the annual ritual is to be performed to take away the sins of the people. On that day do not eat anything at all; come together for worship, and present a food-offering to the Lord. 28 Do no work on that day, because it is the day for performing the ritual to take away sin. 29 Anyone who eats anything on that day will no longer be considered one of God's people. 30 And if anyone does any work on that day, the LORD himself will put him to death. 31 This regulation applies to all your descendants, no matter where they live. 32 From sunset on the ninth day of the month to sunset on the tenth observe this day as a special day of rest, during which nothing may be eaten.

The Festival of Shelters
(Num 29.12-40)

33-34 The Festival of Shelters begins on the fifteenth day of the seventh month and continues for seven days. 35 On the first of these days come together for worship and do none of your daily work. 36 Each day for seven days you shall present a food-offering. On the eighth day

come together again for worship and present a food-offering. It is a day for worship, and you shall do no work.

37 (These are the religious festivals on which you honour the LORD by gathering together for worship and presenting food-offerings, burnt-offerings, grain-offerings, sacrifices, and wine-offerings, as required day by day. 38 These festivals are in addition to the regular Sabbaths, and these offerings are in addition to your regular gifts, your offerings in fulfilment of vows, and your freewill offerings that you give to the LORD.)

39 When you have harvested your fields, celebrate this festival for seven days, beginning on the fifteenth day of the seventh month. The first day shall be a special day of rest. 40 On that day take some of the best fruit from your trees, take palm branches and the branches of leafy trees, and begin a religious festival to honour the LORD your God. 41 Celebrate it for seven days. This regulation is to be kept by your descendants for all time to come. 42 All the people of Israel shall live in shelters for seven days, 43 so that your descendants may know that the LORD made the people of Israel live in simple shelters when he led them out of Egypt. He is the LORD your God.

44 So in this way Moses gave the people of Israel the regulations for observing the religious festivals to honour the LORD.

Taking Care of the Lamps
(Ex 27.20-21)

24 The LORD told Moses 2 to give the following orders to the people of Israel: Bring pure olive-oil of the finest quality for the lamps in the Tent, so that a light may be kept burning regularly. 3 Each evening Aaron shall light them and

23.26-32: Lev 16.29-34   **23.33-36:** Deut 16.13-15

keep them burning until morning, there in the LORD's presence outside the curtain in front of the Covenant Box, which is in the Most Holy Place. This regulation is to be observed for all time to come. [4] Aaron shall take care of the lamps on the lampstand of pure gold and must see that they burn regularly in the LORD's presence.

The Bread Offered to God

5 Take twelve kilogrammes of flour and bake twelve loaves of bread. [6] Put the loaves in two rows, six in each row, on the table covered with pure gold, which is in the LORD's presence. [7] Put some pure incense on each row, as a token food-offering to the LORD to take the place of the bread. [8] Every Sabbath, for all time to come, the bread must be placed in the presence of the LORD. This is Israel's duty for ever. [9] The bread belongs to Aaron and his descendants, and they shall eat it in a holy place, because this is a very holy part of the food offered to the LORD for the priests.

An Example of Just and Fair Punishment

10-11 There was a man whose father was an Egyptian and whose mother was an Israelite named Shelomith, the daughter of Dibri from the tribe of Dan. There in the camp this man quarrelled with an Israelite. During the quarrel he cursed God, so they took him to Moses, [12] put him under guard, and waited for the LORD to tell them what to do with him.

13 The LORD said to Moses, [14] "Take that man out of the camp. Everyone who heard him curse shall put his hands on the man's head to testify that he is guilty, and then the whole community shall stone him to death. [15] Then tell the people of Israel that anyone who curses God must suffer the consequences [16] and be put to death. Any Israelite or any foreigner living in Israel who curses the LORD shall be stoned to death by the whole community.

17 "Anyone who commits murder shall be put to death, [18] and anyone who kills an animal belonging to someone else must replace it. The principle is a life for a life.

19 "If anyone injures another person, whatever he has done shall be done to him. [20] If he breaks a bone, one of his bones shall be broken; if he blinds him in one eye, one of his eyes shall be blinded;

if he knocks out a tooth, one of his teeth shall be knocked out. Whatever injury he causes another person shall be done to him in return. [21] Whoever kills an animal shall replace it, but whoever kills a man shall be put to death. [22] This law applies to all of you, to Israelites and to foreigners living among you, because I am the LORD your God."

23 When Moses had said this to the people of Israel, they took the man outside the camp and stoned him to death. In this way the people of Israel did what the LORD had commanded Moses.

The Seventh Year
(Deut 15.1-11)

25 The LORD spoke to Moses on Mount Sinai and commanded him [2] to give the following regulations to the people of Israel. When you enter the land that the LORD is giving you, you shall honour the LORD by not cultivating the land every seventh year. [3] You shall sow your fields, prune your vineyards, and gather your crops for six years. [4] But the seventh year is to be a year of complete rest for the land, a year dedicated to the LORD. Do not sow your fields or prune your vineyards. [5] Do not even harvest the corn that grows by itself without being sown, and do not gather the grapes from your unpruned vines; it is a year of complete rest for the land. [6] Although the land has not been cultivated during that year, it will provide food for you, your slaves, your hired men, the foreigners living with you, [7] your domestic animals, and the wild animals in your fields. Everything that it produces may be eaten.

The Year of Restoration

8 Count seven times seven years, a total of forty-nine years. [9] Then, on the tenth day of the seventh month, the Day of Atonement, send a man to blow a trumpet throughout the whole land. [10] In this way you shall set the fiftieth year apart and proclaim freedom to all the inhabitants of the land. During this year all property that has been sold shall be restored to the original owner or his descendants, and anyone who has been sold as a slave shall return to his family. [11] You shall not sow your fields or harvest the corn that grows by itself or gather the grapes in your unpruned vineyards. [12] The whole year shall be sacred for you; you shall eat only

24.5-6: Ex 25.30   24.9: Mt 12.4; Mk 2.26; Lk 6.4   24.17: Ex 21.12
24.20: Ex 21.23-25; Deut 19.21; Mt 5.38   24.22: Num 15.16   25.1-7: Ex 23.10-11

what the fields produce of themselves.

13 In this year all property that has been sold shall be restored to its original owner. [14] So when you sell land to your fellow-Israelite or buy land from him, do not deal unfairly. [15] The price is to be fixed according to the number of years the land can produce crops before the next Year of Restoration. [16] If there are many years, the price shall be higher, but if there are only a few years, the price shall be lower, because what is being sold is the number of crops the land can produce. [17] Do not cheat a fellow-Israelite, but obey the LORD your God.

The Problem of the Seventh Year

18 Obey all the LORD's laws and commands, so that you may live in safety in the land. [19] The land will produce its crops, and you will have all you want to eat and will live in safety.

20 But someone may ask what there will be to eat during the seventh year, when no fields are sown and no crops gathered. [21] The LORD will bless the land in the sixth year so that it will produce enough food for two years. [22] When you sow your fields in the eighth year, you will still be eating what you harvested during the sixth year, and you will have enough to eat until the crops you plant that year are harvested.

Restoration of Property

23 Your land must not be sold on a permanent basis, because you do not own it; it belongs to God, and you are like foreigners who are allowed to make use of it.

24 When land is sold, the right of the original owner to buy it back must be recognized. [25] If an Israelite becomes poor and is forced to sell his land, his closest relative is to buy it back. [26] A man who has no relative to buy it back may later become prosperous and have enough to buy it back himself. [27] In that case he must pay to the man who bought it a sum that will make up for the years remaining until the next Year of Restoration, when he would in any event recover his land. [28] But if he does not have enough money to buy the land back, it remains under the control of the man who bought it until the next Year of Restoration. In that year it will be returned to its original owner.

29 If a man sells a house in a walled city, he has the right to buy it back during the first full year from the date of sale. [30] But if he does not buy it back within the year, he loses the right of repurchase, and the house becomes the permanent property of the purchaser and his descendants; it will not be returned in the Year of Restoration. [31] But houses in unwalled villages are to be treated like fields; the original owner has the right to buy them back, and they are to be returned in the Year of Restoration. [32] However, Levites have the right to buy back at any time their property in the cities assigned to them. [33] If a house in one of these cities is sold by a Levite and is not bought back, it must be returned in the Year of Restoration[m] because the houses which the Levites own in their cities are their permanent property among the people of Israel. [34] But the pasture land round the Levite cities shall never be sold; it is their property for ever.

Loans to the Poor

35 If a fellow-Israelite living near you

You must provide for him (25.35)

---

[m] *Probable text* If a house...Restoration; *Hebrew unclear.*
25.35: Deut 15.7–8

becomes poor and cannot support himself, you must provide for him as you would for a hired man, so that he can continue to live near you. 36 Do not charge him any interest, but obey God and let your fellow-Israelite live near you. 37 Do not make him pay interest on the money you lend him, and do not make a profit on the food you sell him. 38 This is the command of the LORD your God, who brought you out of Egypt in order to give you the land of Canaan and to be your God.

Release of Slaves

39 If a fellow-Israelite living near you becomes so poor that he sells himself to you as a slave, you shall not make him do the work of a slave. 40 He shall stay with you as a hired man and serve you until the next Year of Restoration. 41 At that time he and his children shall leave you and return to his family and to the property of his ancestors. 42 The people of Israel are the LORD's slaves, and he brought them out of Egypt; they must not be sold into slavery. 43 Do not treat them harshly, but obey your God. 44 If you need slaves, you may buy them from the nations round you. 45 You may also buy the children of the foreigners who are living among you. Such children born in your land may become your property, 46 and you may leave them as an inheritance to your sons, whom they must serve as long as they live. But you must not treat any of your fellow-Israelites harshly.

47 Suppose a foreigner living with you becomes rich, while a fellow-Israelite becomes poor and sells himself as a slave to that foreigner or to a member of his family. 48 After he is sold, he still has the right to be bought back. One of his brothers 49 or his uncle or his cousin or another of his close relatives may buy him back; or if he himself earns enough, he may buy his own freedom. 50 He must consult the one who bought him, and they must count the years from the time he sold himself until the next Year of Restoration and must set the price for his release on the basis of the wages paid to a hired man. 51-52 He must refund a part of the purchase price according to the number of years left, 53 as if he had been hired on an annual basis. His master must not treat him harshly. 54 If he is not

set free in any of these ways, he and his children must be set free in the next Year of Restoration. 55 An Israelite cannot be a permanent slave, because the people of Israel are the LORD's slaves. He brought them out of Egypt; he is the LORD their God.

Blessings for Obedience
(Deut 7.12–24; 28.1–14)

26 The LORD said, "Do not make idols or set up statues, stone pillars, or carved stones to worship. I am the LORD your God. 2 Keep the religious festivals and honour the place where I am worshipped. I am the LORD.

3 "If you live according to my laws and obey my commands, 4 I will send you rain at the right time, so that the land will produce crops and the trees will bear fruit. 5 Your crops will be so plentiful that you will still be harvesting corn when it is time to pick grapes, and you will still be picking grapes when it is time to sow corn. You will have all that you want to eat, and you will live in safety in your land.

6 "I will give you peace in your land, and you will sleep without being afraid of anyone. I will get rid of the dangerous animals in the land, and there will be no more war there. 7 You will be victorious over your enemies; 8 five of you will be able to defeat a hundred, and a hundred will be able to defeat ten thousand. 9 I will bless you and give you many children; I will keep my part of the covenant that I made with you. 10 Your harvests will be so plentiful that they will last for a year, and even then you will have to throw away what is left of the old harvest to make room for the new. 11 I will live among you in my sacred tent, and I will never turn away from you. 12 I will be with you; I will be your God, and you will be my people. 13 I, the LORD your God, brought you out of Egypt so that you would no longer be slaves. I broke the power that held you down and I let you walk with your head held high."

Punishment for Disobedience
(Deut 28.15–68)

14 The LORD said, "If you will not obey my commands, you will be punished. 15 If you refuse to obey my laws and commands and break the covenant I have

25.37: Ex 22.25; Deut 23.19–20　　**25.39–46:** Ex 21.2–6; Deut 15.12–18
26.1: Ex 20.4; Lev 19.4; Deut 5.8, 16.21–22, 27.1　　**26.3–5:** Deut 11.13–15, 28.1–14
26.12: 2 Cor 6.16

made with you, [16] I will punish you. I will bring disaster on you—incurable diseases and fevers that will make you blind and cause your life to waste away. You will sow your seed, but it will do you no good, because your enemies will conquer you and eat what you have grown. [17] I will turn against you, so that you will be defeated, and those who hate you will rule over you; you will be so terrified that you will run when no one is chasing you.

18 "If even after all this you still do not obey me, I will increase your punishment seven times. [19] I will break your stubborn pride; there will be no rain, and your land will be dry and as hard as iron. [20] All your hard work will do you no good, because your land will not produce crops and the trees will not bear fruit.

21 "If you still continue to resist me and refuse to obey me, I will again increase your punishment seven times. [22] I will send dangerous animals among you, and they will kill your children, destroy your livestock, and leave so few of you that your roads will be deserted.

23 "If after all this punishment you still do not listen to me, but continue to defy me, [24] then I will turn on you and punish you seven times harder than before. [25] I will bring war on you to punish you for breaking our covenant, and if you gather in your cities for safety, I will send incurable diseases among you, and you will be forced to surrender to your enemies. [26] I will cut off your food supply, so that ten women will need only one oven to bake all the bread they have. They will ration it out, and when you have eaten it all, you will still be hungry.

27 "If after all this you still continue to defy me and refuse to obey me, [28] then in my anger I will turn on you and again make your punishment seven times worse than before. [29] Your hunger will be so great that you will eat your own children. [30] I will destroy your places of worship on the hills, tear down your incense-altars, and throw your dead bodies on your fallen idols. In utter disgust [31] I will turn your cities into ruins, destroy your places of worship, and refuse to accept your sacrifices. [32] I will destroy your land so completely that the enemies who occupy it will be shocked at the destruction. [33] I will bring war on you and scatter you in foreign lands. Your land will be deserted, and your cities left in ruins.

[34-35] Then the land will enjoy the years of complete rest that you would not give it; it will lie abandoned and get its rest while you are in exile in the land of your enemies.

36 "I will make those of you who are in exile so terrified that the sound of a leaf blowing in the wind will make you run. You will run as if you were being pursued in battle, and you will fall when there is no enemy near you. [37] You will stumble over one another when no one is chasing you, and you will be unable to fight against any enemy. [38] You will die in exile, swallowed up by the land of your enemies. [39] The few of you who survive in the land of your enemies will waste away because of your own sin and the sin of your ancestors.

40 "But your descendants will confess their sins and the sins of their ancestors, who resisted me and rebelled against me, [41] and made me turn against them and send them into exile in the land of their enemies. At last, when your descendants are humbled and they have paid the penalty for their sin and rebellion, [42] I will remember my covenant with Jacob and with Isaac and with Abraham, and I will renew my promise to give my people the land. [43] First, however, the land must be rid of its people, so that it can enjoy its complete rest, and they must pay the full penalty for having rejected my laws and my commands. [44] But even then, when they are still in the land of their enemies, I will not completely abandon or destroy them. That would put an end to my covenant with them, and I am the LORD their God. [45] I will renew the covenant that I made with their ancestors when I showed all the nations my power by bringing my people out of Egypt, in order that I, the LORD, might be their God."

46 All these are the laws and commands that the LORD gave to Moses on Mount Sinai for the people of Israel.

Laws Concerning Gifts to the LORD

27 The LORD gave Moses [2] the following regulations for the people of Israel. When a person has been given to the LORD in fulfilment of a special vow, that person may be set free by the payment of the following sums of money, [3-7] according to the official standard:

—adult male, twenty to sixty years old:
 50 pieces of silver
—adult female: 30 pieces of silver

26.42: Gen 17.7-8, 26.3-4, 28.13-14

—young male, five to twenty years old:
20 pieces of silver
—young female: 10 pieces of silver
—infant male under five: 5 pieces of
silver
—infant female: 3 pieces of silver
—male above sixty years of age: 15
pieces of silver
—female above sixty: 10 pieces of silver

8 If the man who made the vow is too poor to pay the standard price, he shall bring the person to the priest, and the priest will set a lower price, according to the ability of the man to pay.

9 If the vow concerns an animal that is acceptable as an offering to the LORD, then every gift made to the LORD is sacred, 10 and the man who made the vow may not substitute another animal for it. If he does, both animals belong to the LORD. 11 But if the vow concerns a ritually unclean animal, which is not acceptable as an offering to the LORD, the man shall take the animal to the priest. 12 The priest shall fix a price for it, according to its good or bad qualities, and the price will be final. 13 If the man wishes to buy it back, he must pay the price plus an additional twenty per cent.

14 When someone dedicates his house to the LORD, the priest shall fix the price according to its good or bad points, and the price will be final. 15 If the one who dedicated the house wishes to buy it back, he must pay the price plus an additional twenty per cent.

16 If a man dedicates part of his land to the LORD, the price shall be fixed according to the amount of seed it takes to sow it, at the rate of ten pieces of silver for every twenty kilogrammes of barley. 17 If he dedicates the land immediately after a Year of Restoration, the full price applies. 18 If he dedicates it later, the priest shall estimate the cash value according to the number of years left until the next Year of Restoration, and fix a reduced price. 19 If the man who dedicated the field wishes to buy it back, he must pay the price plus an additional twenty per cent. 20 If he sells the field to someone else without first buying it back from the

LORD, he loses the right to buy it back. 21 At the next Year of Restoration the field will become the LORD's permanent property; it shall belong to the priests.

22 If a man dedicates to the LORD a field that he has bought, 23 the priest shall estimate its value according to the number of years until the next Year of Restoration, and the man must pay the price that very day; the money belongs to the LORD. 24 At the Year of Restoration the field shall be returned to the original owner or to his descendants.

25 All prices shall be fixed according to the official standard.

26 The first-born of an animal already belongs to the LORD, so no one may dedicate it to him as a freewill offering. A calf, a lamb, or a kid belongs to the LORD, 27 but the first-born of an unclean animal may be bought back at the standard price plus an additional twenty per cent. If it is not bought back, it may be sold to someone else at the standard price.

28 No one may sell or buy back what he has unconditionally dedicated[n] to the LORD, whether it is a human being, an animal, or land. It belongs permanently to the LORD. 29 Not even a human being who has been unconditionally dedicated may be bought back; he must be put to death.

30 One-tenth of all the produce of the land, whether grain or fruit, belongs to the LORD. 31 If a man wishes to buy any of it back, he must pay the standard price plus an additional twenty per cent. 32 One out of every ten domestic animals belongs to the LORD. When the animals are counted, every tenth one belongs to the LORD. 33 The owner may not arrange the animals so that the poor animals are chosen, and he may not make any substitutions. If he does substitute one animal for another, then both animals will belong to the LORD and may not be bought back.

34 These are the commands that the LORD gave Moses on Mount Sinai for the people of Israel.

---

[n] UNCONDITIONALLY DEDICATED: *Anything dedicated in this way belonged completely to the LORD and could not be used; it had to be destroyed.*
27.28: Num 18.14   **27.30–33:** Num 18.21; Deut 14.22–29

NUMBERS

INTRODUCTION

The book of *Numbers* tells the story of the Israelites during the nearly forty years from the time they left Mount Sinai until they reached the eastern border of the land that God had promised to give them. The name of the book refers to a prominent feature of the story, that is, the census which Moses took of the Israelites at Mount Sinai before their departure, and again in Moab, east of the Jordan, about a generation later. In the period between the two censuses the Israelites went to Kadesh Barnea on the southern border of Canaan, but failed to enter the promised land from there. After spending many years in that area, they went to the region east of the River Jordan, where part of the people settled and where the rest prepared to cross the river into Canaan.

The book of *Numbers* is an account of a people who were often discouraged and afraid in the face of hardship, and who rebelled against God and against Moses, the man God appointed to lead them. It is the story of God's faithful, persistent care for his people in spite of their weakness and disobedience, and of Moses' steadfast, if sometimes impatient, devotion both to God and to his people.

Outline of Contents

The Israelites prepare to leave Mount Sinai   1.1—9.23
   a. The first census   1.1—4.49
   b. Various laws and rules   5.1—8.26
   c. The second Passover   9.1-23
From Mount Sinai to Moab   10.1—21.35
Events in Moab   22.1—32.42
Summary of the journey from Egypt to Moab   33.1-49
Instructions before crossing the Jordan   33.50—36.13

The First Census of Israel

1 On the first day of the second month in the second year after the people of Israel left Egypt, the LORD spoke to Moses there in the Tent of his presence in the Sinai Desert. He said, ² "You and Aaron are to take a census of the people of Israel by clans and families. List the names of all the men ³ twenty years old or older who are fit for military service. ⁴ Ask one clan chief from each tribe to help you." ⁵⁻¹⁶ These are the men, leaders within their tribes, who were chosen from the community for this work:

Tribe	Clan chief
Reuben	Elizur son of Shedeur
Simeon	Shelumiel son of Zurishaddai
Judah	Nahshon son of Amminadab
Issachar	Nethanel son of Zuar
Zebulun	Eliab son of Helon
Ephraim	Elishama son of Ammihud
Manasseh	Gamaliel son of Pedahzur

1.1-46: Num 26.1-51

Benjamin   Abidan son of Gideoni
Dan   Ahiezer son of
               Ammishaddai
Asher   Pagiel son of Ochran
Gad   Eliasaph son of Deuel
Naphtali   Ahira son of Enan

17 With the help of these twelve men Moses and Aaron 18 called together the whole community on the first day of the second month and registered all the people by clans and families. The names of all the men twenty years old or older were recorded and counted, 19 as the LORD had commanded. In the Sinai Desert, Moses registered the people. 20-46 The men twenty years old or older who were fit for military service were registered by name according to clan and family, beginning with the tribe of Reuben, Jacob's eldest son. The totals were as follows:

Tribe	Number
Reuben	46,500
Simeon	59,300
Gad	45,650
Judah	74,600
Issachar	54,400
Zebulun	57,400
Ephraim	40,500
Manasseh	32,200
Benjamin	35,400
Dan	62,700
Asher	41,500
Naphtali	53,400
Total:	603,550

47 The Levites were not registered with the other tribes, 48 because the LORD had said to Moses, 49 "When you take a census of the men fit for military service, do not include the tribe of Levi. 50 Instead, put the Levites in charge of the Tent of my presence and all its equipment. They shall carry it and its equipment, serve in it, and set up their camp round it. 51 Whenever you move your camp, the Levites shall take the Tent down and set it up again at each new camping place. Anyone else who comes near the Tent shall be put to death. 52 The rest of the Israelites shall set up camp, company by company, each man with his own group and under his own banner. 53 But the Levites shall camp round the Tent to guard it, so that no one may come near and cause my anger to strike the community of Israel." 54 So the people of Israel did everything that the LORD had commanded Moses.

The Arrangement of the Tribes in Camp

2 The LORD gave Moses and Aaron the following instructions. 2 When the Israelites set up camp, each man will camp under the banner of his division and the flag of his own clan. The camp is to be set up all round the Tent.

3-9 On the east side, those under the banner of the division of Judah shall camp in their groups, under their leaders, as follows:

Tribe	Leader	Number
Judah	Nahshon son of Amminadab	74,600
Issachar	Nethanel son of Zuar	54,400
Zebulun	Eliab son of Helon	57,400
Total:		186,400

The division of Judah shall march first.

10-16 On the south, those under the banner of the division of Reuben shall camp in their groups, under their leaders, as follows:

Tribe	Leader	Number
Reuben	Elizur son of Shedeur	46,500
Simeon	Shelumiel son of Zurishaddai	59,300
Gad	Eliasaph son of Deuel	45,650
Total:		151,450

The division of Reuben shall march second.

17 Then, between the first two divisions and the last two the Levites are to march carrying the Tent. Each division shall march in the same order as they camp, each in position under its banner.

18-24 On the west, those under the banner of the division of Ephraim shall camp in their groups, under their leaders, as follows:

Tribe	Leader	Number
Ephraim	Elishama son of Ammihud	40,500
Manasseh	Gamaliel son of Pedahzur	32,200
Benjamin	Abidan son of Gideoni	35,400
Total:		108,100

The division of Ephraim shall march third.

25-31 On the north, those under the banner of the division of Dan shall camp in their groups, under their leaders, as follows:

Tribe	Leader	Number
Dan	Ahiezer son of Ammishaddai	62,700

Asher	Pagiel son of Ochran	41,500
Naphtali	Ahira son of Enan	53,400
Total:		157,600

The division of Dan shall march last.

32 The total number of the people of Israel enrolled in the divisions, group by group, was 603,550. 33 As the LORD had commanded Moses, the Levites were not registered with the rest of the Israelites.

34 So the people of Israel did everything the LORD had commanded Moses. They camped, each under his own banner, and they marched, each with his own clan.

Aaron's Sons

3 This is the family of Aaron and Moses at the time the LORD spoke to Moses on Mount Sinai. 2 Aaron had four sons: Nadab, the eldest, Abihu, Eleazar, and Ithamar. 3 They were anointed and ordained as priests, 4 but Nadab and Abihu were killed when they offered unholy fire to the LORD in the Sinai Desert. They had no children, so Eleazar and Ithamar served as priests during Aaron's lifetime.

The Levites Are Appointed to Serve the Priests

5 The LORD said to Moses, 6 "Bring forward the tribe of Levi and appoint them as servants of Aaron the priest. 7 They shall do the work required for the Tent of my presence and perform duties for the priests and for the whole community. 8 They shall take charge of all the equipment of the Tent and perform the duties for the rest of the Israelites. 9 The only responsibility the Levites have is to serve Aaron and his sons. 10 You shall appoint Aaron and his sons to carry out the duties of the priesthood; anyone else who tries to do so shall be put to death."

11 The LORD said to Moses, 12–13 "The Levites are now to be mine. When I killed all the first-born of the Egyptians, I consecrated as my own the eldest son of each Israelite family and the first-born of every animal. Now, instead of having the first-born sons of Israel as my own, I have the Levites; they will belong to me. I am the LORD."

The Census of the Levites

14 In the Sinai Desert the LORD commanded Moses 15 to register the Levites by clans and families, enrolling every male a month old or older, 16 and

Moses did so. 17–20 Levi had three sons: Gershon, Kohath, and Merari, who were the ancestors of the clans that bear their names. Gershon had two sons: Libni and Shimei; Kohath had four sons: Amram, Izhar, Hebron, and Uzziel; and Merari had two sons: Mahli and Mushi. They were the ancestors of the families that bear their names.

21 The clan of Gershon was composed of the families of Libni and Shimei. 22 The total number of males one month old or older that were enrolled was 7,500. 23 This clan was to camp on the west behind the Tent, 24 with Eliasaph son of Lael as chief of the clan. 25 They were responsible for the Tent, its inner cover, its outer cover, the curtain for the entrance, 26 the curtains for the court which is round the Tent and the altar, and the curtain for the entrance of the court. They were responsible for all the service connected with these items.

27 The clan of Kohath was composed of the families of Amram, Izhar, Hebron, and Uzziel. 28 The total number of males one month old or older that were enrolled was 8,600. 29 This clan was to camp on the south side of the Tent, 30 with Elizaphan son of Uzziel as chief of the clan. 31 They were responsible for the Covenant Box, the table, the lamp-stand, the altars, the utensils the priests use in the Holy Place, and the curtain at the entrance to the Most Holy Place. They were responsible for all the service connected with these items.

32 The chief of the Levites was Eleazar son of Aaron the priest. He was in charge of those who carried out the duties in the Holy Place.

33 The clan of Merari was composed of the families of Mahli and Mushi. 34 The total number of males one month old or older that were enrolled was 6,200. 35 This clan was to camp on the north side of the Tent, with Zuriel son of Abihail as chief of the clan. 36 They were assigned responsibility for the frames for the Tent, its bars, posts, bases, and all its fittings. They were responsible for all the service connected with these items. 37 They were also responsible for the posts, bases, pegs, and ropes for the outer court.

38 Moses and Aaron and his sons were to camp in front of the Tent on the east. They were responsible for carrying out the services performed in the Holy Place for the people of Israel. Anyone else who tried to do so was to be put to death.

3.2: Num 26.60   **3.4:** Lev 10.1-2; Num 26.61   **3.13:** Ex 13.2

[39] The total number of all the Levite males one month old or older that Moses enrolled by clans at the command of the LORD, was 22,000.

The Levites Take the Place of the First-Born Sons

[40-41] The LORD said to Moses, "All of Israel's first-born sons belong to me. So register by name every first-born male Israelite, one month old or older. But in place of them I claim all the Levites as mine! I am the LORD! I also claim the livestock of the Levites in place of all the first-born of the livestock." [42] Moses obeyed, and registered all the first-born males [43] one month old or older; the total was 22,273.

[44] The LORD said to Moses, [45] "Now dedicate the Levites as mine in place of all the first-born Israelite sons, and dedicate the livestock of the Levites in place of the first-born of the Israelites' livestock. [46] Since the first-born Israelite sons outnumber the Levites by 273, you must buy back the extra sons. [47] For each one pay five pieces of silver, according to the official standard, [48] and give this money to Aaron and his sons." [49] Moses obeyed and took [50] the 1,365 pieces of silver [51] and gave them to Aaron and his sons.

The Duties of the Levite Clan of Kohath

4 The LORD told Moses [2] to take a census of the Levite clan of Kohath by sub-clans and families, [3] and to register all the men between the ages of thirty and fifty who were qualified to work in the Tent of the LORD's presence. [4] Their service involves the most holy things.

[5] The LORD gave Moses the following instructions. When it is time to break camp, Aaron and his sons shall enter the Tent, take down the curtain in front of the Covenant Box, and cover the Box with it. [6] They shall put a fine leather cover over it, spread a blue cloth on top, and then insert the carrying-poles.

[7] They shall spread a blue cloth over the table for the bread offered to the LORD and put on it the dishes, the incense bowls, the offering bowls, and the jars for the wine-offering. There shall always be bread on the table. [8] They shall spread a red cloth over all this, put a fine leather cover over it, and then insert the carrying-poles. [9] They shall take a blue cloth and cover the lampstand, with its lamps, tongs, trays, and all the olive-oil containers.

[10] They shall wrap it and all its equipment in a fine leather cover and place it on a carrying-frame.

[11] Next they shall spread a blue cloth over the gold altar, put a fine leather cover over it, and then insert the carrying-poles. [12] They shall take all the utensils used in the Holy Place, wrap them in a blue cloth, put a fine leather cover over them, and place them on a carrying-frame. [13] They shall remove the greasy ashes from the altar and spread a purple cloth over it. [14] They shall put on it all the equipment used in the service at the altar: firepans, hooks, shovels, and basins. Then they shall put a fine leather cover over it and insert the carrying-poles. [15] When it is time to break camp, the clan of Kohath shall come to carry the sacred objects only after Aaron and his sons have finished covering them and all their equipment. The clan of Kohath must not touch the sacred objects, or they will die.

These are the responsibilities of the clan of Kohath whenever the Tent is moved.

[16] Eleazar son of Aaron the priest shall be responsible for the whole Tent and for the oil for the lamps, the incense, the grain-offerings, the anointing oil, and everything else in the Tent that has been consecrated to the LORD.

[17] The LORD said to Moses and Aaron, [18] "Do not let the clan of Kohath [19] be killed by coming near these most sacred objects. To prevent this happening, Aaron and his sons shall go in and assign each man his task and tell him what to carry. [20] But if the Kohathites enter the Tent and see the priests preparing the sacred objects for moving, [a] they will die."

The Duties of the Levite Clan of Gershon

[21] The LORD told Moses [22] to take a census of the Levite clan of Gershon by sub-clans and families, [23] and to register all the men between the ages of thirty and fifty who were qualified to work in the Tent of the LORD's presence. [24] They shall be responsible for carrying the following objects: [25] the Tent, its inner cover, its outer cover, the fine leather cover on top of it, the curtain for the entrance, [26] the curtains and ropes for the court that is round the Tent and the altar, the curtains for the entrance of the court, and all the fittings used in setting up these objects. They shall perform all the tasks required for these things. [27] Moses and Aaron shall see to it that the Gershonites

---

[a] see...moving; or see the sacred objects even for a moment.

They shall be responsible (4.24)

perform all the duties and carry everything that Aaron and his sons assign to them. 28 These are the responsibilites of the Gershon clan in the Tent; they shall carry them out under the direction of Ithamar son of Aaron the priest.

The Duties of the Levite Clan of Merari

29 The LORD told Moses to take a census of the Levite clan of Merari by sub-clans and families, 30 and to register all the men between the ages of thirty and fifty who were qualified to work in the Tent of the LORD's presence. 31 They shall be responsible for carrying the frames, bars, posts, and bases of the Tent, 32 and the posts, bases, pegs, and ropes of the court round the Tent, with all the fittings used in setting them up. Each man will be responsible for carrying specific items. 33 These are the responsibilities of the Merari clan in their service in the Tent: they shall carry them out under the direction of Ithamar son of Aaron the priest.

The Census of the Levites

34-48 Following the LORD's command, Moses, Aaron, and the leaders of the community took a census of the three Levite clans, Kohath, Gershon, and Merari. They did this by sub-clans and families and registered all the men between the ages of thirty and fifty who were qualified to work in the Tent of the LORD's presence, as follows:

Clan	Number
Kohath	2,750
Gershon	2,630
Merari	3,200
Total:	8,580

49 Each man was registered as the LORD had commanded Moses; and at the command of the LORD given through Moses, each man was assigned responsibility for his task of serving or carrying.

Unclean People

5 The LORD said to Moses, 2 "Command the people of Israel to expel from the camp everyone with a dreaded skin disease or a bodily discharge and everyone who is unclean by contact with a corpse. 3 Send all these ritually unclean people out, so that they will not defile the camp, where I live among my people." 4 The Israelites obeyed and expelled them all from the camp.

Repayment for Wrongs Done

5 The LORD gave Moses 6 the following instructions for the people of Israel. When anyone is unfaithful to the LORD and commits a wrong against someone, 7 he must confess his sin and make full repayment, plus an additional twenty per cent, to the person he has wronged. 8 But if that person has died and has no near relative to whom payment can be made, it shall be given to the LORD for the priest. This payment is in addition to the ram used to perform the ritual of purification for the guilty person. 9 Also every special contribution which the Israelites offer to the LORD belongs to the priest to whom they present it. 10 Each priest shall keep the offerings presented to him.

Cases of Wives with Suspicious Husbands

11 The LORD commanded Moses 12-14 to give the Israelites the following instructions. It may happen that a man becomes

5.5-8: Lev 6.1-7

suspicious that his wife is unfaithful to him and has defiled herself by having intercourse with another man. But the husband may not be certain, for his wife may have kept it secret—there was no witness, and she was not caught in the act. Or it may happen that a husband becomes suspicious of his wife, even though she has not been unfaithful. 15 In either case the man shall take his wife to the priest. He shall also take the required offering of one kilogramme of barley flour, but he shall not pour any olive-oil on it or put any incense on it, because it is an offering from a suspicious husband, made to bring the truth to light.

16 The priest shall bring the woman forward and make her stand in front of the altar. 17 He shall pour some holy water into a clay bowl and take some of the earth that is on the floor of the Tent of the LORD's presence and put it in the water to make it bitter. 18 Then he shall loosen the woman's hair and put the offering of flour in her hands. In his hands the priest shall hold the bowl containing the bitter water that brings a curse. 19 Then the priest shall make the woman agree to this oath spoken by the priest: "If you have not committed adultery, you will not be harmed by the curse that this water brings. 20 But if you have committed adultery, 21 may the LORD make your name a curse among your people. May he cause your genital organs to shrink and your stomach to swell up. 22 May this water enter your stomach and cause it to swell up and your genital organs to shrink."

The woman shall respond, "I agree; may the LORD do so."

23 Then the priest shall write this curse down and wash the writing off into the bowl of bitter water. 24 Before he makes the woman drink the water, which may then cause her bitter pain, 25 the priest shall take the offering of flour out of the woman's hands, hold it out in dedication to the LORD, and present it on the altar. 26 Then he shall take a handful of it as a token offering and burn it on the altar. Finally, he shall make the woman drink the water. 27 If she has committed adultery, the water will cause bitter pain; her stomach will swell up and her genital organs will shrink. Her name will become a curse among her people. 28 But if she is innocent, she will not be harmed and will be able to bear children.

29–30 This is the law in cases where

a man is jealous and becomes suspicious that his wife has committed adultery. The woman shall be made to stand in front of the altar, and the priest shall perform this ritual. 31 The husband shall be free of guilt, but the woman, if guilty, must suffer the consequences.

Rules for Nazirites

6 The LORD commanded Moses 2 to give the following instructions to the people of Israel. Any man or woman who makes a special vow to become a Nazirite and dedicates himself to the LORD 3 shall abstain from wine and beer. He shall not drink any kind of drink made from grapes or eat any grapes or raisins. 4 As long as he is a Nazirite, he shall not eat anything that comes from a grapevine, not even the seeds or skins of grapes.

5 As long as he is under the Nazirite vow, he must not cut his hair or shave. He is bound by the vow for the full time that he is dedicated to the LORD, and he shall let his hair and beard grow. 6–7 His hair is the sign of his dedication to God, and so he must not defile himself by going near a corpse, not even that of his father, mother, brother, or sister. 8 As long as he is a Nazirite, he is consecrated to the LORD.

9 If the consecrated hair of a Nazirite is defiled because he is right beside someone who suddenly dies, he must wait seven days and then shave off his hair and beard; and so he becomes ritually clean. 10 On the eighth day he shall bring two doves or two pigeons to the priest at the entrance of the Tent of the LORD's presence. 11 The priest shall offer one as a sin-offering and the other as a burnt-offering, to perform the ritual of purification for him because of his contact with a corpse. On the same day the man shall reconsecrate his hair 12 and rededicate to the LORD his time as a Nazirite. The previous period of time doesn't count, because his consecrated hair was defiled. As a repayment offering he shall bring a one-year-old lamb.

13 When a Nazirite completes his vow, he shall perform the ritual. He shall go to the entrance of the Tent 14 and present to the LORD three animals without any defects: a one-year-old male lamb for a burnt-offering, a one-year-old ewe lamb for a sin-offering, and a ram for a fellowship-offering. 15 He shall also offer a basket of bread made without yeast:

6.3: Lk 1.15   **6.13–21:** Acts 21.23–24

thick loaves made of flour mixed with olive-oil and biscuits brushed with olive-oil, and in addition the required offerings of corn and wine.

16 The priest shall present all these to the LORD and offer the sin-offering and the burnt-offering. 17 He shall sacrifice the ram to the LORD as a fellowship-offering, and offer it with the basket of bread; he shall also present the offerings of corn and wine. 18 At the entrance of the Tent the Nazirite shall shave off his hair and put it on the fire on which the fellowship-offering is being burnt.

19 Then, when the shoulder of the ram is boiled, the priest shall take it and put it, together with one thick loaf of bread and one biscuit from the basket, into the hands of the Nazirite. 20 Next, the priest shall present them as a special gift to the LORD; they are a sacred offering for the priest, in addition to the breast and the leg of the ram which by law belong to the priest. After that, the Nazirite may drink wine.

21 These are the regulations for Nazirites; but if a Nazirite promises an offering beyond what his vow requires him to give, he must fulfil exactly the promise he made.

The Priestly Blessing

22 The LORD commanded Moses 23 to tell Aaron and his sons to use the following words in blessing the people of Israel:
24 May the LORD bless you and take care of you;
25 May the LORD be kind and gracious to you;
26 May the LORD look on you with favour and give you peace.

27 And the LORD said, "If they pronounce my name as a blessing upon the people of Israel, I will bless them."

The Offerings of the Leaders

7 On the day Moses finished setting up the Tent of the LORD's presence, he anointed and dedicated the Tent and all its equipment, and the altar and all its equipment. 2 Then the clan chiefs who were leaders in the tribes of Israel, the same men who were in charge of the census, 3 brought their offerings to the LORD: six wagons and twelve oxen, a wagon for every two leaders and an ox for each leader. After they had presented them, 4 the LORD said to Moses, 5 "Accept these gifts for use in the work to be done for the Tent; give them to the Levites

according to the work they have to do." 6 So Moses gave the wagons and the oxen to the Levites. 7 He gave two wagons and four oxen to the Gershonites, 8 and four wagons and eight oxen to the Merarites. All their work was to be done under the direction of Ithamar son of Aaron. 9 But Moses gave no wagons or oxen to the Kohathites, because the sacred objects they took care of had to be carried on their shoulders.

10 The leaders also brought offerings to celebrate the dedication of the altar. When they were ready to present their gifts at the altar, 11 the LORD said to Moses, "Tell them that each day for a period of twelve days one of the leaders is to present his gifts for the dedication of the altar."

12–83 They presented their offerings in the following order:

Day	Tribe	Leader
1st	Judah	Nahshon son of Amminadab
2nd	Issachar	Nethanel son of Zuar
3rd	Zebulun	Eliab son of Helon
4th	Reuben	Elizur son of Shedeur
5th	Simeon	Shelumiel son of Zurishaddai
6th	Gad	Eliasaph son of Deuel
7th	Ephraim	Elishama son of Ammihud
8th	Manasseh	Gamaliel son of Pedahzur
9th	Benjamin	Abidan son of Gideoni
10th	Dan	Ahiezer son of Ammishaddai
11th	Asher	Pagiel son of Ochran
12th	Naphtali	Ahira son of Enan

The offerings each one brought were identical: one silver bowl weighing 1.5 kilogrammes and one silver basin weighing 800 grammes, by the official standard, both of them full of flour mixed with oil for the grain-offering; one gold dish weighing 110 grammes, full of incense; one young bull, one ram, and a one-year-old lamb, for the burnt-offering; one goat for the sin-offering; and two bulls, five rams, five goats, and five one-year-old lambs for the fellowship-offering.

84–88 The totals of the offerings brought by the twelve leaders for the

dedication of the altar were as follows:
—twelve silver bowls and twelve silver
  basins weighing a total of 27.6
  kilogrammes
—twelve gold dishes weighing a total of
  1.32 kilogrammes, filled with incense
—twelve bulls, twelve rams, and twelve
  one-year-old lambs, together with
  the grain-offerings that go with them,
  for the burnt-offerings
—twelve goats for the sin-offerings
—twenty-four bulls, sixty rams, sixty
  goats, sixty one-year-old lambs, for
  the fellowship-offerings

89 When Moses went into the Tent to talk with the LORD, he heard the LORD speaking to him from above the lid on the Covenant Box, between the two winged creatures. *b*

Placing the Lamps

8 The LORD said to Moses, [2] "Tell Aaron that when he puts the seven lamps on the lamp-stand, he should place them so that the light shines towards the front." [3] Aaron obeyed and placed the lamps facing the front of the lamp-stand. [4] From top to bottom the lamp-stand was made of hammered gold, according to the pattern that the LORD had shown Moses.

The Purification and Dedication of the Levites

5 The LORD said to Moses, [6] "Separate the Levites from the rest of the people of Israel and purify them [7] in the following way: sprinkle them with the water of purification and tell them to shave their whole bodies and to wash their clothes. Then they will be ritually clean. [8] Then they are to take a young bull and the required grain-offering of flour mixed with olive-oil; and you are to take another bull for the sin-offering. [9] Then assemble the whole community of Israel and make the Levites stand in front of the Tent of my presence. [10] The people of Israel are to place their hands on the heads of the Levites, [11] and then Aaron shall dedicate the Levites to me as a special gift from the Israelites, so that they may do my work. [12] The Levites shall then put their hands on the heads of the two bulls; one is to be offered as a sin-offering and the other as a burnt-offering, in order to perform the ritual of purification for the Levites. [13] "Dedicate the Levites as a special

gift to me, and put Aaron and his sons in charge of them. [14] Separate the Levites in this way from the rest of the Israelites, so that they will belong to me. [15] After you have purified and dedicated the Levites, they will be qualified to work in the Tent. [16] I have claimed them in the place of all the first-born sons of the Israelites, and they belong to me alone. [17] When I killed all the first-born in Egypt, I consecrated as my own the eldest son of each Israelite family and the first-born of every animal. [18] I am now taking the Levites instead of all the first-born of the Israelites, [19] and I assign the Levites to Aaron and his sons, as a gift from the Israelites, to work in the Tent for the people of Israel and to protect the Israelites from the disaster that would strike them if they came too near the Holy Place."

20 So Moses, Aaron, and all the people of Israel dedicated the Levites, as the LORD commanded Moses. [21] The Levites purified themselves and washed their clothes, and Aaron dedicated them as a special gift to the LORD. He also performed the ritual of purification for them. [22] The people did everything the LORD had commanded Moses concerning the Levites. And so the Levites were qualified to work in the Tent under Aaron and his sons.

23 The LORD said to Moses, [24] "From the age of twenty-five each Levite shall perform his duties in the Tent of my presence, [25] and at the age of fifty he shall retire. [26] After that, he may help his fellow-Levites in performing their duties in the Tent, but he must not perform any service by himself. This is how you are to regulate the duties of the Levites."

The Second Passover

9 The LORD spoke to Moses in the Sinai Desert in the first month of the second year after the people of Israel had left Egypt. He said, [2-3] "On the fourteenth day of this month, beginning at sunset, the people of Israel are to observe the Passover according to all the rules and regulations for it." [4] So Moses told the people to observe the Passover, [5] and on the evening of the fourteenth day of the first month they did so in the Sinai Desert. The people did everything just as the LORD had commanded Moses.

6 But there were some men who were ritually unclean because they had touched a corpse, and they were not able to keep

---

b WINGED CREATURES: *See Word List.*
8.1-4: Ex 25.31-40, 37.17-24   **8.17:** Ex 13.2   **9.1-5:** Ex 12.1-13

the Passover on that day. They went to Moses and Aaron 7 and said, "We are unclean because we have touched a corpse, but why should we be excluded from presenting the LORD's offering with the rest of the Israelites?"

8 Moses answered, "Wait until I receive instructions from the LORD."

9 The LORD told Moses 10 to say to the people of Israel, "When any of you or your descendants are unclean from touching a corpse or are far away on a journey, but still want to keep the Passover, 11 you are permitted to observe it one month later instead, on the evening of the fourteenth day of the second month. Celebrate it with unleavened bread and bitter herbs. 12 Do not leave any of the food until the following morning and do not break any of the animal's bones. Observe the Passover according to all the regulations. 13 But anyone who is ritually clean and not away on a journey and who does not observe the Passover, shall no longer be considered one of my people, because he did not present the offering to me at the appointed time. He must suffer the consequences of his sin.

14 "If a foreigner living among you wants to keep the Passover, he must observe it according to all the rules and regulations. The same law applies to everyone, whether native or foreigner."

The Fiery Cloud
(Ex 40.34-38)

15-16 On the day the Tent of the Lord's presence was set up, a cloud came and covered it. At night the cloud looked like fire. 17 Whenever the cloud lifted, the people of Israel broke camp, and they set up camp again in the place where the cloud came down. 18 The people broke camp at the command of the LORD, and at his command they set up camp. As long as the cloud stayed over the Tent, they stayed in the same camp. 19 When the cloud stayed over the Tent for a long time, they obeyed the LORD and did not move on. 20 Sometimes the cloud remained over the Tent for only a few days; in any case, they remained in camp or moved, according to the command of the LORD. 21 Sometimes the cloud remained only from evening until morning, and they moved on as soon as the cloud lifted. Whenever the cloud lifted, they moved on. 22 Whether it was two days, a month, a year, or longer, as long as the cloud

remained over the Tent, they did not move on; but when it lifted, they moved. 23 They set up camp and broke camp in obedience to the commands which the LORD gave through Moses.

The Silver Trumpets

10 The LORD said to Moses, 2 "Make two trumpets of hammered silver to use for calling the people together and for breaking camp. 3 When long blasts are sounded on both trumpets, the whole community is to gather round you at the entrance to the Tent of my presence. 4 But when only one trumpet is sounded, then only the leaders of the clans are to gather round you. 5 When short blasts are sounded, the tribes camped on the east will move out. 6 When short blasts are sounded a second time, the tribes on the south will move out. So short blasts are to be sounded to break camp, 7 but in order to call the community together, long blasts are to be sounded. 8 The trumpets are to be blown by Aaron's sons, the priests.

"The following rule is to be observed for all time to come. 9 When you are at war in your land, defending yourselves against an enemy who has attacked you, sound the signal for battle on these trumpets. I, the LORD your God, will help you and save you from your enemies. 10 Also on joyful occasions—at your New Moon Festivals and your other religious festivals—you are to blow the trumpets when you present your burnt-offerings and your fellowship-offerings. Then I will help you. I am the LORD your God."

The Israelites Break Camp

11 On the twentieth day of the second month in the second year after the people left Egypt, the cloud over the Tent of the LORD's presence lifted, 12 and the Israelites started on their journey out of the Sinai Desert. The cloud came to rest in the wilderness of Paran.

13 They began to march at the command of the LORD through Moses, 14 and each time they moved, they were in the same order. Those under the banner of the division led by the tribe of Judah started out first, company by company, with Nahshon son of Amminadab in command. 15 Nethanel son of Zuar was in command of the tribe of Issachar, 16 and Eliab son of Helon was in command of the tribe of Zebulun.

9.12: Ex 12.46; Jn 19.36

When only one trumpet is sounded (10.4)

17 Then the Tent would be taken down, and the clans of Gershon and Merari, who carried it, would start out.

18 Next, those under the banner of the division led by the tribe of Reuben would start out, company by company, with Elizur son of Shedeur in command. 19 Shelumiel son of Zurishaddai was in command of the tribe of Simeon, 20 and Eliasaph son of Deuel was in command of the tribe of Gad.

21 Then the Levite clan of Kohath would start out, carrying the sacred objects. By the time they arrived at the next camp, the Tent had been set up again.

22 Next, those under the banner of the division led by the tribe of Ephraim would start out, company by company, with Elishama son of Ammihud in command. 23 Gamaliel son of Pedahzur was in command of the tribe of Manasseh, 24 and Abidan son of Gideoni was in command of the tribe of Benjamin.

25 Finally, those under the banner of the division led by the tribe of Dan, serving as the rearguard of all the divisions, would start out, company by company, with Ahiezer son of Ammishaddai in command. 26 Pagiel son of Ochran was in command of the tribe of Asher, 27 and Ahira son of Enan was in command of the tribe of Naphtali. 28 This, then, was the order of march, company by company, whenever the Israelites broke camp and set out.

29 Moses said to his brother-in-law Hobab son of Jethro the Midianite, "We are about to start out for the place which the LORD said he would give us. He has promised to make Israel prosperous, so come with us, and we will share our prosperity with you."

30 Hobab answered, "No, I am going back to my native land."

31 "Please don't leave us," Moses said. "You know where we can camp in the wilderness, and you can be our guide. 32 If you come with us, we will share with you all the blessings that the LORD gives us."

The People Set Out

33 When the people left Sinai, the holy mountain, they travelled for three days. The LORD's Covenant Box always went ahead of them to find a place for them to camp. 34 As they moved on from each camp, the cloud of the LORD was over them by day.

35 Whenever the Covenant Box started out, Moses would say, "Arise, LORD; scatter your enemies and put to flight those who hate you!" 36 And whenever it stopped, he would say, "Return, LORD, to the thousands of families of Israel." c

The Place Named Taberah

11 The people began to complain to the LORD about their troubles. When the LORD heard them, he was angry and sent fire on the people. It burnt among them and destroyed one end of the camp. 2 The people cried out to Moses for help; he prayed to the LORD, and the fire died

c Return...Israel; *or* Return, LORD, you who are like an army of millions for Israel.
10.35: Ps 68.1

I can't be responsible for all these people (11.14)

down. ³ So the place was named Taberah,ᵈ because there the fire of the LORD burnt among them.

Moses Chooses Seventy Leaders

4 There were some foreigners travelling with the Israelites. They had a strong craving for meat, and even the Israelites themselves began to complain: "If only we could have some meat! ⁵ In Egypt we used to eat all the fish we wanted, and it cost us nothing. Remember the cucumbers, the water-melons, the leeks, the onions, and the garlic we had? ⁶ But now our strength is gone. There is nothing at all to eat—nothing but this manna day after day!"

7 (Manna was like small seeds, whitish yellow in colour. ⁸⁻⁹ It fell on the camp at night along with the dew. The next morning the people would go round and gather it, grind it or pound it into flour, and then boil it and make it into flat cakes. It tasted like bread baked with olive-oil.)

10 Moses heard all the people complaining as they stood about in groups at the entrances of their tents. He was distressed because the LORD was angry with them, ¹¹ and he said to the LORD, "Why have you treated me so badly? Why are you displeased with me? Why have you given me the responsibility for all these people? ¹² I didn't create them or bring them to birth! Why should you ask me to act like a nurse and carry them in my arms like babies all the way to the land you promised to their ancestors? ¹³ Where could I get enough meat for all these people? They keep whining and asking for meat. ¹⁴ I can't be responsible for all these people by myself; it's too much for me! ¹⁵ If you are going to treat me like this, take pity on me and kill me, so that I won't have to endure your cruelty any longer."

16 The LORD said to Moses, "Assemble seventy respected men who are recognized as leaders of the people, bring them to me at the Tent of my presence, and tell them to stand there beside you. ¹⁷ I will come down and speak with you there, and I will take some of the spirit I have given you and give it to them. Then they can help you to bear the responsibility for these people, and you will not have to bear it alone. ¹⁸ Now tell the people, 'Purify yourselves for tomorrow; you will have meat to eat. The LORD has heard you whining and saying that you wished you had some meat and that you were better off in Egypt. Now the LORD will give you meat, and you will have to eat it. ¹⁹ You will have to eat it not just for one or two days, or five, or ten, or even twenty days, ²⁰ but for a whole month, until it comes out of your ears, until you

ᵈTABERAH: *This name sounds like the Hebrew for "burning."*
11.7–8: Ex 16.31   **11.9:** Ex 16.13–15

are sick of it. This will happen because you have rejected the Lord who is here among you and have complained to him that you should never have left Egypt.'"

21 Moses said to the Lord, "Here I am leading 600,000 people, and you say that you will give them enough meat for a month? 22 Could enough cattle and sheep be killed to satisfy them? Are all the fish in the sea enough for them?"

23 "Is there a limit to my power?" the Lord answered. "You will soon see whether what I have said will happen or not!"

24 So Moses went out and told the people what the Lord had said. He assembled seventy of the leaders and placed them round the Tent. 25 Then the Lord came down in the cloud and spoke to him. He took some of the spirit he had given to Moses and gave it to the seventy leaders. When the spirit came on them, they began to shout like prophets, but not for long.

26 Two of the seventy leaders, Eldad and Medad, had stayed in the camp and had not gone out to the Tent. There in the camp the spirit came on them, and they too began to shout like prophets. 27 A young man ran out to tell Moses what Eldad and Medad were doing.

28 Then Joshua son of Nun, who had been Moses' helper since he was a young man, spoke up and said to Moses, "Stop them, sir!"

29 Moses answered, "Are you concerned about my interests? I wish that the Lord would give his spirit to all his people and make all of them shout like prophets!" 30 Then Moses and the seventy leaders of Israel went back to camp.

The Lord Sends Quails

31 Suddenly the Lord sent a wind that brought quails from the sea, flying less than a metre above the ground. They settled on the camp and all round it for many kilometres in every direction. e 32 So all that day, all night, and all the next day, the people worked catching quails;

e sea, flying...direction; or sea. They settled in the camp and all round it for many kilometres in every direction, until they were piled up nearly a metre deep on the ground.

Catching quails (11.32)

O God, heal her! (12.13)

no one gathered less than a thousand kilogrammes. They spread them out to dry all round the camp. ³³While there was still plenty of meat for them to eat, the LORD became angry with the people and caused an epidemic to break out among them. ³⁴That place was named Kiboth Hattaavah (which means "Graves of Craving"), because there they buried the people who had craved meat.

35 From there the people moved to Hazeroth, where they made camp.

Miriam Is Punished

12 Moses had married a Cushite*ᶠ* woman, and Miriam and Aaron criticized him for it. ²They said, "Has the LORD spoken only through*ᵍ* Moses? Hasn't he also spoken through*ᵍ* us?" The LORD heard what they said. ³(Moses was a humble man, more humble than anyone else on earth.)

4 Suddenly the LORD said to Moses, Aaron, and Miriam, "I want the three of you to come out to the Tent of my presence." They went, ⁵and the LORD came down in a pillar of cloud, stood at the entrance of the Tent, and called out, "Aaron! Miriam!" The two of them stepped forward, ⁶and the LORD said, "Now hear what I have to say! When

there are prophets among you,*ʰ* I reveal myself to them in visions and speak to them in dreams. ⁷It is different when I speak with my servant Moses; I have put him in charge of all my people Israel.*ⁱ* ⁸So I speak to him face to face, clearly and not in riddles; he has even seen my form! How dare you speak against my servant Moses?"

9 The LORD was angry with them; and so as he departed ¹⁰and the cloud left the Tent, Miriam's skin was suddenly covered with a dreaded disease and turned as white as snow. When Aaron looked at her and saw that she was covered with the disease, ¹¹he said to Moses, "Please, sir, do not make us suffer this punishment for our foolish sin. ¹²Don't let her become like something born dead with half its flesh eaten away."

13 So Moses cried out to the LORD, "O God, heal her!"

14 The LORD answered. "If her father had spat in her face, she would have to bear her disgrace for seven days. So let her be shut out of the camp for a week, and after that she can be brought back in." ¹⁵Miriam was shut out of the camp for seven days, and the people did not move on until she was brought back in. ¹⁶Then they left Hazeroth and set up camp in the wilderness of Paran.

*ᶠ*Cushite *(compare Hab 3.7);* or Midianite; *or* Sudanese.   *ᵍ*through; *or to.*
*ʰ*Some ancient translations When...you; *Hebrew unclear.*
*ⁱ*I have put...Israel; *or he can be trusted with all my affairs.*
12.7: Heb 3.2   **12.14:** Num 5.2-3

It took two men to carry it (13.23)

The Spies
(Deut 1.19-33)

13 The LORD said to Moses, 2 "Choose one of the leaders from each of the twelve tribes and send them as spies to explore the land of Canaan, which I am giving to the Israelites." 3-15 Moses obeyed and from the wilderness of Paran he sent out leaders, as follows;

Tribe	Leader
Reuben	Shammua son of Zaccur
Simeon	Shaphat son of Hori
Judah	Caleb son of Jephunneh
Issachar	Igal son of Joseph
Ephraim	Hoshea son of Nun
Benjamin	Palti son of Raphu
Zebulun	Gaddiel son of Sodi
Manasseh	Gaddi son of Susi
Dan	Ammiel son of Gemalli
Asher	Sethur son of Michael
Naphtali	Nahbi son of Vophsi
Gad	Geuel son of Machi

16 These are the spies Moses sent to explore the land. He changed the name of Hoshea son of Nun to Joshua.

17 When Moses sent them out, he said to them, "Go north from here into the southern part of the land of Canaan and then on into the hill-country. 18 Find out what kind of country it is, how many people live there, and how strong they are. 19 Find out whether the land is good or bad and whether the people live in open towns or in fortified cities. 20 Find out whether the soil is fertile and whether the land is wooded. And be sure to bring back some of the fruit that grows there."

(It was the season when grapes were beginning to ripen.)

21 So the men went north and explored the land from the wilderness of Zin in the south all the way to Rehob, near Hamath Pass in the north. 22 They went first into the southern part of the land and came to Hebron, where the clans of Ahiman, Sheshai, and Talmai, the descendants of a race of giants called the Anakim, lived. (Hebron was founded seven years before Zoan in Egypt.) 23 They came to the Valley of Eshcol, and there they cut off a branch which had one bunch of grapes on it so heavy that it took two men to carry it on a pole between them. They also brought back some pomegranates and figs. 24 (That place was named the Valley of Eshcol*j* because of the bunch of grapes the Israelites cut off there.)

25 After exploring the land for forty days, the spies returned 26 to Moses, Aaron, and the whole community of Israel at Kadesh in the wilderness of Paran. They reported what they had seen and showed them the fruit they had brought. 27 They said to Moses, "We explored the land and found it to be rich and fertile; and here is some of its fruit. 28 But the people who live there are powerful, and their cities are very large and well fortified. Even worse, we saw the descendants of the giants there. 29 Amalekites live in the southern part of the land; Hittites, Jebusites, and Amorites live in the hill-country; and Canaanites live by the Mediterranean Sea and along the River Jordan."

30 Caleb silenced the people who were

j ESHCOL: *This name in Hebrew means "bunch of grapes."*

complaining against *k* Moses, and said, "We should attack now and take the land; we are strong enough to conquer it."

31 But the men who had gone with Caleb said, "No, we are not strong enough to attack them; the people there are more powerful than we are." 32 So they spread a false report among the Israelites about the land they had explored. They said, "That land doesn't even produce enough to feed the people who live there. Everyone we saw was very tall, 33 and we even saw giants there, the descendants of Anak. We felt as small as grasshoppers, and that is how we must have looked to them."

The People Complain

14 All night long the people cried out in distress. 2 They complained against Moses and Aaron, and said, "It would have been better to die in Egypt or even here in the wilderness! 3 Why is the LORD taking us into that land? We will be killed in battle, and our wives and children will be captured. Wouldn't it be better to go back to Egypt?" 4 So they said to one another, "Let's choose a leader and go back to Egypt!"

5 Then Moses and Aaron bowed to the ground in front of all the people. 6 And Joshua son of Nun and Caleb son of Jephunneh, two of the spies, tore their clothes in sorrow 7 and said to the people, "The land we explored is an excellent land. 8 If the LORD is pleased with us, he will take us there and give us that rich and fertile land. 9 Do not rebel against the LORD and don't be afraid of the people who live there. We will conquer them easily. The LORD is with us and has defeated the gods who protected them; so don't be afraid." 10 The whole community was threatening to stone them to death, but suddenly the people saw the dazzling light of the LORD's presence appear over the tent.

Moses Prays for the People

11 The LORD said to Moses, "How much longer will these people reject me? How much longer will they refuse to trust in me, even though I have performed so many miracles among them? 12 I will send an epidemic and destroy them, but I will make you the father of a nation that is larger and more powerful than they are!"

13 But Moses said to the LORD, "You brought these people out of Egypt by your power. When the Egyptians hear what you have done to your people, 14 they will tell it to the people who live in this land. These people have already heard that you, LORD, are with us, that you are plainly seen when your cloud stops over us, and that you go before us in a pillar of cloud by day and a pillar of fire by night. 15 Now if you kill all your people, the nations who have heard of your fame will say 16 that you killed your people in the wilderness because you were not able to bring them into the land you promised to give them. 17 So now LORD, I pray, show us your power and do what you promised when you said, 18 'I, the LORD, am not easily angered, and I show great love and faithfulness and forgive sin and rebellion. Yet I will not fail to punish children and grandchildren to the third and fourth generation for the sins of their parents.' 19 And now, LORD, according to the greatness of your unchanging love, forgive, I pray, the sin of these people, just as you have forgiven them ever since they left Egypt."

20 The LORD answered, "I will forgive them, as you have asked. 21 But I promise that as surely as I live and as surely as my presence fills the earth, 22 none of these people will live to enter that land. They have seen the dazzling light of my presence and the miracles that I performed in Egypt and in the wilderness, but they have tried my patience over and over again and have refused to obey me. 23 They will never enter the land which I promised to their ancestors. None of those who have rejected me will ever enter it. 24 But because my servant Caleb has a different attitude and has remained loyal to me, I will bring him into the land which he explored, and his descendants will possess the land 25 in whose valleys the Amalekites and the Canaanites now live. Turn back tomorrow and go into the wilderness in the direction of the Gulf of Aqaba."

The Lord Punishes the People for Complaining

26 The LORD said to Moses and Aaron, 27 "How much longer are these wicked people going to complain against me? I have heard enough of these complaints!

k complaining against; *or* gathered round.
13.33: Gen 6.4   **14.9:** Heb 3.16   **14.13–19:** Ex 32.11–14
14.18: Ex 20.5–6, 34.6–7; Deut 5.9–10, 7.9–10   **14.21–23:** Heb 3.18   **14.24:** Josh 14.9–12

²⁸ Now give them this answer: 'I swear that as surely as I live, I will do to you just what you have asked. I, the LORD, have spoken. ²⁹ You will die and your corpses will be scattered across this wilderness. Because you have complained against me, none of you over twenty years of age will enter that land. ³⁰ I promised to let you live there, but not one of you will, except Caleb and Joshua. ³¹ You said that your children would be captured, but I will bring them into the land that you rejected, and it will be their home. ³² You will die here in this wilderness. ³³ Your children will wander in the wilderness for forty years, suffering for your unfaithfulness, until the last one of you dies. ³⁴ You will suffer the consequences of your sin for forty years, one year for each of the forty days you spent exploring the land. You will know what it means to have me against you! ³⁵ I swear that I will do this to you wicked people who have gathered together against me. Here in the wilderness every one of you will die. I, the LORD, have spoken.' "

36-37 The men Moses had sent to explore the land brought back a false report which caused the people to complain against the LORD. And so the LORD struck them with a disease, and they died. ³⁸ Of the twelve spies only Joshua and Caleb survived.

The First Attempt to Invade the Land
(Deut 1.41-46)

39 When Moses told the Israelites what the LORD had said, they mourned bitterly. ⁴⁰ Early the next morning they started out to invade the hill-country, saying, "Now we are ready to go to the place which the LORD told us about. We admit that we have sinned."

41 But Moses said, "Then why are you disobeying the LORD now? You will not succeed! ⁴² Don't go. The LORD is not with you, and your enemies will defeat you. ⁴³ When you face the Amalekites and the Canaanites, you will die in battle; the LORD will not be with you, because you have refused to follow him."

44 Yet they still dared to go up into the hill-country, even though neither the LORD's Covenant Box nor Moses left the camp. ⁴⁵ Then the Amalekites and the Canaanites who lived there attacked and defeated them, and pursued them as far as Hormah.

Laws about Sacrifice

15 The LORD gave Moses ² the following regulations for the people of Israel to observe in the land that he was going to give them. ³ A bull, a ram, a sheep, or a goat may be presented to the LORD as a burnt-offering or as a sacrifice in fulfilment of a vow or as a freewill offering or as an offering at your regular religious festivals; the smell of these food-offerings is pleasing to the LORD. ⁴⁻⁵ Whoever presents a sheep or a goat as a burnt-offering to the LORD is to bring with each animal a kilogramme of flour mixed with a litre of olive-oil as a grain-offering, together with a litre of wine. ⁶ When a ram is offered, two kilogrammes of flour mixed with one and a half litres of olive-oil are to be presented as a grain-offering, ⁷ together with one and a half litres of wine. The smell of these sacrifices is pleasing to the LORD. ⁸ When a bull is offered to the LORD as a burnt-offering or as a sacrifice in fulfilment of a vow or as a fellowship-offering, ⁹ a grain-offering of three kilogrammes of flour mixed with two litres of olive-oil is to be presented, ¹⁰ together with two litres of wine. The smell of this sacrifice is pleasing to the LORD.

11 That is what shall be offered with each bull, ram, sheep, or goat. ¹² When more than one animal is offered, the accompanying offering is to be increased proportionately. ¹³ Every native Israelite is to do this when he presents a food-offering, a smell pleasing to the LORD. ¹⁴ And if at any time a foreigner living among you, whether on a temporary or a permanent basis, makes a food-offering, a smell that pleases the LORD, he is to observe the same regulations. ¹⁵ For all time to come, the same*ᴵ* rules are binding on you and on the foreigners who live among you. You and they are alike in the LORD's sight; ¹⁶ the same laws and regulations apply to you and to them.

17 The LORD gave Moses ¹⁸ the following regulations for the people of Israel to observe in the land that he was going to give them. ¹⁹ When any food produced there is eaten, some of it is to be set aside as a special contribution to the LORD. ²⁰ When you bake bread, the first loaf of the first bread made from the new corn is to be presented as a special contribution to the LORD. This is to be presented in

ᴵ Some ancient translations the same; *Hebrew* the congregation the same.
14.29: Heb 3.17   **14.33:** Acts 7.36   **15.16:** Lev 24.22

the same way as the special contribution you make from the corn you thresh. 21 For all time to come, this special gift is to be given to the LORD from the bread you bake.

22 But suppose someone unintentionally fails to keep some of these regulations which the LORD has given Moses. 23 And suppose that in the future the community fails to do everything that the LORD commanded through Moses. 24 If the mistake was made because of the ignorance of the community, they are to offer a bull as a burnt-offering, a smell that pleases the LORD, with the proper grain-offering and wine-offering. In addition, they are to offer a male goat as a sin-offering. 25 The priest shall perform the ritual of purification for the community, and they will be forgiven, because the mistake was unintentional and they brought their sin-offering as a food-offering to the LORD. 26 The whole community of Israel and the foreigners living among them will be forgiven, because everyone was involved in the mistake.

27 If an individual sins unintentionally, he is to offer a one-year-old female goat as a sin-offering. 28 At the altar the priest shall perform the ritual of purification to purify the man from his sin, and he will be forgiven. 29 The same regulation applies to everyone who unintentionally commits a sin, whether he is a native Israelite or a resident foreigner.

30 But any person who sins deliberately, whether he is a native or a foreigner, is guilty of treating the LORD with contempt, and he shall be put to death, 31 because he has rejected what the LORD said and has deliberately broken one of his commands. He is responsible for his own death.

The Man Who Broke the Sabbath

32 Once, while the Israelites were still in the wilderness, a man was found gathering firewood on the Sabbath. 33 He was taken to Moses, Aaron, and the whole community, 34 and was put under guard, because it was not clear what should be done with him. 35 Then the LORD said to Moses, "The man must be put to death; the whole community is to stone him to death outside the camp." 36 So the whole community took him outside the camp and stoned him to death, as the LORD had commanded.

Rules about Tassels

37 The LORD commanded Moses 38 to say to the people of Israel: "Make tassels on the corners of your garments and put a blue cord on each tassel. You are to do this for all time to come. 39 The tassels will serve as reminders, and each time you see them you will remember all my commands and obey them; then you will not turn away from me and follow your own wishes and desires. 40 The tassels will remind you to keep all my commands, and you will belong completely to me. 41 I am the LORD your God; I brought you out of Egypt to be your God. I am the LORD."

The Rebellion of Korah, Dathan, and Abiram

16 1-2 Korah son of Izhar, from the Levite clan of Kohath, rebelled against the leadership of Moses. He was joined by three members of the tribe of Reuben—Dathan and Abiram, the sons of Eliab, and On son of Peleth—and by 250 other Israelites, well-known leaders chosen by the community. 3 They assembled before Moses and Aaron and said to them, "You have gone too far! All the members of the community belong to the LORD, and the LORD is with all of us. Why, then, Moses, do you set yourself above the LORD's community?"

4 When Moses heard this, he threw himself on the ground and prayed. 5 Then he said to Korah and his followers, "Tomorrow morning the LORD will show us who belongs to him; he will let the one who belongs to him, that is, the one he has chosen, approach him at the altar. 6-7 Tomorrow morning you and your followers take firepans, put live coals and incense on them, and take them to the altar. Then we will see which of us the LORD has chosen. You Levites are the ones who have gone too far!"

8 Moses continued to speak to Korah. "Listen, you Levites! 9 Do you consider it a small matter that the God of Israel has set you apart from the rest of the community, so that you can approach him, perform your service in the LORD's Tent, and minister to the community and serve them? 10 He has let you and all the other Levites have this honour—and now you are trying to get the priesthood too! 11 When you complain against Aaron, it

is really against the LORD that you and your followers are rebelling."

12 Then Moses sent for Dathan and Abiram, but they said, "We will not come! 13 Isn't it enough that you have brought us out of the fertile land of Egypt to kill us here in the wilderness? Do you also have to lord it over us? 14 You certainly have not brought us into a fertile land or given us fields and vineyards as our possession, and now you are trying to deceive us. We will not come!"

15 Moses was angry and said to the LORD, "Do not accept any offerings these men bring. I have not wronged any of them; I have not even taken one of their donkeys."

16 Moses said to Korah, "Tomorrow you and your 250 followers must come to the Tent of the LORD's presence; Aaron will also be there. 17 Each of you will take his firepan, put incense on it, and then present it at the altar." 18 So every man took his firepan, put live coals and incense on it, and stood at the entrance of the Tent with Moses and Aaron. 19 Then Korah gathered the whole community, and they stood facing Moses and Aaron at the entrance of the Tent. Suddenly the dazzling light of the LORD's presence appeared to the whole community, 20 and the LORD said to Moses and Aaron, 21 "Stand back from these people, and I will destroy them immediately."

22 But Moses and Aaron bowed down with their faces to the ground and said, "O, God, you are the source of all life. When one man sins, do you get angry with the whole community?"

23 The LORD said to Moses, 24 "Tell the people to move away from the tents of Korah, Dathan, and Abiram."

25 Then Moses, accompanied by the leaders of Israel, went to Dathan and Abiram. 26 He said to the people, "Stand away from the tents of these wicked men and don't touch anything that belongs to them. Otherwise, you will be wiped out with them for all their sins." 27 So they moved away from the tents of Korah, Dathan, and Abiram.

Dathan and Abiram had come out and were standing at the entrance of their tents, with their wives and children. 28 Moses said to the people, "This is how you will know that the LORD has sent me to do all these things and that it is not by my own choice that I have done them. 29 If these men die a natural death without some punishment from God, then the

LORD did not send me. 30 But if the LORD does something unheard of, and the earth opens up and swallows them with all they own, so that they go down alive to the world of the dead, you will know that these men have rejected the LORD."

31 As soon as he had finished speaking, the ground under Dathan and Abiram split open 32 and swallowed them and their families, together with all of Korah's followers and their possessions. 33 So they went down alive to the world of the dead, with their possessions. The earth closed over them, and they vanished. 34 All the people of Israel who were there fled when they heard their cry. They shouted, "Run! The earth might swallow us too!"

35 Then the LORD sent a fire that blazed out and burnt up the 250 men who had presented the incense.

The Firepans

36 Then the LORD said to Moses, 37 "Tell Eleazar son of Aaron the priest to remove the bronze firepans from the remains of the men who have been burnt, and scatter the coals from the firepans somewhere else, because the firepans are holy. 38 They became holy when they were presented at the LORD's altar. So take the firepans of these men who were put to death for their sin, beat them into thin plates, and make a covering for the altar. It will be a warning to the people of Israel." 39 So Eleazar the priest took the firepans and had them beaten into thin plates to make a covering for the altar. 40 This was a warning to the Israelites that no one who was not a descendant of Aaron should come to the altar to burn incense for the LORD. Otherwise he would be destroyed like Korah and his men. All this was done as the LORD had commanded Eleazar through Moses.

Aaron Saves the People

41 The next day the whole community complained against Moses and Aaron and said, "You have killed some of the LORD's people." 42 After they had all gathered to protest to Moses and Aaron, they turned towards the Tent and saw that the cloud was covering it and that the dazzling light of the LORD's presence had appeared. 43 Moses and Aaron went and stood in front of the Tent, 44 and the LORD said to Moses, 45 "Stand back from these people, and I will destroy them on the spot!"

The two of them bowed down with their

The earth opens up and swallows them (16.30)

faces to the ground, ⁴⁶and Moses said to Aaron, "Take your firepan, put live coals from the altar in it, and put some incense on the coals. Then hurry with it to the people and perform the ritual of purification for them. Hurry! The LORD's anger has already broken out and an epidemic has already begun." ⁴⁷Aaron obeyed, took his firepan and ran into the middle of the assembled people. When he saw that the plague had already begun, he put the incense on the coals and performed the ritual of purification for the people. ⁴⁸This stopped the plague, and he was left standing between the living and the dead. ⁴⁹The number of people who died was 14,700, not counting those who died in Korah's rebellion. ⁵⁰When the plague had stopped, Aaron returned to Moses at the entrance of the Tent.

Aaron's Stick

17 The LORD said to Moses, ²"Tell the people of Israel to give you twelve sticks, one from the leader of each tribe. Write each man's name on his stick ³and then write Aaron's name on the stick representing Levi. There will be one stick for each tribal leader. ⁴Take them to the Tent of my presence and put them in front of the Covenant Box, where I meet you. ⁵Then the stick of the man I have chosen will sprout. In this way I will put a stop to the constant complaining of these Israelites against you."

6 So Moses spoke to the Israelites, and each of their leaders gave him a stick, one for each tribe, twelve in all, and Aaron's stick was put with them. ⁷Moses then put all the sticks in the Tent in front of the LORD's Covenant Box.

8 The next day, when Moses went into the Tent, he saw that Aaron's stick, representing the tribe of Levi, had sprouted. It had budded, blossomed, and produced ripe almonds! ⁹Moses took all the sticks and showed them to the Israelites. They saw what had happened, and each leader took his own stick back. ¹⁰The LORD said to Moses, "Put Aaron's stick back in front of the Covenant Box. It is to be kept as a warning to the rebel

17.8–10: Heb 9.4

Between the living and the dead (16.48)

Israelites that they will die unless their complaining stops." [11] Moses did as the LORD commanded.

12 The people of Israel said to Moses, "Then that's the end of us! [13] If anyone who even comes near the Tent must die, then we are all as good as dead!"

Duties of Priests and Levites

18 The LORD said to Aaron, "You, your sons, and the Levites must suffer the consequences of any guilt connected with serving in the Tent of my presence; but only you and your sons will suffer the consequences of service in the priesthood. [2] Bring in your relatives, the tribe of Levi, to work with you and help you while you and your sons are serving at the Tent. [3] They are to fulfil their duties to you and their responsibilities for the Tent, but they must not have any contact with sacred objects in the Holy Place or with the altar. If they do, both they and you will be put to death. [4] They are to work with you and fulfil their responsibilities for all the service in the Tent, but no unqualified person may work with you. [5] You and your sons alone must fulfil the responsibilities for the Holy Place and the altar, so that my anger will not again break out against the people of Israel. [6] I am the one who has chosen your relatives the Levites from among the Israelites as a gift to you. They are dedicated to me, so that they can carry out their duties in the Tent. [7] But you and your sons alone shall fulfil all the responsibilities of the priesthood that concern the altar and what is in the Most Holy Place. These things are your responsibility, because I have given you the gift of the priesthood. Any unqualified person who comes near the sacred objects shall be put to death."

The Share of the Priests

8 The LORD said to Aaron, "Remember that I am giving you all the special contributions made to me that are not burnt as sacrifices. I am giving them to you and to your descendants as the part assigned to you for ever. [9] Of the most sacred offerings not burnt on the altar, the following belong to you: the grain-offerings, the sin-offerings, and the repayment offerings. Everything that is presented to me as a sacred offering belongs to you

Aaron's stick...produced ripe almonds (17.8)

and your sons. 10 You must eat these things in a holy place, and only males may eat them; consider them holy.

11 "In addition, any other special contributions that the Israelites present to me shall be yours. I am giving them to you, your sons, and your daughters for all time to come. Every member of your family who is ritually clean may eat them.

12 "I am giving you all the best of the first produce which the Israelites give me each year: olive-oil, wine, and corn. 13 It all belongs to you. Every member of your family who is ritually clean may eat it.

14 "Everything in Israel that has been unconditionally dedicated to me belongs to you.

15 "Every first-born child or animal that the Israelites present to me belongs to you. But you must accept payment to buy back every first-born child, and must also accept payment for every first-born animal that is ritually unclean. 16 Children shall be bought back at the age of one month for the fixed price of five pieces of silver, according to the official standard. 17 But the first-born of cows, sheep, and goats are not to be bought back; they belong completely to me and are to be sacrificed. Throw their blood against the altar and burn their fat as a food-offering, a smell pleasing to me. 18 The meat from them belongs to you, like the breast and the right hind leg of the special offering.

19 "I am giving to you, to your sons, and to your daughters, for all time to come, all the special contributions which the Israelites present to me. This is an unbreakable covenant that I have made with you and your descendants."

20 The LORD said to Aaron, "You will not receive any property that can be inherited, and no part of the land of Israel will be assigned to you. I, the LORD, am all you need."

The Share of the Levites

21 The LORD said, "I have given to the Levites every tithe that the people of Israel present to me. This is in payment for their service in taking care of the Tent of my presence. 22 The other Israelites must no longer approach the Tent and in this way bring on themselves the penalty of death. 23 From now on only the Levites will take care of the Tent and bear the full responsibility for it. This is

a permanent rule that applies also to your descendants. The Levites shall have no permanent property in Israel, 24 because I have given to them as their possession the tithe which the Israelites present to me as a special contribution. That is why I told them that they would have no permanent property in Israel."

The Levites' Tithe

25 The LORD commanded Moses 26 to say to the Levites: "When you receive from the Israelites the tithe that the LORD gives you as your possession, you must present a tenth of it as a special contribution to the LORD. 27 This special contribution will be considered as the equivalent of the offering which the farmer makes of new corn and new wine. 28 In this way you also will present the special contribution that belongs to the LORD from all the tithes which you receive from the Israelites. You are to give this special contribution for the LORD to Aaron the priest. 29 Give it from the best that you receive. 30 When you have presented the best part, you may keep the rest, just as the farmer keeps what is left after he makes his offering. 31 You and your families may eat the rest anywhere, because it is your wages for your service in the Tent. 32 You will not become guilty when you eat it, as long as you have presented the best of it to the LORD. But be sure not to profane the sacred gifts of the Israelites by eating any of the gifts before the best part is offered; if you do, you will be put to death."

Ashes of the Red Cow

19 The LORD commanded Moses and Aaron 2 to give the Israelites the following regulations. Bring to Moses and Aaron a red cow which has no defects and which has never been put to work, 3 and they will give it to Eleazar the priest. It is to be taken outside the camp and killed in his presence.m 4 Then Eleazar is to take some of its blood and with his finger sprinkle it seven times in the direction of the Tent. 5 The whole animal, including skin, meat, blood, and intestines, is to be burnt in the presence of the priest. 6 Then he is to take some cedar-wood, a sprig of hyssop, and a red cord and throw them into the fire. 7 After that, he is to wash his clothes and pour water over himself, and then he may enter the camp; but he remains ritually unclean

m It...presence; or He is to take it outside to the east of the camp and kill it.
18.14: Lev 27.28   **18.21:** Lev 27.30-33; Deut 14.22-29

until evening. [8]The man who burnt the cow must also wash his clothes and pour water over himself, but he also remains unclean until evening. [9]Then a man who is ritually clean is to collect the ashes of the cow and put them in a ritually clean place outside the camp, where they are to be kept for the Israelite community to use in preparing the water for removing ritual uncleanness. This ritual is performed to remove sin. [10]The man who collected the ashes must wash his clothes, but he remains unclean until evening. This regulation is valid for all time to come, both for the Israelites and for the foreigners living among them.

Contact with a Corpse

[11] Whoever touches a corpse is ritually unclean for seven days. [12]He must purify himself with the water for purification on the third day and on the seventh day, and then he will be clean. But if he does not purify himself on both the third and the seventh day, he will not be clean. [13]Whoever touches a corpse and does not purify himself remains unclean, because the water for purification has not been thrown over him. He defiles the LORD'S Tent, and he will no longer be considered one of God's people.

[14] If someone dies in a tent, anyone who is in the tent at the time of death or who enters it becomes ritually unclean for seven days. [15]Every jar and pot in the tent that has no lid[n] on it also becomes unclean. [16]If someone touches a person who has been killed or has died a natural death out of doors or if someone touches a human bone or a grave, he becomes unclean for seven days.

[17] To remove the uncleanness, some ashes from the red cow which was burnt to remove sin shall be taken and put in a pot, and fresh water added. [18]In the first case, someone who is ritually clean is to take a sprig of hyssop, dip it in the water, and sprinkle the tent, everything in it, and the people who were there. In the second case, someone who is ritually clean is to sprinkle the water on the man who had touched the human bone or the dead body or the grave. [19]On the third day and on the seventh the person who is ritually clean is to sprinkle the water on the unclean person. On the seventh day he is to purify the man, who, after washing his clothes and pouring water over himself, becomes ritually clean at sunset.

[20] Anyone who has become ritually unclean and does not purify himself remains unclean, because the water for purification has not been thrown over him. He defiles the LORD'S Tent and will no longer be considered one of God's people. [21]You are to observe this rule for all time to come. The person who sprinkles the water for purification must also wash his clothes; anyone who touches the water remains ritually unclean until evening. [22]Whatever an unclean person touches is unclean, and anyone else who touches it remains unclean until evening.

Events at Kadesh
(Ex 17.1-7)

20 In the first month the whole community of Israel came to the wilderness of Zin and camped at Kadesh. There Miriam died and was buried.

[2] There was no water where they camped, so the people gathered round Moses and Aaron [3]and complained: "It would have been better if we had died in front of the LORD'S Tent along with our fellow-Israelites. [4]Why have you brought us out into this wilderness? Just so that we can die here with our animals? [5]Why did you bring us out of Egypt into this miserable place where nothing will grow? There's no corn, no figs, no grapes, no pomegranates. There is not even any water to drink!" [6]Moses and Aaron moved away from the people and stood at the entrance of the Tent. They bowed down with their faces to the ground, and the dazzling light of the LORD'S presence appeared to them.

[7] The LORD said to Moses, [8]"Take the stick that is in front of the Covenant Box, and then you and Aaron assemble the whole community. There in front of them all speak to that rock over there, and water will gush out of it. In this way you will bring water out of the rock for the people, for them and their animals to drink." [9]Moses went and got the stick, as the LORD had commanded.

[10] He and Aaron assembled the whole community in front of the rock, and Moses said, "Listen, you rebels! Do we have to get water out of this rock for you?" [11]Then Moses raised the stick and struck the rock twice with it, and a great stream

[n]no lid; or no lid fastened.
19.9: Heb 9.13

A great stream of water gushed out (20.11)

of water gushed out, and all the people and animals drank.

12 But the LORD reprimanded Moses and Aaron. He said, "Because you did not have enough faith to acknowledge my holy power before the people of Israel, you will not lead them into the land that I promised to give them."

13 This happened at Meribah,*o* where the people of Israel complained against the LORD and where he showed them that he was holy.

The King of Edom Refuses to Let Israel Pass

14 Moses sent messengers from Kadesh to the king of Edom. They said, "This message is from your kinsmen, the tribes of Israel. You know the hardships we have suffered, 15 how our ancestors went to Egypt, where we lived many years. The Egyptians ill-treated our ancestors and us, 16 and we cried to the LORD for help. He

heard our cry and sent an angel, who led us out of Egypt. Now we are at Kadesh, a town at the border of your territory. 17 Please permit us to pass through your land. We and our cattle will not leave the road or go into your fields or vineyards, and we will not drink from your wells. We will stay on the main road*p* until we are out of your territory."

18 But the Edomites answered, "We refuse to let you pass through our country! If you try, we will march out and attack you."

19 The people of Israel said, "We will stay on the main road, and if we or our animals drink any of your water, we will pay for it—all we want is to pass through."

20 The Edomites repeated, "We refuse!" and they marched out with a powerful army to attack the people of Israel. 21 Because the Edomites would not let the Israelites pass through their

o MERIBAH: *This name in Hebrew means "complaining."* *p* main road; *or* king's highway.

Anyone who was bitten could look at it and be healed (21.8)

territory, the Israelites turned and went another way.

The Death of Aaron

22 The whole community of Israel left Kadesh and arrived at Mount Hor, 23 on the border of Edom. There the LORD said to Moses and Aaron, 24 "Aaron is not going to enter the land which I promised to give to Israel; he is going to die, because the two of you rebelled against my command at Meribah. 25 Take Aaron and his son Eleazar up Mount Hor, 26 and there remove Aaron's priestly robes and put them on Eleazar. Aaron is going to die there." 27 Moses did what the LORD had commanded. They went up Mount Hor in the sight of the whole community, 28 and Moses removed Aaron's priestly robes and put them on Eleazar. There on the top of the mountain Aaron died, and Moses and Eleazar came back down. 29 The whole community learnt that Aaron had died, and they all mourned for him for thirty days.

Victory over the Canaanites

21 When the Canaanite king of Arad in the southern part of Canaan heard that the Israelites were coming by way of Atharim, he attacked them and captured some of them. 2 Then the

Israelites made a vow to the LORD: "If you will let us conquer these people, we will unconditionally dedicate*q* them and their cities to you and will destroy them." 3 The LORD heard them and helped them to conquer the Canaanites. So the Israelites completely destroyed them and their cities, and named the place Hormah.*r*

The Snake Made of Bronze

4 The Israelites left Mount Hor by the road that leads to the Gulf of Aqaba, in order to go round the territory of Edom. But on the way the people lost their patience 5 and spoke against God and Moses. They complained, "Why did you bring us out of Egypt to die in this desert, where there is no food or water? We can't stand any more of this miserable food!" 6 Then the LORD sent poisonous snakes among the people, and many Israelites were bitten and died. 7 The people came to Moses and said, "We sinned when we spoke against the LORD and against you. Now pray to the LORD to take these snakes away." So Moses prayed for the people. 8 Then the LORD told Moses to make a metal snake and put it on a pole, so that anyone who was bitten could look at it and be healed. 9 So Moses made a bronze snake and put it on a pole. Anyone who

q UNCONDITIONALLY DEDICATE: *Anything dedicated in this way belonged completely to the LORD and could not be used; it had to be destroyed.*
r HORMAH: *This name in Hebrew means "destruction."*
20.28: Ex 29.29; Num 33.38; Deut 10.6   **21.1:** Num 33.40   **21.4:** Deut 2.1
21.5-6: 1 Cor 10.9   **21.9:** 2 Kgs 18.4; Jn 3.14

had been bitten would look at the bronze snake and be healed.

From Mount Hor to the Valley of the Moabites

10 The Israelites moved on and camped at Oboth. [11] After leaving that place, they camped at the ruins of Abarim in the wilderness east of Moabite territory. [12] Then they camped in the Valley of Zered. [13] From there they moved again and camped on the north side of the River Arnon, in the wilderness which extends into Amorite territory. (The Arnon was the border between the Moabites and the Amorites.) [14] That is why *The Book of the* LORD's *Battles* speaks of ". . .the town of Waheb in the area of Suphah, and the valleys; the River Arnon, [15] and the slope of the valleys that extend to the town of Ar and towards the border of Moab."

16 From there they went on to a place called Wells, where the LORD said to Moses, "Bring the people together, and I will give them water." [17] At that time the people of Israel sang this song:

"Wells, produce your water;
And we will greet it with a song—
[18] The well dug by princes
And by leaders of the people,
Dug with a royal sceptre
And with their sticks."

They moved from the wilderness to Mattanah, [19] and from there they went on to Nahaliel, and from Nahaliel to Bamoth, [20] and from Bamoth to the valley in the territory of the Moabites, below the top of Mount Pisgah, looking out over the desert.

Victory over King Sihon and King Og
(Deut 2.26—3.11)

21 Then the people of Israel sent messengers to the Amorite king Sihon to say: [22] "Let us pass through your land. We and our cattle will not leave the road and go into your fields or vineyards, and we will not drink water from your wells; we will stay on the main road[s] until we are out of your territory." [23] But Sihon would not permit the people of Israel to pass through his territory. He gathered his army and went out to Jahaz in the wilderness and attacked the Israelites. [24] But the Israelites killed many of the enemy in battle and occupied their land

from the River Arnon north to the Jabbok, that is, to the Ammonites, because the Ammonite border was strongly defended.[t] [25] So the people of Israel captured all the Amorite cities, including Heshbon and all the surrounding towns, and settled in them. [26] Heshbon was the capital city of the Amorite king Sihon, who had fought against the former king of Moab and had captured all his land as far as the River Arnon. [27] That is why the poets sing,

"Come to Heshbon, to King Sihon's city!
We want to see it rebuilt and restored.
[28] Once from this city of Heshbon
Sihon's army went forth like a fire;
It destroyed the city of Ar in Moab
And devoured[u] the hills of the upper
        Arnon.
[29] How terrible for you, people of Moab!
You worshippers of Chemosh are
        brought to ruin!
Your god let the men become refugees,
And the women became captives of the
        Amorite king.
[30] But now their descendants are
        destroyed,
All the way from Heshbon to Dibon,
From Nashim to Nophah, near
        Medeba."[v]

31 So the people of Israel settled in the territory of the Amorites, [32] and Moses sent men to find the best way to attack the city of Jazer. The Israelites captured it and its surrounding towns and drove out the Amorites living there.

33 Then the Israelites turned and took the road to Bashan, and King Og of Bashan marched out with his army to attack them at Edrei. [34] The LORD said to Moses, "Do not be afraid of him. I will give you victory over him, all his people, and his land. Do to him what you did to Sihon, the Amorite king who ruled at Heshbon." [35] So the Israelites killed Og, his sons, and all his people, leaving no survivors, and then they occupied his land.

The King of Moab Sends for Balaam

22 The Israelites moved on and set up camp in the plains of Moab east of the Jordan and opposite Jericho.

2 When the king of Moab, Balak son of Zippor, heard what the Israelites had done to the Amorites and how many Israelites there were, [3] he and all his people became terrified. [4] The Moabites

---

[s] main road; *or* king's highway.
[t] because...strongly defended: *Some ancient translations* as far as Jazer on the Ammonite border.
[u] *One ancient translation* devoured; *Hebrew* the lords of.
[v] *Verse 30 in Hebrew is unclear.*
21.28–29: Jer 48.45–46

HIGHLIGHTS FROM THE STORY OF BALAAM (Chapters 22,23,24)

said to the leaders of the Midianites, "This horde will soon destroy everything round us, like a bull eating the grass in a pasture." So King Balak [5] sent messengers to summon Balaam son of Beor, who was at Pethor near the River Euphrates in the land of Amaw. They brought him this message from Balak: "I want you to know that a whole nation has come from Egypt; its people are spreading out everywhere and threatening to take over our land. [6] They outnumber us, so please come and put a curse on them for me. Then perhaps we will be able to defeat them and drive them out of the land. I know that when you pronounce a blessing, people are blessed, and when you pronounce a curse, they are placed under a curse."

7 So the Moabite and Midianite leaders took with them the payment for the curse, went to Balaam, and gave him Balak's message. [8] Balaam said to them, "Spend the night here, and tomorrow I will report to you whatever the Lord tells me." So the Moabite leaders stayed with Balaam.

9 God came to Balaam and asked, "Who are these men that are staying with you?"

10 He answered, "King Balak of Moab has sent them to tell me [11] that a people who came from Egypt has spread out over the whole land. He wants me to curse them for him, so that he can fight them and drive them out."

12 God said to Balaam, "Do not go with these men, and do not put a curse on the people of Israel, because they have my blessing."

13 The next morning Balaam went to Balak's messengers and said, "Go back home; the Lord has refused to let me go with you." [14] So they returned to Balak and told him that Balaam had refused to come with them.

15 Then Balak sent a larger number of leaders, who were more important than the first. [16] They went to Balaam and gave him this message from Balak: "Please don't let anything prevent you from coming to me! [17] I will reward you richly and do anything you say. Please come and curse these people for me."

18 But Balaam answered, "Even if Balak gave me all the silver and gold in his palace, I could not disobey the command of the Lord my God in even the smallest matter. [19] But please stay the night, as the others did, so that I may learn whether or not the Lord has something else to tell me."

20 That night God came to Balaam and said, "If these men have come to ask you to go with them, get ready to go, but do only what I tell you." [21] So the next morning Balaam saddled his donkey and went with the Moabite leaders.

Balaam and His Donkey

22 God was angry that Balaam was going, and as Balaam was riding along on his donkey, accompanied by his two servants, the angel of the Lord stood in the road to bar his way. [23] When the donkey saw the angel standing there holding a sword, it left the road and turned into the fields. Balaam beat the donkey and brought it back on to the road. [24] Then the angel stood where the road narrowed between two vineyards and had a stone wall on each side. [25] When the donkey saw the angel, it moved over against the wall and crushed Balaam's foot against it. Again Balaam beat the donkey. [26] Once more the angel moved ahead; he stood in a narrow place where there was no room at all to pass on either side. [27] This time, when the donkey saw the angel, it lay down. Balaam lost his temper and began to beat the donkey with his stick. [28] Then the Lord gave the donkey the power of speech, and it said to Balaam, "What have I done to you? Why have you beaten me these three times?"

29 Balaam answered, "Because you have made a fool of me! If I had a sword, I would kill you."

30 The donkey replied, "Am I not the same donkey on which you have ridden all your life? Have I ever treated you like this before?"

"No," he answered.

31 Then the Lord let Balaam see the angel standing there with his sword; and Balaam threw himself face downwards on the ground. [32] The angel demanded, "Why have you beaten your donkey three times like this? I have come to bar your way, because you should not be making this journey. [w] [33] But your donkey saw me and turned aside three times. If it hadn't, I would have killed you and spared the donkey."

34 Balaam replied, "I have sinned. I did not know that you were standing in the road to oppose me; but now if you think

---

[w] *Probable text* you should...journey; *Hebrew unclear.*
22.5: Num 31.8; 2 Pet 2.15-16; Jude 11

it is wrong for me to go on, I will return home."

35 But the angel said, "Go on with these men, but say only what I tell you to say." So Balaam went on with them.

Balak Welcomes Balaam

36 When Balak heard that Balaam was coming, he went to meet him at Ar, a city on the River Arnon at the border of Moab. 37 Balak said to him, "Why didn't you come when I sent for you the first time? Did you think I wasn't able to reward you enough?"

38 Balaam answered, "I came, didn't I? But now, what power have I got? I can say only what God tells me to say." 39 So Balaam went with Balak to the town of Huzoth, 40 where Balak slaughtered cattle and sheep and gave some of the meat to Balaam and the leaders who were with him.

Balaam's First Prophecy

41 Next morning Balak took Balaam up to Bamoth Baal, from where Balaam could see a part of the people of Israel.

23 1 He said to Balak, "Build seven altars here for me, and bring me seven bulls and seven rams."

2 Balak did as he was told, and he and Balaam offered a bull and a ram on each altar. 3 Then Balaam said to Balak, "Stand here by your burnt-offering, while I go to see whether or not the LORD will meet me. I will tell you whatever he reveals to me." So he went alone to the top of a hill, 4 and God met him. Balaam said to him, "I have built the seven altars and offered a bull and a ram on each."

5 The LORD told Balaam what to say and sent him back to Balak to give him his message. 6 So he went back and found Balak still standing by his burnt-offering, with all the leaders of Moab.

7 Balaam uttered this prophecy:
"Balak king of Moab has brought me
From Syria, from the eastern mountains.
'Come and speak for me,' he said.
'Put a curse on the people of Israel.'
8 How can I curse what God has not cursed,
Or speak of doom when the LORD has not?
9 From the high rocks I can see them;
I can watch them from the hills.
They are a nation that lives alone;
They know they are blessed more than other nations.
10 The descendants of Israel are like the dust—
There are too many of them to be counted.
Let me end my days like one of God's people;
Let me die in peace like the righteous."

11 Then Balak said to Balaam, "What have you done to me? I brought you here to curse my enemies, but all you have done is bless them."

12 He answered, "I can say only what the LORD tells me to say."

Balaam's Second Prophecy

13 Then Balak said to Balaam, "Come with me to another place from which you can see only some of the Israelites. Curse them for me from there." 14 He took him to the field of Zophim on the top of Mount Pisgah. There also he built seven altars and offered a bull and a ram on each of them.

15 Balaam said to Balak, "Stand here by your burnt-offering, and I will meet God over there."

16 The LORD met Balaam, told him what to say, and sent him back to Balak to give him his message. 17 So he went back and found Balak still standing by his burnt-offering, with the leaders of Moab. Balak asked what the LORD had said, 18 and Balaam uttered this prophecy:
"Come, Balak son of Zippor,
And listen to what I have to say.
19 God is not like men, who lie;
He is not a human who changes his mind.
Whatever he promises, he does;
He speaks, and it is done.
20 I have been instructed to bless,
And when God blesses, I cannot call it back.
21 I foresee that Israel's future
Will bring her no misfortune or trouble.
The LORD their God is with them;
They proclaim that he is their king.
22 God has brought them out of Egypt;
He fights for them like a wild ox.
23 There is no magic charm, no witchcraft,
That can be used against the nation of Israel. x
Now people will say about Israel,
'Look what God has done!'
24 The nation of Israel is like a mighty lion:
It doesn't rest until it has torn and devoured,

_____

x There...Israel; or No magic charms are used in Israel, no witchcraft is practised there.

Until it has drunk the blood of those
  it has killed."
25 Then Balak said to Balaam, "You
refuse to curse the people of Israel, but
at least don't bless them!"
26 Balaam answered, "Didn't I tell you
that I had to do everything that the LORD
told me?"

Balaam's Third Prophecy

27 Balak said, "Come with me, and I
will take you to another place. Perhaps
God will be willing to let you curse them
for me from there." 28 So he took Balaam
to the top of Mount Peor overlooking the
desert. 29 Balaam said to him, "Build seven
altars for me here and bring me seven
bulls and seven rams." 30 Balak did as he
was told, and offered a bull and a ram
on each altar.

24 By now Balaam knew that the
LORD wanted him to bless the
people of Israel, so he did not go to look
for omens, as he had done before. He
turned towards the desert 2 and saw the
people of Israel camped tribe by tribe.
The spirit of God took control of him,
3 and he uttered this prophecy:
  "The message of Balaam son of Beor,
  The words of the man who can see
    clearly, y
4 Who can hear what God is saying.
  With staring eyes I see in a trance
  A vision from Almighty God.
5 The tents of Israel are beautiful,
6 Like long rows of palms
  Or gardens beside a river,
  Like aloes planted by the LORD
  Or cedars beside the water.
7 They will have abundant rainfall
  And plant their seed in well-watered
    fields. z
  Their king shall be greater than Agag,
  And his rule shall be extended far and
    wide.
8 God brought them out of Egypt;
  He fights for them like a wild ox.
  They devour their enemies,
  Crush their bones, smash their arrows.
9 The nation is like a mighty lion;
  When it is sleeping, no one dares wake
    it.
  Whoever blesses Israel will be blessed,
  And whoever curses Israel will be
    cursed."

10 Balak clenched his fists in anger and
said to Balaam, "I called you to curse
my enemies, but three times now you have
blessed them instead. 11 Now go off home!
I promised to reward you, but the LORD
has kept you from getting the reward."
12 Balaam answered, "I told the messengers you sent to me that 13 even if you
gave me all the silver and gold in your
palace, I could not disobey the command
of the LORD by doing anything of myself.
I will say only what the LORD tells me
to say."

Balaam's Final Prophecies

14 Balaam said to Balak, "Now I am
going back to my own people, but before
I go, I am warning you what the people
of Israel will do to your people in the
future." 15 Then he uttered this prophecy:
  "The message of Balaam son of Beor,
  The words of the man who can see
    clearly, a
16 Who can hear what God is saying
  And receive the knowledge that comes
    from the Most High.
  With staring eyes I see in a trance
  A vision from Almighty God.
17 I look into the future,
  And I see the nation of Israel.
  A king, like a bright star, will arise in
    that nation.
  Like a comet he will come from Israel.
  He will strike the leaders of Moab
  And beat down all the people of Seth. b
18 He will conquer his enemies in Edom
  And make their land his property,
  While Israel continues victorious.
19 The nation of Israel will trample them
    down
  And wipe out the last survivors."
20 Then in his vision Balaam saw the
Amalekites and uttered this prophecy:
  "Amalek was the most powerful nation
    of all,
  But at the end it will perish for ever."
21 In his vision he saw the Kenites, and
uttered this prophecy:
  "The place where you live is secure,
  Safe as a nest set high on a cliff,
22 But you Kenites will be destroyed
  When Assyria takes you captive." c
23 Balaam uttered this prophecy:
  "Who are these people gathering in the
    north? d

y who can see clearly; or whose eyes are closed.
z One ancient translation They...fields; Hebrew unclear.
a who can see clearly; or whose eyes are closed.
b the people of Seth; or who are proud and violent.
c Verse 22 in Hebrew is unclear.
d Probable text Who...north; Hebrew unclear.
24.9: Gen 12.3, 49.9

24 Invaders will sail from Cyprus;
  They will conquer Assyria and Eber,
  But they, in turn, will perish for ever."
25 Then Balaam got ready and went back home, and Balak went on his way.

The People of Israel at Peor

25 When the Israelites were camped in the Valley of Acacia, the men began to have sexual intercourse with the Moabite women who were there. 2 These women invited them to sacrificial feasts, where the god of Moab was worshipped. The Israelites ate the food and worshipped the god 3 Baal of Peor. So the LORD was angry with them 4 and said to Moses, "Take all the leaders of Israel and, in obedience to me, execute them in broad daylight,e and then I will no longer be angry with the people." 5 Moses said to the officials, "Each of you is to kill every man in your tribe who has become a worshipper of Baal of Peor."

6 One of the Israelites took a Midianite woman into his tent in the sight of Moses and the whole community, while they were mourning at the entrance of the Tent of the LORD's presence. 7 When Phinehas, the son of Eleazar and grandson of Aaron the priest, saw this, he got up and left the assembly. He took a spear, 8 followed the man and the woman into the tent, and drove the spear through both of them. In this way the epidemic that was destroying Israel was stopped, 9 but it had already killed twenty-four thousand people.

10 The LORD said to Moses, 11 "Because of what Phinehas has done, I am no longer angry with the people of Israel. He refused to tolerate the worship of any god but me, and that is why I did not destroy them in my anger. 12 So tell him that I am making a covenant with him that is valid for all time to come. 13 He and his descendants are permanently established as priests, because he did not tolerate any rivals to me and brought about forgiveness for the people's sin."

14 The name of the Israelite who was killed with the Midianite woman was Zimri son of Salu, the head of a family in the tribe of Simeon. 15 The woman's name was Cozbi. Zur, her father, was chief of a group of Midianite clans.

16 The LORD commanded Moses, 17 "Attack the Midianites and destroy them, 18 because of the evil they did to you when they deceived you at Peor, and because of Cozbi, who was killed at the time of the epidemic at Peor."

The Second Census

26 After the epidemic the LORD said to Moses and Eleazar son of Aaron, 2 "Take a census by families of the whole community of Israel, of all men twenty years old or older who are fit for military service." 3-4 Moses and Eleazar obeyed, and called together all the men of that age group. They assembled in the plains of Moab across the River Jordan from Jericho.

These were the Israelites who came out of Egypt:

5 The tribe of Reuben (Reuben was the eldest son of Jacob): the clans of Hanoch, Pallu, 6 Hezron, and Carmi. 7 These clans numbered 43,730 men. 8 The descendants of Pallu were Eliab 9 and his sons Nemuel, Dathan, and Abiram. (These are the Dathan and Abiram who were chosen by the community. They defied Moses and Aaron and joined the followers of Korah when they rebelled against the LORD. 10 The ground opened and swallowed them, and they died with Korah and his followers when fire destroyed 250 men; they became a warning to the people. 11 But the sons of Korah were not killed.)

12 The tribe of Simeon: the clans of Nemuel, Jamin, Jachin, 13 Zerah, and Shaul. 14 These clans numbered 22,200 men.

15 The tribe of Gad: the clans of Zephon, Haggi, Shuni, 16 Ozni, Eri, 17 Arod, and Areli. 18 These clans numbered 40,500 men.

19-21 The tribe of Judah: the clans of Shelah, Perez, Zerah, Hezron, and Hamul. (Two of Judah's sons, Er and Onan, had died in the land of Canaan.) 22 These clans numbered 76,500 men.

23 The tribe of Issachar: the clans of Tola, Puah, 24 Jashub, and Shimron. 25 These clans numbered 64,300 men.

26 The tribe of Zebulun: the clans of Sered, Elon, and Jahleel. 27 These clans numbered 60,500 men.

28 The tribes of Joseph, who was the father of two sons, Manasseh and Ephraim.

29 The tribe of Manasseh: Machir son of Manasseh was the father of Gilead, and the following clans traced their ancestry to Gilead: 30 the clans of Iezer,

e in broad daylight; or publicly.
26.1-51: Num 1.1-46

Helek, [31] Asriel, Shechem, [32] Shemida, and Hepher. [33] Zelophehad son of Hepher had no sons, but only daughters; their names were Mahlah, Noah, Hoglah, Milcah, and Tirzah. [34] These clans numbered 52,700 men.

35 The tribe of Ephraim: the clans of Shuthelah, Becher, and Tahan. [36] The clan of Eran traced its descent from Shuthelah. [37] These clans numbered 32,500 men.

These are the clans descended from Joseph.

38 The tribe of Benjamin: the clans of Bela, Ashbel, Ahiram, [39] Shephupham, and Hupham. [40] The clans of Ard and Naaman traced their descent from Bela. [41] These clans numbered 45,600 men.

42 The tribe of Dan: the clan of Shuham, [43] which numbered 64,400 men.

44 The tribe of Asher: the clans of Imnah, Ishvi, and Beriah. [45] The clans of Heber and Malchiel traced their descent from Beriah. [46] Asher had a daughter named Serah. [47] These clans numbered 53,400 men.

48 The tribe of Naphtali: the clans of Jahzeel, Guni, [49] Jezer, and Shillem. [50] These clans numbered 45,400 men.

51 The total number of the Israelite men was 601,730.

52 The LORD said to Moses, [53] "Divide the land among the tribes, according to their size. [54-56] Divide the land by drawing lots, and give a large share to a large tribe and a small one to a small tribe."

57 The tribe of Levi consisted of the clans of Gershon, Kohath, and Merari. [58] Their descendants included the subclans of Libni, Hebron, Mahli, Mushi, and Korah. Kohath was the father of Amram, [59] who was married to Levi's daughter Jochebed, who was born in Egypt. She bore Amram two sons, Aaron and Moses, and a daughter, Miriam. [60] Aaron had four sons, Nadab, Abihu, Eleazar, and Ithamar. [61] Nadab and Abihu died when they offered unholy fire to the LORD. [62] The male Levites who were one month old or older numbered 23,000. They were listed separately from the rest of the Israelites, because they were not given any property in Israel.

63 All these clans were listed by Moses and Eleazar when they took a census of the Israelites in the plains of Moab across the River Jordan from Jericho. [64] There was not even one man left among those whom Moses and Aaron had listed in the first census in the Sinai Desert. [65] The LORD had said that all of them would die in the wilderness, and except for Caleb son of Jephunneh and Joshua son of Nun they all did.

The Daughters of Zelophehad

27 Mahlah, Noah, Hoglah, Milcah, and Tirzah were the daughters of Zelophehad son of Hepher, son of Gilead, son of Machir, son of Manasseh, son of Joseph. [2] They went and stood before Moses, Eleazar the priest, the leaders, and the whole community at the entrance of the Tent of the LORD's presence and said, [3] "Our father died in the wilderness without leaving any sons. He was not among the followers of Korah, who rebelled against the LORD; he died because of his own sin. [4] Just because he had no sons, why should our father's name disappear from Israel? Give us property among our father's relatives."

5 Moses presented their case to the LORD, [6] and the LORD said to him, [7] "What the daughters of Zelophehad request is right; give them property among their father's relatives. Let his inheritance pass on to them. [8] Tell the people of Israel that whenever a man dies without leaving a son, his daughter is to inherit his property. [9] If he has no daughter, his brothers are to inherit it. [10] If he has no brothers, his father's brothers are to inherit it. [11] If he has no brothers or uncles, then his nearest relative is to inherit it and hold it as his own property. The people of Israel are to observe this as a legal requirement, just as I, the LORD, have commanded you."

Joshua Is Chosen as Successor to Moses
(Deut 31.1-8)

12 The LORD said to Moses, "Go up the Abarim Mountains and look out over the land that I am giving to the Israelites. [13] After you have seen it, you will die, as your brother Aaron did, [14] because both of you rebelled against my command in the wilderness of Zin. When the whole community complained against me at Meribah, you refused to acknowledge my holy power before them." (Meribah is the spring at Kadesh in the wilderness of Zin.)

15 Moses prayed, [16] "LORD God, source of all life, appoint, I pray, a man who can lead the people [17] and can command

26.52–56: Num 34.13; Josh 14.1–2   26.60: Num 3.2   26.61: Lev 10.1–2; Num 3.4
26.65: Num 14.26–35   27.7: Num 36.2   27.12–14: Deut 3.23–27, 32.48–52
27.17: 1 Kgs 22.17; Ezek 34.5; Mt 9.36; Mk 6.34

Take Joshua...a capable man (27.18)

them in battle, so that your community will not be like sheep without a shepherd."

18 The LORD said to Moses, "Take Joshua son of Nun, a capable man, and place your hands on his head. ¹⁹Make him stand in front of Eleazar the priest and the whole community, and there before them all proclaim him as your successor. ²⁰Give him some of your own authority, so that the whole community of Israel will obey him. ²¹He will depend on Eleazar the priest, who will learn my will by using the Urim and Thummim.*ᶠ* In this way Eleazar will direct Joshua and the whole community of Israel in all their affairs." ²²Moses did as the LORD had commanded him. He made Joshua stand before Eleazar the priest and the whole community. ²³As the LORD had commanded, Moses put his hands on Joshua's head and proclaimed him as his successor.

The Regular Offerings
(Ex 29.38–46)

28 The LORD commanded Moses ²to instruct the Israelites to present to God at the appointed times the required food-offerings that are pleasing to him.

3 These are the food-offerings that are to be presented to the LORD: for the daily burnt-offering, two one-year-old male lambs without any defects. ⁴Offer the first lamb in the morning, and the second in the evening, ⁵each with a grain-offering of one kilogramme of flour, mixed with one litre of the best olive-oil. ⁶This is the daily offering that is completely burnt, which was first offered at Mount Sinai as a food-offering, a smell pleasing to the LORD. ⁷As the wine-offering with the first lamb, pour out at the altar one litre of wine. ⁸In the evening offer the second lamb in the same way as the morning offering, together with its wine-offering. It also is a food-offering, a smell pleasing to the LORD.

The Sabbath Offering

9 On the Sabbath day offer two one-year-old male lambs without any defects, two kilogrammes of flour mixed with olive-oil as a grain-offering, and the wine-offering. ¹⁰This burnt-offering is to be offered every Sabbath in addition to the daily offering with its wine-offering.

The Offering on the First Day of the Month

11 Present a burnt-offering to the LORD at the beginning of each month: two young bulls, one ram, seven one-year-old

*ᶠ*URIM AND THUMMIM: *Two objects used by the priest to determine God's will; it is not known precisely how they were used.*
27.18: Ex 24.13   **27.21:** Ex 28.30; 1 Sam 14.41, 28.6   **27.23:** Deut 31.23

male lambs, all without any defects. ¹²As a grain-offering, offer flour mixed with olive-oil: with each bull, three kilogrammes of flour; with the ram, two kilogrammes; ¹³and with each lamb, one kilogramme. These burnt-offerings are food-offerings, a smell pleasing to the LORD. ¹⁴The proper wine-offering is two litres of wine with each bull, one and a half litres with the ram, and one litre with each lamb. This is the regulation for the burnt-offering for the first day of each month throughout the year. ¹⁵And in addition to the daily burnt-offering with its wine-offering, offer one male goat as a sin-offering.

The Offerings at the Festival of Unleavened Bread
(Lev 23.5–14)

16 The Passover Festival in honour of the LORD is to be held on the fourteenth day of the first month. ¹⁷On the fifteenth day a religious festival begins which lasts seven days, during which only bread prepared without yeast is to be eaten. ¹⁸On the first day of the festival you are to gather for worship, and no work is to be done. ¹⁹Offer a burnt-offering as a food-offering to the LORD: two young bulls, one ram, and seven one-year-old male lambs, all without any defects. ²⁰Offer the proper grain-offering of flour mixed with olive-oil: three kilogrammes with each bull, two kilogrammes with the ram, ²¹and one kilogramme with each lamb. ²²Also offer one male goat as a sin-offering, and in this way perform the ritual of purification for the people. ²³Offer these in addition to the regular morning burnt-offering. ²⁴In the same way, for seven days offer to the LORD a food-offering, a smell pleasing to him. Offer this in addition to the daily burnt-offering and wine-offering. ²⁵Meet for worship on the seventh day and do no work.

The Offerings at the Harvest Festival
(Lev 23.15–22)

26 On the first day of the Harvest Festival, when you present the offering of new corn to the LORD, you are to gather for worship, and no work is to be done. ²⁷Offer a burnt-offering as a smell pleasing to the LORD: two young bulls, one ram, and seven one-year-old male lambs, all without any defects. ²⁸Offer the proper grain-offering of flour mixed with olive-oil: three kilogrammes with each bull, two kilogrammes with the ram, ²⁹and one kilogramme with each lamb. ³⁰Also offer one male goat as a sin-offering, and in this way perform the ritual of purification for the people. ³¹Offer these and the wine-offering in addition to the daily burnt-offering and grain-offering.

The Offerings at the New Year Festival
(Lev 23.23–25)

29 On the first day of the seventh month you are to gather for worship, and no work is to be done. On that day trumpets are to be blown. ²Present a burnt-offering to the LORD, a smell pleasing to him: one young bull, one ram, and seven one-year-old male lambs, all without any defects. ³Offer the proper grain-offering of flour mixed with olive-oil: three kilogrammes of flour with the bull, two kilogrammes with the ram, ⁴and one kilogramme with each lamb. ⁵Also offer one male goat as a sin-offering, and in this way perform the ritual of purification for the people. ⁶Offer these in addition to the regular burnt-offering for the first day of the month with its grain-offering, and the daily burnt-offering with its grain-offering and wine-offering. These food-offerings are a smell pleasing to the LORD.

The Offerings at the Day of Atonement
(Lev 23.26–32)

7 Gather for worship on the tenth day of the seventh month; eat no food and do no work. ⁸Offer a burnt-offering to the LORD, a smell pleasing to him: one young bull, one ram, and seven one-year-old male lambs, all without any defects. ⁹Offer the proper grain-offering of flour mixed with olive-oil: three kilogrammes of flour with the bull, two kilogrammes with the ram, ¹⁰and one kilogramme with each lamb. ¹¹Also offer one male goat as a sin-offering, in addition to the goat offered in the ritual of purification for the people, and the daily burnt-offering with its grain-offering and wine-offering.

The Offerings at the Festival of Shelters
(Lev 23.33–44)

12 Gather for worship on the fifteenth day of the seventh month. Celebrate this festival in honour of the LORD for seven days and do no work. ¹³On this first day

28.16: Ex 12.1–13; Deut 16.1–2   **28.17–25:** Ex 12.14–20, 23.15, 34.18; Deut 16.3–8
28.26–31: Ex 23.16, 34.22; Deut 16.9–12   **29.7–11:** Lev 16.29–34

offer a food-offering to the LORD, a smell pleasing to him: thirteen young bulls, two rams, and fourteen one-year-old male lambs, all without any defects. ¹⁴Offer the proper grain-offering of flour mixed with olive-oil: three kilogrammes of flour with each bull, two kilogrammes with each ram, ¹⁵and one kilogramme with each lamb, with the required wine-offerings. ¹⁶Also offer one male goat as a sin-offering. Offer these in addition to the daily burnt-offering with its grain-offering and wine-offering.

17 On the second day offer twelve young bulls, two rams, and fourteen one-year-old male lambs, all without any defects. ¹⁸⁻¹⁹Offer with them all the other offerings required for the first day.

20 On the third day offer eleven young bulls, two rams, and fourteen one-year-old male lambs, all without any defects. ²¹⁻²²Offer with them all the other offerings required for the first day.

23 On the fourth day offer ten young bulls, two rams, and fourteen one-year-old male lambs, all without any defects. ²⁴⁻²⁵Offer with them all the other offerings required for the first day.

26 On the fifth day offer nine young bulls, two rams, and fourteen one-year-old male lambs, all without any defects. ²⁷⁻²⁸Offer with them all the other offerings required for the first day.

29 On the sixth day offer eight young bulls, two rams, and fourteen one-year-old male lambs, all without any defects. ³⁰⁻³¹Offer with them all the other offerings required for the first day.

32 On the seventh day offer seven young bulls, two rams, and fourteen one-year-old male lambs, all without any defects. ³³⁻³⁴Offer with them all the other offerings required for the first day.

35 On the eighth day gather for worship and do no work. ³⁶Offer a burnt-offering as a food-offering to the LORD, a smell pleasing to him: one young bull, one ram, and seven one-year-old male lambs, all without any defects. ³⁷⁻³⁸Offer with them all the other offerings required for the first day.

39 These are the regulations concerning the burnt-offerings, grain-offerings, wine-offerings, and fellowship-offerings that you are to make to the LORD at your appointed festivals. These are in addition to the offerings you give in fulfilment of a vow or as freewill offerings.

40 So Moses told the people of Israel

everything that the LORD had commanded him.

Rules about Vows

30 Moses gave the following instructions to the leaders of the tribes of Israel. ²When a man makes a vow to give something to the LORD or takes an oath to abstain from something, he must not break his promise, but must do everything that he said he would.

3 When a young woman still living in her father's house makes a vow to give something to the LORD or promises to abstain from something, ⁴she must do everything that she vowed or promised unless her father raises an objection when he hears about it. ⁵But if her father forbids her to fulfil the vow when he hears about it, she is not required to keep it. The LORD will forgive her, because her father refused to let her keep it.

6 If an unmarried woman makes a vow, whether deliberately or carelessly, or promises to abstain from something, and then marries, ⁷she must do everything that she vowed or promised unless her husband raises an objection when he hears about it. ⁸But if her husband forbids her to fulfil the vow when he hears about it, she is not required to keep it. The LORD will forgive her.

9 A widow or a divorced woman must keep every vow she makes and every promise to abstain from something.

10 If a married woman makes a vow or promises to abstain from something, ¹¹she must do everything that she vowed or promised unless her husband raises an objection when he hears about it. ¹²But if her husband forbids her to fulfil the vow when he hears about it, she is not required to keep it. The LORD will forgive her, because her husband prevented her from keeping her vow. ¹³Her husband has the right to affirm or to annul any vow or promise that she has made. ¹⁴But if, by the day after he hears of the vow, he has raised no objection, she must do everything that she has vowed or promised. He has affirmed the vow by not objecting on the day he heard of it. ¹⁵But if he later annuls the vow, he must suffer the consequences for the failure to fulfil the vow.

16 These are the rules that the LORD gave Moses concerning vows made by an unmarried woman living in her father's house or by a married woman.

30.2: Deut 23.21–23; Mt 5.33

The Holy War against Midian

31 The LORD said to Moses, [2]"Punish the Midianites for what they did to the people of Israel. After you have done that, you will die."

3 So Moses said to the people, "Get ready for war, so that you can attack Midian and punish them for what they did to the LORD. [4]From each tribe of Israel send a thousand men to war."

5 So a thousand men were chosen from each tribe, a total of twelve thousand men ready for battle. [6]Moses sent them to war under the command of Phinehas son of Eleazar the priest, who took charge of the sacred objects and the trumpets for giving signals. [7]They attacked Midian, as the LORD had commanded Moses, and killed all the men, [8]including the five kings of Midian: Evi, Rekem, Zur, Hur, and Reba. They also killed Balaam son of Beor.

9 The people of Israel captured the Midianite women and children, took their cattle and their flocks, plundered all their wealth, [10]and burnt all their cities and camps. [11]They took all the loot that they had captured, including the prisoners and the animals, [12]and brought them to Moses and Eleazar and to the community of the people of Israel, who were at the camp on the plains of Moab across the Jordan from Jericho.

The Army Returns

13 Moses, Eleazar, and all the other leaders of the community went out of the camp to meet the army. [14]Moses was angry with the officers, the commanders of battalions and companies, who had returned from the war. [15]He asked them, "Why have you kept all the women alive? [16]Remember that it was the women who followed Balaam's instructions and at Peor led the people to be unfaithful to the LORD. That was what brought the epidemic on the LORD's people. [17]So now kill every boy and kill every woman who has had sexual intercourse, [18]but keep alive for yourselves all the girls and all the women who are virgins. [19]Now all of you who have killed anyone or have touched a corpse must stay outside the camp for seven days. On the third day and on the seventh day purify yourselves and the women you have captured. [20]You must also purify every piece of clothing and everything made of leather, goats' hair, or wood."

31.16: Num 25.1–9

21 Eleazar the priest said to the men who had returned from battle, "These are the regulations that the LORD has given to Moses. [22-23]Everything that will not burn, such as gold, silver, bronze, iron, tin, or lead, is to be purified by passing it through fire. Everything else is to be purified by the water for purification. [24]On the seventh day you must wash your clothes; then you will be ritually clean and will be permitted to enter the camp."

Division of the Loot

25 The LORD said to Moses, [26]"You and Eleazar, together with the other leaders of the community, are to count everything that has been captured, including the prisoners and the animals. [27]Divide what was taken into two equal parts, one part for the soldiers and the other part for the rest of the community. [28]From the part that belongs to the soldiers, withhold as a tax for the LORD one out of every five hundred prisoners and the same proportion of the cattle, donkeys, sheep, and goats. [29]Give them to Eleazar the priest as a special contribution to the LORD. [30]From the part given to the rest of the people, take one out of every fifty prisoners and the same proportion of the cattle, donkeys, sheep, and goats. Give them to the Levites who are in charge of the LORD's Tent." [31]Moses and Eleazar did what the LORD commanded.

32-35 The following is a list of what was captured by the soldiers, in addition to what they kept for themselves: 675,000 sheep and goats, 72,000 cattle, 61,000 donkeys, and 32,000 virgins. [36-40]The half-share of the soldiers was 337,500 sheep and goats, of which 675 were the tax for the LORD; 36,000 cattle for the soldiers, of which 72 were the tax for the LORD; 30,500 donkeys for the soldiers, of which 61 were the tax for the LORD; and 16,000 virgins for the soldiers, of which 32 were the tax for the LORD. [41]So Moses gave Eleazar the tax as a special contribution to the LORD, as the LORD had commanded.

42-46 The share of the community was the same as that for the soldiers: 337,500 sheep and goats, 36,000 cattle, 30,500 donkeys, and 16,000 virgins. [47]From this share Moses took one out of every fifty prisoners and animals, and as the LORD had commanded, gave them to the Levites who were in charge of the LORD's Tent.

48 Then the officers who had commanded the army went to Moses [49]and

reported, "Sir, we have counted the soldiers under our command and not one of them is missing. 50 So we are bringing the gold ornaments, armlets, bracelets, rings, earrings, and necklaces that each of us has taken. We offer them to the LORD as a payment for our lives, so that he will protect us." 51 Moses and Eleazar received the gold, all of which was in the form of ornaments. 52 The total contribution of the officers weighed nearly two hundred kilogrammes. 53 Those who were not officers kept the loot they had taken. 54 So Moses and Eleazar took the gold to the Tent, so that the LORD would protect the people of Israel.

The Tribes East of the Jordan
(Deut 3.12-22)

32 The tribes of Reuben and Gad had a lot of livestock. When they saw how suitable the land of Jazer and Gilead was for cattle, 2 they went to Moses, Eleazar, and the other leaders of the community and said, 3-4 "This region which the LORD has helped the Israelites to occupy—the towns of Ataroth, Dibon, Jazer, Nimrah, Heshbon, Elealeh, Sibmah, Nebo, and Beon—is good land for livestock, and we have so much livestock. 5 Please give us this land as our property, and do not make us cross the River Jordan and settle there."

6 Moses replied, "Do you want to stay here while your fellow-Israelites go to war? 7 How dare you try to discourage the people of Israel from crossing the Jordan into the land which the LORD has given them? 8 That is what your fathers did when I sent them from Kadesh Barnea to explore the land. 9 They went as far as the Valley of Eshcol and saw the land, but when they returned, they discouraged the people from entering the land which the LORD had given them. 10 The LORD was angry that day and made a promise: 11 'I swear that because they did not remain loyal to me, none of the men twenty years old or older who came out of Egypt will enter the land that I promised to Abraham, Isaac, and Jacob.' 12 This included everyone, except Caleb son of Jephunneh the Kenizzite and Joshua son of Nun; they remained loyal to the LORD. 13 The LORD was angry with the people and made them wander in the wilderness for forty years until that whole generation that had displeased him was dead. 14 And now you have taken your fathers' place,

a new generation of sinful men ready to bring down the fierce anger of the LORD on Israel again. 15 If you people of Reuben and Gad refuse to follow him now, he will once again abandon all these people in the wilderness, and you will be responsible for their destruction."

16 They approached Moses and said, "First, allow us to build stone enclosures here for our sheep and fortified towns for our dependants. 17 Then we will be ready to go with our fellow-Israelites into battle and lead the attack until we have settled them in the land that will be theirs. In the meantime, our dependants can live here in the fortified towns, safe from the people of this land. 18 We will not return to our homes until all the other Israelites have taken possession of the land assigned to them. 19 We will not take possession of any property among them on the other side of the Jordan, because we have received our share here east of the Jordan."

20 Moses answered, "If you really mean what you say, then here in the presence of the LORD get ready to go into battle. 21 All your fighting men are to cross the Jordan and under the command of the LORD they are to attack our enemies until the LORD defeats them 22 and takes possession of the land. After that, you may return, because you will have fulfilled your obligation to the LORD and to your fellow-Israelites. Then the LORD will acknowledge that this land east of the Jordan is yours. 23 But if you do not keep your promise, I warn you that you will be sinning against the LORD. Make no mistake about it; you will be punished for your sin. 24 So build your towns and the enclosures for your sheep, but do what you have promised!"

25 The men of Gad and Reuben said, "Sir, we will do as you command. 26 Our wives and children and our cattle and sheep will remain here in the towns of Gilead. 27 But all of us are ready to go into battle under the LORD's command. We will cross the Jordan and fight, just as you have said."

28 So Moses gave these commands to Eleazar, Joshua, and the other leaders of Israel: 29 "If the men of Gad and Reuben cross the Jordan ready for battle at the LORD's command and if with their help you are able to conquer the land, then give them the land of Gilead as their property. 30 But if they do not cross the

32.8-9: Num 13.17-33 **32.10-13:** Num 14.26-35 **32.28-32:** Josh 1.12-15

Jordan and go into battle with you, they are to receive their share of the property in the land of Canaan, as you do."

31 The men of Gad and Reuben answered, "Sir, we will do as the LORD has commanded. 32 Under his command we will cross into the land of Canaan and go into battle, so that we can retain our property here east of the Jordan."

33 So Moses assigned to the tribes of Gad and Reuben and to half the tribe of Manasseh all the territory of King Sihon of the Amorites and King Og of Bashan, including the towns and the country round them. 34 The tribe of Gad rebuilt the fortified towns of Dibon, Ataroth, Aroer, 35 Atroth Shophan, Jazer, Jogbehah, 36 Beth Nimrah, and Beth Haran. 37 The tribe of Reuben rebuilt Heshbon, Elealeh, Kiriathaim, 38 Nebo, Baal Meon (this name was changed), and Sibmah. They gave new names to the towns they rebuilt.

39 The clan of Machir son of Manasseh invaded the land of Gilead, occupied it, and drove out the Amorites who were there. 40 So Moses gave Gilead to the clan of Machir, and they lived there. 41 Jair, of the tribe of Manasseh, attacked and captured some villages and named them "Villages of Jair." 42 Nobah attacked and captured Kenath and its villages, and he renamed it Nobah, after himself.

The Journey from Egypt to Moab

33 The following account gives the names of the places where the Israelites set up camp after they left Egypt in their tribes under the leadership of Moses and Aaron. 2 At the command of the LORD, Moses wrote down the name of the place each time they set up camp.

3 The people of Israel left Egypt on the fifteenth day of the first month of the year, the day after the first Passover. Under the LORD's protection they left the city of Rameses in full view of the Egyptians, 4 who were burying the first-born sons that the LORD had killed. By doing this, the LORD showed that he was more powerful than the gods of Egypt.

5 The people of Israel left Rameses and set up camp at Sukkoth. 6 Their next camp was at Etham on the edge of the desert. 7 From there they turned back to Pi Hahiroth, east of Baal Zephon, and camped near Migdol. 8 They left Pi Hahiroth and passed through the Red Sea g into the desert of Shur; after a three

days' march they camped at Marah. 9 From there they went to Elim, where they camped, because there were twelve springs of water and seventy palm-trees there.

10 They left Elim and camped near the Gulf of Suez. 11 Their next camp was in the desert of Sin. 12 Then they camped at Dophkah, 13 and after that at Alush. 14 Next was Rephidim, where there was no water for them to drink.

15-37 From Rephidim to Mount Hor they set up camp at the following places: the Sinai Desert, Kibroth Hattaavah (or "Graves of Craving"), Hazeroth, Rithmah, Rimmon Perez, Libnah, Rissah, Kehelathath, Mount Shepher, Haradah, Makheloth, Tahath, Terah, Mithkah, Hashmonah, Moseroth, Bene Jaakan, Hor Haggidgad, Jotbathah, Abronah, Eziongeber, the wilderness of Zin (that is, Kadesh), and Mount Hor, at the edge of the land of Edom.

38-39 At the command of the LORD, Aaron the priest climbed Mount Hor. At the age of 123 he died there on the first day of the fifth month of the fortieth year after the Israelites had left Egypt.

40 The king of Arad in southern Canaan heard that the Israelites were coming.

41-49 From Mount Hor to the plains of Moab the Israelites set up camp at the following places: Zalmonah, Punon, Oboth, the ruins of Abarim in the territory of Moab, Dibon Gad, Almon Diblathaim, the Abarim Mountains near Mount Nebo, and in the plains of Moab across the River Jordan from Jericho, between Beth Jeshimoth and the Valley of Acacia.

Instructions before Crossing the Jordan

50 There in the plains of Moab across the Jordan from Jericho the LORD gave Moses 51 the following instructions for Israel: "When you cross the Jordan into the land of Canaan, 52 you must drive out all the inhabitants of the land. Destroy all their stone and metal idols and all their places of worship. 53 Occupy the land and settle in it, because I am giving it to you. 54 Divide the land among the various tribes and clans by drawing lots, giving a large piece of property to a large clan and a small one to a small clan. 55 But if you do not drive out the inhabitants of the land, those that are left will be as troublesome as splinters in your eyes and thorns in your sides, and they will fight

g RED SEA: *See Word List.*
33.38: Num 20.22-28; Deut 10.6, 32.50   **33.40:** Num 21.1   **33.54:** Num 26.54-56

against you. 56 If you do not drive them out, I will destroy you, as I planned to destroy them."

The Boundaries of the Land

34 The LORD gave Moses 2 the following instructions for the people of Israel: "When you enter Canaan, the land which I am giving you, the borders of your territory will be as follows. 3 The southern border will extend from the wilderness of Zin along the border of Edom. It will begin on the east at the southern end of the Dead Sea. 4 Then it will turn southwards towards Akrabbim Pass and continue on through Zin as far south as Kadesh Barnea. Then it will turn northwest to Hazar Addar and on to Azmon, 5 where it will turn towards the valley at the border of Egypt and end at the Mediterranean.

6 "The western border will be the Mediterranean Sea.

7 "The northern border will follow a line from the Mediterranean to Mount Hor 8 and from there to Hamath Pass. It will continue to Zedad 9 and to Ziphron, and will end at Hazar Enan.

10 "The eastern border will follow a line from Hazar Enan to Shepham. 11 It will then go south to Harbel, east of Ain, and on to the hills on the eastern shore of Lake Galilee, 12 then south along the River Jordan to the Dead Sea.

"These will be the four borders of your land."

13 So Moses said to the Israelites, "This is the land that you will receive by drawing lots, the land that the LORD has assigned to the nine and a half tribes. 14 The tribes of Reuben and Gad and the eastern half of Manasseh have received their property, divided according to their families, 15 on the eastern side of the Jordan, opposite Jericho."

The Leaders Responsible for Dividing the Land

16 The LORD said to Moses, 17 "Eleazar the priest and Joshua son of Nun will divide the land for the people. 18 Take also one leader from each tribe to help them divide it." 19-28 These are the men the LORD chose:

Tribe	Leader
Judah	Caleb son of Jephunneh
Simeon	Shelumiel son of Ammihud
Benjamin	Elidad son of Chislon

Dan	Bukki son of Jogli
Manasseh	Hanniel son of Ephod
Ephraim	Kemuel son of Shiphtan
Zebulun	Elizaphan son of Parnach
Issachar	Paltiel son of Azzan
Asher	Ahihud son of Shelomi
Naphtali	Pedahel son of Ammihud

29 These are the men that the LORD assigned to divide the property for the people of Israel in the land of Canaan.

The Cities Assigned to the Levites

35 In the plains of Moab across the Jordan from Jericho the LORD said to Moses, 2 "Tell the Israelites that from the property they receive they must give the Levites some cities to live in and pasture land round the cities. 3 These cities will belong to the Levites, and they will live there. The pasture land will be for their cattle and all their other animals. 4 The pasture land is to extend outwards from the city walls 450 metres in each direction, 5 so that there is a square area measuring 900 metres on each side, with the city in the middle. 6 You are to give the Levites six cities of refuge to which a man can escape if he kills someone accidentally. In addition, give them forty-two other cities 7 with their pasture land, making a total of forty-eight. 8 The number of Levite cities in each tribe is to be determined according to the size of its territory."

The Cities of Refuge
(Deut 19.1–13; Josh 20.1–9)

9 The LORD told Moses 10 to say to the people of Israel: "When you cross the River Jordan and enter the land of Canaan, 11 you are to choose cities of refuge to which a man can escape if he kills someone accidentally. 12 There he will be safe from the dead man's relative who seeks revenge. A man accused of manslaughter is not to be put to death without a public trial. 13 Choose six cities, 14 three east of the Jordan and three in the land of Canaan. 15 These will serve as cities of refuge for Israelites and for foreigners who are temporary or permanent residents. Anyone who kills someone accidentally can escape to one of them.

16–18 "If, however, a man uses a weapon of iron or stone or wood to kill someone, he is guilty of murder and is to be put to death. 19 The dead man's nearest relative has the responsibility for

34.13–15: Josh 14.1–5   **35.1–8:** Josh 21.1–42

putting the murderer to death. When he finds him, he is to kill him.

20 "If a man hates someone and kills him by pushing him down or by throwing something at him 21or by striking him with his fist, he is guilty of murder and is to be put to death. The dead man's nearest relative has the responsibility for putting the murderer to death. When he finds him, he is to kill him.

22 "But suppose a man accidentally kills someone he does not hate, whether by pushing him down or by throwing something at him. 23Or suppose that, without looking, a man throws a stone that kills someone whom he did not intend to hurt and who was not his enemy. 24In such cases the community shall judge in favour of the man who caused the death and not in favour of the dead man's relative who is seeking revenge. 25The community is to rescue the man guilty of manslaughter from the dead man's relative, and they are to return him to the city of refuge to which he had escaped. He must live there until the death of the man who is then High Priest. 26If the man guilty of manslaughter leaves the city of refuge to which he has escaped 27and if the dead man's relative finds him and kills him, this act of revenge is not murder. 28The man guilty of manslaughter must remain in the city of refuge until the death of the High Priest, but after that he may return home. 29These rules apply to you and your descendants wherever you may live.

30 "A man accused of murder may be found guilty and put to death only on the evidence of two or more witnesses; the evidence of one witness is not sufficient to support an accusation of murder. 31A murderer must be put to death. He cannot escape this penalty by the payment of money. 32If a man has fled to a city of refuge, do not allow him to make a payment in order to return home before the death of the High Priest. 33If you did this, you would defile the land where you are living. Murder defiles the land, and except by the death of the murderer there is no way to perform the ritual of purification for the land where a man has been murdered. 34Do not defile the land where you are living, because I am the LORD and I live among the people of Israel."

The Inheritance of Married Women

36 The heads of the families in the clan of Gilead, the son of Machir and grandson of Manasseh son of Joseph, went to Moses and the other leaders. 2They said, "The LORD commanded you to distribute the land to the people of Israel by drawing lots. He also commanded you to give the property of our relative Zelophehad to his daughters. 3But remember, if they marry men of another tribe, their property will then belong to that tribe, and the total allotted to us will be reduced. 4In the Year of Restoration, when all property that has been sold is restored to its original owners, the property of Zelophehad's daughters will be permanently added to the tribe into which they marry and will be lost to our tribe."

5 So Moses gave the people of Israel the following command from the LORD. He said, "What the tribe of Manasseh says is right, 6and so the LORD says that the daughters of Zelophehad are free to marry anyone they wish but only within their own tribe. 7The property of every Israelite will remain attached to his tribe. 8Every woman who inherits property in an Israelite tribe must marry a man belonging to that tribe. In this way each Israelite will inherit the property of his ancestors, 9and the property will not pass from one tribe to another. Each tribe will continue to possess its own property."

10-11 So Mahlah, Tirzah, Hoglah, Milcah, and Noah, the daughters of Zelophehad, did as the LORD had commanded Moses, and they married their cousins. 12They married within the clans of the tribe of Manasseh son of Joseph, and their property remained in their father's tribe.

13 These are the rules and regulations that the LORD gave the Israelites through Moses in the plains of Moab across the River Jordan from Jericho.

35.30: Deut 17.6, 19.15   **36.2:** Num 27.7

DEUTERONOMY

INTRODUCTION

The book of *Deuteronomy* is organized as a series of addresses given by Moses to the people of Israel in the land of Moab, where they had stopped at the end of the long wilderness journey and were about to enter and occupy Canaan.

Some of the most important matters recorded in the book are as follows: (1) Moses recalls the great events of the past forty years. He appeals to the people to remember how God has led them through the wilderness and to be obedient and loyal to God. (2) Moses reviews the Ten Commandments and emphasizes the meaning of the First Commandment, calling the people to devotion to the Lord alone. Then he reviews the various laws that are to govern Israel's life in the promised land. (3) Moses reminds the people of the meaning of God's covenant with them, and calls for them to renew their commitment to its obligations. (4) Joshua is commissioned as the next leader of God's people. After singing a song celebrating God's faithfulness, and pronouncing a blessing on the tribes of Israel, Moses dies in Moab, east of the River Jordan.

The great theme of the book is that God has saved and blessed his chosen people, whom he loves; his people are to remember this, and love and obey him, so that they may have life and continued blessing.

The key verses of the book are 6.4–6, and contain the words that Jesus called the greatest of all commandments: "Love the LORD your God with all your heart, with all your soul, and with all your strength."

Outline of Contents
Moses' first discourse   1.1—4.49
Moses' second discourse   5.1—26.19
  a. The Ten Commandments   5.1—10.22
  b. Laws, rules, and warnings   11.1—26.19
Instructions for entering Canaan   27.1—28.68
The covenant renewed   29.1—30.20
Moses' last words   31.1—33.29
The death of Moses   34.1-12

Introduction

1 In this book are the words that Moses spoke to the people of Israel when they were in the wilderness east of the River Jordan. They were in the Jordan Valley near Suph, between the town of Paran on one side and the towns of

Tophel, Laban, Hazeroth, and Dizahab on the other. [2](It takes eleven days to travel from Mount Sinai to Kadesh Barnea by way of the hill-country of Edom.) [3]On the first day of the eleventh month of the fortieth year after they had left Egypt, Moses told the people everything the LORD had commanded him to tell them. [4]This was after the LORD[a] had defeated King Sihon of the Amorites, who ruled in the town of Heshbon, and King Og of Bashan, who ruled in the towns of Ashtaroth and Edrei. [5]It was while the people were east of the Jordan in the territory of Moab that Moses began to explain God's laws and teachings.

He said, [6]"When we were at Mount Sinai, the LORD our God said to us, 'You have stayed long enough at this mountain. [7]Break camp and move on. Go to the hill-country of the Amorites and to all the surrounding regions—to the Jordan Valley, to the hill-country and the lowlands, to the southern region, and to the Mediterranean coast. Go to the land of Canaan and on beyond the Lebanon Mountains as far as the great River Euphrates. [8]All of this is the land which I, the LORD, promised to give to your ancestors, Abraham, Isaac, and Jacob, and to their descendants. Go and occupy it.'"

Moses Appoints Judges
(Ex 18.13-27)

[9]Moses said to the people, "While we were still at Mount Sinai, I told you, 'The responsibility for leading you is too much for me. I can't do it alone. [10]The LORD your God has made you as numerous as the stars in the sky. [11]May the LORD, the God of your ancestors, make you increase a thousand times more and make you prosperous, as he promised! [12]But how can I alone bear the heavy responsibility for settling your disputes? [13]Choose some wise, understanding, and experienced men from each tribe, and I will put them in charge of you.' [14]And you agreed that this was a good thing to do. [15]So I took the wise and experienced leaders you chose from your tribes, and I placed them in charge of you. Some were responsible for a thousand people, some for a hundred, some for fifty, and some for ten. I also appointed other officials throughout the tribes.

[16]"At that time I instructed them, 'Listen to the disputes that come up among your people. Judge every dispute fairly, whether it concerns only your own people or involves foreigners who live among you. [17]Show no partiality in your decisions; judge everyone on the same basis, no matter who he is. Do not be afraid of anyone, for the decisions you make come from God. If any case is too difficult for you, bring it to me, and I will decide it.' [18]At the same time I gave you instructions for everything else you were to do.

The Spies Are Sent Out from Kadesh Barnea
(Num 13.1-33)

[19]"We did what the LORD our God commanded us. We left Mount Sinai and went through that vast and fearful desert on the way to the hill-country of the Amorites. When we reached Kadesh Barnea, [20-21]I said, 'You have now come to the hill-country of the Amorites, which the LORD our God, the God of our ancestors, is giving us. Look, there it is. Go and occupy it as he commanded. Do not hesitate or be afraid.'

[22]"But you came to me and said, 'Let's send men ahead of us to spy out the land, so that they can tell us the best route to take and what kind of cities are there.'

[23]"That seemed a good thing to do, so I selected twelve men, one from each tribe. [24]They went into the hill-country as far as the Valley of Eshcol and explored it. [25]They brought us back some fruit they found there, and reported that the land which the LORD our God was giving us was very fertile.

[26]"But you rebelled against the command of the LORD your God, and you would not enter the land. [27]You grumbled to one another: 'The LORD hates us. He brought us out of Egypt just to hand us over to these Amorites, so that they could kill us. [28]Why should we go there? We are afraid. The men we sent tell us that the people there are stronger and taller than we are, and that they live in cities with walls that reach the sky. They saw giants there!'

[29]"But I said, 'Don't be afraid of those people. [30]The LORD your God will lead you, and he will fight for you, just as you saw him do in Egypt [31]and in the desert. You saw how he brought you safely all the way to this place, just as

[a]the LORD; or Moses.
1.4: Num 2.21-35   1.26: Deut 9.23; Heb 3.16   1.31: Acts 13.18

a father would carry his son.' ³²But in spite of what I said, you still would not trust the LORD, ³³even though he always went ahead of you to find a place for you to camp. To show you the way, he went in front of you in a pillar of fire by night and in a pillar of cloud by day.

The LORD Punishes Israel
(Num 14.20–45)

34 "The LORD heard your complaints and became angry, and so he solemnly declared, ³⁵'Not one of you from this evil generation will enter the fertile land that I promised to give your ancestors. ³⁶Only Caleb son of Jephunneh will enter it. He has remained faithful to me, and I will give him and his descendants the land that he has explored.' ³⁷Because of you the LORD also became angry with me and said, 'Not even you, Moses, will enter the land. ³⁸But strengthen the determination of your helper, Joshua son of Nun. He will lead Israel to occupy the land.'

39 "Then the LORD said to all of us, 'Your children, who are still too young to know right from wrong, will enter the land—the children you said would be seized by your enemies. I will give the land to them, and they will occupy it. ⁴⁰But as for you people, turn round and go back into the desert along the road to the Gulf of Aqaba.'

41 "You replied, 'Moses, we have sinned against the LORD. But now we will attack, just as the LORD our God commanded us.' Then each one of you got ready to fight, thinking it would be easy to invade the hill-country.

42 "But the LORD said to me, 'Warn them not to attack, for I will not be with them, and their enemies will defeat them.' ⁴³I told you what the LORD had said, but you paid no attention. You rebelled against him, and in your pride you marched into the hill-country. ⁴⁴Then the Amorites who lived in those hills came out against you like a swarm of bees. They chased you as far as Hormah and defeated you there in the hill-country of Edom. ⁴⁵So you cried out to the LORD for help, but he would not listen to you or pay any attention to you.

The Years in the Desert

⁴⁶"So then, after we had stayed at Kadesh **2** for a long time, ¹we finally turned and went into the desert, along the road to the Gulf of Aqaba, as the LORD had commanded, and we spent a long time wandering about in the hill-country of Edom.

2 "Then the LORD told me ³that we had spent enough time wandering about in those hills and that we should go north. ⁴He told me to give you the following instructions: 'You are about to go through the hill-country of Edom, the territory of your distant relatives, the descendants of Esau. They will be afraid of you, ⁵but you must not start a war with them, because I am not going to give you so much as a square metre of their land. I have given Edom to Esau's descendants. ⁶You may buy food and water from them.'

7 "Remember how the LORD your God has blessed you in everything that you have done. He has taken care of you as you wandered through this vast desert. He has been with you these forty years, and you have had everything you needed.

8 "So we moved on and left the road that goes from the towns of Elath and Eziongeber to the Dead Sea, and we turned north-east towards Moab. ⁹The LORD said to me, 'Don't trouble the people of Moab, the descendants of Lot, or start a war against them. I have given them the city of Ar, and I am not going to give you any of their land.' "

¹⁰(A mighty race of giants called the Emim used to live in Ar. They were as tall as the Anakim, another race of giants. ¹¹Like the Anakim they were also known as Rephaim; but the Moabites called them Emim. ¹²The Horites used to live in Edom, but the descendants of Esau chased them out, destroyed their nation, and settled there themselves, just as the Israelites later chased their enemies out of the land that the LORD gave them.)

13 "Then we crossed the River Zered as the LORD told us to do. ¹⁴This was thirty-eight years after we had left Kadesh Barnea. All the fighting men of that generation had died, as the LORD had said they would. ¹⁵The LORD kept on opposing them until he had destroyed them all.

16 "After they had all died, ¹⁷the LORD said to us, ¹⁸'Today you are to pass through the territory of Moab by way of Ar. ¹⁹You will then be near the land of the Ammonites, the descendants of Lot. Don't trouble them or start a war against them, because I am not going to give you any of the land that I have given them.' "

1.32: Heb 3.19   **1.34–35:** Heb 3.18   **2.1:** Num 21.4   **2.4:** Gen 36.8   **2.9:** Gen 19.37
2.14: Num 14.28–35   **2.19:** Gen 19.38

20 (This territory is also known as the land of the Rephaim, the name of the people who used to live there; the Ammonites called them Zamzummim. 21 They were as tall as the Anakim. There were many of them, and they were a mighty race. But the LORD destroyed them, so that the Ammonites took over their land and settled there. 22 The LORD had done the same thing for the Edomites, the descendants of Esau, who live in the hill-country of Edom. He destroyed the Horites, so that the Edomites took over their land and settled there, where they still live. 23 The land along the Mediterranean coast had been settled by people from the island of Crete. They had destroyed the Avvim, the original inhabitants, and had taken over all their land as far south as the city of Gaza.)

24 "After we had passed through Moab, the LORD said to us, 'Now, start out and cross the River Arnon. I am placing in your power Sihon, the Amorite king of Heshbon, along with his land. Attack him, and begin occupying his land. 25 From today on I will make people everywhere afraid of you. Everyone will tremble with fear at the mention of your name.'

Israel Defeats King Sihon
(Num 21.21–30)

26 "Then I sent messengers from the desert of Kedemoth to King Sihon of Heshbon with the following offer of peace: 27 'Let us pass through your country. We will go straight through and not leave the road. 28 We will pay for the food we eat and the water we drink. All we want to do is to pass through your country, 29 until we cross the River Jordan into the land that the LORD our God is giving us. The descendants of Esau, who live in Edom, and the Moabites, who live in Ar, allowed us to pass through their territory.'

30 "But King Sihon would not let us pass through his country. The LORD your God had made him stubborn and rebellious, so that we could defeat him and take his territory, which we still occupy.

31 "Then the LORD said to me, 'Look, I have made King Sihon and his land helpless before you; take his land and occupy it.' 32 Sihon came out with all his men to fight us near the town of Jahaz, 33 but the LORD our God put him in our power, and we killed him, his sons, and

all his men. 34 At the same time we captured and destroyed every town, and put everyone to death, men, women, and children. We left no survivors. 35 We took the livestock and plundered the towns. 36 The LORD our God let us capture all the towns from Aroer, on the edge of the valley of the Arnon, and the city in the middle of that valley, all the way to Gilead. No town had walls too strong for us. 37 But we did not go near the territory of the Ammonites or to the banks of the River Jabbok or to the towns of the hill-country or to any other place where the LORD our God had commanded us not to go.

Israel Conquers King Og
(Num 21.31–35)

3 "Next, we moved north towards the region of Bashan, and King Og came out with all his men to fight us near the town of Edrei. 2 But the LORD said to me, 'Don't be afraid of him. I am going to give you him, his men, and all his territory to you. Do the same to him as you did to Sihon the Amorite king who ruled in Heshbon.'

3 "So the LORD also placed King Og and his people in our power, and we slaughtered them all. 4 At the same time we captured all his towns—there was not one that we did not take. In all we captured sixty towns—the whole region of Argob, where King Og of Bashan ruled. 5 All these towns were fortified with high walls, gates, and bars to lock the gates, and there were also many villages without walls. 6 We destroyed all the towns and put to death all the men, women, and children, just as we did in the towns that belonged to King Sihon of Heshbon. 7 We took the livestock and plundered the towns.

8 "At that time we took from those two Amorite kings the land east of the River Jordan, from the River Arnon to Mount Hermon. 9 (Mount Hermon is called Sirion by the Sidonians, and Senir by the Amorites.) 10 We took all the territory of King Og of Bashan: the cities on the plateau, the regions of Gilead and of Bashan, as far east as the towns of Salecah and Edrei."

11 (King Og was the last of the Rephaim. His coffin,[b] made of stone,[c] was four metres long and almost two metres wide according to standard measurements. It can still be seen in the Ammonite city of Rabbah.)

[b] coffin; *or* bed.   [c] stone; *or* iron.

The Tribes That Settled East of the Jordan
(Num 32.1–42)

12 "When we took possession of the land, I assigned to the tribes of Reuben and Gad the territory north of the town of Aroer near the River Arnon and part of the hill-country of Gilead, along with its towns. 13 To half the tribe of Manasseh I assigned the rest of Gilead and also all of Bashan, where Og had ruled, that is, the entire Argob region."

(Bashan was known as the land of the Rephaim. 14 Jair, from the tribe of Manasseh, took the entire region of Argob, that is, Bashan, as far as the border of Geshur and Maacah. He named the villages after himself, and they are still known as the villages of Jair.)

15 "I assigned Gilead to the clan of Machir of the tribe of Manasseh. 16 And to the tribes of Reuben and Gad I assigned the territory from Gilead to the River Arnon. The middle of the river was their southern boundary, and their northern boundary was the River Jabbok, part of which formed the Ammonite border. 17 On the west their territory extended to the River Jordan, from Lake Galilee in the north down to the Dead Sea in the south and to the foot of Mount Pisgah on the east.

18 "At the same time, I gave them the following instructions: 'The LORD our God has given you this land east of the Jordan to occupy. Now arm your fighting men and send them across the Jordan ahead of the other tribes of Israel, to help them to occupy their land. 19 Only your wives, children, and livestock—I know you have a lot of livestock—will remain behind in the towns that I have assigned to you. 20 Help your fellow-Israelites until they occupy the land that the LORD is giving them west of the Jordan and until the LORD lets them live there in peace, as he has already done here for you. After that, you may return to this land which I have assigned to you.'

21 "Then I instructed Joshua: 'You have seen all that the LORD your God did to those two kings, Sihon and Og; and he will do the same to everyone else whose land you invade. 22 Don't be afraid of them, for the LORD your God will fight for you.'

Moses Is Not Permitted to Enter Canaan

23 "At that time I earnestly prayed, 24 'Sovereign LORD, I know that you have shown me only the beginning of the great and wonderful things you are going to do. There is no god in heaven or on earth who can do the mighty things that you have done! 25 Let me cross the River Jordan, LORD, and see the fertile land on the other side, the beautiful hill-country and the Lebanon Mountains.'

26 "But because of you people the LORD was angry with me and would not listen. Instead, he said, 'That's enough! Don't mention this again! 27 Go to the peak of Mount Pisgah and look to the north and to the south, to the east and to the west. Look carefully at what you see, because you will never go across the Jordan. 28 Give Joshua his instructions. Strengthen his determination, because he will lead the people across to occupy the land that you see.'

29 "So we remained in the valley opposite the town of Bethpeor."

Moses Urges Israel to Be Obedient

4 Then Moses said to the people, "Obey all the laws that I am teaching you, and you will live and occupy the land which the LORD, the God of your ancestors, is giving you. 2 Do not add anything to what I command you, and do not take anything away. Obey the commands of the LORD your God that I have given you. 3 You yourselves saw what the LORD did at Mount Peor. He destroyed everyone who worshipped Baal there, 4 but those of you who were faithful to the LORD your God are still alive today.

5 "I have taught you all the laws, as the LORD my God told me to do. Obey them in the land that you are about to invade and occupy. 6 Obey them faithfully, and this will show the people of other nations how wise you are. When they hear of all these laws, they will say, 'What wisdom and understanding this great nation has!'

7 "No other nation, no matter how great, has a god who is so near when they need him as the LORD our God is to us. He answers us whenever we call for help. 8 No other nation, no matter how great, has laws so just as those that I have taught you today. 9 Be on your guard! Make certain that you do not forget, as long as you live, what you have seen with your own eyes. Tell your children and your grandchildren 10 about the day you stood in the presence of the

3.18–20: Josh 1.12–15   3.23–27: Num 27.12–14; Deut 32.48–52   4.2: Rev 22.18–19
4.3: Num 25.1–9

LORD your God at Mount Sinai,^{x} when he said to me, 'Assemble the people. I want them to hear what I have to say, so that they will learn to obey me as long as they live and so that they will teach their children to do the same.'

11 "Tell your children how you went and stood at the foot of the mountain which was covered with thick clouds of dark smoke and fire blazing up to the sky. 12 Tell them how the LORD spoke to you from the fire, how you heard him speaking but did not see him in any form at all. 13 He told you what you must do to keep the covenant he made with you— you must obey the Ten Commandments, which he wrote on two stone tablets. 14 The LORD told me to teach you all the laws that you are to obey in the land that you are about to invade and occupy.

Warning against Idolatry

15 "When the LORD spoke to you from the fire on Mount Sinai, you did not see any form. For your own good, then, make certain 16 that you do not sin by making for yourselves an idol in any form at all— whether man or woman, 17 animal or bird, 18 reptile or fish. 19 Do not be tempted to worship and serve what you see in the sky—the sun, the moon, and the stars. The LORD your God has given these to all other peoples for them to worship. 20 But you are the people he rescued from Egypt, that blazing furnace. He brought you out to make you his own people, as you are today. 21 Because of you the LORD your God was angry with me and solemnly declared that I would not cross the River Jordan to enter the fertile land which he is giving you. 22 I will die in this land and never cross the river, but you are about to go across and occupy that fertile land. 23 Be certain that you do not forget the covenant that the LORD your God made with you. Obey his command not to make yourselves any kind of idol, 24 because the LORD your God is like a flaming fire; he tolerates no rivals.

25 "Even when you have been in the land a long time and have children and grandchildren, do not sin by making for yourselves an idol in any form at all. This is evil in the LORD's sight, and it will make him angry. 26 I call heaven and earth as witnesses against you today that, if you

disobey me, you will soon disappear from the land. You will not live very long in the land across the Jordan that you are about to occupy. You will be completely destroyed. 27 The LORD will scatter you among other nations, where only a few of you will survive. 28 There you will serve gods made by human hands, gods of wood and stone, gods that cannot see or hear, eat or smell. 29 There you will look for the LORD your God, and if you search for him with all your heart, you will find him. 30 When you are in trouble and all those things happen to you, then you will finally turn to the LORD and obey him. 31 He is a merciful God. He will not abandon you or destroy you, and he will not forget the covenant that he himself made with your ancestors.

32 "Search the past, the time before you were born, all the way back to the time when God created man on the earth. Search the entire earth. Has anything as great as this ever happened before? Has anyone ever heard of anything like this? 33 Have any people ever lived after hearing a god speak to them from a fire, as you have? 34 Has any god ever dared to go and take a people from another nation and make them his own, as the LORD your God did for you in Egypt? Before your very eyes he used his great power and strength; he brought plagues and war, worked miracles and wonders, and caused terrifying things to happen. 35 The LORD has shown you this, to prove to you that he alone is God and that there is no other. 36 He let you hear his voice from heaven so that he could instruct you; and here on earth he let you see his holy fire, and he spoke to you from it. 37 Because he loved your ancestors, he chose you, and by his great power he himself brought you out of Egypt. 38 As you advanced, he drove out nations greater and more powerful than you, so that he might bring you in and give you their land, the land which still belongs to you. 39 So remember today and never forget: the LORD is God in heaven and on earth. There is no other god. 40 Obey all his laws that I have given you today, and all will go well with you and your descendants. You will continue to live in the land which the LORD your God is giving you to be yours for ever."

^{x} Sinai; or Horeb.

4.11–12: Ex 19.16–18; Heb 12.18–19   **4.13:** Ex 31.18, 34.28; Deut 9.10   **4.14:** Ex 21.1
4.16: Ex 20.4; Lev 26.1; Deut 5.8, 27.15   **4.17–18a:** Rom 1.23
4.20: Ex 19.5; Deut 7.6, 14.2, 26.18; Tit 2.14; 1 Pet 2.9   **4.21:** Num 20.12   **4.24:** Heb 12.29
4.27–28: Deut 28.36   **4.29:** Jer 29.13   **4.35:** Mk 12.32

The Cities of Refuge East of the Jordan

41 Then Moses set aside three cities east of the River Jordan 42 to which a man could escape and be safe if he had accidentally killed someone who had not been his enemy. He could escape to one of these cities and not be put to death. 43 For the tribe of Reuben there was the city of Bezer, on the desert plateau; for the tribe of Gad there was Ramoth, in the territory of Gilead; and for the tribe of Manasseh there was Golan, in the territory of Bashan.

Introduction to the Giving of God's Law

44 Moses gave God's laws and teachings to the people of Israel. 45-46 It was after they had come out of Egypt and were in the valley east of the River Jordan, opposite the town of Bethpeor, that he gave them these laws. This was in the territory that had belonged to King Sihon of the Amorites, who had ruled in the town of Heshbon. Moses and the people of Israel defeated him when they came out of Egypt. 47 They occupied his land and the land of King Og of Bashan, the other Amorite king who lived east of the Jordan. 48 This land extended from the town of Aroer, on the edge of the River Arnon, all the way north to Mount Sirion,d that is, Mount Hermon. 49 It also included all the region east of the River Jordan as far south as the Dead Sea and east to the foot of Mount Pisgah.

The Ten Commandments
(Ex 20.1–17)

5 Moses called together all the people of Israel and said to them, "People of Israel, listen to all the laws that I am giving you today. Learn them and be sure that you obey them. 2 At Mount Sinai the LORD our God made a covenant, 3 not only with our fathers, but with all of us who are living today. 4 There on the mountain the LORD spoke to you face-to-face from the fire. 5 I stood between you and the LORD at that time to tell you what he said, because you were afraid of the fire and would not go up the mountain.

"The LORD said, 6 'I am the LORD your God, who rescued you from Egypt, where you were slaves.

The LORD our God made a covenant (5.2)

7 "'Worship no god but me.

8 "'Do not make for yourselves images of anything in heaven or on earth or in the water under the earth. 9 Do not bow down to any idol or worship it, for I am the LORD your God and I tolerate no rivals. I bring punishment on those who hate me and on their descendants down to the third and fourth generation. 10 But I show my love to thousands of generationse of those who love me and obey my laws.

11 "'Do not use my name for evil purposes, for I, the LORD your God, will punish anyone who misuses my name.

12 "'Observe the Sabbath and keep it holy, as I, the LORD your God, have commanded you. 13 You have six days in which to do your work, 14 but the seventh day is a day of rest dedicated to me. On that day no one is to work—neither you, your children, your slaves, your animals, nor the foreigners who live in your country. Your slaves must rest just as you do. 15 Remember that you were slaves in Egypt, and that I, the LORD your God, rescued you by my great power and strength. That is why I command you to observe the Sabbath.

d One ancient translation Sirion; Hebrew Sion.   e thousands of generations; or thousands.
4.41–43: Josh 20.8–9   **5.8–9:** Lev 26.1; Deut 4.15–18, 27.15
5.9–10: Ex 34.6–7; Num 14.18; Deut 7.9–10   **5.11:** Lev 19.12   **5.12:** Ex 16.23–30, 31.12–14
5.13–14: Ex 23.12, 31.15, 34.21, 35.2; Lev 23.3

16 " 'Respect your father and your mother, as I, the LORD your God, command you, so that all may go well with you and so that you may live a long time in the land that I am giving you.

17 " 'Do not commit murder.

18 " 'Do not commit adultery.

19 " 'Do not steal.

20 " 'Do not accuse anyone falsely.

21 " 'Do not desire another man's wife; do not desire his house, his land, his slaves, his cattle, his donkeys, or anything else that he owns.'

22 "These are the commandments the LORD gave to all of you when you were gathered at the mountain. When he spoke with a mighty voice from the fire and from the thick clouds, he gave these commandments and no others. Then he wrote them on two stone tablets and gave them to me.

The People's Fear
(Ex 20.18-21)

23 "When the whole mountain was on fire and you heard the voice from the darkness, your leaders and the chiefs of your tribes came to me 24 and said, 'The LORD our God showed us his greatness and his glory when we heard him speak from the fire! Today we have seen that it is possible for a man to continue to live, even though God has spoken to him. 25 But why should we risk death again? That terrible fire will destroy us. We are sure to die if we hear the LORD our God speak again. 26 Has any human being ever lived after hearing the living God speak from a fire? 27 Go back, Moses, and listen to everything that the LORD our God says. Then return and tell us what he said to you. We will listen and obey.'

28 "When the LORD heard this, he said to me, 'I have heard what these people said, and they are right. 29 If only they would always feel like this! If only they would always honour me and obey all my commands, so that everything would go well with them and their descendants for ever. 30 Go and tell them to return to their tents. 31 But you, Moses, stay here with me, and I will give you all my laws and commands. Teach them to the people, so that they will obey them in the land that I am giving them.'

32 "People of Israel, be sure that you do everything that the LORD your God has commanded you. Do not disobey any of his laws. 33 Obey them all, so that everything will go well with you and so that you will continue to live in the land that you are going to occupy.

The Great Commandment

6 "These are all the laws that the LORD your God commanded me to teach you. Obey them in the land that you are about to enter and occupy. 2 As long as you live, you and your descendants are to honour the LORD your God and obey all his laws that I am giving you, so that you may live in that land a long time. 3 Listen to them, people of Israel, and obey them! Then all will go well with you, and you will become a mighty nation and live in that rich and fertile land, just as the LORD, the God of our ancestors, has promised.

4 "Israel, remember this! The LORD— and the LORD alone—is our God.[f] 5 Love the LORD your God with all your heart, with all your soul, and with all your strength. 6 Never forget these commands that I am giving you today. 7 Teach them to your children. Repeat them when you are at home and when you are away, when you are resting and when you are working. 8 Tie them on your arms and wear them on your foreheads as a reminder. 9 Write them on the door-posts of your houses and on your gates.

Warning against Disobedience

10 "Just as the LORD your God promised your ancestors, Abraham, Isaac, and Jacob, he will give you a land with large and prosperous cities which you did not build. 11 The houses will be full of good things which you did not put in them, and there will be wells that you did not dig, and vineyards and olive orchards that you did not plant. When the LORD brings you into this land and you have all you want to eat, 12 make certain that you do not forget the LORD who rescued you from Egypt, where you were slaves. 13 Honour

f The LORD...is our God; *or* The LORD, our God, is the only God; *or* The LORD our God is one.
5.16: Deut 27.16; Mt 15.4, 19.19; Mk 7.10, 10.19; Lk 18.20; Eph 6.2,3
5.17: Gen 9.6; Lev 24.17; Mt 5.21, 19.18; Mk 10.19; Lk 18.20; Rom 13.9; Jas 2.11
5.18: Lev 20.10; Mt 5.27, 19.18; Mk 10.19; Lk 18.20; Rom 13.9; Jas 2.11
5.19: Lev 19.11; Mt 19.18; Mk 10.19; Lk 18.20; Rom 13.9
5.20: Ex 23.1; Mt 19.18; Mk 10.19; Lk 18.20   **5.21:** Rom 7.7, 13.9   **5.22-27:** Heb 12.18-19
6.4: Mk 12.29   **6.5:** Mt 22.37; Mk 12.30; Lk 10.27   **6.6-9:** Deut 11.18-20
6.10: Gen 12.7, 26.3, 28.13   **6.13:** Mt 4.10; Lk 4.8

Write them on the door-posts (6.9)

the LORD your God, worship only him, and make your promises in his name alone. ¹⁴Do not worship other gods, any of the gods of the peoples around you. ¹⁵If you do worship other gods, the LORD's anger will come against you like fire and will destroy you completely, because the LORD your God, who is present with you, tolerates no rivals.

16 "Do not put the LORD your God to the test, as you did at Massah. ¹⁷Be sure that you obey all the laws that he has given you. ¹⁸Do what the LORD says is right and good, and all will go well with you. You will be able to take possession of the fertile land that the LORD promised your ancestors, ¹⁹and you will drive out your enemies, as he promised.

20 "In time to come your children will ask you, 'Why did the LORD our God command us to obey all these laws?' ²¹Then tell them, 'We were slaves of the king of Egypt, and the LORD rescued us by his great power. ²²With our own eyes we saw him work miracles and do terrifying things to the Egyptians and to their king and to all his officials. ²³He freed us from Egypt to bring us here and give us this land, as he had promised our ancestors he would. ²⁴Then the LORD our God commanded us to obey all these laws

and to honour him. If we do, he will always watch over our nation and keep it prosperous. ²⁵If we faithfully obey everything that God has commanded us, he will be pleased with us.'ᵍ

The Lord's Own People
(Ex 34.11-16)

7 "The LORD your God will bring you into the land which you are going to occupy, and he will drive many nations out of it. As you advance, he will drive out seven nations larger and more powerful than you: the Hittites, the Girgashites, the Amorites, the Canaanites, the Perizzites, the Hivites, and the Jebusites. ²When the LORD your God places these people in your power and you defeat them, you must put them all to death. Do not make an alliance with them or show them any mercy. ³Do not marry any of them, and do not let your children marry any of them, ⁴because then they would lead your children away from the LORD to worship other gods. If that happens, the LORD will be angry with you and destroy you at once. ⁵So then, tear down their altars, break their sacred stone pillars in pieces, cut down the symbols of their goddess Asherah, and burn their idols. ⁶Do this because you belong to the LORD your God. From all the peoples on earth he chose you to be his own special people.

7 "The LORD did not love you and choose you because you outnumbered other peoples; you were the smallest nation on earth. ⁸But the LORD loved you and wanted to keep the promise that he made to your ancestors. That is why he saved you by his great might and set you free from slavery to the king of Egypt. ⁹Remember that the LORD your God is the only God and that he is faithful. He will keep his covenant and show his constant love to a thousand generations of those who love him and obey his commands, ¹⁰but he will not hesitate to punish those who hate him. ¹¹So now, obey what you have been taught; obey all the laws that I have given you today.

The Blessings of Obedience
(Deut 28.1-14)

12 "If you listen to these commands and

ᵍ If we faithfully...with us; *or* The right thing for us to do is to obey faithfully everything that God has commanded us.
6.16: Ex 17.1-7; Mt 4.7; Lk 4.12   **7.1:** Acts 13.19   **7.5:** Deut 12.3
7.6: Ex 19.5; Deut 4.20, 14.2, 26.18; Tit 2.14; 1 Pet 2.9
7.9-10: Ex 20.5-6, 34.6-7; Num 14.18; Deut 5.9-10   **7.12-16:** Deut 11.13-17

obey them faithfully, then the LORD your God will continue to keep his covenant with you and will show you his constant love, as he promised your ancestors. ¹³ He will love you and bless you, so that you will increase in number and have many children; he will bless your fields, so that you will have corn, wine, and olive-oil; and he will bless you by giving you a lot of livestock and sheep. He will give you all these blessings in the land that he promised your ancestors he would give to you. ¹⁴ No people in the world will be as richly blessed as you. None of you nor any of your livestock will be sterile. ¹⁵ The LORD will protect you from all sickness, and he will not bring on you any of the dreadful diseases that you experienced in Egypt, but he will bring them on all your enemies. ¹⁶ Destroy every nation that the LORD your God places in your power, and do not show them any mercy. Do not worship their gods, for that would be fatal.

17 "Do not tell yourselves that these peoples outnumber you and that you cannot drive them out. ¹⁸ Do not be afraid of them; remember what the LORD your God did to the king of Egypt and to all his people. ¹⁹ Remember the terrible plagues that you saw with your own eyes, the miracles and wonders, and the great power and strength by which the LORD your God set you free. In the same way that he destroyed the Egyptians, he will destroy all these people that you now fear. ²⁰ He will even cause panic ʰ among them and will destroy those who escape and go into hiding. ²¹ So do not be afraid of these people. The LORD your God is with you; he is a great God and one to be feared. ²² Little by little he will drive out these nations as you advance. You will not be able to destroy them all at once, for, if you did, the number of wild animals would increase and be a threat to you. ²³ The LORD will put your enemies in your power and make them panic until they are destroyed. ²⁴ He will put their kings in your power. You will kill them, and they will be forgotten. No one will be able to stop you; you will destroy everyone. ²⁵ Burn their idols. Do not desire the silver or gold that is on them, and do not take it for yourselves. If you do, that will be fatal, because the LORD hates idolatry. ²⁶ Do not bring any of these idols into your homes, or the same curse will be on you that is on them. You must hate

and despise these idols, because they are under the LORD's curse.

A Good Land to Be Possessed

8 "Obey faithfully all the laws that I have given you today, so that you may live, increase in number, and occupy the land which the LORD promised to your ancestors. ² Remember how the LORD your God led you on this long journey through the desert these past forty years, sending hardships to test you, so that he might know what you intended to do and whether you would obey his commands. ³ He made you go hungry, and then he gave you manna to eat, food that you and your ancestors had never eaten before. He did this to teach you that man must not depend on bread alone to sustain him, but on everything that the LORD says. ⁴ During these forty years your clothes have not worn out, nor have your feet swollen up. ⁵ Remember that the LORD your God corrects and punishes you just as a father disciplines his children. ⁶ So then, do as the LORD has commanded you: live according to his laws and obey him. ⁷ The LORD your God is bringing you into a fertile land—a land that has rivers and springs, and underground streams gushing out into the valleys and hills; ⁸ a land that produces wheat and barley, grapes, figs, pomegranates, olives, and honey. ⁹ There you will never go hungry or ever be in need. Its rocks have iron in them, and from its hills you can mine copper. ¹⁰ You will have all you want to eat, and you will give thanks to the LORD your God for the fertile land that he has given you.

Warnings against Forgetting the Lord

11 "Make certain that you do not forget the LORD your God; do not fail to obey any of his laws that I am giving you today. ¹² When you have all you want to eat and have built good houses to live in ¹³ and when your cattle and sheep, your silver and gold, and all your other possessions have increased, ¹⁴ make sure that you do not become proud and forget the LORD your God who rescued you from Egypt, where you were slaves. ¹⁵ He led you through that vast and terrifying desert where there were poisonous snakes and scorpions. In that dry and waterless land he made water flow out of solid rock for you. ¹⁶ In the desert he gave you manna

ʰcause panic; *or* send hornets, *or* send plagues.
8.3: Mt 4.4; Lk 4.4   **8.11-16:** Hos 13.5-6

to eat, food that your ancestors had never eaten. He sent hardships on you to test you, so that in the end he could bless you with good things. [17] So then, you must never think that you have made yourselves wealthy by your own power and strength. [18] Remember that it is the LORD your God who gives you the power to become rich. He does this because he is still faithful today to the covenant that he made with your ancestors. [19] Never forget the LORD your God or turn to other gods to worship and serve them. If you do, then I warn you today that you will certainly be destroyed. [20] If you do not obey the LORD, then you will be destroyed just like those nations that he is going to destroy as you advance.

The People's Disobedience

9 "Listen, people of Israel! Today you are about to cross the River Jordan and occupy the land belonging to nations greater and more powerful than you. Their cities are large, with walls that reach the sky. [2] The people themselves are tall and strong; they are giants, and you have heard it said that no one can stand against them. [3] But now you will see for yourselves that the LORD your God will go ahead of you like a raging fire. He will defeat them as you advance, so that you will drive them out and destroy them quickly, as he promised.

4 "After the LORD your God has driven them out for you, do not say to yourselves that he brought you in to possess this land because you deserved it. No, the LORD is going to drive these people out for you because they are wicked. [5] It is not because you are good and do what is right that the LORD is letting you take their land. He will drive them out because they are wicked and because he intends to keep the promise that he made to your ancestors, Abraham, Isaac, and Jacob. [6] You can be sure that the LORD is not giving you this fertile land because you deserve it. No, you are a stubborn people.

7 "Never forget how you made the LORD your God angry in the desert. From the day that you left Egypt until the day you arrived here, you have rebelled against him. [8] Even at Mount Sinai you made the LORD angry—angry enough to destroy you. [9] I went up the mountain to receive the stone tablets on which was written the covenant that the LORD had made with

you. I stayed there forty days and nights and did not eat or drink anything. [10] Then the LORD gave me the two stone tablets on which he had written with his own hand what he had said to you from the fire on the day that you were gathered there at the mountain. [11] Yes, after those forty days and nights the LORD gave me the two stone tablets on which he had written the covenant.

12 "Then the LORD said to me, 'Go down the mountain at once, because your people, whom you led out of Egypt, have become corrupt and have done evil. They have already turned away from what I commanded them to do, and they have made an idol for themselves.'

13 "The LORD also said to me, 'I know how stubborn these people are. [14] Don't try to stop me. I intend to destroy them so that no one will remember them any longer. Then I will make you the father of a nation larger and more powerful than they are.'

15 "So I turned and went down the mountain, carrying the two stone tablets on which the covenant was written. Flames of fire were coming from the mountain. [16] I saw that you had already disobeyed the command that the LORD your God had given you, and that you had sinned against him by making yourselves a metal idol in the form of a bull-calf. [17] So there in front of you I threw the stone tablets down and broke them to pieces. [18] Then once again I lay face downwards in the LORD's presence for forty days and nights and did not eat or drink anything. I did this because you had sinned against the LORD and had made him angry. [19] I was afraid of the LORD's fierce anger, because he was furious enough to destroy you; but once again the LORD listened to me. [20] The LORD was also angry enough with Aaron to kill him, so I prayed for Aaron at the same time. [21] I took that sinful thing that you had made—that metal bull-calf—and threw it into the fire. Then I broke it in pieces, ground it to dust, and threw the dust into the stream that flowed down the mountain.

22 "You also made the LORD your God angry when you were at Taberah, Massah, and Kibroth Hattaavah. [23] And when he sent you from Kadesh Barnea with orders to go and take possession of the land that he was giving you, you rebelled against him; you did not trust him or obey him.

9.9: Ex 24.18   **9.19:** Heb 12.21   **9.22:** Num 11.3,34; Ex 17.7
9.23: Num 13.25—14.38; Deut 1.21,26; Heb 3.16

So I turned and went down the mountain (9.15)

24 Ever since I have known you, you have rebelled against the LORD.

25 "So I lay face downwards in the LORD's presence those forty days and nights, because I knew that he was determined to destroy you. 26 And I prayed, 'Sovereign LORD, don't destroy your own people, the people you rescued and brought out of Egypt by your great strength and power. 27 Remember your servants, Abraham, Isaac, and Jacob, and do not pay any attention to the stubbornness, wickedness, and sin of this people. 28 Otherwise, the Egyptians will say that you were unable to take your people into the land that you had promised them. They will say that you took your people out into the desert to kill them, because you hated them. 29 After all, these are the people whom you chose to be your own and whom you brought out of Egypt by your great power and might.'

Moses Receives the Commandments Again
(Ex 34.1-10)

10 "Then the LORD said to me, 'Cut two stone tablets like the first ones and make a wooden box to put them in. Come up to me on the mountain, 2 and I will write on those tablets what I wrote on the tablets that you broke, and then you are to put them in the box.'

3 "So I made a box of acacia-wood and cut two stone tablets like the first ones and took them up the mountain. 4 Then the LORD wrote on those tablets the same words that he had written the first time, the Ten Commandments that he gave you when he spoke from the fire on the day you were gathered at the mountain. The LORD gave me the tablets, 5 and I turned and went down the mountain. Then, just as the LORD had commanded, I put them in the box that I had made—and they have been there ever since."

6 (The Israelites set out from the wells that belonged to the people of Jaakan, and went to Moserah. There Aaron died and was buried, and his son Eleazar succeeded him as priest. 7 From there they went to Gudgodah and then on to Jotbathah, a well-watered place. 8 At the mountain[i] the LORD appointed the men of the tribe of Levi to be in charge of the Covenant Box, to serve him as priests, and to pronounce blessings in his name. And these are still their duties. 9 That is why the tribe of Levi received no land as the other tribes did; what they received was the privilege of being the LORD's priests, as the LORD your God promised.)

10 "I stayed on the mountain forty days

---

[i] the mountain; *or* that time.

10.6: Num 20.28, 33.38   **10.8:** Num 3.5-8   **10.10:** Ex 34.28

and nights, as I did the first time. The LORD listened to me once more and agreed not to destroy you. [11] Then he told me to go and lead you, so that you could take possession of the land that he had promised to give to your ancestors.

What God Demands

12 "Now, people of Israel, listen to what the LORD your God demands of you: Worship the LORD and do all that he commands. Love him, serve him with all your heart, [13] and obey all his laws. I am giving them to you today for your benefit. [14] To the LORD belong even the highest heavens; the earth is his also, and everything on it. [15] But the LORD's love for your ancestors was so strong that he chose you instead of any other people, and you are still his chosen people. [16] So then, from now on be obedient to the LORD and stop being stubborn. [17] The LORD your God is supreme over all gods and over all powers. He is great and mighty, and he is to be feared. He does not show partiality, and he does not accept bribes. [18] He makes sure that orphans and widows are treated fairly; he loves the foreigners who live with our people, and gives them food and clothes. [19] So then, show love for those foreigners, because you were once foreigners in Egypt. [20] Obey the LORD your God and worship only him. Be faithful to him and make your promises in his name alone. [21] Praise him—he is your God, and you have seen with your own eyes the great and astounding things that he has done for you. [22] When your ancestors went to Egypt, there were only seventy of them. But now the LORD your God has made you as numerous as the stars in the sky.

The LORD's Greatness

11 "Love the LORD your God and always obey all his laws. [2] Remember today what you have learned about the LORD through your experiences with him. It was you, not your children, who had these experiences. You saw the LORD's greatness, his power, his might, [3] and his miracles. You saw what he did to the king of Egypt and to his entire country. [4] You saw how the LORD completely wiped out the Egyptian army, along with their horses and chariots, by drowning them in the Red Sea[j] when they were pursuing you. [5] You know what the LORD did for you in the desert before you arrived here. [6] You recall what he did to Dathan and Abiram, the sons of Eliab of the tribe of Reuben. In the sight of everyone the earth opened up and swallowed them, along with their families, their tents, and all their servants and animals. [7] Yes, you are the ones who have seen all these great things that the LORD has done.

The Blessings of the Promised Land

8 "Obey all the laws that I have given you today. Then you will be able to cross the river and occupy the land that you are about to enter. [9] And you will live a long time in the rich and fertile land that the LORD promised to give your ancestors and their descendants. [10] The land that you are about to occupy is not like the land of Egypt, where you lived before. There, when you sowed seed, you had to work hard to irrigate the fields; [11] but the land that you are about to enter is a land of mountains and valleys, a land watered by rain. [12] The LORD your God takes care of this land and watches over it throughout the year.

13 "So then, obey the commands that I have given you today; love the LORD your God and serve him with all your heart. [14] If you do, he will send rain on your land when it is needed, in the autumn and in the spring, so that there will be corn, wine, and olive-oil for you, [15] and grass for your livestock. You will have all the food you want. [16] Do not let yourselves be led away from the LORD to worship and serve other gods. [17] If you do, the LORD will become angry with you. He will hold back the rain, and your ground will become too dry for crops to grow. Then you will soon die there, even though it is a good land that he is giving you.

18 "Remember these commands and cherish them. Tie them on your arms and wear them on your foreheads as a reminder. [19] Teach them to your children. Talk about them when you are at home and when you are away, when you are resting and when you are working. [20] Write them on the door-posts of your houses and on your gates. [21] Then you and your children will live a long time in the

---

[j] RED SEA: *See Word List.*
10.17: 1 Tim 6.15; Rev 17.14, 19.16; Acts 10.34; Rom 2.11; Gal 2.6; Eph 6.9
10.22: Gen 15.5, 22.17, 46.27   **11.3:** Ex 7.8—12.13   **11.4:** Ex 14.28   **11.6:** Num 16.31-32
11.13–17: Lev 26.3-5; Deut 7.12-16, 28.1-14   **11.20:** Deut 6.6-9

Teach them to your children (11.19)

occupy, you are to proclaim the blessing from Mount Gerizim and the curse from Mount Ebal. ³⁰(These two mountains are west of the River Jordan in the territory of the Canaanites who live in the Jordan Valley. They are towards the west, not far from the sacred trees of Moreh near the town of Gilgal.) ³¹You are about to cross the River Jordan and occupy the land that the LORD your God is giving you. When you take it and settle there, ³²be sure to obey all the laws that I am giving you today.

The One Place for Worship

12 "Here are the laws that you are to obey as long as you live in the land that the LORD, the God of your ancestors, is giving you. Listen to them! ²In the land that you are taking, destroy all the places where the people worship their gods on high mountains, on hills, and under green trees. ³Tear down their

Tear down their altars (12.3)

land that the LORD your God promised to give to your ancestors. You will live there as long as there is a sky above the earth.

22 "Obey faithfully all the laws that I have given you: Love the LORD your God, do everything he commands, and be faithful to him. ²³Then he will drive out all those nations as you advance, and you will occupy the land belonging to nations greater and more powerful than you. ²⁴All the ground that you march over will be yours. Your territory will extend from the desert in the south to the Lebanon Mountains in the north, and from the River Euphrates in the east to the Mediterranean Sea in the west. ²⁵Wherever you go in that land, the LORD your God will make the people fear you, as he has promised, and no one will be able to stop you.

26 "Today I am giving you the choice between a blessing and a curse—²⁷a blessing, if you obey the commands of the LORD your God that I am giving you today; ²⁸but a curse, if you disobey these commands and turn away to worship other gods that you have never worshipped before. ²⁹When the LORD brings you into the land that you are going to

altars and smash their sacred stone pillars to pieces. Burn their symbols of the goddess Asherah and chop down their idols, so that they will never again be worshipped at those places.

4 "Do not worship the LORD your God in the way that these people worship their gods. ⁵Out of the territory of all your tribes the LORD will choose the one place where the people are to come into his presence and worship him. ⁶There you are to offer your sacrifices that are to be burnt and your other sacrifices, your tithes and your offerings, the gifts that you promise to the LORD, your freewill offerings, and the first-born of your cattle and sheep. ⁷There, in the presence of the

11.24-25: Josh 1.3-5   **11.29:** Deut 27.11-14; Josh 8.33-35   **12.3:** Deut 7.5

LORD your God, who has blessed you, you and your families will eat and enjoy the good things that you have worked for.

8 "When that time comes, you must not do as you have been doing. Until now you have all been worshipping as you please, ⁹because you have not yet entered the land that the LORD your God is giving you, where you can live in peace. ¹⁰When you cross the River Jordan, the LORD will let you occupy the land and live there. He will keep you safe from all your enemies, and you will live in peace. ¹¹The LORD will choose a single place where he is to be worshipped, and there you must bring to him everything that I have commanded: your sacrifices that are to be burnt and your other sacrifices, your tithes and your offerings, and those special gifts that you have promised to the LORD. ¹²Be joyful there in his presence, together with your children, your servants, and the Levites who live in your towns; remember that the Levites will have no land of their own. ¹³You are not to offer your sacrifices wherever you choose; ¹⁴you must offer them only in the one place that the LORD will choose in the territory of one of your tribes. Only there are you to offer your sacrifices that are to be burnt and do all the other things that I have commanded you.

15 "But you are free to kill and eat your animals wherever you live. You may eat as many as the LORD gives you. All of you, whether ritually clean or unclean, may eat them, just as you would eat the meat of deer or antelope. ¹⁶But you must not use their blood as food; you must pour it out on the ground like water. ¹⁷Nothing that you offer to the LORD is to be eaten in the places where you live: neither the tithes of your corn, your wine, or your olive-oil, nor the first-born of your cattle and sheep, the gifts that you promise to the LORD, your freewill offerings, or any other offerings. ¹⁸You and your children, together with your servants and the Levites who live in your towns, are to eat these offerings only in the presence of the LORD your God, in the one place of worship chosen by the LORD your God. And you are to be happy there over everything that you have done. ¹⁹Be sure, also, not to neglect the Levites, as long as you live in your land.

20 "When the LORD your God enlarges your territory, as he has promised, you may eat meat whenever you wish. ²¹If the one place of worship is too far away, then, whenever you wish, you may kill any of the cattle or sheep that the LORD has given you, and you may eat the meat at home, as I have told you. ²²Anyone, ritually clean or unclean, may eat that meat, just as he would eat the meat of deer or antelope. ²³Only do not eat meat with blood still in it, for the life is in the blood, and you must not eat the life with the meat. ²⁴Do not use the blood for food; instead pour it out on the ground like water. ²⁵If you obey this command, the LORD will be pleased, and all will go well for you and your descendants. ²⁶Take to the one place of worship your offerings and the gifts that you have promised the LORD. ²⁷Offer there the sacrifices which are to be completely burnt on the LORD's altar. Also offer those sacrifices in which you eat the meat and pour the blood out on the altar. ²⁸Obey faithfully everything that I have commanded you, and all will go well for you and your descendants for ever, because you will be doing what is right and what pleases the LORD your God.

Warning against Idolatry

29 "The LORD your God will destroy the nations as you invade their land, and you will occupy it and settle there. ³⁰After the LORD destroys those nations, make sure that you don't follow their religious practices, because that would be fatal. Don't try to find out how they worship their gods, so that you can worship in the same way. ³¹Do not worship the LORD your God in the way they worship their gods, for in the worship of their gods they do all the disgusting things that the LORD hates. They even sacrifice their children in the fires on their altars.

32 "Do everything that I have commanded you; do not add anything to it or take anything from it.

13 "A prophet or an interpreter of dreams may promise a miracle or a wonder, ²in order to lead you to worship and serve gods that you have not worshipped before. Even if what he promises comes true, ³do not pay any attention to him. The LORD your God is using him to test you, to see if you love the LORD with all your heart. ⁴Follow the LORD and honour him; obey him and keep his commands; worship him and be faithful to him. ⁵But put to death any interpreter

12.16: Gen 9.4; Lev 7.26–27, 17.10–14, 19.26; Deut 15.23   **12.23–24:** Lev 17.10–14
12.32: Deut 4.2; Rev 22.18–19

Do not even listen to him (13.8)

of dreams or prophet that tells you to rebel against the LORD, who rescued you from Egypt, where you were slaves. Such a man is evil and is trying to lead you away from the life that the LORD has commanded you to live. He must be put to death, in order to rid yourselves of this evil.

6 "Even your brother or your son or your daughter or the wife you love or your closest friend may secretly encourage you to worship other gods, gods that you and your ancestors have never worshipped. 7 One of them may encourage you to worship the gods of the people who live near you or the gods of those who live far away. 8 But do not let him persuade you; do not even listen to him. Show him no mercy or pity, and do not protect him. 9 Kill him! Be the first to stone him, and then let everyone else stone him too. 10 Stone him to death! He tried to lead you away from the LORD your God, who rescued you from Egypt, where you were slaves. 11 Then all the people of Israel will hear what happened; they will be afraid, and no one will ever again do such an evil thing.

12 "When you are living in the towns that the LORD your God gives you, you may hear 13 that some worthless men of your nation have misled the people of their town to worship gods that you have never worshipped before. 14 If you hear such a rumour, investigate it thoroughly; and if it is true that this evil thing did happen, 15 then kill all the people in that town and all their livestock too. Destroy that town completely. 16 Bring together all the possessions of the people who live there and pile them up in the town square. Then burn the town and everything in it as an offering to the LORD your God. It must be left in ruins for ever and never again be rebuilt. 17 Do not keep for yourselves anything that was condemned to destruction, and then the LORD will turn from his fierce anger and show you mercy. He will be merciful to you and make you a numerous people, as he promised your ancestors, 18 if you obey all his commands that I have given you today, and do what he requires.

A Forbidden Mourning Practice

14 "You are the people of the LORD your God. So when you mourn for the dead, don't gash yourselves or shave the front of your head, as other people do. 2 You belong to the LORD your God;

14.1: Lev 19.28, 21.5   **14.2:** Ex 19.5–6; Deut 4.20, 7.6, 26.18; Tit 2.14; 1 Pet 2.9

he has chosen you to be his own people from among all the peoples who live on earth.

Clean and Unclean Animals
(Lev 11.1-47)

3 "Do not eat anything that the LORD has declared unclean. 4 You may eat these animals: cattle, sheep, goats, 5 deer, wild sheep, wild goats, or antelopes—6 any animals that have divided hoofs and that also chew the cud. 7 But no animals may be eaten unless they have divided hoofs and also chew the cud. You may not eat camels, rabbits, or rock-badgers. They must be considered unclean; they chew the cud but do not have divided hoofs. 8 Do not eat pigs. They must be considered unclean; they have divided hoofs but do not chew the cud. Do not eat any of these animals or even touch their dead bodies.

9 "You may eat any kind of fish that has fins and scales, 10 but anything living in the water that does not have fins and scales may not be eaten; it must be considered unclean.

11 "You may eat any clean bird. 12-18 But these are the kinds of birds you are not to eat: eagles, owls, hawks, falcons; buzzards, vultures, crows; ostriches; sea-gulls, storks, herons, pelicans, cormorants; k hoopoes; and bats. 19 "All winged insects are unclean; do not eat them. 20 You may eat any clean insect.

21 "Do not eat any animal that dies a natural death. You may let the foreigners who live among you eat it, or you may sell it to other foreigners. But you belong to the LORD your God; you are his people.

"Do not cook a young sheep or goat in its mother's milk.

The Law of the Tithe

22 "Set aside a tithe—a tenth of all that your fields produce each year. 23 Then go to the one place where the LORD your God has chosen to be worshipped; and there in his presence eat the tithes of your corn, wine, and olive-oil, and the first-born of your cattle and sheep. Do this so that you may learn to honour the LORD your God always. 24 If the place of worship is too far from your home for you to carry there the tithe of the produce that the LORD has blessed you with, then do this: 25 Sell your produce and take the money with you to the one place of worship. 26 Spend it on whatever you want—beef, lamb, wine, beer—and there, in the presence of the LORD your God, you and your families are to eat and enjoy yourselves.

27 "Do not neglect the Levites who live in your towns; they have no property of their own. 28 At the end of every third year bring the tithe of all your crops and store it in your towns. 29 This food is for the Levites, since they own no property, and for the foreigners, orphans, and widows who live in your towns. They are to come and get all they need. Do this, and the LORD your God will bless you in everything you do.

The Seventh Year
(Lev 25.1-7)

15 "At the end of every seventh year you are to cancel the debts of those who owe you money. 2 This is how it is to be done. Everyone who has lent money to a fellow-Israelite is to cancel the debt; he must not try to collect the money; the LORD himself has declared the debt cancelled. 3 You may collect what a foreigner owes you, but you must not collect what any of your own people owe you.

4 "The LORD your God will bless you in the land that he is giving you. Not one of your people will be poor 5 if you obey him and carefully observe everything that I command you today. 6 The LORD will bless you, as he has promised. You will lend money to many nations, but you will not have to borrow from any; you will have control over many nations, but no nation will have control over you.

7 "If in any of the towns in the land that the LORD your God is giving you there is a fellow-Israelite in need, then do not be selfish and refuse to help him. 8 Instead, be generous and lend him as much as he needs. 9 Do not refuse to lend him something, just because the year when debts are cancelled is near. Do not let such an evil thought enter your mind. If you refuse to make the loan, he will cry out to the LORD against you, and you will be held guilty. 10 Give to him freely and unselfishly, and the LORD will bless you in everything you do. 11 There will always be some Israelites who are poor and in

---

k The identification of some of these birds is uncertain.
14.21: Ex 23.19, 34.26   **14.22–29:** Lev 27.30-33; Num 18.21   **15.7–8:** Lev 25.35
15.11: Mt 26.11; Mk 14.7; Jn 12.8

need, and so I command you to be generous to them.

The Treatment of Slaves
(Ex 21.1–11)

12 "If a fellow-Israelite, man or woman, sells himself[l] to you as a slave, you are to release him after he has served you for six years. When the seventh year comes, you must let him go free. 13 When

Do not send him away empty-handed (15.13)

you set him free, do not send him away empty-handed. 14 Give to him generously from what the LORD has blessed you with—sheep, corn, and wine. 15 Remember that you were slaves in Egypt and the LORD your God set you free; that is why I am now giving you this command.

16 "But your slave may not want to leave; he may love you and your family and be content to stay. 17 Then take him to the door of your house and there pierce his ear; he will then be your slave for life. Treat your female slave in the same way. 18 Do not be resentful when you set a slave free; after all, he has served you for six years at half the cost of a hired servant.[m] Do this, and the LORD your God will bless you in all that you do.

The First-Born Cattle and Sheep

19 "Set aside for the LORD your God all the first-born males of your cattle and

sheep; don't use any of these cattle for work and don't shear any of these sheep. 20 Each year you and your family are to eat them in the LORD's presence at the one place of worship. 21 But if there is anything wrong with the animals, if they are crippled or blind or have any other serious defect, you must not sacrifice them to the LORD your God. 22 You may eat such animals at home. All of you, whether ritually clean or unclean, may eat them, just as you eat deer or antelope. 23 But do not use their blood for food; instead, you must pour it out on the ground like water.

The Passover
(Ex 12.1–20)

16 "Honour the LORD your God by celebrating Passover in the month of Abib; it was on a night in that month that he rescued you from Egypt. 2 Go to the one place of worship and slaughter there one of your sheep or cattle for the Passover meal to honour the LORD your God. 3 When you eat this meal, do not eat bread prepared with yeast. For seven days you are to eat bread prepared without yeast, as you did when you had to leave Egypt in such a hurry. Eat this bread—it will be called the bread of suffering—so that as long as you live you will remember the day you came out of Egypt, that place of suffering. 4 For seven days no one in your land is to have any yeast in his house; and the meat of the animal killed on the evening of the first day must be eaten that same night.

5–6 "Slaughter the Passover animals at the one place of worship—and nowhere else in the land that the LORD your God will give you. Do it at sunset, the time of day when you left Egypt. 7 Boil the meat and eat it at the one place of worship; and the next morning return home. 8 For the next six days you are to eat bread prepared without yeast, and on the seventh day assemble to worship the LORD your God, and do no work on that day.

The Harvest Festival
(Ex 34.22; Lev 23.15–21)

9 "Count seven weeks from the time that you begin to harvest the corn, 10 and then celebrate the Harvest Festival, to

[l] sells himself; *or* is sold.
[m] at half...servant; *or* and has worked twice as hard as a hired servant.
15.12–18: Lev 25.39–46   **15.19:** Ex 13.12
15.23: Gen 9.4; Lev 7.26–27, 17.10–14, 19.26; Deut 12.16,23
16.1–8: Lev 23.5–8; Num 28.16–25   **16.9–12:** Num 28.26–31

Each man is to bring a gift (16.17)

honour the LORD your God, by bringing him a freewill offering in proportion to the blessing he has given you. [11] Be joyful in the LORD's presence, together with your children, your servants, and the Levites, foreigners, orphans, and widows who live in your towns. Do this at the one place of worship. [12] Be sure that you obey these commands; do not forget that you were slaves in Egypt.

The Festival of Shelters
(Lev 23.33–43)

13 "After you have threshed all your corn and pressed all your grapes, celebrate the Festival of Shelters for seven days. [14] Enjoy it with your children, your servants, and the Levites, foreigners, orphans, and widows who live in your towns. [15] Honour the LORD your God by celebrating this festival for seven days at the one place of worship. Be joyful, because the LORD has blessed your harvest and your work.

16 "All the men of your nation are to come to worship the LORD three times a year at the one place of worship: at Passover, Harvest Festival, and the Festival of Shelters. Each man is to bring a gift [17] as he is able, in proportion to the blessings that the LORD your God has given him.

The Administration of Justice

18 "Appoint judges and other officials in every town that the LORD your God gives you. These men are to judge the people impartially. [19] They are not to be unjust or show partiality in their judge-ments; and they are not to accept bribes, for gifts blind the eyes even of wise and honest men, and cause them to give wrong decisions. [20] Always be fair and just, so that you will occupy the land that the LORD your God is giving you and will continue to live there.

21 "When you make an altar for the LORD your God, do not put beside it a wooden symbol of the goddess Asherah. [22] And do not set up any stone pillar for idol worship; the LORD hates them.

17 "Do not sacrifice to the LORD your God cattle or sheep that have any defects; the LORD hates this.

2 "Suppose you hear that in one of your towns some man or woman has sinned against the LORD and broken his covenant [3] by worshipping and serving other gods or the sun or the moon or the stars, contrary to the LORD's command. [4] If you hear such a report, then investigate it thoroughly. If it is true that this evil thing has happened in Israel, [5] then take that person outside the town and stone him to death. [6] However, he may be put to death only if two or more witnesses testify against him; he is not to be put to death if there is only one witness. [7] The witnesses are to throw the first stones, and then the rest of the people are to stone that person; in this way you will get rid of this evil.

8 "It may be that some cases will be too difficult for the local judges to decide, such as certain cases of property rights or of bodily injury or those cases that involve a distinction between murder and manslaughter. When this happens, go to

16.13–15: Num 29.12–38   **16.19:** Ex 23.6–8; Lev 19.15   **16.21:** Ex 34.13   **16.22:** Lev 26.1
17.3: Ex 22.20   **17.6:** Num 35.30; Deut 19.15; Mt 18.16; 2 Cor 13.1; 1 Tim 5.19; Heb 10.28
17.7: 1 Cor 5.13

the one place of worship chosen by the LORD your God, [9] and present your case to the levitical priests and to the judge who is in office at that time, and let them decide the case. [10] They will give their decision, and you are to do exactly as they tell you. [11] Accept their verdict and follow their instructions in every detail. [12] Anyone who dares to disobey either the judge or the priest on duty is to be put to death; in this way you will remove this evil from Israel. [13] Then everyone will hear of it and be afraid, and no one else will dare to act in such a way.

Instructions Concerning a King

[14] "After you have taken possession of the land that the LORD your God is going to give you and have settled there, then you will decide you need a king like all the nations round you. [15] Make sure that the man you choose to be king is the one whom the LORD has chosen. He must be one of your own people; do not make a foreigner your king. [16] The king is not to have a large number of horses for his army, and he is not to send people to Egypt to buy horses, [n] because the LORD has said that his people are never to return there. [17] The king is not to have many wives, because this would make him turn away from the LORD; and he is not to make himself rich with silver and gold. [18] When he becomes king, he is to have a copy of the book of God's laws and teachings made from the original copy kept by the levitical priests. [19] He is to keep this book near him and read from it all his life, so that he will learn to honour the LORD and to obey faithfully everything that is commanded in it. [20] This will keep him from thinking that he is better than his fellow-Israelites and from disobeying the LORD's commands in any way. Then he will reign for many years, and his descendants will rule Israel for many generations.

The Share of the Priests

18 "The priestly tribe of Levi is not to receive any share of land in Israel; instead, they are to live on the offerings and other sacrifices given to the LORD. [2] They are to own no land, as the other tribes do; their share is the privilege of being the LORD's priests, as the LORD has promised.

3 "Whenever cattle or sheep are sacrificed, the priests are to be given the shoulder, the jaw, and the stomach. [4] They are to receive the first share of the corn, wine, olive-oil, and wool. [5] The LORD chose from all your tribes the tribe of Levi to serve him as priests for ever.

6 "Any Levite who wants to may come from any town in Israel to the one place of worship [7] and may serve there as a priest of the LORD his God, like the other Levites who are serving there. [8] He is to receive the same amount of food as the other priests, and he may keep whatever his family sends him. [o]

Warning against Pagan Practices

9 "When you come into the land that the LORD your God is giving you, don't follow the disgusting practices of the nations that are there. [10] Don't sacrifice your children in the fires on your altars; and don't let your people practise divination or look for omens or use spells [11] or charms, and don't let them consult the spirits of the dead. [12] The LORD your God hates people who do these disgusting things, and that is why he is driving those nations out of the land as you advance. [13] Be completely faithful to the LORD."

The Promise to Send a Prophet

14 Then Moses said, "In the land you are about to occupy, people follow the advice of those who practise divination and look for omens, but the LORD your God does not allow you to do this. [15] Instead, he will send you a prophet like me from among your own people, and you are to obey him. [p]

16 "On the day that you were gathered at Mount Sinai, you begged not to hear the LORD speak again or to see his fiery presence any more, because you were afraid you would die. [17] So the LORD said to me, 'They have made a wise request. [18] I will send them a prophet like you from among their own people; I will tell him what to say, and he [q] will tell the people

---

[n] to buy horses; *or* in exchange for horses.
[o] *Probable text* and he may keep...sends him; *Hebrew unclear.*
[p] a prophet...him; *or* prophets...them. [q] a prophet...him...he; *or* prophets...them...they.
17.14: 1 Sam 8.5   **17.16:** 1 Kgs 10.28; 2 Chr 1.16, 9.28
17.17: 1 Kgs 10.14–22,27, 11.1–8; 2 Chr 1.15, 9.27   **18.2:** Num 18.20
18.10: Lev 19.26; Ex 22.18   **18.11:** Lev 19.31   **18.13:** Mt 5.48   **18.15:** Acts 3.22, 7.37

It was by accident that he killed a man (19.6)

everything I command. ¹⁹He will speak in my name, and I͏ʳ will punish anyone who refuses to obey him. ²⁰But if any prophet dares to speak a message in my name when I did not command him to do so, he must die for it, and so must any prophet who speaks in the name of other gods.'

21 "You may wonder how you can tell when a prophet's message does not come from the LORD. ²²If a prophet speaks in the name of the LORD and what he says does not come true, then it is not the LORD's message. That prophet has spoken on his own authority, and you are not to fear him.

The Cities of Refuge
(Num 35.9–28; Josh 20.1–9)

19 "After the LORD your God has destroyed the people whose land he is giving you and after you have taken their cities and houses and settled there, ²⁻³divide the territory into three parts, each with a city that can be easily reached. Then a man who kills someone will be able to escape to one of them for protection. ⁴If a man accidentally kills someone who is not his enemy, he may escape to any of these cities and be safe. ⁵For example, if two men go into the forest together to cut wood and if, as one of them is chopping down a tree, the head

of the axe comes off the handle and kills the other, he can run to one of those three cities and be safe. ⁶If there were only one city, the distance to it might be too great, and the relative who is responsible for taking revenge for the killing might catch him and in his anger kill an innocent man. After all, it was by accident that he killed a man who was not his enemy. ⁷This is why I order you to set aside three cities.

8 "When the LORD your God enlarges your territory, as he told your ancestors he would, and gives you all the land he has promised, ⁹then you are to select three more cities. (He will give you this land if you do everything that I command you today and if you love the LORD your God and live according to his teachings.) ¹⁰Do this, so that innocent people will not die and so that you will not be guilty of putting them to death in the land that the LORD is giving you.

11 "But suppose a man deliberately murders his enemy in cold blood and then escapes to one of those cities for protection. ¹²In that case, the leaders of his own town are to send for him and hand him over to the relative responsible for taking revenge for the murder, so that he may be put to death. ¹³Show him no mercy. Rid Israel of this murderer, so that all will go well with you.

ʳHe will speak...and I; *or* When a prophet speaks in my name, I.
18.19: Acts 3.23

Ancient Boundaries

14 "Do not move your neighbour's boundary mark, established long ago in the land that the LORD your God is giving you.

Concerning Witnesses

15 "One witness is not enough to convict a man of a crime; at least two witnesses are necessary to prove that a man is guilty. 16 If one man tries to harm another by falsely accusing him of a crime, 17 both are to go to the one place of worship and be judged by the priests and judges who are then in office. 18 The judges will investigate the case thoroughly; and if the man has made a false accusation against his fellow-Israelite, 19 he is to receive the punishment the accused man would have received. In this way you will get rid of this evil. 20 Then everyone else will hear what happened; they will be afraid, and no one will ever again do such an evil thing. 21 In such cases show no mercy; the punishment is to be a life for a life, an eye for an eye, a tooth for a tooth, a hand for a hand, and a foot for a foot.

Concerning War

20 "When you go out to fight against your enemies and you see chariots and horses and an army that outnumbers yours, do not be afraid of them. The LORD your God, who rescued you from Egypt, will be with you. 2 Before you start fighting, a priest is to come forward and say to the army, 3 'Men of Israel, listen! Today you are going into battle. Do not be afraid of your enemies, or lose courage, or panic. 4 The LORD your God is going with you, and he will give you victory.'

5 "Then the officers will address the men and say, 'Is there any man here who has just built a house, but has not yet dedicated it? If so, he is to go home. Otherwise, if he is killed in battle, someone else will dedicate his house. 6 Is there any man here who has just planted a vineyard, but has not yet had the chance to harvest its grapes? If so, he is to go home. Otherwise, if he is killed in battle, someone else will enjoy the wine. 7 Is there anyone here who is engaged to be married? If so, he is to go home. Otherwise, if he is killed in battle, someone else will marry the woman he is engaged to.'

8 "The officers will also say to the men, 'Is there any man here who has lost his nerve and is afraid? If so, he is to go home. Otherwise, he will destroy the morale of the others.' 9 When the officers have finished speaking to the army, leaders are to be chosen for each unit.

10 "When you go to attack a city, first give its people a chance to surrender. 11 If they open the gates and surrender, they are all to become your slaves and do forced labour for you. 12 But if the people of that city will not surrender, but choose to fight, surround it with your army. 13 Then, when the LORD your God lets you capture the city, kill every man in it. 14 You may, however, take for yourselves the women, the children, the livestock, and everything else in the city. You may use everything that belongs to your enemies. The LORD has given it to you. 15 That is how you are to deal with those cities that are far away from the land you will settle in.

16 "But when you capture cities in the land that the LORD your God is giving you, kill everyone. 17 Completely destroy all the people: the Hittites, the Amorites, the Canaanites, the Perizzites, the Hivites, and the Jebusites, as the LORD ordered you to do. 18 Kill them, so that they will not make you sin against the LORD by teaching you to do all the disgusting things that they do in the worship of their gods.

19 "When you are trying to capture a city, do not cut down its fruit-trees, even though the siege lasts a long time. Eat the fruit, but do not destroy the trees; the trees are not your enemies. 20 You may cut down the other trees and use them in the siege mounds until the city is captured.

Concerning Unsolved Murders

21 "Suppose a man is found murdered in a field in the land that the LORD your God is going to give you, and you do not know who killed him. 2 Your leaders and judges are to go out and measure the distance from the place where the body was found to each of the nearby towns. 3 Then the leaders of the town nearest to where the body was found are to select a young cow that has never

19.14: Deut 27.17
19.15: Num 35.30; Deut 17.6; Mt 18.16; Jn 8.17; 2 Cor 13.1; 1 Tim 5.19; Heb 10.28
19.21: Ex 21.23–25; Lev 24.19–20; Mt 5.38

been used for work. 4 They are to take it down to a spot near a stream that never runs dry and where the ground has never been ploughed or planted, and there they are to break its neck. 5 The levitical priests are to go there also, because they are to decide every legal case involving violence. The LORD your God has chosen them to serve him and to pronounce blessings in his name. 6 Then all the leaders from the town nearest the place where the murdered man was found are to wash their hands over the cow 7 and say, 'We did not murder the man, and we do not know who did it. 8 LORD, forgive your people Israel, whom you rescued from Egypt. Forgive us and do not hold us responsible for the murder of an innocent man.' 9 And so, by doing what the LORD requires, you will not be held responsible for the murder.

Concerning Women Prisoners of War

10 "When the LORD your God gives you victory in battle and you take prisoners, 11 you may see among them a beautiful woman that you like and want to marry. 12 Take her to your home, where she will shave her head,^{s} cut her fingernails, 13 and change her clothes. She is to stay in your home and mourn for her parents for a month; after that, you may marry her. 14 Later, if you no longer want her, you are to let her go free. Since you forced her to have intercourse with you, you cannot treat her as a slave and sell her.

Concerning the First Son's Inheritance

15 "Suppose a man has two wives and they both bear him sons, but the first son is not the child of his favourite wife. 16 When the man decides how he is going to divide his property among his children, he is not to show partiality to the son of his favourite wife by giving him the share that belongs to the first-born son. 17 He is to give a double share of his possessions to his first son, even though he is not the son of his favourite wife. A man must acknowledge his first son and give him the share he is legally entitled to.

Concerning a Disobedient Son

18 "Suppose a man has a son who is stubborn and rebellious, a son who will not obey his parents, even though they punish him. 19 His parents are to take him

before the leaders of the town where he lives and make him stand trial. 20 They are to say to them, 'Our son is stubborn and rebellious and refuses to obey us; he wastes money and is a drunkard.' 21 Then the men of the city are to stone him to death, and so you will get rid of this evil. Everyone in Israel will hear what has happened and be afraid.

Various Laws

22 "If a man has been put to death for a crime and his body is hung on a post, 23 it is not to remain there overnight. It must be buried the same day, because a dead body hanging on a post brings God's curse on the land. Bury the body, so that you will not defile the land that the LORD your God is giving you.

22 "If you see a fellow-Israelite's cow or sheep running loose, do not ignore it; take it back to him. 2 But if its owner lives a long way off or if you don't know who owns it, then take it home with you. When its owner comes looking for it, give it to him. 3 Do the same thing if you find a donkey, a piece of clothing, or anything else that your fellow-Israelite may have lost.

4 "If a fellow-Israelite's donkey or cow

If a...donkey...has fallen down (22.4)

has fallen down, don't ignore it; help him to get the animal to its feet again.

5 "Women are not to wear men's clothing, and men are not to wear women's clothing; the LORD your God hates people who do such things.

---

^{s} shave her head; *or* trim her hair.
21.23: Gal 3.13   **22.1–4:** Ex 23.4–5

6 "If you happen to find a bird's nest in a tree or on the ground with the mother bird sitting either on the eggs or with her young, you are not to take the mother bird. ⁷ You may take the young birds, but you must let the mother bird go, so that you will live a long and prosperous life.

8 "When you build a new house, be sure to put a railing round the edge of the roof. Then you will not be responsible if someone falls off and is killed.

9 "Do not plant any crop in the same field as your grapevines; if you do, you are forbidden to use either the grapes or the produce of the other crop.

10 "Do not hitch an ox and a donkey together for ploughing.

11 "Do not wear cloth made by weaving wool and linen together.

12 "Sew tassels on the four corners of your clothes.

Laws Concerning Sexual Purity

13 "Suppose a man marries a girl and later he decides he doesn't want her. ¹⁴ So he makes up false charges against her, accusing her of not being a virgin when they got married.

15 "If this happens, the girl's parents are to take the blood-stained wedding sheet that proves the girl was a virgin, and they are to show it in court to the town leaders. ¹⁶ The girl's father will say to them, 'I gave my daughter to this man in marriage, and now he doesn't want her. ¹⁷ He has made false charges against her, saying that she was not a virgin when he married her. But here is the proof that my daughter was a virgin; look at the bloodstains on the wedding sheet!' ¹⁸ Then the town leaders are to take the husband and beat him. ¹⁹ They are also to fine him a hundred pieces of silver and give the money to the girl's father, because the man has brought disgrace on an Israelite girl. Moreover, she will continue to be his wife, and he can never divorce her as long as he lives.

20 "But if the charge is true and there is no proof that the girl was a virgin, ²¹ then they are to take her out to the entrance of her father's house, where the men of her city are to stone her to death. She has done a shameful thing among our people by having intercourse before she was married, while she was still living in her father's house. In this way you will get rid of this evil.

22 "If a man is caught having intercourse with another man's wife, both of them are to be put to death. In this way you will get rid of this evil.

23 "Suppose a man is caught in a town having intercourse with a girl who is engaged to someone else. ²⁴ You are to take them outside the town and stone them to death. The girl is to die because she did not cry out for help, although she was in a town, where she could have been heard. And the man is to die because he had intercourse with a girl who was engaged. In this way you will get rid of this evil.

25 "Suppose a man out in the countryside rapes a girl who is engaged to someone else. Then only the man is to be put to death; ²⁶ nothing is to be done to the girl, because she has not committed a sin worthy of death. This case is the same as when one man attacks another man and murders him. ²⁷ The man raped the engaged girl in the countryside, and although she cried for help, there was no one to help her.

28 "Suppose a man is caught raping a girl who is not engaged. ²⁹ He is to pay the girl's father the bride price of fifty pieces of silver, and she is to become his wife, because he forced her to have intercourse with him. He can never divorce her as long as he lives.

30 "No man is to disgrace his father by having intercourse with any of his father's wives.

Exclusion from the LORD's People

23 "No man who has been castrated or whose penis has been cut off may be included among the LORD's people.

2 "No one born out of wedlock or any descendant of such a person, even in the tenth generation, may be included among the LORD's people.

3 "No Ammonite or Moabite—or any of their descendants, even in the tenth generation—may be included among the LORD's people. ⁴ They refused to provide you with food and water when you were on your way out of Egypt, and they hired Balaam son of Beor, from the city of Pethor in Mesopotamia, to curse you. ⁵ But the LORD your God would not listen to Balaam; instead he turned the curse into

22.9-11: Lev 19.19   **22.12:** Num 15.37-41   **22.28-29:** Ex 22.16-17
22.30: Lev 18.8, 20.11; Deut 27.20   **23.3-5:** Neh 13.1-2   **23.4:** Num 22.1-6
23.5: Num 23.7—24.9

a blessing, because he loved you. ⁶As long as you are a nation, never do anything to help these nations or to make them prosperous.

7 "Do not despise the Edomites; they are your relatives. And do not despise the Egyptians; you once lived in their land. ⁸From the third generation onward their descendants may be included among the LORD's people.

Keeping the Military Camp Clean

9 "When you are in camp in time of war, you are to avoid anything that would make you ritually unclean. ¹⁰If a man becomes unclean because he has had a wet dream during the night, he is to go outside the camp and stay there. ¹¹Towards evening he is to wash himself, and at sunset he may come back into camp.

12 "You are to have a place outside the camp where you can go when you need to relieve yourselves. ¹³Carry a stick as part of your equipment, so that when you have a bowel movement you can dig a hole and cover it up. ¹⁴Keep your camp ritually clean, because the LORD your God is with you in your camp to protect you and to give you victory over your enemies. Do not do anything indecent that would cause the LORD to turn his back on you.

Various Laws

15 "If a slave runs away from his owner and comes to you for protection, do not send him back. ¹⁶He may live in any of your towns that he chooses, and you are not to treat him harshly.

17 "No Israelite, man or woman, is to become a temple prostitute. ¹⁸Also, no money earned in this way may be brought into the house of the LORD your God in fulfilment of a vow. The LORD hates temple prostitutes.

19 "When you lend money or food or anything else to a fellow-Israelite, do not charge him interest. ²⁰You may charge interest on what you lend to a foreigner, but not on what you lend to a fellow-Israelite. Obey this rule, and the LORD your God will bless everything you do in the land that you are going to occupy.

21 "When you make a vow to the LORD your God, do not put off doing what you promised; the LORD will hold you to your vow, and it is a sin not to keep it. ²²It is no sin not to make a vow to the LORD, ²³but if you make one voluntarily, be sure that you keep it.

24 "When you walk along a path in someone else's vineyard, you may eat all the grapes you want, but you must not carry any away in a container. ²⁵When you walk along a path in someone else's cornfield, you may eat all the corn you can pull off with your hands, but you must not cut any corn with a sickle.

Divorce and Remarriage

24 "Suppose a man marries a woman and later decides that he doesn't want her, because he finds something about her that he doesn't like.ᵗ So he writes out divorce papers, gives them to her, and sends her away from his home. ²Then suppose she marries another man, ³and he also decides that he doesn't want her, so he also writes out divorce papers, gives them to her, and sends her away from his home. Or suppose her second husband dies. ⁴In either case, her first husband is not to marry her again; he is to consider her defiled. If he married her again, it would be offensive to the LORD. You are not to commit such a terrible sin in the land that the LORD your God is giving you.

Various Laws

5 "When a man is newly married, he is not to be drafted into military service or any other public duty; he is to be excused from duty for one year, so that he can stay at home and make his wife happy.ᵘ

6 "When you lend a man something, you are not to take as security his millstones used for grinding his corn. This would take away the family's means of preparing food to keep alive.

7 "Whoever kidnaps a fellow-Israelite and makes him his slave or sells him into slavery is to be put to death. In this way you will get rid of this evil.

8 "When you are suffering from a dreaded skin-disease, be sure to do exactly what the levitical priests tell you; follow the instructions that I have given them. ⁹Remember what the LORD your God did

---

ᵗ something...like; or that she is guilty of some shameful conduct.
ᵘ make his wife happy; or be happy with his wife.
23.17: Lev 19.29   **23.19–20:** Ex 22.25; Lev 25.36–37; Deut 15.7–11
23.21: Num 30.1–16; Mt 5.33   **24.1:** Mt 5.31, 19.7; Mk 10.4   **24.7:** Ex 21.16
24.8: Lev 13.1—14.54   **24.9:** Num 12.10

You may eat all the grapes you want (23.24)

But you must not carry any away in a container (23.24)

to Miriam as you were coming from Egypt.

10 "When you lend a man something, do not go into his house to get the garment he is going to give you as security; 11 wait outside and let him bring it to you himself. 12 If he is a poor man, do not keep it

overnight; 13 return it to him each evening, so that he can have it to sleep in. Then he will be grateful, and the LORD your God will be pleased with you.

14 "Do not cheat a poor and needy hired servant, whether he is a fellow-Israelite or a foreigner living in one of your towns. 15 Each day before sunset pay him for that day's work; he needs the money and has counted on getting it. If you do not pay him, he will cry out against you to the LORD, and you will be guilty of sin.

16 "Parents are not to be put to death for crimes committed by their children, and children are not to be put to death for crimes committed by their parents; a person is to be put to death only for a crime he himself has committed.

17 "Do not deprive foreigners and orphans of their rights; and do not take a widow's garment as security for a loan. 18 Remember that you were slaves in Egypt and that the LORD your God set you free; that is why I have given you this command.

19 "When you gather your crops and fail to bring in some of the corn that you have cut, do not go back for it; it is to be left for the foreigners, orphans, and widows, so that the LORD your God will bless you in everything you do. 20 When you have picked your olives once, do not go back and get those that are left; they are for the foreigners, orphans, and widows. 21 When you have gathered your grapes once, do not go back over the vines a second time; the grapes that are left are for the foreigners, orphans, and widows. 22 Never forget that you were slaves in Egypt; that is why I have given you this command.

25 "Suppose two Israelites go to court to settle a dispute, and one is declared innocent and the other guilty. 2 If the guilty man is sentenced to be beaten, the judge is to make him lie face downwards and have him whipped. The number of lashes will depend on the crime he has committed. 3 He may be given as many as forty lashes, but no more; more than that would humiliate him publicly.

4 "Do not muzzle an ox when you are using it to thresh corn.

Duty to a Dead Brother

5 "If two brothers live on the same property and one of them dies, leaving

24.10-13: Ex 22.26-27   24.14-15: Lev 19.13   24.16: 2 Kgs 14.6; 2 Chr 25.4; Ezek 18.20
24.17-18: Ex 23.9; Lev 19.33-34; Deut 27.19   24.19-21: Lev 19.9-10, 23.22
25.3: 2 Cor 11.24   25.4: 1 Cor 9.9; 1 Tim 5.18   25.5-6: Mt 22.24; Mk 12.19; Lk 20.28

no son, then his widow is not to be married to someone outside the family; it is the duty of the dead man's brother to marry her. ⁶The first son that they have will be considered the son of the dead man, so that his family line will continue in Israel. ⁷But if the dead man's brother does not want to marry her, she is to go before the town leaders and say, 'My husband's brother will not do his duty; he refuses to give his brother a descendant among the people of Israel.' ⁸Then the town leaders are to summon him and speak to him. If he still refuses to marry her, ⁹his brother's widow is to go up to him in the presence of the town leaders, take off one of his sandals, spit in his face, and say, 'This is what happens to the man who refuses to give his brother a descendant.' ¹⁰His family will be known in Israel as 'the family of the man who had his sandal pulled off.'

Other Laws

11 "If two men are having a fight and the wife of one tries to help her husband by grabbing hold of the other man's genitals, ¹²show her no mercy; cut off her hand.

13-14 "Do not cheat when you use weights and measures. ¹⁵Use true and honest weights and measures, so that you may live a long time in the land that the LORD your God is giving you. ¹⁶The LORD hates people who cheat.

The Command to Kill the Amalekites

17 "Remember what the Amalekites did to you as you were coming from Egypt. ¹⁸They had no fear of God, and so they attacked you from the rear when you were tired and exhausted, and killed all who were straggling behind. ¹⁹So then, when the LORD your God has given you the land and made you safe from all your enemies who live around you, be sure to kill all the Amalekites, so that no one will remember them any longer. Do not forget!

Harvest Offerings

26 "After you have occupied the land that the LORD your God is giving you and have settled there, ²each of you must place in a basket the first part of each crop that you harvest and you must take it with you to the one place of worship. ³Go to the priest in charge at

that time and say to him, 'I now acknowledge to the LORD my God that I have entered the land that he promised our ancestors to give us.'

4 "The priest will take the basket from you and place it before the altar of the LORD your God. ⁵Then, in the LORD's presence you will recite these words: 'My ancestor was a wandering Aramean, who took his family to Egypt to live. They were few in number when they went there, but they became a large and powerful nation. ⁶The Egyptians treated us harshly and forced us to work as slaves. ⁷Then we cried out for help to the LORD, the God of our ancestors. He heard us and saw our suffering, hardship, and misery. ⁸By his great power and strength he rescued us from Egypt. He worked miracles and wonders, and caused terrifying things to happen. ⁹He brought us here and gave us this rich and fertile land. ¹⁰So now I bring to the LORD the first part of the harvest that he has given me.'

"Then set the basket down in the LORD's presence and worship there. ¹¹Be grateful for the good things that the LORD your God has given you and your family; and let the Levites and the foreigners who live among you join in the celebration.

12 "Every third year give the tithe—a tenth of your crops—to the Levites, the foreigners, the orphans, and the widows, so that in every community they will have all they need to eat. When you have done this, ¹³say to the LORD, 'None of the sacred tithe is left in my house; I have given it to the Levites, the foreigners, the orphans, and the widows, as you commanded me to do. I have not disobeyed or forgotten any of your commands concerning the tithe. ¹⁴I have not eaten any of it when I was mourning; I have not taken any of it out of my house when I was ritually unclean; and I have not given any of it as an offering for the dead. ᵛ I have obeyed you, O LORD; I have done everything you commanded concerning the tithe. ¹⁵Look down from your holy place in heaven and bless your people Israel; bless also the rich and fertile land that you have given us, as you promised our ancestors.'

The LORD's Own People

16 "Today the LORD your God com-

ᵛfor the dead; *or* to the dead.
25.7-10: Ruth 4.7-8   **25.13-16:** Lev 19.35-36   **25.17-19:** Ex 17.8-14; 1 Sam 15.2-9
26.2: Ex 23.19   **26.12:** Deut 14.28-29

People of Israel...listen to me (27.9)

mands you to obey all his laws; so obey them faithfully with all your heart. ¹⁷ Today you have acknowledged the LORD as your God; you have promised to obey him, to keep all his laws, and to do all that he commands. ¹⁸ Today the LORD has accepted you as his own people, as he promised you; and he commands you to obey all his laws. ¹⁹ He will make you greater than any other nation that he has created, and you will bring praise and honour to his name. *ʷ* You will be his own people, as he promised."

God's Laws Written on Stones

27 Then Moses, together with the leaders of Israel, said to the people, "Obey all the instructions that I am giving you today. ² On the day you cross the River Jordan and enter the land that the LORD your God is giving you, you are to set up some large stones, cover them with plaster, ³ and write on them all these laws and teachings. When you have entered the rich and fertile land that the LORD, the God of your ancestors, promised you, ⁴ and you are on the other side of the Jordan, set up these stones on Mount Ebal, as I am instructing you today, and cover them with plaster. ⁵ Build an altar there made of stones that have had no iron tools used on them, ⁶ because any altar you build for the LORD your God must be made of uncut stones. There you are to offer the sacrifices that are to be burnt, ⁷ and there you are to sacrifice and

eat your fellowship-offerings and be grateful in the presence of the LORD your God. ⁸ On the stones covered with plaster write clearly every word of God's laws."

9 Then Moses, together with the levitical priests, said to all the people of Israel, "Give me your attention, people of Israel, and listen to me. Today you have become the people of the LORD your God; ¹⁰ so obey him and keep all his laws that I am giving you today."

The Curses on Disobedience

11 Then Moses said to the people of Israel, ¹² "After you have crossed the Jordan, the following tribes are to stand on Mount Gerizim when the blessings are pronounced on the people: Simeon, Levi, Judah, Issachar, Joseph, and Benjamin. ¹³ And the following tribes will stand on Mount Ebal when the curses are pronounced: Reuben, Gad, Asher, Zebulun, Dan, and Naphtali. ¹⁴ The Levites will speak these words in a loud voice:

15 " 'God's curse on anyone who makes an idol of stone, wood, or metal and secretly worships it; the LORD hates idolatry.'

"And all the people will answer, 'Amen!'
16 " 'God's curse on anyone who dishonours his father or mother.'

"And all the people will answer, 'Amen!'
17 " 'God's curse on anyone who moves a neighbour's boundary mark.'

"And all the people will answer, 'Amen!'
18 " 'God's curse on anyone who leads

ʷ bring praise...name; *or* receive praise and honour.
26.18: Ex 19.5; Deut 4.20, 7.6, 14.2; Tit 2.14; 1 Pet 2.9
27.5–6: Ex 20.25   **27.12:** Deut 11.29; Josh 8.33–35
27.15: Ex 20.4, 34.17; Lev 19.4, 26.1; Deut 4.15–18, 5.8
27.17: Deut 19.14   **27.18:** Lev 19.14

27.2–8: Josh 8.30–32

27.16: Ex 20.12; Deut 5.16

a blind man in the wrong direction.'

"And all the people will answer, 'Amen!'

19 "'God's curse on anyone who deprives foreigners, orphans, and widows of their rights.'

"And all the people will answer, 'Amen!'

20 "'God's curse on anyone who disgraces his father by having intercourse with any of his father's wives.'

"And all the people will answer, 'Amen!'

21 "'God's curse on anyone who has sexual relations with an animal.'

"And all the people will answer, 'Amen!'

22 "'God's curse on anyone who has intercourse with his sister or half sister.'

"And all the people will answer, 'Amen!'

23 "'God's curse on anyone who has intercourse with his mother-in-law.'

"And all the people will answer, 'Amen!'

24 "'God's curse on anyone who secretly commits murder.'

"And all the people will answer, 'Amen!'

25 "'God's curse on anyone who accepts money to murder an innocent person.'

"And all the people will answer, 'Amen!'

26 "'God's curse on anyone who does not obey all of God's laws and teachings.'

"And all the people will answer, 'Amen!'

The Blessings of Obedience
(Lev 26.3–13; Deut 7.12–24)

28 "If you obey the LORD your God and faithfully keep all his commands that I am giving you today, he will make you greater than any other nation on earth. 2 Obey the LORD your God and all these blessings will be yours:

3 "The LORD will bless your towns and your fields.

4 "The LORD will bless you with many children, with abundant crops, and with many cattle and sheep.

5 "The LORD will bless your corn crops and the food you prepare from them.

6 "The LORD will bless everything you do.

7 "The LORD will defeat your enemies when they attack you. They will attack from one direction, but they will run from you in all directions.

8 "The LORD your God will bless your work and fill your barns with corn. He will bless you in the land that he is giving you.

9 "If you obey the LORD your God and do everything he commands, he will make

you his own people, as he has promised. 10 Then all the peoples on earth will see that the LORD has chosen you to be his own people, and they will be afraid of you. 11 The LORD will give you many children, many cattle, and abundant crops in the land that he promised your ancestors to give you. 12 He will send rain in season from his rich storehouse in the sky and bless all your work, so that you will lend to many nations, but you will not have to borrow from any. 13 The LORD your God will make you the leader among the nations and not a follower; you will always prosper and never fail if you obey faithfully all his commands that I am giving you today. 14 But you must never disobey them in any way, or worship and serve other gods.

The Consequences of Disobedience
(Lev 26.14–46)

15 "But if you disobey the LORD your God and do not faithfully keep all his commands and laws that I am giving you today, all these evil things will happen to you:

16 "The LORD will curse your towns and your fields.

17 "The LORD will curse your corn crops and the food you prepare from them.

18 "The LORD will curse you by giving you only a few children, poor crops, and few cattle and sheep.

19 "The LORD will curse everything you do.

20 "If you do evil and reject the LORD, he will bring on you disaster, confusion, and trouble in everything you do, until you are quickly and completely destroyed. 21 He will send disease after disease on you until there is not one of you left in the land that you are about to occupy. 22 The LORD will strike you with infectious diseases, with swelling and fever; he will send drought and scorching winds to destroy your crops. These disasters will be with you until you die. 23 No rain will fall, and your ground will become as hard as iron. 24 Instead of rain, the LORD will send down duststorms and sandstorms until you are destroyed.

25 "The LORD will give your enemies victory over you. You will attack them from one direction, but you will run from them in all directions, and all the people on earth will be terrified when they see

27.19: Ex 22.21, 23.9; Lev 19.33–34; Deut 24.17–18   **27.20:** Lev 18.8, 20.11; Deut 22.30
27.21: Ex 22.19; Lev 18.23, 20.15   **27.22:** Lev 18.9, 20.17   **27.23:** Lev 18.17, 20.14
27.26: Gal 3.10   **28.1–14:** Deut 11.13–17

But if you disobey the LORD (28.15)

what happens to you. 26 When you die, birds and wild animals will come and eat your bodies, and there will be no one to scare them off. 27 The LORD will send boils on you, as he did on the Egyptians. He will make your bodies break out with sores. You will be covered with scabs, and you will itch, but there will be no cure. 28 The LORD will make you lose your mind; he will strike you with blindness and confusion. 29 You will grope about in broad daylight like a blind man, and you will not be able to find your way. You will not prosper in anything you do. You will be constantly oppressed and robbed, and there will be no one to help you.

30 "You will be engaged to a girl—but someone else will marry her. You will build a house—but never live in it. You will plant a vineyard—but never eat its grapes. 31 Your cattle will be butchered before your very eyes, but you will not eat any of the meat. Your donkeys will be dragged away while you look on, and they will not be given back to you. Your sheep will be given to your enemies, and there will be no one to help you. 32 Your

sons and daughters will be given as slaves to foreigners while you look on. Every day you will strain your eyes, looking in vain for your children to return. 33 A foreign nation will take all the crops that you have worked so hard to grow, while you receive nothing but constant oppression and harsh treatment. 34 Your sufferings will make you lose your mind. 35 The LORD will cover your legs with incurable, painful sores; boils will cover you from head to foot.

36 "The LORD will take you and your king away to a foreign land, where neither you nor your ancestors ever lived before; there you will serve gods made of wood and stone. 37 In the countries to which the LORD will scatter you, the people will be shocked at what has happened to you; they will make fun of you and ridicule you.

38 "You will sow plenty of seed, but reap only a small harvest, because the locusts will eat your crops. 39 You will plant vineyards and take care of them, but you will not gather their grapes or drink wine from them, because worms will eat the vines. 40 Olive-trees will grow everywhere in your land, but you will not have any olive-oil, because the olives will drop off. 41 You will have sons and daughters, but you will lose them, because they will be taken away as prisoners of war. 42 All your trees and crops will be devoured by insects.

43 "Foreigners who live in your land will gain more and more power, while you gradually lose yours. 44 They will have money to lend you, but you will have none to lend them. In the end they will be your rulers.

45 "All these disasters will come on you, and they will be with you until you are destroyed, because you did not obey the LORD your God and keep all the laws that he gave you. 46 They will be the evidence of God's judgement on you and your descendants for ever. 47 The LORD blessed you in every way, but you would not serve him with glad and joyful hearts. 48 So then, you will serve the enemies that the LORD is going to send against you. You will be hungry, thirsty, and naked—in need of everything. The LORD *x* will oppress you harshly until you are destroyed. 49 The LORD will bring against you a nation from the ends of the earth, a nation whose language you do not know. They will swoop down on you like an

x The LORD; *or* Your enemies.

eagle. ⁵⁰They will be ruthless and show no mercy to anyone, young or old. ⁵¹They will eat your livestock and your crops, and you will starve to death. They will not leave you any corn, wine, olive-oil, livestock, or sheep; and you will die. ⁵²They will attack every town in the land that the LORD your God is giving you, and the high, fortified walls in which you trust will fall.

53 "When your enemies are besieging your towns, you will become so desperate for food that you will even eat the children that the LORD your God has given you. ⁵⁴⁻⁵⁵Even the most refined man of noble birth will become so desperate during the siege that he will eat some of his own children because he has no other food. He will not even give any to his brother or to the wife he loves or to any of his children who are left. ⁵⁶⁻⁵⁷Even the most refined woman of noble birth, so rich that she has never had to walk anywhere, will behave in the same way. When the enemy besieges her town, she will become so desperate for food that she will secretly eat her newborn child and the afterbirth as well. She will not share them with the husband she loves or with any of her children.

58 "If you do not obey faithfully all God's teachings that are written in this book and if you do not honour the wonderful and awesome name of the LORD your God, ⁵⁹he will send on you and on your descendants incurable diseases and horrible epidemics that can never be stopped. ⁶⁰He will bring on you once again all the dreadful diseases you experienced in Egypt, and you will never recover. ⁶¹He will also send all kinds of diseases and epidemics that are not mentioned in this book of God's laws and teachings, and you will be destroyed. ⁶²Although you become as numerous as the stars in the sky, only a few of you will survive, because you did not obey the LORD your God. ⁶³Just as the LORD took delight in making you prosper and in making you increase in number, so he will take delight in destroying you and in bringing ruin on you. You will be uprooted from the land that you are about to occupy.

64 "The LORD will scatter you among all the nations, from one end of the earth to the other, and there you will serve gods made of wood and stone, gods that neither you nor your ancestors have ever worshipped before. ⁶⁵You will find no peace anywhere, no place to call your own; the LORD will overwhelm you with anxiety, hopelessness, and despair. ⁶⁶Your life will always be in danger. Day and night you will be filled with terror, and you will live in constant fear of death. ⁶⁷Your hearts will pound with fear at everything you see. Every morning you will wish for evening; every evening you will wish for morning. ⁶⁸The LORD will send you back to Egypt in ships, even though heʸ said that you would never have to go there again. There you will try to sell yourselves to your enemies as slaves, but no one will want to buy you."

The LORD's Covenant with Israel in the Land of Moab

29 These are the terms of the covenant that the LORD commanded Moses to make with the people of Israel in the land of Moab; all this was in addition to the covenant which the LORD had made with them at Mount Sinai.

2 Moses called together all the people of Israel and said to them, "You saw for yourselves what the LORD did to the king of Egypt, to his officials, and to his entire country. ³You saw the terrible plagues, the miracles, and the great wonders that the LORD performed. ⁴But to this very day he has not let you understand what you have experienced. ⁵For forty years the LORD led you through the desert, and your clothes and sandals never wore out. ⁶You did not have bread to eat or wine or beer to drink, but the LORD provided for your needs in order to teach you that he is your God. ⁷And when we came to this place, King Sihon of Heshbon and King Og of Bashan came out to fight against us. But we defeated them, ⁸took their land, and divided it among the tribes of Reuben and Gad, and half the tribe of Manasseh. ⁹Obey faithfully all the terms of this covenant, so that you will be successful in everything you do.

10 "Today you are standing in the presence of the LORD your God, all of you—your leaders and officials, your men, ¹¹women, and children, and the foreigners who live among you and cut wood and carry water for you. ¹²You are here today to enter into this covenant that the LORD your God is making with you and to accept its obligations, ¹³so that the LORD may now confirm you as his people and be your God, as he promised you and

your ancestors, Abraham, Isaac, and Jacob. 14 You are not the only ones with whom the LORD is making this covenant with its obligations. 15 He is making it with all of us who stand here in his presence today and also with our descendants who are not yet born.

16 "You remember what life was like in Egypt and what it was like to travel through the territory of other nations. 17 You saw their disgusting idols made of wood, stone, silver, and gold. 18 Make sure that no man, woman, family, or tribe standing here today turns from the LORD our God to worship the gods of other nations. This would be like a root that grows to be a bitter and poisonous plant. 19 Make sure that there is no one here today who hears these solemn demands and yet convinces himself that all will be well with him, even if he stubbornly goes his own way. That would destroy all of you, good and evil alike. 20 The LORD will not forgive such a man. Instead, the LORD's burning anger will flame up against him, and all the disasters written in this book will fall on him until the LORD has destroyed him completely. 21 The LORD will make an example of him before all the tribes of Israel and will bring disaster on him in accordance with all the curses listed in the covenant that is written in this book of the LORD's teachings.

22 "In future generations your descendants and foreigners from distant lands will see the disasters and sufferings that the LORD has brought on your land. 23 The fields will be a barren waste, covered with sulphur and salt; nothing will be planted, and not even weeds will grow there. Your land will be like the cities of Sodom and Gomorrah, of Admah and Zeboiim, which the LORD destroyed when he was furiously angry. 24 Then the whole world will ask, 'Why did the LORD do this to their land? What was the reason for his fierce anger?' 25 And the answer will be, 'It is because the LORD's people broke the covenant they had made with him, the God of their ancestors, when he brought them out of Egypt. 26 They served other gods that they had never worshipped before, gods that the LORD had forbidden them to worship. 27 And so the LORD became angry with his people and brought on their land all the disasters written in this book. 28 The LORD became furiously angry, and in his great anger

he uprooted them from their land and threw them into a foreign land, and there they are today.'

29 "There are some things that the LORD our God has kept secret; but he has revealed his Law, and we and our descendants are to obey it for ever.

Conditions for Restoration and Blessing

30 "I have now given you a choice between a blessing and a curse. When all these things have happened to you, and you are living among the nations where the LORD your God has scattered you, you will remember the choice I gave you. 2 If you and your descendants will turn back to the LORD and with all your heart obey his commands that I am giving you today, 3 then the LORD your God will have mercy on you. He will bring you back from the nations where he has scattered you, and he will make you prosperous again. 4 Even if you are scattered to the farthest corners of the earth, the LORD your God will gather you together and bring you back, 5 so that you may again take possession of the land where your ancestors once lived. And he will make you more prosperous and more numerous than your ancestors ever were. 6 The LORD your God will give you and your descendants obedient hearts, so that you will love him with all your heart, and you will continue to live in that land. 7 He will turn all these curses against your enemies, who hated you and oppressed you, 8 and you will again obey him and keep all his commands that I am giving you today. 9 The LORD will make you prosperous in all that you do; you will have many children and a lot of livestock, and your fields will produce abundant crops. He will be as glad to make you prosperous as he was to make your ancestors prosperous, 10 but you will have to obey him and keep all his laws that are written in this book of his teachings. You will have to turn to him with all your heart.

11 "The command that I am giving you today is not too difficult or beyond your reach. 12 It is not up in the sky. You do not have to ask, 'Who will go up and bring it down for us, so that we can hear it and obey it?' 13 Nor is it on the other side of the ocean. You do not have to ask, 'Who will go across the ocean and bring it to us, so that we may hear it and obey it?' 14 No, it is here with you.

29.18: Heb 12.15   **29.23:** Gen 19.24-25   **30.12-14:** Rom 10.6-8

You know it and can quote it, so now obey it.

15 "Today I am giving you a choice between good and evil, between life and death. [16] If you obey the commands of the LORD your God,[z] which I give you today, if you love him, obey him, and keep all his laws, then you will prosper and become a nation of many people. The LORD your God will bless you in the land that you are about to occupy. [17] But if you disobey and refuse to listen, and are led away to worship other gods, [18] you will be destroyed—I warn you here and now. You will not live long in that land across the Jordan that you are about to occupy. [19] I am now giving you the choice

Choose life (30.19)

between life and death, between God's blessing and God's curse, and I call heaven and earth to witness the choice you make. Choose life. [20] Love the LORD your God, obey him and be faithful to him, and then you and your descendants will live long in the land that he promised to give your ancestors, Abraham, Isaac, and Jacob."

Joshua Becomes Moses' Successor

31 Moses continued speaking to the people of Israel, [2] and said, "I am now a hundred and twenty years old and am no longer able to be your leader. And besides this, the LORD has told me that I will not cross the Jordan. [3] The LORD your God himself will go before you and destroy the nations living there, so that you can occupy their land; and Joshua will be your leader, as the LORD has said. [4] The LORD will destroy those people, just as he defeated Sihon and Og, kings of the Amorites, and destroyed their country. [5] The LORD will give you victory over them, and you are to treat them exactly as I have told you. [6] Be determined and confident. Do not be afraid of them. Your God, the LORD himself, will be with you. He will not fail you or abandon you."

7 Then Moses called Joshua and said to him in the presence of all the people of Israel, "Be determined and confident; you are the one who will lead these people to occupy the land that the LORD promised to their ancestors. [8] The LORD himself will lead you and be with you. He will not fail you or abandon you, so do not lose courage or be afraid."

The Law Is to Be Read Every Seven Years

9 So Moses wrote down God's Law and gave it to the levitical priests, who were in charge of the LORD's Covenant Box, and to the leaders of Israel. [10] He commanded them, "At the end of every seven years, when the year that debts are cancelled comes round, read this aloud at the Festival of Shelters. [11] Read it to the people of Israel when they come to worship the LORD your God at the one place of worship. [12] Call together all the men, women, and children, and the foreigners who live in your towns, so that everyone may hear it and learn to honour the LORD your God and to obey his teachings faithfully. [13] In this way your descendants who have never heard the Law of the LORD your God will hear it. And so they will learn to obey him as long as they live in the land that you are about to occupy across the Jordan."

The LORD's Last Instruction to Moses

14 Then the LORD said to Moses, "You haven't much longer to live. Call Joshua and bring him to the Tent, so that I may give him his instructions." Moses and Joshua went to the Tent, [15] and the LORD appeared to them there in a pillar of cloud that stood by the door of the Tent.

[z] *One ancient translation* If you obey the commands of the LORD your God; *Hebrew does not have these words.*
30.20: Gen 12.7, 26.3, 28.13   **31.2:** Num 20.12   **31.4:** Num 21.21-35
31.8: Josh 1.5; Heb 13.5   **31.10:** Deut 15.1, 16.13-15

16 The LORD said to Moses, "You will soon die, and after your death the people will become unfaithful to me and break the covenant that I made with them. They will abandon me and worship the pagan gods of the land they are about to enter. 17 When that happens, I will become angry with them; I will abandon them, and they will be destroyed. Many terrible disasters will come upon them, and then they will realize that these things are happening to them because I, their God, am no longer with them. 18 And I will refuse to help them then, because they have done evil and worshipped other gods.

19 "Now, write down this song. Teach it to the people of Israel, so that it will stand as evidence against them. 20 I will take them into this rich and fertile land, as I promised their ancestors. There they will have all the food they want, and they will live comfortably. But they will turn away and worship other gods. They will reject me and break my covenant, 21 and many terrible disasters will come on them. But this song will still be sung, and it will stand as evidence against them. Even now, before I take them into the land that I promised to give them, I know what they are thinking."

22 That same day Moses wrote down the song and taught it to the people of Israel.

23 Then the LORD spoke to Joshua son of Nun and said to him, "Be confident and determined. You will lead the people of Israel into the land that I promised them, and I will be with you."

24 Moses wrote God's Law in a book, taking care not to leave out anything. 25 When he finished, he said to the levitical priests, who were in charge of the LORD's Covenant Box, 26 "Take this book of God's Law and place it beside the Covenant Box of the LORD your God, so that it will remain there as a witness against his people. 27 I know how stubborn and rebellious they are. They have rebelled against the LORD during my lifetime, and they will rebel even more after I am dead. 28 Assemble all your tribal leaders and officials before me, so that I can tell them these things; I will call heaven and earth to be my witnesses against them. 29 I know that after my death the people will become wicked and reject what I have taught them. And in time to come they will meet with disaster, because they will have made the LORD angry by doing what he has forbidden."

The Song of Moses

30 Then Moses recited the entire song while all the people of Israel listened.

32 "Earth and sky, hear my words,
　　　listen closely to what I say.
2 My teaching will fall like drops of rain
　　and form on the earth like dew.
My words will fall like showers on
　　young plants,
　　like gentle rain on tender grass.
3 I will praise the name of the LORD,
　　and his people will tell of his
　　greatness.

4 "The LORD is your mighty defender,
　　perfect and just in all his ways;
Your God is faithful and true;
　　he does what is right and fair.
5 But you are unfaithful, unworthy to be
　　his people,a
　　a sinful and deceitful nation.
6 Is this the way you should treat the
　　LORD,
　　you foolish, senseless people?
He is your father, your Creator,
　　he made you into a nation.

7 "Think of the past, of the time long ago;
　　ask your fathers to tell you what
　　happened,
　　ask the old men to tell of the past.
8 The Most High assigned nations their
　　lands;
　　he determined where peoples should
　　live.
He assigned to each nation a god,
9 　　but Jacob's descendants he chose for
　　himself.

10 "He found them wandering through
　　the desert,
　　a desolate, wind-swept wilderness.
He protected them and cared for them,
　　as he would protect himself.
11 Like an eagle teaching its young to
　　fly,b
　　catching them safely on its spreading
　　wings,
　　the LORD kept Israel from falling.
12 The LORD alone led his people
　　without the help of a foreign god.

---

a Probable text But you...people; Hebrew unclear.
b teaching its young to fly; or watching over its young.
31.23: Num 27.23; Josh 1.6　　**32.8:** Acts 17.26

13 "He let them rule the highlands,
and they ate what grew in the fields.
They found wild honey among the rocks;
their olive-trees flourished in stony
ground.
14 Their cows and goats gave plenty of
milk;
they had the best sheep, goats, and
cattle,
the finest wheat, and the choicest
wine.

15 "The LORD's people grew rich, but
rebellious;
they were fat and stuffed with food.
They abandoned God their Creator
and rejected their mighty saviour.
16 Their idolatry made the LORD jealous;
the evil they did made him angry.
17 They sacrificed to gods that are not
real,
new gods their ancestors had never
known,
gods that Israel had never obeyed.
18 They forgot their God, their mighty
saviour,
the one who had given them life.

19 "When the LORD saw this, he was
angry
and rejected his sons and daughters.
20 'I will no longer help them,' he said;
'then I will see what happens to them,
those stubborn, unfaithful people.
21 With their idols they have made me
angry,
jealous with their so-called gods,
gods that are really not gods.
So I will use a so-called nation to make
them angry;
I will make them jealous with a nation
of fools.
22 My anger will flame up like fire
and burn everything on earth.
It will reach to the world below c
and consume the roots of the
mountains.

23 " 'I will bring on them endless disasters
and use all my arrows against them.
24 They will die from hunger and fever;
they will die from terrible diseases.
I will send wild animals to attack them,
and poisonous snakes to bite them.
25 War will bring death in the streets;
terrors will strike in the homes.
Young men and young women will die;

neither babies nor old men will be
spared.
26 I would have destroyed them
completely,
so that no one would remember them.
27 But I could not let their enemies boast
that they had defeated my people,
when it was I myself who had crushed
them.'

28 "Israel is a nation without sense;
they have no wisdom at all.
29 They fail to see why they were
defeated;
they cannot understand what
happened.
30 Why were a thousand defeated by one,
and ten thousand by only two?
The LORD, their God, had abandoned
them;
their mighty God had given them up.
31 Their enemies know that their own
gods are weak,
not mighty like Israel's God.
32 Their enemies, corrupt as Sodom and
Gomorrah,
are like vines that bear bitter and
poisonous grapes,
33 like wine made from the venom of
snakes.

34 "The LORD remembers what their
enemies have done;
he waits for the right time to punish
them.
35 The LORD will take revenge and punish
them;
the time will come when they will
fall;
the day of their doom is near.
36 The LORD will rescue his people
when he sees that their strength is
gone.
He will have mercy on those who serve
him,
when he sees how helpless they are.
37 Then the LORD will ask his people,
'Where are those mighty gods you
trusted?
38 You fed them with the fat of your
sacrifices
and offered them wine to drink.
Let them come and help you now;
let them run to your rescue.
39 " 'I, and I alone, am God;
no other god is real.

c THE WORLD BELOW: *This refers to the world of the dead.*
32.17: 1 Cor 10.20   **32.21:** 1 Cor 10.22; Rom 10.19   **32.35:** Rom 12.19; Heb 10.30
32.36a: Ps 135.14

I kill and I give life, I wound and I
   heal,
   and no one can oppose what I do.
40 As surely as I am the living God,
   I raise my hand and I vow
41   that I will sharpen my flashing sword
   and see that justice is done.
I will take revenge on my enemies
   and punish those who hate me.
42 My arrows will drip with their blood,
   and my sword will kill all who oppose
   me.
I will spare no one who fights against
   me;
   even the wounded and prisoners will
   die.'

43 "Nations, you must praise the LORD's
   people—
he punishes all who kill them.
He takes revenge on his enemies
   and forgives the sins of his people."

44 Moses and Joshua son of Nun recited
this song, so that the people of Israel could
hear it.

Moses' Final Instructions

45 When Moses had finished giving
God's teachings to the people, 46 he said,
"Make sure you obey all these commands
that I have given you today. Repeat them
to your children, so that they may
faithfully obey all God's teachings.
47 These teachings are not empty words;
they are your very life. Obey them and
you will live long in that land across the
Jordan that you are about to occupy."

48 That same day the LORD said to
Moses, 49 "Go to the Abarim Mountains
in the land of Moab opposite the city of
Jericho; climb Mount Nebo and look at
the land of Canaan that I am about to
give the people of Israel. 50 You will die
on that mountain as your brother Aaron
died on Mount Hor, 51 because both of you
were unfaithful to me in the presence of
the people of Israel. When you were at
the waters of Meribah, near the town of
Kadesh in the wilderness of Zin, you
dishonoured me in the presence of the
people. 52 You will look at the land from

a distance, but you will not enter the land
that I am giving the people of Israel."

Moses Blesses the Tribes of Israel

33 These are the blessings that Moses,
the man of God, pronounced on the
people of Israel before he died.

2 The LORD came from Mount Sinai;
   he rose like the sun over Edom
   and shone on his people from Mount
     Paran.
Ten thousand angels were with him,
   a flaming fire at his right hand. d
3 The LORD loves his people e
   and protects those who belong to him.
So we bow at f his feet
   and obey his commands.
4 We obey the Law that Moses gave us,
   our nation's most treasured
     possession.
5 The LORD became king of his people
     Israel
   when their tribes and leaders were
     gathered together.

6 Moses said about the tribe of Reuben:
"May Reuben never die out,
Although their people are few."

7 About the tribe of Judah he said:
"LORD, listen to their cry for help;
Unite them again with the other tribes.
Fight for them, LORD,
And help them against their enemies." g

8 About the tribe of Levi he said:
"You, LORD, reveal your will by the
     Urim and Thummim h
Through your faithful servants, the
     Levites;
You put them to the test at Massah
And proved them true at the waters
     of Meribah.
9 They showed greater loyalty to you
Than to parents, brothers, or children.
They obeyed your commands
And were faithful to your covenant.
10 They will teach your people to obey
     your Law;
They will offer sacrifices on your altar.
11 Lord, help their tribe to grow strong;

---

d Probable text Ten thousand...right hand; Hebrew unclear.
e One ancient translation his people; Hebrew the peoples.
f Probable text bow at; Hebrew unclear.
g Probable text Fight for...enemies; Hebrew The tribe of Judah will fight for itself, and the Lord
will help it against its enemies.
h URIM AND THUMMIM: Two objects used by the priest to determine God's will; it is not known
precisely how they were used.
32.43: Rom 15.10; Rev 19.2   **32.48–52:** Num 27.12–14; Deut 3.23–27
33.8: Ex 17.7, 28.30; Num 20.13

Be pleased with what they do.
Crush all their enemies;
Let them never rise again."

12 About the tribe of Benjamin he said:
"This is the tribe the LORD loves and
    protects;
He guards them all the day long,
And he dwells in their midst."[i]

13 About the tribe of Joseph he said:
"May the LORD bless their land with
    rain
And with water from under the earth.
14 May their land be blessed with sun-
    ripened fruit,
Rich with the best fruits of each season.
15 May their ancient hills be covered with
    choice fruit.
16 May their land be filled with all that
    is good,
Blessed by the goodness of the LORD,
Who spoke from the burning bush.
May these blessings come to the tribe
    of Joseph,
Because he was the leader among his
    brothers.
17 Joseph has the strength of a bull,
The horns of a wild ox.
His horns are Manasseh's thousands
And Ephraim's ten thousands.
With them he gores the nations
And pushes them to the ends of the
    earth."

18 About the tribes of Zebulun and
Issachar he said:
"May Zebulun be prosperous in their
    trade on the sea,
And may Issachar's wealth increase at
    home.
19 They invite foreigners to their
    mountain
And offer the right sacrifices there.
They get their wealth from the sea
And from the sand along the shore."

20 About the tribe of Gad he said:
"Praise God, who made their territory
    large.
Gad waits like a lion
To tear off an arm or a scalp.
21 They took the best of the land for
    themselves;
A leader's share was assigned to them.
They obeyed the LORD's commands and
    laws

When the leaders of Israel were
    gathered together."[j]

22 About the tribe of Dan he said:
"Dan is a young lion;
He leaps out from Bashan."

23 About the tribe of Naphtali he said:
"Naphtali is richly blessed by the LORD's
    good favour;
Their land reaches to the south from
    Lake Galilee."

24 About the tribe of Asher he said:
"Asher is blessed more than the other
    tribes.
May he be the favourite of his brothers,
And may his land be rich with olive-
    trees.
25 May his towns be protected with iron
    gates,
And may he always live secure."

26 People of Israel, no god is like your
    God,
    riding in splendour across the sky,
    riding through the clouds to come to
        your aid.
27 God has always been your defence;
    his eternal arms are your support.
He drove out your enemies as you
    advanced,
    and told you to destroy them all.
28 So Jacob's descendants live in peace,
    secure in a land full of corn and wine,
    where dew from the sky waters the
        ground.
29 Israel, how happy you are!
    There is no one like you,
    a nation saved by the LORD.
The LORD himself is your shield and your
    sword,
    to defend you and give you victory.
Your enemies will come begging for
    mercy,
    and you will trample them down.

The Death of Moses

34 Moses went up from the plains of
Moab to Mount Nebo, to the top
of Mount Pisgah east of Jericho, and there
the LORD showed him the whole land: the
territory of Gilead as far north as the town
of Dan; 2 the entire territory of Naphtali;
the territories of Ephraim and Manasseh;
the territory of Judah as far west as the

---

[i] And he...midst; or They live under his protection.
[j] One ancient translation When the leaders...together; Hebrew unclear.

The LORD showed him the whole land (34.1)

Mediterranean Sea; ³the southern part of Judah; and the plain that reaches from Zoar to Jericho, the city of palm-trees. ⁴Then the LORD said to Moses, "This is the land that I promised Abraham, Isaac, and Jacob I would give to their descendants. I have let you see it, but I will not let you go there."

5 So Moses, the LORD's servant, died there in the land of Moab, as the LORD had said he would. ⁶The LORD buried him in a valley in Moab, opposite the town of Bethpeor, but to this day no one knows the exact place of his burial. ⁷Moses was a hundred and twenty years old when he died; he was as strong as ever, and his eyesight was still good. ⁸The people of Israel mourned for him for thirty days in the plains of Moab.

9 Joshua son of Nun was filled with wisdom, because Moses had appointed him to be his successor. The people of Israel obeyed Joshua and kept the commands that the LORD had given them through Moses.

10 There has never been a prophet in Israel like Moses; the LORD spoke with him face to face. ¹¹No other prophet has ever done miracles and wonders like those that the LORD sent Moses to perform against the king of Egypt, his officials, and the entire country. ¹²No other prophet has been able to do the great and terrifying things that Moses did in the sight of all Israel.

34.4: Gen 12.7, 26.3, 28.13   **34.10:** Ex 33.11

THE BOOK OF

JOSHUA

INTRODUCTION

The book of *Joshua* is the story of the Israelite invasion of Canaan under the leadership of Joshua, the successor of Moses. Notable events recorded in this book include the crossing of the Jordan, the fall of Jericho, the battle at Ai, and the renewal of the covenant between God and his people. One of the best-known passages in the book is, "Decide today whom you will serve... As for my family and me, we will serve the Lord" (24.15).

Outline of Contents

The conquest of Canaan 1.1—12.24
The division of the land 13.1—21.45
  a. The land east of the Jordan 13.1-33
  b. The land west of the Jordan 14.1—19.51
  c. The cities of refuge 20.1-9
  d. The cities of the Levites 21.1-45
The eastern tribes return to their territory 22.1-34
Joshua's farewell address 23.1-16
The covenant renewed at Shechem 24.1-33

God Commands Joshua to Conquer Canaan

1 After the death of the Lord's servant Moses, the Lord spoke to Moses' helper, Joshua son of Nun. [2] He said, "My servant Moses is dead. Get ready now, you and all the people of Israel, and cross the River Jordan into the land that I am giving them. [3] As I told Moses, I have given you and all my people the entire land that you will be marching over. [4] Your borders will reach from the desert in the south to the Lebanon Mountains in the north; from the great River Euphrates in the east, through the Hittite country, to the Mediterranean Sea in the west. [5] Joshua, no one will be able to defeat you as long as you live. I will be with you as I was

with Moses. I will always be with you; I will never abandon you. [6] Be determined and confident, for you will be the leader of these people as they occupy this land which I promised their ancestors. [7] Just be determined, be confident; and make sure that you obey the whole Law that my servant Moses gave you. Do not neglect any part of it and you will succeed wherever you go. [8] Be sure that the book of the Law is always read in your worship. Study it day and night, and make sure that you obey everything written in it. Then you will be prosperous and successful. [9] Remember that I have commanded you to be determined and confident! Don't be afraid or discouraged, for I, the Lord your God, am with you wherever you go."

1.3-5: Deut 11.24-25   1.5: Deut 31.6,8; Heb 13.5   1.6: Deut 31.6,7,23

Explore the land...especially the city of Jericho (2.1)

Joshua Gives Orders to the People

10 Then Joshua ordered the leaders to
11 go through the camp and say to the
people, "Get some food ready, because
in three days you are going to cross the
River Jordan to occupy the land that the
LORD your God is giving you."

12 Joshua said to the tribes of Reuben
and Gad and to half the tribe of Manasseh,
13 "Remember how Moses, the LORD's
servant, told you that the LORD your God
would give you this land on the east side
of the Jordan as your home. 14 Your wives,
your children, and your livestock will stay
here, but your soldiers, armed for battle,
will cross over ahead of their fellow-
Israelites in order to help them 15 until
they have occupied the land west of the
Jordan that the LORD your God has given
them. When he has given safety to all
the tribes of Israel, then you may come
back and settle here in your own land
east of the Jordan, which Moses, the
LORD's servant, gave to you."

16 They answered Joshua, "We will do
everything you have told us and will go
wherever you send us. 17 We will obey
you, just as we always obeyed Moses,
and may the LORD your God be with you
as he was with Moses! 18 Whoever questions your authority or disobeys any of
your orders will be put to death. Be
determined and confident!"

Joshua Sends Spies into Jericho

2 Then Joshua sent two spies from the
camp at Acacia with orders to go and
secretly explore the land of Canaan,
especially the city of Jericho. When they

came to the city, they went to spend the
night in the house of a prostitute named
Rahab. 2 The king of Jericho heard that
some Israelites had come that night to
spy out the country, 3 so he sent word
to Rahab: "The men in your house have
come to spy out the whole country! Bring
them out!"

4-6 "Some men did come to my house,"
she answered, "but I don't know where
they were from. They left at sunset before
the city gate was closed. I didn't find out
where they were going, but if you start
after them quickly, you can catch them."
(Now Rahab had taken the two spies up
on the roof and hidden them under some
stalks of flax that she had put there.) 7 The
king's men left the city, and then the gate
was shut. They went looking for the
Israelite spies as far as the place where
the road crosses the Jordan.

8 Before the spies settled down for the
night, Rahab went up on the roof 9 and
said to them, "I know that the LORD has
given you this land. Everyone in the
country is terrified of you. 10 We have
heard how the LORD dried up the Red
Sea in front of you when you were leaving
Egypt. We have also heard how you killed
Sihon and Og, the two Amorite kings east
of the Jordan. 11 We were afraid as soon
as we heard about it; we have all lost
our courage because of you. The LORD
your God is God in heaven above and
here on earth. 12 Now swear by him that
you will treat my family as kindly as I
have treated you, and give me some sign
that I can trust you. 13 Promise me that
you will save my father and mother, my

1.12-15: Num 32.28-32; Deut 3.18-20; Josh 22.1-6   **2.1:** Heb 11.31; Jas 2.25
2.10: Ex 14.21; Num 21.21-35

brothers and sisters, and all their families! Don't let us be killed!''

14 The men said to her, "May God take our lives if we don't do as we say![a] If you do not tell anyone what we have been doing, we promise you that when the LORD gives us this land, we will treat you well."

15 Rahab lived in a house built into the city wall, so she let the men down from the window by a rope. 16 "Go into the hill country," she said, "or the king's men will find you. Hide there for three days until they come back. After that you can go on your way."

17 The men said to her, "We will keep the promise that you have made us give. 18 This is what you must do. When we invade your land, tie this red cord to the window you let us down from. Get your father and mother, your brothers, and all your father's family together in your house. 19 If anyone goes out of the house, his death will be his own fault, and we will not be responsible; but if anyone in the house with you is harmed, then we will be responsible. 20 However, if you tell anyone what we have been doing, then we will not have to keep our promise which you have made us give." 21 She agreed and sent them away. When they had gone, she tied the red cord to the window.

22 The spies went into the hills and hid. The king's men looked for them all over the countryside for three days, but they did not find them, so they returned to Jericho. 23 Then the two spies came down from the hills, crossed the river, and went back to Joshua. They told him everything that had happened, 24 and then said, "We are sure that the LORD has given us the whole country. All the people there are terrified of us."

The People of Israel Cross the Jordan

3 The next morning Joshua and all the people of Israel got up early, left the camp at Acacia, and went to the Jordan, where they camped while waiting to cross it. 2 Three days later the leaders went through the camp 3 and said to the people, "When you see the priests carrying the Covenant Box of the LORD your God, break camp and follow them. 4 You have never been here before, so they will show you the way to go. But do not get near the Covenant Box; stay about a kilometre behind it."

5 Joshua said to the people, "Purify

yourselves, because tomorrow the LORD will perform miracles among you." 6 Then he told the priests to take the Covenant Box and go with it ahead of the people. They did as he said.

7 The LORD said to Joshua, "What I do today will make all the people of Israel begin to honour you as a great man, and they will realize that I am with you as I was with Moses. 8 Tell the priests carrying the Covenant Box that when they reach the river, they must wade in and stand near the bank."

9 Then Joshua said to the people, "Come here and listen to what the LORD your God has to say. 10 As you advance, he will surely drive out the Canaanites, the Hittites, the Hivites, the Perizzites, the Girgashites, the Amorites, and the Jebusites. You will know that the living God is among you 11 when the Covenant Box of the Lord of all the earth crosses the Jordan ahead of you. 12 Now choose twelve men, one from each of the tribes of Israel. 13 When the priests who carry the Covenant Box of the LORD of all the earth put their feet in the water, the Jordan will stop flowing, and the water coming downstream will pile up in one place."

14-15 It was harvest time, and the river was in flood.

When the people left the camp to cross the Jordan, the priests went ahead of them, carrying the Covenant Box. As soon as the priests stepped into the river, 16 the water stopped flowing and piled up, far upstream at Adam, the city beside Zarethan. The flow downstream to the Dead Sea was completely cut off, and the people were able to cross over near Jericho. 17 While the people walked across on dry ground, the priests carrying the LORD's Covenant Box stood on dry ground in the middle of the Jordan until all the people had crossed over.

Memorial Stones Are Set Up

4 When the whole nation had crossed the Jordan, the LORD said to Joshua, 2 "Choose twelve men, one from each tribe, 3 and command them to take twelve stones out of the middle of the Jordan, from the very place where the priests were standing. Tell them to carry these stones with them and to put them down where you camp tonight."

4 Then Joshua called the twelve men he had chosen, 5 and said, "Go into the

---

[a] May God...say; or We will protect you if you protect us.

Twelve stones in the middle of the Jordan (4.9)

Jordan ahead of the Covenant Box of the LORD your God. Each one of you take a stone on your shoulder, one for each of the tribes of Israel. ⁶These stones will remind the people of what the LORD has done. In the future, when your children ask what these stones mean to you, ⁷you will tell them that the water of the Jordan stopped flowing when the LORD's Covenant Box crossed the river. These stones will always remind the people of Israel of what happened here."

8 The men followed Joshua's orders. As the LORD had commanded Joshua, they took twelve stones from the middle of the Jordan, one for each of the tribes of Israel, carried them to the camping place, and put them down there. ⁹Joshua also set up twelve stones in the middle of the Jordan, where the priests carrying the Covenant Box had stood. (Those stones are still there.) ¹⁰The priests stood in the middle of the Jordan until everything had been done that the LORD ordered Joshua to tell the people to do. This is what Moses had commanded.

The people hurried across the river. ¹¹When they were all on the other side, the priests with the LORD's Covenant Box went on ahead of the people. ¹²The men of the tribes of Reuben and Gad and of half the tribe of Manasseh, ready for battle, crossed ahead of the rest of the people, as Moses had told them to do. ¹³In the presence of the LORD about forty thousand men ready for war crossed over to the plain near Jericho. ¹⁴What the LORD did that day made the people of Israel consider Joshua a great man. They honoured him all his life, just as they had honoured Moses.

15 Then the LORD told Joshua ¹⁶to command the priests carrying the Covenant Box to come up out of the Jordan. ¹⁷Joshua did so, ¹⁸and when the priests reached the river bank, the river began flowing once more and flooded its banks again.

19 The people crossed the Jordan on the tenth day of the first month and made camp at Gilgal, east of Jericho. ²⁰There Joshua set up the twelve stones taken from the Jordan. ²¹He said to the people of Israel, "In the future, when your children ask you what these stones mean, ²²you will tell them about the time when Israel crossed the Jordan on dry ground. ²³Tell them that the LORD your God dried up the water of the Jordan for you until you had crossed, just as he dried up the Red Sea for us. ²⁴Because of this everyone on earth will know how great the LORD's power is, and you will honour the LORD your God for ever."

5 All the Amorite kings west of the Jordan and all the Canaanite kings along the Mediterranean Sea heard that the LORD had dried up the Jordan until the people of Israel had crossed it. They became afraid and lost their courage because of the Israelites.

The Circumcision at Gilgal

2 Then the LORD told Joshua, "Make some knives out of flint and circumcise the Israelites." ³So Joshua did as the LORD had commanded, and he circumcised the Israelites at a place called Circumcision Hill. ⁴⁻⁶When the people of Israel left Egypt, all the males were already circumcised. However, during the forty years the people spent crossing the desert, none of the baby boys had been circumcised. Also, by the end of that time all the men who were of fighting age when they left Egypt had died because they had

5.6: Num 14.28-35

The people hurried across the river (4.10)

disobeyed the LORD. Just as he had sworn, they were not allowed to see the rich and fertile land that he had promised their ancestors. ⁷The sons of these men had never been circumcised, and it was this new generation that Joshua circumcised.

8 After the circumcision was completed, the whole nation stayed in the camp until the wounds had healed. ⁹The LORD said to Joshua, "Today I have removed from you the disgrace of being slaves in Egypt." That is why the place was named Gilgal, *b* the name it still has.

10 While the Israelites were camping at Gilgal on the plain near Jericho, they observed Passover on the evening of the fourteenth day of the month. ¹¹The next day was the first time they ate food grown in Canaan: roasted grain and bread made without yeast. ¹²The manna stopped falling then, and the Israelites no longer had any. From that time on they ate food grown in Canaan.

Joshua and the Man with a Sword

13 While Joshua was near Jericho, he suddenly saw a man standing in front of him, holding a sword. Joshua went up to him and asked, "Are you one of our soldiers, or an enemy?"

14 "Neither," the man answered. "I am here as the commander of the LORD's army."

Joshua threw himself on the ground in worship and said, "I am your servant, sir. What do you want me to do?"

15 And the commander of the LORD's army told him, "Take your sandals off; you are standing on holy ground." And Joshua did as he was told.

The Fall of Jericho

6 The gates of Jericho were kept shut and guarded to keep the Israelites out. No one could enter or leave the city. ²The LORD said to Joshua, "I am putting into your hands Jericho, with its king and all its brave soldiers. ³You and your soldiers are to march round the city once a day for six days. ⁴Seven priests, each carrying a trumpet, are to go in front of the Covenant Box. On the seventh day you and your soldiers are to march round the city seven times while the priests blow the trumpets. ⁵Then they are to sound one long note. As soon as you hear it, all the men are to give a loud shout, and

---

*b*GILGAL: *This name sounds like the Hebrew for "removed."*
5.10: Ex 12.1–13   **5.12:** Ex 16.35

the city walls will collapse. Then the whole army will go straight into the city."

6 Joshua called the priests and said to them, "Take the Covenant Box, and seven of you go in front of it, carrying trumpets." 7 Then he ordered his men to start marching round the city, with an advance guard going on ahead of the LORD's Covenant Box.

8-9 So, just as Joshua had ordered, an advance guard started out ahead of the priests who were blowing trumpets; behind these came the priests who were carrying the Covenant Box, followed by a rearguard. All this time the trumpets were sounding. 10 But Joshua had ordered his men not to shout, not to say a word until he gave the order. 11 So he told this group of men to take the LORD's Covenant Box round the city once. Then they came back to camp and spent the night there.

12-13 Joshua got up early the next morning, and for the second time the priests and soldiers marched round the city in the same order as the day before: first, the advance guard; next, the seven priests blowing the seven trumpets; then, the priests carrying the LORD's Covenant Box; and finally, the rearguard. All this time the trumpets were sounding. 14 On this second day they again marched round the city once and then returned to camp. They did this for six days.

15 On the seventh day they got up at daybreak and marched seven times round

the city in the same way—this was the only day that they marched round it seven times. 16 The seventh time round, when the priests were about to sound the trumpets, Joshua ordered his men to shout, and he said, "The LORD has given you the city! 17 The city and everything in it must be totally destroyed as an offering to the LORD. Only the prostitute Rahab and her household will be spared, because she hid our spies. 18 But you are not to take anything that is to be destroyed; if you do, you will bring trouble and destruction on the Israelite camp. 19 Everything made of silver, gold, bronze, or iron is set apart for the LORD. It is to be put in the LORD's treasury."

20 So the priests blew the trumpets. As soon as the men heard it, they gave a loud shout, and the walls collapsed. Then all the army went straight up the hill into the city and captured it. 21 With their swords they killed everyone in the city, men and women, young and old. They also killed the cattle, sheep, and donkeys.

22 Joshua then told the two men who had served as spies, "Go into the prostitute's house and bring her and her family out, as you promised her." 23 So they went and brought Rahab out, along with her father and mother, her brothers, and the rest of her family. They took them all, family and slaves, to safety near the Israelite camp. 24 Then they set fire to the city and burnt it to the ground, along with

6.20: Heb 11.30

They gave a loud shout, and the walls collapsed (6.20)

everything in it, except the things made of gold, silver, bronze, and iron, which they took and put in the LORD's treasury. ²⁵ But Joshua spared the lives of the prostitute Rahab and all her relatives, because she had hidden the two spies that he had sent to Jericho. (Her descendants have lived in Israel to this day.)

26 At that time Joshua issued a solemn warning: "Anyone who tries to rebuild the city of Jericho will be under the LORD's curse.

Whoever lays the foundation will lose
     his eldest son;
Whoever builds the gates will lose his
     youngest."

27 So the LORD was with Joshua, and his fame spread through the whole country.

Achan's Sin

7 The LORD's command to Israel not to take from Jericho anything that was to be destroyed was not obeyed. A man named Achan disobeyed that order, and so the LORD was furious with the Israelites. (Achan was the son of Carmi and grandson of Zabdi, and belonged to the clan of Zerah, a part of the tribe of Judah.)

2 Joshua sent some men from Jericho to Ai, a city east of Bethel, near Bethaven, with orders to go and explore the land. When they had done so, ³ they reported back to Joshua: "There is no need for everyone to attack Ai. Send only about two or three thousand men. Don't send the whole army up there to fight; it is not a large city." ⁴ So about three thousand Israelites made the attack, but they were forced to retreat. ⁵ The men of Ai chased them from the city gate as far as some quarries and killed about thirty-six of them on the way down the hill. Then the Israelites lost their courage and were afraid.

6 Joshua and the leaders of Israel tore their clothes in grief, threw themselves to the ground before the LORD's Covenant Box, and lay there till evening, with dust on their heads to show their sorrow. ⁷ And Joshua said, "Sovereign LORD! Why did you bring us across the Jordan at all? To hand us over to the Amorites? To destroy us? Why didn't we just stay on the other side of the Jordan? ⁸ What can I say, O Lord, now that Israel has retreated from the enemy? ⁹ The Canaanites and everyone else in the country will hear about it.

They will surround us and kill every one of us! And then what will you do to protect your honour?"

10 The LORD said to Joshua, "Get up! Why are you lying on the ground like this? ¹¹ Israel has sinned! They have broken the agreement with me that I ordered them to keep. They have taken some of the things condemned to destruction. They stole them, lied about it, and put them with their own things. ¹² This is why the Israelites cannot stand against their enemies. They retreat from them because they themselves have now been condemned to destruction! I will not stay with you any longer unless you destroy the things you were ordered not to take! ¹³ Get up! Purify the people and get them ready to come before me. Tell them to be ready tomorrow, because I, the LORD God of Israel, have this to say: 'Israel, you have in your possession some things that I ordered you to destroy! You cannot stand against your enemies until you get rid of these things!' ¹⁴ So tell them that in the morning they will be brought forward, tribe by tribe. The tribe that I pick out will then come forward, clan by clan. The clan that I pick out will come forward, family by family. The family that I pick out will come forward, man by man. ¹⁵ The one who is then picked out and found with the condemned goods will be burnt, along with his family and everything he owns, for he has brought terrible shame on Israel and has broken my covenant."

16 Early the next morning Joshua brought Israel forward, tribe by tribe, and the tribe of Judah was picked out. ¹⁷ He brought the tribe of Judah forward, clan by clan, and the clan of Zerah was picked out. Then he brought the clan of Zerah forward, family by family, and the family of Zabdi was picked out. ¹⁸ He then brought Zabdi's family forward, man by man, and Achan, the son of Carmi and grandson of Zabdi, was picked out. ¹⁹ Joshua said to him, "My son, tell the truth here before the LORD, the God of Israel, and confess. Tell me now what you have done. Don't try to hide it from me."

20 "It's true," Achan answered. "I have sinned against the LORD, Israel's God, and this is what I did. ²¹ Among the things we seized I saw a beautiful Babylonian cloak, about two kilogrammes of silver, and a bar of gold weighing over half a kilogramme. I wanted them so much that

6.25: Heb 11.31   **6.26:** 1 Kgs 16.34

I took them. You will find them buried inside my tent, with the silver at the bottom."

22 So Joshua sent some men, who ran to the tent and found that the condemned things really were buried there, with the silver at the bottom. 23 They brought them out of the tent, took them to Joshua and all the Israelites, and laid them down in the presence of the LORD. 24 Joshua, along with all the people of Israel, seized Achan, the silver, the cloak, and the bar of gold, together with Achan's sons and daughters, his cattle, donkeys, and sheep, his tent, and everything else he owned; and they took them to Trouble Valley. 25 And Joshua said, "Why have you brought such trouble on us? The LORD will now bring trouble on you!" All the people then stoned Achan to death; they also stoned and burnt his family and possessions. 26 They put a huge pile of stones over him, which is there to this day. That is why that place is still called Trouble Valley.

Then the LORD was no longer furious.

The Capture and Destruction of Ai

8 The LORD said to Joshua, "Take all the soldiers with you and go on up to Ai. Don't be afraid or discouraged. I will give you victory over the king of Ai; his people, city, and land will be yours. 2 You are to do to Ai and its king what you did to Jericho and its king, but this time you may keep its goods and livestock for yourselves. Prepare to attack the city by surprise from the rear."

3 So Joshua got ready to go to Ai with all his soldiers. He picked out thirty thousand of his best troops and sent them out at night 4 with these orders: "Hide on the other side of the city, but not too far away from it; be ready to attack. 5 My men and I will approach the city. When the men of Ai come out against us, we will turn and run, just as we did the first time. 6 They will pursue us until we have led them away from the city. They will think that we are running away from them, as we did before. 7 Then you will come out of hiding and capture the city. The LORD your God will give it to you. 8 After you have taken the city, set it on fire, just as the LORD has commanded. These are your orders." 9 So Joshua sent them out, and they went to their hiding place and waited there, west of Ai,

between Ai and Bethel. Joshua spent the night in camp.

10 Early in the morning Joshua got up and called the soldiers together. Then he and the leaders of Israel led them to Ai. 11 The soldiers with him went towards the main entrance to the city and set up camp on the north side, with a valley between themselves and Ai. 12 He took about five thousand men and put them in hiding west of the city, between Ai and Bethel. 13 The soldiers were arranged for battle with the main camp north of the city and the rest of the men to the west. Joshua spent the night in the valley. 14 When the king of Ai saw Joshua's men, he acted quickly. He and all his men went out towards the Jordan Valley to fight the Israelites at the same place as before, not knowing that he was about to be attacked from the rear. 15 Joshua and his men pretended that they were retreating, and ran away towards the barren country. 16 All the men in the city had been called together to go after them, and as they pursued Joshua, they kept getting farther away from the city. 17 Every man in Ai[c] went after the Israelites, and the city was left wide open, with no one to defend it.

18 Then the LORD said to Joshua, "Point your spear at Ai; I am giving it to you." Joshua did as he was told, 19 and as soon as he lifted his hand, the men who had been hiding got up quickly, ran into the city and captured it. They immediately set the city on fire. 20 When the men of Ai looked back, they saw the smoke rising to the sky. There was no way for them to escape, because the Israelites who had run towards the barren country now turned round to attack them. 21 When Joshua and his men saw that the others had taken the city and that it was on fire, they turned round and began killing the men of Ai. 22 The Israelites in the city now came down to join the battle. So the men of Ai found themselves completely surrounded by Israelites, and they were all killed. No one got away, and no one lived through it 23 except the king of Ai. He was captured and taken to Joshua.

24 The Israelites killed every one of the enemy in the barren country where they had chased them. Then they went back to Ai and killed everyone there. 25-26 Joshua kept his spear pointed at Ai and did not put it down until every person there had been killed. The whole population of Ai was killed that day—twelve

c One ancient translation Ai; _Hebrew_ Ai and Bethel.

thousand men and women. 27 The Israelites kept for themselves the livestock and goods captured in the city, as the LORD had told Joshua. 28 Joshua burnt Ai and left it in ruins. It is still like that today. 29 He hanged the king of Ai from a tree and left his body there until evening. At sunset Joshua gave orders for the body to be removed, and it was thrown down at the entrance to the city gate. They covered it with a huge pile of stones, which is still there today.

The Law Is Read at Mount Ebal

30 Then Joshua built on Mount Ebal an altar to the LORD, the God of Israel. 31 He made it according to the instructions that Moses, the LORD's servant, had given the Israelites, as it says in the Law of Moses: "an altar made of stones which have not been cut with iron tools." On it they offered burnt sacrifices to the LORD, and they also presented their fellowship-offerings. 32 There, with the Israelites looking on, Joshua made on the stones^d a copy of the Law which Moses had written. 33 The Israelites, with their leaders, officers, and judges, as well as the foreigners among them, stood on two sides of the LORD's Covenant Box, facing the levitical priests who carried it. Half the people stood with their backs to Mount Gerizim and the other half with their backs to Mount Ebal. The LORD's servant Moses had commanded them to do this when the time came for them to receive the blessing. 34 Joshua then read aloud the whole Law, including the blessings and the curses, just as they are written in the book of the Law. 35 Every one of the commandments of Moses was read by Joshua to the whole gathering, which included women and children, as well as the foreigners living among them.

The Gibeonites Deceive Joshua

9 The victories of Israel became known to all the kings west of the Jordan—in the hills, in the foothills, and all along the coastal plain of the Mediterranean Sea as far north as Lebanon; these were the kings of the Hittites, the Amorites, the Canaanites, the Perizzites, the Hivites, and the Jebusites. 2 They all came together and joined forces to fight against Joshua and the Israelites.

3 But the people of Gibeon, who were

Hivites, heard what Joshua had done to Jericho and Ai, 4 and they decided to deceive him. They went and got some food and loaded their donkeys with worn-out sacks and patched-up wineskins. 5 They put on ragged clothes and worn-out sandals that had been mended. The bread they took with them was dry and mouldy. 6 Then they went to the camp at Gilgal and said to Joshua and the men of Israel, "We have come from a distant land. We want you to make a treaty with us."

7 But the men of Israel said, "Why should we make a treaty with you? Maybe you live nearby."

8 They said to Joshua, "We are at your service."

Joshua asked them, "Who are you? Where do you come from?"

9 Then they told him this story: "We have come from a very distant land, sir, because we have heard of the LORD your God. We have heard about everything that he did in Egypt 10 and what he did to the two Amorite kings east of the Jordan: King Sihon of Heshbon and King Og of Bashan, who lived in Ashtaroth. 11 Our leaders and all the people that live in our land told us to get some food ready for a journey and to go and meet you. We were told to put ourselves at your service and ask you to make a treaty with us. 12 Look at our bread. When we left home with it and started out to meet you, it was still warm. But look! Now it is dry and mouldy. 13 When we filled these wineskins, they were new, but look! They are torn. Our clothes and sandals are worn out from the long journey."

14 The men of Israel accepted some food from them, but did not consult the LORD about it. 15 Joshua made a treaty of friendship with the people of Gibeon and allowed them to live. The leaders of the community of Israel gave their solemn promise to keep the treaty.

16 Three days after the treaty had been made, the Israelites learnt that these people did indeed live nearby. 17 So the people of Israel started out and three days later arrived at the cities where these people lived: Gibeon, Chephirah, Beeroth, and Kiriath Jearim. 18 But the Israelites could not kill them, because their leaders had made a solemn promise to them in the name of the LORD, Israel's God. All the people complained to the leaders

---

^dthe stones; or stones.
8.30–32: Deut 27.2–8   **8.31:** Ex 20.25   **8.33–35:** Deut 11.29, 27.11–14
9.7: Ex 23.32, 34.12; Deut 7.2   **9.10:** Num 21.21–35

But look! They are torn (9.13)

about this, [19] but they answered, "We have made our solemn promise to them in the name of the LORD God of Israel. Now we cannot harm them. [20] We must let them live because of our promise; if we don't, God will punish us. [21] Let them live, but they will have to cut wood and carry water for us." This was what the leaders suggested.

[22] Joshua ordered the people of Gibeon to be brought to him, and he asked them, "Why did you deceive us and tell us that you were from far away, when you live right here? [23] Because you did this, God has condemned you. Your people will always be slaves, cutting wood and carrying water for the sanctuary of my God."

[24] They answered, "We did it, sir, because we learnt that it was really true that the LORD your God had commanded his servant Moses to give you the whole land and to kill the people living in it as you advanced. We did it because we were terrified of you; we were in fear of our lives. [25] Now we are in your power; do with us what you think is right." [26] So this is what Joshua did: he protected them and did not allow the people of Israel to kill them. [27] But at the same time he made them slaves, to cut wood and carry water for the people of Israel and for the LORD's altar. To this day they have continued to do this work in the place where the LORD has chosen to be worshipped.

[e] JERUSALEM: *At that time it was a Jebusite city.*

The Amorites Are Defeated

10 Adonizedek, the king of Jerusalem, [e] heard that Joshua had captured and totally destroyed Ai and had killed its king, just as he had done to Jericho and its king. He also heard that the people of Gibeon had made peace with the Israelites and were living among them. [2] The people of Jerusalem were greatly alarmed at this because Gibeon was as large as any of the cities that had a king; it was larger than Ai, and its men were good fighters. [3] So Adonizedek sent the following message to King Hoham of Hebron, King Piram of Jarmuth, King Japhia of Lachish, and to King Debir of Eglon: [4] "Come and help me attack Gibeon, because its people have made peace with Joshua and the Israelites." [5] These five Amorite kings, the kings of Jerusalem, Hebron, Jarmuth, Lachish, and Eglon, joined forces, surrounded Gibeon, and attacked it.

[6] The men of Gibeon sent word to Joshua at the camp in Gilgal: "Do not abandon us, sir! Come at once and help us! Save us! All the Amorite kings in the hill-country have joined forces and have attacked us!"

[7] So Joshua and his whole army, including the best troops, started out from Gilgal. [8] The LORD said to Joshua, "Do not be afraid of them. I have already given you the victory. Not one of them will be able to stand against you." [9] All night

Bring those five kings out to me (10.22)

Joshua and his army marched from Gilgal to Gibeon, and they made a surprise attack on the Amorites. ¹⁰The LORD made the Amorites panic at the sight of Israel's army. The Israelites slaughtered them at Gibeon and pursued them down the mountain pass at Beth Horon, keeping up the attack as far south as Azekah and Makkedah. ¹¹While the Amorites were running down the pass from the Israelite army, the LORD made large hailstones fall down on them all the way to Azekah. More were killed by the hailstones than by the Israelites.

12 On the day that the LORD gave the men of Israel victory over the Amorites, Joshua spoke to the LORD. In the presence of the Israelites he said,

"Sun, stand still over Gibeon;
Moon, stop over Aijalon Valley."

¹³The sun stood still and the moon did not move until the nation had conquered its enemies. This is written in *The Book of Jashar.* The sun stood still in the middle of the sky and did not go down for a whole day. ¹⁴Never before, and never since, has there been a day like it, when the LORD obeyed a human being. The LORD fought on Israel's side!

15 After this, Joshua and his army went back to the camp at Gilgal.

Joshua Captures the Five Amorite Kings

16 The five Amorite kings, however, had escaped and were hiding in the cave at Makkedah. ¹⁷Someone found them, and Joshua was told where they were hiding.

¹⁸He said, "Roll some big stones in front of the entrance to the cave. Place some guards there, ¹⁹but don't stay there yourselves. Keep on after the enemy and attack them from the rear; don't let them get to their cities! The LORD your God has given you victory over them." ²⁰Joshua and the men of Israel slaughtered them, although some managed to find safety inside their city walls and were not killed. ²¹Then all of Joshua's men came back safe to him at the camp at Makkedah.

No one in the land dared even to speak against the Israelites.

22 Then Joshua said, "Open the entrance to the cave and bring those five kings out to me." ²³So the cave was opened, and the kings of Jerusalem, Hebron, Jarmuth, Lachish, and Eglon were brought out ²⁴and taken to Joshua. Joshua then called all the men of Israel to him and ordered the officers who had gone with him to come and put their feet on the necks of the kings. They did so. ²⁵Then Joshua said to his officers, "Don't be afraid or discouraged. Be determined and confident because this is what the LORD is going to do to all your enemies." ²⁶Then Joshua killed the kings and hanged them on five trees, where their bodies stayed until evening. ²⁷At sunset Joshua gave orders, and their bodies were taken down and thrown into the same cave where they had hidden earlier. Large stones were placed at the entrance to the cave, and they are still there.

10.13: 2 Sam 1.18

Joshua Captures More Amorite Territory

28 Joshua attacked and captured Makkedah and its king that day. He put everyone in the city to death; no one was left alive. He did to the king of Makkedah what he had done to the king of Jericho.

29 After this, Joshua and his army went on from Makkedah to Libnah and attacked it. 30 The LORD also gave the Israelites victory over this city and its king. They spared no one, but killed every person in it. They did to the king what they had done to the king of Jericho.

31 After this, Joshua and his army went on from Libnah to Lachish, surrounded it and attacked it. 32 The LORD gave the Israelites victory over Lachish on the second day of the battle. Just as they had done at Libnah, they spared no one, but killed every person in the city. 33 King Horam of Gezer came to the aid of Lachish, but Joshua defeated him and his army and left none of them alive.

34 Next, Joshua and his army went on from Lachish to Eglon, surrounded it and attacked it. 35 They captured it the same day and put everyone there to death, just as they had done at Lachish.

36 After this, Joshua and his army went from Eglon up into the hills to Hebron, attacked it 37 and captured it. They killed the king and everyone else in the city as well as in the nearby towns. Joshua condemned the city to total destruction, just as he had done to Eglon. No one in it was left alive.

38 Then Joshua and his army turned back to Debir and attacked it. 39 He captured it, with its king and all the nearby towns. They put everyone there to death. Joshua did to Debir and its king what he had done to Hebron and to Libnah and its king.

40 Joshua conquered the whole land. He defeated the kings of the hill-country, the eastern slopes, and the western foothills, as well as those of the dry country in the south. He spared no one; everyone was put to death. This was what the LORD God of Israel had commanded. 41 Joshua's campaign took him from Kadesh Barnea in the south to Gaza near the coast, including all the area of Goshen, and as far north as Gibeon. 42 Joshua conquered all these kings and their territory in one campaign because the LORD, Israel's God, was fighting for Israel. 43 After this, Joshua and his army went back to the camp at Gilgal.

Joshua Defeats Jabin and His Allies

11 When the news of Israel's victories reached King Jabin of Hazor, he sent word to King Jobab of Madon, to the kings of Shimron and Achshaph, 2 and to the kings in the hill-country in the north, in the Jordan Valley south of Lake Galilee, in the foothills, and on the coast near Dor. 3 He also sent word to the Canaanites on both sides of the Jordan, to the Amorites, the Hittites, the Perizzites, and the Jebusites in the hill-country, as well as to the Hivites who lived at the foot of Mount Hermon in the land of Mizpah. 4 They came with all their soldiers—an army with as many men as there are grains of sand on the seashore. They also had many horses and chariots. 5 All these kings joined forces and came together and set up camp at Merom Brook to fight against Israel.

6 The LORD said to Joshua, "Do not be afraid of them. By this time tomorrow I will have killed all of them for Israel. You are to cripple their horses and burn their chariots." 7 So Joshua and all his men attacked them by surprise at Merom Brook. 8 The LORD gave the Israelites victory over them; the Israelites attacked and pursued them as far north as Misrephoth Maim and Sidon, and as far east as the valley of Mizpah. The fight continued until none of the enemy was left alive. 9 Joshua did to them what the LORD had commanded: he crippled their horses and burnt their chariots.

10 Joshua then turned back, captured Hazor and killed its king. (At that time Hazor was the most powerful of all those kingdoms.) 11 They put everyone there to death; no one was left alive, and the city was burnt.

12 Joshua captured all these cities and their kings, putting everyone to death, just as Moses, the LORD's servant, had commanded. 13 However, the Israelites did not burn any of the cities built on mounds, except Hazor, which Joshua did burn. 14 The people of Israel took all the valuables and livestock from these cities and kept them for themselves. But they put every person to death; no one was left alive. 15 The LORD had given his commands to his servant Moses, Moses had given them to Joshua, and Joshua obeyed them. He did everything that the LORD had commanded Moses.

THE DIVISION
OF CANAAN

MEDITERRANEAN SEA

Sidon
Mount Lebanon
Mount Hermon
Damascus

Tyre

Dan (Laish)
DAN
Kedesh
Hazor

ASHER

ZEBULUN

NAPHTALI

Mount Tabor

LAKE GALILEE

Ashtaroth

Golan

EAST MANASSEH

Dor

ISSACHAR

Megiddo

Valley of Jezreel

VILLAGES OF JAIR

Jezreel

Ramoth in Gilead

WEST MANASSEH

GILEAD

Mount Ebal

Shechem

Mount Gerizim

River Jordan

GAD

River Jabbok

AMMON

Timnath Serah

Shiloh

EPHRAIM

Bethel Ai

Gibeon

Jericho

Gilgal

Ashdod

DAN

BENJAMIN

Ekron

Jerusalem

Bezer

PHILISTIA

Ashkelon

Libnah

Gath

Lachish

JUDAH

Hebron

REUBEN

DEAD SEA

Gaza

Debir

Engedi

River Arnon

Beersheba

Hormah

SIMEON

MOAB

0   20   40   60
Kilometres

EDOM

The Territory Taken by Joshua

16 Joshua captured all the land—the hill-country and foothills, both north and south, all the area of Goshen and the dry country south of it, as well as the Jordan Valley. 17-18 The territory extended from Mount Halak in the south near Edom, as far as Baalgad in the north, in the valley of Lebanon south of Mount Hermon. Joshua was at war with the kings of this territory for a long time, but he captured them all and put them to death. 19 The only city that made peace with the people of Israel was Gibeon, where some of the Hivites lived. All the others were conquered in battle. 20 The LORD had made them determined to fight the Israelites, so that they would be condemned to total destruction and all be killed without mercy. This was what the LORD had commanded Moses.

21 At this time Joshua went and destroyed the race of giants called the Anakim who lived in the hill-country—in Hebron, Debir, Anab, and in all the hill-country of Judah and Israel. Joshua completely destroyed them and their cities. 22 None of the Anakim were left in the land of Israel; a few, however, were left in Gaza, Gath, and Ashdod.

23 Joshua captured the whole land, as the LORD had commanded Moses. Joshua gave it to the Israelites as their own and divided it into portions, one for each tribe.

So the people rested from war.

The Kings Defeated by Moses

12 The people of Israel had already conquered and occupied the land east of the Jordan, from the Arnon Valley up the Jordan Valley and as far north as Mount Hermon. They defeated two kings. 2 One was Sihon, the Amorite king who ruled at Heshbon. His kingdom included half of Gilead: from Aroer (on the edge of the valley of the Arnon) and the city in *f* the middle of that valley, as far as the River Jabbok, the border of Ammon; 3 it included the Jordan Valley from Lake Galilee south to Beth Jeshimoth (east of the Dead Sea) and on towards the foot of Mount Pisgah.

4 They also defeated King Og of Bashan, who was one of the last of the Rephaim; he ruled at Ashtaroth and Edrei. 5 His kingdom included Mount Hermon, Salecah, and all of Bashan as far as the boundaries of Geshur and Maacah, as well as half of Gilead, as far as the territory of King Sihon of Heshbon.

6 These two kings were defeated by Moses and the people of Israel. Moses, the LORD's servant, gave their land to the tribes of Reuben and Gad and to half the tribe of Manasseh, to be their possession.

The Kings Defeated by Joshua

7 Joshua and the people of Israel defeated all the kings in the territory west of the Jordan, from Baalgad in the valley of Lebanon to Mount Halak in the south near Edom. Joshua divided this land among the tribes and gave it to them as a permanent possession. 8 This portion included the hill-country, the western foothills, the Jordan Valley and its foothills, the eastern slopes, and the dry country in the south. This land had been the home of the Hittites, the Amorites, the Canaanites, the Perizzites, the Hivites, and the Jebusites. 9 The people of Israel defeated the kings of the following cities: Jericho, Ai (near Bethel), 10 Jerusalem, Hebron, 11 Jarmuth, Lachish, 12 Eglon, Gezer, 13 Debir, Geder, 14 Hormah, Arad, 15 Libnah, Adullam, 16 Makkedah, Bethel, 17 Tappuah, Hepher, 18 Aphek, Lasharon, 19 Madon, Hazor, 20 Shimron Meron, Achshaph, 21 Taanach, Megiddo, 22 Kedesh, Jokneam (in Carmel), 23 Dor (on the coast), Goiim (in Galilee *g*), 24 and Tirzah—thirty-one kings in all.

The Land Still to Be Taken

13 Joshua was now very old. The LORD said to him, "You are very old, but there is still much land to be taken: 2 all the territory of Philistia and Geshur, 3 as well as all the territory of the Avvim to the south. (The land from the stream of Shihor, at the Egyptian border, as far north as the border of Ekron was considered Canaanite; the kings of the Philistines lived at Gaza, Ashdod, Ashkelon, Gath, and Ekron.) 4 There is still all the Canaanite country, and Mearah (which belonged to the Sidonians), as far as Aphek, at the Amorite border; 5 the land of the Gebalites; all of Lebanon to the east, from Baalgad, which is south of Mount Hermon, to Hamath Pass. 6 This

---

f Probable text (see 13.16; Deut 2.36) the city in; Hebrew does not have these words.
g One ancient translation Galilee; Hebrew Gilgal.
11.20: Deut 7.16   **12.1–5:** Num 21.21–35; Deut 2.26—3.11   **12.6:** Num 32.33; Deut 3.12
13.6: Num 33.54

includes all the territory of the Sidonians, who live in the hill-country between the Lebanon Mountains and Misrephoth Maim. I will drive all these peoples out as the people of Israel advance. You must divide the land among the Israelites, just as I have commanded you to do. 7 Now then, divide this land among the other nine tribes and half of the tribe of Manasseh, for them to possess as their own."

The Division of the Territory East of the Jordan

8 The tribes of Reuben and Gad and the other half of the tribe of Manasseh had already received the land that Moses, the LORD's servant, had given them; it was on the east side of the River Jordan. 9 Their territory extended to Aroer (on the edge of the Arnon Valley) and the city in the middle of that valley and included all the plateau from Medeba to Dibon. 10 It went as far as the border of Ammon and included all the cities that had been ruled by the Amorite king Sihon, who had ruled at Heshbon. 11 It included Gilead, the regions of Geshur and Maacah, all Mount Hermon, and all of Bashan as far as Salecah. 12 It included the kingdom of Og, the last of the Rephaim, who had ruled at Ashtaroth and Edrei. Moses had defeated these people and driven them out. 13 However, the Israelites did not drive out the people of Geshur and Maacah; they still live in Israel.

14 Moses had given no land to the tribe of Levi. As the LORD had told Moses, they were to receive as their possession a share of the sacrifices burnt on the altar to the LORD God of Israel.

The Territory Assigned to Reuben

15 Moses had given a part of the land to the families of the tribe of Reuben as their possession. 16 Their territory extended to Aroer (on the edge of the Arnon Valley) and the city in the middle of that valley and included all the plateau round Medeba. 17 It included Heshbon and all the cities on the plateau: Dibon, Bamoth Baal, Beth Baalmeon, 18 Jahaz, Kedemoth, Mephaath, 19 Kiriathaim, Sibmah, Zereth-shahar on the hill in the valley, 20 Beth-peor, the slopes of Mount Pisgah, and Beth Jeshimoth. 21 It included all the cities

of the plateau and the whole kingdom of the Amorite king Sihon, who had ruled at Heshbon. Moses defeated him, as well as the rulers of Midian: Evi, Rekem, Zur, Hur, and Reba. All of them had ruled the land for King Sihon. 22 Among those whom the people of Israel killed was the fortune-teller Balaam son of Beor. 23 The Jordan was the western border of the tribe of Reuben. These were the cities and towns given to the families of the tribe of Reuben as their possession.

The Territory Assigned to Gad

24 Moses had also given a part of the land to the families of the tribe of Gad as their possession. 25 Their territory included Jazer and all the cities of Gilead, half the land of Ammon as far as Aroer, which is east of Rabbah; 26 their land extended from Heshbon to Ramath Mizpeh and Betonim, from Mahanaim to the border of Lodebar. 27 In the Jordan Valley it included Beth Haram, Bethnim-rah, Sukkoth, and Zaphon, the rest of the kingdom of King Sihon of Heshbon. Their western border was the River Jordan as far north as Lake Galilee. 28 These were the cities and towns given to the families of the tribe of Gad as their possession.

The Territory Assigned to East Manasseh

29 Moses had given a part of the land to the families of half the tribe of Manasseh as their possession. 30 Their territory extended to Mahanaim and included all of Bashan—the whole kingdom of Og, the king of Bashan, as well as all sixty of the villages of Jair in Bashan. 31 It included half of Gilead, as well as Ashtaroth and Edrei, the capital cities of Og's kingdom in Bashan. All this was given to half the families descended from Machir son of Manasseh.

32 That is how Moses divided the land east of Jericho and the Jordan when he was in the plains of Moab. 33 But Moses did not assign any land to the tribe of Levi. He told them that their possession was to be a share of the offerings to the LORD God of Israel.

The Division of the Territory West of the Jordan

14 What follows is an account of how the land of Canaan west of the

---

13.8: Num 32.33; Deut 3.12   **13.14:** Deut 18.1   **13.33:** Num 18.20; Deut 18.2

Jordan was divided among the people of Israel. Eleazar the priest, Joshua son of Nun, and the leaders of the families of the Israelite tribes divided it among the population. [2] As the LORD had commanded Moses, the territories of the nine and a half tribes west of the Jordan were determined by drawing lots.[h] [3-4] Moses had already assigned the land east of the Jordan to the other two and a half tribes. (The descendants of Joseph were divided into two tribes: Manasseh and Ephraim.) However, Moses gave the Levites no portion of the territory. Instead, they received cities to live in, with fields for their cattle and flocks. [5] The people of Israel divided the land as the LORD had commanded Moses.

Hebron Is Given to Caleb

6 One day some people from the tribe of Judah came to Joshua at Gilgal. One of them, Caleb son of Jephunneh the Kenizzite, said to him, "You know what the LORD said in Kadesh Barnea about you and me to Moses, the man of God. [7] I was forty years old when the LORD's servant Moses sent me from Kadesh Barnea to spy out this land. I brought an honest report back to him. [8] The men who went with me, however, made our people afraid. But I faithfully obeyed the LORD my God. [9] Because I did, Moses promised me that my children and I would certainly receive as our possession the land which I walked over. [10] But now, look. It has been forty-five years since the LORD said that to Moses. That was when Israel was going through the desert, and the LORD, as he promised, has kept me alive ever since. Look at me! I am eighty-five years old [11] and I'm just as strong today as I was when Moses sent me out. I am still strong enough for war or for anything else. [12] Now then, give me the hill-country that the LORD promised me on that day when my men and I reported. We told you then that the race of giants called the Anakim were there in large walled cities. Maybe the LORD will be with me, and I will drive them out, just as the LORD said."

13 Joshua blessed Caleb son of Jephunneh and gave him the city of Hebron as his possession. [14] Hebron still belongs to the descendants of Caleb son

of Jephunneh the Kenizzite, because he faithfully obeyed the LORD, the God of Israel. [15] Before this, Hebron was called the city of Arba. (Arba had been the greatest of the Anakim.)

There was now peace in the land.

The Territory Assigned to Judah

15 The families of the tribe of Judah received a part of the land described as follows:

The land reached south to the southernmost point of the wilderness of Zin, at the border of Edom. [2] This southern border ran from the south end of the Dead Sea, [3] went southwards from the Akrabbim Pass and on to Zin. It ran south of Kadesh Barnea, past Hezron and up to Addar, turned towards Karka, [4] went on to Azmon, and followed the stream on the border of Egypt to the Mediterranean Sea, where the border ended. That was the southern border of Judah.

5 The eastern border was the Dead Sea, all the way up to the inlet where the Jordan empties into it.

The northern border began there, [6] extended up to Beth Hoglah, and went north of the ridge overlooking the Jordan Valley. Then it went up to the Stone of Bohan (Bohan was a son of Reuben), [7] from Trouble Valley up to Debir, and then turned north towards Gilgal, which faces Adummim Pass on the south side of the valley. It then went on to the springs of Enshemesh, out to Enrogel, [8] and up through the Valley of Hinnom on the south side of the hill where the Jebusite city of Jerusalem was located. The border then proceeded up to the top of the hill on the west side of the Valley of Hinnom, at the northern end of the Valley of Rephaim. [9] From there it went to the Springs of Nephtoah and out to the cities near Mount Ephron. There it turned towards Baalah (or Kiriath Jearim), [10] where it circled west of Baalah towards the hill-country of Edom, went on the north side of Mount Jearim (or Chesalon), down to Beth Shemesh, and on past Timnah. [11] The border then went out to the hill north of Ekron, turned towards Shikkeron, past Mount Baalah, and on to Jamnia. It ended at the Mediterranean Sea, [12] which formed the western border.

---

[h] DRAWING LOTS: *This was usually done by using specially marked stones to determine God's will.*
14.2: Num 26.52-56, 34.13   **14.3:** Num 32.33, 34.14-15; Deut 3.12-17   **14.6:** Num 14.30
14.7: Num 13.1-30   **14.9:** Num 14.24

Within these borders lived the people of the families of Judah.

Caleb Conquers Hebron and Debir
(Judg 1.11–15)

13 As the LORD commanded Joshua, part of the territory of Judah was given to Caleb son of Jephunneh, from the tribe of Judah. He received Hebron, the city belonging to Arba, father of Anak. 14 Caleb drove the descendants of Anak out of the city—the clans of Sheshai, Ahiman, and Talmai. 15 From there he went to attack the people living in Debir. (This city used to be called Kiriath Sepher.) 16 Caleb said, "I will give my daughter Achsah in marriage to the man who succeeds in capturing Kiriath Sepher." 17 Othniel, the son of Caleb's brother Kenaz, captured the city, so Caleb gave him his daughter Achsah in marriage. 18 On the wedding day Othniel urged her[i] to ask her father for a field. She got down from her donkey, and Caleb asked her what she wanted. 19 She answered, "I want some pools of water. The land you have given me is in the dry country." So Caleb gave her the upper and lower springs.

The Cities of Judah

20 This is the land that the families of the tribe of Judah received as their possession. 21 The cities farthest south that belonged to them, those that were near the border of Edom, were Kabzeel, Eder, Jagur, 22 Kinah, Dimonah, Adadah, 23 Kedesh, Hazor, Ithnan, 24 Ziph, Telem, Bealoth, 25 Hazor Hadattah, Kerioth Hezron (or Hazor), 26 Amam, Shema, Moladah, 27 Hazar Gaddah, Heshmon, Bethpelet, 28 Hazar Shual, Beersheba, Biziothiah, 29 Baalah, Iim, Ezem, 30 Eltolad, Chesil, Hormah, 31 Ziklag, Madmannah, Sansannah, 32 Lebaoth, Shilhim, Ain, and Rimmon: twenty-nine cities in all, along with the towns round them.

33 The cities in the foothills were Eshtaol, Zorah, Ashnah, 34 Zanoah, Engannim, Tappuah, Enam, 35 Jarmuth, Adullam, Socoh, Azekah, 36 Shaaraim, Adithaim, Gederah, and Gederothaim: fourteen cities, along with the towns round them.

37 There were also Zenan, Hadashah, Migdalgad, 38 Dilean, Mizpah, Joktheel, 39 Lachish, Bozkath, Eglon, 40 Cabbon, Lahmam, Chitlish, 41 Gederoth, Bethdagon, Naamah, and Makkedah: sixteen

cities, along with the towns round them.

42 There were also Libnah, Ether, Ashan, 43 Iphtah, Ashnah, Nezib, 44 Keilah, Achzib, and Mareshah: nine cities, along with the towns round them.

45 There was Ekron with its towns and villages, 46 and all the cities and towns near Ashdod, from Ekron to the Mediterranean Sea.

47 There were Ashdod and Gaza, with their towns and villages, reaching to the stream on the border of Egypt and the coast of the Mediterranean Sea.

48 In the hill-country there were Shamir, Jattir, Socoh, 49 Dannah, Kiriath Sepher (or Debir), 50 Anab, Eshtemoa, Anim, 51 Goshen, Holon, and Giloh: eleven cities, along with the towns round them.

52 There were Arab, Dumah, Eshan, 53 Janim, Beth Tappuah, Aphekah, 54 Humtah, Hebron, and Zior: nine cities, along with the towns round them.

55 There were Maon, Carmel, Ziph, Juttah, 56 Jezreel, Jokdeam, Zanoah, 57 Kain, Gibeah, and Timnah: ten cities, along with the towns round them.

58 There were Halhul, Bethzur, Gedor, 59 Maarath, Bethanoth, and Eltekon: six cities, along with the towns round them.

60 There were Kiriath Baal (or Kiriath Jearim) and Rabbah: two cities, along with the towns round them.

61 In the desert there were Beth Arabah, Middin, Secacah, 62 Nibshan, the city of Salt, and Engedi: six cities, along with the towns round them.

63 But the people of Judah were not able to drive out the Jebusites, who lived in Jerusalem. The Jebusites still live there with the people of Judah.

The Territory Assigned to Ephraim and West Manasseh

16 The southern boundary of the land assigned to the descendants of Joseph started from the Jordan near Jericho, at a point east of the springs of Jericho, and went into the desert. It went from Jericho up into the hill-country as far as Bethel. 2 From Bethel it went to Luz, passing on to Ataroth Addar, where the Archites lived. 3 It then went west to the area of the Japhletites, as far as the area of Lower Beth Horon. It went on from there to Gezer and ended at the Mediterranean Sea.

4 The descendants of Joseph, the tribes

---

[i] *Probable text (see Judg 1.14)* Othniel urged her; *Hebrew* she urged Othniel.
15.13–14: Judg 1.20   **15.63:** Judg 1.21; 2 Sam 5.6; 1 Chr 11.4

of Ephraim and West Manasseh, received this land as their possession.

Ephraim

5 This was the territory of the Ephraimite families: their border ran from Ataroth Addar eastwards to Upper Beth Horon, ⁶and from there to the Mediterranean Sea. Michmethath was on their north. East of there the border bent towards Taanath Shiloh and went past it on the east to Janoah. ⁷Then it went down from Janoah to Ataroth and Naarah, reaching Jericho and ending at the Jordan. ⁸The border went west from Tappuah to the stream of Kanah and ended at the Mediterranean Sea. This was the land given to the families of the tribe of Ephraim as their possession, ⁹along with some towns and villages that were within the borders of Manasseh, but given to the Ephraimites. ¹⁰But they did not drive out the Canaanites who lived in Gezer, so the Canaanites have lived among the Ephraimites to this day, but they have been forced to work as slaves.

West Manasseh

17 A part of the land west of the Jordan was assigned to some of the families descended from Joseph's elder son Manasseh. Machir, the father of Gilead, was Manasseh's eldest son and a military hero, so Gilead and Bashan, east of the Jordan, were assigned to him. ²Land west of the Jordan was assigned to the rest of the families of Manasseh: Abiezer, Helek, Asriel, Shechem, Hepher, and Shemida. These were male descendants of Manasseh son of Joseph, and they were heads of families. ³Zelophehad, son of Hepher, son of Gilead, son of Machir, son of Manasseh, did not have any sons, but only daughters. Their names were Mahlah, Noah, Hoglah, Milcah, and Tirzah. ⁴They went to Eleazar the priest and to Joshua son of Nun and to the leaders, and said, "The Lord commanded Moses to give us, as well as our male relatives, a part of the land to possess." So, as the Lord had commanded, they were given land along with their male relatives. ⁵That is why Manasseh received ten shares in addition to Gilead and Bashan on the east side of the Jordan, ⁶since his female descendants as well as his male descendants were assigned land. The land of Gilead was assigned to the

rest of the descendants of Manasseh.

7 The territory of Manasseh reached from Asher to Michmethath, east of Shechem. The border then went south to include the people of Entappuah. ⁸The land round Tappuah belonged to Manasseh, but the town of Tappuah, on the border, belonged to the descendants of Ephraim. ⁹The border then went down to the stream of Kanah. The cities south of the stream belonged to Ephraim, even though they were in the territory of Manasseh. The border of Manasseh proceeded along the north side of the stream and ended at the Mediterranean Sea. ¹⁰Ephraim was to the south, and Manasseh was to the north, with the Mediterranean Sea as their western border. Asher was to the north-west, and Issachar to the north-east. ¹¹Within the territories of Issachar and Asher, Manasseh possessed Beth Shan and Ibleam, along with their surrounding towns, as well as Dor (the one on the coast),ʲ Endor, Taanach, Megiddo, and their surrounding towns. ¹²The people of Manasseh, however, were not able to drive out the people living in those cities, so the Canaanites continued to live there. ¹³Even when the Israelites became stronger, they did not drive out all the Canaanites, but they did force them to work for them.

Ephraim and West Manasseh Request More Land

14 The descendants of Joseph said to Joshua, "Why have you given us only one part of the land to possess as our own? There are very many of us because the Lord has blessed us."

15 Joshua answered, "If there are so many of you and the hill-country of Ephraim is too small for you, then go into the forests and clear ground for yourselves in the land of the Perizzites and the Rephaim."

16 They replied, "The hill-country is not big enough for us, but the Canaanites in the plains have iron chariots, both those who live in Beth Shan and its surrounding towns and those who live in the Valley of Jezreel."

17 Joshua said to the tribes of Ephraim and West Manasseh, "There are indeed many of you, and you are very powerful. You shall have more than one share. ¹⁸The hill-country will be yours. Even though

---

ʲ *Probable text* Dor (the one on the coast); *Hebrew unclear.*
16.10: Judg 1.29   **17.4:** Num 27.1–7   **17.12–13:** Judg 1.27–28

Go all over the land and map it out (18.8)

it is a forest, you will clear it and take possession of it from one end to the other. As for the Canaanites, you will drive them out, even though they do have iron chariots and are a strong people."

The Division of the Rest of the Land

18 After they had conquered the land, the entire community of Israel assembled at Shiloh and set up the Tent of the LORD's presence. ²There were still seven tribes of the people of Israel who had not yet been assigned their share of the land. ³So Joshua said to the people of Israel, "How long are you going to wait before you go in and take the land that the LORD, the God of your ancestors, has given you? ⁴Let me have three men from each tribe. I will send them out over the whole country to map out the territory that they would like to have as their possession. Then they are to come back to me. ⁵The land will be divided among them in seven parts; Judah will stay in its territory in the south, and Joseph in its territory in the north. ⁶Write down a description of these seven divisions and bring it to me. Then I will draw lots*ᵏ* to consult the LORD our God for you. ⁷The Levites, however, will not receive a share of the land with the rest of you, because their share is to serve as the LORD's priests. And of course, the tribes of Gad, Reuben, and East Manasseh have already received their land east of the Jordan, which Moses, the LORD's servant, gave to them."

8 The men went on their way to map out the land after Joshua had given them

these instructions: "Go all over the land and map it out, and come back to me. And then here in Shiloh I will consult the LORD for you by drawing lots." ⁹So the men went all over the land and set down in writing how they divided it into seven parts, making a list of the towns. Then they went back to Joshua in the camp at Shiloh. ¹⁰Joshua drew lots to consult the LORD for them, and assigned each of the remaining tribes of Israel a certain part of the land.

The Territory Assigned to Benjamin

11 The territory belonging to the families of the tribe of Benjamin was the first to be assigned. Their land lay between the tribes of Judah and Joseph. ¹²On the north their border began at the Jordan and then went up the slope north of Jericho and westwards through the hill-country as far as the desert of Bethaven. ¹³The border then went to the slope on the south side of Luz (also called Bethel), then down to Ataroth Addar, on the mountain south of Lower Beth Horon. ¹⁴The border then went in another direction, turning south from the western side of this mountain and going to Kiriath Baal (or Kiriath Jearim), which belongs to the tribe of Judah. This was the western border. ¹⁵The southern border started on the edge of Kiriath Jearim and went*ˡ* to the Springs of Nephtoah. ¹⁶It then went down to the foot of the mountain that overlooks the Valley of Hinnom, at the north end of the Valley of Rephaim. It then went south through the Valley of Hinnom, south of the Jebusite ridge,

---

ᵏ DRAW LOTS: *See 14.2.*   *ˡ Probable text* and went; *Hebrew* and went westwards.

towards Enrogel. [17] It then turned north to Enshemesh and then on to Geliloth, opposite Adummim Pass. The border then went down to the Stone of Bohan (Bohan was a son of Reuben) [18] and passed north of the ridge overlooking the Jordan Valley. It then went down into the valley, [19] passing north of the ridge of Beth Hoglah, and ended at the northern inlet on the Dead Sea, where the River Jordan empties into it. This was the southern border. [20] The Jordan was the eastern border. These were the borders of the land which the families of the tribe of Benjamin received as their possession.

21 The cities belonging to the families of the tribe of Benjamin were Jericho, Beth Hoglah, Emek Keziz, [22] Beth Arabah, Zemaraim, Bethel, [23] Avvim, Parah, Ophrah, [24] Chepharammoni, Ophni, and Geba: twelve cities, along with the towns round them. [25] There were also Gibeon, Ramah, Beeroth, [26] Mizpah, Chephirah, Mozah, [27] Rekem, Irpeel, Taralah, [28] Zela, Haeleph, Jebus (or Jerusalem), Gibeah, and Kiriath Jearim: fourteen cities, along with the towns round them. This is the land which the families of the tribe of Benjamin received as their possession.

The Territory Assigned to Simeon

19 The second assignment made was for the families of the tribe of Simeon. Its territory extended into the land assigned to the tribe of Judah. [2] It included Beersheba, Sheba, Moladah, [3] Hazar Shual, Balah, Ezem, [4] Eltolad, Bethul, Hormah, [5] Ziklag, Beth Marcaboth, Hazar Susah, [6] Beth Lebaoth, and Sharuhen: thirteen cities, along with the towns round them.

7 There were also Ain, Rimmon, Ether, and Ashan: four cities, along with the towns round them. [8] This included all the towns round these cities as far as Baalath Beer (or Ramah), in the south. This was the land which the families of the tribe of Simeon received as their possession. [9] Since Judah's assignment was larger than was needed, part of its territory was given to the tribe of Simeon.

The Territory Assigned to Zebulun

10 The third assignment made was for the families of the tribe of Zebulun. The land which they received reached as far as Sarid. [11] From there the border went west to Mareal, touching Dabbesheth and

the stream east of Jokneam. [12] On the other side of Sarid it went east to the border of Chisloth Tabor, then to Daberath and up to Japhia. [13] It continued east from there to Gath Hepher and Ethkazin, turning in the direction of Neah on the way to Rimmon. [14] On the north the border turned towards Hannathon, ending at the Valley of Iphtahel. [15] It included Kattath, Nahalal, Shimron, Idalah, and Bethlehem: twelve cities, along with the towns round them. [16] These cities and their towns were in the land which the families of the tribe of Zebulun received as their possession.

The Territory Assigned to Issachar

17 The fourth assignment made was for the families of the tribe of Issachar. [18] Its area included Jezreel, Chesulloth, Shunem, [19] Hapharaim, Shion, Anaharath, [20] Rabbith, Kishion, Ebez, [21] Remeth, Engannim, Enhaddah, and Bethpazzez. [22] The border also touched Tabor, Shahazumah, and Beth Shemesh, ending at the Jordan. It included sixteen cities along with the towns round them. [23] These cities and their towns were in the land which the families of the tribe of Issachar received as their possession.

The Territory Assigned to Asher

24 The fifth assignment made was for the families of the tribe of Asher. [25] Its area included Helkath, Hali, Beten, Achshaph, [26] Allam Melech, Amad, and Mishal. On the west it touched Carmel and Shihor Libnath. [27] As it turned east, the border went to Bethdagon, touching Zebulun and the Valley of Iphtahel on the way north to Bethemek and Neiel. It continued north to Cabul, [28] Ebron, Rehob, Hammon, and Kanah, as far as Sidon. [29] The border then turned to Ramah, reaching the fortified city of Tyre; then it turned to Hosah and ended at the Mediterranean Sea. It included Mahalab, Achzib, [30] Ummah, Aphek, and Rehob: twenty-two cities, along with the towns round them. [31] These cities and their towns were in the land which the families of the tribe of Asher received as their possession.

The Territory Assigned to Naphtali

32 The sixth assignment made was for the families of the tribe of Naphtali. [33] Its border went from Heleph to the oak in

Zaanannim, on to Adaminekeb and to Jamnia, as far as Lakkum, and ended at the Jordan. 34 There the border turned west to Aznoth Tabor, from there to Hukkok, touching Zebulun on the south, Asher on the west, and the Jordan m on the east. 35 The fortified cities were Ziddim, Zer, Hammath, Rakkath, Chinnereth, 36 Adamah, Ramah, Hazor, 37 Kedesh, Edrei, Enhazor, 38 Yiron, Migdalel, Horem, Bethanath, and Beth Shemesh: nineteen cities, along with the towns round them. 39 These cities and their towns were in the land which the families of the tribe of Naphtali received as their possession.

The Territory Assigned to Dan

40 The seventh assignment made was for the families of the tribe of Dan. 41 Its area included Zorah, Eshtaol, Irshemesh, 42 Shaalbim, Aijalon, Ithlah, 43 Elon, Timnah, Ekron, 44 Eltekeh, Gibbethon, Baalath, 45 Jehud, Beneberak, Gathrimmon, 46 Mejarkon, and Rakkon, as well as the territory round Joppa. 47 When the people of Dan lost their land, they went to Laish and attacked it. They captured it, killed its people, and claimed it for themselves. They settled there and changed the name of the city from Laish to Dan, naming it after their ancestor Dan. 48 These cities and their towns were in the land which the families of the tribe of Dan received as their possession.

The Final Assignment of the Land

49 When the people of Israel finished dividing up the land, they gave Joshua son of Nun a part of the land as his own. 50 As the LORD had commanded, they gave him the city he asked for: Timnath Serah, in the hill-country of Ephraim. He rebuilt the city and settled there.

51 Eleazar the priest, Joshua son of Nun, and the leaders of the families of the tribes of Israel assigned these parts of the land by drawing lots n to consult the LORD at Shiloh, at the entrance of the Tent of the LORD's presence. In this way they finished dividing the land.

The Cities of Refuge

20 Then the LORD told Joshua 2 to say to the people of Israel, "Choose the cities of refuge that I commanded Moses to tell you about. 3 A person who kills someone accidentally can go there

and escape the man who is looking for revenge. 4 He can run away to one of these cities, go to the place of judgement at the entrance to the city, and explain to the leaders what happened. Then they will let him into the city and give him a place to live in, so that he can stay there. 5 If the man looking for revenge follows him there, the people of the city must not hand him over to him. They must protect him because he killed the person accidentally and not out of anger. 6 He may stay in the city until he has received a public trial and until the death of the man who is then the High Priest. Then the man may go back home to his own town, from which he had run away."

7 So, on the west side of the Jordan they set aside Kedesh in Galilee, in the hill-country of Naphtali; Shechem, in the hill-country of Ephraim; and Hebron, in the hill-country of Judah. 8 East of the Jordan, on the desert plateau east of Jericho, they chose Bezer in the territory of Reuben; Ramoth in Gilead, in the territory of Gad; and Golan in Bashan, in the territory of Manasseh. 9 These were the cities of refuge chosen for all the people of Israel and for any foreigner living among them. Anyone who killed a person accidentally could find protection there from the man looking for revenge; he could not be killed unless he had first received a public trial.

The Cities of the Levites

21 The leaders of the Levite families went to Eleazar the priest, Joshua son of Nun, and to the heads of the families of all the tribes of Israel. 2 There at Shiloh in the land of Canaan they said to them, "The LORD commanded through Moses that we were to be given cities to live in, as well as pasture land round them for our livestock." 3 So in accordance with the LORD's command the people of Israel gave the Levites certain cities and pasture lands out of their own territories.

4 The families of the Levite clan of Kohath were the first to be assigned cities. The families who were descended from Aaron the priest were assigned thirteen cities from the territories of Judah, Simeon, and Benjamin. 5 The rest of the clan of Kohath was assigned ten cities from the territories of Ephraim, Dan, and West Manasseh.

---

m *One ancient translation* the Jordan; *Hebrew* Judah at the Jordan.
n DRAWING LOTS: *See 14.2.*
19.47: Judg 18.27-29   **20.1-9:** Num 35.6-32; Deut 4.41-43, 19.1-13   **21.2:** Num 35.1-8

6 The clan of Gershon was assigned thirteen cities from the territories of Issachar, Asher, Naphtali, and East Manasseh.

7 The families of the clan of Merari were assigned twelve cities from the territories of Reuben, Gad, and Zebulun.

8 By drawing lots, *o* the people of Israel assigned these cities and their pasture lands to the Levites, as the LORD had commanded through Moses.

9 These are the names of the cities from the territories of Judah and Simeon which were given 10 to the descendants of Aaron who were of the clan of Kohath, which was descended from Levi. Their assignment was the first to be made. 11 They were given the city of Arba (Arba was Anak's father), now called Hebron, in the hill-country of Judah, along with the pasture land surrounding it. 12 However, the fields of the city, as well as its towns, had already been given to Caleb son of Jephunneh as his possession.

13 In addition to Hebron (one of the cities of refuge), the following cities were assigned to the descendants of Aaron the priest: Libnah, 14 Jattir, Eshtemoa, 15 Holon, Debir, 16 Ain, Juttah, and Beth Shemesh, with their pasture lands: nine cities from the tribes of Judah and Simeon. 17 From the territory of Benjamin they were given four cities: Gibeon, Geba, 18 Anathoth, and Almon, with their pasture lands. 19 Thirteen cities in all, with their pasture lands, were given to the priests, the descendants of Aaron.

20 The other families of the Levite clan of Kohath were assigned some cities from the territory of Ephraim. 21 They were given four cities: Shechem and its pasture lands in the hill-country of Ephraim (one of the cities of refuge), Gezer, 22 Kibzaim, and Beth Horon, with their pasture lands. 23 From the territory of Dan they were given four cities: Eltekeh, Gibbethon, 24 Aijalon, and Gathrimmon, with their pasture lands. 25 From the territory of West Manasseh they were given two cities: Taanach and Gathrimmon, with their pasture lands. 26 These families of the clan of Kohath received ten cities in all, with their pasture lands.

27 Another group of Levites, the clan of Gershon, received from the territory of East Manasseh two cities: Golan in Bashan (one of the cities of refuge) and Beeshterah, with their pasture lands.

28 From the territory of Issachar they received four cities: Kishion, Daberath, 29 Jarmuth, and Engannim, with their pasture lands. 30 From the territory of Asher they received four cities: Mishal, Abdon, 31 Helkath, and Rehob, with their pasture lands. 32 From the territory of Naphtali they received three cities: Kedesh in Galilee, with its pasture lands (one of the cities of refuge), Hammoth Dor, and Kartan, with their pasture lands. 33 The various families of the clan of Gershon received a total of thirteen cities with their pasture lands.

34 The rest of the Levites, the clan of Merari, received from the territory of Zebulun four cities: Jokneam, Kartah, 35 Dimnah, and Nahalal, with their pasture lands. 36 From the territory of Reuben they received four cities: Bezer, Jahaz, 37 Kedemoth, and Mephaath, with their pasture lands. 38 From the tribe of Gad they received four cities: Ramoth in Gilead, with its pasture lands (one of the cities of refuge), Mahanaim, 39 Heshbon, and Jazer, with their pasture lands. 40 So the clan of Merari was assigned a total of twelve cities.

41-42 From the land that the people of Israel possessed, a total of forty-eight cities, with the pasture lands round them, was given to the Levites.

Israel Takes Possession of the Land

43 So the LORD gave to Israel all the land that he had solemnly promised their ancestors he would give them. When they had taken possession of it, they settled down there. 44 The LORD gave them peace throughout the land, just as he had promised their ancestors. Not one of all their enemies had been able to stand against them, because the LORD gave the Israelites the victory over all their enemies. 45 The LORD kept every one of the promises that he had made to the people of Israel.

Joshua Sends the Eastern Tribes Home

22 Then Joshua called together the people of the tribes of Reuben, Gad, and East Manasseh. 2 He said to them, "You have done everything that Moses the LORD's servant ordered you to do, and you have obeyed all my commands. 3 All this time you have never once deserted your fellow-Israelites. You have been careful to obey the commands of

o DRAWING LOTS: *See 14.2.*
22.2: Num 32.20-32; Josh 1.12-15

the LORD your God. 4 Now, as he promised, the LORD your God has given your fellow-Israelites peace. So go back home to the land which you claimed for your own, the land on the east side of the Jordan, that Moses, the LORD's servant, gave you. 5 Make sure you obey the law that Moses commanded you: love the LORD your God, do his will, obey his commandments, be faithful to him, and serve him with all your heart and soul." 6-8 Joshua sent them home with his blessing and with these words: "You are going back home very rich, with a lot of livestock, silver, gold, bronze, iron, and many clothes. Share with your fellow-tribesmen what you took from your enemies." Then they left for home.

Moses had given land east of the Jordan to one half of the tribe of Manasseh, but to the other half Joshua had given land west of the Jordan, along with the other tribes.

9 So the people of the tribes of Reuben, Gad, and East Manasseh went back home. They left the rest of the people of Israel at Shiloh in the land of Canaan and started out for their own land, the land of Gilead, which they had taken as the LORD had commanded them through Moses.

The Altar by the Jordan

10 When the tribes of Reuben, Gad, and East Manasseh arrived at Geliloth, still on the west side p of the Jordan, they built a large, impressive altar there by the river. 11 The rest of the people of Israel were told, "Listen! The people of the tribes of Reuben, Gad, and East Manasseh have built an altar at Geliloth, on our side of the Jordan!" 12 When the people of Israel heard this, the whole community came together at Shiloh to go to war against the eastern tribes.

13 Then the people of Israel sent Phinehas, the son of Eleazar the priest, to the people of the tribes of Reuben, Gad, and East Manasseh in the land of Gilead. 14 Ten leading men went with Phinehas, one from each of the western tribes and each one the head of a family among the clans. 15 They came to the land of Gilead, to the people of Reuben, Gad, and East Manasseh, 16 and speaking for the whole community of the LORD, they said to them, "Why have you done this evil thing against the God of Israel? You have rebelled against the LORD by building this

altar for yourselves! You are no longer following him! 17 Remember our sin at Peor, when the LORD punished his own people with an epidemic? We are still suffering because of that. Wasn't that sin enough? 18 Are you going to refuse to follow him now? If you rebel against the LORD today, he will be angry with everyone in Israel tomorrow. 19 Now then, if your land is not fit to worship in, come over into the LORD's land, where his Tent is. Claim some land among us. But don't rebel against the LORD or make rebels out of us by building an altar in addition to the altar of the LORD our God. 20 Remember how Achan son of Zerah refused to obey the command about the things condemned to destruction; the whole community of Israel was punished for that. Achan was not the only one who died because of his sin."

21 The people of the tribes of Reuben, Gad, and East Manasseh answered the heads of the families of the western tribes: 22 "The Mighty One is God! He is the LORD! The Mighty One is God! He is the LORD! He knows why we did this, and we want you to know too! If we rebelled and did not keep faith with the LORD, do not let us live any longer! 23 If we disobeyed the LORD and built our own altar to burn sacrifices on or to use for grain-offerings or fellowship-offerings, let the LORD himself punish us. 24 No! We did it because we were afraid that in the future your descendants would say to ours, 'What do you have to do with the LORD, the God of Israel? 25 He made the Jordan a boundary between us and you people of Reuben and Gad. You have nothing to do with the LORD.' Then your descendants might make our descendants stop worshipping the LORD. 26 So we built an altar, not to burn sacrifices or make offerings, 27 but instead, as a sign for our people and yours, and for the generations after us, that we do indeed worship the LORD before his sacred Tent with our offerings to be burnt and with sacrifices and fellowship-offerings. This was to keep your descendants from saying that ours have nothing to do with the LORD. 28 It was our idea that, if this should ever happen, our descendants could say, 'Look! Our ancestors made an altar just like the LORD's altar. It was not for burning offerings or for sacrifice, but as a sign for our people and yours.' 29 We

---

p still on the west side; or on the east side.

22.16: Deut 12.13-14   **22.17:** Num 25.1-9   **22.20:** Josh 7.1-26 would certainly not rebel against the LORD or stop following him now by building an altar to burn offerings on or for grain-offerings or sacrifices. We would not build any other altar than the altar of the LORD our God that stands in front of the Tent of his presence."

30 Phinehas the priest and the ten leading men of the community who were with him, the heads of families of the western tribes, heard what the people of the tribes of Reuben, Gad, and East Manasseh had to say, and they were satisfied. 31 Phinehas, the son of Eleazar the priest, said to them, "Now we know that the LORD is with us. You have not rebelled against him, and so you have saved the people of Israel from the LORD's punishment."

32 Then Phinehas and the leaders left the people of Reuben and Gad in the land of Gilead and went back to Canaan, to the people of Israel, and reported to them. 33 The Israelites were satisfied and praised God. They no longer talked about going to war to devastate the land where the people of Reuben and Gad had settled.

34 The people of Reuben and Gad said, "This altar is a witness to all of us that the LORD is God." And so they named it "Witness."

Joshua's Farewell Address

23 Much later the LORD gave Israel security from their enemies around them. By that time Joshua was very old, 2 so he called all Israel, the elders, leaders, judges, and officers of the people, and said, "I am very old now. 3 You have seen everything that the LORD your God has done to all these nations because of you. The LORD your God has been fighting for you. 4 I have assigned as the possession of your tribes the land of the nations that are still left, as well as of all the nations that I have already conquered, from the River Jordan in the east to the Mediterranean Sea in the west. 5 The LORD your God will make them retreat from you, and he will drive them away as you advance. You shall have their land, as the LORD your God has promised you. 6 So be careful to obey and do everything that is written in the book of the Law of Moses. Do not neglect any part of it, 7 and then you will not associate with these peoples left among you or speak the names of their gods or use those names in taking

vows or worship those gods or bow down to them. 8 Instead, be faithful to the LORD, as you have been till now. 9 The LORD has driven great and powerful nations out as you advanced and no one has ever been able to stand against you. 10 Any one of you can make a thousand men run away, because the LORD your God is fighting for you, just as he promised. 11 Be careful, then, to love the LORD your God. 12 If you are disloyal and join with the nations that are still left among you and intermarry with them, 13 you may be sure that the LORD your God will no longer drive these nations out as you advance. Rather, they will be as dangerous for you as a trap or a pit and as painful as a whip on your back or thorns in your eyes. And this will last until none of you are left in this good land which the LORD your God has given you.

14 "Now my time has come to die. Every one of you knows in his heart and soul that the LORD your God has given you all the good things that he promised. Every promise he made has been kept; not one has failed. 15 But just as he kept every promise that he made to you, so he will carry out every threat. 16 If you do not keep the covenant which the LORD your God commanded you to keep and if you serve and worship other gods, then in his anger he will punish you, and soon none of you will be left in this good land that he has given you."

Joshua Speaks to the People at Shechem

24 Joshua gathered all the tribes of Israel together at Shechem. He called the elders, the leaders, the judges, and the officers of Israel, and they came into the presence of God. 2 Joshua said to all the people, "This is what the LORD, the God of Israel, has to say: 'Long ago your ancestors lived on the other side of the River Euphrates and worshipped other gods. One of those ancestors was Terah, the father of Abraham and Nahor. 3 Then I took Abraham, your ancestor, from the land beyond the Euphrates and led him through the whole land of Canaan. I gave him many descendants. I gave him Isaac, 4 and to Isaac I gave Jacob and Esau. I gave Esau the hill-country of Edom as his possession, but your ancestor Jacob and his children went down to Egypt. 5 Later I sent Moses and Aaron, and I brought great trouble on Egypt. But I led

23.10: Deut 3.22, 32.30   **24.2:** Gen 11.27   **24.3:** Gen 12.1-9, 21.1-3
24.4: Gen 25.24-26, 36.8, 46.1-7; Deut 2.5   **24.5:** Ex 3.1—12.42

you out; [6]I brought your ancestors out of Egypt, and the Egyptians pursued them with chariots and cavalry. But when your ancestors got to the Red Sea [7]they cried out to me for help, and I put darkness between them and the Egyptians. I made the sea come rolling over the Egyptians and drown them. You know what I did to Egypt.

"'You lived in the desert a long time. [8]Then I brought you to the land of the Amorites, who lived on the east side of the Jordan. They fought you, but I gave you victory over them. You took their land, and I destroyed them as you advanced. [9]Then the king of Moab, Balak son of Zippor, fought against you. He sent word to Balaam son of Beor and asked him to put a curse on you. [10]But I would not listen to Balaam, so he blessed you, and in this way I rescued you from Balak. [11]You crossed the Jordan and came to Jericho. The men of Jericho fought against you, as did the Amorites, the Perizzites, the Canaanites, the Hittites, the Girgashites, the Hivites, and the Jebusites. But I gave you victory over them all. [12]As you advanced, I threw them into panic in order to drive out the two Amorite kings. Your swords and bows had nothing to do with it. [13]I gave you a land that you had never cultivated and cities that you had not built. Now you are living there and eating grapes from vines that you did not plant, and olives from trees that you did not plant.'"

[14]"Now then," Joshua continued, "honour the LORD and serve him sincerely and faithfully. Get rid of the gods which your ancestors used to worship in Mesopotamia and in Egypt, and serve only the LORD. [15]If you are not willing to serve him, decide today whom you will serve, the gods your ancestors worshipped in Mesopotamia or the gods of the Amorites, in whose land you are now living. As for my family and me, we will serve the LORD."

[16]The people replied, "We would never leave the LORD to serve other gods! [17]The LORD our God brought our fathers and us out of slavery in Egypt, and we saw the miracles that he performed. He kept us safe wherever we went among all the nations through which we passed. [18]As we advanced into this land, the LORD drove out all the Amorites who lived here.

As for my family and me, we will serve the LORD (24.15)

So we also will serve the LORD; he is our God."

[19]Joshua said to the people, "But you may not be able to serve the LORD. He is a holy God and will not forgive your sins. He will tolerate no rivals, [20]and if you leave him to serve foreign gods, he will turn against you and punish you. He will destroy you, even though he was good to you before."

[21]The people said to Joshua, "No! We *will* serve the LORD."

[22]Joshua said to them, "You are your own witnesses to the fact that you have chosen to serve the LORD."

"Yes," they said, "we are witnesses."

[23]"Then get rid of those foreign gods that you have," he demanded, "and pledge your loyalty to the LORD, the God of Israel."

[24]The people then said to Joshua, "We will serve the LORD our God. We will obey his commands."

[25]So Joshua made a covenant for[q] the people that day, and there at Shechem he gave them laws and rules to follow.

[q]for; *or* with.

24.6-7: Ex 14.1-31   **24.8:** Num 21.21-35   **24.9-10:** Num 22.1—24.25
24.11: Josh 3.14-17, 6.1-21   **24.12:** Ex 23.28; Deut 7.20   **24.13:** Deut 6.10-11

26 Joshua wrote these commands in the book of the Law of God. Then he took a large stone and set it up under the oak-tree in the LORD's sanctuary. 27 He said to all the people, "This stone will be our witness. It has heard all the words that the LORD has spoken to us. So it will be a witness against you, to keep you from rebelling against your God." 28 Then Joshua sent the people away, and everyone returned to his own part of the land.

Joshua and Eleazar Die

29 After that, the LORD's servant Joshua son of Nun died at the age of a hundred and ten. 30 They buried him on his own land at Timnath Serah in the hill-country of Ephraim north of Mount Gaash.

31 As long as Joshua lived, the people of Israel served the LORD, and after his death they continued to do so as long as those leaders were alive who had seen for themselves everything that the LORD had done for Israel.

32 The body of Joseph, which the people of Israel had brought from Egypt, was buried at Shechem, in the piece of land that Jacob had bought from the sons of Hamor, the father of Shechem, for a hundred pieces of silver. This land was inherited by Joseph's descendants.

33 Eleazar son of Aaron died and was buried at Gibeah, the town in the hill-country of Ephraim which had been given to his son Phinehas.

24.30: Josh 19.49-50   **24.32:** Gen 33.19, 50.24-25; Ex 13.19; Jn 4.5; Acts 7.16

THE BOOK OF

JUDGES

INTRODUCTION

The book of *Judges* is composed of stories from the lawless period of Israel's history between the invasion of Canaan and the establishment of the monarchy. These stories are about the exploits of national heroes called "judges," most of whom were military leaders, rather than judges in the legal sense of the word. One of the better known of them was Samson, whose deeds are recorded in chapters 13-16.

The great lesson of the book is that Israel's survival depended on loyalty to God, while disloyalty always led to disaster. But there was more than this: even when the nation was disloyal to God, and disaster came, God was always ready to save his people when they repented and turned to him again.

Outline of Contents

Events up to the death of Joshua   1.1—2.10
The judges of Israel   2.11—16.31
Various incidents   17.1—21.25

The Tribes of Judah and Simeon Capture Adonibezek

1 After Joshua's death the people of Israel asked the LORD, "Which of our tribes should be the first to go and attack the Canaanites?"

2 The LORD answered, "The tribe of Judah will go first. I am giving them control of the land."

3 The people of Judah said to the people of Simeon, "Go with us into the territory assigned to us, and we will fight the Canaanites together. Then we will go with you into the territory assigned to you." So the tribes of Simeon [4] and Judah went into battle together. The LORD gave them victory over the Canaanites and the Perizzites, and they defeated ten thousand men at Bezek. [5] They found Adonibezek there and fought against him. [6] He ran away, but they chased him, caught him, and cut off his thumbs and big toes. [7] Adonibezek said, "Seventy kings with their thumbs and big toes cut off have picked up scraps under my table. God has now done to me what I did to them." He was taken to Jerusalem, where he died.

The Tribe of Judah Conquers Jerusalem and Hebron

8 The men of Judah attacked Jerusalem and captured it. They killed its people and set fire to the city. [9] After this they went on to fight the Canaanites who lived in the hill-country, in the foothills, and in the dry country to the south. [10] They marched against the Canaanites living in the city of Hebron, which used to be called Kiriath Arba. There they defeated the clans of Sheshai, Ahiman, and Talmai.

Othniel Conquers the City of Debir
(Josh 15.13–19)

11 From there the men of Judah marched against the city of Debir, at that time called Kiriath Sepher. [12] One of them, called Caleb, said, "I will give my daughter Achsah in marriage to the man who succeeds in capturing Kiriath Sepher." [13] Othniel, the son of Caleb's younger brother Kenaz, captured the city, so Caleb gave him his daughter Achsah in marriage. [14] On the wedding day Othniel urged her [a] to ask her father for a field. She got down from her donkey, and Caleb asked her what she wanted. [15] She answered, "I want some pools of water. The land you have given me is in the dry country." So Caleb gave her the upper and lower springs.

The Victories of the Tribes of Judah and Benjamin

16 The descendants of Moses' father-in-law, the Kenite, went on with the people of Judah from Jericho, the city of palm-trees, into the barren country south of Arad in Judah. There they settled among the Amalekites. [b] [17] The people of Judah went with the people of Simeon, and together they defeated the Canaanites who lived in the city of Zephath. They put a curse on the city, destroyed it, and named it Hormah. [c] [18-19] The LORD helped the people of Judah, and they took possession of the hill-country. But they did not capture [d] Gaza, Ashkelon, or Ekron, with their surrounding territories. These people living along the coast had iron chariots, and so the people of Judah were not able to drive them out. [20] As Moses had commanded, Hebron was given to Caleb, who drove out of the city the three clans descended from Anak. [21] But the people of the tribe of Benjamin did not drive out the Jebusites living in Jerusalem, and the Jebusites have continued to live there with the people of Benjamin ever since.

The Tribes of Ephraim and Manasseh Conquer Bethel

22–23 The tribes of Ephraim and Manasseh went to attack the city of Bethel, at that time called Luz. The LORD helped them. They sent spies to the city, [24] who saw a man leaving and said to him, "Show us how to get into the city, and we won't hurt you." [25] So he showed them, and the people of Ephraim and Manasseh killed everyone in the city, except this man and his family. [26] He later went to the land of the Hittites, built a city there, and named it Luz, which is still its name.

People Who Were not Driven Out by the Israelites

27 The tribe of Manasseh did not drive out the people living in the cities of Beth Shan, Taanach, Dor, Ibleam, Megiddo, and the nearby towns; the Canaanites continued to live there. [28] When the Israelites became stronger, they forced the Canaanites to work for them, but still they did not drive them all out.
29 The tribe of Ephraim did not drive out the Canaanites living in the city of Gezer, and so the Canaanites continued to live there with them.

---

[a] Some ancient translations Othniel urged her; Hebrew she urged Othniel.
[b] Some ancient translations Amalekites; Hebrew people.
[c] HORMAH: This name in Hebrew means "destruction."
[d] One ancient translation But they did not capture; Hebrew And they captured.
1.21: Josh 15.63; 2 Sam 5.6; 1 Chr 11.4   **1.27–28:** Josh 17.11–13   **1.29:** Josh 16.10

30 The tribe of Zebulun did not drive out the people living in the cities of Kitron and Nahalal, and so the Canaanites continued to live there with them and were forced to work for them.

31 The tribe of Asher did not drive out the people living in the cities of Acco, Sidon, Ahlab, Achzib, Helbah, Aphek, and Rehob. 32 The people of Asher lived with the local Canaanites, since they did not drive them out.

33 The tribe of Naphtali did not drive out the people living in the cities of Beth Shemesh and Bethanath. The people of Naphtali lived with the local Canaanites, but forced them to work for them.

34 The Amorites forced the people of the tribe of Dan into the hill-country and did not let them come down to the plain. 35 The Amorites continued to live at Aijalon, Shaalbim, and Mount Heres, but the tribes of Ephraim and Manasseh kept them under their rule and forced them to work for them.

36 North of Sela, the Edomite*e* border ran through Akrabbim Pass.

The Angel of the LORD at Bochim

2 The angel of the LORD went from Gilgal to Bochim and said to the Israelites, "I took you out of Egypt and brought you to the land that I promised to your ancestors. I said, 'I will never break my covenant with you. 2 You must not make any covenant with the people who live in this land. You must tear down their altars.' But you have not done what I told you. You have done just the opposite! 3 So I tell you now that I will not drive these people out as you advance. They will be your enemies,*f* and you will be trapped by the worship of their gods." 4 When the angel had said this, all the people of Israel began to cry, 5 and that is why the place is called Bochim.*g* There they offered sacrifices to the LORD.

The Death of Joshua

6 Joshua sent the people of Israel on their way, and each man went to take possession of his own share of the land. 7 As long as Joshua lived, the people of Israel served the LORD, and after his death they continued to do so as long as the leaders were alive who had seen for themselves all the great things that the

LORD had done for Israel. 8 The LORD's servant Joshua son of Nun died at the age of a hundred and ten. 9 He was buried in his own part of the land at Timnath Serah in the hill-country of Ephraim north of Mount Gaash. 10 That whole generation also died, and the next generation forgot the LORD and what he had done for Israel.

Israel Stops Worshipping the LORD

11 Then the people of Israel sinned against the LORD and began to serve the Baals. 12 They stopped worshipping the LORD, the God of their ancestors, the God who had brought them out of Egypt, and they began to worship other gods, the gods of the peoples round them. They bowed down to them and made the LORD angry. 13 They stopped worshipping the LORD and served the Baals and the Astartes. 14 And so the LORD became furious with Israel and let raiders attack and rob them. He let enemies all around overpower them, and the Israelites could no longer protect themselves. 15 Every time they went into battle, the LORD was against them, just as he had said he would be. They were in great distress.

16 Then the LORD gave the Israelites leaders who saved them from the raiders. 17 But the Israelites paid no attention to their leaders. Israel was unfaithful to the LORD and worshipped other gods. Their fathers had obeyed the LORD's commands, but this new generation soon stopped doing so. 18 Whenever the LORD gave Israel a leader, the LORD would help him and would save the people from their enemies as long as that leader lived. The LORD would have mercy on them because they groaned under their suffering and oppression. 19 But when the leader died, the people used to return to the old ways and behave worse than the previous generation. They would serve and worship other gods, and refused to give up their own evil ways. 20 Then the LORD would become furious with Israel and say, "This nation has broken the covenant that I commanded their ancestors to keep. Because they have not obeyed me, 21 I will no longer drive out any of the nations that were still in the land when Joshua died. 22 I will use them to find out whether or not these Israelites will follow my ways, as their ancestors did." 23 So the LORD

e One ancient translation Edomite; *Hebrew* Amorite.
f Some ancient translations enemies; *Hebrew* sides.
g BOCHIM: *This name in Hebrew means "those who cry."*
2.2: Ex 34.12–13; Deut 7.2–5   **2.9:** Josh 19.49–50

Israel...worshipped other gods (2.17)

allowed those nations to remain in the land; he did not give Joshua victory over them, nor did he drive them out soon after Joshua's death.

The Nations Remaining in the Land

3 So then, the LORD left some nations in the land to test the Israelites who had not been through the wars in Canaan. ² He did this only in order to teach each generation of Israelites about war, especially those who had never been in battle before. ³ Those left in the land were the five Philistine cities, all the Canaanites, the Sidonians, and the Hivites who lived in the Lebanon Mountains from Mount Baal Hermon as far as Hamath Pass. ⁴ They were to be a test for Israel, to find out whether or not the Israelites would obey the commands that the LORD had given their ancestors through Moses. ⁵ And so the people of Israel settled down among the Canaanites, the Hittites, the Amorites, the Perizzites, the Hivites, and the Jebusites. ⁶ They intermarried with them and worshipped their gods.

Othniel

7 The people of Israel forgot the LORD their God; they sinned against him and worshipped the idols of Baal and Asherah. ⁸ So the LORD became angry with Israel and let King Cushan Rishathaim of Mesopotamia conquer them, and he ruled over them for eight years. ⁹ Then the Israelites cried out to the LORD, and he sent a man who freed them. This was Othniel, the son of Caleb's younger brother Kenaz. ¹⁰ The spirit of the LORD came upon him, and he became Israel's leader. Othniel went to war, and the LORD gave him victory over the king of Mesopotamia. ¹¹ There was peace in the land for forty years, and then Othniel died.

Ehud

12 The people of Israel sinned against the LORD again. Because of this the LORD made King Eglon of Moab stronger than Israel. ¹³ Eglon joined the Ammonites and the Amalekites; they defeated Israel and captured Jericho, the city of palm-trees. ¹⁴ The Israelites were subject to Eglon for eighteen years.

15 Then the Israelites cried out to the LORD, and he sent a man to free them. This was Ehud, a left-handed man, who was the son of Gera, from the tribe of Benjamin. The people of Israel sent Ehud to King Eglon of Moab with gifts for him. ¹⁶ Ehud had made himself a double-edged sword nearly fifty centimetres long. He had it fastened on his right side under his clothes. ¹⁷ Then he took the gifts to Eglon, who was a very fat man. ¹⁸ When Ehud had given him the gifts, he told the men who had carried them to go back home. ¹⁹ But Ehud himself turned back at the carved stones near Gilgal, went back to Eglon, and said, "Your Majesty, I have a secret message for you."

So the king ordered his servants, "Leave us alone!" And they all went out.

20 Then, as the king was sitting there

alone in his cool room on the roof, Ehud went over to him and said, "I have a message from God for you." The king stood up. 21 With his left hand Ehud took the sword from his right side and plunged it into the king's belly. 22 The whole sword went in, handle and all, and the fat covered it up. Ehud did not pull it out of the king's belly, and it stuck out behind, between his legs. *h* 23 Then Ehud went outside, closed the doors behind him, locked them, 24 and left. The servants came and saw that the doors were locked, but they only thought that the king was inside, relieving himself. 25 They waited as long as they thought they should, but when he still did not open the door, they took the key and opened it. And there was their master, lying dead on the floor.

26 Ehud got away while they were waiting. He went past the carved stones and escaped to Seirah. 27 When he arrived there in the hill-country of Ephraim, he blew a trumpet to call the men of Israel to battle; then he led them down from the hills. 28 He said, "Follow me! The LORD has given you victory over your enemies, the Moabites." So they followed Ehud down and captured the place where the Moabites were to cross the Jordan; they did not allow a single man to cross. 29 That day they killed about ten thousand of the best Moabite soldiers; none of them escaped. 30 That day the Israelites defeated Moab, and there was peace in the land for eighty years.

Shamgar

31 The next leader was Shamgar son of Anath. He too rescued Israel, and did so by killing six hundred Philistines with an ox-goad.

Deborah and Barak

4 After Ehud died, the people of Israel sinned against the LORD again. 2 So the LORD let them be conquered by Jabin, a Canaanite king who ruled in the city of Hazor. The commander of his army was Sisera, who lived at Harosheth-of-the-Gentiles. 3 Jabin had nine hundred iron chariots, and he ruled the people of Israel with cruelty and violence for twenty years. Then the people of Israel cried out to the LORD for help.

4 Now Deborah, the wife of Lappidoth, was a prophet, and she was serving as a judge for the Israelites at that time. 5 She used to sit under a certain palm-tree between Ramah and Bethel in the hill-country of Ephraim, and the people of Israel would go there for her decisions. 6 One day she sent for Barak son of Abinoam from the city of Kedesh in Naphtali and said to him, "The LORD, the God of Israel, has given you this command: 'Take ten thousand men from the tribes of Naphtali and Zebulun and lead them to Mount Tabor. 7 I will bring Sisera, the commander of Jabin's army, to fight against you at the River Kishon. He will have his chariots and soldiers, but I will give you victory over him.' "

8 Then Barak replied, "I will go if you go with me, but if you don't go with me, I won't go either."

9 She answered, "All right, I will go with you, but you won't get any credit for the victory, because the LORD will hand Sisera over to a woman." So Deborah set off for Kedesh with Barak. 10 Barak called the tribes of Zebulun and Naphtali to Kedesh, and ten thousand men followed him. Deborah went with him.

11 In the meantime Heber the Kenite had set up his tent close to Kedesh near the oak-tree at Zanannim. He had moved away from the other Kenites, the descendants of Hobab, the brother-in-law of Moses.

12 When Sisera learnt that Barak had gone up to Mount Tabor, 13 he called out his nine hundred iron chariots and all his men, and sent them from Harosheth-of-the-Gentiles to the River Kishon.

14 Then Deborah said to Barak, "Go! The LORD is leading you! Today he has given you victory over Sisera." So Barak went down from Mount Tabor with his ten thousand men. 15 When Barak attacked with his army, the LORD threw Sisera into confusion together with all his chariots and men. Sisera got down from his chariot and fled on foot. 16 Barak pursued the chariots and the army to Harosheth-of-the-Gentiles, and Sisera's whole army was killed. Not a man was left.

17 Sisera ran away to the tent of Jael, the wife of Heber the Kenite, because King Jabin of Hazor was at peace with Heber's family. 18 Jael went out to meet Sisera and said to him, "Come in, sir; come into my tent. Don't be afraid." So he went in, and she hid him behind a curtain. *i* 19 He said to her, "Please give me a drink of water; I'm thirsty." She opened a leather bag

---

h Probable text it stuck...legs; Hebrew unclear.
i hid him behind a curtain; or covered him with a rug.

The LORD threw...into confusion...all his chariots and men (4.15)

of milk, gave him a drink, and hid him again. 20 Then he told her, "Stand at the door of the tent, and if anyone comes and asks you if someone is here, say no."

21 Sisera was so tired that he fell sound asleep. Then Jael took a hammer and a tent-peg, went up to him quietly, and killed him by driving the peg right through the side of his head and into the ground. 22 When Barak came looking for Sisera, Jael went out to meet him and said to him, "Come here! I'll show you the man you're looking for." So he went in with her, and there was Sisera on the ground, dead, with the tent-peg through his head.

23 That day God gave the Israelites victory over Jabin, the Canaanite king. 24 They pressed harder and harder against him until they destroyed him.

The Song of Deborah and Barak

5 On that day Deborah and Barak son of Abinoam sang this song:

2 Praise the LORD!
　　The Israelites were determined to
　　　fight;
　　the people gladly volunteered.
3 Listen, you kings!
　　Pay attention, you rulers!
　　I will sing, I will play music
　　　to Israel's God, the LORD.
4 LORD, when you left the mountains of
　　　Seir,
　　when you came out of the region of
　　　Edom,

the earth shook, and rain fell from
　　the sky.
Yes, water poured down from the
　　clouds.

5 The mountains quaked before the LORD
　　of Sinai,
　　before the LORD, the God of Israel.

6 In the days of Shamgar son of Anath,
　　in the days of Jael,
caravans no longer went through the
　　land,
　　and travellers used the side roads.
7 The towns of Israel stood abandoned,
　　Deborah;
　　they stood empty until you came,*j*
　　came like a mother for Israel.
8 Then there was war in the land
　　when the Israelites chose new gods.
　　Of the forty thousand men in Israel,
　　did anyone carry shield or spear?
9 My heart is with the commanders of
　　Israel,
　　with the people who gladly
　　　volunteered.
　　Praise the LORD!
10 Tell of *k* it, you that ride on white
　　donkeys,
　　sitting on saddles,
　　and you that must walk wherever you
　　　go.
11 Listen! The noisy crowds round the
　　wells
　　are telling of the LORD's victories,
　　the victories of Israel's people!

j abandoned, Deborah...you came; *or* abandoned; they stood empty until I, Deborah, came.
k Tell of; *or* Think about.
5.5: Ex 19.18

Then the LORD's people marched down
from their cities. [l]
12 Lead on, Deborah, lead on!
Lead on! Sing a song! Lead on!
Forward, Barak son of Abinoam,
lead your captives away!
13 Then the faithful ones came down to
their leaders;
the LORD's people came to him [m] ready
to fight.
14 They came [n] from Ephraim into the
valley, [o]
behind the tribe of Benjamin and its
people.
The commanders came down from
Machir,
the officers down from Zebulun.
15 The leaders of Issachar came with
Deborah;
yes, Issachar came and Barak too,
and they followed him into the valley.
But the tribe of Reuben was divided;
they could not decide whether to
come.
16 Why did they stay behind with the
sheep?
To listen to shepherds calling the
flocks?
Yes, the tribe of Reuben was divided;
they could not decide whether to
come.
17 The tribe of Gad stayed east of the
Jordan,
and the tribe of Dan remained by the
ships.
The tribe of Asher stayed by the seacoast;
they remained along the shore.
18 But the people of Zebulun and Naphtali
risked their lives on the battlefield.

19 At Taanach, by the stream of Megiddo,
the kings came and fought;
the kings of Canaan fought,
but they took no silver away.
20 The stars fought from the sky;
as they moved across the sky,
they fought against Sisera.
21 A flood in the Kishon swept them
away—
the onrushing River Kishon.
I shall march, march on, with strength!
22 Then the horses came galloping on,
stamping the ground with their
hooves.

23 "Put a curse on Meroz," says the angel
of the LORD,
"a curse, a curse on those who live
there.
They did not come to help the LORD,
come as soldiers to fight for him."

24 The most fortunate of women is Jael,
the wife of Heber the Kenite—
the most fortunate of women who live
in tents.
25 Sisera asked for water, but she gave
him milk;
she brought him cream in a beautiful
bowl.
26 She took a tent peg in one hand,
a workman's hammer in the other;
she struck Sisera and crushed his skull;
she pierced him through the head.
27 He sank to his knees,
fell down and lay still at her feet.
At her feet he sank to his knees and
fell;
he fell to the ground, dead.

28 Sisera's mother looked out of the
window;
she gazed [p] from behind the lattice.
"Why is his chariot so late in coming?"
she asked.
"Why are his horses so slow to
return?"
29 Her wisest ladies answered her,
and she told herself over and over,
30 "They are only finding things to
capture and divide,
a girl or two for every soldier,
rich cloth for Sisera,
embroidered pieces for the neck of
the queen." [q]

31 May all your enemies die like that,
O LORD,
but may your friends shine like the
rising sun!

And there was peace in the land for
forty years.

Gideon

6 Once again the people of Israel sinned
against the LORD, so he let the people
of Midian rule them for seven years. [2] The
Midianites were stronger than Israel, and
the people of Israel hid from them in caves
and other safe places in the hills. [3] When-

---

[l] *from their cities; or to their gates.*
[m] *One ancient translation him; Hebrew me.*   [n] *Probable text They came; Hebrew Their root.*
[o] *One ancient translation into the valley; Hebrew in Amalek.*
[p] *Some ancient translations gazed; Hebrew cried out.*
[q] *Probable text queen, Hebrew plunder.*

ever the Israelites sowed any seed, the
Midianites would come with the Amalekites and the desert tribes and attack
them. ⁴They would camp on the land and
destroy the crops as far south as the area
round Gaza. They would take all the
sheep, cattle, and donkeys, and leave
nothing for the Israelites to live on. ⁵They
would come with their livestock and tents,
as thick as locusts. They and their camels
were too many to count. They came and
devastated the land, ⁶and Israel was
helpless against them.

7 Then the people of Israel cried out
to the LORD for help against the Midianites, ⁸and he sent them a prophet who
brought them this message from the LORD,
the God of Israel: "I brought you out of
slavery in Egypt. ⁹I rescued you from the
Egyptians and from the people who fought
against you here in this land. I drove them
out as you advanced, and I gave you their
land. ¹⁰I told you that I am the LORD your
God and that you should not worship the
gods of the Amorites, whose land you are
now living in. But you did not listen to
me."

11 Then the LORD's angel came to the
village of Ophrah and sat under the oak-
tree that belonged to Joash, a man of the
clan of Abiezer. His son Gideon was
threshing some wheat secretly in a
winepress, so that the Midianites would
not see him. ¹²The LORD's angel appeared
to him there and said, "The LORD is with
you, brave and mighty man!"

13 Gideon said to him, "If I may ask,
sir, why has all this happened to us if
the LORD is with us? What about all the
wonderful things that our fathers told us
the LORD used to do—how he brought
them out of Egypt? The LORD has
abandoned us and left us to the mercy
of the Midianites."

14 Then the LORD ordered him, "Go with
all your great strength and rescue Israel
from the Midianites. I myself am sending
you."

15 Gideon replied, "But LORD, how can
I rescue Israel? My clan is the weakest
in the tribe of Manasseh, and I am the
least important member of my family."

16 The LORD answered, "You can do it
because I will help you. You will crush
the Midianites as easily as if they were
only one man."

17 Gideon replied, "If you are pleased
with me, give me some proof that you

The LORD is with you, brave and mighty
man! (6.12)

are really the LORD. ¹⁸Please do not leave
until I bring you an offering of food."

He said, "I will stay until you come
back."

19 So Gideon went into his house and
cooked a young goat and used ten
kilogrammes of flour to make bread
without any yeast. He put the meat in
a basket and the broth in a pot, brought
them to the LORD's angel under the oak-
tree, and gave them to him. ²⁰The angel
ordered him, "Put the meat and the bread
on this rock, and pour the broth over
them." Gideon did so. ²¹Then the LORD's
angel reached out and touched the meat
and the bread with the end of the stick
he was holding. Fire came out of the rock
and burnt up the meat and the bread.
Then the angel disappeared.

22 Gideon then realized that it was the
LORD's angel he had seen, and he said
in terror, "Sovereign LORD! I have seen
your angel face to face!"

23 But the LORD said to him, "Peace.
Don't be afraid. You will not die."
²⁴Gideon built an altar to the LORD there
and named it "The LORD is Peace." (It
is still standing at Ophrah, which belongs
to the clan of Abiezer.)

25 That night the LORD told Gideon,
"Take your father's bull and another bull

seven years old,*r* tear down your father's altar to Baal, and cut down the symbol of the goddess Asherah, which is beside it. 26 Build a well-constructed altar to the LORD your God on top of this mound. Then take the second bull*s* and burn it whole as an offering, using for firewood the symbol of Asherah you have cut down." 27 So Gideon took ten of his servants and did what the LORD had told him. He was too afraid of his family and the people of the town to do it by day, so he did it at night.

28 When the people of the town got up early the next morning, they found that the altar to Baal and the symbol of Asherah had been cut down, and that the second bull had been burnt on the altar that had been built there. 29 They asked each other, "Who did this?" They investigated and found out that Gideon son of Joash had done it. 30 Then they said to Joash, "Bring your son out here, so that we can kill him! He tore down the altar to Baal and cut down the symbol of Asherah beside it."

31 But Joash said to all those who confronted him, "Are you standing up for Baal? Are you defending him? Anyone who stands up for him will be killed before morning. If Baal is a god, let him defend himself. It is his altar that was torn down." 32 From then on Gideon was known as Jerubbaal,*t* because Joash said, "Let Baal defend himself; it is his altar that was torn down."

33 Then all the Midianites, the Amalekites, and the desert tribes assembled, crossed the River Jordan, and camped in the Valley of Jezreel. 34 The spirit of the LORD took control of Gideon, and he blew a trumpet to call the men of the clan of Abiezer to follow him. 35 He sent messengers throughout the territory of both parts of Manasseh to call them to follow him. He sent messengers to the tribes of Asher, Zebulun, and Naphtali, and they also came to join him.

36 Then Gideon said to God, "You say that you have decided to use me to rescue Israel. 37 Well, I am putting some wool on the ground where we thresh the wheat. If in the morning there is dew only on the wool but not on the ground, then I will know that you are going to use me to rescue Israel." 38 That is exactly what happened. When Gideon got up early the

next morning, he squeezed the wool and wrung enough dew out of it to fill a bowl with water. 39 Then Gideon said to God, "Don't be angry with me; let me speak just once more. Please let me make one more test with the wool. This time let the wool be dry, and the ground be wet." 40 That night God did that very thing. The next morning the wool was dry, but the ground was wet with dew.

Gideon Defeats the Midianites

7 One day Gideon and all his men got up early and camped beside the Spring of Harod. The Midianite camp was in the valley to the north of them by Moreh Hill.

2 The LORD said to Gideon, "The men you have are too many for me to give them victory over the Midianites. They might think that they had won by themselves, and so give me no credit. 3 Announce to the people, 'Anyone who is afraid should go back home, and we will stay here at Mount Gilead.'" So twenty-two thousand went back, but ten thousand stayed.

4 Then the LORD said to Gideon, "You still have too many men. Take them down to the water, and I will separate them for you there. If I tell you a man should go with you, he will go. If I tell you a man should not go with you, he will not go." 5 Gideon took the men down to the water, and the LORD said to him, "Separate everyone who laps up the water with his tongue like a dog, from everyone who gets down on his knees to drink." 6 There were three hundred men who scooped up water in their hands and lapped it; all the others got down on their knees to drink. 7 The LORD said to Gideon, "I will rescue you and give you victory over the Midianites with the three hundred men who lapped the water. Tell everyone else to go home." 8 So Gideon sent all the Israelites home, except the three hundred, who kept all the supplies and trumpets. The Midianite camp was below them in the valley.

9 That night the LORD commanded Gideon, "Get up and attack the camp; I am giving you victory over it. 10 But if you are afraid to attack, go down to the camp with your servant Purah. 11 You will hear what they are saying, and then you will have the courage to attack." So Gideon and his servant Purah went down

---

r bull and another bull seven years old; *or* bull, the seven-year-old one.
s the second bull; *or* the bull.
t JERUBBAAL: *This name in Hebrew means "Let Baal defend himself."*
7.3: Deut 20.8

Separate everyone who laps up the water (7.5)

to the edge of the enemy camp. [12] The Midianites, the Amalekites, and the desert tribesmen were spread out in the valley like a swarm of locusts, and they had as many camels as there were grains of sand on the seashore.

13 When Gideon arrived, he heard a man telling a friend about a dream. He was saying, "I dreamt that a loaf of barley bread rolled into our camp and hit a tent. The tent collapsed and lay flat on the ground."

14 His friend replied, "It's the sword of the Israelite, Gideon son of Joash! It can't mean anything else! God has given him victory over Midian and our whole army!"

15 When Gideon heard about the man's dream and what it meant, he fell to his knees and worshipped the LORD. Then he went back to the Israelite camp and said, "Get up! The LORD is giving you victory over the Midianite army!" [16] He divided his three hundred men into three groups and gave each man a trumpet and a jar with a torch inside it. [17] He told them, "When I get to the edge of the camp, watch me, and do what I do. [18] When my group and I blow our trumpets, then you blow yours all round the camp and shout, 'For the LORD and for Gideon!'"

19 Gideon and his hundred men came to the edge of the camp a short while before midnight, just after the guard had been changed. Then they blew the trumpets and broke the jars they were holding, [20] and the other two groups did the same. They all held the torches in their left hands, the trumpets in their right, and shouted, "A sword for the LORD and for Gideon!" [21] Every man stood in his place round the camp, and the whole

enemy army ran away yelling. [22] While Gideon's men were blowing their trumpets, the LORD made the enemy troops attack each other with their swords. They ran towards Zarethan as far as Beth Shittah, as far as the town of Abel Meholah near Tabbath.

23 Then men from the tribes of Naphtali, Asher, and both parts of Manasseh were called out, and they pursued the Midianites. [24] Gideon sent messengers through all the hill-country of Ephraim to say, "Come down and fight the Midianites. Hold the River Jordan and the streams as far as Bethbarah, to keep the Midianites from crossing them." The men of Ephraim were called together, and they held the River Jordan and the streams as far as Bethbarah. [25] They captured the two Midianite chiefs, Oreb and Zeeb; they killed Oreb at Oreb Rock, and Zeeb at the Winepress of Zeeb. They continued to pursue the Midianites and brought the heads of Oreb and Zeeb to Gideon, who was now east of the Jordan.

The Final Defeat of the Midianites

8 Then the men of Ephraim said to Gideon, "Why didn't you call us when you went to fight the Midianites? Why did you treat us like this?" They complained bitterly about it.

2 But he said, "What I was able to do is nothing compared with what you have done. Even the little that you men of Ephraim did is worth more than what my whole clan has done. [3] After all, through the power of God you killed the two Midianite chiefs, Oreb and Zeeb. What have I done to compare with that?" When he said this, they were no longer so angry.

4 By this time Gideon and his three

8.3–5: Ps 83.11

hundred men had come to the River Jordan and had crossed it. They were exhausted, but were still pursuing the enemy. [5] When they arrived at Sukkoth, he said to the men of the town, "Please give my men some loaves of bread. They are exhausted, and I am pursuing Zebah and Zalmunna, the Midianite kings."

6 But the leaders of Sukkoth said, "Why should we give your army any food? You haven't captured Zebah and Zalmunna yet."

7 So Gideon said, "All right! When the LORD has handed Zebah and Zalmunna over to me, I will beat you with thorns and briars from the desert!" [8] Gideon went on to Penuel and made the same request of the people there, but the men of Penuel gave the same answer as the men of Sukkoth. [9] So he said to them, "I am going to come back safe and sound, and when I do, I will tear your tower down!"

10 Zebah and Zalmunna were at Karkor with their army. Of the whole army of desert tribesmen, only about 15,000 were left; 120,000 soldiers had been killed.

[11] Gideon went along the road by the edge of the desert, east of Nobah and Jogbehah, and attacked the army by surprise. [12] The two Midianite kings, Zebah and Zalmunna, ran away, but he pursued them and captured them, and caused their whole army to panic.

13 When Gideon was returning from the battle by way of Heres Pass, [14] he captured a young man from Sukkoth and questioned him. The young man wrote down for Gideon the names of the seventy-seven leading men of Sukkoth. [15] Then Gideon went to the men of Sukkoth and said, "Remember when you refused to help me? You said that you couldn't give any food to my exhausted army because I hadn't captured Zebah and Zalmunna yet. Well, here they are!" [16] He then took thorns and briars from the desert and used them to punish the leaders of Sukkoth. [17] He also tore down the tower at Penuel and killed the men of that city.

18 Then Gideon asked Zebah and Zalmunna, "What about the men you killed at Tabor?"

They answered, "They looked like you—

The whole enemy army ran away yelling (7.21)

every one of them like the son of a king."

19 Gideon said, "They were my brothers, my own mother's sons. I solemnly swear that if you had not killed them, I would not kill you." 20 Then he said to Jether, his eldest son, "Go ahead, kill them!" But the boy did not draw his sword. He hesitated, because he was still only a boy.

21 Then Zebah and Zalmunna said to Gideon, "Come on, kill us yourself. It takes a man to do a man's job." So Gideon killed them and took the ornaments that were on the necks of their camels.

22 After that, the Israelites said to Gideon, "Be our ruler—you and your descendants after you. You have saved us from the Midianites."

23 Gideon answered, "I will not be your ruler, nor will my son. The LORD will be your ruler." 24 But he went on to say, "Let me ask one thing of you. Every one of you give me the earrings you took." (The Midianites, like other desert people, wore gold earrings.)

25 The people answered, "We'll be glad to give them to you." They spread out a cloth, and everyone put on it the earrings that he had taken. 26 The gold earrings that Gideon received weighed nearly twenty kilogrammes, and this did not include the ornaments, necklaces, and purple clothes that the kings of Midian wore, nor the collars that were round the necks of their camels. 27 Gideon made an idol from the gold and put it in his home town, Ophrah. All the Israelites abandoned God and went there to worship the idol. It was a trap for Gideon and his family.

28 So Midian was defeated by the Israelites and was no longer a threat. The land was at peace for forty years, until Gideon died.

The Death of Gideon

29 Gideon went back to his own home and lived there. 30 He had seventy sons, because he had many wives. 31 He also had a concubine in Shechem; she bore him a son, and he named him Abimelech. 32 Gideon son of Joash died at a ripe old age and was buried in the tomb of his father Joash, at Ophrah, the town of the clan of Abiezer.

33 After Gideon's death the people of Israel were again unfaithful to God and worshipped the Baals. They made Baal-of-the-Covenant their god, 34 and no longer served the LORD their God, who had saved them from all their enemies round them. 35 They were not grateful to the family of Gideon for all the good that he had done for Israel.

Abimelech

9 Gideon's son Abimelech went to the town of Shechem, where all his mother's relatives lived, and told them 2 to ask the men of Shechem, "Which would you prefer? To be governed by all seventy of Gideon's sons or by just one man? Remember that Abimelech is your own flesh and blood." 3 His mother's relatives talked to the men of Shechem about this for him, and the men of Shechem decided to follow Abimelech because he was their relative. 4 They gave him seventy pieces of silver from the temple of Baal-of-the-Covenant, and with this money he hired a bunch of worthless scoundrels to join him. 5 He went to his father's house at Ophrah, and there on the top of a single stone he killed his seventy brothers, Gideon's sons. But Jotham, Gideon's youngest son, hid and was not killed. 6 Then all the men of Shechem and Bethmillo got together and went to the sacred oak-tree at Shechem, where they made Abimelech king.

7 When Jotham heard about this, he went and stood on top of Mount Gerizim and shouted out to them, "Listen to me, you men of Shechem, and God may listen to you! 8 Once upon a time the trees got together to choose a king for themselves. They said to the olive-tree, 'Be our king.' 9 The olive-tree answered, 'In order to govern you, I would have to stop producing my oil, which is used to honour gods and men.' 10 Then the trees said to the fig-tree, 'You come and be our king.' 11 But the fig-tree answered, 'In order to govern you, I would have to stop producing my good sweet fruit.' 12 So the trees then said to the grapevine, 'You come and be our king.' 13 But the vine answered, 'In order to govern you, I would have to stop producing my wine, that makes gods and men happy.' 14 So then all the trees said to the thorn-bush, 'You come and be our king.' 15 The thorn-bush answered, 'If you really want to make me your king, then come and take shelter in my shade. If you don't, fire will blaze out of my thorny branches and burn up the cedars of Lebanon.'

16 "Now then," Jotham continued, "were you really honest and sincere when you made Abimelech king? Did you

respect Gideon's memory and treat his family properly, as his actions deserved? 17 Remember that my father fought for you. He risked his life to save you from the Midianites. 18 But today you turned against my father's family. You killed his sons—seventy men on a single stone—and just because Abimelech, his son by his servant-girl, is your relative, you have made him king of Shechem. 19 Now then, if what you did today to Gideon and his family was sincere and honest, then be happy with Abimelech and let him be happy with you. 20 But if not, may fire blaze out from Abimelech and burn up the men of Shechem and Bethmillo. May fire blaze out from the men of Shechem and Bethmillo and burn Abimelech up." 21 Then because he was afraid of his brother Abimelech, Jotham ran away and went to live at Beer.

22 Abimelech ruled Israel for three years. 23 Then God made Abimelech and the men of Shechem hostile to each other, and they rebelled against him. 24 This happened so that Abimelech and the men of Shechem, who encouraged him to murder Gideon's seventy sons, would pay for their crime. 25 The men of Shechem put men in ambush against Abimelech on the mountain-tops, and they robbed everyone who passed their way. Abimelech was told about this.

26 Then Gaal son of Ebed came to Shechem with his brothers, and the men of Shechem put their confidence in him. 27 They all went out into their vineyards and picked the grapes, made wine from them, and held a festival. They went into the temple of their god, where they ate and drank and spoke scornfully of Abimelech. 28 Gaal said, "What kind of men are we in Shechem? Why are we serving Abimelech? Who is he, anyway? The son of Gideon! And Zebul takes orders from him, but why should we serve him? Be loyal to your ancestor Hamor, who founded your clan! 29 I wish I were leading this people! I would get rid of Abimelech! I would say^u to him, 'Reinforce your army, come on out and fight!'"

30 Zebul, the ruler of the city, became angry when he heard what Gaal had said. 31 He sent messengers to Abimelech at Arumah^v to say, "Gaal son of Ebed and his brothers have come to Shechem, and they are not going to let you into the city. 32 Now then, you and your men should move by night and hide in the fields. 33 Get up tomorrow morning at sunrise and make a sudden attack on the city. Then when Gaal and his men come out against you, hit them as hard as you can!"

34 So Abimelech and all his men made their move at night and hid outside Shechem in four groups. 35 When Abimelech and his men saw Gaal come out and stand at the city gate, they got up from their hiding places. 36 Gaal saw them and said to Zebul, "Look! There are men coming down from the mountain-tops!"

"Those are not men," Zebul answered. "They are just shadows on the mountains."

37 Gaal said again, "Look! There are men coming down the crest of the mountain and one group is coming along the road from the oak-tree of the fortune-tellers!"

38 Then Zebul said to him, "Where is all your big talk now? You were the one who asked why we should serve this man Abimelech. These are the men you were treating so scornfully. Go on out now and fight them." 39 Gaal led the men of Shechem out and fought Abimelech. 40 Gaal fled, and Abimelech pursued him. Many were wounded, even at the city gate. 41 Abimelech lived in Arumah, and Zebul drove Gaal and his brothers out of Shechem, so that they could no longer live there.

42 The next day Abimelech found out that the people of Shechem were planning to go out into the fields, 43 so he took his men, divided them into three groups, and hid in the fields, waiting. When he saw the people coming out of the city, he came out of hiding to kill them. 44 While Abimelech and his group hurried forward to guard the city gate, the other two companies attacked the people in the fields and killed them all. 45 The fighting continued all day long. Abimelech captured the city, killed its people, tore it down, and covered the ground with salt.

46 When all the leading men in the fort at Shechem heard about this, they sought safety in the stronghold of the temple of Baal-of-the-Covenant. 47 Abimelech was told that they had gathered there, 48 so he went up to Mount Zalmon with his men. There he took an axe, cut a branch off a tree, and put it on his shoulder.

^{u} One ancient translation I would say; Hebrew He said.
^{v} Probable text Arumah; Hebrew unclear.

He told his men to be quick and do the same thing. 49 So every man cut off a branch of a tree; then they followed Abimelech and piled the wood up against the stronghold. They set it on fire, with the people inside, and all the people of the fort died—about a thousand men and women.

50 Then Abimelech went to Thebez, surrounded that city, and captured it. 51 There was a strong tower there, and every man and woman in the city, including the leaders, ran to it. They locked themselves in and went up to the roof. 52 When Abimelech came to attack the tower, he went up to the door to set the tower on fire. 53 But a woman threw a millstone down on his head and fractured his skull. 54 Then he quickly called the young man who was carrying his weapons and ordered, "Draw your sword and kill me. I don't want it said that a woman killed me." So the young man ran him through, and he died. 55 When the Israelites saw that Abimelech was dead, they all went home.

56 In this way God paid Abimelech back for the crime that he committed against his father in killing his seventy brothers. 57 God also made the men of Shechem suffer for their wickedness, just as Jotham, Gideon's son, said they would when he cursed them.

Tola

10 After Abimelech's death Tola, the son of Puah and grandson of Dodo, came to free Israel. He was from the tribe of Issachar and lived at Shamir in the hill-country of Ephraim. 2 He was Israel's leader for twenty-three years. Then he died and was buried at Shamir.

Jair

3 After Tola came Jair from Gilead. He led Israel for twenty-two years. 4 He had thirty sons who rode thirty donkeys. They had thirty cities in the land of Gilead, which are still called the villages of Jair. 5 Jair died and was buried at Kamon.

Jephthah

6 Once again the Israelites sinned against the LORD by worshipping the Baals and the Astartes, as well as the gods of Syria, of Sidon, of Moab, of Ammon, and of Philistia. They abandoned the LORD and stopped worshipping him. 7 So the LORD became angry with the Israelites, and let

the Philistines and the Ammonites conquer them. 8 For eighteen years they oppressed and persecuted all the Israelites who lived in Amorite country east of the River Jordan in Gilead. 9 The Ammonites even crossed the Jordan to fight the tribes of Judah, Benjamin, and Ephraim. Israel was in great distress.

10 Then the Israelites cried out to the LORD and said, "We have sinned against you, for we left you, our God, and worshipped the Baals."

11 The LORD gave them this answer: "The Egyptians, the Amorites, the Ammonites, the Philistines, 12 the Sidonians, the Amalekites, and the Maonites oppressed you in the past, and you cried out to me. Did I not save you from them? 13 But you still left me and worshipped other gods, so I am not going to rescue you again. 14 Go and cry out to the gods you have chosen. Let them rescue you when you get into trouble."

15 But the people of Israel said to the LORD, "We have sinned. Do whatever you like, but please, save us today." 16 So they got rid of their foreign gods and worshipped the LORD; and he became troubled over Israel's distress.

17 Then the Ammonite army prepared for battle and made camp in Gilead. The men of Israel came together and camped at Mizpah in Gilead. 18 There the people and the leaders of the Israelite tribes asked one another, "Who will lead the fight against the Ammonites? Whoever does will be the leader of everyone in Gilead."

11 Jephthah, a brave soldier from Gilead, was the son of a prostitute. His father Gilead 2 had other sons by his wife, and when they grew up, they forced Jephthah to leave home. They said to him, "You will not inherit anything from our father; you are the son of another woman." 3 Jephthah fled from his brothers and lived in the land of Tob. There he attracted a group of worthless men, and they went round with him.

4 It was some time later that the Ammonites went to war against Israel. 5 When this happened, the leaders of Gilead went to bring Jephthah back from the land of Tob. 6 They said, "Come and lead us, so that we can fight the Ammonites."

7 But Jephthah answered, "You hated me so much that you forced me to leave my father's house. Why come to me now that you're in trouble?"

9.53: 2 Sam 11.21

8 They said to Jephthah, "We are turning to you now because we want you to go with us and fight the Ammonites and lead all the people of Gilead."

9 Jephthah said to them, "If you take me back home to fight the Ammonites and the LORD gives me victory, I will be your ruler."

10 They replied, "We agree. The LORD is our witness." 11 So Jephthah went with the leaders of Gilead, and the people made him their ruler and leader. Jephthah stated his terms at Mizpah in the presence of the LORD.

12 Then Jephthah sent messengers to the king of Ammon to say, "What is your quarrel with us? Why have you invaded my country?"

13 The king of Ammon answered Jephthah's messengers, "When the Israelites came out of Egypt, they took away my land from the River Arnon to the River Jabbok and the River Jordan. Now you must give it back peacefully."

14 Jephthah sent messengers back to the king of Ammon 15 with this answer: "It is not true that Israel took away the land of Moab or the land of Ammon. 16 This is what happened: when the Israelites left Egypt, they went through the desert to the Gulf of Aqaba and came to Kadesh. 17 Then they sent messengers to the king of Edom to ask permission to go through his land. But the king of Edom would not let them. They also asked the king of Moab, but neither would he let them go through his land. So the Israelites stayed at Kadesh. 18 Then they went on through the desert, going round the land of Edom and the land of Moab until they came to the east side of Moab, on the other side of the River Arnon. They made camp there, but they did not cross the Arnon because it was the boundary of Moab. 19 Then the Israelites sent messengers to Sihon, the Amorite king of Heshbon, and asked him for permission to go through his country to their own land. 20 But Sihon would not let Israel do it. He brought his whole army together, made camp at Jahaz, and attacked Israel. 21 But the LORD, the God of Israel, gave the Israelites victory over Sihon and his army. So the Israelites took possession of all the territory of the Amorites who lived in that country. 22 They occupied all the Amorite territory from the Arnon in the south to the Jabbok in the north and from

the desert on the east to the Jordan on the west. 23 So it was the LORD, the God of Israel, who drove out the Amorites for his people, the Israelites. 24 Are you going to try to take it back? You can keep whatever your god Chemosh has given you. But we are going to keep everything that the LORD, our God, has given us. 25 Do you think you are any better than Balak son of Zippor, king of Moab? He never challenged Israel, did he? Did he ever go to war against us? 26 For three hundred years Israel has occupied Heshbon and Aroer, and the towns round them, and all the cities on the banks of the River Arnon. Why haven't you taken them back in all this time? 27 No, I have not done you any wrong. You are doing wrong by making war on me. The LORD is the judge. He will decide today between the Israelites and the Ammonites." 28 But the king of Ammon paid no attention to this message from Jephthah.

29 Then the spirit of the LORD came upon Jephthah. He went through Gilead and Manasseh and returned to Mizpah in Gilead and went on to Ammon. 30 Jephthah promised the LORD: "If you give me victory over the Ammonites, 31 I will burn as an offering the first person that comes out of my house to meet me, when I come back from the victory. I will offer that person to you as a sacrifice."

32 So Jephthah crossed the river to fight the Ammonites, and the LORD gave him victory. 33 He struck at them from Aroer to the area round Minnith, twenty cities in all, and as far as Abel Keramim. There was a great slaughter, and the Ammonites were defeated by Israel.

Jephthah's Daughter

34 When Jephthah went back home to Mizpah, there was his daughter coming out to meet him, dancing and playing the tambourine. She was his only child. 35 When he saw her, he tore his clothes in sorrow and said, "Oh, my daughter! You are breaking my heart! Why must it be you that causes me pain? I have made a solemn promise to the LORD, and I cannot take it back!"

36 She said to him, "If you have made a promise to the LORD, do what you said you would do to me, since the LORD has given you revenge on your enemies, the Ammonites." 37 But she asked her father, "Do this one thing for me. Leave me alone

11.17: Num 20.14–21   **11.18:** Num 21.4   **11.19–22:** Num 21.21–24   **11.25:** Num 22.1–6
11.35: Num 30.2

*Dancing and playing the tambourine
(11.34)*

for two months, so that I can go with
my friends to wander in the mountains
and grieve that I must die a virgin." 38 He
told her to go and sent her away for two
months. She and her friends went up into
the mountains and grieved because she
was going to die unmarried and childless.
39 After two months she came back to her
father. He did what he had promised the
LORD, and she died still a virgin.

This was the origin of the custom in
Israel 40 that the young women would go
away for four days every year to grieve
for the daughter of Jephthah of Gilead.

Jephthah and the Ephraimites

12 The men of Ephraim prepared for
battle; they crossed the River
Jordan to Zaphon and said to Jephthah,
"Why did you cross the border to fight
the Ammonites without calling us to go
with you? We'll burn the house down over
your head!"
2 But Jephthah said to them, "My
people and I had a serious quarrel with
the Ammonites. I did call you, but you
would not rescue me from them. 3 When
I saw that you were not going to, I risked
my life and crossed the border to fight
them, and the LORD gave me victory over
them. So why are you coming to fight
me now?" 4 Then Jephthah brought all
the men of Gilead together, fought the

men of Ephraim and defeated them. (The
Ephraimites had said, "You Gileadites in
Ephraim and Manasseh, you are deserters
from Ephraim!") 5 In order to keep the
Ephraimites from escaping, the Gileadites
captured the places where the Jordan
could be crossed. When any Ephraimite
who was trying to escape asked permission to cross, the men of Gilead would
ask, "Are you an Ephraimite?" If he said,
"No," 6 they would tell him to say
"Shibboleth." But he would say "Sibbo-
leth," because he could not pronounce it
correctly. Then they would seize him and
kill him there at one of the crossings of
the Jordan. At that time forty-two
thousand of the Ephraimites were killed.

7 Jephthah led Israel for six years. Then
he died and was buried in his home town w
in Gilead.

Ibzan, Elon, and Abdon

8 After Jephthah, Ibzan from Bethlehem led Israel. 9 He had thirty sons and
thirty daughters. He gave his daughters
in marriage outside the clan and brought
thirty girls from outside the clan for his
sons to marry. Ibzan led Israel for seven
years, 10 then he died and was buried at
Bethlehem.

11 After Ibzan, Elon from Zebulun led
Israel for ten years. 12 Then he died and
was buried at Aijalon in the territory of
Zebulun.

13 After Elon, Abdon son of Hillel from
Pirathon led Israel. 14 He had forty sons
and thirty grandsons, who rode on
seventy donkeys. Abdon led Israel for
eight years, 15 then he died and was buried
at Pirathon in the territory of Ephraim
in the hill-country of the Amalekites.

The Birth of Samson

13 The Israelites sinned against the
LORD again, and he let the Philistines rule them for forty years.
2 At that time there was a man named
Manoah from the town of Zorah. He was
a member of the tribe of Dan. His wife
had never been able to have children. 3 The
LORD's angel appeared to her and said,
"You have never been able to have
children, but you will soon be pregnant
and have a son. 4 Take care not to drink
any wine or beer, or eat any forbidden
food; 5 and after your son is born, you

w *One ancient translation* his home town; *Hebrew* the towns.
13.5: Num 6.1–5

must never cut his hair, because from the day of his birth he will be dedicated to God as a Nazirite. [x] He will begin the work of rescuing Israel from the Philistines."

6 Then the woman went and said to her husband, "A man of God has come to me, and he looked as frightening as the angel [y] of God. I didn't ask him where he came from, and he didn't tell me his name. [7] But he did tell me that I would become pregnant and have a son. He told me not to drink any wine or beer, or eat any forbidden food, because the boy is to be dedicated to God as a Nazirite as long as he lives."

8 Then Manoah prayed to the LORD, "Please, LORD, let the man of God that you sent come back to us and tell us what we must do with the boy when he is born."

9 God did what Manoah asked, and his angel came back to the woman while she was sitting in the fields. Her husband Manoah was not with her, [10] so she ran at once and said to him, "Look! The man who came to me the other day has appeared to me again."

11 Manoah got up and followed his wife. He went to the man and asked, "Are you the man who was talking to my wife?"

"Yes," he answered.

12 Then Manoah asked, "When your words come true, what must the boy do? What kind of a life must he lead?"

13 The LORD's angel answered, "Your wife must be sure to do everything that I have told her. [14] She must not eat anything that comes from the grapevine; she must not drink any wine or beer, or eat any forbidden food. She must do everything that I have told her."

15-16 Manoah did not know that it was the LORD's angel, so he said to him, "Please do not go yet. Let us cook a young goat for you."

But the angel said, "If I do stay, I will not eat your food. But if you want to prepare it, burn it as an offering to the LORD."

17 Manoah replied, "Tell us your name, so that we can honour you when your words come true."

18 The angel asked, "Why do you want to know my name? It is a name of wonder." [z]

19 So Manoah took a young goat and some grain, and offered them on the rock altar to the LORD who works wonders. [a]

Manoah and his wife saw the LORD's angel (13.20)

20-21 While the flames were going up from the altar, Manoah and his wife saw the LORD's angel go up towards heaven in the flames. Manoah realized then that the man had been the LORD's angel, and he and his wife threw themselves face downwards on the ground. They never saw the angel again.

22 Manoah said to his wife, "We are sure to die, because we have seen God!"

23 But his wife answered, "If the LORD had wanted to kill us, he would not have accepted our offerings; he would not have shown us all this or told us such things now."

24 The woman gave birth to a son and named him Samson. The child grew and the LORD blessed him. [25] And the LORD's power began to strengthen him while he

[x] NAZIRITE: *A person who showed his devotion to God by taking vows not to drink wine or beer or cut his hair or touch corpses (see Num 6.1-8).*
[y] the angel; *or* an angel.   [z] name of wonder; *or* mysterious name.
[a] *Some ancient translations* who works wonders; *Hebrew and* working wonders while Manoah and his wife watched.   **13.18:** Gen 32.29

was between Zorah and Eshtaol in the Camp of Dan.

Samson and the Girl from Timnah

14 One day Samson went down to Timnah, where he noticed a certain Philistine girl. 2 He went back home and said to his father and mother, "There is a Philistine girl down at Timnah who has caught my attention. Get her for me; I want to marry her."

3 But his father and mother asked him, "Why do you have to go to those heathen Philistines to get a wife? Can't you find a girl in our own clan, among all our people?"

But Samson said to his father, "She is the one I want you to get for me. I like her."

4 His parents did not know that it was the LORD who was leading Samson to do this, for the LORD was looking for a chance to fight the Philistines. At this time the Philistines were ruling Israel.

5 So Samson went down to Timnah with his father and mother. As they were going through the vineyards there, he heard a young lion roaring. 6 Suddenly the power of the LORD made Samson strong, and he tore the lion apart with his bare hands, as if it were a young goat. But he did not tell his parents what he had done.

7 Then he went and talked to the girl, and he liked her. 8 A few days later Samson went back to marry her. On the way he left the road to look at the lion he had killed, and he was surprised to find a swarm of bees and some honey inside the dead body. 9 He scraped the honey out into his hands and ate it as he walked along. Then he went to his father and mother and gave them some. They ate it, but Samson did not tell them that he had taken the honey from the dead body of a lion.

10 His father went to the girl's house, and Samson gave a banquet there. This was a custom among the young men. 11 When the Philistines saw him, they sent thirty young men to stay with him. 12-13 Samson said to them, "Let me ask you a riddle. I'll bet each one of you a piece of fine linen and a change of fine clothes that you can't tell me its meaning before the seven days of the wedding feast are over."

"Tell us your riddle," they said. "Let's hear it."

14 He said,

"Out of the eater came something to eat;
Out of the strong came something sweet."

Three days later they had still not solved the riddle.

15 On the fourth[b] day they said to Samson's wife, "Trick your husband into telling us what the riddle means. If you don't, we'll set fire to your father's house and burn you with it.[c] You two invited us so that you could rob us, didn't you?"

16 So Samson's wife went to him in tears and said, "You don't love me! You just hate me! You asked my friends a riddle and didn't tell me what it means!"

He said, "Look, I haven't even told my father and mother. Why should I tell you?" 17 She cried about it for the whole seven days of the feast. But on the seventh day he told her what the riddle meant, for she nagged him about it so much. Then she told the Philistines. 18 So on the seventh day, before Samson went into the bedroom,[d] the men of the city said to him,

"What could be sweeter than honey?
What could be stronger than a lion?"

Samson replied,

"If you hadn't been ploughing with my cow,
You wouldn't know the answer now."

19 Suddenly the power of the LORD made him strong, and he went down to Ashkelon, where he killed thirty men, stripped them, and gave their fine clothes to the men who had solved the riddle. After that, he went back home, furious about what had happened, 20 and his wife was given to the man that had been his best man at the wedding.

15 Some time later Samson went to visit his wife during the wheat harvest and took her a young goat. He said to her father, "I want to go to my wife's room."

But he wouldn't let him go in. 2 He said to Samson, "I really thought that you hated her, so I gave her to your friend. But her younger sister is prettier, anyway. You can have her, instead."

3 Samson said, "This time I'm not going to be responsible for what I do to the Philistines!" 4 So he went and caught three hundred foxes. Two by two, he tied

---

b Some ancient translations fourth; *Hebrew* seventh.
c set fire...you with it; *or* burn you and your family.
d Probable text bedroom; *Hebrew* sun.

He tied their tails together and put torches in the knots (15.4)

their tails together and put torches in the knots. ⁵Then he set fire to the torches and turned the foxes loose in the Philistine cornfields. In this way he burnt up not only the corn that had been harvested but also the corn that was still in the fields, and the olive orchards as well. ⁶When the Philistines asked who had done this, they learnt that Samson had done it because his father-in-law, a man from Timnah, had given Samson's wife to a friend of Samson's. So the Philistines went and burnt the woman to death and burnt down her father's house. ᵉ

7 Samson told them, "So this is how you act! I swear that I won't stop until I pay you back!" ⁸He attacked them fiercely and killed many of them. Then he went and stayed in the cave in the cliff at Etam.

Samson Defeats the Philistines

9 The Philistines came and made camp in Judah, and attacked the town of Lehi. ¹⁰The men of Judah asked them, "Why are you attacking us?"

They answered, "We came to take Samson prisoner and to treat him as he treated us." ¹¹So three thousand men of Judah went to the cave in the cliff at Etam and said to Samson, "Don't you know that the Philistines are our rulers? What have you done to us?"

He answered, "I did to them just what they did to me."

12 They said, "We have come here to

tie you up, so that we can hand you over to them."

Samson said, "Give me your word that you won't kill me yourselves."

13 "All right," they said, "we are only going to tie you up and hand you over to them. We won't kill you." So they tied him up with two new ropes and brought him back from the cliff.

14 When he got to Lehi, the Philistines

He broke the ropes round his arms (15.14)

came running towards him, shouting at him. Suddenly the power of the LORD made him strong, and he broke the ropes round his arms and hands as if they were burnt thread. ¹⁵Then he found the jaw-bone of a donkey that had recently died. He bent down and picked it up, and killed a thousand men with it. ¹⁶So Samson sang,

"With the jaw-bone of a donkey I killed a thousand men;
With the jaw-bone of a donkey I piled them up in piles." ᶠ

¹⁷After that, he threw the jaw-bone away. The place where this happened was named Ramath Lehi. ᵍ

ᵉ burnt the woman...house; *or* burnt the woman and her family to death.
ᶠ PILES: This word sounds like the Hebrew for "donkey."
ᵍ RAMATH LEHI: *This name in Hebrew means "Jaw-bone Hill."*

18 Then Samson became very thirsty, so he called to the LORD and said, "You gave me this great victory; am I now going to die of thirst and be captured by these heathen Philistines?" 19 Then God opened a hollow place in the ground there at Lehi, and water came out of it. Samson drank it and began to feel much better. So the spring was named Hakkore; *h* it is still there at Lehi.

20 Samson led Israel for twenty years while the Philistines ruled the land.

Samson at Gaza

16 One day Samson went to the Philistine city of Gaza, where he met a prostitute and went to bed with her. 2 The people of Gaza found out that Samson was there, so they surrounded the place and waited for him all night long at the city gate. They were quiet all night, thinking to themselves, "We'll wait until daybreak, and then we'll kill him." 3 But Samson stayed in bed only until midnight. Then he got up and took hold of the city gate and pulled it up—doors, posts, lock, and all. He put them on his shoulders and carried them all the way to the top of the hill overlooking Hebron.

Samson and Delilah

4 After this, Samson fell in love with a woman named Delilah, who lived in the Valley of Sorek. 5 The five Philistine kings went to her and said, "Trick Samson into telling you why he is so strong and how we can overpower him, tie him up, and make him helpless. Each one of us will give you eleven hundred pieces of silver."

6 So Delilah said to Samson, "Please tell me what makes you so strong. If someone wanted to tie you up and make you helpless, how could he do it?"

7 Samson answered, "If they tie me up with seven new bowstrings that are not dried out, I'll be as weak as anybody else."

8 So the Philistine kings brought Delilah seven new bowstrings that were not dried out, and she tied Samson up. 9 She had some men waiting in another room, so she shouted, "Samson! The Philistines are coming!" But he snapped the bowstrings just as thread breaks when fire touches it. So they still did not know the secret of his strength.

10 Delilah said to Samson, "Look, you've been making a fool of me and not telling me the truth. Please tell me how someone could tie you up."

11 He answered, "If they tie me with new ropes that have never been used, I'll be as weak as anybody else."

12 So Delilah got some new ropes and tied him up. Then she shouted, "Samson! The Philistines are coming!" The men were waiting in another room. But he snapped the ropes off his arms like thread.

13 Delilah said to Samson, "You're still making a fool of me and not telling me the truth. Tell me how someone could tie you up."

He answered, "If you weave my seven locks of hair into a loom, and make it tight with a peg, I'll be as weak as anybody else."

14 Delilah then lulled him to sleep, took his seven locks of hair, and wove them into the loom. *i* She made it tight with a peg and shouted, "Samson! The Philistines are coming!" But he woke up and pulled his hair loose from the loom.

15 So she said to him, "How can you say you love me, when you don't mean it? You've made a fool of me three times, and you still haven't told me what makes you so strong." 16 She kept on asking him, day after day. He got so sick and tired of her nagging him about it 17 that he finally told her the truth. "My hair has never been cut," he said. "I have been dedicated to God as a Nazirite *j* from the time I was born. If my hair were cut, I would lose my strength and be as weak as anybody else."

18 When Delilah realized that he had told her the truth, she sent a message to the Philistine kings and said, "Come back just once more. He has told me the truth." Then they came and brought the money with them. 19 Delilah lulled Samson to sleep in her lap and then called a man, who cut off *k* Samson's seven locks of hair. Then she began to torment him, for he had lost his strength. 20 Then she shouted, "Samson! The Philistines are coming!" He woke up and thought, "I'll get loose and go free, as always." He did not know that the LORD had left him. 21 The Philistines captured him and put his eyes out. They took him to Gaza, chained him with bronze chains, and put him to work

---

h HAKKORE: *This name in Hebrew means "caller."*
i *One ancient translation* and make it tight *(in verse 13)...into the loom (in verse 14); Hebrew does not have these words.*
j NAZIRITE: *See 13.5.*
k *Probable text* who cut off; *Hebrew* and she cut off.

grinding at the mill in the prison. ²²But
his hair started growing again.

The Death of Samson

23 The Philistine kings met together to
celebrate and offer a great sacrifice to
their god Dagon. They sang, "Our god
has given us victory over our enemy
Samson!" ²⁴⁻²⁵They were enjoying themselves, so they said, "Call Samson, and
let's make him entertain us!"ˡ When they
brought Samson out of the prison, they
made him entertain themᵐ and made him
stand between the pillars. When the
people saw him, they sang praise to their
god: "Our god has given us victory over
our enemy, who devastated our land and
killed so many of us!" ²⁶Samson said to
the boy who was leading him by the hand,
"Let me touch the pillars that hold up
the building. I want to lean on them."
²⁷The building was crowded with men and
women. All five Philistine kings were
there, and there were about three thousand men and women on the roof,
watching Samson entertain them.ⁿ

28 Then Samson prayed, "Sovereign
Lord, please remember me; please, God,
give me my strength just once more, so
that with this one blow I can get even
with the Philistines for putting out my
two eyes." ²⁹So Samson took hold of the
two middle pillars holding up the building.
Putting one hand on each pillar, he pushed
against them ³⁰and shouted, "Let me die
with the Philistines!" He pushed with all
his might, and the building fell down on
the five kings and everyone else. Samson
killed more people at his death than he
had killed during his life.

31 His brothers and the rest of his
family came down to get his body. They
took him back and buried him between
Zorah and Eshtaol in the tomb of his
father Manoah. He had been Israel's
leader for twenty years.

Micah's Idols

17 There was once a man named
Micah, who lived in the hill-
country of Ephraim. ²He said to his
mother, "When someone stole those
eleven hundred pieces of silver from you,
you put a curse on the thief. I heard you

He pushed with all his might (16.30)

do it. Look, I have the money. I am the
one who took it."

His mother said, "May the Lord bless
you, my son!" ³He gave the money back
to his mother, and she said, "To stop the
curse from falling on my son, I myself
am solemnly dedicating the silver to the
Lord. It will be used to make a wooden
idol covered with silver. So now I will
give the pieces of silver back to you."
⁴Then he gave them back to his mother.
She took two hundred of the pieces of
silver and gave them to a metal-worker,
who made an idol, carving it from wood
and covering it with the silver. It was
placed in Micah's house.

5 This man Micah had his own place
of worship. He made some idols and an
ephod,ᵒ and appointed one of his sons
as his priest. ⁶There was no king in Israel
at that time; everyone did just as he
pleased.

7 At that same time there was a young
Levite who had been living in the town
of Bethlehem in Judah. ⁸He left Bethlehem
to find somewhere else to live. While he
was travelling, he came to Micah's house
in the hill-country of Ephraim. ⁹Micah
asked him, "Where do you come from?"

He answered, "I am a Levite from
Bethlehem in Judah. I am looking for
somewhere to live."

10 Micah said, "Stay with me. Be my

ˡmake him entertain us; or make fun of him.   ᵐmade him entertain them; or jeered at him.
ⁿentertain them; or and jeering at him.   ᵒEPHOD: See Word List.
17.6: Judg 21.25

adviser and priest, and I will give you ten pieces of silver a year, some clothes, and your food."*p* 11 The young Levite agreed to stay with Micah and became like a son to him. 12 Micah appointed him as his priest, and he lived in Micah's home. 13 Micah said, "Now that I have a Levite as my priest, I know that the LORD will make things go well for me."

Micah and the Tribe of Dan

18 There was no king in Israel at that time. In those days the tribe of Dan was looking for territory to claim and occupy because they had not yet received any land of their own among the tribes of Israel. 2 So the people of Dan chose five qualified*q* men out of all the families in the tribe and sent them from the towns of Zorah and Eshtaol with instructions to explore the land. When they arrived in the hill-country of Ephraim, they stayed at Micah's house. 3 While they were there, they recognized the accent of the young Levite, so they went up to him and asked, "What are you doing here? Who brought you here?"

4 He answered, "I have an arrangement with Micah, who pays me to serve as his priest."

5 They said to him, "Please ask God if we are going to be successful on our journey."

6 The priest answered, "You have nothing to worry about. The LORD is taking care of you on this journey."

7 So the five men left and went to the town of Laish. They saw how safely the people there were living, like the Sidonians. They were a peaceful, quiet people, with no disputes with anyone; they had all they needed.*r* They lived far away from the Sidonians and had no dealings with any other people. 8 When the five men returned to Zorah and Eshtaol, their countrymen asked them what they had found out. 9 "Come on," they replied. "Let's attack Laish. We saw the land, and it's very good. Don't stay here doing nothing; hurry! Go on in and take it over! 10 When you get there, you will find that the people don't suspect a thing. It is a big country; it has everything a person could want, and God has given it to you."

11 So six hundred men from the tribe of Dan left Zorah and Eshtaol, ready for battle. 12 They went up and made camp west of Kiriath Jearim in Judah. That is why the place is still called Camp of Dan.

13 They went on from there and came to Micah's house in the hill-country of Ephraim.

14 Then the five men who had gone to explore the country round Laish said to their companions, "Did you know that here in one of these houses there is a wooden idol covered with silver? There are also other idols and an ephod. What do you think we should do?" 15 So they went into Micah's house, where the young Levite lived, and asked the Levite how he was getting on. 16 Meanwhile the six hundred soldiers from Dan, ready for battle, were standing at the gate. 17 The five spies went straight on into the house and took the wooden idol covered with silver, the other idols, and the ephod, while the priest stayed at the gate with the six hundred armed men.

18 When the men went into Micah's house and took the sacred objects, the priest asked them, "What are you doing?"

19 They said, "Keep quiet. Don't say a word. Come with us and be our priest and adviser. Wouldn't you rather be a priest for a whole Israelite tribe than for the family of one man?" 20 This made the priest very happy, so he took the sacred objects and went along with them.

21 They turned round and started off, with their children, their livestock, and their belongings going ahead. 22 They had travelled a good distance from the house when Micah called his neighbours out for battle. They caught up with the men from Dan 23 and shouted at them. The men from Dan turned round and asked Micah, "What's the matter? Why all this mob?"

24 Micah answered, "What do you mean, 'What's the matter?' You take my priest and the gods that I made, and walk off! What have I got left?"

25 The men from Dan said, "You had better not say anything else unless you want these men to get angry and attack you. Then you and your whole family would die." 26 Then they went on. Micah saw that they were too strong for him, so he turned and went back home.

27–28 After the men from Dan had taken the priest and the things that Micah had made, they went and attacked Laish, that town of peaceful, quiet people which was in the same valley as Bethrehob. They killed the inhabitants and burnt the town. There was no one to save them, because Laish was a long way from Sidon, and they had no dealings with any other

---

p Probable text your food; *Hebrew* your food. So the Levite went.
q qualified; *or* brave.   *r Probable text* They were...needed; *Hebrew unclear.*

people. The men from Dan rebuilt the town and settled down there. ²⁹ They changed its name from Laish to Dan, after their ancestor Dan, the son of Jacob. ³⁰ The men from Dan set up the idol to be worshipped, and Jonathan, the son of Gershom and grandson of Moses, served as a priest for the tribe of Dan, and his descendants served as their priests until the people were taken away into exile. ³¹ Micah's idol remained there all the time that the Tent where God was worshipped remained at Shiloh.

The Levite and His Concubine

19 In those days, before Israel had a king, there was a Levite living far back in the hill-country of Ephraim. He took a girl from Bethlehem in Judah to be his concubine, ² but she became angry with him, went back to her father's house in Bethlehem, and stayed there four months. ³ Then the man decided to go after her and try to persuade her to return to him. He took his servant and two donkeys with him. The girl showed the Levite into the house, and when her father saw him, he gave him a warm welcome. ⁴ The father insisted that he stay, and so he stayed for three days. The couple had their meals and spent the nights there. ⁵ On the morning of the fourth day they woke up early and got ready to go. But the girl's father said to the Levite, "Have something to eat first. It will do you good. You can go later."

6 So the two men sat down and ate and drank together. Then the girl's father said to him, "Please spend the night here and enjoy yourself."

7 The Levite got up to go, but the father urged him to stay, so he spent another night there. ⁸ Early in the morning of the fifth day he started to leave, but the girl's father said, "Eat something, please. Wait until later in the day." So the two men ate together.

9 When the man, his concubine, and the servant once more started to leave, the father said, "Look, it's almost evening now; you might as well stay all night. It will be dark soon; stay here and have a good time. Tomorrow you can get up early for your journey and go home."

10-11 But the man did not want to spend another night there, so he and his concubine started on their way, with their servant and two donkeys with pack saddles. It was late in the day when they came near Jebus (that is, Jerusalem), so the servant said to his master, "Why don't we stop and spend the night here in this Jebusite city?"

12-13 But his master said, "We're not going to stop in a city where the people are not Israelites. We'll pass on and go a little farther and spend the night at Gibeah or Ramah." ¹⁴ So they went past Jebus and continued on their way. It was sunset when they came to Gibeah in the territory of the tribe of Benjamin. ¹⁵ They turned off the road to go and spend the night there. They went into the city and sat down in the square, but no one offered to take them home for the night.

16 While they were there, an old man came by at the end of a day's work in the fields. He was originally from the hill-country of Ephraim, but he was now living in Gibeah. (The other people there were from the tribe of Benjamin.) ¹⁷ The old man noticed the traveller in the city square and asked him, "Where do you come from? Where are you going?"

18 The Levite answered, "We have been to Bethlehem in Judah, and now we are on our way home ˢ deep in the hill-country of Ephraim. No one will put us up for the night, ¹⁹ even though we have fodder and straw for our donkeys, as well as bread and wine for my concubine and me and for my servant. We have everything we need."

20 The old man said, "You are welcome in my home! I'll take care of you; you don't have to spend the night in the square." ²¹ So he took them home with him and fed their donkeys. His guests washed their feet and had a meal.

22 They were enjoying themselves when all of a sudden some sexual perverts from the town surrounded the house and started beating on the door. They said to the old man, "Bring out that man that came home with you! We want to have sex with him!"

23 But the old man went outside and said to them, "No, my friends! Please! Don't do such an evil, immoral thing! This man is my guest. ²⁴ Look! Here is his concubine and my own daughter, who is a virgin. I'll bring them out now, and you can do with them whatever you want. But don't do such an awful thing to this man!" ²⁵ But the men would not listen to him. So the Levite took his

ˢ *One ancient translation* home; *Hebrew* to the house of the LORD.
19.22–24: Gen 19.5–8

concubine and put her outside with them. They raped her and abused her all night long and didn't stop until morning.

26 At dawn the woman came and fell down at the door of the old man's house, where her husband was. She was still there when daylight came. 27 Her husband got up that morning, and when he opened the door to go on his way, he found his concubine lying in front of the house with her hands reaching for the door. 28 He said, "Get up. Let's go." But there was no answer. So he put her body across the donkey and started on his way home. 29 When he arrived, he went into the house and got a knife. He took his concubine's body, cut it into twelve pieces, and sent one piece to each of the twelve tribes of Israel. 30 Everyone who saw it said, "We have never heard of such a thing! Nothing like this has ever happened since the Israelites left Egypt! We have to do something about this! What will it be?"

Israel Prepares for War

20 All the people of Israel from Dan in the north to Beersheba in the south, as well as from the land of Gilead in the east, answered the call. They gathered in one body in the LORD's presence at Mizpah. 2 The leaders of all the tribes of Israel were present at this gathering of God's people, and there were 400,000 foot-soldiers. 3 Meanwhile the people of Benjamin heard that all the other Israelites had gathered at Mizpah.

The Israelites asked, "Tell us, how was this crime committed?" 4 The Levite whose concubine had been murdered answered, "My concubine and I went to Gibeah in the territory of Benjamin to spend the night. 5 The men of Gibeah came to attack me and surrounded the house at night. They intended to kill me; instead they raped my concubine, and she died. 6 I took her body, cut it in pieces, and sent one piece to each of the twelve tribes of Israel. These people have committed an evil and immoral act among us. 7 All of you here are Israelites. What are we going to do about this?"

8 All the people stood up together and said, "None of us, whether he lives in a tent or in a house, will go home. 9 This is what we will do: we will draw lots and choose some men to attack Gibeah.[t] 10 One tenth of the men in Israel will provide food for the army, and the others will go and punish Gibeah[u] for this immoral act that they have committed in Israel." 11 So all the men in Israel assembled with one purpose—to attack the town.

12 The Israelite tribes sent messengers all through the territory of the tribe of Benjamin to say, "What is this crime that you have committed? 13 Now hand over those perverts in Gibeah, so that we can kill them and remove this evil from Israel." But the people of Benjamin paid no attention to the other Israelites. 14 From all the cities of Benjamin they came to Gibeah to fight against the other people of Israel. 15-16 They called out twenty-six thousand soldiers from their cities that day. Besides these, the citizens of Gibeah gathered seven hundred specially chosen men[v] who were left-handed. Every one of them could sling a stone at a strand of hair and never miss. 17 The rest of the Israelite tribes gathered 400,000 trained soldiers.

The War against the Benjaminites

18 The Israelites went to the place of worship at Bethel, and there they asked God, "Which tribe should attack the Benjaminites first?"

The LORD answered, "The tribe of Judah."

19 So the Israelites started out the next morning and made camp near the city of Gibeah. 20 They went to attack the army of Benjamin, and placed the soldiers in position facing the city. 21 The army of Benjamin came out of the city, and before the day was over they had killed twenty-two thousand Israelite soldiers. 22-23 Then the Israelites went to the place of worship and mourned in the presence of the LORD until evening. They asked him, "Should we go again into battle against our brothers the Benjaminites?"

The LORD answered, "Yes."

So the Israelite army was encouraged, and they placed their soldiers in the same position as they had been the day before. 24 They marched against the army of Benjamin a second time. 25 And for the second time the Benjaminites came out

---

t One ancient translation to attack Gibeah; *Hebrew* to Gibeah.
u One ancient translation Gibeah; *Hebrew* Geba.
v Some ancient translations men; *Hebrew* men. In all this number there were seven hundred specially chosen men.
19.29: 1 Sam 11.7

of Gibeah, and this time they killed eighteen thousand trained Israelite soldiers. 26 Then all the people of Israel went up to Bethel and mourned. They sat there in the LORD's presence and did not eat until evening. They offered fellowship sacrifices and burnt some sacrifices whole—all in the presence of the LORD. 27-28 God's Covenant Box was there at Bethel in those days, and Phinehas, the son of Eleazar and grandson of Aaron, was in charge of it. The people asked the LORD, "Should we go out to fight our brothers the Benjaminites again, or should we give up?"

The LORD answered, "Fight. Tomorrow I will give you victory over them."

29 So the Israelites put some soldiers in hiding round Gibeah. 30 Then for the third successive day they marched against the army of Benjamin and placed their soldiers in battle position facing Gibeah, as they had done before. 31 The Benjaminites came out to fight and were led away from the city. As before, they began killing some Israelites in the open country on the road to Bethel and on the road to Gibeah. They killed about thirty Israelites. 32 The Benjaminites said, "We've beaten them just as we did before."

But the Israelites had planned to retreat and lead them away from the city on to the roads. 33 So when the main army of the Israelites pulled back and regrouped at Baaltamar, the men surrounding Gibeah suddenly rushed out of their hiding places in the rocky country round the city.w 34 Ten thousand men, specially chosen out of all Israel, attacked Gibeah, and the fighting was hard. The Benjaminites had not realized that they were about to be destroyed. 35 The LORD gave Israel victory over the army of Benjamin. The Israelites killed 25,100 of the enemy that day, 36 and the Benjaminites realized they were defeated.

How the Israelites Won

The main body of the Israelite army had retreated from the Benjaminites because they were relying on the men that they had put in hiding round Gibeah. 37 These men ran quickly towards Gibeah; they spread out in the city and killed everyone there. 38 The main Israelite army and the men in hiding had arranged a signal. When they saw a big cloud of smoke going up from the town, 39 the

Israelites out on the battlefield were to turn round. By this time the Benjaminites had already killed the thirty Israelites. They told themselves, "Yes, we've beaten them just as we did before." 40 Then the signal appeared; a cloud of smoke began to go up from the town. The Benjaminites looked behind them and were amazed to see the whole city going up in flames. 41 Then the Israelites turned round, and the Benjaminites were thrown into a panic because they realized that they were about to be destroyed. 42 They retreated from the Israelites and ran towards the open country, but they could not escape. They were caught between the main army and the men who were now coming out of the city,x and they were destroyed. 43 The Israelites had the enemy trapped, and without stopping they pursued them as far as a point east of Gibeah, killing them as they went.y 44 Eighteen thousand of the best Benjaminite soldiers were killed. 45 The others turned and ran towards the open country to the Rock of Rimmon. Five thousand of them were killed along the road. The Israelites continued to pursue the rest to Gidom, killing two thousand. 46 In all, twenty-five thousand Benjaminites were killed that day—all of them brave soldiers.

47 But six hundred men were able to escape to the open country to the Rock of Rimmon, and they stayed there four months. 48 The Israelites turned back against the rest of the Benjaminites and killed them all—men, women, and children, and animals as well. They burnt every town in the area.

Wives for the Tribe of Benjamin

21 When the Israelites had gathered at Mizpah, they had made a solemn promise to the LORD: "None of us will allow a Benjaminite to marry a daughter of ours." 2 So now the people of Israel went to Bethel and sat there in the presence of God until evening. Loudly and bitterly they mourned: 3 "LORD God of Israel, why has this happened? Why is the tribe of Benjamin about to disappear from Israel?"

4 Early the next morning the people built an altar there, offered fellowship sacrifices and burnt some sacrifices whole. 5 They asked, "Is there any group out of all the tribes of Israel that did not go to the gathering in the LORD's presence

---

w One ancient translation the city (that is, Gibeah); Hebrew Geba.
x Probable text city; Hebrew cities.   y Verse 43 in Hebrew is unclear.

at Mizpah?" (They had taken a solemn oath that anyone who had not gone to Mizpah would be put to death.) 6 The people of Israel felt sorry for their brothers the Benjaminites and said, "Today Israel has lost one of its tribes. 7 What shall we do to provide wives for the men of Benjamin who are left? We have made a solemn promise to the LORD that we will not give them any of our daughters."

8 When they asked if there was some group out of the tribes of Israel that had not gone to the gathering at Mizpah, they found out that no one from Jabesh in Gilead had been there; 9 at the roll call of the army no one from Jabesh had responded. 10 So the assembly sent twelve thousand of their bravest men with the orders, "Go and kill everyone in Jabesh, including the women and children. 11 Kill all the males, and also every woman who is not a virgin." 12 Among the people in Jabesh they found four hundred young virgins, so they brought them to the camp at Shiloh, which is in the land of Canaan.

13 Then the whole assembly sent word to the Benjaminites who were at the Rock of Rimmon and offered to end the war. 14 The Benjaminites came back, and the other Israelites gave them the girls from Jabesh whom they had not killed. But there were not enough of them.

15 The people felt sorry for the Benjaminites because the LORD had broken the unity of the tribes of Israel. 16 So the leaders of the gathering said, "There are no more women in the tribe of Benjamin.

What shall we do to provide wives for the men who are left? 17 Israel must not lose one of its twelve tribes. We must find a way for the tribe of Benjamin to survive, 18 but we cannot allow them to marry our daughters, because we have put a curse on anyone of us who allows a Benjaminite to marry one of our daughters."

19 Then they thought, "The yearly festival of the LORD at Shiloh is coming soon." (Shiloh is north of Bethel, south of Lebonah, and east of the road between Bethel and Shechem.) 20 They said to the Benjaminites, "Go and hide in the vineyards 21 and watch. When the girls of Shiloh come out to dance during the festival, you come out of the vineyards. Each of you take a wife by force from among the girls and take her back to the territory of Benjamin with you. 22 If their fathers or brothers come to you[z] and protest, you[a] can say, 'Please let us keep them, because we did not take them from you in battle to be our wives. And since you did not give them to us, you are not guilty of breaking your promise.' "

23 The Benjaminites did this; each of them chose a wife from the girls who were dancing at Shiloh and carried her away. Then they went back to their own territory, rebuilt their towns, and lived there. 24 At the same time the rest of the Israelites left, and every man went back to his own tribe and family and to his own property.

25 There was no king in Israel at that time. Everyone did just as he pleased.

---

[z] One ancient translation you; Hebrew us.   [a] Probable text you; Hebrew we.
21.25: Judg 17.6

THE BOOK OF
RUTH

INTRODUCTION

The peaceful story of *Ruth* is set in the violent times of the book of *Judges*. Ruth, a Moabite woman, is married to an Israelite. When he dies, Ruth shows uncommon loyalty to her Israelite mother-in-law and deep devotion to the God of Israel. In the end, she finds a new husband among her former husband's relatives, and through this marriage becomes the great-grandmother of David, Israel's greatest king.

The stories of *Judges* show the disaster that came when God's people turned away from him. *Ruth* shows the blessing that came to a foreigner who turned to Israel's God, and so became part of his faithful people.

Outline of Contents
Naomi returns to Bethlehem with Ruth   1.1–22
Ruth meets Boaz   2.1—3.18
Boaz marries Ruth   4.1–22

Elimelech and His Family Move to Moab

1 ¹⁻² Long ago, in the days before Israel had a king, there was a famine in the land. So a man named Elimelech, who belonged to the clan of Ephrath and who lived in Bethlehem in Judah, went with his wife Naomi and their two sons Mahlon and Chilion to live for a while in the country of Moab. While they were living there, ³ Elimelech died, and Naomi was left alone with her two sons, ⁴ who married Moabite girls, Orpah and Ruth. About ten years later ⁵ Mahlon and Chilion also died, and Naomi was left all alone, without husband or sons.

Naomi and Ruth Return to Bethlehem

6 Some time later Naomi heard that the LORD had blessed his people by giving them a good harvest; so she got ready to leave Moab with her daughters-in-law.

⁷ They started out together to go back to Judah, but on the way ⁸ she said to them, "Go back home and stay with your mothers. May the LORD be as good to you as you have been to me and to those who have died. ⁹ And may the LORD make it possible for each of you to marry again and have a home."

So Naomi kissed them good-bye. But they started crying ¹⁰ and said to her, "No! We will go with you to your people."

11 "You must go back, my daughters," Naomi answered. "Why do you want to come with me? Do you think I could have sons again for you to marry? ¹² Go back home, for I am too old to get married again. Even if I thought there was still hope, and so got married tonight and had sons, ¹³ would you wait until they had grown up? Would this keep you from marrying someone else? No, my daughters, you know that's impossible.

They went on until they came to Bethlehem (1.19)

The LORD has turned against me, and I feel very sorry for you." [a]

14 Again they started crying. Then Orpah kissed her mother-in-law good-bye and went back home, [b] but Ruth held on to her. 15 So Naomi said to her, "Ruth, your sister-in-law has gone back to her people and to her god. [c] Go back home with her."

16 But Ruth answered, "Don't ask me to leave you! Let me go with you. Wherever you go, I will go; wherever you live, I will live. Your people will be my people, and your God will be my God. 17 Wherever you die, I will die, and that is where I will be buried. May the LORD's worst punishment come upon me if I let anything but death [d] separate me from you!"

18 When Naomi saw that Ruth was determined to go with her, she said nothing more.

19 They went on until they came to Bethlehem. When they arrived, the whole town got excited, and the women there exclaimed, "Is this really Naomi?"

20 "Don't call me Naomi," she answered; "call me Marah, [e] because

Almighty God has made my life bitter. 21 When I left here, I had plenty, but the LORD has brought me back without a thing. Why call me Naomi when the LORD Almighty has condemned me and sent me trouble?"

22 This, then, was how Naomi came back from Moab with Ruth, her Moabite daughter-in-law. The barley harvest was just beginning when they arrived in Bethlehem.

Ruth Works in the Field of Boaz

2 Naomi had a relative named Boaz, a rich and influential man who belonged to the family of her husband Elimelech. 2 One day Ruth said to Naomi, "Let me go to the fields to gather the corn that the harvest workers leave. I am sure to find someone who will let me work with him."

Naomi answered, "Go ahead, my daughter."

3 So Ruth went out to the fields and walked behind the workers, picking up the corn which they left. It so happened that she was in a field that belonged to Boaz.

---

[a] sorry for you; *or* bitter about what has happened to you.
[b] *One ancient translation* and went back home; *Hebrew does not have these words.*
[c] god; *or* gods.   [d] anything but death; *or* even death.
[e] NAOMI...MARAH: *In Hebrew Naomi means "pleasant" and Marah means "bitter."*
2.2: Lev 19.9–10; Deut 24.19

4 Some time later Boaz himself arrived from Bethlehem and greeted the workers. "The Lord be with you!" he said.

"The Lord bless you!" they answered.

5 Boaz asked the man in charge, "Who is that young woman?"

6 The man answered, "She is the foreign girl who came back from Moab with Naomi. 7 She asked me to let her follow the workers and pick up the corn. She has been working since early morning and has just now stopped to rest for a while under the shelter."

8 Then Boaz said to Ruth, "Let me give you some advice. Don't pick up corn anywhere except in this field. Work with the women here; 9 watch them to see where they are reaping and stay with them. I have ordered my men not to molest you. And whenever you are thirsty, go and drink from the water jars that they have filled."

10 Ruth bowed down with her face touching the ground, and said to Boaz, "Why should you be so concerned about me? Why should you be so kind to a foreigner?"

11 Boaz answered, "I have heard about

everything that you have done for your mother-in-law since your husband died. I know how you left your father and mother and your own country and how you came to live among a people you had never known before. 12 May the Lord reward you for what you have done. May you have a full reward from the Lord God of Israel, to whom you have come for protection!"

13 Ruth answered, "You are very kind*f* to me, sir. You have made me feel better by speaking gently to me, even though I am not the equal of one of your servants."

14 At meal-time Boaz said to Ruth, "Come and have a piece of bread, and dip it in the sauce." So she sat with the workers, and Boaz passed some roasted grain to her. She ate until she was satisfied, and she still had some food left over. 15-16 After she had left to go on picking up corn, Boaz ordered the workers, "Let her pick it up even where the bundles are lying, and don't say anything to stop her. Besides that, pull out some corn from the bundles and leave it for her to pick up."

17 So Ruth went on gathering corn in

*f*You are very kind; *or* Please be kind.

Ruth went out...picking up the corn (2.3)

the field until evening, and when she had beaten it out, she found she had nearly ten kilogrammes. ¹⁸ She took the corn back into town and showed her mother-in-law how much she had gathered. She also gave her the food left over from the meal. ¹⁹ Naomi asked her, "Where did you gather all this? Whose field have you been working in? May God bless the man who took an interest in you!"

So Ruth told Naomi that she had been working in a field belonging to a man named Boaz.

20 "May the LORD bless Boaz!" Naomi exclaimed. "The LORD always keeps his promises to the living and the dead." And she went on, "That man is a close relative of ours, one of those responsible for taking care of us."

21 Then Ruth said, "Best of all, he told me to keep picking up corn with his workers until they finish the harvest."

22 Naomi said to Ruth, "Yes, my daughter, it will be better for you to work with the women in Boaz' field. You might be molested if you went to someone else's field." ²³ So Ruth worked with them and gathered corn until all the barley and wheat had been harvested. And she continued to live with her mother-in-law.

Ruth Finds a Husband

3 Some time later Naomi said to Ruth, "I must find a husband for you, so that you will have a home of your own. ² Remember that this man Boaz, whose women you have been working with, is our relative. Now listen. This evening he will be threshing the barley. ³ So wash yourself, put on some perfume, and get dressed in your best clothes. Then go where he is threshing, but don't let him know you are there until he has finished eating and drinking. ⁴ Be sure to notice where he lies down, and after he falls asleep go and lift the covers and lie down at his feet. He will tell you what to do."

5 Ruth answered, "I will do everything you say."

6 So Ruth went to the threshing-place and did just what her mother-in-law had told her. ⁷ When Boaz had finished eating and drinking, he was in a good mood. He went to the pile of barley and lay down to sleep. Ruth slipped over quietly, lifted the covers and lay down at his feet. ⁸ During the night he woke up suddenly, turned over, and was surprised to find a woman lying at his feet. ⁹ "Who are you?" he asked.

"It's Ruth, sir," she answered. "Because you are a close relative, you are responsible for taking care of me. So please marry me."

10 "The LORD bless you," he said. "You are showing even greater family loyalty in what you are doing now than in what you did for your mother-in-law. You might have gone looking for a young man, either rich or poor, but you didn't. ¹¹ Now don't worry, Ruth. I will do everything you ask; as everyone in town knows, you are a fine woman. ¹² It is true that I am a close relative and am responsible for you, but there is a man who is a closer relative than I am. ¹³ Stay here the rest of the night, and in the morning we will find out whether or not he will take responsibility for you. If so, well and good; if not, then I swear by the living LORD that I will take the responsibility. Now lie down and stay here till morning."

14 So she lay there at his feet, but she got up before it was light enough for her to be seen, because Boaz did not want anyone to know that she had been there. ¹⁵ Boaz said to her, "Take off your cloak and spread it out here." She did, and he poured out nearly twenty kilogrammes of barley and helped her to lift it on her shoulder. Then she returned to the town with it. ¹⁶ When she arrived home, her mother-in-law asked her, "How did you get on, my daughter?"

Ruth told her everything that Boaz had done for her. ¹⁷ She added, "He told me I must not come back to you empty-handed, so he gave me all this barley."

18 Naomi said to her, "Now be patient, Ruth, until you see how this all turns out. Boaz will not rest today until he settles the matter."

Boaz Marries Ruth

4 Boaz went to the meeting place at the town gate and sat down there. Then Elimelech's nearest relative, the man whom Boaz had mentioned, came by, and Boaz called to him, "Come over here, my friend, and sit down." So he went over and sat down. ² Then Boaz got ten of the leaders of the town and asked them to sit down there too. When they were seated, ³ he said to his relative, "Now that Naomi has come back from Moab, she wants to sell the field that belonged to our relative Elimelech, ⁴ and I think you ought

2.20: Lev 25.25   **3.12:** Ruth 2.20

It was the custom for the seller to take off his sandal (4.7)

to know about it. Now then, if you want it, buy it in the presence of these men sitting here. But if you don't want it, say so, because the right to buy it belongs first to you and then to me."

The man said, "I will buy it."

5 Boaz said, "Very well, but if you buy the field from Naomi, then you are also buying Ruth,*g* the Moabite widow, so that the field will stay in the dead man's family."

6 The man answered, "In that case I will give up my right to buy the field, because it would mean that my own children would not inherit it. You buy it; I would rather not."

7 Now in those days, to settle a sale or an exchange of property, it was the custom for the seller to take off his sandal and give it to the buyer. In this way the Israelites showed that the matter was settled.

8 So when the man said to Boaz, "You buy it," he took off his sandal and gave it to Boaz. *h* 9 Then Boaz said to the leaders and all the others there, "You are all witnesses today that I have bought from Naomi everything that belonged to Elimelech and to his sons Chilion and Mahlon. 10 In addition, Ruth the Moabite, Mahlon's widow, becomes my wife. This will keep the property in the dead man's family, and his family line will continue among his people and in his town. You are witnesses to this today."

11 The leaders and the others said, "Yes, we are witnesses. May the LORD make your wife become like Rachel and Leah, who bore many children to Jacob. May you become rich in the clan of Ephrath and famous in Bethlehem. 12 May the children that the LORD will give you by this young woman make your family like the family of Perez, the son of Judah and Tamar."

g Some ancient translations Naomi...Ruth; *Hebrew* Naomi and from Ruth.
h One ancient translation and gave it to Boaz; *Hebrew does not have these words.*
4.7–8: Deut 25.9   **4.10:** Deut 25.5–6   **4.11:** Gen 29.31   **4.12:** Gen 38.27–30

Boaz and His Descendants

13 So Boaz took Ruth home as his wife. The LORD blessed her, and she became pregnant and had a son. 14 The women said to Naomi, "Praise the LORD! He has given you a grandson today to take care of you. May the boy become famous in Israel! 15 Your daughter-in-law loves you, and has done more for you than seven sons. And now she has given you a grandson, who will bring new life to you and give you security in your old age." 16 Naomi took the child, held him close, *i* and took care of him.

17 The women of the neighbourhood named the boy Obed. They told everyone, "A son has been born to Naomi!"

Obed became the father of Jesse, who was the father of David.

18-22 This is the family line from Perez to David: Perez, Hezron, Ram, Amminadab, Nahshon, Salmon, Boaz, Obed, Jesse, David.

THE FIRST BOOK OF
SAMUEL

INTRODUCTION

The book of *First Samuel* records the transition in Israel from the period of the judges to the monarchy. This change in Israel's national life revolved mainly around three men: Samuel, the last of the great judges; Saul, Israel's first king; and David, whose early adventures before coming to power are interwoven with the accounts of Samuel and Saul.

The theme of this book, like that of other historical writings in the Old Testament, is that faithfulness to God brings success, while disobedience brings disaster. This is stated clearly in the Lord's message to the priest Eli in 2.30: "I will honour those who honour me, and I will treat with contempt those who despise me."

The book records mixed feelings about the establishment of the monarchy. The Lord himself was regarded as the real king of Israel, but in response to the people's request, the Lord chose a king for them. The important fact was that both the king and the people of Israel lived under the sovereignty and judgement of God (2.7-10). Under God's laws the rights of all people, rich and poor alike, were to be maintained.

Outline of Contents
Samuel as judge of Israel 1.1—7.17
Saul becomes king 8.1—10.27
The first years of Saul's reign 11.1—15.35
David and Saul 16.1—30.31
The death of Saul and his sons 31.1-13

Elkanah and His Family at Shiloh

1 There was a man named Elkanah, from the tribe of Ephraim, who lived in the town of Ramah in the hill-country of Ephraim. He was the son of Jeroham and grandson of Elihu, and belonged to the family of Tohu, a part of the clan of Zuph. ²Elkanah had two wives, Hannah and Peninnah. Peninnah had children, but Hannah had none. ³Every year Elkanah went from Ramah to worship and offer sacrifices to the LORD Almighty at Shiloh, where Hophni and Phinehas, the two sons of Eli, were priests of the LORD. ⁴Each time Elkanah offered his sacrifice, he would give one share of the meat to Peninnah and one share to each of her children. ⁵And even though he loved Hannah very much he would give her only one share, because ᵃ the LORD had kept her from having children. ⁶Peninnah, her rival, would torment and humiliate her, because the LORD had kept her childless. ⁷This went on year after year; whenever they went to the house of the LORD, Peninnah would upset Hannah so much that she would cry and refuse to eat anything. ⁸Her husband Elkanah would ask her, "Hannah, why are you crying? Why won't you eat? Why are you always so sad? Don't I mean more to you than ten sons?"

Hannah and Eli

9–10 One day, after they had finished their meal in the house of the LORD at Shiloh, Hannah got up. She was deeply distressed, and she cried bitterly as she prayed to the LORD. Meanwhile, Eli the priest was sitting in his place by the door. ¹¹Hannah made a solemn promise: "Almighty LORD, look at me, your servant! See my trouble and remember me! Don't forget me! If you give me a son, I promise that I will dedicate him to you for his whole life and that he will never have his hair cut." ᵇ

12 Hannah continued to pray to the LORD for a long time, and Eli watched her lips. ¹³She was praying silently; her lips were moving, but she made no sound.

So Eli thought that she was drunk, ¹⁴and said to her, "Stop making a drunken show of yourself! Stop your drinking and sober up!"

15 "No, I'm not drunk, sir," she answered. "I haven't been drinking! I am desperate, and I have been praying, pouring out my troubles to the LORD. ¹⁶Don't think I am a worthless woman. I have been praying like this because I'm so miserable."

17 "Go in peace," Eli said, "and may the God of Israel give you what you have asked him for."

18 "May you always think kindly of me," she replied. Then she went away, ate some food, and was no longer sad.

Samuel's Birth and Dedication

19 The next morning Elkanah and his family got up early, and after worshipping the LORD, they went back home to Ramah. Elkanah had intercourse with his wife Hannah, and the LORD answered her prayer. ²⁰So it was that she became pregnant and gave birth to a son. She named him Samuel, ᶜ and explained, "I asked the LORD for him."

21 The time came again for Elkanah and his family to go to Shiloh and offer to the LORD the yearly sacrifice and the special sacrifice he had promised. ²²But this time Hannah did not go. She told her husband, "As soon as the child is weaned, I will take him to the house of the LORD, where he will stay all his life."

23 Elkanah answered, "All right, do whatever you think best; stay at home until you have weaned him. And may the LORD make your ᵈ promise come true." So Hannah stayed at home and nursed her child.

24 After she had weaned him, she took him to Shiloh, taking along a three-year-old bull, ᵉ ten kilogrammes of flour, and a leather bag full of wine. She took Samuel, young as he was, to the house of the LORD at Shiloh. ²⁵After they had killed the bull, they took the child to Eli. ²⁶Hannah said to him, "Excuse me, sir. Do you remember me? I am the woman you saw standing here, praying to the

---

ᵃ And...because; or To Hannah, however, he would give a special share, because he loved her very much, even though.
ᵇ NEVER HAVE HIS HAIR CUT: A sign of dedication to the LORD (see Num 6.5).
ᶜ SAMUEL: This name, which in Hebrew means "name of God," is here related to the Hebrew verb for "ask." ᵈ Some ancient translations your; Hebrew his.
ᵉ Some ancient translations a three-year-old bull; Hebrew three bulls.
1.11: Num 6.5

Stop making a drunken show of yourself! (1.14)

LORD. ²⁷I asked him for this child, and he gave me what I asked for. ²⁸So I am dedicating him to the LORD. As long as he lives, he will belong to the LORD."

Then they *f* worshipped the LORD there.

Hannah's Prayer

2 Hannah prayed:
　"The LORD has filled my heart with joy;
　　how happy I am because of what he has done!
I laugh at my enemies;
　　how joyful I am because God has helped me!

² "No one is holy like the LORD;
　　there is none like him,
　　no protector like our God.

³ Stop your loud boasting;
　　silence your proud words.
For the LORD is a God who knows,
　　and he judges all that people do.
⁴ The bows of strong soldiers are broken,
　　but the weak grow strong.
⁵ The people who once were well fed
　　now hire themselves out to get food,
　　but the hungry are hungry no more.
The childless wife has borne seven children,
　　but the mother of many is left with none.
⁶ The LORD kills and restores to life;
　　he sends people to the world of the dead
　　and brings them back again.
⁷ He makes some men poor and others rich;

f Some ancient translations they; *Hebrew* he.
2.1–10: Lk 1.46–55

he humbles some and makes others
   great.
8 He lifts the poor from the dust
   and raises the needy from their
     misery.
He makes them companions of princes
   and puts them in places of honour.
The foundations of the earth belong to
   the Lord;
   on them he has built the world.

9 "He protects the lives of his faithful
   people,
   but the wicked disappear in darkness;
   a man does not triumph by his own
     strength.
10 The Lord's enemies will be destroyed;
   he will thunder against them from
     heaven.
The Lord will judge the whole world;
   he will give power to his king,
   he will make his chosen king
     victorious."

11 Then Elkanah went back home to
Ramah, but the boy Samuel stayed in
Shiloh and served the Lord under the
priest Eli.

The Sons of Eli

12 The sons of Eli were scoundrels.
They paid no attention to the Lord 13 or
to the regulations concerning what the
priests could demand from the people.
Instead, when a man was offering his
sacrifice, the priest's servant would come
with a three-pronged fork. While the meat
was still cooking, 14 he would stick the
fork into the cooking-pot, and whatever
the fork brought out belonged to the
priest. All the Israelites who came to
Shiloh to offer sacrifices were treated like
this. 15 In addition, even before the fat was
taken off and burnt, the priest's servant
would come and say to the man offering
the sacrifice, "Give me some meat for the
priest to roast; he won't accept boiled
meat from you, only raw meat."
16 If the man answered, "Let us do what
is right and burn the fat first; then take
what you want," the priest's servant
would say, "No! Give it to me now! If
you don't, I will have to take it by force!"
17 This sin of the sons of Eli was
extremely serious in the Lord's sight,
because they treated the offerings to the
Lord with such disrespect.

Samuel at Shiloh

18 In the meantime the boy Samuel

continued to serve the Lord, wearing a
sacred linen apron. 19 Each year his

*Each year his mother would make a little
robe (2.19)*

mother would make a little robe and take
it to him when she accompanied her
husband to offer the yearly sacrifice.
20 Then Eli would bless Elkanah and his
wife, and say to Elkanah, "May the Lord
give you other children by this woman
to take the place of the one you dedicated
to him."
After that they would go back home.
21 The Lord did bless Hannah, and she
had three more sons and two daughters.
The boy Samuel grew up in the service
of the Lord.

Eli and His Sons

22 Eli was now very old. He kept
hearing about everything his sons were
doing to the Israelites and that they were

even sleeping with the women who worked at the entrance to the Tent of the LORD's presence. 23 So he said to them, "Why are you doing these things? Everybody tells me about the evil you are doing. 24 Stop it, my sons! This is an awful thing the people of the LORD are talking about! 25 If a man sins against another man, God can defend him; but who can defend a man who sins against the LORD?"

But they would not listen to their father, for the LORD had decided to kill them.

26 The boy Samuel continued to grow and to gain favour both with the LORD and with men.

The Prophecy against Eli's Family

27 A prophet came to Eli with this message from the LORD: "When your ancestor Aaron and his family were slaves of the king of Egypt, I revealed myself to Aaron. 28 From all the tribes of Israel I chose his family to be my priests, to serve at the altar, to burn the incense, and to wear the ephod^g to consult me. And I gave them the right to keep a share of the sacrifices burnt on the altar. 29 Why, then, do you look with greed^h at the sacrifices and offerings which I require from my people? Why, Eli, do you honour your sons more than me by letting them fatten themselves on the best parts of all the sacrifices my people offer to me? 30 I, the LORD God of Israel, promised in the past that your family and your clan would serve me as priests for all time. But now I say that I won't have it any longer! Instead, I will honour those who honour me, and I will treat with contempt those who despise me. 31 Listen, the time is coming when I will kill all the young men in your family and your clan, so that no man in your family will live to be old. 32 You will be troubled and look with envy^i on all the blessings I will give to the other people of Israel, but no one in your family will ever again live to old age. 33 Yet I will keep one of your descendants alive, and he will serve me as priest. But he^j will become blind and lose all hope, and all your other descendants will die a violent death. 34 When your two sons Hophni and Phinehas both die on the same day, this will show you that everything I have said will come true. 35 I will choose a priest who will be faithful to me and

do everything I want him to. I will give him descendants, who will always serve in the presence of my chosen king. 36 Any of your descendants who survive will have to go to that priest and ask him for money and food, and beg to be allowed to help the priests, in order to have something to eat."

The LORD Appears to Samuel

3 In those days, when the boy Samuel was serving the LORD under the direction of Eli, there were very few messages from the LORD, and visions from him were quite rare. 2 One night Eli, who was now almost blind, was sleeping in his own room; 3 Samuel was sleeping in the sanctuary, where the sacred Covenant Box was. Before dawn, while the lamp was still burning, 4 the LORD called Samuel. He answered, "Yes, sir!" 5 and ran to Eli and said, "You called me, and here I am."

But Eli answered, "I didn't call you; go back to bed." So Samuel went back to bed.

6-7 The LORD called Samuel again. The boy did not know that it was the LORD, because the LORD had never spoken to him before. So he got up, went to Eli, and said, "You called me, and here I am."

But Eli answered, "My son, I didn't call you; go back to bed."

8 The LORD called Samuel a third time; he got up, went to Eli, and said, "You called me, and here I am."

Then Eli realized that it was the LORD who was calling the boy, 9 so he said to him, "Go back to bed; and if he calls you again, say, 'Speak, LORD, your servant is listening.'" So Samuel went back to bed.

10 The LORD came and stood there, and called as he had before, "Samuel! Samuel!"

Samuel answered, "Speak; your servant is listening."

11 The LORD said to him, "Some day I am going to do something to the people of Israel that is so terrible that everyone who hears about it will be stunned. 12 On that day I will carry out all my threats against Eli's family, from beginning to end. 13 I have already told him^k that I am going to punish his family for ever because his sons have spoken evil things

---

^{g} EPHOD: See Word List.　　^{h} One ancient translation look with greed ; Hebrew unclear.
^{i} Probable text look with envy; Hebrew unclear.　　^{j} One ancient translation he; Hebrew you.
^{k} One ancient translation I have already told him; Hebrew I will tell him.
2.26: Lk 2.52　　**2.28:** Ex 28.1–4; Lev 7.35–36　　**2.34:** 1 Sam 4.11

Speak; your servant is listening (3.10)

against me. Eli knew they were doing this, but he did not stop them. ¹⁴So I solemnly declare to the family of Eli that no sacrifice or offering will ever be able to remove the consequences of this terrible sin."

15 Samuel stayed in bed until morning; then he got up and opened the doors of the house of the LORD. He was afraid to tell Eli about the vision. ¹⁶Eli called him, "Samuel, my boy!"

"Yes, sir," answered Samuel.

17 "What did the LORD tell you?" Eli asked. "Don't keep anything from me. God will punish you severely if you don't tell me everything he said." ¹⁸So Samuel told him everything; he did not keep anything back. Eli said, "He is the LORD; he will do whatever seems best to him."

19 As Samuel grew up, the LORD was with him and made everything that Samuel said come true. ²⁰So all the people of Israel, from one end of the country to the other, knew that Samuel was indeed a prophet of the LORD. ²¹The LORD continued to reveal himself at Shiloh, where he had appeared to Samuel and had spoken to him. And when Samuel spoke, all Israel listened.

The Capture of the Covenant Box

4 At that time the Philistines gathered to go to war against Israel, so*ˡ* the Israelites set out to fight them. The Israelites set up their camp at Ebenezer and the Philistines at Aphek. ²The Philistines attacked, and after fierce fighting they defeated the Israelites and killed about four thousand men on the battle-field. ³When the survivors came back to camp, the leaders of Israel said, "Why did the LORD let the Philistines defeat us today? Let's go and bring the LORD's Covenant Box from Shiloh, so that he*ᵐ* will go with us and save us from our enemies." ⁴So they sent messengers to Shiloh and fetched the Covenant Box of the LORD Almighty, who is enthroned above the winged creatures.*ˣ* And Eli's two sons, Hophni and Phinehas, came along with the Covenant Box.

5 When the Covenant Box arrived, the Israelites gave such a loud shout of joy that the earth shook. ⁶The Philistines heard the shouting and said, "Listen to all that shouting in the Hebrew camp! What does it mean?" When they found out that the LORD's Covenant Box had arrived in the Hebrew camp, ⁷they were afraid, and said, "A god has come into their camp! We're lost! Nothing like this has ever happened to us before! ⁸Who can save us from those powerful gods? They are the gods who slaughtered the Egyptians in the desert! ⁹Be brave, Philistines! Fight like men, or we will become slaves to the Hebrews, just as they were our slaves. So fight like men!"

10 The Philistines fought hard and defeated the Israelites, who went running to their homes. There was a great slaughter: thirty thousand Israelite soldiers were killed. ¹¹God's Covenant Box was captured, and Eli's sons, Hophni and Phinehas, were both killed.

The Death of Eli

12 A man from the tribe of Benjamin ran all the way from the battlefield to Shiloh and arrived there the same day. To show his grief, he had torn his clothes and put earth on his head. ¹³Eli, who was very anxious about the Covenant Box, was sitting on a seat beside the road, staring. The man spread the news throughout the town, and everyone cried out in fear. ¹⁴Eli heard the noise and asked, "What is all this noise about?" The man hurried to Eli to tell him the news. ¹⁵(Eli was now ninety-eight years old and almost completely blind.) ¹⁶The man said, "I have escaped from the battle and have run all the way here today."

Eli asked him, "What happened, my son?"

17 The messenger answered, "Israel ran away from the Philistines; it was a terrible

---

ˡOne ancient translation the Philistines...so; *Hebrew does not have these words.*
*ᵐ*he; *or* it.
*ˣ*WINGED CREATURES: *See Word List.*
4.4: Ex 25.22

defeat for us! Besides that, your sons Hophni and Phinehas were killed, and God's Covenant Box was captured!"

18 When the man mentioned the Covenant Box, Eli fell backwards from his seat beside the gate. He was so old and fat that the fall broke his neck, and he died. He had been a leader in Israel for forty years.

The Death of the Widow of Phinehas

19 Eli's daughter-in-law, the wife of Phinehas, was pregnant, and it was almost time for her baby to be born. When she heard that God's Covenant Box had been captured and that her father-in-law and her husband were dead, she suddenly went into labour and gave birth. 20 As she was dying, the women helping her said to her, "Be brave! You have a son!" But she paid no attention and did not answer. 21 She named the boy Ichabod,[n] explaining, "God's glory has left Israel"—referring to the capture of the Covenant Box and the death of her father-in-law and her husband. 22 "God's glory has left Israel," she said, "because God's Covenant Box has been captured."

The Covenant Box among the Philistines

5 After the Philistines captured the Covenant Box, they carried it from Ebenezer to their city of Ashdod, 2 took it into the temple of their god Dagon, and set it up beside his statue. 3 Early next morning the people of Ashdod saw that the statue of Dagon had fallen face downwards on the ground in front of the LORD's Covenant Box. So they lifted it up and put it back in its place. 4 Early the following morning they saw that the statue had again fallen down in front of the Covenant Box. This time its head and both its arms were broken off and were lying in the doorway; only the body was left. 5 (That is why even today the priests of Dagon and all his worshippers in Ashdod step over that place and do not walk on it.)

6 The LORD punished the people of Ashdod severely and terrified them. He punished them and the people in the surrounding territory by causing them to have tumours.[o] 7 When they saw what was happening, they said, "The God of Israel is punishing us and our god Dagon. We can't let the Covenant Box stay here

any longer." 8 So they sent messengers and called together all five of the Philistine kings and asked them, "What shall we do with the Covenant Box of the God of Israel?"

"Take it over to Gath," they answered; so they took it to Gath, another Philistine city. 9 But after it arrived there, the LORD punished that city too and caused a great panic. He punished them with tumours which developed in all the people of the city, young and old alike. 10 So they sent the Covenant Box to Ekron, another Philistine city; but when it arrived there, the people cried out, "They have brought the Covenant Box of the God of Israel here, in order to kill us all!" 11 So again they sent for all the Philistine kings and said, "Send the Covenant Box of Israel back to its own place, so that it won't kill us and our families." There was panic throughout the city because God was punishing them so severely. 12 Even those who did not die developed tumours and the people cried out to their gods for help.

The Return of the Covenant Box

6 After the LORD's Covenant Box had been in Philistia for seven months, 2 the people called the priests and the magicians and asked, "What shall we do with the Covenant Box of the LORD? If we send it back where it belongs, what shall we send with it?"

3 They answered, "If you return the Covenant Box of the God of Israel, you must, of course, send with it a gift to him to pay for your sin. The Covenant Box must not go back without a gift. In this way you will be healed, and you will find out why he has kept on punishing you."

4 "What gift shall we send him?" the people asked.

They answered, "Five gold models of tumours and five gold mice, one of each for each Philistine king. The same plague was sent on all of you and on the five kings. 5 You must make these models of the tumours and of the mice that are ravaging your country, and you must give honour to the God of Israel. Perhaps he will stop punishing you, your gods, and your land. 6 Why should you be stubborn, as the king of Egypt and the Egyptians were? Don't forget how God made fools of them until they let the Israelites leave

---

[n] ICHABOD: *This name in Hebrew means "no glory."*
[o] TUMOURS: *The association of tumours with an abundance of mice suggests that this was a case of bubonic plague (see 6.5).*

The wagon came to a field belonging to a man named Joshua (6.14)

Egypt. ⁷So prepare a new wagon and two cows that have never been yoked; hitch them to the wagon and drive their calves back to the barn. ⁸Take the LORD's Covenant Box, put it on the wagon, and place in a box beside it the gold models that you are sending to him as a gift to pay for your sins. Start the wagon on its way and let it go by itself. ⁹Then watch it go; if it goes towards the town of Beth Shemesh, this means that it is the God of the Israelites who has sent this terrible disaster on us. But if it doesn't, then we will know that he did not send the plague; it was only a matter of chance."

10 They did what they were told: they took two cows and hitched them to the wagon, and shut the calves in the barn. ¹¹They put the Covenant Box in the wagon, together with the box containing the gold models of the mice and of the tumours. ¹²The cows started off on the road to Beth Shemesh and headed straight towards it, without turning off the road. They were mooing as they went. The five Philistine kings followed them as far as the border of Beth Shemesh.

13 The people of Beth Shemesh were harvesting wheat in the valley, when suddenly they looked up and saw the Covenant Box. They were overjoyed at the sight. ¹⁴The wagon came to a field belonging to a man named Joshua, who lived in Beth Shemesh, and it stopped there near a large rock. The people chopped up the wooden wagon and killed the cows and offered them as a burnt-sacrifice to the LORD. ¹⁵The Levites lifted off the Covenant Box of the LORD and the box with the gold models in it, and placed them on the large rock. Then the people of Beth Shemesh offered burnt-sacrifices and other sacrifices to the LORD. ¹⁶The five Philistine kings watched them do this and then went back to Ekron that same day.

17 The Philistines sent the five gold tumours to the LORD as a gift to pay for their sins, one each for the cities of Ashdod, Gaza, Ashkelon, Gath, and Ekron. ¹⁸They also sent gold mice, one for each of the cities ruled by the five Philistine kings, both the fortified towns and the villages without walls. The large rock in the field of Joshua of Beth Shemesh, on which they placed the LORD's Covenant Box, is still there as a witness to what happened.

19 The LORD killed seventy of the men of Beth Shemesh because they looked inside the Covenant Box. And the people mourned because the LORD had caused such a great slaughter among them.

The Covenant Box at Kiriath Jearim

20 So the men of Beth Shemesh said, "Who can stand before the LORD, this holy God? Where can we send him to get him

away from us?" ²¹They sent messengers to the people of Kiriath Jearim to say, "The Philistines have returned the LORD's Covenant Box. Come down and fetch it."

7 So the people of Kiriath Jearim fetched the LORD's Covenant Box and took it to the house of a man named Abinadab, who lived on a hill. They consecrated his son Eleazar to be in charge of it.

Samuel Rules Israel

2 The Covenant Box of the LORD stayed in Kiriath Jearim a long time, some twenty years. During this time all the Israelites cried to the LORD for help.

3 Samuel said to the people of Israel, "If you are going to turn to the LORD with all your hearts, you must get rid of all the foreign gods and the images of the goddess Astarte. Dedicate yourselves completely to the LORD and worship only him, and he will rescue you from the power of the Philistines." ⁴So the Israelites got rid of their idols of Baal and Astarte, and worshipped only the LORD.

5 Then Samuel sent for all the Israelites to meet at Mizpah, saying, "I will pray to the LORD for you there." ⁶So they all gathered at Mizpah. They drew some water and poured it out as an offering to the LORD and fasted that whole day. They said, "We have sinned against the LORD." (It was at Mizpah that Samuel settled disputes among the Israelites.)

7 When the Philistines heard that the Israelites had gathered at Mizpah, the five Philistine kings started out with their men to attack them. The Israelites heard about it and were afraid, ⁸and said to Samuel, "Keep praying to the LORD our God to save us from the Philistines." ⁹Samuel killed a young lamb and burnt it whole as a sacrifice to the LORD. Then he prayed to the LORD to help Israel, and the LORD answered his prayer. ¹⁰While Samuel was offering the sacrifice, the Philistines moved forward to attack; but just then the LORD thundered from heaven against them. They became completely confused and fled in panic. ¹¹The Israelites marched out from Mizpah and pursued the Philistines almost as far as Bethcar, killing them along the way.

12 Then Samuel took a stone, set it up between Mizpah and Shen, and said, "The LORD has helped us all the way"—and he named it "Stone of Help." ¹³So the Philistines were defeated, and the LORD prevented them from invading Israel's territory as long as Samuel lived. ¹⁴All the cities which the Philistines had captured between Ekron and Gath were returned to Israel, and so Israel got back all its territory. And there was peace also between the Israelites and the Canaanites.

15 Samuel ruled Israel as long as he lived. ¹⁶Every year he would go round to Bethel, Gilgal, and Mizpah, and in these places he would settle disputes. ¹⁷Then he would go back to his home in Ramah, where also he would serve as judge. In Ramah he built an altar to the LORD.

The People Ask for a King

8 When Samuel grew old, he made his sons judges in Israel. ²The elder son was named Joel and the younger one Abijah; they were judges in Beersheba. ³But they did not follow their father's example; they were interested only in making money, so they accepted bribes and did not decide cases honestly.

4 Then all the leaders of Israel met together, went to Samuel in Ramah, ⁵and said to him, "Look, you are getting old and your sons don't follow your example. So then, appoint a king to rule over us, so that we will have a king, as other countries have." ⁶Samuel was displeased with their request for a king; so he prayed to the LORD, ⁷and the LORD said, "Listen to everything the people say to you. You are not the one they have rejected; I am the one they have rejected as their king. ⁸Ever since I brought them out of Egypt, they have turned away from me and worshipped other gods; and now they are doing to you what they have always done to me. ⁹So then, listen to them, but give them strict warnings and explain how their kings will treat them."

10 Samuel told the people who were asking him for a king everything that the LORD had said to him. ¹¹"This is how your king will treat you," Samuel explained. "He will make soldiers of your sons; some of them will serve in his war chariots, others in his cavalry, and others will run before his chariots. ¹²He will make some of them officers in charge of a thousand men, and others in charge of fifty men. Your sons will have to plough his fields, harvest his crops, and make his weapons and the equipment for his chariots. ¹³Your daughters will have to make perfumes for him and work as his cooks and his bakers.

7.1: 2 Sam 6.2-4; 1 Chr 13.5-7   **8.5:** Deut 17.14

14 He will take your best fields, vineyards, and olive-groves, and give them to his officials. 15 He will take a tenth of your corn and of your grapes for his court officers and other officials. 16 He will take your servants and your best cattle[p] and donkeys, and make them work for him. 17 He will take a tenth of your flocks. And you yourselves will become his slaves. 18 When that time comes, you will complain bitterly because of your king, whom you yourselves chose, but the LORD will not listen to your complaints."

19 The people paid no attention to Samuel, but said "No! We want a king, 20 so that we will be like other nations, with our own king to rule us and to lead us out to war and to fight our battles." 21 Samuel listened to everything they said and then went and told the LORD. 22 The LORD answered, "Do what they want and give them a king." Then Samuel told all the men of Israel to go back home.

Saul Meets Samuel

9 There was a wealthy and influential man named Kish, from the tribe of Benjamin; he was the son of Abiel and grandson of Zeror, and belonged to the family of Becorath, a part of the clan of Aphiah. 2 He had a son named Saul, a handsome man in the prime of life. Saul was a head taller than anyone else in Israel and more handsome as well.

3 Some donkeys belonging to Kish had wandered off, so he said to Saul, "Take one of the servants with you and go and look for the donkeys." 4 They went through the hill-country of Ephraim and the region of Shalishah, but did not find them; so they went on through the region of Shaalim, but the donkeys were not there. Then they went through the territory of Benjamin, but still did not find them. 5 When they came into the region of Zuph, Saul said to his servant, "Let's go back home, or my father might stop thinking about the donkeys and start worrying about us."

6 The servant answered, "Wait! In this town there is a holy man who is highly respected because everything he says comes true. Let's go to him, and maybe he can tell us where we can find the donkeys."

7 "If we go to him, what can we give him?" Saul asked. "There is no food left in our packs, and we haven't anything to give him, have we?"

8 The servant answered, "I have a small silver coin. I can give him that, and then he will tell us where we can find them."

9–11 Saul replied, "A good idea! Let's go." So they went to the town where the holy man lived. As they were going up the hill to the town, they met some girls who were coming out to draw water. They asked the girls, "Is the seer in town?"

(At that time a prophet was called a seer, and so whenever someone wanted to ask God a question, he would say, "Let's go to the seer.")

12–13 "Yes, he is," the girls answered. "In fact, he is just ahead of you. If you hurry, you will catch up with him. As soon as you go into the town, you will find him. He arrived in town today because the people are going to offer a sacrifice on the altar on the hill. The people who are invited won't start eating until he gets there, because he has to bless the sacrifice first. If you go now, you will find him before he goes up the hill to eat." 14 So Saul and his servant went on to the town, and as they were going in, they saw Samuel coming out towards them on his way to the place of worship.

15 Now on the previous day the LORD had said to Samuel, 16 "Tomorrow about this time I will send you a man from the tribe of Benjamin; anoint him as ruler of my people Israel, and he will rescue them from the Philistines. I have seen the suffering of my people and have heard their cries for help."

17 When Samuel caught sight of Saul, the LORD said to him, "This is the man I told you about. He will rule my people." 18 Then Saul went over to Samuel, who was near the gate, and asked, "Tell me, where does the seer live?"

19 Samuel answered, "I am the seer. Go on ahead of me to the place of worship. Both of you are to eat with me today. Tomorrow morning I will answer all your questions and send you on your way. 20 As for the donkeys that were lost three days ago, don't worry about them; they have already been found. But who is it that the people of Israel want so much?[q] It is you—you and your father's family."

21 Saul answered, "I belong to the tribe of Benjamin, the smallest tribe in Israel, and my family is the least important one

---

[p] One ancient translation cattle; Hebrew young men.
[q] who is it...much?; or who is to have the most desirable thing in Israel?

I am the seer (9.19)

in the tribe. Why, then, do you talk like this to me?"

22 Then Samuel led Saul and his servant into the large room and gave them a place at the head of the table where the guests, about thirty in all, were seated. 23 Samuel said to the cook, "Bring the piece of meat I gave you, which I told you to set aside." 24 So the cook brought the choice piece of the leg and placed it before Saul. Samuel*r* said, "Look, here is the piece that was kept for you. Eat it. I saved it for you to eat at this time with the people I invited."*s*

So Saul ate with Samuel that day. 25 When they went down from the place of worship to the town, they made up a bed for Saul*t* on the roof,*u* 26 and he slept there.*v*

Samuel Anoints Saul as Ruler

At dawn Samuel called to Saul on the roof, "Get up, and I will send you on your way." Saul got up, and he and Samuel went out to the street together.

27 When they arrived at the edge of the town, Samuel said to Saul, "Tell the servant to go on ahead of us." The servant left, and Samuel continued, "Stay here a minute, and I will tell you what God has said."

10 Then Samuel took a jar of olive-oil and poured it on Saul's head, kissed him, and said, "The LORD anoints you as ruler of his people Israel. You will rule his people and protect them from all their enemies. And this is the proof to you that the LORD has chosen you*w* to be the ruler of his people: 2 When you

The LORD anoints you as ruler of his people (10.1)

leave me today, you will meet two men near Rachel's tomb at Zelzah in the territory of Benjamin. They will tell you that the donkeys you were looking for have been found, so that your father isn't worried any more about them but about you, and he keeps asking, 'What shall I do about my son?' 3 You will go on from there until you come to the sacred tree at Tabor, where you will meet three men

r Some ancient translations Samuel; *Hebrew* He (that is, the cook).
s Probable text I saved it...invited; *Hebrew unclear.*
t One ancient translation they made up a bed for Saul; *Hebrew* he spoke with Saul.
u ON THE ROOF: *At that time houses had flat roofs, and it was common for people to sleep on them.*
v Some ancient translations and he slept there; *Hebrew* and they got up early.
w Some ancient translations as ruler of his people...the LORD has chosen you; *Hebrew does not have these words.*

on their way to offer a sacrifice to God at Bethel. One of them will be leading three young goats, another one will be carrying three loaves of bread, and the third one will have a leather bag full of wine. ⁴They will greet you and offer you two of the loaves, which you are to accept. ⁵Then you will go to the Hill of God in Gibeah, where there is a Philistine camp. At the entrance to the town you will meet a group of prophets coming down from the altar on the hill, playing harps, drums, flutes, and lyres. They will be dancing and shouting. ⁶Suddenly the spirit of the LORD will take control of you, and you will join in their religious dancing and shouting and will become a different person. ⁷When these things happen, do whatever God leads you to do. ⁸You will go ahead of me to Gilgal, where I will meet you and offer burnt-sacrifices and fellowship-sacrifices. Wait there seven days until I come and tell you what to do."

9 When Saul turned to leave Samuel, God gave Saul a new nature. And everything Samuel had told him happened that day. ¹⁰When Saul and his servant arrived at Gibeah, a group of prophets met him. Suddenly the spirit of God took control of him, and he joined in their ecstatic dancing and shouting. ¹¹People who had known him before saw him doing this and asked one another, "What has happened to the son of Kish? Has Saul become a prophet?" ¹²A man who lived there asked, "How about these other prophets—who do you think their fathers are?" This is how the saying originated, "Has even Saul become a prophet?" ¹³When Saul finished his ecstatic dancing and shouting, he went to the altar on the hill.

14 Saul's uncle saw him and the servant, and he asked them, "Where have you been?"

"Looking for the donkeys," Saul answered. "When we couldn't find them, we went to see Samuel."

15 "And what did he tell you?" Saul's uncle asked.

16 "He told us that the animals had been found," Saul answered—but he did not tell his uncle what Samuel had said about his becoming king.

Saul Is Acclaimed as King

17 Samuel called the people together for a religious gathering at Mizpah ¹⁸and said to them, "The LORD, the God of Israel, says, 'I brought you out of Egypt and rescued you from the Egyptians and all the other peoples who were oppressing you. ¹⁹I am your God, the one who rescues you from all your troubles and difficulties, but today you have rejected me and have asked me to give you a king. Very well, then, gather yourselves before the LORD by tribes and by clans.'"

20 Then Samuel made each tribe come forward, and the LORD picked the tribe of Benjamin. ²¹Then Samuel made the families of the tribe of Benjamin come forward, and the family of Matri was picked out. Then the men of the family of Matri came forward,ˣ and Saul son of Kish was picked out. They looked for him, but when they could not find him, ²²they asked the LORD, "Is there still someone else?"

The LORD answered, "Saul is over there, hiding behind the supplies."

23 So they ran and brought Saul out to the people, and they could see that he was a head taller than anyone else. ²⁴Samuel said to the people, "Here is the man the LORD has chosen! There is no one else among us like him."

All the people shouted, "Long live the king!"

25 Samuel explained to the people the rights and duties of a king, and then wrote them in a book, which he deposited in a holy place. Then he sent everyone home. ²⁶Saul also went back home to Gibeah. Some powerful men,ʸ whose hearts God had touched, went with him. ²⁷But some worthless people said, "How can this fellow do us any good?" They despised Saul and did not bring him any gifts.

Saul Defeats the Ammonites

11 About a month later King Nahash of Ammon led his army against the town of Jabesh in the territory of Gilead and besieged it. The men of Jabesh said to Nahash, "Make a treaty with us, and we will accept you as our ruler."

2 Nahash answered, "I will make a treaty with you on one condition: I will put out everyone's right eye and so bring disgrace on all Israel."

3 The leaders of Jabesh said, "Give us seven days to send messengers throughout the land of Israel. If no one will help us, then we will surrender to you."

ˣ *One ancient translation* Then the men of the family of Matri came forward; *Hebrew does not have these words.*   ʸ *One ancient translation* Some powerful men; *Hebrew* The army.
10.12: 1 Sam 19.23-24

4 The messengers arrived at Gibeah, where Saul lived, and when they told the news, the people started crying in despair. 5 Saul was just coming in from the field with his oxen, and he asked, "What's wrong? Why is everyone crying?" They told him what the messengers from Jabesh had reported. 6 When Saul heard this, the spirit of God took control of him, and he became furious. 7 He took two oxen, cut them in pieces, and sent messengers to carry the pieces throughout the land of Israel with this warning: "Whoever does not follow Saul and Samuel into battle will have this done to his oxen!"

The people of Israel were afraid of what the LORD might do, and all of them, without exception, came out together. 8 Saul gathered them at Bezek: there were 300,000 from Israel and 30,000 from Judah. 9 They said to the messengers from Jabesh, "Tell your people that before noon tomorrow they will be rescued." When the people of Jabesh received the message, they were overjoyed 10 and said to Nahash, "Tomorrow we will surrender to you, and you can do with us whatever you wish."

11 That night Saul divided his men into three groups, and at dawn they rushed into the enemy camp and attacked the Ammonites. By noon they had slaughtered them. The survivors scattered, each man running off by himself.

12 Then the people of Israel said to Samuel, "Where are the people who said that Saul should not be our king? Hand them over to us, and we will kill them!" 13 But Saul said, "No one will be put to death today, for this is the day the LORD rescued Israel." 14 And Samuel said to them, "Let us all go to Gilgal and once more proclaim Saul as our king." 15 So they all went to Gilgal, and there at the holy place they proclaimed Saul king. They offered fellowship-sacrifices, and Saul and all the people of Israel celebrated the event.

Samuel Addresses the People

12 Then Samuel said to the people of Israel, "I have done what you asked me to do. I have given you a king

to rule you, 2 and now you have him to lead you. As for me, I am old and grey, and my sons are with you. I have been your leader from my youth until now. 3 Here I am. If I have done anything wrong, accuse me now in the presence of the LORD and the king he has chosen. Have I taken anybody's cow or anybody's donkey? Have I cheated or oppressed anyone? Have I accepted a bribe from anyone? If I have done any of these things, I will pay back what I have taken."

4 The people answered, "No, you have not cheated us or oppressed us; you have not taken anything from anyone."

5 Samuel replied, "The LORD and the king he has chosen are witnesses today that you have found me to be completely innocent."

"Yes, the LORD is our witness," they answered.

6 Samuel continued, "The LORD is the one who chose Moses and Aaron and who brought your ancestors out of Egypt. 7 Now stand where you are, and I will accuse you before the LORD by reminding you *z* of all the mighty actions the LORD did to save you and your ancestors. 8 When Jacob and his family went to Egypt and the Egyptians oppressed them, *a* your ancestors cried to the LORD for help, and he sent Moses and Aaron, who brought them out of Egypt and settled them in this land. 9 But the people forgot the LORD their God, and so he let the Philistines and the king of Moab and Sisera, commander of the army of the city of Hazor, fight against your ancestors and conquer them. 10 Then they cried to the LORD for help and said, 'We have sinned, because we turned away from you, LORD, and worshipped the idols of Baal and Astarte. Rescue us from our enemies, and we will worship you!' 11 And the LORD sent Gideon, Barak, *b* Jephthah, and finally me. Each of us rescued you from your enemies, and you lived in safety. 12 But when you saw that King Nahash of Ammon was about to attack you, you rejected the LORD as your king and said to me, 'We want a king to rule us.'

13 "Now here is the king you chose; you asked for him, and now the LORD has given him to you. 14 All will go well with you if you honour the LORD your

z One ancient translation by reminding you; *Hebrew does not have these words.*
a One ancient translation and the Egyptians oppressed them; *Hebrew does not have these words.*
b Some ancient translations Barak; *Hebrew* Bedan.
12.6: Ex 6.26   **12.8:** Ex 2.23   **12.9:** Judg 3.12, 4.2, 13.1   **12.10:** Judg 10.10–15
12.11: 1 Sam 3.20; Judg 4.6, 7.1, 11.29   **12.12:** 1 Sam 8.19

God, serve him, listen to him, and obey his commands, and if you and your king follow him. [15] But if you do not listen to the LORD but disobey his commands, he will be against you and your king. [c] [16] So then, stand where you are, and you will see the great thing which the LORD is going to do. [17] It's the dry season, isn't it? But I will pray, and the LORD will send thunder and rain. When this happens, you will realize that you committed a great sin against the LORD when you asked him for a king."

18 So Samuel prayed, and on that same day the LORD sent thunder and rain. Then all the people became afraid of the LORD and of Samuel, [19] and they said to Samuel, "Please, sir, pray to the LORD your God for us, so that we won't die. We now realize that, besides all our other sins, we have sinned by asking for a king."

20 "Don't be afraid," Samuel answered. "Even though you have done such an evil thing, do not turn away from the LORD, but serve him with all your heart. [21] Don't go after [d] false gods; they cannot help you or save you, for they are not real. [22] The LORD has made a solemn promise, and he will not abandon you, for he has decided to make you his own people. [23] As for me, the LORD forbid that I should sin against him by no longer praying for you. Instead, I will teach you what is good and right for you to do. [24] Obey the LORD and serve him faithfully with all your heart. Remember the great things he has done for you. [25] But if you continue to sin, you and your king will be destroyed."

War against the Philistines

13 [e] [2] Saul picked three thousand men, keeping two thousand of them with him in Michmash and in the hill-country of Bethel and sending one thousand with his son Jonathan to Gibeah, in the territory of the tribe of Benjamin. The rest of the men Saul sent home.

3 Jonathan killed the Philistine commander [f] in Geba, and all the Philistines heard about it. Then Saul sent messengers to call the Hebrews to war by blowing a trumpet throughout the whole country. [4] All the Israelites were told that Saul had

killed the Philistine commander and that the Philistines hated them. So the people answered the call to join Saul at Gilgal.

5 The Philistines assembled to fight the Israelites; they had thirty thousand war chariots, six thousand horsemen, and as many soldiers as there are grains of sand on the seashore. They went to Michmash, east of Bethaven, and camped there. [6] Then they launched a strong attack against the Israelites, putting them in a desperate situation. Some of the Israelites hid in caves and holes or among the rocks or in pits and wells; [7] others crossed the River Jordan into the territories of Gad and Gilead.

Saul was still at Gilgal, and the people with him were trembling with fear. [8] He waited seven days for Samuel, as Samuel had instructed him to do, but Samuel still had not come to Gilgal. The people began to desert Saul, [9] so he said to them, "Bring me the burnt-sacrifices and the fellowship-sacrifices." He offered a burnt-sacrifice, [10] and just as he was finishing, Samuel arrived. Saul went out to meet him and welcome him, [11] but Samuel said, "What have you done?"

Saul answered, "The people were deserting me, and you had not come when you said you would; besides that, the Philistines are gathering at Michmash. [12] So I thought, 'The Philistines are going to attack me here in Gilgal, and I have not tried to win the LORD's favour.' So I felt I had to offer a sacrifice."

13 "That was a foolish thing to do," Samuel answered. "You have not obeyed the command the LORD your God gave you. If you had obeyed, he would have let you and your descendants rule over Israel for ever. [14] But now your rule will not continue. Because you have disobeyed him, the LORD will find the kind of man he wants and make him ruler of his people."

15 Samuel left Gilgal and went on his way. The rest of the people followed Saul as he went to join his soldiers. They went from Gilgal [g] to Gibeah in the territory of Benjamin. Saul inspected his troops, about six hundred men. [16] Saul, his son Jonathan, and their men camped in Geba

---

[c] *One ancient translation* your king; *Hebrew* your ancestors.
[d] *Some ancient translations* after; *Hebrew* because after.
[e] *One ancient translation does not have verse 1; Hebrew has as verse 1* Saul was...years old when he became king, and he was king of Israel for two years. *The Hebrew text is defective at two points in this verse.*
[f] killed the Philistine commander; *or* defeated the Philistines camping.
[g] *Some ancient translations* on his way...went from Gilgal; *Hebrew does not have these words.*

13.8: 1 Sam 10.8   **13.14:** Acts 13.22

THE UNITED ISRAELITE KINGDOM

Sidon

Damascus

△ Mount Lebanon

SYRIA

BETHREHOB

△ Mount Hermon

Abel Beth Maacah

Tyre

ASHER

Dan

NAPHTALI

MEDITERRANEAN SEA

Cabul

ZEBULUN

Hazor

GESHUR

LAKE GALILEE

Endor

ISSACHAR

Megiddo

Valley of Jezreel

Lodebar

Ramoth in Gilead

Jezreel

△ Mount Gilboa

Beth Shan

Jabesh in Gilead

Socoh

GAD

River Jordan

GILEAD

Shechem

AMMON

EPHRAIM

Mahanaim

Shiloh

Beth Horon

Bethel

Gilgal

Gibeon

Mizpah

Rabbah

Kiriath Jearim

Gibeah

BENJAMIN

Ekron

Jerusalem

PHILISTIA

Ashdod

Libnah

Bethlehem

Adullam

Tekoa

DEAD SEA

Gath

JUDAH

Ashkelon

Hebron

Gaza

Ziklag

Carmel

MOAB

Beersheba

0   20   40   60
Kilometres

E D O M

in the territory of Benjamin; the Philistine camp was at Michmash. ¹⁷The Philistine soldiers went out on raids from their camp in three groups: one group went towards Ophrah in the territory of Shual, ¹⁸another went towards Beth Horon, and the other one went to the border overlooking the Valley of Zeboim and the wilderness.

19 There were no blacksmiths in Israel because the Philistines were determined to keep the Hebrews from making swords and spears. ²⁰(The Israelites had to go to the Philistines to get their ploughs, hoes, axes, and sickles *h* sharpened; ²¹the charge was one small coin for sharpening axes and for repairing ox-goads, *i* and two coins for sharpening ploughs or hoes.) ²²And so on the day of battle none of the Israelite soldiers except Saul and his son Jonathan had swords or spears.

23 The Philistines sent a group of soldiers to defend the pass of Michmash.

Jonathan's Daring Deed

14 One day Jonathan said to the young man who carried his weapons, "Let's go across to the Philistine camp." But Jonathan did not tell his father Saul, ²who was camping under a pomegranate-tree in Migron, not far from Gibeah; he had about six hundred men with him. ³(The priest carrying the ephod was Ahijah, the son of Ichabod's brother Ahitub, who was the son of Phinehas and grandson of Eli, the priest of the LORD in Shiloh.) The men did not know that Jonathan had left.

4 In the pass of Michmash, which Jonathan had to go through to get over to the Philistine camp, there were two large jagged rocks, one on each side of the pass: one was called Bozez and the other Seneh. ⁵One was on the north side of the pass, facing Michmash, and the other was on the south side, facing Geba.

6 Jonathan said to the young man, "Let's cross over to the camp of those heathen Philistines. Maybe the LORD will help us; if he does, nothing can keep him from giving us the victory, no matter how few of us there are."

7 The young man answered, "Whatever you want to do,ʲ I'm with you."

8 "All right," Jonathan said. "We will go across and let the Philistines see us. ⁹If they tell us to wait for them to come to us, then we will stay where we are. ¹⁰But if they tell us to go to them, then we will, because that will be the sign that the LORD has given us victory over them."

11 So they let the Philistines see them, and the Philistines said, "Look! Some Hebrews are coming out of the holes they have been hiding in!" ¹²Then they called out to Jonathan and the young man, "Come on up here! We have something to tellᵏ you!"

Jonathan said to the young man, "Follow me. The LORD has given Israel victory over them." ¹³Jonathan climbed up out of the pass on his hands and knees, and the young man followed him. Jonathan attacked the Philistines and knocked them down, and the young man killed them. ¹⁴In that first slaughter Jonathan and the young man killed about twenty men in an area of about a quarter of a hectare.ˡ ¹⁵All the Philistines in the countryside were terrified; the raiders and the soldiers in the camp trembled with fear; the earth shook, and there was great panic.

The Defeat of the Philistines

16 Saul's men on watch at Gibeah in the territory of Benjamin saw the Philistines running in confusion. ¹⁷So Saul said to his men, "Count the soldiers and find out who is missing." They did so and found that Jonathan and the young man who carried his weapons were missing. ¹⁸"Bring the ephodᵐ here," Saul said to Ahijah the priest. (On that day Ahijah was carrying it in front of the people of Israel.)ⁿ ¹⁹As Saul was speaking to the priest, the confusion in the Philistine camp got worse and worse, so Saul said to him, "There's no time to consult the LORD!" ²⁰Then he and his men marched into battle against the Philistines, who were fighting each other in complete confusion. ²¹Some Hebrews, who had been on the Philistine side and had gone with them to the camp, changed sides againᵒ and joined Saul and Jonathan. ²²Others, who had been hiding in the hills of Ephraim, heard that the

Philistines were running away, so they also joined in and attacked the Philistines, 23 fighting all the way beyond Bethaven. The LORD saved Israel that day.

Events after the Battle

24 The Israelites were weak with hunger that day, because Saul, with a solemn oath, had given the order: "A curse be on anyone who eats any food today before I take revenge on my enemies." So nobody had eaten anything all day. 25 They all *p* came into a wooded area and found honey everywhere. 26 The woods were full of honey, but no one ate any of it because they were all afraid of Saul's curse. 27 But Jonathan had not heard his father threaten the people with a curse; so he reached out with the stick he was carrying, dipped it in a honeycomb, and ate some honey. At once he felt much better. 28 But one of the men said, "We are all weak with hunger, but your father threatened us and said, 'A curse be on anyone who eats any food today.' "

29 Jonathan answered, "What a terrible thing my father has done to our people! See how much better I feel because I ate some honey! 30 How much better it would have been today if our people had eaten the food they took when they defeated the enemy. Just think how many more Philistines they would have killed!"

31 That day the Israelites defeated the Philistines, fighting all the way from Michmash to Aijalon. By this time the Israelites were very weak with hunger, 32 and so they rushed over to what they had captured from the enemy, took sheep and cattle, slaughtered them on the spot, and ate the meat with the blood still in it. 33 Saul was told, "Look, the people are sinning against the LORD by eating meat with the blood in it."

"You are traitors!" Saul cried out. "Roll a big stone over here *q* to me." 34 Then he gave another order: "Go among the people and tell them all to bring their cattle and sheep here. They are to slaughter them and eat them here; they must not sin against the LORD by eating meat with blood in it." So that night they

all brought their cattle and slaughtered them there. 35 Saul built an altar to the LORD, the first one that he built.

36 Saul said to his men, "Let's go down and attack the Philistines in the night, plunder them until dawn, and kill them all."

"Do whatever you think best," they answered.

But the priest said, "Let's consult God first."

37 So Saul asked God, "Shall I attack the Philistines? Will you give us victory?" But God did not answer that day. 38 Then Saul said to the leaders of the people, "Come here and find out what sin was committed today. 39 I promise by the living LORD, who gives Israel victory, that the guilty one will be put to death, even if he is my son Jonathan." But no one said anything. 40 Then Saul said to them, "All of you stand over there, and Jonathan and I will stand over here."

"Do whatever you think best," they answered.

41 Saul said to the LORD, the God of Israel, "LORD, why have you not answered me today? LORD, God of Israel, answer me by the sacred stones. If the guilt is Jonathan's or mine, answer by the Urim; but if it belongs to your people Israel, *r* answer by the Thummim." *s* The answer indicated Jonathan and Saul; and the people were cleared. 42 Then Saul said, "Decide between my son Jonathan and me." And Jonathan was indicated. 43 Then Saul asked Jonathan, "What have you done?"

Jonathan answered, "I ate a little honey with the stick I was holding. Here I am—I am ready to die."

44 Saul said to him, "May God strike me dead if you are not put to death!"

45 But the people said to Saul, "Will Jonathan, who won this great victory for Israel, be put to death? No! We promise by the living LORD that he will not lose even a hair from his head. What he did today was done with God's help." So the people saved Jonathan from being put to death.

46 After that, Saul stopped pursuing the Philistines, and they went back to their own territory.

---

p Probable text They all; *Hebrew* All the land.   *q One ancient translation* here; *Hebrew* today.
r Some ancient translations answer me by the sacred stones....your people Israel; *Hebrew does not have these words.*
s URIM...THUMMIM: Two stones used by the priest to determine God's will; it is not known precisely how they were used.
14.33: Gen 9.4; Lev 7.26-27, 17.10-14, 19.26; Deut 12.16,23, 15.23
14.41: Num 27.21; 1 Sam 28.6

Saul's Reign and Family

47 After Saul became king of Israel, he fought against all his enemies everywhere: the people of Moab, of Ammon, and of Edom, the kings of Zobah, and the Philistines. Wherever he fought he was victorious. [t] 48 He fought heroically and defeated even the people of Amalek. He saved the Israelites from all attacks.

49 Saul's sons were Jonathan, Ishvi, and Malchishua. His elder daughter was named Merab, and the younger one Michal. 50 His wife was Ahinoam, the daughter of Ahimaaz; his army commander was his cousin Abner, the son of his uncle Ner. 51 Saul's father Kish and Abner's father Ner were sons of Abiel.

52 As long as he lived, Saul had to fight fiercely against the Philistines. So whenever he found a man who was strong or brave, he would enlist him in his army.

War against the Amalekites

15 Samuel said to Saul, "I am the one whom the LORD sent to anoint as king of his people Israel. Now listen to what the LORD Almighty says. 2 He is going to punish the people of Amalek because their ancestors opposed the Israelites when they were coming from Egypt. 3 Go and attack the Amalekites and completely destroy everything they have. Don't leave a thing; kill all the men, women, children, and babies; the cattle, sheep, camels, and donkeys."

4 Saul called his forces together and inspected them at Telem: there were 200,000 soldiers from Israel and 10,000 from Judah. 5 Then he and his men went to the city of Amalek and waited in ambush in a dry river-bed. 6 He sent a warning to the Kenites, a people whose ancestors had been kind to the Israelites when they came from Egypt: "Go away and leave the Amalekites, so that I won't kill you along with them." So the Kenites left.

7 Saul defeated the Amalekites, fighting all the way from Havilah to Shur, east of Egypt; 8 he captured King Agag of Amalek alive and killed all the people. 9 But Saul and his men spared Agag's life and did not kill the best sheep and cattle, the best calves and lambs, [u] or anything else that was good; they destroyed only what was useless or worthless. [v]

Saul Is Rejected as King

10 The LORD said to Samuel, 11 "I am sorry that I made Saul king; he has turned away from me and disobeyed my commands." Samuel was angry, and all night long he pleaded with the LORD. 12 Early the following morning he went off to find Saul. He heard that Saul had gone to the town of Carmel, where he had built a monument to himself, and then had gone on to Gilgal. 13 Samuel went up to Saul, who greeted him, saying, "The LORD bless you, Samuel! I have obeyed the LORD's command."

14 Samuel asked, "Why, then, do I hear cattle mooing and sheep bleating?"

15 Saul answered, "My men took them from the Amalekites. They kept the best sheep and cattle to offer as a sacrifice to the LORD your God, and the rest we have destroyed completely." [w]

16 "Stop," Samuel ordered, "and I will tell you what the LORD said to me last night."

"Tell me," Saul said.

17 Samuel answered, "Even though you consider yourself of no importance, you are the leader of the tribes of Israel. The LORD anointed you king of Israel, 18 and he sent you out with orders to destroy those wicked people of Amalek. He told you to fight until you had killed them all. 19 Why, then, did you not obey him? Why did you rush to seize the loot, and so do what displeases the LORD?"

20 "I did obey the LORD," Saul replied. "I went out as he told me to, brought back King Agag, and killed all the Amalekites. 21 But my men did not kill the best sheep and cattle that they captured; instead, they brought them here to Gilgal to offer as a sacrifice to the LORD your God."

22 Samuel said, "Which does the LORD prefer: obedience or offerings and sacrifices? It is better to obey him than to sacrifice the best sheep to him. 23 Rebellion against him is as bad as witchcraft, and arrogance is as sinful as idolatry. Because you rejected the LORD's command, he has rejected you as king."

24 "Yes, I have sinned," Saul replied.

[t] *One ancient translation* was victorious; *Hebrew* acted wickedly.
[u] *One ancient translation* the best calves and lambs; *Hebrew unclear.*
[v] *Some ancient translations* useless or worthless; *Hebrew unclear.*
[w] DESTROYED COMPLETELY: *These animals had been unconditionally dedicated to the* LORD *and had to be destroyed (see* Lev 27.28).
15.1: 1 Sam 10.1   **15.2:** Ex 17.8–14; Deut 25.17–19

The LORD has torn the kingdom of Israel (15.28)

"I disobeyed the LORD's command and your instructions. I was afraid of my men and did what they wanted. 25 But now I beg you, forgive my sin and go back with me, so that I can worship the LORD."

26 "I will not go back with you," Samuel answered. "You rejected the LORD's command, and he has rejected you as king of Israel."

27 Then Samuel turned to leave, but Saul caught hold of his cloak, and it tore. 28 Samuel said to him, "The LORD has torn the kingdom of Israel away from you today and given it to someone who is a better man than you. 29 Israel's majestic God does not lie or change his mind. He is not a man—he does not change his mind."

30 "I have sinned," Saul replied. "But at least show me respect in front of the leaders of my people and all Israel. Go back with me so that I can worship the LORD your God." 31 So Samuel went back with him, and Saul worshipped the LORD.

32 "Bring King Agag here to me," Samuel ordered. Agag came to him, trembling with fear, thinking to himself, "What a bitter thing it is to die!"*x* 33 Samuel said, "As your sword has made many mothers childless, so now will your mother become childless." And he cut Agag to pieces in front of the altar in Gilgal.

34 Then Samuel went to Ramah, and King Saul went home to Gibeah. 35 As long as Samuel lived, he never again saw the king; but he grieved over him. The LORD was sorry that he had made Saul king of Israel.

David Is Anointed King

16 The LORD said to Samuel, "How long will you go on grieving over Saul? I have rejected him as king of Israel. But now get some olive-oil and go to Bethlehem, to a man named Jesse, because I have chosen one of his sons to be king."

2 "How can I do that?" Samuel asked. "If Saul hears about it, he will kill me!"

The LORD answered, "Take a calf with you and say that you are there to offer a sacrifice to the LORD. 3 Invite Jesse to the sacrifice, and I will tell you what to do. You will anoint as king the man I tell you to."

4 Samuel did what the LORD told him to do and went to Bethlehem, where the city leaders came trembling to meet him and asked, "Is this a peaceful visit, seer?"

5 "Yes," he answered. "I have come to offer a sacrifice to the LORD. Purify yourselves and come with me." He also told Jesse and his sons to purify themselves, and he invited them to the sacrifice.

6 When they arrived, Samuel saw Jesse's son Eliab and said to himself, "This man standing here in the LORD's presence is surely the one he has chosen." 7 But the LORD said to him, "Pay no attention

x trembling with fear...die; *or* confidently, thinking to himself, "Surely the bitter danger of death is past!"
15.27-28: 1 Sam 28.17; 1 Kgs 11.30-31

David would get his harp and play it (16.23)

to how tall and handsome he is. I have rejected him, because I do not judge as man judges. Man looks at the outward appearance, but I look at the heart."

8 Then Jesse called his son Abinadab and brought him to Samuel. But Samuel said, "No, the LORD hasn't chosen him either." 9 Jesse then brought Shammah. "No, the LORD hasn't chosen him either," Samuel said. 10 In this way Jesse brought seven of his sons to Samuel. And Samuel said to him, "No, the LORD hasn't chosen any of these." 11 Then he asked him, "Have you any more sons?"

Jesse answered, "There is still the youngest, but he is out taking care of the sheep."

"Tell him to come here," Samuel said. "We won't offer the sacrifice until he comes." 12 So Jesse sent for him. He was a handsome, healthy young man, and his eyes sparkled. The LORD said to Samuel, "This is the one—anoint him!" 13 Samuel took the olive-oil and anointed David in front of his brothers. Immediately the spirit of the LORD took control of David and was with him from that day on. Then Samuel returned to Ramah.

David in Saul's Court

14 The LORD's spirit left Saul, and an evil spirit sent by the LORD tormented him. 15 His servants said to him, "We know that an evil spirit sent by God is tormenting you. 16 So give us the order, sir, and we will look for a man who knows how to play the harp. Then when the evil spirit comes on you, the man can play his harp, and you will be all right again."

17 Saul ordered them, "Find me a man who plays well and bring him to me."

18 One of his attendants said, "Jesse, of the town of Bethlehem, has a son who is a good musician. He is also a brave and handsome man, a good soldier, and an able speaker. The LORD is with him."

19 So Saul sent messengers to Jesse to say, "Send me your son David, the one who takes care of the sheep." 20 Jesse sent David to Saul with a young goat, a donkey loaded with bread, and a leather bag full of wine. 21 David came to Saul and entered his service. Saul liked him very much and chose him as the man to carry his weapons. 22 Then Saul sent a message to Jesse: "I like David. Let him stay here in my service." 23 From then on, whenever the evil spirit sent by God came on Saul, David would get his harp and play it. The evil spirit would leave, and Saul would feel better and be all right again.

Goliath Challenges the Israelites

17 The Philistines gathered for battle in Socoh, a town in Judah; they camped at a place called Ephes Dammim, between Socoh and Azekah. 2 Saul and the Israelites assembled and camped in the Valley of Elah, where they got ready to fight the Philistines. 3 The Philistines lined up on one hill and the Israelites on another, with a valley between them.

4 A man named Goliath, from the city of Gath, came out from the Philistine camp to challenge the Israelites. He was nearly three metres[y] tall 5 and wore

[y] *Hebrew* nearly three metres; *one ancient Hebrew manuscript and one ancient translation* about two metres.

I dare you to pick someone to fight me!
(17.10)

bronze armour that weighed about fifty-seven kilogrammes and a bronze helmet. [6]His legs were also protected by bronze armour, and he carried a bronze javelin slung over his shoulder. [7]His spear was as thick as the bar on a weaver's loom, and its iron head weighed about seven kilogrammes. A soldier walked in front of him carrying his shield. [8]Goliath stood and shouted at the Israelites, "What are you doing there, lined up for battle? I am a Philistine, you slaves of Saul! Choose one of your men to fight me. [9]If he wins and kills me, we will be your slaves; but if I win and kill him, you will be our slaves. [10]Here and now I challenge the Israelite army. I dare you to pick someone to fight me!" [11]When Saul and his men heard this, they were terrified.

David in Saul's Camp

12 David was the son of Jesse, who was an Ephrathite from Bethlehem in Judah. Jesse had eight sons, and at the time Saul was king, he was already a very old man. [z] [13]His three eldest sons had gone with Saul to war. The eldest was Eliab, the next was Abinadab, and the third was Shammah. [14]David was the youngest son, and while the three eldest brothers stayed with Saul, [15]David would go back to Bethlehem from time to time, to take care of his father's sheep.

16 Goliath challenged the Israelites every morning and evening for forty days. 17 One day Jesse said to David, "Take ten kilogrammes of this roasted grain and these ten loaves of bread, and hurry with them to your brothers in the camp. [18]And take these ten cheeses to the commanding officer. Find out how your brothers are getting on and bring back something to show that you saw them and that they are well. [19]King Saul, your brothers, and all the other Israelites are in the Valley of Elah fighting the Philistines."

20 David got up early the next morning, left someone else in charge of the sheep, took the food, and went as Jesse had told him to. He arrived at the camp just as the Israelites were going out to their battle line, shouting the war-cry. [21]The Philistine and the Israelite armies took up positions for battle, facing each other. [22]David left the food with the officer in charge of the supplies, ran to the battle line, went to his brothers, and asked how they were getting on. [23]As he was talking to them, Goliath came forward and challenged the Israelites as he had done before. And

---

[z] *Some ancient translations* a very old man; *Hebrew unclear.*

David heard him. 24 When the Israelites saw Goliath, they ran away in terror. 25 "Look at him!" they said to each other. "Listen to his challenge! King Saul has promised to give a big reward to the man who kills him; the king will also give him his daughter to marry and will not require his father's family to pay taxes." a

26 David asked the men who were near him, "What will the man get who kills this Philistine and frees Israel from this disgrace? After all, who is this heathen Philistine to defy the army of the living God?" 27 They told him what would be done for the man who killed Goliath.

28 Eliab, David's eldest brother, heard David talking to the men. He was angry with David and said, "What are you doing here? Who is taking care of those sheep of yours out there in the wilderness? You cheeky brat, you! You just came to watch the fighting!"

29 "Now what have I done?" David asked. "Can't I even ask a question?" 30 He turned to another man and asked him the same question, and every time he asked, he got the same answer.

31 Some men heard what David had said, and they told Saul, who sent for him. 32 David said to Saul, "Your Majesty, no one should be afraid of this Philistine! I will go and fight him."

33 "No," answered Saul. "How could you fight him? You're just a boy, and he has been a soldier all his life!"

34 "Your Majesty," David said, "I take care of my father's sheep. Whenever a lion or a bear carries off a lamb, 35 I go after it, attack it, and rescue the lamb. And if the lion or bear turns on me, I grab it by the throat and beat it to death. 36 I have killed lions and bears, and I will do the same to this heathen Philistine, who has defied the army of the living God. 37 The LORD has saved me from lions and bears; he will save me from this Philistine."

"All right," Saul answered. "Go, and the LORD be with you." 38 He gave his own armour to David for him to wear: a bronze helmet, which he put on David's head, and a coat of armour. 39 David strapped Saul's sword over the armour and tried to walk, but he couldn't, because he wasn't used to wearing them. "I can't fight with all this," he said to Saul. "I'm not used to it." So he took it all off. 40 He took his shepherd's stick and then picked up five smooth stones from the stream and put them in his bag. With his catapult ready, he went out to meet Goliath.

David Defeats Goliath

41 The Philistine started walking towards David, with his shield-bearer walking in front of him. He kept coming closer, 42 and when he got a good look at David, he was filled with scorn for him because he was just a nice, good-looking boy. 43 He said to David, "What's that stick for? Do you think I'm a dog?" And he called down curses from his god on David. 44 "Come on," he challenged David, "and I will give your body to the birds and animals to eat."

45 David answered, "You are coming against me with sword, spear, and javelin, but I come against you in the name of the LORD Almighty, the God of the Israelite armies, which you have defied. 46 This very day the LORD will put you in my power; I will defeat you and cut off your head. And I will give the bodies of the Philistine soldiers to the birds and animals to eat. Then the whole world will know that Israel has a God, 47 and everyone here will see that the LORD does not need swords or spears to save his people. He is victorious in battle, and he will put all of you in our power."

48 Goliath started walking towards David again, and David ran quickly towards the Philistine battle line to fight him. 49 He put his hand into his bag and took out a stone, which he slung at Goliath. It hit him on the forehead and broke his skull, and Goliath fell face downwards on the ground. 50 And so, without a sword, David defeated and killed Goliath with a catapult and a stone! 51 He ran to him, stood over him, took Goliath's sword out of its sheath, and cut off his head and killed him.

When the Philistines saw that their hero was dead, they ran away. 52 The men of Israel and Judah shouted and ran after them, pursuing them all the way to Gath b and to the gates of Ekron. The Philistines fell wounded all along the road that leads to Shaaraim, as far as Gath and Ekron. 53 When the Israelites came back from pursuing the Philistines, they looted their camp. 54 David picked up Goliath's head and took it to Jerusalem, but he kept

---

a to pay taxes; or either to pay taxes or serve him.
b One ancient translation Gath; Hebrew a valley.
17.50: 2 Sam 21.19   **17.51:** 1 Sam 21.29

David defeated and killed Goliath (17.50)

Goliath's weapons in his own tent.

David Is Presented to Saul

55 When Saul saw David going out to fight Goliath, he asked Abner, the commander of his army, "Abner, whose son is he?"

"I have no idea, Your Majesty," Abner answered.

56 "Then go and find out," Saul ordered.

57 So when David returned to camp after killing Goliath, Abner took him to Saul. David was still carrying Goliath's head. 58 Saul asked him, "Young man, whose son are you?"

"I am the son of your servant Jesse from Bethlehem," David answered.

18 Saul and David finished their conversation. After that, Saul's son Jonathan was deeply attracted to David and came to love him as much as he loved himself. 2 Saul kept David with him from that day on and did not let him go back home. 3 Jonathan swore eternal friendship with David because of his deep affection for him. 4 He took off the robe he was wearing and gave it to David, together with his armour and also his sword, bow, and belt. 5 David was successful in all the missions on which Saul sent him, and so Saul made him an officer in his army. This pleased all of Saul's officers and men.

18.7: 1 Sam 21.11, 29.5

Saul Becomes Jealous of David

6 As David was returning after killing Goliath and as the soldiers were coming back home, women from every town in Israel came out to meet King Saul. They were singing joyful songs, dancing, and playing tambourines and lyres. 7 In their celebration the women sang, "Saul has killed thousands, but David tens of thousands." 8 Saul did not like this, and he became very angry. He said, "For David they claim tens of thousands, but only thousands for me. They will be making him king next!" 9 And so he was jealous and suspicious of David from that day on.

10 The next day an evil spirit from God suddenly took control of Saul, and he raved in his house like a madman. David was playing the harp, as he did every day, and Saul was holding a spear. 11 "I'll pin him to the wall," Saul said to himself, and he threw the spear at him twice; but David dodged each time.

12 Saul was afraid of David because the LORD was with David but had abandoned him. 13 So Saul sent him away and put him in command of a thousand men. David led his men in battle 14 and was successful in all he did, because the LORD was with him. 15 Saul noticed David's success and became even more afraid of

I'll pin him to the wall (18.11)

him. [16] But everyone in Israel and Judah loved David because he was such a successful leader.

David Marries Saul's Daughter

17 Then Saul said to David, "Here is my elder daughter Merab. I will give her to you as your wife on condition that you serve me as a brave and loyal soldier, and fight the LORD's battles." (Saul was thinking that in this way the Philistines would kill David, and he would not have to do it himself.)

18 David answered, "Who am I and what is my family that I should become the king's son-in-law?" [19] But when the time came for Merab to be given to David, she was given instead to a man named Adriel from Meholah.

20 Saul's daughter Michal, however, fell in love with David, and when Saul heard of this, he was pleased. [21] He said to himself, "I'll give Michal to David; I will use her to trap him, and he will be killed by the Philistines." So for the second time Saul said to David, "You will be my son-in-law." [22] He ordered his officials to speak privately to David and tell him, "The king is pleased with you and all his officials like you; now is a good time for you to marry his daughter."

23 So they told David this, and he answered, "It's a great honour to become the king's son-in-law, too great for someone poor and insignificant like me."

24 The officials told Saul what David had said, [25] and Saul ordered them to tell David: "All the king wants from you as payment for the bride is the foreskins of a hundred dead Philistines, as revenge on his enemies." (This was how Saul planned

to have David killed by the Philistines.) [26] Saul's officials reported to David what Saul had said, and David was delighted with the thought of becoming the king's son-in-law. Before the day set for the wedding, [27] David and his men went and killed two hundred Philistines. He took their foreskins to the king and counted them all out to him, so that he might become his son-in-law. So Saul had to give his daughter Michal in marriage to David.

28 Saul realized clearly that the LORD was with David and also that his daughter Michal loved him. [29] So he became even more afraid of David and was his enemy as long as he lived.

30 The Philistine armies would come and fight, but in every battle David was more successful than any of Saul's other officers. As a result David became very famous.

David Is Persecuted by Saul

19 Saul told his son Jonathan and all his officials that he planned to kill[c] David. But Jonathan was very fond of David, [2] and so he said to him, "My father is trying to kill you. Please be careful tomorrow morning; hide in some secret place and stay there. [3] I will go and stand by my father in the field where you are hiding, and I will speak to him about you. If I find out anything, I will let you know."

4 Jonathan praised David to Saul and said, "Sir, don't do wrong to your servant David. He has never done you any wrong; on the contrary, everything he has done has been a great help to you. [5] He risked his life when he killed Goliath, and the LORD won a great victory for Israel. When

[c] that he planned to kill; *or* to kill.

you saw it, you were glad. Why, then, do you now want to do wrong to an innocent man and kill David for no reason at all?''

6 Saul was convinced by what Jonathan said and made a vow in the LORD's name that he would not kill David. 7 So Jonathan called David and told him everything; then he took him to Saul, and David served the king as he had before.

8 War with the Philistines broke out again. David attacked them and defeated them so thoroughly that they fled.

9 One day an evil spirit from the LORD took control of Saul. He was sitting in his house with his spear in his hand, and David was there, playing his harp. 10 Saul tried to pin David to the wall with his spear, but David dodged, and the spear stuck in the wall. David ran away and escaped.

11 That same night Saul sent some men to watch David's house and kill him the next morning. Michal, David's wife, warned him, "If you don't get away tonight, tomorrow you will be dead.'' 12 She let him down from a window, and he ran away and escaped. 13 Then she took the household idol, laid it on the bed, put a pillow made of goats'-hair at its head, and put a cover over it. 14 When Saul's men came to get David, Michal told them that he was ill. 15 But Saul sent them back to see David for themselves. He ordered them, "Carry him here in his bed, and I will kill him.'' 16 They went inside and found the household idol in the bed and the goats'-hair pillow at its head. 17 Saul asked Michal, "Why have you tricked me like this and let my enemy escape?''

She answered, "He said he would kill me if I didn't help him to escape.''

18 David escaped and went to Samuel in Ramah and told him everything that Saul had done to him. Then he and Samuel went to Naioth and stayed there. 19 Saul was told that David was in Naioth in Ramah, 20 so he sent some men to arrest him. They saw *d* the group of prophets dancing and shouting, with Samuel as their leader. Then the spirit of God took control of Saul's men, and they also began to dance and shout. 21 When Saul heard of this, he sent more messengers, and they also began to dance and shout. He sent messengers the third time, and the same thing happened to them. 22 Then he him-

self started out for Ramah. When he came to the large well in Secu, he asked where Samuel and David were and was told that they were at Naioth. 23 As he was going there, the spirit of God took control of him also, and he danced and shouted all the way to Naioth. 24 He took off his clothes and danced and shouted in Samuel's presence, and lay naked all that day and all that night. (This is how the saying originated, "Has even Saul become a prophet?'')

Jonathan Helps David

20 Then David fled from Naioth in Ramah and went to Jonathan. "What have I done?'' he asked. "What crime have I committed? What wrong have I done to your father to make him want to kill me?''

2 Jonathan answered, "God forbid that you should die! My father tells me everything he does, important or not, and he would not hide this from me. It isn't true!''

3 But David answered, *e* "Your father knows very well how much you like me, and he has decided not to let you know what he plans to do, because you would be deeply hurt. I swear to you by the living LORD that I am only a step away from death!''

4 Jonathan said, "I'll do anything you want.''

5 "Tomorrow is the New Moon Festival,'' David replied, "and I am supposed to eat with the king. But if it's all right with you, I will go and hide in the fields until the evening of the day after tomorrow. 6 If your father notices that I am not at table, tell him that I begged your permission to hurry home to Bethlehem, since it's the time for the annual sacrifice there for my whole family. 7 If he says, 'All right,' I will be safe; but if he becomes angry, you will know that he is determined to harm me. 8 Please do me this favour, and keep the sacred promise you made to me. But if I'm guilty, kill me yourself! Why take me to your father to be killed?''

9 "Don't even think such a thing!'' Jonathan answered. "If I knew for certain that my father was determined to harm you, wouldn't I tell you?''

d Some ancient translations They saw; *Hebrew* He saw.
e One ancient translation answered; *Hebrew* made a vow again.
19.11: Ps 59 (Title)   **19.24:** 1 Sam 10.11–12   **20.5:** Num 28.11

10 David then asked, "Who will let me know if your father answers you angrily?"

11 "Let's go out to the fields," Jonathan answered. So they went, 12 and Jonathan said to David, "May the LORD God of Israel be our witness!*f* At this time tomorrow and on the following day I will question my father. If his attitude towards you is good, I will send you word. 13 If he intends to harm you, may the LORD strike me dead if I don't let you know about it and get you safely away. May the LORD be with you as he was with my father! 14 And if I remain alive, please keep your sacred promise and be loyal to me; but if I die,*g* 15 show the same kind of loyalty to my family for ever. And when the LORD has completely destroyed all your enemies, 16 may our promise to each other still be unbroken. If it is broken, the LORD will punish you."*h*

17 Once again Jonathan made David promise to love him, for Jonathan loved David as much as he loved himself. 18 Then Jonathan said to him, "Since tomorrow is the New Moon Festival, your absence will be noticed if you aren't at the meal. 19 The day after tomorrow your absence will be noticed*i* even more; so go to the place where you hid the other time, and hide behind the pile of stones there.*j* 20 I will then shoot three arrows at it, as though it were a target. 21 Then I will tell my servant to go and find them. And if I tell him, 'Look, the arrows are on this side of you; get them,' that means that you are safe and can come out. I swear by the living LORD that you will be in no danger. 22 But if I tell him, 'The arrows are on the other side of you,' then leave, because the LORD is sending you away. 23 As for the promise we have made to each other, the LORD will make sure that we will keep it for ever."

24 So David hid in the fields. At the New Moon Festival, King Saul came to the meal 25 and sat in his usual place by the wall. Abner sat next to him, and Jonathan sat opposite him.*k* David's place was empty, 26 but Saul said nothing that day, because he thought, "Something has happened to him, and he is not ritually pure." 27 On the following day, the day after the New Moon Festival, David's place was still empty, and Saul asked Jonathan, "Why didn't David come to the meal either yesterday or today?"

28 Jonathan answered, "He begged me to let him go to Bethlehem. 29 'Please let me go,' he said, 'because our family is celebrating the sacrificial feast in town, and my brother ordered me to be there. So then, if you are my friend, let me go and see my relatives.' That is why he isn't in his place at your table."

30 Saul was furious with Jonathan and said to him, "How rebellious and faithless your mother was! Now I know you are taking sides with David and are disgracing yourself and that mother of yours! 31 Don't you realize that as long as David is alive, you will never be king of this country? Now go and bring him here—he must die!"

32 "Why should he die?" Jonathan replied. "What has he done?"

33 At that, Saul threw his spear at Jonathan to kill him, and Jonathan realized that his father was really determined to kill David. 34 Jonathan got up from the table in a rage and ate nothing that day—the second day of the New Moon Festival. He was deeply distressed about David, because Saul had insulted him. 35 The following morning Jonathan went to the fields to meet David, as they had agreed. He took a young boy with him 36 and said to him, "Run and find the arrows I'm going to shoot." The boy ran, and Jonathan shot an arrow beyond him. 37 When the boy reached the place where the arrow had fallen, Jonathan shouted to him, "The arrow is further on! 38 Don't just stand there! Hurry up!" The boy picked up the arrow and returned to his master, 39 not knowing what it all meant; only Jonathan and David knew. 40 Jonathan gave his weapons to the boy and told him to take them back to the town.

41 After the boy had left, David got up from behind the pile of stones,*l* fell on his knees and bowed with his face to the ground three times. Both he and Jonathan were crying as they kissed each other; David's grief was even greater than Jonathan's.*m* 42 Then Jonathan said to

---

f One ancient translation be our witness; *Hebrew does not have these words.*
g Some ancient translations if I die; *Hebrew that I may not die.*
h Verses 15-16 in Hebrew are unclear.
i Some ancient translations your absence will be noticed; *Hebrew* go down.
j Probable text the pile of stones there; *Hebrew* the Ezel Stone.
k One ancient translation sat opposite him; *Hebrew* stood up.
l Probable text the pile of stones; *Hebrew* the south.
m Probable text David's grief was even greater than Jonathan's; *Hebrew unclear.*
20.15: 2 Sam 9.1

God be with you (20.42)

David, "God be with you. The LORD will make sure that you and I, and your descendants and mine, will for ever keep the sacred promise we have made to each other." Then David left, and Jonathan went back to the town.

David Flees from Saul

21 David went to the priest Ahimelech in Nob. Ahimelech came out trembling to meet him and asked, "Why did you come here all by yourself?"

2 "I am here on the king's business," David answered. "He told me not to let anyone know what he sent me to do. As for my men, I have told them to meet me at a certain place. 3 Now, then, what supplies have you got? Give me five loaves of bread or anything else you have."

4 The priest said, "I haven't any ordinary bread, only sacred bread; you can have it if your men haven't had sexual relations recently."

5 "Of course they haven't," answered David. "My men always keep themselves ritually pure even when we go out on an ordinary mission; how much more this time when we are on a special mission!"

6 So the priest gave David the sacred bread, because the only bread he had was the loaves offered to God, which had been removed from the sacred table and replaced by fresh bread.

7 (Saul's chief herdsman, Doeg, who was from Edom, happened to be there that day, because he had to fulfil a religious obligation.)

8 David said to Ahimelech, "Have you got a spear or a sword you can give me? The king's orders made me leave in such a hurry that I didn't have time to get my sword or any other weapon."

9 Ahimelech answered, "I have the sword of Goliath the Philistine, whom you killed in the Valley of Elah; it is behind the ephod, wrapped in a cloth. If you want it, take it—it's the only weapon here."

"Give it to me," David said. "There is not a better sword anywhere!"

10 So David left, fleeing from Saul, and went to King Achish of Gath. 11 The king's officials said to Achish, "Isn't this David, the king of his country? This is the man about whom the women sang, as they danced, 'Saul has killed thousands, but David has killed tens of thousands.'"

12 Their words made a deep impression on David, and he became very much afraid of King Achish. 13 So whenever they were around, David pretended to be insane and acted like a madman when they tried to restrain him; he would scribble on the city[n] gates and dribble down his beard. 14 So Achish said to his officials, "Look! The man is mad! Why did you bring him to me? 15 Haven't I got enough madmen already? Why bring another one to annoy me with his daft actions right here in my own house?"

[n] city; *or* palace.
21.1–6: Mt 12.3–4; Mk 2.25–26; Lk 6.3   **21.6:** Lev 24.5–9   **21.9:** 1 Sam 17.51
21.11: 1 Sam 18.7, 29.5   **21.12:** Ps 56 (Title)   **21.13:** Ps 34 (Title)

The Slaughter of the Priests

22 David fled from the city of Gath and went to a cave near the town of Adullam. When his brothers and the rest of the family heard that he was there, they joined him. ²People who were oppressed or in debt or dissatisfied went to him, about four hundred men in all, and he became their leader.

3 David went on from there to Mizpah in Moab and said to the king of Moab, "Please let my father and mother come and stay with you until I find out what God is going to do for me." ⁴So David left his parents with the king of Moab, and they stayed there as long as David was hiding in the cave.

5 Then the prophet Gad came to David and said, "Don't stay here; go at once to the land of Judah." So David left and went to the forest of Hereth.

6 One day Saul was in Gibeah, sitting under a tamarisk-tree on a hill, with his spear in his hand, and all his officers were standing round him. He was told that David and his men had been found, ⁷and he said to his officers, "Listen, men of Benjamin! Do you think that David will give fields and vineyards to all of you, and make you officers in his army? ⁸Is that why you are plotting against me? Not one of you told me that my own son had made an alliance with David. No one is concerned about me or tells me that David, one of my own men, is at this moment looking for a chance to kill me, and that my son has encouraged him!"

9 Doeg was standing there with Saul's officers, and he said, "I saw David when he went to Ahimelech son of Ahitub in Nob. ¹⁰Ahimelech asked the LORD what David should do, and then he gave David some food and the sword of Goliath the Philistine."

11 So King Saul sent for the priest Ahimelech and all his relatives, who were also priests in Nob, and they came to him. ¹²Saul said to Ahimelech, "Listen, Ahimelech!"

"At your service, sir," he answered.

13 Saul asked him, "Why are you and David plotting against me? Why did you give him some food and a sword, and consult God for him? Now he has turned against me and is waiting for a chance to kill me!"

14 Ahimelech answered, "David is the most faithful officer you have! He is your own son-in-law, captain of⁰ your bodyguard, and highly respected by everyone in the royal court. ¹⁵Yes, I consulted God for him, and it wasn't the first time.ᵖ As for plotting against you, Your Majesty must not accuse me or anyone else in my family. I don't know anything about this matter!"

16 The king said, "Ahimelech, you and all your relatives must die." ¹⁷Then he said to the guards standing near him, "Kill the LORD's priests! They conspired with David and did not tell me that he had run away, even though they knew it all along." But the guards refused to lift a hand to kill the LORD's priests. ¹⁸So Saul said to Doeg, "You kill them!"—and Doeg killed them all. On that day he killed eighty-five priests who were qualified to carry the ephod. ¹⁹Saul also ordered all the other inhabitants of Nob, the city of priests, to be put to death: men and women, children and babies, cattle, donkeys, and sheep—they were all killed.

20 But Abiathar, one of Ahimelech's sons, escaped, and went and joined David. ²¹He told him how Saul had slaughtered the priests of the LORD. ²²David said to him, "When I saw Doeg there that day, I knew that he would be sure to tell Saul. So I am responsibleʳ for the death of all your relatives. ²³Stay with me and don't be afraid. Saul wants to kill both you and me, but you will be safe with me."

David Saves the Town of Keilah

23 David heard that the Philistines were attacking the town of Keilah and were stealing the newly-harvested corn. ²So he asked the LORD, "Shall I go and attack the Philistines?"

"Yes," the LORD answered. "Attack them and save Keilah."

3 But David's men said to him, "We have enough to be afraid of here in Judah; it will be much worse if we go to Keilah and attack the Philistine forces!" ⁴So David consulted the LORD again, and the LORD said to him, "Go and attack Keilah, because I will give you victory over the Philistines." ⁵So David and his men went to Keilah and attacked the Philistines;

⁰Some ancient translations captain of; Hebrew he turned to.
ᵖYes, I consulted...time; or Now, have I done something wrong today by consulting God for him? Not at all!   ʳSome ancient translations I am responsible; Hebrew I have turned.
22.1: Ps 57 (Title); Ps 142 (Title)   **22.9-10:** 1 Sam 21.7-9; Ps 52 (Title)

they killed many of them and took their livestock. And that was how David saved the town.

6 When Abiathar son of Ahimelech escaped and joined David in Keilah, he took the ephod with him.

7 Saul was told that David had gone to Keilah, and he said, "God has put him in my power. David has trapped himself by going into a walled town with fortified gates." 8 So Saul called his troops to war, to march against Keilah and besiege David and his men.

9 When David heard that Saul was planning to attack him, he said to the priest Abiathar, "Bring the ephod here." 10 Then David said, "LORD, God of Israel, I have heard that Saul is planning to come to Keilah and destroy it on account of me, your servant. 11 Will the citizens of Keilah hand me over to Saul? Will Saul really come, as I have heard? LORD, God of Israel, I beg you to answer me!"

The LORD answered, "Saul will come."

12 "And will the citizens of Keilah hand my men and me over to Saul?" David asked again.

"They will," the LORD answered.

13 So David and his men—about six hundred in all—left Keilah at once and kept on the move. When Saul heard that David had escaped from Keilah, he gave up his plan.

David in the Hill-Country

14 David stayed in hiding in the hill-country, in the wilderness near Ziph. Saul was always trying to find him, but God did not hand David over to him. 15 David saw that Saul was out to kill him.

David was at Horesh, in the wilderness near Ziph. 16 Jonathan went to him there and encouraged him with assurances of God's protection, 17 saying to him, "Don't be afraid. My father Saul won't be able to harm you. He knows very well that you are the one who will be the king of Israel and that I will be next in rank to you." 18 The two of them made a sacred promise of friendship to each other. David stayed at Horesh, and Jonathan went home.

19 Some people from Ziph went to Saul at Gibeah and said, "David is hiding in our territory at Horesh on Mount Hachilah, in the southern part of the Judaean wilderness. 20 We know, Your Majesty, how much you want to capture him; so come to our territory, and we will make sure that you catch him."

21 Saul answered, "May the LORD bless you for being so kind to me! 22 Go and make sure once more; find out for certain where he is and who has seen him there. I hear that he is very cunning. 23 Find out exactly the places where he hides, and be sure to bring back a report to me straight away. Then I will go with you, and if he is still in the region, I will hunt him down, even if I have to search the whole land of Judah."

24 So they left and returned to Ziph ahead of Saul. David and his men were in the wilderness of Maon, in a desolate valley in the southern part of the Judaean wilderness. 25 Saul and his men set out to look for David, but he heard about it and went to a rocky hill in the wilderness of Maon and stayed there. When Saul heard about this, he went after David. 26 Saul and his men were on one side of the hill, separated from David and his men, who were on the other side. They were hurrying to get away from Saul and his men, who were closing in on them and were about to capture them. 27 Just then a messenger arrived and said to Saul, "Come back at once! The Philistines are invading the country!" 28 So Saul stopped pursuing David and went to fight the Philistines. That is why that place is called Separation Hill. 29 David left and went to the region of Engedi, where he stayed in hiding.

David Spares Saul's Life

24 When Saul came back from fighting the Philistines, he was told that David was in the wilderness near Engedi. 2 Saul took three thousand of the best soldiers in Israel and went looking for David and his men east of Wild Goat Rocks. 3 He came to a cave close to some sheep pens by the road and went in to relieve himself. It happened to be the very cave in which David and his men were hiding far back in the cave. 4 They said to him, "This is your chance! The LORD has told you that he would put your enemy in your power and you could do to him whatever you wanted to." David crept over and cut off a piece of Saul's robe without Saul's knowing it. 5 But then David's conscience began to trouble him, 6 and he said to his men, "May the LORD keep me from doing any harm to my

David...cut off a piece of Saul's robe (24.4)

master, whom the LORD chose as king! I must not harm him in the least, because he is the king chosen by the LORD!'' ⁷ So David convinced his men that they should not attack Saul.

Saul got up, left the cave, and started on his way. ⁸ Then David went out after him and called to him, "Your Majesty!" Saul turned round, and David bowed down to the ground in respect ⁹ and said, "Why do you listen to people who say that I am trying to harm you? ¹⁰ You can see for yourself that just now in the cave the LORD put you in my power. Some of my men told me to kill you, but I felt sorry for you and said that I would not harm you in the least, because you are the one whom the LORD chose to be king. ¹¹ Look, my father, look at the piece of your robe I am holding! I could have killed you, but instead I only cut this off. This should convince you that I have no thought of rebelling against you or of harming you. You are hunting me down to kill me, even though I have not done you any wrong. ¹² May the LORD judge which one of us is wrong! May he punish you for your action against me, for I will not harm you in the least. ¹³ You know the old saying, 'Evil is done only by evil men.' And so I will not harm you. ¹⁴ Look at what the king of Israel is trying to kill! Look at what he is chasing! A dead

dog, a flea! ¹⁵ The LORD will judge, and he will decide which one of us is wrong. May he look into the matter, defend me, and save me from you."

16 When David had finished speaking, Saul said, "Is that really you, David my son?" And he started crying. ¹⁷ Then he said to David, "You are right, and I am wrong. You have been so good to me, while I have done such wrong to you! ¹⁸ Today you have shown how good you are to me, because you did not kill me, even though the LORD put me in your power. ¹⁹ How often does a man catch his enemy and then let him get away unharmed? The LORD bless you for what you have done to me today! ²⁰ Now I am sure that you will be king of Israel and that the kingdom will continue under your rule. ²¹ But promise me in the LORD's name that you will spare my descendants, so that my name and my family's name will not be completely forgotten." ²² David promised that he would.

Then Saul went back home, and David and his men went back to their hiding place.

The Death of Samuel

25 Samuel died, and all the Israelites came together and mourned for him. Then they buried him at his home in Ramah.

24.14: 1 Sam 26.20

David and Abigail

After this, David went to the wilderness of Paran. ²⁻³ There was a man of the clan of Caleb named Nabal, who was from the town of Maon, and who owned land near the town of Carmel. He was a very rich man, the owner of three thousand sheep and one thousand goats. His wife Abigail was beautiful and intelligent, but he was a mean, bad-tempered man.

Nabal was shearing his sheep in Carmel, ⁴ and David, who was in the wilderness, heard about it, ⁵ so he sent ten young men with orders to go to Carmel, find Nabal, and give him his greetings. ⁶ He instructed them to say to Nabal: "David sends you greetings, my friend, with his best wishes for you, your family, and all that is yours. ⁷ He heard that you were shearing your sheep, and he wants you to know that your shepherds have been with us and we did not harm them. Nothing that belonged to them was stolen all the time they were at Carmel. ⁸ Just ask them, and they will tell you. We have come on a feast day, and David asks you to receive us kindly. Please give what you can to us your servants and to your dear friend David."

9 David's men delivered this message to Nabal in David's name. Then they waited there, ¹⁰ and Nabal finally answered, "David? Who is he? I've never heard of him! The country is full of runaway slaves nowadays! ¹¹ I'm not going to take my bread and water, and the animals I have slaughtered for my shearers, and give them to men who come from I don't know where!"

12 David's men went back to him and told him what Nabal had said. ¹³ "Buckle on your swords!" he ordered, and they all did. David also buckled on his sword and left with about four hundred of his men, leaving two hundred behind with the supplies.

14 One of Nabal's servants said to Nabal's wife Abigail, "Have you heard? David sent some messengers from the wilderness with greetings for our master, but he insulted them. ¹⁵ Yet they were very good to us; they never bothered us, and all the time we were with them in the fields, nothing that belonged to us was stolen. ¹⁶ They protected us day and night the whole time we were with them looking after our flocks. ¹⁷ Please think this over and decide what to do. This could be disastrous for our master and all his family. He is so pigheaded that he won't listen to anybody!"

18 Abigail quickly collected two hundred loaves of bread, two leather bags full of wine, five roasted sheep, seventeen kilogrammes of roasted grain, a hundred bunches of raisins, and two hundred cakes of dried figs, and loaded them on donkeys. ¹⁹ Then she said to the servants, "You go on ahead and I will follow you." But she said nothing to her husband.

20 She was riding her donkey round a bend on a hillside when suddenly she met David and his men coming towards her. ²¹ David had been thinking, "Why did I ever protect that fellow's property out here in the wilderness? Not a thing that belonged to him was stolen, and this is how he pays me back for the help I gave him! ²² May God strike me ˢ dead if I don't kill every last one of those men before morning!"

23 When Abigail saw David, she quickly dismounted and threw herself on the ground ²⁴ at David's feet, and said to him, "Please, sir, listen to me! Let me take the blame. ²⁵ Please, don't pay any attention to Nabal, that good-for-nothing! He is exactly what his name means—a fool! ᵗ I wasn't there when your servants arrived, sir. ²⁶ It is the LORD who has kept you from taking revenge and killing your enemies. And now I swear to you by the living LORD that your enemies and all who want to harm you will be punished like Nabal. ²⁷ Please, sir, accept this present I have brought you, and give it to your men. ²⁸ Please forgive me, sir, for any wrong I have done. The LORD will make you king, and your descendants also, because you are fighting his battles; and you will not do anything evil ᵘ as long as you live. ²⁹ If anyone should attack you and try to kill you, the LORD your God will keep you safe, as a man guards a precious treasure. As for your enemies, however, he will throw them away, as a man hurls stones with his catapult. ³⁰ And when the LORD has done all the good things he has promised you and has made you king of Israel, ³¹ then you will not have to feel regret or remorse, sir, for having killed without cause or for having taken your own revenge. And

ˢ One ancient translation me; Hebrew my enemies.
ᵗ A FOOL: This is the meaning of the Hebrew name Nabal.
ᵘ you will not do anything evil; or no evil will happen to you.

When Abigail saw David (25.23)

when the LORD has blessed you, sir, please do not forget me."

32 David said to her, "Praise the LORD, the God of Israel, who sent you today to meet me! 33 Thank God for your good sense and for what you have done today in keeping me from the crime of murder and from taking my own revenge. 34 The LORD has kept me from harming you. But I swear by the living God of Israel that if you had not hurried to meet me, all of Nabal's men would have been dead by morning!" 35 Then David accepted what she had brought him and said to her, "Go back home and don't worry. I will do what you want."

36 Abigail went back to Nabal, who was at home having a feast fit for a king. He was drunk and in a good mood, so she did not tell him anything until the next morning. 37 Then, after he had sobered up, she told him everything. He suffered a stroke and was completely paralysed. 38 Some ten days later the LORD struck Nabal and he died.

39 When David heard that Nabal had died, he said, "Praise the LORD! He has taken revenge on Nabal for insulting me and has kept me his servant from doing wrong. The LORD has punished Nabal for his evil."

Then David sent a proposal of marriage to Abigail. 40 His servants went to her at Carmel and said to her, "David sent us to take you to him to be his wife."

41 Abigail bowed down to the ground and said, "I am his servant, ready to wash the feet of his servants." 42 She rose quickly and mounted her donkey. Accompanied by her five maids, she went with David's servants and became his wife.

43 David had married Ahinoam from Jezreel, and now Abigail also became his wife. 44 Meanwhile, Saul had given his daughter Michal, who had been David's wife, to Palti son of Laish, who was from the town of Gallim.

David Spares Saul's Life Again

26 Some men from Ziph came to Saul at Gibeah and told him that David was hiding on Mount Hachilah at the edge of the Judaean wilderness. 2 Saul went at once with three thousand of the best soldiers in Israel to the wilderness of Ziph to look for David, 3 and camped by the road on Mount Hachilah. David was still in the wilderness, and when he learnt that Saul had come to look for him, 4 he sent spies and found out that Saul was indeed there. 5 He went at once and located the exact place where Saul and Abner son

25.44: 2 Sam 3.14–16   **26.1:** Ps 54 (Title)

of Ner, commander of Saul's army, slept. Saul slept inside the camp, and his men camped round him.

6 Then David asked Ahimelech the Hittite, and Abishai the brother of Joab (their mother was Zeruiah), "Which of you two will go to Saul's camp with me?"

"I will," Abishai answered.

7 So that night David and Abishai entered Saul's camp and found Saul sleeping in the centre of the camp with his spear stuck in the ground near his head. Abner and the troops were sleeping round him. 8 Abishai said to David, "God has put your enemy in your power tonight. Now let me plunge his own spear through him and pin him to the ground with just one blow—I won't have to strike twice!"

9 But David said, "You must not harm him! The LORD will certainly punish whoever harms his chosen king. 10 By the living LORD," David continued, "I know that the LORD himself will kill Saul, either when his time comes to die a natural death or when he dies in battle. 11 The LORD forbid that I should try to harm the one whom the LORD has made king! Let's take his spear and his water jar, and go." 12 So David took the spear and the water jar from just beside Saul's head, and he and Abishai left. No one saw it or knew what had happened or even woke up—they were all sound asleep, because the LORD had sent a heavy sleep on them all.

13 Then David crossed over to the other side of the valley to the top of the hill, a safe distance away, 14 and shouted to Saul's troops and to Abner, "Abner! Can you hear me?"

"Who is that shouting and waking up the king?" Abner asked.

15 David answered, "Abner, aren't you the greatest man in Israel? So why aren't you protecting your master, the king? Just now someone entered the camp to kill your master. 16 You failed in your duty, Abner! I swear by the living LORD that all of you deserve to die, because you have not protected your master, whom the LORD made king. Look! Where is the king's spear? Where is the water jar that was beside his head?"

17 Saul recognized David's voice and asked, "David, is that you, my son?"

"Yes, Your Majesty," David answered. 18 And he added, "Why, sir, are you still pursuing me, your servant? What have I done? What crime have I committed? 19 Your Majesty, listen to what I have to say. If it is the LORD who has turned you against me, an offering to him will make him change his mind; but if men have done it, may the LORD's curse fall on them. For they have driven me out from the LORD's land to a country where I can only worship foreign gods. 20 Don't let me be killed on foreign soil, away from the LORD. Why should the king of Israel come to kill a flea like me? Why should he hunt me down like a wild bird?"

21 Saul answered, "I have done wrong. Come back, David, my son! I will never harm you again, because you have spared my life tonight. I have been a fool! I have done a terrible thing!"

22 David replied, "Here is your spear, Your Majesty. Let one of your men come over and get it. 23 The LORD rewards those who are faithful and righteous. Today he put you in my power, but I did not harm you, whom the LORD made king. 24 Just as I have spared your life today, may the LORD do the same to me and free me from all troubles!"

25 Saul said to David, "God bless you, my son! You will succeed in everything you do!"

So David went on his way, and Saul returned home.

David among the Philistines

27 David said to himself, "One of these days Saul will kill me. The best thing for me to do is to escape to Philistia. Then Saul will give up looking for me in Israel, and I will be safe." 2 So David and his six hundred men went over at once to Achish son of Maoch, king of Gath. 3 David and his men settled there in Gath with their families. David had his two wives with him, Ahinoam from Jezreel, and Abigail, Nabal's widow, from Carmel. 4 When Saul heard that David had fled to Gath, he gave up trying to find him.

5 David said to Achish, "If you are my friend, let me have a small town to live in. There is no need, sir, for me to live with you in the capital city." 6 So Achish gave him the town of Ziklag, and for this reason Ziklag has belonged to the kings of Judah ever since. 7 David lived in Philistia for sixteen months.

8 During that time David and his men would attack the people of Geshur, Girzi, and Amalek, who had been living in the region a very long time. He would raid their land as far as Shur, all the way down

26.11: 1 Sam 24.6

to Egypt, [9]killing all the men and women and taking the sheep, cattle, donkeys, camels, and even the clothes. Then he would come back to Achish, [10]who would ask him, "Where did you go on a raid this time?" and David would tell him that he had gone to the southern part of Judah or to the territory of the clan of Jerahmeel or to the territory where the Kenites lived. [11]David would kill everyone, men and women, so that no one could go back to Gath and report what he and his men had really done. This is what David did the whole time he lived in Philistia. [12]But Achish trusted David and said to himself, "He is hated so much by his own people the Israelites that he will have to serve me all his life."

28 Some time later, the Philistines gathered their troops to fight Israel, and Achish said to David, "Of course you understand that you and your men are to fight on my side."

2 "Of course," David answered. "I am your servant, and you will see for yourself what I can do."

Achish said, "Good! I will make you my permanent bodyguard."

Saul Consults a Medium

3 Now Samuel had died, and all the Israelites had mourned for him and had buried him in his own city of Ramah. Saul had forced all the fortune-tellers and mediums to leave Israel.

4 The Philistine troops assembled and camped near the town of Shunem; Saul gathered the Israelites and camped at Mount Gilboa. [5]When Saul saw the Philistine army, he was terrified, [6]and so he asked the LORD what to do. But the LORD did not answer him at all, either by dreams or by the use of Urim and Thummim or by prophets. [7]Then Saul ordered his officials, "Find me a woman who is a medium, and I will go and consult her."

"There is one in Endor," they answered.

8 So Saul disguised himself; he put on different clothes, and after dark he went with two of his men to see the woman. "Consult the spirits for me and tell me what is going to happen," he said to her. "Call up the spirit of the man I name."

9 The woman answered, "Surely you know what King Saul has done, how he forced the fortune-tellers and mediums to

leave Israel.[v] Why, then, are you trying to trap me and get me killed?"

10 Then Saul made a sacred vow. "By the living LORD I promise that you will not be punished for doing this," he told her.

11 "Whom shall I call up for you?" the woman asked.

"Samuel," he answered.

12 When the woman saw Samuel, she screamed and said to Saul, "Why have you tricked me? You are King Saul!"

13 "Don't be afraid!" the king said to her. "What do you see?"

"I see a spirit coming up from the earth," she answered.

14 "What does it look like?" he asked.

"It's an old man coming up," she answered. "He is wearing a cloak."

Then Saul knew that it was Samuel, and he bowed to the ground in respect.

15 Samuel said to Saul, "Why have you disturbed me? Why did you make me come back?"

Saul answered, "I am in great trouble! The Philistines are at war with me, and God has abandoned me. He doesn't answer me any more, either by prophets or by dreams. And so I have called you, for you to tell me what I must do."

16 Samuel said, "Why do you call me when the LORD has abandoned you and become your enemy? [17]The LORD has done to you what he told you through me: he has taken the kingdom away from you and given it to David instead. [18]You disobeyed the LORD's command and did not completely destroy the Amalekites and all they had. That is why the LORD is doing this to you now. [19]He will hand you and Israel over to the Philistines. Tomorrow you and your sons will join me, and the LORD will also hand the army of Israel over to the Philistines."

20 At once Saul fell down and lay stretched out on the ground, terrified by what Samuel had said. He was weak, because he had not eaten anything all day and all night. [21]The woman went over to him and saw that he was terrified, so she said to him, "Please, sir, I risked my life by doing what you asked. [22]Now please do what I ask. Let me prepare some food for you. You must eat so that you will be strong enough to travel."

23 Saul refused and said he would not eat anything. But his officers also urged

[v]he forced...Israel; *or* he put to death the fortune-tellers and mediums in Israel.
28.3: Lev 20.27; Deut 18.10–11; 1 Sam 25.1   **28.6:** Num 27.21   **28.17:** 1 Sam 15.28
28.18: 1 Sam 15.3–9

him to eat. He finally gave in, got up from the ground, and sat on the bed. ²⁴ The woman quickly killed a calf which she had been fattening. Then she took some flour, prepared it, and baked some bread without yeast. ²⁵ She set the food before Saul and his officers, and they ate it. And they left that same night.

David Is Rejected by the Philistines

29 The Philistines brought all their troops together at Aphek, while the Israelites camped at the spring in the Valley of Jezreel. ² The five Philistine kings marched out with their units of a hundred and of a thousand men; David and his men marched in the rear with King Achish. ³ The Philistine commanders saw them and asked, "What are these Hebrews doing here?"

Achish answered, "This is David, an official of King Saul of Israel. He has been with me for quite a long time now. He has done nothing I can find fault with since the day he came over to me."

4 But the Philistine commanders were angry with Achish and said to him, "Send that fellow back to the town you gave him. Don't let him go into battle with us; he might turn against us during the fighting. What better way is there for him to win back his master's favour than by the death of our men? ⁵ After all, this is David, the one about whom the women sang, as they danced, 'Saul has killed thousands, but David has killed tens of thousands.'"

6 Achish called David and said to him, "I swear by the living GOD of Israel that you have been loyal to me; and I would be pleased to let you go with me and fight in this battle. I have not found any fault in you from the day you came over to me. But the other kings don't approve of you. ⁷ So go back home in peace, and don't do anything that would displease them."

8 David answered, "What have I done wrong, sir? If, as you say, you haven't found any fault in me since the day I started serving you, why shouldn't I go with you, my master and king, and fight your enemies?"

9 "I agree," Achish replied. "I consider you as loyal as an angel of God. But the other kings have said that you can't go with us into battle. ¹⁰ So then, David, tomorrow morning all of you who left Saul and came over to me will have to get up early and leave as soon as it's light."

11 So David and his men started out early the following morning to go back to Philistia, and the Philistines went on to Jezreel.

The War against the Amalekites

30 Two days later David and his men arrived back at Ziklag. The Amalekites had raided southern Judah and attacked Ziklag. They had burnt down the town ² and captured all the women; they had not killed anyone, but had taken everyone with them when they left. ³ When David and his men arrived, they found that the town had been burnt down and that their wives, sons, and daughters had been carried away. ⁴ David and his men started crying and did not stop until they were completely exhausted. ⁵ Even David's two wives, Ahinoam and Abigail, had been taken away.

6 David was now in great trouble, because his men were all very bitter about losing their children, and they were threatening to stone him; but the LORD his God gave him courage. ⁷ David said to the priest Abiathar son of Ahimelech, "Bring me the ephod," and Abiathar brought it to him. ⁸ David asked the LORD, "Shall I go after those raiders? And will I catch them?"

He answered, "Go after them; you will catch them and rescue the captives."

9 So David and his six hundred men started out, and when they arrived at the brook of Besor, some of them stayed there. ¹⁰ David continued on his way with four hundred men; the other two hundred men were too tired to cross the brook and so stayed behind. ¹¹ The men with David found an Egyptian boy out in the country and brought him to David. They gave him some food and water, ¹² some dried figs, and two bunches of raisins. After he had eaten, his strength returned; he had not had anything to eat or drink for three full days. ¹³ David asked him, "Who is your master, and where are you from?"

"I am an Egyptian, the slave of an Amalekite," he answered. "My master left me behind three days ago because I was ill. ¹⁴ We had raided the territory of the Cherethites in the southern part of Judah and the territory of the clan of Caleb, and we burnt down Ziklag."

15 "Will you lead me to those raiders?" David asked him.

29.5: 1 Sam 18.7, 21.11　　**30.5:** 1 Sam 25.42–43　　**30.7:** 1 Sam 22.20–23

He answered, "I will if you promise me in God's name that you will not kill me or hand me over to my master." [16] And he led David to them.

The raiders were scattered all over the place, eating, drinking, and celebrating because of the enormous amount of loot they had captured from Philistia and Judah. [17] At dawn the next day David attacked them and fought until evening. Except for four hundred young men who mounted camels and got away, none of them escaped. [18] David rescued everyone and everything the Amalekites had taken, including his two wives; [19] nothing at all was missing. David got back all his men's sons and daughters, and all the loot the Amalekites had taken. [20] He also recovered all the flocks and herds; his men drove all the livestock in front of them[w] and said, "This belongs to David!"

21 Then David went back to the two hundred men who had been too weak to go with him and had stayed behind at the brook of Besor. They came forward to meet David and his men, and David went up to them and greeted them warmly. [22] But some mean and worthless men who had gone with David said, "They didn't go with us, and so we won't give them any of the loot. They can take their wives and children and go away."

23 But David answered, "My brothers, you can't do this with what the LORD has given us! He kept us safe and gave us victory over the raiders. [24] No one can agree with what you say! All must share alike: whoever stays behind with the supplies gets the same share as the one who goes into battle." [25] David made this a rule, and it has been followed in Israel ever since.

26 When David returned to Ziklag, he sent part of the loot to his friends, the leaders of Judah, with the message, "Here is a present for you from the loot we took from the LORD's enemies." [27] He sent it to the people in Bethel, to the people in Ramah in the southern part of Judah, and to the people in the towns of Jattir, [28] Aroer, Siphmoth, Eshtemoa, [29] and Racal; to the clan of Jerahmeel, to the Kenites, [30] and to the people in the towns

of Hormah, Borashan, Athach, [31] and Hebron. He sent it to all the places where he and his men had roamed.

The Death of Saul and His Sons
(1 Chr 10.1-12)

31 The Philistines fought a battle against the Israelites on Mount Gilboa. Many Israelites were killed there, and the rest of them, including King Saul and his sons, fled. [2] But the Philistines caught up with them and killed three of Saul's sons, Jonathan, Abinadab, and Malchishua. [3] The fighting was heavy round Saul, and he himself was hit by enemy arrows and badly wounded. [4] He said to the young man carrying his weapons, "Draw your sword and kill me, so that these godless Philistines won't gloat over me and kill me." But the young man was too terrified to do it. So Saul took his own sword and threw himself on it. [5] The young man saw that Saul was dead, so he too threw himself on his own sword and died with Saul. [6] And that is how Saul, his three sons, and the young man died; all of Saul's men died that day. [7] When the Israelites on the other side of the Valley of Jezreel and east of the River Jordan heard that the Israelite army had fled and that Saul and his sons had been killed, they abandoned their towns and fled. Then the Philistines came and occupied them.

8 The day after the battle the Philistines went to plunder the corpses, and they found the bodies of Saul and his three sons lying on Mount Gilboa. [9] They cut off Saul's head, stripped off his armour, and sent messengers with them throughout Philistia to tell the good news to their idols and to their people. [10] Then they put his weapons in the temple of the goddess Astarte, and they nailed his body to the wall of the city of Beth Shan.

11 When the people of Jabesh in Gilead heard what the Philistines had done to Saul, [12] the bravest men started out and marched all night to Beth Shan. They took down the bodies of Saul and his sons from the wall, brought them back to Jabesh, and burnt them there. [13] Then they took the bones and buried them under the tamarisk-tree in the town, and fasted for seven days.

---

w Probable text his men...front of them; *Hebrew unclear.*

THE SECOND BOOK OF
SAMUEL

INTRODUCTION

Second Samuel, the sequel to *First Samuel,* is the history of David's reign as king, first over Judah in the south (chapters 1-4), and then over the whole nation, including Israel in the north (chapters 5-24). It is a vivid account of how David, in order to extend his kingdom and consolidate his position, had to struggle with enemies within the nation as well as with foreign powers. David is shown to be a man of deep faith and devotion to God, and one who was able to win the loyalty of his people. Yet he is also shown as being sometimes ruthless, and willing to commit terrible sins to serve his own desires and ambitions. But when he is confronted with his sins, by the Lord's prophet Nathan, he confesses them and accepts the punishment that God sends.

The life and achievements of David impressed the people of Israel so much that in later times of national distress, when they longed for another king, it was for one who would be "a son of David," that is, a descendant of David who would be like him.

Outline of Contents
David's reign over Judah 1.1—4.12
David's reign over all Israel 5.1—24.25
  a. The early years 5.1—10.19
  b. David and Bathsheba 11.1—12.25
  c. Troubles and difficulties 12.26—20.26
  d. The later years 21.1—24.25

David Learns of Saul's Death

1 After Saul's death David came back from his victory over the Amalekites and stayed in Ziklag for two days. ²The next day a young man arrived from Saul's camp. To show his grief, he had torn his clothes and put earth on his head. He went to David and bowed to the ground in respect. ³David asked him, "Where have you come from?"

"I have escaped from the Israelite camp," he answered.

4 "Tell me what happened," David said.

"Our army ran away from the battle," he replied, "and many of our men were killed. Saul and his son Jonathan were also killed."

5 "How do you know that Saul and Jonathan are dead?" David asked him.

6 He answered, "I happened to be on Mount Gilboa, and I saw that Saul was leaning on his spear and that the chariots and horsemen of the enemy were closing in on him. ⁷Then he turned round, saw me, and called to me. I answered, 'Yes,

1.6–10: 1 Sam 31.1-6; 1 Chr 10.1-6

sir!' [8]He asked who I was, and I told him that I was an Amalekite. [9]Then he said, 'Come here and kill me! I have been badly wounded, and I'm about to die.' [10]So I went up to him and killed him, because I knew that he would die anyway as soon as he fell. Then I took the crown from his head and the bracelet from his arm, and I have brought them to you, sir.''

11 David tore his clothes in sorrow, and

David tore his clothes in sorrow (1.11)

all his men did the same. [12]They grieved and mourned and fasted until evening for Saul and Jonathan and for Israel, the people of the LORD, because so many had been killed in battle.

13 David asked the young man who had brought him the news, "Where are you from?"

He answered, "I'm an Amalekite, but I live in your country."

14 David asked him, "How is it that you dared to kill the LORD's chosen king?" [15]Then David called one of his men and said, "Kill him!" The man struck the Amalekite and mortally wounded him,

[16]and David said to the Amalekite, "You brought this on yourself. You condemned yourself when you admitted that you killed the one whom the LORD chose to be king."

David's Lament for Saul and Jonathan

17 David sang this lament for Saul and his son Jonathan, [18]and ordered it[a] to be taught to the people of Judah. (It is recorded in *The Book of Jashar.*)

[19] "On the hills of Israel our leaders are dead!
The bravest of our soldiers have fallen!
[20] Do not announce it in Gath
or in the streets of Ashkelon.
Do not make the women of Philistia glad;
do not let the daughters of pagans rejoice.

[21] "May no rain or dew fall on Gilboa's hills;
may its fields be always barren!
For the shields of the brave lie there in disgrace;
the shield of Saul is no longer polished with oil.
[22] Jonathan's bow was deadly,
the sword of Saul was merciless,
striking down the mighty, killing the enemy.

[23] "Saul and Jonathan, so wonderful and dear;
together in life, together in death;
swifter than eagles, stronger than lions.

[24] "Women of Israel, mourn for Saul!
He clothed you in rich scarlet dresses
and adorned you with jewels and gold.

[25] "The brave soldiers have fallen,
they were killed in battle.
Jonathan lies dead in the hills.

[26] "I grieve for you, my brother Jonathan;
how dear you were to me!
How wonderful was your love for me,
better even than the love of women.

[27] "The brave soldiers have fallen,
their weapons abandoned and useless."

[a] *One ancient translation* it; *Hebrew* the bow.
1.18: Josh 10.13

David Is Made King of Judah

2 After this, David asked the LORD, "Shall I go and take control of one of the towns of Judah?"

"Yes," the LORD answered.

"Which one?" David asked.

"Hebron," the LORD said. [2] So David went to Hebron, taking with him his two wives: Ahinoam, who was from Jezreel, and Abigail, Nabal's widow, who was from Carmel. [3] He also took his men and their families, and they settled in the towns round Hebron. [4] Then the men of Judah came to Hebron and anointed David as king of Judah.

When David heard that the people of Jabesh in Gilead had buried Saul, [5] he sent some men there with the message: "May the LORD bless you for showing your loyalty to your king by burying him. [6] And now may the LORD be kind and faithful to you. I too will treat you well because of what you have done. [7] Be strong and brave! Saul your king is dead, and the people of Judah have anointed me as their king."

Ishbosheth Is Made King of Israel

8 The commander of Saul's army, Abner son of Ner, had fled with Saul's son Ishbosheth across the Jordan to Mahanaim. [9] There Abner made Ishbosheth king of the territories of Gilead, Asher,[b] Jezreel, Ephraim, and Benjamin, and indeed over all Israel. [10] He was forty years old when he was made king of Israel, and he ruled for two years.

But the tribe of Judah was loyal to David, [11] and he ruled in Hebron over Judah for seven and a half years.

War between Israel and Judah

12 Abner and the officials of Ishbosheth went from Mahanaim to the city of Gibeon. [13] Joab, whose mother was Zeruiah, and David's other officials met them at the pool, where they all sat down, one group on one side of the pool and the other group on the opposite side. [14] Abner said to Joab, "Let's get some of the young men from each side to fight an armed contest."

"All right," Joab answered.

15 So twelve men, representing Ishbosheth and the tribe of Benjamin, fought twelve of David's men. [16] Each man caught his opponent by the head and plunged his sword into his opponent's side, so that all twenty-four of them fell down dead together. And so that place in Gibeon is called "Field of Swords."

17 Then a furious battle broke out, and Abner and the Israelites were defeated by David's men. [18] The three sons of Zeruiah were there: Joab, Abishai, and Asahel. Asahel, who could run as fast as a wild deer, [19] started chasing Abner, running straight for him. [20] Abner looked back and said, "Is that you, Asahel?"

"Yes," he answered.

21 "Stop chasing me!" Abner said. "Run after one of the soldiers and take what he has." But Asahel kept on chasing him. [22] Once more Abner said to him, "Stop chasing me! Why force me to kill you? How could I face your brother Joab?" [23] But Asahel would not give up; so Abner, with a backward thrust[c] of his spear, struck him through the belly so that the spear came out at his back. Asahel dropped to the ground dead, and everyone who came to the place where he was lying stopped and stood there.

24 But Joab and Abishai started out after Abner, and at sunset they came to the hill of Ammah, which is to the east of Giah on the road to the wilderness of Gibeon. [25] The men from the tribe of Benjamin gathered round Abner again and took their stand on the top of a hill. [26] Abner called out to Joab, "Do we have to go on fighting for ever? Can't you see that in the end there will be nothing but bitterness? We are your fellow-countrymen. How long will it be before you order your men to stop chasing us?"

27 "I swear by the living God," Joab answered, "that if you had not spoken, my men would have kept on chasing you until tomorrow morning." [28] Then Joab blew the trumpet as a signal for his men to stop pursuing the Israelites; and so the fighting stopped.

29 Abner and his men marched through the Jordan Valley all that night; they crossed the River Jordan, and after marching all the next morning, they arrived back at Mahanaim.

30 When Joab gave up the chase, he gathered all his men and found that nineteen of them were missing, in addition to Asahel. [31] David's men had killed 360

---

[b] *One ancient translation* Asher; *Hebrew* Assyria.
[c] *Probable text* with a backward thrust; *Hebrew unclear.*
2.2: 1 Sam 25.42–43   **2.4:** 1 Sam 31.11–13

of Abner's men from the tribe of Benjamin. 32 Joab and his men took Asahel's body and buried it in the family tomb at Bethlehem. Then they marched all night and at dawn arrived back at Hebron.

3 The fighting between the forces supporting Saul's family and those supporting David went on for a long time. As David became stronger and stronger, his opponents became weaker and weaker.

David's Sons

2 The following six sons, in the order of their birth, were born to David at Hebron: Amnon, whose mother was Ahinoam, from Jezreel; 3 Chileab, whose mother was Abigail, Nabal's widow, from Carmel; Absalom, whose mother was Maacah, the daughter of King Talmai of Geshur; 4 Adonijah, whose mother was Haggith; Shephatiah, whose mother was Abital; 5 Ithream, whose mother was Eglah. All of these sons were born in Hebron.

Abner Joins David

6 As the fighting continued between David's forces and the forces loyal to Saul's family, Abner became more and more powerful among Saul's followers.

7 One day Ishbosheth son of Saul accused Abner of sleeping with Saul's concubine Rizpah, the daughter of Aiah. 8 This made Abner furious. "Do you think that I would betray Saul? Do you really think I'm serving Judah?" he exclaimed. "From the very first I have been loyal to the cause of your father Saul, his brothers, and his friends, and I have saved you from being defeated by David; yet today you find fault with me about a woman! 9-10 The LORD promised David that he would take the kingdom away from Saul and his descendants and would make David king of both Israel and Judah, from one end of the country to the other. Now may God strike me dead if I don't make this come true!" 11 Ishbosheth was so afraid of Abner that he could not say a word.

12 Abner sent messengers to David, who at that time was at Hebron,*d* to say, "Who is going to rule this land? Make an agreement with me, and I will help you win all Israel over to your side."

13 "Good!" David answered. "I will make an agreement with you on one condition: you must bring Saul's daughter Michal to me when you come to see me."

14 And David also sent messengers to Ishbosheth to say, "Give me back my wife Michal. I paid a hundred Philistine foreskins in order to marry her." 15 So Ishbosheth took her away from her husband Paltiel son of Laish. 16 Paltiel followed her all the way to the town of Bahurim, crying as he went. But when Abner said, "Go back home," he did.

17 Abner went to the leaders of Israel and said to them, "For a long time you have wanted David to be your king. 18 Now here is your chance. Remember that the LORD has said, 'I will use my servant David to rescue my people Israel from the Philistines and from all their other enemies.'" 19 Abner spoke also to the people of the tribe of Benjamin and then went to Hebron to tell David what the people of Benjamin and of Israel had agreed to do.

20 When Abner came to David at Hebron with twenty men, David gave a feast for them. 21 Abner told David, "I will go now and win all Israel over to Your Majesty. They will accept you as king, and then you will get what you have wanted and will rule over the whole land." David gave Abner a guarantee of safety and sent him on his way.

Abner Is Murdered

22 Later on Joab and David's other officials returned from a raid, bringing a large amount of loot with them. Abner, however, was no longer there at Hebron with David, because David had sent him away with a guarantee of safety. 23 When Joab and his men arrived, he was told that Abner had come to King David and had been sent away with a guarantee of safety. 24 So Joab went to the king and said to him, "What have you done? Abner came to you—why did you let him go like that? 25 He came here to deceive you and to find out everything you do and everywhere you go. Surely you know that!"

26 After leaving David, Joab sent messengers to get Abner, and they brought him back from the well of Sirah; but David knew nothing about it. 27 When Abner arrived in Hebron, Joab took him aside at the gate, as though he wanted to speak privately with him, and there he stabbed him in the belly. And so Abner was murdered because he had killed Joab's brother Asahel. 28 When David

d One ancient translation at Hebron; *Hebrew* where he (Abner) was.
3.9-10: 1 Sam 15.28   **3.14:** 1 Sam 18.27

heard the news, he said, "The LORD knows that my subjects and I are completely innocent of the murder of Abner. ²⁹May the punishment for it fall on Joab and all his family! In every generation may there be some man in his family who has gonorrhoea or a dreaded skin disease or is fit only to do a woman's work or is killed in battle or hasn't enough to eat!" ³⁰So Joab and his brother Abishai took revenge on Abner for killing their brother Asahel in the battle at Gibeon.

Abner Is Buried

31 Then David ordered Joab and his men to tear their clothes, wear sackcloth, and mourn for Abner. And at the funeral King David himself walked behind the coffin. ³²Abner was buried at Hebron, and the king wept aloud at the grave, and so did all the people. ³³David sang this lament for Abner:

"Why did Abner have to die like a fool?
³⁴ His hands were not tied,
   And his feet were not bound;
   He died like someone killed by
       criminals!"
And the people wept for him again.

35 All day long the people tried to get David to eat something, but he made a solemn promise, "May God strike me dead if I eat anything before the day is over!" ³⁶They took note of this and were pleased. Indeed, everything the king did pleased the people. ³⁷All David's people and all the people in Israel understood that the king had no part in the murder of Abner. ³⁸The king said to his officials, "Don't you realize that this day a great leader in Israel has died? ³⁹Even though I am the king chosen by God, I feel weak today. These sons of Zeruiah are too violent for me. May the LORD punish these criminals as they deserve!"

Ishbosheth Is Murdered

4 When Saul's son Ishbosheth heard that Abner had been killed in Hebron, he was afraid, and all the people of Israel were alarmed. ²Ishbosheth had two officers who were leaders of raiding parties, Baanah and Rechab, sons of Rimmon, from Beeroth in the tribe of Benjamin. (Beeroth is counted as part of Benjamin. ³Its original inhabitants had fled to Gittaim, where they have lived ever since.) 4 Another descendant of Saul was

Jonathan's son Mephibosheth, who was five years old when Saul and Jonathan were killed. When the news about their death came from the city of Jezreel, his nurse picked him up and fled; but she was in such a hurry that she dropped him, and he became crippled.

5 Rechab and Baanah set out for Ishbosheth's house and arrived there about noon, while he was taking his midday rest. ⁶The woman at the door had become drowsy while she was sifting wheat and had fallen asleep, so Rechab and Baanah slipped in.ᵉ ⁷Once inside, they went to Ishbosheth's bedroom, where he was sound asleep, and killed him. Then they cut off his head, took it with them, and walked all night through the Jordan Valley. ⁸They presented the head to King David at Hebron and said to him, "Here is the head of Ishbosheth, the son of your enemy Saul, who tried to kill you. Today the LORD has allowed Your Majesty to take revenge on Saul and his descendants."

9 David answered them, "I make a vow by the living LORD, who has saved me from all dangers! ¹⁰The messenger who came to me at Ziklag and told me of Saul's death thought he was bringing good news. I seized him and had him put to death. That was the reward I gave him for his good news! ¹¹How much worse it will be for evil men who murder an innocent man asleep in his own house! I will now take revenge on you for murdering him and will wipe you off the face of the earth!" ¹²David gave the order, and his soldiers killed Rechab and Baanah and cut off their hands and feet, which they hung up near the pool in Hebron. They took Ishbosheth's head and buried it in Abner's tomb there at Hebron.

David Becomes King of Israel and Judah
(1 Chr 11.1-9; 14.1-7)

5 Then all the tribes of Israel came to David at Hebron and said to him, "We are your own flesh and blood. ²In the past, even when Saul was still our king, you led the people of Israel in battle, and the LORD promised you that you would lead his people and be their ruler." ³So all the leaders of Israel came to King David at Hebron. He made a sacred alliance with them, they anointed him, and he became king of Israel. ⁴David was

---

ᵉ *Verse 6 follows one ancient translation; Hebrew* They went on into the house carrying wheat, and struck him in the belly. Then Rechab and his brother Baanah escaped.
4.4: 2 Sam 9.3   **4.10:** 2 Sam 1.1-16   **5.4-5:** 1 Kgs 2.11; 1 Chr 3.4, 29.27

thirty years old when he became king, and he ruled for forty years. [5] He ruled in Hebron over Judah for seven and a half years, and in Jerusalem over all Israel and Judah for thirty-three years.

6 The time came when King David and his men set out to attack Jerusalem. The Jebusites, who lived there, thought that David would not be able to conquer the city, and so they said to him, "You will never get in here; even the blind and the crippled could keep you out." [7] (But David did capture their fortress of Zion, and it became known as "David's City.")

8 That day David said to his men, "Does anybody here hate the Jebusites as much as I do? Enough to kill them? Then go up through the water tunnel and attack those poor blind cripples." (That is why it is said, "The blind and the crippled cannot enter the LORD's house.")[f]

9 After capturing the fortress, David lived in it and named it "David's City." He built the city round it, starting at the place where land was filled in on the east side of the hill. [10] He grew stronger all the time, because the LORD God Almighty was with him.

11 King Hiram of Tyre sent a trade mission to David; he provided him with cedar logs and with carpenters and stone-masons to build a palace. [12] And so David realized that the LORD had established him as king of Israel and was making his kingdom prosperous for the sake of his people.

13 After moving from Hebron to Jerusalem, David took more concubines and wives, and had more sons and daughters. [14] The following children were born to him in Jerusalem: Shammua, Shobab, Nathan, Solomon, [15] Ibhar, Elishua, Nepheg, Japhia, [16] Elishama, Eliada, and Eliphelet.

Victory over the Philistines
(1 Chr 14.8–17)

17 The Philistines were told that David had been made king of Israel, so their army set out to capture him. When David heard of it, he went down to a fortified place. [18] The Philistines arrived at the Valley of Rephaim and occupied it. [19] David asked the LORD, "Shall I attack the Philistines? Will you give me the victory?"

"Yes, attack!" the LORD answered. "I will give you the victory!"

20 So David went to Baal Perazim and there he defeated the Philistines. He said, "The LORD has broken through my enemies like a flood." And so that place is called Baal Perazim.[g] [21] When the Philistines fled, they left their idols behind, and David and his men carried them away.

22 Then the Philistines went back to the Valley of Rephaim and occupied it again. [23] Once more David consulted the LORD, who answered, "Don't attack them from here, but go round and get ready to attack them from the other side, near the balsam-trees. [24] When you hear the sound of marching in the tree-tops, then attack because I will be marching ahead of you to defeat the Philistine army." [25] David did what the LORD had commanded, and was able to drive the Philistines back from Geba all the way to Gezer.

The Covenant Box Is Brought to Jerusalem
(1 Chr 13.1–14; 15.25—16.6, 43)

6 Once more David called together the best soldiers in Israel, a total of thirty thousand men, [2] and led them to Baalah[h] in Judah, in order to bring from there God's Covenant Box, bearing the name of the LORD Almighty, who is enthroned above the winged creatures.[x] [3] They took it from Abinadab's home on the hill and placed it on a new cart. Uzzah and Ahio, sons of Abinadab, were guiding the cart, [4] with Ahio walking in front. [5] David and all the Israelites were dancing and singing with all their might[i] to honour the LORD. They were playing harps, lyres, drums, rattles, and cymbals.

6 As they came to the threshing-place of Nacon, the oxen stumbled, and Uzzah reached out and took hold of the Covenant Box. [7] At once the LORD God became angry with Uzzah and killed him because of his irreverence.[j] Uzzah died there beside the Covenant Box, [8] and so that place has been called Perez Uzzah[k] ever since. David was furious because the LORD had punished Uzzah in anger.

9 Then David was afraid of the LORD and said, "How can I take the Covenant

---

[f] Verse 8 in Hebrew is unclear.
[g] BAAL PERAZIM: This name in Hebrew means "Lord of the Break-through."
[h] Probable text (see 1 Chr 13.6) to Baalah; Hebrew from Baaley, or from the leaders.
[x] WINGED CREATURES: See Word List.
[i] One ancient translation (and see 1 Chr 13.8) and singing with all their might; Hebrew with all the fir-trees.
[j] Probable text his irreverence; Hebrew unclear.
[k] PEREZ UZZAH: This name in Hebrew means "Punishment of Uzzah."
5.6: Josh 15.63; Judg 1.21 **6.2:** Ex 25.22 **6.3:** 1 Sam 7.1-2

The Israelites were dancing and singing (6.5)

Box with me now?" ¹⁰ So he decided not to take it with him to Jerusalem; instead, he turned off the road and took it to the house of Obed Edom, a native of the city of Gath. ¹¹ It stayed there three months, and the LORD blessed Obed Edom and his family.

12 King David heard that because of the Covenant Box the LORD had blessed Obed Edom's family and all that he had; so he fetched the Covenant Box from Obed's house to take it to Jerusalem with a great celebration. ¹³ After the men carrying the Covenant Box had gone six steps, David made them stop while he offered the LORD a sacrifice of a bull and a fattened calf. ¹⁴ David, wearing only a linen cloth round his waist, danced with all his might to honour the LORD. ¹⁵ And so he and all the Israelites took the Covenant Box up to Jerusalem with shouts of joy and the sound of trumpets.

16 As the Box was being brought into the city, Michal, Saul's daughter, looked out of the window and saw King David dancing and jumping around in the sacred dance, and she was disgusted with him. ¹⁷ They brought the Box and put it in its place in the Tent that David had set up for it. Then he offered sacrifices and fellowship-offerings to the LORD. ¹⁸ When he had finished offering the sacrifices, he blessed the people in the name of the LORD Almighty ¹⁹ and distributed food to them

all. He gave each man and woman in Israel a loaf of bread, a piece of roasted meat,ˡ and some raisins. Then everyone went home.

20 Afterwards, when David went home to greet his family, Michal came out to meet him. "The king of Israel made a big name for himself today!" she said. "He exposed himself like a fool in the sight of the servant-girls of his officials!"

21 David answered, "I was dancing to honour the LORD, who chose me instead of your father and his family to make me the leader of his people Israel. And I will go on dancing to honour the LORD, ²² and will disgrace myself even more. Youᵐ may think I am nothing, but those girls will think highly of me!"

23 Michal, Saul's daughter, never had any children.

Nathan's Message to David
(1 Chr 17.1-15)

7 King David was settled in his palace, and the LORD kept him safe from all his enemies. ² Then the king said to the prophet Nathan, "Here I am living in a house built of cedar, but God's Covenant Box is kept in a tent!"

3 Nathan answered, "Do whatever you have in mind, because the LORD is with you." ⁴ But that night the LORD said to Nathan, ⁵ "Go and tell my servant David that I say to him, 'You are not the one

---

ˡ a piece of roasted meat; *or a cake of dates.*   ᵐ *One ancient translation* You; *Hebrew* I.
6.11: 1 Chr 26.4-5   **6.19-20:** 1 Chr 16.43

to build a temple for me to live in. [6]From the time I rescued the people of Israel from Egypt until now, I have never lived in a temple; I have travelled round living in a tent. [7]In all my travelling with the people of Israel I never asked any of the leaders[n] that I appointed why they had not built me a temple made of cedar.'

[8] "So tell my servant David that I, the Lord Almighty, say to him, 'I took you from looking after sheep in the fields and made you the ruler of my people Israel. [9]I have been with you wherever you have gone, and I have defeated all your enemies as you advanced. I will make you as famous as the greatest leaders in the world. [10-11]I have chosen a place for my people Israel and have settled them there, where they will live without being oppressed any more. Ever since they entered this land, they have been attacked by violent people, but this will not happen again. I promise to keep you safe from all your enemies and to give you descendants. [12]When you die and are buried with your ancestors, I will make one of your sons king and will keep his kingdom strong. [13]He will be the one to build a temple for me, and I will make sure that his dynasty continues for ever. [14]I will be his father, and he will be my son. When he does wrong, I will punish him as a father punishes his son. [15]But I will not withdraw my support from him as I did from Saul, whom I removed so that you could be king. [16]You will always have descendants, and I will make your kingdom last for ever. Your dynasty will never end.' "

[17]Nathan told David everything that God had revealed to him.

David's Prayer of Thanksgiving
(1 Chr 17.16-27)

[18]Then King David went into the Tent of the Lord's presence, sat down and prayed, "I am not worthy of what you have already done for me, Sovereign Lord, nor is my family. [19]Yet now you are doing even more, Sovereign Lord; you have made promises about my descendants in the years to come. And you let a man see this,[o] Sovereign Lord! [20]What

more can I say to you! You know me, your servant. [21]It was your will and purpose to do this; you have done all these great things in order to teach me. [22]How great you are, Sovereign Lord! There is none like you; we have always known that you alone are God. [23]There is no other nation on earth like Israel, whom you rescued from slavery to make them your own people. The great and wonderful things you did for them[p] have spread your fame throughout the world. You drove out[q] other nations and their gods as your people advanced, the people whom you set free from Egypt to be your own. [24]You have made Israel your own people for ever, and you, Lord, have become their God.

[25] "And now, Lord God, fulfil for all time the promise you made about me and my descendants, and do what you said you would. [26]Your fame will be great, and people will for ever say, 'The Lord Almighty is God over Israel.' And you will preserve my dynasty for all time. [27]Almighty Lord, God of Israel! I have the courage to pray this prayer to you, because you have revealed all this to me, your servant, and have told me that you will make my descendants kings.

[28] "And now, Sovereign Lord, you are God; you always keep your promises, and you have made this wonderful promise to me. [29]I ask you to bless my descendants so that they will continue to enjoy your favour. You, Sovereign Lord, have promised this, and your blessing will rest on my descendants for ever."

David's Military Victories
(1 Chr 18.1-17)

8 Some time later King David attacked the Philistines again, defeated them, and ended their control over the land.[r]

2 Then he defeated the Moabites. He made the prisoners lie down on the ground and put two out of every three of them to death. So the Moabites became his subjects and paid taxes to him.

3 Then he defeated the king of the Syrian state of Zobah, Hadadezer son of Rehob, as Hadadezer was on his way to restore his control over the territory by

---

[n] *Probable text (see 1 Chr 17.6)* leaders; *Hebrew* tribes.
[o] *Probable text* you let a man see this; *Hebrew* this is a law for men.
[p] *Probable text* them; *Hebrew* you (plural).
[q] *One ancient translation (and see 1 Chr 17.21);* You drove out; *Hebrew* for your land.
[r] *Probable text* over the land; *Hebrew unclear.*
7.12: Ps 89.3-4, 132.11; Jn 7.42; Acts 2.30   **7.14:** Ps 89.26-27; 2 Cor 6.18; Heb 1.5
7.16: Ps 89.36-37   **7.23:** Deut 4.34

the upper Euphrates. ⁴David captured seventeen hundred of his horsemen and twenty thousand of his foot soldiers. He kept enough horses for a hundred chariots and crippled all the rest.

5 When the Syrians of Damascus sent an army to help King Hadadezer, David attacked it and killed twenty-two thousand men. ⁶Then he set up military camps in ˢ their territory, and they became his subjects and paid taxes to him. The LORD made David victorious everywhere. ⁷David captured the gold shields carried by Hadadezer's officials and took them to Jerusalem. ⁸He also took a great quantity of bronze from Betah and Berothai, cities ruled by Hadadezer.

9 King Toi of Hamath heard that David had defeated all of Hadadezer's army. ¹⁰So he sent his son Joram to greet King David and congratulate him on his victory over Hadadezer, against whom Toi had fought many times. Joram took David presents made of gold, silver, and bronze. ¹¹King David dedicated them for use in worship, along with the silver and gold he took from the nations he had conquered—¹²Edom, Moab, Ammon, Philistia, and Amalek—as well as part of the loot he had taken from Hadadezer.

13 David became even more famous when he returned from killing eighteen thousand Edomites in the Valley of Salt. ¹⁴He set up military camps ᵗ throughout Edom, and the people there became his subjects. The LORD made David victorious everywhere.

15 David ruled over all Israel and made sure that his people were always treated fairly and justly. ¹⁶Joab, whose mother was Zeruiah, was the commander of the army; Jehoshaphat son of Ahilud was in charge of the records; ¹⁷Zadok son of Ahitub and Ahimelech son of Abiathar were priests; Seraiah was the court secretary; ¹⁸Benaiah son of Jehoiada was in charge of ᵘ David's bodyguard and David's sons were priests.

David and Mephibosheth

9 One day David asked, "Is there anyone left of Saul's family? If there is, I would like to show him kindness for Jonathan's sake."

2 There was a servant of Saul's family named Ziba, and he was told to go to

David. "Are you Ziba?" the king asked.

"At your service, sir," he answered.

3 The king asked him, "Is there anyone

He is crippled (9.3)

left of Saul's family to whom I can show loyalty and kindness, as I promised God I would?"

Ziba answered, "There is still one of Jonathan's sons. He is crippled."

4 "Where is he?" the king asked.

"At the home of Machir son of Ammiel in Lodebar," Ziba answered. ⁵So King David sent for him.

6 When Mephibosheth, the son of Jonathan and grandson of Saul, arrived, he bowed down before David in respect. David said, "Mephibosheth," and he

---

ˢset up military camps in; *or* placed military commanders over.
ᵗset up military camps; *or* placed military commanders over.
ᵘ*Some ancient translations* was in charge of; *Hebrew does not have these words.*
8.13: Ps 60 (Title)   **9.1:** 1 Sam 20.15-17   **9.3:** 2 Sam 4.4

answered, "At your service, sir."

7 "Don't be afraid," David replied. "I will be kind to you for the sake of your father Jonathan. I will give you back all the land that belonged to your grandfather Saul, and you will always be welcome at my table."

8 Mephibosheth bowed again and said, "I am no better than a dead dog, sir! Why should you be so good to me?"

9 Then the king called Ziba, Saul's servant, and said, "I am giving Mephibosheth, your master's grandson, everything that belonged to Saul and his family. 10 You, your sons, and your servants will farm the land for your master Saul's family and bring in the harvest, to provide food for them. But Mephibosheth himself will always be a guest at my table." (Ziba had fifteen sons and twenty servants.)

11 Ziba answered, "I will do everything Your Majesty commands."

So Mephibosheth ate at the king's v table, just like one of the king's sons. 12 Mephibosheth had a young son named Mica. All the members of Ziba's family became servants of Mephibosheth. 13 So Mephibosheth, who was crippled in both feet, lived in Jerusalem, eating all his meals at the king's table.

David Defeats the Ammonites and the Syrians
(1 Chr 19.1–19)

10 Some time later King Nahash of Ammon died, and his son Hanun became king. 2 King David said, "I must show loyal friendship to Hanun, as his father Nahash did to me." So David sent messengers to express his sympathy.

When they arrived in Ammon, 3 the Ammonite leaders said to the king, "Do you think that it is in your father's honour that David has sent these men to express sympathy to you? Of course not! He has sent them here as spies to explore the city, so that he can conquer us!"

4 Hanun seized David's messengers, shaved off one side of their beards, cut off their clothes at the hips, and sent them away. 5 They were too ashamed to return home. When David heard about what had happened, he sent word that they should stay in Jericho and not return until their beards had grown again.

6 The Ammonites realized that they had made David their enemy, so they hired twenty thousand Syrian soldiers from Bethrehob and Zobah, twelve thousand men from Tob, and the king of Maacah with a thousand men. 7 David heard of it and sent Joab against them with the whole army. 8 The Ammonites marched out and took up their position at the entrance to Rabbah, their capital city, while the others, both the Syrians and the men from Tob and Maacah, took up their position in the open countryside.

9 Joab saw that the enemy troops would attack him in front and from the rear, so he chose the best of Israel's soldiers and put them in position facing the Syrians. 10 He placed the rest of his troops under the command of his brother Abishai, who put them in position facing the Ammonites. 11 Joab said to him, "If you see that the Syrians are defeating me, come and help me, and if the Ammonites are defeating you, I will go and help you. 12 Be strong and courageous! Let's fight hard for our people and for the cities of our God. And may the LORD's will be done!"

13 Joab and his men advanced to attack, and the Syrians fled. 14 When the Ammonites saw the Syrians running away, they fled from Abishai and retreated into the city. Then Joab turned back from fighting the Ammonites and went back to Jerusalem.

15 The Syrians realized that they had been defeated by the Israelites, so they called all their troops together. 16 King Hadadezer sent for the Syrians who were on the east side of the River Euphrates, and they came to Helam under the command of Shobach, commander of the army of King Hadadezer of Zobah. 17 When David heard of it, he gathered the Israelite troops, crossed the River Jordan, and marched to Helam, where the Syrians took up their position facing him. The fighting began, 18 and the Israelites drove the Syrian army back. David and his men killed seven hundred Syrian chariot drivers and forty thousand horsemen, and they wounded Shobach, the enemy commander, who died on the battlefield. 19 When the kings who were subject to Hadadezer realized that they had been defeated by the Israelites, they made peace with them and became their subjects. And the Syrians were afraid to help the Ammonites any more.

---

v One ancient translation the king's; Hebrew my.

The rich man had many cattle and sheep (12.2)
The lamb was like a daughter to him (12.3)

David and Bathsheba

11 The following spring, at the time of the year when kings usually go to war, David sent out Joab with his officers and the Israelite army; they defeated the Ammonites and besieged the city of Rabbah. But David himself stayed in Jerusalem.

2 One day, late in the afternoon, David got up from his nap and went to the palace roof. As he walked about up there, he saw a woman having a bath. She was very beautiful. ³ So he sent a messenger to find out who she was, and learnt that she was Bathsheba, the daughter of Eliam and the wife of Uriah the Hittite. ⁴ David sent messengers to fetch her; they brought her to him and he made love to her. (She had just finished her monthly ritual of purification.) Then she went back home. ⁵ Afterwards she discovered that she was pregnant and sent a message to David to tell him.

6 David then sent a message to Joab: "Send me Uriah the Hittite." So Joab sent him to David. ⁷ When Uriah arrived, David asked him if Joab and the troops were well, and how the fighting was going. ⁸ Then he said to Uriah, "Go home and rest a while." Uriah left, and David sent a present to his home. ⁹ But Uriah did not go home; instead he slept at the palace gate with the king's guards. ¹⁰ When David heard that Uriah had not gone home, he asked him, "You have just returned after a long absence; why didn't you go home?"

11 Uriah answered, "The men of Israel and Judah are away at the war, and the Covenant Box is with them; my commander Joab and his officers are camping out in the open. How could I go home, eat and drink, and sleep with my wife? By all that's sacred, I swear that I could never do such a thing!"

12 So David said, "Then stay here the rest of the day, and tomorrow I'll send you back." So Uriah stayed in Jerusalem that day and the next. ¹³ David invited him to supper and made him drunk. But again that night Uriah did not go home; instead he slept on his blanket*ʷ* in the palace guardroom.

14 The next morning David wrote a letter to Joab and sent it by Uriah. ¹⁵ He wrote: "Put Uriah in the front line, where the fighting is heaviest, then retreat and let him be killed." ¹⁶ So while Joab was besieging the city, he sent Uriah to a place where he knew the enemy was strong. ¹⁷ The enemy troops came out of the city and fought Joab's forces; some of David's officers were killed, and so was Uriah.

18 Then Joab sent a report to David telling him about the battle, ¹⁹ and he instructed the messenger, "After you have told the king all about the battle, ²⁰ he may get angry and ask you, 'Why did you go so near the city to fight them? Didn't you realize that they would shoot arrows from the walls? ²¹ Don't you remember how Abimelech son of Gideon was killed? It was at Thebez, where a woman threw a millstone down from the wall and killed him. Why, then, did you go so near the wall?' If the king asks you this, tell him, 'Your officer Uriah was also killed.' "

22 So the messenger went to David and told him what Joab had commanded him to say. ²³ He said, "Our enemies were stronger than we were and came out of

ʷ blanket; *or* bunk.
11.1: 1 Chr 20.1   **11.21:** Judg 9.53

He took the poor man's lamb (12.4)

the city to fight us in the open, but we drove them back to the city gate. ²⁴Then they shot arrows at us from the wall, and some of Your Majesty's officers were killed; your officer Uriah was also killed."

25 David said to the messenger, "Encourage Joab and tell him not to be upset, since you never can tell who will die in battle. Tell him to launch a stronger attack on the city and capture it."

26 When Bathsheba heard that her husband had been killed, she mourned for him. ²⁷When the time of mourning was over, David sent for her to come to the palace; she became his wife and bore him a son. But the LORD was not pleased with what David had done.

Nathan's Message and David's Repentance

12 The LORD sent the prophet Nathan to David. Nathan went to him and said, "There were two men who lived in the same town; one was rich and the other poor. ²The rich man had many cattle and sheep, ³while the poor man had only one lamb, which he had bought. He took care of it, and it grew up in his home with his children. He would feed it with some of his own food, let it drink from his cup, and hold it in his lap. The lamb was like a daughter to him. ⁴One day a visitor arrived at the rich man's home. The rich man didn't want to kill one of his own animals to prepare a meal for him; instead, he took the poor man's lamb and cooked a meal for his guest."

5 David was very angry with the rich man and said, "I swear by the living LORD that the man who did this ought to die! ⁶For having done such a cruel thing, he must pay back four times as much as he took."

7 "You are that man," Nathan said to David. "And this is what the LORD God of Israel says: 'I made you king of Israel and rescued you from Saul. ⁸I gave you his kingdom and his wives; I made you king over Israel and Judah. If this had not been enough, I would have given you twice as much. ⁹Why, then, have you disobeyed my commands? Why did you do this evil thing? You had Uriah killed in battle; you let the Ammonites kill him, and then you took his wife! ¹⁰Now, in every generation some of your descendants will die a violent death because you have disobeyed me and have taken Uriah's wife. ¹¹I swear to you that I will cause someone from your own family to bring trouble on you. You will see it when I take your wives from you and give them to another man; and he will have intercourse with them in broad daylight. ¹²You sinned in secret, but I will make this happen in broad daylight for all Israel to see.'"

13 "I have sinned against the LORD," David said.

Nathan replied, "The LORD forgives you; you will not die. ¹⁴But because you

You are that man (12.7)

12.1: Ps 51 (Title)   **12.11–12:** 2 Sam 16.22

have shown such contempt for the LORD in doing this, your child will die." ¹⁵ Then Nathan went home.

David's Son Dies

The LORD caused the child that Uriah's wife had borne to David to become very ill. ¹⁶ David prayed to God that the child would get well. He refused to eat anything, and every night he went into his room and spent the night lying on the floor. ¹⁷ His court officials went to him and tried to make him get up, but he refused and would not eat anything with them. ¹⁸ A week later the child died, and David's officials were afraid to tell him the news. They said, "While the child was living, David wouldn't answer us when we spoke to him. How can we tell him that his child is dead? He might do himself some harm!"

19 When David noticed them whispering to each other, he realized that the child had died. So he asked them, "Is the child dead?"

"Yes, he is," they answered.

20 David got up from the floor, had a bath, combed his hair, and changed his clothes. Then he went and worshipped in the house of the LORD. When he returned to the palace, he asked for food and ate it as soon as it was served. ²¹ "We don't understand this," his officials said to him. "While the child was alive, you wept for him and would not eat; but as soon as he died, you got up and ate!"

22 "Yes," David answered, "I did fast and weep while he was still alive. I thought that the LORD might be merciful to me and not let the child die. ²³ But now that he is dead, why should I fast? Could I bring the child back to life? I will some day go to where he is, but he can never come back to me."

Solomon Is Born

24 Then David comforted his wife Bathsheba. He had intercourse with her, and she bore a son, whom David named Solomon. The LORD loved the boy ²⁵ and commanded the prophet Nathan to name the boy Jedidiah,ˣ because the LORD loved him.

David Captures Rabbah
(1 Chr 20.1-3)

26 Meanwhile Joab continued his campaign against Rabbah, the capital city of Ammon, and was about to capture it. ²⁷ He sent messengers to David to report: "I have attacked Rabbah and have captured its water supply. ²⁸ Now gather the rest of your forces, attack the city and take it yourself. I don't want to get the credit for capturing it." ²⁹ So David gathered his forces, went to Rabbah, attacked it, and conquered it. ³⁰ From the head of the idol of the Ammonite god Molechʸ David took a gold crown which weighed about thirty-five kilogrammes and had a jewel in it. David took the jewel and put it in his own crown.ᵐ He also took a large amount of loot from the city ³¹ and put its people to work with saws, iron hoes, and iron axes, and forced them to work atᶻ making bricks. He did the same to the people of all the other towns of Ammon. Then he and his men returned to Jerusalem.

Amnon and Tamar

13 David's son Absalom had a beautiful unmarried sister named Tamar. Amnon, another of David's sons, fell in love with her. ² He was so much in love with her that he became ill, because it seemed impossible for him to have her; as a virgin, she was kept from meeting men. ³ But he had a friend, a very shrewd man named Jonadab, the son of David's brother Shammah. ⁴ Jonadab said to Amnon, "You are the king's son, yet day after day I see you looking sad. What's the matter?"

"I'm in love with Tamar, the sister of my half-brother Absalom," he answered.

5 Jonadab said to him, "Pretend that you are ill and go to bed. When your father comes to see you, say to him, 'Please ask my sister Tamar to come and feed me. I want her to prepare the food here where I can see her, and then serve it to me herself.'" ⁶ So Amnon pretended that he was ill and went to bed.

King David went to see him, and Amnon said to him, "Please let Tamar come and make a few cakes here where I can see her, and then serve them to me herself."

7 So David sent word to Tamar in the palace: "Go to Amnon's house and prepare some food for him." ⁸ She went there and found him in bed. She took some dough, prepared it, and made some cakes there where he could see her. Then she baked the cakes ⁹ and emptied them out

---

ˣ JEDIDIAH: *This name in Hebrew means "Beloved of the LORD."*
ʸ idol of the Ammonite god Molech; *or* Ammonite king.
ᵐ jewel...crown; *or* crown and put it on his own head.
ᶻ *Probable text (see 1 Chr 20.3)* work at; *Hebrew* pass through.

of the pan for him to eat, but he wouldn't. He said, "Send everyone away"—and they all left. [10]Then he said to her, "Bring the cakes here to my bed and serve them to me yourself." She took the cakes and went over to him. [11]As she offered them to him, he grabbed her and said, "Come to bed with me!"

[12]"No," she said. "Don't force me to do such a degrading thing! That's awful! [13]How could I ever hold up my head in public again? And you—you would be completely disgraced in Israel. Please, speak to the king, and I'm sure that he will give me to you." [14]But he would not listen to her; and since he was stronger than she was, he overpowered her and raped her.

[15]Then Amnon was filled with a deep hatred for her; he hated her now even more than he had loved her before. He said to her, "Get out!"

[16]"No," she answered. "To send me away like this is a greater crime[a] than what you just did!"

But Amnon would not listen to her; [17]he called in his personal servant and said, "Get this woman out of my sight! Throw her out and lock the door!" [18]The servant put her out and locked the door.

Tamar was wearing a long robe with full sleeves,[b] the usual clothing for an unmarried princess in those days.[c] [19]She sprinkled ashes on her head, tore her robe, and with her face buried in her hands went away crying. [20]When her brother Absalom saw her, he asked, "Has Amnon molested you? Please, sister, don't let it upset you so much. He is your half-brother, so don't tell anyone about it." So Tamar lived in Absalom's house, sad and lonely.

[21]When King David heard what had happened, he was furious. [22]And Absalom hated Amnon so much for having raped his sister Tamar that he would no longer even speak to him.

Absalom's Revenge

[23]Two years later Absalom was having his sheep sheared at Baal Hazor, near the town of Ephraim, and he invited all the king's sons to be there. [24]He went to King David and said, "Your Majesty, I am having my sheep sheared. Will you and your officials come and take part in the festivities?"

[25]"No, my son," the king answered. "It would be too much trouble for you if we all went." Absalom insisted, but the king would not give in, and he asked Absalom to leave.

[26]But Absalom said, "Well, then, will you at least let my brother Amnon come?"

"Why should he?" the king asked. [27]But Absalom kept on insisting until David finally let Amnon and all his other sons go with Absalom.

Absalom prepared a banquet fit for a king[d] [28]and instructed his servants: "Notice when Amnon has had too much to drink, and then when I give the order, kill him. Don't be afraid. I will take the responsibility myself. Be brave and don't hesitate!" [29]So the servants followed Absalom's instructions and killed Amnon. All the rest of David's sons mounted their mules and fled.

[30]While they were on their way home, David was told: "Absalom has killed all your sons—not one of them is left!" [31]The king stood up, tore his clothes in sorrow, and threw himself to the ground. The servants who were there with him tore their clothes also. [32]But Jonadab, the son of David's brother Shammah, said, "Your Majesty, they haven't killed all your sons. Only Amnon is dead. You could tell by looking at Absalom that he had made up his mind to do this from the time that Amnon raped his sister Tamar. [33]So don't believe the news that all your sons are dead; only Amnon was killed."

[34]In the meantime Absalom had fled.

Just then the soldier on sentry duty saw a large crowd coming down the hill on the road from Horonaim.[e] He went to the king and reported what he had seen.[f] [35]Jonadab said to David, "Those are your sons coming, just as I said they would." [36]As soon as he finished saying this, David's sons came in; they started crying, and David and his officials also wept bitterly.

[37-38]Absalom fled and went to the king of Geshur, Talmai son of Ammihud, and stayed there three years. David mourned a long time for his son Amnon;

---

[a] *Probable text* To send me...crime; *Hebrew unclear.*
[b] long robe with full sleeves; *or* decorated robe *(see Gen 37.3).*
[c] *Probable text* in those days; *Hebrew garments.*
[d] *Some ancient translations* Absalom prepared a banquet fit for a king; *Hebrew does not have these words.* [e] *Probable text* from Horonaim; *Hebrew behind him.*
[f] *One ancient translation* He went...had seen; *Hebrew does not have these words.*
13.37: 2 Sam 3.3

Those are your sons coming (13.35)

39 but when he got over Amnon's death, he was filled with longing for his son Absalom.

Joab Arranges for Absalom's Return

14 Joab knew that King David missed Absalom very much, 2 so he sent for a clever woman who lived in Tekoa. When she arrived, he said to her, "Pretend that you are in mourning; put on your mourning clothes, and don't comb your hair. Act like a woman who has been in mourning for a long time. 3 Then go to the king and say to him what I tell you to say." Then Joab told her what to say.

4 The woman went to the king, bowed down to the ground in respect, and said, "Help me, Your Majesty!"

5 "What do you want?" he asked her.

"I am a poor widow, sir," she answered. "My husband is dead. 6 Sir, I had two sons, and one day they got into a quarrel out in the fields, where there was no one to separate them, and one of them killed the other. 7 And now, sir, all my relatives have turned against me and are demanding that I hand my son over to them, so that they can kill him for murdering his brother. If they do this, I will be left without a son. They will destroy my last hope and leave my husband without a son to keep his name alive."

8 "Go back home," the king answered, "and I will take care of the matter."

9 "Your Majesty," she said, "whatever you do, my family and I will take the blame; you and the royal family are innocent."

10 The king replied, "If anyone threatens you, bring him to me, and he will never trouble you again."

11 She said, "Your Majesty, please pray to the LORD your God, so that my relative who is responsible for avenging the death of my son will not commit a greater crime by killing my other son."

"I promise by the living LORD," David replied, "that your son will not be harmed in the least."

12 "Please, Your Majesty, let me say just one more thing," the woman said.

"All right," he answered.

13 She said to him, "Why have you done such a wrong to God's people? You have not allowed your own son to return from exile, and so you have condemned yourself by what you have just said. 14 We will all die; we are like water spilt on the ground, which can't be gathered again. Even God does not bring the dead back to life, but the king can at least find a way to bring a man back from exile. *g* 15 Now, Your Majesty, the reason I have come to speak to you is that the people threatened me, and so I said to myself that I would speak to you in the hope that you would do what I ask. 16 I thought you would listen to me and save me from the one who is trying to kill my son and me and so remove us from the land God gave his people. 17 I said to myself that your promise, sir, would make me safe, because the king is like God's angel and can distinguish good from evil. *h* May the LORD your God be with you!"

18 The king answered, "I'm going to ask you a question, and you must tell me the whole truth."

"Ask me anything, Your Majesty," she answered.

19 "Did Joab put you up to this?" he asked her.

She answered, "I swear by all that is sacred, Your Majesty, that there is no way to avoid answering your question. *i* It was indeed your officer Joab who told me what

---

g Probable text Even God...from exile; *Hebrew unclear.*
h can distinguish good from evil; *or* knows everything.
i there is...question; *or* you are absolutely right.
14.17: 2 Sam 19.27

to do and what to say. 20 But he did it in order to straighten out this whole matter. Your Majesty is as wise as the angel of God and knows everything that happens."

21 Later on the king said to Joab, "I have decided to do what you want. Go and get the young man Absalom and bring him back here."

22 Joab threw himself to the ground in front of David in respect, and said, "God bless you, Your Majesty! Now I know that you are pleased with me, because you have granted my request." 23 Then he got up and went to Geshur and brought Absalom back to Jerusalem. 24 The king, however, gave orders that Absalom should not live in the palace. "I don't want to see him," the king said. So Absalom lived in his own house and did not appear before the king.

Absalom Is Reconciled to David

25 There was no one in Israel as famous for his good looks as Absalom; he had no defect from head to foot. 26 His hair was very thick, and he had to cut it once a year, when it grew too long and heavy. It would weigh more than two kilogrammes according to the royal standard of weights. 27 Absalom had three sons and one daughter named Tamar, a very beautiful woman.

28 Absalom lived two years in Jerusalem without seeing the king. 29 Then he sent for Joab, to ask him to go to the king for him; but Joab would not come. Again Absalom sent for him, and again Joab refused to come. 30 So Absalom said to his servants, "Look, Joab's field is next to mine, and it has barley growing in it. Go and set fire to it." So they went and set the field on fire.

31 Joab went to Absalom's house and demanded, "Why did your servants set fire to my field?"

32 Absalom answered, "Because you wouldn't come when I sent for you. I wanted you to go to the king and ask him from me: 'Why did I leave Geshur and come here? It would have been better for me to have stayed there.'" And Absalom went on, "I want you to arrange for me to see the king, and if I'm guilty, then let him put me to death."

33 So Joab went to King David and told him what Absalom had said. The king sent for Absalom, who went to him and bowed down to the ground in front of him. The king welcomed him with a kiss.

Absalom Plans Rebellion

15 After this, Absalom provided a chariot and horses for himself, and an escort of fifty men. 2 He would get up early and go and stand by the road at the city gate. Whenever someone came there with a dispute that he wanted the king to settle, Absalom would call him over and ask him where he was from. And after the man had told him what tribe he was from, 3 Absalom would say, "Look, the law is on your side, but there is no representative of the king to hear your case." 4 And he would add, "How I wish I were a judge! Then anyone who had a dispute or a claim could come to me, and I would give him justice." 5 When the man approached Absalom to bow down before him, Absalom would reach out, take hold of him, and kiss him. 6 Absalom did this with every Israelite who came to the king for justice, and so he won their loyalty.

7 After four*j* years Absalom said to King David, "Sir, let me go to Hebron and keep a promise I made to the LORD. 8 While I was living in Geshur in Syria, I promised the LORD that if he would take me back to Jerusalem, I would worship him in Hebron."*k*

9 "Go in peace," the king said. So Absalom went to Hebron. 10 But he sent messengers to all the tribes of Israel to say, "When you hear the sound of trumpets, shout, 'Absalom has become king at Hebron!'" 11 There were two hundred men who at Absalom's invitation had gone from Jerusalem with him; they knew nothing of the plot and went in all good faith. 12 And while he was offering sacrifices, Absalom also sent to the town of Gilo for Ahithophel, who was one of King David's advisers. The plot against the king gained strength, and Absalom's followers grew in number.

David Flees from Jerusalem

13 A messenger reported to David, "The Israelites are pledging their loyalty to Absalom."

14 So David said to all his officials who were with him in Jerusalem, "We must get away at once if we want to escape from Absalom! Hurry! Or else he will

---

j Some ancient translations four; *Hebrew* forty.
k One ancient translation in Hebron; *Hebrew does not have these words.*

So the king left, accompanied by all his family (15.16)

soon be here and defeat us and kill everyone in the city!"

15 "Yes, Your Majesty," they answered. "We are ready to do whatever you say." 16 So the king left, accompanied by all his family and officials, except for ten concubines, whom he left behind to take care of the palace.

17 As the king and all his men were leaving the city, they stopped at the last house. 18 All his officials stood*l* next to him as the royal bodyguard passed by in front of him. The six hundred soldiers who had followed him from Gath also passed by, 19 and the king said to Ittai, their leader, "Why are you going with us? Go back and stay with the new king. You are a foreigner, a refugee away from your own country. 20 You have lived here only a short time, so why should I make you wander round with me? I don't even know where I'm going. Go back and take your fellow-countrymen with you—and may the LORD be kind and faithful to you."*m*

21 But Ittai answered, "Your Majesty, I swear to you in the LORD's name that I will always go with you wherever you go, even if it means death."

22 "Fine!" David answered. "March on!" So Ittai went on with all his men and their dependants. 23 The people cried loudly as David's followers left. The king crossed the brook of Kidron, followed by his men, and together they went out towards the wilderness.

24 Zadok the priest was there, and with him were the Levites, carrying the sacred Covenant Box. They set it down*n* and didn't pick it up again until all the people had left the city. The priest Abiathar was there too. *o* 25 Then the king said to Zadok, "Take the Covenant Box back to the city. If the LORD is pleased with me, some day he will let me come back to see it and the place where it stays. 26 But if he isn't pleased with me—well, then, let him do to me what he wishes." 27 And he went on to say to Zadok, "Look,*p* take your son Ahimaaz and Abiathar's son Jonathan and go back to the city in peace. 28 Meanwhile, I will wait at the river crossings in the wilderness until I receive news from you." 29 So Zadok and Abiathar took the Covenant Box back into Jerusalem and stayed there.

30 David went on up the Mount of Olives weeping; he was barefoot and had his head covered as a sign of grief. All who followed him covered their heads and wept also. 31 When David was told*q* that Ahithophel had joined Absalom's rebellion, he prayed, "Please, LORD, turn Ahithophel's advice into nonsense!"

l Probable text stood; *Hebrew* passed.
m One ancient translation and may the LORD be kind and faithful to you; *Hebrew* kindness and faithfulness. *n Probable text* set it down; *Hebrew* poured it out.
o Probable text was there too; *Hebrew* went up.
p Some ancient translations Look; *Hebrew* Are you the seer?
q One ancient translation was told; *Hebrew* told.

David went on up the Mount of Olives weeping (15.30)

32 When David reached the top of the hill, where there was a place of worship, his trusted friend Hushai the Archite met him with his clothes torn and with earth on his head. 33 David said to him, "You will be of no help to me if you come with me, 34 but you can help me by returning to the city and telling Absalom that you will now serve him as faithfully as you served his father. And do all you can to oppose any advice that Ahithophel gives. 35 The priests Zadok and Abiathar will be there; tell them everything you hear in the king's palace. 36 They have their sons Ahimaaz and Jonathan with them, and you can send them to me with all the information you gather."

37 So Hushai, David's friend, returned to the city just as Absalom was arriving.

David and Ziba

16 When David had gone a little beyond the top of the hill, he was suddenly met by Ziba, the servant of Mephibosheth, who had with him a couple of donkeys loaded with two hundred loaves of bread, a hundred bunches of raisins, a hundred bunches of fresh fruit, and a leather bag full of wine. 2 King David asked him, "What are you going to do with all that?"

Ziba answered, "The donkeys are for Your Majesty's family to ride, the bread and the fruit are for the men to eat, and the wine is for them to drink when they get tired in the wilderness."

3 "Where is Mephibosheth, the grandson of your master Saul?" the king asked him.

"He is staying in Jerusalem," Ziba answered, "because he is convinced that the Israelites will now restore to him the kingdom of his grandfather Saul."

4 The king said to Ziba, "Everything that belonged to Mephibosheth is yours."

"I am your servant," Ziba replied. "May I always please Your Majesty!"

David and Shimei

5 When King David arrived at Bahurim, one of Saul's relatives, Shimei son of Gera, came out to meet him, cursing him as

16.1: 2 Sam 9.9-10   **16.3:** 2 Sam 19.26-27

Shimei kept up with them...cursing and throwing stones (16.13)

he came. 6 Shimei started throwing stones at David and his officials, even though David was surrounded by his men and his bodyguard. 7 Shimei cursed him and said, "Get out! Get out! Murderer! Criminal! 8 You took Saul's kingdom, and now the LORD is punishing you for murdering so many of Saul's family. The LORD has given the kingdom to your son Absalom, and you are ruined, you murderer!"

9 Abishai, whose mother was Zeruiah, said to the king, "Your Majesty, why do you let this dog curse you? Let me go over there and cut off his head!"

10 "This is none of your business," the king said to Abishai and his brother Joab. "If he curses me because the LORD told him to, who has the right to ask why he does it?" 11 And David said to Abishai and to all his officials, "My own son is trying to kill me; so why should you be surprised at this Benjaminite? The LORD told him to curse; so leave him alone and let him do it. 12 Perhaps the LORD will notice my misery[r] and give me some blessings to take the place of his curse."

13 So David and his men continued along the road. Shimei kept up with them, walking on the hillside; he was cursing and throwing stones and earth at them as he went. 14 The king and all his men were worn out when they reached the Jordan,[s] and there they rested.

Absalom in Jerusalem

15 Absalom and all the Israelites with him entered Jerusalem, and Ahithophel was with them. 16 When Hushai, David's trusted friend, met Absalom, he shouted, "Long live the king! Long live the king!"

17 "What has happened to your loyalty to your friend David?" Absalom asked him. "Why didn't you go with him?"

18 Hushai answered, "How could I? I am on the side of the one chosen by the LORD, by these people, and by all the Israelites. I will stay with you. 19 After all, whom should I serve, if not my master's son? As I served your father, so now I will serve you."

20 Then Absalom turned to Ahithophel and said, "Now that we are here, what do you advise us to do?"

21 Ahithophel answered, "Go and have intercourse with your father's concubines whom he left behind to take care of the palace. Then everyone in Israel will know that your father regards you as his enemy, and your followers will be greatly encouraged." 22 So they set up a tent for Absalom on the palace roof, and in the sight of everyone Absalom went in and had intercourse with his father's concubines.

23 Any advice that Ahithophel gave in those days was accepted as though it were the very word of God; both David and Absalom followed it.

---

[r] *Some ancient translations* misery; *Hebrew* wickedness.
[s] *One ancient translation* the Jordan; *Hebrew does not have these words.*
16.22: 2 Sam 12.11–12

Hushai Misleads Absalom

17 Not long after that, Ahithophel said to Absalom, "Let me choose twelve thousand men, and tonight I will set out after David. ²I will attack him while he is tired and discouraged. He will be frightened, and all his men will run away. I will kill only the king ³and then bring back all his men to you, like a bride returning to her husband. You want to kill only one man; ᵗ the rest of the people will be safe." ⁴This seemed like good advice to Absalom and all the Israelite leaders.

5 Absalom said, "Now call Hushai, and let us hear what he has to say." ⁶When Hushai arrived, Absalom said to him, "This is the advice that Ahithophel has given us; shall we follow it? If not, you tell us what to do."

7 Hushai answered, "The advice Ahithophel gave you this time is no good. ⁸You know that your father David and his men are hard fighters and that they are as fierce as a mother bear robbed of her cubs. Your father is an experienced soldier and does not stay with his men at night. ⁹Just now he is probably hiding in a cave or some other place. As soon as David attacks your men, whoever hears about it will say that your men have been defeated. ¹⁰Then even the bravest men, as fearless as lions, will be afraid because everyone in Israel knows that your father is a great soldier and that his men are hard fighters. ¹¹My advice is that you bring all the Israelites together from one end of the country to the other, as many as the grains of sand on the sea-shore, and that you lead them personally in battle. ¹²We will find David wherever he is, and attack him before he knows what's happening. Neither he nor any of his men will survive. ¹³If he retreats into a city, our people will all bring ropes and just pull the city ᵘ into the valley below. Not a single stone will be left there on top of the hill."

14 Absalom and all the Israelites said, "Hushai's advice is better than Ahithophel's." The LORD had decided that Ahithophel's good advice would not be followed, so that disaster would come on Absalom.

David Is Warned and Escapes

15 Then Hushai told the priests Zadok and Abiathar what advice he had given to Absalom and the Israelite leaders and what advice Ahithophel had given. ¹⁶Hushai added, "Quick, now! Send a message to David not to spend the night at the river crossings in the wilderness, but to cross the Jordan at once, so that he and his men won't all be caught and killed."

17 Abiathar's son Jonathan and Zadok's son Ahimaaz were waiting at the spring of Enrogel, on the outskirts of Jerusalem, because they did not dare to be seen entering the city. A servant-girl would regularly go and tell them what was happening, and then they would go and tell King David. ¹⁸But one day a boy happened to see them, and he told Absalom; so they hurried off to hide in the house of a certain man in Bahurim. He had a well near his house, and they got down into it. ¹⁹The man's wife took a covering, spread it over the opening of the well and scattered grain over it, so that no one would notice anything. ²⁰Absalom's officials came to the house and asked the woman, "Where are Ahimaaz and Jonathan?"

"They crossed the river," she answered. The men looked for them but could not find them, and so they returned to Jerusalem. ²¹After they left, Ahimaaz and Jonathan came up out of the well and went and reported to King David. They told him what Ahithophel had planned against him and said, "Hurry up and cross the river." ²²So David and his men started crossing the Jordan, and by daybreak they had all gone across.

23 When Ahithophel saw that his advice had not been followed, he saddled his donkey and went back to his own city. After putting his affairs in order, he hanged himself. He was buried in the family grave.

24 David had reached the town of Mahanaim by the time Absalom and the Israelites had crossed the Jordan. ²⁵(Absalom had put Amasa in command of the army in the place of Joab. Amasa was the son of Jether the Ishmaelite; ᵛ his mother was Abigail, the daughter of Nahash and the sister of Joab's mother

---

ᵗ *One ancient translation* like a bride...only one man; *Hebrew* like the return of the whole, so is the man you seek.   ᵘ *Some ancient translations* the city; *Hebrew* him.
ᵛ *One ancient translation (and see 1 Chr 2.17)* Ishmaelite; *Hebrew* Israelite.

Zeruiah.) ²⁶ Absalom and his men camped in the land of Gilead.

27 When David arrived at Mahanaim, he was met by Shobi son of Nahash, from the city of Rabbah in Ammon, and by Machir son of Ammiel, from Lodebar, and by Barzillai, from Rogelim in Gilead. ²⁸⁻²⁹ They brought bowls, clay pots, and bedding, and also food for David and his men: wheat, barley, meal, roasted grain, beans, peas, ʷ honey, cheese, cream, and some sheep. They knew that David and his men would be hungry, thirsty, and tired in the wilderness.

Absalom Is Defeated and Killed

18 King David brought all his men together, divided them into units of a thousand and of a hundred, and placed officers in command of them. ² Then he sent them out in three groups, with Joab and Joab's brother Abishai and Ittai from Gath, each in command of a group. And the king said to his men, "I will go with you myself."

3 "You mustn't go with us," they answered. "It won't make any difference to the enemy if the rest of us turn and run, or even if half of us are killed; but you are worth ten thousand of us. It will be better if you stay here in the city and send us help."

4 "I will do whatever you think best," the king answered. Then he stood by the side of the gate as his men marched out in units of a thousand and of a hundred. ⁵ He gave orders to Joab, Abishai, and Ittai: "For my sake don't harm the young man Absalom." And all the troops heard David give this command to his officers.

6 David's army went out into the countryside and fought the Israelites in the forest of Ephraim. ⁷ The Israelites were defeated by David's men; it was a terrible defeat, with twenty thousand men killed that day. ⁸ The fighting spread over the countryside, and more men died in the forest than were killed in battle.

9 Suddenly Absalom met some of David's men. Absalom was riding a mule, and as it went under a large oak-tree, Absalom's head got caught in the branches. The mule ran on and Absalom was left hanging in mid air. ¹⁰ One of David's men saw him and reported to Joab, "Sir, I saw Absalom hanging in an oak-tree!"

11 Joab answered, "If you saw him, why didn't you kill him on the spot? I myself would have given you ten pieces of silver and a belt."

12 But the man answered, "Even if you gave me a thousand pieces of silver, I wouldn't lift a finger against the king's son. We all heard the king command you and Abishai and Ittai, 'For my sake don't harm the young man Absalom.' ¹³ But if I had disobeyed the king and killed Absalom, the king would have heard about it—he hears about everything—and you would not have defended me."

14 "I'm not going to waste any more time with you," Joab said. He took three spears and plunged them into Absalom's chest while he was still alive, hanging in the oak-tree. ¹⁵ Then ten of Joab's soldiers closed in on Absalom and finished killing him.

16 Joab ordered the trumpet to be blown to stop the fighting, and his troops

---

ʷ *Some ancient translations* peas; *Hebrew* peas and roasted grain.

For David and his men (17.29)

Don't harm the young man Absalom (18.5)

came back from pursuing the Israelites.
17 They took Absalom's body, threw it into
a deep pit in the forest, and covered it
with a huge pile of stones. All the
Israelites fled, each man to his own home.

18 During his lifetime Absalom had
built a monument for himself in King's
Valley, because he had no son to keep
his name alive. So he named it after
himself, and to this day it is known as
Absalom's Monument.

David Is Told of Absalom's Death

19 Then Ahimaaz son of Zadok said to
Joab, "Let me run to the king with the
good news that the LORD has saved him
from his enemies."

20 "No," Joab said, "today you will not
take any good news. Some other day you
may do so, but not today, for the king's
son is dead." 21 Then he said to his
Sudanese slave, "Go and tell the king
what you have seen." The slave bowed
and ran off.

22 Ahimaaz insisted, "I don't care what
happens; please let me take the news
also."

"Why do you want to do it, my son?"
Joab asked. "You will get no reward for
it."

23 "Whatever happens," Ahimaaz said
again, "I want to go."

"Then go," Joab said. So Ahimaaz ran
off down the road through the Jordan
Valley, and soon he passed the slave.

24 David was sitting in the space
between the inner and outer gates of the
city. The watchman went up to the top
of the wall and stood on the roof of the
gateway; he looked out and saw a man
running alone. 25 He called down and told
the king, and the king said, "If he is alone,
he is bringing good news." The runner
came nearer and nearer.

26 Then the watchman saw another
man running alone, and he called down
to the gatekeeper, "Look! There's another
man running!"

The king answered, "This one also is
bringing good news."

27 The watchman said, "I can see that
the first man runs like Ahimaaz."

"He's a good man," the king said, "and
he is bringing good news."

28 Ahimaaz called out a greeting to the
king, threw himself down to the ground
before him, and said, "Praise the LORD
your God, who has given you victory over
the men who rebelled against Your
Majesty!"

29 "Is the young man Absalom safe?"
the king asked.

Ahimaaz answered, "Sir, when your
officer Joab sent me, I saw a great

Absalom's head got caught in the branches (18.9)

commotion, but I couldn't tell what it was."

30 "Stand over there," the king said; and he went over and stood there.

31 Then the Sudanese slave arrived and said to the king, "I have good news for Your Majesty! Today the LORD has given you victory over all who rebelled against you!"

32 "Is the young man Absalom safe?" the king asked.

The slave answered, "I wish that what has happened to him would happen to all your enemies, sir, and to all who rebel against you."

33 The king was overcome with grief. He went up to the room over the gateway and wept. As he went, he cried, "O my son! My son Absalom! Absalom, my son! If only I had died in your place, my son! Absalom, my son!"

Joab Reprimands David

19 Joab was told that King David was weeping and mourning for Absalom. ² And so the joy of victory was turned into sadness for all David's troops that day, because they heard that the king was mourning for his son. ³ They went back into the city quietly, like soldiers who are ashamed because they are running away from battle. ⁴ The king covered his face

and cried loudly, "O my son! My son Absalom! Absalom, my son!"

5 Joab went to the king's house and said to him, "Today you have humiliated your men—the men who saved your life and the lives of your sons and daughters and of your wives and concubines. ⁶ You oppose those who love you and support those who hate you! You have made it clear that your officers and men mean nothing to you. I can see that you would be quite happy if Absalom were alive today and all of us were dead. ⁷ Now go and reassure your men. I swear by the LORD's name that if you don't, not one of them will be with you by tomorrow morning. That would be the worst disaster you have suffered in all your life." ⁸ Then the king got up, and went and sat near the city gate. His men heard that he was there, and they all gathered round him.

David Starts Back to Jerusalem

Meanwhile all the Israelites had fled, each man to his own home. ⁹ All over the country they started quarrelling among themselves. "King David saved us from our enemies," they said to one another. "He rescued us from the Philistines, but now he has fled from Absalom and left the country. ¹⁰ We anointed Absalom as our king, but he has been killed in battle.

O my son! My son Absalom! (19.4)

and they arrived at the Jordan before the king. 18 They crossed[y] the river to escort the royal party across and to do whatever the king wanted.

David Shows Kindness to Shimei

As the king was getting ready to cross, Shimei threw himself down in front of him 19 and said, "Your Majesty, please forget the wrong I did that day you left Jerusalem. Don't hold it against me or think about it any more. 20 I know, sir, that I have sinned, and this is why I am the first one from the northern tribes to come and meet Your Majesty today."

21 Abishai son of Zeruiah spoke up: "Shimei should be put to death because he cursed the one whom the LORD chose as king."

22 But David said to Abishai and his brother Joab, "Who asked your opinion? Are you going to give me trouble? I am the one who is king of Israel now, and no Israelite will be put to death today." 23 And he said to Shimei, "I give you my word that you will not be put to death."

David Shows Kindness to Mephibosheth

24 Then Mephibosheth, Saul's grandson, came down to meet the king. He had not washed his feet, trimmed his beard, or washed his clothes from the time the king left Jerusalem until he returned victorious. 25 When Mephibosheth arrived from[z] Jerusalem to meet the king, the king said to him, "Mephibosheth, you didn't go with me. Why not?"

26 He answered, "As you know, Your Majesty, I am crippled. I told my servant to saddle my donkey so that I could ride along with you, but he betrayed me. 27 He lied about me to Your Majesty, but you are like God's angel, so do what seems right to you. 28 All my father's family deserved to be put to death by Your Majesty, but you gave me the right to eat at your table. I have no right to ask for any more favours from Your Majesty."

29 The king answered, "You don't have to say anything more. I have decided that you and Ziba will share Saul's property."

30 "Let Ziba have it all," Mephibosheth answered. "It's enough for me that Your Majesty has come home safely."

So why doesn't somebody try to bring King David back?"

11 The news of what the Israelites were saying reached King David.[x] So he sent the priests Zadok and Abiathar to ask the leaders of Judah, "Why should you be the last to help bring the king back to his palace? 12 You are my relatives, my own flesh and blood; why should you be the last to bring me back?" 13 David also told them to say to Amasa, "You are my relative. From now on I am putting you in charge of the army in place of Joab. May God strike me dead if I don't!" 14 David's words won the complete loyalty of all the men of Judah, and they sent him word to return with all his officials.

15 On his way back the king was met at the River Jordan by the men of Judah, who had come to Gilgal to escort him across the river. 16 At the same time the Benjaminite Shimei son of Gera from Bahurim hurried to the Jordan to meet King David. 17 He had with him a thousand men from the tribe of Benjamin. And Ziba, the servant of Saul's family, also came with his fifteen sons and twenty servants,

x *Some ancient translations* The news...David; *Hebrew* The news...David, to his palace, *and places this sentence at the end of the verse.*
y *Probable text* They crossed; *Hebrew* The crossing crossed.
z *One ancient translation* from; *Hebrew* at.
19.16: 2 Sam 16.5-13   **19.24:** 2 Sam 9.1-13, 16.1-4

It's enough for me that Your Majesty has come home safely (19.30)

David Shows Kindness to Barzillai

31 Barzillai, from Gilead, had also come down from Rogelim to escort the king across the Jordan. 32 Barzillai was a very old man, eighty years old. He was very rich and had supplied the king with food while he was staying at Mahanaim. 33 The king said to him, "Come with me to Jerusalem, and I will take care of you."

34 But Barzillai answered, "I haven't long to live; why should I go with Your Majesty to Jerusalem? 35 I am already eighty years old, and nothing gives me pleasure any more. I can't taste what I eat and drink, and I can't hear the voices of singers. I would only be a burden to Your Majesty. 36 I don't deserve such a great reward. So I will go just a little way with you beyond the Jordan. 37 Then let me go back home and die near my parents' grave. Here is my son Chimham, who will serve you; take him with you, Your Majesty, and do for him as you think best."

38 The king answered, "I will take him with me and do for him whatever you want. And I will do for you anything you

ask." 39 Then David and all his men crossed the Jordan. He kissed Barzillai and gave him his blessing, and Barzillai went back home.

Judah and Israel Argue over the King

40 When the king had crossed, escorted by all the men of Judah and half the men of Israel, he went on to Gilgal, and Chimham went with him. 41 Then all the Israelites went to the king and said to him, "Your Majesty, why did our brothers, the men of Judah, think they had the right to take you away and escort you, your family, and your men across the Jordan?"

42 The men of Judah answered, "We did it because the king is one of us. So why should this make you angry? He hasn't paid for our food nor has he given us anything."

43 The Israelites replied, "We have ten times as many claims on King David as you have, even if he is one of you. Why do you look down on us? Don't forget that we were the first to talk about bringing the king back!"

But the men of Judah were more violent in making their claims than the men of Israel.

Sheba's Rebellion

20 There happened to be in Gilgal a worthless character named Sheba son of Bikri, of the tribe of Benjamin. He blew the trumpet and called out, "Down with David! We won't follow him! Men of Israel, let's go home!" 2 So the Israelites deserted David and went with Sheba, but the men of Judah remained loyal and followed David from the Jordan to Jerusalem.

3 When David arrived at his palace in Jerusalem, he took the ten concubines he had left to take care of the palace, and put them under guard. He provided for their needs, but did not have intercourse with them. They were kept confined for the rest of their lives, living like widows.

4 The king said to Amasa, "Call the men of Judah together and be back here with them by the day after tomorrow." 5 Amasa went to call them, but he did not get back by the time the king had set. 6 So the king said to Abishai, "Sheba will give us more trouble than Absalom. Take my men and go after him, or else he may occupy some fortified towns and escape from us." 7 So Joab's men, the royal bodyguard, and all the other soldiers left Jerusalem with

19.31: 2 Sam 17.27-29   **20.1:** 1 Kgs 12.16; 2 Chr 10.16   **20.3:** 2 Sam 16.22

Abishai to go after Sheba. ⁸When they reached the large rock at Gibeon, Amasa met them. Joab was dressed for battle, with a sword in its sheath fastened to his belt. As he came forward, the sword fell out. ⁹Joab said to Amasa, "How are you, my friend?" and took hold of his beard with his right hand in order to kiss him. ¹⁰Amasa was not on guard against the sword that Joab was holding in his other hand, and Joab stabbed him in the belly, and his entrails spilt out on the ground. He died immediately, and Joab did not have to strike again.

Then Joab and his brother Abishai went on after Sheba. ¹¹One of Joab's men stood by Amasa's body and called out, "Everyone who is for Joab and David follow Joab!" ¹²Amasa's body, covered with blood, was lying in the middle of the road. Joab's man saw that everybody was stopping, so he dragged the body from the road into the field and threw a blanket over it. ¹³After the body had been removed from the road, everyone followed Joab in pursuit of Sheba.

14 Sheba passed through the territory of all the tribes of Israel and came to the city of Abel Beth Maacah, and all the members of the clan of Bikriᵃ assembled and followed him into the city. ¹⁵Joab's men heard that Sheba was there, and so they went and besieged the city. They built ramps of earth against the outer wall and also began to dig under the wall to make it fall down. ¹⁶There was a wise woman in the city who shouted from the wall, "Listen! Listen! Tell Joab to come here; I want to speak with him." ¹⁷Joab went, and she asked, "Are you Joab?"

"Yes, I am," he answered.

"Listen to me, sir," she said.

"I'm listening," he answered.

18 She said, "Long ago they used to say, 'Go and get your answer in the city of Abel'—and that's just what they did. ¹⁹Ours is a great city, one of the most peaceful and loyal in Israel. Why are you trying to destroy it? Do you want to ruin what belongs to the LORD?"

20 "Never!" Joab answered. "I will never ruin or destroy your city! ²¹That is not our plan. A man named Sheba son of Bikri, who is from the hill-country of Ephraim, started a rebellion against King David. Hand over this one man, and I will withdraw from the city."

"We will throw his head over the wall to you," she said. ²²Then she went to the people of the city with her plan, and they cut off Sheba's head and threw it over the wall to Joab. He blew the trumpet as a signal for his men to leave the city, and they went back home. And Joab returned to Jerusalem to the king.

David's Officials

23 Joab was in command of the army of Israel; Benaiah son of Jehoiada was in charge of David's bodyguard; ²⁴Adoniram was in charge of the forced labour; Jehoshaphat son of Ahilud was in charge of the records; ²⁵Sheva was the court secretary; Zadok and Abiathar were the priests, ²⁶and Ira from the town of Jair was also one of David's priests.

Saul's Descendants Are Put to Death

21 During David's reign there was a severe famine which lasted for three full years. So David consulted the LORD about it, and the LORD said, "Saul and his family are guilty of murder; he put the people of Gibeon to death." ²(The people of Gibeon were not Israelites; they were a small group of Amorites whom the Israelites had promised to protect, but Saul had tried to destroy them because of his zeal for the people of Israel and Judah.) ³So David summoned the people of Gibeon and said to them, "What can I do for you? I want to make up for the wrong that was done to you, so that you will bless the LORD's people."

4 They answered, "Our quarrel with Saul and his family can't be settled with silver or gold, nor do we want to kill any Israelite."

"What, then, do you think I should do for you?" David asked.

5 They answered, "Saul wanted to destroy us and leave none of us alive anywhere in Israel. ⁶So hand over seven of his male descendants, and we will hang them before the LORD at Gibeah, the town of Saul, the LORD's chosen king."

"I will hand them over," the king answered.

7 But because of the sacred promise that he and Jonathan had made to each other, David spared Jonathan's son Mephibosheth, the grandson of Saul. ⁸However, he took Armoni and Mephibosheth, the two sons that Rizpah the daughter of Aiah had borne to Saul; he also took the five sons of Saul's daughter

---

ᵃ *Probable text* Bikri; *Hebrew* Beri.
21.2: Josh 9.3-15   **21.7:** 1 Sam 20.15-17; 2 Sam 9.1-7   **21.8:** 1 Sam 18.19

Merab, whom she had borne to Adriel son of Barzillai, who was from Meholah. 9 David handed them over to the people of Gibeon, who hanged them on the mountain before the LORD—and all seven of them died together. It was late in the spring, at the beginning of the barley harvest, when they were put to death.

10 Then Saul's concubine Rizpah, the daughter of Aiah, used sackcloth to make a shelter for herself on the rock where the corpses were, and she stayed there from the beginning of harvest until the autumn rains came. During the day she would keep the birds away from the corpses, and at night she would protect them from wild animals.

11 When David heard what Rizpah had done, 12 he went and got the bones of Saul and of his son Jonathan from the people of Jabesh in Gilead. (They had stolen them from the public square in Beth Shan, where the Philistines had hanged the bodies on the day they killed Saul on Mount Gilboa.) 13 David took the bones of Saul and Jonathan and also gathered up the bones of the seven men who had been hanged. 14 Then they buried the bones of Saul and Jonathan in the grave of Saul's father Kish, in Zela in the territory of Benjamin, doing all that the king had commanded. And after that, God answered their prayers for the country.

Battles against Philistine Giants
(1 Chr 20.4-8)

15 There was another war between the Philistines and Israel, and David and his men went and fought the Philistines. During one of the battles David grew tired. 16 A giant named Ishbibenob, who was carrying a bronze spear that weighed about three and a half kilogrammes and who was wearing a new sword, thought he could kill David. 17 But Abishai son of Zeruiah came to David's help, attacked the giant, and killed him. Then David's men made David promise that he would never again go out with them to battle. "You are the hope of Israel, and we don't want to lose you," they said.

18 After this there was a battle with the Philistines at Gob, during which Sibbecai from Hushah killed a giant named Saph.

19 There was another battle with the Philistines at Gob, and Elhanan son of Jair b from Bethlehem killed Goliath from

Gath, whose spear had a shaft as thick as the bar on a weaver's loom.

20 Then there was another battle at Gath, where there was a giant who loved to fight. He had six fingers on each hand and six toes on each foot. 21 He defied the Israelites, and Jonathan, the son of David's brother Shammah, killed him.

22 These four were descendants of the giants of Gath, and they were killed by David and his men.

David's Song of Victory
(Psalm 18)

22 When the LORD saved David from Saul and his other enemies, David sang this song to the LORD:

2 The LORD is my protector;

The LORD is my protector (22.2)

    he is my strong fortress.
3 My God is my protection,
    and with him I am safe.
He protects me like a shield;
    he defends me and keeps me safe.
He is my saviour;

---

b *Probable text (see 1 Chr 20.5)* Jair; *Hebrew* Jaareoregim.
21.12: 1 Sam 31.8-13   **21.17:** 1 Kgs 11.36; Ps 132.17

he protects me and saves me from
   violence.
4 I call to the LORD,
   and he saves me from my enemies.
   Praise the LORD!

5 The waves of death were all round me;
   the waves of destruction rolled over
   me.
6 The danger of death was round me,
   and the grave set its trap for me.
7 In my trouble I called to the LORD;
   I called to my God for help.
   In his temple he heard my voice;
   he listened to my cry for help.

8 Then the earth trembled and shook;
   the foundations of the sky rocked and
      quivered
   because God was angry!
9 Smoke poured out of his nostrils,
   a consuming flame and burning coals
      from his mouth.
10 He tore the sky apart and came down,
   with a dark cloud under his feet.
11 He flew swiftly on his winged
      creature; [x]
   he travelled on the wings of the wind.
12 He covered himself with darkness;
   thick clouds, full of [d] water,
   surrounded him;
13   burning coals flamed up from the
      lightning before him.

14 Then the LORD thundered from the sky,
   and the voice of Almighty God was
      heard.
15 He shot his arrows and scattered his
      enemies;
   with flashes of lightning he sent them
      running.
16 The floor of the ocean was laid bare,
   and the foundations of the earth were
      uncovered
   when the LORD rebuked his enemies
   and roared at them in anger.

17 The LORD reached down from above
      and took hold of me;
   he pulled me out of the deep waters.
18 He rescued me from my powerful
      enemies
   and from all those who hate me—
   they were too strong for me.
19 When I was in trouble, they attacked
      me,
   but the LORD protected me.

20 He helped me out of danger;
   he saved me because he was pleased
      with me.

21 The LORD rewards me because I do
      what is right;
   he blesses me because I am innocent.
22 I have obeyed the law of the LORD;
   I have not turned away from my God.
23 I have observed all his laws;
   I have not disobeyed his commands.
24 He knows that I am faultless,
   that I have kept myself from doing
      wrong.
25 And so he rewards me because I do
      what is right,
   because he knows that I am innocent.

26 O LORD, you are faithful to those who
      are faithful to you,
   and completely good to those [f] who
      are perfect.
27 You are pure to those who are pure,
   but hostile to those who are wicked.
28 You save those who are humble,
   but you humble those who are proud.

29 You, LORD, are my light;
   you dispel my darkness.
30 You give me strength to attack my
      enemies
   and power to overcome their defences.

31 This God—how perfect are his deeds,
   how dependable his words!
   He is like a shield
   for all who seek his protection.
32 The LORD alone is God;
   God alone is our defence.
33 This God is my strong refuge;
   he makes [g] my pathway safe.
34 He makes me sure-footed as a deer;
   he keeps me safe on the mountains.
35 He trains me for battle,
   so that I can use the strongest bow.

36 O LORD, you protect me and save me;
   your help has made me great.
37 You have kept me from being
      captured,
   and I have never fallen.
38 I pursue my enemies and defeat them;
   I do not stop until I destroy them.
39 I strike them down, and they cannot
      rise;
   they lie defeated before me.
40 You give me strength for the battle

[x] WINGED CREATURE: *See Word List.*
[d] *Some ancient translations (and see Ps 18.11)* full of; *Hebrew unclear.*
[f] *Probable text (see Ps 18.25)* those; *Hebrew* the strong.
[g] *Probable text (see Ps 18.32)* he makes; *Hebrew unclear.*   **22.34:** Hab 3.19

and victory over my enemies.
41 You make my enemies run from me;
   I destroy those who hate me.
42 They look for help, but no one saves
      them;
   they call to the LORD, but he does
      not answer.
43 I crush them, and they become like
      dust;
   I trample on them like mud in the
      streets.

44 You saved me from my rebellious
      people
   and maintained my rule over the
      nations;
   people I did not know have now
      become my subjects.
45 Foreigners bow before me;
   when they hear me, they obey.
46 They lose their courage
   and come trembling *h* from their
      fortresses.

47 The LORD lives! Praise my defender!
   Proclaim the greatness of the strong
      God who saves me!
48 He gives me victory over my enemies;
   he subdues the nations under me
49   and saves me from my foes.

   O LORD, you give me victory over my
      enemies
   and protect me from violent men.
50 And so I praise you among the nations;
   I sing praises to you.
51 God gives great victories to his king;
   he shows constant love to the one
      he has chosen,
   to David and his descendants for ever.

David's Last Words

23 David son of Jesse was the man
   whom God made great, whom the
God of Jacob chose to be king, and who
was the composer of beautiful songs for
Israel. These are David's last words:

2 The spirit of the LORD speaks through
      me;
   his message is on my lips.
3 The God of Israel has spoken;
   the protector of Israel said to me:
   "The king who rules with justice,
   who rules in obedience to God,

4 is like the sun shining on a cloudless
      dawn,
   the sun that makes the grass sparkle
      after rain."

5 And that is how God will bless my
      descendants,
   because he has made an eternal
      covenant with me,
   an agreement that will not be broken,
   a promise that will not be changed.
   That is all I desire;
   that will be my victory,
   and God will surely bring it about.
6 But godless men are like thorns that
      are thrown away;
   no one can touch them with bare
      hands.
7 You must use an iron tool or a spear;
   they will be burnt completely. *i*

David's Famous Soldiers
(1 Chr 11.10–41)

8 These are the names of David's
famous soldiers: the first was Josheb
Basshebeth from Tachemon, who was the
leader of "The Three"; *j* he fought with
his spear *k* against eight hundred men and
killed them all in one battle.

9 The second of the famous three was
Eleazar son of Dodo, of the clan of Ahoh.
One day he and David challenged the
Philistines who had gathered for battle.
The Israelites fell back, 10 but he stood
his ground and fought the Philistines until
his hand was so stiff that he could not
let go of his sword. The LORD won a great
victory that day. After it was over, the
Israelites returned to where Eleazar was
and stripped the armour from the dead.

11 The third of the famous three was
Shammah son of Agee, from Harar. The
Philistines had gathered at Lehi, where
there was a field of peas. The Israelites
fled from the Philistines, 12 but Shammah
stood his ground in the field, defended
it, and killed the Philistines. The LORD won
a great victory that day.

13 Near the beginning of harvest time *l*
three of "The Thirty" went down to the
cave of Adullam, where David was, while
a band of Philistines was camping in the
Valley of Rephaim. 14 At that time David
was on a fortified hill, and a group of
Philistines had occupied Bethlehem.

---

h Probable text (see Ps 18.45) come trembling; Hebrew come ready to fight.
i Verses 6–7 in Hebrew are unclear.   j One ancient translation "The Three"; Hebrew the third.
k Probable text (see 1 Chr 11.11) he fought with his spear; Hebrew unclear.
l Probable text Near the beginning of harvest time; Hebrew unclear.
22.50: Rom 15.9

15 David felt homesick and said, "How I wish someone would bring me a drink of water from the well by the gate at Bethlehem!" 16 The three famous soldiers forced their way through the Philistine camp, drew some water from the well, and brought it back to David. But he would not drink it; instead he poured it out as an offering to the LORD 17 and said, "LORD, I could never drink this! It would be like drinking the blood of these men who risked their lives!" So he refused to drink it.

Those were the brave deeds of the three famous soldiers.

18 Joab's brother Abishai (their mother was Zeruiah) was the leader of "The Famous Thirty." He fought with his spear against three hundred men and killed them, and became famous among "The Thirty."*m* 19 He was the most famous of "The Thirty"*m* and became their leader, but he was not as famous as "The Three."

20 Benaiah son of Jehoiada, from Kabzeel, was another famous soldier; he did many brave deeds, including killing two great Moabite warriors. He once went down into a pit on a snowy day and killed a lion. 21 He also killed an Egyptian, a huge man who was armed with a spear. Benaiah attacked him with his club, snatched the spear from the Egyptian's hand, and killed him with it. 22 Those were the brave deeds of Benaiah, who was one of "The Thirty."*m* 23 He was outstanding among them, but was not as famous as "The Three." David put him in charge of his bodyguard.

24-39 Other members of "The Thirty" included:

Asahel, Joab's brother
Elhanan son of Dodo from Bethlehem
Shammah and Elika from Harod
Helez from Pelet
Ira son of Ikkesh from Tekoa
Abiezer from Anathoth
Mebunnai from Hushah
Zalmon from Ahoh
Maharai from Netophah
Heleb son of Baanah from Netophah
Ittai son of Ribai from Gibeah in Benjamin
Benaiah from Pirathon
Hiddai from the valleys near Gaash
Abialbon from Arabah

Azmaveth from Bahurim
Eliahba from Shaalbon
The sons of Jashen
Jonathan
Shammah from Harar
Ahiam son of Sharar from Harar
Eliphelet son of Ahasbai from Maacah
Eliam son of Ahithophel from Gilo
Hezro from Carmel
Paarai from Arab
Igal son of Nathan from Zobah
Bani from Gad
Zelek from Ammon
Naharai from Beeroth, Joab's armour bearer
Ira and Gareb from Jattir
Uriah the Hittite.

There were thirty-seven famous soldiers in all.

David Takes a Census
(1 Chr 21.1-27)

24 The LORD was angry with Israel once more, and he made David bring trouble on them. The LORD said to him, "Go and count the people of Israel and Judah." 2 So David gave orders to Joab, the commander of his army: "Go with your officers through all the tribes of Israel from one end of the country to the other, and count the people. I want to know how many there are."

3 But Joab answered the king, "Your Majesty, may the LORD your God make the people of Israel a hundred times more numerous than they are now, and may you live to see him do it. But why does Your Majesty want to do this?" 4 But the king made Joab and his officers obey his order; they left his presence and went out to count the people of Israel.

5 They crossed the Jordan and camped south of Aroer, the city in the middle of the valley, in the territory of Gad.*p* From there they went north to Jazer, 6 and on to Gilead and to Kadesh, in Hittite territory.*q* Then they went to Dan, and from Dan they went *r* west to Sidon. 7 Then they went south to the fortified city of Tyre, on to all the cities of the Hivites and the Canaanites, and finally to Beersheba, in the southern part of Judah. 8 So after nine months and twenty days they returned to Jerusalem, having travelled through the whole country. 9 They

---

m One ancient translation "The Thirty"; *Hebrew* "The Three."
p Probable text Aroer...Gad; *Hebrew unclear.*
q One ancient translation Kadesh, in Hittite territory; *Hebrew* to the land of Tahtim, Hodshi.
r Probable text and from Dan they went; *Hebrew unclear.*

reported to the king the total number of men capable of military service: 800,000 in Israel and 500,000 in Judah.

10 But after David had taken the census, his conscience began to trouble him, and he said to the LORD, "I have committed a terrible sin in doing this! Please forgive me. I have acted foolishly."

11-12 The LORD said to Gad, David's prophet, "Go and tell David that I am giving him three choices. I will do whichever he chooses." The next morning, after David got up, 13 Gad went to him, told him what the LORD had said, and asked, "Which is it to be? Three *s* years of famine in your land or three months of running away from your enemies or three days of an epidemic in your land? Now think it over, and tell me what answer to take back to the LORD."

14 David answered, "I am in a desperate situation! But I don't want to be punished by men. Let the LORD himself be the one to punish us, for he is merciful." 15 So the LORD sent an epidemic on Israel, which lasted from that morning until the time that he had chosen. From one end of the country to the other seventy thousand Israelites died. 16 When the LORD's angel was about to destroy Jerusalem, the LORD changed his mind about punishing the people and said to the angel who was killing them, "Stop! That's enough!" The angel was by the threshing-place of Araunah, a Jebusite.

17 David saw the angel who was killing the people, and said to the LORD, "I am the guilty one. I am the one who did wrong. What have these poor people done? You should punish me and my family."

18 That same day Gad went to David and said to him, "Go up to Araunah's threshing-place and build an altar to the LORD." 19 David obeyed the LORD's command and went as Gad had told him. 20 Araunah looked down and saw the king and his officials coming up to him. He threw himself on the ground in front of David 21 and asked, "Your Majesty, why are you here?"

David answered, "To buy your threshing-place and build an altar for the LORD, in order to stop the epidemic."

22 "Take it, Your Majesty," Araunah said, "and offer to the LORD whatever you wish. Here are these oxen to burn as an offering on the altar; here are their yokes and the threshing-boards to use as fuel." 23 Araunah gave it all to the king *t* and said to him, "May the LORD your God accept your offering."

24 But the king answered, "No, I will pay you for it. I will not offer to the LORD my God sacrifices that have cost me nothing." And he bought the threshing-place and the oxen for fifty pieces of silver. 25 Then he built an altar to the LORD and offered burnt-offerings and fellowship-offerings. The LORD answered his prayer, and the epidemic in Israel was stopped.

---

s Some ancient translations (and see 1 Chr 21.12) Three; Hebrew Seven.
t Probable text to the king; Hebrew to the king the king.

THE FIRST BOOK OF
KINGS

INTRODUCTION

The *First book of Kings* continues the history of the Israelite monarchy begun in the books of *Samuel*. It may be divided into three parts: (1) The succession of Solomon as king of Israel and Judah, and the death of his father David. (2) The reign and achievements of Solomon. Especially noteworthy is the building of the Temple in Jerusalem. (3) The division of the nation into the northern and southern kingdoms, and the stories of the kings who ruled them down to the middle of the ninth century B.C.

In the two books of *Kings* each ruler is judged according to his loyalty to God, and national success is seen as depending on this loyalty. Idolatry and disobedience, on the other hand, lead to disaster. The kings of the northern kingdom all fail the test, while the record of Judah's kings is mixed.

Prominent in *First Kings* are the prophets of the Lord, those courageous spokesmen for God who warned the people not to worship idols and not to disobey God. Especially notable is Elijah and the story of his contest with the priests of Baal (chapter 18).

Outline of Contents

The end of David's reign   1.1—2.12
Solomon becomes king   2.13-46
Solomon's reign   3.1—11.43
   a. The early years   3.1—4.34
   b. The Temple is built   5.1—8.66
   c. The later years   9.1—11.43
The divided kingdom   12.1—22.53
   a. The revolt of the northern tribes   12.1—14.20
   b. The kings of Judah and of Israel   14.21—16.34
   c. The Prophet Elijah   17.1—19.21
   d. King Ahab of Israel   20.1—22.40
   e. Jehoshaphat of Judah and Ahaziah of Israel   22.41-53

King David in His Old Age

1 King David was now a very old man, and although his servants covered him with blankets, he could not keep warm. ² So his officials said to him, "Your Majesty, let us find a young woman to stay with you and take care of you. She will lie close to you and keep you warm." ³ A search was made all over Israel for a beautiful girl, and in Shunem they found such a girl named Abishag, and brought

JERUSALEM IN OLD TESTAMENT TIMES

Tower of Hananel

East wall of Nehemiah's City

Solomon's Wall

THE TEMPLE

THE ALTAR

THE PALACE

Solomon's Wall

Manasseh's Wall

UPPER CITY

NEW CITY

CENTRAL VALLEY

KIDRON VALLEY

Gate

Water Tunnel

Gihon

CITY OF DAVID

Upper Pool

Wall of Zion

OPHEL

Tunnel

Old Ditch

Hezekiah's

Manasseh's Wall

Lower Pool

Old Pool

Steps from David's City

Gate

VALLEY OF HINNOM

Spring of Enrogel

0   100   200   300

Metres

her to the king. ⁴ She was very beautiful, and waited on the king and took care of him, but he did not have intercourse with her.

Adonijah Claims the Throne

5-6 Now that Absalom was dead, Adonijah, the son of David and Haggith, was the eldest surviving son. He was a very handsome man. David had never reprimanded him about anything, and he was ambitious to be king. He provided for himself chariots, horses, and an escort of fifty men. ⁷ He talked with Joab (whose mother was Zeruiah) and with Abiathar the priest, and they agreed to support his cause. ⁸ But Zadok the priest, Benaiah son of Jehoiada, Nathan the prophet, Shimei, Rei, and David's bodyguard were not on Adonijah's side.

9 One day Adonijah offered a sacrifice of sheep, bulls, and fattened calves at Snake Rock, near the spring of Enrogel. He invited the other sons of King David and the king's officials who were from Judah to come to this sacrificial feast, ¹⁰ but he did not invite his half brother Solomon or Nathan the prophet, or Benaiah, or the king's bodyguard.

Solomon Is Made King

11 Then Nathan went to Bathsheba, Solomon's mother, and asked her, "Haven't you heard that Haggith's son Adonijah has made himself king? And King David doesn't know anything about it! ¹² If you want to save your life and the life of your son Solomon, I would advise you ¹³ to go at once to King David and ask him, 'Your Majesty, didn't you solemnly promise me that my son Solomon would succeed you as king? How is it, then, that Adonijah has become king?'" ¹⁴ And Nathan added, "Then, while you are still talking with King David, I will come in and confirm your story."

15 So Bathsheba went to see the king in his bedroom. He was very old, and Abishag, the girl from Shunem, was taking care of him. ¹⁶ Bathsheba bowed low before the king, and he asked, "What do you want?"

17 She answered, "Your Majesty, you made me a solemn promise in the name of the LORD your God that my son Solomon would be king after you. ¹⁸ But Adonijah has already become king, and

you don't know anything about it. ¹⁹ He has offered a sacrifice of many bulls, sheep, and fattened calves, and he invited your sons, and Abiathar the priest, and Joab the commander of your army to the feast, but he did not invite your son Solomon. ²⁰ Your Majesty, all the people of Israel are looking to you to tell them who is to succeed you as king. ²¹ If you don't, as soon as you are dead my son Solomon and I will be treated as traitors."

22 She was still speaking, when Nathan arrived at the palace. ²³ The king was told that the prophet was there, and Nathan went in and bowed low before the king. ²⁴ Then he said, "Your Majesty, have you announced that Adonijah would succeed you as king? ²⁵ This very day he has gone and offered a sacrifice of many bulls, sheep, and fattened calves. He invited all your sons, Joab the commander of your army,ᵃ and Abiathar the priest, and just now they are feasting with him and shouting, 'Long live King Adonijah!' ²⁶ But he did not invite me, sir, or Zadok the priest, or Benaiah, or Solomon. ²⁷ Did Your Majesty approve all this and not even tell your officials who is to succeed you as king?"

28 King David said, "Ask Bathsheba to come back in"—and she came and stood before him. ²⁹ Then he said to her, "I promise you by the living LORD, who has rescued me from all my troubles, ³⁰ that today I will keep the promise I made to you in the name of the LORD, the God of Israel, that your son Solomon would succeed me as king."

31 Bathsheba bowed low and said, "May my lord the king live for ever!"

32 Then King David sent for Zadok, Nathan, and Benaiah. When they came in, ³³ he said to them, "Take my court officials with you; let my son Solomon ride my own mule, and escort him down to the spring of Gihon, ³⁴ where Zadok and Nathan are to anoint him as king of Israel. Then blow the trumpet and shout, 'Long live King Solomon!' ³⁵ Follow him back here when he comes to sit on my throne. He will succeed me as king, because he is the one I have chosen to be the ruler of Israel and Judah."

36 "It shall be done," answered Benaiah, "and may the LORD your God confirm it. ³⁷ As the LORD has been with Your Majesty, may he also be with

---

ᵃ *One ancient translation* Joab the commander of your army; *Hebrew* your army commanders.

1.5: 2 Sam 3.4   **1.11**: 2 Sam 12.24

Solomon, and make his reign even more prosperous than yours."

38 So Zadok, Nathan, Benaiah, and the royal bodyguard put Solomon on King David's mule, and escorted him to the spring of Gihon. 39 Zadok took the container of olive-oil which he had brought from the Tent of the LORD's presence, and anointed Solomon. They blew the trumpet, and all the people shouted, "Long live King Solomon!" 40 Then they all followed him back, shouting for joy and playing flutes, making enough noise to shake the ground.

41 As Adonijah and all his guests were finishing the feast, they heard the noise. And when Joab heard the trumpet, he asked, "What's the meaning of all that noise in the city?" 42 Before he finished speaking, Jonathan, the son of the priest Abiathar, arrived. "Come in," Adonijah said. "You're a good man—you must be bringing good news."

43 "I'm afraid not," Jonathan answered. "His Majesty King David has made Solomon king. 44 He sent Zadok, Nathan, Benaiah, and the royal bodyguard to escort him. They made him ride on the king's mule, 45 and Zadok and Nathan anointed him as king at the spring of Gihon. Then they went into the city, shouting for joy, and the people are now in an uproar. That's the noise you just heard. 46 Solomon is now the king. 47 What is more, the court officials went in to pay their respects to His Majesty King David, and said, 'May your God make Solomon even more famous than you, and may Solomon's reign be even more prosperous than yours.' Then King David bowed in worship on his bed 48 and prayed, 'Let us praise the LORD, the God of Israel, who has today made one of my descendants succeed me as king, and has let me live to see it!'"

49 Then Adonijah's guests were afraid, and they all got up and left, each going his own way. 50 Adonijah, in great fear of Solomon, went to the Tent of the LORD's presence and took hold of the corners of the altar. [b] 51 King Solomon was told that Adonijah was afraid of him and that he was holding on to the corners of the altar and had said, "First, I want King Solomon

to swear to me that he will not have me put to death."

52 Solomon replied, "If he is loyal, not even a hair on his head will be touched; but if he is not, he will die." 53 King Solomon then sent for Adonijah and had him brought down from the altar. Adonijah went to the king and bowed low before him, and the king said to him, "You may go home."

David's Last Instructions to Solomon

2 When David was about to die, he called his son Solomon and gave him his last instructions: 2 "My time to die has come. Be confident and determined, 3 and do what the LORD your God orders you to do. Obey all his laws and commands, as written in the Law of Moses, so that wherever you go you may prosper in everything you do. 4 If you obey him, the LORD will keep the promise he made when he told me that my descendants would rule Israel as long as they were careful to obey his commands faithfully with all their heart and soul.

5 "There is something else. You remember what Joab did to me by killing the two commanders of Israel's armies, Abner son of Ner and Amasa son of Jether. You remember how he murdered them in time of peace in revenge for deaths they had caused in time of war. He killed innocent men [c] and now I bear the responsibility for what he did, and I suffer [d] the consequences. 6 You know what to do; you must not let him die a natural death.

7 "But show kindness to the sons of Barzillai from Gilead and take care of them, because they were kind to me when I was fleeing from your brother Absalom.

8 "There is also Shimei son of Gera, from the town of Bahurim in Benjamin. He cursed me bitterly the day I went to Mahanaim, but when he met me at the River Jordan, I gave him my solemn promise in the name of the LORD that I would not have him killed. 9 But you must not let him go unpunished. You know what to do, and you must see to it that he is put to death."

The Death of David

10 David died and was buried in David's

---

[b] CORNERS OF THE ALTAR: *Small projections at the four corners of the altar that looked like horns. Anyone holding on to them was safe from being killed.*
[c] *Some ancient translations* innocent men; *Hebrew* men in battle.
[d] *Some ancient translations* I bear...and I suffer; *Hebrew* he bears...and he suffers.
2.5: 2 Sam 3.27, 20.10　　**2.7:** 2 Sam 17.27-29　　**2.8:** 2 Sam 16.5-13, 19.16-23

City. [11] He had been king of Israel for forty years, ruling seven years in Hebron and thirty-three years in Jerusalem. [12] Solomon succeeded his father David as king, and his royal power was firmly established.

The Death of Adonijah

13 Then Adonijah, whose mother was Haggith, went to Bathsheba, who was Solomon's mother. "Is this a friendly visit?" she asked.

"It is," he answered, [14] and then he added, "I have something to ask of you."

"What is it?" she asked.

15 He answered, "You know that I should have become king and that everyone in Israel expected it. But it happened differently, and my brother became king, because it was the LORD's will. [16] And now I have one request to make; please do not refuse me."

"What is it?" Bathsheba asked.

17 He answered, "Please ask King Solomon—I know he won't refuse you—to let me have Abishag, the girl from Shunem, as my wife."

18 "Very well," she answered. "I will speak to the king for you."

19 So Bathsheba went to the king to speak to him on behalf of Adonijah. The king stood up to greet his mother and bowed to her. Then he sat on his throne and had another one brought in on which she sat at his right. [20] She said, "I have a small favour to ask of you; please do not refuse me."

"What is it, mother?" he asked. "I will not refuse you."

21 She answered, "Let your brother Adonijah have Abishag as his wife."

22 "Why do you ask me to give Abishag to him?" the king asked. "You might as well ask me to give him the throne too. After all, he is my elder brother, and Abiathar the priest and Joab are on his side!" [e] [23] Then Solomon made a solemn promise in the LORD's name, "May God strike me dead if I don't make Adonijah pay with his life for asking this! [24] The LORD has firmly established me on the throne of my father David; he has kept his promise and given the kingdom to me and my descendants. I swear by the living LORD that Adonijah will die this very day!"

25 So King Solomon gave orders to Benaiah, who went out and killed Adonijah.

Abiathar's Banishment and Joab's Death

26 Then King Solomon said to Abiathar the priest, "Go to your country home in Anathoth. You deserve to die, but I will not have you put to death now, for you were in charge of the LORD's Covenant Box while you were with my father David, and you shared in all his troubles." [27] Then Solomon dismissed Abiathar from serving as a priest of the LORD, and so he made what the LORD had said in Shiloh about the priest Eli and his descendants come true.

28 Joab heard what had happened. (He had supported Adonijah, but not Absalom.) So he fled to the Tent of the LORD's presence and took hold of the corners of the altar. [f] [29] When the news reached King Solomon that Joab had fled to the Tent and was by the altar, Solomon sent a messenger to Joab to ask him why he had fled to the altar. Joab answered that he had fled to the LORD because he was afraid of Solomon. So King Solomon sent Benaiah [g] to kill Joab. [30] He went to the Tent of the LORD's presence and said to Joab, "The king orders you to come out."

"No," Joab answered. "I will die here."

Benaiah went back to the king and told him what Joab had said.

31 "Do what Joab says," Solomon answered. "Kill him and bury him. Then neither I nor any other of David's descendants will any longer be held responsible for what Joab did when he killed innocent men. [32] The LORD will punish Joab for those murders, which he committed [h] without my father David's knowledge. Joab killed two innocent men who were better men than he: Abner, commander of the army of Israel, and Amasa, commander of the army of Judah. [33] The punishment for their murders will fall on Joab and on his descendants for ever. But the LORD will always give success to David's descendants who sit on his throne."

34 So Benaiah went to the Tent of the LORD's presence and killed Joab, and he was buried at his home in the open

---

[e] Some ancient translations and Abiathar the priest...on his side; Hebrew unclear.

[f] CORNERS OF THE ALTAR: See 1.50.

[g] One ancient translation Solomon sent a messenger...sent Benaiah; Hebrew Solomon sent Benaiah.   [h] will punish...committed; or will kill Joab, because he committed those murders.

2.11: 2 Sam 5.4–5; 1 Chr 3.4   **2.12:** 1 Chr 29.23   **2.17:** 1 Kgs 1.3–4

2.26: 1 Sam 22.20–23; 2 Sam 15.24   **2.27:** 1 Sam 2.27–36 country. ³⁵The king made Benaiah commander of the army in Joab's place and put Zadok the priest in Abiathar's place.

The Death of Shimei

36 Then the king sent for Shimei and said to him, "Build a house for yourself here in Jerusalem. Live in it and don't leave the city. ³⁷If you ever leave and go beyond the brook of Kidron, you will certainly die—and you yourself will be to blame."

38 "Very well, Your Majesty," Shimei answered. "I will do what you say." So he lived in Jerusalem a long time.

39 Three years later, however, two of Shimei's slaves ran away to the king of Gath, Achish son of Maacah. When Shimei heard that they were in Gath, ⁴⁰he saddled his donkey and went to King Achish in Gath, to find his slaves. He found them and brought them back home. ⁴¹When Solomon heard what Shimei had done, ⁴²he sent for him and said, "I made you promise in the LORD's name not to leave Jerusalem. And I warned you that if you ever did, you would certainly die. Did you not agree to it and say that you would obey me? ⁴³Why, then, have you broken your promise and disobeyed my command? ⁴⁴You know very well all the wrong that you did to my father David. The LORD will punish you for it. ⁴⁵But he will bless me and he will make David's kingdom secure for ever."

46 Then the king gave orders to Benaiah, who went out and killed Shimei. Solomon was now in complete control.

Solomon Prays for Wisdom
(2 Chr 1.3–12)

3 Solomon made an alliance with the king of Egypt by marrying his daughter. He brought her to live in David's City until he had finished building his palace, the Temple, and the wall round Jerusalem. ²A temple had not yet been built for the LORD, and so the people were still offering sacrifices at many different altars. ³Solomon loved the LORD and followed the instructions of his father David, but he also slaughtered animals and offered them as sacrifices on various altars.

4 On one occasion he went to Gibeon to offer sacrifices because that was where the most famous altar was. He had offered hundreds of burnt-offerings there in the past. ⁵That night the LORD appeared to him in a dream and asked him, "What

would you like me to give you?"

6 Solomon answered, "You always showed great love for my father David, your servant, and he was good, loyal, and honest in his relations with you. And you have continued to show him your great and constant love by giving him a son who today rules in his place. ⁷O LORD God, you have let me succeed my father as king, even though I am very young and don't know how to rule. ⁸Here I am among the people you have chosen to be your own, a people who are so many that they cannot be counted. ⁹So give me the

Give me the wisdom I need (3.9)

wisdom I need to rule your people with justice and to know the difference between good and evil. Otherwise, how would I ever be able to rule this great people of yours?"

10 The LORD was pleased that Solomon had asked for this, ¹¹and so he said to him, "Because you have asked for the wisdom to rule justly, instead of long life for yourself or riches or the death of your enemies, ¹²I will do what you have asked. I will give you more wisdom and understanding than anyone has ever had before or will ever have again. ¹³I will also give you what you have not asked for: all your life you will have wealth and honour, more than that of any other king. ¹⁴And if you obey me and keep my laws and commands, as your father David did, I will give you a long life."

15 Solomon woke up and realized that God had spoken to him in the dream. Then he went to Jerusalem and stood in front of the LORD's Covenant Box and offered burnt-offerings and fellowship-offerings

Don't kill the child (3.27)

to the LORD. After that he gave a feast for all his officials.

Solomon Judges a Difficult Case

16 One day two prostitutes came and presented themselves before King Solomon. 17 One of them said, "Your Majesty, this woman and I live in the same house, and I gave birth to a baby boy at home while she was there. 18 Two days after my child was born she also gave birth to a baby boy. Only the two of us were there in the house—no one else was present. 19 Then one night she accidentally rolled over on her baby and smothered it. 20 She got up during the night, took my son from my side while I was asleep, and carried him to her bed; then she put the dead child in my bed. 21 The next morning, when I woke up and was going to feed my baby, I saw that it was dead. I looked at it more closely and saw that it was not my child."

22 But the other woman said, "No! The living child is mine, and the dead one is yours!"

The first woman answered, "No! The dead child is yours, and the living one is mine!"

And so they argued before the king.

23 Then King Solomon said, "Each of you claims that the living child is hers and that the dead child belongs to the other one." 24 He sent for a sword, and when it was brought, 25 he said, "Cut the living child in two and give each woman half of it."

26 The real mother, her heart full of love for her son, said to the king, "Please, Your Majesty, don't kill the child! Give it to her!"

But the other woman said, "Don't give it to either of us; go ahead and cut it in two."

27 Then Solomon said, "Don't kill the child! Give it to the first woman—she is its real mother."

28 When the people of Israel heard of Solomon's decision, they were all filled with deep respect for him, because they knew then that God had given him the wisdom to settle disputes fairly.

Solomon's Officials

4 Solomon was king of all Israel, 2 and these were his high officials:

The priest: Azariah son of Zadok

3 The court secretaries: Elihoreph and Ahijah, sons of Shisha

In charge of the records: Jehoshaphat
son of Ahilud
⁴ Commander of the army: Benaiah son
of Jehoiada
Priests: Zadok and Abiathar
⁵ Chief of the district governors: Azariah
son of Nathan
Royal adviser: the priest Zabud son of
Nathan
⁶ In charge of the palace servants:
Ahishar
In charge of the forced labour:
Adoniram son of Abda

7 Solomon appointed twelve men as
district governors in Israel. They were to
provide food from their districts for the
king and his household, each man being
responsible for one month out of the year.
⁸ The following are the names of these
twelve officers and the districts they were
in charge of:

Benhur: the hill-country of Ephraim
⁹ Bendeker: the cities of Makaz,
Shaalbim, Beth Shemesh, Elon,
and Beth Hanan
¹⁰ Benhesed: the cities of Arubboth and
Socoh and all the territory of
Hepher
¹¹ Benabinadab, who was married to
Solomon's daughter Taphath: the
whole region of Dor
¹² Baana son of Ahilud: the cities of
Taanach, Megiddo, and all the
region near Beth Shan, near the
town of Zarethan, south of the
town of Jezreel, as far as the city
of Abel Meholah and the city of
Jokmeam
¹³ Bengeber: the city of Ramoth in
Gilead, and the villages in Gilead
belonging to the clan of Jair, a
descendant of Manasseh, and the
region of Argob in Bashan, sixty
large towns in all, fortified with
walls and with bronze bars on the
gates
¹⁴ Ahinadab son of Iddo: the district of
Mahanaim
¹⁵ Ahimaaz, who was married to
Basemath, another of Solomon's
daughters: the territory of Naphtali
¹⁶ Baana son of Hushai: the region of
Asher and the town of Bealoth
¹⁷ Jehoshaphat son of Paruah: the
territory of Issachar
¹⁸ Shimei son of Ela: the territory of
Benjamin

¹⁹ Geber son of Uri: the region of Gilead,
which had been ruled by King
Sihon of the Amorites and King
Og of Bashan

Besides these twelve, there was one
governor over the whole land.

Solomon's Prosperous Reign

20 The people of Judah and Israel were
as numerous as the grains of sand on
the seashore; they ate and drank, and
were happy. ²¹ Solomon's kingdom
included all the nations from the River
Euphrates to Philistia and the Egyptian
border. They paid him taxes and were
subject to him all his life.

22 The supplies Solomon needed each
day were five thousand litres of fine flour
and ten thousand litres of meal; ²³ ten stall-
fed cattle, twenty pasture-fed cattle, and
a hundred sheep, besides deer, gazelles,
roebucks, and poultry.

24 Solomon ruled over all the land west
of the River Euphrates, from Tiphsah on
the Euphrates as far west as the city of
Gaza. All the kings west of the Euphrates
were subject to him, and he was at peace
with all the neighbouring countries. ²⁵ As
long as he lived, the people throughout
Judah and Israel lived in safety, each
family with its own grapevines and fig-
trees.

26 Solomon had forty thousand stalls
for his chariot-horses and twelve thousand cavalry horses. ²⁷ His twelve
governors, each one in the month assigned
to him, supplied the food King Solomon
needed for himself and for all who ate
in the palace; they always supplied
everything needed. ²⁸ Each governor also
supplied his share of barley and straw,
where it was needed,ⁱ for the chariot-
horses and the draught animals.

29 God gave Solomon unusual wisdom
and insight, and knowledge too great to
be measured. ³⁰ Solomon was wiser than
the wise men of the East or the wise men
of Egypt. ³¹ He was the wisest of all men:
wiser than Ethan the Ezrahite, and
Heman, Calcol, and Darda, the sons of
Mahol, and his fame spread throughout
all the neighbouring countries. ³² He composed three thousand proverbs and more
than a thousand songs. ³³ He spoke of
trees and plants, from the Lebanon cedars
to the hyssop that grows on walls; he
talked about animals, birds, reptiles, and

ⁱwhere it was needed; or wherever King Solomon was.
4.21: Gen 15.18; 2 Chr 9.26   **4.26:** 1 Kgs 10.26; 2 Chr 1.14, 9.25   **4.31:** Ps 89 (Title)
4.32: Prov 1.1, 10.1, 25.1; Song 1.1

fish. [34] Kings all over the world heard of his wisdom and sent people to listen to him.

Solomon Prepares to Build the Temple
(2 Chr 2.1–18)

5 King Hiram of Tyre had always been a friend of David's, and when he heard that Solomon had succeeded his father David as king he sent ambassadors to him. [2] Solomon sent back this message to Hiram: [3] "You know that because of the constant wars my father David had to fight against the enemy countries all round him, he could not build a temple for the worship of the LORD his God until the LORD had given him victory over all his enemies. [4] But now the LORD my God has given me peace on all my borders. I have no enemies, and there is no danger of attack. [5] The LORD promised my father David, 'Your son, whom I will make king after you, will build a temple for me.' And I have now decided to build that temple for the worship of the LORD my God. [6] So send your men to Lebanon to cut down cedars for me. My men will work with them, and I will pay your men whatever you decide. As you well know, my men don't know how to cut down trees as well as yours do."

[7] Hiram was extremely pleased when he received Solomon's message, and he said, "Praise the LORD today for giving David such a wise son to succeed him as king of that great nation!" [8] Then Hiram sent Solomon the following message: "I have received your message and I am ready to do what you ask. I will provide the cedars and the pine-trees. [9] My men will bring the logs down from Lebanon to the sea, and will tie them together in rafts to float them down the coast to the place you choose. There my men will untie them, and your men will take charge of them. On your part, I would like you to supply the food for my men."

[10] So Hiram supplied Solomon with all the cedar and pine logs that he wanted, [11] and Solomon provided Hiram with two thousand metric tons of wheat and four hundred thousand litres[j] of pure olive-oil every year to feed his men.

[12] The LORD kept his promise and gave Solomon wisdom. There was peace between Hiram and Solomon, and they made a treaty with each other.

[13] King Solomon drafted 30,000 men as forced labour from all over Israel, [14] and put Adoniram in charge of them. He divided them into three groups of 10,000 men, and each group spent one month in Lebanon and two months back home. [15] Solomon also had 80,000 men in the hill-country quarrying stone, with 70,000 men to carry it, [16] and he placed 3,300 foremen in charge of them to supervise their work. [17] At King Solomon's command they quarried fine large stones for the foundation of the Temple. [18] Solomon's and Hiram's workmen and men from the city of Byblos prepared the stones and the timber to build the Temple.

Solomon Builds the Temple

6 Four hundred and eighty years after the people of Israel left Egypt, during the fourth year of Solomon's reign over Israel, in the second month, the month of Ziv, Solomon began work on the Temple. [2] Inside it was 27 metres long, 9 metres wide, and 13.5 metres high. [3] The entrance room was 4.5 metres deep and 9 metres wide, as wide as the sanctuary itself. [4] The walls of the Temple had openings in them, narrower on the outside than on the inside. [5] Against the outside walls, on the sides and the back of the Temple, a three-storied annexe was built, each storey 2.2 metres high. [6] Each room in the lowest storey was 2.2 metres wide, in the middle storey 2.7 metres wide, and in the top storey 3.1 metres wide. The temple wall on each floor was thinner than on the floor below so that the rooms could rest on the wall without having their beams built into it.

[7] The stones with which the Temple was built had been prepared at the quarry, so that there was no noise made by hammers, axes, or any other iron tools as the Temple was being built.

[8] The entrance to the lowest[k] storey of the annexe was on the south side of the Temple, with stairs leading up to the second and third storeys. [9] So King Solomon finished building the Temple. He put in a ceiling made of beams and boards of cedar. [10] The three-storied annexe, each storey[l] 2.2 metres high, was built against

[j] Some ancient translations (and see 2 Chr 2.10) four hundred thousand litres; Hebrew four thousand litres.   [k] Some ancient translations lowest; Hebrew middle.
[l] Probable text three-storied annexe, each storey; Hebrew three-storied annexe.
5.5: 2 Sam 7.12–13; 1 Chr 17.11–12   **5.14:** 1 Kgs 12.18

Hiram supplied Solomon with cedar and pine logs (5.10)

the outside walls of the Temple, and was joined to them by cedar beams.

11 The LORD said to Solomon, 12 "If you obey all my laws and commands, I will do for you what I promised your father David. 13 I will live among my people Israel in this Temple that you are building, and I will never abandon them."

14 So Solomon finished building the Temple.

The Interior Furnishings of the Temple
(2 Chr 3.8–14)

15 The inside walls were covered with cedar panels from the floor to the ceiling, and the floor was made of pine. 16 An inner room, called the Most Holy Place, was built in the rear of the Temple. It was

nine metres long and was partitioned off by cedar boards reaching from the floor to the ceiling. *m* 17 The room in front of the Most Holy Place was eighteen metres long. 18 The cedar panels were decorated with carvings of gourds and flowers; the whole interior was covered with cedar, so that the stones of the walls could not be seen.

19 In the rear of the Temple an inner room was built, where the LORD's Covenant Box was to be placed. 20 This inner room was nine metres long, nine metres wide, and nine metres high, all covered with pure gold. The altar was covered with cedar panels. *n* 21 The inside of the Temple was covered with gold, and gold chains were placed across the entrance of the

m One ancient translation ceiling; *Hebrew* walls.
6.16: Ex 26.33–34

n Verse 20 in Hebrew is unclear.

inner room, which was also covered with gold. ²²The whole interior of the Temple was covered with gold, as well as the altar in the Most Holy Place.

23 Two winged creatures were made of olive wood and placed in the Most Holy Place, each one 4.4 metres tall. ²⁴⁻²⁶Both were of the same size and shape. Each had two wings, each wing 2.2 metres long, so that the distance from one wing-tip to the other was 4.4 metres. ²⁷They were placed side by side in the Most Holy Place, so that two of their outstretched wings touched each other in the middle of the room, and the other two wings touched the walls. ²⁸The two winged creatures were covered with gold.

29 The walls of the main room and of the inner room were all decorated with carved figures of winged creatures, palm-trees, and flowers. ³⁰Even the floor was covered with gold.

31 A double door made of olive wood was set in place at the entrance of the Most Holy Place; the top of the doorway was a pointed arch. ³²The doors were decorated with carved figures of winged creatures, palm-trees, and flowers. The doors, the winged creatures, and the palm-trees were covered with gold. ³³For the entrance to the main room a rectangular door-frame of olive wood was made. ³⁴There were two folding doors made of pine ³⁵and decorated with carved figures of winged creatures, palm-trees, and flowers, which were evenly covered with gold.

36 An inner court was built in front of the Temple, enclosed with walls which had one layer of cedar beams for every three layers of stone.

37 The foundation of the Temple was laid in the second month, the month of Ziv, in the fourth year of Solomon's reign. ³⁸In the eighth month, the month of Bul, in the eleventh year of Solomon's reign, the Temple was completely finished exactly as it had been planned. It had taken Solomon seven years to build it.

Solomon's Palace

7 Solomon also built a palace for himself, and it took him thirteen years. ²⁻³The Hall of the Forest of Lebanon[o] was 44 metres long, 22 metres wide, and 13.5 metres high. It had three[p] rows of cedar pillars, fifteen in each row, with cedar beams resting on them. The ceiling was of cedar, extending over store-rooms, which were supported by the pillars. ⁴In each of the two side walls there were three rows of windows. ⁵The door-ways and the windows[q] had rectangular frames, and the three rows of windows in each wall faced the opposite rows.

6 The Hall of Columns was 22 metres long and 13.5 metres wide. It had a covered porch, supported by columns.

7 The Throne Room, also called the Hall of Judgement, where Solomon decided cases, had cedar panels from the floor to the rafters.[r]

8 Solomon's own quarters, in another court behind the Hall of Judgement, were made like the other buildings. He also built the same kind of house for his wife, the daughter of the king of Egypt.

9 All these buildings and the great court were made of fine stones from the foundations to the eaves. The stones were prepared at the quarry and cut to measure, with their inner and outer sides trimmed with saws. ¹⁰The foundations were made of large stones prepared at the quarry, some of them three and a half metres long and others four metres long. ¹¹On top of them were other stones, cut to measure, and cedar beams. ¹²The palace court, the inner court of the Temple, and the entrance room of the Temple had walls with one layer of cedar beams for every three layers of cut stones.

Huram's Task

13 King Solomon sent for a man named Huram, a craftsman living in the city of Tyre, who was skilled in bronze work. ¹⁴His father, who was no longer living, was from Tyre, and had also been a skilled bronze craftsman; his mother was from the tribe of Naphtali. Huram was an intelligent and experienced craftsman. He accepted King Solomon's invitation to be in charge of all the bronze work.

The Two Bronze Columns
(2 Chr 3.15-17)

15 Huram cast two bronze columns,

---

o HALL OF THE FOREST OF LEBANON: *A large ceremonial hall in the palace, probably so called because it was panelled in cedar.*   p *One ancient translation* three; *Hebrew* four.
q *One ancient translation* windows; *Hebrew* doorposts.
r *Some ancient translations* rafters; *Hebrew* floor.
6.22: Ex 30.1-3   **6.23-28:** Ex 25.18-20   **7.8:** 1 Kgs 3.1

each one 8 metres tall and 5.3 metres in circumference,[s] and placed them at the entrance of the Temple. [16]He also made two bronze capitals, each one 2.2 metres tall, to be placed on top of the columns. [17]The top of each column was decorated with a design of interwoven chains,[t] [18]and two rows of bronze pomegranates.

19 The capitals were shaped like lilies, 1.8 metres tall, [20]and were placed on a rounded section which was above the chain design. There were two hundred pomegranates in two rows round each[u] capital.

21 Huram placed these two bronze columns in front of the entrance of the Temple: the one on the south side was named Jachin,[v] and the one on the north was named Boaz.[w] [22]The lily-shaped bronze capitals were on top of the columns.

And so the work on the columns was completed.

The Bronze Tank
(2 Chr 4.2-5)

23 Huram made a round tank of bronze, 2.2 metres deep, 4.4 metres in diameter, and 13.2 metres in circumference. [24]All round the outer edge of the rim of the tank[x] were two rows of bronze gourds, which had been cast all in one piece with the rest of the tank. [25]The tank rested on the backs of twelve bronze bulls that faced outwards, three facing in each direction. [26]The sides of the tank were 75 millimetres thick. Its rim was like the rim of a cup, curving outwards like the petals of a lily. The tank held about forty thousand litres.

The Bronze Carts

27 Huram also made ten bronze carts; each was 1.8 metres long, 1.8 metres wide, and 1.3 metres high. [28]They were made of square panels which were set in frames, [29]with the figures of lions, bulls, and winged creatures on the panels; and on the frames, above and underneath the lions and bulls, there were spiral figures in relief. [30]Each cart had four bronze wheels with bronze axles. At the four corners were bronze supports for a basin;

the supports were decorated with spiral figures in relief. [31]There was a circular frame on top for the basin. It projected upwards 45 centimetres from the top of the cart and 18 centimetres down into it. It had carvings round it. [32]The wheels were 66 centimetres high; they were under the panels, and the axles were of one piece with the carts. [33]The wheels were like chariot wheels; their axles, rims, spokes, and hubs were all of bronze. [34]There were four supports at the bottom corners of each cart, which were of one piece with the cart. [35]There was a 22 centimetre band round the top of each cart; its supports and the panels were of one piece with the cart. [36]The supports and panels were decorated with figures of winged creatures, lions, and palm-trees, wherever there was space for them, with spiral figures all round. [37]This, then, is how the carts were made; they were all alike, having the same size and shape.

38 Huram also made ten basins, one for each cart. Each basin was 1.8 metres in diameter, and held about 800 litres. [39]He placed five of the carts on the south side of the Temple, and the other five on the north side; the tank he placed at the south-east corner.

Summary List of Temple Furnishings
(2 Chr 4.11-5.1)

40-45 Huram also made pots, shovels, and bowls. He completed all his work for King Solomon for the LORD's Temple. This is what he made:
The two columns
The two bowl-shaped capitals on top of the columns
The design of interwoven chains on each capital
The four hundred bronze pomegranates, in two rows of a hundred each round the design on each capital
The ten carts
The ten basins
The tank
The twelve bulls supporting the tank
The pots, shovels, and bowls
All this equipment for the Temple, which Huram made for King Solomon, was of polished bronze. [46]The king had

---

[s] *Some ancient translations* each one...circumference; *Hebrew* the first column was 8 metres tall and the second column was 5.3 metres in circumference.   [t] *Verse 17 in Hebrew is unclear.*
[u] *One ancient translation* each; *Hebrew* the second.
[v] JACHIN: *This name sounds like the Hebrew for "he (God) establishes."*
[w] BOAZ: *This name sounds like the Hebrew for "by his (God's) strength."*
[x] *Probable text* All round...tank; *Hebrew unclear.*
7.38: Ex 30.17-21

it all made in the foundry between Sukkoth and Zarethan, in the Jordan Valley. 47 Solomon did not have these bronze objects weighed, because there were too many of them, and so their weight was never determined.

48 Solomon also had gold furnishings made for the Temple: the altar, the table for the bread offered to God, 49 the ten lamp-stands that stood in front of the Most Holy Place, five on the south side and five on the north; the flowers, lamps, and tongs; 50 the cups, lamp snuffers, bowls, dishes for incense, and the pans used for carrying live coals; and the hinges for the doors of the Most Holy Place and of the outer doors of the Temple. All these furnishings were made of gold.

51 When King Solomon finished all the work on the Temple, he placed in the temple storerooms all the things that his father David had dedicated to the LORD— the silver, gold, and other articles.

The Covenant Box Is Brought to the Temple
(2 Chr 5.2–6.2)

8 Then King Solomon summoned all the leaders of the tribes and clans of Israel to come to him in Jerusalem in order to take the LORD's Covenant Box from Zion, David's City, to the Temple. 2 They all assembled during the Festival of Shelters in the seventh month, in the month of Ethanim. 3 When all the leaders had gathered, the priests lifted the Covenant Box 4 and carried it to the Temple. The Levites and the priests also moved the Tent of the LORD's presence and all its equipment to the Temple. 5 King Solomon and all the people of Israel assembled in front of the Covenant Box and sacrificed a large number of sheep and cattle—too many to count. 6 Then the priests carried the Covenant Box into the Temple and put it in the Most Holy Place, beneath the winged creatures. 7 Their outstretched wings covered the box and the poles it was carried by. 8 The ends of the poles could be seen by anyone standing directly in front of the Most Holy Place, but from nowhere else. (The poles are still there today.) 9 There was nothing inside the Covenant Box except the two stone tablets which Moses had placed

there at Mount Sinai, when the LORD made a covenant with the people of Israel as they were coming from Egypt.

10 As the priests were leaving the Temple, it was suddenly filled with a cloud 11 shining with the dazzling light of the LORD's presence, and they could not go back in to perform their duties. 12 Then Solomon prayed:

"You, LORD, have placed the sun in the sky,*y*
    yet you have chosen to live in clouds and darkness.
13 Now I have built a majestic temple for you,
    a place for you to live in for ever."

Solomon's Address to the People
(2 Chr 6.3–11)

14 As the people stood there, King Solomon turned to face them, and he asked God's blessing on them. 15 He said, "Praise the LORD God of Israel! He has kept the promise he made to my father David, when he said, 16 'From the time I brought my people out of Egypt, I have not chosen any city in all the land of Israel in which a temple should be built where I would be worshipped. But I chose you, David, to rule my people.' "

17 And Solomon continued, "My father David planned to build a temple for the worship of the LORD God of Israel, 18 but the LORD said to him, 'You were right in wanting to build a temple for me, 19 but you will never build it. It is your son, your own son, who will build my temple.'

20 "And now the LORD has kept his promise. I have succeeded my father as king of Israel, and I have built the Temple for the worship of the LORD God of Israel. 21 I have also provided a place in the Temple for the Covenant Box containing the stone tablets of the covenant which the LORD made with our ancestors when he brought them out of Egypt."

Solomon's Prayer
(2 Chr 6.12–42)

22 Then in the presence of the people Solomon went and stood in front of the altar, where he raised his arms 23 and prayed, "LORD God of Israel, there is no god like you in heaven above or on earth below! You keep your covenant with your

---

y One ancient translation You...sky; *Hebrew does not have these words.*
7.48: Ex 25.23–30, 30.1–3   **7.49:** Ex 25.31–40   **7.51:** 2 Sam 8.11; 1 Chr 18.11
8.1: 2 Sam 6.12–16; 1 Chr 15.25–29   **8.2:** Lev 23.24   **8.9:** Deut 10.5   **8.10–11:** Ex 40.34–35
8.12: Ps 18.11, 97.2   **8.16:** 2 Sam 7.4–11; 1 Chr 17.3–10   **8.17–18:** 2 Sam 7.1–3; 1 Chr 17.1–2
8.19: 2 Sam 7.12–13; 1 Chr 17.11–12

people and show them your love when they live in whole-hearted obedience to you. 24 You have kept the promise you made to my father David; today every word has been fulfilled. 25 And now, LORD God of Israel, I pray that you will also keep the other promise you made to my father when you told him that there would always be one of his descendants ruling as king of Israel, provided they obeyed you as carefully as he did. 26 So now, O God of Israel, let everything come true that you promised to my father David, your servant.

27 "But can you, O God, really live on earth? Not even all heaven is large enough to hold you, so how can this Temple that I have built be large enough? 28 LORD my God, I am your servant. Listen to my prayer, and grant the requests I make to you today. 29 Watch over this Temple day and night, this place where you have chosen to be worshipped. Hear me when I face this Temple and pray. 30 Hear my prayers and the prayers of your people when they face this place and pray. In your home in heaven hear us and forgive us.

31 "When a person is accused of wronging another and is brought to your altar in this Temple to take an oath that he is innocent, 32 O LORD, listen in heaven and judge your servants. Punish the guilty one as he deserves, and acquit the one who is innocent.

33 "When your people Israel are defeated by their enemies because they have sinned against you, and then when they turn to you and come to this Temple, humbly praying to you for forgiveness, 34 listen to them in heaven. Forgive the sins of your people, and bring them back to the land which you gave to their ancestors.

35 "When you hold back the rain because your people have sinned against you, and then when they repent and face this Temple, humbly praying to you, 36 listen to them in heaven. Forgive the sins of the king and of the people of Israel. Teach them to do what is right. Then, O LORD, send rain on this land of yours, which you gave to your people as a permanent possession.

37 "When there is famine in the land or an epidemic, or the crops are destroyed by scorching winds or swarms of locusts, or when your people are attacked by their enemies, or when there is disease or sickness among them, 38 listen to their prayers. If any of your people Israel, out of heartfelt sorrow, stretch out their hands in prayer towards this Temple, 39 hear their prayer. Listen to them in your home in heaven, forgive them, and help them. You alone know the thoughts of the human heart. Deal with each person as he deserves, 40 so that your people may obey you all the time they live in the land which you gave to our ancestors.

41-42 "When a foreigner who lives in a distant land hears of your fame and of the great things you have done for your people, and comes to worship you and to pray at this Temple, 43 listen to his prayer. In heaven, where you live, hear him and do what he asks you to do, so that all the peoples of the world may know you and obey you, as your people Israel do. Then they will know that this Temple I have built is the place where you are to be worshipped.

44 "When you command your people to go into battle against their enemies and they pray to you, wherever they are, facing this city which you have chosen and this Temple which I have built for you, 45 listen to their prayers. Hear them in heaven, and give them victory.

46 "When your people sin against you— and there is no one who does not sin—and in your anger you let their enemies defeat them and take them as prisoners to some other land, even if that land is far away, 47 listen to your people's prayers. If there in that land they repent and pray to you, confessing how sinful and wicked they have been, hear their prayers O LORD. 48 If in that land they truly and sincerely repent, and pray to you as they face towards this land which you gave to our ancestors, this city which you have chosen, and this Temple which I have built for you, 49 then listen to their prayers. In your home in heaven hear them and be merciful to them. 50 Forgive all their sins and their rebellion against you, and make their enemies treat them with kindness. 51 They are your own people, whom you brought out of Egypt, that blazing furnace.

52 "Sovereign LORD, may you always look with favour on your people Israel and their king, and hear their prayer whenever they call to you for help. 53 You chose them from all the peoples to be your own people, as you told them through your servant Moses when you brought our ancestors out of Egypt."

8.25: 1 Kgs 2.4   **8.27:** 2 Chr 2.6   **8.29:** Deut 12.11

The Final Prayer

54 After Solomon had finished praying to the LORD, he stood up in front of the altar, where he had been kneeling with uplifted hands. 55 In a loud voice he asked God's blessings on all the people assembled there. He said, 56 "Praise the LORD who has given his people peace, as he promised he would. He has kept all the generous promises he made through his servant Moses. 57 May the LORD our God be with us, as he was with our ancestors; may he never leave us, or abandon us; 58 may he make us obedient to him, so that we will always live as he wants us to live, and keep all the laws and commands he gave our ancestors. 59 May the LORD our God remember at all times this prayer and these petitions I have made to him. May he always be merciful to the people of Israel and to their king, according to their daily needs. 60 And so all the nations of the world will know that the LORD alone is God—there is no other. 61 May you, his people, always be faithful to the LORD our God, obeying all his laws and commands, as you do today."

The Dedication of the Temple
(2 Chr 7.4-10)

62 Then King Solomon and all the people there offered sacrifices to the LORD. 63 He sacrificed 22,000 head of cattle and 120,000 sheep as fellowship-offerings. And so the king and all the people dedicated the Temple. 64 That same day he also consecrated the central part of the courtyard, the area in front of the Temple, and then he offered there the sacrifices burnt whole, the grain-offerings, and the fat of the animals for the fellowship-offerings. He did this because the bronze altar was too small for all these offerings.

65 There at the Temple, Solomon and all the people of Israel celebrated the Festival of Shelters for seven z days. There was a huge crowd of people from as far away as Hamath Pass in the north and the Egyptian border in the south. 66 On the eighth day Solomon sent the people home. They all praised him and went home happy because of all the blessings that the LORD had given his servant David and his people Israel.

God Appears to Solomon Again
(2 Chr 7.11-22)

9 After King Solomon had finished building the Temple and the palace and everything else he wanted to build, 2 the LORD appeared to him again, as he had in Gibeon. 3 The LORD said to him, "I have heard your prayer. I consecrate this Temple which you have built as the place where I shall be worshipped for ever. I will watch over it and protect it for all time. 4 If you will serve me in honesty and integrity, as your father David did, and if you obey my laws and do everything I have commanded you, 5 I will keep the promise I made to your father David when I told him that Israel would always be ruled by his descendants. 6 But if you or your descendants stop following me, if you disobey the laws and commands I have given you, and worship other gods, 7 then I will remove my people Israel from the land that I have given them. I will also abandon this Temple which I have consecrated as the place where I am to be worshipped. People everywhere will ridicule Israel and treat her with contempt. 8 This Temple will become a pile of ruins, a and everyone who passes by will be shocked and amazed. 'Why did the LORD do this to this land and this Temple?' they will ask. 9 People will answer, 'It is because they abandoned the LORD their God, who brought their ancestors out of Egypt. They gave their allegiance to other gods and worshipped them. That is why the LORD has brought this disaster on them.' "

Solomon's Agreement with Hiram
(2 Chr 8.1-2)

10 It took Solomon twenty years to build the Temple and his palace. 11 King Hiram of Tyre had provided him with all the cedar and pine and with all the gold he wanted for this work. After it was finished, King Solomon gave Hiram twenty towns in the region of Galilee. 12 Hiram went to see them, and he did not like them. 13 So he said to Solomon, "So these, my brother, are the towns you have given me!" For this reason the area

z One ancient translation seven; Hebrew fourteen.
a Some ancient translations a pile of ruins; Hebrew high.
8.56: Deut 12.10; Josh 21.44-45 **9.2:** 1 Kgs 3.5; 2 Chr 1.7 **9.5:** 1 Kgs 2.4
9.8: 2 Kgs 25.9; 2 Chr 36.19

is still called Cabul.*b* ¹⁴Hiram had sent Solomon more than four thousand kilogrammes of gold.

Further Achievements of Solomon
(2 Chr 8.3–18)

15 King Solomon used forced labour to build the Temple and the palace, to fill in land on the east side of the city, and to build the city wall. He also used it to rebuild the cities of Hazor, Megiddo, and Gezer. ¹⁶(The king of Egypt had attacked Gezer and captured it, killing its inhabitants and setting fire to the city. Then he gave it as a wedding present to his daughter when she married Solomon, ¹⁷and Solomon rebuilt it.) Using his forced labour, Solomon also rebuilt Lower Beth Horon, ¹⁸Baalath, Tamar in the wilderness of Judah, ¹⁹the cities where his supplies were kept, the cities for his horses and chariots, and everything else he wanted to build in Jerusalem, in Lebanon, and elsewhere in his kingdom. ²⁰⁻²¹For his forced labour Solomon used the descendants of the people of Canaan whom the Israelites had not killed when they took possession of their land. These included Amorites, Hittites, Perizzites, Hivites, and Jebusites, whose descendants continue to be slaves down to the present time. ²²Solomon did not make slaves of Israelites; they served as his soldiers, officers, commanders, chariot captains, and horsemen.

23 There were 550 officials in charge of the forced labour working on Solomon's various building projects.

24 Solomon filled in the land on the east side of the city, after his wife, the daughter of the king of Egypt, had moved from David's City to the palace Solomon built for her.

25 Three times a year Solomon offered burnt-offerings and fellowship-offerings on the altar he had built to the LORD. He also burnt incense*c* to the LORD. And so he finished building the Temple.

26 King Solomon also built a fleet of ships at Eziongeber, which is near Elath, on the shore of the Gulf of Aqaba, in the land of Edom. ²⁷King Hiram sent some experienced seamen from his fleet to serve with Solomon's men. ²⁸They sailed to the land of Ophir, and brought back to Solomon more than fourteen thousand kilogrammes of gold.

The Visit of the Queen of Sheba
(2 Chr 9.1–12)

10 The queen of Sheba heard of Solomon's fame,*d* and she travelled to Jerusalem to test him with difficult questions. ²She brought with her a large group of attendants, as well as camels loaded with spices, jewels, and a large amount of gold. When she and Solomon met, she asked him all the questions that she could think of. ³He answered them all; there was nothing too difficult for him to explain. ⁴The queen of Sheba heard Solomon's wisdom and saw the palace he had built. ⁵She saw the food that was served at his table, the living quarters for his officials, the organization of his palace staff and the uniforms they wore, the servants who waited on him at feasts, and the sacrifices he offered in the Temple. It left her breathless and amazed. ⁶She said to King Solomon, "What I heard in my own country about you*e* and your wisdom is true! ⁷But I couldn't believe it until I had come and seen it all for myself. But I didn't hear even half of it; your wisdom and wealth are much greater than what I was told. ⁸How fortunate are your wives!*f* And how fortunate your servants, who are always in your presence and are privileged to hear your wise sayings! ⁹Praise the LORD your God! He has shown how pleased he is with you by making you king of Israel. Because his love for Israel is eternal, he has made you their king so that you can maintain law and justice."

10 She presented to King Solomon the gifts she had brought: more than four thousand kilogrammes of gold and a very large amount of spices and jewels. The amount of spices she gave him was by far the greatest that he ever received at any time.

11 (Hiram's fleet, which had brought gold from Ophir, also brought from there a large amount of juniper wood and jewels. ¹²Solomon used the wood to build railings in the Temple and the palace, and also to make harps and lyres for the musicians. It was the finest juniper wood

---

*b*CABUL: *This name sounds like "ke-bal," the Hebrew for "worthless."*
*c*Hebrew has two additional words, the meaning of which is unclear.
*d*Probable text (see 2 Chr. 9.1) Solomon's fame; Hebrew Solomon's fame concerning the name of the LORD.　　*e*you; *or your deeds.*　　*f*Some ancient translations wives; Hebrew men.
9.25: Ex 23.17, 34.23; Deut 16.16　　　**10.1–10:** Mt 12.42; Lk 11.31

The queen of Sheba heard of Solomon's fame (10.1)

ever imported into Israel; none like it has ever been seen again.)

13 King Solomon gave the queen of Sheba everything she asked for, besides all the other customary gifts that he had generously given her. Then she and her attendants returned to the land of Sheba.

King Solomon's Wealth
(2 Chr 9.13–28)

14 Every year King Solomon received almost twenty-three thousand kilogrammes of gold 15 in addition to the taxes *g* paid by merchants, the profits from trade, and tribute paid by the Arabian kings and the governors of the Israelite districts.

16 Solomon made two hundred large shields, and had each one overlaid with almost seven kilogrammes of gold. 17 He also made three hundred smaller shields, overlaying each one of them with almost two kilogrammes of gold. He had all these shields placed in the Hall of the Forest of Lebanon. *h*

18 He also had a large throne made. Part of it was covered with ivory and the rest of it was covered with the finest gold. 19-20 The throne had six steps leading

up to it, with the figure of a lion at each end of every step, a total of twelve lions. At the back of the throne was the figure of a bull's head, and beside each of the two arms was the figure of a lion. No throne like this had ever existed in any other kingdom.

21 All of Solomon's drinking cups were made of gold, and all the utensils in the Hall of the Forest of Lebanon were of pure gold. No silver was used, since it was not considered valuable in Solomon's day. 22 He had a fleet of ocean-going ships sailing with Hiram's fleet. Every three years his fleet would return, bringing gold, silver, ivory, apes, and monkeys.

23 King Solomon was richer and wiser than any other king, 24 and the whole world wanted to come and listen to the wisdom that God had given him. 25 Everyone who came brought him a gift— articles of silver and gold, robes, weapons, spices, horses, and mules. This continued year after year.

26 Solomon built up a force of fourteen hundred chariots and twelve thousand cavalry horses. Some of them he kept in Jerusalem and the rest he stationed in various other cities. 27 During his reign

g Some ancient translations taxes; *Hebrew* men.
h HALL OF THE FOREST OF LEBANON: *See 7.2–3.*
10.26: 1 Kgs 4.26

silver was as common in Jerusalem as stone, and cedar was as plentiful as ordinary sycomore in the foothills of Judah. 28 The king's agents controlled the export of horses from Musri[i] and Cilicia,[j] 29 and the export of chariots from Egypt. They supplied the Hittite and Syrian kings with horses and chariots, selling chariots for 600 pieces of silver each and horses for 150 each.

Solomon Turns Away from God

11 Solomon loved many foreign women. Besides the daughter of the king of Egypt he married Hittite women and women from Moab, Ammon, Edom, and Sidon. 2 He married them even though the LORD had commanded the Israelites not to intermarry with these people, because they would cause the Israelites to give their loyalty to other gods. 3 Solomon married seven hundred princesses and also had three hundred concubines. They made him turn away from God, 4 and by the time he was old they had led him into the worship of foreign gods. He was not faithful to the LORD his God, as his father David had been. 5 He worshipped Astarte the goddess of Sidon, and Molech the disgusting god of Ammon. 6 He sinned against the LORD and was not true to him as his father David had been. 7 On the mountain east of Jerusalem he built a place to worship Chemosh, the disgusting god of Moab, and a place to worship Molech, the disgusting god of Ammon. 8 He also built places of worship where all his foreign wives could burn incense and offer sacrifices to their own gods.

9-10 Even though the LORD, the God of Israel, had appeared to Solomon twice and had commanded him not to worship foreign gods, Solomon did not obey the LORD, but turned away from him. So the LORD was angry with Solomon 11 and said to him, "Because you have deliberately broken your covenant with me and disobeyed my commands, I promise that I will take the kingdom away from you and give it to one of your officials. 12 However, for the sake of your father David I will not do this in your lifetime, but during the reign of your son. 13 And I will not take the whole kingdom away

from him; instead, I will leave him one tribe for the sake of my servant David and for the sake of Jerusalem, the city I have made my own."

Solomon's Enemies

14 So the LORD caused Hadad, of the royal family of Edom, to turn against Solomon. 15-16 Long before this, when David had conquered Edom, Joab the commander of his army had gone there to bury the dead. He and his men remained in Edom six months, and during that time they killed every male in Edom 17 except Hadad and some of his father's Edomite servants, who escaped to Egypt. (At that time Hadad was just a child.) 18 They left Midian and went to Paran, where some other men joined them. Then they travelled to Egypt and went to the king, who gave Hadad some land and a house and provided him with food. 19 Hadad won the friendship of the king, and the king gave his sister-in-law, the sister of Queen Tahpenes, to Hadad in marriage. 20 She bore him a son, Genubath, who was brought up by the queen in the palace, where he lived with the king's sons.

21 When the news reached Hadad in Egypt that David had died and that Joab the commander of the army was dead, Hadad said to the king, "Let me go back to my own country."

22 "Why?" the king asked. "Have I failed to give you something? Is that why you want to go back home?"

"Just let me go," Hadad answered the king. And he went back to his country.[k]

As king of Edom, Hadad was an evil, bitter enemy of Israel.[l]

23 God also caused Rezon son of Eliada to turn against Solomon. Rezon had fled from his master, King Hadadezer of Zobah, 24 and had become the leader of a gang of outlaws. (This happened after David had defeated Hadadezer and had slaughtered his Syrian allies.) Rezon and his men went and lived in Damascus, where his men made him king of Syria. 25 He was an enemy of Israel during the lifetime of Solomon.

God's Promise to Jeroboam

26 Another man who turned against

---

[i] Probable text Musri; Hebrew Egypt.
[j] MUSRI AND CILICIA: Two ancient countries in what is now south-east Turkey, which were centres of horse breeding in Solomon's time.
[k] One ancient translation And he went back to his country; Hebrew does not have these words.
[l] One ancient translation As king...Israel; in Hebrew this sentence, with some differences, comes at the end of verse 25.
10.28: Deut 17.16   **11.1:** Deut 17.17   **11.2:** Ex 34.16; Deut 7.3-4

Take ten pieces for yourself (11.31)

King Solomon was one of his officials, Jeroboam son of Nebat, from Zeredah in Ephraim. His mother was a widow named Zeruah. 27 This is the story of the revolt.

Solomon was filling in the land on the east side of Jerusalem and repairing the city walls. 28 Jeroboam was an able young man, and when Solomon noticed how hard he worked, he put him in charge of all the forced labour in the territory of the tribes of Manasseh and Ephraim. 29 One day, as Jeroboam was travelling from Jerusalem, the prophet Ahijah, from Shiloh, met him alone on the road in the open country. 30 Ahijah took off the new robe he was wearing, tore it into twelve pieces, 31 and said to Jeroboam, "Take ten pieces for yourself, because the LORD, the God of Israel, says to you, 'I am going to take the kingdom away from Solomon, and I will give you ten tribes. 32 Solomon will keep one tribe, for the sake of my servant David and for the sake of Jerusalem, the city I have chosen to be my own from the whole land of Israel. 33 I am going to do this because Solomon has rejected me and has*m* worshipped foreign gods: Astarte, the goddess of Sidon; Chemosh, the god of Moab; and Molech, the god of Ammon. Solomon has*n* disobeyed me; he has done wrong, and has not kept my laws and commands as his father David

did. 34 But I will not take the whole kingdom away from Solomon, and I will keep him in power as long as he lives. This I will do for the sake of my servant David, whom I chose and who obeyed my laws and commands. 35 I will take the kingdom away from Solomon's son and will give you ten tribes, 36 but I will let Solomon's son keep one tribe, so that I will always have a descendant of my servant David ruling in Jerusalem, the city I have chosen as the place where I am worshipped. 37 Jeroboam, I will make you king of Israel, and you will rule over all the territory that you want. 38 If you obey me completely, live by my laws, and win my approval by doing what I command, as my servant David did, I will always be with you. I will make you king of Israel and will make sure that your descendants rule after you, just as I have done for David. 39 Because of Solomon's sin I will punish the descendants of David, but not for all time.' "

40 And so Solomon tried to kill Jeroboam, but he escaped to King Shishak of Egypt and stayed there until Solomon's death.

The Death of Solomon
(2 Chr 9.29–31)

41 Everything else that Solomon did, his

m Some ancient translations Solomon has...and has; *Hebrew* they have...and have.
n Some ancient translations Solomon has; *Hebrew* They have.

THE DIVIDED
ISRAELITE KINGDOMS

Sidon

Mount Lebanon

Damascus

SYRIA

Zarephath

Ijon

Abel Beth Maacah

Dan

NAPHTALI

BASHAN

Kedesh

Hazor

GALILEE

River Kishon

Mount Carmel

Gath Hepher

Aphek

LAKE GALILEE

EAST MANASSEH

Megiddo

Shunem

Jezreel

Ramoth in Gilead

MEDITERRANEAN SEA

Dothan

Beth Shan

ISRAEL

Tishbe

GILEAD

Samaria

Tirzah

Brook of Cherith

River Jordan

AMMON

Shechem

Tappuah

Penuel

Shiloh

EPHRAIM

Bethel

Gilgal

Gezer

Ramah

Anathoth

Ekron

Gibbethon

BENJAMIN

Beth Shemesh

Jerusalem

Libnah

JUDAH

REUBEN

Gath

Lachish

Gaza

JUDAH

PHILISTIA

DEAD SEA

Aroer

River Arnon

MOAB

Beersheba

0   20   40   60
Kilometres

E D O M

career and his wisdom, are all recorded in *The History of Solomon.* 42 He was king in Jerusalem over all Israel for forty years. 43 He died and was buried in David's City, and his son Rehoboam succeeded him as king.

The Northern Tribes Revolt
(2 Chr 10.1–19)

12 Rehoboam went to Shechem, where all the people of northern Israel had gathered to make him king. 2 When Jeroboam son of Nebat, who had gone to Egypt to escape from King Solomon, heard this news, he returned from o Egypt. 3 The people of the northern tribes sent for him, and then they all went together to Rehoboam and said to him, 4 "Your father Solomon treated us harshly and placed heavy burdens on us. If you make these burdens lighter and make life easier for us, we will be your loyal subjects."

5 "Come back in three days and I will give you my answer," he replied. So they left.

6 King Rehoboam consulted the older men who had served as his father Solomon's advisers. "What answer do you advise me to give these people?" he asked.

7 They replied, "If you want to serve this people well, give a favourable answer to their request, and they will always serve you loyally."

8 But he ignored the advice of the older men and went instead to the young men who had grown up with him and who were now his advisers. 9 "What do you advise me to do?" he asked. "What shall I say to the people who are asking me to make their burdens lighter?"

10 They replied, "This is what you should tell them: 'My little finger is thicker than my father's waist!' 11 Tell them, 'My father placed heavy burdens on you; I will make them even heavier. He beat you with a whip; I'll flog you with a horsewhip!'"

12 Three days later Jeroboam and all the people returned to King Rehoboam, as he had instructed them. 13 The king ignored the advice of the older men and spoke harshly to the people, 14 as the younger men had advised. He said, "My father placed heavy burdens on you; I will make them even heavier. He beat you with a whip; I'll flog you with a horsewhip!"

15 It was the will of the LORD to bring about

what he had spoken to Jeroboam son of Nebat through the prophet Ahijah from Shiloh. This is why the king did not pay any attention to the people.

16 When the people saw that the king would not listen to them, they shouted, "Down with David and his family! What have they ever done for us? Men of Israel, let's go home! Let Rehoboam look out for himself!"

So the people of Israel rebelled, 17 leaving Rehoboam as king only of the people who lived in the territory of Judah.

18 Then King Rehoboam sent Adoniram, who was in charge of the forced labour, to go to the Israelites, but they stoned him to death. At this, Rehoboam hurriedly got into his chariot and escaped to Jerusalem. 19 Ever since that time the people of the northern kingdom of Israel have been in rebellion against the dynasty of David.

20 When the people of Israel heard that Jeroboam had returned from Egypt, they invited him to a meeting of the people and made him king of Israel. Only the tribe of Judah remained loyal to David's descendants.

Shemaiah's Prophecy
(2 Chr 11.1–4)

21 When Rehoboam arrived in Jerusalem, he called together 180,000 of the best soldiers from the tribes of Judah and Benjamin. He intended to go to war and restore his control over the northern tribes of Israel. 22 But God told the prophet Shemaiah 23 to give this message to Rehoboam and to all the people of the tribes of Judah and Benjamin: 24 "Do not attack your own brothers, the people of Israel. Go home, all of you. What has happened is my will." They all obeyed the LORD's command and went back home.

Jeroboam Turns Away from the LORD

25 King Jeroboam of Israel fortified the town of Shechem in the hill-country of Ephraim and lived there for a while. Then he left and fortified the town of Penuel. 26-27 He said to himself, "As things are now, if my people go to Jerusalem and offer sacrifices to the LORD in the Temple there, they will transfer their allegiance to King Rehoboam of Judah and will kill me."

28 After thinking it over, he made two bull-calves of gold and said to his people, "You have been going long enough to

---

o *Some ancient translations (and see 2 Chr 10.2)* returned from; *Hebrew* remained in.
12.16: 2 Sam 20.1   **12.28:** Ex 32.4

Jerusalem to worship. People of Israel, here are your gods who brought you out of Egypt!" ²⁹ He placed one of the gold bull-calves in Bethel and the other in Dan. ³⁰ And so the people sinned, going to worship in Bethel and in Dan. *p* ³¹ Jeroboam also built places of worship on hilltops, and he chose priests from families who were not of the tribe of Levi.

Worship at Bethel Is Condemned

32 Jeroboam also instituted a religious festival on the fifteenth day of the eighth month, like the festival in Judah. On the altar in Bethel he offered sacrifices to the gold bull-calves he had made, and he placed there in Bethel the priests serving at the places of worship he had built. ³³ And on the fifteenth day of the eighth month, the day that he himself had set, he went to Bethel and offered a sacrifice on the altar in celebration of the festival he had instituted for the people of Israel.

13 At the LORD's command a prophet from Judah went to Bethel and arrived there as Jeroboam stood at the altar to offer the sacrifice. ² Following the LORD's command, the prophet denounced the altar: "O altar, altar, this is what the LORD says: A child, whose name will be Josiah, will be born to the family of David. He will slaughter on you the priests serving at the pagan altars who offer sacrifices on you, and he will burn human bones on you." ³ And the prophet went on to say, "This altar will fall apart, and the ashes on it will be scattered. Then you will know that the LORD has spoken through me."

4 When King Jeroboam heard this, he pointed at him and ordered, "Seize that man!" At once the king's arm became paralysed so that he couldn't pull it back. ⁵ The altar suddenly fell apart and the ashes spilt to the ground, as the prophet had predicted in the name of the LORD. ⁶ King Jeroboam said to the prophet, "Please pray for me to the LORD your God, and ask him to heal my arm!"

The prophet prayed to the LORD, and the king's arm was healed. ⁷ Then the king said to the prophet, "Come home with me and have something to eat. I will reward you for what you have done."

8 The prophet answered, "Even if you gave me half your wealth, I would not go with you or eat or drink anything with you. ⁹ The LORD has commanded me not to eat or drink a thing, and not to return home the same way I came." ¹⁰ So he did not go back the same way he had come, but by another road.

The Old Prophet of Bethel

11 At that time there was an old prophet living in Bethel. His sons *q* came and told him what the prophet from Judah had done in Bethel that day and what he had said to King Jeroboam. ¹² "Which way did he go when he left?" the old prophet asked them. They showed him *r* the road ¹³ and he told them to saddle his donkey for him. They did so, and he rode off ¹⁴ down the road after the prophet from Judah and found him sitting under an oak. "Are you the prophet from Judah?" he asked.

"I am," the man answered.

15 "Come home and have a meal with me," he said.

16 But the prophet from Judah answered, "I can't go home with you or accept your hospitality. And I won't eat or drink anything with you here, ¹⁷ because the LORD has commanded me not to eat or drink a thing, and not to return home the same way I came."

18 Then the old prophet from Bethel said to him, "I, too, am a prophet just like you, and at the LORD's command an angel told me to take you home with me and offer you my hospitality." But the old prophet was lying.

19 So the prophet from Judah went home with the old prophet and had a meal with him. ²⁰ As they were sitting at the table, the word of the LORD came to the old prophet, ²¹ and he cried out to the prophet from Judah, "The LORD says that you disobeyed him and did not do what he commanded. ²² Instead, you returned and ate a meal in a place he had ordered you not to eat in. Because of this you will be killed, and your body will not be buried in your family grave."

23 After they had finished eating, the old prophet saddled the donkey for the prophet from Judah, ²⁴ who rode off. On the way, a lion met him and killed him. His body lay on the road, and the donkey and the lion stood beside it. ²⁵ Some men passed by and saw the body on the road,

---

p One ancient translation in Bethel and in Dan; *Hebrew* in Dan.
q Some ancient translations sons; *Hebrew* son.
r Some ancient translations showed him; *Hebrew* saw.
12.32–33: Lev 23.33–34   **13.2:** 2 Kgs 23.15–16

with the lion standing near by. They went on into Bethel and reported what they had seen.

26 When the old prophet heard about it, he said, "That is the prophet who disobeyed the LORD's command! And so the LORD sent the lion to attack and kill him, just as the LORD said he would." 27 Then he said to his sons, "Saddle my donkey for me." They did so, 28 and he rode off and found the prophet's body lying on the road, with the donkey and the lion still standing by it. The lion had not eaten the body or attacked the donkey. 29 The old prophet picked up the body, put it on the donkey, and brought it back to Bethel to mourn over it and bury it. 30 He buried it in his own family grave, and he and his sons mourned over it, saying, "Oh my brother, my brother!" 31 After the burial, the prophet said to his sons, "When I die, bury me in this grave and lay my body next to his. 32 The words that he spoke at the LORD's command against the altar in Bethel and against all the places of worship in the towns of Samaria will surely come true."

Jeroboam's Fatal Sin

33 King Jeroboam of Israel still did not turn from his evil ways, but continued to choose priests from ordinary families to serve at the altars he had built. He ordained as priest anyone who wanted to be one. 34 This sin on his part brought about the ruin and total destruction of his dynasty.

The Death of Jeroboam's Son

14 At that time King Jeroboam's son Abijah fell ill. 2 Jeroboam said to his wife, "Disguise yourself so that no one will recognize you, and go to Shiloh, where the prophet Ahijah lives, the one who said I would be king of Israel. 3 Take him ten loaves of bread, some cakes, and a jar of honey. Ask him what is going to happen to our son, and he will tell you."

4 So she went to Ahijah's home in Shiloh. Old age had made Ahijah blind. 5 The LORD had told him that Jeroboam's wife was coming to ask him about her son, who was ill. And the LORD told Ahijah what to say.

When Jeroboam's wife arrived, she pretended to be someone else. 6 But when Ahijah heard her coming in the door, he said, "Come in. I know you are Jeroboam's wife. Why are you pretending to be someone else? I have bad news for you. 7 Go and tell Jeroboam that this is what the LORD, the God of Israel, says to him: 'I chose you from among the people and made you the ruler of my people Israel. 8 I took the kingdom away from David's descendants and gave it to you. But you have not been like my servant David, who was completely loyal to me, obeyed my commands, and did only what I approve of. 9 You have committed far greater sins than those who ruled before you. You have rejected me and have aroused my anger by making idols and metal images to worship. 10 Because of this I will bring disaster on your dynasty and will kill all your male descendants, young and old alike. I will get rid of your family; they will be swept away like dung. 11 Any members of your family who die in the city will be eaten by dogs, and any who die in the open country will be eaten by vultures. I, the LORD, have spoken.'"

12 And Ahijah went on to say to Jeroboam's wife, "Now go back home. As soon as you enter the town your son will die. 13 All the people of Israel will mourn for him and bury him. He will be the only member of Jeroboam's family who will be properly buried, because he is the only one with whom the LORD, the God of Israel, is pleased. 14 The LORD is going to place a king over Israel who will put an end to Jeroboam's dynasty.* 15 The LORD will punish Israel, and she will shake like a reed shaking in a stream. He will uproot the people of Israel from this good land which he gave to their ancestors, and will scatter them beyond the River Euphrates, because they have aroused his anger by making idols of the goddess Asherah. 16 The LORD will abandon Israel because Jeroboam sinned and led the people of Israel into sin."

17 Jeroboam's wife went back to Tirzah. Just as she entered her home, the child died. 18 The people of Israel mourned for him and buried him, as the LORD had said through his servant, the prophet Ahijah.

The Death of Jeroboam

19 Everything else that King Jeroboam did, the wars he fought and how he ruled, are all recorded in *The History of the*

---

s Hebrew has five additional words, the meaning of which is unclear.
14.10: 1 Kgs 15.29

They built places of worship for false gods (14.23)

Kings of Israel. ²⁰ Jeroboam ruled as king for twenty-two years. He died and was buried, and his son Nadab succeeded him as king.

King Rehoboam of Judah
(2 Chr 11.5—12.15)

21 Solomon's son Rehoboam was forty-one years old when he became king of Judah, and he ruled for seventeen years in Jerusalem, the city which the LORD had chosen from all the territory of Israel as the place where he was to be worshipped. Rehoboam's mother was Naamah from Ammon.

22 The people of Judah sinned against the LORD and did more to arouse his anger against them than all their ancestors had done. ²³ They built places of worship for false gods, and put up stone pillars and symbols of Asherah to worship on the hills and under shady trees. ²⁴ Worst of all, there were men and women who served as prostitutes at those pagan places of worship. The people of Judah practised all the shameful things done by the people whom the LORD had driven out of the land as the Israelites advanced into the country.

25 In the fifth year of Rehoboam's reign King Shishak of Egypt attacked Jerusalem. ²⁶ He took away all the treasures in the Temple and in the palace, including the gold shields Solomon had made. ²⁷ To replace them, King Rehoboam made bronze shields and entrusted them to the officers responsible for guarding the palace gates. ²⁸ Every time the king went to the Temple, the guards carried the shields, and then returned them to the guard-room.

29 Everything else that King Rehoboam did is recorded in *The History of the Kings of Judah.* ³⁰ During all this time Rehoboam and Jeroboam were constantly at war with each other. ³¹ Rehoboam died and was buried in the royal tombs in David's City, and his son Abijah succeeded him as king.

King Abijah of Judah
(2 Chr 13.1—14.1)

15 In the eighteenth year of the reign of King Jeroboam of Israel, Abijah became king of Judah, ²and he ruled for three years in Jerusalem. His mother was Maacah, the daughter of Absalom. ³ He committed the same sins as his father and was not completely loyal to the LORD his God, as his great-grandfather David had been. ⁴ But for David's sake, the LORD his God gave Abijah a son to rule after him in Jerusalem and to keep Jerusalem secure. ⁵ The LORD did this because David had done what pleased him and had never disobeyed any of his commands, except in the case of Uriah the Hittite. ⁶ The war which had begun between Rehoboam and

14.23: 2 Kgs 17.9–10   **14.24:** Deut 23.17   **14.26:** 1 Kgs 10.16–17; 2 Chr 9.15–16
15.4: 1 Kgs 11.36   **15.5:** 2 Sam 11.1–27

Jeroboam continued throughout Abijah's lifetime. ⁷And everything else that Abijah did is recorded in *The History of the Kings of Judah.*

8 Abijah died and was buried in David's City, and his son Asa succeeded him as king.

King Asa of Judah
(2 Chr 15.16—16.6)

9 In the twentieth year of the reign of King Jeroboam of Israel, Asa became king of Judah, ¹⁰and he ruled for forty-one years in Jerusalem. His grandmother was Maacah, the daughter of Absalom. ¹¹Asa did what pleased the Lord, as his ancestor David had done. ¹²He expelled from the country all the male and female prostitutes serving at the pagan places of worship, and he removed all the idols his predecessors had made. ¹³He removed his grandmother Maacah from her position as queen mother, because she had made an obscene idol of the fertility goddess Asherah. Asa cut down the idol and burnt it in the valley of the Kidron. ¹⁴Even though Asa did not destroy all the pagan places of worship, he remained faithful to the Lord all his life. ¹⁵He placed in the Temple all the objects his father had dedicated to God, as well as the gold and silver objects that he himself dedicated.

16 King Asa of Judah and King Baasha of Israel were constantly at war with each other as long as they were in power. ¹⁷Baasha invaded Judah and started to fortify Ramah in order to cut off all traffic in and out of Judah. ¹⁸So King Asa took all the silver and gold that was left in the Temple and the palace, and sent it by some of his officials to Damascus, to King Benhadad of Syria, the son of Tabrimmon and grandson of Hezion, with this message: ¹⁹"Let us be allies, as our fathers were. This silver and gold is a present for you. Now break your alliance with King Baasha of Israel, so that he will have to pull his troops out of my territory."

20 King Benhadad agreed to Asa's proposal and sent his commanding officers and their armies to attack the cities of Israel. They captured Ijon, Dan, Abel Beth Maacah, the area near Lake Galilee, and the whole territory of Naphtali. ²¹When King Baasha heard what had happened, he stopped fortifying Ramah and went to Tirzah.

22 Then King Asa sent out an order throughout all Judah requiring everyone,

without exception, to help carry away from Ramah the stones and timber that Baasha had been using to fortify it. With this material Asa fortified Mizpah and Geba, a city in the territory of Benjamin.

23 Everything else that King Asa did, his brave deeds and the towns he fortified, are all recorded in *The History of the Kings of Judah.* But in his old age he was crippled by a foot disease. ²⁴Asa died and was buried in the royal tombs in David's City, and his son Jehoshaphat succeeded him as king.

King Nadab of Israel

25 In the second year of the reign of King Asa of Judah, King Jeroboam's son Nadab became king of Israel, and he ruled for two years. ²⁶Like his father before him, he sinned against the Lord and led Israel into sin.

27 Baasha son of Ahijah, of the tribe of Issachar, plotted against Nadab and killed him as Nadab and his army were besieging the city of Gibbethon in Philistia. ²⁸This happened during the third year of the reign of King Asa of Judah. And so Baasha succeeded Nadab as king of Israel. ²⁹At once he began killing all the members of Jeroboam's family. In accordance with what the Lord had said through his servant, the prophet Ahijah from Shiloh, all Jeroboam's family were killed; not one survived. ³⁰This happened because Jeroboam aroused the anger of the Lord, the God of Israel, by the sins that he committed and that he caused Israel to commit.

31 Everything else that Nadab did is recorded in *The History of the Kings of Israel.* ³²King Asa of Judah and King Baasha of Israel were constantly at war with each other as long as they were in power.

King Baasha of Israel

33 In the third year of the reign of King Asa of Judah, Baasha son of Ahijah became king of all Israel, and he ruled in Tirzah for twenty-four years. ³⁴Like King Jeroboam before him, he sinned against the Lord and led Israel into sin.

16 The Lord spoke to the prophet Jehu son of Hanani and gave him this message for Baasha: ²"You were a nobody, but I made you the leader of my people Israel. And now you have sinned like Jeroboam and have led my people into sin. Their sins have aroused my anger, [3] and so I will do away with you and your family, just as I did with Jeroboam. [4] Any members of your family who die in the city will be eaten by dogs, and any who die in the open country will be eaten by vultures."

5 Everything else that Baasha did and all his brave deeds are recorded in *The History of the Kings of Israel.* [6] Baasha died and was buried in Tirzah, and his son Elah succeeded him as king.

7 That message from the LORD against Baasha and his family was given by the prophet Jehu because of the sins that Baasha committed against the LORD. He aroused the LORD's anger not only because of the evil he did, just as King Jeroboam had done before him, but also because he killed all Jeroboam's family.

King Elah of Israel

8 In the twenty-sixth year of the reign of King Asa of Judah, Elah son of Baasha became king of Israel, and he ruled in Tirzah for two years. [9] Zimri, one of his officers who was in charge of half the king's chariots, plotted against him. One day in Tirzah, Elah was getting drunk in the home of Arza, who was in charge of the palace. [10] Zimri entered the house, assassinated Elah, and succeeded him as king. This happened in the twenty-seventh year of the reign of King Asa of Judah.

11 As soon as Zimri became king he killed off all the members of Baasha's family. Every male relative and friend was put to death. [12] And so, in accordance with what the LORD had said against Baasha through the prophet Jehu, Zimri killed all the family of Baasha. [13] Because of their idolatry and because they led Israel into sin, Baasha and his son Elah had aroused the anger of the LORD, the God of Israel. [14] Everything else that Elah did is recorded in *The History of the Kings of Israel.*

King Zimri of Israel

15 In the twenty-seventh year of the reign of King Asa of Judah, Zimri ruled in Tirzah over Israel for seven days. The Israelite troops were besieging the city of Gibbethon in Philistia, [16] and when they heard that Zimri had plotted against the king and assassinated him, then and there they all proclaimed their commander Omri king of Israel. [17] Omri and his troops left Gibbethon and went and besieged Tirzah. [18] When Zimri saw that the city had fallen, he went into the palace's inner fortress, set the palace on fire, and died in the flames. [19] This happened because of his sins against the LORD. Like his predecessor Jeroboam he displeased the LORD by his own sins and by leading Israel into sin. [20] Everything else that Zimri did, including the account of his conspiracy, is recorded in *The History of the Kings of Israel.*

King Omri of Israel

21 The people of Israel were divided: some of them wanted to make Tibni son of Ginath king, and the others were in favour of Omri. [22] In the end, those in favour of Omri won; Tibni died and Omri became king. [23] So in the thirty-first year of the reign of King Asa of Judah, Omri became king of Israel, and he ruled for twelve years. The first six years he ruled in Tirzah, [24] and then he bought the hill of Samaria for six thousand pieces of silver from a man named Shemer. Omri fortified the hill, built a town there, and named it Samaria, after Shemer, the former owner of the hill.

25 Omri sinned against the LORD more than any of his predecessors. [26] Like Jeroboam before him, he aroused the anger of the LORD, the God of Israel, by his sins and by leading the people into sin and idolatry. [27] Everything else that Omri did and all his accomplishments are recorded in *The History of the Kings of Israel.* [28] Omri died and was buried in Samaria, and his son Ahab succeeded him as king.

King Ahab of Israel

29 In the thirty-eighth year of the reign of King Asa of Judah, Ahab son of Omri became king of Israel, and he ruled in Samaria for twenty-two years. [30] He sinned against the LORD more than any of his predecessors. [31] It was not enough for him to sin like King Jeroboam; he went further and married Jezebel, the daughter of King Ethbaal of Sidon, and worshipped Baal. [32] He built a temple to Baal in Samaria, made an altar for him, and put it in the temple. [33] He also put up an image of the goddess Asherah. He did more to arouse the anger of the LORD, the God of Israel, than all the kings of Israel before him. [34] During his reign Hiel from Bethel rebuilt Jericho. As the LORD had foretold through Joshua son of Nun, Hiel lost his eldest son Abiram when he laid the foundation of Jericho, and his

16.34: Josh 6.26

I have commanded ravens to bring you food (17.4)

youngest son Segub when he built the gates.

Elijah and the Drought

17 A prophet named Elijah, from Tishbe in Gilead, said to King Ahab, "In the name of the LORD, the living God of Israel, whom I serve, I tell you that there will be no dew or rain for the next two or three years until I say so."

2 Then the LORD said to Elijah, 3 "Leave this place and go east and hide yourself near the brook of Cherith, east of the Jordan. 4 The brook will supply you with water to drink, and I have commanded ravens to bring you food there."

5 Elijah obeyed the LORD's command, and went and stayed by the brook of Cherith. 6 He drank water from the brook, and ravens brought him bread and meat every morning and every evening. 7 After a while the brook dried up because of the lack of rain.

Elijah and the Widow in Zarephath

8 Then the LORD said to Elijah, 9 "Now go to the town of Zarephath, near Sidon, and stay there. I have commanded a widow who lives there to feed you." 10 So Elijah went to Zarephath, and as he came to the gate of the town, he saw a widow gathering firewood. "Please bring me a

drink of water," he said to her. 11 And as she was going to get it, he called out, "And please bring me some bread, too."

12 She answered, "By the living LORD your God I swear that I haven't got any bread. All I have is a handful of flour in a bowl and a drop of olive-oil in a jar. I came here to gather some firewood to take back home and prepare what little I have for my son and me. That will be our last meal, and then we will starve to death."

13 "Don't worry," Elijah said to her. "Go ahead and prepare your meal. But first make a small loaf from what you have and bring it to me, and then prepare the rest for you and your son. 14 For this is what the LORD, the God of Israel, says: 'The bowl will not run out of flour or the jar run out of oil before the day that I, the LORD, send rain.'"

15 The widow went and did as Elijah had told her, and all of them had enough food for many days. 16 As the LORD had promised through Elijah, the bowl did not run out of flour nor did the jar run out of oil.

17 Some time later the widow's son fell ill; he got worse and worse, and finally he died. 18 She said to Elijah, "Man of God, why did you do this to me? Did

17.1: Jas 5.17   **17.9:** Lk 4.25–26

Go ahead and prepare your meal (17.13)

you come here to remind God of my sins
and so cause my son's death?''

19 "Give the boy to me," Elijah said.
He took the boy from her arms, carried
him upstairs to the room where he was
staying, and laid him on the bed. ²⁰Then
he prayed aloud, "O LORD my God, why
have you done such a terrible thing to
this widow? She has been kind enough
to take care of me, and now you kill her
son!" ²¹Then Elijah stretched himself out
on the boy three times and prayed, "O
LORD my God, restore this child to life!"
²²The LORD answered Elijah's prayer; the
child started breathing again and revived.

23 Elijah took the boy back downstairs
to his mother and said to her, "Look, your
son is alive!"

24 She answered, "Now I know that you
are a man of God and that the LORD really
speaks through you!"

Elijah and the Prophets of Baal

18 After some time, in the third year
of the drought, the LORD said to
Elijah, "Go and present yourself to King
Ahab, and I will send rain." ²So Elijah
started out.

The famine in Samaria was at its worst,
³so Ahab called in Obadiah, who was in
charge of the palace. (Obadiah was a
devout worshipper of the LORD, ⁴and
when Jezebel was killing the LORD's
prophets, Obadiah took a hundred of
them, hid them in caves in two groups
of fifty, and provided them with food and
water.) ⁵Ahab said to Obadiah, "Let us
go and look*ᵗ* at every spring and every
river-bed in the land to see if we can find
enough grass to keep the horses and
mules alive. Maybe we won't have to kill
any of our animals." ⁶They agreed on
which part of the land each one would
explore, and set off in different directions.

7 As Obadiah was on his way, he
suddenly met Elijah. He recognized him,
bowed low before him, and asked, "Is it
really you, sir?"

8 "Yes, I'm Elijah," he answered. "Go
and tell your master the king that I am
here."

9 Obadiah answered, "What have I
done that you want to put me in danger
of being killed by King Ahab? ¹⁰By the
living LORD, your God, I swear that the
king has made a search for you in every

ᵗ One ancient translation Let us go and look; *Hebrew* You go and look.
17.21: 2 Kgs 4.34–35

country in the world. Whenever the ruler of a country reported that you were not in his country, Ahab would require that ruler to swear that you could not be found. 11 And now you want me to go and tell him that you are here? 12 What if the spirit of the LORD carries you off to some unknown place as soon as I leave? Then, when I tell Ahab that you are here, and he can't find you, he will put me to death. Remember that I have been a devout worshipper of the LORD ever since I was a boy. 13 Haven't you heard that when Jezebel was killing the prophets of the LORD I hid a hundred of them in caves, in two groups of fifty, and supplied them with food and water? 14 So how can you order me to go and tell the king that you are here? He will kill me!"

15 Elijah answered, "By the living LORD, whom I serve, I promise that I will present myself to the king today."

16 So Obadiah went to King Ahab and told him, and Ahab set off to meet Elijah. 17 When Ahab saw him, he said, "So there you are—the worst troublemaker in Israel!"

18 "I'm not the troublemaker," Elijah answered. "You are—you and your father. You are disobeying the LORD's commands and worshipping the idols of Baal. 19 Now order all the people of Israel to meet me at Mount Carmel. Bring along the 450 prophets of Baal and the 400 prophets of the goddess Asherah who are supported by Queen Jezebel."

20 So Ahab summoned all the Israelites and the prophets of Baal to meet at Mount Carmel. 21 Elijah went up to the people and said, "How much longer will it take you to make up your minds? If the LORD is God, worship him; but if Baal is God, worship him!" But the people didn't say a word. 22 Then Elijah said, "I am the only prophet of the LORD still left, but there are 450 prophets of Baal. 23 Bring two bulls; let the prophets of Baal take one, kill it, cut it in pieces, and put it on the wood—but don't light the fire. I will do the same with the other bull. 24 Then let the prophets of Baal pray to their god, and I will pray to the LORD, and the one who answers by sending fire—he is God." The people shouted their approval.

25 Then Elijah said to the prophets of Baal, "Since there are so many of you, you take a bull and prepare it first. Pray to your god, but don't set fire to the wood."

26 They took the bull that was brought to them, prepared it, and prayed to Baal until noon. They shouted, "Answer us, Baal!" and kept dancing round the altar they had built. But no answer came. 27 At noon Elijah started making fun of them: "Pray louder! He is a god! Maybe he is day-dreaming or relieving himself, or perhaps he's gone on a journey! Or maybe he's sleeping, and you've got to wake him up!" 28 So the prophets prayed louder and cut themselves with knives and daggers, according to their ritual, until blood flowed. 29 They kept on ranting and raving until the middle of the afternoon; but no answer came, not a sound was heard.

30 Then Elijah said to the people, "Come closer to me," and they all gathered round him. He set about repairing the altar of the LORD which had been torn down. 31 He took twelve stones, one for each of the twelve tribes named after the sons of Jacob, the man to whom the LORD had given the name Israel. 32 With these stones he rebuilt the altar for the worship of the LORD. He dug a trench round it, large enough to hold almost fourteen litres of water. 33 Then he placed the wood on the altar, cut the bull in pieces, and laid it on the wood. He said, "Fill four jars with water and pour it on the offering and the wood." They did so, 34 and he said, "Do it again"—and they did. "Do it once more," he said—and they did. 35 The water ran down round the altar and filled the trench.

36 At the hour of the afternoon sacrifice the prophet Elijah approached the altar and prayed, "O LORD, the God of Abraham, Isaac, and Jacob, prove now that you are the God of Israel and that I am your servant and have done all this at your command. 37 Answer me, LORD, answer me, so that this people will know that you, the LORD, are God, and that you are bringing them back to yourself." u

38 The LORD sent fire down, and it burnt up the sacrifice, the wood, and the stones, scorched the earth and dried up the water in the trench. 39 When the people saw this, they threw themselves on the ground and exclaimed, "The LORD is God; the LORD alone is God!"

40 Elijah ordered, "Seize the prophets of Baal; don't let any of them get away!" The people seized them all, and Elijah led

u you are bringing them back to yourself; *or* you yourself made them turn away from you.
18.31: Gen 32.28, 35.10

The Lord sent fire down (18.38)

them down to the River Kishon and killed them.

The End of the Drought

41 Then Elijah said to King Ahab, "Now, go and eat. I hear the roar of rain approaching." ⁴²While Ahab went to eat, Elijah climbed to the top of Mount Carmel, where he bowed down to the ground, with his head between his knees. ⁴³He said to his servant, "Go and look towards the sea."

The servant went and returned, saying, "I didn't see anything." Seven times in all Elijah told him to go and look. ⁴⁴The seventh time he returned and said, "I saw a little cloud no bigger than a man's hand, coming up from the sea."

Elijah ordered his servant, "Go to King Ahab and tell him to get into his chariot and go back home before the rain stops him."

45 In a little while the sky was covered with dark clouds, the wind began to blow, and heavy rain began to fall. Ahab got into his chariot and started back to Jezreel. ⁴⁶The power of the Lord came on Elijah; he fastened his clothes tight round his waist and ran ahead of Ahab all the way to Jezreel.

Elijah on Mount Sinai

19 King Ahab told his wife Jezebel everything that Elijah had done and how he had put all the prophets of Baal to death. ²She sent a message to Elijah: "May the gods strike me dead if by this time tomorrow I don't do the same thing to you that you did to the prophets." ³Elijah was afraid, and fled for his life; he took his servant and went to Beersheba in Judah.

Leaving the servant there, ⁴Elijah walked a whole day into the wilderness. He stopped and sat down in the shade of a tree and wished he would die. "It's too much, Lord," he prayed. "Take away my life; I might as well be dead!"

5 He lay down under the tree and fell asleep. Suddenly an angel touched him and said, "Wake up and eat." ⁶He looked round, and saw a loaf of bread and a

18.42–45: Jas 5.18   **19.4:** Jon 4.3

jar of water near his head. He ate and drank, and lay down again. 7 The Lord's angel returned and woke him up a second time, saying, "Get up and eat, or the journey will be too much for you." 8 Elijah got up, ate and drank, and the food gave him enough strength to walk forty days to Sinai, the holy mountain. 9 There he went into a cave to spend the night.

Suddenly the Lord spoke to him, "Elijah, what are you doing here?"

10 He answered, "Lord God Almighty, I have always served you—you alone. But the people of Israel have broken their covenant with you, torn down your altars, and killed all your prophets. I am the only one left—and they are trying to kill me!"

11 "Go out and stand before me on top of the mountain," the Lord said to him. Then the Lord passed by and sent a furious wind that split the hills and shattered the rocks—but the Lord was not in the wind. The wind stopped blowing, and then there was an earthquake—but the Lord was not in the earthquake. 12 After the earthquake, there was a fire—but the Lord was not in the fire. And after the fire, there was the soft whisper of a voice.

13 When Elijah heard it, he covered his face with his cloak and went out and stood at the entrance of the cave. A voice said to him, "Elijah, what are you doing here?"

14 He answered, "Lord God Almighty, I have always served you—you alone. But the people of Israel have broken their covenant with you, torn down your altars, and killed all your prophets. I am the only one left—and they are trying to kill me."

15 The Lord said, "Return to the wilderness near Damascus, then enter the city and anoint Hazael as king of Syria; 16 anoint Jehu son of Nimshi as king of Israel, and anoint Elisha son of Shaphat from Abel Meholah to succeed you as prophet. 17 Anyone who escapes being put to death by Hazael will be killed by Jehu, and anyone who escapes Jehu will be killed by Elisha. 18 Yet I will leave seven thousand people alive in Israel—all those who are loyal to me and have not bowed to Baal or kissed his idol."

The Call of Elisha

19 Elijah left and found Elisha ploughing with a team of oxen; there were eleven teams ahead of him, and he was ploughing with the last one. Elijah took off his cloak and put it on Elisha. 20 Elisha then left his oxen, ran after Elijah, and said, "Let me kiss my father and mother good-bye, and then I will go with you."

Elijah answered, "All right, go back. I'm not stopping you!" v

21 Then Elisha went to his team of oxen, killed them, and cooked the meat, using the yoke as fuel for the fire. He gave the meat to the people, and they ate it. Then he went and followed Elijah as his helper.

War with Syria

20 King Benhadad of Syria gathered all his troops, and supported by thirty-two other rulers with their horses and chariots, he marched up, laid siege to Samaria, and launched attacks against it. 2 He sent messengers into the city to King Ahab of Israel to say, "King Benhadad demands that 3 you surrender to him your silver and gold, your women and the strongest of your children."

4 "Tell my lord, King Benhadad, that I agree; he can have me and everything I own," Ahab answered.

5 Later the messengers came back to Ahab with another demand from Benhadad: "I sent you word that you were to hand over to me your silver and gold, your women and your children. 6 Now, however, I will send my officers to search your palace and the homes of your officials, and to take everything they w consider valuable. They will be there about this time tomorrow."

7 King Ahab called in all the leaders of the country and said, "You see that this man wants to ruin us. He sent me a message demanding my wives and children, my silver and gold, and I agreed."

8 The leaders and the people answered, "Don't pay any attention to him; don't give in."

9 So Ahab replied to Benhadad's messengers, "Tell my lord the king that I agreed to his first demand, but I cannot agree to the second."

The messengers left and then returned with another message 10 from Benhadad: "I will bring enough men to destroy this city of yours and carry off the rubble in their hands. May the gods strike me dead if I don't!"

11 King Ahab answered, "Tell King Benhadad that a real soldier does his

---

v All right...you; or Go on, but come back, because what I have just done to you is important.
w Some ancient translations they; Hebrew you.
19.10: Rom 11.3   **19.15:** 2 Kgs 8.7–13   **19.16:** 2 Kgs 9.1–6   **19.18:** Rom 11.4

boasting *after* a battle, not before it."

12 Benhadad received Ahab's answer as he and his allies, the other rulers, were drinking in their tents. He ordered his men to get ready to attack the city, so they moved into position.

13 Meanwhile, a prophet went to King Ahab and said, "The LORD says, 'Don't be afraid of that huge army! I will give you victory over it today, and you will know that I am the LORD.'"

14 "Who will lead the attack?" Ahab asked.

The prophet answered, "The LORD says that the young soldiers under the command of the district governors are to do it."

"Who will command the main force?" the king asked.

"You," the prophet answered.

15 So the king called out the young soldiers who were under the district commanders, 232 in all. Then he called out the Israelite army, a total of seven thousand men.

16 The attack began at noon, as Benhadad and his thirty-two allies were getting drunk in their tents. 17 The young soldiers advanced first. Scouts sent out by Benhadad reported to him that a group of soldiers was coming out of Samaria. 18 He ordered, "Take them alive, no matter whether they are coming to fight or to ask for peace."

19 The young soldiers led the attack, followed by the Israelite army, 20 and each one killed the man he fought. The Syrians fled, with the Israelites in hot pursuit, but Benhadad escaped on horseback, accompanied by some of the cavalry. 21 King Ahab took to the field, captured[x] the horses and chariots, and inflicted a severe defeat on the Syrians.

22 Then the prophet went to King Ahab and said, "Go back and build up your forces, and make careful plans, because the king of Syria will attack again next spring."

The Second Syrian Attack

23 King Benhadad's officials said to him, "The gods of Israel are mountain gods, and that is why the Israelites defeated us. But we will certainly defeat them if we fight them in the plains. 24 Now, remove the thirty-two rulers from their commands and replace them with field commanders. 25 Then call up an army as large as the one that deserted you, with the same number of horses and chariots. We will fight the Israelites in the plains, and this time we will defeat them."

King Benhadad agreed and followed their advice. 26 The following spring he called up his men and marched with them to the city of Aphek to attack the Israelites. 27 The Israelites were called up and equipped; they marched out and camped in two groups facing the Syrians. The Israelites looked like two small flocks of goats compared with the Syrians, who spread out over the countryside.

28 A prophet went to King Ahab and said, "This is what the LORD says: 'Because the Syrians say that I am a god of the hills and not of the plains, I will give you victory over their huge army, and you and your people will know that I am the LORD.'"

29 For seven days the Syrians and the Israelites stayed in their camps, facing each other. On the seventh day they started fighting, and the Israelites killed a hundred thousand Syrians. 30 The survivors fled into the city of Aphek, where the city walls fell on twenty-seven thousand of them.

Benhadad also escaped into the city and took refuge in the back room of a house. 31 His officials went to him and said, "We have heard that the Israelite kings are merciful. Give us permission to go to the king of Israel with sackcloth round our waists and ropes round our necks, and maybe he will spare your life." 32 So they wrapped sackcloth round their waists and ropes round their necks, went to Ahab and said, "Your servant Benhadad pleads with you for his life."

Ahab answered, "Is he still alive? Good! He's like a brother to me!"

33 Benhadad's officials were watching for a good sign, and when Ahab said "brother," they took it up at once, and said, "As you say, Benhadad is your brother!"

"Bring him to me," Ahab ordered. When Benhadad arrived, Ahab invited him to get in the chariot with him. 34 Benhadad said to him, "I will restore to you the towns my father took from your father, and you may set up a commercial centre for yourself in Damascus, just as my father did in Samaria."

Ahab replied, "On these terms, then, I will set you free." He made a treaty with him and let him go.

---

[x] *One ancient translation* captured; *Hebrew* destroyed.

They wrapped...ropes round their necks (20.32)

A Prophet Condemns Ahab

35 At the LORD's command a member of a group of prophets ordered a fellow-prophet to hit him. But he refused, ³⁶ so he said to him, "Because you have disobeyed the LORD's command, a lion will kill you as soon as you leave me." And as soon as he left, a lion came along and killed him.

37 Then this same prophet went to another man and said, "Hit me!" This man did so; he hit him a hard blow and hurt him. ³⁸ The prophet bandaged his face with a cloth, to disguise himself, and went and stood by the road, waiting for the king of Israel to pass. ³⁹ As the king was passing by, the prophet called out to him and said, "Your Majesty, I was fighting in the battle when a soldier brought a captured enemy to me and said, 'Guard this man; if he escapes, you will pay for it with your life or else pay a fine of three thousand pieces of silver.' ⁴⁰ But I got busy with other things, and the man escaped."

The king answered, "You have pronounced your own sentence, and you will have to pay the penalty."

41 The prophet tore the cloth from his face, and at once the king recognized him as one of the prophets. ⁴² The prophet then said to the king, "This is the word of the LORD: 'Because you allowed the man to escape whom I had ordered to be killed, you will pay for it with your life, and your army will be destroyed for letting his army escape.'"

43 The king went back home to Samaria, worried and depressed.

Naboth's Vineyard

21 Near King Ahab's palace in Jezreel there was a vineyard owned by a man named Naboth. ² One day Ahab said to Naboth, "Let me have your vineyard; it is close to my palace, and I want to use the land for a vegetable garden. I will give you a better vineyard for it, or, if you prefer, I will pay you a fair price."

3 "I inherited this vineyard from my ancestors," Naboth replied. "The LORD forbid that I should let you have it!"

4 Ahab went home, depressed and angry over what Naboth had said to him. He lay down on his bed, facing the wall, and would not eat. ⁵ His wife Jezebel went to him and asked, "Why are you so depressed? Why won't you eat?"

6 He answered, "Because of what Naboth said to me. I offered to buy his vineyard, or, if he preferred, to give him another one for it, but he told me that I couldn't have it!"

7 "Well, are you the king or aren't you?" Jezebel replied. "Get out of bed, cheer up and eat. I will get you Naboth's vineyard!"

8 Then she wrote some letters, signed them with Ahab's name, sealed them with his seal, and sent them to the officials and leading citizens of Jezreel. ⁹ The letters said: "Proclaim a day of fasting, call the people together, and give Naboth the place of honour. ¹⁰ Get a couple of scoundrels to accuse him to his face of cursing God and the king. Then take him out of the city and stone him to death."

11 The officials and leading citizens of Jezreel did what Jezebel had commanded. ¹² They proclaimed a day of fasting, called the people together, and gave Naboth the place of honour. ¹³ The two scoundrels publicly accused him of cursing God and the king, and so he was taken outside the city and stoned to death. ¹⁴ The message was sent to Jezebel: "Naboth has been put to death."

15 As soon as Jezebel received the message, she said to Ahab, "Naboth is dead. Now go and take possession of the vineyard which he refused to sell to you." ¹⁶ At once Ahab went to the vineyard to take possession of it.

17 Then the LORD said to Elijah, the

20.36: 1 Kgs 13.24

prophet from Tishbe, [18]"Go to King Ahab of Samaria. You will find him in Naboth's vineyard, about to take possession of it. [19]Tell him that I, the LORD, say to him, 'After murdering the man, are you taking over his property as well?' Tell him that this is what I say: 'In the very place that the dogs licked up Naboth's blood they will lick up your blood!'"

20 When Ahab saw Elijah, he said, "Have you caught up with me, my enemy?"

"Yes, I have," Elijah answered. "You have devoted yourself completely to doing what is wrong in the LORD's sight. [21]So the LORD says to you, 'I will bring disaster on you. I will do away with you and get rid of every male in your family, young and old alike. [22]Your family will become like the family of King Jeroboam son of Nebat and like the family of King Baasha son of Ahijah, because you have stirred up my anger by leading Israel into sin.' [23]And concerning Jezebel, the LORD says that dogs will eat her body in the city of Jezreel. [24]Any of your relatives who die in the city will be eaten by dogs, and any who die in the open country will be eaten by vultures."

25 (There was no one else who had devoted himself so completely to doing wrong in the LORD's sight as Ahab—all at the urging of his wife Jezebel. [26]He committed the most shameful sins by worshipping idols, as the Amorites had done, whom the LORD had driven out of the land as the people of Israel advanced.)

27 When Elijah finished speaking, Ahab tore his clothes, took them off, and put on sackcloth. He refused food, slept in the sackcloth, and went about gloomy and depressed.

28 The LORD said to the prophet Elijah, [29]"Have you noticed how Ahab has humbled himself before me? Since he has done this, I will not bring disaster on him during his lifetime; it will be during his son's lifetime that I will bring disaster on Ahab's family."

The Prophet Micaiah Warns Ahab
(2 Chr 18.2-27)

22 There was peace between Israel and Syria for the next two years, [2]but in the third year King Jehoshaphat of Judah went to see King Ahab of Israel.

3 Ahab asked his officials, "Why is it that we have not done anything to get back Ramoth in Gilead from the king of Syria? It belongs to us!" [4]And Ahab asked Jehoshaphat, "Will you go with me to attack Ramoth?"

"I am ready when you are," Jehoshaphat answered, "and so are my soldiers and my cavalry. [5]But first let's consult the LORD."

6 So Ahab called in the prophets, about four hundred of them, and asked them, "Should I go and attack Ramoth, or not?"

"Attack it," they answered. "The Lord will give you victory."

7 But Jehoshaphat asked, "Isn't there another prophet through whom we can consult the LORD?"

8 Ahab answered, "There is one more, Micaiah son of Imlah. But I hate him, because he never prophesies anything good for me; it's always something bad."

"You shouldn't say that!" Jehoshaphat replied.

9 Then Ahab called in a court official and told him to go and fetch Micaiah at once.

10 The two kings, dressed in their royal robes, were sitting on their thrones at the threshing-place just outside the gate of Samaria, and all the prophets were prophesying in front of them. [11]One of them, Zedekiah son of Chenaanah, made iron horns and said to Ahab, "This is what the LORD says: 'With these you will fight the Syrians and totally defeat them.'" [12]All the other prophets said the same thing. "March against Ramoth and you will win," they said. "The LORD will give you victory."

13 Meanwhile, the official who had gone to get Micaiah said to him, "All the other prophets have prophesied success for the king, and you had better do the same."

14 But Micaiah answered, "By the living LORD I promise that I will say what he tells me to!"

15 When he appeared before King Ahab, the king asked him, "Micaiah, should King Jehoshaphat and I go and attack Ramoth, or not?"

"Attack!" Micaiah answered. "Of course you'll win. The LORD will give you victory."

16 But Ahab replied, "When you speak to me in the name of the LORD, tell the truth! How many times do I have to tell you that?"

17 Micaiah answered, "I can see the army of Israel scattered over the hills like sheep without a shepherd. And the LORD

21.19: 1 Kgs 22.38　　**21.23:** 2 Kgs 9.36　　**22.17:** Num 27.17; Mt 9.36; Mk 6.34

said, 'These men have no leader; let them go home in peace.'"

18 Ahab said to Jehoshaphat, "Didn't I tell you that he never prophesies anything good for me? It's always something bad!"

19 Micaiah went on: "Now listen to what the LORD says! I saw the LORD sitting on his throne in heaven, with all his angels standing beside him. 20 The LORD asked, 'Who will deceive Ahab so that he will go and be killed at Ramoth?' Some of the angels said one thing, and others said something else, 21 until a spirit stepped forward, approached the LORD, and said, 'I will deceive him.' 22 'How?' the LORD asked. The spirit replied, 'I will go and make all Ahab's prophets tell lies.' The LORD said, 'Go and deceive him. You will succeed.'"

23 And Micaiah concluded: "This is what has happened. The LORD has made these prophets of yours lie to you. But he himself has decreed that you will meet with disaster!"

24 Then the prophet Zedekiah went up to Micaiah, slapped his face, and asked, "Since when did the LORD's spirit leave me and speak to you?"

25 "You will find out when you go into some back room to hide," Micaiah replied.

26 Then King Ahab ordered one of his officers, "Arrest Micaiah and take him to Amon, the governor of the city, and to Prince Joash. 27 Tell them to throw him in prison and to put him on bread and water until I return safely."

28 "If you return safely," Micaiah exclaimed, "then the LORD has not spoken through me!" And he added, "Listen, everyone, to what I have said!"

The Death of Ahab
(2 Chr 18.28–34)

29 Then King Ahab of Israel and King Jehoshaphat of Judah went to attack the city of Ramoth in Gilead. 30 Ahab said to Jehoshaphat, "As we go into battle, I will disguise myself, but you wear your royal garments." So the king of Israel went into battle in disguise.

31 The king of Syria had ordered his thirty-two chariot commanders to attack no one else except the king of Israel. 32 So when they saw King Jehoshaphat, they all thought that he was the king of Israel, and they turned to attack him. But when he cried out, 33 they realized that he was not the king of Israel, and they stopped

their attack. 34 By chance, however, a Syrian soldier shot an arrow which struck King Ahab between the joints of his armour. "I'm wounded!" he cried out to his chariot driver. "Turn round and pull out of the battle!"

35 While the battle raged on, King Ahab remained propped up in his chariot, facing the Syrians. The blood from his wound ran down and covered the bottom of the chariot, and at evening he died. 36 Near sunset the order went out through the Israelite ranks: "Every man go back to his own country and city!"

37 So died King Ahab. His body was taken to Samaria and buried. 38 His chariot was cleaned up at the pool of Samaria, where dogs licked up his blood and prostitutes washed themselves, as the LORD had said would happen.

39 Everything else that King Ahab did, including an account of his palace decorated with ivory and all the cities he built, is recorded in *The History of the Kings of Israel.* 40 At his death his son Ahaziah succeeded him as king.

King Jehoshaphat of Judah
(2 Chr 20.31—21.1)

41 In the fourth year of the reign of King Ahab of Israel, Jehoshaphat son of Asa became king of Judah 42 at the age of thirty-five, and he ruled in Jerusalem for twenty-five years. His mother was Azubah, the daughter of Shilhi. 43 Like his father Asa before him, he did what was right in the sight of the LORD; but the pagan places of worship were not destroyed, and the people continued to offer sacrifices and burn incense there. 44 Jehoshaphat made peace with the king of Israel.

45 Everything else that Jehoshaphat did, all his bravery and his battles, are recorded in *The History of the Kings of Judah.* 46 He got rid of all the male and female prostitutes serving at the pagan altars who were still left from the days of his father Asa.

47 The land of Edom had no king; it was ruled by a deputy appointed by the king of Judah.

48 King Jehoshaphat built ocean-going ships to sail to the land of Ophir for gold; but they were wrecked at Eziongeber and never sailed. 49 Then King Ahaziah of Israel offered to let his men sail with Jehoshaphat's men, but Jehoshaphat refused the offer.

22.19: Is 6.1; Job 1.6

50 Jehoshaphat died and was buried in the royal tombs in David's City, and his son Jehoram succeeded him as king.

King Ahaziah of Israel

51 In the seventeenth year of the reign of King Jehoshaphat of Judah, Ahaziah son of Ahab became king of Israel, and he ruled in Samaria for two years. 52 He sinned against the LORD, following the wicked example of his father Ahab, his mother Jezebel, and King Jeroboam, who had led Israel into sin. 53 He worshipped and served Baal, and like his father before him, he aroused the anger of the LORD, the God of Israel.

THE SECOND BOOK OF
KINGS

INTRODUCTION

The *Second book of Kings* continues the history of the two Israelite kingdoms where *First Kings* leaves off. The book may be divided into two parts: (1) The story of the two kingdoms from the middle of the ninth century B.C. down to the fall of Samaria and the end of the northern kingdom in 722 B.C. (2) The story of the kingdom of Judah from the fall of the kingdom of Israel down to the capture and destruction of Jerusalem by King Nebuchadnezzar of Babylonia in 586 B.C. The book ends with an account of Gedaliah as governor of Judah under the Babylonians, and a report of the release of King Jehoiachin of Judah from prison in Babylon.

These national disasters took place because of the unfaithfulness of the kings and people of Israel and Judah. The destruction of Jerusalem and the exile of many of the people of Judah was one of the great turning points of Israelite history.

The prophet who stands out in *Second Kings* is Elijah's successor Elisha.

Outline of Contents
The divided kingdom   1.1—17.41
   a. The prophet Elisha   1.1—8.15
   b. The kings of Judah and of Israel   8.16—17.4
   c. The fall of Samaria   17.5-41
The kingdom of Judah   18.1—25.30
   a. From Hezekiah to Josiah   18.1—21.26
   b. Josiah's reign   22.1—23.30
   c. The last kings of Judah   23.31—24.20
   d. The fall of Jerusalem 25.1-30

Elijah and King Ahaziah

1 After the death of King Ahab of Israel, the country of Moab rebelled against Israel.

2 King Ahaziah of Israel fell off the balcony on the roof of his palace in Samaria and was seriously injured. So he sent some messengers to consult Baalzebub, the god of the Philistine city of Ekron, in order to find out whether or not he would recover. 3 But an angel of the LORD commanded Elijah, the prophet from Tishbe, to go and meet the messengers of King Ahaziah and ask them, "Why are you going to consult Baalzebub, the god of Ekron? Is it because you think there is no god in Israel? 4 Tell the king that the LORD says, 'You will not recover from your injuries; you will die!' "

Elijah did as the LORD commanded, 5 and the messengers returned to the king. "Why have you come back?" he asked.

6 They answered, "We were met by a man who told us to come back and tell you that the LORD says to you, 'Why are you sending messengers to consult Baalzebub, the god of Ekron? Is it because you think there is no god in Israel? You will not recover from your injuries; you will die!' "

7 "What did the man look like?" the king asked.

8 "He was wearing a cloak made of animal skins, tied with[a] a leather belt," they answered.

"It's Elijah!" the king exclaimed.

9 Then he sent an officer with fifty men to get Elijah. The officer found him sitting on a hill and said to him, "Man of God, the king orders you to come down."

10 "If I am a man of God," Elijah answered, "may fire come down from heaven and kill you and your men!" At once fire came down and killed the officer and his men.

11 The king sent another officer with fifty men, who went up[b] and said to Elijah, "Man of God, the king orders you to come down at once!"

12 "If I am a man of God," Elijah answered, "may fire come down from heaven and kill you and your men!" At once the fire of God came down and killed the officer and his men.

13 Once more the king sent an officer with fifty men. He went up the hill, fell on his knees in front of Elijah, and pleaded, "Man of God, be merciful to me and my men. Spare our lives! 14 The two other officers and their men were killed by fire from heaven; but please be merciful to me!"

15 The angel of the LORD said to Elijah, "Go down with him, and don't be afraid." So Elijah went with the officer to the king 16 and said to him, "This is what the LORD says: 'Because you sent messengers to consult Baalzebub, the god of Ekron—as if there were no god in Israel to consult—you will not get well; you will die!' "

17 Ahaziah died, as the LORD had said through Elijah. Ahaziah had no sons, so his brother[c] Joram succeeded him as king in the second year of the reign of Jehoram son of Jehoshaphat, king of Judah.

18 Everything else that King Ahaziah did is recorded in *The History of the Kings of Israel.*

Elijah Is Taken Up to Heaven

2 The time came for the LORD to take Elijah up to heaven in a whirlwind. Elijah and Elisha set out from Gilgal, 2 and on the way Elijah said to Elisha, "Now stay here; the LORD has ordered me to go to Bethel."

But Elisha answered, "I swear by my loyalty to the living LORD and to you that I will not leave you." So they went on to Bethel.

3 A group of prophets who lived there went to Elisha and asked him, "Do you know that the LORD is going to take your master away from you today?"

"Yes, I know," Elisha answered. "But let's not talk about it."

4 Then Elijah said to Elisha, "Now stay here; the LORD has ordered me to go to Jericho."

But Elisha answered, "I swear by my loyalty to the living LORD and to you that I will not leave you." So they went on to Jericho.

5 A group of prophets who lived there went to Elisha and asked him, "Do you know that the LORD is going to take your master away from you today?"

"Yes, I know," Elisha answered. "But let's not talk about it."

6 Then Elijah said to Elisha, "Now stay

---

[a] *was wearing...with;* or *was a hairy man and wore.*
[b] *One ancient translation* went up; *Hebrew* answered.
[c] *Some ancient translations* his brother; *Hebrew does not have these words.*

1.8: Mt 3.4; Mk 1.6   **1.10–12:** Lk 9.54

My father!...You are gone! (2.12)

here; the LORD has ordered me to go to the River Jordan."

But Elisha answered, "I swear by my loyalty to the living LORD and to you that I will not leave you." So they went on, [7] and fifty of the prophets followed them to the Jordan. Elijah and Elisha stopped by the river, and the fifty prophets stood a short distance away. [8] Then Elijah took off his cloak, rolled it up, and struck the water with it; the water divided, and he and Elisha crossed to the other side on dry ground. [9] There, Elijah said to Elisha, "Tell me what you want me to do for you before I am taken away."

"Let me receive the share of your power that will make me your successor," [d] Elisha answered.

[10] "That is a difficult request to grant," Elijah replied. "But you will receive it if you see me as I am being taken away from you; if you don't see me, you won't receive it."

[11] They kept talking as they walked on; then suddenly a chariot of fire pulled by horses of fire came between them, and Elijah was taken up to heaven by a whirlwind. [12] Elisha saw it and cried out to Elijah, "My father! My father! Mighty defender of Israel! You are gone!" And he never saw Elijah again.

In grief, Elisha tore his cloak in two. [13] Then he picked up Elijah's cloak that had fallen from him, and went back and stood on the bank of the Jordan. [14] He struck the water with Elijah's cloak, and said, "Where is the LORD, the God of Elijah?" Then he struck the water again, and it divided, and he walked over to the other side. [15] The fifty prophets from Jericho saw him and said, "The power of Elijah is on Elisha!" They went to meet him, bowed down before him, [16] and said, "There are fifty of us here, all strong men. Let us go and look for your master. Maybe the spirit of the LORD has carried him away and left him on some mountain or in some valley."

"No, you must not go," Elisha answered.

17 But they insisted until he gave in and let them go. The fifty of them went and looked high and low for Elijah for three days, but didn't find him. [18] Then they returned to Elisha, who had waited

[d] THE SHARE...SUCCESSOR: *Elisha asked for the share that the first-born son inherited by law from his father (see Deut 21.17).*
2.9: Deut 21.17   **2.12:** 2 Kgs 13.14

at Jericho, and he said to them, "Didn't I tell you not to go?"

Miracles of Elisha

19 Some men from Jericho went to Elisha and said, "As you know, sir, this is a fine city, but the water is bad and causes miscarriages."

20 "Put some salt in a new bowl, and bring it to me," he ordered. They brought it to him, 21 and he went to the spring, threw the salt in the water, and said, "This is what the LORD says: 'I make this water pure, and it will not cause any more deaths or miscarriages.'" 22 And that water has been pure ever since, just as Elisha said it would be.

23 Elisha left Jericho to go to Bethel, and on the way some boys came out of a town and made fun of him. "Get out of here, baldy!" they shouted.

24 Elisha turned round, glared at them, and cursed them in the name of the LORD. Then two she-bears came out of the woods and tore forty-two of the boys to pieces.

25 Elisha went on to Mount Carmel, and later returned to Samaria.

War between Israel and Moab

3 In the eighteenth year of the reign of King Jehoshaphat of Judah, Joram son of Ahab became king of Israel, and he ruled in Samaria for twelve years. 2 He sinned against the LORD, but he was not as bad as his father or his mother Jezebel; he pulled down the image his father had made for the worship of Baal. 3 Yet, like King Jeroboam son of Nebat before him, he led Israel into sin, and would not stop.

4 King Mesha of Moab bred sheep, and every year he gave as tribute to the king of Israel 100,000 lambs, and the wool from 100,000 sheep. 5 But when King Ahab of Israel died, Mesha rebelled against Israel. 6 At once King Joram left Samaria and gathered all his troops. 7 He sent word to King Jehoshaphat of Judah: "The king of Moab has rebelled against me; will you join me in war against him?"

"I will," King Jehoshaphat replied. "I am at your disposal, and so are my men and my horses. 8 What route shall we take for the attack?"

"We will go the long way, through the wilderness of Edom," Joram answered.

9 So King Joram and the kings of Judah and Edom set out. After marching for seven days, they ran out of water, and there was none left for the men or the pack-animals. 10 "We're done for!" King Joram exclaimed. "The LORD has put the three of us at the mercy of the king of Moab!"

11 King Jehoshaphat asked, "Is there a prophet here through whom we can consult the LORD?"

An officer of King Joram's forces answered, "Elisha son of Shaphat is here. He was Elijah's assistant."

12 "He is a true prophet," King Jehoshaphat said. So the three kings went to Elisha.

13 "Why should I help you?" Elisha said to the king of Israel. "Go and consult those prophets that your father and mother consulted."

"No!" Joram replied. "It is the LORD who has put us three kings at the mercy of the king of Moab."

14 Elisha answered, "By the living LORD, whom I serve, I swear that I would have nothing to do with you if I didn't respect your ally King Jehoshaphat of Judah. 15 Now get me a musician."

As the musician played his harp, the power of the LORD came on Elisha, 16 and he said, "This is what the LORD says: 'Dig ditches all over this dry stream bed. 17 Even though you will not see any rain or wind, this stream bed will be filled with water, and you, your livestock, and your pack-animals will have plenty to drink.'" 18 And Elisha continued, "But this is an easy thing for the LORD to do; he will also give you victory over the Moabites. 19 You will conquer all their beautiful fortified cities; you will cut down all their fruit-trees, stop all their springs, and ruin all their fertile fields by covering them with stones."

20 The next morning, at the time of the regular morning sacrifice, water came flowing from the direction of Edom, and covered the ground.

21 When the Moabites heard that the three kings had come to attack them, all the men who could bear arms, from the oldest to the youngest, were called out and stationed at the border. 22 When they got up the following morning, the sun was shining on the water, making it look as red as blood. 23 "It's blood!" they exclaimed. "The three enemy armies must have fought and killed each other! Let's go and loot their camp!"

24 But when they reached the camp,

This is what the LORD says (3.16)

the Israelites attacked them and drove them back. The Israelites kept up the pursuit,*e* slaughtering the Moabites 25 and destroying their cities. As they passed a fertile field, every Israelite would throw a stone on it until finally all the fields were covered; they also stopped up the springs and cut down the fruit-trees. At last only the capital city of Kir Heres*f* was left, and the slingers surrounded it and attacked it.

26 When the king of Moab realized that he was losing the battle, he took seven hundred swordsmen with him and tried to force his way through the enemy lines and escape to the king of Syria,*g* but he failed. 27 So he took his eldest son, who was to succeed him as king, and offered him on the city wall as a sacrifice to the god of Moab. The Israelites were terrified*h* and so they drew back from the city and returned to their own country.

Elisha Helps a Poor Widow

4 The widow of a member of a group of prophets went to Elisha and said, "Sir, my husband has died! As you know, he was a God-fearing man, but now a man he owed money to has come to take away my two sons as slaves in payment for my husband's debt."

2 "What shall I do for you?" he asked. "Tell me, what have you got at home?"

"Nothing at all, except a small jar of olive-oil," she answered.

3 "Go to your neighbours and borrow as many empty jars as you can," Elisha told her. 4 "Then you and your sons go into the house, close the door, and start pouring oil into the jars. Set each one aside as soon as it is full."

5 So the woman went into her house with her sons, closed the door, took the small jar of olive-oil, and poured oil into the jars as her sons brought them to her. 6 When they had filled all the jars, she asked if there were any more. "That was the last one," one of her sons answered. And the olive-oil stopped flowing. 7 She went back to Elisha, the prophet, who said to her, "Sell the olive-oil and pay all your debts, and there will be enough money left over for you and your sons to live on."

Elisha and the Rich Woman from Shunem

8 One day Elisha went to Shunem, where a rich woman lived. She invited him to a meal, and from then on every time he went to Shunem he would have his meals at her house. 9 She said to her husband, "I am sure that this man who comes here so often is a holy man. 10 Let's build a small room on the roof, put a bed, a table, a chair, and a lamp in it, and he can stay there whenever he visits us."

11 One day Elisha returned to Shunem and went up to his room to rest. 12 He told his servant Gehazi to go and call the woman. When she came, 13 he said to Gehazi, "Ask her what I can do for her

---

e One ancient translation kept up the pursuit; *Hebrew unclear.*
f Probable text only the capital city of Kir Heres; *Hebrew unclear.*
g One ancient translation Syria; *Hebrew* Edom.
h TERRIFIED, *either because of what Chemosh, the god of the Moabites, might do, or because of what the LORD, the God of the Israelites, might do.*

So the woman...poured oil into the jars (4.5)

in return for all the trouble she has had in providing for our needs. Maybe she would like me to go to the king or the army commander and put in a good word for her."

"I have all I need here among my own people," she answered.

14 Elisha asked Gehazi, "What can I do for her then?"

He answered, "Well, she has no son, and her husband is an old man."

15 "Tell her to come here," Elisha ordered. She came and stood in the doorway, 16 and Elisha said to her, "By this time next year you will be holding a son in your arms."

"Oh!" she exclaimed. "Please, sir, don't lie to me. You are a man of God!"

17 But, as Elisha had said, at about that time the following year she gave birth to a son.

18 Some years later, at harvest time, the boy went out one morning to join his father, who was in the field with the harvest workers. 19 Suddenly he cried out to his father, "My head hurts! My head hurts!"

"Carry the boy to his mother," the father said to a servant. 20 The servant carried the boy back to his mother, who held him in her lap until noon, at which time he died. 21 She carried him up to Elisha's room, put him on the bed and left, closing the door behind her. 22 Then she called her husband and said to him, "Send a servant here with a donkey. I need to go to the prophet Elisha. I'll be back as soon as I can."

23 "Why do you have to go today?" her husband asked. "It's neither a Sabbath nor a New Moon Festival." *i*

"Never mind," she answered. 24 Then she had the donkey saddled, and ordered the servant, "Make the donkey go as fast as it can, and don't slow down, unless I tell you to." 25 So she set out, and went to Mount Carmel, where Elisha was.

Elisha saw her coming while she was still some distance away, and said to his servant Gehazi, "Look—there comes the woman from Shunem! 26 Hurry to her and find out if everything is all right with her, her husband, and her son."

She told Gehazi that everything was all

i SABBATH...NEW MOON FESTIVAL: *Such holy days were thought to be the best time to consult a prophet.*
4.16: Gen 18.14

Make the donkey go as fast as it can (4.24)

right, ²⁷but when she came to Elisha she bowed down before him and took hold of his feet. Gehazi was about to push her away, but Elisha said, "Leave her alone. Can't you see she's deeply distressed? And the LORD has not told me a thing about it."

28 The woman said to him, "Sir, did I ask you for a son? Didn't I tell you not to raise my hopes?"

29 Elisha turned to Gehazi and said, "Hurry! Take my stick and go. Don't stop to greet anyone you meet, and if anyone greets you, don't take time to answer. Go straight to the house and hold my stick over the boy."

30 The woman said to Elisha, "I swear by my loyalty to the living LORD and to you that I will not leave you!" So the two of them started back together. ³¹Gehazi went on ahead and held Elisha's stick over the child, but there was no sound or any other sign of life. So he went back to meet Elisha and said, "The boy didn't wake up."

32 When Elisha arrived, he went alone into the room and saw the boy lying dead on the bed. ³³He closed the door and prayed to the LORD. ³⁴Then he lay down on the boy, placing his mouth, eyes, and hands on the boy's mouth, eyes, and hands. As he lay stretched out over the boy, the boy's body started to get warm. ³⁵Elisha got up, walked about the room, and then went back and again stretched

4.34–35: 1 Kgs 17.21

himself over the boy. The boy sneezed seven times, and then opened his eyes. ³⁶Elisha called Gehazi and told him to call the boy's mother. When she came in, he said to her, "Here's your son." ³⁷She fell at Elisha's feet, with her face touching the ground; then she took her son and left.

Two More Miracles

38 Once, when there was a famine throughout the land, Elisha returned to Gilgal. While he was teaching a group of prophets, he told his servant to put a big pot on the fire and make some stew for them. ³⁹One of them went out in the fields to get some herbs. He found a wild vine, and picked as many gourds as he could carry. He brought them back and sliced them up into the stew, not knowing what they were. ⁴⁰The stew was poured out for the men to eat, but as soon as they tasted it they exclaimed to Elisha, "It's poisoned!"—and wouldn't eat it. ⁴¹Elisha asked for some meal, threw it into the pot, and said, "Pour out some more stew for them." And then there was nothing wrong with it.

42 Another time, a man came from Baal Shalishah, bringing Elisha twenty loaves of bread made from the first barley harvested that year, and some freshly-cut ears of corn. Elisha told his servant to feed the group of prophets with this, ⁴³but he

If the prophet had told you to do something difficult, you would have done it (5.13)

answered, "Do you think this is enough for a hundred men?"

Elisha replied, "Give it to them to eat, because the LORD says that they will eat and still have some left over." ⁴⁴ So the servant set the food before them, and, as the LORD had said, they all ate and there was still some left over.

Naaman Is Cured

5 Naaman, the commander of the Syrian army, was highly respected and esteemed by the king of Syria, because through Naaman the LORD had given victory to the Syrian forces. He was a great soldier, but he suffered from a dreaded skin-disease. ² In one of their raids against Israel, the Syrians had carried off a little Israelite girl, who became a servant of Naaman's wife. ³ One day she said to her mistress, "I wish that my master could go to the prophet who lives in Samaria! He would cure him of his disease." ⁴ When Naaman heard of this, he went to the king and told him what the girl had said. ⁵ The king said, "Go to the king of Israel and take this letter to him."

So Naaman set out, taking thirty thousand pieces of silver, six thousand pieces of gold, and ten changes of fine clothes. ⁶ The letter that he took read: "This letter will introduce my officer Naaman. I want you to cure him of his disease."

⁷ When the king of Israel read the letter, he tore his clothes in dismay and exclaimed, "How can the king of Syria expect me to cure this man? Does he think that I am God,ʲ with the power of life and death? It's plain that he is trying to start a quarrel with me!"

⁸ When the prophet Elisha heard what had happened, he sent word to the king: "Why are you so upset? Send the man to me, and I'll show him that there is a prophet in Israel!"

⁹ So Naaman went with his horses and chariot, and stopped at the entrance to Elisha's house. ¹⁰ Elisha sent a servant out to tell him to go and wash himself seven times in the River Jordan, and he would be completely cured of his disease. ¹¹ But Naaman left in a rage, saying, "I thought that he would at least come out to me, pray to the LORD his God, wave his hand over the diseased spot,ᵏ and cure me! ¹² Besides, aren't the rivers Abana and Pharpar, back in Damascus, better than any river in Israel? I could have washed in them and been cured!"

¹³ His servants went up to him and said, "Sir, if the prophet had told you to do something difficult, you would have done it. Now why can't you just wash yourself, as he said, and be cured?" ¹⁴ So Naaman went down to the Jordan, dipped himself in it seven times, as Elisha had instructed, and he was completely cured. His flesh became firm and healthy, like that of a child. ¹⁵ He returned to Elisha with all his men and said, "Now I know that there is no god but the God of Israel; so please, sir, accept a gift from me."

ʲGod; *or* a god.   ᵏthe diseased spot; *or* this place.
5.1-14: Lk 4.27

16 Elisha answered, "By the living Lord, whom I serve, I swear that I will not accept a gift."

Naaman insisted that he accept it, but he would not. 17 So Naaman said, "If you won't accept my gift, then let me have two mule-loads of earth to take home with me,[1] because from now on I will not offer sacrifices or burnt-offerings to any god except the Lord. 18 So I hope that the Lord will forgive me when I accompany my king to the temple of Rimmon, the god of Syria, and worship him. Surely the Lord will forgive me!"

19 "Go in peace," Elisha said. And Naaman left.

He had gone only a short distance, 20 when Elisha's servant Gehazi said to himself, "My master has let Naaman get away without paying a thing! He should have accepted what that Syrian offered him. By the living Lord, I will run after him and get something from him." 21 So he set off after Naaman. When Naaman saw a man running after him, he got down from his chariot to meet him, and asked, "Is something wrong?"

22 "No," Gehazi answered. "But my master sent me to tell you that just now two members of the group of prophets in the hill-country of Ephraim arrived, and he would like you to give them three thousand pieces of silver and two changes of fine clothes."

23 "Please take six thousand pieces of silver," Naaman replied. He insisted on it, tied up the silver in two bags, gave them and two changes of fine clothes to two of his servants, and sent them on ahead of Gehazi. 24 When they reached the hill where Elisha lived, Gehazi took the two bags and carried them into the house. Then he sent Naaman's servants back. 25 He went back into the house, and Elisha asked him, "Where have you been?"

"Oh, nowhere, sir," he answered.

26 But Elisha said, "Wasn't I there in spirit when the man got out of his chariot to meet you? This is no time to accept money and clothes, olive-groves and vineyards, sheep and cattle, or servants! 27 And now Naaman's disease will come upon you, and you and your descendants will have it for ever!"

When Gehazi left, he had the disease—his skin was as white as snow.

The Recovery of the Axe-head

6 One day the group of prophets that Elisha was in charge of complained to him, "The place where we live is too small! 2 Give us permission to go to the Jordan and cut down some trees, so that we can build a place to live."

"All right," Elisha answered.

3 One of them urged him to go with them; he agreed, 4 and they set out together. When they arrived at the Jordan, they began to work. 5 As one of them was cutting down a tree, suddenly his iron axehead fell in the water. "What shall I do, sir?" he exclaimed to Elisha. "It was a borrowed axe!"

6 "Where did it fall?" Elisha asked.

The man showed him the place, and Elisha cut off a stick, threw it in the water, and made the axe-head float. 7 "Take it out," he ordered, and the man bent down and picked it up.

The Syrian Army Is Defeated

8 The king of Syria was at war with Israel. He consulted his officers and chose a place to set up his camp. 9 But Elisha sent word to the king of Israel, warning him not to go near that place, because the Syrians were waiting in ambush there. 10 So the king of Israel warned the men who lived in that place, and they were on guard. This happened several times.

11 The Syrian king became greatly upset over this; he called in his officers and asked them, "Which one of you is on the side of the king of Israel?"

12 One of them answered, "No one is, Your Majesty. The prophet Elisha tells the king of Israel what you say even in the privacy of your own room."

13 "Find out where he is," the king ordered, "and I will capture him."

When he was told that Elisha was in Dothan, 14 he sent a large force there with horses and chariots. They reached the town at night and surrounded it. 15 Early the next morning Elisha's servant got up, went out of the house, and saw the Syrian troops with their horses and chariots surrounding the town. He went back to Elisha and exclaimed, "We are doomed, sir! What shall we do?"

16 "Don't be afraid," Elisha answered. "We have more on our side than they have on theirs." 17 Then he prayed, "O

[1] EARTH TO TAKE HOME WITH ME: *It was then believed that a god could be worshipped only on his own land.*

LORD, open his eyes and let him see!" The LORD answered his prayer, and Elisha's servant looked up and saw the hillside covered with horses and chariots of fire all round Elisha.

18 When the Syrians attacked, Elisha prayed, "O LORD, strike these men blind!" The LORD answered his prayer and struck them blind. 19 Then Elisha went to them and said, "You are on the wrong road; this is not the town you are looking for. Follow me, and I will lead you to the man you are after." And he led them to Samaria.

20 As soon as they had entered the city, Elisha prayed, "Open their eyes, LORD, and let them see." The LORD answered his prayer; he restored their sight, and they saw that they were inside Samaria.

21 When the king of Israel saw the Syrians, he asked Elisha, "Shall I kill them, sir? Shall I kill them?"

22 "No," he answered. "Not even soldiers you had captured in combat would you put to death. Give them something to eat and drink, and let them return to their king." 23 So the king of Israel provided a great feast for them; and after they had eaten and drunk, he sent them back to the king of Syria. From then on the Syrians stopped raiding the land of Israel.

The Siege of Samaria

24 Some time later King Benhadad of Syria led his entire army against Israel and laid siege to the city of Samaria. 25 As a result of the siege the food shortage in the city was so severe that a donkey's head cost eighty pieces of silver, and two hundred grammes of dove's dung [m] cost five pieces of silver.

26 The king of Israel was walking by on the city wall when a woman cried out, "Help me, Your Majesty!"

27 He replied, "If the LORD won't help you, what help can I provide? Have I got any wheat or wine? 28 What's your trouble?"

She answered, "The other day this woman here suggested that we eat my child, and then eat her child the next day. 29 So we cooked my son and ate him. The next day I told her that we would eat her son, but she had hidden him!"

30 Hearing this, the king tore his clothes in dismay, and the people who were close

to the wall could see that he was wearing sackcloth under his clothes. 31 He exclaimed, "May God strike me dead if Elisha is not beheaded before the day is over!" 32 And he sent a messenger to get Elisha.

Meanwhile, Elisha was at home with some elders who were visiting him. Before the king's messenger arrived, Elisha said to the elders, "That murderer is sending someone to kill me! Now, when he gets here, shut the door and don't let him come in. The king himself will be just behind him." 33 He had hardly finished saying this, when the king [n] arrived and said, "It's the LORD who has brought this trouble on us! Why should I wait any longer for him to do something?"

7 Elisha answered, "Listen to what the LORD says! By this time tomorrow you will be able to buy in Samaria three kilogrammes of the best wheat or six kilogrammes of barley for one piece of silver."

2 The personal attendant of the king said to Elisha, "That can't happen—not even if the LORD himself were to send grain [x] at once!"

"You will see it happen, but you will never eat any of the food," Elisha replied.

The Syrian Army Leaves

3 Four men who were suffering from a dreaded skin-disease were outside the gates of Samaria, and they said to one another, "Why should we wait here until we die? 4 It's no use going into the city, because we would starve to death in there; but if we stay here, we'll die also. So let's go to the Syrian camp; the worst they can do is kill us, but maybe they will spare our lives." 5 So, as it began to get dark, they went to the Syrian camp, but when they reached it, no one was there. 6 The Lord had made the Syrians hear what sounded like the advance of a large army, with horses and chariots, and the Syrians thought that the king of Israel had hired Hittite and Egyptian kings and their armies to attack them. 7 So that evening the Syrians had fled for their lives, abandoning their tents, horses, and donkeys, and leaving the camp just as it was.

8 When the four men reached the edge of the camp, they went into a tent, ate and drank what was there, grabbed the

[m] DOVE'S DUNG: *This may be a popular term for a vegetable such as wild onions.*
[n] *Probable text* king; *Hebrew* messenger.   [x] grain; *or* rain.
6.29: Deut 28.57; Lam 4.10

silver, gold, and clothing they found, and went off and hid them; then they returned, entered another tent, and did the same thing. 9 But then they said to each other, "We shouldn't be doing this! We have good news and we shouldn't keep it to ourselves. If we wait until morning to tell it, we are sure to be punished. Let's go at once and tell the king's officers!" 10 So they left the Syrian camp, went back to Samaria and called out to the guards at the gates: "We went to the Syrian camp and didn't see or hear anybody; the horses and donkeys have not been untied, and the tents are just as the Syrians left them."

11 The guards announced the news, and it was reported in the palace. 12 It was still night, but the king got out of bed and said to his officials, "I'll tell you what the Syrians are planning! They know about the famine here, so they have left their camp to go and hide in the country-side. They think that we will leave the city to find food, and then they will take us alive and capture the city."

13 One of his officials said, "The people here in the city are doomed anyway, like those that have already died. So let's send some men with five of the horses that are left, so that we can find out what has happened." ⁰ 14 They chose some men, and the king sent them in two chariots with instructions to go and find out what had happened to the Syrian army. 15 The men went as far as the Jordan, and all along the road they saw the clothes and equipment that the Syrians had abandoned as they fled. Then they returned and reported to the king. 16 The people of Samaria rushed out and looted the Syrian camp. And, as the LORD had said, three kilogrammes of the best wheat or six kilogrammes of barley were sold for one piece of silver.

17 It so happened that the king of Israel had put the city gate under the command of the officer who was his personal attendant. The officer was trampled to death there by the people and died, as Elisha had predicted when the king went to see him. 18 Elisha had told the king that by that time the following day three kilogrammes of the best wheat or six kilogrammes of barley would be sold in Samaria for one piece of silver, 19 to which the officer had answered, "That can't happen—not even if the LORD himself were to send grain ˣ at once!" And Elisha

had replied, "You will see it happen, but you will never eat any of the food." 20 And that is just what happened to him—he died, trampled to death by the people at the city gate.

The Woman from Shunem Returns

8 Now Elisha had told the woman who lived in Shunem, whose son he had brought back to life, that the LORD was sending a famine on the land, which would last for seven years, and that she should leave with her family and go and live somewhere else. 2 She had followed his instructions, and had gone with her family to live in Philistia for the seven years.

3 At the end of the seven years, she returned to Israel and went to the king to ask for her house and her land to be restored to her. 4 She found the king talking with Gehazi, Elisha's servant; the king wanted to know about Elisha's miracles. 5 While Gehazi was telling the king how Elisha had brought a dead person back to life, the woman made her appeal to the king. Gehazi said to him, "Your Majesty, here is the woman and here is her son whom Elisha brought back to life!" 6 In answer to the king's question, she confirmed Gehazi's story, and so the king called an official and told him to give back to her everything that was hers, including the value of all the crops that her fields had produced during the seven years she had been away.

Elisha and King Benhadad of Syria

7 Elisha went to Damascus at a time when King Benhadad of Syria was ill. When the king was told that Elisha was there, 8 he said to Hazael, one of his officials, "Take a gift to the prophet, and ask him to consult the LORD to find out whether or not I am going to get well." 9 So Hazael loaded forty camels with all kinds of the finest products of Damascus and went to Elisha. When Hazael met him, he said, "Your servant King Benhadad has sent me to ask you whether or not he will recover from his illness."

10 Elisha answered, "The LORD has revealed to me that he will die; but go to him and tell him that he will recover." 11 Then Elisha stared at him with a horrified look on his face until Hazael became ill at ease. Suddenly Elisha burst into tears. 12 "Why are you crying, sir?" Hazael asked.

⁰ Verse 13 in Hebrew is unclear.   ˣ grain; or rain.
8.1: 2 Kgs 4.8-37

"Because I know the horrible things you will do against the people of Israel," Elisha answered. "You will set their fortresses on fire, slaughter their finest young men, batter their children to death, and rip open their pregnant women."

13 "How could I ever be that powerful?" Hazael asked. "I'm a nobody!"

"The LORD has shown me that you will be king of Syria," Elisha replied.

14 Hazael went back to Benhadad, who asked him, "What did Elisha say?"

"He told me that you would certainly get well," Hazael answered. 15 But on the following day Hazael took a blanket, soaked it in water, and smothered the king. And Hazael succeeded Benhadad as king of Syria.

King Jehoram of Judah
(2 Chr 21.1–20)

16 In the fifth year of the reign of Joram son of Ahab as king of Israel, p Jehoram son of Jehoshaphat became king of Judah 17 at the age of thirty-two, and he ruled in Jerusalem for eight years. 18 His wife was Ahab's daughter, and like the family of Ahab he followed the evil ways of the kings of Israel. He sinned against the LORD, 19 but the LORD was not willing to destroy Judah, because he had promised his servant David that his descendants would always continue to rule.

20 During Jehoram's reign Edom revolted against Judah and became an independent kingdom. 21 So Jehoram set out with all his chariots for Zair, where the Edomite army surrounded them. During the night he and his chariot commanders managed to break out and escape, and his soldiers scattered to their homes. 22 Edom has been independent of q Judah ever since. During this same period the city of Libnah also revolted.

23 Everything else that Jehoram did is recorded in The History of the Kings of Judah. 24 Jehoram died and was buried in the royal tombs in David's City, and his son Ahaziah succeeded him as king.

King Ahaziah of Judah
(2 Chr 22.1–6)

25 In the twelfth year of the reign of Joram son of Ahab as king of Israel, Ahaziah son of Jehoram became king of Judah 26 at the age of twenty-two, and he ruled in Jerusalem for one year. His mother was Athaliah, the daughter of King Ahab and granddaughter of King Omri of Israel. 27 Since Ahaziah was related to King Ahab by marriage, he sinned against the LORD, just as Ahab's family did.

28 King Ahaziah joined King Joram of Israel in a war against King Hazael of Syria. The armies clashed at Ramoth in Gilead, and Joram was wounded in battle. 29 He returned to the city of Jezreel to recover from his wounds, and Ahaziah went there to visit him.

Jehu Is Anointed King of Israel

9 Meanwhile the prophet Elisha called one of the young prophets and said to him, "Get ready and go to Ramoth in Gilead. Take this jar of olive-oil with you, 2 and when you get there look for Jehu, the son of Jehoshaphat and grandson of Nimshi. Take him to a private room away from his companions, 3 pour his olive-oil on his head, and say, 'The LORD proclaims that he anoints you king of Israel.' Then leave there as fast as you can."

4 So the young prophet went to Ramoth, 5 where he found the army officers in a conference. He said, "Sir, I have a message for you."

Jehu asked, "Which one of us are you speaking to?"

"To you, sir," he replied. 6 Then the two of them went indoors, and the young prophet poured the olive-oil on Jehu's head and said to him, "The LORD, the God of Israel, proclaims: 'I anoint you king of my people Israel. 7 You are to kill your master the king, that son of Ahab, so that I may punish Jezebel for murdering my prophets and my other servants. 8 All Ahab's family and descendants are to die; I will get rid of every male in his family, young and old alike. 9 I will treat his family as I did the families of King Jeroboam of Israel and of King Baasha of Israel. 10 Jezebel will not be buried; her body will be eaten by dogs in the territory of Jezreel.'" After saying this, the young prophet left the room and fled.

11 Jehu went back to his fellow-officers, who asked him, "Is everything all right? What did that crazy fellow want with you?"

p Some ancient translations Israel; Hebrew Israel, Jehoshaphat being king of Judah.
q independent of; or in revolt against.
8.13: 1 Kgs 19.15   **8.19:** 1 Kgs 11.36   **8.20:** Gen 27.40   **9.6:** 1 Kgs 19.16
9.10: 1 Kgs 21.23

"You know what he wanted," Jehu answered.

12 "No we don't!" they replied. "Tell us what he said!"

"He told me that the LORD proclaims: 'I anoint you king of Israel.'"

13 At once Jehu's fellow-officers spread their cloaks at the top of the steps for Jehu to stand on, blew trumpets, and shouted, "Jehu is king!"

King Joram of Israel Is Killed

14–15 Then Jehu plotted against King Joram, who was in Jezreel, where he had gone to recover from the wounds which he had received in the battle at Ramoth against King Hazael of Syria. So Jehu said to his fellow-officers, "If you are with me, make sure that no one slips out of Ramoth to go and warn the people in Jezreel." 16 Then he got into his chariot and set off for Jezreel. Joram had still not recovered, and King Ahaziah of Judah was there, visiting him.

17 A guard on duty in the watch-tower at Jezreel saw Jehu and his men approaching. "I see some men riding up!" he called out.

Joram replied, "Send a horseman to find out if they are friends or enemies."

18 The messenger rode out to Jehu and said to him, "The king wants to know if you come as a friend."

"That's none of your business!" Jehu answered. "Fall in behind me."

The guard on the watch-tower reported that the messenger had reached the group but was not returning. 19 Another messenger was sent out, who asked Jehu the same question. Again Jehu answered, "That's none of your business! Fall in behind me."

20 Once more the guard reported that the messenger had reached the group but was not returning. And he added, "The leader of the group is driving his chariot like a madman, just like Jehu!"

21 "Get my chariot ready," King Joram ordered. It was done, and he and King Ahaziah rode out, each in his own chariot, to meet Jehu. They met him at the field which had belonged to Naboth. 22 "Are you coming in peace?" Joram asked him.

"How can there be peace," Jehu answered, "when we still have all the witchcraft and idolatry that your mother Jezebel started?"

23 "It's treason, Ahaziah!" Joram cried out, as he turned his chariot round and fled. 24 Jehu drew his bow, and with all his strength shot an arrow that struck Joram in the back and pierced his heart. Joram fell dead in his chariot, 25 and Jehu said to his aide Bidkar, "Get his body and throw it in the field that belonged to Naboth. Remember that when you and I were riding together behind King Joram's father Ahab, the LORD spoke these words against Ahab: 26 'I saw the murder of Naboth and his sons yesterday. And I promise that I will punish you here in this same field.' So take Joram's body," Jehu ordered his aide, "and throw it in the field that belonged to Naboth, so as to fulfil the LORD's promise."

King Ahaziah of Judah Is Killed

27 King Ahaziah saw what happened, so he fled in his chariot towards the town of Beth Haggan, pursued by Jehu. "Kill him too!" Jehu ordered his men, and they wounded him[s] as he drove his chariot on the road up to Gur, near the town of Ibleam. But he managed to keep going until he reached the city of Megiddo, where he died. 28 His officials took his body back to Jerusalem in a chariot and buried him in the royal tombs in David's City.

29 Ahaziah had become king of Judah in the eleventh year that Joram son of Ahab was king of Israel.

Queen Jezebel Is Killed

30 Jehu arrived in Jezreel. Jezebel, having heard what had happened, put on eyeshadow, arranged her hair, and stood looking down at the street from a window in the palace. 31 As Jehu came through the gate, she called out, "You Zimri![t] You assassin! Why are you here?"

32 Jehu looked up and shouted, "Who is on my side?" Two or three palace officials looked down at him from a window, 33 and Jehu said to them, "Throw her down!" They threw her down, and her blood spattered the wall and the horses. Jehu drove his horses and chariot over her body, 34 entered the palace, and had a meal. Only then did he say, "Take that damned woman and bury her; after all, she is a king's daughter." 35 But the men who went out to bury her found nothing except her skull, and the bones

---

[s] *Some ancient translations* and they wounded him; *Hebrew does not have these words.*
[t] ZIMRI: *An Israelite army officer who assassinated the king of Israel (see 1 Kgs 16.8–12).*
9.26: 1 Kgs 21.19

of her hands and feet. 36 When they reported this to Jehu, he said, "This is what the LORD said would happen, when he spoke through his servant Elijah: 'Dogs will eat Jezebel's body in the territory of Jezreel. 37 Her remains will be scattered there like dung, so that no one will be able to identify them.'"

The Descendants of Ahab Are Killed

10 There were seventy descendants of King Ahab living in the city of Samaria. Jehu wrote a letter and sent copies to the rulers of the city, u to the leading citizens, and to the guardians of Ahab's descendants. The letter read: 2 "You are in charge of the king's descendants and you have at your disposal chariots, horses, weapons, and fortified cities. So then, as soon as you receive this letter, 3 you are to choose the best qualified of the king's descendants, make him king, and fight to defend him."

4 The rulers of Samaria were terrified. "How can we oppose Jehu," they said, "when neither King Joram nor King Ahaziah could?" 5 So the officer in charge of the palace and the official in charge of the city, together with the leading citizens and the guardians, sent this message to Jehu: "We are your servants and we are ready to do anything you say. But we will not make anyone king; do whatever you think best."

6 Jehu wrote them another letter: "If you are with me, and are ready to follow my orders, bring the heads of King Ahab's descendants to me at Jezreel by this time tomorrow."

The seventy descendants of King Ahab were under the care of the leading citizens of Samaria, who were bringing them up. 7 When Jehu's letter was received, the leaders of Samaria killed all seventy of Ahab's descendants, put their heads in baskets, and sent them to Jehu at Jezreel.

8 When Jehu was told that the heads of Ahab's descendants had been brought, he ordered them to be piled up in two heaps at the city gate and to be left there until the following morning. 9 In the morning, he went out to the gate and said to the people who were there, "I was the one who plotted against King Joram and killed him; you are not responsible for that. But who killed all these? 10 This proves that everything that the LORD said about the descendants of Ahab will come

true. The LORD has done what he promised through his prophet Elijah." 11 Then Jehu put to death all the other relatives of Ahab living in Jezreel, and all his officers, close friends, and priests; not one of them was left alive.

The Relatives of King Ahaziah Are Killed

12 Jehu left Jezreel to go to Samaria. On the way, at a place called "Shepherds' Camp," 13 he met some relatives of the late King Ahaziah of Judah and asked them, "Who are you?"

"Ahaziah's relatives," they answered. "We are going to Jezreel to pay our respects to the children of Queen Jezebel and to the rest of the royal family." 14 Jehu ordered his men, "Take them alive!" They seized them, and he put them to death near a pit there. There were forty-two people in all, and not one of them was left alive.

All Remaining Relatives of Ahab Are Killed

15 Jehu started out again, and on his way he was met by Jonadab son of Rechab. Jehu greeted him and said, "You and I think alike. Will you support me?"

"I will," Jonadab answered.

"Give me your hand, then," Jehu replied. They clasped hands, and Jehu helped him up into the chariot, 16 saying, "Come with me and see for yourself how devoted I am to the LORD." And they rode on together to Samaria. 17 When they arrived there, Jehu killed all of Ahab's relatives, not sparing even one. This is what the LORD had told Elijah would happen.

The Worshippers of Baal Are Killed

18 Jehu called the people of Samaria together and said, "King Ahab served the god Baal a little, but I will serve him much more. 19 Call together all the prophets of Baal, all his worshippers, and all his priests. No one is excused; I am going to offer a great sacrifice to Baal, and whoever is not present will be put to death." (This was a trick on the part of Jehu by which he meant to kill all the worshippers of Baal.) 20 Then Jehu ordered, "Proclaim a day of worship in honour of Baal!" The proclamation was made, 21 and Jehu sent word throughout all the land of Israel. All who worshipped Baal came; not one of them failed to come. They all went into the temple of Baal,

u *Some ancient translations* the city; *Hebrew* Jezreel.
9.36: 1 Kgs 21.23   **10.11:** Hos 1.4

filling it from one end to the other. 22 Then Jehu ordered the priest in charge of the sacred robes to bring the robes out and give them to the worshippers. 23 After that, Jehu himself went into the temple with Jonadab son of Rechab and said to the people there, "Make sure that only worshippers of Baal are present and that no worshipper of the LORD has come in." 24 Then he and Jonadab went in to offer sacrifices and burnt-offerings to Baal. He had stationed eighty men outside the temple and had instructed them: "You are to kill all these people; anyone who lets one of them escape will pay for it with his life!"

25 As soon as Jehu had presented the offerings, he said to the guards and officers, "Go in and kill them all; don't let anyone escape!" They went in with drawn swords, killed them all, and dragged the bodies outside. Then they went on into the inner sanctuary of the temple, 26 brought out the sacred pillar that was there, and burnt it. 27 So they destroyed the sacred pillar and the temple, and turned the temple into a latrine—which it still is today.

28 That was how Jehu wiped out the worship of Baal in Israel. 29 But he imitated the sin of King Jeroboam, who led Israel into the sin of worshipping the gold bull-calves he set up in Bethel and in Dan. 30 The LORD said to Jehu, "You have done to Ahab's descendants everything I wanted you to do. So I promise you that your descendants, down to the fourth generation, will be kings of Israel." 31 But Jehu did not obey with all his heart the law of the LORD, the God of Israel; instead, he followed the example of Jeroboam, who led Israel into sin.

The Death of Jehu

32 At that time the LORD began to reduce the size of Israel's territory. King Hazael of Syria conquered all the Israelite territory 33 east of the Jordan, as far south as the town of Aroer on the River Arnon—this included the territories of Gilead and Bashan, where the tribes of Gad, Reuben, and East Manasseh lived.

34 Everything else that Jehu did, including his brave deeds, is recorded in *The History of the Kings of Israel*. 35 He died and was buried in Samaria, and his son Jehoahaz succeeded him as king. 36 Jehu

had ruled in Samaria as king of Israel for twenty-eight years.

Queen Athaliah of Judah
(2 Chr 22.10—23.15)

11 As soon as King Ahaziah's mother Athaliah learnt of her son's murder, she gave orders for all the members of the royal family to be killed. 2 Only Ahaziah's son Joash escaped. He was about to be killed with the others, but was rescued by his aunt Jehosheba, who was King Jehoram's daughter and Ahaziah's half-sister. She took him and his nurse into a bedroom in the Temple and hid him from Athaliah, so that he was not killed. 3 For six years Jehosheba took care of the boy and kept him hidden in the Temple, while Athaliah ruled as queen.

4 But in the seventh year Jehoiada the priest sent for the officers in charge of the royal bodyguard and of the palace guards, and told them to come to the Temple, where he made them agree under oath to what he planned to do. He showed them King Ahaziah's son Joash 5 and gave them the following orders: "When you come on duty on the Sabbath, one third of you are to guard the palace; 6 another third are to stand guard at the Sur Gate, and the other third are to stand guard at the gate behind the other guards. v 7 The two groups that go off duty on the Sabbath are to stand guard at the Temple to protect the king. 8 You are to guard King Joash with drawn swords and stay with him wherever he goes. Anyone who comes near you is to be killed."

9 The officers obeyed Jehoiada's instructions and brought their men to him—those going off duty on the Sabbath and those going on duty. 10 He gave the officers the spears w and shields that had belonged to King David and had been kept in the Temple, 11 and he stationed the men with drawn swords all round the front of the Temple, to protect the king. 12 Then Jehoiada led Joash out, placed the crown on his head, and gave him a copy of the laws governing kingship. Then Joash was anointed and proclaimed king. The people clapped their hands and shouted, "Long live the king!"

13 Queen Athaliah heard the noise being made by the guards and the people, so she hurried to the Temple, where the

---

v *Hebrew has an additional word, the meaning of which is unclear.*
w *Some ancient translations (and see 2 Chr 23.9) spears; Hebrew spear.*
10.29: 1 Kgs 12.28–30

Athaliah tore her clothes in distress (11.14)

crowd had gathered. ¹⁴There she saw the new king standing by the column at the entrance of the Temple, as was the custom. He was surrounded by the officers and the trumpeters, and the people were all shouting joyfully and blowing trumpets. Athaliah tore her clothes in distress and shouted, "Treason! Treason!"

15 Jehoiada did not want Athaliah killed in the temple area, so he ordered the army officers: "Take her out between the rows of guards, and kill anyone who tries to rescue her." ¹⁶They seized her, took her to the palace, and there at the Horse Gate they killed her.

Jehoiada's Reforms
(2 Chr 23.16-21)

17 The priest Jehoiada made King Joash and the people enter into a covenant with the LORD that they would be the LORD's people; he also made a covenant between the king and the people. ¹⁸Then the people went to the temple of Baal and tore it

down; they smashed the altars and the idols, and killed Mattan, the priest of Baal, in front of the altars.

Jehoiada put guards on duty at the Temple, ¹⁹and then he, the officers, the royal bodyguard, and the palace guards escorted the king from the Temple to the palace, followed by all the people. Joash entered by the Guard Gate and took his place on the throne. ²⁰All the people were filled with happiness, and the city was quiet, now that Athaliah had been killed in the palace.

21 Joash became king of Judah at the age of seven.

King Joash of Judah
(2 Chr 24.1-16)

12 In the seventh year of the reign of King Jehu of Israel, Joash became king of Judah, and he ruled in Jerusalem for forty years. His mother was Zibiah from the city of Beersheba. ²Throughout his life he did what pleased the LORD, because Jehoiada the priest

11.14: 2 Kgs 23.3

instructed him. ³ However, the pagan places of worship were not destroyed, and the people continued to offer sacrifices and burn incense there.

4 Joash called the priests and ordered them to save up the money paid in connection with the sacrifices in the Temple, both the dues paid for the regular sacrifices and the money given as free-will gifts. ⁵ Each priest was to be responsible for the money brought by those he served, and the money was to be used to repair the Temple, as needed.

6 But by the twenty-third year of Joash's reign the priests still had not made any repairs to the Temple. ⁷ So he called in Jehoiada and the other priests and asked them, "Why aren't you repairing the Temple? From now on you are not to keep the money you receive; you must hand it over, so that the repairs can be made." ⁸ The priests agreed to this and also agreed not to make the repairs in the Temple.

9 Then Jehoiada took a box, made a hole in the lid, and placed the box by the altar, on the right side as one enters the Temple. The priests on duty at the entrance put in the box all the money given by the worshippers. ¹⁰ Whenever there was a large amount of money in the box, the royal secretary and the High Priest would come, melt down the silver, and weigh it.ˣ ¹¹ After recording the exact amount, they would hand the silver over to the men in charge of the work in the Temple, and these would pay the carpenters, the builders, ¹² the masons, and the stone-cutters, buy the timber and the stones used in the repairs, and pay all other necessary expenses. ¹³ None of the money, however, was used to pay for making silver cups, bowls, trumpets, or tools for tending the lamps, or any other article of silver or of gold. ¹⁴ It was all used to pay the workmen and to buy the materials used in the repairs. ¹⁵ The men in charge of the work were thoroughly honest, so there was no need to require them to account for the funds. ¹⁶ The money given for the repayment offerings and for the offerings for sin was not deposited in the box; it belonged to the priests.

17 At that time King Hazael of Syria attacked the city of Gath and conquered it; then he decided to attack Jerusalem.

¹⁸ King Joash of Judah took all the offerings that his predecessors Jehoshaphat, Jehoram, and Ahaziah had dedicated to the LORD, added to them his own offerings and all the gold in the treasuries of the Temple and the palace, and sent them all as a gift to King Hazael, who then led his army away from Jerusalem.

19 Everything else that King Joash did is recorded in *The History of the Kings of Judah.*

20–21 King Joash's officials plotted against him, and two of them, Jozacar son of Shimeath and Jehozabad son of Shomer, killed him at the house built on the land that was filled in on the east side of Jerusalem, on the road that goes down to Silla. Joash was buried in the royal tombs in David's City, and his son Amaziah succeeded him as king.

King Jehoahaz of Israel

13 In the twenty-third year of the reign of Joash son of Ahaziah as king of Judah, Jehoahaz son of Jehu became king of Israel, and he ruled in Samaria for seventeen years. ² Like King Jeroboam before him he sinned against the LORD and led Israel into sin; he never gave up his evil ways. ³ So the LORD was angry with Israel, and he allowed King Hazael of Syria and his son Benhadad to defeat Israel time after time. ⁴ Then Jehoahaz prayed to the LORD, and the LORD, seeing how harshly the king of Syria was oppressing the Israelites, answered his prayer. ⁵ The LORD sent Israel a leader, who freed them from the Syrians, and so the Israelites lived in peace, as before. ⁶ But they still did not give up the sins into which King Jeroboam had led Israel, but kept onʸ committing them; and the image of the goddess Asherah remained in Samaria.

7 Jehoahaz had no armed forces left except fifty horsemen, ten chariots, and ten thousand men on foot, because the king of Syria had destroyed the rest, trampling them down like dust.

8 Everything else that Jehoahaz did and all his brave deeds are recorded in *The History of the Kings of Israel.* ⁹ He died and was buried in Samaria, and his son Jehoash succeeded him as king.

King Jehoash of Israel

10 In the thirty-seventh year of the reign

ˣ melt down the silver, and weigh it; *or* count the money, and tie it up in bags.
ʸ *Some ancient translations* kept on; *Hebrew* he kept on.
12.4: Ex 30.11–16   **12.15:** 2 Kgs 22.7   **12.16:** Lev 7.7

of King Joash of Judah, Jehoash son of Jehoahaz became king of Israel, and he ruled in Samaria for sixteen years. [11] He too sinned against the LORD and followed the evil example of King Jeroboam, who had led Israel into sin. [12] Everything else that Jehoash did, including his bravery in the war against King Amaziah of Judah, is recorded in *The History of the Kings of Israel.* [13] Jehoash died and was buried in the royal tombs in Samaria, and his son Jeroboam II succeeded him as king.

The Death of Elisha

[14] The prophet Elisha fell ill with a fatal disease, and as he lay dying King Jehoash of Israel went to visit him. "My father, my father!" he exclaimed as he wept. "You have been the mighty defender of Israel!"

[15] "Get a bow and some arrows," Elisha ordered him. Jehoash got them, [16] and Elisha told him to get ready to shoot. The king did so, and Elisha placed his hands on the king's hands. [17] Then, following the prophet's instructions, the king opened the window that faced towards Syria. "Shoot the arrow!" Elisha ordered. As soon as the king shot the arrow, the prophet exclaimed, "You are the LORD's arrow, with which he will win victory over Syria. You will fight the Syrians in Aphek until you defeat them."

[18] Then Elisha told the king to take the other arrows and strike the ground with them. The king struck the ground three times, and then stopped. [19] This made Elisha angry, and he said to the king, "You should have struck five or six times, and then you would have won complete victory over the Syrians; but now you will defeat them only three times."

[20] Elisha died and was buried.

Every year bands of Moabites used to invade the land of Israel. [21] Once, during a funeral, one of those bands was seen, and the people threw the corpse into Elisha's tomb and ran off.[z] As soon as the body came into contact with Elisha's bones, the man came back to life and stood up.

War between Israel and Syria

[22] King Hazael of Syria oppressed the Israelites during all of Jehoahaz' reign, [23] but the LORD was kind and merciful to them. He would not let them be destroyed, but helped them, because of his covenant with Abraham, Isaac, and Jacob. He has never forgotten his people.

[24] At the death of King Hazael of Syria his son Benhadad became king. [25] Then King Jehoash of Israel defeated Benhadad three times and recaptured the cities that had been taken by Benhadad during the reign of Jehoahaz, the father of Jehoash.

King Amaziah of Judah
(2 Chr 25.1-24)

14 In the second year of the reign of Jehoash son of Jehoahaz as king of Israel, Amaziah son of Joash became king of Judah [2] at the age of twenty-five, and he ruled in Jerusalem for twenty-nine years. His mother was Jehoaddin, from Jerusalem. [3] He did what was pleasing to the LORD, but he was not like his ancestor King David; instead, he did what his father Joash had done. [4] He did not tear down the pagan places of worship, and the people continued to offer sacrifices and burn incense there.

[5] As soon as Amaziah was firmly in power, he executed the officials who had killed his father, the king. [6] However, he did not kill their children but followed what the LORD had commanded in the Law of Moses: "Parents are not to be put to death for crimes committed by their children, and children are not to be put to death for crimes committed by their parents; a person is to be put to death only for a crime he himself has committed."

[7] Amaziah killed ten thousand Edomite soldiers in Salt Valley; he captured the city of Sela in battle and called it Joktheel, the name it still has.

[8] Then Amaziah sent messengers to King Jehoash of Israel, challenging him to fight.[a] [9] But King Jehoash sent back the following reply: "Once a thorn bush on the Lebanon Mountains sent a message to a cedar: 'Give your daughter in marriage to my son.' A wild animal passed by and trampled the bush down. [10] Now Amaziah, you have defeated the Edomites, and you are filled with pride. Be satisfied with your fame and stay at home. Why stir up trouble that will only bring disaster on you and your people?"

[11] But Amaziah refused to listen, so King Jehoash marched out with his men and fought against him at Beth Shemesh

---

[z] *One ancient translation* and ran off; *Hebrew* and he ran off.
[a] challenging him to fight; *or* inviting him to a conference.
13.14: 2 Kgs 2.12   **14.6:** Deut 24.16

in Judah. [12] Amaziah's army was defeated, and all his soldiers fled to their homes. [13] Jehoash took Amaziah prisoner, advanced on Jerusalem, and tore down the city wall from Ephraim Gate to the Corner Gate, a distance of nearly two hundred metres. [14] He took all the silver and gold he could find, all the temple equipment and all the palace treasures, and carried them back to Samaria. He also took hostages with him.

15 Everything else that Jehoash did, including his bravery in the war against King Amaziah of Judah, is recorded in *The History of the Kings of Israel.* [16] Jehoash died and was buried in the royal tombs in Samaria, and his son Jeroboam II succeeded him as king.

The Death of King Amaziah of Judah
(2 Chr 25.25–28)

17 King Amaziah of Judah lived fifteen years after the death of King Jehoash of Israel. [18] Everything else that Amaziah did is recorded in *The History of the Kings of Judah.*

19 There was a plot in Jerusalem to assassinate Amaziah, so he fled to the city of Lachish, but his enemies followed him there and killed him. [20] His body was carried back to Jerusalem on a horse and was buried in the royal tombs in David's City. [21] The people of Judah then crowned his sixteen-year-old son Uzziah as king. [22] Uzziah reconquered and rebuilt Elath after his father's death.

King Jeroboam II of Israel

23 In the fifteenth year of the reign of Amaziah son of Joash as king of Judah, Jeroboam son of Jehoash became king of Israel, and he ruled in Samaria for forty-one years. [24] He sinned against the LORD, following the wicked example of his predecessor King Jeroboam son of Nebat, who led Israel into sin. [25] He reconquered all the territory that had belonged to Israel, from Hamath Pass in the north to the Dead Sea in the south. This was what the LORD, the God of Israel, had promised through his servant the prophet Jonah son of Amittai, from Gath Hepher. [26] The LORD saw the terrible[b] suffering of the Israelites; there was no one at all to help them. [27] But it was not the LORD's

purpose to destroy Israel completely and for ever, so he rescued them through King Jeroboam II.

28 Everything else that Jeroboam II did, his brave battles, and how he restored Damascus and Hamath to Israel,[c] are all recorded in *The History of the Kings of Israel.* [29] Jeroboam died and was buried in the royal tombs, and his son Zechariah succeeded him as king.

King Uzziah of Judah
(2 Chr 26.1–23)

15 In the twenty-seventh year of the reign of King Jeroboam II of Israel, Uzziah son of Amaziah became king of Judah [2] at the age of sixteen, and he ruled in Jerusalem for fifty-two years. His mother was Jecoliah from Jerusalem. [3] Following the example of his father, he did what was pleasing to the LORD. [4] But the pagan places of worship were not destroyed, and the people continued to offer sacrifices and burn incense there. [5] The LORD struck Uzziah with a dreaded skin-disease that stayed with him the rest of his life. He lived in a house on his own, relieved of all duties, while his son Jotham governed the country.

6 Everything else that Uzziah did is recorded in *The History of the Kings of Judah.* [7] Uzziah died and was buried in the royal burial ground in David's City, and his son Jotham succeeded him as king.

King Zechariah of Israel

8 In the thirty-eighth year of the reign of King Uzziah of Judah, Zechariah son of Jeroboam II became king of Israel, and he ruled in Samaria for six months. [9] He, like his predecessors, sinned against the LORD. He followed the wicked example of King Jeroboam son of Nebat, who led Israel into sin. [10] Shallum son of Jabesh conspired against King Zechariah, assassinated him at Ibleam,[d] and succeeded him as king.

11 Everything else that Zechariah did is recorded in *The History of the Kings of Israel.*

12 So the promise was fulfilled which the LORD had made to King Jehu: "Your descendants, down to the fourth generation,[e] will be kings of Israel."

---

[b] *Some ancient translations* terrible; *Hebrew* rebellious.
[c] *One ancient translation* to Israel; *Hebrew* for Judah in Israel.
[d] *One ancient translation* at Ibleam; *Hebrew* before people.
[e] FOURTH GENERATION: *Zechariah was Jehu's great-great-grandson.*
14.25: Jon 1.1   **15.7:** Is 6.1   **15.12:** 2 Kgs 10.30

King Shallum of Israel

13 In the thirty-ninth year of the reign of King Uzziah of Judah, Shallum son of Jabesh became king of Israel, and he ruled in Samaria for one month.

14 Menahem son of Gadi went from Tirzah to Samaria, assassinated Shallum, and succeeded him as king. 15 Everything else that Shallum did, including an account of his conspiracy, is recorded in *The History of the Kings of Israel.* 16 As Menahem was on his way from Tirzah, he completely destroyed the city of Tappuah,*f* its inhabitants, and the surrounding territory, because the city did not surrender to him. He even ripped open the bellies of all the pregnant women.

King Menahem of Israel

17 In the thirty-ninth year of the reign of King Uzziah of Judah, Menahem son of Gadi became king of Israel, and he ruled in Samaria for ten years. 18 He sinned against the LORD, for until the day of his death he followed the wicked example of King Jeroboam son of Nebat, who led Israel into sin till the day of his death. 19 Tiglath Pileser, the emperor of Assyria, invaded Israel, and Menahem gave him thirty-four thousand kilogrammes of silver to gain his support in strengthening Menahem's power over the country. 20 Menahem got the money from the rich men of Israel by forcing each one to contribute fifty pieces of silver. So Tiglath Pileser went back to his own country.

21 Everything else that Menahem did is recorded in *The History of the Kings of Israel.* 22 He died and was buried, and his son Pekahiah succeeded him as king.

King Pekahiah of Israel

23 In the fiftieth year of the reign of King Uzziah of Judah, Pekahiah son of Menahem became king of Israel, and he ruled in Samaria for two years. 24 He sinned against the LORD, following the wicked example of King Jeroboam son of Nebat, who led Israel into sin. 25 An officer of Pekahiah's forces, Pekah son of Remaliah, plotted with fifty men from Gilead, assassinated Pekahiah in the palace's inner fortress*g* in Samaria, and succeeded him as king.

26 Everything else that Pekahiah did is recorded in *The History of the Kings of Israel.*

King Pekah of Israel

27 In the fifty-second year of the reign of King Uzziah of Judah, Pekah son of Remaliah became king of Israel, and he ruled in Samaria for twenty years. 28 He sinned against the LORD, following the wicked example of King Jeroboam son of Nebat, who led Israel into sin.

29 It was while Pekah was king that Tiglath Pileser, the emperor of Assyria, captured the cities of Ijon, Abel Beth Maacah, Janoah, Kedesh, and Hazor, and the territories of Gilead, Galilee, and Naphtali, and took the people to Assyria as prisoners.

30 In the twentieth year of the reign of Jotham son of Uzziah as king of Judah, Hoshea son of Elah plotted against King Pekah, assassinated him, and succeeded him as king. 31 Everything else that Pekah did is recorded in *The History of the Kings of Israel.*

King Jotham of Judah
(2 Chr 27.1–9)

32 In the second year of the reign of Pekah son of Remaliah as king of Israel, Jotham son of Uzziah became king of Judah 33 at the age of twenty-five, and he ruled in Jerusalem for sixteen years. His mother was Jerusha, the daughter of Zadok. 34 Following the example of his father Uzziah, Jotham did what was pleasing to the LORD. 35 But the pagan places of worship were not destroyed, and the people continued to offer sacrifices and burn incense there. It was Jotham who built the North Gate of the Temple.

36 Everything else that Jotham did is recorded in *The History of the Kings of Judah.* 37 It was while he was king that the LORD first sent King Rezin of Syria and King Pekah of Israel to attack Judah. 38 Jotham died and was buried in the royal tombs in David's City, and his son Ahaz succeeded him as king.

King Ahaz of Judah
(2 Chr 28.1–27)

16 In the seventeenth year of the reign of Pekah son of Remaliah as king of Israel, Ahaz son of Jotham became king of Judah 2 at the age of twenty, and he ruled in Jerusalem for sixteen years. He

---

f One ancient translation Tappuah; *Hebrew* Tiphṣah.
g Hebrew has two additional words, the meaning of which is unclear.

did not follow the good example of his ancestor King David; instead, he did what was not pleasing to the LORD his God ³and followed the example of the kings of Israel. He even sacrificed his own son as a burnt-offering to idols, imitating the disgusting practice of the people whom the LORD had driven out of the land as the Israelites advanced. ⁴At the pagan places of worship, on the hills, and under every shady tree, Ahaz offered sacrifices and burnt incense.

5 King Rezin of Syria and King Pekah of Israel attacked Jerusalem and beseiged it, but could not defeat Ahaz. ⁶(At the same time, the king of Edom ʰ regained control of the city of Elath, and drove out the Judaeans who lived there. The Edomites settled in Elath, and still live there.) ⁷Ahaz sent men to Tiglath Pileser, the emperor of Assyria, with this message: "I am your devoted servant. Come and rescue me from the kings of Syria and of Israel, who are attacking me." ⁸Ahaz took the silver and gold from the Temple and the palace treasury and sent it as a present to the emperor. ⁹Tiglath Pileser, in answer to Ahaz' plea, marched out with his army against Damascus, captured it, killed King Rezin, and took the people to Kir as prisoners.

10 When King Ahaz went to Damascus to meet Emperor Tiglath Pileser, he saw the altar there and sent back to Uriah the priest an exact model of it, down to the smallest details. ¹¹So Uriah built an altar just like it, and finished it before Ahaz returned. ¹²On his return from Damascus, Ahaz saw that the altar was finished, ¹³so he burnt animal sacrifices and grain-offerings on it, and poured a wine-offering and the blood of a fellowship-offering on it. ¹⁴The bronze altar dedicated to the LORD was between the new altar and the Temple, so Ahaz moved it to the north side of his new altar. ¹⁵Then he ordered Uriah: "Use this large altar of mine for the morning burnt-offerings and the evening grain-offerings, for the burnt-offerings and grain-offerings of the king and the people, and for the people's wine-offerings. Pour on it the blood of all the animals that are sacrificed. But keep the bronze altar for me to use for

divination." ¹⁶Uriah did as the king commanded.

17 King Ahaz took apart the bronze carts used in the Temple and removed the basins that were on them; he also took the bronze tank from the backs of the twelve bronze bulls, and placed it on a stone foundation. ¹⁸And in order to please the Assyrian emperor, Ahaz also removed from the Temple the platform for the royal throne and closed up the king's private entrance to the Temple. ⁱ

19 Everything else that King Ahaz did is recorded in *The History of the Kings of Judah.* ²⁰Ahaz died and was buried in the royal tombs in David's City, and his son Hezekiah succeeded him as king.

King Hoshea of Israel

17 In the twelfth year of the reign of King Ahaz of Judah, Hoshea son of Elah became king of Israel, and he ruled in Samaria for nine years. ²He sinned against the LORD, but not as much as the kings who had ruled Israel before him. ³Emperor Shalmaneser of Assyria made war against him; Hoshea surrendered to Shalmaneser and paid him tribute every year. ⁴But one year Hoshea sent messengers to So, king of Egypt, ʲ asking for his help, and stopped paying the annual tribute to Assyria. When Shalmaneser learnt of this, he had Hoshea arrested and put in prison.

The Fall of Samaria

5 Then Shalmaneser invaded Israel and besieged Samaria. In the third year of the siege, ⁶which was the ninth year of the reign of Hoshea, the Assyrian emperor ᵏ captured Samaria, took the Israelites to Assyria as prisoners, and settled some of them in the city of Halah, some near the River Habor in the district of Gozan, and some in the cities of Media.

7 Samaria fell because the Israelites sinned against the LORD their God, who had rescued them from the king of Egypt and had led them out of Egypt. They worshipped other gods, ⁸followed the customs of the people whom the LORD had driven out as his people advanced, and adopted customs introduced by the kings of Israel. ˡ ⁹The Israelites did ᵐ

ʰ *Probable text* the king of Edom; *Hebrew* King Rezin of Syria.
ⁱ *Verse 18 in Hebrew is unclear.* ʲ So, king of Egypt; *or* the king of Egypt at Sais.
ᵏ ASSYRIAN EMPEROR: *Probably Sargon II, the successor of Shalmaneser.*
ˡ *Probable text* and adopted...Israel; *Hebrew unclear.* ᵐ did; *or* said.
16.3: Deut 12.31　　**16.5:** Is 7.1　　**16.14:** Ex 27.1–2; 2 Chr 4.1
16.17: 1 Kgs 7.23–39; 2 Chr 4.2–6　　**16.20:** Is 14.28

They worshipped other gods (17.7)

things that the LORD their God disapproved of. They built pagan places of worship in all their towns, from the smallest village to the largest city. 10 On all the hills and under every shady tree they put up stone pillars and images of the goddess Asherah, 11 and they burnt incense on all the pagan altars, following the practice of the people whom the LORD had driven out of the land. They aroused the LORD's anger with all their wicked deeds 12 and disobeyed the LORD's command not to worship idols.

13 The LORD had sent his messengers and prophets to warn Israel and Judah: "Abandon your evil ways and obey my commands, which are contained in the Law I gave to your ancestors and which I handed on to you through my servants the prophets." 14 But they would not obey; they were stubborn like their ancestors, who had not trusted in the LORD their God. 15 They refused to obey his instructions, they did not keep the covenant he had made with their ancestors, and they disregarded his warnings. They worshipped worthless idols and became worthless themselves, and they followed the customs of the surrounding nations, disobeying the LORD's command not to imitate them. 16 They broke all the laws of the LORD their God and made two metal bull-calves to worship; they also made an image of the goddess Asherah, worshipped the stars, and served the god Baal. 17 They sacrificed their sons and daughters as burnt-offerings to pagan gods; they consulted mediums and fortune-tellers, and they devoted themselves completely to doing what is wrong in the LORD's sight, and so aroused his anger. 18 The LORD was angry with the Israelites and banished them from his sight, leaving only the kingdom of Judah.

19 But even the people of Judah did not obey the laws of the LORD their God; they imitated the customs adopted by the people of Israel. 20 The LORD rejected all the Israelites, punishing them and handing them over to cruel enemies until at last he had banished them from his sight.

21 After the LORD had separated Israel from Judah, the Israelites made Jeroboam son of Nebat their king. Jeroboam made them abandon the LORD and led them into terrible sins. 22 They followed Jeroboam and continued to practise all the sins he had committed, 23 until at last the LORD banished them from his sight, as he had warned through his servants the prophets that he would do. So the people of Israel were taken into exile to Assyria, where they still live.

The Assyrians Settle in Israel

24 The emperor of Assyria took people from the cities of Babylon, Cuth, Ivvah, Hamath, and Sepharvaim, and settled them in the cities of Samaria,[n] in place of the exiled Israelites. They took possession of these cities and lived there.

[n] SAMARIA: *The name of its capital city was applied to the territory of the former kingdom of Israel.*
17.10: 1 Kgs 14.23   **17.16:** 1 Kgs 12.28   **17.17:** Deut 18.10

They disregarded his warnings (17.15)

25 When they first settled there, they did not worship the LORD, and so he sent lions, which killed some of them. 26 The emperor of Assyria was told that the people had settled in the cities of Samaria did not know the law of the god of that land, and so the god had sent lions, which were killing them. 27 So the emperor commanded: "Send back one of the priests we brought as prisoners; make him *o* go back and live there, in order to teach the people the law of the god of that land." 28 So an Israelite priest who had been deported from Samaria went and lived in Bethel, where he taught the people how to worship the LORD.

29 But the people who settled in Samaria continued to make their own idols, and they placed them in the shrines that the Israelites had built. Each different group made idols in the cities they were living in: 30 The people of Babylon made idols of the god Succoth Benoth; the people of Cuth, idols of Nergal; the people of Hamath, idols of Ashima; 31 the people of Ivvah, idols of Nibhaz and Tartak; and the people of Sepharvaim sacrificed their children as burnt-offerings to their gods Adrammelech and Anammelech. 32 These people also worshipped the LORD and chose from among their own number all sorts of people to serve as priests at the pagan places of worship and to offer sacrifices for them there. 33 So they worshipped the LORD, but they also

worshipped their own gods according to the customs of the countries from which they had come.

34 They still carry on their old customs to this day. They do not worship the LORD nor do they obey the laws and commands which he gave to the descendants of Jacob, whom he named Israel. 35 The LORD had made a covenant with them and had ordered them: "Do not worship other gods; do not bow down to them or serve them or offer sacrifices to them. 36 You shall obey me, the LORD, who brought you out of Egypt with great power and strength; you are to bow down to me and offer sacrifices to me. 37 You shall always obey the laws and commands that I wrote for you. You shall not obey other gods, 38 and you shall not forget the covenant I made with you. 39 You shall obey me, the LORD your God, and I will rescue you from your enemies." 40 But those people would not listen, and they continued to follow their old customs.

41 So those people worshipped the LORD, but they also worshipped their idols; and to this day their descendants continue to do the same.

King Hezekiah of Judah
(2 Chr 29.1–2; 31.1)

18 In the third year of the reign of Hoshea son of Elah as king of Israel, Hezekiah son of Ahaz became king of Judah 2 at the age of twenty-five, and

o Some ancient translations him; *Hebrew* them.
17.34: Gen 32.28, 35.10   **17.35:** Ex 20.5; Deut 5.9   **17.36:** Deut 6.13

he ruled in Jerusalem for twenty-nine years. His mother was Abijah, the daughter of Zechariah. ³ Following the example of his ancestor King David, he did what was pleasing to the LORD. ⁴ He destroyed the pagan places of worship, broke the stone pillars, and cut down the images of the goddess Asherah. He also broke in pieces the bronze snake that Moses had made, which was called Nehushtan. Up to that time the people of Israel had burnt incense in its honour. ⁵ Hezekiah trusted in the LORD, the God of Israel; Judah never had another king like him, either before or after his time. ⁶ He was faithful to the LORD and never disobeyed him, but carefully kept all the commands that the LORD had given Moses. ⁷ So the LORD was with him, and he was successful in everything he did. He rebelled against the emperor of Assyria and refused to submit to him. ⁸ He defeated the Philistines, and raided their settlements, from the smallest village to the largest city, including Gaza and its surrounding territory.

9 In the fourth year of Hezekiah's reign—which was the seventh year of King Hoshea's reign over Israel— Emperor Shalmaneser of Assyria invaded Israel and besieged Samaria. ¹⁰ In the third year of the siege, Samaria fell; this was the sixth year of Hezekiah's reign, and

ᵖ ASSYRIAN EMPEROR: *See 17.6.*
18.4: Num 21.9

the ninth year of Hoshea's reign. ¹¹ The Assyrian emperor ᵖ took the Israelites to Assyria as prisoners and settled some of them in the city of Halah, some near the River Habor in the district of Gozan, and some in the cities of Media.

12 Samaria fell because the Israelites did not obey the LORD their God, but broke the covenant he had made with them and disobeyed all the laws given by Moses, the servant of the LORD. They would not listen and they would not obey.

The Assyrians Threaten Jerusalem
(2 Chr 32.1-19; Is 36.1-22)

13 In the fourteenth year of the reign of King Hezekiah, Sennacherib, the emperor of Assyria, attacked the fortified cities of Judah and conquered them. ¹⁴ Hezekiah sent a message to Sennacherib, who was in Lachish: "I have done wrong; please stop your attack, and I will pay whatever you demand." The emperor's answer was that Hezekiah should send him ten thousand kilogrammes of silver and a thousand kilogrammes of gold. ¹⁵ Hezekiah sent him all the silver in the Temple and in the palace treasury; ¹⁶ he also stripped the gold from the temple doors and the gold with which he himself had covered the doorposts, and he sent it all to Sennacherib. ¹⁷ The Assyrian emperor sent a large army from

Sennacherib...attacked the fortified cities (18.13)

Lachish to attack Hezekiah at Jerusalem; it was commanded by his three highest officials. When they arrived at Jerusalem, they occupied the road where the cloth-makers work, by the ditch that brings water from the upper pond. 18 Then they sent for King Hezekiah, and three of his officials went out to meet them: Eliakim son of Hilkiah, who was in charge of the palace; Shebna, the court secretary; and Joah son of Asaph, who was in charge of the records. 19 One of the Assyrian officials told them that the emperor wanted to know what made King Hezekiah so confident. 20 He demanded, "Do you think that words can take the place of military skill and might? Who do you think will help you rebel against Assyria? 21 You are expecting Egypt to help you, but that would be like using a reed as a walking-stick—it would break and jab your hand. That is what the king of Egypt is like when anyone relies on him."

22 The Assyrian official went on, "Or will you tell me that you are relying on the LORD your God? It was the LORD's shrines and altars that Hezekiah de-stroyed, when he told the people of Judah and Jerusalem to worship only at the altar in Jerusalem. 23 I will make a bargain with you in the name of the emperor. I will give you two thousand horses if you can find that many men to ride them! 24 You are no match for even the lowest ranking Assyrian official, and yet you expect the Egyptians to send you chariots and horsemen! 25 Do you think I have attacked your country and destroyed it without the LORD's help? The LORD himself told me to attack it and destroy it."

26 Then Eliakim, Shebna, and Joah told the official, "Speak Aramaic to us, sir. We understand it. Don't speak Hebrew; all the people on the wall are listening."

27 He replied, "Do you think you and the king are the only ones the emperor sent me to say all these things to? No, I am also talking to the people who are sitting on the wall, who will have to eat their excrement and drink their urine, just as you will."

28 Then the official stood up and shouted in Hebrew, "Listen to what the emperor of Assyria is telling you! 29 He warns you not to let Hezekiah deceive you. Hezekiah can't save you. 30 And don't let him persuade you to rely on the LORD. Don't think that the LORD will save you, and that he will stop our Assyrian army

from capturing your city. 31 Don't listen to Hezekiah. The emperor of Assyria commands you to come out of the city and surrender. You will all be allowed to eat grapes from your own vines, and figs from your own trees, and to drink water from your own wells—32 until the emperor resettles you in a country much like your own, where there are vineyards to give wine and there is corn for making bread; it is a land of olives, olive-oil, and honey. If you do what he commands, you will not die, but live. Don't let Hezekiah fool you into thinking that the LORD will rescue you. 33 Did the gods of any other nations save their countries from the emperor of Assyria? 34 Where are they now, the gods of Hamath and Arpad? Where are the gods of Sepharvaim, Hena, and Ivvah? Did anyone save Samaria? 35 When did any of the gods of all these countries ever save their country from our emperor? Then what makes you think the LORD can save Jerusalem?"

36 The people kept quiet, just as King Hezekiah had told them to; they did not say a word. 37 Then Eliakim, Shebna, and Joah tore their clothes in grief, and went and reported to the king what the Assyrian official had said.

The King Asks Isaiah's Advice
(Is 37.1–7)

19 As soon as King Hezekiah heard their report, he tore his clothes in grief, put on sackcloth, and went to the Temple of the LORD. 2 He sent Eliakim, the official in charge of the palace, Shebna, the court secretary, and the senior priests to the prophet Isaiah son of Amoz. They also were wearing sack-cloth. 3 This is the message which he told them to give Isaiah: "Today is a day of suffering; we are being punished and are in disgrace. We are like a woman who is ready to give birth, but is too weak to do it. 4 The Assyrian emperor has sent his chief official to insult the living God. May the LORD your God hear these insults and punish those who spoke them. So pray to God for those of our people who survive."

5 When Isaiah received King Hez-ekiah's message, 6 he sent back this answer: "The LORD tells you not to let the Assyrians frighten you with their claims that he cannot save you. 7 The LORD will cause the emperor to hear a rumour that will make him go back to his own

The official stood up and shouted in Hebrew (18.28)

country, and the LORD will have him killed there."

The Assyrians Send Another Threat
(Is 37.8-20)

8 The Assyrian official learnt that the emperor had left Lachish and was fighting against the nearby city of Libnah; so he went there to consult him. 9 Word reached the Assyrians that the Egyptian army, led by King Tirhakah of Sudan, was coming to attack them. When the emperor heard this, he sent a letter to King Hezekiah of Judah 10 to say to him, "The god you are trusting in has told you that you will not fall into my hands, but don't let that deceive you. 11 You have heard what an Assyrian emperor does to any country he decides to destroy. Do you think that you can escape? 12 My ancestors destroyed the cities of Gozan, Haran, and Rezeph, and killed the people of Betheden who lived in Telassar, and none of their gods could save them. 13 Where are the kings of the cities of Hamath, Arpad, Sepharvaim, Hena, and Ivvah?"

14 King Hezekiah took the letter from the messengers and read it. Then he went to the Temple, placed the letter there in the presence of the LORD, 15 and prayed, "O LORD, the God of Israel, enthroned above the winged creatures, you alone are God, ruling all the kingdoms of the world. You created the earth and the sky. 16 Now, LORD, look at what is happening to us. Listen to all the things that Sennacherib is saying to insult you, the living God. 17 We all know, LORD, that the emperors of Assyria have destroyed many nations, made their lands desolate, 18 and burnt up their gods—which were no gods at all, only images of wood and stone made by human hands. 19 Now, LORD our God, rescue us from the Assyrians, so that all the nations of the world will know that only you, O LORD, are God."

Isaiah's Message to the King
(Is 37.21-38)

20 Then Isaiah sent a message telling King Hezekiah that in answer to the king's prayer 21 the LORD had said, "The city of Jerusalem laughs at you, Sennacherib, and despises you. 22 Whom do you think you have been insulting and ridiculing? You have been disrespectful to me, the holy God of Israel. 23 You sent your messengers to boast to me that with all

19.15: Ex 25.22

your chariots you had conquered the highest mountains of Lebanon. You boasted that there you cut down the tallest cedars and the finest cypress-trees and that you reached the deepest parts of the forests. [24] You boasted that you dug wells and drank water in foreign lands and that the feet of your soldiers tramped the River Nile dry.

25 "Have you never heard that I planned all this long ago? And now I have carried it out. I gave you the power to turn fortified cities into piles of rubble. [26] The people who lived there were powerless; they were frightened and stunned. They were like grass in a field or weeds growing on a roof when the hot east wind blasts them. [p]

27 "But I know everything about you, what you do and where you go. I know how you rage against me. [28] I have received the report of that rage and that pride of yours, and now I will put a hook through your nose and a bit in your mouth, and take you back by the same road you came."

29 Then Isaiah said to King Hezekiah, "This is a sign of what will happen. This year and next you will have only wild grain to eat, but the following year you will be able to sow your corn and harvest it, and plant vines and eat grapes. [30] Those in Judah who survive will flourish like plants that send roots deep into the ground and produce fruit. [31] There will be people in Jerusalem and on Mount Zion who will survive, because the LORD is determined to make this happen.

32 "This is what the LORD has said about the Assyrian emperor: 'He will not enter this city or shoot a single arrow against it. No soldiers with shields will come near the city, and no siege-mounds will be built round it. [33] He will go back by the same road he came, without entering this city. I, the LORD, have spoken. [34] I will defend this city and protect it, for the sake of my own honour and because of the promise I made to my servant David.' "

35 That night an angel of the LORD went to the Assyrian camp and killed 185,000 soldiers. At dawn the next day, there they lay, all dead! [36] Then the Assyrian emperor Sennacherib withdrew and returned to Nineveh. [37] One day, when he was worshipping in the temple of his god Nisroch, two of his sons, Adrammelech and Sharezer, killed him with their swords, and then escaped to the land of Ararat. Another of his sons, Esarhaddon, succeeded him as emperor.

King Hezekiah's Illness and Recovery
(Is 38.1-8, 21-22; 2 Chr 32.24-26)

20 About this time King Hezekiah fell ill and almost died. The prophet Isaiah son of Amoz went to see him and said to him, "The LORD tells you that you are to put everything in order, because you will not recover. Get ready to die."

2 Hezekiah turned his face to the wall and prayed: 3 "Remember, LORD, that I have served you faithfully and loyally, and that I have always tried to do what you wanted me to." And he began to cry bitterly.

4 Isaiah left the king, but before he had passed through the central courtyard of the palace the LORD told him 5 to go back to Hezekiah, ruler of the LORD's people, and say to him, "I, the LORD, the God of your ancestor David, have heard your prayer and seen your tears. I will heal you, and in three days you will go to the Temple. 6 I will let you live fifteen years longer. I will rescue you and this city of Jerusalem from the emperor of Assyria. I will defend this city, for the sake of my own honour and because of the promise I made to my servant David."

7 Then Isaiah told the king's attendants to put on his boil a paste made of figs, and he would get well. [q] 8 King Hezekiah asked, "What is the sign to prove that the LORD will heal me and that three days later I will be able to go to the Temple?"

9 Isaiah replied, "The LORD will give you a sign to prove that he will keep his promise. Now, would you prefer the shadow on the stairway to go forward ten steps or go back ten steps?" [r]

10 Hezekiah answered, "It's easy to make the shadow go forward ten steps! [s] Make it go back ten steps." [s]

11 Isaiah prayed to the LORD, and the LORD made the shadow go back ten steps [s] on the stairway [t] set up by King Ahaz.

---

[p] *Probable text* when the hot east wind blasts them; *Hebrew* blasted before they are grown.
[q] *One ancient translation (and see Is 38.21)* figs, and he would get well; *Hebrew* figs. They did so, and he got well.   [r] stairway...steps...steps; *or* sundial...divisions...divisions.
[s] steps; *or* divisions.
[t] stairway; *or* sundial. *Archaeological evidence suggests that the stairway referred to in this passage was one specially constructed to tell the time.*

Messengers from Babylonia
(Is 39.1-8)

12 About that same time the king of Babylonia, Merodach Baladan, the son of Baladan, heard that King Hezekiah had been ill, so he sent him a letter and a present. ¹³Hezekiah welcomed the messengers and showed them his wealth—his silver and gold, his spices and perfumes, and all his military equipment. There was nothing in his storerooms or anywhere in his kingdom that he did not show them. ¹⁴Then the prophet Isaiah went to King Hezekiah and asked, "Where did these men come from and what did they say to you?"

Hezekiah answered, "They came from a very distant country, from Babylonia."

15 "What did they see in the palace?"

"They saw everything. There is nothing in the storerooms that I didn't show them."

16 Isaiah then said to the king, "The LORD Almighty says that ¹⁷a time is coming when everything in your palace, everything that your ancestors have stored up to this day, will be carried off to Babylonia. Nothing will be left. ¹⁸Some of your own direct descendants will be taken away and made eunuchs to serve in the palace of the king of Babylonia."

19 King Hezekiah understood this to mean that there would be peace and security during his lifetime, so he replied, "The message you have given me from the LORD is good."

The End of Hezekiah's Reign
(2 Chr 32.32-33)

20 Everything else that King Hezekiah did, his brave deeds, and an account of how he built a reservoir and dug a tunnel to bring water into the city, are all recorded in *The History of the Kings of Judah.* ²¹Hezekiah died, and his son Manasseh succeeded him as king.

King Manasseh of Judah
(2 Chr 33.1-20)

21 Manasseh was twelve years old when he became king of Judah, and he ruled in Jerusalem for fifty-five years. His mother was Hephzibah. ²Following the disgusting practices of the nations whom the LORD had driven out of the land as his people advanced, Manasseh sinned against the LORD. ³He rebuilt the pagan places of worship that his father Hezekiah had destroyed; he built altars for the worship of Baal and made an image of the goddess Asherah, as King Ahab of Israel had done. Manasseh also worshipped the stars. ⁴He built pagan altars in the Temple, the place that the LORD had said was where he should be worshipped. ⁵In the two courtyards of the Temple he built altars for the worship of the stars. ⁶He sacrificed his son as a burnt-offering. He practised divination and magic and consulted[u] fortune-tellers and mediums. He sinned greatly against the LORD and stirred up his anger. ⁷He placed the symbol of the goddess Asherah in the Temple, the place about which the LORD had said to David and his son Solomon: "Here in Jerusalem, in this Temple, is the place that I have chosen out of all the territory of the twelve tribes of Israel as the place where I am to be worshipped. ⁸And if the people of Israel will obey all my commands and keep the whole Law that my servant Moses gave them, then I will not allow them to be driven out of the land that I gave to their ancestors." ⁹But the people of Judah did not obey the LORD, and Manasseh led them to commit even greater sins than those committed by the nations whom the LORD had driven out of the land as his people advanced.

10 Through his servants the prophets the LORD said, ¹¹"King Manasseh has done these disgusting things, things far worse than what the Canaanites did; and with his idols he has led the people of Judah into sin. ¹²So I, the LORD God of Israel, will bring such a disaster on Jerusalem and Judah that everyone who hears about it will be stunned. ¹³I will punish Jerusalem as I did Samaria, as I did King Ahab of Israel and his descendants. I will wipe Jerusalem clean of its people, as clean as a plate that has been wiped and turned upside down. ¹⁴I will abandon the people who survive, and will hand them over to their enemies, who will conquer them and plunder their land. ¹⁵I will do this to my people because they have sinned against me and have stirred up my anger from the time their ancestors came out of Egypt to this day."

16 Manasseh killed so many innocent people that the streets of Jerusalem were flowing with blood; he did this in addition

[u] consulted; *or* brought back.
20.17: 2 Kgs 24.13; 2 Chr 36.10   **20.18:** 2 Kgs 24.14-15; Dan 1.1-7   **21.2:** Jer 15.4
21.4: 2 Sam 7.13   **21.7-8:** 1 Kgs 9.3-5; 2 Chr 7.12-18

to leading the people of Judah into idolatry, causing them to sin against the LORD.

17 Everything else that Manasseh did, including the sins he committed, is recorded in *The History of the Kings of Judah*. 18 Manasseh died and was buried in the palace garden, the garden of Uzza, and his son Amon succeeded him as king.

King Amon of Judah
(2 Chr 33.21–25)

19 Amon was twenty-two years old when he became king of Judah, and he ruled in Jerusalem for two years. His mother was Meshullemeth, the daughter of Haruz, from the town of Jotbah. 20 Like his father Manasseh, he sinned against the LORD; 21 he imitated his father's actions, and he worshipped the idols that his father had worshipped. 22 He rejected the LORD, the God of his ancestors, and disobeyed the LORD's commands.

23 Amon's officials plotted against him and assassinated him in the palace. 24 The people of Judah killed Amon's assassins and made his son Josiah king.

25 Everything else that Amon did is recorded in *The History of the Kings of Judah*. 26 Amon was buried in the tomb in the garden of Uzza, and his son Josiah succeeded him as king.

King Josiah of Judah
(2 Chr 34.1–2)

22 Josiah was eight years old when he became king of Judah, and he ruled in Jerusalem for thirty-one years. His mother was Jedidah, the daughter of Adaiah, from the town of Bozkath. 2 Josiah did what was pleasing to the LORD; he followed the example of his ancestor King David, strictly obeying all the laws of God.

The Book of the Law Is Discovered
(2 Chr 34.8–28)

3 In the eighteenth year of his reign, King Josiah sent the court secretary Shaphan, the son of Azaliah and grandson of Meshullam, to the Temple with the order: 4 "Go to the High Priest Hilkiah and get a report on the amount of money that the priests on duty at the entrance to the Temple have collected from the people. 5 Tell him to give the money to the men who are in charge of the repairs in the Temple. They are to pay 6 the carpenters, the builders, and the masons,

and buy the timber and the stones used in the repairs. 7 The men in charge of the work are thoroughly honest, so there is no need to require them to account for the funds."

8 Shaphan delivered the king's order to Hilkiah, and Hilkiah told him that he had found the book of the Law in the Temple. Hilkiah gave him the book, and Shaphan read it. 9 Then he went back to the king and reported: "Your servants have taken the money that was in the Temple and have handed it over to the men in charge of the repairs." 10 And then he said, "I have here a book that Hilkiah gave me." And he read it aloud to the king.

11 When the king heard the book being read, he tore his clothes in dismay, 12 and gave the following order to Hilkiah the priest, to Ahikam son of Shaphan, to Achbor son of Micaiah, to Shaphan, the court secretary, and to Asaiah, the king's attendant: 13 "Go and consult the LORD for me and for all the people of Judah about the teachings of this book. The LORD is angry with us because our ancestors have not done what this book says must be done."

14 Hilkiah, Ahikam, Achbor, Shaphan, and Asaiah went to consult a woman named Huldah, a prophet who lived in the newer part of Jerusalem. (Her husband Shallum, the son of Tikvah and grandson of Harhas, was in charge of the temple robes.) They described to her what had happened, 15 and she told them to go back to the king and give him 16 the following message from the LORD: "I am going to punish Jerusalem and all its people, as written in the book that the king has read. 17 They have rejected me and have offered sacrifices to other gods, and so have stirred up my anger by all they have done. My anger is aroused against Jerusalem, and it will not die down. 18 As for the king himself, this is what I, the LORD God of Israel, say: You listened to what is written in the book, 19 and you repented and humbled yourself before me, tearing your clothes and weeping, when you heard how I threatened to punish Jerusalem and its people. I will make it a terrifying sight, a place whose name people will use as a curse. But I have heard your prayer, 20 and the punishment which I am going to bring on Jerusalem will not come until after your death. I will let you die in peace."

22.1: Jer 3.6　　**22.7**: 2 Kgs 12.15

The king burnt all these objects outside the city (23.4)

The men returned to King Josiah with this message.

Josiah Does Away with Pagan Worship
(2 Chr 34.3-7, 29-33)

23 King Josiah summoned all the leaders of Judah and Jerusalem, ² and together they went to the Temple, accompanied by the priests and the prophets and all the rest of the people, rich and poor alike. Before them all, the king read aloud the whole book of the covenant which had been found in the Temple. ³ He stood by the royal column and made a covenant with the LORD to obey him, to keep his laws and commands with all his heart and soul, and to put into practice the demands attached to the covenant, as written in the book. And all the people promised to keep the covenant.

⁴ Then Josiah ordered the High Priest Hilkiah, his assistant priests, and the guards on duty at the entrance to the Temple to bring out of the Temple all the objects used in the worship of Baal, of the goddess Asherah, and of the stars. The king burnt all these objects outside the city near the valley of the Kidron, and then had the ashes taken to Bethel. ⁵ He removed from office the priests that the kings of Judah had ordained to offer sacrifices ᵛ on the pagan altars in the cities of Judah and in places near Jerusalem— all the priests who offered sacrifices to Baal, to the sun, the moon, the planets, and the stars. ⁶ He removed from the Temple the symbol of the goddess Asherah, took it out of the city to the valley of the Kidron, burnt it, pounded its ashes to dust, and scattered it over the public burial-ground. ⁷ He destroyed the living-quarters in the Temple occupied by the temple prostitutes. ʷ (It was there that women wove robes used in the worship of Asherah.) ⁸ He brought to Jerusalem the priests who were in the cities of Judah, and throughout the whole country he desecrated the altars where they had

ᵛ *Some ancient translations* to offer sacrifices; *Hebrew* and he offered sacrifices.
ʷ TEMPLE PROSTITUTES: *Men and women who practised prostitution in the worship of fertility gods.*
23.4-6: 2 Kgs 21.3; 2 Chr 33.3

offered sacrifices. He also tore down the altars dedicated to the goat-demons near the gate built by Joshua, the city governor, which was to the left of the main gate as one enters the city. ⁹Those priests were not allowed to serve in the Temple, but they could eat the unleavened bread provided for their fellow-priests.

10 King Josiah also desecrated Topheth, the pagan place of worship in the Valley of Hinnom, so that no one could sacrifice his son or daughter as a burnt-offering to the god Molech. ¹¹He also removed the horses that the kings of Judah had dedicated to the worship of the sun, and he burnt the chariots used in this worship. (These were kept in the temple courtyard, near the gate and not far from the living-quarters of Nathan Melech, a high official.) ¹²The altars which the kings of Judah had built on the palace roof above King Ahaz' quarters, King Josiah tore down, along with the altars put up by King Manasseh in the two courtyards of the Temple; he smashed the altars to bits ˣ and threw them into the valley of the Kidron. ¹³Josiah desecrated the altars that King Solomon had built east of Jerusalem, south of the Mount of Olives, ʸ for the worship of disgusting idols—Astarte the goddess of Sidon, Chemosh the god of Moab, and Molech the god of Ammon. ¹⁴King Josiah broke the stone pillars to pieces, cut down the symbols of the goddess Asherah, and the ground where they had stood he covered with human bones.

15 Josiah also tore down the place of worship in Bethel which had been built by King Jeroboam son of Nebat, who led Israel into sin. Josiah pulled down the altar, broke its stones into pieces, ᶻ and pounded them to dust; he also burnt the image of Asherah. ¹⁶Then Josiah looked round and saw some tombs there on the hill; he had the bones taken out of them and burnt on the altar. In this way he desecrated the altar, doing what the prophet had predicted long before during the festival as King Jeroboam was standing by the altar. King Josiah looked round and saw the tomb of the prophet ᵃ who had made this prediction. ¹⁷"Whose tomb is that?" he asked.

The people of Bethel answered, "It is

the tomb of the prophet who came from Judah and predicted these things that you have done to this altar."

18 "Leave it as it is," Josiah ordered. "His bones are not to be moved."

So his bones were not moved, neither were those of the prophet who had come from Samaria.

19 In every city of Israel King Josiah tore down all the pagan places of worship which had been built by the kings of Israel, who thereby aroused the LORD's anger. He did to all those altars what he had done in Bethel. ²⁰He killed all the pagan priests on the altars where they served, and he burnt human bones on every altar. Then he returned to Jerusalem.

Josiah Celebrates the Passover
(2 Chr 35.1–19)

21 King Josiah ordered the people to celebrate the Passover in honour of the LORD their God, as written in the book of the covenant. ²²No Passover like this one had ever been celebrated by any of the kings of Israel or of Judah, since the time when judges ruled the nation. ²³Now at last, in the eighteenth year of the reign of Josiah, the Passover was celebrated in Jerusalem.

Other Changes Made by Josiah

24 In order to enforce the laws written in the book that the High Priest Hilkiah had found in the Temple, King Josiah removed from Jerusalem and the rest of Judah all the mediums and fortune-tellers, and all the household gods, idols, and all other pagan objects of worship. ²⁵There had never been a king like him before, who served the LORD with all his heart, mind, and strength, obeying all the Law of Moses; nor has there been a king like him since.

26 But the LORD's fierce anger had been aroused against Judah by what King Manasseh had done, and even now it did not die down. ²⁷The LORD said, "I will do to Judah what I have done to Israel: I will banish the people of Judah from my sight, and I will reject Jerusalem, the city I chose, and the Temple, the place I said was where I should be worshipped."

ˣ Probable text smashed...to bits; Hebrew unclear.
ʸ MOUNT OF OLIVES: Hebrew here refers to it as "Mount of Destruction" or "Mount of Sin."
ᶻ One ancient translation broke its stones into pieces; Hebrew burnt the altar.
ᵃ One ancient translation during the festival...the prophet; Hebrew does not have these words.
23.10: Lev 18.21; Jer 7.31, 19.1–6, 32.35   **23.12:** 2 Kgs 21.5; 2 Chr 33.5   **23.13:** 1 Kgs 11.7
23.15: 1 Kgs 12.33   **23.16:** 1 Kgs 13.2   **23.17:** 1 Kgs 13.30–32

There had never been a king like him before (23.25)

The End of Josiah's Reign
(2 Chr 35.20—36.1)

28 Everything else that King Josiah did is recorded in *The History of the Kings of Judah*. 29 While Josiah was king, King Neco of Egypt led an army to the River Euphrates to help the emperor of Assyria. King Josiah tried to stop the Egyptian army at Megiddo and was killed in battle. 30 His officials placed his body in a chariot and took it back to Jerusalem, where he was buried in the royal tombs.

The people of Judah chose Josiah's son Joahaz and anointed him king.

King Joahaz of Judah
(2 Chr 36.2-4)

31 Joahaz was twenty-three years old when he became king of Judah, and he ruled in Jerusalem for three months. His mother was Hamutal, the daughter of Jeremiah from the city of Libnah. 32 Following the example of his ancestors, he sinned against the LORD. 33 His reign ended when King Neco of Egypt took him prisoner in Riblah, in the land of Hamath, and made Judah pay 3,400 kilogrammes of silver and thirty-four kilogrammes of gold as tribute. 34 King Neco made Josiah's son Eliakim king of Judah as successor to Josiah, and changed his name to Jehoiakim. Joahaz was taken to Egypt by King Neco, and there he died.

King Jehoiakim of Judah
(2 Chr 36.5-8)

35 King Jehoiakim collected a tax from the people in proportion to their wealth, in order to raise the amount needed to pay the tribute demanded by the king of Egypt.

36 Jehoiakim was twenty-five years old when he became king of Judah, and he ruled in Jerusalem for eleven years. His mother was Zebidah, the daughter of Pedaiah from the town of Rumah. 37 Following the example of his ancestors, Jehoiakim sinned against the LORD.

24 While Jehoiakim was king, King Nebuchadnezzar of Babylonia invaded Judah, and for three years Jehoiakim was forced to submit to his rule; then he rebelled. 2 The LORD sent armed bands of Babylonians, Syrians, Moabites, and Ammonites against Jehoiakim to destroy Judah, as the LORD had said through his servants the prophets that he would do. 3 This happened at the LORD's command, in order to banish the people of Judah from his sight because of all the sins that King Manasseh had committed, 4 and especially because of all the innocent people he had killed. The LORD could not forgive Manasseh for that.

5 Everything else that Jehoiakim did is recorded in *The History of the Kings of Judah*. 6 Jehoiakim died, and his son Jehoiachin succeeded him as king.

23.34: Jer 22.11-12   **23.36:** Jer 22.18-19, 26.1-6, 35.1-19   **24.1:** Jer 25.1-38; Dan 1.1-2

7 The king of Egypt and his army never marched out of Egypt again, because the king of Babylonia now controlled all the territory that had belonged to Egypt, from the River Euphrates to the northern border of Egypt.

King Jehoiachin of Judah
(2 Chr 36.9–10)

8 Jehoiachin was eighteen years old when he became king of Judah, and he ruled in Jerusalem for three months. His mother was Nehushta, the daughter of Elnathan from Jerusalem. 9 Following the example of his father, Jehoiachin sinned against the LORD.

10 It was during his reign that the Babylonian army, commanded by King Nebuchadnezzar's officers, marched against Jerusalem and besieged it. 11 During the siege Nebuchadnezzar himself came to Jerusalem, 12 and King Jehoiachin, along with his mother, his sons, his officers, and the palace officials, surrendered to the Babylonians. In the eighth year of Nebuchadnezzar's reign he took Jehoiachin prisoner 13 and carried off to Babylon all the treasures in the Temple and the palace. As the LORD had foretold, Nebuchadnezzar broke up all the gold utensils which King Solomon had made for use in the Temple. 14 Nebuchadnezzar carried away as prisoners the people of Jerusalem, all the royal princes, and all the leading men, ten thousand in all. He also deported all the skilled workmen, including the blacksmiths, leaving only the poorest of the people behind in Judah.

15 Nebuchadnezzar took Jehoiachin to Babylon as a prisoner, together with Jehoiachin's mother, his wives, his officials, and the leading men of Judah. 16 Nebuchadnezzar deported all the important men to Babylonia, seven thousand in all, and one thousand skilled workers, including the blacksmiths, all of them able-bodied men fit for military duty.

17 Nebuchadnezzar made Jehoiachin's uncle Mattaniah king of Judah and changed his name to Zedekiah.

King Zedekiah of Judah
(2 Chr 36.11–12; Jer 52.1–3a)

18 Zedekiah was twenty-one years old when he became king of Judah, and he ruled in Jerusalem for eleven years. His mother was Hamutal, the daughter of Jeremiah from the city of Libnah. 19 King Zedekiah sinned against the LORD, just as King Jehoiakim had done. 20 The LORD became so angry with the people of Jerusalem and Judah that he banished them from his sight.

The Fall of Jerusalem
(2 Chr 36.13–21; Jer 52.3b–11)

25 Zedekiah rebelled against King Nebuchadnezzar of Babylonia, so Nebuchadnezzar came with all his army and attacked Jerusalem on the tenth day of the tenth month of the ninth year of Zedekiah's reign. They set up camp outside the city, built siege walls round it, 2 and kept it under siege until Zedekiah's eleventh year. 3 On the ninth day of the fourth month b of that same year, when the famine was so bad that the people had nothing left to eat, 4 the city walls were broken through. Although the Babylonians were surrounding the city, all the soldiers escaped during the night. They left by way of the royal garden, went through the gateway connecting the two walls, and fled in the direction of the Jordan Valley. 5 But the Babylonian army pursued King Zedekiah, captured him in the plains near Jericho, and all his soldiers deserted him. 6 Zedekiah was taken to King Nebuchadnezzar, who was in the city of Riblah, and there Nebuchadnezzar passed sentence on him. 7 While Zedekiah was looking on, his sons were put to death; then Nebuchadnezzar had Zedekiah's eyes put out, placed him in chains, and took him to Babylon.

The Destruction of the Temple
(Jer 52.12–23)

8 On the seventh day of the fifth month of the nineteenth year of King Nebuchadnezzar of Babylonia, Nebuzaradan, adviser to the king and commander of his army, entered Jerusalem. 9 He burnt down the Temple, the palace, and the houses of all the important people in Jerusalem, 10 and his soldiers tore down the city walls. 11 Then Nebuzaradan took away to Babylonia the people who were left in the city, the remaining skilled workmen, c and those who had deserted to

---

b Probable text (see Jer. 52.6) the fourth month; Hebrew the month.
c Probable text (see Jer. 52.15) skilled workmen; Hebrew crowd.
24.12: Jer 22.24–30, 24.1–10, 29.1–2   **24.15:** Ezek 17.12   **24.17:** Jer 37.1; Ezek 17.13
24.18: Jer 27.1–22, 28.1–17   **24.20:** Ezek 17.15   **25.1:** Jer 21.1–10, 34.1–5; Ezek 24.2
25.4: Ezek 33.21   **25.7:** Ezek 12.13

So the people of Judah were carried away from their land into exile (25.21)

the Babylonians. 12 But he left in Judah some of the poorest people, who owned no property, and put them to work in the vineyards and fields.

13 The Babylonians broke in pieces the bronze columns and the carts that were in the Temple, together with the large bronze tank, and they took all the bronze to Babylon. 14 They also took away the shovels and the ash containers used in cleaning the altar, the tools used in tending the lamps, the bowls used for catching the blood from the sacrifices, the bowls used for burning incense, and all the other bronze articles used in the temple service. 15 They took away everything that was made of gold or silver, including the small bowls and the pans used for carrying live coals. 16 The bronze objects that King Solomon had made for the Temple—the two columns, the carts, and the large tank—were too heavy to weigh. 17 The two columns were identical: each one was eight metres high, with a bronze capital on top, 1.3 metres high. All round each capital was a bronze grating decorated with pomegranates made of bronze.

The People of Judah Are Taken to Babylonia
(Jer 52.24–27)

18 In addition, Nebuzaradan, the commanding officer, took away as prisoners Seraiah the High Priest, Zephaniah the

priest next in rank, and the three other important temple officials. 19 From the city he took the officer who had been in command of the troops, five of the king's personal advisers who were still in the city, the commander's assistant, who was in charge of military records, and sixty other important men. 20 Nebuzaradan took them to the king of Babylonia, who was in the city of Riblah 21 in the territory of Hamath. There the king had them beaten and put to death.

So the people of Judah were carried away from their land into exile.

Gedaliah, Governor of Judah
(Jer 40.7-9; 41.1-3)

22 King Nebuchadnezzar of Babylonia made Gedaliah, the son of Ahikam and grandson of Shaphan, governor of Judah, and placed him in charge of all those who had not been taken away to Babylonia. 23 When the Judaean officers and soldiers who had not surrendered heard about this, they joined Gedaliah at Mizpah. These officers were Ishmael son of Nethaniah, Johanan son of Kareah, Seraiah son of Tanhumeth, from the town of Netophah, and Jezaniah from Maacah. 24 Gedaliah said to them, "I give you my word that there is no need for you to be afraid of the Babylonian officials. Settle in this land, serve the king of Babylonia, and all will go well with you."

25 But in the seventh month of that

25.13: 1 Kgs 7.15-26; 2 Chr 3.15-17   **25.14:** 1 Kgs 7.45; 2 Chr 4.16

year, Ishmael, the son of Nethaniah and grandson of Elishama, a member of the royal family, went to Mizpah with ten men, attacked Gedaliah and killed him. He also killed the Israelites and Babylonians who were there with him. 26 Then all the Israelites, rich and poor alike, together with the army officers, left and went to Egypt, because they were afraid of the Babylonians.

Jehoiachin Is Released from Prison
(Jer 52.31-34)

27 In the year that Evilmerodach

25.26: Jer 43.5-7

became king of Babylonia, he showed kindness to King Jehoiachin of Judah by releasing him from prison. This happened on the twenty-seventh day of the twelfth month of the thirty-seventh year after Jehoiachin had been taken away as prisoner. 28 Evilmerodach treated him kindly, and gave him a position of greater honour than he gave the other kings who were exiles with him in Babylonia. 29 So Jehoiachin was permitted to change from his prison clothes and to dine at the king's table for the rest of his life. 30 Each day, for as long as he lived, he was given a regular allowance for his needs.

THE FIRST BOOK OF
CHRONICLES

INTRODUCTION

The books of *Chronicles* are largely a retelling of events recorded in the books of *Samuel* and *Kings,* but from a different point of view. Two main purposes govern the account of the history of the Israelite monarchy in the books of *Chronicles:*

1. To show that in spite of the disasters that had fallen upon the kingdoms of Israel and Judah, God was still keeping his promises to the nation and was working out his plan for his people through those who were living in Judah. As a basis for this assurance, the writer looked to the great achievements of David and Solomon, to the reforms of Jehoshaphat, Hezekiah, and Josiah, and to the people who remained faithful to God.

2. To describe the origin of the worship of God in the Temple at Jerusalem, and especially the organization of the priests and Levites, by which the worship was carried out. David is presented as the real founder of the Temple and its ritual, even though it is Solomon who builds the Temple.

Outline of Contents

Genealogies and lists   1.1—9.44
The death of Saul   10.1-14
The reign of David   11.1—29.30
   a. Troubles and achievements   11.1—22.1
   b. Preparations for building the Temple   22.2—29.30

From Adam to Abraham
(Gen 5.1-32; 10.1-32; 11.10-26)

1 Adam was the father of Seth, Seth was the father of Enosh, Enosh the father of Kenan, 2 Kenan the father of Mahalalel, Mahalalel the father of Jared. 3 Jared was the father of Enoch, who was the father of Methuselah; Methuselah was the father of Lamech, 4 who was the father of Noah. Noah had three sons: Shem, Ham, and Japheth.

5 The sons of Japheth—Gomer, Magog, Madai, Javan, Tubal, Meshech, and Tiras—were the ancestors of the peoples who bear their names. 6 The descendants of Gomer were the people of Ashkenaz, Riphath, and Togarmah. 7 The descendants of Javan were the people of Elishah, Spain, Cyprus, and Rhodes.

8 The sons of Ham—Cush, Egypt, Libya, and Canaan—were the ancestors of the peoples who bear their names. 9 The descendants of Cush were the people of Seba, Havilah, Sabtah, Raamah, and Sabteca. The descendants of Raamah were the people of Sheba and Dedan. 10 (Cush had a son named Nimrod, who became the world's first great conqueror.) 11 The descendants of Egypt were the people of Lydia, Anam, Lehab, Naphtuh, 12 Pathrus, Casluh, and of Crete (from whom the Philistines were descended). 13 Canaan's sons—Sidon, the eldest, and Heth—were the ancestors of the peoples who bear their names. 14 Canaan was also the ancestor of the Jebusites, the Amorites, Girgashites, 15 Hivites, Arkites, Sinites, 16 Arvadites, Zemarites, and Hamathites.

17 Shem's sons—Elam, Asshur, Arpachshad, Lud, Aram, Uz, Hul, Gether, and Meshek—were the ancestors of the peoples who bear their names. 18 Arpachshad was the father of Shelah, who was the father of Eber. 19 Eber had two sons; one was named Peleg,[a] because during his time the people of the world were divided, and the other was named Joktan. 20 The descendants of Joktan were the people of Almodad, Sheleph, Hazarmaveth, Jerah, 21 Hadoram, Uzal, Diklah, 22 Ebal, Abimael, Sheba, 23 Ophir, Havilah, and Jobab.

24 The family line from Shem to Abram is as follows: Shem, Arpachshad, Shelah, 25 Eber, Peleg, Reu, 26 Serug, Nahor, Terah, 27 and Abram (also known as Abraham).

The Descendants of Ishmael
(Gen 25.12-16)

28 Abraham had two sons, Isaac and Ishmael. 29 The sons of Ishmael became the heads of twelve tribes: Nebaioth (from the name of Ishmael's eldest son), Kedar, Adbeel, Mibsam, 30 Mishma, Dumah, Massa, Hadad, Tema, 31 Jetur, Naphish, and Kedemah.

32 Abraham had a concubine named Keturah, who bore him six sons: Zimran, Jokshan, Medan, Midian, Ishbak, and Shuah. Jokshan had two sons: Sheba and Dedan. 33 Midian had five sons: Ephah, Epher, Hanoch, Abida, and Eldaah.

The Descendants of Esau
(Gen 36.1-19)

34 Abraham's son Isaac had two sons, Esau and Jacob. 35 Esau's sons were Eliphaz, Reuel, Jeush, Jalam, and Korah. 36 Eliphaz became the ancestor of the following tribes: Teman, Omar, Zephi, Gatam, Kenaz, Timna, and Amalek. 37 And Reuel became the ancestor of the tribes of Nahath, Zerah, Shammah, and Mizzah.

The Original Inhabitants of Edom
(Gen 36.20-30)

38-42 The original inhabitants of Edom were descended from the following sons of Seir:

Lotan, who was the ancestor of the clans of Hori and Homam. (Lotan had a sister named Timna.)

Shobal, who was the ancestor of the clans of Alvan, Manahath, Ebal, Shephi, and Onam.

Zibeon, who had two sons, Aiah and Anah. Anah was the father of Dishon, and Dishon was the ancestor of the clans of Hamran, Eshban, Ithran, and Cheran.

Ezer, who was the ancestor of the clans of Bilhan, Zaavan, and Jaakan.

Dishan, who was the ancestor of the clans of Uz and Aran.

The Kings of Edom
(Gen 36.31-43)

43-50 The following kings ruled the land of Edom one after the other, in the time before there were any kings in Israel:

Bela son of Beor from Dinhabah

Johab son of Zerah from Bozrah

Husham from the region of Teman

Hadad son of Bedad from Avith (he defeated the Midianites in a battle in the country of Moab)

[a] PELEG: This name sounds like the Hebrew for "divide."

Samlah from Masrekah
Shaul from Rehoboth-on-the-River
Baal Hanan son of Achbor
Hadad from Pau (his wife was
    Mehetabel, the daughter of Matred
    and granddaughter of Mezahab)
51 The people of Edom were divided
into the following tribes: Timna, Alvah,
Jetheth, 52 Oholibamah, Elah, Pinon,
53 Kenaz, Teman, Mibzar, 54 Magdiel, and
Iram.

The Descendants of Judah

2 Jacob had twelve sons: Reuben, Simeon, Levi, Judah, Issachar, Zebulun, 2 Dan, Joseph, Benjamin, Naphtali, Gad, and Asher.

3 Judah had five sons in all. By his wife Bathshua, a Canaanite, he had three sons: Er, Onan, and Shelah. His eldest son, Er, was so evil that the LORD killed him. 4 By his daughter-in-law Tamar, Judah had two more sons, Perez and Zerah.

5 Perez had two sons, Hezron and Hamul. 6 His brother Zerah had five sons: Zimri, Ethan, Heman, Calcol, and Darda. 7 Achan b son of Carmi, one of Zerah's descendants, brought disaster on the people of Israel by keeping loot that had been devoted to God.

8 Ethan had one son, Azariah.

The Family Tree of King David

9 Hezron had three sons: Jerahmeel, Ram, and Caleb.

10 The family line from Ram to Jesse is as follows: Ram, Amminadab, Nahshon (a prominent man of the tribe of Judah), 11 Salmon, Boaz, 12 Obed, and Jesse.

13 Jesse had seven sons. In order of age they were: Eliab, Abinadab, Shammah, 14 Nethanel, Raddai, 15 Ozem, and David. 16 He also had two daughters, Zeruiah and Abigail.

Jesse's daughter Zeruiah had three sons: Abishai, Joab, and Asahel. 17 His other daughter Abigail married Jether, a descendant of Ishmael, and they had a son named Amasa.

The Descendants of Hezron

18 Hezron's son Caleb married Azubah and had a daughter named Jerioth. She had c three sons: Jesher, Shobab, and Ardon. 19 After the death of Azubah, Caleb

married Ephrath, and they had a son named Hur. 20 Hur's son was Uri, and his grandson was Bezalel.

21 When Hezron was sixty years old, he married Machir's daughter, the sister of Gilead. They had a son named Segub, 22 and Segub had a son named Jair. Jair ruled d twenty-three cities in the territory of Gilead. 23 But the kingdoms of Geshur and Aram conquered sixty towns there, including the villages of Jair and Kenath, and the towns near by. All the people who lived there were descendants of Machir, the father of Gilead. 24 After Hezron died, his son Caleb married Ephrath, his father's widow. e They had a son named Ashhur, who founded the town of Tekoa.

The Descendants of Jerahmeel

25 Jerahmeel, the eldest son of Hezron, had five sons: Ram, the eldest, Bunah, Oren, Ozem, and Ahijah. 26-27 Ram had three sons: Maaz, Jamin, and Eker. Jerahmeel had another wife, a woman named Atarah, and they had a son, Onam. 28 Onam had two sons, Shammai and Jada, and Shammai also had two sons, Nadab and Abishur.

29 Abishur married a woman named Abihail, and they had two sons, Ahban and Molid. 30 Abishur's brother Nadab had two sons, Seled and Appaim, but Seled died without having any sons. 31 Appaim was the father of Ishi, Ishi was the father of Sheshan, and Sheshan the father of Ahlai.

32 Jada, the brother of Shammai, had two sons, Jether and Jonathan, but Jether died without having any sons. 33 Jonathan had two sons, Peleth and Zaza. All these were descendants of Jerahmeel.

34 Sheshan had no sons, only daughters. He had an Egyptian servant named Jarha, 35 to whom he gave one of his daughters in marriage. They had a son named Attai. 36 The family line from Attai to Elishama is as follows: Attai, Nathan, Zabad, 37 Ephlal, Obed, 38 Jehu, Azariah, 39 Helez, Eleasah, 40 Sismai, Shallum, 41 Jekamiah, and Elishama.

Other Descendants of Caleb

42 The eldest son of Caleb, Jerahmeel's brother, was named Mesha. Mesha was

b ACHAN: This is his name in Josh 7.1. The Hebrew text here calls him "Achar," which means "disaster."   c Some ancient translations had a daughter... She had; Hebrew unclear.
d ruled; or owned.   e Some ancient translations his son...widow; Hebrew unclear.
2.7: Josh 7.1

the father of Ziph, who was the father of Mareshah, who was the father of Hebron. *f* 43 Hebron had four sons: Korah, Tappuah, Rekem, and Shema. 44 Shema was the father of Raham and the grandfather of Jorkeam. Rekem, Shema's brother, was the father of Shammai, 45 who was the father of Maon, who was the father of Bethzur.

46 Caleb had a concubine named Ephah, and by her he had three more sons: Haran, Moza, and Gazez. Haran also had a son named Gazez.

47 (A man named Jahdai had six sons: Regem, Jotham, Geshan, Pelet, Ephah, and Shaaph.)

48 Caleb had another concubine, Maacah, who bore him two sons, Sheber and Tirhanah. 49 Later she had two more sons: Shaaph, who founded the town of Madmannah; and Shevah, who founded the towns of Machbenah and Gibea.

In addition, Caleb had a daughter named Achsah.

50 The following are also descendants of Caleb.

Hur was the eldest son of Caleb and his wife Ephrath. Hur's son Shobal founded Kiriath Jearim, 51 his second son Salma founded Bethlehem, and his third son Hareph founded Bethgader.

52 Shobal, the founder of Kiriath Jearim, was the ancestor of the people of Haroeh, of half the inhabitants of Menuhoth, 53 and of the following clans that lived in Kiriath Jearim: the Ithrites, Puthites, Shumathites, and Mishraites. (The people of the cities of Zorah and Eshtaol were members of these clans.)

54 Salma, the founder of Bethlehem, was the ancestor of the people of Netophath, of Atroth Beth Joab, and of the Zorites, who were one of the two clans in Manahath.

55 (The following clans of experts in writing and copying documents lived in the town of Jabez: the Tirathites, Shimeathites, and Sucathites. They were Kenites who had intermarried with the Rechabites.)

King David's Children

3 1-3 The following, in order of age, are David's sons who were born while he was in Hebron:

Amnon, whose mother was Ahinoam from Jezreel

Daniel, whose mother was Abigail from Carmel

Absalom, whose mother was Maacah, daughter of King Talmai of Geshur

Adonijah, whose mother was Haggith

Shephatiah, whose mother was Abital

Ithream, whose mother was Eglah

4 All six were born in Hebron during the seven and a half years that David ruled there.

In Jerusalem he ruled as king for thirty-three years, 5 and many sons were born to him there.

His wife Bathsheba, daughter of Ammiel, bore him four sons: Shimea, Shobab, Nathan, and Solomon.

6 He had nine other sons: Ibhar, Elishua, Elpelet, 7 Nogah, Nepheg, Japhia, 8 Elishama, Eliada, and Eliphelet. 9 In addition to all these sons, David had sons by his concubines. He also had a daughter, Tamar.

The Descendants of King Solomon

10 This is the line of King Solomon's descendants from father to son: Solomon, Rehoboam, Abijah, Asa, Jehoshaphat, 11 Jehoram, Ahaziah, Joash, 12 Amaziah, Uzziah, Jotham, 13 Ahaz, Hezekiah, Manasseh, 14 Amon, and Josiah. 15 Josiah had four sons: Johanan, Jehoiakim, Zedekiah, and Joahaz. 16 Jehoiakim had two sons: Jehoiachin and Zedekiah.

The Descendants of King Jehoiachin

17 These are the descendants of King Jehoiachin, who was taken prisoner by the Babylonians. Jehoiachin had seven sons: Shealtiel, 18 Malchiram, Pedaiah, Shenazzar, Jekamiah, Hoshama, and Nedabiah. 19 Pedaiah had two sons, Zerubbabel and Shimei. Zerubbabel was the father of two sons, Meshullam and Hananiah, and one daughter, Shelomith. 20 He had five other sons: Hashubah, Ohel, Berechiah, Hasadiah, and Jushab Hesed.

21 Hananiah had two sons, Pelatiah and Jeshaiah. Jeshaiah was the father of Rephaiah, who was the father of Arnan, the father of Obadiah, the father of Shecaniah. *g* 22 Shecaniah had one son, Shemaiah, and five grandsons: Hattush, Igal, Bariah, Neariah, and Shaphat. 23 Neariah had three sons: Elioenai, Hizkiah, and Azrikam. 24 Elioenai had seven sons: Hodaviah, Eliashib, Pelaiah, Akkub, Johanan, Delaiah, and Anani.

---

f Probable text father of Mareshah...Hebron; *Hebrew unclear.*
g Verse 21 in Hebrew is unclear.   **3.4:** 2 Sam 5.4–5; 1 Kgs 2.11; 1 Chr 29.27   **3.5:** 2 Sam 11.3

The Descendants of Judah

4 These are some of the descendants of Judah: Perez, Hezron, Carmi, Hur, and Shobal. ² Shobal was the father of Reaiah, who was the father of Jahath, the father of Ahumai and Lahad, the ancestors of the people who lived in Zorah.

3-4 Hur was the eldest son of his father Caleb's wife Ephrath, and his descendants founded the city of Bethlehem. Hur had three sons: Etam, Penuel, and Ezer. Etam had three sons:*h* Jezreel, Ishma, and Idbash, and one daughter, Hazzelelponi. Penuel founded the city of Gedor, and Ezer founded Hushah.

5 Ashhur, who founded the town of Tekoa, had two wives, Helah and Naarah. ⁶ He and Naarah had four sons: Ahuzzam, Hepher, Temeni, and Haahashtari. ⁷ Ashhur and Helah had three sons: Zereth, Izhar, and Ethnan.

8 Koz was the father of Anub and Zobebah, and the ancestor of the clans descended from Aharhel son of Harum.

9 There was a man named Jabez, who was the most respected member of his family. His mother had given him the name Jabez,*i* because his birth had been very painful. ¹⁰ But Jabez prayed to the God of Israel, "Bless me, God, and give me much land. Be with me and keep me from anything evil that might cause me pain." And God gave him what he prayed for.

Other Family Lists

11 Caleb, the brother of Shuhah, had a son, Mehir. Mehir was the father of Eshton, ¹² who had three sons: Bethrapha, Paseah, and Tehinnah. Tehinnah was the founder of the city of Nahash. The descendants of these men lived in Recah.

13 Kenaz had two sons, Othniel and Seraiah. Othniel also had two sons, Hathath and Meonothai.*j* ¹⁴ Meonothai was the father of Ophrah.

Seraiah was the father of Joab, the founder of the Valley of Craftsmen, where all the people were skilled workmen.

15 Caleb son of Jephunneh had three sons: Iru, Elah, and Naam. And Elah was the father of Kenaz.

16 Jehallelel had four sons: Ziph, Ziphah, Tiria, and Asarel.

17-18 Ezrah had four sons: Jether, Mered, Epher, and Jalon. Mered married Bithiah, a daughter of the king of Egypt, and they had a daughter, Miriam, and two sons, Shammai and Ishbah. Ishbah founded the town of Eshtemoa. Mered also married a woman from the tribe of Judah, and they had three sons: Jered, who founded the town of Gedor; Heber, founder of the town of Soco; and Jekuthiel, founder of the town of Zanoah.

19 Hodiah married the sister of Naham. Their descendants founded the clan of Garm, which lived in the town of Keilah, and the clan of Maacath, which lived in the town of Eshtemoa.*k*

20 Shimon had four sons: Amnon, Rinnah, Benhanan, and Tilon.

Ishi had two sons: Zoheth and Benzoheth.

The Descendants of Shelah

21 Shelah was one of Judah's sons. His descendants included Er, who founded the town of Lecah; Laadah, founder of the town of Mareshah; the clan of linen-weavers, who lived in the town of Beth Ashbea; ²² Jokim and the people who lived in the town of Cozeba; and Joash and Saraph, who married Moabite women and then settled in Bethlehem.*l* (These traditions are very old.) ²³ They were potters in the service of the king and lived in the towns of Netaim and Gederah.

The Descendants of Simeon

24 Simeon had five sons: Nemuel, Jamin, Jarib, Zerah, and Shaul. ²⁵ Shaul's son was Shallum, his grandson was Mibsam, and his great-grandson was Mishma. ²⁶ Then from Mishma the line descended through Hamuel, Zaccur, and Shimei. ²⁷ Shimei had sixteen sons and six daughters, but his relatives had fewer children, and the tribe of Simeon did not grow as much as the tribe of Judah did.

28 Down to the time of King David the descendants of Simeon lived in the following towns: Beersheba, Moladah, Hazarshual, ²⁹ Bilhah, Ezem, Tolad, ³⁰ Bethuel, Hormah, Ziklag, ³¹ Beth Marcaboth, Hazarsusim, Bethbiri, and Shaaraim. ³² They also lived in five other places: Etam, Ain, Rimmon, Tochen, and Ashan, ³³ and the surrounding villages, as far

---

h Some ancient translations sons; Hebrew fathers.
i JABEZ: This name sounds like the Hebrew for "pain."
j Some ancient translations Meonothai; Hebrew does not have this name.
k Verse 19 in Hebrew is unclear.   l Probable text settled in Bethlehem; Hebrew unclear.
4.28-33: Josh 19.2-8

Potters in the service of the king (4.23)

south-west as the town of Baalath. These are the records which they kept of their families and of the places where they lived.

34-38 The following men were the heads of their clans:

Meshobab, Jamlech, Joshah son of Amaziah, Joel,

Jehu (the son of Joshibiah, the son of Seraiah, the son of Asiel),

Elioenai, Jaakobah, Jeshohaiah, Asaiah, Adiel, Jesimiel, Benaiah,

Ziza (the son of Shiphi, the son of Allon, a descendant of Jedaiah, Shimri, and Shemaiah).

Because their families continued to grow, [39] they spread out westwards almost to Gerar[m] and pastured their sheep on the eastern side of the valley in which that city is located. [40] They found plenty of fertile pasture lands there in a stretch of open country that was quiet and peaceful. The people who had lived there before were Hamites.

41 In the time of King Hezekiah of Judah, the men named above went to Gerar and destroyed the tents and huts of the people who lived there. [n] They drove the people out and settled there permanently because there was plenty of pasture for their sheep. [42] Five hundred other members of the tribe of Simeon went east to Edom. They were led by the sons of Ishi: Pelatiah, Neariah, Rephaiah, and Uzziel. [43] There they killed the surviving Amalekites, and they have lived there ever since.

The Descendants of Reuben

5 These are the descendants of Reuben, the eldest of Jacob's sons. (Because he had intercourse with one of his father's concubines, he lost the rights belonging to the first-born son, and those rights were given to Joseph. [2] It was the tribe of Judah, however, that became the strongest and provided a ruler for all the tribes.) [3] Reuben, the eldest of Jacob's sons, had four sons: Hanoch, Pallu, Hezron, and Carmi.

4-6 These are the descendants of Joel from generation to generation: Shemaiah, Gog, Shimei, Micah, Reaiah, Baal, and Beerah. The Assyrian emperor, Tiglath Pileser, captured Beerah, a leader of the tribe, and deported him.

7 The family records list the following clan leaders in the tribe of Reuben: Jeiel, Zechariah, [8] and Bela, the son of Azaz and grandson of Shema, of the clan of Joel. This clan lived in Aroer and in the territory from there north to Nebo and Baal Meon. [9] They had large herds in the land of Gilead, and so they occupied the land as far east as the desert that stretches all the way to the River Euphrates.

10 In the time of King Saul the tribe of Reuben attacked the Hagrites, killed them in battle, and occupied their land in the eastern part of Gilead.

The Descendants of Gad

11 The tribe of Gad lived to the north of Reuben in the land of Bashan as far

---

[m] *Some ancient translations* Gerar; *Hebrew* Gedor.
[n] the tents and huts...there; *or* the tents of the people who lived there, and the Meunites also.
5.1: Gen 35.22, 49.3-4   **5.2:** Gen 49.8-10   **5.6:** 2 Kgs 15.29

And pastured their sheep (4.39)

east as Salecah. [12] Joel was the founder of the leading clan, and Shapham of the second most important clan. Janai and Shaphat were founders of other clans in Bashan. [13] The other members of the tribe belonged to the following seven clans: Michael, Meshullam, Sheba, Jorai, Jacan, Zia, and Eber. [14] They were descendants of Abihail son of Huri, whose ancestors were traced back as follows: Abihail, Huri, Jaroah, Gilead, Michael, Jeshishai, Jahdo, Buz. [15] Ahi, the son of Abdiel and grandson of Guni, was head of these clans. [16] They lived in the territory of Bashan and Gilead, in the towns there and all over the pasture lands of Sharon. [17] (These records were compiled in the days of King Jotham of Judah and King Jeroboam II of Israel.)

The Armies of the Eastern Tribes

18 In the tribes of Reuben, Gad, and East Manasseh there were 44,760 soldiers, well-trained in the use of shields, swords, and bows. [19] They went to war against the Hagrite tribes of Jetur, Naphish, and Nodab. [20] They put their trust in God and prayed to him for help, and God answered their prayers and made them victorious over the Hagrites and their allies. [21] They captured from the enemy 50,000 camels, 250,000 sheep, and 2,000 donkeys, and took 100,000 prisoners of war. [22] They killed many of the enemy, because the

war was God's will. And they went on living in that territory until the exile. [o]

The People of East Manasseh

23 The people of East Manasseh settled in the territory of Bashan as far north as Baal Hermon, Senir, and Mount Hermon, and their population increased greatly. [24] The following were the heads of their clans: Epher, Ishi, Eliel, Azriel, Jeremiah, Hodaviah, and Jahdiel. They were all outstanding soldiers, well-known leaders of their clans.

The Eastern Tribes Are Deported

25 But the people were unfaithful to the God of their ancestors and deserted him to worship the gods of the nations whom God had driven out of the land. [26] So God made Emperor Pul of Assyria (also known as Tiglath Pileser) invade their country. He deported the tribes of Reuben, Gad, and East Manasseh and settled them permanently in Halah, Habor, and Hara, and by the River Gozan.

The Family Line of the High Priests

6 Levi had three sons: Gershon, Kohath, and Merari.

2 Kohath had four sons: Amram, Izhar, Hebron, and Uzziel.

3 Amram had two sons, Aaron and Moses, and one daughter, Miriam.

[o] THE EXILE: *About 733 B.C. the Assyrians conquered northern Israel and the Israelite territory east of the River Jordan and deported the people (see 2 Kgs 15.29).*
5.26: 2 Kgs 15.19,29, 17.6

Aaron had four sons: Nadab, Abihu, Eleazar, and Ithamar.

4 The descendants of Eleazar from generation to generation are as follows: Phinehas, Abishua, 5 Bukki, Uzzi, 6 Zerahiah, Meraioth, 7 Amariah, Ahitub, 8 Zadok, Ahimaaz, 9 Azariah, Johanan, 10 Azariah (the one who served in the Temple which King Solomon built in Jerusalem), 11 Amariah, Ahitub, 12 Zadok, Shallum, 13 Hilkiah, Azariah, 14 Seraiah, Jehozadak. 15 King Nebuchadnezzar deported Jehozadak along with the other people of Judah and Jerusalem whom the LORD sent into exile.

Other Descendants of Levi

16 Levi had three sons: Gershon, Kohath, and Merari. 17 Each of them also had sons. Gershon was the father of Libni and Shimei; 18 Kohath was the father of Amram, Izhar, Hebron, and Uzziel; 19 and Merari was the father of Mahli and Mushi.

20 These are the descendants of Gershon from generation to generation: Libni, Jahath, Zimmah, 21 Joah, Iddo, Zerah, Jeatherai.

22 These are the descendants of Kohath from generation to generation: Amminadab, Korah, Assir, 23 Elkanah, Ebiasaph, Assir, 24 Tahath, Uriel, Uzziah, Shaul.

25 Elkanah had two sons, Amasai and Ahimoth. 26 These are Ahimoth's descendants from generation to generation: Elkanah, Zophai, Nahath, 27 Eliab, Jeroham, Elkanah.

28 Samuel had two sons: Joel,p the elder, and Abijah, the younger.

29 These are the descendants of Merari from generation to generation: Mahli, Libni, Shimei, Uzzah, 30 Shimea, Haggiah, Asaiah.

The Temple Musicians

31 These are the men whom King David put in charge of the music at the place of worship in Jerusalem after the Covenant Box was moved there. 32 They took regular turns of duty at the Tent of the LORD's presence during the time before King Solomon built the Temple. 33 The family lines of those who held this office are as follows:

The clan of Kohath: Heman, the leader of the first choir, was the son of Joel. His family line went back to Jacob as follows: Heman, Joel, Samuel, 34 Elkanah, Jeroham, Eliel, Toah, 35 Zuph, Elkanah, Mahath, Amasai, 36 Elkanah, Joel, Azariah, Zephaniah, 37 Tahath, Assir, Ebiasaph, Korah, 38 Izhar, Kohath, Levi, Jacob.

39 Asaph was leader of the second choir. His family line went back to Levi as follows: Asaph, Berechiah, Shimea, 40 Michael, Baaseiah, Malchijah, 41 Ethni, Zerah, Adaiah, 42 Ethan, Zimmah, Shimei, 43 Jahath, Gershon, Levi.

44 Ethan of the clan of Merari was the leader of the third choir. His family line went back to Levi as follows: Ethan, Kishi, Abdi, Malluch, 45 Hashabiah, Amaziah, Hilkiah, 46 Amzi, Bani, Shemer, 47 Mahli, Mushi, Merari, Levi.

48 Their fellow-Levites were assigned all the other duties at the place of worship.

The Descendants of Aaron

49 Aaron and his descendants presented the offerings of incense and offered the sacrifices that were burnt on the altar. They were responsible for all the worship in the Most Holy Place and for the sacrifices by which God forgives Israel's sins. They did all this in accordance with the instructions given by Moses, God's servant. 50 This is the line of Aaron's descendants: Eleazar, Phinehas, Abishua, 51 Bukki, Uzzi, Zerahiah, 52 Meraioth, Amariah, Ahitub, 53 Zadok, Ahimaaz.

Where the Levites Lived

54 This is the territory assigned to the descendants of Aaron of the clan of Kohath. They received the first share of the land assigned to the Levites. 55 This included Hebron in the territory of Judah and the pasture lands round it. 56 The fields and villages, however, that belonged to the city were assigned to Caleb son of Jephunneh. 57-59 The following towns were assigned to Aaron's descendants: Hebron, a city of refuge,q Jattir, and the towns of Libnah, Eshtemoa, Hilen, Debir, Ashan, and Beth Shemesh, with their pasture lands. 60 In the territory of Benjamin they were assigned the following towns with their pasture lands: Geba, Alemeth, and Anathoth. This made a total of thirteen towns for all their families to live in. 61 Ten towns in the territory of West Manasseh were assigned by lot to the rest of the

p Some ancient translations (see also 1 Sam 8.2) Joel; Hebrew does not have this name.
q CITY OF REFUGE: If anyone accidentally killed someone, he could escape to one of these cities and be safe from revenge (see Josh 20.1-9).
6.16-19: Ex 6.16-19

clan of Kohath, family by family.

62 To the clan of Gershon, family by family, were assigned thirteen towns in the territories of Issachar, Asher, Naphtali, and East Manasseh in Bashan. 63 In the same way, twelve towns in the territories of Reuben, Gad, and Zebulun were assigned to the clan of Merari, family by family. 64 In this way the people of Israel assigned towns for the Levites to live in, together with the pasture lands round the towns. 65 (The towns in the territories of Judah, Simeon, and Benjamin, mentioned above, were also assigned by drawing lots.)

66 Some of the families of the clan of Kohath were assigned towns and pasture lands in the territory of Ephraim: 67 Shechem, the city of refuge in the hills of Ephraim, Gezer, 68 Jokmeam, Beth Horon, 69 Aijalon, and Gath Rimmon. 70 In the territory of West Manasseh they were assigned the towns of Aner and Bileam with the surrounding pasture lands.

71 The families of the clan of Gershon were assigned the following towns, with the surrounding pasture lands:

In the territory of East Manasseh: Golan in Bashan, and Ashtaroth.

72 In the territory of Issachar: Kedesh, Daberath, 73 Ramoth, and Anem.

74 In the territory of Asher: Mashal, Abdon, 75 Hukok, and Rehob.

76 In the territory of Naphtali: Kedesh in Galilee, Hammon, and Kiriathaim.

77 The remaining families of the clan of Merari were assigned the following towns with the surrounding pasture lands:

In the territory of Zebulun: Rimmono and Tabor.

78 In the territory of Reuben, east of the River Jordan beyond Jericho: Bezer on the plateau, Jahzah, 79 Kedemoth, and Mephaath.

80 In the territory of Gad: Ramoth in Gilead, Mahanaim, 81 Heshbon, and Jazer.

The Descendants of Issachar

7 Issachar had four sons: Tola, Puah, Jashub, and Shimron.

2 Tola had six sons: Uzzi, Rephaiah, Jeriel, Jahmai, Ibsam, and Shemuel. They were heads of families of the clan of Tola and were famous soldiers. At the time of King David their descendants numbered 22,600.

3 Uzzi had one son, Izrahiah. Izrahiah

and his four sons, Michael, Obadiah, Joel, and Isshiah, were all heads of families. 4 They had so many wives and children that their descendants were able to provide 36,000 men for military service.

5 The official records of all the families of the tribe of Issachar listed 87,000 men eligible for military service.

The Descendants of Benjamin and Dan

6 Benjamin had three sons: Bela, Becher, and Jediael.

7 Bela had five sons: Ezbon, Uzzi, Uzziel, Jerimoth, and Iri. They were heads of families in the clan and were all famous soldiers. Their descendants included 22,034 men eligible for military service.

8 Becher had nine sons: Zemirah, Joash, Eliezer, Eleoenai, Omri, Jeremoth, Abijah, Anathoth, and Alemeth. 9 The official record of their descendants by families listed 20,200 men eligible for military service.

10 Jediael had one son, Bilhan, and Bilhan had seven sons: Jeush, Benjamin, Ehud, Chenaanah, Zethan, Tarshish, and Ahishahar. 11 They were heads of families in the clan and were all famous soldiers. Their descendants included 17,200 men eligible for military service. 12 Shuppim and Huppim also belonged to this tribe.

Dan had one son, Hushim. r

The Descendants of Naphtali

13 Naphtali had four sons: Jahziel, Guni, Jezer, and Shallum. (They were descendants of Bilhah.) s

The Descendants of Manasseh

14 By his Aramean concubine, Manasseh had two sons, Asriel and Machir. Machir was the father of Gilead. 15 Machir found a wife for Huppim and one for Shuppim. His sister's name was Maacah. Machir's second son was Zelophehad, and he had only daughters.

16 Maacah, Machir's wife, gave birth to two sons, whom they named Peresh and Sheresh. Peresh had two sons, Ulam and Rakem, 17 and Ulam had a son named Bedan. These are all descendants of Gilead, the son of Machir and grandson of Manasseh.

18 Gilead's sister Hammolecheth had three sons: Ishod, Abiezer, and Mahlah. 19 (Shemida had four sons: Ahian, Shechem, Likhi, and Aniam.)

---

r Probable text Shuppim...Hushim (see Gen 46.23; Num 26.39,42); Hebrew And Shuppim and Huppim, sons of Ir; Hushim sons of Aher.
s BILHAH: A concubine of Jacob and the mother of his two sons Dan and Naphtali.

The Descendants of Ephraim

20 These are the descendants of Ephraim from generation to generation: Shuthelah, Bered, Tahath, Eleadah, Tahath, 21 Zabad, Shuthelah. Ephraim had two other sons besides Shuthelah: Ezer and Elead, who were killed when they tried to steal the livestock belonging to the native inhabitants of Gath. 22 Their father Ephraim mourned for them for many days, and his relatives came to comfort him. 23 Then he had intercourse with his wife again, and she became pregnant and had a son. They named him Beriah, *t* because of the trouble that had come to their family.

24 Ephraim had a daughter named Sheerah. She built the towns of Upper and Lower Beth Horon, and Uzzen Sheerah.

25 Ephraim also had a son named Rephah, whose descendants were as follows: Resheph, Telah, Tahan, 26 Ladan, Ammihud, Elishama, 27 Nun, Joshua.

28 The territory which they took and settled in included Bethel and the towns round it, as far east as Naaran and as far west as Gezer and the towns round it. It also included the cities of Shechem and Ayyah, and the towns round them.

29 The descendants of Manasseh controlled the cities of Beth Shan, Taanach, Megiddo, and Dor, and the towns round them.

All these are the places where the descendants of Joseph son of Jacob lived.

The Descendants of Asher

30 These are the descendants of Asher. He had four sons: Imnah, Ishvah, Ishvi, and Beriah; and one daughter, Serah.

31 Beriah had two sons, Heber and Malchiel. (Malchiel founded the city of Birzaith.)

32 Heber had three sons: Japhlet, Shomer, and Hotham; and one daughter, Shua.

33 Japhlet also had three sons: Pasach, Bimhal, and Ashvath.

34 His brother Shomer had three sons: Rohgah, Jehubbah, and Aram.

35 His brother Hotham *u* had four sons: Zophah, Imna, Shelesh, and Amal.

36 The descendants of Zophah were Suah, Harnepher, Shual, Beri, Imrah, 37 Bezer, Hod, Shamma, Shilshah, Ithran, and Beera.

38 The descendants of Jether were Jephunneh, Pispa, and Ara, 39 and the descendants of Ulla were Arah, Hanniel, and Rizia.

40 All these were descendants of Asher. They were heads of families, famous fighting men, outstanding leaders. Asher's descendants included 26,000 men eligible for military service.

The Descendants of Benjamin

8 Benjamin had five sons. In order of age they were Bela, Ashbel, Aharah, 2 Nohah, and Rapha.

3 The descendants of Bela were Addar, Gera, Abihud, 4 Abishua, Naaman, Ahoah, 5 Gera, Shephuphan, and Huram.

6–7 The descendants of Ehud were Naaman, Ahijah, and Gera. They were heads of families that lived in Geba, but which were forced out and went to live in Manahath. Gera, the father of Uzza and Ahihud, led them in this move.

8–9 Shaharaim divorced two wives, Hushim and Baara. Later, when he lived in the country of Moab, he married Hodesh and had seven sons: Jobab, Zibia, Mesha, Malcam, 10 Jeuz, Sachia, and Mirmah. His sons all became heads of families.

11 He also had two sons by Hushim: Abitub and Elpaal.

12 Elpaal had three sons: Eber, Misham, and Shemed. It was Shemed who built the cities of Ono and Lod and the surrounding villages.

The Benjaminites in Gath and Aijalon

13 Beriah and Shema were heads of families that settled in the city of Aijalon and drove out the people who lived in the city of Gath. 14 Beriah's descendants included Ahio, Shashak, Jeremoth, 15 Zebadiah, Arad, Eder, 16 Michael, Ishpah, and Joha.

The Benjaminites in Jerusalem

17 Elpaal's descendants included Zebadiah, Meshullam, Hizki, Heber, 18 Ishmerai, Izliah, and Jobab.

19 Shimei's descendants included Jakim, Zichri, Zabdi, 20 Elienai, Zillethai, Eliel, 21 Adaiah, Beraiah, and Shimrath.

22 Shashak's descendants included Ishpan, Eber, Eliel, 23 Abdon, Zichri, Hanan, 24 Hananiah, Elam, Anthothijah, 25 Iphdeiah, and Penuel.

26 Jeroham's descendants included

---

t BERIAH: *This name sounds like the Hebrew for "in trouble."*
u *Probable text (see verse 32)* Hotham; *Hebrew* Helem.

Shamsherai, Shehariah, Athaliah, 27 Jaareshiah, Elijah, and Zichri.

28 These were the ancestral heads of families and their principal descendants who lived in Jerusalem.

The Benjaminites in Gibeon and Jerusalem

29 Jeiel [v] founded the city of Gibeon and settled there. His wife was named Maacah, 30 and his eldest son, Abdon. His other sons were Zur, Kish, Baal, Ner, [w] Nadab, 31 Gedor, Ahio, Zecher, 32 and Mikloth, the father of Shimeah. Their descendants lived in Jerusalem near other families of their clan.

The Family of King Saul

33 Ner was the father of Kish, and Kish was the father of King Saul. Saul had four sons: Jonathan, Malchishua, Abinadab, and Eshbaal. [a] 34 Jonathan was the father of Meribbaal, [b] who was the father of Micah.

35 Micah had four sons: Pithon, Melech, Tarea, and Ahaz. 36 Ahaz was the father of Jehoaddah, who was the father of three sons: Alemeth, Azmaveth, and Zimri. Zimri was the father of Moza, 37 Moza the father of Binea, Binea of Raphah, Raphah of Eleasah, and Eleasah of Azel.

38 Azel had six sons: Azrikam, Bocheru, Ishmael, Sheariah, Obadiah, and Hanan. 39 Azel's brother Eshek had three sons: Ulam, Jeush, and Eliphelet.

40 Ulam's sons were outstanding soldiers and archers. He had a hundred and fifty sons and grandsons in all. All those named above were members of the tribe of Benjamin.

The People Who Returned from Captivity

9 All the people of Israel were listed according to their families, and this information was recorded in *The Book of the Kings of Israel.*

The people of Judah had been deported to Babylon as punishment for their sins. 2 The first to return to their property in the cities included Israelite laymen, priests, Levites, and temple workmen. 3 People from the tribes of Judah, Benjamin, Ephraim, and Manasseh went to live in Jerusalem.

4-6 There were 690 families of the tribe of Judah who lived in Jerusalem.

The descendants of Judah's son Perez had as their leader Uthai, the son of Ammihud and grandson of Omri. His other ancestors included Imri and Bani.

The descendants of Judah's son Shelah had as their leader Asaiah, who was the head of his family.

The descendants of Judah's son Zerah had Jeuel as their leader.

7-8 The following members of the tribe of Benjamin lived in Jerusalem:

Sallu son of Meshullam, who was the son of Hodaviah, the son of Hassenuah

Ibneiah son of Jeroham

Elah, the son of Uzzi and grandson of Michri

Meshullam son of Shephatiah, who was the son of Reuel, the son of Ibnijah

9 There were 956 families of this tribe living there. All the men named above were heads of families.

The Priests Who Lived in Jerusalem

10-12 The following priests lived in Jerusalem:

Jedaiah, Jehoiarib, and Jachin

Azariah son of Hilkiah (the chief official in the Temple), whose ancestors included Meshullam, Zadok, Meraioth, and Ahitub

Adaiah son of Jeroham, whose ancestors included Pashhur and Malchijah

Maasai son of Adiel, whose ancestors included Jahzerah, Meshullam, Meshillemith, and Immer

13 The priests who were heads of families totalled 1,760. They were experts in all the work carried on in the Temple.

The Levites Who Lived in Jerusalem

14-16 The following Levites lived in Jerusalem:

Shemaiah son of Hasshub, whose ancestors included Azrikam and Hashabiah, of the clan of Merari

Bakbakkar, Heresh, and Galal

Mattaniah son of Mica, whose ancestors included Zichri and Asaph

Obadiah son of Shemaiah, whose ancestors included Galal and Jeduthun

Berechiah, the son of Asa and grandson

---

[v] *Probable text (and see 9.35)* Jeiel; *Hebrew does not have this name.*
[w] *One ancient translation (and see 9.36)* Ner; *Hebrew does not have this name.*
[a] ESHBAAL: *Called Ishbosheth in 2 Sam 2.8 and elsewhere in 2 Sam.*
[b] MERIBBAAL: *Called Mephibosheth in 2 Sam 4.4 and elsewhere in 2 Sam.*
9.2–3: Ezra 2.27; Neh 7.73

of Elkanah, who lived in the territory that belonged to the town of Netophah

The Temple Guards Who Lived in Jerusalem

17 The following temple guards lived in Jerusalem: Shallum, Akkub, Talmon, and Ahiman. Shallum was their leader. 18 Down to that time members of their clans had been stationed at the eastern entrance to the King's Gate.[x] Formerly they had stood guard at the gates to the camps of the Levites.

19 Shallum, the son of Kore and grandson of Ebiasaph, together with his fellow-members of the clan of Korah, was responsible for guarding the entrance to the Tent of the LORD's presence, just as their ancestors had been when they were in charge of the LORD's camp. 20 Phineas son of Eleazar—may the LORD be with him!—had supervised them at one time.

21 Zechariah son of Meshelemiah was also a guard at the entrance to the Tent of the LORD's presence.

22 In all, 212 men were chosen as guards for the entrances and gates. They were registered according to the villages where they lived. It was King David and the prophet Samuel who had put their ancestors in these responsible positions. 23 They and their descendants continued to guard the gates to the Temple. 24 There was a gate facing in each direction, north, south, east, and west, and each had a chief guard. 25 These guards were assisted by their relatives, who lived in the villages and who had to take turns at guard duty for seven days at a time. 26 The four chief guards were Levites and had the final responsibility. They were also responsible for the rooms in the Temple and for the supplies kept there. 27 They lived near the Temple, because it was their duty to guard it and to open the gates every morning.

The Other Levites

28 Other Levites were responsible for the utensils used in worship. They checked them out and checked them back in every time they were used. 29 Others were in charge of the other sacred equipment, and of the flour, wine, olive-oil, incense, and spices. 30 But the responsibility for mixing the spices belonged to the priests.

31 A Levite named Mattithiah, eldest son of Shallum, of the clan of Korah, was responsible for preparing the baked offerings.[y] 32 Members of the clan of Kohath were responsible for preparing the sacred bread[z] for the Temple every Sabbath.

33 Some Levite families were responsible for the temple music. The heads of these families lived in some of the temple buildings and were free from other duties, because they were on call day and night.

34 The men named above were heads of Levite families, according to their ancestral lines. They were the leaders who lived in Jerusalem.

The Ancestors and Descendants of King Saul
(8.29-38)

35 Jeiel founded the city of Gibeon and settled there. His wife was named Maacah. 36 His eldest son was Abdon, and his other sons were Zur, Kish, Baal, Ner, Nadab, 37 Gedor, Ahio, Zechariah, and Mikloth, 38 the father of Shimeah. Their descendants lived in Jerusalem near other families of their clan.

39 Ner was the father of Kish, and Kish was the father of Saul. Saul had four sons: Jonathan, Malchishua, Abinadab, and Eshbaal.[m] 40 Jonathan was the father of Meribbaal,[n] who was the father of Micah. 41 Micah had four sons: Pithon, Melech, Tarea, and Ahaz.[a] 42 Ahaz was the father of Jarah, who was the father of three sons: Alemeth, Azmaveth, and Zimri. Zimri was the father of Moza, 43 Moza the father of Binea, Binea of Rephaiah, Rephaiah of Eleasah, and Eleasah of Azel.

44 Azel had six sons: Azrikam, Bocheru, Ishmael, Sheariah, Obadiah, and Hanan.

The Death of King Saul
(1 Sam 31.1-13)

10 The Philistines fought a battle against the Israelites on Mount

---

[x] KING'S GATE: *The east gate of the Temple, through which the king usually entered.*
[y] BAKED OFFERINGS: *Thin cakes of flour and olive-oil which were baked and then presented as offerings to God (see Lev 2.4-6).*
[z] SACRED BREAD: *Twelve loaves of bread which were placed on a table in the Temple each Sabbath as an offering to God (see Lev 24.5-9).*
[m] ESHBAAL: *Called Ishbosheth in 2 Sam 2.8 and elsewhere in 2 Sam.*
[n] MERIBBAAL: *Called Mephibosheth in 2 Sam 4.4 and elsewhere in 2 Sam.*
[a] *Some ancient translations Ahaz (see 1 Chr 8.35); Hebrew does not have this name.*

Gilboa. Many Israelites were killed there, and the rest of them, including King Saul and his sons, fled. ²But the Philistines caught up with them and killed three of Saul's sons, Jonathan, Abinadab, and Malchishua. ³The fighting was heavy round Saul, and he was hit by enemy arrows and badly wounded. ⁴He said to the young man carrying his weapons, "Draw your sword and kill me, to keep these godless Philistines from gloating over me." But the young man was too terrified to do it. So Saul took his own sword and threw himself on it. ⁵The young man saw that Saul was dead, so he too threw himself on his sword and died. ⁶So Saul and his three sons all died together and none of his descendants ever ruled. ⁷When the Israelites who lived in the Valley of Jezreel heard that the army had fled and that Saul and his sons had died, they abandoned their towns and ran off. Then the Philistines came and occupied them.

8 The day after the battle, the Philistines went to plunder the corpses, and they found the bodies of Saul and his sons lying on Mount Gilboa. ⁹They cut off Saul's head, stripped off his armour, and sent messengers with them throughout Philistia to tell the good news to their idols and to their people. ¹⁰They put his weapons in one of their temples and hung his head in the temple of their god Dagon. ¹¹When the people of Jabesh in Gilead heard what the Philistines had done to Saul, ¹²the bravest men went and fetched the bodies of Saul and his sons and took them to Jabesh. They buried them there under an oak and fasted for seven days.

13 Saul died because he was unfaithful to the LORD. He disobeyed the LORD's commands; he tried to find guidance by consulting the spirits of the dead ¹⁴instead of consulting the LORD. So the LORD killed him and gave control of the kingdom to David son of Jesse.

David Becomes King of Israel and Judah
(2 Sam 5.1-10)

11 All the people of Israel went to David at Hebron and said to him, "We are your own flesh and blood. ²In the past, even when Saul was still our king, you led the people of Israel in battle, and the LORD your God promised you that you would lead his people and be their ruler." ³So all the leaders of Israel came to King David at Hebron. He made a

sacred alliance with them, they anointed him, and he became king of Israel, just as the LORD had promised through Samuel.

4 King David and all the Israelites went and attacked the city of Jerusalem. It was then known as Jebus, and the Jebusites, the original inhabitants of the land, were still living there. ⁵The Jebusites told David he would never get inside the city, but David captured their fortress of Zion, and it became known as "David's City." ⁶David said, "The first man to kill a Jebusite will be commander of the army!" Joab, whose mother was Zeruiah, led the attack and became commander. ⁷Because David went to live in the fortress, it came to be called "David's City." ⁸He rebuilt the city, starting at the place where land was filled in on the east side of the hill, and Joab restored the rest of the city. ⁹David grew stronger and stronger, because the LORD Almighty was with him.

David's Famous Soldiers
(2 Sam 23.8-39)

10 This is the list of David's famous soldiers. Together with the rest of the people of Israel, they helped him to become king, as the LORD had promised, and they kept his kingdom strong.

11 First was Jashobeam of the clan of Hachmon, the leader of "The Three." *ᵇ* He fought with his spear against three hundred men and killed them all in one battle. ¹²Next among the famous "Three" was Eleazar son of Dodo, of the clan of Ahoh. ¹³He fought on David's side against the Philistines at the battle of Pas Dammim. He was in a barley-field when the Israelites started to run away, ¹⁴so he and his men made a stand in the middle of the field and fought the Philistines. The LORD gave him a great victory.

15 One day three of the thirty leading soldiers went to a rock where David was staying near the cave of Adullam, while a band of Philistines was camping in the Valley of Rephaim. ¹⁶At that time David was on a fortified hill, and a group of Philistines had occupied Bethlehem. ¹⁷David got homesick and said, "How I wish someone would bring me a drink of water from the well by the gate in Bethlehem!" ¹⁸The three famous soldiers forced their way through the Philistine camp, drew some water from the well, and brought it back to David. But he would not drink it; instead he poured it

---

ᵇ One ancient translation (see also 2 Sam 23.8) "The Three"; *Hebrew* "The Thirty".
10.13: Lev 19.31, 20.6; 1 Sam 13.8-14, 15.1-24, 28.7-8   **11.4:** Josh 15.63; Judg 1.21

The three famous soldiers (11.18)

out as an offering to the LORD [19] and said, "I could never drink this! It would be like drinking the blood of these men who risked their lives!" So he refused to drink it. These were the brave deeds of the three famous soldiers.

20 Joab's brother Abishai was the leader of "The Famous Thirty."[c] He fought with his spear against three hundred men and killed them, and became famous among "The Thirty."[d] [21] He was the most famous of "The Thirty"[e] and became their leader, but he was not as famous as "The Three."

22 Benaiah son of Jehoiada from Kabzeel was a famous soldier; he did many brave deeds, including killing two great Moabite warriors. He once went down into a pit on a snowy day and killed a lion. [23] He also killed an Egyptian, a huge man over two metres tall, who was armed with a gigantic spear. Benaiah attacked him with a club, snatched the spear from the Egyptian's hand, and killed him with it. [24] Those were the brave deeds of Benaiah, who was one of "The Thirty."[f] [25] He was outstanding among "The Thirty," but not as famous as "The Three." David put him in charge of his bodyguard.

26-47 These are the other outstanding soldiers:

Asahel, Joab's brother
Elhanan son of Dodo from Bethlehem
Shammoth from Harod
Helez from Pelet
Ira son of Ikkesh from Tekoa
Abiezer from Anathoth
Sibbecai from Hushah
Ilai from Ahoh
Maharai from Netophah
Heled son of Baanah from Netophah
Ithai son of Ribai from Gibeah in Benjamin
Benaiah from Pirathon
Hurai from the valleys near Gaash
Abiel from Arbah
Azmaveth from Bahurum
Eliahba from Shaalbon
Hashem[g] from Gizon
Jonathan son of Shagee from Harar
Ahiam son of Sachar from Harar
Eliphal son of Ur
Hepher from Mecherah
Ahijah from Pelon
Hezro from Carmel
Naarai son of Ezbai
Joel brother of Nathan
Mibhar son of Hagri
Zelek from Ammon
Naharai, Joab's armour-bearer, from Beeroth
Ira and Gareb from Jattir
Uriah the Hittite
Zabad son of Ahlai
Adina son of Shiza (a leading member of the tribe of Reuben, with his own group of thirty soldiers)

[c] *One ancient translation* Thirty; *Hebrew* Three.
[d] *One ancient translation (see also 2 Sam 23.18)* "The Thirty"; *Hebrew* "The Three".
[e] *Probable text (see 2 Sam 23.19)* most famous of "The Thirty"; *Hebrew unclear.*
[f] *Probable text* "The Thirty"; *Hebrew* "The Three".
[g] *Probable text* Hashem; *Hebrew* the sons of Hashem.

Hanan son of Maacah
Joshaphat from Mithan
Uzzia from Ashterah
Shamma and Jeiel, sons of Hotham,
    from Aroer
Jediael and Joha, sons of Shimri, from
    Tiz
Eliel from Mahavah
Jeribai and Joshaviah, sons of Elnaam
Ithmah from Moab
Eliel, Obed, and Jaasiel from Zobah[h]

David's Early Followers from the Tribe of Benjamin

12 David was living in Ziklag, where he had gone to escape from King Saul. There he was joined by many experienced, reliable soldiers, [2] members of the tribe of Benjamin, to which Saul belonged. They could shoot arrows and sling stones either right-handed or left-handed. [3-7] They were under the command of Ahiezer and Joash, sons of Shemaah, from Gibeah.

These were the soldiers:
Jeziel and Pelet, sons of Azmaveth
Beracah and Jehu from Anathoth
Ishmaiah from Gibeon, a famous soldier
    and one of the leaders of "The
    Thirty"
Jeremiah, Jahaziel, Johannan, and
    Jozabad, from Gederah
Eluzai, Jerimoth, Bealiah, Shemariah,
    and Shephatiah, from Hariph
Elkanah, Isshiah, Azarel, Joezer, and
    Jashobeam, of the clan of Korah
Joelah and Zebadiah, sons of Jeroham,
    from Gedor

David's Followers from the Tribe of Gad

[8] These are the names of the famous, experienced soldiers from the tribe of Gad who joined David's troops when he was at the desert fort. They were experts with shields and spears, as fierce-looking as lions and as quick as mountain deer. [9-13] They were ranked in the following order: Ezer, Obadiah, Eliab, Mishmannah, Jeremiah, Attai, Eliel, Johanan, Elzabad, Jeremiah, and Machbannai.

[14] Some of these men from the tribe of Gad were senior officers in command of a thousand men, and others were junior officers in command of a hundred. [15] In the first month of one year, the time when the River Jordan overflowed its banks, they crossed the river, scattering the people who lived in the valleys both east and west of the river.

Followers from Benjamin and Judah

[16] Once a group of men from the tribes of Benjamin and Judah went out to the fort where David was. [17] David went to meet them and said, "If you are coming as friends to help me, you are welcome here. Join us! But if you intend to betray me to my enemies, even though I have not tried to hurt you, the God of our ancestors will know it and punish you."

[18] God's spirit took control of one of them, Amasai, who later became the commander of "The Thirty," and he called out,

"David son of Jesse, we are yours!
Success to you and those who help you!
God is on your side."

David welcomed them and made them officers in his army.

Followers from Manasseh

[19] Some soldiers from the tribe of Manasseh went over to David's side when he was marching out with the Philistines to fight King Saul. Actually he did not help the Philistines, for their kings were afraid that he would betray them to his former master Saul, so they sent him back to Ziklag. [20] These are the soldiers from Manasseh who went over to David's side when he was returning: Adnah, Jozabad, Jediael, Michael, Jozabad, Elihu, and Zillethai. In Manasseh they had all commanded units of a thousand men. [21] They served David as officers over his troops,[i] because they were all outstanding soldiers. Later they were officers in the Israelite army. [22] Almost every day new men joined David's forces, so that his army was soon enormous.

List of David's Forces

[23-37] When David was at Hebron, many trained soldiers joined his army to help make him king in place of Saul, as the LORD had promised. Their numbers were as follows:
Judah: 6,800 well-equipped men, armed
    with shields and spears;
    Simeon: 7,100 well-trained men;
    Levi: 4,600 men;
    Followers of Jehoiada, descendant of
        Aaron: 3,700 men;
    Relatives of Zadok, an able young
        fighter: 22 leading men;
    Benjamin (Saul's own tribe): 3,000 men
    (most of the people of Benjamin had
    remained loyal to Saul);

---

[h] *Probable text* from Zobah; *Hebrew unclear.*
[i] They served David...troops; *or* They helped David fight against the bands of raiders.

Donkeys, camels...loaded with food (12.40)

Ephraim: 20,800 men famous in their own clans;

West Manasseh: 18,000 men chosen to go and make David king;

Issachar: 200 leaders, together with the men under their command (these leaders knew what Israel should do and the best time to do it);

Zebulun: 50,000 loyal and reliable men ready to fight, trained to use all kinds of weapons;

Naphtali: 1,000 leaders, together with 37,000 men armed with shields and spears;

Dan: 28,600 trained men;

Asher: 40,000 men ready for battle;

Tribes east of the Jordan—Reuben, Gad, and East Manasseh: 120,000 men trained to use all kinds of weapons.

38 All these soldiers, ready for battle, went to Hebron, determined to make David king over all Israel. All the rest of the people of Israel were united in the same purpose. ³⁹ They spent three days there with David, feasting on the food and drink which their fellow-countrymen had prepared for them. ⁴⁰ From as far away as the northern tribes of Issachar, Zebulun, and Naphtali, people came bringing donkeys, camels, mules, and oxen loaded with food—flour, figs, raisins, wine, and olive-oil. They also brought cattle and sheep to kill and eat. All this was an expression of the joy that was felt throughout the whole country.

13.5: 1 Sam 7.1-2   13.6: Ex 25.22

The Covenant Box Is Moved from Kiriath Jearim
(2 Sam 6.1-11)

13 King David consulted with all the officers in command of units of a thousand men and units of a hundred men. ²Then he announced to all the people of Israel, "If you give your approval and if it is the will of the LORD our God, let us send messengers to the rest of our countrymen and to the priests and Levites in their towns, and tell them to assemble here with us. ³Then we will go and fetch God's Covenant Box, which was ignored while Saul was king." ⁴The people were pleased with the suggestion and agreed to it.

5 So David assembled the people of Israel from all over the country, from the Egyptian border in the south to Hamath Pass in the north, in order to bring the Covenant Box from Kiriath Jearim to Jerusalem. ⁶David and the people went to the city of Baalah, that is, to Kiriath Jearim, in the territory of Judah, to fetch the Covenant Box of God, which bears the name of the LORD enthroned above the winged creatures. ⁷At Abinadab's house they brought out the Covenant Box and put it on a new cart. Uzzah and Ahio guided the cart, ⁸while David and all the people danced with all their might to honour God. They sang and played

While David and all the people danced (13.8)

musical instruments—harps, drums, cymbals, and trumpets.

9 As they came to the threshing-place of Chidon, the oxen stumbled, and Uzzah stretched out his hand and took hold of the Covenant Box. 10 At once the Lord became angry with Uzzah and killed him for touching the box. He died there in God's presence, 11 and so that place has been called Perez Uzzah *j* ever since. David was furious because the Lord had punished Uzzah in anger.

12 Then David was afraid of God and said, "How can I take the Covenant Box with me now?" 13 So David did not take it with him to Jerusalem. Instead, he left it at the house of a man named Obed Edom, a native of the city of Gath. 14 It stayed there three months, and the Lord blessed Obed Edom's family and everything that belonged to him.

David's Activities in Jerusalem
(2 Sam 5.11-16)

14 King Hiram of Tyre sent a trade mission to David; he provided him with cedar logs and with stone-masons and carpenters to build a palace. 2 And so David realized that the Lord had established him as king of Israel and was making his kingdom prosperous for the sake of his people.

3 There in Jerusalem, David married more wives and had more sons and daughters. 4 The following children were born to him in Jerusalem: Shammua, Shobab, Nathan, Solomon, 5 Ibhar,

Elishua, Elpelet, 6 Nogah, Nepheg, Japhia, 7 Elishama, Beeliada, *x* and Eliphelet.

Victory over the Philistines
(2 Sam 5.17-25)

8 When the Philistines heard that David had now been made king over the whole country of Israel, their army went out to capture him. So David marched out to meet them. 9 The Philistines arrived at the Valley of Rephaim and began plundering. 10 David asked God, "Shall I attack the Philistines? Will you give me the victory?"

The Lord answered, "Yes, attack! I will give you the victory!"

11 So David attacked them at Baal Perazim and defeated them. He said, "God has used me to break through the enemy army like a flood." So that place is called Baal Perazim. *k* 12 When the Philistines fled, they left their idols behind, and David gave orders for them to be burnt.

13 Soon the Philistines returned to the valley and started plundering it again. 14 Once more David consulted God, who answered, "Don't attack them from here, but go round and get ready to attack them from the other side, near the balsam-trees. 15 When you hear the sound of marching in the tree-tops, then attack, because I will be marching ahead of you to defeat the Philistine army." 16 David did what God had commanded, and so he drove the Philistines back from Gibeon all the way to Gezer. 17 David's fame spread

j PEREZ UZZAH: *This name in Hebrew means "Punishment of Uzzah."*
x BEELIADA: *Called Eliada in 3.8.*
k BAAL PERAZIM: *This name in Hebrew means "Lord of the Break-through."*
13.14: 1 Chr 26.4-5

everywhere, and the LORD made every nation afraid of him.

Getting Ready to Move the Covenant Box

15 For his own use, David built houses in David's City.[1] He also prepared a place for God's Covenant Box and put up a tent for it. [2] Then he said, "Only Levites should carry the Covenant Box, because they are the ones the LORD chose to carry it and to serve him for ever." [3] So David summoned all the people of Israel to Jerusalem in order to bring the Covenant Box to the place he had prepared for it. [4] Next he sent for the descendants of Aaron and for the Levites. [5] From the Levite clan of Kohath came Uriel, in charge of 120 members of his clan; [6] from the clan of Merari came Asaiah, in charge of 220; [7] from the clan of Gershon, Joel, in charge of 130; [8] from the clan of Elizaphan, Shemaiah, in charge of 200; [9] from the clan of Hebron, Eliel, in charge of 80; [10] and from the clan of Uzziel, Amminadab, in charge of 112.

[11] David called in the priests Zadok and Abiathar and the six Levites, Uriel, Asaiah, Joel, Shemaiah, Eliel, and Amminadab. [12] He said to the Levites, "You are the leaders of the Levite clans. Purify yourselves and your fellow-Levites, so that you can bring the Covenant Box of the LORD God of Israel to the place I have prepared for it. [13] Because you were not there to carry it the first time, the LORD our God punished us for not worshipping him as we should have done."

[14] Then the priests and the Levites purified themselves in order to move the Covenant Box of the LORD God of Israel. [15] The Levites carried it on poles on their shoulders, as the LORD had commanded through Moses.

[16] David commanded the leaders of the Levites to assign various Levites to sing and to play joyful music on harps and cymbals. [17-21] From the clans of singers they chose the following men to play the brass cymbals: Heman son of Joel, his relative Asaph son of Berechiah, and Ethan son of Kushaiah, of the clan of Merari. To assist them they chose the following Levites to play the high-pitched harps: Zechariah, Jaaziel, Shemiramoth, Jehiel, Unni, Eliab, Maaseiah, and Benaiah.

To play the low-pitched harps they chose the following Levites: Mattithiah,

The Levites carried it on poles (15.15)

Eliphelehu, Mikneiah, Âzaziah, and the temple guards, Obed Edom and Jeiel.

[22] Because of his skill in music Chenaniah was chosen to be in charge of the levitical musicians. [23-24] Berechiah and Elkanah, along with Obed Edom and Jehiah, were chosen as guards for the Covenant Box. The priests Shebaniah, Joshaphat, Nethanel, Amasai, Zechariah, Benaiah, and Eliezer were chosen to blow trumpets in front of the Covenant Box.

Moving the Covenant Box to Jerusalem
(2 Sam 6.12-22)

[25] So King David, the leaders of Israel, and the military commanders went to the house of Obed Edom to fetch the Covenant Box, and they had a great celebration. [26] They sacrificed seven bulls and seven sheep, to make sure that God would help the Levites who were carrying the Covenant Box. [27] David was wearing a robe made of the finest linen, and so were the musicians, Chenaniah their leader, and the Levites who carried the Box. David also wore a linen ephod. [28] So all the Israelites accompanied the Covenant Box up to Jerusalem with shouts of joy, the sound of trumpets, horns, and cymbals, and the music of harps.

[29] As the Box was being brought into the city, Michal, Saul's daughter, looked out of the window and saw King David dancing and leaping for joy, and she was disgusted with him.

16 They took the Covenant Box to the tent which David had prepared for it and put it inside. Then they offered

---

[1] DAVID'S CITY: *That part of Jerusalem which David had captured from the original inhabitants, the Jebusites (see 2 Sam 5.6–10).*
15.2: Deut 10.8   **15.15:** Ex 25.14

sacrifices and fellowship-offerings to God.
² After David had finished offering the
sacrifices, he blessed the people in the
name of the LORD ³ and distributed food
to them all. He gave each man and woman
in Israel a loaf of bread, a piece of roasted
meat, ᵐ and some raisins.

4 David appointed some of the Levites
to lead the worship of the LORD, the God
of Israel, in front of the Covenant Box,
by singing and praising him. ⁵ Asaph was
appointed leader, with Zechariah as his
assistant. Jeiel, Shemiramoth, Jehiel,
Mattithiah, Eliab, Benaiah, Obed Edom,

With shouts of joy (15.28)

and Jeiel were to play harps. Asaph was
to sound the cymbals, ⁶ and two priests,
Benaiah and Jahaziel, were to blow
trumpets regularly in front of the
Covenant Box. ⁷ It was then that David
first gave Asaph and his fellow-Levites
the responsibility for singing praises to
the LORD.

A Song of Praise
(Ps 105.1-15; 96.1-13; 106.1,47-48)

⁸ Give thanks to the LORD, proclaim his
   greatness;
  tell the nations what he has done.
⁹ Sing praise to the LORD;
  tell the wonderful things he has done.
¹⁰ Be glad that we belong to him;
  let all who worship him rejoice!
¹¹ Go to the LORD for help,
  and worship him continually.
¹²⁻¹³ You descendants of Jacob, God's
   servant,
  descendants of Israel, whom God
   chose,

  remember the miracles that God
   performed
  and the judgements that he gave.
¹⁴ The LORD is our God;
  his commands are for all the world.
¹⁵ Never forget God's covenant,
  which he made to last for ever,
¹⁶ the covenant he made with Abraham,
  the promise he made to Isaac.
¹⁷ The LORD made a covenant with Jacob,
  one that will last for ever.
¹⁸ "I will give you the land of Canaan,"
   he said.
  "It will be your own possession."
¹⁹ God's people were few in number,
  strangers in the land of Canaan.
²⁰ They wandered from country to
   country,
  from one kingdom to another.
²¹ But God let no one oppress them;
  to protect them, he warned the kings:
²² "Don't harm my chosen servants;
  do not touch my prophets."

ᵐ a piece of roasted meat; *or* a cake of dates.
16.16: Gen 12.7, 26.3   **16.17-18:** Gen 28.13   **16.21-22:** Gen 20.3-7

23 Sing to the LORD, all the world!
  Proclaim every day the good news
    that he has saved us.
24 Proclaim his glory to the nations,
  his mighty deeds to all peoples.
25 The LORD is great and is to be highly
    praised;
  he is to be honoured more than all
    the gods.
26 The gods of all other nations are only
    idols,
  but the LORD created the heavens.
27 Glory and majesty surround him,
  power and joy fill his Temple.

28 Praise the LORD, all people on earth,
  praise his glory and might.
29 Praise the LORD's glorious name;
  bring an offering and come into his
    Temple.
  Bow down before the Holy One when
    he appears; [n]
30 tremble before him, all the earth!
  The earth is set firmly in place and
    cannot be moved.
31 Be glad, earth and sky!
  Tell the nations that the LORD is king.
32 Roar, sea, and every creature in you;
  be glad, fields, and everything in you!
33 The trees in the woods will shout for
    joy
  when the LORD comes to rule the earth.

34 Give thanks to the LORD, because he
    is good;
  his love is eternal.
35 Say to him, "Save us, O God our
    Saviour;
  gather us together; rescue us from
    the nations,
  so that we may be thankful
  and praise your holy name."
36 Praise the LORD, the God of Israel!
  Praise him now and for ever!

Then all the people said, "Amen," and
praised the LORD.

Worship at Jerusalem and Gibeon

37 King David put Asaph and his fellow-
Levites in permanent charge of the
worship that was held at the place where
the Covenant Box was kept. They were
to perform their duties there day by day.
38 Obed Edom son of Jeduthun and sixty-
eight men of his clan were to assist them.

Hosah and Obed Edom were in charge
of guarding the gates.
39 Zadok the priest and his fellow-
priests, however, were in charge of the
worship of the LORD at the place of
worship in Gibeon. 40 Every morning and
evening they were to burn sacrifices
whole on the altar in accordance with
what was written in the Law which the
LORD gave to Israel. 41 There with them
were Heman and Jeduthun and the others
who were specifically chosen to sing
praises to the LORD for his eternal love.
42 Heman and Jeduthun also had charge
of the trumpets and cymbals and the other
instruments which were played when the
songs of praise were sung. The members
of Jeduthun's clan were in charge of
guarding the gates.
43 Then everyone went home, and
David went home to spend some time with
his family.

Nathan's Message to David
(2 Sam 7.1–17)

17 King David was now living in his
palace. One day he sent for the
prophet Nathan and said to him, "Here
I am living in a house built of cedar, but
the LORD's Covenant Box is kept in a
tent!"
2 Nathan answered, "Do whatever you
have in mind, because God is with you."
3 But that night God said to Nathan,
4 "Go and tell my servant David that I
say to him, 'You are not the one to build
a temple for me to live in. 5 From the
time I rescued the people of Israel from
Egypt until now, I have never lived in
a temple; I have always lived in tents
and moved from place to place. 6 In all
my travelling with the people of Israel
I never asked any of the leaders that I
appointed why they had not built me a
temple made of cedar.'
7 "So tell my servant David that I, the
LORD Almighty, say to him, 'I took you
from looking after sheep in the fields and
made you the ruler of my people Israel.
8 I have been with you wherever you have
gone, and I have defeated all your enemies
as you advanced. I will make you as
famous as the greatest leaders in the
world. 9-10 I have chosen a place for my
people Israel and have settled them there,
where they will live without being
oppressed any more. Ever since they

[n] when he appears; *or* in garments of worship.
16.34: 2 Chr 5.13, 7.3; Ezra 3.11; Ps 100.5, 106.1, 107.1, 118.1, 136.1; Jer 33.11
16.43: 2 Sam 6.19–20

entered this land they have been attacked by violent people, but this will not happen again. I promise to defeat all your enemies and to give you descendants. ¹¹When you die and are buried with your ancestors, I will make one of your sons king and will keep his kingdom strong. ¹²He will be the one to build a temple for me, and I will make sure that his dynasty continues for ever. ¹³I will be his father and he will be my son. I will not withdraw my support from him as I did from Saul, whom I removed so that you could be king. ¹⁴I will put him in charge of my people and my kingdom for ever. His dynasty will never end.' "

15 Nathan told David everything that God had revealed to him.

David's Prayer of Thanksgiving
(2 Sam 7.18-29)

16 Then King David went into the Tent of the LORD's presence, sat down, and prayed, "I am not worthy of what you have already done for me, LORD God, nor is my family. ¹⁷Yet now you are doing even more; you have made promises about my descendants in the years to come, and you, LORD God, are already treating me like a great man.ᵒ ¹⁸What more can I say to you! You know me well, and yet you honour me, your servant. ¹⁹It was your will and purpose to do this for me and to show me my future greatness. ²⁰LORD, there is none like you; we have always known that you alone are God. ²¹There is no other nation on earth like Israel, whom you rescued from slavery to make them your own people. The great and wonderful things you did for them spread your fame throughout the world. You rescued your people from Egypt and drove out other nations as your people advanced. ²²You have made Israel your own people for ever, and you, LORD, have become their God.

23 "And now, O LORD, fulfil for all time the promise you made about me and my descendants, and do what you said you would. ²⁴Your fame will be great, and people will for ever say, 'The LORD Almighty is God over Israel.' And you will preserve my dynasty for all time. ²⁵I have the courage to pray this prayer to you, my God, because you have revealed all this to me, your servant, and have told me that you will make my descendants kings. ²⁶You, LORD, are God, and you have

made this wonderful promise to me. ²⁷I ask you to bless my descendants so that they will continue to enjoy your favour. You, LORD, have blessed them, and your blessing will rest on them for ever."

David's Military Victories
(2 Sam 8.1-18)

18 Some time later King David attacked the Philistines again and defeated them. He took out of their control the city of Gath and its surrounding villages. ²He also defeated the Moabites, who became his subjects and paid taxes to him.

3 Next, David attacked King Hadadezer of the Syrian state of Zobah, near the territory of Hamath, because Hadadezer was trying to gain control of the territory by the upper Euphrates. ⁴David captured a thousand of his chariots, seven thousand horsemen, and twenty thousand foot soldiers. He kept enough horses for a hundred chariots and crippled all the rest.

5 When the Syrians of Damascus sent an army to help King Hadadezer, David attacked it and killed twenty-two thousand men. ⁶Then he set up military camps in their territory, and they became his subjects and paid taxes to him. The LORD made David victorious everywhere. ⁷David captured the gold shields carried by Hadadezer's officials and took them to Jerusalem. ⁸He also took a great quantity of bronze from Tibhath and Kun, cities ruled by Hadadezer. (Solomon later used this bronze to make the tank, the columns, and the bronze utensils for the Temple.)

9 King Toi of Hamath heard that David had defeated Hadadezer's entire army. ¹⁰So he sent his son Joram to greet King David and congratulate him for his victory over Hadadezer, against whom Toi had fought many times. Joram brought David presents made of gold, silver, and bronze. ¹¹King David dedicated them for use in worship, along with the silver and gold he took from the nations he conquered—Edom, Moab, Ammon, Philistia, and Amalek.

12 Abishai, whose mother was Zeruiah, defeated the Edomites in the Valley of Salt and killed eighteen thousand of them. ¹³He set up military camps throughout Edom, and the people there became King David's subjects. The LORD made David victorious everywhere.

ᵒ *Probable text* and you, LORD God...man; *Hebrew unclear.*
17.13: 2 Cor 6.18; Heb 1.5   **18.8:** 1 Kgs 7.40-47; 2 Chr 4.11-18   **18.12:** Ps 60 (Title)

14 David ruled over all Israel and made sure that his people were always treated fairly and justly. 15 Abishai's brother Joab was commander of the army; Jehoshaphat son of Ahilud was in charge of the records; 16 Zadok son of Ahitub and Ahimelech son of Abiathar were priests; Seraiah*p* was court secretary; 17 Benaiah son of Jehoiada was in charge of David's bodyguard; and King David's sons held high positions in his service.

David Defeats the Ammonites and the Syrians
(2 Sam 10.1-19)

19 Some time later King Nahash of Ammon died, and his son Hanun became king. 2 King David said, "I must show loyal friendship to Hanun, as his father Nahash did to me." So David sent messengers to express his sympathy.

When they arrived in Ammon and called on King Hanun, 3 the Ammonite leaders said to the king, "Do you think that it is in your father's honour that David has sent these men to express sympathy to you? Of course not! He has sent them here as spies to explore the land, so that he can conquer it!"

4 Hanun seized David's messengers, shaved off their beards, cut off their clothes at the hips, and sent them away. 5 They were too ashamed to return home. When David heard what had happened, he sent word for them to stay in Jericho and not return until their beards had grown again.

6 King Hanun and the Ammonites realized that they had made David their enemy, so they paid thirty-four thousand kilogrammes of silver to hire chariots and charioteers from Upper Mesopotamia and from the Syrian states of Maacah and Zobah. 7 The thirty-two thousand chariots they hired and the army of the king of Maacah came and camped near Medeba. The Ammonites too came out from all their cities and got ready to fight.

8 When David heard what was happening, he sent out Joab and the whole army. 9 The Ammonites marched out and took up their position at the entrance to Rabbah, their capital city, and the kings who had come to help took up their position in the open countryside.

10 Joab saw that the enemy troops would attack him in front and from the rear, so he chose the best of Israel's soldiers and put them in position facing the Syrians. 11 He placed the rest of his troops under the command of his brother Abishai, who put them in position facing the Ammonites. 12 Joab said to him, "If you see that the Syrians are defeating me, come and help me, and if the Ammonites are defeating you, I will go and help you. 13 Be strong and courageous! Let's fight hard for our people and for the cities of our God. And may the LORD's will be done."

14 Joab and his men advanced to attack, and the Syrians fled. 15 When the Ammonites saw the Syrians running away, they fled from Abishai and retreated into the city. Then Joab went back to Jerusalem.

16 The Syrians realized that they had been defeated by the Israelites, so they brought troops from the Syrian states on the east side of the River Euphrates and placed them under the command of Shobach, commander of the army of King Hadadezer of Zobah. 17 When David heard of it, he gathered the Israelite troops, crossed the Jordan, and put them in position facing the Syrians. The fighting began, 18 and the Israelites drove the Syrian army back. David and his men killed seven thousand Syrian chariot drivers and forty thousand foot-soldiers. They also killed the Syrian commander, Shobach. 19 When the kings who were subject to Hadadezer realized that they had been defeated by Israel, they made peace with David and became his subjects. The Syrians were never again willing to help the Ammonites.

David Captures Rabbah
(2 Sam 12.26-31)

20 The following spring, at the time of the year when kings usually go to war, Joab led out the army and invaded the land of Ammon; King David, however, stayed in Jerusalem. They besieged the city of Rabbah, attacked it, and destroyed it. 2 The Ammonite idol Molech*q* had a gold crown which weighed about thirty-four kilogrammes. In it there was a jewel, which David took and put in his own crown. He also took a large amount of loot from the city. 3 He took the people of the city and put them to work with saws, iron hoes, and axes. He did the same to the people of all the other towns of

p Probable text (see 2 Sam 8.17) Seraiah; Hebrew Shavsha
q Ammonite idol Molech; or Ammonite king.
20.1: 2 Sam 11.1

Ammon. Then he and his men returned to Jerusalem.

Battles against Philistine Giants
(2 Sam 21.15–22)

4 Later on, war broke out again with the Philistines at Gezer. This was when Sibbecai from Hushah killed a giant named Sippai, and the Philistines were defeated.

5 There was another battle with the Philistines, and Elhanan son of Jair killed Lahmi, the brother of Goliath from Gath, whose spear had a shaft as thick as the bar on a weaver's loom.

6 Another battle took place at Gath, where there was a giant with six fingers on each hand and six toes on each foot. He was a descendant of the ancient giants. 7 He defied the Israelites, and Jonathan, the son of David's brother Shammah, killed him.

8 These three, who were killed by David and his men, were descendants of the giants at Gath.

David Takes a Census
(2 Sam 24.1–25)

21 Satan wanted to bring trouble on the people of Israel, so he made David decide to take a census. 2 David gave orders to Joab and the other officers, "Go through Israel, from one end of the country to the other, and count the people. I want to know how many there are."

3 Joab answered, "May the LORD make the people of Israel a hundred times more numerous than they are now! Your Majesty, they are all your servants. Why do you want to do this and make the whole nation guilty?" 4 But the king made Joab obey the order. Joab went out, travelled through the whole country of Israel, and then returned to Jerusalem. 5 He reported to King David the total number of men capable of military service: 1,100,000 in Israel, and 470,000 in Judah. 6 Because Joab disapproved of the king's command, he did not take any census of the tribes of Levi and Benjamin.

7 God was displeased with what had been done, so he punished Israel. 8 David said to God, "I have committed a terrible sin in doing this! Please forgive me. I have acted foolishly."

9 Then the LORD said to Gad, David's prophet, 10 "Go and tell David that I am giving him three choices. I will do whichever he chooses."

11 Gad went to David, told him what the LORD had said, and asked, "Which is it to be? 12 Three years of famine? Or three months of running away from the armies of your enemies? Or three days during which the LORD attacks you with his sword and sends an epidemic on your land, using his angel to bring death throughout Israel? What answer shall I give the LORD?"

13 David replied to Gad, "I am in a desperate situation! But I don't want to be punished by men. Let the LORD himself be the one to punish me, because he is merciful."

14 So the LORD sent an epidemic on the people of Israel, and seventy thousand of them died. 15 Then he sent an angel to destroy Jerusalem, but he changed his mind and said to the angel, "Stop! That's enough!" The angel was standing by the threshing-place of Araunah, a Jebusite.

16 David saw the angel standing in mid air, holding his sword in his hand, ready to destroy Jerusalem. Then David and the leaders of the people—all of whom were wearing sackcloth—bowed low, with their faces touching the ground. 17 David prayed, "O God, I am the one who did wrong. I am the one who ordered the census. What have these poor people done? LORD, my God, punish me and my family, and spare your people."

18 The angel of the LORD told Gad to command David to go and build an altar to the LORD at Araunah's threshing-place. 19 David obeyed the LORD's command and went, as Gad had told him to. 20 There at the threshing-place Araunah and his four sons were threshing wheat, and when they saw the angel, the sons ran and hid. 21 As soon as Araunah saw King David approaching, he left the threshing-place and bowed low, with his face touching the ground. 22 David said to him, "Sell me your threshing-place, so that I can build an altar to the LORD, to stop the epidemic. I'll give you the full price."

23 "Take it, Your Majesty," Araunah said, "and do whatever you wish. Here are these oxen to burn as an offering on the altar, and here are the threshing-boards to use as fuel, and wheat to give as an offering. I give it all to you."

24 But the king answered, "No, I will pay you the full price. I will not give as an offering to the LORD something that belongs to you, something that costs me nothing." 25 And he paid Araunah six

20.5: 1 Sam 17.4–7

hundred gold coins for the threshing-place. ²⁶He built an altar to the LORD there and offered burnt-offerings and fellowship-offerings. He prayed, and the LORD answered him by sending fire from heaven to burn the sacrifices on the altar.

²⁷The LORD told the angel to put his sword away, and the angel obeyed. ²⁸David saw by this that the LORD had answered his prayer, so he offered sacrifices on the altar at Araunah's threshing-place. ²⁹The Tent of the LORD's presence which Moses had made in the wilderness, and the altar on which sacrifices were burnt were still at the place of worship at Gibeon at this time; ³⁰but David was not able to go there to worship God, because he was afraid of the sword of the LORD's angel.

22 So David said, "This is where the Temple of the LORD God will be. Here is the altar where the people of Israel are to offer burnt-offerings."

Preparations for Building the Temple

2 King David gave orders for all the foreigners living in the land of Israel to assemble, and he put them to work. Some of them prepared stone blocks for building the Temple. ³He supplied a large amount of iron for making nails and clamps for the wooden gates, and so much bronze that no one could weigh it. ⁴He arranged for the people of Tyre and Sidon to bring him a large number of cedar logs. ⁵David thought, "The Temple that my son Solomon is to build must be splendid and world-famous. But he is young and inexperienced, so I must make preparations for it." So David got large amounts of the materials ready before he died.

6 He sent for his son Solomon and commanded him to build a temple for the LORD, the God of Israel. ⁷David said to him, "My son, I wanted to build a temple to honour the LORD my God. ⁸But the LORD told me that I had killed too many people and fought too many wars. And so, because of all the bloodshed I have caused, he would not let me build a temple for him. ⁹He did, however, make me a promise. He said, 'You will have a son who will rule in peace, because I will give him peace from all his enemies. His name will be Solomon,ʳ because during his reign I will give Israel peace and security. ¹⁰He will build a temple for me. He will be

my son, and I will be his father. His dynasty will rule Israel for ever.' "

11 David continued, "Now, my son, may the LORD your God be with you, and may he keep his promise to make you successful in building a temple for him. ¹²And may the LORD your God give you insight and wisdom so that you may govern Israel according to his Law. ¹³If you obey all the laws which the LORD gave to Moses for Israel, you will be successful. Be determined and confident, and don't let anything make you afraid. ¹⁴As for the Temple, by my efforts I have accumulated more than 3,400 metric tons of gold and over 34,000 metric tons of silver to be used in building it. Besides that, there is an unlimited supply of bronze and iron. I also have wood and stone ready, but you must get more. ¹⁵You have many workmen. There are men to work in the stone quarries, and there are masons and carpenters, as well as a large number of craftsmen of every sort who can work ¹⁶with gold, silver, bronze, and

Now begin the work (22.16)

iron. Now begin the work, and may the LORD be with you."

17 David commanded all the leaders of Israel to help Solomon. ¹⁸He said, "The LORD your God has been with you and given you peace on all sides. He let me conquer all the people who used to live in this land, and they are now subject to you and to the LORD. ¹⁹Now serve the LORD your God with all your heart and soul. Start building the Temple, so that you can place in it the Covenant Box of

---

ʳ SOLOMON: *This name is formed from the Hebrew word "shalom," which means "peace and security."*

22.7-10: 2 Sam 7.1-16; 1 Chr 17.1-14   **22.13:** Josh 1.6-9 the LORD and all the other sacred objects used in worshipping him."

23

When David was very old, he made his son Solomon king of Israel.

The Work of the Levites

2 King David brought together all the Israelite leaders and all the priests and Levites. ³He took a census of all the male Levites aged thirty or older. The total was thirty-eight thousand. ⁴The king assigned twenty-four thousand to administer the work of the Temple, six thousand to keep records and decide disputes, ⁵four thousand to do guard duty, and four thousand to praise the LORD, using the musical instruments provided by the king for this purpose.

6 David divided the Levites into three groups, according to their clans: Gershon, Kohath, and Merari.

7 Gershon had two sons: Ladan and Shimei. ⁸Ladan had three sons: Jehiel, Zetham, and Joel, ⁹who were the heads of the clans descended from Ladan. (Shimei had three sons: Shelomoth, Haziel, and Haran.)ˢ ¹⁰⁻¹¹Shimei had four sons: Jahath, Zina, Jeush, and Beriah, in order of age. Jeush and Beriah did not have many descendants, so they were counted as one clan.

12 Kohath had four sons: Amram, Izhar, Hebron, and Uzziel. ¹³His eldest son, Amram, was the father of Aaron and Moses. (Aaron and his descendants were set apart to be in charge of the sacred objects for ever, to burn incense in the worship of the LORD, to serve him, and to bless the people in his name. ¹⁴But the sons of Moses, the man of God, were included among the Levites.) ¹⁵Moses had two sons, Gershom and Eliezer. ¹⁶The leader among Gershom's sons was Shebuel. ¹⁷Eliezer had only one son, Rehabiah, but Rehabiah had many descendants.

18 Kohath's second son, Izhar, had a son, Shelomith, the head of the clan. ¹⁹Kohath's third son, Hebron, had four sons: Jeriah, Amariah, Jehaziel, and Jekameam. ²⁰Kohath's fourth son, Uzziel, had two sons, Micah and Isshiah.

21 Merari had two sons, Mahli and Mushi. Mahli also had two sons, Eleazar and Kish, ²²but Eleazar died without having any sons, only daughters. His daughters married their cousins, the sons

of Kish. ²³Merari's second son, Mushi, had three sons: Mahli, Eder, and Jeremoth.

24 These were the descendants of Levi, by clans and families, every one of them registered by name. Each of his descendants, twenty years of age or older, had a share in the work of the LORD's Temple.

25 David said, "The LORD God of Israel has given peace to his people, and he himself will live in Jerusalem for ever. ²⁶So there is no longer any need for the Levites to carry the Tent of the LORD's presence and all the equipment used in worship." ²⁷On the basis of David's final instructions all Levites were registered for service when they reached the age of twenty, ²⁸and were assigned the following duties: to help the priests descended from Aaron with the temple worship, to take care of its courtyards and its rooms, and to keep undefiled everything that is sacred; ²⁹to be responsible for the bread offered to God, the flour used in offerings, the wafers made without yeast, the baked offerings, and the flour mixed with olive-oil; to weigh and measure the temple offerings; ³⁰and to praise and glorify the LORD every morning and every evening ³¹and whenever offerings to the LORD are burnt on the Sabbath, the New Moon Festival, and other festivals. Rules were made specifying the number of Levites assigned to do this work each time. The Levites were assigned the duty of worshipping the LORD for all time. ³²They were given the responsibility of taking care of the Tent of the LORD's presence and the Temple, and of assisting their relatives, the priests descended from Aaron, in the temple worship.

The Work Assigned to the Priests

24

These are the groups to which the descendants of Aaron belong. Aaron had four sons: Nadab, Abihu, Eleazar, and Ithamar. ²Nadab and Abihu died before their father did, and left no descendants, so their brothers Eleazar and Ithamar became priests. ³King David organized the descendants of Aaron into groups according to their duties. He was assisted in this by Zadok, a descendant of Eleazar, and by Ahimelech, a descendant of Ithamar. ⁴The descendants of Eleazar were organized into sixteen groups, while the descendants of Ithamar were organized into eight; this was done

---

ˢ SHIMEI..HARAN: *The relation of this list to the list of Shimei's sons in verse 10 is not clear.*
23.1: 1 Kgs 1.1–40   **23.13:** Ex 28.1   **23.26:** Deut 10.8   **23.28–32:** Num 3.5–9
24.2: Lev 10.1–2

because there were more male heads of families among the descendants of Eleazar. 5 Since there were temple officials and spiritual leaders among the descendants of both Eleazar and Ithamar, assignments were made by drawing lots. 6 The descendants of Eleazar and of Ithamar took turns in drawing lots. Then they were registered by Shemaiah son of Nethanel, a Levite secretary. The king, his officials, the priest Zadok, Ahimelech son of Abiathar, and the heads of the priestly families and of the Levite families, were all witnesses.

7-18 This is the order in which the twenty-four family groups were given their assignments:

1. Jehoiarib
2. Jedaiah
3. Harim
4. Seorim
5. Malchijah
6. Mijamin
7. Hakkoz
8. Abijah
9. Jeshua
10. Shecaniah
11. Eliashib
12. Jakim
13. Huppah
14. Jeshebeab
15. Bilgah
16. Immer
17. Hezir
18. Happizzez
19. Pethahiah
20. Jehezkel
21. Jachin
22. Gamul
23. Delaiah
24. Maaziah

19 These men were registered according to their assignments for going to the Temple and performing the duties established by their ancestor Aaron in obedience to the commands of the LORD God of Israel.

The List of the Levites

20 These are other heads of families descended from Levi:

Jehdeiah, a descendant of Amram through Shebuel;

21 Isshiah, a descendant of Rehabiah;

22 Jahath, a descendant of Izhar through Shelomith;

23 Jeriah, Amariah, Jehaziel, and Jekameam, sons of Hebron, in order of age;

24 Shamir, a descendant of Uzziel through Micah;

25 Zechariah, a descendant of Uzziel through Isshiah, Micah's brother;

26 Mahli, Mushi, and Jaaziah, descendants of Merari. 27 Jaaziah had three sons: Shoham, Zaccur, and Ibri. 28-29 Mahli had two sons, Eleazar and Kish. Eleazar had no sons, but Kish had one son, Jerahmeel. 30 Mushi had three sons: Mahli, Eder, and Jeremoth.

These are the families of the Levites.

31 The head of each family and one of his younger brothers drew lots for their assignments, just as their relatives, the priests descended from Aaron, had done. King David, Zadok, Ahimelech, and the heads of families of the priests and of the Levites were witnesses.

The Temple Musicians

25 King David and the leaders of the Levites chose the following Levite clans to lead the services of worship: Asaph, Heman, and Jeduthun. They were to proclaim God's messages, accompanied by the music of harps and cymbals. This is the list of persons chosen to lead the worship, with the type of service that each group performed:

2 The four sons of Asaph: Zaccur, Joseph, Nethaniah, and Asharelah. They were under the direction of Asaph, who proclaimed God's messages whenever the king commanded.

3 The six sons of Jeduthun: Gedaliah, Zeri, Jeshaiah, Shimei, Hashabiah, and Mattithiah. Under the direction of their father they proclaimed God's message, accompanied by the music of harps, and sang praise and thanks to the LORD.

4 The fourteen sons of Heman: Bukkiah, Mattaniah, Uzziel, Shebuel, Jerimoth, Hananiah, Hanani, Eliathah, Giddalti, Romamti Ezer, Joshbekashah, Mallothi, Hothir, and Mahazioth. 5 God gave to Heman, the king's prophet, these fourteen sons and also three daughters, as he had promised, in order to give power to Heman. 6 All his sons played cymbals and harps under their father's direction, to accompany the temple worship. And Asaph, Jeduthun, and Heman were under orders from the king.

7 All these twenty-four men were experts; and their fellow-Levites were trained musicians. There were 288 men in all.

8 To determine the assignment of duties they all drew lots, whether they were

young or old, experts or beginners.

9–31 These 288 men were divided according to families into twenty-four groups of twelve, with a leader in charge of each group. This is the order in which they were on duty:

1. Joseph of the family of Asaph
2. Gedaliah
3. Zaccur
4. Zeri
5. Nethaniah
6. Bukkiah
7. Asharelah
8. Jeshaiah
9. Mattaniah
10. Shimei
11. Uzziel
12. Hashabiah
13. Shebuel
14. Mattithiah
15. Jerimoth
16. Hananiah
17. Joshbekashah
18. Hanani
19. Mallothi
20. Eliathah
21. Hothir
22. Giddalti
23. Mahazioth
24. Romamti Ezer

The Temple Guards

26 These are the assignments of work for the Levites who served as temple guards. From the clan of Korah there was Meshelemiah son of Kore, of the family of Asaph. [2] He had seven sons, listed in order of age: Zechariah, Jediael, Zebadiah, Jathniel, [3] Elam, Jehohanan, and Eliehoenai.

4 There was also Obed Edom, whom God blessed by giving him eight sons, listed in order of age: Shemaiah, Jehozabad, Joah, Sachar, Nethanel, [5] Ammiel, Issachar, and Peullethai.

6–7 Obed Edom's eldest son, Shemaiah, had six sons: Othni, Rephael, Obed, Elzabad, Elihu, and Semachiah. They were important men in their clan because of their great ability; the last two were especially talented.

8 Obed Edom's family furnished a total of sixty-two highly qualified men for this work.

9 Meshelemiah's family furnished eighteen qualified men.

10 From the clan of Merari there was Hosah, who had four sons: Shimri (his father made him the leader, even though he was not the eldest son), [11] Hilkiah, Tebaliah, and Zechariah. In all there were thirteen members of Hosah's family who were temple guards.

12 The temple guards were divided into groups, according to families, and they were assigned duties in the Temple, just as the other Levites were. [13] Each family, regardless of size, drew lots to see which gate it would be responsible for. [14] Shelemiah drew the east gate, and his son Zechariah, a man who always gave good advice, drew the north gate. [15] Obed Edom was allotted the south gate, and his sons were allotted to guard the storerooms. [16] Shuppim and Hosah were allotted the west gate and the Shallecheth Gate on the upper road. Guard duty was divided into assigned periods, one after another. [17] On the east, six guards were on duty each day, on the north, four, and on the south, four. Four guards were stationed at the storerooms daily, two at each storeroom. [18] Near the western pavilion there were four guards by the road and two at the pavilion itself. [19] This is the assignment of guard duty to the clan of Korah and the clan of Merari.

Other Temple Duties

20 Others of their fellow-Levites[t] were in charge of the temple treasury and the storerooms for gifts dedicated to God. [21] Ladan, one of the sons of Gershon, was the ancestor of several family groups, including the family of his son Jehiel. [22] Ladan's two other sons, Zetham and Joel, had charge of the temple treasury and storerooms.

23 Duties were also assigned to the descendants of Amram, Izhar, Hebron, and Uzziel.

24 Shebuel, of the clan of Moses' son Gershom, was the chief official responsible for the temple treasury. [25] Through Gershom's brother Eliezer he was related to Shelomith. Eliezer was the father of Rehabiah, who was the father of Jeshiah, the father of Joram, the father of Zichri, the father of Shelomith. [26] Shelomith and the members of his family were in charge of all the gifts dedicated to God by King David, the heads of families, leaders of clan groups, and army officers. [27] They took some of the loot they captured in battle and dedicated it for use in the Temple. [28] Shelomith and his family were

---

[t] *One ancient translation* fellow-Levites; *Hebrew* Levites, Ahijah.
26.4–5: 2 Sam 6.11; 1 Chr 13.14

in charge of everything that had been dedicated for use in the Temple, including the gifts brought by the prophet Samuel, by King Saul, by Abner son of Ner, and by Joab son of Zeruiah.

Duties of Other Levites

29 Among the descendants of Izhar, Chenaniah and his sons were assigned administrative duties: keeping records and settling disputes for the people of Israel.

30 Among the descendants of Hebron, Hashabiah and seventeen hundred of his relatives, all outstanding men, were put in charge of the administration of all religious and civil matters in Israel west of the River Jordan. 31 Jeriah was the leader of the descendants of Hebron. In the fortieth year that David was king, an investigation was made of the family line of Hebron's descendants, and outstanding soldiers belonging to this family were found living at Jazer in the territory of Gilead. 32 King David chose two thousand seven hundred outstanding heads of families from Jeriah's relatives and put them in charge of administering all religious and civil matters in Israel east of the River Jordan—the territories of Reuben, Gad, and East Manasseh.

Military and Civil Organization

27 This is the list of the Israelite heads of families and clan leaders and their officials who administered the work of the kingdom. Each month of the year a different group of twenty-four thousand men was on duty under the commander for that month.

2-15 The following were the commanders for each month:

First month: Jashobeam son of Zabdiel (he was a member of the clan of Perez, a part of the tribe of Judah)

Second month: Dodai, a descendant of Ahohi (Mikloth was his second in command) u

Third month: Benaiah son of Jehoiada the priest; he was the leader of "The Thirty" (his son Amizzabad succeeded him as commander of this group)

Fourth month: Asahel, brother of Joab (his son Zebadiah succeeded him)

Fifth month: Shamhuth, a descendant of Izhar

Sixth month: Ira son of Ikkesh from Tekoa

Seventh month: Helez, an Ephraimite from Pelon

Eighth month: Sibbecai from Hushah (he was a member of the clan of Zerah, a part of the tribe of Judah)

Ninth month: Abiezer from Anathoth in the territory of the tribe of Benjamin

Tenth month: Maharai from Netophah (he was a member of the clan of Zerah)

Eleventh month: Benaiah from Pirathon in the territory of the tribe of Ephraim

Twelfth month: Heldai from Netophah (he was a descendant of Othniel)

Administration of the Tribes of Israel

16-22 This is the list of the administrators of the tribes of Israel:

Tribe	Administrator
Reuben	Eliezer son of Zichri
Simeon	Shephatiah son of Maacah
Levi	Hashabiah son of Kemuel
Aaron	Zadok
Judah	Elihu, one of King David's brothers
Issachar	Omri son of Michael
Zebulun	Ishmaiah son of Obadiah
Naphtali	Jeremoth son of Azriel
Ephraim	Hoshea son of Azaziah
West Manasseh	Joel son of Pedaiah
East Manasseh	Iddo son of Zechariah
Benjamin	Jaasiel son of Abner
Dan	Azarel son of Jeroham

23 King David did not take a census of the people who were under the age of twenty, because of the LORD's promise to make the people of Israel as numerous as the stars in the sky. 24 Joab, whose mother was Zeruiah, began to take a census, but he did not complete it. God punished Israel because of this census, so the final figures were never recorded in King David's official records.

Administrators of the Royal Property

25-31 This is the list of those who administered the royal property:

Royal storerooms: Azmaveth son of Adiel

u Probable text Mikloth...command; Hebrew unclear.
27.23: Gen 15.5, 22.17, 26.4   **27.24:** 2 Sam 24.1-15; 1 Chr 21.1-14

Local storerooms: Jonathan son of Uzziah

Farm labour: Ezri son of Chelub

Vineyards: Shimei from Ramah

Wine cellars: Zabdi from Shepham

Olives and sycomore-trees (in the western foothills): Baal Hanan from Geder

Olive-oil storage: Joash

Cattle in the Plain of Sharon: Shirtai from Sharon

Cattle in the valleys: Shaphat son of Adlai

Camels: Obil, an Ishmaelite

Donkeys: Jehdeiah from Meronoth

Sheep and goats: Jaziz, a Hagrite

David's Personal Advisers

32 Jonathan, King David's uncle, was a skilful adviser and a scholar. He and Jehiel son of Hachmoni were in charge of the education of the king's sons. 33 Ahithophel was adviser to the king, and Hushai the Archite was the king's friend and counsellor. 34 After Ahithophel died, Abiathar and Jehoiada son of Benaiah became advisers. Joab was commander of the royal army.

David's Instructions for the Temple

28 King David commanded all the officials of Israel to assemble in Jerusalem. So all the officials of the tribes, the officials who administered the work of the kingdom, the leaders of the clans, the supervisors of the property and livestock that belonged to the king and his sons—indeed all the palace officials, leading soldiers, and important men—gathered in Jerusalem.

2 David stood before them and addressed them: "My countrymen, listen to me. I wanted to build a permanent home for the Covenant Box, the footstool of the LORD our God. I have made preparations for building a temple to honour him, 3 but he has forbidden me to do it, because I am a soldier and have shed too much blood. 4 The LORD, the God of Israel, chose me and my descendants to rule Israel for ever. He chose the tribe of Judah to provide leadership, and out of Judah he chose my father's family. From all that family it was his pleasure to take me and make me king over all Israel. 5 He gave me many sons, and out of them all he chose Solomon to rule over Israel, the LORD's kingdom.

6 "The LORD said to me, 'Your son

Solomon is the one who will build my Temple. I have chosen him to be my son, and I will be his father. 7 I will make his kingdom last for ever if he continues to obey carefully all my laws and commands as he does now.'

8 "So now, my people, in the presence of our God and of this assembly of all Israel, the LORD's people, I charge you to obey carefully everything that the LORD our God has commanded us, so that you may continue to possess this good land and so that you may hand it on to succeeding generations for ever."

9 And to Solomon he said, "My son, I charge you to acknowledge your father's God and to serve him with an undivided heart and a willing mind. He knows all our thoughts and desires. If you go to him, he will accept you; but if you turn away from him, he will abandon you for ever. 10 You must realize that the LORD has chosen you to build his holy Temple. Now do it—and do it with determination."

11 David gave Solomon the plans for all the temple buildings, for the storerooms and all the other rooms, and for the Most Holy Place, where sins are forgiven. 12 He also gave him the plans for all he had in mind for the courtyards and the rooms around them, and for the storerooms for the temple equipment and the gifts dedicated to the LORD. 13 David also gave him the plans for organizing the priests and Levites to perform their duties, to do the work of the Temple, and to take care of all the temple utensils. 14 He gave instructions as to how much silver and gold was to be used for making the utensils, 15 for each lamp and lampstand, 16 for the silver tables, and for each gold table on which were placed the loaves of bread offered to God. 17 He also gave instructions as to how much pure gold was to be used in making forks, bowls, and jars, how much silver and gold in making dishes, 18 and how much pure gold in making the altar on which incense was burnt and in making the chariot for the winged creatures that spread their wings over the LORD's Covenant Box. 19 King David said, "All this is contained in the plan written according to the instructions which the LORD himself gave me to carry out."

20 King David said to his son Solomon, "Be confident and determined. Start the work and don't let anything stop you. The LORD God, whom I serve, will be with

28.2–7: 2 Sam 7.1–16; 1 Chr 17.1–14

My son Solomon is the one (29.1)

you. He will not abandon you, but he will stay with you until you finish the work to be done on his Temple. 21 The priests and the Levites have been assigned duties to perform in the Temple. Workmen with every kind of skill are eager to help you, and all the people and their leaders are at your command."

Gifts for Building the Temple

29 King David announced to the whole assembly: "My son Solomon is the one whom God has chosen, but he is still young and lacks experience. The work to be done is tremendous, because this is not a palace for men but a temple for the LORD God. 2 I have made every effort to prepare materials for the Temple—gold, silver, bronze, iron, timber, precious stones and gems, stones for mosaics, and quantities of marble. 3 Over and above all this that I have provided, I have given silver and gold from my personal property because of my love for God's Temple. 4 I have given more than a hundred metric tons of the finest gold and almost two hundred and forty metric tons of pure silver for decorating the walls

of the Temple 5 and for all the objects which the craftsmen are to make. Now who else is willing to give a generous offering to the LORD?"

6 Then the heads of the clans, the officials of the tribes, the commanders of the army, and the administrators of the royal property volunteered to give 7 the following for the work on the Temple: more than 170 metric tons of gold, over 340 metric tons of silver, almost 620 metric tons of bronze, and more than 3,400 metric tons of iron. 8 Those who had precious stones gave them to the temple treasury, which was administered by Jehiel of the Levite clan of Gershon. 9 The people had given willingly to the LORD, and they were happy that so much had been given. King David also was extremely happy.

David Praises God

10 There in front of the whole assembly King David praised the LORD. He said, "LORD God of our ancestor Jacob, may you be praised for ever and ever! 11 You are great and powerful, glorious, splendid, and majestic. Everything in heaven and

29.1–2: 1 Chr 22.5   **29.11:** Mt 6.13

earth is yours, and you are king, supreme ruler over all. ¹²All riches and wealth come from you; you rule everything by your strength and power; and you are able to make anyone great and strong. ¹³Now, our God, we give you thanks, and we praise your glorious name.

14 "Yet my people and I cannot really give you anything, because everything is a gift from you, and we have only given back what is yours already. ¹⁵You know, O LORD, that we pass through life like exiles and strangers, as our ancestors did. Our days are like a passing shadow, and we cannot escape death. ¹⁶O LORD, our God, we have brought together all this wealth to build a temple to honour your holy name, but it all came from you and all belongs to you. ¹⁷I know that you test everyone's heart and are pleased with people of integrity. In honesty and sincerity I have willingly given all this to you, and I have seen how your people who are gathered here have been happy to bring offerings to you. ¹⁸LORD God of our ancestors Abraham, Isaac, and Jacob, keep such devotion for ever strong in your people's hearts and keep them always faithful to you. ¹⁹Give my son Solomon a wholehearted desire to obey everything that you command and to build the Temple for which I have made these preparations."

20 Then David commanded the people, "Praise the LORD your God!" And the whole assembly praised the LORD, the God of their ancestors, and they bowed low and gave honour to the LORD and also to the king.

21 The following day they killed animals as sacrifices, dedicating them to the LORD, and then gave them to the people to eat. In addition, they sacrificed a thousand bulls, a thousand rams, and a thousand lambs, which they burnt whole on the altar. They also brought the offerings of wine. ²²So that day they were very happy as they ate and drank in the presence of the LORD.

For a second time they proclaimed Solomon king. In the name of the LORD they anointed him as their ruler and Zadok as priest. ²³So Solomon succeeded his father David on the throne which the LORD had established. He was a successful king, and the whole nation of Israel obeyed him. ²⁴All the officials and soldiers, and even all of David's other sons promised to be loyal to Solomon as king. ²⁵The LORD made the whole nation stand in awe of Solomon, and he made him more glorious than any other king that had ruled Israel.

Summary of David's Reign

26 David son of Jesse ruled over all Israel ²⁷for forty years. He ruled in Hebron for seven years and in Jerusalem for thirty-three. ²⁸He died at a ripe old age, wealthy and respected, and his son Solomon succeeded him as king. ²⁹The history of King David from beginning to end is recorded in the records of the three prophets, Samuel, Nathan, and Gad. ³⁰The records tell how he ruled, how powerful he was, and all the things that happened to him, to Israel, and to the surrounding kingdoms.

THE SECOND BOOK OF
CHRONICLES

INTRODUCTION

Second Chronicles begins where *First Chronicles* ends, starting with the account of the rule of King Solomon until his death. After recording the revolt of the northern tribes led by Jeroboam against Rehoboam, King Solomon's son and successor, the account confines itself to the history of the southern kingdom of Judah until the fall of Jerusalem in 586 B.C.

Outline of Contents

The reign of Solomon 1.1—9.31
  a. The early years 1.1-17
  b. The Temple is built 2.1—7.10
  c. The later years 7.11—9.31
The revolt of the northern tribes 10.1-19
The kings of Judah 11.1—36.12
The fall of Jerusalem 36.13-23

King Solomon Prays for Wisdom
(1 Kgs 3.1-15)

1 Solomon, the son of King David, took firm control of the kingdom of Israel, and the LORD his God blessed him and made him very powerful.

2 King Solomon gave an order to all the officers in charge of units of a thousand men and of a hundred men, all the government officials, all the heads of families, and all the rest of the people, 3 commanding them to go with him to the place of worship at Gibeon. They went there because that was where the Tent of the LORD's presence was located, which Moses, the LORD's servant, had made in the wilderness. 4 (The Covenant Box, however, was in Jerusalem, kept in a tent which King David had set up when he brought the Box from Kiriath Jearim.) 5 The bronze altar which had been made by Bezalel, the son of Uri and grandson of Hur, was also in Gibeon in front of the Tent of the LORD's presence. King Solomon and all the people worshipped the LORD there. 6 In front of the Tent the king worshipped the LORD by offering sacrifices on the bronze altar; he had a thousand animals killed and burnt whole on it.

7 That night God appeared to Solomon and asked, "What would you like me to give you?"

8 Solomon answered, "You always showed great love for my father David, and now you have let me succeed him as king. 9 O LORD God, fulfil the promise you made to my father. You have made me king over a people who are so many that they cannot be counted, 10 so give me the wisdom and knowledge I need to rule over them. Otherwise, how would I ever be able to rule this great people of yours?"

11 God replied to Solomon, "You have

1.4: 2 Sam 6.1-17; 1 Chr 13.5-14, 15.25—16.1   **1.5:** Ex 38.1-7   **1.9:** Gen 13.16, 28.14

made the right choice. Instead of asking for wealth or treasure or fame or the death of your enemies or even for long life for yourself, you have asked for wisdom and knowledge so that you can rule my people, over whom I have made you king. [12] I will give you wisdom and knowledge. And in addition, I will give you more wealth, treasure, and fame than any king has ever had before or will ever have again."

King Solomon's Power and Wealth
(1 Kgs 10.26-29)

13 So Solomon left[a] the place of worship at Gibeon, where the Tent of the LORD's presence was, and returned to Jerusalem. There he ruled over Israel. [14] He built up a force of fourteen hundred chariots and twelve thousand cavalry horses. Some of them he kept in Jerusalem, and the rest he stationed in various other cities. [15] During his reign silver and gold became as common in Jerusalem as stone, and cedar was as plentiful as ordinary sycamore. [16] The king's agents controlled the export of horses from Musri[b] and Cilicia,[c] [17] and the export of chariots from Egypt. They supplied the Hittite and Syrian kings with horses and chariots, selling chariots for six hundred pieces of silver each and horses for a hundred and fifty each.[d]

Preparations for Building the Temple
(1 Kgs 5.1-18)

2 King Solomon decided to build a temple where the LORD would be worshipped, and also to build a palace for himself. [2] He put seventy thousand men to work transporting materials, and eighty thousand men to work quarrying stone. There were three thousand six hundred men responsible for supervising the work.

3 Solomon sent a message to King Hiram of Tyre: "Do business with me as you did with my father, King David, when you sold him cedar logs for building his palace. [4] I am building a temple to honour the LORD my God. It will be a holy place where my people and I will worship him by burning incense of fragrant spices, where we will present offerings of sacred bread to him continuously, and where we will offer burnt-offerings every morning and evening, as well as on Sabbaths, New

Moon Festivals, and other holy days honouring the LORD our God. He has commanded Israel to do this for ever. [5] I intend to build a great temple, because our God is greater than any other god. [6] Yet no one can really build a temple for God, because even all the vastness of heaven cannot contain him. How then can I build a temple that would be anything more than a place to burn incense to God? [7] Now send me a man with skill in engraving, in working gold, silver, bronze, and iron, and in making blue, purple and red cloth. He will work with the craftsmen of Judah and Jerusalem whom my father David selected. [8] I know how skilful your woodmen are, so send me cedar, cypress, and juniper logs from Lebanon. I am ready to send my men to assist yours [9] in preparing large quantities of timber, because this temple I intend to build will be large and magnificent. [10] As provisions for your workmen, I will send you two thousand metric tons of wheat, two thousand metric tons of barley, four hundred thousand litres of wine, and four hundred thousand litres of olive-oil."

11 King Hiram sent Solomon a letter in reply. He wrote, "Because the LORD loves his people, he has made you their king. [12] Praise the LORD God of Israel, Creator of heaven and earth! He has given King David a wise son, full of understanding and skill, who now plans to build a temple for the LORD and a palace for himself. [13] I am sending you a wise and skilful master craftsman named Huram. [14] His mother was a member of the tribe of Dan and his father was a native of Tyre. He knows how to make things out of gold, silver, bronze, iron, stone, and wood. He can work with blue, purple, and red cloth, and with linen. He can do all sorts of engraving and can follow any design suggested to him. Let him work with your craftsmen and with those who worked for your father, King David. [15] So now send us the wheat, barley, wine, and olive-oil that you promised. [16] In the mountains of Lebanon we will cut down all the cedars you need, bind them together in rafts, and float them by sea as far as Joppa. From there you can take them to Jerusalem."

---

[a] *Some ancient translations* left; *Hebrew* came to.   [b] *Probable text* Musri; *Hebrew* Egypt.
[c] MUSRI AND CILICIA: *Two ancient countries in what is now south-east Turkey which were centres of horse-breeding in Solomon's time.*   [d] *Verses 16–17 in Hebrew are unclear.*
1.14: 1 Kgs 4.26   **1.16:** Deut 17.16   **2.6:** 1 Kgs 8.27; 2 Chr 6.18

Construction of the Temple Begins
(1 Kgs 6.1–38)

17 King Solomon took a census of all the foreigners living in the land of Israel, similar to the census his father David had taken. There were 153,600 resident foreigners. 18 He assigned 70,000 of them to transport materials and 80,000 to cut stones in the mountains, and appointed 3,600 supervisors to make sure the work was done.

3 King David, Solomon's father, had already prepared a place for the Temple. It was in Jerusalem, on Mount Moriah, where the LORD appeared to David, the place which Araunah the Jebusite had used as a threshing-place. King Solomon began the construction 2 in the second month of the fourth year that he was king. 3 The Temple which King Solomon built was twenty-seven metres long and nine metres wide. 4 The entrance room was the full width of the Temple, nine metres, and was fifty-four metres high. The inside of the room was overlaid with pure gold. 5 The main room was panelled with cedar and overlaid with fine gold, in which were worked designs of palm-trees and chain patterns. 6 The king decorated the Temple with beautiful precious stones and with gold imported from the land of Parvaim. 7 He used the gold to overlay the temple walls, the rafters, the thresholds, and the doors. On the walls the workmen carved designs of winged creatures. e 8 The inner room, called the Most Holy Place, was nine metres long and nine metres wide, which was the full width of the Temple. Over twenty metric tons of gold were used to cover the walls of the Most Holy Place; 9 570 grammes of gold were used for making nails, and the walls of the upper rooms were also covered with gold.

10 The king also ordered his workmen to make two winged creatures out of metal, cover them with gold, and place them in the Most Holy Place, 11–13 where they stood side by side facing the entrance. Each had two wings, each wing 2.2 metres long, which were spread out so that they touched each other in the centre of the room and reached the wall on either side of the room, stretching across the

full width of about nine metres. 14 A curtain for the Most Holy Place was made of linen and of other material, which was dyed blue, purple, and red, with designs of the winged creatures worked into it.

The Two Bronze Columns
(1 Kgs 7.15–22)

15 The king made two columns, each one fifteen and a half metres tall, and placed them in front of the Temple. Each one had a capital 2.2 metres tall. 16 The tops of the columns were decorated with a design of interwoven chains and one hundred bronze pomegranates. f 17 The columns were set at the sides of the temple entrance: the one on the south side was named Jachin, g and the one on the north side was named Boaz. h

Equipment for the Temple
(1 Kgs 7.23–51)

4 King Solomon had a bronze altar made, which was nine metres square and four and a half metres high. 2 He also made a round tank of bronze, 2.2 metres deep, 4.4 metres in diameter, and 13.2 metres in circumference. 3 All round the outer edge of the rim of the tank i were two rows of decorations, one above the other. The decorations were in the shape of bulls, which had been cast all in one piece with the rest of the tank. 4 The tank rested on the backs of twelve bronze bulls that faced outwards, three facing in each direction. 5 The sides of the tank were 75 millimetres thick. Its rim was like the rim of a cup, curving outwards like the petals of a flower. The tank held about sixty thousand litres. 6 They also made ten basins, five to be placed on the south side of the Temple and five on the north side. They were to be used to rinse the parts of the animals that were burnt as sacrifices. The water in the large tank was for the priests to use for washing.

7–8 They made ten gold lampstands according to the usual pattern, and ten tables, and placed them in the main room of the Temple, five lampstands and five tables on each side. They also made a hundred gold bowls.

9 They made an inner courtyard for the priests, and also an outer courtyard. The

---

e WINGED CREATURES: See Word List.   f Verse 16 in Hebrew is unclear.
g JACHIN: This name sounds like the Hebrew for "he (God) establishes."
h BOAZ: This name sounds like the Hebrew for "by his (God's) strength."
i Probable text All round...tank; Hebrew unclear.

3.1: Gen 22.2   **3.8:** Ex 26.33–34   **3.10–13:** Ex 25.18–20   **3.14:** Ex 26.31   **4.1:** Ex 27.1–2
4.6: Ex 30.17–21   **4.7:** Ex 25.31–40   **4.8:** Ex 25.23–30

doors in the gates between the courtyards were covered with bronze. ¹⁰The tank was placed near the south-east corner of the Temple.

11–16 Huram also made pots, shovels, and bowls. He completed all the objects that he had promised King Solomon he would make for the Temple:

The two columns

The two bowl-shaped capitals on top of the columns

The design of interwoven chains on each capital

The four hundred bronze pomegranates arranged in two rows round the design of each capital

The ten*ʲ* carts

The ten basins

The tank

The twelve bulls supporting the tank

The pots, shovels, and forks

Huram the master craftsman made all these objects*ᵏ* out of polished bronze, as King Solomon had commanded, for use in the Temple of the LORD.

17 The king had them all made in the foundry between Sukkoth and Zeredah*ˡ* in the Jordan Valley. ¹⁸So many objects were made that no one determined the total weight of the bronze used.

19 King Solomon also had gold furnishings made for the Temple: the altar and the tables for the bread offered to God; ²⁰the lampstands and the lamps of fine gold that were to burn in front of the Most Holy Place, according to plan; ²¹the flower decorations, the lamps, and the tongs; ²²the lamp snuffers, the bowls, the dishes for incense, and the pans used for carrying live coals. All these objects were made of pure gold. The outer doors of the Temple and the doors to the Most Holy Place were overlaid with gold.

5 When King Solomon finished all the work on the Temple, he placed in the temple storerooms all the things that his father David had dedicated to the LORD—the silver, gold, and other articles.

The Covenant Box Is Brought to the Temple
(1 Kgs 8.1–9)

2 Then King Solomon summoned all the leaders of the tribes and clans of Israel to assemble in Jerusalem, in order to take the LORD's Covenant Box from Zion, David's City, *ᵐ* to the Temple. ³They all assembled at the time of the Festival of Shelters. ⁴When all the leaders had gathered, then the Levites lifted the Covenant Box ⁵and carried it to the Temple. The priests and the Levites also moved the Tent of the LORD's presence and all its equipment to the Temple. ⁶King Solomon and all the people of Israel assembled in front of the Covenant Box and sacrificed a large number of sheep and cattle—too many to count. ⁷Then the priests carried the Covenant Box of the LORD into the Temple and put it in the Most Holy Place, beneath the winged creatures. ⁸Their outstretched wings covered the Box and the carrying-poles. ⁹The ends of the poles could be seen by anyone standing directly in front of the Most Holy Place, but from nowhere else. (The poles are still there today.) ¹⁰There was nothing inside the Covenant Box except the two stone tablets which Moses had placed there at Mount Sinai, when the LORD made a covenant with the people of Israel as they were coming from Egypt.

The Glory of the Lord

11–14 All the priests present, regardless of the group to which they belonged, had consecrated themselves. And all the Levite musicians—Asaph, Heman, and Jeduthun, and the members of their clans—were wearing linen clothing. The Levites stood near the east side of the altar with cymbals and harps, and with them were a hundred and twenty priests playing trumpets. The singers were accompanied in perfect harmony by trumpets, cymbals, and other instruments, as they praised the LORD, singing:

"Praise the LORD, because he is good,
And his love is eternal."

As the priests were leaving the Temple, it was suddenly filled with a cloud shining with the dazzling light of the LORD's presence, and they could not continue the service of worship.

Solomon's Address to the People
(1 Kgs 8.12–21)

6 Then King Solomon prayed,
"LORD, you have chosen to live in clouds and darkness.

ʲ Probable text (see 1 Kgs 7.40–45) ten; Hebrew he made.
ᵏ One ancient translation all these objects; Hebrew all their objects.
ˡ Zeredah; or Zarethan (see 1 Kgs 7.46). *ᵐ DAVID'S CITY: See Word List.*
5.1: 2 Sam 8.11; 1 Chr 18.11   **5.2:** 2 Sam 6.12–15; 1 Chr 15.25–28   **5.10:** Deut 10.5
5.13: 1 Chr 16.34; 2 Chr 7.3; Ezra 3.11; Ps 100.5, 106.1, 107.1, 116.1, 136.1; Jer 33.11
5.13–14: Ex 40.34–35

2 Now I have built a majestic temple for you,

a place for you to live in for ever."

3 All the people of Israel were standing there. The king turned to face them and asked God's blessing on them. 4 He said, "Praise the LORD God of Israel! He has kept the promise he made to my father David when he said to him, 5 'From the time I brought my people out of Egypt until now, I did not choose any city in the land of Israel as the place to build a temple where I would be worshipped, and I did not choose anyone to lead my people Israel. 6 But now I have chosen Jerusalem as the place where I will be worshipped, and you, David, to rule my people.'"

7 And Solomon continued, "My father David planned to build a temple for the worship of the LORD God of Israel, 8 but the LORD said to him, 'You were right in wanting to build a temple for me, 9 but you will never build it. It is your son, your own son, who will build my temple.'

10 "Now the LORD has kept his promise: I have succeeded my father as king of Israel, and I have built a temple for the worship of the LORD God of Israel. 11 I have placed in the Temple the Covenant Box, which contains the stone tablets of the covenant which the LORD made with the people of Israel."

Solomon's Prayer
(1 Kgs 8.22-53)

12 Then in the presence of the people Solomon went and stood in front of the altar and raised his arms in prayer. 13 (Solomon had made a bronze platform and put it in the middle of the courtyard. It was 2.2 metres square and 1.3 metres high. He mounted this platform, knelt down where everyone could see him, and raised his hands towards heaven.) 14 He prayed, "LORD God of Israel, in all heaven and earth there is no god like you. You keep your covenant with your people and show them your love when they live in wholehearted obedience to you. 15 You have kept the promise you made to my father David; today every word has been fulfilled. 16 Now, LORD God of Israel, keep the other promise you made to my father when you told him that there would always be one of his descendants ruling as king of Israel, provided that they carefully obeyed your Law just as he did. 17 So now, LORD God of Israel, let every-

thing come true that you promised to your servant David.

18 "But can you, O God, really live on earth among men and women? Not even all heaven is large enough to hold you, so how can this Temple that I have built be large enough? 19 LORD my God, I am your servant. Listen to my prayer and grant the requests I make to you. 20 Watch over this Temple day and night. You have promised that this is where you will be worshipped, so hear me when I face this Temple and pray. 21 Hear my prayers and the prayers of your people Israel when they face this place and pray. In your home in heaven hear us and forgive us.

22 "When a person is accused of wronging another and is brought to your altar in this Temple to take an oath that he is innocent, 23 O LORD, listen in heaven and judge your servants. Punish the guilty one as he deserves and acquit the one who is innocent.

24 "When your people Israel are defeated by their enemies because they have sinned against you and then when they turn to you and come to this Temple, humbly praying to you for forgiveness, 25 listen to them in heaven. Forgive the sins of your people and bring them back to the land which you gave to them and to their ancestors.

26 "When you hold back the rain because your people have sinned against you and then when they repent and face this Temple, humbly praying to you, 27 O LORD, listen to them in heaven and forgive the sins of your servants, the people of Israel, and teach them to do what is right. Then, O LORD, send rain on this land of yours, which you gave to your people as a permanent possession.

28 "When there is famine in the land or an epidemic or the crops are destroyed by scorching winds or swarms of locusts, or when your people are attacked by their enemies, or when there is disease or sickness among them, 29 listen to their prayers. If any of your people Israel, out of heartfelt sorrow, stretch out their hands in prayer towards this Temple, 30 hear their prayer. Listen to them in your home in heaven and forgive them. You alone know the thoughts of the human heart. Deal with each person as he deserves, 31 so that your people may honour you and obey you all the time they live in the land which you gave to our ancestors.

6.4-9: 2 Sam 7.1-13; 1 Chr 17.1-12 **6.16:** 1 Kgs 2.4 **6.18:** 2 Chr 2.6 **6.20:** Deut 12.11

32 "When a foreigner who lives in a distant land hears how great and powerful you are and how you are always ready to act, and then he comes to pray at this Temple, 33 listen to his prayer. In heaven, where you live, hear him and do what he asks you to do, so that all the peoples of the world may know you and obey you, as your people Israel do. Then they will know that this Temple I have built is where you are to be worshipped.

34 "When you command your people to go into battle against their enemies and they pray to you, wherever they are, facing this city which you have chosen and this Temple which I have built for you, 35 listen to their prayers. Hear them in heaven and give them victory.

36 "When your people sin against you— and there is no one who does not sin—and in your anger you let their enemies defeat them and take them as prisoners to some other land, even if that land is far away, 37 listen to your people's prayers. If there in that land they repent and pray to you, confessing how sinful and wicked they have been, hear their prayers, O LORD. 38 If in that land they truly and sincerely repent and pray to you as they face towards this land which you gave to our ancestors, this city which you have chosen, and this Temple which I have built for you, 39 then listen to their prayers. In your home in heaven hear them and be merciful to them and forgive all the sins of your people.

40 "Now, O my God, look on us and listen to the prayers offered in this place. 41 Rise up now, LORD God, and with the Covenant Box, the symbol of your power, enter the Temple and stay here for ever. Bless your priests in all they do, and may all your people be happy because of your goodness to them. 42 LORD God, do not reject the king you have chosen. Remember the love you had for your servant David." [n]

The Dedication of the Temple
(1 Kgs 8.62–66)

7 When King Solomon finished his prayer, fire came down from heaven and burnt up the sacrifices that had been offered, and the dazzling light of the LORD's presence filled the Temple. 2 Because the Temple was full of the dazzling light, the priests could not enter

it. 3 When the people of Israel saw the fire fall from heaven and the light fill the Temple, they fell face downwards on the pavement, worshipping God and praising him for his goodness and his eternal love. 4 Then Solomon and all the people offered sacrifices to the LORD. 5 He sacrificed 22,000 head of cattle and 120,000 sheep as fellowship-offerings. And so he and all the people dedicated the Temple. 6 The priests stood in the places that were assigned to them, and facing them stood the Levites, praising the LORD with the musical instruments that King David had provided and singing the hymn, "His Love Is Eternal!" as they had been commissioned by David. The priests blew trumpets while all the people stood.

7 Solomon consecrated the central part of the courtyard, the area in front of the Temple, and then offered there the sacrifices burnt whole, the grain-offerings, and the fat from the fellowship-offerings. He did this because the bronze altar which he had made was too small for all these offerings.

8 Solomon and all the people of Israel celebrated the Festival of Shelters for seven days. There was a huge crowd of people from as far away as Hamath Pass in the north and the Egyptian border in the south. 9 They had spent seven days for the dedication of the altar and then seven more days for the festival. On the last day they had a closing celebration, 10 and on the following day, the twenty-third day of the seventh month, Solomon sent the people home. They were happy about all the blessings that the LORD had given to his people Israel, to David, and to Solomon.

God Appears to Solomon Again
(1 Kgs 9.1–9)

11 After King Solomon had finished the Temple and the palace, successfully completing all his plans for them, 12 the LORD appeared to him at night. He said to him, "I have heard your prayer, and I accept this Temple as the place where sacrifices are to be offered to me. 13 Whenever I hold back the rain or send locusts to eat up the crops or send an epidemic on my people, 14 if they pray to me and repent and turn away from the evil they have been doing, then I will hear them in heaven, forgive their sins, and make their

[n] the love you...David; or your servant David's loyal service.
6.41–42: Ps 132.8–10   **7.1:** Lev 9.23–24
7.3: 1 Chr 16.34; 2 Chr 5.13; Ezra 3.11; Ps 100.5, 106.1, 107.1, 118.1, 136.1; Jer 33.11

land prosperous again. [15] I will watch over this Temple and be ready to hear all the prayers that are offered here, [16] because I have chosen it and consecrated it as the place where I will be worshipped for ever. I will watch over it and protect it for all time. [17] If you serve me faithfully as your father David did, obeying my laws and doing everything I have commanded you, [18] I will keep the promise I made to your father David when I told him that Israel would always be ruled by his descendants. [19] But if you and your people ever disobey the laws and commands I have given you, and worship other gods, [20] then I will remove you from the land that I gave you, and I will abandon this Temple that I have consecrated as the place where I am to be worshipped. People everywhere will ridicule it and treat it with contempt.

21 "The Temple is now greatly honoured, but then everyone who passes by it will be amazed and will ask, 'Why did the LORD do this to this land and this Temple?' [22] People will answer, 'It is because they abandoned the LORD their God, who brought their ancestors out of Egypt. They gave their allegiance to other gods and worshipped them. That is why the LORD has brought this disaster on them.'"

Solomon's Achievements
(1 Kgs 9.10-28)

8 It took Solomon twenty years to build the Temple and his palace. [2] He also rebuilt the cities that King Hiram had given him, and sent Israelites to settle in them. [3] He captured the territory of Hamath and Zobah [4] and fortified the city of Palmyra in the desert. He rebuilt all the cities in Hamath that were centres for storing supplies. [5] Solomon also rebuilt the following cities: Upper Beth Horon and Lower Beth Horon (fortified cities with gates that could be barred), [6] the city of Baalath, all the cities where he stored supplies, and the cities where his horses and chariots were stationed. He carried out all his plans for building in Jerusalem, in Lebanon, and throughout the territory that he ruled over. [7-8] Solomon employed in forced labour all the descendants of the people of Canaan whom the Israelites had not killed when they took possession of the land. These included Hittites, Amorites, Perizzites, Hivites, and Jebu-

sites, whose descendants continue to be slaves down to the present time. [9] Israelites were not used in forced labour, but served as soldiers, officers, chariot commanders, and horsemen. [10] There were 250 officials in charge of the forced labour working on the various building projects.

11 Solomon moved his wife, the daughter of the king of Egypt, from David's City to a house he built for her. He said, "She must not live in the palace of King David of Israel, because any place where the Covenant Box has been is holy."

12 Solomon offered sacrifices to the LORD on the altar which he had built in front of the Temple. [13] He offered burnt-offerings according to the requirements of the Law of Moses for each holy day: Sabbaths, New Moon Festivals, and the three annual festivals—the Festival of Unleavened Bread, the Harvest Festival, and the Festival of Shelters. [14] Following the rules laid down by his father David, he organized the daily work of the priests and of the Levites who assisted the priests in singing hymns and in doing their work. He also organized the temple guards in sections for performing their daily duties at each gate, in accordance with the commands of David, the man of God. [15] The instructions which David had given the priests and the Levites concerning the storehouses and other matters were carried out in detail.

16 By this time all Solomon's projects had been completed. From the laying of the foundation of the LORD's Temple to its completion, all the work had been successful.

17 Then Solomon went to Eziongeber and Elath, ports on the shore of the Gulf of Aqaba, in the land of Edom. [18] King Hiram sent him ships under the command of his own officers and manned by experienced sailors. They sailed with Solomon's officers to the land of Ophir and brought back to Solomon more than fifteen thousand kilogrammes of gold.

The Visit of the Queen of Sheba
(1 Kgs 10.1-13)

9 The queen of Sheba heard of King Solomon's fame, and she travelled to Jerusalem to test him with difficult questions. She brought with her a large group of attendants, as well as camels loaded with spices, jewels, and a large amount of gold. When she and Solomon

---

7.18: 1 Kgs 2.4   **8.13:** Ex 23.14-17, 34.22-23; Num 28.9, 29.39; Deut 16.16
9.1-9: Mt 12.42; Lk 11.31

met, she asked him all the questions that she could think of. ²He answered them all; there was nothing too difficult for him to explain. ³The queen of Sheba heard Solomon's wisdom and saw the palace he had built. ⁴She saw the food that was

It left her breathless and amazed (9.4)

served at his table, the living-quarters for his officials, the organization of his palace staff and the uniforms they wore, the clothing of the servants who waited on him at feasts, and the sacrifices he offered⁰ in the Temple. It left her breathless and amazed.

5 She said to the king, "What I heard in my own country about you𝑃 and your wisdom is true! ⁶I did not believe what they told me until I came and saw for myself. I had not heard of even half your wisdom. You are even wiser than people say. ⁷How fortunate are the men who serve you, who are always in your presence and are privileged to hear your wise sayings! ⁸Praise the LORD your God! He has shown how pleased he is with you by making you king, to rule in his name. Because he loves his people Israel and wants to preserve them for ever, he has made you their king so that you can maintain law and justice."

9 She presented to King Solomon the gifts she had brought: more than four thousand kilogrammes of gold and a very large amount of spices and jewels. There have never been any other spices as fine as those that the queen of Sheba gave to King Solomon.

10 (The men of King Hiram and of King Solomon who brought gold from Ophir also brought juniper wood and jewels. ¹¹Solomon used the wood to make stairs for the Temple and for his palace, and to make harps and lyres for the musicians. Nothing like that had ever been seen before in the land of Judah.)

12 King Solomon gave the queen of Sheba everything she asked for. This was in addition to what he gave her in exchange for the gifts𝑞 she brought to him. Then she and her attendants returned to the land of Sheba.

King Solomon's Wealth
(1 Kgs 10.14–25)

13 Every year King Solomon received almost twenty-three thousand kilogrammes of gold, ¹⁴in addition to the taxes paid by the traders and merchants. The kings of Arabia and the governors of the Israelite districts also brought him silver and gold. ¹⁵Solomon made two hundred large shields, each of which was covered with about seven kilogrammes of beaten gold, ¹⁶and three hundred smaller shields, each covered with about three kilogrammes of beaten gold. He had them all placed in the Hall of the Forest of Lebanon.𝑟

17 The king also had a large throne made. Part of it was covered with ivory and the rest of it was covered with pure gold. ¹⁸Six steps led up to the throne, and there was a footstool attached to it, covered with gold. There were arms on each side of the throne, and the figure of a lion stood at each side. ¹⁹Twelve figures of lions were on the steps, one at either end of each step. No throne like this had ever existed in any other kingdom.

20 All King Solomon's cups were made of gold, and all the utensils in the Hall of the Forest of Lebanon were of pure gold. Silver was not considered valuable in Solomon's day. ²¹He had a fleet of ocean-going ships sailing with King Hiram's fleet. Every three years his fleet would return, bringing gold, silver, ivory, apes, and monkeys.

⁰ *Probable text (see 1 Kgs 10.5)* sacrifices he offered; *Hebrew* his upper rooms.
𝑃you; *or* your deeds.   𝑞 *Probable text* he gave her in exchange for the gifts; *Hebrew unclear.*
𝑟HALL OF THE FOREST OF LEBANON: *A large ceremonial hall in the palace, probably so called because it was panelled in cedar.*

22 King Solomon was richer and wiser than any other king in the world. 23 They all consulted him, to hear the wisdom that God had given him. 24 Each of them brought Solomon gifts—articles of silver and gold, robes, weapons, spices, horses, and mules. This continued year after year.

25 King Solomon also had four thousand stalls for his chariots and horses, and had twelve thousand cavalry horses. Some of them he kept in Jerusalem and the rest he stationed in various other cities. 26 He was supreme ruler of all the kings in the territory from the River Euphrates to Philistia and the Egyptian border. 27 During his reign silver was as common in Jerusalem as stone, and cedar was as plentiful as ordinary sycomore in the foothills of Judah. 28 Solomon imported horses from Musri s and from every other country.

Summary of Solomon's Reign
(1 Kgs 11.41–43)

29 The rest of the history of Solomon from beginning to end is recorded in *The History of Nathan the Prophet,* in *The Prophecy of Ahijah of Shiloh,* and in *The Visions of Iddo the Prophet,* which also deal with the reign of King Jeroboam of Israel. 30 Solomon ruled in Jerusalem over all Israel for forty years. 31 He died and was buried in David's City, and his son Rehoboam succeeded him as king.

The Northern Tribes Revolt
(1 Kgs 12.1–20)

10 Rehoboam went to Shechem, where all the people of northern Israel had gathered to make him king. 2 When Jeroboam son of Nebat, who had gone to Egypt to escape from King Solomon, heard this news, he returned home. 3 The people of the northern tribes sent for him, and they all went together to Rehoboam and said to him, 4 "Your father placed heavy burdens on us. If you make these burdens lighter and make life easier for us, we will be your loyal subjects."

5 Rehoboam replied, "Give me three days to consider the matter. Then come back." So the people left.

6 King Rehoboam consulted the older men who had served as his father Solomon's advisers. "What answer do you advise me to give these people?" he asked.

7 They replied, "If you are kind to these people and try to please them by giving

a considerate answer, they will always serve you loyally."

8 But he ignored the advice of the older men and went instead to the young men who had grown up with him and who were now his advisers. 9 "What do you advise me to do?" he asked. "What shall I say to the people who are asking me to make their burdens lighter?"

10 They replied, "This is what you should tell them: 'My little finger is thicker than my father's waist.' 11 Tell them, 'My father placed heavy burdens on you; I will make them even heavier. He beat you with a whip; I'll flog you with a horsewhip!'"

12 Three days later Jeroboam and all the people returned to King Rehoboam, as he had instructed them. 13 The king ignored the advice of the older men and spoke harshly to the people, 14 as the younger men had advised. He said, "My father placed heavy burdens on you; I will make them even heavier. He beat you with a whip; I'll flog you with a horsewhip!" 15 It was the will of the LORD God to bring about what he had spoken to Jeroboam son of Nebat through the prophet Ahijah from Shiloh. This is why the king did not pay any attention to the people.

16 When the people saw that the king would not listen to them, they shouted, "Down with David and his family! What have they ever done for us? Men of Israel, let's go home! Let Rehoboam look out for himself!"

So the people of Israel rebelled, 17 leaving Rehoboam as king only of the people who lived in the territory of Judah.

18 Then King Rehoboam sent Adoniram, who was in charge of the forced labour, to go to the Israelites, but they stoned him to death. At this, Rehoboam hurriedly got into his chariot and escaped to Jerusalem. 19 Ever since that time the people of the northern kingdom of Israel have been in rebellion against the dynasty of David.

Shemaiah's Prophecy
(1 Kgs 12.21–24)

11 When King Rehoboam arrived in Jerusalem, he called together a hundred and eighty thousand of the best soldiers from the tribes of Benjamin and Judah. He intended to go to war and restore his control over the northern tribes

---

s *Probable text (see 1.16)* Musri; *Hebrew* Egypt.
9.25: 1 Kgs 4.26　　**9.26:** Gen 15.18; 1 Kgs 4.21　　**9.28:** Deut 17.16　　**10.16:** 2 Sam 20.1

of Israel. ²But the LORD told the prophet Shemaiah ³to give this message to King Rehoboam and to all the people of the tribes of Judah and Benjamin: ⁴"Do not attack your fellow-Israelites. Go home, all of you. What has happened is my will." They obeyed the LORD's command and did not go to fight Jeroboam.

Rehoboam Fortifies the Cities

5 Rehoboam remained in Jerusalem and had fortifications built for the following cities of Judah and Benjamin: ⁶Bethlehem, Etam, Tekoa, ⁷Bethzur, Soco, Adullam, ⁸Gath, Mareshah, Ziph, ⁹Adoraim, Lachish, Azekah, ¹⁰Zorah, Aijalon, and Hebron. ¹¹He had them strongly fortified and appointed a commander for each of them, and in each one he placed supplies of food, olive-oil, and wine, ¹²and also shields and spears. In this way he kept Judah and Benjamin under his control.

Priests and Levites Come to Judah

13 From all the territory of Israel priests and Levites came south to Judah. ¹⁴The Levites abandoned their pastures and other land and moved to Judah and Jerusalem, because King Jeroboam of Israel and his successors would not let them serve as priests of the LORD. ¹⁵Jeroboam appointed priests of his own to serve at the pagan places of worship and to worship demons and the idols he made in the form of bull-calves. ¹⁶From all the tribes of Israel people who sincerely wanted to worship the LORD, the God of Israel, followed the Levites to Jerusalem, so that they could offer sacrifices to the LORD, the God of their ancestors. ¹⁷This strengthened the kingdom of Judah, and for three years they supported Rehoboam son of Solomon and lived as they had under the rule of King David and King Solomon.

Rehoboam's Family

18 Rehoboam married Mahalath, whose father was Jerimoth son of David, and whose mother was Abihail, the daughter of Eliab and granddaughter of Jesse. ¹⁹They had three sons, Jeush, Shemariah, and Zaham. ²⁰Later he married Maacah, the daughter of Absalom, and they had four sons: Abijah, Attai, Ziza, and Shelomith. ²¹In all, Rehoboam had eighteen wives and sixty concubines, and he fathered twenty-eight sons and sixty

daughters. Of all his wives and concubines he loved Maacah best, ²²and he favoured her son Abijah over all his other children, choosing him as the one to succeed him as king. ²³Rehoboam wisely assigned responsibilities to his sons, and stationed them throughout Judah and Benjamin in the fortified cities. He provided generously for them and also secured many wives for them.

An Egyptian Invasion of Judah
(1 Kgs 14.25–28)

12 As soon as Rehoboam had established his authority as king, he and all his people abandoned the Law of the LORD. ²In the fifth year of Rehoboam's reign their disloyalty to the LORD was punished. King Shishak of Egypt attacked Jerusalem ³with an army of twelve hundred chariots, sixty thousand horsemen, and more soldiers than could be counted, including Libyan, Sukkite, and Sudanese troops. ⁴He captured the fortified cities of Judah and advanced as far as Jerusalem.

5 Shemaiah the prophet went to King Rehoboam and the Judaean leaders who had gathered in Jerusalem to escape Shishak. He said to them, "This is the LORD's message to you: 'You have abandoned me, so now I have abandoned you to Shishak.'"

6 The king and the leaders admitted that they had sinned, and they said, "What the LORD is doing is just."

7 When the LORD saw this, he spoke again to Shemaiah and said to him, "Because they admit their sin, I will not destroy them. But when Shishak attacks, they will barely survive. Jerusalem will not feel the full force of my anger, ⁸but Shishak will conquer them, and they will learn the difference between serving me and serving earthly rulers."

9 King Shishak came to Jerusalem and took the treasures from the Temple and from the palace. He took everything, including the gold shields that King Solomon had made. ¹⁰To replace them, Rehoboam made bronze shields and entrusted them to the officers responsible for guarding the palace gates. ¹¹Every time the king went to the Temple, the guards carried the shields and then returned them to the guardroom. ¹²Because he submitted to the LORD, the LORD's anger did not completely destroy him, and things went well for Judah.

Summary of Rehoboam's Reign

13 Rehoboam ruled in Jerusalem and increased his power as king. He was forty-one years old when he became king, and he ruled for seventeen years in Jerusalem, the city which the LORD had chosen from all the territory of Israel as the place where he was to be worshipped. Rehoboam's mother was Naamah, from the land of Ammon. 14 He did what was evil, because he did not try to find the LORD's will.

15 Rehoboam's acts from beginning to end and his family records are found in *The History of Shemaiah the Prophet* and *The History of Iddo the Prophet.* Rehoboam and Jeroboam were constantly at war with each other. 16 Rehoboam died and was buried in the royal tombs in David's City and his son Abijah succeeded him as king.

Abijah's War with Jeroboam
(1 Kgs 15.1-8)

13 In the eighteenth year of the reign of King Jeroboam of Israel, Abijah became king of Judah, 2 and he ruled for three years in Jerusalem. His mother was Micaiah daughter of Uriel, from the city of Gibeah.

War broke out between Abijah and Jeroboam. 3 Abijah raised an army of 400,000 soldiers, and Jeroboam opposed him with an army of 800,000.

4 The armies met in the hill-country of Ephraim. King Abijah went up Mount Zemaraim and called out to Jeroboam and the Israelites: "Listen to me!" he said. 5 "Don't you know that the LORD, the God of Israel, made an unbreakable covenant with David, giving him and his descendants kingship over Israel for ever? 6 Jeroboam son of Nebat rebelled against Solomon, his king. 7 Later he gathered together a group of worthless scoundrels, and they forced their will on Rehoboam son of Solomon, who was too young and inexperienced to resist them. 8 Now you propose to fight against the royal authority that the LORD gave to David's descendants. You have a huge army and have with you the gold bull-calves that Jeroboam made to be your gods. 9 You drove out the LORD's priests, the descendants of Aaron, and you drove out the Levites. In their place you appointed priests in the same way that other nations do. Anybody who comes along with a bull or seven sheep can get himself conse-crated as a priest of those so-called gods of yours.

10 "But we still serve the LORD our God and have not abandoned him. Priests descended from Aaron perform their duties, and Levites assist them. 11 Every morning and every evening they offer him incense and animal sacrifices burnt whole. They present the offerings of bread on a table that is ritually clean, and every evening they light the lamps on the gold lampstand. We do what the LORD has commanded, but you have abandoned him. 12 God himself is our leader and his priests are here with trumpets, ready to blow them and call us to battle against you. People of Israel, don't fight against the LORD, the God of your ancestors! You can't win!"

13 Meanwhile Jeroboam had sent some of his troops to ambush the Judaean army from the rear, while the rest faced them from the front. 14 The Judaeans looked round and saw that they were surrounded. They cried to the LORD for help, and the priests blew the trumpets. 15 The Judaeans gave a loud shout, and led by Abijah, they attacked; God defeated Jeroboam and the Israelite army. 16 The Israelites fled from the Judaeans, and God let the Judaeans overpower them. 17 Abijah and his army dealt the Israelites a crushing defeat—half a million of Israel's best soldiers were killed. 18 And so the people of Judah were victorious over Israel, because they relied on the LORD, the God of their ancestors.

19 Abijah pursued Jeroboam's army and occupied some of his cities: Bethel, Jeshanah, and Ephron, and the villages near each of these cities. 20 Jeroboam never regained his power during Abijah's reign. Finally the LORD struck him down, and he died.

21 Abijah, however, grew more powerful. He had fourteen wives and fathered twenty-two sons and sixteen daughters. 22 The rest of the history of Abijah, what he said and what he did, is written in *The History of Iddo the Prophet.*

King Asa Defeats the Sudanese

14 King Abijah died and was buried in the royal tombs in David's City. His son Asa succeeded him as king, and under Asa the land enjoyed peace for ten years. 2 Asa pleased the LORD, his God, by doing what was right and good. 3 He removed the foreign altars and the pagan places of worship, broke down the sacred stone columns, and cut down the symbols of the goddess Asherah. [4] He commanded the people of Judah to do the will of the LORD, the God of their ancestors, and to obey his teachings and commands. [5] Because he abolished the pagan places of worship and the incense-altars from all the cities of Judah, the kingdom was at peace under his rule. [6] He built fortifications for the cities of Judah during this time, and for several years there was no war, because the LORD gave him peace. [7] He said to the people of Judah, "Let us fortify the cities by building walls and towers, and gates that can be shut and barred. We have control of the land because we have done the will of the LORD our God. He has protected us and given us security on every side." And so they built and prospered. [8] King Asa had an army of 300,000 men from Judah, armed with shields and spears, and 280,000 men from Benjamin, armed with shields and bows. All of them were brave, well-trained men.

9 A Sudanese named Zerah invaded Judah with an army of a million men and three hundred chariots and advanced as far as Mareshah. [10] Asa went out to fight him, and both sides took up their positions in the Valley of Zephathah near Mareshah. [11] Asa prayed to the LORD his God, "O LORD, you can help a weak army as easily as a powerful one. Help us now, O LORD our God, because we are relying on you, and in your name we have come out to fight against this huge army. LORD, you are our God; no one can hope to defeat you."

12 The LORD defeated the Sudanese army when Asa and the Judaean army attacked them. They fled, [13] and Asa and his troops pursued them as far as Gerar. So many of the Sudanese were killed that the army was unable to rally and fight. [t] They were overpowered by the LORD and his army, and the army took large amounts of loot. [14] Then they were able to destroy the cities in the area around Gerar, because the people there were terrified of the LORD. The army plundered all those cities and captured large amounts of loot. [15] They also attacked the camps of some shepherds, capturing large numbers of sheep and camels. Then they returned to Jerusalem.

Asa's Reforms

15 The spirit of God came upon Azariah son of Oded, [2] and he went to meet King Asa. He called out, "Listen to me, King Asa, and all you people of Judah and Benjamin! The LORD is with you as long as you are with him. If you look for him, he will let you find him, but if you turn away, he will abandon you. [3] For a long time Israel lived without the true God, without priests to teach them, and without a law. [4] But when trouble came, they turned to the LORD, the God of Israel. They searched for him and found him. [5] In those days no one could come and go in safety, because there was trouble and disorder in every land. [6] One nation oppressed another nation, and one city oppressed another city, because God was bringing trouble and distress on them. [7] But you must be strong and not be discouraged. The work that you do will be rewarded."

8 When Asa heard the prophecy that Azariah son of [u] Oded had spoken, he was encouraged. He did away with all the idols in the land of Judah and Benjamin and all the idols in the cities he had captured in the hill-country of Ephraim. He also repaired the altar of the LORD that stood in the temple courtyard.

9 Many people had come over to Asa's side from Ephraim, Manasseh, and Simeon, and were living in his kingdom, because they had seen that the LORD was with him. Asa summoned all of them and the people of Judah and Benjamin. [10] They assembled in Jerusalem in the third month of the fifteenth year that Asa was king. [11] On that day they offered sacrifices to the LORD from the loot they had brought back: seven hundred head of cattle and seven thousand sheep. [12] They made a covenant in which they agreed to worship the LORD, the God of their ancestors, with all their heart and soul. [13] Anyone, young or old, male or female, who did not worship him was to be put to death. [14] In a loud voice they took an oath in the LORD's name that they would keep the covenant, and then they shouted and blew trumpets. [15] All the people of Judah were happy because they had made this covenant with all their heart. They took delight in worshipping the LORD, and he

---

[t] So many of the Sudanese...fight; *or* The Sudanese were completely defeated; not one of them was left alive.
[u] *Some ancient translations* Azariah son of; *Hebrew does not have these words.*

accepted them and gave them peace on every side.

16 King Asa removed his grandmother Maacah from her position as queen mother, because she had made an obscene idol of the fertility goddess Asherah. Asa cut down the idol, chopped it up, and burnt the pieces in the valley of the Kidron. 17 Even though Asa did not destroy all the pagan places of worship in the land, he remained faithful to the LORD all his life. 18 He placed in the Temple all the objects his father Abijah had dedicated to God, as well as the gold and silver objects that he himself dedicated. 19 There was no more war until the thirty-fifth year of his reign.

Troubles with Israel
(1 Kgs 15.17–22)

16 In the thirty-sixth year of the reign of King Asa of Judah, King Baasha of Israel invaded Judah and started to fortify Ramah in order to cut off all traffic in and out of Judah. 2 So Asa took silver and gold from the treasuries of the Temple and the palace and sent it to Damascus, to King Benhadad of Syria, with this message: 3 "Let us be allies, as our fathers were. This silver and gold is a present for you. Now break your alliance with King Baasha of Israel so that he will have to pull his troops out of my territory."
4 Benhadad agreed to Asa's proposal and sent his commanding officers and their armies to attack the cities of Israel. They captured Ijon, Dan, Abel Beth Maacah, and all the cities of Naphtali where supplies were stored. 5 When King Baasha heard what was happening, he stopped fortifying Ramah and abandoned the work. 6 Then King Asa gathered men from throughout Judah and ordered them to carry off the stones and timber that Baasha had been using at Ramah, and they used them to fortify the cities of Geba and Mizpah.

The Prophet Hanani

7 At that time the prophet Hanani went to King Asa and said, "Because you relied on the king of Syria instead of relying on the LORD your God, the army of the king of Israel v has escaped from you. 8 Didn't the Sudanese and the Libyans have large armies with many chariots and horsemen? But because you relied on the LORD, he gave you victory over them. 9 The LORD keeps close watch over the whole

world, to give strength to those whose hearts are loyal to him. You have acted foolishly, and so from now on you will always be at war." 10 This made Asa so angry with the prophet that he had him put in chains. It was at this same time that Asa began treating some of the people cruelly.

The End of Asa's Reign
(1 Kgs 15.23–24)

11 All the events of Asa's reign from beginning to end are recorded in *The History of the Kings of Judah and Israel.* 12 In the thirty-ninth year that Asa was king, he was crippled by a severe foot disease; but even then he did not turn to the LORD for help, but to doctors. 13 Two years later he died 14 and was buried in the rock tomb which he had carved out for himself in David's City. They used spices and perfumed oils to prepare his body for burial, and they built a huge bonfire to mourn his death.

Jehoshaphat Becomes King

17 Jehoshaphat succeeded his father Asa as king and strengthened his position against Israel. 2 He stationed troops in the fortified cities of Judah, in the Judaean countryside, and in the cities which Asa had captured in the territory of Ephraim. 3 The LORD blessed Jehoshaphat because he followed the example of his father's early life and did not worship Baal. 4 He served his father's God, obeyed God's commands, and did not act in the way the kings of Israel did. 5 The LORD gave Jehoshaphat firm control over the kingdom of Judah, and all the people brought him gifts, so that he became wealthy and highly honoured. 6 He took pride in serving the LORD and destroyed all the pagan places of worship and the symbols of the goddess Asherah in Judah.

7 In the third year of his reign he sent out the following officials to teach in the cities of Judah: Benhail, Obadiah, Zechariah, Nethanel, and Micaiah. 8 They were accompanied by nine Levites and two priests. The Levites were Shemaiah, Nethaniah, Zebadiah, Asahel, Shemiramoth, Jehonathan, Adonijah, Tobijah, and Tobadonijah; and the priests were Elishama and Jehoram. 9 They took the book of the Law of the LORD and went through all the towns of Judah, teaching it to the people.

v *One ancient translation* Israel; *Hebrew* Syria.

Jehoshaphat's Greatness

10 The LORD made all the surrounding kingdoms afraid to go to war against King Jehoshaphat. 11 Some of the Philistines brought Jehoshaphat a large amount of silver and other gifts, and some Arabs brought him 7,700 sheep and 7,700 goats. 12 So Jehoshaphat continued to grow more and more powerful. Throughout Judah he built fortifications and cities, 13 where supplies were stored in huge amounts.

In Jerusalem he stationed outstanding officers, 14 according to their clans. Adnah was the commander of the troops from the clans of Judah, and he had 300,000 soldiers under him. 15 Second in rank was Jehohanan, with 280,000 soldiers, 16 and third was Amasiah son of Zichri, with 200,000. (Amasiah had volunteered to serve the LORD.) 17 The commander of the troops from the clans of Benjamin was Eliada, an outstanding soldier, in command of 200,000 men armed with shields and bows. 18 His second in command was Jehozabad with 180,000 men, well-equipped for battle. 19 These men served the king in Jerusalem, and in addition he stationed other soldiers in the other fortified cities of Judah.

The Prophet Micaiah Warns Ahab
(1 Kgs 22.1-28)

18 When King Jehoshaphat of Judah became rich and famous, he arranged a marriage between a member of his family and the family of King Ahab of Israel. 2 A number of years later Jehoshaphat went to the city of Samaria to visit Ahab. To honour Jehoshaphat and those with him, Ahab had a large number of sheep and cattle slaughtered for a feast. He tried to persuade Jehoshaphat to join him in attacking the city of Ramoth in Gilead. 3 He asked, "Will you go with me to attack Ramoth?"

Jehoshaphat replied, "I am ready when you are, and so is my army. We will join you." 4 Then he added, "But first let's consult the LORD."

5 So Ahab called in the prophets, about four hundred of them, and asked them, "Should I go and attack Ramoth, or not?"

"Attack it," they answered. "God will give you victory."

6 But Jehoshaphat asked, "Isn't there another prophet through whom we can consult the LORD?"

7 Ahab answered, "There is one more,

18.16: Num 27.17; Ezek 34.5; Mt 9.36; Mk 6.34

Micaiah son of Imlah. But I hate him because he never prophesies anything good for me; it's always something bad."

"You shouldn't say that!" Jehoshaphat replied.

8 So King Ahab called in a court official and told him to go and fetch Micaiah at once.

9 The two kings, dressed in their royal robes, were sitting on their thrones at the threshing-place just outside the gate of Samaria, and all the prophets were prophesying in front of them. 10 One of them, Zedekiah son of Chenaanah, made iron horns and said to Ahab, "This is what the LORD says, 'With these you will fight the Syrians and totally defeat them.'" 11 All the other prophets said the same thing. "March against Ramoth and you will win," they said. "The LORD will give you victory."

12 Meanwhile, the official who had gone to fetch Micaiah said to him, "All the other prophets have prophesied success for the king, and you had better do the same."

13 But Micaiah answered, "By the living LORD, I will say what my God tells me to!"

14 When he appeared before King Ahab, the king asked him, "Micaiah, should King Jehoshaphat and I go and attack Ramoth, or not?"

"Attack!" Micaiah answered. "Of course you'll win. The LORD will give you victory."

15 But Ahab replied, "When you speak to me in the name of the LORD, tell the truth! How many times do I have to tell you that?"

16 Micaiah answered, "I can see the army of Israel scattered over the hills like sheep without a shepherd. And the LORD said, 'These men have no leader; let them go home in peace.'"

17 Ahab said to Jehoshaphat, "I told you that he never prophesies anything good for me; it's always something bad!"

18 Micaiah went on: "Now listen to what the LORD says! I saw the LORD sitting on his throne in heaven, with all his angels standing beside him. 19 The LORD asked, 'Who will deceive Ahab so that he will go and get killed at Ramoth?' Some of the angels said one thing, and others said something else, 20 until a spirit stepped forward, approached the LORD, and said, 'I will deceive him.' 'How?' the LORD asked. 21 The spirit replied, 'I will go and

All the prophets were prophesying in front of them (18.9)

make all Ahab's prophets tell lies.' The LORD said, 'Go and deceive him. You will succeed.' "

22 And Micaiah concluded: "This is what has happened. The LORD has made these prophets of yours lie to you. But he himself has decreed that you will meet with disaster!"

23 Then the prophet Zedekiah went up to Micaiah, slapped his face, and asked, "Since when did the LORD's spirit leave me and speak to you?"

24 "You will find out when you go into some back room to hide," Micaiah replied.

25 Then King Ahab ordered one of his officers, "Arrest Micaiah and take him to Amon, the governor of the city, and to Prince Joash. 26 Tell them to throw him in prison and to put him on bread and water until I return safely."

27 "If you return safely," Micaiah exclaimed, "then the LORD has not spoken through me!" And he added, "Listen, everyone, to what I have said!"

The Death of Ahab
(1 Kgs 22.29–35)

28 Then King Ahab of Israel and King Jehoshaphat of Judah went to attack the city of Ramoth in Gilead. 29 Ahab said to Jehoshaphat, "As we go into battle, I will disguise myself, but you wear your royal garments." So the king of Israel went into battle in disguise.

30 The king of Syria had ordered his chariot commanders to attack no one else except the king of Israel. 31 So when they saw King Jehoshaphat, they all thought that he was the king of Israel, and they turned to attack him. But Jehoshaphat gave a shout, and the LORD God rescued him and turned the attack away from him. 32 The chariot commanders saw that he was not the king of Israel, so they stopped pursuing him. 33 By chance, however, a Syrian soldier shot an arrow which struck King Ahab between the joints of his armour. "I'm wounded!" he cried out to his chariot driver. "Turn round and pull out of the battle!" 34 While the battle raged on, King Ahab remained propped up in his chariot, facing the Syrians. At sunset he died.

A Prophet Reprimands Jehoshaphat

19 King Jehoshaphat of Judah returned safely to his palace in Jerusalem. 2 A prophet, Jehu son of Hanani, went to meet the king and said to him, "Do you think it is right to help those who are wicked and to take the side of those who hate the LORD? What you have done has brought the LORD's anger on you. 3 But even so, there is some good in you. You have removed all the symbols of the goddess Asherah which people worshipped, and you have tried to follow God's will."

Jehoshaphat's Reforms

4 Even though King Jehoshaphat lived in Jerusalem, he travelled regularly among the people, from Beersheba in the south to the edge of the hill-country of Ephraim in the north, in order to call the people back to the LORD, the God of their ancestors. 5 He appointed judges in each of the fortified cities of Judah 6 and instructed them: "Be careful in pronouncing judgement; you are not acting on human authority, but on the authority of the LORD, and he is with you when you pass sentence. 7 Honour the LORD and act carefully, because the LORD our God does not tolerate fraud or partiality or the taking of bribes."

8 In Jerusalem Jehoshaphat appointed Levites, priests, and some of the leading citizens as judges in cases involving a violation of the Law of the LORD or legal disputes between inhabitants of the city. w 9 He gave them the following instructions: "You must perform your duties in reverence for the LORD, faithfully obeying him in everything you do. 10 Whenever your fellow-citizens from any of the cities bring before you a case of homicide or any other violation of a law or commandment, you must instruct them carefully how to conduct themselves during the trial, so that they do not become guilty of sinning against the LORD. Unless you do, you and your fellow-citizens will feel the force of the LORD's anger. But if you do your duty, you will not be guilty. 11 Amariah the High Priest will have final authority in all religious cases, and Zebadiah son of Ishmael, governor of Judah, will have final authority in all civil cases. The Levites have the responsibility of seeing that the decisions of the courts are carried out. Be courageous and carry out these instructions, and may the LORD be on the side of the right!"

War against Edom

20 Some time later the armies of Moab and Ammon, together with their allies, the Meunites, x invaded Judah. 2 Some messengers came and announced to King Jehoshaphat: "A large army from Edom has come from the other side of the Dead Sea to attack you. They have already captured Hazazon Tamar." (This

is another name for Engedi.) 3 Jehoshaphat was frightened and prayed to the LORD for guidance. Then he gave orders for a fast to be observed throughout the country. 4 From every city of Judah people hurried to Jerusalem to ask the LORD for guidance, 5 and they and the people of Jerusalem gathered in the new courtyard of the Temple. King Jehoshaphat went and stood before them 6 and prayed aloud, "O LORD God of our ancestors, you rule in heaven over all the nations of the world. You are powerful and mighty, and no one can oppose you. 7 You are our God. When your people Israel moved into this land, you drove out the people who were living here and gave the land to the descendants of Abraham, your friend, to be theirs for ever. 8 They have lived here and have built a temple to honour you, knowing 9 that if any disaster struck them to punish them—a war, y an epidemic, or a famine—then they could come and stand in front of this Temple where you are worshipped. They could pray to you in their trouble, and you would hear them and rescue them.

10 "Now the people of Ammon, Moab, and Edom have attacked us. When our ancestors came out of Egypt, you did not allow them to enter those lands, so our ancestors went round them and did not destroy them. 11 This is how they repay us—they come to drive us out of the land that you gave us. 12 You are our God! Punish them, for we are helpless in the face of this large army that is attacking us. We do not know what to do, but we look to you for help."

13 All the men of Judah, with their wives and children, were standing there at the Temple. 14 The spirit of the LORD came upon a Levite who was present in the crowd. His name was Jahaziel son of Zechariah; he was a member of the clan of Asaph and was descended from Asaph through Mattaniah, Jeiel, and Benaiah. 15 Jahaziel said, "Your Majesty and all you people of Judah and Jerusalem, the LORD says that you must not be discouraged or be afraid to face this large army. The battle depends on God, not on you. 16 Attack them tomorrow as they come up the pass at Ziz. You will meet them at the end of the valley that leads to the wild country near Jeruel. 17 You will not have to fight this battle.

---

w Some ancient translations between...city; Hebrew unclear.
x One ancient translation Meunites; Hebrew Ammonites.
y struck...war; or struck them—a devastating war.
20.7: Is 41.8; Jas 2.23   **20.10:** Deut 2.4–19   **20.15–17:** Deut 20.1–4   **20.17:** Ex 14.13–14

They...saw that they were all lying on the ground, dead (20.24)

Just take up your positions and wait; you will see the LORD give you victory. People of Judah and Jerusalem, do not hesitate or be afraid. Go out to battle, and the LORD will be with you!''

18 Then King Jehoshaphat bowed low, with his face touching the ground, and all the people bowed with him and worshipped the LORD. 19 The members of the Levite clans of Kohath and Korah stood up and with a loud shout praised the LORD, the God of Israel.

20 Early the next morning the people went out to the wild country near Tekoa. As they were starting out, Jehoshaphat addressed them with these words: "Men of Judah and Jerusalem! Put your trust in the LORD your God, and you will stand firm. Believe what his prophets tell you, and you will succeed." 21 After consulting with the people, the king ordered some musicians to put on the robes they wore on sacred occasions and to march ahead of the army, singing: "Praise the LORD! His love is eternal!"

22 When they began to sing, the LORD threw the invading armies into a panic. 23 The Ammonites and the Moabites attacked the Edomite army and completely destroyed it, and then they turned on each other in savage fighting. 24 When the Judaean army reached a tower that was in the desert, they looked towards the enemy and saw that they were all lying on the ground, dead. Not one had escaped.

25 Jehoshaphat and his troops moved in to take the loot, and they found many cattle,z supplies, clothing, and other valuable objects. They spent three days gathering the loot, but there was so much that they could not take everything. 26 On the fourth day they assembled in the Valley of Beracah and praised the LORD for all he had done. That is why the valley is called "Beracah."a 27 Jehoshaphat led his troops back to Jerusalem in triumph,

because the LORD had defeated their enemies. 28 When they reached the city, they marched to the Temple, to the music of harps and trumpets. 29 Every nation that heard how the LORD had defeated Israel's enemies was terrified, 30 so Jehoshaphat ruled in peace, and God gave him security on every side.

The End of Jehoshaphat's Reign
(1 Kgs 22.41–50)

31 Jehoshaphat had become king of Judah at the age of thirty-five and had ruled in Jerusalem for twenty-five years. His mother was Azubah, the daughter of Shilhi. 32 Like his father Asa before him, he did what was right in the sight of the LORD; 33 but the pagan places of worship were not destroyed. The people still did not turn wholeheartedly to the worship of the God of their ancestors.

34 Everything else that Jehoshaphat did, from the beginning of his reign to its end, is recorded in *The History of Jehu Son of Hanani*, which is a part of *The History of the Kings of Israel*.

35 At one time King Jehoshaphat of Judah made an alliance with King Ahaziah of Israel, who did many wicked things. 36 At the port of Eziongeber they built ocean-going ships. 37 But Eliezer son of Dodavahu, from the town of Mareshah, warned Jehoshaphat, "Because you have made an alliance with Ahaziah, the LORD will destroy what you have built." And the ships were wrecked and never sailed.

21 Jehoshaphat died and was buried in the royal tombs in David's City and his son Jehoram succeeded him as king.

King Jehoram of Judah
(2 Kgs 8.17–24)

2 Jehoram son of King Jehoshaphat of Judah had six brothers: Azariah, Jehiel, Zechariah, Azariahu, Michael, and Shephatiah. 3 Their father gave them large

---

z *One ancient translation* cattle; *Hebrew* among them.
a BERACAH: *This name in Hebrew means "praise."*

amounts of gold, silver, and other valuable possessions, and placed each one in charge of one of the fortified cities of Judah. But because Jehoram was the eldest, Jehoshaphat made him his successor. ⁴When Jehoram was in firm control of the kingdom, he had all his brothers killed, and also some Israelite officials.

5 Jehoram became king at the age of thirty-two, and he ruled in Jerusalem for eight years. ⁶He followed the wicked example of King Ahab and the other kings of Israel, because he had married one of Ahab's daughters. He sinned against the LORD, ⁷but the LORD was not willing to destroy the dynasty of David, because he had made a covenant with David and promised that his descendants would always continue to rule.

8 During Jehoram's reign Edom revolted against Judah and became an independent kingdom. ⁹So Jehoram and his officers set out with chariots and invaded Edom. There the Edomite army surrounded them, but during the night they managed to break out and escape. ¹⁰Edom has been independent of ᵇ Judah ever since. During this same period, the city of Libnah also revolted, because Jehoram had abandoned the LORD, the God of his ancestors. ¹¹He even built pagan places of worship in the Judaean highlands and led the people of Judah and Jerusalem to sin against the LORD.

12 The prophet Elijah sent Jehoram a letter, which read as follows: "The LORD, the God of your ancestor David, condemns you, because you did not follow the example of your father, King Jehoshaphat, or that of your grandfather, King Asa. ¹³Instead, you have followed the example of the kings of Israel and have led the people of Judah and Jerusalem into being unfaithful to God, just as Ahab and his successors led Israel into unfaithfulness. You even murdered your brothers, who were better men than you are. ¹⁴As a result, the LORD will severely punish your people, your children, and your wives, and will destroy your possessions. ¹⁵You yourself will suffer a painful disease of the intestines that will grow worse day by day."

16 Some Philistines and Arabs lived near where some Sudanese had settled along the coast. The LORD incited them

to go to war against Jehoram. ¹⁷They invaded Judah, looted the royal palace, and carried off as prisoners all the king's wives and sons except Ahaziah, his youngest son.

18 Then after all this, the LORD brought on the king a painful disease of the intestines. ¹⁹For almost two years it grew steadily worse until finally the king died in agony. His subjects did not light a bonfire in mourning for him as had been done for his ancestors.

20 Jehoram had become king at the age of thirty-two and had ruled in Jerusalem for eight years. Nobody was sorry when he died. They buried him in David's City, but not in the royal tombs.

King Ahaziah of Judah
(2 Kgs 8.25-29; 9.21-28)

22 Some Arabs had led a raid and killed all King Jehoram's sons except Ahaziah, the youngest. So now the people of Jerusalem made Ahaziah king as his father's successor. ²⁻³Ahaziah became king at the age of twenty-two,ᶜ and he ruled in Jerusalem for one year. Ahaziah also followed the example of King Ahab's family, since his mother Athaliah—the daughter of King Ahab and granddaughter of King Omri of Israel— gave him advice that led him into evil. ⁴He sinned against the LORD, because after his father's death other members of King Ahab's family became his advisers, and they led to his downfall. ⁵Following their advice, he joined King Joram of Israel in a war against King Hazael of Syria. The armies clashed at Ramoth in Gilead, and Joram was wounded in battle. ⁶He returned to the city of Jezreel to recover from his wounds, and Ahaziah went there to visit him.

7 God used this visit to Joram to bring about Ahaziah's downfall. While Ahaziah was there, he and Joram were confronted by a man named Jehu son of Nimshi, whom the LORD had chosen to destroy the dynasty of Ahab. ⁸As Jehu was carrying out God's sentence on the dynasty, he came across a group made up of Judaean leaders and of Ahaziah's nephews that had accompanied Ahaziah on his visit. Jehu killed them all. ⁹A search was made for Ahaziah, and he was found hiding in Samaria. They took him to Jehu and put him to death. But they did bury

ᵇindependent of; *or* in revolt against.
ᶜ *Some ancient translations (and see 2 Kgs 8.26)* twenty-two; *Hebrew* forty-two.
21.7: 1 Kgs 11.36   **21.8:** Gen 27.40

his body out of respect for his grandfather King Jehoshaphat, who had done all he could to serve the LORD.

No member of Ahaziah's family was left who could rule the kingdom.

Queen Athaliah of Judah
(2 Kgs 11.1-3)

10 As soon as King Ahaziah's mother Athaliah learnt of her son's murder, she gave orders for all the members of the royal family of Judah to be killed. 11 Ahaziah had a half-sister, Jehosheba, who was married to a priest named Jehoiada. She secretly rescued one of Ahaziah's sons, Joash, took him away from the other princes who were about to be murdered and hid him and a nurse in a bedroom at the Temple. By keeping him hidden, she saved him from death at the hands of Athaliah. 12 For six years he remained there in hiding, while Athaliah ruled as queen.

The Revolt against Athaliah
(2 Kgs 11.4-16)

23 After waiting six years Jehoiada the priest decided that it was time to take action. He made a pact with five army officers: Azariah son of Jeroham, Ishmael son of Jehohanan, Azariah son of Obed, Maaseiah son of Adaiah, and Elishaphat son of Zichri. 2 They travelled to all the cities of Judah and brought back with them to Jerusalem the Levites and all the heads of the clans.

3 They all gathered in the Temple, and there they made a covenant with Joash, the king's son. Jehoiada said to them, "Here is the son of the late king! He is now to be king, as the LORD promised that King David's descendants would be. 4 This is what we will do. When the priests and Levites come on duty on the Sabbath, one third of them will guard the temple gates, 5 another third will guard the royal palace, and the rest will be stationed at the Foundation Gate. All the people will assemble in the temple courtyard. 6 No one is to enter the temple buildings except the priests and the Levites who are on duty. They may enter, because they are consecrated, but the rest of the people must obey the LORD's instructions and stay outside. 7 The Levites are to stand guard round the king, with their swords drawn, and are to stay with the king wherever he goes. Anyone who tries to enter the Temple is to be killed."

8 The Levites and the people of Judah carried out Jehoiada's instructions. The men were not dismissed when they went off duty on the Sabbath, so the commanders had available both those coming on duty and those going off. 9 Jehoiada gave the officers the spears and shields that had belonged to King David and had been kept in the Temple. 10 He stationed the men with drawn swords all round the front of the Temple, to protect the king. 11 Then Jehoiada led Joash out, placed the crown on his head, and gave him a copy of the laws governing kingship. And so he was made king. Jehoiada the priest and his sons anointed Joash, and everyone shouted, "Long live the king!"

12 Athaliah heard the people cheering for the king, so she hurried to the Temple, where the crowd had gathered. 13 There she saw the new king at the temple entrance, standing by the column reserved for kings and surrounded by the army officers and the trumpeters. All the people were shouting joyfully and blowing trumpets, and the temple musicians with their instruments were leading the celebration. She tore her clothes in distress and shouted, "Treason! Treason!"

14 Jehoiada did not want Athaliah killed in the temple area, so he called out the army officers and said, "Take her out between the rows of guards, and kill anyone who tries to rescue her."

15 They seized her, took her to the palace, and there at the Horse Gate they killed her.

Jehoiada's Reforms
(2 Kgs 11.17-20)

16 The priest Jehoiada got King Joash and the people to join him in making a covenant that they would be the LORD's people. 17 Then they all went to the temple of Baal and tore it down. They smashed the altars and idols there and killed Mattan, the priest of Baal, in front of the altars. 18 Jehoiada put the priests and Levites in charge of the work of the Temple. They were to carry out the duties assigned to them by King David and to burn the sacrifices offered to the LORD in accordance with the Law of Moses. They were also in charge of the music and the celebrations. 19 Jehoiada also put guards on duty at the temple gates to keep out anyone who was ritually unclean.

20 The army officers, the leading citizens, the officials, and all the rest of

23.3: 2 Sam 7.12

And so he was made king (23.11)

the people joined Jehoiada in a procession that brought the king from the Temple to the palace. They entered by the main gate, and the king took his place on the throne. 21 All the people were filled with happiness, and the city was quiet, now that Athaliah had been killed.

King Joash of Judah
(2 Kgs 12.1–16)

24 Joash became king of Judah at the age of seven, and he ruled in Jerusalem for forty years. His mother was Zibiah from the city of Beersheba. 2 He did what was pleasing to the LORD as long as Jehoiada the priest was alive. 3 Jehoiada chose two wives for King Joash, and they bore him sons and daughters.

4 After he had been king for a while, Joash decided to have the Temple repaired. 5 He ordered the priests and the Levites to go to the cities of Judah and collect from all the people enough money to make the annual repairs on the Temple. He told them to act promptly, but the Levites delayed, 6 so he called in Jehoiada, their leader, and demanded, "Why haven't you seen to it that the Levites collect from Judah and Jerusalem the tax which Moses, the servant of the LORD, required the people *d* to pay for support of the Tent of the LORD's presence?"

7 (The followers of Athaliah, that corrupt woman, *e* had damaged the Temple and had used many of the sacred objects in the worship of Baal.)

8 The king ordered the Levites to make a box for contributions and to place it at the temple gate. 9 They sent word throughout Jerusalem and Judah for everyone to bring to the LORD the tax which Moses, God's servant, had first collected in the wilderness. 10 This pleased the people and their leaders, and they brought their tax money and filled the box with it. 11 Every day the Levites would take the box to the royal official who was in charge of it. Whenever it was full, the royal secretary and the High Priest's representative would take the money out and return the box to its place. And so they collected a large sum of money.

12 The king and Jehoiada would give the money to those who were in charge of repairing the Temple, and they hired stonemasons, carpenters, and metalworkers to make the repairs. 13 All the workmen worked hard, and they restored the Temple to its original condition, as solid as ever. 14 When the repairs were finished, the remaining gold and silver was given to the king and Jehoiada, who used it to have bowls and other utensils made for the Temple.

d Probable text required the people; *Hebrew unclear.*
e that corrupt woman; *or* whom she corrupted.
24.6: Ex 30.11–16

Brought their tax money (24.10)

Jehoiada's Policies Are Reversed

As long as Jehoiada was alive, sacrifices were offered regularly at the Temple. ¹⁵ After reaching the very old age of a hundred and thirty, he died. ¹⁶ They buried him in the royal tombs in David's City in recognition of the service he had done for the people of Israel, for God, and for the Temple.

17 But once Jehoiada was dead, the leaders of Judah persuaded King Joash to listen to them instead. ¹⁸ So the people stopped worshiping in the Temple of the LORD, the God of their ancestors, and began to worship idols and the images of the goddess Asherah. Their guilt for these sins brought the LORD's anger on Judah and Jerusalem. ¹⁹ The LORD sent prophets to warn them to return to him, but the people refused to listen. ²⁰ Then the spirit of God took control of Zechariah son of Jehoiada the priest. He stood where the people could see him and called out, "The LORD God asks why you have disobeyed his commands and are bringing disaster on yourselves! You abandoned him, so he has abandoned you!" ²¹ King Joash joined in a conspiracy against Zechariah, and on the king's orders the people stoned Zechariah in the temple courtyard. ²² The king forgot about the

loyal service that Zechariah's father Jehoiada had given him, and he had Zechariah killed. As Zechariah was dying, he called out, "May the LORD see what you are doing and punish you!"

The End of Joash's Reign

23 When autumn came that year, the Syrian army attacked Judah and Jerusalem, killed all the leaders, and took large amounts of loot back to Damascus. ²⁴ The Syrian army was small, but the LORD let them defeat a much larger Judaean army because the people had abandoned him, the LORD God of their ancestors. In this way King Joash was punished. ²⁵ He was severely wounded, and when the enemy withdrew, two of his officials plotted against him and killed him in his bed to avenge the murder of the son *f* of Jehoiada the priest. He was buried in David's City, but not in the royal tombs. ²⁶ (Those who plotted against him were Zabad, the son of an Ammonite woman named Shimeath, and Jehozabad, the son of a Moabite woman named Shimrith). ²⁷ The *Commentary on the Book of Kings* contains the stories of the sons of Joash, the prophecies spoken against him, and the record of how he rebuilt the Temple. His son Amaziah succeeded him as king.

f Some ancient translations son; *Hebrew* sons.
24.20–21: Mt 23.35; Lk 11.51

King Amaziah of Judah
(2 Kgs 14.2-6)

25 Amaziah became king at the age of twenty-five, and he ruled in Jerusalem for twenty-nine years. His mother was Jehoaddin from Jerusalem. [2] He did what was pleasing to the LORD, but did it reluctantly. [3] As soon as he was firmly in power, he executed the officials who had murdered his father. [4] He did not, however, execute their children, but followed what the LORD had commanded in the Law of Moses: "Parents are not to be put to death for crimes committed by their children, and children are not to be put to death for crimes committed by their parents; a person is to be put to death only for a crime he himself has committed."

War against Edom
(2 Kgs 14.7)

[5] King Amaziah organized all the men of the tribes of Judah and Benjamin into army units, according to the clans they belonged to, and placed officers in command of units of a thousand men and units of a hundred men. This included all men twenty years of age or older, 300,000 in all. They were picked troops, ready for battle, skilled in using spears and shields. [6] In addition, he hired 100,000 soldiers from Israel at a cost of about 3,400 kilogrammes of silver. [7] But a prophet went to the king and said to him, "Don't take these Israelite soldiers with you. The LORD is not with these men from the Northern Kingdom. [8] You may think that they will make you stronger[g] in battle, but it is God who has the power to give victory or defeat, and he will let your enemies defeat you."

[9] Amaziah asked the prophet, "But what about all that silver I have already paid for them?"

The prophet replied, "The LORD can give you back more than that!" [10] So Amaziah sent the hired troops away and told them to go home. At this they went home, bitterly angry with the people of Judah.

[11] Amaziah summoned up his courage and led his army to the Valley of Salt. There they fought and killed ten thousand Edomite soldiers [12] and captured another ten thousand. They took the prisoners to the top of the cliff at the city of Sela

and threw them off, so that they were killed on the rocks below.

[13] Meanwhile the Israelite soldiers that Amaziah had not allowed to go into battle with him attacked the Judaean cities between Samaria and Beth Horon, killed three thousand men, and captured quantities of loot.

[14] When Amaziah returned from defeating the Edomites, he brought their idols back with him, set them up, worshipped them, and burnt incense to them. [15] This made the LORD angry, so he sent a prophet to Amaziah. The prophet demanded, "Why have you worshipped foreign gods that could not even save their own people from your power?"

[16] "Since when," Amaziah interrupted, "have we made you adviser to the king? Stop talking, or I'll have you killed!"

The prophet stopped, but not before saying, "Now I know that God has decided to destroy you because you have done all this and have ignored my advice."

War against Israel
(2 Kgs 14.8-20)

[17] King Amaziah of Judah and his advisers plotted against Israel. He then sent a message to King Jehoash of Israel, who was the son of Jehoahaz and grandson of Jehu, challenging him to fight.[h] [18] Jehoash sent this answer to Amaziah: "Once, a thorn bush in the Lebanon Mountains sent a message to a cedar: 'Give your daughter in marriage to my son.' A wild animal passed by and trampled the bush down. [19] Now Amaziah, you boast that you have defeated the Edomites, but I advise you to stay at home. Why stir up trouble that will only bring disaster on you and your people?"

[20] But Amaziah refused to listen. It was God's will for Amaziah to be defeated, because he had worshipped the Edomite idols. [21] So King Jehoash of Israel went into battle against King Amaziah of Judah. They met at Beth Shemesh in Judah, [22] the Judaean army was defeated, and the soldiers fled to their homes. [23] Jehoash captured Amaziah and took him to Jerusalem. There he tore down the city wall from Ephraim Gate to the Corner Gate, a distance of nearly two hundred metres. [24] He took back to Samaria as loot all the gold and silver in the Temple, the temple equipment

[g] *Some ancient translations* You may...stronger; *Hebrew unclear.*
[h] challenging him to fight; *or* inviting him to a conference.
25.4: Deut 24.16

guarded by the descendants of Obed Edom, and the palace treasures. He also took hostages with him.

25 King Amaziah of Judah outlived King Jehoash of Israel by fifteen years. 26 All the other things that Amaziah did from the beginning to the end of his reign are recorded in *The History of the Kings of Judah and Israel.* 27 Ever since the time when he rebelled against the LORD, there had been a plot against him in Jerusalem. Finally he fled to the city of Lachish, but his enemies followed him there and killed him. 28 His body was carried to Jerusalem on a horse, and he was buried in the royal tombs in David's City.

King Uzziah of Judah
(2 Kgs 14.21–22; 15.1–7)

26 All the people of Judah chose Amaziah's sixteen-year-old son Uzziah to succeed his father as king. 2 (It was after the death of Amaziah that Uzziah recaptured Elath and rebuilt the city.)

3 Uzziah became king at the age of sixteen, and he ruled in Jerusalem for fifty-two years. His mother was Jecoliah from Jerusalem. 4 Following the example of his father, he did what was pleasing to the LORD. 5 As long as Zechariah, his religious adviser, was living, he served the LORD faithfully, and God blessed him.

6 Uzziah went to war against the Philistines. He tore down the walls of the cities of Gath, Jamnia, and Ashdod, and built fortified cities near Ashdod and in the rest of Philistia. 7 God helped him to defeat the Philistines, the Arabs living at Gurbaal, and the Meunites. 8 The Ammonites paid tribute to Uzziah, and he became so powerful that his fame spread even to Egypt.

9 Uzziah strengthened the fortifications of Jerusalem by building towers at the Corner Gate, at the Valley Gate, and where the wall turned. 10 He also built fortified towers in the open country and dug many cisterns, because he had large herds of livestock in the western foothills and plains. Because he loved farming, he encouraged the people to plant vineyards in the hill-country and to farm the fertile land.

11 He had a large army ready for battle. Its records were kept by his secretaries Jeiel and Maaseiah under the supervision of Hananiah, a member of the king's staff.

12 The army was commanded by 2,600 officers. 13 Under them were 307,500 soldiers able to fight effectively for the king against his enemies. 14 Uzziah supplied the army with shields, spears, helmets, coats of armour, bows and arrows, and stones for slinging. 15 In Jerusalem his inventors made equipment for shooting arrows and for throwing large stones from the towers and corners of the city wall. His fame spread everywhere, and he became very powerful because of the help he received from God.

Uzziah Is Punished for His Pride

16 But when King Uzziah became strong, he grew arrogant, and that led to his downfall. He defied the LORD his God by going into the Temple to burn incense on the altar of incense. 17 Azariah the priest, accompanied by eighty strong and courageous priests, followed the king 18 to resist him. They said, "Uzziah! You have no right to burn incense to the LORD. Only the priests who are descended from Aaron have been consecrated to do this. Leave this holy place. You have offended the LORD God, and you no longer have his blessing."

19 Uzziah was standing there in the Temple beside the incense altar and was holding an incense burner. He became angry with the priests, and immediately a dreaded skin-disease broke out on his forehead. 20 Azariah and the other priests stared at the king's forehead in horror, and then forced him to leave the Temple. He hurried to get out, because the LORD had punished him.

21 For the rest of his life King Uzziah was ritually unclean because of his disease. Unable to enter the Temple again, he lived in his own house, relieved of all duties, while his son Jotham governed the country.

22 The prophet Isaiah son of Amoz recorded all the other things that King Uzziah did during his reign. 23 Uzziah died and was buried in the royal burial-ground, but because of his disease he was not buried in the royal tombs. His son Jotham succeeded him as king.

King Jotham of Judah
(2 Kgs 15.32–38)

27 Jotham became king at the age of twenty-five, and he ruled in Jerusalem for sixteen years. His mother was

26.18: Ex 30.7–8; Num 3.10   **26.23:** Is 6.1

A dreaded skin-disease broke out on his forehead (26.19)

Jerushah, the daughter of Zadok. [2] He did what was pleasing to the LORD, just as his father had done; but unlike his father he did not sin by burning incense*i* in the Temple. The people, however, went on sinning.

[3] It was Jotham who built the North Gate of the Temple and did extensive work on the city wall in the area of Jerusalem called Ophel. [4] In the mountains of Judah he built cities, and in the forests he built forts and towers. [5] He fought against the king of Ammon and his army and defeated them. Then he forced the Ammonites to pay him the following tribute each year for three years: 3,400 kilogrammes of silver, 1,000 metric tons of wheat, and 1,000 metric tons of barley. [6] Jotham grew powerful because he faithfully obeyed the LORD his God. [7] The other events of Jotham's reign, his wars, and his policies, are all recorded in *The History of the Kings of Israel and Judah.* [8] Jotham was twenty-five years old when he became king, and he ruled in Jerusalem for sixteen years. [9] He died and was buried in David's City and his son Ahaz succeeded him as king.

King Ahaz of Judah
(2 Kgs 16.1-4)

28 Ahaz became king at the age of twenty, and he ruled in Jerusalem for sixteen years. He did not follow the good example of his ancestor King David; instead, he did what was not pleasing to the LORD [2] and followed the example of the kings of Israel. He had metal images of Baal made, [3] burnt incense in the Valley of Hinnom, and even sacrificed his own sons as burnt-offerings to idols, imitating the disgusting practice of the people whom the LORD had driven out of the land as the Israelites advanced. [4] At the pagan places of worship, on the hills, and under every shady tree Ahaz offered sacrifices and burnt incense.

War with Syria and Israel
(2 Kgs 16.5)

[5-6] Because King Ahaz sinned, the LORD his God let the king of Syria defeat him and take a large number of Judaeans back to Damascus as prisoners. The LORD also let the king of Israel, Pekah son of Remaliah, defeat Ahaz and kill 120,000 of the bravest Judaean soldiers in one day. The LORD, the God of their ancestors, permitted this to happen, because the people of Judah had abandoned him. [7] An Israelite soldier named Zichri killed King Ahaz' son Maaseiah, the palace administrator Azrikam, and Elkanah, who was second in command to the king. [8] Even though the Judaeans were their fellow-countrymen, the Israelite army captured 200,000 women and children as prisoners and took them back to Samaria, along with large amounts of loot.

The Prophet Oded

[9] A man named Oded, a prophet of the LORD, lived in the city of Samaria. He met the returning Israelite army with its Judaean prisoners as it was about to enter the city, and he said, "The LORD God of your ancestors was angry with Judah and let you defeat them, but now he has heard of the vicious way you slaughtered them. [10] And now you intend to make the men and women of Jerusalem and Judah your slaves. Don't you know that you also have committed sins against the LORD your God? [11] Listen to me! These prisoners are your brothers and sisters. Let them go, or the LORD will punish you in his anger."

i he did not sin by burning incense; *or* he did not take part in the worship.
28.5-6: Is 7.1

Those who were too weak to walk (28.15)

12 Four of the leading men of the Northern Kingdom, Azariah son of Jehohanan, Berechiah son of Meshillemoth, Jehizkiah son of Shallum, and Amasa son of Hadlai also opposed the actions of the army. ¹³They said, "Don't bring those prisoners here! We have already sinned against the LORD and made him angry enough to punish us. Now you want to do something that will increase our guilt." ¹⁴So then the army handed the prisoners and the loot over to the people and their leaders, ¹⁵and the four men were appointed to provide the prisoners with clothing from the captured loot. They gave them clothes and sandals to wear, gave them enough to eat and drink, and put olive-oil on their wounds. Those who were too weak to walk were put on donkeys, and all the prisoners were taken back to Judaean territory at Jericho, the city of palm-trees. Then the Israelites returned home to Samaria.

Ahaz Asks Assyria for Help
(2 Kgs 16.7-9)

16-17 The Edomites began to raid Judah again and captured many prisoners, so King Ahaz asked Tiglath Pileser, the emperor of Assyria, to send help. ¹⁸At this same time the Philistines were raiding the towns in the western foothills and in southern Judah. They captured the cities of Beth Shemesh, Aijalon, and Gederoth, and the cities of Soco, Timnah, and Gimzo with their villages, and settled there permanently. ¹⁹Because King Ahaz of Judah had violated the rights of his people and had defied the LORD, the LORD brought troubles on Judah. ²⁰The Assyrian emperor, instead of helping Ahaz, opposed him and caused him trouble. ²¹So Ahaz took the gold from the Temple, the palace, and the homes of the leaders of the people, and gave it to the emperor, but even this did not help.

The Sins of Ahaz

22 When his troubles were at their worst, that man Ahaz sinned against the LORD more than ever. 23 He offered sacrifices to the gods of the Syrians, who had defeated him. He said, "The Syrian gods helped the kings of Syria, so if I sacrifice to them, they may help me too." This brought disaster on him and on his nation. 24 In addition, he took all the temple equipment and broke it in pieces. He closed the Temple and set up altars in every part of Jerusalem. 25 In every city and town in Judah, he built pagan places of worship, where incense was to be burnt to foreign gods. In this way he brought on himself the anger of the LORD, the God of his ancestors.

26 All the other events of his reign, from beginning to end, are recorded in *The History of the Kings of Judah and Israel.* 27 King Ahaz died and was buried in Jerusalem, but not in the royal tombs. His son Hezekiah succeeded him as king.

King Hezekiah of Judah
(2 Kgs 18.1–3)

29 Hezekiah became king of Judah at the age of twenty-five, and he ruled in Jerusalem for twenty-nine years. His mother was Abijah, the daughter of Zechariah. 2 Following the example of his ancestor King David, he did what was pleasing to the LORD.

The Purification of the Temple

3 In the first month of the year after Hezekiah became king, he re-opened the gates of the Temple and had them repaired. 4 He assembled a group of priests and Levites in the east courtyard of the Temple 5 and spoke to them there. He said, "You Levites are to consecrate yourselves and purify the Temple of the LORD, the God of your ancestors. Remove from the Temple everything that defiles it. 6 Our ancestors were unfaithful to the LORD our God and did what was displeasing to him. They abandoned him and turned their backs on the place where he dwells. 7 They closed the doors of the Temple, let the lamps go out, and failed to burn incense or offer burnt-offerings in the Temple of the God of Israel. 8 Because of this the LORD has been angry with Judah and

Jerusalem, and what he has done to them has shocked and frightened everyone. You know this very well. 9 Our fathers were killed in battle, and our wives and children have been taken away as prisoners.

10 "I have now decided to make a covenant with the LORD, the God of Israel, so that he will no longer be angry with us. 11 My sons, do not lose any time. You are the ones that the LORD has chosen to burn incense to him and to lead the people in worshipping him."

12–14 The following Levites were there:
From the clan of Kohath, Mahath son
　　of Amasai and Joel son of Azariah
From the clan of Merari, Kish son of
　　Abdi and Azariah son of Jehallelel
From the clan of Gershon, Joah son of
　　Zimnah and Eden son of Joah
From the clan of Elizaphan, Shimri and
　　Jeuel
From the clan of Asaph, Zechariah and
　　Mattaniah
From the clan of Heman, Jehuel and
　　Shimei
From the clan of Jeduthun, Shemaiah
　　and Uzziel

15 These men assembled their fellow-Levites, and they all made themselves ritually clean. Then, as the king had commanded them to do, they began to make the Temple ritually clean, according to the Law of the LORD.*j* 16 The priests went inside the Temple to purify it, and they carried out into the temple courtyard everything that was ritually unclean. From there the Levites took it all outside the city to the valley of the Kidron.

17 The work was begun on the first day of the first month, and by the eighth day they had finished it all, including the entrance room to the Temple. Then they worked for the next eight days, until the sixteenth of the month, preparing the Temple for worship.

The Temple Is Rededicated

18 The Levites made the following report to King Hezekiah: "We have completed the ritual purification of the whole Temple, including the altar for burnt-offerings, the table for the sacred bread, and all their equipment. 19 We have also brought back all the equipment which King Ahaz took away during those years he was unfaithful to God, and we have

---

*j*Then, as the king...LORD; *or* Then they began to make the Temple ritually clean, as the king, who was acting at the LORD's command, had ordered them to do.
28.27: Is 14.28

rededicated it. It is all in front of the LORD's altar."

20 Without delay King Hezekiah assembled the leading men of the city, and together they went to the Temple. 21 As an offering to take away the sins of the royal family and of the people of Judah and to purify the Temple, they took seven bulls, seven sheep, seven lambs, and seven goats. The king told the priests, who were descendants of Aaron, to offer the animals as sacrifices on the altar. 22 The priests killed the bulls first, then the sheep, and then the lambs, and sprinkled the blood of each sacrifice on the altar. 23 Finally they took the goats to the king and to the other worshippers, who laid their hands on them. 24 Then the priests killed the goats and poured their blood on the altar as a sacrifice to take away the sin of all the people, for the king had commanded burnt-offerings and sin-offerings to be made for all Israel.

25 The king followed the instructions that the LORD had given to King David through Gad, the king's prophet, and through the prophet Nathan; he stationed Levites in the Temple, with harps and cymbals, 26 instruments like those that King David had used. The priests also stood there with trumpets. 27 Hezekiah gave the order for the burnt-offering to be presented; and as the offering began, the people sang praise to the LORD, and the musicians began to play the trumpets and all the other instruments. 28 Everyone who was there joined in worship, and the singing and the rest of the music continued until all the sacrifices had been burnt. 29 Then King Hezekiah and all the people knelt down and worshipped God. 30 The king and the leaders of the nation told the Levites to sing to the LORD the songs of praise that were written by David and by Asaph the prophet. So everyone sang with great joy as they knelt and worshipped God.

31 Hezekiah said to the people, "Now that you are ritually clean, bring sacrifices as offerings of thanksgiving to the LORD." They obeyed, and some of them also voluntarily brought animals to be sacrificed as burnt-offerings. 32 They brought seventy bulls, a hundred sheep, and two hundred lambs as burnt-offerings for the LORD; 33 they also brought six hundred bulls and three thousand sheep as sacrifices for the people to eat. 34 Since there were not enough priests to kill all these animals, the Levites helped them until the work was finished. By then more priests had made themselves ritually clean. (The Levites were more faithful in keeping ritually clean than the priests were.) 35 In addition to offering the sacrifices that were burnt whole, the priests were responsible for burning the fat that was offered from the sacrifices which the people ate, and for pouring out the wine that was presented with the burnt-offerings.

And so worship in the Temple was begun again. 36 King Hezekiah and the people were happy, because God had helped them to do all this so quickly.

Preparations for Passover

30 1-3 The people had not been able to celebrate the Passover Festival at the proper time, in the first month, because not enough priests were ritually clean and not many people had assembled in Jerusalem. So King Hezekiah, his officials, and the people of Jerusalem agreed to celebrate it in the second month, and the king sent word to all the people of Israel and Judah. He took special care to send letters to the tribes of Ephraim and Manasseh, inviting them to come to the Temple in Jerusalem to celebrate the Passover in honour of the LORD, the God of Israel. 4 The king and the people were pleased with their plan, 5 so they invited all the Israelites, from Dan in the north to Beersheba in the south, to come together in Jerusalem and celebrate the Passover according to the Law, in larger numbers than ever before. 6 Messengers went out at the command of the king and his officials through all Judah and Israel with the following invitation:

"People of Israel, you have survived the Assyrian conquest of the land. Now return to the LORD, the God of Abraham, Isaac, and Jacob, and he will return to you. 7 Do not be like your ancestors and your fellow-Israelites who were unfaithful to the LORD their God. As you can see, he punished them severely. 8 Do not be stubborn as they were, but obey the LORD. Come to the Temple in Jerusalem, which the LORD your God has made holy for ever, and worship him so that he will no longer be angry with you. 9 If you return to the LORD, then those who have taken your relatives away as prisoners will take pity on them and let them come back home. The LORD your God is kind and

Messengers went out (30.6)

merciful, and if you return to him, he will accept you."

10 The messengers went to every city in the territory of the tribes of Ephraim and Manasseh, and as far north as the tribe of Zebulun, but people laughed at them and ridiculed them. ¹¹ Still, there were some from the tribes of Asher, Manasseh, and Zebulun who were willing to come to Jerusalem. ¹² God was also at work in Judah and united the people in their determination to obey his will by following the commands of the king and his officials.

Passover Is Celebrated

13 A great number of people gathered in Jerusalem in the second month to celebrate the Festival of Unleavened Bread. ¹⁴ They took all the altars that had been used in Jerusalem for offering sacrifices and burning incense and threw them into the valley of the Kidron. ¹⁵ And on the fourteenth day of the month they killed the lambs for the Passover sacrifice. The priests and Levites who were not ritually clean were so ashamed that they dedicated themselves to the LORD, and now they could sacrifice burnt-offerings in the Temple. ¹⁶ They took their places in the Temple according to the instructions in the Law of Moses, the man of God. The Levites gave the blood of the sacrifices to the priests, who sprinkled it on the altar. ¹⁷ Because many of the people were not ritually clean, they could not kill the Passover lambs, so the Levites

did it for them, and dedicated the lambs to the LORD. ¹⁸ In addition, many of those who had come from the tribes of Ephraim, Manasseh, Issachar, and Zebulun had not performed the ritual of purification, and so they were observing Passover improperly. King Hezekiah offered this prayer for them: ¹⁹ "O LORD, the God of our ancestors, in your goodness forgive those who are worshipping you with all their heart, even though they are not ritually clean." ²⁰ The LORD answered Hezekiah's prayer; he forgave the people and did not harm them. ²¹ For seven days the people who had gathered in Jerusalem celebrated the Festival of Unleavened Bread with great joy, and day after day the Levites and the priests praised the LORD with all their strength. *ᵏ* ²² Hezekiah praised the Levites for their skill in conducting the worship of the LORD.

A Second Celebration

After the seven days during which they offered sacrifices in praise of the LORD, the God of their ancestors, ²³ they all decided to celebrate for another seven days. So they celebrated with joy. ²⁴ King Hezekiah contributed a thousand bulls and seven thousand sheep for the people to kill and eat, and the officials gave them another thousand bulls and ten thousand sheep. A large number of priests went through the ritual of purification. ²⁵ So everyone was happy—the people of Judah, the priests, the Levites, the people who had come from the north, and the

ᵏ *Probable text* with all their strength; *Hebrew* with mighty instruments.

foreigners who had settled permanently in Israel and Judah. 26 The city of Jerusalem was filled with joy, because nothing like this had happened since the days of King Solomon, the son of David. 27 The priests and the Levites asked the LORD's blessing on the people. In his home in heaven God heard their prayers and accepted them.

Hezekiah Reforms Religious Life

31 After the festival ended, all the people of Israel went to every city in Judah and broke the stone pillars, cut down the symbols of the goddess Asherah, and destroyed the altars and the pagan places of worship. They did the same thing throughout the rest of Judah, and the territories of Benjamin, Ephraim, and Manasseh; then they all returned home.

2 King Hezekiah re-established the organization of the priests and Levites, under which they each had specific duties. These included offering the burnt-offerings and the fellowship-offerings, taking part in the temple worship, and giving praise and thanks in the various parts of the Temple. 3 From his own flocks and herds he provided animals for the burnt-offerings each morning and evening, and for those offered on the Sabbath, at the New Moon Festival, and at the other festivals which are required by the Law of the LORD.

4 In addition, the king told the people of Jerusalem to bring the offerings to which the priests and the Levites were entitled, so that they could give all their time to the requirements of the Law of the LORD. 5 As soon as the order was given, the people of Israel brought gifts of their finest corn, wine, olive-oil, honey, and other farm produce, and they also brought the tithes[l] of everything they had. 6 All the people who lived in the cities of Judah brought tithes of their cattle and sheep, and they also brought large quantities of gifts, which they dedicated to the LORD their God. 7 The gifts started arriving in the third month and continued to pile up for the next four months. 8 When King Hezekiah and his officials saw how much had been given, they praised the LORD and praised his people Israel. 9 The king spoke to the priests and the Levites about these gifts, 10 and Azariah the High Priest,

a descendant of Zadok, said to him, "Since the people started bringing their gifts to the Temple, there has been enough to eat and a large surplus besides. We have all this because the LORD has blessed his people."

11 On the king's orders they prepared storerooms in the Temple area 12 and put all the gifts and tithes in them for safekeeping. They placed a Levite named Conaniah in charge and made his brother Shimei his assistant. 13 Ten Levites were assigned to work under them: Jehiel, Azaziah, Nahath, Asahel, Jerimoth, Jozabad, Eliel, Ismachiah, Mahath, and Benaiah. All this was done under the authority of King Hezekiah and Azariah the High Priest. 14 Kore son of Imnah, a Levite who was chief guard at the East Gate of the Temple, was in charge of receiving the gifts offered to the LORD and of distributing them. 15 In the other cities where priests lived, he was faithfully assisted in this by other Levites: Eden, Miniamin, Jeshua, Shemaiah, Amariah, and Shecaniah. They distributed the food equally to their fellow-Levites according to what their duties were, 16 and not by clans. They gave a share to all males thirty[m] years of age or older who had daily responsibilities in the Temple in accordance with their positions. 17 The priests were assigned their duties by clans, and the Levites twenty years of age or older were assigned theirs by work groups. 18 They were all registered together with their wives, children, and other dependants, because they were required to be ready to perform their sacred duties at any time. 19 Among the priests who lived in the cities assigned to Aaron's descendants, or in the pasture lands belonging to these cities, there were responsible men who distributed the food to all the males in the priestly families and to everyone who was on the rolls of the Levite clans.

20 Throughout all Judah, King Hezekiah did what was right and what was pleasing to the LORD his God. 21 He was successful, because everything he did for the Temple or in observance of the Law, he did in a spirit of complete loyalty and devotion to his God.

---

[l] GIFTS...TITHES: *The gifts were for the priests, and the tithes for the Levites (see Num 18).*
[m] *Probable text* thirty; *Hebrew* three.
31.3: Num 28.1—29.39   **31.4-5:** Num 18.12-13,21

Receiving the gifts offered to the LORD and...distributing them (31.14)

The Assyrians Threaten Jerusalem
(2 Kgs 18.13–37; 19.14–19, 35–37;
Is 36.1–22; 37.8–38)

32 After these events, in which King Hezekiah served the LORD faithfully, Sennacherib, the emperor of Assyria, invaded Judah. He besieged the fortified cities and gave orders for his army to break their way through the walls. ² When Hezekiah saw that Sennacherib intended to attack Jerusalem also, ³–⁴ he and his officials decided to cut off the supply of water outside the city in order to prevent the Assyrians from having any water when they got near Jerusalem. The officials led a large number of people out and stopped up all the springs, so that no more water flowed out of them. ⁵ The king strengthened the city's defences by repairing the wall, building towers on it,ⁿ and building an outer wall. In addition, he repaired the defences built on the land that was filled in on the east side of the old part of Jerusalem. He also had a large number of spears and shields made. ⁶ He placed all the men in the city under the command of army officers and ordered them to assemble in the open square at the city gate. He said to them, ⁷ "Be determined and confident, and don't be afraid of the Assyrian emperor or of the army he is leading. We have more power on our side than he has on his. ⁸ He has human power, but we have the LORD our God to help us and to fight our battles." The people were encouraged by these words of their king.

⁹ Some time later, while Sennacherib and his army were still at Lachish, he sent the following message to Hezekiah and the people of Judah who were with him in Jerusalem: ¹⁰ "I, Sennacherib, Emperor of Assyria, ask what gives you people the confidence to remain in Jerusalem under siege. ¹¹ Hezekiah tells you that the LORD your God will save you from our power, but Hezekiah is deceiving you and will let you die of hunger and thirst. ¹² He is the one who destroyed the LORD's shrines and altars and then told the people of Judah and Jerusalem to worship and burn incense at one altar only. ¹³ Don't you know what my ancestors and I have done to the people of other nations? Did the gods of any other nation save their people from the emperor of Assyria? ¹⁴ When did any of the gods of all those countries ever save their country from us? Then what makes you think that your god can save you? ¹⁵ Now don't let Hezekiah deceive you or mislead you like that. Don't believe him! No god of any nation has ever been able to save his people from any Assyrian emperor. So certainly this god of yours can't save you!"

¹⁶ The Assyrian officials said even worse things about the LORD God and Hezekiah, the LORD's servant. ¹⁷ The letter that the emperor wrote defied the LORD, the God of Israel. It said, "The gods of the nations have not saved their people

ⁿ *Some ancient translations* building towers on it; *Hebrew* building on the towers.

from my power, and neither will Hezekiah's god save his people from me." [18]The officials shouted this in Hebrew in order to frighten and discourage the people of Jerusalem who were on the city wall, so that it would be easier to capture the city. [19]They talked about the God of Jerusalem in the same way that they talked about the gods of the other peoples, idols made by human hands.

20 Then King Hezekiah and the prophet Isaiah son of Amoz prayed to God and cried out to him for help. [21]The LORD sent an angel that killed the soldiers and officers of the Assyrian army. So the emperor went back to Assyria disgraced. One day when he was in the temple of his god, some of his sons killed him with their swords.

22 In this way the LORD rescued King Hezekiah and the people of Jerusalem from the power of Sennacherib, the emperor of Assyria, and also from their other enemies. He let the people live in peace[o] with all the neighbouring countries. [23]Many people came to Jerusalem, bringing offerings to the LORD and gifts to Hezekiah, so that from then on all the nations held Hezekiah in honour.

Hezekiah's Illness and Pride
(2 Kgs 20.1-3, 12-19; Is 38.1-3; 39.1-8)

24 About this time King Hezekiah fell ill and almost died. He prayed, and the LORD gave him a sign that he would recover. [25]But Hezekiah was too proud to show gratitude for what the LORD had done for him, and Judah and Jerusalem suffered for it. [26]Finally, however, Hezekiah and the people of Jerusalem humbled themselves, and so the LORD did not punish the people until after Hezekiah's death.

Hezekiah's Wealth and Splendour

27 King Hezekiah became very wealthy, and everyone held him in honour. He had storerooms built for his gold, silver, precious stones, spices, shields, and other valuable objects. [28]In addition, he had storehouses built for his corn, wine, and olive-oil; barns for his cattle; and enclosures for his sheep. [29]Besides all this, God gave him sheep and cattle and so much other wealth that he built many cities. [30]It was King Hezekiah who blocked the outlet for the Spring of Gihon and channelled the water to flow through

a tunnel to a point inside the walls of Jerusalem. Hezekiah succeeded in everything he did, [31]and even when the Babylonian ambassadors came to inquire about the unusual event that had happened in the land, God let Hezekiah go his own way only in order to test his character.

The End of Hezekiah's Reign
(2 Kgs 20.20-21)

32 Everything else that King Hezekiah did and his devotion to the LORD are recorded in *The Vision of the Prophet Isaiah Son of Amoz* and in *The History of the Kings of Judah and Israel*. [33]Hezekiah died and was buried in the upper section of the royal tombs. All the people of Judah and Jerusalem paid him great honour at his death. His son Manasseh succeeded him as king.

King Manasseh of Judah
(2 Kgs 21.1-9)

33 Manasseh was twelve years old when he became king of Judah, and he ruled in Jerusalem for fifty-five years. [2]Following the disgusting practices of the nations whom the LORD had driven out of the land as his people advanced, Manasseh sinned against the LORD. [3]He rebuilt the pagan places of worship that his father Hezekiah had destroyed. He built altars for the worship of Baal, made images of the goddess Asherah, and worshipped the stars. [4]He built pagan altars in the Temple, the place that the LORD had said was where he should be worshipped for ever. [5]In the two courtyards of the Temple he built altars for the worship of the stars. [6]He sacrificed his sons in the Valley of Hinnom as burnt-offerings. He practised divination and magic and consulted fortune-tellers and mediums. He sinned greatly against the LORD and stirred up his anger. [7]He placed an image in the Temple, the place about which God had said to David and his son Solomon: "Here in Jerusalem, in this Temple, is the place that I have chosen out of all the territory of the twelve tribes of Israel as the place where I am to be worshipped. [8]And if the people of Israel will obey all my commands and keep the whole Law that my servant Moses gave them, then I will not allow them to be driven out of the land that I gave to their ancestors." [9]Manasseh led the people of

---

[o] *Some ancient translations* He let the people live in peace; *Hebrew* He led the people.
33.2: Jer 15.4   **33.4:** 2 Chr 6.6   **33.7-8:** 1 Kgs 9.3-5; 2 Chr 7.12-18

He sinned greatly against the LORD (33.6)

Judah to commit even greater sins than those committed by the nations whom the LORD had driven out of the land as his people advanced.

Manasseh Repents

10 Although the LORD warned Manasseh and his people, they refused to listen. 11 So the LORD let the commanders of the Assyrian army invade Judah. They captured Manasseh, stuck hooks in him, put him in chains, and took him to Babylon. 12 In his suffering he became humble, turned to the LORD his God, and begged him for help. 13 God accepted Manasseh's prayer and answered it by letting him go back to Jerusalem and rule again. This convinced Manasseh that the LORD was God.

14 After this, Manasseh increased the height of the outer wall on the east side of David's City, from a point in the valley near the spring of Gihon north to the Fish Gate and the area of the city called Ophel. He also stationed an army officer in command of a unit of troops in each of the fortified cities of Judah. 15 He removed from the Temple the foreign gods and the image that he had placed there, and the pagan altars that were on the hill where the Temple stood and in other places in Jerusalem; he took all these things outside the city and threw them away. 16 He also

repaired the altar where the LORD was worshipped, and he sacrificed fellowship-offerings and thanksgiving-offerings on it. He commanded all the people of Judah to worship the LORD, the God of Israel. 17 Although the people continued to offer sacrifices at other places of worship, they offered them only to the LORD.

The End of Manasseh's Reign
(2 Kgs 21.17-18)

18 Everything else that Manasseh did, the prayer he made to his God, and the messages of the prophets who spoke to him in the name of the LORD, the God of Israel, are all recorded in *The History of the Kings of Israel.* 19 The king's prayer and God's answer to it, and an account of the sins he committed before he repented—the evil he did, the pagan places of worship and the symbols of the goddess Asherah that he made and the idols that he worshipped—are all recorded in *The History of the Prophets.* 20 Manasseh died and was buried at the palace, and his son Amon succeeded him as king.

King Amon of Judah
(2 Kgs 21.19-26)

21 Amon was twenty-two years old when he became king of Judah, and he ruled in Jerusalem for two years. 22 Like

his father Manasseh, he sinned against the LORD, and he worshipped the idols that his father had worshipped. 23 But unlike his father, he did not become humble and turn to the LORD; he was even more sinful than his father had been.

24 Amon's officials plotted against him and assassinated him in the palace. 25 The people of Judah killed Amon's assassins and made his son Josiah king.

King Josiah of Judah
(2 Kgs 22.1–2)

34 Josiah was eight years old when he became king of Judah, and he ruled in Jerusalem for thirty-one years. 2 He did what was pleasing to the LORD; he followed the example of his ancestor King David, strictly obeying all the laws of God.

Josiah Attacks Pagan Worship

3 In the eighth year that Josiah was king, while he was still very young, he began to worship the God of his ancestor King David. Four years later he began to destroy the pagan places of worship, the symbols of the goddess Asherah, and all the other idols. 4 Under his direction his men smashed the altars where Baal was worshipped and tore down the incense-altars near them. They ground to dust the images of Asherah and all the other idols and then scattered the dust on the graves of the people who had sacrificed to them. 5 He burnt the bones of the pagan priests on the altars where they had worshipped. By doing all this, he made Judah and Jerusalem ritually clean again. 6 He did the same thing in the cities and the devastated areas of Manasseh, Ephraim, and Simeon, and as far north as Naphtali. 7 Throughout the territory of the Northern Kingdom he smashed the altars and the symbols of Asherah, ground the idols to dust, and broke in pieces all the incense-altars. Then he returned to Jerusalem.

The Book of the Law Is Discovered
(2 Kgs 22.3–20)

8 In the eighteenth year of his reign, after he had purified the land and the Temple by ending pagan worship, King Josiah sent three men to repair the Temple of the LORD God: Shaphan son of Azaliah, Maaseiah, the governor of Jerusalem, and Joah son of Joahaz, a high official. 9 The money that the Levite guards had collected in the Temple was handed over to Hilkiah the High Priest. (It had been collected from the people of Ephraim and Manasseh and the rest of the Northern Kingdom, and from the people of Judah, Benjamin, and Jerusalem.) 10 This money was then handed over to the three men in charge of the temple repairs, and they gave it to 11 the carpenters and the builders to buy the stones and the timber used to repair the buildings that the kings of Judah had allowed to decay. 12 The men who did the work were thoroughly honest. They were supervised by four Levites: Jahath and Obadiah of the clan of Merari, and Zechariah and Meshullam of the clan of Kohath. (The Levites were all skilful musicians.) 13 Other Levites were in charge of transporting materials and supervising the workmen on various jobs, and others kept records or served as guards.

14 While the money was being taken out of the storeroom, Hilkiah found the book of the Law of the LORD, the Law that God had given to Moses. 15 He said to Shaphan, "I have found the book of the Law here in the Temple." He gave Shaphan the book, 16 and Shaphan took it to the king. He reported, "We have done everything that you commanded. 17 We have taken the money that was kept in the Temple and handed it over to the workmen and their supervisors." 18 Then he added, "I have here a book that Hilkiah gave me." And he read it aloud to the king.

19 When the king heard the book being read, he tore his clothes in dismay 20 and gave the following order to Hilkiah, to Ahikam son of Shaphan, to Abdon p son of Micaiah, to Shaphan, the court secretary, and to Asaiah, the king's attendant: 21 "Go and consult the LORD for me and for the people who still remain in Israel and Judah. Find out about the teachings of this book. The LORD is angry with us because our ancestors have not obeyed the word of the LORD and have not done what this book says must be done."

22 At the king's command, Hilkiah and the others went to consult a woman named Huldah, a prophet who lived in the newer part of Jerusalem. (Her husband Shallum, the son of Tikvah and grandson of Harhas, was in charge of the

p ABDON: Achbor in 2 Kgs 22.12.
34.1: Jer 3.6   **34.4:** 2 Kgs 21.3; 2 Chr 33.3   **34.5:** 1 Kgs 13.2

temple robes.) They described to her what had happened, 23 and she told them to go back to the king and give him 24 the following message from the LORD: "I am going to punish Jerusalem and all its people with the curses written in the book that was read to the king. 25 They have rejected me and have offered sacrifices to other gods, and so have stirred up my anger by all they have done. My anger is aroused against Jerusalem, and it will not die down. 26 As for the king himself, this is what I, the LORD God of Israel, say: You listened to what is written in the book, 27 and you repented and humbled yourself before me, tearing your clothes and weeping, when you heard how I threatened to punish Jerusalem and its people. I have heard your prayer, 28 and the punishment which I am going to bring on Jerusalem will not come until after your death. I will let you die in peace."

The men returned to King Josiah with this message.

Josiah Makes a Covenant to Obey The LORD
(2 Kgs 23.1-20)

29 King Josiah summoned all the leaders of Judah and Jerusalem, 30 and together they went to the Temple, accompanied by the priests and the Levites and all the rest of the people, rich and poor alike. Before them all, the king read aloud the whole book of the covenant, which had been found in the Temple. 31 He stood by the royal column*q* and made a covenant with the LORD to obey him, to keep his laws and commands with all his heart and soul, and to put into practice the demands attached to the covenant, as written in the book. 32 He made the people of Benjamin and everyone else present in Jerusalem promise to keep the covenant. And so the people of Jerusalem obeyed the requirements of the covenant they had made with the God of their ancestors. 33 King Josiah destroyed all the disgusting idols that were in the territory belonging to the people of Israel, and as long as he lived, he required the people to serve the LORD, the God of their ancestors.

Josiah Celebrates the Passover
(2 Kgs 23.21-23)

35 King Josiah celebrated the Passover at Jerusalem in honour

of the LORD; on the fourteenth day of the first month they killed the animals for the festival. 2 He assigned to the priests the duties they were to perform in the Temple and encouraged them to do them well. 3 He also gave these instructions to the Levites, the teachers of Israel, who were dedicated to the LORD: "Put the sacred Covenant Box in the Temple that King Solomon, the son of David, built. You are no longer to carry it from place to place, but you are to serve the LORD your God and his people Israel. 4 Take your places in the Temple by clans, according to the responsibilities assigned to you by King David and his son King Solomon, 5 and arrange yourselves so that some of you will be available to help each family of the people of Israel. 6 You are to kill the Passover lambs and goats. Now make yourselves ritually clean and prepare the sacrifices in order that your fellow-Israelites may follow the instructions which the LORD gave through Moses."

7 For the use of the people at the Passover, King Josiah contributed from his own herds and flocks thirty thousand sheep, lambs, and young goats, and three thousand bulls. 8 His officials also made contributions for the people, the priests, and the Levites to use. And the officials in charge of the Temple—Hilkiah, the High Priest, Zechariah, and Jehiel—gave the priests two thousand six hundred lambs and young goats and three hundred bulls for sacrifices during the festival. 9 The leaders of the Levites—Conaniah, Shemaiah and his brother Nethanel, Hashabiah, Jeiel, and Jozabad—contributed five thousand lambs and young goats and five hundred bulls for the Levites to offer as sacrifices.

10 When everything was arranged for the Passover, the priests and the Levites took their places, as commanded by the king. 11 After the lambs and goats had been killed, the Levites skinned them, and the priests sprinkled the blood on the altar. 12 Then they divided among the people, by family groups, the animals for burnt-offerings, so that they could offer them according to the instructions in the Law of Moses. 13 The Levites roasted the Passover sacrifices over the fire, according to the regulations, and boiled the sacred offerings in pots, cauldrons, and pans, and quickly distributed the meat to

---

q Probable text (see 2 Kgs 23.3) by the royal column; *Hebrew* in his place.
35.4: 2 Chr 8.14   **35.13:** Ex 12.8-9

the people. 14 After this was done, the Levites provided meat for themselves and for the priests descended from Aaron, for the priests were kept busy until night, burning the animals that were burnt whole and the fat of the sacrifices. 15 The following musicians of the Levite clan of Asaph were in the places assigned to them by King David's instructions: Asaph, Heman, and Jeduthun, the king's prophet. The guards at the temple gates did not need to leave their posts, because the other Levites prepared the Passover for them. 16 So, as King Josiah had commanded, everything was done that day for the worship of the LORD, the keeping of the Passover Festival, and the offering of burnt-offerings on the altar. 17 For seven days all the people of Israel who were present celebrated the Passover and the Festival of Unleavened Bread. 18 Since the days of the prophet Samuel, the Passover had never been celebrated like this. None of the former kings had ever celebrated a Passover like this one celebrated by King Josiah, the priests, the Levites, and the people of Judah, Israel, and Jerusalem 19 in the eighteenth year of Josiah's reign.

The End of Josiah's Reign
(2 Kgs 23.28–30)

20 After King Josiah had done all this for the Temple, King Neco of Egypt led an army to fight at Carchemish on the River Euphrates. Josiah tried to stop him, 21 but Neco sent Josiah this message: "This war I am fighting does not concern you, King of Judah. I have not come to fight you, but to fight my enemies, and God has told me to hurry. God is on my side, so don't oppose me, or he will destroy you." 22 But Josiah was determined to fight. He refused to listen to what God was saying through King Neco, so he disguised himself and went into battle on the plain of Megiddo. 23 During the battle King Josiah was struck by Egyptian arrows. He ordered his servants, "Take me away; I'm badly hurt!" 24 They lifted him out of his chariot, placed him in a second chariot which he had there, and took him to Jerusalem. There he died and was buried in the royal tombs. All the people of Judah and Jerusalem mourned his death.

25 The prophet Jeremiah composed a lament for King Josiah. It has become a custom in Israel for the singers, both men and women, to use this song when they mourn for him. The song is found in the collection of laments.

26 Everything that Josiah did—his devotion to the LORD, his obedience to the Law, 27 and his history from beginning to end—is all recorded in *The History of the Kings of Israel and Judah.*

King Joahaz of Judah
(2 Kgs 23.30–35)

36 The people of Judah chose Josiah's son Joahaz and anointed him king in Jerusalem. 2 Joahaz was twenty-three years old when he became king of Judah, and he ruled in Jerusalem for three months. 3 King Neco of Egypt took him prisoner and made Judah pay 3,400 kilogrammes of silver and 34 kilogrammes of gold as tribute. 4 Neco made Joahaz' brother Eliakim king of Judah and changed his name to Jehoiakim. Joahaz was taken to Egypt by Neco.

King Jehoiakim of Judah
(2 Kgs 23.36—24.7)

5 Jehoiakim was twenty-five years old when he became king of Judah, and he ruled in Jerusalem for eleven years. He sinned against the LORD his God. 6 King Nebuchadnezzar of Babylonia invaded Judah, captured Jehoiakim, and took him to Babylonia in chains. 7 Nebuchadnezzar carried off some of the treasures of the Temple and put them in his palace in Babylon. 8 Everything that Jehoiakim did, including his disgusting practices and the evil he committed, is recorded in *The History of the Kings of Israel and Judah.* His son Jehoiachin succeeded him as king.

King Jehoiachin of Judah
(2 Kgs 24.8–17)

9 Jehoiachin was eighteen x years old when he became king of Judah, and he ruled in Jerusalem for three months and ten days. He too sinned against the LORD. 10 When spring came, King Nebuchadnezzar took Jehoiachin to Babylonia as a prisoner, and carried off the treasures of the Temple. Then Nebuchadnezzar made Jehoiachin's uncle r Zedekiah king of Judah and Jerusalem.

x *Some ancient translations (and see 2 Kgs 24.8)* eighteen; *Hebrew* eight.
r *Some ancient translations (and see 2 Kgs 24.17)* uncle; *Hebrew* brother.
35.15: 1 Chr 25.1   **35.17:** Ex 12.1-20   **36.4:** Jer 22.11–12
36.5: Jer 22.18-19, 26.1-6, 35.1-19   **36.6:** Jer 25.1-38, 36.1-32, 45.1-5; Dan 1.1-2
36.10: Jer 22.24-30, 24.1-10, 29.1-2, 37.1; Ezek 17.12,13

King Zedekiah of Judah
(2 Kgs 24.18-20; Jer 52.1-3a)

11 Zedekiah was twenty-one years old when he became king of Judah, and he ruled in Jerusalem for eleven years. 12 He sinned against the LORD and did not listen humbly to the prophet Jeremiah, who spoke the word of the LORD.

The Fall of Jerusalem
(2 Kgs 25.1-21; Jer 52.3b-11)

13 Zedekiah rebelled against King Nebuchadnezzar, who had forced him to swear in God's name that he would be loyal. He stubbornly refused to repent and return to the LORD, the God of Israel. 14 In addition, the leaders of Judah, the priests, and the people followed the sinful example of the nations round them in worshipping idols, and so they defiled the Temple, which the LORD himself had made holy. 15 The LORD, the God of their ancestors, had continued to send prophets to warn his people, because he wanted to spare them and the Temple. 16 But they ridiculed God's messengers, ignoring his words and laughing at his prophets, until at last the LORD's anger against his people was so great that there was no escape.

17 So the LORD brought the king of Babylonia to attack them. The king killed the young men of Judah, even in the Temple. He had no mercy on anyone, young or old, man or woman, sick or healthy. God handed them all over to him. 18 The king of Babylon looted the Temple, the temple treasury, and the wealth of the king and his officials, and took everything back to Babylon. 19 He burnt down the Temple and the city, with all its palaces and its wealth, and broke down the city wall. 20 He took all the survivors to Babylonia, where they served him and his descendants as slaves until the rise of the Persian Empire. 21 And so what the LORD had foretold through the prophet Jeremiah was fulfilled: "The land will lie desolate for seventy years, to make up for the Sabbath rest *s* that has not been observed."

Cyrus Commands the Jews to Return
(Ezra 1.1-4)

22 In the first year that Cyrus of Persia was emperor, *t* the LORD made what he had said through the prophet Jeremiah come true. He prompted Cyrus to issue the following command and send it out in writing to be read aloud everywhere in his empire:

23 "This is the command of Cyrus, Emperor of Persia. The LORD, the God of Heaven, has made me ruler over the whole world and has given me the responsibility of building a temple for him in Jerusalem in Judah. Now, all of you who are God's people, go there, and may the LORD your God be with you."

---

s SABBATH REST: *A reference to the requirement of the Law that every seventh year the land was not to be farmed (see Lev 25.1-7).*
t EMPEROR: *King Cyrus of Persia occupied the city of Babylon in 539 B.C. and began to reign as the emperor of Babylonia.*
36.11: Jer 27.1-22, 28.1-17　　**36.13:** Ezek 17.15　　**36.17:** Jer 21.1-10, 34.1-5
36.21: Jer 25.11, 29.10　　**36.23:** Is 44.28

THE BOOK OF
EZRA

INTRODUCTION

The book of *Ezra* is a sequel to *Chronicles,* describing the return of some of the Jewish exiles from Babylon and the restoration of life and worship in Jerusalem. These events are presented in the following stages: (1) The first group of Jewish exiles returns from Babylonia at the order of Cyrus, the Persian emperor. (2) The Temple is rebuilt and dedicated, and the worship of God restored in Jerusalem. (3) Years later another group of Jews returns to Jerusalem under the leadership of Ezra, an expert in the Law of God, who helps the people reorganize their religious and social life in order to safeguard the spiritual heritage of Israel.

Outline of Contents

The first return from exile   1.1—2.70
The Temple is rebuilt and dedicated   3.1—6.22
Ezra returns with other exiles   7.1—10.44

Cyrus Commands the Jews to Return

1 In the first year that Cyrus of Persia was emperor,[a] the LORD made what he had said through the prophet Jeremiah come true. He prompted Cyrus to issue the following command and send it out in writing to be read aloud everywhere in his empire:

2 "This is the command of Cyrus, Emperor of Persia. The LORD, the God of Heaven, has made me ruler over the whole world and has given me the responsibility of building a temple for him in Jerusalem in Judah. 3 May God be with all of you who are his people. You are to go to Jerusalem and rebuild the Temple of the LORD, the God of Israel, the God who is worshipped in Jerusalem. 4 If any of his people in exile need help to return, their neighbours are to give them this help. They are to provide them with silver and gold, supplies and pack animals, as well as offerings to present in the Temple of God in Jerusalem."

5 Then the heads of the clans of the tribes of Judah and Benjamin, the priests and Levites, and everyone else whose heart God had moved got ready to go and rebuild the LORD's Temple in Jerusalem. 6 All their neighbours helped them by giving them many things: silver utensils, gold, supplies, pack animals, other valuables, and offerings for the Temple.

7 Cyrus gave them back the bowls and cups that King Nebuchadnezzar had taken from the Temple in Jerusalem and had put in the temple of his gods. 8 He handed them over to Mithredath, chief of the royal treasury, who made an inventory

---

a EMPEROR: *King Cyrus of Persia occupied the city of Babylon in 539 B.C. and began to reign as the emperor of Babylonia.*
1.1: Jer 25.11, 29.10   **1.2:** Is 44.28

Many of the exiles left (2.1)

of them for Sheshbazzar, the governor of Judah, 9-10 as follows:

gold bowls for offerings	30
silver bowls for offerings	1,000
other bowls	29
small gold bowls	30
small silver bowls	410
other utensils	1,000

11 In all there were 5,400 gold and silver bowls and other articles which Sheshbazzar took with him when he and the other exiles went from Babylon to Jerusalem.

The List of Those Who Returned from Exile
(Neh 7.4-73)

2 Many of the exiles left the province of Babylon and returned to Jerusalem and Judah, each to his own city. Their families had been living in exile in Babylonia ever since King Nebuchadnezzar had taken them there as prisoners. 2 Their leaders were Zerubbabel, Joshua, Nehemiah, Seraiah, Reelaiah, Mordecai, Bilshan, Mispar, Bigvai, Rehum, and Baanah.

This is the list of the clans of Israel, with the number of those from each clan who returned from exile:

3-20 Parosh	2,172
Shephatiah	372
Arah	775
Pahath Moab (descendants of Jeshua and Joab)	2,812
Elam	1,254
Zattu	945
Zaccai	760
Bani	642
Bebai	623
Azgad	1,222
Adonikam	666
Bigvai	2,056
Adin	454
Ater (also called Hezekiah)	98
Bezai	323
Jorah	112
Hashum	223
Gibbar	95

21-35 People whose ancestors had lived in the following towns also returned:

Bethlehem	123
Netophah	56
Anathoth	128
Azmaveth	42
Kiriath Jearim, Chephirah, and Beeroth	743
Ramah and Geba	621
Michmash	122
Bethel and Ai	223
Nebo	52
Magbish	156
The other Elam	1,254
Harim	320
Lod, Hadid, and Ono	725
Jericho	345
Senaah	3,630

36-39 This is the list of the priestly clans that returned from exile:

Jedaiah (descendants of Jeshua)	973
Immer	1,052
Pashhur	1,247

Harim - 1,017

40-42 Clans of Levites who returned from exile:

Jeshua and Kadmiel (descendants of Hodaviah) - 74

Temple musicians (descendants of Asaph) - 128

Temple guards (descendants of Shallum, Ater, Talmon, Akkub, Hatita, and Shobai) - 139

43-54 Clans of temple workmen who returned from exile:

Ziha, Hasupha, Tabbaoth,
Keros, Siaha, Padon,
Lebanah, Hagabah, Akkub,
Hagab, Shamlai, Hanan,
Giddel, Gahar, Reaiah,
Rezin, Nekoda, Gazzam,
Uzza, Paseah, Besai,
Asnah, Meunim, Nephisim,
Bakbuk, Hakupha, Harhur,
Bazluth, Mehida, Harsha,
Barkos, Sisera, Temah,
Neziah, and Hatipha

55-57 Clans of Solomon's servants who returned from exile:

Sotai, Hassophereth, Peruda,
Jaalah, Darkon, Giddel,
Shephatiah, Hattil, Pochereth Hazzebaim, and Ami

58 The total number of descendants of the temple workmen and of Solomon's servants who returned from exile was 392.

59-60 There were 652 belonging to the clans of Delaiah, Tobiah, and Nekoda who returned from the towns of Tel Melah, Tel Harsha, Cherub, Addan, and Immer; but they could not prove that they were descendants of Israelites.

61-62 The following priestly clans could find no record to prove their ancestry: Habaiah, Hakkoz, and Barzillai. (The ancestor of the priestly clan of Barzillai had married a woman from the clan of Barzillai of Gilead and had taken the name of his father-in-law's clan.) Since they were unable to prove who their ancestors were, they were not accepted as priests. 63 The Jewish governor told them that they could not eat the food offered to God until there was a priest who could use the Urim and Thummim.b

64-67 Total number of exiles who returned - 42,360

Their male and female servants - 7,337

Male and female musicians - 200

Horses - 736

Mules - 245

Camels - 435

Donkeys - 6,720

68 When the exiles arrived at the LORD's Temple in Jerusalem, some of the leaders of the clans gave freewill offerings to help rebuild the Temple on its old site. 69 They gave as much as they could for this work, and the total came to 500 kilogrammes of gold, 2,800 kilogrammes of silver, and 100 robes for priests.

70 The priests, the Levites, and some of the people settled in or near Jerusalem;c the musicians, the temple guards, and the temple workmen settled in nearby towns; and the rest of the Israelites settled in the towns where their ancestors had lived.

Worship Begins Again

3 By the seventh month the people of Israel were all settled in their towns. Then they all assembled in Jerusalem, 2 and Joshua son of Jehozadak, his fellow-priests, and Zerubbabel son of Shealtiel, together with his relatives, rebuilt the altar of the God of Israel, so that they could burn sacrifices on it according to the instructions written in the Law of Moses, the man of God. 3 Even thoughd the returning exiles were afraid of the people who were living in the land, they rebuilt the altar where it had stood before. Then they began once again to burn on it the regular morning and evening sacrifices. 4 They celebrated the Festival of Shelters according to the regulations; each day they offered the sacrifices required for that day; 5 and in addition they offered the regular sacrifices to be burnt whole and those to be offered at the New Moon Festival and at all the other regular assemblies at which the LORD is worshipped, as well as all the offerings that were given to the LORD voluntarily. 6 Although the people had not yet started to rebuild the Temple, they began on the first day of the seventh month to burn sacrifices to the LORD.

The Rebuilding of the Temple Begins

7 The people gave money to pay the stonemasons and the carpenters and gave

---

b URIM AND THUMMIM: *Two objects used by the priest to determine God's will; it is not known precisely how they were used.*
c *One ancient translation* in or near Jerusalem; *Hebrew does not have these words.*
d *Even though; or Because.*

2.63: Num 27.21   **2.70:** 1 Chr 9.2; Neh 11.3   **3.2:** Ex 27.1   **3.3:** Num 28.1-8
3.4: Num 29.12-38   **3.5:** Num 28.11—29.39

The foundation of the Temple had been started (3.11)

food, drink, and olive-oil to be sent to the cities of Tyre and Sidon in exchange for cedar-trees from Lebanon, which were to be brought by sea to Joppa. All this was done with the permission of Cyrus, emperor of Persia. 8 So in the second month of the year after they came back to the site of the Temple in Jerusalem, they began work. Zerubbabel, Joshua, and the rest of their fellow-countrymen, the priests, and the Levites, in fact all the exiles who had come back to Jerusalem, joined in the work. All the Levites twenty years of age or older were put in charge of the work of rebuilding the Temple. 9 The Levite Joshua and his sons and relatives, and Kadmiel and his sons (the clan of Hodaviah)*e* joined together in taking charge of the rebuilding of the Temple. (They were helped by the Levites of the clan of Henadad.)

10 When the men started to lay the foundation of the Temple, the priests in their robes took their places with trumpets in their hands, and the Levites of the clan of Asaph stood there with cymbals. They praised the LORD according to the instructions handed down from the time of King David. 11 They sang the LORD's praises, repeating the refrain:

"The LORD is good, and his love for
    Israel is eternal."

Everyone shouted with all his might, praising the LORD, because the work on the foundation of the Temple had been started. 12 Many of the older priests, Levites, and heads of clans had seen the first Temple, and as they watched the foundation of this Temple being laid, they cried and wailed. But the others who were there shouted for joy. 13 No one could distinguish between the joyful shouts and the crying, because the noise they made was so loud that it could be heard far and wide.

Opposition to the Rebuilding of the Temple

4 The enemies of the people of Judah and Benjamin heard that those who had returned from exile were rebuilding the Temple of the LORD, the God of Israel. 2 So they went to see Zerubbabel and the heads of the clans and said, "Let us join you in building the Temple. We worship the same God you worship, and we have been offering sacrifices to him ever since Esarhaddon, emperor of Assyria, sent us here to live."

3 Zerubbabel, Joshua, and the heads of the clans said to them, "We don't need

e Probable text (see 2.40) Hodaviah; *Hebrew* Judah.
3.10: 1 Chr 25.1
3.11: 1 Chr 16.34; 2 Chr 5.13, 7.3; Ps 100.5, 106.1, 107.1, 118.1, 136.1; Jer 33.11
4.2: 2 Kgs 17.24–41

your help to build a temple for the LORD our God. We will build it ourselves, just as Cyrus, emperor of Persia, commanded us."

4 Then the people who had been living in the land tried to discourage and frighten the Jews and keep them from building. 5 They also bribed Persian government officials to work against them. They kept on doing this throughout the reign of Cyrus and into the reign of Darius. *f*

Opposition to the Rebuilding of Jerusalem

6 At the beginning of the reign of Xerxes the emperor, the enemies of the people living in Judah and Jerusalem brought written charges against them.

7 Again, in the reign of Artaxerxes, emperor of Persia, Bishlam, Mithredath, Tabeel, and their associates wrote a letter to the emperor. The letter was written in Aramaic *h* and was to be translated when read. *i*

8 Also Rehum, the governor, and Shimshai, the secretary of the province, wrote the following letter to Artaxerxes about Jerusalem:

9 "From Rehum, the governor, from Shimshai, secretary of the province, from their associates, the judges, and from all the other officials, who are men originally from Erech, Babylon, and Susa in the land of Elam, 10 together with the other peoples whom the great and powerful Ashurbanipal moved from their homes and settled in the city of Samaria and elsewhere in the province of West Euphrates." *j*

11 This is the text of the letter:

"To Emperor Artaxerxes from his servants, the men of West Euphrates.

12 "We want Your Majesty to know that the Jews who came here from your other territories have settled in Jerusalem and are rebuilding that evil and rebellious city. They have begun to rebuild the walls and will soon finish them. 13 Your Majesty, if this city is rebuilt and its walls are completed, the people will stop paying taxes, and your royal revenues will decrease. 14 Now, because we are

under obligation to Your Majesty, we do not want to see this happen, and so we suggest 15 that you order a search to be made in the records your ancestors kept. If you do, you will discover that this city has always been rebellious and that from ancient times it has given trouble to kings and to rulers of provinces. Its people have always been hard to govern. This is why the city was destroyed. 16 We therefore are convinced that if this city is rebuilt and its walls are completed, Your Majesty will no longer be able to control the province of West Euphrates."

17 The emperor sent this answer:

"To Rehum, the governor, to Shimshai, secretary of the province, and to their associates who live in Samaria and in the rest of West Euphrates, greetings.

18 "The letter which you sent has been translated and read to me. 19 I gave orders for an investigation to be made, and it has indeed been found that from ancient times Jerusalem has revolted against royal authority and that it has been full of rebels and troublemakers. 20 Powerful kings have reigned there and have ruled over the entire province of West Euphrates, collecting taxes and revenue. 21 Therefore you are to issue orders that those men are to stop rebuilding the city until I give further commands. 22 Do this at once, so that no more harm may be done to my interests."

23 As soon as this letter from Artaxerxes was read to Rehum, Shimshai, and their associates, they hurried to Jerusalem and forced the Jews to stop rebuilding the city.

Work on the Temple Begins Again

24 Work on the Temple had been stopped and had remained at a standstill until the second year of the reign of **5** Darius, emperor of Persia. 1 At that time two prophets, Haggai and Zechariah son of Iddo, began to speak in the name of the God of Israel to the

---

f DARIUS: *The account of these events is continued at verse 24. The material in verses 6–23 describes events which took place almost a century later.*
h ARAMAIC: *From 4.8 to 6.18 this book is not in Hebrew, but Aramaic, the official language of the Persian Empire.*
i The letter...read; *or It was in Aramaic and was written in the Aramaic script.*
j PROVINCE OF WEST EUPHRATES: *Under Persian rule the land of Judah was part of this large Persian province west of the River Euphrates.*
4.6: Esth 1.1   **4.24—5.1:** Hag 1.1; Zech 1.1

Jews who lived in Judah and Jerusalem. ²When Zerubbabel son of Shealtiel and Joshua son of Jehozadak heard their messages, they began to rebuild the Temple in Jerusalem, and the two prophets helped them.

3 Almost at once Tattenai, governor of West Euphrates, Shethar Bozenai, and their fellow-officials came to Jerusalem and demanded: "Who gave you orders to build this Temple and equip it?" ⁴They*k* also asked for the names of all the men who were helping to build the Temple. ⁵But God was watching over the Jewish leaders, and the Persian officials decided to take no action until they could write to Darius and receive a reply. ⁶This is the report that they sent to the emperor:

⁷"To Emperor Darius, may you rule in peace.

⁸"Your Majesty should know that we went to the province of Judah and found that the Temple of the great God is being rebuilt with large stone blocks and with wooden beams set in the wall. The work is being done with great care and is moving ahead steadily.

⁹"We then asked the leaders of the people to tell us who had given them authority to rebuild the Temple and to equip it. ¹⁰We also asked them their names so that we could inform you who the leaders of this work are.

¹¹"They answered, 'We are servants of the God of heaven and earth, and we are rebuilding the Temple which was originally built and equipped many years ago by a powerful king of Israel. ¹²But because our ancestors made the God of Heaven angry, he let them be conquered by King Nebuchadnezzar of Babylonia, a king of the Chaldean dynasty. The Temple was destroyed, and the people were taken into exile in Babylonia. ¹³Then in the first year of the reign of King Cyrus as emperor of Babylonia, Cyrus issued orders for the Temple to be rebuilt. ¹⁴He restored the gold and silver temple utensils which Nebuchadnezzar had taken from the Temple in Jerusalem and had placed in the temple in Babylon. Cyrus handed these utensils over to a man named Sheshbazzar, whom he appointed governor of Judah. ¹⁵The

emperor told him to take them and return them to the Temple in Jerusalem, and to rebuild the Temple where it had stood before. ¹⁶So Sheshbazzar came and laid its foundation; construction has continued from then until the present, but the Temple is still not finished.'

¹⁷"Now, if it please Your Majesty, let a search be made in the royal records in Babylon to find whether or not Cyrus gave orders for this Temple in Jerusalem to be rebuilt, and then inform us what your will is in this matter."

Cyrus' Order Is Rediscovered

6 So Darius the emperor issued orders for a search to be made in the royal records that were kept in Babylon. ²But it was in the city of Ecbatana in the province of Media that a scroll was found, containing the following record:

³"In the first year of his reign Cyrus the emperor commanded that the Temple in Jerusalem be rebuilt as a place where sacrifices are made and offerings are burnt. The Temple is to be twenty-seven metres high and twenty-seven metres wide. ⁴The walls are to be built with one layer of wood on top of every three layers of stone. All expenses are to be paid by the royal treasury. ⁵Also the gold and silver utensils which King Nebuchadnezzar brought to Babylon from the Temple in Jerusalem are to be returned to their proper place in the Jerusalem Temple."

Darius Orders the Work to Continue

6 Then Darius sent the following reply:

"To Tattenai, governor of West Euphrates, Shethar Bozenai, and your fellow-officials in West Euphrates.

"Stay away from the Temple ⁷and do not interfere with its construction. Let the governor of Judah and the Jewish leaders rebuild the Temple of God where it stood before. ⁸I hereby command you to help them rebuild it. Their expenses are to be paid promptly out of the royal funds received from taxes in West Euphrates, so that the work is not interrupted. ⁹Day by day, without fail, you are to give the priests in

---

k Some ancient translations They; *Aramaic* We.
5.2: Hag 1.12; Zech 4.6–9   **5.12:** 2 Kgs 25.8–12; 2 Chr 36.17–20; Jer 52.12–15
5.13: Ezra 1.2–11

Joyfully dedicated the Temple (6.16)

Jerusalem whatever they tell you they need: young bulls, sheep, or lambs to be burnt as offerings to the God of Heaven, or wheat, salt, wine, or olive-oil. [10]This is to be done so that they can offer sacrifices that are acceptable to the God of Heaven and pray for his blessing on me and my sons. [11]I further command that if anyone disobeys this order, a wooden beam is to be torn out of his house, sharpened at one end, and then driven through his body. And his house is to be made a rubbish heap. [12]May the God who chose Jerusalem as the place where he is to be worshipped overthrow any king or nation that defies this command and tries to destroy the Temple there. I, Darius, have given this order. It is to be fully obeyed."

The Temple Is Dedicated

13 Then Tattenai the governor, Shethar Bozenai, and their fellow-officials did exactly as the emperor had commanded. [14]The Jewish leaders made good progress with the building of the Temple, encouraged by the prophets Haggai and Zechariah. They completed the Temple as they had been commanded by the God of Israel and by Cyrus, Darius, and Artaxerxes, emperors of Persia. [15]They finished the Temple on the third day of the month Adar in the sixth year of the reign of Darius the emperor. [16]Then the people of Israel—the priests, the Levites, and all the others who had returned from exile—joyfully dedicated the Temple. [17]For the dedication they offered a hundred bulls, two hundred sheep, and four hundred lambs as sacrifices, and twelve goats as offerings for sin, one for each tribe of Israel. [18]They also organized the priests and the Levites for the temple services in Jerusalem, according to the instructions contained in the book of Moses.

The Passover

19 The people who had returned from exile celebrated Passover on the fourteenth day of the first month of the following year. [20]All the priests and the Levites had purified themselves and were ritually clean. The Levites killed the animals for the Passover sacrifices for all the people who had returned, for the priests, and for themselves. [21]The sacrifices were eaten by all the Israelites who had returned from exile and by all those who had given up the pagan ways of the other people who were living in the land and who had come to worship the LORD God of Israel. [22]For seven days they joyfully celebrated the Festival of Unleavened Bread. They were full of joy because the LORD had made the emperor of Assyria[l] favourable to them, so that he supported them in their work of rebuilding the Temple of the God of Israel.

[l]EMPEROR OF ASSYRIA: *Apparently a reference to the Persian emperor who then also ruled the territory once occupied by Assyria, Israel's ancient enemy.*
6.14: Hag 1.1; Zech 1.1   **6.19:** Ex 12.1–20

Ezra Arrives in Jerusalem

7 Many years later, when Artaxerxes was emperor of Persia, there was a man named Ezra. He traced his ancestors back to Aaron, the High Priest, as follows: Ezra was the son of Seraiah, son of Azariah, son of Hilkiah, [2] son of Shallum, son of Zadok, son of Ahitub, [3] son of Amariah, son of Azariah, son of Meraioth, [4] son of Zerahiah, son of Uzzi, son of Bukki, [5] son of Abishua, son of Phinehas, son of Eleazar, son of Aaron.

6-7 Ezra was a scholar with a thorough knowledge of the Law which the LORD, the God of Israel, had given to Moses. Because Ezra had the blessing of the LORD his God, the emperor gave him everything he asked for. In the seventh year of the reign of Artaxerxes, Ezra set out from Babylonia for Jerusalem with a group of Israelites which included priests, Levites, temple musicians, temple guards, and workmen. [8-9] They left Babylonia on the first day of the first month, and with God's help they arrived in Jerusalem on the first day of the fifth month. [10] Ezra had devoted his life to studying the Law of the LORD, to practising it, and to teaching all its laws and regulations to the people of Israel.

The Document Which Artaxerxes Gave to Ezra

11 Artaxerxes gave the following document to Ezra, the priest and scholar, who had a thorough knowledge of the laws and commands which the LORD had given to Israel:

[12] "From Artaxerxes[m] the emperor to Ezra the priest, scholar in the Law of the God of Heaven.[n]

[13] "I command that throughout my empire all the Israelite people, priests, and Levites that so desire be permitted to go with you to Jerusalem. [14] I, together with my seven counsellors, send you to investigate the conditions in Jerusalem and Judah in order to see how well the Law of your God, which has been entrusted to you, is being obeyed. [15] You are to take with you the gold and silver offerings which I and my counsellors desire to give to the God of Israel, whose Temple is in Jerusalem. [16] You are also to take all the silver and gold which you collect throughout the province

of Babylon and the offerings which the Israelite people and their priests give for the Temple of their God in Jerusalem.

[17] "You are to spend this money carefully and buy bulls, rams, lambs, corn, and wine and offer them on the altar of the Temple in Jerusalem. [18] You may use the silver and gold that is left over for whatever you and your fellow-countrymen desire, in accordance with the will of your God. [19] You are to present to God in Jerusalem all the utensils that have been given to you for use in the temple services. [20] And anything else which you need for the Temple, you may get from the royal treasury.

[21] "I command all the treasury officials in the province of West Euphrates to provide promptly for Ezra, the priest and scholar in the Law of the God of Heaven, everything he asks you for, [22] up to a limit of 3,400 kilogrammes of silver, 10,000 kilogrammes of wheat, 2,000 litres of wine, 2,000 litres of olive-oil, and as much salt as necessary. [23] You must be careful to provide everything which the God of Heaven requires for his Temple, and so make sure that he is never angry with me or with those who reign after me. [24] You are forbidden to collect any taxes from the priests, Levites, musicians, guards, workmen, or anyone else connected with this Temple.

[25] "You, Ezra, using the wisdom which your God has given you, are to appoint administrators and judges to govern all the people in West Euphrates who live by the Law of your God. You must teach that Law to anyone who does not know it. [26] If anyone disobeys the laws of your God or the laws of the empire, he is to be punished promptly: by death or by exile or by confiscation of his property or by imprisonment."

Ezra Praises God

27 Ezra said, "Praise the LORD, the God of our ancestors! He has made the emperor willing to honour in this way the Temple of the LORD in Jerusalem. [28] By God's grace I have won the favour of the emperor, of his counsellors, and of all his powerful officials; the LORD my God has

---

[m] Verses 12–26 are in Aramaic (see also 4.7).
[n] Aramaic has an additional word, the meaning of which is unclear.

I have been able to persuade many...to return with me (7.28)

given me courage, and I have been able to persuade many of the heads of the clans of Israel to return with me."

The People Who Returned from Exile

8 This is the list of the heads of the clans who had been in exile in Babylonia and who returned with Ezra to Jerusalem when Artaxerxes was emperor:

²⁻¹⁴ Gershom, of the clan of Phinehas
Daniel, of the clan of Ithamar
Hattush son of Shecaniah, of the clan of David
Zechariah, of the clan of Parosh, with 150 men of his clan (there were records of their ancestry)
Eliehoenai son of Zerahiah, of the clan of Pahath Moab, with 200 men
Shecaniah son of Jahaziel, of the clan of Zattu,ᵒ with 300 men
Ebed son of Jonathan, of the clan of Adin, with 50 men
Jeshaiah son of Athaliah, of the clan of Elam, with 70 men
Zebadiah son of Michael, of the clan of Shephatiah, with 80 men
Obadiah son of Jehiel, of the clan of Joab, with 218 men
Shelomith son of Josiphiah, of the clan of Bani,ᵖ with 160 men
Zechariah son of Bebai, of the clan of Bebai, with 28 men
Johanan son of Hakkatan, of the clan of Azgad, with 110 men
Eliphelet, Jeuel, and Shemaiah, of the clan of Adonikam, with 60 men (they returned at a later date)
Uthai and Zaccur, of the clan of Bigvai, with 70 men

Ezra Finds Levites for the Temple

15 I assembled the entire group by the canal that runs to the town of Ahava, and we camped there three days. I found that there were priests in the group, but no Levites. ¹⁶ I sent for nine of the leaders: Eliezer, Ariel, Shemaiah, Elnathan, Jarib, Elnathan, Nathan, Zechariah, and Meshullam, and for two teachers, Joiarib and Elnathan. ¹⁷ I sent them to Iddo, head of the community at Casiphia, to ask him and his associates, the temple workmen, to send us people to serve God in the Temple. ¹⁸ Through God's grace they sent us Sherebiah, an able man, a Levite from the clan of Mahli, and eighteen of his sons and brothers came with him. ¹⁹ They also sent Hashabiah and Jeshaiah of the clan of Merari, with twenty of their relatives. ²⁰ In addition there were 220 temple workmen whose ancestors had been designated by King David and his officials to assist the Levites. They were all listed by name.

Ezra Leads the People in Fasting and Prayer

21 There by the Ahava Canal I gave orders for us all to fast and humble

ᵒ *One ancient translation (see also 2.8) Zattu; Hebrew does not have this name.*
ᵖ *One ancient translation (see also 2.10) Bani; Hebrew does not have this name.*

ourselves before our God and to ask him to lead us on our journey and protect us and our children and all our possessions. 22 I would have been ashamed to ask the emperor for a troop of cavalry to guard us from any enemies during our journey, because I had told him that our God blesses everyone who trusts him, but that he is displeased with and punishes anyone who turns away from him. 23 So we fasted and prayed for God to protect us, and he answered our prayers.

The Gifts for the Temple

24 From among the leading priests I chose Sherebiah, Hashabiah, and ten others. 25 Then I weighed out the silver, the gold, and the utensils which the emperor, his advisers and officials, and the people of Israel had given to be used in the Temple, and I gave it to the priests. 26-27 This is what I gave them:

silver – 22 metric tons
100 silver utensils – 70 kilogrammes
gold – 3,400 kilogrammes
20 gold bowls – 8.4 kilogrammes
2 fine bronze bowls, equal in value to
gold bowls

28 I said to them, "You are sacred to the LORD, the God of your ancestors, and so are all the silver and gold utensils brought to him as freewill offerings. 29 Guard them carefully until you reach the Temple. There in the priests' room weigh them and hand them over to the leaders of the priests and of the Levites, and to the leaders of the people of Israel in Jerusalem." 30 So the priests and the Levites took charge of the silver, the gold, and the utensils, to take them to the Temple in Jerusalem.

The Return to Jerusalem

31 It was on the twelfth day of the first month that we left the Ahava Canal to go to Jerusalem. Our God was with us and protected us from enemy attacks and from ambush as we travelled. 32 When we reached Jerusalem, we rested for three days. 33 Then on the fourth day we went to the Temple, weighed the silver, the gold, and the utensils, and handed them over to Meremoth the priest, son of Uriah. With him were Eleazar son of Phinehas and two Levites, Jozabad son of Jeshua and Noadiah son of Binnui. 34 Everything was counted and weighed, and a complete record was made at the same time.

35 All those who had returned from exile then brought offerings to be burnt as sacrifices to the God of Israel. They offered 12 bulls for all Israel, 96 rams, and 77 lambs; they also offered 12 goats to purify themselves from sin. All these animals were burnt as sacrifices to the LORD. 36 They also took the document the emperor had given them and gave it to the governors and officials of the province of West Euphrates, who then gave their support to the people and the temple worship.

Ezra Learns of Intermarriages with Non-Jews

9 After all this had been done, some of the leaders of the people of Israel came and told me that the people, the priests, and the Levites had not kept themselves separate from the people in the neighbouring countries of Ammon, Moab, and Egypt or from the Canaanites, Hittites, Perizzites, Jebusites, and Amorites. They were doing the same disgusting things that those people did. 2 Jewish men were marrying foreign women, and so God's holy people had become contaminated. The leaders and officials were the chief offenders. 3 When I heard this, I tore my clothes in despair, tore my hair and my beard, and sat down crushed with grief. 4 I sat there grieving until the time for the evening sacrifice to be offered, and people began to gather round me—all those who were frightened because of what the God of Israel had said about the sins of those who had returned from exile.

5 When the time came for the evening sacrifice, I got up from where I had been grieving, and still wearing my torn clothes, I knelt in prayer and stretched out my hands to the LORD my God. 6 I said, "O God, I am too ashamed to raise my head in your presence. Our sins pile up, high above our heads; they reach as high as the heavens. 7 From the days of our ancestors until now, we, your people, have sinned greatly. Because of our sins we, our kings, and our priests have fallen into the hands of foreign kings, and we have been slaughtered, robbed, and carried away as prisoners. We have been totally disgraced, as we still are today. 8 Now for a short time, O LORD our God, you have been gracious to us and have let some of us escape from slavery and live in safety in this holy place. You have freed us from slavery and given us new life. 9 We were slaves, but you did not leave us in slavery. You made the emperors of

Persia favour us and permit us to go on living and to rebuild your Temple, which was in ruins, and to find safety here in Judah and Jerusalem.

10 "But now, O God, what can we say after all that has happened? We have again disobeyed the commands [11]that you gave us through your servants, the prophets. They told us that the land we were going to occupy was an impure land because the people who lived in it filled it from one end to the other with disgusting, filthy actions. [12]They told us that we were never to intermarry with those people and never to help them prosper or succeed if we wanted to enjoy the land and pass it on to our descendants for ever. [13]Even after everything that has happened to us in punishment for our sins and wrongs, we know that you, our God, have punished us less than we deserve and have allowed us to survive. [14]Then how can we ignore your commandments again and intermarry with these wicked people? If we do, you will be so angry that you will destroy us completely and let no one survive. [15]LORD God of Israel, you are just, but you have let us survive. We confess our guilt to you; we have no right to come into your presence."

The Plan for Ending Mixed Marriages

10 While Ezra was bowing in prayer in front of the Temple, weeping and confessing these sins, a large group of Israelites—men, women, and children—gathered round him, weeping bitterly. [2]Then Shecaniah son of Jehiel, of the clan of Elam, said to Ezra, "We have broken faith with God by marrying foreign women, but even so there is still hope for Israel. [3]Now we must make a solemn promise to our God that we will send these women and their children away. We will do what you and the others who honour God's commands advise us to do. We will do what God's Law demands. [4]It is your responsibility to act. We are behind you, so go ahead and get it done."

[5]So Ezra began by making the leaders of the priests, of the Levites, and of the rest of the people take an oath that they would do what Shecaniah had proposed. [6]Then he went from in front of the Temple into the living-quarters of Jehohanan son of Eliashib, and spent the night[r] there grieving over the unfaithfulness of the

exiles. He did not eat or drink anything.

[7]A message was sent throughout Jerusalem and Judah that all those who had returned from exile were to meet in Jerusalem [8]by order of the leaders of the people. If anyone failed to come within three days, all his property would be confiscated, and he would lose his right to be a member of the community. [9]Within the three days, on the twentieth day of the ninth month, all the men living in the territory of Judah and Benjamin came to Jerusalem and assembled in the temple square. It was raining hard, and because of the weather and the importance of the meeting everyone was trembling.

[10]Ezra the priest stood up and spoke to them. He said, "You have been faithless and have brought guilt on Israel by marrying foreign women. [11]Now then, confess your sins to the LORD, the God of your ancestors, and do what pleases him. Separate yourselves from the foreigners living in our land and get rid of your foreign wives."

[12]The people shouted in answer, "We will do whatever you say." [13]But they added, "The crowd is too big, and it's raining hard. We can't stand here in the open like this. This isn't something that can be done in one or two days, because so many of us are involved in this sin. [14]Let our officials stay in Jerusalem and take charge of the matter. Then let anyone who has a foreign wife come at a set time, together with the leaders and the judges of his city. In this way God's anger over this situation will be turned away." [15]No one was opposed to the plan except Jonathan son of Asahel and Jahzeiah son of Tikvah, who had the support of Meshullam and of Shabbethai, a Levite.

[16]The returned exiles accepted the plan, so Ezra the priest appointed[s] men from among the heads of the clans and recorded their names. On the first day of the tenth month they began their investigation, [17]and within the next three months they investigated all the cases of men with foreign wives.

The Men Who Had Foreign Wives

[18]This is the list of the men who had foreign wives:

Priests, listed by clans:

Clan of Joshua and his brothers, sons of Jehozadak: Maaseiah, Eliezer, Jarib,

---

[r] *One ancient translation* spent the night; *Hebrew* went.
[s] *Some ancient translations* appointed; *Hebrew unclear.*
9.12: Ex 34.11–16; Deut 7.1–5

The crowd is too big, and it's raining hard (10.13)

and Gedaliah. ¹⁹They promised to divorce their wives, and they offered a ram as a sacrifice for their sins.

20 Clan of Immer: Hanani and Zebadiah
21 Clan of Harim: Maaseiah, Elijah, Shemaiah, Jehiel, and Uzziah
22 Clan of Pashhur: Elioenai, Maaseiah, Ishmael, Nethanel, Jozabad, and Elasah
²³ *Levites:*
Jozabad, Shimei, Kelaiah (also called Kelita), Pethahiah, Judah, and Eliezer
²⁴ *Musicians:*
Eliashib
Temple guards:
Shallum, Telem, and Uri
²⁵ *Others:*
Clan of Parosh: Ramiah, Izziah, Malchijah, Mijamin, Eleazar, Malchijah, and Benaiah
26 Clan of Elam: Mattaniah, Zechariah, Jehiel, Abdi, Jeremoth, and Elijah
27 Clan of Zattu: Elioenai, Eliashib, Mattaniah, Jeremoth, Zabad, and Aziza
28 Clan of Bebai: Jehohanan, Hananiah, Zabbai, and Athlai

29 Clan of Bani: Meshullam, Malluch, Adaiah, Jashub, Sheal, and Jeremoth
30 Clan of Pahath Moab: Adna, Chelal, Benaiah, Maaseiah, Mattaniah, Bezalel, Binnui, and Manasseh
31-32 Clan of Harim: Eliezer, Isshijah, Malchijah, Shemaiah, Shimeon, Benjamin, Malluch, and Shemariah
33 Clan of Hashum: Mattenai, Mattattah, Zabad, Eliphelet, Jeremai, Manasseh, and Shimei
34-37 Clan of Bani: Maadai, Amram, Uel, Benaiah, Bedeiah, Cheluhi, Vaniah, Meremoth, Eliashib, Mattaniah, Mattenai, and Jaasu
38-42 Clan of Binnui: Shimei, Shelemiah, Nathan, Adaiah, Machnadebai, Shashai, Sharai, Azarel, Shelemiah, Shemariah, Shallum, Amariah, and Joseph
43 Clan of Nebo: Jeiel, Mattithiah, Zabad, Zebina, Jaddai, Joel, and Benaiah
44 All these men had foreign wives. They divorced them and sent them and their children away. ᵗ

ᵗ *Verse 44 in Hebrew is unclear.*

THE BOOK OF
NEHEMIAH

INTRODUCTION

The book of *Nehemiah* may be divided into four parts: (1) The return of Nehemiah to Jerusalem, where he has been sent by the Persian emperor to govern Judah. (2) The rebuilding of the walls of Jerusalem. (3) The solemn reading of the Law of God by Ezra, and the people's confession of sin. (4) Further activities of Nehemiah as governor of Judah.

A notable feature of the book is the record of Nehemiah's deep dependence on God and his frequent prayers to him.

Outline of Contents

Nehemiah returns to Jerusalem   1.1—2.20
The walls of Jerusalem are rebuilt   3.1—7.73
The Law is read and the covenant is renewed   8.1—10.39
Further activities of Nehemiah   11.1—13.31

1 This is the account of what Nehemiah son of Hacaliah accomplished.

Nehemiah's Concern for Jerusalem

In the month of Kislev in the twentieth year that Artaxerxes was emperor of Persia, I, Nehemiah, was in Susa, the capital city. ² Hanani, one of my brothers, arrived from Judah with a group of other men, and I asked them about Jerusalem and about our fellow-Jews who had returned from exile in ᵃ Babylonia. ³ They told me that those who had survived and were back in the homeland ᵇ were in great difficulty and that the foreigners who lived near by looked down on them. They also told me that the walls of Jerusalem were still broken down and that the gates had not been restored since the time they were burnt. ⁴ When I heard all this, I sat down and wept.

For several days I mourned and did not eat. I prayed to God, ⁵ "LORD God of Heaven! You are great, and we stand in fear of you. You faithfully keep your covenant with those who love you and do what you command. ⁶ Look at me, LORD, and hear my prayer, as I pray day and night for your servants, the people of Israel. I confess that we, the people of Israel, have sinned. My ancestors and I have sinned. ⁷ We have acted wickedly against you and have not done what you commanded. We have not kept the laws which you gave us through Moses, your servant. ⁸ Remember now what you told Moses: 'If you people of Israel are unfaithful to me, I will scatter you among the other nations. ⁹ But then if you turn back to me and do what I have commanded you, I will bring you back to the place where I have chosen to be worshipped, even though you are scattered to the ends of the earth.'

ᵃ had returned from exile in; *or* had not been exiled to.
ᵇ had survived and...homeland; *or* had remained in the homeland and had not gone into exile.
1.8: Lev 26.33   **1.9:** Deut 30.1–5

Why are you looking so sad? (2.2)

10 "Lord, these are your servants, your own people. You rescued them by your great power and strength. [11] Listen now to my prayer and to the prayers of all your other servants who want to honour you. Give me success today and make the emperor merciful to me."

In those days I was the emperor's wine steward.

Nehemiah Goes to Jerusalem

2 One day four months later, when Emperor Artaxerxes was dining, I took the wine to him. He had never seen me look sad before, [2] so he asked, "Why are you looking so sad? You aren't ill, so it must be that you're unhappy."

I was startled [3] and answered, "May Your Majesty live for ever! How can I help looking sad when the city where my ancestors are buried is in ruins and its gates have been destroyed by fire?"

[4] The emperor asked, "What is it that you want?"

I prayed to the God of Heaven, [5] and then I said to the emperor, "If Your Majesty is pleased with me and is willing to grant my request, let me go to the land of Judah, to the city where my ancestors are buried, so that I can rebuild the city."

[6] The emperor, with the empress sitting at his side, approved my request. He asked me how long I would be gone and when I would return, and I told him.

[7] Then I asked him to grant me the favour of giving me letters to the governors of West Euphrates Province,[c] instructing them to let me travel to Judah. [8] I asked also for a letter to Asaph, keeper of the royal forests, instructing him to supply me with timber for the gates of the fort that guards the Temple, for the city walls, and for the house I was to live in. The emperor gave me all I asked for, because God was with me.

[9] The emperor sent some army officers and a troop of horsemen with me, and I made the journey to West Euphrates. There I gave the emperor's letters to the governors. [10] But Sanballat, from the town of Beth Horon, and Tobiah, an official in the province of Ammon, heard that someone had come to work for the good of the people of Israel, and they were highly indignant.

[11] I went on to Jerusalem, and for three days [12] I did not tell anyone what God had inspired me to do for Jerusalem. Then in the middle of the night I got up and went out, taking a few of my companions with me. The only animal we took was the donkey that I rode on. [13] It was still night as I left the city through the Valley Gate on the west and went south past Dragon's Fountain to the Rubbish Gate. As I went, I inspected the broken walls of the city and the gates that had been destroyed by fire. [14] Then on the east side of the city I went north to the Fountain Gate and the King's Pool. The donkey I was riding could not find any path through

[c] WEST EUPHRATES PROVINCE: *Under Persian rule the land of Israel was part of this large Persian province west of the River Euphrates.*
2.3: 2 Kgs 25.8-10; 2 Chr 36.19; Jer 52.12-14

I inspected the broken walls (2.13)

the rubble, ¹⁵ so I went down into the valley of the Kidron and rode along, looking at the wall. Then I returned the way I had come and went back into the city through the Valley Gate.

16 None of the local officials knew where I had been or what I had been doing. So far I had not said anything to any of my fellow-Jews—the priests, the leaders, the officials, or anyone else who would be taking part in the work. ¹⁷ But now I said to them, "See what trouble we are in because Jerusalem is in ruins and its gates are destroyed! Let's rebuild the city walls and put an end to our disgrace." ¹⁸ And I told them how God had been with me and helped me, and what the emperor had said to me.

They responded, "Let's start rebuilding!" And they got ready to start the work.

19 When Sanballat, Tobiah, and an Arab named Geshem heard what we were planning to do, they laughed at us and said, "What do you think you're doing? Are you going to rebel against the emperor?"

20 I answered, "The God of Heaven will give us success. We are his servants, and we are going to start building. But you have no right to any property in Jerusalem, and you have no share in its traditions."

Rebuilding the Wall of Jerusalem

3 This is how the city wall was rebuilt. ^d The High Priest Eliashib and his fellow-priests rebuilt the Sheep Gate, dedicated it, and put the gates in place. They dedicated the wall as far as the Tower of the Hundred and the Tower of Hananel.

2 The men of Jericho built the next section.

Zaccur son of Imri built the next section.

3 The clan of Hassenaah built the Fish Gate. They put the beams and the gates in place, and put in the bolts and bars for locking the gate.

4 Meremoth, the son of Uriah and grandson of Hakkoz, built the next section.

Meshullam, the son of Berechiah and grandson of Meshezabel, built the next section.

Zadok son of Baana built the next section.

5 The men of Tekoa built the next section, but the leading men of the town refused to do the manual labour assigned to them by the supervisors.

6 Joiada son of Paseah and Meshullam son of Besodeiah rebuilt Jeshanah Gate. ^e They put the beams and the gates in place, and put in the bolts and bars for locking the gate.

---

^dCITY WALL WAS REBUILT: *According to the following report, the rebuilding of the wall started at the middle of the north side and proceeded anti-clockwise round the city. Many of the places mentioned cannot be identified.*   ^eJeshanah Gate; *or* the Old Gate.

This is how the city wall was rebuilt (3.1)

7 Melatiah from Gibeon, Jadon from Meronoth, and the men of Gibeon and Mizpah built the next section, as far as the residence of the governor of West Euphrates.

8 Uzziel son of Harhaiah, a goldsmith, built the next section.

Hananiah, a maker of perfumes, built the next section, as far as Broad Wall.

9 Rephaiah son of Hur, ruler of half the Jerusalem District, built the next section.

10 Jedaiah son of Harumaph built the next section, which was near his own house.

Hattush son of Hashabneiah built the next section.

11 Malchijah son of Harim and Hasshub son of Pahath Moab built both the next section and the Tower of the Ovens.

12 Shallum son of Hallohesh, ruler of the other half of the Jerusalem District, built the next section. (His daughters helped with the work.)

13 Hanun and the inhabitants of the city of Zanoah rebuilt the Valley Gate. They put the gates in place, put in the bolts and the bars for locking the gate, and repaired the wall for 440 metres, as far as the Rubbish Gate.

14 Malchijah son of Rechab, ruler of the Beth Haccherem District, rebuilt the Rubbish Gate. He put the gates in place, and put in the bolts and the bars for locking the gate.

15 Shallum son of Colhozeh, ruler of the Mizpah District, rebuilt the Fountain Gate. He covered the gateway, put the gates in place, and put in the bolts and the bars. At the Pool of Shelah he built the wall next to the royal garden, as far as the steps leading down from David's City.

16 Nehemiah son of Azbuk, ruler of half the Bethzur District, built the next section, as far as David's tomb, the pool, and the barracks.

Levites Who Worked on the Wall

17 The following Levites rebuilt the next several sections of the wall:

Rehum son of Bani built the next section;

Hashabiah, ruler of half the Keilah District, built the next section on behalf of his district;

18 Bavvai son of Henadad, ruler of the other half of the Keilah District, built the next section;

19 Ezer son of Jeshua, ruler of Mizpah, built the next section in front of the armoury, as far as the place where the wall turns;

20 Baruch son of Zabbai built the next section, as far as the entrance to the house of the High Priest Eliashib;

21 Meremoth, the son of Uriah and grandson of Hakkoz, built the next section, up to the far end of Eliashib's house.

Priests Who Worked on the Wall

22 The following priests rebuilt the next several sections of the wall:

Priests from the area around Jerusalem built the next section;

23 Benjamin and Hasshub built the next section, which was in front of their houses;

Azariah, the son of Maaseiah and grandson of Ananiah, built the next section, which was in front of his house;

24 Binnui son of Henadad built the next section, from Azariah's house to the corner of the wall;

25-26 Palal son of Uzai built the next section, beginning at the corner of the wall and the tower of the upper palace near the court of the guard;

Pedaiah son of Parosh built the next section, to a point on the east near the Water Gate and the tower guarding the Temple. (This was near that part of the city called Ophel, where the temple workmen lived.)

Other Builders

27 The men of Tekoa built the next section, their second one, from a point opposite the large tower guarding the Temple as far as the wall near Ophel.

28 A group of priests built the next section, going north from the Horse Gate, each one building in front of his own house.

29 Zadok son of Immer built the next section, which was in front of his house.

Shemaiah son of Shecaniah, keeper of the East Gate, built the next section.

30 Hananiah son of Shelemiah and Hanun, the sixth son of Zalaph, built the next section, their second one.

Meshullam son of Berechiah built the next section, which was in front of his house.

31 Malchijah, a goldsmith, built the next section, as far as the building used by the temple workmen and the merchants, which was by the Miphkad[f] Gate, near the room on top of the north-east corner of the wall.

32 The goldsmiths and the merchants built the last section, from the room at the corner as far as the Sheep Gate.

Nehemiah Overcomes Opposition to His Work

4 When Sanballat heard that we Jews had begun rebuilding the wall, he was furious and began to ridicule us. 2 In front of his companions and the Samaritan troops he said, "What do these miserable Jews think they're doing? Do they intend to rebuild the city? Do they think that by offering sacrifices they can finish the work in one day? Can they make building-stones out of heaps of burnt rubble?"

3 Tobiah was standing there beside him, and he added, "What kind of wall could they ever build? Even a fox could knock it down!"

4 I prayed, "Listen to them mocking us, O God! Let their ridicule fall on their own heads. Let them be robbed of everything they have, and let them be taken as prisoners to a foreign land. 5 Don't forgive the evil they do and don't forget their sins, for they have insulted us who are building."

6 So we went on rebuilding the wall, and soon it was half its full height, because the people were eager to work.

7 Sanballat, Tobiah, and the people of Arabia, Ammon, and Ashdod heard that we were making progress in rebuilding the wall of Jerusalem and that the gaps in the wall were being closed, and they were very angry. 8 So they all plotted together to come and attack Jerusalem and create confusion, 9 but we prayed to our God and kept men on guard against them day and night.

10 The people of Judah had a song they sang:

"We grow weak carrying burdens;
There's so much rubble to take away.
How can we build the wall today?"

11 Our enemies thought we would not see them or know what was happening until they were already upon us, killing us and putting an end to our work. 12 But time after time Jews who were living among our enemies came to warn us of the plans our enemies were making against us.[g] 13 So I armed the people with swords, spears, and bows, and stationed them by clans behind the wall, wherever it was still unfinished.

14 I saw that the people were worried, so I said to them and to their leaders and officials, "Don't be afraid of our enemies. Remember how great and terrifying the Lord is, and fight for your fellow-countrymen, your children, your wives, and your homes." 15 Our enemies heard that we had found out what they were plotting, and they realized that God had defeated their plans. Then all of us went back to rebuilding the wall.

16 From then on half my men worked and half stood guard, wearing coats of armour and armed with spears, shields, and bows. And our leaders gave their full

---

[f] Miphkad; or Mustering, or Watch.
[g] Probable text the plans our enemies were making against us; Hebrew unclear.

Worked with one hand and kept a weapon in the other (4.17)

support to the people [17] who were rebuilding the wall. Even those who carried building materials worked with one hand and kept a weapon in the other, [18] and everyone who was building kept a sword strapped to his waist. The man who was to sound the alarm on the bugle stayed with me. [19] I told the people and their officials and leaders, "The work is spread out over such a distance that we are widely separated from one another on the wall. [20] If you hear the bugle, gather round me. Our God will fight for us." [21] So every day, from dawn until the stars came out at night, half of us worked on the wall, while the other half stood guard with spears.

22 During this time I told the men in charge that they and all their helpers had to stay in Jerusalem at night, so that we could guard the city at night as well as work in the daytime. [23] I didn't take off my clothes even at night, neither did any of my companions nor my servants nor my bodyguard. And we all kept our weapons to hand. [h]

Oppression of the Poor

5 Some time later many of the people, both men and women, began to complain against their fellow-Jews. [2] Some said, "We have large families, we need corn to keep us alive."

3 Others said, "We have had to mortgage our fields and vineyards and houses to get enough corn to keep us from starving."

4 Still others said, "We had to borrow money to pay the royal tax on our fields and vineyards. [5] We are of the same race as our fellow-Jews. Aren't our children just as good as theirs? But we have to make slaves of our children. Some of our daughters have already been sold as slaves. We are helpless because our fields and vineyards have been taken away from us."

6 When I heard their complaints, I was angry [7] and decided to act. I denounced the leaders and officials of the people and told them, "You are oppressing your brothers!"

I called a public assembly to deal with the problem [8] and said, "As far as we have been able, we have been buying back our Jewish brothers who had to sell themselves to foreigners. Now you are forcing your own brothers to sell themselves to you, their fellow-Jews!" The leaders were silent and could find nothing to say.

9 Then I said, "What you are doing is wrong! You ought to obey God and do what's right. Then you would not give our enemies, the Gentiles, any reason to ridicule us. [10] I have let the people borrow money and corn from me, and so have my companions and the men who work for me. Now let's give up all our claims to repayment. [11] Cancel all the debts [i] they

---

[h] *Probable text* weapons to hand; *Hebrew unclear.*
[i] *One ancient translation* debts; *Hebrew unclear.*
5.7: Ex 22.25; Lev 25.35–37; Deut 23.19–20

owe you—money or corn or wine or olive-oil. And give them back their fields, vineyards, olive-groves, and houses at once!"

12 The leaders replied, "We'll do as you say. We'll give the property back and not try to collect the debts."

I called in the priests and made the leaders swear in front of them to keep the promise they had just made. 13 Then I took off the sash[j] I was wearing round my waist and shook it out. "This is how God will shake any of you who don't keep your promise," I said. "God will take away your houses and everything you own, and will leave you with nothing."

Everyone who was present said, "Amen!" and praised the LORD. And the leaders kept their promise.

Nehemiah's Unselfishness

14 During all the twelve years that I was governor of the land of Judah, from the twentieth year that Artaxerxes was emperor until his thirty-second year, neither my relatives nor I ate the food I was entitled to have as governor. 15 Every governor who had been in office before me had been a burden to the people and had demanded forty silver coins a day[k] for food and wine. Even their servants had oppressed the people. But I acted differently, because I honoured God. 16 I put all my energy into rebuilding the wall and did not acquire any property. Everyone who worked for me joined in the rebuilding. 17 I regularly fed at my table a hundred and fifty of the Jewish people and their leaders, besides all the people who came to me from the surrounding nations. 18 Every day I served one ox, six of the best sheep, and many chickens, and every ten days I provided a fresh supply of wine. But I knew what heavy burdens the people had to bear, so I did not claim the allowance that the governor is entitled to.

19 I pray you, O God, remember to my credit everything that I have done for this people.

Plots against Nehemiah

6 Sanballat, Tobiah, Geshem, and the rest of our enemies heard that we had finished building the wall and that there were no gaps left in it, although we still had not set up the gates in the gateways. 2 So Sanballat and Geshem sent me a message, suggesting that I meet with them in one of the villages in the Plain of Ono. This was a trick of theirs to try to harm me. 3 I sent messengers to say to them, "I am doing important work and can't go down there. I am not going to let the work stop just to go and see you."

4 They sent me the same message four times, and each time I sent them the same reply.

5 Then Sanballat sent one of his servants to me with a fifth message, this one in the form of an unsealed letter.[l] 6 It read:

"Geshem tells me that a rumour is going round among the neighbouring peoples that you and the Jewish people intend to revolt and that this is why you are rebuilding the wall. He also says you plan to make yourself king 7 and that you have arranged for some prophets to proclaim in Jerusalem that you are the king of Judah. His Majesty is certain to hear about this, so I suggest that you and I meet to talk the situation over."

8 I sent a reply to him: "Nothing of what you are saying is true. You have made it all up yourself."

9 They were trying to frighten us into stopping work. I prayed, "But now, God, make me strong!"

10 About this time I went to visit Shemaiah, the son of Delaiah and grandson of Mehetabel, who was unable to leave his house. He said to me, "You and I must go and hide together in the Holy Place of the Temple and lock the doors, because they are coming to kill you. Any night now they will come to kill you."

11 I answered, "I'm not the kind of man that runs and hides. Do you think I would try to save my life by hiding in the Temple? I won't do it."

12 When I thought it over, I realized that God had not spoken to Shemaiah, but that Tobiah and Sanballat had bribed him to give me this warning. 13 They hired him to frighten me into sinning, so that they could ruin my reputation and humiliate me.

14 I prayed, "God, remember what Tobiah and Sanballat have done and

---

[j] SASH: *Clothing in those days had no pockets, so small items were tucked into the sash that was worn like a belt round the waist. Shaking it out was a symbol of losing everything.*
[k] *One ancient translation* a day; *Hebrew unclear.*
[l] UNSEALED LETTER: *Leaving a letter unsealed was a deliberate way of making certain that its contents would become widely known.*

punish them. Remember that woman Nodiah and all the other prophets who tried to frighten me."

The Conclusion of the Work

15 After fifty-two days of work the entire wall was finished on the twenty-fifth day of the month of Elul. 16 When our enemies in the surrounding nations heard this, they realized that they had lost face, since everyone knew that the work had been done with God's help.

17 During all this time the Jewish leaders had been in correspondence with Tobiah. 18 Many people in Judah were on his side because of his Jewish father-in-law, Shecaniah son of Arah. In addition, his son Jehohanan had married the daughter of Meshullam son of Berechiah. 19 People would talk in front of me about all the good deeds Tobiah had done and would tell him everything I said. And he kept sending me letters to try to frighten me.

7 And now the wall had been rebuilt, the gates had all been put in place, and the temple guards, the members of the sacred choir, and the other Levites had been assigned their work. 2 I put two men in charge of governing the city of Jerusalem: my brother Hanani and Hananiah, commanding officer of the fortress. Hananiah was a reliable and God-fearing man without an equal. 3 I told them not to have the gates of Jerusalem opened in the morning until well after sunrise and to have them closed and barred before the guards went off duty at sunset. I also told them to appoint guards from among the people who lived in Jerusalem and to assign some of them to specific posts and others to patrol the area round their own houses.

The List of Those Who Returned from Exile
(Ezra 2.1-70)

4 Jerusalem was a large city, but not many people were living in it, and not many houses had been built yet. 5 God inspired me to assemble the people and their leaders and officials and to check their family records. I located the records of those who had first returned from captivity, and this is the information I found:

6 Many of the exiles left the province of Babylon and returned to Jerusalem and Judah, each to his own city. Their families had been living in exile in Babylonia ever since King Nebuchadnezzar had taken them there as prisoners. 7 Their leaders were Zerubbabel, Joshua, Nehemiah, Azariah, Raamiah, Nahamani, Mordecai, Bilshan, Mispereth, Bigvai, Nehum, and Baanah.

8-25 This is the list of the clans of Israel, with the number of those from each clan who returned from exile:

Parosh – 2,172
Shephatiah – 372
Arah – 652
Pahath Moab (descendants of Jeshua and Joab) – 2,818
Elam – 1,254
Zattu – 845
Zaccai – 760
Binnui – 648
Bebai – 628
Azgad – 2,322
Adonikam – 667
Bigvai – 2,067
Adin – 655
Ater (also called Hezekiah) – 98
Hashum – 328
Bezai – 324
Hariph – 112
Gibeon – 95

26-38 People whose ancestors had lived in the following towns also returned:

Bethlehem and Netophah – 188
Anathoth – 128
Beth Azmaveth – 42
Kiriath Jearim, Chephirah, and Beeroth – 743
Ramah and Geba – 621
Michmash – 122
Bethel and Ai – 123
The other Nebo – 52
The other Elam – 1,254
Harim – 320
Jericho – 345
Lod, Hadid, and Ono – 721
Senaah – 3,930

39-42 This is the list of the priestly clans that returned from exile:

Jedaiah (descendants of Jeshua) – 973
Immer – 1,052
Pashhur – 1,247
Harim – 1,017

43-45 Clans of Levites who returned from exile:

Jeshua and Kadmiel (descendants of Hodaviah) – 74
Temple musicians (descendants of Asaph) – 148
Temple guards (descendants of Shallum, Ater, Talmon, Akkub, Hatita, and Shobai) – 138

46-56 Clans of temple workmen who returned from exile:

Ziha, Hasupha, Tabbaoth,
Keros, Sia, Padon,
Lebana, Hagaba, Shalmai,
Hanan, Giddel, Gahar,
Reaiah, Rezin, Nekoda,
Gazzam, Uzza, Paseah,
Besai, Meunim, Nephushesim,
Bakbuk, Hakupha, Harhur,
Bazlith, Mehida, Harsha,
Barkos, Sisera, Temah,
Neziah, and Hatipha.

57-59 Clans of Solomon's servants who returned from exile:

Sotai, Sophereth, Perida,
Jaalah, Darkon, Giddel,
Shephatiah, Hattil, Pochereth
  Hazzebaim, and Amon.

60 The total number of descendants of the temple workmen and of Solomon's servants who returned from exile was 392.

61-62 There were 642 belonging to the clans of Delaiah, Tobiah, and Nekoda who returned from the towns of Tel Melah, Tel Harsha, Cherub, Addon, and Immer; but they could not prove that they were descendants of Israelites.

63-64 The following priestly clans could find no record to prove their ancestry: Hobaiah, Hakkoz, and Barzillai. (The ancestor of the priestly clan of Barzillai had married a woman from the clan of Barzillai of Gilead and taken the name of his father-in-law's clan.) Since they were unable to prove who their ancestors were, they were not accepted as priests. 65 The Jewish governor told them that they could not eat the food offered to God until there was a priest who could use the Urim and Thummim. *m*

66-69 Total number of exiles who
  returned - 42,360
Their male and female servants - 7,337
Male and female musicians - 245
Horses - 736
Mules - 245
Camels - 435
Donkeys - 6,720

70-72 Many of the people contributed to help pay the cost of restoring the Temple:

The governor   8 kilogrammes of gold
                 50 ceremonial bowls
                 530 robes for priests

Heads of clans 168 kilogrammes of gold
                1,250 kilogrammes of
                  silver
The rest of the people
                168 kilogrammes of gold
                140 kilogrammes of
                  silver
                67 robes for priests

73 The priests, the Levites, the temple guards, the musicians, many of the ordinary people, the temple workmen—all the people of Israel—settled in the towns and cities of Judah.

Ezra Reads the Law to the People

8 By the seventh month the people of Israel were all settled in their towns. On the first day of that month they all assembled in Jerusalem, in the square just inside the Water Gate. They asked Ezra, the priest and scholar of the Law which the LORD had given Israel through Moses, to get the book of the Law. ² So Ezra brought it to the place where the people had gathered—men, women, and the children who were old enough to understand. ³ There in the square by the gate he read the Law to them from dawn until noon, and they all listened attentively.

4 Ezra was standing on a wooden platform that had been built for the occasion. The following men stood at his right: Mattithiah, Shema, Anaiah, Uriah, Hilkiah, and Maaseiah; and the following stood at his left: Pedaiah, Mishael, Malchijah, Hashum, Hashbaddanah, Zechariah, and Meshullam.

5 As Ezra stood there on the platform high above the people, they all kept their eyes fixed on him. As soon as he opened the book, they all stood up. 6 Ezra said, "Praise the LORD, the great God!"

All the people raised their arms in the air and answered, "Amen! Amen!" They knelt in worship, with their faces to the ground.

7 Then they rose and stood in their places, and the following Levites explained the Law to them: Jeshua, Bani, Sherebiah, Jamin, Akkub, Shabbethai, Hodiah, Maaseiah, Kelita, Azariah, Jozabad, Hanan, and Pelaiah. ⁸ They gave an oral translation *n* of God's Law and explained *o* it so that the people could understand it.

---

m URIM AND THUMMIM: *Two objects used by the priest to determine God's will; it is not known precisely how they were used.*
n TRANSLATION: *The Law was written in Hebrew, but in Babylonia the Jews had adopted Aramaic as the language for daily life. Because of this a translation was necessary.*
o They gave...explained; *or* They read God's Law and then translated it, explaining.
7.65: Ex 28.30; Deut 33.8   **7.73:** 1 Chr 9.2; Neh 11.3

9 When the people heard what the Law required, they were so moved that they began to cry. So Nehemiah, who was the governor, Ezra, the priest and scholar of the Law, and the Levites who were explaining the Law told all the people, "This day is holy to the LORD your God, so you are not to mourn or cry. 10 Now go home and have a feast. Share your food and wine with those who haven't enough. Today is holy to our Lord, so don't be sad. The joy that the LORD gives you will make you strong."

11 The Levites went about calming the people and telling them not to be sad on such a holy day. 12 So all the people went home and ate and drank joyfully and shared what they had with others, because they understood what had been read to them.

The Festival of Shelters

13 The next day the heads of the clans, together with the priests and the Levites, went to Ezra to study the teachings of the Law. 14 They discovered that the Law, which the LORD gave through Moses, ordered the people of Israel to live in temporary shelters during the Festival of Shelters. 15 So they gave the following instructions and sent them*p* all through Jerusalem and the other cities and towns: "Go out to the hills and get branches from pines, olives, myrtles, palms, and other trees to make shelters according to the instructions written in the Law."

16 So the people got branches and built shelters on the flat roofs of their houses, in their yards, in the temple courtyard, and in the public squares by the Water Gate and by the Ephraim Gate. 17 All the people who had come back from captivity built shelters and lived in them. This was the first time it had been done since the days of Joshua son of Nun, and everybody was excited and happy. 18 From the first day of the festival to the last they read a part of God's Law every day. They celebrated for seven days, and on the eighth day there was a closing ceremony, as required in the Law.

The People Confess Their Sins

9 1-2 On the twenty-fourth day of the same month the people of Israel assembled to fast in order to show sorrow

for their sins. They had already separated themselves from all foreigners. They wore sackcloth and put dust on their heads as signs of grief. Then they stood and began to confess the sins that they and their ancestors had committed. 3 For about three hours the Law of the LORD their God was read to them, and for the next three hours they confessed their sins and worshipped the LORD their God.

4 There was a platform for the Levites, and on it stood Jeshua, Bani, Kadmiel, Shebaniah, Bunni, Sherebiah, Bani, and Chenani. They prayed aloud to the LORD their God.

5 The following Levites gave a call to worship: Jeshua, Kadmiel, Bani, Hashabneiah, Sherebiah, Hodiah, Shebaniah, and Pethahiah. They said:

"Stand up and praise the LORD your
    God;
  praise him for ever and ever!
Let everyone praise his glorious name,
    although no human praise is great
    enough."

The Prayer of Confession

6 And then the people of Israel prayed this prayer:
"You, LORD, you alone are LORD;
  you made the heavens and the stars
    of the sky.
You made land and sea and everything
    in them;
  you gave life to all.
The heavenly powers bow down and
    worship you.
7 You, LORD God, chose Abram
  and led him out of Ur in Babylonia;
  you changed his name to Abraham.
8 You found that he was faithful to you,
  and you made a covenant with him.
You promised to give him the land of
    the Canaanites,
  the land of the Hittites and the
    Amorites,
  the land of the Perizzites, the
    Jebusites, and the Girgashites,
  to be a land where his descendants
    would live.
You kept your promise, because you
    are faithful.

9 "You saw how our ancestors suffered
    in Egypt;

---

p Probable text So they...sent them; *Hebrew* It also ordered that the following instructions be sent.
8.14–15: Lev 23.33–36,39–43; Deut 16.13–15   **9.7:** Gen 11.31, 12.1, 17.5   **9.8:** Gen 15.18–21
9.9: Ex 3.7, 14.10–12

you heard their call for help at the
Red Sea.
10 You worked amazing miracles against
the king,
against his officials and the people
of his land,
because you knew how they
oppressed your people.
You won then the fame you still have
today.
11 Through the sea you made a path for
your people
and led them through on dry ground.
Those who pursued them drowned in
deep water,
as a stone sinks in the raging sea.
12 With a cloud you led them in day-time,
and at night you lighted their way
with fire.
13 At Mount Sinai you came down from
heaven;
you spoke to your people
and gave them good laws and sound
teachings.
14 You taught them to keep your
Sabbaths holy,
and through your servant Moses you
gave them your laws.

15 "When they were hungry, you gave
them bread from heaven,
and water from a rock when they
were thirsty.
You told them to take control of the
land
which you had promised to give them.
16 But our ancestors grew proud and
stubborn
and refused to obey your commands.
17 They refused to obey; they forgot all
you did;
they forgot the miracles you had
performed.
In their pride they chose a leader
to take them back to slavery in Egypt.
But you are a God who forgives;
you are gracious and loving, slow to
be angry.
Your mercy is great; you did not forsake
them.
18 They made an idol in the shape of
a bull-calf
and said it was the god who led them
from Egypt!
How much they insulted you, LORD!

19 But you did not abandon them there
in the desert,
for your mercy is great.
You did not take away the cloud or
the fire
that showed them the path by day
and night.
20 In your goodness you told them what
they should do;
you fed them with manna and gave
them water to drink.
21 Through forty years in the desert
you provided all that they needed;
their clothing never wore out,
and their feet were not swollen with
pain.

22 "You let them conquer nations and
kingdoms,
lands that bordered their own.
They conquered the land of Heshbon,
where Sihon ruled,
and the land of Bashan, where Og
was king.
23 You gave them as many children as
there are stars in the sky,
and let them conquer and live in the
land
that you had promised their ancestors
to give them.
24 They conquered the land of Canaan;
you overcame the people living there.
You gave your people the power to do
as they pleased
with the people and kings of Canaan.
25 Your people captured fortified cities,
fertile land, houses full of wealth,
cisterns already dug,
olive-trees, fruit-trees, and vineyards.
They ate all they wanted and grew fat;
they enjoyed all the good things you
gave them.

26 "But your people rebelled and
disobeyed you;
they turned their backs on your Law.
They killed the prophets who warned
them,
who told them to turn back to you.
They insulted you time after time,
27   so you let their enemies conquer and
rule them.
In their trouble they called to you for
help,
and you answered them from heaven.

9.10: Ex 7.8—12.32   **9.11:** Ex 14.21-29, 15.4-5   **9.12:** Ex 13.21-22
9.13-14: Ex 19.18—23.33   **9.15:** Ex 16.4-15, 17.1-7; Deut 1.21
9.16-17: Num 14.1-4; Deut 1.26-33   **9.17:** Ex 34.6; Num 14.18   **9.18:** Ex 32.1-4
9.19-21: Deut 8.2-4   **9.22:** Num 21.21-35   **9.23:** Gen 15.5, 22.17; Josh 3.14-17
9.24: Josh 11.23   **9.25:** Deut 6.10-11   **9.26-28:** Judg 2.11-16

In your great mercy you sent them
leaders
who rescued them from their foes.
28 When peace returned, they sinned
again,
and again you let their enemies
conquer them.
Yet when they repented and asked you
to save them,
in heaven you heard, and time after
time
you rescued them in your great mercy.
29 You warned them to obey your
teachings,
but in pride they rejected your laws,
although keeping your Law is the way
to life.
Obstinate and stubborn, they refused to
obey.
30 Year after year you patiently warned
them.
You inspired your prophets to speak,
but your people were deaf,
so you let them be conquered by other
nations.
31 And yet, because your mercy is great,
you did not forsake or destroy them.
You are a gracious and merciful God!

32 "O God, our God, how great you are!
How terrifying, how powerful!
You faithfully keep your covenant
promises.
From the time when Assyrian kings
oppressed us,
even till now, how much we have
suffered!
Our kings, our leaders, our priests and
prophets,
our ancestors, and all our people have
suffered.
Remember how much we have suffered!
33 You have done right to punish us;
you have been faithful, even though
we have sinned.
34 Our ancestors, our kings, leaders, and
priests
have not kept your Law.
They did not listen to your commands
and warnings.
35 With your blessing, kings ruled your
people
when they lived in the broad, fertile
land you gave them;
but they failed to turn from sin and
serve you.
36 And now we are slaves in the land
that you gave us,

this fertile land which gives us food.
37 What the land produces goes to the
kings
that you put over us because we
sinned.
They do as they please with us and our
livestock,
and we are in deep distress!"

The People Sign an Agreement

38 Because of all that has happened,
we, the people of Israel, hereby make a
solemn written agreement, and our
leaders, our Levites, and our priests put
their seals to it.

10 The first to sign was the governor,
Nehemiah son of Hacaliah, and
then Zedekiah signed. The following also
signed:
2-8 *Priests:*
Seraiah, Azariah, Jeremiah,
Pashhur, Amariah, Malchijah,
Hattush, Shebaniah, Malluch,
Harim, Meremoth, Obadiah,
Daniel, Ginnethon, Baruch,
Meshullam, Abijah, Mijamin,
Maaziah, Bilgai, and Shemaiah.
9-13 *Levites:*
Jeshua son of Azaniah,
Binnui of the clan of Henadad,
Kadmiel, Shebaniah, Hodiah,
Kelita, Pelaiah, Hanan,
Mica, Rehob, Hashabiah,
Zaccur, Sherebiah, Shebaniah,
Hodiah, Bani, and Beninu.
14-27 *Leaders of the people:*
Parosh, Pahath Moab,
Elam, Zattu, Bani,
Bunni, Azgad, Bebai,
Adonijah, Bigvai, Adin,
Ater, Hezekiah, Azzur,
Hodiah, Hashum, Bezai,
Hariph, Anathoth, Nebai,
Magpiash, Meshullam, Hezir,
Meshezabel, Zadok, Jaddua,
Pelatiah, Hanan, Anaiah,
Hoshea, Hananiah, Hasshub,
Hallohesh, Pilha, Shobek,
Rehum, Hashabnah, Maaseiah,
Ahiah, Hanan, Anan,
Malluch, Harim, and Baanah.

The Agreement

28 We, the people of Israel, the priests,
the Levites, the temple guards, the temple
musicians, the temple workmen, and all
others who in obedience to God's Law
have separated themselves from the

9.29: Lev 18.5   9.30: 2 Kgs 17.13-18; 2 Chr 36.15-16
9.32: 2 Kgs 15.19,29, 17.3-6; Ezra 4.2,10

foreigners living in our land, we, together with our wives and all our children old enough to understand, 29 do hereby join with our leaders in an oath, under penalty of a curse if we break it, that we will live according to God's Law, which God gave through his servant Moses; that we will obey all that the LORD, our Lord, commands us; and that we will keep all his laws and requirements.

30 We will not intermarry with the foreigners living in our land.

31 If foreigners bring corn or anything else to sell to us on the Sabbath or on any other holy day, we will not buy from them.

Every seventh year we will not farm the land, and we will cancel all debts.

32 Every year we will each contribute five grammes of silver to help pay the expenses of the Temple.

33 We will provide for the temple worship the following: the sacred bread, the daily grain-offering, the animals to be burnt each day as sacrifices, the sacred offerings for Sabbaths, New Moon Festivals, and other festivals, the other sacred offerings, the offerings to take away the sins of Israel, and anything else needed for the Temple.

34 We, the people, priests, and Levites, will draw lots each year to determine which clans are to provide wood to burn the sacrifices offered to the LORD our God, according to the requirements of the Law.

35 We will take to the Temple each year an offering of the first corn we harvest and of the first fruit that ripens on our trees.

36 The first son born to each of us we will take to the priests in the Temple and there, as required by the Law, dedicate him to God. We will also dedicate the first calf born to each of our cows, and the first lamb or kid born to each of our sheep or goats.

37 We will take to the priests in the Temple the dough made from the first corn harvested each year and our other offerings of wine, olive-oil, and all kinds of fruit.

We will take to the Levites, who collect tithes in our farming villages, the tithes from the crops that grow on our land. 38 Priests who are descended from Aaron are to be with the Levites when tithes

are collected, and for use in the Temple the Levites are to take to the temple storerooms one tenth of all the tithes they collect. 39 The people of Israel and the Levites are to take the contributions of corn, wine, and olive-oil to the storerooms where the utensils for the Temple are kept and where the priests who are on duty, the temple guards, and the members of the temple choir have their quarters.

We will not neglect the house of our God.

The People Who Lived in Jerusalem

11 The leaders settled in Jerusalem, and the rest of the people drew lots to choose one family out of every ten to go and live in the holy city of Jerusalem, while the rest were to live in the other cities and towns. 2 The people praised anyone else who volunteered to live in Jerusalem. 3 In the other towns and cities the people of Israel, the priests, the Levites, the temple workmen, and the descendants of Solomon's servants lived on their own property in their own towns.

The following is the list of the leading citizens of the province of Judah who lived in Jerusalem:

4 *Members of the tribe of Judah:*

Athaiah, the son of Uzziah and grandson of Zechariah. His other ancestors included Amariah, Shephatiah, and Mahalalel, descendants of Judah's son Perez.

5 Maaseiah, the son of Baruch and grandson of Colhozeh. His other ancestors included Hazaiah, Adaiah, Joiarib, and Zechariah, descendants of Judah's son Shelah.

6 Of the descendants of Perez, 468 outstanding men lived in Jerusalem.

7 *Members of the tribe of Benjamin:*

Sallu, the son of Meshullam and grandson of Joed. His other ancestors included Pedaiah, Kolaiah, Maaseiah, Ithiel, and Jeshaiah.

8 Gabbai and Sallai, close relatives q of Sallu.

In all, 928 Benjaminites lived in Jerusalem. 9 Joel son of Zichri was their leader, and Judah son of Hassenuah was the second senior official in the city.

10 *Priests:*

Jedaiah son of Joiarib, and Jachin.

11 Seraiah, the son of Hilkiah and

q *One ancient translation* close relatives; *Hebrew* after him.
10.30: Ex 34.16; Deut 7.3   **10.31:** Ex 23.10–11; Lev 25.1–7; Deut 15.1–2   **10.32:** Ex 30.11–16
10.35: Ex 23.19, 34.26; Deut 26.2   **10.36:** Ex 13.2   **10.37:** Num 18.21   **10.38:** Num 18.26
11.3: Neh 7.73

grandson of Meshullam. His ancestors included Zadok, Meraioth, and Ahitub, who was the High Priest. [12] In all, 822 members of this clan served in the Temple.

Adaiah, the son of Jeroham and grandson of Pelaliah. His ancestors included Amzi, Zechariah, Pashhur, and Malchijah. [13] In all, 242 members of this clan were heads of families.

Amashsai, the son of Azarel and grandson of Ahzai. His ancestors included Meshillemoth and Immer. [14] There were 128 members of this clan who were outstanding soldiers. Their leader was Zabdiel, a member of a leading family. [r]

[15] *Levites:*

Shemaiah, the son of Hasshub and grandson of Azrikam. His ancestors included Hashabiah and Bunni.

16 Shabbethai and Jozabad, prominent Levites in charge of the work outside the Temple.

17 Mattaniah, the son of Mica and grandson of Zabdi, a descendant of Asaph. He led the temple choir in singing the prayer of thanksgiving.

Bakbukiah, who was Mattaniah's assistant.

Abda, the son of Shammua and grandson of Galal, a descendant of Jeduthun.

18 In all, 284 Levites lived in the holy city of Jerusalem.

[19] *Temple guards:*

Akkub, Talmon, and their relatives, 172 in all.

20 The rest of the people of Israel and the remaining priests and Levites lived on their own property in the other cities and towns of Judah. [21] The temple workmen lived in the part of Jerusalem called Ophel and worked under the supervision of Ziha and Gishpa.

22 The supervisor of the Levites who lived in Jerusalem was Uzzi, the son of Bani and grandson of Hashabiah. His ancestors included Mattaniah and Mica, and he belonged to the clan of Asaph, the clan that was responsible for the music in the temple services. [23] There were royal regulations stating how the clans should take turns in leading the temple music each day.

24 Pethahiah son of Meshezabel, of the clan of Zerah and the tribe of Judah, represented the people of Israel at the Persian court.

The People in Other Towns and Cities

25 Many of the people lived in towns near their farms. Those who were of the tribe of Judah lived in Kiriath Arba, Dibon, and Jekabzeel, and in the villages near these cities. [26] They also lived in the cities of Jeshua, Moladah, Bethpelet, [27] and Hazarshual, and in Beersheba and the villages around it. [28] They lived in the city of Ziklag, in Meconah and its villages, [29] in Enrimmon, in Zorah, in Jarmuth, [30] in Zanoah, in Adullam, and in the villages near these towns. They lived in Lachish and on the farms near by, and in Azekah and its villages. That is to say, the people of Judah lived in the territory between Beersheba in the south and the Valley of Hinnom in the north.

31 The people of the tribe of Benjamin lived in Geba, Michmash, Ai, Bethel and the nearby villages, [32] Anathoth, Nob, Ananiah, [33] Hazor, Ramah, Gittaim, [34] Hadid, Zeboim, Neballat, [35] Lod, and Ono, and in the Valley of Craftsmen. [36] Some groups of Levites that had lived in the territory of Judah were assigned to live with the people of Benjamin.

List of Priests and Levites

12 The following is a list of the priests and Levites who returned from exile with Zerubbabel son of Shealtiel and with the High Priest Joshua:

[2-7] *Priests:*

Seraiah, Jeremiah, Ezra, Amariah, Malluch, Hattush, Shecaniah, Rehum, Meremoth, Iddo, Ginnethoi, Abijah, Mijamin, Maadiah, Bilgah, Shemaiah, Joiarib, Jedaiah, Sallu, Amok, Hilkiah, and Jedaiah.

These men were leaders among all their fellow-priests in the days of Joshua.

[8] *Levites:*

The following were in charge of the singing of hymns of thanksgiving: Jeshua, Binnui, Kadmiel, Sherebiah, Judah, and Mattaniah.

9 The following formed the choir that sang the responses: Bakbukiah, Unno, and their fellow-Levites.

Descendants of the High Priest Joshua

10 Joshua was the father of Joiakim; Joiakim was the father of Eliashib; Eliashib was the father of Joiada; [11] Joiada

---

[r] a member of a leading family; *or* son of Haggedolim.

was the father of Jonathan; and Jonathan was the father of Jaddua.

Heads of the Priestly Clans

12-21 When Joiakim was High Priest, the following priests were the heads of the priestly clans:

Priest	Clan
Meraiah	Seraiah
Hananiah	Jeremiah
Meshullam	Ezra
Jehohanan	Amariah
Jonathan	Malluchi
Joseph	Shebaniah
Adna	Harim
Helkai	Meraioth
Zechariah	Iddo
Meshullam	Ginnethon
Zichri	Abijah
...s	Miniamin
Piltai	Moadiah
Shammua	Bilgah
Jehonathan	Shemaiah
Mattenai	Joiarib
Uzzi	Jedaiah
Kallai	Sallai
Eber	Amok
Hashabiah	Hilkiah
Nethanel	Jedaiah

Record of the Priestly and Levite Families

22 A record was kept of the heads of the Levite families and of the priestly families during the lifetimes of the following High Priests: Eliashib, Joiada, Jonathan, and Jaddua. This record was finished when Darius was emperor of Persia.

23 The heads of the Levite families, however, were recorded in the official records only until the time of Jonathan, the grandson of Eliashib.

Assignment of Duties in the Temple

24 Under the direction of Hashabiah, Sherebiah, Jeshua, Binnui,t and Kadmiel, the Levites were organized into groups. Two groups at a time praised God responsively and gave thanks to him, in accordance with the instructions given by King David, the man of God.

25 The following temple guards were in charge of guarding the storerooms by the gates to the Temple: Mattaniah, Bakbukiah, Obadiah, Meshullam, Talmon, and Akkub.

26 These people lived during the time of Joiakim, the son of Joshua and grandson of Jehozadak, and the time of Nehemiah the governor, and the time of Ezra, the priest who was a scholar of the Law.

Nehemiah Dedicates the City Wall

27 When the city wall of Jerusalem was dedicated, the Levites were brought in from wherever they were living, so that they could join in celebrating the dedication with songs of thanksgiving and with the music of cymbals and harps. 28 The Levite families of singers gathered from the area where they had settled round Jerusalem and from the towns round Netophah, 29 and from Bethgilgal, Geba, and Azmaveth. 30 The priests and the Levites performed ritual purification for themselves, the people, the gates, and the city wall.

31 I assembled the leaders of Judah on top of the wall and put them in charge of two large groups to march round the city, giving thanks to God.

The first group went to the right on top of the wall towards the Rubbish Gate. u 32 Hoshaiah marched behind the singers, followed by half the leaders of Judah. 33-35 The following priests, blowing trumpets, marched next: Azariah, Ezra, Meshullam, Judah, Benjamin, Shemaiah, and Jeremiah. Next came Zechariah, the son of Jonathan and grandson of Shemaiah. (His ancestors also included Mattaniah, Micaiah, and Zaccur, of the clan of Asaph.) 36 He was followed by other members of his clan—Shemaiah, Azarel, Milalai, Gilalai, Maai, Nethanel, Judah, and Hanani—all of whom carried musical instruments of the kind played by King David, the man of God. Ezra the scholar led this group in the procession. 37 At the Fountain Gate they went up the steps that led to David's City, past David's palace, and back to the wall at the Water Gate, on the east side of the city.

38 The other group of those who gave thanks went to the left along the top of the wall, and I followed with half the people. We marched past the Tower of the Ovens to the Broad Wall, 39 and from

---

s In Hebrew a name is missing from the list.
t Probable text (see 10.9 and 12.8) Binnui; Hebrew son of.
u RUBBISH GATE: The two groups started somewhere on the south-western part of the city wall and went in opposite directions until they met in front of the Temple in the north-eastern part of the city.

The other group...went to the left (12.38)

there we went past Ephraim Gate, Jeshanah Gate, [v] the Fish Gate, the Tower of Hananel, and the Tower of the Hundred, to the Sheep Gate. We ended our march near the gate to the Temple.

40 So both the groups that were giving thanks to God reached the temple area.

In addition to the leaders who were with me, [41] my group included the following priests, blowing trumpets: Eliakim, Maaseiah, Miniamin, Micaiah, Elioenai, Zechariah, and Hananiah; [42] and they were followed by Maaseiah, Shemaiah, Eleazar, Uzzi, Jehohanan, Malchijah, Elam, and Ezer. The singers, led by Jezrahiah, sang at the top of their voices.

43 That day many sacrifices were offered, and the people were full of joy because God had made them very happy. The women and the children joined in the celebration, and the noise they all made could be heard far and wide.

Providing for Worship in the Temple

44 At that time men were put in charge of the storerooms where contributions for the Temple were kept, including the tithes and the first corn and fruit that ripened each year. These men were responsible for collecting from the farms near the various cities the contributions for the priests and the Levites which the Law required. All the people of Judah were pleased with the priests and the Levites, [45] because they performed the ceremonies of purification and the other rituals that God had commanded. The temple mu-

sicians and the temple guards also performed their duties in accordance with the regulations made by King David and his son Solomon. [46] From the time of King David and the musician Asaph long ago, the musicians have led songs of praise and thanksgiving to God. [47] In the time of Zerubbabel and also in the time of Nehemiah, all the people of Israel gave daily gifts for the support of the temple musicians and the temple guards. The people gave a sacred offering to the Levites, and the Levites gave the required portion to the priests.

Separation from Foreigners

13 When the Law of Moses was being read aloud to the people, they came to the passage that said that no Ammonite or Moabite was ever to be permitted to join God's people. [2] This was because the people of Ammon and Moab did not give food and water to the Israelites on their way out of Egypt. Instead, they paid money to Balaam to curse Israel, but our God turned the curse into a blessing. [3] When the people of Israel heard this law read, they excluded all foreigners from the community.

Nehemiah's Reforms

4 The priest Eliashib, who was in charge of the temple storerooms, had for a long time been on good terms with Tobiah. [5] He allowed Tobiah to use a large room that was intended only for storing offerings of corn and incense, the equipment

[v] Ephraim Gate, Jeshanah Gate; *or* Ephraim Gate (also called the Old Gate).
12.45: 1 Chr 25.1–8, 26.12   **13.1–2:** Deut 23.3–5   **13.2:** Num 22.1–6

used in the Temple, the offerings for the priests, and the tithes of corn, wine, and olive-oil given to the Levites, to the temple musicians, and to the temple guards. [6] While this was going on, I was not in Jerusalem, because in the thirty-second year that Artaxerxes[w] was king of Babylon I had gone back to report to him. After some time I received his permission [7] and returned to Jerusalem. There I was shocked to find that Eliashib had allowed Tobiah to use a room in the Temple. [8] I was furious and threw out all Tobiah's belongings. [9] I gave orders for the rooms to be ritually purified and for the temple equipment, grain-offerings, and incense to be put back.

[10] I also learnt that the temple musicians and other Levites had left Jerusalem and gone back to their farms, because the people had not been giving them enough to live on. [11] I reprimanded the officials for letting the Temple be neglected. And I brought the Levites and musicians back to the Temple and put them to work again. [12] Then all the people of Israel again started bringing to the temple storerooms their tithes of corn, wine, and olive-oil. [13] I put the following men in charge of the storerooms: Shelemiah, a priest; Zadok, a scholar of the Law; and Pedaiah, a Levite. Hanan, the son of Zaccur and grandson of Mattaniah, was to be their assistant. I knew I could trust these men to be honest in distributing the supplies to their fellow-workers.

14 Remember, my God, all these things that I have done for your Temple and its worship.

15 At that time I saw people in Judah pressing juice from grapes on the Sabbath. Others were loading corn, wine, grapes, figs, and other things on their donkeys and taking them into Jerusalem; I warned them not to sell anything on the Sabbath. [16] Some men from the city of Tyre were living in Jerusalem, and they brought fish and all kinds of goods into the city to sell to our people on the Sabbath. [17] I reprimanded the Jewish leaders and said, "Look at the evil you're doing! You're making the Sabbath unholy. [18] This is exactly why God punished your ancestors when he brought destruction on this city. And yet you insist on bringing more of God's anger down on Israel by profaning the Sabbath."

19 So I gave orders for the city gates to be shut at the beginning of every Sabbath, as soon as evening[x] began to fall, and not to be opened again until the Sabbath was over. I stationed some of my men at the gates to make sure that nothing was brought into the city on the Sabbath. [20] Once or twice merchants who sold all kinds of goods spent Friday night outside the city walls. [21] I warned them, "It's no use waiting out there for morning to come. If you try this again, I'll use force against you." From then on they did not come back on the Sabbath. [22] I ordered the Levites to purify themselves and to go and guard the gates to make sure that the Sabbath was kept holy.

Remember me, O God, for this also, and

---

[w] ARTAXERXES: *As emperor of Persia, Artaxerxes also had the title "King of Babylon."*
[x] EVENING: *The Jewish day begins at sunset.*
13.10: Deut 12.19   **13.12:** Mal 3.10   **13.15:** Ex 20.8-10; Deut 5.12-14; Jer 17.21-22

You're making the Sabbath unholy (13.17)

spare me because of your great love.

23 At that time I also discovered that many of the Jewish men had married women from Ashdod, Ammon, and Moab. [24] Half their children spoke the language of Ashdod or some other language and didn't know how to speak our language. [25] I reprimanded the men, called down curses on them, beat them, and pulled out their hair. Then I made them take an oath in God's name that never again would they or their children intermarry with foreigners. [26] I said, "It was foreign women that made King Solomon sin. He was a man who was greater than any of the kings of other nations. God loved him and made him king over all Israel, and yet he fell into this sin. [27] Are we then to follow your example and disobey our God by marrying foreign women?"

28 Joiada was the son of Eliashib the High Priest, but one of Joiada's sons married the daughter of Sanballat, from the town of Beth Horon, so I made Joiada leave Jerusalem.

29 Remember, O God, how those people defiled both the office of priest and the covenant you made with the priests and the Levites.

30 I purified the people from everything foreign; I prepared regulations for the priests and the Levites so that each one would know his duty; [31] I arranged for the wood used for burning the offerings to be brought at the proper times, and for the people to bring their offerings of the first corn and the first fruits that ripened.

Remember all this, O God, and give me credit for it.

13.23-25: Ex 34.11-16; Deut 7.1-5 **13.26:** 2 Sam 12.24-25; 1 Kgs 11.1-8 **13.28:** Neh 4.1

THE BOOK OF
ESTHER

INTRODUCTION

The events of the book of *Esther,* which take place at the winter residence of the Persian emperor, centre round a Jewish heroine named Esther, who by her great courage and devotion to her people saved them from being exterminated by their enemies. The book explains the background and meaning of the Jewish festival of Purim.

Outline of Contents

Esther becomes queen 1.1—2.23
Haman's plots 3.1—5.14
Haman is put to death 6.1—7.10
The Jews defeat their enemies 8.1—10.3

Queen Vashti Defies King Xerxes

1 [1-2] From his royal throne in Persia's capital city of Susa, King Xerxes ruled over 127 provinces, all the way from India to Sudan.

3 In the third year of his reign he gave a banquet for all his officials and administrators. The armies of Persia and Media were present, as well as the governors and noblemen of the provinces. [4] For six whole months he made a show of the

1.1: Ezra 4.6

riches of the imperial court with all its splendour and majesty.

5 After that, the king gave a banquet for all the men in the capital city of Susa, rich and poor alike. It lasted a whole week and was held in the gardens of the royal palace. 6 The courtyard there was decorated with blue and white cotton curtains, tied by cords of fine purple linen to silver rings on marble columns. Couches made of gold and silver had been placed in the courtyard, which was paved with white marble, red feldspar, shining mother-of-pearl, and blue turquoise. 7 Drinks were served in gold cups, no two of them alike, and the king was generous with the royal wine. 8 There were no limits on the drinks; the king had given orders to the palace servants that everyone could have as much as he wanted. [a]

9 Meanwhile, inside the royal palace Queen Vashti was giving a banquet for the women.

10 On the seventh day of his banquet the king was drinking and feeling merry, so he called in the seven eunuchs who were his personal servants, Mehuman, Biztha, Harbona, Bigtha, Abagtha, Zethar, and Carkas. 11 He ordered them to bring in Queen Vashti, wearing her royal crown. The queen was a beautiful woman, and the king wanted to show off her beauty to the officials and all his guests. 12 But when the servants told Queen Vashti of the king's command, she refused to come. This made the king furious.

13 Now it was the king's custom to ask for expert opinion on questions of law and order, so he called for his advisers, who would know what should be done. 14 Those he most often turned to for advice were Carshena, Shethar, Admatha, Tarshish, Meres, Marsena, and Memucan—seven officials of Persia and Media who held the highest offices in the kingdom. 15 He said to these men, "I, King Xerxes, sent my servants to Queen Vashti with a command, and she refused to obey it! What does the law say that we should do with her?"

16 Then Memucan declared to the king and his officials: "Queen Vashti has insulted not only the king but also his officials—in fact, every man in the empire! 17 Every woman in the empire will begin to look down on her husband as

soon as she hears what the queen has done. They'll say, 'King Xerxes commanded Queen Vashti to come to him, and she refused.' 18 When the wives of the royal officials of Persia and Media hear about the queen's behaviour they will be telling their husbands about it before the day is out. Wives everywhere will have no respect for their husbands, and husbands will be angry with their wives. 19 If it please Your Majesty, issue a royal proclamation that Vashti may never again appear before the king. Order it to be written into the laws of Persia and Media, so that it can never be changed. Then give her place as queen to some better woman. 20 When your proclamation is made known all over this huge empire, every woman will treat her husband with proper respect, whether he's rich or poor."

21 The king and his officials liked this idea, and the king did what Memucan suggested. 22 To each of the royal provinces he sent a message in the language and the system of writing of that province, saying [b] that every husband should be the master of his home and speak with final authority.

Esther Becomes Queen

2 Later, even after the king's anger had cooled down, he kept thinking about what Vashti had done and about his proclamation against her. 2 So some of the king's advisers who were close to him suggested, "Why don't you make a search to find some beautiful young virgins? 3 You can appoint officials in every province of the empire and order them to bring all these beautiful young girls to your harem here in Susa, the capital city. Put them in the care of Hegai, the eunuch who is in charge of your women, and let them be given a beauty treatment. 4 Then take the girl you like best and make her queen in Vashti's place."

The king thought this was good advice, so he followed it.

5 There in Susa lived a Jew named Mordecai son of Jair; he was from the tribe of Benjamin and was a descendant of Kish and Shimei. 6 When King Nebuchadnezzar of Babylon took King Jehoiachin of Judah into exile from Jerusalem, along with a group of captives, Mordecai was among them. 7 He had a

---

[a] There were no limits...wanted; or But no one was forced to drink; the king had given orders to the palace servants that everyone could have as much or as little as he wanted.
[b] saying; or in order.
2.6: 2 Kgs 24.10–16; 2 Chr 36.10

cousin, Esther, whose Hebrew name was Hadassah; she was a beautiful girl, and had a good figure. At the death of her parents, Mordecai had adopted her and brought her up as his own daughter.

8 When the king had issued his new proclamation and many girls were being brought to Susa, Esther was among them. She too was put in the royal palace in the care of Hegai, who had charge of the harem. ⁹Hegai liked Esther, and she won his favour. He lost no time in beginning her beauty treatment of massage and special diet. He gave her the best place in the harem and assigned seven girls specially chosen from the royal palace to serve her.

10 Now, on the advice of Mordecai, Esther had kept it secret that she was Jewish. ¹¹Every day Mordecai would walk to and fro in front of the courtyard of the harem, in order to find out how she was getting on and what was going to happen to her.

12 The regular beauty treatment for the women lasted a year—massages with oil of myrrh for six months and with oil of balsam for six more. After that, each girl would be taken in turn to King Xerxes. ¹³When she went from the harem to the palace, she could wear whatever she wanted. ¹⁴She would go there in the evening, and the next morning she would be taken to another harem and put in the care of Shaashgaz, the eunuch in charge of the king's concubines. She would not go to the king again unless he liked her enough to ask for her by name.

15 The time came for Esther to go to the king. Esther—the daughter of Abihail and the cousin of Mordecai, who had adopted her as his daughter; Esther—admired by everyone who saw her. When her turn came, she wore just what Hegai, the eunuch in charge of the harem, advised her to wear. ¹⁶So in Xerxes' seventh year as king, in the tenth month, the month of Tebeth, Esther was brought to King Xerxes in the royal palace. ¹⁷The king liked her more than any of the other girls, and more than any of the others she won his favour and affection. He placed the royal crown on her head and made her queen in place of Vashti. ¹⁸Then the king gave a great banquet in Esther's honour and invited all his officials and administrators. He proclaimed a holiday [c]

Esther was brought to King Xerxes (2.16)

for the whole empire and distributed gifts worthy of a king.

Mordecai Saves the King's Life

19 Meanwhile Mordecai had been appointed by the king to an administrative position. ²⁰As for Esther, she had still not let it be known that she was Jewish. Mordecai had told her not to tell anyone, and she obeyed him in this, just as she had obeyed him when she was a little girl under his care.

21 During the time that Mordecai held office in the palace, Bigthana and Teresh, two of the palace eunuchs who guarded the entrance to the king's rooms, became hostile to King Xerxes and plotted to assassinate him. ²²Mordecai learnt about it and told Queen Esther, who then told the king what Mordecai had found out. ²³There was an investigation, and it was discovered that the report was true, so both men were hanged on the gallows. The king ordered an account of this to be written down in the official records of the empire.

Haman Plots to Destroy the Jews

3 Some time later King Xerxes promoted a man named Haman to the position of prime minister. Haman was the son of Hammedatha, a descendant of Agag. [d] ²The king ordered all the officials in his service to show their respect for Haman by kneeling and bowing to him.

[c]holiday; *or* remission of taxes.
[d]AGAG: *An Amalekite king; his people were traditional enemies of the people of Israel.*

They all did so, except for Mordecai, who refused to do it. ³The other officials in the royal service asked him why he was disobeying the king's command; ⁴day after day they urged him to give in, but he would not listen to them. "I am a Jew," he explained, "and I cannot bow to Haman." So they told Haman about this, wondering if he would tolerate Mordecai's conduct. ⁵Haman was furious when he realized that Mordecai was not going to kneel and bow to him, ⁶and when he learnt that Mordecai was a Jew, he decided to do more than punish Mordecai alone. He made plans to kill every Jew in the whole Persian Empire.

7 In the twelfth year of King Xerxes' rule, in the first month, the month of Nisan, Haman ordered the lots to be cast ("purim," they were called) to find out the right day and month to carry out his plot. The thirteenth day of the twelfth month, the month of Adar, was decided on.

8 So Haman told the king, "There is a certain race of people scattered all over your empire and found in every province. They observe customs that are not like those of any other people. Moreover, they do not obey the laws of the empire, so it is not in your best interests to tolerate them. ⁹If it please Your Majesty, issue a decree that they are to be put to death. If you do, I guarantee that I will be able to put more than 340,000 kilogrammes of silver into the royal treasury for the administration of the empire."

10 The king took off his ring, which was used to stamp proclamations and make them official, and gave it to the enemy of the Jewish people, Haman son of Hammedatha, the descendant of Agag. ¹¹The king told him, "The people and their money are yours; do as you like with them."

12 So on the thirteenth day of the first month Haman called the king's secretaries and dictated a proclamation to be translated into every language and system of writing used in the empire and to be sent to all the rulers, governors, and officials. It was issued in the name of King Xerxes and stamped with his ring. ¹³Runners took this proclamation to every province of the empire. It contained the instructions that on a single day, the thirteenth day of Adar, all Jews—young and old, women and children—were to be killed. They were to be slaughtered without mercy and their belongings were to be taken. ¹⁴The contents of the proclamation were to be made public in every province, so that everyone would be prepared when that day came.

15 At the king's command the decree was made public in the capital city of Susa, and runners carried the news to the provinces. The king and Haman sat down and had a drink while the city of Susa was being thrown into confusion.

Mordecai Asks for Esther's Help

4 When Mordecai learnt of all that had been done, he tore his clothes in anguish. Then he dressed in sackcloth, covered his head with ashes, and walked through the city, wailing loudly and bitterly, ²until he came to the entrance of the palace. He did not go in because no one wearing sackcloth was allowed inside. ³Throughout all the provinces, wherever the king's proclamation was made known, there was loud mourning among the Jews. They fasted, wept and wailed, and most of them put on sackcloth and lay in ashes.

4 When Esther's servant-girls and eunuchs told her what Mordecai was doing, she was deeply disturbed. She sent Mordecai some clothes to put on instead of the sackcloth, but he would not accept them. ⁵Then she called Hathach, one of the palace eunuchs appointed as her servant by the king, and told him to go to Mordecai and find out what was happening and why. ⁶Hathach went to Mordecai in the city square at the entrance of the palace. ⁷Mordecai told him everything that had happened to him and just how much money Haman had promised to put into the royal treasury if all the Jews were killed. ⁸He gave Hathach a copy of the proclamation that had been issued in Susa, ordering the destruction of the Jews. Mordecai asked him to take it to Esther, explain the situation to her, and ask her to go and plead with the king and beg him to have mercy on her people. ⁹Hathach did this, ¹⁰and Esther gave him this message to take back to Mordecai: ¹¹"If anyone, man or woman, goes to the inner courtyard and sees the king without being summoned, that person must die. That is the law; everyone, from the king's advisers to the people in the provinces, knows that. There is only one way to get round this law: if the king holds out his gold sceptre to someone, then that person's life is spared. But it has been a month since the king sent for me."

There was loud mourning among the Jews (4.3)

12 When Mordecai received Esther's message, 13 he sent her this warning: "Don't imagine that you are safer than any other Jew just because you are in the royal palace. 14 If you keep quiet at a time like this, help will come from heaven to the Jews, and they will be saved, but you will die and your father's family will come to an end. Yet who knows—maybe it was for a time like this that you were made queen!"

15 Esther sent Mordecai this reply: 16 "Go and gather all the Jews in Susa together; hold a fast and pray for me. Don't eat or drink anything for three days and nights. My servant-girls and I will be doing the same. After that, I will go to the king, even though it is against the law. If I must die for doing it, I will die."

17 Mordecai then left and did everything that Esther had told him to do.

Esther Invites the King and Haman to a Banquet

5 On the third day of her fast Esther put on her royal robes and went and stood in the inner courtyard of the palace, facing the throne room. The king was inside, seated on the royal throne, facing the entrance. 2 When the king saw Queen Esther standing outside, she won his favour, and he held out to her the gold sceptre. She then came up and touched the tip of it. 3 "What is it, Queen Esther?" the king asked. "Tell me what you want, and you shall have it—even if it is half my empire."

4 Esther replied, "If it please Your Majesty, I would like you and Haman to be my guests tonight at a banquet I am preparing for you."

5 The king then ordered Haman to come quickly, so that they could be Esther's guests. So the king and Haman went to Esther's banquet. 6 Over the wine the king asked her, "Tell me what you want, and you shall have it. I will grant your request, even if you ask for half my empire."

7 Esther replied, 8 "If Your Majesty is kind enough to grant my request, I would like you and Haman to be my guests tomorrow at another banquet that I will prepare for you. At that time I will tell you what I want."

Haman Plots to Kill Mordecai

9 When Haman left the banquet he was happy and in a good mood. But then he saw Mordecai at the entrance of the palace, and when Mordecai did not rise or show any sign of respect as he passed, Haman was furious with him. 10 But he controlled himself and went home. Then he invited his friends to his house and asked his wife Zeresh to join them. 11 He boasted to them how rich he was, how many sons he had, how the king had promoted him to high office, and how much more important he was than any of the king's other officials. 12 "What is more," Haman went on, "Queen Esther gave a banquet for no one but the king and me, and we are invited back tomorrow. 13 But none of this means a thing to me as long as I see that Jew Mordecai sitting at the entrance of the palace."

14 So his wife and all his friends suggested, "Why don't you have a gallows built, twenty-two metres tall? Tomorrow morning you can ask the king to have Mordecai hanged on it, and then you can go to the banquet happy." Haman thought this was a good idea, so he had the gallows built.

See how the king rewards a man he wishes to honour! (6.11)

The King Honours Mordecai

6 That same night the king could not get to sleep, so he ordered the official records of the empire to be brought and read to him. [2] The part they read included the account of how Mordecai had uncovered a plot to assassinate the king—the plot made by Bigthana and Teresh, the two palace eunuchs who had guarded the king's rooms. [3] The king asked, "How have we honoured and rewarded Mordecai for this?"

His servants answered, "Nothing has been done for him."

[4] "Are any of my officials in the palace?" the king asked.

Now Haman had just entered the courtyard; he had come to ask the king to have Mordecai hanged on the gallows that was now ready. [5] So the servants answered, "Haman is here, waiting to see you."

"Show him in," said the king.

[6] So Haman came in, and the king said to him, "There is someone I wish very much to honour. What should I do for this man?"

Haman thought to himself, "Now who could the king want to honour so much? Me, of course."

[7-8] So he answered the king, "Order royal robes to be brought for this man—robes that you yourself wear. Order a royal ornament[e] to be put on your own horse. [9] Then get one of your highest

noblemen to dress the man in these robes and lead him, mounted on the horse, through the city square. Let the nobleman announce as they go: 'See how the king rewards a man he wishes to honour!'"

[10] Then the king said to Haman, "Hurry and get the robes and the horse, and provide these honours for Mordecai the Jew. Do everything for him that you have suggested. You will find him sitting at the entrance of the palace."

[11] So Haman got the robes and the horse, and he put the robes on Mordecai. Mordecai got on the horse, and Haman led him through the city square, announcing to the people as they went: "See how the king rewards a man he wishes to honour!"

[12] Mordecai then went back to the palace entrance while Haman hurried home, covering his face in embarrassment. [13] He told his wife and all his friends everything that had happened to him. Then she and those wise friends of his said to him, "You are beginning to lose power to Mordecai. He is a Jew, and you cannot overcome him. He will certainly defeat you."

Haman Is Put to Death

[14] While they were still talking, the palace eunuchs arrived in a hurry to take **7** Haman to Esther's banquet. [1] And so the king and Haman went to eat with Esther [2] for a second time. Over the wine the king asked her again, "Now, Queen

[e]ORNAMENT: *Probably a type of crown.*
6.2: Esth 2.21-22

Esther, what do you want? Tell me and you shall have it. I'll even give you half the empire."

3 Queen Esther answered, "If it please Your Majesty to grant my humble request, my wish is that I may live and that my people may live. 4 My people and I have been sold for slaughter. If it were nothing more serious than being sold into slavery, I would have kept quiet and not bothered you about it; f but we are about to be destroyed—exterminated!"

5 Then King Xerxes asked Queen Esther, "Who dares to do such a thing? Where is this man?"

6 Esther answered, "Our enemy, our persecutor, is this evil man Haman!"

Haman stared at the king and queen in terror. 7 The king got up in a fury, left the room, and went outside to the palace gardens. Haman could see that the king was determined to punish him for this, so he stayed behind to beg Queen Esther for his life. 8 He had just thrown himself down on Esther's couch to beg for mercy, when the king came back into the room from the gardens. Seeing this, the king cried out, "Is this man going to rape the queen right here in front of me, in my own palace?"

The king had no sooner said this than the eunuchs covered Haman's head. 9 Then one of them, who was named Harbonah, said, "Haman even went so far as to build a gallows at his house so that he could hang Mordecai, who saved Your Majesty's life. And it's twenty-two metres tall!"

"Hang Haman on it!" the king commanded.

10 So Haman was hanged on the gallows that he had built for Mordecai. Then the king's anger cooled down.

The Jews Are Told to Fight Back

8 That same day King Xerxes gave Queen Esther all the property of Haman, the enemy of the Jews. Esther told the king that Mordecai was related to her, and from then on Mordecai was allowed to enter the king's presence. 2 The king took off his ring with his seal on it (which he had taken back from Haman) and gave it to Mordecai. Esther put Mordecai in charge of Haman's property.

3 Then Esther spoke to the king again, throwing herself at his feet and crying. She begged him to do something to stop the evil plot that Haman, the descendant

of Agag, g had made against the Jews. 4 The king held out the gold sceptre to her, so she stood up and said, 5 "If it please Your Majesty, and if you care about me and if it seems right to you, please issue a proclamation to prevent Haman's orders from being carried out—those orders that the son of Hammedatha the descendant of Agag gave for the destruction of all the Jews in the empire. 6 How can I endure it if this disaster comes on my people, and my own relatives are killed?"

7 King Xerxes then said to Queen Esther and Mordecai, the Jew, "Look, I have hanged Haman for his plot against the Jews, and I have given Esther his property. 8 But a proclamation issued in the king's name and stamped with the royal seal cannot be revoked. You may, however, write to the Jews whatever you wish; and you may write it in my name and stamp it with the royal seal."

9 This happened on the twenty-third day of the third month, the month of Sivan. Mordecai called the king's secretaries and dictated letters to the Jews and to the governors, administrators, and officials of all the 127 provinces from India to Sudan. The letters were written to each province in its own language and system of writing and to the Jews in their language and system of writing. 10 Mordecai had the letters written in the name of King Xerxes, and he stamped them with the royal seal. They were delivered by riders mounted on fast horses from the royal stables.

11 These letters explained that the king would allow the Jews in every city to organize themselves for self-defence. If armed men of any nationality in any province attacked the Jewish men, their children or their women, the Jews could fight back and destroy the attackers; they could slaughter them to the last man and take their possessions. 12 This decree was to take effect throughout the Persian Empire on the day set for the slaughter of the Jews, the thirteenth of Adar, the twelfth month. 13 It was to be proclaimed as law and made known to everyone in every province, so that the Jews would be ready to take revenge on their enemies when that day came. 14 At the king's command the riders mounted royal horses and rode off at top speed. The decree was also made public in Susa, the capital city.

15 Mordecai left the palace, wearing royal robes of blue and white, a cloak

---

f Probable text and not...it; Hebrew unclear.　　g AGAG: See 3.1.

of fine purple linen, and a magnificent gold crown. Then the streets of Susa rang with cheers and joyful shouts. ¹⁶For the Jews there was joy and relief, happiness and a sense of victory. ¹⁷In every city and province, wherever the king's proclamation was read, the Jews held a joyful holiday with feasting and happiness. In fact, many other people became Jews, because they were afraid of them now.

The Jews Destroy Their Enemies

9 The thirteenth day of Adar came, the day on which the royal proclamation was to take effect, the day when the enemies of the Jews were hoping to get them in their power. But instead, the Jews triumphed over them. ²In the Jewish quarter of every city*ʰ* in the empire the Jews organized themselves to attack anyone who tried to harm them. People everywhere were afraid of them, and no one could stand against them. ³In fact, all the provincial officials—governors, administrators, and royal representatives—helped the Jews because they were all afraid of Mordecai. ⁴It was well known throughout the empire that Mordecai was now a powerful man in the palace and was growing more powerful. ⁵So the Jews could do what they wanted with their enemies. They attacked them with swords and slaughtered them.

6 In Susa, the capital city itself, the Jews killed five hundred men. ⁷⁻¹⁰Among them were the ten sons of Haman son of Hammedatha, the enemy of the Jews: Parshandatha, Dalphon, Aspatha, Poratha, Adalia, Aridatha, Parmashta, Arisai, Aridai, and Vaizatha. However, there was no looting.

11 That same day the number of people killed in Susa was reported to the king. ¹²He then said to Queen Esther, "In Susa alone the Jews have killed five hundred men, including Haman's ten sons. What must they have done out in the provinces! What do you want now? You shall have it. Tell me what else you want, and you shall have it."

13 Esther answered, "If it please Your Majesty, let the Jews in Susa do again tomorrow what they were allowed to do today. And order the bodies of Haman's ten sons to be hung from the gallows." ¹⁴The king ordered this to be done, and the proclamation was issued in Susa. The bodies of Haman's ten sons were publicly displayed. ¹⁵On the fourteenth day of Adar the Jews of Susa got together again and killed three hundred more men in the city. But again, they did no looting.

16 The Jews in the provinces also organized and defended themselves. They rid themselves of their enemies by killing seventy-five thousand people who hated them. But they did no looting. ¹⁷This was on the thirteenth day of Adar. On the next day, the fourteenth, there was no more killing, and they made it a joyful day of feasting. ¹⁸The Jews of Susa, however, made the fifteenth a holiday, since they had slaughtered their enemies on the thirteenth and fourteenth and then stopped on the fifteenth. ¹⁹This is why Jews who live in small towns observe the fourteenth day of the month of Adar as a joyous holiday, a time for feasting and giving gifts of food to one another.

The Festival of Purim

20 Mordecai had these events written down and sent letters to all the Jews, near and far, throughout the Persian Empire, ²¹telling them to observe the fourteenth and fifteenth days of Adar as holidays every year. ²²These were the days on which the Jews had rid themselves of their enemies; this was a month that had been turned from a time of grief and despair into a time of joy and happiness. They were told to observe these days with feasts and parties, giving gifts of food to one another and to the poor. ²³So the Jews followed Mordecai's instructions, and the celebration became an annual custom.

24 Haman son of Hammedatha—the descendant of Agag and the enemy of the Jewish people—had cast lots (or "purim," as they were called) to determine the day for destroying the Jews; he had planned to wipe them out. ²⁵But Esther went to the king, and the king issued written orders with the result that Haman suffered the fate he had planned for the Jews—he and his sons were hanged from the gallows. ²⁶That is why the holidays are called Purim. Because of Mordecai's letter and because of all that had happened to them, ²⁷the Jews made it a rule for themselves, their descendants, and anyone who might become a Jew, that at the proper time each year these two days would be regularly observed according to Mordecai's instructions. ²⁸It was

*ʰ*In the Jewish quarter of every city; *or* In every Jewish city.
9.24: Esth 3.7

resolved that every Jewish family of every future generation in every province and every city should remember and observe the days of Purim for all time to come.

29 Then Queen Esther, the daughter of Abihail, along with Mordecai, also wrote a letter, putting her full authority behind the letter about Purim, which Mordecai had written earlier. 30 The letter was addressed to all the Jews, and copies were sent to all the 127 provinces of the Persian Empire. It wished the Jews peace and security 31 and directed them and their descendants to observe the days of Purim at the proper time, just as they had adopted rules for the observance of fasts and times of mourning. This was commanded by both Mordecai and Queen Esther. 32 Esther's command, confirming the rules for Purim, was written down on a scroll.

The Greatness of Xerxes and Mordecai

10 King Xerxes imposed forced labour on the people of the coastal regions of his empire as well as on those of the interior. 2 All the great and wonderful things he did, as well as the whole story of how he promoted Mordecai to high office, are recorded in the official records of the kings of Persia and Media. 3 Mordecai the Jew was second in rank only to King Xerxes himself. He was honoured and well-liked by his fellow-Jews. He worked for the good of his people and for the security of all their descendants.

THE BOOK OF
JOB

INTRODUCTION

The book of *Job* is the story of a good man who suffers total disaster—he loses all his children and property and is afflicted with a repulsive disease. Then in three series of poetic dialogues the author shows how Job's friends and Job himself react to these calamities. In the end, God himself, whose dealings with mankind have been a prominent part of the discussion, appears to Job.

The friends of Job explain his suffering in traditional religious terms. Since God, so they assume, always rewards good and punishes evil, the sufferings of Job can only mean that he has sinned. But for Job this is too simple; he does not deserve such cruel punishment, because he has been an unusually good and righteous man. He cannot understand how God can let so much evil happen to one like himself, and he boldly challenges God. Job does not lose his faith, but he does long to be justified before God and to regain his honour as a good man.

God does not give an answer to Job's questions, but he does respond to Job's faith by overwhelming him with a poetic picture of his divine power and wisdom. Job then humbly acknowledges God as wise and great, and repents of the wild and angry words he had used.

The prose conclusion records how Job is restored to his former condition, with even greater prosperity than before. God reprimands Job's friends for failing to understand the meaning of Job's suffering. Only Job had really sensed that God is greater than traditional religion had depicted him.

Outline of Contents

Prologue 1.1—2.13
Job and his friends 3.1—31.40
  a. Job's complaint 3.1-26
  b. The first dialogue 4.1—14.22
  c. The second dialogue 15.1—21.34
  d. The third dialogue 22.1—27.23
  e. In praise of wisdom 28.1-28
  f. Job's final statement 29.1—31.40
The speeches of Elihu 32.1—37.24
The Lord answers Job 38.1—42.6
Epilogue 42.7-17

Satan Tests Job

1 There was a man named Job, living in the land of Uz, *a* who worshipped God and was faithful to him. He was a good man, careful not to do anything evil. ² He had seven sons and three daughters, ³ and owned seven thousand sheep, three thousand camels, one thousand head of cattle, and five hundred donkeys. He also had a large number of servants and was the richest man in the East.

4 Job's sons used to take it in turns to give a feast, to which all the others would come, and they always invited their three sisters to join them. ⁵ The morning after each feast, Job would get up early and offer sacrifices for each of his children in order to purify them. He always did this because he thought that one of them might have sinned by insulting God unintentionally.

6 When the day came for the heavenly beings *b* to appear before the LORD, Satan *c* was there among them. ⁷ The LORD asked him, "What have you been doing?"

Satan answered, "I have been walking here and there, roaming round the earth."

8 "Did you notice my servant Job?" the LORD asked. "There is no one on earth as faithful and good as he is. He worships me and is careful not to do anything evil."

9 Satan replied, "Would Job worship you if he got nothing out of it? ¹⁰ You have always protected him and his family and everything he owns. You bless every-thing he does, and you have given him enough cattle to fill the whole country. ¹¹ But now suppose you take away everything he has—he will curse you to your face!"

12 "All right," the LORD said to Satan, "everything he has is in your power, but you must not hurt Job himself." So Satan left.

Job's Children and Wealth Are Destroyed

13 One day when Job's children were having a feast at the home of their eldest brother, ¹⁴ a messenger came running to Job. "We were ploughing the fields with the oxen," he said, "and the donkeys were in a nearby pasture. ¹⁵ Suddenly the Sabeans *d* attacked and stole them all. They killed every one of your servants except me. I am the only one who escaped to tell you."

16 Before he had finished speaking, another servant came and said, "Light-ning struck the sheep and the shepherds and killed them all. I am the only one who escaped to tell you."

17 Before he had finished speaking, another servant came and said, "Three bands of Chaldean *e* raiders attacked us, took away the camels, and killed all your servants except me. I am the only one who escaped to tell you."

18 Before he had finished speaking, another servant came and said, "Your children were having a feast at the home of your eldest son, ¹⁹ when a storm swept

---

a UZ: *An area whose exact location is unknown.*
b HEAVENLY BEINGS: *Supernatural beings who serve God in heaven.*
c SATAN: *A supernatural being whose name indicates he was regarded as man's opponent.*
d SABEANS: *A tribe of wandering raiders from the south.*
e CHALDEANS: *A tribe of wandering raiders from the north.*
1.6: Gen 6.2   **1.9-11:** Rev 12.10

The LORD gave, and now he has taken away (1.21)

in from the desert. It blew the house down and killed them all. I am the only one who escaped to tell you."

20 Then Job stood up and tore his clothes in grief. He shaved his head and threw himself face downwards on the ground. 21 He said, "I was born with nothing, and I will die with nothing. The LORD gave, and now he has taken away. May his name be praised!"

22 In spite of everything that had happened, Job did not sin by blaming God.

Satan Tests Job Again

2 When the day came for the heavenly beings to appear before the LORD again, Satan was there among them. 2 The LORD asked him, "Where have you been?"

Satan answered, "I have been walking here and there, roaming round the earth."

3 "Did you notice my servant Job?" the LORD asked. "There is no one on earth as faithful and good as he is. He worships me and is careful not to do anything evil. You persuaded me to let you attack him for no reason at all, but Job is still as faithful as ever."

4 Satan replied, "A man will give up everything in order to stay alive. 5 But now suppose you hurt his body—he will curse you to your face!"

6 So the LORD said to Satan, "All right, he is in your power, but you are not to kill him."

7 Then Satan left the LORD's presence and made sores break out all over Job's body. 8 Job went and sat by the rubbish heap and took a piece of broken pottery to scrape his sores. 9 His wife said to him, "You are still as faithful as ever, aren't you? Why don't you curse God and die?"

10 Job answered, "You are talking nonsense! When God sends us something good, we welcome it. How can we complain when he sends us trouble?" In spite of everything he suffered, Job said nothing against God.

Job's Friends Come

11 Three of Job's friends were Eliphaz, from the city of Teman, Bildad, from the land of Shuah, and Zophar, from the land of Naamah. When they heard how much Job had been suffering, they decided to go and comfort him. 12 While they were still a long way off they saw Job, but did not recognize him. When they did, they began to weep and wail, tearing their

Why don't you curse God and die? (2.9)

clothes in grief and throwing dust into the air and on their heads. 13 Then they sat there on the ground with him for seven days and nights without saying a word, because they saw how much he was suffering.

Job's Complaint to God

3 Finally Job broke the silence and cursed the day on which he had been born.

Job

2-3 O God, put a curse on the day I was
    born;
    put a curse on the night when I was
    conceived!
4 Turn that day into darkness, God.
  Never again remember that day;
    never again let light shine on it.
5 Make it a day of gloom and thick
    darkness;
    cover it with clouds, and blot out the
    sun.
6 Blot that night out of the year,
    and never let it be counted again;
7   make it a barren, joyless night.
8 Tell the sorcerers to curse that day,
    those who know how to control
    Leviathan.*f*
9 Keep the morning star from shining;
    give that night no hope of dawn.
10 Curse that night for letting me be born,
    for exposing me to trouble and grief.

11 I wish I had died in my mother's womb
    or died the moment I was born.
12 Why did my mother hold me on her
    knees?
    Why did she feed me at her breast?
13 If I had died then, I would be at rest
    now,
14   sleeping like the kings and rulers
    who rebuilt ancient palaces,
15 Then I would be sleeping like princes
    who filled their houses with gold and
    silver,
16   or sleeping like a still-born child.
17 In the grave wicked men stop their
    evil,
    and tired workmen find rest at last.
18 Even prisoners enjoy peace,
    free from shouts and harsh
    commands.
19 Everyone is there, the famous and the
    unknown,
    and slaves at last are free.

20 Why let men go on living in misery?
    Why give light to men in grief?
21 They wait for death, but it never
    comes;

they prefer a grave to any treasure.
22 They are not happy till they are dead
    and buried;
23   God keeps their future hidden
    and hems them in on every side.
24 Instead of eating, I mourn,
    and I can never stop groaning.
25 Everything I fear and dread comes
    true.
26 I have no peace, no rest,
    and my troubles never end.

The First Dialogue
(4.1—14.22)

4 *Eliphaz*
1-2 Job, will you be annoyed if I
    speak?
    I can't keep quiet any longer.
3 You have taught many people
    and given strength to feeble hands.
4 When someone stumbled, weak and
    tired,
    your words encouraged him to stand.
5 Now it's your turn to be in trouble,
    and you are too stunned to face it.
6 You worshipped God, and your life was
    blameless;
    and so you should have confidence
    and hope.
7 Think back now. Name a single case
    where a righteous man met with
    disaster.
8 I have seen people plough fields of evil
    and sow wickedness like seed;
    now they harvest wickedness and evil.
9 Like a storm, God destroys them in his
    anger.
10 The wicked roar and growl like lions,
    but God silences them and breaks
    their teeth.
11 Like lions with nothing to kill and eat,
    they die, and all their children are
    scattered.

12 Once a message came quietly,
    so quietly I could hardly hear it.
13 Like a nightmare it disturbed my sleep.
14   I trembled and shuddered;
    my whole body shook with fear.
15 A light breeze touched my face,
    and my hair bristled with fright.
16 I could see something standing there;
    I stared, but couldn't tell what it was.
    Then I heard a voice out of the silence:
17 "Can anyone be righteous in the sight
    of *g* God

*f*LEVIATHAN: *Some take this to be the crocodile, others a legendary monster. Magicians were thought to be able to make him cause eclipses of the sun.*
*g*righteous in the sight of; *or* more righteous than.
3.1–19: Jer 20.14–18   **3.21:** Rev 9.6   **4.13:** Job 33.15

or be pure before[h] his Creator?
18 God does not trust his heavenly
   servants;
   he finds fault even with his angels.
19 Do you think he will trust a creature
   of clay,
   a thing of dust that can be crushed
   like a moth?
20 A man may be alive in the morning,
   but die unnoticed before evening
   comes.
21 All that he has is taken away;
   he dies, still lacking wisdom."

5 Call out, Job. See if anyone answers.
   Is there any angel to whom you can
   turn?
2 To worry yourself to death with
   resentment
   would be a foolish, senseless thing
   to do.
3 I have seen fools who looked secure,
   but I called down a sudden curse on
   their homes.
4 Their sons can never find safety;
   no one stands up to defend them in
   court.
5 Hungry people will eat the fool's crops—
   even the grain growing among
   thorns[i]—
   and thirsty people will envy his
   wealth.
6 Evil does not grow in the soil,
   nor does trouble grow out of the
   ground.
7 No indeed! Man brings trouble on
   himself,
   as surely as sparks fly up from a fire.[j]

8 If I were you, I would turn to God
   and present my case to him.
9 We cannot understand the great things
   he does,
   and to his miracles there is no end.
10 He sends rain on the land
   and he waters the fields.
11 Yes, it is God who raises the humble
   and gives joy to all who mourn.
12-13 He upsets the plans of cunning men,
   and traps wise men in their own
   schemes,
   so that nothing they do succeeds;
14   even at noon they grope in darkness.
15 But God saves the poor[k] from death;
   he saves the needy from oppression.

16 He gives hope to the poor and silences
   the wicked.
17 Happy is the person whom God
   corrects!
   Do not resent it when he rebukes you.
18 God bandages the wounds he makes;
   his hand hurts you, and his hand heals.
19 Time after time he will save you from
   harm;
20   when famine comes, he will keep
   you alive,
   and in war protect you from death.
21 God will rescue you from slander;
   he will save you when destruction
   comes.
22 You will laugh at violence and hunger
   and not be afraid of wild animals.
23 The fields you plough will be free of
   rocks;
   wild animals will never attack you.
24 Then you will live at peace in your
   tent;
   when you look at your sheep, you
   will find them safe.
25 You will have as many children
   as there are blades of grass in a
   pasture.
26 Like wheat that ripens till harvest time,
   you will live to a ripe old age.
27 Job, we have learnt this by long study.
   It is true, so now accept it.

6 *Job*
1-2 If my troubles and griefs were
   weighed on scales,
3   they would weigh more than the sands
   of the sea,
   so my wild words should not surprise
   you.
4 Almighty God has pierced me with
   arrows,
   and their poison spreads through my
   body.
   God has lined up his terrors against me.

5 A donkey is content when eating grass,
   and a cow is quiet when eating hay.
6 But who can eat tasteless, unsalted
   food?
   What flavour is there in the white
   of an egg?
7 I have no appetite for food like that,
   and everything I eat makes me sick.[l]

8 Why won't God give me what I ask?

---

[h] be pure before; *or* be more pure than.
[i] *Probable text* even...thorns; *Hebrew unclear.*
[j] sparks fly up from a fire; *or* birds fly up to the sky.   [k] *Probable text* poor; *Hebrew unclear.*
[l] *Probable text* sick; *Hebrew unclear.*
5.13: 1 Cor 3.19   **5.17:** Prov 3.11; Heb 12.5–6   **5.18:** Hos 6.1

Why won't he answer my prayer?
9 If only he would go ahead and kill me!
10 If I knew he would, I would leap for
         joy,
   no matter how great my pain.
   I know that God is holy;
      I have never opposed what he
      commands.
11 What strength have I got to keep on
      living?
   Why go on living when I have no
      hope?
12 Am I made of stone? Is my body
      bronze?
13 I have no strength left to save myself;
   there is nowhere I can turn for help.

14 In trouble *m* like this I need loyal
      friends—
   whether I've forsaken God or not.
15 But you, my friends, you deceive me
      like streams
   that go dry when no rain comes.
16 The streams are choked with snow and
      ice,
17   but in the heat they disappear,
   and the stream beds lie bare and dry.
18 Caravans get lost looking for water;
   they wander and die in the desert.
19 Caravans from Sheba and Tema
      search,
20   but their hope dies beside dry
      streams.
21 You are like *n* those streams to me, *o*
   you see my fate and draw back in
      fear.
22 Have I asked you to give me a gift
   or to bribe someone on my behalf
23   or to save me from some enemy or
      tyrant?

24 All right, teach me; tell me my faults.
   I will be quiet and listen to you.
25 Honest words are convincing,
   but you are talking nonsense.
26 You think I am talking nothing but
      wind;
   then why do you answer my words
      of despair?
27 You would even throw dice for orphan
      slaves
   and make yourselves rich off your
      closest friends!
28 Look me in the face. I won't lie.

You think I am talking nothing but wind
(6.26)

29 You have gone far enough. Stop being
      unjust.
   Don't condemn me. I'm in the right.
30 But you think I am lying—
   you think I can't tell right from wrong.

7 Human life is like forced army service,
      like a life of hard manual labour,
2   like a slave longing for cool shade;
   like a worker waiting for his pay.
3 Month after month I have nothing to
      live for;
   night after night brings me grief.
4 When I lie down to sleep, the hours
      drag;
   I toss all night and long for dawn.
5 My body is full of worms;
   it is covered with scabs;
   pus runs out of my sores.
6 My days pass by without hope,
   pass faster than a weaver's shuttle. *p*

7 Remember, O God, my life is only a
      breath;
   my happiness has already ended.
8 You see me now, but never again.
   If you look for me, I'll be gone.
9-10 Like a cloud that fades and is gone,
   a man dies and never returns;
   he is forgotten by all who knew him.

m Probable text trouble; *Hebrew unclear.*   *n Probable text* like; *Hebrew* because.
o Some ancient translations and one Hebrew manuscript to me; *most Hebrew manuscripts have
two different expressions:* nothing *in the text and* to him *in the margin.*
*p WEAVER'S SHUTTLE: A small device in the loom which carries threads to and fro rapidly in
weaving cloth.*

¹¹ No! I can't be quiet!
I am angry and bitter.
I have to speak.

¹² Why do you keep me under guard?
Do you think I am a sea-monster?�q
¹³ I lie down and try to rest;
I look for relief from my pain.
¹⁴ But you—you terrify me with dreams;
you send me visions and nightmares
¹⁵ until I would rather be strangled
than live in this miserable body.
¹⁶ I give up; I am tired of living.

I give up; I am tired of living (7.16)

Leave me alone. My life makes no sense.

¹⁷ Why is man so important to you?
Why pay attention to what he does?
¹⁸ You inspect him every morning
and test him every minute.
¹⁹ Won't you look away long enough
for me to swallow my spittle?
²⁰ Are you harmed by my sin, you jailer?
Why use me for your target-practice?
Am I so great a burden to you?
²¹ Can't you ever forgive my sin?
Can't you pardon the wrong I do?
Soon I will be in my grave,
and I'll be gone when you look for
me.

8 *Bildad*
¹⁻² Are you finally through with
your windy speech?
³ God never twists justice;
he never fails to do what is right.
⁴ Your children must have sinned against
God,
and so he punished them as they
deserved.
⁵ But turn now and plead with Almighty
God;
⁶ if you are so honest and pure,
then God will come and help you
and restore your household as your
reward.
⁷ All the wealth you lost will be nothing
compared with what God will give
you then.

⁸ Look for a moment at ancient wisdom;
consider the truths our fathers learnt.
⁹ Our life is short, we know nothing at
all;
we pass like shadows across the earth.
¹⁰ But let the ancient wise men teach
you;
listen to what they had to say:

¹¹ "Reeds can't grow where there is no
water;
they are never found outside a swamp.
¹² If the water dries up, they are the first
to wither,
while still too small to be cut and
used.
¹³ Godless men are like those reeds;
their hope is gone, once God is
forgotten.
¹⁴ They trust a thread—a spider's web.
¹⁵ If they lean on a web, will it hold
them up?
If they grab for a thread, will it help
them stand?"

¹⁶ Evil men sprout like weeds in the sun,
like weeds that spread all through the
garden.
¹⁷ Their roots wrap round the stones
and hold fast toʳ every rock.
¹⁸ But then pull them up—
no one will ever know they were there.
¹⁹ Yes, that's all the joy evil men have;
others now come and take their
places.

²⁰ But God will never abandon the
faithful

�q SEA-MONSTER: *A reference to ancient stories in which sea-monsters had to be guarded so that they would not escape and do damage.*   ʳ *Probable text* hold fast to; *Hebrew* see.
7.17: Ps 8.4, 144.3

or ever give help to evil men.
²¹ He will let you laugh and shout again,
²² but he will bring disgrace on those
      who hate you,
    and the homes of the wicked will
      vanish.

9

Job
¹⁻² Yes, I've heard all that before.
    But how can a man win his case
      against God?
³ How can anyone argue with him?
    He can ask a thousand questions
    that no one could ever answer. ˢ
⁴ God is so wise and powerful;
    no man can stand up against him.
⁵ Without warning he moves mountains
    and in anger he destroys them.
⁶ God sends earthquakes and shakes the
      ground;
    he rocks the pillars that support the
      earth.
⁷ He can keep the sun from rising,
    and the stars from shining at night.
⁸ No one helped God spread out the
      heavens
    or trample the sea-monster's back. ᵗ
⁹ God hung the stars in the sky—the
      Great Bear,
    Orion, the Pleiades, and the stars of
      the south.
¹⁰ We cannot understand the great
      things he does,
    and to his miracles there is no end.

¹¹ God passes by, but I cannot see him.
¹² He takes what he wants, and no one
      can stop him;
    no one dares ask him, "What are you
      doing?"
¹³ God's anger is constant. He crushed
      his enemies
    who helped Rahab, ᵘ the sea-monster,
      oppose him.
¹⁴ So how can I find words to answer
      God?
¹⁵ Though I am innocent, all I can do
    is beg for mercy from God my judge.
¹⁶ Yet even then, if he lets me speak,
    I can't believe he would listen to me.
¹⁷ He sends storms to batter and bruise
      me
    without any reason at all.
¹⁸ He won't let me get my breath;
    he has filled my life with bitterness.

¹⁹ Should I try force? Try force on God?
    Should I take him to court? Could
      anyone make him go? ᵛ
²⁰ I am innocent and faithful, but my
      words sound guilty,
    and everything I say seems to
      condemn me.
²¹⁻²² I am innocent, but I no longer care.
    I am sick of living. Nothing matters;
    innocent or guilty, God will destroy
      us.
²³ When an innocent man suddenly dies,
    God laughs.
²⁴ God gave the world to the wicked.
    He made all the judges blind.
    And if God didn't do it, who did?

²⁵ My days race by, not one of them good.
²⁶ My life passes like the swiftest boat,
    as fast as an eagle swooping down
      on a rabbit.
²⁷⁻²⁸ If I smile and try to forget my
      pain,
    all my suffering comes back to haunt
      me;
    I know that God does hold me guilty.
²⁹ Since I am held guilty, why should
      I bother?
³⁰   No soap can wash away my sins.
³¹ God throws me into a pit of filth,
    and even my clothes are ashamed of
      me.
³² If God were human, I could answer
      him;
    we could go to court to decide our
      quarrel.
³³ But there is no one to step between
      us—
    no one to judge both God and me.
³⁴ Stop punishing me, God!
    Keep your terrors away!
³⁵ I am not afraid. I am going to talk
    because I know my own heart.

10

I am tired of living.
    Listen to my bitter complaint.
² Don't condemn me, God.
    Tell me! What is the charge against
      me?
³ Is it right for you to be so cruel?
    To despise what you yourself have
      made?
    And then to smile on the schemes
      of wicked men?
⁴ Do you see things as we do?

ˢHe can ask...answer; or A man could ask him a thousand questions, and he would not answer.
ᵗTRAMPLE THE SEA-MONSTER'S BACK: A reference to ancient stories in which a sea-monster was
  killed and then trampled on (see also 26.13).
ᵘRAHAB: A legendary sea-monster which represented the forces of chaos and evil.
ᵛProbable text make him go; Hebrew make me go.
9.2: Job 4.17   **9.9:** Job 38.31; Amos 5.8

5 Is your life as short as ours?
6 Then why do you track down all my
  sins
    and hunt down every fault I have?
7 You know that I am not guilty,
    that no one can save me from you.

8 Your hands formed and shaped me,
    and now *w* those same hands destroy
      me.
9 Remember that you made me from
    clay; *x*
    are you going to crush me back to
      dust?
10 You gave my father strength to beget
    me;
    you made me grow in my mother's
      womb.
11 You formed my body with bones and
    sinews
    and covered the bones with muscles
      and skin.
12 You have given me life and constant
    love,
    and your care has kept me alive.
13 But now I know that all that time
    you were secretly planning to harm
      me.
14 You were watching to see if I would
    sin,
    so that you could refuse to forgive
      me.
15 As soon as I sin, I'm in trouble with
    you,
    but when I do right, I get no credit.
  I am miserable and covered with
    shame. *y*
16 If I have any success at all,
    you hunt me down like a lion;
    to hurt me you even work miracles.
17 You always have some witness against
    me;
    your anger towards me grows and
      grows;
    you always plan some new attack.

18 Why, God, did you let me be born?
    I should have died before anyone saw
      me.
19 To go from the womb straight to the
    grave
    would have been as good as never
      existing.
20 Isn't my life almost over? Leave me
    alone!
    Let me enjoy the time I have left.

21 I am going soon and will never come
    back—
    going to a land that is dark and
      gloomy,
22 a land of darkness, shadows, and
    confusion,
    where the light itself is darkness.

11

Zophar
1-2 Will no one answer all this
    nonsense?
  Does talking so much put a man in
    the right?
3 Job, do you think we can't answer you?
    That your mocking words will leave
      us speechless?
4 You claim that what you say is true;
    you claim you are pure in the sight
      of God.
5 How I wish God would answer you!
6 He would tell you there are many sides
    to wisdom;
    there are things too deep for human
      knowledge.
  God is punishing you less than you
    deserve.

7 Can you discover the limits and bounds
    of the greatness and power of God?
8 The sky is no limit for God,
    but it lies beyond your reach.
  God knows the world of the dead,
    but you do not know it.
9 God's greatness is broader than the
    earth,
    wider than the sea.
10 If God arrests you and brings you to
    trial,
    who is there to stop him?
11 God knows which men are worthless;
    he sees all their evil deeds.
12 Stupid men will start being wise
    when wild donkeys are born tame.

13 Put your heart right, Job. Reach out
    to God.
14 Put away evil and wrong from your
    home.
15 Then face the world again, firm and
    courageous.
16 Then all your troubles will fade from
    your memory,
    like floods that are past and
      remembered no more.
17 Your life will be brighter than
    sunshine at noon,

---

w Some ancient translations and now; *Hebrew* together.
x One ancient translation from clay; *Hebrew* like clay.
y Probable text covered with shame; *Hebrew* see my shame.

and life's darkest hours will shine like
the dawn.
18 You will live secure and full of hope;
God will protect you and give you
rest.
19 You won't be afraid of your enemies;
many people will ask you for help.
20 But the wicked will look round in
despair
and find that there is no way to escape.
Their one hope is that death will come.

12 *Job*
1-2 Yes, you are the voice of the
people.
When you die, wisdom will die with
you.
3 But I have as much sense as you have;
I am in no way inferior to you;
everyone knows all that you have said.
4 Even my friends laugh at me now;
they laugh, although I am righteous
and blameless;
but there was a time when God
answered my prayers.
5 You have no troubles, and yet you make
fun of me;
you hit a man who is about to fall.
6 But thieves and godless men live in
peace,
though their only god is their own
strength.

7 Even birds and animals have much they
could teach you;
8   ask the creatures of earth and sea
for their wisdom.
9 All of them know that the LORD's hand
made them.
10 It is God who directs the lives of his
creatures;
every man's life is in his power.
11 But just as your tongue enjoys tasting
food,
your ears enjoy hearing words.

12-13 Old men have wisdom,
but God has wisdom and power.
Old men have insight;
God has insight and power to act.
14 When God tears down, who can
rebuild,
and who can free the man God
imprisons?
15 Drought comes when God withholds
rain;
floods come when he turns water
loose.

16 God is strong and always victorious;
both deceived and deceiver are in his
power.
17 He takes away the wisdom of rulers
and makes leaders act like fools.
18 He dethrones kings and makes them
prisoners;
19   he humbles priests and men of
power.
20 He silences men who are trusted,
and takes the wisdom of old men
away.
21 He disgraces those in power
and puts an end to the strength of
rulers.
22 He sends light to places dark as death.
23 He makes nations strong and great,
but then he defeats and destroys them.
24 He makes their leaders foolish
and lets them wander confused and
lost;
25   they grope in the dark and stagger
like drunkards.

13 1-2 Everything you say, I have
heard before.
I understand it all; I know as much
as you do.
I'm not your inferior.
3 But my dispute is with God, not you;
I want to argue my case with him.
4 You cover up your ignorance with lies;
you are like doctors who can't heal
anyone.
5 Say nothing, and someone may think
you are wise!

6 Listen while I state my case.
7   Why are you lying?
Do you think your lies will benefit
God?
8 Are you trying to defend him?
Are you going to argue his case in
court?
9 If God looks at you closely, will he find
anything good?
Do you think you can fool God as
you fool men?
10 Even though your prejudice is hidden,
he will reprimand you,
11   and his power will fill you with
terror.
12 Your proverbs are as useless as ashes;
your arguments crumble like clay.
13 Be quiet and give me a chance to speak,
and let the results be what they will.

14 I am z ready to risk my life.

z *One ancient translation* I am; *Hebrew* Why am I...?

Be quiet and give me a chance to speak (13.13)

because I know I am in the right.

19 Are you coming to accuse me, God?
  If you do, I am ready to be silent
    and die.
20 Let me ask for two things; agree to
    them,
  and I will not try to hide from you:
21   stop punishing me, and don't crush
    me with terror.

22 Speak first, O God, and I will answer.
  Or let me speak, and you answer me.
23 What are my sins? What wrongs have
    I done?
  What crimes am I charged with?

24 Why do you avoid me?
  Why do you treat me like an enemy?
25 Are you trying to frighten me? I'm
    nothing but a leaf;
  you are attacking a piece of dry straw.

26 You bring bitter charges against me,
  even for what I did when I was young.
27 You bind chains on my feet;
  you watch every step I take,
  and even examine my footprints.
28 As a result, I crumble like rotten wood,
  like a moth-eaten coat.

14 We are all born weak and helpless.
    All lead the same short, troubled
      life.
2 We grow and wither as quickly as
    flowers;
  we disappear like shadows.
3 Will you even look at me, God,
  or put me on trial and judge me?
4 Nothing clean can ever come
  from anything as unclean as man.
5 The length of his life is decided
    beforehand—
  the number of months he will live.
  You have settled it, and it can't be
    changed.
6 Look away from him and leave him
    alone;a
  let him enjoy his hard life—if he can.b

7 There is hope for a tree that has been
    cut down;
  it can come back to life and sprout.
8 Even though its roots grow old,
  and its stump dies in the ground,
9   with water it will sprout like a young
    plant.

15 I've lost all hope, so what if God kills
    me?
  I am going to state my case to him.
16 It may even be that my boldness will
    save me,
  since no wicked man would dare to
    face God.
17 Now listen to my words of explanation.
18 I am ready to state my case,

---

aOne Hebrew manuscript and leave him alone; most Hebrew manuscripts so that he may rest.
blet him...can; or until he finishes his day of hard work.
13.27: Job 33.11

*Hope for a tree that has been cut down
(14.7)*

10 But a man dies, and that is the end
of him;
he dies, and where is he then?

11 Like rivers that stop running,
and lakes that go dry,
12   people die, never to rise.
They will never wake up while the sky
endures;
they will never stir from their sleep.

13 I wish you would hide me in the world
of the dead;
let me be hidden until your anger is
over,
and then set a time to remember me.
14 If a man dies, can he come back to
life?
But I will wait for better times,
wait till this time of trouble is ended.
15 Then you will call, and I will answer,
and you will be pleased with me, your
creature.
16 Then you will watch every step I take,
but you will not keep track of my
sins.
17 You will forgive them and put them
away;
you will wipe out all the wrongs I
have done.

18 There comes a time when mountains
fall

15.14–16: Job 25.4–6

and solid cliffs are moved away.
19 Water will wear down rocks,
and heavy rain will wash away the
soil;
so you destroy man's hope for life.
20 You overpower a man and send him
away for ever;
his face is twisted in death.
21 His sons win honour, but he never
knows it,
nor is he told when they are disgraced.
22 He feels only the pain of his own body
and the grief of his own mind.

The Second Dialogue
(15.1—21.34)

15 *Eliphaz*
1-2 Empty words, Job! Empty
words!
3 No wise man would talk as you do
or defend himself with such
meaningless words.
4 If you had your way, no one would fear
God;
no one would pray to him.
5 Your wickedness is evident by what you
say;
you are trying to hide behind clever
words.
6 There is no need for me to condemn
you;
you are condemned by every word
you speak.

7 Do you think you were the first man
born?
Were you there when God made the
mountains?
8 Did you overhear the plans God made?
Does human wisdom belong to you
alone?
9 There is nothing you know that we don't
know.
10 We learnt our wisdom from grey-
haired men—
men born before your father.

11 God offers you comfort; why still
reject it?
We have spoken for him with calm,
even words.
12 But you are excited and glare at us
in anger.
13 You are angry with God and denounce
him.

14 Can any man be really pure?
Can anyone be right with God?

¹⁵ Why, God does not trust even his
angels;
even they are not pure in his sight.
¹⁶ And man drinks evil as if it were water;
yes, man is corrupt; man is worthless.

¹⁷ Now listen, Job, to what I know.
¹⁸ Wise men have taught me truths
which they learnt from their fathers,
and they kept no secrets hidden.
¹⁹ Their land was free from foreigners;
there was no one to lead them away
from God.

²⁰ A wicked man who oppresses others
will be in torment as long as he lives.
²¹ Voices of terror will scream in his ears,
and robbers attack when he thinks
he is safe.
²² He has no hope of escaping from
darkness,
for somewhere a sword is waiting to
kill him,
²³ and vultures ^c are waiting ^d to eat
his corpse.
He knows his future is dark;
²⁴ disaster, like a powerful king,
is waiting to attack him.

²⁵ That is the fate of the man
who shakes his fist at God
and defies the Almighty.
²⁶⁻²⁷ That man is proud and rebellious;
he stubbornly holds up his shield
and rushes to fight against God.

²⁸ That is the man who captured cities
and seized houses whose owners had
fled,
but war will destroy those cities and
houses.
²⁹ He will not remain rich for long;
nothing he owns will last.
Even his shadow ^e will vanish,
³⁰ and he will not escape from
darkness.
He will be like a tree
whose branches are burnt by fire,
whose blossoms ^f are blown away by
the wind.
³¹ If he is foolish enough to trust in evil,
then evil will be his reward.
³² Before his time is up he will wither, ^g
wither like a branch and never be
green again.

³³ He will be like a vine that loses its
unripe grapes;
like an olive-tree that drops its
blossoms.
³⁴ There will be no descendants for
godless men,
and fire will destroy the homes built
by bribery.
³⁵ These are the men who plan trouble
and do evil;
their hearts are always full of deceit.

16

Job
¹⁻² I have heard words like that
before;
the comfort you give is only torment.
³ Are you going to keep on talking for
ever?
Do you always have to have the last
word?
⁴ If you were in my place and I in yours,
I could say everything you are saying.
I could shake my head wisely
and drown you with a flood of words.
⁵ I could strengthen you with advice
and keep talking to comfort you.

⁶ But nothing I say helps,
and being silent does not calm my
pain.
⁷ You have worn me out, God;
you have let my family be killed.
⁸ You have seized me; you are my
enemy.
I am skin and bones,
and people take that as proof of my
guilt. ^h

⁹ In anger God tears me limb from limb;
he glares at me with hate.
¹⁰ People sneer at me;
they crowd round me and slap my
face.
¹¹ God has handed me over to evil men.
¹² I was living in peace,
but God took me by the throat
and battered me and crushed me.
God uses me for target-practice
¹³ and shoots arrows at me from every
side—
arrows that pierce and wound me;
and even then he shows no pity.
¹⁴ He wounds me again and again;
he attacks like a soldier gone mad
with hate.

---

^c *One ancient translation* vultures; *Hebrew* where is he?
^d *One ancient translation* are waiting; *Hebrew* he wanders.
^e *One ancient translation* shadow; *Hebrew* unclear.
^f *One ancient translation* blossoms; *Hebrew* mouth.
^g *Some ancient translations* wither; *Hebrew* be filled.
^h *Verses 7–8 in Hebrew are unclear.*

The comfort you give is only torment (16.1)

15 I mourn and wear clothes made of
    sackcloth,
  and I sit here in the dust defeated.
16 I have cried until my face is red,
  and my eyes are swollen and circled
    with shadows,
17   but I am not guilty of any violence,
  and my prayer to God is sincere.

18 O Earth, don't hide the wrongs done
    to me!
  Don't let my call for justice be silenced!
19 There is someone in heaven
  to stand up for me and take my side.
20 My friends scorn me;
  my eyes pour out tears to God.
21 I want someone to plead with God
    for me,
  as a man pleads for his friend.
22 My years are passing now,
  and I walk the road of no return.

17 The end of my life is near. I can
      hardly breathe;
  there is nothing left for me but the
    grave.
2 I watch how bitterly everyone mocks
  me.
3 I am being honest, God. Accept my word.

There is no one else to support what
  I say.
4 You have closed their minds to reason;
  don't let them triumph over me now.
5 In the old proverb a man betrays his
    friends for money,
  and his children suffer for it. *i*
6 And now people use this proverb
    against me;
  they come and spit in my face.
7 My grief has almost made me blind;
  my arms and legs are as thin as
    shadows.
8 Those who claim to be honest are
    shocked,
  and they all condemn me as godless.
9 Those who claim to be respectable
  are more and more convinced they
    are right.
10 But if all of them came and stood
    before me,
  I would not find even one of them
    wise.

11 My days have passed; my plans have
    failed;
  my hope is gone.
12 But my friends say night is daylight;
  they say that light is near,

i a man...suffer for it; *or* a man entertains his friends while his children go hungry.
16.19: Job 19.25

but I know I remain in darkness.
¹³ My only hope is the world of the dead,
    where I will lie down to sleep in the
        dark.
¹⁴ I will call the grave my father,
    and the worms that eat me
    I will call my mother and my sisters.
¹⁵ Where is there any hope for me?
    Who sees any?
¹⁶ Hope will not go with me*j*
    when I go down to the world of the
        dead.

18   Bildad

¹⁻² Job, can't people like you ever
    be quiet?
If you stopped to listen, we could talk
    to you.
³ What makes you think we are as stupid
    as cattle?
⁴ You are only hurting yourself with your
    anger.
Will the earth be deserted because
    you are angry?
Will God move mountains to satisfy
    you?

⁵ The wicked man's light will still be put
    out;
    its flame will never burn again.
⁶ The lamp in his tent will be darkened.
⁷ His steps were firm, but now he
    stumbles;
    he falls—a victim of his own advice.
⁸ He walks into a net, and his feet are
    caught;
⁹   a trap catches his heels and holds him.
¹⁰ On the ground a snare is hidden;
    a trap has been set in his path.

¹¹ All round him terror is waiting;
    it follows him at every step.
¹² He used to be rich, but now he goes
    hungry;
    disaster stands and waits at his side.
¹³ A deadly disease spreads over his body
    and causes his arms and legs to rot.
¹⁴ He is torn from the tent where he lived
    secure,
    and is dragged off to face King Death.
¹⁵ Now anyone may live in his tent—*k*
    after sulphur is sprinkled to disinfect
        it!*l*
¹⁶ His roots and branches are withered
    and dry.

¹⁷ His fame is ended at home and abroad;
    no one remembers him any more.
¹⁸ He will be driven out of the land of
    the living,
    driven from light into darkness.
¹⁹ He has no descendants, no survivors.
²⁰ From east to west, all who hear of
    his fate
    shudder and tremble with fear.
²¹ That is the fate of evil men,
    the fate of those who care nothing
        for God.

19   Job

¹⁻² Why do you keep tormenting
    me with words?
³ Time after time you insult me
    and show no shame for the way you
        abuse me.
⁴ Even if I have done wrong,
    how does that hurt you?
⁵ You think you are better than I am,
    and regard my troubles as proof of
        my guilt.
⁶ Can't you see it is God who has done
    this?
    He has set a trap to catch me.
⁷ I protest against his violence,
    but no one is listening;
    no one hears my cry for justice.
⁸ God has blocked the way, and I can't
    get through;
    he has hidden my path in darkness.
⁹ He has taken away all my wealth
    and destroyed my reputation.
¹⁰ He batters me from every side.
    He uproots my hope
    and leaves me to wither and die.
¹¹ God is angry and rages against me;
    he treats me like his worst enemy.
¹² He sends his army to attack me;
    they dig trenches and lay siege to my
        tent.

¹³ God has made my brothers forsake
    me;
    I am a stranger to those who knew
        me;
¹⁴   my relatives and friends are gone.
¹⁵ Those who were guests in my house
    have forgotten me;
    my servant-girls treat me like a
        stranger and a foreigner.
¹⁶ When I call a servant, he doesn't
    answer—

---

j One ancient translation with me; *Hebrew unclear.*
k Now anyone may live in his tent; *Hebrew unclear.*
l TO DISINFECT IT: *Sulphur was used in the ancient world as a disinfectant and to clean rooms
that had contained corpses.*
18.5–6: Job 21.17

even when I beg him to help me.

17 My wife can't stand the smell of my
    breath,
    and my own brothers won't come
      near me.
18 Children despise me and laugh when
    they see me.
19 My closest friends look at me with
    disgust;
    those I loved most have turned
      against me.
20 My skin hangs loose on my bones;
    I have barely escaped with my life. *m*

21 You are my friends! Take pity on me!

You are my friends! Take pity on me!
(19.21)

    The hand of God has struck me down.
22 Why must you persecute me as God
    does?
    Haven't you tormented me enough?

23 How I wish that someone would
    remember my words
    and record them in a book!
24 Or with a chisel carve my words in
    stone
    and write them so that they would
      last for ever. *n*
25 But I know there is someone in heaven
    who will come at last to my defence.
26 Even after my skin is eaten by disease,
    while still in this body *o* I will see God. *p*
27 I will see him with my own eyes,

and he will not be a stranger.

My courage failed because you said,
28   "How can we torment him?"
    You looked for some excuse to attack
    me.
29 But now, be afraid of the sword—
    the sword that brings God's wrath on
    sin,
    so that you will know there is one
      who judges. *q*

20   *Zophar*
1-2 Job, you upset me. Now I'm
     impatient to answer.
3   What you have said is an insult,
    but I know how to reply to you.

4 Surely you know that from ancient
    times,
    when man was first placed on earth,
5   no wicked man has been happy for
    long.
6 He may grow great, towering to the sky,
    so great that his head reaches the
      clouds,
7   but he will be blown away like dust.
  Those who used to know him
    will wonder where he has gone.
8 He will vanish like a dream, like a vision
    at night,
    and never be seen again.
9 He will disappear from the place where
    he used to live;
10   and his sons will make good what
    he stole from the poor.
11 His body used to be young and
    vigorous,
    but soon it will turn to dust.

12-13 Evil tastes so good to him
    that he keeps some in his mouth to
    enjoy its flavour.
14 But in his stomach the food turns
    bitter,
    as bitter as any poison could be.
15 The wicked man vomits up the wealth
    he stole;
    God takes it back, even out of his
      stomach.
16 What the evil man swallows is like
    poison;
    it kills him like the bite of a deadly
      snake.
17 He will not live to see rivers of olive-
    oil *r*

m Verse 20 in Hebrew is unclear.   *n last for ever; or be on record.*
o while still in this body; or although not in this body.   *p Verse 26 in Hebrew is unclear.*
q one who judges; or a judgement.   *r Probable text He will...olive-oil; Hebrew unclear.*

or streams that flow with milk and
honey.

18 He will have to give up all he has
worked for;

he will have no chance to enjoy his
wealth,

19 because he oppressed and neglected
the poor

and seized houses someone else had
built.

20 His greed is never satisfied.

21 When he eats, there is nothing left
over,

but now his prosperity comes to an
end.

22 At the height of his success
all the weight of misery will crush
him.

23 Let him eat all he wants!
God will punish him in fury and anger.

24 When he tries to escape from an iron
sword,

a bronze bow will shoot him down.

25 An arrow sticks through his body;
its shiny point drips with his blood,
and terror grips his heart.

26 Everything he has saved is destroyed;
a fire not lit by human hands
burns him and all his family.

27 Heaven reveals this man's sin,
and the earth gives testimony against
him.

28 All his wealth will be destroyed
in the flood of God's anger.

29 This is the fate of wicked men,
the fate that God assigns to them.

21 Job

1-2 Listen to what I am saying;
that is all the comfort I ask from you.

3 Give me a chance to speak and then,
when I am through, sneer if you like.

4 My quarrel is not with mortal men;
I have good reason to be impatient.

5 Look at me. Isn't that enough
to make you stare in shocked silence?

6 When I think of what has happened to
me,

I am stunned, and I tremble and shake.

7 Why does God let evil men live,
let them grow old and prosper?

8 They have children and grandchildren,
and live to watch them all grow up.

9 God does not bring disaster on their
homes;

they never have to live in terror.

10 Yes, all their cattle breed

and give birth without trouble.

11 Their children run and play like lambs

12 and dance to the music of harps and
flutes.

13 They live out their lives in peace
and quietly die without suffering.

14 The wicked tell God to leave them
alone;

they don't want to know his will for
their lives.

15 They think there is no need to serve
God

nor any advantage in praying to him.

16 They claim they succeed by their own
strength,

but their way of thinking I can't
accept.

17 Was a wicked man's light ever put
out?

Did one of them ever meet with
disaster?

Did God ever punish the wicked in anger

18 and blow them away like straw in
the wind,

or like dust carried away in a storm?

19 You claim God punishes a child for
the sins of his father.

No! Let God punish the sinners
themselves;

let him show that he does it because
of *their* sins.

20 Let sinners bear their own
punishment;

let them feel the wrath of Almighty
God.

21 When a man's life is over,
does he really care whether his
children are happy?

22 Can a man teach God,
who judges even those in high places?

23-24 Some men stay healthy till the day
they die;

they die happy and at ease,
their bodies well-nourished.

25 Others have no happiness at all;
they live and die with bitter hearts.

26 But all alike die and are buried;
they all are covered with worms.

27 I know what spiteful thoughts you
have.

28 You ask, "Where is the house of the
great man now,

the man who practised evil?"

29 Haven't you talked with people who
    travel?
    Don't you know the reports they bring
    back?
30 On the day God is angry and punishes,
    it is the wicked man who is always
    spared.
31 There is no one to accuse a wicked
    man
    or pay him back for all he has done.
32 When he is carried to the graveyard,
    to his well-guarded tomb,
33   thousands join the funeral
        ʾprocession,
    and even the earth lies gently on his
    body.

34 And you! You try to comfort me with
    nonsense!
    Every answer you give is a lie!

The Third Dialogue
(22.1—27.23)

22 *Eliphaz*
    1-2 Is there any man, even the
        wisest,
    who could ever be of use to God?
3 Does your doing right benefit God,
    or does your being good help him at
    all?
4 It is not because you stand in awe of
    God
    that he reprimands you and brings
    you to trial.
5 No, it's because you have sinned so
    much;
    it's because of all the evil you do.
6 To make your brother repay you the
    money he owed,
    you took away his clothes and left
    him nothing to wear.
7 You refused water to those who were
    tired,
    and refused to feed those who were
    hungry.
8 You used your power and your position
    to take over the whole land.
9 You not only refused to help widows,
    but you also robbed and ill-treated
    orphans.
10 So now there are pitfalls all round you,
    and suddenly you are full of fear.
11 It has grown so dark that you cannot
    see,

and a flood overwhelms you.
12 Doesn't God live in the highest heavens
    and look down on the stars, even
    though they are high?
13 And yet you ask, "What does God
    know?
    He is hidden by clouds—how can he
    judge us?"
14 You think the thick clouds keep him
    from seeing,
    as he walks on the dome of the sky.

15 Are you determined to walk in the
    paths
    that evil men have always followed?
16 Even before their time had come,
    they were washed away by a flood.
17 These are the men who rejected God
    and believed that he could do nothing
    to them.
18 And yet it was God who made them
    prosperous—
    I can't understand the thoughts of the
    wicked.
19 Good men are glad and innocent men
    laugh
    when they see the wicked punished.
20 All that the wicked own is destroyed,
    and fire burns up anything that is left.

21 Now, Job, make peace with God
    and stop treating him like an enemy;
    if you do, then he will bless you.
22 Accept the teaching he gives;
    keep his words in your heart.
23 Yes, you must humbly*s* return to God
    and put an end to all the evil
    that is done in your house.
24 Throw away your gold;
    dump your finest gold in the dry
    stream bed.
25 Let Almighty God be your gold,
    and let him be silver, piled high for
    you.
26 Then you will always trust in God
    and find that he is the source of your
    joy.
27 When you pray, he will answer you,
    and you will keep the vows you made.
28 You will succeed in all you do,
    and light will shine on your path.
29 God brings down the proud*t*
    and saves the humble.
30 He will rescue you if you are innocent*u*,
    if what you do is right. *v*

---

s One ancient translation humbly; *Hebrew* be built up.
t Probable text proud; *Hebrew unclear.*
u Some ancient translations innocent; *Hebrew* not innocent.
v Verse 30 in Hebrew is unclear.
22.2–3: Job 35.6–8

23

Job

¹⁻² I still rebel and complain
　　against God;
　I can't hold back my groaning.
³ How I wish I knew where to find him,
　and knew how to go where he is.
⁴ I would state my case before him
　and present all the arguments in my
　　favour.
⁵ I want to know what he would say
　and how he would answer me.
⁶ Would God use all his strength against
　　me?
　No, he would listen as I spoke.
⁷ I am honest; I could reason with God;
　he would declare me innocent *w* once
　　and for all.

⁸ I have searched in the east, but God
　　is not there;
　I have not found him when I searched
　　in the west.
⁹ God has been at work in the north and
　　the south,
　but still I have not seen him.
¹⁰ Yet God knows every step I take;
　if he tests me, he will find me pure.
¹¹ I follow faithfully the road he chooses,
　and never wander to either side.
¹² I always do what God commands;
　I follow his will, not my own desires.

¹³ He never changes. No one can oppose
　　him
　or stop him from doing what he wants
　　to do.
¹⁴ He will fulfil what he has planned for
　　me;
　that plan is just one of the many he
　　has;
¹⁵ 　I tremble with fear before him.
¹⁶⁻¹⁷ Almighty God has destroyed my
　　courage.
　It is God, not the dark, that makes me
　　afraid—
　even though the darkness has made
　　me blind.

24

Why doesn't God set a time for
　　judging,
　a day of justice for those who serve
　　him?

² Men move boundary stones to get more
　　land;
　they steal sheep and put them with
　　their own flocks.

I tremble with fear before him (23.15)

³ They take donkeys that belong to
　　orphans,
　and keep a widow's ox till she pays
　　her debts.
⁴ They prevent the poor from getting their
　　rights
　and force the needy to run and hide.

⁵ So the poor, like wild donkeys,
　search for food in the dry wilderness;
　nowhere else can they find food for
　　their children.
⁶ They have to harvest fields they don't
　　own, *x*
　and gather grapes in wicked men's
　　vineyards.
⁷ At night they sleep with nothing to
　　cover them,
　nothing to keep them from the cold.
⁸ They are drenched by the rain that falls
　　on the mountains,
　and they huddle beside the rocks for
　　shelter.

⁹ Evil men make slaves of fatherless
　　infants
　and take the poor man's children in
　　payment for debts.
¹⁰ But the poor must go out with no
　　clothes to protect them;
　they must go hungry while harvesting
　　wheat.
¹¹ They press olives for oil, and grapes
　　for wine,
　but they themselves are thirsty.

---

w he would declare me innocent; *or* then my rights would be safe.
x FIELDS THEY DON'T OWN: *Having been cheated out of their own land, the poor are forced to work
for others for very small pay.*

12 In the cities the wounded and dying
         cry out,
     but God ignores their prayers.

13 There are men who reject the light;
     they don't understand it or go where
         it leads.
14 At dawn the murderer gets up
     and goes out to kill the poor,
     and at night he steals.
15 The adulterer waits for twilight to
         come;
     he covers his face so that no one can
         see him.
16 At night thieves break into houses,
     but by day they hide and avoid the
         light.
17 They fear the light of day,
     but darkness holds no terror for them.

[Zophar]y
18 The wicked man is swept away by
         floods,
     and the land he owns is under God's
         curse;
     he no longer goes to work in his
         vineyards.
19 As snow vanishes in heat and drought,
     so a sinner vanishes from the land
         of the living.
20 Not even his mother remembers him
         now;
     he is eaten by worms and destroyed
         like a fallen tree.
21 That happens because he ill-treated
         widows
     and showed no kindness to childless
         women.
22 God, in his strength, destroys the
         mighty;
     God acts—and the wicked man dies.
23 God may let him live secure,
     but keeps an eye on him all the time.
24 For a while the wicked man prospers,
     but then he withers like a weed,
     like an ear of corn that has been cut
         off.
25 Can anyone deny that this is so?
     Can anyone prove that my words are
         not true?

25   *Bildad*
         1-2 God is powerful; all must
                 stand in awe of him;
     he keeps his heavenly kingdom in
         peace.

3 Can anyone count the angels who serve
         him?
     Is there any place where God's light
         does not shine?
4 Can anyone be righteous or pure in
         God's sight?
5 In his eyes even the moon is not bright,
     nor the stars pure.
6 Then what about man, that worm, that
         insect?
     What is man worth in God's eyes?

26   *Job*
         1-2 What a fine help you are to
                 me—
     poor, weak man that I am!
3 You give such good advice
     and share your knowledge with a fool
         like me!
4 Who do you think will hear all your
         words?
     Who inspired you to speak like this?

[Bildad]z
5 The spirits of the dead tremble
     in the waters under the earth.
6 The world of the dead lies open to God;
     no covering shields it from his sight.
7 God stretched out the northern sky
     and hung the earth in empty space.
8 It is God who fills the clouds with water
     and keeps them from bursting with
         the weight.
9 He hides the full moon behind a cloud.
10 He divided light from darkness
     by a circle drawn on the face of the
         sea.
11 When he threatens the pillars that hold
         up the sky,
     they shake and tremble with fear.
12 It is his strength that conquered the
         sea;a
     by his skill he destroyed the monster
         Rahab.b
13 It is his breath that made the sky clear,
     and his hand that killed the escaping
         monster.c
14 But these are only hints of his power,
     only the whispers that we have heard.
     Who can know how truly great God
         is?

27   *Job*
         1-2 I swear by the living Almighty
                 God,

yZophar *is not named in the text, but this speech is usually assigned to him.*
zBildad *is not named in the text, but this speech is usually assigned to him.*
aCONQUERED THE SEA: *A reference to an ancient story in which the sea fought against God.*
bRAHAB: *See 9.13.*   cESCAPING MONSTER: *See 9.8.*

who refuses me justice and makes my
life bitter—
3 as long as God gives me breath,
4 my lips will never say anything evil,
my tongue will never tell a lie.
5 I will never say that you men are right;
I will insist on my innocence to my
dying day.
6 I will never give up my claim to be
right;
my conscience is clear.

7 May all who oppose me and fight
against me
be punished like wicked, unrighteous
men.
8 What hope is there for godless men
in the hour when God demands their
life?
9 When trouble comes, will God hear their
cries?
10 They should have desired the joy he
gives;
they should have constantly prayed
to him.

11 Let me teach you how great is God's
power,
and explain what Almighty God has
planned.
12 But no, after all, you have seen for
yourselves;
so why do you talk such nonsense?

[Zophar]d
13 This is how Almighty God
punishes wicked, violent men.
14 They may have many sons,
but all will be killed in war;
their children never have enough to
eat.
15 Those who survive will die from
disease,
and even their widows will not mourn
their death.
16 The wicked may have too much silver
to count
and more clothes than anyone needs;
17 but some good man will wear the
clothes,
and some honest man will get the
silver.
18 The wicked build houses like a spider's
webe

or like the hut of a slave guarding
the fields.
19 One last timef they will lie down rich,
and when they wake up, they will
find their wealth gone.
20 Terror will strike like a sudden flood;
a wind in the night will blow them
away;
21 the east wind will sweep them from
their homes;
22 it will blow down on them without
pity
while they try their best to escape.
23 The wind howls at them as they run,
frightening them with destructive
power.

In Praise of Wisdomg

28 There are mines where silver is
dug;
There are places where gold is refined.
2 Men dig iron out of the ground
And melt copper out of the stones.
3 Men explore the deepest darkness.
They search the depths of the earth
And dig for rocks in the darkness.
4 Far from where anyone lives
Or human feet ever travel,
Men dig the shafts of mines.
There they work in loneliness,
Clinging to ropes in the pits.
5 Food grows out of the earth,
But underneath the same earth
All is torn up and crushed.
6 The stones of the earth contain
sapphires,
And its dust contains gold.
7 No hawk sees the roads to the mines,
And no vulture ever flies over them.
8 No lion or other fierce beast
Ever travels those lonely roads.

9 Men dig the hardest rocks,
Dig mountains away at their base.
10 As they tunnel through the rocks,
They discover precious stones.
11 They dig to the sources ofh rivers
And bring to light what is hidden.
12 But where can wisdom be found?
Where can we learn to understand?

13 Wisdom is not to be found among men;
No one knows its true value.
14 The depths of the oceans and seas
Say that wisdom is not found there.

---

dZophar is not named in the text, but this speech is usually assigned to him.
e Some ancient translations spider's web; Hebrew moth or bird's nest.
f Some ancient translations One last time; Hebrew They will not be gathered.
g The Hebrew text does not indicate who is speaking in this chapter.
h Some ancient translations dig to the sources of; Hebrew bind from trickling.

15 It cannot be bought with silver or gold.
16 The finest gold and jewels
Cannot equal its value.
17 It is worth more than gold,
Than a gold vase or finest glass.
18 The value of wisdom is more
Than coral or crystal or rubies.
19 The finest topaz and the purest gold
Cannot compare with the value of
wisdom.

20 Where, then, is the source of wisdom?
Where can we learn to understand?
21 No living creature can see it,
Not even a bird in flight.
22 Even death and destruction
Admit they have heard only rumours.

23 God alone knows the way,
Knows the place where wisdom is found,
24 Because he sees the ends of the earth,
Sees everything under the sky.
25 When God gave the wind its power
And determined the size of the sea;
26 When God decided where the rain
would fall,
And the path that the thunderclouds
travel;
27 It was then he saw wisdom and tested
its worth—
He gave it his approval.

28 God said to men,
"To be wise, you must have reverence
for the Lord.
To understand, you must turn from
evil."

Job's Final Statement of His Case

29 Job began speaking again.

Job

2 If only my life could once again
be as it was when God watched over
me.
3 God was always with me then
and gave me light as I walked through
the darkness.
4 Those were the days when I was
prosperous,
and the friendship of God protected
my home.
5 Almighty God was with me then,
and I was surrounded by all my
children.
6 My cows and goats gave plenty of milk,
and my olive-trees grew in the
rockiest soil.
7 Whenever the city elders met
and I took my place among them,

28.28: Ps 111.10; Prov 1.7, 9.10

8 young men stepped aside as soon as
they saw me,
and old men stood up to show me
respect.
9 The leaders of the people would stop
talking;
10 even the most important men kept
silent.
11 Everyone who saw me or heard of me
had good things to say about what
I had done.
12 When the poor cried out, I helped
them;
I gave help to orphans who had
nowhere to turn.
13 Men who were in deepest misery
praised me,
and I helped widows find security.
14 I have always acted justly and fairly.
15 I was eyes for the blind,
and feet for the lame.
16 I was like a father to the poor
and took the side of strangers in
trouble.
17 I destroyed the power of cruel men
and rescued their victims.

18 I always expected to live a long life
and to die at home in comfort.
19 I was like a tree whose roots always
have water
and whose branches are wet with dew.
20 Everyone was always praising me,
and my strength never failed me.
21 When I gave advice, people were silent
and listened carefully to what I said;
22 they had nothing to add when I had
finished.
My words sank in like drops of rain;
23 everyone welcomed them
just as farmers welcome rain in
spring.
24 I smiled on them when they had lost
confidence;
my cheerful face encouraged them.
25 I took charge and made the decisions;
I led them as a king leads his troops,
and gave them comfort in their
despair.

30 But men younger than I am make
fun of me now!
Their fathers have always been so
worthless
that I wouldn't let them help my dogs
guard sheep.
2 They were a bunch of worn-out men,
too weak to do any work for me.

³ They were so poor and hungry
     that they would gnaw dry roots—
     at night, in wild, desolate places.
⁴ They pulled up the plants of the desert
     and ate them,
     even the tasteless roots of the broom-
     tree!
⁵ Everyone drove them away with shouts,
     as if they were shouting at thieves.
⁶ They had to live in caves,
     in holes dug in the sides of cliffs.
⁷ Out in the wilds they howled like animals
     and huddled together under the
     bushes.
⁸ A worthless bunch of nameless
     nobodies!
     They were driven out of the land.

⁹ Now they come and laugh at me;
     I am nothing but a joke to them.
¹⁰ They treat me with disgust;
     they think they are too good for me,
     and even come and spit in my face.
¹¹ Because God has made me weak and
     helpless,
     they turn against me with all their
     fury.
¹² This mob attacks me head-on;
     they send me running; they prepare
     their final assault.
¹³ They cut off my escape and try to
     destroy me;
     and there is no one to stop *i* them.
¹⁴ They pour through the holes in my
     defences
     and come crashing down on top of
     me;
¹⁵ I am overcome with terror;
     my dignity is gone like a puff of wind,
     and my prosperity like a cloud.

¹⁶ Now I am about to die;
     there is no relief for my suffering.
¹⁷ At night my bones all ache;
     the pain that gnaws me never stops.
¹⁸ God seizes me by my collar
     and twists my clothes out of shape.
¹⁹ He throws me down in the mud;
     I am no better than dirt.

²⁰ I call to you, O God, but you never
     answer;
     and when I pray, you pay no attention.
²¹ You are treating me cruelly;
     you persecute me with all your power.
²² You let the wind blow me away;
     you toss me about in a raging storm.
²³ I know you are taking me off to my
     death,

He throws me down in the mud (30.19)

     to the fate in store for everyone.
²⁴ Why do you attack a ruined man,
     one who can do nothing but beg for
     pity?*j*
²⁵ Didn't I weep with people in trouble
     and feel sorry for those in need?
²⁶ I hoped for happiness and light,
     but trouble and darkness came
     instead.
²⁷ I am torn apart by worry and pain;
     I have had day after day of suffering.
²⁸ I go about in gloom, without any
     sunshine;
     I stand up in public and plead for
     help.
²⁹ My voice is as sad and lonely
     as the cries of a jackal or an ostrich.
³⁰ My skin has turned dark; I am burning
     with fever.
³¹ Where once I heard joyful music,
     now I hear only mourning and
     weeping.

31   I have made a solemn promise
     never to look with lust at a girl.

² What does Almighty God do to us?
     How does he repay human deeds?
³ He sends disaster and ruin
     to those who do wrong.
⁴ God knows everything I do;
     he sees every step I take.

⁵ I swear I have never acted wickedly
     and never tried to deceive others.
⁶ Let God weigh me on honest scales,

---

i Probable text stop; *Hebrew* help.   *j Verse 24 in Hebrew is unclear.*

and he will see how innocent I am.
7 If I have turned from the right path
or let myself be attracted to evil,
if my hands are stained with sin,
8 then let my crops be destroyed,
or let others eat the food I grow.

9 If I have been attracted to my
neighbour's wife,
and waited, hidden, outside her door,
10 then let my wife cook another man's
food
and sleep in another man's bed.
11 Such wickedness should be punished
by death.
12 It would be like a destructive, hellish
fire,
consuming everything I have.

13 When one of my servants complained
against me,
I would listen and treat him fairly.
14 If I did not, how could I then face
God?
What could I say when God came
to judge me?
15 The same God who created me
created my servants also.

16 I have never refused to help the poor;
never have I let widows live in despair
17 or let orphans go hungry while I ate.
18 All my life I have taken care of them. *k*

19 When I found someone in need,
too poor to buy clothes,
20 I would give him clothing made of
wool
that had come from my own flock
of sheep.
Then he would praise me with all his
heart.

21 If I have ever cheated an orphan,
knowing I could win in court,
22 then may my arms be broken;
may they be torn from my shoulders.
23 Because I fear God's punishment,
I could never do such a thing.

24 I have never trusted in riches
25 or taken pride in my wealth.
26 I have never worshipped the sun in
its brightness
or the moon in all its beauty.
27 I have not been led astray to honour
them
by kissing my hand in reverence to
them.

28 Such a sin should be punished by
death;
it denies Almighty God.

29 I have never been glad when my
enemies suffered,
or pleased when they met with
disaster;
30 I never sinned by praying for their
death.
31 All the men who work for me know
that I have always welcomed
strangers.
32 I invited travellers into my home
and never let them sleep in the streets.

33 Other men try to hide their sins,
but I have never concealed mine.
34 I have never feared what people would
say;
I have never kept quiet or stayed
indoors
because I feared their scorn.

35 Will no one listen to what I am saying?
I swear that every word is true.
Let Almighty God answer me.

If the charges my opponent brings
against me
were written down so that I could
see them,
36 I would wear them proudly on my
shoulder
and place them on my head like a
crown.
37 I would tell God everything I have
done,
and hold my head high in his presence.

38 If I have stolen the land I farm
and taken it from its rightful owners—
39 if I have eaten the food that grew
there
but let the farmers that grew it
starve—
40 then instead of wheat and barley,
may weeds and thistles grow.

The words of Job are ended.

Elihu's Speech
(32.1—37.24)

32 Because Job was convinced of his
own innocence, the three men gave
up trying to answer him. 2 But a bystander
named Elihu could not control his anger
any longer, because Job was justifying
himself and blaming God. (Elihu was the

k All my life...them; *Hebrew unclear.*

son of Barakel, a descendant of Buz, and belonged to the clan of Ram.) ³He was also angry with Job's three friends. They could find no way to answer Job, and this made it appear that God was in the wrong. ⁴Because Elihu was the youngest one there, he had waited until everyone finished speaking. ⁵When he saw that the three men could not answer Job, he was angry ⁶and began to speak.

Elihu

I am young, and you are old,
　　so I was afraid to tell you what I
　　think.
⁷I told myself that you ought to speak,
　　that you older men should share your
　　wisdom.
⁸But it is the spirit of Almighty God
　　that comes to men and gives them
　　wisdom.
⁹It is not growing old that makes men
　　wise
　　or helps them to know what is right.
¹⁰So now I want you to listen to me;
　　let me tell you what I think.

¹¹I listened patiently while you were
　　speaking
　　and waited while you searched for
　　wise phrases.
¹²I paid close attention and heard you
　　fail;
　　you have not disproved what Job has
　　said.
¹³How can you claim you have
　　discovered wisdom?
　　God must answer Job, for you have
　　failed.
¹⁴Job was speaking to you, not to me,
　　but I would never answer as you did.

¹⁵Words have failed them, Job;
　　they have no answer for you.
¹⁶Shall I go on waiting when they are
　　silent?
　　They stand there with nothing more
　　to say.
¹⁷No, I will give my own answer now
　　and tell you what I think.
¹⁸I can hardly wait to speak.
　　I can't hold back the words.
¹⁹If I don't get a chance to speak,
　　I will burst like a wineskin full of
　　new wine.
²⁰I can't stand it; I have to speak.
²¹I will not take sides in this debate;
　　I am not going to flatter anyone.
²²I don't know how to flatter,

and God would quickly punish me if
　　I did.

33 And now, Job, listen carefully
　　to all that I have to say.
²I am ready to say what's on my mind.
³All my words are sincere,
　　and I am speaking the truth.
⁴God's spirit made me and gave me life.

⁵Answer me if you can. Prepare your
　　arguments.
⁶You and I are the same in God's sight,
　　both of us were formed from clay.
⁷So you have no reason to fear me;
　　I will not overpower you.

⁸Now this is what I heard you say:
⁹"I am not guilty; I have done nothing
　　wrong.
　　I am innocent and free from sin.
¹⁰But God finds excuses for attacking
　　me
　　and treats me like an enemy.
¹¹He binds chains on my feet;
　　he watches every move I make."

¹²But I tell you, Job, you are wrong.
　　God is greater than any man.
¹³Why do you accuse God
　　of never answering a man's
　　complaints?
¹⁴Although God speaks again and again,
　　no one pays attention to what he says.
¹⁵At night when men are asleep,
　　God speaks in dreams and visions.
¹⁶He makes them listen to what he says,
　　and they are frightened at his
　　warnings.
¹⁷God speaks to make them stop their
　　sinning
　　and to save them from becoming
　　proud.
¹⁸He will not let them be destroyed;
　　he saves them from death itself.
¹⁹God corrects a man by sending
　　sickness
　　and filling his body with pain.
²⁰The sick man loses his appetite,
　　and even the finest food looks
　　revolting.
²¹His body wastes away to nothing;
　　you can see all his bones;
²² he is about to go to the world of
　　the dead.

²³Perhaps an angel may come to his
　　aid—
　　one of God's thousands of angels,

who remind men of their duty.

24 In mercy the angel will say, "Release him!
He is not to go down to the world of the dead.
Here is the ransom to set him free."

25 His body will grow young and strong again;

26 when he prays, God will answer him;
he will worship God with joy;
God will set things right for him again.

27 He will say in public, "I have sinned.
I have not done right, but God spared me.

28 He kept me from going to the world of the dead,
and I am still alive."

29 God does all this again and again;

30 he saves a person's life,
and gives him the joy of living.

31 Now, Job, listen to what I am saying;
be quiet and let me speak.

32 But if you have something to say, let me hear it;
I would gladly admit you are in the right.

33 But if not, be quiet and listen to me,
and I will teach you how to be wise.

34

1-2 You men are so wise, so clever;
listen now to what I am saying.

3 You know good food when you taste it,
but not wise words when you hear them.

4 It is up to us to decide the case.

5 Job claims that he is innocent,
that God refuses to give him justice.

6 He asks, "How could I lie and say I am wrong?
I am fatally wounded, but I am sinless."

7 Have you ever seen anyone like this man Job?
He never shows respect for God.

8 He likes the company of evil men
and goes about with sinners.

9 He says that it never does any good
to try to follow God's will.

10 Listen to me, you men who understand!
Will Almighty God do what is wrong?

11 He rewards people for what they do
and treats them as they deserve.

12 Almighty God does not do evil;
he is never unjust to anyone.

13 Did God get his power from someone else?
Did someone put him in charge of the world?

14 If God took back the breath of life,

15 then everyone living would die
and turn into dust again.

16 Now listen to me, if you are wise.

17 Are you condemning the righteous God?
Do you think that he hates justice?

18 God condemns kings and rulers
when they are worthless or wicked.

19 He does not take the side of rulers
nor favour the rich against the poor,
for he created everyone.

20 A man may suddenly die at night.
God strikes men down and they perish;
he kills the mighty with no effort at all.

21 He watches every step men take.

22 There is no darkness dark enough
to hide a sinner from God.

23 God does not need to set a time[1]
for men to go and be judged by him.

24 He does not need an investigation
to remove leaders and replace them with others.

25 Because he knows what they do
he overthrows them and crushes them by night.

26 He punishes sinners where all can see it,

27 because they have stopped following him
and ignored all his commands.

28 They forced the poor to cry out to God,
and he heard their calls for help.

29 If God decided to do nothing at all,
no one could criticize him.
If he hid his face, men would be helpless.

30 There would be nothing that nations could do
to keep godless oppressors from ruling them.

31 Job, have you confessed your sins to God
and promised not to sin again?

32 Have you asked God to show you your faults,

---

l Probable text a time; Hebrew yet.
34.3: Job 12.11   **34.11:** Ps 62.12

and have you agreed to stop doing evil?

33 Since you object to what God does,
can you expect him to do what you want?
The decision is yours, not mine;
tell us now what you think.

34 Any sensible person will surely agree;
any wise man who hears me will say

35 that Job is speaking from ignorance
and that nothing he says makes sense.

36 Think through everything that Job says;
you will see that he talks like an evil man.

37 To his sins he adds rebellion;
in front of us all he mocks God.

35

1-2 It is not right, Job, for you to say
that you are innocent in God's sight,

3 or to ask God, "How does my sin affect you?
What have I gained by not sinning?"

4 I am going to answer you and your friends too.

5 Look at the sky! See how high the clouds are!

6 If you sin, that does no harm to God.
If you do wrong many times, does that affect him?

7 Do you help God by being so righteous?
There is nothing God needs from you.

8 It is your fellow-man who suffers from your sins,
and the good you do helps him.

9 When men are oppressed, they groan;
they cry for someone to save them.

10 But they don't turn to God, their Creator,
who gives them hope in their darkest hours.

11 They don't turn to God, who makes us wise,
wiser than any animal or bird.

12 They cry for help, but God doesn't answer,
for they are proud and evil men.

13 It is useless for them to cry out;
Almighty God does not see or hear them.

14 Job, you say you can't see God;
but wait patiently—your case is before him.

15 You think that God does not punish,

35.6-8: Job 22.2-3

that he pays little attention to sin.

16 It is useless for you to go on talking;
it is clear you don't know what you are saying.

36

1-2 Be patient and listen a little longer
to what I am saying on God's behalf.

3 My knowledge is wide; I will use what I know
to show that God, my Creator, is just.

4 Nothing I say to you is false;
you see before you a truly wise man.

5 How strong God is! He despises no one;
there is nothing he doesn't understand.

6 He does not let sinners live on,
and he always treats the poor with justice.

7 He protects those who are righteous;
he allows them to rule like kings
and lets them be honoured for ever.

8 But if people are bound in chains,
suffering for what they have done,

9 God shows them their sins and their pride.

10 He makes them listen to his warning
to turn away from evil.

11 If they obey God and serve him,
they live out their lives in peace and prosperity.

12 But if not, they will die in ignorance
and cross the stream into the world of the dead.

13 Those who are godless keep on being angry,
and even when punished, they don't pray for help.

14 They die while they are still young,
worn out by a life of disgrace.

15 But God teaches men through suffering
and uses distress to open their eyes.

16 God brought you out of trouble,
and let you enjoy security;
your table was piled high with food.

17 But now you are being punished as you deserve.

18 Be careful not to let bribes deceive you,
or riches lead you astray.

19 It will do you no good to cry out for help;
all your strength can't help you now.

20 Don't wish for night to come,
the time when nations will perish.

21 Be careful not to turn to evil;

Everyone has seen what he has done (36.25)

your suffering was sent to keep you
   from it.
²² Remember how great is God's power;
   he is the greatest teacher of all.
²³ No one can tell God what to do
   or accuse him of doing evil.
²⁴ He has always been praised for what
   he does;
   you also must praise him.
²⁵ Everyone has seen what he has done;
   but we can only watch from a
   distance. ᵐ
²⁶ We cannot fully know his greatness
   or count the number of his years.

²⁷ It is God who takes water from the
   earth
   and turns it into drops of rain.
²⁸ He lets the rain pour from the clouds
   in showers for all mankind.
²⁹ No one knows how the clouds move
   or how the thunder roars
   through the sky, where God dwells.
³⁰ He sends lightning through all the sky,
   but the depths of the sea remain dark.
³¹ This is how he feeds ⁿ the people
   and provides an abundance of food.
³² He seizes the lightning with his hands
   and commands it to hit the mark.
³³ Thunder announces the approaching
   storm,

and the cattle know it is coming.
37 The storm makes my heart beat
   wildly.
² Listen, all of you, to the voice of God,
   to the thunder that comes from his
   mouth.
³ He sends the lightning across the sky,
   from one end of the earth to the other.
⁴ Then the roar of his voice is heard,
   the majestic sound of thunder,
   and all the while the lightning flashes.
⁵ At God's command amazing things
   happen,
   wonderful things that we can't
   understand.
⁶ He commands snow to fall on the earth,
   and sends torrents of drenching rain.
⁷ He brings the work of men to a stop;
   he shows them what he can do. ˣ
⁸ The wild animals go to their dens.
⁹ The storm winds come from the south,
   and the biting cold from the north.
¹⁰ The breath of God freezes the waters,
   and turns them to solid ice.
¹¹ Lightning flashes from the clouds, ᵒ
¹²   as they move at God's will.
   They do all that God commands,
   everywhere throughout the world.
¹³ God sends rain to water the earth;
   he may send it to punish men,
   or to show them his favour.

ᵐ but we can only watch from a distance; *or* no one understands it all.
ⁿ *Probable text* feeds; *Hebrew* judges.
ˣ *One ancient translation* them what he can do; *Hebrew* this to those whom he has made.
ᵒ *Verse 11 in Hebrew is unclear.*

14 Pause a moment, Job, and listen;
      consider the wonderful things God
      does.
15 Do you know how God gives the
      command
      and makes lightning flash from the
      clouds?
16 Do you know how clouds float in the
      sky,
      the work of God's amazing skill?
17 No, you can only suffer in the heat
      when the south wind oppresses the
      land.
18 Can you help God stretch out the sky
      and make it as hard as polished
      metal?
19 Teach us what to say to God;
      our minds are blank; we have nothing
      to say.
20 I won't ask to speak with God;
      why should I give him a chance to
      destroy me?

21 And now the light in the sky is
      dazzling,
      too bright for us to look at it;
      and the sky has been swept clean by
      the wind.
22 A golden glow is seen in the north,
      and the glory of God fills us with awe.
23 God's power is so great that we cannot
      come near him;
      he is righteous and just in his dealings
      with men.
24 No wonder, then, that everyone stands
      in awe of him,
      and that he ignores those who claim
      to be wise.

The LORD Answers Job

38 Then out of the storm the LORD
      spoke to Job.

The LORD
2 Who are you to question my wisdom
      with your ignorant, empty words?
3 Stand up now like a man
      and answer the questions I ask you.
4 Were you there when I made the world?
      If you know so much, tell me about
      it.
5 Who decided how large it would be?
      Who stretched the measuring-line
      over it?
      Do you know all the answers?
6 What holds up the pillars *p* that support
      the earth?

Who laid the corner-stone of the
      world?
7 In the dawn of that day the stars sang
      together,
      and the heavenly beings *q* shouted for
      joy.
8 Who closed the gates to hold back the
      sea *r*
      when it burst from the womb of the
      earth?
9 It was I who covered the sea with clouds
      and wrapped it in darkness.
10 I marked a boundary for the sea
      and kept it behind bolted gates.
11 I told it, "So far and no farther!
      Here your powerful waves must stop."
12 Job, have you ever in all your life
      commanded a day to dawn?
13 Have you ordered the dawn to seize
      the earth
      and shake the wicked from their
      hiding places?
14 Daylight makes the hills and valleys
      stand out
      like the folds of a garment,
      clear as the imprint of a seal on clay.
15 The light of day is too bright for the
      wicked
      and restrains them from deeds of
      violence.

16 Have you been to the springs in the
      depths of the sea?
      Have you walked on the floor of the
      ocean?
17 Has anyone ever shown you the gates
      that guard the dark world of the dead?
18 Have you any idea how big the world
      is?
      Answer me if you know.

19 Do you know where the light comes
      from
      or what the source of darkness is?
20 Can you show them how far to go,
      or send them back again?
21 I am sure you can, because you're so
      old
      and were there when the world was
      made!

22 Have you ever visited the storerooms,
      where I keep the snow and the hail?
23 I keep them ready for times of trouble,
      for days of battle and war.
24 Have you been to the place where the
      sun comes up,

---

p PILLARS: *See 9.6.*   *q* HEAVENLY BEINGS: *See 1.6.*   *r* TO HOLD BACK THE SEA: *See 26.12.*
38.8–11: Jer 5.22

or the place from which the east wind
blows?

25 Who dug a channel for the pouring
rain
and cleared the way for the
thunderstorm?
26 Who makes rain fall where no one
lives?
27 Who waters the dry and thirsty land,
so that grass springs up?
28 Does either the rain or the dew have
a father?
29 Who is the mother of the ice and the
frost,
30 which turn the waters to stone
and freeze the face of the sea?

31 Can you tie the Pleiades together
or loosen the bonds that hold Orion?
32 Can you guide the stars season by
season
and direct the Great and the Little
Bear?
33 Do you know the laws that govern
the skies,
and can you make them apply to the
earth?

34 Can you shout orders to the clouds
and make them drench you with rain?
35 And if you command the lightning to
flash,
will it come to you and say, "At your
service"?
36 Who tells the ibis *s* when the Nile will
flood,
or who tells the cock that rain will
fall? *t*
37 Who is wise enough to count the
clouds
and tilt them over to pour out the
rain,
38 rain that hardens the dust into
lumps?

39 Do you find food for lions to eat,
and satisfy hungry young lions
40 when they hide in their caves,
or lie in wait in their dens?
41 Who is it that feeds the ravens
when they wander about hungry,
when their young cry to me for food?

39 Do you know when mountain-
goats are born?
Have you watched wild deer give
birth?

2 Do you know how long they carry their
young?
Do you know the time for their birth?
3 Do you know when they will crouch
down
and bring their young into the world?
4 In the wilds their young grow strong;
they go away and don't come back.

5 Who gave the wild donkeys their
freedom?
Who turned them loose and let them
roam?
6 I gave them the desert to be their home,
and let them live on the salt plains.
7 They keep far away from the noisy cities,
and no one can tame them and make
them work.
8 The mountains are the pastures where
they feed,
where they search for anything green
to eat.

9 Will a wild ox work for you?
Is he willing to spend the night in
your stable?
10 Can you hold one with a rope and
make him plough?
Or make him pull a harrow in your
fields?
11 Can you rely on his great strength
and expect him to do your heavy
work?
12 Do you expect him to bring in your
harvest
and gather the grain from your
threshing-place?

13 How fast the wings of an ostrich beat!
But no ostrich can fly like a stork. *u*
14 The ostrich leaves her eggs on the
ground
for the heat in the soil to warm them.
15 She is unaware that a foot may crush
them
or a wild animal break them.
16 She acts as if the eggs were not hers,
and is unconcerned that her efforts
were wasted.
17 It was I who made her foolish
and did not give her wisdom.
18 But when she begins to run, *v*
she can laugh at any horse and rider.

*s*IBIS: *A bird in ancient Egypt that was believed to announce the flooding of the River Nile.*
t Verse 36 in Hebrew is unclear.   *u* Verse 13 in Hebrew is unclear.
v Probable text* run; *Hebrew unclear.*
38.31: Job 9.9; Amos 5.8

*The ostrich...the horses...an eagle
...the monster (39.14,24,27; 40.15)*

¹⁹ Was it you, Job, who made horses so
    strong
    and gave them their flowing manes?
²⁰ Did you make them leap like locusts
    and frighten men with their snorting?
²¹ They eagerly paw the ground in the
    valley;
    they rush into battle with all their
    strength.
²² They do not know the meaning of fear,
    and no sword can turn them back.
²³ The weapons which their riders carry
    rattle and flash in the sun.
²⁴ Trembling with excitement, the horses
    race ahead;
    when the trumpet blows, they can't
    stand still.
²⁵ At each blast of the trumpet they
    snort;
    they can smell a battle before they
    get near,
    and they hear the officers shouting
    commands.

39.30: Mt 24.28; Lk 17.37

²⁶ Does a hawk learn from you how to
    fly
    when it spreads its wings towards the
    south?
²⁷ Does an eagle wait for your command
    to build its nest high in the
    mountains?
²⁸ It makes its home on the highest rocks
    and makes the sharp peaks its
    fortress.
²⁹ From there it watches near and far
    for something to kill and eat.
³⁰ Around dead bodies the eagles gather,
    and the young eagles drink the blood.

40 ¹⁻² Job, you challenged Almighty
        God;
    will you give up now, or will you
    answer?

Job
³⁻⁴ I spoke foolishly, LORD. What can I
    answer?
    I will not try to say anything else.

5 I have already said more than I should.

6 Then out of the storm the LORD spoke to Job once again.

The LORD

7 Stand up now like a man,
   and answer my questions.
8 Are you trying to prove that I am unjust—
   to put me in the wrong and yourself in the right?
9 Are you as strong as I am?
   Can your voice thunder as loud as mine?
10 If so, stand up in your honour and pride;
   clothe yourself with majesty and glory.
11 Look at those who are proud;
   pour out your anger and humble them.
12 Yes, look at them and bring them down;
   crush the wicked where they stand.
13 Bury them all in the ground;
   bind them in the world of the dead.
14 Then I will be the first to praise you
   and admit that you won the victory yourself.

15 Look at the monster Behemoth; *w*
   I created him and I created you.
   He eats grass like a cow,
16   but what strength there is in his body,
   and what power there is in his muscles!
17 His tail stands up like a cedar,
   and the muscles in his legs are strong.
18 His bones are as strong as bronze,
   and his legs are like iron bars.

19 The most amazing of all my creatures!
   Only his Creator can defeat him.
20 Grass to feed him grows
   on the hills where wild beasts play. *x*
21 He lies down under the thorn-bushes,
   and hides among the reeds in the swamp.
22 The thorn-bushes and the willows by the stream
   give him shelter in their shade.
23 He is not afraid of a rushing river;

he is calm when the Jordan dashes in his face.
24 Who can blind his eyes and capture him?
   Or who can catch his snout in a trap?

41 Can you catch Leviathan *y* with a fish-hook
   or tie his tongue down with a rope?
2 Can you put a rope through his snout
   or put a hook through his jaws?
3 Will he beg you to let him go?
   Will he plead with you for mercy?
4 Will he make an agreement with you
   and promise to serve you for ever?
5 Will you tie him up like a pet bird,
   like something to amuse your servant-girls?
6 Will fishermen bargain over him?
   Will merchants cut him up to sell?
7 Can you fill his hide with fishing-spears
   or pierce his head with a harpoon?
8 Touch him once and you'll never try it again;
   you'll never forget the fight!

9 Anyone who sees Leviathan
   loses courage and falls to the ground.
10 When he is aroused, he is fierce;
   no one would dare to stand before him.
11 Who can attack him and still be safe?
   No one in all the world can do it. *z*

12 Let me tell you about Leviathan's legs
   and describe how great and strong he is.
13 No one can tear off his outer coat
   or pierce the armour *a* he wears.
14 Who can make him open his jaws,
   ringed with those terrifying teeth?
15 His back *b* is made of rows of shields,
   fastened together and hard as stone.
16 Each one is joined so tight to the next,
   not even a breath can come between.
17 They all are fastened so firmly together
   that nothing can ever pull them apart.
18 Light flashes when he sneezes,
   and his eyes glow like the rising sun.
19 Flames blaze from his mouth,
   and streams of sparks fly out.
20 Smoke comes pouring out of his nose,
   like smoke from weeds burning under a pot.
21 His breath starts fires burning;

---

w BEHEMOTH: *Some identify this with the hippopotamus, others with a legendary creature.*
x *Verse 20 in Hebrew is unclear.*   *y* LEVIATHAN: *See 3.8.*   *z* *Verse 11 in Hebrew is unclear.*
a *One ancient translation* armour; *Hebrew* bridle.
b *Some ancient translations* back; *Hebrew* pride.
41.1: Ps 74.14, 104.26; Is 27.1

The LORD made him prosperous again (42.10)

flames leap out of his mouth.
[22] His neck is so powerful
that all who meet him are terrified.
[23] There is not a weak spot in his skin;
it is as hard and unyielding as iron.
[24] His stony heart is without fear,
as unyielding and hard as a millstone.
[25] When he rises up, even the strongest[c]
are frightened;
they are helpless with fear.
[26] There is no sword that can wound him;
no spear or arrow or lance that can
harm him.
[27] For him iron is as flimsy as straw,
and bronze as soft as rotten wood.
[28] There is no arrow that can make him
run;
rocks thrown at him are like bits of
straw.
[29] To him a club is a piece of straw,
and he laughs when men throw
spears.
[30] The scales on his belly are like jagged
pieces of pottery;

they tear up the muddy ground like
a threshing-sledge.[d]
[31] He churns up the sea like boiling water
and makes it bubble like a pot of oil.
[32] He leaves a shining path behind him
and turns the sea to white foam.
[33] There is nothing on earth to compare
with him;
he is a creature that has no fear.
[34] He looks down on even the proudest
animals;
he is king of all wild beasts.

42

Then Job answered the LORD.

Job

[2] I know, LORD, that you are all-powerful;
that you can do everything you want.
[3] You ask how I dare question your
wisdom
when I am so very ignorant.
I talked about things I did not
understand,
about marvels too great for me to
know.

[c] strongest; *or* gods.
[d] THRESHING SLEDGES: *These had sharp pieces of iron or stone fastened beneath them.*
42.3: Job 38.2

4 You told me to listen while you spoke
  and to try to answer your questions.
5 In the past I knew only what others
    had told me,
  but now I have seen you with my
    own eyes.
6 So I am ashamed of all I have said
  and repent in dust and ashes.

Conclusion

7 After the LORD had finished speaking to Job, he said to Eliphaz, "I am angry with you and your two friends, because you did not speak the truth about me, as my servant Job did. 8 Now take seven bulls and seven rams to Job and offer them as a sacrifice for yourselves. Job will pray for you, and I will answer his prayer and not disgrace you as you deserve. You did not speak the truth about me as he did."

9 Eliphaz, Bildad, and Zophar did what the LORD had told them to do, and the LORD answered Job's prayer.

10 Then, after Job had prayed for his three friends, the LORD made him prosperous again and gave him twice as much as he had had before. 11 All Job's brothers and sisters and former friends came to visit him and feasted with him in his house. They expressed their sympathy and comforted him for all the troubles the LORD had brought on him. Each of them gave him some money and a gold ring.

12 The LORD blessed the last part of Job's life even more than he had blessed the first. Job owned fourteen thousand sheep, six thousand camels, two thousand head of cattle, and one thousand donkeys. 13 He was the father of seven sons and three daughters. 14 He called the eldest daughter Jemimah, the second Keziah, and the youngest Keren Happuch. e 15 There were no other women in the whole world as beautiful as Job's daughters. Their father gave them a share of the inheritance along with their brothers.

16 Job lived a hundred and forty years after this, long enough to see his grandchildren and great-grandchildren. 17 And then he died at a very great age.

---

e In Hebrew the names of Job's daughters suggest beauty both by their sound and by their meaning. JEMIMAH means "dove"; KEZIAH means "cassia," a variety of cinnamon used as a perfume; and KEREN HAPPUCH means a small box used for eye make-up.
42.4: Job 38.3   **42.10:** Job 1.1–3

THE PSALMS

INTRODUCTION

The book of *Psalms* is the hymn book and prayer book of the Bible. Composed by different authors over a long period of time, these hymns and prayers were collected and used by the people of Israel in their worship, and eventually this collection was included in their Scriptures.

These religious poems are of many kinds: there are hymns of praise and worship of God; prayers for help, protection, and salvation; pleas for forgiveness; songs of thanksgiving for God's blessings; and petitions for the punishment of enemies. These prayers are both personal and national; some portray the most intimate feelings of one person, while others represent the needs and feelings of all the people of God.

The psalms were used by Jesus, quoted by the writers of the New Testament, and became the treasured book of worship of the Christian Church from its beginning.

Outline of Contents

The 150 psalms are grouped into five collections, or books, as follows:

Psalms   1—41
Psalms 42—72
Psalms 73—89
Psalms 90—106
Psalms 107—150

BOOK ONE
(Psalms 1-41)

True Happiness

1 Happy are those
  who reject the advice of evil men,
who do not follow the example of
  sinners
or join those who have no use for
  God.
² Instead, they find joy in obeying the
  Law of the LORD,
and they study it day and night.

³ They are like trees that grow beside a
  stream,
  that bear fruit at the right time,
  and whose leaves do not dry up.
They succeed in everything they do.

⁴ But evil men are not like this at all;
  they are like straw that the wind
    blows away.
⁵ Sinners will be condemned by God
  and kept apart from God's own
    people.
⁶ The righteous are guided and protected
  by the LORD,

1.3: Jer 17.8

but the evil are on the way to their doom.

God's Chosen King

2 Why do the nations plan rebellion?
Why do people make their useless plots?
2 Their kings revolt,
their rulers plot together against the LORD
and against the king he chose.
3 "Let us free ourselves from their rule," they say;
"let us throw off their control."

4 From his throne in heaven the Lord laughs
and mocks their feeble plans.
5 Then he warns them in anger
and terrifies them with his fury.
6 "On Zion,*a* my sacred hill," he says,
"I have installed my king."

7 "I will announce," says the king, "what the LORD has declared.
He said to me: 'You are my son;
today I have become your father.
8 Ask, and I will give you all the nations;
the whole earth will be yours.
9 You will break them with an iron rod;
you will shatter them in pieces like a clay pot.'"

10 Now listen to this warning, you kings;
learn this lesson, you rulers of the world:
11 Serve the LORD with fear;
12 tremble and bow down to him;*b*
or else his anger will be quickly aroused,
and you will suddenly die.
Happy are all who go to him for protection.

Morning Prayer for Help*c*

3 I have so many enemies, LORD,
so many who turn against me!
2 They talk about me and say,
"God will not help him."

3 But you, O LORD, are always my shield from danger;
you give me victory
and restore my courage.

4 I call to the LORD for help,
and from his sacred hill*d* he answers me.

5 I lie down and sleep,
and all night long the LORD protects me.
6 I am not afraid of the thousands of enemies
who surround me on every side.

7 Come, LORD! Save me, my God!
You punish all my enemies
and leave them powerless to harm me.
8 Victory comes from the LORD—
may he bless his people.

Evening Prayer for Help*e*

4 Answer me when I pray,
O God, my defender!
When I was in trouble, you helped me.
Be kind to me now and hear my prayer.

2 How long will you people insult me?
How long will you love what is worthless
and go after what is false?

3 Remember that the LORD has chosen the righteous for his own,
and he hears me when I call to him.

4 Tremble with fear and stop sinning;
think deeply about this,
when you lie in silence on your beds.
5 Offer the right sacrifices to the LORD,
and put your trust in him.

6 There are many who pray:
"Give us more blessings, O LORD.
Look on us with kindness!"
7 But the joy that you have given me
is more than they will ever have
with all their corn and wine.

8 When I lie down, I go to sleep in peace;
you alone, O LORD, keep me perfectly safe.

A Prayer for Protection*f*

5 Listen to my words, O LORD,
and hear my sighs.

---

*a*ZION: *See Zion in Word List.*
*b*Probable text tremble...him; *Some other possible texts* with trembling kiss his feet *and with trembling kiss the Son* and tremble and kiss the mighty one; *Hebrew unclear.*
*c*HEBREW TITLE: *A psalm by David, after he ran away from his son Absalom.*
*d*SACRED HILL: *See 2.6.*   *e*HEBREW TITLE: *A psalm by David.*
*f*HEBREW TITLE: *A psalm by David.*
2.1–2: Acts 4.25-26   **2.7:** Acts 13.33; Heb 1.5, 5.5   **2.9:** Rev 2.26–27, 12.5, 19.15
3 Title: 2 Sam 15.13—17.22   **4.4:** Eph 4.26

2 Listen to my cry for help,
　my God and king!

I pray to you, O LORD;
3 　you hear my voice in the morning;
at sunrise I offer my prayer[g]
　and wait for your answer.

4 You are not a God who is pleased with
　wrongdoing;
　you allow no evil in your presence.
5 You cannot stand the sight of proud
　men;
　you hate all wicked people.
6 You destroy all liars
　and despise violent, deceitful men.

7 But because of your great love
　I can come into your house;
I can worship in your holy Temple
　and bow down to you in reverence.
8 LORD, I have so many enemies!
　Lead me to do your will;
　make your way plain for me to follow.

9 What my enemies say can never be
　trusted;
　they only want to destroy.
Their words are flattering and smooth,
　but full of deadly deceit.
10 Condemn and punish them, O God;
　may their own plots cause their ruin.
Drive them out of your presence
　because of their many sins
　and their rebellion against you.

11 But all who find safety in you will
　rejoice;
　they can always sing for joy.
Protect those who love you;
　because of you they are truly happy.
12 You bless those who obey you, LORD;
　your love protects them like a shield.

A Prayer for Help in Time of Trouble[h]

6 LORD, don't be angry and rebuke me!
　　Don't punish me in your anger!
2 I am worn out, O LORD; have pity on
　me!
　Give me strength; I am completely
　　exhausted
3 　and my whole being is deeply troubled.
How long, O LORD, will you wait to help
　me?

4 Come and save me, LORD;
　in your mercy rescue me from death.
5 In the world of the dead you are not
　remembered;
　no one can praise you there.

6 I am worn out with grief;
　every night my bed is damp from my
　　weeping;
　my pillow is soaked with tears.
7 I can hardly see;
　my eyes are so swollen
　from the weeping caused by my
　　enemies.

8 Keep away from me, you evil men!
　The LORD hears my weeping;
9 　he listens to my cry for help
　and will answer my prayer.
10 My enemies will know the bitter
　　shame of defeat;
　in sudden confusion they will be
　　driven away.

A Prayer for Justice[i]

7 O LORD, my God, I come to you for
　　protection;
　rescue me and save me from all who
　　pursue me,
2 or else like a lion they will carry me
　　off
　where no one can save me,
　and there they will tear me to pieces.

3-4 O LORD, my God, if I have wronged
　　anyone,
　if I have betrayed a friend
　or without cause done violence to my
　　enemy[j]—
　if I have done any of these things—
5 then let my enemies pursue me and
　　catch me,
　let them cut me down and kill me
　and leave me lifeless on the ground!

6 Rise in your anger, O LORD!
　Stand up against the fury of my
　　enemies;
　rouse yourself and help me!
　Justice is what you demand,
7 　so bring together all the peoples round
　　you,
　and rule over them from above.[k]
8 You are the judge of all mankind.
　Judge in my favour, O LORD;

[g] prayer; or sacrifice.　[h] HEBREW TITLE: A psalm by David.
[i] HEBREW TITLE: A song which David sang to the LORD because of Cush the Benjaminite.
[j] without...enemy; or shown mercy to someone who wronged me unjustly.
[k] Probable text rule over them from above; Hebrew return above over them.
5.9: Rom 3.13　　**6.1:** Ps 38.1　　**6.8:** Mt 7.23; Lk 13.27

you know that I am innocent.
9 You are a righteous God
and judge our thoughts and desires.
Stop the wickedness of evil men
and reward those who are good.

10 God is my protector;
he saves those who obey him.
11 God is a righteous judge
and always condemns the wicked.
12 If they do not change their ways,
God will sharpen his sword.
He bends his bow and makes it ready;
13 he takes up his deadly weapons
and aims his burning arrows.

14 See how wicked people think up evil;
they plan trouble and practise
deception.
15 But in the traps they set for others,
they themselves get caught.
16 So they are punished by their own
evil
and are hurt by their own violence.

17 I thank the LORD for his justice,
I sing praises to the LORD, the Most
High.

God's Glory and Man's Dignity [l]

8 O LORD, our Lord,
your greatness is seen in all the
world!
Your praise reaches up to the heavens;
2 it is sung by children and babies.
You are safe and secure from all your
enemies;
you stop anyone who opposes you.

3 When I look at the sky, which you have
made,
at the moon and the stars, which you
set in their places—
4 what is man, that you think of him;
mere man, that you care for him?

5 Yet you made him inferior only to
yourself; [m]
you crowned him with glory and
honour.
6 You appointed him ruler over
everything you made;
you placed him over all creation:
7 sheep and cattle, and the wild animals
too;
8 the birds and the fish

and the creatures in the seas.

9 O LORD, our Lord,
your greatness is seen in all the world!

Thanksgiving to God for His Justice [n]

9 I will praise you, LORD, with all my
heart;
I will tell of all the wonderful things
you have done.
2 I will sing with joy because of you.
I will sing praise to you, Almighty
God.

3 My enemies turn back when you appear;
they fall down and die.
4 You are fair and honest in your
judgements,
and you have judged in my favour.

5 You have condemned the heathen
and destroyed the wicked;
they will be remembered no more.
6 Our enemies are finished for ever;
you have destroyed their cities,
and they are completely forgotten.

7 But the LORD is king for ever;
he has set up his throne for judgement.
8 He rules the world with righteousness;
he judges the nations with justice.

9 The LORD is a refuge for the oppressed,
a place of safety in times of trouble.
10 Those who know you, LORD, will trust
you;
you do not abandon anyone who
comes to you.

11 Sing praise to the LORD, who rules in
Zion!
Tell every nation what he has done!
12 God remembers those who suffer;
he does not forget their cry,
and he punishes those who wrong
them.

13 Be merciful to me, O LORD!
See the sufferings my enemies cause
me!
Rescue me from death, O LORD,
14 that I may stand before the people
of Jerusalem
and tell them all the things for which
I praise you.
I will rejoice because you saved me.

---

[l] HEBREW TITLE: *A psalm by David.*   [m] yourself; *or* the gods, *or* the angels.
[n] HEBREW TITLE: *A psalm by David.*
7.9: Rev 2.23   **8.2:** Mt 21.16   **8.4:** Job 7.17–18; Ps 144.3; Heb 2.6–8
8.6: 1 Cor 15.27; Eph 1.22; Heb 2.8

I will praise you, Lord (9.1)

¹⁵ The heathen have dug a pit and fallen
   in;
   they have been caught in their own
   trap.
¹⁶ The Lord has revealed himself by his
   righteous judgements,
   and the wicked are trapped by their
   own deeds.

¹⁷ Death is the destiny of all the wicked,
   of all those who reject God.
¹⁸ The needy will not always be
   neglected;
   the hope of the poor will not be
   crushed for ever.

¹⁹ Come, Lord! Do not let men defy you!
   Bring the heathen before you
   and pronounce judgement on them.
²⁰ Make them afraid, O Lord;
   make them know that they are only
   mortal beings.

A Prayer for Justice

10 Why are you so far away, O Lord?
   Why do you hide yourself when
   we are in trouble?
² The wicked are proud and persecute the
   poor;

10.7: Rom 3.14

catch them in the traps they have
made.

³ The wicked man is proud of his evil
   desires;
   the greedy man curses and rejects the
   Lord.
⁴ A wicked man does not care about the
   Lord;
   in his pride he thinks that God doesn't
   matter.

⁵ A wicked man succeeds in everything.
   He cannot understand God's
   judgements;
   he sneers at his enemies.
⁶ He says to himself, "I will never fail;
   I will never be in trouble."
⁷ His speech is filled with curses, lies, and
   threats;
   he is quick to speak hateful, evil
   words.

⁸ He hides himself in the villages,
   waiting to murder innocent people.
   He spies on his helpless victims;
⁹ he waits in his hiding place like a
   lion.
   He lies in wait for the poor;

he catches them in his trap and drags
them away.

10 The helpless victims lie crushed;
brute strength has defeated them.
11 The wicked man says to himself, "God
doesn't care!
He has closed his eyes and will never
see me!"

12 O LORD, punish those wicked men!
Remember those who are suffering!
13 How can a wicked man despise God
and say to himself, "He will not
punish me"?

14 But you do see; you take notice of
trouble and suffering
and are always ready to help.
The helpless man commits himself to
you;
you have always helped the needy.

15 Break the power of wicked and evil
men;
punish them for the wrong they have
done
until they do it no more.

16 The LORD is king for ever and ever.
Those who worship other gods
will vanish from his land.

17 You will listen, O LORD, to the prayers
of the lowly;
you will give them courage.
18 You will hear the cries of the
oppressed and the orphans;
you will judge in their favour,
so that mortal men may cause terror
no more.

Confidence in the LORD [o]

11 I trust in the LORD for safety.
How foolish of you to say to me,
"Fly away like a bird to the mountains, [p]
2 because the wicked have drawn their
bows and aimed their arrows
to shoot from the shadows at good
men.
3 There is nothing a good man can do
when everything falls apart."

4 The LORD is in his holy temple;
he has his throne in heaven.
He watches people everywhere
and knows what they are doing.

*Those who do them will live in his
presence (11.7)*

5 He examines the good and the wicked
alike;
the lawless he hates with all his heart.

6 He sends down flaming coals [q] and
burning sulphur on the wicked;
he punishes them with scorching
winds.
7 The LORD is righteous and loves good
deeds;
those who do them will live in his
presence.

A Prayer for Help [r]

12 Help us, LORD!
There is not a good man left;
honest men can no longer be found.
2 All of them lie to one another;
they deceive each other with flattery.

3 Silence those flattering tongues, O
LORD!
Close those boastful mouths that say,
4 "With our words we get what we want.
We will say what we wish,
and no one can stop us."

5 "But now I will come," says the LORD,
"because the needy are oppressed
and the persecuted groan in pain.
I will give them the security they long
for."

6 The promises of the LORD can be trusted;
they are as genuine as silver
refined seven times in the furnace.

7-8 Wicked men are everywhere,
and everyone praises what is evil.
Keep us always safe, O LORD,

---

[o] HEBREW TITLE: *By David.*
[p] *Some ancient translations* like a bird to the mountains; *Hebrew* bird, to your *(plural)* mountains.
[q] *One ancient translation* coals; *Hebrew* traps. [r] HEBREW TITLE: *A psalm by David.*

and preserve us from such people.

A Prayer for Help[s]

13 How much longer will you forget
me, LORD? For ever?
How much longer will you hide
yourself from me?
2 How long must I endure trouble?
How long will sorrow fill my heart
day and night?
How long will my enemies triumph
over me?

3 Look at me, O LORD my God, and answer
me.
Restore my strength; don't let me die.
4 Don't let my enemies say, "We have
defeated him."
Don't let them gloat over my downfall.

5 I rely on your constant love;
I will be glad, because you will rescue
me.
6 I will sing to you, O LORD,
because you have been good to me.

The Wickedness of Men[t]
(Ps 53)

14 Fools say to themselves,
"There is no God."
They are all corrupt,
and they have done terrible things;
there is no one who does what is right.

2 The LORD looks down from heaven at
mankind
to see if there are any who are wise,
any who worship him.
3 But they have all gone wrong;
they are all equally bad.
Not one of them does what is right,
not a single one.

4 "Don't they know?" asks the LORD.
"Are all these evildoers ignorant?
They live by robbing my people,
and they never pray to me."

5 But then they will be terrified,
for God is with those who obey him.
6 Evildoers frustrate the plans of the
humble man,
but the LORD is his protection.

7 How I pray that victory
will come to Israel from Zion.

How happy the people of Israel will be
when the LORD makes them
prosperous again!

What God Requires[u]

15 LORD, who may enter your
Temple?
Who may worship on Zion, your
sacred hill?[v]

2 A person who obeys God in everything
and always does what is right,
whose words are true and sincere,
3 and who does not slander others.
He does no wrong to his friends
nor spreads rumours about his
neighbours.
4 He despises those whom God rejects,
but honours those who obey the LORD.
He always does what he promises,
no matter how much it may cost.
5 He makes loans without charging
interest
and cannot be bribed to testify against
the innocent.

Whoever does these things will always
be secure.

A Prayer of Confidence[w]

16 Protect me, O God; I trust in you
for safety.
2 I say to the LORD, "You are my Lord;
all the good things I have come from
you."

3 How excellent are the LORD's faithful
people!
My greatest pleasure is to be with
them.

4 Those who rush to other gods
bring many troubles on themselves.[x]
I will not take part in their sacrifices;
I will not worship their gods.

5 You, LORD, are all I have,
and you give me all I need;
my future is in your hands.
6 How wonderful are your gifts to me;
how good they are!

7 I praise the LORD, because he guides
me,
and in the night my conscience warns
me.

---

[s] HEBREW TITLE: *A psalm by David.*
[u] HEBREW TITLE: *A psalm by David.*
[w] HEBREW TITLE: *A psalm by David.*
14.1–3: Rom 3.10–12
[t] HEBREW TITLE: *By David.*
[v] SACRED HILL: *See 2.6.*
[x] *Probable text* Those...themselves; *Hebrew unclear.*

8 I am always aware of the LORD's
    presence;
    he is near, and nothing can shake me.

9 And so I am thankful and glad,
    and I feel completely secure,
10 because you protect me from the
    power of death.
I have served you faithfully,
    and you will not abandon me to the
    world of the dead.

11 You will show me the path that leads
    to life;
    your presence fills me with joy
    and brings me pleasure for ever.

The Prayer of an Innocent Man[y]

17 Listen, O LORD, to my plea for
    justice;
    pay attention to my cry for help!
Listen to my honest prayer.
2 You will judge in my favour,
    because you know what is right.

3 You know my heart.
    You have come to me at night;
    you have examined me completely
    and found no evil desire in me.
4 I speak no evil as others do;
    I have obeyed your command
    and have not followed paths of
    violence.
5 I have always walked in your way
    and have never strayed from it.

6 I pray to you, O God, because you
    answer me;
    so turn to me and listen to my words.
7 Reveal your wonderful love and save
    me;
    at your side I am safe from my
    enemies.

8 Protect me as you would your very eyes;
    hide me in the shadow of your wings
9   from the attacks of the wicked.

Deadly enemies surround me;
10   they have no pity and speak proudly.
11 They are round me now, wherever I
    turn,
    watching for a chance to pull me
    down.
12 They are like lions, waiting for me,
    wanting to tear me to pieces.

13 Come, LORD! Oppose my enemies and
    defeat them!
Save me from the wicked by your
    sword;
14   save me from those who in this life
    have all they want.
Punish them with the sufferings you
    have stored up for them;
    may there be enough for their children
    and some left over for their children's
    children!

15 But I will see you, because I have done
    no wrong;
    and when I awake, your presence will
    fill me with joy.

David's Song of Victory[z]
(2 Sam 22.1-51)

18 How I love you, LORD!
    You are my defender.

2 The LORD is my protector;
    he is my strong fortress.
My God is my protection,
    and with him I am safe.
He protects me like a shield;
    he defends me and keeps me safe.
3 I call to the LORD,
    and he saves me from my enemies.
Praise the LORD!

4 The danger of death was all round me;
    the waves of destruction rolled over
    me.
5 The danger of death was round me,
    and the grave set its trap for me.
6 In my trouble I called to the LORD;
    I called to my God for help.
In his temple he heard my voice;
    he listened to my cry for help.

7 Then the earth trembled and shook;
    the foundations of the mountains
    rocked and quivered,
    because God was angry.
8 Smoke poured out of his nostrils,
    a consuming flame and burning coals
    from his mouth.
9 He tore the sky apart and came down
    with a dark cloud under his feet.
10 He flew swiftly on a winged creature;[x]
    he travelled on the wings of the wind.
11 He covered himself with darkness;

---

y HEBREW TITLE: *A prayer by David.*
z HEBREW TITLE: *The words that David, the LORD's servant, sang to the LORD on the day the LORD*
saved him from Saul and all his other enemies.   x WINGED CREATURE: *See Word List.*
16.8-11: Acts 2.25-28   **16.10:** Acts 13.35

thick clouds, full of water, surrounded him.

12 Hailstones and flashes of fire
came from the lightning before him
and broke through the dark clouds.

13 Then the LORD thundered from the sky;
and the voice of the Most High was
heard. [a]

14 He shot his arrows and scattered his
enemies;
with flashes of lightning he sent them
running.

15 The floor of the ocean was laid bare,
and the foundations of the earth were
uncovered,
when you rebuked your enemies, LORD,
and roared at them in anger.

16 The LORD reached down from above
and took hold of me;
he pulled me out of the deep waters.

17 He rescued me from my powerful
enemies
and from all those who hate me—
they were too strong for me.

18 When I was in trouble, they attacked
me,
but the LORD protected me.

19 He helped me out of danger;
he saved me because he was pleased
with me.

20 The LORD rewards me because I do
what is right;
he blesses me because I am innocent.

21 I have obeyed the law of the LORD;
I have not turned away from my God.

22 I have observed all his laws;
I have not disobeyed his commands.

23 He knows that I am faultless,
that I have kept myself from doing
wrong.

24 And so he rewards me because I do
what is right,
because he knows that I am innocent.

25 O LORD, you are faithful to those who
are faithful to you;
completely good to those who are
perfect.

26 You are pure to those who are pure,
but hostile to those who are wicked.

27 You save those who are humble,
but you humble those who are proud.

28 O LORD, you give me light;

you dispel my darkness.

29 You give me strength to attack my
enemies
and power to overcome their defences.

30 This God—how perfect are his deeds!
How dependable his words!
He is like a shield
for all who seek his protection.

31 The LORD alone is God;
God alone is our defence.

32 He is the God who makes me strong,
who makes my pathway safe.

33 He makes me sure-footed as a deer;
he keeps me safe on the mountains.

34 He trains me for battle,
so that I can use the strongest bow.

35 O LORD, you protect me and save me;
your care has made me great,
and your power has kept me safe.

36 You have kept me from being
captured,
and I have never fallen.

37 I pursue my enemies and catch them;
I do not stop until I destroy them.

38 I strike them down, and they cannot
rise;
they lie defeated before me.

39 You give me strength for the battle
and victory over my enemies.

40 You make my enemies run from me;
I destroy those who hate me.

41 They cry for help, but no one saves
them;
they call to the LORD, but he does
not answer.

42 I crush them, so that they become like
dust
which the wind blows away.
I trample on them like mud in the
streets.

43 You saved me from a rebellious people
and made me ruler over the nations;
people I did not know have now
become my subjects.

44 Foreigners bow before me;
when they hear me, they obey.

45 They lose their courage
and come trembling from their
fortresses.

46 The LORD lives! Praise my defender!
Proclaim the greatness of the God
who saves me.

47 He gives me victory over my enemies;

---

[a] One ancient translation (and see 2 Sam 22.14) was heard; Hebrew was heard hailstones and flashes of fire.
18.33: Hab 3.19

he subdues the nations under me
48 and saves me from my foes.

O Lord, you give me victory over my
enemies
and protect me from violent men.
49 And so I praise you among the nations;
I sing praises to you.

50 God gives great victories to his king;
he shows constant love to the one
he has chosen,
to David and his descendants for ever.

God's Glory in Creation[b]

19 How clearly the sky reveals God's
glory!
How plainly it shows what he has
done!
2 Each day announces it to the following
day;
each night repeats it to the next.
3 No speech or words are used,
no sound is heard;
4 yet their message[c] goes out to all the
world
and is heard to the ends of the earth.
God made a home in the sky for the
sun;
5   it comes out in the morning like a
happy bridegroom,
like an athlete eager to run a race.
6 It starts at one end of the sky
and goes across to the other.
Nothing can hide from its heat.

The Law of the Lord

7 The law of the Lord is perfect;
it gives new strength.
The commands of the Lord are
trustworthy,
giving wisdom to those who lack it.
8 The laws of the Lord are right,
and those who obey them are happy.
The commands of the Lord are just
and give understanding to the mind.
9 Reverence for the Lord is good;
it will continue for ever.
The judgements of the Lord are just;
they are always fair.
10 They are more desirable than the
finest gold;
they are sweeter than the purest
honey.
11 They give knowledge to me, your
servant;

I am rewarded for obeying them.

12 No one can see his own errors;
deliver me, Lord, from hidden faults!
13 Keep me safe, also, from wilful sins;
don't let them rule over me.
Then I shall be perfect
and free from the evil of sin.

14 May my words and my thoughts be
acceptable to you,
O Lord, my refuge and my redeemer!

A Prayer for Victory[d]

20 May the Lord answer you when
you are in trouble!
May the God of Jacob protect you!
2 May he send you help from his Temple
and give you aid from Mount Zion.
3 May he accept all your offerings
and be pleased with all your sacrifices.
4 May he give you what you desire
and make all your plans succeed.
5 Then we will shout for joy over your
victory
and celebrate your triumph by
praising our God.
May the Lord answer all your requests.

6 Now I know that the Lord gives victory
to his chosen king;
he answers him from his holy heaven
and by his power gives him great
victories.
7 Some trust in their war-chariots
and others in their horses,
but we trust in the power of the Lord
our God.
8 Such people will stumble and fall,
but we will rise and stand firm.

9 Give victory to the king, O Lord;
answer[e] us when we call.

Praise for Victory[f]

21 The king is glad, O Lord, because
you gave him strength;
he rejoices because you made him
victorious.
2 You have given him his heart's desire;
you have answered his request.

3 You came to him with great blessings
and set a crown of gold on his head.
4 He asked for life, and you gave it,

[b]HEBREW TITLE: A psalm by David.   [c]Some ancient translations message; Hebrew line.
[d]HEBREW TITLE: A psalm by David.
[e]Some ancient translations answer; Hebrew he will answer.
[f]HEBREW TITLE: A psalm by David.
18.49: Rom 15.9   **19.4:** Rom 10.18

a long and lasting life.

5 His glory is great because of your help;
    you have given him fame and majesty.
6 Your blessings are with him for ever
    and your presence fills him with joy.

7 The king trusts in the LORD Almighty;
    and because of the LORD's constant
      love
    he will always be secure.
8 The king will capture all his enemies;
    he will capture everyone who hates
      him.
9 He will destroy them like a blazing fire
    when he appears.

The LORD will devour them in his anger,
    and fire will consume them.
10 None of their descendants will survive;
    the king will kill them all.

11 They make their plans, and plot
      against him,
    but they will not succeed.
12 He will shoot his arrows at them
    and make them turn and run.

13 We praise you, LORD, for your great
      strength!
    We will sing and praise your power.

A Cry of Anguish and a Song of Praise[g]

22   My God, my God, why have you
      abandoned me?
I have cried desperately for help,
    but still it does not come.
2 During the day I call to you, my God,
    but you do not answer;
I call at night,
    but get no rest.
3 But you are enthroned as the Holy One,
    the one whom Israel praises.
4 Our ancestors put their trust in you;
    they trusted you, and you saved them.
5 They called to you and escaped from
      danger;
    they trusted you and were not
      disappointed.

6 But I am no longer a man; I am a worm,
    despised and scorned by everyone!
7 All who see me jeer at me;
    they stick out their tongues and shake
      their heads.

8 "You relied on the LORD," they say.
    "Why doesn't he save you?
If the LORD likes you,
    why doesn't he help you?"

9 It was you who brought me safely
      through birth,
    and when I was a baby, you kept me
      safe.
10 I have relied on you since the day I
      was born,
    and you have always been my God.
11 Do not stay away from me!
    Trouble is near,
    and there is no one to help.

12 Many enemies surround me like bulls;
    they are all round me,
    like fierce bulls from the land of
      Bashan.
13 They open their mouths like lions,
    roaring and tearing at me.

14 My strength is gone,
    gone like water spilt on the ground.
All my bones are out of joint;
    my heart is like melted wax.
15 My throat[h] is as dry as dust,
    and my tongue sticks to the roof of
      my mouth.
You have left me for dead in the dust.

16 A gang of evil men is round me;
    like a pack of dogs they close in on
      me;
    they tear at[i] my hands and feet.
17 All my bones can be seen.
    My enemies look at me and stare.
18 They gamble for my clothes
    and divide them among themselves.

19 O LORD, don't stay away from me!
    Come quickly to my rescue!
20 Save me from the sword;
    save my life from these dogs.
21 Rescue me from these lions;
    I am helpless[j] before these wild bulls.

22 I will tell my people what you have
      done;
    I will praise you in their assembly:
23 "Praise him, you servants of the LORD!
    Honour him, you descendants of
      Jacob!
    Worship him, you people of Israel!

[g] HEBREW TITLE: *A psalm by David.* [h] *Probable text* throat; *Hebrew* strength.
[i] *Some ancient translations* they tear at; *others* they tie; *Hebrew* like a lion.
[j] *Some ancient translations* I am helpless; *Hebrew* you answered me.
22.1: Mt 27.46; Mk 15.34   **22.7:** Mt 27.39; Mk 15.29; Lk 23.35   **22.8:** Mt 27.43
22.18: Mt 27.35; Mk 15.24; Lk 23.34; Jn 19.24   **22.22:** Heb 2.12

24 He does not neglect the poor or ignore
   their suffering;
  he does not turn away from them,
   but answers when they call for help."

25 In the full assembly I will praise you
   for what you have done;
  in the presence of those who worship
   you
  I will offer the sacrifices I promised.
26 The poor will eat as much as they
   want;
  those who come to the LORD will
   praise him.
  May they prosper for ever!

27 All nations will remember the LORD.
   From every part of the world they
   will turn to him;
  all races will worship him.
28 The LORD is king,
   and he rules the nations.

29 All proud men will bow down to him; [k]
   all mortal men will bow down before
   him.
30 Future generations will serve him;
   men will speak of the Lord to the
   coming generation.
31 People not yet born will be told:
   "The Lord saved his people."

The LORD Our Shepherd [l]

23 The LORD is my shepherd;
      I have everything I need.
2 He lets me rest in fields of green grass
  and leads me to quiet pools of fresh
   water.
3 He gives me new strength.
  He guides me in the right paths,
   as he has promised.
4 Even if I go through the deepest
   darkness,
  I will not be afraid, LORD,
   for you are with me.
  Your shepherd's rod and staff protect
   me.

5 You prepare a banquet for me,
  where all my enemies can see me;
  you welcome me as an honoured guest
   and fill my cup to the brim.
6 I know that your goodness and love will
   be with me all my life;
  and your house will be my home as
   long as I live.

*Even if I go through the deepest darkness
(23.4)*

The Great King [m]

24 The world and all that is in it
      belong to the LORD;
  the earth and all who live on it are
   his.
2 He built it on the deep waters beneath
   the earth
  and laid its foundations in the ocean
   depths.

3 Who has the right to go up the LORD's
   hill? [n]
  Who may enter his holy Temple?
4 Those who are pure in act and in
   thought,
  who do not worship idols
   or make false promises.
5 The LORD will bless them and save them;
   God will declare them innocent.
6 Such are the people who come to God,
   who come into the presence of the
   God of Jacob.

7 Fling wide the gates,
  open the ancient doors,
  and the great king will come in.
8 Who is this great king?
  He is the LORD, strong and mighty,
   the LORD, victorious in battle.

9 Fling wide the gates,
  open the ancient doors,
  and the great king will come in.

¹⁰ Who is this great king?
The triumphant LORD—he is the great
king!

A Prayer for Guidance and Protection°

25 To you, O LORD, I offer my prayer;
² in you, my God, I trust.
Save me from the shame of defeat;
don't let my enemies gloat over me!
³ Defeat does not come to those who trust
in you,
but to those who are quick to rebel
against you.

⁴ Teach me your ways, O LORD;
make them known to me.
⁵ Teach me to live according to your truth,
for you are my God, who saves me.
I always trust in you.

⁶ Remember, O LORD, your kindness and
constant love
which you have shown from long ago.
⁷ Forgive the sins and errors of my youth.
In your constant love and goodness,
remember me, LORD!

⁸ Because the LORD is righteous and good,
he teaches sinners the path they
should follow.
⁹ He leads the humble in the right way
and teaches them his will.
¹⁰ With faithfulness and love he leads
all who keep his covenant and obey
his commands.

¹¹ Keep your promise, LORD, and forgive
my sins,
for they are many.
¹² Those who have reverence for the LORD
will learn from him the path they
should follow.
¹³ They will always be prosperous,
and their children will possess the
land.
¹⁴ The LORD is the friend of those who
obey him
and he affirms his covenant with
them.

¹⁵ I look to the LORD for help at all times,
and he rescues me from danger.
¹⁶ Turn to me, LORD, and be merciful to
me,
because I am lonely and weak.
¹⁷ Relieve me of my worries
and save me from all my troubles.
¹⁸ Consider my distress and suffering

and forgive all my sins.

¹⁹ See how many enemies I have;
see how much they hate me.
²⁰ Protect me and save me;
keep me from defeat.
I come to you for safety.
²¹ May my goodness and honesty
preserve me,
because I trust in you.

²² From all their troubles, O God,
save your people Israel!

The Prayer of a Good Man ᴾ

26 Declare me innocent, O LORD,
because I do what is right
and trust you completely.
² Examine me and test me, LORD;
judge my desires and thoughts.
³ Your constant love is my guide;
your faithfulness always leads me. �q

⁴ I do not keep company with worthless
people;
I have nothing to do with hypocrites.
⁵ I hate the company of evil men
and avoid the wicked.

⁶ LORD, I wash my hands to show that
I am innocent
and march in worship round your
altar.
⁷ I sing a hymn of thanksgiving
and tell of all your wonderful deeds.

⁸ I love the house where you live, O LORD,
the place where your glory dwells.
⁹ Do not destroy me with the sinners;
spare me from the fate of murderers—
¹⁰ men who do evil all the time
and are always ready to take bribes.

¹¹ As for me, I do what is right;
be merciful to me and save me!

¹² I am safe from all dangers;
in the assembly of his people I praise
the LORD.

A Prayer of Praise ʳ

27 The LORD is my light and my
salvation;
I will fear no one.
The LORD protects me from all danger;
I will never be afraid.

ᵒHEBREW TITLE: *By David.*   ᴾHEBREW TITLE: *By David.*
q your faithfulness always leads me; *or* I live in loyalty to you.   ʳHEBREW TITLE: *By David.*

2 When evil men attack me and try to
kill me,
  they stumble and fall.
3 Even if a whole army surrounds me,
  I will not be afraid;
even if enemies attack me,
  I will still trust God. *s*

4 I have asked the LORD for one thing;
  one thing only do I want:
to live in the LORD's house all my life,
  to marvel there at his goodness,
  and to ask for his guidance.
5 In times of trouble he will shelter me;
  he will keep me safe in his Temple
  and make me secure on a high rock.
6 So I will triumph over my enemies
  around me.
  With shouts of joy I will offer
    sacrifices in his Temple;
  I will sing, I will praise the LORD.

7 Hear me, LORD, when I call to you!
  Be merciful and answer me!
8 When you said, "Come and worship
  me,"
  I answered, "I will come, LORD;
9   don't hide yourself from me!"

Don't be angry with me;
  don't turn your servant away.
You have been my help;
  don't leave me, don't abandon me,
  O God, my saviour.
10 My father and mother may abandon
  me,
  but the LORD will take care of me.

11 Teach me, LORD, what you want me
  to do,
  and lead me along a safe path,
  because I have many enemies.
12 Don't abandon me to my enemies,
  who attack me with lies and threats.

13 I know that I will live to see
  the LORD's goodness in this present
  life.
14 Trust in the LORD.
  Have faith, do not despair.
  Trust in the LORD.

A Prayer for Help *t*

28   O LORD, my defender, I call to you.
    Listen to my cry!

If you do not answer me,
  I will be among those who go down
  to the world of the dead.
2 Hear me when I cry to you for help,
  when I lift my hands towards your
  holy Temple.
3 Do not condemn me with the wicked,
  with those who do evil—
  men whose words are friendly,
  but who have hatred in their hearts.

4 Punish them for what they have done,
  for the evil they have committed.
Punish them for all their deeds;
  give them what they deserve!
5 They take no notice of what the LORD
  has done
  or of what he has made;
so he will punish them
  and destroy them for ever.

6 Give praise to the LORD;
  he has heard my cry for help.
7 The LORD protects and defends me;
  I trust in him.
He gives me help and makes me glad;
  I praise him with joyful songs.

8 The LORD protects his people;
  he defends and saves his chosen king.
9 Save your people, LORD,
  and bless those who are yours.
Be their shepherd,
  and take care of them for ever.

The Voice of the LORD in the Storm *u*

29   Praise the LORD, you heavenly
    beings;
  praise his glory and power.
2 Praise the LORD's glorious name;
  bow down before the Holy One when
  he appears. *v*

3 The voice of the LORD is heard on the
  seas;
  the glorious God thunders,
  and his voice echoes over the ocean.
4 The voice of the LORD is heard
  in all its might and majesty.

5 The voice of the LORD breaks the cedars,
  even the cedars of Lebanon.
6 He makes the mountains of Lebanon
  jump like calves

s still trust God; *or* not lose courage.
t HEBREW TITLE: *By David.*
u HEBREW TITLE: *A psalm by David.*
v when he appears; *or* in garments of worship; *or* in his beautiful Temple.
28.4: Rev 22.12   **29.1-2:** Ps 96.7-9

and makes Mount Hermon leap like
a young bull.

7 The voice of the LORD makes the
lightning flash.
8 His voice makes the desert shake;
he shakes the desert of Kadesh.
9 The LORD's voice shakes the oaks w
and strips the leaves from the trees
while everyone in his Temple shouts,
"Glory to God!"

10 The LORD rules over the deep waters;
he rules as king for ever.
11 The LORD gives strength to his people
and blesses them with peace.

A Prayer of Thanksgiving x

30 I praise you, LORD, because you
have saved me
and kept my enemies from gloating
over me.
2 I cried to you for help, O LORD my God,
and you healed me;
3 you kept me from the grave.
I was on my way to the depths below, y
but you restored my life.

4 Sing praise to the LORD,
all his faithful people!
Remember what the Holy One has done,
and give him thanks!
5 His anger lasts only a moment,
his goodness for a lifetime.
Tears may flow in the night,
but joy comes in the morning.

6 I felt secure and said to myself,
"I will never be defeated."
7 You were good to me, LORD;
you protected me like a mountain
fortress.
But then you hid yourself from me,
and I was afraid.

8 I called to you, LORD;
I begged for your help:
9 "What will you gain from my death?
What profit from my going to the
grave?
Are dead people able to praise you?
Can they proclaim your unfailing
goodness?
10 Hear me, LORD, and be merciful!
Help me, LORD!"

11 You have changed my sadness into
a joyful dance;
you have taken away my sorrow
and surrounded me with joy.
12 So I will not be silent;
I will sing praise to you.
LORD, you are my God,
I will give you thanks for ever.

A Prayer of Trust in God z

31 I come to you, LORD, for protection;
never let me be defeated.
You are a righteous God;
save me, I pray!
2 Hear me! Save me now!
Be my refuge to protect me;
my defence to save me.

3 You are my refuge and defence;
guide me and lead me as you have
promised.
4 Keep me safe from the trap that has
been set for me;
shelter me from danger.
5 I place myself in your care.
You will save me, LORD;
you are a faithful God.

6 You hate those who worship false gods,
but I trust in you.
7 I will be glad and rejoice
because of your constant love.
You see my suffering;
you know my trouble.
8 You have not let my enemies capture
me;
you have given me freedom to go
where I wish.

9 Be merciful to me, LORD,
for I am in trouble;
my eyes are tired from so much crying;
I am completely worn out.
10 I am exhausted by sorrow,
and weeping has shortened my life.
I am weak from all my troubles; a
even my bones are wasting away.

11 All my enemies, and especially my
neighbours,
treat me with contempt;
those who know me are afraid of me;
when they see me in the street, they
run away.

w *Probable text* shakes the oaks; *Hebrew* makes the deer give birth.
x HEBREW TITLE: *A song for the dedication of the Temple; a psalm by David.*
y THE DEPTHS BELOW: *The world of the dead (see 6.5).*   z HEBREW TITLE: *A psalm by David.*
a *Some ancient translations* troubles; *Hebrew* iniquity.
31.5: Lk 23.46

¹² Everyone has forgotten me, as though
    I were dead;
  I am like something thrown away.
¹³ I hear many enemies whispering;
    terror is all round me.
They are making plans against me,
    plotting to kill me.

¹⁴ But my trust is in you, O LORD;
    you are my God.
¹⁵ I am always in your care;
    save me from my enemies,
    from those who persecute me.
¹⁶ Look on your servant with kindness;
    save me in your constant love.
¹⁷ I call to you, LORD;
    don't let me be disgraced.
May the wicked be disgraced;
    may they go silently down to the
    world of the dead.
¹⁸ Silence those liars—
    all the proud and arrogant
    who speak with contempt about
    righteous men.

¹⁹ How wonderful are the good things
    you keep for those who honour you!
Everyone knows how good you are,
    how securely you protect those who
    trust you.
²⁰ You hide them in the safety of your
    presence
    from the plots of men;
in a safe shelter you hide them
    from the insults of their enemies.

²¹ Praise the LORD!
How wonderfully he showed his love
    for me
    when I was surrounded and attacked!
²² I was afraid and thought
    that he had driven me out of his
    presence.
But he heard my cry,
    when I called to him for help.

²³ Love the LORD, all his faithful people.
The LORD protects the faithful,
    but punishes the proud as they
    deserve.
²⁴ Be strong, be courageous,
    all you that hope in the LORD.

Confession and Forgiveness *b*

32 Happy are those whose sins are
    forgiven,
whose wrongs are pardoned.
² Happy is the man whom the LORD does

    not accuse of doing wrong
    and who is free from all deceit.

³ When I did not confess my sins,
    I was worn out from crying all day
    long.
⁴ Day and night you punished me, LORD;
    my strength was completely drained,
    as moisture is dried up by the summer
    heat.

⁵ Then I confessed my sins to you;
    I did not conceal my wrongdoings.
I decided to confess them to you,
    and you forgave all my sins.

⁶ So all your loyal people should pray to
    you in times of need; *c*
when a great flood of trouble comes
    rushing in,
    it will not reach them.
⁷ You are my hiding place;
    you will save me from trouble.
I sing aloud of your salvation,
    because you protect me.

⁸ The LORD says, "I will teach you the
    way you should go;
    I will instruct you and advise you.
⁹ Don't be stupid like a horse or a mule,
    which must be controlled with a bit
    and bridle
    to make it submit."

¹⁰ The wicked will have to suffer,
    but those who trust in the LORD
    are protected by his constant love.
¹¹ You that are righteous, be glad and
    rejoice
because of what the LORD has done.
You that obey him, shout for joy!

A Song of Praise

33 All you that are righteous,
    shout for joy for what the LORD
    has done;
praise him, all you that obey him.
² Give thanks to the LORD with harps,
    sing to him with stringed instruments.
³ Sing a new song to him,
    play the harp with skill, and shout
    for joy!

⁴ The words of the LORD are true
    and all his works are dependable.
⁵ The LORD loves what is righteous and
    just;
    his constant love fills the earth.

---

b HEBREW TITLE: *A poem by David.*   *c Some ancient translations* need; *Hebrew* finding only.
32.1–2: Rom 4.7–8

⁶ The LORD created the heavens by his
command,
the sun, moon, and stars by his
spoken word.
⁷ He gathered all the seas into one place;
he shut up the ocean depths in
storerooms.

⁸ Worship the LORD, all the earth!
Honour him, all peoples of the world!
⁹ When he spoke, the world was created;
at his command everything appeared.

¹⁰ The LORD frustrates the purposes of
the nations;
he keeps them from carrying out their
plans.
¹¹ But his plans endure for ever;
his purposes last eternally.
¹² Happy is the nation whose God is the
LORD;
happy are the people he has chosen
for his own!

¹³ The LORD looks down from heaven
and sees all mankind.
¹⁴ From where he rules, he looks down
on all who live on earth.
¹⁵ He forms all their thoughts
and knows everything they do.

¹⁶ A king does not win because of his
powerful army;
a soldier does not triumph because
of his strength.
¹⁷ War-horses are useless for victory;
their great strength cannot save.

¹⁸ The LORD watches over those who
obey him,
those who trust in his constant love.
¹⁹ He saves them from death;
he keeps them alive in times of famine.

²⁰ We put our hope in the LORD;
he is our protector and our help.
²¹ We are glad because of him;
we trust in his holy name.

²² May your constant love be with us,
LORD,
as we put our hope in you.

In Praise of God's Goodness ᵈ

34 I will always thank the LORD;
I will never stop praising him.
² I will praise him for what he has done;

may all who are oppressed listen and
be glad!
³ Proclaim with me the LORD's greatness;
let us praise his name together!

⁴ I prayed to the LORD, and he answered
me;
he freed me from all my fears.
⁵ The oppressed look to him and are glad;
they will never be disappointed.
⁶ The helpless call to him, and he answers;
he saves them from all their troubles.
⁷ His angel guards those who honour the
LORD
and rescues them from danger.

⁸ Find out for yourself how good the LORD
is.
Happy are those who find safety with
him.
⁹ Honour the LORD, all his people;
those who obey him have all they
need.
¹⁰ Even lions go hungry for lack of food,
but those who obey the LORD lack
nothing good.

¹¹ Come, my young friends, and listen
to me,
and I will teach you to honour the
LORD.
¹² Would you like to enjoy life?
Do you want long life and happiness?
¹³ Then hold back from speaking evil
and from telling lies.
¹⁴ Turn away from evil and do good;
strive for peace with all your heart.

¹⁵ The LORD watches over the righteous
and listens to their cries;
¹⁶ but he opposes those who do evil,
so that when they die, they are soon
forgotten.
¹⁷ The righteous call to the LORD, and
he listens;
he rescues them from all their
troubles.
¹⁸ The LORD is near to those who are
discouraged;
he saves those who have lost all hope.

¹⁹ The good man suffers many troubles,
but the LORD saves him from them
all;
²⁰ the LORD preserves him completely;
not one of his bones is broken.
²¹ Evil will kill the wicked;

ᵈHEBREW TITLE: *By David, who left the presence of Abimelech after pretending to be mad and being sent away by him.*
34 Title: 1 Sam 21.13–15   **34.8:** 1 Pet 2.3   **34.12–16:** 1 Pet 3.10–12   **34.20:** Jn 19.36

those who hate the righteous will be
punished.

22 The LORD will save his people;
those who go to him for protection
will be spared.

A Prayer for Help e

35 Oppose those who oppose me,
LORD,
and fight those who fight against me!
2 Take your shield and armour
and come to my rescue.
3 Lift up your spear and your axe
against those who pursue me.
Promise that you will save me.

4 May those who try to kill me
be defeated and disgraced!
May those who plot against me
be turned back and confused!
5 May they be like straw blown by the
wind
as the angel of the LORD pursues
them!
6 May their path be dark and slippery
while the angel of the LORD strikes
them down!

7 Without any reason they laid a trap for
me
and dug a deep hole to catch me.
8 But destruction will catch them before
they know it;
they will be caught in their own trap
and fall to their destruction!

9 Then I will be glad because of the LORD;
I will be happy because he saved me.
10 With all my heart I will say to the
LORD,
"There is no one like you.
You protect the weak from the strong,
the poor from the oppressor."

11 Evil men testify against me
and accuse me of crimes I know
nothing about.
12 They pay me back evil for good,
and I sink in despair.
13 But when they were sick, I dressed
in mourning;
I deprived myself of food;
I prayed with my head bowed low,
14   as I would pray for a friend or a
brother.
I went about bent over in mourning,

as one who mourns for his mother.

15 But when I was in trouble, they were
all glad
and gathered round to mock me;
strangers beat me
and kept striking me.
16 Like men who would mock a cripple, f
they glared at me with hate.

17 How much longer, Lord, will you just
look on?
Rescue me from their attacks;
save my life from these lions!
18 Then I will thank you in the assembly
of your people;
I will praise you before them all.

19 Don't let my enemies, those liars,
gloat over my defeat.
Don't let those who hate me for no
reason
smirk with delight over my sorrow.

20 They do not speak in a friendly way;
instead they invent all kinds of lies
about peace-loving people.
21 They accuse me, shouting,
"We saw what you did!"
22 But you, O LORD, have seen this.
So don't be silent, Lord;
don't keep yourself far away!
23 Rouse yourself, O Lord, and defend
me;
rise up, my God, and plead my cause.
24 You are righteous, O LORD, so declare
me innocent;
don't let my enemies gloat over me.
25 Don't let them say to themselves,
"We are rid of him!
That's just what we wanted!"

26 May those who gloat over my suffering
be completely defeated and confused;
may those who claim to be better than
I am
be covered with shame and disgrace.

27 May those who want to see me
acquitted
shout for joy and say again and again,
"How great is the LORD!
He is pleased with the success of his
servant."
28 Then I will proclaim your
righteousness,
and I will praise you all day long.

---

e HEBREW TITLE: *By David.*   f *Probable text* Like men...cripple; *Hebrew unclear.*
35.19: Ps 69.4; Jn 15.25

The Wickedness of Man[g]

36 Sin speaks to the wicked man deep
in his heart;
he rejects God and has no reverence
for him.
2 Because he thinks so highly of himself,
he thinks that God will not discover
his sin and condemn it.
3 His speech is wicked and full of lies;
he no longer does what is wise and
good.
4 He makes evil plans as he lies in bed;
nothing he does is good,
and he never rejects anything evil.

The Goodness of God

5 LORD, your constant love reaches the
heavens;
your faithfulness extends to the skies.
6 Your righteousness is towering like the
mountains;
your justice is like the depths of the
sea.
Men and animals are in your care.

7 How precious, O God, is your constant
love!
We find[x] protection under the
shadow of your wings.
8 We feast on the abundant food you
provide;
you let us drink from the river of your
goodness.
9 You are the source of all life,
and because of your light we see the
light.

10 Continue to love those who know you
and to do good to those who are
righteous.
11 Do not let proud men attack me
or wicked men make me run away.

12 See where evil men have fallen.
There they lie, unable to rise.

The Destiny of the Wicked and
of the Good[h]

37 Don't be worried on account of the
wicked;
don't be jealous of those who do
wrong.
2 They will soon disappear like grass that
dries up;
they will die like plants that wither.

3 Trust in the LORD and do good;

live in the land and be safe.
4 Seek your happiness in the LORD,
and he will give you your heart's
desire.

5 Give yourself to the LORD;
trust in him, and he will help you;
6 he will make your righteousness shine
like the noonday sun.

7 Be patient and wait for the LORD to act;
don't be worried about those who
prosper
or those who succeed in their evil
plans.

8 Don't give in to worry or anger;
it only leads to trouble.
9 Those who trust in the LORD will possess
the land,
but the wicked will be driven out.

10 Soon the wicked will disappear;
you may look for them, but you won't
find them;
11 the humble will possess the land
and enjoy prosperity and peace.

12 The wicked man plots against the good
man
and glares at him with hate.
13 But the Lord laughs at wicked men,
because he knows they will soon be
destroyed.

14 The wicked draw their swords and
bend their bows
to kill the poor and needy,
to slaughter those who do what is
right;
15 but they will be killed by their own
swords,
and their bows will be smashed.

16 The little that a good man owns
is worth more than the wealth of all
the wicked,
17 because the LORD will take away the
strength of the wicked,
but protect those who are good.

18 The LORD takes care of those who obey
him,
and the land will be theirs for ever.
19 They will not suffer when times are
bad;
they will have enough in time of
famine.

[g] HEBREW TITLE: *By David, the LORD's servant.*
[x] precious, O God, is...find; *or* precious is your constant love! Gods and men find.
[h] HEBREW TITLE: *By David.*
36.1: Rom 3.18　　　**37.11:** Mt 5.5

20 But the wicked will die;
  the enemies of the LORD will vanish
    like wild flowers;
  they will disappear like smoke.

21 The wicked man borrows and never
    pays back,
  but the good man is generous with
    his gifts.
22 Those who are blessed by the LORD
    will possess the land,
  but those who are cursed by him will
    be driven out.

23 The LORD guides a man in the way
    he should go
  and protects those who please him.
24 If they fall, they will not stay down,
  because the LORD will help them up.

25 I am an old man now; I have lived
    a long time,
  but I have never seen a good man
    abandoned by the LORD
  or his children begging for food.
26 At all times he gives freely and lends
    to others,
  and his children are a blessing.

27 Turn away from evil and do good,
  and your descendants will always live
    in the land;
28 for the LORD loves what is right
  and does not abandon his faithful
    people.
  He protects them for ever,
  but the descendants of the wicked will
    be driven out.
29 The righteous will possess the land
  and live in it for ever.

30 A good man's words are wise,
  and he is always fair.
31 He keeps the law of his God in his
    heart
  and never departs from it.

32 A wicked man watches a good man
  and tries to kill him;
33 but the LORD will not abandon him
    to his enemy's power
  or let him be condemned when he
    is on trial.

34 Put your hope in the LORD and obey
    his commands;
  he will honour you by giving you the
    land,

and you will see the wicked driven
    out.

35 I once knew a wicked man who was
    a tyrant;
  he towered over everyone like a cedar
    of Lebanon; [i]
36 but later I [j] passed by, and he wasn't
    there;
  I looked for him, but couldn't find
    him.

37 Notice the good man, observe the
    righteous man;
  a peaceful man has descendants,
38 but sinners are completely destroyed,
  and their descendants are wiped out.

39 The LORD saves righteous men
  and protects them in times of trouble.
40 He helps them and rescues them;
  he saves them from the wicked,
  because they go to him for protection.

The Prayer of a Suffering Man [k]

38 O LORD, don't punish me in your
    anger!
2 You have wounded me with your
    arrows;
  you have struck me down.

3 Because of your anger, I am in great
    pain;
  my whole body is diseased because
    of my sins.
4 I am drowning in the flood of my sins;
  they are a burden too heavy to bear.

5 Because I have been foolish,
  my sores stink and rot.
6 I am bowed down, I am crushed;
  I mourn all day long.
7 I am burning with fever
  and I am near to death.
8 I am worn out and utterly crushed;
  my heart is troubled, and I groan with
    pain.

9 O Lord, you know what I long for;
  you hear all my groans.
10 My heart is pounding, my strength is
    gone,
  and my eyes have lost their brightness.
11 My friends and neighbours will not
    come near me,
  because of my sores;
  even my family keeps away from me.

[i] *One ancient translation* like a cedar of Lebanon; *Hebrew unclear.*
[j] *Some ancient translations* I; *Hebrew* he.   [k] HEBREW TITLE: *A psalm by David; a lament.*

12 Those who want to kill me lay traps
      for me,
    and those who want to hurt me
      threaten to ruin me;
    they never stop plotting against me.

13 I am like a deaf man and cannot hear,
    like a dumb man and cannot speak.
14 I am like a man who does not answer,
    because he cannot hear.

15 But I trust in you, O LORD;
    and you, O Lord my God, will answer
      me.
16 Don't let my enemies gloat over my
      distress;
    don't let them boast about my
      downfall!
17 I am about to fall
    and am in constant pain.

18 I confess my sins;
    they fill me with anxiety.
19 My enemies are healthy and strong;
    there are many who hate me for no
      reason.
20 Those who pay back evil for good
    are against me because I try to do
      right.

21 Do not abandon me, O LORD;
    do not stay away, my God!
22 Help me now, O Lord my saviour!

The Confession of a Suffering Man [l]

39 I said, "I will be careful what I
      do
    and will not let my tongue make me
      sin;
    I will not say anything
      while evil men are near."
2 I kept quiet, not saying a word,
    not even about anything good!
    But my suffering only grew worse,
3   and I was overcome with anxiety.
    The more I thought, the more troubled
      I became;
    I could not keep from asking:
4 "LORD, how long will I live?
    When will I die?
    Tell me how soon my life will end."

5 How short you have made my life!
    In your sight my lifetime seems
      nothing.
    Indeed every living man is no more than
      a puff of wind,
6   no more than a shadow.

All he does is for nothing;
    he gathers wealth, but doesn't know
      who will get it.

7 What, then, can I hope for, Lord?
    I put my hope in you.
8 Save me from all my sins,
    and don't let fools laugh at me.
9 I will keep quiet, I will not say a word,
    for you are the one who made me
      suffer like this.
10 Don't punish me any more!
    I am about to die from your blows.
11 You punish a man's sins by your
      rebukes,
    and like a moth you destroy what he
      loves.
    Indeed a man is no more than a puff
      of wind!

12 Hear my prayer, LORD,
    and listen to my cry;
    come to my aid when I weep.
    Like all my ancestors
    I am only your guest for a little while.
13 Leave me alone so that I may have
      some happiness
    before I go away and am no more.

A Song of Praise [m]

40 I waited patiently for the LORD's
      help;
    then he listened to me and heard my
      cry.
2 He pulled me out of a dangerous pit,
    out of the deadly quicksand.
    He set me safely on a rock
    and made me secure.
3 He taught me to sing a new song,
    a song of praise to our God.
    Many who see this will take warning
    and will put their trust in the LORD.

4 Happy are those who trust the LORD,
    who do not turn to idols
    or join those who worship false gods.
5 You have done many things for us, O
      LORD our God;
    there is no one like you!
    You have made many wonderful
      plans for us.
    I could never speak of them all—
      their number is so great!

6 You do not want sacrifices and
      offerings;
    you do not ask for animals burnt
      whole on the altar

[l] HEBREW TITLE: *A psalm by David.*   [m] HEBREW TITLE: *A psalm by David.*
40.6–8: Heb 10.5–7

or for sacrifices to take away sins.
Instead, you have given me ears to hear
you,
7 and so I answered, "Here I am;
your instructions for me are in the
book of the Law.[n]
8 How I love to do your will, my God!
I keep your teaching in my heart."

9 In the assembly of all your people, LORD,
I told the good news that you save
us.
You know that I will never stop telling
it.
10 I have not kept the news of salvation
to myself;
I have always spoken of your
faithfulness and help.
In the assembly of all your people I
have not been silent
about your loyalty and constant love.

11 LORD, I know you will never stop being
merciful to me.
Your love and loyalty will always
keep me safe.

A Prayer for Help
(Ps 70)

12 I am surrounded by many troubles—
too many to count!
My sins have caught up with me,
and I can no longer see;
they are more than the hairs of my head,
and I have lost my courage.
13 Save me, LORD! Help me now!
14 May those who try to kill me
be completely defeated and confused.
May those who are happy because of
my troubles
be turned back and disgraced.
15 May those who jeer at me
be dismayed by their defeat.

16 May all who come to you
be glad and joyful.
May all who are thankful for your
salvation
always say, "How great is the LORD!"

17 I am weak and poor, O Lord,
but you have not forgotten me.
You are my saviour and my God—
hurry to my aid!

The Prayer of a Sick Man[o]

41 Happy are those who are
concerned for the poor;
the LORD will help them when they
are in trouble.
2 The LORD will protect them and preserve
their lives;
he will make them happy in the land;
he will not abandon them to the power
of their enemies.
3 The LORD will help them when they are
sick
and will restore them to health.

4 I said, "I have sinned against you, LORD;
be merciful to me and heal me."
5 My enemies say cruel things about me.
They want me to die and be forgotten.
6 Those who come to see me are not
sincere;
they gather bad news about me
and then go out and tell it everywhere.
7 All who hate me whisper to each other
about me,
they imagine the worst about[p] me.
8 They say, "He is fatally ill;
he will never leave his bed again."
9 Even my best friend, the one I trusted
most,
the one who shared my food,
has turned against me.

10 Be merciful to me, LORD, and restore
my health,
and I will pay my enemies back.
11 They will not triumph over me,
and I will know that you are pleased
with me.
12 You will help me, because I do what
is right;
you will keep me in your presence
for ever.

13 Praise the LORD, the God of Israel!
Praise him now and for ever!

Amen! Amen!

BOOK TWO
(Psalms 42–72)

The Prayer of a Man in Exile[q]

42 As a deer longs for a stream of
cool water,

[n] your instructions...Law; or my devotion to you is recorded in your book.
[o] HEBREW TITLE: A psalm by David.
[p] imagine the worst about; or make evil plans to harm.
[q] HEBREW TITLE: A poem by the clan of Korah.
41.9: Mt 26.23; Mk 14.18; Lk 22.21; Jn 13.18   **41.13:** Ps 106.48

so I long for you, O God.
2 I thirst for you, the living God;
    when can I go and worship in your
        presence?
3 Day and night I cry,
    and tears are my only food;
all the time my enemies ask me,
    "Where is your God?"

4 My heart breaks when I remember the
        past,
    when I went with the crowds to the
        house of God
    and led them as they walked along,
    a happy crowd, singing and shouting
        praise to God.
5 Why am I so sad?
    Why am I so troubled?
I will put my hope in God,
    and once again I will praise him,
    my saviour and my God.

6-7 Here in exile my heart is breaking,
    and so I turn my thoughts to him.
He has sent waves of sorrow over my
        soul;
    chaos roars at me like a flood,
    like waterfalls thundering down to the
        Jordan
    from Mount Hermon and Mount
        Mizar.
8 May the Lord show his constant love
        during the day,
    so that I may have a song at night,
    a prayer to the God of my life.

9 To God, my defender, I say,
    "Why have you forgotten me?
Why must I go on suffering
    from the cruelty of my enemies?"
10 I am crushed by their insults,
    as they keep on asking me,
    "Where is your God?"

11 Why am I so sad?
    Why am I so troubled?
I will put my hope in God,
    and once again I will praise him,
    my saviour and my God.

The Prayer of a Man in Exile
(Continuation of Psalm 42)

43 O God, declare me innocent,
    and defend my cause against the
        ungodly;
    deliver me from lying and evil men!
2 You are my protector;
    why have you abandoned me?

Why must I go on suffering
    from the cruelty of my enemies?

3 Send your light and your truth;
    may they lead me
    and bring me back to Zion, your
        sacred hill, r
    and to your Temple, where you live.
4 Then I will go to your altar, O God;
    you are the source of my happiness.
I will play my harp and sing praise to
        you,
    O God, my God.

5 Why am I so sad?
    Why am I so troubled?
I will put my hope in God,
    and once again I will praise him,
    my saviour and my God.

A Prayer for Protection s

44 With our own ears we have heard
        it, O God—
our ancestors have told us about it,
about the great things you did in their
        time,
    in the days of long ago:
2 how you yourself drove out the heathen
    and established your people in their
        land;
how you punished the other nations
    and caused your own to prosper.
3 Your people did not conquer the land
    with their swords;
    they did not win it by their own
        power;
it was by your power and your strength,
    by the assurance of your presence,
    which showed that you loved them.

4 You are my king and my God;
    you give t victory to your people,
5   and by your power we defeat our
        enemies.
6 I do not trust in my bow
    or in my sword to save me;
7 but you have saved us from our enemies
    and defeated those who hate us.
8 We will always praise you
    and give thanks to you for ever.

9 But now you have rejected us and let
        us be defeated;
    you no longer march out with our
        armies.
10 You made us run from our enemies,
    and they took for themselves what
        was ours.

---

r SACRED HILL: See 2.6.
s HEBREW TITLE: A poem by the clan of Korah.
t Some ancient translations and my God; you give; Hebrew O God; give.

11 You allowed us to be slaughtered like
  sheep;
  you scattered us in foreign countries.
12 You sold your own people for a small
  price
  as though they had little value. *m*

13 Our neighbours see what you did to
  us,
  and they mock us and laugh at us.
14 You have made us an object of
  contempt among the nations;
  they shake their heads at us in scorn.
15 I am always in disgrace;
  I am covered with shame
16   from hearing the sneers and insults
  of my enemies and those who hate
  me.

17 All this has happened to us,
  even though we have not forgotten
  you
  or broken the covenant you made
  with us.
18 We have not been disloyal to you;
  we have not disobeyed your
  commands.
19 Yet you left us helpless among wild
  animals;
  you abandoned us in deepest
  darkness.

20 If we had stopped worshipping our
  God
  and prayed to a foreign god,
21 you would surely have discovered it,
  because you know our secret
  thoughts.
22 But it is on your account that we are
  being killed all the time,
  that we are treated like sheep to be
  slaughtered.

23 Wake up, Lord! Why are you asleep?
  Rouse yourself! Don't reject us for
  ever!
24 Why are you hiding from us?
  Don't forget our suffering and
  trouble!

25 We fall crushed to the ground;
  we lie defeated in the dust.
26 Come to our aid!

Because of your constant love save
  us!

A Royal Wedding Song *u*

45 Beautiful words fill my mind,
  as I compose this song for the
  king.
Like the pen of a good writer
  my tongue is ready with a poem.

2 You are the most handsome of men;
  you are an eloquent speaker.
  God has always blessed you.
3 Buckle on your sword, mighty king;
  you are glorious and majestic.

4 Ride on in majesty to victory
  for the defence of truth and justice! *v*
  Your strength will win you great
  victories!
5 Your arrows are sharp,
  they pierce the hearts of your
  enemies;
  nations fall down at your feet.

6 The kingdom that God has given you *w*
  will last for ever and ever.
  You rule over your people with justice;
7   you love what is right and hate what
  is evil.
  That is why God, your God, has chosen
  you
  and has poured out more happiness
  on you
  than on any other king.
8 The perfume of myrrh and aloes is on
  your clothes;
  musicians entertain you in palaces
  decorated with ivory.
9 Among the ladies of your court are
  daughters of kings,
  and on the right of your throne stands
  the queen,
  wearing ornaments of finest gold.

10 Bride of the king, listen to what I say—
  forget your people and your relatives.
11 Your beauty will make the king desire
  you;
  he is your master, so you must obey
  him.
12 The people of Tyre will bring you gifts;
  rich people will try to win your favour.

m as...value; *or* and made no profit from the sale.
u HEBREW TITLE: *A poem by the clan of Korah; a love song.*
v *Probable text* and justice; *Hebrew* and meekness of justice.
w The kingdom that God has given you; *or* Your kingdom, O God; *or* Your divine kingdom.
44.22: Rom 8.36   **45.6–7:** Heb 1.8–9

¹³ The princess is in the palace—how
   beautiful she is!
   Her gown is made of gold thread.
¹⁴ In her colourful gown she is led to
   the king,
   followed by her bridesmaids,
   and they also are brought to him.
¹⁵ With joy and gladness they come
   and enter the king's palace.

¹⁶ You, my king, will have many sons
   to succeed your ancestors as kings,
   and you will make them rulers over
   the whole earth.
¹⁷ My song will keep your fame alive
   for ever,
   and everyone will praise you for all
   time to come.

God Is with Us *x*

46 God is our shelter and strength,
      always ready to help in times
      of trouble.
² So we will not be afraid, even if the
   earth is shaken
   and mountains fall into the ocean
   depths;
³ even if the seas roar and rage,
   and the hills are shaken by the
   violence.

⁴ There is a river that brings joy to the
   city of God,
   to the sacred house of the Most High.
⁵ God is in that city, and it will never
   be destroyed;
   at early dawn he will come to its aid.

x HEBREW TITLE: *A song by the clan of Korah.*
y HEBREW TITLE: *A psalm by the clan of Korah.*

⁶ Nations are terrified, kingdoms are
   shaken;
   God thunders, and the earth dissolves.

⁷ The Lord Almighty is with us;
   the God of Jacob is our refuge.

⁸ Come and see what the Lord has done.
   See what amazing things he has done
   on earth.
⁹ He stops wars all over the world;
   he breaks bows, destroys spears,
   and sets shields on fire.
¹⁰ "Stop fighting," he says, "and know
   that I am God,
   supreme among the nations,
   supreme over the world."

¹¹ The Lord Almighty is with us;
   the God of Jacob is our refuge.

The Supreme Ruler *y*

47 Clap your hands for joy, all
      peoples!
      Praise God with loud songs!
² The Lord, the Most High, is to be feared;
   he is a great king, ruling over all the
   world.
³ He gave us victory over the peoples;
   he made us rule over the nations.
⁴ He chose for us the land where we live,
   the proud possession of his people,
   whom he loves.

⁵ God goes up to his throne.
   There are shouts of joy and the blast
   of trumpets,

We will not be afraid (46.2)

Clap your hands for joy (47.1)

as the LORD goes up.
⁶ Sing praise to God;
   sing praise to our king!
⁷ God is king over all the world;
   praise him with songs!

⁸ God sits on his sacred throne;
   he rules over the nations.
⁹ The rulers of the nations assemble
   with the people *z* of the God of
      Abraham.
More powerful than all armies is he;
   he rules supreme.

Zion, the City of God *a*

48 The LORD is great and is to be
      highly praised
in the city of our God, on his sacred
   hill. *b*
² Zion, the mountain of God, is high and
      beautiful;
   the city of the great king brings joy
      to all the world.
³ God has shown that there is safety with
      him
   inside the fortresses of the city.

⁴ The kings gathered together
   and came to attack Mount Zion.
⁵ But when they saw it, they were
      amazed;
   they were afraid and ran away.

⁶ There they were seized with fear and
      anguish,
   like a woman about to bear a child,
⁷   like ships tossing in a furious storm.

⁸ We have heard what God has done,
   and now we have seen it
   in the city of our God, the LORD
      Almighty;
he will keep the city safe for ever.

⁹ Inside your Temple, O God,
   we think of your constant love.
¹⁰ You are praised by people everywhere,
   and your fame extends over all the
      earth.
You rule with justice;
¹¹   let the people of Zion be glad!
You give right judgements;
   let there be joy in the cities of Judah!

¹² People of God, walk round Zion and
      count the towers;
¹³   take notice of the walls and examine
      the fortresses,
so that you may tell the next generation:
¹⁴   "This God is our God for ever and
      ever;
   he will lead us for all time to come."

The Foolishness of Trusting in Riches *c*

49 Hear this, everyone!
      Listen, all people everywhere,

---

z Probable text with the people; *Hebrew* the people.
a HEBREW TITLE: *A psalm by the clan of Korah; a song.*
c HEBREW TITLE: *A psalm by the clan of Korah.*
48.2: Mt 5.35

b SACRED HILL: *See 2.6.*

² great and small alike,
  rich and poor together.
³ My thoughts will be clear;
  I will speak words of wisdom.
⁴ I will turn my attention to proverbs
  and explain their meaning as I play
  the harp.

⁵ I am not afraid in times of danger
  when I am surrounded by enemies,
⁶ by evil men who trust in their riches
  and boast of their great wealth.
⁷ A person can never redeem himself;
  he cannot pay God the price for his
  life,
⁸ because the payment for a human life
  is too great.
  What he could pay would never be
  enough
⁹ to keep him from the grave,
  to let him live for ever.

¹⁰ Anyone can see that even wise men
  die,
  as well as foolish and stupid men.
  They all leave their riches to their
  descendants.
¹¹ Their graves *d* are their homes for ever;
  there they stay for all time,
  though they once had lands of their
  own.
¹² A man's greatness cannot save him
  from death;
  he will still die like the animals.

¹³ See what happens to those who trust
  in themselves,
  the fate of those *e* who are satisfied
  with their wealth—
¹⁴ they are doomed to die like sheep,
  and Death will be their shepherd.
  The righteous will triumph over them,
  as their bodies quickly decay
  in the world of the dead far from their
  homes. *x*
¹⁵ But God will rescue me;
  he will save me from the power of
  death.

¹⁶ Don't be upset when a man becomes
  rich,
  when his wealth grows even greater;
¹⁷ he cannot take it with him when he
  dies;
  his wealth will not go with him to
  the grave.
¹⁸ Even if a man is satisfied with this
  life
  and is praised because he is
  successful,
¹⁹ he will join all his ancestors in death,
  where the darkness lasts for ever.
²⁰ A man's greatness cannot save him
  from death;
  he will still die like the animals.

True Worship *f*

50 The Almighty God, the LORD,
  speaks;
  he calls to the whole earth from east
  to west.

---

d Some ancient translations graves; *Hebrew* inner thoughts.
e One ancient translation the fate of those; *Hebrew* after them.
x in...homes; *Hebrew unclear.*
f HEBREW TITLE: *A psalm by Asaph.*

He cannot take it with him when he dies (49.17)

All the animals in the forest are mine (50.10)

2 God shines from Zion,
  the city perfect in its beauty.

3 Our God is coming, but not in silence;
  a raging fire is in front of him,
  a furious storm is round him.
4 He calls heaven and earth as witnesses
  to see him judge his people.
5 He says, "Gather my faithful people to
    me,
  those who made a covenant with me
    by offering a sacrifice."
6 The heavens proclaim that God is
    righteous,
  that he himself is judge.

7 "Listen, my people, and I will speak;
  I will testify against you, Israel.
  I am God, your God.
8 I do not reprimand you because of your
    sacrifices
  and the burnt-offerings you always
    bring me.
9 And yet I do not need bulls from your
    farms
  or goats from your flocks;
10 all the animals in the forest are mine
  and the cattle on thousands of hills.
11 All the wild birds are mine

and all living things in the fields.

12 "If I were hungry, I would not ask
    you for food,
  for the world and everything in it is
    mine.
13 Do I eat the flesh of bulls
  or drink the blood of goats?
14 Let the giving of thanks be your
    sacrifice to God,*g*
  and give the Almighty all that you
    promised.
15 Call to me when trouble comes;
  I will save you,
  and you will praise me."

16 But God says to the wicked,
  "Why should you recite my
    commandments?
  Why should you talk about my
    covenant?
17 You refuse to let me correct you;
  you reject my commands.
18 You become the friend of every thief
    you see
  and you associate with adulterers.

19 "You are always ready to speak evil;
  you never hesitate to tell lies.

g Let the giving...to God; *or* Offer your thanksgiving sacrifice to God.

20 You are ready to accuse your own
     brothers
     and to find fault with them.
21 You have done all this, and I have
     said nothing,
     so you thought that I was like you.
   But now I reprimand you
     and make the matter plain to you.

22 "Listen to this, you that ignore me,
     or I will destroy you,
     and there will be no one to save you.
23 Giving thanks is the sacrifice that
     honours me,
     and I will surely save all who obey
     me."

A Prayer for Forgiveness[h]

51 Be merciful to me, O God,
       because of your constant love.
   Because of your great mercy
     wipe away my sins!
2 Wash away all my evil
     and make me clean from my sin!

3 I recognize my faults;
     I am always conscious of my sins.
4 I have sinned against you—only against
     you—
   and done what you consider evil.
   So you are right in judging me;
     you are justified in condemning me.
5 I have been evil from the day I was
     born;
     from the time I was conceived, I have
     been sinful.

6 Sincerity and truth are what you
     require;
     fill my mind with your wisdom.
7 Remove my sin, and I will be clean;
     wash me, and I will be whiter than
     snow.
8 Let me hear the sounds of joy and
     gladness;
     and though you have crushed me and
     broken me,
     I will be happy once again.
9 Close your eyes to my sins
     and wipe out all my evil.

10 Create a pure heart in me, O God,
     and put a new and loyal spirit in me.
11 Do not banish me from your presence;

do not take your holy spirit away from
     me.
12 Give me again the joy that comes from
     your salvation,
     and make me willing to obey you.
13 Then I will teach sinners your
     commands,
     and they will turn back to you.

14 Spare my life, O God, and save me,[i]
     and I will gladly proclaim your
     righteousness.
15 Help me to speak, Lord,
     and I will praise you.

16 You do not want sacrifices,
     or I would offer them;
   you are not pleased with burnt-offerings.
17 My sacrifice is a humble spirit, O God;
     you will not reject a humble and
     repentant heart.

18 O God, be kind to Zion and help her;
     rebuild the walls of Jerusalem.
19 Then you will be pleased with proper
     sacrifices
     and with our burnt-offerings;
     and bulls will be sacrificed on your
     altar.

God's Judgement and Grace[j]

52 Why do you boast, great man, of
       your evil?
   God's faithfulness is eternal.
2 You make plans to ruin others;
     your tongue is like a sharp razor.
   You are always inventing lies.
3 You love evil more than good
     and falsehood more than truth.
4 You love to hurt people with your
     words, you liar!

5 So God will ruin you for ever;
     he will take hold of you and snatch
     you from your home;
   he will remove you from the world
     of the living.
6 Righteous people will see this and be
     afraid;
     then they will laugh at you and say,
7 "Look, here is a man who did not depend
     on God for safety,
     but trusted instead in his great wealth
     and looked for security in being
     wicked."

[h] HEBREW TITLE: *A psalm by David, after the prophet Nathan had spoken to him about his adultery with Bathsheba.*
[i] Spare my life...me; *or* O God my saviour, keep me from the crime of murder.
[j] HEBREW TITLE: *A poem by David, after Doeg the Edomite went to Saul and told him that David had gone to the house of Ahimelech.*
51 Title: 2 Sam 12.1–15   **51.4:** Rom 3.4   **52** Title: 1 Sam 22.9–10

8 But I am like an olive-tree growing in
the house of God;
I trust in his constant love for ever
and ever.
9 I will always thank you, God, for what
you have done;
in the presence of your people
I will proclaim that you are good.

The Wickedness of Men [k]
(Ps 14)

53 Fools say to themselves,
"There is no God."
They are all corrupt,
and they have done terrible things;
there is no one who does what is right.

2 God looks down from heaven at
mankind
to see if there are any who are wise,
any who worship him.
3 But they have all turned away;
they are all equally bad.
Not one of them does what is right,
not a single one.

4 "Don't they know?" God asks.
"Are these evildoers ignorant?
They live by robbing my people,
and they never pray to me."

5 But then they will be terrified,
as they have never been before,
for God will scatter the bones of the
enemies of his people.
God has rejected them,
and so Israel will totally defeat them.

6 How I pray that victory
will come to Israel from Zion.
How happy the people of Israel will be
when God makes them prosperous
again!

A Prayer for Protection from Enemies [l]

54 Save me by your power, O God;
set me free by your might!
2 Hear my prayer, O God;
listen to my words!
3 Proud men are coming to attack me;
cruel men are trying to kill me—
men who do not care about God.

4 But God is my helper.
The Lord is my defender.

5 May God use their own evil to punish
my enemies.
He will destroy them because he is
faithful.

6 I will gladly offer you a sacrifice, O
LORD;
I will give you thanks
because you are good.
7 You have rescued me from all my
troubles,
and I have seen my enemies defeated.

The Prayer of a Man Betrayed
by a Friend [m]

55 Hear my prayer, O God;
don't turn away from my plea!
2 Listen to me and answer me;
I am worn out by my worries.
3 I am terrified by the threats of my
enemies,
crushed by the oppression of the
wicked.
They bring trouble on me;
they are angry with me and hate me.

4 I am terrified,
and the terrors of death crush me.
5 I am gripped by fear and trembling;
I am overcome with horror.
6 I wish I had wings, like a dove.
I would fly away and find rest.
7 I would fly far away
and live in the wilderness.
8 I would quickly find myself a shelter
from the raging wind and the storm.
9 Confuse the speech of my enemies, O
Lord!

I see violence and riots in the city,
10   surrounding it day and night,
filling it with crime and trouble.
11 There is destruction everywhere;
the streets are full of oppression and
fraud.

12 If it were an enemy that mocked me,
I could endure it;
if it were an opponent boasting over
me,
I could hide myself from him.
13 But it is you, my companion,
my colleague and close friend.
14 We had intimate talks with each other
and worshipped together in the
Temple.

[k] HEBREW TITLE: *A poem by David.*
[l] HEBREW TITLE: *A poem by David, after the men from Ziph went to Saul and told him that David
was hiding in their territory.* [m] HEBREW TITLE: *A poem by David.*
53.1–3: Rom 3.10–12   **54 Title:** 1 Sam 23.19, 26.1

¹⁵ May my enemies die before their time;
    may they go down alive into the world
      of the dead!
Evil is in their homes and in their hearts.

¹⁶ But I call to the LORD God for help,
    and he will save me.
¹⁷ Morning, noon, and night
    my complaints and groans go up to
      him,
    and he will hear my voice.
¹⁸ He will bring me safely back
    from the battles that I fight
    against so many enemies.
¹⁹ God, who has ruled from eternity,
    will hear me and defeat them;
for they refuse to change,
    and they do not fear him.

²⁰ My former companion attacked his
    friends;
    he broke his promises.
²¹ His words were smoother than cream,
    but there was hatred in his heart;
his words were as soothing as oil,
    but they cut like sharp swords.

²² Leave your troubles with the LORD,
    and he will defend you;
he never lets honest men be defeated.

²³ But you, O God, will bring those
    murderers and liars to their graves
    before half their life is over.
As for me, I will trust in you.

A Prayer of Trust in God ⁿ

56 Be merciful to me, O God,
    because I am under attack;
my enemies persecute me all the time.
² All day long my opponents attack me.
    There are so many who fight against
      me.
³ When I am afraid, O LORD Almighty,
    I put my trust in you.
⁴ I trust in God and am not afraid;
    I praise him for what he has promised.
    What can a mere human being do
      to me?

⁵ My enemies make trouble for me all
    day long;
    they are always planning how to hurt
      me!
⁶ They gather in hiding-places
    and watch everything I do,

    hoping to kill me.
⁷ Punish ᵒ them, O God, for their evil;
    defeat those people in your anger!

⁸ You know how troubled I am;
    you have kept a record of my tears.
    Aren't they listed in your book?
⁹ The day I call to you,
    my enemies will be turned back.
I know this: God ᵖ is on my side—
¹⁰   the LORD, whose promises I praise.
¹¹ In him I trust, and I will not be afraid.
    What can a mere human being do
      to me?

¹² O God, I will offer you what I have
    promised;
    I will give you my offering of
      thanksgiving,
¹³ because you have rescued me from
    death
    and kept me from defeat.
And so I walk in the presence of God,
    in the light that shines on the living.

A Prayer for Help �q

57 Be merciful to me, O God, be
    merciful,
because I come to you for safety.
In the shadow of your wings I find
    protection
    until the raging storms are over.

² I call to God, the Most High,
    to God, who supplies my every need.
³ He will answer from heaven and save
    me;
    he will defeat my oppressors.
    God will show me his constant love
      and faithfulness.

⁴ I am surrounded by enemies,
    who are like man-eating lions.
Their teeth are like spears and arrows;
    their tongues are like sharp swords.

⁵ Show your greatness in the sky, O God,
    and your glory over all the earth.

⁶ My enemies have spread a net to catch
    me;
    I am overcome with distress.
They dug a pit in my path,
    but fell into it themselves.

⁷ I have complete confidence, O God;

ⁿ HEBREW TITLE: *A psalm by David, after the Philistines captured him in Gath.*
ᵒ *Probable text* Punish; *Hebrew* Save.   ᵖ I know this: God; *or* Because I know that God.
q HEBREW TITLE: *A psalm by David, after he fled from Saul in the cave.*
56 Title: 1 Sam 21.13–15   **57 Title:** 1 Sam 22.1, 24.3

I will sing and praise you!
8 Wake up, my soul!
Wake up, my harp and lyre!
I will wake up the sun.
9 I will thank you, O Lord, among the
nations.
I will praise you among the peoples.
10 Your constant love reaches the
heavens;
your faithfulness touches the skies.
11 Show your greatness in the sky, O
God,
and your glory over all the earth.

A Prayer for God to Punish the Wicked [r]

58 Do you rulers [s] ever give a just
decision?
Do you judge all men fairly?
2 No! You think only of the evil you can
do,
and commit crimes of violence in the
land.

3 Evil men go wrong all their lives;
they tell lies from the day they are
born.
4 They are full of poison like snakes;
they stop up their ears like a deaf
cobra,
5 which does not hear the voice of the
snake-charmer,
or the chant of the clever magician.

6 Break the teeth of these fierce lions,
O God.
7 May they disappear like water draining
away;
may they be crushed like weeds on
a path. [t]
8 May they be like snails that dissolve
into slime;
may they be like a baby born dead
that never sees the light.
9 Before they know it, they are cut down
like weeds;
in his fierce anger God will blow them
away
while they are still living. [u]

10 The righteous will be glad when they
see sinners punished;
they will wade through the blood of
the wicked.
11 People will say, "The righteous are
indeed rewarded;

there is indeed a God who judges the
world."

A Prayer for Safety [v]

59 Save me from my enemies, my
God;
protect me from those who attack me!
2 Save me from those evil men;
rescue me from those murderers!

3 Look! They are waiting to kill me;
cruel men are gathering against me.
It is not because of any sin or wrong
I have done,
4 nor because of any fault of mine, O
LORD,
that they hurry to their places.

5 Rise, LORD God Almighty, and come to
my aid;
see for yourself, God of Israel!
Wake up and punish the heathen;
show no mercy to evil traitors!

6 They come back in the evening,
snarling like dogs as they go about
the city.
7 Listen to their insults and threats.
Their tongues are like swords in their
mouths,
yet they think that no one hears them.

8 But you laugh at them, LORD;
you mock all the heathen.
9 I have confidence in your strength;
you are my refuge, O God.
10 My God loves me and will come to
me;
he will let me see my enemies
defeated.

11 Do not kill them, O God, or my people
may forget.
Scatter them by your strength and
defeat them,
O Lord, our protector.
12 Sin is on their lips; all their words
are sinful;
may they be caught in their pride!
Because they curse and lie,
13 destroy them in your anger;
destroy them completely.
Then everyone will know that God rules
in Israel,
that his rule extends over all the earth.

[r] HEBREW TITLE: *A psalm by David.*   [s] rulers; *or gods.*
[t] *Probable text* may...path; *Hebrew unclear.*   [u] *Verse 9 in Hebrew is unclear.*
[v] HEBREW TITLE: *A psalm by David, after Saul sent men to watch his house in order to kill him.*
59 Title: 1 Sam 19.11

14 My enemies come back in the evening,
   snarling like dogs as they go about
     the city,
15   like dogs roaming about for food
   and growling if they do not find
     enough.

16 But I will sing about your strength;
   every morning I will sing aloud of
     your constant love.
  You have been a refuge for me,
   a shelter in my time of trouble.
17 I will praise you, my defender.
  My refuge is God,
   the God who loves me.

A Prayer for Deliverance [w]

60 You have rejected us, God, and
     defeated us;
  you have been angry with us—but
   now turn back to us. [x]
2 You have made the land tremble, and
   you have cut it open;
  now heal its wounds, because it is
   falling apart.
3 You have made your people suffer
   greatly;
  we stagger around as though we were
   drunk.
4 You have warned those who show you
   reverence,
  so that they might escape destruction.
5 Save us by your might; answer our
   prayer,
  so that the people you love may be
   rescued.

6 From his sanctuary [y] God has said,
  "In triumph I will divide Shechem
  and distribute the Valley of Sukkoth
   to my people.
7 Gilead is mine, and Manasseh too;
  Ephraim is my helmet
  and Judah my royal sceptre.
8 But I will use Moab as my wash-basin
  and I will throw my sandals on Edom,
   as a sign that I own it.
  Did the Philistines think they would
   shout in triumph over me?"

9 Who, O God, will take me into the
   fortified city?
  Who will lead me to Edom?
10 Have you really rejected us?

Aren't you going to march out with
   our armies?
11 Help us against the enemy;
  human help is worthless.
12 With God on our side we will win;
  he will defeat our enemies.

A Prayer for Protection [z]

61 Hear my cry, O God;
     listen to my prayer!
2 In despair and far from home
  I call to you!

  Take me to a safe refuge,
3   for you are my protector,
  my strong defence against my
   enemies.

4 Let me live in your sanctuary all my
   life;
  let me find safety under your wings.
5 You have heard my promises, O God,
  and you have given me what belongs
   to those who honour you.

6 Add many years to the king's life;
  let him live on and on!
7 May he rule for ever in your presence,
   O God;
  protect him with your constant love
   and faithfulness.

8 So I will always sing praises to you,
  as I offer you daily what I have
   promised.

Confidence in God's Protection [a]

62 I wait patiently for God to save
     me;
  I depend on him alone.
2 He alone protects and saves me;
  he is my defender,
  and I shall never be defeated.

3 How much longer will all of you attack
   a man
  who is no stronger than a broken-
   down fence?
4 You only want to bring him down from
   his place of honour;
  you take pleasure in lies.
  You speak words of blessing,
  but in your heart you curse him.

5 I depend on God alone;

---

[w] HEBREW TITLE: *A psalm by David, for teaching, when he fought against the Arameans from Naharaim and from Zobah, and Joab turned back and killed 12,000 Edomites in the Valley of Salt.*
[x] angry with us...us; *or* angry with us and turned your back on us.
[y] From his sanctuary; *or* In his holiness.   [z] HEBREW TITLE: *By David.*
[a] HEBREW TITLE: *A psalm by David.*
60 Title: 2 Sam 8.13; 1 Chr 18.12

Take me to a safe refuge (61.2)

I put my hope in him.
6 He alone protects and saves me;
  he is my defender,
  and I shall never be defeated.
7 My salvation and honour depend on
    God;
  he is my strong protector;
  he is my shelter.

8 Trust in God at all times, my people.
  Tell him all your troubles,
  for he is our refuge.

9 Men are all like a puff of breath;
  great and small alike are worthless.
  Put them on the scales, and they weigh
    nothing;
  they are lighter than a mere breath.
10 Don't put your trust in violence;
  don't hope to gain anything by
    robbery;
  even if your riches increase,
  don't depend on them.

11 More than once I have heard God say
  that power belongs to him
12 and that his love is constant.

You yourself, O Lord, reward everyone
  according to his deeds.

Longing for God [b]

63 O God, you are my God,
    and I long for you.
My whole being desires you;
  like a dry, worn-out, and waterless
    land,
  my soul is thirsty for you.
2 Let me see you in the sanctuary;
  let me see how mighty and glorious
    you are.
3 Your constant love is better than life
    itself,
  and so I will praise you.
4 I will give you thanks as long as I live;
  I will raise my hands to you in prayer.
5 My soul will feast and be satisfied,
  and I will sing glad songs of praise
    to you.

6 As I lie in bed, I remember you;
  all night long I think of you,
7 because you have always been my
    help.

[b] HEBREW TITLE: A psalm by David, when he was in the desert of Judah.
62.12: Job 34.11; Jer 17.10; Mt 16.27; Rom 2.6; Rev 2.23   **63 Title:** 1 Sam 23.14

In the shadow of your wings I sing for joy.
⁸ I cling to you,
and your hand keeps me safe.

⁹ Those who are trying to kill me
will go down into the world of the dead.
¹⁰ They will be killed in battle,
and their bodies eaten by wolves.
¹¹ Because God gives him victory,
the king will rejoice.
Those who make promises in God's name will praise him,
but the mouths of liars will be shut.

A Prayer for Protection *c*

64 I am in trouble, God—listen to my prayer!
I am afraid of my enemies—save my life!
² Protect me from the plots of the wicked,
from mobs of evil men.
³ They sharpen their tongues like swords
and aim cruel words like arrows.
⁴ They are quick to spread their shameless lies;
they destroy good men with cowardly slander.
⁵ They encourage each other in their evil plots;
they plan where to place their traps.
"No one can see them," they say.
⁶ They make evil plans and say,
"We have planned a perfect crime."
The heart and mind of man are a mystery.

⁷ But God shoots his arrows at them,
and suddenly they are wounded.
⁸ He will destroy them because of those words; *d*
all who see them will shake their heads.
⁹ They will all be afraid;
they will think about what God has done
and tell about his deeds.
¹⁰ All righteous people will rejoice
because of what the LORD has done.
They will find safety in him;
all good people will praise him.

Praise and Thanksgiving *e*

65 O God, it is right for us to praise you in Zion

and keep our promises to you,
² because you answer prayers.
People everywhere will come to you
³ on account of their sins.
Our faults defeat us, *f*
but you forgive them.
⁴ Happy are those whom you choose,
whom you bring to live in your sanctuary.
We shall be satisfied with the good things of your house,
the blessings of your sacred Temple.

⁵ You answer us by giving us victory
and you do wonderful things to save us.
People all over the world
and across the distant seas trust in you.
⁶ You set the mountains in place by your strength,
showing your mighty power.
⁷ You calm the roar of the seas
and the noise of the waves;
you calm the uproar of the peoples.
⁸ The whole world stands in awe
of the great things that you have done.
Your deeds bring shouts of joy
from one end of the earth to the other.

⁹ You show your care for the land by sending rain;
you make it rich and fertile.
You fill the streams with water;
you provide the earth with crops.
This is how you do it:
¹⁰ you send abundant rain on the ploughed fields
and soak them with water;
you soften the soil with showers
and cause the young plants to grow.
¹¹ What a rich harvest your goodness provides!
Wherever you go there is plenty.
¹² The pastures are filled with flocks;
the hillsides are full of joy.
¹³ The fields are covered with sheep;
the valleys are full of wheat.
Everything shouts and sings for joy.

A Song of Praise and Thanksgiving *g*

66 Praise God with shouts of joy, all people!
² Sing to the glory of his name;
offer him glorious praise!

---

c HEBREW TITLE: *A psalm by David.*
d Probable text He will destroy them because of those words; *Hebrew* They will destroy him, those words are against them.   *e* HEBREW TITLE: *A psalm by David; a song.*
f One ancient translation us; *Hebrew* me.   *g* HEBREW TITLE: *A song.*

3 Say to God, "How wonderful are the
  things you do!
    Your power is so great
    that your enemies bow down in fear
    before you.
4 Everyone on earth worships you;
    they sing praises to you,
    they sing praises to your name."

5 Come and see what God has done,
    his wonderful acts among men.
6 He changed the sea into dry land;
    our ancestors crossed the river on
    foot.
  There we rejoiced because of what he
    did.
7 He rules for ever by his might
    and keeps his eyes on the nations.
    Let no rebels rise against him.
8 Praise our God, all nations;
    let your praise be heard.
9 He has kept us alive
    and has not allowed us to fall.

10 You have put us to the test, God;
    as silver is purified by fire
    so you have tested us.
11 You let us fall into a trap
    and placed heavy burdens on our
    backs.
12 You let our enemies trample over us;
    we went through fire and flood,
    but now you have brought us to a
    place of safety. h

13 I will bring burnt-offerings to your
    house;
    I will offer you what I promised.
14 I will give you what I said I would
    when I was in trouble.
15 I will offer sheep to be burnt on the
    altar;
    I will sacrifice bulls and goats,
    and the smoke will go up to the sky.

16 Come and listen, all who honour God,
    and I will tell you what he has done
    for me.
17 I cried to him for help;
    I praised him with songs.
18 If I had ignored my sins,
    the Lord would not have listened to
    me.
19 But God has indeed heard me;
    he has listened to my prayer.

20 I praise God,

because he did not reject my prayer
or keep back his constant love from
me.

A Song of Thanksgiving i

67 God, be merciful to us and bless
    us;
    look on us with kindness,
2 so that the whole world may know your
    will;
    so that all nations may know your
    salvation.

3 May the peoples praise you, O God;
    may all the peoples praise you!

4 May the nations be glad and sing for
    joy,
    because you judge the peoples with
    justice
    and guide every nation on earth.

5 May the peoples praise you, O God;
    may all the peoples praise you!

6 The land has produced its harvest;
    God, our God, has blessed us.
7 God has blessed us;
    may all people everywhere honour
    him.

A National Song of Triumph j

68 God rises up and scatters his
    enemies.
    Those who hate him run away in
    defeat.
2 As smoke is blown away, so he drives
    them off;
    as wax melts in front of the fire,
    so do the wicked perish in God's
    presence.
3 But the righteous are glad and rejoice
    in his presence;
    they are happy and shout for joy.

4 Sing to God, sing praises to his name;
    prepare a way for him who rides on
    the clouds. k
    His name is the LORD—be glad in his
    presence!

5 God, who lives in his sacred Temple,
    cares for orphans and protects
    widows.
6 He gives the lonely a home to live in
    and leads prisoners out into happy
    freedom,

h *Some ancient translations* safety; *Hebrew* overflowing.   i HEBREW TITLE: *A psalm; a song.*
j HEBREW TITLE: *A psalm by David; a song.*   k on the clouds; *or* across the desert.
66.6: Ex 14.21; Josh 3.14–17

but rebels will have to live in a
desolate land.

7 O God, when you led your people,
when you marched across the desert,
8 the earth shook, and the sky poured
down rain,
because of the coming of the God of
Sinai,[l]
the coming of the God of Israel.
9 You caused abundant rain to fall
and restored your worn-out land;
10 your people made their home there;
in your goodness you provided for the
poor.

11 The Lord gave the command,
and many women carried the news:
12 "Kings and their armies are running
away!"
The women at home divided what was
captured:
13 figures of doves covered with silver,
whose wings glittered with fine gold.
(Why did some of you stay among the
sheep pens on the day of battle?)
14 When Almighty God scattered the
kings on Mount Zalmon,
he caused snow to fall there.

15 What a mighty mountain is Bashan,
a mountain of many peaks!
16 Why from your mighty peaks do you
look with scorn
on the mountain[m] on which God
chose to live?
The LORD will live there for ever!

17 With his many thousands of mighty
chariots
the Lord comes from Sinai[n] into the
holy place.
18 He goes up to the heights,
taking many captives with him;
he receives gifts from rebellious men.
The LORD God will live there.

19 Praise the Lord,
who carries our burdens day after
day;
he is the God who saves us.
20 Our God is a God who saves;
he is the LORD, our Lord,
who rescues us from death.

21 God will surely break the heads of his
enemies,
of those who persist in their sinful
ways.
22 The Lord has said, "I will bring your
enemies back from Bashan;
I will bring them back from the depths
of the ocean,
23 so that you may wade in their blood,
and your dogs may lap up as much
as they want."

24 O God, your march of triumph is seen
by all,
the procession of God, my king, into
his sanctuary.
25 The singers are in front, the musicians
are behind,
in between are the girls beating the
tambourines.
26 "Praise God in the meeting of his
people;
praise the LORD, all you descendants
of Jacob!"
27 First comes Benjamin, the smallest
tribe,
then the leaders of Judah with their
group,
followed by the leaders of Zebulun
and Naphtali.

28 Show your power, O God,
the power you have used on our behalf
29 from your Temple in Jerusalem,
where kings bring gifts to you.
30 Rebuke Egypt, that wild animal in the
reeds;
rebuke the nations, that herd of bulls
with their calves,
until they all bow down and offer you
their silver.
Scatter those people who love to make
war![o]
31 Ambassadors[p] will come from Egypt;
the Sudanese will raise their hands
in prayer to God.

32 Sing to God, kingdoms of the world,
sing praise to the Lord,
33 to him who rides in the sky,
the ancient sky.
Listen to him shout with a mighty roar.
34 Proclaim God's power;
his majesty is over Israel,
his might is in the skies.

[l] GOD OF SINAI: *As the people of Israel went from Egypt to Canaan, God revealed himself to them
at Mount Sinai (see Ex 19.16–25).* [m] MOUNTAIN: *See 2.6.*
[n] *Probable text* comes from Sinai; *Hebrew* in them, Sinai. [o] *Verse 30 in Hebrew is unclear.*
[p] *Some ancient translations* Ambassadors; *Hebrew unclear.*
68.8: Ex 19.18   **68.18**: Eph 4.8

35 How awesome is God as he comes
  from his sanctuary—
  the God of Israel!
He gives strength and power to his
  people.

Praise God!

A Cry for Help [q]

69 Save me, O God!
  The water is up to my neck;
2 I am sinking in deep mud,
  and there is no solid ground;
I am out in deep water,
  and the waves are about to drown
  me.
3 I am worn out from calling for help,
  and my throat is aching.
I have strained my eyes,
  looking for your help.

4 Those who hate me for no reason
  are more numerous than the hairs of
  my head.
My enemies tell lies against me;
  they are strong and want to kill me.
They made me give back things I did
  not steal.
5 My sins, O God, are not hidden from
  you;
  you know how foolish I have been.
6 Don't let me bring shame on those who
  trust in you,
  Sovereign LORD Almighty!
Don't let me bring disgrace to those
  who worship you,
  O God of Israel!
7 It is for your sake that I have been
  insulted
  and that I am covered with shame.
8 I am like a stranger to my brothers,
  like a foreigner to my family.

9 My devotion to your Temple burns in
  me like a fire;
  the insults which are hurled at you
  fall on me.
10 I humble myself [r] by fasting,
  and people insult me;
11 I dress myself in clothes of mourning,
  and they laugh at me.
12 They talk about me in the streets,
  and drunkards make up songs about
  me.

13 But as for me, I will pray to you, LORD;

answer me, God, at a time you choose.
Answer me because of your great love,
  because you keep your promise to
  save.
14 Save me from sinking in the mud;
  keep me safe from my enemies,
  safe from the deep water.
15 Don't let the flood come over me;
  don't let me drown in the depths
  or sink into the grave.

16 Answer me, LORD, in the goodness of
  your constant love;
  in your great compassion turn to me!
17 Don't hide yourself from your servant;
  I am in great trouble—answer me
  now!
18 Come to me and save me;
  rescue me from my enemies.

19 You know how I am insulted,
  how I am disgraced and dishonoured;
  you see all my enemies.
20 Insults have broken my heart,
  and I am in despair.
I had hoped for sympathy, but there
  was none;
  for comfort, but I found none.
21 When I was hungry, they gave me
  poison;
  when I was thirsty, they offered me
  vinegar.
22 May their banquets cause their ruin;
  may their sacred feasts cause their
  downfall.
23 Strike them with blindness!
  Make their backs always weak!
24 Pour out your anger on them;
  let your indignation overtake them.
25 May their camps be left deserted;
  may no one be left alive in their tents.
26 They persecute those whom you have
  punished;
  they talk about the sufferings of those
  you have wounded.
27 Keep a record of all their sins;
  don't let them have any part in your
  salvation.
28 May their names be erased from the
  book of the living;
  may they not be included in the list
  of your people.

29 But I am in pain and despair;
  lift me up, O God, and save me!

---

q HEBREW TITLE: *By David.*   r *Some ancient translations* humble myself; *Hebrew* cry.
69.4: Ps 35.19; Jn 15.25   **69.9:** Jn 2.17; Rom 15.3
69.21: Mt 27.48; Mk 15.36; Lk 23.36; Jn 19.28-29   **69.22-23:** Rom 11.9-10   **69.25:** Acts 1.20
69.28: Ex 32.32; Rev 3.5. 13.8, 17.8

30 I will praise God with a song;
   I will proclaim his greatness by giving
      him thanks.
31 This will please the LORD more than
      offering him cattle,
   more than sacrificing a full-grown
      bull.
32 When the oppressed see this, they will
      be glad;
   those who worship God will be
      encouraged.
33 The LORD listens to those in need
   and does not forget his people in
      prison.

34 Praise God, O heaven and earth,
   seas and all creatures in them.
35 He will save Jerusalem
   and rebuild the towns of Judah.
   His people will live there and possess
      the land;
36   the descendants of his servants will
         inherit it,
   and those who love him will live there.

A Prayer for Help [s]
(Ps 40.13–17)

70 Save me, O God!
   LORD, help me now!
2 May those who try to kill me
   be defeated and confused.
   May those who are happy because of
      my troubles
   be turned back and disgraced.
3 May those who jeer at me
   be dismayed by their defeat.

4 May all who come to you
   be glad and joyful.
   May all who are thankful for your
      salvation
   always say, "How great is God!"

5 I am weak and poor;
   come to me quickly, O God.
   You are my saviour, O LORD—
   hurry to my aid!

An Old Man's Prayer

71 LORD, I have come to you for
      protection;
   never let me be defeated!
2 Because you are righteous, help me and
      rescue me.
   Listen to me and save me!
3 Be my secure shelter
   and a strong fortress [t] to protect me;

you are my refuge and defence.

4 My God, rescue me from wicked men,
   from the power of cruel and evil men.
5 Sovereign LORD, I put my hope in you;
   I have trusted in you since I was
      young.
6 I have relied on you all my life;
   you have protected [u] me since the day
      I was born.
   I will always praise you.

7 My life has been an example to many,
   because you have been my strong
      defender.
8 All day long I praise you
   and proclaim your glory.
9 Do not reject me now that I am old;
   do not abandon me now that I am
      feeble.
10 My enemies want to kill me;
   they talk and plot against me.
11 They say, "God has abandoned him;
   let's go after him and catch him;
   there is no one to rescue him."

12 Don't stay so far away, O God;
   my God, hurry to my aid!
13 May those who attack me
   be defeated and destroyed.
   May those who try to hurt me
   be shamed and disgraced.
14 I will always put my hope in you;
   I will praise you more and more.
15 I will tell of your goodness;
   all day long I will speak of your
      salvation,
   though it is more than I can
      understand.
16 I will praise your power, Sovereign
      LORD;
   I will proclaim your goodness, yours
      alone.

17 You have taught me ever since I was
      young,
   and I still tell of your wonderful acts.
18 Now that I am old and my hair is
      grey,
   do not abandon me, O God!
   Be with me while I proclaim your power
      and might
   to all generations to come.

19 Your righteousness, God, reaches the
      skies.
   You have done great things;

[s] HEBREW TITLE: *A psalm by David; a lament.*
[t] *One ancient translation* a strong fortress; *Hebrew* to go always you commanded.
[u] *Some ancient translations* protected; *Hebrew unclear.*

there is no one like you.
20 You have sent troubles and suffering
    on me,
    but you will restore my strength;
    you will keep me from the grave.
21 You will make me greater than ever;
    you will comfort me again.

22 I will indeed praise you with the harp;

Now that I am old (71.18)

I will praise your faithfulness, my God.
On my harp I will play hymns to you,
    the Holy One of Israel.
23 I will shout for joy as I play for you;
    with my whole being I will sing
    because you have saved me.
24 I will speak of your righteousness all
        day long,
    because those who tried to harm me
    have been defeated and disgraced.

A Prayer for the King [v]

72 Teach the king to judge with your
        righteousness, O God;
    share with him your own justice,
2 so that he will rule over your people
        with justice
    and govern the oppressed with
        righteousness.
3 May the land enjoy prosperity;
    may it experience righteousness.
4 May the king judge the poor fairly;
    may he help the needy
    and defeat their oppressors.

5 May your people worship you as long
    as the sun shines,
    as long as the moon gives light, for
    ages to come.

6 May the king be like rain on the fields,
    like showers falling on the land.
7 May righteousness flourish in his
        lifetime,
    and may prosperity last as long as
    the moon gives light.

8 His kingdom will reach from sea to sea,
    from the Euphrates to the ends of
    the earth.
9 The peoples of the desert will bow down
        before him;
    his enemies will throw themselves to
    the ground.
10 The kings of Spain and of the islands
    will offer him gifts;
    the kings of Sheba and Seba [a] will
    bring him offerings.
11 All kings will bow down before him;
    all nations will serve him.

12 He rescues the poor who call to him,
    and those who are needy and
        neglected.
13 He has pity on the weak and poor;
    he saves the lives of those in need.
14 He rescues them from oppression and
        violence;
    their lives are precious to him.

15 Long live the king!
    May he be given gold from Arabia;
    may prayers be said for him at all
        times;
    may God's blessings be on him
        always!
16 May there be plenty of corn in the
        land;
    may the hills be covered with crops,
    as fruitful as those of Lebanon.
    May the cities be filled with people,
    like fields full of grass.
17 May the king's name never be
        forgotten;
    may his fame last as long as the sun.
    May all nations ask God to bless them
    as he has blessed the king. [b]

18 Praise the LORD, the God of Israel!
    He alone does these wonderful things.
19 Praise his glorious name for ever!

[v] HEBREW TITLE: *By Solomon.*
[a] SHEBA AND SEBA: *Sheba was towards the south in Arabia and Seba was on the opposite side
of the Red Sea.*   [b] as he...king; *or* and may they wish happiness for the king.
72.8: Zech 9.10

May his glory fill the whole world.

Amen! Amen!

²⁰ This is the end of the prayers of David son of Jesse.

BOOK THREE
(Psalms 73–89)

The Justice of God ᵂ

73
God is indeed good to Israel,
to those who have pure hearts.
² But I had nearly lost confidence;
my faith was almost gone
³ because I was jealous of the proud
when I saw that things go well for
the wicked.

⁴ They do not suffer pain;
they are strong and healthy.
⁵ They do not suffer as other people do;
they do not have the troubles that
others have.
⁶ And so they wear pride like a necklace
and violence like a robe;
⁷ their hearts pour out evil, ˣ
and their minds are busy with wicked
schemes.
⁸ They laugh at other people and speak
of evil things;
they are proud and make plans to
oppress others.
⁹ They speak evil of God in heaven
and give arrogant orders to men on
earth,
¹⁰ so that even God's people turn to them
and eagerly believe whatever they
say. ʸ
¹¹ They say, "God will not know;
the Most High will not find out."
¹² That is what the wicked are like.
They have plenty and are always
getting more.

¹³ Is it for nothing, then, that I have kept
myself pure
and have not committed sin?
¹⁴ O God, you have made me suffer all
day long;
every morning you have punished me.
¹⁵ If I had said such things,
I would not be acting as one of your
people.

¹⁶ I tried to think this problem through,
but it was too difficult for me
¹⁷ until I went into your Temple.
Then I understood what will happen to
the wicked.

¹⁸ You will put them in slippery places
and make them fall to destruction!
¹⁹ They are instantly destroyed;
they go down to a horrible end.
²⁰ They are like a dream that goes away
in the morning;
when you rouse yourself, O Lord, they
disappear.

²¹ When my thoughts were bitter
and my feelings were hurt,
²² I was as stupid as an animal;
I did not understand you.
²³ Yet I always stay close to you,
and you hold me by the hand.
²⁴ You guide me with your instruction
and at the end you will receive me
with honour.
²⁵ What else have I in heaven but you?
Since I have you, what else could I
want on earth?
²⁶ My mind and my body may grow weak,
but God is my strength;
he is all I ever need.

²⁷ Those who abandon you will certainly
perish;
you will destroy those who are
unfaithful to you.
²⁸ But as for me, how wonderful to be
near God,
to find protection with the Sovereign
LORD
and to proclaim all that he has done!

A Prayer for National Deliverance ᶻ

74
Why have you abandoned us like
this, O God?
Will you be angry with your own
people for ever?
² Remember your people, whom you
chose for yourself long ago,
whom you brought out of slavery to
be your own tribe.
Remember Mount Zion, where once
you lived.
³ Walk over these total ruins;
our enemies have destroyed
everything in the Temple.

ᵂ HEBREW TITLE: *By Asaph.*
ˣ *Some ancient translations* their hearts pour out evil; *Hebrew unclear.*
ʸ *Verse 10 in Hebrew is unclear.*   ᶻ HEBREW TITLE: *A poem by Asaph.*

4 Your enemies have shouted in triumph
  in your Temple;
    they have placed their flags there as
    signs of victory.
5 They looked like woodmen
    cutting down trees with their axes. *a*
6 They smashed all the wooden panels
    with their axes and sledge-hammers.
7 They wrecked your Temple and set it
  on fire;
    they desecrated the place where you
    are worshipped.
8 They wanted to crush us completely;
    they burnt down every holy place in
    the land.

9 All our sacred symbols are gone;
    there are no prophets left,
    and no one knows how long this will
    last.
10 How long, O God, will our enemies
    laugh at you?
    Will they insult your name for ever?
11 Why have you refused to help us?
    Why do you keep your hands behind
    you? *b*

12 But you have been our king from the
    beginning, O God;
    you have saved us many times.
13 With your mighty strength you divided
    the sea
    and smashed the heads of the sea-
    monsters;
14 you crushed the heads of the monster
    Leviathan *c*
    and fed his body to desert animals. *d*
15 You made springs and fountains flow;
    you dried up large rivers.
16 You created the day and the night;
    you set the sun and the moon in their
    places;
17 you set the limits of the earth;
    you made summer and winter.

18 But remember, O Lord, that your
    enemies laugh at you,
    that they are godless and despise you.
19 Don't abandon your helpless people
    to their cruel enemies;
    don't forget your persecuted people!

20 Remember the covenant you made
    with us.
    There is violence in every dark corner
    of the land.
21 Don't let the oppressed be put to
    shame;
    let those poor and needy people praise
    you.

22 Rouse yourself, God, and defend your
    cause!
    Remember that godless people laugh
    at you all day long.
23 Don't forget the angry shouts of your
    enemies,
    the continuous noise made by your
    foes.

God the Judge *e*

75 We give thanks to you, O God,
    we give thanks to you!
  We proclaim how great you are
  and tell of *f* the wonderful things you
    have done.

2 "I have set a time for judgement," says
    God,
    "and I will judge with fairness.
3 Though every living creature tremble
    and the earth itself be shaken,
    I will keep its foundations firm.
4 I tell the wicked not to be arrogant;
5   I tell them to stop their boasting."

6 Judgement does not come from the east
    or from the west,
    from the north or from the south; *g*
7 it is God who is the judge,
    condemning some and acquitting
    others.
8 The Lord holds a cup in his hand,
    filled with the strong wine of his
    anger.
  He pours it out, and all the wicked drink
    it;
    they drink it down to the last drop.

9 But I will never stop speaking of the
    God of Jacob
    or singing praises to him.
10 He will break the power of the wicked,
    but the power of the righteous will
    be increased.

a Verse 5 in Hebrew is unclear.
b Probable text Why do you keep your hands behind you; *Hebrew unclear.*
c LEVIATHAN: *A legendary monster which was a symbol of the forces of chaos and evil.*
d animals; *or* people.   *e* HEBREW TITLE: *A psalm by Asaph; a song.*
f Some ancient translations We proclaim how great you are and tell of; *Hebrew* Your name is
near and they tell of.
g Probable text from the north or from the south; *Hebrew* from the wilderness of the mountains.
74.13: Ex 14.21   **74.14:** Job 41.1; Ps 104.26; Is 27.1

God the Victor [h]

76 God is known in Judah;
his name is honoured in Israel.
2 He has his home in Jerusalem;
he lives on Mount Zion.
3 There he broke the arrows of the enemy,
their shields and swords, yes, all their
weapons.

4 How glorious you are, O God!
How majestic, as you return from the
mountains
where you defeated your foes.
5 Their brave soldiers have been stripped
of all they had
and now are sleeping the sleep of
death;
all their strength and skill was useless.
6 When you threatened them, O God of
Jacob,
the horses and their riders fell dead.

7 But you, LORD, are feared by all.
No one can stand in your presence
when you are angry.
8 You made your judgement known from
heaven;
the world was afraid and kept silent,
9 when you rose up to pronounce
judgement,
to save all the oppressed on earth.

10 Men's anger only results in more
praise for you;
those who survive the wars will keep
your festivals. [i]

11 Give the LORD your God what you
promised him;
bring gifts to him, all you nearby
nations.
God makes men fear him;
12 he humbles proud princes
and terrifies great kings.

Comfort in Time of Distress [j]

77 I cry aloud to God;
I cry aloud, and he hears me.
2 In times of trouble I pray to the Lord;
all night long I lift my hands in prayer,
but I cannot find comfort.
3 When I think of God, I sigh;
when I meditate, I feel discouraged.

4 He keeps me awake all night;
I am so worried that I cannot speak.
5 I think of days gone by
and remember years of long ago.
6 I spend the night in deep thought; [k]
I meditate, and this is what I ask
myself:
7 "Will the Lord always reject us?
Will he never again be pleased with
us?
8 Has he stopped loving us?
Does his promise no longer stand?
9 Has God forgotten to be merciful?
Has anger taken the place of his
compassion?"
10 Then I said, "What hurts me most is
this—
that God is no longer powerful." [l]

11 I will remember your great deeds,
LORD;
I will recall the wonders you did in
the past.
12 I will think about all that you have
done;
I will meditate on all your mighty acts.

13 Everything you do, O God, is holy.
No god is as great as you.
14 You are the God who works miracles;
you showed your might among the
nations.
15 By your power you saved your people,
the descendants of Jacob and of
Joseph.

16 When the waters saw you, O God, they
were afraid,
and the depths of the sea trembled.
17 The clouds poured down rain;
thunder crashed from the sky,
and lightning flashed in all directions.
18 The crash of your thunder rolled out,
and flashes of lightning lit up the
world;
the earth trembled and shook.
19 You walked through the waves;
you crossed the deep sea,
but your footprints could not be seen.
20 You led your people like a shepherd,
with Moses and Aaron in charge.

God and His People [m]

78 Listen, my people, to my teaching,
and pay attention to what I say.

---

[h] HEBREW TITLE: *A psalm by Asaph; a song.*
[i] *One ancient translation* will keep your festivals; *verse 10 in Hebrew is unclear.*
[j] HEBREW TITLE: *A psalm by Asaph.*   [k] *Some ancient translations* deep thought; *Hebrew* song.
[l] *Verse 10 in Hebrew is unclear.*   [m] HEBREW TITLE: *A poem by Asaph.*

2 I am going to use wise sayings
   and explain mysteries from the past,
3 things we have heard and known,
   things that our fathers told us.
4 We will not keep them from our
      children;
   we will tell the next generation
      about the LORD's power and his great
      deeds
   and the wonderful things he has done.

5 He gave laws to the people of Israel
   and commandments to the
      descendants of Jacob.
   He instructed our ancestors
      to teach his laws to their children,
6 so that the next generation might learn
      them
   and in turn should tell their children.
7 In this way they also would put their
      trust in God
   and not forget what he has done,
   but always obey his commandments.
8 They would not be like their ancestors,
   a rebellious and disobedient people,
   whose trust in God was never firm
   and who did not remain faithful to
      him.

9 The Ephraimites, armed with bows and
      arrows,
   ran away on the day of battle.
10 They did not keep their covenant with
      God;
   they refused to obey his law.
11 They forgot what he had done,
   the miracles they had seen him
      perform.
12 While their ancestors watched, God
      performed miracles
   in the plain of Zoan in the land of
      Egypt.
13 He divided the sea and took them
      through it;
   he made the waters stand like walls.
14 By day he led them with a cloud
   and all night long with the light of
      a fire.
15 He split rocks open in the desert
   and gave them water from the depths.
16 He caused a stream to come out of
      the rock
   and made water flow like a river.

17 But they continued to sin against God,
   and in the desert they rebelled against
      the Most High.

18 They deliberately put God to the test
   by demanding the food they wanted.
19 They spoke against God and said,
   "Can God supply food in the desert?
20 It is true that he struck the rock,
   and water flowed out in a torrent;
   but can he also provide us with bread
   and give his people meat?"

21 And so the LORD was angry when he
      heard them;
   he attacked his people with fire,
   and his anger against them grew,
22 because they had no faith in him
   and did not believe that he would save
      them.
23 But he spoke to the sky above
   and commanded its doors to open;
24 he gave them grain from heaven,
   by sending down manna for them to
      eat.
25 So they ate the food of angels,
   and God gave them all they wanted.
26 He also caused the east wind to blow,
   and by his power he stirred up the
      south wind;
27 and to his people he sent down birds,
   as many as the grains of sand on the
      shore;
28 they fell in the middle of the camp
   all round the tents.
29 So the people ate and were satisfied;
   God gave them what they wanted.
30 But they had not yet satisfied their
      craving
   and were still eating,
31 when God became angry with them
   and killed their strongest men,
   the best young men of Israel.

32 In spite of all this the people kept
      sinning;
   in spite of his miracles they did not
      trust him.
33 So he ended their days like a breath
   and their lives with sudden disaster.
34 Whenever he killed some of them,
   the rest would turn to him;
   they would repent and pray earnestly
      to him.
35 They remembered that God was their
      protector,
   that the Almighty came to their aid.
36 But their words were all lies;
   nothing they said was sincere.
37 They were not loyal to him;

78.2: Mt 13.35   78.12: Ex 7.8—12.32   78.13: Ex 14.21-22   78.14: Ex 13.21-22
78.15-16: Ex 17.1-7; Num 20.2-13   78.18-31: Ex 16.2-15; Num 11.4-23,31-35
78.24: Jn 6.31

they were not faithful to their
    covenant with him.

38 But God was merciful to his people.
    He forgave their sin
    and did not destroy them.
  Many times he held back his anger
    and restrained his fury.
39 He remembered that they were only
    mortal beings,
    like a wind that blows by and is gone.

40 How often they rebelled against him
    in the desert;
    how many times they made him sad!
41 Again and again they put God to the
    test
    and brought pain to the Holy God of
    Israel.
42 They forgot his great power
    and the day when he saved them from
    their enemies
43   and performed his mighty acts and
    miracles
    in the plain of Zoan in the land of
    Egypt.
44 He turned the rivers into blood,
    and the Egyptians had no water to
    drink.
45 He sent flies among them, that
    tormented them,
    and frogs that ruined their land.
46 He sent locusts to eat their crops
    and to destroy their fields.
47 He killed their grapevines with hail
    and their fig-trees with frost.
48 He killed their cattle with hail
    and their flocks with lightning. [n]
49 He caused them great distress
    by pouring out his anger and fierce
    rage,
    which came as messengers of death.
50 He did not restrain his anger
    or spare their lives,
    but killed them with a plague.
51 He killed the first-born sons
    of all the families of Egypt.

52 Then he led his people out like a
    shepherd
    and guided them through the desert.
53 He led them safely, and they were not
    afraid;
    but the sea came rolling over their
    enemies.

54 He brought them to his holy land,
    to the mountains which he himself
    conquered.
55 He drove out the inhabitants as his
    people advanced;
    he divided their land among the tribes
    of Israel
    and gave their homes to his people.

56 But they rebelled against Almighty
    God
    and put him to the test.
  They did not obey his commandments,
57   but were rebellious and disloyal like
    their fathers,
    unreliable as a crooked arrow.
58 They angered him with their heathen
    places of worship,
    and with their idols they made him
    furious.
59 God was angry when he saw it,
    so he rejected his people completely.
60 He abandoned his tent in Shiloh, [o]
    the home where he had lived among
    us.
61 He allowed our enemies to capture the
    Covenant Box,
    the symbol of his power and glory.
62 He was angry with his own people
    and let them be killed by their
    enemies.
63 Young men were killed in war,
    and young women had no one to
    marry.
64 Priests died by violence,
    and their widows were not allowed
    to mourn.

65 At last the Lord woke up as though
    from sleep;
    he was like a strong man excited by
    wine.
66 He drove his enemies back
    in lasting and shameful defeat.
67 But he rejected the descendants of
    Joseph;
    he did not select the tribe of Ephraim.
68 Instead he chose the tribe of Judah
    and Mount Zion, which he dearly
    loves.
69 There he built his Temple
    like his home in heaven;
    he made it firm like the earth itself,
    secure for all time.

[n] hail...lightning; or terrible disease...deadly plague.
[o] SHILOH: *The central place of worship for the people of Israel before the time of King David.*
78.44: Ex 7.17-21   **78.45:** Ex 8.1-6,20-24   **78.46:** Ex 10.12-15   **78.47-48:** Ex 9.22-25
78.51: Ex 12.29   **78.52:** Ex 13.17-22   **78.53:** Ex 14.26-28   **78.54:** Ex 15.17; Josh 3.14-17
78.55: Josh 11.16-23   **78.56:** Judg 2.11-15   **78.60:** Josh 18.1; Jer 7.12-14, 26.6
78.61: 1 Sam 4.4-22

70 He chose his servant David;
   he took him from the pastures,
71 where he looked after his flocks,
   and he made him king of Israel,
   the shepherd of the people of God.
72 David took care of them with unselfish
      devotion
   and led them with skill.

A Prayer for the Nation's Deliverance[p]

79 O God, the heathen have invaded
      your land.
   They have desecrated your holy
      Temple
   and left Jerusalem in ruins.
2 They left the bodies of your people for
      the vultures,
   the bodies of your servants for wild
      animals to eat.
3 They shed your people's blood like
      water;
   blood flowed like water all through
      Jerusalem,
   and no one was left to bury the dead.
4 The surrounding nations insult us;
   they laugh at us and mock us.

5 LORD, will you be angry with us for ever?
   Will your anger continue to burn like
      fire?
6 Turn your anger on the nations that do
      not worship you,
   on the people who do not pray to
      you.
7 For they have killed your people;
   they have ruined your country.

8 Do not punish us for the sins of our
      ancestors.
   Have mercy on us now;
   we have lost all hope.
9 Help us, O God, and save us;
   rescue us and forgive our sins
   for the sake of your own honour.
10 Why should the nations ask us,
   "Where is your God?"
   Let us see you punish the nations
   for shedding the blood of your
      servants.

11 Listen to the groans of the prisoners,
   and by your great power free those
      who are condemned to die.
12 Lord, pay the other nations back seven
      times
   for all the insults they have hurled
      at you.

13 Then we, your people, the sheep of
      your flock,
   will thank you for ever
   and praise you for all time to come.

A Prayer for the Nation's Restoration[q]

80 Listen to us, O Shepherd of Israel;
      hear us, leader of your flock.
   Seated on your throne above the winged
      creatures,
2   reveal yourself to the tribes of
      Ephraim, Benjamin, and Manasseh.
   Show us your strength;
   come and save us!

3 Bring us back, O God!
   Show us your mercy, and we will be
      saved!

4 How much longer, LORD God Almighty,
   will you be angry with your people's
      prayers?
5 You have given us sorrow to eat,
   a large cup of tears to drink.
6 You let the surrounding nations fight
      over our land;
   our enemies insult us.

7 Bring us back, Almighty God!
   Show us your mercy, and we will be
      saved!

8 You brought a grapevine out of Egypt;
   you drove out other nations and
      planted it in their land.
9 You cleared a place for it to grow;
   its roots went deep, and it spread out
      over the whole land.
10 It covered the hills with its shade;
   its branches overshadowed the giant
      cedars.
11 It extended its branches to the
      Mediterranean Sea
   and as far as the River Euphrates.
12 Why did you break down the fences
      round it?
   Now anyone passing by can steal its
      grapes;
13   wild pigs trample it down,
   and wild animals feed on it.

14 Turn to us, Almighty God!
   Look down from heaven at us;
   come and save your people!
15 Come and save this grapevine that you
      planted,

---

p HEBREW TITLE: *A psalm by Asaph.*   *q* HEBREW TITLE: *A psalm by Asaph; a testimony.*
78.70-71: 1 Sam 16.11-12; 2 Sam 7.8; 1 Chr 17.7   **80.1:** Ex 25.22
79.1: 2 Kgs 25.8-10; 2 Chr 36.17-19; Jer 52.12-14

this young vine you made grow so
strong!

16 Our enemies have set it on fire and
cut it down;
look at them in anger and destroy
them!
17 Preserve and protect the people you
have chosen,
the nation you made so strong.
18 We will never turn away from you
again;
keep us alive, and we will praise you.

19 Bring us back, LORD God Almighty.
Show us your mercy, and we will be
saved.

A Song for a Festival [r]

81 Shout for joy to God our defender;
sing praise to the God of Jacob!
2 Start the music and beat the
tambourines;
play pleasant music on the harps and
the lyres.
3 Blow the trumpet for the festival,
when the moon is new and when the
moon is full.
4 This is the law in Israel,
an order from the God of Jacob.
5 He gave it to the people of Israel
when he attacked the land of Egypt.

I hear an unknown voice saying,
6 "I took the burdens off your backs;
I let you put down your loads of bricks.
7 When you were in trouble, you called
to me, and I saved you.
From my hiding-place in the storm,
I answered you.
I put you to the test at the springs
of Meribah.
8 Listen, my people, to my warning;
Israel, how I wish you would listen
to me!
9 You must never worship another god.
10 I am the LORD your God,
who brought you out of Egypt.
Open your mouth, and I will feed you.

11 "But my people would not listen to
me;
Israel would not obey me.
12 So I let them go their stubborn ways
and do whatever they wanted.

13 How I wish my people would listen
to me;
how I wish they would obey me!
14 I would quickly defeat their enemies
and conquer all their foes.
15 Those who hate me would bow in fear
before me;
their punishment would last for ever.
16 But I would feed you with the finest
wheat
and satisfy you with wild honey."

God the Supreme Ruler [s]

82 God presides in the heavenly
council;
in the assembly of the gods he gives
his decision:
2 "You must stop judging unjustly;
you must no longer be partial to the
wicked!
3 Defend the rights of the poor and the
orphans;
be fair to the needy and the helpless.
4 Rescue them from the power of evil men.

5 "How ignorant you are! How stupid!
You are completely corrupt,
and justice has disappeared from the
world.
6 'You are gods,' I said;
'all of you are sons of the Most High.'
7 But you will die like men;
your life will end like that of any
prince."

8 Come, O God, and rule the world;
all the nations are yours.

A Prayer for the Defeat of
Israel's Enemies [t]

83 O God, do not keep silent;
do not be still, do not be quiet!
2 Look! Your enemies are in revolt,
and those who hate you are rebelling.
3 They are making secret plans against
your people;
they are plotting against those you
protect.
4 "Come," they say, "let us destroy their
nation,
so that Israel will be forgotten for
ever."

5 They agree on their plan
and form an alliance against you:
6 the people of Edom and the Ishmaelites;

---

[r] HEBREW TITLE: By Asaph.　　[s] HEBREW TITLE: A psalm by Asaph.
[t] HEBREW TITLE: A psalm by Asaph; a song.
81.3: Num 10.10　　**81.7:** Ex 17.7; Num 20.13　　**81.9–10:** Ex 20.2–3; Deut 5.6–7
82.6: Jn 10.34

the people of Moab and the Hagrites;
⁷ the people of Gebal, Ammon, and
  Amalek,
  and of Philistia and Tyre.
⁸ Assyria has also joined them
  as a strong ally of the Ammonites
  and Moabites, the descendants of
  Lot.

⁹ Do to them what you did to the
  Midianites,
  and to Sisera and Jabin at the River
  Kishon.
¹⁰ You defeated them at Endor,
  and their bodies rotted on the ground.
¹¹ Do to their leaders what you did to
  Oreb and Zeeb;
  defeat all their rulers as you did Zebah
  and Zalmunna,
¹² who said, "We will take for our own
  the land that belongs to God."

¹³ Scatter them like dust, O God,
  like straw blown away by the wind.
¹⁴ As fire burns the forest,
  as flames set the hills on fire,
¹⁵ chase them away with your storm
  and terrify them with your fierce
  winds.
¹⁶ Cover their faces with shame, O LORD,
  and make them acknowledge your
  power.
¹⁷ May they be defeated and terrified for
  ever;
  may they die in complete disgrace.
¹⁸ May they know that you alone are
  the LORD,
  supreme ruler over all the earth.

Longing for God's House ᵘ

84 How I love your Temple, LORD
      Almighty!
² How I want to be there!
  I long to be in the LORD's Temple.
  With my whole being I sing for joy
  to the living God.
³ Even the sparrows have built a nest,
  and the swallows have their own
  home;
  they keep their young near your altars,
  LORD Almighty, my king and my God.
⁴ How happy are those who live in your
  Temple,
  always singing praise to you.

⁵ How happy are those whose strength
  comes from you,

who are eager to make the pilgrimage
  to Mount Zion.
⁶ As they pass through the dry valley of
  Baca,
  it becomes a place of springs;
  the autumn rain fills it with pools.
⁷ They grow stronger as they go;
  they will see the God of gods on Zion.

⁸ Hear my prayer, LORD God Almighty.
  Listen, O God of Jacob!
⁹ Bless our king, O God,
  the king you have chosen.

¹⁰ One day spent in your Temple
  is better than a thousand anywhere
  else;
  I would rather stand at the gate of the
  house of my God
  than live in the homes of the wicked.
¹¹ The LORD is our protector and glorious
  king,
  blessing us with kindness and honour.
  He does not refuse any good thing
  to those who do what is right.
¹² LORD Almighty, how happy are those
  who trust in you!

A Prayer for the Nation's Welfare ᵛ

85 LORD, you have been merciful to
      your land;
  you have made Israel prosperous
  again.
² You have forgiven your people's sins
  and pardoned all their wrongs.
³ You stopped being angry with them
  and held back your furious rage.

⁴ Bring us back, O God our saviour,
  and stop being displeased with us!
⁵ Will you be angry with us for ever?
  Will your anger never cease?
⁶ Make us strong again,
  and we, your people, will praise you.
⁷ Show us your constant love, O LORD,
  and give us your saving help.

⁸ I am listening to what the LORD God
  is saying;
  he promises peace to us, his own
  people,
  if we do not go back to our foolish
  ways.
⁹ Surely he is ready to save those who
  honour him,
  and his saving presence will remain
  in our land.

ᵘ HEBREW TITLE: *A psalm by the clan of Korah.*
ᵛ HEBREW TITLE: *A psalm by the clan of Korah.*
83.9: Judg 4.6–22, 7.1–23   **83.11:** Judg 7.25, 8.12

10 Love and faithfulness will meet;
  righteousness and peace will embrace.
11 Man's loyalty will reach up from the
  earth,
  and God's righteousness will look
    down from heaven.
12 The LORD will make us prosperous,
  and our land will produce rich
    harvests.
13 Righteousness will go before the LORD
  and prepare the path for him.

A Prayer for Help[w]

86 Listen to me, LORD, and answer
    me,
  for I am helpless and weak.
2 Save me from death, because I am loyal
  to you;
  save me, for I am your servant and
    I trust in you.

3 You are my God, so be merciful to me;
  I pray to you all day long.
4 Make your servant glad, O Lord,
  because my prayers go up to you.
5 You are good to us and forgiving,
  full of constant love for all who pray
    to you.

6 Listen, LORD, to my prayer;
  hear my cries for help.
7 I call to you in times of trouble,
  because you answer my prayers.

8 There is no god like you, O Lord,
  not one has done what you have done.
9 All the nations that you have created
  will come and bow down to you;
  they will praise your greatness.
10 You are mighty and do wonderful
    things;
  you alone are God.

11 Teach me, LORD, what you want me
    to do,
  and I will obey you faithfully;
  teach me to serve you with complete
    devotion.
12 I will praise you with all my heart,
  O Lord my God;
  I will proclaim your greatness for ever.
13 How great is your constant love for
    me!
  You have saved me from the grave
    itself.

14 Proud men are coming against me, O
    God;
  a gang of cruel men is trying to kill
    me—
  people who pay no attention to you.
15 But you, O Lord, are a merciful and
    loving God,
  always patient, always kind and
    faithful.
16 Turn to me and have mercy on me;
  strengthen me and save me,
  because I serve you, just as my
    mother did.
17 Show me proof of your goodness,
    LORD;
  those who hate me will be ashamed
  when they see that you have given
    me comfort and help.

In Praise of Jerusalem[x]

87 The LORD built his city on the
    sacred hill;[y]
2   more than any other place in Israel
  he loves the city of Jerusalem.
3 Listen, city of God,
  to the wonderful things he says about
    you:

4 "I will include Egypt and Babylonia
  when I list the nations that obey me;
  I will number among the inhabitants of
    Jerusalem
  the people of Philistia, Tyre, and
    Sudan."

5 Of Zion it will be said
  that all nations belong there
  and that the Almighty will make her
    strong.
6 The LORD will write a list of the peoples
  and include them all as citizens of
    Jerusalem.
7 They dance and sing,
  "In Zion is the source of all our
    blessings."

A Cry for Help[z]

88 LORD God, my saviour, I cry out
    all day,
  and at night I come before you.
2 Hear my prayer;
  listen to my cry for help!

3 So many troubles have fallen on me
  that I am close to death.

---

[w] HEBREW TITLE: *A prayer by David.*   [x] HEBREW TITLE: *A psalm by the clan of Korah; a song.*
[y] SACRED HILL: *See 2.6.*
[z] HEBREW TITLE: *A psalm by the clan of Korah; a song. A poem by Heman the Ezrahite.*
86.9: Rev 15.4

⁴ I am like all others who are about to
  die;
  all my strength is gone. ᵃ
⁵ I am abandoned among the dead;
  I am like the slain lying in their graves,
  those you have forgotten completely,
  who are beyond your help.
⁶ You have thrown me into the depths
  of the tomb,
  into the darkest and deepest pit.
⁷ Your anger lies heavy on me,
  and I am crushed beneath its waves.

⁸ You have caused my friends to abandon
  me;
  you have made me repulsive to them.
  I am closed in and cannot escape;
⁹   my eyes are weak from suffering.
  LORD, every day I call to you
  and lift my hands to you in prayer.

¹⁰ Do you perform miracles for the dead?
  Do they rise up and praise you?
¹¹ Is your constant love spoken of in the
  grave
  or your faithfulness in the place of
  destruction?
¹² Are your miracles seen in that place
  of darkness
  or your goodness in the land of the
  forgotten?

¹³ LORD, I call to you for help;
  every morning I pray to you.
¹⁴ Why do you reject me, LORD?
  Why do you turn away from me?
¹⁵ Ever since I was young, I have suffered
  and been near death;
  I am worn out ᵇ from the burden of
  your punishments.
¹⁶ Your furious anger crushes me;
  your terrible attacks destroy me.
¹⁷ All day long they surround me like
  a flood;
  they close in on me from every side.
¹⁸ You have made even my closest
  friends abandon me,
  and darkness is my only companion.

A Hymn in Time of National Trouble ᶜ

89 O LORD, I will always sing of your
  constant love;
  I will proclaim your faithfulness for
  ever.

² I know that your love will last for all
  time,
  that your faithfulness is as permanent
  as the sky.
³ You said, "I have made a covenant with
  the man I chose;
  I have promised my servant David,
⁴ 'A descendant of yours will always be
  king;
  I will preserve your dynasty for
  ever.'"

⁵ The heavens sing of the wonderful
  things you do;
  the holy ones sing of your
  faithfulness, LORD.
⁶ No one in heaven is like you, LORD;
  none of the heavenly beings is your
  equal.
⁷ You are feared in the council of the
  holy ones;
  and all of them stand in awe of you.

⁸ LORD God Almighty, none is as mighty
  as you;
  in all things you are faithful, O LORD.
⁹ You rule over the powerful sea;
  you calm its angry waves.
¹⁰ You crushed the monster Rahab ᵈ and
  killed it;
  with your mighty strength you
  defeated your enemies.
¹¹ Heaven is yours, the earth also;
  you made the world and everything
  in it.
¹² You created the north and the south;
  Mount Tabor and Mount Hermon sing
  to you for joy.
¹³ How powerful you are!
  How great is your strength!
¹⁴ Your kingdom is founded on
  righteousness and justice;
  love and faithfulness are shown in all
  you do.

¹⁵ How happy are the people who
  worship you with songs,
  who live in the light of your kindness!
¹⁶ Because of you they rejoice all day
  long,
  and they praise you for your goodness.
¹⁷ You give us great victories;
  in your love you make us triumphant.
¹⁸ You, O LORD, chose our protector;
  you, the Holy God of Israel, gave us
  our king.

ᵃ all my strength is gone; *or there is no help for me.*
ᵇ *Probable text* I am worn out; *Hebrew unclear.*
ᶜ HEBREW TITLE: *A poem by Ethan the Ezrahite.*
ᵈ RAHAB: *A legendary sea-monster which represented the forces of chaos and evil.*
89.Title: 1 Kgs 4.31   **89.4:** 2 Sam 7.12–16; 1 Chr 17.11–14; Ps 132.11; Acts 2.30

God's Promise to David

19 In a vision long ago you said to your
    faithful servants,
  "I have given help to a famous soldier;
  I have given the throne to one I chose
    from the people.
20 I have made my servant David king
  by anointing him with holy oil.
21 My strength will always be with him,
  my power will make him strong.
22 His enemies will never succeed against
    him;
  the wicked will not defeat him.
23 I will crush his foes
  and kill everyone who hates him.
24 I will love him and be loyal to him;
  I will make him always victorious.
25 I will extend his kingdom
  from the Mediterranean to the River
    Euphrates.
26 He will say to me,
  'You are my father and my God;
  you are my protector and saviour.'
27 I will make him my first-born son,
  the greatest of all kings.
28 I will always keep my promise to him,
  and my covenant with him will last
    for ever.
29 His dynasty will be as permanent as
    the sky;
  a descendant of his will always be
    king.

30 "But if his descendants disobey my
    law
  and do not live according to my
    commands,
31 if they disregard my instructions
  and do not keep my commandments,
32 then I will punish them for their sins;
  I will make them suffer for their
    wrongs.
33 But I will not stop loving David
  or fail to keep my promise to him.
34 I will not break my covenant with him
  or take back even one promise I made
    him.

35 "Once and for all I have promised by
    my holy name:
  I will never lie to David.
36 He will always have descendants,
  and I will watch over his kingdom
    as long as the sun shines.
37 It will be as permanent as the moon,
  that faithful witness in the sky."

Lament over the Defeat of the King

38 But you are angry with your chosen
    king;
  you have deserted and rejected him.
39 You have broken your covenant with
    your servant
  and thrown his crown in the mud.
40 You have torn down the walls of his
    city
  and left his forts in ruins.
41 All who pass by steal his belongings;
  all his neighbours laugh at him.
42 You have given the victory to his
    enemies;
  you have made them all happy.
43 You have made his weapons useless
  and let him be defeated in battle.
44 You have taken away his royal
    sceptre [e]
  and hurled his throne to the ground.
45 You have made him old before his time
  and covered him with disgrace.

A Prayer for Deliverance

46 LORD, will you hide yourself for ever?
  How long will your anger burn like
    fire?
47 Remember how short my life is;
  remember that you created all of us
    mortal!
48 Who can live and never die?
  How can man keep himself from the
    grave?

49 Lord, where are the former proofs of
    your love?
  Where are the promises you made to
    David?
50 Don't forget how I, your servant, am
    insulted,
  how I endure all the curses [f] of the
    heathen.
51 Your enemies insult your chosen king,
    O LORD!
  They insult him wherever he goes.

52 Praise the LORD for ever!

Amen! Amen!

e *Probable text* royal sceptre; *Hebrew* purity.
89.20: 1 Sam 13.14; Acts 13.22; 1 Sam 16.12

f *Probable text* curses; *Hebrew* crowds.
89.27: Rev 1.5

BOOK FOUR
(Psalms 90–106)
Of God and Man[g]

90
O Lord, you have always been our home.
2 Before you created the hills
  or brought the world into being,
  you were eternally God,
  and will be God for ever.

3 You tell man to return to what he was;
  you change him back to dust.
4 A thousand years to you are like one day;
  they are like yesterday, already gone,
  like a short hour in the night.
5 You carry us away like a flood;
  we last no longer than a dream.
  We are like weeds that sprout in the morning,
6   that grow and burst into bloom,
    then dry up and die in the evening.

7 We are destroyed by your anger;
  we are terrified by your fury.
8 You place our sins before you,
  our secret sins where you can see them.

9 Our life is cut short by your anger;
  it fades away like a whisper.
10 Seventy years is all we have—
   eighty years, if we are strong;
   yet all they bring us is trouble and sorrow;
   life is soon over, and we are gone.

11 Who has felt the full power of your anger?
   Who knows what fear your fury can bring?
12 Teach us how short our life is,
   so that we may become wise.

13 How much longer will your anger last?
   Have pity, O Lord, on your servants!
14 Fill us each morning with your constant love,
   so that we may sing and be glad all our life.
15 Give us now as much happiness as
   the sadness you gave us
   during all our years of misery.
16 Let us, your servants, see your mighty deeds;
   let our descendants see your glorious might.

17 Lord our God, may your blessings be with us.
   Give us success in all we do!

God Our Protector

91
Whoever goes to the Lord for safety,
  whoever remains under the protection of the Almighty,
2 can say to him,
  "You are my defender and protector.
  You are my God; in you I trust."
3 He will keep you safe from all hidden dangers
  and from all deadly diseases.
4 He will cover you with his wings;
  you will be safe in his care;
  his faithfulness will protect and defend you.
5 You need not fear any dangers at night
  or sudden attacks during the day
6   or the plagues that strike in the dark
    or the evils that kill in daylight.

7 A thousand may fall dead beside you,
  ten thousand all round you,
  but you will not be harmed.
8 You will look and see
  how the wicked are punished.

9 You have made the Lord your[x] defender,
  the Most High your protector,
10 and so no disaster will strike you,
   no violence will come near your home.
11 God will put his angels in charge of you
   to protect you wherever you go.
12 They will hold you up with their hands
   to keep you from hurting your feet on the stones.
13 You will trample down lions and snakes,
   fierce lions and poisonous snakes.

14 God says, "I will save those who love me
   and will protect those who acknowledge me as Lord.
15 When they call to me, I will answer them;
   when they are in trouble, I will be with them.
   I will rescue them and honour them.
16 I will reward them with long life;
   I will save them."

[g]HEBREW TITLE: *A prayer by Moses, the man of God.* [x]*Probable text* your; *Hebrew* my.
90.4: 2 Peter 3.8   **91.11:** Mt 4.6; Lk 4.10   **91.12:** Mt 4.6; Lk 4.11   **91.13:** Lk 10.19

A Song of Praise [h]

92 How good it is to give thanks to you, O LORD,
to sing in your honour, O Most High God,
[2] to proclaim your constant love every morning
and your faithfulness every night,
[3] with the music of stringed instruments
and with melody on the harp.
[4] Your mighty deeds, O LORD, make me glad;
because of what you have done, I sing for joy.

[5] How great are your actions, LORD!
How deep are your thoughts!
[6] This is something a fool cannot know;
a stupid man cannot understand:
[7] the wicked may grow like weeds,
those who do wrong may prosper;
yet they will be totally destroyed,
[8] because you, LORD, are supreme for ever.

[9] We know that your enemies will die,
and all the wicked will be defeated.
[10] You have made me as strong as a wild ox;
you have blessed me with happiness.
[11] I have seen the defeat of my enemies
and heard the cries of the wicked.

[12] The righteous will flourish like palm-trees;
they will grow like the cedars of Lebanon.
[13] They are like trees planted in the house of the LORD,
that flourish in the Temple of our God,
[14] that still bear fruit in old age
and are always green and strong.
[15] This shows that the LORD is just,
that there is no wrong in my protector.

God the King

93 The LORD is king.
He is clothed with majesty and strength.
The earth is set firmly in place
and cannot be moved.
[2] Your throne, O LORD, has been firm from the beginning,
and you existed before time began.

[3] The ocean depths raise their voice, O LORD;

they raise their voice and roar.
[4] The LORD rules supreme in heaven,
greater than the roar of the ocean,
more powerful than the waves of the sea.

[5] Your laws are eternal, LORD,
and your Temple is holy indeed,
for ever and ever.

God the Judge of All

94 LORD, you are a God who punishes;
reveal your anger!
[2] You are the judge of all men;
rise and give the proud what they deserve!
[3] How much longer will the wicked be glad?
How much longer, LORD?
[4] How much longer will criminals be proud
and boast about their crimes?

[5] They crush your people, LORD;
they oppress those who belong to you.
[6] They kill widows and orphans,
and murder the strangers who live in our land.
[7] They say, "The LORD does not see us;
the God of Israel does not notice."

[8] My people, how can you be such stupid fools?
When will you ever learn?
[9] God made our ears—can't he hear?
He made our eyes—can't he see?
[10] He scolds the nations—won't he punish them? [x]
He is the teacher of all men—hasn't he any knowledge?
[11] The LORD knows what they think;
he knows how senseless their reasoning is.

[12] LORD, how happy is the person you instruct,
the one to whom you teach your law!
[13] You give him rest from days of trouble
until a pit is dug to trap the wicked.
[14] The LORD will not abandon his people;
he will not desert those who belong to him.
[15] Justice will again be found in the courts,
and all righteous people will support it.

[h] HEBREW TITLE: *A psalm; a song for the Sabbath.*
[x] them; *or* our wicked leaders.
94.11: 1 Cor 3.20

Let us...worship him (95.6)

16 Who stood up for me against the
 wicked?
 Who took my side against the
 evildoers?
17 If the LORD had not helped me,
 I would have gone quickly to the land
 of silence.*i*
18 I said, "I am falling";
 but your constant love, O LORD, held
 me up.
19 Whenever I am anxious and worried,
 you comfort me and make me glad.

20 You have nothing to do with corrupt
 judges,
 who make injustice legal,
21 who plot against good men
 and sentence the innocent to death.
22 But the LORD defends me;
 my God protects me.
23 He will punish them for their
 wickedness
 and destroy them for their sins;
 the LORD our God will destroy them.

A Song of Praise

95 Come, let us praise the LORD!
 Let us sing for joy to God, who
 protects us!
2 Let us come before him with
 thanksgiving
 and sing joyful songs of praise.
3 For the LORD is a mighty God,
 a mighty king over all the gods.
4 He rules over the whole earth,
 from the deepest caves to the highest
 hills.
5 He rules over the sea, which he made;
 the land also, which he himself
 formed.

6 Come, let us bow down and worship
 him;
 let us kneel before the LORD, our
 Maker!
7 He is our God;
 we are the people he cares for,
 the flock for which he provides.

*i*LAND OF SILENCE: *The world of the dead (see 6.5).*
95.7–8: Heb 3.15, 4.7 **95.7–11:** Heb 3.7–11

Listen today to what he says:

⁸ "Don't be stubborn, as your ancestors
 were at Meribah,
 as they were that day in the desert
 at Massah.
⁹ There they put me to the test and tried
 me,
 although they had seen what I did
 for them.
¹⁰ For forty years I was disgusted with
 those people.
 I said, 'How disloyal they are!
 They refuse to obey my commands.'
¹¹ I was angry and made a solemn
 promise:
 'You will never enter the land
 where I would have given you rest.' "

God the Supreme King
(1 Chr 16.23-33)

96 Sing a new song to the LORD!
 Sing to the LORD, all the world!
² Sing to the LORD, and praise him!
 Proclaim every day the good news
 that he has saved us.
³ Proclaim his glory to the nations,
 his mighty deeds to all peoples.

⁴ The LORD is great and is to be highly
 praised;
 he is to be honoured more than all
 the gods.
⁵ The gods of all other nations are only
 idols,
 but the LORD created the heavens.
⁶ Glory and majesty surround him;
 power and beauty fill his Temple.

⁷ Praise the LORD, all people on earth;
 praise his glory and might.
⁸ Praise the LORD's glorious name;
 bring an offering and come into his
 Temple.
⁹ Bow down before the Holy One when
 he appears;ʲ
 tremble before him, all the earth!

¹⁰ Say to all the nations, "The LORD is
 king!
 The earth is set firmly in place and
 cannot be moved;
 he will judge the peoples with justice."
¹¹ Be glad, earth and sky!
 Roar, sea, and every creature in you;
¹² be glad, fields, and everything in
 you!

*The trees in the woods will shout for joy
(96.12)*

The trees in the woods will shout for
 joy
¹³ when the LORD comes to rule the
 earth.
 He will rule the peoples of the world
 with justice and fairness.

God the Supreme Ruler

97 The LORD is king! Earth, be glad!
 Rejoice, you islands of the seas!
² Clouds and darkness surround him;
 he rules with righteousness and
 justice.
³ Fire goes in front of him
 and burns up his enemies round him.
⁴ His lightning lights up the world;
 the earth sees it and trembles.
⁵ The hills melt like wax before the LORD,
 before the Lord of all the earth.
⁶ The heavens proclaim his righteousness,
 and all the nations see his glory.

ʲwhen he appears; *or* in garments of worship.
95.8-9: Ex 17.1-7; Num 20.2-13   **95.11:** Num 14.20-23; Deut 1.34-36, 12.9-10; Heb 4.3-5
96.7-9: Ps 29.1-2

7 Everyone who worships idols is put to
   shame;
     all the gods bow down *k* before the
     LORD.
8 The people of Zion are glad,
     and the cities of Judah rejoice
     because of your judgements, O LORD.
9 LORD Almighty, you are ruler of all the
   earth;
     you are much greater than all the
     gods.

10 The LORD loves those who hate evil; *l*
     he protects the lives of his people;
     he rescues them from the power of
     the wicked.
11 Light shines on the righteous,
     and gladness on the good.
12 All you that are righteous be glad
     because of what the LORD has done!
   Remember what the holy God has done,
     and give thanks to him.

God the Ruler of the World *x*

98 Sing a new song to the LORD;
       he has done wonderful things!
   By his own power and holy strength
     he has won the victory.
2 The LORD announced his victory;
     he made his saving power known to
     the nations.
3 He kept his promise to the people of
   Israel
     with loyalty and constant love for
     them.
   All people everywhere have seen the
     victory of our God.

4 Sing for joy to the LORD, all the earth;
     praise him with songs and shouts of
     joy!
5 Sing praises to the LORD!
     Play music on the harps!
6 Blow trumpets and horns,
     and shout for joy to the LORD, our
     king.

7 Roar, sea, and every creature in you;
     sing, earth, and all who live on you!
8 Clap your hands, you rivers;
     you hills, sing together with joy before
     the LORD,
9   because he comes to rule the earth.
   He will rule the peoples of the world
     with justice and fairness.

God the Supreme King

99 The LORD is king;
       and the people tremble.
   He is enthroned above the winged
     creatures
     and the earth shakes.
2 The LORD is mighty in Zion;
     he is supreme over all the nations.
3 Everyone will praise his great and
     majestic name.
   Holy is he!

4 Mighty king, *m* you love what is right;
     you have established justice in Israel;
     you have brought righteousness and
     fairness.
5 Praise the LORD our God;
     worship before his throne!
   Holy is he!

6 Moses and Aaron were his priests,
     and Samuel was one who prayed to
     him;
     they called to the LORD, and he
     answered them.
7 He spoke to them from the pillar of
     cloud;
     they obeyed the laws and commands
     that he gave them.

8 O LORD, our God, you answered your
     people;
     you showed them that you are a God
     who forgives,
     even though you punished them for
     their sins.
9 Praise the LORD our God,
     and worship at his sacred hill! *n*
   The LORD our God is holy.

A Hymn of Praise *o*

100 Sing to the LORD, all the world!
       2 Worship the LORD with joy;
   come before him with happy songs!

3 Acknowledge that the LORD is God.
   He made us, and we belong to him;
     we are his people, we are his flock.

4 Enter the temple gates with
     thanksgiving,
     go into its courts with praise.
   Give thanks to him and praise him.

k all the gods bow down; *or* bow down, all gods.
l *Probable text* The LORD loves those who hate evil; *Hebrew* Hate evil, you who love the LORD.
x HEBREW TITLE: *A psalm.*
m *Probable text* Mighty king; *Hebrew* The might of the king.
n SACRED HILL: *See 2.6.*
o HEBREW TITLE: *A psalm of thanksgiving.*
99.1: Ex 25.22   **99.7:** Ex 33.9

Enter the temple gates with thanksgiving (100.4)

⁵ The LORD is good;
  his love is eternal.
  and his faithfulness lasts for ever.

A King's Promise ᵖ

101 My song is about loyalty and
    justice,
  and I sing it to you, O LORD.
² My conduct will be faultless.
  When will you come to me?

I will live a pure life in my house,
³   and will never tolerate evil.
I hate the actions of those who turn
    away from God;
  I will have nothing to do with them.
⁴ I will not be dishonest, �q
  and will have no dealings with evil. ʳ

⁵ I will get rid of anyone
  who whispers evil things about
    someone else;
I will not tolerate a man
  who is proud and arrogant.

⁶ I will approve of those who are faithful
    to God
  and will let them live in my palace.
Those who are completely honest
  will be allowed to serve me.

⁷ No liar will live in my palace;
  no hypocrite will remain in my
    presence.
⁸ Day after day I will destroy
  the wicked in our land;
I will expel all evil men
  from the city of the LORD.

The Prayer of a Troubled Young Man ˢ

102 Listen to my prayer, O LORD,
    and hear my cry for help!
² When I am in trouble,
  don't turn away from me!
Listen to me,
  and answer me quickly when I call!

³ My life is disappearing like smoke;
  my body is burning like fire.
⁴ I am beaten down like dry grass;
  I have lost my desire for food.
⁵ I groan aloud;
  I am nothing but skin and bones.
⁶ I am like a wild bird in the desert,
  like an owl in abandoned ruins.
⁷ I lie awake;
  I am like a lonely bird on a house-top.
⁸ All day long my enemies insult me;
  those who mock me use my name
    in cursing.

⁹⁻¹⁰ Because of your anger and fury,
  ashes are my food,
  and my tears are mixed with my drink.
You picked me up and threw me away.
¹¹ My life is like the evening shadows;
  I am like dry grass.

¹² But you, O LORD, are king for ever;
  all generations will remember you.
¹³ You will rise and take pity on Zion;
  the time has come to have mercy on
    her;
  this is the right time.
¹⁴ Your servants love her,

ᵖ HEBREW TITLE: *A psalm by David.*   q not be dishonest; *or stay away from dishonest people.*
ʳ evil; *or evil men.*
ˢ HEBREW TITLE: *A prayer by a weary sufferer who pours out his complaints to the LORD.*
100.5: 1 Chr 16.34; 2 Chr 5.13, 7.3; Ezra 3.11; Ps 106.1, 107.1, 118.1, 136.1; Jer 33.11

even though she is destroyed;
they have pity on her,
even though she is in ruins.

15 The nations will fear the LORD;
all the kings of the earth will fear
his power.
16 When the LORD rebuilds Zion,
he will reveal his greatness.
17 He will hear his forsaken people
and listen to their prayer.

18 Write down for the coming generation
what the LORD has done,
so that people not yet born will praise
him.
19 The LORD looked down from his holy
place on high,
he looked down from heaven to earth.
20 He heard the groans of prisoners
and set free those who were
condemned to die.
21 And so his name will be proclaimed
in Zion,
and he will be praised in Jerusalem
22   when nations and kingdoms come
together
and worship the LORD.

23 The LORD has made me weak while
I am still young;
he has shortened my life.
24 O God, do not take me away now
before I grow old.

O LORD, you live for ever;
25   long ago you created the earth,
and with your own hands you made
the heavens.
26 They will disappear, but you will
remain;
they will all wear out like clothes.
You will discard them like clothes,
and they will vanish.
27 But you are always the same,
and your life never ends.
28 Our children will live in safety,
and under your protection
their descendants will be secure.

The Love of God [t]

103 Praise the LORD, my soul!
All my being, praise his holy
name!
2 Praise the LORD, my soul,
and do not forget how kind he is.
3 He forgives all my sins
and heals all my diseases.

4 He keeps me from the grave
and blesses me with love and mercy.
5 He fills my life [u] with good things,
so that I stay young and strong like
an eagle.

6 The LORD judges in favour of the
oppressed
and gives them their rights.
7 He revealed his plans to Moses
and let the people of Israel see his
mighty deeds.
8 The LORD is merciful and loving,
slow to become angry and full of
constant love.
9 He does not keep on rebuking;
he is not angry for ever.
10 He does not punish us as we deserve
or repay us according to our sins and
wrongs.
11 As high as the sky is above the earth,
so great is his love for those who
honour him.
12 As far as the east is from the west,
so far does he remove our sins from
us.
13 As a father is kind to his children,
so the LORD is kind to those who
honour him.
14 He knows what we are made of;
he remembers that we are dust.

15 As for us, our life is like grass.
We grow and flourish like a wild flower;
16   then the wind blows on it, and it
is gone—
no one sees it again.
17 But for those who honour the LORD,
his love lasts for ever,
and his goodness endures for all
generations
18 of those who are true to his covenant
and who faithfully obey his
commands.

19 The LORD placed his throne in heaven;
he is king over all.
20 Praise the LORD, you strong and
mighty angels,
who obey his commands,
who listen to what he says.
21 Praise the LORD, all you heavenly
powers,
you servants of his, who do his will!
22 Praise the LORD, all his creatures
in all the places he rules.
Praise the LORD, my soul!

[t] HEBREW TITLE: *By David.*   [u] *Probable text* my life; *Hebrew unclear.*
102.25–27: Heb 1.10–12   **103.8**: Jas 5.11

In Praise of the Creator

104 Praise the LORD, my soul!
O LORD, my God, how great
you are!
You are clothed with majesty and glory;
2 you cover yourself with light.
You have spread out the heavens like
a tent
3 and built your home on the waters
above. *v*
You use the clouds as your chariot
and ride on the wings of the wind.
4 You use the winds as your messengers
and flashes of lightning as your
servants.

5 You have set the earth firmly on its
foundations,
and it will never be moved.
6 You placed the ocean over it like a robe,
and the water covered the mountains.
7 When you rebuked the waters, they fled;
they rushed away when they heard
your shout of command.
8 They flowed over the mountains and
into the valleys,
to the place you had made for them.
9 You set a boundary they can never pass,
to keep them from covering the earth
again.

10 You make springs flow in the valleys,
and rivers run between the hills.
11 They provide water for the wild
animals;
there the wild donkeys quench their
thirst.
12 In the trees near by,
the birds make their nests and sing.
13 From the sky you send rain on the
hills,
and the earth is filled with your
blessings.
14 You make grass grow for the cattle
and plants for man to use,
so that he can grow his crops
15 and produce wine to make him
happy,
olive-oil to make him cheerful,
and bread to give him strength.

16 The cedars of Lebanon get plenty of
rain—
the LORD's own trees, which he
planted.

17 There the birds build their nests;
the storks nest in the fir-trees.
18 The wild goats live in the high
mountains,
and the rock-badgers hide in the cliffs.

19 You created the moon to mark the
months;
the sun knows the time to set.
20 You made the night, and in the
darkness
all the wild animals come out.
21 The young lions roar while they hunt,
looking for the food that God provides.
22 When the sun rises, they go back
and lie down in their dens.
23 Then people go out to do their work
and keep working until evening.

24 LORD, you have made so many things!
How wisely you made them all!
The earth is filled with your creatures.
25 There is the ocean, large and wide,
where countless creatures live,
large and small alike.
26 The ships sail on it, and in it plays
Leviathan,
that sea-monster which you made. *w*

27 All of them depend on you
to give them food when they need
it.
28 You give it to them, and they eat it;
you provide food, and they are
satisfied.
29 When you turn away, they are afraid;
when you take away your breath,
they die
and go back to the dust from which
they came.
30 But when you give them breath, *x* they
are created;
you give new life to the earth.

31 May the glory of the LORD last for
ever!
May the LORD be happy with what
he has made!
32 He looks at the earth, and it trembles;
he touches the mountains, and they
pour out smoke.

33 I will sing to the LORD all my life;
as long as I live I will sing praises
to my God.
34 May he be pleased with my song,

---

*v*THE WATERS ABOVE: *A reference to the waters above the celestial dome (Gen 1.6–7).*
*w*in it plays...made; *or* Leviathan is there, that sea-monster you made to amuse you.
*x*give them breath; *or* send out your spirit.
104.4: Heb 1.7   **104.26:** Job 41.1; Ps 74.14; Is 27.1

for my gladness comes from him.
35 May sinners be destroyed from the earth;
may the wicked be no more.

Praise the LORD, my soul!
Praise the LORD!

God and His People
(1 Chr 16.8-22)

105 Give thanks to the LORD,
proclaim his greatness;
tell the nations what he has done.
2 Sing praise to the LORD;
tell of the wonderful things he has done.
3 Be glad that we belong to him;
let all who worship him rejoice.
4 Go to the LORD for help;
and worship him continually.
5-6 You descendants of Abraham, his servant;
you descendants of Jacob, the man he chose:
remember the miracles that God performed
and the judgements that he gave.

7 The LORD is our God;
his commands are for all the world.
8 He will keep his covenant for ever,
his promises for a thousand generations.
9 He will keep the agreement he made with Abraham
and his promise to Isaac.
10 The LORD made a covenant with Jacob,
one that will last for ever.
11 "I will give you the land of Canaan," he said.
"It will be your own possession."

12 God's people were few in number,
strangers in the land of Canaan.
13 They wandered from country to country,
from one kingdom to another.
14 But God let no one oppress them;
to protect them, he warned the kings:
15 "Don't harm my chosen servants;
do not touch my prophets."

16 The LORD sent famine to their country
and took away all their food.

17 But he sent a man ahead of them,
Joseph, who had been sold as a slave.
18 His feet were kept in chains,
and an iron collar was round his neck,
19 until what he had predicted came true.
The word of the LORD proved him right.
20 Then the king of Egypt had him released;
the ruler of nations set him free.
21 He put him in charge of his government
and made him ruler over all the land,
22 with power over the king's officials
and authority to instruct his advisers.

23 Then Jacob went to Egypt
and settled in that country.
24 The LORD gave many children to his people
and made them stronger than their enemies.
25 He made the Egyptians hate his people
and treat his servants with deceit.

26 Then he sent his servant Moses,
and Aaron, whom he had chosen.
27 They did God's mighty acts
and performed miracles in Egypt.
28 God sent darkness on the country,
but the Egyptians did not obey[y] his command.
29 He turned their rivers into blood
and killed all their fish.
30 Their country was overrun with frogs,
even the palace was filled with them.
31 God commanded, and flies and gnats swarmed throughout the whole country.
32 He sent hail and lightning on their land
instead of rain;
33 he destroyed their grapevines and fig-trees
and broke down all the trees.
34 He commanded, and the locusts came,
countless millions of them;
35 they ate all the plants in the land;
they ate all the crops.
36 He killed the first-born sons
of all the families of Egypt.

37 Then he led the Israelites out;
they carried silver and gold,
and all of them were healthy and strong.

y Some ancient translations did not obey; Hebrew obeyed.
105.9: Gen 12.7, 17.8, 26.3   **105.10-11:** Gen 28.13   **105.14-15:** Gen 20.3-7
105.16: Gen 41.53-57   **105.17:** Gen 37.28, 45.5   **105.18-19:** Gen 39.20—40.23
105.20: Gen 41.14   **105.21:** Gen 41.39-41   **105.23:** Gen 46.6, 47.11   **105.24-25:** Ex 1.7-14
105.26: Ex 3.1—4.17   **105.28:** Ex 10.21-23   **105.29:** Ex 7.17-21   **105.30:** Ex 8.1-6
105.31: Ex 8.16-17,20-24   **105.32-33:** Ex 9.22-25   **105.34-35:** Ex 10.12-15
105.36: Ex 12.29   **105.37-38:** Ex 12.33-36

³⁸ The Egyptians were afraid of them
and were glad when they left.
³⁹ God put a cloud over his people
and a fire at night to give them light.
⁴⁰ They^z asked, and he sent quails;
he gave them food from heaven to
satisfy them.
⁴¹ He opened a rock, and water gushed
out,
flowing through the desert like a river.
⁴² He remembered his sacred promise
to Abraham his servant.

⁴³ So he led his chosen people out,
and they sang and shouted for joy.
⁴⁴ He gave them the lands of other
peoples
and let them take over their fields,
⁴⁵ so that his people would obey his laws
and keep all his commands.

Praise the LORD!

The LORD's Goodness to His People

106
Praise the LORD!

Give thanks to the LORD, because he
is good;
his love is eternal.
² Who can tell all the great things he has
done?
Who can praise him enough?
³ Happy are those who obey his
commands,
who always do what is right.

⁴ Remember me, LORD, when you help
your people;
include me when you save them.
⁵ Let me see the prosperity of your people
and share in the happiness of your
nation,
in the glad pride of those who belong
to you.

⁶ We have sinned as our ancestors did;
we have been wicked and evil.
⁷ Our ancestors in Egypt did not
understand God's wonderful acts;
they forgot the many times he showed
them his love,
and they rebelled against the
Almighty^a at the Red Sea.
⁸ But he saved them, as he had promised,

in order to show his great power.
⁹ He gave a command to the Red Sea,
and it dried up;
he led his people across on dry land.
¹⁰ He saved them from those who hated
them;
he rescued them from their enemies.
¹¹ But the water drowned their enemies;
not one of them was left.
¹² Then his people believed his promises
and sang praises to him.

¹³ But they quickly forgot what he had
done
and acted without waiting for his
advice.
¹⁴ They were filled with craving in the
desert
and put God to the test;
¹⁵ so he gave them what they asked for,
but also sent a terrible disease among
them.

¹⁶ There in the desert they were jealous
of Moses
and of Aaron, the LORD's holy servant.
¹⁷ Then the earth opened up and
swallowed Dathan
and buried Abiram and his family;
¹⁸ fire came down on their followers
and burnt up those wicked people.

¹⁹ They made a gold bull-calf at Sinai
and worshipped that idol;
²⁰ they exchanged the glory of God
for the image of an animal that eats
grass.
²¹ They forgot the God who had saved
them
by his mighty acts in Egypt.
²² What wonderful things he did there!
What amazing things at the Red Sea!
²³ When God said that he would destroy
his people,
his chosen servant, Moses, stood up
against God
and prevented his anger from
destroying them.

²⁴ Then they rejected the pleasant land,
because they did not believe God's
promise.
²⁵ They stayed in their tents and
grumbled

^z *Some ancient translations* They; *Hebrew* He.
^a *Probable text* the Almighty; *Hebrew* the sea.
105.39: Ex 13.21-22   **105.40:** Ex 16.2-15   **105.41:** Ex 17.1-7; Num 20.2-13
105.44: Josh 11.16-23
106.1: 1 Chr 16.34; 2 Chr 5.13, 7.3; Ezra 3.11; Ps 100.5, 107.1, 118.1, 136.1; Jer 33.11
106.7: Ex 14.10-12   **106.9-12:** Ex 14.21-31   **106.12:** Ex 15.1-21   **106.14-15:** Num 11.4-34
106.16-18: Num 16.1-35   **106.19-23:** Ex 32.1-14   **106.24-26:** Num 14.1-35

and would not listen to the LORD.
26 So he gave them a solemn warning
  that he would make them die in the
  desert
27 and scatter their descendants among
  the heathen,
  letting them die in foreign countries.

28 Then at Peor, God's people joined in
  the worship of Baal,
  and ate sacrifices offered to lifeless
  gods.
29 They stirred up the LORD's anger by
  their actions,
  and a terrible disease broke out
  among them.
30 But Phinehas stood up and punished
  the guilty,
  and the plague was stopped.
31 This has been remembered in his
  favour ever since
  and will be for all time to come.

32 At the springs of Meribah the people
  made the LORD angry,
  and Moses was in trouble on their
  account.
33 They made him so bitter
  that he spoke without stopping to
  think.

34 They did not kill the heathen,
  as the LORD had commanded them
  to do,
35 but they intermarried with them
  and adopted their pagan ways.
36 God's people worshipped idols,
  and this caused their destruction.
37 They offered their own sons and
  daughters
  as sacrifices to the idols of Canaan.
38 They killed those innocent children,
  and the land was defiled by those
  murders.
39 They made themselves impure by their
  actions
  and were unfaithful to God.

40 So the LORD was angry with his people;
  he was disgusted with them.
41 He abandoned them to the power of
  the heathen,
  and their enemies ruled over them.
42 They were oppressed by their enemies

and were in complete subjection to
  them.
43 Many times the LORD rescued his
  people,
  but they chose to rebel against him
  and sank deeper into sin.
44 Yet the LORD heard them when they
  cried out,
  and he took notice of their distress.
45 For their sake he remembered his
  covenant,
  and because of his great love he
  relented.
46 He made all their oppressors
  feel sorry for them.

47 Save us, O LORD our God,
  and bring us back from among the
  nations,
  so that we may be thankful
  and praise your holy name.

48 Praise the LORD, the God of Israel;
  praise him now and for ever!
  Let everyone say, "Amen!"

Praise the LORD!

BOOK FIVE
(Psalms 107–150)
In Praise of God's Goodness

107 "Give thanks to the LORD,
    because he is good;
  his love is eternal!"
2 Repeat these words in praise to the
  LORD,
  all you whom he has saved.
  He has rescued you from your enemies
3 and has brought you back from
  foreign countries,
  from east and west, from north and
  south. b

4 Some wandered in the trackless desert
  and could not find their way to a city
  to live in.
5 They were hungry and thirsty
  and had given up all hope.
6 Then in their trouble they called to the
  LORD,
  and he saved them from their distress.
7 He led them by a straight road
  to a city where they could live.

b Probable text south; Hebrew the Mediterranean Sea (meaning "west").
106.27: Lev 26.33　106.28–31: Num 25.1–13　106.32–33: Num 20.2–13
106.34–36: Judg 2.1–3, 3.5–6　106.37: 2 Kgs 17.17　106.38: Num 35.33
106.40–46: Judg 2.14–18　106.47–48: 1 Chr 16.35–36
107.1: 1 Chr 16.34; 2 Chr 5.13, 7.3; Ezra 3.11; Ps 100.5, 106.1, 118.1, 136.1; Jer 33.11

He brought them safe to the port (107.30)

8 They must thank the LORD for his
　　constant love,
　　for the wonderful things he did for
　　them.
9 He satisfies those who are thirsty
　　and fills the hungry with good things.

10 Some were living in gloom and
　　darkness,
　　prisoners suffering in chains,
11 because they had rebelled against the
　　commands of Almighty God
　　and had rejected his instructions.
12 They were worn out from hard work;
　　they would fall down, and no one
　　would help.
13 Then in their trouble they called to
　　the LORD,
　　and he saved them from their distress.
14 He brought them out of their gloom
　　and darkness
　　and broke their chains in pieces.
15 They must thank the LORD for his
　　constant love,
　　for the wonderful things he did for
　　them.
16 He breaks down doors of bronze
　　and smashes iron bars.

17 Some were fools, suffering because of
　　their sins
　　and because of their evil;
18 they couldn't stand the sight of food
　　and were close to death.
19 Then in their trouble they called to
　　the LORD,
　　and he saved them from their distress.
20 He healed them with his command

　　and saved them from the grave.
21 They must thank the LORD for his
　　constant love,
　　for the wonderful things he did for
　　them.
22 They must thank him with sacrifices,
　　and with songs of joy must tell all
　　that he has done.

23 Some sailed over the ocean in ships,
　　earning their living on the seas.
24 They saw what the LORD can do,
　　his wonderful acts on the seas.
25 He commanded, and a mighty wind
　　began to blow
　　and stirred up the waves.
26 The ships were lifted high in the air
　　and plunged down into the depths.
　In such danger the men lost their
　　courage;
27 　they stumbled and staggered like
　　drunken men—
　　all their skill was useless.
28 Then in their trouble they called to
　　the LORD,
　　and he saved them from their distress.
29 He calmed the raging storm,
　　and the waves became quiet.
30 They were glad because of the calm,
　　and he brought them safe to the port
　　they wanted.
31 They must thank the LORD for his
　　constant love,
　　for the wonderful things he did for
　　them.
32 They must proclaim his greatness in
　　the assembly of the people

and praise him before the council of
the leaders.

33 The LORD made rivers dry up
completely
and stopped springs from flowing.
34 He made rich soil become a salty
wilderness
because of the wickedness of those
who lived there.
35 He changed deserts into pools of water
and dry land into flowing springs.
36 He let hungry people settle there,
and they built a city to live in.
37 They sowed the fields and planted
grapevines
and reaped an abundant harvest.
38 He blessed his people, and they had
many children;
he kept their herds of cattle from
decreasing.

39 When God's people were defeated and
humiliated
by cruel oppression and suffering,
40 he showed contempt for their
oppressors
and made them wander in trackless
deserts.
41 But he rescued the needy from their
misery
and made their families increase like
flocks.
42 The righteous see this and are glad,
but all the wicked are put to silence.

43 May those who are wise think about
these things;
may they consider the LORD's
constant love.

A Prayer for Help against Enemies [d]
(Ps 57.7–11; 60.5–12)

108 I have complete confidence, O
God!
I will sing and praise you!
Wake up, my soul!
2 Wake up, my harp and lyre!
I will wake up the sun.
3 I will thank you, O LORD, among the
nations.
I will praise you among the peoples.
4 Your constant love reaches above the
heavens;
your faithfulness touches the skies.

5 Show your greatness in the sky, O God,
and your glory over all the earth.
6 Save us by your might; answer my
prayer,
so that the people you love may be
rescued.

7 From his sanctuary [e] God has said,
"In triumph I will divide Shechem
and distribute the Valley of Sukkoth
to my people.
8 Gilead is mine, and Manasseh too;
Ephraim is my helmet
and Judah my royal sceptre.
9 But I will use Moab as my wash-basin
and I will throw my sandals on Edom,
as a sign that I own it.
I will shout in triumph over the
Philistines."

10 Who, O God, will take me into the
fortified city?
Who will lead me to Edom?
11 Have you really rejected us?
Aren't you going to march out with
our armies?
12 Help us against the enemy;
human help is worthless.
13 With God on our side we will win;
he will defeat our enemies.

The Complaint of a Man in Trouble [f]

109 I praise you, God; don't remain
silent!
2 Wicked men and liars have attacked me.
They tell lies about me
3 and they say evil things about me,
attacking me for no reason.
4 They oppose me, even though I love
them
and have prayed for them. [g]
5 They pay me back evil for good
and hatred for love.

6 Choose some corrupt judge to try my
enemy,
and let one of his own enemies accuse
him.
7 May he be tried and found guilty;
may even his prayer be considered
a crime!
8 May his life soon be ended;
may another man take his job!
9 May his children become orphans,
and his wife a widow!
10 May his children be homeless beggars;

---

[d] HEBREW TITLE: *A psalm by David; a song.*   [e] From his sanctuary; *or* In his holiness.
[f] HEBREW TITLE: *A psalm by David.*   [g] *Probable text* have prayed for them; *Hebrew unclear.*
109.8: Acts 1.20

may they be driven from *h* the ruins
    they live in!
11 May his creditors take away all his
    property,
    and may strangers get everything he
    worked for.
12 May no one ever be kind to him
    or care for the orphans he leaves
    behind.
13 May all his descendants die,
    and may his name be forgotten in the
    next generation.
14 May the LORD remember the evil of
    his ancestors
    and never forgive his mother's sins.
15 May the LORD always remember their
    sins,
    but may they themselves be
    completely forgotten!

16 That man never thought of being kind;
    he persecuted and killed
    the poor, the needy, and the helpless.
17 He loved to curse—may he be cursed!
    He hated to give blessings—may no
    one bless him!
18 He cursed as naturally as he dressed
    himself;
    may his own curses soak into his body
    like water
    and into his bones like oil!
19 May they cover him like clothes
    and always be round him like a belt!

20 LORD, punish my enemies in that
    way—
    those who say such evil things against
    me!
21 But my Sovereign LORD, help me as
    you have promised,
    and rescue me because of the
    goodness of your love.
22 I am poor and needy;
    I am hurt to the depths of my heart.
23 Like an evening shadow I am about
    to vanish;
    I am blown away like an insect.
24 My knees are weak from lack of food;
    I am nothing but skin and bones.
25 When people see me, they laugh at
    me;
    they shake their heads in scorn.

26 Help me, O LORD my God;

because of your constant love, save
    me!
27 Make my enemies know
    that you are the one who saves me.
28 They may curse me, but you will bless
    me.
    May my persecutors be defeated, *i*
    and may I, your servant, be glad.
29 May my enemies be covered with
    disgrace;
    may they wear their shame like a robe.

30 I will give loud thanks to the LORD;
    I will praise him in the assembly of
    the people,
31 because he defends the poor man
    and saves him from those who
    condemn him to death.

The LORD and His Chosen King *j*

110 The LORD said to my lord, the
    king,
    "Sit here at my right
    until I put your enemies under your
    feet."
2 From Zion the LORD will extend your
    royal power.
    "Rule over your enemies," he says.
3 On the day you fight your enemies,
    your people will volunteer.
Like the dew of early morning
    your young men will come to you on
    the sacred hills. *k*

4 The LORD made a solemn promise and
    will not take it back:
    "You will be a priest for ever
    in the priestly order of Melchizedek." *l*

5 The Lord is at your right side;
    when he becomes angry, he will
    defeat kings.
6 He will pass judgement on the nations
    and fill the battlefield with corpses;
    he will defeat kings all over the earth.
7 The king will drink from the stream by
    the road,
    and strengthened, he will stand
    victorious.

In Praise of the LORD

111 Praise the LORD!

With all my heart I will thank the LORD

---

h One ancient translation be driven from; *Hebrew* seek.
i One ancient translation May my persecutors be defeated; *Hebrew* They persecuted me and
were defeated.   *j* HEBREW TITLE: A psalm by David.   *k* Verse 3 in Hebrew is unclear.
l in...Melchizedek; *or* like Melchizedek; *or* in the line of succession to Melchizedek.
109.25: Mt 27.39; Mk 15.29
110.1: Mt 22.44; Mk 12.36; Lk 20.42–43; Acts 2.34–35; 1 Cor 15.25; Eph 1.20–22; Col 3.1;
110.1: Heb 1.13, 8.1, 10.12-13   **110.4:** Heb 5.6, 6.20, 7.17,21

in the assembly of his people.

2 How wonderful are the things the LORD
does!
All who are delighted with them want
to understand them.

3 All he does is full of honour and majesty;
his righteousness is eternal.

4 The LORD does not let us forget his
wonderful actions;
he is kind and merciful.

5 He provides food for those who honour
him;
he never forgets his covenant.

6 He has shown his power to his people
by giving them the lands of foreigners.

7 In all he does he is faithful and just;
all his commands are dependable.

8 They last for all time;
they were given in truth and
righteousness.

9 He set his people free
and made an eternal covenant with
them.
Holy and mighty is he!

10 The way to become wise is to honour
the LORD; m
he gives sound judgement to all who
obey his commands.
He is to be praised for ever.

The Happiness of a Good Person

112 Praise the LORD!

Happy is the person who honours the
LORD,
who takes pleasure in obeying his
commands.

2 The good man's children will be
powerful in the land;
his descendants will be blessed.

3 His family will be wealthy and rich,
and he will be prosperous for ever.

4 Light shines in the darkness for good
men,
for those who are merciful, kind, and
just.

5 Happy is the person who is generous
with his loans,
who runs his business honestly.

6 A good person will never fail;
he will always be remembered.

7 He is not afraid of receiving bad news;

his faith is strong, and he trusts in
the LORD.

8 He is not worried or afraid;
he is certain to see his enemies
defeated.

9 He gives generously to the needy,
and his kindness never fails;
he will be powerful and respected.

10 The wicked see this and are angry;
they glare in hate and disappear;
their hopes are gone for ever.

In Praise of the LORD's Goodness

113 Praise the LORD!

You servants of the LORD,
praise his name!

2 May his name be praised,
now and for ever.

3 From the east to the west
praise the name of the LORD!

4 The LORD rules over all nations;
his glory is above the heavens.

5 There is no one like the LORD our God.
He lives in the heights above,

6 but he bends down
to see the heavens and the earth.

7 He raises the poor from the dust;
he lifts the needy from their misery

8 and makes them companions of princes,
the princes of his people.

9 He honours the childless wife in her
home;
he makes her happy by giving her
children.

Praise the LORD!

A Passover Song

114 When the people of Israel left
Egypt,
when Jacob's descendants left that
foreign land,

2 Judah became the Lord's holy people,
Israel became his own possession.

3 The Red Sea looked and ran away;
the River Jordan stopped flowing.

4 The mountains skipped like goats;
the hills jumped about like lambs.

5 What happened, Sea, to make you run
away?
And you, O Jordan, why did you stop
flowing?

m The way...the LORD; or The most important part of wisdom is honouring the LORD
111.10: Job 28.28; Prov 1.7, 9.10　　**112.9:** 2 Cor 9.9　　**114.1:** Ex 12.51
114.3: Ex 14.21; Josh 3.16

6 You mountains, why did you skip like
  goats?
  You hills, why did you jump about
  like lambs?

7 Tremble, earth, at the Lord's coming,
  at the presence of the God of Jacob,
8 who changes rocks into pools of water
  and solid cliffs into flowing springs.

The One True God

115
To you alone, O LORD, to you
alone,
and not to us, must glory be given
because of your constant love and
faithfulness.

2 Why should the nations ask us,
  "Where is your God?"
3 Our God is in heaven;
  he does whatever he wishes.
4 Their gods are made of silver and gold,
  formed by human hands.
5 They have mouths, but cannot speak,
  and eyes, but cannot see.
6 They have ears, but cannot hear,
  and noses, but cannot smell.
7 They have hands, but cannot feel,
  and feet, but cannot walk;
  they cannot make a sound.
8 May all who made them and who trust
  in them
  become[n] like the idols they have
  made.

9 Trust in the LORD, you people of Israel.
  He helps you and protects you.
10 Trust in the LORD, you priests of God.
   He helps you and protects you.
11 Trust in the LORD, all you that worship
   him.
   He helps you and protects you.

12 The LORD remembers us and will bless
   us;
   he will bless the people of Israel
   and all the priests of God.
13 He will bless everyone who honours
   him,
   the great and the small alike.

14 May the LORD give you children—
   you and your descendants!
15 May you be blessed by the LORD,
   who made heaven and earth!

16 Heaven belongs to the LORD alone,
   but he gave the earth to man.
17 The LORD is not praised by the dead,
   by any who go down to the land of
   silence.[o]
18 But we, the living, will give thanks
   to him
   now and for ever.

Praise the LORD!

A Man Saved from Death Praises God

116
I love the LORD, because he
hears me;
he listens to my prayers.
2 He listens to me
  every time I call to him.
3 The danger of death was all round me;
  the horrors of the grave closed in on
  me;
  I was filled with fear and anxiety.
4 Then I called to the LORD,
  "I beg you, LORD, save me!"

5 The LORD is merciful and good;
  our God is compassionate.
6 The LORD protects the helpless;
  when I was in danger, he saved me.
7 Be confident, my heart,
  because the LORD has been good to
  me.

8 The LORD saved me from death;
  he stopped my tears
  and kept me from defeat.
9 And so I walk in the presence of the
  LORD
  in the world of the living.
10 I kept on believing, even when I said,
   "I am completely crushed,"
11 even when I was afraid and said,
   "No one can be trusted."

12 What can I offer the LORD
   for all his goodness to me?
13 I will bring a wine-offering to the LORD,
   to thank him for saving me.
14 In the assembly of all his people
   I will give him what I have promised.

15 How painful it is to the LORD
   when one of his people dies!
16 I am your servant, LORD;
   I serve you, just as my mother did.
   You have saved me from death.

---

[n] May all...become; or All who made them and who trust in them will become.
[o] LAND OF SILENCE: The world of the dead (see 6.5).
114.8: Ex 17.1–7; Num 20.2–13   **115.4–8:** Ps 135.15–18; Rev 9.20   **115.13:** Rev 11.18, 19.5
116.10: 2 Cor 4.13

Praise the LORD, all nations! (117.1)

¹⁷ I will give you a sacrifice of
    thanksgiving
  and offer my prayer to you.
¹⁸⁻¹⁹ In the assembly of all your people,
  in the sanctuary of your Temple in
    Jerusalem,
  I will give you what I have promised.

Praise the LORD!

In Praise of the LORD

117 Praise the LORD, all nations!
    Praise him, all peoples!
² His love for us is strong
  and his faithfulness is eternal.

Praise the LORD!

A Prayer of Thanks for Victory

118 Give thanks to the LORD,
    because he is good,
  and his love is eternal.

² Let the people of Israel say,
  "His love is eternal."
³ Let the priests of God say,
  "His love is eternal."
⁴ Let all who worship him say,
  "His love is eternal."

⁵ In my distress I called to the LORD;
  he answered me and set me free.
⁶ The LORD is with me, I will not be afraid;
  what can anyone do to me?
⁷ It is the LORD who helps me,
  and I will see my enemies defeated.
⁸ It is better to trust in the LORD
  than to depend on man.
⁹ It is better to trust in the LORD
  than to depend on human leaders.

¹⁰ Many enemies were round me;
  but I destroyed them by the power
    of the LORD!
¹¹ They were round me on every side;

117.1: Rom 15.11
118.1: 1 Chr 16.34; 2 Chr 5.13, 7.3; Ezra 3.11; Ps 100.5, 106.1, 107.1, 136.1; Jer 33.11
118.6: Heb 13.6

but I destroyed them by the power
of the LORD!
¹² They swarmed round me like bees,
but they burnt out as quickly as a
fire among thorns;
by the power of the LORD I destroyed
them.
¹³ I was fiercely attacked and was being
defeated,
but the LORD helped me.
¹⁴ The LORD makes me powerful and
strong;
he has saved me.

¹⁵ Listen to the glad shouts of victory
in the tents of God's people:
"The LORD's mighty power has done
it!
¹⁶   His power has brought us victory—
his mighty power in battle!"

¹⁷ I will not die; instead, I will live
and proclaim what the LORD has done.
¹⁸ He has punished me severely,
but he has not let me die.

¹⁹ Open to me the gates of the Temple;
I will go in and give thanks to the
LORD!

²⁰ This is the gate of the LORD;
only the righteous can come in.

²¹ I praise you, LORD, because you heard
me,
because you have given me victory.

²² The stone which the builders rejected
as worthless
turned out to be the most important
of all.
²³ This was done by the LORD;
what a wonderful sight it is!
²⁴ This is the day of the LORD's victory;
let us be happy, let us celebrate!
²⁵ Save us, LORD, save us!
Give us success, O LORD!

²⁶ May God bless the one who comes
in the name of the LORD!
From the Temple of the LORD we bless
you.
²⁷ The LORD is God; he has been good
to us.
With branches in your hands, start the
festival
and march round the altar.

²⁸ You are my God, and I give you thanks;
I will proclaim your greatness.

²⁹ Give thanks to the LORD, because he
is good,
and his love is eternal.

The Law of the LORD

119 Happy are those whose lives are
faultless,
who live according to the law of the
LORD.
² Happy are those who follow his
commands,
who obey him with all their heart.
³ They never do wrong;
they walk in the LORD's ways.
⁴ LORD, you have given us your laws
and told us to obey them faithfully.
⁵ How I hope that I shall be faithful
in keeping your instructions!
⁶ If I pay attention to all your commands,
then I will not be put to shame.
⁷ As I learn your righteous judgements,
I will praise you with a pure heart.
⁸ I will obey your laws;
never abandon me!

Obedience to the Law of the LORD

⁹ How can a young man keep his life
pure?
By obeying your commands.
¹⁰ With all my heart I try to serve you;
keep me from disobeying your
commandments.
¹¹ I keep your law in my heart,
so that I will not sin against you.
¹² I praise you, O LORD;
teach me your ways.
¹³ I will repeat aloud
all the laws you have given.
¹⁴ I delight in following your commands
more than in having great wealth.
¹⁵ I study your instructions;
I examine your teachings.
¹⁶ I take pleasure in your laws;
your commands I will not forget.

Happiness in the Law of the LORD

¹⁷ Be good to me, your servant,
so that I may live and obey your
teachings.
¹⁸ Open my eyes, so that I may see
the wonderful truths in your law.
¹⁹ I am here on earth for just a little
while;

118.14: Ex 15.2; Is 12.2   **118.22:** Lk 20.17; Acts 4.11; 1 Pet 2.7
118.22–23: Mt 21.42; Mk 12.10–11   **118.25:** Mt 21.9; Mk 11.9; Jn 12.13
118.26: Mt 21.9, 23.39; Mk 11.9; Lk 13.35, 19.38; Jn 12.13

do not hide your commands from me.
20 My heart aches with longing;
   I want to know your judgements at
       all times.
21 You reprimand the proud;
   cursed are those who disobey your
       commands.
22 Free me from their insults and scorn,
   because I have kept your laws.
23 The rulers meet and plot against me,
   but I will study your teachings.
24 Your instructions give me pleasure;
   they are my advisers.

Determination to Obey the Law of the LORD

25 I lie defeated in the dust;
   revive me, as you have promised.
26 I confessed all I have done, and you
       answered me;
   teach me your ways.
27 Help me to understand your laws,
   and I will meditate on your wonderful
       teachings. P
28 I am overcome by sorrow;
   strengthen me, as you have promised.
29 Keep me from going the wrong way,
   and in your goodness teach me your
       law.
30 I have chosen to be obedient;
   I have paid attention to your
       judgements.
31 I have followed your instructions,
   LORD;
   don't let me be put to shame.
32 I will eagerly obey your commands,
   because you will give me more
       understanding.

A Prayer for Understanding

33 Teach me, LORD, the meaning of your
       laws,
   and I will obey them at all times.
34 Explain your law to me, and I will
       obey it;
   I will keep it with all my heart.
35 Keep me obedient to your
       commandments,
   because in them I find happiness.
36 Give me the desire to obey your laws
   rather than to get rich.
37 Keep me from paying attention to
       what is worthless;
   be good to me, as you have promised.
38 Keep your promise to me, your
       servant—
   the promise you make to those who
       obey you.
39 Save me from the insults I fear;

P teachings; or deeds.

how wonderful are your judgements!
40 I want to obey your commands;
   give me new life, for you are righteous.

Trusting the Law of the LORD

41 Show me how much you love me,
   LORD,
   and save me according to your
       promise.
42 Then I can answer those who insult
       me
   because I trust in your word.
43 Enable me to speak the truth at all
       times,
   because my hope is in your
       judgements.
44 I will always obey your law,
   for ever and ever.
45 I will live in perfect freedom,
   because I try to obey your teachings.
46 I will announce your commands to
       kings
   and I will not be ashamed.
47 I find pleasure in obeying your
       commands,
   because I love them.
48 I respect and love your
       commandments;
   I will meditate on your instructions.

Confidence in the Law of the LORD

49 Remember your promise to me, your
       servant;
   it has given me hope.
50 Even in my suffering I was comforted
   because your promise gave me life.
51 The proud are always scornful of me,
   but I have not departed from your
       law.
52 I remember your judgements of long
       ago,
   and they bring me comfort, O LORD.
53 When I see the wicked breaking your
       law,
   I am filled with anger.
54 During my brief earthly life
   I compose songs about your
       commands.
55 In the night I remember you, LORD,
   and I think about your law.
56 I find my happiness
   in obeying your commands.

Devotion to the Law of the LORD

57 You are all I want, O LORD;
   I promise to obey your laws.
58 I ask you with all my heart
   to have mercy on me, as you have
       promised!

⁵⁹ I have considered my conduct,
   and I promise to follow your
      instructions.
⁶⁰ Without delay I hurry
   to obey your commands.
⁶¹ The wicked have laid a trap for me,
   but I do not forget your law.
⁶² In the middle of the night I wake up
   to praise you for your righteous
      judgements.
⁶³ I am a friend of all who serve you,
   of all who obey your laws.
⁶⁴ LORD, the earth is full of your constant
      love;
   teach me your commandments.

The Value of the Law of the LORD

⁶⁵ You have kept your promise, LORD,
   and you are good to me, your servant.
⁶⁶ Give me wisdom and knowledge,
   because I trust in your commands.
⁶⁷ Before you punished me, I used to go
      wrong,
   but now I obey your word.
⁶⁸ How good you are—how kind!
   Teach me your commands.
⁶⁹ Proud men have told lies about me,
   but with all my heart I obey your
      instructions.
⁷⁰ These men have no understanding,
   but I find pleasure in your law.
⁷¹ My punishment was good for me,
   because it made me learn your
      commands.
⁷² The law that you gave means more
      to me
   than all the money in the world.

The Justice of the Law of the LORD

⁷³ You created me, and you keep me safe;
   give me understanding, so that I may
      learn your laws.
⁷⁴ Those who honour you will be glad
      when they see me,
   because I trust in your promise.
⁷⁵ I know that your judgements are
      righteous, LORD,
   and that you punished me because
      you are faithful.
⁷⁶ Let your constant love comfort me,
   as you have promised me, your
      servant.
⁷⁷ Have mercy on me, and I will live
   because I take pleasure in your law.
⁷⁸ May the proud be ashamed for falsely
      accusing me;
   as for me, I will meditate on your
      instructions.
⁷⁹ May those who honour you come to
      me—

all those who know your commands.
⁸⁰ May I perfectly obey your
      commandments
   and be spared the shame of defeat.

A Prayer for Deliverance

⁸¹ I am worn out, LORD, waiting for you
      to save me;
   I place my trust in your word.
⁸² My eyes are tired from watching for
      what you promised,
   while I ask, "When will you help me?"
⁸³ I am as useless as a discarded
      wineskin;
   yet I have not forgotten your
      commands.
⁸⁴ How much longer must I wait?
   When will you punish those who
      persecute me?
⁸⁵ Proud men, who do not obey your law,
   have dug pits to trap me.
⁸⁶ Your commandments are all
      trustworthy;
   men persecute me with lies—help me!
⁸⁷ They have almost succeeded in killing
      me,
   but I have not neglected your
      commands.
⁸⁸ Because of your constant love be good
      to me,
   so that I may obey your laws.

Faith in the Law of the LORD

⁸⁹ Your word, O LORD, will last for ever;
   it is eternal in heaven.
⁹⁰ Your faithfulness endures through all
      the ages;
   you have set the earth in place, and
      it remains.
⁹¹ All things remain to this day because
      of your command,
   because they are all your servants.
⁹² If your law had not been the source
      of my joy,
   I would have died from my sufferings.
⁹³ I will never neglect your instructions,
   because by them you have kept me
      alive.
⁹⁴ I am yours—save me!
   I have tried to obey your commands.
⁹⁵ Wicked men are waiting to kill me,
   but I will meditate on your laws.
⁹⁶ I have learnt that everything has
      limits;
   but your commandment is perfect.

Love for the Law of the LORD

⁹⁷ How I love your law!
   I think about it all day long.
⁹⁸ Your commandment is with me all the
      time

and makes me wiser than my enemies.
99 I understand more than all my
teachers,
because I meditate on your
instructions.
100 I have greater wisdom than old men,
because I obey your commands.
101 I have avoided all evil conduct,
because I want to obey your word.
102 I have not neglected your
instructions,
for you yourself are my teacher.
103 How sweet is the taste of your
instructions—
sweeter even than honey!
104 I gain wisdom from your laws,
and so I hate all bad conduct.

Light from the Law of the LORD

105 Your word is a lamp to guide me
and a light for my path.
106 I will keep my solemn promise
to obey your just instructions.
107 My sufferings, LORD, are terrible
indeed;
keep me alive, as you have promised.
108 Accept my prayer of thanks, O LORD,
and teach me your commands.
109 I am always ready to risk my life;
I q have not forgotten your law.
110 Wicked men lay a trap for me,
but I have not disobeyed your
commands.
111 Your commandments are my eternal
possession;
they are the joy of my heart.
112 I have decided to obey your laws
until the day I die.

Safety in the Law of the LORD

113 I hate those who are not completely
loyal to you,
but I love your law.
114 You are my defender and protector;
I put my hope in your promise.
115 Go away from me, you sinful people.
I will obey the commands of my God.
116 Give me strength, as you promised,
and I shall live;
don't let me be disappointed in my
hope!
117 Hold me, and I will be safe,
and I will always pay attention to your
commands.
118 You reject everyone who disobeys
your laws;
their deceitful schemes are useless.

119 You treat all the wicked like rubbish,
and so I love your instructions.
120 Because of you I am afraid;
I am filled with fear because of your
judgements.

Obedience to the Law of the LORD

121 I have done what is right and good;
don't abandon me to my enemies!
122 Promise that you will help your
servant;
don't let arrogant men oppress me!
123 My eyes are tired from watching for
your saving help,
for the deliverance you promised.
124 Treat me according to your constant
love,
and teach me your commands.
125 I am your servant; give me
understanding,
so that I may know your teachings.
126 LORD, it is time for you to act,
because people are disobeying your
law.
127 I love your commands more than
gold,
more than the finest gold.
128 And so I follow all your instructions; r
I hate all wrong ways.

Desire to Obey the Law of the LORD

129 Your teachings are wonderful;
I obey them with all my heart.
130 The explanation of your teachings
gives light
and brings wisdom to the ignorant.
131 In my desire for your commands
I pant with open mouth.
132 Turn to me and have mercy on me
as you do on all those who love you.
133 As you have promised, keep me from
falling;
don't let me be overcome by evil.
134 Save me from those who oppress me,
so that I may obey your commands.
135 Bless me with your presence
and teach me your laws.
136 My tears pour down like a river,
because people do not obey your law

The Justice of the Law of the LORD

137 You are righteous, LORD,
and your laws are just.
138 The rules that you have given
are completely fair and right.
139 My anger burns in me like a fire,
because my enemies disregard your
commands.

q I am always ready to risk my life; I; or My life is in constant danger, but I.
r Some ancient translations all your instructions; Hebrew unclear.

140 How certain your promise is!
How I love it!
141 I am unimportant and despised,
but I do not neglect your teachings.
142 Your righteousness will last for ever,
and your law is always true.
143 I am filled with trouble and anxiety,
but your commandments bring me
joy.
144 Your instructions are always just;
give me understanding, and I shall
live.

A Prayer for Deliverance

145 With all my heart I call to you;
answer me, LORD, and I will obey your
commands!
146 I call to you;
save me, and I will keep your laws.
147 Before sunrise I call to you for help;
I place my hope in your promise.
148 All night long I lie awake,
to meditate on your instructions.
149 Because your love is constant, hear
me, O LORD;
show your mercy, and preserve my
life!
150 My cruel persecutors are coming
closer,
people who never keep your law.
151 But you are near to me, LORD,
and all your commands are
permanent.
152 Long ago I learnt about your
instructions;
you made them to last for ever.

A Plea for Help

153 Look at my suffering, and save me,
because I have not neglected your law.
154 Defend my cause, and set me free;
save me, as you have promised.
155 The wicked will not be saved,
for they do not obey your laws.
156 But your compassion, LORD, is great;
show your mercy and save me!
157 I have many enemies and oppressors,
but I do not fail to obey your laws.
158 When I look at those traitors, I am
filled with disgust,
because they do not keep your
commands.
159 See how I love your instructions,
LORD.
Your love never changes, so save me!
160 The heart of your law is truth,
and all your righteous judgements are
eternal.

Dedication to the Law of the LORD

161 Powerful men attack me unjustly,
but I respect your law.
162 How happy I am because of your
promises—
as happy as someone who finds rich
treasure.
163 I hate and detest all lies,
but I love your law.
164 Seven times each day I thank you
for your righteous judgements.
165 Those who love your law have
perfect security,
and there is nothing that can make
them fall.
166 I wait for you to save me, LORD,
and I do what you command.
167 I obey your teachings;
I love them with all my heart.
168 I obey your commands and your
instructions;
you see everything I do.

A Prayer for Help

169 Let my cry for help reach you, LORD!
Give me understanding, as you have
promised.
170 Listen to my prayer,
and save me according to your
promise!
171 I will always praise you,
because you teach me your laws.
172 I will sing about your law,
because your commands are just.
173 Always be ready to help me,
because I follow your commands.
174 How I long for your saving help, O
LORD!
I find happiness in your law.
175 Give me life, so that I may praise
you;
may your instructions help me.
176 I wander about like a lost sheep;
so come and look for me, your servant,
because I have not neglected your
laws.

A Prayer for Help

120 When I was in trouble, I called
to the LORD,
and he answered me.
2 Save me, LORD,
from liars and deceivers.

3 You liars, what will God do to you?
How will he punish you?
4 With a soldier's sharp arrows,
with red-hot charcoal!

⁵ Living among you is as bad as living
    in Meshech
    or among the people of Kedar.ˢ
⁶ I have lived too long
    with people who hate peace!
⁷ When I speak of peace,
    they are for war.

The LORD Our Protector

121 I look to the mountains;
      where will my help come
       from?
² My help will come from the LORD,
    who made heaven and earth.

³ He will not let you fall;
    your protector is always awake.

⁴ The protector of Israel
    never dozes or sleeps.
⁵ The LORD will guard you;
    he is by your side to protect you.
⁶ The sun will not hurt you during the
    day,
    nor the moon during the night.

⁷ The LORD will protect you from all
    danger;
    he will keep you safe.
⁸ He will protect you as you come and
    go
    now and for ever.

In Praise of Jerusalem ᵗ

122 I was glad when they said to
      me,
    "Let us go to the LORD's house."
² And now we are here,
    standing inside the gates of
    Jerusalem!

³ Jerusalem is a city restored
    in beautiful order and harmony.
⁴ This is where the tribes come,
    the tribes of Israel,
    to give thanks to the LORD
    according to his command.
⁵ Here the kings of Israel
    sat to judge their people.

⁶ Pray for the peace of Jerusalem:
    "May those who love you prosper.
⁷   May there be peace inside your walls
    and safety in your palaces."
⁸ For the sake of my relatives and friends
    I say to Jerusalem, "Peace be with
    you!"

Let us go to the LORD's house (122.1)

⁹ For the sake of the house of the LORD
    our God
    I pray for your prosperity.

A Prayer for Mercy

123 LORD, I look up to you,
      up to heaven, where you rule.
² As a servant depends on his master,
    as a maid depends on her mistress,
    so we will keep looking to you, O LORD
    our God,
    until you have mercy on us.

³ Be merciful to us, LORD, be merciful;
    we have been treated with so much
    contempt.
⁴ We have been mocked too long by the
    rich
    and scorned by proud oppressors.

God the Protector of His People ᵘ

124 What if the LORD had not been
      on our side?
    Answer, O Israel!

² "If the LORD had not been on our side
    when our enemies attacked us,

ˢ MESHECH...KEDAR: *Two distant regions, whose people were regarded as savages.*
ᵗ HEBREW TITLE: *By David.*   ᵘ HEBREW TITLE: *By David.*

Gather the harvest with joy! (126.5)

3 then they would have swallowed us alive
    in their furious anger against us;
4 then the flood would have carried us
    away,
    the water would have covered us,
5   the raging torrent would have
    drowned us."

6 Let us thank the LORD,
    who has not let our enemies destroy
    us.
7 We have escaped like a bird from a
    hunter's trap;
    the trap is broken, and we are free!
8 Our help comes from the LORD,
    who made heaven and earth.

The Security of God's People

125 Those who trust in the LORD are
    like Mount Zion,
which can never be shaken, never be
    moved.
2 As the mountains surround Jerusalem,
    so the LORD surrounds his people
    now and for ever.

3 The wicked will not always rule over
    the land of the righteous;
    if they did, the righteous themselves
    might do evil.
4 LORD, do good to those who are good,
    to those who obey your commands.

5 But when you punish the wicked,
    punish also those who abandon your
    ways.

Peace be with Israel!

A Prayer for Deliverance

126 When the LORD brought us back
    to Jerusalem, *v*
it was like a dream!
2 How we laughed, how we sang for joy!
    Then the other nations said about us,
    "The LORD did great things for them."
3 Indeed he did great things for us;
    how happy we were!

4 LORD, make us prosperous again, *m*
    just as the rain brings water back to
    dry river-beds.
5 Let those who wept as they sowed their
    seed,
    gather the harvest with joy!

6 Those who wept as they went out
    carrying the seed
will come back singing for joy,
    as they bring in the harvest.

In Praise of God's Goodness *w*

127 If the LORD does not build the
    house,
    the work of the builders is useless;

v brought us back to Jerusalem; *or* made Jerusalem prosperous again.
m make...again; *or* take us back to our land.
w HEBREW TITLE: *By Solomon.*

if the LORD does not protect the city,
　it is useless for the sentries to stand
　　guard.
2 It is useless to work so hard for a living,
　getting up early and going to bed late.
For the LORD provides for those he loves,
　while they are asleep.

3 Children are a gift from the LORD;
　they are a real blessing.
4 The sons a man has when he is young
　are like arrows in a soldier's hand.
5 Happy is the man who has many such
　arrows.
He will never be defeated
　when he meets his enemies in the
　　place of judgement.

The Reward of Obedience to the LORD

128 Happy are those who obey the
LORD,
　who live by his commands.

2 Your work will provide for your needs;
　you will be happy and prosperous.
3 Your wife will be like a fruitful vine
　in your home,
　and your sons will be like young olive-
　　trees round your table.
4 A man who obeys the LORD
　will surely be blessed like this.

5 May the LORD bless you from Zion!
May you see Jerusalem prosper
　all the days of your life!
6 May you live to see your grandchildren!

Peace be with Israel!

A Prayer against Israel's Enemies

129 Israel, tell us how your enemies
have persecuted you
ever since you were young.

2 "Ever since I was young,
　my enemies have persecuted me
　　cruelly,
　but they have not overcome me.
3 They cut deep wounds in my back
　and made it like a ploughed field.
4 But the LORD, the righteous one,
　has freed me from slavery."

5 May everyone who hates Zion
　be defeated and driven back.
6 May they all be like grass growing on
　　the house-tops,
　which dries up before it can grow;

7 no one gathers it up
　or carries it away in bundles.
8 No one who passes by will say,
　"May the LORD bless you!
　We bless you in the name of the
　　LORD."

A Prayer for Help

130 From the depths of my despair
I call to you, LORD.
2 Hear my cry, O Lord;
　listen to my call for help!
3 If you kept a record of our sins,
　who could escape being condemned?
4 But you forgive us,
　so that we should stand in awe of
　　you.

5 I wait eagerly for the LORD's help,
　and in his word I trust.
6 I wait for the Lord
　more eagerly than watchmen wait for
　　the dawn—
　than watchmen wait for the dawn.

7 Israel, trust in the LORD,
　because his love is constant
　and he is always willing to save.
8 He will save his people Israel
　from all their sins.

A Prayer of Humble Trust [x]

131 LORD, I have given up my pride
and turned away from my
arrogance.
I am not concerned with great matters
　or with subjects too difficult for me.
2 Instead, I am content and at peace.
As a child lies quietly in its mother's
　　arms,
　so my heart is quiet within me.
3 Israel, trust in the LORD
　now and for ever!

In Praise of the Temple

132 LORD, do not forget David
and all the hardships he
endured.
2 Remember, LORD, what he promised,
　the vow he made to you, the Mighty
　　God of Jacob:
3 "I will not go home or go to bed;
4 　I will not rest or sleep,
5 　until I provide a place for the LORD,
　a home for the Mighty God of Jacob."

6 In Bethlehem we heard about the
　Covenant Box,

More eagerly than watchmen wait (130.6)

and we found it in the fields of Jearim.
⁷ We said, "Let us go to the LORD's house;
let us worship before his throne."

⁸ Come to the Temple, LORD, with the
Covenant Box,
the symbol of your power,
and stay here for ever.
⁹ May your priests do always what is
right;
may your people shout for joy!

¹⁰ You made a promise to your servant
David;
do not reject your chosen king, LORD.
¹¹ You made a solemn promise to
David—
a promise you will not take back:
"I will make one of your sons king,
and he will rule after you.
¹² If your sons are true to my covenant
and to the commands I give them,
their sons, also, will succeed you for
all time as kings."

¹³ The LORD has chosen Zion;
he wants to make it his home:
¹⁴ "This is where I will live for ever;
this is where I want to rule.
¹⁵ I will richly provide Zion with all she
needs;
I will satisfy her poor with food.
¹⁶ I will bless her priests in all they do,

and her people will sing and shout
for joy.
¹⁷ Here I will make one of David's
descendants a great king;
here I will preserve the rule of my
chosen king.
¹⁸ I will cover his enemies with shame,
but his kingdom will prosper and
flourish."

In Praise of Brotherly Love ʸ

133 How wonderful it is, how
pleasant,
for God's people to live together in
harmony!
² It is like the precious anointing oil
running down from Aaron's head and
beard,
down to the collar of his robes.
³ It is like the dew on Mount Hermon,
falling on the hills of Zion.
That is where the LORD has promised
his blessing—
life that never ends.

A Call to Praise God

134 Come, praise the LORD,
all his servants,
all who serve in his Temple at night.
² Raise your hands in prayer in the
Temple,
and praise the LORD!

ʸHEBREW TITLE: *By David.*
132.11: 2 Sam 7.12-16; 1 Chr 17.11-14; Ps 89.3-4; Acts 2.30   **132.17:** 1 Kgs 11.36

3 May the LORD, who made heaven and
 earth,
 bless you from Zion!

A Hymn of Praise

135 Praise the LORD!

Praise his name, you servants of the
 LORD,
2   who stand in the LORD's house,
 in the Temple of our God.
3 Praise the LORD, because he is good;
 sing praises to his name, because he
 is kind. z
4 He chose Jacob for himself,
 the people of Israel for his own.

5 I know that our LORD is great,
 greater than all the gods.
6 He does whatever he wishes
 in heaven and on earth,
 in the seas and in the depths below.
7 He brings storm clouds from the ends
 of the earth;
 he makes lightning for the storms,
 and he brings out the wind from his
 storeroom.

8 In Egypt he killed all the first-born
 of men and animals alike.
9 There he performed miracles and
 wonders
 to punish the king and all his officials.
10 He destroyed many nations

and killed powerful kings:
11 Sihon, king of the Amorites,
 Og, king of Bashan,
 and all the kings in Canaan.
12 He gave their lands to his people;
 he gave them to Israel.

13 LORD, you will always be proclaimed
 as God;
 all generations will remember you.
14 The LORD will defend his people;
 he will take pity on his servants.

15 The gods of the nations are made of
 silver and gold;
 they are formed by human hands.
16 They have mouths, but cannot speak,
 and eyes, but cannot see.
17 They have ears, but cannot hear;
 they are not even able to breathe.
18 May all who made them and who trust
 in them
 become a like the idols they have
 made!

19 Praise the LORD, people of Israel;
 praise him, you priests of God!
20 Praise the LORD, you Levites;
 praise him, all you that worship him!
21 Praise the LORD in Zion,
 in Jerusalem, his home.

Praise the LORD!

z he is kind; *or* it is pleasant to do so.
a May all...become; *or* All who made them and who trust in them will become.
135.15–18: Ps 115.4–8; Rev 9.20

How wonderful...for God's people to live together in harmony (133.1)

A Hymn of Thanksgiving

136 Give thanks to the LORD,
because he is good;
his love is eternal.

2 Give thanks to the greatest of all gods;
his love is eternal.

3 Give thanks to the mightiest of all lords;
his love is eternal.

4 He alone performs great miracles;
his love is eternal.

5 By his wisdom he made the heavens;
his love is eternal;

6 he built the earth on the deep waters;
his love is eternal.

7 He made the sun and the moon;
his love is eternal;

8 the sun to rule over the day;
his love is eternal;

9 the moon and the stars to rule over the
night;
his love is eternal.

10 He killed the first-born sons of the
Egyptians;
his love is eternal.

11 He led the people of Israel out of
Egypt;
his love is eternal;

12 with his strong hand, his powerful
arm;
his love is eternal.

13 He divided the Red Sea;
his love is eternal;

14 he led his people through it;
his love is eternal;

15 but he drowned the king of Egypt and
his army;
his love is eternal.

16 He led his people through the desert;
his love is eternal.

17 He killed powerful kings;
his love is eternal;

18 he killed famous kings;
his love is eternal;

19 Sihon, king of the Amorites;
his love is eternal;

20 and Og, king of Bashan;
his love is eternal.

21 He gave their lands to his people;
his love is eternal;

22 he gave them to Israel, his servant;
his love is eternal.

23 He did not forget us when we were
defeated;
his love is eternal;

24 he freed us from our enemies;
his love is eternal.

25 He gives food to every living creature;
his love is eternal.

26 Give thanks to the God of heaven;
his love is eternal.

A Lament of Israelites in Exile

137 By the rivers of Babylon we sat
down;
there we wept when we remembered
Zion.

2 On the willows near by
we hung up our harps.

3 Those who captured us told us to sing;
they told us to entertain them:
"Sing us a song about Zion."

4 How can we sing a song to the LORD
in a foreign land?

5 May I never be able to play the harp
again
if I forget you, Jerusalem!

6 May I never be able to sing again
if I do not remember you,
if I do not think of you as my greatest
joy!

7 Remember, LORD, what the Edomites did
the day Jerusalem was captured.
Remember how they kept saying,
"Tear it down to the ground!"

8 Babylon, you will be destroyed.
Happy is the man who pays you back
for what you have done to us—

9 who takes your babies
and smashes them against a rock.

A Prayer of Thanksgiving [b]

138 I thank you, LORD, with all my
heart;
I sing praise to you before the gods.

2 I face your holy Temple,
bow down, and praise your name
because of your constant love and
faithfulness,
because you have shown that your
name and your commands are
supreme. [c]

[b] HEBREW TITLE: *By David.*
[c] *Probable text* your name and your commands are supreme; *Hebrew* your command is greater
than all your name.
136.1: 1 Chr 16.34; 2 Chr 5.13, 7.3; Ezra 3.11; Ps 100.5, 106.1, 107.1, 118.1; Jer 33.11
136.5: Gen 1.1   **136.6:** Gen 1.2   **136.7–9:** Gen 1.16   **136.10:** Ex 12.29   **136.11:** Ex 12.51
136.13–15: Ex 14.21–29   **136.19:** Num 21.21–30   **136.20:** Num 21.31–35   **137.8:** Rev 18.6

3 You answered me when I called to you;
  with your strength you strengthened
    me.

4 All the kings in the world will praise
    you, LORD,
  because they have heard your
    promises.
5 They will sing about what you have done
  and about your great glory.
6 Even though you are so high above,
    you care for the lowly,
  and the proud cannot hide from you.

7 When I am surrounded by troubles,
    you keep me safe.
  You oppose my angry enemies
  and save me by your power.
8 You will do everything you have
    promised;
  LORD, your love is eternal.
  Complete the work that you have
    begun.

God's Complete Knowledge and Care [d]

139 LORD, you have examined me
          and you know me.
2 You know everything I do;
  from far away you understand all my
    thoughts.
3 You see me, whether I am working or
    resting;
  you know all my actions.
4 Even before I speak,
  you already know what I will say.
5 You are all round me on every side;
  you protect me with your power.
6 Your knowledge of me is too deep;
  it is beyond my understanding.

7 Where could I go to escape from you?
  Where could I get away from your
    presence?
8 If I went up to heaven, you would be
    there;
  if I lay down in the world of the dead,
    you would be there.
9 If I flew away beyond the east
  or lived in the farthest place in the
    west,
10 you would be there to lead me,
  you would be there to help me.
11 I could ask the darkness to hide me
  or the light round me to turn into
    night,

12 but even darkness is not dark for you,
  and the night is as bright as the day.
  Darkness and light are the same to
    you.

13 You created every part of me;
  you put me together in my mother's
    womb.
14 I praise you because you are to be
    feared;
  all you do is strange and wonderful.
  I know it with all my heart.
15 When my bones were being formed,
  carefully put together in my mother's
    womb,
  when I was growing there in secret,
  you knew that I was there—
16   you saw me before I was born.
  The days allotted to me
  had all been recorded in your book,
  before any of them ever began.
17 O God, how difficult I find your
    thoughts; [e]
  how many of them there are!
18 If I counted them, they would be more
    than the grains of sand.
  When I awake, I am still with you.

19 O God, how I wish you would kill the
    wicked!
  How I wish violent men would leave
    me alone!
20 They say wicked things about you;
  they speak evil things against your
    name. [f]
21 O LORD, how I hate those who hate
    you!
  How I despise those who rebel against
    you!
22 I hate them with a total hatred;
  I regard them as my enemies.

23 Examine me, O God, and know my
    mind;
  test me, and discover my thoughts.
24 Find out if there is any evil in me
  and guide me in the everlasting way. [g]

A Prayer for Protection [h]

140 Save me, LORD, from evil men;
          keep me safe from violent
            men.
2 They are always plotting evil,
  always stirring up quarrels.
3 Their tongues are like deadly snakes;

---

[d] HEBREW TITLE: *A psalm by David.*
[e] how difficult I find your thoughts; *or* how precious are your thoughts to me.
[f] *Probable text* they speak...name; *Hebrew unclear.*
[g] the everlasting way; *or* the ways of my ancestors.   [h] HEBREW TITLE: *A psalm by David.*
140.3: Rom 3.13

their words are like a cobra's poison.

4 Protect me, LORD, from the power of
   the wicked;
  keep me safe from violent men
   who plot my downfall.
5 Proud men have set a trap for me;
  they have laid their snares
  and along the path they have set traps
   to catch me.

6 I say to the LORD, "You are my God."
  Hear my cry for help, LORD!
7 My Sovereign LORD, my strong defender,
  you have protected me in battle.
8 LORD, don't give the wicked what they
   want;
  don't let their plots succeed.

9 Don't let my enemies be victorious;[i]
  make their threats against me fall
   back on them.
10 May red-hot coals fall on them;
  may they be thrown into a pit and
   never get out.
11 May those who accuse others falsely
   not succeed;
  may evil overtake violent men and
   destroy them.

12 LORD, I know that you defend the
   cause of the poor
  and the rights of the needy.
13 The righteous will praise you indeed;
  they will live in your presence.

An Evening Prayer[j]

141 I call to you, LORD; help me now!
     Listen to me when I call to
     you.
2 Receive my prayer as incense,
  my uplifted hands as an evening
   sacrifice.

3 LORD, place a guard at my mouth,
  a sentry at the door of my lips.
4 Keep me from wanting to do wrong
  and from joining evil men in their
   wickedness.
  May I never take part in their feasts.

5 A good man may punish me and rebuke
   me in kindness,
  but I will never accept honour from
   evil men,

because I am always praying against
  their evil deeds.
6 When their rulers are thrown down
   from rocky cliffs,
  the people will admit that my words
   were true.
7 Like wood that is split and chopped into
   bits,
  so their bones are scattered at the
   edge of the grave.[k]

8 But I keep trusting in you, my Sovereign
   LORD.
  I seek your protection;
  don't let me die!
9 Protect me from the traps they have
   set for me,
  from the snares of those evildoers.
10 May the wicked fall into their own
   traps
  while I go by unharmed.

A Prayer for Help[l]

142 I call to the LORD for help;
     I plead with him.
2 I bring him all my complaints;
  I tell him all my troubles.
3 When I am ready to give up,
  he knows what I should do.
In the path where I walk,
  my enemies have hidden a trap for
   me.
4 When I look beside me,
  I see that there is no one to help me,
  no one to protect me.
No one cares for me.

5 LORD, I cry to you for help;
  you, LORD, are my protector;
  you are all I want in this life.
6 Listen to my cry for help,
  for I am sunk in despair.
Save me from my enemies;
  they are too strong for me.
7 Set me free from my distress;[m]
  then in the assembly of your people
   I will praise you
  because of your goodness to me.

A Prayer for Help[n]

143 LORD, hear my prayer!
     In your righteousness listen to
     my plea;
  answer me in your faithfulness!
2 Don't put me, your servant, on trial;

---

[i] *Probable text* Don't let my enemies be victorious; *Hebrew unclear.*
[j] HEBREW TITLE: *A psalm by David.*   [k] *Verses 5–7 in Hebrew are unclear.*
[l] HEBREW TITLE: *A poem by David, when he was in the cave; a prayer.*   [m] distress; *or* prison.
[n] HEBREW TITLE: *A psalm by David.*
141.2: Rev 5.8   **142 Title:** 1 Sam 22.1, 24.3   **143.2:** Rom 3.20; Gal 2.16

no one is innocent in your sight.

3 My enemy has hunted me down
and completely defeated me.
He has put me in a dark prison,
and I am like those who died long
ago.
4 So I am ready to give up;
I am in deep despair.

5 I remember the days gone by;
I think about all that you have done,
I bring to mind all your deeds.
6 I lift up my hands to you in prayer;
like dry ground my soul is thirsty for
you.

7 Answer me now, LORD!
I have lost all hope.
Don't hide yourself from me,
or I will be among those who go down
to the world of the dead.
8 Remind me each morning of your
constant love,
for I put my trust in you.
My prayers go up to you;
show me the way I should go.

9 I go to you for protection, LORD;
rescue me from my enemies.
10 You are my God;
teach me to do your will.
Be good to me, and guide me on a safe
path.

11 Rescue me, LORD, as you have
promised;
in your goodness save me from my
troubles!
12 Because of your love for me, kill my
enemies
and destroy all my oppressors,
for I am your servant.

A King Thanks God for Victory[o]

144 Praise the LORD, my protector!
He trains me for battle
and prepares me for war.
2 He is my protector and defender,
my shelter and saviour,
in whom I trust for safety.
He subdues the nations under me.

3 LORD, what is man, that you notice him;
mere man, that you pay attention to
him?
4 He is like a puff of wind;
his days are like a passing shadow.

5 O LORD, tear the sky apart and come
down;
touch the mountains, and they will
pour out smoke.
6 Send flashes of lightning and scatter
your enemies;
shoot your arrows and send them
running.
7 Reach down from above,
pull me out of the deep water, and
rescue me;
save me from the power of foreigners,
8 who never tell the truth
and lie even under oath.

9 I will sing you a new song, O God;
I will play the harp and sing to you.
10 You give victory to kings
and rescue your servant David.
11 Save me from my cruel enemies;
rescue me from the power of
foreigners,
who never tell the truth
and lie even under oath.

12 May our sons in their youth
be like plants that grow up strong.
May our daughters be like stately pillars
which adorn the corners of a palace.
13 May our barns be filled
with crops of every kind.
May the sheep in our fields
bear young by the tens of thousands.
14 May our cattle reproduce plentifully
without miscarriage or loss.
May there be no cries of distress in
our streets.

15 Happy is the nation of whom this is
true;
happy are the people whose God is
the LORD!

A Hymn of Praise[p]

145 I will proclaim your greatness,
my God and king;
I will thank you for ever and ever.
2 Every day I will thank you;
I will praise you for ever and ever.
3 The LORD is great and is to be highly
praised;
his greatness is beyond
understanding.

4 What you have done will be praised
from one generation to the next;
they will proclaim your mighty acts.

[o] HEBREW TITLE: *By David.*   [p] HEBREW TITLE: *A song of praise by David.*
144.3: Job 7.17–18; Ps 8.4

⁵ They will speak of your glory and
majesty,
    and I will meditate on your wonderful
    deeds.
⁶ People will speak of your mighty deeds,
    and I will proclaim your greatness.
⁷ They will tell about all your goodness
    and sing about your kindness.
⁸ The Lord is loving and merciful,
    slow to become angry and full of
    constant love.
⁹ He is good to everyone
    and has compassion on all he made.

¹⁰ All your creatures, Lord, will praise
you,
    and all your people will give you
    thanks.
¹¹ They will speak of the glory of your
    royal power
    and tell of your might,
¹² so that everyone will know your
    mighty deeds
    and the glorious majesty of your
    kingdom.
¹³ Your rule is eternal,
    and you are king for ever.

The Lord is faithful to his promises,
    and he is merciful in all his acts.
¹⁴ He helps those who are in trouble;
    he lifts those who have fallen.

¹⁵ All living things look hopefully to you,
    and you give them food when they
    need it.
¹⁶ You give them enough
    and satisfy the needs of all.

¹⁷ The Lord is righteous in all he does,
    merciful in all his acts.
¹⁸ He is near to those who call to him,
    who call to him with sincerity.
¹⁹ He supplies the needs of those who
    honour him;
    he hears their cries and saves them.
²⁰ He protects everyone who loves him,
    but he will destroy the wicked.

²¹ I will always praise the Lord;
    let all his creatures praise his holy
    name for ever.

In Praise of God the Saviour

146 Praise the Lord!
        Praise the Lord, my soul!
² I will praise him as long as I live;
    I will sing to my God all my life.

146.6: Acts 4.24, 14.15

³ Don't put your trust in human leaders;
    no human being can save you.
⁴ When they die, they return to the dust;
    on that day all their plans come to
    an end.

⁵ Happy is the man who has the God of
    Jacob to help him
    and who depends on the Lord his God,
⁶   the Creator of heaven, earth, and sea,
    and all that is in them.
He always keeps his promises;
⁷   he judges in favour of the oppressed
    and gives food to the hungry.

The Lord sets prisoners free
⁸   and gives sight to the blind.
He lifts those who have fallen;
    he loves his righteous people.
⁹ He protects the strangers who live in
    our land;
    he helps widows and orphans,
    but takes the wicked to their ruin.

¹⁰ The Lord is king for ever.
    Your God, O Zion, will reign for all
    time.

Praise the Lord!

In Praise of God the Almighty

147 Praise the Lord!

It is good to sing praise to our God;
    it is pleasant and right to praise him.
² The Lord is restoring Jerusalem;
    he is bringing back the exiles.
³ He heals the broken-hearted
    and bandages their wounds.

⁴ He has decided the number of the stars
    and calls each one by name.
⁵ Great and mighty is our Lord;
    his wisdom cannot be measured.
⁶ He raises the humble,
    but crushes the wicked to the ground.

⁷ Sing hymns of praise to the Lord;
    play music on the harp to our God.
⁸ He spreads clouds over the sky;
    he provides rain for the earth
    and makes grass grow on the hills.
⁹ He gives animals their food
    and feeds the young ravens when they
    call.

¹⁰ His pleasure is not in strong horses,
    nor his delight in brave soldiers;

11 but he takes pleasure in those who
    honour him,
  in those who trust in his constant love.

12 Praise the LORD, O Jerusalem!
  Praise your God, O Zion!
13 He keeps your gates strong;
  he blesses your people.
14 He keeps your borders safe
  and satisfies you with the finest
    wheat.

15 He gives a command to the earth,
  and what he says is quickly done.
16 He spreads snow like a blanket
  and scatters frost like dust.
17 He sends hail like gravel;
  no one can endure the cold he sends!
18 Then he gives a command, and the
    ice melts;
  he sends the wind, and the water
    flows.

19 He gives his message to his people,
  his instructions and laws to Israel.
20 He has not done this for other nations;
  they do not know his laws.

Praise the LORD!

A Call for the Universe to Praise God

148 Praise the LORD!

Praise the LORD from heaven,
  you that live in the heights above.
2 Praise him, all his angels,
  all his heavenly armies.

3 Praise him, sun and moon;
  praise him, shining stars.
4 Praise him, highest heavens,
  and the waters above the sky. *q*

5 Let them all praise the name of the
    LORD!
  He commanded, and they were created;
6   by his command they were fixed in
      their places for ever,
    and they cannot disobey. *r*

7 Praise the LORD from the earth,
  sea-monsters and all ocean depths;
8 lightning and hail, snow and clouds,
  strong winds that obey his command.

9 Praise him, hills and mountains,
  fruit-trees and forests;

10 all animals, tame and wild,
  reptiles and birds.

11 Praise him, kings and all peoples,
  princes and all other rulers;
12 girls and young men,
  old people and children too.

13 Let them all praise the name of the
    LORD!
  His name is greater than all others;
    his glory is above earth and heaven.
14 He made his nation strong,
  so that all his people praise him—
    the people of Israel, so dear to him.

Praise the LORD!

A Hymn of Praise

149 Praise the LORD!

Sing a new song to the LORD;
  praise him in the assembly of his
    faithful people!
2 Be glad, Israel, because of your Creator;
  rejoice, people of Zion, because of
    your king!
3 Praise his name with dancing;
  play drums and harps in praise of him.

4 The LORD takes pleasure in his people;
  he honours the humble with victory.
5 Let God's people rejoice in their triumph
  and sing joyfully all night long.
6 Let them shout aloud as they praise God,
  with their sharp swords in their hands
7   to defeat the nations
    and to punish the peoples;
8   to bind their kings in chains,
    their leaders in chains of iron;
9   to punish the nations as God has
      commanded.
  This is the victory of God's people.

Praise the LORD!

Praise the LORD!

150 Praise the LORD!

Praise God in his Temple!
  Praise his strength in heaven!
2 Praise him for the mighty things he has
    done.
  Praise his supreme greatness.

3 Praise him with trumpets.

---

q WATERS ABOVE THE SKY: *See Gen 1.6–7.*
r by his command...disobey; *or* he has fixed them in their places for all time, by a command that
lasts for ever.

Praise him with harps and lyres.
4 Praise him with drums and dancing.
Praise him with harps and flutes.
5 Praise him with cymbals.

Praise him with loud cymbals.
6 Praise the LORD, all living creatures!

Praise the LORD!

THE BOOK OF
PROVERBS

INTRODUCTION

The book of *Proverbs* is a collection of moral and religious teachings in the form of sayings and proverbs. Much of it has to do with practical, everyday concerns. It begins with the reminder that "To have knowledge, you must first have reverence for the LORD," and then goes on to deal with matters not only of religious morality, but also of common sense and good manners. Its many short sayings reveal the insights of ancient Israelite teachers about what a wise person will do in certain situations. Some of these concern family relations, others business dealings. Some deal with matters of etiquette in social relationships, and others with the need for self-control. Much is said about such qualities as humility, patience, respect for the poor, and loyalty to friends.

Outline of Contents
In praise of wisdom   1.1—9.18
The proverbs of Solomon   10.1—29.27
The words of Agur   30.1-33
Various sayings   31.1-31

The Value of Proverbs

1 The proverbs of Solomon, son of David and king of Israel.

2 Here are proverbs that will help you to recognize wisdom and good advice, and understand sayings with deep meaning. 3 They can teach you how to live intelligently and how to be honest, just, and fair. 4 They can make an inexperienced person clever and teach young men how to be resourceful. 5 These proverbs can even add to the knowledge of wise men and give guidance to the educated, 6 so that they can understand the hidden meanings of proverbs and the problems that wise men raise.

Advice to Young Men

7 To have knowledge, you must first have reverence for the LORD.[a] Stupid people have no respect for wisdom and refuse to learn.

8 Pay attention to what your father and mother tell you, my son. 9 Their teaching will improve your character as a handsome turban or a necklace improves your appearance.

10 When sinners tempt you, my son, don't give in. 11 Suppose they say, "Come on; let's find someone to kill! Let's attack

[a] To...LORD; *or* The most important part of knowledge is having reverence for the LORD.
1.1: 1 Kgs 4.32   **1.7:** Job 28.28; Ps 111.10; Prov 9.10

1.9   *1.11–15*   *1.28*   *1.33*   *2.2*

some innocent people for the fun of it! [12]They may be alive and well when we find them, but they'll be dead when we're through with them! [13]We'll find all kinds of riches and fill our houses with loot! [14]Come and join us, and we'll all share what we steal."

[15]Don't go with people like that, my son. Stay away from them. [16]They can't wait to do something bad. They're always ready to kill. [17]It does no good to spread a net when the bird you want to catch is watching, [18]but men like that are setting a trap for themselves, a trap in which they will die. [19]Robbery always claims the life of the robber—this is what happens to[b] anyone who lives by violence.

Wisdom Calls

[20]Listen! Wisdom is calling out in the streets and market-places, [21]calling loudly at the city gates and wherever people come together:

[22]"Foolish people! How long do you want to be foolish? How long will you enjoy pouring scorn on knowledge? Will you never learn? [23]Listen when I reprimand you; I will give you good advice and share my knowledge with you. [24]I have been calling you, inviting you to come, but you would not listen. You paid no attention to me. [25]You have ignored all my advice and have not been willing to let me correct you. [26]So when you get into trouble, I will laugh at you. I will mock you when terror strikes—[27]when it comes on you like a storm, bringing fierce winds of trouble, and you are in pain and misery. [28]Then you will call for wisdom, but I will not answer. You may look for me everywhere, but you will not find me. [29]You have never had any use for knowledge and have always refused to obey the LORD. [30]You have never wanted my advice or paid any attention when I corrected you. [31]So then, you will get what you deserve, and your own actions will make you sick. [32]Inexperi-

enced people die because they reject wisdom. Stupid people are destroyed by their own lack of concern. [33]But whoever listens to me will have security. He will be safe, with no reason to be afraid."

The Rewards of Wisdom

2 Learn what I teach you, my son, and never forget what I tell you to do. [2]Listen to what is wise and try to understand it. [3]Yes, beg for knowledge; plead for insight. [4]Look for it as hard as you would for silver or some hidden treasure. [5]If you do, you will know what it means to fear the LORD and you will succeed in learning about God. [6]It is the LORD who gives wisdom; from him come knowledge and understanding. [7]He provides help and protection for righteous, honest men. [8]He protects those who treat others fairly, and guards those who are devoted to him.

[9]If you listen to me, you will know what is right, just, and fair. You will know what you should do. [10]You will become wise, and your knowledge will give you pleasure. [11]Your insight and understanding will protect you [12]and prevent you from doing the wrong thing. They will keep you away from people who stir up trouble by what they say—[13]men who have abandoned a righteous life to live in the darkness of sin, [14]men who find pleasure in doing wrong and who enjoy senseless evil, [15]unreliable men who cannot be trusted.

[16]You will be able to resist any immoral woman who tries to seduce you with her smooth talk, [17]who is faithless to her own husband and forgets her sacred vows. [18]If you go to her house, you are travelling the road to death. To go there is to approach the world of the dead. [19]No one who visits her ever comes back. He never returns to the road to life. [20]So you must follow the example of good men and live a righteous life. [21]Righteous men—men of integrity—will live in this land

---

[b] *One ancient translation* what happens to; *Hebrew* the path of.
1.20–21: Prov 8.1–3

2.16   3.12   3.20   3.23   3.29

of ours. ²²But God will snatch wicked men from the land and pull sinners out of it like plants from the ground.

Advice to Young Men

3 Don't forget what I teach you, my son. Always remember what I tell you to do. ²My teaching will give you a long and prosperous life. ³Never let go of loyalty and faithfulness. Tie them round your neck; write them on your heart. ⁴If you do this, both God and man will be pleased with you.

5 Trust in the LORD with all your heart. Never rely on what you think you know. ⁶Remember the LORD in everything you do, and he will show you the right way. ⁷Never let yourself think that you are wiser than you are; simply obey the LORD and refuse to do wrong. ⁸If you do, it will be like good medicine, healing your wounds and easing your pains. ⁹Honour the LORD by making him an offering from the best of all that your land produces. ¹⁰If you do, your barns will be filled with grain, and you will have too much wine to be able to store it all.

11 When the LORD corrects you, my son, pay close attention and take it as a warning. ¹²The LORD corrects those he loves, as a father corrects a son of whom he is proud. ¹³Happy is the man who becomes wise—who gains understanding. ¹⁴There is more profit in it than there is in silver; it is worth more to you than gold. ¹⁵Wisdom is more valuable than jewels; nothing you could want can compare with it. ¹⁶Wisdom offers you long life, as well as wealth and honour. ¹⁷Wisdom can make your life pleasant and lead you safely through it. ¹⁸Those who become wise are happy; wisdom will give them life.

¹⁹The LORD created the earth by his wisdom;

by his knowledge he set the sky in place.

²⁰His wisdom caused the rivers to flow
and the clouds to give rain to the earth.

21 Hold on to your wisdom and insight, my son. Never let them get away from you. ²²They will provide you with life—a pleasant and happy life. ²³You can go safely on your way and never even stumble. ²⁴You will not be afraid when you go to bed, and you will sleep soundly through the night. ²⁵You will not have to worry about sudden disasters, such as come on the wicked like a storm. ²⁶The LORD will keep you safe. He will not let you fall into a trap.

27 Whenever you possibly can, do good to those who need it. ²⁸Never tell your neighbour to wait until tomorrow if you can help him now. ²⁹Don't plan anything that will hurt your neighbour; he lives beside you, trusting you. ³⁰Don't argue with someone for no reason when he has never done you any harm. ³¹Don't be jealous of violent people or decide to act as they do, ³²because the LORD hates people who do evil, but he takes righteous men into his confidence. ³³The LORD puts a curse on the homes of wicked men, but blesses the homes of the righteous. ³⁴He has no use for conceited people, but shows favour to those who are humble. ³⁵Wise men will gain an honourable reputation, but stupid men will only add to their own disgrace.

The Benefits of Wisdom

4 Listen to what your father teaches you, my sons. Pay attention, and you will have understanding. ²What I am teaching you is good, so remember it all. ³When I was only a little boy, my parents' only son, ⁴my father would teach me. He would say, "Remember what I say and never forget it. Do as I tell you, and you will live. ⁵Get wisdom and insight! Do not forget or ignore what I say. ⁶Do not abandon wisdom, and she will protect you; love her, and she will keep you safe.

3.4: Lk 2.52   **3.7:** Rom 12.16   **3.11:** Job 5.17
3.34: Jas 4.6; 1 Pet 5.5   **3.11–12:** Heb 12.5–6   **3.12:** Rev 3.19

4.14–15   4.25   5.3   5.8   5.13

⁷Getting wisdom is the most important thing you can do. Whatever else you get, get insight. ⁸Love wisdom, and she will make you great. Embrace her,ᶜ and she will bring you honour. ⁹She will be your crowning glory."

10 Listen to me, my son. Take seriously what I am telling you, and you will live a long life. ¹¹I have taught you wisdom and the right way to live. ¹²Nothing will stand in your way if you walk wisely, and you will not stumble when you run. ¹³Always remember what you have learnt. Your education is your life—guard it well. ¹⁴Do not go where evil men go. Do not follow the example of the wicked. ¹⁵Don't do it! Keep away from evil! Refuse it and go on your way. ¹⁶Wicked people cannot sleep unless they have done something wrong. They lie awake unless they have hurt someone. ¹⁷Wickedness and violence are like food and drink to them.

18 The road the righteous travel is like the sunrise, getting brighter and brighter until daylight has come. ¹⁹The road of the wicked, however, is dark as night. They fall, but cannot see what they have stumbled over.

20 Pay attention to what I say, my son. Listen to my words. ²¹Never let them get away from you. Remember them and keep them in your heart. ²²They will give life and health to anyone who understands them. ²³Be careful how you think; your life is shaped by your thoughts. ²⁴Never say anything that isn't true. Have nothing to do with lies and misleading words. ²⁵Look straight ahead with honest confidence; don't hang your head in shame. ²⁶Plan carefully what you do, and whatever you do will turn out right. ²⁷Avoid evil and walk straight ahead. Don't go one step off the right way.

Warning against Adultery

5 Pay attention, my son, and listen to my wisdom and insight. ²Then you

will know how to behave properly, and your words will show that you have knowledge. ³The lips of another man's wife may be as sweet as honey and her kisses as smooth as olive-oil, ⁴but when it is all over, she leaves you nothing but bitterness and pain. ⁵She will take you down to the world of the dead; the road she walks is the road to death. ⁶She does not stay on the road to life; but wanders off, and does not realize what is happening.

7 Now listen to me, my sons, and never forget what I am saying. ⁸Keep away from such a woman! Don't even go near her door! ⁹If you do, others will gain the respect that you once had, and you will die young at the hands of merciless men. ¹⁰Yes, strangers will take all your wealth, and what you have worked for will belong to someone else. ¹¹You will lie groaning on your deathbed, your flesh and muscles being eaten away, ¹²and you will say, "Why would I never learn? Why would I never let anyone correct me? ¹³I wouldn't listen to my teachers. I paid no attention to them. ¹⁴And suddenly I found myselfᵈ publicly disgraced."

15 Be faithful to your own wife and give your love to her alone. ¹⁶Children that you have by other women will do you no good. ¹⁷Your children should grow up to help you, not strangers. ¹⁸So be happy with your wife and find your joy with the girl you married—¹⁹pretty and graceful as a deer. Let her charms keep you happy; let her surround you with her love. ²⁰Why should you give your love to another woman, my son? Why should you prefer the charms of another man's wife? ²¹The LORD sees everything you do. Wherever you go, he is watching. ²²The sins of a wicked man are a trap. He gets caught in the net of his own sin. ²³He dies because he has no self-control. His utter stupidity will send him to his grave.

ᶜEmbrace her; *or* Prize her highly.   ᵈAnd suddenly...myself; *or* I was about to be.
4.26: Heb 12.13

5.15   6.5   6.6   6.13   6.23

More Warnings

6 Have you promised to be responsible for someone else's debts, my son? ²Have you been caught by your own words, trapped by your own promises? ³Well then, my son, you are in that man's power, but this is how to get out of it: hurry to him, and beg him to release you. ⁴Don't let yourself go to sleep or even stop to rest. ⁵Get out of the trap like a bird or a deer escaping from a hunter.

6 Lazy people should learn a lesson from the way ants live. ⁷They have no leader, chief, or ruler, ⁸but they store up their food during the summer, getting ready for winter. ⁹How long is the lazy man going to lie in bed? When is he ever going to get up? ¹⁰"I'll just take a short nap," he says; "I'll fold my hands and rest a while." ¹¹But while he sleeps, poverty will attack him like an armed robber.

12 Worthless, wicked people go around telling lies. ¹³They wink and make gestures to deceive you, ¹⁴all the while planning evil in their perverted minds, stirring up trouble everywhere. ¹⁵Because of this, disaster will strike them without warning, and they will be fatally wounded.

16–19 There are seven things that the Lord hates and cannot tolerate:
A proud look,
 a lying tongue,
  hands that kill innocent people,
   a mind that thinks up wicked plans,
    feet that hurry off to do evil,
     a witness who tells one lie after
      another,
   and a man who stirs up
     trouble among friends.

Warning against Adultery

20 Do what your father tells you, my son, and never forget what your mother taught you. ²¹Keep their words with you always, locked in your heart. ²²Their teaching will lead you when you travel,

protect you at night, and advise you during the day. ²³Their instructions are a shining light; their correction can teach you how to live. ²⁴It can keep you away from bad women, from the seductive words of other men's wives. ²⁵Don't be tempted by their beauty; don't be trapped by their flirting eyes. ²⁶A man can hire a prostitute for the price of a loaf of bread, but adultery will cost him all he has.

27 Can you carry fire against your chest without burning your clothes? ²⁸Can you walk on hot coals without burning your feet? ²⁹It is just as dangerous to sleep with another man's wife. Whoever does it will suffer. ³⁰People don't despise a thief if he steals food when he is hungry; ᵉ ³¹yet if he is caught, he must pay back seven times more—he must give up everything he has. ³²But a man who commits adultery hasn't any sense. He is just destroying himself. ³³He will be dishonoured and beaten up; he will be permanently disgraced. ³⁴A husband is never angrier than when he is jealous; his revenge knows no limits. ³⁵He will not accept any payment; no amount of gifts will satisfy his anger.

7 Remember what I say, my son, and never forget what I tell you to do. ²Do what I say, and you will live. Be as careful to follow my teaching as you are to protect your eyes. ³Keep my teaching with you all the time; write it on your heart. ⁴Treat wisdom as your sister, and insight as your closest friend. ⁵They will keep you away from other men's wives, from women with seductive words.

The Immoral Woman

6 Once I was looking out of the window of my house, ⁷and I saw many inexperienced young men, but noticed one foolish fellow in particular. ⁸He was walking along the street near the corner where a certain woman lived. He was passing near her house ⁹in the evening after it

---

ᵉPeople don't despise...hungry; *or* Don't people despise...hungry?
6.10–11: Prov 24.33–34

7.6   7.10   7.13   7.22   8.13

was dark. ¹⁰ And then she met him; she
was dressed like a prostitute and was
making plans. ¹¹ She was a bold and
shameless woman who always walked the
streets ¹² or stood waiting at a corner,
sometimes in the streets, sometimes in
the market-place. ¹³ She threw her arms
round the young man, kissed him, looked
him straight in the eye, and said, ¹⁴ "I
made my offerings today and have the
meat from the sacrifices. ¹⁵ So I came out
looking for you. I wanted to find you,
and here you are! ¹⁶ I've covered my bed
with sheets of coloured linen from Egypt.
¹⁷ I've perfumed it with myrrh, aloes, and
cinnamon. ¹⁸ Come on! Let's make love
all night long. We'll be happy in each
other's arms. ¹⁹ My husband isn't at home.
He's gone away on a long journey. ²⁰ He
took plenty of money with him and won't
be back for two weeks." ²¹ So she tempted
him with her charms, and he gave in to
her smooth talk. ²² Suddenly he was going
with her like an ox on the way to be
slaughtered, like a deer prancing into a
trap ᶠ ²³ where an arrow would pierce its
heart. He was like a bird going into a
net—he did not know that his life was in
danger.

24 Now then, my sons, listen to me. Pay
attention to what I say. ²⁵ Do not let such
a woman win your heart; don't go
wandering after her. ²⁶ She has been the
ruin of many men and caused the death
of too many to count. ²⁷ If you go to her
house, you are on the way to the world
of the dead. It is a short cut to death.

In Praise of Wisdom

8 Listen! Wisdom is calling out.
Reason is making herself heard.
² On the hilltops near the road
and at the cross-roads she stands.
³ At the entrance to the city,
beside the gates, she calls:
⁴ "I appeal to you, mankind;
I call to everyone on earth.
⁵ Are you immature? Learn to be mature.

Are you foolish? Learn to have sense.
⁶ Listen to my excellent words;
all I tell you is right.
⁷ What I say is the truth;
lies are hateful to me.
⁸ Everything I say is true;
nothing is false or misleading.
⁹ To the man with insight, it is all clear;
to the well-informed, it is all plain.
¹⁰ Choose my instruction instead of
silver;
choose knowledge rather than the
finest gold.

¹¹ "I am Wisdom, I am better than jewels;
nothing you want can compare with
me.
¹² I am Wisdom, and I have insight;
I have knowledge and sound
judgement.
¹³ To honour the LORD is to hate evil;
I hate pride and arrogance,
evil ways and false words.
¹⁴ I make plans and carry them out.
I have understanding, and I am strong.
¹⁵ I help kings to govern
and rulers to make good laws.
¹⁶ Every ruler on earth governs with my
help,
statesmen and noblemen alike.
¹⁷ I love those who love me;
whoever looks for me can find me.
¹⁸ I have riches and honour to give,
prosperity and success.
¹⁹ What you get from me is better than
the finest gold,
better than the purest silver.
²⁰ I walk the way of righteousness;
I follow the paths of justice,
²¹ giving wealth to those who love me,
filling their houses with treasures.

²² "The LORD created me first of all,
the first of his works, long ago.
²³ I was made in the very beginning,
at the first, before the world began.
²⁴ I was born before the oceans,
when there were no springs of water.

ᶠ *Probable text* like a deer prancing into a trap; *Hebrew unclear.*
8.1–3: Prov 1.20–21   **8.22:** Rev 3.14

8.34   9.9   9.13,14   10.5   10.26

25 I was born before the mountains,
  before the hills were set in place,
26 before God made the earth and its
    fields
  or even the first handful of soil.
27 I was there when he set the sky in
    place,
  when he stretched the horizon across
    the ocean,
28 when he placed the clouds in the sky,
  when he opened the springs of the
    ocean
29 and ordered the waters of the sea
  to rise no further than he said.
  I was there when he laid the earth's
    foundations.
30 I was beside him like an architect,g
  I was his daily source of joy,
  always happy in his presence—
31 happy with the world
  and pleased with the human race.

32 "Now, young men, listen to me.
  Do as I say, and you will be happy.
33 Listen to what you are taught.
  Be wise; do not neglect it.
34 The man who listens to me will be
    happy—
  the man who stays at my door every
    day,
  waiting at the entrance to my home.
35 The man who finds me finds life,
  and the LORD will be pleased with him.
36 The man who does not find me hurts
    himself;
  anyone who hates me loves death."

Wisdom and Stupidity

9 Wisdom has built her house and
made seven pillars for it. 2 She has
had an animal killed for a feast, mixed
spices in the wine, and laid the table. 3 She
has sent her servant-girls to call out from
the highest place in the town: 4 "Come
in, ignorant people!" And to the foolish
man she says, 5 "Come, eat my food and
drink the wine that I have mixed. 6 Leave

the company of ignorant people, and live.
Follow the way of knowledge."

7 If you correct a conceited man, you
will only be insulted. If you reprimand
an evil man, you will only get hurt. 8 Never
correct a conceited man; he will hate you
for it. But if you correct a wise man, he
will respect you. 9 Anything you say to
a wise man will make him wiser. Whatever you tell a righteous man will add
to his knowledge.

10 To be wise you must first have
reverence for the LORD. If you know the
Holy One, you have understanding. 11 Wisdom will add years to your life. 12 You are
the one who will profit if you have
wisdom, and if you reject it, you are the
one who will suffer.

13 Stupidity is like a loud, ignorant,
shameless woman.h 14 She sits at the door
of her house or on a seat in the highest
part of the town, 15 and calls out to people
passing by, who are minding their own
business: 16 "Come in, ignorant people!"
To the foolish man she says, 17 "Stolen
water is sweeter. Stolen bread tastes
better." 18 Her victims do not know that
the people die who go to her house, that
those who have already entered are now
deep in the world of the dead.

Solomon's Proverbs

10 These are Solomon's proverbs:
  A wise son makes his father proud
of him; a foolish one brings his mother
grief.

2 Wealth that you get by dishonesty will
do you no good, but honesty can save
your life.

3 The LORD will not let good people go
hungry, but he will keep the wicked from
getting what they want.

4 Being lazy will make you poor, but
hard work will make you rich.

5 A sensible man gathers the crops
when they are ready; it is a disgrace to
sleep through the time of harvest.

6 A good man will receive blessings. A
wicked man's words hide a violent nature.

g an architect; or a little child. h Verse 13 in Hebrew is unclear.
9.10: Job 28.28; Ps 111.10; Prov 1.7

11.1   11.12   11.22   11.25   11.28

7 Good people will be remembered as a blessing, but the wicked will soon be forgotten.

8 Sensible people accept good advice. People who talk foolishly will come to ruin.

9 Honest people are safe and secure, but the dishonest will be caught.

10 Someone who holds back the truth causes trouble, but one who openly criticizes works for peace.*i*

11 A good man's words are a fountain of life, but a wicked man's words hide a violent nature.

12 Hate stirs up trouble, but love overlooks all offences.

13 Intelligent people talk sense, but stupid people need to be punished.

14 The wise get all the knowledge they can, but when fools speak, trouble is not far off.

15 Wealth protects the rich; poverty destroys the poor.

16 The reward for doing good is life, but sin leads only to more sin.

17 People who listen when they are corrected will live, but those who will not admit that they are wrong are in danger.

18 A man who hides his hatred is a liar. Anyone who spreads gossip is a fool.

19 The more you talk, the more likely you are to sin. If you are wise, you will keep quiet.

20 A good man's words are like pure silver; a wicked man's ideas are worthless.

21 A good man's words will benefit many people, but you can kill yourself with stupidity.

22 It is the LORD's blessing that makes you wealthy. Hard work can make you no richer.*j*

23 It is foolish to enjoy doing wrong. Intelligent people take pleasure in wisdom.

24 The righteous get what they want, but the wicked will get what they fear most.

25 Storms come, and the wicked are blown away, but honest people are always safe.

26 Never get a lazy man to do something for you; he will be as irritating as vinegar on your teeth or smoke in your eyes.

27 Obey the LORD, and you will live longer. The wicked die before their time.

28 The hopes of good men lead to joy, but wicked people can look forward to nothing.

29 The LORD protects honest people, but destroys those who do wrong.

30 Righteous people will always have security, but the wicked will not survive in the land.

31 Righteous people speak wisdom, but the tongue that speaks evil will be stopped.

32 Righteous people know the kind thing to say, but the wicked are always saying things that hurt.

11 The LORD hates people who use dishonest scales. He is happy with honest weights.

2 People who are proud will soon be disgraced. It is wiser to be modest.

3 If you are good, you are guided by honesty. People who can't be trusted are destroyed by their own dishonesty.

4 Riches will do you no good on the day you face death, but honesty can save your life.

5 Honesty makes a good man's life easier, but a wicked man will cause his own downfall.

6 Righteousness rescues the honest man, but someone who can't be trusted is trapped by his own greed.

7 When a wicked man dies, his hope dies with him. Confidence placed in riches comes to nothing.

8 The righteous are protected from trouble; it comes to the wicked instead.

9 You can be ruined by the talk of godless people, but the wisdom of the righteous can save you.

10 A city is happy when honest people

---

i One ancient translation but one...peace; *Hebrew repeats verse 8b.*
j Hard work...richer; or And the LORD does not add sorrow to your wealth.
10.12: Jas 5.20; 1 Pet 4.8

12.10 *12.18* *12.27* *13.1* *13.9*

have good fortune, and there are joyful shouts when wicked men die.

11 A city becomes great when righteous men give it their blessing; but a city is brought to ruin by the words of the wicked.

12 It is foolish to speak scornfully of others. If you are sensible, you will keep quiet.

13 No one who gossips can be trusted with a secret, but you can put confidence in someone who is trustworthy.

14 A nation will fall if it has no guidance. Many advisers mean security.

15 If you promise to pay a stranger's debt, you will regret it. You are better off if you don't get involved.

16 A gracious lady is respected, but a woman without virtue is a disgrace.
A lazy man will never have money,[k] but an aggressive man will get rich.

17 You do yourself a favour when you are kind. If you are cruel, you only hurt yourself.

18 Wicked people do not really gain anything, but if you do what is right, you are certain to be rewarded.

19 Anyone who is determined to do right will live, but anyone who insists on doing wrong will die.

20 The LORD hates evil-minded people, but loves those who do right.

21 You can be sure that evil men will be punished, but righteous men will escape.

22 Beauty in a woman without good judgement is like a gold ring in a pig's snout.

23 What good people want always results in good; when the wicked get what they want, everyone is angry.[l]

24 Some people spend their money freely and still grow richer. Others are cautious, and yet grow poorer.

25 Be generous, and you will be pros-

perous. Help others, and you will be helped.

26 People curse a man who hoards grain, waiting for a higher price, but they praise the one who puts it up for sale.

27 If your goals are good, you will be respected, but if you are looking for trouble, that is what you will get.

28 Those who depend on their wealth will fall like the leaves of autumn, but the righteous will prosper like the leaves of summer.

29 The man who brings trouble on his family will have nothing at the end.
Foolish men will always be servants to the wise.

30 Righteousness[m] gives life, but violence[n] takes it away.

31 Those who are good are rewarded here on earth, so you can be sure that wicked and sinful people will be punished.

12 Anyone who loves knowledge wants to be told when he is wrong. It is stupid to hate being corrected.

2 The LORD is pleased with good people, but condemns those who plan evil.

3 Wickedness does not give security, but righteous people stand firm.

4 A good wife is her husband's pride and joy; but a wife who brings shame on her husband is like a cancer in his bones.

5 Honest people will treat you fairly; the wicked only want to deceive you.

6 The words of wicked men are murderous, but the words of the righteous rescue those who are threatened.

7 Wicked men meet their downfall and leave no descendants, but the families of righteous men live on.

8 If you are intelligent, you will be praised; if you are stupid, people will look down on you.

9 It is better to be an ordinary man

[k] *One ancient translation* but a woman...money; *Hebrew does not have these words.*
[l] everyone is angry; *or* God punishes them.
[m] *One ancient translation* Righteousness; *Hebrew* A righteous man.
[n] *Probable text* violence; *Hebrew* a wise man.
11.31: 1 Pet 4.18

13.24   14.1   14.4   14.20   14.31

working for a living than to play the part of a great man but go hungry.

10 A good man takes care of his animals, but wicked men are cruel to theirs.

11 A hard-working farmer has plenty to eat, but it is stupid to waste time on useless projects.

12 All that wicked people want is to find evil things to do, but the righteous stand firm. *o*

13 A wicked man is trapped by his own words, but an honest man gets himself out of trouble.

14 Your reward depends on what you say and what you do; you will get what you deserve.

15 Stupid people always think they are right. Wise people listen to advice.

16 When a fool is annoyed, he quickly lets it be known. Sensible people will ignore an insult.

17 When you tell the truth, justice is done, but lies lead to injustice.

18 Thoughtless words can wound as deeply as any sword, but wisely spoken words can heal.

19 A lie has a short life, but truth lives on for ever.

20 Those who plan evil are in for a rude surprise, but those who work for good will find happiness.

21 Nothing bad happens to righteous people, but the wicked have nothing but trouble.

22 The LORD hates liars, but is pleased with those who keep their word.

23 Sensible people keep quiet about what they know, but stupid people advertise their ignorance.

24 Hard work will give you power; being lazy will make you a slave.

25 Worry can rob you of happiness, but kind words will cheer you up.

26 The righteous man is a guide to his friend, but the path of the wicked leads them astray.

27 If you are lazy, you will never get what you are after, but if you work hard, you will get a fortune. *p*

28 Righteousness is the road to life; wickedness *q* is the road to death.

13 A wise son pays attention when his father corrects him, but an arrogant person never admits he is wrong.

2 Good people will be rewarded for what they say, but those who are deceitful are hungry for violence.

3 Be careful what you say and protect your life. A careless talker destroys himself.

4 No matter how much a lazy person may want something, he will never get it. A hard worker will get everything he wants.

5 Honest people hate lies, but the words of wicked people are shameful and disgraceful.

6 Righteousness protects the innocent; wickedness is the downfall of sinners.

7 Some people pretend to be rich, but have nothing. Others pretend to be poor, but own a fortune.

8 A rich man has to use his money to save his life, but no one threatens a poor man.

9 The righteous are like a light shining brightly; the wicked are like a lamp flickering out.

10 Arrogance causes nothing but trouble. It is wiser to ask for advice.

11 The more easily you get your wealth, the sooner you will lose it. The harder it is to earn, the more you will have.

12 When hope is crushed, the heart is crushed, but a wish come true fills you with joy.

13 If you refuse good advice, you are asking for trouble; follow it and you are safe.

14 The teachings of the wise are a fountain of life; they will help you escape when your life is in danger.

15 Intelligence wins respect, but those

---

o Verse 12 in Hebrew is unclear.   *p Verse 27 in Hebrew is unclear.*
q One ancient translation wickedness; *Hebrew* path.

15.1　　　　　15.13　　　　　15.17(1)　　　　　15.17(2)　　　　　15.19

who can't be trusted are on the road to ruin.[r]

16 Sensible people always think before they act, but stupid people advertise their ignorance.

17 Unreliable messengers cause trouble, but those who can be trusted bring peace.

18 Someone who will not learn will be poor and disgraced. Anyone who listens to correction is respected.

19 How good it is to get what you want! Stupid people refuse to turn away from evil.

20 Keep company with the wise and you will become wise. If you make friends with stupid people, you will be ruined.

21 Trouble follows sinners everywhere, but righteous people will be rewarded with good things.

22 A good man will have wealth to leave to his grandchildren, but the wealth of sinners will go to righteous men.

23 Unused fields could yield plenty of food for the poor, but unjust men keep them from being farmed.[s]

24 If you don't punish your son, you don't love him. If you do love him, you will correct him.

25 The righteous have enough to eat, but the wicked are always hungry.

14 Homes are made by the wisdom of women, but are destroyed by foolishness.

2 Be honest and you show that you have reverence for the LORD; be dishonest and you show that you do not.

3 A fool's pride makes him talk too much; a wise man's words protect him.

4 Without any oxen to pull the plough your barn will be empty, but with them it will be full of corn.[t]

5 A reliable witness always tells the truth, but an unreliable one tells nothing but lies.

6 Conceited people can never become wise, but intelligent people learn easily.

7 Stay away from foolish people; they have nothing to teach you.

8 Why is a clever person wise? Because he knows what to do. Why is a stupid person foolish? Because he only thinks he knows.

9 Foolish people don't care if they sin, but good people want to be forgiven.[u]

10 Your joy is your own; your bitterness is your own. No one can share them with you.

11 A good man's house will still be standing after an evil man's house has been destroyed.

12 What you think is the right road may lead to death.

13 Laughter may hide sadness. When happiness is gone, sorrow is always there.

14 Bad people will get what they deserve. Good people will be rewarded for their deeds.[v]

15 A fool will believe anything; sensible people watch their step.

16 Wise people are careful to stay out of trouble, but stupid people are careless and act too quickly.

17 People with a hot temper do foolish things; wiser people remain calm.[w]

18 Ignorant people get what their foolishness deserves, but the clever are rewarded with knowledge.

19 Evil people will have to bow down to the righteous and humbly beg their favour.

20 No one, not even his neighbour, likes a poor man, but the rich have many friends.

21 If you want to be happy, be kind to the poor; it is a sin to despise anyone.

22 You will earn the trust and respect of others if you work for good; if you work for evil, you are making a mistake.

23 Work and you will earn a living; if

---

[r] One ancient translation road to ruin; Hebrew permanent road.
[s] Verse 23 in Hebrew is unclear.
[t] your barn will be...corn; or you may grow a little corn, but with them you can grow much more.
[u] Verse 9 in Hebrew is unclear.　　[v] Probable text for their deeds; Hebrew from upon them.
[w] One ancient translation remain calm; Hebrew are hated.
14.12: Prov 16.25

you sit around talking you will be poor.

24 Wise people are rewarded with wealth, but fools are known by[x] their foolishness.

25 A witness saves lives when he tells the truth; when he tells lies, he betrays people.

26 Reverence for the LORD gives confidence and security to a man and his family.

27 Do you want to avoid death? Reverence for the LORD is a fountain of life.

28 A king's greatness depends on how many people he rules; without them he is nothing.

29 If you stay calm, you are wise, but if you have a hot temper, you only show how stupid you are.

30 Peace of mind makes the body healthy, but jealousy is like a cancer.

31 If you oppress poor people, you insult the God who made them; but kindness shown to the poor is an act of worship.

32 Wicked people bring about their own downfall by their evil deeds, but good people are protected by their integrity.[y]

33 Wisdom is in every thought of an intelligent man; fools know nothing[m] about wisdom.

34 Righteousness makes a nation great; sin is a disgrace to any nation.

35 Kings are pleased with competent officials, but they punish those who fail them.

15 A gentle answer quietens anger, but a harsh one stirs it up.

2 When wise people speak, they make knowledge attractive, but stupid people spout nonsense.

3 The LORD sees what happens everywhere; he is watching us, whether we do good or evil.

4 Kind words bring life, but cruel words crush your spirit.

5 It is foolish to ignore what your father taught you; it is wise to accept his correction.

6 Righteous men keep their wealth, but wicked men lose theirs when hard times come.

7 Knowledge is spread by people who are wise, not by fools.

8 The LORD is pleased when good men pray, but hates the sacrifices that wicked men bring him.

9 The LORD hates the ways of evil people, but loves those who do what is right.

10 If you do what is wrong, you will be severely punished; you will die if you do not let yourself be corrected.

11 Not even the world of the dead can keep the LORD from knowing what is there; how then can a man hide his thoughts from God?

12 Conceited people do not like to be corrected; they never ask for advice from those who are wiser.

13 When people are happy, they smile, but when they are sad, they look depressed.

14 Intelligent people want to learn, but stupid people are satisfied with ignorance.

15 The life of the poor is a constant struggle, but happy people always enjoy life.

16 Better to be poor and fear the LORD than to be rich and in trouble.

17 Better to eat vegetables with people you love than to eat the finest meat where there is hate.

18 Hot tempers cause arguments, but patience brings peace.

19 If you are lazy, you will meet difficulty everywhere, but if you are honest, you will have no trouble.

20 A wise son makes his father happy. Only a fool despises his mother.

21 Stupid people are happy with their foolishness, but the wise will do what is right.

22 Get all the advice you can, and you will succeed; without it you will fail.

23 What a joy it is to find just the right word for the right occasion!

---

[x] *Probable text* are known by; *Hebrew unclear.*
[y] *Some ancient translations* integrity; *Hebrew death.*
[m] *One ancient translation* nothing; *Hebrew does not have this word.*

16.30   16.31   17.6   17.14   17.17

24 Wise people walk the road that leads upwards to life, not the road that leads downwards to death.

25 The LORD will destroy the homes of arrogant men, but he will protect a widow's property.

26 The LORD hates evil thoughts, but he is pleased with friendly words.

27 If you try to make a profit dishonestly, you will get your family into trouble. Don't take bribes and you will live longer.

28 Good people think before they answer. Evil people have a quick reply, but it causes trouble.

29 When good people pray, the LORD listens, but he ignores those who are evil.

30 Smiling faces make you happy, and good news makes you feel better.

31 If you pay attention when you are corrected, you are wise.

32 If you refuse to learn, you are hurting yourself. If you accept correction, you will become wiser.

33 Reverence for the LORD is an education in itself. You must be humble before you can ever receive honours.

16 We may make our plans, but God has the last word. [z]

2 You may think everything you do is right, but the LORD judges your motives.

3 Ask the LORD to bless your plans, and you will be successful in carrying them out.

4 Everything the LORD has made has its destiny; and the destiny of the wicked is destruction.

5 The LORD hates everyone who is arrogant; he will never let them escape punishment.

6 Be loyal and faithful, and God will forgive your sin. Obey the LORD and nothing evil will happen to you.

7 When you please the LORD, you can make [a] your enemies into friends.

8 It is better to have a little, honestly earned, than to have a large income gained dishonestly.

9 You may make your plans, but God directs your actions.

10 The king speaks with divine authority; his decisions are always right.

11 The LORD wants weights and measures to be honest and every sale to be fair.

12 Kings cannot tolerate evil, [b] because justice is what makes a government strong.

13 A king wants to hear the truth and will favour those who speak it.

14 A wise man will try to keep the king happy; if the king becomes angry, someone may die.

15 The king's favour is like the clouds that bring rain in the springtime—life is there.

16 It is better—much better—to have wisdom and knowledge than gold and silver.

17 Those who are good travel a road that avoids evil; so watch where you are going—it may save your life.

18 Pride leads to destruction, and arrogance to downfall.

19 It is better to be humble and stay poor than to be one of the arrogant and get a share of their loot.

20 Pay attention to what you are taught, and you will be successful; trust in the LORD and you will be happy.

21 A wise, mature person is known for his understanding. The more pleasant his words, the more persuasive he is.

22 Wisdom is a fountain of life to the wise, but trying to educate stupid people is a waste of time.

23 Intelligent people think before they speak; what they say is then more persuasive.

24 Kind words are like honey—sweet to the taste and good for your health.

25 What you think is the right road may lead to death.

---

[z] God...word; or God inspires our words.   [a] you can make; or he will make.
[b] Kings...evil; or It is intolerable for kings to do evil.
16.25: Prov 14.12

26 A labourer's appetite makes him work harder, because he wants to satisfy his hunger.

27 Evil people look for ways to harm others; even their words burn with evil.

28 Gossip is spread by wicked people; they stir up trouble and break up friendships.

29 Violent people deceive their friends and lead them to disaster.

30 Watch out for people who grin and wink at you; they have thought of something evil.

31 Long life is the reward of the righteous; grey hair is a glorious crown.

32 It is better to be patient than powerful. It is better to win control over yourself than over whole cities.

33 Men cast lots to learn God's will, but God himself determines the answer.

17 Better to eat a dry crust of bread with peace of mind than to have a banquet in a house full of trouble.

2 A shrewd servant will gain authority over a master's worthless son and receive a part of the inheritance.

3 Gold and silver are tested by fire, and a person's heart is tested by the LORD.

4 Evil people listen to evil ideas, and liars listen to lies.

5 If you laugh at poor people, you insult the God who made them. You will be punished if you take pleasure in someone's misfortune.

6 Old men are proud of their grandchildren, just as boys are proud of their fathers.

7 Respected people do not tell lies, and fools have nothing worthwhile to say.

8 Some people think a bribe works like magic; they believe it can do anything.

9 If you want people to like you, forgive them when they wrong you. Remembering wrongs can break up a friendship.

10 An intelligent person learns more from one rebuke than a fool learns from being beaten a hundred times.

11 Death will come like a cruel messenger to wicked people who are always stirring up trouble.

12 It is better to meet a mother bear robbed of her cubs than to meet some fool busy with a stupid project.

13 If you repay good with evil, you will never get evil out of your house.

14 The start of an argument is like the first break in a dam; stop it before it goes any further.

15 Condemning the innocent or letting the wicked go—both are hateful to the LORD.

16 It does a fool no good to spend money on an education, because he has no common sense.

17 Friends always show their love. What are brothers for if not to share trouble?

18 Only a man with no sense would promise to be responsible for someone else's debts.

19 To like sin is to like making trouble. If you brag all the time,[c] you are asking for trouble.

20 Anyone who thinks and speaks evil can expect to find nothing good—only disaster.

21 There is nothing but sadness and sorrow for a father whose son does foolish things.

22 Being cheerful keeps you healthy. It is slow death to be gloomy all the time.

23 Corrupt judges accept secret bribes, and then justice is not done.

24 An intelligent person aims at wise action, but a fool starts off in many directions.

25 A foolish son brings grief to his father and bitter regrets to his mother.

26 It is not right to make an innocent person pay a fine; justice is perverted when good people are punished.

27 Someone who is sure of himself does not talk all the time. People who stay calm have real insight. 28 After all, even a fool may be thought wise and intelligent if he stays quiet and keeps his mouth shut.

[c]brag...time; *or* make a show of your wealth.

18.14   18.22   18.23   19.3   19.6

18 People who do not get along with others are interested only in themselves; they will disagree with what everyone else knows is right.

2 A fool does not care whether he understands a thing or not; all he wants to do is to show how clever he is.

3 Sin and shame go together. Lose your honour, and you will get scorn in its place.

4 A person's words can be a source of wisdom, deep as the ocean, fresh as a flowing stream.

5 It is not right to favour the guilty and prevent the innocent from receiving justice.

6 When some fool starts an argument, he is asking for a beating.

7 When a fool speaks, he is ruining himself; he gets caught in the trap of his own words.

8 Gossip is so tasty—how we love to swallow it!

9 A lazy person is as bad as someone who is destructive.

10 The LORD is like a strong tower, where the righteous can go and be safe.

11 Rich people, however, imagine that their wealth protects them like high, strong walls round a city.

12 No one is respected unless he is humble; arrogant people are on the way to ruin.

13 Listen before you answer. If you don't you are being stupid and insulting.

14 Your will to live can sustain you when you are sick, but if you lose it, your last hope is gone.

15 Intelligent people are always eager and ready to learn.

16 Do you want to meet an important person? Take him a gift and it will be easy.

17 The first man to speak in court always seems right until his opponent begins to question him.

18 If two powerful men are opposing each other in court, casting lots can settle the issue.

19 Help your brother and he will protect you like a strong city wall,[d] but if you quarrel with him, he will close his doors to you.

20 You will have to live with the consequences of everything you say. 21 What you say can preserve life or destroy it; so you must accept the consequences of your words.

22 Find a wife and you find a good thing; it shows that the LORD is good to you.

23 When the poor man speaks, he has to beg politely, but when the rich man answers, he is rude.

24 Some friendships do[e] not last, but some friends are more loyal than brothers.

19 It is better to be poor but honest than to be a lying fool.

2 Enthusiasm without knowledge is not good; impatience will get you into trouble.

3 Some people ruin themselves by their own stupid actions and then blame the LORD.

4 Rich people are always finding new friends, but the poor cannot keep the few they have.

5 If you tell lies in court, you will be punished—there will be no escape.

6 Everyone tries to gain the favour of important people; everyone claims the friendship of those who give out favours.

7 Even the brothers of a poor man have no use for him; no wonder he has no friends. No matter how hard he tries, he cannot win any.[f]

8 Do yourself a favour and learn all you can; then remember what you learn and you will prosper.

9 No one who tells lies in court can escape punishment; he is doomed.

10 Fools should not live in luxury, and slaves should not rule over noblemen.

11 If you are sensible, you will control

d *Some ancient translations* Help...wall; *Hebrew unclear.*
e *Some ancient translations* Some friendships do; *Hebrew* A man of friends does.
f *Probable text* No matter...any; *Hebrew unclear.*

19.7   19.12   19.13   19.20   19.24

your temper. When someone wrongs you, it is a great virtue to ignore it.

12 The king's anger is like the roar of a lion, but his favour is like welcome rain.

13 A stupid son can bring his father to ruin. A nagging wife is like water going drip-drip-drip.

14 A man can inherit a house and money from his parents, but only the LORD can give him a sensible wife.

15 Be lazy if you want to; sleep on, but you will go hungry.

16 Keep God's laws and you will live longer; if you ignore them, you will die.

17 When you give to the poor, it is like lending to the LORD, and the LORD will pay you back.

18 Discipline your children while they are young enough to learn. If you don't, you are helping them to destroy themselves.[g]

19 If someone has a hot temper, let him take the consequences. If you get him out of trouble once, you will have to do it again.[h]

20 If you listen to advice and are willing to learn, one day you will be wise.

21 People may plan all kinds of things, but the LORD's will is going to be done.

22 It is a disgrace to be greedy;[i] poor people are better off than liars.

23 Obey the LORD and you will live a long life, content and safe from harm.

24 Some people are too lazy to put food in their own mouths.

25 Arrogance should be punished, so that people who don't know any better can learn a lesson. If you are wise, you will learn when you are corrected.

26 Only a shameful, disgraceful person would ill-treat his father or turn his mother away from his home.

27 Son, when you stop learning, you will soon neglect what you already know.

28 There is no justice where a witness is determined to hurt someone. Wicked people love the taste of evil.

29 A conceited fool is sure to get a beating.

20 Drinking too much makes you loud and foolish. It's stupid to get drunk.

2 Fear an angry king as you would a growling lion; making him angry is suicide.

3 Any fool can start arguments; the honourable thing is to stay out of them.

4 A farmer who is too lazy to plough his fields at the right time will have nothing to harvest.

5 A person's thoughts are like water in a deep well, but someone with insight can draw them out.

6 Everyone talks about how loyal and faithful he is, but just try to find someone who really is!

7 Children are fortunate if they have a father who is honest and does what is right.

8 The king sits in judgement and knows evil when he sees it.

9 Can anyone really say that his conscience is clear, that he has got rid of his sin?

10 The LORD hates people who use dishonest weights and measures.

11 Even a child shows what he is by what he does; you can tell if he is honest and good.

12 The LORD has given us eyes to see with and ears to listen with.

13 If you spend your time sleeping, you will be poor. Keep busy and you will have plenty to eat.

14 The customer always complains that the price is too high, but then he goes off and brags about the bargain he got.

15 If you know what you are talking about, you have something more valuable than gold or jewels.

16 Anyone stupid enough to promise to be responsible for a stranger's debts ought to have his own property held to guarantee payment.

17 What you get by dishonesty you may

[g] If you...themselves; or But don't beat them so hard that you kill them.
[h] get him out...again; or try to get him out of trouble, you only make things worse.
[i] It...greedy; or Loyalty is what is desired in a person.

20.1   20.12   20.20   20.29   21.8

enjoy like the finest food, but sooner or later it will be like a mouthful of sand.

18 Get good advice and you will succeed; don't go charging into battle without a plan.

19 A gossip can never keep a secret. Stay away from people who talk too much.

20 If you curse your parents, your life will end like a lamp that goes out in the dark.

21 The more easily you get your wealth, the less good it will do you.

22 Don't take it on yourself to repay a wrong. Trust the LORD and he will make it right.

23 The LORD hates people who use dishonest scales and weights.

24 The LORD has determined our path; how then can anyone understand the direction his own life is taking?

25 Think carefully before you promise an offering to God. You might regret it later.

26 A wise king will find out who is doing wrong, and will punish him without pity.

27 The LORD gave us mind and conscience; we cannot hide from ourselves.

28 A king will remain in power as long as his rule is honest, just, and fair.

29 We admire the strength of youth and respect the grey hair of age.

30 Sometimes it takes a painful experience to make us change our ways.

21 The LORD controls the mind of a king as easily as he directs the course of a stream.

2 You may think that everything you do is right, but remember that the LORD judges your motives.

3 Do what is right and fair; that pleases the LORD more than bringing him sacrifices.

4 Wicked people are controlled by their conceit and arrogance, and this is sinful.

5 Plan carefully and you will have plenty; if you act too quickly, you will never have enough.

6 The riches you get by dishonesty soon disappear, but not before they lead you into the jaws of death.

7 The wicked are doomed by their own violence; they refuse to do what is right.

8 Guilty people walk a crooked path; the innocent do what is right.

9 Better to live on the roof than share the house with a nagging wife.

10 Wicked people are always hungry for evil; they have no mercy on anyone.

11 When someone who is conceited gets his punishment, even an unthinking person learns a lesson. One who is wise will learn from what he is taught.

12 God, the righteous one, knows what goes on in the homes of the wicked, and he will bring the wicked down to ruin.

13 If you refuse to listen to the cry of the poor, your own cry for help will not be heard.

14 If someone is angry with you, a gift given secretly will calm him down.

15 When justice is done, good people are happy, but evil people are brought to despair.

16 Death is waiting for anyone who wanders away from good sense.

17 Indulging in luxuries, wine, and rich food will never make you wealthy.

18 The wicked bring on themselves the suffering they try to cause good people.

19 Better to live out in the desert than with a nagging, complaining wife.

20 Wise people live in wealth and luxury, but stupid people spend their money as fast as they get it.

21 Be kind and honest and you will live a long life; others will respect you and treat you fairly.

22 A shrewd general can take a city defended by strong men, and destroy the walls they relied on.

23 If you want to stay out of trouble, be careful what you say.

24 Show me a conceited person and I will show you someone who is arrogant, proud, and inconsiderate.

25 A lazy man who refuses to work is only killing himself; 26 all he does is think about what he would like to have. A righteous man, however, can give, and give generously.

21.9   21.13   21.14   21.23   21.25

27 The LORD hates it when wicked men offer him sacrifices, especially if they do it from evil motives.

28 The testimony of a liar is not believed, but the word of someone who thinks matters through is accepted.

29 Righteous people are sure of themselves; the wicked have to pretend as best they can.

30 Human wisdom, brilliance, insight— they are of no help if the LORD is against you.

31 You can get horses ready for battle, but it is the LORD who gives victory.

22 If you have to choose between a good reputation and great wealth, choose a good reputation.

2 The rich and the poor have this in common: the LORD made them both.

3 Sensible people will see trouble coming and avoid it, but an unthinking person will walk right into it and regret it later.

4 Obey the LORD, be humble, and you will get riches, honour, and a long life.

5 If you love your life, stay away from the traps that catch the wicked along the way.

6 Teach a child how he should live, and he will remember it all his life.

7 Poor people are the rich man's slaves. Borrow money and you are the lender's slave.

8 If you sow the seeds of injustice, disaster will spring up, and your oppression of others will end.

9 Be generous and share your food with the poor. You will be blessed for it.

10 Get rid of a conceited person, and then there will be no more arguments, quarrelling, or calling of names.

11 If you love purity of heart and graciousness of speech, the king will be your friend.

12 The LORD sees to it that truth is kept safe by disproving the words of liars.

13 The lazy man stays at home; he says a lion might get him if he goes outside.

14 Adultery is a trap—it catches those with whom the LORD is angry.

15 Children just naturally do silly, careless things, but a good spanking will teach them how to behave.

16 If you make gifts to rich people or oppress the poor to get rich, you will become poor yourself.

The Thirty Wise Sayings

17 Listen, and I will teach you what wise men have said. Study their teachings, 18 and you will be glad if you remember them and can quote them. 19 I want you to put your trust in the LORD; that is why I am going to tell them to you now. 20 I have written down thirty sayings for you. They contain knowledge and good advice, 21 and will teach you what the truth really is. Then when you are sent to find it out, you will bring back the right answer.

– 1 –

22 Don't take advantage of the poor just because you can; don't take advantage of those who stand helpless in court. 23 The LORD will argue their case for them and threaten the life of anyone who threatens theirs.

– 2 –

24 Don't make friends with people who have hot, violent tempers. 25 You might learn their habits and not be able to change.

– 3 –

26 Don't promise to be responsible for someone else's debts. 27 If you should be unable to pay, they will take away even your bed.

– 4 –

28 Never move an old boundary-mark that your ancestors established.

21.31　　　　22.5　　　　22.9　　　　22.17　　　　23.1

– 5 –

29 Show me a man who does a good job, and I will show you a man who is better than most and worthy of the company of kings.

– 6 –

23 When you sit down to eat with an important man, keep in mind who he is.*j* ²If you have a big appetite, restrain yourself. ³Don't be greedy for the fine food he serves; he may be trying to trick you.

– 7 –

4 Be wise enough not to wear yourself out trying to get rich. ⁵Your money can be gone in a flash, as if it had grown wings and flown away like an eagle.

– 8 –

6 Don't eat at the table of a stingy man or be greedy for the fine food he serves. ⁷"Come on and have some more," he says, but he doesn't mean it. What he thinks is what he really is. ⁸You will vomit up what you have eaten, and all your flattery will be wasted.

– 9 –

9 Don't try to talk sense to a fool; he can't appreciate it.

– 10 –

10 Never move an old boundary-mark or take over land owned by orphans. ¹¹The LORD is their powerful defender, and he will argue their case against you.

– 11 –

12 Pay attention to your teacher and learn all you can.

j keep...is; *or* notice carefully what is before you.

– 12 –

13 Don't hesitate to discipline a child. A good spanking won't kill him. ¹⁴As a matter of fact, it may save his life.

– 13 –

15 Son, if you become wise, I will be very happy. ¹⁶I will be proud when I hear you speaking words of wisdom.

– 14 –

17 Don't be envious of sinful people; let reverence for the LORD be the concern of your life. ¹⁸If it is, you have a bright future.

– 15 –

19 Listen, my son, be wise and give serious thought to the way you live. ²⁰Don't associate with people who drink too much wine or stuff themselves with food. ²¹Drunkards and gluttons will be reduced to poverty. If all you do is eat and sleep, you will soon be wearing rags.

– 16 –

22 Listen to your father; without him you would not exist. When your mother is old, show her your appreciation.
23 Truth, wisdom, learning, and good sense—these are worth paying for, but too valuable for you to sell.
24 A righteous man's father has good reason to be happy. You can take pride in a wise son.
25 Make your father and mother proud of you; give your mother that happiness.

– 17 –

26 Pay close attention, son, and let my life be your example. ²⁷Prostitutes and immoral women are a deadly trap. ²⁸They

23.6   23.21   23.22   23.31   23.32

wait for you like robbers and cause many men to be unfaithful.

careful plans before you fight a battle, and the more good advice you get, the more likely you are to win.

-18-

29-30 Show me someone who drinks too much, who has to try out some new drink, and I will show you someone miserable and sorry for himself, always causing trouble and always complaining. His eyes are bloodshot, and he has bruises that could have been avoided. 31 Don't let wine tempt you, even though it is rich red, though it sparkles in the cup, and it goes down smoothly. 32 The next morning you will feel as if you had been bitten by a poisonous snake. 33 Weird sights will appear before your eyes, and you will not be able to think or speak clearly. 34 You will feel as if you were out on the ocean, sea-sick, swinging high up in the rigging of a tossing ship. 35 "I must have been hit," you will say; "I must have been beaten up, but I don't remember it. Why can't I wake up? I need another drink."

-19-

24 Don't be envious of evil people, and don't try to make friends with them. 2 Causing trouble is all they ever think about; every time they open their mouth someone is going to be hurt.

-20-

3 Homes are built on the foundation of wisdom and understanding.k 4 Where there is knowledge, the rooms are furnished with valuable, beautiful things.

-21-

5 Being wise is better than being strong;l yes, knowledge is more important than strength. 6 After all, you must make

-22-

7 Wise sayings are too deep for a stupid person to understand. He has nothing to say when important matters are being discussed.

-23-

8 If you are always planning evil, you will earn a reputation as a troublemaker. 9 Any scheme a fool thinks up is sinful. People hate a person who has nothing but scorn for others.

-24-

10 If you are weak in a crisis, you are weak indeed.

-25-

11 Don't hesitate to rescue someone who is about to be executed unjustly. 12 You may say that it is none of your business, but God knows and judges your motives. He keeps watch on you; he knows. And he will reward you according to what you do.

-26-

13 Son, eat honey; it is good. And just as honey from the comb is sweet on your tongue, 14 you may be sure that wisdom is good for the soul. Get wisdom and you have a bright future.

-27-

15 Don't be like the wicked who scheme to rob an honest man or to take away

k Homes...understanding; or It takes care to lay the foundations of a house, and craftsmanship to build it.
l Some ancient translations Being wise is better than being strong; Hebrew A man is wise in strength.

23.34   24.11   25.9   25.13   25.14

his home. ¹⁶ No matter how often an honest man falls, he always gets up again; but disaster destroys the wicked.

-28-

17 Don't be glad when your enemy meets disaster, and don't rejoice when he stumbles. ¹⁸ The LORD will know if you are gloating, and he will not like it; and then he might not punish him.

-29-

19 Don't let evil people worry you; don't be envious of them. ²⁰ A wicked person has no future—nothing to look forward to.

-30-

21 Have reverence for the LORD, my son, and honour the king. Have nothing to do with people who rebel against them; ²² such men could be ruined in a moment. Do you realize the disaster that God or the king can cause?

More Wise Sayings

23 Wise men have also said these things:

It is wrong for a judge to be prejudiced. ²⁴ If he pronounces a guilty person innocent, he will be cursed and hated by everyone. ²⁵ Judges who punish the guilty, however, will be prosperous and enjoy a good reputation.

26 An honest answer is a sign of true friendship.

27 Don't build your house and establish a home until your fields are ready, and you are sure that you can earn a living.

28 Don't give evidence against someone else without good reason, or say misleading things about him. ²⁹ Don't say, "I'll do to him just what he did to me! I'll get even with him!"

30 I walked through the fields and vineyards of a lazy, stupid man. ³¹ They were full of thorn bushes and overgrown with weeds. The stone wall round them had fallen down. ³² I looked at this, thought about it, and learned a lesson from it: ³³ Have a nap and sleep if you want to. Fold your hands and rest awhile, ³⁴ but while you are asleep, poverty will attack you like an armed robber.

More of Solomon's Proverbs

25 Here are more of Solomon's proverbs, copied by men at the court of King Hezekiah of Judah.

2 We honour God for what he conceals; we honour kings for what they explain.

3 You never know what a king is thinking; his thoughts are beyond us, like the heights of the sky or the depths of the ocean.

4 Take the impurities out of silver and the artist can produce a thing of beauty. ⁵ Keep evil advisers away from the king and his government will be known for its justice.

6 When you stand before the king, don't try to impress him and pretend to be important. ⁷ It is better to be asked to take a higher position than to be told to give your place to someone more important.

8 Don't be too quick to go to court about something you have seen. If another witness later proves you wrong, what will you do then?

9 If you and your neighbour have a difference of opinion, settle it between yourselves and do not reveal any secrets. ¹⁰ Otherwise everyone will learn that you can't keep a secret, and you will never live down the shame.

11 An idea well-expressed is like a design of gold, set in silver.

12 A warning given by an experienced person to someone willing to listen is more valuable than gold rings or jewellery made of the finest gold.

13 A reliable messenger is refreshing to the one who sends him, like cold water in the heat of harvest time.

24.33–34: Prov 6.10–11   **25.6–7:** Lk 14.8–10

| 25.18 | 25.25 | 26.3 | 26.11 | 26.17 |

14 People who promise things that they never give are like clouds and wind that bring no rain.

15 Patient persuasion can break down the strongest resistance and can even convince rulers.

16 Never eat more honey than you need; too much may make you vomit. 17 Don't visit your neighbour too often; he may get tired of you and come to hate you.

18 A false accusation is as deadly as a sword, a club, or a sharp arrow.

19 Depending on an unreliable person in a crisis is like trying to chew with a loose tooth or walk with a crippled foot.

20 Singing to a person who is depressed is like taking off his clothes on a cold day or like rubbing salt in a wound.

21 If your enemy is hungry, feed him; if he is thirsty, give him a drink. 22 You will make him burn with shame, and the LORD will reward you.

23 Gossip brings anger just as surely as the north wind brings rain.

24 Better to live on the roof than share the house with a nagging wife.

25 Finally hearing good news from a distant land is like a drink of cold water when you are dry and thirsty.

26 A good person who gives in to someone who is evil reminds you of a polluted spring or a poisoned well.

27 Too much honey is bad for you, and so is trying to win too much praise. _m_

28 If you cannot control your anger, you are as helpless as a city without walls, open to attack.

26 Praise for a fool is out of place, like snow in summer or rain at harvest time.

2 Curses cannot hurt you unless you deserve them. They are like birds that fly by and never settle.

3 You have to whip a horse, you have to bridle a donkey, and you have to beat a fool.

4 If you answer a silly question, you are just as silly as the person who asked it.

5 Give a silly answer to a silly question, and the one who asked it will realize that he's not as clever as he thinks.

6 If you let a fool deliver a message, you might as well cut off your own feet; you are asking for trouble.

7 A fool can use a proverb about as well as a crippled man can use his legs.

8 Praising someone who is stupid makes as much sense as tying a stone in a catapult.

9 A fool quoting a wise saying reminds you of a drunk man trying to pick a thorn out of his hand.

10 An employer who hires any fool that comes along is only hurting everybody concerned. _n_

11 A fool doing some stupid thing a second time is like a dog going back to its vomit.

12 The most stupid fool is better off than someone who thinks he is wise when he is not.

13 Why doesn't the lazy man ever get out of the house? What is he afraid of? Lions?

14 The lazy man turns over in bed. He gets no farther than a door swinging on its hinges.

15 Some people are too lazy to put food in their own mouths.

16 A lazy man will think he is more intelligent than seven men who can give good reasons for their opinions.

17 Getting involved in an argument that is none of your business is like going down the street and grabbing a dog by the ears.

18-19 A man who misleads someone and then claims that he was only joking is like a madman playing with a deadly weapon.

20 Without wood, a fire goes out; without gossip, quarrelling stops.

21 Charcoal keeps the embers glowing,

---

m Probable text and so...praise; _Hebrew unclear._
25.21–22: Rom 12.20

n Verse 10 in Hebrew is unclear.

26.20   26.27   27.9   27.18   27.23

wood keeps the fire burning, and trouble-makers keep arguments alive.

22 Gossip is so tasty! How we love to swallow it!

23 Insincere*o* talk that hides what you are really thinking is like a fine glaze*p* on a cheap clay pot.

24 A hypocrite hides his hate behind flattering words. 25 They may sound fine, but don't believe him, because his heart is filled to the brim with hate. 26 He may disguise his hatred, but everyone will see the evil things he does.

27 People who set traps for others get caught themselves. People who start landslides get crushed.

28 You have to hate someone to want to hurt him with lies. Insincere talk brings nothing but ruin.

27 Never boast about tomorrow. You don't know what will happen between now and then.

2 Let other people praise you—even strangers; never do it yourself.

3 The weight of stone and sand is nothing compared to the trouble that stupidity can cause.

4 Anger is cruel and destructive, but it is nothing compared to jealousy.

5 Better to correct someone openly than to let him think you don't care for him at all.

6 A friend means well, even when he hurts you. But when an enemy puts his arm round your shoulder—watch out!

7 When you are full, you will refuse honey, but when you are hungry, even bitter food tastes sweet.

8 A man away from home is like a bird away from its nest.

9 Perfume and fragrant oils make you feel happier, but trouble shatters your peace of mind.*q*

10 Do not forget your friends or your father's friends. If you are in trouble, don't ask your brother for help; a neighbour near by can help you more than a brother who is far away.

11 Be wise, my son, and I will be happy; I will have an answer for anyone who criticizes me.

12 Sensible people will see trouble coming and avoid it, but an unthinking person will walk right into it and regret it later.

13 Anyone stupid enough to promise to be responsible for a stranger's debts*r* deserves to have his own property held to guarantee payment.

14 You might as well curse your friend as wake him up early in the morning with a loud greeting.

15 A nagging wife is like water going drip-drip-drip on a rainy day. 16 How can you keep her quiet? Have you ever tried to stop the wind or ever tried to hold a handful of oil?*s*

17 People learn from one another, just as iron sharpens iron.

18 Take care of a fig-tree and you will have figs to eat. A servant who takes care of his master will be honoured.

19 It is your own face that you see reflected in the water and it is your own self that you see in your heart.

20 Human desires are like the world of the dead—there is always room for more.

21 Fire tests gold and silver; a person's reputation can also be tested.

22 Even if you beat a fool until he's half dead, you still can't beat his foolishness out of him.

23 Look after your sheep and cattle as carefully as you can, 24 because wealth is not permanent. Not even nations last for ever. 25 You cut the hay and then cut the grass on the hillsides while the next crop of hay is growing. 26 You can make clothes from the wool of your sheep and buy land with the money you get from selling some

---

o One ancient translation Insincere; *Hebrew* Burning.
p Probable text fine glaze; *Hebrew* unrefined silver.
q One ancient translation but trouble...mind; *Hebrew unclear.*
r One ancient translation stranger's debts; *Hebrew* stranger's debts or those of an immoral woman.   *s Probable text* or ever...oil; *Hebrew unclear.*
27.1: Jas 4.13–16

of your goats. ²⁷ The rest of the goats will provide milk for you and your family, and for your servant-girls as well.

28 The wicked run when no one is chasing them, but an honest person is as brave as a lion.

2 When a nation sins, it will have one ruler after another. But a nation will be strong and endure when it has intelligent, sensible leaders.

3 A man in authority who oppresses poor people is like a driving rain that destroys the crops.

4 If you have no regard for the law, you are on the side of the wicked; but if you obey it, you are against them.

5 Evil people do not know what justice is, but those who worship the LORD understand it well.

6 Better to be poor and honest than rich and dishonest.

7 A young man who obeys the law is intelligent. One who makes friends with good-for-nothings is a disgrace to his father.

8 If you get rich by charging interest and taking advantage of people, your wealth will go to someone who is kind to the poor.

9 If you do not obey the law, God will find your prayers too hateful to hear.

10 If you trick an honest person into doing evil, you will fall into your own trap.

The innocent will be well rewarded.

11 Rich people always think they are wise, but a poor person who has insight into character knows better.

12 When good men come to power, everybody celebrates, but when bad men rule, people stay in hiding.

13 You will never succeed in life if you try to hide your sins. Confess them and give them up; then God will show mercy to you.

14 Always obey the LORD and you will be happy. If you are stubborn, you will be ruined.

15 Poor people are helpless against a wicked ruler; he is as dangerous as a growling lion or a prowling bear.

16 A ruler without good sense will be a cruel tyrant. One who hates dishonesty will rule a long time.

17 A man guilty of murder is digging his own grave as fast as he can. Don't try to stop him.

18 Be honest and you will be safe. If you are dishonest, you will suddenly fall.

19 A hard-working farmer has plenty to eat. People who waste time will always be poor.

20 Honest people will lead a full, happy life. But if you are in a hurry to get rich, you are going to be punished.

21 Prejudice is wrong. But some judges will do wrong to get even the smallest bribe.

22 Selfish people are in such a hurry to get rich that they do not know when poverty is about to strike.

23 Correct someone, and afterwards he will appreciate it more than flattery.

24 Anyone who thinks it isn't wrong to steal from his parents is no better than a common thief.

25 Selfishness only causes trouble. You are much better off to trust the LORD.

26 It is foolish to follow your own opinions. Be safe, and follow the teachings of wiser people.

27 Give to the poor and you will never be in need. If you close your eyes to the poor, many people will curse you.

28 People stay in hiding when bad men come to power. But when they fall from power, righteous men will rule again.

29 If you get more stubborn every time you are corrected, one day you will be crushed and never recover.

2 Show me a righteous ruler and I will show you a happy people. Show me a wicked ruler and I will show you a miserable people.

3 If you appreciate wisdom, your father will be proud of you.

It is a foolish waste to spend money on prostitutes.

4 When the king is concerned with justice, the nation will be strong, but when

he is only concerned with money, he will ruin his country.

5 If you flatter your friends, you set a trap for yourself. *t*

6 Evil people are trapped in their own sins, while honest people are happy and free.

7 A good person knows the rights of the poor, but wicked people cannot understand such things.

8 People with no regard for others can throw whole cities into turmoil. Those who are wise keep things calm.

9 When an intelligent man brings a lawsuit against a fool, the fool only laughs and becomes loud and abusive.

10 Bloodthirsty people hate anyone who's honest, but righteous people will protect *u* the life of such a person.

11 Stupid people express their anger openly, but sensible people are patient and hold it back.

12 If a ruler pays attention to false information, all his officials will be liars.

13 A poor man and his oppressor have this in common—the LORD gave eyes to both of them.

14 If a king defends the rights of the poor, he will rule for a long time.

15 Correction and discipline are good for children. If a child has his own way, he will make his mother ashamed of him.

16 When evil men are in power, crime increases. But the righteous will live to see the downfall of such men.

17 Discipline your son and you can always be proud of him. He will never give you reason to be ashamed.

18 A nation without God's guidance is a nation without order. Happy is the man who keeps God's law!

19 You cannot correct a servant just by talking to him. He may understand you, but he will pay no attention.

20 There is more hope for a stupid fool than for someone who speaks without thinking.

21 If you give your servant everything he wants from childhood on, some day he will take over everything you own. *v*

22 People with quick tempers cause a lot of quarrelling and trouble.

23 Arrogance will bring your downfall, but if you are humble, you will be respected.

24 A thief's partner is his own worst enemy. He will be punished if he tells the truth in court, and God will curse him if he doesn't.

25 It is dangerous to be concerned with what others think of you, but if you trust the LORD, you are safe.

26 Everybody wants the good will of the ruler, but only from the LORD can you get justice.

27 The righteous hate the wicked, and the wicked hate the righteous.

The Words of Agur

30 These are the solemn words of Agur son of Jakeh:

"God is not with me, God is not with me,
  and I am helpless. *w*

2 I am more like an animal than a man;
  I do not have the sense a man should have.

3 I have never learned any wisdom,
  and I know nothing at all about God.

4 Who has ever mastered heavenly knowledge?
  Who has ever caught the wind in his hand?
  Or wrapped up water in a piece of cloth?
  Or fixed the boundaries of the earth?
  Who is he, if you know? Who is his son?

5 "God keeps every promise he makes. He is like a shield for all who seek his protection. 6 If you claim that he said something that he never said, he will reprimand you and show that you are a liar."

More Proverbs

7 I ask you, God, to let me have two things before I die: 8 keep me from lying, and let me be neither rich nor poor. So give me only as much food as I need. 9 If I have more, I might say that I do not need you. But if I am poor, I might steal and bring disgrace on my God.

10 Never criticize a servant to his master. You will be cursed and suffer for it.

11 There are people who curse their fathers and do not show their appreciation for their mothers.

12 There are people who think they are pure when they are as filthy as they can be.

13 There are people who think they are

---

t yourself; *or* them.   *u* *Probable text* protect; *Hebrew* seek.
v he...own; *or* you will not be able to control him.
w *Probable text* God...helpless; *Hebrew unclear.*

30.13   30.19   30.32   31.8   31.28

so good—oh, how good they think they are!

14 There are people who take cruel advantage of the poor and needy; that is the way they make their living.

15 A leech has two daughters, and both are named "Give me!"

There are four things that are never satisfied:
16 the world of the dead,
  a woman without children,
    dry ground that needs rain,
      and a fire burning out of control.

17 Anyone who makes fun of his father or despises his mother in her old age[x] ought to be eaten by vultures or have his eyes picked out by wild ravens.

18 There are four things that are too mysterious for me to understand:
19 an eagle flying in the sky,
  a snake moving on a rock,
    a ship finding its way over the sea,
      and a man and a woman falling in love.

20 This is how an unfaithful wife acts: she commits adultery, has a bath, and says, "But I haven't done anything wrong!"

21 There are four things that the earth itself cannot tolerate:
22 a slave who becomes a king,
  a fool who has all he wants to eat,
23   a hateful woman who gets married,
    and a servant-girl who takes the place of her mistress.

24 There are four animals in the world that are small, but very, very clever:
25 Ants: they are weak, but they store up their food in the summer.
26 Rock-badgers: they are not strong either, but they make their homes among the rocks.
27 Locusts: they have no king, but they move in formation.
28 Lizards: you can hold one in your hand, but you can find them in palaces.
29 There are four things that are im-

pressive to watch as they walk:
30 lions, strongest of all animals and afraid of none;
31 goats,
  strutting cocks,
    and kings in front of their people.[y]
32 If you have been foolish enough to be arrogant and plan evil, stop and think! 33 If you churn milk, you get butter. If you hit someone's nose, it bleeds. If you stir up anger, you get into trouble.

Advice to a King

31 These are the solemn words which King Lemuel's mother said to him:
2 "You are my own dear son, the answer to my prayers. What shall I tell you? 3 Don't spend all your energy on sex and all your money on women; they have destroyed kings. 4 Listen, Lemuel. Kings should not drink wine or have a craving for alcohol. 5 When they drink, they forget the laws and ignore the rights of people in need. 6 Alcohol is for people who are dying, for those who are in misery. 7 Let them drink and forget their poverty and unhappiness.

8 "Speak up for people who cannot speak for themselves. Protect the rights of all who are helpless. 9 Speak for them and be a righteous judge. Protect the rights of the poor and needy."

The Capable Wife

10 How hard it is to find a capable wife! She is worth far more than jewels!

11 Her husband puts his confidence in her, and he will never be poor.

12 As long as she lives, she does him good and never harm.

13 She keeps herself busy making wool and linen cloth.

14 She brings home food from out-of-the-way places, as merchant ships do.

15 She gets up before daylight to prepare food for her family and to tell her servant-girls what to do.

16 She looks at land and buys it, and

x One ancient translation mother in her old age; Hebrew mother's obedience.
y Verse 31 in Hebrew is unclear.

with money she has earned she plants a vineyard.

17 She is a hard worker, strong and industrious.

18 She knows the value of everything she makes, and works late into the night.

19 She spins her own thread and weaves her own cloth.

20 She is generous to the poor and needy.

21 She doesn't worry when it snows, because her family has warm clothing.

22 She makes bedspreads and wears clothes of fine purple linen.

23 Her husband is well known, one of the leading citizens.

24 She makes clothes and belts, and sells them to merchants.

25 She is strong and respected and not afraid of the future.

26 She speaks with a gentle wisdom.

27 She is always busy and looks after her family's needs.

28 Her children show their appreciation, and her husband praises her.

29 He says, "Many women are good wives, but you are the best of them all."

30 Charm is deceptive and beauty disappears, but a woman who honours the LORD should be praised.

31 Give her credit for all she does. She deserves the respect of everyone.

ECCLESIASTES

INTRODUCTION

The book of *Ecclesiastes* contains the thoughts of "the Philosopher," a man who reflected deeply on how short and contradictory human life is, with its mysterious injustices and frustrations, and concluded that "life is useless." He could not understand the ways of God, who controls human destiny. Yet, in spite of this, he advised people to work hard, and to enjoy the gifts of God as much and as long as they could.

Many of the Philosopher's thoughts appear negative and even depressing. But the fact that this book is in the Bible shows that biblical faith is broad enough to take into account such pessimism and doubt. Many have taken comfort in seeing themselves in the mirror of *Ecclesiastes,* and have discovered that the same Bible which reflects these thoughts also offers the hope in God that gives life its greater meaning.

Life Is Useless

1 These are the words of the Philosopher, David's son, who was king in Jerusalem.

2 It is useless, useless, said the Philosopher. Life is useless, all useless. 3 You spend your life working, labouring, and what do you have to show for it? 4 Generations come and generations go, but the world stays just the same. 5 The sun still rises, and it still goes down, going wearily back to where it must start all over again. 6 The wind blows south, the wind blows north—round and round and back again. 7 Every river flows into the sea, but the sea is not yet full. The water returns to where the rivers began, and starts all over again. 8 Everything leads to weariness—a weariness too great for words. Our eyes can never see enough to be satisfied; our ears can never hear

enough. ⁹What has happened before will happen again. What has been done before will be done again. There is nothing new in the whole world. ¹⁰"Look," they say, "here is something new!" But no, it has all happened before, long before we were born. ¹¹No one remembers what has happened in the past, and no one in days to come will remember what happens between now and then.

The Philosopher's Experience

12 I, the Philosopher, have been king over Israel in Jerusalem. ¹³I determined that I would examine and study all the things that are done in this world.

God has laid a miserable fate upon us. ¹⁴I have seen everything done in this

I tell you, it is all useless (1.14)

world, and I tell you, it is all useless. It is like chasing the wind. ¹⁵You can't straighten out what is crooked; you can't count things that aren't there.

16 I told myself, "I have become a great man, far wiser than anyone who ruled Jerusalem before me. I know what wisdom and knowledge really are." ¹⁷I was determined to learn the difference between knowledge and foolishness, wisdom and madness. But I found out that I might as well be chasing the wind. ¹⁸The wiser you are, the more worries you have; the more you know, the more it hurts.

2 I decided to enjoy myself and find out what happiness is. But I found that this is useless, too. ²I discovered that laughter is foolish, that pleasure does you no good. ³Driven on by my desire for wisdom, I decided to cheer myself up with wine and have a good time. I thought that this might be the best way people can spend their short lives on earth.

4 I accomplished great things. I built myself houses and planted vineyards. ⁵I planted gardens and orchards, with all kinds of fruit-trees in them; ⁶I dug ponds to irrigate them. ⁷I bought many slaves, and there were slaves born in my household. I owned more livestock than anyone else who had ever lived in Jerusalem. ⁸I also piled up silver and gold from the royal treasuries of the lands I ruled. Men and women sang to entertain me, and I had all the women a man could want.

9 Yes, I was great, greater than anyone else who had ever lived in Jerusalem, and my wisdom never failed me. ¹⁰Anything I wanted, I got. I did not deny myself any pleasure. I was proud of everything I had worked for, and all this was my reward. ¹¹Then I thought about all that I had done and how hard I had worked doing it, and I realized that it didn't mean a thing. It was like chasing the wind—of no use at all. ¹²After all, a king can only do what previous kings have done.

So I started thinking about what it meant to be wise or reckless or foolish. ¹³Oh, I know, "Wisdom is better than foolishness, just as light is better than darkness. ¹⁴Wise men can see where they are going, and fools cannot." But I also know that the same fate is waiting for us all. ¹⁵I thought to myself, "I will suffer the same fate as fools. So what have I gained from being so wise?" "Nothing," I answered, "not a thing." ¹⁶No one remembers wise men, and no one remembers fools. In days to come, we will all be forgotten. We must all die—wise and foolish alike. ¹⁷So life came to mean nothing to me, because everything in it had brought me nothing but trouble. It had all been useless; I had been chasing the wind.

18 Nothing that I had worked for and earned meant a thing to me, because I knew that I would have to leave it to my successor, ¹⁹and he might be wise, or he might be foolish—who knows? Yet he will own everything I have worked for, everything my wisdom has earned for me in this world. It is all useless. ²⁰So I came to regret that I had worked so hard. ²¹You work for something with all your wisdom, knowledge, and skill, and then you have to leave it all to someone who hasn't had to work for it. It is useless, and it isn't right! ²²You work and worry your way

---

1.16: 1 Kgs 4.29-31   **2.4-8:** 1 Kgs 10.23-27; 2 Chr 9.22-27   **2.7:** 1 Kgs 4.23
2.8: 1 Kgs 10.10,14-22   **2.9:** 1 Chr 29.25

Anything I wanted, I got (2.10)

through life, and what do you have to show for it? ²³ As long as you live, everything you do brings nothing but worry and heartache. Even at night your mind can't rest. It is all useless.

24 The best thing a man can do is to

It is like chasing the wind (2.26)

eat and drink and enjoy what he has earned. And yet, I realized that even this comes from God. ²⁵ How else could you have anything to eat or enjoy yourself at all? ²⁶ God gives wisdom, knowledge, and happiness to those who please him, but he makes sinners work, earning and saving, so that what they get can be given to those who please him. It is all useless. It is like chasing the wind.

A Time for Everything

3 Everything that happens in this world happens at the time God chooses. ² He sets the time for birth and the time for death,
　　the time for planting and the time for pulling up,
³ 　the time for killing and the time for healing,
　　the time for tearing down and the time for building.
⁴ He sets the time for sorrow and the time for joy,
　　the time for mourning and the time for dancing,

2.23: Job 5.7, 14.1　　**2.24:** Ecc 3.13, 5.18, 9.7; Lk 12.19; 1 Cor 15.32　　**2.26:** Job 32.8; Prov 2.6

5 the time for making love and the time
for not making love,
the time for kissing and the time for
not kissing.
6 He sets the time for finding and the
time for losing,
the time for saving and the time for
throwing away,
7 the time for tearing and the time for
mending,
the time for silence and the time for
talk.
8 He sets the time for love and the time
for hate,
the time for war and the time for
peace.

9 What do we gain from all our work? 10 I know the heavy burdens that God has laid on us. 11 He has set the right time for everything. He has given us a desire to know the future, but never gives us the satisfaction of fully understanding what he does. 12 So I realized that all we can do is to be happy and do the best we can while we are still alive. 13 All of us should eat and drink and enjoy what we have worked for. It is God's gift.

14 I know that everything God does will last for ever. You can't add anything to it or take anything away from it. And one thing God does is to make us stand in awe of him. 15 Whatever happens or can happen has already happened before. God makes the same thing happen again and again.

Injustice in the World

16 In addition, I have also noticed that in this world you find wickedness where justice and right ought to be. 17 I told myself, "God is going to judge the righteous and the evil alike, because every thing, every action, will happen at its own set time."[a] 18 I concluded that God is testing us, to show us that we are no better than animals. 19 After all, the same fate awaits man and animal alike. One dies just like the other. They are both the same kind of creature. A human being is no better off than an animal, because life has no meaning for either. 20 They are both going to the same place—the dust. They both came from it; they will both go back to it. 21 How can anyone be sure that a man's spirit goes upwards while an animal's spirit goes down into the ground? 22 So I realized then that the best thing we can do is to enjoy what we have worked for. There is nothing else we can

do.[b] There is no way for us to know what will happen after we die.

4 Then I looked again at all the injustice that goes on in this world. The oppressed were weeping, and no one would help them. No one would help them, because their oppressors had power on their side. 2 I envy those who are dead and gone; they are better off than those who are still alive. 3 But better off than either are those who have never been born, who have never seen the injustice that goes on in this world.

4 I have also learnt why people work so hard to succeed: it is because they envy their neighbours. But it is useless. It is like chasing the wind. 5 They say that a man would be a fool to fold his hands and let himself starve to death. 6 Perhaps so, but it is better to have only a little, with peace of mind, than to be busy all the time with both hands, trying to catch the wind.

7 I have noticed something else in life that is useless. 8 Here is a man who lives alone. He has no son, no brother, yet he is always working, never satisfied with the wealth he has. For whom is he working so hard and denying himself any pleasure? This is useless, too—and a miserable way to live.

9 Two are better off than one, because together they can work more effectively. 10 If one of them falls down, the other can help him up. But if someone is alone and falls, it's just too bad, because there is no one to help him. 11 If it is cold, two can sleep together and stay warm, but how can you keep warm by yourself? 12 Two men can resist an attack that would defeat one man alone. A rope made of three cords is hard to break.

13-14 A man may rise from poverty to become king of his country, or go from prison to the throne, but if in his old age he is too foolish to take advice, he is not as well off as a young man who is poor but intelligent. 15 I thought about all the people who live in this world, and I realized that somewhere among them there is a young man who will take the king's place. 16 There may be no limit to the number of people a king rules; when he is gone, no one will be grateful for what he has done. It is useless. It is like chasing the wind.

a *Probable text* its own set time; *Hebrew* its own set time there.
b what we have...do; *or* our work, because we are going to have to do it anyway.

A rich man, however, has so much that he stays awake worrying (5.12)

Don't Make Rash Promises

5 Be careful about going to the Temple. It is better to go there to learn than to offer sacrifices as foolish people do, people who don't know right from wrong. ²Think before you speak, and don't make any rash promises to God. He is in heaven and you are on earth, so don't say any more than you have to. ³The more you worry, the more likely you are to have bad dreams, and the more you talk, the more likely you are to say something foolish. ⁴So when you make a promise to God, keep it as quickly as possible. He has no use for a fool. Do what you promise to do. ⁵Better not to promise at all than to make a promise and not keep it. ⁶Don't let your own words lead you into sin, so that you have to tell God's priest that you didn't mean it. Why make God angry with you? Why let him destroy what you have worked for? ⁷No matter how much you dream, how much useless work you do, or how much you talk, you must still stand in awe of God.

Life Is Useless

8 Don't be surprised when you see that the government oppresses the poor and denies them justice and their rights. Every official is protected by the one over him, and both are protected by still higher officials.

9 Even a king depends on the harvest. *c*

10 If you love money, you will never be satisfied; if you long to be rich, you will never get all you want. It is useless. ¹¹The richer you are, the more mouths you must feed. All you gain is the knowledge that you are rich. ¹²A working man may or may not have enough to eat, but at least he can get a good night's sleep. A rich man, however, has so much that he stays awake worrying.

13 Here is a terrible thing that I have seen in this world: people save up their money for a time when they may need it, *d* ¹⁴and then lose it all in some unlucky deal and end up with nothing left to pass on to their children. ¹⁵We leave this world just as we entered it—with nothing. In spite of all our work there is nothing we can take with us. ¹⁶It isn't right! We go just as we came. We labour, trying to catch the wind, and what do we get? ¹⁷We have to live our lives in darkness and grief, *e* worried, angry, and sick.

18 This is what I have found out: the best thing anyone can do is to eat and drink and enjoy what he has worked for during the short life that God has given him; this is man's fate. ¹⁹If God gives a man wealth and property and lets him enjoy them, he should be grateful and enjoy what he has worked for. It is a gift from God. ²⁰Since God has allowed him to be happy, he will not worry too much about how short life is.

6 I have noticed that in this world a serious injustice is done. ²God will give someone wealth, honour, and property, yes, everything he wants, but then will not let him enjoy it. Some stranger will enjoy it instead. It is useless, and it's all wrong. ³A man may have a hundred children and live a long time, but no matter how long he lives, if he does not get his share of happiness and does not receive a decent burial, then I say that a baby born dead is better off. ⁴It does

c Verse 9 in Hebrew is unclear.   *d for...it; or to their own hurt.*
e Some ancient translations in darkness and grief; Hebrew eating in darkness.
5.4: Ps 66.13–14   **5.15:** Job 1.21; Ps 49.17; 1 Tim 6.7

that baby no good to be born; it disappears into darkness, where it is forgotten. ⁵It never sees the light of day or knows what life is like, but at least it has found rest—⁶more so than the man who never enjoys life, though he may live two thousand years. After all, both of them are going to the same place.

7 A man does all his work just to get something to eat, but he never has enough. ⁸How is a wise man better off than a fool? What good does it do a poor man to know how to face life? ⁹It is useless; it is like chasing the wind. It is better to be satisfied with what you have than to be always wanting something else.

10 Everything that happens was already determined long ago, and we all know that a man*f* cannot argue with someone who is stronger than he. ¹¹The longer you argue, the more useless it is, and you are no better off. ¹²How can anyone know what is best for a man in this short, useless life of his—a life that passes like a shadow? How can anyone know what will happen in the world after he dies?

Than to have stupid people sing your praises (7.5)

Thoughts about Life

7 A good reputation is better than expensive perfume; and the day you die is better than the day you are born.

2 It is better to go to a home where there is mourning than to one where there is a party, because the living should always remind themselves that death is waiting for us all.

3 Sorrow is better than laughter; it may sadden your face, but it sharpens your understanding.

4 Someone who is always thinking about happiness is a fool. A wise person thinks about death.

5 It is better to have wise people reprimand you than to have stupid people sing your praises.

6 When a fool laughs, it is like thorns crackling in a fire. It doesn't mean a thing.

7 When a wise man cheats someone, he is acting like a fool. If you take a bribe, you ruin your character.

8 The end of anything is better than its beginning.

Patience is better than pride.

9 Keep your temper under control; it is foolish to harbour a grudge.

10 Never ask, "Oh, why were things so

If you take a bribe (7.7)

much better in the old days?" It's not an intelligent question.

11 Everyone who lives ought to be wise; it is as good as receiving an inheritance ¹²and will give you as much security as money can. Wisdom keeps you safe—this is the advantage of knowledge.

13 Think about what God has done. How can anyone straighten out what God has made crooked? ¹⁴When things are going well for you, be glad, and when trouble comes, just remember: God sends both happiness and trouble; you never

---

*f*and we...man; *or* and a man's nature is already known; a man.
7.1: Prov 22.1   **7.9:** Jas 1.19

The love she offers you will catch you like a trap (7.26)

26 I found something more bitter than death—woman. The love she offers you will catch you like a trap or like a net; and her arms round you will hold you like a chain. A man who pleases God can get away, but she will catch the sinner. 27 Yes, said the Philosopher, I found this out little by little while I was looking for answers. 28 I have looked for other answers but have found none. I found one man in a thousand that I could respect, but not one woman. 29 This is all that I have learnt: God made us plain and simple, but we have made ourselves very complicated.

8 Only a wise man knows what things really mean. Wisdom makes him smile and makes his frowns disappear.

Obey the King

2 Do what the king says,[h] and don't

know what is going to happen next.[g]

15 My life has been useless, but in it I have seen everything. A good man may die while another man lives on, even though he is evil. 16 So don't be too good or too wise—why kill yourself? 17 But don't be too wicked or too foolish, either—why die before you have to? 18 Avoid both extremes. If you have reverence for God, you will be successful anyway.

19 Wisdom does more for a person than ten rulers can do for a city.

20 There is no one on earth who does what is right all the time and never makes a mistake.

21 Don't pay attention to everything people say—you may hear your servant insulting you, 22 and you know yourself that you have insulted other people many times.

23 I used my wisdom to test all of this. I was determined to be wise, but it was beyond me. 24 How can anyone discover what life means? It is too deep for us, too hard to understand. 25 But I devoted myself to knowledge and study; I was determined to find wisdom and the answers to my questions, and to learn how wicked and foolish stupidity is.

None of us knows what is going to happen (8.7)

make any rash promises to God. 3 The king can do anything he likes, so depart from

[g] you...next; *or* you cannot find fault with him.
[h] *Some ancient translations* Do what the king says; *Hebrew unclear.*

Wise men may claim to know (8.17)

his presence; don't stay in such a dangerous place. ⁴The king acts with authority, and no one can challenge what he does. ⁵As long as you obey his commands, you are safe, and a wise man knows how and when to do it. ⁶There is a right time and a right way to do everything, but we know so little! ⁷None of us knows what is going to happen, and there is no one to tell us. ⁸No one can keep himself from dying or put off the day of his death. That is a battle we cannot escape; we cannot cheat our way out.

The Wicked and the Righteous

9 I saw all this when I thought about the things that are done in this world, a world where some men have power and others have to suffer under them. ¹⁰Yes, I have seen wicked men buried in their graves, but on the way back from the cemetery people praise them in the very city where they did their evil. It is useless.ⁱ

11 Why do people commit crimes so readily? Because crime is not punished quickly enough. ¹²A sinner may commit a hundred crimes and still live. Oh yes, I know what they say: "If you obey God, everything will be all right, ¹³but it will not go well for the wicked. Their life is like a shadow and they will die young, because they do not obey God." ¹⁴But this is nonsense. Look at what happens in the world: sometimes righteous men get the punishment of the wicked, and wicked men get the reward of the righteous. I say it is useless.

15 So I am convinced that a man should enjoy himself, because the only pleasure he has in this life is eating and drinking and enjoying himself. He can at least do this as he labours during the life that God has given him in this world.

16 Whenever I tried to become wise and learn what goes on in the world, I realized that you could stay awake night and day ¹⁷and never be able to understand what God is doing. However hard you try, you will never find out. Wise men may claim to know, but they don't.

9 I thought long and hard about all this and saw that God controls the actions of wise and righteous men, even their love and their hate. No one knows anything about what lies ahead of him. ²It makes no difference.ʲ The same fate comes to the righteous and the wicked, to the good

---

ⁱ *Verse 10 in Hebrew is unclear.*
ʲ men, even their...difference; *or* men, but no one knows whether it is out of love or hate. ²It makes no difference what lies ahead of us.

Better to listen to the quiet words of a wise man (9.17)

and the bad,^{k} to those who are religious and those who are not, to those who offer sacrifices and those who do not. A good man is no better off than a sinner; a man who takes an oath is no better off than one who does not. ³One fate comes to all alike, and this is as wrong as anything that happens in this world. As long as people live, their minds are full of evil and madness, and suddenly they die. ⁴But

A live dog is better off than a dead lion (9.4)

anyone who is alive in the world of the living has some hope; a live dog is better off than a dead lion. ⁵Yes, the living know they are going to die, but the dead know nothing. They have no further reward; they are completely forgotten. ⁶Their loves, their hates, their passions, all died with them. They will never again take part in anything that happens in this world.

7 Go ahead—eat your food and be happy; drink your wine and be cheerful. It's all right with God. ⁸Always look happy and cheerful. ⁹Enjoy life with the woman you love, as long as you live the useless life that God has given you in this world. Enjoy every useless day of it, because that is all you will get for all your trouble. ¹⁰Work hard at whatever you do, because there will be no action, no thought, no knowledge, no wisdom in the world of the dead—and that is where you are going.

11 I realized another thing, that in this world fast runners do not always win the race, and the brave do not always win the battle. Wise men do not always earn a living, intelligent men do not always get rich, and capable men do not always rise to high positions. Bad luck happens to everyone. ¹²You never know when your time is coming. Like birds suddenly caught in a trap, like fish caught in a net, we are trapped at some evil moment when we least expect it.

Thoughts on Wisdom and Foolishness

13 There is something else I saw, a good example of how wisdom is regarded in this world. ¹⁴There was a little town without many people in it. A powerful king attacked it. He surrounded it and prepared to break through the walls. ¹⁵A man lived there who was poor, but so clever that he could have saved the town. But no one thought about him.^{l} ¹⁶I have always said that wisdom is better than

---

^{k} *Some ancient translations* and the bad; *Hebrew does not have these words.*
^{l} he could have...him; *or* he saved the town. But later on no one remembered him.

strength, but no one thinks of a poor man as wise or pays any attention to what he says. ¹⁷It is better to listen to the quiet words of a wise man than to the shouts of a ruler at a council of fools. ¹⁸Wisdom does more good than weapons, but one sinner can undo a lot of good.

10 Dead flies can make a whole bottle of perfume stink, and a little stupidity can cancel out the greatest wisdom.

2 It is natural for a wise man to do the right thing and for a fool to do the wrong thing. ³His stupidity will be evident even to strangers he meets along the way; he lets everyone know that he is a fool.

4 If your ruler becomes angry with you, do not hand in your resignation; serious wrongs may be pardoned if you keep calm. ᵐ

5 Here is an injustice I have seen in the world—an injustice caused by rulers. ⁶Stupid people are given positions of authority while rich men are ignored. ⁷I

I have seen slaves on horseback (10.7)

have seen slaves on horseback while noblemen go on foot like slaves.

8 If you dig a pit, you fall in it; if you break through a wall, a snake bites you. ⁹If you work in a stone quarry, you get hurt by stones. If you split wood, you get hurt doing it. ¹⁰If your axe is blunt and you don't sharpen it, you have to work harder to use it. It is more sensible to plan ahead. ¹¹Knowing how to charm a snake is of no use if you let the snake bite first. ¹²What a wise man says brings him honour, but a fool is destroyed by his own words. ¹³He starts out with silly talk and ends up with pure madness. ¹⁴A fool talks on and on.

ᵐkeep calm; *or* submit to him.
10.8: Ps 7.15; Prov 26.27

No one knows what is going to happen next, and no one can tell us what will happen after we die.

15 Only someone too stupid to find his way home would wear himself out with work.

16 A country is in trouble when its king is a youth and its leaders feast all night long. ¹⁷But a country is fortunate to have a king who makes his own decisions and leaders who eat at the proper time, who control themselves and don't get drunk.

18 When a man is too lazy to repair

When a man is too lazy to repair his roof (10.18)

his roof, it will leak, and the house will fall in.

19 Feasting makes you happy and wine cheers you up, but you can't have either without money.

20 Don't criticize the king, even silently, and don't criticize the rich, even in the privacy of your bedroom. A bird might carry the message and tell them what you said.

What a Wise Man Does

11 Invest your money in foreign trade, and one of these days you will make a profit. ²Put your investments in several places—many places, in fact—because you never know what kind of bad luck you are going to have in this world.

3 No matter in which direction a tree falls, it will lie where it fell. When the clouds are full, it rains. ⁴If you wait until the wind and the weather are just right, you will never sow anything and never harvest anything. ⁵God made everything,

and you can no more understand what he does than you understand how new life begins in the womb of a pregnant woman. 6 Do your sowing in the morning and in the evening, too. You never know whether it will all grow well or whether one sowing will do better than the other.

7 It is good to be able to enjoy the pleasant light of day. 8 Be grateful for every year you live. No matter how long you live, remember that you will be dead much longer. There is nothing at all to look forward to.

Advice to Young People

9 Young people, enjoy your youth. Be happy while you are still young. Do what you want to do, and follow your heart's desire. But remember that God is going to judge you for whatever you do.

10 Don't let anything worry you or cause you pain. You aren't going to be young very long.

12 So remember your Creator[n] while you are still young, before those dismal days and years come when you will say, "I don't enjoy life." 2 That is when

Remember your Creator...before those dismal days...come (12.1)

the light of the sun, the moon, and the stars will grow dim for you, and the rain clouds will never pass away. 3 Then your arms, that have protected you, will tremble, and your legs, now strong, will grow weak. Your teeth will be too few to chew your food, and your eyes too dim to see clearly. 4 Your ears will be deaf to the noise of the street. You will barely be able to hear the mill as it grinds or music as it plays, but even the song of a bird will wake you from sleep. 5 You will be afraid of high places, and walking will be dangerous. Your hair will turn white; you will hardly be able to drag yourself along, and all desire will have gone.

We are going to our final resting place, and then there will be mourning in the streets. 6 The silver chain will snap, and the golden lamp will fall and break; the rope at the well will break, and the water jar will be shattered. 7 Our bodies will return to the dust of the earth, and the breath of life will go back to God, who gave it to us.

8 Useless, useless, said the Philosopher. It is all useless.

The Summing Up

9 But because the Philosopher was wise, he kept on teaching the people what he knew. He studied proverbs and honestly tested their truth. 10 The Philosopher tried to find comforting words, but the words he wrote were honest. 11 The sayings of wise men are like the sharp sticks that shepherds use to guide sheep, and collected proverbs are as lasting as firmly driven nails. They have been given by God, the one Shepherd of us all.

12 My son, there is something else to watch out for. There is no end to the writing of books, and too much study will wear you out.

13 After all this, there is only one thing to say: Have reverence for God, and obey his commands, because this is all that man was created for. 14 God is going to judge everything we do, whether good or bad, even things done in secret.

---

[n] *The Hebrew expression for* your Creator *sounds like the Hebrew for* your grave.

THE SONG OF SONGS

INTRODUCTION

The *Song of Songs* is a series of love poems, for the most part in the form of songs addressed by a man to a woman, and by the woman to the man. In some translations, the book is called *The Song of Solomon,* because it is attributed to Solomon in the Hebrew.

These songs have often been interpreted by Jews as a picture of the relationship between God and his people, and by Christians as a picture of the relationship between Christ and the Church.

Outline of Contents

First song   1.1—2.7
Second song   2.8—3.5
Third song   3.6—5.1
Fourth song   5.2—6.3
Fifth song   6.4—8.4
Sixth song   8.5-14

---

1 The most beautiful of songs, by Solomon. [a]

The First Song

The Woman

2 Your lips cover me with kisses;
    your love is better than wine.
3 There is a fragrance about you;
    the sound of your name recalls it.
    No woman could help loving you.
4 Take me with you, and we'll run away;
    be my king and take me to your room.
  We will be happy together,
    drink deep, and lose ourselves in love.
  No wonder all women love you!
5 Women of Jerusalem, I am dark but [b]
    beautiful,
  dark as the desert tents of Kedar,
  but beautiful as the curtains in
    Solomon's palace.

6 Don't look down on me because of my
    colour,
  because the sun has tanned me.
  My brothers were angry with me
    and made me work in the vineyard.
  I had no time to care for myself.
7 Tell me, my love,
    Where will you lead your flock to
      graze?
    Where will they rest from the
      noonday sun?
  Why should I need to look for you
    among the flocks of the other
      shepherds? [c]

The Man

8 Don't you know the place, loveliest of
    women?
  Go and follow the flock;
    find pasture for your goats
    near the tents of the shepherds.

[a] by Solomon; *or* dedicated to Solomon, *or* about Solomon.   [b] but; *or* and.
[c] *Probable text* Why should I...shepherds; *Hebrew unclear.*
1.1: 1 Kgs 4.32

¹⁷   the cedars will be the beams of our
          house,
      and the cypress-trees the ceiling.
2 I am only a wild flower in Sharon,
      a lily in a mountain valley.

The Man
² Like a lily among thorns
      is my darling among women.

The Woman
³ Like an apple-tree among the trees of
          the forest,
      so is my dearest compared with other
          men.
   I love to sit in its shadow,
      and its fruit is sweet to my taste.
⁴ He brought me to his banqueting hall
      and raised the banner of love over
          me.
⁵ Restore my strength with raisins
      and refresh me with apples!
   I am weak from passion.
⁶ His left hand is under my head,
      and his right hand caresses me.
⁷ Promise me, women of Jerusalem;
      swear by the swift deer and the
          gazelles

Loveliest of women (1.8)

⁹ You, my love, excite men
      as a mare excites the stallions of
          Pharaoh's chariots.
¹⁰ Your hair is beautiful upon your
          cheeks
      and falls along your neck like jewels.
¹¹ But we will make for you a chain of
          gold
      with ornaments of silver.

The Woman
¹² My king was lying on his couch,
      and my perfume filled the air with
          fragrance.
¹³ My lover has the scent of myrrh
      as he lies upon my breasts.
¹⁴ My lover is like the wild flowers
      that bloom in the vineyards at Engedi.

The Man
¹⁵ How beautiful you are, my love;
      how your eyes shine with love!

The Woman
¹⁶ How handsome you are, my dearest;
      how you delight me!
   The green grass will be our bed;

How your eyes shine with love! (1.15)

that you will not interrupt our love.

The Second Song

The Woman

8 I hear my lover's voice.
He comes running over the mountains,
    racing across the hills to me.
9 My lover is like a gazelle,

Like a young stag (2.9)

like a young stag.
There he stands beside the wall.
He looks in through the window
    and glances through the lattice.
10 My lover speaks to me.

The Man

Come then, my love;
    my darling, come with me.
11 The winter is over; the rains have
        stopped;
12   in the countryside the flowers are
        in bloom.
This is the time for singing;
    the song of doves is heard in the fields.
13 Figs are beginning to ripen;
    the air is fragrant with blossoming
        vines.
Come then, my love;
    my darling, come with me.
14 You are like a dove that hides
    in the crevice of a rock.
Let me see your lovely face
    and hear your enchanting voice.

15 Catch the foxes, the little foxes,
    before they ruin our vineyard in
        bloom.

The Woman

16 My lover is mine, and I am his.

*d*mountains of Bether; *or* rugged mountains.

He feeds his flock among the lilies
17   until the morning breezes blow
    and the darkness disappears.
Return, my darling, like a gazelle,
    like a stag on the mountains of
        Bether. *d*

3 Asleep on my bed, night after night
    I dreamt of the one I love;
I was looking for him, but couldn't
    find him.
2 I went wandering through the city,
    through its streets and alleys.
I looked for the one I love.
    I looked, but couldn't find him.
3 The watchmen patrolling the city saw
        me.
    I asked them, "Have you found my
        lover?"
4 As soon as I left them, I found him.
I held him and wouldn't let him go
    until I took him to my mother's house,
    to the room where I was born.

5 Promise me, women of Jerusalem;
    swear by the swift deer and the
        gazelles
    that you will not interrupt our love.

The Third Song

The Woman

6 What is this coming from the desert
    like a column of smoke,
    fragrant with incense and myrrh,
    the incense sold by the traders?
7 Solomon is coming, carried on his
        throne;
    sixty soldiers form the bodyguard,
    the finest soldiers in Israel.
8 All of them are skilful with the sword;
    they are battle-hardened veterans.
Each of them is armed with a sword,
    on guard against a night attack.
9 King Solomon is carried on a throne
    made of the finest wood.
10 Its posts are covered with silver;
    over it is cloth embroidered with gold.
Its cushions are covered with purple
        cloth,
    lovingly woven by the women of
        Jerusalem.
11 Women of Zion, come and see King
        Solomon.
He is wearing the crown that his mother
    placed on his head
    on his wedding day,
    on the day of his gladness and joy.

The Man

4 How beautiful you are, my love!

How your eyes shine with love
  behind your veil.
Your hair dances, like a flock of goats
  bounding down the hills of Gilead.
2 Your teeth are as white as sheep
  that have just been shorn and washed.
Not one of them is missing;
  they are all perfectly matched.
3 Your lips are like a scarlet ribbon;
  how lovely they are when you speak.
Your cheeks glow behind your veil.
4 Your neck is like the tower of David,
  round and smooth,*e*
  with a necklace like a thousand shields
    hung round it.
5 Your breasts are like gazelles,
  twin deer feeding among lilies.
6 I will stay on the hill of myrrh,
  the hill of incense,
  until the morning breezes blow
  and the darkness disappears.
7 How beautiful you are, my love;
  how perfect you are!

8 Come with me from the Lebanon
    Mountains, my bride;
  come with me from Lebanon.
Come down from the top of Mount
    Amana,
  from Mount Senir and Mount Hermon,
  where the lions and leopards live.
9 The look in your eyes, my sweetheart
    and bride,
  and the necklace you are wearing
  have stolen my heart.
10 Your love delights me,
  my sweetheart and bride.
Your love is better than wine;
  your perfume more fragrant than any
    spice.
11 The taste of honey is on your lips,
  my darling;
  your tongue is milk and honey for
    me.
Your clothing has all the fragrance of
  Lebanon.

12 My sweetheart, my bride, is a secret
    garden,
  a walled garden, a private spring;
13   there the plants flourish.
They grow like an orchard of
    pomegranate-trees
  and bear the finest fruits.
There is no lack of henna and nard,
14   of saffron, calamus, and cinnamon,
    or incense of every kind.
Myrrh and aloes grow there
  with all the most fragrant perfumes.

e round and smooth; *Hebrew unclear.*

15 Fountains water the garden,
  streams of flowing water,
  brooks gushing down from the
    Lebanon Mountains.

The Woman
16 Wake up, North Wind.
  South Wind, blow on my garden;
  fill the air with fragrance.
Let my lover come to his garden
  and eat the best of its fruits.

The Man
5 I have entered my garden,
    my sweetheart, my bride.
I am gathering my spices and myrrh;
  I am eating my honey and honeycomb;
  I am drinking my wine and milk.

The Women
Eat, lovers, and drink
  until you are drunk with love!

The Fourth Song
The Woman
2 While I slept, my heart was awake.
  I dreamt my lover knocked at the door.

The Man
Let me come in, my darling,
  my sweetheart, my dove.
My head is wet with dew,
  and my hair is damp from the mist.

The Woman
3 I have already undressed;
  why should I get dressed again?
I have washed my feet;
  why should I get them dirty again?

4 My lover put his hand to the door,
  and I was thrilled that he was near.
5   I was ready to let him come in.
My hands were covered with myrrh,
  my fingers with liquid myrrh,
  as I grasped the handle of the door.
6 I opened the door for my lover,
  but he had already gone.
How I wanted to hear his voice!
I looked for him, but couldn't find him;
  I called to him, but heard no answer.

7 The watchmen patrolling the city found
    me;
  they struck me and bruised me;
  the guards at the city wall tore off
    my cape.
8 Promise me, women of Jerusalem,
  that if you find my lover,

you will tell him I am weak from
   passion.

The Women

9 Most beautiful of women,
   is your lover different from everyone
      else?
   What is there so wonderful about him
      that we should give you our promise?

The Woman

10 My lover is handsome and strong;
   he is one in ten thousand.
11 His face is bronzed and smooth;
   his hair is wavy,
      black as a raven.
12 His eyes are as beautiful as doves by
      a flowing brook,
   doves washed in milk and standing
      by the stream. *f*
13 His cheeks are as lovely as a garden
      that is full of herbs and spices.
   His lips are like lilies,
      wet with liquid myrrh.
14 His hands are well-formed,
      and he wears rings set with gems.
   His body is like smooth ivory, *g*
      with sapphires set in it.
15 His thighs are columns of alabaster
      set in sockets of gold.
   He is majestic, like the Lebanon
      Mountains
      with their towering cedars.
16 His mouth is sweet to kiss;
      everything about him enchants me.
   This is what my lover is like,
      women of Jerusalem.

The Women

6 Most beautiful of women,
      where has your lover gone?
   Tell us which way your lover went,
      so that we can help you find him.

The Woman

2 My lover has gone to his garden,
   where the balsam-trees grow.
   He is feeding his flock in the garden
      and gathering lilies.
3 My lover is mine, and I am his;
   he feeds his flock among the lilies.

The Fifth Song

The Man

4 My love, you are as beautiful as
      Jerusalem,
   as lovely as the city of Tirzah,

as breathtaking as these great cities. *h*
5 Turn your eyes away from me;
   they are holding me captive.
   Your hair dances, like a flock of goats
      bounding down the hills of Gilead.
6 Your teeth are as white as a flock of
      sheep
   that have just been washed.
   Not one of them is missing;
      they are all perfectly matched.
7 Your cheeks glow behind your veil.
8 Let the king have sixty queens, eighty
      concubines,
   young women without number!
9 But I love only one,
   and she is as lovely as a dove.
   She is her mother's only daughter,
      her mother's favourite child.
   All women look at her and praise her;
   queens and concubines sing her
      praises.

10 Who is this whose glance is like the
      dawn?
   She is beautiful and bright,
      as dazzling as the sun or the moon. *i*
11 I have come down among the almond-
      trees
   to see the young plants in the valley,
   to see the new leaves on the vines
   and the blossoms on the pomegranate-
      trees.
12 I am trembling; you have made me
      as eager for love
   as a chariot driver is for battle. *j*

The Women

13 Dance, dance, *k* girl of Shulam.
   Let us watch you as you dance.

The Woman

   Why do you want to watch me
      as I dance between the rows of
         onlookers?

The Man

7 What a wonderful girl you are!
      How beautiful are your feet in
         sandals.
   The curve of your thighs
      is like the work of an artist.
2 A bowl is there,
   that never runs out of spiced wine.
   A sheaf of wheat is there,
      surrounded by lilies.
3 Your breasts are like twin deer,
   like two gazelles.

---

f and standing by the stream; *Hebrew unclear.*   *g* like smooth ivory; *Hebrew unclear.*
h as breathtaking as...cities; *Hebrew unclear.*   *i* as dazzling as...moon; *Hebrew unclear.*
j Verse 12 in Hebrew is unclear.   *k* Dance, dance; *or* Come back, come back.

Let us watch you as you dance (6.13)

4 Your neck is like a tower of ivory.
　Your eyes are like the pools in the city
　　of Heshbon,
　　　near the gate of that great city.
　Your nose is as lovely as the tower of
　　Lebanon
　　　that stands guard at Damascus.
5 Your head is held high like Mount
　　Carmel.
　Your braided hair shines like the finest
　　satin;
　　its beauty*l* could hold a king captive.

6 How pretty you are, how beautiful;
　　how complete the delights of your
　　　love.
7 You are as graceful as a palm-tree,
　　and your breasts are clusters of dates.
8 I will climb the palm-tree
　　and pick its fruit.
　To me your breasts are like bunches
　　of grapes,
　　your breath like the fragrance of
　　　apples,
9　and your mouth like the finest wine.

The Woman
　Then let the wine flow straight to my
　　lover,
　　flowing over his lips and teeth.*m*
10 I belong to my lover, and he desires
　　me.
11 Come, darling, let's go out to the
　　countryside
　　and spend the night in the villages.*n*
12 We will get up early and look at the
　　vines
　　to see whether they've started to
　　　grow,
　　whether the blossoms are opening
　　and the pomegranate-trees are in
　　　bloom.
　There I will give you my love.
13 You can smell the scent of mandrakes,
　　and all the pleasant fruits are near
　　　our door.
　Darling, I have kept for you
　　the old delights and the new.

8 I wish that you were my brother,
　　that my mother had nursed you at
　　　her breast.
　Then, if I met you in the street,
　　I could kiss you and no one would
　　　mind.
2 I would take you to my mother's house,
　　where you could teach me love.
　I would give you spiced wine,
　　my pomegranate wine to drink.

3 Your left hand is under my head,
　　and your right hand caresses me.

4 Promise me, women of Jerusalem,
　　that you will not interrupt our love.

The Sixth Song

The Women
5 Who is this coming from the desert,
　　arm in arm with her lover?

The Woman
　Under the apple-tree I woke you,
　　in the place where you were born.
6 Close your heart to every love but mine;
　　hold no one in your arms but me.
　Love is as powerful as death;
　　passion is as strong as death itself.
　It bursts into flame
　　and burns like a raging fire.
7 Water cannot put it out;
　　no flood can drown it.

*l*beauty; *Hebrew unclear.*
m Some ancient translations lips and teeth; *Hebrew* lips of those who sleep.
n villages; *or* fields.

But if anyone tried to buy love with
    his wealth,
    contempt is all he would get.

The Woman's Brothers
8 We have a young sister,
    and her breasts are still small.
What will we do for her
    when a young man comes courting?
9 If she is a wall,
    we will build her a silver tower.
But if she is a gate,
    we will protect her with panels of
       cedar.

The Woman
10 I am a wall,
    and my breasts are its towers.
My lover knows that with him
    I find contentment and peace.

The Man
11 Solomon has a vineyard
    in a place called Baal Hamon.
There are farmers who rent it from him;
    each one pays a thousand silver coins.
12 Solomon is welcome to his thousand
    coins,
    and the farmers to two hundred as
      their share;
I have a vineyard of my own!

13 Let me hear your voice from the
    garden, my love;
    my companions are waiting to hear
    you speak.

The Woman
14 Come to me, my lover, like a gazelle,
    like a young stag on the mountains
    where spices grow.

THE BOOK OF

ISAIAH

INTRODUCTION

The book of *Isaiah* is named after a great prophet who lived in Jerusalem in the latter half of the eighth century B.C. This book may be divided into three principal parts:

1. *Chapters 1–39* come from a time when Judah, the southern kingdom, was threatened by a powerful neighbour, Assyria. Isaiah saw that the real threat to the life of Judah was not simply the might of Assyria, but the nation's own sin and disobedience to God, and their lack of trust in him. In vivid words and actions the prophet called the people and their leaders to a life of righteousness and justice, and warned that failure to listen to God would bring doom and destruction. Isaiah also foretold a time of world-wide peace and the coming of a descendant of David who would be the ideal king.

2. *Chapters 40–55* come from a time when many of the people of Judah were in exile in Babylon, crushed and without hope. The prophet proclaimed that God would set his people free and take them home to Jerusalem, to begin a new life. A notable theme of these chapters is that God is the Lord of history, and his plan for his people includes their mission to all nations, who will be blessed through Israel. The passages about "the Servant of the Lord" are among the best-known in the Old Testament.

3. *Chapters 56–66* are for the most part addressed to people who were back in Jerusalem, and who needed reassurance that God was going to fulfil his promises to the nation. Concern is expressed for righteousness and justice, and also for Sabbath observance, sacrifice, and prayer. A notable passage

is 61.1-2, words used by Jesus at the beginning of his ministry to express his calling.

Outline of Contents

Warnings and promises 1.1—12.6
Punishment of the nations 13.1—23.18
God's judgement of the world 24.1—27.13
Further warnings and promises 28.1—35.10
King Hezekiah of Judah and the Assyrians 36.1—39.8
Messages of promise and hope 40.1—55.13
Warnings and promises 56.1—66.24

1 This book contains the messages about Judah and Jerusalem which God revealed to Isaiah son of Amoz during the time when Uzziah, Jotham, Ahaz, and Hezekiah were kings of Judah.

God Reprimands His People

2 The LORD said, "Earth and sky, listen to what I am saying! The children I brought up have rebelled against me. ³Cattle know who owns them, and donkeys know where their master feeds them. But that is more than my people Israel know. They don't understand at all."

4 You are doomed, you sinful nation, you corrupt and evil people! Your sins drag you down! You have rejected the LORD, the holy God of Israel, and have turned your backs on him. ⁵Why do you keep on rebelling? Do you want to be punished even more? Israel, your head is already covered with wounds, and your heart and mind are sick. ⁶From head to foot there is not a healthy spot on your body. You are covered with bruises and sores and open wounds. Your wounds have not been cleaned or bandaged. No ointment has been put on them.

7 Your country has been devastated, and your cities have been burnt to the ground. While you look on, foreigners take over your land and bring everything to ruin. ⁸Jerusalem alone is left, a city under siege—as defenceless as a watchman's hut in a vineyard or a shed in a cucumber field. ⁹If the LORD Almighty had not let some of the people survive, Jerusalem would have been totally destroyed, just as Sodom and Gomorrah were.

Why do you keep on rebelling? (1.5)

10 Jerusalem, your rulers and your people are like those of Sodom and Gomorrah. Listen to what the LORD is saying to you. Pay attention to what our God is teaching you. ¹¹He says, "Do you think I want all these sacrifices you keep offering to me? I have had more than enough of the sheep you burn as sacrifices and of the fat of your fine animals. I am tired of the blood of bulls and sheep and goats. ¹²Who asked you to bring me all this when you come to worship me? Who asked you to do all this tramping about in my Temple? ¹³It's useless to bring your

1.1: 2 Kgs 15.1-7, 15.32—16.20, 18.1—20.21; 2 Chr 26.1—32.33   1.9: Gen 19.24; Rom 9.29
1.11-14: Amos 5.21-22

offerings. I am disgusted with the smell of the incense you burn. I cannot stand your New Moon Festivals, your Sabbaths, and your religious gatherings; they are all corrupted by your sins. [14] I hate your New Moon Festivals and holy days; they are a burden that I am tired of bearing.

15 "When you lift your hands in prayer,

When you lift your hands in prayer (1.15)

I will not look at you. No matter how much you pray, I will not listen, for your hands are covered with blood. [16] Wash yourselves clean. Stop all this evil that I see you doing. Yes, stop doing evil [17] and learn to do right. See that justice is done— help those who are oppressed, give orphans their rights, and defend widows."

18 The LORD says, "Now, let's settle the matter. You are stained red with sin, but I will wash you as clean as snow.[a] Although your stains are deep red, you will be as white as wool.[b] [19] If you will only obey me, you will eat the good things the land produces. [20] But if you defy me, you are doomed to die. I, the LORD, have spoken."

The Sinful City

21 The city that once was faithful is behaving like a whore! At one time it was filled with righteous men, but now only murderers remain. [22] Jerusalem, you were once like silver, but now you are worthless; you were like good wine, but now you are only water. [23] Your leaders are rebels and friends of thieves; they are always accepting gifts and bribes. They never defend orphans in court or listen when widows present their case.

24 So now, listen to what the LORD Almighty, Israel's powerful God, is saying: "I will take revenge on you, my enemies, and you will cause me no more trouble. [25] I will take action against you. I will purify you just as metal is refined, and will remove all your impurity. [26] I will give your rulers and advisers like those you had long ago. Then Jerusalem will be called the righteous, faithful city."

27 Because the LORD is righteous, he will save Jerusalem and everyone there who repents. [28] But he will crush everyone who sins and rebels against him; he will kill everyone who forsakes him.

29 You will be sorry that you ever worshipped trees and planted sacred gardens.[c] [30] You will wither like a dying oak, like a garden that no one waters. [31] Just as straw is set on fire by a spark, so powerful men will be destroyed by their own evil deeds, and no one will be able to stop the destruction.

Everlasting Peace
(Mic 4.1-3)

2 This is the message which God gave to Isaiah son of Amoz about Judah and Jerusalem:
[2] In days to come
the mountain where the Temple stands
will be the highest one of all,
towering above all the hills.
Many nations will come streaming to it,
[3]   and their people will say,
"Let us go up the hill of the LORD,[d]
to the Temple of Israel's God.
He will teach us what he wants us to do;
we will walk in the paths he has chosen.
For the LORD's teaching comes from Jerusalem;
from Zion he speaks to his people."

[4] He will settle disputes among great nations.
They will hammer their swords into ploughs
and their spears into pruning-knives.
Nations will never again go to war,
never prepare for battle again.

[a] sin, but...snow; *or* sin; do you think I will wash you as clean as snow?
[b] Although your...wool; *or* Your stains are deep red; do you think you will be as white as wool?
[c] SACRED GARDENS: *People believed that dedicating a garden to a fertility god would cause him to bless their crops.*
[d] HILL OF THE LORD: *Mount Zion, the hill in Jerusalem on which the Temple was built.*
2.4: Joel 3.10

To escape from the LORD's anger (2.19,21)

5 Now, descendants of Jacob, let us walk in the light which the LORD gives us!

Arrogance Will Be Destroyed

6 O God, you have forsaken your people, the descendants of Jacob! The land is full of magic practices from the east and from Philistia.ᵉ The people follow foreign customs. ⁷Their land is full of silver and gold, and there is no end to their treasures. Their land is full of horses, and there is no end to their chariots. ⁸Their land is full of idols, and they worship objects that they have made with their own hands.

9 Everyone will be humiliated and disgraced. Do not forgive them, LORD!

10 They will hide in caves in the rocky hills or dig holes in the ground to try to escape from the LORD's anger and to hide from his power and glory! ¹¹A day is coming when human pride will be ended and human arrogance destroyed. Then the LORD alone will be exalted. ¹²On that day the LORD Almighty will humble everyone who is powerful, everyone who is proud and conceited. ¹³He will destroy the tall cedars of Lebanon and all the oaks in the land of Bashan. ¹⁴He will level the high mountains and hills, ¹⁵every high tower, and the walls of every fortress. ¹⁶He will sink even the largest and most beautiful ships. ¹⁷⁻¹⁸Human pride will be ended, and human arrogance will be destroyed. Idols will completely disappear, and the LORD alone will be exalted on that day.

19 People will hide in caves in the rocky hills or dig holes in the ground to try to escape from the LORD's anger and to hide from his power and glory, when he comes to shake the earth. ²⁰When that day comes, they will throw away the gold and silver idols they have made, and abandon them to the moles and the bats. ²¹When the LORD comes to shake the earth, people will hide in holes and caves in the rocky hills to try to escape from his anger and to hide from his power and glory.

22 Put no more confidence in mortal men. What are they worth?

Chaos in Jerusalem

3 Now the Lord, the Almighty LORD, is about to take away from Jerusalem and Judah everything and everyone that the people depend on. He is going to take away their food and their water, ²their heroes and their soldiers, their judges and their prophets, their fortune-tellers and their statesmen, ³their military and civilian leaders, their politicians and everyone who uses magic to control events. ⁴The LORD will let the people be governed by immature boys. ⁵Everyone will take advantage of everyone else. Young people will not respect their elders, and worthless people will not respect their superiors.

6 A time will come when the members of a clan will choose one of their number

ᵉ *Probable text* The land...Philistia; *Hebrew unclear.*
2.10: Rev 6.15; 2 Thes 1.9

and say to him, "You at least have something to wear, so be our leader in this time of trouble."

7 But he will answer, "Not me! I can't help you. I haven't any food or clothes either. Don't make me your leader!"

8 Yes, Jerusalem is doomed! Judah is collapsing! Everything they say and do is against the LORD; they openly insult God himself. [9] Their prejudices will be held against them. They sin as openly as the people of Sodom did. They are doomed, and they have brought it on themselves.

10 Righteous men will be happy,[f] and things will go well for them. They will be able to enjoy what they have worked for. [11] But evil men are doomed; what they have done to others will now be done to them.

12 Moneylenders oppress my people, and their creditors cheat them.

My people, your leaders are misleading you, so that you do not know which way to turn.

The LORD Judges His People

13 The LORD is ready to state his case; he is ready to judge his people.[g] [14] The LORD is bringing the elders and leaders of his people to judgement. He makes this accusation: "You have plundered vineyards, and your houses are full of what you have taken from the poor. [15] You have no right to crush my people and take advantage of the poor. I, the Sovereign LORD Almighty, have spoken."

A Warning to the Women of Jerusalem

16 The LORD said, "Look how proud the women of Jerusalem are! They walk along with their noses in the air. They are always flirting. They take dainty little steps, and the bracelets on their ankles jingle. [17] But I will punish them—I will shave their heads and leave them bald."

18 A day is coming when the Lord will take away from the women of Jerusalem everything they are so proud of—the ornaments they wear on their ankles, on their heads, on their necks, [19] and on their wrists. He will take away their veils [20] and their hats; the magic charms they wear on their arms and at their waists; [21] the rings they wear on their fingers and in their noses; [22] all their fine robes, gowns, cloaks, and purses; [23] their revealing garments, their linen handkerchiefs, and

With their noses in the air (3.16)

the scarves and long veils they wear on their heads.

24 Instead of using perfumes, they will stink; instead of fine belts, they will wear coarse ropes; instead of having beautiful hair, they will be bald; instead of fine clothes, they will be dressed in rags; their beauty will be turned to shame!

25 The men of the city, yes, even the strongest men, will be killed in war. [26] The city gates will mourn and cry, and the city itself will be like a woman sitting on the ground, stripped naked.

4 When that time comes, seven women will grab hold of one man and say, "We can feed and clothe ourselves, but please let us say you are our husband, so that we won't have to endure the shame of being unmarried."

Jerusalem Will Be Restored

2 The time is coming when the LORD will make every plant and tree in the land

---

[f] *Probable text* Righteous men will be happy; *Hebrew* Say to the righteous.
[g] *Some ancient translations* his people; *Hebrew* the peoples.

He waited for the grapes to ripen,
but every grape was sour.
3 So now my friend says, "You people
who live in Jerusalem and Judah, judge
between my vineyard and me. ⁴Is there
anything I failed to do for it? Then why
did it produce sour grapes and not the
good grapes I expected?
5 "This is what I am going to do to
my vineyard; I will take away the hedge
round it, break down the wall that
protects it, and let wild animals eat it
and trample it down. ⁶I will let it be
overgrown with weeds. I will not prune
the vines or hoe the ground; instead I
will let briars and thorns cover it. I will
even forbid the clouds to let rain fall on
it."
⁷ Israel is the vineyard of the LORD
Almighty;
the people of Judah are the vines he
planted.
He expected them to do what was good,
but instead they committed murder.
He expected them to do what was right,
but their victims cried out for justice.

The Evil That Men Do

8 You are doomed! You buy more
houses and fields to add to those you
already have. Soon there will be nowhere
for anyone else to live, and you alone
will live in the land. ⁹I have heard the
LORD Almighty say, "All these big, fine
houses will be empty ruins. ¹⁰The grapevines growing on ten hectares of land will
yield only eight litres of wine. A hundred
and eighty litres of seed will produce only
eighteen litres of corn."

11 You are doomed! You get up early
in the morning to start drinking, and you
spend long evenings getting drunk. ¹²At
your feasts you have harps and tambourines and flutes—and wine. But you
don't understand what the LORD is doing,
¹³and so you will be carried away as
prisoners. Your leaders will starve to
death, and the common people will die
of thirst. ¹⁴The world of the dead is hungry
for them, and it opens its mouth wide.
It gulps down the nobles of Jerusalem
along with the noisy crowd of common
people.

15 Everyone will be disgraced, and all
who are proud will be humbled. ¹⁶But the
LORD Almighty shows his greatness by
doing what is right, and he reveals his
holiness by judging his people. ¹⁷In the

Dressed in rags (3.24)

grow large and beautiful. All the people
of Israel who survive will take delight and
pride in the crops that the land produces.
³Everyone who is left in Jerusalem, whom
God has chosen for survival, will be called
holy. ⁴By his power the Lord will judge
and purify the nation and wash away the
guilt of Jerusalem and the blood that has
been shed there. ⁵Then over Mount Zion
and over all who are gathered there, the
LORD will send a cloud in the daytime
and smoke and a bright flame at night.
God's glory will cover and protect the
whole city. ⁶His glory will shade the city
from the heat of the day and make it
a place of safety, sheltered from the rain
and storm.

The Song of the Vineyard

5 Listen while I sing you this song,
a song of my friend and his
vineyard:
My friend had a vineyard
on a very fertile hill.
² He dug the soil and cleared it of stones;
he planted the finest vines.
He built a tower to guard them,
dug a pit for treading the grapes.

4.5: Ex 13.21, 24.16   **5.1–2:** Mt 21.33; Mk 12.1; Lk 20.9

A very fertile hill. He dug the soil...cleared it of stones; he planted the finest vines. He

built a tower...dug a pit...He waited for the grapes to ripen, but every grape was sour (5.1-2)

ruins of the cities lambs will eat grass and young goats will find pasture. *h*

18 You are doomed! You are unable to break free from your sins. 19 You say, "Let the LORD hurry up and do what he says he will, so that we can see it. Let Israel's holy God carry out his plans; let's see what he has in mind."

20 You are doomed! You call evil good and call good evil. You turn darkness into light and light into darkness. You make what is bitter sweet, and what is sweet you make bitter.

21 You are doomed! You think you are wise, so very clever.

22 You are doomed! Heroes of the wine bottle! Brave and fearless when it comes to mixing drinks! 23 But for just a bribe you let guilty men go free, and you prevent the innocent from getting justice. 24 So now, just as straw and dry grass shrivel and burn in the fire, your roots will rot and your blossoms will dry up and blow away, because you have rejected what the LORD Almighty, Israel's holy God, has

taught us. 25 The LORD is angry with his people and has stretched out his hand to punish them. The mountains will shake, and the bodies of those who die will be left in the streets like rubbish. Yet even then the LORD's anger will not be ended, but his hand will still be stretched out to punish.

26 The LORD gives a signal to call for a distant nation. *o* He whistles for them to come from the ends of the earth. And here they come, swiftly, quickly! 27 None of them grows tired; none of them stumbles. They never doze or sleep. Not a belt is loose; not a sandal strap is broken. 28 Their arrows are sharp, and their bows are ready to shoot. Their horses' hooves are as hard as flint, and their chariot-wheels turn like a whirlwind. 29 The soldiers roar like lions that have killed an animal and are carrying it off where no one can take it away from them.

30 When that day comes, they will roar over Israel as loudly as the sea. Look at

h Verse 17 in Hebrew is unclear.   *o* Probable text a distant nation; Hebrew distant nations.

In the ruins of the cities (5.17)

this country! Darkness and distress! The light is swallowed by darkness.

God Calls Isaiah to Be a Prophet

6 In the year that King Uzziah died, I saw the Lord. He was sitting on his throne, high and exalted, and his robe filled the whole Temple. ²Round him flaming creatures were standing, each of which had six wings. Each creature covered its face with two wings, and its body with two, and used the other two for flying. ³They were calling out to each other:

"Holy, holy, holy!
The LORD Almighty is holy!
His glory fills the world."

4 The sound of their voices made the foundation of the Temple shake, and the Temple itself was filled with smoke.

5 I said, "There is no hope for me! I am doomed because every word that passes my lips is sinful, and I live among a people whose every word is sinful. And yet, with my own eyes, I have seen the King, the LORD Almighty!"

6 Then one of the creatures flew down to me, carrying a burning coal that he had taken from the altar with a pair of tongs. ⁷He touched my lips with the burning coal and said, "This has touched your lips, and now your guilt is gone, and your sins are forgiven."

8 Then I heard the Lord say, "Whom shall I send? Who will be our messenger?" I answered, "I will go! Send me!"

9 So he told me to go and give the people this message: "No matter how much you listen, you will not understand. No matter

how much you look, you will not know what is happening." ¹⁰Then he said to me, "Make the minds of these people dull, their ears deaf, and their eyes blind, so that they cannot see or hear or understand. If they did, they might turn to me and be healed."

11 I asked, "How long will it be like this, Lord?"

He answered, "Until the cities are ruined and empty—until the houses are uninhabited—until the land itself is a desolate waste. ¹²I will send the people far away and make the whole land desolate. ¹³Even if one person out of ten remains in the land, he too will be destroyed; he will be like the stump of an oak-tree that has been cut down."

(The stump represents a new beginning for God's people.)

A Message for King Ahaz

7 When King Ahaz, the son of Jotham and grandson of Uzziah, ruled Judah, war broke out. Rezin, king of Syria, and Pekah son of Remaliah, king of Israel, attacked Jerusalem, but were unable to capture it.

2 When word reached the king of Judah that the armies of Syria were already in the territory of Israel, he and all his people were so terrified that they trembled like trees shaking in the wind.

3 The LORD said to Isaiah, "Take your son Shear Jashub,ⁱ and go to meet King Ahaz. You will find him on the road where the cloth makers work, at the end of the ditch that brings water from the upper pool. ⁴Tell him to keep alert, to stay calm,

---

ⁱSHEAR JASHUB: *This name in Hebrew means "A few will come back"* (see also 10.20-22).
6.1: 2 Kgs 15.7; 2 Chr 26.23 **6.3:** Rev 4.8 **6.4:** Rev 15.8
6.9-10: Mt 13.14-15; Mk 4.12; Lk 8.10; Jn 12.40; Acts 28.26-27 **7.1:** 2 Kgs 16.5; 2 Chr 28.5-6

Heroes of the wine bottle! (5.22)

and not to be frightened or disturbed. The anger of King Rezin and his Syrians and of King Pekah is no more dangerous than the smoke from two smouldering sticks. 5 Syria, together with Israel and its king, has made a plot. 6 They intend to invade Judah, terrify the people into joining their side, and then put Tabeel's son on the throne.

7 "But I, the LORD, declare that this will never happen. 8 Why? Because Syria is no stronger than Damascus, its capital city, and Damascus is no stronger than King Rezin. As for Israel, within sixty-five years it will be too shattered to survive as a nation. 9 Israel is no stronger than Samaria, its capital city, and Samaria is no stronger than King Pekah.

"If your faith is not enduring, you will not endure."

The Sign of Immanuel

10 The LORD sent another message to Ahaz: 11 "Ask the LORD your God to give you a sign. It can be from deep in the world of the dead or from high up in heaven."

12 Ahaz answered, "I will not ask for a sign. I refuse to put the LORD to the test."

13 To that Isaiah replied, "Listen, now, descendants of King David. It's bad enough for you to wear out the patience of men—must you wear out God's patience too? 14 Well then, the Lord himself will give you a sign: a young woman x who is pregnant will have a son and will name him 'Immanuel.' j 15 By the time he is old enough to make his own decisions, people will be drinking milk and eating honey. k 16 Even before that time comes, the lands of those two kings who terrify you will be deserted.

17 "The LORD is going to bring on you, on your people, and on the whole royal family, days of trouble worse than any that have come since the kingdom of Israel separated from Judah—he is going to bring the king of Assyria.

18 "When that time comes, the LORD will whistle as a signal for the Egyptians to come like flies from the farthest branches of the Nile, and for the Assyrians to come from their land like bees. 19 They will swarm in the rugged valleys and in the caves in the rocks, and they will cover every thorn-bush and every pasture.

20 "When that time comes, the Lord will hire a barber from across the Euphrates—the emperor of Assyria!— and he will shave off your beards, and the hair on your heads and your bodies.

x YOUNG WOMAN: *The Hebrew word here translated "young woman" is not the specific term for "virgin", but refers to any young woman of marriageable age. The use of "virgin" in Mat. 1.23 reflects a Greek translation of the Old Testament, made some 500 years after Isaiah.*
j IMMANUEL: *This name in Hebrew means "God is with us."*
k MILK AND HONEY: *These foods were associated with the earlier days of Israel's history.*
7.14: Mt 1.23

21 "When that time comes, even if a farmer has been able to save only one young cow and two goats, 22 they will give so much milk that he will have all he needs. Yes, the few survivors left in the land will have milk and honey to eat.

23 "When that time comes, the fine vineyards, each with a thousand vines and each worth a thousand pieces of silver, will be overgrown with thorn-bushes and briars. 24 People will go hunting there with bows and arrows. Yes, the whole country will be full of briars and thorn-bushes. 25 All the hills where crops used to grow will be so overgrown with thorns that no one will go there. It will be a place where cattle and sheep graze."

Isaiah's Son as a Sign to the People

8 The LORD said to me, "Take a large piece of writing material and write on it in large letters: *l* 'Quick Loot, Fast Plunder.' 2 Get two reliable men, the priest Uriah and Zechariah son of Jeberechiah, to serve as witnesses."

3 Some time later my wife became pregnant. When our son was born, the LORD said to me, "Name him 'Quick-Loot-Fast-Plunder.' 4 Before the boy is old enough to say 'Mummy' and 'Daddy,' all the wealth of Damascus and all the loot of Samaria will be carried off by the king of Assyria."

The King of Assyria Is Coming

5 The LORD spoke to me again. 6 He said, "Because these people have rejected the quiet waters from the brook of Shiloah, *m* and tremble *n* before King Rezin and King Pekah, 7 I, the Lord, will bring the emperor of Assyria and all his forces to attack Judah. They will advance like the flood waters of the River Euphrates, overflowing all its banks. 8 They will sweep through Judah in a flood, rising shoulder high and covering everything."

God is with us! His outspread wings protect the land. *o*

9 Gather together in fear, you nations! Listen, you distant parts of the earth. Get ready to fight, but be afraid! Yes, get ready, but be afraid! 10 Make your plans! But they will never succeed. Talk as much as you like! But it is all useless, because God is with us.

The LORD Warns the Prophet

11 With his great power the LORD warned me not to follow the path which the people were following. He said, 12 "Do not join in the schemes of the people and do not be afraid of the things that they fear. 13 Remember that I, the LORD Almighty, am holy; I am the one you must fear. 14 Because of my awesome holiness I am like a stone that people stumble over; I am like a trap that will catch the people of the kingdoms of Judah and Israel and the people of Jerusalem. 15 Many will stumble; they will fall and be crushed. They will be caught in a trap."

Warning against Consulting the Dead

16 You, my disciples are to guard and preserve the messages that God has given me. 17 The LORD has hidden himself from his people, but I trust him and place my hope in him.

18 Here I am with the children the LORD has given me. The LORD Almighty, whose throne is on Mount Zion, has sent us as living messages to the people of Israel.

19 But people will tell you to ask for messages from fortune-tellers and mediums, who chirp and mutter. They will say, "After all, people should ask for messages from the spirits and consult the dead on behalf of the living."

20 You are to answer them, "Listen to what the LORD is teaching you! Don't listen to mediums—what they tell you will do you no good." *p*

A Time of Trouble

21 The people will wander through the land, discouraged and hungry. In their hunger and their anger they will curse their king and their God. They may look up to the sky 22 or stare at the ground, but they will see nothing but trouble and darkness, terrifying darkness into which **9** they are being driven. 1 There will be no way for them to escape from this time of trouble.

The Future King

The land of the tribes of Zebulun and

---

l large letters; *or* letters that everyone can read.
m BROOK OF SHILOAH *A stream which flowed from the large spring on the eastern side of Jerusalem.* *n* Probable text tremble; Hebrew rejoice.
o everything." God.....land; *or* everything. They will spread out over the land. God be with us!"
p Verse 20 in Hebrew is unclear.
8.12–13: 1 Pet 3.14–15   **8.14–15:** 1 Pet 2.8   **8.17:** Heb 2.13   **8.18:** Heb 2.13   **9.1:** Mt 4.15

The people who walked in darkness (9.2)

Naphtali was once disgraced, but the future will bring honour to this region, from the Mediterranean eastwards to the land on the other side of the Jordan, and even to Galilee itself, where the foreigners live.

2 The people who walked in darkness
    have seen a great light.
They lived in a land of shadows,
    but now light is shining on them.
3 You have given them great joy, *q* LORD;
    you have made them happy.
They rejoice in what you have done,
    as people rejoice when they harvest
       their corn
    or when they divide captured wealth.
4 For you have broken the yoke that
       burdened them
    and the rod that beat their shoulders.
You have defeated the nation
    that oppressed and exploited your
       people,
    just as you defeated the army of
       Midian long ago.
5 The boots of the invading army
    and all their bloodstained clothing
    will be destroyed by fire.
6 A child is born to us!
    A son is given to us!
    And he will be our ruler.
He will be called, "Wonderful *r*
       Counsellor,"
    "Mighty God," "Eternal Father,"
    "Prince of Peace."
7 His royal power will continue to grow;
    his kingdom will always be at peace.
He will rule as King David's successor,
    basing his power on right and justice,
    from now until the end of time.

The LORD Almighty is determined to do all this.

The LORD Will Punish Israel

8 The Lord has pronounced judgement on the kingdom of Israel, on the descendants of Jacob. 9 All the people of Israel, everyone who lives in the city of Samaria, will know that he has done this. Now they are proud and arrogant. They say, 10 "The brick buildings have fallen down, but we will replace them with stone buildings. The beams of sycamore wood have been cut down, but we will replace them with the finest cedar."

11 The LORD has stirred up their enemies *s* to attack them. 12 Syria on the east and Philistia on the west have opened their mouths to devour Israel. Yet even so the LORD's anger is not ended; his hand is still stretched out to punish.

13 The people of Israel have not repented; even though the LORD Almighty has punished them, they have not returned to him. 14 In a single day the LORD will punish Israel's leaders and its people; he will cut them off, head and tail. 15 The old and honourable men are the head— and the tail is the prophets whose teachings are lies! 16 Those who lead these people have misled them and totally confused them. 17 And so the Lord will not let any of the young men escape, and he will not show pity to any of the widows and orphans, because all the people are godless and wicked and everything they say is evil. Yet even so the LORD's anger will not be ended, but his hand will still be stretched out to punish.

18 The wickedness of the people burns

---

q Probable text You have given them great joy; *Hebrew* You have increased the nation.
r Wonderful; *or* Wise.   *s Probable text* their enemies; *Hebrew* the enemies of Rezin.
9.2: Mt 4.16; Lk 1.79   **9.7:** Lk 1.32–33

Like a forest fire (9.18)

like a fire that destroys thorn-bushes and thistles. It burns like a forest fire that sends up columns of smoke. ¹⁹Because the LORD Almighty is angry, his punishment burns like a fire throughout the land and destroys the people, and it is every man for himself. ²⁰Everywhere in the country people snatch and eat any bit of food they can find, but their hunger is never satisfied. They even eat their own children! ²¹The people of Manasseh and the people of Ephraim attack each other, and together they attack Judah. Yet even so the LORD's anger is not ended; his hand is still stretched out to punish.

10 You are doomed! You make unjust laws that oppress my people. ²That is how you prevent the poor from having their rights and from getting justice. That is how you take the property that belongs to widows and orphans. ³What will you do when God punishes you? What will you do when he brings disaster on you from a distant country? Where will you run to find help? Where will you hide your wealth? ⁴You will be killed in battle or dragged off as prisoners. Yet even so the LORD's anger will not be ended; his hand will still be stretched out to punish.

The Emperor of Assyria as the Instrument of God

5 The LORD said, "Assyria! I use Assyria like a club to punish those with whom I am angry. ⁶I sent Assyria to attack a godless nation, people who have made me angry. I sent them to loot and steal and trample on the people like dirt in the streets."

7 But the Assyrian emperor has his own violent plans in mind. He is determined to destroy many nations. ⁸He boasts, "Every one of my commanders is a king! ⁹I conquered the cities of Calno and Carchemish, the cities of Hamath and Arpad. I conquered Samaria and Damascus. ¹⁰I stretched out my hand to punish those kingdoms that worship idols, idols more numerous than those of Jerusalem and Samaria. ¹¹I have destroyed Samaria and all its idols, and I will do the same to Jerusalem and the images that are worshiped there."

12 But the Lord says, "When I finish what I am doing on Mount Zion and in Jerusalem, I will punish the emperor of Assyria for all his boasting and all his pride."

13 The emperor of Assyria boasts, "I have done it all myself. I am strong and wise and clever. I wiped out the boundaries between nations and took the supplies they had stored. Like a bull I have trampled on the people who live there. ¹⁴The nations of the world were like a bird's nest, and I gathered their wealth as easily as gathering eggs. Not a wing fluttered to scare me off; no beak opened to scream at me!"

15 But the LORD says, "Can an axe claim to be greater than the man who uses it? Is a saw more important than the man who saws with it? A club doesn't lift up a man; a man lifts up a club."

16 The LORD Almighty is going to send disease to punish those who are now well-fed. In their bodies there will be a fire that burns and burns. ¹⁷God, the light of Israel, will become a fire. Israel's holy God will become a flame, which in a single day will burn up everything, even the thorns and thistles. ¹⁸The rich forests and farmlands will be totally destroyed, in the same way that a fatal sickness destroys a man. ¹⁹There will be so few trees left that even a child will be able to count them.

A Few Will Come Back

20 A time is coming when the people

10.5–34: Is 14.24–27; Nah 1.1–3.19; Zeph 2.13–15

of Israel who have survived will no longer rely on the nation that almost destroyed them. They will truly put their trust in the LORD, Israel's holy God. 21 A few of the people of Israel will come back to their mighty God. 22 Even though now there are as many people of Israel as there are grains of sand by the sea, only a few will come back. Destruction is in store for the people, and it is fully deserved. 23 Yes, throughout the whole country the Sovereign LORD Almighty will bring destruction, as he said he would.

The LORD Will Punish Assyria

24 The Sovereign LORD Almighty says to his people who live in Zion, "Do not be afraid of the Assyrians, even though they oppress you as the Egyptians used to do. 25 In only a little while I will finish punishing you, and then I will destroy them. 26 I, the LORD Almighty, will beat them with my whip as I beat the people of Midian at the Rock of Oreb. I will punish Assyria as I punished Egypt. 27 When that time comes, I will free you from the power of Assyria, and their yoke will no longer be a burden on your shoulders." *s*

The Invader Attacks

28 The enemy army has captured the city of Ai! *t* They have passed through Migron! They left their supplies at Michmash! 29 They have crossed the pass and are spending the night at Geba! The people in the town of Ramah are terrified, and the people in King Saul's town of Gibeah have run away. 30 Shout, people of Gallim! Listen, people of Laishah! Answer, people of Anathoth! 31 The people of Madmenah and Gebim are running for their lives. 32 Today the enemy are in the town of Nob, and there they are shaking their fists at Mount Zion, at the city of Jerusalem.

33 The LORD Almighty will bring them crashing down like branches cut off a tree. The proudest and highest of them will be cut down and humiliated. 34 The LORD will cut them down as trees in the heart of the forest are cut down with an axe, as even the finest trees of Lebanon fall!

The Peaceful Kingdom

11 The royal line of David is like a tree that has been cut down; but just as new branches sprout from a stump, so a new king will arise from among David's descendants.
2 The spirit of the LORD will give him wisdom,
    and the knowledge and skill to rule his people.
He will know the LORD's will and have reverence for him,
3   and find pleasure in obeying him.
He will not judge by appearance or hearsay;
4   he will judge the poor fairly
    and defend the rights of the helpless.
At his command the people will be punished,
    and evil persons will die.
5 He will rule his people with justice and integrity.

6 Wolves and sheep will live together in peace,
    and leopards will lie down with young goats.
Calves and lion cubs will feed *u* together,
    and little children will take care of them.
7 Cows and bears will eat together,
    and their calves and cubs will lie down in peace.
Lions will eat straw as cattle do.
8 Even a baby will not be harmed
    if it plays near a poisonous snake.
9 On Zion, God's sacred hill,
    there will be nothing harmful or evil.
The land will be as full of knowledge of the LORD
    as the seas are full of water.

The Exiled People Will Return

10 A day is coming when the new king from the royal line of David will be a symbol to the nations. They will gather in his royal city and give him honour. 11 When that day comes, the Lord will once again use his power and bring back home those of his people who are left in Assyria and Egypt, in the lands of Pathros, Sudan, Elam, Babylonia, and Hamath, and in the coastlands and on the islands of the sea. 12 The LORD will

---

s Hebrew has three additional words, the meaning of which is unclear.
t Ai: This and the other places mentioned in verses 28–32 were located near Jerusalem, along the way by which an invader would come to attack from the north.
u Some ancient translations will feed; Hebrew and well-fed cattle.
10.22–23: Rom 9.27   **11.1:** Rev 5.5, 22.16   **11.4:** 2 Thes 2.8   **11.5:** Eph 6.14
11.6–9: Is 65.25   **11.9:** Hab 2.14   **11.10:** Rom 15.12

And little children will take care of them (11.6)

raise a signal flag to show the nations that he is gathering together again the scattered people of Israel and Judah and bringing them back from the four corners of the earth. ¹³ The kingdom of Israel will not be jealous of Judah any more, and Judah will not be the enemy of Israel. ¹⁴ Together they will attack the Philistines on the west and plunder the people who live to the east. They will conquer the people of Edom and Moab, and the people of Ammon will obey them. ¹⁵ The LORD will dry up the Gulf of Suez, and he will bring a hot wind to dry up the Euphrates, leaving only seven tiny streams, so that anyone will be able to walk across. ¹⁶ There will be a highway out of Assyria for those of his people Israel who have survived there, just as there was for their ancestors when they left Egypt.

Hymn of Thanksgiving

12 A day is coming when people will sing,
"I praise you, LORD! You were angry with me,
  but now you comfort me and are angry no longer.
² God is my saviour;
  I will trust him and not be afraid.
The LORD gives me power and strength;
  he is my saviour.
³ As fresh water brings joy to the thirsty,
  so God's people rejoice when he saves them."

4 A day is coming when people will sing,
"Give thanks to the LORD! Call for him to help you!

Tell all the nations what he has done!
  Tell them how great he is!
⁵ Sing to the LORD because of the great things he has done.
  Let the whole world hear the news.
⁶ Let everyone who lives in Zion shout and sing!
  Israel's holy God is great,
  and he lives among his people."

Tell them how great he is! (12.4)

11.15: Rev 16.12   **12.2:** Ex 15.2; Ps 118.14

God Will Punish Babylon

13 This is a message about Babylon, which Isaiah son of Amoz received from God.

2 On the top of a barren hill raise the battle flag! Shout to the soldiers and raise your arm as the signal for them to attack the gates of the proud city. ³The LORD has called out his proud and confident soldiers to fight a holy war and punish those he is angry with.

4 Listen to the noise on the mountains— the sound of a great crowd of people, the sound of nations and kingdoms gathering. The LORD of Armies is preparing his troops for battle. ⁵They are coming from far-off countries at the ends of the earth. In his anger the LORD is coming to devastate the whole country.

6 Howl in pain! The day of the LORD is near, the day when the Almighty brings destruction. ⁷Everyone's hands will hang limp, and everyone's courage will fail. ⁸They will all be terrified and overcome with pain, like the pain of a woman in labour. They will look at each other in fear, and their faces will burn with shame. ⁹The day of the LORD is coming—that cruel day of his fierce anger and fury. The earth will be made a wilderness, and every sinner will be destroyed. ¹⁰Every star and every constellation will stop shining, the sun will be dark when it rises, and the moon will give no light.

11 The LORD says, "I will bring disaster on the earth and punish all wicked people for their sins. I will humble everyone who is proud and punish everyone who is arrogant and cruel. ¹²Those who survive will be scarcer than gold. ¹³I will make the heavens tremble, and the earth will be shaken out of its place on that day when I, the LORD Almighty, show my anger.

14 "The foreigners living in Babylon will run away to their own countries, scattering like deer escaping from hunters, like sheep without a shepherd. ¹⁵Anyone who is caught will be stabbed to death. ¹⁶While they look on helplessly, their babies will be battered to death, their houses will be looted, and their wives will be raped."

17 The LORD says, "I am stirring up the Medes[v] to attack Babylon. They care nothing for silver and are not tempted by gold. ¹⁸With their bows and arrows they will kill the young men. They will show no mercy to babies and take no pity on children. ¹⁹Babylonia is the most beautiful kingdom of all; it is the pride of its people. But I, the LORD, will overthrow Babylon as I did Sodom and Gomorrah! ²⁰No one will ever live there again. No wandering Arab will ever pitch his tent there, and no shepherd will ever pasture his flock there. ²¹It will be a place where desert animals live and where owls build their nests. Ostriches will live there, and wild goats will prance through the ruins. ²²The towers and palaces will echo with the cries of hyenas and jackals. Babylon's time has come! Her days are almost over."

The Return from Exile

14 The LORD will once again be merciful to his people Israel and choose them as his own. He will let them live in their own land again, and foreigners will come and live there with them. ²Many nations will help the people of Israel to return to the land which the LORD gave them, and there the nations will serve Israel as slaves. Those who once captured Israel will now be captured by Israel, and the people of Israel will rule over those who once oppressed them.

The King of Babylonia in the World of the Dead

3 The LORD will give the people of Israel relief from their pain and suffering, and from the hard work they were forced to do. ⁴When he does this, they are to mock the king of Babylonia and say:

"The cruel king has fallen! He will never oppress anyone again! ⁵The LORD has ended the power of the evil rulers ⁶who angrily oppressed the peoples and never stopped persecuting the nations they had conquered. ⁷Now at last the whole world enjoys rest and peace, and everyone sings for joy. ⁸The cypress-trees and the cedars of Lebanon rejoice over the fallen king, because there is no one to cut them down, now that he is gone!

9 "The world of the dead is getting ready to welcome the king of Babylonia. The ghosts of those who were powerful on earth are stirring about. The ghosts of kings are rising from their thrones.

ᵛMEDES: *People of a nation north-east of Babylonia, which became part of the Persian empire.*
13.1–14.23: Is 47.1–15; Jer 50.1–51.64　　**13.6:** Joel 1.15
13.10: Ezek 32.7; Mt 24.29; Mk 13.24–25; Lk 21.25; Rev 6.12–13　　**13.19:** Gen 19.24
13.21: Is 34.14; Zeph 2.14; Rev 18.2

The people of Moab wail in grief (15.2)

10 They all call out to him, 'Now you are as weak as we are! You are one of us! 11 You used to be honoured with the music of harps, but now here you are in the world of the dead. You lie on a bed of maggots and are covered with a blanket of worms.'

12 "King of Babylonia, bright morning star, you have fallen from heaven! In the past you conquered nations, but now you have been thrown to the ground. 13 You were determined to climb up to heaven and to place your throne above the highest stars. You thought you would sit like a king on that mountain in the north where the gods assemble. 14 You said you would climb to the tops of the clouds and be like the Almighty. 15 But instead, you have been brought down to the deepest part of the world of the dead.

16 "The dead will stare and gape at you. They will ask, 'Is this the man who shook the earth and made kingdoms tremble? 17 Is this the man who destroyed cities and turned the world into a desert? Is this the man who never freed his prisoners or let them go home?' 18 All the kings of the earth lie in their magnificent tombs, 19 but you have no tomb, and your corpse is thrown out to rot. It is covered by the bodies of soldiers killed in battle, thrown with them into a rocky pit, and trampled down. 20 Because you ruined your country and killed your own people, you will not be buried like other kings. None of your evil family will survive. 21 Let the slaughter begin! The sons of this king will die because of their ancestors' sins. None of them will ever rule the earth or cover it with cities."

God Will Destroy Babylon

22 The LORD Almighty says, "I will attack Babylon and bring it to ruin. I will leave nothing—no children, no survivors at all. I, the LORD, have spoken. 23 I will turn Babylon into a marsh, and owls will live there. I will sweep Babylon with a broom that will sweep everything away. I, the LORD Almighty, have spoken."

God Will Destroy the Assyrians

24 The LORD Almighty has sworn an oath: "What I have planned will happen.

14.12: Rev 8.10, 9.1   14.13–15: Mt 11.23; Lk 10.15
14.24–27: Is 10.5–34; Nah 1.1–3.19; Zeph 2.13–15

Trying to escape with all their possessions (15.7)

What I have determined to do will be done. 25 I will destroy the Assyrians in my land of Israel and trample upon them on my mountains. I will free my people from the Assyrian yoke and from the burdens they have had to bear. 26 This is my plan for the world, and my arm is stretched out to punish the nations." 27 The LORD Almighty is determined to do this; he has stretched out his arm to punish, and no one can stop him.

God Will Destroy the Philistines

28 This is a message that was proclaimed in the year that King Ahaz died.

29 People of Philistia, the rod that beat you is broken, but you have no reason to be glad. When one snake dies, a worse one comes in its place. A snake's egg hatches a flying dragon. 30 The LORD will be a shepherd to the poor of his people and will let them live in safety. But he will send a terrible famine on you Philistines, and it will not leave any of you alive.

31 Howl and cry for help, all you Philistine cities! Be terrified, all of you! A cloud of dust is coming from the north— it is an army with no cowards in its ranks.

32 How shall we answer the messengers that come to us from Philistia? We will tell them that the LORD has established Zion and that his suffering people will find safety there.

God Will Destroy Moab

15 This is a message about Moab.

The cities of Ar and Kir are destroyed in a single night, and silence covers the land of Moab. 2 The people of Dibon[w] climb the hill to weep at the shrine. The people of Moab wail in grief over the cities of Nebo and Medeba; they have shaved their heads and their beards in grief. 3 The people in the streets are dressed in sackcloth; in the city squares and on the house-tops people mourn and cry. 4 The people of Heshbon and Elealeh cry out, and their cry can be heard as far away as Jahaz. Even the soldiers tremble; their courage is gone. 5 My heart cries out for Moab! The people have fled to the town of Zoar, and to Eglath Shelishiyah. Some climb the road to Luhith, weeping as they go; some escape to Horonaim, grieving loudly. 6 The brook of Nimrim is dry, the grass beside it has withered, and nothing green is left. 7 The people go across the Valley of Willows, trying to escape with all their possessions. 8 Everywhere at Moab's borders the sound of crying is heard. It is heard at the towns of Eglaim and Beerelim. 9 At the town of Dibon the river is red with blood, and God has something even worse in store for the people there. Yes, there will be a bloody slaughter of everyone left in Moab.

w *Probable text* people of Dibon; *Hebrew* people and Dibon.
14.28: 2 Kgs 16.20; 2 Chr 28.27
14.29–31: Jer 47.1–7; Ezek 25.15–17; Joel 3.4–8; Amos 1.6–8; Zeph 2.4–7; Zech 9.5–7
15.1–16.14: Is 25.10–12; Jer 48.1–47; Ezek 25.8–11; Amos 2.1–3; Zeph 2.8–11

Moab's Hopeless Situation

16 From the city of Sela in the desert the people of Moab send a lamb as a present to the one who rules in Jerusalem. ²They wait on the banks of the River Arnon and move aimlessly to and fro, like birds driven from their nest.

3 They say to the people of Judah, "Tell us what to do. Protect us like a tree that casts a cool shadow in the heat of noon, and let us rest in your shade. We are refugees; hide us where no one can find us. ⁴Let us stay in your land. Protect us from those who want to destroy us."

(Oppression and destruction will end, and those who are devastating the country will be gone. ⁵Then one of David's descendants will be king, and he will rule the people with faithfulness and love. He will be quick to do what is right, and he will see that justice is done.)

6 The people of Judah say, "We have heard how proud the people of Moab are. We know that they are arrogant and conceited, but their boasts are empty."

7 The people of Moab will weep because of the troubles they suffer. They will all weep when they remember the fine food they used to eat in the city of Kir Heres. They will be driven to despair. ⁸The farms near Heshbon and the vineyards of Sibmah are destroyed—those vineyards whose wine used to make the rulers of the nations drunk. At one time the vines spread as far as the city of Jazer, and eastwards into the desert, and westwards to the other side of the Dead Sea. ⁹Now I weep for Sibmah's vines as I weep for Jazer. My tears fall for Heshbon and Elealeh, because there is no harvest to make the people glad. ¹⁰No one is happy now in the fertile fields. No one shouts or sings in the vineyards. No one tramples grapes to make wine; the shouts of joy are ended.ʸ ¹¹I groan with sadness for Moab, with grief for Kir Heres. ¹²The people of Moab wear themselves out going to their mountain shrines and to their temples to pray, but it will do them no good.

13 That is the message the LORD gave earlier about Moab. ¹⁴And now the LORD says, "In exactly three years Moab's great wealth will disappear. Of its many people, only a few will survive, and they will be weak."

God Will Punish Syria and Israel

17 The LORD said, "Damascus will not be a city any longer; it will be only a pile of ruins. ²The cities of Syria will be deserted for ever.ᶻ They will be a pasture for sheep and cattle, and no one will drive them away. ³Israel will be defenceless, and Damascus will lose its independence. Those Syrians who survive will be in disgrace like the people of Israel. I, the LORD Almighty, have spoken."

4 The LORD said, "A day is coming when Israel's greatness will come to an end, and its wealth will be replaced by poverty. ⁵Israel will be like a field where the corn has been cut and harvested, as desolate as a field in the valley of Rephaim when it has been picked bare. ⁶Only a few

Israel will be like an olive-tree (17.6)

people will survive, and Israel will be like an olive-tree from which all the olives have been picked except two or three at the very top, or a few that are left on the lower branches. I, the LORD God of Israel, have spoken."

7 When that day comes, people will turn for help to their Creator, the holy God of Israel. ⁸They will no longer rely on the altars they made with their own hands, or trust in their own handiwork— symbols of the goddess Asherah and altars for burning incense.

9 When that day comes, well-defended cities will be deserted and left in ruins like the cities that the Hivites and the

---

ʸ*One ancient translation* the shouts of joy are ended; *Hebrew* I have ended the shouts of joy.
ᶻ*One ancient translation* The cities...for ever; *Hebrew* The cities of Aroer are deserted.
17.1–3: Jer 49.23–27; Amos 1.3–5; Zech 9.1

Amorites[a] abandoned as they fled from the people of Israel.

10 Israel, you have forgotten the God who rescues you and who protects you like a mighty rock. Instead, you plant sacred gardens[b] in order to worship a foreign god. 11 But even if they sprouted and blossomed the very morning you planted them, there would still be no harvest. There would be only trouble and incurable pain.

Enemy Nations Are Defeated

12 Powerful nations are in commotion with a sound like the roar of the sea, like the crashing of huge waves. 13 The nations advance like rushing waves, but God reprimands them and they retreat, driven away like dust on a hillside, like straw in a whirlwind. 14 In the evening they cause terror, but by morning they are gone. That is the fate of everyone who plunders our land.

God Will Punish Sudan

18 Beyond the rivers of Sudan there is a land where the sound of wings is heard. 2 From that land ambassadors come down the Nile in boats made of reeds. Go back home, swift messengers! Take a message back to your land divided by rivers, to your strong and powerful nation, to your tall and smooth-skinned people, who are feared all over the world.

3 Listen, everyone who lives on earth! Look for a signal flag to be raised on the tops of the mountains! Listen for the blowing of the bugle! 4 The LORD said to me, "I will look down from heaven as quietly as the dew forms in the warm nights of harvest time, as serenely as the sun shines in the heat of the day. 5 Before the grapes are gathered, when the blossoms have all fallen and the grapes are ripening, the enemy will destroy the Sudanese as easily as a knife cuts branches from a vine. 6 The corpses of their soldiers will be left exposed to the birds and the wild animals. In summer the birds will feed on them, and in winter, the animals."

7 A time is coming when the LORD Almighty will receive offerings from this land divided by rivers, this strong and powerful nation, this tall and smooth-skinned people, who are feared all over the world. They will come to Mount Zion, where the LORD Almighty is worshipped.

God Will Punish Egypt

19 This is a message about Egypt.

The LORD is coming to Egypt, riding swiftly on a cloud. The Egyptian idols tremble before him, and the people of Egypt lose their courage. 2 The LORD says, "I will stir up civil war in Egypt and turn brother against brother and neighbour against neighbour. Rival cities will fight each other, and rival kings will struggle for power. 3 I am going to frustrate the plans of the Egyptians and destroy their morale. They will ask their idols to help them, and they will go and consult mediums and ask the spirits of the dead for advice. 4 I will hand the Egyptians over to a tyrant, to a cruel king who will rule them. I, the LORD Almighty, have spoken."

5 The water will be low in the Nile, and the river will gradually dry up. 6 The channels of the river will stink as they slowly go dry. Reeds and rushes will wither, 7 and all the crops sown along the banks of the Nile will dry up and be blown away. 8 Everyone who earns his living by fishing in the Nile will groan and cry; their hooks and their nets will be useless. 9 Those who make linen cloth will be in despair; 10 weavers and skilled workmen will be broken and depressed.

11 The leaders of the city of Zoan are fools! Egypt's wisest men give stupid advice! How dare they tell the king that they are successors to the ancient scholars and kings? 12 King of Egypt, where are those clever advisers of yours? Perhaps they can tell you what plans the LORD Almighty has for Egypt. 13 The leaders of Zoan and Memphis are fools. They were supposed to lead the nation, but they have misled it. 14 The LORD has made them give confusing advice. As a result, Egypt does everything wrong and staggers like a drunken man slipping on his own vomit. 15 No one in Egypt, rich or poor, important or unknown, can offer help.

Egypt Will Worship the LORD

16 A time is coming when the people of Egypt will be as timid as women. They will tremble in terror when they see that the LORD Almighty has stretched out his hand to punish them. 17 The people of Egypt will be terrified of Judah every time they are reminded of the fate that the

---

[a] *One ancient translation* the Hivites and the Amorites; *Hebrew* woodland and hill-country.

[b] SACRED GARDENS: *See 1.29.*

18.1-7: Zeph 2.12   **19.1-25:** Jer 46.2-26; Ezek 29.1-32.32

Their hooks and their nets will be useless (19.8)

LORD Almighty has prepared for them.

18 When that time comes, the Hebrew language will be spoken in five Egyptian cities. The people there will take their oaths in the name of the LORD Almighty. One of the cities will be called, "City of the Sun."

19 When that time comes, there will be an altar to the LORD in the land of Egypt and a stone pillar dedicated to him at the Egyptian border. 20 They will be symbols of the LORD Almighty's presence in Egypt. When the people there are oppressed and call out to the LORD for help, he will send someone to rescue them. 21 The LORD will reveal himself to the Egyptian people, and then they will acknowledge and worship him, and bring him sacrifices and offerings. They will make solemn promises to him and do what they promise. 22 The LORD will punish the Egyptians, but then he will heal them. They will turn to him, and he will hear their prayers and heal them.

23 When that time comes, there will be a highway between Egypt and Assyria. The people of those two countries will travel to and fro between them, and the two nations will worship together. 24 When that time comes, Israel will rank with Egypt and Assyria, and these three nations will be a blessing to all the world. 25 The LORD Almighty will bless them and say, "I will bless you, Egypt, my people; you, Assyria, whom I created; and you, Israel, my chosen people."

The Sign of the Naked Prophet

20 Under the orders of Sargon, emperor of Assyria, the commander-in-chief of the Assyrian army attacked the Philistine city of Ashdod. 2 Three years earlier the LORD had told Isaiah son of Amoz to take off his sandals and the sackcloth he was wearing. He obeyed and went about naked and barefoot. 3 When Ashdod was captured, the LORD said, "My servant Isaiah has been going about naked and barefoot for three years. This is a sign of what will happen to Egypt and Sudan. 4 The emperor of Assyria will lead away naked the prisoners he captures from those two countries. Young and old, they will walk barefoot and naked, with their buttocks exposed, bringing shame on Egypt. 5 Those who have put their trust in Sudan and have boasted about Egypt will be disillusioned, their hopes shattered. 6 When that time comes, the people who live along the coast of Philistia will say, 'Look at what has happened to the people we relied on to protect us from the emperor of Assyria! How will we ever survive?'"

A Vision of the Fall of Babylon

21 This is a message about Babylonia. Like a whirlwind sweeping across the desert, disaster will come from a terrifying land. 2 I have seen a vision of cruel events, a vision of betrayal and destruction.

Army of Elam, attack! Army of Media, lay siege to the cities! God will put an end to the suffering which Babylon has caused.

3 What I saw and heard in the vision has filled me with terror and pain, pain like that of a woman in labour. 4 My head is spinning, and I am trembling with fear. I had been longing for evening to come,

but it has brought me nothing but terror.

5 In the vision a banquet is ready; rugs are spread for the guests to sit on. They are eating and drinking. Suddenly the command rings out: "Officers! Prepare your shields!"

6 Then the Lord said to me, "Go and post a sentry, and tell him to report what he sees. 7 If he sees men coming on horseback, two by two, and men riding on donkeys and camels, he is to observe them carefully."

8 The sentry calls out, "Sir, I have been standing guard at my post day and night."

9 Suddenly, here they come! Men on horseback, two by two. The sentry gives the news, "Babylon has fallen! All the idols they worshipped lie shattered on the ground."

10 My people Israel, you have been threshed like wheat, but now I have announced to you the good news that I have heard from the LORD Almighty, the God of Israel.

A Message about Edom

11 This is a message about Edom.

Someone calls to me from Edom, "Sentry, how soon will the night be over? Tell me how soon it will end."

12 I answer, "Morning is coming, but night will come again. If you want to ask again, come back and ask."

A Message about Arabia

13 This is a message about Arabia.

You people of Dedan, whose caravans camp in the barren country of Arabia, 14 give water to the thirsty people who come to you. You people of the land of Tema, give food to the refugees. 15 People are fleeing to escape from swords that are ready to kill them, from bows that are ready to shoot, from all the dangers of war.

16 Then the Lord said to me, "In exactly one year the greatness of the tribes of Kedar will be at an end. 17 The bowmen are the bravest men of Kedar, but few of them will be left. I, the LORD God of Israel, have spoken."

A Message about Jerusalem

22 This is a message about the Valley of Vision.

What is happening? Why are all the people of the city celebrating on the roofs of the houses? 2 The whole city is in an uproar, filled with noise and excitement.

21.9: Rev 14.8, 18.2   **22.13:** 1 Cor 15.32

Your men who died in this war did not die fighting. 3 All your leaders ran away and were captured before they shot a single arrow. 4 Now leave me alone to weep bitterly over all those of my people who have died. Don't try to comfort me. 5 This is a time of panic, defeat, and confusion in the Valley of Vision, and the Sovereign LORD Almighty has sent it on us. The walls of our city have been battered down, and cries for help have echoed among the hills.

6 The soldiers from the land of Elam came riding on horseback, armed with bows and arrows. Soldiers from the land of Kir had their shields ready. 7 The fertile valleys of Judah were filled with chariots; soldiers on horseback stood in front of Jerusalem's gates. 8 All Judah's defences crumbled.

When that happened, you brought weapons out of the arsenal. 9-10 You found the places where the walls of Jerusalem needed repair. You inspected all the houses in Jerusalem and tore some of them down to get stones to repair the city walls. In order to store water, 11 you built a reservoir inside the city to hold the water flowing down from the old pool. But you paid no attention to God, who planned all this long ago and who caused it to happen.

12 The Sovereign LORD Almighty was calling you then to weep and mourn, to shave your heads and wear sackcloth. 13 Instead, you laughed and celebrated. You killed sheep and cattle to eat, and you drank wine. You said, "We might as well eat and drink! Tomorrow we'll be dead."

14 The Sovereign LORD Almighty himself spoke to me and said, "This evil will never be forgiven them as long as they live. I, the Sovereign LORD Almighty, have spoken."

A Warning to Shebna

15 The Sovereign LORD Almighty told me to go to Shebna, the manager of the royal household, and say to him, 16 "Who do you think you are? What right have you to carve a tomb for yourself out of the rocky hillside? 17 You may be important, but the LORD will pick you up and throw you away. 18 He will pick you up like a ball and throw you into a much larger country. You will die there beside the chariots you were so proud of. You are a disgrace to your master's household.

19 The LORD will remove you from office and bring you down from your high position."

20 The LORD said to Shebna, "When that happens, I will send for my servant Eliakim son of Hilkiah. 21 I will put your official robe and belt on him and give him all the authority you have had. He will be like a father to the people of Jerusalem and Judah. 22 I will give him complete authority under the king, the descendant of David. He will have the keys of office; what he opens, no one will shut, and what he shuts, no one will open. 23 I will fasten him firmly in place like a peg, and he will be a source of honour to his whole family.

24 "But all his relatives and dependants will become a burden to him. They will hang on him like pots and bowls hanging from a peg! 25 When that happens, the peg that was firmly fastened will work loose and fall. And that will be the end of everything that was hanging on it." The LORD has spoken.

A Message about Phoenicia

23 This is a message about Tyre.

Howl with grief, you sailors out on the ocean! Your home port of Tyre has been destroyed; its houses and its harbour are in ruins. As your ships return from Cyprus, you learn the news. 2 Wail, you merchants of Sidon! You sent men 3 across the sea to buy and sell the corn that grew in Egypt and to do business with all the nations.

4 City of Sidon, you are disgraced! The sea and the great ocean depths disown you and say, "I never had any children. I never brought up sons or daughters."

5 Even the Egyptians will be shocked and dismayed when they learn that Tyre has been destroyed.

6 Howl with grief, you people of Phoenicia! Try to escape to Spain! 7 Can this be the joyful city of Tyre, founded so long ago? Is this the city that sent settlers across the sea to establish colonies? 8 Who was it that planned to bring all this on Tyre, that imperial city, whose merchant princes were the most honoured men on earth? 9 The LORD Almighty planned it. He planned it in order to put an end to their pride in what they had done and to humiliate their honoured men.

10 Go and farm the land, you people in the colonies in Spain! There is no one to protect you any more. c 11 The LORD has stretched out his hand over the sea and overthrown kingdoms. He has ordered the Phoenician centres of commerce to be destroyed. 12 City of Sidon, your happiness has ended, and your people are oppressed. Even if they escape to Cyprus, they will still not be safe.

13 (It was the Babylonians, not the Assyrians, who let the wild animals overrun Tyre. It was the Babylonians who put up siege-towers, tore down the fortifications of Tyre, and left the city in ruins. d)

14 Howl with grief, you sailors out on the ocean! The city you relied on has been destroyed.

15 A time is coming when Tyre will be forgotten for seventy years, the lifetime of a king. When those years are over, Tyre will be like the prostitute in the song:

16 Take your harp, go round the town,
     you poor forgotten whore!
Play and sing your songs again
     to bring men back once more.

17 When the seventy years are over, the LORD will let Tyre go back to her old trade, and she will hire herself out to all the kingdoms of the world. 18 The money she earns by commerce will be dedicated to the LORD. She will not store it away, but those who worship the LORD will use her money to buy the food and the clothing they need.

The LORD Will Punish the Earth

24 The LORD is going to devastate the earth and leave it desolate. He will twist the earth's surface and scatter its people. 2 Everyone will meet the same fate—the priests and the people, slaves and masters, buyers and sellers, lenders and borrowers, rich and poor. 3 The earth will lie shattered and ruined. The LORD has spoken and it will be done.

4 The earth dries up and withers; the whole world grows weak; both earth and sky decay. 5 The people have defiled the earth by breaking God's laws and by violating the covenant he made to last for ever. 6 So God has pronounced a curse on the earth. Its people are paying for what they have done. Fewer and fewer remain alive. 7 The grapevines wither, and wine is becoming scarce. Everyone who

---

c Verse 10 in Hebrew is unclear.   d Verse 13 in Hebrew is unclear.
22.22: Rev 3.7
23.1–18: Ezek 26.1–28.19; Joel 3.4–8; Amos 1.9–10; Zech 9.1–4; Mt 11.21–22; Lk 10.13–14

was once happy is now sad, 8 and the joyful music of their harps and drums has ceased. 9 There is no more happy singing over wine; no one enjoys its taste any more. 10 In the city everything is in chaos, and people lock themselves in their houses for safety. 11 People shout in the streets because there is no more wine. Happiness is gone for ever; it has been banished from the land. 12 The city is in ruins, and its gates have been broken down. 13 This is what will happen in every nation all over the world. It will be like the end of harvest, when the olives have been beaten off every tree and the last grapes picked from the vines.

14 Those who survive will sing for joy. Those in the west will tell how great the LORD is, 15 and those in the east will praise him. The people who live along the sea will praise the LORD, the God of Israel. 16 From the most distant parts of the world we will hear songs in praise of Israel, the righteous nation.

But there is no hope for me! I am wasting away! Traitors continue to betray, and their treachery grows worse and worse. 17 Listen to me, everyone! There are terrors, pits, and traps waiting for you. 18 Anyone who tries to escape from the terror will fall into a pit, and anyone who escapes from the pit will be caught in a trap. Torrents of rain will pour from the sky, and earth's foundations will shake. 19 The earth will crack and shatter and split open. 20 The earth itself will stagger like a drunken man and sway like a hut in a storm. The world is weighed down by its sins; it will collapse and never rise again.

21 A time is coming when the LORD will punish the powers above and the rulers of the earth. 22 God will crowd kings together like prisoners in a pit. He will shut them in prison until the time of their punishment comes. 23 The moon will grow dark, and the sun will no longer shine, for the LORD Almighty will be king. He will rule in Jerusalem on Mount Zion, and the leaders of the people will see his glory.

A Hymn of Praise

25 LORD, you are my God;
  I will honour you and praise your
    name.
You have done amazing things;
  you have faithfully carried out
    the plans you made long ago.

Kings...like prisoners in a pit (24.22)

2 You have turned cities into ruins
  and destroyed their fortifications.
The palaces which our enemies built
  are gone for ever.
3 The people of powerful nations will
    praise you;
  you will be feared in the cities of cruel
    nations.
4 The poor and the helpless have fled to
    you
  and have been safe in times of trouble.
You give them shelter from storms
  and shade from the burning heat.
Cruel men attack like a winter storm, [e]
5   like drought in a dry land.
But you, LORD, have silenced our
    enemies;
  you silence the shouts of cruel men,
  as a cloud cools a hot day.

God Prepares a Banquet

6 Here on Mount Zion the LORD Almighty will prepare a banquet for all the nations of the world—a banquet of the richest food and the finest wine. 7 Here he will suddenly remove the cloud of sorrow that has been hanging over all the nations. 8 The Sovereign LORD will destroy death for ever! He will wipe away the tears from everyone's eyes and take away the disgrace his people have suffered throughout the world. The LORD himself has spoken!

9 When it happens, everyone will say, "He is our God! We have put our trust in him, and he has rescued us. He is the LORD! We have put our trust in him, and

e *Probable text* winter storm; *Hebrew* storm against a wall.
25.8: 1 Cor 15.54; Rev 7.17, 21.4

now we are happy and joyful because he
has saved us."

God Will Punish Moab

10 The LORD will protect Mount Zion,
but the people of Moab will be trampled
down, just as straw is trampled in manure.
[11] They will stretch out their hands as if
they were trying to swim, but God will
humiliate them, and their hands will sink
helplessly. [12] He will destroy the fortresses
of Moab with their high walls and bring
them tumbling down into the dust.

God Will Give His People Victory

26 A day is coming when the people
will sing this song in the land of
Judah:
　　Our city is strong!
　　God himself defends its walls!
[2] Open the city gates
　　and let the faithful nation enter,
　　the nation whose people do what is
　　　right.
[3] You, LORD, give perfect peace
　　to those who keep their purpose firm
　　and put their trust in you.
[4] Trust in the LORD for ever;
　　he will always protect us.
[5] He has humbled those who were proud;
　　he destroyed the strong city they lived
　　　in,
　　and sent its walls crashing into the
　　　dust.
[6] Those who were oppressed walk over
　　　it now
　　and trample it under their feet.

[7] LORD, you make the path smooth for
　　　good men;
　　the road they travel is level.
[8] We follow your will and put our hope
　　in you;
　　you are all that we desire.
[9] At night I long for you with all my heart;
　　when you judge the earth and its
　　　people,
　　they will all learn what justice is.
[10] Even though you are kind to wicked
　　　men,
　　they never learn to do what is right.
　　Even here in a land of righteous people
　　　they still do wrong;
　　they refuse to recognize your
　　　greatness.

[11] Your enemies do not know that you
　　will punish them.
LORD, put them to shame and let them
　　suffer;
　　let them suffer the punishment you
　　have prepared.
Show them how much you love your
　　people.

[12] You will give us prosperity, LORD;
　　everything that we achieve
　　is the result of what you do. [f]
[13] LORD our God, we have been ruled
　　by others,
　　but you alone are our LORD.
[14] Now they are dead and will not live
　　again;
　　their ghosts will not rise,
　　for you have punished them and
　　destroyed them.
No one remembers them any more.
[15] LORD, you have made our nation grow,
　　enlarging its territory on every side,
　　and this has brought you honour.
[16] You punished your people, LORD,
　　and in anguish they prayed to you. [g]
[17] You, LORD, have made us cry out,
　　as a woman in labour cries out in
　　pain.
[18] We were in pain and agony,
　　but we gave birth to nothing.
We have won no victory for our land;
　　we have accomplished nothing. [h]

[19] Those of our people who have died
　　will live again!
Their bodies will come back to life.
All those sleeping in their graves
　　will wake up and sing for joy.
As the sparkling dew refreshes the
　　earth,
　　so the LORD will revive those who
　　have long been dead.

Judgement and Restoration

20 Go into your houses, my people, and
shut the door behind you. Hide yourselves
for a little while until God's anger is over.
[21] The LORD is coming from his heavenly
dwelling-place to punish the people of the
earth for their sins. The murders that were
secretly committed on the earth will be
revealed, and the ground will no longer
hide those who have been killed.

[f] everything that...do; or you treat us according to what we do.
[g] Verse 16 in Hebrew is unclear.   [h] We have won...nothing; Hebrew unclear.
25.10–12: Is 15.1–16.14; Jer 48.1–47; Ezek 25.8–11; Amos 2.1–3; Zeph 2.8–11
26.11: Heb 10.27   **26.19:** Dan 12.2

The fortified city lies in ruins (27.10)

27 On that day the LORD will use his powerful and deadly sword to punish Leviathan, that wriggling, twisting dragon, and to kill the monster*i* that lives in the sea.

2 On that day the LORD will say of his pleasant vineyard, 3 "I watch over it and water it continually. I guard it night and day so that no one will harm it. 4 I am no longer angry with the vineyard. If only there were thorns and briars to fight against, then I would burn them up completely. 5 But if the enemies of my people want my protection, let them make peace with me. Yes, let them make peace with me."

6 In days to come the people of Israel, the descendants of Jacob, will take root like a tree, and they will blossom and bud. The earth will be covered with the fruit they produce.

7 Israel has not been punished by the LORD as severely as its enemies, nor has she lost as many men. 8 The LORD punished his people by sending them into exile. He took them away with a cruel wind from the east.*k* 9 But Israel's sins will be forgiven only when the stones of pagan altars are ground up like chalk, and no more incense-altars or symbols of the goddess Asherah are left.

10 The fortified city lies in ruins. It is deserted like an empty wilderness. It has become a pasture for cattle, where they can rest and graze. 11 The branches of the trees are withered and broken, and women gather them for firewood. Because the people have understood nothing, God their Creator will not pity them or show them any mercy.

12 On that day, from the Euphrates to the Egyptian border, the LORD will gather his people one by one, like someone separating the wheat from the chaff.

13 When that day comes, a trumpet will be blown to call back from Assyria and Egypt all the Israelites who are in exile there. They will come and worship the LORD in Jerusalem, on his sacred hill.*l*

A Warning to the Northern Kingdom

28 The kingdom of Israel is doomed! Its glory is fading like the crowns of flowers on the heads of its drunken leaders. Their proud heads are well perfumed, but there they lie, dead drunk. 2 The Lord has someone strong and powerful ready to attack them, someone who will come like a hailstorm, like a torrent of rain, like a rushing, overpowering flood, and will overwhelm the land. 3 The pride of those drunken leaders will be trampled underfoot. 4 The fading glory of those proud leaders will disappear like the first figs of the season, picked and eaten as soon as they are ripe.

5 A day is coming when the LORD Almighty will be like a glorious crown of flowers for his people who survive. 6 He will give a sense of justice to those who serve as judges, and courage to those who defend the city gates from attack.

Isaiah and the Drunken Prophets of Judah

7 Even the prophets and the priests are so drunk that they stagger. They have drunk so much wine and liquor that they stumble in confusion. The prophets are too drunk to understand the visions that God sends, and the priests are too drunk

*i*LEVIATHAN...MONSTER: *Legendary monsters which were symbols of the nations oppressing Israel.*
k Verse 8 in Hebrew is unclear.   *l*SACRED HILL: *See 2.3.*
27.1: Job 41.1; Ps 74.14, 104.26

So drunk that they stagger (28.7)

to decide the cases that are brought to them. ⁸The tables where they sit are all covered with vomit, and not a clean spot is left.

9 They complain about me. They say, "Who does that man think he's teaching? Who needs his message? It's only good for babies that have just been weaned! ¹⁰He is trying to teach us letter by letter, line by line, lesson by lesson."

11 If you won't listen to me, then God will use foreigners speaking some strange-sounding language to teach you a lesson. ¹²He offered rest and comfort to all of you, but you refused to listen to him. ¹³That is why the LORD is going to teach you letter by letter, line by line, lesson by lesson. Then you will stumble with every step you take. You will be wounded, trapped, and taken prisoner.

A Cornerstone for Zion

14 Now you arrogant men who rule here in Jerusalem over this people, listen to what the LORD is saying. ¹⁵You boast that you have made a treaty with death and reached an agreement with the world of the dead. You are certain that disaster will spare you when it comes, because you depend on lies and deceit to keep you safe. ¹⁶This, now, is what the Sovereign LORD says: "I am placing in Zion a foundation that is firm and strong. In it I am putting a solid cornerstone on which are written the words, 'Faith that is firm is also patient.' ¹⁷Justice will be the

measuring-line for the foundation, and honesty will be its plumb-line."

Hailstorms will sweep away all the lies you depend on, and floods will destroy your security. ¹⁸The treaty you have made with death will be abolished, and your agreement with the world of the dead will be cancelled. When disaster sweeps down, you will be overcome. ¹⁹It will strike you again and again, morning after morning. You will have to bear it day and night. Each new message from God will bring new terror! ²⁰You will be like the man

A bed too short...with a blanket too narrow (28.20)

in the proverb, who tries to sleep in a bed too short to stretch out on, with a blanket too narrow to wrap himself in. ²¹The LORD will fight as he did at Mount Perazim and in the valley of Gibeon, in order to do what he intends to do—strange as his actions may seem. He will complete his work, his mysterious work.

22 Don't laugh at the warning I am giving you! If you do, it will be even harder for you to escape. I have heard the LORD Almighty's decision to destroy the whole country.

God's Wisdom

23 Listen to what I am saying; pay attention to what I am telling you. ²⁴No farmer goes on constantly ploughing his fields and getting them ready for sowing. ²⁵Once he has prepared the soil, he sows the seeds of herbs such as dill and cumin. He sows rows of wheat and barley, *m* and at the edges of his fields he sows other grain. ²⁶He knows how to do his work, because God has taught him. ²⁷He never uses a heavy club to beat out dill seeds or cumin seeds; instead he uses light sticks of the proper size. ²⁸He does not ruin the wheat by threshing it endlessly, and he knows how to thresh it by driving

---

m Hebrew has an additional word, the meaning of which is unclear.
28.11-12: 1 Cor 14.21　　**28.16:** Ps 118.22-23; Rom 9.33, 10.11; 1 Pet 2.6
28.21: Josh 10.10-12; 2 Sam 5.20; 1 Chr 14.11

a cart over it without bruising the grains. 29 All this wisdom comes from the LORD Almighty. The plans God makes are wise, and they always succeed!

The Fate of Jerusalem

29 God's altar, Jerusalem itself, is doomed! The city where David camped is doomed! Let another year or two come and go, with its feasts and festivals, 2 and then God will bring disaster on the city that is called "God's altar." There will be weeping and wailing, and the whole city will be like an altar covered with blood. 3 God will attack the city, surround it, and besiege it. 4 Jerusalem will be like a ghost struggling to speak from under the ground, a muffled voice coming from the dust.

5 Jerusalem, all the foreigners who attack you will be blown away like dust, and their terrifying armies will fly away like straw. Suddenly and unexpectedly 6 the LORD Almighty will rescue you with violent thunderstorms and earthquakes. He will send tempests and raging fire; 7 then all the armies of the nations attacking the city of God's altar, all their weapons and equipment—everything—will vanish like a dream, like something imagined in the night. 8 All the nations that assemble to attack Jerusalem will be like a starving man who dreams he is eating and wakes up hungry, or like a man dying of thirst who dreams he is drinking and wakes with a dry throat.

Disregarded Warnings

9 Go ahead and be stupid! Go ahead and be blind! Get drunk without any wine! Stagger without drinking a drop! 10 The LORD has made you drowsy, ready to fall into a deep sleep. The prophets should be the eyes of the people, but God has blindfolded them. 11 The meaning of every prophetic vision will be hidden from you; it will be like a sealed scroll. If you take it to someone who knows how to read and ask him to read it to you, he will say he can't because it is sealed. 12 If you give it to someone who can't read and ask him to read it to you, he will answer that he doesn't know how.

13 The Lord said, "These people claim to worship me, but their words are meaningless, and their hearts are somewhere else. Their religion is nothing but human rules and traditions, which they have simply memorized. 14 So I will startle

them with one unexpected blow after another. Those who are wise will turn out to be fools, and all their cleverness will be useless."

Hope for the Future

15 Those who try to hide their plans from the LORD are doomed! They carry out their schemes in secret and think no one will see them or know what they are doing. 16 They turn everything upside down. Which is more important, the potter or the clay? Can something a man has made say to him, "You didn't make me"? Or can it say to him, "You don't know what you are doing"?

17 As the saying goes, before long the dense forest will become farmland, and the farmland will go back to forest.

18 When that day comes, the deaf will be able to hear a book being read aloud, and the blind, who have been living in darkness, will open their eyes and see. 19 Poor and humble people will once again find the happiness which the LORD, the holy God of Israel, gives. 20 It will be the end of those who oppress others and show contempt for God. Every sinner will be destroyed. 21 God will destroy those who slander others, those who prevent the punishment of criminals, and those who tell lies to keep honest men from getting justice.

22 So now the LORD, the God of Israel, who rescued Abraham from trouble, says, "My people, you will not be disgraced any longer, and your faces will no longer be pale with shame. 23 When you see the children that I will give you, then you will acknowledge that I am the holy God of Israel. You will honour me and stand in awe of me. 24 Foolish people will learn to understand, and those who are always grumbling will be glad to be taught."

A Useless Treaty with Egypt

30 The LORD has spoken: "Those who rule Judah are doomed because they rebel against me. They follow plans that I did not make, and sign treaties against my will, piling one sin on another. 2 They go to Egypt for help without asking for my advice. They want Egypt to protect them, so they put their trust in Egypt's king. 3 But the king will be powerless to help them, and Egypt's protection will end in disaster. 4 Although their ambassadors have already arrived at the Egyptian cities of Zoan and Hanes, 5 the people of Judah

29.10: Rom 11.8   **29.13:** Mt 15.8-9; Mk 7.6-7   **29.14:** 1 Cor 1.19   **29.16:** Is 45.9

will regret that they ever trusted that unreliable nation, a nation that fails them when they expect help."

6 This is God's message about the animals of the southern desert: "The ambassadors travel through dangerous country, where lions live and where there are poisonous snakes and flying dragons. They load their donkeys and camels with expensive gifts for a nation that cannot give them any help. 7 The help that Egypt gives is useless. So I have nicknamed Egypt, 'The Harmless Dragon.'"

The Disobedient People

8 God told me to write down in a book what the people are like, so that there would be a permanent record of how evil they are. 9 They are always rebelling against God, always lying, always refusing to listen to the LORD's teachings. 10 They tell the prophets to keep quiet. They say, "Don't talk to us about what's right. Tell us what we want to hear. Let us keep our illusions. 11 Get out of our way and stop blocking our path. We don't want to hear about your holy God of Israel."

12 But this is what the holy God of Israel says: "You ignore what I tell you and rely on violence and deceit. 13 You are guilty. You are like a high wall with a crack running down it; suddenly you will collapse. 14 You will be shattered like a clay pot, so badly broken that there is no piece big enough to pick up hot coals with, or to scoop water from a cistern."

15 The Sovereign LORD, the holy God of Israel, says to the people, "Come back and quietly trust in me. Then you will be strong and secure." But you refuse to do it! 16 Instead, you plan to escape from your enemies by riding fast horses. And you are right—escape is what you will have to do! You think your horses are fast enough, but those who pursue you will be faster! 17 A thousand of you will run away when you see one enemy soldier, and five soldiers will be enough to make you all run away. Nothing will be left of your army except a lonely flagstaff on the top of a hill! 18 And yet the LORD is waiting to be merciful to you. He is ready to take pity on you because he always does what is right. Happy are those who put their trust in the LORD.

God Will Bless His People

19 You people who live in Jerusalem will not weep any more. The LORD is compassionate, and when you cry to him for help, he will answer you. 20 The Lord will make you go through hard times, but he himself will be there to teach you, and you will not have to search for him any more. 21 If you wander off the road to the right or the left, you will hear his voice behind you, saying, "Here is the road. Follow it." 22 You will take your idols plated with silver and your idols covered with gold, and will throw them away like filth, shouting, "Out of my sight!" 23 Whenever you sow your seeds, the LORD will send rain to make them grow and will give you a rich harvest, and your livestock will have plenty of pasture. 24 The oxen and donkeys that plough your fields will eat the finest and best fodder. 25 On the day when the forts of your enemies are captured and their people are killed, streams of water will flow from every mountain and every hill. 26 The moon will be as bright as the sun, and the sun will be seven times brighter than usual, like the light of seven days in one. This will all happen when the LORD bandages and heals the wounds he has given his people.

God Will Punish Assyria

27 The LORD's power and glory can be seen in the distance. Fire and smoke show his anger. He speaks, and his words burn like fire. 28 He sends the wind in front of him like a flood that carries everything away. It sweeps nations to destruction and puts an end to their evil plans. 29 But you, God's people, will be happy and sing as you do on the night of a sacred festival. You will be as happy as those who walk to the music of flutes on their way to the Temple of the LORD, the defender of Israel.

30 The LORD will let everyone hear his majestic voice and feel the force of his anger. There will be flames, cloudbursts, hailstones, and torrents of rain. 31 The Assyrians will be terrified when they hear the LORD's voice and feel the force of his punishment. 32 As the LORD strikes them again and again, his people will keep time with the music of drums and harps. God himself will fight against the Assyrians. 33 Long ago a place was prepared where a huge fire will burn the emperor of Assyria. It is deep and wide, and piled high with wood. The LORD will breathe out a stream of flame to set it on fire.

God Will Protect Jerusalem

31 Those who go to Egypt for help are doomed! They are relying on

The finest and best fodder (30.24)

Egypt's vast military strength—horses, chariots, and soldiers. But they do not rely on the LORD, the holy God of Israel, or ask him for help. ²He knows what he is doing! He sends disaster. He carries out his threats to punish evil men and those who protect them. ³The Egyptians are not gods—they are only human. Their horses are not supernatural. When the LORD acts, the strong nation will crumble, and the weak nation it helped will fall. Both of them will be destroyed.

4 The LORD said to me, "No matter how shepherds yell and shout, they can't scare away a lion from an animal that it has killed; in the same way, there is nothing that can keep me, the LORD Almighty, from protecting Mount Zion. ⁵Just as a bird hovers over its nest to protect its young, so I, the LORD Almighty, will protect Jerusalem and defend it."

6 The LORD said, "People of Israel, you have sinned against me and opposed me. But now, come back to me! ⁷A time is coming when all of you will throw away the sinful idols you made out of silver and gold. ⁸Assyria will be destroyed in war, but not by human power. The Assyrians will run from battle, and their young men will be made slaves. ⁹Their emperor will run away in terror, and the officers will be so frightened that they will abandon their battle flags." The LORD has spoken—the LORD who is worshipped

in Jerusalem and whose fire burns there for sacrifices.

A King with Integrity

32 Some day there will be a king who rules with integrity, and national leaders who govern with justice. ²Each of them will be like a shelter from the wind and a place to hide from storms. They will be like streams flowing in a desert, like the shadow of a giant rock

As a bird hovers over its nest (31.5)

in a barren land. ³Their eyes and ears will be open to the needs of the people. ⁴They will not be impatient any longer, but they will act with understanding and will say what they mean. ⁵No one will think that a fool is honourable or say that a scoundrel is honest. ⁶A fool speaks foolishly and thinks up evil things to do. What he does and what he says are an insult to the LORD, and he never feeds the hungry or gives thirsty people anything to drink. ⁷A stupid person is evil and does evil things; he plots to ruin the poor with lies and to prevent them getting their rights. ⁸But an honourable person acts honestly and stands firm for what is right.

Judgement and Restoration

9 You women who live an easy life, free from worries, listen to what I am saying. ¹⁰You may be satisfied now, but this time next year you will be in despair because there will be no grapes for you to gather. ¹¹You have been living an easy life, free from worries; but now, tremble with fear! Strip off your clothes and tie rags round your waist. ¹²Beat your breasts in grief because the fertile fields and the vineyards have been destroyed, ¹³and thorn-bushes and briars are growing on my people's land. Weep for all the houses where people were happy and for the city that was full of life. ¹⁴Even the palace will be abandoned and the capital city totally deserted. Homes and the forts that guarded them will be in ruins for ever. Wild donkeys will roam there, and sheep will find pasture there.

15 But once more God will send us his spirit. The waste land will become fertile, and fields will produce rich crops. ¹⁶Everywhere in the land righteousness and justice will be done. ¹⁷Because everyone will do what is right, there will be peace and security for ever. ¹⁸God's people will be free from worries, and their homes peaceful and safe. (¹⁹But hail will fall on the forests, and the city will be torn down.) ²⁰How happy everyone will be with plenty of water for the crops and safe pasture everywhere for the donkeys and cattle.

A Prayer for Help

33 Our enemies are doomed! They have robbed and betrayed, although no one has robbed them or betrayed them. But their time to rob and

betray will end, and they themselves will become victims of robbery and treachery.

2 LORD, have mercy on us. We have put our hope in you. Protect us day by day and save us in times of trouble. ³When you fight for us, nations run away from the noise of battle. ⁴Their belongings are pounced upon and taken as loot.

5 How great the LORD is! He rules over everything. He will fill Jerusalem with justice and integrity ⁶and give stability to the nation. He always protects his people and gives them wisdom and knowledge. Their greatest treasure is their reverence for the LORD.

7 Brave men are calling for help. The ambassadors who tried to bring about peace are crying bitterly. ⁸The highways are so dangerous that no one travels on them. Treaties are broken and agreements are violated. No one is respected any more. ⁹The land lies idle and deserted. The forests of Lebanon have withered, the fertile valley of Sharon is like a desert, and in Bashan and on Mount Carmel the leaves are falling from the trees.

The LORD Warns His Enemies

10 The LORD says to the nations, "Now I will act. I will show how powerful I am. ¹¹You make worthless plans and everything·you do is useless. My spirit is like a fire that will destroy you. ˣ ¹²You will crumble like rocks burnt to make lime, like thorns burnt to ashes. ¹³Let everyone near and far hear what I have done and acknowledge my power."

14 The sinful people of Zion are trembling with fright. They say, "God's judgement is like a fire that burns for ever. Can any of us survive a fire like that?" ¹⁵You can survive if you say and do what is right. Don't use your power to cheat the poor and don't accept bribes. Don't join with those who plan to commit murder or to do other evil things. ¹⁶Then you will be safe; you will be as secure as if you were in a strong fortress. You will have food to eat and water to drink.

The Glorious Future

17 Once again you will see a king ruling in splendour over a land that stretches in all directions. ¹⁸Your old fears of foreign tax-collectors and spies will be only a memory. ¹⁹You will no longer see any arrogant foreigners who speak a language that you can't understand. ²⁰Look at Zion, the city where we

---

ˣ *One ancient translation* My spirit...you; *Hebrew* You are destroying yourselves.

Owls and ravens will take over the land (34.11)

celebrate our religious festivals. Look at Jerusalem! What a safe place it will be to live in! It will be like a tent that is never moved, whose pegs are never pulled up and whose ropes never break. 21 The LORD will show us his glory. We will live beside broad rivers and streams, but hostile ships will not sail on them. [n] 22-23 All the rigging on those ships is useless; the sails cannot be spread! We will seize all the wealth of enemy armies, and there will be so much that even lame men can have a share. The LORD himself will be our king; he will rule over us and protect us. 24 No one who lives in our land will ever again complain of being ill, and all sins will be forgiven.

God Will Punish His Enemies

34 Come, people of all nations! Gather round and listen. Let the whole earth and everyone living on it come here and listen. 2 The LORD is angry with all the nations and all their armies. He has condemned them to destruction. 3 Their corpses will not be buried, but will lie there rotting and stinking; and the mountains will be red with blood. 4 The sun, moon, and stars will crumble to dust. The sky will disappear like a scroll being rolled up, and the stars will fall like leaves dropping from a vine or a fig-tree.

5 The LORD has prepared his sword in heaven, and now it will strike Edom, those people whom he has condemned to destruction. 6 His sword will be covered with their blood and fat, like the blood and fat of lambs and goats that are sacrificed. The LORD will offer this sacrifice in the city of Bozrah; he will make this a great slaughter in the land of Edom. 7 The people will fall like wild oxen and young bulls, and the earth will be red with blood and covered with fat. 8 This is the time when the LORD will rescue Zion and take vengeance on her enemies.

9 The rivers of Edom will turn into tar, and the soil will turn into sulphur. The whole country will burn like tar. 10 It will burn day and night, and smoke will rise from it for ever. The land will lie waste age after age, and no one will ever travel through it again. 11 Owls and ravens will take over the land. The LORD will make it a barren waste again, as it was before the creation. 12 There will be no king to rule the country, and the leaders will all be gone. [o] 13 Thorns and thistles will grow up in all the palaces and walled towns, and jackals and owls will live in them. 14 Wild animals will roam there, and demons will call to each other. The night monster [p] will come there looking for a place to rest. 15 Owls will build their nests, lay eggs, hatch their young, and care for them there. Vultures will gather there, one after another.

16 Search in the LORD's book of living creatures and read what it says. Not one of these creatures will be missing, and not one will be without its mate. The LORD has commanded it to be so; he himself will

---

[n] *Verse 21 in Hebrew is unclear.*
[o] *Verse 12 in Hebrew begins with a word, the meaning of which is unclear.*
[p] NIGHT MONSTER: *A female demon, believed to live in desolate places.*
34.4: Mt 24.29; Mk 13.25; Lk 21.26; Rev 6.13–14
34.5–17: Is 63.1–6; Jer 49.7–22; Ezek 25.12–14, 35.1–15; Amos 1.11–12; Obad 1–14; Mal 1.2–5
34.10: Rev 14.11, 19.3

bring them together. ¹⁷It is the LORD who
will divide the land among them and give
each of them a share. They will live in
the land age after age, and it will belong
to them for ever.

The Road of Holiness

35 The desert will rejoice,
and flowers will bloom in the
wilderness.
² The desert will sing and shout for joy;
it will be as beautiful as the Lebanon
Mountains
and as fertile as the fields of Carmel
and Sharon.
Everyone will see the LORD's splendour,
see his greatness and power.

³ Give strength to hands that are tired
and to knees that tremble with
weakness.
⁴ Tell everyone who is discouraged,
"Be strong and don't be afraid!
God is coming to your rescue,
coming to punish your enemies."

⁵ The blind will be able to see,
and the deaf will hear.
⁶ The lame will leap and dance,
and those who cannot speak will
shout for joy.
Streams of water will flow through the
desert;
⁷ the burning sand will become a lake,
and dry land will be filled with springs.
Where jackals used to live,
marsh grass and reeds will grow.

⁸ There will be a highway there,
called "The Road of Holiness."
No sinner will ever travel that road;
no fools will mislead those who follow
it. ⁹
⁹ No lions will be there,
no fierce animals will pass that way.
Those whom the LORD has rescued
will travel home by that road.
¹⁰ They will reach Jerusalem with
gladness,
singing and shouting for joy.
They will be happy for ever,
for ever free from sorrow and grief.

The Assyrians Threaten Jerusalem
(2 Kgs 18.13-27; 2 Chr 32.1-19)

36 In the fourteenth year that
Hezekiah was king of Judah,
Sennacherib, the emperor of Assyria,
attacked the fortified cities of Judah and

captured them. ²Then he ordered his chief
official to go from Lachish to Jerusalem
with a large military force to demand that
King Hezekiah should surrender. The
official occupied the road where the
clothmakers work, by the ditch that
brings water from the upper pond. ³Three
Judaeans came out to meet him: the
official in charge of the palace, Eliakim
son of Hilkiah; the court secretary,
Shebna; and the official in charge of the
records, Joah son of Asaph. ⁴The Assyrian
official told them that the emperor wanted
to know what made King Hezekiah so
confident. ⁵He demanded, "Do you think
that words can take the place of military
skill and might? Who do you think will
help you rebel against Assyria? ⁶You are
expecting Egypt to help you, but that
would be like using a reed as a walking-
stick—it would break and jab your hand.
That is what the king of Egypt is like
when anyone relies on him."

7 The Assyrian official went on, "Or will
you tell me that you are relying on the
LORD your God? It was the LORD's shrines
and altars that Hezekiah destroyed when
he told the people of Judah and Jerusalem
to worship at one altar only. ⁸I will make
a bargain with you in the name of the
emperor. I will give you two thousand
horses if you can find that many men
to ride them. ⁹You are no match for even
the lowest ranking Assyrian official, and
yet you expect the Egyptians to send you
chariots and cavalry. ¹⁰Do you think I
have attacked your country and destroyed
it without the LORD's help? The LORD
himself told me to attack it and destroy
it."

11 Then Eliakim, Shebna, and Joah said
to the official, "Speak Aramaic to us. We
understand it. Don't speak Hebrew; all
the people on the wall are listening."

12 He replied, "Do you think you and
the king are the only ones the emperor
sent me to say all these things to? No,
I am also talking to the people who are
sitting on the wall, who will have to eat
their excrement and drink their urine, just
as you will."

13 Then the official stood up and
shouted in Hebrew, "Listen to what the
emperor of Assyria is telling you. ¹⁴He
warns you not to let Hezekiah deceive
you. Hezekiah can't save you. ¹⁵And don't
let him persuade you to rely on the LORD.
Don't think that the LORD will save you

---

q *Probable text* no fools...follow it; *Hebrew unclear.*
35.3: Heb 12.12   **35.5-6:** Mt 11.5; Lk 7.22   **36.6:** Ezek 29.6-7

The people kept quiet (36.21)

and that he will stop our Assyrian army from capturing your city. ¹⁶ Don't listen to Hezekiah! The emperor of Assyria commands you to come out of the city and surrender. You will all be allowed to eat grapes from your own vines and figs from your own trees, and to drink water from your own wells—¹⁷ until the emperor resettles you in a country much like your own, where there are vineyards to give wine and there is corn for making bread. ¹⁸ Don't let Hezekiah fool you into thinking that the LORD will rescue you. Did the gods of any other nations save their countries from the emperor of Assyria? ¹⁹ Where are they now, the gods of Hamath and Arpad? Where are the gods of Sepharvaim? Did anyone save Samaria? ²⁰ When did any of the gods of all these countries ever save their country from our emperor? Then what makes you think the LORD can save Jerusalem?"

21 The people kept quiet, just as King Hezekiah had told them to; they did not say a word. ²² Then Eliakim, Shebna, and Joah tore their clothes in grief and went and reported to the king what the Assyrian official had said.

The King Asks Isaiah's Advice
(2 Kgs 19.1–7)

37 As soon as King Hezekiah heard their report, he tore his clothes in grief, put on sackcloth, and went to the Temple of the LORD. ² He sent Eliakim, the official in charge of the palace, Shebna, the court secretary, and the senior priests to the prophet Isaiah son of Amoz. They also were wearing sackcloth. ³ This is the message which he told them to give to Isaiah: "Today is a day of suffering; we are being punished and are in disgrace. We are like a woman who is ready to give birth, but is too weak to do it. ⁴ The Assyrian emperor has sent his chief official to insult the living God. May the LORD your God hear these insults and punish those who spoke them. So pray to God for those of our people who survive."

5 When Isaiah received King Hezekiah's message, ⁶ he sent back this answer: "The LORD tells you not to let the Assyrians frighten you by their claims that he cannot save you. ⁷ The LORD will cause the emperor to hear a rumour that will make him go back to his own country, and the LORD will have him killed there."

The Assyrians Send Another Threat
(2 Kgs 19.8–19)

8 The Assyrian official learnt that the emperor had left Lachish and was fighting against the nearby city of Libnah; so he went there to consult him. ⁹ Word reached the Assyrians that the Egyptian army, led by King Tirhakah of Sudan, was coming to attack them. When the emperor heard this, he sent a letter to King Hezekiah ¹⁰ of Judah to say to him, "The god you are trusting in has told you that you will not fall into my hands, but don't let that deceive you. ¹¹ You have heard what an Assyrian emperor does to any country he decides to destroy. Do you think that you can escape? ¹² My ancestors destroyed the cities of Gozan, Haran, and Rezeph, and killed the people of Betheden who lived in Telassar, and none of their gods could save them. ¹³ Where are the kings of the cities of Hamath, Arpad, Sepharvaim, Hena, and Ivvah?"

14 King Hezekiah took the letter from

the messengers and read it. Then he went to the Temple, placed the letter there in the presence of the LORD, 15 and prayed, 16 "Almighty LORD, God of Israel, enthroned above the winged creatures, you alone are God, ruling all the kingdoms of the world. You created the earth and the sky. 17 Now, LORD, hear us and look at what is happening to us. Listen to all the things that Sennacherib is saying to insult you, the living God. 18 We all know, LORD, that the emperors of Assyria have destroyed many nations, made their lands desolate, 19 and burnt up their gods— which were no gods at all, only images of wood and stone made by human hands. 20 Now, LORD our God, rescue us from the Assyrians, so that all the nations of the world will know that you alone are God."

Isaiah's Message to the King
(2 Kgs 19.20–37)

21 Then Isaiah sent a message telling King Hezekiah that in answer to the king's prayer 22 the LORD had said, "The city of Jerusalem laughs at you, Sennacherib, and despises you. 23 Whom do you think you have been insulting and ridiculing? You have been disrespectful to me, the holy God of Israel. 24 You sent your servants to boast to me that with all your chariots you had conquered the highest mountains of Lebanon. You boasted that there you cut down the tallest cedars and the finest cypress-trees, and that you reached the deepest parts of the forests. 25 You boasted that you dug wells and drank water in foreign lands, and that the feet of your soldiers tramped the River Nile dry.

26 "Have you never heard that I planned all this long ago? And now I have carried it out. I gave you the power to turn fortified cities into piles of rubble. 27 The people who lived there were powerless; they were frightened and stunned. They were like grass in a field or weeds growing on a roof when the hot east wind blasts them. q

28 "But I know everything about you, what you do and where you go. I know how you rage against me. 29 I have received the report of that rage and that pride of yours, and now I will put a hook through your nose and a bit in your mouth

and will take you back by the road on which you came."

30 Then Isaiah said to King Hezekiah, "This is a sign of what will happen. This year and next you will have only wild grain to eat, but the following year you will be able to sow your corn and harvest it, and plant vines and eat grapes. 31 Those in Judah who survive will flourish like plants that send roots deep into the ground and produce fruit. 32 There will be people in Jerusalem and on Mount Zion who will survive, because the LORD Almighty is determined to make this happen.

33 "This is what the LORD has said about the Assyrian emperor: 'He will not enter this city or shoot a single arrow against it. No soldiers with shields will come near the city, and no siege-mounds will be built round it. 34 He will go back by the road on which he came, without entering this city. I, the LORD, have spoken. 35 I will defend this city and protect it, for the sake of my own honour and because of the promise I made to my servant David.' "

36 An angel of the LORD went to the Assyrian camp and killed 185,000 soldiers. At dawn the next day there they lay, all dead! 37 Then the Assyrian emperor Sennacherib withdrew and returned to Nineveh. 38 One day when he was worshipping in the temple of his god Nisroch, two of his sons, Adrammelech and Sharezer, killed him with their swords and then escaped to the land of Ararat. Another of his sons, Esarhaddon, succeeded him as emperor.

King Hezekiah's Illness and Recovery
(2 Kgs 20.1–11; 2 Chr 32.24–26)

38 About this time King Hezekiah fell ill and almost died. The prophet Isaiah son of Amoz went to see him and said to him, "The LORD tells you that you are to put everything in order because you will not recover. Get ready to die."

2 Hezekiah turned his face to the wall and prayed: 3 "Remember, LORD, that I have served you faithfully and loyally, and that I have always tried to do what you wanted me to." And he began to cry bitterly.

---

q *Probable text* when...them; *Hebrew* blasted before they are grown.
37.16: Ex 25.22

An angel of the LORD went to the Assyrian camp (37.36)

4 Then the LORD commanded Isaiah ⁵to go back to Hezekiah and say to him, "I, the LORD, the God of your ancestor David, have heard your prayer and seen your tears; I will let you live fifteen years longer. ⁶I will rescue you and this city of Jerusalem from the emperor of Assyria, and I will continue to protect the city."

21 ʳ Isaiah told the king to put a paste made of figs on his boil, and he would get well. ²²Then King Hezekiah asked, "What is the sign to prove that I will be able to go to the Temple?"

7 Isaiah replied, "The LORD will give you a sign to prove that he will keep his promise. ⁸On the stairway built by King Ahaz, the LORD will make the shadow go back ten steps." And the shadow moved back ten steps. ˢ

9 After Hezekiah recovered from his illness, he wrote this song of praise:
¹⁰ I thought that in the prime of life
    I was going to the world of the dead,
    Never to live out my life.
¹¹ I thought that in this world of the living
    I would never again see the LORD
    Or any living person.
¹² My life was cut off and ended,
    Like a tent that is taken down,
    Like cloth that is cut from a loom.
    I thought that God was ending my life. ᵗ
¹³ All night I cried out with pain,
    As if a lion were breaking my bones.
    I thought that God was ending my life. ᵘ
¹⁴ My voice was thin and weak,
    And I moaned like a dove.

My eyes grew tired from looking to
    heaven.
Lord, rescue me from all this trouble.
¹⁵ What can I say? The LORD has done
    this.
My heart is bitter, and I cannot sleep.

¹⁶ Lord, I will live for you, for you alone;
    Heal me and let me live. ᵛ
¹⁷ My bitterness will turn into peace.
    You save ʷ my life from all danger;
    You forgive all my sins.
¹⁸ No one in the world of the dead can
    praise you;
    The dead cannot trust in your
    faithfulness.
¹⁹ It is the living who praise you,
    As I praise you now.
    Fathers tell their children how faithful
    you are.
²⁰ LORD, you have healed me.
    We will play harps and sing your praise,
    Sing praise in your Temple as long as
    we live. ʸ

Messengers from Babylonia
(2 Kgs 20.12–19)

39 About this time, the king of Babylonia, Merodach Baladan, son of Baladan, heard that King Hezekiah had been ill, so he sent him a letter and a present. ²Hezekiah welcomed the messengers and showed them his wealth—his silver and gold, his spices and perfumes, and all his military equipment. There was nothing in his storerooms or anywhere in his kingdom that he did not show them.

ʳ *Verses 21–22 are moved here from the end of the chapter (see 2 Kgs. 20.6–9).*
ˢ *stairway...ten steps...steps; or sundial...ten degrees...degrees (see 2 Kgs 20.9–11).*
ᵗ *I thought...my life; Hebrew unclear.*   ᵘ *Verse 13 in Hebrew is unclear.*
ᵛ *Verses 15–16 in Hebrew are unclear.*   ʷ *Some ancient translations save; Hebrew love.*
ʸ *Verses 21–22 are placed after verse 6.*

³Then the prophet Isaiah went to King Hezekiah and asked, "Where did these men come from and what did they say to you?"

Hezekiah answered, "They came from a very distant country, from Babylonia."

4 "What did they see in the palace?"

"They saw everything. There is nothing in the storerooms that I didn't show them."

5 Isaiah then told the king, "The LORD Almighty says that ⁶a time is coming when everything in your palace, everything that your ancestors have stored up to this day, will be carried off to Babylonia. Nothing will be left. ⁷Some of your own direct descendants will be taken away and made eunuchs to serve in the palace of the king of Babylonia."

8 King Hezekiah understood this to mean that there would be peace and security during his lifetime, so he replied, "The message you have given me from the LORD is good."

Words of Hope

40 "Comfort my people," says our God. "Comfort them!
² Encourage the people of Jerusalem.
Tell them they have suffered long enough
    and their sins are now forgiven. ᶻ
I have punished them in full for all their sins."

³ A voice cries out,
"Prepare in the wilderness a road for the LORD!
    Clear the way in the desert for our God!
⁴ Fill every valley;
    level every mountain.
The hills will become a plain,
    and the rough country will be made smooth.
⁵ Then the glory of the LORD will be revealed,
    and all mankind will see it.
The LORD himself has promised this."

⁶ A voice cries out, "Proclaim a message!"
"What message shall I proclaim?" I ask.
"Proclaim that all mankind are like grass;
    they last no longer than wild flowers.

⁷ Grass withers and flowers fade,
    when the LORD sends the wind blowing over them.
People are no more enduring than grass.
⁸ Yes, grass withers and flowers fade,
    but the word of our God endures for ever."

⁹ Jerusalem, go up on a high mountain

Tell...that their God is coming! (40.9)

and proclaim the good news!
Call out with a loud voice, Zion;
    announce the good news! ᵃ
Speak out and do not be afraid.
Tell the towns of Judah
    that their God is coming!

¹⁰ The Sovereign LORD is coming to rule with power,
    bringing with him the people he has rescued. ᵇ
¹¹ He will take care of his flock like a shepherd;
    he will gather the lambs together
    and carry them in his arms;
    he will gently lead their mothers.

ᶻ and their sins are now forgiven; *or* they have paid for what they did.
ᵃ Jerusalem, go up...news!; *or* Go up on a high mountain and proclaim the good news to Jerusalem! Call out with a loud voice and announce the good news to Zion!
ᵇ the people he has rescued; *or* the rewards he has for his people.
39.7: Dan 1.1–7; 2 Kgs 24.10–16; 2 Chr 36.10   **40.3:** Mt 3.3; Mk 1.3; Jn 1.23
40.3–5: Lk 3.4–6   **40.6–8:** Jas 1.10–11; 1 Pet 1.24–25   **40.10:** Is 62.11; Rev 22.12
40.11: Ezek 34.15; Jn 10.11

Israel's Incomparable God

12 Can anyone measure the ocean by
     handfuls
     or measure the sky with his hands?
   Can anyone hold the soil of the earth
     in a cup
     or weigh the mountains and hills on
       scales?
13 Can anyone tell the LORD what to do?
     Who can teach him or give him
       advice?
14 With whom does God consult
     in order to know and understand
     and to learn how things should be
       done?

15 To the LORD the nations are nothing,
     no more than a drop of water;
     the distant islands are as light as dust.
16 All the animals in the forests of
     Lebanon
     are not enough for a sacrifice to our
       God,
     and its trees are too few to kindle
       the fire.
17 The nations are nothing at all to him.

18 To whom can God be compared?
     How can you describe what he is like?
19 He is not like an idol that workmen
     make,
     that metalworkers cover with gold
     and set in a base of silver.
20 The man who cannot afford silver or
     gold d
     chooses wood that will not rot.
   He finds a skilful craftsman
     to make an image that won't fall
       down.

21 Do you not know?
     Were you not told long ago?
     Have you not heard how the world
       began?
22 It was made by the one who sits on
     his throne
     above the earth and beyond the sky;
     the people below look as tiny as ants.
   He stretched out the sky like a curtain,
     like a tent in which to live.
23 He brings down powerful rulers
     and reduces them to nothing.
24 They are like young plants,
     just set out and barely rooted.
   When the LORD sends a wind,

they dry up and blow away like straw.

25 To whom can the holy God be
     compared?
     Is there anyone else like him?
26 Look up at the sky!
     Who created the stars you see?
     The one who leads them out like an
       army,
     he knows how many there are
     and calls each one by name!
   His power is so great—
     not one of them is ever missing!

27 Israel, why then do you complain
     that the LORD doesn't know your
       troubles
     or care if you suffer injustice?
28 Don't you know? Haven't you heard?
   The LORD is the everlasting God;
     he created all the world.
   He never grows tired or weary.
   No one understands his thoughts.
29 He strengthens those who are weak
     and tired.
30 Even those who are young grow weak;
     young men can fall exhausted.
31 But those who trust in the LORD for
     help
     will find their strength renewed.
   They will rise on wings like eagles;
     they will run and not get weary;
     they will walk and not grow weak.

God's Assurance to Israel

41 God says,
     "Be silent and listen to me, you
       distant lands!
   Get ready to present your case in
     court;
     you will have your chance to speak.
   Let us come together to decide who is
     right.

2 "Who was it that brought the conqueror
     from the east, e
     and makes him triumphant wherever
     he goes?
   Who gives him victory over kings and
     nations?
     His sword strikes them down as if
       they were dust.
     His arrows scatter them like straw
       before the wind.
3 He follows in pursuit and marches
     safely on,

---

d Verses 19-20a in Hebrew are unclear.
e THE CONQUEROR FROM THE EAST: Cyrus, the emperor of Persia (see 45.1).
40.13: Rom 11.34; 1 Cor 2.16   **40.18–19:** Acts 17.29

so fast that he hardly touches the
    ground!

4 Who was it that made this happen?
    Who has determined the course of
        history?
    I, the LORD, was there at the beginning,
        and I, the LORD, will be there at the
        end.

5 "The people of distant lands have seen
        what I have done;
    they are frightened and tremble with
        fear.
    So they all assemble and come.
6 The craftsmen help and encourage one
        another.
7 The carpenter says to the goldsmith,
        'Well done!'
    The man who beats the idol smooth
        encourages the one who nails it
        together.
    They say, 'The soldering is good'—
        and they fasten the idol in place with
        nails.

8 "But you, Israel my servant,
    you are the people that I have chosen,
        the descendants of Abraham, my
        friend.
9 I brought you from the ends of the earth;
    I called you from its farthest corners
        and said to you, 'You are my servant.'
    I did not reject you, but chose you.
10 Do not be afraid—I am with you!
    I am your God—let nothing terrify
        you!
    I will make you strong and help you;
    I will protect you and save you.

11 "Those who are angry with you
        will know the shame of defeat.
    Those who fight against you will die
12   and will disappear from the earth.
13 I am the LORD your God;
    I strengthen you and say,
        'Do not be afraid; I will help you.'"

14 The LORD says,
    "Small and weak as you are, Israel,
        don't be afraid; I will help you.
    I, the holy God of Israel, am the one
        who saves you.
15 I will make you like a threshing-board,
        with spikes that are new and sharp.
    You will thresh mountains and destroy
        them;
    hills will crumble into dust.
16 You will toss them in the air;
    the wind will carry them off,

and they will be scattered by the
    storm.
Then you will be happy because I am
    your God;
    you will praise me, the holy God of
        Israel.

17 "When my people in their need look
        for water,
    when their throats are dry with thirst,
    then I, the LORD, will answer their
        prayer;
    I, the God of Israel, will never
        abandon them.
18 I will make rivers flow among barren
        hills
    and springs of water run in the valleys.
    I will turn the desert into pools of water
        and the dry land into flowing springs.
19 I will make cedars grow in the desert,
        and acacias and myrtles and olive-
        trees.
    Forests will grow in barren land,
        forests of pine and juniper and
        cypress.
20 People will see this and know
        that I, the LORD, have done it.
    They will come to understand
        that Israel's holy God has made it
        happen."

The LORD's Challenge to False Gods

21 The LORD, the king of Israel, has this
to say:
    "You gods of the nations, present your
        case.
    Bring the best arguments you have!
22 Come here and predict what will
        happen,
    so that we will know it when it takes
        place.
    Explain to the court the events of the
        past,
    and tell us what they mean.
23 Tell us what the future holds—
        then we will know that you are gods!
    Do something good or bring some
        disaster;
    fill us with fear and awe!
24 You and all you do are nothing;
    those who worship you are
        disgusting!

25 "I have chosen a man who lives in
        the east; f
    I will bring him to attack from the
        north.

---

f A MAN WHO LIVES IN THE EAST: See 41.2.
41.8: 2 Chr 20.7; Jas 2.23

I will turn the desert into pools of water (41.18)

He tramples on rulers as if they were
  mud,
  like a potter trampling clay.
²⁶ Which of you predicted that this would
  happen,
    so that we could say that you were
    right?
None of you said a word about it;
  no one heard you say a thing!
²⁷ I, the LORD, was the first to tell Zion
  the news;
    I sent a messenger to Jerusalem to
    say,
    'Your people are coming! They are
    coming home!'ᵍ
²⁸ When I looked among the gods,
  none of them had a thing to say;
    not one could answer the questions
    I asked.
²⁹ All these gods are useless;
  they can do nothing at all—
    these idols are weak and powerless."

The LORD's Servant

42 The LORD says,
  "Here is my servant, whom I
  strengthen—
    the one I have chosen, with whom
    I am pleased.
I have filled him with my spirit,
  and he will bring justice to every
  nation.
² He will not shout or raise his voice
  or make loud speeches in the streets.
³ He will not break off a bent reed

or put out a flickering lamp.
He will bring lasting justice to all.
⁴ He will not lose hope or courage;
  he will establish justice on the earth.
  Distant lands eagerly wait for his
  teaching."

⁵ God created the heavens and stretched
  them out;
    he fashioned the earth and all that
    lives there;
    he gave life and breath to all its people.
And now the LORD God says to his
  servant,
⁶ "I, the LORD, have called you and given
  you power
    to see that justice is done on earth.
Through you I will make a covenant
  with all peoples;
    through you I will bring light to the
    nations.
⁷ You will open the eyes of the blind
  and set free those who sit in dark
  prisons.

⁸ "I alone am the LORD your God.
  No other god may share my glory;
  I will not let idols share my praise.
⁹ The things I predicted have now come
  true.
  Now I will tell you of new things
    even before they begin to happen."

A Song of Praise

¹⁰ Sing a new song to the LORD;

ᵍ *Verse 27 in Hebrew is unclear.*
42.1: Mt 3.17, 17.5; Mk 1.11; Lk 3.22, 9.35   **42.1-4:** Mt 12.18-21   **42.5:** Acts 17.24-25
42.6: Is 49.6; Lk 2.32; Acts 13.47, 26.23

sing his praise, all the world!
Praise him, you that sail the sea;
   praise him, all creatures of the sea!
Sing, distant lands and all who live
   there!
¹¹ Let the desert and its towns praise
      God;
   let the people of Kedar praise him!
Let those who live in the city of Sela
   shout for joy from the tops of the
      mountains!
¹² Let those who live in distant lands
   give praise and glory to the LORD!
¹³ The LORD goes out to fight like a
      warrior;
   he is ready and eager for battle.
He gives a war-cry, a battle-shout;
   he shows his power against his
      enemies.

God Promises to Help His People

14 God says,
"For a long time I kept silent;
   I did not answer my people.
But now the time to act has come;
   I cry out like a woman in labour.
¹⁵ I will destroy the hills and mountains
   and dry up the grass and trees.
I will turn the river valleys into deserts ʰ
   and dry up the pools of water.

¹⁶ "I will lead my blind people
   by roads they have never travelled.
I will turn their darkness into light
   and make rough country smooth
      before them.
These are my promises,
   and I will keep them without fail.
¹⁷ All who trust in idols,
   who call images their gods,
   will be humiliated and disgraced."

Israel's Failure to Learn

18 The LORD says,
"Listen, you deaf people!
   Look closely, you that are blind!
¹⁹ Is anyone more blind than my servant,
   more deaf than the messenger I send?
²⁰ Israel, you have seen so much,
   but what has it meant to you?
You have ears to hear with,
   but what have you really heard?"

²¹ The LORD is a God who is eager to
      save,
   so he exalted his laws and teachings,
   and he wanted his people to honour
      them.

ʰ *Probable text* deserts; *Hebrew* coastlands.

²² But now his people have been
      plundered;
   they are locked up in dungeons
   and hidden away in prisons.
They were robbed and plundered,
   with no one to come to their rescue.

²³ Will any of you listen to this?
   From now on will you listen with
      care?
²⁴ Who gave Israel up to the looters?
   It was the LORD himself, against
      whom we sinned!
We would not live as he wanted us to
      live
   or obey the teachings he gave us.
²⁵ So he made us feel the force of his
      anger
   and suffer the violence of war.
Like fire his anger burned throughout
      Israel,
   but we never knew what was
      happening;
   we learnt from it nothing at all.

God Promises to Rescue His People

43 Israel, the LORD who created you
         says,
"Do not be afraid—I will save you.
   I have called you by name—you are
      mine.
² When you pass through deep waters,
   I will be with you;
   your troubles will not overwhelm you.
When you pass through fire, you will
      not be burnt;
   the hard trials that come will not hurt
      you.
³ For I am the LORD your God,
   the holy God of Israel, who saves you.
I will give up Egypt to set you free;
   I will give up Sudan and Seba.
⁴ I will give up whole nations to save
      your life,
   because you are precious to me
   and because I love you and give you
      honour.
⁵ Do not be afraid—I am with you!

"From the distant east and the farthest
      west,
   I will bring your people home.
⁶ I will tell the north to let them go
   and the south not to hold them back.
Let my people return from distant lands,
   from every part of the world.
⁷ They are my own people,
   and I created them to bring me glory."

I will bring your people home (43.5)

Israel Is the LORD's Witness

8 God says,
"Summon my people to court.
They have eyes, but they are blind;
they have ears, but they are deaf!
9 Summon the nations to come to the trial.
Which of their gods can predict the
future?
Which of them foretold what is
happening now?
Let these gods bring in their witnesses
to prove that they are right,
to testify to the truth of their words.

10 "People of Israel, you are my
witnesses;
I chose you to be my servant,
so that you would know me and believe
in me
and understand that I am the only
God.
Besides me there is no other god;
there never was and never will be.

11 "I alone am the LORD,
the only one who can save you.
12 I predicted what would happen,
and then I came to your aid.
No foreign god has ever done this;
you are my witnesses.
13 I am God and always will be.
No one can escape from my power;
no one can change what I do."

Escape from Babylon

14 Israel's holy God, the LORD who
saves you, says,
"To save you, I will send an army

against Babylon;
I will break down the city gates,
and the shouts of her people will turn
into crying.
15 I am the LORD, your holy God.
I created you, Israel, and I am your
king."

I alone am the LORD (43.11)

The LORD made a road through the sea (43.16)

16 Long ago the LORD made a road
    through the sea,
  a path through the swirling waters.
17 He led a mighty army to destruction,
  an army of chariots and horses.
  Down they fell, never to rise,
    snuffed out like the flame of a lamp!

18 But the LORD says,
  "Do not cling to events of the past
  or dwell on what happened long ago.
19 Watch for the new thing I am going
    to do.
  It is happening already—you can see
    it now!
  I will make a road through the
    wilderness
  and give you streams of water there.
20 Even the wild animals will honour me;
    jackals and ostriches will praise me
  when I make rivers flow in the desert
    to give water to my chosen people.
21 They are the people I made for myself,
  and they will sing my praises!"

Israel's Sin

22 The LORD says,
  "But you were tired of me, Israel;
    you did not worship me.
23 You did not bring me your burnt-
    offerings of sheep;
  you did not honour me with your
    sacrifices.
  I did not burden you by demanding
    offerings

or wear you out by asking for incense.
24 You didn't buy incense for me
  or satisfy me with the fat of your
    animals.
  Instead you burdened me with your sins;
    you wore me out with the wrongs
    you committed.
25 And yet, I am the God who forgives
    your sins,
  and I do this because of who I am.
  I will not hold your sins against you.

26 "Let us go to court; bring your
    accusation!
  Present your case to prove you are
    in the right!
27 Your earliest ancestor[i] sinned;
  your leaders sinned against me,
28 and your rulers profaned[j] my
    sanctuary.
  So I brought destruction on Israel;
  I let my own people be insulted."

The LORD Is the Only God

44 The LORD says,
    "Listen now, Israel, my servant,
  my chosen people, the descendants
    of Jacob.
2 I am the LORD who created you;
  from the time you were born, I have
    helped you.
  Do not be afraid; you are my servant,
    my chosen people whom I love.

3 "I will give water to the thirsty land

---

[i] YOUR EARLIEST ANCESTOR: *A reference either to Jacob or to Abraham, or possibly to Adam.*
[j] *One ancient translation* your rulers profaned; *Hebrew* I profaned the rulers of.

and make streams flow on the dry
ground.
I will pour out my spirit on your
children
and my blessing on your descendants.
4 They will thrive like well-watered grass,
like willows by streams of running
water.

5 "One by one, people will say, 'I am the
LORD's.'
They will come to join the people of
Israel.
Each one will mark the name of the
LORD on his arm
and call himself one of God's people."

6 The LORD, who rules and protects Israel,
the LORD Almighty, has this to say:
"I am the first, the last, the only God;
there is no other god but me.
7 Could anyone else have done what I
did?
Who could have predicted all that
would happen
from the very beginning to the end
of time?^{k}
8 Do not be afraid, my people!
You know that from ancient times until
now
I have predicted all that would
happen,
and you are my witnesses.
Is there any other god?
Is there some powerful god I never
heard of?"

Idolatry Is Ridiculed

9 All those who make idols are worthless, and the gods they prize so highly
are useless. Those who worship these
gods are blind and ignorant—and they will
be disgraced. 10 It's no good making a
metal image to worship as a god!
11 Everyone who worships it will be
humiliated. The people who make idols
are human beings and nothing more. Let
them come and stand trial—they will be
terrified and will suffer disgrace.

12 The metalworker takes a piece of
metal and works with it over a fire. His
strong arm swings a hammer to pound
the metal into shape. As he works, he
gets hungry, thirsty, and tired.

13 The carpenter measures the wood.
He outlines a figure with chalk, carves
it out with his tools, and makes it in the
form of a man, a handsome human figure,

to be placed in his house. 14 He might cut
down cedars to use, or choose oak or
cypress wood from the forest. Or he might
plant a laurel-tree and wait for the rain
to make it grow. 15 A man uses part of
a tree for fuel and part of it for making
an idol. With one part he builds a fire
to warm himself and bake bread; with
the other part he makes a god and
worships it. 16 With some of the wood he
makes a fire; he roasts meat, eats it, and
is satisfied. He warms himself and says,
"How nice and warm! What a beautiful
fire!" 17 The rest of the wood he makes
into an idol, and then he bows down and
worships it. He prays to it and says, "You
are my god—save me!"

18 Such people are too stupid to know
what they are doing. They close their eyes
and their minds to the truth. 19 The maker

Bowing down to a block of wood (44.19)

of idols hasn't the wit or the sense to
say, "Some of the wood I burnt up. I
baked some bread on the embers and I
roasted meat and ate it. And the rest of
the wood I made into an idol. Here I am
bowing down to a block of wood!"

20 It makes as much sense^l as eating
ashes. His foolish ideas have so misled
him that he is beyond help. He won't
admit to himself that the idol he holds
in his hand is not a god at all.

The LORD, the Creator and Saviour

21 The LORD says,
"Israel, remember this;
remember that you are my servant.
I created you to be my servant,

---

^{k} *Verse 7 in Hebrew is unclear.* ^{l} It makes as much sense; *or* It will do as much good.
44.6: Is 48.12; Rev 1.17, 22.13

The idol he holds in his hand is not a god at all (44.20)

and I will never forget you.
22 I have swept your sins away like a
    cloud.
  Come back to me; I am the one who
    saves you."

23 Shout for joy, you heavens!
  Shout, deep places of the earth!
Shout for joy, mountains, and every tree
    of the forest!
The LORD has shown his greatness
  by saving his people Israel.

24 "I am the LORD, your saviour;
  I am the one who created you.
I am the LORD, the Creator of all things.
  I alone stretched out the heavens;
  when I made the earth, no one helped
    me.
25 I make fools of fortune-tellers
  and frustrate the predictions of
    astrologers.
The words of the wise I refute
  and show that their wisdom is
    foolishness.
26 But when my servant makes a
    prediction,

44.25: 1 Cor 1.20   **44.28:** 2 Chr 36.23; Ezra 1.2

when I send a messenger to reveal
    my plans,
  I make those plans and predictions
    come true.
I tell Jerusalem that people will live
    there again,
  and the cities of Judah that they will
    be rebuilt.
Those cities will rise from the ruins.
27 With a word of command I dry up
    the ocean.
28 I say to Cyrus, 'You are the one who
    will rule for me;
  you will do what I want you to do:
  you will order Jerusalem to be rebuilt
  and the Temple foundations to be
    laid.' "

The LORD Appoints Cyrus

45 The LORD has chosen Cyrus to be
    king!
He has appointed him to conquer
    nations;
  he sends him to strip kings of their
    power;
  the LORD will open the gates of cities
    for him.
To Cyrus the LORD says,
2 "I myself will prepare your way,
    levelling mountains and hills.
I will break down bronze gates
  and smash their iron bars.
3 I will give you treasures from dark,
    secret places;
  then you will know that I am the LORD,
  and that the God of Israel has called
    you by name.
4 I appoint you to help my servant Israel,
  the people that I have chosen.
I have given you great honour,
  although you do not know me.

5 "I am the LORD; there is no other god.
  I will give you the strength you need,
  although you do not know me.
6 I do this so that everyone
  from one end of the world to the other
  may know that I am the LORD
  and that there is no other god.
7 I create both light and darkness;
  I bring both blessing and disaster.
  I, the LORD, do all these things.
8 I will send victory from the sky like
    rain;
  the earth will open to receive it
  and will blossom with freedom and
    justice.
I, the LORD, will make this happen."

The LORD of Creation and History

9 Does a clay pot dare to argue with its
maker,
a pot that is like all the others?
Does the clay ask the potter what he
is doing?
Does the pot complain that its maker
has no skill?
10 Does anyone dare to say to his parents,
"Why did you make me like this?"
11 The LORD, the holy God of Israel,
the one who shapes the future, says:
"You have no right to question me
about my children
or to tell me what I ought to do!
12 I am the one who made the earth
and created mankind to live there.
By my power I stretched out the
heavens;
I control the sun, the moon, and the
stars.
13 I myself have stirred Cyrus to action
to fulfil my purpose and put things
right.
I will straighten every road that he
travels.
He will rebuild my city, Jerusalem,
and set my captive people free.
No one has hired him or bribed him
to do this."
The LORD Almighty has spoken.

14 The LORD says to Israel,
"The wealth of Egypt and Sudan will
be yours,
and the tall men of Seba will be your
slaves;
they will follow you in chains.
They will bow down to you and confess,
'God is with you—he alone is God.
15 The God of Israel, who saves his
people,
is a God who conceals himself.
16 Those who make idols will all be
ashamed;
all of them will be disgraced.
17 But Israel is saved by the LORD,
and her victory lasts for ever;
her people will never be disgraced.'"

18 The LORD created the heavens—
he is the one who is God!
He formed and made the earth—
he made it firm and lasting.
He did not make it a desolate waste,
but a place for people to live in.
It is he who says, "I am the LORD,
and there is no other god.

45.9: Rom 9.20   **45.23:** Rom 14.11; Phil 2.10-11

19 I have not spoken in secret
or kept my purpose hidden.
I did not require the people of Israel
to look for me in a desolate waste.
I am the LORD, and I speak the truth;
I make known what is right."

The LORD of the World and
the Idols of Babylon

20 The LORD says,
"Come together, people of the nations,
all who survive the fall of the empire;
present yourselves for the trial!
The people who parade with their idols
of wood
and pray to gods that cannot save
them—
those people know nothing at all!
21 Come and present your case in court;
let the defendants consult one
another.
Who predicted long ago what would
happen?
Was it not I, the LORD, the God who
saves his people?
There is no other god.

22 "Turn to me now and be saved,
people all over the world!
I am the only God there is.
23 My promise is true,
and it will not be changed.
I solemnly promise by all that I am:
Everyone will come and kneel before
me
and vow to be loyal to me.

24 "They will say that only through me
are victory and strength to be found;
but all who hate me will suffer
disgrace.
25 I, the LORD, will rescue all the
descendants of Jacob,
and they will give me praise.

46 "This is the end for Babylon's
gods!
Bel and Nebo once were worshipped,
but now they are loaded on donkeys,
a burden for the backs of tired
animals.
2   The idols cannot save themselves;
they are captured and carried away.
This is the end for Babylon's gods!

3 "Listen to me, descendants of Jacob,
all who are left of my people.
I have cared for you from the time you
were born.

The idols cannot save themselves (46.2)

4 I am your God and will take care of
 you
  until you are old and your hair is grey.
 I made you and will care for you;
  I will give you help and rescue you.

5 "With whom will you compare me?"
  says the LORD.
 "Is there anyone else like me?
6 People open their purses and pour out
  gold;
  they weigh out silver on the scales.
 They hire a goldsmith to make a god;
  then they bow down and worship it!
7 They lift it to their shoulders and carry
  it;
  they put it in place, and there it stands,
  unable to move from where it is.
 If anyone prays to it, it cannot answer
  or save him from disaster.

8 "Remember this, you sinners;
  consider what I have done.
9 Remember what happened long ago;
  acknowledge that I alone am God
  and that there is no one else like me.
10 From the beginning I predicted the
  outcome;
  long ago I foretold what would
  happen.
 I said that my plans would never fail,
  that I would do everything I intended
  to do.
11 I am calling a man to come from the
  east;[m]
  he will swoop down like a hawk
  and accomplish what I have planned.
 I have spoken, and it will be done.

12 "Listen to me, you stubborn people
  who think that victory is far away.
13 I am bringing the day of victory near—
  it is not far away at all.
 My triumph will not be delayed.
 I will save Jerusalem
  and bring honour to Israel there."

Judgement on Babylon

47 The LORD says,
  "Babylon, come down from your
  throne,
  and sit in the dust on the ground.
 You were once like a virgin, a city
  unconquered,
  but you are soft and delicate no
  longer!
 You are now a slave!
2 Turn the millstone! Grind the flour!
 Off with your veil! Strip off your fine
  clothes!
 Lift up your skirts to cross the
  streams![n]
3 People will see you naked;
  they will see you humbled and
  shamed.
 I will take vengeance, and no one will
  stop me."

4 The holy God of Israel sets us free—
  his name is the LORD Almighty.

5 The LORD says to Babylon,
 "Sit in silence and darkness;
  no more will they call you the queen
  of nations!
6 I was angry with my people;
  I treated them as no longer mine:
 I put them in your power,

---

m A MAN TO COME FROM THE EAST: *See 41.2.*
n CROSS THE STREAMS: *This probably refers to going into exile.*
47.1–15: Is 13.1–14.23; Jer 50.1, 51.64

and you showed them no mercy;
even the aged you treated harshly.
7 You thought you would always be a
queen,
and did not take these things to heart
or think how it all would end.

8 "Listen to this, you lover of pleasure,
you that think you are safe and secure.
You claim you are as great as God—
that there is no one else like you.
You thought that you would never be
a widow
or suffer the loss of your children.
9 But in a moment, in a single day,
both of these things will happen.
In spite of all the magic you use,
you will lose your husband and
children.

10 "You felt sure of yourself in your evil;
you thought that no one could see
you.
Your wisdom and knowledge led you
astray,
and you said to yourself, 'I am God—
there is no one else like me.'
11 Disaster will come upon you,
and none of your magic can stop it.
Ruin will come on you suddenly—
ruin you never dreamt of!
12 Keep all your magic spells and charms;
you have used them since you were
young.
Perhaps they will be of some help to
you;
perhaps you can frighten your
enemies.
13 You are powerless in spite of the
advice you get.
Let your astrologers come forward and
save you—
those people who study the stars,
who map out the zones of the heavens
and tell you from month to month
what x is going to happen to you.

14 "They will be like bits of straw,
and a fire will burn them up!
They will not even be able to save
themselves—
the flames will be too hot for them,
not a cosy fire to warm themselves
by.
15 That is all the good they will do you—
those astrologers you've consulted all
your life.

x *Some ancient translations* what; *Hebrew* from what.
47.8-9: Rev 18.7-8

Those people who study the stars (47.13)

They all will leave you and go their own
way,
and none will be left to save you."

God Is LORD of the Future

48 Listen to this, people of Israel,
you that are descended from
Judah:
You swear by the name of the LORD
and claim to worship the God of
Israel—
but you don't mean a word you say.
2 And yet you are proud to say
that you are citizens of the holy city
and that you depend on Israel's God,
whose name is the LORD Almighty.

3 The LORD says to Israel,
"Long ago I predicted what would take
place;
then suddenly I made it happen.
4 I knew that you would prove to be
stubborn,
as rigid as iron and unyielding as
bronze.
5 And so I predicted your future long ago,
announcing events before they took
place,
to prevent you from claiming
that your idols and images made them
happen.

6 "All I foretold has now taken place;
    you have to admit my predictions
        were right.
Now I will tell you of new things to
        come,
    events that I did not reveal before.
7 Only now am I making them happen;
    nothing like this took place in the past.
If it had, you would claim that you knew
        all about it.
8 I knew that you couldn't be trusted,
    that you have always been known as
        a rebel.
That is why you never heard of this
        at all,
    why no word of it ever came to your
        ears.

9 "In order that people will praise my
        name,
    I am holding my anger in check;
    I am keeping it back and will not
        destroy you.
10 I have tested you in the fire of
        suffering,
    as silver is refined in a furnace.
But I have found that you are worthless.
11 What I do is done for my own sake—
    I will not let my name be dishonoured
    or let anyone else share the glory
    that should be mine and mine alone."

Cyrus, the LORD's Chosen Leader

12 The LORD says,
"Listen to me, Israel, the people I have
        called!
I am God, the first, the last, the only
        God!
13 My hands made the earth's
        foundations
    and spread the heavens out.
When I summon earth and sky,
    they come at once and present
        themselves.

14 "Assemble and listen, all of you!
None of the gods could predict
    that the man I have chosen would
        attack Babylon;
    he will do what I want him to do.
15 I am the one who spoke and called
        him;
    I led him out and gave him success.

16 "Now come close to me and hear what
    I say.

From the beginning I have spoken
        openly,
    and have always made my words
        come true."
(Now the Sovereign LORD has given me
his power and sent me.)

The LORD's Plan for His People

17 The holy God of Israel,
    the LORD who saves you, says:
"I am the LORD your God,
    the one who wants to teach you for
        your own good
    and direct you in the way you should
        go.

18 "If only you had listened to my
        commands!
Then blessings would have flowed for
        you
    like a stream that never goes dry!
Victory would have come to you
    like the waves that roll on the shore.
19 Your descendants would be as
        numerous as grains of sand,
    and I would have made sure they were
        never destroyed."

20 Go out from Babylon, go free!
Shout the news gladly; make it known
        everywhere:
    "The LORD has saved his servant
        Israel!"
21 When the LORD led his people through
        a hot, dry desert,
    they did not suffer from thirst.
He made water come from a rock for
        them;
    he split the rock open, and water
        flowed out.

22 "There is no safety for sinners," says
    the LORD.

Israel, A Light to the Nations

49 Listen to me, distant nations,
      you people who live far away!
Before I was born, the LORD chose me
and appointed me to be his servant.
2 He made my words as sharp as a sword.
    With his own hand he protected me. o
He made me like an arrow,
    sharp and ready for use.
3 He said to me, "Israel, you are my
        servant;
    because of you, people will praise
        me."

o With his own hand...me; or He kept me hidden in his hand.
48.12: Is 44.6; Rev 1.17, 22.13   **48.20:** Rev 18.4   **48.22:** Is 57.21   **49.1:** Jer 1.5
49.2: Heb 4.12; Rev 1.16

4 I said, "I have worked, but how hopeless
it is!
  I have used up my strength, but have
  accomplished nothing."
Yet I can trust the LORD to defend my
  cause;
  he will reward me for what I do.

5 Before I was born, the LORD appointed
me;
  he made me his servant to bring back
  his people,
  to bring back the scattered people of
  Israel.
The LORD gives me honour;
  he is the source of my strength.

6 The LORD said to me,
"I have a greater task for you, my
servant.
  Not only will you restore to greatness
  the people of Israel who have
  survived,
but I will also make you a light to the
  nations—
  so that all the world may be saved."

7 Israel's holy God and saviour says
  to the one who is deeply despised,
  who is hated by the nations
  and is the servant of rulers:
"Kings will see you released
  and will rise to show their respect;
princes also will see it,
  and they will bow low to honour you."

This will happen because the LORD has
  chosen his servant;
the holy God of Israel keeps his
  promises.

The Restoration of Jerusalem

8 The LORD says to his people,
"When the time comes to save you, I
  will show you favour
  and answer your cries for help.
I will guard and protect you
  and through you make a covenant
  with all peoples.
I will let you settle once again
  in your land that is now laid waste.
9 I will say to the prisoners, 'Go free!'
  and to those who are in darkness,
  'Come out to the light!'
They will be like sheep that graze on
  the hills;
10   they will never be hungry or thirsty.
  Sun and desert heat will not hurt them,

for they will be led by one who loves
  them.
  He will lead them to springs of water.

11 "I will make a highway across the
  mountains
  and prepare a road for my people to
  travel.
12 My people will come from far away,
  from the north and the west,
  and from Aswan[p] in the south."

13 Sing, heavens! Shout for joy, earth!
  Let the mountains burst into song!
The LORD will comfort his people;
  he will have pity on his suffering
  people.

14 But the people of Jerusalem said,
"The LORD has abandoned us!
  He has forgotten us."
15 So the LORD answers,
"Can a woman forget her own baby
  and not love the child she bore?
Even if a mother should forget her child,
  I will never forget you.
16 Jerusalem, I can never forget you!
  I have written your name on the
  palms of my hands.

17 "Those who will rebuild you are
  coming soon,
  and those who destroyed you will
  leave.
18 Look around and see what is
  happening!
  Your people are assembling—they
  are coming home!
As surely as I am the living God,
  you will be proud of your people,
  as proud as a bride is of her jewels.

19 "Your country was ruined and
  desolate—
  but now it will be too small
  for those who are coming to live there.
And those who left you in ruins
  will be far removed from you.
20 Your people who were born in exile
  will one day say to you,
  'This land is too small—
  we need more room to live in!'
21 Then you will say to yourself,
  'Who bore all these children for me?
  I lost my children and could have no
  more.
  I was exiled and driven away—
  who brought these children up?

p ASWAN: *A city in southern Egypt, where a large Jewish community had settled.*
49.6: Is 42.6; Lk 2.32; Acts 13.47, 26.23   **49.8:** 2 Cor 6.2   **49.10:** Rev 7.16–17

I was left all alone—
where did these children come
from?'"

22 The Sovereign LORD says to his
people:
"I will signal to the nations,
and they will bring your children
home.
23 Kings will be like fathers to you;
queens will be like mothers.
They will bow low before you and
honour you;
they will humbly show their respect
for you.
Then you will know that I am the LORD;
no one who waits for my help will
be disappointed."

24 Can you take away a soldier's loot?
Can you rescue the prisoners of a
tyrant?

25 The LORD replies,
"That is just what is going to happen.
The soldier's prisoners will be taken
away,
and the tyrant's loot will be seized.
I will fight against whoever fights you,
and I will rescue your children.
26 I will make your oppressors kill each
other;
they will be drunk with murder and
rage.
Then all mankind will know that I am
the LORD,
the one who saves you and sets you
free.
They will know that I am Israel's
powerful God."

50

The LORD says,
"Do you think I sent my people
away
like a man who divorces his wife?
Where, then, are the papers of
divorce?
Do you think I sold you into captivity
like a man who sells his children as
slaves?
No, you went away captive because of
your sins;
you were sent away because of your
crimes.

2 "Why did my people fail to respond
when I went to them to save them?
Why did they not answer when I called?
Am I too weak to save them?

I can dry up the sea with a command
and turn rivers into a desert,
so that the fish in them die for lack
of water.
3 I can make the sky turn dark,
as if it were in mourning for the dead."

The Obedience of the LORD's Servant

4 The Sovereign LORD has taught me what
to say,
so that I can strengthen the weary.
Every morning he makes me eager
to hear what he is going to teach me.
5 The LORD has given me understanding,
and I have not rebelled
or turned away from him.
6 I bared my back to those who beat me.
I did not stop them when they insulted
me,
when they pulled out the hairs of my
beard
and spat in my face.

7 But their insults cannot hurt me
because the Sovereign LORD gives me
help.
I brace myself to endure them.
I know that I will not be disgraced,
8 for God is near,
and he will prove me innocent.
Does anyone dare to bring charges
against me?
Let us go to court together!
Let him bring his accusation!
9 The Sovereign LORD himself defends
me—
who, then, can prove me guilty?
All my accusers will disappear;
they will vanish like moth-eaten cloth.

10 All of you that honour the LORD
and obey the words of his servant,
the path you walk may be dark indeed,
but trust in the LORD, rely on your
God.
11 All of you that plot to destroy others
will be destroyed by your own plots.
The LORD himself will make this happen;
you will suffer a miserable fate.

Words of Comfort to Jerusalem

51

The LORD says,
"Listen to me, you that want to
be saved,
you that come to me for help.
Think of the rock from which you came,
the quarry from which you were dug.
2 Think of your ancestor, Abraham,

50.6: Mt 26.67; Mk 14.65   **50.8-9:** Rom 8.33–34

and of Sarah, from whom you are
descended.
When I called Abraham, he was
childless,
but I blessed him and gave him
children;
I made his descendants numerous.

3 "I will show compassion to Jerusalem,
to all who live in her ruins.
Though her land is a desert, I will make
it a garden,
like the garden I planted in Eden.
Joy and gladness will be there,
and songs of praise and thanks to me.

4 "Listen to me, my people,
listen to what I say:
I give my teaching to the nations;
my laws will bring them light.
5 I will come quickly and save them;
the time of my victory is near.
I myself will rule over the nations.
Distant lands wait for me to come;
they wait with hope for me to save
them.
6 Look up at the heavens; look at the
earth!
The heavens will disappear like
smoke;
the earth will wear out like old
clothing,
and all its people will die like flies.
But the deliverance I bring will last for
ever;
my victory will be final.

7 "Listen to me, you that know what is
right,
who have my teaching fixed in your
hearts.
Do not be afraid when people taunt and
insult you;
8   they will vanish like moth-eaten
clothing!
But the deliverance I bring will last for
ever;
my victory will endure for all time."

9 Wake up, LORD, and help us!
Use your power and save us;
use it as you did in ancient times.
It was you that cut the sea-monster
Rahab*q* to pieces.
10 It was you also who dried up the sea
and made a path through the water,

so that those you were saving could
cross.
11 Those whom you have rescued
will reach Jerusalem with gladness,
singing and shouting for joy.
They will be happy for ever,
for ever free from sorrow and grief.

12 The LORD says,
"I am the one who strengthens you.
Why should you fear mortal man,
who is no more enduring than grass?
13 Have you forgotten the LORD who
made you,
who stretched out the heavens
and laid the earth's foundations?
Why should you live in constant fear
of the fury of those who oppress you,
of those who are ready to destroy
you?
Their fury can no longer touch you.
14 Those who are prisoners will soon be
set free;
they will live a long life
and have all the food they need.

15 "I am the LORD your God;
I stir up the sea
and make its waves roar.
My name is the LORD Almighty!
16 I stretched out*r* the heavens
and laid the earth's foundations;
I say to Jerusalem, 'You are my people!
I have given you my teaching,
and I protect you with my hand.'"

The End of Jerusalem's Suffering

17 Jerusalem, wake up!
Rouse yourself and get up!
You have drunk the cup of punishment
that the LORD in his anger gave you
to drink;
you drank it down, and it made you
stagger.
18 There is no one to lead you,
no one among your people
to take you by the hand.

19 A double disaster has fallen on you:
your land has been devastated by war,
and your people have starved.
There is no one to show you sympathy.
20 At the corner of every street
your people collapse from weakness;
they are like deer caught in a hunter's
net.

*q*RAHAB: *A legendary sea-monster, which represented the forces of chaos and evil, and was
sometimes a symbol of Egypt.*   *r One ancient translation* stretched out; *Hebrew* planted.
51.17: Rev 14.10, 16.19

They have felt the force of God's anger.

21 You suffering people of Jerusalem,
  you that stagger as though you were
    drunk,
22 the LORD your God defends you and
    says,
"I am taking away the cup
  that I gave you in my anger.
You will no longer have to drink
  the wine that makes you stagger.
23 I will give it to those who oppressed
    you,
  to those who made you lie down in
    the streets
  and trampled on you as if you were
    dirt."

God Will Rescue Jerusalem

52 Jerusalem, be strong and great
    again!
  Holy city of God, clothe yourself with
    splendour!
The heathen will never enter your gates
  again.
2 Shake yourself free, Jerusalem!
  Rise from the dust and sit on your
    throne!
Undo the chains that bind you,
  captive people of Zion!

3 The Sovereign LORD says to his people, "When you became slaves, no money was paid for you; in the same way nothing will be paid to set you free. 4 When you went to live in Egypt as foreigners, you did so of your own free will; Assyria, however, took you away by force and paid nothing for you. 5 And now in Babylonia the same thing has happened: you are captives, and nothing was paid for you. Those who rule over you boast and brag and constantly show contempt for me. 6 In time to come you will acknowledge that I am God and that I have spoken to you."

7 How wonderful it is to see
  a messenger coming across the
    mountains,
  bringing good news, the news of
    peace!
He announces victory and says to Zion,
  "Your God is king!"
8 Those who guard the city are shouting,
  shouting together for joy!

They can see with their own eyes
  the return of the LORD to Zion!

9 Break into shouts of joy,
  you ruins of Jerusalem!
The LORD will rescue his city
  and comfort his people.
10 The LORD will use his holy power;
  he will save his people,
  and all the world will see it.
11 Make sure you leave Babylonia,
  all you that carry the temple
    equipment!
Touch no forbidden thing; *s*
  keep yourselves holy and leave.
12 This time you will not have to leave
    in a hurry;
  you will not be trying to escape.
The LORD your God will lead you
  and protect you on every side.

The Suffering Servant

13 The LORD says,
"My servant will succeed in his task;
  he will be highly honoured. *t*
14 Many people were shocked when they
    saw him;
  he was so disfigured that he hardly
    looked human.
15 But now many nations will marvel at
    him,
  and kings will be speechless with
    amazement.
They will see and understand
  something they had never known."

*A messenger coming across the
mountains (52.7)*

s FORBIDDEN THING: *Any object that was considered ritually unclean.*
t he will be highly honoured; *or* he will be restored to greatness and honour.
52.1: Rev 21.2, 27   **52.5:** Rom 2.24   **52.7:** Nah 1.15; Rom 10.15; Eph 6.15
52.11: 2 Cor 6.17   **52.15:** Rom 15.21

He never said a word (53.7)

53 The people reply,
"Who would have believed what
we now report?
Who could have seen the LORD's hand
in this?
2 It was the will of the LORD that his
servant
should grow like a plant taking root
in dry ground.
He had no dignity or beauty
to make us take notice of him.
There was nothing attractive about him,
nothing that would draw us to him.
3 We despised him and rejected him;
he endured suffering and pain.
No one would even look at him—
we ignored him as if he were nothing.

4 "But he endured the suffering that
should have been ours,
the pain that we should have borne.
All the while we thought that his
suffering
was punishment sent by God.
5 But because of our sins he was wounded,
beaten because of the evil we did.
We are healed by the punishment he
suffered,
made whole by the blows he received.
6 All of us were like sheep that were lost,
each of us going his own way.
But the LORD made the punishment fall
on him,
the punishment all of us deserved.

7 "He was treated harshly, but endured
it humbly;

he never said a word.
Like a lamb about to be slaughtered,
like a sheep about to be sheared,
he never said a word.
8 He was arrested and sentenced and led
off to die,
and no one cared about his fate.
He was put to death for the sins of
our people.
9 He was placed in a grave with evil men,
he was buried with the rich,
even though he had never committed
a crime
or ever told a lie."

10 The LORD says,
"It was my will that he should suffer;
his death was a sacrifice to bring
forgiveness.
And so he will see his descendants;
he will live a long life,
and through him my purpose will
succeed.
11 After a life of suffering, he will again
have joy;
he will know that he did not suffer
in vain.
My devoted servant, with whom I am
pleased,
will bear the punishment of many
and for his sake I will forgive them.
12 And so I will give him a place of
honour,
a place among great and powerful
men.
He willingly gave his life
and shared the fate of evil men.

53.1: Jn 12.38; Rom 10.16 **53.4:** Mt 8.17 **53.5:** 1 Pet 2.24 **53.6:** 1 Pet 2.25
53.7: Rev 5.6 **53.7–8:** Acts 8.32-33 **53.9:** 1 Pet 2.22 **53.12:** Mk 15.28; Lk 22.37

He took the place of many sinners
and prayed that they might be
forgiven." [u]

The Lord's Love for Israel

54 Jerusalem, you have been like a
childless woman,
but now you can sing and shout for
joy.
Now you will have more children
than a woman whose husband never
left her!

2 Make the tent you live in larger;
lengthen its ropes and strengthen the
pegs!

3 You will extend your boundaries on all
sides;
your people will get back the land
that the other nations now occupy.
Cities now deserted will be filled with
people.

4 Do not be afraid—you will not be
disgraced again;
you will not be humiliated.
You will forget your unfaithfulness as
a young wife,
and your desperate loneliness as a
widow.

5 Your Creator will be like a husband to
you—
the Lord Almighty is his name.
The holy God of Israel will save you—
he is the ruler of all the world.

6 Israel, you are like a young wife,
deserted by her husband and deeply
distressed.
But the Lord calls you back to him and
says:

7 "For one brief moment I left you;
with deep love I will take you back.

8 I turned away angry for only a moment,
but I will show you my love for ever."
So says the Lord who saves you.

9 "In the time of Noah I promised
never again to flood the earth.
Now I promise not to be angry with
you again;
I will not reprimand or punish you.

10 The mountains and hills may crumble,
but my love for you will never end;
I will keep for ever my promise of
peace."
So says the Lord who loves you.

The Future Jerusalem

11 The Lord says,

"O Jerusalem, you suffering, helpless
city,
with no one to comfort you,
I will rebuild your foundations with
precious stones.

12 I will build your towers with rubies,
your gates with stones that glow like
fire,
and the wall around you with jewels.

13 "I myself will teach your people,
and give them prosperity and peace.

14 Justice and right will make you strong.
You will be safe from oppression and
terror.

15 If anyone attacks you,
he does it without my consent;
whoever fights against you will fall.

16 "I create the blacksmith,
who builds a fire and forges weapons.
I also create the soldier,
who uses the weapons to kill.

17 But no weapon will be able to hurt
you;
you will have an answer for all who
accuse you.
I will defend my servants
and give them victory."
The Lord has spoken.

God's Offer of Mercy

55 The Lord says,
"Come, everyone who is
thirsty—
here is water!
Come, you that have no money—
buy corn and eat!
Come! Buy wine and milk—
it will cost you nothing!

2 Why spend money on what does not
satisfy?
Why spend your wages and still be
hungry?
Listen to me and do what I say,
and you will enjoy the best food of
all.

3 "Listen now, my people, and come to
me;
come to me, and you will have life!
I will make a lasting covenant with you
and give you the blessings I promised
to David.

4 I made him a leader and commander
of nations,
and through him I showed them my
power.

---

[u] prayed that they might be forgiven; *or* suffered the punishment they deserved.
54.1: Gal 4.27   **54.9:** Gen 9.8-17   **54.11-12:** Rev 21.18-21   **54.13:** Jn 6.45
55.1: Rev 21.6; 22.17   **55.3:** Acts 13.34

⁵ Now you will summon foreign nations;
    at one time they did not know you,
    but now they will come running to
      join you!
I, the LORD your God, the holy God of
    Israel,
    will make all this happen;
    I will give you honour and glory."

⁶ Turn to the LORD and pray to him,
    now that he is near.
⁷ Let the wicked leave their way of life
    and change their way of thinking.
Let them turn to the LORD, our God;
    he is merciful and quick to forgive.
⁸ "My thoughts," says the LORD, "are not
     like yours,
    and my ways are different from yours.
⁹ As high as the heavens are above the
     earth,
    so high are my ways and thoughts
     above yours.

¹⁰ "My word is like the snow and the
     rain
    that come down from the sky to water
     the earth.
They make the crops grow
    and provide seed for sowing and food
     to eat.
¹¹ So also will be the word that I speak—
    it will not fail to do what I plan for
     it;
    it will do everything I send it to do.

¹² "You will leave Babylon with joy;
    you will be led out of the city in peace.
The mountains and hills will burst into
    singing,
    and the trees will shout for joy.
¹³ Cypress-trees will grow where now
     there are briars;
    myrtle-trees will come up in place of
     thorns.
This will be a sign that will last for
     ever,
    a reminder of what I, the LORD, have
     done."

God's People Will Include All Nations

56 The LORD says to his people, "Do what is just and right, for soon I will save you. ²I will bless those who always observe the Sabbath and do not misuse it. I will bless those who do nothing evil."

3 A foreigner who has joined the LORD's people should not say, "The LORD will not

let me worship with his people."

A man who has been castrated should never think that because he cannot have children, he can never be part of God's people. ⁴The LORD says to such a man, "If you honour me by observing the Sabbath and if you do what pleases me and faithfully keep my covenant, ⁵then your name will be remembered in my Temple and among my people longer than if you had sons and daughters. You will never be forgotten."

6 And the LORD says to those foreigners who become part of his people, who love him and serve him, who observe the Sabbath and faithfully keep his covenant: ⁷"I will bring you to Zion, my sacred hill, ᵛ give you joy in my house of prayer, and accept the sacrifices you offer on my altar. My Temple will be called a house of prayer for the people of all nations."

8 The Sovereign LORD, who has brought his people Israel home from exile, has promised that he will bring still other people to join them.

Israel's Leaders Are Condemned

9 The LORD has told the foreign nations to come like wild animals and devour his people. ¹⁰He says, "All the leaders, who are supposed to warn my people, are blind! They know nothing. They are like watchdogs that don't bark—they only lie about and dream. How they love to sleep! ¹¹They are like greedy dogs that never get enough. These leaders have no understanding. Every one of them does as he pleases and seeks his own advantage. ¹²'Let's get some wine,' these drunkards say, 'and drink all we can hold! Tomorrow will be even better than today!'"

Israel's Idolatry Is Condemned

57 Good people die, and no one understands or even cares. But when they die, no calamity can hurt them. ²Those who live good lives find peace and rest in death.

3 Come here to be judged, you sinners! You are no better than sorcerers, adulterers, and prostitutes. ⁴Who are you making fun of? Who are you liars jeering at? ⁵You worship the fertility gods by having sex under those sacred trees of yours. You offer your children as sacrifices in the rocky caves near the bed of a stream. ⁶You take smooth stones from there and worship them as gods. You pour

---

ᵛSACRED HILL: *See 2.3.*
55.10: 2 Cor 9.10   **56.7:** Mt 21.13; Mk 11.17; Lk 19.46

out wine as offerings to them and bring them grain-offerings. Do you think I am pleased with all this? ⁷You go to the high mountains to offer sacrifices and have sex. ⁸You set up your obscene idols just inside your front doors. You forsake me; you take off your clothes and climb into your large beds with your lovers, whom you pay to sleep with you. And there you satisfy your lust. ⁹You put on your perfumes and ointments and go to worship the god Molech. To find gods to worship, you send messengers far and wide, even to the world of the dead. ¹⁰You wear yourselves out looking for other gods, but you never give up. You think your obscene idols give you strength, and so you never grow weak.

11 The LORD says, "Who are these gods that make you afraid, so that you tell me lies and forget me completely? Have you stopped honouring me because I have kept silent for so long? ¹²You think that what you do is right, but I will expose your conduct, and your idols will not be able to help you. ¹³When you cry for help, let those idols of yours save you! A puff of wind will carry them off! But those who trust in me will live in the land and will worship me in my Temple."

God's Promise of Help and Healing

14 The LORD says, "Let my people return to me. Remove every obstacle from their path! Build the road, and make it ready!

15 "I am the high and holy God, who lives for ever. I live in a high and holy place, but I also live with people who are humble and repentant, so that I can restore their confidence and hope. ¹⁶I gave my people life, and I will not continue

to accuse them or be angry with them for ever. ʷ ¹⁷I was angry with them because of their sin and greed, and so I punished them and abandoned them. But they were stubborn and kept on going their own way. 18 "I have seen how they acted, but I will heal them. I will lead them and help them, and I will comfort those who mourn. ¹⁹I offer peace to all, both near and far! I will heal my people. ²⁰But evil men are like the restless sea, whose waves never stop rolling in, bringing filth and muck. ²¹There is no safety for sinners," says the LORD.

True Fasting

58 The LORD says, "Shout as loud as you can! Tell my people Israel about their sins! ²They worship me every day, claiming that they are eager to know my ways and obey my laws. They say they want me to give them just laws and that they take pleasure in worshipping me."

3 The people ask, "Why should we fast if the LORD never notices? Why should we go without food if he pays no attention?"

The LORD says to them, "The truth is that at the same time as you fast, you pursue your own interests and oppress your workers. ⁴Your fasting makes you violent, and you quarrel and fight. Do you think this kind of fasting will make me listen to your prayers? ⁵When you fast, you make yourselves suffer; you bow your heads low like a blade of grass, and spread out sackcloth and ashes to lie on. Is that what you call fasting? Do you think I will be pleased with that?

6 "The kind of fasting I want is this: Remove the chains of oppression and the

ʷI gave my people...for ever; *or* I will not continue to accuse them or be angry
with them for ever, for then they would die—the very people to whom I gave life.
57.19: Eph 2.17   **57.21:** Is 48.22

How they love to sleep! (56.10)

The kind of fasting I want is this (58.6-7)

yoke of injustice, and let the oppressed go free. [7] Share your food with the hungry and open your homes to the homeless poor. Give clothes to those who have nothing to wear, and do not refuse to help your own relatives.

[8] "Then my favour will shine on you like the morning sun, and your wounds will be quickly healed. I will always be with you to save you; my presence will protect you on every side. [9] When you pray, I will answer you. When you call to me, I will respond.

"If you put an end to oppression, to every gesture of contempt, and to every evil word; [10] if you give food to the hungry and satisfy those who are in need, then the darkness around you will turn to the brightness of noon. [11] And I will always guide you and satisfy you with good things. I will keep you strong and well. You will be like a garden that has plenty of water, like a spring of water that never runs dry. [12] Your people will rebuild what has long been in ruins, building again on the old foundations. You will be known as the people who rebuilt the walls, who restored the ruined houses."

The Reward for Keeping the Sabbath

[13] The LORD says, "If you treat the Sabbath as sacred and do not pursue your own interests on that day; if you value my holy day and honour it by not travelling, working, or talking idly on that day, [14] then you will find the joy that comes from serving me. I will make you honoured all over the world, and you will enjoy the land I gave to your ancestor, Jacob. I, the LORD, have spoken."

The Prophet Condemns the People's Sins

59 Don't think that the LORD is too weak to save you or too deaf to hear your call for help! [2] It is because of your sins that he doesn't hear you. It is your sins that separate you from

God when you try to worship him. [3] You are guilty of lying, violence, and murder.

[4] You go to court, but you haven't got justice on your side. You depend on lies to win your case. You carry out your plans to hurt others. [5-6] The evil plots you make are as deadly as the eggs of a poisonous snake. Crush an egg, out comes a snake! But your plots will do you no good—they are as useless as clothing made of cobwebs! [7] You are always planning something evil, and you can hardly wait to do it. You never hesitate to murder innocent people. You leave ruin and destruction wherever you go, [8] and no one is safe when you are about. Everything you do is unjust. You follow a crooked path, and no one who walks that path will ever be safe.

The People Confess Their Sin

[9] The people say, "Now we know why God does not save us from those who oppress us. We hope for light to walk by, but there is only darkness, [10] and we grope about like blind people. We stumble at noon, as if it were night, as if we were in the dark world of the dead. [11] We are frightened and distressed. We long for God to save us from oppression and wrong, but nothing happens.

[12] "LORD, our crimes against you are many. Our sins accuse us. We are well aware of them all. [13] We have rebelled against you, rejected you, and refused to follow you. We have oppressed others and turned away from you. Our thoughts are false; our words are lies. [14] Justice is driven away, and right cannot come near. Truth stumbles in the public square, and honesty finds no place there. [15] There is so little honesty that anyone who stops doing evil finds himself the victim of crime."

The LORD Prepares to Rescue His People

The LORD has seen this, and he is

58.7: Mt 25.35   59.7-8: Rom 3.15-17

Like a strong wind (59.19)

The Future Glory of Jerusalem

60 Arise, Jerusalem, and shine like
the sun;
The glory of the LORD is shining on you!
2 Other nations will be covered by
darkness,
But on you the light of the LORD will
shine;
The brightness of his presence will be
with you.
3 Nations will be drawn to your light,
And kings to the dawning of your new
day.

4 Look around you and see what is
happening:
Your people are gathering to come
home!
Your sons will come from far away;
Your daughters will be carried like
children.
5 You will see this and be filled with joy;
You will tremble with excitement.
The wealth of the nations will be
brought to you;
From across the sea their riches will
come.

6 Great caravans of camels will come,
from Midian and Ephah.
They will come from Sheba, bringing
gold and incense.
People will tell the good news of what
the LORD has done!
7 All the sheep of Kedar and Nebaioth
Will be brought to you as sacrifices
And offered on the altar to please the
LORD.
The LORD will make his Temple more
glorious than ever.

8 What are these ships that skim along
like clouds,
Like doves returning home?
9 They are ships coming from distant
lands,
Bringing God's people home.
They bring with them silver and gold
To honour the name of the LORD,
The holy God of Israel,
Who has made all nations honour his
people.

displeased that there is no justice. 16 He
is astonished to see that there is no one
to help the oppressed. So he will use his
own power to rescue them and to win
the victory. 17 He will wear justice like a
coat of armour and saving power like a
helmet. He will clothe himself with the
strong desire to set things right and to
punish and avenge the wrongs that people
suffer. 18 He will punish his enemies
according to what they have done, even
those who live in distant lands. 19 From
east to west everyone will fear him and
his great power. He will come like a
rushing river, like a strong wind.

20 The LORD says to his people, "I will
come to Jerusalem to defend you and to
save all of you that turn from your sins.
21 And I make a covenant with you: I have
given you my power and my teachings
to be yours for ever, and from now on
you are to obey me and teach your
children and your descendants to obey me
for all time to come."

10 The LORD says to Jerusalem,
"Foreigners will rebuild your walls,
And their kings will serve you.
In my anger I punished you,

59.16: Is 63.5   **59.17:** Eph 6.14, 17; 1 Thes 5.8   **59.20:** Rom 11.26

Great caravans of camels will come (60.6)

But now I will show you my favour
and mercy.
11 Day and night your gates will be open,
So that the kings of the nations
May bring you their wealth.
12 But nations that do not serve you
Will be completely destroyed.

13 "The wood of the pine, the juniper,
and the cypress,
The finest wood from the forests of
Lebanon,
Will be brought to rebuild you,
Jerusalem,
To make my Temple beautiful,
To make my city glorious.
14 The sons of those who oppressed you
will come
And bow low to show their respect.
All who once despised you will worship
at your feet.
They will call you 'The City of the LORD,'
'Zion, the City of Israel's Holy God.'

15 "You will no longer be forsaken and
hated,
A city deserted and desolate.
I will make you great and beautiful,
A place of joy for ever and ever.
16 Nations and kings will care for you
As a mother nurses her child.
You will know that I, the LORD, have
saved you,
That the mighty God of Israel sets you
free.

17 "I will bring you gold instead of bronze,
Silver and bronze instead of iron and
wood,
And iron instead of stone.
Your rulers will no longer oppress you;
I will make them rule with justice and
peace.

18 The sounds of violence will be heard
no more;
Destruction will not shatter your
country again.
I will protect and defend you like a wall;
You will praise me because I have saved
you.

19 "No longer will the sun be your light
by day
Or the moon be your light by night;
I, the LORD, will be your eternal light;
The light of my glory will shine on you.

I will be your eternal light (60.19)

20 Your days of grief will come to an
end.
I, the LORD, will be your eternal light,
More lasting than the sun and moon.
21 Your people will all do what is right,
And will possess the land for ever.
I planted them, I made them,
To reveal my greatness to all.
22 Even your smallest and humblest
family
Will become as great as a powerful
nation.
When the right time comes,
I will make this happen quickly.
I am the LORD!"

60.11: Rev 21.25-26   **60.14:** Rev 3.9   **60.19:** Rev 21.23, 22.5

The finest wood from the forests of Lebanon (60.13)

The Good News of Deliverance

61 The Sovereign LORD has filled me
with his spirit.
He has chosen me and sent me
To bring good news to the poor,
To heal the broken-hearted,
To announce release to captives
And freedom to those in prison.
2 He has sent me to proclaim
That the time has come
When the LORD will save his people
And defeat their enemies.
He has sent me to comfort all who
mourn,
3 To give to those who mourn in Zion
Joy and gladness instead of grief,
A song of praise instead of sorrow.
They will be like trees
That the LORD himself has planted.
They will all do what is right,
And God will be praised for what he
has done.
4 They will rebuild cities that have long
been in ruins.

5 My people, foreigners will serve you.
They will take care of your flocks
And farm your land and tend your
vineyards.
6 And you will be known as the priests
of the LORD,
The servants of our God.
You will enjoy the wealth of the nations
And be proud that it is yours.
7 Your shame and disgrace are ended.
You will live in your own land,
And your wealth will be doubled;
Your joy will last for ever.

8 The LORD says,
"I love justice and I hate oppression
and crime.
I will faithfully reward my people
And make an eternal covenant with
them.

9 They will be famous among the nations;
Everyone who sees them will know
That they are a people whom I have
blessed."

10 Jerusalem rejoices because of what
the LORD has done.
She is like a bride dressed for her
wedding.
God has clothed her with salvation and
victory.
11 As surely as seeds sprout and grow,
The Sovereign LORD will save his people,
And all the nations will praise him.

62 I will speak out to encourage
Jerusalem;
I will not be silent until she is saved,
And her victory shines like a torch in
the night.
2 Jerusalem, the nations will see you
victorious!
All their kings will see your glory.
You will be called by a new name,
A name given by the LORD himself.
3 You will be like a beautiful crown for
the LORD.
4 No longer will you be called "Forsaken,"
Or your land be called "The Deserted
Wife."
Your new name will be "God Is Pleased
with Her."
Your land will be called "Happily
Married,"
Because the LORD is pleased with you
And will be like a husband to your land.
5 Like a young man taking a virgin as
his bride,
He who formed you will marry you.
As a groom is delighted with his bride,
So your God will delight in you.

6 On your walls, Jerusalem, I have placed
sentries;
They must never be silent day or night.

61.1: Mt 11.5; Lk 7.22   **61.1–2:** Lk 4.18–19   **61.2:** Mt 5.4   **61.10:** Rev 21.2

Like a torch in the night (62.1)

They must remind the LORD of his promises
And never let him forget them.
⁷ They must give him no rest until he restores Jerusalem
And makes it a city the whole world praises.

⁸ The LORD has made a solemn promise,
And by his power he will carry it out:
"Your corn will no longer be food for your enemies,
And foreigners will no longer drink your wine.
⁹ But you that sowed and harvested the corn
Will eat the bread and praise the LORD.
You that tended and gathered the grapes
Will drink the wine in the courts of my Temple."

¹⁰ People of Jerusalem, go out of the city
And build a road for your returning people!
Prepare a highway; clear it of stones!
Put up a signal so that the nations can know
¹¹ That the LORD is announcing to all the earth:
"Tell the people of Jerusalem
That the LORD is coming to save you,
Bringing with him the people he has rescued."
¹² You will be called "God's Holy People,"
"The People the LORD Has Saved."
Jerusalem will be called "The City That God Loves,"
"The City That God Did Not Forsake."

The LORD's Victory over the Nations

63 "Who is this coming from the city of Bozrah in Edom? Who is this so splendidly dressed in red, marching along^x in power and strength?"

^x *Some ancient translations* marching along; *Hebrew* bowed down.
62.11: Is 40.10; Rev 22.12
63.1–6: Is 34.5–17; Jer 49.7–22; Ezek 25.12–14, 35.1–15; Amos 1.11–12; Obad 1–14; Mal 1.2–5

Build a road for your returning people! (62.10)

"It is the LORD, powerful to save, coming to announce his victory."

2 "Why is his clothing so red, like that of a man who tramples grapes to make wine?"

3 The LORD answers, "I have trampled the nations like grapes, and no one came to help me. I trampled them in my anger, and their blood has stained all my clothing. 4 I decided that the time to save my people had come; it was time to punish their enemies. 5 I was amazed when I looked and saw that there was no one to help me. But my anger made me strong, and I won the victory myself. 6 In my anger I trampled whole nations and shattered them. I poured out their life-blood on the ground."

The LORD's Goodness to Israel

7 I will tell of the LORD's unfailing love;
I praise him for all he has done for us.
He has richly blessed the people of Israel because of his mercy and constant love.

8 The LORD said, "They are my people; they will not deceive me." And so he saved them 9 from all their suffering. It was not an angel, but the LORD himself who saved them. In his love and compassion he rescued them. He had always taken care of them in the past, 10 but they rebelled against him and made his holy spirit sad. So the LORD became their enemy and fought against them.

11 But then they y remembered the past, the days of Moses, the servant of the LORD, and they asked, "Where now is the LORD, who saved the leaders of his people from the sea? Where is the LORD, who gave his spirit to Moses? 12-13 Where is the LORD, who by his power did great things through Moses, dividing the waters of the sea and leading his people through the deep water, to win everlasting fame for himself?"

Led by the LORD, they were as sure-footed as wild horses, and never stumbled. 14 As cattle are led into a fertile valley, so the LORD gave his people rest. He led his people and brought honour to his name.

A Prayer for Mercy and Help

15 LORD, look upon us from heaven, where you live in your holiness and glory. Where is your great concern for us? Where is your power? Where are your love and compassion? Do not ignore us. 16 You are our father. Our ancestors Abraham and Jacob do not acknowledge us, but you, LORD, are our father, the one who has always rescued us. 17 Why do you let us stray from your ways? Why do you make us so stubborn that we turn away from you? Come back, for the sake of those who serve you, for the sake of the people who have always been yours.

18 We, your holy people, were driven out by our enemies for a little while: they trampled down your sanctuary. z 19 You treat us as though you had never been our ruler, as though we had never been your people.

64 Why don't you tear the sky apart and come down? The mountains would see you and shake with fear. 2 They would tremble like water boiling over a hot fire. Come and reveal your power to your enemies, and make the nations tremble at your presence! 3 There was a time when you came and did terrifying things that we did not expect; the mountains saw you and shook with fear. 4 No one has ever seen or heard of a God like you, who does such deeds for those who put their hope in him. 5 You welcome those who find joy in doing what is right, those who remember how you want them to live. You were angry with us, but we went on sinning; in spite of your great anger we have continued to do wrong since ancient times. a 6 All of us have been sinful; even our best actions are filthy through and through. Because of our sins we are like leaves that wither and are blown away by the wind. 7 No one turns to you in prayer; no one goes to you for help. You have hidden yourself from us and have abandoned b us because of our sins.

8 But you are our father, LORD. We are like clay, and you are like the potter. You created us, 9 so do not be too angry with us or hold our sins against us for ever. We are your people; be merciful to us. 10 Your sacred cities are like a desert; Jerusalem is a deserted ruin, 11 and our Temple, the sacred and beautiful place where our ancestors praised you, has been destroyed by fire. All the places we loved

---

y Probable text they; Hebrew he.   z Verse 18 in Hebrew is unclear.
a Probable text in spite of...ancient times; Hebrew unclear.
b Some ancient translations abandoned; Hebrew melted.
63.3: Rev 14.20, 19.13, 15   **63.5:** Is 59.16   **63.12:** Ex 14.21   **64.4:** 1 Cor 2.9

are in ruins. ¹²Lᴏʀᴅ, are you unmoved by all this? Are you going to do nothing and make us suffer more than we can endure?

God's Punishment of the Rebellious

65 The Lᴏʀᴅ said, "I was ready to answer my people's prayers, but they did not pray. I was ready for them to find me, but they did not even try. The nation did not pray to me, even though I was always ready to answer, 'Here I am; I will help you.' ²I have always been ready to welcome my people, who stubbornly do what is wrong and go their own way. ³They shamelessly keep on making me angry. They offer pagan sacrifices in sacred gardens ᶜ and burn incense on pagan altars. ⁴At night they go to caves and tombs to consult the spirits of the dead. They eat pork and drink broth made from meat offered in pagan sacrifices. ⁵And then they say to others, 'Keep away from us; we are too holy for you to touch!' I cannot stand people like that—my anger against them is like a fire that never goes out.

6 "I have already decided on their punishment, and their sentence is written down. I will not overlook what they have done, but will repay them ⁷for their sins and the sins of their ancestors. They have burnt incense at pagan hill shrines and spoken evil of me. So I will punish them as their past deeds deserve."

8 The Lᴏʀᴅ says, "No one destroys good grapes; instead, they make wine with them. Neither will I destroy all my people—I will save those who serve me. ⁹I will bless the Israelites who belong to the tribe of Judah, and their descendants will possess my land of mountains. My chosen people, who serve me, will live there. ¹⁰They will worship me and will lead their sheep and cattle to pasture in the Plain of Sharon in the west and in the Valley of Trouble in the east.

11 "But it will be different for you that forsake me, who ignore Zion, my sacred hill, ᵉ and worship Gad and Meni, the gods of luck and fate. ¹²It will be your fate to die a violent death, because you did not answer when I called you or listen when I spoke. You chose to disobey me and do evil. ¹³And so I tell you that those who worship and obey me will have plenty

to eat and drink, but you will be hungry and thirsty. They will be happy, but you will be disgraced. ¹⁴They will sing for joy, but you will cry with a broken heart. ¹⁵My chosen people will use your name as a curse. I, the Sovereign Lᴏʀᴅ, will put you to death. But I will give a new name to those who obey me. ¹⁶Anyone in the land who asks for a blessing will ask to be blessed by the Faithful God. Whoever takes an oath will swear by the name of the Faithful God. The troubles of the past will be gone and forgotten."

The New Creation

17 The Lᴏʀᴅ says, "I am making a new earth and new heavens. The events of the past will be completely forgotten. ¹⁸Be glad and rejoice for ever in what I create. The new Jerusalem I make will be full of joy, and her people will be happy. ¹⁹I myself will be filled with joy because of Jerusalem and her people. There will be no weeping there, no calling for help. ²⁰Babies will no longer die in infancy, and all people will live out their life span. Those who live to be a hundred will be considered young. To die before that would be a sign that I had punished them. ²¹⁻²²People will build houses and live in them themselves—they will not be used by someone else. They will plant vineyards and enjoy the wine—it will not be drunk by others. Like trees, my people will live long lives. They will fully enjoy the things that they have worked for. ²³The work they do will be successful, and their children will not meet with disaster. I will bless them and their descendants for all time to come. ²⁴Even before they finish praying to me, I will answer their prayers. ²⁵Wolves and lambs will eat together; lions will eat straw, as cattle do, and snakes will no longer be dangerous. On Zion, my sacred hill, ᶠ there will be nothing harmful or evil."

The Lᴏʀᴅ Judges the Nations

66 The Lᴏʀᴅ says, "Heaven is my throne, and the earth is my footstool. What kind of house, then, could you build for me, what kind of place for me to live in? ²I myself created the whole universe! I am pleased with those who are humble and repentant, who fear me and obey me.

ᶜ SACRED GARDENS: *See 1.29.*   ᵉ SACRED HILL: *See 2.3.*   ᶠ SACRED HILL: see 2.3.
65.1: Rom 10.20   **65.2:** Rom 10.21   **65.10:** Josh 7.24-26
65.17: Is 66.22; 2 Pet 3.13; Rev 21.1   **65.19:** Rev 21.4   **65.25:** Is 11.6-9
66.1: Mt 5.34, 35, 23.22   **66.1-2a:** Acts 7.49-50

3 "The people do as they please. It's all the same to them whether they kill a bull as a sacrifice or sacrifice a human being; whether they sacrifice a lamb or break a dog's neck; whether they present a grain-offering or offer pigs' blood; whether they offer incense or pray to an idol. They take pleasure in disgusting ways of worship. 4 So I will bring disaster upon them—the very things they are afraid of—because no one answered when I called or listened when I spoke. They chose to disobey me and do evil."

5 Listen to what the LORD says, you that fear him and obey him: "Because you are faithful to me, some of your own people hate you and will have nothing to do with you. They mock you and say, 'Let the LORD show his greatness and save you, so that we may see you rejoice.' But they themselves will be disgraced! 6 Listen! That loud noise in the city, that sound in the Temple, is the sound of the LORD punishing his enemies!

7 "My holy city is like a woman who suddenly gives birth to a child, without ever going into labour. 8 Has anyone ever seen or heard of such a thing? Has a nation ever been born in a day? Zion will not have to suffer long, before the nation is born. 9 Do not think that I will bring my people to the point of birth and not let them be born." The LORD has spoken.

10 Rejoice with Jerusalem; be glad for
      her,
    all you that love this city!
  Rejoice with her now,
    all you that have mourned for her!
11 You will enjoy her prosperity,
    like a child at its mother's breast.

12 The LORD says, "I will bring you lasting prosperity; the wealth of the nations will flow to you like a river that never goes dry. You will be like a child that is nursed by its mother, carried in her arms, and treated with love. 13 I will comfort you in Jerusalem, as a mother comforts her child. 14 When you see this happen, you will be glad; it will make

you strong and healthy. Then you will know that I, the LORD, help those who obey me, and I show my anger against my enemies."

15 The LORD will come with fire. He will ride on the wings of a storm to punish those he is angry with. 16 By fire and sword he will punish all the people of the world whom he finds guilty—and many will be put to death.

17 The LORD says, "The end is near for those who purify themselves for pagan worship, who go in procession to sacred gardens, g and who eat pork and mice and other disgusting foods. 18 I know h their thoughts and their deeds. I am coming i to gather the people of all the nations. When they come together, they will see what my power can do 19 and will know that I am the one who punishes them.

"But I will spare some of them and send them to the nations and the distant lands that have not heard of my fame or seen my greatness and power: to Spain, Libya, j and Lydia, with its skilled bowmen, and to Tubal and Greece. Among these nations they will proclaim my greatness. 20 They will bring back all your fellow-countrymen from the nations as a gift to me. They will bring them to my sacred hill k in Jerusalem on horses, mules, and camels, and in chariots and wagons, just as Israelites bring grain-offerings to the Temple in ritually clean containers. 21 I will make some of them priests and Levites.

22 "Just as the new earth and the new heavens will endure by my power, so your descendants and your name will endure. 23 On every New Moon Festival and every Sabbath, people of every nation will come to worship me here in Jerusalem," says the LORD. 24 "As they leave, they will see the dead bodies of those who have rebelled against me. The worms that eat them will never die, and the fire that burns them will never be put out. The sight of them will be disgusting to all mankind."

---

g SACRED GARDENS: See 1.29.   h Some ancient translations I know; Hebrew I.
i Some ancient translations I am coming; Hebrew He is coming.
j One ancient translation Libya; Hebrew Pul.   k SACRED HILL: See 2.3.
66.7: Rev 12.5   **66.22:** Is 65.17; 2 Pet 3.13; Rev 21.1   **66.24:** Mk 9.48

THE BOOK OF
JEREMIAH

INTRODUCTION

The prophet Jeremiah lived during the latter part of the seventh century and the first part of the sixth century B.C. During his long ministry he warned God's people of the catastrophe that was to fall upon the nation because of their idolatry and sin. He lived to see this prediction come true with the fall of Jerusalem to the Babylonian king, Nebuchadnezzar, the destruction of the city and the Temple, and the exile to Babylonia of Judah's king and many of the people. He also foretold the eventual return of the people from exile and the restoration of the nation.

The book of *Jeremiah* may be divided into the following parts: (1) The call of Jeremiah. (2) Messages from God to the nation of Judah and its rulers during the reigns of Josiah, Jehoiakim, Jehoiachin, and Zedekiah. (3) Material from the memoirs of Baruch, Jeremiah's secretary, including various prophecies and important events from the life of Jeremiah. (4) Messages from the Lord about various foreign nations. (5) A historical appendix, giving an account of the fall of Jerusalem, and the exile to Babylon.

Jeremiah was a sensitive man who deeply loved his people, and who hated to have to pronounce judgement upon them. In many passages he spoke with deep emotion about the things he suffered because God had called him to be a prophet. The word of the Lord was like fire in his heart—he could not keep it back.

Some of the greatest words in the book point beyond Jeremiah's own troubled time to the day when there would be a new covenant, one that God's people would keep without a teacher to remind them, because it would be written on their hearts (31.31-34).

Outline of Contents

The call of Jeremiah 1.1-19
Prophecies during the reigns of Josiah, Jehoiakim, Jehoiachin, and Zedekiah 2.1—25.38
Events in Jeremiah's life 26.1—45.5
Prophecies against the nations 46.1—51.64
The fall of Jerusalem 52.1-34

Jeremiah

1 This book is the account of what was said by Jeremiah son of Hilkiah, one of the priests of the town of Anathoth in the territory of Benjamin. ²The LORD spoke to Jeremiah in the thirteenth year that Josiah son of Amon was king of Judah, ³and he spoke to him again when Josiah's son Jehoiakim was king. After that, the LORD spoke to him many times, until the eleventh year of the reign of Zedekiah son of Josiah. In the fifth month of that year the people of Jerusalem were taken into exile.

The Call of Jeremiah

4 The LORD said to me, ⁵"I chose you before I gave you life, and before you were born I selected you to be a prophet to the nations."

6 I answered, "Sovereign LORD, I don't know how to speak; I am too young."

7 But the LORD said to me, "Do not say that you are too young, but go to the people I send you to, and tell them everything I command you to say. ⁸Do not be afraid of them, for I will be with you to protect you. I, the LORD, have spoken!"

9 Then the LORD stretched out his hand, touched my lips, and said to me, "Listen, I am giving you the words you must speak. ¹⁰Today I give you authority over nations and kingdoms to uproot and to pull down, to destroy and to overthrow, to build and to plant."

Two Visions

11 The LORD asked me, "Jeremiah, what do you see?"

I answered, "A branch of an almond-tree."

12 "You are right," the LORD said, "and I am watching ᵃ to see that my words come true."

13 Then the LORD spoke to me again. "What else do you see?" he asked.

I answered, "I see a pot boiling in the north, and it is about to tip over this way."

14 He said to me, "Destruction will boil over from the north on all who live in this land, ¹⁵because I am calling all the nations in the north to come. Their kings will set up their thrones at the gates of Jerusalem and round its walls, and also round the other cities of Judah. ¹⁶I will

I am giving you the words you must speak (1.9)

punish my people because they have sinned; they have abandoned me, have offered sacrifices to other gods, and have made idols and worshipped them. ¹⁷Get ready, Jeremiah; go and tell them everything I command you to say. Do not be afraid of them now, or I will make you even more afraid when you are with them. ¹⁸⁻¹⁹Listen, Jeremiah! Everyone in this land—the kings of Judah, the officials, the priests, and the people—will be against you. But today I am giving you the strength to resist them; you will be like a fortified city, an iron pillar, and a bronze wall. They will not defeat you, for I will be with you to protect you. I, the LORD, have spoken."

ᵃWATCHING: *This word in Hebrew sounds like the Hebrew for "almond."*
1.2: 2 Kgs 22.3—23.27; 2 Chr 34.8—35.19
1.3: 2 Kgs 23.36—24.7,18—25.21; 2 Chr 36.5-8, 11.21

God's Care for Israel

2 The LORD told me ²to proclaim this message to everyone in Jerusalem.
"I remember how faithful you were
when you were young,
how you loved me when we were first
married;
you followed me through the desert,
through a land that had not been
sown.
³ Israel, you belonged to me alone;
you were my sacred possession.
I sent suffering and disaster
on everyone who hurt you.
I, the LORD, have spoken."

The Sin of Israel's Ancestors

4 Listen to the LORD's message, you descendants of Jacob, you tribes of Israel.
⁵ The LORD says:
"What accusation did your ancestors
bring against me?
What made them turn away from me?
They worshipped worthless idols
and became worthless themselves.
⁶ They did not care about me,
even though I rescued them from
Egypt
and led them through the wilderness:
a land of deserts and sand-dunes,
a dry and dangerous land
where no one lives
and no one will even travel.
⁷ I brought them into a fertile land,
to enjoy its harvests and its other
good things.
But instead they ruined my land;
they defiled the country I had given
them.
⁸ The priests did not ask, 'Where is the
LORD?'
My own priests did not know me.
The rulers rebelled against me;
the prophets spoke in the name of
Baal
and worshipped useless idols.

The LORD's Case against His People

⁹ "And so I, the LORD, will state my case
against my people again.
I will bring charges against their
descendants.
¹⁰ Go west to the island of Cyprus,
and send someone eastwards to the
land of Kedar.
You will see that nothing like this has
ever happened before.
¹¹ No other nation has ever changed its
gods,

even though they were not real.
But my people have exchanged me,
the God who has brought them
honour,
for gods that can do nothing for them.
¹² And so I command the sky to shake
with horror,
to be amazed and astonished,
¹³ for my people have committed two
sins:
they have turned away from me,
the spring of fresh water,
and they have dug cisterns,
cracked cisterns that can hold no
water at all.

The Results of Israel's Unfaithfulness

¹⁴ "Israel is not a slave;
he was not born into slavery.
Why then do his enemies hunt him
down?
¹⁵ They have roared at him like lions;
they have made his land a desert,
and his towns lie in ruins, completely
abandoned.
¹⁶ Yes, the men of Memphis and
Tahpanhes
have cracked his skull.
¹⁷ Israel, you brought this on yourself!
You deserted me, the LORD your God,
while I was leading you along the way.
¹⁸ What do you think you will gain by
going to Egypt
to drink water from the Nile?
What do you think you will gain by
going to Assyria
to drink water from the Euphrates?
¹⁹ Your own evil will punish you,
and your turning from me will
condemn you.
You will learn how bitter and wrong
it is
to abandon me, the LORD your God,
and no longer to remain loyal to
me.
I, the Sovereign LORD Almighty, have
spoken."

Israel Refuses to Worship the LORD

20 The Sovereign LORD says,
"Israel, long ago you rejected my
authority;
you refused to obey me and worship
me.
On every high hill
and under every green tree
you worshipped fertility gods.
²¹ I planted you like a choice vine
from the very best seed.
But look what you have become!

You are like a rotten, worthless vine.
22 Even if you washed with the strongest
      soap,
    I would still see the stain of your guilt.
23 How can you say you have not defiled
      yourself,
    that you have never worshipped Baal?
    Look how you sinned in the valley;
      see what you have done.
    You are like a wild camel on heat,
      running about loose,
24   rushing into the desert. *b*
    When she is on heat, who can control
      her?
    No male that wants her has to trouble
      himself;
    she is always available at mating time.
25 Israel, don't wear your feet out,
      or let your throat become dry
    from chasing after other gods.
    But you say, 'No! I can't turn back.
    I have loved foreign gods
    and will go after them.' "

Israel Deserves to be Punished

26 The LORD says, "Just as a thief is
disgraced when caught, so all you people
of Israel will be disgraced—your kings
and officials, your priests and prophets.
27 You will all be disgraced—you that say
that a tree is your father and that a rock
is your mother. This will happen because
you turned away from me instead of
turning to me. But when you are in
trouble, you ask me to come and save
you.
28 "Where are the gods that you made
for yourselves? When you are in trouble,
let them save you—if they can! Judah,
you have as many gods as you have cities.
29 What is your complaint? Why have you
rebelled against me? 30 I punished you,
but it did no good; you would not let me
correct you. Like a raging lion, you have
murdered your prophets. 31 People of
Israel, listen to what I am saying. Have
I been like a desert to you, like a dark
and dangerous land? Why, then, do you
say that you will do as you please, that
you will never come back to me? 32 Does
a young woman forget her jewellery, or
a bride her wedding-dress? But my people
have forgotten me for more days than
can be counted. 33 You certainly know how
to chase after lovers. Even the worst of
women can learn from you. 34 Your clothes
are stained with the blood of the poor and
innocent, not with the blood of burglars.

"But in spite of all this, 35 you say, 'I
am innocent; surely the LORD is no longer
angry with me.' But I, the LORD, will
punish you because you deny that you
have sinned. 36 You have cheapened yourself by turning to the gods of other
nations. You will be disappointed by
Egypt, just as you were by Assyria. 37 You
will turn away from Egypt, hanging your
head in shame. I, the LORD, have rejected
those you trust; you will not gain anything
from them."

Unfaithful Israel

3 The LORD says, "If a man divorces
   his wife, and she leaves him and
becomes another man's wife, he cannot
take her back again. This would completely defile the land. But, Israel, you
have had many lovers, and now you want
to return to me! 2 Look up at the hill-tops.
Is there any place where you have not
acted like a prostitute? You waited for
lovers along the roadside, as an Arab
waits for victims in the desert. You have
defiled the land with your prostitution.
3 That is why the rains were held back,
and the spring showers did not come. You
even look like a prostitute; you have no
shame.
4 "And now you say to me, 'You are
my father, and you have loved me ever
since I was a child. 5 You won't always
be angry; you won't be cross with me
for ever.' Israel, that is what you said,
but you did all the evil you could."

Israel and Judah Must Repent

6 When Josiah was king, the LORD said
to me, "Have you seen what Israel, that
unfaithful woman, has done? She has
turned away from me, and on every high
hill and under every green tree she has
acted like a prostitute. 7 I thought that
after she had done all this, she would
surely return to me. But she did not return,
and her unfaithful sister Judah saw it all.
8 Judah also saw that I divorced Israel and
sent her away because she had turned
from me and had become a prostitute.
But Judah, Israel's unfaithful sister, was
not afraid. She too became a prostitute
9 and was not at all ashamed. She defiled
the land, and she committed adultery by
worshipping stones and trees. 10 And after
all this, Judah, Israel's unfaithful sister,
only pretended to return to me; she was
not sincere. I, the LORD, have spoken."

b Probable text rushing into the desert; *Hebrew* a wild donkey used to the desert.
3.6: 2 Kgs 22.1—23.30; 2 Chr 34.1—35.27

Worshipping stones and trees (3.9)

11 Then the LORD told me that, even though Israel had turned away from him, she had proved to be better than unfaithful Judah. 12 He told me to go and say to Israel, "Unfaithful Israel, come back to me. I am merciful and will not be angry; I will not be angry with you for ever. 13 Only admit that you are guilty and that you have rebelled against the LORD, your God. Confess that under every green tree you have given your love to foreign gods and that you have not obeyed my commands. I, the LORD, have spoken.

14 "Unfaithful people, come back; you belong to me. I will take one of you from each town and two from each clan, and I will bring you back to Mount Zion. 15 I will give you rulers who obey me, and they will rule you with wisdom and understanding. 16 Then when you have become numerous in that land, people will no longer talk about my Covenant Box. They will no longer think about it or remember it; they will not even need it, nor will they make another one. 17 When that time comes, Jerusalem will be called 'The Throne of the LORD,' and all nations will gather there to worship me. They will no longer do what their stubborn and evil hearts tell them. 18 Israel will join with Judah, and together they will come from exile in the country in the north and will return to the land that I gave your ancestors as a permanent possession."

The Idolatry of God's People

19 The LORD says,
"Israel, I wanted to accept you as my son
and give you a delightful land,
the most beautiful land in all the world.
I wanted you to call me father,
and never again turn away from me.
20 But like an unfaithful wife,
you have not been faithful to me.
I, the LORD, have spoken."

21 A noise is heard on the hill-tops:
it is the people of Israel crying and pleading,
because they have lived sinful lives
and have forgotten the LORD their God.
22 Return, all of you who have turned away from the LORD;
he will heal you and make you faithful.

You say, "Yes, we are coming to the LORD, because he is our God. 23 We were not helped at all by our pagan worship on the hill-tops. Help for Israel comes only from the LORD our God. 24 But the worship of Baal, the god of shame, has made us lose flocks and herds, sons and daughters—everything that our ancestors have worked for since ancient times. 25 We should lie down in shame and let our disgrace cover us. We and our ancestors

The enemy is coming like clouds (4.13)

have always sinned against the LORD our God; we have never obeyed his commands."

A Call to Repentance

4 The LORD says, "People of Israel, if you want to turn, then turn back to me. If you are faithful to me and remove the idols I hate, ²it will be right for you to swear by my name. Then[c] all the nations will ask me to bless them, and they will praise me."

3 The LORD says to the people of Judah and Jerusalem, "Plough up your unploughed fields; do not sow your seeds among thorns. ⁴Keep your covenant with me, your LORD, and dedicate yourselves to me, you people of Judah and Jerusalem. If you don't, my anger will burn like fire because of the evil things you have done. It will burn, and there will be no one to put it out."

Judah Is Threatened with Invasion

⁵ Blow the trumpet throughout the land!
  Shout loud and clear!
  Tell the people of Judah and Jerusalem
    to run to the fortified cities.
⁶ Point the way to Zion!
  Run for safety! Don't delay!
  The LORD is bringing disaster
    and great destruction from the north.
⁷ Like a lion coming from its hiding place,
    a destroyer of nations has set out.
  He is coming to destroy Judah.
  The cities of Judah will be left in ruins,
    and no one will live in them.
⁸ So put on sackcloth, and weep and wail
    because the fierce anger of the LORD
    has not turned away from Judah.

9 The LORD said, "On that day kings and officials will lose their courage; priests will be shocked and prophets will be astonished."

10 Then I said, "Sovereign LORD, you have completely deceived the people of Jerusalem! You have said there would be peace, but a sword is at their throats."

11 The time is coming when the people of Jerusalem will be told that a scorching wind is blowing in from the desert towards them. It will not be a gentle wind that only blows away the chaff—¹²the wind that comes at the LORD's command will be much stronger than that! It is the LORD himself who is pronouncing judgement on his people.

Judah Is Surrounded by Enemies

13 Look, the enemy is coming like clouds. His war-chariots are like a whirlwind, and his horses are faster than eagles. We are lost! We are doomed!

14 Jerusalem, wash the evil from your heart, so that you may be saved. How long will you go on thinking sinful thoughts?

15 Messengers from the city of Dan and from the hills of Ephraim announce the bad news. ¹⁶They have come to warn the nations and to tell Jerusalem that enemies are coming from a country far away. These enemies will shout against the cities of Judah ¹⁷and will surround Jerusalem like men guarding a field, because her people have rebelled against the LORD. The LORD has spoken.

18 Judah, you have brought this on yourself by the way you have lived and by the things you have done. Your sin has caused this suffering; it has stabbed you through the heart.

Jeremiah's Sorrow for His People

¹⁹ The pain! I can't bear the pain!
  My heart! My heart! My heart is beating wildly!

[c]it will be right...name. Then; *or* and if you swear by my name and are truthful, just, and righteous, then.
4.3: Hos 10.12

I can't keep quiet;
I hear the trumpets
and the shouts of battle.

20 One disaster follows another;
the whole country is left in ruins.
Suddenly our tents are destroyed;
their curtains are torn to pieces.

21 How long must I see the battle raging
and hear the blasts of trumpets?

22 The LORD says, "My people are stupid;
they don't know me.
They are like foolish children;
they have no understanding.
They are experts at doing what is evil,
but failures at doing what is good."

Jeremiah's Vision of the Coming Destruction

23 I looked at the earth—it was a barren
waste;
at the sky—there was no light.

24 I looked at the mountains—they were
shaking,
and the hills were rocking to and fro.

25 I saw that there were no people;
even the birds had flown away.

26 The fertile land had become a desert;
its cities were in ruins
because of the LORD's fierce anger.

27 (The LORD has said that the whole
earth will become a wilderness, but that
he will not completely destroy it.)

28 The earth will mourn;
the sky will grow dark.
The LORD has spoken
and will not change his mind.
He has made his decision
and will not turn back.

29 At the noise of the horsemen and
bowmen
everyone will run away.
Some will run to the forest,
others will climb up among the rocks.
Every town will be left empty,
and no one will live in them again.

30 Jerusalem, you are doomed!
Why do you dress in scarlet?
Why do you put on jewellery and
paint your eyes?
You are making yourself beautiful for
nothing!
Your lovers have rejected you
and want to kill you.

31 I heard a cry, like a woman in labour,
a scream like a woman bearing her
first child.
It was the cry of Jerusalem gasping for
breath,
stretching out her hand and saying,
"I am doomed!

They are coming to kill me!"

The Sin of Jerusalem

5 People of Jerusalem, run through
your streets!
Look around! See for yourselves!
Search the market-places!
Can you find one person
who does what is right
and tries to be faithful to God?
If you can, the LORD will forgive
Jerusalem.

2 Even though you claim to worship the
LORD,
you do not mean what you say.

3 Surely the LORD looks for faithfulness.
He struck you, but you paid no
attention;
he crushed you, but you refused to
learn.
You were stubborn and would not turn
from your sins.

4 Then I thought, "These are only the poor
and ignorant.
They behave foolishly;
they don't know what their God
requires,
what the LORD wants them to do.

5 I will go to the people in power,
and talk with them.
Surely they know what their God
requires,
what the LORD wants them to do."
But all of them have rejected the LORD's
authority
and refuse to obey him.

6 That is why lions from the forest will
kill them;
wolves from the desert will tear them
to pieces,
and leopards will prowl through their
towns.
If those people go out, they will be torn
apart
because their sins are numerous
and time after time they have turned
from God.

7 The LORD asked, "Why should I forgive
the sins of my people?
They have abandoned me
and have worshipped gods that are
not real.
I fed my people until they were full,
but they committed adultery
and spent their time with prostitutes.

8 They were like well-fed stallions wild
with desire,
each lusting for his neighbour's wife.

9 Shouldn't I punish them for these things

and take revenge on a nation such
as this?
10 I will send enemies to cut down my
people's vineyards,
but not to destroy them completely.
I will tell them to strip away the
branches,
because those branches are not mine.
11 The people of Israel and Judah
have betrayed me completely.
I, the LORD, have spoken."

The LORD Rejects Israel

12 The LORD's people have denied him
and have said, "He won't really do
anything.*d* We won't have hard times; we
won't have war or famine." 13-14 They
have said that the prophets are nothing
but windbags and that they have no
message from the LORD. The LORD God
Almighty said to me, "Jeremiah, because
these people have said such things, I will
make my words like a fire in your mouth.
The people will be like wood, and the
fire will burn them up."

15 People of Israel, the LORD is bringing
a nation from afar to attack you. It is
a strong and ancient nation, a nation
whose language you do not know. 16 Their
bowmen are mighty soldiers who kill
without mercy. 17 They will devour your
crops and your food; they will kill your
sons and your daughters. They will
slaughter your flocks and your herds and
destroy your vines and fig-trees. The
fortified cities in which you trust will be
destroyed by their army.

18 The LORD says, "Yet even in those
days I will not completely destroy my
people. 19 When they ask why I did all
these things, tell them, Jeremiah, that just
as they turned away from me and served
foreign gods in their own land, so they
will serve strangers in a land that is not
theirs."

God Warns His People

20 The LORD says, "Tell the descendants
of Jacob, tell the people of Judah: 21 Pay
attention, you foolish and stupid people,
who have eyes, but cannot see, and have
ears, but cannot hear. 22 I am the LORD;
why don't you fear me? Why don't you
tremble before me? I placed the sand as
the boundary of the sea, a permanent
boundary that it cannot cross. The sea
may toss, but it cannot go beyond it; the
waves may roar, but they cannot break
through. 23 But you people! You are
stubborn and rebellious; you have turned
aside and left me. 24 You never thought
to honour me, even though I send the
autumn rains and the spring rains and
give you the harvest season each year.
25 Instead, your sins have kept these good
things from you.

26 "Evil men live among my people;
they lie in wait like men who spread nets
to catch birds,*e* but they have set their
traps to catch men. 27 Just as a hunter
fills his cage with birds, they have filled
their houses with loot. That is why they
are powerful and rich, 28 why they are fat
and well fed. There is no limit to their
evil deeds. They do not give orphans their
rights or show justice to the oppressed.

29 "But I, the LORD, will punish them
for these things; I will take revenge on
this nation. 30 A terrible and shocking
thing has happened in the land: 31 prophets speak nothing but lies; priests rule
as the prophets command, and my people
offer no objections. But what will they
do when it all comes to an end?"

Jerusalem Is Surrounded by Enemies

6 People of Benjamin, run for safety!
Escape from Jerusalem! Sound the
trumpet in Tekoa and build a signal fire
in Beth Haccherem. Disaster and destruction are about to come from the north.
2 The city of Zion is beautiful, but it will
be destroyed; 3 kings will camp there with
their armies. They will pitch their tents
round the city, and each one will camp
wherever he wants. 4 They will say,
"Prepare to attack Jerusalem! Get ready!
We'll attack at noon!" But then they will
say, "It's too late, the day is almost over,
and the evening shadows are growing
long. 5 We'll attack by night; we'll destroy
the city's fortresses."

6 The LORD Almighty has ordered these
kings to cut down trees and build mounds
in order to besiege Jerusalem. He has said,
"I will punish this city because it is full
of oppression. 7 As a well keeps its water
fresh, so Jerusalem keeps its evil fresh.
I hear violence and destruction in the city;
sickness and wounds are all I see. 8 People
of Jerusalem, let these troubles be a
warning to you, or else I will abandon
you; I will turn your city into a desert,
a place where no one lives."

---

d He won't...anything; *or* We don't want anything to do with him.
e *Probable text* they...birds; *Hebrew unclear.*
5.21: Is 6.9–10; Ezek 12.2; Mk 8.18   **5.22:** Job 38.8–11

Rebellious Israel

9 The LORD Almighty said to me, "Israel will be stripped clean like a vineyard from which every grape has been picked. So you must rescue everyone you can while there is still time."

10 I answered, "Who would listen to me if I spoke to them and warned them? They are stubborn and refuse to listen to your message; they laugh at what you tell me to say. 11 Your anger against them burns in me too, LORD, and I can't hold it in any longer."

Then the LORD said to me, "Pour out my anger on the children in the streets and on the gatherings of the young men. Husbands and wives will be taken away, and even the very old will not be spared. 12 Their houses will be given to others, and so will their fields and their wives. I am going to punish the people of this land. 13 Everyone, great and small, tries to make money dishonestly; even prophets and priests cheat the people. 14 They act as if my people's wounds were only scratches. 'All is well,' they say, when all is not well. 15 Were they ashamed because they did these disgusting things? No, they were not at all ashamed; they don't even know how to blush. And so they will fall as others have fallen; when I punish them, that will be the end of them. I, the LORD, have spoken."

Israel Rejects God's Way

16 The LORD said to his people, "Stand at the crossroads and look. Ask for the ancient paths and where the best road is. Walk on it, and you will live in peace."

But they said, "No, we will not!" 17 Then the LORD appointed watchmen to listen for the trumpet's warning. But they said, "We will not listen."

18 So the LORD said, "Listen, you nations, and learn what is going to happen to my people. 19 Listen, earth! As punishment for all their schemes I am bringing ruin on these people, because they have rejected my teaching and have not obeyed my words. 20 What do I care about the incense they bring me from Sheba, or the spices from a distant land? I will not accept their offerings or be pleased with their sacrifices. 21 And so I will make these people stumble and fall. Fathers and sons will die, and so will friends and neighbours."

Invasion from the North

22 The LORD says, "People are coming from a country in the north; a mighty nation far away is preparing for war. 23 They have taken up their bows and swords; they are cruel and merciless. They sound like the roaring sea, as they ride their horses. They are ready for battle against Jerusalem."

24 "We have heard the news," say the

We have heard the news...and our hands hang limp (6.24)

people of Jerusalem, "and our hands hang limp; we are seized by anguish and pain like a woman in labour. 25 We dare not go to the countryside or walk on the roads, because our enemies are armed and terror is all round us."

26 The LORD says to his people, "Put on sackcloth and roll in ashes. Mourn with bitter tears as you would for an only son, because the one who comes to destroy you will suddenly attack. 27 Jeremiah, test my people, as you would test metal, and find out what they are like. 28 They are all stubborn rebels, hard as bronze and iron. They are all corrupt, going round and spreading gossip. 29 The furnace burns fiercely, but the waste metals do not melt and run off. It is useless to go on refining

6.12–15: Jer 8.10–12　　**6.14:** Ezek 13.10　　**6.16:** Mt 11.29

my people, because those who are evil are not taken away. ³⁰They will be called worthless dross, because I, the LORD, have rejected them."

Jeremiah Preaches in the Temple

7 ¹⁻³The LORD sent me to the gate of the Temple where the people of Judah went in to worship. He told me to stand there and announce what the LORD Almighty, the God of Israel, had to say to them: "Change the way you are living and the things you are doing, and I will let you go on living here. ⁴Stop believing those deceitful words, 'We are safe! This is the LORD's Temple, this is the LORD's Temple, this is the LORD's Temple!'

5 "Change the way you are living and stop doing the things you are doing. Be fair in your treatment of one another. ⁶Stop taking advantage of aliens, orphans, and widows. Stop killing innocent people in this land. Stop worshipping other gods, for that will destroy you. ⁷If you change, I will let you go on living here in the land which I gave your ancestors as a permanent possession.

8 "Look, you put your trust in deceitful words. ⁹You steal, murder, commit adultery, tell lies under oath, offer sacrifices to Baal, and worship gods that you had not known before. ¹⁰You do these things I hate, and then you come and stand in my presence, in my own Temple, and say, 'We are safe!' ¹¹Do you think that my Temple is a hiding place for robbers? I have seen what you are doing. ¹²Go to Shiloh,ᶠ the first place where I chose to be worshipped, and see what I did to it because of the sins of my people Israel. ¹³You have committed all these sins, and even though I spoke to you over and over again, you refused to listen. You would not answer when I called you. ¹⁴And so, what I did to Shiloh I will do to this Temple of mine, in which you trust. Here in this place that I gave to your ancestors and to you, I will do the same thing that I did to Shiloh. ¹⁵I will drive you out of my sight as I drove out your relatives, the people of Israel. I, the LORD, have spoken."

The People's Disobedience

16 The LORD said, "Jeremiah, do not pray for these people. Do not cry or pray on their behalf; do not plead with me, for I will not listen to you. ¹⁷Don't you see what they are doing in the cities of Judah and in the streets of Jerusalem? ¹⁸The children gather firewood, the men build fires, and the women mix dough to bake cakes for the goddess they call the Queen of Heaven. They also pour out wine-offerings to other gods, in order to hurt me. ¹⁹But am I really the one they are hurting? No, they are hurting themselves and bringing shame on themselves. ²⁰And so I, the Sovereign LORD, will pour out my fierce anger on this Temple. I will pour it out on people and animals alike, and even on the trees and the crops. My anger will be like a fire that no one can put out.

21 "My people, some sacrifices you burn completely on the altar, and some you are permitted to eat. But what I, the LORD, say is that you might as well eat them all. ²²I gave your ancestors no commands about burnt-offerings or any other kinds of sacrifices, when I brought them out of Egypt. ²³But I did command them to obey me, so that I would be their God and they would be my people. And I told them to live as I had commanded them, so that things would go well for them. ²⁴But they did not obey or pay any attention. Instead, they did whatever their stubborn and evil hearts told them to do, and they became worse instead of better. ²⁵From the day that your ancestors came out of Egypt until this very day, I have kept on sending my servants, the prophets, to you. ²⁶Yet no one listened or paid any attention. Instead, you became more stubborn and rebellious than your ancestors.

27 "So, Jeremiah, you will speak all these words to my people, but they will not listen to you; you will call them, but they will not answer. ²⁸You will tell them that their nation does not obey me, the LORD their God, or learn from their punishment. Faithfulness is dead. No longer is it even talked about.

Sinful Deeds in the Valley of Hinnom

29 "Mourn, people of Jerusalem;
  cut off your hair and throw it away.
Sing a funeral song on the hill-tops,
  because I, the LORD, am angry,
  and have rejected my people.

ᶠSHILOH: *The city where the Covenant Box was kept in the time of Eli (see 1 Sam 1.3). The city was destroyed, probably by the Philistines.*

7.11: Mt 21.13; Mk 11.17; Lk 19.46 **7.12–14:** Josh 18.1; Ps 78.60; Jer 26.6 **7.18:** Jer 44.7-19

30 "The people of Judah have done an evil thing. They have placed their idols, which I hate, in my Temple and have defiled it. ³¹In the Valley of Hinnom they have built an altar called Topheth, so that they can sacrifice their sons and daughters in the fire. I did not command them to do this—it did not even enter my mind. ³²And so, the time will come when it will no longer be called Topheth or the Valley of Hinnom, but the Valley of Slaughter. They will bury people there because there will be nowhere else to bury them. ³³The corpses will be food for the birds and wild animals, and there will be no one to scare them off. ³⁴The land will become a desert. In the cities of Judah and in the streets of Jerusalem I will put an end to the sounds of joy and gladness and to the happy sounds of wedding feasts.

8 "At that time the bones of the kings and of the officials of Judah, as well as the bones of the priests, of the prophets, and of the other people who lived in Jerusalem, will be taken out of their graves. ²Instead of being gathered and buried, their bones will be like manure lying on the ground. They will be spread out before the sun, the moon, and the stars, which these people have loved and served, and which they have consulted and worshipped. ³And the people of this evil nation who survive, who live in the places where I have scattered them, will prefer to die rather than to go on living. I, the LORD Almighty, have spoken."

Sin and Punishment

4 The LORD told me to say to his people, "When someone falls down, doesn't he get back up? If someone misses the road, doesn't he turn back? ⁵Why then, my people, do you turn away from me without ever turning back? You cling to your idols and refuse to return to me. ⁶I listened carefully, but you did not speak the truth. Not one of you has been sorry for his wickedness; not one of you has asked, 'What have I done wrong?' Everyone keeps on going his own way, like a horse rushing into battle. ⁷Even storks know when it is time to return; doves, swallows, and thrushes know when it is time to migrate. But, my people, you do not know the laws by which I rule you. ⁸How can you say that you are wise, and that you know my laws? Look, the laws have been

changed by dishonest scribes. ⁹Your wise men are put to shame; they are confused and trapped. They have rejected my words; what wisdom have they got now? ¹⁰So I will give their fields to new owners and their wives to other men. Everyone, great and small, tries to make money dishonestly. Even prophets and priests cheat the people. ¹¹They act as if my people's wounds were only scratches. 'All is well,' they say, when all is not well. ¹²My people, were you ashamed because you did these disgusting things? No, you were not ashamed at all; you don't even know how to blush! And so you will fall as others have fallen; when I punish you, that will be the end of you. I, the LORD, have spoken.

13 "I wanted to gather my people, as a man gathers his harvest; but they are like a vine with no grapes, like a fig-tree with no figs; even the leaves have withered. Therefore, I have allowed outsiders to take over the land."*g*

14 "Why are we sitting still?" God's people ask. "Come on, we will run to the fortified cities, and die there. The LORD our God has condemned us to die; he has given us poison to drink, because we have sinned against him. ¹⁵We hoped for peace and a time of healing, but it was no use; terror came instead. ¹⁶Our enemies are already in the city of Dan; we hear the snorting of their horses. The whole land trembles when their horses neigh. Our enemies have come to destroy our land and everything in it, our city and all its people."

17 "Watch out!" the LORD says, "I am sending snakes among you, poisonous snakes that cannot be charmed, and they will bite you."

Jeremiah's Sorrow for His People

¹⁸ My sorrow cannot be healed;*h*
    I am sick at heart.
¹⁹ Listen! Throughout the land
    I hear my people crying out,
"Is the LORD no longer in Zion?
    Is Zion's king no longer there?"
The LORD, their king, replies,
"Why have you made me angry by
    worshipping your idols
and by bowing down to your useless
    foreign gods?"
²⁰ The people cry out,

---

g Therefore...land; *Hebrew unclear.*   *h* Probable text My sorrow...healed; *Hebrew unclear.*
7.31: Lev 18.21; 2 Kgs 23.10; Jer 32.35   **7.34:** Jer 16.9, 25.10; Rev 18.23
8.10–12: Jer 6.12–15   **8.11:** Ezek 13.10

Like a vine with no grapes, like a fig-tree with no figs (8.13)

"The summer is gone, the harvest is
        over,
    but we have not been saved."

21 My heart has been crushed
    because my people are crushed;
    I mourn; I am completely dismayed.
22 Is there no medicine in Gilead?[i]

I am sick at heart (8.18)

Are there no doctors there?
Why, then, have my people not been
    healed?

9 I wish my head were a well of water,
        and my eyes a fountain of tears,
    so that I could cry day and night
        for my people who have been killed.
2 I wish I had a place to stay in the desert
    where I could get away from my
        people.
    They are all unfaithful,
        a mob of traitors.
3 They are always ready to tell lies;
    dishonesty instead of truth rules the
        land.

The LORD says,
"My people do one evil thing after
        another,
    and do not acknowledge me as their
        God."

4 Everyone must be on guard against his
        friend,
    and no one can trust his brother;
    for every brother is as deceitful as Jacob,
    and everyone slanders his friends.
5-6 They all mislead their friends,
    and no one tells the truth;
    they have taught their tongues to lie
    and will not give up their sinning.
    They do one violent thing after another,
    and one deceitful act follows another.

The LORD says that his people reject
        him.
7 Because of this the LORD Almighty says,
"I will refine my people like metal

---

[i]GILEAD: *A region east of the Jordan, famous for plants that were used for medicinal purposes.*

and put them to the test.
My people have done evil—
    what else can I do with them?
8 Their tongues are like deadly arrows;
    they always tell lies.
Everyone speaks friendly words to his
        neighbour,
    but is really setting a trap for him.
9 Will I not punish them for these things?
    Will I not take revenge on a nation
        like this?
I, the LORD, have spoken."

10 I said, "I will mourn for the mountains
        and weep for the pastures,
because they have dried up,
    and no one travels through them.
The sound of livestock is no longer
        heard;
    birds and wild animals have fled and
        gone."

11 The LORD says, "I will make Jerusalem
        a pile of ruins,
    a place where jackals live;
the cities of Judah will become a desert,
    a place where no one lives."

12 I asked, "LORD, why is the land
devastated and dry as a desert, so that
no one travels through it? Who is wise
enough to understand this? To whom
have you explained it so that he can tell
others?"

13 The LORD answered, "This has happened because my people have abandoned
the teaching that I gave them. They have
not obeyed me or done what I told them.
14 Instead, they have been stubborn and
have worshipped the idols of Baal as their
fathers taught them to do. 15 So then, listen
to what I, the LORD Almighty, the God
of Israel, will do: I will give my people
bitter plants to eat and poison to drink. 16 I
will scatter them among nations that
neither they nor their ancestors have
heard about, and I will send armies
against them until I have completely
destroyed them."

The People of Jerusalem Cry Out for Help

17 The LORD Almighty said,
"Think about what is happening!
Call for the mourners to come,
    for the women who sing funeral
        songs."

18 The people said,

"Tell them to hurry and sing a funeral
        song for us,
    until our eyes fill with tears,
    and our eyelids are wet from crying."

19 Listen to the sound of crying in Zion,
"We are ruined!
    We are completely disgraced!
We must leave our land;
    our homes have been torn down."

20 I said,
"Listen to the LORD, you women,
    and pay attention to his words.
Teach your daughters how to mourn,
    and your friends how to sing a funeral
        song.
21 Death has come in through our
        windows
    and entered our palaces;
it has cut down the children in the
        streets
    and the young men in the market-
        places.
22 Dead bodies are scattered everywhere,
    like piles of manure on the fields,
like corn cut and left behind by the
        reapers,
    corn that no one gathers.
This is what the LORD has told me to
        say."

23 The LORD says,
"Wise men should not boast of their
        wisdom,
    nor strong men of their strength,
    nor rich men of their wealth.
24 If anyone wants to boast,
    he should boast that he knows and
        understands me,
because my love is constant,
    and I do what is just and right.
These are the things that please me.
I, the LORD, have spoken."

25-26 The LORD says, "The time is
coming when I will punish the people of
Egypt, Judah, Edom, Ammon, Moab, and
the desert people, who have their hair
cut short.j All these people are circumcised, but have not kept the covenant it
symbolizes. None of these people and
none of the people of Israel have kept
my covenant."

---

j HAIR CUT SHORT: *The desert people cut their hair short in honour of their god, a pagan practice
forbidden to the Israelites (see Lev 19.27).*
9.24: 1 Cor 1.31; 2 Cor 10.17

Idolatry and True Worship

10 People of Israel, listen to the message that the LORD has for you. ² He says,

"Do not follow the ways of other nations;
do not be disturbed by unusual sights in the sky,
even though other nations are terrified.
³ The religion of these people is worthless.
A tree is cut down in the forest;
it is carved by the tools of the woodcarver,
⁴ and decorated with silver and gold.
It is fastened down with nails
to keep it from falling over.
⁵ Such idols are like scarecrows in a field of melons;

They cannot speak; they have to be carried (10.5).

they cannot speak;
they have to be carried
because they cannot walk.
Do not be afraid of them:
they can cause you no harm,
and they can do you no good."

⁶ LORD, there is no one like you;
you are mighty,
and your name is great and powerful.
⁷ Who would not honour you, the king of all nations?
You deserve to be honoured.

There is no one like you
among all the wise men of the nations
or among any of their kings.
⁸ All of them are stupid and foolish.
What can they learn from wooden idols?ᵏ
⁹ Their idols are covered with silver from Spain
and with gold from Uphaz,
all the work of artists;
they are dressed in violet and purple cloth
woven by skilled weavers.
¹⁰ But you, LORD, are the true God,
you are the living God
and the eternal king.
When you are angry, the world trembles;
the nations cannot endure your anger.

11 (You people must tell them that the gods who did not make the earth and the sky will be destroyed. They will no longer exist anywhere on earth.)

A Hymn of Praise to God

¹² The LORD made the earth by his power;
by his wisdom he created the world
and stretched out the heavens.
¹³ At his command the waters above the sky ˡ roar;
he brings clouds from the ends of the earth.
He makes lightning flash in the rain
and sends the wind from his storeroom.
¹⁴ At the sight of this, men feel stupid and senseless;
those who make idols are disillusioned,
because the gods they make are false and lifeless.
¹⁵ They are worthless and should be despised;
they will be destroyed when the LORD comes to deal with them.
¹⁶ The God of Jacob is not like them;
he is the one who made everything,
and he has chosen Israel to be his very own people.
The LORD Almighty is his name.

The Coming Exile

17 People of Jerusalem, you are under siege! Gather up your belongings. ¹⁸ The LORD is going to throw you out of this land; he is going to crush you until not

---

ᵏ What can...idols?; *or* What their idols teach is worthless.
ˡ WATERS ABOVE THE SKY: *See Gen 1.6–8.*
10.7: Rev 15.4

one of you is left. The LORD has spoken.
19 The people of Jerusalem cried out,
"How badly we are hurt!
Our wounds will not heal.
And we thought this was something we
could endure!
20 Our tents are ruined;
the ropes that held them have broken.
Our children have all gone away;
there is no one left to put up our
tents again;
there is no one to hang their curtains."

21 I answered, "Our leaders are stupid;
they do not ask the LORD for guidance.
This is why they have failed,
and our people have been scattered.
22 Listen! News has come!
There is a great commotion in a nation
to the north;
its army will turn the cities of Judah
into a desert,
a place where jackals live."

23 LORD, I know that no one is the master
of his own destiny;
no person has control over his own
life.
24 Correct your people, LORD;
but do not be too hard on us
or punish us when you are angry;
that would be the end of us.
25 Turn your anger on the nations that
do not worship you
and on the people who reject you.
They have killed your people;
they have destroyed us completely
and left our country in ruins.

Jeremiah and the Covenant

11 The LORD said to me, 2 "Listen to
the terms of the covenant. Tell the
people of Judah and of Jerusalem 3 that
I, the LORD God of Israel, have placed
a curse on everyone who does not obey
the terms of this covenant. 4 It is the
covenant I made with their ancestors
when I brought them out of Egypt, the
land that was like a blazing furnace to
them. I told them to obey me and to do
everything that I had commanded. I told
them that if they obeyed, they would be
my people and I would be their God. 5 Then
I would keep the promise I made to their
ancestors that I would give them the rich
and fertile land which they now have."

I said, "Yes, LORD."

6 Then the LORD said to me, "Go to
the cities of Judah and to the streets of

Jerusalem. Proclaim my message there
and tell the people to listen to the terms
of the covenant and to obey them. 7 When
I brought their ancestors out of Egypt,
I solemnly warned them to obey me, and I
have kept on warning the people until
this day. 8 But they did not listen or obey.
Instead, everyone continued to be as
stubborn and evil as ever. I had commanded them to keep the covenant, but
they refused. So I brought on them all
the punishments described in it."

9 Then the LORD said to me, "The people
of Judah and of Jerusalem are plotting
against me. 10 They have gone back to the
sins of their ancestors, who refused to
do what I said; they have worshipped
other gods. Both Israel and Judah have
broken the covenant that I made with
their ancestors. 11 So now, I, the LORD,
warn them that I am going to bring
destruction on them, and they will not
escape. And when they cry out to me
for help, I will not listen to them. 12 Then
the people of Judah and of Jerusalem will
go to the gods to whom they offer
sacrifices and will cry out to them for
help. But those gods will not be able to
save them when this destruction comes.
13 The people of Judah have as many gods
as they have cities, and the inhabitants
of Jerusalem have set up as many altars
for sacrifices to that disgusting god Baal
as there are streets in the city. 14 Jeremiah,
don't pray to me or plead with me on
behalf of these people. When they are in
trouble and call to me for help, I will
not listen to them."

15 The LORD says, "The people I love
are doing evil things. What right have they
to be in my Temple? Do they think they
can prevent disaster by making promises *m* and by offering animal sacrifices?
Will that make them happy? 16 I once
called them a leafy olive-tree, full of
beautiful fruit; but now, with a roar like
thunder I will set its leaves on fire and
break its branches.

17 "I, the LORD Almighty, planted Israel
and Judah; but now I threaten them with
disaster. They have brought this on
themselves because they have done
wrong; they have made me angry by
offering sacrifices to Baal."

A Plot against Jeremiah's Life

18 The LORD informed me of the plots
that my enemies were making against me.
19 I was like a trusting lamb taken out

---

m One ancient translation promises; *Hebrew* many.

I will set its leaves on fire (11.16)

to be killed, and I did not know that it was against me that they were planning evil things. They were saying, "Let's chop down the tree while it is still healthy; *x* let's kill him so that no one will remember him any more."

20 Then I prayed, "Almighty LORD, you are a just judge; you test people's thoughts and feelings. I have placed my cause in your hands; so let me watch you take revenge on these people."

21 The men of Anathoth wanted me killed, and they told me that they would kill me if I kept on proclaiming the LORD's message. ²²So the LORD Almighty said, "I will punish them! Their young men will be killed in war; their children will die of starvation. ²³I have set a time for bringing disaster on the people of Anathoth, and when that time comes, none of them will survive."

Jeremiah Questions the LORD

12 LORD, if I argued my case with you,
   you would prove to be right.
Yet I must question you about matters
   of justice.
Why are wicked men so prosperous?
   Why do dishonest men succeed?
² You plant them, and they take root;
   they grow and bear fruit.
They always speak well of you,
   yet they do not really care about you.

³ But, LORD, you know me;
   you see what I do,
   and how I love you.
Drag these evil men away like sheep
   to be butchered;
   guard them until it is time for them
   to be slaughtered.
⁴ How long will our land be dry,
   and the grass in every field be
   withered?
Animals and birds are dying
   because of the wickedness of our
   people,
   people who say, 'God doesn't see
   what we are doing.' *n*

5 The LORD said,
"Jeremiah, if you get tired racing
   against men,
   how can you race against horses?
If you can't even stand up in open
   country,
   how will you manage in the jungle
   by the Jordan?
⁶ Even your brothers, members of your
   own family, have betrayed you;
   they join in the attacks against you.
Do not trust them, even though they
   speak friendly words."

The LORD's Sorrow because of His People

7 The LORD says,
"I have abandoned Israel;
   I have rejected my chosen nation.

---

x Probable text while it is still healthy; *Hebrew* with its bread.
n Some ancient translations what we are doing; *Hebrew* our latter end.

I have given the people I love
into the power of their enemies.
8 My chosen people have turned against
me;
like a lion in the forest
they have roared at me,
and so I hate them.
9 My chosen people are like a bird
attacked from all sides by hawks.
Call the wild animals
to come and join in the feast!
10 Many foreign rulers have destroyed
my vineyard;
they have trampled down my fields;
they have turned my lovely land into
a desert.
11 They have made it a wilderness;
it lies desolate before me.
The whole land has become a desert,
and no one cares.
12 Across all the desert highlands
men have come to plunder.
I have sent war to destroy the entire
land;
no one can live in peace.
13 My people sowed wheat, but gathered
weeds;
they have worked hard, but got
nothing for it.
Because of my fierce anger
their crops have failed."

The LORD's Promise to Israel's Neighbours

14 The LORD says, "I have something
to say about Israel's neighbours who have
ruined the land I gave to my people Israel.
I will take those wicked people away from
their countries like an uprooted plant, and
I will rescue Judah from them. 15 But after
I have taken them away, I will have mercy
on them; I will bring each nation back
to its own land and to its own country.
16 If with all their hearts they will accept
the religion of my people and will swear,
'As the LORD lives'—as they once taught
my people to swear by Baal—then they
will also be a part of my people and will
prosper. 17 But if any nation will not obey,
then I will completely uproot it and
destroy it. I, the LORD, have spoken."

The Linen Shorts

13 The LORD told me to go and buy
myself some linen shorts and to
put them on; but he told me not to put
them in water. 2 So I bought them and
put them on. 3 Then the LORD spoke to
me again, and said, 4 "Go to the River
Euphrates and hide the shorts in a hole

in the rocks." 5 So I went and hid them
near the Euphrates.

6 Some time later the LORD told me to
go back to the Euphrates and get the
shorts. 7 So I went back, and when I found
the place where I had hidden them, I saw
that they were ruined and were no longer
any good.

8 Then the LORD spoke to me again. He
said, 9 "This is how I will destroy the pride
of Judah and the great pride of Jerusalem.
10 These evil people have refused to obey
me. They have been as stubborn and
wicked as ever, and have worshipped and
served other gods. So then, they will
become like these shorts that are no
longer any good. 11 Just as shorts fit tightly
round the waist, so I intended all the
people of Israel and Judah to hold tightly
to me. I did this so that they would be
my people and would bring praise and
honour to my name; but they would not
obey me."

The Wine-Jar

12 The LORD God said to me, "Jeremiah,
tell the people of Israel that every wine-jar
should be filled with wine. They will
answer that they know every wine-jar
should be filled with wine. 13 Then tell
them that I, the LORD, am going to fill
the people in this land with wine until
they are drunk: the kings, who are David's
descendants, the priests, the prophets,
and all the people of Jerusalem. 14 Then
I will smash them like jars against one
another, old and young alike. No pity,
compassion, or mercy will stop me from
killing them."

Jeremiah Warns against Pride

15 People of Israel, the LORD has spoken!
Be humble and listen to him.
16 Honour the LORD, your God,
before he brings darkness,
and you stumble on the mountains;
before he turns into deep darkness
the light you hoped for.
17 If you will not listen,
I will cry in secret because of your
pride;
I will cry bitterly, and my tears will
flow
because the LORD's people have been
taken away as captives.

18 The LORD said to me, "Tell the king
and his mother to come down from their
thrones, because their beautiful crowns

They come back with their jars empty (14.3)

have fallen from their heads.⁰ ¹⁹The towns of southern Judah are under siege; no one can get through to them. All the people of Judah have been taken away into exile."

20 Jerusalem, look! Your enemies are coming down from the north! Where are the people entrusted to your care, your people you were so proud of? ²¹What will you say when people you thought were your friends conquer you and rule over you?ᵖ You will be in pain like a woman giving birth. ²²If you ask why all this has happened to you—why your clothes have been torn off and you have been raped—it is because your sin is so terrible. ²³Can a black man change the colour of his skin, or a leopard remove its spots? If they could, then you that do nothing but evil could learn to do what is right. ²⁴The LORD will scatter you like straw that is blown away by the desert wind. ²⁵He has said that this will be your fate. This is what he has decided to do with you, because you have forgotten him and have trusted in false gods. ²⁶The LORD himself will strip off your clothes and expose you to shame. ²⁷He has seen you do the things he hates. He has seen you go after pagan gods on the hills and in the fields, like a man lusting after his

neighbour's wife or like a stallion after a mare. People of Jerusalem, you are doomed! When will you ever be pure?

The Terrible Drought

14 The LORD said to me concerning the drought,
² "Judah is in mourning;
  its cities are dying,
its people lie on the ground in sorrow,
  and Jerusalem cries out for help.
³ The rich people send their servants for water;
  they go to the cisterns,
  but find no water;
  they come back with their jars empty.
Discouraged and confused,
  they hide their faces.
⁴ Because there is no rain
  and the ground is dried up,
the farmers are sick at heart;
  they hide their faces.
⁵ In the field the mother deer
  abandons her new-born fawn
  because there is no grass.
⁶ The wild donkeys stand on the hill-tops
  and pant for breath like jackals;
  their eyesight fails them
  because they have no food.
⁷ My people cry out to me,
  'Even though our sins accuse us,

⁰ *Some ancient translations* from their heads; *Hebrew unclear.*
ᵖ *Probable text* what...over you; *Hebrew unclear.*

help us, LORD, as you have promised.
We have turned away from you many
times;
we have sinned against you.
8 You are Israel's only hope;
you are the one who saves us from
disaster.
Why are you like a stranger in our land,
like a traveller who stays for only one
night?
9 Why are you like a man taken by
surprise,
like a soldier powerless to help?
Surely, LORD, you are with us!
We are your people;
do not abandon us.' "

10 The LORD says about these people,
"They love to run away from me, and
they will not control themselves. So I am
not pleased with them. I will remember
the wrongs they have done and punish
them because of their sins."
11 The LORD said to me, "Do not ask
me to help these people. 12 Even if they
fast, I will not listen to their cry for help;
and even if they offer me burnt-offerings
and grain-offerings, I will not be pleased
with them. Instead, I will kill them in war
and by starvation and disease."
13 Then I said, "Sovereign LORD, you
know that the prophets are telling the
people that there will be no war or
starvation, because you have promised,
they say, that there will be only peace
in our land."
14 But the LORD replied, "The prophets
are telling lies in my name; I did not send
them, nor did I give them any orders or
speak one word to them. The visions they
talk about have not come from me; their
predictions are worthless things that they
have imagined. 15 I, the LORD, tell you what
I am going to do to those prophets whom
I did not send but who speak in my name
and say war and starvation will not strike
this land—I will kill them in war and by
starvation. 16 The people to whom they
have said these things will be killed in
the same way. Their bodies will be thrown
out into the streets of Jerusalem, and there
will be no one to bury them. This will
happen to all of them—including their
wives, their sons, and their daughters. I
will make them pay for their wickedness."
17 The LORD commanded me to tell the
people about my sorrow and to say:

"May my eyes flow with tears day and
night,
may I never stop weeping,
for my people are deeply wounded
and are badly hurt.
18 When I go out into the fields,
I see the bodies of men killed in war;
when I go into the towns,
I see people starving to death.
Prophets and priests carry on their
work,
but they don't know what they are
doing." q

The People Plead with the LORD

19 LORD, have you completely rejected
Judah?
Do you hate the people of Zion?
Why have you hurt us so badly
that we cannot be healed?
We looked for peace, but nothing good
happened;
we hoped for healing, but terror came
instead.
20 We have sinned against you, LORD;
we confess our own sins
and the sins of our ancestors.
21 Remember your promises and do not
despise us;
do not bring disgrace on Jerusalem,
the place of your glorious throne.
Do not break the covenant you made
with us.
22 None of the idols of the nations can
send rain;
the sky by itself cannot make showers
fall.
We have put our hope in you, O LORD
our God,
because you are the one who does
these things.

Doom for the People of Judah

15 Then the LORD said to me, "Even
if Moses and Samuel were standing here pleading with me, I would not
show these people any mercy. Make them
go away; make them get out of my sight.
2 When they ask you where they should
go, tell them that I have said:
Some are doomed to die by disease—
that's where they will go!
Others are doomed to die in war—
that's where they will go!
Some are doomed to die of starvation—
that's where they will go!

q Prophets...doing; or Prophets and priests have been dragged away to a land they know nothing
about.
15.1: Ex 32.11-14; Num 14.13-19; 1 Sam 7.5-9   **15.2:** Rev 13.10

Others are doomed to be taken away
    as prisoners—
    that's where they will go!
3 I, the LORD, have decided that four
terrible things will happen to them: they
will be killed in war; their bodies will
be dragged off by dogs; birds will eat
them, and wild animals will devour what
is left over. 4 I will make all the people
of the world horrified at them because
of what Hezekiah's son Manasseh did in
Jerusalem when he was king of Judah."

5 The LORD says,
"Who will pity you, people of Jerusalem,
    and who will grieve over you?
Who will stop long enough
    to ask how you are?
6 You people have rejected me;
    you have turned your backs on me.
So I stretched out my hand and crushed
    you
    because I was tired of controlling my
    anger.*r*
7 In every town in the land
    I threw you to the wind like straw.
I destroyed you, my people,
    I killed your children
    because you did not stop your evil
    ways.
8 There are more widows in your land
    than grains of sand by the sea.
I killed your young men in their prime
    and made their mothers suffer.
I suddenly struck them
    with anguish and terror.
9 The mother who lost her seven children
    has fainted,
    gasping for breath.
Her daylight has turned to darkness;
    she is disgraced and sick at heart.
I will let your enemies kill
    those of you who are still alive.
I, the LORD, have spoken."

Jeremiah Complains to the LORD

10 What an unhappy man I am! Why
did my mother bring me into the world?
I have to quarrel and argue with everyone
in the land. I have not lent any money
or borrowed any; yet everyone curses me.
11 LORD, may all their curses come true
if I have not served*s* you well, if I have*s*
not pleaded with you on behalf of my
enemies when they were in trouble and
distress. 12 (No one can break iron, especially the iron from the north that is
mixed with bronze.)

13 The LORD said to me, "I will send
enemies to carry away the wealth and
treasures of my people, in order to punish
them for the sins they have committed
throughout the land. 14 I will make them
serve their enemies in a land they know
nothing about, because my anger is like
fire, and it will burn for ever."

15 Then I said, "LORD, you understand.
Remember me and help me. Let me have
revenge on those who persecute me. Do
not be so patient with them that they
succeed in killing me. Remember that it
is for your sake that I am insulted. 16 You
spoke to me, and I listened to every word.
I belong to you, LORD God Almighty, and
so your words filled my heart with joy
and happiness. 17 I did not spend my time
with other people, laughing and having
a good time. In obedience to your orders
I stayed by myself and was filled with
anger. 18 Why do I keep on suffering? Why
are my wounds incurable? Why won't
they heal? Do you intend to disappoint
me like a stream that goes dry in the
summer?"

19 To this the LORD replied, "If you
return, I will take you back, and you will
be my servant again. If instead of talking
nonsense you proclaim a worthwhile
message, you will be my prophet again.
The people will come back to you, and
you will not need to go to them. 20 I will
make you like a solid bronze wall as far
as they are concerned. They will fight
against you, but they will not defeat you.
I will be with you to protect you and
keep you safe. 21 I will rescue you from the
power of wicked and violent men. I, the
LORD, have spoken."

The LORD's Will for Jeremiah's Life

16 Again the LORD spoke to me and
said, 2 "Do not marry or have
children in a place like this. 3 I will tell
you what is going to happen to the
children who are born here and to their
parents. 4 They will die of terrible diseases,
and no one will mourn for them or bury
them. Their bodies will lie like piles of
manure on the ground. They will be killed
in war or die of starvation, and their
bodies will be food for the birds and the
wild animals.

5 "You must not enter a house where
there is mourning. Do not grieve for
anyone. I will no longer bless my people

---

r you because...anger; or you; I was tired of feeling sorry for you.
s Probable text LORD...served; Hebrew unclear.
15.4: 2 Kgs 21.1–16; 2 Chr 33.1–9

with peace or show them love and mercy. 6 The rich and the poor will die in this land, but no one will bury them or mourn for them. No one will gash himself or shave his head to show his grief. 7 No one will eat or drink with anyone to comfort him when a loved one dies. No one will show sympathy, not even for someone who has lost his father or mother.

8 "Do not enter a house where people are feasting. Do not sit down with them to eat and drink. 9 Listen to what I, the LORD Almighty, the God of Israel, have to say. I will silence the sounds of joy and gladness and the happy sounds of wedding feasts. The people here will live to see this happen.

10 "When you tell them all this, they will ask you why I have decided to punish them so harshly. They will ask what crime they are guilty of and what sin they have committed against the LORD their God. 11 Then tell them that the LORD has said, 'Your ancestors turned away from me and worshipped and served other gods. They abandoned me and did not obey my teachings. 12 But you have done even worse than your ancestors. All of you are stubborn and evil, and you do not obey me. 13 So then, I will throw you out of this land into a land that neither you nor your ancestors have ever known. And there you will serve other gods day and night, and I will show you no mercy.'"

The Return from Exile

14 The LORD says, "The time is coming when people will no longer swear by me as the living God who brought the people of Israel out of the land of Egypt. 15 Instead, they will swear by me as the living God who brought the people of Israel out of a northern land and out of all the other countries where I had scattered them. I will bring them back to their own country, to the land that I gave their ancestors. I, the LORD, have spoken."

The Coming Punishment

16 The LORD says, "I am sending for many fishermen to come and catch these people. Then I will send for many hunters to hunt them down on every mountain and hill and in the caves among the rocks. 17 I see everything they do. Nothing is hidden from me; their sins do not escape

my sight. 18 I will make them pay double for their sin and wickedness, because they have defiled my land with idols that are as lifeless as corpses, and have filled it with their false gods."

Jeremiah's Prayer of Confidence in the LORD

19 LORD, you are the one who protects me and gives me strength; you help me in times of trouble. Nations will come to you from the ends of the earth and say, "Our ancestors had nothing but false gods, nothing but useless idols. 20 Can a man make his own gods? No, if he did, they would not really be gods."

21 "So then," says the LORD, "once and for all I will make the nations know my power and my might; they will know that I am the LORD."

The Sin and Punishment of Judah

17 The LORD says, "People of Judah, your sin is written with an iron pen; it is engraved on your hearts with a diamond point and carved on the corners of your altars. 2 Your people worship at the altars and the symbols that have been set up for the goddess Asherah by every green tree, on the hill-tops 3 and on the mountains in the open country. I will make your enemies take away your wealth and your treasures because of all the sins you have committed *t* throughout your land. 4 You will have to give up *u* the land I gave you, and I will make you serve your enemies in a land you know nothing about, because my anger is like a fire, and it will burn for ever."

Various Sayings

5 The LORD says,
"I will condemn the person
  who turns away from me
and puts his trust in the strength of mortal man.
6 He is like a bush in the desert,
  which grows in the dry wilderness,
  on salty ground where nothing else grows.
Nothing good ever happens to him.

7 "But I will bless the person
  who puts his trust in me.
8 He is like a tree growing near a stream
  and sending out roots to the water.
It is not afraid when hot weather comes,

---

t Probable text because of all the sins you have committed; *Hebrew* your high places for sins.
u Probable text You...give up; *Hebrew unclear.*
16.9: Jer 7.34, 25.10; Rev 18.23   **17.8:** Ps 1.3

because its leaves stay green;
it has no worries when there is no rain;
it keeps on bearing fruit.

9 "Who can understand the human heart?
There is nothing else so deceitful;
it is too sick to be healed.

10 I, the LORD, search the minds
and test the hearts of men.
I treat each one according to the way
he lives,
according to what he does."

11 The person who gets money
dishonestly
is like a bird that hatches eggs it didn't
lay.
In the prime of life he will lose his riches,
and in the end he is nothing but a
fool.

12 Our Temple is like a glorious throne,
standing on a high mountain from the
beginning.

13 LORD, you are Israel's hope;
all who abandon you will be put to
shame.
They will disappear like names written
in the dust, *a*
because they have abandoned you,
the LORD,
the spring of fresh water.

Jeremiah Asks the LORD for Help

14 LORD, heal me and I will be completely well; rescue me and I will be perfectly safe. You are the one I praise! 15 The people say to me, "Where are those threats the LORD made against us? Let him carry them out now!" 16 But, LORD, I never urged you to bring disaster on them; *b* I did not wish a time of trouble for them. LORD, you know this; you know what I have said. 17 Do not be a terror to me; you are my place of safety when trouble comes. 18 Bring disgrace on those who persecute me, but spare me, LORD. Fill them with terror, but do not terrify me. Bring disaster on them and break them to pieces.

On Observing the Sabbath

19 The LORD said to me, "Jeremiah, go and announce my message at the People's Gate, through which the kings of Judah enter and leave the city; then go to all

the other gates of Jerusalem. 20 Tell the kings and all the people of Judah and everyone who lives in Jerusalem and enters these gates, to listen to what I say. 21 Tell them that if they love their lives, they must not carry any load on the Sabbath; they must not carry anything in through the gates of Jerusalem 22 or carry anything out of their houses on the Sabbath. They must not work on the Sabbath; they must observe it as a sacred day, as I commanded their ancestors. 23 Their ancestors did not listen to me or pay any attention. Instead, they became stubborn; they would not obey me or learn from me.

24 "Tell these people that they must obey all my commands. They must not carry any load in through the gates of this city on the Sabbath. They must observe the Sabbath as a sacred day and must not do any work at all. 25 Then their kings and princes will enter the gates of Jerusalem and have the same royal power that David had. Together with the people of Judah and of Jerusalem, they will ride in chariots and on horses, and the city of Jerusalem will always be filled with people. 26 People will come from the towns of Judah and from the villages round Jerusalem; they will come from the territory of Benjamin, from the foothills, from the mountains, and from southern Judah. They will bring to my Temple burnt-offerings and sacrifices, grain-offerings and incense, as well as thank-offerings. 27 But they must obey me and observe the Sabbath as a sacred day. They must not carry any load through the gates of Jerusalem on that day, for if they do, I will set the gates of Jerusalem on fire. Fire will burn down the palaces of Jerusalem, and no one will be able to put it out."

Jeremiah at the Potter's House

18 The LORD said to me, 2 "Go down to the potter's house, where I will give you my message." 3 So I went there and saw the potter working at his wheel. 4 Whenever a piece of pottery turned out imperfect, he would take the clay and make it into something else.

5 Then the LORD said to me, 6 "Haven't I the right to do with you people of Israel what the potter did with the clay? You are in my hands just like clay in the

a disappear...dust; *or* go to the world of the dead.
b *Probable text* bring disaster on them; *Hebrew* from being a shepherd after you.
17.10: Ps 62.12; Rev 2.23   **17.21:** Neh 13.15-22   **17.22:** Ex 20.8-10; Deut 5.12-14

potter's hands. ⁷If at any time I say that I am going to uproot, break down, or destroy any nation or kingdom, ⁸but then that nation turns from its evil, I will not do what I said I would. ⁹On the other hand, if I say that I am going to plant or build up any nation or kingdom, ¹⁰but then that nation disobeys me and does evil, I will not do what I said I would. ¹¹Now then, tell the people of Judah and of Jerusalem that I am making plans against them and getting ready to punish them. Tell them to stop living sinful lives— to change their ways and the things they are doing. ¹²They will answer, 'No, why should we? We will all be just as stubborn and evil as we want to be.' "

The People Reject the LORD

13 The LORD says,
"Ask every nation if such a thing
    has ever happened before.
  The people of Israel have done a
    terrible thing!
¹⁴ Are Lebanon's rocky heights ever
    without snow?
  Do its cool mountain streams ever run
    dry?
¹⁵ Yet my people have forgotten me;
    they burn incense to idols.
  They have stumbled in the way they
    should go,
    they no longer follow the old ways;
    they walk on unmarked paths.
¹⁶ They have made this land a thing of
    horror,
    to be despised for ever.
  All who pass by will be shocked at what
    they see;
    they will shake their heads in
    amazement.
¹⁷ I will scatter my people before their
    enemies,
    like dust blown by the east wind.
  I will turn my back on them;
    I will not help them when the disaster
    comes."

A Plot against Jeremiah

18 Then the people said, "Let's do something about Jeremiah! There will always be priests to instruct us, wise men to give us counsel, and prophets to proclaim God's message. Let's bring charges against him, and stop listening to what he says."

19 So I prayed, "LORD, hear what I am saying and listen to what my enemies are saying about me. ²⁰Is evil the payment

19.2: 2 Kgs 23.10; Jer 7.30–32, 32.34–35

LORD, hear what I am saying (18.19)

for good? Yet they have dug a pit for me to fall in. Remember how I came to you and spoke on their behalf, so that you would not deal with them in anger. ²¹But now, LORD, let their children starve to death; let them be killed in war. Let the women lose their husbands and children; let the men die of disease and the young men be killed in battle. ²²Send a mob to plunder their homes without warning; make them cry out in terror. They have dug a pit for me to fall in and have set traps to catch me. ²³But, LORD, you know all their plots to kill me. Do not forgive their evil or pardon their sin. Throw them down in defeat and deal with them while you are angry."

The Broken Jar

19 The LORD told me to go and buy a clay jar. He also told me to take some of the elders of the people and some of the older priests, ²and to go through Potsherd Gate out to the Valley of Hinnom. There I was to proclaim the message that he would give me. ³The LORD told me to say, "Kings of Judah

The LORD told me to break the jar (19.10)

and people of Jerusalem, listen to what I, the LORD Almighty, the God of Israel, have to say. I am going to bring such a disaster on this place that everyone who hears about it will be stunned. 4 I am going to do this because the people have abandoned me and defiled this place by offering sacrifices here to other gods— gods that neither they nor their ancestors nor the kings of Judah have known anything about. They have filled this place with the blood of innocent people, 5 and they have built altars for Baal in order to burn their children in the fire as sacrifices. I never commanded them to do this; it never even entered my mind. 6 So then, the time will come when this place will no longer be called Topheth or the Valley of Hinnom. Instead, it will be known as the Valley of Slaughter. 7 In this place I will frustrate all the plans of the people of Judah and Jerusalem. I will let their enemies triumph over them and kill them in battle. I will give their corpses to the birds and the wild animals as food. 8 I will bring such terrible destruction on this city that everyone who passes by will be shocked and amazed. 9 The enemy will surround the city and try to kill its people. The siege will be

19.5: Lev 18.21

so terrible that the people inside the city will eat one another and even their own children."

10 Then the LORD told me to break the jar in front of the men who had gone with me 11 and to tell them that the LORD Almighty had said, "I will break this people and this city, and it will be like this broken clay jar that cannot be put together again. People will bury their dead even in Topheth because there will be nowhere else to bury them. 12 I promise that I will make this city and its inhabitants like Topheth. 13 The houses of Jerusalem, the houses of the kings of Judah, and indeed all the houses on whose roofs incense has been burnt to the stars and where wine has been poured out as an offering to other gods—they will all be as unclean as Topheth."

14 Then I left Topheth, where the LORD had sent me to proclaim his message. I went and stood in the court of the Temple and told all the people 15 that the LORD Almighty, the God of Israel, had said, "I am going to bring on this city and on every nearby town all the punishment that I said I would, because you are stubborn and will not listen to what I say."

Jeremiah's Conflict with Pashhur the Priest

20 When the priest Pashhur son of Immer, who was the chief officer of the Temple, heard me proclaim these things, ²he ordered me to be beaten and placed in chains near the upper Benjamin Gate in the Temple. ³The next morning, after Pashhur had released me from the chains, I said to him, "The LORD did not name you Pashhur. The name he has given you is 'Terror Everywhere.' ⁴The LORD himself has said, 'I am going to make you a terror to yourself and to your friends, and you will see them all killed by the swords of their enemies. I am going to put all the people of Judah under the power of the king of Babylonia; he will take some away as prisoners to his country and put others to death. ⁵I will also let their enemies plunder all the wealth of this city and seize all its possessions and property, even the treasures of the kings of Judah, and carry everything off to Babylonia. ⁶As for you, Pashhur, you and all your family will also be captured and taken off to Babylonia. There you will die and be buried, along with all your friends to whom you have told so many lies.'"

Jeremiah Complains to the LORD

⁷ LORD, you have deceived me,
  and I was deceived.
You are stronger than I am,
  and you have overpowered me.
Everyone jeers at me;
  they mock me all day long.

⁸ Whenever I speak, I have to cry out
  and shout, "Violence! Destruction!"
LORD, I am ridiculed and scorned all
  the time
  because I proclaim your message.
⁹ But when I say, "I will forget the LORD
  and no longer speak in his name,"
then your message is like a fire
  burning deep within me.
I try my best to hold it in,
  but can no longer keep it back.
¹⁰ I hear everybody whispering,
  "Terror is everywhere!
  So let's report him to the authorities!"
Even my close friends wait for my
  downfall.
"Perhaps he can be tricked," they say;
  "then we can catch him and get
  revenge."

¹¹ But you, LORD, are on my side, strong
  and mighty,
  and those who persecute me will fail.
They will be disgraced for ever,
  because they cannot succeed.
Their disgrace will never be forgotten.
¹² But, Almighty LORD, you test men
  justly;
  you know what is in their hearts and
  minds.
So let me see you take revenge on my
  enemies,
  for I have placed my cause in your
  hands.
¹³ Sing to the LORD!
  Praise the LORD!
He rescues the oppressed from the
  power of evil men.

¹⁴ Curse the day I was born!
Forget the day my mother gave me
  birth!
¹⁵ Curse the man who made my father
  glad
  when he brought him the news,
  "It's a boy! You have a son!"
¹⁶ May he be like those cities
  that the LORD destroyed without
  mercy.
May he hear cries of pain in the morning
  and the battle alarm at noon,
¹⁷   because he didn't kill me before I
  was born.
Then my mother's womb would have
  been my grave.
¹⁸ Why was I born?
  Was it only to have trouble and
  sorrow,
  to end my life in disgrace?

Jerusalem's Defeat Is Predicted

21 King Zedekiah of Judah sent Pashhur son of Malchiah and the priest Zephaniah son of Maaseiah to me with this request: ²"Please speak to the LORD for us, because King Nebuchadnezzar of Babylonia and his army are besieging the city. Maybe the LORD will perform one of his miracles for us and force Nebuchadnezzar to retreat."

³ Then the LORD spoke to me, and I told the men who had been sent to me ⁴to tell Zedekiah that the LORD, the God of Israel, had said, "Zedekiah, I am going to defeat your army that is fighting against the king of Babylonia and his army. I will pile up your soldiers' weapons in the centre of the city. ⁵I will fight against you with all my might, my anger,

20.14–18: Job 3.1–19   **21.2:** 2 Kgs 25.1–11; 2 Chr 36.17–21

my wrath, and my fury. ⁶I will kill everyone living in this city; people and animals alike will die of a terrible disease. ⁷But as for you, your officials, and the people who survive the war, the famine, and the disease—I will let all of you be captured by King Nebuchadnezzar and by your enemies, who want to kill you. Nebuchadnezzar will put you to death. He will not spare any of you or show mercy or pity to any of you. I, the LORD, have spoken."

8 Then the LORD told me to say to the people, "Listen! I, the LORD, am giving you a choice between the way that leads to life and the way that leads to death. ⁹Anyone who stays in the city will be killed in war or by starvation or disease. But whoever goes out and surrenders to the Babylonians, who are now attacking the city, will not be killed; he will at least escape with his life. ¹⁰I have made up my mind not to spare this city, but to destroy it. It will be given over to the king of Babylonia and he will burn it to the ground. I, the LORD, have spoken."

Judgement on the Royal House of Judah

11-12 The LORD told me to give this message to the royal house of Judah, the descendants of David: "Listen to what I, the LORD, am saying. See that justice is done every day. Protect the person who is being cheated from the one who is cheating him. If you don't, the evil you are doing will make my anger burn like a fire that cannot be put out. ¹³You, Jerusalem, are sitting[c] high above the valleys, like a rock rising above the plain. But I will fight against you. You say that no one can attack you or break through your defences. ¹⁴But I will punish you for what you have done. I will set your palace on fire, and the fire will burn down everything round it. I, the LORD, have spoken."

Jeremiah's Message to the Royal House of Judah

22 ¹⁻²The LORD told me to go to the palace of the king of Judah, the descendant of David, and there tell the king, his officials, and the people of Jerusalem to listen to what the LORD had said: ³"I, the LORD, command you to do what is just and right. Protect the person who is being cheated from the one who is cheating him. Do not ill-treat or oppress foreigners, orphans, or widows; and do not kill innocent people in this holy place. ⁴If you really do as I have commanded, then David's descendants will continue to be kings. And they, together with their officials and their people, will continue to pass through the gates of this palace in chariots and on horses. ⁵But if you do not obey my commands, then I swear to you that this palace will fall into ruins. I, the LORD, have spoken.

6 "To me, Judah's royal palace is as beautiful as the land of Gilead and as the Lebanon Mountains; but I will make it a desolate place where no one lives. ⁷I am sending men to destroy it. They will all bring their axes, cut down its beautiful cedar pillars, and throw them into the fire.

8 "Afterwards many foreigners will pass by and ask one another why I, the LORD, have done such a thing to this great city. ⁹Then they will answer that it is because you have abandoned your covenant with me, your God and have worshipped and served other gods."

Jeremiah's Message concerning Joahaz

¹⁰ People of Judah, do not weep for King
    Josiah;
  do not mourn his death.
But weep bitterly for Joahaz, his son;
  they are taking him away, never to
    return,
    never again to see the land where he
      was born.

11 The LORD says concerning Josiah's son Joahaz, who succeeded his father as king of Judah, "He has gone away from here, never to return. ¹²He will die in the country where they have taken him, and he will never again see this land."

Jeremiah's Message concerning Jehoiakim

¹³ Doomed is the man who builds his
      house by injustice
    and enlarges it by dishonesty;
  who makes his countrymen work for
    nothing
    and does not pay their wages.
¹⁴ Doomed is the man who says,
    "I will build myself a mansion
    with spacious rooms upstairs."
  So he puts windows in his house,
    panels it with cedar,
    and paints it red.
¹⁵ Does it make you a better king
    if you build houses of cedar,
    finer than those of others?

ᶜYou, Jerusalem, are sitting; or You are enthroned.
22.5: Mt 23.38; Lk 13.35   **22.11:** 2 Kgs 23.31-34; 2 Chr 36.1-4

Your father enjoyed a full life.
He was always just and fair,
and he prospered in everything he did.
16 He gave the poor a fair trial,
and all went well with him.
That is what it means to know the LORD.
17 But you can only see your selfish
interests;
you kill the innocent
and violently oppress your people.
The LORD has spoken.

18 So then, the LORD says about Josiah's
son Jehoiakim, king of Judah,
"No one will mourn his death or say,
'How terrible, my friend, how
terrible!'
No one will weep for him or cry,
'My lord! My king!'
19 With the funeral honours of a donkey,
he will be dragged away
and thrown outside Jerusalem's
gates."

Jeremiah's Message about the Fate of Jerusalem

20 People of Jerusalem, go to Lebanon
and shout,
go to the land of Bashan and cry;
call out from the mountains of Moab,
because all your allies have been
defeated.
21 The LORD spoke to you when you were
prosperous,
but you refused to listen.
That is what you've done all your life;
you never would obey the LORD.
22 Your leaders will be blown away by
the wind,
your allies taken as prisoners of war,
your city disgraced and put to shame
because of all the evil you have done.
23 You rest secure among the cedars
brought from Lebanon;
but how pitiful you'll be when pains
strike you,
pains like those of a woman in labour.

God's Judgement on Jehoiachin

24 The LORD said to King Jehoiachin,
son of King Jehoiakim of Judah, "As
surely as I am the living God, even if
you were the signet-ring on my right hand,
I would pull you off 25 and give you to
people you are afraid of, people who want
to kill you. I will give you to King
Nebuchadnezzar of Babylonia and his

soldiers. 26 I am going to force you and
your mother into exile. You will go to
a country where neither of you was born,
and both of you will die there. 27 You will
long to see this country again, but you
will never return."

28 I said, "Has King Jehoiachin become
like a broken jar that is thrown away
and that no one wants? Is that why he
and his children have been taken into exile
to a land they know nothing about?"
29 O land, land, land!
Listen to what the LORD has said:
30 "This man is condemned to lose his
children,
to be a man who will never succeed.
He will have no descendants
who will rule in Judah
as David's successors.
I, the LORD, have spoken."

Hope for the Future

23 How terrible will be the LORD's
judgement on those rulers who
destroy and scatter his people! 2 This is
what the LORD, the God of Israel, says
about the rulers who were supposed to
take care of his people: "You have not
taken care of my people; you have
scattered them and driven them away.
Now I am going to punish you for the
evil you have done. 3 I will gather the rest
of my people from the countries where I
have scattered them, and I will bring them
back to their homeland. They will have
many children and increase in number.
4 I will appoint rulers to take care of them.
My people will no longer be afraid or
terrified, and I will not punish them
again. *d* I, the LORD, have spoken."

5 The LORD says, "The time is coming
when I will choose as king a righteous
descendant of David. That king will rule
wisely and do what is right and just
throughout the land. 6 When he is king,
the people of Judah will be safe, and the
people of Israel will live in peace. He will
be called 'The LORD Our Salvation.'

7 "The time is coming," says the LORD,
"when people will no longer swear by me
as the living God who brought the people
of Israel out of the land of Egypt. 8 Instead,
they will swear by me as the living God
who brought the people of Israel out of
a northern land and out of all the other
countries where I had scattered them.
Then they will live in their own land."

---

d I will not punish them again; *or* not one of them will be missing.
22.18: 2 Kgs 23.36—24.6; 2 Chr 36.5-7   **22.24:** 2 Kgs 24.8-15; 2 Chr 36.9-10
23.5-6: Jer 33.14-16

Jeremiah's Message about the Prophets

9 My heart is crushed,
  and I am trembling.
Because of the LORD,
  because of his holy words,
  I am like a man who is drunk,
  a man who has had too much wine.
10 The land is full of people unfaithful
    to the LORD;
  they live wicked lives and misuse
    their power.
Because of the LORD's curse the land
    mourns
  and the pastures are dry.

11 The LORD says,
"The prophets and the priests are
    godless;
  I have caught them doing evil in the
    Temple itself.
12 The paths they follow will be slippery
    and dark;
  I will make them stumble and fall.
I am going to bring disaster on them;
  the time of their punishment is
    coming.
I, the LORD, have spoken.
13 I have seen the sin of Samaria's
    prophets:
  they have spoken in the name of Baal
    and have led my people astray.
14 But I have seen the prophets in
    Jerusalem do even worse:
  they commit adultery and tell lies;
  they help people to do wrong,
  so that no one stops doing what is
    evil.
To me, they are all as bad
  as the people of Sodom and
    Gomorrah.

15 "So then, this is what I, the LORD
Almighty, say about the prophets of
Jerusalem:
  I will give them bitter plants to eat
    and poison to drink,
  because they have spread ungodliness
    throughout the land."

16 The LORD Almighty said to the people
of Jerusalem, "Do not listen to what the
prophets say; they are filling you with
false hopes. They tell you what they have
imagined and not what I have said. 17 To
the people who refuse to listen to what
I have said, they keep saying that all will
go well with them. And they tell everyone
who is stubborn that disaster will never
touch him."

18 I said, "None of these prophets has
ever known the LORD's secret thoughts.
None of them has ever heard or understood his message, or ever listened or paid
attention to what he said. 19 His anger is a
storm, a furious wind that will rage over
the heads of the wicked, 20 and it will not
end until he has done everything he
intends to do. In days to come his people
will understand this clearly."

21 The LORD said, "I did not send these
prophets, but even so they went. I did
not give them any message, but still they
spoke in my name. 22 If they had known
my secret thoughts, then they could have
proclaimed my message to my people and
could have made them give up the evil
lives they live and the wicked things they
do.

23 "I am a God who is everywhere and
not in one place only. 24 No one can hide
where I cannot see him. Do you not know
that I am everywhere in heaven and on
earth? 25 I know what those prophets have
said who speak lies in my name and claim
that I have given them my messages in
their dreams. 26 How much longer will
those prophets mislead my people with
the lies they have invented? 27 They think
that the dreams they tell will make my
people forget me, just as their fathers
forgot me and turned to Baal. 28 The
prophet who has had a dream should say
it is only a dream, but the prophet who
has heard my message should proclaim
that message faithfully. What good is
straw compared with wheat? 29 My
message is like a fire, and like a hammer
that breaks rocks in pieces. 30 I am against
those prophets who take each other's
words and proclaim them as my message.
31 I am also against those prophets who
speak their own words and claim they
came from me. 32 Listen to what I, the
LORD, say! I am against the prophets who
tell their dreams that are full of lies. They
tell these dreams and lead my people
astray with their lies and their boasting.
I did not send them or order them to go,
and they are of no help at all to the people.
I, the LORD, have spoken."

The LORD's Burden

33 The LORD said to me, "Jeremiah,
when one of my people or a prophet or
a priest asks you, 'What is the LORD's

23.14: Gen 18.20; Ezek 16.49

message?' you are to tell him, 'You are a burden[e] to the LORD, and he is going to get rid of you.' [34]If one of my people or a prophet or a priest even uses the words 'the LORD's burden,' I will punish him and his family. [35]Instead, each one should ask his friends and his relatives, 'What answer has the LORD given? What has the LORD said?' [36]So they must no longer use the words 'the LORD's burden,' because if anyone does, I will make my message a real burden to him. The people have perverted the words of their God, the living God, the LORD Almighty. [37]Jeremiah, ask the prophets, 'What answer did the LORD give you? What did the LORD say?' [38]And if they disobey my command and use the words 'the LORD's burden,' then tell them that [39]I will certainly pick them up[f] and throw them far away from me, both them and the city that I gave to them and their ancestors. [40]I will bring on them everlasting shame and disgrace that will never be forgotten."

Two Baskets of Figs

24 The LORD showed me two baskets of figs placed in front of the Temple. (This was after King Nebuchadnezzar of Babylonia had taken away Jehoiakim's son, King Jehoiachin of Judah, as a prisoner from Jerusalem to Babylonia, together with the leaders of Judah, the craftsmen, and the skilled workers.) [2]The first basket contained good figs, those that ripen early; the other one contained bad figs, too bad to eat. [3]Then the LORD said to me, "Jeremiah, what do you see?"

I answered, "Figs. The good ones are very good, and the bad ones are very bad, too bad to eat."

4 So the LORD said to me, [5]"I, the LORD, the God of Israel, consider that the people who were taken away to Babylonia are like these good figs, and I will treat them with kindness. [6]I will watch over them and bring them back to this land. I will build them up and not tear them down; I will plant them and not pull them up. [7]I will give them the desire to know that I am the LORD. Then they will be my people, and I will be their God, because they will return to me with all their heart.

8 "As for King Zedekiah of Judah, the politicians round him, and the rest of the people of Jerusalem who have stayed in this land or moved to Egypt—I, the LORD, will treat them all like these figs that are too bad to be eaten. [9]I will bring such a disaster on them that all the nations of the world will be terrified. People will mock them, make jokes about them, ridicule them, and use their name as a curse everywhere I scatter them. [10]I will bring war, starvation, and disease on them until there is not one of them left in the land that I gave to them and their ancestors."

The Enemy from the North

25 In the fourth year that Jehoiakim son of Josiah was king of Judah, I received a message from the LORD concerning all the people of Judah. (This was the first year that Nebuchadnezzar was king of Babylonia.) [2]I said to all the people of Judah and of Jerusalem, [3]"For twenty-three years, from the thirteenth year that Josiah son of Amon was king of Judah until this very day, the LORD has spoken to me, and I have never failed to tell you what he said. But you have paid no attention. [4]You would not listen or pay attention, even though the LORD has continued to send you his servants the prophets. [5]They told you to turn from your wicked way of life and from the evil things you are doing, so that you could go on living in the land that the LORD gave you and your ancestors as a permanent possession. [6]They told you not to worship and serve other gods and not to make the LORD angry by worshipping the idols you had made. If you had obeyed the LORD, then he would not have punished you. [7]But the LORD himself says that you refused to listen to him. Instead, you made him angry with your idols and have brought his punishment on yourselves.

8 "So then, because you would not listen to him, the LORD Almighty says, [9]'I am going to send for all the peoples from the north and for my servant, King Nebuchadnezzar of Babylonia. I am going to bring them to fight against Judah and its inhabitants and against all the neighbouring nations. I am going to destroy this nation and its neighbours and leave them in ruins for ever, a terrible

---

[e] The Hebrew word for message and burden is the same.
[f] The Hebrew verb for pick up comes from the same root as the Hebrew word for message and burden.
24.1: 2 Kgs 24.12–16; 2 Chr 36.10   **25.1:** 2 Kgs 24.1; 2 Chr 36.5–7; Dan 1.1–2

and shocking sight. I, the LORD, have spoken. ¹⁰I will silence their shouts of joy and gladness and the happy sounds of wedding feasts. They will have no oil for their lamps, and there will be no more corn. ¹¹This whole land will be left in ruins and will be a shocking sight, and the neighbouring nations will serve the king of Babylonia for seventy years. ¹²After that I will punish Babylonia and its king for their sin. I will destroy that country and leave it in ruins for ever. ¹³I will punish Babylonia with all the disasters that I threatened to bring on the nations when I spoke through Jeremiah—all the disasters recorded in this book. ¹⁴I will pay the Babylonians back for what they have done, and many nations and great kings will make slaves of them.' "

God's Judgement on the Nations

15 The LORD, the God of Israel, said to me, "Here is a wine cup filled with my anger. Take it to all the nations to whom I send you, and make them drink from it. ¹⁶When they drink from it, they will stagger and go out of their minds because of the war I am sending against them."

17 So I took the cup from the LORD's hand, gave it to all the nations to whom the LORD had sent me, and made them drink from it. ¹⁸Jerusalem and all the towns of Judah, together with its kings and leaders, were made to drink from it, so that they would become a desert, a terrible and shocking sight, and so that people would use their name as a curse—as they still do.

19–26 Here is the list of all the others who had to drink from the cup:
the king of Egypt, his officials and
  leaders;
all the Egyptians and all the foreigners
  in Egypt;
all the kings of the land of Uz;
all the kings of the Philistine cities of
  Ashkelon, Gaza, Ekron, and what
  remains of Ashdod;
all the people of Edom, Moab, and
  Ammon;
all the kings of Tyre and Sidon;
all the kings of the Mediterranean lands;
the cities of Dedan, Tema, and Buz;
all the people who cut their hair short;
all the kings of Arabia;
all the kings of the desert tribes;

all the kings of Zimri, Elam, and Media;
all the kings of the north, far and near,
  one after another.
Every nation on the face of the earth had to drink from it. Last of all, the king of Babylonia will drink from it.

27 Then the LORD said to me, "Tell the people that I, the LORD Almighty, the God of Israel, am commanding them to drink until they are drunk and vomit, until they fall down and cannot get up, because of the war that I am sending against them. ²⁸And if they refuse to take the cup from your hand and drink from it, then tell them that the LORD Almighty has said that they will still have to drink from it. ²⁹I will begin my work of destruction in my own city. Do they think they will go unpunished? No, they will be punished, for I am going to send war on all the people on earth. I, the LORD Almighty, have spoken.

30 "You, Jeremiah, must proclaim everything I have said. You must tell these people,
'The LORD will roar from heaven
  and thunder from the heights of
    heaven.
He will roar against his people;
  he will shout like a man treading
    grapes.
Everyone on earth will hear him,
³¹ and the sound will echo to the ends
    of the earth.
The LORD has a case against the nations.
  He will bring all people to trial
  and put the wicked to death.
The LORD has spoken.' "

32 The LORD Almighty says that disaster is coming on one nation after another, and a great storm is gathering at the far ends of the earth. ³³On that day the bodies of those whom the LORD has killed will lie scattered from one end of the earth to the other. No one will mourn for them, and they will not be taken away and buried. They will lie on the ground like piles of manure.

34 Cry, you leaders, you shepherds of my people, cry out loud! Mourn and roll in the dust. The time has come for you to be slaughtered,ᵍ and you will be butchered like rams.ʰ ³⁵There will be no way for you to escape. ³⁶⁻³⁷You moan and cry out in distress because the LORD

ᵍ Hebrew has an additional word, the meaning of which is unclear.
ʰ One ancient translation rams; Hebrew vessels.
25.10: Jer 7.34, 16.9; Rev 18.22–23   **25.11:** 2 Chr 36.21; Jer 29.10; Dan 9.2

in his anger has destroyed your nation and left your peaceful country in ruins. [38] The LORD has abandoned his people [i] like a lion that leaves its cave. The horrors of war and the LORD's fierce anger have turned the country into a desert.

Jeremiah Is Brought to Trial

26 Soon after Jehoiakim son of Josiah became king of Judah, [2] the LORD said to me, "Stand in the court of the Temple and proclaim all I have commanded you to say to the people who come from the towns of Judah to worship there. Do not leave out anything. [3] Perhaps the people will listen and give up their evil ways. If they do, then I will change my mind about the destruction I plan to bring on them for all their wicked deeds."

4 The LORD told me to say to the people, "I, the LORD, have said that you must obey me by following the teaching that I gave you, [5] and by paying attention to the words of my servants, the prophets, whom I have kept on sending to you. You have never obeyed what they said. [6] If you continue to disobey, then I will do to this Temple what I did to Shiloh, [j] and all the nations of the world will use the name of this city as a curse."

7 The priests, the prophets, and all the people heard me saying these things in the Temple, [8] and as soon as I had finished all that the LORD had commanded me to speak, they seized me and shouted, "You ought to be killed for this! [9] Why have you said in the LORD's name that this Temple will become like Shiloh and that this city will be destroyed and no one will live in it?" Then the people crowded round me.

10 When the leaders of Judah heard what had happened, they hurried from the royal palace to the Temple and took their places at the New Gate. [11] Then the priests and the prophets said to the leaders and to the people, "This man deserves to be sentenced to death because he has spoken against our city. You heard him with your own ears."

12 Then I said, "The LORD sent me to proclaim everything that you heard me say against this Temple and against this city. [13] You must change the way you are living and the things you are doing, and must obey the LORD your God. If you do,

he will change his mind about the destruction that he said he would bring on you. [14] As for me, I am in your power! Do with me whatever you think is fair and right. [15] But be sure of this: if you kill me, you and the people of this city will be guilty of killing an innocent man, because it is the LORD who sent me to give you this warning."

16 Then the leaders and the people said to the priests and the prophets, "This man spoke to us in the name of the LORD our God; he should not be put to death."

17 After that, some of the elders stood up and said to the people who had assembled, [18] "When Hezekiah was king of Judah, the prophet Micah of Moresheth told all the people that the LORD Almighty had said,

'Zion will be ploughed like a field,
    Jerusalem will become a pile of ruins,
    and the Temple hill will become a
        forest.'

[19] King Hezekiah and the people of Judah did not put Micah to death. Instead, Hezekiah honoured the LORD and tried to win his favour. And the LORD changed his mind about the disaster that he said he would bring on them. Now we are about to bring a terrible disaster on ourselves."

20 (There was another man, Uriah son of Shemaiah from Kiriath Jearim, who spoke in the name of the LORD against this city and nation just as Jeremiah did. [21] When King Jehoiakim and his soldiers and officials heard what Uriah had said, the king tried to have him killed. But Uriah heard about it; so he fled in terror and escaped to Egypt. [22] King Jehoiakim, however, sent Elnathan son of Achbor and some other men to Egypt to get Uriah. [23] They brought him back to King Jehoiakim, who had him killed and his body thrown into the public burial-ground.)

24 But because I had the support of Ahikam son of Shaphan, I was not handed over to the people and killed.

Jeremiah Wears an Ox Yoke

27 Soon after Josiah's son Zedekiah became king of Judah, the LORD told me [2] to make myself a yoke out of leather straps and wooden crossbars and to put it on my neck. [3] Then the LORD

---

[i] The Lord...people; or The Lord's people run away.   [j] SHILOH: See 7.12.
26.1: 2 Kgs 23.36—24.6; 2 Chr 36.5-7   **26.6:** Josh 18.1; Ps 78.60; Jer 7.12-14
26.18: Mic 3.12   **27.1:** 2 Kgs 24.18-20; 2 Chr 36.11-13

told me to send a message[k] to the kings of Edom, Moab, Ammon, Tyre, and Sidon through their ambassadors who had come to Jerusalem to see King Zedekiah. [4]The LORD Almighty, the God of Israel, told me to command them to tell their kings that the LORD had said: [5]"By my great power and strength I created the world, mankind, and all the animals that live on the earth; and I give it to anyone I choose. [6]I am the one who has placed all these nations under the power of my servant, King Nebuchadnezzar of Babylonia, and I have made even the wild animals serve him. [7]All nations will serve him, and they will serve his son and his grandson until the time comes for his own nation to fall. Then his nation will serve powerful nations and great kings.

[8]"But if any nation or kingdom will not submit to his rule, then I will punish that nation by war, starvation, and disease until I have let Nebuchadnezzar destroy it completely. [9]Do not listen to your prophets or to anyone who claims he can predict the future, either by dreams or by calling up the spirits of the dead or by magic. They all tell you not to submit to the king of Babylonia. [10]They are deceiving you and will cause you to be taken far away from your country. I will drive you out, and you will be destroyed. [11]But if any nation submits to the king of Babylonia and serves him, then I will let it stay on in its own land, to farm it and live there. I, the LORD, have spoken."

[12]I said the same thing to King Zedekiah of Judah, "Submit to the king of Babylonia. Serve him and his people, and you will live. [13]Why should you and your people die in war or of starvation or disease? That is what the LORD has said will happen to any nation that does not submit to the king of Babylonia. [14]Do not listen to the prophets who tell you not to surrender to him. They are deceiving you. [15]The LORD himself has said that he did not send them and that they are lying to you in his name. And so he will drive you out, and you will be killed, you and the prophets who are telling you these lies."

[16]Then I told the priests and the people that the LORD had said: "Do not listen to the prophets who say that the temple treasures will soon be brought back from Babylonia. They are lying to you. [17]Don't listen to them! Submit to the king of Babylonia and you will live! Why should this city become a pile of ruins? [18]If they are really prophets and if they have my message, let them ask me, the LORD Almighty, not to allow the treasures that remain in the Temple and in the royal palace to be taken to Babylonia."

[19-20] (When King Nebuchadnezzar took away to Babylonia the king of Judah, Jehoiachin son of Jehoiakim, and the leading men of Judah and Jerusalem, he left the columns, the bronze tank, the carts, and some of the other temple treasures.)

[21]"Listen to what I, the LORD Almighty, the God of Israel, say about the treasures that are left in the Temple and in the royal palace in Jerusalem: [22]They will be taken to Babylonia and will remain there until I turn my attention to them. Then I will bring them back and restore them to this place. I, the LORD, have spoken."

Jeremiah and the Prophet Hananiah

28 That same year,[l] in the fifth month of the fourth year that Zedekiah was king, Hananiah son of Azzur, a prophet from the town of Gibeon, spoke to me in the Temple. In the presence of the priests and of the people he told me [2]that the LORD Almighty, the God of Israel, had said: "I have broken the power of the king of Babylonia. [3]Within two years I will bring back to this place all the temple treasures that King Nebuchadnezzar took to Babylonia. [4]I will also bring back the king of Judah, Jehoiachin son of Jehoiakim, along with all the people of Judah who went into exile in Babylonia. Yes, I will break the power of the king of Babylonia. I, the LORD, have spoken."

[5]Then in the presence of the priests and of all the people who were standing in the Temple, I said to Hananiah: [6]"Wonderful! I hope the LORD will do this! I certainly hope he will make your prophecy come true and will bring back from Babylonia all the temple treasures and all the people who were taken away as prisoners. [7]But listen to what I say to you and to the people. [8]The prophets who spoke long ago, before my time and yours, predicted that war, starvation, and disease would come to many nations and powerful kingdoms. [9]But a prophet who predicts peace can only be recognized as a prophet whom the LORD has truly sent

---

[k] *Probable text* a message; *Hebrew* them.

[l] *One ancient translation* That same year; *Hebrew* That same year at the beginning of his reign.

28.1: 2 Kgs 24.18–20; 2 Chr 36.11-13

when that prophet's predictions come true."

10 Then Hananiah took the yoke off my neck, broke it in pieces, [11] and said in the presence of all the people: "The LORD has said that this is how he will break the yoke that King Nebuchadnezzar has put on the neck of all the nations; and he will do this within two years." Then I left.

12 Some time after this the LORD told me [13] to go and say to Hananiah: "The LORD has said that you may be able to break a wooden yoke, but he[m] will replace it with an iron yoke. [14] The LORD Almighty, the God of Israel, has said that he will put an iron yoke on all these nations and that they will serve King Nebuchadnezzar of Babylonia. The LORD has said that he will make even the wild animals serve Nebuchadnezzar."

15 Then I told Hananiah this, and added, "Listen, Hananiah! The LORD did not send you, and you are making these people believe a lie. [16] And so the LORD himself says that he is going to get rid of you. Before this year is over you will die because you have told the people to rebel against the LORD."

17 And Hananiah died in the seventh month of that same year.

Jeremiah's Letter to the Jews in Babylonia

29 I wrote a letter to the priests, the prophets, the leaders of the people, and to all the others whom Nebuchadnezzar had taken away as prisoners from Jerusalem to Babylonia. [2] I wrote it after King Jehoiachin, his mother, the palace officials, the leaders of Judah and of Jerusalem, the craftsmen, and the skilled workmen had been taken into exile. [3] I gave the letter to Elasah son of Shaphan and to Gemariah son of Hilkiah, whom King Zedekiah of Judah was sending to King Nebuchadnezzar of Babylonia. It said:

[4] "The LORD Almighty, the God of Israel, says to all those people whom he allowed Nebuchadnezzar to take away as prisoners from Jerusalem to Babylonia: [5] 'Build houses and settle down. Plant gardens and eat what you grow in them. [6] Marry and have children. Then let your children get married, so that they also may have

children. You must increase in numbers and not decrease. [7] Work for the good of the cities where I have made you go as prisoners. Pray to me on their behalf, because if they are prosperous, you will be prosperous too. [8] I, the LORD, the God of Israel, warn you not to let yourselves be deceived by the prophets who live among you or by any others who claim they can predict the future. Do not pay any attention to their[x] dreams. [9] They are telling you lies in my name. I did not send them. I, the LORD Almighty, have spoken.'

[10] "The LORD says, 'When Babylonia's seventy years are over, I will show my concern for you and keep my promise to bring you back home. [11] I alone know the plans I have for you, plans to bring you prosperity and not disaster, plans to bring about the future you hope for.[n] [12] Then you will call to me. You will come and pray to me, and I will answer you. [13] You will seek me, and you will find me because you will seek me with all your heart. [14] Yes, I say, you will find me, and I will restore you to your land. I will gather you from every country and from every place to which I have scattered you, and I will bring you back to the land from which I had sent you away into exile. I, the LORD, have spoken.'

[15] "You say that the LORD has given you prophets in Babylonia. [16] Listen to what the LORD says about the king who rules the kingdom that David ruled and about the people of this city, that is, your relatives who were not taken away as prisoners with you. [17] The LORD Almighty says, 'I am bringing war, starvation, and disease on them, and I will make them like figs that are too rotten to be eaten. [18] I will pursue them with war, starvation, and disease, and all the nations of the world will be horrified at what they see. Everywhere I scatter them, people will be shocked and terrified at what has happened to them. People will mock them and use their name as a curse. [19] This will happen to them because they did not obey the message that I kept on sending to

---

[m] One ancient translation he; Hebrew you. [x] Probable text their; Hebrew your.
[n] the future you hope for; or a future full of hope.
29.1–2: 2 Kgs 24.12–16; 2 Chr 36.10   **29.10:** 2 Chr 36.21; Jer 25.11; Dan 9.2
29.13: Deut 4.29

them through my servants the prophets. They refused to listen. ²⁰All of you whom I sent into exile in Babylonia, listen to what I, the LORD, say.'

²¹"The LORD Almighty, the God of Israel, has spoken about Ahab son of Kolaiah and Zedekiah son of Maaseiah, who are telling you lies in his name. He has said that he will hand them over to the power of King Nebuchadnezzar of Babylonia, who will put them to death before your eyes. ²²When the people who were taken away as prisoners from Jerusalem to Babylonia want to bring a curse on someone, they will say, 'May the LORD treat you like Zedekiah and Ahab, whom the king of Babylonia roasted alive!' ²³This will be their fate because they are guilty of terrible sins—they have committed adultery and have told lies in the LORD's name. This was against the LORD's will; he knows what they have done, and he is a witness against them. ᵒ The LORD has spoken."

The Letter of Shemaiah

24-25 The LORD Almighty, the God of Israel, gave me a message for Shemaiah of Nehelam, who had sent a letter in his own name to all the people of Jerusalem and to the priest Zephaniah son of Maaseiah and to all the other priests. In this letter, Shemaiah wrote to Zephaniah:

²⁶"The LORD made you a priest in place of Jehoiada, and you are now the chief officerᵖ in the Temple. It is your duty to see that every madman who pretends to be a prophet is placed in chains with an iron collar round his neck. ²⁷Why haven't you done this to Jeremiah of Anathoth, who has been speaking as a prophet to the people? ²⁸He must be stopped because he told the people in Babylonia that they would be prisoners there a long time and should build houses, settle down, plant gardens, and eat what they grow."

29 Zephaniah read the letter to me, ³⁰and then the LORD told me ³¹⁻³²to send to all the prisoners in Babylon this message about Shemaiah: "I, the LORD, will punish Shemaiah and all his descendants. I did not send him, but he spoke to you as if he were a prophet, and he

made you believe lies. He will have no descendants among you. He will not live to see the good things that I am going to do for my people, because he told them to rebel against me. I, the LORD, have spoken."

The LORD's Promises to His People

30 The LORD, the God of Israel, ²said to me: "Write down in a book everything that I have told you, ³because the time is coming when I will restore my people, Israel and Judah. I will bring them back to the land that I gave their ancestors, and they will take possession of it again. I, the LORD, have spoken."

4 The LORD says to the people of Israel and Judah:

⁵ "I heard a cry of terror,
   a cry of fear and not of peace.
⁶ Now stop and think!
   Can a man give birth to a child?
Why then do I see every man with his
      hands on his stomach
   like a woman in labour?
   Why is everyone so pale?
⁷ A terrible day is coming;
   no other day can compare with it—
   a time of distress for my people,
   but they will survive."

8 The LORD Almighty says: "When that day comes, I will break the yoke that is round their necks and remove their chains, and they will no longer be the slaves of foreigners. ⁹Instead, they will serve me, the LORD their God, and a descendant of David, whom I will enthrone as king.

¹⁰ "My people, do not be afraid;
   people of Israel, do not be terrified.
I will rescue you from that distant land,
   from the land where you are prisoners.
You will come back home and live in
      peace;
   you will be secure, and no one will
      make you afraid.
¹¹ I will come to you and save you.
I will destroy all the nations
   where I have scattered you,
   but I will not destroy you.
I will not let you go unpunished;
   but when I punish you, I will be fair.
I, the LORD, have spoken."

12 The LORD says to his people,
"Your wounds are incurable,
   your injuries cannot be healed.

ᵒdone, and he...them; *or* done; he saw them do it.
ᵖ *Some ancient translations* officer; *Hebrew* officers.
30.10-11: Jer 46.27-28

13 There is no one to take care of you,
　no remedy for your sores,
　no hope of healing for you.
14 All your lovers have forgotten you;
　they no longer care about you.
I have attacked you like an enemy;
　your punishment has been harsh
　because your sins are many
　and your wickedness is great.
15 Complain no more about your injuries;
　there is no cure for you.
I punished you like this
　because your sins are many
　and your wickedness is great.
16 But now, all who devour you will be
　devoured,
　and all your enemies will be taken
　away as prisoners.
All who oppress you will be oppressed,
　and all who plunder you will be
　plundered.
17 I will make you well again;
　I will heal your wounds,
　though your enemies say,
'Zion is an outcast;
　no one cares about her.'
I, the LORD, have spoken."

18 The LORD says,
"I will restore my people to their land
　and have mercy on every family;
Jerusalem will be rebuilt,
　and its palace restored.
19 The people who live there will sing
　praise;
　they will shout for joy.
By my blessing they will increase in
　numbers;
　my blessing will bring them honour.
20 I will restore the nation's ancient
　power
　and establish it firmly again;
I will punish all who oppress them.
21-22 Their ruler will come from their
　own nation,
　their prince from their own people.
He will approach me when I invite him,
　for who would dare come uninvited?
They will be my people,
　and I will be their God.
I, the LORD, have spoken."

23-24 The LORD's anger is a storm, a
furious wind that will rage over the heads
of the wicked. It will not end until he
has done all that he intends to do. In
days to come his people will understand
this clearly.

Israel's Return Home

31 The LORD says, "The time is
coming when I will be the God of
all the tribes of Israel, and they will be
my people. 2 In the desert I showed mercy
to those people who had escaped death.
When the people of Israel longed for rest,
3 I appeared to them q from far away.
People of Israel, I have always loved you,
so I continue to show you my constant
love. 4 Once again I will rebuild you. Once
again you will take up your tambourines
and dance joyfully. 5 Once again you will
plant vineyards on the hills of Samaria,
and those who plant them will eat what
the vineyards produce. 6 Yes, the time is
coming when watchmen will call out on
the hills of Ephraim, 'Let's go up to Zion,
to the LORD our God.' "

7 The LORD says,
"Sing with joy for Israel,
　the greatest of the nations.
Sing your song of praise,
'The LORD has saved his x people;
　he has rescued all who are left.'
8 I will bring them from the north
　and gather them from the ends of the
　earth.
The blind and the lame will come with
　them,
　pregnant women and those about to
　give birth.
They will come back a great nation.
9 My people will return weeping,
　praying as I lead them back.
I will guide them to streams of water,
　on a smooth road where they will not
　stumble.
I am like a father to Israel,
　and Ephraim is my eldest son."
10 The LORD says,
"Nations, listen to me,
　and proclaim my words on the far-off
　shores.
I scattered my people, but I will gather
　them
　and guard them as a shepherd guards
　his flock.
11 I have set Israel's people free
　and have saved them from a mighty
　nation.
12 They will come and sing for joy on
　Mount Zion
　and be delighted with my gifts—
　gifts of corn and wine and olive-oil,
　gifts of sheep and cattle.
They will be like a well-watered garden;
　they will have everything they need.

q One ancient translation them; Hebrew me.
x Some ancient translations The LORD...his; Hebrew LORD, save your.

The girls will dance and be happy, and men, young and old, will rejoice (31.13)

¹³ Then the girls will dance and be happy,
   and men, young and old, will rejoice.
I will comfort them and turn their
     mourning into joy,
   their sorrow into gladness.
¹⁴ I will fill the priests with the richest
     food
   and satisfy all the needs of my people.
I, the LORD, have spoken."

The LORD's Mercy on Israel

15 The LORD says,
"A sound is heard in Ramah,
   the sound of bitter weeping.
Rachel is crying for her children;
   they are gone,
   and she refuses to be comforted.
¹⁶ Stop your crying
   and wipe away your tears.
All that you have done for your children
   will not go unrewarded;
   they will return from the enemy's
     land.

¹⁷ There is hope for your future;
   your children will come back home.
   I, the LORD, have spoken.

¹⁸ "I hear the people of Israel say in grief,
   'LORD, we were like an untamed animal,
   but you taught us to obey.
Bring us back;
   we are ready to return to you,
   the LORD our God.
¹⁹ We turned away from you,
   but soon we wanted to return.
After you had punished us,
   we hung our heads in grief.
We were ashamed and disgraced,
   because we sinned when we were
     young.'

²⁰ "Israel, you are my dearest son,
   the child I love best.
Whenever I mention your name,
   I think ʳ of you with love.
My heart goes out to you;

ʳ I mention...I think; *or* I threaten to punish, I still think.
31.15: Gen 35.16–19; Mt 2.18

I will be merciful.
21 Set up signs and mark the road;
    find again the way by which you left.
Come back, people of Israel,
    come home to the towns you left.
22 How long will you hesitate, faithless
    people?
I have created something new and
    different,
    as different as a woman protecting
    a man." *s*

The Future Prosperity of God's People

23 The LORD Almighty, the God of Israel, says, "When I restore the people to their land, they will once again say in the land of Judah and in its towns,
'May the LORD bless the sacred hill *t* of
    Jerusalem,
    the holy place where he lives.'
24 People will live in Judah and in all its towns, and there will be farmers, and shepherds with their flocks. 25 I will refresh those who are weary and will satisfy with food everyone who is weak from hunger. 26 So then, people will say, 'I went to sleep and woke up refreshed.'
27 "I, the LORD, say that the time is coming when I will fill the land of Israel and Judah with people and animals. 28 And just as I took care to uproot, to pull down, to overthrow, to destroy, and to demolish them, so I will take care to plant them and to build them up. 29 When that time comes, people will no longer say,
'The parents ate the sour grapes,
But the children got the sour taste.'
30 Instead, whoever eats sour grapes will have his own teeth set on edge; and everyone will die because of his own sin."
31 The LORD says, "The time is coming when I will make a new covenant with the people of Israel and with the people of Judah. 32 It will not be like the old covenant that I made with their ancestors when I took them by the hand and led them out of Egypt. Although I was like a husband to them, they did not keep that covenant. 33 The new covenant that I will make with the people of Israel will be this: I will put my law within them and write it on their hearts. I will be their God, and they will be my people. 34 None of them will have to teach his fellow-countryman to know the LORD, because all will know me, from the least to the greatest. I will forgive their sins and I

will no longer remember their wrongs. I, the LORD, have spoken."

35 The LORD provides the sun for light
    by day,
    the moon and the stars to shine at
    night.
He stirs up the sea and makes it roar;
    his name is the LORD Almighty.
36 He promises that as long as the natural
    order lasts,
    so long will Israel be a nation.
37 If one day the sky could be measured
    and the foundations of the earth
    explored,
    only then would he reject the people
    of Israel
    because of all they have done.
The LORD has spoken.

38 "The time is coming," says the LORD, "when all Jerusalem will be rebuilt as my city, from Hananel Tower west to the Corner Gate. 39 And the boundary line will continue from there on the west to the hill of Gareb and then round to Goah. 40 The entire valley, where the dead are buried and refuse is thrown, and all the fields above the brook of Kidron as far as the Horse Gate to the east, will be sacred to me. The city will never again be torn down or destroyed."

Jeremiah Buys a Field

32 The LORD spoke to me in the tenth year that Zedekiah was king of Judah, which was also the eighteenth year of King Nebuchadnezzar of Babylonia. 2 At that time the army of the king of Babylonia was attacking Jerusalem, and I was locked up in the courtyard of the royal palace. 3 King Zedekiah had imprisoned me there and had accused me of announcing that the LORD had said, "I am going to let the king of Babylonia capture this city, 4 and King Zedekiah will not escape. He will be handed over to the king of Babylonia; he will see him face to face and will speak to him in person. 5 Zedekiah will be taken to Babylonia, and he will remain there until I deal with him. Even if he fights the Babylonians, he will not be successful. I, the LORD, have spoken."

6 The LORD told me 7 that Hanamel, my uncle Shallum's son, would come to me with the request to buy his field at

---

s as different...man; *Hebrew unclear.*
t SACRED HILL: *Mount Zion, the hill in Jerusalem which formed part of the Temple and palace area.*
31.29: Ezek 18.2   **31.31:** Mt 26.28; Mk 14.24; Lk 22.20; 1 Cor 11.25; 2 Cor 3.6
31.31–34: Heb 8.8–12   **31.33:** Heb 10.16   **31.34:** Heb 10.17   **32.1:** 2 Kgs 25.1–7

Anathoth in the territory of Benjamin, because I was his nearest relative and had the right to buy it for myself. 8 Then, just as the LORD had said, Hanamel came to me there in the courtyard and asked me to buy the field. So I knew that the LORD had really spoken to me. 9 I bought the field from Hanamel and weighed out the money to him; the price came to seventeen pieces of silver. 10 I signed and sealed the deed, had it witnessed, and weighed out the money on scales. 11 Then I took both copies of the deed of purchase—the sealed copy containing the contract and its conditions, and the open copy—12 and gave them to Baruch, the son of Neriah and grandson of Mahseiah. I gave them to him in the presence of Hanamel and of the witnesses who had signed the deed of purchase and of the men who were sitting in the courtyard. 13 Before them all I said to Baruch, 14 "The LORD Almighty, the God of Israel, has ordered you to take these deeds, both the sealed deed of purchase and the open copy, and to place them in a clay jar, so that they may be preserved for years to come. 15 The LORD Almighty, the God of Israel, has said that houses, fields, and vineyards will again be bought in this land."

Jeremiah's Prayer

16 After I had given the deed of purchase to Baruch, I prayed, 17 "Sovereign LORD, you made the earth and the sky by your great power and might; nothing is too difficult for you. 18 You have shown constant love to thousands, but you also punish people for the sins of their parents. You are a great and powerful God; you are the LORD Almighty. 19 You make wise plans and do mighty things; you see everything that people do, and you reward them according to their actions. 20 Long ago, you performed miracles and wonders in Egypt, and you have continued to perform them to this day, both in Israel and among all the other nations, so that you are now known everywhere. 21 By means of miracles and wonders that terrified our enemies, you used your power and might to bring your people Israel out of Egypt. 22 You gave them this rich and fertile land, as you had promised their ancestors. 23 But when they came into this land and took possession of it, they did not obey your commands or live according to your teaching; they did nothing that you had ordered them to do. And so you brought all this destruction on them.

24 "The Babylonians have built siege mounds round the city to capture it, and they are attacking. War, starvation, and disease will make the city fall into their hands. You can see that all you have said has come true. 25 Yet, Sovereign LORD, you are the one who ordered me to buy the field in the presence of witnesses, even though the city is about to be captured by the Babylonians."

26 Then the LORD said to me, 27 "I am the LORD, the God of all mankind. Nothing is too difficult for me. 28 I am going to give this city over to King Nebuchadnezzar of Babylonia and his army; they will capture it 29 and set it on fire. They will burn it down, together with the houses where people have made me angry by burning incense to Baal on the rooftops and by pouring out wine-offerings to other gods. 30 From the very beginning of their history the people of Israel and the people of Judah have displeased me and made me angry by what they have done. 31 The people of this city have made me angry and furious from the day it was built. I have decided to destroy it 32 because of all the evil that has been done by the people of Judah and Jerusalem, together with their kings and leaders, their priests and prophets. 33 They turned their backs on me; and though I kept on teaching them, they would not listen and learn. 34 They even placed their disgusting idols in the Temple built for my worship, and they have defiled it. 35 They have built altars to Baal in the Valley of Hinnom, to sacrifice their sons and daughters to the god Molech. I did not command them to do this, and it did not even enter my mind that they would do such a thing and make the people of Judah sin."

A Promise of Hope

36 The LORD, the God of Israel, said to me, "Jeremiah, the people are saying that war, starvation, and disease will make this city fall into the hands of the king of Babylonia. Now listen to what else I have to say. 37 I am going to gather the people from all the countries where I have scattered them in my anger and fury, and I am going to bring them back to this place and let them live here in safety.

32.28: 2 Kgs 25.1–11; 2 Chr 36.17–21　　**32.34:** 2 Kgs 23.10; Jer 7.30–31, 19.1–6
32.35: Lev 18.21; 2 Kgs 23.10; Jer 7.31

38 Then they will be my people, and I will be their God. 39 I will give them a single purpose in life: to honour me for all time, for their own good and the good of their descendants. 40 I will make an eternal covenant with them. I will never stop doing good things for them, and I will make them fear me with all their heart, so that they will never turn away from me. 41 I will take pleasure in doing good things for them, and I will establish them permanently in this land.

42 "Just as I have brought this disaster on these people, so I am going to give them all the good things that I have promised. 43 The people are saying that this land will be like a desert where neither people nor animals live, and that it will be given over to the Babylonians. But fields will once again be bought in this land. 44 People will buy them, and the deeds will be signed, sealed, and witnessed. This will take place in the territory of Benjamin, in the villages round Jerusalem, in the towns of Judah, and in the towns in the hill-country, in the foothills, and in southern Judah. I will restore the people to their land. I, the LORD, have spoken."

Another Promise of Hope

33 While I was still in prison in the courtyard, the LORD's message came to me again. 2 The LORD, who made the earth, who formed it and set it in place, spoke to me. He whose name is the LORD said, 3 "Call to me, and I will answer you; I will tell you wonderful and marvellous things that you know nothing about. 4 I, the LORD, the God of Israel, say that the houses of Jerusalem and the royal palace of Judah will be torn down as a result of the siege and the attack. 5 Some will fight against the Babylonians, who will fill the houses w with the corpses of those whom I am going to strike down in my anger and fury. I have turned away from this city because of the evil things that its people have done. 6 But I will heal this city and its people and restore them to health. I will show them abundant peace and security. 7 I will make Judah and Israel prosperous, and I will rebuild them as they were before. 8 I will purify them from the sins that they have committed against me, and I will forgive their sins and their rebellion. 9 Jerusalem

The LORD's message came to me again (33.1)

will be a source of joy, honour, and pride to me; and every nation in the world will fear and tremble when they hear about the good things that I do for the people of Jerusalem and about the prosperity that I bring to the city."

10 The LORD said, "People are saying that this place is like a desert, that it has no people or animals living in it. And they are right; the towns of Judah and the streets of Jerusalem are empty; no people or animals live there. But in these places you will hear again 11 the shouts of gladness and joy and the happy sounds of wedding feasts. You will hear people sing as they bring thank-offerings to my Temple; they will say,

'Give thanks to the LORD Almighty,
    because he is good
    and his love is eternal.'
I will make this land as prosperous as it was before. I, the LORD, have spoken."

12 The LORD Almighty said, "In this land that is like a desert and where no people or animals live, there will once again be pastures where shepherds can take their sheep. 13 In the towns of the hill-country, in the foothills, and in southern Judah, in the territory of

w *as a result...houses; Hebrew unclear.*
33.11: 1 Chr 16.34; 2 Chr 5.13, 7.3; Ezra 3.11; Ps 100.5, 106.1, 107.1, 118.1, 136.1

Benjamin, in the villages round Jerusalem, and in the towns of Judah, shepherds will once again count their sheep. I, the LORD, have spoken."

14 The LORD said, "The time is coming when I will fulfil the promise that I made to the people of Israel and Judah. 15 At that time I will choose as king a righteous descendant of David. That king will do what is right and just throughout the land. 16 The people of Judah and of Jerusalem will be rescued and will live in safety. The city will be called 'The LORD Our Salvation.' 17 I, the LORD, promise that there will always be a descendant of David to be king of Israel 18 and that there will always be priests from the tribe of Levi to serve me and to offer burnt-offerings, grain-offerings, and sacrifices."

19 The LORD said to me, 20 "I have made a covenant with the day and with the night, so that they always come at their proper times; and that covenant can never be broken. 21 In the same way I have made a covenant with my servant David that he would always have a descendant to be king, and I have made a covenant with the priests from the tribe of Levi that they would always serve me; and those covenants can never be broken. 22 I will increase the number of descendants of my servant David and the number of priests from the tribe of Levi, so that it will be as impossible to count them as it is to count the stars in the sky or the grains of sand on the sea-shore."

23 The LORD said to me, 24 "Have you noticed how people are saying that I have rejected Israel and Judah, the two families that I chose? And so they look with contempt on my people and no longer consider them a nation. 25 But I, the LORD, have a covenant with day and night, and I have made the laws that control earth and sky. 26 And just as surely as I have done this, so I will maintain my covenant with Jacob's descendants and with my servant David. I will choose one of David's descendants to rule over the descendants of Abraham, Isaac, and Jacob. I will be merciful to my people and make them prosperous again."

A Message for Zedekiah

34 The LORD spoke to me when King Nebuchadnezzar of Babylonia and his army, supported by troops from all the nations and races that were subject to him, were attacking Jerusalem and its nearby towns. 2 The LORD, the God of Israel, told me to go and say to King Zedekiah of Judah, "I, the LORD, will hand this city over to the king of Babylonia, and he will burn it down. 3 You will not escape; you will be captured and handed over to him. You will see him face to face and talk to him in person; then you will go to Babylonia. 4 Zedekiah, listen to what I say about you. You will not be killed in battle. 5 You will die in peace, and as people burnt incense when they buried your ancestors, who were kings before you, in the same way they will burn incense for you. They will mourn over you and say, 'Our king is dead!' I, the LORD, have spoken."

6 Then I gave this message to King Zedekiah in Jerusalem 7 while the army of the king of Babylonia was attacking the city. The army was also attacking Lachish and Azekah, the only other fortified cities left in Judah.

Deceitful Treatment of Slaves

8 King Zedekiah and the people of Jerusalem had made an agreement to set free 9 their Hebrew slaves, both male and female, so that no one would have a fellow-Israelite as a slave. 10 All the people and their leaders agreed to free their slaves and never to enslave them again. They did set them free, 11 but later they changed their minds, took them back, and forced them to become slaves again.

12 Then the LORD, 13 the God of Israel, told me to say to the people: "I made a covenant with your ancestors when I rescued them from Egypt and set them free from slavery. I told them that 14 every seven years they were to set free any Hebrew slave who had served them for six years. But your ancestors would not pay any attention to me or listen to what I said. 15 Just a few days ago you changed your minds and did what pleased me. All of you agreed to set your fellow-Israelites free, and you made a covenant in my presence, in the Temple where I am worshipped. 16 But then you changed your minds again and dishonoured me. All of you took back the slaves whom you had set free as they desired, and you forced them into slavery again. 17 So now, I, the LORD, say that you have disobeyed me: you have not given your fellow-Israelites their freedom. Very well, then, I will give

33.14–16: Jer 23.5–6   33.17: 2 Sam 7.12–16; 1 Kgs 2.4; 1 Chr 17.11–14   33.18: Num 3.5–10
34.1: 2 Kgs 25.1–11; 2 Chr 36.17–21   34.14: Ex 21.2; Deut 15.12

you freedom: the freedom to die by war, disease, and starvation. I will make every nation in the world horrified at what I do to you. 18-19 The officials of Judah and of Jerusalem, together with the palace officials, the priests, and all the leaders, made a covenant with me by walking between the two halves of a bull that they had cut in two. But they broke the covenant and did not keep its terms. So I will do to these people what they did to the bull. 20 I will hand them over to their enemies, who want to kill them, and their corpses will be eaten by birds and wild animals. 21 I will also hand over King Zedekiah of Judah and his officials to those who want to kill them. I will hand them over to the Babylonian army, which has stopped its attack against you. 22 I will give the order, and they will return to this city. They will attack it, capture it, and burn it down. I will make the towns of Judah like a desert where no one lives. I, the LORD, have spoken."

Jeremiah and the Rechabites

35 When Jehoiakim son of Josiah was king of Judah, the LORD said to me, 2 "Go to the members of the Rechabite clan and talk to them. Then bring them into one of the rooms in the Temple and offer them some wine." 3 So I took the entire Rechabite clan—Jaazaniah (the son of another Jeremiah, who was Habazziniah's son) and all his brothers and sons—4 and brought them to the Temple. I took them into the room of the disciples of the prophet Hanan son of Igdaliah. This room was above the room of Maaseiah son of Shallum, an important official in the Temple, and near the rooms of the other officials. 5 Then I placed cups and bowls full of wine before the Rechabites, and I said to them, "Have some wine."

6 But they answered, "We do not drink wine. Our ancestor Jonadab son of Rechab told us that neither we nor our descendants were ever to drink any wine. 7 He also told us not to build houses or farm the land, and not to plant vineyards or buy them. He commanded us always to live in tents, so that we might remain in this land where we live like strangers. 8 We have obeyed all the instructions that Jonadab gave us. We ourselves never drink wine, and neither do our wives, our sons, or our daughters. 9-10 We do not build houses for homes—we live in tents—and we own no vineyards, fields, or corn.

We have fully obeyed everything that our ancestor Jonadab commanded us. 11 But when King Nebuchadnezzar invaded the country, we decided to come to Jerusalem to get away from the Babylonian and Syrian armies. That is why we are living in Jerusalem."

12-13 Then the LORD Almighty, the God of Israel, told me to go and say to the people of Judah and Jerusalem, "I, the LORD, ask you why you refuse to listen to me and to obey my instructions. 14 Jonadab's descendants have obeyed his command not to drink wine, and to this very day none of them drink any. But I have kept on speaking to you, and you have not obeyed me. 15 I have continued to send you all my servants the prophets, and they have told you to give up your evil ways and to do what is right. They warned you not to worship and serve other gods, so that you could go on living in the land that I gave you and your ancestors. But you would not listen to me or pay attention to me. 16 Jonadab's descendants have obeyed the command that their ancestor gave them, but you people have not obeyed me. 17 So now, I, the LORD Almighty, the God of Israel, will bring on you people of Judah and of Jerusalem all the destruction that I promised. I will do this because you would not listen when I spoke to you, and you would not answer when I called you."

18 Then I told the Rechabite clan that the LORD Almighty, the God of Israel, had said, "You have obeyed the command that your ancestor Jonadab gave you; you have followed all his instructions, and you have done everything he commanded you. 19 So I, the LORD Almighty, the God of Israel, promise that Jonadab son of Rechab will always have a male descendant to serve me."

Baruch Reads the Scroll in the Temple

36 In the fourth year that Jehoiakim son of Josiah was king of Judah, the LORD said to me, 2 "Get a scroll and write on it everything that I have told you about Israel and Judah and all the nations. Write everything that I have told you from the time I first spoke to you, when Josiah was king, up to the present. 3 Perhaps when the people of Judah hear about all the destruction that I intend to bring on them, they will turn from their evil ways. Then I will forgive their wickedness and their sins."

35.1: 2 Kgs 23.36—24.6; 2 Chr 36.5-7   **36.1:** 2 Kgs 24.1; 2 Chr 36.5-7; Dan 1.1-2

Baruch wrote it all down on a scroll... Baruch read from the scroll... Then the officials sent Jehudi (36.4,10,14)

4 So I called Baruch son of Neriah and dictated to him everything that the LORD had said to me. And Baruch wrote it all down on a scroll. 5 Then I gave Baruch the following instructions: "I am no longer allowed to go into the Temple. 6 But I want you to go there the next time the people are fasting. You are to read the scroll aloud, so that they will hear everything that the LORD has said to me and that I have dictated to you. Do this where everyone can hear you, including the people of Judah who have come in from their towns. 7 Perhaps they will pray to the LORD and turn from their evil ways, because the LORD has threatened this people with his terrible anger and fury." 8 So Baruch read the LORD's words in the Temple exactly as I had told him to do.

9 In the ninth month of the fifth year that Jehoiakim was king of Judah, the people fasted to gain the LORD's favour. The fast was kept by all who lived in Jerusalem and by all who came there from the towns of Judah. 10 Then, while all the people were listening, Baruch read from the scroll everything that I had said. He did this in the Temple, from the room of Gemariah son of Shaphan, the court secretary. His room was in the upper court near the entrance of the New Gate of the Temple.

The Scroll Is Read to the Officials

11 Micaiah, the son of Gemariah and grandson of Shaphan, heard Baruch read from the scroll what the LORD had said. 12 Then he went to the royal palace, to the room of the court secretary, where all the officials were in session. Elishama, the court secretary, Delaiah son of Shemaiah, Elnathan son of Achbor, Gemariah son of Shaphan, Zedekiah son of Hananiah, and all the other officials were there. 13 Micaiah told them everything that he had heard Baruch read to the people. 14 Then the officials sent Jehudi (the son of Nethaniah, grandson of Shelemiah, and great-grandson of Cushi) to tell Baruch to bring the scroll that he had read to the people. Baruch brought them the scroll. 15 "Sit down," they said, "and read the scroll to us." So Baruch did. 16 After he had read it, they turned to one another in alarm, and said to Baruch, "We must report this to the king." 17 Then they asked him, "Tell us, now, how did you come to write all this? Did Jeremiah dictate it to you?"

18 Baruch answered, "Jeremiah dictated every word of it to me, and I wrote it down in ink on this scroll."

19 Then they said to him, "You and Jeremiah must go and hide. Don't let anyone know where you are."

The King Burns the Scroll

20 The officials put the scroll in the room of Elishama, the court secretary, and went to the king's court, where they reported everything to the king. 21 Then the king sent Jehudi to get the scroll. He took it from the room of Elishama and read it to the king and all the officials who were standing round him. 22 It was winter and the king was sitting in his winter palace in front of the fire. 23 As soon as Jehudi finished reading three or four

We must report this to the king... As soon as Jehudi finished reading three or four columns, the king cut them off...Then I took another scroll (36.16,23,32)

columns, the king cut them off with a small knife and threw them into the fire. He kept doing this until the entire scroll was burnt up. 24 But neither the king nor any of his officials who heard all this was afraid or showed any sign of sorrow. 25 Although Elnathan, Delaiah, and Gemariah begged the king not to burn the scroll, he paid no attention to them. 26 Then he ordered Prince Jerahmeel, together with Seraiah son of Azriel and Shelemiah son of Abdeel, to arrest me and my secretary Baruch. But the LORD had hidden us.

Jeremiah Writes Another Scroll

27 After King Jehoiakim had burnt the scroll that I had dictated to Baruch, the LORD told me 28 to take another scroll and write on it everything that had been on the first one. 29 The LORD told me to say to the king, "You have burnt the scroll, and you have asked Jeremiah why he wrote that the king of Babylonia would come and destroy this land and kill its people and its animals. 30 So now, I, the LORD, say to you, King Jehoiakim, that no descendant of yours will ever rule over David's kingdom. Your corpse will be thrown out where it will be exposed to the sun during the day and to the frost at night. 31 I will punish you, your descendants, and your officials because of the sins all of you commit. Neither you nor the people of Jerusalem and of Judah have paid any attention to my warnings, and so I will bring on all of you the disaster that I have threatened."

32 Then I took another scroll and gave it to my secretary Baruch, and he wrote down everything that I dictated. He wrote everything that had been on the first scroll and similar messages that I dictated to him.

Zedekiah's Request to Jeremiah

37 King Nebuchadnezzar of Babylonia made Zedekiah son of Josiah king of Judah in the place of Jehoiachin son of Jehoiakim. 2 But neither Zedekiah nor his officials nor the people obeyed the message which the LORD had given me.

3 King Zedekiah sent Jehucal son of Shelemiah and the priest Zephaniah son of Maaseiah to ask me to pray to the LORD our God on behalf of our nation. 4 I had not yet been put in prison and was still moving about freely among the people. 5 The Babylonian army had been besieging Jerusalem, but when they heard that the Egyptian army had crossed the Egyptian border, they retreated.

6 Then the LORD, the God of Israel, told me 7 to say to Zedekiah, "The Egyptian army is on its way to help you, but it will return home. 8 Then the Babylonians will come back, attack the city, capture it, and burn it down. 9 I, the LORD, warn you not to deceive yourselves into thinking that the Babylonians will not come back, because they will. 10 Even if you defeat the whole Babylonian army, so that only wounded men are left, lying in their tents, those men would still get up and burn this city to the ground."

37.1: 2 Kgs 24.17; 2 Chr 36.10

Jeremiah Is Arrested and Imprisoned

11 The Babylonian army retreated from Jerusalem because the Egyptian army was approaching. 12 So I started to leave Jerusalem and go to the territory of Benjamin to take possession of my share of the family property. 13 But when I reached the Benjamin Gate, the officer in charge of the soldiers on duty there, a man by the name of Irijah, the son of Shelemiah and grandson of Hananiah, stopped me and said, "You are deserting to the Babylonians!"

14 I answered, "That's not so! I'm not deserting." But Irijah would not listen to me. Instead, he arrested me and took me to the officials. 15 They were furious with me and ordered me to be beaten and locked up in the house of Jonathan, the court secretary, whose house had been made into a prison. 16 I was put in an underground cell and kept there a long time.

17 Later on King Zedekiah sent for me, and there in the palace he asked me privately, "Is there any message from the LORD?"

"There is," I answered, and added, "You will be handed over to the king of Babylonia." 18 Then I asked, "What crime have I committed against you or your officials or this people, to make you put me in prison? 19 What happened to your prophets who told you that the king of Babylonia would not attack you or the country? 20 And now, Your Majesty, I beg you to listen to me and do what I ask. Please do not send me back to the prison in Jonathan's house. If you do, I will surely die there."

21 So King Zedekiah ordered me to be locked up in the palace courtyard. I stayed there, and each day I was given a loaf of bread from the bakeries until all the bread in the city was gone.

Jeremiah in a Dry Well

38 Shephatiah son of Mattan, Gedaliah son of Pashhur, Jehucal son of Shelemiah, and Pashhur son of Malchiah heard that I was telling the people that 2 the LORD had said, "Whoever stays on in the city will die in war or of starvation or disease. But whoever goes out and surrenders to the Babylonians will not be killed; he will at least escape with his life." 3 I was also telling them that the LORD had said, "I am going to give the city to the Babylonian army, and they will capture it."

4 Then the officials went to the king and said, "This man must be put to death. By talking like this he is making the soldiers in the city lose their courage, and he is doing the same thing to everyone else left in the city. He is not trying to help the people; he only wants to hurt them."

5 King Zedekiah answered, "Very well, then, do what you wish with him; I can't stop you." 6 So they took me and let me down by ropes into Prince Malchiah's well, which was in the palace courtyard. There was no water in the well, only mud, and I sank down in it.

7 However, Ebedmelech the Sudanese, a eunuch who worked in the royal palace, heard that they had put me in the well. At that time the king was holding court at the Benjamin Gate. 8 So Ebedmelech went there and said to the king, 9 "Your Majesty, what these men have done is wrong. They have put Jeremiah in the well, where he is sure to die of starvation, since there is no more food in the city." 10 Then the king ordered Ebedmelech to take with him three men and to pull me out of the well before I died. 11 So Ebedmelech went with the men to the palace storeroom and got some worn-out clothing which he let down to me by ropes. 12 He told me to put the rags under my arms, so that the ropes wouldn't hurt me. I did this, 13 and they pulled me up out of the well. After that I was kept in the courtyard.

Zedekiah Asks Jeremiah's Advice

14 On another occasion King Zedekiah had me brought to him at the third entrance to the Temple, and he said, "I am going to ask you a question, and I want you to tell me the whole truth."

15 I answered, "If I tell you the truth, you will put me to death, and if I give you advice, you won't pay any attention."

16 So King Zedekiah promised me in secret, "I swear by the living God, the God who gave us life, that I will not put you to death or hand you over to the men who want to kill you."

17 Then I told Zedekiah that the LORD Almighty, the God of Israel, had said, "If you surrender to the king of Babylonia's officers, your life will be spared, and this city will not be burnt down. Both you and your family will be spared. 18 But if you do not surrender, then this city will be handed over to the Babylonians, who

And they pulled me up out of the well (38.13)

will burn it down, and you will not escape from them."

19 But the king answered, "I am afraid of our countrymen who have deserted to the Babylonians. I may be handed over to them and tortured."

20 I said, "You will not be handed over to them. I beg you to obey the LORD's message; then all will go well with you, and your life will be spared. 21 But the LORD has shown me in a vision what will happen if you refuse to surrender. 22 In it I saw all the women left in Judah's royal palace being led out to the king of Babylonia's officers. Listen to what they were saying as they went:

'The king's best friends misled him,
   they overruled him.
And now that his feet have sunk in the
   mud,
   his friends have left him.' "

23 Then I added, "All your women and children will be taken out to the Babylonians, and you yourself will not escape from them. You will be taken prisoner by the king of Babylonia, and this city will be burnt to the ground."

24 Zedekiah replied, "Don't let anyone know about this conversation, and your life will not be in danger. 25 If the officials hear that I have talked with you, they will come and ask you what we said. They will promise not to put you to death if you tell them everything. 26 Just tell them you were begging me not to send you back to prison to die there." 27 Then all the officials came and questioned me, and I told them exactly what the king had told me to say. There was nothing else they could do, because no one had overheard the conversation. 28 And I was kept in the palace courtyard until the day Jerusalem was captured.

The Fall of Jerusalem

39 In the tenth month of the ninth year that Zedekiah was king of Judah, King Nebuchadnezzar of Babylonia came with his whole army and attacked Jerusalem. 2 On the ninth day of the fourth month of Zedekiah's eleventh year as king, the city walls were broken through.

3 (When Jerusalem was captured,[z] all the high officials of the king of Babylonia came and took their places at the Middle Gate, including Nergal Sarezer, Samgar Nebo, Sarsechim, and another Nergal Sarezer.)[a]

4 When King Zedekiah and all his soldiers saw what was happening, they tried to escape from the city during the night. They left by way of the royal garden, went through the gateway connecting the two walls, and escaped in the direction of the Jordan Valley. 5 But the Babylonian army pursued them and captured Zedekiah in the plains near Jericho. Then they took him to King Nebuchadnezzar, who was in the city of Riblah in the territory of Hamath, and there Nebuchadnezzar passed sentence on him. 6 At Riblah he put Zedekiah's sons

---

[z] When Jerusalem was captured; *these words are moved here from the end of chapter 38.*
[a] *The names and titles of these men are unclear.*
38.28: Ezek 33.21

to death while Zedekiah was looking on, and he also executed the officials of Judah. ⁷After that, he had Zedekiah's eyes put out and had him placed in chains to be taken to Babylonia. ⁸Meanwhile, the Babylonians burnt down the royal palace and the houses of the people and tore down the walls of Jerusalem. ⁹Finally Nebuzaradan, the commanding officer, took away as prisoners to Babylonia the people who were left in the city, together with those who had deserted to him. ¹⁰He left in the land of Judah some of the poorest people, who owned no property, and he gave them vineyards and fields.

Jeremiah's Release

11 But King Nebuchadnezzar commanded Nebuzaradan, the commanding officer, to give the following order: ¹²"Go and find Jeremiah and take good care of him. Do not harm him, but do for him whatever he wants." ¹³So Nebuzaradan, together with the high officials Nebushazban and Nergal Sarezer and all the other officers of the king of Babylonia, ¹⁴brought me from the palace courtyard. They put me under the care of Gedaliah, the son of Ahikam and grandson of Shaphan, who was to see that I got home safely. And so I stayed there among the people.

Hope for Ebedmelech

15 While I was still imprisoned in the palace courtyard, the Lord told me ¹⁶to tell Ebedmelech the Sudanese that the Lord Almighty, the God of Israel, had said, "Just as I said I would, I am going to bring upon this city destruction and not prosperity. And when this happens, you will be there to see it. ¹⁷But I, the Lord, will protect you, and you will not be handed over to the men you are afraid of. ¹⁸I will keep you safe, and you will not be put to death. You will escape with your life because you have put your trust in me. I, the Lord, have spoken."

Jeremiah Stays with Gedaliah

40 The Lord spoke to me after Nebuzaradan, the commanding officer, had set me free at Ramah. I had been taken there in chains, along with all the other people from Jerusalem and Judah who were being taken away as prisoners to Babylonia.

2 The commanding officer took me

aside and said, "The Lord your God threatened this land with destruction, ³and now he has done what he said he would. All this happened because your people sinned against the Lord and disobeyed him. ⁴Now, I am taking the chains off your wrists and setting you free. If you want to go to Babylonia with me, you may do so, and I will take care of you. But if you don't want to go, you don't have to. You have the whole country to choose from, and you may go wherever you wish."

5 When I did not answer,ᶜ Nebuzaradan said, "Go back to Gedaliah, the son of Ahikam and grandson of Shaphan, whom the king of Babylonia has made governor of the towns of Judah. You may stay with him and live among the people, or you may go anywhere you think you should." Then he gave me a present and some food to take with me, and let me go on my way. ⁶I went to stay with Gedaliah in Mizpah and lived among the people who were left in the land.

Gedaliah, Governor of Judah
(2 Kgs 25.22–24)

7 Some of the Judaean officers and soldiers had not surrendered. They heard that the king of Babylonia had made Gedaliah governor of the land and had placed him in charge of all those who had not been taken away to Babylonia— the poorest people in the land. ⁸So Ishmael son of Nethaniah, Johanan son of Kareah, Seraiah son of Tanhumeth, the sons of Ephai from Netophah, and Jezaniah from Maacah went with their men to Gedaliah at Mizpah. ⁹Gedaliah said to them, "I give you my word that there is no need for you to be afraid to surrender to the Babylonians. Settle down in this land, serve the king of Babylonia, and all will go well with you. ¹⁰I myself will stay in Mizpah and be your representative when the Babylonians come here. But you can gather and store up wine, fruit, and olive-oil, and live in the villages you occupy." ¹¹Meanwhile, all the Israelites who were in Moab, Ammon, Edom, and other countries, heard that the king of Babylonia had allowed some Israelites to stay on in Judah and that he had made Gedaliah their governor. ¹²So they left the places where they had been scattered, and returned to Judah. They came to Gedaliah at Mizpah, and there they gathered in

---

ᶜWhen I did not answer; *or* Then, before he left.
40.7–9: 2 Kgs 25.22–24

large amounts of wine and fruit.

Gedaliah Is Murdered
(2 Kgs 25.25–26)

13 After this, Johanan and the leaders of the soldiers who had not surrendered came to Gedaliah at Mizpah ¹⁴ and said to him, "Don't you know that King Baalis of Ammon has sent Ishmael to murder you?" But Gedaliah did not believe it. ¹⁵ Then Johanan said privately to him, "Let me go and kill Ishmael, and no one will know who did it. Why should he be allowed to murder you? That would cause all the Jews who have gathered round you to be scattered, and it would bring disaster on all the people who are left in Judah."

16 But Gedaliah answered, "Don't do it! What you are saying about Ishmael is not true!"

41 In the seventh month of that year, Ishmael, the son of Nethaniah and grandson of Elishama, a member of the royal family and one of the king's chief officers, went to Mizpah with ten men to see Gedaliah. While they were all eating a meal together, ²Ishmael and the ten men with him pulled out their swords and killed Gedaliah. ³Ishmael also killed all the Israelites who were with Gedaliah at Mizpah and the Babylonian soldiers who happened to be there.

4 The next day, before anyone knew about Gedaliah's murder, ⁵eighty men arrived from Shechem, Shiloh, and Samaria. They had shaved off their beards, torn their clothes, and gashed themselves. They were taking corn and incense to offer in the Temple. ⁶So Ishmael went out from Mizpah to meet them, weeping as he went. When he came to them, he said, "Please come in to see Gedaliah." ⁷As soon as they were inside the city, Ishmael and his men killed them and threw their bodies in a well.

8 But there were ten men in the group who said to Ishmael, "Please don't kill us! We have wheat, barley, olive-oil, and honey hidden in the fields." So he spared them. ⁹The well into which Ishmael threw the bodies of the men he had killed was the large one ᵉ that King Asa had dug when he was being attacked by King Baasha of Israel. Ishmael filled the well with the bodies. ¹⁰Then he made prisoners of the king's daughters and all the rest of the people in Mizpah, whom Nebuzaradan the commanding officer had placed under the care of Gedaliah. Ishmael took them prisoner and started off in the direction of the territory of Ammon.

11 Johanan and all the army leaders with him heard of the crime that Ishmael had committed. ¹²So they went after him with their men and overtook him near the large pool at Gibeon. ¹³When Ishmael's prisoners saw Johanan and the leaders of the forces with him, they were glad, ¹⁴and turned and ran to them. ¹⁵But Ishmael and eight of his men got away from Johanan and escaped to the land of Ammon.

16 Then Johanan and the leaders of the forces with him took charge of the people whom Ishmael had taken away as prisoners from Mizpah after murdering Gedaliah—soldiers, women, children, and eunuchs. ¹⁷⁻¹⁸They were afraid of the Babylonians because Ishmael had murdered Gedaliah, whom the king of Babylonia had made governor of the land. So they set out for Egypt, in order to get away from the Babylonians. On the way, they stopped at Chimham, near Bethlehem.

The People Ask Jeremiah to Pray for Them

42 Then all the army leaders, including Johanan son of Kareah and Azariah ᶠ son of Heshaiah, came with people of every class ²and said to me, "Please do what we ask you! Pray to the LORD our God for us. Pray for all of us who have survived. Once there were many of us; but now only a few of us are left, as you can see. ³Pray that the LORD our God will show us the way we should go and what we should do."

4 I answered, "Very well, then. I will pray to the LORD our God, just as you have asked, and whatever he says, I will tell you. I will not keep back anything from you."

5 Then they said to me, "May the LORD be a true and faithful witness against us if we do not obey all the commands that the LORD our God gives you for us. ⁶Whether it pleases us or not, we will obey the LORD our God, to whom we are asking you to pray. All will go well with us if we obey him."

ᵉ One ancient translation was the large one; Hebrew by means of Gedaliah.
ᶠ One ancient translation (see also 43.2) Azariah; Hebrew Jezaniah.
41.1–3: 2 Kgs 25.25

They disobeyed the LORD's command and went into Egypt (43.7)

The LORD's Answer to Jeremiah's Prayer

7 Ten days later the LORD spoke to me; [8] so I called together Johanan, all the army leaders who were with him, and all the other people. [9] I said to them, "The LORD, the God of Israel, to whom you sent me with your request has said, [10] 'If you are willing to go on living in this land, then I will build you up and not tear you down; I will plant you and not pull you up. The destruction I brought on you has caused me great sorrow. [11] Stop being afraid of the king of Babylonia. I am with you, and I will rescue you from his power. [12] Because I am merciful, I will make him have mercy on you and let you go back home. I, the LORD, have spoken.'

[13-15] "But you people who are left in Judah must not disobey the LORD your God and refuse to live in this land. You must not say, 'No, we will go and live in Egypt, where we won't face war any more or hear the call to battle or go hungry.' If you say this, then the LORD Almighty, the God of Israel, says, 'If you are determined to go and live in Egypt, [16] then the war that you fear will overtake you, and the hunger you dread will follow you, and you will die there in Egypt. [17] All the people who are determined to go and live in Egypt will die either in war or of starvation or disease. Not one of them will survive, not one will escape the disaster that I am going to bring on them.'

18 "The LORD, the God of Israel, says, 'Just as my anger and fury were poured out on the people of Jerusalem, so my fury will be poured out on you if you go to Egypt. You will be a horrifying sight; people will treat you with scorn and use your name as a curse. You will never see this place again.' "

19 Then I continued, "The LORD has told you people who are left in Judah not to go to Egypt. And so I warn you now [20] that

you are making a fatal mistake. You asked me to pray to the LORD our God for you, and you promised that you would do everything that he commands. [21] And now I have told you, but you are disobeying everything that the LORD our God sent me to tell you. [22] So then, remember this: you will die in war or of starvation or disease in the land where you want to go and live."

Jeremiah Is Taken to Egypt

43 I finished telling the people everything that the LORD their God had sent me to tell them. [2] Then Azariah son of Hoshaiah and Johanan son of Kareah and all the other arrogant men said to me, "You are lying. The LORD our God did not send you to tell us not to go and live in Egypt. [3] Baruch son of Neriah has stirred you up against us, so that the Babylonians will gain power over us and can either kill us or take us away to Babylonia." [4] So neither Johanan nor any of the army officers nor any of the people would obey the LORD's command to remain in the land of Judah. [5] Then Johanan and all the army officers took everybody left in Judah away to Egypt, together with all the people who had returned from the nations where they had been scattered: [6] the men, the women, the children, and the king's daughters. They took everyone whom Nebuzaradan the commanding officer had left under the care of Gedaliah, including Baruch and me. [7] They disobeyed the LORD's command and went into Egypt as far as the city of Tahpanhes.

8 There the LORD said to me, [9] "Get some large stones and bury them in the mortar of the pavement[g] in front of the entrance to the government building here in the city, and let some of the Israelites see you do it. [10] Then tell them that I, the LORD Almighty, the God of Israel, am

---

[g] *Probable text* bury them...pavement; *Hebrew unclear.*
43.5-7: 2 Kgs 25.26

going to bring my servant King Nebuchadnezzar of Babylonia to this place, and he [h] will put his throne over these stones that you [i] buried, and will spread the royal tent over them. 11 Nebuchadnezzar will come and defeat Egypt. Those people who are doomed to die of disease will die of disease, those doomed to be taken away as prisoners will be taken away as prisoners, and those doomed to be killed in war will be killed in war. 12 I will set fire to the temples of Egypt's gods, and the king of Babylonia will either burn their gods or carry them off. As a shepherd picks his clothes clean of lice, so the king of Babylonia will pick the land of Egypt clean and then leave victorious. 13 He will destroy the sacred stone monuments at Heliopolis in Egypt and will burn down the temples of the Egyptian gods."

The Lord's Message to the Israelites in Egypt

44 The Lord spoke to me concerning all the Israelites living in Egypt, in the cities of Migdol, Tahpanhes, and Memphis, and in the southern part of the country. 2 The Lord Almighty, the God of Israel, said, "You yourselves have seen the destruction I brought on Jerusalem and all the other cities of Judah. Even now they are still in ruins, and no one lives in them 3 because their people had done evil and had made me angry. They offered sacrifices to other gods and served gods that neither they nor you nor your ancestors ever worshipped. 4 I kept sending you my servants the prophets, who told you not to do this terrible thing that I hate. 5 But you would not listen or pay any attention. You would not give up your evil practice of sacrificing to other gods. 6 So I poured out my anger and fury on the towns of Judah and on the streets of Jerusalem, and I set them on fire. They were left in ruins and became a horrifying sight, as they are today.

7 "And so I, the Lord Almighty, the God of Israel, now ask why you are doing such an evil thing to yourselves. Do you want to bring destruction on men and women, children and babies, so that none of your people will be left? 8 Why do you make me angry by worshipping idols and by sacrificing to other gods here in Egypt, where you have come to live? Are you doing this just to destroy yourselves, so that every nation on earth will treat you with scorn and use your name as a curse?

9 Have you forgotten all the wicked things that have been done in the towns of Judah and in the streets of Jerusalem by your ancestors, by the kings of Judah and their wives, and by you and your wives? 10 But to this day you have not humbled yourselves. You have not honoured me or lived according to all the laws that I gave you and your ancestors.

11 "So then, I, the Lord Almighty, the God of Israel, will turn against you and destroy all Judah. 12 As for the people of Judah who are left and are determined to go and live in Egypt, I will see to it that all of them are destroyed. All of them, great and small, will die in Egypt, either in war or of starvation. They will be a horrifying sight; people will treat them with scorn and use their name as a curse. 13 I will punish those who live in Egypt, just as I punished Jerusalem—with war, starvation, and disease. 14 None of the people of Judah who are left and have come to Egypt to live will escape or survive. Not one of them will return to Judah, where they long to live once again. No one will return except a few refugees."

15 Then all the men who knew that their wives offered sacrifices to other gods, and all the women who were standing there, including the Israelites who lived in southern Egypt—a large crowd in all— said to me, 16 "We refuse to listen to what you have told us in the name of the Lord. 17 We will do everything that we said we would. We will offer sacrifices to our goddess, the Queen of Heaven, and we will pour out wine-offerings to her, just as we and our ancestors, our king and our leaders, used to do in the towns of Judah and in the streets of Jerusalem. Then we had plenty of food, we were prosperous, and had no troubles. 18 But ever since we stopped sacrificing to the Queen of Heaven and stopped pouring out wine-offerings to her, we have had nothing, and our people have died in war and of starvation."

19 And the women added, "When we baked cakes shaped like the Queen of Heaven, offered sacrifices to her, and poured out wine-offerings to her, our husbands approved of what we were doing."

20 Then I said to all the men and the women who had answered me in this way, 21 "As for the sacrifices which you and your ancestors, your kings and your leaders, and the people of the land offered in the towns of Judah and in the streets

---

[h] *Some ancient translations* he; *Hebrew* I.   [i] *Some ancient translations* you; *Hebrew* I.

of Jerusalem—do you think that the LORD did not know about them or that he forgot them? ²²This very day your land lies in ruins and no one lives in it. It has become a horrifying sight, and people use its name as a curse because the LORD could no longer endure your wicked and evil practices. ²³This present disaster has come on you because you offered sacrifices to other gods and sinned against the LORD by not obeying all his commands."

24-25 I told all the people, especially the women, what the LORD Almighty, the God of Israel, was saying to the people of Judah living in Egypt: "Both you and your wives have made solemn promises to the Queen of Heaven. You promised that you would offer sacrifices to her and pour out wine-offerings to her, and you have kept your promises. Very well, then! Keep your promises! Carry out your vows! ²⁶But now listen to the vow that I, the LORD, have made in my mighty name to all you Israelites in Egypt: Never again will I let any of you use my name to make a vow by saying, 'I swear by the living Sovereign LORD!' ²⁷I will see to it that you will not prosper, but will be destroyed. All of you will die, either in war or of disease, until not one of you is left. ²⁸But a few of you will escape death and return from Egypt to Judah. Then the survivors will know whose words have come true, mine or theirs. ²⁹I, the LORD, will give you proof that I will punish you in this place and that my promise to bring destruction on you will come true. ³⁰I will hand over King Hophra of Egypt to his enemies who want to kill him, just as I handed over King Zedekiah of Judah to King Nebuchadnezzar of Babylonia, who was his enemy and wanted to kill him."

God's Promise to Baruch

45 In the fourth year that Jehoiakim son of Josiah was king of Judah, Baruch wrote down what I had dictated to him. Then I told him ²that the LORD, the God of Israel, had said, "Baruch, ³you are saying, 'I give up! The LORD has added sorrow to my troubles. I am worn out from groaning, and I can't find any rest!'

4 "But I, the LORD, am tearing down what I have built and pulling up what I have planted. I will do this to the entire earth. ⁵Are you looking for special treatment for yourself? Don't do it. I am bringing disaster on all mankind, but you will at least escape with your life, wherever you go. I, the LORD, have spoken."

Egypt's Defeat at Carchemish

46 The LORD spoke to me about the nations, ²beginning with Egypt. This is what he said about the army of King Neco of Egypt, which King Nebuchadnezzar of Babylonia defeated at Carchemish near the River Euphrates in the fourth year that Jehoiakim was king of Judah:
³ "The Egyptian officers shout,
   'Get your shields ready
   and march into battle!
⁴ Harness your horses and mount them!
   Fall in line and put on your helmets!
   Sharpen your spears!
   Put on your armour!'

⁵ "But what do I see?" asks the LORD.
   "They are turning back in terror.
   Their soldiers are beaten back;
   overcome with fear, they run as fast
      as they can
   and do not look back.
⁶ Those who run fast cannot get away;
   the soldiers cannot escape.
   In the north, by the Euphrates,
   they stumble and fall.
⁷ Who is this that rises like the Nile,
   like a river flooding its banks?
⁸ It is Egypt, rising like the Nile,
   like a river flooding its banks.
   Egypt said, 'I will rise and cover the
      world;
   I will destroy cities and the people
      who live there.
⁹ Command the horses to go
   and the chariots to roll!
   Send out the soldiers:
   men from Sudan and Libya, carrying
      shields,
   and skilled bowmen from Lydia.' "

¹⁰ This is the day of the Sovereign LORD
      Almighty:
   today he will take revenge;
   today he will punish his enemies.
   His sword will eat them until it is full,
   and drink their blood until it is
      satisfied.
   Today the Almighty sacrifices his
      victims

44.30: 2 Kgs 25.1-7   45.1: 2 Kgs 24.1; 2 Chr 36.5-7; Dan 1.1-2
46.2-26: Is 19.1-25; Ezek 29.1—32.32

Command the horses to go (46.9)

in the north, by the Euphrates.
11 People of Egypt, go to Gilead[j]
and look for medicine!
All your medicine has proved useless;
nothing can heal you.
12 Nations have heard of your shame;
everyone has heard you cry.
One soldier trips over another,
and both of them fall to the ground.

The Coming of Nebuchadnezzar

13 When King Nebuchadnezzar of Babylonia came to attack Egypt, the LORD spoke to me. He said,
14 "Proclaim it in the towns of Egypt,
in Migdol, Memphis, and Tahpanhes:
'Get ready to defend yourselves;
all you have will be destroyed in war!
15 Why has your mighty god Apis fallen?
The LORD has struck him down!'
16 Your soldiers have stumbled and
fallen;[k]
each one says to the other,
'Hurry! Let's go home to our people
and escape the enemy's sword!'

17 "Give the king of Egypt a new name—
'Noisy Braggart Who Missed His
Chance.'
18 I, the LORD Almighty, am king.
I am the living God.
As Mount Tabor towers above the
mountains
and Mount Carmel stands high above
the sea,
so will be the strength of the one who
attacks you.
19 Get ready to be taken prisoner,
you people of Egypt!
Memphis will be made a desert,
a ruin where no one lives.
20 Egypt is like a splendid cow,

attacked by a stinging fly from the
north.
21 Even her hired soldiers
are helpless as calves.
They did not stand and fight;
all of them turned and ran.
The day of their doom had arrived,
the time of their destruction.
22 Egypt runs away, hissing like a snake,
as the enemy's army approaches.
They attack her with axes,
like men cutting down trees
23 and destroying a thick forest.
Their men are too many to count;
their soldiers outnumber the locusts.
24 The people of Egypt are put to shame;
they are conquered by the people of
the north.
I, the LORD, have spoken."

25 The LORD Almighty, the God of Israel, says, "I am going to punish Amon, the god of Thebes, together with Egypt and its gods and kings. I am going to take the king of Egypt and all who put their trust in him, 26 and hand them over to those who want to kill them, to King Nebuchadnezzar of Babylonia and his army. But later on, people will live in Egypt again, as they did in times past. I, the LORD, have spoken."

The LORD Will Save His People

27 "My people, do not be afraid,
people of Israel, do not be terrified.
I will rescue you from that distant land,
from the land where you are prisoners.
You will come back home and live in
peace;
you will be secure, and no one will
make you afraid.
28 I will come to you and save you.

---

[j] GILEAD: *See 8.22.* [k] *Probable text* Your soldiers...fallen; *Hebrew unclear.*
46.13: Jer 43.10-13 **46.27-28:** Jer 30.10-11

I will destroy all the nations
   where I have scattered you,
but I will not destroy you.
I will not let you go unpunished;
   but when I punish you, I will be fair.
I, the LORD, have spoken."

The LORD's Message about Philistia

47 Before the king of Egypt attacked Gaza, the LORD spoke to me about Philistia. [2] He said:
   "Look! Waters are rising in the north
      and will rush like a river in flood.
They will cover the land and everything
      on it,
   cities and the people who live there.
People will call out for help;
   everyone on earth will cry bitterly.
[3] They will hear the hoof beats of horses,
   the clatter of chariots,
   the rumble of wheels.
Fathers will not turn back for their
   children;
   their hands will hang limp at their
   sides.
[4] The time has come to destroy Philistia,
   to cut off from Tyre and Sidon
   all the help that remains.
I, the LORD, will destroy the Philistines,
   all who came from the shores of Crete.
[5] Great sorrow has come to the people
   of Gaza,
   and Ashkelon's people are silent.
How long will the rest of Philistia
   mourn?
[6] You cry out, 'Sword of the LORD!
   How long will you go on slashing?
Go back to your scabbard,
   stay there and rest!'
[7] But how can it rest,
   when I have given it work to do?
I have commanded it to attack Ashkelon
   and the people who live on the coast."

The Destruction of Moab

48 This is what the LORD Almighty said about Moab:
"Pity the people of Nebo—
   their town is destroyed!
Kiriathaim is captured,
   its mighty fortress torn down,
   and its people put to shame;
[2]   the splendour of Moab is gone.
The enemy have captured Heshbon
   and plot to destroy the nation of Moab.
The town of Madmen will be silenced;
   armies will march against it.
[3] The people of Horonaim cry out,

   'Violence! Destruction!'
[4] "Moab has been destroyed;
   listen to the children crying.
[5] Hear the sound of their sobs
   along the road up to Luhith,
   the cries of distress
   on the way down to Horonaim.
[6] 'Quick, run for your lives!' they say.
   'Run like a wild desert donkey!'

[7] "Moab, you trusted in your strength and
   your wealth,
   but now even you will be conquered;
your god Chemosh will go into exile,
   along with his princes and priests.
[8] Not a town will escape the destruction;
   both valley and plain will be ruined.
I, the LORD, have spoken.
[9] Set up a tombstone for Moab;
   it will soon be destroyed.
Its towns will be left in ruins,
   and no one will live there again."
10 (Curse the man who does not do the LORD's work with all his heart! Curse the man who does not slash and kill!)

The Cities of Moab Are Destroyed

11 The LORD said, "Moab has always lived secure and has never been taken into exile. Moab is like wine left to settle undisturbed and never poured from jar to jar. Its flavour has never been ruined, and it tastes as good as ever.

12 "So now, the time is coming when I will send people to pour Moab out like wine. They will empty its wine-jars and break them in pieces. [13] Then the Moabites will be disillusioned with their god Chemosh, just as the Israelites were disillusioned with Bethel, a god in whom they trusted.

14 "Men of Moab, why do you claim to
   be heroes,
   brave soldiers tested in war?
15 Moab and its cities are destroyed;
   its finest young men have been
   slaughtered.
I am the king, the LORD Almighty,
   and I have spoken.
16 Moab's doom approaches;
   its ruin is coming soon.

17 "Mourn for that nation, you that live
   near by,
   all of you that know its fame.
Say, 'Its powerful rule has been broken;
   its glory and might are no more.'

47.1–7: Is 14.29–31; Ezek 25.15–17; Joel 3.4–8; Amos 1.6–8; Zeph 2.4–7; Zech 9.5–7
48.1–47: Is 15.1—16.14, 25.10–12; Ezek 25.8–11; Amos 2.1–3; Zeph 2.8–11

18 You that live in Dibon,
come down from your place of honour
and sit on the ground in the dust;
Moab's destroyer is here
and has left its forts in ruins.
19 You that live in Aroer,
stand by the road and wait;
ask those who are running away,
find out from them what has
happened.
20 'Moab has fallen,' they will answer,
'weep for it; it is disgraced.
Announce along the River Arnon
that Moab is destroyed!'

21 "Judgement has come on the cities of the plateau: on Holon, Jahzah, Mephath, 22 Dibon, Nebo, Beth Diblathaim, 23 Kiriathaim, Bethgamul, Bethmeon, 24 Kerioth, and Bozrah. Judgement has come on all the cities of Moab, far and near. 25 Moab's might has been crushed; its power has been destroyed. I, the LORD, have spoken."

Moab Will Be Humbled

26 The LORD said, "Make Moab drunk, because it has rebelled against me. Moab will roll in its own vomit, and people will laugh. 27 Moab, remember how you jeered at the people of Israel? You treated them as though they had been caught with a gang of robbers.

28 "You people who live in Moab, leave your towns! Go and live on the cliffs! Be like the dove that makes its nest in the sides of a ravine. 29 Moab is very proud! I have heard how proud, arrogant, and conceited the people are, how much they think of themselves. 30 I, the LORD, know of their arrogance. Their boasts amount to nothing, and the things they do will not last. 31 And so I will weep for everyone in Moab and for the people of Kir Heres. 32 I will cry for the people of Sibmah, even more than for the people of Jazer. City of Sibmah, you are like a vine whose branches reach across the Dead Sea and go as far as Jazer. But now your summer fruits and your grapes have been destroyed. 33 Happiness and joy have been taken away from the fertile land of Moab. I have made the wine stop flowing from the winepresses; there is no one to make the wine and shout for joy.

34 "The people of Heshbon and Elealeh cry out,[l] and their cry can be heard as far as Jahaz; it can be heard by the people in Zoar, and it is heard as far as Horonaim and Eglath Shelishiyah. Even the brook of Nimrim has dried up. 35 I will stop the people of Moab from making burnt-offerings at their places of worship and from offering sacrifices to their gods. I, the LORD, have spoken.

36 "So my heart mourns for Moab and for the people of Kir Heres, like someone playing a funeral song on a flute, because everything they owned is gone. 37 All of them have shaved their heads and cut off their beards. They have all made gashes on their hands, and everyone is wearing sackcloth. 38 On all the house-tops of Moab and in all its public squares there is nothing but mourning, because I have broken Moab like a jar that no one wants. 39 Moab has been shattered! Cry out! Moab has been disgraced. It is in ruins, and all the surrounding nations jeer at it. I, the LORD, have spoken."

No Escape for Moab

40 The LORD has promised that a nation will swoop down on Moab like an eagle with its outspread wings, 41 and the towns and fortresses will be captured. On that day Moab's soldiers will be as frightened as a woman in labour. 42 Moab will be destroyed and will no longer be a nation, because it rebelled against me. 43 Terror, pits, and traps are waiting for the people of Moab. The LORD has spoken. 44 Whoever tries to escape the terror will fall into the pits, and whoever climbs out of the pits will be caught in the traps, because the LORD has set the time for Moab's destruction. 45 Helpless refugees try to find protection in Heshbon, the city that King Sihon once ruled, but it is in flames.[m] Fire has burnt up the frontiers and the mountain heights of the war-loving people of Moab. 46 Pity the people of Moab! The people who worshipped Chemosh have been destroyed, and their sons and daughters have been taken away as prisoners.

47 But in days to come the LORD will make Moab prosperous again. All of this is what the LORD has said will happen to Moab.

l Probable text Heshbon...cry out; Hebrew unclear.
m Heshbon, the city...flames; or the city of Heshbon, but it is in flames and the palace of King Sihon is burning.

Hide! (49.8)

The LORD's Judgement on Ammon

49 This is what the LORD said about Ammon: "Where are the men of Israel? Is there no one to defend their land? Why have they let the people who worship Molech take the territory of the tribe of Gad and settle there? [2] But the time is coming when I will make the people of the capital city of Rabbah hear the noise of battle, and it will be left in ruins and its villages burnt to the ground. Then Israel will take its land back from those who took it from them. [3] People of Heshbon, cry out! Ai is destroyed! Women of Rabbah, go into mourning! Put on sackcloth and mourn. Run about in confusion. Your god Molech will be taken into exile, together with his priests and princes. [4] Why do you unfaithful people boast? Your strength is failing. Why do you trust in your power and say that no one would dare attack you? [5] I will bring terror on you from every side. You will all run away. Each one will run for his life, and there will be no one to bring your troops together again.

[6] "But later on I will make Ammon prosperous again. I, the LORD, have spoken."

The LORD's Judgement on Edom

[7] This is what the LORD Almighty said about Edom: "Have the people of Edom lost their good judgement? Can their advisers no longer tell them what to do? Has all their wisdom disappeared? [8] People of Dedan, turn and run! Hide! I am going to destroy Esau's descendants, because the time has come for me to punish them. [9] When men pick grapes, they leave a few on the vines, and when robbers come at night, they take only what they want. [10] But I[o] have stripped Esau's descendants completely and uncovered their hiding places, so that they can no longer hide. All the people of Edom are destroyed. Not one of them is left. [11] Leave your orphans with me, and I will take care of them. Your widows can depend on me.

[12] "If even those who did not deserve to be punished had to drink from the cup of punishment, do you think that you will go unpunished? No, you must drink from the cup! [13] I myself have sworn that the city of Bozrah will become a horrifying sight and a desert; people will jeer at it and use its name as a curse. All the near-by villages will be in ruins for ever. I, the LORD, have spoken."

[14] I said, "Edom, I have received a message from the LORD. He has sent a messenger to tell the nations to assemble their armies and to get ready to attack you. [15] The LORD is going to make you weak, and no one will respect you. [16] Your pride has deceived you. No one fears you

---

[o] they leave a few...they take only what they want.[10] But I; *or* they leave nothing...they take everything.[10] And so I.

49.1–6: Ezek 21.28–32, 25.1–7; Amos 1.13–15; Zeph 2.8–11
49.7–22: Is 34.5–17, 63.1–6; Ezek 25.12–14, 35.1–15; Amos 1.11–12; Obad 1–14; Mal 1.2–5

as much as you think they do. You live on the rocky cliffs, high on top of the mountain; but even though you live as high up as an eagle, the LORD will bring you down. The LORD has spoken."

17 The LORD said, "The destruction that will come on Edom will be so terrible that everyone who passes by will be shocked and terrified. 18 The same thing will happen to Edom as happened to Sodom and Gomorrah, when they and the near-by towns were destroyed. No one will ever live there again. I, the LORD, have spoken. 19 Like a lion coming out of the thick woods along the Jordan up to the green pasture land, I will come and make the Edomites run away suddenly from their country. Then the leader I choose will rule the nation. Who can be compared to me? Who would dare challenge me? What ruler could oppose me? 20 So listen to the plan that I have made against the people of Edom, and to what I intend to do to the people of the city of Teman. Even their children will be dragged off, and everyone will be horrified. 21 When Edom falls, there will be such a noise that the entire earth will shake, and the cries of alarm will be heard as far away as the Gulf of Aqaba. 22 The enemy will attack Bozrah like an eagle swooping down with outspread wings. On that day Edom's soldiers will be as frightened as a woman in labour."

The LORD's Judgement on Damascus

23 This is what the LORD said about Damascus: "The people in the cities of Hamath and Arpad are worried and troubled because they have heard bad news. Anxiety rolls over them like a sea, and they cannot rest. 24 The people of Damascus are weak and have fled in terror. They are in pain and misery like a woman in labour. 25 The famous city that used to be happy[p] is completely deserted. 26 On that day her young men will be killed in the city streets, and all her soldiers destroyed. 27 I will set the walls of Damascus on fire and will burn down King Benhadad's palaces. I, the LORD Almighty, have spoken."

Judgement on the Tribe of Kedar and the City of Hazor

28 This is what the LORD said about the tribe of Kedar and the districts controlled by Hazor, which were conquered by King Nebuchadnezzar of Babylonia: "Attack the people of Kedar and destroy that tribe of eastern people! 29 Seize their tents and their flocks, their tent curtains and everything in their tents. Take their camels and tell the people, 'Terror is all round you!'

30 "People of Hazor, I, the LORD, warn you to run far away and hide. King Nebuchadnezzar of Babylonia has plotted against you, and this is what he says, 31 'Come on! We'll attack those people that feel safe and secure! Their city has no gates or locks and is completely unprotected.'

32 "Take their camels and all their livestock! I will scatter in every direction those people who cut their hair short, and I will bring disaster on them from every side. 33 Hazor will be made a desert for ever, a place where only jackals live. No one will ever live there again. I, the LORD, have spoken."

The LORD's Judgement on Elam

34 Soon after Zedekiah became king of Judah, the LORD Almighty spoke to me about the country of Elam. 35 He said, "I will kill all the bowmen who have made Elam so powerful. 36 I will make winds blow against Elam from all directions, and I will scatter her people everywhere, until there is no country where her refugees have not gone. 37 I will make the people of Elam afraid of their enemies, who want to kill them. In my great anger I will destroy the people of Elam and send armies against them until I have wiped them out. 38 I will destroy their kings and leaders, and set up my throne there. 39 But later on I will make the people of Elam prosperous again. I, the LORD, have spoken."

Babylon's Capture

50 This is the message that the LORD gave me about the city of Babylon and its people:

2 "Tell the news to the nations! Proclaim it!
Give the signal and announce the news!
Do not keep it a secret!
Babylon has fallen!
Her god Marduk has been shattered!
Babylon's idols are put to shame,
her disgusting images are crushed!

---

p *Some ancient translations* happy; *Hebrew* my happiness.
49.18: Gen 19.24–25　　**49.23–27:** Is 17.1–3; Amos 1.3–5; Zech 9.1
50.1–51.64: Is 13.1—14.23, 47.1–15

Like sheep...scattered by lions (50.17)

3 "A nation from the north has come to attack Babylonia and will make it a desert. Men and animals will run away, and no one will live there."

Israel's Return

4 The LORD says, "When that time comes, the people of both Israel and Judah will come weeping, looking for me, their God. 5 They will ask the way to Zion and then go in that direction. They will make an eternal covenant with me and never break it.

6 "My people are like sheep whose shepherds have let them get lost in the mountains. They have wandered like sheep from one mountain to another, and they have forgotten where their home is. 7 They are attacked by all who find them. Their enemies say, 'They sinned against the LORD, and so what we have done is not wrong. Their ancestors trusted in the LORD, and they themselves should have remained faithful to him.'

8 "People of Israel, run away from Babylonia! Leave the country! Be the first to leave! 9 I am going to stir up a group of strong nations in the north and make them attack Babylonia. They will line up in battle against the country and conquer it. They are skilful hunters, shooting arrows that never miss the mark. 10 Babylonia will be looted, and those who loot it will take everything they want. I, the LORD, have spoken."

Babylon's Fall

11 The LORD says, "People of Babylonia, you plundered my nation. You are happy and glad, going about like a cow threshing corn or like a neighing horse, 12 but your own great city will be humiliated and disgraced. Babylonia will be the least important nation of all; it will become a dry and waterless desert. 13 Because of my anger no one will live in Babylon; it will be left in ruins, and all who pass by will be shocked and amazed.

14 "Bowmen, line up for battle against Babylon and surround it. Shoot all your arrows at Babylon, because it has sinned against me, the LORD. 15 Raise the war cry all round the city! Now Babylon has surrendered. Its walls have been broken through and torn down.q I am taking my revenge on the Babylonians. So take your revenge on them, and treat them as they have treated others. 16 Do not let seeds be sown in that country or let a harvest be gathered. Every foreigner living there will be afraid of the attacking army and will go back home."

Israel's Return

17 The LORD says, "The people of Israel are like sheep, chased and scattered by lions. First, they were attacked by the emperor of Assyria, and then King Nebuchadnezzar of Babylonia gnawed their bones. 18 Because of this, I, the LORD Almighty, the God of Israel, will punish

q *Hebrew has an additional word, the meaning of which is unclear.*
50.8: Rev 18.4

King Nebuchadnezzar and his country, just as I punished the emperor of Assyria. 19 I will restore the people of Israel to their land. They will eat the food that grows on Mount Carmel and in the region of Bashan, and they will eat all they want of the crops that grow in the territories of Ephraim and Gilead. 20 When that time comes, no sin will be found in Israel and no wickedness in Judah, because I will forgive those people whose lives I have spared. I, the LORD, have spoken."

God's Judgement on Babylonia

21 The LORD says, "Attack the people of Merathaim and of Pekod. Kill and destroy them.*r* Do everything I command you. I, the LORD, have spoken. 22 The noise of battle is heard in the land, and there is great destruction. 23 Babylonia hammered the whole world to pieces, and now that hammer is shattered! All the nations are shocked at what has happened to that country. 24 Babylonia, you fought against me, and you have been caught in the trap I set for you, even though you did not know it. 25 I have opened the place where my weapons are stored, and in my anger I have taken them out, because I, the Sovereign LORD Almighty, have work to do in Babylonia. 26 Attack it from every side and break open the places where its grain is stored! Pile up the loot like piles of grain! Destroy the country! Leave nothing at all! 27 Kill all their soldiers! Slaughter them! The people of Babylonia are doomed! The time has come for them to be punished!"

28 (Refugees escape from Babylonia and come to Jerusalem, and they tell how the LORD our God took revenge for what the Babylonians had done to his Temple.)

29 "Tell the bowmen to attack Babylon. Send out everyone who knows how to use the bow and arrow. Surround the city and don't let anyone escape. Pay it back for all it has done, and treat it as it has treated others, because it acted with pride against me, the Holy One of Israel. 30 So its young men will be killed in the city streets, and all its soldiers will be destroyed on that day. I, the LORD, have spoken.

31 "Babylonia, you are filled with pride, so I, the Sovereign LORD Almighty, am against you. The time has come for me to punish you. 32 Your proud nation will stumble and fall, and no one will help you up. I will set your cities on fire, and everything around will be destroyed."

33 The LORD Almighty says, "The people of Israel and of Judah are oppressed. All who captured them are guarding them closely and will not let them go. 34 But the one who will rescue them is strong—his name is the LORD Almighty. He himself will take up their cause and will bring peace to the earth, but trouble to the people of Babylonia."

35 The LORD says,
"Death to Babylonia!
    Death to its people,
    to its rulers, to its men of wisdom.
36 Death to its lying prophets—
    what fools they are!
Death to its soldiers—
    how terrified they are!
37 Destroy its horses and chariots!
    Death to its hired soldiers—
    how weak they are!
Destroy its treasures;
    plunder and loot.
38 Bring a drought on its land
    and dry up its rivers.
Babylonia is a land of terrifying idols,
    that have made fools of the people.
39 "And so Babylon will be haunted by demons and evil spirits,*t* and by unclean birds. Never again will people live there, not for all time to come. 40 The same thing will happen to Babylon as happened to Sodom and Gomorrah, when I destroyed them and the near-by towns. No one will ever live there again. I, the LORD, have spoken.
41 "People are coming from a country
    in the north,
    a mighty nation far away;
    many kings are preparing for war.
42 They have taken their bows and
    swords;
    they are cruel and merciless.
They sound like the roaring sea,
    as they ride their horses.
They are ready for battle against
    Babylonia.
43 The king of Babylonia hears the news,
    and his hands hang limp.
    He is seized by anguish,
    by pain like a woman in labour.

44 "Like a lion coming out of the thick woods, along the Jordan up to the green pasture land, I, the LORD, will come and

---

r One ancient translation them; *Hebrew* after them.
t demons and evil spirits; *or* wildcats and jackals.
50.29: Rev 18.6   **50.39:** Rev 18.2   **50.40:** Gen 19.24–25

make the Babylonians run away suddenly from their city. Then the leader I choose will rule the nation. Who can be compared to me? Who would dare challenge me? What ruler could oppose me? ⁴⁵So listen to the plan that I have made against the city of Babylon and to what I intend to do to its people. Even their children will be dragged off, and everyone will be horrified. ⁴⁶When Babylon falls, there will be such a noise that the entire earth will shake, and the cries of alarm will be heard by the other nations."

Further Judgement on Babylonia

51 The LORD says, "I am bringing a destructive wind u against Babylonia and its people. ²I will send foreigners to destroy Babylonia like a wind that blows straw away. When that day of destruction comes, they will attack from every side and leave the land bare. ³Don't give its soldiers time to shoot their arrows or to put on their armour. Do not spare the young men! Destroy the whole army! ⁴They will be wounded and die in the streets of their cities. ⁵I, the LORD God Almighty, have not abandoned Israel and Judah, even though they have sinned against me, the Holy One of Israel. ⁶Run

Run for your lives! (51.6)

away from Babylonia! Run for your lives! Do not be killed because of Babylonia's sin. I am now taking my revenge and punishing it as it deserves. ⁷Babylonia was like a gold cup in my hand, making the whole world drunk. The nations drank its wine and went out of their minds. ⁸Babylonia has suddenly fallen and is destroyed! Mourn over it! Get medicine for its wounds, and perhaps it can be healed. ⁹Foreigners living there said, 'We tried to help Babylonia, but it was too late. Let's leave her now and go back home. God has punished Babylonia with

all his might and has destroyed it completely.' "

10 The LORD says, "My people shout, 'The LORD has shown that we are in the right. Let's go and tell the people in Jerusalem what the LORD our God has done.' "

11 The LORD has stirred up the kings of Media, because he intends to destroy Babylonia. That is how he will take revenge for the destruction of his Temple.

The attacking officers command, "Sharpen your arrows! Get your shields ready! ¹²Give the signal to attack Babylon's walls. Strengthen the guard! Post the sentries! Place men in ambush!"

The LORD has done what he said he would do to the people of Babylonia. ¹³That country has many rivers and rich treasures, but its time is up, and its thread of life is cut. ¹⁴The LORD Almighty has sworn by his own life that he will bring many men to attack Babylonia like a swarm of locusts, and they will shout with victory.

A Hymn of Praise to God

¹⁵ The LORD made the earth by his power;
  by his wisdom he created the world
  and stretched out the heavens.
¹⁶ At his command the waters above the
    sky v roar;
  he brings clouds from the ends of the
    earth.
  He makes lightning flash in the rain
  and sends the wind from his
    storeroom.
¹⁷ At the sight of this, men feel stupid
    and senseless;
  those who make idols are disillusioned
  because the gods they make are false
    and lifeless.
¹⁸ They are worthless and should be
    despised;
  they will be destroyed when the LORD
    comes to deal with them.
¹⁹ The God of Jacob is not like them;
  he is the one who made everything,
  and he has chosen Israel to be his
    very own people.
  The LORD Almighty is his name.

The LORD's Hammer

20 The LORD says,
"Babylonia, you are my hammer, my
    weapon of war.
I used you to crush nations and
    kingdoms,

---

u destructive wind; *or* destroying spirit.   v WATERS ABOVE THE SKY: *See Gen 1.6–8.*
51.7: Rev 17.2–4, 18.3   **51.9:** Rev 18.5   **51.13:** Rev 17.1

Give the signal to attack Babylon's walls (51.12)

21 to shatter horses and riders,
 to shatter chariots and their drivers,
22 to kill men and women,
 to slay old and young,
 to kill boys and girls,
23 to slaughter shepherds and their
   flocks,
 to slaughter ploughmen and their
   horses,
 to crush rulers and high officials."

Babylonia's Punishment

24 The LORD says, "You will see me repay Babylonia and its people for all the evil they did to Jerusalem. 25 Babylonia, you are like a mountain that destroys the whole world, but I, the LORD, am your enemy. I will take hold of you, level you to the ground, and leave you in ashes. 26 None of the stones from your ruins will ever be used again for building. You will be like a desert for ever. I, the LORD, have spoken.

27 "Give the signal to attack! Blow the trumpet so that the nations can hear! Prepare the nations for war against Babylonia! Tell the kingdoms of Ararat, Minni, and Ashkenaz to attack. Appoint an officer to lead the attack. Bring up the horses like a swarm of locusts. 28 Prepare the nations for war against Babylonia. Send for the kings of Media, their leaders and officials, and the armies of all the countries they control. 29 The earth trembles and shakes because the LORD is carrying out his plan to make Babylonia a desert, where no one lives. 30 The Babylonian soldiers have stopped fighting and remain in their forts. They have lost their courage and have become like women. The city gates are broken down, and the houses are on fire. 31 Messenger after messenger runs to tell the king of Babylonia that his city has been broken into from every side. 32 The enemy have captured the river-crossing and have set the fortresses on fire. The Babylonian soldiers have panicked. 33 Soon the enemy will cut them down and trample them like corn on a threshing-place. I, the LORD Almighty, the God of Israel, have spoken."

34 The king of Babylonia cut Jerusalem
   up
   and ate it.
He emptied the city like a jar;
 like a monster he swallowed it.
He took what he wanted
 and threw the rest away.
35 Let the people of Zion say,
 "May Babylonia be held responsible
 for the violence done to us!"
Let the people of Jerusalem say,
 "May Babylonia be held responsible
 for what we have suffered!"

The LORD Will Help Israel

36 And so the LORD said to the people of Jerusalem, "I will take up your cause and will make your enemies pay for what they did to you. I will dry up the source of Babylonia's water and make its rivers go dry. 37 That country will become a pile of ruins where wild animals live. It will be a horrible sight; no one will live there, and all who see it will be terrified. 38 The

That country will become a pile of ruins where wild animals live (51.37)

Babylonians all roar like lions and growl like lion cubs. ³⁹Are they greedy? I will prepare them a feast and make them drunk and happy. They will go to sleep and never wake up. ⁴⁰I will take them to be slaughtered, like lambs, goats, and rams. I, the LORD, have spoken."

Babylon's Fate

41 The LORD says about Babylon: "The city that the whole world praised has been captured! What a horrifying sight Babylon has become to the nations! ⁴²The sea has rolled over Babylon and covered it with roaring waves. ⁴³The towns have become a horrifying sight and are like a waterless desert, where no one lives or even travels. ⁴⁴I will punish Bel, the god of Babylonia, and make him give up his stolen goods; the nations will not worship him any more.

"Babylon's walls have fallen. ⁴⁵People of Israel, run away from there! Run for your life from my fierce anger. ⁴⁶Do not lose courage or be afraid because of the rumours you hear. Every year a different rumour spreads—rumours of violence in the land and of one king fighting another. ⁴⁷And so the time is coming when I will deal with Babylonia's idols. The whole country will be put to shame, and all its people will be killed. ⁴⁸Everything on earth and in the sky will shout for joy when Babylonia falls to the people who come from the north to destroy it. ⁴⁹Babylonia caused the death of people all over the world, and now Babylonia will fall because it caused the death of

so many Israelites. I, the LORD, have spoken."

God's Message to the Israelites in Babylonia

50 The LORD says to his people in Babylonia: "You have escaped death! Now go! Don't wait! Though you are far from home, think about me, your LORD, and remember Jerusalem. ⁵¹You say, 'We've been disgraced and made ashamed; we feel completely helpless because foreigners have taken over the holy places in the Temple.' ⁵²So then, I say that the time is coming when I will deal with Babylon's idols, and the wounded will groan throughout the country. ⁵³Even if Babylon could climb to the sky and build a strong fortress there, I would still send people to destroy it. I, the LORD, have spoken."

Further Destruction of Babylon

54 The LORD says,
"Listen to the sound of crying in Babylon,
  of mourning for the destruction in the land.
⁵⁵I am destroying Babylon
  and putting it to silence.
The armies rush in like roaring waves
  and attack with noisy shouts.
⁵⁶They have come to destroy Babylon;
  its soldiers are captured,
  and their bows are broken.
I am a God who punishes evil,
  and I will treat Babylon as it deserves.
⁵⁷I will make its rulers drunk—
  men of wisdom, leaders, and soldiers.

51.48: Rev 18.20   51.49: Rev 18.24

They will go to sleep and never wake
    up.
  I, the king, have spoken,
  I am the LORD Almighty.
58 The walls of mighty Babylon will be
    thrown to the ground,
  and its towering gates burnt down.
  The work of the nations is all for
    nothing;
  their efforts go up in flames.
  I, the LORD Almighty, have spoken."

Jeremiah's Message Is Sent to Babylonia

59 King Zedekiah's personal attendant
was Seraiah, the son of Neriah and
grandson of Mahseiah. In the fourth year
that Zedekiah was king of Judah, Seraiah
was going to Babylonia with him, and I
gave him some instructions. 60 I wrote in
a book an account of all the destruction
that would come on Babylonia, as well
as all these other things about Babylonia.
61 I told Seraiah, "When you get to
Babylon, be sure to read aloud to the
people everything that is written here.
62 Then pray, 'LORD, you have said that
you would destroy this place, so that there
would be no living creature in it, neither
man nor animal, and it would be like a
desert for ever.' 63 Seraiah, when you
finish reading this book to the people, then
tie it to a stone and throw it into the River
Euphrates, 64 and say, 'This is what will
happen to Babylonia—it will sink and
never rise again, because of the destruction that the LORD is going to bring on
it.' " *w*

The words of Jeremiah end here.

The Fall of Jerusalem
(2 Kgs 24.18—25.7)

52 Zedekiah was twenty-one years
old when he became king of Judah,
and he ruled in Jerusalem for eleven years.
His mother's name was Hamutal, the
daughter of the Jeremiah who lived in
the city of Libnah. 2 King Zedekiah sinned
against the LORD, just as King Jehoiakim
had done. 3 The LORD became so angry
with the people of Jerusalem and Judah
that he banished them from his sight.

Zedekiah rebelled against King Nebuchadnezzar of Babylonia, 4 and so
Nebuchadnezzar came with all his army
and attacked Jerusalem on the tenth day
of the tenth month of the ninth year of
Zedekiah's reign. They set up camp
outside the city, built siege walls round

It will sink and never rise again (51.64)

it, 5 and kept it under siege until
Zedekiah's eleventh year. 6 On the ninth
day of the fourth month of that same year,
when the famine was so bad that the
people had nothing left to eat, 7 the city
walls were broken through. Although the
Babylonians were surrounding the city,
all the soldiers escaped during the night.
They left by way of the royal garden, went
through the gateway connecting the two
walls, and fled in the direction of the
Jordan Valley. 8 But the Babylonian army
pursued King Zedekiah, captured him in
the plains near Jericho, and all his soldiers
deserted him. 9 Zedekiah was taken to
King Nebuchadnezzar, who was in the
city of Riblah in the territory of Hamath,
and there Nebuchadnezzar passed sentence on him. 10 At Riblah he put
Zedekiah's sons to death while Zedekiah
was looking on and he also had the
officials of Judah executed. 11 After that,
he had Zedekiah's eyes put out and had
him placed in chains and taken to
Babylon. Zedekiah remained in prison in
Babylon until the day he died.

w One ancient translation on it; *Hebrew* on it and they will become tired out.
51.63–64: Rev 18.21   **52.4:** Ezek 24.2   **52.7:** Ezek 33.21   **52.11:** Ezek 12.13

So the people of Judah were carried away (52.27)

The Destruction of the Temple
(2 Kgs 25.8–17)

12 On the tenth day of the fifth month of the nineteenth year of King Nebuchadnezzar of Babylonia, Nebuzaradan, adviser to the king and commander of his army, entered Jerusalem. 13 He burnt down the Temple, the palace, and the houses of all the important people in Jerusalem; 14 and his soldiers tore down the city walls. 15 Then Nebuzaradan took away to Babylonia* the people who were left in the city, the remaining skilled workmen, and those who had deserted to the Babylonians. 16 But he left in Judah some of the poorest people, who owned no property, and he put them to work in the vineyards and fields.

17 The Babylonians broke in pieces the bronze columns and the carts that were in the Temple, together with the large bronze tank, and they took all the bronze to Babylon. 18 They also took away the shovels and the ash containers used in cleaning the altar, the tools used in tending the lamps, the bowls used for catching the blood from the sacrifices, the bowls used for burning incense, and all the other bronze articles used in the temple service. 19 They took away everything that was made of gold or silver: the small bowls, the pans used for carrying live coals, the bowls for holding the blood from the sacrifices, the ash containers, the lampstands, the bowls used for incense, and the bowls used for pouring out offerings of wine. 20 The bronze objects that King Solomon had made for the Temple—the two columns, the carts, the large tank, and the twelve bulls that supported it—were too heavy to weigh. 21-22 The two columns were identical: each one was 8 metres high and 5.3 metres round. They were hollow, and the

metal was 75 millimetres thick. On top of each column was a bronze capital 2.2 metres high, and all round it was a grating decorated with pomegranates, all of which was also made of bronze. 23 On the grating of each column there were a hundred pomegranates in all, and ninety-six of these were visible from the ground.

The People of Judah Are Taken to Babylonia
(2 Kgs 25.18–21, 27–30)

24 In addition, Nebuzaradan, the commanding officer, took away as prisoners Seraiah the High Priest, Zephaniah the priest next in rank, and the three other important temple officials. 25 From the city he took the officer who had been in command of the troops, seven of the king's personal advisers who were still in the city, the commander's assistant, who was in charge of military records, and sixty other important men. 26 Nebuzaradan took them to the king of Babylonia, who was in the city of Riblah 27 in the territory of Hamath. There the king had them beaten and put to death.

So the people of Judah were carried away from their land into exile. 28 This is the record of the people that Nebuchadnezzar took away as prisoners: in his seventh year as king he carried away 3,023; 29 in his eighteenth year, 832 from Jerusalem; 30 and in his twenty-third year, 745—taken away by Nebuzaradan. In all, 4,600 people were taken away.

31 In the year that Evilmerodach became king of Babylonia, he showed kindness to King Jehoiachin of Judah by releasing him from prison. This happened on the twenty-fifth day of the twelfth month of the thirty-seventh year after Jehoiachin had been taken away as a prisoner. 32 Evilmerodach treated him kindly and gave him a position of greater

---

x Probable text Babylonia; *Hebrew* Babylonia some of the poorest of the people.
52.13: 1 Kgs 9.8   **52.17–23:** 1 Kgs 7.15–47

honour than he gave the other kings who were exiles with him in Babylonia. ³³ So Jehoiachin was permitted to change from his prison clothes and to dine at the king's table for the rest of his life. ³⁴ Each day for as long as he lived, he was given a regular allowance for his needs.

LAMENTATIONS

INTRODUCTION

The book of *Lamentations* is a collection of five poems lamenting the destruction of Jerusalem in 586 B.C., and its aftermath of ruin and exile. In spite of the mournful nature of most of the book, there is also the note of trust in God and hope for the future. These poems are used by the Jews in worship on the annual days of fasting and mourning which commemorate the national disaster of 586 B.C.

Outline of Contents

The sorrows of Jerusalem   1.1–22
The punishment of Jerusalem   2.1–22
Punishment and hope   3.1–66
Jerusalem in ruins   4.1–22
A prayer for mercy   5.1–22

The Sorrows of Jerusalem

1 How lonely lies Jerusalem, once so full of people!
Once honoured by the world, she is now like a widow;
The noblest of cities has fallen into slavery.

² All night long she cries; tears run down her cheeks.
Of all her former friends, not one is left to comfort her.
Her allies have betrayed her and all are now against her.

³ Judah's people are helpless slaves, forced away from home. *ª*
They live in other lands, with no place to call their own—

Surrounded by enemies, with no way to escape.

⁴ No one comes to the Temple now to worship on the holy days.
The girls who sang there suffer, and the priests can only groan.
The city gates stand empty, and Zion is in agony.

⁵ Her enemies succeeded; they hold her in their power.
The LORD has made her suffer for all her many sins;
Her children have been captured and taken away.

⁶ The splendour of Jerusalem is a thing of the past.
Her leaders are like deer that are weak from hunger,

ª are helpless...home; *or* fled from home, from the misery of slavery.

Like a widow...all night long she cries (1.1,2)

Whose strength is almost gone as
    they flee from the hunters.

7 A lonely ruin now, Jerusalem recalls her
    ancient splendour.
  When she fell to the enemy, there was
    no one to help her;
  Her conquerers laughed at her
    downfall.

8 Her honour is gone; she is naked and
    held in contempt.
  She groans and hides her face in
    shame.
  Jerusalem made herself filthy with
    terrible sin.

9 Her uncleanness was easily seen, but
    she showed no concern for her fate.
  Her downfall was terrible; no one can
    comfort her.
  Her enemies have won, and she cries
    to the LORD for mercy.

10 Her enemies robbed her of all her
    treasures.
  She saw them enter the Temple itself,
  Where the LORD had forbidden
    Gentiles to go.

11 Her people groan as they look for
    something to eat;
  They exchange their treasures for
    food to keep themselves alive.
  "Look at me, LORD," the city cries;
    "see me in my misery."

12 "Look at me!" she cries to everyone
    who passes by. *b*
  "No one has ever had pain like mine,
  Pain that the LORD brought on me
    in the time of his anger.

13 "He sent fire from above, a fire that
    burnt inside me.
  He set a trap for me and brought me
    to the ground.
  Then he abandoned me and left me
    in constant pain.

14 "He took note of all my sins and tied
    them all together;
  He hung them round my neck, and
    I grew weak beneath the weight.
  The Lord gave me to my foes, and
    I was helpless against them.

15 "The Lord jeered at all my strongest
    soldiers;

*b*Look...by; *or* May this not happen to you that pass by; *or* Does this mean nothing to you that
pass by?

He sent an army to destroy my young
men.
He crushed my people like grapes in
a winepress.

16 "That is why my eyes are overflowing
with tears.
No one can comfort me; no one can
give me courage.
The enemy has conquered me; my
people have nothing left.

17 "I stretch out my hands, but no one
will help me.
The LORD has called enemies against
me from every side;
They treat me like some filthy thing.

18 "But the LORD is just, for I have
disobeyed him.
Listen to me, people everywhere; look
at me in my pain.
My young men and women have been
taken away captive.

19 "I called to my allies, but they refused
to help me.
The priests and the leaders died in
the city streets,
Looking for food to keep themselves
alive.

20 "Look, O LORD, at my agony, at the
anguish of my soul!
My heart is broken in sorrow for my
sins.
There is murder in the streets; even
indoors there is death.

21 "Listen c to my groans; there is no one
to comfort me.
My enemies are glad that you brought
disaster on me.
Bring d the day you promised; make
my enemies suffer as I do.

22 "Condemn them for all their
wickedness;
Punish them as you punished me for
my sins.
I groan in misery, and I am sick at
heart."

The LORD's Punishment of Jerusalem

2 The Lord in his anger has covered
Zion with darkness.
Its heavenly splendour he has turned
into ruins.

On the day of his anger he abandoned
even his Temple.

2 The Lord destroyed without mercy
every village in Judah
And tore down the forts that defended
the land.
He brought disgrace on the kingdom
and its rulers.

3 In his fury he shattered the strength
of Israel;
He refused to help us when the enemy
came.
He raged against us like fire,
destroying everything.

4 He aimed his arrows at us like an enemy;
He killed all those who were our joy
and delight.
Here in Jerusalem we felt his burning
anger.

5 Like an enemy, the Lord has destroyed
Israel;
He has left her forts and palaces in
ruins.
He has brought on the people of Judah
unending sorrow.

6 He smashed to pieces the Temple where
we worshipped him;
He has put an end to holy days and
Sabbaths.
King and priest alike have felt the
force of his anger.

7 The Lord rejected his altar and deserted
his holy Temple;
He allowed the enemy to tear down
its walls.
They shouted in victory where once
we had worshipped in joy.

8 The LORD was determined that the walls
of Zion should fall;
He measured them off to make sure
of total destruction.
The towers and walls now lie in ruins
together.

9 The gates lie buried in rubble, their bars
smashed to pieces.
The king and the noblemen now are
in exile.
The Law is no longer taught, and the
prophets have no visions from the
LORD.

c One ancient translation Listen; Hebrew They listened.
d One ancient translation Bring; Hebrew You brought.

794

Get up again...to cry out to the Lord (2.19)

¹⁰ Jerusalem's old men sit on the ground
in silence,
With dust on their heads and
sackcloth on their bodies.
Young girls bow their heads to the
ground.

¹¹ My eyes are worn out with weeping;
my soul is in anguish.
I am exhausted with grief at the
destruction of my people.
Children and babies are fainting in
the streets of the city.

¹² Hungry and thirsty, they cry to their
mothers;
They fall in the streets as though they
were wounded,
And slowly die in their mothers' arms.

¹³ O Jerusalem, beloved Jerusalem, what
can I say?
How can I comfort you? No one has
ever suffered like this.
Your disaster is boundless as the
ocean; there is no possible hope.

¹⁴ Your prophets had nothing to tell you
but lies;
Their preaching deceived you by
never exposing your sin.
They made you think you did not need
to repent.

¹⁵ People passing by the city look at you
in scorn.

They shake their heads and laugh at
the ruins of Jerusalem.
"Is this that lovely city? Is this the
pride of the world?"

¹⁶ All your enemies mock you and glare
at you with hate.
They curl their lips and sneer, "We
have destroyed it!
This is the day we have waited for!"

¹⁷ The LORD has finally done what he
threatened to do:
He has destroyed us without mercy,
as he warned us long ago.
He gave our enemies victory, gave
them joy at our downfall.

¹⁸ O Jerusalem, let your very walls cry
out to the Lord!ᵉ
Let your tears flow like rivers night
and day;
Wear yourself out with weeping and
grief!

¹⁹ All through the night get up again and
again to cry out to the Lord;
Pour out your heart and beg him for
mercy on your children—
Children starving to death on every
street corner!

²⁰ Look, O LORD! Look at those you are
torturing!
Women are eating the bodies of the
children they loved!

ᵉ *Probable text* O Jerusalem...Lord; *Hebrew* Their hearts cried out to the Lord, O wall of
Jerusalem.

Priests and prophets are being killed
in the Temple itself!

21 Young and old alike lie dead in the
streets,
Young men and women, killed by
enemy swords.
You slaughtered them without mercy
on the day of your anger.

22 You invited my enemies to hold a
carnival of terror all round me,
And no one could escape on that day
of your anger.
They murdered my children, whom
I had reared and loved.

Punishment, Repentance, and Hope

3 I am one who knows what it is to
be punished by God.
2   He drove me deeper and deeper into
darkness
3   And beat me again and again with
merciless blows.

4 He has left my flesh open and raw, and
has broken my bones.
5   He has shut me in a prison of misery
and anguish.
6   He has forced me to live in the
stagnant darkness of death.

7 He has bound me in chains; I am a
prisoner with no hope of escape.
8   I cry aloud for help, but God refuses
to listen;
9   I stagger as I walk; stone walls block
me wherever I turn.

10 He waited for me like a bear; he
pounced on me like a lion.
11   He chased me off the road, tore me
to pieces, and left me.
12   He drew his bow and made me the
target for his arrows.

13 He shot his arrows deep into my body.
14   People laugh at me all day long; I
am a joke to them all.
15   Bitter suffering is all he has given
me for food and drink.

16 He rubbed my face in the ground and
broke my teeth on the gravel.
17   I have forgotten what health and
peace and happiness are.
18   I have not much longer to live; my
hope in the LORD is gone.

But God refuses to listen (3.8)

19 The thought of my pain, my
homelessness, is bitter poison;
20   I think of it constantly and my spirit
is depressed.
21   Yet hope returns when I remember
this one thing:

22 The LORD's unfailing love and mercy
still continue,
23   Fresh as the morning, as sure as
the sunrise.
24   The LORD is all I have, and so I put
my hope in him.

25 The LORD is good to everyone who
trusts in him,
26   So it is best for us to wait in
patience—to wait for him to save
us—
27   And it is best to learn this patience
in our youth.

28 When we suffer, we should sit alone
in silent patience;
29   We should bow in submission, for
there may still be hope.
30   Though beaten and insulted, we
should accept it all.

31 The Lord is merciful and will not reject
us for ever.
32   He may bring us sorrow, but his

love for us is sure and strong.
33 He takes no pleasure in causing us
grief or pain.

34 The Lord knows when our spirits are
crushed in prison;
35 He knows when we are denied the
rights he gave us;
36 When justice is perverted in court,
he knows.

37 The will of the Lord alone is always
carried out. [f]
38 Good and evil alike take place at
his command.
39 Why should we ever complain when
we are punished for our sin? [g]

40 Let us examine our ways and turn
back to the LORD.
41 Let us open our hearts to God in
heaven and pray,
42 "We have sinned and rebelled, and
you, O LORD, have not forgiven us.

43 "You pursued us and killed us; your
mercy was hidden by your anger,
44 By a cloud of fury too thick for our
prayers to get through.
45 You have made us the refuse heap
of the world.

46 "We are insulted and mocked by all
our enemies.
47 We have been through disaster and
ruin; we live in danger and fear.
48 My eyes flow with rivers of tears
at the destruction of my people.

49 "My tears will pour out in a ceaseless
stream
50 Until the LORD looks down from
heaven and sees us.
51 My heart is grieved when I see what
has happened to the women of the
city.

52 "I was trapped like a bird by enemies
who had no cause to hate me.
53 They threw me alive into a pit and
closed the opening with a stone.
54 Water began to close over me, and
I thought death was near.

55 "From the bottom of the pit, O LORD,
I cried out to you,

56 And when I begged you to listen
to my cry, you heard.
57 You answered me and told me not
to be afraid.

58 "You came to my rescue, Lord, and
saved my life.
59 Judge in my favour; you know the
wrongs done against me.
60 You know how my enemies hate me
and how they plot against me.

61 "You have heard them insult me, O
LORD; you know all their plots.
62 All day long they talk about me and
make their plans.
63 From morning till night they jeer at
me.

64 "Punish them for what they have
done, O LORD;
65 Curse them and fill them with
despair!
66 Hunt them down and wipe them off
the earth!"

Jerusalem after its Fall

4 Our glittering gold has grown dull;
the stones of the Temple lie
scattered in the streets.

2 Zion's young men were as precious to
us as gold,
but now they are treated like common
clay pots.

3 Even a mother wolf will nurse her cubs,
but my people are like ostriches, cruel
to their young.

4 They let their babies die of hunger and
thirst;
children are begging for food that no
one will give them.

5 People who once ate the finest foods
die starving in the streets;
those raised in luxury are pawing
through refuse for food.

6 My people have been punished even
more than the inhabitants of
Sodom,
which met with a sudden downfall
at the hands of God.

[f] The will...out; or No one can make anything happen unless the LORD is willing.
[g] Why should...sin; or Why should we complain about being punished for sin, as long as we are
still alive?
4.6: Gen 19.24

7 Our princes *i* were undefiled and pure
as snow,
vigorous and strong, glowing with
health.

8 Now they lie unknown in the streets,
their faces blackened in death;
their skin, dry as wood, has shrivelled
on their bones.

9 Those who died in the war were better
off than those who died later,
who starved slowly to death, with no
food to keep them alive.

10 The disaster that came to my people
brought horror;
loving mothers boiled their own
children for food.

11 The LORD turned loose the full force
of his fury;
he lit a fire in Zion that burnt it to
the ground.

12 No one anywhere, not even rulers of
foreign nations,
believed that any invader could enter
Jerusalem's gates.

13 But it happened because her prophets
sinned and her priests were guilty
of causing the death of innocent
people.

14 Her leaders wandered through the
streets like blind men,
so stained with blood that no one
would touch them.

15 "Go away!" people shouted. "You're
defiled! Don't touch me!"
So they wandered from nation to
nation, welcomed by no one.

16 The LORD had no more concern for
them; he scattered them himself.
He showed no regard for our priests
and leaders.

17 We looked until we could look no
longer for help that never came.
We kept waiting for help from a
nation that had none to give.

18 The enemy was watching for us; we
could not even walk in the streets.
Our days were over; the end had
come.

19 Swifter than eagles swooping from the
sky, they chased us down.
They tracked us down in the hills;
they took us by surprise in the
desert.

20 They captured the source of our life,
the king the LORD had chosen,
the one we had trusted to protect us
from every invader.

21 Laugh on, people of Edom and Uz;
be glad while you can.
Your disaster is coming too; you too
will stagger naked in shame.

22 Zion has paid for her sin; the LORD
will not keep us in exile any longer.
But Edom, the LORD will punish you;
he will expose your guilty deeds.

A Prayer for Mercy

5 Remember, O LORD, what has
happened to us.
Look at us, and see our disgrace.

2 Our property is in the hands of
strangers;
foreigners are living in our homes.

3 Our fathers have been killed by the
enemy,
and now our mothers are widows.

4 We must pay for the water we drink;
we must buy the wood we need for
fuel.

5 Driven hard like donkeys or camels,
we are tired, but are allowed no rest.

6 To get food enough to stay alive,
we went begging to Egypt and
Assyria.

7 Our ancestors sinned, but now they are
gone,
and we are suffering for their sins.

8 We are ruled by men who are no better
than slaves,
and no one can save us from their
power.

9 Murderers roam through the
countryside;

---

i princes *or* Nazirites.
4.10: Deut 28.57; Ezek 5.10

we risk our lives when we look for
food.

¹⁰ Hunger has made us burn with fever,
until our skin is as hot as an oven.

¹¹ Our wives have been raped on Mount
Zion itself;
in every Judaean village our
daughters have been forced to
submit.

¹² Our leaders have been taken and
hanged;
our old men are shown no respect.

¹³ Our young men are forced to grind
corn like slaves;
boys go staggering under heavy loads
of wood.

¹⁴ The old people no longer sit at the
city gate,
and the young people no longer make
music.

¹⁵ Happiness has gone out of our lives;
grief has taken the place of our
dances.

¹⁶ Nothing is left of all we were proud
of.
We sinned, and now we are doomed.

¹⁷ We are sick at our very hearts
and can hardly see through our tears,

¹⁸ because Mount Zion lies lonely and
deserted,
and wild jackals prowl through its
ruins.

¹⁹ But you, O LORD, are king for ever,
and will rule to the end of time.

²⁰ Why have you abandoned us so long?
Will you ever remember us again?

²¹ Bring us back to you, LORD! Bring us
back!
Restore our ancient glory.

²² Or have you rejected us for ever?
Is there no limit to your anger?

THE BOOK OF
EZEKIEL

INTRODUCTION

The prophet Ezekiel lived in exile in Babylon during the period before and
after the fall of Jerusalem in 586 B.C. His message was addressed both to
the exiles in Babylonia and to the people of Jerusalem. The book of *Ezekiel*
has six principal parts: (1) God's call to Ezekiel to be a prophet. (2) Warnings
to the people about God's judgement on them and about the coming fall
and destruction of Jerusalem. (3) Messages from the Lord regarding his
judgement upon the various nations that oppressed and misled his people.
(4) Comfort for Israel after the fall of Jerusalem and the promise of a brighter
future. (5) The prophesy against Gog. (6) Ezekiel's picture of a restored Temple
and nation.

Ezekiel was a man of deep faith and great imagination. Many of his insights
came in the form of visions, and many of his messages were expressed in
vivid symbolic actions. Ezekiel emphasized the need for inner renewal of
the heart and spirit, and the responsibility of each individual for his own
sins. He also proclaimed his hope for the renewal of the life of the nation.
As a priest, as well as prophet, he had special interest in the Temple and
in the need for holiness.

Outline of Contents

Ezekiel's call 1.1—3.27
Messages of doom on Jerusalem 4.1—24.27
God's judgement of the nations 25.1—32.32
God's promise to his people 33.1—37.28
Prophecy against Gog 38.1—39.29
A vision of the future Temple and land 40.1—48.35

EZEKIEL'S FIRST VISION OF GOD
(1.1–7.27)

God's Throne

1 On the fifth day of the fourth month of the thirtieth year,[a] I, Ezekiel the priest, son of Buzi, was living with the Jewish exiles by the River Chebar in Babylonia. The sky opened, and I saw a vision of God. [2](It was the fifth year since King Jehoiachin had been taken into exile.) [3]There in Babylonia beside the River Chebar, I heard the LORD speak to me and I felt his power.

4 I looked up and saw a storm coming from the north. Lightning was flashing from a huge cloud, and the sky round it was glowing. Where the lightning was flashing, something shone like bronze. [5]At the centre of the storm, I saw what looked like four living creatures in human form, [6]but each of them had four faces and four wings. [7]Their legs were straight, and they had hoofs like those of a bull. They shone like polished bronze. [8]In addition to their four faces and four wings, they each had four human hands, one under each wing. [9]Two wings of each creature were spread out so that the creatures formed a square with their wing tips touching. When they moved, they moved as a group without turning their bodies.

10 Each living creature had four different faces: a human face in front, a lion's face at the right, a bull's face at the left, and an eagle's face at the back. [11]Two wings[b] of each creature were raised so that they touched the tips of the wings of the creatures next to it, and their other two wings were folded against their bodies. [12]Each creature faced all four directions, and so the group could go wherever they wished, without having to turn.

13 Among[c] the creatures there was something that looked like a blazing torch, constantly moving. The fire would blaze up and shoot out flashes of lightning. [14]The creatures themselves darted to and fro with the speed of lightning.

15 As I was looking at the four creatures, I saw four wheels touching the ground, one beside each of them.[d] [16]All four wheels were alike; each one shone like a precious stone, and each had another wheel intersecting it at right angles, [17]so that the wheels could move in any of the four directions. [18]The rims of the wheels were covered with eyes.[e] [19]Whenever the creatures moved, the wheels moved with them, and if the creatures rose up from the earth, so did the wheels. [20]The creatures went wherever they wished, and the wheels did exactly what the creatures did, because the creatures controlled them. [21]So every time the creatures moved or stopped or rose in the air, the wheels did exactly the same.

22 Above the heads of the creatures there was something that looked like a dome made of dazzling crystal. [23]There under the dome stood the creatures, each stretching out two wings towards the ones next to it and covering its body with the other two wings. [24]I heard the noise their wings made in flight; it sounded like the roar of the sea, like the noise of a huge army, like the voice of Almighty God. When they stopped flying, they folded

---

[a]THIRTIETH YEAR: *It is not known to what year this refers.*
[b]*Some ancient translations* Two wings; *Hebrew* Their faces, their wings.
[c]*Some ancient translations* Among; *Hebrew* And the likeness of.
[d]*Some ancient translations* them; *Hebrew* their faces. [e]*Verse 18 in Hebrew is unclear.*
1.1: Rev 19.11 **1.2:** 2 Kgs 24.10–16; 2 Chr 36.9–10 **1.5:** Rev 4.6
1.10: Ezek 10.14; Rev 4.7 **1.15–21:** Ezek 10.9–13 **1.18:** Rev 4.8 **1.22:** Rev 4.6
1.24: Rev 1.15, 19.6

their wings, 25 but there was still a sound coming from above the dome over their heads.

26 Above the dome there was something that looked like a throne made of sapphire, and sitting on the throne was a figure that looked like a man. 27 The figure seemed to be shining like bronze in the middle of a fire. It shone all over with a bright light 28 that had in it all the colours of the rainbow. This was the dazzling light that shows the presence of the LORD.

God Calls Ezekiel to Be a Prophet

When I saw this, I fell face downwards on the ground. Then I heard a voice

2 1 saying, "Mortal man, stand up. I want to talk to you." 2 While the voice was speaking, God's spirit entered me and raised me to my feet, and I heard the voice continue, 3 "Mortal man, I am sending you to the people of Israel. They have rebelled and turned against me and are still rebels, just as their ancestors were. 4 They are stubborn and do not respect me, so I am sending you to tell them what I, the Sovereign LORD, am saying to them. 5 Whether those rebels listen to you or not, they will know that a prophet has been among them.

6 "But you, mortal man, must not be afraid of them or of anything they say. They will defy and despise you; it will be like living among scorpions. Still, don't be afraid of those rebels or of anything they say. 7 You will tell them whatever I tell you to say, whether they listen or not. Remember what rebels they are.

8 "Mortal man, listen to what I tell you. Don't be rebellious like them. Open your mouth and eat what I am going to give you." 9 I saw a hand stretched out towards me, and it was holding a scroll. 10 The hand unrolled the scroll, and I saw that there was writing on both sides—cries of grief were written there, and wails and groans.

3 God said, "Mortal man, eat this scroll; then go and speak to the people of Israel."

2 So I opened my mouth, and he gave me the scroll to eat. 3 He said, "Mortal man, eat this scroll that I give you; fill your stomach with it." I ate it, and it tasted as sweet as honey.

4 Then God said, "Mortal man, go to the people of Israel and say to them whatever I tell you to say. 5 I am not sending you to a nation that speaks a

I saw a hand stretched out towards me (2.9)

difficult foreign language, but to the Israelites. 6 If I sent you to great nations that spoke difficult languages you didn't understand, they would listen to you. 7 But none of the people of Israel will be willing to listen; they will not even listen to me. All of them are stubborn and defiant. 8 Now I will make you as stubborn and as tough as they are. 9 I will make you as firm as a rock, as hard as a diamond; don't be afraid of those rebels."

10 God continued, "Mortal man, pay close attention and remember everything I tell you. 11 Then go to your countrymen who are in exile and tell them what I, the Sovereign LORD, am saying to them, whether they pay attention to you or not."

12 Then God's spirit lifted me up, and I heard behind me the loud roar of a voice that said, "Praise the glory of the LORD in heaven above!" 13 I heard the wings of the creatures beating together in the air, and the noise of the wheels, as loud as an earthquake. 14 The power of the LORD came on me with great force, and as his spirit carried me off, I felt bitter and angry. 15 So I came to Tel Abib beside the River Chebar, where the exiles were living, and for seven days I stayed there, overcome by what I had seen and heard.

1.26: Ezek 10.1; Rev 4.2-3   **1.27:** Ezek 8.2   **2.9-10:** Rev 5.1   **3.1-3:** Rev 10.9-10

The LORD Appoints Ezekiel as a Watchman
(Ezek 33.1-9)

16 After the seven days had passed, the LORD spoke to me. 17 "Mortal man," he said, "I am making you a watchman for the nation of Israel. You will pass on to them the warnings I give you. 18 If I announce that an evil man is going to die but you do not warn him to change his ways so that he can save his life, he will die, still a sinner, and I will hold you responsible for his death. 19 If you do warn an evil man and he doesn't stop sinning, he will die, still a sinner, but your life will be spared.

20 "If a truly good man starts doing evil and I put him in a dangerous situation, he will die if you do not warn him. He will die because of his sins—I will not remember the good he did—and I will hold you responsible for his death. 21 If you do warn a good man not to sin and he listens to you and doesn't sin, he will stay alive, and your life will also be spared."

Ezekiel Will Be Unable to Talk

22 I felt the powerful presence of the LORD and heard him say to me, "Get up and go out into the valley. I will talk to you there."

23 So I went out into the valley, and there I saw the glory of the LORD, just as I had seen it beside the River Chebar. I fell face downwards on the ground, 24 but God's spirit entered me and raised me to my feet. The LORD said to me, "Go home and shut yourself up in the house. 25 You will be tied with ropes, mortal man, and you will not be able to go out in public. 26 I will paralyse your tongue so that you won't be able to warn these rebellious people. 27 Then, when I speak to you again and give you back the power of speech, you will tell them what I, the Sovereign LORD, am saying. Some of them will listen, but some will ignore you, for they are a nation of rebels."

Ezekiel Acts Out the Siege of Jerusalem

4 God said, "Mortal man, get a brick, put it in front of you, and scratch lines on it to represent the city of Jerusalem. 2 Then, to represent a siege, put trenches, earthworks, camps, and battering-rams all round it. 3 Take an iron

But God's spirit entered me and raised me to my feet (3.24)

pan and set it up like a wall between you and the city. Face the city. It is under siege, and you are the one besieging it. This will be a sign to the nation of Israel.

4-5 "Then lie down on your left side, and I[g] will place on you the guilt of the nation of Israel. For 390 days you will stay there and suffer because of their guilt. I have sentenced you to one day for each year their punishment will last. 6 When you finish that, turn over on your right side and suffer for the guilt of Judah for forty days—one day for each year of their punishment.

7 "Fix your eyes on the siege of Jerusalem. Shake your fist at the city and prophesy against it. 8 I will tie you up so that you cannot turn from one side to the other until the siege is over.

9 "Now take some wheat, barley, beans, peas, millet, and spelt. Mix them all together and make bread. That is what you are to eat during the 390 days you are lying on your left side. 10 You will be allowed 230 grammes of bread a day, and it will have to last until the next day. 11 You will also have a limited amount of water to drink, two cups a day. 12 You are to build a fire out of dried human excrement, bake bread on the fire, and eat it where everyone can see you."

13 The LORD said, "This represents the way the Israelites will have to eat food

---

g *Probable text* I; *Hebrew* you

which the Law forbids, *h* when I scatter them to foreign countries."

14 But I replied, "No, Sovereign LORD! I have never defiled myself. From childhood on I have never eaten meat from any animal that died a natural death or was killed by wild animals. I have never eaten any food considered unclean."

15 So God said, "Very well. I will let you use cow dung instead, and you can bake your bread on that."

16 And he added, "Mortal man, I am going to cut off the supply of bread for Jerusalem. The people there will be distressed and anxious as they measure out the food they eat and the water they drink. 17 They will run out of bread and water; they will be in despair, and they will waste away because of their sins."

Ezekiel Cuts His Hair

5 The LORD said, "Mortal man, take a sharp sword and use it to shave off your beard and all your hair. Then weigh the hair on scales and divide it into three parts. 2 Burn a third of it in the city when the siege is over. Take another third and chop it up with your sword as you move about outside the city. Scatter the remaining third to the winds, and I will pursue it with my sword. 3 Keep back a few hairs and wrap them in the hem of your clothes. 4 Then take a few of them out again, throw them in the fire, and let them burn up. From them fire will spread to the whole nation of Israel."

5 The Sovereign LORD said, "Look at Jerusalem. I put her at the centre of the world, with other countries all round her. 6 But Jerusalem rebelled against my commands and showed that she was more wicked than the other nations, more disobedient than the countries around her. Jerusalem rejected my commands and refused to keep my laws. 7 Now listen, Jerusalem, to what I, the Sovereign LORD, am saying. By not obeying my laws or keeping my commands, you have caused more trouble than the nations around you. You have followed the customs of other nations. 8 And so I, the Sovereign LORD, am telling you that I am your enemy. I will pass judgement on you where all the nations can see it. 9 Because of all the things you do that I hate, I will punish Jerusalem as I have never done before and will never do again. 10 As a result,

parents in Jerusalem will eat their children, and children will eat their parents. I will punish you and scatter in every direction any who are left alive.

11 "Therefore, as I am the living God— this is the word of the Sovereign LORD— because you defiled my Temple with all the evil, disgusting things you did, I will cut you down without mercy. 12 A third of your people will die from sickness and hunger in the city; a third will be cut down by swords outside the city; and I will scatter the last third to the winds and pursue them with a sword.

13 "You will feel all the force of my anger and rage until I am satisfied. When all this happens, you will be convinced that I, the LORD, have spoken to you because I am outraged at your unfaithfulness. 14 Everyone from the nations around you who passes by will sneer at you and keep his distance.

15 "When I am angry and furious with you and punish you, all the nations around you will be terrified. They will look at you with disgust and will mock you. 16 I will cut off your supply of food and let you starve. You *i* will feel the pains of hunger like sharp arrows sent to destroy you. 17 I will send hunger and wild animals to kill your children, and will send sickness, violence, and war to kill you. I, the LORD, have spoken."

The LORD Condemns Idolatry

6 The LORD spoke to me. 2 "Mortal man," he said, "look towards the mountains of Israel and give them my message. 3 Tell the mountains of Israel to hear the word of the LORD—to hear what I, the Sovereign LORD, am telling the mountains, the hills, the gorges, and the valleys: I will send a sword to destroy the places where people worship idols. 4 The altars will be torn down and the incense-altars broken. All the people there will be killed in front of their idols. 5 I will scatter the corpses of the people of Israel; I will scatter their bones all round the altars. 6 All the cities of Israel will be destroyed, so that all their altars and their idols will be smashed to pieces, their incense-altars will be shattered, and everything they made will disappear. 7 People will be killed everywhere, and those who survive will acknowledge that I am the LORD.

---

h FOOD WHICH THE LAW FORBIDS: *The Law of Moses prohibited the eating of certain foods as being ritually unclean (see Lev. 11).* *i* Probable text You; Hebrew They.
5.10: Lam 4.10   **5.17:** Rev 6.8

Corpses will be scattered among the idols (6.13)

8 "I will let some escape the slaughter and be scattered among the nations, 9 where they will live in exile. There they will remember me and know that I have punished them and disgraced them,[j] because their faithless hearts deserted me and they preferred idols to me. And they will be disgusted with themselves because of the evil and degrading things they have done. 10 They will know that I am the LORD and that my warnings were not empty threats."

11 The Sovereign LORD said, "Wring your hands! Stamp your feet! Cry in sorrow because of all the evil, disgusting things the Israelites have done. They are going to die in war, by famine, and by disease. 12 Those far away will fall ill and die; those near by will be killed in war; those who survive will starve to death. They will feel all the force of my anger. 13 Corpses will be scattered among the idols and round the altars, scattered on every high hill, on the top of every mountain, under every green tree and every large oak, in every place where they burnt sacrifices to their idols. Then everyone will know that I am the LORD. 14 Yes, I will stretch out my hand and destroy their country. I will make it a waste from the southern desert to the city of Riblah in the north, not sparing any place where the Israelites live. Then everyone will know that I am the LORD."

The End Is Near for Israel

7 The LORD spoke to me. 2 "Mortal man," he said, "this is what I, the Sovereign LORD, am saying to the land of Israel: This is the end for the whole land!

3 "Israel, the end has come. You will feel my anger, because I am judging you for what you have done. I will pay you back for all your disgusting conduct. 4 I will not spare you or show you any mercy. I am going to punish you for the disgusting things you have done, so that you will know that I am the LORD."

5 This is what the Sovereign LORD is saying, "One disaster after another is coming on you. 6 It's all over. This is the end. You are finished. 7 The end is coming for you people who live in the land. The time is near when there will be no more celebrations at the mountain shrines, only confusion.[k]

8 "Very soon now you will feel all the force of my anger. I am judging you for what you have done, and I will pay you back for all your disgusting conduct. 9 I will not spare you or show you any mercy. I am going to punish you for the disgusting things you have done, so that you will know that I am the LORD, and that I am the one who punishes you."

10 The day of disaster is coming for Israel. Violence is flourishing. Pride is at its height.[l] 11 Violence produces more

[j] *Some ancient translations* disgraced them; *Hebrew* I am disgraced.
[k] *Probable text* celebrations...confusion; *Hebrew unclear.*
[l] *Probable text* Pride is at its height; *Hebrew unclear.*

Some will escape to the mountains (7.16)

wickedness. Nothing of theirs will remain, nothing of their wealth, their splendour, or their glory.

12 The time is coming. The day is near when buying and selling will have no more meaning, because God's punishment will fall on everyone alike. [13] No merchant will live long enough to get back what he has lost, because God's anger is on everyone. Those who are evil cannot survive. [n] [14] The trumpet sounds, and everyone gets ready. But no one goes off to war, for God's anger will fall on everyone alike.

Punishment for Israel's Sins

15 There is fighting in the streets, and sickness and hunger in the houses. Anyone who is out in the country will die in the fighting, and anyone in the city will be a victim of sickness and hunger. [16] Some will escape to the mountains like doves frightened from the valleys. All of them will moan over their sins. [o] [17] Everyone's hands will be weak, and their knees will shake. [18] They will put on sackcloth and they will tremble all over. Their heads will be shaved, and they will all be disgraced. [19] They will throw their gold and silver away in the streets like refuse, because neither silver nor gold can save them when the LORD pours out his fury. They cannot use it to satisfy their desires or fill their stomachs. Gold and silver led them into sin. [20] Once they were proud of their beautiful jewels, but they used them to make disgusting idols. That is why the LORD has made their wealth repulsive to them.

21 "I will let foreigners rob them," says the LORD, "and law-breakers will take all their wealth and defile it. [22] I will not interfere when my treasured Temple is profaned, when robbers break into it and defile it.

23 "Everything is in confusion [q]—the land is full of murders and the cities are full of violence. [24] I will bring the most evil nations here and let them have your homes. Your strongest men will lose their confidence when I let the nations profane the places where you worship. [25] Despair is coming. You will look for peace and never find it. [26] One disaster will follow another, and a steady stream of bad news

They were proud of their beautiful jewels (7.20)

---

[n] *Verse 13 in Hebrew is unclear.*
[o] *Verse 16 in Hebrew is unclear.*
[q] *One ancient translation* Everything is in confusion; *Hebrew unclear.*

will pour in. You will beg the prophets to reveal what they foresee. The priests will have nothing to teach the people, and the elders will have no advice to give. ²⁷The king will mourn, the prince will give up hope, and the people will shake with fear. I will punish you for all you have done, and will judge you in the same way as you have judged others. This will show you that I am the LORD."

EZEKIEL'S SECOND VISION OF GOD
(8.1–10.22)

Idolatry in Jerusalem

8 On the fifth day of the sixth month of the sixth year of our exile, the leaders of the exiles from Judah were sitting in my house with me. Suddenly the power of the Sovereign LORD came on me. ²I looked up and saw a vision of a fiery human form. From the waist down his body looked like fire, and from the waist up he was shining like polished bronze. ³He stretched out what seemed to be a hand and seized me by the hair. Then in this vision God's spirit lifted me high in the air and took me to Jerusalem. He took me to the inner entrance of the north gate of the Temple, where there was an idol that was an outrage to God.

4 There I saw the dazzling light that shows the presence of Israel's God, just as I had seen it when I was by the River Chebar. ⁵God said to me, "Mortal man, look towards the north." I looked, and there near the altar by the entrance of the gateway I saw the idol that was an outrage to God.

6 God said to me, "Mortal man, do you see what is happening? Look at the disgusting things the people of Israel are doing here, driving me farther and farther away from my holy place. You will see even more disgraceful things than this."

7 He took me to the entrance of the outer courtyard and showed me a hole in the wall. ⁸He said, "Mortal man, break through the wall here." I broke through it and found a door. ⁹He said to me, "Go in and look at the evil, disgusting things they are doing there." ¹⁰So I went in and looked. The walls were covered with

drawings of snakes and other unclean animals,ʳ and of the other things which the Israelites were worshipping. ¹¹Seventy Israelite leaders were there, including Jaazaniah son of Shaphan. Each one was holding an incense-burner, and smoke was rising from the incense. ¹²God asked me, "Mortal man, do you see what the Israelite leaders are doing in secret? They are all worshipping in a room full of images. Their excuse is: 'The LORD doesn't see us! He has abandoned the country.'"

13 Then the LORD said to me, "You are going to see them do even more disgusting things than that." ¹⁴So he took me to the north gate of the Temple and showed me women weeping over the death of the god Tammuz.ˢ

15 He asked, "Mortal man, do you see that? You will see even more disgusting things." ¹⁶So he took me to the inner courtyard of the Temple. There near the entrance of the sanctuary, between the altar and the passage, were about twenty-five men. They had turned their backs to the sanctuary and were bowing low towards the east, worshipping the rising sun.

17 The LORD said to me, "Mortal man, do you see that? These people of Judah are not satisfied with merely doing all the disgusting things you have seen here and with spreading violence throughout the country. No, they must come and do them here in the Temple itself and make me even more angry. Look how they insult me in the most offensive way possible!ᵐ ¹⁸They will feel all the force of my anger. I will not spare them or show them any mercy. They will shout prayers to me as loud as they can, but I will not listen to them."

Jerusalem Is Punished

9 Then I heard God shout, "Come here, you men who are going to punish the city. Bring your weapons with you." ²At once six men came from the outer north gate of the Temple, each one carrying a weapon. With them was a man dressed in linen clothes, carrying something to write with. They all came and stood by the bronze altar.

ʳUNCLEAN ANIMALS: *The Law of Moses prohibited the eating of certain animals as being ritually unclean (see 4.13; Lev. 11).*
ˢTAMMUZ: *A god who was thought to die when vegetation died and to come to life the next year. Women would mourn his ritual death.*
ᵐIN THE MOST OFFENSIVE WAY POSSIBLE: *A reference to a pagan rite of putting a branch to the nose.*
8.2: Ezek 1.27   **8.4:** Ezek 1.28

3 Then the dazzling light of the presence of the God of Israel rose up from the winged creatures, [t] where it had been, and moved to the entrance of the Temple. The LORD called to the man dressed in linen, 4 "Go through the whole city of Jerusalem and put a mark on the forehead of everyone who is distressed and troubled because of all the disgusting things being done in the city."

5 And I heard God say to the other men, "Follow him through the city, and kill. Spare no one; have mercy on no one. 6 Kill the old men, young men, young women, mothers, and children. But don't touch anyone who has the mark on his forehead. Start here at my Temple." So they began with the leaders who were standing there at the Temple.

7 God said to them, "Defile the Temple. Fill its courtyards with corpses. Get to work!" So they began to kill the people in the city. [u]

8 While the killing was going on, I was there alone. I threw myself face downwards on the ground and shouted, "Sovereign LORD, are you so angry with Jerusalem that you are going to kill everyone left in Israel?"

9 God answered, "The people of Israel and Judah are guilty of terrible sins. They have committed murder all over the land and have filled Jerusalem with crime. They say that I, the LORD, have abandoned their country and that I don't see them. 10 But I will not have pity on them; I will do to them what they have done to others."

11 Then the man wearing linen clothes returned and reported to the LORD, "I have carried out your orders."

The Glory of the LORD Leaves the Temple

10 I looked at the dome over the heads of the living creatures [x] and above them was something that seemed to be a throne made of sapphire. 2 God said to the man wearing linen clothes, "Go between the wheels under the creatures and fill your hands with burning coals. Then scatter the coals over the city."

I watched him go. 3 The creatures were standing to the south of the Temple when he went in, and a cloud filled the inner courtyard. 4 The dazzling light of the LORD's presence rose up from the creatures and moved to the entrance of the Temple. Then the cloud filled the Temple, and the courtyard was blazing with the light. 5 The noise made by the creatures' wings was heard even in the outer courtyard. It sounded like the voice of Almighty God.

6 When the LORD commanded the man wearing linen clothes to take some fire from between the wheels that were under the creatures, the man went in and stood by one of the wheels. 7 One of the creatures put his hand into the fire that was there among them, picked up some coals, and put them in the hands of the man in linen. The man took the coals and left.

8 I saw that each creature had what looked like a human hand under each of its wings. 9-10 I also saw that there were four wheels, all alike, one beside each creature. The wheels shone like precious stones, and each one had another wheel which intersected it at right angles. 11 When the creatures moved, they could go in any direction without turning. They all moved together in the direction they wanted to go, without having to turn round. 12 Their bodies, backs, hands, wings, and wheels were covered with eyes. 13 These wheels were the same as those I had seen in my first vision.

14 Each creature had four faces. The first was the face of a bull, the second a human face, the third the face of a lion, and the fourth the face of an eagle. 15 (They were the same creatures that I had seen by the River Chebar.) When the creatures rose in the air 16 and moved, the wheels went with them. Whenever they spread their wings to fly, the wheels still went with them. 17 When the creatures stopped, the wheels stopped; and when the creatures flew, the wheels went with them, because the creatures controlled them.

18 Then the dazzling light of the LORD's presence left the entrance of the Temple and moved to a place above the creatures. 19 They spread their wings and flew up from the earth while I was watching, and the wheels went with them. They paused at the east gate of the Temple, and the dazzling light was over them. 20 I recognized them as the same creatures which I had seen beneath the God of Israel at the River Chebar.

21 Each of them had four faces, four

[t] WINGED CREATURES: (see 1.5-12).
[u] work!" So they...city.; or work! Go on and start killing the people in the city!"
[x] LIVING CREATURES: See 1.5-12.

9.4: Rev 7.3, 9.4, 14.1   **10.1:** Ezek 1.26; Rev 4.2   **10.2:** Rev 8.5   **10.9-13:** Ezek 1.15-21
10.12: Rev 4.8   **10.14:** Ezek 1.10; Rev 4.7

wings, and what looked like a human hand under each wing. 22 Their faces looked exactly like the faces *w* I had seen by the River Chebar. Each creature moved straight ahead.

Jerusalem Is Condemned

11 God's spirit lifted me up and took me to the east gate of the Temple. There near the gate I saw twenty-five men, including Jaazaniah son of Azzur and Pelatiah son of Benaiah, two leaders of the nation.

2 God said to me, "Mortal man, these men make evil plans and give bad advice in this city. 3 They say, 'We will soon be building houses again. *x* The city is like a cooking-pot, and we are like the meat in it, but at least it protects us from the fire.' 4 Now then, denounce them, mortal man."

5 The spirit of the LORD took control of me, and the LORD told me to give the people this message: "People of Israel, I know what you are saying and what you are planning. 6 You have murdered so many people here in the city that the streets are full of corpses.

7 "So this is what I, the Sovereign LORD, am saying to you. This city is indeed a cooking-pot, but what is the meat? The corpses of those you have killed! You will not be here—I will throw you out of the city! 8 Are you afraid of swords? I will bring men with swords to attack you. 9 I will take you out of the city and hand you over to foreigners. I have sentenced you to death, 10 and you will be killed in battle in your own country. Then everyone will know that I am the LORD. 11 This city will not protect you as a pot protects the meat in it. I will punish you wherever you may be in the land of Israel. 12 You will know that I am the LORD and that while you were keeping the laws of the neighbouring nations, you were breaking *my* laws and disobeying *my* commands."

13 While I was prophesying, Pelatiah dropped dead. I threw myself face downwards on the ground and shouted, "No, Sovereign LORD! Are you going to kill everyone left in Israel?"

God's Promise to the Exiles

14 The LORD spoke to me. 15 "Mortal man," he said, "the people who live in Jerusalem are talking about you and your fellow-Israelites who are in exile. They say, 'The exiles are too far away to worship the LORD. He has given us possession of the land.'

16 "Now tell your fellow-exiles what I am saying. I am the one who sent them to live in far-off nations and scattered them in other countries. Yet, for the time being I will be present with them in the lands where they have gone.

17 "So tell them what I, the Sovereign LORD, am saying. I will gather them out of the countries where I scattered them, and will give the land of Israel back to them. 18 When they return, they are to get rid of all the filthy, disgusting idols they find. 19 I will give them a new heart and a new mind. I will take away their stubborn heart of stone and will give them an obedient heart. 20 Then they will keep my laws and faithfully obey all my commands. They will be my people, and I will be their God. 21 But I will punish the people who love to worship filthy, disgusting idols. I will punish them for what they have done." The Sovereign LORD has spoken.

God's Glory Leaves Jerusalem

22 The living creatures began to fly, and the wheels went with them. The dazzling light of the presence of the God of Israel was over them. 23 Then the dazzling light left the city and moved to the mountain east of it. 24 In the vision the spirit of God lifted me up and brought me back to the exiles in Babylonia. Then the vision faded, 25 and I told the exiles everything that the LORD had shown me.

The Prophet as a Refugee

12 The LORD spoke to me. 2 "Mortal man," he said, "you are living among rebellious people. They have eyes, but they see nothing; they have ears, but they hear nothing, because they are rebellious.

3 "Now, mortal man, pack a bundle just as a refugee would, and start out before nightfall. Let everyone see you leaving and going to another place. Maybe those rebels will notice you. *y* 4 While it is still daylight, pack your bundle for exile, so that they can see you, and then let them

---

w *Probable text* the faces; *Hebrew* the faces and them.
x We will...again; *or* We won't be building houses for a while.
y Maybe those...you; *or* Maybe they will then realize that they are rebels.
11.19-20: Ezek 36.26–28   **11.22-23:** Ezek 43.2–5   **12.2:** Is 6.9–10; Jer 5.21; Mk 8.18

In the vision (11.24)

watch you leave in the evening as if you were going into exile. ⁵While they are watching, break a hole through the wall of your house and take your pack out through it. ⁶Let them watch you putting your pack on your shoulder and going out into the dark with your eyes covered, so that you can't see where you are going. What you do will be a warning to the Israelites."

7 I did what the LORD told me to do. That day I packed a bundle as a refugee would, and that evening as it was getting dark I dug a hole in the wall with my hands and went out. While everyone watched, I put the pack on my shoulder and left.

8 The next morning the LORD spoke to me. ⁹"Mortal man," he said, "now that those Israelite rebels are asking you what

you're doing, ¹⁰tell them what I, the Sovereign LORD, am saying to them. This message is for the prince ruling in Jerusalem and for all the people who live there. ¹¹Tell them that what you have done is a sign of what will happen to them—they will be refugees and captives. ¹²The prince who is ruling them will shoulder his pack in the dark and escape through a hole that they dig for him in the wall. He will cover his eyes and not see where he is going. ¹³But I will spread out my net and trap him in it. Then I will take him to the city of Babylon, where he will die without having seen it. ¹⁴I will scatter in every direction all the members of his court and his advisers and bodyguard, and people will search for them to kill them.

15 "When I scatter them among the

12.13: 2 Kgs 25.7; Jer 52.11

other nations and in foreign countries, they will know that I am the LORD. [16] I will let a few of them survive the war, the famine, and the diseases, so that there among the nations they will realize how disgusting their actions have been and will acknowledge that I am the LORD."

The Sign of the Trembling Prophet

17 The LORD spoke to me. [18] "Mortal man," he said, "tremble when you eat, and shake with fear when you drink. [19] Tell the whole nation that this is the message of the Sovereign LORD to the people of Jerusalem who are still living in their land: They will tremble when they eat and shake with fear when they drink. Their land will be stripped bare, because everyone who lives there is lawless. [20] Cities that are now full of people will be destroyed, and the country will be made a wilderness. Then they will know that I am the LORD."

A Popular Proverb and an Unpopular Message

21 The LORD spoke to me. [22] "Mortal man," he said, "why do the people of Israel repeat this proverb: 'Time goes by, and predictions come to nothing'? [23] Now tell them what I, the Sovereign LORD, have to say about that. I will put an end to that proverb. It won't be repeated in Israel any more. Tell them instead: The time has come, and the predictions are coming true!

24 "Among the people of Israel there will be no more false visions or misleading prophecies. [25] I, the LORD, will speak to them, and what I say will be done. There will be no more delay. In your own lifetime, you rebels, I will do what I have warned you I would do. I have spoken," says the Sovereign LORD.

26 The LORD said to me, [27] "Mortal man, the Israelites think that your visions and prophecies are about the distant future. [28] So tell them that I, the Sovereign LORD, am saying: There will be no more delay. What I have said will be done. I, the Sovereign LORD, have spoken!"

Prophecy against False Male Prophets

13 The LORD spoke to me. [2] "Mortal man," he said, "denounce the prophets of Israel who make up their own prophecies. Tell them to listen to the word of the LORD."

3 This is what the Sovereign LORD says:

"These foolish prophets are doomed! They provide their own inspiration and invent their own visions. [4] People of Israel, your prophets are as useless as foxes living among the ruins of a city. [5] They don't guard the places where the walls have crumbled, nor do they rebuild the walls, and so Israel cannot be defended when war comes on the day of the LORD. [6] Their visions are false, and their predictions are lies. They claim that they are speaking my message, but I have not sent them. Yet they expect their words to come true! [7] I tell them: Those visions you see are false, and the predictions you make are lies. You say that they are my words, but I haven't spoken to you!"

8 So the Sovereign LORD says to them, "Your words are false, and your visions are lies. I am against you. [9] I am about to punish you prophets who have false visions and make misleading predictions. You will not be there when my people gather to make decisions; your names will not be included in the list of the citizens of Israel; you will never return to your land. Then you will know that I am the Sovereign LORD.

10 "The prophets mislead my people by saying that all is well. All is certainly not well! My people have put up a wall of loose stones, and then the prophets have come and covered it with whitewash. [11] Tell the prophets that their wall is going to fall down. I will send a pouring rain. Hailstones will fall on it, and a strong wind will blow against it. [12] The wall will collapse, and everyone will ask you what good the whitewash did."

13 Now this is what the Sovereign LORD says: "In my anger I will send a strong wind, pouring rain, and hailstones to destroy the wall. [14] I intend to break down the wall they whitewashed, to shatter it, and to leave the foundation stones bare. It will collapse and kill you all. Then everyone will know that I am the LORD.

15 "The wall and those who covered it with whitewash will feel the force of my anger. Then I will tell you that the wall is gone and so are those who whitewashed it— [16] those prophets who assured Jerusalem that all was well, when all was not well!" The Sovereign LORD has spoken.

Prophecy against False Female Prophets

17 The LORD said, "Now, mortal man, look at the women among your people

13.10: Jer 6.14, 8.11

I will send a strong wind, pouring rain, and hailstones to destroy the wall (13.13)

who make up predictions. Denounce them 18 and tell them what the Sovereign LORD is saying to them:

‑ "You women are doomed! You sew magic wristbands for everyone and make magic scarves for everyone to wear on their heads, so that they can have power over other people's lives. You want to possess the power of life and death over my people and to use it for your own benefit. 19 You dishonour me in front of my people in order to get a few handfuls of barley and a few pieces of bread. You kill people who don't deserve to die, and you keep people alive who don't deserve to live. So you tell lies to my people, and they believe you."

20 Now this is what the Sovereign LORD says: "I hate the wristbands that you use in your attempt to control life and death. I will rip them off your arms and set free the people that you were controlling. z 21 I will rip off your scarves and let my people escape from your power once and for all. Then you will know that I am the LORD.

22 "By your lies you discourage good people, whom I do not wish to hurt. You prevent evil people from giving up evil and saving their lives. 23 So now your false visions and misleading predictions are over. I am rescuing my people from your power, so that you will know that I am the LORD."

God Condemns Idolatry

14 Some of the leaders of the Israelites came to consult me about the LORD's will. 2 Then the LORD spoke to me. 3 "Mortal man," he said, "these men have

given their hearts to idols and are letting idols lead them into sin. Do they think I will give them an answer?

4 "Now speak to them and tell them what I, the Sovereign LORD, am saying to them: Every Israelite who has given his heart to idols and lets them lead him into sin and who then comes to consult a prophet, will get an answer from me— the answer that his many idols deserve! 5 All those idols have turned the Israelites away from me, but by my answer I hope to win back their loyalty.

6 "Now then, tell the Israelites what I, the Sovereign LORD, am saying: Turn back and leave your disgusting idols.

7 "Whenever one of the Israelites or one of the foreigners who live in the Israelite community turns away from me and worships idols, and then goes to consult a prophet, I, the LORD, will give him his answer! 8 I will oppose him. I will make an example of him. I will remove him from the community of my people, so that you will know that I am the LORD.

9 "If a prophet is deceived into giving a false answer, it is because I, the LORD, have deceived him. I will remove him from the people of Israel. 10 Both the prophet and the one who consults him will get the same punishment. 11 I will do this to keep the Israelites from deserting me and defiling themselves by their sins. They are to be my people, and I will be their God." The Sovereign LORD has spoken.

Noah, Danel, and Job

12 The LORD spoke to me. 13 "Mortal man," he said, "if a country sins and is

z *In verse 20 in Hebrew a word occurs twice, the meaning of which is unclear.*

unfaithful to me, I will stretch out my hand and destroy its supply of food. I will send a famine and kill people and animals alike. [14] Even if those three men, Noah, Danel, [a] and Job, were living there, their goodness would save only their own lives." The Sovereign LORD has spoken.

15 "Or I might send wild animals to kill the people, making the land so dangerous that no one could travel through it, [16] and even if those three men lived there—as surely as I, the Sovereign LORD, am the living God—they would not be able to save even their own children. They would save only their own lives, and the land would become a wilderness.

17 "Or I might bring war on that country and send destructive weapons to wipe out people and animals alike, [18] and even if those three men lived there—as surely as I, the Sovereign LORD, am the living God—they would not be able to save even their children, but only their own lives.

19 "If I send an epidemic on that country and in my anger take many lives, killing people and animals, [20] even if Noah, Danel, and Job lived there—as surely as I, the Sovereign LORD, am the living God—they would not be able to save even their own children. Their goodness would save only their own lives."

21 This is what the Sovereign LORD is saying: "I will send my four worst punishments on Jerusalem—war, famine, wild animals, and disease—to destroy people and animals alike. [22] If anyone does survive and save his children, look at them when they come to you. See how evil they are, and be convinced that the punishment I am bringing on Jerusalem is justified; [23] then you will know that there was good reason for everything I did." The Sovereign LORD has spoken.

A Parable about a Vine

15 The LORD spoke to me. [2] "Mortal man," he said, "how does a vine compare with a tree? What good is a branch of a grapevine compared with the trees of the forest? [3] Can you use it to make anything? Can you even make a peg out of it to hang things on? [4] It is only good for building a fire. And when the ends are burnt up and the middle is

Can you make anything out of it? (15.4)

charred, can you make anything out of it? [5] It was useless even before it was burnt. Now that the fire has burnt it and charred it, it is even more useless."

6 Now this is what the Sovereign LORD is saying, "Just as a vine is taken from the forest and burnt, so I will take the people who live in Jerusalem [7] and will punish them. They have escaped one fire, but now fire will burn them up. When I punish them, you will know that I am the LORD. [8] They have been unfaithful to me, and so I will make the country a wilderness." The Sovereign LORD has spoken.

Jerusalem the Unfaithful

16 The LORD spoke to me again. [2] "Mortal man," he said, "point out to Jerusalem what disgusting things she has done. [3] Tell Jerusalem what the Sovereign LORD is saying to her:

"You were born in the land of Canaan. Your father was an Amorite, and your mother was a Hittite. [b] [4] When you were born, no one cut your umbilical cord or washed you [c] or rubbed you with salt or wrapped you in cloth. [5] No one took enough pity on you to do any of these things for you. When you were born, no one loved you. You were thrown out in an open field.

6 "Then I passed by and saw you squirming in your own blood. You were covered with blood, but I wouldn't let you die. [7] I made you grow like a healthy plant. You grew strong and tall and became a young woman. [d] Your breasts were well-formed, and your hair had grown, but you were naked.

8 "As I passed by again, I saw that the

---

[a] DANEL: *or* Daniel, *an ancient hero, known for his righteous life.*
[b] AMORITE...HITTITE: *The Israelites regarded these people as immoral and idolatrous.*
[c] *Hebrew has an additional word, the meaning of which is unclear.*
[d] *Probable text* young woman; *Hebrew unclear.*
14.21: Rev 6.8

time had come for you to fall in love. I covered your naked body with my coat and promised to love you. Yes, I made a marriage covenant with you, and you became mine." This is what the Sovereign LORD says.

9 "Then I took water and washed the blood off you. I rubbed olive-oil on your skin. ¹⁰ I dressed you in embroidered gowns and gave you shoes of the best leather, a linen headband, and a silk cloak. ¹¹ I put jewels on you—bracelets and necklaces. ¹² I gave you a nose-ring and earrings and a beautiful crown to wear. ¹³ You had ornaments of gold and silver, and you always wore clothes of embroidered linen and silk. You ate bread made from the best flour, and had honey and olive-oil to eat. Your beauty was dazzling, and you became a queen. ¹⁴ You became famous in every nation for your perfect beauty, because I was the one who made you so lovely." This is what the Sovereign LORD says.

15 "But you took advantage of your beauty and fame to sleep with everyone who came along.^e ¹⁶ You used some of your clothes to decorate your places of worship, and just like a prostitute,^f you gave yourself to everyone. ¹⁷ You took the silver and gold jewellery that I had given you, used it to make male images, and committed adultery with them. ¹⁸ You took the embroidered clothes I gave you and put them on the images, and offered to the images the olive-oil and incense I had given you. ¹⁹ I gave you food—the best flour, olive-oil, and honey—but you offered it as a sacrifice to win the favour of idols." This is what the Sovereign LORD says.

20 "Then you took the sons and the daughters you had borne me and offered them as sacrifices to idols. Wasn't it bad enough to be unfaithful to me, ²¹ without taking my children and sacrificing them to idols? ²² During your disgusting life as a prostitute you never once remembered your childhood—when you were naked, squirming in your own blood."

Jerusalem's Life as a Prostitute

23 The Sovereign LORD said, "You are doomed! Doomed! You did all that evil, and then ²⁴ by the side of every road you built places to worship idols and practise prostitution. ²⁵ You dragged your beauty

through the mud. You offered yourself to everyone who came by, and you were more of a prostitute every day. ²⁶ You let your lustful neighbours, the Egyptians, go to bed with you, and you used your prostitution to make me angry.

27 "Now I have raised my hand to punish you and to take away your share of my blessing. I have handed you over to the Philistines, who hate you and are disgusted with your immoral actions.

28 "Because you were not satisfied by the others, you went running after the Assyrians. You were their prostitute, but they didn't satisfy you either. ²⁹ You were also a prostitute for the Babylonians, that nation of businessmen, but they didn't satisfy you either.

30 ^g This is what the Sovereign LORD is saying: "You have done all this like a shameless prostitute. ³¹ On every street you built places to worship idols and practise prostitution. But you are not out for money like a common prostitute. ³² You are like a woman who commits adultery with strangers instead of loving her husband. ³³ A prostitute is paid, but you gave presents to all your lovers and bribed them to come from everywhere to sleep with you. ³⁴ You are a special kind of prostitute. No one forced you to become one. You didn't get paid; you paid them! Yes, you are different."

God's Judgement on Jerusalem

35 Now then, Jerusalem, you whore! Hear what the LORD is saying.

36 This is what the Sovereign LORD says: "You stripped off your clothes and, like a prostitute, you gave yourself to your lovers and to all your disgusting idols, and you killed your children as sacrifices to idols. ³⁷ Because of this I will bring all your former lovers together—the ones you liked and the ones you hated. I will bring them round you in a circle, and then I will strip off your clothes and let them see you naked. ³⁸ I will condemn you for adultery and murder, and in my anger and fury I will punish you with death. ³⁹ I will put you in their power, and they will tear down the places where you engage in prostitution and worship idols. They will take away your clothes and jewels and leave you completely naked. 40 "They will stir up a crowd to stone you, and they will cut you to pieces with

^e Hebrew has two additional words, the meaning of which is unclear.
^f Hebrew has four additional words, the meaning of which is unclear.
^g Verse 30 in Hebrew begins with three words, the meaning of which is unclear.

their swords. [41] They will burn your houses down and let crowds of women see your punishment. I will make you stop being a prostitute and make you stop giving gifts to your lovers. [42] Then my anger will be over, and I will be calm. I will not be angry or jealous any more. [43] You have forgotten how I treated you when you were young, and you have made me angry by all the things you did. That is why I have made you pay for them all. Why did you add sexual immorality to all the other disgusting things you did?" The Sovereign LORD has spoken.

Like Mother, Like Daughter

44 The LORD said, "People will use this proverb about you, Jerusalem: 'Like mother, like daughter.' [45] You really are your mother's daughter. She detested her husband and her children. You are like your sisters, who hated their husbands and their children. You and your sister cities had a Hittite mother and an Amorite [h] father.

46 "Your elder sister is Samaria, in the north, with her villages. Your younger sister, with her villages, is Sodom, in the south. [47] Were you content to follow in their footsteps and copy their disgusting actions? No, in only a little while you were behaving worse than they were in everything you did.

[48] "As sure as I am the living God," the Sovereign LORD says, "your sister Sodom and her villages never did the evil that you and your villages have done. [49] She and her daughters were proud because they had plenty to eat and lived in peace and quiet, but they did not take care of the poor and the underprivileged. [50] They were proud and stubborn and did the things that I hate, so I destroyed them, as you well know.

51 "Samaria did not sin half as much as you have. You have acted more disgustingly than she ever did. Your corruption makes your sisters look innocent by comparison. [52] And now you will have to endure your disgrace. Your sins are so much worse than those of your sisters that they look innocent beside you. Now blush and bear your shame, because you make your sisters look pure."

Sodom and Samaria Will Be Restored

53 The LORD said to Jerusalem, "I will make them prosperous again—Sodom and her villages and Samaria and her villages. Yes, I will make you prosperous too. [54] You will be ashamed of yourself, and your disgrace will show your sisters how well-off they are. [55] They will become prosperous again, and you and your villages will also be restored. [56] Didn't you joke about Sodom in those days when you were proud [57] and before the evil you did had been exposed? Now you are just like her—a joke to the Edomites, the Philistines, and your other neighbours who hate you. [58] You must suffer for the obscene, disgusting things you have done." The LORD has spoken.

A Covenant That Lasts For Ever

59 The Sovereign LORD says, "I will treat you as you deserve, because you ignored your promises and broke the covenant. [60] But I will honour the covenant I made with you when you were young, and I will make a covenant with you that will last for ever. [61] You will remember how you have acted, and be ashamed of it when you get your elder sister and your younger sister back. I will let them be like daughters to you, even though this was not part of my covenant with you. [62] I will renew my covenant with you, and you will know that I am the LORD. [63] I will forgive all the wrongs you have done, but you will remember them and be too ashamed to open your mouth." The Sovereign LORD has spoken.

The Parable of the Eagles and the Vine

17 The LORD spoke to me. [2] "Mortal man," he said, "tell the Israelites a parable [3] to let them know what I, the Sovereign LORD, am saying to them: There was a giant eagle with beautiful feathers and huge wings, spread wide. He flew to the Lebanon Mountains and broke off the top of a cedar-tree, [4] which he carried to a land of commerce, and placed in a city of merchants. [5] Then he took a young plant from the land of Israel and planted it in a fertile field, [i] where there was always water to make it grow. [6] The plant sprouted and became a low, wide-spreading grapevine. The branches grew upward towards the eagle, and the roots grew deep. The vine was covered with branches and leaves.

7 "There was another giant eagle with huge wings and thick plumage. And now the vine sent its roots towards him and

[h] HITTITE...AMORITE: See 16.3.
[i] Hebrew has an additional word, the meaning of which is unclear.

Yes, it is planted, but will it live and grow? (17.10)

turned its leaves towards him, in the hope that he would give it more water than there was in the garden where it was growing.[j] 8 But the vine had already been planted in a fertile, well-watered field so that it could grow leaves and bear grapes and be a magnificent vine.

9 "So I, the Sovereign LORD, ask: Will this vine live and grow? Won't the first eagle pull it up by its roots, pull off the grapes, and break off the branches and let them wither? It will not take much strength or a mighty nation to pull it up. 10 Yes, it is planted, but will it live and grow? Won't it wither when the east wind strikes it? Won't it wither there where it is growing?"

He...broke off the top of a cedar-tree (17.3)

The Parable Is Explained

11 The LORD said to me, 12 "Ask these rebels if they know what the parable means. Tell them that the king of Babylonia came to Jerusalem and took the king and his officials back with him to Babylonia. 13 He took one of the king's family, made a treaty with him, and made him swear to be loyal. He took important men as hostages 14 to keep the nation from rising again and to make sure that the treaty would be kept. 15 But the king of Judah rebelled and sent agents to Egypt to get horses and a large army. Will he succeed? Can he get away with that? He cannot break the treaty and go unpunished!

16 "As surely as I am the living God," says the Sovereign LORD, "this king will die in Babylonia because he broke his oath and the treaty he had made with the king of Babylonia, who put him on the throne. 17 Even the powerful army of the king of Egypt will not be able to help him fight when the Babylonians build earthworks and dig trenches in order to kill many people. 18 He broke his oath and the treaty he had made. He did all these things, and now he will not escape."

19 The Sovereign LORD says, "As surely as I am the living God, I will punish him for breaking the treaty which he swore in my name to keep. 20 I will spread out a hunter's net and catch him in it. I will take him to Babylonia and punish him there, because he was unfaithful to me. 21 His best soldiers will be killed in battle, and the survivors will be scattered in

[j] And now the vine...growing; *or* And now the vine turned away from the garden where it was growing and sent its roots towards him and turned its leaves towards him, in the hope that he would give it water.
17.12–15: 2 Kgs 24.15–20; 2 Chr 36.10–13

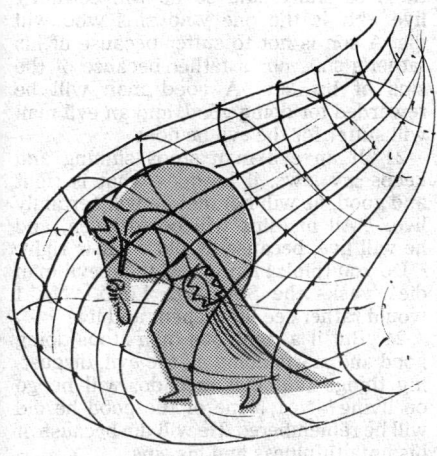

I will spread out a hunter's net and catch him in it (17.20)

every direction. Then you will know that I, the LORD, have spoken."

18.2: Jer 31.29

God's Promise of Hope

22 This is what the Sovereign LORD says:

"I will take the top of a tall cedar
  and break off a tender sprout;
I will plant it on a high mountain,
23 on Israel's highest mountain.
It will grow branches and bear seed
  and become a magnificent cedar.
Birds of every kind will live there
  and find shelter in its shade.
24 All the trees in the land will know
  that I am the LORD.
I cut down the tall trees
  and make the small trees grow tall.
I wither up the green trees
  and make the dry trees become green.
I, the LORD, have spoken. I will do what I have said I would do."

Individual Responsibility

18 The LORD spoke to me ²and said, "What is this proverb people keep repeating in the land of Israel?

'The parents ate the sour grapes,
  But the children got the sour taste.'

3 "As surely as I am the living God," says the Sovereign LORD, "you will not

Birds of every kind will live there (17.23)

repeat this proverb in Israel any more. ⁴The life of every person belongs to me, the life of the parent as well as that of the child. The person who sins is the one who will die.

5 "Suppose there is a truly good man, righteous and honest. He doesn't worship the idols of the Israelites or eat the sacrifices offered at forbidden shrines. He doesn't seduce another man's wife or have intercourse with a woman during her period. ⁷He doesn't cheat or rob anyone. He returns what a borrower gives him as security; he feeds the hungry and gives clothing to the naked. ⁸He doesn't lend money for profit. He refuses to do evil and gives an honest decision in any dispute. ⁹Such a man obeys my commands and carefully keeps my laws. He is righteous, and he will live," says the Sovereign LORD.

10 "Then suppose this man has a son who robs and kills, who does any*k* of these things ¹¹that the father never did. He eats sacrifices offered at forbidden shrines and seduces other men's wives. ¹²He cheats the poor, he robs, he keeps what a borrower gives him as security. He goes to pagan shrines, worships disgusting idols, ¹³and lends money for profit. Will he live? No, he will not. He has done all these disgusting things, and so he will die. He will be to blame for his own death.

14 "Now suppose this second man has a son. He sees all the sins his father practised, but does not follow his example. ¹⁵He doesn't worship the idols of the Israelites or eat the sacrifices offered at forbidden shrines. He doesn't seduce another man's wife ¹⁶or oppress anyone or rob anyone. He returns what a borrower gives him as security. He feeds the hungry and gives clothing to the naked. ¹⁷He refuses to do evil*l* and doesn't lend money for profit. He keeps my laws and obeys my commands. He will not die because of his father's sins, but he will certainly live. ¹⁸His father, on the other hand, cheated and robbed,*m* and always did evil to everyone. And so he died because of the sins he himself had committed.

19 "But you ask:'Why shouldn't the son suffer because of his father's sins?' The answer is that the son did what was right and good. He kept my laws and followed

them carefully, and so he will certainly live. ²⁰It is the one who sins who will die. A son is not to suffer because of his father's sins, nor a father because of the sins of his son. A good man will be rewarded for doing good, and an evil man will suffer for the evil he does.

21 "If an evil man stops sinning and keeps my laws, if he does what is right and good, he will not die; he will certainly live. ²²All his sins will be forgiven, and he will live, because he did what is right. ²³Do you think I enjoy seeing an evil man die?" asks the Sovereign LORD. "No, I would rather see him repent and live.

24 "But if a righteous man stops doing good and starts doing all the evil, disgusting things that evil men do, will he go on living? No! None of the good he did will be remembered. He will die because of his unfaithfulness and his sins.

25 "But you say, 'What the Lord does isn't right.' Listen to me, you Israelites. Do you think my way of doing things isn't right? It is your way that isn't right. ²⁶When a righteous man stops doing good and starts doing evil and then dies, he dies because of the evil he has done. ²⁷When an evil man stops sinning and does what is right and good, he saves his life. ²⁸He realizes what he is doing and stops sinning, so he will certainly not die, but go on living. ²⁹And you Israelites say, 'What the Lord does isn't right.' You think my way isn't right, do you? It is your way that isn't right.

30 "Now I, the Sovereign LORD, am telling you Israelites that I will judge each of you by what he has done. Turn away from all the evil you are doing, and don't let your sin destroy you. ³¹Give up all the evil you have been doing, and get yourselves new minds and hearts. Why do you Israelites want to die? ³²I do not want anyone to die," says the Sovereign LORD. "Turn away from your sins and live."

A Song of Sorrow

19 The LORD told me to sing this song of sorrow for two princes of Israel: ² What a lioness your mother was! She reared her cubs among the fierce male lions. ³ She reared a cub and taught him to hunt;

---

k Some ancient translations who does any; *Hebrew unclear.*
l Some ancient translations (see also v. 8) to do evil; *Hebrew* from the poor.
m Some ancient translations robbed; *Hebrew unclear.*
18.9: Lev 18.5   **18.20:** Deut 24.16

He realizes what he is doing and stops sinning (18.28)

he became a man-eater.
4 The nations heard about him
  and trapped him in a pit.
With hooks they dragged him off to
  Egypt.
5 She waited until she saw all hope was
  gone.
Then she reared another of her cubs,
  and he grew into a fierce lion.
6 When he was full-grown,
  he prowled with the other lions.
He too learnt to hunt and became a
  man-eater.
7 He wrecked forts,^{o} he ruined towns.
The people of the land were terrified
  every time he roared.
8 The nations gathered to fight him;
  people came from everywhere.
They spread their hunting nets
  and caught him in their trap.
9 They put him in a cage
  and took him to the king of Babylonia.
They kept him under guard,
  so that his roar would never be heard
  again
  on the hills of Israel.

10 Your mother was like a grapevine^p
  planted near a stream.

Because there was plenty of water,
  the vine was covered with leaves and
  fruit.
11 Its branches were strong,
  and grew to be royal sceptres.
The vine grew tall enough to reach the
  clouds;
  everyone saw how leafy and tall it
  was.
12 But angry hands pulled it up by the
  roots
  and threw it to the ground.
The east wind dried up its fruit.
Its branches were broken off;
  they dried up and were burnt.
13 Now it is planted in the desert,
  in a dry and waterless land.
14 The stem of the vine caught fire;
  fire burnt up its branches and fruit.
The branches will never again be strong,
  will never be royal sceptres.
This is a song of sorrow; it has been sung
again and again.

The Lord's Will and Man's Defiance

20 It was the tenth day of the fifth
month of the seventh year of our
exile. Some of the leaders of the Israelite
community came to consult me about the

---

^{o} *One ancient translation* wrecked forts; *Hebrew unclear.*
^{p} *Hebrew has an additional word, the meaning of which is unclear.*

LORD's will, and they sat down in front of me. ²Then the LORD spoke to me. ³"Mortal man," he said, "speak to these men and tell them that the Sovereign LORD is saying: You have come to ask my will, have you? As surely as I am the living God, I will not let you ask me anything. I, the Sovereign LORD, have spoken.

4 "Are you ready to pass sentence on them, mortal man? Then do so. Remind them of the disgusting things their fathers did. ⁵Tell them what I am saying. When I chose Israel, I made them a promise. I revealed myself to them in Egypt and told them: I am the LORD your God. ⁶It was then that I promised to take them out of Egypt and lead them to a land I had chosen for them, a rich and fertile land, the finest land of all. ⁷I told them to throw away the disgusting idols they loved and not to make themselves unclean with the false gods of Egypt, because I am the LORD their God. ⁸But they defied me and refused to listen. They did not throw away their disgusting idols or give up the Egyptian gods. I was ready to let them feel the full force of my anger there in Egypt. ⁹But I did not, since that would have brought dishonour to my name, for in the presence of the people among whom they were living I had announced to Israel that I was going to lead them out of Egypt.

10 "And so I led them out of Egypt into the desert. ¹¹I gave them my commands and taught them my laws, which bring life to anyone who obeys them. ¹²I made the keeping of the Sabbath a sign of the agreement between us, to remind them that I, the LORD, make them holy. ¹³But even in the desert they defied me. They broke my laws and rejected my commands, which bring life to anyone who obeys them. They completely profaned the Sabbath. I was ready to let them feel the force of my anger there in the desert and destroy them. ¹⁴But I did not, since that would have brought dishonour to my name among the nations which had seen me lead Israel out of Egypt. ¹⁵So I made a promise in the desert that I would not take them to the land I had given them, a rich and fertile land, the finest land of all. ¹⁶I made the promise because they had rejected my commands, broken my laws, and profaned the Sabbath—they preferred to worship their idols.

17 "But then I took pity on them. I decided not to kill them there in the desert.

I gave them my commands (20.11)

¹⁸Instead, I warned the young people among them: Do not keep the laws your ancestors made; do not follow their customs or defile yourselves with their idols. ¹⁹I am the LORD your God. Obey my laws and my commands. ²⁰Make the Sabbath a holy day, so that it will be a sign of the covenant we made, and will remind you that I am the LORD your God.

21 "But that generation also defied me. They broke my laws and did not keep my commands, which bring life to anyone who obeys them. They profaned the Sabbath. I was ready to let them feel the force of my anger there in the desert and kill them all. ²²But I did not, since that would have brought dishonour to my name among the nations which had seen me bring Israel out of Egypt. ²³So I made another promise in the desert. I vowed that I would scatter them all over the world. ²⁴I did this because they had rejected my commands, broken my laws, profaned the Sabbath, and worshipped the same idols their ancestors had served.

25 "Then I gave them laws that are not good and commands that do not bring life. ²⁶I let them defile themselves with their own offerings, and I let them sacrifice their first-born sons. This was

20.5-6: Ex 6.2-8   20.11, 13: Lev 18.5   20.12: Ex 31.13-17   20.15: Num 14.26-35
20.23: Lev 26.33

to punish them and show them that I am the LORD.

27 "Now then, mortal man, tell the Israelites what I, the Sovereign LORD, am saying to them. This is another way their fathers insulted me by their unfaithfulness. 28 I brought them to the land I had promised to give them. When they saw the high hills and green trees, they offered sacrifices at all of them. They made me angry by the sacrifices they burnt and by the wine they brought as offerings. 29 I asked them: What are these high places where you go? So they have been called 'High Places'q ever since. 30 Now tell the Israelites what I, the Sovereign LORD, am saying: Why must you commit the same sins your fathers did and go running after their idols? 31 Even today you offer the same gifts and defile yourselves with the same idols by sacrificing your children to them in the fire. And then you Israelites still come to ask what my will is! As surely as I, the Sovereign LORD, am the living God, I will not let you ask me anything. 32 You have made up your minds that you want to be like the other nations, like the people who live in other countries and worship trees and rocks. But that will never be.

God Punishes and Forgives

33 "As surely as I, the Sovereign LORD, am the living God, I warn you that in my anger I will rule over you with a strong hand, with all my power. 34 I will show you my power and my anger when I gather you together and bring you back from all the countries where you have been scattered. 35 I will bring you into the 'Desert of the Nations,' and there I will condemn you to your face. 36 I will now condemn you just as I condemned your fathers in the Sinai Desert," says the Sovereign LORD.

37 "I will take firm control of you and make you obey my covenant. 38 I will take away from among you those who are rebellious and sinful. I will take them out of the lands where they are living now, but I will not let them return to the land of Israel. Then you will know that I am the LORD."

39 The Sovereign LORD said, "And now, all you Israelites, please yourselves! Go

on and serve your idols! But I warn you that after this you will have to obey me and stop dishonouring my holy name by offering gifts to your idols. 40 There in the land, on my holy mountain,s the high mountain of Israel, all you people of Israel will worship me. I will be pleased with you and will expect you to bring me your sacrifices, your best offerings, and your holy gifts. 41 After I bring you out of the countries where you have been scattered and gather you together, I will accept the sacrifices that you burn, and the nations will see that I am holy. 42 When I bring you back to Israel, the land that I promised I would give to your ancestors, then you will know that I am the LORD. 43 Then you will remember all the disgraceful things you did and how you defiled yourselves. You will be disgusted with yourselves because of all the evil things you did. 44 When I act to protect my honour, you Israelites will know that I am the LORD, because I do not deal with you as your wicked, evil actions deserve." The Sovereign LORD has spoken.

Fire in the South

45 The LORD spoke to me. 46 "Mortal man," he said, "look towards the south. Speak against the south and prophesy against the forest of the south. 47 Tell the southern forest to hear what the Sovereign LORD is saying: Look! I am starting a fire, and it will burn up every tree in you, whether green or dry. Nothing will be able to put it out. It will spread from south to north, and everyone will feel the heat of the flames. 48 They will all see that I, the LORD, set it on fire and that no one can put it out."

49 But I protested, "Sovereign LORD, don't make me do it! Everyone is already complaining that I always speak in riddles."

The LORD's Sword

21 The LORD spoke to me. 2 "Mortal man," he said, "denounce Jerusalem. Denounce the places where people worship. Warn the land of Israel 3 that I, the LORD, am saying: I am your enemy. I will draw my sword and kill all of you, good and evil alike. 4 I will use my sword against everyone from north to south.

---

q HIGH PLACES: *Pagan places of worship which the Hebrews were forbidden to use. The Hebrew word translated "High Places" sounds like the Hebrew for "where you go."*
s HOLY MOUNTAIN: *Mount Zion, the hill in Jerusalem which formed part of the Temple and palace area.*

5 Everyone will know that I, the LORD, have drawn my sword and that I will not put it away.

6 "Mortal man, groan as if your heart is breaking with despair. Groan in sorrow where everyone can watch you. 7 When they ask you why you are groaning, tell them it is because of the news that is coming. When it comes, their hearts will be filled with fear, their hands will hang limp, their courage will fail, and their knees will tremble. The time has come; it is here." The Sovereign LORD has spoken.

8 The LORD said to me, 9 "Mortal man, prophesy. Tell the people what I, the Lord, am saying:

A sword, a sword is sharpened and
    polished.
10 It is sharpened to kill,
    polished to flash like lightning.
There can be no rejoicing,
    for my people have disregarded every
    warning and punishment. t
11 The sword is being polished,
    to make it ready for use.
It is sharpened and polished,
    to be put in the hands of a killer.
12 Howl in grief, mortal man;
    this sword is meant for my people
    and for all the leaders of Israel.
They are going to be killed
    with all the rest of my people.
Beat your breast in despair!
13 I am testing my people,
    and if they refuse to repent,
    all these things will happen to them. u

14 "Now, mortal man, prophesy. Clap your hands, and the sword will strike again and again. It is a sword that kills, a sword that terrifies v and slaughters. 15 It makes my people lose courage and stumble. I am threatening their city with a sword w that flashes like lightning and is ready to kill. 16 Cut to the right and the left, you sharp sword! Cut wherever you turn. x 17 I also will clap my hands, and my anger will be over. I, the LORD, have spoken."

The Sword of the King of Babylonia

18 The LORD spoke to me. 19 "Mortal

man," he said, "mark out two roads by which the king of Babylonia can come with his sword. Both of them are to start in the same country. Put up a signpost where the roads fork. y 20 One will show the king the way to the Ammonite city of Rabbah, and the other the way to Judah, to the fortified city, Jerusalem. 21 The king of Babylonia stands by the signpost at the fork of the road. To discover which way to go, he shakes the arrows; z he consults his idols; he examines the liver of a sacrificed animal. 22 Now! His right hand holds the arrow marked 'Jerusalem'! It tells him to go and set up battering-rams, to shout the battle-cry, to place battering-rams against the gates, to throw up earthworks, and to dig trenches. 23 The people of Jerusalem won't believe this, because of the treaties they have made. But this prediction is to remind them of their sins and to warn them that they will be captured. 24 This then is what I, the Sovereign LORD, am saying: Your sins are exposed. Everyone knows how guilty you are. You show your sins in your every action. You stand condemned, and I will hand you over to your enemies.

25 "You wicked, unholy ruler of Israel, your day, the day of your final punishment, is coming. 26 I, the Sovereign LORD, have spoken. Take off your crown and your turban. Nothing will be the same again. Raise the poor to power! Bring down those who are ruling! 27 Ruin, ruin! Yes, I will make the city a ruin. But this will not happen until the one whom I have chosen to punish the city has come. Then I will give it to him.

A Sword and the Ammonites

28 "Mortal man, prophesy. Announce what I, the Sovereign LORD, am saying to the Ammonites, who are insulting Israel. Say to them:

'A sword is ready to destroy;
    It is polished to kill, to flash like
    lightning.
29 The visions that you see are false, and the predictions you make are lies. You are wicked and evil, and your day is coming, the day of your final punishment. The sword is going to fall on your necks.

---

t Probable text There...punishment; Hebrew unclear.   u Verse 13 in Hebrew is unclear.
v Some ancient translations terrifies; Hebrew unclear.
w Probable text threatening...sword; Hebrew unclear.   x Verse 16 in Hebrew is unclear.
y Probable text Put...fork; Hebrew unclear.
z SHAKES THE ARROWS: When faced with a decision, people in ancient times would sometimes take a handful of arrows, throw them down, and study the pattern in which they fell, in order to learn what to do.
21.28-32: Jer 49.1-6; Ezek 25.1-7; Amos 1.3-15; Zeph 2.8-11

30 " 'Put up the sword! I will judge you in the place where you were created, in the land where you were born. 31 You will feel my anger when I turn it loose on you like a blazing fire. And I will hand you over to brutal men, experts at destruction. 32 You will be destroyed by fire. Your blood will be shed in your own country, and no one will remember you any more.' " The LORD has spoken.

The Crimes of Jerusalem

22 The LORD spoke to me. 2 "Mortal man," he said, "are you ready to judge the city that is full of murderers? Make clear to her all the disgusting things she has done. 3 Tell the city what I, the Sovereign LORD, am saying: Because you have murdered so many of your own people and have defiled yourself by worshipping idols, your time is coming. 4 You are guilty of those murders and are defiled by the idols you made, and so your day is coming, your time is up! That is why I have let the nations mock you and all the countries sneer at you. 5 Countries near by and countries far away sneer at you because of your lawlessness. 6 All Israel's leaders trust in their own strength and commit murder. 7 No one in the city honours his parents. You cheat foreigners and take advantage of widows and orphans. 8 You have no respect for the holy places, and you don't keep the Sabbath. 9 Some of your people tell lies about others in order to have them put to death. Some of them eat sacrifices offered to idols. Some are always satisfying their lusts. 10 Some of them sleep with their father's wife. Some force women to have intercourse with them during their period. 11 Some commit adultery, and others seduce their daughters-in-law or their half-sisters. 12 Some of your people murder for pay. Some charge interest on the loans they make to their fellow-Israelites and get rich by taking advantage of them. They have forgotten me." The Sovereign LORD has spoken.

13 "I will bring my fist down on your robberies and murders. 14 Do you think you will have any courage left or have strength enough to lift your hand when I am finished with you? I, the LORD, have spoken, and I keep my word. 15 I will scatter your people to every country and nation and will put an end to your evil

actions. 16 And so the other nations will dishonour you, but you will know that I am the LORD."

God's Refining Furnace

17 The LORD said to me, 18 "Mortal man, the Israelites are of no use to me. They are like the waste metal—copper, tin, iron, and lead—left over after silver has been refined in a furnace. 19 So now I, the Sovereign LORD, am telling them that they are just as useless as that. I will bring them all together in Jerusalem 20 in the same way that the ore of silver, copper, iron, lead, and tin is put in a refining furnace. My anger and rage will melt them just as fire melts ore. 21 Yes, I will gather them in Jerusalem, build a fire under them, and melt them with my anger. 22 They will be melted in Jerusalem just as silver is melted in a furnace, and then they will know that they are feeling the anger of the LORD."

The Sins of Israel's Leaders

23 The LORD spoke to me again. 24 "Mortal man," he said, "tell the Israelites that their land is unholy, and so I am punishing it in my anger. 25 The leaders[a] are like lions roaring over the animals they have killed. They kill the people, take all the money and property they can get, and by their murders leave many widows. 26 The priests break my law and have no respect for what is holy. They make no distinction between what is holy and what is not. They do not teach the difference between clean and unclean things, and they ignore the Sabbath. As a result the people of Israel do not respect me. 27 The government officials are like wolves tearing apart the animals they have killed. They commit murder in order to get rich. 28 The prophets have hidden these sins like men covering a wall with whitewash. They see false visions and make false predictions. They claim to speak the word of the Sovereign LORD, but I, the LORD, have not spoken to them. 29 The wealthy cheat and rob. They ill-treat the poor and take advantage of foreigners. 30 I looked for someone who could build a wall, who could stand in the places where the walls have crumbled and defend the land when my anger is about to destroy it, but I could find no one. 31 So I will turn my anger loose on them,

---

a One ancient translation The leaders; *Hebrew* A conspiracy of her prophets.
22.7: Ex 20.12, 22.21–22; Deut 5.16, 24.17   **22.8:** Lev 19.30, 26.2   **22.10–11:** Lev 18.7–20
22.12: Ex 22.25, 23.8; Lev 25.36–37; Deut 16.19, 23.19   **22.26:** Lev 10.10

and like a fire I will destroy them for what they have done." The Sovereign LORD has spoken.

The Sinful Sisters

23 The LORD spoke to me. [2] "Mortal man," he said, "there were once two sisters. [3] When they were young, living in Egypt, they lost their virginity and became prostitutes. [4] The older one was named Oholah[x] (she represents Samaria), and the younger one was named Oholibah[y] (she represents Jerusalem). I married both of them, and they bore me children. [5] Although she was mine, Oholah continued to be a prostitute and was full of lust for her lovers from Assyria. [6] They were soldiers in uniforms of purple, noblemen and high-ranking officers; all of them were handsome young cavalry officers. [7] She was the whore for all the Assyrian officers, and her lust led her to defile herself by worshipping Assyrian idols. [8] She continued what she had begun as a prostitute in Egypt, where she lost her virginity. From the time she was a girl, men slept with her and treated her like a prostitute. [9] So I handed her over to her Assyrian lovers whom she wanted so much. [10] They stripped her naked, seized her sons and daughters, and then killed her with a sword. Women everywhere gossiped about her fate.

[11] "Even though her sister Oholibah saw this, she was wilder and more of a prostitute than Oholah had ever been. [12] She too was full of lust for the Assyrian noblemen and officers—soldiers in bright uniforms—and for the cavalry officers, all those handsome young men. [13] I saw that she was completely immoral, that the second sister was as bad as the first.

[14-15] "She sank deeper and deeper in her immorality. She was attracted by the images of high Babylonian officials carved into the wall and painted bright red, with sashes round their waists and fancy turbans on their heads. [16] As soon as she saw them, she was filled with lust and sent messengers to them in Babylonia. [17] The Babylonians came to have sex with her. They used her and defiled her so much that finally she became disgusted with them. [18] She exposed herself publicly and let everyone know she was a whore. I was as disgusted with her as I had been with her sister. [19] She became more of a prostitute than ever, acting just as she did as a girl, when she was a prostitute in

Egypt. [20] She was filled with lust for oversexed men who had all the lustfulness of donkeys or stallions." [21] (Oholibah, you wanted to repeat the immorality you were guilty of as a girl in Egypt, where men played with your breasts and you lost your virginity.)

God's Judgement on the Younger Sister

22 "Now then, Oholibah, this is what I, the Sovereign LORD, am saying to you. You are tired of those lovers, but I will make them angry with you and bring them to surround you. [23] I will bring all the Babylonians and Chaldeans, men from Pekod, Shoa, and Koa, and all the Assyrians. I will gather all those handsome young noblemen and officers, all those important officials and high-ranking cavalry officers. [24] They will attack you from the north,[b] bringing a large army with chariots and supply wagons. Protected by shields and helmets, they will surround you. I will hand you over to them, and they will judge you by their own laws. [25] Because I am angry with you, I will let them deal with you in their anger. They will cut off your nose and your ears and kill your children. Yes, they will take your sons and daughters from you and burn them alive. [26] They will tear off your clothes and take your jewels. [27] I will put a stop to your lust and to the obscenities you have committed ever since you were in Egypt. You won't look at any more idols or think about Egypt any more."

28 This is what the Sovereign LORD says: "I will hand you over to people you hate and are disgusted with. [29] And because they hate you, they will take away everything you have worked for and leave you stripped naked, exposed like a prostitute. Your lust and your prostitution [30] have brought this on you. You were a prostitute for the nations and defiled yourself with their idols. [31] You followed in your sister's footsteps, and so I will give you the same cup of punishment to drink."

32 The Sovereign LORD says,

"You will drink from your sister's cup;
　　it is large and deep.
Everyone will scorn and mock you;
　　the cup is full.
[33] It will make you miserable and drunk,
　　that cup of fear and ruin,
　　your sister Samaria's cup.
[34] You will drink and drain it dry,
　　and with its broken pieces

---

[x] This name in Hebrew means "her sanctuary".
[y] This name in Hebrew means "my sanctuary is in her".
[b] One ancient translation north; Hebrew unclear.

tear your breast.
I, the Sovereign LORD, have spoken."

35 Now this is what the Sovereign LORD is saying: "Because you forgot me and turned your back on me, you will suffer for your lust and your prostitution."

God's Judgement on Both Sisters

36 The LORD said to me, "Mortal man, are you ready to judge Oholah and Oholibah? Accuse them of the disgusting things they have done. 37 They have committed adultery and murder—adultery with idols and murder of the sons they bore me. They sacrificed my sons to their idols. 38 And that is not all they did. They profaned my Temple and broke the Sabbath, which I had established. 39 The very day that they killed my children as sacrifices to idols, they came to my Temple and profaned it!

40 "Again and again they sent messengers to invite men to come from a great distance, and the men came. The two sisters would bathe and put on eyeshadow and jewellery. 41 They would sit on a beautiful couch, and in front of them they would have a table covered with good things, including the incense and the olive-oil that I had given them. 42 The sound of a carefree crowd could be heard, a group of men brought in from the desert. They put bracelets on the women's arms and beautiful crowns on their heads. 43 And I said to myself that they were using as a prostitute a woman worn out by adultery.c 44 They went back to these prostitutes again and again. They went back to Oholah and Oholibah, those immoral women. 45 Righteous men will condemn them on the charge of adultery and murder, because they practise adultery and their hands are stained with blood."

46 This is what the Sovereign LORD says: "Bring a mob to terrorize them and rob them. 47 Let the mob stone them and attack them with swords, kill their children, and burn down their houses. 48 Throughout the land I will put a stop to immorality, as a warning to every woman not to commit adultery as they did. 49 And you two sisters—I will punish you for your immorality and your sin of worshipping idols. Then you will know that I am the Sovereign LORD."

The Corroded Cooking-Pot

24 On the tenth day of the tenth month of the ninth year of our exile, the LORD spoke to me. 2 "Mortal man," he said, "write down today's date, because this is the day that the king of Babylonia is beginning the siege of Jerusalem. 3 Tell my rebellious people this parable that I, the Sovereign LORD, have for them:

Set the pot on the fire
    and fill it up with water.
4 Put in the best pieces of meat—
    the shoulders and the legs—
    fill it with choice bony pieces too.
5 Use the meat of the finest sheep;
    pile the woodd under the pot.
Let the water boil;
    boil the bones and the meat."

6 This is what the Sovereign LORD is saying: "The city of murderers is doomed! It is like a corroded pot that is never cleaned. Piece after piece of meat is taken out, and not one is left. 7 There was murder in the city, but the blood was not spilt on the ground where the dust could hide it; it was spilt on a bare rock. 8 I have left the blood there, where it cannot be hidden, where it demands angry revenge."

9 This is what the Sovereign LORD is saying: "The city of murderers is doomed! I myself will pile up the firewood. 10 Bring more wood! Fan the flames! Cook the meat! Boil away the broth!e Burn up the bones! 11 Now set the empty bronze pot on the coals and let it get red-hot. Then the pot will be ritually pure again after the corrosion is burnt off, 12 although all that corrosion will not disappear in the flames.f 13 Jerusalem, your immoral actions have defiled you. Although I tried to purify you, you remained defiled. You will not be pure again until you have felt the full force of my anger. 14 I, the Sovereign LORD, have spoken. The time has come for me to act. I will not ignore your sins or show pity or be merciful. You will be punished for what you have done." The Sovereign LORD has spoken.

The Death of the Prophet's Wife

15 The LORD spoke to me. 16 "Mortal man," he said, "with one blow I am going

---

c Verses 42–43 in Hebrew are unclear.   d Probable text wood; Hebrew bones.
e Some ancient translations Boil away the broth; Hebrew unclear.
f Verse 12 in Hebrew begins with two words, the meaning of which is unclear.
24.2: 2 Kgs 25.1; Jer 52.4

Set the pot on the fire (24.3)

to take away the person you love most. You are not to complain or cry or shed any tears. ¹⁷ Don't let your sobbing be heard. Do not go bareheaded or barefoot as a sign of mourning. Don't cover your face or eat the food that mourners eat."

18 Early in the day I was talking with the people. That evening my wife died, and the next day I did as I had been told. ¹⁹ The people asked me, "Why are you acting like this?"

20 So I said to them, "The LORD spoke to me and told me ²¹ to give you Israelites this message: You are proud of the strength of the Temple. You like to look at it and to visit it, but the LORD is going to profane it. And the younger members of your families who are left in Jerusalem will be killed in war. ²² Then you will do what I have done. You will not cover your faces or eat the food that mourners eat. ²³ You will not go bareheaded or barefoot or mourn or cry. You will waste away because of your sins, and you will groan to one another. ²⁴ Then I will be a sign to you; you will do everything I have done. The LORD says that when this happens, you will know that he is the Sovereign LORD."

25 The LORD said, "Now, mortal man, I will take away from them the strong Temple that was their pride and joy, which they liked to look at and to visit. And I will take away their sons and daughters. ²⁶ On the day that I do this, someone who escapes the destruction will come and tell you about it. ²⁷ That same day you will get back the power of speech which you had lost, and you will talk with him. In this way you will be a sign to the people, and they will know that I am the LORD."

Prophecy against Ammon

25 The LORD spoke to me. ² "Mortal man," he said, "denounce the country of Ammon. ³ Tell them to listen to what I, the Sovereign LORD, am saying: You were delighted to see my Temple profaned, to see the land of Israel devastated, to see the people of Judah go into exile. ⁴ Because you were glad, I will let the tribes from the eastern desert conquer you. They will set up their camps in your country and settle there. They will eat the fruit and drink the milk that should have been yours. ⁵ I will turn the city of Rabbah into a place to keep camels, and the whole country of Ammon into a place to keep sheep, so that you will know that I am the LORD.

6 "This is what the Sovereign LORD is saying: You clapped your hands and jumped for joy. You despised the land of Israel. ⁷ Because you did, I will hand you over to other nations who will rob you and plunder you. I will destroy you so completely that you will not be a nation

25.1-7: Jer 49.1-6; Ezek 21.28-32; Amos 1.13-15; Zeph 2.8-11

any more or have a country of your own. Then you will know that I am the LORD."

Prophecy against Moab

8 The Sovereign LORD said, "Because Moab[g] has said that Judah is like all the other nations, 9 I will let the cities that defend the border of Moab be attacked, including even the finest cities—Beth Jeshimoth, Baal Meon, and Kiriathaim. 10 I will let the tribes of the eastern desert conquer Moab, together with Ammon, so that Moab[h] will no longer be a nation. 11 I will punish Moab, and they will know that I am the LORD."

Prophecy against Edom

12 The Sovereign LORD said, "The people of Edom took cruel revenge on Judah, and that revenge has brought lasting guilt on Edom. 13 Now I announce that I will punish Edom and kill every man and animal there. I will make it a waste, from the city of Teman to the city of Dedan, and the people will be killed in battle. 14 My people Israel will take revenge on Edom for me, and they will make Edom feel my furious anger. Edom will know what it means to be the object of my revenge." The Sovereign LORD has spoken.

Prophecy against Philistia

15 The Sovereign LORD said, "The Philistines have taken cruel revenge on their age-long enemies and destroyed them in their hate. 16 And so I am announcing that I will attack the Philistines and wipe them out. I will destroy everyone left living there on the Philistine Plain. 17 I will punish them severely and take full revenge on them. They will feel my anger. Then they will know that I am the LORD."

Prophecy against Tyre

26 On the first day of the ... month[i] of the eleventh year of our exile, the LORD spoke to me. 2 "Mortal man," he said, "this is what the people in the city of Tyre are cheering about. They shout, 'Jerusalem is shattered! Her

commercial power is gone! She won't be our rival any more!'

3 "Now then, this is what I, the Sovereign LORD, am saying: I am your enemy, city of Tyre. I will bring many nations to attack you, and they will come like the waves of the sea. 4 They will destroy your city walls and tear down your towers. Then I will sweep away all the dust and leave only a bare rock. 5 Fishermen will dry their nets on it, there where it stands in the sea. I, the Sovereign LORD, have spoken. The nations will plunder Tyre, 6 and with their swords they will kill those who live in her towns on the mainland. Then Tyre will know that I am the LORD."

7 The Sovereign LORD says, "I am going to bring the greatest king of all—King Nebuchadnezzar of Babylonia—to attack Tyre. He will come from the north with a huge army, with horses and chariots and with cavalry. 8 Those who live in the towns on the mainland will be killed in the fighting. The enemy will dig trenches, build earthworks, and make a solid wall of shields against you. 9 They will pound in your walls with battering-rams and tear down your towers with iron bars. 10 The clouds of dust raised by their horses will cover you. The noise of their horses pulling wagons and chariots will shake your walls as they pass through the gates of the ruined city. 11 Their horsemen will storm through your streets, killing your people with their swords. Your mighty pillars will be thrown to the ground. 12 Your enemies will help themselves to your wealth and merchandise. They will pull down your walls and shatter your luxurious houses. They will take the stones and wood and all the rubble, and dump them into the sea. 13 I will put an end to all your songs, and I will silence the music of your harps. 14 I will leave only a bare rock where fishermen can dry their nets. The city will never be rebuilt. I, the Sovereign LORD, have spoken."

15 The Sovereign LORD has this to say to the city of Tyre: "When you are being conquered, the people who live along the coast will be terrified at the screams of

---

g Some ancient translations Moab; Hebrew Moab and Seir.
h Probable text Moab; Hebrew Ammon.
i month; the Hebrew text does not specify the month.
25.8-11: Is 15.1—16.14, 25.10-12; Jer 48.1-47; Amos 2.1-3; Zeph 2.8-11
25.12-14: Is 34.5-17, 63.1-6; Jer 49.7-22; Ezek 35.1-15; Amos 1.11-12; Obad 1-14; Mal 1.2-5
25.15-17: Is 14.29-31; Jer 47.1-7; Joel 3.4-8; Amos 1.6-8; Zeph 2.4-7; Zech 9.5-7
26.1-28.19: Is 23.1-18; Joel 3.4-8; Amos 1.9-10; Zech 9.1-4; Mt 11.21-22; Lk 10.13-14
26.13: Rev 18.22

That city which stands at the edge of the sea (27.3)

those who are slaughtered. ¹⁶ All the kings of the seafaring nations will come down from their thrones. They will take off their robes and their embroidered clothes and sit trembling on the ground. They will be so terrified at your fate that they will not be able to stop trembling. ¹⁷ They will sing this funeral song for you:

The famous city is destroyed!
Her ships have been swept*ʲ* from the
     seas.
The people of this city ruled the seas
And terrified all who lived on the coast.
¹⁸ Now, on the day it has fallen,
The islands are trembling,
And their people are shocked at such
     destruction."

19 The Sovereign LORD says: "I will make you as desolate as ruined cities where no one lives. I will cover you with the water of the ocean depths. ²⁰ I will send you down to the world of the dead to join the people who lived in ancient times. I will make you stay in that underground world among eternal ruins, keeping company with the dead. As a result you will never again be inhabited and take your place*ˡ* in the land of the living. ²¹ I will make you a terrifying example, and that will be the end of you. People may look for you, but you will

never be found." The Sovereign LORD has spoken.

A Funeral Song for Tyre

27 The LORD said to me, ²"Mortal man, sing a funeral song for Tyre, ³ that city which stands at the edge of the sea and does business with the people living on every seacoast. Tell her what the Sovereign LORD is saying:

Tyre, you boasted of your perfect
     beauty.
⁴ Your home is the sea.
Your builders made you like a beautiful
     ship;
⁵ They used fir-trees from Mount Hermon
     for timber
And a cedar from Lebanon for your
     mast.
⁶ They took oak-trees from Bashan to
     make oars;
They made your deck out of pine from
     Cyprus
And inlaid it with ivory.
⁷ Your sails were made of linen,
Embroidered linen from Egypt,
Easily recognized from afar.
Your awnings were made of finest cloth,
Of purple from the island of Cyprus.
⁸ Your oarsmen were from the cities of
     Sidon and Arvad.
Your own skilful men were the sailors.

ʲ Some ancient translations swept; *Hebrew* inhabited.
ˡ One ancient translation and take your place; *Hebrew unclear.*
26.16–18: Rev 18.9–10   **26.21:** Rev 18.21

⁹ The ship's carpenters
Were well-trained men from Byblos.
Sailors from every sea-going ship
Did business in your shops.

10 "Soldiers from Persia, Lydia, and Libya served in your army. They hung their shields and their helmets in your barracks. They are the men who won glory for you. ¹¹ Soldiers from Arvad guarded your walls, and men from Gamad guarded your towers. They hung their shields on your walls. They are the men who made you beautiful.

12 "You did business in Spain and took silver, iron, tin, and lead in payment for your abundant goods. ¹³ You did business in Greece, Tubal, and Meshech and traded your goods for slaves and for articles of bronze. ¹⁴ You sold your goods for draught-horses, war-horses, and mules from Beth Togarmah. ¹⁵ The people of Rhodes ᵐ traded with you; people of many coastal lands gave you ivory and ebony in exchange for your goods. ¹⁶ The people of Syria bought your merchandise and your many products. They gave emeralds, purple cloth, embroidery, fine linen, coral, and rubies in payment for your wares. ¹⁷ Judah and Israel paid for your goods with wheat, ⁿ honey, olive-oil, and spices. ¹⁸⁻¹⁹ The people of Damascus bought your merchandise and your products, paying for them with wine from Helbon and wool from Sahar. ᵒ They exchanged wrought iron and spices for your goods. ²⁰ The people of Dedan exchanged saddle-cloths for your goods. ²¹ The Arabians and the rulers of the land of Kedar paid for your merchandise with lambs, sheep, and goats. ²² For your goods the merchants of Sheba and Raamah exchanged jewels, gold, and the finest spices. ²³ The cities of Haran, Canneh, and Eden, the merchants of Sheba, the cities of Asshur and Chilmad—they all traded with you. ²⁴ They sold you luxurious clothing, purple cloth, and embroidery, brightly coloured carpets, and well-made cords and ropes. ²⁵ Your merchandise was carried in fleets of the largest cargo ships.

You were like a ship at sea
Loaded with heavy cargo.
²⁶ When your oarsmen brought you out
   to sea,
An east wind wrecked you far from land.
²⁷ All your wealth of merchandise,

All the sailors in your crew,
Your ship's carpenters and your
   merchants,
Every soldier on board the ship—
All, all were lost at sea
When your ship was wrecked.
²⁸ The shouts of the drowning sailors
Echoed on the shore.

²⁹ "Every ship is now deserted,
And every sailor has gone ashore.
³⁰ They all mourn bitterly for you,
Throwing dust on their heads and
   rolling in ashes.
³¹ They shave their heads for you
And dress themselves in sackcloth.
Their hearts are bitter as they weep.
³² They chant a funeral song for you:
'Who can be compared to Tyre,
To Tyre now silent in the sea?
³³ When your merchandise went
   overseas,
You filled the needs of every nation.
Kings were made rich
By the wealth of your goods.
³⁴ Now you are wrecked in the sea;
You have sunk to the ocean depths.
Your goods and all who worked for you
Have vanished with you in the sea.'

35 "Everyone who lives along the coast is shocked at your fate. Even their kings are terrified, and fear is written on their faces. ³⁶ You are gone, gone for ever, and merchants all over the world are terrified, afraid that they will share your fate."

Prophecy against the King of Tyre

28 The LORD spoke to me. ² "Mortal man," he said, "tell the ruler of Tyre what I, the Sovereign LORD, am saying to him: Puffed up with pride, you claim to be a god. You say that like a god you sit on a throne, surrounded by the seas. You may pretend to be a god, but, no, you are mortal, not divine. ³ You think you are wiser than Danel, ᵖ that no secret can be kept from you. ⁴ Your wisdom and skill made you rich with treasures of gold and silver. ⁵ You made clever business deals and kept on making profits. How proud you are of your wealth!

6 "Now then, this is what I, the Sovereign LORD, am saying: Because you think you are as wise as a god, ⁷ I will bring ruthless enemies to attack you. They

---

ᵐ One ancient translation Rhodes; Hebrew Dedan.
ⁿ Hebrew has two additional words, the meaning of which is unclear.
ᵒ Hebrew has three additional words, the meaning of which is unclear.
ᵖ Danel; or Daniel (see 14.14).
27.25–36: Rev 18.11–19

will destroy all the beautiful things you have acquired by your skill and wisdom. 8 They will kill you and send you to a watery grave. 9 When they come to kill you, will you still claim that you are a god? When you face your murderers, you will be mortal and not at all divine. 10 You will die like a dog at the hand of godless foreigners. I, the Sovereign LORD, have given the command."

The Fall of the King of Tyre

11 The LORD spoke to me again. 12 "Mortal man," he said, "grieve for the fate that is waiting for the king of Tyre. Tell him what I, the Sovereign LORD, am saying: You were once an example of perfection. How wise and handsome you were! 13 You lived in Eden, the garden of God, and wore gems of every kind: rubies and diamonds; topaz, beryl, carnelian, and jasper; sapphires, emeralds, and garnets. You had ornaments of gold. They were made for you q on the day you were created. 14 I put a terrifying angel there to guard you. r You lived on my holy mountain and walked among sparkling gems. 15 Your conduct was perfect from the day you were created until you began to do evil. 16 You were busy buying and selling, and this led you to violence and sin. So I forced you to leave my holy mountain, and the angel who guarded you drove you away from the sparkling gems. 17 You were proud of being handsome, and your fame made you act like a fool. Because of this I hurled you to the ground and left you as a warning to other kings. 18 You did such evil in buying and selling that your places of worship were corrupted. So I set fire to the city and burnt it to the ground. All who look at you now see you reduced to ashes. 19 You are gone, gone for ever, and all the nations that had come to know you are terrified, afraid that they will share your fate."

Prophecy against Sidon

20 The LORD said to me, 21 "Mortal man, denounce the city of Sidon. 22 Tell the people there what I, the Sovereign LORD, say about them: I am your enemy, Sidon; people will praise me because of what I do to you. They will know that I am the LORD, when I show how holy I am

by punishing those who live in you. 23 I will send diseases on you and make blood flow in your streets. You will be attacked from every side, and your people will be killed. Then you will know that I am the LORD."

Israel Will Be Blessed

24 The LORD said, "None of the surrounding nations that treated Israel with scorn will ever again be like thorns and briars to hurt Israel. And they will know that I am the Sovereign LORD."

25 The Sovereign LORD said, "I will bring back the people of Israel from the nations where I scattered them, and all the nations will know that I am holy. The people of Israel will live in their own land, the land that I gave to my servant Jacob. 26 They will live there in safety. They will build houses and plant vineyards. I will punish all their neighbours who treated them with scorn, and Israel will be secure. Then they will know that I am the LORD their God."

Prophecy against Egypt

29 On the twelfth day of the tenth month of the tenth year of our exile, the LORD spoke to me. 2 "Mortal man," he said, "denounce the king of Egypt. Tell him how he and all the land of Egypt will be punished. 3 Say that this is what the Sovereign LORD is telling the king of Egypt: I am your enemy, you monster crocodile, lying in the river. You say that the Nile is yours and that you made it. s 4 I am going to put a hook through your jaw and make the fish in your river stick fast to you. Then I will pull you up out of the Nile, with all the fish sticking to you. 5 I will throw you and all those fish into the desert. Your body will fall on the ground and be left unburied. I will give it to the birds and animals for food. 6 Then all the people of Egypt will know that I am the LORD."

The LORD says, "The Israelites relied on you Egyptians for support, but you were no better than a weak stick. 7 When they leaned on you, you broke, pierced their armpits, and made them wrench their backs. t 8 Now then, I, the Sovereign LORD, am telling you that I will get men to attack you with swords, and they will

---

q Probable text They were made for you; Hebrew unclear.
r One ancient translation I put...you; Hebrew unclear.
s Some ancient translations you made it; Hebrew you made yourself.
t One ancient translation wrench their backs; Hebrew make their backs stand.
28.20-26: Joel 3.4-8; Zech 9.1-2; Mt 11.21-22; Lk 10.13-14
29.1-32.32: Is 19.1-25; Jer 46.2-26   **29.6:** Is 36.6

I will pull you up out of the Nile (29.4)

kill your people and your animals. ⁹Egypt will become an empty waste. Then you will know that I am the LORD.

"Because you said that the Nile is yours and you made it, ¹⁰I am your enemy and the enemy of your Nile. I will make all of Egypt an empty waste, from the city of Migdol in the north to the city of Aswan in the south, all the way to the Sudanese border. ¹¹No human being or animal will walk through it. For forty years nothing will live there. ¹²I will make Egypt the most desolate country in the world. For forty years the cities of Egypt will lie in ruins, ruins worse than those of any other city. I will make the Egyptians refugees. They will flee to every country and live among other peoples."

13 The Sovereign LORD says, "After forty years I will bring the Egyptians back from the nations where I have scattered them, ¹⁴and I will let them live in southern Egypt, their original home. There they will be a weak kingdom, ¹⁵the weakest kingdom of all, and they will never again rule over other nations. I will make them so unimportant that they will not be able to bend any other nation to their will. ¹⁶Israel will never again depend on them for help. Egypt's fate will remind Israel how wrong it was to rely on them. Then Israel will know that I am the Sovereign LORD."

King Nebuchadnezzar Will Conquer Egypt

17 On the first day of the first month of the twenty-seventh year of our exile, the LORD spoke to me. ¹⁸"Mortal man," he said, "King Nebuchadnezzar of Babylonia launched an attack on Tyre. He made his soldiers carry such heavy loads that their heads were rubbed bald and their shoulders were worn raw, but neither the

king nor his army got anything for all their trouble. ¹⁹So now this is what I, the Sovereign LORD, am saying: I am giving the land of Egypt to King Nebuchadnezzar. He will loot and plunder it and carry off all the wealth of Egypt as his army's pay. ²⁰I am giving him Egypt in payment for his services, because his army was working for me. I, the Sovereign LORD, have spoken.

21 "When that happens, I will make the people of Israel strong and let you, Ezekiel, speak out where everyone can hear you, so that they will know that I am the LORD."

The LORD Will Punish Egypt

30 The LORD spoke again. ²"Mortal man," he said, "prophesy and announce what I, the Sovereign LORD, am saying. You are to shout these words:

A day of terror is coming!
³ The day is near, the day when the LORD
    will act,
A day of clouds and trouble for the
    nations.
⁴ There will be war in Egypt
And great distress in Sudan.
Many in Egypt will be killed;
The country will be plundered
And left in ruins.
5 "That war will also kill the soldiers hired from Sudan, Lydia, Libya, Arabia, Kub, and even from among my own people."

6 The LORD says, "From Migdol in the north to Aswan in the south, all Egypt's defenders will be killed in battle. Egypt's proud army will be destroyed. I, the Sovereign LORD, have spoken. ⁷The land will be the most desolate in the world, and its cities will be left totally in ruins. ⁸When I set fire to Egypt and all her defenders

are killed, then they will know that I am the LORD.

9 "When that day comes and Egypt is destroyed, I will send messengers in ships to arouse the unsuspecting people of Sudan, and they will be terrified. That day is coming!"

10 The Sovereign LORD says, "I will use King Nebuchadnezzar of Babylonia to put an end to Egypt's wealth. 11 He and his ruthless army will come to devastate the land. They will attack Egypt with swords, and the land will be full of corpses. 12 I will dry up the Nile and put Egypt under the power of evil men. Foreigners will devastate the whole country. I, the LORD, have spoken."

13 The Sovereign LORD says, "I will destroy the idols and the false gods in Memphis. There will be no one to rule over Egypt, and I will terrify all the people. 14 I will make southern Egypt desolate and set fire to the city of Zoan in the north. I will punish the capital city of Thebes. 15 I will let the city of Pelusium, Egypt's great fortress, feel my fury. I will destroy the wealth of Thebes. 16 I will set fire to Egypt, and Pelusium will be in agony. The walls of Thebes will be broken down, and the city will be flooded. u 17 The young men of the cities of Heliopolis and Bubastis will die in the war, and the other people will be taken prisoner. 18 Darkness will fall on Tahpanhes when I break the power of Egypt and put an end to the strength they were so proud of. A cloud will cover Egypt, and the people of all her cities will be taken prisoner. 19 When I punish Egypt in this way, they will know that I am the LORD."

The Broken Power of the King of Egypt

20 On the seventh day of the first month of the eleventh year of our exile, the LORD spoke to me. 21 "Mortal man," he said, "I have broken the arm of the king of Egypt. No one has bandaged it or put it in a sling so that it could heal and be strong enough to hold a sword again. 22 Now then, this is what I, the Sovereign LORD, say: I am the enemy of the king of Egypt. I am going to break both his arms—the good one and the one already broken—and the sword will fall from his hand. 23 I am going to scatter the Egyptians throughout the world. 24 Then I will make the arms of the king of Babylonia

strong and put my sword in his hands. But I will break the arms of the king of Egypt, and he will groan and die in front of his enemy. 25 Yes, I will weaken him and strengthen the king of Babylonia. When I give him my sword and he points it towards Egypt, everyone will know that I am the LORD. 26 I will scatter the Egyptians throughout the world. Then they will know that I am the LORD."

Egypt Is Compared to a Cedar Tree

31 On the first day of the third month of the eleventh year of our exile, the LORD spoke to me. 2 "Mortal man," he said, "say to the king of Egypt and all his people:

How powerful you are!
What can I compare you to?
3 You are like v a cedar in Lebanon,
With beautiful, shady branches,
A tree so tall it reaches the clouds. w
4 There was water to make it grow,
And underground rivers to feed it.
They watered the place where the tree was growing
And sent streams to all the trees of the forest.
5 Because it was well-watered,
It grew taller than other trees.
Its branches grew thick and long.
6 Every kind of bird built nests in its branches;
The wild animals bore their young in its shelter;
The nations of the world rested in its shade.
7 How beautiful the tree was—
So tall, with such long branches.
Its roots reached down to the deep-flowing streams.
8 No cedar in God's garden could compare with it.
No fir-tree ever had such branches,
And no plane-tree such boughs.
No tree in God's own garden was so beautiful.
9 I made it beautiful, with spreading branches.
It was the envy of every tree in Eden, the garden of God.

10 "Now then, I, the Sovereign LORD, will tell you what is going to happen to that tree that grew until it reached the clouds. w As it grew taller it grew proud; 11 so I have rejected it and will let a foreign

---

u One ancient translation flooded; Hebrew unclear.
v Probable text You are like; Hebrew Assyria is.
w One ancient translation clouds; Hebrew thick branches.
31.8: Gen 2.9

No tree...will grow as tall as that again (31.14)

ruler have it. He will give that tree what it deserves for its wickedness. ¹²Ruthless foreigners will cut it down and leave it. Its branches and broken boughs will fall on every mountain and valley in the country. All the nations that have been living in its shade will go away. ¹³The birds will come and perch on the fallen tree, and the wild animals will walk over its branches. ¹⁴And so from now on, no tree, no matter how well-watered it is, will grow as tall as that again or push its top through the clouds*ˣ* and reach such a height. All of them are doomed to die like mortal men, doomed to join those who go down to the world of the dead."

15 This is what the Sovereign Lᴏʀᴅ says: "On the day when the tree goes to the world of the dead, I will make the underground waters cover it as a sign of mourning. I will hold back the rivers and not let the many streams flow out. Because the tree has died, I will bring darkness over the Lebanon Mountains and make all the trees of the forest wither. ¹⁶When I send it down to the world of the dead, the noise of its downfall will shake the nations. All the trees of Eden and all the choice, well-watered trees of Lebanon who have gone to the world below will be pleased at its downfall. ¹⁷They will go with it to the world of the dead to join those that have already fallen. And all who live under its shadow will be scattered among the nations.*ʸ*

18 "The tree is the king of Egypt and all his people. Not even the trees in Eden were so tall and impressive. But now, like the trees of Eden, it will go down to the world of the dead and join the ungodly and those killed in battle. I have spoken," says the Sovereign Lᴏʀᴅ.

The King of Egypt Is Compared to a Crocodile

32 On the first day of the twelfth month of the twelfth year of our exile, the Lᴏʀᴅ spoke to me. ²"Mortal man," he said, "give a solemn warning to the king of Egypt. Give him this message from me: You act like a lion among the nations, but you are more like a crocodile splashing through a river. You muddy the water with your feet and pollute the rivers. ³When many nations gather, I will catch you in my net and let them drag the net ashore. ⁴I will throw you out on the ground and bring all the birds and animals of the world to feed on you. ⁵I will cover mountains and valleys with your rotting corpse. ⁶I will pour out your blood until it spreads over the mountains and fills the streams. ⁷When I destroy you, I will cover the sky and blot out the stars. The sun will hide behind the clouds, and the moon will give no light. ⁸I will put out all the lights of heaven and plunge your world into darkness. I, the Sovereign Lᴏʀᴅ, have spoken.

9 "Many nations will be troubled when I spread the news of your destruction through countries you never heard of. ¹⁰What I do to you will shock many nations. When I swing my sword, kings will shudder with fright. On the day you fall, all of them will tremble in fear for their own lives."

11 The Sovereign Lᴏʀᴅ says to the king of Egypt, "You will face the sword of the king of Babylonia. ¹²I will let soldiers from cruel nations draw their swords and kill all your people. All your people and everything else that you are proud of will be destroyed. ¹³I will slaughter your cattle

ˣclouds; see 31.3   *ʸProbable text And all...nations; Hebrew unclear.*
32.7: Is 13.10; Mt 24.29; Mk 13.24–25; Lk 21.25; Rev 6.12–13, 8.12

at every water-hole. There will be no people or cattle to muddy the water any more. [14] I will let your waters settle and become clear and let your rivers run calm. I, the Sovereign LORD, have spoken. [15] When I make Egypt a desolate waste and destroy all who live there, they will know that I am the LORD. [16] This solemn warning will become a funeral song. The women of the nations will sing it to mourn for Egypt and all its people. I, the Sovereign LORD, have spoken."

The World of the Dead

[17] On the fifteenth day of the first month[z] of the twelfth year of our exile, the LORD spoke to me. [18] "Mortal man," he said, "mourn for all the many people of Egypt. Send them down with the other powerful nations to the world of the dead. [19] Say to them:

"Do you think you are more beautiful than anyone else?
You will go down to the world of the dead
and lie there among the ungodly.

[20] "The people of Egypt will fall with those who are killed in battle. A sword is ready to kill them all.[a] [21] The greatest heroes and those who fought on the Egyptian side welcome the Egyptians to the world of the dead. They shout: 'The ungodly who were killed in battle have come down here, and here they lie!'

[22] "Assyria is there, with the graves of her soldiers all around. They were all killed in battle, [23] and their graves are in the deepest parts of the world of the dead. All her soldiers fell in battle, and their graves surround her tomb. Yet once they terrified the land of the living.

[24] "Elam is there, with the graves of her soldiers all around. They were all killed in battle, and they went down, uncircumcised, to the world of the dead. In life they spread terror, but now they lie dead and disgraced. [25] Elam lies down among those killed in battle, and the graves of her soldiers are all around her. They are all uncircumcised, all killed in battle. In life they spread terror, but now they lie dead and disgraced, sharing the fate of those killed in battle.

[26] "Meshech and Tubal are there, with the graves of their soldiers all around. They are all uncircumcised, all killed in battle. Yet once they terrified the living. [27] They were not given honourable burial like the heroes of ancient times,[b] who went fully armed to the world of the dead, their swords placed under their heads and their shields[c] over their bodies. These heroes were once powerful enough to terrify the living.

[28] "That is how the Egyptians will lie crushed among the uncircumcised who were killed in battle.

[29] "Edom is there with her kings and rulers. They were powerful soldiers, but now they lie in the world of the dead with the uncircumcised who were killed in battle.

[30] "All the princes of the north are there, and so are the Sidonians. Their power once spread terror, but now they go down in disgrace with those killed in battle and are laid to rest, uncircumcised. They share the disgrace of those who go down to the world of the dead.

[31] "The sight of all these who were killed in battle will be a comfort to the king of Egypt and his army," says the Sovereign LORD.

[32] "I made the king of Egypt terrorize the living, but he and all his army will be killed and laid to rest with all the uncircumcised who die in battle." The Sovereign LORD has spoken.

God Appoints Ezekiel as a Watchman
(Ezek 3.16-21)

33 The LORD spoke to me. [2] "Mortal man," he said, "tell your people what happens when I bring war to a land. The people of that country choose one of their number to be a watchman. [3] When he sees the enemy approaching, he sounds the alarm to warn everyone. [4] If someone hears it but pays no attention and the enemy comes and kills him, then he is to blame for his own death. [5] His death is his own fault, because he paid no attention to the warning. If he had paid attention, he could have escaped. [6] If, however, the watchman sees the enemy coming and does not sound the alarm, the enemy will come and kill those sinners, but I will hold the watchman responsible for their death.

[7] "Now, mortal man, I am making you a watchman for the nation of Israel. You must pass on to them the warnings I give

---

[z] One ancient translation of the first month; Hebrew does not have these words.
[a] Probable text A sword...all; Hebrew unclear.
[b] Some ancient translations of ancient times; Hebrew of the uncircumcised.
[c] Probable text shields; Hebrew iniquities.

you. [8] If I announce that an evil man is going to die but you do not warn him to change his ways so that he can save his life, then he will die, still a sinner, and I will hold you responsible for his death. [9] If you do warn an evil man and he doesn't stop sinning, he will die, still a sinner, but your life will be spared."

Individual Responsibility

10 The LORD spoke to me. "Mortal man," he said, "repeat to the Israelites what they are saying: 'We are burdened with our sins and the wrongs we have done. We are wasting away. How can we live?' [11] Tell them that as surely as I, the Sovereign LORD, am the living God, I do not enjoy seeing a sinner die. I would rather see him stop sinning and live. Israel, stop the evil you are doing. Why do you want to die?

12 "Now, mortal man, tell the Israelites that when a good man sins, the good he has done will not save him. If an evil man stops doing evil, he won't be punished, and if a good man starts sinning, his life will not be spared. [13] I may promise life to a good man, but if he starts thinking that his past goodness is enough and begins to sin, I will not remember any of the good he did. He will die because of his sins. [14] I may warn an evil man that he is going to die, but if he stops sinning and does what is right and good— [15] for example, if he returns the security he took for a loan or gives back what he stole—if he stops sinning and follows the laws that give life, he will not die, but live. [16] I will forgive the sins he has committed, and he will live because he has done what is right and good.

17 "And your people say that what I do isn't right! No, it's their way that isn't right. [18] When a righteous man stops doing good and starts doing evil, he will die for it. [19] When an evil man gives up sinning and does what is right and good, he has saved his life. [20] But Israel, you say that what I do isn't right. I am going to judge you by what you do."

The News of Jerusalem's Fall

21 On the fifth day of the tenth month of the twelfth year of our exile, a man who had escaped from Jerusalem came and told me that the city had fallen. [22] The evening before he came, I had felt the powerful presence of the LORD. When the

33.21: 2 Kgs 25.3–10; Jer 39.2–8, 52.4–14

man arrived the next morning, the LORD gave me back the power of speech.

The Sins of the People

23 The LORD spoke to me. [24] "Mortal man," he said, "the people who are living in the ruined cities of the land of Israel are saying: 'Abraham was only one man, and he was given the whole land. There are many of us, so now the land is ours.'

25 "Tell them what I, the Sovereign LORD, am saying: You eat meat with the blood still in it. You worship idols. You commit murder. What makes you think that the land belongs to you? [26] You rely on your swords. Your actions are disgusting. Everyone commits adultery. What makes you think that the land is yours?

27 "Tell them that I, the Sovereign LORD, warn them that as surely as I am the living God, the people who live in the ruined cities will be killed. Those living in the country will be eaten by wild animals. Those hiding in the mountains and in caves will die of disease. [28] I will make the country a desolate waste, and the power they were so proud of will come to an end. The mountains of Israel will be so wild that no one will be able to travel through them. [29] When I punish the people for their sins and make the country a waste, then they will know that I am the LORD."

The Results of the Prophet's Message

30 The LORD said, "Mortal man, your people are talking about you when they meet by the city walls or in the doorways of their houses. They say to one another, 'Let's go and hear what word has come from the LORD now.' [31] So my people crowd in to hear what you have to say, but they don't do what you tell them to do. Loving words are on their lips, but they continue their greedy ways. [32] To them you are nothing more than an entertainer singing love songs or playing a harp. They listen to all your words and don't obey a single one of them. [33] But when all your words come true—and they will come true—then they will know that a prophet has been among them."

The Shepherds of Israel

34 The LORD spoke to me. [2] "Mortal man," he said, "denounce the rulers of Israel. Prophesy to them, and tell them what I, the Sovereign LORD, say

They listen to all your words and don't obey a single one of them (33.32)

to them: You are doomed, you shepherds of Israel! You take care of yourselves, but never tend the sheep. ³ You drink the milk, wear clothes made from the wool, and kill and eat the finest sheep. But you never tend the sheep. ⁴ You have not taken care of the weak ones, healed those that are sick, bandaged those that are hurt, brought back those that wandered off, or looked for those that were lost. Instead, you treated them cruelly. ⁵ Because the sheep had no shepherd, they were scattered, and wild animals killed and ate them. ⁶ So my sheep wandered over the high hills and the mountains. They were scattered over the face of the earth, and no one looked for them or tried to find them.

7 "Now, you shepherds, listen to what I, the LORD, am telling you. ⁸ As surely as I am the living God, you had better listen to me. My sheep have been attacked by wild animals that killed and ate them because there was no shepherd. My shepherds did not try to find the sheep. They were taking care of themselves and not the sheep. ⁹ So listen to me, you shepherds. ¹⁰ I, the Sovereign LORD, declare that I am your enemy. I will take my sheep away from you and never again let you be their shepherds; never again will I let you take care only of yourselves. I will rescue my sheep from you and not let you eat them.

34.5: Num 27.17; 1 Kgs 22.17; Mt 9.36; Mk 6.34

The Good Shepherd

11 "I, the Sovereign LORD, tell you that I myself will look for my sheep and take care of them ¹² in the same way as a shepherd takes care of his sheep that were scattered and are brought together again. I will bring them back from all the places where they were scattered on that dark, disastrous day. ¹³ I will take them out of foreign countries, gather them together, and bring them back to their own land. I will lead them back to the mountains and the streams of Israel and will feed them in pleasant pastures. ¹⁴ I will let them graze in safety in the mountain meadows and the valleys and in all the green pastures of the land of Israel. ¹⁵ I myself will be the shepherd of my sheep, and I will find them a place to rest. I, the Sovereign LORD, have spoken.

16 "I will look for those that are lost, bring back those that wander off, bandage those that are hurt, and heal those that are sick; but those that are fat and strong I will destroy, because I am a shepherd who does what is right.

17 "Now then, my flock, I, the Sovereign LORD, tell you that I will judge each of you and separate the good from the bad, the sheep from the goats. ¹⁸ Some of you are not satisfied with eating the best grass; you even trample down what you don't eat! You drink the clear water and muddy what you don't drink! ¹⁹ My

other sheep have to eat the grass you trample down and drink the water you muddy.

20 "So now, I, the Sovereign LORD, tell you that I will judge between you strong sheep and the weak sheep. ²¹You pushed the sick ones aside and butted them away from the flock. ²²But I will rescue my sheep and not let them be ill-treated any more. I will judge each of my sheep and separate the good from the bad. ²³I will give them a king like my servant David to be their one shepherd, and he will take care of them. ²⁴I, the LORD, will be their God, and a king like my servant David will be their ruler. I have spoken. ²⁵I will make a covenant with them that guarantees their security. I will get rid of all the dangerous animals in the land, so that my sheep can live safely in the fields and sleep in the forests.

26 "I will bless them and let them live round my sacred hill.ᵉ There I will bless them with showers of rain when they need it. ²⁷The trees will bear fruit, the fields will produce crops, and everyone will live in safety on his own land. When I break my people's chains and set them free from those who made them slaves, then they will know that I am the LORD. ²⁸The heathen nations will not plunder them any more, and the wild animals will not kill and eat them. They will live in safety, and no one will terrify them. ²⁹I will give them fertile fields and put an end to hunger

in the land. The other nations will not sneer at them any more. ³⁰Everyone will know that I protect Israel and that they are my people. I, the Sovereign LORD, have spoken.

31 "You, my sheep, the flock that I feed, are my people, and I am your God," says the Sovereign LORD.

God's Punishment of Edom

35 The LORD spoke to me. ²"Mortal man," he said, "denounce the country of Edom. ³Tell the people what I, the Sovereign LORD, am saying:

I am your enemy, mountains of Edom!
I will make you a desolate waste.
⁴ I will leave your cities in ruins
And your land desolate;
Then you will know that I am the LORD.

5 "You were Israel's constant enemy and let her people be slaughtered in the time of her disaster, the time of final punishment for her sins. ⁶So then—as surely as I, the Sovereign LORD, am the living God—death is your fate, and you cannot escape it. You are guilty ofᶠ murder, and murder will follow you. ⁷I will make the hill-country of Edom a waste and kill everyone who travels through it. ⁸I will cover the mountains with corpses, and the bodies of those who are killed in battle will cover the hills and valleys. ⁹I will make you desolate for ever, and no one will live in your cities again. Then you will know that I am the LORD.

ᵉ SACRED HILL: See 20.40.　　ᶠ One ancient translation are guilty of; Hebrew hate.
34.23: Rev 7.17　　**34.24:** Ezek 37.24
35.1–15: Is 34.5–17, 63.1–6; Jer 49.7–22; Ezek 25.12–14; Amos 1.11–12; Obad 1–14; Mal 1.2–5

I myself will be the shepherd of my sheep (34.15)

10 "You said that the two nations, Judah and Israel, together with their lands, belonged to you and that you would possess them, even though I, the Lord, was their GOD. 11 So then, as surely as I, the Sovereign LORD, am the living God, I will pay you back for your anger, your jealousy, and your hatred towards my people. They will know that I am punishing you for what you did to them. 12 Then you will know that I, the LORD, heard you say with contempt that the mountains of Israel were desolate and that they were yours to devour. 13 I have heard the wild, boastful way you have talked against me."

14 The Sovereign LORD says, "I will make you so desolate that the whole world will rejoice at your downfall, 15 just as you rejoiced at the devastation of Israel, my own possession. The mountains of Seir, yes, all the land of Edom, will be desolate. Then everyone will know that I am the LORD."

God's Blessing on Israel

36 The LORD said, "Mortal man, speak to the mountains of Israel and tell them to listen to the message which I, 2 the Sovereign LORD, have for them: Israel's enemies gloated and said, 'Now those ancient hills are ours!'

3 "Prophesy, then, and announce what I, the Sovereign LORD, am saying. When the neighbouring nations captured and plundered the mountains of Israel, all of them insulted Israel. 4 So now listen to what I, the Sovereign LORD, say to you mountains and hills, to you brooks and valleys, to you places that were left in ruins, and to you deserted cities which were plundered and mocked by all the surrounding nations.

5 "I, the Sovereign LORD, have spoken out in the heat of my anger against the surrounding nations, and especially against Edom. With glee and contempt, they captured my land and took possession of its pastures.

6 "So prophesy to the land of Israel; tell the mountains, hills, brooks, and valleys what I, the Sovereign LORD, am saying in jealous anger because of the way the nations have insulted and humiliated them. 7 I, the Sovereign LORD, solemnly promise that the surrounding nations will be humiliated. 8 But on the mountains of Israel the trees will again grow leaves and bear fruit for you, my people Israel. You are going to come home soon. 9 I am on your side, and I will make sure that your land is ploughed again and that seeds are sown there. 10 I will make your population grow. You will live in the cities and rebuild everything that was left in ruins. 11 I will make people and cattle increase in number. There will be more of you than ever before, and you will have many children. I will let you live there as you used to live, and I will make you more prosperous than ever. Then you will know that I am the LORD. 12 I will bring you, my people Israel, back to live again in the land. It will be your own land, and it will never again let your children starve.

13 "I, the Sovereign LORD, say: It is true that people call the land a man-eater, and they say that it robs the nation of its children. 14 But from now on it will no longer be a man-eater who robs you of your children. I, the Sovereign LORD, have spoken. 15 The land will no longer have to listen to the nations mocking it or see the peoples sneer at it. The land will no longer rob the nation of its children. I, the Sovereign LORD, have spoken."

Israel's New Life

16 The LORD spoke to me. 17 "Mortal man," he said, "when the Israelites were living in their land, they defiled it by the way they lived and acted. I regarded their behaviour as being as ritually unclean as a woman is during her monthly period. 8 18 I let them feel the force of my anger because of the murders they had committed in the land and because of the idols by which they had defiled it. 19 I condemned them for the way they lived and acted, and I scattered them through foreign countries. 20 Wherever they went, they brought disgrace on my holy name, because people would say, 'These are the people of the LORD, but they had to leave his land.' 21 That made me concerned for my holy name, since the Israelites brought disgrace on it everywhere they went.

22 "Now then, give the Israelites the message that I, the Sovereign LORD, have for them: What I am going to do is not for the sake of you Israelites, but for the sake of my holy name, which you have disgraced in every country where you have gone. 23 When I demonstrate to the nations the holiness of my great name—the name you disgraced among them—

g RITUALLY UNCLEAN...PERIOD: *This is based on the view of ritual uncleanness described in the Law of Moses (see Lev 15.19).*

I could see that there were very many bones (37.2)

then they will know that I am the Lord. I, the Sovereign Lord, have spoken. I will use you to show the nations that I am holy. 24 I will take you from every nation and country and bring you back to your own land. 25 I will sprinkle clean water on you and make you clean from all your idols and everything else that has defiled you. 26 I will give you a new heart and a new mind. I will take away your stubborn heart of stone and give you an obedient heart. 27 I will put my spirit in you and I will see to it that you follow my laws and keep all the commands I have given you. 28 Then you will live in the land I gave your ancestors. You will be my people, and I will be your God. 29 I will save you from everything that defiles you. I will command the corn to be plentiful, so that you will not have any more famines. 30 I will increase the yield of your fruit-trees and your fields, so that there will be no more famines to disgrace you among the nations. 31 You will remember your evil conduct and the wrongs that you committed, and you will be disgusted with yourselves because of your sins and your iniquities. 32 Israel, I want you to know that I am not doing all this for your sake. I want you to feel the shame and disgrace of what you are doing. I, the Sovereign Lord, have spoken."

33 The Sovereign Lord says, "When I make you clean from all your sins, I will let you live in your cities again and let you rebuild the ruins. 34 Everyone who used to walk by your fields saw how overgrown and wild they were, but I will let you farm them again. 35 Everyone will say how this land, which was once a wilderness, has become like the Garden of Eden, and how the cities which were torn down, looted, and left in ruins, are now inhabited and fortified. 36 Then the neighbouring nations that have survived will know that I, the Lord, rebuild ruined cities and replant waste fields. I, the Lord, have promised that I would do this—and I will."

37 The Sovereign Lord says, "I will once again let the Israelites ask me for help, and I will let them increase in numbers like a flock of sheep. 38 The cities that are now in ruins will then be as full of people as Jerusalem was once full of the sheep which were offered as sacrifices at a festival. Then they will know that I am the Lord."

The Valley of Dry Bones

37 I felt the powerful presence of the Lord, and his spirit took me and set me down in a valley where the ground was covered with bones. 2 He led me all round the valley, and I could see that there were very many bones and that they were very dry. 3 He said to me, "Mortal man, can these bones come back to life?"

I replied, "Sovereign Lord, only you can answer that!"

4 He said, "Prophesy to the bones. Tell these dry bones to listen to the word of the Lord. 5 Tell them that I, the Sovereign Lord, am saying to them: I am going to

36.26–28: Ezek 11.19-20

put breath into you and bring you back to life. [6] I will give you sinews and muscles, and cover you with skin. I will put breath into you and bring you back to life. Then you will know that I am the LORD."

7 So I prophesied as I had been told. While I was speaking, I heard a rattling noise, and the bones began to join together. [8] While I watched, the bones were covered with sinews and muscles, and then with skin. But there was no breath in the bodies.

9 God said to me, "Mortal man, prophesy to the wind. [h] Tell the wind that the Sovereign LORD commands it to come from every direction, to breathe into these dead bodies, and to bring them back to life."

10 So I prophesied as I had been told. Breath entered the bodies, and they came to life and stood up. There were enough of them to form an army.

11 God said to me, "Mortal man, the people of Israel are like these bones. They say that they are dried up, without any hope and with no future. [12] So prophesy to my people Israel and tell them that I, the Sovereign LORD, am going to open their graves. I am going to take them out and bring them back to the land of Israel. [13] When I open the graves where my people are buried and bring them out, they will know that I am the LORD. [14] I will put my breath in them, bring them back to life, and let them live in their own land. Then they will know that I am the LORD. I have promised that I would do this— and I will. I, the LORD, have spoken."

Judah and Israel in One Kingdom

15 The LORD spoke to me again. [16] "Mortal man," he said, "take a wooden stick and write on it the words, 'The kingdom of Judah.' Then take another stick and write on it the words, 'The kingdom of Israel.' [17] Then hold the two sticks end to end in your hand so that they look like one stick. [18] When your people ask you to tell them what this means, [19] tell them that I, the Sovereign LORD, am going to take the stick representing Israel and put it with the one that represents Judah. Out of the two I will make one stick and hold it in my hand.

20 "Hold in your hand the two sticks and let the people see them. [21] Then tell them that I, the Sovereign LORD, am going to take all my people out of the nations

where they have gone, gather them together, and bring them back to their own land. [22] I will unite them into one nation in the land, on the mountains of Israel. They will have one king to rule over them, and they will no longer be divided into two nations or split into two kingdoms. [23] They will not defile themselves with disgusting idols any more or corrupt themselves with sin. I will free them from all the ways in which they sin and betray me. I will purify them; they will be my people, and I will be their God. [24] A king like my servant David will be their king. They will all be united under one ruler and will obey my laws faithfully. [25] They will live on the land I gave to my servant Jacob, the land where their ancestors lived. They will live there for ever, and so will their children and all their descendants. A king like my servant David will rule over them for ever. [26] I will make a covenant with them that guarantees their security for ever. I will establish them and increase their population, and put my Temple in their land, where it will stay for ever. [27] I will live there with them; I will be their God, and they will be my people. [28] When I place my Temple there to be among them for ever, then the nations will know that I, the LORD, have chosen Israel to be my own people."

Gog as the Instrument of God

38 The LORD spoke to me. [2] "Mortal man," he said, "denounce Gog, chief ruler of the nations of Meshech and Tubal in the land of Magog. Denounce him, [3] and tell him that I, the Sovereign LORD, am his enemy. [4] I will turn him round, put hooks in his jaws, and drag him and all his troops away. His army, with its horses and uniformed riders, is enormous, and every soldier carries a shield and is armed with a sword. [5] Men from Persia, Sudan, and Libya are with him, and all have shields and helmets. [6] All the fighting men of the lands of Gomer and Beth Togarmah in the north are with him, and so are men from many other nations. [7] Tell him to get ready and have all his troops ready at his command. [8] After many years I will order him to invade a country where the people were brought back together from many nations and have lived without fear of war. He will invade the mountains of Israel, which

---

[h] wind; or spirit. The same Hebrew word may mean wind, or spirit, or breath.
37.10: Rev 11.11 **37.24:** Ezek 34.24 **37.27:** 2 Cor 6.16; Rev 21.3 **38.2:** Rev 20.8

were desolate and deserted so long, but where all the people now live in safety. [9] He and his army and the many nations with him will attack like a storm and cover the land like a cloud."

10 This is what the Sovereign LORD says to Gog: "When that time comes, you will start thinking up an evil plan. [11] You will decide to invade a helpless country where the people live in peace and security in unwalled towns that have no defences. [12] You will plunder and loot the people who live in cities that were once in ruins. They have been gathered from the nations, and now they have livestock and property and live at the crossroads of the world. [13] The people of Sheba and Dedan and the merchants from the towns of Spain will ask you, 'Have you assembled your army and attacked in order to loot and plunder? Do you intend to get silver and gold, livestock and property, and to march off with all those spoils?'"

14 So the Sovereign LORD sent me to tell Gog what he was saying to him: "Now while my people Israel live in security, you will set out[j] [15] from your place in the far north, leading a large, powerful army of soldiers from many nations, all of them on horseback. [16] You will attack my people Israel like a storm moving across the land. When the time comes, I will send you to invade my land in order to show the nations who I am, to show my holiness by what I do through you. [17] You are the one I was talking about long ago, when I announced through my servants, the prophets of Israel, that in days to come I would bring someone to attack Israel." The Sovereign LORD has spoken.

God's Punishment of Gog

18 The Sovereign LORD says, "On the day when Gog invades Israel, I will be furious. [19] I declare in the heat of my anger that on that day there will be a severe earthquake in the land of Israel. [20] Every fish and bird, every animal large and small, and every human being on the face of the earth will tremble for fear of me. Mountains will fall, cliffs will crumble, and every wall will collapse. [21] I will terrify Gog with all sorts of calamities.[k] I, the Sovereign LORD, have spoken. His men will turn their swords against one another.

[22] I will punish him with disease and bloodshed. Torrents of rain and hail, together with fire and sulphur, will pour down on him and his army and on the many nations that are on his side. [23] In this way I will show all the nations that I am great and that I am holy. They will know then that I am the LORD."

The Defeat of Gog

39 The Sovereign LORD said, "Mortal man, denounce Gog, the chief ruler of the nations of Meshech and Tubal, and tell him that I am his enemy. [2] I will turn him in a new direction and lead him out of the far north until he comes to the mountains of Israel. [3] Then I will knock his bow out of his left hand and his arrows out of his right hand. [4] Gog and his army and his allies will fall dead on the mountains of Israel, and I will let their bodies be food for all the birds and wild animals. [5] They will fall dead in the open field. I, the Sovereign LORD, have spoken. [6] I will start a fire in the land of Magog and along all the coasts where people live undisturbed, and everyone will know that I am the LORD. [7] I will make sure that my people Israel know my holy name, and I will not let my name be disgraced any more. Then the nations will know that I, the LORD, am the Holy God of Israel."

8 The Sovereign LORD said, "The day I spoke about is certain to come. [9] The people who live in the cities of Israel will go out and collect the abandoned weapons for firewood. They will build fires with the shields, bows, arrows, spears, and clubs, and will have enough to last for seven years. [10] They will not have to gather firewood in the fields or cut down trees in the forest, because they will have the abandoned weapons to burn. They will loot and plunder those who looted and plundered them." The Sovereign LORD has spoken.

The Burial of Gog

11 The LORD said, "When all this happens, I will give Gog a burial-ground there in Israel, in Travellers' Valley, east of the Dead Sea.[l] Gog and all his army will be buried there, and the valley will be called 'The Valley of Gog's Army.' [12] It will take the Israelites seven months to bury all

---

[j] One ancient translation set out; Hebrew know.
[k] One ancient translation terrify...calamities; Hebrew unclear.
[l] Hebrew has four additional words, the meaning of which is unclear.

the corpses and make the land clean again. [13] Everyone in the land will help to bury them, and they will be honoured for this on the day of my victory. I, the Sovereign LORD, have spoken. [14] After the seven months are over, men will be chosen to travel through the land in order to find and bury those bodies[m] remaining on the ground, so that they can make the land clean. [15] As they go up and down the country, every time they find a human bone, they will put a marker beside it so that the grave-diggers can come and bury it in the Valley of Gog's Army. [16] (There will be a town near by named after the army.) And so the land will be made clean again."

17 The Sovereign LORD said to me, "Mortal man, call all the birds and animals to come from all round to eat the sacrifice I am preparing for them. It will be a huge feast on the mountains of Israel, where they can eat meat and drink blood. [18] They are to eat the bodies of soldiers and drink the blood of the rulers of the earth, all of whom will be killed like rams or lambs or goats or fat bulls. [19] When I kill these people like sacrifices, the birds and animals are to eat all the fat they can hold and to drink blood until they are drunk. [20] At my table they will eat all they can hold of horses and their riders and of soldiers and fighting men. I, the Sovereign LORD, have spoken."

The Restoration of Israel

21 The LORD said, "I will let the nations see my glory and show them how I use my power to carry out my just decisions. [22] The Israelites will know from then on that I am the LORD their God. [23] And the nations will know that the Israelites went into exile because of the sins which they committed against me. I turned away from them and let their enemies defeat them and kill them in battle. [24] I gave them what they deserved for their uncleanness and their wickedness, and I turned away from them."

25 The Sovereign LORD said, "But now I will be merciful to Jacob's descendants, the people of Israel, and make them prosperous again. I will protect my holy name. [26] When they are once more living in safety in their own land, with no one

to threaten them, they will be able to forget how they were disgraced for having betrayed me. [27] In order to show the many nations that I am holy, I will bring my people back from all the countries where their enemies live. [28] Then my people will know that I am the LORD their God. They will know this, because I sent them into captivity and now gather them and bring them back into their own land, not leaving even one of them behind. [29] I will pour out my spirit on the people of Israel and never again turn away from them. I, the Sovereign LORD, have spoken."

A VISION OF THE FUTURE TEMPLE
(40.1–48.35)

Ezekiel Is Taken to Jerusalem

40 It was the tenth day of the new year, which was the twenty-fifth year after we had been taken into exile and the fourteenth year after Jerusalem was captured. On that day I felt the powerful presence of the LORD, and he carried me away. [2] In a vision God took me to the land of Israel and put me on a high mountain. I saw in front of me[n] a group of buildings that looked like a city. [3] He took me closer, and I saw a man who shone like bronze. He was holding a linen tape-measure and a measuring-rod and was standing by a gateway.

4 He said to me, "Watch, mortal man. Listen carefully and pay close attention to everything I show you, because this is why you were brought here. You are to tell the people of Israel everything you see."

The East Gate

5 What I saw was the Temple, and there was a wall round it. The man took his measuring-rod, which was three metres long, and measured the wall. It was three metres high and three metres thick. [6] Then he went to the gateway that faced east. He went up the steps, and at the top he measured the entrance; it was three metres deep.[o] [7] Beyond it there was a passage, which had three guardrooms on each side. Each of the rooms was square, three metres on each side, and the walls between them were two and a half metres

---

[m] Some ancient translations those bodies; Hebrew the travellers.
[n] One ancient translation in front of me; Hebrew in the south.
[o] One ancient translation deep; Hebrew deep, one entrance three metres deep.
39.17-20: Rev 19.17-18　　**40.2:** Rev 21.10　　**40.3:** Rev 11.1, 21.15
40.5–42.20: 1 Kgs 6.1-38; 2 Chr 3.1-9

He was holding a linen tape-measure and a measuring-rod (40.3)

thick. Beyond the guardrooms there was a passage three metres long that led to an entrance room which faced the Temple. 8-9 He measured this room, and found it was four metres deep. It formed that end of the gateway which was nearest the Temple, and at its far end the walls were one metre thick. 10 (These guardrooms on each side of the passage were all the same size, and the walls between them were all of the same thickness.)

11 Next, the man measured the width of the passage in the gateway. It was six and a half metres altogether, and the space between the open gates was five metres. 12 In front of each of the guard-rooms there was a low wall fifty centi-metres high and fifty centimetres thick. (The rooms were three metres square.) 13 Then he measured the distance from the back wall *x* of one room to the back wall *x* of the room across the passage from it, and it was twelve and a half metres. 14 The room at the far end led out to a courtyard. He measured that room and found it was ten metres wide. *p* 15 The total length of the gateway from the outside wall of the gate to the far side of the last room was twenty-five metres. 16 There were small openings in the outside walls of all the rooms and also in the inner walls between

the rooms. There were palm-trees carved on the inner walls that faced the passage.

The Outer Courtyard

17 The man took me through the gateway into the courtyard. There were thirty rooms built against the outer wall, and in front of them there was an area paved with stones, 18 which extended round the courtyard. This outer courtyard was at a lower level than the inner courtyard.

19 There was a gateway at a higher level that led to the inner courtyard. The man measured the distance between the two gateways, and it was fifty metres. *q*

The North Gate

20 Then the man measured the gateway on the north side that led into the outer courtyard. 21 The three guardrooms on each side of the passage, the walls between them, and the entrance room all had the same measurements as those in the east gateway. The total length of the gateway was twenty-five metres and the width twelve and a half metres. 22 The entrance room, the windows, and the carved palm-trees were like those in the east gate. Here seven steps led up to the gate, and the entrance room was at the

x Probable text back wall; Hebrew roof.
p Verse 14 in Hebrew is unclear.
q Hebrew has two additional words, the meaning of which is unclear.

end facing the courtyard. 23 Across the courtyard from this north gateway was another gateway leading to the inner courtyard, just as there was on the east side. The man measured the distance between these two gateways, and it was fifty metres.

The South Gate

24 Next, the man took me to the south side, and there we saw another gateway. He measured its inner walls and its entrance room, and they were the same as the others. 25 There were windows in the rooms of this gateway just as in the others. The total length of the gateway was twenty-five metres, and the width twelve and a half metres. 26 Seven steps led up to it, and its entrance room was also at the end facing the courtyard. There were palm-trees carved on the inner walls that faced the passage. 27 Here, too, there was a gateway leading to the inner courtyard. The man measured the distance to this second gateway, and it was fifty metres.

The Inner Courtyard: The South Gate

28 The man took me through the south gateway into the inner courtyard. He measured the gateway, and it was the same size as the gateways in the outer wall. 29-30 Its guardrooms, its entrance room, and its inner walls were the same size as those in the other gateways. There were also windows in the rooms of this gateway. The total length was twenty-five metres and the width twelve and a half metres. 31 Its entrance room faced the other courtyard, and palm-trees were carved on the walls along the passage. Eight steps led up to this gate.

The Inner Courtyard: The East Gate

32 The man took me through the east gateway into the inner courtyard. He measured the gateway, and it was the same size as the others. 33 Its guardrooms, its entrance room, and its inner walls measured the same as those in the other gateways. There were windows all round, and in the entrance room also. The total length was twenty-five metres and the width twelve and a half metres. 34 The entrance room faced the outer courtyard. Palm-trees were carved on the walls along the passage. Eight steps led up to this gate.

The Inner Courtyard: The North Gate

35 Then the man took me to the north gateway. He measured it, and it was the same size as the others. 36 Like them, it also had guardrooms, decorated inner walls, an entrance room, and windows all round. Its total length was twenty-five metres and its width twelve and a half metres. 37 The entrance room *r* faced the outer courtyard. Palm-trees were carved on the walls along the passage. Eight steps led up to this gate.

Buildings Near the North Gate

38 In the outer courtyard there was an annexe attached to the inner gateway on the north side. It opened into the entrance room that faced the courtyard, and there they washed the carcasses of the animals to be burnt whole as sacrifices. 39 In this entrance room there were four tables, two on each side of the room. It was on these tables that they killed the animals to be offered as sacrifices, either to be burnt whole or to be sacrifices for sin or as repayment-offerings. 40 Outside the room there were four similar tables, two on either side of the entrance of the north gate. 41 Altogether there were eight tables on which the animals to be sacrificed were killed: four inside the room and four out in the courtyard. 42 The four tables in the annexe, used to prepare the offerings to be burnt whole, were of cut stone. They were fifty centimetres high, and their tops were seventy-five centimetres square. All the equipment used in killing the sacrificial animals was kept on these tables. 43 Ledges seventy-five millimetres wide ran round the edge of the tables. All the meat to be offered in sacrifice was placed on the tables. *s*

44 Then he brought me into the inner courtyard. There were two rooms opening on the inner courtyard, one facing south beside the north gateway and the other facing north beside the south gateway. *t* 45 The man told me that the room which faced south was for the priests who served in the Temple, 46 and the room which faced north was for the priests who served at the altar. All the priests are descended from Zadok; they are the only members of the tribe of Levi who are permitted to go into the LORD's presence to serve him.

r Some ancient translations entrance room; *Hebrew* inner wall.
s Verse 43 in Hebrew is unclear.
t One ancient translation Then...south gateway; *verse 44 in Hebrew is unclear.*

The Inner Courtyard and the Temple Building

47 The man measured the inner courtyard, and it was fifty metres square. The Temple was on the west side, and in front of it was an altar. [48] Then he took me into the entrance room of the Temple. He measured the entrance: it was two and a half metres deep and seven metres wide, [u] with walls one and a half metres thick on either side. [49] Steps led up to the entrance room, which was ten metres wide and six metres deep. There were two columns, one on each side of the entrance.

41 Next, the man took me into the central room, the Holy Place. He measured the passage leading into it: it was three metres deep [v] [2] and five metres wide, with walls two and a half metres thick on either side. He measured the room itself: it was twenty metres long, and ten metres wide.

3 Then he went to the innermost room. He measured the passage leading into it: it was one metre deep and three metres wide, with walls on either side three and a half metres thick. [w] [4] He measured the room itself, and it was ten metres square. This room was beyond the central room. Then he said to me, "This is the Most Holy Place."

The Rooms Built against the Temple Walls

5 The man measured the thickness of the inner wall of the temple building, and it was three metres. Against this wall, all round the Temple, was a series of small rooms two metres wide. [6] These rooms were in three storeys, with thirty rooms on each floor. The Temple's outer wall on each floor was thinner than on the floor below, so that the rooms could rest on the wall without being anchored into it. [7] And so the temple walls, when seen from the outside, seemed to have the same thickness all the way to the top. Against the Temple's outer wall, on the outside of the rooms, two wide stairways were built, so that it was possible to go from the lower storey to the middle and the upper storeys. [x] [8-11] The outside wall of these rooms was two and a half metres thick; there was one door into the rooms on the north side of the Temple, and one into those on the south side. I saw that

there was a terrace two and a half metres wide all round the Temple; it was three metres above the ground and it was level with the foundation of the rooms by the temple walls. Between the terrace and the buildings used by the priests there was an open space ten metres across, along the sides of the Temple.

The Building on the West

12 At the far end of the open space on the west side of the Temple there was a building forty-five metres long and thirty-five metres wide; its walls were two and a half metres thick all round.

The Total Measurements of the Temple Building

13 The man measured the outside of the Temple, and it was fifty metres long. And from the back of the Temple, across the open space to the far side of the building to the west, the distance was also fifty metres. [14] The distance across the front of the Temple, including the open space on either side, was also fifty metres. [15] He measured the length of the building to the west, including its corridors on both sides, and it was also fifty metres.

Details of the Temple Building

The entrance room of the Temple, the Holy Place, and the Most Holy Place [16] were all panelled with wood from the floor to the windows. These windows could be covered. [z] [17] The inside walls of the Temple, up as high as above the doors, were completely covered with carvings [a] [18] of palm-trees and winged creatures. Palm-trees alternated with creatures, one following the other, all the way round the room. Each creature had two faces: [19] a human face that was turned towards the palm-tree on one side, and a lion's face that was turned towards the tree on the other side. It was like this all round the wall, [20] from the floor to above the doors. [21] The door-posts of the Holy Place were square.

The Wooden Altar

In front of the entrance of the Most Holy Place there was something that looked like [22] a wooden altar. It was one and a half metres high and one metre wide. Its corner-posts, its base, [c] and its

[u] *One ancient translation* and seven metres wide; *Hebrew does not have these words.*
[v] *Hebrew has two additional words, the meaning of which is unclear.*
[w] *One ancient translation* with walls on either side three and a half metres thick; *Hebrew and three and a half metres thick.*   [x] *Verse 7 in Hebrew is unclear.*
[z] *Verse 16 in Hebrew is unclear.*   [a] *Verse 17 in Hebrew is unclear.*
[c] *Some ancient translations* base; *Hebrew length.*

sides were all made of wood. The man said to me, "This is the table which stands in the presence of the LORD."

The Doors

23 There was a door at the end of the passage leading to the Holy Place and one also at the end of the passage leading to the Most Holy Place. 24 They were double doors that swung open in the middle. 25 There were palm-trees and winged creatures carved on the doors of the Holy Place, just as there were on the walls. And there was a wooden covering over the outside of the doorway of the entrance room. 26 At the sides of this room there were windows, and the walls were decorated with palm-trees. e

Two Buildings Near the Temple

42 Then the man took me into the outer courtyard and led me to a building on the north side of the Temple, not far from the building at the west end of the Temple. 2 This building was fifty metres long and twenty-five metres wide. 3 On one side it faced the space ten metres wide which was alongside the Temple, and on the other side it faced the pavement of the outer court. It was built on three levels, each one set further back than the one below it. 4 Along the north side of this building was a passage five metres wide and fifty metres long, f with entrances on that side. 5 The rooms at the upper level of the building were narrower than those at the middle and lower levels because they were set further back. 6 The rooms at all three levels were on terraces and were not supported by columns like the other buildings in the courtyard. 7-8 At the lower level the outer wall of the building was solid for twenty-five metres, half its length; and there were rooms in the remaining twenty-five metres. At the top level there were rooms in the entire length of the building. 9-10 Below these two rooms at the east end of the building, where the wall of the courtyard began, g there was an entrance into the outer courtyard.

At the south h side of the Temple there was an identical building not far from the building at the west end of the Temple. 11 In front of the rooms there was a passage just like the one on the north side. It had the same measurements, the same design, and the same kind of entrances. 12 There was a door under the rooms on the south side of the building, at the east end where the wall began.

13 The man said to me, "Both these buildings are holy. In them the priests who enter the LORD's presence eat the holiest offerings. Because the rooms are holy, the priests will place the holiest offerings there: the grain-offerings and the sacrifices offered for sin or as repayment-offerings. 14 When priests have been in the Temple and want to go to the outer courtyard, they must leave in these rooms the holy clothing they wore while serving the LORD. They must put on other clothes before going out to the area where the people gather."

The Measurements of the Temple Area

15 When the man had finished measuring inside the temple area, he took me out through the east gate and then measured the outside of the area. 16 He took the measuring-rod and measured the east side, and it was 250 metres. 17-19 Then he measured the north side, the south side, and the west side; each side had the same length, 250 metres, i 20 so that the wall enclosed a square 250 metres on each side. The wall served to separate what was holy from what was not.

The LORD Returns to the Temple

43 The man took me to the gate that faces east, 2 and there I saw coming from the east the dazzling light of the presence of the God of Israel. God's voice sounded like the roar of the sea, and the earth shone with the dazzling light. 3 This vision was like the one I had seen when God came to destroy Jerusalem, and the one I saw by the River Chebar. Then I threw myself face downwards on the ground. 4 The dazzling light passed through the east gate and went into the Temple.

5 The LORD's spirit lifted me up and took me into the inner courtyard, where I saw that the Temple was filled with the glory of the LORD. 6 The man stood beside me there, and I heard the LORD speak to me out of the Temple: 7 "Mortal man, here is my throne. I will live here among the

---

e Hebrew has three additional words, the meaning of which is unclear.
f Some ancient translations fifty metres long; Hebrew a way of fifty centimetres.
g One ancient translation where...began; Hebrew in the breadth of the wall of the courtyard.
h One ancient translation south; Hebrew east. i Verses 16–19 in Hebrew are unclear.
43.2: Ezek 10.3–4, 18–19, 11.22–23; Rev 1.15

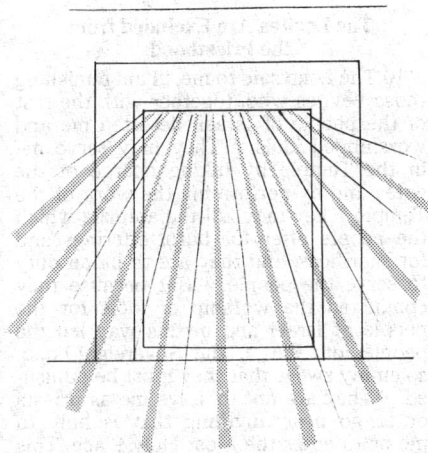

The dazzling light passed through the east gate (43.4)

as in measuring the Temple. All round the base of the altar there was a gutter fifty centimetres deep and fifty centimetres wide, with a rim at the outside edge twenty-five centimetres high. [14]The lowest section of the altar, from the top of the base, was one metre high. The next section was set back from the edge fifty centimetres all round, and was two metres high. The section after that was also set back from the edge fifty centimetres all round. [15]This top section, on which the sacrifices were burnt, was also two metres high. The projections on the four corners were higher than the rest of the top. [16]The top of the altar was a square, six metres on each side. [17]The middle section was also a square, seven metres on each side, with a rim at the outside edge twenty-five centimetres high. (The gutter was fifty centimetres wide.) The steps going up the altar were on the east side.

The Consecration of the Altar

18 The Sovereign LORD said to me, "Mortal man, listen to what I tell you. When the altar is built, you are to dedicate it by burning sacrifices on it and by sprinkling on it the blood of the animals that were sacrificed. [19]Those priests belonging to the tribe of Levi who are descended from Zadok are the only ones who are to come into my presence to serve me. I, the Sovereign LORD, command this. You will give them a young bull to offer as a sacrifice for sin. [20]You are to take some of its blood and put it on the projections on the top corners of the altar, and on the corners of the middle section of the altar, and all round its edges. In this way you will purify the altar and consecrate it. [21]You are to take the bull that is offered as a sacrifice for sin and burn it at the specified place outside the temple area. [22]The next day you are to take a male goat without any defects and offer it as a sacrifice for sin. Purify the altar with its blood in the same way as you did with the bull. [23]When you have finished doing that, take a young bull and a young ram, both of them without any defects, [24]and bring them to me. The priests will sprinkle salt on them and burn them as an offering to me. [25]Each day for seven days you are to offer a goat, a bull, and a ram as sacrifices for sin. All of them must be without any defects. [26]For seven days the priests are to

people of Israel and rule over them for ever. Neither the people of Israel nor their kings will ever again disgrace my holy name by worshipping other gods or by burying the corpses of[j] their kings in this place. [8]The kings built the thresholds and door-posts of their palace right against the thresholds and door-posts of my Temple, so that there was only a wall between us. They disgraced my holy name by all the disgusting things they did, and so in my anger I destroyed them. [9]Now they must stop worshipping other gods and remove the corpses of[k] their kings. If they do, I will live among them for ever."

10 And the LORD continued, "Mortal man, tell the people of Israel about the Temple, and let them study its plan. Make them ashamed of their sinful actions. [11]Then if they are ashamed of what they have done, explain the plan of the Temple to them: its design, its entrances and exits, its shape, the arrangement of everything, and all its rules and regulations. Write all this down for them so that they can see how everything is arranged and can carry out all the rules. [12]This is the law of the Temple: All the area surrounding it on the top of the mountain is sacred and holy."

The Altar

13 These are the measurements of the altar, using the same unit of measurement

---

[j]by burying the corpses of; *or* putting up monuments to.
[k]remove the corpses of; *or* remove the monuments to.
43.13–17: Ex 27.1–2; 2 Chr 4.1

consecrate the altar and make it ready for use. 27 When the week is over, the priests are to begin offering on the altar the burnt-offerings and the fellowship-offerings of the people. Then I will be pleased with all of you. I, the Sovereign LORD, have spoken."

The Use of the East Gate

44 The man led me to the outer gate at the east side of the temple area. The gate was closed, 2 and the LORD said to me, "This gate will stay closed and will never be opened. No human being is allowed to use it, because I, the LORD God of Israel, have entered through it. It is to remain closed. 3 The ruling prince, however, may go there to eat a holy meal in my presence. He is to enter and leave the gateway through the entrance room at the inner end."

Rules for Admission to the Temple

4 Then the man took me through the north gate to the front of the Temple. As I looked, I saw that the Temple of the LORD was filled with the dazzling light of his presence. I threw myself face downwards on the ground, 5 and the LORD said to me, "Mortal man, pay attention to everything you see and hear. I am going to tell you the rules and regulations for the Temple. Note carefully which persons are allowed to go in and out of the Temple and which persons are not.

6 "Tell those rebellious people of Israel that I, the Sovereign LORD, will no longer tolerate the disgusting things they have been doing. 7 They have profaned my Temple by letting uncircumcised foreigners, people who do not obey me, enter the Temple when the fat and the blood of the sacrifices are being offered to me. So my people have broken my covenant by all the disgusting things they have done. 8 They have not taken charge of the sacred rituals in my Temple, but instead have put foreigners in charge.

9 "I, the Sovereign LORD, declare that no uncircumcised foreigner, no one who disobeys me, will enter my Temple, not even a foreigner who lives among the people of Israel."

The Levites Are Excluded from the Priesthood

10 The LORD said to me, "I am punishing those Levites who, together with the rest of the people of Israel, deserted me and worshipped idols. 11 They may serve me in the Temple by taking charge of the gates and by performing the work of the Temple. They may kill the animals which the people offer for burnt-offerings and for sacrifices, and they are to be on duty to serve the people. 12 But because they conducted the worship of idols for the people of Israel and in this way led the people into sin, I, the Sovereign LORD, solemnly swear that they must be punished. 13 They are not to serve me as priests or to go near anything that is holy to me or to enter the Most Holy Place. This is the punishment for the disgusting things they have done. 14 I am assigning to them the menial work that is to be done in the Temple."

The Priests

15 The Sovereign LORD said, "Those priests belonging to the tribe of Levi who are descended from Zadok, however, continued to serve me faithfully in the Temple when the rest of the people of Israel turned away from me. So now they are the ones who are to serve me and come into my presence to offer me the fat and the blood of the sacrifices. 16 They alone will enter my Temple, serve at my altar, and conduct the temple worship. 17 When they enter the gateway to the inner courtyard of the Temple, they are to put on linen clothing. They must not wear anything made of wool when they are on duty in the inner courtyard or in the Temple. 18 So that they won't perspire, they are to wear linen turbans and linen trousers, but no belt. 19 Before they go to the outer courtyard where the people are, they must first take off the clothes they wore on duty in the Temple and leave them in the holy rooms. They are to be put on other clothing in order to keep their sacred clothing from harming the people.[1]

20 "Priests must neither shave their heads nor let their hair grow long. They are to keep it a proper length. 21 Priests must not drink any wine before going into the inner courtyard. 22 No priest may

---

[1] HARMING THE PEOPLE: *It was believed that ordinary people would be harmed by touching something holy.*

43.27: Ex 29.35-37   **44.17-18:** Ex 28.39-43; Lev 16.4   **44.19:** Lev 16.23   **44.20:** Lev 21.5
44.21: Lev 10.9   **44.22:** Lev 21.7, 13-14

marry a divorced woman; he is to marry only an Israelite virgin or the widow of another priest.

23 "The priests are to teach my people the difference between what is holy and what is not, and between what is ritually clean and what is not. 24 When a legal dispute arises, the priests are to decide the case according to my laws. They are to keep the religious festivals according to my rules and regulations, and they are to keep the Sabbaths holy.

25 "A priest is not to become ritually unclean by touching a corpse, unless it is one of his parents, one of his children or a brother or an unmarried sister. 26 After he has become clean again, he must wait seven days 27 and then go into the inner courtyard of the Temple and offer a sacrifice for his purification, so that he can serve in the Temple again. I, the Sovereign LORD, have spoken.

28 "The priests have the priesthood as their share of what I have given Israel to be handed down from one generation to another. They are not to hold property in Israel; I am all they need. 29 The grain-offerings, the sin-offerings and the repayment-offerings will be the priests' food, and they are to receive everything in Israel that is set apart for me. 30 The priests are to have the best of all the first harvest and of everything else that is offered to me. Each time the people bake bread, they are to give the priests the first loaf as an offering, and my blessing will rest on their homes. 31 The priests must not eat any bird or animal that dies a natural death or is killed by another animal."

The LORD's Portion of the Country

45 When the land is divided to give each tribe a share, one part is to be dedicated to the LORD. It is to be twelve and a half kilometres long by ten kilometres ^{m} wide. The entire area will be holy. 2 In this area there is to be a square plot of land for the Temple, 250 metres along each side, entirely surrounded by an open space twenty-five metres wide. 3 Half of this area, a section twelve and a half kilometres by five kilometres, is to be measured off; it will contain the Temple, the holiest place of all. 4 It will

be a holy part of the country, set aside for the priests who serve the LORD in his Temple. It will contain their houses and the section of land for the Temple. 5 The other half of the area is to be set aside as the possession of the Levites, who do the work in the Temple. There will be towns there for them to live in. ^{n}

6 Next to the holy area, another section, twelve and a half kilometres long and two and a half kilometres wide, is to be set aside for a city where any of the people of Israel may live.

Land for the Prince

7 Land is also to be set aside for the ruling prince. From the western boundary of the holy area it will extend west to the Mediterranean Sea; and from the eastern boundary it will extend to the eastern border of the country, so that its length will be the same as the length of one of the areas allotted to the tribes of Israel. 8 This area will be the share the ruling prince will have in the land of Israel, so that he will no longer oppress the people, but will let the rest of the country belong to the tribes of Israel.

Rules for the Prince

9 The Sovereign LORD said, "You have sinned too long, you rulers of Israel! Stop your violence and oppression. Do what is right and just. You must never again drive my people off their land. I, the Sovereign LORD, am telling you this.

10 "Everyone must use honest weights and measures:

11 "The *ephah* for dry measure is to be equal to the *bath* for liquid measure. The standard is the *homer*. ^{o} The resulting measures are as follows:

    1 *homer* = 10 *ephahs* = 10 *baths*

12 "Your weights are to be as follows:

    20 *gerahs* = 1 *shekel* ^{p}

    60 *shekels* = 1 *mina*

13–15 "This is the basis on which you are to make your offerings:

    Wheat: $\frac{1}{60}$th of your harvest

    Barley: $\frac{1}{60}$th of your harvest

    Olive-oil: $\frac{1}{100}$th of the yield of your trees

(Measure it by the *bath*: 10 *baths* = 1 *homer* = 1 *kor*.)

---

^{m} One ancient translation ten kilometres; Hebrew five kilometres.
^{n} One ancient translation towns there for them to live in; Hebrew twenty rooms.
^{o} HOMER: A unit of dry or liquid measure, about 175 litres; so an ephah or a bath would be about 17.5 litres. ^{p} SHEKEL: In Ezekiel's time this unit of weight was about 11.4 grammes.
44.23: Lev 10.10   **44.25:** Lev 21.1–4   **44.28:** Num 18.20   **44.29–30:** Num 18.8–19
44.31: Lev 22.8   **45.10:** Lev 19.36

Sheep: 1 sheep out of every 200 from the meadows of Israel.

"You are to bring grain-offerings, animals to be burnt whole, and animals for fellowship-offerings, so that your sins will be forgiven. I, the Sovereign LORD, command it.

16 "All the people of the land must take q these offerings to the ruling prince of Israel. 17 It will be his duty to provide the animals to be burnt whole, the grain-offerings, and the wine-offerings for the whole nation of Israel at the New Moon Festivals, the Sabbaths, and the other festivals. He is to provide the sin-offerings, the grain-offerings, the offerings to be burnt whole, and the fellowship-offerings, to take away the sins of the people of Israel."

The Festivals
(Ex 12.1–20; Lev 23.33–43)

18 The Sovereign LORD said, "On the first day of the first month you are to sacrifice a bull without any defects and purify the Temple. 19 The priest will take some of the blood of this sin-offering and put it on the door-posts of the Temple, on the four corners of the altar, and on the posts of the gateways to the inner courtyard. 20 On the seventh day of the month you are to do the same thing on behalf of anyone who sins unintentionally or through ignorance. In this way, you will keep the Temple holy.

21 "On the fourteenth day of the first month you will begin the celebration of the Passover Festival. For seven days everyone will eat bread made without yeast. 22 On the first day of the festival the ruling prince must offer a bull as a sacrifice for his sins and for those of all the people. 23 On each of the seven days of the festival he is to sacrifice to the LORD seven bulls and seven rams without any defects and burn them whole. He is also to sacrifice a male goat each day as a sin-offering. 24 For each bull and each ram that is sacrificed, there is to be an offering of seventeen and a half litres of corn and three litres of olive-oil.

25 "For the Festival of Shelters, which begins on the fifteenth day of the seventh month, the prince will offer on each of the seven days the same sacrifice for sin, the same offerings to be burnt whole, and the same offerings of corn and olive-oil."

The Prince and the Festivals

46 The Sovereign LORD says, "The east gateway to the inner courtyard must be kept closed during the six working days, but it is to be opened on the Sabbath and at the New Moon Festival. 2 The ruling prince will go from the outer courtyard into the entrance room by the gateway and stand beside the posts of the gate while the priests burn his sacrifices whole and offer his fellowship-offerings. There at the gate he must worship and then go out again. The gate must not be shut until evening. 3 Each Sabbath and each New Moon Festival all the people are also to bow down and worship the LORD in front of the gate.

4 "On the Sabbath the prince is to bring to the LORD, as sacrifices to be burnt whole, six lambs and one ram, all without any defects. 5 With each ram he is to bring an offering of seventeen and a half litres of corn, and with each lamb he is to bring whatever he wants to give. For each such grain-offering he is to bring three litres of olive-oil. 6 At the New Moon Festival he will offer a young bull, six lambs, and a ram, all without any defects. 7 With each bull and each ram the offering is to be seventeen and a half litres of corn, and with each lamb the offering is to be whatever the prince wants to give. Three litres of olive-oil are to be offered with each such grain-offering of corn. 8 The prince must leave the entrance room of the gateway and go out by the same way as he went in.

9 "When the people come to worship the LORD at any festival, those who enter by the north gate are to leave by the south gate after they have worshipped, and those who enter by the south gate are to leave by the north gate. No one may go out by the same way as he entered, but must leave by the opposite gate. 10 The prince is to come in when the people come, and leave when they leave. 11 On the feast days and at the festivals the grain-offering will be seventeen and a half litres with each bull or ram, and whatever the worshipper wants to give with each lamb. Three litres of olive-oil are to be offered with each such grain-offering.

12 "When the ruling prince wants to make a voluntary offering to the LORD, either an offering to be burnt whole or a fellowship-offering, the east gate to the

---

q Probable text must take; Hebrew unclear.
45.21: Ex 12.1–20; Num 28.16–25   **45.25:** Lev 23.33–36; Num 29.12–38

inner courtyard will be opened for him. He is to make the offering in the same way as he does on the Sabbath, and the gate is to be closed after he goes out again."

The Daily Offering

13 The LORD says, "Every morning a one-year-old lamb without any defects is to be burnt whole as an offering to the LORD. This offering must be made every day. ¹⁴Also an offering of two kilogrammes of flour is to be made every morning, together with one litre of olive-oil for mixing with the flour. The rules for this offering to the LORD are to be in force for ever. ¹⁵The lamb, the flour, and the olive-oil are to be offered to the LORD every morning for ever."

The Prince and the Land

16 The Sovereign LORD commands: "If the ruling prince gives any of the land he owns to one of his sons as a present, it will belong to that son as a part of his family property. ¹⁷But if the ruling prince gives any of his land to anyone who is in his service, it will become the prince's property again when the Year of Restoration⁵ comes round. It belongs to him, and only he and his sons can own it permanently. ¹⁸The ruling prince must not take any of the people's property away from them. Any land he gives to his sons must be from the land that is assigned to him, so that he will not oppress any of my people by taking their land."

The Temple Kitchens

19 Then the man took me to the entrance of the rooms facing north near the gate on the south side of the inner courtyard. These are holy rooms for the priests. He pointed out a place on the west side of the rooms ²⁰and said, "This is the place where the priests are to boil the meat offered as sacrifices for sin or as repayment-offerings, and to bake the offerings of flour, so that nothing holy is carried to the outer courtyard, where it might harm the people." ᵗ

21-22 Then he led me to the outer courtyard and showed me that in each of its four corners there was a smaller ᵘ courtyard, twenty metres long and fifteen

metres wide. ²³Each one had a stone wall round it, with fireplaces built against the wall. ²⁴The man told me, "These are the kitchens where the temple servants are to boil the sacrifices the people offer."

The Stream Flowing from the Temple

47 The man led me back to the entrance of the Temple. Water was coming out from under the entrance and flowing east, the direction the Temple faced. It was flowing down from under the south part of the temple past the south side of the altar. ²The man then took me out of the temple area by way of the north gate and led me round to the gate that faces east. A small stream of water was flowing out at the south side of the gate. ³With his measuring-rod the man measured five hundred metres downstream to the east and told me to wade through the stream there. The water came only to my ankles. ⁴Then he measured another five hundred metres, and the water came up to my knees. Another five hundred metres further down, the water was up to my waist. ⁵He measured five hundred metres more, and there the stream was so deep I could not wade through it. It was too deep to cross except by swimming. ⁶He said to me, "Mortal man, note all this carefully."

Then the man took me back to the bank of the river, ⁷and when I got there I saw that there were very many trees on each bank. ⁸He said to me, "This water flows through the land to the east and down into the Jordan Valley and to the Dead Sea. When it flows into the Dead Sea, it replaces the salt water of that sea with fresh water. ⁹Wherever the stream flows, there will be all kinds of animals and fish. The stream will make the water of the Dead Sea fresh, and wherever it flows, it will bring life. ¹⁰From the Springs of Engedi all the way to the Springs of Eneglaim, there will be fishermen on the shore of the sea, and they will spread out their nets there to dry. There will be as many different kinds of fish there as there are in the Mediterranean Sea. ¹¹But the water in the marshes and ponds along the shore will not be made fresh. They will remain there as a source of salt. ¹²On each bank of the stream all kinds of trees

---

ˢ YEAR OF RESTORATION: *Every fifty years, all Israelites were required to give freedom to any of their fellow-countrymen who had become slaves because of debts; they were also to give back to the original owner, or his heirs, any ancestral land that had been sold for debt (see Lev 25.8–55).*
ᵗ HARM THE PEOPLE: *See 44.19.*
ᵘ *One ancient translation* smaller; *Hebrew* enclosed.
46.17: Lev 25.10   **47.1:** Zech 14.8; Jn 7.38; Rev 22.1   **47.12:** Rev 22.2

The man...told me to wade through the stream there (47.3)

will grow to provide food. Their leaves will never wither, and they will never stop bearing fruit. They will have fresh fruit every month, because they are watered by the stream that flows from the Temple. The trees will provide food, and their leaves will be used for healing people."

The Boundaries of the Land

13 The Sovereign LORD said, "These are the boundaries of the land that is to be divided among the twelve tribes, with the tribe of Joseph receiving two sections. [v] [14] I solemnly promised your ancestors that I would give them possession of this land; now divide it equally among you.

15 "The northern boundary runs eastwards from the Mediterranean Sea to the city of Hethlon, to Hamath Pass, to the city of Zedad, [w] [16] to the cities of Berothah and Sibraim (they are located between the territory of the kingdom of Damascus and that of the kingdom of Hamath), and to the city of Ticon (located by the border of the district of Hauran). [17] So the northern boundary runs from the Mediterranean eastwards to the city of Enon, with the border regions of Damascus and Hamath to the north of it.

18 "The eastern boundary runs south from a point between the territory of Damascus and that of Hauran, with the River Jordan forming the boundary between the land of Israel on the west and Gilead on the east, as far as Tamar [y] on the Dead Sea.

19 "The southern boundary runs south-west from Tamar to the oasis of Kadesh Meribah, and then north-west along the Egyptian border to the Mediterranean Sea.

20 "The western boundary is formed by the Mediterranean and runs north to a point west of Hamath Pass.

21 "Divide this land among your tribes; [22] it is to be your permanent possession. The foreigners who are living among you and who have had children born here are also to receive their share of the land when you divide it. They are to be treated like full Israelite citizens and are to draw lots for shares of the land along with the tribes of Israel. [23] Each foreign resident will receive his share with the people of the tribe among whom he is living. I, the Sovereign LORD, have spoken."

The Division of the Land among the Tribes

48 [1-7] The northern boundary of the land runs eastwards from the Mediterranean Sea to the city of Hethlon, to Hamath Pass, to the city of Enon, to the boundary between the kingdoms of Damascus and Hamath. Each tribe is to receive one section of land extending from the eastern boundary westwards to the Mediterranean Sea, [z] in the following order from north to south:

Dan
Asher
Naphtali
Manasseh
Ephraim
Reuben
Judah

The Special Section in the Centre of the Land

8 The next section of the land is to be

---

[v] TWO SECTIONS: *The tribes of Manasseh and Ephraim, the sons of Joseph, were each given one section.*
[w] *One ancient translation* Hamath...Zedad; *Hebrew* Zedad Pass to the city of Hamath.
[y] *Some ancient translations* Tamar; *Hebrew unclear.*
[z] *One ancient translation* extending...Sea; *Hebrew* having an eastern boundary and a western boundary.

set apart for special use. It is to be twelve and a half kilometres wide from north to south, and the same length from east to west as the sections given to the tribes. The Temple will be in this section.

9 In the centre of this section, a special area twelve and a half kilometres by ten kilometres[x] is to be dedicated to the LORD. 10 The priests are to have a portion of this holy area. From east to west their portion is to measure twelve and a half kilometres, and from north to south, five kilometres. The Temple of the LORD is to be in the middle of this area. 11 This holy area is to be for the priests who are descendants of Zadok. They served me faithfully and did not join the rest of the Israelites in doing wrong, as the other members of the tribe of Levi did. 12 So they are to have a special area next to the area belonging to the Levites, and it will be the holiest of all. 13 The Levites also are to have a special area, south of that of the priests. It too is to be twelve and a half kilometres from east to west, by five kilometres from north to south. 14 The area dedicated to the LORD is the best part of all the land, and none of it may be sold or exchanged or transferred to anyone else. It is holy and belongs to the LORD.

15 The part of the special area that is left, twelve and a half kilometres by two and a half kilometres, is not holy, but is for the general use of the people. They may live there and use the land. The city is to be in the centre of it, 16 and it will be a square, measuring 2,250 metres on each side. 17 All round the city on each side there will be an open space 125 metres across. 18 The land that is left after the city has been built in the area immediately to the south of the holy area—five kilometres by two and a half kilometres on the east and five kilometres by two and a half kilometres on the west— is to be used as farm land by the people who live in the city. 19 Anyone who lives in the city, no matter which tribe he comes from, may farm that land.

20 And so the total area in the centre of the section which was set apart will

be a square measuring twelve and a half kilometres on each side, and it will include the area occupied by the city.

21-22 To the east and to the west of this area which contains the Temple, the priests' land, the Levites' land, and the city, the remaining land belongs to the ruling prince. It extends eastwards to the eastern boundary and westwards to the Mediterranean Sea, and is bounded on the north by the section belonging to Judah and on the south by the section belonging to Benjamin.

Land for the Other Tribes

23-27 South of this special section, each of the remaining tribes is to receive one section of land running from the eastern boundary westwards to the Mediterranean Sea, in the following order from north to south:

> Benjamin
> Simeon
> Issachar
> Zebulun
> Gad

28 On the south side of the portion given to the tribe of Gad, the boundary runs south-west from Tamar to the oasis of Kadesh, and then north-west along the Egyptian border to the Mediterranean Sea. 29 The Sovereign LORD said, "That is the way the land is to be divided into sections for the tribes of Israel to possess."

The Gates of Jerusalem

30-34 There are twelve entrances to the city of Jerusalem. Each of the four walls measures 2,250 metres and has three gates in it, each named after one of the tribes. The gates in the north wall are named after Reuben, Judah, and Levi; those in the east wall, after Joseph, Benjamin, and Dan; those in the south wall, after Simeon, Issachar, and Zebulun; and those in the west wall are named after Gad, Asher, and Naphtali. 35 The total length of the wall on all four sides of the city is nine thousand metres. The name of the city from now on will be, "The-LORD-Is-Here!"

---

[x] *Probable text (see 45.1)* ten kilometres; *Hebrew* five kilometres.
48.30-34: Rev 21.12-13

THE BOOK OF
DANIEL

INTRODUCTION

The book of *Daniel* was written during a time when the Jews were suffering greatly under the persecution and oppression of a pagan king. Using stories and accounts of visions, the writer encourages the people of his time with the hope that God will bring the tyrant down and restore sovereignty to God's people.

The book has two main parts: (1) Stories about Daniel and some of his fellow-exiles, who through their faith in God and obedience to him triumph over their enemies. These stories are set in the time of the Babylonian and Persian Empires. (2) A series of visions seen by Daniel, which in the form of symbols present the successive rise and fall of several empires, beginning with Babylonia, and predict the downfall of the pagan oppressor and the victory of God's people.

Outline of Contents
Daniel and his friends 1.1—6.28
Daniel's visions 7.1—11.45
  a. The four beasts 7.1–28
  b. The ram and the goat 8.1—9.27
  c. The heavenly messenger 10.1—11.45
  d. The time of the end 12.1–13

THE STORY OF DANIEL AND HIS FRIENDS
(1.1—6.28)

The Young Men at Nebuchadnezzar's Court

1 In the third year that Jehoiakim was king of Judah, King Nebuchadnezzar of Babylonia attacked Jerusalem and surrounded the city. ²The Lord let him capture King Jehoiakim and seize some of the temple treasures. He took some prisoners back with him to the temple of his gods in Babylon, and put the captured treasures in the temple storerooms.

3 The king ordered Ashpenaz, his chief official, to select from among the Israelite exiles some young men of the royal family and of the noble families. ⁴They had to be handsome, intelligent, well-trained, quick to learn, and free from physical defects, so that they would be qualified to serve in the royal court. Ashpenaz was to teach them to read and write the Babylonian language. ⁵The king also gave orders that every day they were to be given the same food and wine as the members of the royal court. After three years of this training they were to appear before the king. ⁶Among those chosen were Daniel, Hananiah, Mishael, and Azariah, all of whom were from the tribe

1.1: 2 Kgs 24.1; 2 Chr 36.5-7   **1.2-4:** 2 Kgs 20.17-18, 24.10-16; 2 Chr 36.10; Is 39.7-8

of Judah. 7 The chief official gave them new names: Belteshazzar, Shadrach, Meshach, and Abednego.

8 Daniel made up his mind not to let himself become ritually unclean by eating the food and drinking the wine of the royal court, so he asked Ashpenaz to help him, 9 and God made Ashpenaz sympathetic to Daniel. 10 Ashpenaz, however, was afraid of the king, so he said to Daniel, "The king has decided what you are to eat and drink, and if you don't look as fit as the other young men, he may kill me."

11 So Daniel went to the guard whom Ashpenaz had placed in charge of him and his three friends. 12 "Test us for ten days," he said. "Give us vegetables to eat and water to drink. 13 Then compare us with the young men who are eating the food of the royal court, and base your decision on how we look."

14 He agreed to let them try it for ten days. 15 When the time was up, they looked healthier and stronger than all those who had been eating the royal food. 16 So from then on the guard let them continue to eat vegetables instead of what the king provided.

17 God gave the four young men knowledge and skill in literature and philosophy. In addition, he gave Daniel skill in interpreting visions and dreams.

18 At the end of the three years set by the king, Ashpenaz took all the young men to Nebuchadnezzar. 19 The king talked with them all, and Daniel, Hananiah, Mishael, and Azariah impressed him more than any of the others. So they became members of the king's court. 20 No matter what question the king asked, or what problem he raised, these four knew ten times more than any fortune-teller or magician in his whole kingdom. 21 Daniel remained at the royal court until Cyrus the emperor of Persia conquered Babylonia.

Nebuchadnezzar's Dream

2 In the second year that Nebuchadnezzar was king, he had a dream. It worried him so much that he couldn't sleep, 2 so he sent for his fortune-tellers, magicians, sorcerers, and wizards to come and explain the dream to him. When they came and stood before the king, 3 he said to them, "I'm worried about a dream I have had. I want to know what it means."

4 They answered the king in Aramaic, a "May Your Majesty live for ever! Tell

us your dream, and we will explain it to you."

5 The king said to them, "I have made up my mind that you must tell me the dream and then tell me what it means. If you can't, I'll have you torn limb from limb and make your houses a pile of ruins. 6 But if you can tell me both the dream and its meaning, I will reward you with gifts and great honour. Now then, tell me what the dream was and what it means."

7 They answered the king again, "If Your Majesty will only tell us what the dream was, we will explain it."

8 At that, the king exclaimed, "Just as I thought! You are trying to gain time, because you see that I have made up my mind 9 to give all of you the same punishment if you don't tell me the dream. You have agreed among yourselves to go on telling me lies because you hope that in time things will change. Tell me what the dream was, and then I will know that you can also tell me what it means."

10 The advisers replied, "There is no one on the face of the earth who can tell Your Majesty what you want to know. No king, not even the greatest and most powerful, has ever made such a demand of his fortune-tellers, magicians, and wizards. 11 What Your Majesty is asking for is so difficult that no one can do it for you except the gods, and they do not live among human beings."

12 At that, the king flew into a rage and ordered the execution of all the royal advisers in Babylon. 13 So the order was issued for all of them to be killed, including Daniel and his friends.

God Shows Daniel What the Dream Means

14 Then Daniel went to Arioch, commander of the king's bodyguard, who had been ordered to carry out the execution. Choosing his words carefully, 15 he asked Arioch why the king had issued such a harsh order. So Arioch told Daniel what had happened.

16 Daniel went at once and obtained royal permission for more time, so that he could tell the king what the dream meant. 17 Then Daniel went home and told his friends Hananiah, Mishael, and Azariah what had happened. 18 He told them to pray to the God of heaven for mercy and to ask him to explain the mystery to them so that they would not be killed along with the other advisers in Babylon.

---

a From here to the end of chapter 7, the language used is Aramaic, not Hebrew.
2.2: Gen 41.8

CHAPTER 2 v.3

v.10

v.12

v.15

v.17

v.19

v.28

v.31

v.34

v.35

v.36

v.46

v.47

19 Then that same night the mystery was revealed to Daniel in a vision, and he praised the God of heaven:
20 "God is wise and powerful!
   praise him for ever and ever.
21 He controls the times and the seasons;
   he makes and unmakes kings;
   it is he who gives wisdom and
      understanding.
22 He reveals things that are deep and
      secret;
   he knows what is hidden in darkness,
      and he himself is surrounded by light.
23 I praise you and honour you, God of
      my ancestors.
   You have given me wisdom and
      strength;
   you have answered my prayer
   and shown us what to tell the king."

Daniel Tells the King the Dream and Explains It

24 So Daniel went to Arioch, whom the king had commanded to execute the royal advisers. He said to him, "Don't put them to death. Take me to the king, and I will tell him what his dream means."
25 At once Arioch took Daniel into King Nebuchadnezzar's presence and told the king, "I have found one of the Jewish exiles, who can tell Your Majesty the meaning of your dream."
26 The king said to Daniel (who was also called Belteshazzar), "Can you tell me what I dreamt and what it means?"
27 Daniel replied, "Your Majesty, there is no wizard, magician, fortune-teller, or astrologer who can tell you that. 28 But there is a God in heaven, who reveals mysteries. He has informed Your Majesty what will happen in the future. Now I will tell you the dream, the vision you had while you were asleep.
29 "While Your Majesty was sleeping, you dreamt about the future; and God, who reveals mysteries, showed you what is going to happen. 30 Now, this mystery was revealed to me, not because I am wiser than anyone else, but so that Your Majesty may learn the meaning of your dream and understand the thoughts that have come to you.
31 "Your Majesty, in your vision you saw standing before you a giant statue, bright and shining, and terrifying to look at. 32 Its head was made of the finest gold; its chest and arms were made of silver; its waist and hips of bronze; 33 its legs of iron, and its feet partly of iron and partly of clay. 34 While you were looking

at it, a great stone broke loose from a cliff without anyone touching it, struck the iron and clay feet of the statue, and shattered them. 35 At once the iron, clay, bronze, silver, and gold crumbled and became like the dust on a threshing-place in summer. The wind carried it all away, leaving not a trace. But the stone grew to be a mountain that covered the whole earth.
36 "This was the dream. Now I will tell Your Majesty what it means. 37 Your Majesty, you are the greatest of all kings. The God of heaven has made you emperor and given you power, might, and honour. 38 He has made you ruler of all the inhabited earth and ruler over all the animals and birds. You are the head of gold. 39 After you there will be another empire, not as great as yours, and after that a third, an empire of bronze, which will rule the whole earth. 40 And then there will be a fourth empire, as strong as iron, which shatters and breaks everything. And just as iron shatters everything, it will shatter and crush all the earlier empires. 41 You also saw that the feet and the toes were partly clay and partly iron. This means that it will be a divided empire. It will have something of the strength of iron, because there was iron mixed with the clay. 42 The toes—partly iron and partly clay—mean that part of the empire will be strong and part of it weak. 43 You also saw that the iron was mixed with the clay. This means that the rulers of that empire will try to unite their families by intermarriage, but they will not be able to, any more than iron can mix with clay. 44 At the time of those rulers the God of heaven will establish a kingdom that will never end. It will never be conquered, but will completely destroy all those empires, and then last for ever. 45 You saw how a stone broke loose from a cliff without anyone touching it and how it struck the statue made of iron, bronze, clay, silver, and gold. The great God is telling Your Majesty what will happen in the future. I have told you exactly what you dreamt, and have given you its true meaning."

The King Rewards Daniel

46 Then King Nebuchadnezzar bowed to the ground and gave orders for sacrifices and offerings to be made to Daniel. 47 The king said, "Your God is the greatest of all gods, the Lord over kings, and the one who reveals mysteries. I know this because you have been able to explain

this mystery." ⁴⁸Then he gave Daniel a high position, presented him with many splendid gifts, put him in charge of the province of Babylon, and made him the head of all the royal advisers. ⁴⁹At Daniel's request the king put Shadrach, Meshach, and Abednego in charge of the affairs of the province of Babylon; Daniel, however, remained at the royal court.

Nebuchadnezzar Commands Everyone to Worship a Gold Statue

3 King Nebuchadnezzar had a gold statue made, twenty-seven metres high and nearly three metres wide, and he had it set up in the plain of Dura in the province of Babylon. ²Then the king gave orders for all his officials to come together—the princes, governors, lieutenant-governors, commissioners, treasurers, judges, magistrates, and all the other officials of the provinces. They were to attend the dedication of the statue which King Nebuchadnezzar had set up. ³When all these officials gathered for the dedication and stood in front of the statue, ⁴a herald announced in a loud voice, "People of all nations, races, and languages! ⁵You will hear the sound of the trumpets, followed by the playing of oboes, lyres, zithers, and harps; and then all the other instruments will join in. As soon as the music starts, you are to bow down and worship the gold statue that King Nebuchadnezzar has set up. ⁶Anyone who does not bow down and worship will immediately be thrown into a blazing furnace." ⁷And so, as soon as they heard the sound of the instruments, the people of all the nations, races, and languages bowed down and worshipped the gold statue which King Nebuchadnezzar had set up.

Daniel's Three Friends Are Accused of Disobedience

8 It was then that some Babylonians took the opportunity to denounce the Jews. ⁹They said to King Nebuchadnezzar, "May Your Majesty live for ever! ¹⁰Your Majesty has issued an order that as soon as the music starts, everyone is to bow down and worship the gold statue, ¹¹and that anyone who does not bow down and worship it is to be thrown into a blazing furnace. ¹²There are some Jews whom you put in charge of the province

of Babylon—Shadrach, Meshach, and Abednego—who are disobeying Your Majesty's orders. They do not worship your god or bow down to the statue you set up."

13 At that, the king flew into a rage and ordered the three men to be brought before him. ¹⁴He said to them, "Shadrach, Meshach, and Abednego, is it true that you refuse to worship my god and to bow down to the gold statue I have set up? ¹⁵Now then, as soon as you hear the sound of the trumpets, oboes, lyres, zithers, harps, and all the other instruments, bow down and worship the statue. If you do not, you will immediately be thrown into a blazing furnace. Do you think there is any god who can save you?"

16 Shadrach, Meshach, and Abednego answered, "Your Majesty, we will not try to defend ourselves. ¹⁷If the God whom we serve is able to save us from the blazing furnace and from your power, then he will. ᵈ ¹⁸But even if he doesn't, Your Majesty may be sure that we will not worship your god, and we will not bow down to the gold statue that you have set up."

Daniel's Three Friends Are Sentenced to Death

19 Then Nebuchadnezzar lost his temper, and his face turned red with anger at Shadrach, Meshach, and Abednego. So he ordered his men to heat the furnace seven times hotter than usual. ²⁰And he commanded the strongest men in his army to tie the three men up and throw them into the blazing furnace. ²¹So they tied them up, fully dressed—shirts, robes, caps, and all—and threw them into the blazing furnace. ²²Now because the king had given strict orders for the furnace to be made extremely hot, the flames burnt up the guards who took the men to the furnace. ²³Then Shadrach, Meshach, and Abednego, still tied up, fell into the heart of the blazing fire.

24 Suddenly Nebuchadnezzar leapt to his feet in amazement. He asked his officials, "Didn't we tie up three men and throw them into the blazing furnace?"

They answered, "Yes, we did, Your Majesty."

25 "Then why do I see four men walking about in the fire?" he asked. "They are not tied up, and they show no sign of

ᵈIf the God...will; or If it is true that we refuse to worship your god or bow down to the gold statue you set up, the God whom we serve is able to save us from the blazing furnace and from your power—and he will.

The fourth one looks like an angel (3.25)

being hurt—and the fourth one looks like an angel."[x]

The Three Men Are Released and Promoted

26 So Nebuchadnezzar went up to the door of the blazing furnace and called out, "Shadrach! Meshach! Abednego! Servants of the Supreme God! Come out!" And they came out at once. [27] All the princes, governors, lieutenant-governors, and other officials of the king gathered to look at the three men, who had not been harmed by the fire. Their hair was not singed, their clothes were not burnt, and there was no smell of smoke on them. 28 The king said, "Praise the God of Shadrach, Meshach, and Abednego! He sent his angel and rescued these men who serve and trust him. They disobeyed my orders and risked their lives rather than bow down and worship any god except their own.

29 "And now I command that if anyone of any nation, race, or language speaks disrespectfully of the God of Shadrach, Meshach, and Abednego, he is to be torn limb from limb, and his house is to be made a pile of ruins. There is no other god who can rescue like this."

30 And the king promoted Shadrach, Meshach, and Abednego to higher pos-

itions in the province of Babylon.

Nebuchadnezzar's Second Dream

4 King Nebuchadnezzar sent the following message to the people of all nations, races, and languages in the world:

"Greetings! [2] Listen to my account of the wonders and miracles which the Supreme God has shown me.

3 "How great are the wonders God shows us!
How powerful are the miracles he performs!
God is king for ever; he will rule for all time.

4 "I was living comfortably in my palace, enjoying great prosperity. [5] But I had a frightening dream and saw terrifying visions while I was asleep. [6] I ordered all the royal advisers in Babylon to be brought to me so that they could tell me what the dream meant. [7] Then all the fortune-tellers, magicians, wizards, and astrologers were brought in, and I told them my dream, but they could not explain it to me. [8] Then Daniel came in. (He is also called Belteshazzar, after the name of my god.) The spirit of the holy gods[e] is in him, so I told him what I had dreamt. I said to him: [9] Belteshazzar, chief of the fortune-tellers, I know that the spirit of the holy gods[f] is in you, and

[x] an angel; *or* a son of the gods; *or* a son of God.
[e] gods; *or* God.
[f] gods; *or* God.

that you understand all mysteries. This is [g] my dream. Tell me what it means.

10 "While I was asleep, I had a vision of a huge tree in the middle of the earth. [11] It grew bigger and bigger until it reached the sky and could be seen by everyone in the world. [12] Its leaves were beautiful, and it was loaded down with fruit— enough for the whole world to eat. Wild animals rested in its shade, birds built nests in its branches, and every kind of living being ate its fruit.

13 "While I was thinking about the vision, I saw coming down from heaven an angel, alert and watchful. [14] He proclaimed in a loud voice, 'Cut the tree down and chop off its branches; strip off its leaves and scatter its fruit. Drive the animals from under it and the birds out of its branches. [15] But leave the stump in the ground with a band of iron and bronze round it. Leave it there in the field with the grass.

" 'Now let the dew fall on this man, and let him live with the animals and the plants. [16] For seven years he will not have a human mind, but the mind of an animal. [17] This is the decision of the alert and watchful angels. So then, let all people everywhere know that the Supreme God has power over human kingdoms and that he can give them to anyone he chooses— even to the least important of men.'

18 "This is the dream I had," said King Nebuchadnezzar. "Now, Belteshazzar, tell me what it means. None of my royal advisers could tell me, but you can, because the spirit of the holy gods [h] is in you."

Daniel Explains the Dream

19 At this, Daniel, who is also called Belteshazzar, was so alarmed that he could not say anything. The king said to him, "Belteshazzar, don't let the dream and its message alarm you."

Belteshazzar replied, "Your Majesty, I wish that the dream and its explanation applied to your enemies and not to you. [20] The tree, so tall that it reached the sky, could be seen by everyone in the world. [21] Its leaves were beautiful, and it had enough fruit on it to feed the whole world. Wild animals rested under it, and birds made their nests in its branches.

22 "Your Majesty, you are the tree, tall and strong. You have grown so great that you reach the sky, and your power extends over the whole world. [23] While

So tall that it reached the sky (4.20)

Leave the stump in the ground (4.23)

Your Majesty was watching, an angel came down from heaven and said, 'Cut the tree down and destroy it, but leave the stump in the ground. Wrap a band of iron and bronze round it, and leave it in the field with the grass. Let the dew fall on this man, and let him live there with the animals for seven years.'

24 "This, then, is what it means, Your Majesty, and this is what the Supreme

[g] *Probable text* This is; *Aramaic* Visions of.   [h] gods; *or* God.

God has declared will happen to you. ²⁵You will be driven away from human society and will live with wild animals. For seven years you will eat grass like an ox, and sleep in the open air, where the dew will fall on you. Then you will admit that the Supreme God controls all human kingdoms, and that he can give them to anyone he chooses. ²⁶The angel ordered the stump to be left in the ground. This means that you will become king again when you acknowledge that God rules all the world. ²⁷So then, Your Majesty, follow my advice. Stop sinning, do what is right, and be merciful to the poor.ⁱ Then you will continue to be prosperous."

28 All this did happen to King Nebuchadnezzar. ²⁹Only twelve months later, while he was walking about on the roof of his royal palace in Babylon, ³⁰he said, "Look how great Babylon is! I built it as my capital city to display my power and might, my glory and majesty."

31 Before the words were out of his mouth, a voice spoke from heaven, "King Nebuchadnezzar, listen to what I say! Your royal power is now taken away from you. ³²You will be driven away from human society, live with wild animals, and eat grass like an ox for seven years. Then you will acknowledge that the Supreme God has power over human kingdoms and that he can give them to anyone he chooses."

33 The words came true immediately. Nebuchadnezzar was driven out of human society and ate grass like an ox. The dew fell on his body, and his hair grew as long as eagles' feathers and his nails as long as birds' claws.

Nebuchadnezzar Praises God

34 "When the seven years had passed," said the king, "I looked up at the sky, and my sanity returned. I praised the Supreme God and gave honour and glory to the one who lives for ever.

"He will rule for ever,
    and his kingdom will last for all time.
³⁵ He looks on the people of the earth
    as nothing;
    angels in heaven and people on earth
    are under his control.
No one can oppose his will
    or question what he does.

36 "When my sanity returned, my honour, my majesty, and the glory of my kingdom were given back to me. My officials and my noblemen welcomed me, and I was given back my royal power, with even greater honour than before.

37 "And now, I, Nebuchadnezzar, praise, honour, and glorify the King of Heaven. Everything he does is right and just, and he can humble anyone who acts proudly."

Belshazzar's Banquet

5 One night King Belshazzar invited a thousand noblemen to a great banquet, and they drank wine together. ²While they were drinking, Belshazzar gave orders to bring in the gold and silver cups and bowls which his fatherˣ Nebuchadnezzar had carried off from the Temple in Jerusalem. The king sent for them so that he, his noblemen, his wives, and his concubines could drink out of them. ³At once the gold cups and bowls were brought in, and they all drank wine out of them ⁴and praised gods made of gold, silver, bronze, iron, wood, and stone.

5 Suddenly a human hand appeared and

Suddenly a human hand appeared (5.5)

began writing on the plaster wall of the palace, where the light from the lamps was shining most brightly. And the king saw the hand as it was writing. ⁶He turned pale and was so frightened that his knees began to shake. ⁷He shouted for someone to bring in the magicians, wizards, and astrologers. When they came in, the king said to them, "Anyone who can read this writing and tell me what it means will be dressed in robes of royal purple, wear a gold chain of honour round his neck, and be the third in power in the kingdom."

ⁱ Stop sinning...to the poor; *or* Make up for your sins by doing what is right and by being merciful to the poor.   ˣ *There were several kings of Babylonia between Nebuchadnezzar and Belshazzar. Father may mean predecessor, or the name Nebuchadnezzar may be used for Nabinodus.*

⁸The royal advisers came forward, but none of them could read the writing or tell the king what it meant. ⁹In his distress King Belshazzar grew even paler, and his noblemen had no idea what to do.

10 The queen mother heard the noise made by the king and his noblemen and entered the banqueting-hall. She said, "May Your Majesty live for ever! Please do not be so disturbed and look so pale. ¹¹There is a man in your kingdom who has the spirit of the holy gods ᵏ in him. When your father was king, this man showed good sense, knowledge, and wisdom like the wisdom of the gods. And King Nebuchadnezzar, your father, ˣ made him chief of the fortune-tellers, magicians, wizards, and astrologers. ¹²He has unusual ability and is wise and skilful in interpreting dreams, solving riddles, and explaining mysteries; so send for this man Daniel, whom the king named Belteshazzar, and he will tell you what all this means."

Daniel Explains the Writing

13 Daniel was brought at once into the king's presence, and the king said to him, "Are you Daniel, that Jewish exile whom my father the king brought here from Judah? ¹⁴I have heard that the spirit of the holy gods ᵏ is in you and that you are skilful and have knowledge and wisdom. ¹⁵The advisers and magicians were brought in to read this writing and tell me what it means, but they could not discover the meaning. ¹⁶Now I have heard that you can find hidden meanings and explain mysteries. If you can read this writing and tell me what it means, you will be dressed in robes of royal purple, wear a gold chain of honour round your neck, and be the third in power in the kingdom."

17 Daniel replied, "Keep your gifts for yourself or give them to someone else. I will read for Your Majesty what has been written and tell you what it means.

18 "The Supreme God made your father Nebuchadnezzar a great king and gave him dignity and majesty. ¹⁹He was so great that people of all nations, races, and languages were afraid of him and trembled. If he wanted to kill someone, he did; if he wanted to keep someone alive, he did. He honoured or disgraced anyone he wanted to. ²⁰But because he

became proud, stubborn, and cruel, he was removed from his royal throne and lost his place of honour. ²¹He was driven away from human society, and his mind became like that of an animal. He lived with wild donkeys, ate grass like an ox, and slept in the open air with nothing to protect him from the dew. Finally he admitted that the Supreme God controls all human kingdoms and can give them to anyone he chooses.

22 "But you, his son, have not humbled yourself, even though you knew all this. ²³You acted against the Lord of heaven and brought in the cups and bowls taken from his Temple. You, your noblemen, your wives, and your concubines drank wine out of them and praised gods made of gold, silver, bronze, iron, wood, and stone—gods that cannot see or hear and that do not know anything. But you did not honour the God who determines whether you live or die and who controls everything you do. ²⁴That is why God has sent the hand to write these words.

25 "This is what was written: 'Number, number, weight, divisions.' ²⁶And this is what it means: *number,* God has numbered the days of your kingdom and brought it to an end; ²⁷*weight,* you have been weighed on the scales and found to be too light; ²⁸*divisions,* your kingdom is divided up and given to the Medes and Persians." ˡ

29 Immediately Belshazzar ordered his servants to dress Daniel in a robe of royal purple and to hang a gold chain of honour round his neck. And he made him the third in power in the kingdom. ³⁰That same night Belshazzar, the king of Babylonia, was killed; ³¹and Darius the Mede, who was then sixty-two years old, seized the royal power.

Daniel in the Pit of Lions

6 Darius decided to appoint a hundred and twenty governors to hold office throughout his empire. ²In addition, he chose Daniel and two others to supervise the governors and to look after the king's interests. ³Daniel soon showed that he could do better work than the other supervisors or the governors. Because he was so outstanding, the king considered putting him in charge of the whole empire. ⁴Then the other supervisors and the governors tried to find something wrong

---

ᵏ gods; *or God.*   ˣ *your father (see 5.2).*
ˡ PERSIANS: *In Aramaic the word for "Persians" sounds like the word for "division."*
5.29: Gen 41.42

with the way Daniel administered the empire, but they couldn't, because Daniel was reliable and did not do anything wrong or dishonest. 5 They said to one another, "We are not going to find anything of which to accuse Daniel unless it is something in connection with his religion."

6 So they went to see the king and said, "King Darius, may Your Majesty live for ever! 7 All of us who administer your empire—the supervisors, the governors, the lieutenant-governors, and the other officials—have agreed that Your Majesty should issue an order and enforce it strictly. Give orders that for thirty days no one be permitted to request anything from any god or from any man except from Your Majesty. Anyone who violates this order is to be thrown into a pit filled with lions. 8 So let Your Majesty issue this order and sign it, and it will be in force, a law of the Medes and Persians, which cannot be changed." 9 And so King Darius signed the order. 10 When Daniel learnt

He knelt down at the open windows (6.10)

that the order had been signed, he went home. In an upstairs room of his house there were windows that faced towards Jerusalem. There, just as he had always done, he knelt down at the open windows and prayed to God three times a day.

11 When Daniel's enemies observed him praying to God, 12 all of them went together to the king to accuse Daniel.

They said, "Your Majesty, you signed an order that for the next thirty days anyone who requested anything from any god or from any man except you, would be thrown into a pit filled with lions."

The king replied, "Yes, a strict order, a law of the Medes and Persians, which cannot be changed."

13 Then they said to the king, "Daniel, one of the exiles from Judah, does not respect Your Majesty or obey the order you issued. He prays regularly three times a day."

14 When the king heard this, he was upset and did his best to find some way to rescue Daniel. He kept trying until sunset. 15 Then the men came back to the king and said to him, "Your Majesty knows that according to the laws of the Medes and Persians no order which the king issues can be changed."

16 So the king gave orders for Daniel to be arrested and he was thrown into the pit filled with lions. He said to Daniel, "May your God, whom you serve so loyally, rescue you." 17 A stone was put over the mouth of the pit, and the king placed his own royal seal and the seal of his noblemen on the stone, so that no one could rescue Daniel. 18 Then the king returned to the palace and spent a sleepless night, without food or any form of entertainment.

19 At dawn the king got up and hurried to the pit. 20 When he got there, he called out anxiously, "Daniel, servant of the living God! Was the God you serve so loyally able to save you from the lions?"

21 Daniel answered, "May Your Majesty live for ever! 22 God sent his angel to shut the mouths of the lions so that they would not hurt me. He did this because he knew that I was innocent and because I have not wronged you, Your Majesty."

23 The king was overjoyed and gave orders for Daniel to be pulled up out of the pit. So they pulled him up and saw that he had not been hurt at all, for he trusted God. 24 Then the king gave orders to arrest all the men who had accused Daniel, and they were thrown, together with their wives and their children, into the pit filled with lions. Before they even reached the bottom of the pit, the lions pounced on them and broke all their bones.

25 Then King Darius wrote to the people of all nations, races, and languages on earth:

He knew that I was innocent (6.22)

"Greetings! 26 I command that throughout my empire everyone should fear and respect Daniel's God.

"He is a living God,
  and he will rule for ever.
His kingdom will never be destroyed,
  and his power will never come to an
    end.
27 He saves and rescues;
  he performs wonders and miracles
    in heaven and on earth.
He saved Daniel from being killed by
    the lions."

28 Daniel prospered during the reign of Darius and the reign of Cyrus the Persian.

DANIEL DESCRIBES HIS VISIONS
(7.1—12.13)

Daniel's Vision of the Four Beasts

7 In the first year that Belshazzar was king of Babylonia, I had a dream and saw a vision in the night. I wrote the dream down, and this is the record ²of what I saw that night:

Winds were blowing from all directions and lashing the surface of the ocean. ³Four huge beasts came up out of the ocean, each one different from the others. ⁴The first one looked like a lion, but had wings like an eagle. While I was watching, the wings were torn off. The beast was lifted up and made to stand like a man. And then a human mind was given to it.

5 The second beast looked like a bear standing on its hind legs. It was holding three ribs between its teeth, and a voice said to it, "Go on, eat as much meat as you can!"

6 While I was watching, another beast appeared. It looked like a leopard, but on its back there were four wings, like the wings of a bird, and it had four heads. It had a look of authority about it.

7 As I was watching, a fourth beast appeared. It was powerful, horrible, terrifying. With its huge iron teeth it crushed its victims, and then it trampled on them. Unlike the other beasts, it had ten horns. ⁸While I was staring at the horns, I saw a little horn coming up among the others. It tore out three of the horns that were already there. This horn had human eyes and a mouth that was boasting proudly.

The Vision of the One Who Has Been Living For Ever

9 While I was looking, thrones were put in place. One who had been living for ever sat down on one of the thrones. His clothes were white as snow, and his hair was like pure wool. His throne, mounted on fiery wheels, was blazing with fire, ¹⁰and a stream of fire was pouring out from it. There were many thousands of people there to serve him, and millions of people stood before him. The court began its session, and the books were opened.

11 While I was looking, I could still hear the little horn bragging and boasting. As I watched, the fourth beast was killed,

7.3: Rev 13.1, 17.8   **7.4–6:** Rev 13.2   **7.7:** Rev 12.3, 13.1   **7.8:** Rev 13.5–6
7.9: Rev 20.4, 1.14   **7.10:** Rev 5.11, 20.12

and its body was thrown into the flames and destroyed. [12] The other beasts had their power taken away, but they were permitted to go on living for a limited time.

13 During this vision in the night, I saw what looked like a human being. He was approaching me, surrounded by clouds, and he went to the one who had been living for ever and was presented to him. [14] He was given authority, honour, and royal power, so that the people of all nations, races, and languages would serve him. His authority would last for ever, and his kingdom would never end.

The Visions Are Explained

15 The visions I saw alarmed me, and I was deeply disturbed.[m] [16] I went up to one of those standing there and asked him to explain it all. So he told me the meaning. [17] He said, "These four huge beasts are four empires which will arise on earth. [18] And the people of the Supreme God will receive royal power and keep it for ever and ever."

19 Then I wanted to know more about the fourth beast, which was not like any of the others—the terrifying beast which crushed its victims with its bronze claws and iron teeth and then trampled on them. [20] And I wanted to know about the ten horns on its head and the horn that had come up afterwards and had made three of the horns fall. It had eyes and a mouth and was boasting proudly. It was more terrifying than any of the others.

21 While I was looking, that horn made war on God's people and conquered them. [22] Then the one who had been living for ever came and pronounced judgement in favour of[n] the people of the Supreme God. The time had arrived for God's people to receive royal power.

23 This is the explanation I was given: "The fourth beast is a fourth empire that will be on the earth and will be different from all other empires. It will crush the whole earth and trample it down. [24] The ten horns are ten kings who will rule that empire. Then another king will appear; he will be very different from the earlier ones and will overthrow three kings. [25] He will speak against the Supreme God and

oppress God's people. He will try to change their religious laws and festivals, and God's people will be under his power for three and a half years. [26] Then the heavenly court will sit in judgement, take away his power, and destroy him completely. [27] The power and greatness of all the kingdoms on earth will be given to the people of the Supreme God. Their royal power will never end and all rulers on earth will serve and obey them."

28 This is the end of the account. I was so frightened that I turned pale, and I kept everything to myself.

Daniel's Vision of a Ram and a Goat

8 In the third year that Belshazzar was king, I saw a second vision.[o] [2] In the vision I suddenly found myself in the walled city of Susa in the province of Elam. I was standing by the River Ulai, [3] and there beside the river I saw a ram that had two long horns, one of which was longer and newer than the other. [4] I watched the ram butting with his horns to the west, the north, and the south. No animal could stop him or escape his power. He did as he pleased and grew arrogant.

5 While I was wondering what this meant, a goat came rushing out of the west, moving so fast that his feet didn't touch the ground. He had one prominent horn between his eyes. [6] He came towards the ram, which I had seen standing beside the river, and rushed at him with all his force. [7] I watched him attack the ram. He was so angry that he smashed into him and broke the two horns. The ram had no strength to resist. He was thrown to the ground and trampled on, and there was no one who could save him.

8 The goat grew more and more arrogant, but at the height of his power his horn was broken. In its place four prominent horns came up, each pointing in a different direction. [9] Out of one of these four horns grew a little horn, whose power extended towards the south and the east and towards the Promised Land. [10] It grew strong enough to attack the army of heaven, the stars themselves, and it threw some of them to the ground and trampled on them. [11] It even defied the

---

[m] Aramaic has two additional words, the meaning of which is unclear.
[n] pronounced judgement in favour of; or gave the right to judge to.
[o] Beginning at 8.1, the rest of this book is in Hebrew (see 2.4).
7.13: Mt 24.30, 26.64; Mk 13.26, 14.62; Lk 21.27; Rev 1.7,13, 14.14   **7.14:** Rev 11.15
7.18: Rev 22.5   **7.21:** Rev 13.7   **7.22:** Rev 20.4   **7.24:** Rev 17.12   **7.25:** Rev 12.14, 13.5–6
7.27: Rev 20.4, 22.5   **8.10:** Rev 12.4

Prince of the heavenly army, stopped the daily sacrifices offered to him, and desecrated the Temple. ¹²People sinned there instead of offering the proper daily sacrifices,ᵖ and true religion was thrown to the ground. The horn was successful in everything it did.

13 Then I heard one angel ask another, "How long will these things that were seen in the vision continue? How long will an awful sin replace the daily sacrifices? How long will the army of heaven and the Temple be trampled on?"

14 I heard the other angel answer, "It will continue for 1,150 days, during which evening and morningˣ sacrifices will not be offered. Then the Temple will be restored."

The Angel Gabriel Explains the Vision

15 I was trying to understand what the vision meant, when suddenly someone was standing in front of me. ¹⁶I heard a voice call out over the River Ulai, "Gabriel, explain to him the meaning of what he saw." ¹⁷Gabriel came and stood beside me, and I was so terrified that I fell to the ground.

He said to me, "Mortal man, understand the meaning. The vision has to do with the end of the world." ¹⁸While he was talking, I fell to the ground unconscious. But he took hold of me, raised me to my feet, ¹⁹and said, "I am showing you what the result of God's anger will be. The vision refers to the time of the end.

20 "The ram you saw that had two horns represents the kingdoms of Media and Persia. ²¹The goat represents the kingdom of Greece, and the prominent horn between his eyes is the first king. ²²The four horns that came up when the first horn was broken represent the four kingdoms into which that nation will be divided and which will not be as strong as the first kingdom.

23 "When the end of those kingdoms is near and they have become so wicked that they must be punished, there will be a stubborn, vicious, and deceitful king. ²⁴He will grow strong—but not by his own power. He will cause terrible destruction and be successful in everything he does. He will bring destruction on powerful men and on God's own people. ²⁵Because he is cunning, he will succeed in his deceitful ways. He will be proud of himself and destroy many people without

warning. He will even defy the greatest King of all, but he will be destroyed without the use of any human power. ²⁶This vision about the evening and morning sacrifices which has been explained to you will come true. But keep it secret now, because it will be a long time before it does come true."

27 I was depressed and ill for several days. Then I got up and went back to the work that the king had assigned to me, but I was puzzled by the vision and could not understand it.

Daniel Prays for His People

9 Darius the Mede, who was the son of Xerxes, ruled over the kingdom of Babylonia. ²In the first year of his reign, I was studying the sacred books and thinking about the seventy years that Jerusalem would be in ruins, according to what the LORD had told the prophet Jeremiah. ³And I prayed earnestly to the Lord God, pleading with him, fasting, wearing sackcloth, and sitting in ashes. ⁴I prayed to the LORD my God and confessed the sins of my people.

I said, "Lord God, you are great, and we honour you. You are faithful to your covenant and show constant love to those who love you and do what you command.

5 "We have sinned, we have been evil, we have done wrong. We have rejected what you commanded us to do and have turned away from what you showed us was right. ⁶We have not listened to your servants the prophets, who spoke in your name to our kings, our rulers, our ancestors, and our whole nation. ⁷You, Lord, always do what is right, but we have always brought disgrace on ourselves. This is true of all of us who live in Judaea and in Jerusalem and of all the Israelites whom you scattered in countries near and far because they were unfaithful to you. ⁸Our kings, our rulers, and our ancestors have acted shamefully and sinned against you, Lord. ⁹You are merciful and forgiving, although we have rebelled against you. ¹⁰We did not listen to you, O LORD our God, when you told us to live according to the laws which you gave us through your servants the prophets. ¹¹All Israel broke your laws and refused to listen to what you said. We sinned against you, and so you brought on us the curses that are written in the Law of Moses, your servant. ¹²You did

ᵖPeople...sacrifices; *Hebrew unclear.* ˣ1,150 days...morning; *or* 2,300 days, during which.
8.16: Lk 1.19,26 **9.2:** Jer 25.11, 29.10

what you said you would do to us and our rulers. You punished Jerusalem more severely than any other city on earth, [13] giving us all the punishment described in the Law of Moses. But even now, O LORD our God, we have not tried to please you by turning from our sins or by following your truth. [14] You, O LORD our God, were prepared to punish us, and you did, because you always do what is right, and we did not listen to you.

15 "O Lord our God, you showed your power by bringing your people out of Egypt, and your power is still remembered. We have sinned; we have done wrong. [16] You have defended us in the past, so do not be angry with Jerusalem any longer. It is your city, your sacred hill. [q] All the people in the neighbouring countries look down on Jerusalem and on your people because of our sins and the evil our ancestors did. [17] O God, hear my prayer and pleading. Restore your Temple, which has been destroyed; restore it so that everyone will know that you are God. [18] Listen to us, O God; look at us, and see the trouble we are in and the suffering of the city that bears your name. We are praying to you because you are merciful, not because we have done right. [19] Lord, hear us. Lord, forgive us. Lord, listen to us, and act! In order that everyone will know that you are God, do not delay! This city and these people are yours."

Gabriel Explains the Prophecy

20 I went on praying, confessing my sins and the sins of my people Israel, and pleading with the LORD my God to restore his holy Temple. [21] While I was praying, Gabriel, whom I had seen in the earlier vision, came flying down to where I was. It was the time for the evening sacrifice to be offered. [22] He explained, "Daniel, I have come here to help you understand the prophecy. [23] When you began to plead with God, he answered you. He loves you, and so I have come to tell you the answer. Now pay attention while I explain the vision.

24 "Seven times seventy years is the length of time God has set for freeing your people and your holy city from sin and evil. Sin will be forgiven and eternal

God, do not delay! (9.19)

justice established, so that the vision and the prophecy will come true, and the holy Temple[r] will be rededicated. [25] Note this and understand it: From the time the command is given to rebuild Jerusalem, until God's chosen leader comes, seven times seven years will pass. Jerusalem will be rebuilt with streets and strong defences, and will stand for seven times sixty-two years, but this will be a time of troubles. [26] And at the end of that time God's chosen leader will be killed unjustly.[s] The city and the Temple will be destroyed by the invading army of a powerful ruler. The end will come like a flood, bringing the war and destruction which God has prepared. [27] That ruler will have a firm agreement with many people for seven years, and when half this time is past, he will put an end to sacrifices and offerings. The Awful Horror[t] will be placed on the highest point of the Temple and will remain there until the one who put it there meets the end which God has prepared for him."

---

[q] SACRED HILL: *Mount Zion (see Zion in Word List)*.
[r] Temple; *or altar*.
[s] *One ancient translation* unjustly; *Hebrew unclear*.
[t] THE AWFUL HORROR: *A pagan image set up in the Jerusalem Temple by foreign conquerors (see 1 Macc 1.54–61)*.
9.21: Lk 1.19,26   **9.27:** Dan 11.31, 12.11; Mt 24.15; Mk 13.14

Daniel's Vision by the River Tigris

10 (In the third year that Cyrus was emperor of Persia, a message was revealed to Daniel, who is also called Belteshazzar. The message was true but extremely hard to understand. [u] It was explained to him in a vision.)

2 At that time, I was mourning for three weeks. 3 I did not eat any rich food or any meat, drink any wine, or comb my hair until the three weeks were past.

4 On the twenty-fourth day of the first month of the year, I was standing on the bank of the mighty River Tigris. 5 I looked up and saw someone who was wearing linen clothes and a belt of fine gold. 6 His body shone like a jewel. His face was as bright as a flash of lightning, and his eyes blazed like fire. His arms and legs shone like polished bronze, and his voice sounded like the roar of a great crowd.

7 I was the only one who saw the vision. The men who were with me did not see anything, but they were terrified and ran and hid. 8 I was left there alone, watching this amazing vision. I had no strength left, and my face was so changed that no one could have recognized me. 9 When I heard his voice, I fell to the ground unconscious and lay there face downwards. 10 Then a hand took hold of me and raised me to my hands and knees; I was still trembling.

11 The angel said to me, "Daniel, God loves you. Stand up and listen carefully to what I am going to say. I have been sent to you." When he had said this, I stood up, still trembling.

12 Then he said, "Daniel, don't be afraid. God has heard your prayers ever since the first day you decided to humble yourself in order to gain understanding. I have come in answer to your prayer. 13 The angel prince of the kingdom of Persia opposed me for twenty-one days. Then Michael, one of the chief angels, came to help me, because I had been left there alone in Persia. 14 I have come to make you understand what will happen to your people in the future. This is a vision about the future."

15 When he said this, I stared at the ground, speechless. 16 Then the angel, who looked like a man, stretched out his hand and touched my lips. I said to him, "Sir,

this vision makes me so weak that I can't stop trembling. 17 I am like a slave standing before his master. How can I talk to you? I have no strength or breath left in me."

18 Once more he took hold of me, and I felt stronger. 19 He said, "God loves you, so don't let anything worry you or frighten you."

When he had said this, I felt even stronger and said, "Sir, tell me what you have to say. You have made me feel better."

20-21 He said, "Do you know why I came to you? It is to reveal to you what is written in the Book of Truth. Now I have to go back and fight the guardian angel of Persia. After that, the guardian angel of Greece will appear. There is no one to help me except Michael, Israel's guardian angel. [v]

11 1 He is [w] responsible for helping and defending me. 2 And what I am now going to tell you is true."

The Kingdoms of Egypt and Syria

The angel said, "Three more kings will rule over Persia, followed by a fourth, who will be richer than all the others. At the height of his power and wealth he will challenge the kingdom of Greece.

3 "Then a heroic king will appear. He will rule over a huge empire and do whatever he wants. 4 But at the height of his power his empire will break up and be divided into four parts. Kings not descended from him will rule in his place, but they will not have the power that he had.

5 "The king of Egypt will be strong. One of his generals, however, will be even stronger and rule a greater kingdom. 6 After a number of years the king of Egypt will make an alliance with the king of Syria and give him his daughter in marriage. But the alliance will not last, and she, her husband, her child, [x] and the servants who went with her will all be killed. 7 Soon afterwards, one of her relatives will become king. He will attack the army of the king of Syria, enter their fortress, and defeat them. 8 He will carry back to Egypt the images of their gods and the articles of gold and silver dedicated to those gods. After several years

---

[u] but extremely hard to understand; or and it was about a great war.
[v] Probable text guardian angel; Hebrew guardian angel. And I, in the first year of Darius the Mede.
[w] One ancient translation He is; Hebrew I am.
[x] Some ancient translations her child; Hebrew her father.
10.5-6: Rev 1.13-15, 2.18, 19.12　　　**10.13,21:** Rev 12.7

of peace [9] the king of Syria will invade Egypt, but he will be forced to retreat.

10 "The sons of the king of Syria will prepare for war and gather a large army. One of them will sweep on like a flood and attack an enemy fortress. [11] In his anger the king of Egypt will go to war against the king of Syria and capture his huge army. [12] He will be proud of his victory and of the many soldiers he has killed, but he will not continue to be victorious.

13 "The king of Syria will go back and gather a larger army than he had before. When the proper time comes, he will return with a large, well-equipped army. [14] Then many people will rebel against the king of Egypt. And some violent men from your nation, Daniel, will rebel because of a vision they have seen, but they will be defeated. [15] So the king of Syria will lay siege to a fortified city and capture it. The soldiers of Egypt will not continue to fight; even the best of them will not have enough strength. [16] The Syrian invader will do with them as he pleases, without opposition. He will stand in the Promised Land and have it completely in his power.

17 "The king of Syria will plan an expedition, using his whole army. Then, in order to destroy his enemy's kingdom, he will make an alliance with him and offer him his daughter[y] in marriage; but his plan will not succeed. [18] After that he will attack the nations by the sea and conquer many of them. But a foreign leader will defeat him and put an end to his arrogance; indeed he will turn the arrogance of Syria's king back on him.[z] [19] The king will return to the fortresses of his own land, but he will be defeated, and that will be the end of him.

20 "He will be followed by another king, who will send an officer to oppress the people with taxes in order to increase the wealth of his kingdom. In a short time that king will be killed, but not publicly and not in battle."

The Evil King of Syria

21 The angel went on to explain: "The next king of Syria will be an evil man who has no right to be king, but he will come unexpectedly and seize power by trickery. [22] Anyone who opposes him, even God's High Priest, will be swept away and wiped out. [23] By making treaties, he will deceive other nations, and he will grow stronger and stronger, even though he rules only a small nation. [24] He will invade a wealthy province without warning and will do things that none of his ancestors ever did. Then he will divide among his followers the goods and property he has captured in war. He will make plans to attack fortresses, but his time will soon run out.

25 "He will boldly raise a large army to attack the king of Egypt, who will prepare to fight back with a huge and powerful army. But the king of Egypt will be deceived and will not be successful. [26] His closest advisers will ruin him. Many of his soldiers will be killed, and his army will be wiped out. [27] Then the two kings will sit down to eat at the same table, but their motives will be evil, and they will lie to each other. They will not get what they want, because the time for it has not yet come. [28] The king of Syria will return home with all the loot he has captured, determined to destroy the religion of God's people. He will do as he pleases and then return to his own land.

29 "Later on he will invade Egypt again, but this time things will turn out differently. [30] The Romans will come in ships and oppose him, and he will be frightened.

"Then he will turn back in a rage and try to destroy the religion of God's people. He will follow the advice of those who have abandoned that religion. [31] Some of his soldiers will desecrate the Temple. They will stop the daily sacrifices and set up The Awful Horror.[a] [32] By deceit the king will win the support of those who have already abandoned their religion, but those who follow God will fight back. [33] Wise leaders of the people will share their wisdom with many others. But for a while some of them will be killed in battle or be burnt to death, and some will be robbed and made prisoners. [34] While the killing is going on, God's people will receive a little help, even though many who join them will do so for selfish reasons. [35] Some of those wise leaders will be killed, but as a result of this the people will be purified. This will continue until the end comes, the time that God has set.

y his daughter; *or* a young woman.   z *Probable text* his arrogance...on him: *Hebrew unclear.*
a THE AWFUL HORROR: *See 9.27.*
11.31: Dan 9.27, 12.11; Mt 24.15; Mk 13.14

36 "The king of Syria will do as he pleases. He will boast that he is greater than any god, superior even to the Supreme God. He will be able to do this until the time when God punishes him. God will do exactly what he has planned. 37 The king will ignore the god his ancestors served, and also the god that women love. In fact, he will ignore every god, because he will think he is greater than any of them. 38 Instead, he will honour the god who protects fortresses. He will offer gold, silver, jewels, and other rich gifts to a god his ancestors never worshipped. 39 To defend his fortresses, he will use people who worship a foreign god. He will give great honour to those who accept him as ruler, put them into high offices, and give them land as a reward.

40 "When the king of Syria's final hour has almost come, the king of Egypt will attack him, and the king of Syria will fight back with all his power, using chariots, horses, and many ships. He will invade many countries, like the waters of a flood. 41 He will even invade the Promised Land and kill tens of thousands, but the countries of Edom, Moab, and what is left of Ammon will escape. 42 When he invades all those countries, even Egypt will not be spared. 43 He will take away Egypt's hidden treasures of gold and silver and its other prized possessions. He will conquer Libya and Sudan. 44 Then news that comes from the east and the north will frighten him, and he will fight furiously, killing many people. 45 He will even set up his huge royal tents between the sea and the mountain on which the Temple stands. But he will die, with no one there to help him."

The Time of the End

12 The angel wearing linen clothes said, "At that time the great angel Michael, who guards your people, will appear. Then there will be a time of troubles, the worst since nations first came into existence. When that time comes, all the people of your nation whose names are written in God's book will be saved. 2 Many of those who have already died will live again: some will enjoy eternal life, and some will suffer eternal disgrace. 3 The wise leaders will shine with all the brightness of the sky. And those who have taught many people to do what is right will shine like the stars for ever."

4 He said to me, "And now, Daniel,

Daniel, close the book (12.4)

close the book and put a seal on it until the end of the world. Meanwhile, many people will waste their efforts trying to understand what is happening."

5 Then I saw two men standing by a river, one on each bank. 6 One of them asked the angel who was standing further upstream, "How long will it be until these amazing events come to an end?"

7 The angel raised both hands towards the sky and made a solemn promise in the name of the Eternal God. I heard him say, "It will be three and a half years. When the persecution of God's people ends, all these things will have happened."

8 I heard what he said, but I did not understand it. So I asked, "But, sir, how will it all end?"

9 He answered, "You must go now, Daniel, because these words are to be kept secret and hidden until the end comes. 10 Many people will be purified. Those who are wicked will not understand but will go on being wicked; only those who are wise will understand.

11 "From the time the daily sacrifices are stopped, that is, from the time of The Awful Horror,*b* 1,290 days will pass. 12 Happy are those who remain faithful until 1,335 days are over!

13 "And you, Daniel, be faithful to the end. Then you will die, but you will rise to receive your reward at the end of time."

*b*THE AWFUL HORROR: See 9.27.
11.36: 2 Thes 2.3–4; Rev 13.5–6   **12.1:** Mt 24.21; Mk 13.19; Rev 7.14, 12.7
12.2: Is 26.19; Mt 25.46; Jn 5.29   **12.4:** Rev 22.10   **12.7:** Rev 10.5, 12.14   **12.10:** Rev 22.11
12.11: Dan 9.27, 11.31; Mt 24.15; Mk 13.14

THE BOOK OF
HOSEA

INTRODUCTION

The prophet Hosea preached in the northern kingdom of Israel, after the prophet Amos, during the troubled times before the fall of Samaria in 721 B.C. He was especially concerned about the idolatry of the people and their faithlessness towards God. Hosea boldly pictured this faithlessness in terms of his own disastrous marriage to an unfaithful woman. Just as his wife Gomer turned out to be unfaithful to him, so God's people had deserted the Lord. For this, judgement would fall on Israel. Yet in the end God's constant love for his people would prevail, and he would win the nation back to himself and restore the relationship. This love is expressed in the moving words: "How can I give you up, Israel? How can I abandon you?...My heart will not let me do it! My love for you is too strong" (11.8).

Outline of Contents
Hosea's marriage and family   1.1—3.5
Messages against Israel   4.1—13.16
A message of repentance and promise   14.1-9

1 This is the message which the LORD gave Hosea son of Beeri during the time that Uzziah, Jotham, Ahaz, and Hezekiah were kings of Judah, and Jeroboam son of Jehoash was king of Israel.

Hosea's Wife and Children

2 When the LORD first spoke to Israel through Hosea, he said to Hosea, "Go and get married; your wife will be unfaithful, and your children will be just like her.[a] In the same way, my people have left me and become unfaithful."

3 So Hosea married a woman named Gomer, the daughter of Diblaim. After the birth of their first child, a son, 4 the LORD said to Hosea, "Name him 'Jezreel,' because it will not be long before I punish the king of Israel for the murders that his ancestor Jehu committed at Jezreel.[b] I am going to put an end to Jehu's dynasty.[x] 5 And in the Valley of Jezreel I will at that time destroy Israel's military power."

6 Gomer had a second child—this time it was a girl. The LORD said to Hosea, "Name her 'Unloved,' because I will no longer show love to the people of Israel or forgive them. 7 But to the people of Judah I will show love. I, the LORD their God, will save them, but I will not do

[a] get married; your wife...her; *or* marry a prostitute, and have children by her who will be just as bad as she is.
[b] JEZREEL: *At this city Jehu assassinated the king of Israel and all the rest of the royal family, and became the first king of a new dynasty (see 2 Kgs 9—10).*
[x] Jehu's dynasty; *or* the kingdom of Israel.
1.1: 2 Kgs 14.23—15.7, 15.32—16.20, 18.1—20.21; 2 Chr 26.1—27.8, 28.1—32.33
1.4: 2 Kgs 10.11

it by war—with swords or bows and arrows or with horses and horsemen."

8 After Gomer had weaned her daughter, she became pregnant again and had another son. ⁹ The LORD said to Hosea, "Name him 'Not-My-People,' because the people of Israel are not my people, and I am not their God."

Israel Is to Be Restored

10 The people of Israel will become like the sand of the sea, more than can be counted or measured. Now God says to them, "You are not my people," but the day is coming when he will say to them, "You are the children of the living God!" ¹¹ The people of Judah and the people of Israel will be reunited. They will choose for themselves a single leader, and once again they will grow and prosper in their land. Yes, the day of Jezreel ᶜ will be a **2** great day! ¹ So call your fellow-Israel-ites "God's People" and "Loved-by-the-Lord."

Unfaithful Gomer—Unfaithful Israel

2 My children, plead with your mother—though she is no longer a wife to me, and I am no longer her husband. Plead with her to stop her adultery and prostitution. ³ If she does not, I will strip her as naked as she was on the day she was born. I will make her like a dry and barren land, and she will die of thirst. ⁴⁻⁵ I will not show mercy to her children; they are the children of a shameless prostitute. ᵈ She herself said, "I will go to my lovers—they give me food and water, wool and linen, olive-oil and wine." ⁶ So I am going to fence her in with thorn-bushes and build a wall to block her way. ⁷ She will run after her lovers but will not catch them. She will look for them but will not find them. Then she will say, "I am going back to my first husband—I was better off then than I am now." ⁸ She would never acknowledge that I am the one who gave her the corn, the wine, the olive-oil, and all the silver and gold that she used in the worship of Baal. ⁹ So at harvest time I will take back my gifts of corn and wine, and will take away the wool and the linen I gave her for clothing. ¹⁰ I will strip her naked in front of her lovers, and no one will be able to save her from my power. ¹¹ I will put an end to all her festivities—her annual and monthly festivals and her Sabbath celebrations—all her religious meetings. ¹² I will destroy her grapevines and her fig-trees, which she said her lovers gave her for serving them. I will turn her vineyards and orchards into a wilderness; wild animals will destroy them. ¹³ I will punish her for the times that she forgot me when she burnt incense to Baal and put on her jewellery to go chasing after her lovers. The LORD has spoken.

The LORD's Love for His People

14 So I am going to take her into the desert again; there I will win her back with words of love. ¹⁵ I will give back to her the vineyards she had and make Trouble Valley a door of hope. She will respond to me there as she did when she was young, when she came from Egypt. ¹⁶ Then once again she will call me her husband—she will no longer call me her Baal. ᵉ ¹⁷ I will never let her speak the name of Baal again.

18 At that time I will make a covenant with all the wild animals and birds, so that they will not harm my people. I will also remove all weapons of war from the land, all swords and bows, and will let my people live in peace and safety.

¹⁹ Israel, I will make you my wife;
   I will be true and faithful;
   I will show you constant love and
      mercy
   and make you mine for ever.
²⁰ I will keep my promise and make you
      mine,
   and you will acknowledge me as LORD.
²¹⁻²² At that time I will answer the
      prayers of my people Israel. ᶠ
   I will make rain fall on the earth,
   and the earth will produce corn and
      grapes and olives.
²³ I will establish my people in the land
      and make them prosper.
   I will show love to those who were
      called "Unloved,"
   and to those who were called "Not-
      My-People"

ᶜ JEZREEL: *This name in Hebrew means "God sows" and suggests growth and prosperity.*
ᵈ the children of a shameless prostitute; *or* as shameless as their mother, a prostitute.
ᵉ BAAL: *This title of the Canaanite god means "Lord"; another meaning of the word is "husband."*
ᶠ ISRAEL: *The Hebrew text here refers to Israel as Jezreel (see 1.4,11).*
1.10: Rom 9.26   **2.15:** Josh 7.24-26   **2.23:** Rom 9.25; 1 Pet 2.10

Let my people live in peace (2.18)

I will say, "You are my people,"
and they will answer, "You are our
   God."

Hosea and the Unfaithful Woman

3 The LORD said to me, "Go again[x] and show your love for a woman who is committing adultery with a lover. You must love her just as I still love the people of Israel, even though they turn to other gods and like to take offerings of raisins to idols." [g]

2 So I paid fifteen pieces of silver and 150 kilogrammes of barley to buy her. 3 I told her that for a long time she would have to wait for me without being a prostitute or committing adultery; and during this time I would wait for her. 4 In just this way the people of Israel will have to live for a long time without kings or leaders, without sacrifices or sacred stone pillars, without idols or images to use for divination. 5 But the time will come when the people of Israel will once again turn to the LORD their God, and to a descendant of David their king. Then they will fear the LORD and will receive his good gifts.

The LORD's Accusation against Israel

4 The LORD has an accusation to bring against the people who live in this land. Listen, Israel, to what he says: "There is no faithfulness or love in the land, and the people do not acknowledge me as God. 2 They make promises and break them; they lie, murder, steal, and commit adultery. Crimes increase, and there is one murder after another. 3 And so the land will dry up, and everything that lives on it will die. All the animals and birds, and even the fish, will die."

The LORD Accuses the Priests

4 The LORD says, "Let no one accuse the people or reprimand them—my complaint is against you priests. [h] 5 Night and day you blunder on, and the prophets do no better than you. I am going to destroy Israel, your mother. 6 My people are doomed because they do not acknowledge me. You priests have refused to acknowledge me and have rejected my teaching, and so I reject you and will not acknowledge your sons as my priests.

7 "The more of you priests there are,

---

[x] The LORD...again; *or* The LORD spoke to me again. He said, "Go..."
[g] OFFERINGS OF RAISINS TO IDOLS: *Dried grapes were used in the worship of fertility gods, who were believed to give abundant harvests to their worshippers.*
[h] *Probable text* my complaint is against you priests; *Hebrew* your people are like those with a complaint against the priests.

the more you sin against me, and so I will turn your honour into disgrace. ⁸ You grow rich from the sins of my people, and so you want them to sin more and more. ⁹ You will suffer the same punishment as the people! I will punish you and make you pay for the evil you do. ¹⁰ You will eat your share of the sacrifices, but still be hungry. You will worship the fertility gods, but still have no children, because you have turned away from me to follow other gods."

The Lord Condemns Pagan Worship

11 The Lord says, "Wine, both old and new, is robbing my people of their senses! ¹² They ask for revelations from a piece

They ask for revelations from a piece of wood (4.12)

of wood! A stick tells them what they want to know! They have left me. Like a woman who becomes a prostitute, they have given themselves to other gods. ¹³ At sacred places on the mountain-tops they offer sacrifices, and on the hills they burn

incense under tall, spreading trees, because the shade is so pleasant!

"As a result, your daughters serve as prostitutes, and your daughters-in-law commit adultery. ¹⁴ Yet I will not punish them for this, because you yourselves go off with temple prostitutes,ⁱ and together with them you offer pagan sacrifices. As the proverb says, 'A people without sense will be ruined.'

15 "Even though you people of Israel are unfaithful to me, may Judah not be guilty of the same thing. Don't worship at Gilgal or Bethaven,ʲ or make promises there in the name of the living Lord. ¹⁶ The people of Israel are as stubborn as mules. How can I feed them like lambs in a meadow? ¹⁷ The people of Israel are under the spell of idols. Let them go their own way. ¹⁸ After drinking much wine, they delight in their prostitution, preferring disgrace to honour. ¹⁹ They will be carried away as by the wind, and they will be ashamed of their pagan sacrifices.ᵏ

5 "Listen to this, you priests! Pay attention, people of Israel! Listen, you that belong to the royal family! You are supposed to judge with justice—so judgement will fall on you! You have become a trap at Mizpah, a net spread on Mount Tabor, ²a deep pit at Acacia City,ˡ and I will punish all of you. ³ I know what Israel is like—she cannot hide from me. She has been unfaithful, and her people are unfit to worship me."

Hosea Warns against Idolatry

4 The evil that the people have done prevents them from returning to their God. Idolatry has a powerful hold on them, and they do not acknowledge the Lord. ⁵ The arrogance of the people of Israel cries out against them. Their sins make them stumble and fall, and the people of Judah fall with them. ⁶ They take their sheep and cattle to offer as sacrifices to the Lord, but it does them no good. They cannot find him, for he has left them. ⁷ They have been unfaithful to the Lord; their children do not belong to him. So now they and their lands will soon be destroyed.

War between Judah and Israel

8 Blow the war trumpets in Gibeah!

ⁱ TEMPLE PROSTITUTES: *These women were found in Canaanite temples, where fertility gods were worshipped. It was believed that intercourse with these prostitutes assured fertile fields and herds.*
ʲ BETHAVEN: *This name means "house of evil" or "house of idolatry" and in this passage refers to the city of Bethel, a name which means "house of God." See also 5.8 and 10.8*
ᵏ sacrifices; *some ancient translations* altars. *Verses 17–19 in Hebrew are unclear.*
ˡ *Probable text* a deep pit at Acacia City; *Hebrew unclear.*

Sound the alarm in Ramah! Raise the war-cry at Bethaven! Into battle, men of Benjamin! ⁹The day of punishment is coming, and Israel will be ruined. People of Israel, this will surely happen!

10 The LORD says, "I am angry because the leaders of Judah have invaded Israel and stolen land from her. So I will pour out punishment on them like a flood. ¹¹Israel is suffering oppression; she has lost land that was rightfully hers, because she insisted on going for help to those who had none to give.ᵐ ¹²I will bring destruction on Israel and ruin on the people of Judah.

13 "When Israel saw how sick she was and when Judah saw her own wounds, then Israel went to Assyria to ask the great emperor for help, but he could not cure them or heal their wounds. ¹⁴I will attack the people of Israel and Judah like a lion. I myself will tear them to pieces and then leave them. When I drag them off, no one will be able to save them.

15 "I will abandon my people until they have suffered enough for their sins and come looking for me. Perhaps in their suffering they will try to find me."

The People's Insincere Repentance

6 The people say, "Let's return to the LORD! He has hurt us, but he will be sure to heal us; he has wounded us, but he will bandage our wounds, won't he? ²In two or three days he will revive us, and we will live in his presence. ³Let us try to know the LORD. He will come to us as surely as the day dawns, as surely as the spring rains that water the earth."

4 But the LORD says, "Israel and Judah, what am I going to do with you? Your love for me disappears as quickly as morning mist; it is like dew, that vanishes early in the day. ⁵That is why I have sent my prophets to you with my message of judgement and destruction. What I want from you is plain and clear: ⁶I want your constant love, not your animal sacrifices. I would rather have my people know me than burn offerings to me.

7 "But as soon as they entered the land at Adam,ⁿ they broke the covenant I had made with them. ⁸Gilead is a city full of evil men and murderers. ⁹The priests are like a gang of robbers who wait in ambush for a man. Even on the road to

the holy place at Shechem they commit murder. And they do all this evil deliberately! ¹⁰I have seen a horrible thing in Israel: my people have defiled themselves by worshipping idols.

11 "And as for you, people of Judah, I have set a time to punish you also for what you are doing.

7 "Whenever I want to heal my people Israel and make them prosperous again, all I can see is their wickedness and the evil they do. They cheat one another; they break into houses and steal; they rob people in the streets. ²It never enters their heads that I will remember all this evil; but their sins surround them, and I cannot avoid seeing them."

Conspiracy in the Palace

3 The LORD says, "People deceive the king and his officers by their evil plots. ⁴They are all treacherous and disloyal. Their hatred smoulders like the fire in an oven, which is not stirred by the baker until the dough is ready to bake. ⁵On the day of the king's celebration they made the king and his officials drunk and foolish with wine. ⁶Yes, they burnedᵒ like an oven with their plotting. All night their anger smouldered, and in the morning it burst into flames.

7 "In the heat of their anger they murdered their rulers. Their kings have been assassinated one after another, but no one prays to me for help."

Israel and the Nations

8 The LORD says, "The people of Israel are like a half-baked loaf of bread. They rely on the nations around them ⁹and do not realize that this reliance on foreigners has robbed them of their strength. Their days are numbered, but they don't even know it. ¹⁰The arrogance of the people of Israel cries out against them. In spite of everything that has happened, they have not returned to me, the LORD their God. ¹¹Israel flits about like a silly pigeon; first her people call on Egypt for help, and then they run to Assyria! ¹²But I will spread out a net and catch them like birds as they go by. I will punish them for the evil they have done.ᵖ

13 "They are doomed! They have left me and rebelled against me. They will be destroyed. I wanted to save them, but

---

ᵐ *Probable text* those who had none to give; *Hebrew* command.
ⁿ *Probable text* But...at Adam; *Hebrew* But like Adam.
ᵒ *One ancient translation* burned; *Hebrew* drew near.
ᵖ *Probable text* the evil they have done; *Hebrew* the report to their congregation.
6.6: Mt 9.13, 12.7

their worship of me was false. [14] They have not prayed to me sincerely, but instead they throw themselves down and wail as the heathen do. When they pray for corn and wine, they gash themselves like pagans. What rebels they are! [15] Even though I was the one who brought them up and made them strong, they plotted against me. [16] They keep on turning away from me to a god that is powerless. [q] They are as unreliable as a crooked bow. Because their leaders talk arrogantly, they will die a violent death, and the Egyptians will laugh."

The LORD Condemns Israel for Idol Worship

8 The LORD says, "Sound the alarm! Enemies are swooping down on my land like eagles! My people have broken the covenant I made with them and have rebelled against my teaching. [2] Even though they call me their God and claim that they are my people and that they know me, [3] they have rejected what is good. Because of this their enemies will pursue them.

4 "My people chose kings, but they did it on their own. They appointed leaders, but without my approval. They took their silver and gold and made idols—for their own destruction. [5] I hate the gold bull worshipped by the people of the city of Samaria. I am furious with them. How long will it be before they give up their idolatry? [6] An Israelite craftsman made the idol, and it is not a god at all! The gold bull worshipped in Samaria will be smashed to pieces! [7] When they sow the wind, they will reap a storm! A field of corn that doesn't ripen can never produce any bread. But even if it did, foreigners would eat it up. [8] Israel has become like any other nation and is as useless as a broken pot. [9] Stubborn as wild donkeys, the people of Israel go their own way. They have gone off to seek help from Assyria, and have paid other nations to protect them. [10] But now I am going to gather them together and punish them. Soon they will writhe in pain, when the emperor of Assyria oppresses them.

11 "The more altars the people of Israel build for removing sin, the more places

they have for sinning! [12] I write down countless teachings for the people, but they reject them as strange and foreign. [13] They offer sacrifices to me and eat the meat of the sacrifices. [r] But I, the LORD, am not pleased with them, and now I will remember their sin and punish them for it; I will send them back to Egypt!

14 "The people of Israel have built palaces, but they have forgotten their own Maker. The people of Judah have built fortified cities. But I will send fire that will burn down their palaces and their cities."

Hosea Announces Punishment for Israel

9 People of Israel, stop celebrating your festivals like pagans. You have turned away from your God and have been unfaithful to him. All over the land you have sold yourselves like prostitutes to the god Baal and have loved the corn you thought he paid you with! [2] But soon you will not have enough corn and olive-oil, and there will be no wine. [3] The people of Israel will not remain in the LORD's land, but will have to go back to Egypt and will have to eat forbidden food [s] in Assyria. [4] In those foreign lands they will not be able to make offerings of wine to the LORD, or bring their sacrifices to him. Their food will defile everyone who eats it, like food eaten at funerals. It will be used only to satisfy their hunger; none of it will be taken as an offering to the LORD's Temple. [5] And when the time comes for the appointed festivals in honour of the LORD, what will they do then? [6] When the disaster comes and the people are scattered, the Egyptians will gather them up—gather them for burial there at Memphis! Their treasures of silver and the places where their homes once stood will be overgrown with weeds and thorn-bushes.

7 The time for punishment has come, the time when people will get what they deserve. When that happens, Israel will know it! "This prophet," you say, "is a fool. This inspired man is insane." You people hate me so much because your sin is so great. [8] God has sent me as a prophet to warn his people Israel. Yet wherever I go, you try to trap me like

---

[q] *Probable text* a god...powerless; *Hebrew unclear.*
[r] *They offer...the sacrifices; Hebrew unclear.*
[s] FORBIDDEN FOOD: *The Law of Moses prohibited the eating of certain foods as being ritually unclean (see Lev 11).*
9.7: Lk 21.22

a bird. Even in God's Temple the people are the prophet's enemies. [9] They are hopelessly evil in what they do, just as they were at Gibeah. [t] God will remember their sin and punish them for it.

Israel's Sin and Its Consequences

10 The LORD says, "When I first found Israel, it was like finding grapes growing in the desert. When I first saw your ancestors, it was like seeing the first ripe figs of the season. But when they came to Mount Peor, they began to worship Baal, and soon became as disgusting as the gods they loved. [11] Israel's greatness will fly away like a bird, and there will be no more children born to them, no more women pregnant, no more children conceived. [12] But even if they did bring up children, I would take them away and not leave one alive. When I abandon these people, terrible things will happen to them."

13 LORD, I can see their children being hunted down [u] and killed. [14] What shall I ask you to do to these people? Make their women barren! Make them unable to nurse their babies!

The LORD's Judgement on Israel

15 The LORD says, "All their evil-doing began in Gilgal. It was there that I began to hate them. And because of the evil they have done, I will drive them out of my land. I will not love them any more; all their leaders have rebelled against me. [16] The people of Israel are like a plant whose roots have dried up and which bears no fruit. They will have no children, but even if they did, I would kill the children so dear to them."

The Prophet Speaks about Israel

17 The God I serve will reject his people, because they have not listened to him. They will become wanderers among the nations. [1] The people of Israel were like a grapevine that was full of grapes. The more prosperous they were, the more altars they built. The more productive their land was, the more beautiful they made the sacred stone pillars they worship. [2] The people whose

10

hearts are deceitful must now suffer for their sins. God will break down their altars and destroy their sacred pillars.

3 These people will soon be saying, "We have no king because we did not fear the LORD. But what could a king do for us anyway?" [4] They utter empty words and make false promises and useless treaties. Justice has become injustice, growing like poisonous weeds in a ploughed field.

5 The people who live in the city of Samaria will be afraid and will mourn the loss of the gold bull [a] at Bethel. They and the priests who serve the idol will weep over it. They will wail when it is stripped of its golden splendour. [6] The idol will be carried off to Assyria as tribute to the great emperor. Israel will be disgraced and put to shame because of the advice she followed. [7] Her king will be carried off, like a chip of wood on water. [8] The hilltop shrines of Aven, [b] where the people of Israel worship idols, will be destroyed. Thorns and weeds will grow up over their altars. The people will call out to the mountains, "Hide us!" and to the hills, "Cover us!"

The LORD Pronounces Judgement on Israel

9 The LORD says, "The people of Israel have not stopped sinning against me since the time of their sin at Gibeah. [v] So at Gibeah war will catch up with them. [10] I will attack [w] this sinful people and punish them. Nations will join together against them, and they will be punished for their many sins.

11 "Israel was once like a well-trained young cow, ready and willing to thresh grain. But I decided to put a yoke [x] on her beautiful neck and to harness her for harder work. I made Judah pull the plough and Israel pull the harrow. [12] I said, 'Plough new ground for yourselves, plant righteousness, and reap the blessings that your devotion to me will produce. It is time for you to turn to me, your LORD, and I will come and pour out blessings upon you.' [13] But instead you planted evil and reaped its harvest. You have eaten the fruit produced by your lies.

"Because you trusted in your chariots [y] and in the large number of your soldiers,

---

[t] GIBEAH: *At this city some Israelites of the tribe of Benjamin raped a Levite's concubine; this caused a civil war that almost wiped out the Benjaminites (see Judg 19—21).*
[u] *Probable text* being hunted down; *Hebrew unclear.*
[a] *Some ancient translations* bull; *Hebrew* cows.
[b] AVEN: *This name means "evil" or "idolatry" and in this passage refers to the city of Bethel, a name which means "house of God." See also 4.15 and 5.8.*
[v] GIBEAH: *See 9.9.*   [w] *One ancient translation* I will attack; *Hebrew* In my desire.
[x] *Probable text* put a yoke; *Hebrew* spare.   [y] *One ancient translation* chariots; *Hebrew* way.
9.9: Judg 19.1–30   **9.10:** Num 25.1–5   **10.8:** Lk 23.30; Rev 6.16   **10.9:** Judg 19.1–30
10.12: Jer 4.3

Thorns and weeds will grow up over their altars (10.8)

14 war will come to your people, and all your fortresses will be destroyed. It will be like the day when King Shalman destroyed the city of Betharbel in battle, and mothers and their children were crushed to death. 15 That is what will happen to you, people of Bethel, because of the terrible evil that you have done. As soon as the battle begins, the king of Israel will die."

God's Love for His Rebellious People

11 The LORD says,
    "When Israel was a child, I loved
        him
and called him out of Egypt as my
    son. *z*
2 But the more I *a* called to him,
    the more he turned away from me. *b*
My people sacrificed to Baal;
    they burnt incense to idols.
3 Yet I was the one who taught Israel
    to walk.
I took my people up in my arms, *c*
    but they did not acknowledge that I
    took care of them.
4 I drew them to me with affection and
    love.
I picked them up and held them to
    my cheek;
I bent down to them and fed them. *d*

5 "They refuse to return to me, and so they must return to Egypt, and Assyria will rule them. 6 War will sweep through their cities and break down the city gates.

It will destroy my people because they do what they themselves think best. 7 They insist on turning away from me. They will cry out because of the yoke that is on them, but no one will lift it from them. *e*

8 "How can I give you up, Israel?
    How can I abandon you?
Could I ever destroy you as I did Admah,
    or treat you as I did Zeboiim?
My heart will not let me do it!
    My love for you is too strong.
9 I will not punish you in my anger;
    I will not destroy Israel again.
For I am God and not man.
    I, the Holy One, am with you.
I will not come to you in anger.

10 "My people will follow me when I roar like a lion at their enemies. They will hurry to me from the west. 11 They will come from Egypt, as swiftly as birds, and from Assyria, like doves. I will bring them to their homes again. I, the LORD, have spoken."

Israel and Judah Are Condemned

12 The LORD says, "The people of Israel have surrounded me with lies and deceit, and the people of Judah are still rebelling against me, the faithful and holy God.

12 1 Everything that the people of Israel do from morning to night is useless and destructive. Treachery and acts of violence increase among them.

z him, and called him...son; *or* him; from the time he left Egypt I have called him my son.
a *One ancient translation* I; *Hebrew* they.   *b* *One ancient translation* me; *Hebrew* them.
c *One ancient translation* I...my arms; *Hebrew* He...his arms.   *d* *Verse 4 in Hebrew is unclear.*
e *Verse 7 in Hebrew is unclear.*
11.1: Ex 4.22; Mt 2.15   **11.8:** Deut 29.23

The altars there will become piles of stone (12.11)

They make treaties with Assyria and do business with Egypt."

2 The LORD has an accusation to bring against the people of Judah; he is also going to punish Israel for the way her people act. He will pay them back for what they have done. ³Their ancestor Jacob struggled with his twin brother Esau while the two of them were still in their mother's womb; when Jacob grew up, he fought against God—⁴he fought against an angel and won. He wept and asked for a blessing. And at Bethel God came to our ancestor Jacob and spoke with him.ᶠ ⁵This was the LORD God Almighty—the LORD is the name by which he is to be worshipped. ⁶So now, descendants of Jacob, trust in your God and return to him. Be loyal and just, and wait patiently for your God to act.

Further Words of Judgement

7 The LORD says, "The people of Israel are as dishonest as the Canaanites; they love to cheat their customers with false scales. ⁸'We are rich,' they say. 'We've made a fortune. And no one can accuse us of getting rich dishonestly.' ⁹But I, the LORD your God who led you out of Egypt, I will make you live in tents again, as you did when I came to you in the desert.

10 "I spoke to the prophets and gave them many visions, and through the prophets I gave my people warnings. ¹¹Yet idols are worshipped in Gilead, and those who worship them will die. Bulls are sacrificed in Gilgal, and the altars there will become piles of stone in the open fields."

12 Our ancestor Jacob had to flee to Mesopotamia, where, in order to get a wife, he worked for another man and took care of his sheep. ¹³The LORD sent a prophet to rescue the people of Israel from slavery in Egypt and to take care of them. ¹⁴The people of Israel have made the LORD bitterly angry; they deserve death for their crimes. The LORD will punish them for the disgrace they have brought on him.

Final Judgement on Israel

13 In the past, when the tribe of Ephraim spoke, the other tribes of Israel were afraid; they looked up to Ephraim. But the people sinned by worshipping Baal, and for this they will die. ²They still keep on sinning by making metal images to worship—idols of silver, designed by human minds, made by human hands. And then they say, "Offer sacrifices to them!" How can men kiss those idols—idols in the shape of bulls!ᵍ ³And so these people will disappear like morning mist, like the dew that vanishes early in the day. They will be like chaff which the wind blows from the threshing-place, like smoke from a chimney.

4 The LORD says, "I am the LORD your God, who led you out of Egypt. You have no God but me. I alone am your saviour. ⁵I took care of you in a dry, desert land. ⁶But when you entered the good land, you became full and satisfied, and then you grew proud and forgot me. ⁷So I will

ᶠ *Some ancient translations* him; *Hebrew* us.
ᵍ *Probable text* And then they...bulls; *Hebrew unclear.*
12.3: Gen 25.26   **12.3–4:** Gen 32.24–26   **12.4:** Gen 28.10–22   **12.9:** Lev 23.42–43
12.12: Gen 29.1–20   **12.13:** Ex 12.50–51   **13.5–6:** Deut 8.11–17

Like a leopard I will lie in wait (13.7)

attack you like a lion. Like a leopard I will lie in wait along your path. ⁸I will attack you like a bear that has lost her cubs, and I will tear you open. Like a lion I will devour you on the spot, and will tear you to pieces like a wild animal.

9 "I will destroy you, people of Israel! Then who can help you?ʰ ¹⁰You asked for a king and for leaders, but how can they save the nation?ⁱ ¹¹In my anger I have given you kings, and in my fury I have taken them away.

12 "Israel's sin and guilt are on record, and the records are safely stored away. ¹³Israel has a chance to live, but is too foolish to take it—like a child about to be born, who refuses to come out of the womb. ¹⁴I will not save this people from the world of the dead or rescue them from the power of death. Bring onᵏ ·your plagues, death! Bring onᵏ your destruction, world of the dead! I will no longer have pity for this people. ¹⁵Even though Israel flourishes like weeds,ˡ I will send a hot east wind from the desert, and it will dry up their springs and wells. It will take away everything of value. ¹⁶Samaria must be punished for rebelling against me. Her people will die in war; babies will

be dashed to the ground, and pregnant women will be ripped open."

Hosea's Plea to Israel

14 Return to the LORD your God, people of Israel. Your sin has made you stumble and fall. ²Return to the LORD, and let this prayer be your offering to him: "Forgive all our sins and accept our prayer, and we will praise you as we have promised. ³Assyria can never save us, and war-horses cannot protect us. We will never again say to our idols that they are our God. O LORD, you show mercy to those who have no one else to turn to."

The LORD Promises New Life for Israel

4 The LORD says,
"I will bring my people back to me.
I will love them with all my heart;
    no longer am I angry with them.
⁵ I will be to the people of Israel
    like rain in a dry land.
They will blossom like flowers;
    they will be firmly rooted
    like the trees of Lebanon.
⁶ They will be alive with new growth,
    and beautiful like olive-trees.
They will be fragrant
    like the cedars of Lebanon.
⁷ Once again they will live under my
        protection.
They will grow corn
    and be fruitful like a vineyard.
    They will be as famous as the wine
        of Lebanon.
⁸ The people of Israelⁿ will have nothing
        more to do with idols;
    I will answer their prayers and take
        care of them;
Like an evergreen tree I will shelter
        them;
    I am the source of all their blessings."

Conclusion

9 May those who are wise understand what is written here, and may they take it to heart. The LORD's ways are right, and righteous people live by following them, but sinners stumble and fall because they ignore them.

ʰ *One ancient translation* who can help you?; *Hebrew* in me is your help.
ⁱ *Verse 10 in Hebrew is unclear.*   ᵏ *Some ancient translations* Bring on; *Hebrew* I will be.
ˡ *Probable text* like weeds; *Hebrew* among brothers.
ⁿ *One ancient translation* The people of Israel; *Hebrew* Israel, I.
13.10: 1 Sam 8.5–6   **13.11:** 1 Sam 10.17–24, 15.26   **13.14:** 1 Cor 15.55

THE BOOK OF
JOEL

INTRODUCTION

Little is known about the prophet Joel, and it is not clear just when he lived. But it seems likely that the book comes from the fifth or fourth century B.C. during the time of the Persian Empire. Joel describes a terrible invasion of locusts and a devastating drought in Palestine. In these events he sees a sign of the coming Day of the Lord, a time when the Lord will punish those who oppose his righteous will. The prophet conveys the Lord's call to the people to repent, and his promise of restoration and blessing for his people. Noteworthy is the promise that God will send his spirit upon all the people, men and women, young and old alike.

Outline of Contents

The plague of locusts   1.1—2.17
Promise of restoration   2.18-27
The day of the Lord   2.28—3.21

---

1 This is the LORD's message to Joel son of Pethuel.

The People Mourn the Destruction of the Crops

2 Pay attention, you older people;
  everyone in Judah, listen.
Has anything like this ever happened
  in your time or the time of your
    fathers?
3 Tell your children about it;
  they will tell their children,
  who in turn will tell the next
    generation.

4 Swarm after swarm of locusts settled
    on the crops;
  what one swarm left, the next swarm
    devoured.
5 Wake up and weep, you drunkards;
  cry, you wine-drinkers;
  the grapes for making new wine have
    been destroyed.

6 An army of locusts has attacked our
    land;
  they are powerful and too many to
    count;
  their teeth are as sharp as those of
    a lion.
7 They have destroyed our grapevines
  and chewed up our fig-trees.
They have stripped off the bark,
  till the branches are white.

8 Cry, you people, like a girl who mourns
    the death
  of the man she was going to marry.
9 There is no corn or wine to offer in
    the Temple;
  the priests mourn because they have
    no offerings for the LORD.
10 The fields are bare;
  the ground mourns
    because the corn is destroyed,
    the grapes are dried up,

1.6: Rev 9.8

The ground mourns (1.10)

and the olive-trees are withered.

¹¹ Grieve, you farmers;
  cry, you that take care of the vineyards,
    because the wheat, the barley,
    yes all the crops are destroyed.
¹² The grapevines and fig-trees have
      withered;
    all the fruit-trees have wilted and died.
  The joy of the people is gone.
¹³ Put on sackcloth and weep,
    you priests who serve at the altar!
  Go into the Temple and mourn all night!
  There is no corn or wine to offer your
      God.
¹⁴ Give orders for a fast;
    call an assembly!
  Gather the leaders
    and all the people of Judah
  into the Temple of the LORD your God
    and cry out to him.
¹⁵ The day of the LORD is near;
    the day when the Almighty brings
      destruction.
  What terror that day will bring!

¹⁶ We look on helpless as our crops are
      destroyed.
    There is no joy in the Temple of our
      God.
¹⁷ The seeds die in the dry earth.
  There is no grain to be stored,
    and so the empty granaries are in
      ruins.

¹⁸ The cattle are bellowing in distress
    because there is no pasture for them;
    the flocks of sheep also suffer.
¹⁹ I cry out to you, LORD,
    because the pastures and trees are
      dried up,
    as though a fire had burnt them.
²⁰ Even the wild animals cry out to you
    because the streams have become dry.

The Locusts as a Warning of the Day of the LORD

2 Blow the trumpet; sound the alarm
    on Zion, God's sacred hill. *a*
  Tremble, people of Judah!
    The day of the LORD is coming soon.
² It will be a dark and gloomy day,
    a black and cloudy day.
  The great army of locusts advances
    like darkness spreading over the
      mountains.
  There has never been anything like it,
    and there never will be again.

³ Like fire they eat up the plants.
    In front of them the land is like the
      Garden of Eden,
    but behind them it is a barren desert.
  Nothing escapes them.
⁴ They look like horses;
    they run like war-horses.
⁵ As they leap on the tops of the
      mountains,
    they rattle like chariots;

a SACRED HILL: *Mount Zion (see Zion in Word List).*
1.15: Is 13.6   **2.4–5:** Rev 9.7–9

they crackle like dry grass on fire.
They are lined up like a great army
    ready for battle.
6 As they approach, everyone is terrified;
    every face turns pale.
7 They attack like warriors;
    they climb the walls like soldiers.
They all keep marching straight ahead
    and do not change direction
8   or get in each other's way.
They swarm through defences,
    and nothing can stop them.
9 They rush against the city;
    they run over the walls;
    they climb up the houses
    and go in through the windows like
        thieves.

10 The earth shakes as they advance;
    the sky trembles.
The sun and the moon grow dark,
    and the stars no longer shine.
11 The LORD thunders commands to his
    army.
    The troops that obey him
    are many and mighty.
How terrible is the day of the LORD!
    Who will survive it?

A Call to Repentance

12 "But even now," says the LORD,
    "repent sincerely and return to me
    with fasting and weeping and
        mourning.

2.10: Rev 8.12   **2.11:** Rev 6.17

13 Let your broken heart show your
    sorrow;
    tearing your clothes is not enough."

Come back to the LORD your God.
    He is kind and full of mercy;
    he is patient and keeps his promise;
    he is always ready to forgive and not
        punish.
14 Perhaps the LORD your God will
    change his mind
    and bless you with abundant crops.
Then you can offer him corn and wine.

15 Blow the trumpet on Mount Zion;
    give orders for a fast and call an
        assembly!
16 Gather the people together;
    prepare them for a sacred meeting;
    bring the old people;
    gather the children
    and the babies too.
    Even newly married couples
    must leave their room and come.
17 The priests, serving the LORD
    between the altar and the entrance
        of the Temple,
    must weep and pray:
    "Have pity on your people, LORD.
    Do not let other nations despise us
        and mock us
    by saying, 'Where is your God?' "

Let your broken heart show your sorrow (2.13)

God Restores Fertility to the Land

18 Then the LORD showed concern for his
   land;
   he had mercy on his people.
19 He answered them:
   "Now I am going to give you
   corn and wine and olive-oil,
   and you will be satisfied.
   Other nations will no longer despise
   you.
20 I will remove the locust army that
   camp from the north
   and will drive some of them into the
   desert.
   Their front ranks will be driven into
   the Dead Sea,
   their rear ranks into the
   Mediterranean.
   Their dead bodies will stink.
   I will destroy them because of all they
   have done to you.

21 "Fields, don't be afraid,
   but be joyful and glad
   because of all the LORD has done for
   you.
22 Animals, don't be afraid.
   The pastures are green;
   the trees bear their fruit,
   and there are plenty of figs and grapes.

23 "Be glad, people of Zion,
   rejoice at what the LORD your God
   has done for you.
   He has given you the right amount
   of autumn rain; b
   he has poured down the winter rain
   for you
   and the spring rain as before.
24 The threshing-places will be full of
   corn;
   the pits beside the presses will
   overflow with wine and olive-oil.
25 I will give you back what you lost
   in the years when swarms of locusts
   ate your crops.
   It was I who sent this army against
   you.
26 Now you will have plenty to eat, and
   be satisfied.
   You will praise the LORD your God,
   who has done wonderful things for
   you.

My people will never be despised
   again.
27 Then, Israel, you will know that I am
   among you,
   and that I, the LORD, am your God
   and there is no other.
   My people will never be despised
   again.

The Day of the LORD

28 "Afterwards I will pour out my spirit
   on everyone:
   your sons and daughters will proclaim
   my message;
   your old men will have dreams,
   and your young men will see visions.
29 At that time I will pour out my spirit
   even on servants, both men and
   women.

30 "I will give warnings of that day
   in the sky and on the earth;
   there will be bloodshed, fire, and
   clouds of smoke.
31 The sun will be darkened,
   and the moon will turn red as blood
   before the great and terrible day of
   the LORD comes.
32 But all who ask the LORD for help will
   be saved.
   As the LORD has said,
   'Some in Jerusalem will escape;
   those whom I choose will survive.'"

God Will Judge the Nations

3 The LORD says,
   "At that time I will restore
   the prosperity of Judah and
   Jerusalem.
2 I will gather all the nations
   and bring them to the Valley of
   Judgement.
   There I will judge them
   for all they have done to my people.
   They have scattered the Israelites in
   foreign countries
   and divided up Israel, my land.
3 They threw dice to decide
   who would get the captives.
   They sold boys and girls into slavery
   to pay for prostitutes and wine.
4 "What are you trying to do to me,
Tyre, Sidon, and all the regions of
Philistia? Are you trying to pay me back
for something? If you are, I will quickly

---

b right amount of autumn rain; or autumn rain because he is just.
2.28–32: Acts 2.17–21   **2.31:** Mt 24.29; Mk 13.24–25; Lk 21.25; Rev 6.12–13
2.32: Rom 10.13
3.4–8: Is 14.29–31, 23.1–18; Jer 47.1–7; Ezek 25.15—28.26; Amos 1.6–10; Zeph 2.4–7; Zech 9.1–7;
Mt 11.21–22; Lk 10.13–14

pay you back! ⁵ You have taken my silver and gold and carried my rich treasures into your temples. ⁶ You have taken the people of Judah and Jerusalem far from their own country and sold them to the Greeks. ⁷ Now I am going to bring them out of the places to which you have sold them. I will do to you what you have done to them. ⁸ I will let your sons and daughters be sold to the people of Judah; they will sell them to the far-off Sabeans. I, the LORD, have spoken.

⁹ "Make this announcement among the
    nations:
  'Prepare for war;
  call your warriors;
  gather all your soldiers and march!
¹⁰ Hammer the points of your ploughs
    into swords
  and your pruning-knives into spears.
Even the weak must fight.
¹¹ Hurry ᶜ and come,
  all you surrounding nations,
  and gather in the valley.' "

  Send down, O LORD, your army to attack
    them.

¹² "The nations must get ready
  and come to the Valley of Judgement.
There I, the LORD, will sit to judge
  all the surrounding nations.
¹³ They are very wicked;
cut them down like corn
  at harvest time;
crush them as grapes are crushed
  in a full winepress
  until the wine runs over."

¹⁴ Thousands and thousands
  are in the Valley of Judgement.
It is there that the day of the LORD
  will soon come.
¹⁵ The sun and the moon grow dark,
  and the stars no longer shine.

God Will Bless His People

¹⁶ The LORD roars from Mount Zion;
  his voice thunders from Jerusalem;
  earth and sky tremble.
But he will defend his people.
¹⁷ "Then, Israel, you will know that I
    am the LORD your God.
I live on Zion, my sacred hill.
Jerusalem will be a sacred city;
  foreigners will never conquer it again.

¹⁸ "At that time the mountains will be
    covered with vineyards,
  and cattle will be found on every hill;
  there will be plenty of water for all
    the streams of Judah.
A stream will flow from the Temple of
    the LORD,
  and it will water the Valley of Acacia.

¹⁹ "Egypt will become a desert,
  and Edom a ruined waste,
because they attacked the land of Judah
  and killed its innocent people.
²⁰⁻²¹ I will avenge ᵉ those who were
    killed;
  I will not spare the guilty.
But Judah and Jerusalem will be
    inhabited for ever,
  and I the LORD, will live on Mount
    Zion."

ᶜ *Probable text* Hurry; *Hebrew* Help.
ᵉ *Some ancient translations* avenge; *Hebrew* declare innocent.
3.10: Is 2.4; Mic 4.3　　**3.13:** Rev 14.14–16,19–20, 19.15　　**3.16:** Amos 1.2

THE BOOK OF

AMOS

INTRODUCTION

Amos was the first prophet in the Bible whose message was recorded at length. Although he came from a town in Judah, he preached to the people of the northern kingdom of Israel, about the middle of the eighth century B.C. It was a time of great prosperity, notable religious piety, and apparent security. But Amos saw that prosperity was limited to the wealthy, and that it fed on injustice and on oppression of the poor. Religious observance was insincere, and security more apparent than real. With passion and courage he preached that God would punish the nation. He called for justice to "flow like a stream," and said, "Perhaps the Lord will be merciful to the people of this nation who are still left alive" (5.15).

Outline of Contents
Judgement on Israel's neighbours 1.1—2.5
Judgement on Israel 2.6—6.14
Five visions 7.1—9.15

---

1 These are the words of Amos, a shepherd from the town of Tekoa. Two years before the earthquake, when Uzziah was king of Judah and Jeroboam son of Jehoash was king of Israel, God revealed to Amos all these things about Israel.

2 Amos said,

"The LORD roars from Mount Zion;
    his voice thunders from Jerusalem.
The pastures dry up,
    and the grass on Mount Carmel turns
        brown."

God's Judgement on Israel's Neighbours

Syria

3 The LORD says, "The people of Damascus have sinned again and again, and for this I will certainly punish them.

They treated the people of Gilead with savage cruelty. ⁴So I will send fire upon the palace built by King Hazael and I will burn down the fortresses of King Benhadad. ⁵I will smash the city gates of Damascus and remove the inhabitants of the Valley of Aven and the ruler of Betheden. The people of Syria will be taken away as prisoners to the land of Kir."

Philistia

6 The LORD says, "The people of Gaza have sinned again and again, and for this I will certainly punish them. They carried off a whole nation and sold them as slaves to the people of Edom. ⁷So I will send fire upon the city walls of Gaza and burn down its fortresses. ⁸I will remove the rulers of the cities of Ashdod and

1.1: 2 Kgs 15.1-7; 2 Chr 26.1-23; 2 Kgs 14.23-29   **1.2:** Joel 3.16
1.3-5: Is 17.1-3; Jer 49.23-27; Zech 9.1
1.6-8: Is 14.29-31; Jer 47.1-7; Ezek 25.15-17; Joel 3.4-8; Zeph 2.4-7; Zech 9.5-7

I will send fire (1.4—2.5)

Ashkelon. I will punish the city of Ekron, and all the Philistines who are left will die."

Tyre

9 The LORD says, "The people of Tyre have sinned again and again, and for this I will certainly punish them. They carried off a whole nation into exile in the land of Edom, and did not keep the treaty of friendship they had made. ¹⁰ So I will send fire upon the city walls of Tyre and burn down its fortresses."

Edom

11 The LORD says, "The people of Edom have sinned again and again, and for this I will certainly punish them. They hunted down their brothers,[b] the Israelites, and showed them no mercy. Their anger had no limits, and they never let it die. ¹² So I will send fire upon the city of Teman and burn down the fortresses of Bozrah."

Ammon

13 The LORD says, "The people of Ammon have sinned again and again, and for this I will certainly punish them. In their wars for more territory they even ripped open pregnant women in Gilead. ¹⁴ So I will send fire upon the city walls of Rabbah and burn down its fortresses.

Then there will be shouts on the day of battle, and the fighting will rage like a storm. ¹⁵ Their king and his officers will go into exile."

Moab

2 The LORD says, "The people of Moab have sinned again and again, and for this I will certainly punish them. They dishonoured the bones of the king of Edom by burning them to ashes. ² I will send fire upon the land of Moab and burn down the fortresses of Kerioth. The people of Moab will die in the noise of battle while soldiers are shouting and trumpets are sounding. ³ I will kill the ruler of Moab and all the leaders of the land."

Judah

4 The LORD says, "The people of Judah have sinned again and again, and for this I will certainly punish them. They have despised my teachings and have not kept my commands. They have been led astray by the same false gods that their ancestors served. ⁵ So I will send fire upon Judah and burn down the fortresses of Jerusalem."

God's Judgement on Israel

6 The LORD says, "The people of Israel have sinned again and again, and for this

---

[b] THEIR BROTHERS: *The Israelites were descended from Jacob, who was the brother of Esau, the ancestor of the Edomites.*
1.9-10: Is 23.1-18; Ezek 26.1—28.19; Joel 3.4-8; Zech 9.1-4; Mt 11.21-22; Lk 10.13-14
1.11-12: Is 34.5-17, 63.1-6; Jer 49.7-22; Ezek 25.12-14, 35.1-15; Obad 1-14; Mal 1.2-5
1.13-15: Jer 49.1-6; Ezek 21.28-32, 25.1-7; Zeph 2.8-11
2.1-3: Is 15.1—16.14, 25.10-12; Jer 48.1-47; Ezek 25.8-11; Zeph 2.8-11

I will certainly punish them. They sell into slavery honest men who cannot pay their debts, poor men who cannot repay even the price of a pair of sandals. 7 They trample [c] down the weak and helpless and push the poor out of the way. A man and his father have intercourse with the same slave-girl, and so profane my holy name. 8 At every place of worship men sleep on clothing that they have taken from the poor as security for debts. In the temple of their God they drink wine which they have taken from those who owe them money.

9 "And yet, my people, it was for your sake that I totally destroyed the Amorites, men who were as tall as cedar-trees and as strong as oaks. 10 I brought you out of Egypt, led you through the desert for forty years, and gave you the land of the Amorites to be your own. 11 I chose some of your sons to be prophets, and some of your young men to be Nazirites. [e] Isn't this true, people of Israel? I, the LORD, have spoken. 12 But you made the Nazirites drink wine, and ordered the prophets not to speak my message. 13 And now I will crush you to the ground, and you will groan like a cart loaded with corn. 14 Not even fast runners will escape; strong men will lose their strength, and soldiers will not be able to save their own lives. 15 Bowmen will not stand their ground, fast runners will not get away, and men on horses will not escape with their lives. 16 On that day even the bravest soldiers will drop their weapons and run." The LORD has spoken.

3 People of Israel, listen to this message which the LORD has spoken about you, the entire nation that he brought out of Egypt; 2 "Of all the nations on earth, you are the only one I have known and cared for. That is what makes your sins so terrible, and that is why I must punish you for them."

The Prophet's Task

3 Do two men start travelling together without arranging to meet?

4 Does a lion roar in the forest unless he has found a victim?

Does a young lion growl in his den unless he has caught something?

5 Does a bird get caught in a trap if the trap has not been baited?

Does a trap spring unless something sets it off?

6 Does the war trumpet sound in a city without making the people afraid?

Does disaster strike a city unless the LORD sends it?

7 The Sovereign LORD never does anything without revealing his plan to his servants, the prophets.

8 When a lion roars, who can avoid being afraid?

When the Sovereign LORD speaks, who can avoid proclaiming his message?

The Doom of Samaria

9 Announce to those who live in the palaces of Egypt and Ashdod: "Gather together in the hills surrounding Samaria and see the great disorder and the crimes being committed there."

10 The LORD says, "These people fill their mansions with things taken by crime and violence. They don't even know how to be honest. 11 And so an enemy will surround their land, destroy their defences, and plunder their mansions."

12 The LORD says, "As a shepherd recovers only two legs or an ear of a sheep that a lion has eaten, so only a few will survive of Samaria's people, who now recline on luxurious couches. [f] 13 Listen now, and warn the descendants of Jacob," says the Sovereign LORD Almighty. 14 "On the day when I punish the people of Israel for their sins, I will destroy the altars of Bethel. The corners of every altar will be broken off and will fall to the ground. 15 I will destroy winter houses and summer houses. The houses decorated with ivory will fall in ruins; every large house will be destroyed."

4 Listen to this, you women of Samaria, who grow fat like the well-fed cows of Bashan, who ill-treat the weak, oppress the poor, and demand that your husbands keep you supplied with liquor! 2 As the Sovereign LORD is holy, he has promised, "The days will come when they will drag you away with hooks; every one of you will be like a fish on a hook. 3 You will be dragged to the nearest break in the wall and thrown out." [g]

---

[c] trample; *Hebrew unclear.*
[e] NAZIRITES: *Israelites who showed their devotion to God by taking vows not to drink wine or beer or cut their hair or touch corpses (See Num 6.1–8).* [f] luxurious couches; *Hebrew unclear.*
[g] *Hebrew has an additional word, the meaning of which is unclear.*
2.9: Deut 3.8–11 **2.11:** Num 6.1–8 **3.14:** 2 Kgs 23.15

Still you did not come back to me (4.9)

Israel's Failure to Learn

4 The Sovereign LORD says, "People of Israel, go to the holy place in Bethel and sin, if you must! Go to Gilgal and sin with all your might! Go ahead and bring animals to be sacrificed morning after morning, and bring your tithes every third day. 5 Go ahead and offer your bread in thanksgiving to God, and boast about the extra offerings you bring! This is the kind of thing you love to do.

6 "I was the one who brought famine to all your cities, yet you did not come back to me. 7 I held back the rain when your crops needed it most. I sent rain on one city, but not on another. Rain fell on one field, but another field dried up. 8 Weak with thirst, the people of several cities went to a city where they hoped to find water, but there was not enough to drink. Still you did not come back to me.

9 "I sent a scorching wind to dry up your crops. The locusts ate up all your gardens and vineyards, your fig-trees and olive-trees. Still you did not come back to me.

10 "I sent a plague on you like the one I sent on Egypt. I killed your young men in battle and took your horses away. I filled your nostrils with the stink of dead bodies in your camps. Still you did not come back to me.

11 "I destroyed some of you as I destroyed Sodom and Gomorrah. Those of you who survived were like a burning stick saved from a fire. Still you did not come back to me," says the LORD. 12 "So then, people of Israel, I am going to punish you. And because I am going to do this,

get ready to face my judgement!"

13 God is the one who made the mountains
  and created the winds.
He makes his thoughts known to man;
  he changes day into night.
He walks on the heights of the earth.
This is his name: the LORD God
  Almighty!

A Call to Repentance

5 Listen, people of Israel, to this funeral song which I sing over you:

2 Virgin Israel has fallen,
  Never to rise again!
She lies abandoned on the ground,
  And no one helps her up.

3 The Sovereign LORD says, "A city in Israel sends out a thousand soldiers, but only a hundred return; another city sends out a hundred, but only ten come back."

4 The LORD says to the people of Israel, "Come to me, and you will live. 5 Do not go to Beersheba to worship. Do not try to find me at Bethel—Bethel will come to nothing. Do not go to Gilgal—her people are doomed to exile."

6 Go to the LORD, and you will live. If you do not go, he will sweep down like fire on the people of Israel. The fire will burn up the people of Bethel, and no one will be able to put it out. 7 You are doomed, you that twist justice and cheat people out of their rights!

8 The LORD made the stars,
  the Pleiades and Orion.
He turns darkness into daylight,

4.11: Gen 19.24   **5.8:** Job 9.9, 38.31

and day into night.
He calls for the waters of the sea
and pours them out on the earth.
His name is the LORD.
⁹ He brings destruction on the mighty and
their strongholds.

10 You people hate anyone who challenges injustice and speaks the whole truth in court. ¹¹ You have oppressed the poor and robbed them of their grain. And so you will not live in the fine stone houses you build or drink wine from the beautiful vineyards you plant. ¹² I know how terrible your sins are and how many crimes you have committed. You persecute good men, take bribes, and prevent the poor from getting justice in the courts. ¹³ And so, keeping quiet in such evil times is the clever thing to do!

14 Make it your aim to do what is right, not what is evil, so that you may live. Then the LORD God Almighty really will be with you, as you claim he is. ¹⁵ Hate what is evil, love what is right, and see that justice prevails in the courts. Perhaps the LORD will be merciful to the people of this nation who are still left alive.

16 And so the Sovereign LORD Almighty says, "There will be wailing and cries of sorrow in the city streets. Even farmers will be called to mourn the dead along with those who are paid to mourn. ¹⁷ There will be wailing in all the vineyards. All this will take place because I am coming to punish you." The LORD has spoken.

5.21-22: Is 1.11-14   **5.25-27:** Acts 7.42-43

18 How terrible it will be for you who long for the day of the LORD! What good will that day do you? For you it will be a day of darkness and not of light. ¹⁹ It will be like a man who runs from a lion and meets a bear! Or like a man who comes home and puts his hand on the wall—only to be bitten by a snake! ²⁰ The day of the LORD will bring darkness and not light; it will be a day of gloom, without any brightness.

21 The LORD says, "I hate your religious festivals; I cannot stand them! ²² When you bring me burnt-offerings and grain-offerings, I will not accept them; I will not accept the animals you have fattened to bring me as offerings. ²³ Stop your noisy songs; I do not want to listen to your harps. ²⁴ Instead, let justice flow like a stream, and righteousness like a river that never goes dry.

25 "People of Israel, I did not demand sacrifices and offerings during those forty years that I led you through the desert. ²⁶ But now, because you have worshipped images of Sakkuth, your king god, and of Kaiwan, your star god, you will have to carry those images ²⁷ when I take you into exile in a land beyond Damascus," says the LORD, whose name is Almighty God.

The Destruction of Israel

6 How terrible it will be for you that have such an easy life in Zion and for you that feel safe in Samaria—you

There will be wailing and cries of sorrow (5.16)

Like a man who runs from a lion (5.19)

great men of this great nation Israel, you to whom the people go for help! ²Go and look at the city of Calneh. Then go on to the great city of Hamath and on down to the Philistine city of Gath. Were they any better than the kingdoms of Judah and Israel? Was their territory larger than yours? ³You refuse to admit that a day of disaster is coming, but what you do only brings that day closer. ⁴How terrible it will be for you that stretch out on your luxurious couches, feasting on veal and lamb! ⁵You like to compose songs, as David did, and play them on harps. ⁶You drink wine by the bowlful and use the finest perfumes, but you do not mourn over the ruin of Israel. ⁷So you will be the first to go into exile. Your feasts and banquets will come to an end.

8 The Sovereign LORD Almighty has given this solemn warning: "I hate the pride of the people of Israel; I despise their luxurious mansions. I will give their capital city and everything in it to the enemy."

9 If there are ten men left in a family, they will die. ¹⁰The dead man's relative, the one in charge of the funeral, will take the body out of the house. The relative will call to whoever is still left in the house, "Is anyone else there with you?"

A voice will answer, "No!"

Then the relative will say, "Be quiet! We must be careful not even to mention the LORD's name."ʰ

11 When the LORD gives the command, houses large and small will be smashed to pieces. ¹²Do horses gallop on rocks? Do men plough the sea with oxen? Yet

you have turned justice into poison, and right into wrong.

13 You boast about capturing the town of Lodebar.ⁱ You boast, "We were strong enough to take Karnaim."ʲ

14 The LORD God Almighty himself says, "People of Israel, I am going to send a foreign army to occupy your country. It will oppress you from Hamath Pass in the north to the brook of the Arabah in the south."

A Vision of Locusts

7 I had a vision from the Sovereign LORD. In it I saw him create a swarm of locusts just after the king's share of the hay had been cut and the grass was starting to grow again. ²In my vision I saw the locusts eat up every green thing in the land, and then I said, "Sovereign LORD, forgive your people! How can they survive? They are so small and weak!"

3 The LORD changed his mind and said, "What you saw will not take place."

A Vision of Fire

4 I had another vision from the Sovereign LORD. In it I saw him preparing to punish his people with fire. The fire burnt up the great ocean under the earth, and started to burn up the land. ⁵Then I said, "Stop, Sovereign LORD! How can your people survive? They are so small and weak!"

6 The LORD changed his mind again and said, "This will not take place either."

A Vision of a Plumb-Line

7 I had another vision from the Lord. In it I saw him standing beside a wall

---

ʰ Verse 10 in Hebrew is unclear.
ⁱ LODEBAR: *This name sounds like the Hebrew for "nothing."*
ʲ KARNAIM: *The name of this small town means "horns," a symbol of strength.*

that had been built with the help of a plumb-line, and there was a plumb-line in his hand. ⁸He asked me, "Amos, what do you see?"

"A plumb-line," I answered.

Then he said, "I am using it to show that my people are like a wall that is out of line. I will not change my mind again about punishing them. ⁹The places where Isaac's descendants worship will be destroyed. The holy places of Israel will be left in ruins. I will bring the dynasty of King Jeroboam to an end."

Amos and Amaziah

10 Amaziah, the priest of Bethel, then sent a report to King Jeroboam of Israel: "Amos is plotting against you among the people. His speeches will destroy the country. ¹¹This is what he says: 'Jeroboam will die in battle, and the people of Israel will be taken away from their land into exile.'"

12 Amaziah then said to Amos, "That's enough, prophet! Go on back to Judah and do your preaching there. Let *them* pay you for it. ¹³Don't prophesy here at Bethel any more. This is the king's place of worship, the national temple."

14 Amos answered, "I am not the kind of prophet who prophesies for pay. I am a herdsman, and I take care of fig-trees. ¹⁵But the LORD took me from my work as a shepherd and ordered me to come

and prophesy to his people Israel. ¹⁶So now listen to what the LORD says. You tell me to stop prophesying, to stop raving against the people of Israel. ¹⁷And so, Amaziah, the LORD says to you, 'Your wife will become a prostitute on the streets, and your children will be killed in war. Your land will be divided up and given to others, and you yourself will die in a heathen country. And the people of Israel will certainly be taken away from their own land into exile.'"

A Vision of a Basket of Fruit

8 I had another vision from the Sovereign LORD. In it I saw a basket of fruit. ²The LORD asked, "Amos, what do you see?"

"A basket of fruit," I answered.

The LORD said to me, "The end*ˡ* has come for my people Israel. I will not change my mind again about punishing them. ³On that day the songs in the palace will become cries of mourning. There will be dead bodies everywhere. They will be thrown out in silence."*ᵐ*

Israel's Doom

4 Listen to this, you that trample on the needy and try to destroy the poor of the country. ⁵You say to yourselves, "We can hardly wait for the holy days to be over so that we can sell our corn. When will the Sabbath end, so that we

*ˡ*END: *The Hebrew words for "end" and "fruit" sound alike.*   *ᵐ*out in silence; *or* out. Silence!

I hate the pride of the people of Israel (6.8)

Stop, O Sovereign L<small>ORD</small> (7.5)

can start selling again? Then we can overcharge, use false measures, and tamper with the scales to cheat our customers. 6 We can sell worthless wheat at a high price. We'll find a poor man who can't pay his debts, not even the price of a pair of sandals, and we'll buy him as a slave."

7 The L<small>ORD</small>, the God of Israel, has sworn, "I will never forget their evil deeds. 8 And so the earth will quake, and everyone in the land will be in distress. The whole country will be shaken; it will rise and fall like the River Nile. 9 The time is coming when I will make the sun go down at noon and the earth grow dark in daytime. I, the Sovereign L<small>ORD</small>, have spoken. 10 I will turn your festivals into funerals and change your glad songs into cries of grief. I will make you shave your heads and wear sackcloth, and you will be like parents mourning for their only son. That day will be bitter to the end.

11 "The time is coming when I will send famine on the land. People will be hungry, but not for bread; they will be thirsty, but not for water. They will hunger and thirst for a message from the L<small>ORD</small>. I, the Sovereign L<small>ORD</small>, have spoken. 12 People will wander from the Dead Sea to the Mediterranean and then on from the north to the east. They will look everywhere for a message from the L<small>ORD</small>, but they will not find it. 13 On that day even healthy young men and women will collapse from thirst. 14 Those who swear by the idols of Samaria, who say, 'By the god of Dan,' or, 'By the god of Beersheba'—those people will fall and not rise again."

The Lord's Judgements

9 I saw the Lord standing by the altar. He gave the command: "Strike the tops of the temple columns so hard that the whole porch will shake. Break them off and let them fall on the heads of the people. I will kill the rest of the people in war. No one will get away; not one will escape. 2 Even if they dig their way down to the world of the dead, I will catch them. Even if they climb up to heaven, I will bring them down. 3 If they hide on the top of Mount Carmel, I will search for them and catch them. If they hide from me at the bottom of the sea, I will command the sea-monster *o* to bite them. 4 If they are taken away into captivity by their enemies, I will order them to be put to death. I am determined to destroy them, not to help them."

Amos, what do you see? (8.2)

---

o SEA-MONSTER: *It was believed that the sea was inhabited by a great monster. This creature, like all others, was regarded as under God's control.*

5 The Sovereign Lord Almighty touches
　　the earth,
　　and it quakes;
　　all who live there mourn.
The whole world rises and falls like the
　　River Nile.

6 The Lord builds his home in the heavens,
　　and over the earth he puts the dome
　　of the sky.
He calls for the waters of the sea
　　and pours them out on the earth.
His name is the Lord!

7 The Lord says, "People of Israel, I
think as much of the people of Sudan
as I do of you. I brought the Philistines
from Crete and the Syrians from Kir, just
as I brought you from Egypt. 8 I, the
Sovereign Lord, am watching this sinful
kingdom of Israel, and I will destroy it
from the face of the earth. But I will not
destroy all the descendants of Jacob.

9 "I will give the command and shake
the people of Israel like corn in a sieve.
I will shake them among the nations to
remove all who are worthless. 10 The
sinners among my people will be killed
in war—all those who say, 'God will not
let any harm come near us.' "

The Future Restoration of Israel

11 The Lord says, "A day is coming
when I will restore the kingdom of David,
which is like a house fallen into ruins.
I will repair its walls and restore it. I
will rebuild it and make it as it was long
ago. 12 And so the people of Israel will
conquer what is left of the land of Edom
and all the nations that were once mine,"
says the Lord, who will cause this to
happen.
13 "The days are coming," says the Lord,
　　"when corn will grow faster than it
　　can be harvested,
　　and grapes will grow faster than the
　　wine can be made.
The mountains will drip with sweet
　　wine,
　　and the hills will flow with it.
14 I will bring my people back to their
　　land.
They will rebuild their ruined cities
　　and live there;
they will plant vineyards and drink
　　the wine;
they will plant gardens and eat what
　　they grow.
15 I will plant my people on the land I
　　gave them,
　　and they will not be pulled up again."
The Lord your God has spoken.

9.11-12: Acts 15.16-18

THE BOOK OF
OBADIAH

INTRODUCTION

This short book comes from some undetermined time after the fall of Jerusalem in 586 B.C., when Edom, Judah's age-old enemy to the south-east, not only rejoiced over the fall of Jerusalem, but took advantage of Judah's plight to loot the city and help the invader. Obadiah prophesied that Edom would be punished and defeated, along with other nations that were the enemies of Israel.

Outline of Contents

The punishment of Edom 1–14
The day of the Lord 15–21

---

1 This is the prophecy of Obadiah—what the Sovereign LORD said about the nation of Edom.

The Lord Will Punish Edom

The LORD has sent his messenger to the nations,
and we have heard his message:
"Get ready! Let us go to war against Edom!"
2 The LORD says to Edom,
"I will make you weak;
everyone will despise you.
3 Your pride has deceived you.
Your capital is a fortress of solid rock;
your home is high in the mountains,
and so you say to yourself,
'Who can ever pull me down?'
4 Even though you make your home
as high as an eagle's nest,
so that it seems to be among the stars,
yet I will pull you down.

5 "When thieves come at night,
they take only what they want.
When people gather grapes,

they always leave a few.
But your enemies have wiped you out
completely.
6 Descendants of Esau, your treasures
have been looted.
7 Your allies have deceived you;
they have driven you from your
country.
People who were at peace with you have
now conquered you.
Those friends who ate with you have
laid a trap for you;
they say of you, 'Where is all that
cleverness he had?'

8 "On the day I punish Edom,
I will destroy their clever men
and wipe out all their wisdom.
9 The fighting men of Teman will be
terrified,
and every soldier in Edom will be
killed.

Reasons for Edom's Punishment

10 "Because you robbed and killed
your brothers,[a] the descendants of
Jacob,

a YOUR BROTHERS: *The Israelites were descended from Jacob, who was the brother of Esau, the ancestor of the Edomites.*
1–14: Is 34.5–17, 63.1–6; Jer 49.7–22; Ezek 25.12–14, 35.1–15; Amos 1.11–12; Mal 1.2–5

You should not have gloated (v.12)

you will be destroyed and
 dishonoured for ever.
¹¹ You stood aside on that day
 when enemies broke down their gates.
 You were as bad as those strangers
 who carried off Jerusalem's wealth
 and divided it among themselves.
¹² You should not have gloated
 over the misfortune of your brothers
 in Judah.
 You should not have been glad
 on the day of their ruin.
 You should not have laughed at them
 in their distress.
¹³ You should not have entered the city
 of my people
 to gloat over their suffering
 and to seize their riches
 on the day of their disaster.
¹⁴ You should not have stood at the cross-
 roads
 to catch those trying to escape.
 You should not have handed them over
 to the enemy
 on the day of their distress.

God Will Judge the Nations

¹⁵ "The day is near when I, the LORD,
 will judge all nations.
 Edom, what you have done
 will be done to you.
 You will get back what you have
 given.
¹⁶ My people have drunk a bitter cup
 of punishment
 on my sacred hill. ᵇ

But all the surrounding nations will
 drink
 a still more bitter cup of punishment;
 they will drink it all and vanish away.

The Victory of Israel

¹⁷ "But on Mount Zion some will escape,
 and it will be a sacred place.
 The people of Jacob will possess
 the land that is theirs by right.

¹⁸ The people of Jacob and of Joseph
 will be like fire;
 they will destroy the people of Esau
 as fire burns stubble.
 No descendant of Esau will survive.
 I, the LORD, have spoken.

¹⁹ "People from southern Judah will
 occupy Edom;
 those from the western foothills will
 capture Philistia;
 Israelites will possess the territory of
 Ephraim and Samaria;
 the people of Benjamin will take
 Gilead.
²⁰ The army of exiles from northern Israel
 will return and conquer Phoenicia
 as far north as Zarephath.
 The exiles from Jerusalem who are in
 Sardis
 will capture the towns of southern
 Judah.
²¹ The victorious men of Jerusalem
 will attack Edom and rule over it.
 And the LORD himself will be King."

ᵇ SACRED HILL: *Mount Zion (see Zion in Word List).*

THE BOOK OF
JONAH

INTRODUCTION

The book of *Jonah* is unlike other prophetic books of the Bible in that it is a narrative, describing the adventures of a prophet who tried to disobey God's command. God told him to go to Nineveh, the capital of the great empire of Assyria, Israel's deadly enemy. But Jonah did not want to go there with God's message, because he was convinced that God would not carry out his threat to destroy the city. After a series of dramatic events, he reluctantly obeyed, and finally sulked when his message of doom did not come true.

The book portrays God's absolute sovereignty over his creation. But above all it portrays God as a God of love and mercy, who would rather forgive and save even the enemies of his people, than punish and destroy them.

Outline of Contents
Jonah's call and disobedience   1.1–17
Jonah's repentance and deliverance   2.1–10
Jonah's message against Nineveh   3.1–10
God's mercy on Nineveh   4.1–11

Jonah Disobeys the LORD

1 One day, the LORD spoke to Jonah son of Amittai. 2 He said, "Go to Nineveh, that great city, and speak out against it; I am aware how wicked its people are." 3 Jonah, however, set out in the opposite direction in order to get away from the LORD. He went to Joppa, where he found a ship about to go to Spain. He paid his fare and went aboard with the crew to sail to Spain, where he would be away from the LORD. 4 But the LORD sent a strong wind on the sea, and the storm was so violent that the ship was in danger of breaking up. 5 The sailors were terrified and cried out for help, each one to his own god. Then, in order to lessen the danger[a], they threw the cargo[b] over-board. Meanwhile, Jonah had gone below and was lying in the ship's hold, sound asleep.

6 The captain found him there and said to him, "What are you doing asleep? Get up and pray to your god for help. Maybe he will feel sorry for us and spare our lives."

7 The sailors said to one another, "Let's draw lots and find out who is to blame for getting us into this danger." They did so, and Jonah's name was drawn. 8 So they said to him: "Now then, tell us! Who is to blame for this? What are you doing here? What country do you come from? What is your nationality?"

9 "I am a Hebrew," Jonah answered. "I worship the LORD, the God of heaven, who made land and sea." 10 Jonah went

[a] lessen the danger; *or* lighten the ship.   [b] cargo; *or* equipment.
1.1: 2 Kgs 14.25

1.1-2

1.3

1.3

1.4

1.5

1.6

1.7-8

1.9-12

1.13-14

1.15

on to tell them that he was running away from the LORD.

The sailors were terrified, and said to him, "That was an awful thing to do!"[c] 11 The storm was getting worse all the time, so the sailors asked him, "What should we do to you to stop the storm?"

12 Jonah answered, "Throw me into the sea, and it will calm down. I know it is my fault that you are caught in this violent storm."

13 Instead, the sailors tried to get the ship to shore, rowing with all their might. But the storm was getting worse and worse, and they got nowhere. 14 So they cried out to the LORD, "O LORD, we pray, don't punish us with death for taking this man's life! You, O LORD, are responsible for all this; it is your doing." 15 Then they picked Jonah up and threw him into the sea, and it calmed down at once. 16 This made the sailors so afraid of the LORD that they offered a sacrifice and promised to serve him.

17 At the LORD's command a large fish swallowed Jonah, and he was inside the fish for three days and nights.

Jonah's Prayer

2 From deep inside the fish Jonah prayed to the LORD his God:

2 "In my distress, O LORD, I called to you,
and you answered me.
From deep in the world of the dead
I cried for help, and you heard me.
3 You threw me down into the depths,
to the very bottom of the sea,
where the waters were all round me,
and all your mighty waves rolled over me.
4 I thought I had been banished from your presence
and would never see your holy Temple again.
5 The water came over me and choked me;
the sea covered me completely,
and seaweed was wrapped round my head.
6 I went down to the very roots of the mountains,
into the land whose gates lock shut for ever.[e]
But you, O LORD my God,
brought me back from the depths alive.
7 When I felt my life slipping away,

then, O LORD, I prayed to you,
and in your holy Temple you heard me.
8 Those who worship worthless idols
have abandoned their loyalty to you.
9 But I will sing praises to you;
I will offer you a sacrifice
and do what I have promised.
Salvation comes from the LORD!"

10 Then the LORD ordered the fish to spew Jonah up on the beach, and it did.

Jonah Obeys the LORD

3 Once again the LORD spoke to Jonah. 2 He said, "Go to Nineveh, that great city, and proclaim to the people the message I have given you." 3 So Jonah obeyed the LORD and went to Nineveh, a city so large that it took three days to walk through it. 4 Jonah started through the city, and after walking a whole day, he proclaimed, "In forty days Nineveh will be destroyed!"

5 The people of Nineveh believed God's message. So they decided that everyone should fast, and all the people, from the greatest to the least, put on sackcloth to show that they had repented.

6 When the king of Nineveh heard about it, he got up from his throne, took off his robe, put on sackcloth, and sat down in ashes. 7 He sent out a proclamation to the people of Nineveh: "This is an order from the king and his officials: No one is to eat anything; all persons, cattle, and sheep are forbidden to eat or drink. 8 All persons and animals must wear sackcloth. Everyone must pray earnestly to God and must give up his wicked behaviour and his evil actions. 9 Perhaps God will change his mind; perhaps he will stop being angry, and we will not die!"

10 God saw what they did; he saw that they had given up their wicked behaviour. So he changed his mind and did not punish them as he had said he would.

Jonah's Anger and God's Mercy

4 Jonah was very unhappy about this and became angry. 2 So he prayed, "LORD, didn't I say before I left home that this is just what you would do? That's why I did my best to run away to Spain! I knew that you are a loving and merciful God, always patient, always kind, and always ready to change your mind and

c and said...to do; *or* and asked him, "Why did you have to run away like that?"
e THE LAND WHOSE GATES LOCK SHUT FOR EVER: *A reference to the world of the dead (see 2.2).*
1.17: Mt 12.40   **3.4–5:** Mt 12.41; Lk 11.32   **4.2:** Ex 34.6

1.15

2.10

3.3

3.4

3.5

4.1

4.5

4.6

4.7

4.8

4.9-11

not punish. ³Now, LORD, let me die. I am better off dead than alive."

4 The LORD answered, "What right have you to be angry?"

5 Jonah went out east of the city and sat down. He made a shelter for himself and sat in its shade, waiting to see what would happen to Nineveh. ⁶Then the LORD God made a plant grow up over Jonah to give him some shade, so that he would be more comfortable. Jonah was extremely pleased with the plant. ⁷But at dawn the next day, at God's command, a worm attacked the plant, and it died. ⁸After the sun had risen, God sent a hot east wind, and Jonah was about to faint from the heat of the sun beating down on his head. So he wished he were dead.ᶠ "I am better off dead than alive," he said.

9 But God said to him, "What right have you to be angry about the plant?"

Jonah replied, "I have every right to be angry—angry enough to die!"

10 The LORD said to him, "This plant grew up in one night and disappeared the next; you didn't do anything for it, and you didn't make it grow—yet you feel sorry for it! ¹¹How much more, then, should I have pity on Nineveh, that great city. After all, it has more than 120,000 innocent children in it, as well as many animals!"

ᶠwished he were dead; or prayed that he would die.
4.3: 1 Kgs 19.4

THE BOOK OF

MICAH

INTRODUCTION

The prophet Micah, a contemporary of Isaiah, was from a country town in Judah, the southern kingdom. He was convinced that Judah was about to face the same kind of national catastrophe that Amos had predicted for the northern kingdom, and for the same reason—God would punish the hateful injustice of the people. Micah's message, however, contains more clear and notable signs of hope for the future.

Passages especially worth noting are the picture of universal peace under God (4.1-4); the prediction of a great king who would come from the family line of David and bring peace to the nation (5.2-5a); and, in a single verse (6.8), the summary of much that the prophets of Israel had to say: "What he requires of us is this: to do what is just, to show constant love, and to live in humble fellowship with our God."

Outline of Contents
Judgement on Israel and Judah   1.1—3.12
Restoration and peace   4.1—5.15
Message of warning and hope   6.1—7.20

---

1 During the time that Jotham, Ahaz, and Hezekiah were kings of Judah, the LORD gave this message to Micah, who was from the town of Moresheth. The LORD revealed to Micah all these things about Samaria and Jerusalem.

1.1: 2 Kgs 15.32—16.20, 18.1—20.21; 2 Chr 27.1-7, 28.1—32.33

A Lament for Samaria and Jerusalem

2 Hear this, all you nations;
   listen to this, all who live on earth!
The Sovereign LORD will testify against
      you.
   Listen! He speaks from his heavenly
      temple.
3 The LORD is coming from his holy place;
   he will come down and walk on the
      tops of the mountains.
4 Then the mountains will melt under him
      like wax in a fire;
   they will pour down into the valleys
      like water pouring down a hill.

5 All this will happen because the
people of Israel have sinned and rebelled
against God. Who is to blame for Israel's
rebellion? Samaria, the capital city itself!
Who is guilty of idolatry in Judah?
Jerusalem itself! 6 So the LORD says, "I
will make Samaria a pile of ruins in the
open country, a place for planting grapevines. I will pour the rubble of the city
down into the valley, and will lay bare
the city's foundations. 7 All its precious
idols will be smashed to pieces, everything
given to its temple prostitutes will be
destroyed by fire, and all its images will
become a desolate heap. Samaria acquired
these things for its fertility rites, and now
her enemies will carry them off for temple
prostitutes elsewhere."

8 Then Micah said, "Because of this I
will mourn and lament. To show my
sorrow, I will walk about barefoot and
naked. I will howl like a jackal and wail
like an ostrich. 9 Samaria's wounds cannot
be healed, and Judah is about to suffer
in the same way; destruction has reached
the gates of Jerusalem itself, where my
people live."

The Enemy Approaches Jerusalem

10 Don't tell our enemies in Gath about
our defeat; don't let them see you
weeping. People of Beth Leaphrah, [a] show
your despair by rolling in the dust! 11 You
people of Shaphir, go into exile, naked
and ashamed. Those who live in Zaanan
dare not come out of their city. When
you hear the people of Bethezel mourn,
you will know that there is no refuge
there. 12 The people of Maroth wait

anxiously for relief, because the LORD has
brought disaster close to Jerusalem.
13 You that live in Lachish, hitch the
horses to the chariots. You imitated the
sins of Israel and so caused Jerusalem
to sin. 14 And now, people of Judah, say
good-bye to the town of Moresheth Gath.
The kings of Israel will get no help from
the town of Achzib.

15 People of Mareshah, the LORD will
hand you over to an enemy, who is going
to capture your town. The leaders of Israel
will go and hide in the cave at Adullam.
16 People of Judah, cut off your hair in
mourning for the children you love. Make
yourselves as bald as vultures, because
your children will be taken away from
you into exile.

The Fate of Those Who Oppress the Poor

2 How terrible it will be for those who
lie awake and plan evil! When
morning comes, as soon as they have the
chance, they do the evil they planned.
2 When they want fields, they seize them;
when they want houses, they take them.
No man's family or property is safe.

3 And so the LORD says, "I am planning
to bring disaster on you, and you will
not be able to escape it. You are going
to find yourselves in trouble, and then
you will not walk so proudly any more.
4 When that time comes, people will use
your story as an example of disaster, and
they will sing this song of despair about
your experience:

   We are completely ruined!
   The LORD has taken our land away
   And given it to those who took us
      captive." [b]

5 So then, when the time comes for the
land to be given back to the LORD's people,
there will be no share for any of you.

6 The people preach at me and say,
"Don't preach at us. Don't preach about
all that. God is not going to disgrace us.
7 Do you think the people of Israel are
under a curse? [c] Has the LORD lost his
patience? Would he really do such
things? Doesn't he [d] speak kindly to those
who do right?"

8 The LORD replies, "You attack my
people [e] like enemies. Men return from

---

[a] BETH LEAPHRAH: *The prophet speaks of outlying towns (verses 10–14) which an enemy army
approaching Jerusalem would attack.*
[b] *Probable text* those who took us captive; *Hebrew* rebels.
[c] *Probable text* under a curse; *Hebrew unclear.*
[d] *Probable text* Doesn't he; *Hebrew* Don't I.
[e] *Probable text* You attack my people; *Hebrew* Recently my people have attacked.

Don't preach at us (2.6)

battle, thinking they are safe at home, but there you are, waiting to steal the coats off their backs. ⁹You drive the women of my people out of the homes they love, and you have robbed their children of my blessings for ever. ¹⁰Get up and go; there is no safety here any more. Your sins have doomed this place to destruction.

11 "These people want the kind of prophet who goes about full of lies and deceit and says, 'I prophesy that wine and liquor will flow for you.'

12 "But I will gather you together, all you people of Israel that are left. I will bring you together like sheep returning to the fold. Like a pasture full of sheep, your land will once again be filled with many people."

13 God will open the way for them and lead them out of exile. They will break out of the city gates and go free. Their king, the LORD himself, will lead them out.

Micah Denounces Israel's Leaders

3 Listen, you rulers of Israel! You are supposed to be concerned about justice, ²yet you hate what is good and you love what is evil. You skin my people alive and tear the flesh off their bones. ³You eat my people up. You strip off their skin, break their bones, and chop them up like meat for the pot. ⁴The time is

coming when you will cry out to the LORD, but he will not answer you. He will not listen to your prayers, for you have done evil.

5 My people are deceived by prophets who promise peace to those who pay them, but threaten war for those who don't. To these prophets the LORD says, ⁶"Prophets, your day is almost over; the sun is going down on you. Because you mislead my people, you will have no more prophetic visions, and you will not be able to predict anything." ⁷Those who predict the future will be disgraced by their failure. They will all be humiliated because God does not answer them.

8 But as for me, the LORD fills me with his spirit and power, and gives me a sense of justice and the courage to tell the people of Israel what their sins are. ⁹Listen to me, you rulers of Israel, you that hate justice and turn right into wrong. ¹⁰You are building God's city, Jerusalem, on a foundation of murder and injustice. ¹¹The city's rulers govern for bribes, the priests interpret the Law for pay, the prophets give their revelations for money—and they all claim that the LORD is with them. "No harm will come to us," they say. "The LORD is with us."

12 And so, because of you, Zion will be ploughed like a field, Jerusalem will become a pile of ruins, and the Temple hill will become a forest.

3.12: Jer 26.18

The prophets give their revelations for money (3.11)

The LORD's Universal Reign of Peace
(Is 2.1–4)

4 In days to come
the mountain where the Temple stands ·
will be the highest one of all,
towering above all the hills.
Many nations will come streaming to it,
² and their people will say,
"Let us go up the hill of the LORD,[f]
to the Temple of Israel's God.
For he will teach us what he wants us to do;
we will walk in the paths he has chosen.
For the LORD's teaching comes from Jerusalem;
from Zion he speaks to his people."

³ He will settle disputes among the nations,
among the great powers near and far.
They will hammer their swords into ploughs
and their spears into pruning-knives.
Nations will never again go to war,
never prepare for battle again.
⁴ Everyone will live in peace
among his own vineyards and fig-trees,
and no one will make him afraid.
The LORD Almighty has promised this.

5 Each nation worships and obeys its own god, but we will worship and obey the LORD our God for ever and ever.

Israel Will Return from Exile

6 "The time is coming," says the LORD, "when I will gather together the people I punished, those who have suffered in exile. ⁷They are crippled and far from home, but I will make a new beginning with those who are left, and they will become a great nation. I will rule over them on Mount Zion from that time on and for ever."

8 And you, Jerusalem, where God, like a shepherd, watches over his people, will once again be the capital of the kingdom that was yours. ⁹Why do you cry out so loudly? Why are you suffering like a woman in labour? Is it because you have no king, and your counsellors are dead? ¹⁰Twist and groan,[g] people of Jerusalem, like a woman giving birth, for now you will have to leave the city and live in the open country. You will have to go to Babylon, but there the LORD will save you from your enemies. ¹¹Many nations have gathered to attack you. They say, "Jerusalem must be destroyed! We will see this city in ruins!" ¹²But these nations do not know what is in the LORD's mind. They do not realize that they have been gathered together to be punished in the same way that corn is brought in to be threshed.

13 The LORD says, "People of Jerusalem, go and punish your enemies! I will make you as strong as a bull with iron horns and bronze hoofs. You will crush many nations, and the wealth they got by violence you will present to me, the Lord of the whole world."

5 People of Jerusalem, gather your forces![h] We are besieged! They are attacking the leader of Israel!

God Promises a Ruler from Bethlehem

2 The LORD says, "Bethlehem Ephra-

---

[f] HILL OF THE LORD: *Mount Zion (see Zion in Word List).*
[g] *Probable text* groan; *Hebrew* bring forth.
[h] *Probable text* People...forces; *Hebrew unclear.*
4.3: Joel 3.10   **4.4:** Zech 3.10   **5.2:** Mt 2.6; Jn 7.42

thah, you are one of the smallest towns in Judah, but out of you I will bring a ruler for Israel, whose family line goes back to ancient times."

3 So the LORD will abandon his people to their enemies until the woman who is to give birth has her son. Then his fellow-countrymen who are in exile will be reunited with their own people. ⁴When he comes, he will rule his people with the strength that comes from the LORD and with the majesty of the LORD God himself. His people will live in safety because people all over the earth will acknowledge his greatness, ⁵and he will bring peace.

Deliverance and Punishment

When the Assyrians invade our country and break through our defences, we will send our strongest leaders to fight them. ⁶By force of arms they will conquer Assyria, the land of Nimrod, and they*ⁱ* will save us from the Assyrians when they invade our territory.

7 The people of Israel who survive will be like refreshing dew sent by the LORD for many nations, like showers on growing plants. They will depend on God, not man. ⁸Those who are left among the nations will be like a lion hunting for food in a forest or a pasture: he gets in among the sheep, pounces on them, and tears them to pieces—and there is no hope of rescue. ⁹Israel will conquer her enemies and destroy them all.

10 The LORD says, "At that time I will take away your horses and destroy your chariots. ¹¹I will destroy the cities in your land and tear down all your defences. ¹²I will destroy the magic charms you use and leave you without any fortune-tellers. ¹³I will destroy your idols and sacred stone pillars; no longer will you worship the things that you yourselves have made. ¹⁴I will pull down the images of the goddess Asherah in your land and destroy your cities. ¹⁵And in my great anger I will take revenge on all nations that have not obeyed me."

The LORD's Case Against Israel

6 Listen to the LORD's case against Israel.
Arise, O LORD, and present your case;

let the mountains and the hills hear what you say.

2 You mountains, you everlasting foundations of the earth, listen to the LORD's case! The LORD has a case against his people. He is going to bring an accusation against Israel.

3 The LORD says, "My people, what have I done to you? How have I been a burden to you? Answer me. ⁴I brought you out of Egypt; I rescued you from slavery; I sent Moses, Aaron, and Miriam to lead you. ⁵My people, remember what King Balak of Moab planned to do to you and how Balaam son of Beor answered him. Remember the things that happened on the way from the camp at Acacia to Gilgal. Remember these things and you will realize what I did in order to save you."

What the LORD Requires

6 What shall I bring to the LORD, the God of heaven, when I come to worship him? Shall I bring the best calves to burn as offerings to him? ⁷Will the LORD be pleased if I bring him thousands of sheep or endless streams of olive-oil? Shall I offer him my first-born child to pay for my sins? ⁸No, the LORD has told us what is good. What he requires of us is this: to do what is just, to show constant love, and to live in humble fellowship with our God.

9 It is wise to fear the LORD. He calls to the city, "Listen, you people who assemble in the city!*ʲ* ¹⁰In the houses of evil men are treasures which they got dishonestly. They use false measures, a thing that I hate.*ᵏ* ¹¹How can I forgive men who use false scales and weights? ¹²Your rich men exploit the poor, and all of you are liars. ¹³So I have already begun*ˡ* your ruin and destruction because of your sins. ¹⁴You will eat, but not be satisfied—in fact you will still be hungry. You will carry things off, but you will not be able to save them; anything you do save I will destroy in war. ¹⁵You will sow corn, but not harvest the crop. You will press oil from olives, but never be able to use it. You will make wine, but never drink it. ¹⁶This will happen because you have followed the evil practices of King Omri

---

ⁱ Probable text they; *Hebrew* he.
ʲ Probable text who assemble in the city; *Hebrew* and who appointed it. Yet.
ᵏ Verse 10 in Hebrew is unclear. *ˡ Some ancient translations* begun; *Hebrew* made ill.
5.6: Gen 10.8-11 **6.4:** Ex 4.10-16, 12.50-51, 15.20
6.5: Num 22.2—24.25; Josh 3.1—4.19 **6.16:** 1 Kgs 16.23-34, 21.25-26

How can I forgive men who use false scales and weights? (6.11)

and of his son, King Ahab. You have continued their policies, and so I will bring you to ruin, and everyone will despise you. People[m] everywhere will treat you with contempt."[n]

Israel's Moral Corruption

7 It's hopeless! I am like a hungry man who finds no fruit left on the trees and no grapes on the vines. All the grapes and all the tasty figs have been picked. [2] There is not an honest person left in the land, no one loyal to God. Everyone is waiting for a chance to commit murder. Everyone hunts down his fellow-countryman. [3] They are all experts at doing evil. Officials and judges ask for bribes. The influential man tells them what he wants, and so they scheme together.[o] [4] Even the best and most honest of them are as worthless as weeds.

The day has come when God will punish the people, as he warned them through their watchmen, the prophets. Now they are in confusion. [5] Don't believe your neighbour or trust your friend. Be careful what you say even to your wife. [6] In these times sons treat their fathers like fools, daughters oppose their mothers, and young women quarrel with their mothers-

in-law; a man's enemies are the members of his own family.

[7] But I will watch for the LORD; I will wait confidently for God, who will save me. My God will hear me.

The LORD Brings Salvation

8 Our enemies have no reason to gloat over us. We have fallen, but we will rise again. We are in darkness now, but the LORD will give us light. [9] We have sinned against the LORD, so now we must endure his anger for a while. But in the end he will defend us and right the wrongs that have been done to us. He will bring us out to the light; we will live to see him save us. [10] Then our enemies will see this and be disgraced—the same enemies who taunted us by asking, "Where is the LORD your God?" We will see them defeated, trampled[p] down like mud in the streets.

11 People of Jerusalem, the time to rebuild the city walls is coming. At that time your territory will be enlarged. [12] Your people will return to you from everywhere—from Assyria in the east, from Egypt in the south, from the region of the Euphrates, from distant seas and far-off mountains. [13] But the earth will become a desert because of the wickedness of those who live on it.

[m] *One ancient translation* People; *Hebrew* My people.
[n] People...contempt; *or* As my people you will everywhere be treated with contempt.
[o] and so they scheme together; *Hebrew unclear.*
[p] We will see...trampled; *or* We will gloat over them as they lie trampled.
7.6: Mt 10.35–36; Lk 12.53

The LORD's Compassion on Israel

14 Be a shepherd to your people, LORD, the people you have chosen. Although they live apart in the wilderness, there is fertile land around them. Let them go and feed in the rich pastures of Bashan and Gilead, as they did long ago.

15 Work miracles for us,*q* LORD, as you did in the days when you brought us out of Egypt. 16 The nations will see this and be frustrated in spite of all their strength. In dismay they will close their mouths and cover their ears. 17 They will crawl in the dust like snakes; they will come from their fortresses, trembling and afraid. They will turn in fear to the LORD our God.

18 There is no other god like you, O LORD; you forgive the sins of your people who have survived. You do not stay angry for ever, but you take pleasure in showing us your constant love. 19 You will be merciful to us once again. You will trample our sins underfoot and send them to the bottom of the sea! 20 You will show your faithfulness and constant love to your people, the descendants of Abraham and of Jacob, as you promised our ancestors long ago.

q Probable text Work miracles for us; *Hebrew* I will work miracles for him.

Your people will return to you from everywhere (7.12)

THE BOOK OF

NAHUM

INTRODUCTION

The book of *Nahum* is a poem celebrating the fall of Nineveh, the capital city of Israel's ancient and oppressive enemy, the Assyrians. The fall of Nineveh, near the end of the seventh century B.C., is seen as the judgement of God upon a cruel and arrogant nation.

Outline of Contents
Judgement on Nineveh   1.1–15
The fall of Nineveh   2.1—3.19

1 This is a message about Nineveh, the account of a vision seen by Nahum, who was from Elkosh.

The Lord's Anger against Nineveh

² The Lord God tolerates no rivals;
he punishes those who oppose him.
In his anger he pays them back.
³ The Lord does not easily become angry,
but he is powerful
and never lets the guilty go
unpunished.

Where the Lord walks, storms arise;
the clouds are the dust raised by his
feet!
⁴ He commands the sea, and it dries up!
He makes the rivers go dry.
The fields of Bashan wither,
Mount Carmel turns brown,
and the flowers of Lebanon fade.
⁵ Mountains quake in the presence of the
Lord;
hills melt before him.
The earth shakes when the Lord
appears;
the world and all its people tremble.
⁶ When he is angry, who can survive?
Who can survive his terrible fury?
He pours out his flaming anger;

rocks crumble to dust before him.

⁷ The Lord is good;
he protects his people in times of
trouble;
he takes care of those who turn to
him.
⁸ Like a great rushing flood he completely
destroys his enemies;[a]
he sends to their death those who
oppose him.
⁹ What are you plotting against the Lord?
He will destroy you.
No one opposes him more than once.
¹⁰ Like tangled thorns and dry straw,
you drunkards will be burnt up![b]

11 From you, Nineveh, there came a man full of wicked schemes, who plotted against the Lord. ¹² This is what the Lord says to his people Israel: "Even though the Assyrians are strong and numerous, they will be destroyed and disappear. My people, I made you suffer, but I will not do it again. ¹³ I will now end Assyria's power over you and break the chains that bind you."

14 This is what the Lord has decreed about the Assyrians: "They will have no descendants to carry on their name. I will

---

ᵃ *Some ancient translations* his enemies; *Hebrew* its place.   ᵇ *Verse 10 in Hebrew is unclear.*
1.1—3.19: Is 10.5–34, 14.24–27; Zeph 2.13–15

destroy the idols that are in the temples of their gods. I am preparing a grave for the Assyrians—they don't deserve to live!"

15 Look, a messenger is coming over

Look, a messenger is coming (1.15)

the mountains with good news! He is on his way to announce the victory! People of Judah, celebrate your festivals and give God what you solemnly promised him. The wicked will never invade your land again. They have been totally destroyed!

The Fall of Nineveh

2 Nineveh, you are under attack!
The power that will shatter you has come.
Man the defences!
Guard the road!
Prepare for battle!

2 (The LORD is about to restore the glory of Israel, as it was before her enemies plundered her.)

3 The enemy soldiers carry red shields
and wear uniforms of red.
They are preparing to attack!
Their chariots flash like fire!
Their horses *c* prance!

4 Chariots dash wildly through the streets,
rushing to and fro through the city
squares.

They flash like torches
and dart about like lightning.
5 The officers are summoned;
they stumble as they press forward.

The attackers rush to the wall
and set up the shield for the battering-
ram.
6 The gates by the river burst open;
the palace is filled with terror.
7 The queen is taken captive;
her servants moan like doves
and beat their breasts in sorrow.
8 Like water from a broken dam
the people rush from Nineveh! *e*
"Stop! Stop!" the cry rings out—
but no one turns back.

9 Plunder the silver!
Plunder the gold!
The city is full of treasure!

10 Nineveh is destroyed, deserted,
desolate!
Hearts melt with fear;
knees tremble, strength is gone;
faces grow pale.

11 Where now is the city
that was like a den of lions,
the place where young lions were fed,
where the lion and the lioness would
go
and their cubs would be safe?
12 The lion killed his prey
and tore it to pieces for his mate and
her cubs;
he filled his den with torn flesh.

13 "I am your enemy!" says the LORD Almighty. "I will burn up your chariots. Your soldiers will be killed in war, and I will take away everything that you took from others. The demands of your envoys will no longer be heard."

3 Doomed is the lying, murderous city,
full of wealth to be looted and
plundered!

2 Listen! The crack of the whip,
the rattle of wheels,
the gallop of horses,
the jolting of chariots!
3 Horsemen charge,
swords flash, spears gleam!
Corpses are piled high,
dead bodies without number—

c Some ancient translations horses; *Hebrew* cypresses.
e Probable text Like water...Nineveh; *Hebrew unclear.*
1.15: Is 52.7

The fall of Nineveh (chapter 2)

men stumble over them!
⁴ Nineveh the whore is being punished.
Attractive and full of deadly charms,
   she enchanted nations and enslaved[f]
   them.

5 The LORD Almighty says,
"I will punish you, Nineveh!
I will strip you naked
   and let the nations see you,
   see you in all your shame.
⁶ I will treat you with contempt
   and cover you with filth.
People will stare at you in horror.
⁷ All who see you will shrink back.
They will say, 'Nineveh lies in ruins!
Who has any sympathy for her?
Who will want to comfort her?'"

8 Nineveh, are you any better than
Thebes, the capital of Egypt? She too had
a river to protect her like a wall—the
Nile was her defence. ⁹ She ruled Sudan
and Egypt, there was no limit to her
power; Libya was her ally. ¹⁰ Yet the
people of Thebes were carried off into
exile. At every street corner their children
were beaten to death. Their leading men
were carried off in chains and divided
among their captors.

11 Nineveh, you too will fall into a
drunken stupor! You too will try to escape
from your enemies. ¹² All your fortresses
will be like fig-trees with ripe figs: shake
the trees, and the fruit falls right into your
mouth! ¹³ Your soldiers are like women,
and your country stands defenceless
before your enemies. Fire will destroy the
bars across your gates. ¹⁴ Draw water to
prepare for a siege, and strengthen your
fortresses! Trample the clay to make
bricks, and get the brick moulds ready!
¹⁵ No matter what you do, you will still
be burnt to death or killed in battle. You
will be wiped out like crops eaten up by
locusts.

You multiplied like locusts! ¹⁶ You
produced more merchants than there are
stars in the sky! But now they are gone,
like locusts that spread their wings and
fly away. ¹⁷ Your officials are like a swarm
of locusts that stay in the walls on a cold
day. But when the sun comes out, they
fly away, and no one knows where they
have gone!

18 Emperor of Assyria, your governors
are dead, and your noblemen are asleep
for ever! Your people are scattered on
the mountains, and there is no one to
bring them home again. ¹⁹ There is no
remedy for your injuries, and your
wounds cannot be healed. All those who
hear the news of your destruction clap
their hands for joy. Did anyone escape
your endless cruelty?

[f]enslaved; *or* seduced.

THE BOOK OF
HABAKKUK

INTRODUCTION

The words of the prophet Habakkuk come from near the end of the seventh century B.C., at a time when the Babylonians were in power. He was deeply disturbed by the violence of these cruel people, and asked the Lord, "So why are you silent while they destroy people who are more righteous than they are?" (1.13). The Lord's answer was that he would take action in his own good time, and meanwhile "those who are righteous will live because they are faithful to God" (2.4).

The rest of the book is a prophecy of doom on the unrighteous, with a concluding psalm celebrating the greatness of God and expressing the undying faith of the poet.

Outline of Contents

Habakkuk's complaints and the Lord's replies 1.1—2.4
Doom on the unrighteous 2.5-20
Habakkuk's prayer 3.1-19

---

1 This is the message that the LORD revealed to the prophet Habakkuk.

Habakkuk Complains of Injustice

2 O LORD, how long must I call for help before you listen, before you save us from violence? 3 Why do you make me see such trouble? How can you endure to look on such wrongdoing? Destruction and violence are all round me, and there is fighting and quarrelling everywhere. 4 The law is weak and useless, and justice is never done. Evil men get the better of the righteous, and so justice is perverted.

The LORD's Reply

5 Then the LORD said to his people, "Keep watching the nations round you, and you will be astonished at what you see. I am going to do something that you will not believe when you hear about it. 6 I am bringing the Babylonians to power, those fierce, restless people. They are marching out across the world to conquer other lands. 7 They spread fear and terror, and in their pride they are a law to themselves.

8 "Their horses are faster than leopards, fiercer than hungry wolves. Their horsemen come riding from distant lands; their horses paw the ground. They come swooping down like eagles attacking their prey.

9 "Their armies advance in violent conquest, and everyone is terrified as they approach. [b] Their captives are as numerous as grains of sand. 10 They treat kings with contempt and laugh at high officials. No fortress can stop them—they pile up earth against it and capture it.

---

b Probable text and everyone...approach; *Hebrew unclear.*
1.5: Acts 13.41   **1.6:** 2 Kgs 24.2

LORD... how can you stand these treacherous, evil men? (1.12,13)

11 Then they sweep on like the wind and are gone, these men whose power is their god."

Habakkuk Complains to the LORD Again

12 LORD, from the very beginning you are God. You are my God, holy and eternal. LORD, my God and protector, you have chosen the Babylonians and made them strong so that they can punish us. 13 But how can you stand these treacherous, evil men? Your eyes are too holy to look at evil, and you cannot stand the sight of people doing wrong. So why are you silent while they destroy people who are more righteous than they are?

14 How can you treat people like fish or like a swarm of insects that have no ruler to direct them? 15 The Babylonians catch people with hooks, as though they were fish. They drag them off in nets and shout for joy over their catch! 16 They even worship their nets and offer sacrifices to them, because their nets provide them with the best of everything.

17 Are they going to use their swords for ever and keep on destroying nations without mercy?

The LORD's Answer to Habakkuk

2 I will climb my watch-tower and wait to see what the LORD will tell me to say and what answer he x will give to my complaint.

2 The LORD gave me this answer: "Write down clearly on clay tablets what I reveal to you, so that it can be read at a glance. 3 Put it in writing, because it is not yet time for it to come true. But the time is coming quickly, and what I show you will come true. It may seem slow in coming, but wait for it; it will certainly take place, and it will not be delayed. 4 And this is the message: 'Those who are evil will not survive, c but those who are righteous will live because they are faithful to God.'"

Doom on the Unrighteous

5 Wealth is deceitful. Greedy men are proud and restless—like death itself they are never satisfied. That is why they conquer nation after nation for themselves. 6 The conquered people will taunt their conquerors and show their scorn for them. They will say, "You take what isn't yours, but you are doomed! How long will you go on getting rich by forcing your debtors to pay up?"

7 But before you know it, you that have conquered others will be in debt yourselves and be forced to pay interest. Enemies will come and make you tremble. They will plunder you! 8 You have plundered the people of many nations, but now those who have survived will plunder you

x *One ancient translation* he; *Hebrew* I.
c *Probable text* will not survive; *Hebrew unclear.*
2.3: Heb 10.37
2.4: Rom 1.17; Gal 3.11; Heb 10.38

because of the murders you have committed and because of your violence against the people of the world and its cities. *d*

9 You are doomed! You have made your family rich with what you took by violence, and have tried to make your own home safe from harm and danger! 10 But your schemes have brought shame on your family; by destroying many nations you have only brought ruin on yourself. 11 Even the stones of the walls cry out against you, and the rafters echo the cry.

12 You are doomed! You founded a city on crime and built it up by murder. 13 The nations you conquered wore themselves out in useless labour, and all they have built goes up in flames. The LORD Almighty has done this. 14 But the earth will be as full of the knowledge of the LORD's glory as the seas are full of water.

15 You are doomed! In your fury you humiliated and disgraced your neighbours; you made them stagger as though they were drunk. 16 You in turn will be covered with shame instead of honour. You yourself will drink and stagger. The LORD will make you drink your own cup of punishment, and your honour will be turned to disgrace. 17 You have cut down the forests of Lebanon; now you will be cut down. You killed its animals; now animals will terrify you. This will happen because of the murders you have committed and because of your violence against the people of the world and its cities. *d*

18 What's the use of an idol? It is only something that a man has made, and it tells you nothing but lies. What good does it do for its maker to trust it—a god that can't even talk! 19 You are doomed! You say to a piece of wood, "Wake up!" or to a block of stone, "Get up!" Can an idol reveal anything to you? It may be covered with silver and gold, but there is no life in it.

20 The LORD is in his holy Temple; let everyone on earth be silent in his presence.

A Prayer of Habakkuk

3 This is a prayer of the prophet Habakkuk: *e*

2 O LORD, I have heard of what you have done,
  and I am filled with awe.
Now do again in our times
  the great deeds you used to do.
Be merciful, even when you are angry.

3 God is coming again from Edom;
  the holy God is coming from the hills of Paran.
His splendour covers the heavens;
  and the earth is full of his praise.
4 He comes with the brightness of lightning;
  light flashes from his hand,
  there where his power is hidden.
5 He sends disease before him
  and commands death to follow him.
6 When he stops, the earth shakes;
  at his glance the nations tremble.
The eternal mountains are shattered;
  the everlasting hills sink down,
  the hills where he walked in ancient times.

7 I saw the people of Cushan afraid
  and the people of Midian tremble.
8 Was it the rivers that made you angry, LORD?
  Was it the sea that made you furious?
You rode upon the clouds;
  the storm cloud was your chariot,
  as you brought victory to your people.
9 You got ready to use your bow,
  ready to shoot your arrows. *f*
Your lightning split open the earth.
10 When the mountains saw you, they trembled;
  water poured down from the skies.
The waters under the earth roared,
  and their waves rose high.
11 At the flash of your speeding arrows
  and the gleam of your shining spear,
  the sun and the moon stood still.
12 You marched across the earth in anger;
  in fury you trampled the nations.
13 You went out to save your people,
  to save your chosen king.
You struck down the leader of the wicked
  and completely destroyed his followers. *h*
14 Your arrows pierced the commander of his army

---

d the people...cities; *or* the land, the city, and those who live in it.
e Hebrew has an additional phrase, the meaning of which is unclear.
f Probable text ready to shoot your arrows; Hebrew unclear.
h Probable text completely...followers; Hebrew unclear.
2.14: Is 11.9

when it came like a storm to scatter
us,
gloating like those who secretly
oppress the poor. [i]
15 You trampled the sea with your horses,
and the mighty waters foamed.

16 I hear all this, and I tremble;
my lips quiver with fear.
My body goes limp,
and my feet stumble[j] beneath me.

I will quietly wait for the time to come

when God will punish those who
attack us.

17 Even though the fig-trees have no fruit
and no grapes grow on the vines,
even though the olive-crop fails
and the fields produce no corn,
even though the sheep all die
and the cattle-stalls are empty,
18 I will still be joyful and glad,
because the LORD God is my saviour.
19 The Sovereign LORD gives me strength.
He makes me sure-footed as a deer,
and keeps me safe on the mountains.

[i] Verse 14 in Hebrew is unclear.   [j] Probable text my feet stumble; Hebrew I am excited, because.
3.19: 2 Sam 22.34; Ps 18.33

THE BOOK OF
ZEPHANIAH

INTRODUCTION

The prophet Zephaniah preached in the latter part of the seventh century B.C., probably in the decade before King Josiah's religious reforms of 621 B.C. The book contains the familiar prophetic themes: A day of doom and destruction is threatened, when Judah will be punished for her worship of other gods. The Lord will punish other nations also. Although Jerusalem is doomed, in time the city will be restored, with a humble and righteous people living there.

Outline of Contents
The day of the Lord's judgement 1.1—2.3
The doom of Israel's neighbours 2.4–15
Jerusalem's doom and redemption 3.1–20

1 This is the message that the LORD gave to Zephaniah during the time that Josiah son of Amon was king of Judah. (Zephaniah was descended from King Hezekiah through Amariah, Gedaliah, and Cushi.)

The Day of the LORD's Judgement

2 The LORD said, "I am going to destroy everything on earth, 3 all human beings

and animals, birds and fish. I will bring about the downfall of[a] the wicked. I will destroy all mankind, and no survivors will be left. I, the LORD, have spoken.

4 "I will punish the people of Jerusalem and of all Judah. I will destroy the last trace of the worship of Baal there, and no one will even remember the pagan priests who serve him. 5 I will destroy anyone who goes up on the roof and

[a] Probable text I will bring about the downfall of; Hebrew the stumbling blocks.
1.1: 2 Kgs 22.1—23.30; 2 Chr 34.1—35.27

worships the sun, the moon, and the stars. I will also destroy those who worship me and swear loyalty to me, but then take oaths in the name of the god Molech. 6 I will destroy those who have turned back and no longer follow me, those who do not come to me or ask me to guide them."

7 The day is near when the LORD will sit in judgement; so be silent in his presence. The LORD is preparing to sacrifice his people and has invited enemies to plunder Judah. 8 "On that day of slaughter," says the LORD, "I will punish the officials, the king's sons, and all who practise foreign customs. 9 I will punish all who worship like pagans and who steal and kill in order to fill their master's house[b] with loot.

10 "On that day," says the LORD, "you will hear the sound of crying at the Fish Gate in Jerusalem. You will hear wailing in the newer part of the city and a great crashing sound in the hills. 11 Wail and cry when you hear this, you that live in the lower part of the city, because all the merchants will be dead!

12 "At that time I will take a lamp and

The LORD never does anything, one way or the other (1.12)

search Jerusalem. I will punish the people

who are self-satisfied and confident, who say to themselves, 'The LORD never does anything, one way or the other.' 13 Their wealth will be looted and their houses destroyed. They will never live in the houses they are building or drink wine from the vineyards they are planting."

14 The great day of the LORD is near— very near and coming fast! That will be a bitter day, for even[c] the bravest soldiers will cry out in despair! 15 It will be a day of fury, a day of trouble and distress, a day of ruin and destruction, a day of darkness and gloom, a black and cloudy day, 16 a day filled with the sound of war-trumpets and the battle-cry of soldiers attacking fortified cities and high towers.

17 The LORD says, "I will bring such disasters on mankind that everyone will grope about like a blind man. They have sinned against me, and now their blood will be poured out like water, and their dead bodies will lie rotting on the ground."

18 On the day when the LORD shows his fury, not even all their silver and gold will save them. The whole earth will be destroyed by the fire of his anger. He will put an end—a sudden end—to everyone who lives on earth.

A Plea for Repentance

2 Shameless nation, come to your senses 2 before you are driven away like chaff blown by the wind, before the burning anger of the LORD comes upon you, before the day when he shows his fury. 3 Turn to the LORD, all you humble people of the land, who obey his commands. Do what is right, and humble yourselves before the LORD. Perhaps you will escape punishment on the day when the LORD shows his anger.

The Doom of the Nations round Israel

4 No one will be left in the city of Gaza. Ashkelon will be deserted. The people of Ashdod will be driven out in half a day,[x] and the people of Ekron will be driven from their city. 5 You Philistines are doomed, you people who live along the coast. The LORD has passed sentence on you. He will destroy you, and not one of you will be left. 6 Your land by the sea will become open fields with shepherds' huts and sheep pens. 7 The people of Judah who survive will occupy your

[b] their master's house; *or* the temple of their god.
[c] That...even; *or* Listen! That terrible day is coming when even.
[x] in half a day; *or* by a surprise attack at noon.
2.4–7: Is 14.29–31; Jer 47.1–7; Ezek 25.15–17; Joel 3.4–8; Amos 1.6–8; Zech 9.5–7

Everyone who passes by will shrink back in horror (2.15)

land. They will pasture their flocks there and sleep in the houses of Ashkelon. The LORD their God will be with them and make them prosper again.

8 The LORD Almighty says, "I have heard the people of Moab and Ammon insulting and taunting my people, and boasting that they would seize their land. 9 As surely as I am the living LORD, the God of Israel, I swear that Moab and Ammon are going to be destroyed like Sodom and Gomorrah. They will become a place of salts pits and everlasting ruin, overgrown with weeds. Those of my people who survive will plunder them and take their land."

10 That is how the people of Moab and Ammon will be punished for their pride and arrogance and for insulting the people of the LORD Almighty. 11 The LORD will terrify them. He will reduce the gods of the earth to nothing, and then every nation will worship him, each in its own land.

12 The LORD will also put the people of Sudan to death.

13 The LORD will use his power to destroy Assyria. He will make the city of Nineveh a deserted ruin, a waterless desert. 14 It will be a place where flocks, herds, and animals of every kind will lie down. Owls will live among its ruins and hoot from the windows. Crows[e] will caw on the doorsteps. The cedar-wood of her buildings will be stripped away. 15 That is what will happen to the city that is so proud of its own power and thinks

it is safe. Its people think that their city is the greatest in the world. What a desolate place it will become, a place where wild animals will rest! Everyone who passes by will shrink back in horror.

Jerusalem's Sin and Redemption

3 Jerusalem is doomed, that corrupt, rebellious city that oppresses its own people. 2 It has not listened to the LORD or accepted his discipline. It has not put its trust in the LORD or asked for his help. 3 Its officials are like roaring lions; its judges are like hungry wolves, too greedy to leave a bone until morning. 4 The prophets are irresponsible and treacherous; the priests defile what is sacred, and twist the law of God to their own advantage. 5 But the LORD is still in the city; he does what is right and never what is wrong. Every morning without fail, he brings justice to his people. And yet the unrighteous people there keep on doing wrong and are not ashamed.

6 The LORD says, "I have wiped out whole nations; I have destroyed their cities and left their walls and towers in ruins. The cities are deserted; the streets are empty—no one is left. 7 I thought that then my people would have reverence for me and accept my discipline, that they would never forget[f] the lesson I taught them. But soon they were behaving as badly as ever.

8 "Just wait," the LORD says. "Wait for

---

e Some ancient translations Crows; *Hebrew* Desolation.
f Some ancient translations they would never forget; *Hebrew* their dwelling would not be cut off.
2.8-11: Is 15.1—16.14, 25.10-12; Jer 48.1—49.6; Ezek 21.28-32, 25.1-11; Amos 1.13-15
2.9: Gen 19.24   **2.12:** Is 18.1-7   **2.13-15:** Is 10.5-34, 14.24-27; Nah 1.1—3.19

the day when I rise to accuse the nations. I have made up my mind to gather nations and kingdoms, in order to let them feel the force of my anger. The whole earth will be destroyed by the fire of my fury.

9 "Then I will change the people of the nations, and they will pray to me alone and not to other gods. They will all obey me. ¹⁰ Even from distant Sudan my scattered people will bring offerings to me. ¹¹ At that time you, my people, will no longer need to be ashamed that you rebelled against me. I will remove everyone who is proud and arrogant, and you will never again rebel against me on my sacred hill.ᵍ ¹² I will leave there a humble and lowly people, who will come to me for help. ¹³ The people of Israel who survive will do no wrong to anyone, tell no lies, nor try to deceive. They will be prosperous and secure, afraid of no one."

A Song of Joy

¹⁴ Sing and shout for joy, people of
    Israel!
  Rejoice with all your heart,
    Jerusalem!
¹⁵ The LORD has ended your punishment;
  he has removed all your enemies.

The LORD, the king of Israel, is with
    you;
  there is no reason now to be afraid.
¹⁶ The time is coming when they will
    say to Jerusalem,
  "Do not be afraid, city of Zion!
  Do not let your hands hang limp!
¹⁷ The LORD your God is with you;
  his power gives you victory.
The LORD will take delight in you,
  and in his love he will give you new
    life.ʰ
He will sing and be joyful over you,
¹⁸ as joyful as people at a festival."
The LORD says,
  "I have ended the threat of doom
    and taken away your disgrace.ⁱ
¹⁹ The time is coming!
I will punish your oppressors;
  I will rescue all the lame
  and bring the exiles home.
I will turn their shame to honour,
  and all the world will praise them.
²⁰ The time is coming!
I will bring your scattered people home;
  I will make you famous throughout
    the world
  and make you prosperous once
    again."
The LORD has spoken.

ᵍ SACRED HILL: *Mount Zion (see Zion in Word List).*
ʰ *Some ancient translations* give you new life; *Hebrew* be silent.
ⁱ *Verse 18 in Hebrew is unclear.*
3.13: Rev 14.5

THE BOOK OF
HAGGAI

INTRODUCTION

The book of *Haggai* is a collection of brief messages that came from the Lord through the prophet Haggai in 520 B.C. The people had returned from exile and had lived in Jerusalem for some years, but the Temple still lay in ruins. The messages urge the leaders of the people to rebuild the Temple, and the Lord promises prosperity and peace in the future for a renewed and purified people.

Outline of Contents

The command to rebuild the Temple   1.1-15
Messages of comfort and hope   2.1-23

The LORD's Command to Rebuild the Temple

1 During the second year that Darius was emperor of Persia, on the first day of the sixth month, the LORD spoke through the prophet Haggai. The message was for the governor of Judah, Zerubbabel son of Shealtiel, and for the High Priest, Joshua son of Jehozadak.

2 The LORD Almighty said to Haggai, "These people say that this is not the right time to rebuild the Temple." 3 The LORD then gave this message to the people through the prophet Haggai: 4 "My people, why should you be living in well-built houses while my Temple lies in ruins? 5 Don't you see what is happening to you? 6 You have sown much corn, but have harvested very little. You have food to eat, but not enough to make you full. You have wine to drink, but not enough to get drunk on! You have clothing, but not enough to keep you warm. And the working man cannot earn enough to live on. 7 Can't you see why this has happened? 8 Now go up into the hills, get timber, and rebuild the Temple; then I will be pleased and will be worshipped as I should be.

9 "You hoped for large harvests, but they turned out to be small. And when you brought the harvest home, I blew it away.*a* Why did I do that? Because my Temple lies in ruins while every one of you is busy working on his own house. 10 That is why there is no rain and nothing can grow. 11 I have brought drought on the land—on its hills, cornfields, vineyards, and olive orchards—on every crop the ground produces, on men and animals, on everything you try to grow."

The People Obey the LORD's Command

12 Then Zerubbabel and Joshua and all the people who had returned from the exile*b* in Babylonia, did what the LORD their God told them to do. They were afraid and obeyed the prophet Haggai, the LORD's messenger. 13 Then Haggai gave the LORD's message to the people: "I will be with you—that is my promise." 14 The

---

a I blew it away; *or* I spoilt it.
b who had returned from the exile; *or* who had not gone into exile.
1.1: Ezra 4.24—5.2, 6.14

Why should you be living in well-built houses while my Temple lies in ruins? (1.4)

LORD inspired everyone to work on the Temple: Zerubbabel, the governor of Judah; Joshua, the High Priest, and all the people who had returned from the exile. *b* They began working on the Temple of the LORD Almighty, their God, 15 on the twenty-fourth day of the sixth month of the second year that Darius was emperor.

The Splendour of the New Temple

2 On the twenty-first day of the seventh month of that same year, the LORD spoke again through the prophet Haggai. 2 He told Haggai to speak to Zerubbabel, the governor of Judah, to Joshua, the High Priest, and to the people, and to say to them, 3 "Is there anyone among you who can still remember how splendid the Temple used to be? How does it look to you now? It must seem like nothing at all. 4 But now don't be discouraged, any of you. Do the work, for I am with you. 5 When you came out of Egypt, I promised that I would always be with you. I am still with you, so do not be afraid.

6 "Before long I will shake heaven and earth, land and sea. 7 I will overthrow all the nations here, and their treasures will be brought here, and the Temple will be filled with wealth. 8 All the silver and gold of the world is mine. 9 The new Temple will be more splendid than the old one, and there I will give my people prosperity and peace." The LORD Almighty has spoken.

The Prophet Consults the Priests

10 On the twenty-fourth day of the ninth month of the second year that Darius was emperor, the LORD Almighty spoke again to the prophet Haggai. 11 He said, "Ask the priests for a ruling on this question: 12 Suppose someone takes a piece of consecrated meat from a sacrifice and carries it in a fold of his robe. If he then lets his robe touch any bread, cooked food, wine, olive-oil, or any kind of food at all, will it make that food consecrated also?"

When the question was asked, the priests answered, "No."

13 Then Haggai asked, "Suppose a man is defiled because he has touched a dead body. If he then touches any of these foods, will that make them defiled too?"

The priests answered, "Yes."

14 Then Haggai said, "The LORD says that the same thing applies to the people of this nation and to everything they produce; and so everything they offer on the altar is defiled."

2.3: Ezra 3.12   **2.5:** Ex 29.45–46   **2.6:** Heb 12.26   **2.13:** Num 19.11–22

The LORD Promises His Blessing

15 The LORD says, "Can't you see what has happened to you? Before you started to rebuild the Temple, 16 you would go to a heap of corn expecting to find two hundred kilogrammes, but there would be only a hundred. You would go to draw a hundred litres of wine from a vat, but find only forty. 17 I sent scorching winds and hail to ruin everything you tried to grow, but still you did not repent. 18 Today is the twenty-fourth day of the ninth month, the day that the foundation of the Temple has been completed. See what is going to happen from now on. 19 Although there is no corn left, and the grapevines, fig-trees, pomegranates, and olive-trees have not yet produced, yet from now on I will bless you."

The LORD's Promise to Zerubbabel

20 On that same day, the twenty-fourth of the month, the LORD gave Haggai a second message 21 for Zerubbabel, the governor of Judah: "I am about to shake heaven and earth 22 and overthrow kingdoms and end their power. I will overturn chariots and their drivers; the horses will die, and their riders will kill one another. 23 On that day I will take you, Zerubbabel my servant, and I will appoint you to rule in my name. You are the one I have chosen." The LORD Almighty has spoken.

THE BOOK OF

ZECHARIAH

INTRODUCTION

The book of *Zechariah* has two distinct parts: (1) *Chapters 1–8* Prophecies from the prophet Zechariah, dated at various times in the years from 520 to 518 B.C. These are largely in the form of visions, and deal with the restoration of Jerusalem, the rebuilding of the Temple, the purification of God's people, and the messianic age to come. (2) *Chapters 9–14* A collection of messages about the expected Messiah and the final judgement.

Outline of Contents

Messages of warning and hope   1.1—8.23
Judgement on Israel's neighbours   9.1–8
Future prosperity and peace   9.9—14.21

The LORD Calls His People to Return to Him

1 In the eighth month of the second year that Darius was emperor of Persia, the LORD gave this message to the prophet Zechariah, the son of Berechiah and grandson of Iddo. 2 The LORD Almighty told Zechariah to say to the people, "I, the LORD, was very angry with your ancestors, 3 but now I say to you, 'Return to me, and I will return to you. 4 Do not be like your ancestors. Long ago the prophets gave them my message, telling them not to live evil, sinful lives any longer. But they would not listen to me or obey me. 5 Your ancestors and those prophets are no longer alive. 6 Through my servants the prophets I gave your ancestors commands and warnings, but

1.1: Ezra 4.24—5.1, 6.14

they disregarded them and suffered the consequences. Then they repented and acknowledged that I, the LORD Almighty, had punished them as they deserved and as I had determined to do."

The Prophet's Vision of the Horses

7 In the second year that Darius was emperor, on the twenty-fourth day of the eleventh month (the month of Shebat), the LORD gave me a message in a vision at night. 8 I saw an angel of the LORD riding a red horse. He had stopped among some myrtle-trees in a valley, and behind him were other horses—red, dappled, and white. 9 I asked him, "Sir, what do these horses mean?"

He answered, "I will show you what they mean. 10 The LORD sent them to go and inspect the earth."

11 They reported to the angel: "We have been all over the world and have found that the whole world lies helpless and subdued."

12 Then the angel said, "Almighty LORD, you have been angry with Jerusalem and the cities of Judah for seventy years now. How much longer will it be before you show them mercy?"

13 The LORD answered the angel with comforting words, 14 and the angel told me to proclaim what the LORD Almighty had said: "I have a deep love and concern for Jerusalem, my holy city, 15 and I am very angry with the nations that enjoy quiet and peace. For while I was holding back my anger against my people, those nations made the sufferings of my people worse. 16 So I have come back to Jerusalem to show mercy to the city. My Temple will be restored, and the city will be rebuilt."

17 The angel also told me to proclaim: "The LORD Almighty says that his cities will be prosperous again and that he will once again help Jerusalem and claim the city as his own."

The Vision of the Horns

18 In another vision I saw four ox horns. 19 I asked the angel that had been speaking to me, "What do these horns mean?"

He answered, "They stand for the world powers that have scattered the people of Judah, Israel, and Jerusalem."

20 Then the LORD showed me four workmen with hammers. 21 I asked, "What have these men come to do?"

He answered, "They have come to terrify and overthrow the nations that completely crushed the land of Judah and scattered its people."

The Vision of the Measuring-Line

2 In another vision I saw a man with a measuring-line in his hand. 2 "Where are you going?" I asked.

"To measure Jerusalem," he answered, "to see how long and how wide it is."

3 Then I saw the angel who had been speaking to me step forward, and another angel came to meet him. 4 The first one said to the other, "Run and tell that young man with the measuring-line that there are going to be so many people and so much livestock in Jerusalem that it will be too big to have walls. 5 The LORD has promised that he himself will be a wall of fire round the city to protect it and that he will live there in all his glory."

The Exiles Are Called to Come Home

6-7 The LORD said to his people, "I scattered you in all directions. But now, you exiles, escape from Babylonia and return to Jerusalem. 8 Anyone who strikes you strikes what is most precious to me."

So the LORD Almighty[a] sent me with this message for the nations that had plundered his people: 9 "The LORD himself will fight against you, and you will be plundered by the people who were once your servants."

When this happens, everyone will know that the LORD Almighty sent me.

10 The LORD said, "Sing for joy, people of Jerusalem! I am coming to live among you!"

11 At that time many nations will come to the LORD and become his people. He will live among you, and you will know that he has sent me to you. 12 Once again Judah will be the special possession of the LORD in his sacred land, and Jerusalem will be the city he loves most of all.

13 Be silent, everyone, in the presence of the LORD, for he is coming from his holy dwelling-place.

The Prophet's Vision of the High Priest

3 In another vision the LORD showed me the High Priest Joshua standing

---

[a] Hebrew has two additional words, the meaning of which is unclear.
1.8: Rev 6.2–8   **3.1:** Ezra 5.2; Rev 12.10

before the angel of the LORD. And there beside Joshua stood Satan,[b] ready to bring an accusation against him. 2 The angel of the LORD[c] said to Satan, "May the LORD condemn you, Satan! May the LORD, who loves Jerusalem, condemn you. This man is like a stick snatched from the fire."

3 Joshua was standing there, wearing filthy clothes. 4 The angel said to his heavenly attendants, "Take away the filthy clothes this man is wearing." Then he said to Joshua, "I have taken away your sin and will give you new clothes to wear."

5 He commanded the attendants to put[d] a clean turban on Joshua's head. They did so, and then they put the new clothes on him while the angel of the LORD stood there.

6 Then the angel told Joshua that 7 the LORD Almighty had said: "If you obey my laws and perform the duties I have assigned to you, then you will continue to be in charge of my Temple and its courts, and I will hear your prayers, just as I hear the prayers of the angels who are in my presence. 8 Listen then, Joshua, you who are the High Priest; and listen, you fellow-priests of his, you that are the sign of a good future: I will reveal my servant, who is called The Branch! 9 I am placing in front of Joshua a single stone with seven facets. I will engrave an inscription on it, and in a single day I will take away the sin of this land. 10 When that day comes, each of you will invite his neighbour to come and enjoy peace and security, surrounded by your vineyards and fig-trees."

The Vision of the Lamp-stand

4 The angel who had been speaking to me came again and roused me as if I had been sleeping. 2 "What do you see?" he asked.

"A lamp-stand made of gold," I answered. "At the top is a bowl for the oil. On the lamp-stand are seven lamps, each one with places for seven wicks. 3 There are two olive-trees beside the lamp-stand, one on each side of it." 4 Then I asked the angel, "What do these things stand for, sir?"

5 "Don't you know?" he asked me.

In front of Joshua (3.9)

"No, I don't, sir," I replied.[e]

10b The angel said to me, "The seven lamps are the seven eyes of the LORD, which see all over the earth."

11 Then I asked him, "What do the two olive-trees on either side of the lamp-stand mean? 12 And what is the meaning of the two olive branches beside the two gold pipes from which the olive-oil pours?"

13 He asked me, "Don't you know?"

"No, I don't, sir," I answered.

14 Then he said, "These are the two men whom God has chosen and anointed to serve him, the Lord of the whole earth."

God's Promise to Zerubbabel

6 The angel told me to give Zerubbabel this message from the LORD: "You will succeed, not by military might or by your own strength, but by my spirit. 7 Obstacles as great as mountains will disappear before you. You will rebuild the Temple, and as you put the last stone in place, the

---

[b] SATAN: *A supernatural being whose name indicates he was regarded as man's opponent.*
[c] *One ancient translation* The angel of the LORD; *Hebrew* The LORD.
[d] *Some ancient translations* He commanded the attendants to put; *Hebrew* I said, "Let them put."
[e] *Verses 10b–14 are moved here from the end of the chapter in order to retain the natural order of the narrative.*
3.2: Jude 9   **3.8:** Jer 23.5, 33.15; Zech 6.12   **3.10:** Mic 4.4   **4.3:** Rev 11.4   **4.6:** Ezra 5.2
4.10: Rev 5.6   **4.11:** Rev 11.4

people will shout, 'Beautiful, beautiful!'"

8 Another message came to me from the LORD. ⁹He said, "Zerubbabel has laid the foundation of the Temple, and he will finish the building. When this happens, my people will know that it is I who sent you to them. ¹⁰They are disappointed because so little progress is being made. But they will see Zerubbabel continuing to build the Temple, and they will be glad."

The Vision of the Flying Scroll

5 I looked again, and this time I saw a scroll flying through the air. ²The angel asked me what I saw. I answered, "A scroll flying through the air; it is nine metres long and four and a half metres wide."

3 Then he said to me, "On it is written the curse that is to go out over the whole land. On one side of the scroll it says that every thief will be removed from the land; and on the other side it says that everyone who tells lies under oath will also be taken away. ⁴The LORD Almighty says that he will send this curse out, and it will enter the house of every thief and the house of everyone who tells lies under oath. It will remain in their houses and leave them in ruins."

The Vision of the Woman in the Basket

5 The angel appeared again and said, "Look! Something else is coming!"

6 "What is it?" I asked.

He replied, "It is a basket, and it stands for the sin ᶠ of the whole land."

7 The basket had a lid made of lead. As I watched, the lid was raised, and there in the basket sat a woman!

8 The angel said, "This woman represents wickedness." Then he pushed her down into the basket and put the lid back down. ⁹I looked up and saw two women flying towards me with powerful wings like those of a stork. They picked up the basket and flew off with it.

10 I asked the angel, "Where are they taking it?"

11 He answered, "To Babylonia, where they will build a temple for it. When the temple is finished, the basket will be placed there to be worshipped."

The Vision of the Four Chariots

6 I had another vision. This time I saw four chariots coming out from between two bronze mountains. ²The first

There in the basket sat a woman! (5.7)

chariot was pulled by red horses, the second by black horses, ³the third by white horses, and the fourth by dappled horses. ⁴Then I asked the angel, "Sir, what do these chariots mean?"

5 He answered, "These are the four winds; they have just come from the presence of the Lord of all the earth."

6 The chariot pulled by the black horses was going north to Babylonia, the white horses were going to the west, and the dappled horses were going to the country in the south. ⁷As the dappled horses came out, they were impatient to go and inspect the earth. The angel said, "Go and inspect the earth!"—and they did. ⁸Then the angel cried out to me, "The horses that went north to Babylonia have calmed down the LORD's anger."

The Command to Crown Joshua

9 The LORD gave me this message. ¹⁰He said, "Take the gifts given by the exiles Heldai, Tobijah, and Jedaiah, and go at once to the home of Josiah son of Zephaniah. All these men have returned from exile in Babylonia. ¹¹Make a crown out of the silver and gold they have given, and put it on the head of the High Priest,

---

ᶠ *Some ancient translations* sin; *Hebrew* eye.
6.2: Rev 6.4,5   **6.3:** Rev 6.2   **6.5:** Rev 7.1

Joshua son of Jehozadak. 12 Tell him that the LORD Almighty says, 'The man who is called The Branch will flourish where he is and rebuild the LORD's Temple. 13 He is the one who will build it and receive the honour due to a king, and he will rule his people. A priest will stand by his throne, and they will work together in peace and harmony.' 14 The crown will be a memorial in the LORD's Temple in honour of Heldai, g Tobijah, Jedaiah, and Josiah." h

15 Men who live far away will come and help to rebuild the Temple of the LORD. And when it is rebuilt, you will know that the LORD Almighty sent me to you. This will all happen if you fully obey the commands of the LORD your God.

The LORD Condemns Insincere Fasting

7 In the fourth year that Darius was emperor, on the fourth day of the ninth month (the month of Kislev), the LORD gave me a message.
2 The people of Bethel had sent Sharezer and Regemmelech and their men to the Temple of the LORD Almighty to pray for the LORD's blessing 3 and to ask the priests and the prophets this question: "Should we continue to mourn because of the destruction of the Temple, by fasting in the fifth month as we have done for so many years now?"
4 This is the message of the LORD that came to me. 5 He said, "Tell the people of the land and the priests that when they fasted and mourned in the fifth and seventh months during these seventy years, it was not in honour of me. 6 And when they ate and drank, it was for their own satisfaction."
7 This is what the LORD said through the earlier prophets at the time when Jerusalem was prosperous and filled with people and when there were many people living not only in the towns round the city but also in the southern region and in the western foothills.

Disobedience, the Cause of Exile

8 The LORD gave this message to Zechariah: 9 "Long ago I gave these commands to my people: 'You must see that justice is done, and must show kindness and mercy to one another. 10 Do not oppress widows, orphans, foreigners who live among you, or anyone else in need. And do not plan ways of harming one another.'
11 "But my people stubbornly refused to listen. They closed their minds 12 and made their hearts as hard as rock. Because they would not listen to the teaching which I sent through the prophets who lived long ago, I became very angry. 13 Because they did not listen when I spoke, I did not answer when they prayed. 14 Like a storm I swept them away to live in foreign countries. This good land was left a desolate place, with no one living in it."

The LORD Promises to Restore Jerusalem

8 The LORD Almighty gave this message to Zechariah: 2 "I have longed to help Jerusalem because of my deep love for her people, a love which has made me angry with her enemies. 3 I will return to Jerusalem, my holy city, and live there. It will be known as the faithful city, and the hill of the LORD Almighty i will be called the sacred hill. 4 Once again old men and women, so old that they use a stick when they walk, will be sitting in the city squares. 5 And the streets will again be full of boys and girls playing.
6 "This may seem impossible to those of the nation who are now left, but it's not impossible for me. 7 I will rescue my people from the lands where they have been taken, 8 and will bring them back from east and west to live in Jerusalem. They will be my people, and I will be their God, ruling over them faithfully and justly.
9 "Have courage! You are now hearing the same words the prophets spoke at the time the foundation was being laid for rebuilding my Temple. 10 Before that time no one could afford to hire either men or animals, and no one was safe from his enemies. I turned people against one another. 11 But now I am treating the survivors of this nation differently. 12 They will sow their crops in peace. Their vines will bear grapes, the earth will produce crops, and there will be plenty of rain. I will give all these blessings to the people of my nation who survive. 13 People of Judah and Israel! In the past foreigners have cursed one another by saying, 'May the same disasters fall on you that fell on Judah and Israel!' But I will save you,

g One ancient translation Heldai; Hebrew Helem.
h One ancient translation Josiah; Hebrew Hen.
i HILL OF THE LORD ALMIGHTY: Mount Zion (see Zion in Word List).
6.12: Jer 23.5, 33.15; Zech 3.8

May you receive the same blessings that came to Judah and Israel (8.13)

and then those foreigners will say to one another, 'May you receive the same blessings that came to Judah and Israel!' So have courage and don't be afraid."

14 The LORD Almighty says, "When your ancestors made me angry, I planned disaster for them and did not change my mind, but carried out my plans. 15 But now I am planning to bless the people of Jerusalem and Judah. So don't be afraid. 16 These are the things you should do: Speak the truth to one another. In the courts, give real justice—the kind that brings peace. 17 Do not plan ways of harming one another. Do not give false testimony under oath. I hate lying, injustice, and violence."

18 The LORD Almighty gave this message to Zechariah: 19 "The fasts held in the fourth, fifth, seventh, and tenth months will become festivals of joy and gladness for the people of Judah. You must love truth and peace."

20 The LORD Almighty says, "The time is coming when people from many *x* cities will come to Jerusalem. 21 Those from one city will say to those from another, 'We are going to worship the LORD Almighty and pray for his blessing. Come with us!'

22 Many *x* peoples and powerful nations will come to Jerusalem to worship the LORD Almighty, and to pray for his blessing. 23 In those days ten foreigners will come to one Jew and say, 'We want to share in your destiny, because we have heard that God is with you.'"

Judgement on Neighbouring Nations

9 This is the LORD's message:
He has decreed punishment for the land of Hadrach and for the city of Damascus. Not only the tribes of Israel, but also the capital of Syria belong to the LORD. 2 Hamath, which borders on Hadrach, also belongs to him, and so do the cities of Tyre and Sidon, with all their skill. 3 Tyre has built fortifications for herself and has piled up so much silver and gold that it is as common as dirt! 4 But the Lord will take away everything she has. He will throw her wealth into the sea, and the city will be burnt to the ground.

5 The city of Ashkelon will see this and be afraid. The city of Gaza will see it and suffer great pain. So will Ekron, and her hopes will be shattered. Gaza will lose her king, and Ashkelon will be left

*x*many; *or* great.
8.16: Eph 4.25   **9.1:** Is 17.1-3; Jer 49.23-27; Amos 1.3-5
9.1-4: Is 23.1-18; Ezek 26.1—28.26; Joel 3.4-8; Amos 1.9-10; Mt 11.21-22; Lk 10.13-14
9.5-7: Is 14.29-31; Jer 47.1-7; Ezek 25.15-17; Joel 3.4-8; Amos 1.6-8; Zeph 2.4-7

deserted. ⁶People of mixed race will live in Ashdod. The LORD says, "I will humble all these proud Philistines. ⁷They will no longer eat meat with blood in it, or other forbidden food. All the survivors will become part of my people and be like a clan in the tribe of Judah. Ekron will become part of my people, as the Jebusites*ʲ* did. ⁸I will guard my land and keep armies from passing through it. I will not allow tyrants to oppress my people any more. I have seen how my people have suffered."

The Future King

⁹ Rejoice, rejoice, people of Zion!

Look, your king is coming to you! (9.9)

Shout for joy, you people of
    Jerusalem!
Look, your king is coming to you!
He comes triumphant and victorious,
    but humble and riding on a donkey—
    on a colt, the foal of a donkey.
10 The LORD says,
"I will remove the war-chariots from
    Israel
and take the horses from Jerusalem;
    the bows used in battle will be
      destroyed.
Your king will make peace among the
    nations;
he will rule from sea to sea,
    from the River Euphrates to the ends
      of the earth."

The Restoration of God's People

11 The LORD says,
"Because of my covenant with you
    that was sealed by the blood of
      sacrifices,
I will set your people free—
    free from the waterless pit of exile.
¹² Return, you exiles who now have hope;
    return to your place of safety.
I tell you now, I will repay you twice
    over
    with blessing for all you have suffered.
¹³ I will use Judah like a soldier's bow
    and Israel like the arrows.
I will use the men of Zion like a sword,
    to fight the men of Greece."

¹⁴ The LORD will appear above his people;
    he will shoot his arrows like lightning.
The Sovereign LORD will sound the
      trumpet;
    he will march in the storms from the
      south.
¹⁵ The LORD Almighty will protect his
    people,
    and they will destroy their enemies.
They will shout in battle like drunken
      men
    and will shed the blood of their
      enemies;
    it will flow like the blood of a sacrifice
      poured on the altar from a bowl.ᵏ

¹⁶ When that day comes, the LORD will
    save his people,
    as a shepherd saves his flock from
      danger.
They will shine in his land
    like the jewels of a crown.
¹⁷ How good and beautiful the land will
    be!
    The young people will grow strong
      on its corn and wine.

The LORD Promises Deliverance

10 Ask the LORD for rain in the spring of the year. It is the LORD who sends rain clouds and showers, making the fields green for everyone. ²People consult idols and fortune-tellers, but the answers they get are lies and nonsense. Some interpret dreams, but only mislead you; the comfort they give is useless. So the people wander about like lost sheep.

ʲ JEBUSITES: *The original inhabitants of Jerusalem, who became David's subjects after he captured the city.*   ᵏ *Verse 15 in Hebrew is unclear.*
9.9: Mt 21.5; Jn 12.15   **9.10:** Ps 72.8   **9.11:** Ex 24.8

They are in trouble because they have no leader.

3 The LORD says, "I am angry with those foreigners who rule my people, and I am going to punish them. The people of Judah are mine, and I, the LORD Almighty, will take care of them. They will be my powerful war-horses. [4] From among them will come rulers, leaders, and commanders to govern my people.[l] [5] The people of Judah will be victorious like soldiers who trample their enemies into the mud of the streets. They will fight because the LORD is with them, and they will defeat even the enemy horsemen.

[6] "I will make the people of Judah strong;
  I will rescue the people of Israel.
I will have compassion on them
  and bring them all back home.
They will be as though I had never
    rejected them.
  I am the LORD their God; I will answer
    their prayers.
[7] The people of Israel will be strong like
    soldiers,
  happy like men who have been
    drinking wine.
Their descendants will remember this
    victory
  and be glad because of what the LORD
    has done.

[8] "I will call my people
  and gather them together.
I will rescue them
  and make them as numerous as they
    used to be.
[9] Though I have scattered them among
    the nations,
  yet in far-off places they will
    remember me.
They and their children will survive
  and return home together.
[10] From Egypt and Assyria I will bring
    them home
  and settle them in their own country.
I will settle them in Gilead and Lebanon
    also;
  the whole land will be filled with
    people.
[11] When they pass through their sea of
    trouble,
  I, the LORD, will strike the waves,

and the depths of the Nile will go
    dry.
Proud Assyria will be humbled,
  and mighty Egypt will lose her power.
[12] I will make my people strong;
  they will worship and obey me."
The LORD has spoken.

The Fall of the Tyrants

11 Open your doors, Lebanon,
  so that fire can burn down your
    cedar-trees![m]
[2] Weep and wail, cypress-trees—
  the cedars have fallen;
  those glorious trees have been
    destroyed!
Weep and wail, oaks of Bashan—
  the dense forest has been cut down!
[3] The rulers cry out in grief;
  their glory is gone!
Listen to the roaring of the lions;
  their forest home along the Jordan is
    destroyed!

The Two Shepherds

4 The LORD my God said to me, "Act the part of the shepherd[n] of a flock of sheep that are going to be butchered. [5] Their owners kill them and go unpunished. They sell the meat and say, 'Praise the LORD! We are rich!' Even their own shepherds have no pity on them."

6 (The LORD said, "I will no longer pity anyone on earth. I myself will put all the people in the power of their rulers. Those rulers will devastate the earth, and I will not save it from their power.")

7 Those who bought and sold the sheep hired me, and I became the shepherd of the sheep that were going to be butchered. I took two sticks: one I called "Favour," and the other "Unity." And I took care of the flock. [8] I lost patience with three other shepherds, who hated me, and I got rid of them all in a single month. [9] Then I said to the flock, "I will not be your shepherd any longer. Let those who are to die, die. Let those who are to be destroyed, be destroyed. Those who are left will destroy one another." [10] Then I took the stick called "Favour" and broke it, to cancel the covenant which the LORD had made with all the nations. [11] So the covenant was cancelled on that day

[l] From among...people; or All oppressors—rulers, leaders, and commanders—will depart together from Judah.
[m] CEDAR-TREES: *Trees are used here as symbols of powerful nations or their kings.*
[n] SHEPHERD: *Shepherd is used here as a symbol of a king or leader, and sheep as symbols of his people or followers.*

He has abandoned his flock (11.17)

Those who bought and sold the sheep were watching me, and they knew that the LORD was speaking through what I did. ¹²I said to them, "If you are willing, give me my wages. But if not, keep them." So they paid me thirty pieces of silver as my wages.

13 The LORD said to me, "Put them in the temple treasury."ᵒ So I took the thirty pieces of silver—the magnificent sum they thought I was worth—and put them in the temple treasury. ¹⁴Then I broke the second stick, the one called "Unity," and the unity of Judah and Israel was shattered.

15 Then the LORD said to me, "Once again act the part of a shepherd, this time a worthless one. ¹⁶I have put a shepherd in charge of my flock, but he does not help the sheep that are threatened by destruction; nor does he look for the lost, or heal those that are hurt, or feed the healthy. Instead, he eats the meat of the fattest sheep and tears off their hoofs. ¹⁷That worthless shepherd is doomed! He has abandoned his flock. War will totally destroy his power. His arm will wither, and his right eye will go blind."

The Future Deliverance of Jerusalem

12 This is a message about Israel from the LORD, the LORD who spread out the skies, created the earth, and gave life to man. He says, ²"I will make Jerusalem like a cup of wine; the nations round her

will drink and stagger like drunken men. And when they besiege Jerusalem, the cities of the rest of Judah will also be besieged. ³But when that time comes, I will make Jerusalem like a heavy stone—any nation that tries to lift it will be hurt. All the nations of the world will join forces to attack her. ⁴At that time I will terrify all their horses and make all their riders go mad. I will watch over the people of Judah, but I will make the horses of their enemies blind. ⁵Then the clans of Judah will say to themselves, 'The LORD God Almighty gives strength to his people who live in Jerusalem.'

6 "At that time I will make the clans of Judah like a fire in a forest or in a field of ripe corn—they will destroy all the surrounding nations. The people of Jerusalem will remain safe in the city.

7 "I, the LORD, will give victory to the armies of Judah first, so that the honour which the descendants of David and the people of Jerusalem will receive will be no greater than that of the rest of Judah. ⁸At that time the LORD will protect those who live in Jerusalem, and even the weakest among them will become as strong as David was. The descendants of David will lead them like the angel of the LORD, like God himself. ⁹At that time I will destroy every nation that tries to attack Jerusalem.

10 "I will fill the descendants of David and the other people of Jerusalem with

ᵒ*Some ancient translations* Put them in the temple treasury; *Hebrew* Give them to the potter.
11.12: Mt 26.15   **11.12-13:** Mt 27.9-10   **12.10:** Jn 19.37; Rev 1.7
12.10-14: Mt 24.30; Rev 1.7

the spirit of mercy and the spirit of prayer. They will look at the one whom they stabbed to death, and they will mourn for him like those who mourn for an only child. They will mourn bitterly, like those who have lost their first-born son. ¹¹ At that time the mourning in Jerusalem will be as great as the mourning for Hadad-rimmon ᵖ in the plain of Megiddo. ¹²⁻¹⁴ Each family in the land will mourn by itself: the family descended from David, the family descended from Nathan, the family descended from Levi, the family descended from Shimei, and all the other families. Each family will mourn by itself, and the men of each family will mourn separately from the women.

13 "When that time comes," says the LORD Almighty, "a fountain will be opened to purify the descendants of David and the people of Jerusalem from their sin and idolatry. ² At that time I will remove the names of the idols from the land, and no one will remember them any more. I will get rid of anyone who claims to be a prophet and will take away the desire to worship idols. ³ Then if anyone still insists on prophesying, his own father and mother will tell him that he must be put to death, because he claimed to speak the LORD's word, but spoke lies instead. When he prophesies, his own father and mother will stab him to death. ⁴ When that time comes, no prophet will be proud of his visions, or act like a prophet, or wear a prophet's coarse garment in order to deceive people. ⁵ Instead, he will say, 'I am not a prophet. I am a farmer—I have farmed the land all my life.' ⁶ Then if someone asks him, 'What are those wounds on your chest?' he will answer, 'I got them at a friend's house.' "

The Command to Kill God's Shepherd

7 The LORD Almighty says, "Wake up, sword, and attack the shepherd �q who works for me! Kill him, and the sheep will be scattered. I will attack my people ⁸ and throughout the land two-thirds of the people will die. ⁹ And I will test the third that survives and will purify them as silver is purified by fire. I will test them as gold is tested. Then they will pray to me, and I will answer them. I will tell them that they are my people,

and they will confess that I am their God."

Jerusalem and the Nations

14 The day when the LORD will sit in judgement is near. Then Jerusalem will be looted, and the loot will be divided up before your eyes. ² The LORD will bring all the nations together to make war on Jerusalem. The city will be taken, the houses looted, and the women raped. Half the people will go into exile, but the rest of them will not be taken away from the city. ³ Then the LORD will go out and fight against those nations, as he has fought in times past. ⁴ At that time he will stand on the Mount of Olives, to the east of Jerusalem. Then the Mount of Olives will be split in two from east to west by a large valley. Half the mountain will move northwards and half of it southwards. ⁵ You will escape through this valley that divides the mountain in two. ʳ You will flee as your ancestors did when the earthquake struck in the time of King Uzziah of Judah. The LORD my God will come, bringing all the angels with him.

6 When that time comes, there will no longer be cold or frost, ˢ ⁷ nor any darkness. There will always be daylight, even at night-time. When this will happen is known only to the LORD.

8 When that day comes, fresh water will flow from Jerusalem, half of it to the Dead Sea and the other half to the Mediterranean. It will flow all the year round, in the dry season as well as the wet. ⁹ Then the LORD will be king over all the earth; everyone will worship him as God and know him by the same name.

10 The whole region, from Geba in the north to Rimmon in the south, will be made level. Jerusalem will tower above the land round it; the city will reach from the Benjamin Gate to the Corner Gate, where there had been an earlier gate, and from the Tower of Hananel to the royal winepresses. ¹¹ The people will live there in safety, no longer threatened by destruction.

12 The LORD will bring a terrible disease on all the nations that make war on Jerusalem. Their flesh will rot away while they are still alive; their eyes and their tongues will rot away.

13 At that time the LORD will make them

ᵖ HADAD-RIMMON: *Probably a name for Baal, the god of vegetation in Canaan and Syria. When the vegetation died each year, the worshippers thought that the god had died too, and they mourned his death.*   �q SHEPHERD: *See 11.4.*

ʳ *Probable text* You will escape...in two; *Hebrew unclear.*

ˢ *Probable text* cold or frost; *Hebrew unclear.*

13.7: Mt 26.31; Mk 14.27   **14.8:** Ezek 47.1; Jn 7.38; Rev 22.1   **14.11:** Rev 22.3

so confused and afraid that everyone will seize the man next to him and attack him. [14]The men of Judah will fight to defend Jerusalem. They will take as loot the wealth of all the nations—gold, silver, and clothing in great abundance.

15 A terrible disease will also fall on the horses, the mules, the camels, and the donkeys—on all the animals in the camps of the enemy.

16 Then all the survivors from the nations that have attacked Jerusalem will go there each year to worship the LORD Almighty as king, and to celebrate the Festival of Shelters. [17]If any nation refuses to go and worship the LORD Almighty as king, then rain will not fall on their land. [18]If the Egyptians refuse to celebrate the Festival of Shelters, then they will be struck by the same disease that the LORD will send on every nation that refuses to go. [19]This will be the punishment that will fall on Egypt and on all the other nations if they do not celebrate the Festival of Shelters.

20 At that time even the harness bells of the horses will be inscribed with the words "Dedicated to the LORD." The cooking-pots in the Temple will be as sacred as the bowls before the altar. [21]Every cooking-pot in Jerusalem and in all Judah will be set apart for use in the worship of the LORD Almighty. The people who offer sacrifices will use them for boiling the meat of the sacrifices. When that time comes, there will no longer be any merchant in the Temple of the LORD Almighty.

14.16: Lev 23.39–43

THE BOOK OF
MALACHI

INTRODUCTION

The book of *Malachi* comes from some time in the fifth century B.C. after the Temple in Jerusalem was rebuilt. The prophet's main concern is to call priests and people to renew their faithfulness to their covenant with God. It is clear that there is laxity and corruption in the life and worship of God's people. Priests and people are cheating God by not giving him the offerings that are rightly due to him, and by not living according to his teaching. But the Lord will come to judge and purify his people, sending ahead of him his messenger to prepare the way and to proclaim his covenant.

Outline of Contents

Israel's sins 1.1—2.16
God's judgement and his mercy 2.17—4.6

1 This is the message that the LORD gave Malachi to tell the people of Israel.

The LORD's Love for Israel

2 The LORD says to his people, "I have always loved you."

But they reply, "How have you shown your love for us?"

The LORD answers, "Esau and Jacob were brothers, but I have loved Jacob and his descendants, ³ and have hated Esau and his descendants. I have devastated Esau's hill-country and abandoned the land to jackals."

4 If Esau's descendants, the Edomites, say, "Our towns have been destroyed, but we will rebuild them," then the LORD will reply, "Let them rebuild—I will tear them down again. People will call them 'The evil country' and 'The nation with whom the LORD is angry for ever.'"

5 The people of Israel are going to see this with their own eyes, and they will say, "The LORD is mighty even outside the land of Israel!"

The LORD Reprimands the Priests

6 The LORD Almighty says to the priests, "A son honours his father, and a servant honours his master. I am your father—why don't you honour me? I am your master—why don't you respect me? You despise me, and yet you ask, 'How have we despised you?' ⁷This is how—by offering worthless food on my altar. Then you ask, 'How have we failed to respect you?' I will tell you—by showing contempt for my altar. ⁸When you bring a blind or sick or lame animal to sacrifice to me, do you think there's nothing wrong with that? Try giving an animal like that to the governor! Would he be pleased with you or grant you any favours?"

9 Now, you priests, try asking God to be good to us. He will not answer your prayer, and it will be your fault. ¹⁰The LORD Almighty says, "I wish one of you would close the temple doors so as to prevent you from lighting useless fires on my altar. I am not pleased with you; I will not accept the offerings you bring me. ¹¹People from one end of the world to the other honour me. Everywhere they burn incense to me and offer acceptable sacrifices. All of them honour me! ¹²But

you dishonour me when you say that my altar is worthless and when you offer on it food that you despise. ¹³You say, 'How tired we are of all this!' and you turn up your nose at me. As your offering to me you bring a stolen animal or one that is lame or sick. Do you think I will accept that from you? ¹⁴A curse on the cheat who sacrifices a worthless animal to me, when he has in his flock a good animal that he promised to give me! For I am a great king, and people of all nations fear me."

2 The LORD Almighty says to the priests, "This command is for you: ²You must honour me by what you do. If you will not listen to what I say, then I will bring a curse on you. I will put a curse on the things you receive for your support. In fact, I have already put a curse on them, because you do not take my command seriously. ³I will punish your children and rub your faces in the dung of the animals you sacrifice—and you will be taken out to the dunghill. ⁴Then you will know that I have given you this command, so that my covenant with the priests, the descendants of Levi, will not be broken.

5 "In my covenant I promised them life and well-being, and this is what I gave them, so that they might respect me. In those days they did respect and fear me. ⁶They taught what was right, not what was wrong. They lived in harmony with me; they not only did what was right themselves, but they also helped many others to stop doing evil. ⁷It is the duty of priests to teach the true knowledge of God. People should go to them to learn my will, because they are the messengers of the LORD Almighty.

8 "But now you priests have turned away from the right path. Your teaching has led many to do wrong. You have broken the covenant I made with you. ⁹So I, in turn, will make the people of Israel despise you because you do not obey my will, and when you teach my people, you do not treat everyone alike."

The People's Unfaithfulness to God

10 Don't we all have the same father? Didn't the same God create us all? Then why do we break our promises to one another, and why do we despise the

1.2-3: Rom 9.13
1.2-5: Is 34.5-17, 63.1-6; Jer 49.7-22; Ezek 25.12-14, 35.1-15; Amos 1.11-12; Obad 1-14
1.8: Deut 15.21   **2.4:** Num 3.11-13   **2.5:** Num 25.12

covenant that God made with our ancestors? [11] The people of Judah have broken their promise to God and done a horrible thing in Jerusalem and all over the country. They have defiled the Temple which the LORD loves. Men have married women who worship foreign gods. [12] May the LORD remove from the community of Israel those who do this, and never again let them participate in the offerings our nation brings to the LORD Almighty.[a]

13 This is another thing you do. You drown the LORD's altar with tears, weeping and wailing because he no longer accepts the offerings you bring him. [14] You ask why he no longer accepts them. It is because he knows you have broken your promise to the wife you married when you were young. She was your partner, and you have broken your promise to her, although you promised before God that you would be faithful to her. [15] Didn't God make you one body and spirit with her?[b] What was his purpose in this? It was that you should have children who are truly God's people. So make sure that none of you breaks his promise to his wife. [16] "I hate divorce," says the LORD God of Israel. "I hate it when one of you does such a cruel thing to his wife. Make sure that you do not break your promise to be faithful to your wife."

The Day of Judgement Is Near

17 You have tired the LORD out with your talk. But you ask, "How have we tired him?" By saying, "The LORD Almighty thinks all evildoers are good; in fact he likes them." Or by asking, "Where is the God who is supposed to be just?"

3 The LORD Almighty answers, "I will send my messenger to prepare the way for me. Then the Lord you are looking for will suddenly come to his Temple. The messenger you long to see will come and proclaim my covenant."

2 But who will be able to endure the day when he comes? Who will be able to survive when he appears? He will be like strong soap, like a fire that refines metal. [3] He will come to judge like one who refines and purifies silver. As a metalworker refines silver and gold, so the LORD's messenger will purify the priests, so that they will bring to the LORD the right kind of offerings. [4] Then the offerings

which the people of Judah and Jerusalem bring to the LORD will be pleasing to him, as they used to be in the past.

5 The LORD Almighty says, "I will appear among you to judge, and I will testify at once against those who practise magic, against adulterers, against those who give false testimony, those who cheat employees out of their wages, and those who take advantage of widows, orphans, and foreigners—against all who do not respect me.

The Payment of Tithes

6 "I am the LORD, and I do not change.

I am the Lord, and I do not change (3.6)

And so you, the descendants of Jacob, are not yet completely lost. [7] You, like your ancestors before you, have turned away from my laws and have not kept them. Turn back to me, and I will turn to you. But you ask, 'What must we do to turn back to you?' [8] I ask you, is it right for a person to cheat God? Of course not, yet you are cheating me. 'How?' you ask. In the matter of tithes and offerings. [9] A curse is on all of you because the whole nation is cheating me. [10] Bring the full amount of your tithes to the Temple, so that there will be plenty of food there. Put me to the test and you will see that

[a] *One ancient translation* May...Almighty; *Hebrew unclear.*
[b] *Probable text* Didn't God...her; *Hebrew unclear.*
3.1: Mt 11.10; Mk 1.2; Lk 1.76, 7.27   **3.2:** Joel 2.11; Rev 6.17
3.10: Lev 27.30; Num 18.21-24; Deut 12.6, 14.22-29; Neh 13.12

My saving power will rise on you like the sun (4.2)

I will open the windows of heaven and pour out on you in abundance all kinds of good things. ¹¹I will not let insects destroy your crops, and your grapevines will be loaded with grapes. ¹²Then the people of all nations will call you happy, because your land will be a good place to live in.

God's Promise of Mercy

13 "You have said terrible things about me," says the LORD. "But you ask, 'What have we said about you?' ¹⁴You have said, 'It's useless to serve God. What's the use of doing what he says or of trying to show the LORD Almighty that we are sorry for what we have done? ¹⁵As we see it, proud people are the ones who are happy. Evil men not only prosper, but they test God's patience with their evil deeds and get away with it.'"

16 Then the people who feared the LORD spoke to one another, and the LORD listened and heard what they said. In his presence, there was written down in a book a record of those who feared the LORD and respected him. ¹⁷"They will be my people," says the LORD Almighty. "On the day when I act, they will be my very own. I will be merciful to them, as a father

is merciful to the son who serves him. ¹⁸Once again my people will see the difference between what happens to the righteous and to the wicked, to the person who serves me and the one who does not."

The Day of the LORD Is Coming

4 The LORD Almighty says, "The day is coming when all proud and evil people will burn like straw. On that day they will burn up, and there will be nothing left of them. ²But for you who obey me, my saving power will rise on you like the sun and bring healing like the sun's rays. You will be as free and happy as calves let out of a stall. ³On the day when I act, you will overcome the wicked, and they will be like dust under your feet.

4 "Remember the teachings of my servant Moses, the laws and commands which I gave him at Mount Sinai for all the people of Israel to obey.

5 "But before the great and terrible day of the LORD comes, I will send you the prophet Elijah. ⁶He will bring fathers and children together again; otherwise I would have to come and destroy your country."

4.5: Mt 11.14, 17.10-13; Mk 9.11-13; Lk 1.17; Jn 1.21

DEUTEROCANONICAL BOOKS/ APOCRYPHA

Introduction

The following books: Tobit, Judith, Esther (the Greek text), Wisdom of Solomon, Sirach, Baruch, Letter of Jeremiah, Song of the Three Young Men, Susanna, Bel and the Dragon, 1 Maccabees, and 2 Maccabees, formed part of the Septuagint Greek text and were interspersed among other books of the Old Testament.

This Greek text was not only widely used by Jews but was known as well by numerous "God-fearing" Gentiles who were attracted to the high moral teachings of the Old Testament, even though they had not themselves become converts to Judaism. One can thus readily understand how and why early Christianity, as it spread among Greek-speaking Jews and Gentiles, employed this Greek text. In fact, the majority of Old Testament quotations in the New Testament are based on this translation.

Precisely when Jewish leadership officially adopted the traditional 39 books of the so-called "Hebrew Canon" is not known; nor is there agreement as to exactly what criteria were used in determining the canon. According to tradition the determination of the books of the Hebrew canon was made about A.D. 90, but there is evidence to believe that official and widespread agreement on this issue came somewhat later.

Among Christians it was apparently only in the fourth century that the issue of the canonicity of these books arose, a situation which is reflected in Jerome's denying their canonicity and Augustine's affirming it.

In 1546 at the Council of Trent the Roman Catholic Church officially declared these books to be sacred and canonical and to be accepted "with equal devotion and reverence."

At the time of the Reformation Martin Luther did not regard these books as Scripture but as "useful and good for reading." In his German translation of the Bible he accepted the view of Jerome denying their canonicity and placed them at the end of the Old Testament with the superscription "Apocrypha." Protestants generally continued this practice in their translations of the Bible into such languages as Swedish, Norwegian, Danish, Slovenian, French, Spanish and English.

Among Christians who do not accept these books as Scripture there is, however, widespread agreement as to their importance in providing much valuable information on Jewish history, life, thought, worship, and religious practice during the centuries immediately prior to the time of Christ. Accordingly, they make possible a clearer understanding of the historical and cultural situation in which Jesus lived and taught.

Catholics speak of these books as "deuterocanonical" to indicate that their canonical status as Scripture was settled later than that of the protocanonical books. Others usually refer to these books as Apocrypha.

PALESTINE
IN THE TIME
OF THE MACCABEES

Damascus

Sidon

Tyre

Kedesh

Hazor

Seleucia

Maked

Ptolemais

Baskama

Dathema

GALILEE

Arbela

Chaspho

Karnaim

Bosor

MEDITERRANEAN
SEA

LAKE
GALILEE

Alema

Dor

V. of Jezreel

Ephron

GILEAD

ARBATTA

Beth Shan

Bozrah

Samaria

SAMARIA

River Jordan

Pirathon

△ Mt. Gerizim

Joppa

Modein

Jazer

Bethel

AMMON

JUDAEA

Jericho

Ashdod

Jerusalem

Medeba

Gaza

Hebron

PHILISTIA

Adora

DEAD
SEA

Gerar

(For inset showing places
in Judaea see next map)

0   20   40   60

Kilometres

iv

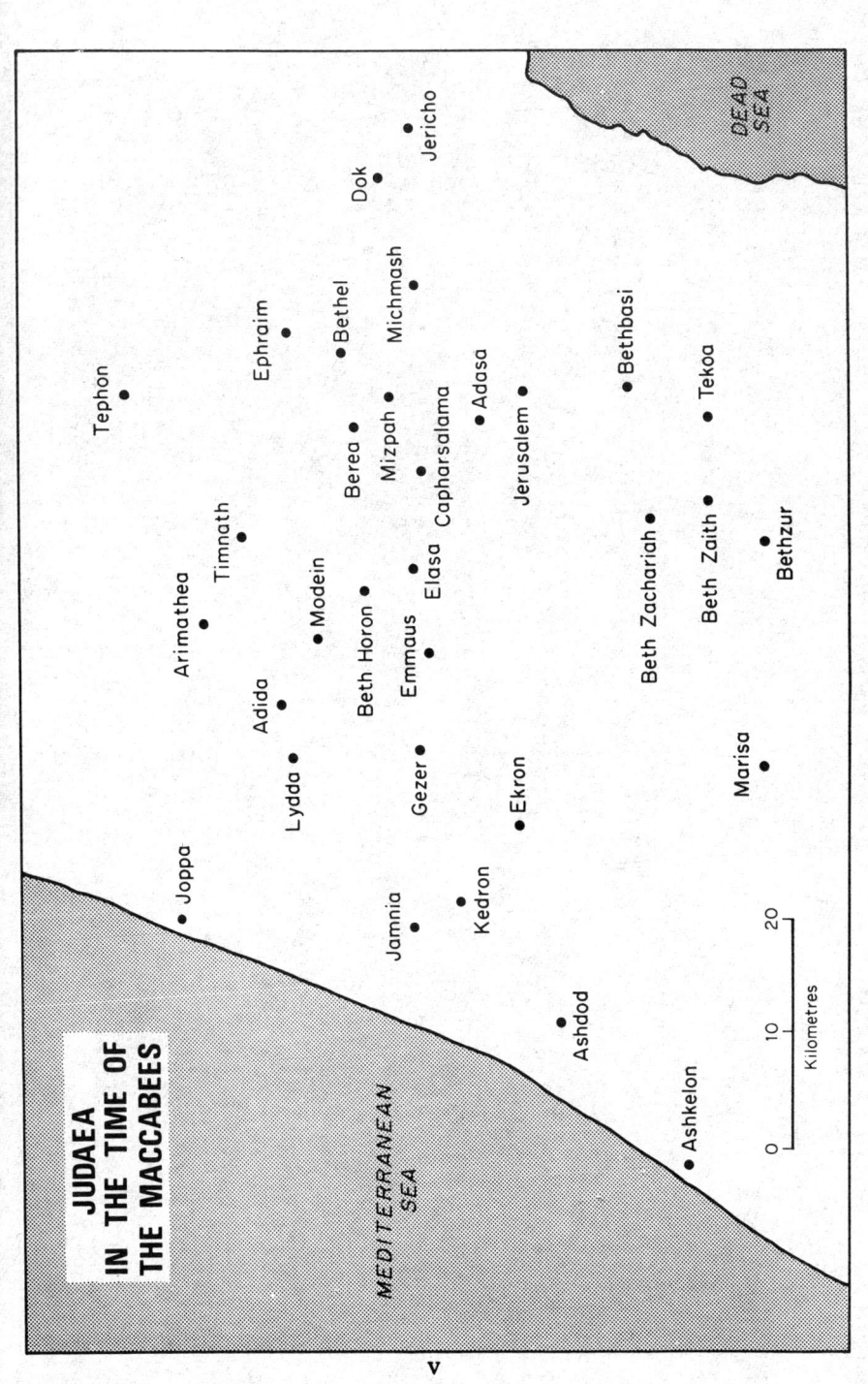

JUDAEA
IN THE TIME OF
THE MACCABEES

MEDITERRANEAN SEA

DEAD SEA

Jericho

Dok

Bethel

Michmash

Ephraim

Adasa

Bethbasi

Tephon

Berea

Mizpah

Capharsalama

Elasa

Tekoa

Jerusalem

Timnath

Beth Zachariah

Beth Zaith

Arimathea

Modein

Bethzur

Adida

Beth Horon

Emmaus

Lydda

Gezer

Ekron

Marisa

Joppa

Kedron

Jamnia

Ashdod

Ashkelon

0   10   20
Kilometres

v

THE BOOK OF
TOBIT

INTRODUCTION

The book of *Tobit,* originally written in Hebrew or Aramaic, is a story which tells of miraculous help to God's faithful people and teaches Jewish piety and morality. The book offers a vivid picture of Jewish religion and culture in the period prior to the New Testament.

Outline of Contents

Tobit in Nineveh and Sarah in Media suffer and pray   1.1—3.15
Their prayers are answered   3.16—11.18
  a. In answer to their prayers God sends the angel Raphael   3.16,17
  b. Tobit gives advice to his son, Tobias   4.1-21
  c. Raphael travels with Tobias to Media   5.1—7.12
  d. Tobias marries Sarah   7.13—9.6
  e. Raphael returns with Tobias and Sarah, and cures Tobit's
    blindness   10.1—11.18
The angel Raphael reveals who he is   12.1—22
Tobit praises God and gives advice to Tobias   13.1—14.15

---

1 I am Tobit and this is the story of my life. My father was Tobiel, my grandfather was Ananiel, and my great-grandfather was Aduel. Aduel's father was Gabael; his grandfather was Raphael; and his great-grandfather was Raguel, who belonged to the clan of Asiel, a part of the tribe of Naphtali. ² During the time that Shalmaneser was emperor of Assyria, I was taken captive in my home town of Thisbe, located in northern Galilee, south of Kadesh in Naphtali, north-west of Hazor, and north of Phogor.

Tobit's Early Life

3 All my life I have been honest and have tried to do what was right. I have often given money to help needy relatives and fellow Jews who were deported with me to Nineveh, the capital of Assyria.

4 When I was young, I lived in northern Israel. All the tribes in Israel were supposed to offer sacrifices in Jerusalem.

It was the one city that God had chosen from among all the Israelite cities as the place where his Temple was to be built for his holy and eternal home. But my entire tribe of Naphtali rejected the city of Jerusalem and the kings descended from David. ⁵ Like everyone else in this tribe, my own family used to go to the city of Dan in the mountains of northern Galilee to offer sacrifices to the gold bull-calf which King Jeroboam of Israel had set up there.

Tobit's Faithfulness to His Religion

6 I was the only one in my family who regularly went to Jerusalem to celebrate the religious festivals, as the Law of Moses commands everyone to do. I would hurry off to Jerusalem with the first part of my harvest, the first-born of my animals, a tenth of my cattle, and the freshly clipped wool from my sheep. Then I would stand before the altar in the

1.2: 2 Kgs 17.3; 18.9   **1.5:** 1 Kgs 12.28–29   **1.6:** Deut 16.16

I would hurry off to Jerusalem with the first part of my harvest (1.6)

Temple, and give these offerings to the priests, the descendants of Aaron. [7] I would give a tenth of my grain, wine, olive-oil, pomegranates, figs, and other fruits to the Levites who served God in Jerusalem. Every year, except the seventh year when the land was at rest,[a] I would sell a second tenth of my possessions and spend the money in Jerusalem on the festival meal.

8 But every third year, I would give a third tithe[b] to widows and orphans and to foreigners living among my people, and we would eat the festival meal together. I did this in keeping with the Law of Moses, which Deborah, the mother of my grandfather Ananiel, had taught me to obey. (I had been left an orphan when my father died.)

Tobit's Faithfulness In Exile

9 When I grew up, I married Anna, a member of my own tribe. We had a son and named him Tobias. [10] Later, I was taken captive and deported to Assyria, and that is how I came to live in Nineveh.

While we lived in Nineveh, all my relatives and fellow Jews used to eat the same kind of food as the other people who lived there, [11] but I refused to do so. [12] Since I took seriously the commands of

the Most High God, [13] he made Emperor Shalmaneser respect me, and I was placed in charge of purchasing all the emperor's supplies.

14 Before the emperor died, I made regular visits to the land of Media to buy things for him there. Once, when I was in the city of Rages in Media, I left some bags of money there with Gabael, Gabrias's brother, and asked him to keep them for me. There were more than 300 kilogrammes of silver coins in those bags. [15] When Shalmaneser died, his son Sennacherib succeeded him as emperor. It soon became so dangerous to travel on the roads in Media that I could no longer go there.

Tobit Buries the Dead

16 While Shalmaneser was still emperor, I took good care of my fellow Jews whenever they were in need. [17] If they were hungry, I shared my food with them; if they needed clothes, I gave them some of my own. Whenever I saw that the dead body of one of my people had been thrown outside the city wall, I gave it a decent burial.

18 One day Sennacherib cursed God, the King of Heaven; God punished him, and Sennacherib had to retreat from Judah. On his way back to Media he was so furious that he killed many Israelites. But I secretly removed the bodies and buried them; and when Sennacherib later searched for the bodies, he could not find them.

19 Then someone from Nineveh told the emperor that I was the one who had been burying his victims. As soon as I realized that the emperor knew all about me and that my life was in danger, I became frightened. So I ran away and hid. [20] Everything I owned was seized and put in the royal treasury. My wife Anna and my son Tobias were all I had left.

Tobit's Nephew Rescues Him

21 About six weeks later, two of Sennacherib's sons assassinated him and then escaped to the mountains of Ararat. Another son, Esarhaddon, became emperor and put Ahikar, my brother Anael's son, in charge of all the financial affairs of the empire. [22] This was actually the second time Ahikar was appointed to this position, for when Sennacherib was emperor of Assyria, Ahikar had been wine

---

[a] THE LAND WAS AT REST: *See Lev 25.1–7.*   [b] a third tithe; *some manuscripts have* the money.
1.17: Job 31.16–20

steward, treasurer, and accountant, and had been in charge of the official seal. Since Ahikar was my nephew, he put in a good word for me with the emperor, and I was allowed to return to Nineveh.

A Family Celebration

2 When I returned home I was reunited with my wife Anna and my son Tobias. At the Harvest Festival, which is also called the Festival of Weeks, I sat down to a delicious meal. ² When I saw how much food there was on the table, I said to Tobias, "My son, go out and find some fellow Jew who is living in poverty here in exile, someone who takes God's commands seriously. Bring him back with you, so that he can share this festival meal with us. I won't start eating until you come back."

A Murder in Nineveh

3 So Tobias went out to look for such a person. But he quickly returned, shouting, "Father! Father!"

"Yes, what is it?" I asked.

"One of our people has just been murdered! Someone strangled him and threw his body into the market-place."

4 I jumped up and left the table without even touching my food. I removed the body from the street and carried it to a little shed, where I left it until sunset, when I could bury it. ⁵ Then I returned home and washed, so as to purify myself. In deep sorrow I ate my dinner. ⁶ I was reminded of what the prophet Amos had said to the people of Bethel,

"Your festivals will be turned into funerals,
    and your glad songs will become cries of grief."

I began to weep.

7 After sunset I went out, dug a grave, and buried the man. ⁸ My neighbours thought I was mad. "Haven't you learnt anything?" they asked. "You have already been in danger once for burying the dead, and you would have been killed if you had not run away. But here you are doing the same thing all over again."

Tobit Is Blinded

9 That night I washed, so as to purify myself, and went out into my courtyard to sleep by the wall. It was a hot night, and I did not pull the cover up over my head. ¹⁰ Sparrows were on the wall right above me, but I did not know it. Their warm droppings fell into my eyes, causing a white film to form on them. I went to one doctor after another, but the more they treated me with their medicines, the worse my eyes became, until finally I was completely blind.

For four years I could see nothing. My relatives were deeply concerned about my condition, and Ahikar supported me for two years before he went to the land of Elam.

A Family Quarrel

11 After Ahikar left, my wife Anna had to go to work, so she took up weaving, like many other women. ¹² The people she worked for would pay her when she delivered the cloth. One spring day, she cut a finished piece of cloth from the loom and took it to the people who had ordered it. They paid her the full price and also gave her a goat.

13 When Anna came home with the goat, it began to bleat. I called out, "Where did that goat come from? You stole it, didn't you? Take it straight back to its owners. It's not right to eat stolen food!"

14 "No!" she replied. "It was given to me as a gift in addition to what I got for the cloth." But I didn't believe her, and I blushed for shame for what she had done. I ordered her to return the goat to its owners, but she had the last word. "Now I see what you are really like!" she shouted. "Where is all that concern of yours for others? What about all those good deeds you used to do?"

Tobit's Prayer

3 I was so embarrassed and ashamed that I sighed and began to cry. Then, as I choked back my tears, I prayed:
² "You are righteous, O Lord!
You are merciful ᶜ in all you do,
    faithful in all your ways.
You are the judge of this world. ᵈ
³⁻⁴ I beg you, treat me with kindness.
Do not punish me for my sins,
    not even for sins of which I am unaware.
My ancestors rebelled and disobeyed ᵉ
    your commands,

ᶜ merciful; *some manuscripts add* and just.
ᵈ You are the judge of this world; *some manuscripts have* You are always fair and just when you judge.   ᵉ My ancestors...disobeyed; *some manuscripts have* I disobeyed.
2.1: Ex 23.16   **2.5:** Num 19.11–13   **2.6:** Amos 8.10

but do not punish me for their sins.
You let our people be plundered,
  taken captive and killed.
You made an example of our people,
  an object of contempt and disgrace
  in all the nations where you scattered
    us.
5 You have often judged my ancestors for
    their sins
  and punished me for mine.
We were disloyal and rejected your
    commands,
  so our punishment has always been
    just.

6 "Now treat me as you please.
Take my life away and free me from
    this world;
  let my body return to the earth.
  I would be better off dead.
I am tormented by insults I don't
    deserve,
  and weighed down with despair.
Lord, give the command—
  bring all my troubles to an end,
  take me to my eternal rest.
Don't reject my prayer.
I would rather die than live in misery
  and face such cruel insults."

Sarah's Troubles

7 That same day in the city of Ecbatana
in Media, it happened that Sarah, the
daughter of a man named Raguel, was
insulted by one of her father's servant
girls. 8 Sarah had been married seven
times, but the evil demon, Asmodeus,
killed each husband before the marriage
could be consummated. The servant girl
said to Sarah, "You husband-killer! Look
at you! You've already had seven
husbands, but not one of them lived long
enough to give you a son.*f* 9 Why should
you take it out on us? Why don't you
go and join your dead husbands? I hope
we never see a child of yours!"

10 Sarah was so depressed that she
burst into tears and went upstairs
determined to hang herself. But when she
thought it over, she said to herself, "No,
I won't do it! People would insult my
father and say, 'You had only one child,
a daughter whom you loved dearly, but
she hanged herself because she felt so
miserable.' Such grief would bring my
grey-haired father to his grave, and I

would be responsible. I won't kill myself;
I'll just beg the Lord to let me die. Then
I won't have to listen to those insults any
longer!"

Sarah's Prayer

11 Then Sarah stood by the window,
raised her arms in prayer, and said,
"God of mercy, worthy of our praise,
  may your name always be honoured,
  may all your creation praise you for
    ever.

Sarah's prayer (3.11)

12 "Lord, I look to you for help.
13 Speak the word and set me free from
    this life;
  then I will no longer have to hear
    these insults.
14 You know, O Lord, that I'm still a
    virgin;
  I have never been defiled by a man.
15 Never have I disgraced myself or my
    father's name,
  as long as we have lived in this land
    of exile.
My father has no other child to be his
    heir,
  and there is no relative*g* whom I can
    marry.
I have already lost seven husbands,
  so why should I live any longer?
But if it is not your will to take my
    life,
  at least show mercy to me.
Don't let me hear those insults again!"*h*

f but...son; *some manuscripts have* but it hasn't done you a bit of good.
g RELATIVE: *In Israel it was customary to marry within one's own tribe.*
h at least...again; *some manuscripts have* at least listen to my complaint.

God Hears the Prayers of Tobit and Sarah

16 As Tobit and Sarah were praying, God in heaven heard their prayers [17] and sent his angel Raphael to help them. He was sent to remove the white film from Tobit's eyes, so that he could see again, and to arrange a marriage between Sarah and Tobit's son Tobias, who, as her cousin, had the right to marry her. Raphael was also ordered to expel the demon Asmodeus from Sarah. At the very moment that Tobit went back into his house from the courtyard, Sarah, in her house in Ecbatana, was coming downstairs.

Tobit's Advice to Tobias

4 That same day, Tobit remembered the money that he had left with Gabael at Rages in Media. [2] He thought to himself, "Now that I have asked God to let me die, I should call my son Tobias and tell him about the money."

3-4 So Tobit called Tobias and said to him, "My son, when I die, give me a proper burial. And after I'm gone, show respect to your mother. Take care of her for the rest of her life, and when she dies, bury her beside me. Remember, she risked her life to bring you into this world, so try to make her happy and never do anything that would worry her.

5 "Every day of your life, keep the Lord our God in mind. Never sin deliberately or disobey any of his commands. Always do what is right and never get involved in anything evil. [6] Be honest, and you will succeed in whatever you do.

7 "Give generously to anyone who faithfully obeys God.[i] If you are stingy in giving to the poor, God will be stingy in giving to you. [8] Give according to what you have. The more you have, the more you should give. Even if you have only a little, be sure to give something. [9] This is as good as money saved. You will have your reward in a time of trouble. [10-11] Taking care of the poor is the kind of offering that pleases God in heaven. Do this, and you will be kept safe from the dark world of the dead.

12 "My son, be on your guard against prostitutes. Above all, marry a woman of our tribe, because we are descendants of the prophets. Do not marry anyone who is not related to us. Remember that Noah, Abraham, Isaac and Jacob, our earliest ancestors, all married relatives. God blessed them with children, and so their descendants will inherit the land of Israel. [13] Be loyal to your own relatives, my son. Don't be too proud to marry one of them. Such pride leads to terrible frustration and ruin, just as laziness brings on severe poverty and causes starvation.

14 "Pay your workers each day; never keep back their wages overnight. Honour God in this way, and he will reward you. Behave properly at all times. [15] Never do to anyone else anything that you would not want someone to do to you.

"Do not drink so much wine that you get drunk, and do not let drinking become a habit.

16 "Give food to the hungry and clothes to people in need. If you are prosperous, give generously, and do it gladly!

17 "When one of God's faithful people has died, prepare food for the family,[j] but never do this when an evil man dies.

18 "Take the advice of sensible people, and never treat any useful advice lightly.

19 "Take advantage of every opportunity to praise the Lord your God. Ask him to make you prosper in whatever you set out to do. He does not give his wisdom to the people of any other nation. He is the source of all good things, but he can also destroy you and bring you to certain death, if he wishes.

"Remember all my instructions. Don't forget them for one minute.

20 "Tobias, I want you to know that I once left a large sum of money with Gabrias's son, Gabael, at Rages in Media. [21] We're poor now, but don't worry. If you obey God and avoid sin, he will be pleased with you and make you prosperous."

Travel Preparations

5 Then Tobias answered his father, "I'll do everything you told me. [2] But how can I get the money back from Gabael? We have never even met each other. How can I prove to him who I am, so that he will trust me and give me the money? Besides that, I don't know how to get to Media."

3 Tobit replied, "Gabael and I both

---

[i] *The translation of verses 7b–19b, accidentally omitted in the Greek manuscript that this translation normally follows, is based on other Greek manuscripts.*
[j] *prepare...family; or put food on his grave.*
3.17: Num 36.6–9; Tob 6.10–12   **4.7:** Deut 15.7–8; Prov 19.17; Sir 3.30—4.6; 1 Jn 3.17
4.15: Mt 7.12; Lk 6.31   **4.17:** Deut 26.14   **4.21:** 1 Tim 6.6–8

signed a document. I then tore it in two, and we each took a half. I put his half with the money. That was twenty years ago! Now, go and find a reliable person to travel with you to Media and back, and we will pay him when you return. But you must get the money that I left with Gabael."

Tobias Meets Raphael

4 Tobias then went out to look for someone who knew the way to Media and would travel with him. Almost as soon as he left the house, he found himself face to face with Raphael. Tobias did not know that Raphael was an angel of God, 5 so he asked him where he was from.

"I am an Israelite," Raphael answered, "one of your distant relatives, and I have come here to Nineveh to find work."

"Do you know the way to Media?" Tobit asked.

6 "Yes, I do," Raphael replied. "I have been there many times, and I know all the roads well. I used to stay with our relative Gabael, who lives there in the town of Rages. k It takes at least two days to travel there from Ecbatana, the capital city, because Rages is up in the mountains."

7 Then Tobias said to Raphael, "Wait here for me, my friend, while I go in and tell my father. I would like you to travel with me, and I will pay you for the journey."

8 "All right," Raphael said, "I'll wait, but don't take too long."

9 Tobias went in and told his father, "I have found a fellow Israelite to travel with me."

"Call the man in," Tobit replied. "I would like to know what family and tribe he belongs to, and whether he is a reliable travelling companion for you."

Tobit Meets Raphael

So Tobias went out and called to Raphael, "My father would like to meet you." When Raphael came in, Tobit greeted him first.

Then Raphael returned the greeting, "I hope all is well with you."

But Tobit replied, "How can all be well with me? I'm blind and can't see a thing. It's like being dead and no longer able to see the light. I might as well be dead! I can hear people talking, but I can't see them."

"Cheer up!" Raphael said to him. "God is going to cure you soon, so don't worry!"

Tobit then said, "My son Tobias wants to go to Media. Can you go with him and show him the way? I will pay you, of course."

Raphael replied, "Certainly I can go with him. I have travelled there many times, and I know all the roads in the mountains and on the plains."

10 Tobit questioned him further, "Tell me, my friend, what family and tribe do you belong to?"

11 But Raphael asked, "Why do you need to know that?"

"Tell me the truth," said Tobit. "What is your name, and who are you?"

12 Raphael replied, "My name is Azarias, and I am the son of the older Ananias, one of your relatives."

13 Then Tobit said to him, "Welcome to our home! God bless you, my son. Please don't be offended because I wanted to know the truth about you and your family. As it turns out, you are from a good family and a relative at that! I knew Ananias and Nathan, the two sons of the older Shemaiah. They were always loyal to their religion. We used to travel together to Jerusalem and worship there. Your relatives are fine people, and you come from good stock. Have a safe journey."

14 Tobit continued, "I will pay the normal daily wage plus expenses for both of you. 15 Be a good companion to Tobias, and I will add a bonus to your wages."

16 "I will go with him," Raphael said. "And don't worry; we will get there and back safely. The roads are not dangerous."

"God be with you!" Tobit replied. Then he called Tobias and said to him, "My son, get everything ready that you need for the journey, so that the two of you can be on your way. May God and his angel watch over you both and bring you back to me safe and sound."

Before leaving for Media, Tobias kissed his father and mother good-bye. Tobit said again, "Have a safe journey!"

17 Then his mother began to cry. "How could you send my son away like this?" she complained. "He's our only means of support. Who will take care of us now? 18 Is that money so important to you that you are willing to risk your own son's life to get it back? 19 Why can't we be

content to live on what the Lord has given us?"

20 "Calm down," Tobit said to her. "He will get there and back safely, and with your own eyes you will see him return home safe and sound. 21 Now stop worrying about them, dear. A good angel will go with Tobias. He will have a successful journey and will come back in good health." At that, Anna calmed down and stopped crying.

Tobias Catches a Fish

6 So Tobias and the angel started out towards Media, taking Tobias's dog along with them. They walked on until sunset, then camped by the River Tigris. 2 Tobias had gone down to wash his feet in the river, when suddenly a huge fish jumped up out of the water and tried to swallow one of his feet. Tobias let out

Grab that fish! (6.3)

a yell, 3 and the angel called to him, "Grab that fish! Don't let it get away."

Then Tobias grabbed the fish and dragged it up on the bank.

4 "Cut the fish open," the angel instructed, "and take out its gall-bladder, heart, and liver. Keep these with you; they can be used for medicine, but throw away the guts."

5 Tobias did as the angel had told him. Then he cooked the fish, ate part of it, and salted the rest to take along with him.

The two continued on together until they were near Media. 6 Then Tobias asked, "Azarias, my friend, what diseases

can be cured by this gall-bladder, heart, and liver?"

7 The angel answered, "The heart and liver can be burnt and used to chase away a demon or an evil spirit that is tormenting someone. The attacks will stop immediately, and the person will never be troubled again. 8 You can use the gall-bladder to treat a man whose eyes are covered with a white film. Just rub it on his eyes and blow on the film, and he will be able to see again."

On the Way to Ecbatana

9 When they had reached Media and were approaching the city of Ecbatana, 10 Raphael said, "Tobias, my friend."

"Yes, what is it?" Tobias asked.

Raphael continued, "Tonight we will stay at the home of your relative Raguel. He has only one child, a daughter named Sarah, 11 and since you are her closest relative, you have the right to marry her. You also have the right to inherit all her father's property. 12 She is sensible, brave, and very beautiful; and her father is a good man. Tonight I'll discuss the marriage proposal with her father, and he will consent to give her to you as your bride. Then, when we return home from the town of Rages, we will celebrate the marriage. Raguel cannot refuse to let you marry her, and he cannot let any other man have her. If he did, then according to the Law of Moses he would deserve the death penalty. He knows that you are the only man who has the right to marry his daughter and receive the inheritance, so follow my advice. Raguel and I will discuss the matter tonight and arrange your engagement to Sarah. When we get back from the city of Rages, we will take her home with us."

13 Tobias then said to Raphael, "Azarias, my friend, I have already heard about Sarah's seven former husbands, and how each one dropped dead on his wedding night, even before he could get to bed. 14 According to the story I heard, a demon killed them. He doesn't harm Sarah, but he kills every man who tries to get near her. I am afraid of this demon. I am an only child, and if I were to die, the sorrow would send my parents to their graves. They haven't even got another son to bury them."

15 The angel replied, "Have you already forgotten your father's instructions? He told you to marry a woman from your own tribe. So, listen carefully to what I

say. Don't worry about the demon. Marry Sarah! I know that tonight Raguel will let Sarah marry you. [16] When you go into the bedroom, take the fish's heart and liver with you and place them on the burning incense, [17] so that the odour will spread throughout the room. When the demon smells it, he will leave and never come near Sarah again. But before you consummate the marriage, both of you must get up and pray for the Lord in heaven to be merciful to you and to protect you. Don't be afraid. Sarah was meant to be yours from the beginning of creation. You will rescue her from the demon, and she will go with you to your home. You and Sarah will have many children, whom you will love very much. So don't worry!"

Tobias listened very carefully to what Raphael had to say. He knew that Sarah was a relative on his father's side of the family. He began to fall in love with her and looked forward to marrying her.

At Raguel's House

7 When Tobias and the angel Raphael had entered the city of Ecbatana, Tobias said, "Azarias, my friend, take me to see Raguel as quickly as you can." The angel brought him to Raguel's house, where they found him sitting at the entrance to his courtyard. Raphael and Tobias greeted him first; then he replied, "Come in, my friends. You are welcome in my home."

Raguel brought them into his house [2] and said to his wife Edna, "Doesn't this young man look just like my cousin Tobit?"

[3] Edna asked them, "Where do you come from?"

"We are Israelites of the tribe of Naphtali," Tobias and Raphael answered, "but we are now living in exile in the city of Nineveh in Assyria."

[4] Edna said, "Do you know our cousin Tobit?"

"We certainly do know him," they answered.

"How is he?" she asked.

[5] "He is alive and well," they replied. Then Tobias added, "Tobit is my father." [6] At that Raguel got up, and with tears of joy in his eyes he kissed Tobias. [7] Then he said, "God bless you, my child. Your father is a good and noble man. What a terrible tragedy that such an

honest and generous man should have lost his sight!" He threw his arms round Tobias's neck and wept on his shoulder. [8] His wife Edna and his daughter Sarah also wept for Tobit.

Raguel gave Tobias and Raphael a warm welcome and had one of his rams slaughtered. After the guests had bathed and were about to sit down to eat, Tobias said to Raphael, "Azarias, my friend, when are you going to ask Raguel to let me marry Sarah?"

[9] But Raguel overheard the question and said to Tobias, [10] "Eat and drink something first and enjoy yourself this evening. You have the right to marry Sarah, and I cannot let anyone else marry her, because you are my closest relative. But I must tell you the truth, my son. [11] I have already given her to seven men, all of them relatives. Each one died on his wedding night, as soon as he entered the bedroom. But now, my son, have something to eat and drink. The Lord will take care of you both."

Tobias replied, "I won't eat or drink until you give me your word."

[12] Raguel agreed. "Certainly I will," he said. "I will give her to you just as the Law of Moses commands. God in heaven has arranged this marriage, so take her as your wife. From now on, you belong to each other. Sarah is yours today and for ever. May the Lord of heaven keep both of you safe tonight. May he be merciful and kind to you."

The Marriage Ceremony

[13] Then Raguel called his daughter. When she came in, he took her by the hand and gave her to Tobias with his blessing, "Take her to be your wife according to the teachings in the Law of Moses. Take her safely with you to your father's house. May the God of heaven give you a happy life together."

[14] Raguel asked his wife to bring him a blank scroll so that he could write out the marriage contract. Edna brought him the scroll, and Raguel wrote out the agreement, saying that Sarah was given to Tobias according to the teachings in the Law of Moses. [15] After the ceremony they began the meal.

[16] Raguel called his wife and said, "Get the spare room ready, my dear, and take Sarah there."

[17] Edna made up the bed as Raguel had

7.6: Gen 33.4; 45.14; Lk 15.20

They went out to dig a grave (8.9)

told her. Then she took Sarah into the room with her, and Sarah began to cry.[l] But Edna wiped away her tears and said, [18] "Don't worry, Sarah. I'm sure the Lord of heaven will make you happy this time and not sad. So cheer up, my dear." Then Edna left the room.

The Demon Is Expelled

8 When they had finished the meal, and it was time to go to bed, Sarah's parents led young Tobias to the bedroom. [2] He remembered Raphael's instructions, so he took the fish's liver and heart out of the bag where he had been keeping them. Then he placed them on the burning incense. [3] The smell drove the demon away from them, and he fled to Egypt.[m] Raphael chased after him and caught him there. At once he bound him hand and foot.

The Prayer of Tobias

[4] When Tobias and Sarah were alone behind closed doors, Tobias got up from the bed and said to his wife, "Get up, dear. Let's pray for the Lord to be merciful and protect us." [5] Sarah got up so that they could pray together and ask God for his protection. Then Tobias prayed:

"God of our ancestors, you are worthy
      of praise.
May your name be honoured for ever
      and ever
      by all your creatures in heaven and
      on earth.
[6] You created Adam and gave him his
      wife Eve
      to be his helper and support.
They became the parents of all mankind.
You said, 'It is not good for man to
      live alone.
   I will make a suitable helper for him.'
[7] Lord, I have chosen Sarah because it
      is right,
      not because I lusted for her.
Please be merciful to us
      and grant that we may grow old
      together."
[8] Then they both said "Amen" [9] and went to bed for the night.

Anxious Parents

Later that night, Raguel called his servants, and together they went out to dig a grave, [10] because Raguel thought, "Tobias will probably die too, and people will laugh and make fun of us." [11] When they had finished digging the grave, Raguel went back into the house and said to his wife, [12] "Send one of the servant

---

[l]and Sarah began to cry; *some manuscripts have* and she began to cry.
[m] EGYPT: *Egypt was thought of as the most remote part of the world and the home of demons and evil spirits.*
8.3: Mt 12.43   **8.5:** S of 3Y 3   **8.6:** Gen 2.18

girls to find out if Tobias is still alive. If he isn't, then we will bury him before anyone finds out." [13] They then sent a servant girl to take a lamp and see if he was still alive. As she opened the door, she could see that both of them were sound asleep. [14] So she went back and told Raguel and Edna that Tobias was alive and unharmed. [15] Then Raguel[n] praised the God of heaven:

Raguel's Prayer

"You are worthy of our praise, O God.
May your people praise you for ever,
    may they praise you with pure hearts.
[16] I praise you because you have made
    me glad;
    you have been merciful to us,
    and my worst fears did not come true.
[17] You deserve our praise, O Lord;
    you were merciful to this young
    couple,
    the only children of their parents.
Now, grant them your mercy and
    protection.
Let them live out their lives in happiness
    and love."
[18] Then Raguel ordered his servants to fill in the grave before dawn.

The Wedding Feast

19 Raguel told his wife to bake enough bread for a big feast. Then he went out to the herd and brought back two oxen and four rams, which he ordered his servants to slaughter in preparation for the wedding feast. [20] He called for Tobias and vowed[o] that he would not let him leave for two weeks. "Stay, and we will eat and drink together," he said. "It will do my daughter good after her terrible suffering. [21] Then you may take half of what I own and go back to your father safe and sound. You will inherit the other half when Edna and I die. Have no doubts about our love for you; from now on you are as much our son as Sarah is our daughter. You can be sure of that, my son."

The Journey to Rages

9 Then Tobias called Raphael and said to him, [2] "Azarias, take four of the servants with you, and two camels, and go to Gabael's house in the town of Rages. Give him the signed document, so that he will give you the money. Then bring him back with you for the wedding feast. [3-4] You know that my father is counting the days until I come home, and he will be very upset if I am even one day late. You know, too, how Raguel insists that I must stay, and I cannot disappoint him."

5 So Raphael and the four servants went to Rages in Media, where they stayed at Gabael's house. Raphael gave him the signed document and told him that Tobit's son Tobias had recently married, and that Gabael was invited to the wedding feast. At once Gabael counted out the bags of money, which were still sealed, and they loaded them on the camels.[p] [6] Very early the next morning, they set out for the wedding feast. When Raphael and Gabael came to Raguel's house, they found Tobias at dinner. Tobias immediately got up and greeted Gabael. With tears in his eyes Gabael returned the greeting and added, "You are just like your honest and generous father. May the Lord in heaven bless you and your wife, your mother-in-law, and your father. Praise God! He has let me live to see my cousin Tobias, who looks so much like his father."

Tobit and Anna Are Worried

10 Meanwhile, every day Tobit was keeping count of the time needed to travel to Rages and back. When the time was up and his son had not returned, Tobit said to his wife, [2] "What can be keeping him? Do you suppose Gabael has died? Maybe there is no one to give him the money." [3] Tobit was very worried.

4 Then Anna said, "My son is dead. I'm sure of it." She began to weep and to mourn for Tobias, [5] "Oh, my son, the joy of my life, why did I ever let you leave home?"

6 Tobit tried to comfort her. "Calm down, my dear," he said. "Don't worry. He will be all right. Something unexpected is probably keeping them longer than we counted on. Besides, his companion is a reliable man and a relative at that. Don't let yourself get so upset over him, dear. I'm sure he is already on his way home."

7 But she replied, "Be quiet and leave me alone! Don't try to fool me. My son is dead." Each day she would rush out

---

[n] Raguel; *some manuscripts have* they.   [o] vowed; *some manuscripts have* said.
[p] loaded them on the camels; *some manuscripts have* stacked them up.
8.20: Gen 24.55

Each day she would...watch for him until sunset (10.7)

of the house to the road which Tobias had taken and would watch for him until sunset. She would let no one comfort her,*q* and when she returned home she would weep and mourn for her son all night long, without sleeping.

Departure from Ecbatana

The two-week wedding feast which Raguel had promised to hold for his daughter Sarah came to an end. So Tobias went to him and asked, "Please let me go home now. I'm certain my parents have given up all hope of ever seeing me again. Please, Raguel, let me go home to my father. I have already told you the condition he was in when I left."

8 But Raguel answered, "Stay, my son. Stay here with me. I will send messengers to your father to tell him that you are all right."

9 But Tobit insisted, "No, I can't! Please let me go back to my father."

10 So Raguel gave Tobias his bride Sarah without further delay. He also gave Tobias half of everything he owned: slaves, cattle, sheep, donkeys, camels, clothes, money, and furniture. 11 Raguel embraced Tobias and sent them on their way with his blessing, "Good-bye, my son. Have a safe journey. May the Lord of heaven protect you and Sarah. And may I live to see your children." 12 Raguel then said to Sarah, "Go with your husband and live in his parents' house. From now

on they are as much your parents as your own mother and I are. Let me hear only good things about you as long as I live." After saying good-bye he sent them on their way.

Then Edna said to Tobias, "Tobias my dear child, may the Lord bring you safely home. And may he let me live to see your children. The Lord is my witness; I am placing my daughter in your care. Never, at any time in your life, do anything that would break her heart. Have a safe journey, Tobias. From now on, Sarah is your wife and I am your mother. May we all prosper as long as we live." Then Edna kissed them both and sent them safely on their way.

11 When Tobias left, he was as happy as could be. He praised the Lord of heaven and earth, the King of all the world, because his journey had been so successful, and he promised to honour Raguel and his wife as long as they lived.*r*

The Homecoming

As they came near the city of Kaserin, just outside Nineveh, 2 Raphael said, "Tobias, you know the condition your father was in when we left him. 3 We should go on ahead of your wife and get the house ready before everyone else arrives. 4 Be sure to bring the fish's gall-bladder with you." So they went on ahead, and Tobias's dog ran along with*s* them.

5 Meanwhile, Anna sat looking down

---

*q*She would let no one comfort her; *some manuscripts have* She would not eat a bite.
*r*successful, and...lived; *or* successful. And Raguel made Tobias promise to honour him and Edna as long as they lived.   *s*Tobias's dog...with; *some manuscripts have* the Lord accompanied.

the road for her son. 6 Suddenly she saw him coming and shouted out to Tobit, "Look! Our son is coming, and his friend is with him!"

7 Before they reached Tobit, Raphael said to Tobias, "Your father will be able to see again. 8 Just put the fish's gall-bladder on his eyes like a plaster. The medicine will make the white film shrivel up so that you can peel it off, and your father will then regain his eyesight."

9 Anna ran to her son, threw her arms round him, and exclaimed, "Now that I have seen you alive, my child, I can die in peace!" And she wept for joy.

Tobit's Cure

10 Tobit got up and stumbled out through the entrance of the courtyard. 11 Tobias went up to him, holding the fish's gall-bladder in his hand. He blew on his father's eyes and steadied him. "Don't worry now, father," he said. 12-13 Tobias then applied the gall, and beginning from the corners of Tobit's eyes, he peeled away the white film. 14 Tobit threw his arms round Tobias's neck and wept for joy. Then he exclaimed, "I can see you! My son, the light of my eyes!

"Praise God. Praise him for his
    greatness.
Praise all his holy angels.
May he continue to bless us.
Praise all his angels for ever.
15 He brought this illness upon me,
    but now I can see my son Tobias!"

Then Tobias went happily into the house, praising God at the top of his voice. He told his father how successful he had been, that he had not only brought back the money, but had married Raguel's daughter Sarah, who was on her way and would soon arrive.

Sarah's Arrival

16 Tobit was excited and praised God as he went out to meet his son's bride at the city gate. When the people of Nineveh saw him, they were amazed, because he was walking on his own, with no one leading him by the hand. 17 Tobit praised God and told everyone how God in his mercy had restored his sight.

When Tobit met Sarah, he greeted her, "Welcome, daughter! Praise God for bringing you to us, my daughter. May God bless your father, as well as you and my son Tobias. Welcome to your new home.

May you always be blessed with good health and happiness. Come in, my daughter!"

It was a day of great joy for all the Jews of Nineveh. 18 Tobit's nephews Ahikar and Nadab called in to share Tobit's happiness with him.

The Angel Raphael

12 When the wedding feast was over, Tobit called his son Tobias and said to him, "My son, be sure to pay your travelling companion, and don't forget to give him a bonus."

2 Tobias asked him, "Father, how much do you think I should pay him? I wouldn't mind giving him half of everything we brought back with us. 3 He brought me home safe and sound; he went to get the money for me from Gabael; he rid my wife of a demon; and he cured your blindness. How much of a bonus should I give him?"

4 Tobit answered, "Give him half of what he helped you bring back. He well deserves that."

5 Tobias then called Raphael and said to him, "Here is half of what you helped me bring back. You have earned it; have a safe journey home."

6 Then Raphael called the two men aside and said to them, "Praise God and tell everyone about the good things he has done for you, so that they too will honour him and sing his praises. Let everyone know what God has done. Never stop praising him.

7 "It's a good idea to keep a king's secret, but what God does should be told everywhere, so that he may be praised and honoured.

"If you do good, no harm will come to you.

8 "It is better to pray sincerely and to please God by helping the poor than to be rich and dishonest. It is better to give to the poor than to store up gold. 9 Such generosity will save you from death and will wash away all your sins. Those who give to the poor will live full lives, 10 but those who live a life of sin and wickedness are their own worst enemies.

11 "I have already told you that a king's secret ought to be kept, but the things God does should be told to everyone. Now I will reveal to you the full truth and keep nothing back. 12 Tobit, when you and Sarah prayed to the Lord, I was the one

Tobit and Tobias were terrified (12.16)

who brought your prayers into his glorious presence. I did the same thing each time you buried the dead. 13 On the day you got up from the table without eating your meal in order to bury that corpse, God sent me to test you. 14 But he also sent me to cure you and to rescue your daughter-in-law, Sarah, from her troubles. 15 I am Raphael, one of the seven angels who stand in the glorious presence of the Lord, ready to serve him."

16 Tobit and Tobias were terrified and fell to the ground, trembling with fear. 17 But Raphael said to them, "Don't be afraid; everything is all right. Always remember to praise God. 18 He wanted me to come and help you; I did not come on my own. So sing God's praises as long as you live. 19 When you thought you saw me eating, I did not really eat anything; it only seemed as if I did. 20 While you are on this earth, you must praise the Lord God and give him thanks. Now I must go back to him who sent me. Write down everything that has happened to you."

21 Then Raphael disappeared into the sky. Tobit and Tobias stood up, but they could no longer see him. 22 They began to sing hymns of praise, giving thanks for all the mighty deeds God had done while his angel Raphael had been with them.

Tobit's Song of Praise

13 Then Tobit prayed:
    "Praise the eternal God,
    praise the one who rules.
2 He punishes us; then he shows us mercy.
    He sends us down to the world of
        the dead,
    then he brings us up from the grave.
No one can escape his power.

3 "People of Israel, give thanks among
        the nations,
    where he sent you into exile;
4   even there he showed his great power.
Let all who live hear your praise.
The Lord is our God and father for ever.

5 "Though he punished you for your
        wickedness,
    he will be merciful and bring you home
    from among the nations where he
        scattered you.

6 "Turn to him with all your heart and
        soul,
    live in loyal obedience to him.
    Then he will turn to you to help you
    and will no longer hide himself.
Remember what God has done for you,
    and give thanks with all your heart.
Praise the righteous Lord;
    honour the eternal King.

12.15: Zech 4.10; Lk 1.19; Rev 8.2   **13.4:** Is 63.16; Jer 3.4; Wis 14.3; Sir 23.1,4; Mt 6.9

"Although I live in exile in a foreign
land,
  I will give thanks to the Lord
  and will speak of his great strength
    to a nation of sinners.
'Turn away from your sins, and do what
pleases God!
Perhaps he will be gracious
  and show you his mercy.'

7 "I praise my God and rejoice in his
    greatness;
  my whole being honours the King of
    Heaven.

8 "Let everyone tell of his greatness
  and sing his praises in Jerusalem.

9 "Jerusalem, holy city of our God,
  he will punish you for the sins of your
    people,
  but he will be merciful to all who
    do right.
10 So give thanks to the Lord, for he is
    good.
  Praise the eternal King. *t*
  Your Temple will be rebuilt,
  and your people will be happy again.

"May the Lord make all your exiles glad,
  may he take care of your suffering
    people
    for as long as time shall last.

11 "Jerusalem, your light will shine
    brightly for all the world,
  and from far away many nations will
    come to you.
Their people will come to honour the
    Lord your God,
  they will bring gifts for the King of
    Heaven.
In your streets many generations will
    sing joyful praise,
  your name will endure for ever as
    God's chosen city.
12 A curse will be on all who make
    threats against you,
  on all who destroy you and tear down
    your walls,
  on all who demolish your towers and
    burn your homes.
But all who honour you will be blessed
    for ever.

13 "Rejoice, Jerusalem, because of your
    righteous people;

they will be gathered together from
    exile
  to praise the Lord of the ages.

14 "Happy are all who love you
  and are pleased to see you prosper.
Those who mourn over your suffering
    now
  will one day be happy;
  your happiness will bring them joy
    for ever.

15 "I praise the Lord, the great King;
16   Jerusalem will be rebuilt
  and will be his home for ever.

"Jerusalem, how happy I will be
  when my descendants can see your
    splendour
  and give thanks to the King of Heaven.

"Your gates will be built with sapphires
    and emeralds,
  and all your walls with precious
    stones.
Your towers will be made of gold,
  and their fortifications of pure gold.
17 Your streets will be paved with rubies
    and precious jewels.
18 Joyful songs will ring out from your
    gates,
  and from all your houses people will
    shout,
  'Praise the Lord! Praise the God of
    Israel!'

"Jerusalem, God will bless your people,
  and they will praise his holy name
    for ever."
With these words Tobit ended his song
of praise.

Tobit's Final Advice

14 ¹⁻²Tobit was 62 years old when he
became blind, but after his sight
had been restored, he lived a very full
life. Once again he gave generously to
the poor, and he continued to praise God
and tell of his greatness. Tobit died a
peaceful death at the age of 112, and was
given an honourable burial in Nineveh.

3 But just before Tobit died, he sent
for his son Tobias and told him, 4 "My
son, take your children and go at once
to Media. I believe that God's judgement
which his prophet Nahum announced
against Nineveh is about to take place.
Everything that God's prophets told Israel

t Some manuscripts do not have verses 6b–10a Although I live...Praise the eternal King.
13.9–18: Is 60.1–22; Rev 21.9—22.5   **14.4:** Neh 1.2—3.19

about Nineveh and Assyria will happen. It will all come true, every word of it, when the right time comes. I am absolutely convinced that everything God has said is sure to come true. God does not break his promises. It will be safer for you in Media than in Assyria or Babylon.

"Our fellow Jews who live in Israel will all be scattered and taken from that good land into exile. All Israel will become a wilderness; Samaria and Jerusalem will be abandoned cities. God's Temple will be burnt to the ground and will lie in complete ruin for a while. 5 But God will have mercy on his people again, and he will bring them back to the land of Israel. They will rebuild the Temple, but it will not be as splendid as the first Temple, not until the proper time has come. But when that time does come, all the people of Israel will return from exile, and they will rebuild the city of Jerusalem in all its former splendour. They will rebuild God's Temple in Jerusalem, just as Israel's prophets have foretold.

6 "Then all the nations in the world will come back to God. They will worship him as the only true God and give up the idols that led them into false worship. 7 The nations of the world will praise the everlasting God by doing what he demands.

"At that time God will save all the people of Israel who have been faithful to him. He will bring them together to Jerusalem, and let them take possession of the land of Abraham, and there they will live securely for ever. All who love God with their heart and soul will rejoice, but all sinners and evil people will be wiped off the face of the earth.

8 "Now, my children, follow my instructions. Worship God sincerely and do what is pleasing to him. 9 Bring up your children to do what is right. Teach them that they must give to the poor and must always remember to praise God with all sincerity.

10 "Tobias, my son, leave Nineveh now. Do not stay here. As soon as you bury your mother beside me, leave; do not stay another night within the city limits. It is a wicked city and full of immorality; the people here have no sense of shame. Remember what Nadab did to Ahikar his own uncle who had brought him up. He tried to kill Ahikar and forced him to go into hiding in a tomb. Ahikar came back into the light of day, but God sent Nadab down into everlasting darkness for what he had done. Ahikar escaped the deadly trap which Nadab had set for him, because Ahikar u had given generously to the poor. But Nadab fell into that fatal trap and it destroyed him. 11 So now, my children, you see what happens to those who show their concern for others, and how death awaits those who treat others unjustly. But now I am very weak."

Then they laid Tobit on his bed. He died and was given an honourable burial. 12 Later on, Tobit's wife died and was buried beside her husband. Then Tobias and his wife moved to Ecbatana in Media, where they lived with Raguel, Tobias's father-in-law. 13 Tobias took care of Edna and Raguel in their old age and showed them great respect. When at last they died, he buried them at Ecbatana. Tobias inherited Raguel's estate, as he had inherited the estate of his father Tobit.

14 At the ripe old age of 117 Tobias died, 15 having lived long enough to hear about the destruction of Nineveh and to see King Cyaxares v of Media take the people away as captives. Tobias praised God for the way that he had punished the people of Nineveh and Assyria. As long as he lived he gave thanks for what God had done to Nineveh.

---

u Ahikar; or I.   v Probable text Cyaxares; Greek unclear.

THE BOOK OF
JUDITH

INTRODUCTION

The book of *Judith* depicts a time when the Jewish nation was about to be crushed by an enemy army. Judith, the heroine of the story, is a deeply religious widow who observes all the requirements of the Law of Moses. She depends on God to help her complete the dramatic rescue of the nation by killing Holofernes.

Outline of Contents

The Jews are threatened with destruction   1.1—7.32
Judith saves the nation   8.1—14.19
The Jews are victorious   15.1—16.25

The War between Nebuchadnezzar and Arphaxad

1 While King Nebuchadnezzar was ruling over the Assyrians from his capital city of Nineveh, King Arphaxad ruled over the Medes from his capital city of Ecbatana. ² Round Ecbatana King Arphaxad built a wall 30 metres high and 22 metres thick of cut stones; each stone was 130 centimetres thick and 260 centimetres long. ³ At each gate he built a tower 44 metres high, with a foundation 26 metres thick. ⁴ Each gateway was 30 metres high and 18 metres wide—wide enough for his whole army to march through, with the infantry in formation.

5 In the twelfth year of his reign King Nebuchadnezzar went to war against King Arphaxad in the large plain round the city of Rages. ⁶ Many nations joined forces with King Arphaxad—all the people who lived in the mountains, those who lived along the rivers Tigris, Euphrates, and Hydaspes, as well as those who lived in the plain ruled by King Arioch of Elam. Many nations joined this Chelodite alliance.

7 Then King Nebuchadnezzar of Assyria sent a message to the Persians and to the people to the west, in the regions of Cilicia, Damascus, Lebanon, Antilebanon, to those along the coast, ⁸ and in the regions of Carmel, Gilead, northern Galilee, and the Valley of Jezreel. ⁹⁻¹⁰ The message also went to the people living in Samaria and the nearby towns, to those in the area west of the River Jordan as far as the cities of Jerusalem, Bethany, Chelous, and Kadesh, and to the district of Goshen. The message was also taken to the Egyptian cities of Tahpanhes, Rameses, Tanis, and Memphis, and the district up the River Nile to the Sudan border. ¹¹ But everyone in this whole region ignored King Nebuchadnezzar's appeal and refused to take part in the war. They thought that he had no chance of winning the war, so they were not afraid of him and sent his messengers back disgraced and empty-handed.

12 This made Nebuchadnezzar so furious that he vowed he would risk his entire kingdom to take revenge on all those people. He vowed that he would put to death the entire population of Cilicia, Damascus, Syria, Moab, Ammon, Judah, and Egypt—everyone from the Mediterranean Sea to the Persian Gulf.

13 In the seventeenth year of his reign King Nebuchadnezzar led his army into battle against King Arphaxad. He defeated all Arphaxad's forces, including his entire cavalry, and all his charioteers.

[14] Then Nebuchadnezzar occupied all the towns in the land of Media and advanced against the city of Ecbatana. He captured the city's towers, looted its markets, and made that beautiful city a ruin. [15] He captured King Arphaxad in the mountains round Rages and killed him. After Arphaxad's death, [16] Nebuchadnezzar and his entire army returned to Nineveh with all the loot taken in battle. There they relaxed and feasted for four months.

The War against the Nations in the West

2 In the eighteenth year of Nebuchadnezzar's reign, on the twenty-second day of the first month of that year, he and his advisers decided to carry out his threat to take revenge on all those countries that had refused to help him. [2-3] The king called his general staff and senior officers together and reported in detail how those countries had betrayed him. He and his officers agreed that everyone who had refused to help him in the war should be put to death. Then he described to them his plan of attack.

Holofernes, who was the general in command (2.4)

[4] At the close of the meeting, Nebuchadnezzar gave the following command to Holofernes, who was the general in command of his armies and second in command to the king: [5] "I, Nebuchadnezzar, the great king and ruler of all the earth, command you to choose some experienced soldiers: 120,000 infantry and 12,000 cavalry. [6] Then attack the lands to the west because they refused to respond to my appeal for help. [7] Warn them that they must prepare their offerings of earth and water to show that

2.20: Judg 7.12; Joel 2.2–11;

they have surrendered unconditionally. I will make them feel the full force of my anger and completely destroy them. My armies will march over every foot of their land and plunder it as they go. [8] I will fill the valleys with their dead bodies and will choke up every stream and river with so many corpses that they will all overflow. [9] I will take captive all those who are left alive and carry them off to the ends of the earth.

[10] "But you, Holofernes, are ordered to go ahead of me and occupy all their territories in advance. If they surrender to you, hold them for me until I come to punish them. [11] But if they resist, do not spare them. Kill them and loot the entire region under your control. [12] I have taken a solemn vow, and at the risk of my life and my royal power I am determined to do what I have vowed to do. [13] Do not disobey me in any way. I am your king; remember that, and carry out without delay every order that I have given you."

The Campaign of Holofernes

14 So Holofernes left the king and called together all the commanders, generals, and officers of the Assyrian army. [15] Just as the king had ordered, he chose 120,000 of the best infantrymen and 12,000 of the best mounted archers [16] and arranged them in battle formation. [17] He also took along a very large number of camels, donkeys, and mules to carry the equipment, as well as many sheep, cattle, and goats for food. [18] Every soldier received plenty of rations and a large payment of gold and silver from the royal treasury.

19 Then Holofernes and his entire army set out, advancing ahead of King Nebuchadnezzar. The chariots, the cavalry, and the infantry marched out to overrun the entire western region. [20] Other troops went with them. There were so many that it was impossible to count them—they were like a swarm of locusts or like grains of sand in the desert.

21 Three days after they had left the city of Nineveh, they reached the plains round Bectileth near the mountains north of Cilicia, where they set up camp. [22] From there Holofernes advanced into the hill-country with his entire army, his infantry, cavalry, and chariots. [23] He totally destroyed the countries of Libya and Lydia, then plundered all the people of Rassis and the Ishmaelites who lived on

the edge of the desert, south of the land of the Chelleans.

24 Then Holofernes crossed the River Euphrates and marched through the land of Mesopotamia, completely destroying all the walled towns along the River Abron as far as the sea. 25 He seized the territory of Cilicia, killing everyone who resisted him, and went as far as the southern borders of the land of Japheth, near Arabia. 26 He surrounded the Midianites, burnt down their tents, and slaughtered their sheep.

27 Holofernes went down into the plains round Damascus during the wheat harvest, burnt all the fields, slaughtered the flocks and herds, looted the towns, devastated the entire countryside, and killed all the young men. 28 Panic seized all the people who lived along the Mediterranean Sea, and they shook with fear. Everyone in the towns of Tyre, Sidon, Sur, Ocina, Jamnia, Ashdod, and Ashkelon was terrified.

The Peace Delegation to King Nebuchadnezzar

3 All these nations sent a peace delegation to King Nebuchadnezzar with this message: 2 "We remain loyal to you, great King Nebuchadnezzar; we are ready to serve you and obey any command that you may wish to give us. 3 Our buildings, all our land, our wheat fields, our livestock, and our tents are at your disposal; use them in any way you wish. 4 Our people will be your slaves, and you may use our towns as you please."

5 After the peace delegation had brought this message, 6 Holofernes led Nebuchadnezzar's army down to the Mediterranean coast. He stationed guards in all the walled towns and selected certain local men in each of the towns as reserve troops. 7 The people in the towns and in the surrounding countryside welcomed Holofernes by wearing wreaths of flowers and dancing to the beat of drums. 8 But Holofernes destroyed all their places of worship[a] and cut down their sacred trees. He had been ordered to destroy all the gods of the land so that all the nations and tribes would worship only Nebuchadnezzar and pray to him as a god.

9 Then Holofernes passed through the Valley of Jezreel near Dothan, which faces the main ridge of the mountains of Judah,

10 and set up camp between Geba and Scythopolis. He stayed there for a month in order to get supplies for his army.

The Israelite Plan for Defence

4 The people of Judah heard what Holofernes, the commander of King Nebuchadnezzar's armies, had done to the other nations. They heard how he had looted and destroyed all their temples, 2 and they were terrified of him and afraid of what he might do to Jerusalem and to the Temple of the Lord their God. 3 They had only recently returned home to Judah from exile and had just rededicated the Temple and its utensils and its altar after they had been defiled. 4 So they sent a warning to the whole region of Samaria and to the towns of Kona, Beth Horon, Belmain, Jericho, Choba, and Aesora, and to the Valley of Salem. 5 They immediately occupied the mountaintops, fortified the villages on the mountains, and stored up food in preparation for war. It was fortunate that they had recently harvested their fields.

6 The High Priest Joakim, who was in Jerusalem at that time, wrote to the people in the towns of Bethulia and Betomesthaim, which face the Valley of Jezreel near Dothan. 7 He ordered them to occupy the mountain passes which led into the land of Judah, where it would be easy to withstand an attack, since the approach was only wide enough for two men at a time to pass. 8 The Israelites carried out the orders given to them by the High Priest Joakim and the Council which met in Jerusalem.

Prayer before the War

9 The men of Israel prayed earnestly to God and fasted. 10 They put on sackcloth—they and their wives, their children, their livestock, and every resident foreigner, every slave and hired labourer. 11-12 They also covered the altar with sackcloth. Then all the men, women, and children in Jerusalem lay face down on the ground in front of the Temple; they lay there in the Lord's presence, all in sackcloth, their heads covered with ashes. They joined together in earnest prayer to the God of Israel, begging him not to let their children be captured, their wives carried off, or their home towns destroyed. They pleaded with him not to give the Gentiles the satisfaction of

---

[a] One ancient translation places of worship; Greek territory.
3.8: Ex 34.13; 2 Chr 17.6   **4.10-12:** Jon 3.7-8; Esth 4.1-3

destroying the Temple and dishonouring it. [13] The Lord heard their prayers and saw their distress. For many days the people of Judah and Jerusalem continued their fast in front of the Temple of the Lord Almighty. [14] The High Priest Joakim, the priests, and all the others who served in the Lord's Temple, wore sackcloth when they offered the daily burnt-offering, the freewill offerings of the people, and the offerings made to fulfil a vow. [15] They put ashes on their turbans and cried out in prayer to the Lord, begging him to have mercy on the whole nation.

The War Council in the Camp of Holofernes

5 When Holofernes, the Assyrian general, heard that the Israelites had prepared for war, blocked the mountain passes, fortified the mountaintops, and set up roadblocks in the plains, [2] he boiled over with anger. He called together all the Moabite rulers, all the Ammonite generals, and all the governors of the region along the Mediterranean coast [3] and said to them, "You live in Canaan, so tell me about the people who live in these mountains. Which cities do they occupy? How large is their army? What is the source of their power and strength? Who is the king who leads their army? [4] Why have they alone, of all the people in the west, refused to come out and surrender to me?"

The Speech of Achior

[5] Then Achior, the leader of all the Ammonites, answered Holofernes, "Sir, if you will please be so kind as to listen to me, I will tell you the truth about these people who live in the mountains near your camp. I will not lie to you. [6] These people are the descendants of some Babylonians [7-8] who abandoned the ways of their ancestors in order to worship the God of heaven. Finally, they were driven out of their land because they refused to worship their ancestors' gods. Then they fled to Mesopotamia, where they settled and lived for a long time.

[9] "Afterwards, their god told them to leave Mesopotamia and go to the land of Canaan, where they settled and became very rich in gold, silver, and livestock. [10] Later, when a famine struck all the land of Canaan, these Israelites, as they were later called, went down to Egypt and stayed there as long as there was enough food. While they were there, they became a large nation with so many people that they could not be counted. [11] So the king of Egypt turned against them. He took advantage of them and put them to work making bricks. He oppressed them and made them slaves. [12] But they prayed to their god, and he sent disasters that left the Egyptians helpless. When the Egyptians drove them out of the country, [13] their god dried up the Red Sea in front of them, [14] and then led them along the way to Sinai and Kadesh Barnea.

"The Israelites drove out all the people who lived in the southern part of Canaan, [15] occupied the land of the Amorites, wiped out the people of Heshbon, crossed the River Jordan, and took possession of the entire mountain region. [16] They drove out the Canaanites, the Perizzites, the Jebusites, the Shechemites, and all the Girgashites. The Israelites have now lived in these mountains for a long time.

[17] "Their god hates wickedness, and as long as they did not sin against him, they prospered. [18] But when they disobeyed him, they suffered heavy losses in many wars and were finally taken away as captives to a foreign country. The temple of their god was levelled to the ground and their cities were occupied by their enemies. [19] But now that they have returned to their god, they have come back home from the countries where they had been scattered. They have again taken possession of the city of Jerusalem, where their temple is, and have resettled in the mountains that had remained uninhabited.

[20] "Sir, if these people are now sinning against their god, even unknowingly, and if we can be sure that they are guilty of some offence, we can successfully attack them. [21] But if they have not disobeyed the law of their god, then you should leave them alone, or he will defend them, and we will be disgraced before the whole world."

The Reaction of the Crowd

[22] When Achior had finished his speech, all the people standing round the tent began to protest. Holofernes' own senior officers, as well as the Moabites and the men from the Mediterranean coast, demanded that Achior be put to death.

[23] "Why should we be afraid of these

4.13: Esth 4.16   **4.14:** Joel 2.17   **5.9:** Gen 11.31—12.5   **5.10:** Gen 42.1-5; Ex 1.7
5.11: Ex 1.8-14   **5.12:** Ex 7.1-12, 29.46   **5.13:** Ex 14.21-22   **5.17:** Deut 28.1-68

Israelites?" they asked. "They are weak; they can't put up a strong defence. ²⁴Let's go ahead! General Holofernes, your great army will slaughter them easily."

The Speech of Holofernes

6 When the noise of the crowd round the council had subsided, Holofernes spoke to Achior in front of the entire group, the men from the Mediterranean coast, the Moabites, and the Ammonite mercenaries.ᵇ

2 "Achior,ᶜ who do you think you are, acting like a prophet? Who are you to tell us not to go to war against the Israelites because some god will defend them? Nebuchadnezzar is our god, and that's all that matters. He will send his army and wipe these Israelites off the face of the earth. Their god can't help them. ³But we serve Nebuchadnezzar, and we will beat them as easily as if their whole army were one man. They will not be able to hold their ground against our cavalry; ⁴it will overwhelm them. The mountains will be soaked with their blood, and the valleys will be filled with their corpses. After our attack, they will be completely wiped out; not a trace of them will be left. This is the command of Nebuchadnezzar, the lord of the whole earth, and he doesn't speak idle words. ⁵Achior, you are nothing but an Ammonite mercenary, and you talk like a traitor. You will not see me again until I come and punish this race of runaway slaves. ⁶And when I do, my soldiers will put you to death. You will be just another name on the casualty list.

7 "Now my men will take you into the mountains and leave you in one of the Israelite towns, ⁸and you will die with the people there. ⁹Why look so worried, Achior? Don't you think the town can stand against me? I will carry out all my threats; you can be sure of that!"

Achior Is Brought to Bethulia

10 Then Holofernes ordered his men, who were waiting in his tent, to seize Achior, take him to Bethulia, and hand him over to the Israelites. ¹¹So the men seized Achior and took him out of the camp into the valley. From there they led him into the mountains, as far as the spring which was below Bethulia.

12 When the men of that town saw them approaching, they picked up their weapons and ran to the top of the hill. Every man who used a sling as a weapon rained stones down on Holofernes' soldiers, and this stopped them from coming any farther up the mountain. ¹³The Assyrians were forced to take cover along the mountainside, where they tied Achior up and left him lying at the foot of the mountain. Then they returned to Holofernes.

14 Later, when the Israelites came down from Bethulia, they untied Achior, brought him into the town, and took him before the town officials, ¹⁵who at that time were Uzziah son of Micah, of the tribe of Simeon, Chabris son of Gothoniel, and Charmis son of Melchiel. ¹⁶The officials called together the town elders, and all the women and the young men also ran to the assembly. Achior was brought before the people, and Uzziah began questioning him. ¹⁷Achior told them what had been said at Holofernes' war council, what he himself had said to the Assyrian officers, and how Holofernes had boasted about what he would do to the Israelites. ¹⁸When the people heard this, they fell on their knees and worshipped God. They prayed: ¹⁹"O Lord God of heaven, look how our boastful enemies have humiliated your people! Have pity on us and help us." ²⁰Then they reassured Achior and praised him for what he had done. ²¹After the assembly was over, Uzziah took Achior home with him, and gave a banquet there for the elders. All that night they prayed to the God of Israel for help.

The Siege of Bethulia

7 ¹⁻²The next day Holofernes gathered his whole army together, as well as his allied forces. It was an immense army, consisting of 170,000 infantry and 12,000 cavalry, not counting the support troops who took care of the equipment. He ordered them to march on Bethulia, seize the mountain passes, and attack the Israelites. So they moved out ³and set up camp beside the spring in the valley near Bethulia. The camp was so wide that it spread out towards the town of Dothan as far as Balbaim, and so long that it stretched from Bethulia to Cyamon, which faces the Valley of Jezreel.

4 When the Israelites saw the size of

ᵇthe Ammonite mercenaries; *some manuscripts do not have these words.*
ᶜAchior; *some manuscripts add* you and your hired soldiers from Ephraim; *others add* you and your mercenaries from Ammon.

the army, they were terrified and said to one another, "Those soldiers are going to eat up everything in sight. There's not enough food in the mountains, valleys, and hills put together to feed an army like that." ⁵ But in spite of their fear, all the Israelites took up their weapons, lighted signal fires on the towers, and remained on guard duty all night. ⁶ The next day Holofernes led out his entire cavalry so that the Israelites in Bethulia could see them. ⁷ He inspected the approaches to the town and the springs that supplied its water. He seized the springs and stationed guards there, before returning to camp.

8 All the leaders of the Edomite and Moabite forces, along with the commanders of the troops from the Mediterranean coast, came to Holofernes and said, ⁹ "Sir, if you listen to our advice, your troops will not suffer heavy losses. ¹⁰ These Israelites do not rely on their weapons for defence but rather on the height of the mountains where they live, since the mountains are not easy to climb. ¹¹ So then, General Holofernes, if you do not make a direct attack on them, your whole army will suffer no casualties. ¹² Stay in your camp and keep your soldiers in their quarters. Just command your men to blockade the springs at the foot of the mountains, ¹³ because that's where the people of Bethulia come to draw their water. Then, when they are dying of thirst, they will surrender their town to you. Meanwhile, we and our men will go up to the tops of the surrounding mountains, where we will set up camp and keep anyone from leaving the town. ¹⁴ Everyone will starve to death—men, women, and children. Even before they attack, the streets will be littered with their corpses. ¹⁵ In this way you can make them pay for their rebellion and for refusing to surrender peacefully to you."

16 Holofernes and his entire staff were pleased with this suggestion, so he gave orders to put the plan into action. ¹⁷ The Moabites and 5,000 Assyrians moved their camp into the valley to control the source of the town's water. ¹⁸ The Edomites and the Ammonites went up into the mountains and set up their camp opposite the town of Dothan. They sent some of their men to the south-east in the direction of Acraba, near Chusi, which is beside the River Mochmur. The rest of the Assyrian army set up camp in the valley.

Their camp was spread out over the whole countryside, because the number of tents and the amount of equipment needed for such a large army were immense.

19 Then the Israelites cried out to the Lord their God for help. They had lost their courage, for with the enemy all round them there was no way to escape. ²⁰ The entire Assyrian army—infantry, chariots, and cavalry—blockaded Bethulia for thirty-four days until the town ran out of water. ²¹ All the reservoirs and cisterns went dry, so that the drinking water had to be rationed, and not a day passed when there was enough water to

No one had any strength left (7.22)

go round. ²² Children were becoming weak; everywhere throughout the town women and young people were collapsing. No one had any strength left.

23 All the people of the town—men, women, and children alike—gathered round Uzziah and the town officials and shouted in protest, ²⁴ "God will punish you for what you have done to us! You are to blame for what is happening, because you did not make peace with the Assyrians. ²⁵ There is no one to help us now! God has put us in their power. We are exhausted and dying of thirst. ²⁶ Call the Assyrians now and surrender to them, and let Holofernes and his army take the town and loot it. ²⁷ We are better off as

7.5: 1 Macc 12.28-29

prisoners of war. They will make us slaves, but at least we will be alive, and we won't have to watch our wives and children dying before our eyes. 28 Heaven and earth are witnesses against you, and so is our God, the Lord of our ancestors, who is punishing us for their sins as well as ours. We can only hope and pray that he will not let these terrible things happen to us today." *d*

29 Everyone there began to weep loudly and to pray to the Lord their God. 30 Then Uzziah said to them, "Don't give up, my friends! Let's wait five more days to see if the Lord our God will be merciful to us. Surely he will not abandon us completely. 31 But if no help comes after five days, then I will do as you say." 32 So Uzziah dismissed the people. All the men returned to their guard posts on the walls and towers, while the women and children went back to their homes. The morale of the entire town was very low.

Judith, the Israelite Widow

8 At that time, Judith heard about Uzziah's decision. She was the daughter of Merari, the granddaughter of Ox and the great-granddaughter of Joseph. Joseph's ancestors were Oziel, Elkiah, Ananias, Gideon, Raphaim, Ahitub, Elijah, Hilkiah, Eliab, Nathanael, Salamiel, Sarasadai, and Israel. 2 Judith's husband Manasseh, who belonged to the same tribe and clan, had died during the barley harvest. 3 He had got sunstroke while in the fields supervising the farm workers and later died in bed at home in Bethulia. He was buried in the family tomb in the field between Dothan and Balamon.

4 For three years and four months, Judith had lived as a widow. 5 In her grief she built a little shelter on the roof of her house and lived there, wearing sackcloth. 6 She fasted during that entire period except when fasting was forbidden: the day before the Sabbath and the Sabbath itself, the eve of the New Moon Festival and the Festival itself, and all the festivals and holidays observed by the people of Israel. 7 Judith was a very beautiful woman. Her husband had left her gold and silver, servants and slaves, livestock and fields. She continued to supervise the estate, 8 and no one ever said anything bad about Judith. She was a very religious woman.

Judith Meets with the Town Officials

9 Judith heard how the people were complaining bitterly against Uzziah, now that the water shortage had broken their morale. She learnt that in answer to their complaints he had promised to surrender the town to the Assyrians after five days. 10 Judith sent a slave, the woman who managed her business affairs, to invite Uzziah, *e* Chabris, and Charmis, the town officials, to her home.

11 When the officials arrived, Judith said to them, "Please listen to me. You are the leaders of the people of Bethulia, but you were wrong to speak to the people as you did today. You should not have made a solemn promise before God that you would surrender the town to our enemies if the Lord did not come to our aid within a few days. 12 What right have you to put God to the test as you have done today? Who are you to put yourselves in God's place in dealing with human affairs? 13 It is the Lord Almighty that you are putting to the test! Will you never learn? 14 There is no way that you can understand what is in the depths of a human heart or find out what a person is thinking. Yet you dare to read God's mind and interpret his thoughts! How can you claim to understand God, the Creator? No, my friends, you must stop arousing the anger of the Lord our God! 15 If he decides not to come to our aid within five days, he still may rescue us at any time he chooses. Or he may let our enemies destroy us. 16 But you must not lay down conditions for the Lord our God! Do you think that he is like one of us? Do you think you can bargain with him or force him to make a decision? 17 No! Instead, we should ask God for his help and wait patiently for him to rescue us. If he wants to, he will answer our cry for help. 18 We do not worship gods made with human hands. Not one of our clans, tribes, towns, or cities has ever done that, even though our ancestors used to do so. 19 That is why God let their enemies kill them and take everything they had. It was a great defeat! 20 But since we worship no other God but the

---

d We can...today; *some Greek manuscripts and ancient translations have* We demand that you surrender, as we have asked you to do today.
e Uzziah; *some Greek manuscripts do not have this word.*
8.5: Judg 3.20; 2 Kgs 4.10   **8.12:** Deut 6.16; Job 38.2   **8.14:** Rom 11.33–34; 1 Cor 2.11

Lord, we can hope that he will not reject us or any of our people.

21 If our town is taken by the enemy, the entire region of Judah will then fall, and our Temple in Jerusalem will be looted. And God will make us pay with our lives for allowing the Temple to be defiled. 22 He will hold us responsible for the slaughter and captivity of our people and for the destruction of the land we have inherited. We will be despised and mocked by the people in those nations to which we will be taken as slaves. 23 We are not going to win the favour of our enemies by surrendering to them now. *f* If we do surrender, the Lord our God will see that we are put to shame.

24 "No, my friends, we should set an example for our fellow countrymen. Not only their lives, but the fate of the Temple and the altar depend on us. 25 The Lord our God is putting us to the test, just as he tested our ancestors, and we should be thankful for that. 26 Remember how he put Abraham and Isaac to the test, and what happened to Jacob while he was working as a shepherd for his uncle Laban in Mesopotamia. 27 God is not testing our loyalty as severely as he did theirs. God is not sending this punishment on us as revenge, but as a warning to us who worship him."

28 Then Uzziah answered Judith, "Everything you have said makes good sense, and no one can argue with it. 29 This is not the first time you have shown wisdom. Ever since you were a child, all of us have recognized the soundness and maturity of your judgement. 30 But our people are dying of thirst. They forced us to say what we did and to make a solemn promise, which we cannot break. 31 So now, since you are a deeply religious woman, pray for our people; ask the Lord to send rain to fill our cisterns, so that we can get our strength back."

32 "All right," Judith replied, "I am going to do something which our Jewish people will never forget. 33 Tonight, the three of you must stand guard at the gate so that my slave-woman and I can leave the town. And before the day comes on which you have promised to surrender, the Lord will use me to rescue the people of Israel. 34 But you must not ask me what I am going to do; I will explain it to you when it is all over."

35 Uzziah and the other officials said to her, "You have our blessing. May the Lord our God guide you as you take revenge on our enemies." Then they left Judith's roof-top shelter and returned to their posts.

Judith's Prayer

9 Then Judith put ashes on her head, opened her robe to reveal the sackcloth she was wearing under her clothes, and bowed down with her face to the floor. It was the time that the evening incense was being offered in the Temple in Jerusalem, and Judith prayed in a loud voice: 2 "O Lord, the God of my ancestor Simeon, remember how you armed Simeon with a sword to take revenge on those foreigners who seized Dinah, who was a virgin, tore off her clothes, *g* and defiled her; they stripped her naked and shamed her; they raped her and disgraced her, even though you had forbidden this. 3 That is why you let their leaders be killed—put to death on the same bed where they had raped the girl. *h* You destroyed them all, slaves, princes, and rulers on their thrones. 4 You let their wives be carried off, their daughters taken captive, and their possessions plundered by the Israelites, your chosen people, who were eager to do your will. Dinah's brothers were furious because of this disgrace to their family, so they called on you for help.

"O my God, listen to my prayer, the prayer of a widow. 5 Your hand guided all that happened then, and all that happened before and after. You have planned it all—what is happening now, and what is yet to be. Your plans have always been carried out. 6 Whatever you want to be done is as good as done. You know in advance all that you will do and what decisions you will make. 7 Now the Assyrians are stronger than ever; they take pride in their cavalry and their infantry. They rely on their weapons, but they do not know that you, O Lord, are a warrior who ends war. The Lord is your name. 8 In your anger, use your power to shatter their mighty army. They plan to defile your Temple, where you are worshipped, and to hack off the corners of your altar with their swords. 9 Look how proud and boastful they are! Pour out your fury upon them! I am only a

---

f We are not...now; *or* No good will ever come out of our slavery.
g *Probable text* clothes; *Greek unclear.*   *h* *Probable text* put to death...girl; *Greek unclear.*
8.26: Gen 22.1–18; 29.1—31.55   **9.2:** Gen 34.1–31

widow, but give me the strength to carry out my plan. ¹⁰Use my deceitful words to strike them all dead, master and slave alike. Let a woman's strength break their pride. ¹¹Your power does not depend on the size and strength of an army. You are a God who cares for the humble and helps the oppressed. You give support and protection to people who are weak and helpless; you save those who have lost hope. ¹²Now hear my prayer, O God of my ancestor Simeon, the God in whom Israel trusts, ruler of heaven and earth, creator of the rivers and the seas, king of all creation. Hear my prayer and ¹³let my deceitful words wound and kill those who have planned such cruelty against your covenant and your holy Temple, against Mount Zion and the land you have given to your people. ¹⁴Make your whole nation and every tribe recognize that you are God, almighty and all-powerful, and that you alone protect the people of Israel!"

Judith Goes to the Camp of Holofernes

10 When Judith had finished her prayer to the God of Israel, ²she stood up, called her slave-woman, and went down into the house as she always did on Sabbaths and festival days. ³She took off her sackcloth and her widow's clothes, had a bath, and put on rich perfumes. She brushed her hair, tied a ribbon round it, and dressed herself in the fine clothes she used to wear on joyful occasions when her husband Manasseh was still alive. ⁴She put on sandals and all her finest jewellery: rings and earrings, and bracelets on her wrists and ankles. She made herself so beautiful that she was sure to attract the attention of any man who saw her. ⁵Judith gave her slave-woman a leather bag of wine and a jar of oil to carry. She filled a bag with roasted barley, cakes of dried figs, and several loaves of bread baked according to Jewish food laws. She carefully wrapped all the food and dishes and gave them to her slave. ⁶Then the two women left the house and went to the gates of Bethulia, where they found Uzziah and the town officials, Chabris and Charmis, standing guard. ⁷When the men saw Judith after she had changed her clothes and put on make-up, they were struck by her beauty and said to her, ⁸"May the God of our fathers bless you and make your plan successful, so that you may bring glory to Jerusalem and victory to Israel."

Judith prayed ⁹and then said, "Tell the men to open the gates for me. I am on my way to do what we were talking about." Then they ordered the young men to open the gates for her, ¹⁰and Judith and her slave left the city. The men watched her as she went down the mountain into the valley, until she was out of sight.

11 As the two women were walking through the valley, an Assyrian patrol met them. ¹²They arrested Judith and questioned her, "What is your nationality? Where did you come from, and where are you going?"

"I am a Hebrew," she answered, "but I am running away from the Israelites because God is going to let you destroy them. ¹³I am on my way to see Holofernes, the general in command of your army, to give him some reliable information. I can show him how to advance into the mountains and take control of the entire region without a single casualty."

14 The men stared at her because she was so beautiful. They listened to her story and said, ¹⁵"You have saved your life by coming down here to see our general. Some of our men will take you to his headquarters and present you to him. ¹⁶Do not be afraid of him. Just tell him what you have told us, and he will treat you well." ¹⁷They assigned a hundred men to escort Judith and her slave to the headquarters of Holofernes.

18 There was great commotion in the Assyrian camp as news of Judith's arrival spread from tent to tent. While she stood outside the tent of Holofernes waiting to be presented to him, many Assyrian soldiers came and stood round her. ¹⁹They were greatly impressed by her beauty and wondered what kind of people the Israelites were. "Who can feel contempt for people whose women are so beautiful?" they asked one another. "We had better kill all the men, or else these Jews will be able to charm the whole world."

20 Then Holofernes' bodyguard and his personal servants came out and led Judith into the tent. ²¹Holofernes was resting on his bed under a mosquito net woven of purple and gold thread and decorated with emeralds and other precious stones. ²²When the men told him that Judith had arrived, he came to the outer part of the

9.13: Gk Est C.24–25

They were greatly impressed by her beauty (10.19)

tent. Silver lamps were carried ahead of him. 23 When Judith came towards him and his servants, they were all astonished at her beauty. She bowed down to the ground before Holofernes, but his servants helped her to her feet.

11 Holofernes said to Judith, "Don't worry; there's no need for you to be afraid. I have never hurt anyone who was willing to serve Nebuchadnezzar, king of the whole world. 2 Even now, if your people up in the mountains had not insulted me, I would not have declared war on them. They have brought all this trouble on themselves. 3 But tell me, why have you left them and come to us? You will be safe here. There's no need to be afraid! We have spared your life tonight, and you are in no danger for the future. 4 No one here will harm you; everyone will treat you well, like all other servants of my master, Nebuchadnezzar."

5 Then Judith said to Holofernes, "Allow me to speak to you, my lord, and please listen to what I have to say. I will tell you the truth. 6 If you follow my advice, God will do something great with you, and my lord will not fail in his plan. 7 For I swear to you by the life and strength of Nebuchadnezzar, king of the whole world, who sent you to bring order to all the subjects of his kingdom, that not only have you made people serve him, but because of you even the wild animals, the livestock, and the birds obey him. Because of you, Nebuchadnezzar and his entire kingdom will prosper.*i* 8 We have heard how wise and clever you are. The whole world knows that you are the most competent, skilled, and accomplished general in the whole Assyrian Empire. 9 Achior was rescued by the men of Bethulia, and has told us what he said at your war council. 10 Please, sir, do not dismiss lightly what Achior told you, but take it seriously, because it is true. No one can harm or conquer our people unless they sin against their God.

11 "But you will not suffer any setbacks, nor will you fail to achieve your goal. When the Israelites sin and make their God angry, they will die. 12 Their food

i not only...prosper; *Greek unclear.*
11.7: Jer 27.6; Dan 2.38

supply has already run out, and the water shortage has become serious, so they have decided to kill their livestock and eat foods that God's Law clearly forbids them to eat. [13]They have decided to eat the wheat set aside from the early harvest and the tithes of wine and oil, which are holy and are reserved for the priests who serve God in Jerusalem. The rest of us are forbidden even to touch this sacred food, [14]but since the people in Jerusalem have already broken this law, the people of our town have sent messengers to the Council there requesting permission to do the same. [15]On the day that they receive permission and actually eat the food, you will be able to destroy them. [16]As soon as I learnt about this, I ran away from my people. God has sent me to do something with you that will amaze everyone in the entire world who hears about it. [17]Sir, I am a religious woman; I worship the God of Heaven day and night. I will stay here in your camp, and each night I will go out into the valley to pray to God, and he will tell me when the Israelites have sinned. [18]As soon as I find out, I will come and tell you, and you can march out with your whole army. The Israelites will not be able to defend themselves against you. [19]I will guide you through the central part of the land of Judah until we come to Jerusalem, where I will crown you king in the centre of the city. You will scatter the people of Jerusalem like sheep without a shepherd. Not even a dog will dare to growl at you. God has revealed these things to me in advance and has sent me to report them to you."

20 Holofernes and his personal servants were pleased with what Judith had said, and they admired her wisdom. [21]"She must be the wisest and most beautiful woman in the world," they commented one to another.

22 Then Holofernes said to her, "It's a good thing that God has sent you here to bring us victory and to destroy those who have insulted King Nebuchadnezzar. [23]Not only are you beautiful, but you know how to make a speech. If you do as you have promised, your God will be my God. You will live in King Nebuchadnezzar's palace and will be famous throughout the world."

Judith Remains Faithful to Her Religion

12 Holofernes commanded his men to take Judith to the table on which

his silver was set out and to serve her with some of his own special food and wine. [2]But Judith refused. "I cannot eat your food," she said, "for I would be breaking the laws of my God. I will eat only what I have brought with me."

3 "But what will you do when your food and wine are gone?" Holofernes asked. "Where will we get more food for you? There are no Israelites here in our camp."

4 "Sir," Judith answered, "as surely as you live, I have more than enough food to last until the Lord has used me to carry out his plan."

5 Then Holofernes' personal servants led Judith to a tent. She slept there until the time of the morning watch just before dawn, when she got up [6]and sent a message to Holofernes requesting permission to go out into the valley to pray. [7]Holofernes ordered his guards to let Judith leave the camp. So for three days Judith lived in the camp, and each night she would go out to the valley near Bethulia and bathe at the spring. [8]After she had bathed, she would pray to the Lord God to guide her in her plan to bring victory to Israel. [9]Then she would return to the camp ritually pure and remain in her tent until after the evening meal.

Holofernes' Banquet

10 On the fourth day of Judith's stay in the camp, Holofernes gave a banquet for his highest-ranking officers, but he did not invite any of the officers who were on duty. [11]He said to Bagoas, the eunuch who was in charge of his personal affairs, "Go and persuade the Hebrew woman, who is in your care, to come to my tent to eat and drink with us. [12]It would be a disgrace to let slip an opportunity to make love to a woman like that. If I don't try to seduce her, she will laugh at me."

13 So Bagoas left Holofernes and went to Judith. "Lovely lady," he said, "the general invites you to his tent for some drinks. Come and enjoy yourself like the Assyrian women who serve in Nebuchadnezzar's palace. This is a great honour."

14 "I shall be glad to accept," Judith answered. "How could I refuse? I'll remember this happy night as long as I live."

15 So Judith got up and put on her prettiest clothes. Her slave-woman went ahead of her and placed on the ground in front of Holofernes the lambskins that

11.13: Ex 23.19; Lev 27.30   12.2: Dan 1.8; Gk Est C.28

O Lord...help me with what I am about to do (13.4)

Bagoas had given Judith to sit on when she ate. ¹⁶ Judith came into the tent and sat down there. Holofernes was aroused when he saw her and had an uncontrollable desire to make love to her. From the first day he had seen her, he had been waiting for a chance to seduce her. ¹⁷ "Join us for a drink and enjoy yourself," he said to her.

18 "I'll be glad to, sir," Judith replied; "this is the happiest day of my life." ¹⁹ But even then Judith ate and drank only what her slave had prepared. ²⁰ Holofernes was so charmed by her that he drank more wine than he had ever drunk at one time in his whole life.

13 Finally, when it got late, the guests excused themselves and left. Bagoas then closed up the tent from the outside and prevented Holofernes' servants from going in. So they all went to bed; everyone was very tired because the banquet had lasted so long. ² Judith was left alone in the tent with Holofernes who was lying drunk on his bed. ³ Judith's slave-woman was waiting outside the tent for Judith to go and pray, as she had done each night. Judith had also told Bagoas that she would be going out to pray as usual.

4 All the guests and servants were now gone, and Judith and Holofernes were alone in the tent. Judith stood by Holofernes' bed and prayed silently, "O Lord, God Almighty, help me with what I am about to do for the glory of Jerusalem. ⁵ Now is the time to rescue your chosen people and to help me carry out my plan to destroy the enemies who are threatening us." ⁶ Judith went to the bedpost by Holofernes' head and took down his sword. ⁷ She came closer, seized Holofernes by the hair of his head, and said, "O Lord, God of Israel, give me strength now." ⁸ Then Judith raised the sword and struck him twice on the neck as hard as she could, chopping off his head. ⁹ She rolled his body off the bed and took down the mosquito net from the bedposts. Then she came out and gave Holofernes' head to her slave, ¹⁰ who put it in the food bag.

Judith and Her Slave Return to Bethulia

Then the two women left together, as they always did when they went to pray. After they had walked through the Assyrian camp, they crossed the valley and went up the mountainside until they came to the gates of Bethulia. ¹¹ When they were a short distance away, Judith called out to the guards at the gate, "Open the gate! Open the gate! Our God is still with us. Today he has once again shown his strength in Israel and used his power against our enemies."

12 When the men heard her voice, they hurried down to the gates and called for the town officials. 13 Everyone, young and old, ran together to the gate. No one could believe that Judith had come back. They opened the gate for her and her slave and welcomed them. Then, when they had lit a fire to give some light and had gathered round the two women, 14 Judith shouted, "Praise God, give him praise! Praise God, who has not held back his mercy from the people of Israel. Tonight he has used me to destroy our enemies." 15 She then took the head out of the food bag and showed it to the people. "Here," she said, "is the head of Holofernes, the general of the Assyrian army, and here is the mosquito net from his bed, where he lay in a drunken stupor. The Lord has used a woman to kill him. 16 As the Lord lives, I swear that Holofernes never touched me, although my beauty deceived him and brought him to his ruin. I was not defiled or disgraced; the Lord took care of me through it all."

17 Everyone in the city was utterly amazed. They bowed down and worshipped God, praying together, "Our God, you are worthy of great praise. Today you have triumphed over the enemies of your people."

18 Then Uzziah said, "Judith, my dear, the Most High God has blessed you more than any other woman on earth. How worthy of praise is the Lord God who created heaven and earth! He guided you as you cut off the head of our deadliest enemy. 19 Your trust in God will never be forgotten by those who tell of God's power. 20 May God give you everlasting honour for what you have done. May he reward you with blessings, because you remained faithful to him and did not hesitate to risk your own life to relieve the oppression of your people."

All the people replied, "Amen, amen!"

Judith's Plan

14 Then Judith said to them, "My friends, please follow my advice. In the morning, take this head and hang it on the town wall. 2 Appoint a leader for yourselves, and at sunrise get all your able-bodied men to take their weapons and march out of the town with him, as if they were going down into the valley to attack the Assyrian outpost. 3 The

Assyrian guards will grab their weapons and rush back to camp to wake up their officers. The officers will run to Holofernes' tent but will not find him, and the whole army will be terrified and retreat as you advance against them. 4 Then you and all the other Israelites will be able to follow them and kill them as they retreat. 5 But before you do any of this, send Achior the Ammonite to me. I want to see if he recognizes Holofernes, the man who spoke of Israel with contempt and sent Achior to us, thinking he would be killed along with the rest of us."

Achior's Conversion

6 So they called Achior from Uzziah's house. But when he came and saw the head of Holofernes in the hands of one of the men, Achior fainted and fell to the floor. 7 When they had helped him up, Achior bowed at Judith's feet in respect. "May every family in the land of Judah praise you," he said, "and may every nation tremble with terror when they hear your name. 8 Please tell me how you managed to do this."

While all the people were gathered round, Judith told him everything that she had done from the day she left the town until that moment. 9 When she had finished her story, the people cheered so loudly that the whole town echoed with sounds of joy. 10 When Achior heard all that the God of Israel had done, he became a firm believer. He was circumcised and made a member of the Israelite community, as his descendants are to the present day.

Panic in Holofernes' Camp

11 The next morning the Israelites hung the head of Holofernes on the wall of the town. All of them took up their weapons and went out in companies to the slopes in front of the town. 12 When the Assyrians saw what was happening, they sent word to their officers, and these reported the matter to their superiors. 13 These men then went to Holofernes' tent and said to Bagoas, "Wake up the general! Those worthless Israelites have dared to come down from the mountain to attack us; they are just asking to be destroyed."

14 Bagoas went in and clapped his hands in front of the sleeping quarters of the tent, thinking that Holofernes was in bed with Judith. 15 When there was no

13.18: Judg 5.24; Lk 1.28,42

answer, he drew the curtain aside and went in, and there he found the headless body sprawled over a footstool. [16] Bagoas let out a yell. He screamed, tore his clothes, and started groaning and weeping. [17] He went into the tent where Judith had stayed, but of course he did not find her. He rushed out and shouted to the officers, [18] "They have tricked us! One Israelite woman has disgraced Nebuchadnezzar's whole kingdom. Look in there! Holofernes is lying dead on the ground and his head is gone!" [19] When the officers heard this, they tore their clothes in grief; and as the panic spread, wild cries and shouts were heard throughout the camp.

Israel's Victory

15 When the soldiers heard what had happened, they were horrified [2] and began to tremble with fear. They all scattered in different directions from the camp, making no effort to stay together as they tried to escape along the paths in the mountains and valleys. [3] The soldiers who had camped in the mountains round Bethulia also began to retreat. Then all the Israelite soldiers came charging down on them.

4 Uzziah sent messengers to the towns of Betomesthaim, Bebai, Choba, and Kola, and throughout the land of Israel to tell everyone what had happened and to urge them to join in pursuing and destroying the enemy. [5] When they received the message, they all attacked the Assyrians and chased them as far as Choba, slaughtering them as they went. Even the people of Jerusalem and others living in the mountains joined the attack when the messengers told them what had happened in the Assyrian camp. The people of the regions of Gilead and Galilee blocked the path of the retreating Assyrians and inflicted heavy losses on them. They pursued them as far as the region round Damascus.

6 The rest of the people in Bethulia went down to the Assyrian camp, plundered it and carried away enough loot to make themselves very rich. [7] When the Israelite soldiers returned from the slaughter, they helped themselves to what was left. There was so much of it that the people of the towns and villages in the hill-country also shared in the loot.

Israel Celebrates the Victory

8 The High Priest Joakim and the Council of Israel came from Jerusalem to see for themselves what great things the Lord had done for his people and to

You are...the heroine of Israel (15.9)

meet Judith and congratulate her. [9] When they arrived, they all praised her, "You are Jerusalem's crowning glory, the heroine of Israel, the pride and joy of our people! [10] You have won this great victory for Israel by yourself. God, the Almighty, is pleased with what you have done. May he bless you as long as you live."

All the people responded, "Amen."

11 It took the people thirty days to finish looting the camp of the Assyrians. Judith was given Holofernes' tent, all his silver, his bowls, his couches, and all his furniture. She took them and loaded as much as she could on her mule; then she brought her waggons and loaded them too. [12] All the Israelite women came to see her; they sang her praises and danced in her honour. On this joyful occasion Judith and the other women waved ivy-covered branches [13] and wore wreaths of olive leaves on their heads. Judith took her place at the head of the procession to lead the women as they danced. All the men of Israel followed, wearing wreaths of flowers on their heads, carrying their weapons, and singing songs of praise.

Judith's Song of Praise

16 Then Judith sang a song of thanksgiving there with all Israel present, and the people joined in this song of praise. [2] She sang,

"Praise my God and sing to him;

praise the Lord with drums and
   cymbals;
   play a new song for him.
Praise him and call on him for help.
3 The Lord is a warrior who ends war.
   He rescued me from my pursuers
   and brought me back to his people's
      camp.
4 Down from the mountains of the north
      came the Assyrians,
   with their tens of thousands of
      soldiers.
Their troops blocked the rivers in the
      valleys;
   their cavalry covered the mountains.
5 They threatened to set fire to our
      country,
   slaughter our young men,
   dash our babies to the ground,
   take our children away as captives,
   and carry off all our young women.
6 But the Lord Almighty tricked them;
   he used a woman to stop them.
7 Their hero was not slain by young
      soldiers
   or attacked and killed by mighty
      giants.
It was Judith, the daughter of Merari,
   who brought him down with her
      beauty.
8 She gave victory to the oppressed
      people of Israel,
   when she took off her widow's clothes,
   and put on a linen dress to entice
      him.
She put on her rich perfumes
   and tied a ribbon round her hair.
9 Her dainty sandal caught his eye;
   her beauty captured his heart.
Then the sword slashed through his
      neck.
10 The Persians trembled at her daring;
   the Medes were amazed at her
      bravery.
11 Then our people shouted in victory.
   They had been weak and oppressed,
   but they forced the enemy to retreat
      in panic and fear.
12 We are descendants of slaves,
   but our enemies turned and ran;
   we killed them like runaway slaves.
They were destroyed by the army of
      the Lord.

13 "I will sing a new song to my God.
   O Lord, you are strong and glorious!
   You have never been defeated.

14 Let all your creatures serve you.
   You gave the command,
   and all of them came into being;
   you breathed on them,
   and all of them were created.
   No one can oppose your command.
15 The mountains and the seas tremble,
   and rocks melt like wax when you
      come near.
But there is mercy for all who obey
      you.
16 The Lord is more pleased with those
      who obey him
   than with all the choice meat on the
      altar,
   or with all the most fragrant sacrifices.
17 The nations who rise up against my
      people are doomed.
   The Lord Almighty will punish them
      on Judgement Day.
   He will send fire and worms to devour
      their bodies,
   and they will weep in pain for ever."

Judith's Fame

18 When the people arrived in
Jerusalem, they purified themselves and
worshipped God. They presented their
burnt-offerings, freewill offerings, and
gifts. 19 Judith dedicated to God all
Holofernes' property, which the people
had given to her. And as a special offering
in fulfilment of a vow, she presented to the
Lord the mosquito net which she had
taken from Holofernes' bed. 20 For three
months the people continued to celebrate
in front of the Temple in Jerusalem, and
Judith stayed there with them.

21 When the celebrations had ended,
everyone returned home, and Judith went
back to Bethulia to live on her own estate.
For the rest of her life she was famous
throughout the land of Israel. 22 Many men
wanted to marry her, but she never
remarried after the death of her husband
Manasseh. 23-24 Her fame continued to
spread, and she lived in the house her
husband had left her. Before she died,
Judith divided her property among her
husband's and her own close relatives and
set her slave-woman free. When she died
in Bethulia at the age of 105, she was
buried beside her husband, and the people
of Israel mourned her death for seven
days. 25 As long as Judith lived, and for
many years after her death, no one dared
to threaten the people of Israel.

16.13: Ps 144.9   **16.16:** Is 15.22; Ps 51.16,17; Hos 6.6

THE BOOK OF

ESTHER

(THE GREEK VERSION)

INTRODUCTION

The book of *Esther* in Greek is a translation, adaptation, and expansion of the book of *Esther* in Hebrew. The chain of events is much the same, but there are many variations in text, including different proper names and a strong religious tone. The six additions, shown as Chapters A-F in this translation, provide a different introduction and conclusion, introduce documents in an official style, and emphasize the religious elements by the addition of prayers and accounts of how they were answered.

Outline of Contents

Esther becomes queen   A.1—2.23
Haman's plot against the Jews   3.1—5.14
Haman is put to death   6.1—7.10
The Jews defeat their enemies   8.1—F.10
Postscript

Mordecai's Strange Dream

A ^{a1-3} Mordecai, a Jew who belonged to the tribe of Benjamin, was taken into exile, along with King Jehoiachin of Judah, when King Nebuchadnezzar of Babylonia captured Jerusalem. Mordecai was the son of Jair, a descendant of Kish and Shimei. He now lived in the Persian city of Susa, where he was an important official in the royal court of Xerxes the great king.

During the second year of Xerxes' reign, on the first day of the month of Nisan, Mordecai had a dream. ⁴ He dreamt that there was great noise and confusion, loud thunder, and an earthquake, with terrible turmoil on the earth. ⁵ Then two huge dragons appeared, ready to fight each other. ⁶ They made a dreadful noise, and all the nations got ready to make war against God's nation of righteous people. ⁷ For the world it was a day of darkness and gloom, trouble and distress, destruction and ruin. ⁸ All God's righteous people were troubled, in great fear of what was about to happen to them. They prepared for death, ⁹ but they cried out to God for help. In the dream their prayer was answered by a great river which came flowing out of a small spring. ¹⁰ The day dawned, the sun rose, and the humble people were made strong and destroyed their arrogant enemies.

¹¹ Mordecai woke up from this dream in which he saw what God planned to do. He thought about it all day and tried to understand what it meant.

Mordecai Saves the King's Life

¹² While Mordecai was resting in the courtyard of the palace, where two of the king's eunuchs, Gabatha and Tharra, were on guard, ¹³ he overheard them plotting together. He listened carefully to what

---

^a *Chapter A 1-17 corresponds to Chapter 11.2—12.6 in a number of English translations.*
A.1-3: 2 Kgs 24.10-16

*He overheard them plotting together
(A.13)*

they were saying and learnt that they were making plans to kill the king. So Mordecai went to King Xerxes and told him about the plot of the two eunuchs. ¹⁴The king had them questioned, and when they confessed, they were led away and executed.

15 The king ordered an account of this to be written in the official records, and Mordecai also wrote an account of it. ¹⁶Then the king appointed Mordecai to a position at court and gave him many gifts as a reward for what he had done.

17 But Haman son of Hammedatha, a Bougaean who was respected by the king, tried to cause trouble for Mordecai and his people the Jews, because Mordecai had been responsible for the death of the two eunuchs.

Queen Vashti Defies King Xerxes

1 ¹⁻²These things happened in the time of King Xerxes, who ruled over 127 provinces, all the way from India to Sudan, from his royal throne in Susa, Persia's capital city. ³In the third year of his reign, the king gave a banquet for all his advisers, the representatives of other countries, the noblemen from Persia and Media, and the governors of the provinces. ⁴For six whole months he made a show of the riches of the imperial court

with magnificent and expensive celebrations.

5 After the feast ᵇ the king gave a banquet for the people of other nations who were in the city. It lasted a week and was held in the palace courtyard, ⁶which was decorated with linen and cotton curtains, held by cords of purple linen attached to silver and gold blocks on marble and stone columns. Couches made of gold and silver had been placed in the courtyard, which was paved with green and white marble and mother-of-pearl. The couches were spread with a fine, thin fabric of many colours, with roses round the edges. ⁷There were gold and silver cups, and one of them, decorated with jewels worth more than a thousand metric tons of silver, had been set out for display. There was plenty of good wine from the king's own supply. ⁸There were no limits on the drinks. The king had given orders to the palace servants that they should provide him and his guests with as much as they wanted.

9 Meanwhile, inside the royal palace Queen Vashti was giving a banquet for the women.

10 On the seventh day of his banquet the king was feeling happy, so he called in the seven eunuchs who were his personal servants, Haman, Bazan, Tharra, Boraze, Zatholta, Abataza, and Tharaba. ¹¹He ordered them to bring in the queen, so that he could place the royal crown on her head and show her off to the officials and all his guests, for she was a beautiful woman. ¹²But Queen Vashti refused to obey and would not come with the servants. This embarrassed the king and made him furious.

13 He told his advisers about Vashti's reply and asked them to give a legal opinion about what he should do. ¹⁴⁻¹⁵Three of them, who were closest to the king and held the highest offices, came and told him what the law required and what should be done to Queen Vashti for disobeying the command he had given her through his servants. They were Arkesaeus, Sarsathaeus, and Malesear, officials of Persia and Media.

16 Then the king told his officials and the governors of Media and Persia how the queen had defied him. So Muchaeus said to the king and everyone present: "Queen Vashti has insulted not only you but all of us as well. ¹⁷⁻¹⁸As soon as our

---

ᵇfeast; *some manuscripts have* wedding feast.
1.1–2: Ezra 4.6

wives hear what the queen has done, they will be bold enough to defy their husbands and treat them with disrespect in the same way that Vashti has treated you. ¹⁹ If, then, it please Your Majesty, issue a royal proclamation that Vashti may never again appear before the king. Let it be written into the laws of Media and Persia. Then give her place as queen to some better woman. There is no other way. ²⁰ When your proclamation is made known all over this empire, then every woman will treat her husband with proper respect, whether he is rich or poor."

21 The king and his officials liked this idea, and the king did as Muchaeus suggested. ²² To each of the royal provinces he sent a message in the language of that province, saying that every husband must be respected in his own home.

Esther Becomes Queen

2 Later the king's anger cooled down. Although he no longer mentioned Vashti, he kept thinking of how he had condemned her. ² So some of the king's advisers suggested, "Why don't you make a search to find some beautiful young girls of good character? ³ You can appoint officials in every province of the empire and get them to bring all these beautiful young virgins to your harem here in Susa. Put them in the care of Hegai, the eunuch who is in charge of your women, and let them be given cosmetics and whatever else they may need. ⁴ Then take the girl you like best and make her queen in Vashti's place."

The king thought this was good advice, so he followed it.

5 There in Susa lived a Jew named Mordecai son of Jair; he belonged to the tribe of Benjamin and was a descendant of Kish and Shimei. ⁶ He was among the captives whom King Nebuchadnezzar of Babylonia had taken into exile from Jerusalem. ⁷ Mordecai was the guardian of Esther, the daughter of his uncle Aminadab. She was a beautiful girl, and after the death of her parents, Mordecai brought her up until she was of age. ᶜ

8 When the king had issued his new proclamation, many girls were being brought to Susa, and Esther was among them. She too was put in the royal palace in the care of Hegai, who had charge of the harem. ⁹ Hegai liked Esther, and she

won his favour. He lost no time in beginning her beauty treatment of massage and special diet. He assigned seven girls specially chosen from the royal palace to serve her, and he treated her and her servants well.

10 Now, on the advice of Mordecai, Esther had kept secret the fact that she was Jewish. ¹¹ Every day Mordecai would walk to and fro in front of the courtyard of the harem, watching to see what was going to happen to her.

12 The regular beauty treatment for the young women lasted a year: massages with oil of myrrh for six months and with beauty creams and cosmetics for six more. ¹³ After that, each girl was handed over to the person appointed to conduct her from the harem to the palace, and she was taken to the king. ¹⁴ She would go there in the evening, and the next morning she would be taken to another harem and put in the care of Hegai, the eunuch in charge. She would not go to the king again unless he asked for her by name.

15 The time came for Esther, the daughter of Aminadab the uncle of Mordecai, to go to the king. She had done everything that Hegai had advised, and she was admired by everyone who saw her. ¹⁶ So in Xerxes' seventh year as king, in the twelfth month, the month of Adar, she was brought to the king. ¹⁷ He fell in love with Esther, who pleased him more than any of the others, and he placed the queen's crown on her head. ¹⁸ Then the king gave a week-long banquet for all his advisers and administrators to celebrate his marriage to Esther. He also granted a reduction of taxes for the whole empire.

Mordecai Saves the King's Life

19 Meanwhile Mordecai had been appointed to a high administrative position. ²⁰ As for Esther, she had still not let it be known that she was Jewish. Mordecai had told her not to tell anyone, and she obeyed him in this, just as she had obeyed him when she was a little girl under his care. She continued to worship God and carry out God's commands, without abandoning her Jewish ways.

21 When the king promoted Mordecai to a higher position, the two palace eunuchs who were officers of the king's bodyguard became angry and plotted to assassinate the king. ²² Mordecai learnt

---

ᶜ until she was of age *or* and planned to marry her.
2.6: 2 Kgs 24.10–16; 2 Chr 36.10

The regular beauty treatment...lasted a year (2.12)

about it and told Queen Esther, who then told the king the details of the plot. ²³ The king had the two men questioned, and both men were hanged. To honour Mordecai, the king ordered an account of this to be written down in the royal records, so that his valuable service would be remembered.

Haman Plots to Destroy the Jews

3 Some time later King Xerxes honoured a man named Haman son of Hammedatha, a Bougaean, by promoting him to the position of prime minister. ² The king ordered all the officials in his service to show their respect for Haman by bowing to him. They all did so, except Mordecai, who refused to bow to Haman. ³ The other officials in the royal service asked him why he was disobeying the king's command. ⁴ Day after day they urged him to give in, but he would not listen to them. "I am a Jew," he explained, "and I cannot bow to Haman." So they told Haman how Mordecai was defying the king's orders. ⁵ Haman was furious when he realized that Mordecai was not going to bow to him, ⁶ and so he made plans to kill every Jew in the whole Persian Empire.

⁷ In the twelfth year of King Xerxes' reign, Haman ordered the lots to be cast to find out the right day and month to destroy the Jews, all in a single day. The fourteenth day of the month of Adar was the date chosen.

⁸ So Haman told the king, "There is a certain race of people scattered among the nations all over your empire. They observe customs that are not like those of any other people. Moreover, they do not obey the laws of the empire, so it is not in your best interest to tolerate them. ⁹ If it please Your Majesty, issue a decree that they are to be put to death. If you do this, I promise to put 340 metric tons of silver into the royal treasury."

¹⁰ The king took off his ring, which was used to stamp official proclamations, and gave it to Haman to seal the decree that was to be written against the Jews. ¹¹ The king told him, "Keep the money, and do whatever you want with that race of people."

¹² So on the thirteenth day of the first month, Haman called the king's secretaries and dictated a proclamation to be translated into every language in the empire and to be sent to all rulers and governors. It was issued in the name of King Xerxes and sent to all the 127 provinces, which stretched from India to Sudan. ¹³ Runners took this proclamation to every province of the empire. It

contained the instructions that on a single day in the twelfth month, the month of Adar, all Jews were to be killed and their belongings confiscated. *d*

Xerxes' Proclamation against the Jews

B *e*This is a copy of the decree: "King Xerxes the Great sends the following decree to the governors of his 127 provinces, from India to Sudan, and to their subordinate officials:

2 "After I became ruler of many nations and master of the whole world, I resolved that my subjects should always live at peace. I wanted this, not because of pride in my power but because I was always reasonable and governed my subjects with kindness. I determined to renew the peace that everyone longs for and to do what was necessary to create a civilized kingdom, safe for travel from one border to another.

3 "I asked my advisers how to accomplish this goal, and Haman made a suggestion. He is distinguished among us as a man of great wisdom, and at all times he has demonstrated his concern for the welfare of the kingdom. Because of his unfailing loyalty, he has been raised to the second highest position in the empire. *4*Recently Haman told us about a certain unruly people scattered among all the other peoples of the empire. He explained to us that these people have their own laws, are opposed to every other nation, and constantly ignore royal commands. As a result of their attitude, we are not able to establish the kind of unified government which we earnestly intend for the empire.

5 "These people are hostile to our government and commit terrible crimes which threaten the security of the empire. They follow strange customs, obey their own laws, and stand alone in their constant opposition to all mankind. *6*In the light of these facts, we recommend the slaughter of the people referred to by Haman, our prime minister. All of them, including women and children, must be put to death; no one is to be spared. They are our enemies; we will show them no pity. This order is to be carried out this year on the fourteenth day of the twelfth month, the month of Adar. *7*These people, who have caused so

much trouble for so long, will all die a violent death in a single day. From then on, our government will be secure and stable."

3 *14*The contents of the proclamation were made public in every province, and everyone was ordered to be prepared for that day.

15 The decree was also rapidly made public in the capital city of Susa. And while the king and Haman got drunk, the city of Susa was thrown into confusion.

Mordecai Asks for Esther's Help

4 When Mordecai learnt of all that had been done, he tore his clothes in anguish. Then he dressed in sackcloth, covered his head with ashes, and ran through the city crying loudly, "An innocent nation is being destroyed!" *2*When he came to the entrance of the palace, he stopped. He did not go in because no one covered in sackcloth and ashes was allowed inside. *3*Throughout all the provinces, wherever the king's proclamation was made known, there was loud mourning among the Jews. They wept, wailed, and put on sackcloth and ashes.

4 When Esther's servant girls and eunuchs told her what Mordecai was doing, she was deeply disturbed. She sent Mordecai some clothes to put on instead of the sackcloth, but he would not accept them. *5*Then she called Hathach, one of the palace eunuchs appointed as her servant, and told him to go to Mordecai and get the details of what was happening. *f* *7*Mordecai told him everything that had happened and how Haman had promised to put 340 metric tons of silver into the royal treasury if all the Jews were killed. *8*He gave Hathach a copy of the proclamation that had been issued in Susa, ordering the destruction of the Jews. Mordecai asked him to take it to Esther so that she might go and plead with the king and beg him to have mercy on her people. "Tell her," he said, "to remember the days when she was just an ordinary person being brought up under my care. Now, since Haman, the king's prime minister, has spoken against us and demands our death, she must pray to the Lord and then speak to the king about us. She must save us from death."

---

d Chapter 3 continues after Chapter B.
e Chapter B 1–7 corresponds to Chapter 13.1–7 in a number of English translations.
f Some manuscripts add verse 6: Hathach went to Mordecai in the city square at the entrance to the palace.

9 So Hathach did this, 10 and Esther gave him this message to take back to Mordecai: 11 "If anyone, man or woman, goes to the inner courtyard and sees the king without being summoned, that person will be sentenced to death. Everyone in the empire knows that. Only if the king holds out his gold sceptre to him can his life be spared. But it has been a month now since the king has sent for me."

12 When Mordecai received Esther's message, 13 he sent her this warning: "Esther, don't imagine that you are safer than any of the other Jews in the empire. 14 If you keep quiet at a time like this, help will come to the Jews in some other way and they will be saved, but you will die and your father's family will come to an end. Yet, who knows? Maybe it was for a time like this that you were made queen!"

15 Esther sent Mordecai this reply: 16 "Go and gather all the Jews in Susa together; hold a fast and pray for me. Don't eat or drink anything for three days and nights. My servant girls and I will be doing the same. After that, I will go to the king, even though it is against the law. If I must die for doing it, I will die."

17 Mordecai then left and did everything that Esther had told him to do.

Mordecai's Prayer

C gMordecai prayed to the Lord, calling to mind what the Lord had done in the past: 2 "O Lord, you are the Lord and King of all creation, and everything obeys your commands. If you wish to save Israel, no one can stop you. 3 You made heaven and earth and all the wonderful things on earth. 4 You are the Lord of all, and there is no one who can stand against you. 5 You know all things. You know, Lord, that when I refused to bow to that arrogant Haman, it was not because I was arrogant or trying to impress people. 6-7 I simply did not want to honour any man more than I honour God. I refuse to bow to anyone but you, my Lord; and this is not because of pride. If it would help to save Israel, I would be willing even to kiss the soles of his feet.

8-9 "And now, O Lord, God and King, God of Abraham, spare your people; save us from our enemies. They are determined

to destroy us; they are looking for a chance. Long ago you chose us to be your people and rescued us from the land of Egypt. Do not abandon us now. 10 We are your chosen people, so listen to my prayer and be gracious to us. Turn our misfortune into joy so that we may live to sing your praises. Save us from death so that we can keep on praising you."

11 And all the people of Israel prayed loudly and earnestly because they were sure that they were going to die.

Esther's Prayer

12 Queen Esther, in deep agony, turned

Esther's prayer (C.12)

to the Lord. 13 She took off her splendid robes and put on garments of mourning and grief. Instead of her rich perfumes, she put ashes and dung on her head. She did all she could to destroy any dignity in her appearance. She let her tangled and uncombed hair hang down over her body that she had always taken such care to beautify. 14 She prayed to the Lord God of Israel, "My Lord and King, only you are God. I am all alone, and I have no one to turn to but you. Help me! 15 I am about to risk my life. 16 O Lord, as long as I can remember, my family has told me how you chose Israel from all the nations and how in ancient times you singled out our ancestors to be your people for ever. You have kept all your promises to them.

17 "But we sinned against you. You

---

g Chapter C 1–30 corresponds to Chapter 13.8—14.19 in a number of English translations.
C.8–9: Ex 3.6

handed us over to our enemies because we worshipped their gods. [18] We deserved your punishment, O Lord. [19] But our enemies are no longer satisfied just to see us in slavery. They have made a solemn promise to their idols [20] not only to destroy the people who praise you, but to do away with your Law and to remove for ever the glory of your house and altar. [21] They want the whole world to praise worthless idols and stand in awe of mortal kings for ever.

[22] "Lord, these gods are nothing; do not surrender your power to them or give our enemies the chance to laugh at our downfall. Instead, turn their evil plans against them, and make an example of that man who first planned our destruction.

[23] "Remember us, O Lord. Come to us in this time of trouble. Give me courage, King of all gods and Ruler over all earthly powers. [24] Give me the right words to say when I go in to face Xerxes, that savage lion. Change his heart so that he will turn against Haman, our enemy, and destroy him and his gang. [25] Come to our rescue, O Lord. Help me; I am all alone, and I have no one to turn to but you.

[26] "You know everything, Lord. You know that I hate the honour I receive from these Gentiles. I detest the thought of having sex with any of these uncircumcised heathen. [27] But you know that I have no choice. I hate the crown I have to wear as queen on official occasions. I never wear it unless I have to; it's as disgusting as last month's rag. [28] I refuse to eat at Haman's table or honour the king by attending his parties, and I have never drunk any of the wine dedicated to his gods. [29] Since I came here, the only thing that has brought me joy is my worship of you, Lord God of Abraham.

[30] "Almighty God, listen to the prayer of your people. Rescue us from these evil men, and take away my fear."

Esther Goes to the King

D [h] Queen Esther prayed for three days. Then she took off the clothes she had been wearing and put on her splendid robes again. [2-3] In all her royal splendour, she prayed again to her God and saviour, who sees everything. Walking like a queen, she left her room accompanied by two servant girls, one of

them escorting her by the arm and [4] the other holding up the train of her robe. [5] Queen Esther's face was radiantly beautiful. She looked as cheerful as she was lovely, but in her heart she was terror-stricken. [6] She passed through all the doors and entered the throne room, where she stood before the king. He was seated on his royal throne, dressed in his glorious robes, which were covered with gold and precious jewels. It was an awe-inspiring sight. [7] His face glowed with splendour, but when he saw Esther, he stared at her with fierce anger. She grew weak and turned pale; she almost fainted and had to lean her head on her attendant's shoulder.

[8] But God changed the king's anger into tender concern. He quickly rose from his throne and took her in his arms until she was able to stand. He calmed her with comforting words. [9] "What is it, Esther?" he said to her. "I am your husband. There's no need to be afraid. [10] Our law applies only to ordinary people; you will not die. [11] Come here to me." [12] He lifted his gold sceptre and touched her on the neck with it. Then he kissed her and said, "Tell me what you want."

[13] "When I looked at you, my lord, I thought I was seeing an angel of God," the queen answered, "and I was overcome by your awesome majesty. [14] You are so marvellous and your face is so full of kindness."

[15] But while she was speaking, she fainted again. [16] The king was concerned about her, and all his attendants tried to revive her.

Esther Invites the King and Haman to a Banquet

5 [i3] "What is it, Esther?" the king asked. "Tell me what you want, and you shall have it—even if it is half my empire."

[4] Esther replied, "Today is a special day for me. If it please my lord, I would like you and Haman to be my guests tonight at a banquet I am preparing for you."

[5] The king then ordered Haman to come quickly, so that they could be Esther's guests. So the king and Haman went to Esther's banquet. [6] Over the wine the king again said to her, "Tell me what you want, Queen Esther."

[7] Esther replied, [8] "If my lord is kind

---

[h] *Chapter D 1–16 corresponds to Chapter 15.1–16 in a number of English translations.*
[i] *In Greek, Chapter D replaces verses 1 and 2 in Hebrew.*
C.24–25: Jdt 9.13   **C.28:** Dan 1.8; Jdt 12.2   **5.3:** Mk 6.23

enough to grant my request, I would like you and Haman to be my guests tomorrow at another banquet that I will prepare for you. It will be just like this one."

Haman Plots to Kill Mordecai

9 When Haman left the king he was happy and in a good mood, until he saw Mordecai the Jew in the courtyard of the palace. That made him furious, 10 but he went home. Then he invited his friends to his house and asked his wife Zeresh to join them. 11 He boasted to them about how rich he was and about the honour the king had paid him when he promoted him to high office and made him prime minister. 12 "What is more," Haman said, "Queen Esther gave a banquet for no one but the king and me, and we are invited back tomorrow. 13 But none of this means a thing to me as long as I see that Jew Mordecai sitting in the courtyard of the palace."

14 Then his wife and all his friends suggested, "Why don't you have a gallows put up, twenty-two metres high? Tomorrow morning you can ask the king to have Mordecai hanged on it, and then you can go with the king to the banquet and enjoy yourself." Haman thought it was a good idea, so he had the gallows built.

The King Honours Mordecai

6 That night the Lord kept the king from sleeping, so the king ordered his private secretary to bring the official records of the empire and read them to him. 2 He read the account of how Mordecai had uncovered a plot to assassinate the king—the plot made by the two eunuchs who served as palace guards. 3 The king asked, "How have we honoured and rewarded Mordecai for this?"

His servants answered, "You have done nothing for him."

4 Now just as the king was inquiring about Mordecai's good deed, Haman entered the courtyard. He had come to ask the king to have Mordecai hanged on the gallows that was now ready.

"Who is that in the courtyard?" the king asked.

5 The servants answered, "It is Haman; he is waiting to see you."

"Show him in," said the king.

6 So Haman came in, and the king said to him, "There is someone I wish very

much to honour. What should I do for this man?"

Haman thought to himself, "Now who could the king want to honour so much? Me, of course."

7-8 So he answered the king, "Let the royal servants bring a fine linen robe for this man—one that you yourself wear. And let them bring a horse that you yourself ride. 9 Then get one of your highest noblemen to put that robe on the man you like so much and then get the nobleman to lead him, mounted on the horse, through the city square. Let the nobleman announce as they go: 'See how the king rewards a man whom he wishes to honour!' "

10 Then the king said to Haman, "Fine! Do all that for Mordecai the Jew, who holds a high position in the palace; don't leave out anything."

11 So Haman got the robe and the horse, and he put the robe on Mordecai. Mordecai got on the horse, and Haman led him through the city square, announcing to the people as they went: "See how the king rewards a man whom he wishes to honour!"

12 Mordecai then went back to the courtyard while Haman hurried home, covering his face in embarrassment. 13 He told his wife and all his friends everything that had happened to him. Then they all said to him, "You are beginning to lose power to Mordecai. He is a Jew, and you cannot overcome him. He will certainly defeat you, for the living God is with him!"

Haman Is Put Death

14 While they were still talking, the palace eunuchs arrived to take Haman to Esther's banquet.

7 And so the king and Haman went to eat with Esther 2 for a second time. Over the wine the king asked her again, "Now, Queen Esther, what do you want? Tell me and you shall have it. I'll even give you half the empire."

3 Queen Esther answered, "If it please Your Majesty to grant my humble request, my wish is that I may live and that my people may live. 4 My people and I have been sold into slavery; our possessions have been plundered, and now we are to be destroyed—all of us, including our children, will be slaves—and so far I have kept quiet. It isn't right that our enemy should be a member of the royal court."

5 Then King Xerxes asked Esther, "Who dares to do such a thing?"

Our enemy is this evil man Haman! (7.6)

6 Esther answered, "Our enemy is this evil man Haman!"

In terror Haman faced the king and queen. 7 The king got up from the table and went outside to the palace gardens. Haman could see that he was in a dangerous situation, so he stayed behind to beg the queen for his life. 8 He had just thrown himself down on Esther's couch to beg for mercy, when the king came back into the room from the gardens. Seeing this, the king cried out, "Are you going to rape my wife here in my own palace?"

When Haman heard this, he turned away in despair. 9 Then one of the eunuchs, whose name was Bougathan, said, "Haman has even gone so far as to build a gallows at his house so that he can hang Mordecai, who warned Your Majesty about the plot. And it's twenty-two metres high!"

"Hang Haman on it!" the king commanded.

10 So Haman was hanged on the gallows that he had built for Mordecai. Then the king's anger cooled down.

The Jews Are Told to Fight Back

8 That same day King Xerxes gave Queen Esther all the property of Haman, the enemy of the Jews. Esther told the king that Mordecai was related to her, and Mordecai was invited to enter the king's presence. 2 The king took off his ring with his seal on it (which he had

taken back from Haman) and gave it to Mordecai. Esther put Mordecai in charge of Haman's property.

3 Then Esther spoke to the king again, throwing herself at his feet. She begged him to do something to stop the evil plot that Haman had made against the Jews. 4 The king held out the gold sceptre to her, so she stood up 5 and said, "If it please Your Majesty and if you care about me, please issue a proclamation to prevent Haman's orders from being carried out— those orders he gave for the destruction of all the Jews in the empire. 6 How can I endure it if this disaster comes on my people? How can I go on living if my whole nation is destroyed?"

7 Then the king said to Esther, "I have hanged Haman for his plot against the Jews, and I have given you his property. If that is not enough, 8 you may write to the Jews whatever you like; and you may write it in my name and stamp it with the royal seal, for a proclamation issued in the king's name and stamped with the royal seal cannot be revoked."

9 On the twenty-third day of the first month, the month of Nisan, the king's secretaries were called and letters were written to the Jews and to the governors and administrators of all 127 provinces from India to Sudan. The letters were written to each province in its own language. 10 They were written in the name of the king and stamped with the

8.8: Dan 6.8

royal seal, and they were delivered by runners.

11 These letters explained that the king would allow the Jews in every city of the empire to live by their own laws and organize for self-defence. They were permitted to treat their opponents and enemies in any way they liked. 12 This decree was to take effect throughout the Persian Empire on the thirteenth day of Adar, the twelfth month.*j*

The King's Decree in Favour of the Jews

E *k*This is a copy of the decree: "Greetings from King Xerxes the Great to the governors of the 127 provinces, which extend from India to Sudan, and to all those who are loyal to us.

2 "Many men become increasingly arrogant when honours are given to them and favours are done for them. 3 They do not know what to do with so much good fortune, so they not only try to harm our subjects, but they even scheme against those who grant them favours. 4 They are never grateful for what people do for them, and they even think they can escape the judgement of God, who hates evil and sees everything. In their arrogance they listen to the flattery of ignorant, sinful men.

5 "It often happens also that friends who have been entrusted with administrative responsibilities exert pressure on those in authority. They make their leaders their partners in killing people and bring about misfortunes that can never be remedied. 6 These friends, by their lies and deceitful ways, take advantage of the good will of their rulers.

7 "You can see examples of this misuse of power not only in the stories that have been handed down to us from the past, but in the more recent outrageous things which have happened among you.

8 "I intend to make sure that in future my kingdom will remain untroubled and peaceful for all mankind. 9 This can be done by changing certain policies and by judging fairly each situation that comes to my attention.

10 "Consider, for example, the case of Haman son of Hammedatha, a Macedonian. He is a foreigner with no Persian blood and with no trace of my generosity; but I welcomed him, 11 and he received the benefit of my concern and love for all mankind. He was, in fact, proclaimed 'Father' of the empire and received more honour than anyone else, except the king.

12 "But his arrogance knew no limits, and he tried to murder me and take over the empire. 13 In his crafty and deceitful way, he asked that Mordecai be put to death—Mordecai, who once saved my life and who has always supported me. He even asked for the death of Esther, our blameless queen, and in fact, the death of all the Jewish people. 14 His purpose was to leave us helpless and to allow the Macedonians to take over the Persian Empire. 15 Even though this wicked criminal plotted to wipe out the Jews, I find that they are not traitors at all but are governed by very just laws. 16 They worship the living God, the highest and greatest God, who has kept our empire in its excellent condition from the time of our ancestors until our own day.

17 "Therefore I advise you not to carry out the instructions issued in the letters sent out by Haman. 18 He is the person responsible for all of this, and he has been hanged, along with his entire family, at the gates of Susa. God, who governs all things, has given him the speedy punishment that he deserved.

19 "I order you to post copies of this decree in every public place. Permit the Jews to live by their own customs, 20 and give them support when they defend themselves against those who attack them on the day set for their destruction, the thirteenth day of Adar, the twelfth month. 21 God, who governs all things, has turned that day of destruction into a day of celebration for his chosen people.

22 "Include this day among your national holidays and celebrate it as a festival. 23 Now and in the future it will remind us and all our allies of the way God watches over our nation, and those who plot against us will be reminded of God's threat of destruction.

24 "Every province, every city, without exception, which does not obey these orders will feel my anger. It will be destroyed in battle and burnt to the ground. No human being will ever go there again, and even the birds and wild animals will avoid it for ever.

8 *l*13 "Post copies of this decree where it can be clearly seen in every

---

*j Chapter 8 continues after Chapter E.
k Chapter E 1–24 corresponds to Chapter 16.1–24 in a number of English translations.
l Verses 1–12 precede Chapter E.*

Post copies of this decree...in every province (8.13)

Messengers on horses rode off (8.14)

province, so that all the Jews can be ready to fight their enemies when that day comes."

14 Messengers on horses rode off at top speed to carry out the orders of the king, and the decree was also made public in Susa.

15 Mordecai left the palace, wearing royal robes, a turban of fine purple linen, and a gold crown. When the people of Susa saw him, they cheered, 16 and the Jews were happy and joyful. 17 They held a joyful holiday with feasting and happiness in every city and province, wherever the king's proclamation was posted. In fact, many Gentiles were circumcised and became Jews, because they were now afraid of them.

The Jews Destroy Their Enemies

9 On the thirteenth day of Adar, the day on which the royal proclamation was to take effect, 2 it was the enemies of the Jews who were wiped out. People everywhere were afraid of the Jews, and no one could stand against them. 3 In fact, the provincial governors, the administrators, and the royal scribes showed respect for the Jews, because they were all afraid of Mordecai. 4-5 The royal decree had made his name known throughout the empire.

6 In Susa, the capital city itself, the Jews killed five hundred people 7-10 and

9.1: 1 Macc 7.49; 2 Macc 15.36

looted their property. Among them were the ten sons of Haman son of Hammedatha, a Bougaean, the enemy of the Jews: Pharsannestain, Delphon, Phasga, Pharadatha, Barea, Sarbacha, Marmasima, Arouphaeus, Arsaeus, and Zabouthaeus.

11 That same day the number of people killed in Susa was reported to the king. 12 He then said to Esther, "In Susa alone the Jews have killed five hundred people. What must they have done out in the provinces! Tell me what else you want, and you shall have it."

13 Esther answered, "Let the Jews in Susa do again tomorrow what they were allowed to do today. And order the bodies of Haman's ten sons to be hung up." 14 The king agreed, and permitted the Jews to put the bodies of Haman's ten sons on public display. 15 On the fourteenth day of Adar the Jews of Susa got together again and killed three hundred more people in the city. But they did no looting.

16 The Jews in the provinces also organized and defended themselves. They rid themselves of their enemies by killing 15,000 people on the thirteenth day of Adar, but they did no looting. 17 On the next day, the fourteenth, there was no more killing, and the Jews made it a joyful holiday of rest and feasting. 18 The Jews of Susa, however, made the fifteenth a holiday, since they had slaughtered their enemies on the thirteenth and fourteenth and did not stop until the fifteenth. 19 This is why Jews who live in small towns observe the fourteenth day of the month of Adar as a holiday, a time of giving gifts of food to one another, while the Jews in the large cities celebrate the holiday in the same way on the fifteenth.

The Festival of Purim

20 Mordecai had these events written down in a book and sent it to all the Jews, near and far, throughout the Persian Empire, 21 telling them to observe the fourteenth and fifteenth days of Adar as holidays. 22 These were the days on which the Jews had rid themselves of their enemies. The Jews were to observe the whole month as a holiday, for this was a month that had been turned from a time of grief and despair into a time of joy and happiness. They were told to observe these days with feasts and parties, giving gifts of food to friends and to the poor. 23 So the Jews accepted all that Mordecai had written.

24 Mordecai had recorded how Haman son of Hammedatha, the Macedonian, had fought against the Jewish people, how he had made a decree and cast lots to determine the day he would destroy them, 25 and how he had gone to the king to request that Mordecai be hanged. But Haman suffered the same fate he had planned for the Jews—he and his sons were hanged from the gallows. 26-28 Because of Mordecai's letter, because of all they had suffered, and because of all that had happened to them, the Jews accepted Mordecai's suggestion and made it a rule for themselves, their descendants, and anyone that might become a Jew, that these days should be properly observed as a memorial, generation after generation, in every city, province, and country. The Jews were to remember and observe these days of Purim for all time to come and never neglect them. (The holidays are called Purim because "purim" in their language is the word for "lots.")

29-30 Then Queen Esther, the daughter of Aminadab, along with Mordecai the Jew, wrote down what they had done, putting the queen's full authority behind the letter about Purim. 31 They both took responsibility for establishing the festival and made up their minds to observe it at all costs. m 32 Esther established the festival for ever, and a written record was made of her official decree.

The Greatness of Xerxes and Mordecai

10 King Xerxes imposed taxes on the people of the coastal regions of his empire as well as on those of the interior. 2 His power and virtue, as well as the wealth and splendour of his empire, are recorded in the official records of the kings of Persia and Media. 3 Mordecai was second in rank only to King Xerxes himself. He was a great man in the empire and was honoured by his fellow Jews. He was greatly loved, for he sought the welfare of his people.

Mordecai Remembers His Dream

F n Then Mordecai said, "God has caused all these things to happen! 2 And I am reminded of the dream I had about all this. Every detail of the dream has come true: 3 the small spring that became a river, the dawn that turned into sunlight, and the abundance of water. The river is Esther, whom the king married and made his queen. 4 The two dragons represent Haman and me. 5 The nations are all those who have gathered together to destroy the Jews. 6 My nation is Israel, which cried out to God for help and was saved. The Lord saved his people! He rescued us from all these evils and performed great miracles and wonders that have never happened among other nations. 7 That is because God prepared one destiny for his own people and another for all other nations. 8 Then came the day and the hour when these two destinies were to be decided; the time had come for God to make a decision about the nations. 9 God remembered his chosen people and gave the verdict in their favour. 10 So each year for all time to come God's people will gather together in his presence on the fourteenth and fifteenth of the month of Adar, and celebrate with joy and happiness."

Postscript

During the fourth year of the reign of Ptolemy and Cleopatra, a man named Dositheus, who claimed to be a levitical priest, brought the preceding letter about the Purim festival. He was accompanied by his son Ptolemy, and they declared that the letter was genuine and that it had been translated by Lysimachus, son of Ptolemy, a member of a Jerusalem family.

---

m at all costs; Greek unclear.
n Chapter F 1–10 corresponds to Chapter 10.4—11.1 in a number of English translations.
9.24–26: Esth 3.7

THE WISDOM
OF SOLOMON

INTRODUCTION

This book was originally written in Greek by an unknown Jewish author. The book makes use of traditional Jewish material, as well as ideas borrowed from Greek philosophy, in order to teach that God rewards those who are faithful to him.

Outline of Contents

Immortality for the righteous and punishment for the wicked   1.1—5.23
In praise of wisdom   6.1—9.18
Wisdom's protection of God's people and punishment of enemies   10.1—12.27
The foolishness of idolatry   13.1—15.13
Blessing and punishment when the Israelites left Egypt   15.14—19.22

The Search for Justice

1 Love justice, you rulers of the world. Set your minds sincerely on the Lord, and look for him with all honesty. ²Those who do not try to test him will find him; he will show himself to those who trust him. ³Dishonest thoughts separate people from God, and if we are foolish enough to test him, his power will put us to shame. ⁴Wisdom will never be at home with anyone who is deceitful or who is a slave of sin. ⁵Everyone who is holy has learnt to stay away from deceitful people. He will not stay around when foolish thoughts are being expressed; he will not feel comfortable when injustice is done.

God Is Aware of What We Say

6 Wisdom is a spirit that is friendly to people, but she will not forgive anyone who speaks against God, for God knows our feelings and thoughts, and hears our every word. ⁷Since the Lord's spirit fills the entire world, and holds everything in it together, she knows every word that people say. ⁸No one who speaks wickedly will escape notice; sooner or later he will receive just punishment. ⁹The intentions of ungodly people will be closely examined; their words will be reported to the Lord, and then they will get the punishment that their wickedness deserves. ¹⁰God will tolerate no challenge, and since he hears everything, you cannot hide your complaining from him. ¹¹So be sure that you do not go about complaining—it does no good—and don't engage in bitter talk. The most secret things you say will have their consequences, and lying will destroy your soul.

God Did Not Create Death

12 Do not bring on your own death by sinful actions. ¹³God did not invent death, and when living creatures die, it gives him

1.1: Wis 6.1–11   **1.13:** Ezek 18.32; 33.11; 2 Esd 3.7; 2 Pet 3.9

no pleasure. [14] He created everything so that it might continue to exist, and everything he created is wholesome and good. There is no deadly poison in it. No, death does not rule this world, [15] for God's justice does not die.

16 Ungodly people have brought death on themselves by the things they have said and done. They yearn for death as if it were a lover. They have gone into partnership with death, and it is just what they deserve.

Wicked Thinking

2 Wicked people are wrong when they say to themselves, "Our life is short and full of sorrow, and when its end comes, there is no escape. No one has ever been known to come back from the world of the dead. [2] We were born by chance, and after life is over, we will be as if we had never been born at all. Our breath is no more than a puff of smoke; our mind is nothing more than a spark thrown off by the beating of our heart. [3] When that spark dies, our body will crumble into ashes, and our breath will become part of the empty air. [4] In time, no one will remember anything we ever did, and even our names will be forgotten. Our lives will pass away like traces of clouds and vanish like mist in the heat of the sun. [5] Our time on earth is like a passing shadow. There is no escape from the day of our death; it is fixed, and no one can postpone it."

6 The wicked say, "Come on, then, let's enjoy the good things of life, and live in this world just as we did when we were young and free of care! [7] Let's drink the most expensive wines and use the finest perfumes. Let's not miss a single flower in the springtime! [8] Before the roses wither, let's pick them and wear them in our hair! [9] Let's all join in and leave signs everywhere of our carefree revelry! Life owes us that much!

10 "We'll oppress the poor, even if they are righteous. We'll show no respect for widows or old people. [11] We'll call ourselves right if we are strong enough to get what we want. No one ever got anywhere by being weak! [12] Righteous people are nothing but a nuisance, so let's look for chances to get rid of them. They are against what we do; they accuse us of breaking the Law of Moses and

violating the traditions of our ancestors. [13] They claim to know God, and they call themselves the Lord's children. [14] We can't stand the sight of people like that; what they are contradicts our whole way of thinking. [15] They are not like other people; they have strange ways. [16] They think that our moral standards are so corrupt that everything we do should be avoided. They boast of having God for their Father, and believe that only the righteous will die happy. [17] But we'll see if that's true! Let's see what will happen when it's time for them to die! [18] If the righteous really are God's children, God will save them from their enemies. [19] So let's put them to the test. We'll be cruel to them, and torment them; then we'll find out how calm and reasonable they are! We'll find out just how much they can stand! [20] We'll condemn them to a shameful death. After all, they say that God will protect them."

21 That is how evil people think, but they are wrong. They are blinded by their own wickedness. [22] They have never known God's secrets, never hoped for the rewards of a holy and blameless life. [23] When God created us, he did not intend that we should die; he made us like himself. [24] It was the Devil's jealousy that brought death into the world, and those who belong to the Devil are the ones who will die.

The Destiny of the Righteous

3 But righteous people are protected by God and will never suffer torment. [2] It is a foolish mistake to think that righteous people die and that their death is a terrible evil. [3] They leave us, but it is not a disaster. In fact, the righteous are at peace. [4] It might appear that they have suffered punishment, but they have the confident hope of immortality. [5-6] Their sufferings were light compared with the blessings they will receive. God has tested them, like gold in a furnace, and found them worthy to be with him. He has accepted them, just as he accepts the sacrifices which his worshippers burn on the altar.

7 When God comes to reward the righteous, they will blaze out against the wicked like fire in dry straw. [8] They will rule over nations and peoples, and the Lord will be their king for ever. [9] Those

1.16: Prov 8.36; Is 28.15; Sir 14.12   **2.6:** Is 22.13; 1 Cor 15.32   **2.23:** Gen 1.26-27
3.2: Wis 4.17   **3.5-6:** Rom 8.18; 2 Cor 4.17

who have put their trust in God will come to understand the truth of his ways. Those who have been faithful will live with him in his love, for he is kind and merciful to the ones whom he has chosen. [a]

The Destiny of the Wicked

10 The ungodly, however, will get the punishment their wicked thoughts deserve, because they rebelled against the Lord and ignored what was right. [b] 11 A man who has no use for wisdom or education has a miserable life in store for him. He has nothing to hope for. His labours are useless, and he will never accomplish anything worth while. 12 The woman he marries will turn out to be irresponsible, and his children will go wrong. 13 All his descendants will be under a curse.

The Importance of Virtue

On Judgement Day God will reward the woman who has never been able to have a child, provided she has not been guilty of adultery. Then she will be happy. 14 On that day, even the man who has been castrated will be rewarded with happiness, if he has kept the Law and has not stored up resentment against the Lord. Because he has been faithful, he will receive a special reward more precious than having children: a place in the Lord's

Wisdom is like a root that is alive and can always send up new shoots (3.15)

heavenly Temple. 15 Honest deeds are like a tree that bears marvellous fruit. Wisdom is like a root that is alive and can always send up new shoots.

16 But children born of adultery or of a forbidden union will die an early death. 17 Yet even if they do live a long time,

they will never amount to anything. They will not be respected in their old age, 18 and if they die young, they will have no hope or comfort on Judgement Day. 19 Children born of a forbidden union suffer a miserable fate.

4 It is better to have virtue, even if it means having no children. Your virtue will be recognized by other people and by God, and you will be remembered for it for ever. 2 Virtue provides an example for people to follow; when it is not there, they miss it. It has always been the finest prize a person can win, and it always will be so. It is the noblest of all the good qualities a person can have.

3 No matter how many children are born of a forbidden union, none of them will ever amount to anything. They are illegitimate; they can never lay a firm foundation for themselves, never take deep root. 4 Like trees with shallow roots, they put out leaves for a while, but they sway in the wind, and storms uproot them. 5 Their branches snap off before they mature; their fruit never ripens, and it is good for nothing. 6 On Judgement Day children born of a forbidden union will testify to the sin of their parents and act as witnesses against them.

7 Righteous people, however, will find rest, even if they die young. 8 We honour old age, but not just because a person has lived a long time. 9 Wisdom and righteousness are signs of the maturity that should come with old age.

The Example of Enoch

10 Once there was a man named Enoch who pleased God, and God loved him. While Enoch was still living among sinners, God took him away, 11 so that evil and falsehood could not corrupt his mind and soul. 12 (We all know that people can be so fascinated by evil that they cannot recognize what is good even when they are looking right at it. Innocent people can be so corrupted with desire that they can think of nothing but what they want.) 13 This man Enoch achieved in a few years' time a perfection that other people could never attain in a complete lifetime. 14 The Lord was pleased with Enoch's life and quickly took him out of this wicked world. People were aware of his departure but didn't understand. They never seemed to learn the lesson 15 that

[a] *Some manuscripts add* and he protects his own people *(see 4.15).*
[b] what was right; *or* righteous people.
4.1: Sir 16.3   **4.10–14:** Gen 5.21–24; Sir 44.16; Heb 11.5

This is the man we made fun of (5.4)

God is kind and merciful to his own people; he protects those whom he has chosen.

The Fate of the Wicked

16 Even when righteous people are dead and gone, they put to shame the wicked people who live on after them. In their old age the wicked will be disgraced by young people who have already achieved perfection. 17 The wise may die young, but the wicked will never understand that this is the Lord's way of taking them off to safety. 18 They make light of a wise person's death, but the Lord will soon be laughing at them. When they die, they will not be given an honourable burial. Even the dead will hold them in scorn and disgust for ever. 19 God will throw them to the ground and make them speechless. Like buildings shaken from their foundations, they will be reduced to piles of ruins. They will be in torment. People will soon forget all about them. 20 They will come in fear to the Judgement, where their sins will be counted; they will stand condemned by their own lawless actions.

The Regrets of the Wicked

5 On that day the righteous man, full of confidence, will stand before those who oppressed him and made light of his labours. 2 They will be amazed to see him safe and will tremble with terrible fear. 3 Then they will regret what they did, and groaning in anguish they will say to one another: 4 "This is the man we made fun of. We thought he was a joke. What fools we were! We thought he was mad to live in the way he did, and when he died, we didn't honour him. 5 And now here he is, one of God's own children, with a place of his own among God's people. 6 We were the ones who wandered off the right road. We never lived in the light of righteousness; we never caught the first glimmer of its light. 7 All our lives we wandered across unmarked deserts, instead of following the road which the Lord wanted us to travel. And this lawlessness led us to ruin. 8 We were so proud of ourselves—we bragged about how rich we were—and now, what good has it done us? 9 All those things are gone now; they have disappeared like a

shadow, like something you hear and then forget.

10 "A ship sails across the waves of the ocean, but when it is gone, it leaves no trace. You cannot tell it was ever there. [11] A bird flies through the air, but leaves no sign that it has been there. It speeds along, riding through the thin air by the force of its wings, leaving behind no trace of its passing. [12] An arrow splits the air when it is shot at a target, but at once the air closes up behind it, and no one can tell where it passed. [13] It is the same with us—we were born, and then we ceased to be. We left no sign of virtue behind us; we were destroyed by our wickedness."

14 What hope do wicked people have? Only the hope of straw blown about in the wind, the hope of ocean foam[c] that disappears in the storm, the hope of smoke in the breeze. Their hope lasts no longer than our memory of a guest who stays one day and leaves the next.

15 But the righteous live on for ever. The Lord will reward them; the Most High will protect them. [16] He will give them royal splendour and a magnificent crown. He will shield them with his powerful arm. [17] He will go out into battle determined to defeat his enemies, and use the creation itself as a weapon. [18] Righteousness will be his armour, genuine justice will be his helmet, [19] holiness will be his invincible shield. [20] He will sharpen his stern anger into a sword, and the forces of nature will join him in battle against those who are foolish enough to oppose him. [21] Bolts of lightning will strike right on target, as if the Lord had made a bow out of the clouds and was shooting arrows. [22] Hailstones will beat down on his enemies with terrible force. The oceans and rivers will come rushing over them in a devastating flood. [23] Great wind-storms will blow them away like straw. Lawlessness will be the ruin of the whole world. Evil actions will cause governments to fall.

The Responsibility of Rulers

6 So then, you kings, you rulers the world over, listen to what I say, and learn from it. [2] You govern many lands and are proud that so many people are under your rule, [3] but this authority has been given to you by the Lord Most High. He will examine what you have done and

what you plan to do. [4] You rule on behalf of God and his kingdom, and if you do not govern justly, if you do not uphold the law, if you do not live according to God's will, [5] you will suffer sudden and terrible punishment. Judgement is especially severe on those in power. [6] Common people may be mercifully forgiven for their wrongs, but those in power will face a severe judgement. [7] The Lord of all is not afraid of anyone, no matter how great he is. He himself made everyone, great and common alike, and he provides for all equally, [8] but he will judge the conduct of rulers more strictly. [9] It is for you, mighty kings, that I write these words, so that you may know how to act wisely and avoid mistakes. [10] These are holy matters, and if you treat them in a holy manner, you yourselves will be considered holy. If you have learnt this lesson, you will be able to defend yourselves at the Judgement. [11] So then, make my teaching your treasure and joy, and you will be well instructed.

The Value of Wisdom

12 Wisdom shines bright and never grows dim; those who love her and look for her can easily find her. [13] She is quick to make herself known to anyone who desires her. [14] Get up early in the morning to find her, and you will have no problem; you will find her sitting at your door. [15] To fasten your attention on Wisdom is to gain perfect understanding. If you look for her, you will soon find peace of mind, [16] because she will be looking for those who are worthy of her, and she will find you wherever you are. She is kind and will be with you in your every thought.

17 Wisdom begins when you sincerely want to learn. To desire Wisdom is to love her; [18] to love her is to keep her laws; to keep her laws is to be certain of immortality; [19] immortality will bring you close to God. [20] This desire for Wisdom can prepare you to rule a kingdom. [21] So then, you that rule the nations, if you value your thrones and symbols of authority, honour Wisdom so that you may rule for ever.

Solomon Wishes to Share His Wisdom

22 I will tell you what Wisdom is, and how she came to be. I will not keep anything secret. I will trace her history from the beginning and make knowledge

---

[c] ocean foam; *some manuscripts have* frost.
5.17–23: Eph 6.11–17   **6.3:** Rom 13.1

of her open to all. I will not ignore any part of the truth. 23 No jealous desire to guard my own knowledge will make me hold back anything. Wisdom has nothing in common with such an attitude. 24 No indeed—the more wise people there are, the safer the world will be. A sensible king can be depended on to give his people this kind of security. 25 So then, learn what I am about to teach you, and you will profit from it.

A King Is Like Everyone Else

7 1-2 Like every human being, I am mortal. I am a descendant of that first man, who was made from the soil. I was conceived from the sperm of a man, in the pleasure of intercourse. For nine months my flesh took shape in the blood of my mother's womb. 3 When I was born, I came into the world like anyone else. I began to breathe the same air we all breathe; and like everyone else, the first sound I made was a cry. 4 I was wrapped in cloths and cared for. 5 No king ever began life differently. 6 For all of us, there is one way into life, and there is one way out.

Solomon Declares His Love for Wisdom

7 Realizing that I was only a man, I prayed and was given understanding. The spirit of Wisdom came to me. 8 I regarded her more highly than any throne or crown. Wealth was nothing compared to her. 9 Precious jewels could not equal her worth; beside Wisdom all the gold in the world is a handful of sand, and silver is nothing more than clay. 10 I valued her more than health and good looks. Hers is a brightness that never grows dim, and I preferred it to any other light.

11 When Wisdom came to me, all good things came with her. She brought me untold riches. 12 I was happy with them all, because Wisdom had brought them to me. I had not realized before that she was the source of all these things. 13 I was sincere in learning from her, and now I am glad to share what I learnt. 14 No one can ever exhaust the treasures of Wisdom. Use those treasures and you are God's friends; he approves of what you learn from her.

15 I pray to God that my thoughts may be worthy of what I have learnt, and that I may speak according to his will. He is Wisdom's guide; he gives correction to those who are wise. 16 We are under his power and authority—we ourselves, our words, all our understanding and skills. 17 It is he who gave me true knowledge of the forces of nature: what the world is made of; how the elements behave; 18 how the calendar is determined by the movements of the sun, the changing seasons, 19 the constellations, and the cycles of years. 20 He has taught me about the nature of living creatures, the behaviour of wild animals, the force of the winds, the reasoning powers of human beings, the different kinds of plants, and the use of their roots as medicine. 21 I learnt things that were well known and things that had never been known before, 22 because Wisdom, who gave shape to everything that exists, was my teacher.

The Nature of Wisdom

The spirit of Wisdom is intelligent and holy. It is of one nature but reveals itself in many ways. It is not made of any material substance, and it moves about freely. It is clear, clean, and confident; it cannot be harmed. d It loves what is good. It is sharp and unconquerable, 23 kind, and a friend of humanity. It is dependable and sure, and has no worries. It has power over everything, and sees everything. It penetrates every spirit that is intelligent and pure, no matter how delicate its substance may be.

24 Wisdom moves more easily than motion itself; she is so pure that she penetrates everything. 25 She is a breath of God's power—a pure and radiant stream of glory from the Almighty. Nothing that is defiled can ever steal its way into Wisdom. 26 She is a reflection of eternal light, a perfect mirror of God's activity and goodness. 27 Even though Wisdom acts alone, she can do anything. She makes everything new, although she herself never changes. From generation to generation she enters the souls of holy people, and makes them God's friends and prophets. 28 There is nothing that God loves more than people who are at home with Wisdom. 29 Wisdom is more beautiful than the sun and all the constellations. She is better than light itself, 30 because night always follows day, but evil will never

8 overcomes Wisdom. 1 Her great power reaches into every part of the world, and she sets everything in useful order.

---

d cannot be harmed; or does no harm.
7.7: 1 Kgs 3.6–9; Wis 9.1–18

Solomon's Love for Wisdom

2 Wisdom has been my love. I courted her when I was young and wanted to make her my bride. I fell in love with her beauty. ³ She glorifies her noble origin by living with God, the Lord of all, who loves her. ⁴ She is familiar with God's mysteries and helps to determine his course of action.

5 Is it good to have riches in this life? Nothing can make you richer than Wisdom, who makes everything function. ⁶ Is knowledge a useful thing to have? Nothing is better than Wisdom, who has given shape to everything that exists. ⁷ Do you love justice? All the virtues are the result of Wisdom's work: justice and courage, self-control and understanding. Life can offer us nothing more valuable than these. ⁸ Do you want to have wide experience? Wisdom knows the lessons of history and can anticipate the future. She knows how to interpret what people say and how to solve problems. She knows the miracles that God will perform, and how the movements of history will develop.

9 So I decided to take Wisdom home to live with me, because I knew that she would give me good advice and encourage me in times of trouble and grief. ¹⁰ I thought to myself, "Because of her I will be honoured wherever people come together. The old men will respect me, even though I am young. ¹¹ They will find that my opinions show deep insight, and those in power will admire me. ¹² When I am silent, they will wait for me to speak, and when I speak, they will pay attention. Even when I speak at length, they will listen with concentration. ¹³ Because of Wisdom I will gain immortality; I will live for ever in the memory of those who come after me. ¹⁴ I will hold power over nations and peoples; ¹⁵ dreaded tyrants will be seized with fear at the mention of my name. I will be famous, as a good king and as a brave soldier. ¹⁶ When I come home to Wisdom, I will find contentment because there is no conflict or pain in living with her, only happiness and joy."

17 And so I thought it over: to be wedded to Wisdom is to live for ever, ¹⁸ to love her is to be perfectly happy, to do her work is to be rich beyond measure, to share her company is to have sound judgement, to converse with her is to be honoured. Then I was determined

to take Wisdom as my bride. ¹⁹ I had a pleasant personality, even as a child. I had been fortunate enough to receive a good soul, or rather, I was given a sound body to live in because I was already good. ²⁰ Still, I realized that I would never receive Wisdom unless God gave her to me—and knowing that only God could give her to me was itself a sign of understanding. So I prayed, begging the Lord with all my heart:

Solomon Prays for Wisdom

9 "God of my ancestors, merciful Lord, by your word you created everything. ² By your Wisdom you made man to rule all creation, ³ to govern the world with holiness and righteousness, to administer justice with integrity. ⁴ Give me the Wisdom that sits beside your throne; give me a place among your children. ⁵ I am your slave, as was my mother before me. I am only human. I am not strong, and my life will be short. I have little understanding of the Law or of how to apply it. ⁶ Even if a man is perfect, he will be thought of as nothing without the Wisdom that comes from you. ⁷ You chose me rather than anyone else to be the king of your own people, to judge your sons and daughters. ⁸ You told me to build a temple on your sacred mountain, an altar in Jerusalem, the city you chose as your home. It is a copy of that temple in heaven, which you prepared at the beginning. ⁹ Wisdom is with you and knows your actions; she was present when you made the world. She knows what pleases you, what is right and in accordance with your commands. ¹⁰ Send her from the holy heavens, down from your glorious throne, so that she may work at my side, and I may learn what pleases you. ¹¹ She knows and understands everything, and will guide me intelligently in what I do. Her glory will protect me. ¹² Then I will judge your people fairly, and be worthy of my father's throne. My actions will be acceptable.

13 "Who can ever learn the will of God? ¹⁴ Human reason is not adequate for the task, and our philosophies tend to mislead us, ¹⁵ because our mortal bodies weigh our souls down. The body is a temporary structure made of earth, a burden to the active mind. ¹⁶ All we can do is make guesses about things on earth; we must struggle to learn about things that are close to us. Who, then, can ever hope

8.2: Sir 15.2   **8.4:** Prov 8.27–30   **9.1–18:** 1 Kgs 3.6–9; Wis 7.7

V. 3

V. 4

V. 6

V. 10

V. 13

V. 15

to understand heavenly things? 17 No one has ever learnt your will, unless you first gave him Wisdom, and sent your holy spirit down to him. 18 In this way people on earth have been set on the right path, have learnt what pleases you, and have been kept safe by Wisdom.''

Wisdom Protected Adam

10 Wisdom protected the father of the world, the first man that was ever formed, when he alone had been created. She saved him from his own sinful act 2 and gave him the strength to master everything on earth.

Cain Abandoned Wisdom

3 But there was an unrighteous man who abandoned Wisdom; he destroyed himself by killing his brother in a fit of anger.

Wisdom Protected Noah

4 Because of that sin, the earth was flooded, but Wisdom saved it again. She guided a righteous man in his flimsy wooden boat.

Wisdom Helped Abraham

5 Once when the nations were frustrated in their wicked plans, Wisdom recognized a righteous man and kept him innocent in God's sight. She gave him strength to obey God's command in spite of his love for his son.

Wisdom Rescued Lot

6 Wisdom rescued a righteous man while ungodly people were dying. He escaped the flames that destroyed the Five Cities. 7 You can still see the evidence of their wickedness. The land there is barren and smoking. The plants bear fruit that never ripens, and a pillar of salt stands as a monument to one who did not believe. 8 The people of those cities ignored Wisdom and could not tell right from wrong. Not only that, but the remains of their cities still remind us of the foolish way they lived, so that their failure can never be forgotten. 9 But Wisdom rescued her servants from the danger.

Wisdom Protected Jacob

10 A righteous man once had to escape from his brother's anger, and Wisdom guided him in the right way. She showed him God's kingdom and allowed him to know about holy things. e She made him prosperous and successful in his work. 11 When others were greedy for what he had, and wanted to take it away from him, Wisdom stood by him and made him rich. 12 She protected him from his enemies who were waiting for a chance to attack him. She gave him victory in a hard fight, so that he might realize that nothing can make a person stronger than serving God.

Wisdom Rescued Joseph

13 There was once a righteous man who was sold into slavery, but Wisdom did not abandon him. She kept him safe from sin. She went to prison with him 14 and never left him until she had given him power over an empire and made him the ruler of people who had once oppressed him. She let it be known that a false accusation had been made against him, and she gave him eternal honour.

Wisdom Led the Israelites Out of Egypt

15 Wisdom once rescued an innocent and holy people from a nation of oppressors. 16 She entered the soul of one of God's servants and f stood up to dreaded kings by performing miracles. 17 She rewarded God's people for their hardships. She guided them on a miraculous journey. She gave them shade during the day and brilliant starlight at night. 18 She led them through the deep waters of the Red Sea, 19 but she drowned their enemies and washed their bodies up on the shore. 20 And so the righteous looted the ungodly. They sang hymns to your holy name, O Lord; together they praised you for defending them. 21 Wisdom gave speech to those who could not speak; she even caused babies to speak clearly.

Wisdom Led the Israelites through the Desert

11 Wisdom brought success to the people of Israel through a holy prophet. 2 They travelled across a desert where no one lived and camped in places where no human being had ever been.

---

e holy things; or angels.   f and; or who.
10.1–2: Gen 1.26–28   **10.3:** Gen 4.8–13   **10.4:** Gen 7.1—8.22
10.5: Gen 11.1–9; 12.1–3; 22.1–19   **10.6–9:** Gen 19.1–29
10.10–12: Gen 27.43; 28.10–22; 32.24–30   **10.13–14:** Gen 37.12–36; 39.1–23; 41.37–44
10.15–21: Ex 1.1—15.21   **11.1–5:** Ex 15.22—17.16

³They stood up to their enemies and fought them off. ⁴When your people grew thirsty, they called to you, Lord, and you gave them water flowing out of solid rock. ⁵The disasters that punished the Egyptians saved your people when they were in trouble.

The Punishment of the Egyptians

6–8 Because those enemies decreed that the babies of your people should be killed, you stirred up the sources of their ever-flowing river and made it foul with blood.

In the desert you let your people go thirsty, to give them a taste of how you had punished their enemies. And then, when they least expected it, you gave them plenty of water. ⁹When they were being tested, even though it was a merciful discipline, they learnt how wicked people were tortured when you judged them in anger. ¹⁰You tested your people, as a father tests his children, to warn them. But you judged their enemies like a stern king and condemned them. ¹¹They suffered, whether they were near your people or far from them. ¹²Their sorrow was doubled; they groaned as they looked back on what had happened. ¹³When they learnt that their punishment had been of benefit to your people, they realized that it was your work, Lord. ¹⁴The Egyptians had refused to have anything to do with that man who, long before, as a baby, had been thrown out and exposed; but as things worked out, they ended by being amazed at him. The righteous never suffered a thirst like theirs.

15 Their wickedness misled them into silly ideas, so that they worshipped snakes and other disgusting animals, creatures without any powers of reason. Because of this, you punished them with millions of such animals, ¹⁶and taught them that punishment for sin takes the same form as the sin itself. ¹⁷Your almighty power, Lord, created the world out of material that had no form at all. You could easily have punished those people by sending an invasion of bears or savage lions. ¹⁸You could have created new and terrible animals, that could breathe fire or roar and send out clouds of smoke, or shoot out fearful sparks from their eyes. ¹⁹You could have made animals like these that would not have to attack those people to kill them, but could scare them to death just by looking at them. ²⁰But this was not necessary. You could have pursued them with your justice or struck them dead at the slightest hint of your power. But you have chosen to measure, count, and weigh everything you do.

God Is Powerful and Merciful

21 You can show your great power whenever you wish, and no one can stand up against it. ²²In your sight the whole world is a grain of sand, barely heavy enough to tip a pair of scales, a drop of dew on the ground in the morning. ²³You are powerful enough to do anything, but you are merciful to everyone; you overlook our sins and give us time to repent. ²⁴You love everything that exists; you do not despise anything that you have made. If you had not liked it, you would not have made it in the first place. ²⁵How could anything last, if you did not want it to? How could it endure, if you had not created it? ²⁶You have allowed it all to exist, O Lord, because it is yours, and you love every **12** living thing. ¹Your immortal spirit is in every one of them, ²and so you gently correct those who sin against you. You remind them of what they are doing, and warn them about it, so that they may abandon their evil ways and put their trust in you, Lord.

The Sins of the Canaanites

3–4 You hated the people who lived in your holy land long ago, because they did horrible things: they practised magic and conducted unholy worship; ⁵they killed children without mercy and ate the flesh and blood of human beings. They were initiated into secret rituals*ᵍ* ⁶in which parents murdered their own defenceless children. It was your will that our ancestors should destroy those people, ⁷so that the land which you consider the most precious of all lands would be a suitable home for your people. ⁸But even in this you showed mercy towards their enemies, since they too were human beings. You sent hornets ahead of your army, to destroy the enemy gradually. ⁹You could have allowed the righteous to destroy those ungodly people in battle; you could have wiped them out immediately with wild animals or with

*ᵍ*They were...rituals; *Greek unclear.*
11.15–16: Ex 8.1–24; 10.12–15   **12.3–7:** Deut 12.31; 18.9–13   **12.8:** Ex 23.28

one harsh command. ¹⁰But instead, you carried out your sentence gradually, to give them a chance to repent, even though you knew that they came from evil stock, that they had been wicked since birth, and that they would never change their way of thinking. ¹¹Their whole nation was cursed from the start, and though you had not punished them for their sins, it was not because you were afraid of anyone.

God Is Sovereign

12 You created those wicked people, and no one can speak in their defence or condemn you for destroying them. No one can question what you have done or challenge your judgement. ¹³All things are under your care, and there is no other god to whom you must justify your decisions. ¹⁴No king or ruler on earth can accuse you of punishing those people unfairly. ¹⁵You are righteous, and you rule everything righteously. You have never used your power to condemn a person who does not deserve to be punished. ¹⁶Your strength is the source of justice. You can show mercy to everyone, because you are the Lord of all. ¹⁷You show your strength when people doubt that your power is perfect, and you punish anyone who knows your power but dares to ignore it. ¹⁸Even though you have absolute power, you are a merciful judge. You could take action against us whenever you choose, but instead, you rule us with great patience.

19 By the things you have done you have taught your people that a person who is righteous must also be kind. You have given your people abundant hope by allowing them to repent of their sins. ²⁰You were very careful and patient in punishing your people's enemies; even when they deserved to die, you gave them every opportunity to give up their sinful ways. ²¹But you judged your own people very strictly, even though you had made covenants with their ancestors and had solemnly promised to give them good things.

22 Yes, you punish us, but you punish our enemies ten thousand times more, so that when we judge others, we may remember your goodness, and when we are being judged, we may look for mercy.

The Punishment of the Egyptians

23 And so you tormented those who

were foolish enough to live wickedly—you tormented them with the horrible things they worshipped. ²⁴They had wandered far away from the truth and worshipped the most disgusting and horrible animals. They were deceived as easily as little children. ²⁵And so you punished them for their stupidity, and your judgement made them look like fools. ²⁶It was a light punishment, but those who pay no attention to such warnings deserve to feel the full weight of God's judgement. ²⁷When they were punished with those creatures they considered gods, they became bitterly disillusioned and recognized that the true God was the one they had always refused to acknowledge. That is why they suffered the final punishment.

The Foolishness of Nature Worship

13 Anyone who does not know God is simply foolish. Such people look at the good things around them and still fail to see the living God. They have studied the things he made, but they have not recognized the one who made them. ²Instead, they suppose that the gods who rule the world are fire or wind or storm or the circling stars or rushing water or the heavenly bodies. ³People were so delighted with the beauty of these things that they thought they must be gods, but they should have realized that these things have a master and that he is much greater than all of them, for he is the creator of beauty, and he created them. ⁴Since people are amazed at the power of these things, and how they behave, they ought to learn from them that their maker is far more powerful. ⁵When we realize how vast and beautiful the creation is, we are learning about the Creator at the same time.

6 But maybe we are too harsh with these people. After all, they may have really wanted to find God, but they couldn't. ⁷Surrounded by God's works, they keep on looking at them, until they are finally convinced that because the things they see are so beautiful, they must be gods. ⁸But still, these people really have no excuse. ⁹If they had enough intelligence to speculate about the nature of the universe, why did they never find the Lord of all things?

The Foolishness of Idolatry

10 But the most miserable people of all

are those who rest their hopes on lifeless things, who worship things that have been made by human hands—images of animals artistically made from gold and silver, or some useless stone carved by someone long ago. ¹¹A skilled wood-worker may saw down some suitable tree, carefully strip off the bark, and then, with skilful craftsmanship, make from it an object that will serve some useful purpose. ¹²He will take the pieces left over and use them as firewood to cook a meal that he can sit down to and enjoy. ¹³But out of that scrap wood he may take one piece that isn't good for anything—maybe it's crooked and full of knots—and carefully carve it in his leisure time, using spare moments to shape it into the crude image of a person, ¹⁴or perhaps of some worthless animal. He paints it all over with red, covering up every flaw in the work. ¹⁵Then he prepares a suitable place in the wall for it and fastens it in place with iron nails. ¹⁶He is careful to keep it from falling, because he knows it is only an idol and needs help; it cannot help itself. ¹⁷But he is not ashamed to pray to this lifeless thing about his marriage, his children, and his pos-

It is dead, but he prays to it for life (13.18)

sessions. ¹⁸It is weak, but he prays to it for health. It is dead, but he prays to it for life. It has no experience, but he prays to it for help. It cannot walk, but he prays to it for a successful journey. ¹⁹Its hands have no power, but he asks it to help him—in business, in making money, and in his work.

Wooden Idols Compared with Noah's Wooden Boat

14 In the same way, a man getting ready to sail on the raging sea will call for help from a piece of wood that is not as strong as the ship he is about to

board. ²Someone designed the ship out of a desire for profit, and a craftsman built it with skill. ³But it is your care, O Father, that steers it; you give it a safe path through the waves of the sea. ⁴People may go to sea even if they have no skill, because you can save them from any danger. ⁵It is your will that the things you have made by your wisdom should be put to use. And so people can cross the sea in a boat and come safely to land, because they trust their lives to that small piece of wood.

6 This is what happened in ancient times, when a proud race of giants was dying away. The hope of the world escaped on such a boat under your guidance and left the world a new generation to carry on the human race. ⁷A blessing was on Noah's wooden boat that allowed righteousness to survive, ⁸but a curse is on an idol made by human hands. A curse is also on the one who makes it, because he works on this perishable thing and then calls it a god. ⁹Ungodly people and these ungodly things they make are equally hated by God, ¹⁰who will punish both the things made and the people who made them. ¹¹And so God's judgement will fall on pagan idols, because, even though they are made from something God created, they become horrible things that trap the souls of foolish people.

The Origins of Idolatry

12 Sexual immorality began when idols were invented. They have corrupted human life ever since they were first made. ¹³Idols have not always existed, nor will they exist for ever. ¹⁴It was human pride that brought them into the world, and that is why a quick end has been planned for them.

15 Once there was a father who was overwhelmed with grief at the untimely death of his child, so he made an image of that child who had been suddenly taken from him. He then honoured a dead human being as a god, and handed on secret rituals and ceremonies to those who were under his authority. ¹⁶As time went on, this ungodly custom became stronger. Finally it became law, and idols were being worshipped at the command of powerful rulers. ¹⁷When people lived too far away to honour a ruler in his presence but were eager to pay honour to this absent king, they would imagine what he must look like, and would then

make a likeness of him. ¹⁸The ambitious artists who made these likenesses caused this worship to spread, even among people who did not know the king. ¹⁹An artist might want to please some ruler, and so he would use his skill to make the likeness better looking than the man himself. ²⁰Then people would be so attracted by the work of art, that the man whom they had earlier honoured now became the object of their worship. ²¹So all this became a deadly trap, because people who were grieving, or under royal authority, would take objects of stone or wood, and give them the honour reserved for the one God.

The Results of Idolatry

22 One thing led to another. It was not enough to be wrong about the knowledge of God. They lived in a state of evil warfare, but they were so ignorant that they called it peace. ²³They murdered children in their initiation rituals, celebrated secret mysteries, and held wild ceremonial orgies with unnatural practices. ²⁴They no longer kept their lives or their marriages pure. A man might kill another by an act of treachery or cause him grief by committing adultery with his wife. ²⁵Everything was a complete riot of bloody murder, robbery, deceit, corruption, faithlessness, disorder, falsehood, ²⁶harassment of innocent people, ingratitude, moral decay, sexual perversion, broken marriages, adultery, and immorality. ²⁷The worship of idols, whose names should never be spoken, is the beginning and the end, the cause and the result of every evil. ²⁸People who worship them lose control of themselves in ecstasy, or pass off lies as prophecies, or live wickedly, or break their word without hesitation. ²⁹They tell lies under oath and expect no punishment, because the idols they put their trust in are lifeless. ³⁰But punishment will finally catch up with them, for two reasons: first, they were in error about God when they worshipped idols, and secondly, they had so little regard for holiness that they made false statements to deceive people. ³¹When unrighteous people commit sin, they will be hunted down, not by the power of whatever thing they swear by, but by the punishment that sinners deserve.

The True God Gives Immortality

15 But you, our God, are kind and true and patient. You rule the

You rule the universe with mercy (15.1)

universe with mercy. ²Even if we sin, we know your power and are still yours. But because we know that we belong to you, we will not sin. ³Knowing you is perfect righteousness. Recognizing your power is where immortality begins. ⁴We have not been misled by any evil product of human skill, by any useless object painted by some artist, or by any idol smeared with different colours. ⁵The sight of such things arouses the passions of foolish people and makes them desire a dead, lifeless image. ⁶Anyone who makes such a thing or desires it or worships it is in love with something evil, and gets what he deserves when he places his hopes in it.

The Foolishness of Worshipping Clay Idols

7 A potter works the soft clay and carefully shapes each object for our use. Some things he makes are put to good use, and some are not, but he makes them all from the same clay, and shapes them in the same manner. The potter himself decides which objects shall be used for what purposes. ⁸He is a human being who was himself formed from earth only a

short while earlier, and after a little while, when he must return the soul that was lent to him, he will go back to the same earth. He is a human being, but he wastes his labour shaping a useless god out of the same clay that he uses to make pots. 9His life will be short, and he will soon have to die, but he is not concerned about that. He wants to compete with those who work in gold, silver, and bronze, and make the same things as they do. He takes great pride in the things he makes, but they are counterfeit. 10His heart is made of ashes. His hope is cheaper than dirt. His life is not worth as much as his clay, 11because he never came to know the God who shaped him, who breathed into him an active soul and a living spirit. 12He thinks of human life as just a game, a market where he can make a profit. He believes that he must make money however he can, even by evil ways. 13This man, who makes idols and fragile pots from the same clay, knows better than anyone else that he is sinning.

The Punishment of the Egyptians

14 But the most foolish of all people, showing less sense than babies, were the enemies who oppressed your people, O Lord. 15They thought that all their pagan idols were gods, even though idols cannot see with their eyes, cannot breathe through their nose, cannot hear with their ears, cannot feel with their fingers, and cannot walk on their legs. 16Some man whose spirit is only borrowed made them. No one can ever make a god that is equal to a human being. 17Every person will die sooner or later, but anything he makes with his wicked hands is dead from the start. He himself is better than what he worships. He at least is alive, but what he worships is not, and never has been. 18Such people worship the most disgusting animals, including even the least intelligent ones. 19Even as animals they are not attractive enough to make anyone want them. God himself passed them by when he put his approval and blessing on the rest of creation.

16 1And so it was appropriate that these people were punished by such creatures—tormented by swarms of them.

2 But you, O Lord, did not punish your people in this way; instead, you showed them kindness. You sent them quails to eat, a rare, delicious food to satisfy their hunger. 3You did all this so that the idolaters, when they were hungry, would be unable to eat because of the disgusting creatures sent to them. Your people, however, suffered hunger for only a short while, and then they ate the finest food. 4It was necessary for the oppressors to suffer relentless need, while your people saw how their enemies were being tormented.

5 When terrible, fierce snakes attacked your people and were killing them with their poison, you did not remain angry long enough to destroy your people. 6This trouble lasted for only a little while, as a warning. Then you gave them a healing symbol, the bronze snake, to remind them of what your Law requires. 7If a person looked at that symbol, he was cured of the snakebite—not by what he saw, but by you, the saviour of all mankind. 8By doing this, you also convinced our enemies that you are the one who rescues people from every evil. 9Our enemies died from the bites of locusts and flies; no way was found to cure them, because they deserved to be punished by such creatures. 10But even poisonous snakes could not overcome your people, because you had mercy, helped them, and cured them. 11They were bitten so that they would remember your commands, but they were quickly rescued, in order to keep them from forgetting you completely and depriving themselves of your kindness. 12No medicine or ointment cured them. They were restored to health by your word, O Lord, the word which heals all humanity. 13You have power over life and death; you can bring a person to the brink of death and back again. 14A wicked man may kill someone, but he cannot bring the dead person back to life or rescue a soul imprisoned in the world of the dead.

Disastrous Storms Hit Egypt

15 No one can possibly escape from you. 16Look at those ungodly people: they refused to recognize you as God, so you punished them with your great power. They were overtaken by terrible storms of rain and hail and were completely destroyed by fire. 17The most amazing thing was that the fire burned all the more fiercely in the water, which usually puts fire out. All the forces of nature fight to defend those who are righteous. 18At one point the flames died down, so that they wouldn't destroy the creatures sent to

16.2: Ex 16.11–13; Num 11.31–32   **16.5–7:** Num 21.6–9

punish the ungodly. Those people had to learn that they were being overtaken by your judgement. ¹⁹But at another point, when surrounded by water, the flames burned more fiercely than fire had ever burned before, and so destroyed the crops on the land where those unrighteous people lived.

The Israelites Receive Manna to Eat

20 But this disaster did not strike your people. Instead, you gave them the food of angels. From heaven you sent down bread that was ready to eat, and they did not have to prepare it. The food you gave delighted everyone, no matter what his taste. ²¹All this showed how lovingly you care for your children. That food satisfied the desire of everyone who ate it; it was changed to suit each person's taste. ²²It was food that under normal circumstances would vanish away like snow or ice, but now it did not melt even in the fire. This was meant to teach your people that the same fire that was destroying their enemies' crops during the heavy downpour of rain and hail ²³held back its power, so that your own righteous people might have food.

24 You created the universe; it is at your command. All creation uses its power to punish unrighteous people, but it becomes mild and kind to those who put their trust in you. ²⁵Creation assumed all kinds of forms to show how you provide generously for all who pray to you.ʰ ²⁶This happened so that the people whom you loved, O Lord, might learn that they are not fed by what they can grow. It is your word that maintains those who put their trust in you. ²⁷The food that was not destroyed by the fire melted when the first ray of sunlight warmed it. ²⁸This was to teach us that we must get up before daybreak to give you thanks, and pray as the sun comes up. ²⁹But an ungrateful person's hope will melt away like frost, and drain away like water that is not being used.

Terror Strikes the Egyptians at Night

17 O Lord, your acts of judgement are marvellous and hard to explain; that is why people who had not been taught about them went astray. ²When lawless people imagined that they had your holy nation in their power, they were themselves imprisoned in a long night of darkness. They lay in their own houses, shut off from your eternal care. ³They thought that their sins had been secret and unnoticed, shielded from view by a dark curtain of forgetfulness, but now they were horribly afraid, confused, and terrified by ghostly forms. ⁴Not even the dark corners where they lay could protect them from fear. They were surrounded by horrible noises; grim ghosts with gloomy faces appeared before their eyes. ⁵No fire had power to give them light, and the brilliant stars could do nothing to relieve that deathly darkness. ⁶There was only a dreadful fire, lit by no human hand, that shone on them, and in their terror they believed that the real world was even worse than the things they imagined. ⁷The illusions produced by their magic tricks were put to shame, and all the wisdom they had boasted of came to nothing. ⁸They had claimed they could drive away all the fears and illnesses of sick minds, but now they themselves were sick with silly, groundless fears. ⁹Even though nothing dangerous had actually happened, they were terrified by hissing snakes and animals advancing on them. ¹⁰And so they died, shaking with fear, afraid even to open their eyes, yet unable to keep them shut.

11 Wickedness is cowardly in itself and stands self-condemned.ⁱ Someone with a guilty conscience will always imagine things to be worse than they really are. ¹²Fear is nothing but the failure to use the help that reason gives. ¹³When you lack the confidence to rely on reason, you give in to the fears caused by ignorance.

14 All night long those people slept the same restless sleep, even though the night held no power over them, since it came from the powerless depths of the world of the dead. ¹⁵They were chased by hideous forms and lay paralysed as they surrendered themselves to the sudden, unexpected fear that came over them. ¹⁶People would suddenly collapse and lie locked in the chains of their own fear. ¹⁷Farmers, shepherds, and labourers out in the countryside were captured by the same inevitable fate and bound in the darkness by the same invisible chain. ¹⁸⁻¹⁹They were panic-stricken by the sighing of the wind or by the singing of birds in the trees or by the roar of rushing water or by the rumble of falling rocks or by the sound of unseen creatures

ʰpray to you; *or* are in need.   ⁱWickedness...self-condemned; *Greek unclear.*
16.20–29: Ex 16.1–36

running about or by the savage roaring of wild animals or by the echoes from the mountains. 20 In the full light of day, the rest of the world went about its business undisturbed. 21 Only those people were covered by this heavy night, a foretaste of the darkness of death that was waiting for them. They were a burden to themselves that was even heavier than the darkness.

Light Shines On The Israelites

18 Yet all the while a brilliant light was shining for your holy people. Their enemies heard their voices, but couldn't see them. They envied the good fortune of your people, who were not suffering. 2 Those enemies could at least be thankful that the people they had wronged were not taking vengeance on them now, and so they begged them to leave. *j*

3 Then you guided your people as they travelled through a country they did not know. You guided them with a pillar of fire. It was like a sun that would not harm them on that glorious journey. 4 But their enemies, who were not allowed to see the light, deserved to be prisoners in darkness, because they had made prisoners of your people. And it was through your people that the eternal light of the Law was going to be given to the world.

The Death of the Egyptian First-born

5 When your enemies were carrying out their resolve to kill the babies of your holy people, there was one child who was abandoned but later rescued. Then you punished your enemies by killing a great number of their own children. You drowned their whole army at one time in the rushing waters. 6 But our ancestors had been told in advance of what would happen that night, so that they would be cheered and encouraged by confident trust in your promises to them. 7 Your people knew that you would rescue the righteous nation and destroy their enemies. 8 With the same act you punished our enemies and did us the glorious honour of calling us to yourself.

9 During all this time devout men from this righteous nation were secretly offering sacrifices, giving their word to each other that they would keep God's law and share each other's blessings and dangers. Already they were chanting those ancient hymns of praise. 10 But their enemies' pitiful cries of grief echoed everywhere, as they mourned for their dead children. 11 Masters suffered the same punishment as their slaves; the king endured the same loss as the common people. 12 There were too many dead bodies to count. There were not enough people left to bury them all. In a single moment their dearest children died; all of them met death in the same way. 13 These people had paid no attention to any warning, but relied instead on their magical powers. But when their first-born sons were killed, then they recognized that Israel was God's son.

14 The short night was half over, and all was quiet and peaceful, 15 when suddenly your threats were carried out! An invincible word of judgement sped from your royal throne in heaven, straight down to that doomed land. It came like a soldier charging to attack, 16 carrying out your firm command with a fearful weapon, standing with feet on the ground and head touching the sky, filling the land with death. 17 At that moment the people who were about to die had terrible nightmares and were seized by sudden fear. 18 All over the land they lay half-dead and let it be known why they were dying. 19 They knew why they were dying, because their horrible dreams had told them.

Aaron's Prayer Saves the Israelites from Death

20 Death also came to the righteous nation, for an epidemic struck many of them while they were in the desert, but your anger did not last long. 21 There was a certain blameless man who quickly took action to defend them. Acting as their priest, Aaron offered prayers and burnt the incense used in asking forgiveness of sins. With prayers and incense as his weapons, he withstood your anger and ended the disaster. By doing this he proved that he was your servant. 22 He overcame the bitter difficulty, *k* but not by his own strength or by military force. Instead, he used prayer to stop the punishment, appealing to the promises you solemnly made to our ancestors. 23 Dead bodies were already lying in piles,

---

j begged them to leave *or* begged their forgiveness for their past hostility.
k *Probable text* bitter difficulty; *Greek* crowd.
18.1–4: Ex 13.17–22   **18.20–25:** Num 16.41–50

but he stepped in to hold your anger back and to keep it from harming those who were left alive. 24 He wore a long robe decorated with symbols of the universe. In honour of our ancestors he wore four rows of engraved stones on his chest, and your own majesty was represented by the ornament on his turban. 25 The Angel of Death was afraid of these things, and gave in. It was only a slight experience of your wrath, but it was enough.

The Suicidal Stupidity of the Egyptians

19 But the godless continued to feel your pitiless anger until the very end. You knew what they would do before they did it. 2 You knew that even though they let your people go and made them leave quickly, they would change their minds and pursue them. 3-4 While the Egyptians were still mourning at the graves of their dead, they forgot why all this had happened, and they foolishly decided that the people they had begged to leave were runaways. So they chased after them. They were led into this as part of the punishment they deserved, so that they would suffer the rest of the torments they were due to receive. 5 They were to meet a strange death, while your people continued on their miraculous journey.

God Guides and Protects His People

6 The whole nature of the universe was changed at your command so that your people would not be harmed. 7 They saw the cloud over their camp and dry land where water had been. There was a grass-covered plain between the stormy waves of the Red Sea, making it easy for them to cross over. 8 All your people, under your protection, saw this miracle and went across. 9 They pranced about like horses let out to pasture; they skipped about like lambs and praised you, Lord, for saving them. 10 They still remembered what life had been like when they were slaves—how the earth bred gnats instead of cattle,

how the river produced huge numbers of frogs instead of fish. 11-12 Later, when they desperately wanted better food, quails came up from the sea to satisfy their hunger. The quail was a bird they had never seen before.

The Punishment of the Egyptians

13 But violent thunder gave warning of the punishment that was coming on those sinners. They suffered a well-deserved punishment for their great wickedness. No nation had ever hated strangers so bitterly. 14 Other people had been known to refuse welcome to strangers who came to them, but these people made slaves of those who were their guests and who had shown them kindness. 15 Any nation will be punished if it does not welcome foreigners, 16 but these people, who had earlier welcomed the foreigners with happy celebrations and treated them as equals, later made them suffer cruelly. 17 These people were also struck with blindness, like the men of Sodom who came to the door of that righteous man Lot. They found themselves in total darkness, as each one groped around to find his own door.

God's Miraculous Power

18 On a harp each string keeps its own pitch, but each sound can be combined with others to make different melodies. That is how it was in those days, when the very elements entered into new combinations. Look at what happened! 19 Land animals took to the water, and swimming creatures came up on the land. 20 Fire burned even in water, which could not put it out. 21 And yet the flames could not burn the flesh of the perishable creatures walking in them, and did not melt that heavenly food that would ordinarily have melted like frost.

22 Lord, you have made your people great—glorious in all respects. You have never neglected them. You have given them help, always, everywhere.

THE WISDOM OF JESUS SON OF

SIRACH

(ECCLESIASTICUS)

INTRODUCTION

The Wisdom of Jesus, Son of Sirach, also known as *Ecclesiasticus,* was written in Hebrew by a man named Joshua (or Jesus) and was later translated into Greek by his grandson. The book includes traditional Jewish wisdom material and makes a defence of Judaism by showing that God has given true wisdom to his people. Many subjects of a religious, moral, and practical nature are presented, sometimes at length and sometimes in short proverbial sayings.

Outline of Contents

Foreword
In praise of wisdom (Part 1) 1.1—23.27
  a. Duty, reward, and practical advice 1.1—16.23
  b. God's wisdom and human response 16.24—23.27
In praise of wisdom (Part 2) 24.1—50.21
  a. Wisdom and virtue 24.1—32.13
  b. God's wisdom and man's worship and work 32.14—42.14
  c. God's glory in nature 42.15—43.33
  d. In praise of ancestors 44.1—50.21
Epilogue and Appendices 50.22—51.30

Foreword

The Law, the Prophets, and the later writers have left us a wealth of valuable teachings, and we should praise Israel for the instruction and wisdom they provide. But it is not enough that those who read them should gain understanding for themselves. Anyone who values learning should be able to help others by what he himself says and writes. That is why my grandfather Jesus devoted himself to reading the Law, the Prophets, and the other books of our ancestors. After he had mastered them, he was led to write a book of his own in order to share his wisdom and learning with others, so that anyone who shared his love for learning should have his book available as well, and be all the more able to live according to the Law.

Let me urge you, then, to read this book carefully and with an open mind. And please be patient in those places where, in spite of all my diligent efforts, I may not have translated some phrases very well. What was originally written in Hebrew does not always have exactly the same sense when it is translated into another language. [a] That is true not only of this book, but even of the Law itself,

---

[a] *The book of Sirach was written in Hebrew, but the writer of this foreword translated it into Greek.*

Who can count raindrops? (1.2)

the Prophets, and the other books. The translations differ quite a bit from the original.

I came to Egypt in the thirty-eighth year of King Euergetes' reign and stayed for some time. While I was there, I had the opportunity for a good deal of study and felt the necessity of translating the following book. I wanted to use all my diligence and skill to complete it and make it available for all those living in foreign lands who wish to learn and who have the strength of character to live by the Law of Moses.

In Praise of Wisdom

1 All wisdom comes from the Lord,
    and Wisdom is with him for ever.
² Who can count raindrops or the sand
    along the shore?
    Who can count the days of eternity?
³ How high is the sky? How wide is the
    earth?
    How deep is the ocean? How
    profound is Wisdom?
    Can anyone find answers to these
    questions?
⁴ Wisdom was created before anything
    else;

understanding has always existed. *b*
⁶ Has anyone ever been shown where
    Wisdom originates?
    Does anyone understand her subtle
    cleverness? *c*
⁸ There is only one who is wise,
    and we must stand in awe before his
    throne.
⁹ The Lord himself created Wisdom;
    he saw her and recognized her value,
    and so he filled everything he made
    with Wisdom.
¹⁰ He gave some measure of Wisdom to
    everyone,
    but poured her out on those who love
    him.

¹¹ If you fear the Lord, honour and pride
    will be yours;
    you will be crowned with happiness
    and joy.
¹² To honour the Lord is a heartfelt
    delight;
    it will give you a long and happy life,
¹³ and at the end of your days all will
    go well for you.
    God will bless you on the day of your
    death.
¹⁴ To fear the Lord is the first step to
    Wisdom.

b Some manuscripts add verse 5: The source of Wisdom is the word of God on high; her ways are eternal commands.
c Some manuscripts add verse 7: To whom has the knowledge of Wisdom been revealed? Who has understood her great experience?
1.1: Prov 2.6   **1.9:** Prov 8.22–31; Sir 29.9

Wisdom is given to the faithful in their mothers' wombs.

¹⁵ She has lived with us from ancient times,
and generations to come will rely on her.

¹⁶ To fear the Lord is Wisdom at her fullest;
she satisfies us completely with her gifts

¹⁷ and fills our homes and our barns
with all that our hearts can desire.

¹⁸ To fear the Lord is the flower of Wisdom
that blossoms with peace and good health. ᵈ

¹⁹ She sends knowledge and understanding like the rain,
and increases the honour of those who receive her.

²⁰ To fear the Lord is the root of Wisdom;
her branches are long life. ᵉ

Self-control

22 There is no excuse for unjustified anger; it can bring about your downfall. ²³ Wait and be patient, and later you will be glad you did. ²⁴ Keep quiet until the right time to speak, and you will gain a reputation for good sense.

Wisdom and Reverence for God

25 Wisdom has a treasury of wise sayings, but sinners have nothing but contempt for godliness. ²⁶ If you want to be wise, keep the Lord's commands, and he will give you Wisdom in abundance. ²⁷ Fearing the Lord is Wisdom and an education in itself. He is pleased by loyalty and humility. ²⁸ Be faithful in the practice of your religion; when you worship the Lord, do it with all your heart. ²⁹ Be careful about what you say, and don't be a hypocrite. ³⁰ Don't be arrogant; you may suffer a fall and be disgraced. The Lord will reveal your secrets and humble you in front of everyone in the synagogue, because you did not come there with reverence for the Lord, but with a heart full of hypocrisy.

Faithfulness to God

2 My son, if you are going to serve the Lord, be prepared for times when you will be put to the test. ² Be sincere and determined. Keep calm when trouble comes. ³ Stay with the Lord; never abandon him, and you will be prosperous at the end of your days. ⁴ Accept whatever happens to you. Even if you suffer humiliation, be patient. ⁵ Gold is tested by fire, and human character is tested in the furnace of humiliation. ⁶ Trust the Lord, and he will help you. Walk straight in his ways, and put your hope in him.

7 All you that fear the Lord, wait for him to show you his mercy. Do not turn away from him, or you will fall. ⁸ All you that fear the Lord, trust him, and you will certainly be rewarded. ⁹ All you that fear the Lord, look forward to his blessings of mercy and eternal happiness.

10 Think back to the ancient generations and consider this: has the Lord ever disappointed anyone who put his hope in him? Has the Lord ever abandoned anyone who held him in constant reverence? Has the Lord ever ignored anyone who prayed to him? ¹¹ The Lord is kind and merciful; he forgives our sins and keeps us safe in time of trouble. ¹² But those who lose their nerve are doomed— all those sinners who try to have it both ways! ¹³ Doom is sure to come for those who lose their courage; they have no faith, and so they will have no protection. ¹⁴ Doom is sure to come for those who lose their hope. What will they do when the Lord comes to judge them?

15 Those who fear the Lord do not disobey his commands; those who love him will live as he wants them to live. ¹⁶ Those who fear and love the Lord will try to please him and devote themselves to the Law. ¹⁷ Those who fear the Lord are always ready to serve him. They humble themselves before him, and say, ¹⁸ "We place our destiny in the hands of the Lord, not in the hands of men, because his mercy is as great as his majesty."

Duties to Parents

3 Children, listen to me; I am your father. Do what I tell you and you will be safe, ² for the Lord has given fathers authority over their children and given children the obligation to obey their mothers. ³ If you respect your father, you can make up for your sins, ⁴ and if you honour your mother, you are earning

---

ᵈ Some manuscripts add: He saw her and recognized her value (see 1.9).
ᵉ Some manuscripts add verse 21: Honouring the Lord takes sin away; where the fear of the Lord is found, it turns away anger.
1.17: Wis 7.11　　**1.20**: Prov 3.16; 4.10　　**2.5**: Wis 3.5–6; 1 Pet 1.7
2.5–6: Wis 6.18; Jn 14.15,21,23

If you obey the Lord by...making your mother happy (3.6)

great wealth. ⁵ If you respect your father, one day your own children will make you happy; the Lord will hear your prayers. ⁶ If you obey the Lord by honouring your father and making your mother happy, you will live a long life. ⁷ Obey your parents as if you were their slave. ⁸ Honour your father in everything you do and say, so that you may receive his blessing. ⁹ When parents give their blessing, they give strength to their children's homes, but when they curse their children, they destroy the very foundations.

10 Never seek honour for yourself at your father's expense; it is not to your credit if he is dishonoured. ¹¹ Your own honour comes from the respect that you show to your father. If children do not honour their mothers, it is their own disgrace. ¹² My son, take care of your father when he grows old; give him no cause for worry as long as he lives. ¹³ Be sympathetic even if his mind fails him; don't look down on him just because you are strong and healthy. ¹⁴ The Lord will not forget the kindness you show to your father; it will help you to make up for your sins. ¹⁵ When you are in trouble, the Lord will remember your kindness and will help you; your sins will melt away like frost in warm sunshine. ¹⁶ Whoever abandons his parents or gives them cause for anger may as well be cursing the Lord; he is already under the Lord's curse.

Humility

17 My son, be humble in everything you do, and people will appreciate it more than gifts. *f* ¹⁸ The greater you become, the more humble you should be; then the Lord will be pleased with you. *g* ²⁰ The Lord's power is great, and he is honoured by those who are humble. ²¹ Don't try to understand things that are too hard for you, or investigate matters that are beyond your power to know. ²² Concentrate on the Law, which has been given to you. You do not need to know about things which the Lord has not revealed, ²³ so don't concern yourself with them. After all, what has been shown to you is beyond human power to understand. ²⁴ Many people have been misled by their own opinions; their wrong ideas have warped their judgement. *h*

26 Stubbornness will get you into trouble in the end. If you live dangerously, it will kill you. ²⁷ A stubborn person will be burdened down with troubles. Sinners go on adding one sin to another. ²⁸ There is no cure for the troubles that arrogant people have; wickedness has taken deep root in them. ²⁹ Intelligent people will learn from proverbs and parables. They listen well because they want to learn.

Giving to the Poor

30 Giving to the poor can make up for sin, just as water can put out a blazing fire. ³¹ Anyone who responds to others with acts of kindness is thinking of the future, because he will find help if he ever

4 falls on hard times. ¹ My son, don't prevent the poor from making a living, or keep them waiting in their need. ² Never give a hungry person any cause for resentment or anger. ³ Don't add to the troubles of someone who is already desperate. If he is in need, don't put off giving to him. ⁴⁻⁵ Don't refuse to help a beggar who is in distress. Don't turn your

---

f Hebrew *people...gifts; Greek* those whom the Lord approves will love you.
g Some Greek manuscripts add verse 19: Many are exalted and esteemed, but God's secrets are revealed to the humble; Hebrew: God's mercy is great, and he reveals his secrets to those who are humble.
h Some Greek manuscripts add verse 25: If you have no eyes, you cannot see; don't claim to have knowledge if you don't have it; Hebrew has, after verse 27: If you have no eyes, you cannot see; if you have no knowledge, you cannot have Wisdom.
3.8: Ex 20.12   **3.18:** Phil 2.3   **3.22:** Deut 29.29

The greater you become, the more humble you should be (3.18)

back on a poor person or give him any reason to curse you. ⁶If he becomes so bitter that he does curse you, his Creator will hear his prayer.

7 Make yourself popular in the synagogue. Bow your head to men of authority. ⁸Listen to what the poor have to say, and answer them politely. ⁹Protect people from those who want to wrong them, and be firm in your judgements. ¹⁰Be like a father to orphans, and provide widows with the help their husbands can no longer give them. Then you will be like a son of the Most High, and he will love you more than your own mother does.

Wisdom as a Teacher

11 Wisdom takes care of those who look for her; she raises them to greatness. ¹²Loving her is loving life itself; rising early to look for her is pure joy. ¹³Anyone who obtains Wisdom will be greatly honoured. Wherever he goes, the Lord will bless him. ¹⁴Wisdom's servants are the servants of the Holy One, and the Lord

loves everyone who loves her. ¹⁵Those who obey her will give sound judgements;*ⁱ* those who pay attention to her have true security. ¹⁶Put your trust in Wisdom, and you will possess her and pass her on to your descendants. ¹⁷At first, Wisdom will lead you along difficult paths. She will make you so afraid that you will think you cannot go on. The discipline she demands will be tormenting, and she will put you to the test with her requirements until she trusts you*ʲ* completely. ¹⁸Then she will come to you with no delay, reveal her secrets to you, and make you happy. ¹⁹But if you go astray, she will abandon you and let you go to your own ruin.

Self-confidence

20 Take advantage of opportunities, but guard yourself against evil. Don't under-rate yourself. ²¹Humility deserves honour and respect, but a low opinion of yourself leads to sin. ²²Do not let others have their way at your expense; do not bring on

ⁱ Hebrew give sound judgements; *Greek* judge nations.   *ʲ* she trusts you; *or* you trust her.

your own ruin by giving up your rights.
²³Never hesitate to speak out when the
occasion ᵏ calls for it. Don't hide your
wisdom. ˡ ²⁴Your wisdom and education
can be known only by what you say. ²⁵Do
not, however, go against the truth, and
remember that you do not know
everything. ²⁶Don't be ashamed to confess
your sins; there's no point in trying to
stop a river from flowing. ²⁷Don't allow
yourself to be dominated by someone who
is stupid or show partiality to influential
people. ²⁸Stand up for what is right, even
if it costs you your life; the Lord God
will be fighting on your side.

29 Don't be quick to speak or lazy and
negligent in your work. ³⁰Don't act like
a lion at home or be suspicious of your
servants. ³¹Don't stick out your hand to
get something if you're going to be
tightfisted when the time comes to pay
it back.

Don't Be Presumptuous

5 Don't rely on money to make you
independent. ²Don't think you have
everything you want, and then spend your
energy trying to get it. ³Don't think that
no one can exercise authority over you; if
you do, the Lord is certain to punish you.
⁴Don't think that you can sin and get
away with it; the Lord does not mind
waiting to punish you. ⁵Don't be so
certain of the Lord's forgiveness that you
go on committing one sin after another.
⁶Don't think that his mercy is so great
that he will forgive your sins no matter
how many they are. He does show mercy,
but he also shows his furious anger with
sinners. ⁷Come back to the Lord quickly.
Don't think that you can keep putting it
off. His anger can come upon you
suddenly, and you will die under his
punishment. ⁸Don't rely on dishonest
wealth; it will do you no good on that
day of disaster.

Sincerity and Self-control

9-10 Be certain about what you believe
and consistent in what you say. Don't try
to please everyone or agree with
everything people say.ᵐ ¹¹Always be
ready to listen, but take your time in
answering. ¹²Answer only if you know

*Answer only if you know what to say,
and if you don't...keep quiet (5.12)*

what to say, and if you don't know what
to say, keep quiet. ¹³Speaking can bring
you either honour or disgrace; what you
say can ruin you.

14 Don't get a reputation for being a
gossip, and don't tell tales that will hurt
people. Just as thieves will suffer disgrace,
so liars will suffer severe condemnation.
¹⁵Do nothing destructive,ⁿ whether it

6 seems insignificant or not, ¹and do
not be an enemy when you should
be a friend. A bad reputation brings you
the disgrace that lying sinners deserve.
²Do not let your passions carry you away;
this can tear your soul to pieces like a
bull. ᵒ ³You will be left like a dead tree
without any leaves or fruit. ⁴Evil desire
will destroy you and make you a joke
to your enemies.

Friendship

5 If you are polite and courteous, you
will enjoy the friendship of many people.
⁶Exchange greetings with many, but take
advice from only one person out of a
thousand. ⁷When you make friends, don't
be too quick to trust them; make sure
that they have proved themselves. ⁸Some
people will be your friends only when it
is convenient for them, but they won't
stand by you in trouble. ⁹Others will fall
out with you over some argument, and
then embarrass you by letting everyone
know about it. ¹⁰⁻¹¹Others will sit at your

ᵏ *Probable text* the occasion; *Greek* safety.
ˡ *Hebrew* Don't hide your wisdom; *most Greek manuscripts do not have these words; other Greek
manuscripts* Don't hide your wisdom for the sake of appearances.
ᵐ *Hebrew* everything people say; *Greek adds* That is what double-tongued sinners do.
ⁿ *Hebrew* Do nothing destructive; *Greek* Do not be ignorant in anything.
ᵒ *Verse 2 in both Greek and Hebrew is unclear.*
4.31: Acts 20.35   **5.4:** Ecc 8.11

table as long as things are going well; they will stick to you like your shadow and give orders to your servants, but they will not stand by you in trouble. ¹²If your situation takes a turn for the worse, they will turn against you, and you won't be able to find them anywhere.

13 Stay away from your enemies and be on guard against your friends. ¹⁴A loyal friend is like a safe shelter; find one, and you have found a treasure. ¹⁵Nothing else is as valuable; there is no way of putting a price on it. ¹⁶A loyal friend is like a medicine that keeps you in good health. Only those who fear the Lord can find such a friend. ¹⁷A person who fears the Lord can make real friendships, because he will treat his friends as he does himself. *p*

Learn from Wisdom

18 My son, learn to value Wisdom while you are young, and you will still be able to find her when you grow old. ¹⁹Work as hard to find Wisdom as a farmer works to plough and sow his fields; then you can expect a good harvest. You will have to work at it for a while, but you will soon be enjoying what you have earned. ²⁰Undisciplined people find Wisdom's demands too hard and don't have enough determination to meet them. ²¹Her requirements are a burden heavier than they are willing to bear, and they quickly lay them aside. ²²"Discipline" means just that—discipline, *q* and not many people are able to discipline themselves.

23 My son, listen to me and take my advice. ²⁴Put Wisdom's chains round your feet and her yoke round your neck. ²⁵Carry her on your shoulder and don't be resentful of her bonds. ²⁶Follow Wisdom, and keep to her ways with all your heart. ²⁷Go looking for her, and she will reveal herself to you. Take hold of her and don't let go. ²⁸Then you will discover the peace of mind she offers, and she will become your joy. ²⁹⁻³⁰The signs of slavery you wear will become signs of royal majesty. Her chains will be your protection, and you will wear her yoke like a magnificent robe. ³¹You will wear Wisdom like a splendid crown.

32 My son, you can learn if you want to. You can be clever if you are determined to be. ³³If you are willing to listen, you will learn and become wise. ³⁴Go where the old people are; find a man who is wise, and stay with him. ³⁵Be ready to listen when religious people speak, and don't miss anything that shows insight. ³⁶If you find a man with understanding, get up early to call on him; wear out his doorstep with your visits.

37 Devote all your time to studying the Lord's commands and thinking about them. He will give you the insight and wisdom you are looking for.

Miscellaneous Advice

7 ¹⁻²If you do no wrong, no wrong will ever come to you. ³Do not plough the ground to sow seeds of injustice; you may reap a bigger harvest than you expect.

4 Don't ask the Lord for a place of honour or ask the king for an important position. ⁵Don't try to convince the Lord that you are righteous or make a show of your wisdom before the king. ⁶Don't set your heart on being a judge, unless you have the strength of character needed to put an end to injustice. If you let yourself be influenced by someone in a position of power, your integrity will be damaged. ⁷Don't commit any crime against the general public, and don't disgrace yourself among your fellow citizens.

8 Don't commit the same sin twice. The punishment you get the first time ought to be enough.

9 Don't think that God Most High is going to take into account how very generous you are and so accept any offering you decide to make.

10 Never get tired of praying, and never miss a chance to give to the poor.

11 Don't laugh at a man who has been humiliated. It is the Lord who humbles a person, but the Lord also raises him up again.

12 Don't think up lies to tell about your friends. ¹³Don't tell lies at all. It never does any good.

14 In an official assembly, don't get up and talk a lot of nonsense. And don't repeat yourself when you pray.

15 Don't try to avoid farm work or other hard labour; the Most High has given us these jobs to do.

16 Don't join forces with a crowd of

p because...himself; *or* because his friends will also fear the Lord.
q Hebrew "Discipline"...discipline; *Greek* "Wisdom"...wisdom.
6.19: Jas 5.7–8   **6.37:** Josh 1.8; Ps 1.2

sinners; remember that the Lord's punishment is sure to come.

17 Be very humble, because the decay of death awaits us all.*r*

Relations with Others

18 Don't betray a friend for money. Don't betray a real friend for all the gold in the world.

19 Don't miss your chance to marry a wise and good woman. A gracious wife is worth more than gold.

20 Don't ill-treat a servant who does his work well, or an employee who does his best for you.

21 Show the same love to a wise servant that you would show to yourself,*s* and let him have his freedom.

22 Take good care of any animals you own. If they make money for you, keep them.

Teach them self-discipline while they are young (7.23)

23 If you have sons, educate them. Teach them self-discipline while they are young.

24 If you have daughters, keep them virtuous, and don't be too indulgent with them. 25 When you give your daughter in marriage, you have finished a great task, but give her to a sensible man.

26 If you have a good wife, do not divorce her, but do not trust yourself to someone you don't love.

27 Honour your father with all your heart, and never forget how your mother suffered when you were born. 28 Remember that you owe your life to them. How can you ever repay them for all they have done for you?

29 Fear the Lord with all your heart, and have respect for his priests. 30 Love your Creator with all your strength, and give his ministers your support. 31 Honour the Lord and respect the priests. Supply them with what you have been commanded to give: the first produce, the offering for sin, the shoulder of the sacrificial animal—all the required sacrifices and offerings.

32 Give your help to the poor, and the Lord will give you his perfect blessing. 33 Be generous to every living soul, and be gracious to the memory of the dead. 34 Show sympathy to those who have lost a loved one, and mourn with them. 35 Do not hesitate to visit the sick. You will be loved for things like these. 36 Whatever you do, remember that some day you must die. As long as you keep this in mind, you will never sin.

Using Common Sense

8 Do not challenge a person who has influence; you may fall into his power. 2 Do not quarrel with a rich man; he may bribe people to turn against you. Gold has destroyed many people and corrupted kings. 3 Don't argue with someone who talks too much; you will just be adding fuel to his fire. 4 Don't make fun of someone who has bad manners; he may insult your ancestors. 5 Don't criticize someone if he is already turning away from sin. Remember that we are all guilty. 6 Never think less of someone because he is old; some of us are growing old, too. 7 Don't be happy over the death of anyone; remember that all of us must die.

8 Do not disregard what wise men have said. Study their proverbs; from them you can learn to be cultured and to serve great men. 9 Pay attention to what old people say, for they learnt from those who came before them. You can learn from them, and they can teach you how to have an answer ready when you need one.

10 You should not provide a sinner with more opportunity to sin. You might get hurt yourself; it's as easy as getting burnt while adding logs to a fire. 11 You should not get up and walk out on someone who

---

r Hebrew the decay...all; *Greek* the punishment of the ungodly is fire and worms.
s Hebrew Show the same love...yourself; *Greek* Show love to a wise servant.
7.21: Ex 21.2; Deut 15.12–15   **7.27–28:** Ex 20.12

is insolent. He might twist your words and use them against you. ¹²You should not lend anything to someone more powerful than you. If you do, you might as well consider it lost. ¹³You should not guarantee anyone else's loan to an extent that you cannot afford. You must be prepared to pay any such guarantee. ¹⁴You should not bring a lawsuit against a judge. He will win because of his position. ¹⁵You should not travel with anyone who is reckless. It will cause you nothing but trouble. He will do any foolish thing he pleases, and you will die with him.

16 You should not get into an argument with anyone who has a hot temper or go to a place where the two of you will be alone. Violence means nothing to such a person, and he will attack you when there is no one to help you. ¹⁷You should not ask a stupid person for advice. He will not be able to keep secret what you tell him. ¹⁸You should not do anything in front of a stranger that should be kept secret. There is no way of knowing what will happen if you do. ¹⁹You should not reveal your most private thoughts to anyone. If you do, you may as well throw away any chance of happiness. ᵗ

Women

9 Don't be jealous of the wife you love. You will only be teaching her how to do you harm. ²Do not surrender your dignity to a woman. ³Keep away from other men's wives ᵘ or they will trap you. ⁴Don't keep company with female musicians; they will trick you. ⁵Don't look too intently at a virgin, or you may find yourself forced to pay a bride price. ⁶Don't give yourself to prostitutes, or you may lose everything you own. ⁷So don't go looking about in the streets or wandering round in the run-down parts of town. ⁸When you see a good-looking woman, look the other way; don't let your mind dwell on the beauty of any woman who is not your wife. Many men have been led astray by a woman's beauty. It kindles passion as if it were fire. ⁹Don't sit down to eat with another man's wife or join her for a drink. You may give in to the temptation of her charms and be destroyed by your passion.

When you see a good-looking woman, look the other way (9.8)

Friendships with Other Men

10 Never abandon an old friend; you will never find a new one who can take his place. Friendship is like wine; it gets better as it grows older. ¹¹Don't be jealous of a sinner's success; you don't know what kind of disaster is in store for him. ¹²Don't take pleasure in the things that make ungodly people happy; remember that they will be held guilty as long as they live. ¹³If you keep away from a man who has the power to put you to death, you will not have to fear for your life; but if you must go near him, be very careful, or he may kill you. Be conscious that you are walking among hidden traps, that you are an easy target.

14 Get to know the people round you as well as you can, and take advice only from those who are qualified to give it. ¹⁵Engage in conversation with intelligent men, and let the Law of the Most High be the topic of your discussions. ¹⁶Choose righteous people for your dinner companions. Your chief pride should be your fear of the Lord.

Rulers

17 A skilled craftsman is admired for the things he makes, and a leader's wisdom is proved by his words. ¹⁸Someone who speaks rashly and recklessly is

ᵗ *Hebrew* If...happiness; *Greek* And don't let anyone do you a favour.
ᵘ *Hebrew* other men's wives; *Greek* immoral women.
9.1: Num 5.12–15

feared and hated by everyone in town.

10

¹A wise ruler will educate his people, and his government will be orderly. ²All the officials and all the citizens will be like their ruler. ³An uneducated king will ruin his people, but a government will grow strong if its rulers are wise. ⁴The Lord sees to the government of the world and brings the right person to power at the right time. ⁵The success of that person is in the Lord's hands. The Lord is the source of the honour given to any official.

Pride

6 Don't be angry with someone for every little thing he does wrong. Don't do anything out of injured pride. ⁷Arrogance and injustice are hated by both the Lord and man. ⁸Injustice, arrogance, and wealth cause nations to fall from power, and others then rise to take their place. ⁹We are only dust and ashes; what have we got to be proud of? Our body decays even while we are alive. ᵛ ¹⁰A long illness puzzles the doctor. ʷ Even a king may be alive today and dead tomorrow. ¹¹When a person dies, all he then possesses is worms, flies, and maggots.

12 Pride has its beginning when a person abandons the Lord, his maker. ¹³Pride is like a fountain pouring out sin, and whoever persists in it will be filled with wickedness. That is why the Lord brought terrible punishments on some people and completely destroyed them. ¹⁴The Lord has overthrown kings and put humbler people in their place. ¹⁵The Lord has pulled up nations by the roots and established humbler ones in their place. ¹⁶The Lord has overthrown empires and completely devastated their lands. ¹⁷He destroyed some so completely that they are not even remembered any more. ¹⁸The Creator never intended human beings to be arrogant and violent.

People Who Should Be Honoured

19 Who deserves honour? The human race does, because people fear the Lord. Who does not deserve honour? The human race does not, because people break the Lord's commands. ²⁰A leader should be honoured by those who follow him, and the Lord honours those who fear him. ˣ

22 Rich people, famous people, and poor people all take pride in their fear of the Lord. ²³It is not right to refuse honour to a poor person who is intelligent, and it is not right to give honour to a sinner. ²⁴Men of influence, rulers, and judges will be honoured, but none of them is greater than a person who fears the Lord. ²⁵A slave who is wise will have free citizens serving him; and if they are sensible, they will not resent it.

Humility and Self-respect

26 When you do your work, don't make a show of your skill, and don't try to put on an act when you are in trouble. ²⁷It is better to work and have more than you need than to go about boasting but hungry.

28 My son, keep your self-respect, but remain modest. Value yourself at your true worth. ²⁹There is no excuse for a person who runs himself down. No one respects a person who has no respect for himself. ³⁰Poor people can be honoured for their good sense, and rich people can be honoured for their wealth. ³¹If someone is honoured while he is poor, think how much he will be honoured if he becomes rich! If someone is despised while he is rich, think how much more he will be

11

despised if he becomes poor! ¹If a poor man is wise, he has good reason to be proud, and he will be thought of as a great man.

Appearances

2 Do not compliment a person on his good looks. On the other hand, do not look down on someone who is unattractive. ³Compared with most flying things, a bee is very small, but the honey it makes is the sweetest of foods. ⁴Don't make fun of someone who has fallen on hard times and is dressed in rags. ʸ The Lord does wonderful things that human beings never notice. ⁵Many are the kings who have ended their careers sitting on the ground, while their crowns were worn by men no one had heard of before. ⁶Many are the rulers who have suffered disgrace.

ᵛ Our body...alive; *this sentence in both Greek and Hebrew is unclear.*
ʷ A long...doctor; *this sentence in both Greek and Hebrew is unclear.*
ˣ *Some manuscripts add verse 21*: Success begins with fear of the Lord, but failure begins with stubbornness and arrogance.
ʸ *Hebrew* Don't...rags; *Greek* Don't take pride in fine clothes, and don't let compliments go to your head.
10.14: 1 Sam 2.8; Lk 1.52

Many are the famous men who have fallen into the power of others.

Be Cautious

7 Before you start criticizing, get your facts straight and think the matter through. 8 Don't interrupt while someone is speaking; hear what he has to say before you answer. 9 Don't get into an argument over something that is none of your business. Don't take part in decisions that are being made by sinners.

10 My son, don't get involved in too many things. If you try to do too much, you will suffer for it. You won't be able to finish your work, and you won't be able to get away from it either. 11 For instance, here is a man who never stops working like a slave, but gets further behind all the time. 12 On the other hand, another man may be very poor and not up to his task. He may be slow, and he may need help, but the Lord is pleased with him and pulls him out of his bad situation. 13 When he is back on his feet again, everyone is astounded.

14 Everything comes from the Lord: success and failure, poverty and wealth, life and death. 15 Wisdom, understanding, knowledge of the Law, love, and the doing of good deeds—all these come from the Lord. 16 Error and darkness have been with sinners from the beginning, and those who enjoy evil will have it with them into their old age. 17 The Lord's gifts to religious people are gifts that endure. If he approves of you, you will always be successful. 18 A man may grow rich by working hard and denying himself pleasure, but what does he get for it? 19 He says to himself, "Now I can finally sit back and enjoy what I have worked for." But he has no idea how long it will be before he must die and leave his wealth to others.

20 Stand by your duty and stick at it; grow old at your work. 21 Don't be jealous of what sinners achieve; just stick to your own work, and trust the Lord. It is very easy for the Lord to make a poor man suddenly rich. 22 Devout people will receive the Lord's blessing as their reward, and that blessing can be given in a moment. 23 Don't be concerned about what you need, or what success the future holds for you. 24 On the other hand, don't think that you have everything you need or that nothing can go wrong for you in the future. 25 When things are going well, people don't think about hard times; and when things are going badly, they forget about prosperity. 26 The Lord can easily wait until the day of a man's death to reward or punish him. 27 At that time his deeds are revealed for everyone to see; all his happiness can be erased in that one moment of misery. 28 So then, don't think of anyone's life as happy until it is over, because all the evidence is not in until the person is dead. *z*

Be Careful in Choosing Friends

29 Be careful about the kind of person you invite into your home, because clever people can fool you in many ways. 30 A proud man is a decoy to lure you into danger; like a spy, he will look for your weaknesses. *a* 31 He will make good appear evil and find fault with the noblest actions. 32 A single spark can set a pile of coals ablaze, and a sinner is just waiting for a chance to use violence. 33 Watch out for such people and their evil plans; they will ruin you permanently. 34 If you bring a stranger home with you, it will only cause trouble, even between you and your own family.

12 When you do a good deed, make sure you know who is benefiting from it; then what you do will not be wasted. *b* 2 You will be repaid for any kindness you show to a devout person. If he doesn't repay you, the Most High will. 3 No good ever comes to a person who gives comfort to the wicked; it is not a righteous act. *c* 4 Give to religious people, but don't help sinners. 5 Do good to humble people, but don't give anything to those who are not devout. Don't give them food, or they will use your kindness against you. Every good thing you do for such people will bring you twice as much trouble in return. 6 The Most High himself hates sinners, and he will punish them. 7 Give to good people, but do not help sinners.

8 When things are going well, it is hard to tell who your real friends are, but in hard times you can recognize your enemies; 9 even your friends will leave you

---

z Hebrew all...dead; *Greek* a man will be known by his children.
a Hebrew look...weaknesses; *Greek* wait for your downfall.
b what you do...wasted; *or* you will be thanked for what you do.
c Hebrew gives...act; *Greek* makes evil a habit or refuses to give to the poor.
11.18-19: Ps 49.10; Lk 12.16-21   **12.1:** Mt 7.6

But when you are successful, your enemies will act like friends (12.9)

then. But when you are successful, your enemies will act like friends.*d* 10 Never trust an enemy; his wickedness is as destructive as rust. 11 Watch out, and be on guard against him, even if he pretends to be ever so humble. He is like a metal mirror that rusts away if you don't keep it polished. 12 Seat an enemy at your right hand, and the next thing you know he'll be trying to get your own place of honour. Put him next to you, and he will overthrow you. Then you will realize the truth of my words, and be stung with regret when you remember them. 13 Nobody feels sorry for snake charmers or wild animal tamers who get bitten, 14 and nobody will feel sorry for you if you go about with sinners and get involved in their wrongdoing.

15 An enemy will stay with you for a while, but not when trouble comes. 16 He will speak fine words while he plots how to trap you. He will pretend to share your sorrows, but he will kill you if he gets a chance. 17 If trouble comes your way, you will find him waiting, ready to trip you up while he pretends to help you. 18 He will be a different person then, rubbing his hands, nodding his head, and spreading rumours about you.

13 If you touch tar, it will stick to you, and if you keep company with arrogant people, you will come to be just like them. 2 Don't try to lift something too heavy for you, and don't keep company with people who are richer and more powerful than you. You cannot keep a clay pot next to an iron kettle; the pot will break if it hits the kettle. 3 If a rich man wrongs someone, he can afford to add insult to injury; but if a poor man is wronged, he is forced to apologize for himself. 4 A rich man will use you as long as he can profit from it, but when you need him, he will leave you helpless. 5 He will live with you as long as you have anything and will gladly drain you dry. 6 If he needs you, he will trick you with his smiles and cheerful, kindly words. "Do you need anything?" he will ask. 7 He will feed you until you are embarrassed. Finally, when he has drained you two or three times over, he will laugh at you. If you see him later, he will pretend he doesn't know you, and will pass you by.

8 Be careful not to be misled; you can be enjoying yourself and suddenly find yourself humiliated. 9 If you are invited to the home of an influential man, be reserved in your behaviour. Then he will invite you more often. 10 If you push yourself on him, he will put you in your place. On the other hand, if you keep your distance from him, he will forget about you. 11 Don't pretend to be his equal or trust everything he says. In spite of all his long and polite conversation, he is testing you.

12 If a person does not keep confidences, he is cruel; he will not hesitate to hurt you or have you put in jail. 13 Keep your secrets to yourself and be very careful, for you are always walking on dangerous ground.*e*

15 Every creature prefers its own kind,

---

d Hebrew act like friends; *Greek* be sorry.
e Some manuscripts add verses 13b–14: When you hear this in your sleep, wake up! 14 As long as you live, love the Lord and call on him to rescue you.

and people are no different. ¹⁶ Just as animals of the same species flock together, so people keep company with people like themselves. ¹⁷ A sinner has no more in common with a devout person than a wolf has with a lamb. ¹⁸ A rich man has no more in common with a poor man than a hyena has with a dog. ¹⁹ The rich hunt down the poor just as lions hunt down wild donkeys in the open country. ²⁰ Arrogant people have nothing but scorn for the humble, and the rich think of the poor in the same way. ²¹ When a rich man stumbles, his friends will steady him, but if a poor man falls, his friends will have nothing to do with him. ²² When a rich man makes a mistake, there are many people to cover up for him and explain away all the things he never should have said. But let a poor man make a mistake, and he gets nothing but criticism. Even if what he says makes good sense, nobody

When a rich man speaks, everyone is silent...but let a poor man speak...(13.23)

will listen. ²³ When a rich man speaks, everyone is silent, and they praise him to the skies for what he says. But let a poor man speak, and everybody says, "Who is that?" They push him down if he so much as stumbles.

24 There is nothing wrong with being

---

f *Probable text* Greed; *Greek* Wicked injustice.

---

rich if you haven't sinned to get there. But there is nothing sinful about being poor, either. Only the ungodly think so. ²⁵ It's what is in your heart that makes the expression on your face happy or sad. ²⁶ If you feel cheerful, you will look cheerful, although making up proverbs calls for some intense thought.

14 If a person never says anything carelessly, he is to be congratulated; he doesn't need to feel guilty. ² If a person has a clear conscience and never gives up hope, he is certainly to be congratulated!

Responsible Use of Wealth

3 It isn't right for someone who is selfish to be rich. What use is money to a stingy person? ⁴ If you deny yourself in order to accumulate wealth, you are only accumulating it for someone else. Others will use your riches to live in luxury. ⁵ How can you be generous with others if you are stingy with yourself, if you are not willing to enjoy your own wealth? ⁶ No one is worse off than someone who is stingy with himself; it is a sin that brings its own punishment. ⁷ When such a person does something good, it is only by accident; his selfishness will sooner or later be evident. ⁸ A selfish man is an evil man; he turns his back on people's needs ⁹ and is never satisfied with what he has. Greed f will shrivel up a person's soul. ¹⁰ Some people are too stingy to put bread on their own table.

11 My son, treat yourself as well as you can, and bring worthy offerings to the Lord. ¹² Remember that death is coming for you some day, and you haven't been told when that will be. ¹³ Before that day comes, be kind to your friends; be as generous as you can. ¹⁴ Don't deny yourself a single day's happiness. If there is something you want to do and it is lawful, go ahead! ¹⁵ Some day all that you have worked for will be divided up and given to others. ¹⁶ So be generous; but also be willing to receive from others. Enjoy yourself, for you will not find any pleasures in the world of the dead. ¹⁷ The human body wears out like a piece of clothing. The ancient law decrees that we must die. ¹⁸ Human beings are like leaves on a spreading tree. New growth takes the place of the fallen leaves; while some of us die, others are being born. ¹⁹ Everything made by human hands will decay and

perish, along with the person who made it.

The Happiness of Having Wisdom

20 It is a happy person who is concerned with Wisdom and who uses good sense. 21 Anyone who studies the ways of Wisdom will also learn her secrets. 22 Go after Wisdom like a hunter looking for game. 23 Look into her windows and listen at her doors. 24 Camp as close to her house as you can get, 25 and you will have a fine place to live. 26-27 Build your home there, safe beneath her protecting branches, and shaded from the heat. *g*

15 If you fear the Lord, you will do this. Master his Law, and you will find Wisdom. 2 She will come to welcome you, like a mother or a young bride. 3 She will give you wisdom and knowledge like food and drink. 4 Rely on her for support, and you will never know the disgrace of failure. 5 She will make you more honoured than all your neighbours; when you speak in the assembly, she will give you the right words. 6 You will find happiness and genuine joy; your name will be remembered for ever.

7 But people who are foolish or sinful will never even catch sight of Wisdom. 8 She will have nothing to do with conceited people; she never enters the mind of liars. 9 It is not appropriate for a sinner to sing hymns of praise, because his worship is insincere. 10 A hymn should be an expression of wisdom, inspired by the Lord himself.

Free Will

11 Don't blame the Lord for your sin; the Lord does not cause what he hates. *h* 12 Don't claim that he has misled you; he doesn't need the help of sinners to accomplish his purposes. 13 The Lord hates evil in all its forms, and those who fear the Lord find nothing attractive in evil. 14 When, in the beginning, the Lord created human beings, he left them free to do as they wished. 15 If you want to, you can keep the Lord's commands. You can decide whether you will be loyal to him or not. 16 He has placed fire and water before you; reach out and take whichever you want. 17 You have a choice between life and death; you will get whichever you choose. 18 The Lord's wisdom and power are great and he sees everything. 19 He is aware of everything a person does, and he takes care of those who fear him. 20 He has never commanded anyone to be wicked or given anyone permission to sin.

God's Punishment of Sinners

16 A large family is nothing to be desired if the children are worthless. Godless sons are nothing to be proud of. 2 No matter how many children you have, don't look on them with pride unless they fear the Lord. 3 Don't put much hope in their future or expect them to live a long time. One child who does the Lord's will is better than a thousand who do not. *i* It is better to go to your grave with no children at all than to have children who are godless.

4 A city's population may grow because of the wisdom of one person, while a whole tribe of lawless people disappears. 5 I have seen such things many times and have heard of even more striking examples. 6 The Lord's flaming anger will break out against a small gathering of sinners or a disobedient nation. 7 He did not forgive those ancient giants who rebelled against him, confident of their own strength. 8 He detested the arrogance of the people among whom Lot lived, and he did not spare them. 9 He showed no mercy on that nation which he doomed to destruction for its sins, 10 nor on those 600,000 people on the march through the wilderness who gathered together in stubborn rebellion. 11 Even if there had been only one stubborn person, it would have been a miracle if he had escaped punishment. The Lord is merciful, but he can also become angry. He can be overwhelming in his forgiveness or in his anger. 12 His punishment is as severe as his mercy is great. He judges people by what they have done. 13 No sinner can escape with what he has stolen. The Lord will reward the patience of devout people. 14 Every righteous person will be

---

g Hebrew Build...heat; *Greek* Let her protect your children. Live safe beneath her branches, shaded from the heat, surrounded by her glory.
h Hebrew the Lord does not cause what he hates; *Greek* do not do what the Lord hates.
i Hebrew who does...do not; *Greek* is better than a thousand.

14.20-25: Prov 8.32-35   **15.11-20:** Sir 17.1-12   **16.7:** Gen 6.4; Wis 14.6

rewarded;[j] everyone will get what he deserves.[k]

17 Never say, "I will hide from the Lord. Nobody up there is going to give me a thought. How can I be noticed among so many people? The creation is so enormous, what am I worth? 18 When the Lord comes, everything will tremble: the earth and the great waters beneath it, the sky and the heavens above it. 19 The mountains will shake, and the foundations of the earth will shudder when he looks at them. 20 The Lord isn't going to give me a thought. Nobody cares what I do. 21 If I sin and am secretly disloyal, nobody will know it.[l] 22 If I do what is right, nobody will tell the Lord about it. Who wants to wait for him, anyway? He is too slow in doing what he has said he would." 23 Only someone with very little sense, and foolishly misguided, would think things like that.

God's Wisdom in Creation

24 My son, listen and pay attention to me; you will gain knowledge if you do. 25 I will give you diligent and accurate instruction.
26 In the beginning the Lord did his work of creation,[m]
    and he gave everything a place of its own.
27 He arranged everything in an eternal order
    and decreed that it should be that way for ever.
Not one part of creation ever grows hungry;
    no part grows tired or stops its work.
28 The parts do not crowd one another,
    and they never disobey his word.
29 When the Lord had made all this,

he looked at the earth and filled it with good things.
30 He covered it with all kinds of creatures
    that must die and return to the dust.

17 Then the Lord formed human beings from the dust
    and sent each of them back to it again.
2 He gave them only a limited time to live,
    but he gave them authority over everything on earth.
3 He made them to be like himself,
    and gave them his[n] own strength.
4 He made all other creatures afraid of them;
    he gave them authority over all the animals and birds.[o]
6 He gave them their tongues, their eyes, their ears, their minds, and their consciences.
7 He filled them with knowledge and understanding
    and showed them the difference between good and evil.
8 He gave them his own insight
    to let them see the majesty of his creation.[p]
10 They will praise his holy name
    and proclaim the greatness of all he does.
11 He made knowledge available to them
    and gave them the Law as a source of life.
12 He made an eternal covenant with them
    and revealed his commands to them.
13 They saw the splendour of his majesty
    and heard the glory of his voice.
14 He warned them against unrighteousness
    and taught each person how to treat others.

---

[j] Hebrew Every...rewarded; Greek He makes room for every act of mercy.
[k] Some manuscripts add verses 15-16: The Lord made the king of Egypt so stubborn that he would not acknowledge the Lord, in order that the world might know the Lord's works. 16 He shows his mercy to all creation; he has divided his light from darkness with a plumb-line.
[l] Hebrew 20-21 The Lord...know it; Greek 20 It is altogether too big for the human mind to handle. No one can understand his ways. 21 Most of his works are just as invisible as the storm wind.
[m] Hebrew In...creation; Greek In the judgement of the Lord his works are from the beginning.
[n] Probable text his; Greek their.
[o] Some manuscripts add verse 5: The Lord gave them the five senses, but he also gave them a sixth—intelligence, and a seventh—reason, which enables them to interpret what comes to them through the senses.
[p] Some manuscripts add verse 9: and he allowed them to take pride for ever in his marvellous deeds.
17.1-3: Gen 1.26-28; 2.7   **17.7:** Gen 2.17

God Is Judge

15 The Lord is always aware of what people do; there is no way to hide from him. *q* 17 He gave each nation its own ruler, but Israel is the Lord's own possession. *r* 19 The Lord is always watching what people do; everything they do is as clear as day to him. 20 None of their sins are hidden from him; he is aware of them all. *s* 22 When we give to the poor, the Lord considers it as precious as a valuable ring. Human kindness is as precious to him as life itself. 23 Later he will judge the wicked and punish them; they will get what they deserve. 24 But the Lord will allow those who repent to return to him. He always gives encouragement to those who are losing hope.

A Call to Repentance

25 Come to the Lord, and leave your sin behind. Pray sincerely that he will help you to live a better life. 26 Return to the Most High and turn away from sin. Have an intense hatred for wickedness. 27 Those who are alive can give thanks to the Lord, but can anyone in the world of the dead sing praise to the Most High? 28 A person who is alive and well can sing the Lord's praises, but the dead, who no longer exist, have no way to give him thanks. 29 How great is the Lord's merciful forgiveness of those who turn to him! 30 But this is not the nature of human beings; *t* not one of us is immortal. 31 Nothing is brighter than the sun, but even the sun's light fails during an eclipse. How much easier it is for human thoughts to be eclipsed by evil! 32 The Lord can look out over all the stars in the sky. Human beings? They are dust and ashes.

The Greatness of God

18 The Lord, who lives for ever, created the whole universe, 2 and he alone is just. *u* 4 He has given no one enough power to describe what he has done, and no one can investigate it completely. 5 Who can measure his majestic power? Who can tell the whole story of his merciful actions? 6 We cannot add to them; we cannot subtract from them. There is no way to comprehend the marvellous things the Lord has done. 7 When we come to the end of that story, we have not even begun; we are simply at a loss for words.

Man Is Nothing

8 What is man? Of what use is he? The good that he does—the evil that he does—what does it all mean? 9 If a person lives a hundred years, he has lived an unusually long time, 10 but compared with all eternity, those years are like a drop of water in the ocean, like a single grain of sand. 11 That is why the Lord is so patient with us, why he is so free with his mercy. 12 He looks at us and knows that we are doomed to die; that is why he is so willing to forgive us. 13 A person can show compassion to someone he knows, but the Lord shows compassion for all humanity. He corrects us; he disciplines us; he teaches us. Like a shepherd tending sheep, he brings us back to himself. 14 He will have compassion on us if we accept his guidance and are eager for him to show us where we are wrong.

Kindness and Charity

15 My son, when you help someone, don't reprimand him at the same time. When you make a gift, don't say anything that hurts. 16 Your words count for more than what you give. Even dew gives some relief during a spell of hot weather. 17 Yes, kind words are more effective than the best of gifts, and if you are really concerned, you will give both. 18 It is stupid to be unkind and insulting. No one's eyes are going to sparkle at a gift that you resent giving.

Self-examination

19 Know what you are talking about before you speak, and give attention to

---

q Some manuscripts add verses 16–17a: From childhood on they tend to be evil; their heart is like stone, and they don't seem to be able to make it more human. 17 He divided the nations of the whole earth.
r Some manuscripts add verse 18: Israel is his first-born, whom he disciplines as he brings him up. He gives him the light of his love and never neglects him.
s Some manuscripts add verse 21: But the Lord is gracious and knows his creatures; so he has spared them rather than abandon them.
t But...human beings; or People cannot have everything.
u Some manuscripts add verses 2b–3: and there is no other beside him. 3 He guides the world with his hand, and everything obeys him. He is the king of all things, and his power separates what is holy from what is not.
17.25–26: Jer 3.12   **17.27–28:** Ps 6.5; Is 38.18; Bar 2.17–18

your health before you get ill. ²⁰Examine your conscience before the Lord judges you; then when that time comes, he will forgive you. ²¹Humble yourself before you are punished with sickness. When you have sinned, show repentance. ²²If you make a promise to the Lord, keep it as soon as you can. Don't wait until you are about to die to set things straight. ²³But before you make such a promise, be prepared to keep it. Don't try to test the Lord's patience. ²⁴Think! Do you want him to be angry with you on the day you die? When you face his judgement, do you want him to turn his back on you? ²⁵When you have all you want, think what it is like to be hungry, what it is to be poor. ²⁶Things can change in a single day; the Lord can act very quickly. ²⁷If you are wise, you will be careful in everything you do. When sin is all round you, be especially careful that you do not become guilty. ²⁸Every intelligent person can recognize wisdom and will honour anyone who shows it. ²⁹If you appreciate wisdom when you hear it, you will become wise yourself, and your words will be a source of wisdom for others.

Self-control

30 Don't be controlled by your lust; keep your passions in check. ³¹If you allow yourself to satisfy your every desire, you will be a joke to your enemies. ³²Don't indulge in luxurious living; the expense of it will ruin you. ³³Don't make yourself a beggar by borrowing for expensive banquets when you haven't enough

19 money of your own. ¹If you do, you ᵛ will never get rich; if you don't pay attention to small matters, you will gradually ruin yourself. ²Wine and women make sensible men do foolish things. A man who goes to prostitutes gets more and more careless, ³and that carelessness will cost him his life. Worms will feed on his decaying body.

4 It is silly to trust people too quickly. If you sin, you are hurting yourself. ⁵If wickedness makes you happy, you will be condemned.

Loose Talk

6 Avoid idle talk, and you will avoid a lot of trouble. ⁷Never repeat what you hear, and you will have no regrets. ⁸Don't tell it to your friends or your enemies unless it would be sinful to keep it to yourself. ⁹Whoever hears you will take note of it, and sooner or later will hate you for it. ¹⁰Have you heard a rumour? Let it die with you. Be brave! It won't make you explode. ¹¹A foolish person trying to keep a secret suffers like a woman in labour. ¹²Whenever he hears a secret, it's like an arrow stuck in his leg.

13 If you hear that a friend has done something wrong, ask him about it. Maybe it isn't true. If it is true, he won't do it again. ¹⁴If you hear that a neighbour has said something he shouldn't, ask him about it. Maybe he didn't say it. If he did, he won't say it again. ¹⁵If you hear something bad about a friend, ask him about it. It might be a lie. Don't believe everything you hear. ¹⁶A person may say something carelessly and not really mean it. Everyone has sinned in this way at one time or another. ¹⁷If you hear something that makes you angry with your neighbour, ask him about it before you threaten him. Leave the matter to the Law of the Most High. ʷ

Recognizing Real Wisdom

20 Fear the Lord and keep his Law; that is what Wisdom is all about. ˣ ²²You may know everything there is to know about wickedness, but that does not make you wise. It is not sensible to follow the advice of sinners. ²³It is possible to use cleverness for wicked purposes, but some people act like fools because they don't know any better. ²⁴A devout person, even if he is not very intelligent, is better off than the cleverest of sinners. ²⁵It is possible to be marvellously clever and still be dishonest, or to get what you want by being absurdly polite.

26 Then there are those wicked people who go about looking very solemn and mournful, but who are only trying to deceive you. ²⁷They will turn their faces away and pretend not to hear you, but they'll take advantage of you when you least expect it. ²⁸If for some reason they are unable to sin now, they'll get round

---

ᵛ Hebrew If you do, you; Greek A worker who drinks too much.
ʷ Some manuscripts add verses 17c–19: and don't be angry. ¹⁸Fearing the Lord is the first step towards his accepting you; he will love you if you are wise. ¹⁹Learn the Lord's commands. It is a discipline that gives life. Those who do what pleases him enjoy the fruit of the tree of immortality.
ˣ Some manuscripts add verses 20b–21: and what the knowledge of his omnipotence means. ²¹If a servant refuses to obey his master, but later does obey, the master is still angry.

...and pretend not to hear you (19.27)

to it at the first opportunity. 29 You can know a man by his appearance. The first time you look at him, you can tell if he has good sense. 30 His character shows in the way he dresses, the way he laughs, and the way he walks.

Knowing When to Talk

20 A person can be rebuked in the wrong way; it may be wiser to keep quiet than to speak. 2 But it is much better to rebuke the person than to keep your anger bottled up. 3 Admit when you are wrong, and you will avoid embarrassment. 4 Using force to get a point across is like a castrated man trying to rape a girl. 5 Some people are thought to be wise because they don't talk much; others are disliked because they talk too much. 6 Some people keep quiet because they don't have anything to say; others keep quiet because they know the right time to speak. 7 A wise person will not speak until the right moment, but a bragging fool doesn't know when that time is. 8 No one can stand a person who talks too long and will not give others a chance to speak.

Sudden Changes of Fortune

9 Bad luck can sometimes lead to success, and a stroke of good luck can sometimes lead to loss.

10 Generosity will sometimes do you no good, but at other times it will repay you double.

11 Honour can be followed by disgrace, but there are people who have risen from obscurity to places of honour.

12 Sometimes what seems like a real bargain can turn out to be a very expensive mistake.

13 When a person with good judgement speaks, he wins friends. A stupid person, though, can shower compliments on everybody, and it won't help him a bit. 14 If such a person gives you something, it won't do any good; it won't be as valuable as he thinks it is.*y* 15 He isn't generous with anything but criticism, which he will shout for all the world to hear. If he lends you something today, he'll want it back tomorrow. (Don't you hate people like that?) 16 Then that fool will say, "Nobody likes me. Nobody appreciates what I do for them. They'll take what I give them, but then talk about me behind my back." 17 And he's right—he's a constant joke to everyone.

Inappropriate Talk

18 A slip of the tongue is worse than a slip on the pavement; the wicked will go to ruin just as suddenly as a person slips and falls.

19 An impolite person is like one of those indecent stories that ignorant people are always telling.

20 Nobody takes a proverb seriously when some fool quotes it at the wrong time.

21 If a person is too poor to afford sin, he can rest without a guilty conscience.

22 You can lose all your self-respect by being reluctant to speak up in the presence of stupidity.

23 If you promise a friend something because you are too bashful to say no, you're making an enemy needlessly.

24 Lying is an ugly blot on a person's character, but ignorant people do it all the time. 25 A thief is better than a habitual liar, but both are headed for ruin. 26 A liar has no honour. He lives in constant disgrace.

Stewardship of Wisdom

27 Speak wisely, and you will get ahead in the world. Influential people appreciate good sense. 28 They will excuse your errors if they like you, so cultivate the soil and reap the harvest!

29 Gifts and bribes make even wise men blind to the truth, and prevent them from being honest in their criticism.

30 Wisdom that is not expressed is like a treasure that has been hidden—both are useless. 31 But a person who covers up

y it won't be...it is; *or* he only expects to be repaid.

his foolishness is better than one who
keeps his wisdom to himself.

Sin

21 Have you sinned, my son? Don't
do it again, and pray for forgiveness for what you have already done.
² Avoid sin as if it were a snake. If you
get too near, it will sink its teeth into
your soul like a lion, and destroy you.
³ Every lawless act leaves an incurable
wound, like one left by a double-edged
sword.

4 If a person is insolent and arrogant,
he may lose everything he has.

5 When poor people pray, God hears
them and quickly answers their prayers.

6 If you refuse to accept correction, you
are committing a sin; and if you fear the
Lord, you will make a sincere change in
your ways.

7 A man may be famous as a good
speaker, but when he is wrong, a sensible
person will detect it.

8 A man who borrows money to build
a house is just collecting stones for his
own tomb.ᶻ

9 A group of people who have no
respect for the Law is like a pile of
kindling; they will meet a fiery end. ¹⁰ The
road that sinners walk is smooth and
paved, but it leads to the world of the
dead.

Wisdom and Foolishness

11 Whoever wants to keep the Law
must learn what the Law means. If you
fear the Lord in every sense of the term,
you will have wisdom. ¹² You have to be
intelligent to learn anything; but there is
such a thing as just pretending to be
intelligent, which only makes people
bitter. ¹³ A wise man's knowledge is like
a river that never runs dry, like an ever-
flowing stream of good advice.

14 A fool, on the other hand, has a mind
like a jar with a hole in it; anything he
learns is soon lost.

15 When an educated person hears
something that shows insight, it
stimulates his mind and leads him on to
other ideas. But when someone who is
satisfied with ignorance hears it, he won't
like it, and will forget it as soon as he
can. ¹⁶ Listening to a foolish person talk
is like travelling with a heavy load on

*A fool...has a mind like a jar with a hole
in it (21.14)*

your back, but it is a pleasure to hear
what intelligent people have to say. ¹⁷ The
assembly will be eager to hear from an
intelligent person and will take his opinion
seriously.

18 To an ignorant person, wisdom is as
useless as a house gone to ruin. He has
never even thought about the things he
is so sure of. ¹⁹ To a person without any
sense, an education is like handcuffs,
²⁰⁻²¹ but to a sensible person, it is like
gold bracelets. An intelligent person will
smile quietly while a fool roars with
laughter. ²²⁻²³ A stupid person will peep
into someone's house through the door
and then march right in, but someone with
experience and good manners will have
enough respect to wait outside.
²⁴ Eavesdropping at doors is bad manners,
and anyone with a sense of decency would
be ashamed to do it.

25 Presumptuous people talk about
things that are none of their business,ᵃ
but the wise will consider the consequences of what they say. ²⁶ Fools say
whatever comes to mind; wise people
think before they speak.

27 When a wicked man curses his
enemyᵇ he is cursing himself.

28 A gossip ruins his own character,
and everyone in the neighbourhood hates
him.

Laziness and Foolishness

22 ¹⁻² Lazy people are no better than
dung; they are repulsive, and no
one wants to get near them.

3 It is a disgrace to a father to have
an undisciplined child, especially if it is
a daughter. ⁴ A sensible daughter will get

ᶻ his own tomb; *some manuscripts have* the winter.
ᵃ *Probable text* Presumptuous...business; *Greek* The lips of strangers speak of these things.
ᵇ his enemy; *or* Satan.
21.5: Sir 35.17–19

a husband, but a shameless daughter brings her father grief. ⁵A girl with no sense of propriety will disgrace both her husband and her father; neither will have any respect for her.

6 Lecturing your children can sometimes be as out of place as singing to people in mourning, but a whipping is a wise choice of discipline at any time.

7 Trying to teach a fool is like gluing a broken pot together again, like waking someone out of a deep sleep. ⁸Explaining something to a fool is like explaining it to a sleepy man; when you have finished, he'll say, "What was that again?"ᶜ

11 We mourn for the dead because they have no access to light. We ought to mourn for fools, because they have no access to intelligence. In fact, we should go into deeper mourning for fools, because the life they lead is worse than death. The dead are at least at rest. ¹²For seven days we mourn the dead, but a foolish or ungodly person causes a lifetime of grief.

13 Don't visit stupid people or spend a lot of time talking with them. Avoid them; then they can't contaminate you, and you can live in peace without being troubled or worn down by their foolishness. ¹⁴Such people are a heavier burden to bear than lead; and the only word that fits them is "fools." ¹⁵It is easier to carry a load of sand, salt, and iron than to put up with a stupid person.

16 A wooden beam can be put into a building so firmly that an earthquake cannot shake it loose; a person can be trained to use reason and good sense so well that he keeps his head when a crisis comes. ¹⁷A mind that thinks things through intelligently is like a firm wall, finely decorated. ¹⁸Small stones on top of a wallᵈ will not stay put when the wind blows, and a person whose stupid ideas have made him timid will not be able to stand up to frightening situations.

Friendship

19 If you stick something in your eye, tears will flow; and if you hurt a person deeply, you will discover his true feelings. ²⁰If you throw stones at birds, you will scare them away; and if you insult a friend, you will break up the friendship.

²¹⁻²²Even if you have a violent argument with a friend, and speak sharply, all is not lost. You can still make it up with him. But any friend will leave you if you insult him, if you are arrogant, if you reveal his secrets, or if you turn on him unexpectedly.

23 Gain the confidence of your neighbour if he is poor; then you can share his happiness if he becomes successful. Stand by him when he is in trouble if you want to share with him when better times come his way.

24 Fumes and smoke appear before the flames do; insults come before violence.

25 I will never be afraid to protect a friend, and I will never turn a friend away if he needs me. ²⁶If I suffer because of him, everyone who learns of it will be on guard against him.

A Prayer for Help against Sin

27 I wish that a guard could be placed at my mouth, that my lips could be wisely sealed. It would keep me from making mistakes and prevent me from destroying myself with my own tongue!

23 O Lord, my Father and master of my life, do not leave me at the mercy of my own words; don't let them cause my downfall. ²I wish I could be whipped for my thoughts, so that Wisdom could discipline my mind. I would not want to be spared when I am wrong; I would not want a single sin to be overlooked! ³Then I would not keep on sinning, making one mistake after another. I could not fall to my enemies and be humiliated by them.

4 O Lord, my Father, God of my life, keep me from being arrogant; ⁵protect me from evil desires. ⁶Keep me from being overcome by greed or lust; do not leave me at the mercy of these shameless passions.

Taking Oaths

7 My children, listen to what I have to say about proper speech; do as I teach you and you will never get trapped. ⁸Sinners are caught by their own arrogant, insulting words.

9 Don't fall into the habit of taking oaths, and don't use God's holy name too freely. ¹⁰A slave who is constantly beaten

---

ᶜ *Some manuscripts add verses 9-10*: Children who are brought up well do not show the humble origin of their parents. ¹⁰Children who are not brought up well, who are arrogant and conceited, are a stain on the noblest family.
ᵈ Small...wall; *some manuscripts have* A fence on top of a hill.
22.12: Gen 50.10; Jdt 16.24 **23.9:** Mt 5.34; Jas 5.12

will never be free of bruises; someone who is always taking an oath by the Holy Name will never be free of sin. ¹¹ A man who takes oaths all the time is sinful to the core, and punishment is never far away from his household. If he fails to fulfil his oath, he is guilty. If he ignores his oath, he is twice as guilty. If his oath was insincere in the first place, he cannot be pardoned and will have a house full of trouble.

Filthy Talk

12 There is one way of speaking that is like death itself—may no Israelite ever be guilty of it! Devout people do not wallow in such sin, and they will keep away from such behaviour. ¹³ Don't fall into the habit of coarse, profane talk; it is sinful. ¹⁴ You might forget yourself while in the company of important people and make a fool of yourself with some foul word that comes to you naturally. Think how your parents would feel! You would curse the day you were born and wish you were dead! ¹⁵ If you fall into the habit of using offensive language, you will never break yourself of it as long as you live.

Sexual Sins

16 There are any number of ways to sin and bring down the Lord's anger, but sexual passion is a hot, blazing fire that cannot be put out at will; it can only burn itself out. A man who lives for nothing but sexual enjoyment will keep on until that fire destroys him. ¹⁷ To such a man all women are desirable, and he can never get enough as long as he lives.

18 The man who is unfaithful to his wife thinks to himself, "No one will ever know. It's dark in here, and no one sees me. I have nothing to worry about. As for the Most High, he won't even notice." ¹⁹ This man is only afraid of other people. He doesn't realize that the eyes of the Lord are ten thousand times brighter than the sun, that he sees everything we do, even when we try to hide it. ²⁰ He knew everything before he created the world, as well as after. ²¹ That sinful man will be caught when he least expects it, and punished publicly.

22 The same is true of a woman who is unfaithful to her husband and presents him with a child by another man. ²³ In the first place, she has broken the Law of the Most High. In the second place, she has wronged her husband. And in the third place, she has made a whore of herself by committing adultery and bearing the child of a man not her husband. ²⁴⁻²⁵ The children will suffer for her sin. They will not be able to find a place in society or establish families. She herself will be brought before the assembly ²⁶ and permanently disgraced. There will be a curse on her memory. After she is gone, ²⁷ everyone will realize that nothing is better than fearing the Lord, nothing is sweeter than keeping his commands.

In Praise of Wisdom

24 Listen to Wisdom! She proudly sings her own praises among the Israelites, her own people, ² in the assembly of the Most High, in the presence of his power. ᵉ
³ "I am the word spoken by the Most High.
　　I covered the earth like a mist.
⁴ I made my home in highest heaven,
　　my throne on a pillar of cloud.
⁵ Alone I walked round the circle of the sky
　　and walked through the ocean
　　beneath the earth.
⁶ I ruled over ᶠ all the earth and the ocean waves,
　　over every nation, over every people.
⁷ I looked everywhere for a place to settle,
　　some part of the world to make my home.
⁸ Then my Creator, who created the universe,
　　told me where I was to live.
　'Make your home in Israel,' he said.
　　'The descendants of Jacob will be your people.'
⁹ He created me in eternity, before time began,
　　and I will exist for all eternity to come.
¹⁰ I served him in the sacred Tent
　　and then made my home on Mount Zion.
¹¹ He settled me in the Beloved City
　　and gave me authority over Jerusalem.
¹² I put down roots among an honoured people
　　whom the Lord had chosen as his own.
¹³ I grew tall, like the cedars in Lebanon,
　　like the cypresses on Mount Hermon,
¹⁴ like the palm-trees of Engedi, ᵍ

ᵉ power; *or* angels. 　ᶠ ruled over; *some manuscripts have* gained possession of.
ᵍ of Engedi; *some manuscripts have* on the seashore.
24.4: Ex 33.9-10

like the roses of Jericho,
like beautiful olive-trees in the fields,
like plane-trees growing by the water.
¹⁵ My breath was the spicy smell of
cinnamon,
of sweet perfume and finest myrrh,
of stacte, onycha, and galbanum,
the fragrant incense in the sacred
Tent.
¹⁶ Like an oak I spread out my branches,
magnificent and graceful.
¹⁷ Like a grapevine I put out lovely
shoots;
my blossoms gave way to rich and
glorious fruit. ʰ
¹⁹ Come to me, all you that want me,
and eat your fill of my fruit.
²⁰ You will remember me as sweeter than
honey,
better then honey from the comb.
²¹ Eat me, and you will hunger for more;
drink me, and you will thirst for more.
²² Obey me, and you will never have
cause for embarrassment;
do as I say, and you will be safe from
sin."

Wisdom and the Law

23 Wisdom is the Law, the Law which
Moses commanded us to keep, the
covenant of God Most High, the
inheritance of the synagogues of Israel. ⁱ
²⁵ The Law overflows with Wisdom like
the River Pishon, like the Tigris at fruit-
picking time. ²⁶ The Law brims over with
understanding like the Euphrates, like the
Jordan at harvest time. ²⁷ It sparkles with
teachings like the Nile, ʲ like the Gihon
at grape-picking time.
28 The first man ever created never
knew Wisdom completely, and the last
person on earth will be no more
successful. ²⁹ The possibilities of Wisdom
are vaster than the ocean; her resources
are more profound than the deepest
waters beneath the earth.
30 As for me, I thought of myself as
an irrigation canal bringing water from
a river into a garden. ³¹ I only intended
to water my orchard and flower beds, but
the canal soon became a river, and the
river became a sea. ³² And so I present

you with my learning; I hold it high, so
that its light can be seen everywhere, like
that of the rising sun. ³³ Like an inspired
prophet, I pour out my teachings, so that
future generations can benefit from them.
³⁴ Please realize that I have not done all
this hard work for myself alone, but to
help anyone who wants to be wise.

People Who Deserve Praise

25 There are three things in which I
take special delight—things that
are beautiful to the Lord and man alike ᵏ
brothers who get along with each other,
neighbours who are friends,
and a married couple who are
happy together.
2 There are three kinds of people I
cannot stand, whose behaviour I find
highly offensive:
poor people who are arrogant,
rich people who lie,
and foolish old men who commit
adultery.
3 Unless you learn what you can while
you are young, you will never be wise
when you reach old age. ⁴ Sound
judgement, good advice, and grey hair go
together beautifully. ⁵ Wisdom, understanding, and sound counsel are appropriate to the aged and the respected.
⁶ Elderly people wear the crown of long
experience, and they can boast of nothing
finer than their fear of the Lord.
7 I will tell you about ten kinds of people
that I feel fortunate to know, especially
fortunate in the case of the tenth:
someone who takes pride in his children,
someone who lives to see his enemies
fall,
⁸ a man fortunate enough to have an
understanding wife,
a married couple who are well-matched, ˡ
a person who never speaks sinfully,
a person who doesn't have to work for
someone less competent than
himself,
⁹ someone fortunate enough to have a real
friend, ᵐ
a person that people are happy to listen
to,

ʰ Some manuscripts add verse 18: I am the mother of beautiful love, of fear, knowledge, and holy
hope. Since I am eternal, I am given to all my children, who are named by him.
ⁱ Some manuscripts add verse 24: Always be strong in the Lord; stay with him, so that he may
make you strong. There is no God but the Lord Almighty, and no saviour except him.
ʲ One ancient translation It sparkles...Nile; Greek It makes teachings shine like light.
ᵏ Some ancient translations There are...alike; Greek I was made beautiful in three ways and I
stood before the Lord and man in beauty.
ˡ Hebrew and one ancient translation a married couple... well-matched; Greek does not have these
words.   ᵐ Some ancient translations real friend; Greek good sense.

Women

13 No wound is as serious as wounded love. No troubles are as serious as the troubles that women cause. [14] No sufferings are worse than the sufferings caused by people who hate you. No revenge is worse than revenge taken by an enemy. [15] No poison is deadlier than the poison of a snake, and no anger is deadlier than the anger of a woman. [o]

16 I would rather live in the same house with a lion or a dragon than with a bad wife. [17] When a wife is in a bad mood, her expression changes until she looks like an angry bear. [18] Her husband has to go and eat with the neighbours, where he can't hold back his bitter sighs.

19 Compared with the troubles caused by a woman, any other trouble looks small. May such women suffer the fate of sinners!

20 A quiet man living with a nagging wife is like an old man climbing up a sandy hill.

21 Never lose your head over a woman's beauty, and don't try to win a woman because she is wealthy. [p] [22] When a man is supported by his wife, there is sure to be anger, arrogance, and humiliation. [23] A bad wife will make her husband gloomy and depressed, and break his heart. Show me a timid man who can never make up his mind, and I will show you a wife who doesn't make her husband happy. [24] Sin began with a woman, and we must all die because of her. [25] Don't let a bad wife have her way, any more than you would allow water to leak from your cistern. [26] If she won't do as you tell her, divorce her.

26 The husband of a good wife is a fortunate man; he will live twice as long because of her. [2] A fine wife is a joy to her husband, and he can live out his years in peace. [3] A good wife is among the precious blessings given to those who fear the Lord. [4] Whether such men are rich or poor, they will be happy and always look cheerful.

5 There are four things that scare me; vicious rumours spread around town, a gathering mob, false accusations—these are all worse than death. [6] But a woman jealous of another woman causes heartache and grief; her tongue lashes out at everyone.

There are three things in which I take special delight (25.1)

[10] and the really great one: someone who is wise.

But the greatest one of all is the person who fears the Lord.

11 Such a person has no equal, because the fear of the Lord is the most important thing in the world. [n]

---

[n] *Some manuscripts add verse 12: Fearing the Lord is the first step towards loving him, and faith is the first step towards loyalty to him.* [o] *Some ancient translations* woman; *Greek* enemy.
[p] *Hebrew* because she is wealthy; *Greek does not have these words.*

7 A bad wife is like a yoke that doesn't fit. Trying to control her is like holding a scorpion. ⁸A drunken woman is an infuriating sight; she can't conceal her shameless behaviour. ⁹You can tell an unfaithful wife by the bold and flirting look in her eyes.

10 If your daughter is determined to have her own way, keep a close watch on her. If you don't, she'll take advantage of any chance she gets. ¹¹If she is too self-willed, be on guard, and don't be surprised if she disappoints you. ¹²She'll spread her legs anywhere for any man who wants her, just as a thirsty traveller will drink whatever water is available.

13 A gracious wife is her husband's delight; her abilities make him a stronger man. q ¹⁴A wife who doesn't talk too much is a gift from the Lord. Such restraint is admirable beyond words. ¹⁵A modest wife has endless charm; it is a quality too precious to measure. ¹⁶The beauty of a good wife in her well-kept home is like the noonday sun shining in the Lord's sky. ¹⁷Her beautiful face and attractive figure are r as lovely as the light from the sacred lampstand in the Temple, ¹⁸and like its gold shaft set on its silver base are her shapely legs and strong ankles. s t

Sad Observations

28 There are two things that make me sad, and a third that makes me angry:

a soldier who has become poor,
  intelligent people who are not
    respected,
and a righteous person who turns
    to evil.

The Lord will punish such a person with death!

29 A merchant can hardly avoid doing wrong; every salesman is guilty of sin.

27 ¹Many people have sinned while looking for a profit; if you want to be rich you have to keep blinkers on your eyes. ²It is hard to remove a peg that is stuck between two stones of a house, and it is just as hard to remove dishonesty from buying and selling. ³Unless you are determined in your fear of the Lord, your house is going to come down on you.

Speech Reflects True Feelings

4 A person's talk shows his faults; it is like a sieve that separates out the rubbish. ⁵The way you think shows your character just as surely as a kiln shows any flaws in the pottery being fired. ⁶You can tell how well a tree has been cared for by the fruit it bears, and you can tell a person's feelings by the way he expresses himself. ⁷Never praise anyone before you hear him talk; that is the real test.

Honesty

8 If you try to be honest, you can be, and it will improve your character as handsome clothing improves your appearance. ⁹Birds come to roost with those of their own kind, and the habit of honesty comes to those who try to be honest. ¹⁰Sin waits for those looking for a chance to sin, just as a lion waits for prey.

Foolish Talk

11 When devout people talk, what they say always makes sense, but foolish people are always contradicting themselves. ¹²When you find yourself with stupid people, look for some excuse to leave, but when you are with serious-minded people, stay as long as you can.

13 The stories that foolish people tell are offensive, and they make jokes about the worst kinds of sin. ¹⁴When such people curse, it is enough to make your hair stand on end, and when they start arguing among themselves, all you can

---

q her abilities...man; or she knows how to keep him well-fed.
r and attractive figure are; or as she grows older is.
s strong ankles; some manuscripts have firm breasts or determined heart.
t Some manuscripts add verses 19–27: My son, stay healthy while you are young, and don't give your strength to strangers. ²⁰Search the whole land for a fertile field, and plant it with your own seed, trusting your own good stock. ²¹Then your children will survive and grow up confident of their good family. ²²A prostitute is like spittle; a married woman who has affairs brings death to her lovers. ²³A lawless man will get a godless wife, as he deserves, but a man who honours the Lord will have a devout wife. ²⁴A shameless wife enjoys making a disgrace of herself, but a modest wife will act modestly even alone with her husband. ²⁵A self-willed woman is a bitch, but a woman with a sense of decency honours the Lord. ²⁶A wife who honours her husband will seem wise to everyone; but if she dishonours him by her overbearing attitude, everyone will know that she is ungodly. Fortunate is the husband of a good wife, because he will live twice as long. ²⁷A loud-mouthed, talkative woman is like a trumpet sounding the signal for attack, and any man who has such a wife will spend his life at war.

27.6: Mt 7.14; 12.33; Lk 6.44

do is to stop up your ears. ¹⁵ It is painful to listen to them insult each other, and such blustering can lead to violence.

Betraying Secrets

16 If you repeat secrets that have been told to you, you are destroying the confidence others have in you, and you will never have a close friend. ¹⁷ Respect your friends, and keep faith with them. If you do betray a friend's confidence, you may as well forget you have a friend. ¹⁸ You have killed that friendship just as surely as if you had taken a weapon and killed an enemy. ¹⁹ Your friend is gone. You can no more get him back than you can get a bird to come back to your hand once you let it go. ²⁰ Don't bother going after him. It's too late. He is gone, like a deer escaped from a trap. ²¹ Wounds can be bandaged and insults can be forgiven, but if you betray a confidence, it is hopeless.

Hypocrisy

22 When someone starts winking at you, he has something bad in mind, and nothing can stop him from going through with it. ²³ When he's with you, his talk is so nice! He compliments you on every word you say. But behind your back it's a different story; he will take what you have said and turn it against you. ²⁴ There is nothing in the world that I hate as much as a person like that—and the Lord hates him too.

25 Throw a stone straight up in the air and it will come down on your head. Strike a blow, and you yourself will be wounded. ²⁶ People who set traps fall into them themselves. ²⁷ People who hurt others will be hurt by their own actions and will have no idea why.

28 Arrogant people insult others and make fun of them,ᵘ but someone is waiting like a lion for a chance to take revenge on them. ²⁹ Those who are happy to witness the downfall of devout people are going to fall into a trap and die a painful death.

Resentment

30 Anger and a hot temper are horrible things, but sinners have both. ¹ The **28** Lord is taking note of your sins, and if you take vengeance on someone, the Lord will take vengeance on you. ² But if you forgive someone who has wronged

you, your sins will be forgiven when you pray. ³ You cannot expect the Lord to pardon you while you are bearing a grudge against someone else. ⁴ You yourself are a sinner, and if you won't forgive another person, you have no right to pray that the Lord will forgive your sins. ⁵ If you cannot get rid of your anger, you have no hope of forgiveness—you are only a human being. ⁶ Think about it! Some day you will die, and your body will decay. So give up hate and live by the Lord's commands, ⁷ the commands in the covenant of the Most High. Instead of getting upset over your neighbour's faults, overlook them.

Arguments

8 If you stay out of arguments, you will not sin so much, because a hot temper gets them started. ⁹ It is sinful to break up a friendship by creating hostility among people who get along well together. ¹⁰ The more fuel, the hotter the fire. The more stubbornness, the hotter the argument. And the stronger or richer a man is, the angrier he can afford to become. ¹¹ An argument that blazes out suddenly can lead to violence. ¹² You can blow on a spark to make it glow, or you can spit on it to put it out. Either way, you do it with your mouth.

Vicious Talk

13 Gossips and liars deserve to be cursed, because they have been the ruin of many people who were minding their own business. ¹⁴ Many have had their lives ruined and have been driven from their homes because of people who meddled in their business. Such unwanted interference has resulted in the destruction of strong cities and the homes of respected men. ¹⁵ Meddlers have caused faithful wives to be divorced, robbed of everything they had worked for. ¹⁶ Anyone who pays attention to slander can never find peace of mind. ¹⁷ A whip can raise a welt, but a vicious tongue can break bones. ¹⁸ More people have died as a result of loose talk than were ever killed by swords. ¹⁹⁻²⁰ Count yourself lucky if you have been spared the experience of having irresponsible talk directed against you—if you have never had that iron yoke round your neck or those heavy chains on your legs. ²¹ Slander leads to a miserable death; but in fact, you'd be better off dead.

ᵘ insult others...them; *or* will be insulted and mocked.
27.16-21: Prov 20.19; 25.9   **28.2:** Mt 6.17; Mk 11.25   **28.13-26:** Sir 51.2-6; Jas 3.5-12

It is sinful to break up a friendship (28.9)

22 Devout people, however, cannot be overcome by slander; they cannot be burnt by its flames. 23 Its victims are those who have abandoned the Lord; once the fire of slander has been lit among them, it cannot be put out. Slander will pounce on them like a lion and tear them to pieces like a leopard.

24 Don't you fence in your property? Don't you lock up your money? 25 Well, be just as careful with what you say. Weigh every word, and have a lock ready for your mouth. 26 Someone may be waiting for you to slip, and if you are not careful, you will stumble over your own words and fall down in front of him.

Loans and Repayment

29 Be kind enough to lend to your neighbour when he needs help. You are keeping the Lord's commands if you help him. 2 If he needs something, lend it to him. And when you are in debt, pay it back as soon as you can. 3 If you meet your obligations, you will always be able to borrow what you need. 4 Many people treat a loan as something they found and can keep, causing embarrassment to those who helped them. 5 Some people will speak politely, bow, and scrape until they get the loan they want, but when the time comes to pay it back, they'll put it off, say that it's inconvenient, and make a lot of worthless excuses. 6 If the lender insists on being paid, he can count himself lucky to get back half. If he doesn't insist, the borrower has robbed him and made an unnecessary enemy. All the lender will get from him are curses, insults, and disrespect, but never any gratitude.

7 Many people refuse to lend at all, not because they are stingy, but because *v* they don't want to be cheated if they can avoid it.

Generosity

8 Nevertheless, be understanding with those who are poor. Don't keep them waiting for your generosity. 9 The Lord has commanded us to help the poor; don't refuse them the help they need. 10 It is better to lose your money by helping a brother or a friend than to lose it by letting it rust away under a rock somewhere. 11 Use your wealth as the Most High has commanded; this will do you more good than keeping your money for yourself. 12 Count among your treasures the fact that you give to the poor. It will save you from all kinds of trouble 13 and will be a better defence against your enemies than the strongest shield or stoutest spear.

Guaranteeing Debts

14 A good man is willing to guarantee his neighbour's debts. Only someone who has lost all sense of decency would refuse to do so. 15 If someone does this favour for you, don't forget it; he has risked his good name for you. 16 There are some ungrateful sinners who abandon those who stand behind them, and they cause them loss of property. 17 Guaranteeing loans has ruined many prosperous men and caused them unsettling storms of trouble. 18 Influential people have lost their homes over it and have had to go wandering in foreign countries. 19 A sinner who hopes to make a profit by guaranteeing a loan is going to find

v not because…stingy, but because; *some manuscripts have* therefore, because of this wickedness.
29.1-7: Ex 22.25; Lev 25.35-38

Going from house to house is a miserable way to live (29.24)

himself involved in lawsuits. ²⁰ So help your neighbour as much as you can, but protect yourself against the dangers involved.

Home and Hospitality

21 The necessities of life are water, food, clothing, and a home where you can have privacy. ²² It is better to be poor and live under your own crude roof than to enjoy lavish banquets in other people's homes. ²³ Be happy with what you have, even if it isn't very much, and don't listen to anyone who would insult your home and family. *ʷ* ²⁴ Going from house to house is a miserable way to live. Anywhere you go, you don't dare to speak. ²⁵ You welcome the guests and pour the drinks, and nobody thanks you. Instead, people humiliate you by saying things like: ²⁶ "Stranger! Come here and lay the table! I want to eat what you've got there! Give it here! ²⁷ Go away, stranger! I've got an important guest! My brother is coming to visit, and I need the room!"

28 Being denied hospitality or having a moneylender hound him—these are hard things for any sensitive person to endure.

Bringing Up Children

30 A father who loves his son will whip him often, so that he can be proud of him later. ²If a son is disciplined, he will be of some use, and his father can boast of him to his friends. ³ A man who gives good guidance to his son can not only take pride in him among his friends, but he can make his enemies jealous. ⁴⁻⁵ While the father is alive, the sight of his son makes him happy, and when he dies, he has no regrets. He is not really dead, because his son is like him. ⁶ He has left someone to take vengeance on his enemies and to return the favours he owes his friends.

7 But a man who spoils his son will have to bandage his wounds. *ˣ* His heart will stop every time he hears a shout. ⁸ An untamed horse is going to be stubborn, and an undisciplined son is no different. ⁹ If you pamper your child and play with him, he will be a disappointment and a source of grief. ¹⁰ Laugh with him now, and one day you will have to cry over him, grinding your teeth in regret. ¹¹ Don't give him freedom while he is young, and don't overlook what he does wrong. ¹² Beat him while he is still a child, and make him respect your authority. If you don't, he will be stubborn and

---

ʷ don't listen...family; *or* don't listen to insults from your family; *some manuscripts do not have these words; one ancient translation has* don't get a reputation for living off other people.
ˣ will have...wounds; *or* is going to be hurt.

...so that he can be proud of him later (30.1)

disobedient and cause you nothing but sorrow. ¹³ So discipline your son and give him work to do, or else he will be an embarrassment to you.

Health

14 It is better to be poor, but strong and healthy, than to be rich, but in poor health. ¹⁵ A sound, healthy body and a cheerful attitude[y] are more valuable than gold and jewels. ¹⁶ Nothing can make you richer or give you greater happiness than those two things. ¹⁷ It would be better to be dead, asleep for ever, than to live in the misery of chronic illness. ¹⁸ The finest food means nothing if you are too ill to eat it; it might as well be offered to an idol.[z] ¹⁹ But there is no point in offering food to an idol; it can't eat it or smell it. It is just the same with someone whom the Lord has afflicted. ²⁰ He looks at his food and sighs, like a castrated man hugging a girl.

Cheerfulness and Sadness

21 Don't deliberately torture yourself by giving in to depression. ²² Happiness makes for a long life and makes it worth living. ²³ Enjoy yourself and be happy; don't worry all the time. Worry never did anybody any good, and it has destroyed many people. ²⁴ It will make you old before your time. Jealousy and anger will shorten your life. ²⁵ A cheerful person with a good attitude will have a good appetite and enjoy his food.

Problems Caused by Money

31 Worrying about money will make you lose weight and lose sleep. ² Worrying about business[a] will keep you from sleeping just as surely as a serious illness does.

3 Rich people work hard to make a lot of money; then they can sit back and live in luxury. ⁴ Poor people work hard and have nothing to show for it, and when they rest, they are still poor.

5 No one who loves money can be judged innocent; his efforts to get rich have led him into sin.[b] ⁶ Many people have been ruined because of money, brought face to face with disaster. ⁷ Money is a trap

Money is a trap for those who are fascinated by it (31.7)

---

[y] *Hebrew* a cheerful attitude; *Greek* a strong body.
[z] *Hebrew* offered to an idol; *Greek* placed on a grave.
[a] *Hebrew* Worrying about business; *Greek* Sleepless worry.
[b] *Hebrew* have...sin; *Greek* will destroy him.
30.21–25: Ecc 11.9–10

for those who are fascinated by it, a trap that every fool falls into.

8 A person who gets rich without sinfully chasing after money is fortunate. 9 Do you know anyone like that? If so, we will congratulate him for performing a miracle that no one else has ever been able to do. 10 If anyone has ever passed this test, he can well be proud. Has anyone ever known that he could get away with cheating someone, and not taken advantage of it? 11 If so, he deserves his wealth, and everyone will praise him for his generosity.

Behaviour at Dinner Parties

12 When you sit down at a fancy banquet, don't let your mouth hang open, and don't say, "Look at all that food!" 13 It is impolite to have a greedy eye; remember that. Nothing in creation is greedier than the eye; that is why it sheds tears so often.c 14 Don't reach out for everything you see, and don't elbow people out of the way to get at the food. 15 Be considerate of the other people at the table and treat them the way you want to be treated. 16 When you get your food, eat it like a human being. Don't smack your lips and slurp; nobody can stand that. 17 It's good manners to be the first to stop eating; stuffing yourself is offensive. 18 If there are many people present, don't try to be the first to be served. 19 A little bit is plenty for anyone with good manners. Besides, you won't be short of breath when you go to bed. 20 People who eat too much get stomach-ache and cannot sleep. If you don't overeat, you can get a good night's sleep and wake up early the next morning feeling fine. 21 But if you do get a stomach-ache from eating too much, go off and vomitd and you will feel better. 22 My son, if you listen to what I am saying and put it into practice, one of these days you will thank me for it. Be moderatee in everything you do, and you will never be sick.

23 People appreciate a generous host, and he deserves their praise. 24 But everybody in town will complain about a host who is stingy with his food, and their complaints are justified.

25 Don't try to prove your manhood by

how much you can drink. Wine has been the ruin of many. 26 An arrogant man's character shows through when he is in a drunken argument, in the same way that iron is tested when it is heated red-hot and then dipped in water. 27 Wine can put new life into you if you drink it in moderation. What would life be like without it? Wine was created to make us happy. 28 If you drink it in moderation and at the right time, it can raise your spirits and make you cheerful, 29 but if you drink when you are angry and upset, it leads to headaches, embarrassment, and disgrace.f 30 A drunken fool can lose his temper and hurt himself. His drinking makes him weak and an easy target for angry blows. 31 Never rebuke a person when you have both been drinking. Don't hurt his feelings while he is having a good time. It's not the time to criticize anyone, or to ask him to pay back a debt.

32 If you are chosen to preside at a banquet, don't put on airs. Just be like everyone else. Look after the guests before you sit down. 2 After you have performed your duties, you can sit down and enjoy yourself with the others. They will respect you for doing a good job.

3 If you are older than most of the guests, you may talk; that is your right. But you should know what you are talking about and not interrupt the music. 4 If entertainment is being provided, don't keep up a steady conversation; it's the wrong time to show off your wit. 5 Music at a banquet where wine is served is like a ruby set in gold. 6 Good music and good wine—an emerald set in gold.

7 If you are young, don't speak unless you have to, but never more than twice, and only if someone speaks to you first. 8 Come to the point and say it all in a few words. Show that you are well-informed, but stay quiet. 9 Don't treat important people as if you were their equal and don't make a nuisance of yourself by asking them a lot of questions.g 10 The reputation of a modest person goes before him, as lightning before thunder.

11 Leave the party at the right time and never be the last to go. Don't linger at the door; just go straight home. 12 There you can enjoy yourself as you wish, but

c Hebrew so often; Greek on every face.
d go off and vomit; some manuscripts have get up in the middle of the meal.
e Hebrew moderate; Greek industrious.
f Hebrew when you are...disgrace; Greek too much, it leads to bitterness, offence, and stumbiing.
g Hebrew make...questions; Greek keep talking when someone else is speaking.

don't commit the sin of bragging. [13] And don't forget to thank your Creator for letting you enjoy so many good things.

Interpreting the Law

[14] If you fear the Lord, you will accept his correction. He will bless those who get up early in the morning to pray. [15] Study his Law, and you will master it, unless you are insincere about it, in which case you will fail. [16] If you fear the Lord, you will know what is right, and you will be famous for your fairness. [17] Sinners have no use for correction, and will interpret the Law to suit themselves.

[18] Sensible people will consider every opinion, but arrogant[h] people will let nothing stand in their way. [19] Never do anything without thinking it through, and once you have done something, don't look back and wish you had done something else. [20] Don't take a course of action that is dangerous, and don't make the same mistake twice.[i] [21] Don't be too sure of yourself, even when the way looks easy. [22] Always watch where you are going.[j] [23] Whatever you do be careful;[k] this is keeping the Lord's commands.

[24] Believing in the Law means keeping the Lord's commands. If you trust the Lord, you cannot lose. [1] No evil will ever come to a person who fears the Lord; however often danger comes, the Lord will come to his rescue. [2] A person who has no use for the Law hasn't any sense, and anyone who is insincere about it is going to be tossed about like a boat in a storm. [3] If you are wise, you will believe in the Law; you will find it as reliable as the sacred lots.

[4] Prepare what you are going to say and people will listen to you. Use what you have learnt before you start talking. [5] A foolish person's mind works like a cartwheel, going round and round in circles. [6] A sarcastic friend is like a wild horse that neighs no matter who tries to ride him.

People Are Not Alike

[7] Why are some days holier than others, even though the same sun rises on every day of the year? [8] It is because the Lord made them different by setting them apart as religious holidays and festivals. [9] He made some days holy and important, and made other days ordinary.

[10] Every human being was made from the earth, just as Adam was. [11] But the Lord, in his wisdom, made them all different and gave them different tasks. [12] He blessed some, making them honoured and holy, keeping them near him. Others he cursed, humbling them and removing them from their positions. [13] Just as clay is in the potter's hands for him to shape as he pleases, so we are in the hands of our Creator for him to do with as he wishes.

[14] Good is the opposite of evil, life is the opposite of death, and sin is the opposite of devotion to the Lord. [15] Think about it: the Most High has made everything in pairs, each thing the opposite of something else.

[16] As for me, I have been the last to come on duty, as if going through vineyards to gather whatever the grape-pickers had left behind. But the Lord blessed me, and I did well,[l] like a grape-picker who has filled his winepress. [17] But I want you to know that I have not done all this work for myself alone, but for everyone who wants to learn. [18] Listen to me, all you great leaders! All you leaders of the assemblies, hear what I have to say!

Be Independent

[19] Never, as long as you live, give anyone power over you—whether son, wife, brother, or friend. Don't give your property to anyone; you might change your mind and have to ask for it back. [20] As long as you have breath in your body, don't let anyone lead your life for you. [21] It is better that your children be dependent on you than the other way round. [22] Keep control over all that you do; don't let anything stain your reputation. [23] Wait until the last moment of your life, when you are breathing your last, and then divide your property among your heirs.

Treatment of Slaves

[24] A donkey should be given his fodder and his burden, and he should be beaten. A slave should be given his food and his work, and he should be disciplined. [25] If

---

[h] *Hebrew* arrogant; *Greek* foreign and arrogant.
[i] *Hebrew* make...twice; *Greek* stumble on stones.
[j] *Hebrew* watch...going; *Greek* look out for your children.
[k] *Hebrew* be careful; *Greek* have confidence in yourself.   [l] did well; *or* overtook the others.
33.3: Ex 28.30; Sir 45.10

you make your slave work, you can set your mind at ease. If you don't keep him busy, he will be looking for freedom. ²⁶You can use harness and yoke to tame an animal, and a slave can be tortured in the stocks. ²⁷Keep him at work, and don't let him be idle; idleness can only teach him how to make trouble. ²⁸Work is what he needs. If he won't obey you, put him in chains.

29 But don't be too severe with anyone, and never be unfair. ³⁰If you have a slave, treat him as you would want to be treated; you bought him with your hard-earned money. ³¹Treat him as a brother; you need him as you need yourself. If you ill-treat him and he runs away, where are you going to look for him?

Dreams Mean Nothing

34 Foolish people are deceived by vain hopes, and dreams get them all excited. ²A person who pays any attention at all to dreams is like someone who tries to catch shadows or chase the wind. ³What you see in a dream is no more real than the reflection of your face in a mirror. ⁴What is unreal can no more produce something real than what is dirty can produce something clean. ⁵Dreams, divination, and omens are all nonsense. You see in them only what you want to see. ᵐ ⁶Unless the Most High has sent you the dream, pay no attention to it. ⁷Dreams have misled many people; they put their faith in them, only to be disappointed. ⁸The Law is complete without such falsehood. Wisdom, as spoken by the righteous, is also complete without it.

Travel

9 A well-travelled ⁿ man with wide experience knows many things and talks sense. ¹⁰You can't know much if you haven't experienced much, but travel can make you cleverer. ¹¹In my own travels I have seen many things and learnt more than I can put into words. ¹²I have been in danger of death many times, but I have always been able to escape by relying on past experience.

Fear the Lord

13 Those who fear the Lord will live, because they have put their trust in the one who can save them. ¹⁴Fear the Lord, and you will have nothing else to fear.

If your trust is in him, you will never act like a coward. ¹⁵People who fear the Lord are fortunate, because they know where they can look for help. ¹⁶The Lord watches over those who love him; he is their strong protection and firm support. He shelters them from the heat, shades them from the noonday sun, and keeps them from stumbling and falling. ¹⁷He makes them cheerful and puts a sparkle in their eyes. He blesses them with life and health.

Offering Sacrifices

18 If you offer as a sacrifice an animal that you have obtained dishonestly, it is defective and unacceptable. ¹⁹The Most High gets no pleasure from sacrifices made by ungodly people; no amount of sacrifices can make up for their sins. ²⁰A man who steals an animal from the poor to offer as a sacrifice is like a man who kills a boy before his father's eyes. ²¹Food means life itself to poor people, and taking it away from them is murder. ²²It is murder to deprive someone of his living or to cheat an employee of his wages.

23 When one man builds and somebody else tears down, has anything been accomplished but hard work? ²⁴When one man blesses and somebody else curses, which one is the Lord going to listen to? ²⁵If you touch a dead body and then purify yourself by washing, but then go and touch it again, what good did the washing do? ²⁶If you fast because of your sins, and then go out and commit the same sins over again, what have you gained by going without food? Who do you think is going to listen to your prayers?

35 Keeping the Law is worth many offerings; it is a fellowship-offering in itself. ²Returning a kindness is like a grain-offering; giving to the poor is like a thanksgiving-offering. ³Keeping away from sin will please the Lord and make atonement for sin. ⁴But don't come to the Temple without an offering; ⁵the Law requires that you bring one. ⁶When a righteous man offers a sacrifice and the fat drips down on the altar, a pleasant smell rises to the Most High. ⁷The Lord will accept the offerings made by a righteous man and will not forget them. ⁸Praise the Lord by making generous offerings to him; don't be stingy with the first of your crops. ⁹Be cheerful with every gift you make, and when you pay your

---

ᵐ *Probable text* You see...to see; *Greek* The mind has an imagination like a woman in labour.
ⁿ A well-travelled; *some manuscripts have* An educated.
34.1–8: Deut 13.1–5; 18.9–14　　**35.9:** 2 Cor 9.7

tithes, do it gladly. [10] Give to the Most High as he has given to you, just as generously as you can. [11] The Lord always repays and will do it many times over. [12] But don't try to bribe him or rely on offerings that you have obtained dishonestly. He will not accept them.

God's Justice

The Lord is fair[o] and does not show partiality. [13] He is not prejudiced against the poor; when someone prays who has been wronged, the Lord listens. [14] When orphans and widows pour out their prayers, he does not ignore them. [15] The tears running down a widow's cheek cry out in accusation against the one who has caused her distress.

16 Serve the Lord willingly, and the Lord will accept you; your prayers will reach the skies. [17] The prayer of a humble person goes past the clouds and keeps on going until it reaches the Lord Most High, where it stays until he answers by seeing that justice is done and that the guilty are punished.

18 And the Lord will act quickly. He will show no patience with wicked people. He will take vengeance by crushing the heathen. He will completely wipe out the merciless and the arrogant, and will destroy the authority of the wicked. [19] He will give every person what his thoughts and actions deserve. Because of the Lord's mercy, his people will be happy when he has judged their case. [20] In times of trouble his mercy is as welcome as rain after a long drought.

A Prayer for Israel

36 O Lord God of the universe, look upon us and have mercy. [2] Make every nation stand in fear of you. [3] Take action against the foreign nations, and let them witness your power! [4] You have used us to show them how holy you are; now use them to show us how great you are. [5] Let them learn, as we have learnt, that there is no God, O Lord, but you. [6] Give new signs, perform new miracles; show us your glorious strength! [7-9] Bring on that appointed time when everyone can talk about the great things you do. Pour out your furious, flaming anger, and let none of our enemies survive. Destroy those who have oppressed your people. [10] Crush all those enemy rulers who think

they are the only people in the world who matter! [11] Gather the tribes of Israel together again, and give them back their land as you gave it to them long ago. [12] Lord, have mercy on Israel, the people who are known by your name, whom you called your first-born son. [13] Take pity on Jerusalem, your holy city, where you chose to stay. [14] Fill your Temple[p] on Mount Zion with your glory and with hymns of praise. [15] Testify for your people, whom you created in the beginning; fulfil the prophecies that have been spoken in your name. [16] Reward those who have put their faith in you, and vindicate your prophets. [17] You have always been gracious to your people;[q] listen to your servants as we pray. Then everyone on earth will recognize that you are the Lord, the God of the ages.

Choosing a Wife

18 Any kind of food can be eaten, but some foods are better than others. [19] And just as the tongue can distinguish the flavours of different kinds of meat, so a sharp mind can detect lies. [20] A person with a warped mind causes trouble, but an experienced person knows how to pay it back.

21 A woman has to take any man as a husband, but a man must choose his wife carefully. [22] A woman's beauty makes a man happy; there is no fairer sight for the human eye to see. [23] If the woman is kind and gentle in her speech, her husband is the most fortunate of men. [24] When a man marries, he gets the finest thing he will ever have—a wife to help and encourage him.

25 If property is not fenced in, thieves will wander in and help themselves. And if a man has no wife, he is a sighing wanderer; [26] people have no more trust in a homeless man who sleeps in a different place every night than they have in a wandering thief who goes from town to town.

False Friends

37 Anyone can claim to be your friend, but some people are friends in name only. [2] The grief caused when a close friendship turns sour is as bad as death. [3] This evil impulse we have! Why was it ever formed? How did it manage to cover the earth with deceit? [4] Some

---

[o] Hebrew fair; Greek judge.　　[p] Hebrew Temple; Greek people.
[q] Hebrew You have...people; Greek According to the blessing of Aaron on your people.

people will be your friend as long as things are going well, but they will turn against you when trouble comes. 5 A real*r* friend will help you against your enemies*s* and protect you in the fight. 6 Never forget such a companion in battle;*t* share the results of your victory with him.

Caution in Taking Advice

7 Anyone can give advice, but some people do so only in their own interest. 8 Be careful when somebody offers you advice. Find out first what his interest in the matter is, because you can be sure that he is thinking primarily of himself. Why should he come out on top instead of you?*u* 9 He will assure you that things look good, and then stand back to watch what happens to you.

10 Don't ask advice of anyone who doesn't trust you, and don't give advice to anyone who is jealous of you.

11 Don't ask a woman for advice about a rival of hers,

a coward about war,

a merchant about a bargain,

a buyer about selling,

a stingy person about gratitude,

a cruel person about kindness,

a lazy person about work,

a casual worker about finishing a job,

a lazy slave about a difficult task.

Pay no attention to any advice they may give.

12 Instead, rely on someone who is religious and known to keep the Lord's commands, someone who is sympathetic with you, who will be sorry to see you fail. 13 And trust your own judgement; no one's advice is more reliable. 14 Sometimes your own intuition can tell you more than seven watchmen on a high tower. 15 Above all, pray to the Most High that he will show you the right thing to do.

Wisdom and Confidence

16 Planning and thought lie behind everything that is done. 17-18 The mind concerns itself with four things: these are good and evil, life and death. They all begin in the mind,*v* but the tongue is their absolute ruler.

19 A man may have the ability to teach, but still not be of much use to himself. 20 He may be clever with words, but end up starving because people hate him. 21 This may happen if he hasn't any sense, if the Lord has not given him tact. 22 A man may consider himself wise and let you know that he is certain about what he knows. 23 Anyone who really is wise will be the teacher of his people, and they can be certain that what he teaches is the truth. 24 Everyone will praise such a man and speak of him as fortunate. 25 A person's life has only a limited number of days, but the life of Israel cannot be measured in days at all. 26 A wise man will win the confidence of his people, and they will remember him for ever.

Controlling the Appetite

27 My son, as you go through life, keep your appetite under control, and don't eat anything that you know is bad for you. 28 All food doesn't agree with everyone, and everyone doesn't like the same kinds of food. 29 Don't feel that you just have to have all sorts of fancy food, and don't be a glutton over any food. 30 If you eat too much, you'll be sick; if you do it all the time, you'll always have stomach trouble. 31 Gluttony has been the death of many people. Avoid it and live longer.

Sickness and Medicine

38 Give doctors the honour they deserve, for the Lord gave them their work to do.*w* 2 Their skill came from the Most High, and kings reward them for it. 3 Their knowledge gives them a position of importance, and powerful people hold them in high regard.

4 The Lord created medicines from the earth, and a sensible person will not hesitate to use them. 5 Didn't a tree once make bitter water fit to drink, so that the Lord's power*x* might be known? 6 He gave medical knowledge to human beings, so that we would praise him for the miracles he performs. 7-8 The chemist mixes these medicines, and the doctor will use them to cure diseases and ease pain. There is no end to the activities of the Lord, who gives health to the people of the world.

---

r Hebrew real; Greek does not have this word.
s Hebrew against your enemies; Greek hoping to get a meal.
t Hebrew in battle; Greek in your soul.
u Hebrew Why...you?; Greek He may use his influence against you.
v Hebrew The mind...the mind; Greek There are four things that show the changes of the heart:
good and evil, life and death.   *w Hebrew gave them their work to do; Greek created them.*
x the Lord's power; or its healing properties.
38.5: Ex 15.23–25

9 My son, when you feel ill, don't ignore it. Pray to the Lord, and he will make you well. ¹⁰Confess all your sins and determine that in the future you will live a righteous life. ¹¹Offer incense and a grain-offering, as fine as you can afford.ʸ ¹²Then call the doctor—for the Lord created him—and keep him at your side; you need him. ¹³There are times when you have to depend on his skill. ¹⁴The doctor's prayer is that the Lord will make him able to ease his patients' pain and make them well again. ¹⁵As for the person who sins against his Creator, he deserves to be sick.

Mourning for the Dead

16 My son, when someone dies, you should mourn. Weep and wail to show how deeply you feel the loss. Prepare the body in the proper way, and be present at the burial. ¹⁷Weep bitterly and passionately; observe the proper period of mourning for the person. Mourn for a whole day or maybe two, to keep people from talking, but then pull yourself together and reconcile yourself to the loss. ¹⁸Grief can undermine your health and even lead to your own death. ¹⁹Grief lingers on after the death of a loved one, but it is not wise to let it lead you into poverty.

20 Don't lose yourself in sorrow; drive it away.ᶻ Remember that we must all die sometime. ²¹There is no way to bring the dead person back. All your sorrow does him no good, and it hurts you. Don't forget that. ²²You will die, just as he did. Today it was his turn; tomorrow it will be yours. ²³When the dead have been laid to rest, let the memory of them fade. Once they are gone, take courage.

Scholarship and Other Occupations

24 A scholar must have time to study if he is going to be wise; he must be relieved of other responsibilities. ²⁵How can a farmhand gain knowledge, when his only ambition is to drive the oxen and make them work, when all he is able to talk about is livestock? ²⁶He takes great pains to plough a straight furrow and will work far into the night to feed the animals.

27 It is the same with the artist and the craftsman, who work night and day engraving precious stones, carefully working out new designs. They take great pains to produce a lifelike image, and will work far into the night to finish the work.

28 It is the same with the blacksmith at his anvil, planning what he will make from a piece of iron. The heat from the fire sears his skin as he sweats away at the forge. The clanging of the hammer deafens himᵃ as he carefully watches the object he is working take shape. He takes great pains to complete his task, and will work far into the night to bring it to perfection.

29 It is the same with the potter, sitting at his wheel and turning it with his feet, always concentrating on his work, concerned with how many objects he can

He works the clay with his feet until he can shape it with his hands (38.30)

produce. ³⁰He works the clay with his feet until he can shape it with his hands; then he takes great pains to glaze it properly, and will work far into the night to clean out the kiln.

31 All these people are skilled with their hands, each of them an expert at his own craft. ³²Without such people there could be no cities; no one would live or visit where these services were not available. ³³These people are not sought out to serve on the public councils, and they never attain positions of great importance. They do not serve as judges, and they do not understand legal matters. They have no

ʸ Hebrew as fine as you can afford; Greek unclear.
ᶻ drive it away; or put the memory of the person aside.
ᵃ Probable text deafens him; Greek renews his ears.
38.16–23: Sir 22.11–12

education and are not known for their
wisdom. You never hear them quoting
proverbs. 34 But the work they do holds
this world together. When they do their
work, it is the same as offering prayer. b

39 But it is different with the man
who devotes himself to studying
the Law of the Most High. He examines
the wisdom of all the ancient writers and
concerns himself with the prophecies. 2 He
memorizes the sayings of famous men and
is a skilled interpreter of parables. 3 He
studies the hidden meaning of proverbs
and is able to discuss the obscure points of
parables. 4 Great men call on him for his
services, and he is seen in the company
of rulers. He travels to foreign lands in
his efforts to learn about human good and
evil. 5 It is his practice to get up early and
pray aloud to the Lord his Creator, asking
the Most High to forgive his sins. 6 Then,
if the great Lord is willing, he will be
filled with understanding. He will pour
out a stream of wise sayings, and give
thanks to the Lord in prayer. 7 He will
have knowledge to share and good advice
to give, as well as insight into the Lord's
secrets. 8 He will demonstrate his learning
in what he teaches, c and his pride will be
in the Lord's Law and covenant. 9 He will
be widely praised for his wisdom, and it
will never be lost, because people for
generations to come will remember him.
10 The Gentiles will talk about his wisdom,
and he will be praised aloud in the
assembly. 11 If he lives to old age, he will
die a famous man, but if he is laid to
rest before he is famous, he will be
content. d

A Hymn in Praise of God

12 Like the moon, I am full—full of
more ideas to be discussed. 13 Listen to
me, you devout sons of mine, and blossom
like a rosebush by a stream. 14 Bloom like
a sweet-smelling lily, and send your
fragrance into the air like incense. Sing
the Lord's praises, and thank him for all
that he has done. 15 Proclaim his glory
in grateful praise! To the music of the
harp, sing this song:
16 All that the Lord has done is very good;
    all that he commands is sooner or
        later done.

17 No one should ask why things are as
        they are;
    these questions will be answered at
        the right time.
He commanded, and the water piled up
        high,
    great walls of water arose when he
        spoke.
18 Whatever he commands is promptly
        done;
    there are no limits to his power to
        save.
19 He sees all that every human being
        does;
    there is no way to hide from his sight
20 He sees the whole of time, from
        beginning to end,
    and nothing takes him by surprise. e
21 No one should ask why things are as
        they are;
    everything in creation has its purpose.

22 His blessings overflow like the Nile,
    enriching the world in a fertile flood. f
23 He turns fresh water into salt water,
    and he turns his anger on the nations.
24 For the devout, his ways are straight;
    for the wicked, they are laid with
        traps.
25 From the beginning he has made good
        things for the good
    and terrible things for sinners.
26 The basic needs of life are these:
    water, fire, iron, and salt,
    flour, honey, and milk,
    wine, clothing, and oil.
27 All these things are good for those
        who are devout,
    but they turn into evils for sinners.

28 There are winds that were created to
        bring punishment,
    fierce enough to move mountains. g
In times of judgement, they unleash
        their strength
    and calm the anger of their maker.
29-30 Vicious animals, scorpions, and
        snakes;
    the sword that destroys the wicked;
fire, hail, famine, and disease;
    these have all been created as
        punishments.
31 They are all glad to obey the Lord's
        command

---

b When...prayer or When they pray, it is about their work.
c his learning...teaches; or the wisdom of what he has been taught.
d if he is...content; Greek unclear.   e takes him by surprise; or is too marvellous for him.
f Hebrew overflow...flood; Greek cover the dry land like a river and drench it like a flood.
g Hebrew move mountains; Greek lash heavily.

and are ready to serve him here on
earth.
When their times of duty come,
they never disobey.
[32] (I was long convinced of this, so after
thinking it over I put *h* it in writing.)
[33] Everything made by the Lord is good;
he meets every need at the proper
time.
[34] No one can claim that some things
are worse than others,
for everything is good in its proper
place.
[35] Now then, sing praises with all your
heart,
and praise the name of the Lord!

The Misery of Human Life

40 Every person has been given a
great deal of work to do. A heavy
burden lies on all of us from the day of
our birth until the day we go back to
the earth, the mother of us all. [2] We are
confused and fearful, dreading the day of
our death—[3-4] all of us from the king on
his splendid throne wearing royal robes
and a crown, to the humblest person
dressed in sacking and living in poverty.
[5] All through our lives we meet anger,
jealousy, and trouble. Things disturb us;
we live with furious conflicts and with the
fear of death. Even when we go to bed,
we think up new troubles in our sleep.
[6] We get little rest, if any at all. When
we sleep, it is as if we were awake,
disturbed by our imaginations. If we
dream that we are running from an
enemy, [7] just as we are about to be
caught, *i* we wake up and are relieved to
find there is nothing to be afraid of.

[8] These are what all creatures, both
human and animal, must face (but it is
seven times worse for sinners): [9] death,
violence, conflict, murder, disaster,
famine, sickness, epidemic. [10] All these
things were created because of the
wicked; they are the ones who have
caused destruction. *j* [11] Everything that
comes from the earth goes back to the
earth, just as all water flows into the sea.

The Results of Evil

[12] Nothing that comes from bribery or
injustice will last, but the effects of loyalty
will remain for ever. [13] Wealth that has
been obtained dishonestly is like a stream
that runs full during a thunderstorm,
[14] tumbling rocks along as it flows, but
then suddenly goes dry. *k* [15] The children
of ungodly people will not leave large
families; they are like plants trying to take
root on rock, [16] like reeds along a river
bank, withering *l* before any other plant.
[17] Acts of kindness and charity are as
lasting as eternity. *m*

The Joys of Human Life

[18] Having independent means or
working for a living—both can make life
pleasant, but it is better to find a treasure.

[19] A man's name can be preserved if
he has children or if he establishes a city,
but finding Wisdom is a better way.

Owning livestock and orchards will
make you famous, *n* but it is better to have
a wife you love. *o*

[20] Wine and music can make you
happy, but a happy marriage *p* is even
better.

[21] Flutes and harps make fine music,
but a pleasant voice is better than either.

[22] Gracefulness and beauty please the
eye, but not as much as new growth in
the spring.

[23] You can't go wrong with a good
friend or neighbour, but an intelligent wife
is *q* better than either.

[24] Brothers and helpers are good to
have in times of trouble, but it will be
an even greater help if you have made
a practice of giving to the poor.

[25] Gold and silver provide security, but
good advice is better.

[26] Wealth and strength give confidence,
but the fear of the Lord can give you
even greater confidence. When you fear
the Lord you need nothing more; it is
all the support you need. [27] The fear of
the Lord is like a rich garden of blessings;
you could not want a more glorious
shelter.

---

h put; *or* left.   *i* *Probable text* caught; *Greek* rescued.
j *Hebrew* have caused destruction; *Greek* caused the flood.
k *Verses 13–14 are translated from Hebrew; verse 14 in Greek is unclear.*
l *Hebrew* withering; *Greek* pulled up.
m *Hebrew* Acts...eternity; *Greek* Kindness is a blessed garden, and charity lasts for ever.
n *Hebrew* but finding Wisdom...famous; *Greek does not have these words.*
o *Hebrew* wife you love; *Greek* blameless wife.
p *Hebrew* a happy marriage; *Greek* the love of Wisdom.
q *Hebrew* an intelligent wife is; *Greek* a wife and a husband are.

Begging

28 My son, don't live the life of a beggar; it is better to die than to beg. [29] If you have to depend on someone else for your food, you are not really living your own life. You pollute yourself by accepting food from another. Begging is torture to the soul of any sensitive person. [r] [30] A shameless person can make begging sound sweet, but something inside him burns.

Death

41 Death! The very thought of it is bitter to someone who is prosperous, living peacefully with his possessions, free of worries, and still able to enjoy his food.

2 Death! Its sentence is welcome to someone living in poverty, with failing health, very old, burdened with worries, blind, and without hope. [s]

3 Do not be afraid of death's decree. Remember that it came to those before you and will come to those after you. [4] The Lord has decreed it for every living creature. Who are you to object to what the Most High wishes? In the world of the dead no one will care whether you lived ten years, a hundred, or a thousand.

The Fate of the Wicked

5 The children of sinners, brought up in ungodly surroundings, turn out to be hateful people. [6] They will lose whatever they inherit, and their own descendants will live in permanent disgrace. [7] The children will put the blame for their disgrace on their ungodly parents.

8 You are doomed, you irreligious men who have abandoned the Law of the Most High God. [9] When you have children, disaster will strike them and you will be left with nothing but sorrow. There will be great joy whenever you stumble, [t] and even after your death you will be cursed. [10] What comes into being from nothing [u] will return to nothing; [u] so it will be with the godless, doomed to extinction.

11 A person's body amounts to nothing, [v] but a good reputation will last for ever. [12] Protect your reputation; it will outlive you and last longer than a thousand treasures of gold. [13] A good life lasts only a short time, but a good reputation will last for ever.

A Sense of Decency

14 My children, do as I teach you and live at peace. Wisdom that is not expressed is like a treasure that has been hidden—both are useless. [15] A person who covers up his foolishness is better than one who keeps his wisdom to himself.

16 My children, listen and I will teach you the circumstances when it is proper to be ashamed. [w] Sometimes it is entirely out of place.

[17] Before your parents, be ashamed of immoral behaviour.

Before a ruler or an important person, be ashamed of a lie.

[18] Before a judge, be ashamed of criminal behaviour.

Before a public assembly, be ashamed of breaking the law.

Before a friend or partner, be ashamed of dishonesty.

[19] Before your neighbours, be ashamed of theft.

Be ashamed of breaking a promise, [x] of leaning on the dinner table with your elbows,

of stinginess when you are asked for something,

[20] of not returning a greeting, of staring at a prostitute,

[21] of turning down a relative's request, of depriving someone of what is rightly his,

of staring at another man's wife,

[22] of playing around with his slave girl (keep away from her bed!)

of insulting your friends, of following up your gifts with criticism,

[23] of betraying secrets.

These are times when it is proper for you to be ashamed, and people will respect you for it.

A Sense of Pride

42 On the other hand, it is possible to sin by giving in to other people too much. Here are some things you should not be ashamed of:

---

[r] *Hebrew* Begging...person; *Greek* An intelligent and understanding person will avoid it.
[s] *Hebrew* blind, and without hope; *Greek* rebellious and without patience.
[t] *Hebrew* When you have...stumble; *Greek* You are born under a curse.
[u] *Hebrew* nothing; *Greek* earth.
[v] *Hebrew* A person's...nothing; *Greek* The death of a person's body is mourned.
[w] *Hebrew* My children...ashamed; *Greek* Show respect for what I say.
[x] *Hebrew* of breaking a promise; *Greek* of yourself before the truth of God.

² the Law of the Most High and his
      covenant,
   judging even godless people fairly,
³ sharing expenses with a business
      partner or a travelling companion,
   sharing an inheritance,
⁴ using accurate weights and measures,
⁵ making a profit, whether great or small,
   bargaining with a merchant,
   disciplining your children often,
   beating a disloyal slave until the blood
      flows.
6 It is wise to lock things up if you
cannot trust your wife or if too many
people are around. ⁷Keep an accurate
record of any deposits you make or of
anything you give or receive. ⁸Don't
hesitate to correct someone who is acting
foolishly or an old man who goes about
with prostitutes. All this is worthwhile
advice, and if you follow it, everyone will
approve of your behaviour.

Fathers and Daughters

9 Although he will not let his daughter
know it, a father will lie awake at night
worrying about her. If she is young, he
worries that she might not get married.
If she is already married, he worries about
her happiness. ¹⁰If she is a virgin, he
worries that she might be seduced and
become pregnant while living in his house.
If she is married, he worries that she might
be unfaithful, or that she might not be
able to have children.

11 Keep a close watch over your
daughter if she is determined to have her
own way. If you don't, she may make
a fool of you in front of your enemies. You
will be a constant joke to everyone in
town, a public disgrace. Make sure that
her room has no windows or any place
where she can look out to the entrance
of the house.ʸ ¹²Don't let her show off
her beauty in front of men, or spend her
time talking with the women.ᶻ ¹³Women
hurt other women just as moths damage
clothing.

14 A man's wickedness is better than
a woman's goodness; women bring shame
and disgrace.

The Glory of God in Nature

¹⁵ Now I will remind you of the works
   of the Lord
and describe the things I have seen.
The words of the Lord brought his
      works into being,
   and the whole creation obeys his
      commands.
¹⁶ The light of the sun shines down on
      everything,
   and everything is filled with the
      Lord's glory.
¹⁷ Not even to his holy angels has the
      Lord given power
   to describe all his mighty deeds,
even though he has given them power
   to stand unharmed in his glorious
      presence.ᵃ
¹⁸ He sees into the oceans and into the
      human heart,
   and he knows the secrets of both.
The Most High knows everything that
      can be known
   and understands the signs of the ages.
¹⁹ He knows all that has ever been and
      all that ever will be;
   he uncovers the deepest of mysteries.
²⁰ He takes notice of our every thought
   and hears our every word.
²¹ The orderly world shows the greatness
      of his wisdom;
   he is the same for ever and ever.ᵇ
Nothing can be added to him, and
      nothing taken away;
   he needs no one to give him advice.
²² All his works are beautiful,
   down to the smallest and faintest
      spark of light.ᶜ
²³ All these things go on for ever,
   and all of them have their purpose.
²⁴ All things are in pairs, each the
      opposite of the other,
   but nothing the Lord made is
      incomplete.
²⁵ Everything completes the goodness of
      something else.
   Could anyone ever see enough of this
      splendour?

43 How beautiful is the bright, clear
         sky above us!
   What a glorious sight it is!
² The sun, when it appears, proclaims as
      it rises
   how marvellous a thing it is, made
      by the Most High.
³ At noon it dries up the land;
   no one can stand its blazing heat.

ʸ Hebrew Make sure...house; *Greek does not have these words.*
ᶻ Hebrew Don't let...women; *Greek unclear.*
ᵃ Hebrew even though...presence; *Greek* which the Lord Almighty established so that everything
may stand firm in his glory.   ᵇ Hebrew he is...ever; *Greek* he is before eternity and is eternal.
ᶜ Hebrew down to...spark of light; *Greek unclear.*
42.9–11: Sir 7.24–25; 26.10–12

It spans the horizon in a circle of glory (43.12)

⁴ The setting sun sets fire to the hilltops,
　like a metal furnace glowing from the
　heat. ᵈ
　It sends out fiery rays,
　blinding the eyes with its brightness.
⁵ The Lord, who made it, is great;
　it speeds on its way at his command.

⁶ There is also the moon, marking the
　passage of time, ᵉ
　an eternal sign of the changing
　seasons.
⁷ The moon determines the holy days.
　Its light grows full and then grows
　dim.
⁸ The "month" is named after the moon,
　marvellous to watch as it grows fuller
　each night,
　a signal light for the heavenly armies,
　shining out in the dome of the sky.

⁹ The shining stars make the night sky
　lovely,
brilliant ornaments in the Lord's high
　heavens.
¹⁰ They stay in the places assigned to
　them by the Holy One
　and never relax their dutiful watch.

¹¹ Look at the rainbow and praise its
　Creator!
　How magnificent, how radiant, its
　beauty!
¹² Like a bow bent by the hands of the
　Most High,
　it spans the horizon in a circle of glory.

¹³ He commands, and snow begins to fall;
　lightning strikes to carry out his
　judgements.
¹⁴ The storerooms of the sky are thrown
　open,
　and the clouds roll out like flying birds.
¹⁵ With his power he forms great masses
　of clouds
　and shatters the ice into hailstones.

ᵈ *Hebrew* The setting...heat; *Greek* A man at a furnace works with scorching heat, but the sun
burns the hills three times as much.　ᵉ *Hebrew* marking...time; *Greek unclear.*

16-17 He speaks, and thunder twists the
earth in pain;
the mountains are shaken by his
strength. *f*
Whenever he wishes, the south wind
blows,
whirlwinds come, and windstorms
from the north.
He sends the snow fluttering down like
birds,
like locusts alighting on the ground.
18 We marvel at its beautiful whiteness,
and in fascination we watch it fall.
19 He sprinkles frost over the ground like
salt,
and it freezes into thorny flowers of
ice. *g*
20 He sends the cold north wind blowing
and the water hardens into ice;
every lake and pond freezes over,
putting on a coat of icy armour.
21 He scorches the hills of the wilderness
with drought,
and the grass turns brown from its
heat;
22 but a cloudy mist restores it all to
life
as the weather cools and dew appears.

23 By his wisdom he calmed the great
oceans
and placed the islands there.
24 Sailors tell about the dangers of the
sea,
and we listen to their tales in
amazement.
25 In the sea are strange and marvellous
creatures:
huge monsters and all kinds of living
things.
26 Each of the Lord's messengers
succeeds at its task.
Everything is held together by his
word.

27 We could say much more and never
finish,
but it all means this: the Lord is
everything.
28 How can we find the power to praise
him?
He is greater than all his creation.
29 The Lord is awesome in his greatness;
his power is overwhelming.
30 Though you do your best to praise him,

he is greater than you can ever
express.
Though you honour him tirelessly and
with all your strength,
you still cannot praise him enough.
31 No one has seen him, no one can
describe him;
no one can praise him as he deserves.
32 Mysteries greater than these are still
unknown;
we know only a fraction of his works.
33 The Lord made the universe
and then gave wisdom to devout men.

The Glory of God in History

44 So let us now give praise to godly *h*
men,
our ancestors of generations past,
2 men whom the Lord honoured with
great glory,
in whom his greatness has been seen
from the beginning of time.
3 There were some who ruled kingdoms,
and some who were known for their
strength.
Some were wise advisers,
and some spoke prophecies.
4 There were statesmen whose policies
governed the people,
rulers who issued decrees, *i*
scholars who spoke wise words, *j*
and those who used pointed
proverbs, *k*
5 poets, and composers of music,
6 rich and powerful men living
peacefully at home.
7 All these were famous in their own
times,
honoured by the people of their day.
8 Some men left a reputation,
and people still praise them today.
9 There are others who are not
remembered,
as if they had never lived,
they died and were forgotten,
they, and their children after them.

10 But we will praise these godly men,
whose righteous deeds have never
been forgotten.
11 Their reputations will be passed on
to their descendants,
and this will be their inheritance. *l*
12 Their descendants continue to keep
the covenant

---

f Hebrew by his strength; Greek when he appears.   g Hebrew flowers of ice; Greek points.
h Hebrew godly; Greek famous.
i Probable Hebrew text rulers who issued decrees; Greek unclear.
j Hebrew scholars...words; Greek unclear.
k Hebrew and those...proverbs; Greek does not have these words.
l Verse 11 in Greek is unclear.

NOAH

ABRAHAM

JACOB

MOSES

AARON

JOSHUA

SAMUEL

DAVID

SOLOMON

ELIJAH

JOSIAH

NEHEMIAH

SIMON

and always will, because of what their ancestors did.
13 Their family line will go on for ever,
    and their fame will never fade.
14 Their bodies were laid to rest,
    but their reputations will live for ever.
15 Nations will tell about the wisdom of these men,
    and God's people will praise them.

Enoch

16 Enoch pleased the Lord and was taken up into heaven. He became an inspiration for repentance for all time to come.

Noah

17 Noah was a perfectly righteous man. After destruction came, he gave the human race a new start. *m* Because of him there were people left on earth when the flood was over. 18 The Lord made an eternal covenant with him, promising that life would never again be destroyed by a flood.

Abraham

19 Abraham was the great ancestor of many nations; his reputation was faultless. *n* 20 He kept the Law of the Most High and made a covenant with him, a covenant marked on his body. When he was put to the test, he was found faithful. 21 And so the Lord made him a solemn promise that his descendants would be a blessing to the world; that their number would be countless, like the dust of the earth; that they would be honoured more than any other people on earth; and that their land would extend from sea to sea, from the Euphrates to the ends of the earth.

Isaac and Jacob

22-23 The Lord renewed that covenant with Isaac, and then again with Jacob, repeating the promise that Abraham's descendants would be a blessing to all mankind. The Lord assured Jacob that he would bless him; he gave him the land that would be his, dividing it into twelve parts, one for each of the tribes.

Moses

45 From Jacob's descendants the Lord raised up a godly man who won the favour of everyone, loved by God and man alike. This man was Moses, whose very memory is a blessing. 2 The Lord made him as glorious as the angels and made his enemies fear him. 3 There in Egypt at his command the disaster struck. *o* The Lord made kings hold him in respect. The Lord gave him his commands for his people and showed him the dazzling light of his presence. 4 The Lord chose Moses out of all mankind and consecrated him because of his loyalty and humility. 5 He let him hear his voice and led him into the dark cloud, where, face to face, he gave him the commandments, the Law that gives life and knowledge, so that Moses might teach the covenant regulations to the Israelites.

Aaron

6 The Lord raised up Aaron, a holy man like his brother Moses, of the tribe of Levi. 7 He made an eternal covenant with him, giving him the privilege of serving as priest to the Lord's people. He honoured him by clothing him with magnificent robes and fine ornaments, 8 perfect in their splendour. He granted him the symbols of authority: the linen shorts, the shirt, and the robe with the pomegranates round the hem. 9 Gold bells were also round its hem, so that when he walked, their ringing would be heard in the Temple, and the Lord would remember his people. 10 The Lord gave Aaron the sacred robe with the gold, blue, and purple embroidery; the breastpiece with the Urim and Thummim, *p* 11 the red yarn, spun by an expert; the precious stones with names engraved on them, mounted in a gold setting by a jeweller, placed on the breastpiece to remind the Lord of the twelve tribes of Israel. 12 He gave him the turban with the gold ornament engraved with the words "Dedicated to the Lord." It was expertly crafted, a beautiful work of art, and it was a high honour to wear it. 13 Before Aaron's time such beautiful things were never seen. No one but Aaron and his

---

m Hebrew gave...start; *Greek* was taken in exchange for the human race.
n Hebrew his reputation was faultless; *Greek* there was no one like him in reputation.
o Hebrew struck; *Greek* stopped.
p URIM AND THUMMIM: *Two objects used by the priest to determine God's will; it is not known precisely how they were used.*
44.16: Gen 5.24; Heb 11.5; Jude 14   **44.17-18:** Gen 6.9—9.17
44.19-21: Gen 15.1—17.27; 22.1-18   **44.22-23:** Gen 17.19; 26.3-5; 27.28; 28.14
45.1-5: Ex 6.28—11.10; 20.1-21   **45.6:** Ex 4.14   **45.7-13:** Ex 28.1-43

descendants ever wore them, or ever will.
14 The grain-offering is to be presented
twice a day and burnt completely.

15 Moses ordained Aaron to office by
pouring the sacred anointing oil over his
head. An eternal covenant was made with
him and his descendants, that they would
serve the Lord as his priests and bless
the people in the Lord's name. 16 The Lord
chose Aaron out of all mankind to offer
sacrifices, to burn fragrant incense to
remind the Lord of his people, and to take
away their sins. 17 He entrusted the
commandments to Aaron's keeping and
gave him the authority to make legal
decisions and to teach Israel the Law.

18 Once, while the people were in the
wilderness, an angry group of jealous
outsiders conspired against Moses. These
were Dathan, Abiram, and Korah with
their supporters. 19 The Lord saw what
they were doing and became angry, so
furious that he performed a miracle and
destroyed them in a blazing fire. 20 Then he
rewarded Aaron again, giving him a
special honour: the right to the offerings
of the first produce, so that the priests
should have enough to eat. 21 Their food
is the sacrifices offered to the Lord; the
Lord gave this to Aaron and his
descendants. 22 But Aaron, unlike the rest
of the people, was to inherit no land, no
special portion of his own. The Lord
himself would be all he needed.

Phinehas

23 Only Moses and Aaron were more
famous for their intense devotion to the
Lord than Phinehas son of Eleazar. He
brought about forgiveness for Israel's sin
by standing firm in brave determination
when everyone else was in revolt. 24 And
so the Lord made a covenant with him,
valid for all time to come, that he should
be in charge of the sanctuary and of his
people, that he and his descendants
should hold the office of High Priest for
ever. 25 Unlike the covenant made with
David son of Jesse, from the tribe of
Judah, where the kingship passed only
from father to son, the priesthood was
to pass from Aaron to all his descendants.

26 Now praise the Lord, who is good,
who has crowned you with glory! q May
he give you wisdom to judge his people
fairly, so that their success and your
authority r may continue for all time to
come.

Joshua

46 Joshua s son of Nun was a great
soldier and the next of the
prophets after Moses. He lived up to the
meaning of his name as the great deliverer
of the Lord's chosen people. He defeated
the enemies that attacked them, so that
Israel could claim its land. 2 How
magnificent it was when he raised his arm
and then led the attack on the cities! 3 No
one could stand up to him; t he was
fighting a holy war for the Lord. 4 Remember how he held back the sun and
made one day as long as two? 5 When
his enemies were threatening him from
every side, he prayed to the mighty Lord
Most High, and his prayer was answered
with a hailstorm of devastating force.
6 The Lord hurled the hail down on the
enemy u and destroyed them at the pass
at Beth Horon, so that the nations would
realize how strong Joshua was, since he
was fighting as a devoted follower of the
Lord.

Caleb

7 Joshua was loyal as long as Moses
lived, both he and Caleb son of Jephunneh.
They stood up to the whole community,
made them stop their ungrateful
complaining, and kept them from sinning.
8 Out of the 600,000 Israelites who
marched through the wilderness, these
two were the only ones spared and
allowed to enter the rich and fertile land
that was to be theirs. 9 The Lord made
Caleb strong, and when he was an old
man, he was still strong enough to go
up into the hill country and capture it
for himself and his descendants. 10 Then
all Israel could see how good it is to follow
the Lord.

The Judges

11 Then there were the judges, each one

---

q Hebrew Now praise...glory; *Greek does not have these words.*
r *Probable Hebrew text* and your authority; *Greek unclear.*
s JOSHUA: *This name in Hebrew means "the Lord saves."*
t *Hebrew* No one...to him; *Greek* No one before had ever been so brave.
u *Probable text* The Lord hurled...enemy; *Greek unclear.*
45.15: Lev 8.1-36   **45.18-19:** Num 16.1-35   **45.22:** Num 18.20; Deut 12.12
45.23-26: Num 25.7-13   **46.1-6:** Josh 1.1—11.23
46.7-10: Num 14.6-10; 11.21; Josh 14.6.11   **46.11:** Judg 1.1—16.31

famous in his own right, who never fell into idolatry and never abandoned the Lord. 12 May their memory be honoured! May these whom we honour spring from the grave to new life in their descendants!

Samuel

13 Samuel was loved by the Lord. As the Lord's prophet he established the kingdom and appointed rulers for the people. 14 He judged the nation in accordance with the Law of the Lord, and the Lord protected Israel. 15 Because Samuel was faithful, he was accepted as a true prophet. People trusted him as a seer because of his words. 16 When his enemies were threatening him from every side, he called upon the mighty Lord and offered him a young lamb as a sacrifice. 17 Then the Lord thundered from heaven with a mighty roar 18 and destroyed all the enemy v rulers of Philistia. 19 When Samuel was about to die, he gave assurances before the Lord and the anointed king that he had never taken anyone's property, not even so much as a pair of shoes, and no one contradicted him. 20 Even after he died, he prophesied to King Saul how he would die. Out of the grave he spoke as a prophet, to blot out his people's wickedness.

Nathan

47 After him came Nathan, who was a prophet at the time of David.

David

2 As the choice fat portion of the fellowship-offering is reserved for the Lord, so David was chosen from among the Israelites. 3 He played with lions and bears as if they were lambs or little goats. 4 When he was still a boy, he killed a giant to rescue his people. He put a stone in his sling, took aim, and put an end to Goliath's bragging. 5 He prayed to the Lord, the Most High, and was given the strength to kill that famous soldier, so that the nations would have respect for the power of his people. 6 The people honoured him for killing his tens of thousands, and when he was crowned king, they praised him for being chosen

by the Lord. 7 He wiped out all his enemies and permanently crushed the Philistines, so that they never again became a threat.

8 In everything David did, he gave thanks and praise to the Holy Lord, the Most High. He loved his Creator and sang praises to him with all his heart. 9 He put singers at the altar to provide beautiful music. 10 He set the times of the festivals throughout the year and made them splendid occasions; the Temple rang with the Lord's praises all day long. 11 The Lord forgave David's sin and established his power for ever. He made a covenant with him that he and his descendants would reign in splendour over Israel.

Solomon

12 David prepared the way well for his son, a wise man, to rule after him. 13 There was no war while Solomon was king. God gave him peace on all his borders, so that he could build for the Lord a Temple which would stand for ever. 14 How wise you were, Solomon, when you were young! Your knowledge was like the Nile w in flood. 15 Your influence reached over all the world; your proverbs and riddles were known everywhere. 16 You were famous everywhere, and people loved you for bringing peace. 17 Nations round the world held you in admiration for your songs, proverbs, parables, and witty sayings. 18 You gathered silver and gold as if it were tin or lead, all in the name of the Lord God of Israel.

19 But your lust for women was your downfall. 20 You stained your reputation and that of your descendants. They suffered punishment for that foolishness of yours, which caused them so much grief. 21 It divided the nation, and a rival kingdom arose in northern Israel. 22 But the Lord will always be merciful and keep all his promises. x He will never destroy the descendants of David, whom he chose and who loved him. So for Israel's sake he allowed David's family to survive.

Rehoboam and Jeroboam

23 Solomon followed his ancestors in death and left one of his sons to rule after him. This was Rehoboam, a man of little

v Hebrew enemy; Greek rulers of Tyre and.   w Hebrew the Nile; Greek a river.
x Hebrew keep all his promises; Greek will not destroy what he made.
46.13–20: 1 Sam 3.19–20; 7.9–11; 10.1; 12.3; 16.13; 28.18–19   **47.1:** 2 Sam 7.2–3; 12.1
47.2–11: 1 Sam 17.34—18.7; 2 Sam 5.7; 8.1; 12.13   **47.13–17:** 1 Kgs 4.21–32
47.18: 1 Kgs 10.21,27   **47.19:** 1 Kgs 11.1   **47.21:** 1 Kgs 12.15-20   **47.22:** 2 Sam 7.15
47.23-25: 1 Kgs 11.43; 12.10-30; 2 Kgs 17.6,18

intelligence and great foolishness,[y] whose policies caused a rebellion.

There was also the unspeakable Jeroboam,[z] who led northern Israel in sinful ways. 24 His people became so sinful that they were exiled from their land. 25 They tried all kinds of wickedness, until the Lord took vengeance on them.

Elijah

48 Then there arose the fiery prophet Elijah, whose words blazed like a torch. 2 He brought a famine on the people, and many of them died because of his persistence. 3 Speaking in the name of the Lord, he kept the rain from coming, and on three occasions he called down fire. 4 Elijah, your miracles were marvellous! No one else can boast of such deeds! 5 In the name of the Most High, you brought a dead man back to life. 6 You brought a famous king down to sickness and death. 7 At Sinai you heard the Lord rebuke you and declare his determination to punish his enemies. 8 You anointed a king to be the instrument of that punishment, and a prophet to take your place. 9 You were taken up to heaven in a fiery whirlwind, a chariot drawn by fiery horses. 10 The scripture says that you are ready to appear at the designated time,[a] to cool God's anger before it breaks out in fury; that you "will bring fathers and children together again," and restore the tribes of Israel. 11 Fortunate are those who live to see you come, as well as those who have already died in love, for we too shall live.[b]

Elisha

12 When Elijah was hidden by the whirlwind, Elisha was filled with his spirit. As long as he lived, he was not afraid of rulers, and they could not make him do as they wished. 13 Nothing was too hard for him. Even when he was dead, his body worked a miracle. 14 In life and in death he performed amazing miracles.

15 But in spite of all this, the people did not abandon their sinful ways until they were taken from their land as prisoners and scattered all over the world.

This left the nation few in number, but those who remained were still ruled by the descendants of David. 16 Some of the people did what was pleasing to the Lord, but others committed sin after sin.

Hezekiah

17 Hezekiah prepared his city to resist a siege and provided it with a water supply. He had a tunnel built through solid rock with iron tools and had cisterns built to hold the water. 18 During his reign Sennacherib attacked the city and sent his chief official from Lachish. He challenged Jerusalem and boasted arrogantly. 19 The people lost their courage and shook with fear; they were in pain, like a woman in labour. 20 But they prayed to the merciful Lord, the Holy One in heaven, who quickly answered their prayers and sent Isaiah to save them. 21 The Lord struck the Assyrian camp; his angel wiped them out. 22 Yes, Hezekiah did what was pleasing to the Lord and firmly followed the example of his ancestor David. This was what was commanded by the great prophet Isaiah, whose visions were trusted. 23 He made the sun move backward and lengthened the king's life. 24 He comforted the mourners in Jerusalem. His powerful spirit looked into the future, 25 and he predicted what was to happen before the end of time, hidden things that had not yet occurred.

Josiah

49 The memory of Josiah is as sweet as the fragrance of expertly blended incense, sweet as honey to the taste,[c] like music with wine at a banquet. 2 He followed the correct policy of reforming the nation and removed the horrors of idolatry. 3 He was completely loyal to the Lord and strengthened true religion in those wicked times.

Jeremiah

4 All the kings, except David, Hezekiah, and Josiah, were terrible sinners, because they abandoned the Law of the Most High to the very end of the kingdom.[d] 5 They surrendered their power and honour to

---

[y] Hebrew great foolishness; Greek the people's fool.
[z] Hebrew the unspeakable (one); Greek Jeroboam son of Nebat.
[a] Hebrew you are...time; Greek unclear.　　[b] Verse 11 in Greek is unclear.
[c] Hebrew to the taste; Greek to everyone.
[d] Hebrew to the very end of the kingdom; Greek and failed.

48.1–11: 1 Kgs 17.1–24; 18.38; 19.15–16; 2 Kgs 1.10–16; 2.11; Mal 4.5–6　　**48.12:** 2 Kgs 2.9,13
48.13: 2 Kgs 13.20–21　　**48.15:** 2 Kgs 18.11–12　　**48.17:** 2 Kgs 20.20　　**48.18:** 2 Kgs 18.13–17
48.20–21: 2 Kgs 19.15–20,35　　**48.23:** 2 Kgs 20.10–11　　**49.1–3:** 2 Kgs 22.1,11–13; 23.3,25

foreigners, [6] who set fire to the holy city and left its streets deserted, just as Jeremiah had predicted. [7] Jeremiah had been badly treated, even though he was chosen as a prophet before he was born, "to uproot and to pull down, to destroy and to overthrow," but also "to build and to plant."

Ezekiel

8 It was Ezekiel who was shown the vision of the divine glory over the chariot and the living creatures. [9] He also referred to the prophet Job, who always did the right thing. [e]

The Twelve Prophets

10 May the bones of the twelve prophets rise to new life, because these men encouraged the people of Israel and saved them with confident hope.

Zerubbabel and Joshua

11 How can we praise Zerubbabel? He was like a signet ring on the Lord's right hand, [12] as was Joshua son of Jehozadak. They rebuilt the Lord's holy Temple, destined for eternal fame.

Nehemiah

13 The memory of Nehemiah is also great. He rebuilt the ruined walls of Jerusalem, installing the gates and bars. He rebuilt our homes.

The Patriarchs

14 No one else like Enoch has ever walked the face of the earth, for he was taken up from the earth. [15] No one else like Joseph has ever been born; [f] even his bones were honoured. [g] [16] Shem, Seth, and Enosh [h] were highly honoured, but Adam's glory was above that of any other living being.

Simon Son of Onias

50 The greatest of his brothers and the pride of his people [i] was the High Priest Simon son of Onias, who repaired the Temple [2] and laid the foundation for the high double wall and the fortifications of the Temple. [j] [3] The

reservoir, as big as the bronze tank, was dug [k] while he was in office. [4] He made plans to protect his people from attack and fortified the city so that it could withstand a siege.

5 How glorious he was when he came out of the Most Holy Place! [l] [6] He was like the morning star shining through the clouds, like the full moon, [7] like the sun shining on the Temple of the Most High, like the rainbow gleaming in glory against the clouds, [8] like roses in springtime, like lilies beside a stream, like the cedars of Lebanon in summer, [9] like burning incense, like a cup made of hammered gold and decorated with all kinds of jewels, [10] like an olive-tree loaded with fruit, like a cypress-tree towering into the clouds.

11 When Simon put on his magnificent robe and went up to the holy altar dressed in perfect splendour, he made the Temple courtyard a majestic sight. [12] When the priests handed him the portions of the sacrifice as he stood beside the altar with his assistants circling him like a wreath, he was like a young cedar of Lebanon surrounded by palm-trees. [13] Those were the descendants of Aaron in their splendid garments, standing before the whole assembly of Israel, holding in their hands the offering made to the Lord. [14] When he had finished the service at the altar and had arranged the sacrifice to the Most High, the Almighty, [15] he reached for a cup and poured out sweet-smelling wine at the foot of the altar as an offering to the Most High, the universal King. [16] Then the priests shouted and blew their trumpets of hammered silver. They made a loud noise that the Most High would hear. [17] All the people immediately bowed down with their faces to the ground to worship their Lord, the Almighty, the Most High. [18] Then the choir began to sing his praises, and the beautiful music rang out. [19] The people kept praying to the merciful Lord Most High until the service of worship had come to a close. [20] Then Simon came down from the altar, raised his hands over the whole assembly of Israel, and reverently pronounced the

---

[e] Probable Hebrew text He also...thing; Greek unclear.
[f] Greek adds the greatest of his brothers and the pride of his people; Hebrew and one ancient translation place these words in 50.1.   [g] even...honoured; or the Lord watched over his body.
[h] Hebrew Shem, Seth, and Enosh; Greek Shem and Seth among men.
[i] The greatest...people; Hebrew and one ancient translation place the words at this point; Greek places them at 49.15.   [j] Verse 2 in Greek is unclear.   [k] Hebrew dug; Greek reduced.
[l] Hebrew Most Holy Place; Greek Most Holy Place among the people.
49.6-7: Jer 1.4-10; 39.8   **49.8-9:** Ezek 1.3-15; 14.14-20   **49.11:** Ezra 3.2; Hag 2.23
49.12: Hag 1.1,12   **49.13:** Neh 6.15   **50.20:** Num 6.24-27

blessing from the Lord, [21] while the people bowed a second time in worship to receive that blessing from the Most High.

A Benediction

22 Now then, give praise to the God of the universe, who has done great things everywhere, who brings us up [m] from the time we are born, and deals with us mercifully. [23] May he give us happiness and allow us to have peace in Israel for ever. [24] May he continue his mercy to us and rescue us in our time of need.

Three Hated Nations

25 There are two nations that I detest, and a third that does not even deserve to be called a nation. [26] These are the Edomites, [n] the inhabitants of the Philistine cities, and the stupid Samaritans.

The Wisdom of Jesus Son of Sirach

27 I, Jesus son of Sirach Eleazar [o] of Jerusalem, put all my wisdom into writing this book to provide instruction and knowledge for others. [28] May God bless everyone who gives attention to these teachings. Whoever takes them to heart will become wise. [29] Whoever lives by them will be strong enough for any occasion, because he will be walking in the light of the Lord.

A Song of Thanksgiving

51 I give you thanks, O Lord and King;
        I praise you as my God and
            Saviour.
I give you thanks,
2   for you have helped me and protected
        me.
You have rescued me from death,
    from dangerous lies and slander.
3 You helped me when no one else would;
    in your great mercy you saved me
        from the many troubles I have known:
from the glaring hatred of my enemies,
    who wanted to put an end to my life;
4 from suffocation in oppressive smoke
    rising from fires that I did not light;
5 from death itself;
    from vicious slander reported to the
        king.
6 I was once brought face to face with
        death;
7   enemies surrounded me everywhere.
I looked for someone to help me,

but there was no one there.
8 But then, O Lord, I remembered how
        merciful you are
    and what you had done in times past.
I remembered that you rescue those
    who rely on you,
    that you save them from their
        enemies.
9 Then from here on earth I prayed to
        you
    to rescue me from death.
10 I prayed, "O Lord, you are my father; [p]
    do not abandon me to my troubles
    when I am helpless against arrogant
        enemies.
11 I will always praise you
    and sing hymns of thanksgiving."
You answered my prayer,
12   and saved me from the threat of
        destruction.
And so I thank you and praise you.
    O Lord, I praise you!

The Search for Wisdom

13 When I was still young, before I started out on my travels, I boldly prayed for Wisdom. [14] I went to the Temple and asked for her, and I will look for her as long as I live. [15] From my blossoming youth to my ripe old age she has been my delight. I have followed directly in her path ever since I was young. [16] I received Wisdom as soon as I began listening for her, and I have been rewarded with great knowledge. [17] I have always been a learner and am grateful to everyone who has been my teacher. [18] I was determined to live wisely and was devoted to the cause of goodness. I have no regrets. [19] I fought for Wisdom and was strict in my conduct. When I prayed, I sadly confessed how far short of Wisdom I fell. [20] But I was determined to have her, and I found her by keeping myself free from sin. I have grown in Wisdom since first I found her, and I will never be without her. [21] Because I was driven by the desire to find her, I have been richly rewarded. [22] The Lord gave me a gift for words, and I have used it in his praise.

23 Come to me, all you that need instruction, and learn in my school. [24] Why do you admit that you are ignorant and do nothing about it? [25] This is what I say: It costs nothing to be wise. [26] Put on the yoke, and be willing to learn. The opportunity is always near. [27] See for

_____

[m] brings us up; _or_ honours us.   [n] _Hebrew_ Edomites; _Greek_ Samaritans.
[o] Sirach Eleazar; _or_ Sirach son of Eleazar.
[p] _Hebrew_ you are my father; _Greek_ father of my Lord.

yourselves! I have really not studied very hard, but I have found great contentment. ²⁸No matter how much it costs you to get Wisdom, it will be well worth it. ²⁹Be joyfully grateful for the Lord's mercy, and never be ashamed to praise him. ³⁰Do your duty at the proper time, and the Lord, at the time he thinks proper, will give you your reward.

THE BOOK OF

BARUCH

INTRODUCTION

The book of *Baruch* is a collection of four distinct, short discourses, attributed to Baruch, the secretary of the prophet Jeremiah (Jeremiah 32.12; 36.4). These discourses, written at various times, probably in Hebrew originally, were later put together into a single document.

Outline of Contents

Historical introduction   1.1–14
A prayer of confession and deliverance   1.15—3.8
In praise of wisdom   3.9—4.4
Comfort and help for Jerusalem   4.5—5.9

Introduction

1 This book was written by Baruch son of Neraiah, grandson of Mahseiah, and a descendant of Zedekiah, Hasadiah, and Hilkiah. It was written in Babylon ²on the seventh day of the month ᵃ in the fifth year after the Babylonians captured Jerusalem and burnt it down. ³⁻⁴Baruch read the book aloud to Jehoiachin son of Jehoiakim, king of Judah, and to all the people who lived in Babylon by the River Sud. Everyone came to hear it read—nobles, children of royal family, elders, in fact, all the people, no matter what their status.

5 When the book was read, everyone cried, fasted, and prayed to the Lord. ⁶Then each one gave as much money as he could, ⁷and the collection was sent to Jerusalem to Jehoiakim the High Priest, son of Hilkiah and grandson of Shallum, and to the other priests and to all the people who were with him in Jerusalem.

8 On the tenth day of the month of Sivan, Baruch took the sacred utensils which had been carried away from the Temple and returned them to Judah. These were the silver utensils which Zedekiah son of King Josiah of Judah had ordered to be made ⁹after King Nebuchadnezzar of Babylonia had deported Jehoiachin, the rulers, the craftsmen, ᵇ the nobles, and the common people and had taken them from Jerusalem to Babylon.

A Letter to Jerusalem

10 The people wrote:

Please use the money we are sending you to buy animals for the burnt-offerings and the sin-offerings, to buy incense, and to provide the grain-offerings. Offer them on the

ᵃTHE MONTH: *The month is probably the fifth month of the Hebrew calendar (see 2 Kgs 25.8; Jer 52.12).* ᵇcraftsmen; *Greek prisoners.*
1.1: Jer 36.4   **1.3–4:** 2 Kgs 24.8-17

Baruch read the book aloud (1.3)

altar of the Lord our God, ¹¹and pray for King Nebuchadnezzar of Babylonia and his son Belshazzar, that they may live as long as the heavens last. ¹²Then the Lord will strengthen us and be our guide. Nebuchadnezzar and his son Belshazzar will protect us, and we will be loyal to them as long as we live; then they will be pleased with us. ¹³We ask you also to pray to the Lord God for us, because we have sinned against him, and he is still angry with us. ¹⁴Please read this book that we are sending you and make your own confession of sin in the Temple on the first day of the Festival of Shelters and on other holy days of assembly.

A Confession of Sin

¹⁵This is the confession you should make: "The Lord our God is righteous, but we are still covered with shame. All of us—the people of Judah, the people of Jerusalem, ¹⁶our kings, our rulers, our priests, our prophets, and our ancestors have been put to shame, ¹⁷because we have sinned against the Lord our God ¹⁸and have disobeyed him. We did not listen to

1.20: Deut 28.15–68

him or live according to his commandments. ¹⁹From the day the Lord brought our ancestors out of Egypt until the present day, we have continued to be unfaithful to him, and we have not hesitated to disobey him. ²⁰Long ago, when the Lord led our ancestors out of Egypt, so that he could give us a rich and fertile land, he pronounced curses against us through his servant Moses. And today we are suffering because of those curses. ²¹We refused to obey the word of the Lord our God which he spoke to us through the prophets. Instead, we all did as we pleased and went on our own evil way. We turned to other gods and did things the Lord hates.

2 "So the Lord carried out the threat he had made against us and against our judges, our kings, our rulers, and the people of Israel and Judah. ²Nowhere else on earth have such things happened as happened in Jerusalem when the Lord carried out the threats written in the Law of Moses. ³Things were so bad that we even ate the flesh of our own sons and daughters. ⁴The Lord scattered our people, handing us over to the control of all the nations around us, and they looked on us with reproach and horror. ⁵We sinned against the Lord our God and refused to obey him. Therefore our nation was conquered, instead of being victorious.

⁶ "The Lord our God is always righteous, but we and our ancestors are still burdened with our guilt. ⁷Even though the Lord punished us as he had threatened, ⁸we still did not turn to him and pray that we might abandon our evil thoughts. ⁹⁻¹⁰We did not obey him or live by his just commands, so the Lord brought on us all the punishments he had kept ready for us.

The Prayer for Deliverance

¹¹ "You, O Lord, are the God of Israel who brought your people out of Egypt with great power and with signs, miracles, and wonders. You showed your mighty strength and gained a glorious reputation, which is still recognized today. ¹²O Lord our God, we have sinned; we have been unfaithful; we have disobeyed all your commands. ¹³But do not be

angry with us any longer. Here among the nations where you have scattered us, only a few of us are left. ¹⁴ Listen to our prayer of petition, Lord, and rescue us for the sake of your own honour. Let those who have taken us into exile be pleased with us. ¹⁵ Then the whole world will know that you are the Lord our God and that you have chosen the nation of Israel to be your own people.

¹⁶ "O Lord, look down from heaven and see our misery. Listen to our prayer. ¹⁷ Open your eyes and look upon us. Those in the world of the dead with no breath left in their bodies cannot offer praises to you or proclaim how just you are. ¹⁸ Only the living, O Lord, can offer you praise and acknowledge your justice, even though they may be suffering greatly, bent and weak, hungry and with failing eyesight.

¹⁹ "O Lord our God, we pray to you for mercy, but not because of any good things done by our ancestors and our kings. ²⁰ You turned your anger and wrath against us, just as you had threatened to do when your servants the prophets spoke your word to us and said, ²¹ 'Bend your backs and serve the king of Babylonia, and you can remain in the land that I gave to your ancestors. ²² But if you refuse to obey my command to serve him, ²³ I will bring to an end every sound of joy and celebration in the towns of Judah and in Jerusalem. Even the happy sounds of wedding feasts will no longer be heard. The whole land will be desolate and uninhabited.'

²⁴ "But we did not obey your command to serve the king of Babylonia, so you carried out the threat that you had made when you spoke through your servants the prophets, when you said that the bones of our kings and of our ancestors would be taken from their tombs and scattered. ²⁵ And now here they lie exposed to the heat of the day and to the frost of the night. They died in torment from famine, war, and disease. ²⁶ And because of the sin of the people of Israel and Judah, you have reduced your own Temple to ruins, even as it is today.

²⁷ "But, Lord, you have been patient with us and have shown us great mercy, ²⁸ as you promised through your servant Moses on the day you commanded him to write your Law in the presence of the Israelites. ²⁹ 'If you do not obey me,' you said, 'you will be reduced to a handful among the nations where I will scatter you. ³⁰ I know that you will not obey me, because you are a stubborn people. But when you are taken into exile in another land, you will come to your senses. ³¹ Then you will realize that I am the Lord your God, and I will give you a desire to know and a mind with which to understand. ³² There in the land of your exile you will praise me and remember me. ³³ You will stop being so stubborn and wicked, for you will remember what happened to your ancestors when they sinned against the Lord. ³⁴ Then I will bring you back to the land that I solemnly promised to give to your ancestors, to Abraham, Isaac, and Jacob, and it will be yours again. I will increase your population, and you will never again be reduced to a small number. ³⁵ I will make an everlasting covenant with you; I will be your God and you will be my people. I will never again remove you, the people of Israel, from the land that I gave you.'

3   "O Lord Almighty, God of Israel, from the depth of our troubled, weary souls we cry out to you. ² Hear us, O Lord, and have mercy on us, because we have sinned against you. ³ You reign as king for ever, but we die and are gone for ever. ⁴ O Lord Almighty, God of Israel, hear our prayer. We are no better than dead men. Our ancestors sinned against you, the Lord their God. They refused to obey you, and we are suffering the consequences of their sin. ⁵ Forget the sinful things that our ancestors did in the past; at a time like this, think only of your power and reputation, ⁶ for you are the Lord our God, and we will praise you. ⁷ You have made us fear you, so that we might pray to you. Here in exile we will praise you because we have turned away from the sins of our ancestors. ⁸ You have scattered us among the nations, and you have made them despise and curse us. You are punishing us for the sins of our ancestors when they

2.21-23: Jer 7.34; 27.10-12   **2.24:** Jer 8.1-2   **2.28-29:** Deut 28.58-62   **2.35:** Jer 32.38-40

rebelled against you, the Lord our God."

In Praise of Wisdom

9 Listen, Israel, to the commands that promise life; pay attention, and you will become wise. 10 Why is it, Israel, that you find yourself in an enemy land? Why have you grown old in a foreign country? You are ritually unclean, like the dead; 11 you are already counted among the dead. But why? 12 It is because you have left the source of Wisdom! 13 If you had walked in God's ways, you would have lived in peace for ever. 14 Learn where understanding, strength, and insight are to be found. Then you will know where to find a long and full life, light to guide you, and peace.

15 No one has ever found where Wisdom lives or has entered her treasure house, 16-17 and those who have tried have vanished: the rulers of the nations, the men who hunted wild animals and birds for sport, those who accumulated vast fortunes of silver and gold, which everyone trusts and will do anything to get, 18 and those who worried and schemed to make money, but who left no trace of their work behind. 19 They have all disappeared and gone down to the world of the dead. Others have come along to take their place. 20 A later generation was born and lived in the land, but they too did not discover the way to knowledge. They did not find the path to Wisdom or ever reach her. 21 Their children also failed. 22 Wisdom was not found by the Canaanites. It has not been discovered by the Edomites 23 although they search after knowledge. The way to Wisdom has not been found by the merchants of Merran and Tema or by those who relate fables or by any others who seek understanding.

24 O Israel, how great is the universe in which God dwells! How vast is all that he possesses! 25 There is no end to it; there is no way to measure how wide or how high it is. 26 Here in early times the famous giants were born, a mighty race skilled in war. 27 But God did not choose them to be his people or show them the way of knowledge. 28 They died out because they had neither understanding nor insight.

29 No one has ever gone up into heaven to get Wisdom and bring her down out of the clouds. 30 No one has sailed across the seas to find Wisdom, or bought her with precious gold. 31 No one knows how to get to her or how to discover the path that leads to her.

32 The only one who knows Wisdom is God, and he knows all things. With his understanding he found her. He established the earth for all time and filled it with all kinds of animals. 33 The light trembled and obeyed when he called. He sent it out, and it appeared. 34 He called the stars, and they promptly answered; they took their places and gladly shone to please the one who made them. 35 He is our God, and there is none like him. 36 He discovered the entire path leading to understanding and gave Wisdom to his servant Israel, whom he loved. 37 From that time on, Wisdom appeared on earth and lived among us.

4 Wisdom is the book of God's commandments, the Law that will last for ever. All who hold on to her will live, but those who abandon her will die. 2 Turn to Wisdom, people of Israel, and take hold of her. Make your way towards the splendour of her light. 3 Do not surrender our glorious privileges to any other people. 4 How happy we are, people of Israel; we have the advantage of knowing what is pleasing to God!

Comfort for Jerusalem

5 Take courage, my people, you are the ones who keep Israel's name alive. 6 You were sold to Gentile nations, but not to be destroyed. Because you made God angry, he handed you over to your enemies. 7 When you offered sacrifices to demons instead of to God, you angered the one who made you. 8 You forgot the Eternal God, who had nourished you as a child, and so you brought grief to Jerusalem, who had been like a mother to you. 9 Jerusalem saw that God was punishing you because he was angry, and she said to all the neighbouring cities, "Look at the great misery that God has brought on me. 10 I saw my sons and daughters taken into captivity, a captivity brought on them by the Eternal God. 11 I brought up my children with great delight, but I cried and mourned when they were taken from me. 12 Let no one take pleasure in my suffering now that I am a widow and so many of my children have been taken from me. They turned away from God's Law, and their sins have made me a deserted city. 13 They had no respect for

3.9: Prov 4.20–22   **3.15:** Job 28.12,20   **3.26:** Gen 6.4; Wis 14.6   **4.1:** Sir 24.23

God has sent my children into exile (4.14)

his commandments and would not live by them; they refused to let him guide them in the way of righteousness.

14 "All you neighbouring cities, come and consider how the Eternal God has sent my children into exile. 15 He brought against them a nation from far away, a shameless nation that speaks a foreign language and has no respect for the elderly and no pity for children. 16 These people carried off my beloved sons and took away my daughters, and I was left a widow, completely alone.

17 "My children in exile, I can do nothing to help you. 18 Only the one who brought this punishment upon you can rescue you from your enemies. 19 Go your own way, my children; live your own life! I am all alone. 20 I have taken off the robes I wore during days of peace, and I have dressed myself like a person in mourning. I will cry out to the Eternal God for help as long as I live.

21 "Take courage, my children, and cry out to God for help. He will rescue you from oppression, from the power of your enemies. 22 I am confident that the Eternal God will soon set you free. The Holy One, your eternal saviour, will make me happy when he shows you mercy. 23 I cried and wailed when you were taken away, but God will bring you back and will make me happy for ever. 24 Just as the neighbouring cities watched as you were taken captive, so they will soon see the Eternal God coming in glorious splendour to rescue you. 25 My children, endure God's punishment with patience. Your enemies have persecuted you, but you will soon see them destroyed and at your mercy. 26 My children, I spoiled you with

love, but you have had to follow rugged paths; you were carried off like sheep caught in an enemy raid.

27 "Take courage, my children, and cry out to God for help. He punished you, but he will not forget you. 28 Just as you were once determined to turn away from God, now turn back and serve him with ten times more determination. 29 The one who brought these calamities upon you will rescue you and bring you everlasting joy."

Jerusalem Is Assured of Help

30 Take courage, Jerusalem. God, who gave you your name, will now bring comfort to you. 31 Misery will come to those who ill-treated you and then rejoiced when you fell. 32 Misery will come to those cities that made your children slaves. Misery will be the fate of Babylon, that city which swallowed up your sons. 33 Just as that city rejoiced when you fell and took delight in your ruin, so now she will mourn when she herself is deserted. 34 I will turn her proud boastings into mourning and take away her large population in which she took pride. 35 I, the Eternal God, will send down fire on her, and it will burn for many days. Her ruins will be haunted by demons for a long time to come.

36 Look to the east, Jerusalem, and see the joy that God is bringing to you. 37 Look, your children are coming home, the children that were taken from you. They have been gathered together from the east and from the west by the command of God, the Holy One. And now they are coming home, rejoicing in the glory of God.

4.19: 2 Esd 2.2

God will lead Israel home...with great joy (5.9)

5 Jerusalem, take off the clothes you have worn in your mourning and distress, and put on the eternal splendour of God's glory. ²Put round you the cloak of God's righteousness. Place on your head the crown of the glory of the Eternal God. ³God will show your splendour to every nation on earth. ⁴For ever he will say to you: "Your security comes from your righteousness, and your splendour from your devotion to me."ᶜ

5 Get up, Jerusalem, stand on the mountaintop; see where God, the Holy One, is bringing your children together from the east and from the west. They are rejoicing that God has remembered them. ⁶Jerusalem, your children were led away by their enemies; they left you on foot, but God is bringing them back to you, carried in royal splendour. ⁷God has commanded that every high mountain and the everlasting hills shall be made low; he has commanded that the valleys shall be filled and the ground levelled, so that the people of Israel may come safely home in the glory of God. ⁸At the command of God, forests of fragrant trees will spring up to provide shade for the people of Israel. ⁹God will lead Israel home. They will return with great joy, guided by his mercy and righteousness, surrounded by the light of his glorious presence.

ᶜFor ever...devotion to me; *or* He will give you this name for ever: "Peace from Righteousness and Glory from Godliness."
5.1–2: Is 52.1; 61.3,10; Rev 21.2

THE LETTER OF
JEREMIAH

INTRODUCTION

The *Letter of Jeremiah* is in the form of a letter claiming to be written by the prophet Jeremiah to Jews who are about to be taken into exile. It consists mainly of a lengthy condemnation of idolatry.

Outline of Contents
The helplessness of idols   1–40
The foolishness of worshipping idols   41–73

1 This is a copy of the letter sent by Jeremiah to the people of Jerusalem just before they were captured by the Babylonian king and taken to Babylon. It contains the message that God had commanded Jeremiah to give them.

The People Face a Long Captivity

2 You have sinned against God. That is why you are about to be taken away as prisoners to Babylon by King Nebuchadnezzar. 3 You will remain there in exile for many years, as long as seven generations; then God will lead you peacefully home from Babylon.

4 There in Babylon you will see gods made of wood, silver, and gold—gods which people carry on their shoulders and which fill the heathen with fear. 5 You must be careful never to imitate those Gentiles. Don't let their gods fill you with fear when you see them being carried in procession and being worshipped. 6 Instead, say to yourselves, "It is you alone, Lord, that we must worship." 7 God's angel will be there with you; he will take care of you.

The Helplessness of Idols

8 Their idols are plated with silver and gold and have tongues that were carved by woodworkers. But they are not real gods, and they cannot speak. 9 The people make gold crowns and put them on the heads of their gods, as if these idols were girls who love jewellery. 10 Sometimes the priests steal the silver and gold from their gods and spend it on themselves; 11 they even give some of it to the temple prostitutes. People take these gods of wood, silver, and gold, and put clothes on them, as if they were human. 12 But even though the gods are dressed in purple robes like kings, they still cannot keep themselves from being tarnished or protect themselves from termites. 13 When dust from the temple settles on their faces, someone has to wipe it off for them. 14 Like human judges they hold sceptres in their hands, but they have no power to punish anyone who wrongs them. 15 Sometimes they have daggers and axes in their hands, but they cannot protect themselves from being destroyed in war or from being carried off by thieves. 16 All this proves that they are not gods—do not worship them.

17 Those gods sitting in their temples are as useless as a broken bowl. Their eyes are filled with the dust that people kick up when they come in. 18 The priests fortify the temples with doors and bars and bolts, so that thieves cannot break in. The gods are locked up as securely as a prisoner about to be executed for a crime against the king. 19 The priests light lamps for the gods, far more than they need for their own use, but the idols

can't see even one of them. ²⁰ Their insides are eaten away by termites, just like the wooden beams of the temple, and their clothing is destroyed, but they don't even know it. ²¹ Their faces are blackened by the smoke in the temple. ²² Bats, swallows, and other birds perch on them, and even cats sit on them. ²³ All this proves that they are not gods—do not worship them.

24 These idols have been plated with gold to make them beautiful, but they do not shine unless someone polishes them. When they were being poured into moulds, they felt nothing. ²⁵ It makes no difference how high a price is paid for them; they are still unable to breathe.

They...must be carried around (v.26)

²⁶ See how useless they are! They can't walk on their own feet, but must be carried around. ²⁷ Even those who take care of them are embarrassed when one of their gods falls to the ground and has to be picked up again. When someone stands one of them in a certain place, it cannot move, and if it is leaning over, it can never straighten itself up. Offering gifts to them is like giving gifts to a corpse. ²⁸ Priests sell what is sacrificed to their gods and use the money on themselves. And the wives of the priests preserve the sacrifices with salt for use later, instead of sharing them with the poor and helpless. ²⁹ Even women who are having their monthly period or women who have just given birth are allowed to touch the sacrifices. All this proves that they are not gods—do not worship them.

30 How can they ever be called gods, when women are allowed to make offerings to these things made of wood, silver, and gold? ³¹ The priests even sit

in the temples when they are in mourning, with torn clothes and shaved, uncovered heads. ³² The priests roar and shout in the presence of their gods as if they were taking part in a funeral feast. ³³ They take the clothing off their gods and give it to their wives and children. ³⁴ It doesn't matter whether a person helps or harms these gods, since they cannot pay him back. They are not able to make anyone a king or to dethrone him, ³⁵ and they cannot make a person wealthy or give him any money. If someone makes a vow to them but does not keep it, they will never make him pay up. ³⁶ They can never rescue a person from death, and they never help a weak person against one who is strong. ³⁷ They cannot restore sight to the blind or save anyone in distress. ³⁸ They cannot offer any mercy or give help to widows or orphans. ³⁹ These things made of wood and covered with silver and gold are as powerless as stone taken from the mountains; and the people who worship them will be put to shame. ⁴⁰ How can anyone think that they are gods or call them gods?

The Foolishness of Worshipping Idols

The Babylonians bring dishonour on their own gods. ⁴¹ When someone cannot speak, they take him to the temple and ask Bel to give him the power of speech, as if Bel could understand anything. ⁴² But even when the people realize that their gods cannot help, they are stupid enough to go on worshipping them. ⁴³ Not only that, but women wrap cords round themselves and sit beside the road burning incense and offering themselves as prostitutes. When one of them is taken off for sex, she returns to ridicule the woman next to her who was not beautiful enough to be chosen. ⁴⁴ Everything about these idols is false. How can anyone think that they are gods or call them gods?

45 Woodworkers and goldsmiths make these gods, so they can never be anything other than what these people want them to be. ⁴⁶ Even their makers do not live long lives, so how are they able to create gods? ⁴⁷ These people leave nothing but deceit and disgrace as an inheritance for future generations. ⁴⁸ When wars and disturbances come, the priests plan where they can go into hiding with their gods. ⁴⁹ These idols are helpless in the face of wars and disturbances. Why can't people realize that these idols are not gods?

41: Is 46.1

50 These idols are nothing more than wood covered with silver and gold; one day it will be clear that they are really not gods at all. 51 All nations and kings will realize that idols are nothing more than the work of human hands. They do not have the power of a god, 52 and anyone should know that they are not really gods.

53 These gods can never make anyone a king or bring rain. 54 They can't make decisions about their own affairs or give justice to someone who has been wronged; they can do absolutely nothing. They are as useless as crows flying about in the air. 55 When a temple catches fire, the priests run away to save themselves, while the gods made of wood and covered with silver and gold are left to burn like wooden beams. 56 They can't fight kings or go to war against enemies. How can anyone believe that they are gods?

57 These gods of wood, covered with silver and gold, cannot protect themselves from thieves and robbers 58 who take off the silver and gold and the gods' clothing and walk away with all of it. The gods can do nothing to stop them. 59 Anything from a courageous king to a useful piece of pottery is better than a false god. Even a door is better than a false god; a door at least protects the things in the house. Even a wooden pillar in a palace is better than a false god.

60 God provided the sun, the moon, and the stars to give light, and they obey him. 61 The same is true of lightning and wind. The lightning can be seen far and wide, and the wind blows everywhere. 62 When God commands clouds to spread out over the whole world, they obey. 63 When God sends down fire from heaven to burn up mountains and forests, it does what it is told. Idols cannot do these things—they can't even do a good imitation. 64 Why should they be called gods, when they are not able to help us or harm us in any way? 65 You know that they are not gods—do not worship them.

66 These gods have no power over kings; they cannot pronounce curses on them or grant them blessings. 67 They cannot produce for the nations any signs in the sky; they cannot shine like the sun or the moon. 68 Even wild animals are better off than these idols; animals can at least run from danger to protect themselves. 69 So it is absolutely clear that they are not gods—do not worship them.

70 These gods of theirs, made of wood and covered with silver and gold, are about as helpful as a scarecrow in a cucumber patch; they are no protection at all. 71 They do as much good as a thorn bush in a garden; instead of keeping birds away, they provide a perch for them. These gods are like a dead body thrown out into the darkness. 72 The purple linen a robes they wear rot away, so we know that they are not gods. Finally they will be eaten by termites, and then no one anywhere will have any use for them.

73 The righteous person has an advantage over others; he does not own any idols, and they can never make a fool of him.

a linen; *Greek* marble.

THE PRAYER OF AZARIAH AND THE SONG OF THE THREE YOUNG MEN

INTRODUCTION

The *Prayer of Azariah* and the *Song of the Three Young Men* is one of the three major additions to the book of *Daniel* in the Greek version. This insertion between 3.23 and 3.24 of *Daniel* gives the prayer of Azariah and the song of the three young men after King Nebuchadnezzar had them thrown into the blazing furnace.

Outline of Contents

Prayer of Azariah   1–22
Description of the furnace   23–27
The song of the three young men   28–68

The Prayer of Azariah

1 The three young men, Hananiah, Mishael, and Azariah,[a] started walking about in the flames, singing hymns to God, and praising him as Lord. 2 Then Azariah stood still and there in the fire he prayed aloud: 3 "O Lord, the God of our ancestors, we praise and adore you; may your name be honoured for ever. 4 You have treated us as we deserve. In everything you have done to us you are always honest, and when you bring us to judgement, you are always fair. 5 You did what was right when you brought disaster upon Jerusalem, the holy city of our ancestors. We deserved that judgement because of our sins. 6 We disobeyed you, we turned our backs on you, and we are guilty of every sin. 7 We did not do the things that you commanded us to do. If we had obeyed your laws, we would have prospered, 8 but now we deserve the judgement and punishment that you have brought upon us. 9 You have handed us over to lawless, hateful, and defiant enemies—to the most wicked king in the world. 10 And now all of us who worship you are humiliated; we are too ashamed to open our mouths.

11 "Yet for the sake of your own honour, do not break your covenant with us and abandon us for ever. 12 Do not withhold your mercy from us. Keep your promises to Abraham, whom you loved, to Isaac, your servant, and to Jacob, the father of your holy people Israel. 13 You promised to give them as many descendants as the stars in the sky or as the grains of sand along the seashore. 14 But now, Lord, we are fewer in number than any other nation; wherever we are, we live in disgrace because of our sins. 15 We are left without a king, without any prophets or leaders. There is no longer a Temple where we can go to offer you burnt-offerings, sacrifices, gifts, or incense, no place where we can make offerings to you and find your mercy. 16 But we come to you with repentant hearts and humble spirits, begging you to accept us just as if we had come with burnt-offerings of rams and bulls and thousands of fat lambs. 17 Accept our

---

[a] HANANIAH, MISHAEL, AND AZARIAH: *These are the original names of Shadrach, Meshach, and Abednego (see Dan 1.6–7).*
1: Dan 3.23

repentance as our sacrifice to you today, so that we may obey you with all our hearts. No one who trusts you will ever be disappointed. 18-19 Now with all our hearts we promise to obey you, worship you, and come to you in prayer. Treat us with kindness and mercy, and let us never be put to shame. 20 O Lord, rescue us with one of your miracles; bring honour to your name.

21 "Bring disgrace and shame on all who harm us. Take away their might and power and crush their strength. 22 Let them know that you alone are Lord and God and that you rule in majesty over the whole world."

23 The king's servants who had thrown the three men into the furnace kept the fire hot by feeding it with oil, tar, flax, and brushwood. 24 The flames blazed up to a height of more than twenty metres 25 and even spread out and burnt up the Babylonians standing near the furnace. 26 But an angel of the Lord came down into the fire where the three men were. He pushed aside the flames 27 so that it felt as if a cool breeze were blowing, and the fire did not touch the men at all or hurt them in any way.

The Song of the Three Young Men

28 There in the furnace the three young men again started singing together in praise of God:

The three young men again started singing (v.28)

29 "We praise you, O Lord, the God of our ancestors.
30 May your glorious, holy name be held in honour and reverence for ever.

26: Tob 5.4

31 May hymns be sung to your glory for ever
and may your holy presence be praised in that temple,
32 where you sit on your heavenly throne above the winged creatures and look down to the world of the dead.
May you be praised and honoured for ever.
33 May you be praised as you sit on your royal throne.
May hymns be sung to your glory for ever.
34 May you be praised in the dome of the heavens.
May hymns be sung to your glory for ever.

35 "Praise the Lord, all creation; sing his praise and honour him for ever.
36 Praise the Lord, skies above; sing his praise and honour him for ever.
37 Praise the Lord, all angels of the Lord; sing his praise and honour him for ever.
38 Praise the Lord, all waters above the sky; sing his praise and honour him for ever.
39 Praise the Lord, all heavenly powers; sing his praise and honour him for ever.
40 Praise the Lord, sun and moon; sing his praise and honour him for ever.
41 Praise the Lord, stars of heaven; sing his praise and honour him for ever.
42 Praise the Lord, rain and dew; sing his praise and honour him for ever.
43 Praise the Lord, all winds; sing his praise and honour him for ever.
44 Praise the Lord, fire and heat; sing his praise and honour him for ever.
45 Praise the Lord, bitter cold and scorching heat; sing his praise and honour him for ever.
46 Praise the Lord, dews and snows; sing his praise and honour him for ever.
47 Praise the Lord, nights and days;

sing his praise and honour him for
ever.

48 Praise the Lord, daylight and darkness;
sing his praise and honour him for
ever.

49 Praise the Lord, ice and cold;
sing his praise and honour him for
ever.

50 Praise the Lord, frost and snow;
sing his praise and honour him for
ever.

51 Praise the Lord, lightning and storm
clouds;
sing his praise and honour him for
ever.

52 "Let the earth praise the Lord;
sing his praise and honour him for
ever.

53 Praise the Lord, mountains and hills;
sing his praise and honour him for
ever.

54 Praise the Lord, everything that grows;
sing his praise and honour him for
ever.

55 Praise the Lord, lakes and rivers;
sing his praise and honour him for
ever.

56 Praise the Lord, springs of water;
sing his praise and honour him for
ever.

57 Praise the Lord, whales and sea
creatures;
sing his praise and honour him for
ever.

58 Praise the Lord, all birds;
sing his praise and honour him for
ever.

59 Praise the Lord, all cattle and wild
animals;

sing his praise and honour him for
ever.

60 "Praise the Lord, all people on earth;
sing his praise and honour him for
ever.

61 Praise the Lord, people of Israel;
sing his praise and honour him for
ever.

62 Praise the Lord, priests of the Lord;
sing his praise and honour him for
ever.

63 Praise the Lord, servants of the Lord;
sing his praise and honour him for
ever.

64 Praise the Lord, all faithful people;
sing his praise and honour him for
ever.

65 Praise the Lord, all who are humble
and holy;
sing his praise and honour him for
ever.

66 Praise the Lord, Hananiah, Azariah,
and Mishael;
sing his praise and honour him for
ever.
He rescued us from the world of the
dead
and saved us from the power of death.
He brought us out from the burning
furnace
and saved us from the fire.

67 Give thanks to the Lord, for he is good
and his mercy lasts for ever.

68 Praise the Lord, all who worship him;
sing praise to the God of gods and
give him thanks,
for his mercy lasts for ever."

THE BOOK OF
SUSANNA

INTRODUCTION

The book of *Susanna* is a story that was added to the book of *Daniel,* evidently when the latter was translated into Greek. The book tells how the beautiful and virtuous Susanna, falsely charged with adultery, is cleared by the wisdom and courage of Daniel.

Outline of Contents

Two wicked judges attempt to seduce Susanna   1–27
Susanna is condemned to death   28–41
Daniel rescues Susanna and the judges are condemned
   to death   42–64

Susanna's Beauty Attracts Two Judges

1 In Babylon there lived a man named Joakim, ²who was married to Susanna, daughter of Hilkiah. Susanna was a beautiful woman and deeply religious. ³Her parents were devout Jews who had brought up their daughter to live according to the Law of Moses. ⁴Her husband Joakim was very wealthy. Lovely gardens surrounded his house, and the other Jews often gathered there for meetings, because they all thought so highly of him. ⁵⁻⁶Everyone who had a legal case to present would also go to Joakim's house, where two judges held court. These two leaders of the Jewish community had recently been appointed to office. They were the ones about whom the Lord said, "There is wickedness in Babylon; judges are failing to give guidance to the people."

7 Every day at noon, when all the people left for lunch, Susanna used to take a walk in the gardens. ⁸The two judges were so attracted to her that they would wait about and watch for her. ⁹They became so obsessed with their desire for her that they lost interest both in prayer and in their responsibility as judges. ¹⁰They each wanted Susanna, but neither told the other how he felt, ¹¹for each was ashamed to admit his lust. ¹²So day after day they watched eagerly to catch sight of her.

13 One day at noon they said to each other, "It's time for lunch; let's go home." ¹⁴So they both left and went their separate ways, but soon each one came back for a look at Susanna, and by accident they met each other. At first each tried to explain what he was doing there, but finally they both confessed their desire for Susanna. They decided to watch for a time when they might find her alone. ¹⁵⁻¹⁷So they kept waiting for the right opportunity.

The Judges Try to Seduce Susanna

One day Susanna went into the garden as usual with her two servant girls. No one else was there, except the two judges, who had hidden and were watching Susanna. It was very hot and she decided to take a bath. So she said to her servants, "Bring me some bath oil and some perfume, and lock the gates, so that I won't be disturbed." ¹⁸The servants locked the main gates and went out by the side door to get what Susanna had asked for. They did not notice the two men.

19 As soon as the servants had left, the two judges jumped out from their hiding-place, ran to Susanna, ²⁰and said to her,

Each one came back for a look at Susanna (v.14)

"The gates are locked and no one will see us. We are burning to have sex with you, so give us what we want. ²¹ If you don't, we will go to court and swear that we saw you send your servants away, so that you could be alone with a young man."

22 "There is no way out," Susanna moaned. "If I give in to you, I could be put to death for adultery. If I refuse, you will still have me trapped. ²³ But I would rather be your innocent victim than sin against the Lord." ²⁴ So she started screaming as loud as she could, and the two judges began shouting accusations, ²⁵ while one of them ran and unlocked the gates.

26 As soon as the servants in the house heard all the noise, they ran into the gardens through the side door to find out what had happened to Susanna. ²⁷ The judges told their story, and the servants were shocked and ashamed. Such a thing had never been said about Susanna before.

The Judges Testify against Susanna

28 The next day, when the people

assembled at Joakim's house, the two judges arrived, fully determined to carry out their wicked plan to have Susanna put to death. ²⁹ In front of all the people they said, "Send for Joakim's wife Susanna, the daughter of Hilkiah." When she was called, ³⁰ she came in with her parents, her children, and all her other relatives. ³¹ Susanna was so graceful and beautiful ³² that the two wicked men ordered her veil to be removed, so that they might enjoy looking at her. ³³ Her family and everyone else were in tears.

34 Then the two judges stood up in front of the people, placed their hands on Susanna's head, and began making their accusations against her. ³⁵ She was crying, but she looked up to heaven because she trusted the Lord. ³⁶ The two men gave the following testimony: "We were walking in the garden when this woman came in with her two servant girls. She locked the main gates and asked the servants to leave. ³⁷ Then a young man who had been hiding in the garden came to her, and they lay down together. ³⁸ We were in a corner of the garden, and when we saw

22: Lev 20.10; Deut 22.22

what was happening, we ran over ³⁹and caught them in the act. We tried to hold on to the man, but he was too strong for us. He ran and opened the gates and got away, ⁴⁰but we were able to hold the woman. We asked her who the man was, but she refused to tell us. We swear that our testimony is true." ⁴¹Because the two men were not only leaders in the community but also judges, the people believed their story and condemned Susanna to death.

Daniel Rescues Susanna

42 Then Susanna cried out in a loud voice, "Eternal God, nothing can be kept secret from you; you know everything before it happens. ⁴³Here I am about to die, but you know that I am innocent, that these men are lying. Why must I die?"

44 The Lord heard her prayer ⁴⁵and led a young man named Daniel to speak out, just as Susanna was being taken away to her death. ⁴⁶He shouted, "I refuse to be a party to her death!"

47 Everyone turned round to look at him and asked, "What are you talking about?"

48 Daniel stood up before them and said, "People of Israel, how foolish can you be? Are you going to condemn an Israelite woman to death on this kind of evidence? You haven't even tried to find out the truth. ⁴⁹Reopen the case. The testimony these men gave was a lie."

50 So all the people hurried back to where the trial had taken place, and the officials said to Daniel, "God has given you wisdom beyond your years, so come and join us and explain to us what you mean."

51 Daniel said to them, "Separate the two judges, and let me question them one at a time." ⁵²Then Daniel called the first judge and said, "You wicked old man, now you will have to answer for all the sins you have committed. ⁵³You have been giving unjust sentences. You have condemned the innocent and released the guilty, even though the Lord has said, 'Do not put an innocent person to death.' ⁵⁴Now if you really did see this couple making love, tell me, what tree were they under?"

"Under a small gum-tree," he answered.

55 Daniel said, "Right! That lie will cost you your life. God's angel has already been given orders to chop^a you in two."

56 Then the first judge was led away and the second one was brought before Daniel. "You are more like a Canaanite than a Jew," Daniel said to him. "This woman's beauty has warped your judgement, and lust has corrupted your thinking. ⁵⁷You are used to having your way with the women of Israel because they have been afraid of you, but here is a Jewish woman, and she would not give in. ⁵⁸Now, tell me what tree you saw them under."

"Under a large oak-tree," he answered.

59 Daniel said, "Right! That lie will cost you your life; God's angel is waiting with his sword in his hand, ready to cut^b you in two. Then we shall be rid of you both."

60 Then all the people shouted and praised God, who saves those who put their trust in him. ⁶¹They turned against the two judges because Daniel had proved that they had lied under oath. ⁶²The Law of Moses states that people who give false testimony shall receive the same punishment that the accused person would have received. And so the two judges were put to death, and the life of an innocent woman was saved. ⁶³Susanna's parents, her husband, and all her relatives praised God because she had been proved innocent of the charges. ⁶⁴From that day on, Daniel was held in high regard.

---

^aCHOP: *This word in Greek sounds like the Greek for "a small gum-tree."*
^bCUT: *This word in Greek sounds like the Greek for "a large oak tree."*
53: Ex 23.7   **62:** Deut 19.16–21

BEL

AND THE DRAGON

INTRODUCTION

Bel and the Dragon consists of two stories which were added to the Greek translation of the book of *Daniel*. The first tells of Daniel's wisdom and courage in revealing the falseness of the idol Bel, and the second describes how he destroyed a dragon which was worshipped by the Babylonians.

Outline of Contents

Daniel's wisdom defeats the priests of Bel   1–22
Daniel kills the dragon   23–32
Daniel is rescued from the pit of lions   33–42

Daniel and the Priests of Bel

1 After the death of King Astyages, Cyrus of Persia took over his kingdom. ²Daniel was one of King Cyrus's closest companions, and the king thought more highly of Daniel than of any other of his advisers.

3 The Babylonians had an idol named Bel. Each day the people had to provide Bel with an offering of four hundred litres of fine flour, forty sheep, and two hundred litres of wine. ⁴King Cyrus believed that Bel was a god, and each day he used to go and worship it. But Daniel worshipped his own God.

5 One day the king asked Daniel, "Why don't you worship Bel?"

Daniel answered, "I do not worship idols made with human hands. I worship only the living God, who created heaven and earth and is the Lord of all mankind."

6 "And don't you believe that our god Bel is really alive?" asked the king. "Haven't you seen how much he eats and drinks every day?"

7 Daniel laughed and said, "Don't be taken in, Your Majesty. This god you call Bel is nothing more than clay covered with bronze; it has never eaten or drunk anything."

8–10 At this the king became angry and called in all seventy of the priests of Bel. He said to them, "I warn you that you will be put to death, unless you can show me that it is Bel who is eating these offerings. If you prove to me that it is Bel, then I will have Daniel put to death for claiming that Bel is not a god."

Daniel agreed to this proposal.

11 Then they all went with the king into Bel's temple, where the priests said to the king, "Your Majesty, we will go out and let you place the food on the table and prepare the wine. When you leave, you may lock the door behind you and seal it with the royal seal. ¹²In the morning when you return, if you find that Bel has not eaten everything, you can put us to death. But if he has, Daniel will die for making false accusations against us."

13 But the priests were not worried, because they had made a secret entrance underneath a table in the temple, so that they could go in every night and eat the offerings.

14 When the priests had left, the king set out the food for Bel. Then Daniel ordered his servants to bring some ashes and scatter them all over the floor of the temple. No one except the king saw them do this. After that they all went out, locked the door, sealed it with the royal seal, and left.

3: Is 46.1; Jer 51.44   **3–32:** Dan 6.16–24

The king set out the food for Bel (v.14)

15 That night, as usual, the priests with their wives and children came into the temple by the secret entrance and ate all the food and drank all the wine.

16 Early the next morning, the king and Daniel went to the temple. 17 The king asked, "Have the seals been broken, Daniel?"

"No, Your Majesty, they have not been broken," he replied.

18 As soon as the door was opened, the king saw the empty table and shouted, "You are great, O Bel! You really are a god."

19 But Daniel began to laugh and said to the king, "Before you enter the temple, look at the floor and tell me whose footprints you see there."

20 "I see the footprints of men, women, and children," said the king, 21 and he became so angry that he had the priests and their families arrested and brought to him. They showed him the secret doors through which they had come in each night to eat the food placed on the table. 22 So the king had the priests put to death, and he gave Bel to Daniel, who destroyed the idol and tore down its temple.

Daniel Kills the Dragon

23 There was also a huge dragon which the Babylonians worshipped. 24 One day the king said to Daniel, "You can't tell me that this god is not alive. So worship him!"

25 "I worship the Lord," replied Daniel. "He is the only living God. 26 And if Your Majesty will give me permission, I will kill this dragon of yours without using a sword or a club."

"You have my permission," answered the king.

27 So Daniel took some tar, some fat, and some hair and boiled them all together. He made cakes out of the mixture and fed them to the dragon. When the dragon ate them, it swelled up and burst open. "That's the kind of thing you Babylonians worship," said Daniel.

28 When the people of Babylon heard what had happened, they staged an angry demonstration against the king. "The king has become a Jew," they shouted. "First he destroyed Bel and slaughtered the priests, and now he has killed our dragon." 29 They went to the king and demanded that Daniel be handed over to them. "If you refuse," they warned the king, "we will put you and your family to death."

O Lord, the God of Daniel, how great you are (v.41)

30 When the king saw that they meant what they said, he was forced to hand Daniel over to them. 31 The men threw him into a pit filled with lions, where they left him for six days. 32 There were seven lions in the pit, and normally they were fed two men and two sheep each day. But they were given nothing to eat during these six days, in order to make sure that Daniel would be eaten.

Daniel Is Rescued from the Pit of Lions

33 At that time the prophet Habakkuk was in the land of Judah. He had cooked a stew and crumbled bread into it. He

was carrying a bowl of it to the men who were out in the fields harvesting corn, [34] when an angel of the Lord said to him, "Take the food you are carrying and give it to Daniel, who is in Babylon in a pit of lions."

35 Habakkuk answered, "Sir, I have never been to Babylon, and I don't know where the pit of lions is."

36 So the angel seized the prophet by the hair and took him to Babylon with the speed of the wind. [a] He set him down near the pit of lions. [37] Habakkuk called out, "Daniel! Daniel! God has sent you some food. Here, take it."

38 When Daniel heard Habakkuk, he prayed, "God, you did remember me; you never abandon those who love you." [39] Then he got up and ate the meal, and God's angel immediately took Habakkuk home.

40 Seven days after Daniel had been thrown to the lions, the king went to the pit to mourn for him. When he got there and looked in, there sat Daniel. [41] The king shouted, "O Lord, the God of Daniel, how great you are. You alone are God." [42] So he pulled Daniel out of the pit and had the men who tried to kill Daniel thrown into it. And the lions ate them immediately, while the king watched.

[a] with the speed of the wind; or by the power of his spirit.
36: Ezek 8.3

THE FIRST BOOK OF THE

MACCABEES

INTRODUCTION

The *First book of the Maccabees* describes events in Jewish history from the time of Antiochus Epiphanes (175 B.C.) to the rise of John Hyrcanus (134 B.C.).

The historical interest of the book centres in the Hasmonaean, or Maccabaean, family, and it supports the view that they are divinely chosen to save Israel. The book also has a strong religious theme: God is at work in history and will give victory as a reward to those who are faithful to him.

Outline of Contents

Persecution and the revolt of Mattathias   1.1—2.70
The leadership of Judas Maccabaeus   3.1—9.22
The leadership of Jonathan   9.23—12.53
The leadership of Simon   13.1—16.24

Alexander the Great

1 This history begins when Alexander the Great, son of Philip of Macedonia, marched from Macedonia and attacked Darius, king of Persia and Media. Alexander enlarged the Greek Empire by defeating Darius and seizing his throne. [2] He fought many battles, captured fortified cities, and put the kings of the region to death. [3] As he advanced to the ends of the earth, he plundered many nations; and when he had conquered the

world, he became proud and arrogant. [4] By building up a strong army, he dominated whole nations and their rulers, and forced everyone to pay him taxes.

5-7 When Alexander had been emperor for twelve years, he fell ill and realized that he was about to die. He called together his generals, noblemen who had been brought up with him since his early childhood, and divided his empire, giving a part to each of them. [8] After his death, the generals took control, [9] and each had himself crowned king of his own territory. The descendants of these kings ruled for many generations and brought a great deal of misery on the world.

Antiochus Epiphanes and the Renegade Jews
(2 Macc 4.7-17)

10 The wicked ruler Antiochus Epiphanes, son of King Antiochus the Third of Syria, was a descendant of one of Alexander's generals. Antiochus Epiphanes had been a hostage in Rome before he became king of Syria in the year 137. [a]

11 At that time there appeared in the land of Israel a group of traitorous Jews who had no regard for the Law and who had a bad influence on many of our people. They said, "Let's come to terms with the Gentiles, for our refusal to associate with them has brought us nothing but trouble." [12] This proposal appealed to many people, [13] and some of them became so enthusiastic about it that they went to the king and received from him permission to follow Gentile customs. [14] They built in Jerusalem a stadium like those in the Greek cities. [15] They had an operation performed to hide their circumcision, abandoned the holy covenant, started associating with [b] Gentiles, and did all sorts of other evil things.

Antiochus Attacks Egypt

16 When Antiochus had firmly established himself as king, he decided to conquer Egypt and rule that country as well as Syria. [17] He invaded Egypt with a large fleet of ships and a powerful army, including chariots, elephants, and cavalry. [18] When the attack came, King Ptolemy of Egypt turned and fled, and many of his soldiers were killed. [19] Antiochus was able to capture the fortified cities of Egypt and plunder the whole land.

Antiochus Persecutes the Jews

20 In the year 143, [c] after the conquest of Egypt, Antiochus marched with a great army against the land of Israel and the city of Jerusalem. [21] In his arrogance, he entered the Temple and took away the gold altar, the lampstand with all its equipment, [22] the table for the bread offered to the Lord, the cups and bowls, the gold fire pans, the curtain, and the crowns. He also stripped all the gold from the front of the Temple [23] and carried off the silver and gold and everything else of value, including all the treasures that he could find stored there. [24] Then he took it all to his own country. He also murdered many people and boasted arrogantly about it. [25] There was great mourning everywhere in the land of Israel.

[26] Rulers and leaders groaned in sorrow.
Young men and young women grew weak.
The beauty of our women faded.
[27] Every bridegroom sang a funeral song,
and every bride sat mourning in her room.
[28] All our people were clothed with shame,
and our land trembled for them.

29 Two years later Antiochus sent a large army from Mysia [d] against the towns of Judaea. When the soldiers entered Jerusalem, [30] their commander spoke to the people, offering them terms of peace, and completely deceiving them. Then he suddenly launched a fierce attack on the city, dealing it a major blow and killing many of the people. [31] He plundered the city, set it on fire, and tore down its buildings and walls. [32] He and his army took the women and children as prisoners and seized the cattle.

33 Then Antiochus and his forces built high walls and strong towers in the area north of the Temple, turning it into a fort. [34] They brought in a group of traitorous Jews and installed them there. [35] They also brought in arms and supplies and stored in the fort all the loot that they had taken in Jerusalem. This fort became a great threat to the city.

36 The fort was a threat to the Temple,

---

[a] THE YEAR 137: *The dates in this book are counted from the beginning of the Syrian Kingdom in 312 B.C. The year 137 corresponds to 175 B.C.*   [b] started associating with; *or married.*
[c] THE YEAR 143: *This corresponds to 169 B.C.*
[d] *Probable text* a large army from Mysia; *Greek* a tax collector with a large army.
1.10: 2 Macc 4.7   **1.15:** 1 Cor 7.18

Then he took it all to his own country (1.24)

a constant, evil menace for Israel.

[37] Innocent people were murdered round
the altar;
the Holy Place was defiled by murderers.

[38] The people of Jerusalem fled in fear,
and the city became a colony of
foreigners.
Jerusalem was foreign to its own people,
who had been forced to abandon the
city.

[39] Her Temple was as empty as a
wilderness;
her festivals were turned into days of
mourning,
her Sabbath joy into shame.
Her honour became an object of ridicule.

[40] Her shame was as great as her former
glory,
and her pride was turned into deepest
mourning.

[41-43] Antiochus now issued a decree
that all nations in his empire should
abandon their own customs and become
one people. All the Gentiles and even
many of the Israelites submitted to this
decree. They adopted the official pagan
religion, offered sacrifices to idols, and
no longer observed the Sabbath.

[44] The king also sent messengers with

e the holy things in it; *or* the priests.

a decree to Jerusalem and all the towns
of Judaea, ordering the people to follow
customs that were foreign to the country.
[45] He ordered them not to offer burnt-
offerings, grain-offerings, or wine-offerings in the Temple, and commanded them
to treat Sabbaths and festivals as ordinary
work days. [46] They were even ordered to
defile the Temple and the holy things in
it. e [47] They were commanded to build
pagan altars, temples, and shrines, and
to sacrifice pigs and other unclean
animals there. [48] They were forbidden to
circumcise their sons and were required
to make themselves ritually unclean in
every way they could, [49] so that they
would forget the Law which the Lord had
given through Moses and would disobey
all its commands. [50] The penalty for
disobeying the king's decree was death.

[51] The king not only issued the same
decree throughout his whole empire, but
he also appointed officials to supervise
the people and commanded each town in
Judaea to offer pagan sacrifices. [52] Many
of the Jews were ready to forsake the
Law and to obey these officials. They
defiled the land with their evil, [53] and their

conduct forced all true Israelites to hide wherever they could.

54 On the fifteenth day of the month of Kislev in the year 145,[f] King Antiochus set up "The Awful Horror" on the altar of the Temple, and pagan altars were built in the towns throughout Judaea. 55 Pagan sacrifices were offered in front of houses and in the streets. 56 Any books of the Law which were found were torn up and burnt, 57 and anyone who was caught with a copy of the sacred books or who obeyed the Law was put to death by order of the king. 58 Month after month these wicked men used their power against the Israelites caught in the towns.

59 On the twenty-fifth of the month, these same evil men offered sacrifices on the pagan altar erected on top of the altar in the Temple. 60 Mothers who had allowed their babies to be circumcised were put to death in accordance with the king's decree. 61 Their babies were hung round their necks, and their families and those who had circumcised them were put to death. 62 But many people in Israel firmly resisted the king's decree and refused to eat food that was ritually unclean. 63 They preferred to die rather than break the holy covenant and eat unclean food—and many did die. 64 In his anger God made Israel suffer terribly.

The Faithfulness of Mattathias

2 During that time, a priest of the Jehoiarib family named Mattathias, who was the son of John and the grandson of Simeon, moved from Jerusalem and settled in Modein. 2 Mattathias had five sons: John (also called Gaddi), 3 Simon (also called Thassi), 4 Judas (also called Maccabaeus), 5 Eleazar (also called Avaran), and Jonathan (also called Apphus).

6 When Mattathias saw all the sins that were being committed in Judaea and Jerusalem, 7 he said:

"Why was I born to see these terrible things,
  the ruin of my people and of the holy city?
Must I sit here helpless
  while the city is surrendered to enemies
  and the Temple falls into the hands of foreigners?

8 The Temple is like a man without honour.
9 Its splendid furnishings
  have been carried away as loot.
Our children have been killed in the streets,
  and our young men by the sword of the enemy.
10 Every nation in the world has occupied the city
  and robbed her of her possessions.
11 All her ornaments have been stripped away;
  she is now a slave, no longer free.
12 Look at our Temple, profaned by the Gentiles,
  emptied of all its splendour.
13 Why should we go on living?"

14 In their grief, Mattathias and his sons tore their clothes, put on sackcloth, and continued in deep mourning.

15 Then the king's officials, who were forcing the people to turn from God, came to the town of Modein to force the people there to offer pagan sacrifices. 16 Many of the Israelites came to meet them, including Mattathias and his sons. 17 The king's officials said to Mattathias, "You are a respected leader in this town, and you have the support of your sons and relatives. 18 Why not be the first one here to do what the king has commanded? All the Gentiles, the people of Judaea, and all the people left in Jerusalem have already done so. If you do, you and your sons will be honoured with the title of 'Friends of the King,' and you will be rewarded with silver and gold and many gifts."

19 Mattathias answered in a loud voice, "I don't care if every Gentile in this empire has obeyed the king and yielded to the command to abandon the religion of his ancestors. 20 My sons, my relatives, and I will continue to keep the covenant that God made with our ancestors. 21 With God's help we will never abandon his Law or disobey his commands. 22 We will not obey the king's decree, and we will not change our way of worship in the least."

23 Just as he finished speaking, one of the men from Modein decided to obey the king's decree and stepped out in front of everyone to offer a pagan sacrifice on the altar that stood there. 24 When Mattathias saw him, he became angry enough to do what had to be done.

---

[f] THE YEAR 145: This corresponds to 167 B.C.
1.54: Dan 9.27; 11.31; 12.11; 1 Macc 6.7; Mt 24.15; Mk 13.14   **1.60:** 2 Macc 6.10

We will not obey the king's decree (2.22)

Shaking with rage, he ran forward and killed the man right there on the altar. ²⁵ He also killed the royal official who was forcing the people to sacrifice, and then he tore down the altar. ²⁶ In this way Mattathias showed his deep devotion for the Law, just as Phinehas had done when he killed Zimri son of Salu.

The Guerrilla Warfare of Mattathias

27 Then Mattathias went through the town shouting, "Everyone who is faithful to God's covenant and obeys his Law, follow me!" ²⁸ With this, he and his sons fled to the mountains, leaving behind all they owned.

29-30 At that time also many of the Israelites who were seeking to be right with God through obedience to the Law went out to live in the wilderness, taking their children, their wives, and their livestock with them, because of the terrible oppression they were suffering. ³¹ The report soon reached the king's officials and the soldiers in the fort at Jerusalem that some men who had defied the king's command had gone into hiding in the wilderness. ³² A large force of soldiers pursued them, caught up with them, set up camp opposite them, and prepared to attack them on the Sabbath. ³³ "There is still time," they shouted out to the Jews. "Come out and obey the king's command, and we will spare your lives."

34 "We will not come out," they answered. "We will not obey the king's command, and we will not profane the Sabbath."

35 The soldiers attacked them immediately, ³⁶ but the Jews did nothing to resist; they did not even throw stones or block the entrances to the caves where they were hiding. ³⁷ They said, "We will all die with a clear conscience. Let heaven and earth bear witness that you are slaughtering us unjustly." ³⁸ So the enemy attacked them on the Sabbath and killed the men, their wives, their children, and their livestock. A thousand people died.

39 When Mattathias and his friends heard about this, they were greatly saddened ⁴⁰ and said to one another, "If all of us do as these fellow Jews of ours have done and refuse to fight the Gentiles to defend our lives and our religion, we will soon be wiped off the face of the earth." ⁴¹ On that day they decided that if anyone attacked them on the Sabbath, they would defend themselves, so that they would not all die as their fellow Jews had died in the caves.

42 Then Mattathias and his friends were joined by a group of devout and patriotic Jews, the strongest and bravest men in Israel, who had all volunteered to defend the Law. ⁴³ In addition, everyone who was fleeing from the persecution joined them and strengthened their forces. ⁴⁴ Now that they had an army, they gave vent to their anger by attacking the renegade Jews. Those who escaped were forced to flee to the Gentiles for safety. ⁴⁵ Mattathias and his friends went everywhere tearing down pagan altars ⁴⁶ and circumcising by force every uncircumcised boy they found within the borders of Israel. ⁴⁷ They were also successful in hunting down the arrogant Gentile officials. ⁴⁸ They rescued the Law of Moses from the Gentiles and their kings and broke the power of the wicked King Antiochus.

The Death of Mattathias

49 When the time came for Mattathias to die, he said to his sons, "These are times of violence and distress. Arrogant men are in control and have made us an object of ridicule. ⁵⁰ But you, my sons, must be devoted to the Law and ready to die to defend God's covenant with our ancestors. ⁵¹ Remember what our ancestors did and how much they accomplished in their day. Follow their example, and you will be rewarded with great glory and undying fame. ⁵² Remember how Abraham put his trust in the Lord when he was tested and how

2.26: Num 25.6–15   **2.32:** 2 Macc 6.11   **2.52:** Gen 15.16; 22.15–18

the Lord was pleased with him and accepted him. [53] Joseph, in his time of trouble, obeyed God's commands and became ruler over the land of Egypt. [54] Phinehas, our ancestor, because of his burning devotion, was given the promise that his descendants would always be priests. [55] Joshua was made a judge in Israel because he obeyed the command of Moses. [56] Caleb brought back a good report to the community and was given a part of the land as a reward. [57] David was made king and was given the promise that his descendants would always be kings because of his steadfast loyalty to God. [58] Elijah, because of his great devotion to the Law, was taken up into heaven. [59] Hananiah, Azariah, and Mishael were saved from the flames because they had faith. [60] Daniel was a man of integrity, and the Lord rescued him from the mouth of the lions. [61] Take each of these ancestors of ours as an example, and you will realize that no one who puts his trust in the Lord will ever lack strength. [62] Don't be afraid of the threats of a wicked man. Remember that he will die and all his splendour will end with worms feeding on his decaying body. [63] Today he may be highly honoured, but tomorrow he will disappear; his body will return to the earth and his scheming will come to an end. [64] But you, my sons, be strong and courageous in defending the Law, because it is through the Law that you will earn great glory.

65 "Your brother Simon is wise, so always listen to him as you would to me. [66] Judas Maccabaeus has been strong all his life; he will be your commander and will lead you in battle against the enemy. [67] Call everyone who obeys God's Law to rally round you; then avenge the wrongs done to your people. [68] Pay the Gentiles back for what they have done, and always obey the Law and its commands."

69 Then Mattathias gave them his blessing and died. [70] He was buried in the family tomb at Modein, and all the people of Israel went into deep mourning for him. This happened in the year 146.[g]

The Early Victories of Judas
(2 Macc 8.1-7)

3 Judas Maccabaeus took the place of his father Mattathias. [2] All his brothers and all the loyal followers of his father gave him their support, and they were happy to carry on Israel's war.
[3] Judas brought greater glory to his
    people.
In his armour, he was like a giant.
He took up his weapons and went to
    war;
    with his own sword he defended his
        camp.
[4] He was like a ferocious lion roaring as
    it attacks.
[5] Judas hunted down those who broke
    the Law
    and set fire to all who oppressed his
        people.
[6] In fear of him, lawless men huddled
    together in terror,
    not knowing which way to turn.
He advanced the cause of freedom by
    what he did.
[7] He made life miserable for many kings,
    but brought joy to the people of Israel.
We will praise him for ever for what
    he did.
[8] He went through the towns of Judaea
    and destroyed all the godless men.
He relieved Israel of its terrible
    suffering.[h]
[9] His fame spread to the ends of the earth,
    as he gathered together those who
        were threatened with death.

10 Then Apollonius assembled a Gentile army, including a large force from Samaria, to attack the people of Israel. [11] When Judas learnt of this, he marched out to battle, defeated the army, and killed Apollonius. Many Gentiles lost their lives, and the rest fled. [12] When the spoils of war were collected, Judas took the sword of Apollonius and used it in battle until the day he died.

13 Seron, the general of the Syrian forces, learnt that Judas had gathered together an army, consisting of a band of loyal men who were ready to fight under his command. [14] Seron said to himself, "I will make a reputation for myself throughout the empire by defeating Judas and his men, who have no respect for the king's command." [15] Then he began a new campaign against Judas and was joined by a strong force of godless men who were eager to help him take vengeance on Israel. [16] When he approached the pass at Beth Horon, Judas

[g] THE YEAR 146: *This corresponds to 166 B.C.*
[h] relieved Israel of its terrible suffering; *or* saved Israel from God's anger.
2.53: Gen 39.1—45.28   **2.55–56:** Num 13.1—14.12   **2.57:** 2 Sam 7.16   **2.58:** 2 Kgs 2.9–12
2.59: Dan 3.8–30   **2.60:** Dan 6.1–24; Bel 31–42

It is the Lord's power that determines the outcome (3.19)

went out to meet him with a small group of men. ¹⁷When Judas's men saw the army coming against them, they asked, "How can our little group of men fight an army as big as that? Besides, we have not eaten all day, and we are tired!"

18 "It is not difficult," Judas answered, "for a small group to overpower a large one. It makes no difference to the Lord whether we are rescued by many people or by just a few. ¹⁹Victory in battle does not depend on who has the largest army; it is the Lord's power that determines the outcome. ²⁰Our enemies are coming against us with great violence, intending to plunder our possessions and kill our wives and children. ²¹But we are fighting for our lives and for our religion. ²²When we attack, the Lord will crush our enemies, so don't be afraid of them."

23 As soon as Judas had finished speaking, he and his men made a sudden attack against Seron and his army and crushed them. ²⁴They pursued them down the pass at Beth Horon to the plain and killed about eight hundred men. Those who escaped fled to Philistia. ²⁵After that, Gentiles everywhere began to be afraid of Judas and his brothers. ²⁶His fame reached the ears of King Antiochus, and people in every nation talked about Judas and his victories.

The King Appoints Lysias as Governor

27 When Antiochus heard what had happened, he was furious. He ordered all the armies of his empire to assemble in one huge force. ²⁸From his treasury he paid a full year's wages to his soldiers and ordered them to be prepared for any emergency. ²⁹But then he found that the funds in his treasury were exhausted. Income from taxes had decreased because of the disorder and the troubles he had brought on the world by doing away with the laws which had been in force from the earliest times. ³⁰Antiochus had always given presents more lavishly than earlier kings, but now he was worried that he might not be able to continue this, or even to meet expenses—this had happened once or twice before. ³¹He was very disturbed; but finally he decided to go to Persia, collect the taxes from the provinces there, and bring together a large sum of ready cash.

32 He appointed Lysias, an important man who had been granted the title "Relative of the King," as governor to take care of the king's affairs in the whole territory between the River Euphrates and the Egyptian border. ³³The king also made Lysias the guardian of his son Antiochus the Fifth until his own return. ³⁴He put Lysias in charge of all the elephants and of half his army, and then gave him detailed instructions about what he wanted done, and in particular, what he wanted done with the inhabitants of Judaea and Jerusalem. ³⁵Lysias was ordered to send an army against the Jews, especially the Jews in Jerusalem, to break

their power and destroy them, so that no trace of them would remain. ³⁶He was ordered to take their land and give it to foreigners, who would settle the whole area. ³⁷Taking the other half of his army, the king set out from Antioch, his capital city, in the year 147.ⁱ He crossed the Euphrates and marched through Mesopotamia.

The Victories of Judas
(2 Macc 8.8-29, 34-36)

38 Lysias chose Nicanor, Gorgias, and Ptolemy son of Dorymenes as army commanders; all three were able men who bore the title "Friend of the King." ³⁹He put them in charge of 40,000 infantry and 7,000 cavalry and ordered them to invade the land of Judaea and destroy it as the king had commanded. ⁴⁰These commanders set out with their entire force, and when they came to the plains near Emmaus, they made camp. ⁴¹A force from Idumeaʲ and Philistia joined them. The merchants of the region heard about the strength of the army, and they came to the camp with chains and a large amount of money, hoping to buy some Jewish slaves.

42 Judas and his brothers saw that their situation was getting more and more difficult, with foreign armies camped within their own borders. They also learnt that the king had commanded the complete destruction of the people. ⁴³So they determined to rebuild their ruined nation and fight for their country and the Temple. ⁴⁴Then the whole community came together to prepare for war and to pray for God's mercy.
⁴⁵Jerusalem was as empty as a
  wilderness;
no citizens left or entered the city.
The holy Temple was profaned by
  foreigners,
and Gentiles camped in the city's fort;
so joy departed from the people of Israel,
and the sound of music was heard no
  more.
46 Then Judas and his men assembled and marched to Mizpah, opposite Jerusalem, because the people of Israel had previously had a place of worship there. ⁴⁷In deep mourning, they fasted all that day, put on sackcloth, threw ashes on their heads, and tore their clothes. ⁴⁸The Gentiles would have consulted their idols in such a situation, but the Israelites

unrolled the book of the Law to search for God's guidance. ⁴⁹They brought the priests' robes, the offerings of the first grain, and the tithes, and then they brought in some Nazirites who had completed their vows. ⁵⁰The whole community prayed, "Lord, what shall we do with these things? Where shall we take them, ⁵¹now that your holy Temple has been trampled and profaned by Gentiles, and your priests mourn in disgrace? ⁵²The Gentiles have come to attack and destroy us. You know what they plan to do! ⁵³If you don't help us, how can we stand up against them?" ⁵⁴Then they blew trumpets and shouted loudly.

55 After that, Judas divided his men into groups of ten, fifty, a hundred, and a thousand, placing officers in charge of each group. ⁵⁶Then, in obedience to the Law, he sent home everyone who had recently been married, or built a house, or planted a vineyard, as well as anyone who was afraid. ⁵⁷Finally, the army marched out and took up positions south of Emmaus, ⁵⁸where Judas said to them: "Prepare yourselves for battle and be courageous! Be ready early tomorrow morning to fight these Gentiles who have joined forces to attack us and destroy us and our Temple. ⁵⁹It is better for us to die fighting than to stand idly by and watch the destruction of our nation and our Temple. ⁶⁰But the Lord will do what he pleases."

4 Gorgias took five thousand infantry and a thousand of his most experienced cavalry and left camp by night, ²with men from the fort in Jerusalem as his guides. He had planned to make a surprise attack on the Jewish army, ³but Judas learnt of the plan and moved out with his men to attack the king's army at Emmaus ⁴while Gorgias and his troops were still away from the camp. ⁵When Gorgias and his army reached Judas's camp that night, they found no one there. They thought Judas and his men were trying to escape, so they started looking for them in the mountains.

6 At dawn Judas appeared in the plain with three thousand men, not all of them as well armed as they would have liked. ⁷They saw the huge Gentile army of experienced troops wearing armour and protected by cavalry. ⁸But Judas said to his men, "Don't worry about the size of

---

ⁱTHE YEAR 147: This corresponds to 165 B.C.   ʲProbable text Idumea; Greek Syria.
3.56: Deut 20.5-8; Judg 7.3

their army, and don't be frightened when they attack. ⁹Remember how our ancestors were saved at the Red Sea when the king of Egypt was pursuing them with his army! ¹⁰Now let us ask the Lord to have mercy on us. Let us pray that he will honour his covenant with our ancestors and crush this army when we attack today. ¹¹Then all the Gentiles will know that Israel has a God who rescues and saves them."

12 When the Gentiles saw Judas and his men preparing for battle, ¹³they moved out of their camp to fight. Then Judas and his men sounded their trumpets ¹⁴and attacked. The Gentiles broke ranks and fled to the plain, ¹⁵but all the stragglers were killed. The Israelites pursued the enemy as far as Gezer, the plains of Idumea, and the towns of Ashdod and Jamnia. Altogether they killed about three thousand of the enemy.

16 When Judas and his army came back from the pursuit, ¹⁷⁻¹⁸he said to his men, "Don't be greedy for loot. Gorgias and his army are near by in the mountains, so there is still heavy fighting ahead of us. We must stand firm and fight. After that, you can safely take all the loot you want." ¹⁹Judas was just finishing his speech when an enemy patrol on a scouting mission looked down from the mountains ²⁰and saw that their army had been put to flight; they could tell from the smoke that their camp was burning. ²¹When they saw all this, they were terrified, and when they also saw that Judas's army was in the plain ready for battle, ²²they all fled to Philistia. ²³Then Judas returned to loot the enemy camp; he took large amounts of gold and silver, blue and purple cloth, and other rich plunder. ²⁴When the Jews came back to their own camp, they sang a hymn: "The Lord is worthy of praise; his mercy endures for ever." ²⁵That day brought a great victory to the people of Israel.

Victory over Lysias
(2 Macc 11.1–12)

26 The Gentile troops that escaped went to Lysias and reported all that had happened. ²⁷When Lysias heard that his troops had lost the battle, he was shocked and disappointed that Israel had not been defeated as the king had commanded.

28 In the following year Lysias gathered an army of sixty thousand well-trained infantry and five thousand cavalry,

intending to conquer the Jews. ²⁹They marched into Idumea and camped at Bethzur. Judas came to meet them with ten thousand men. ³⁰When Judas saw how strong the enemy's army was, he prayed, "We will praise you, Saviour of Israel. You broke the attack of the giant by the hand of your servant David and you let Saul's son Jonathan and the young man who carried his weapons defeat the entire Philistine army. ³¹Now in the same way let your people Israel defeat our enemy. Put them to shame, in spite of all their confidence in their infantry and cavalry. ³²Make them afraid; let their bold strength melt away; let them tremble at the prospect of defeat. ³³We love and worship you; so let us kill our enemies, that we may then sing your praises."

34 The battle began, and in the hand-to-hand fighting about five thousand of Lysias' men were killed. ³⁵When Lysias saw that his army was being defeated and when he saw the reckless courage of Judas and his men, who showed that they were ready to live or die with honour, he returned to Antioch. There he recruited some mercenaries and planned to return to Judaea later with a much larger army.

The Purification of the Temple
(2 Macc 10.1–8)

36 Judas and his brothers said, "Now that our enemies have been defeated, let's go to Jerusalem to purify the Temple and rededicate it." ³⁷So the whole army was assembled and went up to Mount Zion. ³⁸There they found the Temple abandoned, the altar profaned, the gates burnt down, the courtyards overgrown with a forest of weeds, and the priests' rooms torn down. ³⁹In their sorrow, they tore their clothes, cried loudly, threw ashes on their heads, ⁴⁰and fell face downwards on the ground. When the signal was given on the trumpets, everyone cried out to the Lord.

41 Then Judas ordered some of his soldiers to attack the men in the fort, while he purified the Temple. ⁴²He chose some priests who were qualified and who were devoted to the Law. ⁴³They purified the Temple and took the stones that had been defiled and put them in an unclean place. ⁴⁴They discussed what should be done with the altar of burnt-offerings, which had been desecrated ⁴⁵by the Gentiles, and decided to tear it down, so that it would not stand there as a

4.30: 1 Sam 17.41–54; 14.1–23

monument to their shame. So they tore down the altar [46] and put the stones in a suitable place on the Temple hill, where they were to be kept until a prophet should appear and decide what to do with them. [47] Then they took uncut stones, as the Law of Moses required, and built a new altar like the old one. [48] They repaired the Temple, inside and out, and dedicated its courtyards. [49] They made new utensils for worship and brought the lampstand, the altar of incense, and the table for the bread into the Temple. [50] They burnt incense on the altar and lit the lamps on the lampstand, and there was light in the Temple! [51] They placed the loaves of bread on the table, hung the curtains, and completed all the work.

[52-54] The twenty-fifth day of the ninth month, the month of Kislev, in the year 148[k] was the anniversary of the day the Gentiles had desecrated the altar. On that day a sacrifice was offered on the new altar in accordance with the Law of Moses. The new altar was dedicated and hymns were sung to the accompaniment of harps, lutes, and cymbals. [55] All the people bowed down with their faces to the ground and worshipped and praised the Lord for giving them victory.

[56] For eight days they celebrated the rededication of the altar. With great joy they brought burnt-offerings and offered fellowship-offerings and thank-offerings. [57] They decorated the front of the Temple with gold crowns and shields, rebuilt the gates and the priests' rooms and put doors on them. [58] Now that the Jews had removed the shame which the Gentiles had brought, they held a great celebration. [59] Then Judas, his brothers, and the entire community of Israel decreed that the rededication of the altar should be celebrated with a festival of joy and gladness at the same time each year, beginning on the twenty-fifth of the month of Kislev and lasting for eight days.

[60] Then they built high walls and strong towers round Mount Zion, so that the Gentiles could not come in and trample and defile it again. [61] Judas placed a detachment of soldiers there to guard the Temple. He also fortified the town of Bethzur, so that the people of Israel would have a fortress facing Idumea.

Wars with Neighbouring Nations
(2 Macc 10.14–33; 12.10–45)

5 When the neighbouring nations heard that the Jews had built the altar and restored the Temple as it had been before, they were so furious [2] that they made up their minds to destroy all the Jews who were living among them. So they began to murder and kill our people.

[3] The Idumeans were blockading the Israelites, so Judas went to war against them at Akrabattene, crushed them, and looted them. [4] He also dealt with the people of Baean, who were a constant threat to the people of Israel, because they used to lie in ambush waiting to trap Israelite travellers. [5] He shut the Baeanites up in their forts, took a solemn oath that he would destroy them, and burnt their forts with everyone in them. [6] Then he marched against the land of Ammon, where he met a large and powerful army under the command of a man named Timothy. [7] Judas won many battles against them and finally defeated them. [8] He captured Jazer and its surrounding villages and then returned to Judaea.

[9] The Gentiles in Gilead assembled to attack and destroy the Israelites living in their territory. But the Israelites fled to the fortress of Dathema [10-11] and sent the following letter to Judas and his brothers: "The Gentiles round us are joining forces under Timothy. We have fled to this fortress for protection, and now they are getting ready to capture it and destroy us. [12] Many of us have already been killed. Come and rescue us! [13] All the Jewish men in the region of Tob[l] have been killed, their wives and their children have been taken captive, and their possessions have been carried off. A force of about a thousand men has been destroyed there."

[14] This letter was still being read when other messengers, who had torn their clothes in sorrow, arrived with a report from Galilee. [15] They said, "An army from Ptolemais, Tyre, Sidon, and the whole of Galilee has come together to destroy us."

[16] When Judas and the people heard all this, a great assembly was held to decide what should be done to help their countrymen, who were in such difficulty under enemy attack. [17] Judas said to his brother Simon, "Choose some men and go and rescue our fellow Jews in Galilee;

---

[k] THE YEAR 148: *This corresponds to 164 B.C.*
[l] in the region of Tob; *or* who were fighting with Tobias.
4.47: Ex 20.25; Deut 27.5–6   **4.52–54:** 1 Macc 1.54

Judas and his men saw a vast army attacking the fortress (5.30)

our brother Jonathan and I will go to Gilead." 18 Judas left the rest of his army to defend Judaea and put the two leaders, Azariah and Joseph son of Zechariah, in charge of the people. 19 He said to them: "I am leaving you in command here, but don't go out and fight the Gentiles until we get back." 20 Then three thousand men joined Simon for the march into Galilee, and eight thousand remained with Judas for the march into Gilead.

21 Simon went into Galilee and fought many battles with the Gentiles. He defeated them 22 and pursued them all the way to the city of Ptolemais, killing about three thousand of them, and taking the loot. 23 Then he took the Jews who were in Galilee and Arbatta, with their wives, their children, and all they owned, and brought them back to Judaea with him. There was great rejoicing.

24 During this time, Judas Maccabeus and his brother Jonathan had crossed the River Jordan and had marched for three days through the desert. 25 They met some friendly Nabateans who told them all that had happened to the Jews in Gilead. 26 They reported that many Jews were imprisoned in the fortified cities of Bozrah, Bosor, Alema, Chaspho, Maked, and Karnaim, 27 while others were imprisoned in the smaller towns of Gilead. They also reported that the enemy was drawn up to make an attack the next day on· the Jewish fortresses, hoping to destroy all the Jews in a single day.

28 So Judas and his army suddenly turned and attacked Bozrah by the desert road, captured the town, and killed every man in it. They looted the town and set it on fire. 29 They left there and marched

all night to the fortress at Dathema. 30 At dawn Judas and his men saw a vast army attacking the fortress; they were bringing up ladders, siege-platforms, and battering-rams in an effort to capture it. 31 When Judas heard the noise, the shouts, and the sound of trumpets coming from the city, he realized that the battle had begun, 32 so he said to his men, "Fight today for our fellow Jews!"

33 He ordered his men to march in three columns and attack the enemy from the rear. As they moved forward, they blew trumpets and shouted prayers. 34 When the army under Timothy's command saw that it was Judas Maccabeus, the soldiers turned and fled. Judas crushed them and killed about eight thousand men that day.

35 Then Judas turned aside to attack the town of Alema; *m* he captured it and killed all the men in it. He looted the town and set fire to it. 36 From there he went on and captured Chaspho, Maked, Bosor, and the other towns of Gilead.

37 After this, Timothy gathered another army and camped opposite Raphon, on the other side of a river. 38 Judas sent some men to spy out the camp, and they reported back to him that all the Gentiles in the region had joined Timothy and had formed a large army. 39 Timothy had also hired Arab mercenaries to help him, and these were camped on the other side of the river ready to attack Judas. So Judas went out to meet them in battle.

40 As Judas and his army came closer to the water, Timothy said to his officers, "If he keeps on coming and crosses the river, we won't be able to turn back his attack, and he will defeat us. 41 But if he is afraid and stops on the other side of the

m ALEMA: *The name of the town is not certain.*

river, we will cross over to attack and defeat him." 42 When Judas reached the bank of the river, he gave orders to his officers to let no one stop but to push everyone forward into battle. 43 Judas was the first to cross the river against the enemy, and all his men followed him. The Gentiles broke ranks before them, threw away their arms, and fled to the pagan temple at Karnaim. 44 But Judas and his men took the city and burnt down the temple with all who were in it. With Karnaim overthrown, the Gentiles could no longer offer any resistance to Judas.

45 Then Judas gathered together all the Jews in Gilead to take them back to Judaea with him. It was a large group of all kinds of people, together with their wives and children and all that they owned. 46 They went as far as Ephron, a large, well-fortified town. It was impossible to go round it on either side, and the road passed directly through the town. 47 But the people there would not let them pass and blocked the town gates with stones. 48 Then Judas sent a friendly message to them: "Let us pass through your territory to return home. No one will harm you; we will just pass through." But they still refused to open the gates.

49 So Judas told everyone in the group, except the fighting men, to camp where they were. 50 The fighting men were ordered to take up their positions and attack the town. They fought all that day and all night, until they had taken it. 51 Judas had all the men of Ephron put to death, plundered the town, and levelled it. Then he and his army marched through the town over the dead bodies. 52 They crossed the Jordan into the wide plain opposite Beth Shan. 53 Throughout the whole march Judas kept gathering up the stragglers and encouraging the people until they reached the land of Judaea. 54 With thanksgiving and rejoicing, they went up to Mount Zion and sacrificed burnt-offerings because they had returned safely without the loss of a single man.

55 While Judas and Jonathan were in Gilead and their brother Simon was attacking Ptolemais in Galilee, 56 Joseph and Azariah, the commanders of the army in Judaea, heard about their brave deeds and victories. 57 They said to one another, "Let us go to war with the Gentiles around us and win some fame for ourselves." 58 So they and their men attacked Jamnia.

59 Gorgias and his men went out of the town to meet them in battle. 60 They defeated Joseph and Azariah and pursued them as far as the borders of Judaea. At least two thousand Israelite men were killed that day. 61 This great defeat came about because the Jewish commanders wanted to be heroes and refused to obey Judas and his brothers. 62 Besides, they did not belong to the family of the Maccabees, whom God had chosen to bring freedom to the people of Israel.

63 But Judas Maccabaeus and his brothers won great respect among all the Israelites and all the Gentiles. When people heard of their fame, 64 large crowds gathered to praise them.

65 Then Judas and his brothers went to war against the Edomites to the south. He attacked Hebron and its surrounding towns, destroyed its fortifications, and burnt down the towers round it. 66 Then he marched into the land of the Philistines and passed through Marisa. [n] 67 That day a number of priests were killed in battle because they wanted to be heroes and foolishly went out to fight. 68 Judas turned aside to Ashdod in Philistia. He pulled down the altars, burnt the images of their gods, plundered their towns, and then returned to Judaea.

The Death of Antiochus the Fourth
(2 Macc 1.11–17; 9.1–29; 10.9–11)

6 As King Antiochus the Fourth was passing through Mesopotamia, he heard of a city in Persia, named Elymais, which was famous for its riches in silver and gold. 2 The temple was very rich, containing gold shields, armour, and weapons left there by Alexander, son of King Philip of Macedonia, who was the first to rule over the Greek Empire. 3 Antiochus came and tried to take the city and loot it, but he didn't succeed, because the citizens had learnt what he was planning to do, 4 and they drew up their troops to resist him. In great frustration he withdrew to return to Babylonia.

5 In Persia a messenger reached him with the news that the armies he had sent into Judaea had been defeated. 6 Lysias and his strong army had been forced to flee from the Jews, who were now reinforced by the additional weapons, supplies, and loot they had taken from the defeated armies. 7 The Jews had pulled

n Some ancient translations Marisa; _Greek_ Samaria.
6.7: 1 Macc 1.54

1 MACCABEES 6

down the thing they called "The Awful Horror" that Antiochus had built on the altar in Jerusalem. They had also surrounded the Temple with high walls, as it had been before, and had taken and fortified the town of Bethzur, one of the king's own towns.

8 When the king heard this report, he was so dumbfounded and terribly shaken that he went to bed in a fit of deep depression because things had not turned out as he had hoped. 9 He remained ill for a long time, as waves of despair swept over him, until he finally realized that he was going to die. 10 He called together all those to whom he had given the title "Friends of the King" and said to them, "I cannot sleep, and my heart is broken with grief and worry. 11 At first I asked myself why these great waves of trouble were sweeping over me, since I have been kind and well-liked during my reign. 12 But then I remembered the wrongs I did in Jerusalem when I took all the silver and gold objects from the Temple and tried without any good reason to destroy the inhabitants of Judaea. 13 I know this is why all these terrible things have happened to me and I am about to die in deep despair here in this foreign land."

14 Then he called Philip, one of his most trusted advisers, and put him in charge of his whole empire. 15 He gave him his crown, robe, and official ring, and authorized him to educate his son Antiochus the Fifth and bring him up to be king. 16 King Antiochus died there in the year 149. o

17 When Lysias learnt that the king had died, he made the young Antiochus king in place of his father. He had brought up Antiochus from childhood and now gave him the name Eupator.

The Campaign of Antiochus the Fifth and Lysias
(2 Macc 13.1–26; 11.22–26)

18 Meanwhile, the enemies in the fort at Jerusalem had been blockading the people of Israel in the area round the Temple, constantly causing them trouble and giving support to the Gentiles. 19 So Judas decided to get rid of them and called all the people together to besiege the fort. 20 The people assembled and laid siege to the fort in the year 150. P They built siege-platforms and battering-rams.

21 But some of the men under siege escaped, and together with some of the renegade Jews, they went to the king and said, 22 "How long are you going to wait before you take revenge for what was done to our countrymen? 23 We were willing to serve your father, follow his orders, and obey his decrees. 24 But what good did it do us? Now our own countrymen have become our enemies. q In fact, they have killed as many of us as they could find and have stolen our possessions. 25 But we are not the only ones they have harmed; they have attacked all their neighbours. 26 And now they have laid siege to the fort in Jerusalem and are planning to take it. They have also fortified the Temple and Bethzur. 27 Unless you act immediately, they will do even more, and you will not be able to stop them."

28 When the king heard this, he was furious. He brought together all the army commanders, the cavalry officers, and his most trusted advisers. 29 He also hired mercenary soldiers from other countries and from the Greek islands. 30 His forces numbered 100,000 infantry, 20,000 cavalry, and 32 elephants trained for war. 31 The king and his army passed through Idumea and laid siege to Bethzur, where they fought for a long time. They built battering-rams and siege-platforms, but the defenders fought bravely and came out of the town and burnt down the platforms.

32 Then Judas withdrew his troops from the fort in Jerusalem and set up his camp at Beth Zechariah, blocking the advance of the king's army. 33 Early the next morning, the king rapidly moved his army along the road to Beth Zechariah, where his troops took up battle positions and blew trumpets. 34 They got the elephants ready for battle by showing them grape juice and mulberry juice. 35 The huge animals were distributed among the infantry units. A thousand men, protected by chain armour and bronze helmets, were stationed with each elephant. Each animal was also accompanied by a special force of five hundred cavalry, 36 which always remained with the elephant. 37 A strong, protected wooden platform was securely fastened by a special harness to the back of each elephant. Three r soldiers rode on each

animal, in addition to the elephant driver. [38]Lysias placed the rest of the cavalry on the two flanks of the army where they could be protected by the infantry while harassing the enemy. [39] The sunlight, reflected off the bronze and gold shields, shone on the mountains and flashed like burning torches. [40]Part of the king's army was spread out over the higher ground of the mountain slopes and part over the lower land, but they all moved forward steadily and in good order. [41]All the people were terrified when they heard the noise made by the clashing of weapons and the marching of that great and powerful army.

42 Judas and his army advanced into battle, and immediately killed six hundred of the king's army. [43]When Eleazar Avaran saw that one of the elephants was larger than the others and that it was covered with royal armour, he thought that the king was riding on it. [44]Eleazar sacrificed his life to save his people and to gain eternal fame. [45]He ran boldly towards the elephant, which was in the middle of a battalion of infantry. He rushed forward killing men to the right and left, so that the enemy soldiers fell back before him on both sides. [46]He slipped in under the elephant and stabbed it to death, and it fell on him and killed him. [47]But when the Jews realized how strong the royal army was and how determined it was to fight, they retreated.

48 The king and his army advanced to fight the Jews at Jerusalem and laid siege to the whole of Judaea and Jerusalem. [49]He made peace with the Jews of Bethzur, who then left the town. There had not been enough food in the town for them to withstand the siege because it was the sabbatical year, when no fields were sown. [50]The king occupied Bethzur and stationed a body of troops there to guard it. [51]Then he surrounded the Temple and besieged it for a long time. He set up siege-platforms, battering-rams, catapults for throwing fire and stones, and other weapons to throw spears and rocks. [52]The defenders also made war machines to oppose those of the enemy, and so the battle went on for a long time. [53]But there was no food left in the Temple storage bins because it was the sabbatical year, and the people who had fled from the Gentiles and taken refuge in Judaea had eaten up all the food that had been stored there. [54]The shortage of food had been

so severe that many people had scattered to their homes, and only a few men were left in the Temple.

55 Meanwhile, Philip, who had been appointed by King Antiochus before his death to educate his son to be king, [56]returned from Persia and Media. He had come back with the royal army and planned to take control of the government. When Lysias heard this news, [57]he made rapid preparations to depart. He said to the young king, to his officers, and to his men, "We are growing weaker each day; we are short of provisions, and this place we are besieging is strong. Besides, there are pressing government affairs which need our attention. [58]So now let's arrange a truce and make a peace treaty with the Jews and their whole nation. [59]We will allow them to follow their own laws and customs as they did before. All this trouble started when we provoked them by abolishing their laws and customs."

60 This recommendation was well received by the king and the officers, so Lysias proposed peace terms to the Jews, and they accepted them. [61]When the king and his officers solemnly agreed to abide by these terms, the Jews came out of their fortress. [62]But when the king entered the Temple area on Mount Zion and saw the strong fortifications, he broke his word and ordered the walls surrounding the Temple to be torn down. [63]Then he hurriedly left and returned to Antioch, where he found Philip in control of the city. The king attacked the city and took it by force.

The High Priest Alcimus and the Campaign of Nicanor
(2 Macc 14.1–36; 15.1–36)

7 In the year 151,[5] Demetrius son of Seleucus left Rome and with a few men landed at a town on the Mediterranean coast, where he proclaimed himself king. [2]As he was making his way to the royal palace of his ancestors, the soldiers arrested Antiochus the Fifth and Lysias, planning to take them to Demetrius. [3]When Demetrius heard about it, he said, "I don't want to see them." [4]So the soldiers killed them, and Demetrius took the throne.

5 Then all the godless traitorous Jews led by Alcimus, who wanted to be High Priest, went to Demetrius. [6]They brought accusations against the other Jews and

[5]THE YEAR 151: *This corresponds to 161 B.C.*

said, "Judas and his brothers have killed everybody who supported you, and they have driven us out of our country. 7 We advise you to send someone whom you can trust to go and inspect all the damage done to our property and the king's territory and to punish Judas, his brothers, and all who support them."

8 King Demetrius chose one of his advisers, a man by the name of Bacchides, who was the governor of Greater Syria. He was an important man in the empire and loyal to the king. 9 He was sent along with the godless Alcimus, whom the king had appointed High Priest; Alcimus had orders to take revenge on the Jews. 10 They left Antioch and arrived in Judaea with a large army. Bacchides tried to trick Judas and his brothers by sending to them messengers with offers of peace. 11 But when Judas and his brothers saw what a large army they had brought, they did not believe what the messengers said.

12 A group of teachers of the Law came to Alcimus and Bacchides, asking for justice. 13 These devout and patriotic men were the first of the Jews to try to make peace with Alcimus and Bacchides. 14 They trusted Alcimus, who was a priest descended from Aaron, and they thought he would not cause them any harm. 15 Alcimus assured them of his peaceful intentions and solemnly promised that no harm would come to them or their friends. 16 But as soon as they began to trust him, he arrested sixty of them and put them all to death on the same day. As the scripture says,

17 "The blood of your faithful people was
    poured out,
  their bodies were scattered round
    Jerusalem,
  and there was no one left to bury the
    dead."

18 When this happened, all the people were afraid of Alcimus and Bacchides, and they said, "They don't know what truth or justice means. They gave their solemn word and then broke it!" 19 Bacchides left Jerusalem and set up his headquarters at Beth Zaith. He ordered the arrest of some of the faithful Jews and even many of the renegades who had willingly joined him; he had them killed and thrown into a deep pit. 20 Bacchides put the country under the control of Alcimus, left troops there to help him, and returned to the king.

21 Alcimus then began his struggle to establish himself as High Priest. 22 Every troublemaker in the country joined him. They gained control of the land of Judaea and caused great difficulties for the Jews. 23 Judas saw that the trouble Alcimus and his men had caused was even worse than the damage done by the Gentiles. 24 So he went round the whole country of Judaea, taking revenge on all the men who had willingly joined Alcimus and preventing them from leaving the towns and going into the country. 25 When Alcimus saw that Judas and his men were growing more powerful and when he realized that he would not be able to stand against them, he returned to the king and accused them of great crimes.

26 Then the king sent Nicanor, one of his most honoured officers, who hated the Jews, with orders to exterminate them. 27 Nicanor came to Jerusalem with a big army. He tried to trick Judas and his brothers by sending peace offers. He said, 28 "There need not be any quarrel between you and me. I will come to you with a small escort for a friendly private conversation." 29 When he came to Judas, they exchanged polite greetings, but Judas's enemies were ready to kidnap him. 30 When Judas learnt that Nicanor's visit was part of a plot against him, he was afraid and decided not to meet him again. 31 Nicanor realized that his plan had been discovered, so he left Jerusalem to meet Judas in battle near Capharsalama. 32 About five hundred of Nicanor's men were killed, and the rest of the army escaped to the fort in Jerusalem.

33 Some time later Nicanor went to Mount Zion. Some of the priests left the Temple and, along with some of the leaders of the people, went to welcome him with words of peace and to show him the burnt-offering that was being sacrificed on behalf of the king. 34 But he ridiculed them and made them ceremonially unclean by spitting on them. He spoke proudly 35 and angrily threatened them with an oath, "Unless Judas and his army are surrendered to me immediately, I will burn this Temple down as soon as I return after my victory." And he left in a rage.

36 The priests went into the courtyard and stood facing the altar and the Temple. They started weeping and prayed, 37 "Lord, you chose this Temple to bear your name and to be a place of prayer and intercession for your people. 38 Now,

take vengeance on this man and his army; let them die in battle. Remember how they spoke evil of you, and let none of them survive."

39 Nicanor left Jerusalem and set up his headquarters at Beth Horon, where the Syrian army joined him. 40 Meanwhile, Judas set up camp at Adasa with three thousand men. There Judas prayed, 41 "Lord, the Scriptures tell us that when a king sent messengers to insult you, your angel went out and killed 185,000 of his soldiers. 42 Now, in the same way, crush this army before us today and let everyone know that Nicanor is being punished because he insulted your holy Temple. Punish him as his wickedness deserves."

43 The armies met in battle on the thirteenth day of the month of Adar, and Nicanor's army was defeated. Nicanor himself was the first to be killed in the battle, 44 and when his soldiers saw that he was dead, they threw down their weapons and fled. 45 The Jews pursued them all day long from Adasa to Gezer. As they followed, they kept sounding the call to battle on the trumpets, 46 and from all the surrounding villages of Judaea people came out and attacked the fleeing enemy from the sides. This forced them back towards the Jews who were chasing them, and all the enemy were killed in the fight. Not one of them survived.

47 The Jews took the loot and then cut off Nicanor's head and his right arm, which he had extended so arrogantly. They brought his head and his arm to be put on display outside Jerusalem. 48 There was great rejoicing among the Jews. They set that day aside as a special day of celebration, 49 and decreed that the thirteenth day of Adar should be observed as an annual day of celebration. 50 There was peace in the land of Judaea for a little while.

The Treaty with the Romans

8 Judas had heard about the Romans and their reputation as a military power. He knew that they welcomed all those who joined them as allies and that those who came to them could be sure of the friendship of Rome. 2 People had told him about the wars the Romans had fought and their heroic acts among the Gauls, whom they had conquered and forced to pay taxes. 3 He had been told what they had done in Spain when they captured the silver-mines and the gold-mines there. 4 By careful planning and persistence, they had conquered the whole country, even though it was far from Rome. They had overcome the kings from distant lands who had fought against them; they had defeated them so badly that the survivors had to pay annual taxes. 5 They had fought and conquered Philip and Perseus, kings of Macedonia, and all who had joined them against Rome. 6 They had even defeated Antiochus the Great, king of Syria, who had attacked them with 120 elephants, cavalry, chariots, and a powerful army. 7 They had taken him alive and forced him and his successors to pay heavy taxes, to give hostages, and to surrender 8 India, Media, Lydia, and some of their best lands. They took these and gave them to King Eumenes. [t]

9 When the Greeks made plans to attack and destroy them, 10 the Romans learnt of the plans and sent a general to fight against them. The Romans killed many of the Greeks, took their wives and children captive, plundered their possessions, occupied their land, tore down their fortresses, and made them slaves, as they are today. 11 They also destroyed or made slaves of other kingdoms, the islands, and everyone who had ever fought against them. 12 But they maintained their friendship with their allies and those who relied on them for protection. They conquered kings near and far, and everyone who heard of their reputation was afraid of them. 13 They helped some men to become kings, while they deposed others; they had become a world power. 14 In spite of all this, no Roman ever tried to advance his own position by wearing a crown or putting on royal robes. 15 They created a senate, and each day 320 senators came together to deliberate about the affairs of the people and their well-being. 16 Each year they entrusted to one man the responsibility of governing them and controlling their whole territory. Everyone obeyed this one man, and there was no envy or jealousy among them.

17 Judas chose Eupolemus, the son of John and grandson of Accos, and Jason son of Eleazar and sent them to Rome to make a treaty of friendship and alliance with the Romans. 18 He did this to get rid of Syrian oppression, since the Jews clearly saw that they were being reduced

---

[t] KING EUMENES: *This is King Eumenes II, king of Pergamum from 197–158* B.C.
7.41: 2 Kgs 19.35   8.17: 2 Macc 4.11

to slavery. ¹⁹ After a long and difficult journey, Eupolemus and Jason reached Rome and entered the Senate. They addressed the assembly in these terms: ²⁰ "Judas Maccabaeus, his brothers, and the Jewish people have sent us here to make a mutual defence treaty with you, so that we may be officially recorded as your friends and allies."

21 The Romans accepted the proposal, ²² and what follows is a copy of the letter which was engraved on bronze tablets and sent to Jerusalem to remain there as a record of the treaty:

²³ "May things go well for ever for the Romans and for the Jewish nation on land and sea! May they never have enemies, and may they never go to war! ²⁴ But if war is declared first against Rome or any of her allies anywhere, ²⁵ the Jewish nation will come to her aid with whole-hearted support, as the situation may require. ²⁶ And to those at war with her, the Jews shall not give or supply food, arms, money, or ships, as was agreed in Rome. The Jews must carry out their obligations without receiving anything in return.

²⁷ "In the same way, if war is declared first against the Jewish nation, the Romans will come to their aid with hearty support, as the situation may require. ²⁸ And to their enemies there shall not be given or supplied food, arms, money, or ships, as was agreed in Rome. The Romans must carry out their obligations without deception.

²⁹ "These are the terms of the treaty that the Romans have made with the Jewish people. ³⁰ But if, in the future, both parties shall agree to add or remove anything, they shall act on their decision, and whatever they add or remove shall be valid.

³¹ "Furthermore, concerning the wrongs which King Demetrius is doing against the Jews, we have written to him as follows, 'Why have you treated our friends and allies, the Jews, so harshly? ³² If they complain to us about you once more, we will support their cause and go to war against you on land and sea.' "

The Death of Judas

9 When Demetrius heard that Nicanor and his army had been annihilated, he again sent Bacchides and Alcimus to the land of Judaea, this time with the Syrian wing of the army. ² They moved along the Gilgal road, laid siege to Mesaloth in Arbela, captured it, and killed many people. ³ In the first month of the year 152, ᵘ they set up camp opposite Jerusalem. ⁴ From there they marched to Berea with twenty thousand infantry and two thousand cavalry.

5 Judas had camped at Elasa, with three thousand experienced soldiers. ⁶ But when they saw the enormous size of the enemy army, they were terrified. So many men deserted that only eight hundred Jewish soldiers were left. ⁷ When Judas saw that his army was dwindling away and that the battle was about to begin, he was worried because there was not enough time to bring his army together. ⁸ He was discouraged, but he said to those who were still with him, "Let us prepare for the attack; maybe we can still defeat them."

9 His men tried to talk him out of it. "We are not strong enough," they said. "Let's retreat now and save our lives. Then we can return with reinforcements and fight the enemy. We haven't enough men now."

10 Judas replied, "Never let it be said that I ran from a battle. If our time has come, let's die bravely for our fellow Jews and not leave any stain on our honour."

11 The Syrian army came out of the camp and took up battle positions against the Jews. The cavalry was divided into two parts. The shock troops were in the front lines, but the archers and those who used slings went ahead of the main formation. ¹² Bacchides took his position on the right. The infantry advanced, protected on both sides by the cavalry, and the war trumpets were blown. The soldiers of Judas also sounded their trumpets. ¹³ The ground shook from the noise when the two armies met, and they fought from morning until evening.

14 When Judas saw that Bacchides and the main force of the Syrian army was on the right, all his bravest men joined him, ¹⁵ and they crushed the Syrians' right wing. They pursued them as far as the

---

ᵘ THE YEAR 152: *This corresponds to 160 B.C.*
8.22: 1 Macc 14.18

foothills. ^v 16 But when the Syrians on the left wing saw that their right wing had been crushed, they turned to attack Judas and his men from the rear. 17 The fighting became very fierce, and many on both sides were killed. 18 Finally Judas himself was killed. Then all his men fled. 19 Jonathan and Simon took their brother's body and buried it in the family tomb at Modein, 20 and there at the tomb they wept for him. All Israel mourned for him in great sorrow for many days. They said, 21 "It can't be true! The mighty hero and saviour of Israel has been killed!"

22 The other deeds of Judas, his battles, his courageous acts, and his great achievements, were too many to write down.

Jonathan Succeeds Judas

23 After the death of Judas, the lawless traitors began to reappear everywhere in Judaea, and all the wicked men returned. 24 Also at that time there was a severe famine, and the whole country went over to the side of the renegades. 25 Bacchides deliberately appointed some renegade Jews as rulers over the country. 26 These men hunted down the friends of Judas and brought them all before Bacchides, and he subjected them to torture and humiliation. 27 It was a time of great trouble for Israel, worse than anything that had happened to them since the time prophets ceased to appear among them. 28 Then all the friends of Judas came together and said to Jonathan, 29 "Since your brother Judas died, there has been no one like him to lead us against our enemies, against Bacchides and those of our own nation who oppose us. 30 So today we choose you to succeed him as our ruler and commander to carry on our war." 31 Jonathan accepted the leadership that day and took the place of his brother Judas.

The Campaigns of Jonathan

32 When Bacchides learnt of this, he made up his mind to kill Jonathan. 33 But when this news reached Jonathan, he fled, with his brother Simon and their men, to the wilderness of Tekoa and set up camp at the pool of Asphar. 34 (Bacchides learnt about this on the Sabbath and crossed the Jordan with his whole army.) ^w 35 Jonathan sent his brother John, who was responsible for the soldiers'

families, to ask the Nabateans, with whom he was on friendly terms, for permission to store with them the large amount of baggage they had. 36 But the Jambrites from Medeba attacked John, took him captive, and carried off all the baggage. 37 Some time later Jonathan and his brother Simon learnt that the Jambrites were about to celebrate an important wedding and that there would be a bridal procession from the town of Nadabath. The bride was the daughter of one of the great princes of Canaan. 38 Jonathan and Simon had wanted revenge for the death of their brother John, so they and their men went up one of the mountains and hid. 39 They kept watch and saw a noisy crowd loaded down with baggage. The bridegroom, his friends, and his relatives were on their way to meet the bride's party. They were heavily armed and were playing musical instruments and drums. 40 The Jews attacked from their ambush and killed many of them; the rest escaped into the mountains, while the Jews carried off all their possessions. 41 So the wedding was turned into a time of mourning and their joyful music into funeral songs. 42 Jonathan and Simon had taken full revenge for the death of their brother, and they returned to the marshes along the Jordan.

43 Bacchides heard about this and arrived on the Sabbath at the banks of the Jordan with a large army. 44 Jonathan said to his men, "Now we must fight for our lives. We are in a worse situation than we have ever been in before. 45 The enemy is in front of us, the river is behind us, and marshes and thickets are on both sides of us; there is no way out. 46 So pray now for the Lord to save us from our enemies."

47 The battle began and Jonathan and his men were just about to kill Bacchides, when he escaped to the rear of the army. 48 So Jonathan and his men jumped into the Jordan and swam to the other side to escape, and the Syrian army did not cross the river to follow them. 49 That day Bacchides lost about a thousand men.

50 After Bacchides returned to Jerusalem, the Syrians built fortifications with high walls and barred gates for a number of towns in Judaea: Emmaus, Beth Horon, Bethel, Timnath, Pirathon, Tephon, and the fortress in Jericho. 51 In all of these Bacchides placed troops to

^v Probable text the foothills; Greek Mount Ashdod.
^w Verse 34 is probably misplaced and belongs with verse 43.

They kept watch and saw a noisy crowd loaded down with baggage (9.39)

harass the Jews. 52 He also strengthened the fortifications of the towns of Bethzur and Gezer and of the fort in Jerusalem. He placed army units in them and stored up supplies there. 53 Then he took the sons of the leading men of the country as hostages and imprisoned them in the fort.

54 In the second month of the year 153,ˣ the High Priest Alcimus ordered that the wall of the inner court of the Temple must be torn down. This would have destroyed what the prophets had accomplished; but just as the work began, 55 he had a stroke, and work was stopped. Paralysed and unable to open his mouth, he could not speak or even make a will for his family. 56 He died in great torment. 57 When Bacchides learnt that Alcimus was dead, he returned to King Demetrius, and the land of Judaea had peace for two years.

58 Then all the renegades got together and said, "Look, Jonathan and his men are living in peace and security. If we bring Bacchides here now, he can capture them all in a single night." 59 They went to discuss the matter with Bacchides, 60 and he set out with a large army. He sent secret letters to all his allies in Judaea, asking them to seize Jonathan and his men. But they were not able to do so because the plot was discovered. 61 Jonathan and his men captured fifty of the traitorous leaders who had been involved in the plot and put them to death. 62 Then Jonathan, Simon, and their forces

withdrew to Bethbasi in the wilderness. They rebuilt the ruined fortifications and strengthened the defences of the town. 63 When Bacchides learnt about all this, he got his whole army together and alerted his supporters in Judaea. 64 He attacked Bethbasi from all sides and built siege-platforms. After the battle had gone on for a long time, 65 Jonathan slipped out into the country with a small body of men and left his brother Simon in charge of the town. 66 Jonathan defeated Odomera and his people, and then attacked and destroyed the Phasirite camp. Once defeated, they joined Jonathan and advanced with him in his attack against Bacchides. 67 At the same time, Simon and his men rushed from the town and burnt the siege-platforms. 68 In the battle Bacchides was pressed so hard that all his plans came to nothing, and he was defeated. 69 He was so furious with the traitorous Jews who had urged him to come to Judaea that he put many of them to death.

Then Bacchides decided to return to his own country, 70 but when Jonathan learnt of this, he sent ambassadors to Bacchides to arrange for peace terms and the return of Jewish prisoners. 71 Bacchides agreed to do as Jonathan asked and gave him his solemn promise that he would let him live in peace for the rest of his life. 72 Bacchides handed over the prisoners and returned to his own country. Never

ˣTHE YEAR 153: *This corresponds to 159 B.C.*

again did he come into Jewish territory. [73]War came to an end in Israel. Jonathan settled in Michmash and began to govern the people and to eliminate the renegade Jews from Israel.

Alexander Epiphanes Makes Jonathan High Priest

10 In the year 160,[y] Alexander Epiphanes,[z] son of Antiochus the Fourth, landed at Ptolemais and captured it. The people welcomed him as their king. [2]When King Demetrius heard of it, he gathered a large army and went out to meet him in battle. [3]At that time Demetrius sent Jonathan a friendly letter full of flattery, [4]in the hope of winning Jonathan over to his side and making peace with the Jews before Alexander made a treaty with them against him. [5]Demetrius thought that Jonathan would certainly remember all the wrongs he had done to him, his brothers, and the entire Jewish nation. [6]And so Demetrius made Jonathan his ally and gave him authority to raise an army and equip it. He also ordered that the hostages held in the fort at Jerusalem should be handed over to Jonathan. [7]So Jonathan went to Jerusalem and read the letter to all the people and to the men in the fort. [8]These men were terrified when they learnt that the king had given Jonathan authority to raise an army. [9]They handed the hostages over to him, and he returned them to their parents.

10 Jonathan set up his headquarters in Jerusalem and began to rebuild and restore the city. [11]He ordered the builders to use squared stones for the city walls and for the protecting wall round Mount Zion. This was done. [12]The foreigners deserted the fortresses that Bacchides had built; [13]each man left his post and returned to his own country. [14]But some of the Jews who had abandoned the Law of Moses and its commands were still left in Bethzur, which served as their last place of refuge.

15 King Alexander learnt of the promises Demetrius had made to Jonathan and he also learnt about Jonathan himself, about the battles he had fought, his courageous deeds, and the troubles he and his brothers had endured. [16]He was certain that he would never find another man like Jonathan and so decided to make him his friend and ally. [17]He wrote Jonathan a letter:

[18]"King Alexander to his friend Jonathan, greetings. [19]I have heard that you are a brave man who has earned the right to be a friend of the king. [20]I have this day appointed you as High Priest of your nation and conferred upon you the title of 'Friend of the King.' You are to be our ally and give us your support."

He also sent him a royal robe and a gold crown. [21]Jonathan put on the robes of the High Priest in the seventh month of the year 160[a] at the Festival of Shelters. He raised an army and stored up a large supply of weapons.

Jonathan Supports Alexander Epiphanes

22 When Demetrius heard this, he was distressed and said, [23]"How did we manage to let Alexander get ahead of us? He has strengthened his position by making an alliance with the Jews. [24]I also will write them a friendly letter offering high positions and gifts, so that they will support me."

25 He wrote:

"King Demetrius to the nation of the Jews, greetings. [26]We are delighted to learn that you have kept your obligations under our treaty, remained loyal to us, and have not gone over to the side of our enemies. [27]Now if you continue to remain loyal to us, we will reward you well. [28]We will grant you exemptions from many taxes and allow you other privileges. [29]I hereby grant all the Jewish people release and exemption from payment of regular taxes, salt taxes, and other special taxes. [30]Furthermore, from this day I release you from your obligation to pay me one-third of the grain-harvest and half of the fruit-harvest. From now on I will not demand these payments from Judaea or from the three districts that have been added to Judaea from Samaria and Galilee. [31]Jerusalem and its surrounding territory is to be recognized as a holy city and to be exempt from the payment of all taxes. [32]I also give up my authority over the fort in Jerusalem and place it under the High

---

[y]THE YEAR 160: *This corresponds to 152 B.C.*
[z]ALEXANDER EPIPHANES: *Alexander Epiphanes is more widely known as Alexander Balas.*
[a]THE YEAR 160: *This corresponds to 152 B.C.*
10.30: 1 Macc 11.34

Priest, who may station there anyone he wishes to guard it. ³³I freely grant release to all Jews who are prisoners of war anywhere in my kingdom. All of them will be exempt from taxes, even on their livestock.ᵇ ³⁴No taxes shall be collected from any Jew anywhere in my kingdom on Sabbaths, New Moon Festivals, and other holy days. Furthermore, no taxes shall be collected three days before or after the major holy days. ³⁵No one has the right on any of these days to demand payment or to trouble you in any way.

³⁶"Jews may be enlisted in the royal army up to a total of thirty thousand men, and they will receive the same pay as other royal troops. ³⁷Some of them may be stationed in the great royal fortresses, and others assigned to responsible positions in the government. They shall have Jews as their leaders and officers, and they shall be allowed to follow their own laws and customs, just as the king has permitted for the people of Judaea.

³⁸"The three districts added to Judaea from the territory of Samaria will be completely incorporated into Judaea and placed under the authority of the High Priest alone. ³⁹I give to the Temple in Jerusalem for its operating expenses the revenues from the city of Ptolemais and the lands belonging to it. ⁴⁰I also promise to make an annual gift of fifteen thousand silver coins from appropriate accounts within the royal treasury. ⁴¹The total accumulated state subsidy, which we have failed to pay in recent years, shall be paid, and the payments continued from now on for the work of the Temple. ⁴²In addition to this, we will no longer require the five thousand silver coins annually from the Temple income. This money belongs to the priests serving in the Temple. ⁴³Whoever owes a debt to the king or any other debt and takes refuge in the Temple in Jerusalem or in any area that belongs to it may not be arrested, nor may his property anywhere in my kingdom be confiscated. ⁴⁴The expenses for rebuilding and renovating the Temple shall be provided from the royal treasury. ⁴⁵Likewise, the expenses for rebuilding the walls of Jerusalem and its surrounding fortifications, as well as the walls of designated towns in Judaea, shall be provided from the royal treasury."

46 When Jonathan and the people heard the proposals made by King Demetrius, they refused to believe them or accept them, because they remembered how harshly he had treated them and what terrible troubles he had caused them. ⁴⁷They preferred to give their allegiance to Alexander because he had been the first to open peace negotiations, and they remained his allies as long as he lived.

48 King Alexander raised a large army and took up battle positions facing Demetrius. ⁴⁹But when the armies of the two kings met in battle, the army of Alexanderᶜ turned and ran. Demetriusᵈ pursued them and won the battle. ⁵⁰Alexanderᶜ fought bitterly until sundown, but Demetrius was killed that day.

51 Then Alexander sent ambassadors to King Ptolemy the Sixth of Egypt with this message:

⁵²"I have returned to my kingdom and taken my seat on the throne of my ancestors. I have taken over the government, and I am now in control of the country. ⁵³I made war on Demetrius, defeated him and his army, and I have taken over his kingdom. ⁵⁴Now I am ready to make an alliance. Give me your daughter in marriage, and I will give both of you such gifts as you deserve."

55 King Ptolemy replied, "It was a great day when you returned to your country and took the throne of your ancestors. ⁵⁶I agree to your proposals, but first meet me at Ptolemais. We can get acquainted there, and I will give you my daughter in marriage."

57 So in the year 162ᵉ Ptolemy and his daughter Cleopatraᶠ left Egypt and arrived at Ptolemais. ⁵⁸King Alexander met them, and Ptolemy gave him his daughter in marriage. The wedding was

---

ᵇ This sentence in Greek is unclear.   ᶜAlexander; some manuscripts have Demetrius.
ᵈDemetrius; some manuscripts have Alexander.   ᵉTHE YEAR 162: This corresponds to 150 B.C.
ᶠCLEOPATRA: This was Cleopatra Thea, also known as Cleopatra the Third, and not to be confused with Cleopatra the Seventh (69–30 B.C.), who was involved in the history of Caesar and Mark Antony.

Ptolemy and his daughter Cleopatra left Egypt (10.57)

celebrated there in Ptolemais with royal splendour.

59 King Alexander wrote asking Jonathan to come to meet him. 60 So Jonathan, in a show of splendour, went to Ptolemais and met the two kings. He presented them with gifts of silver and gold, and he also gave many gifts to the high officials who had accompanied them. Everyone was favourably impressed with him. 61 At the same time some traitorous Jews who wanted to make trouble for Jonathan made accusations against him, but King Alexander paid no attention to them. 62 He gave orders that Jonathan should be given royal robes to wear, 63 and he honoured him by letting him sit at his side. Alexander told his officers to take Jonathan into the centre of the city and to announce that no one was to bring charges against him for any reason and no one was to cause him any kind of trouble. 64 When his accusers saw the honours given to him, heard the announcement, and saw him clothed in royal robes, they all fled. 65 The king further honoured Jonathan by enrolling him in the First Order of the "Friends of the King" and by making him a general and governor of his province. 66 Jonathan

returned to Jerusalem pleased and successful.

Jonathan's Victory over Apollonius

67 In the year 165 g Demetrius the Second, the son of Demetrius the First, left Crete and arrived in Syria, the land of his ancestors. 68 When King Alexander heard about this, he was worried and returned to Antioch, the capital of Syria. 69 Demetrius reappointed Apollonius governor of Greater Syria. Apollonius raised a large army, set up camp near Jamnia, and sent the following message to Jonathan the High Priest:

70 "Because of you I am being ridiculed, but why do you, there in your mountains, continue this rebellion when no one supports you? 71 If you really have any confidence in your army, come down here on the plain and fight, where we can test each other's strength. Study the situation, and you will find that I have the support of the forces from the cities. 72 You will learn who I am and who our allies are, and you will discover that you have no chance of standing against us. Your predecessors have already been beaten twice on their own ground; 73 so how

g THE YEAR 165: *This corresponds to 147 B.C.*

do you expect to defeat my cavalry and the kind of army I have here on the plain? Down here there is not so much as a pebble to hide behind and no way to escape."

74 When Jonathan received this message from Apollonius, he became angry. He took ten thousand picked troops from Jerusalem; his brother Simon also brought troops, and their two forces ⁷⁵set up camp outside Joppa. The men of the city refused to let them in because there was a detachment of Apollonius's troops there, but Jonathan attacked, ⁷⁶and the men in the city became so frightened that they opened the gates, allowing Jonathan to capture Joppa. ⁷⁷When Apollonius heard what had happened, he took three thousand cavalry and a large army of infantry and pretended to retreat south towards Ashdod. However, relying upon the strength of his cavalry, he marched into the plain with his main force, ⁷⁸⁻⁷⁹positioning a thousand cavalry where they could attack Jonathan's forces from the rear. Jonathan continued his pursuit as far as Ashdod, where the two armies met in battle. ⁸⁰Not until then did Jonathan realize that he was caught in an ambush. His army was surrounded, and enemy arrows rained down on them from morning until evening. ⁸¹But Jonathan's men stood firm, as he had ordered, and the attacking cavalry grew tired. ⁸²Then, when the cavalry was exhausted, Simon appeared on the scene with his forces and attacked and overwhelmed the enemy infantry, who broke ranks and fled. ⁸³The cavalry, which by now was scattered all over the battlefield, fled to Ashdod, where they took refuge in the temple of Dagon, their god. ⁸⁴But Jonathan set fire to the city and to the temple of Dagon, burning to death all those who had taken refuge there. Then he set fire to the surrounding towns and looted them. ⁸⁵That day about eight thousand were either killed in the battle or burnt to death. ⁸⁶Jonathan left and set up camp at Ashkelon, where the men of the city came out to welcome him with great honours. ⁸⁷Jonathan and his men returned to Jerusalem with large quantities of loot.

88 When King Alexander heard what Jonathan had done, he gave him even greater honours. ⁸⁹He sent him a gold shoulder buckle, which is given only to those honoured with the title "Relative of the King." He also gave him the city of Ekron and its surrounding territory.

The Fall of Alexander Epiphanes

11 King Ptolemy the Sixth of Egypt assembled an army of soldiers more numerous than the grains of sand along the sea-shore, and he also gathered a great fleet of ships. He intended to trap Alexander, take his kingdom, and add it to his own, ²so he went to Syria with promises of peace, and the citizens opened their gates to him and welcomed him. King Alexander had ordered them to do this because Ptolemy was his father-in-law. ³But as Ptolemy moved north, he stationed a detachment of troops in each town. ⁴When he reached Ashdod, the people there showed him the burnt ruins of the temple of Dagon and all the destruction in the city and the surrounding towns. There were corpses everywhere. The bodies of the men Jonathan had burnt to death during the battle were now stacked up along Ptolemy's route. ⁵The people told him what Jonathan had done, hoping that he would hold him responsible, but Ptolemy said nothing. ⁶Jonathan, with all the proper ceremony, went to Joppa to meet him. They exchanged greetings and spent the night there. ⁷Jonathan accompanied him as far as the River Eleutherus before returning to Jerusalem. ⁸In this way King Ptolemy, in his plot against Alexander, took control of the towns along the coast as far north as Seleucia-by-the-sea.

9 From there Ptolemy sent this message to King Demetrius: "Let's make a treaty. My daughter is now Alexander's wife, but I will take her back and give her to you and let you rule over your father's kingdom. ¹⁰I regret that I ever gave her to Alexander, because he has tried to kill me." ¹¹Ptolemy made this accusation against Alexander because he wanted to take over his kingdom. ¹²So he took his daughter away from Alexander and gave her to Demetrius; he broke off all relations with Alexander, and they became open enemies. ¹³Then Ptolemy entered Antioch and assumed the crown of Syria; so he wore both the crown of Egypt and the crown of Syria.

14 King Alexander was in Cilicia at the time because the people of that region were in a state of rebellion. ¹⁵But when he heard what Ptolemy had done, he moved to attack him. Ptolemy met him with a large force and won a decisive victory. ¹⁶While Ptolemy reached the

peak of his power, Alexander fled to Arabia to find protection, [17]but an Arab named Zabdiel cut off his head and sent it to Ptolemy. [18]Two days later Ptolemy himself died, and the troops he had left in the fortresses were then killed by the local citizens. [19]So in the year 167[h] Demetrius the Second became king.

Jonathan Wins the Favour of Demetrius the Second

20 About that time Jonathan gathered the men of Judaea to attack the fort in Jerusalem. They built many siege-platforms to use in the attack. [21]But some traitorous Jews who hated their own nation went to King Demetrius the Second and told him that Jonathan was laying siege to the fort in Jerusalem. [22]When Demetrius heard this, he was furious and immediately moved his headquarters to Ptolemais. He wrote to Jonathan and ordered him to lift the siege and to meet him for a conference in Ptolemais without a moment's delay.

23 When Jonathan received the message, he gave orders for the siege to continue, and then chose some Jewish leaders and some priests to go with him. At the risk of his life, [24]he went to the king in Ptolemais, taking along robes, silver and gold, and many other gifts. He made a good impression on the king. [25]Although some lawless traitors of his own nation had made accusations against Jonathan, [26]the king still treated him just as his predecessors had done. He honoured him in the presence of all his advisers, [27]and confirmed him as High Priest, restoring all his former honours and appointing him to the highest rank among the "Friends of the King."

28 Jonathan asked the king to release the territory of Judaea and the three regions of Samaria[i] from the payment of taxes, promising that if Demetrius would do that, he would pay him a lump sum of ten thousand kilogrammes of silver. [29]The king agreed and wrote a letter to Jonathan to confirm all this:

[30]"King Demetrius to King Jonathan and to the Jewish nation, greetings.

[31]"For your information I am sending a copy of the letter I have written to the noble Lasthenes about you:

[32]"'King Demetrius to the noble Lasthenes, greetings. [33]I have decided to grant the Jewish nation certain benefits because they are our loyal allies and keep their treaty obligations. [34]I confirm their rights to the land of Judaea and the three regions of Ephraim, Lydda, and Arimathea, which are hereby annexed to Judaea from Samaria with all the lands belonging to them. This will be of benefit to everyone who goes to Jerusalem to offer sacrifice, since payments of the annual tax on produce and fruit from these lands will no longer be made to the king, but to the Temple. [35]And I also grant them relief from the payment of revenues now due to me from tithes, tolls, salt taxes, and special taxes. [36]None of the provisions mentioned in this letter shall ever be cancelled in the future.

[37]"'You are required to see that a complete copy of this decree is made and given to Jonathan, to be posted in a prominent place on the Temple hill.'"

Jonathan Helps Demetrius the Second

38 When King Demetrius saw that the land was peaceful under his rule and there was no further resistance, he disbanded his whole army and sent everyone home, except the soldiers he had hired from the Greek islands. This made all the soldiers who had served under his predecessors hate him because they had lost their source of income. [39]One of Alexander's former supporters, Trypho, saw that all the soldiers were complaining about Demetrius, so he went to Imalkue, the Arab who was responsible for bringing up Alexander's young son Antiochus. [40]Trypho stayed there for a long time and kept urging Imalkue to hand the boy over to him, so that he could make him king in place of his father. He also told Imalkue about the decrees of Demetrius and how the soldiers hated him.

41 Jonathan sent a message to King Demetrius asking him to remove his troops from the fort in Jerusalem and from the fortresses in Judaea, since they kept harassing the Jews. [42]Demetrius replied: "I will do what you request, and when the opportunity presents itself, I will bestow upon you and your nation the

---

[h]THE YEAR 167: *This corresponds to 145 B.C.*
[i]*Probable text* three regions of Samaria; *Greek* three regions and Samaria.
11.34: 1 Macc 10.30

highest honours. ⁴³But now you can help me by sending soldiers to fight for me, because all my troops have revolted."

44 So Jonathan sent three thousand trained soldiers to Antioch. The king was delighted when they arrived, ⁴⁵because a mob of 120,000 had gathered in the city determined to kill him. ⁴⁶But he escaped to the palace while the mob took control of the streets and began to riot. ⁴⁷Then the king called on the Jewish soldiers for help, and they all rushed to his aid. They went through the whole city and killed at least 100,000 people. ⁴⁸They saved the king's life, but they plundered and burnt the city. ⁴⁹When the people saw that the Jews had complete control of the city, they lost courage and appealed to the king, requesting ⁵⁰him to arrange a truce and stop the Jewish attack. ⁵¹The rebels threw down their arms and surrendered. The king and everyone in his kingdom now had great respect for the Jews, who returned to Jerusalem with a great deal of loot. ⁵²Demetrius was firmly established as king, and the country was at peace under his rule, ⁵³but he broke all his promises and turned against Jonathan. He did not reward him for his loyal service, but instead continued to harass him.

Jonathan Supports Antiochus the Sixth

54 Some time later, Trypho returned with the young boy Antiochus and crowned him king. ⁵⁵All the soldiers that Demetrius had dismissed then came to the support of the young king. They defeated Demetrius, and he fled. ⁵⁶Trypho captured the elephants and took control of Antioch. ⁵⁷The young King Antiochus wrote to Jonathan and confirmed him as High Priest and as ruler over the four regions and gave him the title "Friend of the King." ⁵⁸He sent him a gold dinner-service and authorized him to drink from gold cups, to wear a royal robe, and to wear the gold shoulder buckle awarded to "Relatives of the King." ⁵⁹He also appointed Jonathan's brother Simon as governor of the territory from the Phoenician coast to the Egyptian border. 60 Jonathan then marched with his army through the towns of Greater Syria, and all the Syrian forces joined him as allies. He went to Ashkelon, where the people welcomed him with great honours. ⁶¹Then he went to Gaza, but the people there barred their gates against him. So he laid siege to the city and burnt and looted the surrounding area. ⁶²The people of Gaza then asked for peace, and Jonathan arranged a truce. He took the sons of the leaders and sent them to Jerusalem as hostages. After that he marched on as far as Damascus.

63 Jonathan learnt that the officers of Demetrius had come to Kedesh in Galilee with a large army, intending to keep him from carrying out his plan. ⁶⁴So he left his brother Simon in Judaea and set out to meet them in battle. ⁶⁵Then Simon laid siege to Bethzur and fought against it for a long time. ⁶⁶The people asked for peace terms, and Simon agreed. He then took over the town, drove the people out, and stationed a detachment of troops there.

67 Jonathan and his army set up camp by Lake Galilee. Early the next morning he marched his troops to the plain of Hazor, ⁶⁸where the main force of the foreign army was advancing to meet him. Unknown to Jonathan, they had left a detachment of troops in ambush in the mountains, ⁶⁹and when the men in ambush came out and attacked, ⁷⁰Jonathan's entire army turned and ran. No one was left, except two officers, Mattathias son of Absalom and Judas son of Chalphi. ⁷¹Jonathan was humiliated, so he tore his clothes, threw dust on his head, and prayed. ⁷²Then he turned back to the battle, crushed the enemy, and put them to flight. ⁷³When his own fleeing soldiers saw this, they turned back and joined him in pursuit. They chased the enemy all the way back to their camp at Kedesh and then took over the camp. ⁷⁴At least three thousand enemy soldiers were killed that day. Jonathan then returned to Jerusalem.

Alliances with Rome and Sparta

12 When Jonathan saw that things were working out to his advantage, he chose ambassadors and sent them to Rome to confirm and renew friendship with the Romans. ²He also sent letters with a similar message to Sparta and other places. ³The ambassadors went to Rome, where they were admitted to the Senate chamber, and reported that the High Priest Jonathan and the Jewish nation had sent them to renew the earlier ties of friendship and alliance with Rome. ⁴The Romans provided them with letters to the authorities in each country through which they would pass, guaranteeing them safe conduct in their return to the land of Judaea.

5 This is a copy of the letter Jonathan wrote to the Spartans:

⁶"Jonathan the High Priest, the national council of leaders, the priests, and the rest of the people of Judaea, to our brothers in Sparta, greetings. ⁷At an earlier time, your King Arius sent a letter to our High Priest Onias, stating that our two nations are related, as the attached copy shows. ⁸Onias received your ambassador with full honours and acknowledged receipt of your letter, which declared our alliance and friendship. ⁹And now, although we are not in need of such alliances, since we find our source of strength in the holy books we possess, ¹⁰we have written to renew our ties of brotherhood and friendship with you. We do not wish to become total strangers, and it has now been many years since your last communication. ¹¹Throughout the years we have taken every opportunity, on our festival days and other suitable days, to remember you when we have offered our sacrifices and made our prayers, as it is fitting and proper for brothers to do. ¹²We also are pleased that fame has come to you. ¹³But we have had one series of troubles after another and have had to fight many wars, because we have been under constant attack by surrounding nations. ¹⁴During this time of war, we did not wish to trouble you or our other allies and friends, ¹⁵since we do have the help of the Lord, who has defeated our enemies and rescued us from them. ¹⁶So we have chosen Numenius son of Antiochus together with Antipater son of Jason and sent them as ambassadors to Rome to renew our ties of friendship and alliance with the Romans. ¹⁷We have also ordered them to go to you with our greetings and deliver this letter about the renewal of our ties of brotherhood. ¹⁸And now we request an answer to this letter.

¹⁹"The following is a copy of the earlier letter:

²⁰"'King Arius of Sparta to Onias the High Priest, greetings. ²¹We have found a document about the Spartans and the Jews indicating that we are related and that both our nations are descended from Abraham. ²²Now that we have discovered this, please send us a report about your situation. ²³In reply, we will send you a letter indicating that we are willing to share our possessions, including livestock and property, if you will do the same. We have given orders to our ambassadors to give you a full report about these matters.'"

Campaigns of Jonathan and Simon

²⁴Jonathan learnt that the officers of Demetrius had returned to attack him with an even larger army than before. ²⁵Jonathan did not want to give them an opportunity to penetrate his own territory, so he left Jerusalem and went to meet them in the region of Hamath. ²⁶Jonathan sent spies into the enemy camp, who reported to him that the enemy forces were making plans to attack the Jews by night. ²⁷At sunset Jonathan ordered all his soldiers to be on the alert and to have their weapons ready for a surprise attack any time during the night. He also stationed guards all round the

They were panic-stricken and fled, leaving their campfires burning (12.28)

camp. ²⁸When the enemy soldiers learnt that Jonathan and his men were ready for battle, they were panic-stricken and fled, leaving their campfires burning. ²⁹Jonathan and his men saw the campfires but did not realize what had happened until the next morning. ³⁰Jonathan then set out after them, but he could not overtake them because they had already crossed the River Eleutherus. ³¹Then Jonathan turned aside and attacked a tribe of Arabs called Zabadeans. He defeated them and plundered their possessions. ³²Then he broke camp and went to Damascus, inspecting the entire area along the way.

33 Meanwhile, Simon had also set out on a campaign and had advanced as far as Ashkelon and the neighbouring fortresses. Then he turned aside to Joppa 34 and stationed a detachment of soldiers there because he had heard that the people were planning to hand over the fortress of Joppa to the soldiers of Demetrius.

35 When Jonathan returned, he called the council of the leaders together and made plans with them to build fortresses in Judaea, 36 to increase the height of the walls of Jerusalem, and to build a high wall to separate the fort from the city. This would isolate the fort, making it impossible for the enemy to buy or sell anything. 37 The people worked together to strengthen the city's defences because a part of the east wall along the valley of the Kidron had collapsed and the Chaphenatha section was in need of repair. 38 Simon also rebuilt the town of Adida in the foothills. He fortified it and constructed barred gates for it.

Trypho Captures Jonathan

39 Then Trypho plotted a rebellion against King Antiochus so that he could make himself king of Syria. 40 He was afraid, however, that Jonathan would not agree to this and would go to war against him to prevent it. So Trypho got his army ready and went to Beth Shan in the hope of capturing Jonathan and putting him to death. 41 But Jonathan also came to Beth Shan with forty thousand well-trained soldiers. 42 When Trypho saw how large an army Jonathan had brought with him, he was afraid to take action. 43 So he received Jonathan with all honours, presented him to all his advisers, gave him gifts, and ordered his advisers and soldiers to obey Jonathan as they would obey him. 44 He asked Jonathan, "Why have you put these soldiers to so much trouble when we are not at war? 45 Why don't you send them home? Choose a few men to stay with you, and then accompany me to Ptolemais. I will hand the city over to you, as well as the rest of the fortresses, the troops, and all the officials. Then I will turn round and leave. In fact, that's why I am here." 46 Jonathan believed him, and following his advice, sent his soldiers back to Judaea. 47 He took three thousand men with him, but left two thousand of them in Galilee, while only a thousand accompanied him the rest of the way. 48 But when Jonathan entered Ptolemais, the people of the city locked the gates, arrested him, and killed everyone who had come with him.

49 Trypho sent infantry and cavalry units to Galilee and the Valley of Jezreel to kill the rest of Jonathan's soldiers. 50 The Jewish troops thought that Jonathan had been captured and killed, along with all those who had accompanied him, so they encouraged one another and marched out in battle formation. 51 When the approaching enemy forces saw that the Jews were ready to fight for their lives, they turned back. 52 Then the Jewish soldiers returned to Judaea safely, but terribly afraid. The whole nation was in deep mourning, assuming that Jonathan and all his men had been killed. 53 All the surrounding nations now tried to destroy them. They thought that the Jews had no leaders or allies and that the time was ripe to annihilate them and put an end to their history.

Simon Leads the Jews

13 Simon learnt that Trypho had assembled a large army and that he had plans to invade Judaea and devastate it. 2 He realized that this news had brought panic and fear to the people, so he went to Jerusalem, called the people together, 3 and tried to encourage them by saying, "You know how much my father's family, my brothers, and I have done for the sake of the Law of Moses and the Temple. You also know about the wars we have fought and the troubles we have had. 4 All my brothers have been killed fighting for our Law, our Temple, and our nation, and I am the only one left. 5 But never let it be said that I tried to save my own life in a time of danger; I do not consider myself better than my brothers. 6 Not in the least! It is true that in their hatred all the Gentile nations have gathered together to destroy us, but I will fight to defend my nation, the Temple, and your loved ones."

7 These words immediately revived the morale of the people, 8 and they answered with a loud shout, "You are now our leader in place of your brothers Judas and Jonathan. 9 Fight our wars, and we will do whatever you ask." 10 So Simon gathered together all the soldiers and hurried to complete the walls of Jerusalem and to strengthen all its defences. 11 He sent Jonathan son of Absalom to Joppa with a

large army. This Jonathan drove out the people who were there and occupied the town.

12 Trypho left Ptolemais with a large army to invade Judaea, taking Simon's brother Jonathan along with him as a prisoner. 13 Simon set up camp at Adida at the edge of the plain. 14 When Trypho learnt that Simon had succeeded his brother Jonathan and that he was ready to meet him in battle, he sent this message to him: 15 "I am holding your brother Jonathan under arrest because while he was in office he did not pay his debts to the royal treasury. 16 However, I will release him if you will pay me three thousand kilogrammes of silver and send two of his sons as hostages to guarantee that he will not revolt against us when he is released."

17 Although Simon knew that they were deceiving him, he sent for the money and the two sons because he did not want to arouse the hostility of the Jews. 18 He was afraid that they might later say that Jonathan was put to death because Simon would not send the money and the boys. 19 So he did as Trypho had demanded, but Trypho broke his promise and did not release Jonathan.

20 Then Trypho made a move to invade the land and destroy it, circling round by the road to Adora. But Simon and his army moved along facing him wherever he went. 21 The enemy soldiers in the fort in Jerusalem kept sending messengers to Trypho urging him to come to them quickly by way of the desert and to send them supplies. 22 Trypho got all his cavalry ready for the invasion, but that night there was a heavy snowstorm, and he was not able to move up into the hills. So he withdrew and went into Gilead. 23 When he was near Baskama, he had Jonathan put to death and his body was buried there. 24 Then Trypho turned and went back to his own country.

25 Simon had the body of his brother Jonathan brought to Modein, to be buried in the town of their ancestors. 26 Everyone in Israel was in deep sorrow at the loss of Jonathan, and they mourned for him a long time. 27 Over the tomb of his father and his brothers Simon built a high monument that could be seen from a great distance. It was covered on the front and the back with polished stone. 28 He constructed seven pyramids side by side

for his father, his mother, and his four brothers. 29 For the pyramids he created a setting of tall columns on which there were carvings. Some of these carvings were of suits of armour and some were of ships. It was a monument to their victories, which travellers from overseas could visit. *j* 30 The tomb which he built in Modein is still there today.

31 Meanwhile, Trypho assassinated the young king, Antiochus the Sixth, 32 and took over his kingdom in Syria. He brought great troubles on that country.

33 Simon rebuilt the fortresses of Judaea with high towers, strong walls, and barred gates; then he placed stores of supplies there. 34 He sent ambassadors to King Demetrius the Second to ask for tax relief for the land, since Trypho was doing nothing but rob them. 35 Demetrius sent the following letter in reply:

36 "King Demetrius to the High Priest Simon, the friend of kings, to the Jewish nation, and to their leaders, greetings. 37 I have received the gold crown and the gold palm branch which you sent, and I am prepared to make a peace treaty with you and to instruct our tax officials to grant you exemptions. 38 Our previous agreements with you are confirmed, and the fortresses which you have built are to remain yours. 39 I grant you pardon for treaty violations committed up to the present date, and I release you from payment of the special tax still due and any other taxes that have been collected up to this time in Jerusalem. 40 All Jews who are qualified may enrol in the royal service. Let us have peace."

41 So in the year 170 *k* the yoke of the Gentile oppressors was removed from the Jews. 42 People began to date their documents and contracts with these words: "In the first year of Simon, the great High Priest, commander and leader of the Jews."

43 At that time Simon laid siege to Gezer and surrounded it with his army. He built a movable siege-platform, brought it up to the town wall, attacked one of the towers, and captured it. 44 The men who had been on the siege-platform then moved rapidly into the town, and this created great confusion. 45 The men of the town, their wives, and their children

---

j Verses 28–29 in Greek are unclear.   *k THE YEAR 170: This corresponds to 142 B.C.*
13.43: 2 Macc 10.32–38

tore their clothes in distress and climbed up on the top of the town wall. They pleaded loudly with Simon for a truce. 46"Have mercy on us," they begged. "Don't punish us as we deserve!"

47 So Simon came to terms with them and ended the fighting. He made the people leave the town; then he purified the houses in which there had been idols. When that was done, he and his men entered the town singing hymns and songs of praise. 48He got rid of everything that would make the town ritually unclean and settled it with men who would obey every command contained in the Law of Moses. He strengthened the defences of the town and built himself a palace there.

49 The men in the fort in Jerusalem were now prevented from leaving to buy or sell anything. They were suffering from severe hunger and many of them had died of starvation. 50Finally they appealed to Simon for a truce. He agreed, removed them from the fort, and purified it. 51On the twenty-third day of the second month, in the year 171,¹ there was a great celebration in the city because this terrible threat to the security of Israel had been ended. Simon and his men entered the fort singing hymns of praise and thanksgiving, while carrying palm branches and playing harps, cymbals, and lyres. 52Simon issued a decree that the day should be joyfully celebrated every year. He strengthened the defences of the Temple hill on the side facing the fort, and he and his men made their headquarters there. 53Simon's son John was now a grown man, so Simon made him commander of the whole army, and John set up his headquarters at Gezer.

In Praise of Simon

14 In the year 172ᵐ King Demetrius the Second gathered his army and went to Media to seek additional help for his war against Trypho. 2When King Arsaces the Sixth of Persia and Media heard that Demetrius had entered his territory, he sent one of his commanders with some troops to capture Demetrius alive. 3They attacked and defeated the army of Demetrius, took him captive, and brought him back to King Arsaces, who threw him in prison.

4 The land of Judaea was at peace as long as Simon lived. During his entire reign, he used his position of power and influence to do what was good for his people, and they were always pleased with him as their ruler. 5He added to his reputation when he captured the port of Joppa and opened up the route to the Greek islands. 6He not only enlarged the territory of his nation and gained control of the whole country, 7but he brought back many prisoners of war and captured Gezer, Bethzur, and the fort in Jerusalem. He purified the fort, and there was no one to oppose him.

8 The Jews farmed their land in peace; the land produced its crops and the trees bore fruit. 9The young men showed off their splendid military uniforms, while the old men sat round the city squares and talked about the great things that had happened. 10Simon supplied the cities with food and provided them with weapons of defence. His fame spread everywhere. 11He brought peace to the country, and Israel's joy knew no bounds. 12Everyone lived in peace among his own vineyards and fig-trees, and no one made them afraid. 13In those days all the enemy kings had been defeated, and there was no one left in the land to fight the Jews. 14Simon provided help for all the poor among his people, and guided by the Law of Moses, he got rid of all wicked and lawless men. 15He provided the Temple with splendid furnishings and added a large number of utensils for use in worship.

16 When the news that Jonathan had died reached Rome and Sparta, it brought great sorrow. 17But when the Spartans heard that Simon had succeeded his brother as High Priest and that he was in control of the country and its towns, 18they engraved on bronze tablets a renewal of the treaty of friendship which they had made with his brothers Judas and Jonathan and sent the tablets to him. 19These were read to the assembly in Jerusalem. 20What follows is a copy of the letter sent by the Spartans:

"The people of Sparta and their rulers to Simon the High Priest, to the leaders and the priests of the Jews, and to all our Jewish brothers, greetings. 21The delegation that you sent to our people has told us how respected and renowned you are. Their visit has been a source of joy for us, 22and a report of their visit has been written down in our public

---

¹THE YEAR 171: *This corresponds to 141* B.C.   ᵐTHE YEAR 172: *This corresponds to 140* B.C.
14.18: 1 Macc 8.22

records, as follows: 'Numenius son of Antiochus and Antipater son of Jason, honoured representatives of the Jews, appeared before us to renew their treaty of friendship. [23] The assembly of the people was pleased to receive these men with all honours and to place a copy of their report in the public archives, so that the people of Sparta may have it on record. A copy of this document has been made for the High Priest Simon.' "

24 Later, Simon sent Numenius to Rome with the gift of a large gold shield weighing five hundred kilogrammes, to confirm the Jews' alliance with the Romans.

25 When the people of Israel heard about all this, they asked themselves, "How can we express our thanks to Simon and his sons? [26] He, his brothers, and his father's whole family have been towers of strength for our nation. They have fought off our enemies and set the nation free."

So they recorded this on bronze tablets and set them up on columns on Mount Zion. [27] The inscription read as follows:

"On the eighteenth day of the month of Elul in the year 172,[n] that is, in the third year of Simon, the High Priest,[o] [28] at a great assembly of priests, people, officials, and national leaders the following facts were made known to us: [29] Often when wars broke out in the country, Simon son of Mattathias, a priest of the Jehoiarib family, and his brothers risked their lives in protecting our nation, our Temple, and our Law against our enemies. They have brought great glory to our nation. [30] Jonathan united our people and became the High Priest before he died. [31] The enemies of the Jews plotted to invade the land and defile the Temple. [32] Then Simon assumed command and fought for his country. He spent a large amount of his own money to provide weapons and pay for his nation's armed forces. [33] He fortified the towns of Judaea, and especially Bethzur on the border, where enemy weapons had previously been stored. He stationed a detachment of soldiers there. [34] He fortified the seaport of Joppa as well as the city of Gezer on the border of Ashdod, which was previously occupied by enemy soldiers. He settled Jews there and provided the towns with everything that the people needed.[p] [35] When the people saw Simon's patriotism and how he wanted to bring glory to his nation, they made him their leader and High Priest. They did this because of all that he had accomplished through his loyalty and because he had brought about justice and had tried in every way to bring glory to his nation.

[36] "Under his leadership the Gentiles were driven out of the land. Enemy soldiers were forced out of the area north of the Temple, where they had built the fort, from which the soldiers used to go out and defile the holy Temple. [37] Simon settled Jews in the fort, strengthened it for the security of the country and the city of Jerusalem, and increased the height of the city walls. [38] As a result, King Demetrius confirmed him as High Priest, [39] gave him the title of 'Friend of the King,' and treated him with great honour. [40] Demetrius did this because he had heard that the Romans were calling the Jews their friends, allies, and brothers and that they had received Simon's delegation with full honours.

[41] "Therefore,[q] the Jews and their priests are happy to have Simon and his descendants as their leaders and High Priests, until a true prophet appears. [42] Simon shall govern their country, have charge of the Temple, and shall be their military commander. He shall be in charge of military supplies fortifications, and public works. [43] The people must obey him in everything. All government contracts shall be drawn up in his name. He shall have the right to wear royal robes with the gold shoulder buckle.

[44] "No one, priest or people, shall have the legal right to annul any of these decisions, to alter or change any of Simon's orders, to convene any assembly in the country without his permission, or to wear royal robes

---

[n] THE YEAR 172: *This corresponds to 140 B.C.*
[o] *Greek has an additional word, the meaning of which is unclear.*
[p] that the people needed; *or* that was needed to keep them in repair.
[q] Therefore; *some manuscripts have* and that.

with the gold shoulder buckle. 45 Anyone who disobeys or disregards these regulations shall be subject to punishment.

46 "The people gave their unanimous approval to grant Simon the right to act in accordance with these regulations. 47 Simon consented and agreed to be supreme leader: High Priest, commander of the armies, and governor of the Jews and the priests."

48 It was decided that this declaration should be engraved on bronze tablets and set up in a prominent place within the Temple area 49 and that copies should be placed in the Temple treasury, where Simon and his sons would have access to them.

Antiochus the Seventh Asks for Simon's Support

15 From the Greek islands Antiochus son of King Demetrius wrote the following letter to Simon the High Priest and governor of the Jews and to the whole nation:

2 "King Antiochus to Simon, the High Priest and governor, and to the Jewish nation, greetings. 3 As you know, the kingdom of my ancestors has been seized by traitors. I have decided to reclaim it and restore its former greatness. I have raised a large army of mercenary troops and have fitted out warships. 4 I plan to invade the land and to attack those who have destroyed many of the towns and ruined the country.

5 "Now therefore, I confirm all exemptions from taxes and payments granted to you by former kings. 6 I authorize you to mint your own coins as legal currency in your own country. 7 Jerusalem and the Temple shall be free of taxation. All the weapons that you have manufactured and the defences you have built and now occupy shall remain yours. 8 In addition, all debts now owed to the royal treasury, or which may in the future fall due, are permanently cancelled. 9 As soon as I have regained control of my kingdom, I will confer upon you, your nation, and the Temple such great honours that the glory of your country will be evident to the whole world."

10 In the year 174 r Antiochus invaded the land of his ancestors. Most of the soldiers came over to his side, so that there were very few left with Trypho. 11 Trypho, pursued by Antiochus, fled to the coastal city of Dor, 12 realizing that he was in a desperate situation, now that all his troops had deserted him. 13 Then Antiochus laid siege to Dor with 120,000 well-trained soldiers and 8,000 cavalry. 14 With his ships joining the attack, he completely surrounded the town and brought such pressure on it that no one was able to enter or leave.

Rome Supports the Jews

15 Meanwhile, Numenius and those with him arrived in Jerusalem from Rome with the following letter addressed to various kings and countries:

16 "From Lucius, consul of the Romans, to King Ptolemy, greetings. 17 A delegation from our friends and allies the Jews has come to us to renew the earlier treaty of friendship and alliance. They were sent by the High Priest Simon and the Jewish people, 18 and they have brought as a gift a gold shield weighing five hundred kilogrammes. 19 So we have decided to write to various kings and countries urging them not to harm the Jews, their towns, or their country in any way. They must not make war against the Jews or give support to those who attack them. 20 We have decided to accept the shield and grant them protection. 21 Therefore if any traitors escape from Judaea and seek refuge in your land, hand them over to Simon the High Priest, so that he may punish them according to Jewish law."

22 Lucius wrote the same letter to King Demetrius, to Attalus, Ariarathes, and Arsaces, 23 and to all the following countries: Sampsames, Sparta, Delos, Myndos, Sicyon, Samos, Caria, Pamphylia, Lycia, Halicarnassus, Rhodes, Phaselis, Cos, Side, Aradus, Gortyna, Cnidus, Cyprus, and Cyrene. 24 A copy of the letter was also sent to Simon the High Priest.

Antiochus the Seventh Breaks with Simon

25 King Antiochus laid siege to Dor for the second time, keeping it under constant attack. He built siege-platforms, and his blockade kept Trypho and his men from

---

r THE YEAR 174: This corresponds to 138 B.C.
15.15: 1 Macc 12.16

going in or out. ²⁶ Simon sent two thousand well-trained soldiers to help Antiochus, as well as silver and gold and a great deal of equipment. ²⁷ But Antiochus refused to accept them, cancelled all the previous agreements that he had made with Simon, and became his enemy. ²⁸ Then Antiochus sent his trusted official Athenobius to negotiate with Simon. He said to Simon, "You are occupying Joppa, Gezer, and the fort in Jerusalem, cities that belong to my kingdom. ²⁹ You have devastated those regions and brought great trouble to the country. You have seized control of many places in my kingdom. ³⁰ Now you must hand back the cities that you have captured, and you must give me the tax money that you have taken from places that you occupied outside the territory of Judaea. ³¹ If you are unwilling to do this, then you must pay me seventeen thousand kilogrammes of silver, and seventeen thousand additional kilogrammes of silver to compensate me for damages and for lost taxes. If you refuse to do either of these, we will go to war against you."

32 When Athenobius came to Jerusalem and saw the splendour of Simon's court, the gold and silver dishes in his banqueting-hall, and the rest of the display of great wealth, he was amazed. He delivered the king's message to Simon, ³³ and Simon answered, "We have never taken land away from other nations or confiscated anything that belonged to other people. On the contrary, we have simply taken back property that we inherited from our ancestors, land that had been unjustly taken away from us by our enemies at one time or another. ³⁴ We are now only making use of this opportunity to recover our ancestral heritage. ³⁵ As for Joppa and Gezer, which you claim, we will give you 3,400 kilogrammes of silver, in spite of the fact that the people of those cities have done great harm to our nation."

Athenobius made no reply, ³⁶ but he returned to the king in a rage. When he told the king what Simon had said, and reported on the splendour of Simon's court and all that he had seen, the king became violently angry.

John's Victory over Cendebeus

37 In the meantime, Trypho had boarded a ship and escaped to the town of Orthosia. ³⁸ King Antiochus appointed Cendebeus as commander of the coastal area, provided him with infantry and cavalry, ³⁹ and gave him orders to move against Judaea. He also ordered him to rebuild the town of Kedron and fortify its gates, so that he could fight against the Jewish people. The king himself continued to pursue Trypho.

40 Cendebeus then came to Jamnia and began to harass the Jews by invading Judaea, capturing people, and murdering them. ⁴¹ He rebuilt Kedron and stationed some cavalry and infantry units there, so that they could make attacks and patrol the roads of Judaea, as the king had ordered.

16 Simon's son John left Gezer and went to report to his father what Cendebeus had done. ² Simon said to John and Judas, his two eldest sons, "All my father's family, my brothers, and I have fought Israel's battles all our lives, and many times we have been successful in saving Israel. ³ I am old now, but you, thanks to God, are in the prime of life. You must take my place and that of my brother in fighting for our nation. And may God himself be with you."

4 Then John raised an Israelite army of twenty thousand trained soldiers and cavalry and marched out against Cendebeus. They spent the night in Modein, ⁵ and then early the next morning they moved into the plain. There a large army of infantry and cavalry moved to meet them, but there was a river between the two armies. ⁶ John and his army took up battle positions facing the enemy, but when John saw that his soldiers were afraid to cross the river, he crossed ahead of them, and his men saw him and followed. ⁷ John divided his army and placed his cavalry in the middle of the infantry, because there was a large number of enemy cavalry. ⁸ The trumpets sounded the attack, and Cendebeus and his army were defeated, and many of them were killed. The rest ran back to their fortress at Kedron. ⁹ Judas was wounded in the battle, but his brother John continued to pursue the enemy as far as Kedron, which Cendebeus had rebuilt. ¹⁰ The escaping soldiers fled to the towers in the fields at Ashdod, and John set fire to the city. On that day, two thousand enemy soldiers were killed, and John returned safely to Judaea.

The Murder of Simon and Two of His Sons

11 Simon the High Priest had appointed Ptolemy son of Abubus commander for

the Plain of Jericho. Ptolemy was very rich, [12] because he was Simon's son-in-law. [13] But he became too ambitious and wanted to take over the country. So he devised a plan to assassinate Simon and his sons. [14] Simon, together with his sons Mattathias and Judas, was visiting the towns in the area, in order to see to their needs. They arrived in Jericho in the month of Shebat, the eleventh month, in the year 177. [s] [15] Ptolemy, still plotting to murder Simon and his two sons, received them in a small fortress called Dok, which he had built. He gave a great banquet for them, but he had men hidden within the fortress. [16] When Simon and his sons were drunk, Ptolemy and his men came out of hiding and with swords in their hands rushed into the banqueting-hall, where they killed Simon, his two sons, and some of the servants. [17] By this horrible act of treachery, Ptolemy returned evil for good.

18 Then Ptolemy wrote a report of what

he had done and sent it to the king. In the letter he requested that troops be sent to help him and that the country and the cities be handed over to him. [19] He wrote a letter to the army officers inviting them to join him and promising them silver, gold, and gifts. Then he sent some of his men to Gezer to kill John, [20] and others to take control of Jerusalem and the Temple hill. [21] But someone ran to Gezer ahead of Ptolemy's men and reported to John that his father and his brothers had been killed and that Ptolemy was sending his soldiers to kill him. [22] John was horrified at this news, but, because he had been warned in advance, he was able to capture and put to death the men who had been sent to kill him.

23 Now the rest of what John did from the time he succeeded his father: his wars, his deeds of courage, his rebuilding of walls, and his other achievements, [24] are all written in the chronicles of his reign as High Priest.

[s] THE YEAR 177: *This corresponds to 134 B.C.*

THE SECOND BOOK OF THE

MACCABEES

INTRODUCTION

The *Second book of the Maccabees* is a condensation of a five-volume history by Jason of Cyrene. The book reports events in Jewish history from the time of the High Priest, Onias the Third (about 180 B.C.), to the death of Nicanor (161 B.C.), and parallels in part the events described in the early chapters of *First Maccabees.* There is a strong emphasis on loyalty to the law and on God's reward to martyrs who die for their faith.

Outline of Contents

Letters to the Jews of Egypt and Preface   1.1—2.32
Struggles for the high priesthood   3.1—4.50
Antiochus Epiphanes and the persecution of the Jews   5.1—7.42
The victories of Judas   8.1—15.39

A Letter to the Jews in Egypt

1 "From the Jews of Jerusalem and Judaea to their brothers in Egypt, warm greetings.

2 "May God be good to you and keep the covenant he made with Abraham, Isaac, and Jacob, his faithful servants. 3 May he fill each of you with the desire to worship him and to do his will eagerly with all your heart and soul. 4 May he enable you to understand his Law and his commands. May he give you peace, 5 answer your prayers, forgive your sins, and never abandon you in times of trouble. 6 Here in Judaea we are now praying for you.

7 "In the year 169,[a] when Demetrius the Second was king of Syria, we wrote to tell you about the persecution and the hard times that came upon us in the years after Jason revolted against authority in the Holy Land. 8 Jason and his men set fire to the Temple gates and slaughtered innocent people. Then we prayed to the Lord and he answered our prayers. So we sacrificed animals, gave offerings of grain, lit the lamps in the Temple, and set out the sacred loaves. 9 This is why we urge you to celebrate in the month of Kislev a festival similar to the Festival of Shelters. Written in the year 188."[b]

A LETTER TO ARISTOBULUS
The Death of King Antiochus

10 "From the Jews of Jerusalem and Judaea, the Jewish Senate, and Judas, to Aristobulus, a descendant of priests and the teacher of King Ptolemy, and to the Jews in Egypt, greetings and good health.

11 "We thank God because he saved us from great danger. We were like men ready to fight against a king, 12 but God drove the enemy from our holy city. 13 When King Antiochus arrived in Persia, his army seemed impossible to defeat, but they were cut to pieces in the temple of the goddess Nanea by an act of treachery on the part of her priests. 14 King Antiochus had gone to the temple with some of his most trusted advisers, so that he might marry the goddess and then take away most of the temple treasures as a wedding gift. 15 After the priests had laid out the treasure, he and a few of his men went into the temple to collect it. But the priests closed the doors behind him 16 and stoned him and his men from trapdoors hidden in the ceiling. Then they cut up the bodies and threw the heads to the people outside. 17 Praise God for punishing those evil men! Praise him for everything!

Fire Consumes Nehemiah's Sacrifice

18 "On the twenty-fifth day of the month of Kislev we will celebrate the Festival of Rededication just as we celebrate the Festival of Shelters. We thought it important to remind you of this, so that you too may celebrate this festival. In this way you will remember how fire appeared when Nehemiah offered sacrifices after he had rebuilt the Temple and the altar. 19 At the time when our ancestors were being taken to exile in Persia, a few devout priests took some fire from the altar and secretly hid it in the bottom of a dry cistern. They hid the fire so well that no one ever discovered it. 20 Years later, when it pleased God, the Persian emperor sent Nehemiah back to Jerusalem, and Nehemiah told the descendants of those priests to find the fire. They reported to us that they had found no fire but only some oily liquid. Nehemiah then told them to scoop some up and bring it to him. 21 When everything for the sacrifice had been placed on the altar, he told the priests to pour the liquid over both the wood and the sacrifice. 22 After this was done and some time had passed, the sun appeared from behind the clouds, and suddenly everything on the altar burst into flames. Everyone looked on in amazement. 23 Then, while the fire was consuming the sacrifice, Jonathan the High Priest led the people in prayer, and Nehemiah and all the people responded.

Nehemiah's Prayer

24 "Nehemiah's prayer went something like this: 'Lord God, Creator of all things, you are awesome and strong, yet merciful and just. You alone are king. No one but you is kind; 25 no one but you is gracious and just. You are almighty and eternal, for ever ready to rescue Israel from trouble. You chose our ancestors to be your own special people. 26 Accept this sacrifice which we offer on behalf of all Israel; protect your chosen people and make us holy. 27 Free those who are slaves in foreign lands and gather together our scattered people. Have mercy on our people, who are ill-treated and despised, so that all other nations will know that

---

[a] THE YEAR 169: *This corresponds to 143 B.C.*   [b] THE YEAR 188: *This corresponds to 124 B.C.*
1.13–16: 1 Macc 6.1–4; 2 Macc 9.1–10

Everyone looked on in amazement (1.22)

you are our God. ²⁸ Punish the brutal and
arrogant people who have oppressed us,
²⁹ and then establish your people in your
holy land, as Moses said you would.'

The Persian Emperor Hears about the Fire

30 "Then the priests sang hymns.
³¹ After the sacrifices had been consumed,
Nehemiah gave orders for the rest of the
liquid to be poured over some large stones.
³² Immediately a fire blazed up, but it was
extinguished by a flame from the fire on
the altar.

33 "News of what had happened spread
everywhere. The Persian emperor heard
that a liquid had been found in the place
where the priests had hidden the altar
fire, just before they were taken into exile.
He also heard that Nehemiah and his
friends had used this liquid to burn the
sacrifice on the altar. ³⁴ When the emperor
investigated the matter and found out that
this was true, he had the area fenced off
and made into a shrine. ³⁵ It became a
substantial source of income for him, and
he used the money for gifts to anyone
who was in his good favour. ³⁶ Nehemiah
and his friends called the liquid *nephthar*,
which means 'purification,' but most
people call it 'naphtha.'

Jeremiah Hides the Tent of the Lord's Presence

2 "We know from the records that
Jeremiah the prophet instructed the
people who were being taken into exile
to hide some of the fire from the altar, as
we have just mentioned. ² We also know
that he taught them God's Law and
warned them not to be deceived by the
ornamented gold and silver idols which
they would see in the land of their exile.
³ And then he urged them never to
abandon the Law.

4 "These same records also tell us that
Jeremiah, acting under divine guidance,
commanded the Tent of the Lord's
Presence and the Covenant Box to follow
him to the mountain where Moses had
looked down on the land which God had
promised our people. ⁵ When Jeremiah got
to the mountain, he found a huge cave and
there he hid the Tent of the Lord's
Presence, the Covenant Box, and the altar
of incense. Then he sealed up the entrance.

6 "Some of Jeremiah's friends tried to
follow him and mark the way, but they
could not find the cave. ⁷ When Jeremiah
learnt what they had done, he reprimanded them, saying, 'No one must
know about this place until God gathers
his people together again and shows them

They could not find the cave (2.6)

mercy. ⁸At that time he will reveal where these things are hidden, and the dazzling light of his presence will be seen in the cloud, as it was in the time of Moses and on the occasion when Solomon prayed that the Temple might be dedicated in holy splendour.'

How Solomon Celebrated the Festival

9 "We are also told how the wise King Solomon offered a sacrifice of dedication at the completion of the Temple, ¹⁰and that when he prayed, fire came down from heaven and consumed the sacrifices, just as it had done earlier when Moses prayed. ¹¹Moses had explained that the sin-offering was consumed by fire because it was not eaten. ¹²Solomon celebrated the festival for eight days.

Nehemiah's Library

13 "These same facts are found in the royal records and in the memoirs of Nehemiah, who established a library and collected the writings of David, letters of the kings concerning offerings, and books about the kings and prophets. ¹⁴Judas also collected the books that had been scattered because of the war, and we still have them. ¹⁵If you ever need any of these books, let us know, and we will send them.

An Invitation to Celebrate the Festival

16 "Since we are about to celebrate the Festival of Rededication, we are writing to you, advising you to celebrate it as well. ¹⁷God has saved all his people and has restored to all of us our holy land, the kingship, the priesthood, and the Temple services, ¹⁸just as he promised in his Law. He has rescued us from terrible evils and has purified the Temple, and we are confident that in his mercy he will soon gather us to his holy Temple from every nation under the sun."

Author's Preface

19 Jason of Cyrene has recorded in five volumes the story of Judas Maccabaeus and his brothers, the purification of the great Temple, and the dedication of its altar. ²⁰He has described the battles with Antiochus Epiphanes and with his son Eupator, ²¹and he has told of the heavenly visions that appeared to those who fought bravely and enthusiastically to defend Judaism. Our forces were few in number, but they plundered the entire country and routed the heathen forces. ²²They recaptured the Temple famous throughout the world, liberated Jerusalem, and restored the laws that were in danger of being abolished. They were able to do all these things because the Lord was merciful and kind to them.

23 I will now try to summarize in a single book the five volumes written by Jason. ²⁴The number of details and the

2.8: Ex 16.10; 24.16; 1 Kgs 8.10-11   **2.16:** 1 Macc 4.59

bulk of material can be overwhelming for anyone who wants to read an account of the events. 25 But I have attempted to simplify it for all readers; those who read for sheer pleasure will find enjoyment and those who want to memorize the facts will not find it difficult. 26 Writing such a summary is a difficult task, demanding hard work and sleepless nights. 27 It is as difficult as preparing a banquet that people of different tastes will enjoy. But I am happy to undergo this hardship in order to please my readers. 28 I will leave the matter of detail to the original author and attempt to give only a summary of the events. 29 I am not the builder of a new house who is concerned with every detail of the structure, but simply a painter whose only concern is to make the house look attractive. 30 The historian must master his subject, examine every detail, and then explain it carefully, 31 but whoever is merely writing a summary should be permitted to give a brief account without going into a detailed discussion. 32 So then, without any further comment, I will begin my story. It would be foolish to write such a long introduction that the story itself would have to be cut short.

The Argument between Onias and Simon

3 When Onias c was High Priest in Jerusalem, the holy city enjoyed peace and prosperity, and its laws were strictly obeyed, because he was devout and hated evil. 2 The kings of Syria and Egypt honoured the Temple and presented it with expensive gifts, 3 and King Seleucus, d ruler of all Asia, even used to pay the costs of the Temple sacrifices from the revenues he collected.

4 But a man by the name of Simon, of the tribe of Bilgah, e the chief administrative official of the Temple, lost an argument he had with Onias over the regulations governing the city market. 5 At this time Apollonius son of Thraseus was the governor of Greater Syria. Simon went to him 6 and said that there was so much money in the Temple treasury that it could not be counted, and since the money was not needed for sacrifices, it might as well be placed under the king's control.

Heliodorus Is Sent to Jerusalem

7 When Apollonius met the king, he told him about the money, and the king

ordered Heliodorus, his chief minister, to get it for him. 8 Heliodorus set out at once on his mission, but he claimed that he was only making a tour of inspection of the cities of Greater Syria. 9 After he had arrived in Jerusalem and had been warmly received by the High Priest, he explained the real reason for his visit and asked if what he had been told was true. 10-11 The High Priest then stated that Simon, that devil of a man, had not been telling the truth. There was indeed some money in the Temple treasury, but part of it was set aside for widows and orphans and part of it belonged to Hyrcanus son of Tobias, a very important man. He also pointed out that the total amount was only thirteen thousand kilogrammes of silver and six thousand five hundred kilogrammes of gold. 12 He added that it was absolutely impossible that anyone should be permitted to take the money of those people who had placed their trust in the sanctity and safety of this world-famous Temple.

Heliodorus Plans to Enter the Temple

13 But Heliodorus insisted that the money should be taken for the royal treasury, as the king had ordered. 14 So he fixed a day and went into the Temple to supervise the counting of the money. This caused an uproar throughout the entire city. 15 Priests, wearing their priestly robes, threw themselves face downwards before the altar and begged God to keep the money safe, since he had given the laws designed to protect the money that people deposited in the Temple. 16 It was heartbreaking to see the High Priest. His face turned pale, revealing the agony of his soul, 17 and his body was trembling with fear, reflecting the pain in his heart. 18 People ran from their houses to join together in prayer that the Temple might not be defiled. 19 Women, wearing nothing but skirts of sackcloth, crowded the streets. Young girls whose parents had never allowed them to be seen in public ran to the gates or to the walls of the city, or just stared out of their windows. 20 But wherever they went, they lifted their hands to God in prayer. 21 What a pitiful sight it was to see the High Priest in such great agony and frustration and to see everyone in the

c ONIAS: This is Onias the Third, son of Simon the Second (see 4.4–6; Sir 50.1–21).
d SELEUCUS: This is Seleucus the Fourth, known as Philopator, son of Antiochus the Third, 187–175 B.C. e Some ancient translations Bilgah (see Neh 12.5,18); Greek Benjamin.

city confused and lying face downwards on the ground.

The Lord Protects His Temple

22 While everyone was begging the Lord Almighty to protect the money that had been entrusted to his care, 23 Heliodorus went on with his plan. 24 But at the very moment that he and his bodyguard arrived at the treasury, the Lord of all supernatural powers caused such a vision to appear that everyone who had dared to enter with Heliodorus was panic-stricken and weak with fear at this display of the Lord's power. 25 In the vision they saw a horse and a rider. The horse had a richly decorated bridle, and its rider, dressed in gold armour, was frightening. Suddenly the horse rushed at Heliodorus, then reared up and struck at him with its hoofs. 26 Heliodorus also saw two unusually strong and handsome young men, wearing very fine clothes. They stood on either side of him and beat him unmercifully. 27 He immediately fell to the ground unconscious, and his men put him on a stretcher 28 and carried him out. Only a moment earlier this man had entered the treasury with a large group of men, including all his bodyguard, but now he was being carried away helpless. So they all[f] openly acknowledged the mighty power of God.

Onias Prays for Heliodorus's Recovery

29 Heliodorus lay there unable to speak and without hope of recovery from this demonstration of God's power. 30 But the Jews praised Almighty God because he had miraculously protected his Temple and had brought great happiness where only minutes before there had been fear and confusion. 31 Some of Heliodorus's friends quickly asked Onias the High Priest to pray that the Most High would spare the life of this man who was at the point of death. 32 So the High Priest offered a sacrifice in the hope that God would save Heliodorus, for he did not want the king to think that the Jews had done this to the man he had sent. 33 While Onias was offering the sacrifice, the two young men, wearing the same clothes as before, again appeared to Heliodorus and said, "Be grateful to the High Priest; the Lord has spared your life because of him. 34 Remember that it was the Lord of heaven who punished you. Now go and

tell everyone of his great power." When they had said this, they disappeared.

Heliodorus Praises God

35 So Heliodorus offered a sacrifice to the Lord and made many promises, because the Lord had spared his life. Then he said good-bye to Onias and returned with his army to the king. 36 There he told everyone what the Lord, the most powerful of all gods, had done.

37 When the king asked Heliodorus who would be the best man to send on the next mission to Jerusalem, Heliodorus replied, 38 "If you have an enemy or know of someone plotting against your government, send him. He will come back badly beaten, if he comes back at all, for some strange power from God is at work there. 39 The God of Heaven watches over the Temple; he strikes down and destroys anyone who comes to harm it." 40 That is the story of how the Temple treasury was protected from Heliodorus.

Simon Accuses Onias

4 But Simon (mentioned earlier as the one who informed Apollonius about the money and brought trouble on the nation) also lied about Onias, claiming that he was responsible for the attack on Heliodorus and for the difficulties that followed. 2 He dared to accuse Onias of plotting against the government—Onias who not only had made donations to Jerusalem and had protected the Temple, but who was eager to see that all our laws were obeyed. 3-4 Apollonius son of Menestheus, the governor of Greater Syria, encouraged Simon in every evil thing he did, and Simon's opposition finally grew so strong that one of his trusted followers committed several murders. Onias realized how dangerous the situation had become, 5 so he went to the king, not for the purpose of making accusations against his fellow-countrymen, but for the common good of all Jews, both in their private and public lives. 6 He realized that without the king's cooperation there was no hope for peace, and Simon would keep on with his foolishness.

Jason Introduces Greek Customs

7 Later, when King Seleucus died and Antiochus (known as Epiphanes) became king, Jason the brother of Onias became

[f]they all; *some manuscripts have* he.
4.7: 1 Macc 1.10

High Priest by corrupt means. ⁸He went to see *g* the king and offered him 12,000 kilogrammes of silver with 2,700 more kilogrammes to be paid later. ⁹Jason also offered him an additional 5,000 kilogrammes of silver for the authority to establish a stadium where young men could train and to enrol the people of Jerusalem as citizens of Antioch. *h*

10 The king gave his approval, and just as soon as Jason took over the office of High Priest, he made the people of Jerusalem change to the Greek way of life. ¹¹He began by abolishing the favours that John had secured for the Jews from previous Syrian kings. (John was the father of the Eupolemus who later went to Rome to make an alliance and to establish ties of friendship.) Jason also did away with our Jewish customs and introduced new customs that were contrary to our Law. ¹²With great enthusiasm he built a stadium near the Temple hill and led our finest young men to adopt the Greek custom of participating in athletic events. ¹³Because of the unrivalled wickedness of Jason, that ungodly and illegitimate High Priest, the craze for the Greek way of life and for foreign customs reached such a point ¹⁴that even the priests lost all interest in their sacred duties. They lost interest in the Temple services and neglected the sacrifices. Just as soon as the signal was given, they would rush off to take part in the games that were forbidden by our Law. ¹⁵They did not care about anything their ancestors had valued; they prized only Greek honours. ¹⁶And this turned out to be the source of all their troubles, for the very people whose ways they admired and whose customs they tried to imitate became their enemies and oppressed them. ¹⁷It is a serious thing to disregard God's law, as you will see from the following events.

Jerusalem under Syrian Influence

18 Once when the king was present for the athletic games that were held every five *i* years in the city of Tyre, ¹⁹that worthless Jason sent some men there from Jerusalem, who were also enrolled as citizens of Antioch, to take ten thousand kilogrammes of silver to pay for a sacrifice to the god Hercules. But even

these men did not think it was fitting to use such a large sum of money for a sacrifice, and ²⁰so the money originally intended as a sacrifice to Hercules was used for the construction of warships.

21 When Apollonius son of Menestheus was sent to Egypt to attend the crowning of Philometor as king, Antiochus learnt that Philometor was opposed to his policies. Antiochus became concerned about the security of his own kingdom, so he went to Joppa and then on to Jerusalem. ²²There he was welcomed with great splendour by Jason and the people of the city who went out to greet him, shouting and carrying torches. From Jerusalem Antiochus led his army to Phoenicia.

Menelaus Becomes High Priest

23 Three years later, Jason sent Menelaus (brother of the Simon *j* mentioned earlier) to take some money to the king and to get his decision on several important matters. ²⁴But when he stood before the king, Menelaus impressed him with his show of authority and offered ten thousand kilogrammes of silver more than Jason had offered for his appointment to the office of High Priest. ²⁵As a result Menelaus returned to Jerusalem with papers from the king, confirming him as High Priest. But he possessed no other qualifications; he had the temper of a cruel tyrant and could be as fierce as a wild animal. ²⁶So Jason, who had cheated his own brother out of the office of High Priest, was now forced to flee to the land of Ammon. ²⁷Menelaus continued to be High Priest, but he never paid any of the money he had promised the king. ²⁸However, Sostratus, the captain of the fort in Jerusalem, kept demanding the money, since it was his responsibility to collect it. So finally, the two men were summoned to appear before the king concerning the matter. ²⁹Menelaus left his brother Lysimachus as acting High Priest, while Sostratus left the fort under the command of Crates, the commander of the mercenary troops from Cyprus.

The Murder of Onias

30 Meanwhile, there was a revolt in the Cilician cities of Tarsus and Mallus,

---

g went to see; *or* wrote to.
h the people...Antioch; *or* the men of Jerusalem as supporters of King Antiochus.
i five; *or* four.   *j* SIMON: See 3.4.
4.11: 1 Macc 8.17

because the king had given those cities to Antiochis, his mistress. ³⁶ So the king left Andronicus, one of his high officials, in command, while he hurried off to Cilicia to restore order. ³²Menelaus took advantage of this opportunity and presented Andronicus with some of the gold objects he had removed from the Temple in Jerusalem. He had already sold some of them to the city of Tyre and to other nearby cities. ³³When Onias heard about this, he fled for safety to a temple at Daphne near the city of Antioch and openly accused Menelaus. ³⁴Then Menelaus secretly persuaded Andronicus to kill Onias. So Andronicus went to Onias and deceived him with a friendly greeting and with promises of safety. Although Onias was suspicious, Andronicus finally lured him away from the safety of the temple and immediately murdered him in cold blood.

Andronicus Is Punished

35 The Jews and Gentiles were very angry because Onias had been murdered. ³⁶So when the king returned from the territory of Cilicia, the Jews of Antioch went to him and protested against this senseless killing. Many Gentiles felt the same way about the crime. ³⁷King Antiochus was deeply grieved and was so filled with sorrow that he was moved to tears when he recalled the wisdom and self-control that Onias had shown throughout his life. ³⁸Antiochus became so angry that he tore off Andronicus's royal robe, stripped him naked, and marched him round the city to the very spot where Onias had been murdered. Then Antiochus had this bloodthirsty murderer put to death. This was how the Lord gave him the punishment he deserved.

Lysimachus Is Killed

39 Meanwhile, with the support of his brother Menelaus, Lysimachus had on numerous occasions robbed the Jerusalem Temple and had taken many of its gold objects. When word of this spread round, crowds began to gather in protest against Lysimachus. ⁴⁰Finally, the crowds were becoming dangerous and were beginning to get out of control, so Lysimachus sent three thousand armed men to attack them. They were led by Auranus, a man as stupid as he was old. ⁴¹When the Jews in

the Temple courtyard realized what was happening, they picked up stones, pieces of wood, or simply handfuls of ashes from the altar and threw them at Lysimachus and his men in the confusion. ⁴²They killed a few of Lysimachus's men, wounded many of them, and all the rest ran for their lives. Lysimachus himself, that temple robber, was killed near the Temple treasury.

Menelaus Is Brought to Trial

43 Because of this incident Menelaus was brought to trial. ⁴⁴When the king came to the city of Tyre, the Jewish authorities in Jerusalem sent three men to bring charges against Menelaus. ⁴⁵When Menelaus saw that he was losing the case, he offered Ptolemy son of Dorymenes a large bribe to persuade the king to decide in his favour. ⁴⁶Ptolemy then asked the king to go outside the courtroom with him, as though to get some fresh air, and there he persuaded him to change his mind ⁴⁷and declare Menelaus innocent of the charges against him. So Menelaus was set free, although he had caused all the trouble; but the three men, whom even the cruel Scythians would have declared innocent, were sentenced to death. ⁴⁸The three men had spoken in defence of Jerusalem, its people,ᵏ and the sacred untensils stolen from the Temple, but they were quickly and unjustly executed. ⁴⁹Some of the people of Tyre, however, showed their disgust with this crime and their respect for these men by giving them a splendid funeral. ⁵⁰Menelaus stayed on in his position because of the greed of those in power. He grew more evil every day and became the worst enemy of his own people.

Visions of a Battle

5 About this time Antiochus the Fourth made a second attack against Egypt. ²For nearly forty days people all over Jerusalem saw visions of cavalry troops in gold armour charging across the sky. The horsemen were armed with spears and their swords were drawn. ³They were lined up in battle against one another, attacking and counterattacking. Shields were clashing, there was a rain of spears, and arrows flew through the air. All the different kinds of armour and the gold bridles on the horses flashed in the

ᵏits people; *some manuscripts also have* the surrounding villages.
4.34: Dan 9.26

sunlight. 4 Everyone in the city prayed that these visions might be a good sign.

Jason Attacks Jerusalem

5 When a false report began to spread that Antiochus had died, Jason took more than a thousand men and suddenly attacked Jerusalem. They drove back the men stationed on the city walls and finally captured the city. Menelaus fled for safety to the fort, near the Temple hill, 6 while Jason and his men went on slaughtering their fellow Jews without mercy. Jason did not realize that success against one's own people is the worst kind of failure. He even considered his success a victory over enemies, rather than a defeat of his own people. 7 But Jason did not take over the government. Instead he was forced to flee once again to the territory of the Ammonites, and in the end his evil plot brought him nothing but shame and disgrace, 8 and he died in misery. Aretas, the ruler of the Arabs, imprisoned him; he was looked upon as a criminal and despised because he had betrayed his own people; everyone was hunting for him, and he had to run from town to town. He fled to Egypt for safety, 9 then to Greece, hoping to find refuge among the Spartans, who were related to the Jews. Finally, this man, who had forced so many others to flee from their own country, died as a fugitive in a foreign land. 10 Jason had killed many people and left their bodies unburied, but now his own death was unmourned. He was not given a funeral or even buried with his ancestors.

Antiochus Attacks Jerusalem
(1 Macc 1.20–63)

11 When the news of what had happened in Jerusalem reached Antiochus, he thought the whole country of Judaea was in revolt, and he became as furious as a wild animal. So he left Egypt and took Jerusalem by storm, 12 giving his men orders to cut down without mercy everyone they met and to slaughter anyone they found hiding in the houses. 13 They murdered everyone—men and women, boys and girls; even babies were butchered. 14 Three days later Jerusalem had lost eighty thousand people: forty thousand killed in the attack and at least that many taken away to be sold as slaves.

15 But Antiochus was still not satisfied. He even dared to enter the holiest Temple in all the world, guided by Menelaus, who had become a traitor both to his religion and to his people. 16 With his filthy and unholy hands, Antiochus swept away the sacred utensils and the gifts which other kings had given to increase the glory and honour of the Temple. 17 He was so thrilled with his conquest that he did not realize that the Lord had let his holy Temple be defiled because the sin of the people of Jerusalem had made him angry for a while. 18 If the people of Jerusalem had not been involved in so many sins, Antiochus would have been punished immediately and prevented from taking such a foolish action. He would have suffered the same fate as Heliodorus, who was sent by King Seleucus to inspect the treasury. 19 But the Lord did not choose his people for the sake of his Temple; he established his Temple for the sake of his people. 20 So the Temple shared in the people's suffering but also later shared in their prosperity. The Lord abandoned it when he became angry, but restored it when his anger had cooled down.

Another Attack against Jerusalem

21 Antiochus took 62,000 kilogrammes of silver from the Temple and hurried off to Antioch. Such was his arrogance that he felt he could make ships sail across dry land or troops march across the sea. 22 He appointed governors to cause trouble for the people. In Jerusalem he placed Philip, a man from Phrygia who was more evil than Antiochus himself. 23 At Mount Gerizim he placed Andronicus. In addition to these, there was Menelaus, who ill-treated his fellow Jews far worse than the governors did. Antiochus hated the Jews so much 24 that he sent an army of 22,000 mercenary troops from Mysia to Jerusalem under the command of a man named Apollonius, with orders to kill every man in the city and to sell the women and boys as slaves. 25 Apollonius arrived in Jerusalem, pretending to be on a peace mission. Then on a Sabbath, when all the Jews were observing the day of rest, he led his troops, who were fully armed, in a parade outside the city. 26 Suddenly he commanded his men to kill everyone who had come out to see them. They rushed into the city and murdered a great many people.

27 But Judas Maccabeus and about nine others escaped into the barren mountains, where they lived like wild animals. In order not to defile themselves, they ate only the plants which they found growing there.

The Jews Are Persecuted Because of Their Faith

6 Not long after that, the king sent an elderly Athenian[1] to force the Jews to abandon their religion and the customs of their ancestors. [2] He was also to defile their Temple by dedicating it to the Olympian god Zeus.[m] The temple on Mount Gerizim was to be officially named "Temple of Zeus the God of Hospitality," as the people who lived there had requested.

[3] The oppression was harsh and almost intolerable. [4] Gentiles filled the Temple with drinking parties and all sorts of immorality. They even had intercourse with prostitutes there. Forbidden objects were brought into the Temple, [5] and the altar was covered with detestable sacrifices prohibited by our Law. [6] It was impossible to observe the Sabbath, to celebrate any of the traditional festivals, or even so much as to admit to being a Jew. [7] Each month when the king's birthday was celebrated, the Jews were compelled by brute force to eat the intestines of sacrificial animals. Then, during the festival in honour of the wine god Dionysus, they were required to wear ivy wreaths on their heads and march in procession. [8] On the advice of Ptolemy,[n] the neighbouring Greek cities were also instructed to require Jews to eat the sacrifices; [9] they were told to put to death every Jew who refused to adopt the Greek way of life. It was easy to see that hard times were ahead. [10] For example, two women were arrested for having their babies circumcised. They were paraded round the city with their babies hung from their breasts; then they were thrown down from the city wall. [11] On another occasion, Philip was told that some Jews had gathered in a nearby cave to observe the Sabbath in secret. Philip attacked and burnt them all alive. They had such respect for the Sabbath that they would not fight to defend themselves.

The Lord Punishes and Shows Mercy

[12] I beg you not to become discouraged as you read about the terrible things that happened. Consider that this was the Lord's way of punishing his people, not of destroying them. [13] In fact, it is a sign of kindness to punish a person immediately for his sins, rather than to wait a long time. [14] The Lord does not treat us as he does other nations: he waits patiently until they have become deeply involved in sin before he punishes them, [15] but he punishes us before we have sinned too much. [16] So the Lord is always merciful to us, his own people. Although he punishes us with disasters, he never abandons us. [17] I have made these few observations by way of reminder. We will now get on with the story.

Eleazar Dies for His Faith

[18] There was an elderly and highly respected teacher of the Law by the name of Eleazar, whose mouth was being forced open to make him eat pork. [19-20] But he preferred an honourable death rather than a life of disgrace. So he spat out the meat and went willingly to the place of torture, showing how people should have courage to refuse unclean food, even if it costs them their lives. [21-22] The men in charge of the sacrifice had been friends of Eleazar for a long time, and because of this friendship they told him privately to bring meat that was lawful for him to eat. He need only pretend to eat the pork, they said, and in this way he would not be put to death.

[23] But Eleazar made a decision worthy of his grey hair and advanced age. All his life he had lived in perfect obedience to God's holy laws, so he replied, "Kill me, here and now. [24] Such deception is not worthy of a man of my years. Many young people would think that I had denied my faith after I was ninety years old. [25] If I pretended to eat this meat, just to live a little while longer, it would bring shame and disgrace on me and lead many young people astray. [26] For the present I might be able to escape what you could do to me, but whether I live or die, I cannot escape Almighty God. [27] If I die bravely now, it will show that I deserved my long life. [28] It will also set a good example of the way young people should be willing and glad to die for our sacred and respected laws."

As soon as he said these things, he went[o] off to be tortured, [29] and the very

---

[l]elderly Athenian; *or* an elder of Athens, *or* Athenaios the elder, *or* Geron an Athenian; *some manuscripts have* an elderly Antiochean, *or* an elder of Antioch.
[m]ZEUS: *The supreme god of the Greeks; Mount Olympus was thought to be his home.*
[n]Ptolemy *(see 4.45); some manuscripts have* the people of Ptolemais.
[o]went; *some manuscripts have* was dragged.
6.10: 1 Macc 1.60–61   **6.11:** 1 Macc 2.32–38   **6.18:** Lev 11.7–8; Heb 11.35

His courageous death was remembered as a glorious example (6.31)

people who had treated him kindly a few minutes before, now turned against him, because they thought he had spoken like a madman. 30 When they had beaten him almost to the point of death, he groaned and said, "The Lord possesses all holy knowledge. He knows I could have escaped these terrible sufferings and death, yet he also knows that I gladly suffer these things, because I fear him."

31 So Eleazar died. But his courageous death was remembered as a glorious example, not only by young people, but by the entire nation as well.

A Mother and Her Sons Die for Their Faith

7 On another occasion a Jewish mother and her seven sons were arrested. The king was having them beaten to force them to eat pork. 2 Then one of the young men said, "What do you hope to gain by doing this? We would rather die than abandon the traditions of our ancestors."

3 This made the king so furious that he gave orders for huge pans and cauldrons to be heated red-hot, 4 and it was done immediately. Then he told his men to cut off the tongue of the one who had spoken and to scalp him and chop off his hands and feet, while his mother and six brothers looked on. 5 After the young man had been reduced to a helpless mass of breathing flesh, the king gave orders for him to be carried over and thrown into one of the pans. As a cloud

of smoke streamed up from the pan, the brothers and their mother encouraged one another to die bravely, saying, 6 "The Lord God is looking on and understands our suffering. Moses made this clear when he wrote a song condemning those who had abandoned the Lord. He said, 'The Lord will have mercy on those who serve him.'"

7 After the first brother had died in this way, the soldiers started amusing themselves with the second one by tearing the hair and skin from his head. Then they asked him, "Now will you eat this pork, or do you want us to chop off your hands and feet one by one?"

8 He replied in his native language, "I will never eat it!" So the soldiers tortured him, just as they had the first one, 9 but with his dying breath he cried out to the king, "You butcher! You may kill us, but the King of the universe will raise us from the dead and give us eternal life, because we have obeyed his laws."

10 The soldiers began entertaining themselves with the third brother. When he was ordered to stick out his tongue, he quickly did so. Then he bravely held out his hands 11 and courageously said, "God gave these to me. But his laws mean more to me than my hands, and I know God will give them back to me again." 12 The king and those with him were amazed at his courage and at his willingness to suffer.

13 After he had died, the soldiers

7.1–42: Heb 11.35–36   **7.6:** Deut 32.36

tortured the fourth one in the same cruel way, ¹⁴but his final words were, "I am glad to die at your hands, because we have the assurance that God will raise us from death. But there will be no resurrection to life for you, Antiochus!"

15 When the soldiers took the fifth boy and began torturing him, ¹⁶he looked the king squarely in the eye and said, "You have the power to do whatever you want with us, even though you also are mortal. But do not think that God has abandoned our people. ¹⁷Just wait. God will use his great power to torture you and your descendants."

18 Then the soldiers took the sixth boy, and just before he died he said, "Make no mistake. We are suffering what we deserve, because we have sinned against our God. That's why all these terrible things are happening to us. ¹⁹But don't think for a minute that you will avoid being punished for fighting against God."

20 The mother was the most amazing one of them all, and she deserves a special place in our memory. Although she saw her seven sons die in a single day, she endured it with great courage because she trusted in the Lord. ²¹She combined womanly emotion with manly courage and spoke words of encouragement to each of her sons in their native language. ²²"I do not know how your life began in my womb," she would say. "I was not the one who gave you life and breath and put together each part of your body. ²³It was God who did it, God who created the universe, the human race, and all that exists. He is merciful and he will give you back life and breath again, because you love his laws more than you love yourself."

24 Antiochus was sure that the mother was mocking him, so he did his best to persuade her youngest son to abandon the traditions of his ancestors. He promised not only to make the boy rich and famous, but to place him in a position of authority and to give him the title "Friend of the King." ²⁵But the boy paid no attention to him, so Antiochus tried to persuade the boy's mother to talk him into saving his life, ²⁶and after much persuasion she agreed to do so. ²⁷Leaning over her son, she fooled the cruel tyrant by saying in her native language, "My son, have pity on me. Remember that I carried you in my womb for nine months and nursed you for three years. I have taken care of you and looked after all your needs up to the present day. ²⁸So I urge you, my child, to look at the sky and the earth. Consider everything you see there, and realize that God made it all from nothing, just as he made the human race. ²⁹Don't be afraid of this butcher. Give up your life willingly and prove yourself worthy of your brothers, so that by God's mercy I may receive you back with them at the resurrection."

King Antiochus...I refuse to obey your orders (7.30)

30 Before she could finish speaking, the boy said, "King Antiochus, what are you waiting for? I refuse to obey your orders. I only obey the commands in the Law which Moses gave to our ancestors. ³¹You have thought up all kinds of cruel things to do to our people, but you won't escape the punishment that God has in store for you. ³²⁻³³It is true that our living Lord is angry with us and is making us suffer because of our sins, in order to correct and discipline us. But this will last only a short while, for we are still his servants, and he will forgive us. ³⁴But you are the cruellest and most disgusting thing that ever lived. So don't fool yourself with illusions of greatness while you punish God's people. ³⁵There is no way for you to escape punishment at the hands of the almighty and all-seeing God. ³⁶My brothers suffered briefly because of our faithfulness to God's covenant, but now they have entered eternal life.ᵖ But you will fall under God's judgement and be punished as you deserve for your arrogance. ³⁷I now give up my body and my life for the laws of our ancestors, just as my brothers did. But I also beg God

ᵖbriefly...life; *or* briefly, but now they have entered eternal life because of our covenant with God.

to show mercy to his people quickly and to torture you until you are forced to acknowledge that he alone is God. [38] May my brothers and I be the last to suffer the anger of Almighty God, which he has justly brought upon our entire nation."

[39] These words of ridicule made Antiochus so furious that he had the boy tortured even more cruelly than his brothers. [40] And so the boy died, with absolute trust in the Lord, never unfaithful for a minute.

[41] Last of all, the mother was put to death.

[42] But I have said enough about the Jews being tortured and being forced to eat the intestines of sacrificial animals.

Judas Maccabaeus Revolts
(1 Macc 3.1–26)

8 Judas Maccabaeus and his friends went secretly from village to village until they had gathered a force of about six thousand Jewish men who had remained faithful to their religion. [2] They begged the Lord to help his people, now trampled under foot by all nations, to take pity on the Temple, now defiled by pagans, [3] and to have mercy on Jerusalem, now destroyed and almost levelled to the ground. [4] They also asked the Lord to show his hatred of evil by taking revenge on those who were murdering his people, mercilessly slaughtering innocent children, and saying evil things against the Lord.

[5] When Judas had finally organized his forces, the Gentiles were unable to stand against him, because the Lord's anger against Israel had now turned to mercy. [6–7] Judas would make sudden attacks on towns and villages and burn them. He captured strategic positions and routed many enemy troops, finding that he was most successful at night. People everywhere spoke of his bravery.

Ptolemy Sends Nicanor to Attack Judas
(1 Macc 3. 38–41)

[8] When Philip, governor of Jerusalem, realized that Judas was gaining ground little by little and that his victories were becoming more and more frequent, he wrote a letter to Ptolemy, governor of Greater Syria, requesting his help in defending the royal interests. [9] Ptolemy immediately appointed Nicanor son of Patroclus, who was also in the closest circle of the King's Friends, and sent him with more than twenty thousand troops

of various nationalities to wipe out the entire Jewish race. Ptolemy also appointed Gorgias, a general of wide military experience, to go with him. [10] King Antiochus owed the Romans 68,000 kilogrammes of silver; Nicanor planned to pay off the debt by selling Jewish prisoners of war as slaves.

[11] So he at once sent word to the towns along the coast, informing them that he would be selling Jews for less than a kilogramme of silver each. But he did not know of the judgement that Almighty God had in store for him.

Judas Learns of Nicanor's Plans
(1 Macc 3.42–54)

[12] Judas learnt that Nicanor was advancing with his army towards Judaea, so he informed his men. [13] Some were cowardly and did not believe in the justice of God, and they ran away as fast as they could. [14] But others sold all their remaining possessions so that the Lord would consider them worthy to be saved from the godless Nicanor, who had sold them as slaves even before the battle had taken place. [15] They prayed that if God was not willing to do this for their sake alone, he might be willing to rescue them because of the covenants he had made with their ancestors, and because he, the great and wonderful God, had called them to be his people. [16] Judas brought together all six thousand of his men and encouraged them not to be frightened or to flee in panic at the sight of the large number of Gentile troops who were marching against them without cause. Instead they should fight bravely, [17] never forgetting the crimes the Gentiles had committed against the Temple, and how they had made Jerusalem suffer terribly and had done away with Jewish traditions. [18] "They rely on their weapons and their daring," Judas said, "but we trust in Almighty God, who is able to destroy not only these troops, but, if necessary, the entire world, with a mere nod of his head."

[19] Then Judas went on to remind them of the ways God had helped their ancestors: during the time of Sennacherib 185,000 of the enemy had been destroyed; [20] and once in Babylonia 8,000 Jews came to the aid of 4,000 Macedonians, defeating 120,000 Galatians and taking a great deal of loot, all because of God's help.

Judas Defeats Nicanor
(1 Macc 3.55—4.27)

21 Judas's words encouraged his men and made them willing to die for their religion and their country. He then divided his army into four divisions 22 of about fifteen hundred men each, with himself and his brothers Simon, Joseph, and Jonathan each in charge of a division. 23 After ordering Eleazar to read aloud q from the holy book, he gave his men the battle-cry: "God will help us," and personally led the attack against Nicanor.

24 Almighty God fought on their side, and they killed more than nine thousand of the enemy. They wounded many others and put the entire enemy army to flight. 25 They seized the money from the people who had come to buy them as slaves. Then they pursued the enemy a long way, until they had to return, 26 because it was almost time for the Sabbath to begin. 27 When they had collected the enemy's weapons and looted the dead, they celebrated the Sabbath, praising the Lord and giving thanks to him, because he had brought them safely to that day and had given them the first sign of his mercy. 28 When the Sabbath was over, they gave some of the loot to the victims of persecution and to the widows and orphans; then they divided the rest among their own families. 29 Afterwards they joined together in prayer to the merciful Lord, asking him to look favourably upon his servants.

Judas Defeats Timothy and Bacchides

30 The Jews later fought against the forces of Timothy and Bacchides and killed more than twenty thousand of them. They captured some very high fortresses and took a lot of loot, which they divided equally among themselves and the widows, orphans, old men, and the victims of persecution. 31 They carefully collected all the enemy's weapons and stored them in strategic places, but the rest of the loot was taken to Jerusalem. 32 They executed the commanding officer of Timothy's forces, a godless man who had caused the Jews much suffering. 33 While celebrating their victory in the city of their ancestors, they burnt alive those men who had set fire to the Temple gates. The dead included Callisthenes, who had hidden in a small house; and so he received the

q Probable text After...aloud; Greek unclear.
8.23: 1 Macc 3.48

punishment he deserved for his evil deeds.

34 In this way, the evil Nicanor, who had brought a thousand merchants to buy the Jews, 35 was defeated with the help of the Lord by the very people he despised so much. He threw off his splendid uniform and fled all alone like a runaway slave, until he reached Antioch. He had succeeded only in destroying his entire army. 36 This man, who had tried to pay a debt to Rome by selling the people of Jerusalem, showed that the Jews could not be defeated. God was their mighty defender, because they obeyed the laws he had given them.

The Lord Punishes Antiochus
(1 Macc 6.1-7; 2 Macc 1.11-17)

9 About this time Antiochus was retreating in disorder from Persia, 2 where he had entered the city of Persepolis and had attempted to rob a temple and take control of the city. The people took up arms and attacked Antiochus, forcing his army to retreat in disgrace. 3 When he reached Ecbatana, he was told what had happened to the forces of Nicanor and Timothy. 4 He was furious and decided to make the Jews pay for the defeat he had suffered. So he ordered his chariot driver not to stop until they reached Jerusalem. With great arrogance he said, "I will turn Jerusalem into a graveyard full of Jews."

But he did not know that he was heading straight for God's judgement. 5 In fact, as soon as he had said these words, the all-seeing Lord, the God of Israel, struck him down with an invisible but fatal blow. He was seized with sharp intestinal pains for which there was no relief—6 a fitting punishment for the man who had tortured others in so many terrible ways! 7 But this in no way caused him to give up his pride. Instead he became more arrogant than ever, and breathing out fiery threats against the Jews, he gave orders to drive even faster. As a result he fell out of his chariot with such a thud that it made every bone in his body ache. 8 His arrogant pride made him think he had the superhuman strength to make ocean waves obey him and to weigh high mountains on a pair of scales. But suddenly he fell flat on the ground and had to be carried off on a stretcher, a clear sign to everyone of God's power. 9 Even the eyes of this godless man were crawling with worms and he lived in terrible pain and agony. The stink was so bad that his entire army was sickened, [10] and no one was able to come close enough to carry him about. Yet only a short while before, he thought he could take hold of the stars.

Antiochus Makes a Promise to God
(1 Macc 6.8–17)

[11] Antiochus was deeply depressed and suffered constant pain because of the punishment that God had brought on him, so he finally came to his senses and gave up his arrogant pride. [12] Then, when he could no longer endure his own stench, he said, "It is right that all mortals should be subject to God and not think that they are his equal." [13] The time of the Lord's mercy had come to an end for Antiochus, but this worthless man made the Lord a promise: [14] "I once intended to level Jerusalem to the ground and make that holy city a graveyard full of Jews," he said, "but now I declare it a free city. [15] I had planned to throw out the dead bodies of the Jews and their children for the wild animals and the birds to eat, for I did not consider them worth burying. But now I intend to grant them the same privileges as the citizens of Athens enjoy. [16] I once looted the Temple and took its sacred utensils, but I will fill it with splendid gifts and with better utensils than before, and I will pay the cost of the sacrifices from my own resources. [17] Besides all this, I will become a Jew myself and go wherever people live, telling them of God's power."

Antiochus's Letter to the Jews

[18] Antiochus was in despair and could find no relief from his pain, because God was punishing him as he deserved, so he wrote the following letter to the Jews:

[19] "King Antiochus to the Jews, my most distinguished subjects. Warm greetings and best wishes for your health and prosperity.

[20] "I hope that you and your families are in good health and that all goes well with you. My hope is in God, [21] and I remember with a deep sense of joy the respect and kindness that you have shown me.

"On my way home from Persia I fell violently ill, and so I thought it best to begin making plans for the general welfare of the people. [22] I have not given up hopes of getting well; in fact I am fully confident that I will recover. [23] But I recall that my father used to appoint a successor whenever he went on a military campaign east of the Euphrates. [24] He did this so that if something unexpected happened, or if some bad news came back, then his subjects would not be afraid, for they knew who had been left in command. [25] Also, I know how the rulers along the frontiers of my kingdom are constantly on the lookout for any opportunity that may come along. That is why I have appointed my son Antiochus to succeed me as king. I have frequently entrusted him to your care and recommended him to you when I went on my regular visits to the provinces east of the Euphrates. (He is receiving a copy of the letter which follows.) [26] Now I strongly urge each of you to keep in mind the good things that I have done for you, both individually and as a nation, and to continue in your goodwill towards me and my son. [27] I am confident that he will treat you with fairness and kindness, just as I have always done."

[28] And so, this murderer, who had cursed God, suffered the same terrible agonies he had brought on others, and then died a miserable death in the mountains of a foreign land. [29] One of his close friends, Philip, took his body home; but, because he was afraid of Antiochus's son, he went on to King Ptolemy Philometor of Egypt.

The Rededication of the Temple
(1 Macc 4.36–61)

10 Judas Maccabaeus and his followers, under the leadership of the Lord, recaptured the Temple and the city of Jerusalem. [2] They tore down the altars which foreigners had set up in the marketplace and destroyed the other places of worship that had been built. [3] They purified the Temple and built a new altar. Then, with new fire started by striking flint, they offered sacrifice for the first time in two years, burnt incense, lit the lamps, and set out the sacred loaves. [4] After they had done all this, they lay face downwards on the ground and prayed that the Lord would never again let such disasters strike them. They begged him to be merciful when he punished them for future sins and not hand them over any more to barbaric, pagan Gentiles. ⁵They rededicated the Temple on the twenty-fifth day of the month of Kislev, the same day of the same month on which the Temple had been desecrated by the Gentiles. ⁶The happy celebration lasted eight days, like the Festival of Shelters, and the people remembered how only a short time before, they had spent the Festival of Shelters wandering like wild animals in the mountains and living in caves. ⁷But now, carrying green palm branches and sticks decorated with ivy, they paraded round, singing grateful praises to him who had brought about the purification of his own Temple. ⁸Everyone agreed that the entire Jewish nation should celebrate this festival each year.

Ptolemy Macron Commits Suicide

9 The days of Antiochus Epiphanes had come to an end. ¹⁰Now we will tell about Antiochus Eupator, the son of this godless man, and give a summary of the evil effects of his wars. ¹¹When he became king he appointed a man by the name of Lysias to be in charge of the affairs of state and to be chief governor of Greater Syria, ¹²replacing Ptolemy Macron, who had been the first governor to treat the Jews fairly. Macron had established peaceful relations with them in an attempt to make up for the wrongs they had suffered. ¹³As a result, the King's Friends went to Eupator and accused Macron of treachery, because he had abandoned the island of Cyprus, which King Philometor of Egypt had placed under his command, and had gone over to Antiochus Epiphanes. In fact, everyone called Macron a traitor. No longer able to maintain the respect that his office demanded, he committed suicide by taking poison.

Judas Maccabaeus Defeats the Idumeans
(1 Macc 5.1-8)

14 When Gorgias became governor of Idumea, he kept a force of mercenaries and attacked the Jews at every opportunity. ¹⁵Not only this, but the Idumeans themselves controlled certain strategic fortresses and were constantly harassing the Jews. They welcomed those who fled from Jerusalem and did everything they could to keep the country in a perpetual state of war. ¹⁶So Judas Maccabaeus and his men, after offering prayers for God's help, rushed out and

made a vigorous attack against the Idumean fortresses. ¹⁷They beat back those who were defending the walls and captured the fortresses, killing everyone they found, a total of about twenty thousand people.

18 About nine thousand of the enemy, however, managed to take refuge in two easily defended forts, with everything they needed to withstand a siege. ¹⁹Judas had to go on to some other places in the country, where he was more urgently needed, but he left behind Simon and Joseph, together with Zacchaeus and his men. This force was large enough to continue the siege, ²⁰but some of Simon's men were greedy, and when they were offered 64 kilogrammes of silver, they let some of the enemy escape from the forts. ²¹When Judas heard what had happened, he called together the leaders of his troops and accused those men of selling their brothers by setting their enemies free to fight against them. ²²Then he executed the traitors and immediately captured the two forts. ²³Judas was always successful in battle, and in his assault on those two forts he killed more than twenty thousand men.

Judas Defeats Timothy

24 Timothy, who had been defeated by the Jews once before, had gathered a large number of cavalry from Asia and a tremendous force of mercenary troops and was now advancing to take Judaea by armed attack. ²⁵But as the enemy forces were approaching, Judas and his men prayed to God. They put on sackcloth, threw earth on their heads, ²⁶and lay face downwards on the steps of the altar, begging God to help them by fighting against their enemies, as he had promised in his Law. ²⁷When they had finished praying, they took up their weapons, went out a good distance from Jerusalem, and stopped for the night not far from the enemy. ²⁸At daybreak the two armies joined in battle. The Jewish forces depended upon both their bravery and their trust in the Lord for victory, while the enemy relied only on their ability to fight fiercely. ²⁹When the fighting was at its worst, the enemy saw five handsome men riding on horses with gold bridles and leading the Jewish forces. ³⁰These five men surrounded Judas, protecting him with their own armour and showering the

enemy with arrows and thunderbolts. The enemy forces then became so confused and bewildered that they broke ranks, and the Jews cut them to pieces, 31 slaughtering 20,500 infantry and 600 cavalry.

32 Timothy himself escaped to the strongly defended fort of Gezer, where his brother Chaereas was in command. 33 Judas and his men besieged the fort for four days with great enthusiasm, 34 but the men inside trusted to the security of their positions and shouted all sorts of terrible insults against the Jews and their God. 35 At dawn on the fifth day, twenty of Judas's men, burning with anger at these insults, bravely climbed the wall and with savage fury chopped down everyone they met. 36 At the same time, others climbed the walls on the other side of the fort and set the towers on fire. Many of the enemy were burnt to death as the flames spread. A third force broke down the gates and let in the rest of Judas's men to capture the city. 37 Timothy had hidden in a cistern, but they killed him, as well as his brother Chaereas and Apollophanes.

38 When it was over, the Jews celebrated by singing hymns and songs of thanksgiving to the Lord, who had shown them great kindness and had given them victory.

Judas Maccabaeus Defeats Lysias
(1 Macc 4.26-35)

11 Not long after Timothy was defeated, Lysias, the king's guardian and relative, and head of the government, heard what had happened. He became angry 2 and led eighty thousand infantry and all his cavalry against the Jews with the intention of turning Jerusalem into a Greek city. 3 The Temple would be taxed, as were all Gentile places of worship, and the office of High Priest would be up for sale each year. 4 Lysias was so pleased with his tens of thousands of infantry, his thousands of cavalry, and his eighty elephants that he failed to take into account the power of God. 5 He invaded Judaea and attacked the fort of Bethzur, about thirty kilometres south of Jerusalem.

6 When Judas and his men heard that Lysias was laying siege to their forts, they and all the people cried and wept, begging the Lord to send a good angel to save

them. 7 Judas was the first to take up his weapons, and he urged the others to join him in risking their lives to help their fellow Jews. So with great eagerness they all set out together. 8 But they had not gone far from Jerusalem, when suddenly they noticed that they were being led by a horseman dressed in white and carrying gold weapons. 9 Immediately all of them together thanked God for his mercy; he had made them brave enough to attack not only men, but also the most savage animals or even walls of iron. 10 So they marched in battle formation, and with them went the one whom the Lord in his mercy had sent to fight on their side. 11 Then they charged into the enemy like lions, killing 11,000 infantry and 1,600 cavalry, and forcing the rest to run for their lives. 12 Most of those who ran were wounded and had lost their weapons, and Lysias himself managed to escape only because he ran away like a coward.

Lysias Makes Peace with the Jews
(1 Macc 6.56-61)

13 Lysias was no fool. As he thought about the defeat he had suffered, he realized it was because the mighty God had fought for the Jews, making it impossible for them to be defeated. So he sent a message to the Jews, 14 trying to persuade them to agree to a just settlement and promising to do all he could to make the king friendly towards them.r 15 Judas Maccabaeus considered what would be best for the people, and so he agreed to all the proposals Lysias had made, since the king had granted every written request that Judas had presented to Lysias.s

The Letter of Lysias to the Jews

16 Here is a copy of the letter which Lysias wrote to the Jews:

"Lysias to the Jewish people, greetings. 17 Your representatives John and Absalom have delivered to me the official document which you sent with them, and they have asked me to agree to what is contained in it. 18 I have informed the king of the matters that needed to be brought to his attention, and he has agreed to do whatever is possible. 19 If you continue to be loyal to the government, I will do everything I can in the future to benefit your nation. 20 I

---

r to do...them; *Greek unclear.*

s since...Lysias; *or* and the king granted every written request that Judas presented to Lysias.

have instructed your representatives and mine to meet with you to discuss the details of these matters. ²¹May all go well with you. Dated the twenty-fourth day of the month of Dioscorinthius in the year 148."ᵗ

The King's Letter to Lysias

22 This is a copy of the king's letter:
"King Antiochus to the honourable Lysias, greetings. ²³Now that my father has gone to be with the gods, I want the subjects of my kingdom to conduct their own affairs without interference. ²⁴I understand that the Jews do not wish to adopt the Greek way of life, as my father had intended, but prefer their own way of life and have requested that they be allowed to live according to their own customs. ²⁵Since I desire that they live undisturbed like the other nations in my empire, I hereby decree that their Temple be restored to them and that they be allowed to live according to the customs of their ancestors. ²⁶Please inform them of this decision and assure them of my friendship, so that they may conduct their own affairs in peace, without anything to worry about."

27 Here is a copy of the king's letter to the Jewish people:
"King Antiochus to the Jewish leaders and all the Jews, greetings. ²⁸I hope that all is going well for you. I am in good health. ²⁹Menelaus has informed me of your desire to return home and attend to your own affairs. ³⁰So then, those of you who return home by the thirtieth of the month of Xanthicus may rest assured that you have nothing to fear. ³¹You may continue to observe your food laws and other laws, as you used to do, and no Jew will be punished for any crime done in ignorance. ³²I am sending Menelaus to set your minds at ease. ³³May all go well with you. Dated the fifteenth day of the month of Xanthicus in the year 148."ᵘ

The Letter of the Romans to the Jews

34 The Romans also sent the Jews the following letter:
"Quintus Memmius and Titus Manius, representatives of the Romans, to the Jews, greetings. ³⁵We are in complete agreement with all

that has been granted to you by the noble Lysias. ³⁶We are now on our way to Antioch, so please examine carefully those matters that Lysias referred to the king. Then send a reply to us immediately so that we can represent your best interests before him. Do this as soon as you can, ³⁷without delay, so that we may know what you have decided. ³⁸May all go well with you. Dated the fifteenth day of the month of Xanthicus in the year 148."

The Jews of Joppa Are Murdered

12 When the peace agreement between the Jews and the Syrians was completed, Lysias returned to the king, and the Jews went back to their farming. ²But some of the local governors, Timothy and Apollonius son of Gennaeus, as well as Hieronymus and Demophon, would not let them live in peace; and neither would Nicanor, the commander of the mercenaries from Cyprus.

3 About this time, the people of Joppa did a cruel thing to the Jews of their city. They pretended to be friendly to the Jews and invited them and their families to go sailing with them on ships they had provided. ⁴Since all the people of the town had decided to do this, the Jews suspected nothing and accepted the invitation out of a feeling of good will. But when they were out at sea, the people of Joppa drowned all two hundred of them.

5 As soon as Judas heard of this inhuman thing that had been done to his fellow Jews, he informed his men. ⁶After they had prayed to God, the just judge, they attacked the murderers. Under cover of darkness they set fire to the harbour, burning all the ships, and killing everyone they found hiding there. ⁷The gates of the city were locked, so Judas withdrew; but he was determined to return at some other time and wipe out everyone living there.

8 Judas heard that the people of Jamnia had plans to kill the Jews of their city also. ⁹So he attacked Jamnia at night, setting fire to its harbour and the ships there. The flames could be seen as far as Jerusalem, fifty kilometres away.

Judas's Victories in the Region of Gilead
(1 Macc 5.9-54)

10 When Judas and his men were about two kilometres away from Jamnia on their

ᵗTHE YEAR 148: *This corresponds to 164 B.C.*   ᵘTHE YEAR 148: *This corresponds to 164 B.C.*

He sent the women and the children on ahead with the baggage (12.21)

way to meet Timothy in battle, they were attacked by more than five thousand Arabs, supported by five hundred cavalry. ¹¹It was a hard fight, but with the help of God they defeated those desert tribesmen, who then asked to be on friendly terms with the Jews, promising to give them some livestock and offering to help them in other ways as well. ¹²Judas thought their friendship might prove useful in many ways, so he agreed to make peace with them; after that the Arabs returned to their tents.

13 Judas also attacked the heavily fortified walled city of Caspin. The people who lived there were a mixed population of Gentiles ¹⁴who relied on the strength of their walls and felt confident that they had enough food stored up to last through a siege. So they made fun of Judas and his men, shouting out insults against them and profanities against their God. ¹⁵But the Jews prayed to the Almighty Lord of the universe, who had torn down the walls of Jericho in the days of Joshua without using battering-rams or siege-weapons. Then they made a fierce attack against the wall ¹⁶and because it was God's will, they captured the city. The Jews slaughtered so many people that a nearby lake, which was about a quarter of a mile wide, seemed to be overflowing with blood.

Judas Defeats Timothy's Army
(1 Macc 5.37–44)

17 From the city of Caspin, Judas and his men marched about 150 kilometres, until they came to the Jewish settlement of Charax, near the city of Tob. ¹⁸But they did not find Timothy there, because he had already left the region. He had been able to do nothing there except leave behind a strong garrison in one place. ¹⁹Two of Judas's generals, Dositheus and Sosipater, attacked the garrison and killed all ten thousand men stationed there. ²⁰Then Judas divided his army into several divisions, placing Dositheus and Sosipater each in command of a division, and hurried after Timothy, who had a force of 120,000 infantry and 2,500 cavalry. ²¹When Timothy found out that Judas was coming after him, he sent the women and the children on ahead with the baggage to the city of Karnaim, which was almost impossible to besiege or even to reach, because of the narrow passes that led up to it. ²²But at the moment that Judas's first division came into sight, the enemy forces were thrown into panic by a vision sent by God, who sees everything. In their terror they began to run wildly about and many of them were wounded by the swords of their own men. ²³So Judas and his men pursued them as hard as they could, killing at least thirty thousand of the enemy. ²⁴Timothy himself was captured by the troops of Dositheus and Sosipater. But he was very shrewd and managed to convince them that many of their relatives were his prisoners and would be put to death if anything happened to him. ²⁵Finally, after he had

promised to send their relatives home safely, they let him go free.

Judas Wins Other Victories
(1 Macc 5.45–54)

26 Next, Judas attacked the city of Karnaim and the temple of the goddess Atargatis there, killing 25,000 people [27] and completely destroying both the city and the temple. Then he attacked the fortified city of Ephron where Lysias and [v] people of all nationalities were living. Strong young men took up their positions in front of the walls and fought bravely, while inside the city were stored large quantities of military supplies and weapons. [28] But the Jews prayed for help to the Lord, who crushes the power of his enemies. So they captured the city and killed about 25,000 people. [29] From there they hurried on to the city of Beth Shan, 120 kilometres north of Jerusalem. [30] The Jews there told Judas how kindly the people of the city had treated them, especially during hard times. [31] So Judas and his men thanked the people and urged them to show the same good will towards the Jews in the future. Then they left for Jerusalem, where they arrived shortly before the Harvest Festival.

Judas Defeats Gorgias

32 After Pentecost (as the Harvest Festival is called in Greek) Judas and his men quickly marched out against Gorgias, the governor of Idumea, [33] who met them with three thousand infantry and four hundred cavalry. [34] In the battle that followed, a few Jews were killed. [35] Then a Jew from the city of Tob, [w] a powerful horseman by the name of Dositheus, grabbed Gorgias by his cloak and started dragging him away by brute force, intending to take the worthless man alive. But suddenly one of the Thracian horsemen rushed at Dositheus and chopped off his arm, allowing Gorgias to escape to the city of Marisa.

36 By now the Jewish men under the command of Esdrias had been fighting for a long time and were exhausted. So Judas prayed that the Lord would show that he was on their side and in command of their troops. [37] Then, while Judas sang a hymn in his native language as a battle-cry, the Jews made a surprise attack against Gorgias and his men and put them to flight.

Prayers for Men Killed in Battle

38 After the battle Judas led his men to the town of Adullam. It was the day before the Sabbath, so they purified themselves according to Jewish custom and then observed the holy day. [39] By the following day it was urgent that they gather up the bodies of the men who had been killed in battle and bury them in their family tombs. [40] But on each of the dead, hidden under their clothes, they found small images of the gods worshipped in Jamnia, which the Law forbids Jews to wear. Everyone then knew why these men had been killed. [41] So they praised the ways of the Lord, the just judge, who reveals what is hidden, [42] and they begged him that this sin might be completely blotted out. Then, Judas, that great man, urged the people to keep away from sin, because they had seen for themselves what had happened to those men who had sinned. [43] He also took up a collection from all his men, totalling about two kilogrammes of silver, and sent it to Jerusalem to provide for a sin-offering. Judas did this noble thing because he believed in the resurrection of the dead. [44] If he had not believed that the dead would be raised, it would have been foolish and useless to pray for them. [45] In his firm and devout conviction that all God's faithful people would receive a wonderful reward, Judas made provision for a sin-offering to set free from their sin those who had died.

Menelaus Is Put to Death

13 In the year 149 [x] Judas Maccabaeus and his followers found out that Antiochus Eupator was marching against Judaea with a large army [2] and that Lysias, the young king's guardian and the head of his government, was with him. They [y] had a force of Greek troops consisting of 110,000 infantry, 5,300 cavalry, 22 elephants, and 300 chariots with sharp blades attached to their wheels.

3 Menelaus, trying to take advantage of the situation, went over to their side and urged them on, not because he was concerned for the country, but because he hoped to be confirmed as High Priest.

---

[v] Lysias and; *some manuscripts do not have these words.*
[w] a Jew from the city of Tob; *some manuscripts have* one of Bacenor's men.
[x] THE YEAR 149: *This corresponds to 163* B.C.   [y] They; *Greek unclear.*
12.32: Ex 23.16   **12.40:** Deut 7.25

4 But God, the King of kings, made Antiochus furious with Menelaus. Lysias proved to Antiochus that this criminal had been the source of all his troubles, so Antiochus ordered him to be taken to the city of Berea and put to death in the way that it was done there. 5 In that city there is a tower about 22 metres high. It is filled with ashes, and all round the inside of the tower is a platform sloping down into the ashes. 6 People accused of crimes against the gods or of any other serious crime are taken there and thrown down to their death. 7 Menelaus was put to death in that way, without even having the privilege of a burial, 8 and that was just what he deserved. He had often profaned the sacred ashes of the altar fire in the Temple, and now he met his death in ashes.

A Battle Near the City of Modein

9 King Antiochus arrogantly continued his barbaric invasion of Judaea, intending to deal with the Jews more harshly than his father had ever done. 10 When Judas learnt of this, he told the people to pray to the Lord day and night, because they were in danger of losing their Law, their country, and their holy Temple. As never before, they needed his help and protection 11 to keep their newly restored country from falling into the hands of godless Gentiles. 12 For three days the people did nothing but lie face downwards on the ground, fasting and crying, begging the merciful Lord for his help. Then Judas spoke words of encouragement to the people, urging them to get ready for action.

13 Afterwards, Judas met privately with the Jewish leaders and decided to march out with God's help to battle against the king, rather than wait for Antiochus to invade Judaea and besiege Jerusalem. 14 Then, leaving the outcome of the battle to the Creator of the world, Judas encouraged his men to fight bravely and to be willing to die for their laws, the Temple, Jerusalem, their country, and their whole way of life. They set up camp near the city of Modein. 15 Judas gave his men the battle-cry, "Victory comes from God," and that night, with a picked force of his bravest young men, he attacked the area near the king's tent and killed as many as two thousand men. They also stabbed to death z the leading elephant and its keeper. 16 Everyone in camp was terrified and in panic when Judas and his men finally left victoriously 17 just before dawn. The help and protection of the Lord had made all this possible.

Antiochus the Fifth Makes a Treaty with the Jews
(1 Macc 6.48-63)

18 This taste of Jewish daring was enough to convince King Antiochus that he had to find some better way of capturing the Jewish positions. 19 He attacked the strong Jewish fort of Bethzur, but was repeatedly beaten back and finally defeated. 20 Judas sent supplies to the men who were defending the fort, 21 but a Jewish soldier by the name of Rhodocus gave some secret information to the enemy. He was found out, however, caught, and put to death. 22 The king made a second attempt to come to terms with the people of Bethzur, and when he had reached an agreement with them, he withdrew his forces. Then he went to attack Judas, but again he was defeated. 23 Meanwhile, Philip had been left at Antioch in charge of the government, but King Antiochus learnt that he had revolted. The king did not know what to do, so he initiated peace talks with the Jews, agreed to their terms, and promised to be just in his treatment of them. To put the treaty into effect, he offered a sacrifice, gave a generous gift to show his respect for the Temple, 24 and graciously received Judas Maccabaeus. After that, the king appointed Hegemonides to be governor of the territory between the cities of Ptolemais and Gerar, 25 and then he himself went on to Ptolemais. The people there were angry because of the treaty he had made with the Jews—so angry, in fact, that they wanted the treaty cancelled. 26 But Lysias made a public speech, defending the treaty as well as he could. After he had calmed the people down and convinced them that he was right, he returned to Antioch.

In this way King Antiochus's invasion was turned into a retreat.

Alcimus Speaks against Judas
(1 Macc 7.1-21)

14 Three years later, Judas and his men learnt that Demetrius son of Seleucus had sailed into the port of Tripolis with a powerful army and a fleet. 2 It was reported that he had killed King

---

z *Probable text* stabbed to death; *Greek unclear.*

Antiochus and his guardian Lysias and had taken over the country.

3 There was a man by the name of Alcimus, who had formerly been High Priest but who had gladly adopted the Greek way of life during the revolt. Realizing that he could never again be High Priest and fearful of what the Jews might do to him, ⁴he went to see King Demetrius in the year 151.ᵃ On this occasion he presented the king with a gold crown and a palm branch, together with some olive branches traditionally presented to the Temple, but he said nothing about his plans. ⁵Later, however, he got the chance to put his foolish plans into effect when Demetrius summoned him to a meeting of his advisers and asked him what the Jews were intending to do.

Alcimus said, ⁶"The followers of Judas Maccabaeus think of themselves as devout and patriotic; they love war and are constantly inciting the people to rebellion and will never leave the nation in peace. ⁷It is their fault that I no longer hold the glorious position of High Priest, to which I am entitled by birth. And so I have come here, ⁸primarily out of a genuine concern for your interests as king, but also out of consideration for my own countrymen, for the foolish policies of Judas and his followers have brought terrible suffering on our entire nation. ⁹When Your Majesty has examined all the details of these matters, please act in your usual kind and generous manner to relieve the oppression of our nation and its people. ¹⁰As long as Judas is alive, it will be impossible for our nation to enjoy peace."

Demetrius Sends Nicanor to Attack Judas

11 As soon as Alcimus had finished his speech, the other advisers quickly seized this opportunity to arouse Demetrius's anger against Judas, because they also hated him. ¹²So King Demetrius immediately appointed Nicanor, who was the commander of his elephant forces, to be governor of Judaea, and sent him there ¹³with orders to kill Judas, scatter his followers, and make Alcimus High Priest of the greatest Temple in all the world. ¹⁴All the foreigners in Judaea, who had fled from Judas's attacks, now rushed to join forces with Nicanor, because they thought that any defeat or trouble that came to the Jews would be to their own advantage.

15 The Jews heard that Nicanor was attacking and that the foreigners in their country were giving him their support. So they threw earth on themselves and prayed to their God, who had chosen their nation as his possession for ever and had never failed to help them in time of need. ¹⁶Then Judas, their leader, gave the order, and they immediately marched out to engage the enemy in battle near the village of Adasa.ᵇ ¹⁷Judas's brother Simon was fighting Nicanor but was gradually losing the battle because of an unexpected move on the part of the enemy. ¹⁸However, when Nicanor heard how bravely and courageously Judas and his men were fighting for their country, he decided not to settle the matter in battle. ¹⁹Instead, he sent Posidonius, Theodotus, and Mattathias to make a treaty with the Jews.

20 After the terms of the treaty had been worked out in detail, Nicanor informed his troops, and they unanimously agreed. ²¹Then a day was set on which the leaders would meet in private. Ceremonial chairs were brought out from each camp and set up. ²²Judas had taken the precaution of placing fully-armed troops in strategic places, in case of sudden treachery on the part of the enemy. But the two leaders had a friendly meeting. ²³Nicanor stayed on in Jerusalem for some time after that. He did not ill-treat the Jews in any way, and even sent away the people who had come over to his side. ²⁴The two men became the best of friends, and Judas was Nicanor's constant companion. ²⁵Nicanor urged him to marry and start a family. So Judas did this and settled down to a peaceful life.

Nicanor Turns against Judas

26 When Alcimus noticed how well Nicanor and Judas were getting along, he obtained a copy of the treaty and went to see King Demetrius. He told the king that Nicanor was disloyal to the government, because he had appointed the traitor Judas to be his successor. ²⁷These false accusations infuriated the king, and in his anger he wrote to Nicanor, informing him that he was dissatisfied with the treaty and ordering him to arrest Judas Maccabaeus and send him to Antioch at once.

ᵃTHE YEAR 151: *This corresponds to 161* B.C.   ᵇ*Probable text* Adasa; *Greek* Dessau.
14.15–25: 1 Macc 7.27–28

28 When this message reached Nicanor, he was hurt and didn't know what to do, because he did not like having to break an agreement with a man who had kept his part of the bargain. 29 Yet it was impossible for him to ignore the king's command, so he began looking for a way to trap Judas. 30 Judas, however, noticed that Nicanor was becoming hostile and rude towards him, and he knew that this was a bad sign. So he gathered a large number of his followers and went into hiding.

31 When Nicanor realized that Judas had been too clever for him, he went to the great and holy Temple at the time when the priests were offering sacrifice and ordered them to surrender Judas to him. 32 But the priests declared under oath that they had no idea where Judas was hiding. 33 Then Nicanor raised his right arm in the direction of the Temple and made a solemn threat: "If you do not hand Judas over to me as a prisoner, I will level God's Temple to the ground, demolish this altar, and on this spot build a glorious temple to Dionysus." 34 Then he left, and immediately the priests raised their arms towards heaven and prayed to God, the faithful Defender of our nation: 35 "Lord, you are in need of nothing, yet it has pleased you to place your Temple here and to live among us. 36 You alone are holy, and your Temple has only recently been purified, so now protect its holiness for ever."

Razis Dies for His Country

37 One of the leaders in Jerusalem, a man by the name of Razis, was denounced to Nicanor. It was said that he had helped his people in many ways and was so highly respected by them that he was known as "the Father of the Jews." 38 During the early days of the revolution he had risked his life for Judaism and had been brought to trial because of his loyalty. 39 Wishing to show clearly how much he disliked the Jews, Nicanor sent more than five hundred soldiers to arrest Razis, 40 because he thought his arrest would be a crippling blow to the Jews. 41 The soldiers were about to capture the tower where Razis had gone. They were forcing open the gates to the courtyard, and the order had been given to set the door on fire. Razis realized there was no escape, so he tried to commit suicide with his sword, 42 preferring to die with honour

rather than suffer humiliation at the hands of evil men.

43 Under the pressure of the moment, Razis misjudged the thrust of the sword, and it did not kill him. So, while the soldiers were swarming into the room, he rushed to the wall and jumped off like a brave hero into the crowd below. 44 The crowd quickly moved back, and he fell in the space they left. 45 Still alive, and burning with courage, he got up, and with blood gushing from his wounds, he ran through the crowd and finally climbed a steep rock. 46 Now completely drained of blood, he tore out his intestines with both hands and threw them at the crowd, and as he did so, he prayed for the Lord of life and breath to give them back to him. That was how he died.

Nicanor's Cruel Plan

15 Nicanor learnt that Judas and his men were in the region of Samaria, so he decided to attack them on the Sabbath, when he could do so without any danger to himself. 2 The Jews who were forced to accompany his army begged him not to do such a cruel and savage thing, but to respect the day that the all-seeing God had honoured and made the most holy of all days. 3 Then Nicanor, the lowest creature on earth, asked if there was some sovereign ruler in heaven who had commanded them to honour the Sabbath. 4 And the Jews replied, "Yes; the living Lord, who rules in heaven, commanded us to honour the Sabbath."

5 But Nicanor answered, "I am the ruler on earth, and I order you to take up your weapons and to do what the king commands." However, he did not succeed in carrying out his cruel plan.

Judas Prepares His Troops for Battle

6 In his arrogance Nicanor had boasted that he would set up a monument in honour of his victory over Judas. 7 But Judas was fully confident that the Lord would help him, 8 so he urged his men not to be afraid of the enemy. He encouraged them to remember how the Almighty had helped them in times past and to rest assured that he would give them victory this time also. 9 He renewed their hope by reading to them from the Law and the Prophets and by reminding them of the battles they had already won. 10 When his men were ready for battle, he gave them their orders and at the same

time pointed out how the Gentiles could not be trusted, because they never kept their treaties. [11]He armed all his men, not by encouraging them to trust in shields and spears, but by inspiring them with courageous words. He also raised their morale by telling them about his dream, a kind of vision that they could trust in.

12 He told them that he had seen a vision of Onias, the former High Priest, that great and wonderful man of humble and gentle disposition, who was an outstanding orator and who had been taught from childhood how to live a virtuous life. With outstretched arms Onias was praying for the entire Jewish nation. [13]Judas then saw an impressive white-haired man of great dignity and authority. [14]Onias said: "This is God's prophet Jeremiah, who loves his fellow Jews and offers many prayers for us and for Jerusalem, the holy city."

15 Then Jeremiah stretched out his right hand and gave Judas a gold sword, saying as he did so, [16]"This holy sword is a gift from God. Take it and destroy your enemies."

17 The eloquent words that Judas spoke encouraged everyone to be brave, and inspired boys to fight like men. Their city, their religion, and their Temple were in danger. So the Jews made up their minds not to waste any time, but to make a daring attack against the enemy and bravely decide their fate in hand-to-hand combat. [18]They were not so concerned about their own families and relatives as they were about their sacred Temple. [19]And the people who had to stay in Jerusalem were deeply concerned about how a battle on open ground would turn out.

The Defeat and Death of Nicanor

20 Everyone was waiting to see who would win the battle. The enemy troops were already moving forward, with their cavalry on each side of them, and their elephants placed in strategic positions. [21]Judas Maccabeus looked at the huge enemy force, the variety of their weapons, and their fierce elephants. Then he raised his hands towards heaven and prayed to the Lord, who works miracles, because he knew that the Lord gives victory to those who deserve it, not to those who have a strong army. [22]Judas said: "Lord, when Hezekiah was king of Judah, you

sent your angel, who killed 185,000 of King Sennacherib's men. [23]Now once again, Lord of heaven, send your good angel to make our enemies shake and tremble with fear. [24]By your great power, destroy these people who have slandered you and have come out to attack your chosen people." So Judas ended his prayer.

25 Nicanor and his army moved forward to the sound of trumpets and battle-songs, [26]but Judas and his men went into battle calling on God for help. [27]So by fighting with their hands and praying to God in their hearts, the Jews killed more than 35,000 of the enemy. How grateful they were for the help they had received from God! [28]When the battle was over and they were going home celebrating their victory, they noticed Nicanor in full armour lying dead on the battlefield. [29]Then with loud shouts they praised the Lord in their native language.

30 Judas Maccabaeus, who had always fought with all his body and soul for his fellow Jews, never losing the patriotism of his youth, ordered his men to cut off Nicanor's head and right arm and to take them to Jerusalem. [31]When they arrived in the city, he called together all the people, stationed the priests before the altar, and sent for the men in the fort. [32]He showed them the head of the evil Nicanor and the arm which that wicked man had arrogantly stretched out against the sacred Temple of the Almighty God. [33]Then he cut out the tongue of that godless man, promising to feed it bit by bit to the birds and to hang up his head opposite the Temple, as evidence of what his foolishness did for him. [34]Everyone there looked up to heaven and praised the Lord, who had revealed his power and had kept his Temple from being defiled. [35]Judas hung Nicanor's head from the wall of the fort, as a clear proof to everyone of the Lord's help. [36]By unanimous vote it was decided that this day would never be forgotten, but would be celebrated each year on the eve of Mordecai's Day, [c] which is the thirteenth day of the twelfth month, called Adar in Aramaic.

Concluding Words

37 That is how things turned out for Nicanor. The city of Jerusalem remained in the possession of the Hebrew people

---

[c]MORDECAI'S DAY: *The Festival of Purim (see Esth 9.17–22).*
15.22: 2 Kgs 19.35   **15.25–35:** 1 Macc 7.43–50   **15.36:** 1 Macc 7.49

from that time on, so I will end my story here. [38] If it is well written and to the point, I am pleased; if it is poorly written and uninteresting, I have still done my best. [39] We know it is unhealthy to drink wine or water alone, whereas wine mixed with water makes a delightfully tasty drink. So also a good story skilfully written gives pleasure to those who read it. With this I conclude.

SOME ADDITIONAL
BOOKS

Introduction

The following books: 1 Esdras, 2 Esdras, and the Prayer of Manasseh, are accepted by many (especially Anglicans) as a part of the Apocrypha. 1 Esdras and the Prayer of Manasseh constituted a part of the Septuagint Greek text of the Old Testament used by Christians during the early centuries of Christianity. The book of 2 Esdras may not have been in its final form until towards the end of the second century A.D.

THE FIRST BOOK OF
ESDRAS

INTRODUCTION

The *First book of Esdras* parallels the account given in *Second Chronicles* 35-36, *Ezra*, and *Nehemiah* 6-8, although there are omissions, additions, and variations in both order and detail. The most distinctive new material is the debate before the emperor in chapters 3 and 4.

Outline of Contents

Josiah and the fall of Jerusalem   1.1-58
The return from exile   2.1-30
The debate of the bodyguards before the emperor   3.1—4.63
The Temple rebuilt and dedicated   5.1—7.15
Ezra returns with other exiles   8.1—9.55

Josiah Celebrates the Passover
(2 Kgs 23.21-23; 2 Chr 35.1-9)

1 King Josiah celebrated the Passover at Jerusalem in honour of the Lord; on the fourteenth day of the first month they killed the animals for the festival. ²Josiah organized the priests, dressed in their priestly robes, to serve in the Temple according to the daily order. ³He also instructed the Levites, the Temple servants, to purify themselves for the Lord's service, so that they could put the sacred Covenant Box of the Lord in the Temple that King Solomon, the son of David, had built. ⁴Josiah said to them, "You must no longer carry it from place to place, but you are to serve the Lord your God and minister to his people Israel. Get ready by family and clan to carry out your duties ⁵according to the directions given by King David and the splendid way that they were carried out by his son King Solomon. Take your places in the Temple in proper order according to your family divisions as Levites serving the Lord for the people of Israel. ⁶Kill the Passover lambs and goats and prepare the sacrifices for your fellow Israelites. Then celebrate the Passover according to the instructions that the Lord gave to Moses."

7 Josiah gave to the people who were present thirty thousand young sheep and goats and three thousand calves. These were a gift from the royal estates to carry out the promise he had made to the people, the priests, and the Levites. ⁸The officials in charge of the Temple—Hilkiah, Zechariah, and Jehiel—also gave the priests two thousand six hundred sheep and three hundred calves for sacrifices during the festival. ⁹And the army commanders—Conaniah, Shemaiah and his brother Nethanel, Hashabiah, Ochiel, and Joram—contributed five thousand sheep and seven hundred calves for the Levites to offer as sacrifices.

10-11 This is what happened. The priests and the Levites, dressed in the proper manner and carrying the unleavened bread, came that morning to present the offerings to the Lord according to the instructions in the Law of Moses. They took their positions in front of the people in the order of tribal and family divisions. ¹²The Levites roasted the Passover sacrifices and ʻhen boiled them in pots and cauldrons, r͏   ͺg

1.5: 2 Chr 8.14   **1.12:** Ex 12.8-9

The priests and the Levites...carrying the unleavened bread (1.10)

a pleasant smell. [13] Then they distributed the meat to all the people. After that was done, they took meat for themselves and for the priests, the descendants of Aaron, [14] because the priests were kept busy until night burning the fat of the sacrifices. [15-16] The guards at the Temple gates and the Temple singers of the Levite clan of Asaph (with Asaph, Zechariah, and Eddinus, who were representatives of the king) remained at the places assigned to them by King David's instructions. They did not need to leave their posts, because the other Levites prepared the Passover for them.

[17-18] So, as King Josiah had commanded, everything that related to the sacrifices offered to the Lord was done that day; the Passover Festival was celebrated, and the sacrifices were offered on the altar. [19] All the people of Israel who were present at that time kept the Passover and observed the Festival of Unleavened Bread for seven days. [20] Since the days of the prophet Samuel, the Passover had never been celebrated so faithfully. [21-22] None of the former kings of Israel had ever celebrated a Passover like this one celebrated by King Josiah in Jerusalem in the eighteenth year of his

reign; it was celebrated by the priests, the Levites, and all the people of Judah and Israel.

The End of Josiah's Reign
(2 Kgs 23.28–30; 2 Chr 35.20–27)

23 The Lord was pleased with everything Josiah did, for he was a deeply religious man. [24] But the ancient records also tell the story of those who sinned and rebelled against the Lord during Josiah's reign. They sinned more than any other nation or kingdom and did things that offended the Lord so much that his judgement fell on the people of Israel.

25 After Josiah had done all these things, the king of Egypt led an army to fight at Carchemish on the River Euphrates. Josiah tried to stop him, [26] but the king of Egypt sent Josiah this message: "The war I am fighting does not concern you, King of Judah. [27] The Lord God did not send me to fight you; my battle is on the Euphrates. The Lord is with me, and he is urging me on; so withdraw your troops and don't oppose the Lord." [28] But Josiah did not go back to his chariot and withdraw. He refused to listen to what the Lord had said through the prophet Jeremiah and decided to fight.

1.19: Ex 12.1–20

29 He went into battle on the plain of Megiddo, and the Egyptian commanders attacked him.

30 King Josiah ordered his servants, "Take me off the battlefield; I'm badly wounded." So they took him out of the line of battle immediately, 31 and he got into a second chariot and was taken back to Jerusalem. There he died and was buried in the royal tomb. 32 All the people of Judah mourned for him.

The prophet Jeremiah composed a lament for King Josiah. It has become a custom in Israel for the leaders and their wives to sing this song when they mourn for him. 33 These things are recorded in *The History of the Kings of Judah*. Everything that Josiah did, how he gained his fame and his understanding of the Law, what he did èarlier and what is told here, is all recorded in *The History of the Kings of Israel and Judah*.

King Joahaz of Judah
(2 Kgs 23.30–35; 2 Chr 36.1–4)

34 The people of Judah chose Josiah's son Joahaz *a* and made him king. Joahaz was twenty-three years old, 35 and he ruled over Judah and Jerusalem for three months. Then the king of Egypt deposed him 36 and made the nation pay 3,400 kilogrammes of silver and 34 kilogrammes of gold as tribute. 37 The king of Egypt appointed Joahaz's brother Jehoiakim king of Judah and Jerusalem. 38 Jehoiakim put the leading men of the nation in prison, then had his brother Zarius arrested and brought back from Egypt.

King Jehoiakim of Judah
(2 Kgs 23.36—24.7; 2 Chr 36.5–8)

39 Jehoiakim was twenty-five years old when he became king of Judah and Jerusalem. He sinned against the Lord. 40 King Nebuchadnezzar of Babylonia invaded Judah, captured Jehoiakim, and took him to Babylonia in bronze chains. 41 Nebuchadnezzar also carried off some of the sacred utensils from the Temple and put them in his own temple in Babylon. 42 The stories about Jehoiakim, his depravity, and the godless way he lived are recorded in *The Chronicles of the Kings*.

King Jehoiachin of Judah
(2 Kgs 24.8–17; 2 Chr 36.9–10)

43 Jehoiachin was eighteen years old when he succeeded his father Jehoiakim as king, 44 and he ruled in Jerusalem for three months and ten days. He too sinned against the Lord. 45 A year later King Nebuchadnezzar had Jehoiachin taken to Babylonia as a prisoner; Nebuchadnezzar also carried off sacred utensils from the Temple. 46 Then he made Zedekiah king of Judah and Jerusalem.

King Zedekiah of Judah
(2 Kgs 24.18–20; 2 Chr 36.11–12; Jer 52.1–3a)

Zedekiah was then twenty-one years old, and he ruled for eleven years. 47 He sinned against the Lord and refused to listen to the prophet Jeremiah, who spoke the word of the Lord.

The Fall of Jerusalem
(2 Kgs 25.1–21; 2 Chr 36.13–21; Jer 52.3b–11)

48 Although King Nebuchadnezzar had forced Zedekiah to swear in the Lord's name that he would be loyal to him, Zedekiah broke his oath and rebelled against him. He stubbornly refused to obey the commands of the Lord, the God of Israel. 49 In addition, the leaders of the people and even the chief priests did more godless and lawless things than all the corrupt heathen; they defiled the Temple of the Lord, which he had made holy. 50 The God of their ancestors had continued to send prophets to call them back from their sins, because he wanted to spare them and the Temple. 51 But when the Lord spoke through his prophets, the people ridiculed them and laughed. 52 At last the Lord became so angry with his people and their depraved ways that he ordered the kings of Babylonia to attack them. 53 The Babylonians killed the young men of Judah all round the Temple and did not spare anyone, young or old, man or woman. The Lord handed them all over to their enemies. 54 The Babylonians carried off all the sacred utensils from the Temple, the treasure chests, *b* and the wealth of the king; they took everything away to Babylon, leaving nothing behind. 55 They burnt down the Temple, broke down the city wall, set fire to its towers, 56 and completely destroyed all its beauty.

a Joahaz; *some manuscripts have* Jeconiah.
b treasure chests; *some manuscripts have* the equipment of the Covenant Box.
1.37: Jer 22.11-12   **1.39:** Jer 22.18-19; 26.1   **1.40:** Dan 1.1-2
1.45: Jer 22.24-30; 24.1; 29.1-2; Ezek 17.12   **1.48:** Ezek 17.15

Nebuchadnezzar forced all the survivors to be led away to Babylon, [57] where they served him and his descendants as slaves until the rise of the Persian Empire. And so what the Lord had foretold through the prophet Jeremiah was fulfilled: [58] "The land will lie desolate for seventy years to make up for the Sabbath rest[c] that has not been observed."

Cyrus Commands the Jews to Return
(2 Chr 36.22–23; Ezra 1.1–11)

2 In the first year that Cyrus of Persia was emperor,[d] the Lord made what he had said through the prophet Jeremiah come true. [2] He prompted Cyrus to issue the following command and send it out in writing to be read aloud everywhere in his empire:

[3] "This is the command of Cyrus, emperor of Persia. The Lord of Israel, the Lord Most High, has appointed me ruler over the whole world [4] and has given me the responsibility of building a temple for him in Jerusalem in Judah. [5] May the Lord be with those of you who are his people. You are to go to Jerusalem and rebuild the Temple of the Lord of Israel, the Lord who lives in Jerusalem. [6] If any of his people in exile need help to return, their neighbours must give them this help, and provide them with silver and gold [7] and other gifts, with horses and pack animals, as well as anything else offered for the Temple of the Lord in Jerusalem in fulfilment of a vow."

[8] Then the heads of the clans of the tribes of Judah and Benjamin, the priests and the Levites, and everyone else whose heart the Lord had moved, got ready to go and rebuild the Lord's Temple in Jerusalem. [9] Their neighbours helped them with everything, giving them silver, gold, horses, and pack animals. Many of their neighbours were also led to give a large number of other things, in fulfilment of vows.

[10] Cyrus gave them back the sacred utensils that King Nebuchadnezzar had taken from Jerusalem and had put in the temple of his idols. [11] He brought them out and handed them over to Mithredath, chief of the royal treasury, [12] who delivered them to Sheshbazzar, the governor of Judah. [13] Here is the inventory of the utensils:

gold bowls for offerings	1,000
silver bowls for offerings	1,000
silver fire pans	29
small gold bowls	30
small silver bowls	2,410
other utensils	1,000

[14] In all there were 5,469 gold and silver bowls and other utensils, [15] and Sheshbazzar took these with him when he and the other exiles went from Babylon to Jerusalem.

Opposition to Rebuilding Jerusalem
(Ezra 4.7–24)

[16] In the reign of Emperor Artaxerxes of Persia, Bishlam, Mithredath, Tabeel, Rehum, Beltethmus, Shimshai the secretary of the province, and their associates who lived in Samaria and elsewhere wrote the following letter of protest against the Jews who were living in Judah and Jerusalem:

[17] "To His Majesty Emperor Artaxerxes from your servants, the official correspondent Rehum, the secretary Shimshai, the other members of the council, and the judges of Greater Syria and Phoenicia.

[18] "We want Your Majesty to know that the Jews who came here from your other territories have settled in Jerusalem and are rebuilding that evil and rebellious city. They are restoring the marketplaces, repairing the walls, and laying the foundations for a temple. [19] If this city is rebuilt and its walls are completed, the people will stop paying taxes and will even rebel against royal authority. [20] Since work on the Temple has already begun, we consider it appropriate not to overlook such an important matter [21] but to bring it to the attention of Your Majesty. Then, if it seems proper to you, a search may be made in the records your ancestors kept. [22] You will find information about these matters in the historical records, and you will discover that this city has always been rebellious and given trouble to other cities and kings. [23] The Jews have used it from ancient times as a base for rebellions and

---

[c] SABBATH REST: *A reference to the requirement of the Law that every seventh year the land was not to be farmed (see Lev 25.1–7).*
[d] EMPEROR: *King Cyrus of Persia occupied the city of Babylon in 539 B.C. and began to reign as the emperor of Babylonia.*
1.58: Jer 25.11; 29.10   **2.3:** Is 44.28

wars. That is why the city was destroyed. 24 We therefore declare to you that if this city is rebuilt and its walls are restored, Your Majesty will no longer be able to enter Greater Syria and Phoenicia."

25 The emperor sent the following answer to the official correspondent Rehum, Beltethmus, the secretary Shimshai, and their associates who lived in Samaria, Syria, and Phoenicia:

26 "After reading the letter which you sent me, I gave orders for an investigation to be made, and it has indeed been found that from ancient times Jerusalem has revolted against royal authority, 27 and its people have been involved in insurrections and wars. Powerful and cruel kings have reigned there and have ruled over Greater Syria and Phoenicia, from which they collected taxes. 28 Therefore I am now issuing orders that those men be prevented from rebuilding the city and that necessary steps be taken to ensure that these orders will not be disobeyed, 29 so that this trouble spot will no longer be a threat to the royal interests."

They hurried to Jerusalem...and began interfering with the rebuilding (2.30)

30 As soon as this letter from Artaxerxes was read, Rehum, Shimshai the secretary, and their associates hurried to Jerusalem with a force of cavalry and a large number of armed troops and began interfering with the rebuilding of the Temple. The work had to stop, and no more was done until the second year of the reign of Darius, emperor of Persia.

The Debate of the Bodyguards before the Emperor

3 Darius the emperor gave a great banquet for all those under him, all the members of his family and staff, all the leading officials of Persia and Media, 2 all his chief officers, administrators, and the governors of the 127 provinces stretching from India to Sudan. 3 When everyone had had enough to eat and drink, they left, and Darius went to bed. He fell asleep but soon awoke.

A Contest Is Proposed

4 Then the three young men who served Emperor Darius as his personal bodyguard said to one another, 5 "Let each of us name the one thing that he considers the strongest thing in the world. The emperor will decide who has given the wisest answer to this question and will give magnificent gifts and prizes to the winner. 6 He will wear royal robes, drink from a gold cup, and sleep in a gold bed. He will have a chariot with gold-studded bridles, wear a fine linen turban, and have a gold necklace. 7 Because of his wisdom he will be an adviser to the emperor and will be given the title 'Relative of the Emperor.'"

8 Then each of them wrote down the best answer he could think of, sealed it, and put it under the emperor's pillow. They said to one another, 9 "When the emperor wakes up, the statements will be given to him. He and the three leading officials of Persia will decide who gave the wisest answer. The winner will be given the prize on the basis of what he has written." 10 The first wrote, "There is nothing stronger than wine." 11 The second wrote, "There is nothing stronger than the emperor." 12 And the third wrote, "There is nothing stronger than a woman, but truth can conquer anything."

13 When the emperor woke up, the written statements were given to him, and he read them. 14 Then he sent messengers and called together all the leading officials of Persia and Media, including the chief officers, administrators, governors, and commissioners. 15 He took his seat in the council chamber and had the three statements read aloud. 16 "Bring in the three young men," he said, "and let them explain their answers." So when they

were brought in, [17] they were asked to explain what they had written.

The Speech about Wine

The bodyguard who had written about the strength of wine spoke first: [18] "Gentlemen," he began, "wine is clearly the strongest thing in the world. It confuses the mind of everyone who drinks it. [19] It has exactly the same effect on everyone: king or orphan, slave or free, rich or poor. [20] It makes every thought happy and carefree, and makes one forget every sorrow and responsibility. [21] It makes everyone feel rich, ignore the power of kings and officials, and talk as if he owned the whole world. [22] When men drink wine, they forget who their friends and neighbours are, and then they are soon drawing their swords to fight them. [23] Then, when they sober up, they don't remember what they have done. [24] Gentlemen," he finished by saying, "if wine makes men act in this way, it certainly must be the strongest thing in the world."

The Speech about the Emperor

4 The bodyguard who had written about the strength of the emperor spoke next. [2] "Gentlemen," he began, "nothing in the world is stronger than men, since they rule over land and sea and, in fact, over everything in the world. [3] But the emperor is the strongest of them all; he is their lord and master, and men obey him, no matter what he commands. [4] If he tells them to make war on one another, they do it. If he sends them out against his enemies, they go, even if they have to break down mountains, walls, or towers. [5] They may kill or be killed, but they never disobey the emperor's orders. If they are victorious, they bring him all their loot and everything else they have taken in battle. [6] Farmers do not go out to war, but even when they bring to the emperor a part of everything that they harvest, and they compel one another to pay taxes to the emperor. [7] Although the emperor is only one man, if he orders people to kill, they kill; if he orders them to set prisoners free, they do it; [8] if he orders them to attack, they do; if he orders destruction, they destroy; if he orders them to build, they build; [9] if he orders crops to be destroyed or fields to be planted, it is done. [10] Everybody, soldier or civilian, obeys the emperor. And when he sits down to eat or drink and then falls asleep,

[11] his servants stand guard round him, without being able to go and take care of their own affairs, for they never disobey him. [12] Gentlemen," he ended by saying, "since people obey the emperor like this, certainly nothing in the world is stronger than he is."

The Speech about Women

13 The bodyguard who had written about the women and the truth—it was Zerubbabel—spoke last. [14] "Gentlemen," he began, "the emperor is certainly powerful, men are numerous, and wine is strong, but who rules and controls them all? It is women! [15] Women gave birth to the emperor and all the men who rule over land and sea. [16] Women brought them into the world. Women brought up the men who planted the vineyards from which wine comes. [17] Women make the clothes that men wear; women bring honour to men; in fact, without women, men couldn't live.

18 "Men may accumulate silver or gold or other beautiful things, but if they see a woman with a pretty face or a good figure, [19] they will leave it all to gape and stare, and they will desire her more than their wealth. [20] A man will leave his own father, who brought him up, and leave his own country to get married. [21] He will forget his father, his mother, and his country to spend the rest of his life with his wife. [22] So you must recognize that women are your masters. Don't you work and sweat and then take all that you have earned and give it to your wives? [23] A man will take his sword and go out to attack, rob and steal, and sail the seas and rivers. [24] He may have to face lions or travel in the dark, but when he has robbed, stolen, and plundered, he will bring the loot home to the woman he loves.

25 "A man loves his wife more than his parents. [26] Some men are driven out of their minds on account of a woman, and others become slaves for the sake of a woman. [27] Others have been put to death, have ruined their lives, or have committed crimes because of a woman. [28] So now do you believe me?

"The emperor's power is certainly great—no nation has the courage to attack him. [29] But once I saw him with Apame, his concubine, the daughter of the famous Bartacus. While she was sitting at the emperor's right, [30] she took his crown off his head, put it on her own, and then slapped his face with her left hand. ³¹All the emperor did was look at her with his mouth open. Whenever she smiles at him, he smiles back; and when she gets angry with him, he flatters her and teases her until she is in a good mood again. ³²Gentlemen, if women can do all that, surely there can be nothing stronger in the world." ³³The emperor and his officials just looked at one another.

The Speech about Truth

Then Zerubbabel began to speak about truth. ³⁴"Yes, gentlemen," he said, "women are very strong. But think how big the earth is, how high the sky is; think how fast the sun moves, as it rapidly circles the whole sky in a single day. ³⁵If the sun can do this, it is certainly great. But truth is greater and stronger than all of these things. ³⁶Everyone on earth honours truth; heaven praises it; all creation trembles in awe before it.

"There is not the slightest injustice in truth. ᵉ ³⁷You will find injustice in wine, the emperor, women, all human beings, in all they do, and in everything else. There is no truth in them; they are unjust and they will perish. ³⁸But truth endures and is always strong; it will continue to live and reign for ever. ³⁹Truth shows no partiality or favouritism; it does what is right, rather than what is unjust or evil. Everyone approves what truth does; ⁴⁰its decisions are always fair. Truth is strong, royal, powerful, and majestic for ever. Let all things praise the God of truth!"

The Response

41 When Zerubbabel had finished speaking, all the people shouted, "Truth is great—there is nothing stronger!"
42 Then the emperor said to him, "You may ask anything you want, even more than what was agreed, and I will give it to you. You will be my adviser, and you will be granted the title 'Relative of the Emperor.'"
43 Zerubbabel replied, "Your Majesty, permit me to remind you of the solemn vow you took on the day you became emperor. You promised to rebuild Jerusalem ⁴⁴and to send back all the treasures that had been taken from the city. Remember that when Cyrus made a vow to destroy Babylon, he set these things aside and solemnly promised to send them back to Jerusalem. ⁴⁵You also promised to rebuild the Temple, which

the Edomites burnt down when the Babylonians devastated the land of Judah. ⁴⁶So, Your Majesty, because you are a man of generosity, I beg you to fulfil the solemn promise you made to the King of Heaven."

47 Then Darius the emperor stood up, kissed Zerubbabel, and wrote letters for him to all the treasurers, governors, and administrators in the provinces, ordering them to provide safe conduct for him and all those going with him to rebuild Jerusalem. ⁴⁸He also wrote letters to all the governors in Greater Syria and Phoenicia, with special instructions to those in Lebanon, to transport cedar logs to Jerusalem and help Zerubbabel rebuild the city.

49 The emperor also provided letters for all the Jews who wished to return to Jerusalem. These letters guaranteed their freedom and ordered all governors, treasurers, and other administrators not to interfere with them in any way. ⁵⁰All the land that they acquired was to be exempt from taxation, and the Edomites were to surrender the villages they had taken from the Jews. ⁵¹Each year 680 kilogrammes of silver would be given for the construction of the Temple until it was finished. ⁵²In addition, 340 kilo-grammes of silver would be given each year to provide for the seventeen burnt-offerings to be offered in the Temple each day. ⁵³All the Jews who left Babylonia to build the city of Jerusalem would be granted their freedom, together with their children and the priests.

54 The emperor's orders gave specific instructions, as follows: the priests were to be supported, their robes for the Temple service were to be provided, ⁵⁵the Levites were to be supported until the Temple and Jerusalem were completely rebuilt, ⁵⁶and land and wages were to be provided for all the guards of the city. ⁵⁷He also reaffirmed Cyrus' instructions that all the small utensils and Temple treasures that Cyrus had set aside should be returned to Jerusalem.

58 Then the young man Zerubbabel left the council chamber, turned towards Jerusalem, looked up to heaven, and praised the King of Heaven: ⁵⁹"Lord, all praise belongs to you; you are the source of all victory and wisdom, ⁶⁰and I thank you, O Lord of our ancestors, for giving wisdom to me, your servant."

ᵉin truth; *some manuscripts have* with God.
4.45: Obad 10–14

61 Zerubbabel took the emperor's letters and went to Babylon, where he told his fellow Jews everything that had happened. 62 They praised the God of their ancestors because he had made it possible for them 63 to go and rebuild Jerusalem and the Temple which bears his name. For seven days they held a joyful celebration, accompanied by music.

The List of Those Who Returned from Exile
(Ezra 2.1–70; Neh 7.4–73)

5 After this, the heads of clans were chosen, tribe by tribe, to go to Jerusalem with their wives, children, slaves, and animals. 2 Darius sent a thousand cavalry troops to escort them safely back to Jerusalem. 3 He sent them off to the music of drums and flutes, while all their fellow-countrymen danced for joy.

4 These are the names, by tribes, clans, and families, of the men who returned: 5 Among the priests, descendants of Phinehas son of Aaron, was Joshua, son of Jozadak and grandson of Seraiah. He was accompanied by Zerubbabel,f who was the son of Shealtiel of the family of David, of the line of Perez, of the tribe of Judah. 6 He was the one who had spoken the wise words before Darius, emperor of Persia. They left Babylon in the second year of his reign in Nisan, the first month.

7 These are the Jewish men who returned from exile. Their families had been living in Babylonia since King Nebuchadnezzar had taken them there as prisoners. 8 They returned to Jerusalem and the rest of Judah, each to his own home town. Their leaders were Zerubbabel, Joshua, Nehemiah, Seraiah, Resaiah, Eneneus, Mordecai, Beelsarus, Aspharasus, Reeliah, Rehum, and Baanah.

9–17a The following is a list of the clans of Israel, with the number of those from each clan who returned with their leaders from exile:

Parosh — 2,172
Shephatiah — 472
Arah — 756
Pahath Moab (descendants of Jeshua and Joab) — 2,812
Elam — 1,254
Zattu — 945
Chorbe — 705
Bani — 648
Bebai — 623
Azgad — 1,322

Adonikam — 667
Bigvai — 2,066
Adin — 454
Ater (also called Hezekiah) — 92
Kilan and Azetas — 67
Azaru — 432
Annias — 101
Arom — ...
Bezai — 323
Arsiphurith — 112
Baiterus — 3,005

17b–23 People whose ancestors had lived in the following towns also returned:

Bethlehem — 123
Netophah — 55
Anathoth — 158
Beth Azmaveth — 42
Kiriath Jearim — 25
Chephirah and Beeroth — 743
The towns of the Chadiasans and the Ammidians — 422
Ramah and Geba — 621
Michmash — 122
Bethel — 52
Magbish — 156
The other Elam and Ono — 725
Jericho — 345
Senaah — 3,330

24–25 The following is the list of the priestly clans that returned from exile:

Jedaiah (descendants of Jeshua and Anasib) — 972
Immer — 1,052
Pashhur — 1,247
Harim — 1,017

26–28 Clans of Levites who returned from exile:

Jeshua, Kadmiel, Bannas, and Sudias — 74
Temple musicians (descendants of Asaph) — 128
Temple guards (descendants of Shallum, Ater, Talmon, Akkub, Hatita, and Shobai) — 139

29–32 Clans of Temple workmen who returned from exile:

Esau, Hasupha, Tabbaoth,
Keros, Siaha, Padon,
Lebanah, Hagabah, Akkub,
Uthai, Ketab, Hagab,
Shamlai, Hanan, Cathua,
Geddur, Jairus, Daisan,
Noeba, Chaseba, Gazera,
Uzza, Phinoe, Asara,
Besai, Asnah, Meunim,
Nephisim, Akub, Hakupha,
Asur, Pharakim, Bazluth,
Mehida, Cutha, Charea,
Barkos, Sisera, Temah,

---

f Probable text He was accompanied by Zerubbabel; Greek and Joakim son of Zerubbabel.

Neziah, Hatipha

33-34 Clans of Solomon's servants who returned from exile:

Hassophereth, Peruda, Jaalah,
Lozon, Giddel, Shephatiah,
Agia, Phochereth Hazzebaim,
Sarothie, Masiah, Gas,
Addus, Subas, Apherra,
Barodis, Shaphat, Adlon

35 The total number of descendants of the Temple workmen and of Solomon's servants who returned from exile was 372.

36-37 There were 652 belonging to the clans of Delaiah (descendants of Tobiah) and Nekoda who returned from the towns of Tel Melah and Tel Harsha, with their leaders Cherub, Addan, and Immer; but these could not prove that they were descendants of the Israelites.

38-39 The following clans, who claimed to be priestly clans, could find no record to prove their ancestry: Habaiah, Hakkoz, Jaddus (the ancestor of the clan of Jaddus had married Agia, one of the daughters of Barzillai, and had taken the name of his father-in-law's clan). Since they were unable to prove who their ancestors were, they were not allowed to function as priests. [40]Nehemiah the governor[g] told them that they could not eat the food offered to God until there was a High Priest who could use the Revelation and Truth.[h]

41-43 The total number of Israelites (twelve years old or older, not counting servants) — 42,360

Male and female servants — 7,337
Male and female musicians — 245
Camels — 435
Horses — 7,036
Mules — 245
Donkeys — 5,525

44 When the exiles arrived at the place of God's Temple in Jerusalem, some of the leaders of the clans took a vow to rebuild the Temple on its old site, to the best of their ability. [45]They promised to contribute for the rebuilding and the service of the Temple 500 kilogrammes of gold, 2,500 kilogrammes of silver, and 100 robes for priests.

46 The priests, the Levites, and some of the people settled in or near Jerusalem; the musicians and the Temple guards settled in nearby towns; and the rest of the Israelites settled in the towns where their ancestors had lived.

Worship Begins Again
(Ezra 3.1-6)

47 By the seventh month the people of Israel were all settled in their towns. Then they all assembled in the open square in front of the first gate on the east side of the Temple area. [48]Joshua son of Jehozadak, his fellow-priests, and Zerubbabel son of Shealtiel, together with his relatives, prepared the altar of the God of Israel, [49]so that they could burn sacrifices on it according to the instructions written in the Law of Moses, the man of God. [50]Some of the local people, even though they were stronger than the Jews and opposed to them, joined them[i] in rebuilding the altar where it had stood before. Then the Jews began once again to burn the regular morning and evening sacrifices on the altar. [51]They celebrated the Festival of Shelters, according to the regulations, each day offering the sacrifices required for that day. [52]They also offered the normal daily sacrifices, as well as those required for the Sabbath, the New Moon Festival, and the other regular assemblies for worship. [53]Although the people had not yet rebuilt God's Temple, everyone who had made a vow to God began to offer sacrifices on the first day of the seventh month.

The Rebuilding of the Temple Begins
(Ezra 3.7-13)

54 The people gave money to pay the stonemasons and the carpenters; they gave food, drink, [55]and carts to be sent to the cities of Tyre and Sidon in exchange for cedar logs from Lebanon, which were to be floated to the harbour at Joppa. All this was done according to the orders given by Cyrus, emperor of Persia.

56-57 So in the second month of the year after they came back to the site of the Temple in Jerusalem, they started the work and began laying the foundation. Zerubbabel, Joshua, and the rest of their fellow-countrymen, the priests, and the Levites—in fact, all the exiles who had come back to Jerusalem, joined in the work. [58]The Levites twenty years of age or older were put in charge of rebuilding

---

[g]Probable meaning the governor; Greek and Attharias.
[h]REVELATION AND TRUTH: This is the Greek translation of Urim and Thummim, two objects used by the priest to determine God's will; it is not known precisely how they were used.
[i]Some of...joined them; Greek unclear.
5.40: Num 27.21   **5.46:** 1 Chr 9.2; Neh 11.3   **5.52:** Num 28.11—29.39

the Temple for the Lord. The Levite Jeshua and his sons and relatives, his brother Kadmiel, the sons of Jeshua Emadabun, the sons of Joda son of Iliadun, and all their sons and relatives— in fact, all the Levites joined together to take charge of the rebuilding of the Temple.

While the workmen were building the Temple of the Lord, 59 the priests in their robes took their places with trumpets and other musical instruments in their hands, and the Levites of the clan of Asaph stood there with cymbals. 60 They praised the Lord and gave thanks to him according to the instructions handed down from the time of King David. 61 They sang psalms praising the Lord, repeating the refrain: "The goodness of the Lord and his glorious presence are with all Israel for ever." 62 All the people blew trumpets and shouted with all their might, praising the Lord because the Temple was being rebuilt. 63 Some of the older priests, Levites, and heads of clans had seen the first Temple, and when they came and saw the building of this Temple, they cried and wailed. 64 Others who were there blew trumpets and shouted for joy. 65 The crowd blew the trumpets so loudly that the blast could be heard far away, but no one near by could hear the blast of the trumpets because the sound made by those who were crying and wailing was so loud.

Opposition to the Rebuilding of the Temple
(Ezra 4.1-5)

66 The enemies of the tribes of Judah and Benjamin heard the sound of the trumpets and came to see what it meant. 67 When they learnt that those who had returned from exile were rebuilding the Temple of the Lord, the God of Israel, 68 they went to Zerubbabel, Joshua, and the heads of the clans and said, "Let us join you in building the Temple. 69 We worship the same Lord you worship and we have been offering sacrifices to him ever since Esarhaddon,[j] emperor of Assyria, sent us here to live."

70 Zerubbabel, Joshua, and the heads of the clans said to them, "We don't need your help in building the Temple for the Lord our God. 71 We will build it ourselves, just as Cyrus, emperor of Persia, commanded us."

72 Then the people who had been living in the land began to harass[k] the Jews; they cut off their supplies and kept them from building. 73 These people plotted, agitated, and rioted so much that they prevented the Temple from being completed during the reign of Cyrus. The work was halted until Darius became emperor, two years later.

Work on the Temple Begins Again
(Ezra 5.1-17)

6 In the second year of the reign of Darius, the two prophets, Haggai and Zechariah son of Iddo, began to speak in the name of the Lord God of Israel to the Jews who lived in Judah and Jerusalem. 2 When Zerubbabel son of Shealtiel and Joshua son of Jehozadak heard their messages, they began to rebuild the Temple in Jerusalem, and the two prophets helped them.

3 Almost at once Sisinnes, governor of Greater Syria and Phoenicia, with Shethar Bozenai and their fellow-officials, came to Jerusalem and demanded: 4 "Who gave you orders to build this temple and complete this roof and everything else? Who is doing this ˌwork?" 5 But the Lord was with the people who had returned from exile and was watching over the Jewish leaders, 6 and they were allowed to continue building until Darius could be informed and his reply received. 7 This is the report that the Persian officials sent to the emperor:

8 "To Emperor Darius, greetings.

"Your Majesty should know that we went to Judah and to Jerusalem and there we found the leaders of the Jews who have returned from exile 9 building a large new temple for the Lord with expensive, shaped stone blocks and with wooden beams set in the walls. 10 The work is being done rapidly and is moving ahead steadily; yet they are taking great care and making their work look beautiful.

11 "We then asked the leaders of the people to tell us who had given them orders to rebuild the Temple and lay the foundations for the buildings. 12 We also asked them who their leaders were and demanded a list of their names, so that we could inform you.

---

[j] ESARHADDON: *Greek* Asbasareth.   [k] *Probable text* harass; *Greek unclear.*
5.59-60: 1 Chr 25.1   **5.61:** 1 Chr 16.34; 2 Chr 5.11-14; Ps 100.5; 106.1; 118.1; 136.1; Jer 33.11
5.67-68: 2 Kgs 17.24-41   **6.1:** Zech 1.1   **6.2:** Hag 1.12; Zech 4.6-9

13 "They answered, 'We are servants of the Lord who created heaven and earth. 14 This Temple was built and equipped many years ago by a very powerful king of Israel. 15 But because our ancestors sinned against Israel's Lord in heaven and made him angry, he let them be conquered by King Nebuchadnezzar of Babylonia, a king of the Chaldean dynasty. 16 The Temple was demolished and burnt, and the people were taken into exile in Babylonia. 17 Then, in the first year of his reign as emperor of Babylonia, Cyrus issued orders for the Temple to be rebuilt. 18 He gave back the sacred gold and silver utensils which Nebuchadnezzar had taken from the Temple in Jerusalem and had placed in his own temple in Babylon. Cyrus handed these utensils over to Zerubbabel and the governor, Sheshbazzar. 19 The Emperor told Sheshbazzar to take them and return them to the Temple in Jerusalem, and to rebuild the Temple where it had stood before. 20 So Sheshbazzar came and laid its foundation, and construction has continued from then until the present, but the Temple is still not finished.'

21 "Now, if it please Your Majesty, have a search made in the royal records in Babylon 22 to find whether or not the building of this Temple in Jerusalem had the approval of Emperor Cyrus, and then, if it please Your Majesty, inform us what your will is in this matter."

Emperor Cyrus' Order Is Rediscovered
(Ezra 6.1-5)

23 So Darius the emperor ordered a search to be made in the royal records that were kept in Babylon. It was, however, in the fortress of Ecbatana in the province of Media that a scroll was found, containing the following record:
24 "In the first year of his reign Cyrus the emperor ordered the rebuilding of the Temple in Jerusalem, where sacrifices are continually offered. 25 The Temple is to be 27 metres high and 27 metres wide. The walls must be built with one layer of new local wood on top of every three layers of shaped stone. All expenses are to be paid by the royal

treasury. 26 Also the gold and silver utensils which King Nebuchadnezzar brought to Babylon from the Temple in Jerusalem are to be returned to their proper place in the Jerusalem Temple."

Darius Orders the Work to Continue
(Ezra 6.6-12)

27 Then Darius gave strict orders to Sisinnes, governor of Greater Syria and Phoenicia, Shethar Bozenai, their fellow-officials, and the local officials to stay away from Jerusalem and let Zerubbabel, the servant of the Lord and governor of Judah, and the other Jewish leaders rebuild the Temple of the Lord where it stood before. 28 "And I also command," he continued, "that it be completely rebuilt and that, until it is finished, every effort be made to help the Jews who have returned from exile. 29 From the taxes received in Greater Syria and Phoenicia a contribution shall be made on a regular basis to these men, payable to Zerubbabel, the governor, for bulls, sheep, and lambs to be used in their sacrifices to the Lord. 30 In the same way, each year and without further question, wheat, salt, wine, and olive-oil are to be supplied, according to the daily needs indicated by the priests. 31 This must be done so that they can make wine-offerings to God Most High for me and my children and pray for his blessing on our lives." 32 He also gave these orders: "If anyone disobeys the commands as written above or fails to carry them out, he is to be hanged on a wooden beam taken from his own house, and his property is to be handed over to the emperor. 33 May the Lord who is worshipped at Jerusalem destroy any king or nation that tries to stop the work or damage the Temple there. 34 I, Darius, issue the command that these orders be carried out in every detail."

The Temple Is Dedicated
(Ezra 6.13-18)

7 Then Sisinnes, the governor, Shethar Bozenai, and their fellow-officials did exactly as the emperor had commanded 2 and gave careful supervision to the work on the Temple, helping the Jewish leaders and Temple officials. 3 The workers made good progress with the building of the Temple, encouraged by the prophets

6.15-16: 2 Kgs 25.8-12; 2 Chr 36.17-20; Jer 52.12-15   **6.17:** Ezra 1.2-11; 1 Esd 2.3-15
7.3: Hag 1.1

Haggai and Zechariah. ⁴The Jews completed the building according to the command of the Lord, the God of Israel, and with the permission of Cyrus, Darius, and Artaxerxes, emperors of Persia. ⁵The Temple was completed on the twenty-third day of the month of Adar in the sixth year of the reign of Darius the emperor. ⁶Then the people of Israel—the priests, the Levites, and all the others who had returned from exile and joined them—carried out all the commands in the Law of Moses. ⁷For the dedication they offered a hundred bulls, two hundred rams, and four hundred lambs as sacrifices, ⁸and twelve goats as offerings for sin, one goat for the leader of each tribe of Israel. ⁹The priests in their robes and the Levites took their positions, family by family, for the Temple services of the Lord, the God of Israel, according to the instructions contained in the book of Moses. The Temple guards stood at each gate.

The Passover
(Ezra 6.19–22)

10 The people of Israel who had returned from exile celebrated the Passover on the fourteenth day of the first month of the following year. The priests and Levites had purified themselves at the same time. ¹¹Not all the Jews who had returned purified themselves at that time, but the Levites did.ˡ ¹²The Levites killed the animals for the Passover sacrifices for all the people who had returned, for the priests, and for themselves. ¹³The sacrifices were eaten by all the Israelites who had returned from exile; they worshipped the Lord and rejected the pagan ways of the other people who were living in the land. ¹⁴For seven days they celebrated the Festival of Unleavened Bread. They rejoiced in the presence of the Lord, ¹⁵the God of Israel, because he had made the plans of the emperor of Assyriaᵐ favourable to them and had supported them in their work.

Ezra Arrives in Jerusalem
(Ezra 7.1–10)

8 Many years later, when Artaxerxes was emperor of Persia, a man named Ezra came from Babylon. He traced his ancestry back to Aaron, the High Priest, as follows: Ezra was the son of Seraiah,

son of Azariah, son of Hilkiah, son of Shallum, ²son of Zadok, son of Ahitub, son of Amariah, son of Azariah, son of Bukki, son of Abishua, son of Phinehas, son of Eleazar, son of Aaron.

3-4 Ezra was a scholar with a thorough knowledge of the Law which the God of Israel had given to Moses. The emperor had a high regard for him and approved all the requests he made. Ezra set out from Babylonia ⁵for Jerusalem with a group of Israelites which included priests, Levites, Temple musicians, Temple guards, and workmen. ⁶They left Babylonia on the first day of the first month in the seventh year of the reign of Artaxerxes. God gave them a safe journey, and they arrived in Jerusalem on the first day of the fifth month. ⁷Ezra had a thorough knowledge of the Law of the Lord and neglected none of its details. As a result he could teach all its laws and regulations to all the people of Israel.

The Document That Artaxerxes Gave to Ezra
(Ezra 7.11–26)

8 The following is a copy of the decree that Artaxerxes gave to Ezra, the priest and scholar of the Law of the Lord:

⁹"From Artaxerxes the emperor to Ezra the priest, scholar of the Law of the Lord, greetings.

¹⁰ "In my generosity I have decided to decree that throughout my empire any of the Jews who so desire, including priests and Levites, may go with you to Jerusalem. ¹¹I and the seven counsellors who have the title 'Friends of the Emperor' have decided that all who wish to do so may go with you. ¹²Let them investigate the conditions in Jerusalem and Judah to see how well the Law of the Lord is being obeyed. ¹³Let them also take with them to Jerusalem the gifts which I and my counsellors have vowed to give to the Lord of Israel, including all the silver and gold belonging to the Lord which may be found in Babylonia, ¹⁴and all that is given by the people of Israel for the temple of their Lord. The silver and gold are to be collected to buy bulls, rams, lambs, and everything else that

---

ˡ Verse 11 in Greek is unclear.
ᵐ EMPEROR OF ASSYRIA: Apparently a reference to the Persian emperor who then also ruled the territory once occupied by Assyria, Israel's ancient enemy.
7.10: Ex 12.1–20

is necessary, [15]so that sacrifices may be offered on the altar of the Lord in Jerusalem.

[16] "You may use the silver and gold for whatever you and your fellow-countrymen desire, in accordance with the will of your God. [17-18]You may obtain from the royal treasury the sacred vessels of the Lord that are being entrusted to you for use in the temple of your God in Jerusalem, as well as anything else you may need for the Temple service.

[19] "I command all the treasury officials in Greater Syria and Phoenicia to provide promptly for Ezra, the priest and scholar of the Law of God Most High, everything he asks for, [20]up to a limit of 3,400 kilogrammes of silver, 10,000 kilogrammes of wheat, 2,000 litres of wine, and as much salt as may be needed. [21]You must be careful to do everything that the Law requires in order to honour God Most High and so make sure that he is never angry with me or with those who reign after me. [22]You are forbidden to collect any taxes from the priests, Levites, musicians, guards, workmen, or anyone else connected with this temple. No one has the right to impose any burden on them.

[23] "You, Ezra, using the wisdom that comes from God, shall appoint administrators and judges to govern all the people in Greater Syria and Phoenicia who live by the Law of your God. You must teach that Law to anyone who does not know it. [24]If anyone disobeys the laws of your God or the laws of the empire, he is to be punished promptly: by death, by fine, by exile, or by some other punishment."

Ezra Praises God
(Ezra 7.27–28)

[25] Ezra said, "Praise the Lord, the Lord alone! He has made the emperor willing to restore the glory of the Temple of the Lord in Jerusalem. [26]By God's grace, I have won the respect of the emperor, his counsellors, all his Friends, and all his powerful officials. [27]The Lord my God has given me courage, and I have been able to persuade many men to return with me."

The People Who Returned from Exile
(Ezra 8.1–14)

[28] This is the list of the leaders of the clans and families who had been in exile in Babylonia and returned with Ezra to Jerusalem when Artaxerxes was emperor: [29-40]Gershom, of the clan of Phinehas

Gamael, of the clan of Ithamar

Hattush son of Shecaniah, of the clan of David

Zechariah, of the clan of Parosh, with 150 men of his clan (there were records of their family line)

Eliehoenai son of Zechariah, of the clan of Pahath Moab, with 200 men

Shecaniah son of Jehaziel, of the clan of Zattu, with 300 men

Ebed son of Jonathan, of the clan of Adin, with 250 men

Jeshaiah son of Gotholiah, of the clan of Elam, with 70 men

Zeraiah son of Michael, of the clan of Shephatiah, with 70 men

Obadiah son of Jehiel, of the clan of Joab, with 212 men

Shelomith son of Josiphiah, of the clan of Bani, with 160 men

Zechariah son of Bebai, of the clan of Bebai, with 28 men

Johanan son of Hakkatan, of the clan of Azgad, with 110 men

Eliphelet, Jeuel, and Shemaiah, of the clan of Adonikam, with 70 men (they returned at a later date)

Uthai son of Istalcurus, of the clan of Bigvai, with 70 men

Ezra Finds Priests and Levites for the Temple
(Ezra 8.15–20)

[41] I assembled the entire group at the River Theras, and we camped there for three days. I inspected them [42]and found that there were no priests or Levites in the group, [43-44]so I sent a message to ten of the leaders who were competent men: Eliezer, Iduel, Maasmas, Elnathan, Shemaiah, Jarib, Nathan, Elnathan, Zechariah, and Meshullam. [45]I told them to go to Iddo, the chief official at the treasury, [46]and ask him, his associates, and the treasury officials to send us priests to serve in the Temple of our Lord. [47]With God's help, they sent us some able men: Sherebiah, a Levite from the clan of Mahli, with eighteen of his sons and relatives, [48]and Hashabiah, Annunus, and his brother Jeshaiah of the clan of Hananiah, with twenty of their sons.

49 There were also 220 Temple workmen whose ancestors had been designated by King David and his officials to assist the Levites. They were all listed in the register by name.

Ezra Leads the People in Fasting and Prayer
(Ezra 8.21-23)

50 There by the River Theras I made a vow that the young men should fast in the presence of our Lord and ask him for a safe journey for us, our children, and our animals. 51 I would have been ashamed to ask the emperor for infantry and cavalry to accompany us and protect us from our enemies, 52 because I had told him that our Lord by his strength blesses and protects those who trust him. 53 So once again we prayed for our Lord to protect us, and he answered our prayers.

The Gifts for the Temple
(Ezra 8.24-30)

54 From among the leading priests I chose Sherebiah, Hashabiah, and ten others. 55 Then I weighed out the silver, the gold, and the sacred utensils which the emperor, his advisers and officials, and the people of Israel had given to be used in the Temple, and I gave it to the priests. 56-57 This is what I gave them:

silver	22,000 kilogrammes
silver utensils	3,400 kilogrammes
gold	3,400 kilogrammes
gold bowls	20
fine bronze bowls that looked like gold	12

58 I said to the priests, "You are sacred to the Lord, the Lord of our ancestors, and so are the utensils and the silver and gold brought to him in fulfilment of a vow. 59 Guard them carefully until you reach the Temple. There in the priests' rooms, hand them over to the leaders of the priests and the Levites and to the leaders of the people of Israel in Jerusalem." 60 So the priests and the Levites took charge of the silver, the gold, and the utensils for Jerusalem and brought them to the Temple.

The Return to Jerusalem
(Ezra 8.31-36)

61 It was on the twelfth day of the first month that we left the River Theras, and with the Lord's presence and protection we reached Jerusalem. He protected us from all our enemies on our journey, and we arrived safely. 62 After we had been

there three days, we went to the Temple, weighed the silver and gold and handed it all over to Meremoth the priest, son of Uriah. 63 With him were Eleazar son of Phinehas and two Levites, Jozabad son of Jeshua and Moeth son of Sabannus. 64 Everything was counted and weighed, and a complete record was made at the same time.

65 All those who had returned from exile then offered sacrifices to the Lord, the God of Israel. They offered twelve bulls for all Israel, ninety-six rams, 66 and seventy-two lambs; they also offered twelve goats as a fellowship-offering. They sacrificed all these animals to the Lord. 67 Then they took the decree the emperor had given them and gave it to the governors and officials of Greater Syria and Phoenicia, who then honoured the Jewish people and the Temple of the Lord.

Ezra Learns of Intermarriages with Non-Jews
(Ezra 9.1-15)

68 After all this had been done, some of the leaders of the people of Israel came and told me that 69 the people, the leaders, the priests, and the Levites had not kept themselves separate from the people in the neighbouring countries of Edom, Moab, and Egypt, or from the Canaanites, Hittites, Perizzites, and Jebusites. They were doing the same disgusting things that those people did. 70 God's holy people had become contaminated because Jewish men were marrying foreign women. Even the leaders and the officials had taken part in this breaking of the Law from the very beginning. 71 As soon as I heard this, I tore my clothes and my sacred robe in despair. I also tore my hair and my beard, and sat down crushed with anxiety and grief. 72 I sat there grieving about this sin until it was time for the evening sacrifice to be offered, when people began to gather round me—all those who were disturbed by what the Lord of Israel had said.

73 Then I got up from where I had been fasting, and still wearing my torn clothes, I knelt in prayer and stretched out my hands to the Lord. 74 I said, "O Lord, I am ashamed and confused in your presence. 75 Our sins tower over our heads; they reach as high as the heavens. 76 This has been true from the days of our ancestors until now; we, your people, have sinned greatly. 77 Because of our sins

and the sins of our ancestors, we and our relatives, our kings, and our priests have fallen into the hands of foreign kings, and we have been slaughtered, robbed, and carried away as prisoners. We have been totally disgraced, as we still are today. 78 Now, Lord, for a short time you have shown us great mercy. You have allowed just a few of us to survive in order to carry on the name of Israel here in your holy Temple. 79 You have let the light of our nation shine again, after feeding us and taking care of us during the time of our slavery. 80 Even when we were slaves you did not abandon us; you made the emperors of Persia favour us, so that they gave us food, 81 restored the glory of your Temple, rebuilt the city of Jerusalem out of its ruins, and gave us a place of security here in Judah and Jerusalem.

82 "But now, Lord, what can we say, after you have done all this for us? We have again disobeyed the commands that you gave us through your servants, the prophets. They told us that 83 the land we were to occupy was an impure land because the heathen people who lived in it filled it with their disgusting deeds. 84 They told us that we should never intermarry with those people 85 and never seek peaceful relations with them if we wanted to be strong and enjoy the land and pass it on to our descendants for ever. 86 Even after everything that has happened to us in punishment for our sins, we know that you, Lord, have punished us less than we deserve 87 and have allowed us to survive. But we have rebelled again, broken your Law, and intermarried with these wicked people. 88 Yet you were not angry enough to destroy us completely and leave none of us alive, with no descendants and without our name. 89 Lord of Israel, you are faithful; you have allowed us to survive. 90 We confess our guilt to you; we have no right to come into your presence."

The Plan for Ending Mixed Marriages
(Ezra 10.1-17)

91 While Ezra was bowing in prayer in front of the Temple, weeping and confessing these sins, a large group of people from Jerusalem—men, women, and children—gathered round him, all of them weeping bitterly. 92 Then Shecaniah son of Jehiel, one of the Israelites, said to Ezra, "We have sinned against the Lord

by marrying foreign women, but even so, there is still hope for Israel. 93 Now we must make a solemn promise to the Lord that we will send all these foreign women and their children away. 94 We will do what you and the others who obey the Law of the Lord advise us to do. 95 It is your responsibility to act. We are behind you, so go ahead and get it done."

96 So Ezra began by making the leaders of the priests, of the Levites, and of the rest of the people take an oath that they would divorce their foreign wives.

9 Then Ezra went from the court of the Temple into the living quarters of Jehohanan son of Eliashib 2 and spent the night there grieving over the people's terrible violation of the Law. He did not eat or drink anything.

3 A message was sent throughout Jerusalem and Judah, calling all those who had returned from exile to meet in Jerusalem, 4 by order of the leaders of the people. If anyone failed to come within two or three days, his cattle would be confiscated, and he would lose his right to be a member of the community.

5 Within the three days, on the twentieth day of the ninth month, all the men of the tribes of Judah and Benjamin came to Jerusalem 6 and assembled in the Temple square. Everyone was shivering with the cold because it was wintertime.

7 Then Ezra stood up and spoke to them, "You have broken the Law and brought guilt on Israel by marrying foreign women. 8 Now then, tell the truth and confess your sins to the Lord, the God of our ancestors, 9 and do what he requires. Separate yourselves from the foreigners living in our land and get rid of your foreign wives."

10 The people shouted in reply, "We will do whatever you say." 11 But they added, "The crowd is too big, and it's wintertime. We can't stand here in the open like this. This isn't something that can be settled in one or two days, since so many of us are involved in this sin. 12 Let our officials stay in Jerusalem and take charge of the matter. Then let anyone who has a foreign wife come at an appointed time, 13 together with the leaders and the judges of his city. In this way God's anger over this situation will be turned away." 14 Jonathan son of Asahel and Jahzeiah son of Tikvah assumed responsibility for the plan; and

8.84-85: Ex 34.11-16; Deut 7.1-5

Meshullam, Levi, and Shabbethai served with them as judges.

15 The returned exiles carried out the investigation in full. [16] Ezra the priest appointed men from among the heads of the clans and recorded their names. On the first day of the tenth month they began their investigation, [17] and within the next three months they investigated all the cases of men with foreign wives.

The Men Who Had Foreign Wives
(Ezra 10.18–44)

18 The following is a list of the men who had foreign wives:

Priests, listed by clans:

19 Clan of Joshua and his brothers, sons of Jozadak: Maaseiah, Eliezar, Jarib, and Jodan. [20] They promised to divorce their wives, and they offered rams as a sacrifice for their sins.

21 Clan of Immer: Hanani, Zebadiah, Manes, Shemaiah, Jehiel, and Azariah

22 Clan of Pashhur: Elioenai, Maaseiah, Ishmael, Nathanael, Okidelus, and Elasah

23 Levites:

Jozabad, Shimei, Kelaiah (also called Kelita), Pethahiah, Judah, and Jonah

24 Musicians:

Eliashib and Bacchurus

25 Temple guards:

Shallum and Telem

26 Others:

Clan of Parosh: Ramiah, Izziah, Malchijah, Milelos, Eleazar, Asebiah, and Benaiah

27 Clan of Elam: Mattaniah, Zechariah, Jezriel, Abdi, Jeremoth, and Elijah

28 Clan of Zattu: Elioenai, Eliashib, Othoniah, Jeremoth, Zabad, and Zerdaiah

29 Clan of Bebai: Jehohanan, Hananiah, Zabbai, and Emathis

30 Clan of Bani: Meshullam, Malluch, Adaiah, Jashub, Sheal, and Jeremoth

31 Clan of Addi: Naathus, Moossias, Laccunus, Naidus, Bescaspasmys, Sesthel, Belnuus, and Manesseas

32 Clan of Annan: Elionas, Asiah, Melchiah, Sabbaiah, and Simon Chosemaeus

33 Clan of Hashum: Mattenai, Mattattah, Zabad, Eliphelet, Manasseh, and Shimei

34 Clan of Bani: Jeremai, Maadai, Amram, Joel, Mamdai, Bedeiah, Vaniah, Carabasion, Eliashib, Machnadebai, Eliasis, Binnui, Elialis, Shimei, Shelemiah, and Nathaniah

Clan of Ezora: Shashai, Azarel, Azael, Shemaiah, Amariah, and Joseph

35 Clan of Nebo: Mattithiah, Zabad, Iddo, Joel, and Benaiah

36 All these men had foreign wives. They divorced them and sent them and their children away.

Ezra Reads the Law to the People
(Neh 7.73—8.12)

37 The priests, the Levites, and many of the ordinary people of Israel settled in Jerusalem and its vicinity. By the seventh month the other Israelites were all settled in their towns. On the first day of that month [38] they all assembled in Jerusalem in the square just inside the east gate of the Temple. [39] They asked Ezra, the High Priest and scholar of the Law which the Lord had given Israel through Moses, to bring the book of the Law. [40] So Ezra brought it to the place where all the people—men, women, and all the priests—had gathered to hear it. [41] There in the square by the gate he read the Law to them from dawn until noon, and they all listened attentively.

42 Ezra was standing on a wooden platform that had been built for the occasion. [43] The following men stood at his right: Mattathiah, Shema, Ananiah, Azariah, Uriah, Hezekiah, and Baalsamos; [44] and the following stood at his left: Pedaiah, Mishael, Malchijah, Lothasubus, Nabariah, and Zechariah.

45 Ezra took his seat on the platform in a prominent place where everyone could see him. As soon as he took the book of the Law [46] and opened it, all the people stood up. Ezra said, "Praise the Lord, God Most High, God Almighty, Ruler of all."

47 All the people raised their arms in the air and answered, "Amen!" They knelt down in worship, with their faces to the ground.

48 The following Levites taught the Law of the Lord to the people: Jeshua, Anniuth, Sherebiah, Jamin, Akkub, Shabbethai, Hodiah, Maiannas, Kelita, Azariah, Jozabad, Hanan, and Peliah. They read the Law to the people and explained what was read.

49–50 When the people heard what the Law required, they were so moved that they began to weep. The governor[n] said to Ezra, the priest and scholar of the Law, and to all the Levites who were teaching

---

[n] Probable meaning The governor; Greek Attharates.
9.37: 1 Chr 9.2; Neh 11.3

All the people...had gathered to hear it (9.40)

the people, "This day is holy to the Lord;
⁵¹ go home and have a feast. Share your
food and wine with those who have none.
⁵² Today is holy to the Lord, so don't be
sad. He will restore your former glory."

53 The Levites gave the command to
all the people: "This day is holy; do not
be sad." ⁵⁴ So all the people went home
and ate and drank joyfully and shared
what they had with those who had
nothing. They celebrated ⁵⁵ because they
understood what had been read to them.

Then they assembled.... *o*

---

o Originally the Greek text must have continued (see Neh 8.13).

THE SECOND BOOK OF
ESDRAS

INTRODUCTION

The *Second book of Esdras* is primarily an apocalypse (or series of visions and revelations) that was written by an unknown Jewish author in Hebrew or Aramaic. This was translated into Greek, and an introduction and appendix of Christian origin were added. The original and the Greek translation have disappeared, and the text is now preserved primarily in Latin. The main part of the work reports seven revelations that were given to Shealtiel (identified with Ezra) and answers questions about the problem of evil, suffering, persecution, the end of the world, judgement, and the new world.

Outline of Contents

Introduction   1.1—2.48
The first vision   3.1—5.19
The second vision   5.20—6.34
The third vision   6.35—9.25
The fourth vision   9.26—10.59
The fifth vision   11.1—12.50
The sixth vision   12.51—13.56
The seventh vision   13.57—14.48
Additional prophecies   15.1—16.78

1 This is the second book of the prophet Ezra. He was the son of Seraiah, the grandson of Azariah, and a descendant of Hilkiah, Shallum, Zadok, Ahitub, ² Ahijah, Phinehas, Eli, Amariah, Azariah, Meraioth, Arna, Uzzi, Borith, Abishua, Phinehas, Eleazar, ³ and Aaron, of the tribe of Levi.

The Rejection of Israel

When I, Ezra, was a captive in Media during the reign of Artaxerxes, king of Persia, ⁴ the Lord said to me, ⁵ "Go and remind my people and their children of the sins they have committed against me, and let them tell their grandchildren. ⁶ My people have sinned even more than their ancestors, for they have forgotten me and offered sacrifices to foreign gods. ⁷ I

rescued them from Egypt, where they were slaves, but they have done things that made me angry and have refused to listen to my warnings.

8 "Ezra, tear your hair in grief and call down on these people all the disasters they deserve. They are rebellious and refuse to obey my Law. ⁹ How much longer can I tolerate these people for whom I have done so much? ¹⁰ For their sake I overthrew many kings and crushed the king of Egypt together with his officials and all his army. ¹¹ I destroyed all the nations that opposed them, and in the east I scattered the people of the provinces of Tyre and Sidon and killed all the enemies of Israel.

12 "Ezra, tell them that the Lord says: ¹³ I brought you across the Red Sea and

1.1–3: Ezra 7.1–5; 1 Esd 8.1–2   **1.5:** Is 58.1   **1.10:** Ex 14.28   **1.13:** Ex 14.29

made safe roads for you where there were none. I made Moses your leader and gave you Aaron as your priest. 14 I provided you with light from a pillar of fire and performed great miracles among you, but you have forgotten me. I, the Lord, have spoken.

15 "The Lord Almighty says: I sent you quails as a sign of my care for you. I provided you with camps where you could be safe, but all you did there was complain. 16 Even when I destroyed your enemies, you did not appreciate what I had done. You have never done anything but complain. 17 Have you forgotten the blessings I gave you? There in the desert when you were hungry and thirsty you cried out to me: 18 'Why have you brought us out to this desert to kill us? Being slaves to the Egyptians was better than coming here to die.' 19 I was moved by your bitter groans and gave you manna, the bread of angels. 20 When you were thirsty, I split the rock and all the water you needed flowed out. To protect you from the heat, I provided you with shady trees. 21 I divided fertile lands among you and drove out the Canaanites, the Perizzites, and the Philistines, who opposed your advance. What more could I have done for you?

22 "The Lord Almighty says: There in the desert by the river of bitter water when you were thirsty and cursed me, 23 in spite of your insults I did not send fire upon you. Instead, I made the water fit to drink by throwing wood into the river. 24 People of Israel, what can I do with you? People of Judah, you refuse to obey me. So I will turn to other nations and make them my people. They will keep my laws. 25 Because you have abandoned me, I will abandon you. You will beg me for mercy, but I will show you none. 26 When you pray to me, I will not hear you. You never hesitate to commit murder; your hands are stained with the blood of those you have killed. 27 It is not me that you have betrayed; you have betrayed yourselves.

Israel Is to Be Replaced

28 "The Lord Almighty says: I have pleaded with you as a father pleads with his sons, as a mother pleads with her daughters, or as a nursemaid pleads with her small children. 29 I begged you to be

my people so that I could be your God, to be my children so that I could be your father. 30 I gathered you together as a hen gathers her chicks under her wings. But now what can I do with you? I will banish you from my sight; 31 and even when you offer sacrifices to me, I will turn away from you. Your religious festivals, your New Moon celebrations, or your circumcision ceremonies mean nothing to me. 32 I sent you my servants, the prophets, but you killed them and mutilated their corpses. I will make you pay for murdering them.

33 "The Lord Almighty says: Your Temple is abandoned. I will scatter you like straw blown away by the wind. 34 Your children will have no descendants because they rejected my commandments and did what I hated, just as you did. 35 I will give your home to a people that is about to appear. They will believe me, even though they have not yet heard of me. They will do what I command, even though I never performed any miracles for them. 36 They have not seen the prophets, but they will live by their ancient teachings. 37 I give my solemn promise that I will bless those people, and their little children will laugh and shout for joy. Those people have never seen me, but deep within them they will believe my words.

38 "Now, Father Ezra, look with pride at the people you see coming from the east. 39 Look at the leaders I have given them: Abraham, Isaac, Jacob, Hosea, Amos, Micah, Joel, Obadiah, Jonah, 40 Nahum, Habakkuk, Zephaniah, Haggai, Zechariah, and Malachi (who is also called the Lord's messenger).

2 "The Lord says: I led my people out of slavery in Egypt; I gave them commandments through my servants, the prophets, but they refused to listen and ignored my teachings. 2 Jerusalem, the mother who brought them into the world, says to them, 'Go your own way, my children; I am now a widow left completely alone. 3 I took great delight in bringing you up, but you sinned against the Lord God and did what I knew was wrong, so I mourned in deep grief when I lost you. 4 What can I do for you, now that I am a widow and left completely alone? Go, my children, and ask the Lord for mercy.'

5 "Father Ezra, I call on you to testify against these people as their mother has done, because they have refused to keep my covenant. 6 Now bring confusion on them and ruin on their mother, so that they will have no descendants. 7 They will be scattered among the nations, and no one on earth will remember them any longer, for they have despised my covenant.

8 "How terrible will be your punishment, Assyria. You have let wicked people hide within your borders. Remember, sinful nation, what I did to Sodom and Gomorrah. 9 Their land now lies covered with lumps of tar and heaps of ashes. That is what I do to people who do not obey me.

10 "The Lord says to Ezra: Announce to my new people that I will give them the kingdom of Jerusalem, which I had planned to give to Israel. 11 I will take the dazzling light of my presence away from Israel and will give to my new people the eternal Temple that I had prepared for Israel. 12 The tree of life will fill the air round them with its fragrance. They will never have to work; they will never grow tired. 13 Ask, and you will receive. Pray that the number of the days you have to wait will be reduced. Even now the kingdom has been prepared for you, so stay alert. 14 Call heaven and earth to witness that I, the living God, have abolished evil and created good.

15 "Mother Jerusalem, take your children in your arms. Guide their steps in safe paths; rear them with the same delight as a dove has in rearing her young. I, the Lord, have chosen you. 16 I will raise your dead from their graves because I recognize them as my people. 17 Jerusalem, mother of these people, do not be afraid; I, the Lord, have chosen you.

18 "I will send my servants Isaiah and Jeremiah to help you. At their request I have consecrated and prepared for you twelve trees, heavy with different kinds of fruit, 19 twelve fountains flowing with milk and honey, and seven high mountains covered with roses and lilies. I will make your children very happy there. 20 Now, Jerusalem, come to the defence of widows, take the side of the fatherless, give to the poor, protect orphans, give clothing to those who have none, 21 take care of those who are broken and weak, do not make fun of those who are crippled,

protect the disabled, and help the blind to catch the vision of my dazzling splendour. 22 Keep both the old and the young safe within your walls. 23 Whenever you find a dead body, bury it and mark the grave, and I will give you a place of honour when I raise the dead.

24 "Be calm, my people; your time to rest will come. 25 Take care of your children like a faithful nursemaid and guide their steps in safe paths, 26 so that none of them will be lost. When the time comes, I will hold you responsible for them. 27 Don't worry; when the day of trouble and distress comes, others will cry and mourn, but you will be happy and rich. 28 The other nations will be jealous of you, but they will not be able to harm you.

29 "I will protect you with my power and save your children from hell. 30 Be happy, Jerusalem, you and your children, because I, the Lord, will rescue you. 31 Remember your children who are asleep in their graves; I, the Lord Almighty, am merciful, and I will bring them out from the place where they lie hidden in the earth. 32 Until I come, hold your children close and tell them about my grace and mercy, which are like a spring that never runs dry."

Ezra on Mount Sinai

33 I, Ezra, was on Mount Sinai when the Lord ordered me to go to the people of Israel. But when I went to them, they rejected me and refused to listen to what the Lord commanded. 34 That is why I am speaking to you Gentiles. You are ready to listen and understand: "Wait for your shepherd who is coming very soon, at the end of the age, to give you eternal rest. 35 Be ready to receive the blessings of the kingdom, for eternal light will shine on you for ever. 36 Flee from the darkness of this present age and accept the joyful splendour prepared for you. I testify publicly for my saviour. 37 The Lord has appointed him, so accept him and be happy. Give thanks to God, who has called you into his heavenly kingdom. 38 Stand up and see the number of those who have received the Lord's mark and who share in his banquet. 39 They have left the darkness of this age and have received shining white robes from the Lord. 40 So now, Jerusalem, welcome these people who have kept the Law of the Lord, and

2.8: Gen 19.24　　2.12: Rev 2.7; 22.2,14　　2.13: Mt 7.7–8; 25.34　　2.18: Rev 22.2
2.23: Tob 1.17–19　　2.26: Jn 17.12

this will complete the list of those whom God has assigned to you. 41 The children you longed for have returned; their number is now complete. So pray that the Lord's kingdom may come and that your people, whom God chose before he created the world, may become holy."

Ezra on Mount Zion

42 I, Ezra, saw an enormous crowd on Mount Zion, too many people to count. They were all singing and praising the Lord. 43 Standing in the middle of this crowd was a very tall young man, taller than any of the others. He was placing a crown on the head of each person, but he towered above them all. I was spellbound by the sight, 44 and I asked the angel, "Who are these people, sir?"

45 He replied, "These are people who have taken off their mortal robes and have put on immortal ones. They have confessed their faith in God, and now they are being given crowns and palm branches as symbols of their victory."

46 Then I asked the angel, "Who is the young man who is putting the crowns on their heads and giving them the palms?"

47 "He is the Son of God," the angel replied, "and all these people confessed their faith in him while they lived on earth." Then I began to praise those who had stood for the Lord so bravely. 48 And the angel said to me, "Go and tell my people what you have seen, the many marvellous wonders of the Lord."

THE FIRST VISION
Ezra's Prayer of Complaint

3 Thirty years after the fall of Jerusalem, I, Shealtiel (also known as Ezra), was in Babylon. I was lying on my bed, troubled and disturbed, 2 as I thought about the ruins of Jerusalem and the prosperity of those who lived in Babylon. 3 I was deeply disturbed and began to express my fears to God Most High. 4 "O Lord and Master," I said, "you, and you alone, spoke the word at the beginning of creation and formed the world. At your command the dust 5 produced the lifeless body of Adam. Then with your hands you shaped it, you breathed into it the breath of life, and he began to live. 6 You brought him into the Garden of Eden, which you yourself had

planted before the earth was made. 7 You gave him just one commandment, but he disobeyed it, and you immediately made him and his descendants subject to death.

"From Adam were born more nations, tribes, clans, and families than can be counted. 8 All the nations did whatever they wished; they sinned against you and rejected your commands. But you did nothing to stop them. 9 Then again, after a while, you brought on the flood and destroyed the world's population. 10 They all suffered the same fate: as death had come to Adam, so now death came to a whole generation in the flood. 11 But you spared one man, Noah, with his family and all his righteous descendants.

12 "The number of people living on earth began to increase, and the number of families, tribes, and nations grew. They too fell into sin and were worse than the generations before them. 13 But then you chose Abraham. 14 You loved him, and to him alone in the dead of night you secretly disclosed how the world would end. 15 You made an everlasting covenant with him and promised him that you would never abandon his descendants. You gave him Isaac, and to Isaac you gave Jacob and Esau. 16 You chose Jacob, and his descendants became a great nation, but you rejected Esau.

17 "You rescued the descendants of Jacob from Egypt and led them to Mount Sinai. 18 There you bent down the skies, shook a the earth, moved the world, made the waters beneath the earth tremble, and brought disorder to the universe. 19 The dazzling light of your presence passed through the four gates of fire, earthquake, wind, and frost, in order to give the Law and its commandments to Jacob's descendants, the people of Israel. 20 Yet you did not remove their evil impulse, but let your Law guide their lives. 21 The first man, Adam, weighed down with an evil impulse, sinned and was defeated, and the same was true of all his descendants. 22 So the disease became permanent, and although the Law was in the hearts of the people, so also was the root of evil! That is why what was good passed away, while what was evil continued.

23 "Many years later you sent your servant David 24 and told him to build a city which would bear your name and in which sacrifices would be offered to you.

---

a Some ancient translations shook; Latin steadied.
2.42: Rev 7.9   **3.1:** Ezra 3.2; 5.2; Neh 12.1   **3.7:** Wis 1.13–14; 2.23–24   **3.8:** Gen 6.12
3.9: Gen 6.9—8.22   **3.20:** Sir 15.14

²⁵This was done for many years, but then the inhabitants of the city disobeyed you ²⁶and sinned just like Adam and all his descendants, because they had the same evil impulse. ²⁷So you handed over your own city to your enemies.

28 "I said to myself, 'Perhaps Babylon has been allowed to conquer Jerusalem because the people who live there are better than we are.' ²⁹But when I got to Babylon, I saw more sins than I could count, and now for thirty years I have seen many sinners here. So I was perplexed ³⁰when I saw how you tolerate sinners and do not punish them, how you protect your enemies and yet destroy your own people. ³¹You haven't given anyone the faintest hint as to how these ways of yours can be changed. Surely Babylon is no better than Jerusalem. ³²No other nation, except Israel, has ever known you or accepted your covenants. ³³But Israel was never rewarded, and never profited from its labour. I have travelled widely in other nations, and I have seen how prosperous they are, although they don't keep your commands. ³⁴Now then, Lord, if you would just weigh our sins on the scales against those of the rest of the world, it would be perfectly clear that their sins are heavier. ³⁵There has never been a time when the people of the world did not sin against you; but has any other nation kept your commands as well as Israel has? ³⁶You may find individuals who have, but you won't find a nation that has done so."

The Human Mind Cannot Understand God's Ways

4 The angel Uriel, who had been sent to me, replied, ²"You can't even understand what happens in this world. Do you think you can understand the ways of God Most High?"

3 "Yes, sir, I do!" I answered.

The angel continued, "I have been sent to ask you to solve three riddles about what happens in this world. ⁴If you can explain even one of them to me, I will answer your questions about God's ways and teach you why the human race has an evil impulse."

5 "I agree, sir," I said.

Then he said to me, "Good! How do you weigh out a kilogramme of fire? How do you measure a cubic metre[b] of wind?

Weigh out a kilogramme of fire...measure a cubic metre of wind (4.5)

How do you bring back a day that has passed?"

6 I answered, "Why do you ask me such questions? No human being could answer them."

7 Then he said, "What if I had asked you how many dwelling places there are at the bottom of the sea? How many rivers flow into the waters beneath the earth? How many rivers are there above the dome of the sky? Where are the exits from the world of the dead? Where are the entrances to[c] Paradise? ⁸If I had asked you these questions, you might have answered, 'I have never gone down into the waters beneath the earth, and I have not yet entered the world of the dead. I have never gone up to heaven.' ⁹But all I have asked you about is fire, wind, and the day that has just passed—things that you have experienced. Yet you have given me no answer. ¹⁰You can't even understand things that you have been familiar with since you were a child. ¹¹How then can your little mind understand the ways of God Most High? Can a man already worn down by this corrupt world understand the ways of the incorruptible God?"

When I heard this, I fell face downwards on the ground[d] ¹²and said to him, "It would have been better if we had never been born than to have to live in a world

---

[b] *Some ancient translations* cubic metre; *Latin* blast.
[c] *Some ancient translations* exits from...entrances to; *Latin* exits from.
[d] *Verse 11 in Latin is unclear.*

of sin and suffering without understanding why things happen as they do."

13 The angel Uriel answered, "I once went into the woods and heard the trees plotting together. 14 They were saying, 'Let's go to war against the sea and push it back, so that we may have more room.' 15 But the waves of the sea also plotted together and said, 'Let's conquer the woods and extend our territory.' 16 But all the plotting of the trees was useless because fire came and destroyed them. 17 And the plotting of the sea was just as useless because the sand stood firm and blocked its advance. 18 Now, if you were the judge and had to decide between them, which would you pronounce right?"

19 I replied, "They were both wrong, because trees belong on the land, and waves belong in the sea."

20 "You have given the right answer," he said. "So why can't you see the answer to your own problems? 21 For just as trees have their place on land, and waves have their place in the sea, so the people of this world can understand only what goes on in this world, and only heavenly beings can understand what goes on in heaven."

The End of the Age

22 "Please tell me, sir," I asked, "why then was I given the ability to understand anything? 23 I am not interested in asking questions about what goes on in the heavens; I am only concerned about things that go on about us. Why has God allowed Israel to be disgraced by foreign nations? Why has he let the nation he loves be handed over to the power of godless nations? Why do the Law and the covenant that were given to our ancestors mean nothing any more? 24 Why do we die as quickly as insects? Why is our life shorter than a breath? Why does God think us unworthy of his mercy? 25 Why doesn't God do something to help his own people? These are the questions that I want to ask."

26 Uriel answered, "If you live long enough, you will be surprised at what you will see, because this age is rapidly passing away. 27 This age is so full of misery and imperfection that it cannot hold all the blessings that God has promised the righteous in the time to come. 28 The evil about which you have asked me has already been planted, but the time for its harvesting has not yet

arrived. 29 This evil must be harvested, and this world where it was planted must be removed, before the new age where the good is to be planted can appear. 30 At the beginning of time one grain of evil seed was sown in the heart of Adam. See how much wickedness it has already produced! Think how much more it will produce before it is cut down and threshed out at Judgement Day. 31 You can see for yourself what a big crop this one evil seed has produced. 32 How terrible will be the harvest on Judgement Day when these countless ears of corn are threshed out!"

33 Then I asked, "How long do we have to wait before this happens? Why are our lives so short and so full of misery?"

34 Uriel answered, "Don't be in a greater hurry than God Most High! You are thinking only of yourself, but God has to be concerned about everybody. e 35 Your questions are the same ones asked by the souls of the righteous dead in the places where God is keeping them waiting: 'How long must we wait here? When will the day of judgement come, when we will get our reward?' 36 The archangel Jeremiel answers them, 'It will happen as soon as the complete number of those who have suffered as you have are here. For God has weighed this age, 37 measured the years, and numbered the days. Nothing will be changed until time has run its predetermined course.'"

38 "But, sir," I replied, "all of us here on earth are such wicked sinners. 39 Is it possible that because of our sin the righteous dead are having to wait for their reward?"

40 His answer was, "Can a pregnant woman keep her child from being born after her nine months are up?"

41 "No, sir, she cannot," I answered.

And he continued, "In the world of the dead, the place where God has stored the souls is like a womb. 42 It is as eager to return the souls entrusted to it from the beginning of the world as a woman is to end her labour pains. 43 When that happens, you will have the answer to all your questions."

44 "Please, sir," I asked, "if you think I am able to understand it, can you 45 tell me one more thing? Is the time that is still to come longer than the past that has already gone by? 46 I know how long the past has been, but I don't know the future."

e *Verse 34 in Latin is unclear.*

4.21: Is 55.8-9; Jn 3.31; 1 Cor 2.14   **4.30:** 2 Esd 3.20   **4.36:** 2 Esd 2.41; Rev 6.11

Wickedness will increase (5.2)

47 "Come here and stand at my right," he commanded, "and I will show you a vision and explain its meaning." ⁴⁸So I stood by him and looked, and I saw a blazing fire pass by in front of me, and when it was gone, I saw that smoke was still there. ⁴⁹Then a rain cloud passed by in front of me, bringing a heavy downpour of rain; and when the downpour was over, there was still a light rain. ⁵⁰"Think about this," said Uriel. "Just as the downpour was greater than the light rain that followed it and the fire was greater than the smoke left behind, in the same way the time that has passed is much longer than the time to come. The time that is left is like the rain and the smoke."

The Signs of the End

51 "Please tell me," I asked, "do you think I will live until that time? If not, who will be alive when it happens?"

52 He answered, "I can tell you some of the signs of the end, if that is what you are asking about; but I am not here to tell you how long you will live, and in any case, I don't know.

5 "But these are the signs: The time will come when all people on earth will be in the grip of great confusion.*f* The way of truth will be hidden, and no faith will be left in the land. ²Wickedness will increase until it has become worse than you have ever known it to be. ³The country that you now see ruling the world will lie in ruins, with no inhabitant or traveller there. ⁴After that,*g* if God Most High lets you live long enough, you will see that country in confusion. The sun will suddenly start shining at night, and the moon in the daytime. ⁵Blood will drip from trees; stones will speak; nations will be in confusion; the movement of the stars will be changed. ⁶A king unwanted by anyone will begin to rule, and the,birds will fly away. ⁷Fish will be washed up on the shores of the Dead Sea. The voice of one whom many do not know will be heard at night; everyone will hear it. ⁸The earth will break open*h* in many places and begin spouting flames. Wild animals will leave the fields and forests. At their monthly periods women will bear monsters. ⁹Fresh water will become salty. Friends everywhere will attack one

ᶠSome ancient translations confusion; Latin unclear.   ᵍAfter that; Latin unclear.
ʰOne ancient translation The earth will break open; Latin Chaos will appear.
4.51—5.19: Mt 24.4–31; Mk 13.5–27; Lk 21.8–28   **5.2:** Mt 24.12   **5.5:** Hab 2.11

another. Then understanding will disappear, and reason will go into hiding, [10] and they will not be found even though many may look for them. Everywhere on earth wickedness and violence will increase. [11] One country will ask a neighbouring country if justice or anyone who does right has come that way, but the answer will always be 'No.' [12] At that time people will hope for much, but will get nothing; they will work hard, but will never succeed at anything. [13] These are the signs of the end that I am permitted to show you. But if you begin to pray again and continue to weep and fast for seven more days, you will hear even greater things."

14 Then I woke up, and I was trembling violently. I was so disturbed that I was about to faint, [15] but the angel that had come to talk with me took hold of me, strengthened me, and set me on my feet.

16 The next night, Phaltiel, who was a leader of the people, came to me and asked, "Where have you been? And why do you look so sad? [17] Don't you know that the people of Israel in the land of their exile have been put in your care? [18] So get up and eat. Do not abandon us like a shepherd leaving his flock to the attacks of savage wolves."

19 "Leave me alone," I answered. "Do not come near me for the next seven days. Then come back." So he left.

THE SECOND VISION
Ezra's Prayer and Uriel's Answer

20 Then, crying and mourning, I fasted for seven days, as the angel Uriel had commanded me to do. [21] At the end of the seven days, I was again deeply troubled, [22] but I recovered my ability to think, and again I began to speak with God Most High. [23] "Lord and Master," I said, "from all the forests and plants on earth you have chosen this one vine. [24] From all the countries of the world, you have chosen this one small land. From all the flowers in the world, you have chosen this one lily. [25] From all the water in the deep oceans, you have filled up this one river. From all the cities that have ever been built, you have set apart this one city, Jerusalem, as your own. [26] From all the birds that were created, you chose this one dove. From all the animals that were made, you chose this one lamb. [27] From all the nations of the world, you

chose this one nation to be your own, and you gave its people your Law, which is honoured by people everywhere.

28 "And now, Lord, since all this is true, why have you dishonoured[i] this one people more than all others by handing them over to many nations? Why have you scattered your own people, [29] who believed in your covenants? Why have you let them be trampled on by people who rejected your promises? [30] If you are so angry with your own people, you yourself ought to punish them."

31 When I had finished speaking, the angel who had come to me on a previous night was sent to me again. [32] He said, "Listen carefully to me, and I will teach you more."

33 "Please go on, sir," I said.

So he continued, "Are you worried about the people of Israel? Do you think you love them more than God, who made them?"

34 "No, sir," I replied. "I spoke as I did because I was so confused and upset. I am always troubled whenever I try to think about the ways of God Most High or to understand even a small part of what he does."

35 "You cannot understand!" he answered.

And I asked, "Why not, sir? In that case, why was I born? Why didn't I die before I was born? Then I wouldn't have seen the sufferings and troubles of the people of Israel."

36 The angel said to me, "I will answer you if you can do the following things: Tell me how many people are yet to be born; collect scattered raindrops for me; make dead flowers bloom again; [37] open the rooms where the winds are locked up and make them blow for me; show me the picture of a sound. If you can do these things, I will answer your questions about the sufferings of the people of Israel."

38 I answered, "Lord and master, no one can do these things, except God, who is not confined to this world. [39] How can I give you any kind of answer? What do I know?"

40 He continued, "You could not do even one of the things that I asked you to do. How can you expect to understand God's judgements or why God has promised his love to his people?"

---

[i] Some ancient translations dishonoured; Latin prepared.
5.35: Job 3.11

Descending Generations

41 Then I said, "But, Lord God, your concern is with the people who will be alive at the end of the world. What will happen to those who live before that time? What about us? What about those who came before us, and those who will live after us?"

42 He answered me, "The final judgement can be compared to a circle, and just as a circle has no beginning or end, so those who come early will not be too early, and those who come late will not be too late."

43 I replied, "But couldn't you have created all human beings, those of the past, the present, and the future, so that they would all live at the same time? In that way, you could have had your final judgement sooner."

44 He answered, "The creation cannot move faster than the Creator. And besides, the world wouldn't have been able to hold all the people if everyone had been created at the same time."

45 "Why, then," I asked, "did you tell me just now that one day you would bring back to life at the same time every creature that ever lived? If the world can hold them all then, it can hold them now."

46 He answered, "That would be like asking a woman who has given birth to ten children why she didn't have them all at once, instead of one at a time."

47 "That would be impossible," I answered. "She can't have them all at once."

48 "In the same way," he continued, "I have made the world like a womb so that it produces human beings at regular intervals. 49 The rule that neither a young child nor an old woman can give birth to a baby also applies to the world that I have created."

50 Then I said, "Since you have brought up the subject, may I ask if the world you have been talking about is still young or is it approaching old age?"

51 He replied, "You can learn the answer from any woman who has given birth to several children. 52 Ask her why her younger children do not grow as tall as her older children. 53 She will tell you that those born while she was young and healthy are much stronger than those born when she was getting old and becoming weak. 54 You will notice that you are smaller than people of earlier generations; 55 those who come later will be smaller still. This shows you that creation is already getting old and losing the strength of her youth."

God Will Bring the End of the World

56 "If you please, Lord," I asked, "will you show me the one through whom you will bring judgement on your creation?"

6 He said to me, "I made this decision before I created the world: before the gates of the world were standing; before the winds were brought together to blow, 2 or the lightning flashed, or the thunder rolled; before the foundations of Paradise were laid, 3 or the beautiful flowers appeared; before the powers that move the stars were established, or the armies of angels assembled; 4 before the air was piled up high, or the divisions of the heavens given their names; before I chose Mount Zion as my footstool; 5 before the present age was planned, or the scheming of its sinners was rejected, or my seal was placed on those who obeyed the Law and laid up a treasure of faithfulness. 6 Even then, I decided that since I, and I alone, had created the world, I, and I alone, would bring it to an end."

7 Then I asked, "How long a period of time will divide the ages? When will the first age end and the next age begin?"

8 He answered, "The interval will be no longer than that between Abraham and Abraham.*j* He was the grandfather of both Jacob and Esau, and when they were born, Jacob was holding Esau's heel. 9 Esau represents the end of this age, and Jacob represents the beginning of the new age. 10 So, if Jacob's hand is the beginning and Esau's heel is the end,*k* do not try to find a space in between."

The Signs of the End

11 "Lord and Master," I said, "please hear my request. 12 On that earlier night you showed me some of the signs of the end; now please show me the rest."

13 "Stand up," he said, "and you will hear a very loud voice. 14 If the place where you are standing is violently shaken 15 while the voice is speaking, don't be afraid. The message will be about the end of the world, and the foundations of the world will understand 16 that the voice is

---

j Abraham; *some manuscripts have* Isaac.
k *Some ancient translations* So...end; *Latin unclear.*
5.52: Gen 6.4; Num 13.33

speaking about them. They will tremble and quake because they know that they will undergo a change when the end comes."

17 When he said this, I stood up and listened. I heard a voice that sounded like a roaring river. [18]It said, "The time is near when I will come to judge the people living on the earth. [19]I will punish those who have hurt others with their injustice. Jerusalem's humiliation will come to an end, [20]and this age which is about to pass away will have the final seal put on it. Then I will give the following signs: the books will be opened across the sky for all to see. [21]Children only a year old will speak. Pregnant women will give birth after only three or four months, and their premature babies will live and run about. [22]Sown fields will suddenly become bare, and full barns will suddenly become empty. [23]Then the trumpet will sound, and sudden terror will grip the heart of everyone when he hears it. [24]Friends will fight like enemies, and the earth and its people will be terrified. Rivers will stop flowing and stand still for three hours.

25 "Those who survive all these things that I have predicted will be rescued when I bring to an end this world that I created. [26]They will see the men who never died but were taken up alive into heaven. The hearts and minds of people on earth will be changed. [27]Evil will be destroyed and deceit eliminated. [28]Faith will grow strong, corruption will be overcome, and truth, which has not produced fruit for so long, will make itself felt again."

29 While the voice was speaking, the ground beneath me began to rock to and fro.[l] [30]Then the angel said to me, "These are the things that I have come to show you tonight.[m] [31]Now if you will pray and fast for seven more days, I will come back and tell you even greater things,[n] [32]because God Most High has heard your prayer; the Mighty God has seen the pure and righteous life that you have lived since your youth. [33]That is why he has sent me to show you all these things and to tell you not to be afraid but to trust him. [34]Do not be so quick to raise useless questions in the present age; then you will not be so quick to do so in the final age."

THE THIRD VISION
Why God's People Suffer

35 After that, I mourned and fasted for seven more days, as I had done before, and so I completed the three weeks of fasting that I had been commanded to observe. [36]On the eighth night I was again deeply troubled, and I began to speak to God Most High. [37]I was very tense and my heart was uneasy, [38]but I said, "O Lord, at the beginning of creation you spoke the word. On the first day you commanded, 'Let the universe be made,' and your word carried out that command. [39]At that time the spirit was moving, darkness and silence were everywhere, and no human voice was yet heard.[o] [40]Then you commanded that a ray of light should shine out of the room where it was stored, so that your works could be seen. [41]On the second day you created the angel of the sky and commanded him to separate the water, so that part of it would move up above the dome of the sky and part remain below. [42]On the third day you commanded the water that covered the earth to come together in one place and cover a seventh of the earth's surface. Then you dried out the rest of the earth's surface to make dry land, so that it might be cultivated and sown and used in your service. [43]Your word went out and completed the work immediately. [44]In an instant all kinds of fruits and vegetables appeared, enough kinds to satisfy every taste. There were flowers of indescribable fragrances and of the most magnificent colours. These things were made on the third day. [45]On the fourth day the brightly-shining sun, the light of the moon, and the arrangement of the stars were created by your command. [46]You commanded them to serve the human race, which would soon be created. [47]On the fifth day you commanded the part of the earth covered by water to produce birds and fish; and it was done. [48]At your command, the still and lifeless water brought forth living creatures, so that the nations might proclaim your wonderful works. [49]Then

[l] *Some ancient translations* the ground...fro; *Latin unclear.*
[m] *One ancient translation* tonight; *Latin unclear.*
[n] *Some ancient translations* things; *Latin adds* in the daytime.
[o] *Some ancient translations* yet heard; *Latin adds* from you.

6.17: Rev 1.15; 14.2; 19.6   **6.20:** Dan 7.10; 12.1; Mal 3.16; Rev 20.12
6.23: 1 Cor 15.51–52; 1 Thes 4.16   **6.26:** Gen 5.24; 2 Kgs 2.11–12; Sir 44.16; Mal 4.5–6
6.38: Ps 33.6; Heb 11.3; 2 Pet 3.5   **6.49–52:** Job 7.12; Ps 74.12–15

you singled out two of the living creatures; you named one of them Behemoth and the other Leviathan. 50 You separated them from each other because the sea wasn't big enough to hold them both. 51 You let Behemoth live on a part of the land that you dried up on the third day of creation; it is a land of a thousand mountains. 52 You let Leviathan live in the sea. You kept them both alive, so that your chosen people may feast on them at the time you choose. 53 On the sixth day you commanded the earth to produce animals, domestic and wild, large and small. 54 More important than all of these, you created Adam and put him in charge of everything that you had made. And all of us, the people you have chosen, are descended from him.

55 "O Lord, I have told you all this because you said that you created this first world for the sake of your people. 56 You said that, in spite of their great numbers, all the other nations descended from Adam are nothing, worth no more than a drop of water, no more than spittle. 57 But now, Lord, those nations that are considered as nothing are ruling over us and destroying us. 58 We are your people, and you have called us your first-born, your only son, your witness, your loved one, but we have been handed over to the power of these other nations. 59 If this world was really created for the sake of your people, why don't we have possession of it? How much longer must we wait?"

7 When I had finished speaking, the same angel that had been sent to me on the earlier nights appeared again. 2 He said, "Stand up, Ezra, and listen to what I have come to tell you."

3 "Go ahead, sir," I said.

He continued, "Picture in your mind a broad,p immense sea spreading over a vast area, 4 but with an entrance no wider than a river. 5 No one who wishes to enter that sea, whether to visit it or control it, can reach its broad expanse of water without passing through the narrow entrance. 6 Or take another example: Picture a city built on a plain. The city is full of all kinds of good things, 7 but the entrance to it is narrow and steep, with fire on one side and deep water on the other. 8 The one path between the fire and the water is so narrow that only one

person at a time may walk on it. 9 If anyone inherits this city, he cannot take possession of his inheritance without passing through this dangerous entrance."

10 "That is right, sir," I said.

"That is how it is with the people of Israel," he added. 11 "I made this world for their sake, but when Adam broke my commands, the world came under my judgement. 12 Then the entrances into this world were made narrow and difficult to travel. They were rough, dangerous, and few in number. 13 But the entrances to the great world to come are wide and safe and lead to immortality. 14 Everyone who lives must walk the narrow and meaningless ways of this world in order to receive the blessings stored up in the world to come. 15 So, Ezra, why are you upset and disturbed by the thought thatq you are mortal and must die? 16 Why don't you think about the age to come, rather than the present age?"

17 I answered, "Lord and master, in your Law you said that the righteous would receive all these blessings, but that the wicked would perish. 18 So the righteous can endure all the difficulties of this narrow way because they look forward to the broad and open life of the future, but the wicked must pass through the narrow way without any hope of seeing the broad open life."

19 The angel replied, "Do you think you are a better judge than God? Do you think you are wiser than God Most High? 20 It is better to let many people of the present age perish than to allow them to neglect the Law that God has given them. 21 God has given clear commandments to everyone coming into this world, telling them what they should do to obtain life and to avoid punishment. 22 But the wicked would not listen and refused to obey him. In their foolishness 23 they have made their own wicked and deceitful plans. They denied the existence of God Most High and refused to follow his ways. 24 They have rejected his Law, refused to accept his promises, disobeyed his decrees, and failed to do what he commanded. 25 That's the reason, Ezra, that there is emptiness for the empty and fullness for the full.

p Some ancient translations broad; Latin deep.
7.11: Rom 5.18–20   7.15–16: 2 Cor 4.18

q by the thought that; or since.

The Messianic Kingdom and the Final Judgement

26 "The time is coming when these signs will take place. The invisible city will appear, [r] and the land that is now hidden will be seen. 27 Everyone who survives the calamities I have predicted will also see the wonderful things I will do. 28 My son the Messiah [s] will be revealed, together with those who come with him. He will bring four hundred years of happiness to all these survivors. 29 At the end of that time, my son the Messiah and all human beings will die. 30 Then the world will return to its original silence, and for seven days it will be like it was at the beginning. No one will be left alive. 31 After seven days this corrupt age will pass out of existence and a new age will be awakened. 32 The ground will give up the dead who sleep there in silence, and the souls of the dead will be released from the places where they have been kept. 33 God Most High will appear on his judgement seat. Mercy and patience will vanish completely 34 and be replaced by judgement. Truth and faithfulness will once again stand firm. 35 The good and bad that people have done will be fully revealed, and reward and punishment will follow immediately. [t] 36 The pit of torment, the fires of hell, will appear, and opposite them the Paradise of joy and rest.

37 "Then God Most High will say to the nations that have been raised from the dead, 'Look! I am the one whom you have denied and refused to serve; it is my commands that you have rejected. 38 Look around you; there is joy and peace in one direction, fire and torment in the other.' That is what he will say to them on Judgement Day.

39 "On Judgement Day there will be no sun, moon, or stars; 40 no cloud, thunder, or lightning; no wind, water, or air; no darkness, evening, or morning; 41 no summer, spring, or winter; no heat, frost, or cold; no hail, rain, or dew; 42 no noon, night, or dawn; no daylight, brightness, or light. The only light will be the dazzling brightness of God Most High, making it possible for everyone to see. 43 The judgement will last seven years. 44 That's the arrangement I have made for Judgement Day, but I have revealed these things only to you."

Only a Few Will Be Saved

45 Then I said, "Lord, I repeat what I said earlier: How fortunate are the people who can live now and obey your commands! 46 But what about those for whom I have been praying? There is no one in the present generation who has not sinned, no one who has not broken your covenant. 47 Now I understand that the world to come will bring joy to only a few, but torment to many. 48 The evil impulse within us has grown and it has led us away from God's ways, brought us to ruin, put us on the way to death and destruction, and taken us far from life. It has destroyed not only a few, but almost everyone who was ever created."

49 "Listen to me," the angel said, "and I will teach you further and correct your thinking. 50 Because only a few will be saved, God created two worlds, instead of only one. 51 As you say, only a few people are righteous, but there are large numbers of wicked people. But listen: 52 If you had only a few precious stones, would you add lumps of lead and clay to them in order to have more?" [u]

53 "Surely no one would do that, sir," I answered.

54 "Take another illustration," he continued. "The earth herself will give you an answer if you humbly ask her 55 whether she produces more gold, silver, copper, iron, lead, or clay. 56 There is more silver than gold, more copper than silver, more iron than copper, more lead than iron, and more clay than lead. 57 So judge for yourself which are more desirable and valuable, common things or rare things."

58 I answered, "Lord and master, the common things are cheap; it is the rare things that are valuable."

59 "All right," he replied, "so draw the logical conclusion: the person who has what is scarce has more reason to be pleased than the person who has what is plentiful. 60 It's the same with the judgement [v] that I have promised: I will be pleased with the few who will be saved, because they are the ones who now praise and honour me and make my name known. 61 I will not be sad about the large

---

[r] *Some ancient translations* The invisible city will appear; *Latin* The bride will appear and the appearing city.   [s] *Some ancient translations* the Messiah; *Latin* Jesus.
[t] *Verses 36–105 are not found in the Authorized Version, but they have been restored from ancient sources.*   [u] *One ancient translation* would you...more; *Latin unclear.*
[v] *Some ancient translations* judgement; *Latin* creation.
7.32: Dan 12.2   **7.36:** Lk 16.23–24; Rev 9.2

number of people who will be lost, because even now they last no longer than a vapour; they disappear like fire and smoke; they catch fire, blaze up, and quickly go out."

62 Then I said to the earth, "Look at what you have done! When you gave birth to the rest of creation you gave birth to reason. 63 It would have been better if you had never been created. Then we humans would never have had the power of reasoning! 64 But as it is now, our reason grows up with us and then torments us, because we realize that we are going to die! 65 Compared with us who must bear this sorrow, the dumb animals must be happy. 66 They are much better off than we are. They do not have to look forward to the judgement; they are not aware of any torment or salvation that is promised to them after death. 67 What good is it to us that we are going to be given life in the future if it is to be a life of terrible torment? 68 Everyone who is born is caught in the web of sin, is full of wickedness and burdened with guilt. 69 I think it would be better if after death we did not have to face judgement."

70 The angel replied, "When God Most High was creating the world, as well as Adam and his descendants, the first thing he did was to get everything ready for the judgement. 71 So you ought to learn from your own words. You said that your reason grows up with you, 72 and that's the point. The people of this world used their reason and sinned; they received God's commands but did not keep them; they accepted the Law and then disobeyed it. And that's why they will suffer torment. 73 What excuse can they offer at the judgement? How can they answer at the last day? 74 God Most High has been very patient with the people of this world for a long time, but it has not been for their sake. He has done it for the sake of the age to come."

The Soul after Death

75 Then I said, "Sir, may I ask you, please, to explain to me what happens when we die, when each of us must give back his soul? Will we be kept at rest until the time when you begin to make your new creation, or will our torment begin immediately?"

76 "I will answer that question also," he replied, "but do not include yourself among those who will be tormented because they have no use for religion. 77 After all, you have a treasure of good works stored up with God Most High, which will not be shown to you until the last days. 78 But to answer your question about death: When God Most High has pronounced the final decree that a person shall die, the soul leaves the body to return to the one who gave it. Immediately it praises the glory of God Most High. 79 Let me explain first about people who had no use for the ways of God Most High and hated those who worshipped him. 80 There is no place where their souls can go for rest; they must wander about for ever in torment, grief, and sorrow. Their torment will progress in seven stages. 81 Firstly, they ignore the Law of God Most High. 82 Secondly, they can no longer make a sincere repentance and obtain life. 83 Thirdly, they see the reward stored up for those who put their faith in the covenants of God Most High. 84 Fourthly, they think about the torment that has been stored up for them in the last days. 85 Fifthly, they see angels guarding the homes of other souls in complete silence. 86 Sixthly, they recognize that they must soon be tormented. w 87 Seventhly, and worst of all, when they see the glory of God Most High, they are sick with remorse and shame. They cringe in fear, because while they were living they sinned against him. And now they are about to come before him to be judged on the last day.

88 "Now let me explain about those who followed the ways of God Most High and what will happen when the time comes for them to leave their mortal bodies. 89 While they lived on earth, through constant difficulty and danger, they served God Most High and carefully kept the Law given by the Lawgiver. 90 This is what they will receive: 91 They will rejoice when they see the great glory of God. He will receive them, and they will enter their rest in seven stages of joy. 92 The first joy is to have struggled hard and won the victory over the evil impulse which was formed in them, but which did not succeed in leading them from life into death. 93 The second is to see the endless wandering of the souls of the wicked and the punishment that is waiting for them. 94 The third is to know what a good report their Maker has given about them, that during their lifetime they kept the Law that was entrusted to them.

w Verse 86 in Latin is unclear.

95 The fourth is to appreciate the rest that they are to enjoy in the places where they have been brought together, guarded by angels, in complete silence, and with the glory that is waiting for them at the last day. 96 The fifth is to rejoice that they have now escaped the corrupt world and will receive the future life as their possession. They can see both the narrow, troubled x world from which they have been freed and the spacious world they will receive and enjoy for ever. 97 The sixth is to be shown how their faces will shine like the sun and how they are to be like the light of the stars that never die. 98 The seventh joy, and best of all, is when they rush to meet God face to face, with perfect trust and happiness, without any fear or shame. They served him during their lifetime and now they will receive from him their reward in glory. 99 These rewards that I have been telling you about are those that have been prepared for the souls of the righteous. I described to you earlier the torment that the rebellious will suffer."

100 Then I asked, "When the souls of the righteous are separated from their bodies, will they be given time to see what you have told me about?"

101 "They will be free for seven days," he answered, "and during that time they will be able to see the things I have told you about. After that they will be brought together with the other souls in their homes."

The Finality of Judgement and the Salvation of the Few

102 Then I said, "Sir, please tell me whether the righteous will be able to ask God Most High to show mercy on the unrighteous on Judgement Day. 103 Will fathers be able to pray for their children, children for parents, brothers for brothers, relatives for those near to them, and friends y for those dear to them?"

104 "I will be happy to tell you," he replied. "Judgement Day is final z and sets the final seal on truth for all to see. You know that in this age a father cannot send his son to be sick a for him or sleep or eat or be healed for him. An owner cannot send his slave to do these things for him, nor can a person send his best friend. 105 In the same way, on that day, no one will be able to pray for another person. Each person will receive the punishment or reward for his own sinfulness or righteousness." b

106 "If that is so," I answered, "how can we explain what we find in the Scriptures? Abraham prayed for the people of Sodom, and Moses for our ancestors who sinned in the desert. 107 Later, Joshua prayed for the people of Israel in the time of Achan, 108 and Samuel prayed for them in the days of Saul. c David prayed at the time of the epidemic, and Solomon prayed for those who were going to worship in the Temple. 109 Elijah prayed that the people might have rain and for a dead person to come back to life. 110 Hezekiah prayed for the people during the time of Sennacherib. And there are many other examples. 111 If righteous people prayed for the unrighteous during such times when corruption increased and injustice multiplied, why won't the same thing happen at the Judgement Day?"

112 "The present age is not the end of everything," the angel answered. "Even in this age, the glorious presence of God is not d always seen. That is why the strong have prayed for the weak during this age. 113 But the Judgement Day will be the end of the present age and the beginning of the future age. Then all corruption will end, 114 self-indulgence and disloyalty will be eliminated. Righteousness and truth will reach their full maturity. 115 So on Judgement Day, no one will be able to have mercy on those who have been condemned, and no one will be able to harm those who have been acquitted."

116 I answered, "I made this point before, and I will make it again. It would have been better if the earth had never produced Adam, or when it had done so,

---

x Some ancient translations troubled; Latin unclear.
y Some ancient translations friends; Latin the confident.
z One ancient translation final; Latin bold.
a Some ancient translations be sick; Latin understand.
b Verses 106–140 are the equivalent of verses 36–70 in the Authorized Version.
c Some ancient translations in the days of Saul; Latin does not have these words.
d Some ancient translations is not; Latin is.

7.97: Dan 12.3; Mt 13.43   **7.98:** Mt 5.8; Heb 12.14; 1 Jn 3.2; Rev 22.4
7.106: Gen 18.23; Ex 32.11   **7.107:** Josh 7.6-7
7.108: 1 Sam 7.9; 2 Sam 24.17; 1 Kgs 8.22-23,30   **7.109:** 1 Kgs 18.42,45; 17.20-21
7.110: 2 Kgs 19.15-19

if it had made him so that he could not sin. ¹¹⁷ What good is it for any of us to have life in the present age, when it is full of misery and when all we can look forward to after death is punishment? ¹¹⁸ O Adam, what have you done? Your sin was not only your own downfall; it was also the downfall of all of us who are your descendants. ¹¹⁹ What good is it to us that we have the promise of immortal life, when we have committed sins that condemn us to death? ¹²⁰ What good is the hope of eternity, when we find ourselves in such a completely hopeless situation? ¹²¹ What good is it that safe and secure homes have been prepared for us in the future world, when we have lived such wicked lives? ¹²² What good is the promise that the glorious presence of God Most High will protect those who have lived pure lives, when our own lives have been so full of sin? ¹²³ What good is it that Paradise is shown to us, that its imperishable fruit can heal us and provide all we need? We can never go there ¹²⁴ because we have lived unacceptable lives.ᵉ ¹²⁵ What good is it that the faces of those who practice self-control will shine more brightly than the stars, when our own faces will be blacker than the night? ¹²⁶ Never in our whole lives, when we sinned, did we think about what we would have to suffer after death."

127 The angel replied, "This is the meaning of the conflict that every person on earth must endure: ¹²⁸ If he is defeated, he must suffer the things you have just told me about, but if he is victorious, he will receive the rewards that I have just mentioned. ¹²⁹ That is why Moses long ago urged the people to choose life so that they might live. ¹³⁰ But they did not believe him or the prophets who came after him, and they did not believe me when I spoke to them. ¹³¹ So the sadness over their destruction is nothing compared with the great joy over the salvation of those who believe."

132 I answered, "Sir, I know that God Most High is spoken of as merciful because he shows mercy to those who have not yet entered this world. ¹³³ He is called compassionate because he shows compassion to those who repent and obey his Law. ¹³⁴ He is thought of as patient because he is patient with his own

creatures who have sinned. ¹³⁵ He is known as generous because he prefers to give rather than to demand. ¹³⁶ And he is known as very forgiving because he continues to forgive sinners of the past, present, and future. ¹³⁷ If he did not continue to forgive, there would be no life for this world or the people in it. ¹³⁸ He is spoken of as pardoning because, if it were not for his goodness in pardoning sinners, not one person in ten thousand would gain life. ¹³⁹ He is called judge because he pardons and blots out the many sins of those who were created by his word. ¹⁴⁰ If he did not, only a handful of the whole human race would be left."ᶠ

8 The angel replied, "God Most High made this world for many people, but the future world for only a few. ²Ezra, let me give you an illustration. If you ask the earth, it will tell you that it produces a large amount of clay for pots but only a small amount of gold dust. And that's how it is with the present world: ³many have been created, but only a few will be saved."

Ezra Prays for His People

4 I said to myself, "I must search for wisdom and try to understand. ⁵I was brought into this world without my consent,ᵍ and I will leave it against my will. God has given me only a few short years as my span of life."

6 Then I prayed, "O Lord above, permit me, your humble servant, to offer this prayer: Sow a seed within us, and let it grow until it produces new hearts and minds, so that sinful humanity may have life. ⁷For you alone are God, and you created all of us, as the scripture says. ⁸You give life and provide arms and legs to the body formed in the womb, where it is kept safe in the elements of fire and water. The body which you form is carried in the womb for nine months, ⁹and you alone provide safety for the protecting womb and the protected body. Then when the womb delivers what was created in it, ¹⁰your command produces milk from the breasts of the human body. ¹¹The infant you created is fed in this way for a while, and then you continue to provide your mercy. ¹²You bring a person up in your righteousness, teach him your Law, and discipline him with your wisdom.

ᵉ Probable text unacceptable lives; Latin in unacceptable places.
ᶠ Verses 106–140 are the equivalent of verses 36–70 in the Authorized Version.
ᵍ One ancient translation without my consent; Latin to obey.
7.123: Ezek 47.12; Rev 22.2   **7.129:** Deut 30.19   **8.3:** Mt 22.14

¹³You are his Creator and, as you wish, you can take away his life or allow him to live. ¹⁴But if you are so ready to destroy a person that was so carefully created at your command, why was he created in the first place?

15 "Now, Lord, I must say this: You may know what is best with regard to the rest of mankind, but I mourn for your own people—¹⁶I am disturbed and grieved for your own nation Israel, the descendants of Jacob. ¹⁷So I want to pray for them and for myself, because I can see how all of us who live on this earth have failed, ¹⁸and I know that judgement will soon come upon us. ¹⁹So please hear me and listen to my prayer."

The prayer that Ezra prayed before he was taken up into heaven begins here. He prayed, ²⁰"O Lord, you live for ever, and the highest heavens are yours. ²¹Your throne is more wonderful than anything we can imagine; your glory surpasses our understanding; the heavenly army of angels stands trembling before you. ²²They are ready to turn themselves into wind or fire at your command. Your word is everlastingly true. ²³Your mighty commands accomplish fearful things. With one look, you dry up the deep oceans, and you can melt the mountains with your anger. Your truth lasts for ever.ʰ ²⁴O Lord, you created me, and I am your servant, so listen to my prayer. ²⁵As long as I have life and understanding, I cannot keep silent.

26 "Do not take account of the sins of your people; rather, consider those who have served you faithfully. ²⁷Pay no attention to godless people and what they do, but take into account those who have kept your covenant in spite of all their sufferings. ²⁸Do not think about those who have lived wicked lives, but remember those who have gladly confessed you as God. ²⁹Do not destroy your people because of those who have lived like animals, but be mindful of those who have taught your Law in such a wonderful way. ³⁰Do not be angry with those you consider worse than animals, but show your love to those who have always trusted in your glorious presence.

31 "It is true that we and our ancestors have lived our lives in ways that bring death, but it is because of us who are sinners that you are called merciful. ³²You

will surely be called merciful if you choose to take pity on us—we are sinners without any righteous deeds to our credit. ³³Those who are righteous will receive their reward on the basis of the many good works that they have stored up with you.

34 "What is man that you should be angry with him? What is this mortal race that you should be so bitter against it? ³⁵To speak the truth, no person was ever born who did not sin; there is no one living who is not guilty. ³⁶Therefore, Lord, your righteousness and goodness will certainly be made known when you show mercy to those who have no treasure of good deeds."

37 The Lord answered me, "Part of what you have said is correct, and things will happen as you have indicated. ³⁸You can be sure that I will give no thought to those who have sinned, or to their creation, death, judgement or destruction. ³⁹Instead, I will find my joy in the creation of the righteous, their earthly journey, their salvation, and their final reward. ⁴⁰Things will happen just as I have said. ⁴¹The farmer sows many seeds and puts out many plants, but not all of them take root or come up at the right time. That's how it is with this world. Not everyone who has been placed in this world will be saved."

42 Then I said, "Please let me speak. ⁴³The farmer's seed may not come up because you did not send rain at the right time, or it may be ruined by too much rain. ⁴⁴But people are different. You formed them with your own hands; you created them to be like you; and you made everything for their benefit. How can you compare them to a farmer's seed? ⁴⁵It's impossible, O Lordⁱ above! Spare the people who are your own. Have pity on them. Show your mercy to the people you have created."

46 He answered, "The present is for those who live now, and the future for those who are to come. ⁴⁷You are certainly not able to love what I have created more than I do. Never again consider yourself among the unrighteous, as you have done so often. ⁴⁸Yet I am very pleased ⁴⁹that you have shown proper humility and not boasted by thinking of yourself as righteous. ⁵⁰The people of this world who have lived their lives in pride and arrogance will suffer

---

ʰ Some ancient translations lasts for ever; Latin testifies.
ⁱ Some ancient translations O Lord; Latin does not have these words.
8.22: Ps 104.4; Heb 1.7

many things in the last days. [51] But, Ezra, you should be thinking about the glory that is waiting for you and those like you. [52] For all of you, Paradise has been opened, the tree of life has been planted, the world to come has been made ready, all your needs have been provided, the heavenly city has been built, full rest from your labours has been offered, goodness and wisdom have been perfected. [53] The source of evil has been sealed off, so that it cannot reach you; all sickness has been removed, death[j] has been taken away, hell is gone, and corruption has disappeared. [54] All suffering has been taken away, and the treasure of immortality is at last revealed.

55 "So don't ask any more questions about the large number of people who are lost. [56] For when they had the opportunity to choose, they despised God Most High, had contempt for his Law, and refused to follow his ways. [57] In addition, they ill-treated the righteous servants of God. [58] They even said to themselves that there was no God, although they knew that they must die. [59] So the joys I have described are waiting for you, while thirst and torment are in store for them. But God Most High did not want anyone to perish. [60] He created everyone and prepared life for everyone, but those he created dishonoured the name of their Creator and were ungrateful to the one who offered them life. [61] That is why the day on which I will judge them is near. [62] I have made this known to you and a few others like you, but not to everyone."

The Signs of the End

I answered, [63] "Sir, you have shown me many signs which you will perform in the last days, but you have not told me how I can know when this will happen."

9 He answered, "Consider all these things very carefully. When you see that some of the signs I have told you about have appeared, [2] you will know that the time has come when God Most High will bring judgement on the world he has created. [3] There will be earthquakes, national rebellions, international intrigues, unstable leaders, and confused rulers. When you see these things

happening, [4] you will know that they are what God Most High has spoken about since the beginning of creation. [5] The beginning and the end[k] of everything that happens in this world are clear. [6] The same is true in the world above:[l] wonders and miracles show the beginning of events, and mighty signs show when they end.

7 "Some people will escape destruction and be saved by their good works or by their faith. All of them [8] will survive the dangers I have described and will enjoy the salvation provided in the land that I have set apart from eternity as my own. [9] Then those who have ignored my ways and held them in contempt will be surprised when they find themselves in continual torment. [10] This will include all those who ignored me while they were alive, even though they accepted the blessings I gave them. [11] It will include all those who scorned my Law during the time they were free to do so and all those who refused to repent when they still had the chance. [12] The torment they will have to suffer after death will force them to recognize the truth. [13] Therefore, Ezra, you should stop asking questions about how the wicked will be punished. Instead, be concerned about how and when the righteous will be saved. The world was created for them and belongs to them."

14 I said, [15] "I must repeat what I said before. The lost far outnumber those who are saved—[16] it is like a wave compared with a drop of water."

17 He answered, "The seed to be sown depends on the soil; the colour of the flower depends on the kind of flower; the quality of a product depends on the skill of the workman; and the size of the harvest depends on how hard the farmer has worked. [18] Before I created this world or the people who would live in it, no one opposed me, because no one existed. [19] When I had created the world, I supplied it with an abundance of food and a Law of profound wisdom, but the people I created lived corrupt lives. [20] I looked at my world and saw that it was ruined. I saw that my earth was in danger of being destroyed by the wicked plans of the people who had come into it. [21] When I saw this, I found it very difficult to spare them, but I saved a few for myself, one

[j] Some ancient translations death; Latin does not have this word.
[k] One ancient translation The beginning and the end; Latin unclear.
[l] The same...above; Latin unclear.
8.52: 1 Pet 1.4   **8.59:** Lk 16.24   **9.11:** Wis 12.10,20; Heb 12.17

grape out of a bunch and one tree out of a great forest. *m* 22 So let them perish— all those people who were born only to be lost. But let my chosen people be kept safe—those for whom I worked so hard to bring them to perfection.

23 "And now, Ezra, you must wait seven more days, but do not fast this time. 24 Go to a field of wild flowers where no one has ever lived and eat nothing but the flowers—do not eat any meat or drink any wine. 25 Pray the whole time to God Most High. Then I will come and talk with you again."

THE FOURTH VISION
The Law Remains

26 I obeyed the angel's command and went to a field called Ardat. I sat there among the flowers and ate the wild plants, and that was enough food for me. 27 After seven days I was lying on the grass, and once again my thoughts began to trouble me. 28 Then I began to speak and said to God Most High, 29 "O Lord, you revealed yourself to our ancestors when they were travelling through the trackless, barren desert after they had left Egypt. You said to them, 30 'Listen to me, people of Israel. 31 I am giving you my Law. It will be like a seed sown among you that produces fruit, and it will be your crowning glory for ever.' 32 Our ancestors received the Law, but they disobeyed its commands. Yet the fruit of the Law was not destroyed—it could not be destroyed because it was yours. 33 Those who had received the Law were destroyed because they did not guard the good seed that was sown in them. 34-35 The usual thing is that the container remains after its contents have been destroyed, for example, seed in the ground, a ship on the sea, or food in a bowl. But this is not the case with us sinners. 36 The Law was placed in our hearts, and we are the ones who will be destroyed because we have sinned. 37 The Law will not be destroyed; it will remain in all its glory."

The Vision of the Weeping Woman

38 While I was saying these things to myself, I looked round and saw a woman on my right. She was weeping and wailing, terribly upset; her clothes were torn, and there were ashes on her head. 39 I immediately put my own troubles out of my mind, turned to the woman, 40 and asked, "Why are you crying? Why are you so upset?"

41 "Please, sir," she answered, "leave me alone and let me go on crying and mourning; I am bitter and depressed."

42 "Tell me what's wrong," I said.

43 She answered, "Sir, I was married for thirty years, but I was never able to have a child. 44 During those thirty years I prayed every day and every hour, day and night, to God Most High for a child. 45 After thirty years God answered my prayer; he saw my suffering, took away my distress, and gave me a son. What great joy this brought to my husband and me and to all our neighbours! We sang the praises of the Almighty. 46 I brought our son up with the greatest care, 47 and when he was grown, I chose a wife for him and prepared for the wedding.

10 "On the wedding night when my son entered the bedroom, he dropped dead. 2 So we put out all the wedding lamps, and all my neighbours came to comfort me. I remained in control of myself until the evening of the second day, 3 when they all left. That night I got up and came out to this field, as you see. 4 I have decided never to return to that town. I am going to stay here in constant mourning, neither eating nor drinking anything until I die."

5 When she told me this, I put aside my own thoughts and spoke sharply to her: 6 "You are the most foolish woman I ever met. Don't you see what our people are suffering? Don't you know all that has happened to us? 7 Jerusalem, the mother of us all, is overcome with grief and shame. You ought to be mourning for her 8 and sharing the grief and sorrow of all of us. But you are mourning for that one son of yours. 9 Ask the earth; let her tell you that she is the one who ought to be mourning for the vast multitudes of people that she has brought to birth. 10 All of us who are living came originally from her, and there are more to come. Almost all of us go straight to destruction—the vast multitude of earth's children are lost. 11 So who has more right to mourn, you for your one son, or the earth, which has lost so many? 12-13 I know what you are thinking; you think that your sorrow is worse than the earth's. You think that it is only natural for earth's multitudes to live and then die, but you have lost your own flesh and blood which

---

m Some ancient translations a great forest; *Latin* great tribes.
9.29: Ex 19.9; 24.10; Deut 4.12   **10.7:** Gal 4.26

you brought to birth with such trouble and pain. But let me tell you [14] that from the time God created the earth she has suffered as much in producing human beings for God as you did in childbirth. [15] So keep your tears to yourself, and be brave about what has happened to you. [16] If you will accept God's decision as just, you will get your son back at the right time, and you will receive the praise due to a mother. [17] Go back to the city and to your husband."

18 "No," she answered, "I will never go back; I am going to stay here and die."

19-20 "Don't do that," I continued. "Consider the misfortunes and sorrows of Jerusalem, and you won't feel so sorry for yourself. [21] You can see that our place of worship is in ruins, our altar has been torn down, our Temple has been destroyed, [22] our musical instruments lie quiet, our hymns have been silenced, our joy has ended, the light of the sacred lamp has been put out, our Covenant Box has been carried off, our sacred utensils have been desecrated, the name of our God has been profaned, our leaders have been dishonoured, our priests have been burnt to death, our Levites have been taken captive, our virgins have been raped, our wives have been violated, our devout men have been carried off, our children have been abandoned, our young people have been made slaves, and our strong soldiers have been made helpless. [23] Worst of all, Jerusalem, once marked as God's own city, has lost its glory and has been handed over to our enemies. [24] So put aside all your sorrow and grief. May God Most High, the Almighty, be merciful to you and give you peace. May he give you rest from your troubles."

25 While I was speaking to the woman, her face suddenly began to shine with a light that flashed like lightning. I was afraid to stand near her and wondered what all this meant. [26] Suddenly she let out a loud and terrifying cry that shook the earth. [27] When I looked up, I could no longer see the woman, but there was a city built [n] on huge foundations. I was afraid and shouted, [28] "Where is the angel Uriel, who came to me earlier? It is his fault that I am so confused. My prayer

is useless, and I have nothing to hope for but death."

Uriel's Interpretation of the Vision

29 I was still speaking when the angel Uriel appeared again. He saw me [30] lying there unconscious like a corpse, so he took hold of my right hand, gave me strength, and stood me on my feet. Then he asked, [31] "What's the matter? Why are you so disturbed and confused?"

32 I answered, "You abandoned me completely! I did as you told me and came out to this field, but I cannot explain what I am seeing.

33 "Stand up like a man," he answered, "and I will explain it to you."

34 "Sir," I answered, "please explain it to me. I will die in my frustration if you leave me, [35] for I cannot understand what I have seen and heard. [36] Or is my mind playing tricks on me, and is this just a bad dream? [37] I beg you, sir, tell me what this vision means."

38 The angel said, "Now listen closely, and I will explain the meaning of these things that you fear. God Most High has revealed many secrets to you [39] because he has seen that you have lived a righteous life and have always grieved and mourned for your people and for Jerusalem. [40] This is what the vision means: A woman appeared to you a little while ago, [41] and when you saw that she was mourning, you tried to console her. [42-43] The woman told you about the death of her son. Then she vanished from your sight, and a whole city [o] appeared. This is the meaning: [44] The woman you saw is Jerusalem, which you now see as a completed city. [45] When she told you that for thirty years she had had no children, it meant that for three thousand [p] years no offerings had yet been made there. [46] Then Solomon built the city, and sacrifices began to be offered there. At that time the childless woman gave birth to her son. [47] When she told you that she took great care in bringing the son up, that referred to the period when Jerusalem was inhabited. [48] When she told you of the death of her son on his wedding day, that meant the destruction of Jerusalem. [49] So in the vision you saw how she mourned for her son, and you tried to console her for what had happened— this is what was to be revealed to you.

---

[n] Some ancient translations built; Latin being built.
[o] Some ancient translations whole city; Latin city being built.
[p] Some ancient translations three thousand; Latin three.
10.27: Heb 11.10; Rev 21.9-27

⁵⁰When God Most High saw that you were grieving for the woman with all your heart and soul, he showed you all her glory and majestic beauty. ⁵¹That is why I told you to go and stay in the field where no one had ever lived, ⁵²for I knew that God Most High was going to show you these things. ⁵³I told you to go to the field where no foundation had ever been built, ⁵⁴because nothing built by man could stand in the place where the city of God Most High was about to be revealed.

55 "So don't be afraid. Go into the city and look at its beautiful and majestic buildings. See as much as you can. ⁵⁶After that, you will hear as much as you can. ⁵⁷You are more fortunate than most people, and only a few have the reputation with God Most High that you have. ⁵⁸Remain here until tomorrow night, ⁵⁹and he will show you in dreams and visions what he plans to do for those who will be living on the earth in the last days." So I slept there that night and the next, as I had been told.

THE FIFTH VISION
The Vision of an Eagle

11 The second night I had a dream. I saw an eagle coming up out of the sea. it had twelve wings and three heads. ²As I looked, it spread out its wings over the whole world. Winds blew on it from every direction, and clouds*q* gathered over it. ³Then from its wings I saw rival wings begin to grow, but they were small and insignificant. ⁴All three heads of the eagle were asleep, even the middle one, which was larger than the others. ⁵While I was watching, the eagle flew up in the air and became ruler of the whole earth and all its people. ⁶I saw how everything on earth was brought under the eagle's control—no one on earth was able to oppose it. ⁷Then I saw the eagle stand up on its claws and say to its wings, ⁸"Not all of you are to wake up at the same time; you must sleep where you are and wake up when your turn comes, ⁹and the heads must wake up last." ¹⁰I looked again and saw that the voice was not coming from any of the eagle's heads but from the middle of its body. ¹¹I counted its rival wings, and there were eight of them.

12 I saw one of the wings on the right side rise up and govern the whole world.

¹³After its rule came to an end, it vanished so completely that it left no trace. Then the next wing rose up and governed for a long time. ¹⁴When its rule was coming to an end and it was about to vanish like the first wing, ¹⁵a voice said to it, ¹⁶"Listen, you have ruled the world for a long time, and I want you to hear this message before you disappear: ¹⁷No one after you will rule as long as you did—not even half as long." ¹⁸The third wing rose up and governed as the earlier ones had done; then it also vanished. ¹⁹The same thing happened to all the other wings: one after the other they rose to power and then vanished.

20 I kept looking, and after a while the other small wings on the right side rose up to seize power. Some of them governed briefly and quickly disappeared, ²¹while others rose up but were never able to govern. ²²Then I noticed that the twelve large wings and two of the small wings had disappeared. ²³Nothing was left on the eagle's body except the three sleeping heads and the six small wings. ²⁴I kept watching, and suddenly two of the six small wings left the others and moved under the head on the right side, while the other four remained where they were. ²⁵Then I saw that these four small wings were plotting to rise up and seize power. ²⁶One of them rose up, but it quickly disappeared. ²⁷The second one also rose up, but it disappeared even more quickly than the first. ²⁸I saw that the two remaining small wings were also plotting to seize control for themselves. ²⁹While they were making their plans, one of the sleeping heads suddenly awoke. It was the one in the middle, the one that was larger than the other two. ³⁰Then I saw that it was joined by the other heads, ³¹and when it turned to eat up the two little wings that were planning to seize power, the other two heads helped it. ³²This head gained power over the whole world, established an oppressive rule over people everywhere, and exercised more power over the world than any of the other wings had done before. ³³Then, as I watched, the middle head disappeared just as suddenly as the wings had done. ³⁴Two heads were left, and they also gained power over the earth and its people; ³⁵but while I was still watching, the head on the right ate up the head on the left.

---

q Some ancient translations clouds; *Latin does not have this word.*
11.1: Dan 7.3–4; Rev 13.1

36 Then I heard a voice which said, "Ezra, look straight ahead and think about what you see."

37 I looked and saw what appeared to be an angry lion come roaring out of the forest. I heard it speak in human language to the eagle and say, 38 "Listen, Eagle, to what I have to say to you; it is the message of God Most High: 39 You are the only one left of the four animals that I appointed to govern my world and to bring the ages of this world to an end. 40 You are the fourth animal and you have conquered all the animals that came before you. As long as you have been in this world, you have ruled it through terror, oppression, and deceit, 41 with a total disregard for truth. 42 You have viciously attacked harmless people who were living in peace; you have hated those who spoke the truth, and you have loved liars. You have destroyed the homes of those who were prosperous and have torn down the walls of those who did you no harm. 43 God Most High knows how proud and arrogant you are. The Almighty One 44 has looked back over the world he established. The end has come; the final age is over. 45 So, Eagle, the time has come for you to vanish, along with your big, terrible wings, your small, wicked wings, your evil heads, your awful claws, and your whole worthless body. 46 The entire world will be set free from your violence and renewed as it sets its hope on the judgement and mercy of God, who created it."

12 While the lion was speaking in this way to the eagle, I looked 2 and saw that the last head of the eagle was gone. Then the two small wings that had moved over to that head rose up to govern, but their rule was short and full of trouble. 3 They disappeared before my eyes, and the whole body of the eagle burst into flames, and the world was terrified.

The Interpretation of the Vision

I was so disturbed and so afraid that I woke up. I said, 4 "I have brought this on myself, because I have tried to study the ways of God Most High. 5 I am mentally exhausted and completely worn out. The terrible fears I have experienced this night have taken my last bit of strength. 6 All I can do now is pray to God Most High to give me strength until the end." 7 Then I prayed, "Master and Lord, if it is true that you consider me more righteous than many others and if you hear my prayers, then I beg you, 8 give me strength. Show me, O Lord, the full meaning of this terrifying vision, and set my mind at ease. 9 After all, you did consider me worthy to be shown the end of this age."

10 God's angel said to me, "Here is the interpretation of the vision you saw. 11 The eagle you saw coming up out of the sea represents the fourth kingdom in the vision that your brother Daniel saw. 12 But he was not given the same interpretation of it that I am giving you. 13 The time is coming when an empire will be established on earth that is more terrible than any before it. 14 Twelve kings will rule over it, one after the other. 15 The second king will rule longer than any of the others. 16 That is the meaning of the twelve wings that you saw.

17 "You heard the voice speaking from the middle of the eagle's body, instead of from its heads. 18 That means that after the rule of the second king, a great struggle for power will take place, and the empire will be in danger of breaking up. But that will not happen, and the empire will regain its earlier power.

19 "You saw the eight small wings growing out of the eagle's big wings. That means 20 that eight kings will rise up in the empire, but their rule will be brief and unimportant. 21 Two of them will appear briefly near the middle of the period, four of them will not appear until near the end, and two will be left until the very end.

22 "You saw the three heads that were asleep. That means 23 that in the last days of the empire, God Most High will raise up three kings; they r will restore much of the empire and rule over the world 24 and its people with more harshness than any before them. The reason they are called the eagle's heads 25 is that these three kings will bring to a head and complete the godless work of the eagle. 26 You saw the largest head disappear. This means that one of the kings will die in his bed, in great agony. 27 The other two will die in battle. 28 One of them will kill the other; then he also will be killed in battle at the end of time.

29 "You saw the two small wings moving under the head on the right side. 30 That means that God Most High has

---

r Some ancient translations they; Latin he.

12.11: Dan 7.7

What wrong have we done to you? (12.41)

kept them until the end, but their rule was short and full of trouble, as you saw.

31 "You saw the angry lion come roaring out of the forest, and you heard it speak to the eagle and rebuke it for the evil that it had done and for all that it had said. 32 The lion represents the Messiah, whom God Most High has held back until the end. He will be a descendant of David and will come and speak[s] to the rulers. He will rebuke them for their wickedness, their sinfulness, and their contempt for God's ways. 33 While they are still living, he will bring them to judgement, condemn them for their sin, and destroy them. 34 But he will have mercy on the rest of my people, those who are left in my land; he will set them free and make them happy until the end comes, the Judgement Day about which I told you at the beginning.

35 "That is the dream you had, and that is its interpretation. 36 But you are the only one that God Most High has considered worthy to reveal this secret to. 37 So write in a book everything you saw, and put it in a safe hiding place. 38 Then teach these secrets to those who are wise among your people, those who will be able to understand them and keep them secret. 39 But you must stay here seven more days, so that God Most High may reveal to you whatever he wishes." Then the angel left me.

The People Come to Ezra

40 When the seven days had passed and all the people heard that I had not yet returned to the city, all of them, rich and poor, came and asked me, 41 "What wrong have we done to you? How have we ill-treated you? Why have you abandoned us and settled down in this place? 42 You are the only one of all our prophets who is left. You are like the last bunch of grapes in a vineyard, like a lantern in a dark place, like a safe harbour for a ship in a storm. 43 Haven't we suffered enough already? 44 If you abandon us, it would have been better if we had died like the others in the fire that destroyed Jerusalem. 45 We are no better than those who died." Then they all started crying loudly.

I answered, 46 "Be brave, Israel, put away your sorrow. 47 God Most High will keep you in mind; the Almighty One has not forgotten you in all your troubles. 48 And I haven't left you or abandoned you. I came here to pray for Jerusalem in her time of trouble and to ask mercy for her and for your Temple, now in disgrace. 49 Please return to your homes, all of you. I will come back to you in a few days." 50 So they left me and went back to the city.

THE SIXTH VISION
The Vision

51 I stayed in the field for seven days, as the angel had commanded me. I ate nothing but wild flowers; I was a vegetarian in those days.

13 The seven days passed, and the following night I had a dream. 2 In

---

[s] *Some ancient translations* He will...speak; *Latin does not have these words.*
12.32: Dan 7.13–14

The wind brought with it out of the sea what looked like a man (13.3)

my dream I saw a wind coming up out of the sea and stirring up great waves. ³ As I watched, the wind brought with it out of the sea what looked like a man, [t] and he was flying [u] on the clouds. When he turned his face, everything he looked at began to tremble, ⁴ and when he spoke, everyone who heard his voice melted like wax in a fire.

5 I looked again and saw a crowd too large to count. They were people gathered together from all parts of the world to fight against the man who had come up out of the sea. ⁶ Then I watched the man carve out a high mountain and fly up onto it. ⁷ I tried to see the place or the region from which the mountain was carved, but I couldn't. ⁸ Then I saw that all the people who had come together to make war against him were terrified, but they still prepared to fight him. ⁹ When the man saw the great crowd advancing to attack him, he did not take up any weapons. ¹⁰ The only thing I saw was what looked like a stream of fire coming out of his mouth. He sent a flaming wind from his lips and a storm of sparks from his tongue. The stream of fire, the flaming wind, and the great storm combined ¹¹ and swept down on the crowd that was coming to attack him, and burnt them all up. In a single moment, that crowd too large to count vanished, and there was nothing left but powdery ashes and the smell of smoke. I was shocked when I saw what had happened.

12 Then I saw the man come down from the mountain and call another large crowd to come to him—this was a peace-loving crowd. ¹³ All sorts of people came: some were happy, some were sad, some had their hands and feet tied, and some brought others as a gift to the Lord.

The Interpretation of the Vision

I was so frightened that I woke up. I prayed to God Most High and said, ¹⁴ "Lord, you have been showing me all

[t] *Some ancient translations* the wind...man; *Latin does not have these words.*
[u] *Some ancient translations* flying; *Latin growing strong.*
13.3: Dan 7.13; 2 Esd 13.32   **13.6:** Dan 2.45   **13.13:** Is 66.20

these marvellous things. You have considered me worthy and have heard my prayers. ¹⁵ Now please show me the meaning of this dream also. ¹⁶ I have been thinking how terrible it will be for the people who will be living in those days, but how much worse for those who do not survive. ¹⁷ They will be in great sorrow ¹⁸ because they will not enjoy any of the pleasures reserved for the last days. ¹⁹ But how terrible also for those who do survive; they will have to face great dangers and many troubles, as these dreams have shown. ²⁰ Nevertheless, it is better to pass through these dangers and reach the end than to disappear like a cloud from this world and never see what takes place in the last days."

He answered, ²¹ "I will explain to you the meaning of the vision and answer the questions you have asked. ²² You have raised questions about those who will survive until the end. The answer is that ²³ the one who brings the dangers in those days will also protect from danger the people who have stored up good works and faithfulness with God the Almighty One. ²⁴ You may be certain that those who survive are far more fortunate than those who die.

25 "This is the meaning of the vision. The man you saw coming up out of the sea ²⁶ represents the one whom God Most High has kept ready for many ages. He will free the world he created and establish the new order for those who survive. ²⁷ You saw the wind, fire, and storm going out of the man's mouth, ²⁸ and you saw that without the use of a spear or any other weapon he destroyed the great crowd that was advancing to attack him. This means that ²⁹ the time is near when God Most High will begin to free the people on earth. ³⁰ At that time everyone will be close to panic. ³¹ They will begin to make war against one another, city against city, region against region, nation against nation, and kingdom against kingdom. ³² When that happens, the signs I told you about earlier will take place, and then I will reveal my son, whom you saw as a man coming out of the sea. ³³ When they hear his voice, all the nations will leave their own territory, forget their wars with one another, ³⁴ and come together in one great crowd too large to count, as you saw in your dream. The nations will unite with

the single purpose of making war on my son. ³⁵ He will take his stand on the top of Mount Zion, ³⁶ and the new Jerusalem will be seen by everyone. It will be completed and fully built, just as in your dream you saw the mountain carved out, but not by human hands. ³⁷ Then my son will condemn the assembled nations for their godlessness. That is what the storm meant. ³⁸ He will confront them with the wicked plans they have made and also with the torments they must endure. That is what the flames meant. Then he will easily destroy them by means of ᵛ the Law. That is what the fire meant.

39 "You saw him gather another great crowd of peace-loving people. ⁴⁰ These are the ten tribes of Israel who were taken away into captivity in the time of King Hoshea. King Shalmaneser of Assyria captured them and deported them to a foreign land east of the River Euphrates. ⁴¹ But the ten tribes decided not to stay in that land among the many Gentiles, so they moved farther east to a country where no human beings had ever lived before. ⁴² There they hoped to keep their laws, which they had failed to keep in their own country. ⁴³ When they had to make the difficult passage across the Euphrates, ⁴⁴ God Most High performed miracles for them and blocked the channels of the river until they had crossed over. ⁴⁵ Their long journey through that region, which is named Arzareth, took a year and a half, ⁴⁶ and they have lived there ever since. Now in these last days they are coming back home, ⁴⁷ and once again God Most High will block the channels of the river, so that they may cross over. That is the meaning of the great crowd of peace-loving people you saw. ⁴⁸ But they will also have with them all your own people who are left and who are found within the borders of my holy land. ⁴⁹ When the time comes for my son to destroy the crowd that has gathered from every nation, he will protect his people who are left ⁵⁰ and perform many great miracles for them."

51 Then I said, "Lord and Master, please tell me why the man came up out of the sea."

52 He answered, "No one can explore the bottom of the sea to find out what is there. In the same way, no human being can see my son or those who come with

ᵛ One ancient translation by means of; Latin and.
13.31: Mt 24.7   13.36: 2 Esd 7.26; Rev 21.2,9   13.40: 2 Kgs 17.1–6

him until the day that has been fixed.
⁵³That is the meaning of your dream. You alone have been given this information, ⁵⁴because you have given up your own interests to devote yourself to mine and to the study of my Law. ⁵⁵You have dedicated your life to wisdom, and understanding has been like a mother to you. ⁵⁶That is why God Most High has rewarded you by showing you these things. After three days, I will come back and tell you about other profound wonders."

THE SEVENTH VISION
The Voice from the Bush

57 I went for a walk in the field, worshipping and praising God Most High for the miracles he performs in his own good time. ⁵⁸For he controls the ages and what happens in them. I remained there for three days.

14 On the third day, while I was sitting under an oak-tree, ²suddenly a voice came out of a bush near me and called, "Ezra! Ezra!"

I stood up and answered, "Here I am, Lord."

3 The voice continued, "I revealed myself from a bush and spoke to Moses when my people were slaves in Egypt. ⁴I sent him to lead them out of Egypt, and I brought them to Mount Sinai. I kept Moses with me there on the mountain for a long time, ⁵while I told him the secrets about the ages and the end of time. I told him ⁶what to make public and what to keep secret. ⁷Now I command you ⁸to memorize the signs, visions, and interpretations that I have given you. ⁹You will be taken out of this world into the heavenly world where you and others like you will live with my son until the end of time. ¹⁰The world is no longer young; it is rapidly approaching old age. ¹¹The whole history of the world is divided into twelve periods, and the tenth period has already arrived ¹²and it is half over; only two and a half parts remain. ¹³So set your house in order, warn your people, comfort those who are humble, and teach those who are wise.^w Then say good-bye to this mortal life. ¹⁴Put earthly cares away from you, throw down your human burdens, and lay aside your weak human nature. ¹⁵Put all your anxieties aside, and

get ready to leave this world quickly. ¹⁶You have seen many evil things already, but far worse things are about to happen. ¹⁷As the world grows older and weaker, the evils that will come upon its people will multiply. ¹⁸Truth will depart and falsehood will draw ever nearer. The eagle you saw in your vision is just about to arrive."

Ezra Reproduces the Sacred Writings

19 I replied, "Let me speak^x in your presence, Lord. ²⁰I am ready to depart, as you have commanded, and I will warn the present generation; but who will warn the people who have not yet been born? This world is a dark place, and its people have no light. ²¹Your Law has been destroyed by fire, so no one can know what you have done in the past or what you are planning to do in the future. ²²Please send your holy spirit to me, so that I can write down everything that has been done in this world from the beginning, everything that was written in your Law. Then in these last days, people will be able to find the right way and obtain life if they want to."

23 He answered, "Go and call the people together and tell them not to look for you for forty days. ²⁴Prepare a large number of writing tablets, and take with you these five men who can write fast: Seraiah, Dabriah, Shelemiah, Ethan, and Asiel. ²⁵Then come here, and I will light the lamp of understanding in your heart, and it will not go out until you have finished what you are supposed to write. ²⁶When you have finished your work, you will make some of it public, and you will give the rest to wise men, who will keep it secret. Tomorrow at this time you will begin to write."

27 I did as I was commanded and called all the people together. I said, ²⁸"Listen to what I have to say, people of Israel. ²⁹At first our ancestors lived as foreigners in Egypt, but then they were set free ³⁰and received from God the life-giving Law. But they did not keep it, and when your turn came, you did not keep it either. ³¹God gave you the holy land as your own possession, but you were as sinful as your ancestors and did not follow the ways that God Most High had commanded. ³²God is a just judge, so after a while

---

^w Some ancient translations teach...wise; Latin does not have these words.
^x Some ancient translations Let me speak; Latin does not have these words.
14.2: Ex 3.4

They took turns at writing down what I said (14.42)

he took away what he had given you.
33 Now you are in exile here, but you are
closer to Jerusalem than some of your
fellow Jews.y 34 But if you will discipline
your thoughts and be willing to learn, you
will be kept safe in this life and will be
granted mercy after death, 35 for
Judgement Day comes after death. We
will be brought back to life, and the
righteous people will be made known,
while what the godless have done will
be exposed. 36 But now for forty days, no
one is to come near me or try to find
me."

37 As I had been commanded, I took
the five men, and we went to the field
and stayed there. 38 On the next day I
suddenly heard a voice saying, "Ezra,
open your mouth and drink what I am
giving you." 39 So I opened my mouth,
and I was handed a cup full of a fiery-
coloured liquid, 40 which I took and drank.
When I had drunk it, my mind overflowed
with understanding, and wisdom
increased within me as my memory
became perfect. 41 I began to speak and
went on talking without stopping. 42 God
Most High also gave wisdom to the five
men with me, and they took turns at

writing down what I said. They used an
alphabet z that they had not known before,
and worked for forty days, writing in the
daytime and eating at night. 43 I spoke
all day long, and I was not silent even
at night. 44 During the forty days, ninety-
four a books were written.

45 At the end of the forty days, God
Most High said to me, "You are now to
make public the first twenty-four b books c
that you wrote, so that everyone, whether
he is worthy or not, may read them. 46 But
the last seventy books that you wrote are
to be held back and to be given only to
the wise men among your people,
47 because these books contain a flood of
understanding, a fountain of wisdom, and
a river of knowledge." 48 Then I did as
I was told.

ADDITIONAL PROPHECIES
The Coming Disasters

15 The Lord says, "Proclaim to my
people the prophetic messages
that I will give you, 2 and then have them
written down, because they are true and
will be fulfilled. 3 Do not be afraid of those
who plot against you or be disturbed by

y but...fellow Jews; *Latin unclear.*   z *Some ancient translations* an alphabet; *Latin unclear.*
a *Some ancient translations* ninety-four; *Latin unclear.*
b *Some ancient translations* twenty-four; *Latin does not have this word.*
c TWENTY-FOUR BOOKS: *The Hebrew Bible contains twenty-four books, corresponding to the
thirty-nine books of the Christian Old Testament.*

their unbelief. ⁴Every unbeliever will die because of his unbelief."

5 The Lord says, "I am going to bring terrible disasters on the whole world— war and famine, death and destruction— ⁶because wickedness has spread everywhere, and evil has reached its limit."

7 "Therefore," the Lord says, ⁸"I will no longer remain silent about the wickedness of these godless people; I will no longer tolerate it. They have murdered innocent people, and the blood they have spilt cries out to me for revenge; the souls of the righteous are constantly pleading for vengeance. ⁹Let there be no doubt," says the Lord, "I will hear the plea of all the innocent people who have been murdered and I will take vengeance for what has been done to them.

10 "My people are being led to the slaughter like a flock of sheep. They will no longer have to live in Egypt; ¹¹I will use all my strength and power to bring them out of that land. I will bring disasters upon the Egyptians, as I did earlier, and I will destroy their country. ¹²The whole land will be in mourning; it will be shaken to its foundations when I, the Lord, strike it and pound on it. ¹³The farmers will mourn because their seed will fail to sprout, and their trees will be destroyed by blight, hail, and terrible storms.

14 "The world and the people in it are doomed. ¹⁵The war that will bring their destruction is very near. Nations will arm themselves and fight against other nations. ¹⁶There will be great political turmoil, with one group trying to overpower another and gain control, while ignoring the legitimate government. ¹⁷There will no longer be free access to the cities, ¹⁸because the struggle for power will bring destruction, terror, and total confusion wherever people live. ¹⁹Driven by famine and terrible suffering, men will assault their neighbours and mercilessly plunder their possessions."

20 God says, "I am calling together all the kings of the earth to come from north, south, east, and west to turn back and restore what they have taken. ²¹I will pay them back with the same harsh treatment they have always given to my chosen people." The Lord says, ²²"I will use my power, and there will be no mercy for sinners; I will put to death all who have murdered innocent people. ²³My anger has become so fierce that fire has blazed out to burn up the foundations of the earth and to burn up sinners like straw. ²⁴Sinners who do not keep my commands are doomed," says the Lord. ²⁵"I will have no mercy on them! Out of my sight, you rebels! Do not defile my holy Temple."

A Terrifying Vision

26 God is aware of all those who sin against him, and he will hand them over to death and destruction. ²⁷Terrible disasters have already come upon the world, and there is no escape. You have sinned against God, and he will not rescue you.

28 Then in the east you will suddenly see a fearsome sight. ²⁹Arab armies with many chariots will advance like dragons. As soon as they start out, the sound of their hissing will spread across the world and bring fear and trembling to everyone who hears it. ³⁰The Carmonians will come out of the forest in a fierce rage like wild boars advancing in full strength to attack the dragons. With their tusks they will tear up a large part of Assyria, ³¹but the dragons will unite their forces, regain their former strength, and win the victory. They will turn and pursue the wild boars, ³²who will be thrown into panic, beaten into silence, and forced to turn and run. ³³The wild boars will be ambushed in Assyria, and one of them will be killed. This will bring fear and panic to their army and indecision to their kings.

34 Then suddenly clouds—terrible, angry storm clouds—will cover the sky from one end to the other. ³⁵They will collide head-on and release their violence upon the earth. The blood of war will be as deep as a horse's belly ³⁶or a man's thigh or a camel's knee. ³⁷Everywhere on earth people will tremble in fear at the horrible sight. ³⁸Then great storm clouds will move in from the north and the south, and others from the west. ³⁹But the winds from the east will prevail and push back those angry storm clouds that were about to bring destruction.ᵈ ⁴⁰⁻⁴¹Huge, powerful, angry storm clouds will arise and ruin the whole world and its people. A terrible storm of fire, hail, and flashing swords will come sweeping down on those who have power and authority.ᵉ Every river will overflow into the fields, and the floods ⁴²will demolish cities, walls, mountains, hills, forests, and crops. ⁴³⁻⁴⁴This destruction will press on until it reaches

---

ᵈ Verse 39 in Latin is unclear.
ᵉ those who have power and authority; or every hill and mountain.

Babylon and engulfs it in a raging storm of ruin. The dust and the smoke will form a great cloud reaching to the sky, and all the neighbouring cities will mourn for Babylon. ⁴⁵Anyone who survives will become a slave to those who destroyed the city.

Asia Is Doomed

46–47 You, Asia, are to be pitied. You are doomed! You have enjoyed the splendour and glory of Babylon. You have imitated her and dressed up your daughters to look like prostitutes to please and gratify your lovers, who have always lusted for you. ⁴⁸Because you have imitated that vile prostitute in everything she has done or planned, God has this to say: ⁴⁹"I will send disasters upon you. I will make you a widow and send poverty, famine, war, and epidemics to destroy your homes and bring ruin and death. ⁵⁰The power of which you boast will wither like a flower when the burning heat is sent upon you. ⁵¹You will be a wretched, weak woman so bruised, beaten, and wounded that you will no longer attract your wealthy lovers. ⁵²I would not punish you so severely," says the Lord, ⁵³"if you had not murdered my chosen people. But you took great delight in striking them, and when you were drunk, you boasted about killing them.

54 "Paint your face! ⁵⁵You will be paid for your work as a prostitute; you will get what you have earned. ⁵⁶I will pay you back," says the Lord, "for what you have done to my chosen people. I will bring disaster on you. ⁵⁷You will be put to death, and your children will starve. Your cities will be torn down, and the people out in the country will be killed. ⁵⁸Those in the mountains will starve; their hunger and thirst will drive them to eat their own flesh and drink their own blood. ⁵⁹You will be more miserable than anyone has ever been, but there will be still more punishment to come. ⁶⁰The army that destroyed Babylon will march back through your country and devastate your peaceful city; they will destroy your beautiful country and leave most of it in ruins. ⁶¹Your country will be destroyed like straw in a fire. ⁶²They will burn up all your forests and orchards. All over your land, your cities and mountains will be covered with ruins. ⁶³Your splendour will vanish; your children will be carried

off as prisoners; your possessions will be plundered."

16 Babylonia, Asia, Egypt, and Syria, you are doomed! ²Put on mourning, your sackcloth and goat's hair. Cry and wail for your children because the time for your destruction is near. ³I am sending war on you, and no one can stop it. ⁴I am sending fire on you, and no one can put it out. ⁵I am sending disasters on you, and no one can stop them from coming. ⁶Can anyone stop a hungry lion in the forest or put out a fire that is burning in straw ⁷or turn back an arrow shot by a strong bowman? ⁸When the Lord God sends disaster, no one can hold it back. ⁹No one can put out the blazing anger of the Lord. ¹⁰When he sends lightning, no one can keep from trembling; and when it thunders, everyone is afraid. ¹¹When the Lord makes his threats, no one can keep from falling to the ground in his presence. ¹²The foundations of the earth tremble. There is violent churning in the deepest part of the sea. Even the creatures in the sea are in turmoil when the Lord makes his glorious power felt. ¹³He is like a mighty bowman whose strong right arm bends the bow. His arrows are sharp and never miss their mark once they are shot out towards any part of the earth. ¹⁴He has already sent out his disasters towards the earth, and they will not miss their target. ¹⁵The fire has been lit, and it cannot be put out until it burns up the foundations of the earth. ¹⁶The disasters are on their way towards the earth, and like an arrow shot by a strong bowman, they cannot be turned back.

17 I am doomed! I am doomed! Who will rescue me in those days? ¹⁸Troubles will come, and many people will groan. Famine will come, and many will die. Wars will come, and the world powers will tremble. Disasters will come, and everyone will be terrified. What will people do when these disasters come? ¹⁹Famine, epidemics, troubles, and suffering are sent to punish and correct people. ²⁰But in spite of all this, they will not turn away from their sins; they soon forget their punishment. ²¹The time is coming when food will be so cheap that people will think a time of peace and plenty has arrived. But then disasters will spring up everywhere—wars, famine, and great confusion. ²²Many people on earth will starve to death, and those who escape

Troubles will come, and many people will groan (16.18)

starvation will be killed in war. ²³ Their corpses will be thrown out like dung, and there will be no one left to comfort the living. The earth will be deserted and its cities demolished. ²⁴ There will be no one left to plough the land or sow it. ²⁵ Trees will bear their fruit, but there will be no one left to pick it. ²⁶ Grapes will ripen, but there will be no one left to make wine. There will be desolation everywhere, ²⁷ and a person will long to see the face of another human being or even to hear another person's voice. ²⁸ Only ten will be left out of a whole city, and in the countryside, only two, who have hidden in the forest or in caves. ²⁹ When an olive-grove is harvested, three or four olives may be left on each tree. ³⁰ When grapes in a vineyard are picked, a few bunches may be left even by those who look carefully. ³¹ That is how it will be in those days. Three or four will be missed by the soldiers who search through the houses to kill everyone. ³² The land will be left empty; the fields will be overgrown with briars; the roads and paths will be covered with weeds and thorns because there will be no sheep to graze along them. ³³ Young women will be in mourning because there is no one to marry them; wives will be in mourning because they have lost their husbands; girls will be in mourning because there is no one to help them. ³⁴ All the young men will be killed in the war,

and all the married men will die in the famine.

God's People Must Prepare for the End

35 Now listen to my message, you people who serve the Lord. ³⁶ It is the Lord's message, so receive it and believe what he says. ³⁷ The disasters are approaching rapidly, and they will not be delayed. ³⁸ A woman in the ninth month of pregnancy may suffer labour pains for several hours, but when the time comes for the baby to be born, there is no longer any delay. ³⁹ In the same way, the disasters that are coming on the earth will not be delayed, and the world will groan when it is caught in its labour pains.

40 Listen to my message, my people, and get ready for the battle. When the disasters come, you must live as people whose home is not in this world. ⁴¹⁻⁴² Merchants must not expect to make a profit from what they sell; they must be ready to run for their lives. Their customers must expect to lose whatever they buy. Whoever builds a house should not plan to live in it. ⁴³ Farmers should not expect to harvest their crops or pick their grapes. ⁴⁴ Those who marry must not expect to have children, and those who don't marry must live as if they had been widowed. ⁴⁵ Everything that is done will be useless. ⁴⁶ Foreigners will harvest the crops, seize the wealth, tear down the houses, and carry off the children as slaves. Anyone who has children will be bringing them up to be slaves or to die of starvation. ⁴⁷ Anyone who makes money will do so only to see it violently taken away. The more possessions people gather, the more they spend on their cities and houses, the more attention they give to their personal appearance, ⁴⁸ the more angry the Lord will become with them because of their sin. This is what the Lord says. ⁴⁹ Just as a respectable woman despises a prostitute, ⁵⁰ so righteousness despises sinfulness, no matter how attractive it may look. Righteousness will expose every sin in the world and condemn it face to face when her Defender comes. ⁵¹ So do not imitate sinfulness or what it does, ⁵² for in a very short time sinfulness will be swept out of the world and righteousness will rule among us.

53 Sinners must not deny their sins. Those who say that they have not sinned against God and his majesty are only bringing fiery shame upon themselves.

54 The Lord certainly knows everything that people do; he knows their plans and innermost thoughts. 55 When the Lord said, "Let the world be created," it was done! When he said, "Let the sky be created," that was done too. 56 He set the stars in place by his command, and he knows how many of them there are. 57 He knows what is in the deepest part of the sea and the treasures that are there. He has measured the sea and everything that is in it. 58 By his word he confined the sea to its place and put the land on top of the water. 59 The Lord stretched out the sky and fixed it firmly over the water like a dome. 60 He put springs of water in the desert and lakes in the high mountains, so that water could flow down in the rivers and water the land. 61 The Lord created human beings and gave each one of them a heart. He gave them life, breath, and understanding, 62 which is the spirit of God the Almighty, who created everything and who knows all secrets and sees into all hidden places. 63 My people, the Lord knows everything you plan and the secret thoughts of your heart. Sinners who try to hide their sins are doomed. 64 The Lord will carefully examine everything you have done and bring you to judgement. 65 On that day you will be thrown into utter confusion; all your sins will be publicly exposed and the wicked things you have done will witness against you. 66 What will you do then? How will you hide your sins from God and his angels? 67 God is your judge, so fear him! Abandon your sins, put away the evil you have done, and never sin again. Then God will save you from all these disasters.

68 A vast mob of people is ready now to descend on you and devour you like flames. They will drag some of you off and force you to eat pagan sacrifices. 69 If you give in to them, they will ridicule you, mock you, and humiliate you. 70 In many places near the cities f there will be violent persecution against those who fear the Lord. 71 The attackers will act like wild men; they will plunder and destroy without pity all those who still fear the Lord. 72 They will turn them out of their homes and take away all their possessions. 73 This will be the time of testing for my chosen people, and they will prove to be as pure as refined gold.

74 But listen to what the Lord says: "My chosen people, the time of terrible suffering is near, but I will rescue you. 75 Don't be afraid or have any doubts; I am your God and I will lead you. 76 If you keep my laws and my commands," says the Lord, "you must not let your sins weigh you down or control you. 77 Those who are chained by their sins, overwhelmed by the evil they have done, are doomed. They will be like a field overgrown with brushwood, with the path across it so choked with thorns that no one can get through. 78 It is abandoned and doomed to be destroyed by fire."

---

f In...cities; *Latin unclear.*
16.73: Zech 13.9; 1 Pet 1.7

THE PRAYER OF
MANASSEH

INTRODUCTION

The *Prayer of Manasseh* is a beautiful short prayer of repentance. It is presented as a prayer by Manasseh, the wicked king of Judah, referred to in *Second Chronicles* 33.12-20.

---

¹ Lord Almighty, God of our fathers,
  God of Abraham, Isaac, and Jacob,
  God of their righteous descendants,
² you created the universe
  and all the splendour that fills it.
³ The sea obeys your command
  and never overflows its bounds.
  The power of your wonderful, glorious name
  keeps the ocean depths in their place.
⁴ When you show your power,
  all creation trembles.
⁵ Your glorious splendour is overwhelming,
  and your anger is more than sinners can endure.
⁶ But the mercy you promise is also greater
  than we can understand or measure.
⁷ For you are the Lord Most High;
  you are patient and show mercy and compassion.
  You make our punishment easier to bear
  when we suffer for our sins.
  O Lord, in your great goodness and mercy
  you promise forgiveness and salvation
  to those who repent of their sin
  against you.ᵃ
⁸ You, Lord, are the God of righteous people.
  Repentance was not necessary
  for Abraham, Isaac, and Jacob,
  for they did not sin against you.
  But for sinners like me
  you have made repentance possible.
⁹ I have committed more sins
  than there are grains of sand along
  the seashore.

They are so many, Lord, they are so many.
  I have done so much that is wrong
  that I am not worthy to turn my face
  towards heaven.
¹⁰ I am crushed beneath the weight of
  my sin;ᵇ
  I am bowed down by its heavy iron chain.
  I can find no relief,
  for I have made you angry.
  I have set up idols everywhere;
  I have done what you hate.
¹¹ But now I bow in deep humility,
  praying for your mercy.
¹² I have sinned, Lord, I have sinned;
  I confess the wicked things I have done.
¹³ I beg you, Lord, I earnestly pray:
  forgive me, forgive me.
  Do not destroy me because of my sins;
  do not be angry with me for ever
  or store up punishment for me.
  Do not condemn me to the world of
  the dead,
  for you, O Lord, forgive those who repent.
¹⁴ Show me all your mercy and kindness
  and save me,
  even though I do not deserve it.
¹⁵ Then I will go on praising you as long
  as I live.
  All the heavenly powers sing your praises,
  and your glory endures for ever.
  Amen.

ᵃO Lord...against you; *some manuscripts do not have these words.*
ᵇcrushed...my sin; *Greek unclear.*
1: 2 Chr 33.11-13,18-19 **9:** 2 Kgs 21.1-18

THE
NEW TESTAMENT

JERUSALEM IN NEW TESTAMENT TIMES

Present City Wall

To Caesarea

Damascus Gate

Pool of Bethzatha

PRAETORIUM

FORT

Ancient City Wall

Gate

TEMPLE

To Bethany

Gethsemane

Golgotha

Gate

Beautiful Gate

Gate

Court of Gentiles

Solomon's Porch

To Joppa

Gennath Gate

Bridge

Gates

To Bethlehem

HEROD'S PALACE

Pool

Present City Wall

KIDRON VALLEY

Pool of Siloam

To Jericho

Gate

0   200   400

Metres

Roads

VALLEY OF HINNOM

To Dead Sea

THE GOSPEL ACCORDING TO
MATTHEW

INTRODUCTION

The Gospel according to Matthew tells the good news that Jesus is the promised Saviour, the one through whom God fulfilled the promises he made to his people in the Old Testament. This good news is not only for the Jewish people, among whom Jesus was born and lived, but for the whole world.

Matthew is carefully arranged. It begins with the birth of Jesus, describes his baptism and temptation, and then takes up his ministry of preaching, teaching, and healing in Galilee. After this the Gospel records Jesus' journey from Galilee to Jerusalem and the events of Jesus' last week, culminating in his crucifixion and resurrection.

This Gospel presents Jesus as the great Teacher, who has the authority to interpret the Law of God, and who teaches about God's kingdom. Much of his teaching is gathered by subject matter into five collections: (1) the Sermon on the Mount, which concerns the character, duties, privileges, and destiny of the citizens of the Kingdom of heaven (chapters 5-7); (2) instructions to the twelve disciples for their mission (chapter 10); (3) parables about the Kingdom of heaven (chapter 13); (4) teaching on the meaning of discipleship (chapter 18); and (5) teaching about the end of the present age and the coming of the Kingdom of heaven (chapters 24-25).

Outline of Contents

Genealogy and birth of Jesus Christ   1.1—2.23
The ministry of John the Baptist   3.1-12
The baptism and temptation of Jesus   3.13—4.11
Jesus' public ministry in Galilee   4.12—18.35
From Galilee to Jerusalem   19.1—20.34
The last week in and near Jerusalem   21.1—27.66
The resurrection and appearances of the Lord   28.1-20

The Ancestors of Jesus Christ
(Luke 3.23-38)

1 This is the list of the ancestors of Jesus Christ, a descendant of David, who was a descendant of Abraham.

2-6a From Abraham to King David, the following ancestors are listed: Abraham, Isaac, Jacob, Judah and his brothers; then Perez and Zerah (their mother was Tamar), Hezron, Ram, Amminadab, Nahshon, Salmon, Boaz (his mother was Rahab), Obed (his mother was Ruth), Jesse, and King David.

6b-11 From David to the time when the people of Israel were taken into exile in Babylon, the following ancestors are listed: David, Solomon (his mother was the woman who had been Uriah's wife), Rehoboam, Abijah, Asa, Jehoshaphat,

1.11: 2 Kgs 24.14-15; 2 Chr 36.10; Jer 27.20

Jehoram, Uzziah, Jotham, Ahaz, Hezekiah, Manasseh, Amon, Josiah, and Jehoiachin and his brothers.

12-16 From the time after the exile in Babylon to the birth of Jesus, the following ancestors are listed: Jehoiachin, Shealtiel, Zerubbabel, Abiud, Eliakim, Azor, Zadok, Achim, Eliud, Eleazar, Matthan, Jacob, and Joseph, who married Mary, the mother of Jesus, who was called the Messiah.

17 So then, there were fourteen generations from Abraham to David, and fourteen from David to the exile in Babylon, and fourteen from then to the birth of the Messiah.

The Birth of Jesus Christ
(Luke 2.1-7)

18 This was how the birth of Jesus Christ took place. His mother Mary was engaged to Joseph, but before they were married, she found out that she was going to have a baby by the Holy Spirit. ¹⁹ Joseph was a man who always did what was right, but he did not want to disgrace Mary publicly; so he made plans to break the engagement privately. ²⁰ While he was thinking about this, an angel of the Lord appeared to him in a dream and said, "Joseph, descendant of David, do not be afraid to take Mary to be your wife. For it is by the Holy Spirit that she has conceived. ²¹ She will have a son, and you will name him Jesus—because he will save his people from their sins."

22 Now all this happened in order to make what the Lord had said through the prophet come true, ²³ "A virgin will become pregnant and have a son, and he will be called Immanuel" (which means, "God is with us").

24 So when Joseph woke up, he married Mary, as the angel of the Lord had told him to do. ²⁵ But he had no sexual relations with her before she gave birth to her son. And Joseph named him Jesus.

Visitors from the East

2 Jesus was born in the town of Bethlehem in Judaea, during the time when Herod was king. Soon afterwards, some men who studied the stars came from the east to Jerusalem ² and asked, "Where is the baby born to be the king of the Jews? We saw his star when it came up in the east, and we have come to worship him."

3 When King Herod heard about this,

he was very upset, and so was everyone else in Jerusalem. ⁴ He called together all the chief priests and the teachers of the Law and asked them, "Where will the Messiah be born?"

5 "In the town of Bethlehem in Judaea," they answered. "For this is what the prophet wrote:
⁶ 'Bethlehem in the land of Judah,
    you are by no means the least of the
      leading cities of Judah;
for from you will come a leader
    who will guide my people Israel.' "

7 So Herod called the visitors from the east to a secret meeting and found out from them the exact time the star had appeared. ⁸ Then he sent them to Bethlehem with these instructions: "Go and make a careful search for the child, and when you find him, let me know, so that I too may go and worship him."

9-10 And so they left, and on their way they saw the same star they had seen in the east. When they saw it, how happy they were, what joy was theirs! It went ahead of them until it stopped over the place where the child was. ¹¹ They went into the house, and when they saw the child with his mother Mary, they knelt down and worshipped him. They brought out their gifts of gold, frankincense, and myrrh, and presented them to him.

12 Then they returned to their country by another road, since God had warned them in a dream not to go back to Herod.

The Escape to Egypt

13 After they had left, an angel of the Lord appeared in a dream to Joseph and said, "Herod will be looking for the child in order to kill him. So get up, take the child and his mother and escape to Egypt, and stay there until I tell you to leave."

14 Joseph got up, took the child and his mother, and left during the night for Egypt, ¹⁵ where he stayed until Herod died. This was done to make what the Lord had said through the prophet come true, "I called my Son out of Egypt."

The Killing of the Children

16 When Herod realized that the visitors from the east had tricked him, he was furious. He gave orders to kill all the boys in Bethlehem and its neighbourhood who were two years old and younger—this was done in accordance with what he had learned from the

1.18: Lk 1.27   **1.21:** Lk 1.31   **1.23:** Is 7.14   **1.25:** Lk 2.21   **2.6:** Mic 5.2   **2.15:** Hos 11.1

The same star . . . went ahead of them (2.9–10)

visitors about the time when the star had appeared.

17 In this way what the prophet Jeremiah had said came true:

18 "A sound is heard in Ramah,
　the sound of bitter weeping.
Rachel is crying for her children;
　she refuses to be comforted,
　for they are dead."

The Return from Egypt

19 After Herod died, an angel of the Lord appeared in a dream to Joseph in Egypt 20 and said, "Get up, take the child and his mother, and go back to the land of Israel, because those who tried to kill the child are dead." 21 So Joseph got up, took the child and his mother, and went back to Israel.

22 But when Joseph heard that Archelaus had succeeded his father Herod as king of Judaea, he was afraid to go there. He was given more instructions in a dream, so he went to the province of Galilee 23 and made his home in a town named Nazareth. And so what the prophets had said came true: "He will be called a Nazarene."

The Preaching of John the Baptist
(Mark 1.1–8; Luke 3.1–18; John 1.19–28)

3 At that time John the Baptist came to the desert of Judaea and started preaching. 2 "Turn away from your sins," he said, "because the Kingdom of heaven is near!" 3 John was the man the prophet Isaiah was talking about when he said,

"Someone is shouting in the desert,
'Prepare a road for the Lord;
make a straight path for him to
　travel!'"

4 John's clothes were made of camel's hair; he wore a leather belt round his waist, and his food was locusts and wild honey. 5 People came to him from Jerusalem, from the whole province of Judaea, and from all the country near the River Jordan. 6 They confessed their sins, and he baptized them in the Jordan.

7 When John saw many Pharisees and Sadducees coming to him to be baptized, he said to them, "You snakes—who told you that you could escape from the punishment God is about to send? 8 Do those things that will show that you have turned from your sins. 9 And don't think you can escape punishment by saying that

2.18: Jer 31.15　　**2.23:** Mk 1.24; Lk 2.39; Jn 1.45　　**3.2:** Mt 4.17; Mk 1.15　　**3.3:** Is 40.3
3.4: 2 Kgs 1.8　　**3.7:** Mt 12.34, 23.33　　**3.9:** Jn 8.33

Order these stones to turn into bread (4.3)

Abraham is your ancestor. I tell you that God can take these stones and make descendants for Abraham! ¹⁰ The axe is ready to cut down the trees at the roots; every tree that does not bear good fruit will be cut down and thrown in the fire. ¹¹ I baptize you with water to show that you have repented, but the one who will come after me will baptize you with the Holy Spirit and fire. He is much greater than I am; and I am not good enough even to carry his sandals. ¹² He has his winnowing shovel with him to thresh out all the grain. He will gather his wheat into his barn, but he will burn the chaff in a fire that never goes out."

The Baptism of Jesus
(Mark 1.9–11; Luke 3.21–22)

13 At that time Jesus arrived from Galilee and came to John at the Jordan to be baptized by him. ¹⁴ But John tried to make him change his mind. "I ought to be baptized by you," John said, "and yet you have come to me!"

15 But Jesus answered him, "Let it be so for now. For in this way we shall do all that God requires." So John agreed.

16 As soon as Jesus was baptized, he came up out of the water. Then heaven was opened to him, and he saw the Spirit of God coming down like a dove and alighting on him. ¹⁷ Then a voice said from heaven, "This is my own dear Son, with whom I am pleased."

The Temptation of Jesus
(Mark 1.12–13; Luke 4.1–13)

4 Then the Spirit led Jesus into the desert to be tempted by the Devil. ² After spending forty days and nights without food, Jesus was hungry. ³ Then the Devil came to him and said, "If you are God's Son, order these stones to turn into bread."

4 But Jesus answered, "The scripture says, 'Man cannot live on bread alone, but needs every word that God speaks.'"

5 Then the Devil took Jesus to Jerusalem, the Holy City, set him on the highest point of the Temple, ⁶ and said to him, "If you are God's Son, throw yourself down, for the scripture says,

'God will give orders to his angels about you;

they will hold you up with their hands, so that not even your feet will be hurt on the stones.'"

7 Jesus answered, "But the scripture also says, 'Do not put the Lord your God to the test.'"

8 Then the Devil took Jesus to a very

3.10: Mt 7.19   **3.17:** Gen 22.2; Ps 2.7; Is 42.1; Mt 12.18, 17.5; Mk 1.11; Lk 9.35
4.1: Heb 2.18, 4.15   **4.4:** Deut 8.3   **4.6:** Ps 91.11–12   **4.7:** Deut 6.16

high mountain and showed him all the kingdoms of the world in all their greatness. 9 "All this I will give you," the Devil said, "if you kneel down and worship me."

10 Then Jesus answered, "Go away, Satan! The scripture says, 'Worship the Lord your God and serve only him!'"

11 Then the Devil left Jesus; and angels came and helped him.

Jesus Begins His Work in Galilee
(Mark 1.14–15; Luke 4.14–15)

12 When Jesus heard that John had been put in prison, he went away to Galilee. 13 He did not stay in Nazareth, but went to live in Capernaum, a town by Lake Galilee, in the territory of Zebulun and Naphtali. 14 This was done to make what the prophet Isaiah had said come true,

15 "Land of Zebulun and land of Naphtali,
on the road to the sea, on the other side of the Jordan,
Galilee, land of the Gentiles!
16 The people who live in darkness
will see a great light.
On those who live in the dark land of death
the light will shine."

17 From that time Jesus began to preach his message: "Turn away from your sins, because the Kingdom of heaven is near!"

Jesus Calls Four Fishermen
(Mark 1.16–20; Luke 5.1–11)

18 As Jesus walked along the shore of Lake Galilee, he saw two brothers who were fishermen, Simon (called Peter) and his brother Andrew, catching fish in the lake with a net. 19 Jesus said to them, "Come with me, and I will teach you to catch men." 20 At once they left their nets and went with him.

21 He went on and saw two other brothers, James and John, the sons of Zebedee. They were in their boat with their father Zebedee, getting their nets ready. Jesus called them, 22 and at once they left the boat and their father, and went with him.

Jesus Teaches, Preaches, and Heals
(Luke 6.17–19)

23 Jesus went all over Galilee, teaching in the synagogues, preaching the Good News about the Kingdom, and healing people who had all kinds of disease and sickness. 24 The news about him spread through the whole country of Syria, so that people brought to him all those who were sick, suffering from all kinds of diseases and disorders: people with demons, and epileptics, and paralytics— and Jesus healed them all. 25 Large crowds followed him from Galilee and the Ten Towns, from Jerusalem, Judaea, and the land on the other side of the Jordan.

The Sermon on the Mount

5 Jesus saw the crowds and went up a hill, where he sat down. His disciples gathered round him, 2 and he began to teach them:

True Happiness
(Luke 6.20–23)

3 "Happy are those who know they are spiritually poor;
the Kingdom of heaven belongs to them!
4 "Happy are those who mourn;
God will comfort them!
5 "Happy are those who are humble;
they will receive what God has promised!
6 "Happy are those whose greatest desire is to do what God requires;
God will satisfy them fully!
7 "Happy are those who are merciful to others;
God will be merciful to them!
8 "Happy are the pure in heart;
they will see God!
9 "Happy are those who work for peace;
God will call them his children!
10 "Happy are those who are persecuted because they do what God requires;
the Kingdom of heaven belongs to them!

11 "Happy are you when people insult you and persecute you and tell all kinds of evil lies against you because you are my followers. 12 Be happy and glad, for a great reward is kept for you in heaven. This is how the prophets who lived before you were persecuted.

4.10: Deut 6.13   **4.12:** Mt 14.3; Mk 6.17; Lk 3.19–20   **4.13:** Jn 2.12   **4.15–16:** Is 9.1–2
4.17: Mt 3.2   **4.23:** Mt 9.35; Mk 1.39   **5.4:** Is 61.2   **5.5:** Ps 37.11   **5.6:** Is 55.1–2
5.8: Ps 24.3–4   **5.10:** 1 Pet 3.14   **5.11:** 1 Pet 4.14   **5.12:** 2 Chr 36.16; Acts 7.52

Salt and Light
(Mark 9.50; Luke 14.34–35)

13 "You are like salt for all mankind. But if salt loses its saltiness, there is no way to make it salty again. It has become worthless, so it is thrown out and people trample on it.

14 "You are like light for the whole world. A city built on a hill cannot be hidden. 15 No one lights a lamp and puts it under a bowl; instead he puts it on the lampstand, where it gives light for everyone in the house. 16 In the same way your light must shine before people, so that they will see the good things you do and praise your Father in heaven.

Teaching about the Law

17 "Do not think that I have come to do away with the Law of Moses and the teachings of the prophets. I have not come to do away with them, but to make their teachings come true. 18 Remember that as long as heaven and earth last, not the least point nor the smallest detail of the Law will be done away with—not until the end of all things. *a* 19 So then, whoever disobeys even the least important of the commandments and teaches others to do the same, will be least in the Kingdom of heaven. On the other hand, whoever obeys the Law and teaches others to do the same, will be great in the Kingdom of heaven. 20 I tell you, then, that you will be able to enter the Kingdom of heaven only if you are more faithful than the teachers of the Law and the Pharisees in doing what God requires.

Teaching about Anger

21 "You have heard that people were told in the past, 'Do not commit murder; anyone who does will be brought to trial.' 22 But now I tell you: whoever is angry *b* with his brother will be brought to trial, whoever calls his brother 'You good-for-nothing!' will be brought before the Council, and whoever calls his brother a worthless fool will be in danger of going to the fire of hell. 23 So if you are about to offer your gift to God at the altar and there you remember that your brother has

something against you, 24 leave your gift there in front of the altar, go at once and make peace with your brother, and then come back and offer your gift to God.

25 "If someone brings a lawsuit against you and takes you to court, settle the dispute with him while there is time, before you get to court. Once you are there, he will hand you over to the judge, who will hand you over to the police, and you will be put in jail. 26 There you will stay, I tell you, until you pay the last penny of your fine.

Teaching about Adultery

27 "You have heard that it was said, 'Do not commit adultery.' 28 But now I tell you: anyone who looks at a woman and wants to possess her is guilty of committing adultery with her in his heart. 29 So if your right eye causes you to sin, take it out and throw it away! It is much better for you to lose a part of your body than to have your whole body thrown into hell. 30 If your right hand causes you to sin, cut it off and throw it away! It is much better for you to lose one of your limbs than for your whole body to go to hell.

Teaching about Divorce
(Matt. 19.9; Mark 10.11–12; Luke 16.18)

31 "It was also said, 'Anyone who divorces his wife must give her a written notice of divorce.' 32 But now I tell you: if a man divorces his wife, for any cause other than her unfaithfulness, then he is guilty of making her commit adultery if she marries again; and the man who marries her commits adultery also.

Teaching about Vows

33 "You have also heard that people were told in the past, 'Do not break your promise, but do what you have vowed to the Lord to do.' 34 But now I tell you: do not use any vow when you make a promise. Do not swear by heaven, for it is God's throne; 35 nor by earth, for it is the resting place for his feet; nor by Jerusalem, for it is the city of the great King. 36 Do not even swear by your head,

---

a the end of all things; *or* all its teachings come true.
b whoever is angry; *some manuscripts have* whoever without cause is angry.
5.14: Jn 8.12, 9.5   **5.15:** Mk 4.21; Lk 8.16, 11.33   **5.16:** 1 Pet 2.12   **5.18:** Lk 16.17
5.21: Ex 20.13; Deut 5.17   **5.27:** Ex 20.14; Deut 5.18   **5.29:** Mt 18.9; Mk 9.47
5.30: Mt 18.8; Mk 9.43   **5.31:** Deut 24.1–4; Mt 19.7; Mk 10.4
5.32: Mt 19.9; Mk 10.11–12; Lk 16.18; 1 Cor 7.10–11   **5.33:** Lev 19.12; Num 30.2; Deut 23.21
5.34: Jas 5.12; Is 66.1; Mt 23.22   **5.35:** Is 66.1; Ps 48.2

because you cannot make a single hair white or black. 37 Just say 'Yes' or 'No'— anything else you say comes from the Evil One.

Teaching about Revenge
(Luke 6.29-30)

38 "You have heard that it was said, 'An eye for an eye, and a tooth for a tooth.' 39 But now I tell you: do not take revenge on someone who wrongs you. If anyone slaps you on the right cheek, let him slap your left cheek too. 40 And if someone takes you to court to sue you for your shirt, let him have your coat as well. 41 And if one of the occupation troops forces you to carry his pack one kilometre, carry it two kilometres. 42 When someone asks you for something, give it to him; when someone wants to borrow something, lend it to him.

Love for Enemies
(Luke 6.27-28, 32-36)

43 "You have heard that it was said, 'Love your friends, hate your enemies.' 44 But now I tell you: love your enemies and pray for those who persecute you, 45 so that you may become the sons of your Father in heaven. For he makes his sun to shine on bad and good people alike, and gives rain to those who do good and to those who do evil. 46 Why should God reward you if you love only the people who love you? Even the tax collectors do that! 47 And if you speak only to your friends, have you done anything out of the ordinary? Even the pagans do that! 48 You must be perfect—just as your Father in heaven is perfect!

Teaching about Charity

6 "Make certain you do not perform your religious duties in public so that people will see what you do. If you do these things publicly, you will not have any reward from your Father in heaven.

2 "So when you give something to a needy person, do not make a big show of it, as the hypocrites do in the houses of worship and on the streets. They do it so that people will praise them. I assure you, they have already been paid in full. 3 But when you help a needy person, do it in such a way that even your closest friend will not know about it. 4 Then it will be a private matter. And your Father,

Do not make a big show of it (6.2)

who sees what you do in private, will reward you.

Teaching about Prayer
(Luke 11.2-4)

5 "When you pray, do not be like the hypocrites! They love to stand up and pray in the houses of worship and on the street corners, so that everyone will see them. I assure you, they have already been paid in full. 6 But when you pray, go to your room, close the door, and pray to your Father, who is unseen. And your Father, who sees what you do in private, will reward you.

7 "When you pray, do not use a lot of meaningless words, as the pagans do, who think that their gods will hear them because their prayers are long. 8 Do not be like them. Your Father already knows what you need before you ask him. 9 This, then, is how you should pray:

'Our Father in heaven:
    May your holy name be honoured;
10   may your Kingdom come;
    may your will be done on earth as
        it is in heaven.
11   Give us today the food we need. c
12   Forgive us the wrongs we have done,
        as we forgive the wrongs that
        others have done to us.
13   Do not bring us to hard testing,

---

c we need; or for today; or for tomorrow.
5.38: Ex 21.24; Lev 24.20; Deut 19.21   **5.43:** Lev 19.18   **5.48:** Lev 19.2; Deut 18.13
6.1: Mt 23.5   **6.5:** Lk 18.10-14

but keep us safe from the Evil One.'ˣ

14 "If you forgive others the wrongs they have done to you, your Father in heaven will also forgive you. ¹⁵But if you do not forgive others, then your Father will not forgive the wrongs you have done.

Teaching about Fasting

16 "And when you fast, do not put on a sad face as the hypocrites do. They neglect their appearance so that everyone will see that they are fasting. I assure you, they have already been paid in full. ¹⁷When you go without food, wash your face and comb your hair, ¹⁸so that others cannot know that you are fasting—only your Father, who is unseen, will know. And your Father, who sees what you do in private, will reward you.

Riches in Heaven
(Luke 12.33–34)

19 "Do not store up riches for yourselves here on earth, where moths and rust destroy, and robbers break in and steal. ²⁰Instead, store up riches for yourselves in heaven, where moths and rust cannot destroy, and robbers cannot break in and steal. ²¹For your heart will always be where your riches are.

The Light of the Body
(Luke 11.34–36)

22 "The eyes are like a lamp for the body. If your eyes are sound, your whole body will be full of light; ²³but if your eyes are no good, your body will be in darkness. So if the light in you is darkness, how terribly dark it will be!

God and Possessions
(Luke 16.13; 12.22–31)

24 "No one can be a slave of two masters; he will hate one and love the other; he will be loyal to one and despise the other. You cannot serve both God and money.

25 "This is why I tell you not to be worried about the food and drink you need in order to stay alive, or about clothes for your body. After all, isn't life worth more than food? And isn't the body worth more than clothes? ²⁶Look at the birds: they do not sow seeds, gather a harvest and put it in barns; yet your Father in heaven takes care of them! Aren't you worth much more than birds? ²⁷Can any

of you live a bit longerᵈ by worrying about it?

28 "And why worry about clothes? Look how the wild flowers grow: they do not work or make clothes for themselves. ²⁹But I tell you that not even King Solomon with all his wealth had clothes as beautiful as one of these flowers. ³⁰It is God who clothes the wild grass—grass that is here today and gone tomorrow, burnt up in the oven. Won't he be all the more sure to clothe you? How little faith you have!

31 "So do not start worrying: 'Where will my food come from? or my drink? or my clothes?' ³²(These are the things the pagans are always concerned about.) Your Father in heaven knows that you need all these things. ³³Instead, be concerned above everything else with the Kingdom of God and with what he requires of you, and he will provide you with all these other things. ³⁴So do not worry about tomorrow; it will have enough worries of its own. There is no need to add to the troubles each day brings.

Judging Others
(Luke 6.37–38, 41–42)

7 "Do not judge others, so that God will not judge you, ²for God will judge you in the same way as you judge others, and he will apply to you the same rules you apply to others. ³Why, then, do you look at the speck in your brother's eye, and pay no attention to the log in your own eye? ⁴How dare you say to your brother, 'Please, let me take that speck out of your eye,' when you have a log in your own eye? ⁵You hypocrite! First take the log out of your own eye, and then you will be able to see clearly to take the speck out of your brother's eye.

6 "Do not give what is holy to dogs—they will only turn and attack you. Do not throw your pearls in front of pigs—they will only trample them underfoot.

Ask, Seek, Knock
(Luke 11.9–13)

7 "Ask, and you will receive; seek, and you will find; knock, and the door will be opened to you. ⁸For everyone who asks will receive, and anyone who seeks will find, and the door will be opened to him who knocks. ⁹Would any of you who are fathers give your son a stone when he

---

ˣ *Some manuscripts add* For yours is the kingdom, and the power, and the glory for ever, Amen.
ᵈlive a bit longer; *or* grow a bit taller.
6.14-15: Mk 11.25-26   **6.19:** Jas 5.2-3   **6.29:** 1 Kgs 10.4-7; 2 Chr 9.3-6   **7.2:** Mk 4.24

Aren't you worth much more than birds? (6.26)

asks for bread? 10 Or would you give him a snake when he asks for a fish? 11 Bad as you are, you know how to give good things to your children. How much more, then, will your Father in heaven give good things to those who ask him!

12 "Do for others what you want them to do for you: this is the meaning of the Law of Moses and of the teachings of the prophets.

The Narrow Gate
(Luke 13.24)

13 "Go in through the narrow gate, because the gate to hell is wide and the road that leads to it is easy, and there are many who travel it. 14 But the gate to life is narrow and the way that leads to it is hard, and there are few people who find it.

A Tree and Its Fruit
(Luke 6.43-44)

15 "Be on your guard against false prophets; they come to you looking like sheep on the outside, but on the inside they are really like wild wolves. 16 You will know them by what they do. Thorn bushes do not bear grapes, and briars do not bear figs. 17 A healthy tree bears good fruit, but a poor tree bears bad fruit. 18 A healthy tree cannot bear bad fruit, and a poor tree cannot bear good fruit. 19 And any tree that does not bear good fruit is cut down and thrown in the fire. 20 So then, you will know the false prophets by what they do.

I Never Knew You
(Luke 13.25-27)

21 "Not everyone who calls me 'Lord, Lord' will enter the Kingdom of heaven, but only those who do what my Father in heaven wants them to do. 22 When Judgement Day comes, many will say to me, 'Lord, Lord! In your name we spoke God's message, by your name we drove out many demons and performed many miracles!' 23 Then I will say to them, 'I never knew you. Get away from me, you wicked people!'

7.12: Lk 6.31   **7.19:** Mt 3.10; Lk 3.9   **7.20:** Mt 12.33   **7.23:** Ps 6.8

The Two House Builders
(Luke 6.47–49)

24 "So then, anyone who hears these words of mine and obeys them is like a wise man who built his house on rock. 25 The rain poured down, the rivers overflowed, and the wind blew hard against that house. But it did not fall, because it was built on rock.

26 "But anyone who hears these words of mine and does not obey them is like a foolish man who built his house on sand. 27 The rain poured down, the rivers overflowed, the wind blew hard against that house, and it fell. And what a terrible fall that was!"

The Authority of Jesus

28 When Jesus finished saying these things, the crowd was amazed at the way he taught. 29 He wasn't like the teachers of the Law; instead, he taught with authority.

Jesus Heals a Man
(Mark 1.40–45; Luke 5.12–16)

8 When Jesus came down from the hill, large crowds followed him. 2 Then a man suffering from a dreaded skin-disease came to him, knelt down before him, and said, "Sir, if you want to, you can make me clean." *e*
3 Jesus stretched out his hand and touched him. "I do want to," he answered. "Be clean!" At once the man was healed of his disease. 4 Then Jesus said to him, "Listen! Don't tell anyone, but go straight to the priest and let him examine you; then in order to prove to everyone that you are cured, offer the sacrifice that Moses ordered."

Jesus Heals a Roman Officer's Servant
(Luke 7.1–10)

5 When Jesus entered Capernaum, a Roman officer met him and begged for help: 6 "Sir, my servant is sick in bed at home, unable to move and suffering terribly."
7 "I will go and make him well," Jesus said.
8 "Oh no, sir," answered the officer. "I do not deserve to have you come into my house. Just give the order, and my servant will get well. 9 I, too, am a man under the authority of superior officers, and I have soldiers under me. I order this one, 'Go!' and he goes; and I order that one, 'Come!' and he comes; and I order my slave, 'Do this!' and he does it."

10 When Jesus heard this, he was surprised and said to the people following him, "I tell you, I have never found anyone in Israel with faith like this. 11 I assure you that many will come from the east and the west and sit down with Abraham, Isaac, and Jacob at the feast in the Kingdom of heaven. 12 But those who should be in the Kingdom will be thrown out into the darkness, where they will cry and grind their teeth." 13 Then Jesus said to the officer, "Go home, and what you believe will be done for you."

And the officer's servant was healed that very moment.

Jesus Heals Many People
(Mark 1.29–34; Luke 4.38–41)

14 Jesus went to Peter's home, and there he saw Peter's mother-in-law sick in bed with a fever. 15 He touched her hand; the fever left her, and she got up and began to wait on him.

16 When evening came, people brought to Jesus many who had demons in them. Jesus drove out the evil spirits with a word and healed all who were sick. 17 He did this to make what the prophet Isaiah had said come true, "He himself took our sickness and carried away our diseases."

The Would-be Followers of Jesus
(Luke 9.57–62)

18 When Jesus noticed the crowd round him, he ordered his disciples to go to the other side of the lake. 19 A teacher of the Law came to him. "Teacher," he said, "I am ready to go with you wherever you go."

20 Jesus answered him, "Foxes have holes, and birds have nests, but the Son of Man has nowhere to lie down and rest."

21 Another man, who was a disciple, said, "Sir, first let me go back and bury my father."

22 "Follow me," Jesus answered, "and let the dead bury their own dead."

Jesus Calms a Storm
(Mark 4.35–41; Luke 8.22–25)

23 Jesus got into a boat, and his disciples went with him. 24 Suddenly a fierce storm hit the lake, and the boat

e MAKE ME CLEAN: *This disease was considered to make a person ritually unclean.*
7.28–29: Mk 1.22; Lk 4.32   **8.4:** Lev 14.1–32   **8.11:** Lk 13.29
8.12: Mt 22.13, 25.30; Lk 13.28   **8.17:** Is 53.4

was in danger of sinking. But Jesus was asleep. 25 The disciples went to him and woke him up. "Save us, Lord!" they said. "We are about to die!"

26 "Why are you so frightened?" Jesus answered. "How little faith you have!" Then he got up and ordered the winds and the waves to stop, and there was a great calm.

27 Everyone was amazed. "What kind of man is this?" they said. "Even the winds and the waves obey him!"

Jesus Heals Two Men with Demons
(Mark 5.1–20; Luke 8.26–39)

28 When Jesus came to the territory of Gadara on the other side of the lake, he was met by two men who came out of the burial caves there. These men had demons in them and were so fierce that no one dared travel on that road. 29 At once they screamed, "What do you want with us, you Son of God? Have you come to punish us before the right time?"

30 Not far away there was a large herd of pigs feeding. 31 So the demons begged Jesus, "If you are going to drive us out, send us into that herd of pigs."

32 "Go," Jesus told them; so they left and went off into the pigs. The whole herd rushed down the side of the cliff into the lake and was drowned.

33 The men who had been taking care of the pigs ran away and went into the town, where they told the whole story and what had happened to the men with the demons. 34 So everyone from the town went out to meet Jesus; and when they saw him, they begged him to leave their territory.

Jesus Heals a Paralysed Man
(Mark 2.1–12; Luke 5.17–26)

9 Jesus got into the boat and went back across the lake to his own town,f 2 where some people brought to him a paralysed man, lying on a bed. When Jesus saw how much faith they had, he said to the paralysed man, "Courage, my son! Your sins are forgiven."

3 Then some teachers of the Law said to themselves, "This man is speaking blasphemy!"

4 Jesus perceived what they were thinking, so he said, "Why are you thinking such evil things? 5 Is it easier to say, 'Your sins are forgiven,' or to say, 'Get up and walk'? 6 I will prove to you,

then, that the Son of Man has authority on earth to forgive sins." So he said to the paralysed man, "Get up, pick up your bed, and go home!"

7 The man got up and went home. 8 When the people saw it, they were afraid, and praised God for giving such authority to men.

Jesus Calls Matthew
(Mark 2.13–17; Luke 5.27–32)

9 Jesus left that place, and as he walked along, he saw a tax collector, named Matthew, sitting in his office. He said to him, "Follow me."

Matthew got up and followed him.

10 While Jesus was having a meal in Matthew's house,g many tax collectors and other outcasts came and joined Jesus and his disciples at the table. 11 Some Pharisees saw this and asked his disciples, "Why does your teacher eat with such people?"

12 Jesus heard them and answered, "People who are well do not need a doctor, but only those who are sick. 13 Go and find out what is meant by the scripture that says: 'It is kindness that I want, not animal sacrifices.' I have not come to call respectable people, but outcasts."

The Question about Fasting
(Mark 2.18–22; Luke 5.33–39)

14 Then the followers of John the Baptist came to Jesus, asking, "Why is it that we and the Pharisees fast often, but your disciples don't fast at all?"

15 Jesus answered, "Do you expect the guests at a wedding party to be sad as long as the bridegroom is with them? Of course not! But the day will come when the bridegroom will be taken away from them, and then they will fast.

16 "No one patches up an old coat with a piece of new cloth, for the new patch will shrink and make an even bigger hole in the coat. 17 Nor does anyone pour new wine into used wineskins, for the skins will burst, the wine will pour out, and the skins will be ruined. Instead, new wine is poured into fresh wineskins, and both will keep in good condition."

The Official's Daughter and the Woman Who Touched Jesus' Cloak
(Mark 5.21–43; Luke 8.40–56)

18 While Jesus was saying this, a Jewish official came to him, knelt down

---

f HIS OWN TOWN: *Capernaum (see 4.13).*   g in Matthew's house; *or* in his *(that is,* Jesus') house.
9.10–11: Lk 15.1–2   **9.13:** Mt 12.7; Hos 6.6

before him, and said, "My daughter has just died; but come and place your hands on her, and she will live."

19 So Jesus got up and followed him, and his disciples went along with him.

20 A woman who had suffered from severe bleeding for twelve years came up behind Jesus and touched the edge of his cloak. ²¹ She said to herself, "If I only

If I only touch his cloak (9.21)

touch his cloak, I will get well."

22 Jesus turned round and saw her, and said, "Courage, my daughter! Your faith has made you well." At that very moment the woman became well.

23 Then Jesus went into the official's house. When he saw the musicians for the funeral and the people all stirred up, ²⁴ he said, "Get out, everybody! The little girl is not dead—she is only sleeping!" Then they all laughed at him. ²⁵ But as soon as the people had been put out, Jesus went into the girl's room and took hold of her hand, and she got up. ²⁶ The news about this spread all over that part of the country.

Jesus Heals Two Blind Men

27 Jesus left that place, and as he walked along, two blind men started following him. "Take pity on us, Son of David!" they shouted.

28 When Jesus had gone indoors, the two blind men came to him, and he asked them, "Do you believe that I can heal you?"

"Yes, sir!" they answered.

29 Then Jesus touched their eyes and said, "Let it happen, then, just as you

believe!"—³⁰ and their sight was restored. Jesus spoke sternly to them, "Don't tell this to anyone!"

31 But they left and spread the news about Jesus all over that part of the country.

Jesus Heals a Dumb Man

32 As the men were leaving, some people brought to Jesus a man who could not talk because he had a demon. ³³ But as soon as the demon was driven out, the man started talking, and everyone was amazed. "We have never seen anything like this in Israel!" they exclaimed.

34 But the Pharisees said, "It is the chief of the demons who gives him the power to drive out demons."

Jesus Has Pity for the People

35 Jesus went round visiting all the towns and villages. He taught in the synagogues, preached the Good News about the Kingdom, and healed people with every kind of disease and sickness. ³⁶ As he saw the crowds, his heart was filled with pity for them, because they were worried and helpless, like sheep without a shepherd. ³⁷ So he said to his disciples, "The harvest is large, but there are few workers to gather it in. ³⁸ Pray to the owner of the harvest that he will send out workers to gather in his harvest."

The Twelve Apostles
(Mark 3.13-19; Luke 6.12-16)

10 Jesus called his twelve disciples together and gave them authority to drive out evil spirits and to heal every disease and every sickness. ² These are the names of the twelve apostles: first, Simon (called Peter) and his brother Andrew; James and his brother John, the sons of Zebedee; ³ Philip and Bartholomew; Thomas and Matthew, the tax collector; James son of Alphaeus, and Thaddaeus; ⁴ Simon the Patriot, and Judas Iscariot, who betrayed Jesus.

The Mission of the Twelve
(Mark 6.7-13; Luke 9.1-6)

5 These twelve men were sent out by Jesus with the following instructions: "Do not go to any Gentile territory or any Samaritan towns. ⁶ Instead, you are to go to the lost sheep of the people of Israel. ⁷ Go and preach, 'The Kingdom of heaven

9.34: Mt 10.25, 12.24; Mk 3.22; Lk 11.15   **9.35:** Mt 4.23; Mk 1.39; Lk 4.44
9.36: Num 27.17; 1 Kgs 22.17; 2 Chr 18.16; Ezek 34.5; Mk 6.34   **9.37-38:** Lk 10.2
10.7-15: Lk 10.4-12

is near!' ⁸Heal the sick, bring the dead back to life, heal those who suffer from dreaded skin-diseases, and drive out demons. You have received without paying, so give without being paid. ⁹Do not carry any gold, silver, or copper money in your pockets; ¹⁰do not carry a beggar's bag for the journey or an extra shirt or shoes or a stick. A worker should be given what he needs.

11 "When you come to a town or village, go in and look for someone who is willing to welcome you, and stay with him until you leave that place. ¹²When you go into a house, say, 'Peace be with you.' ¹³If the people in that house welcome you, let your greeting of peace remain; but if they do not welcome you, then take back your greeting. ¹⁴And if some home or town will not welcome you or listen to you, then leave that place and shake the dust off your feet. ¹⁵I assure you that on the Judgement Day God will show more mercy to the people of Sodom and Gomorrah than to the people of that town!

Coming Persecutions
(Mark 13.9–13; Luke 21.12–17)

16 "Listen! I am sending you out just like sheep to a pack of wolves. You must be as cautious as snakes and as gentle as doves. ¹⁷Watch out, for there will be men who will arrest you and take you to court, and they will whip you in the synagogues. ¹⁸For my sake you will be brought to trial before rulers and kings, to tell the Good News to them and to the Gentiles. ¹⁹When they bring you to trial, do not worry about what you are going to say or how you will say it; when the time comes, you will be given what you will say. ²⁰For the words you will speak will not be yours; they will come from the Spirit of your Father speaking through you.

21 "Men will hand over their own brothers to be put to death, and fathers will do the same to their children; children will turn against their parents and have them put to death. ²²Everyone will hate you because of me. But whoever holds out to the end will be saved. ²³When they persecute you in one town, run away to another one. I assure you that you will

not finish your work in all the towns of Israel before the Son of Man comes.

24 "No pupil is greater than his teacher; no slave is greater than his master. ²⁵So a pupil should be satisfied to become like his teacher, and a slave like his master. If the head of the family is called Beelzebul, the members of the family will be called even worse names!

Whom to Fear
(Luke 12.2–7)

26 "So do not be afraid of people. Whatever is now covered up will be uncovered, and every secret will be made known. ²⁷What I am telling you in the dark you must repeat in broad daylight, and what you have heard in private you must announce from the housetops. ²⁸Do not be afraid of those who kill the body but cannot kill the soul; rather be afraid of God, who can destroy both body and soul in hell. ²⁹For only a penny you can buy two sparrows, yet not one sparrow falls to the ground without your Father's consent. ³⁰As for you, even the hairs of your head have all been counted. ³¹So do not be afraid; you are worth much more than many sparrows!

Confessing and Rejecting Christ
(Luke 12.8–9)

32 "If anyone declares publicly that he belongs to me, I will do the same for him before my Father in heaven. ³³But if anyone rejects me publicly, I will reject him before my Father in heaven.

Not Peace, but a Sword
(Luke 12.51–53; 14.26–27)

34 "Do not think that I have come to bring peace to the world. No, I did not come to bring peace, but a sword. ³⁵I came to set sons against their fathers, daughters against their mothers, daughters-in-law against their mothers-in-law; ³⁶a man's worst enemies will be the members of his own family.

37 "Whoever loves his father or mother more than me is not fit to be my disciple; whoever loves his son or daughter more than me is not fit to be my disciple. ³⁸Whoever does not take up his cross and follow in my steps is not fit to be my disciple. ³⁹Whoever tries to gain his own

10.10: 1 Cor 9.14; 1 Tim 5.18   **10.14:** Acts 13.51   **10.15:** Mt 11.24; Gen 19.24–28
10.16: Lk 10.3   **10.17–20:** Mk 13.9–11; Lk 12.11–12, 21.12–15   **10.21:** Mk 13.12; Lk 21.16
10.22: Mt 24.9,13; Mk 13.13; Lk 21.17   **10.24:** Lk 6.40; Jn 13.16, 15.20
10.25: Mt 9.34, 12.24; Mk 3.22; Lk 11.15   **10.26:** Mk 4.22; Lk 8.17   **10.33:** 2 Tim 2.12
10.35–36: Mic 7.6   **10.38:** Mt 16.24; Mk 8.34; Lk 9.23
10.39: Mt 16.25; Mk 8.35; Lk 9.24, 17.33; Jn 12.25

life will lose it; but whoever loses his life for my sake will gain it.

Rewards
(Mark 9.41)

40 "Whoever welcomes you welcomes me; and whoever welcomes me welcomes the one who sent me. 41 Whoever welcomes God's messenger because he is God's messenger, will share in his reward. And whoever welcomes a good man because he is good, will share in his reward. 42 You can be sure that whoever gives even a drink of cold water to one of the least of these my followers because he is my follower, will certainly receive a reward."

The Messengers from John the Baptist
(Luke 7.18-35)

11 When Jesus finished giving these instructions to his twelve disciples, he left that place and went off to teach and preach in the towns near there.

2 When John the Baptist heard in prison about the things that Christ was doing, he sent some of his disciples to him. 3 "Tell us," they asked Jesus, "are you the one John said was going to come, or should we expect someone else?"

4 Jesus answered, "Go back and tell John what you are hearing and seeing: 5 the blind can see, the lame can walk, those who suffer from dreaded skin-diseases are made clean,h the deaf hear, the dead are brought back to life, and the Good News is preached to the poor. 6 How happy are those who have no doubts about me!"

7 While John's disciples were leaving, Jesus spoke about him to the crowds: "When you went out to John in the desert, what did you expect to see? A blade of grass bending in the wind? 8 What did you go out to see? A man dressed up in fancy clothes? People who dress like that live in palaces? 9 Tell me, what did you go out to see? A prophet? Yes indeed, but you saw much more than a prophet. 10 For John is the one of whom the scripture says: 'God said, I will send my messenger ahead of you to open the way for you.' 11 I assure you that John the Baptist is greater than any man who has ever lived. But he who is least in the

Kingdom of heaven is greater than John. 12 From the time John preached his message until this very day the Kingdom of heaven has suffered violent attacks,i and violent men try to seize it. 13 Until the time of John all the prophets and the Law of Moses spoke about the Kingdom; 14 and if you are willing to believe their message, John is Elijah, whose coming was predicted. 15 Listen, then, if you have ears!

16 "Now, to what can I compare the people of this day? They are like children sitting in the market-place. One group shouts to the other, 17 'We played wedding music for you, but you wouldn't dance! We sang funeral songs, but you wouldn't cry!' 18 When John came, he fasted and drank no wine, and everyone said, 'He has a demon in him!' 19 When the Son of Man came, he ate and drank, and everyone said, 'Look at this man! He is a glutton and a drinker, a friend of tax collectors and other outcasts!' God's wisdom, however, is shown to be true by its results."

The Unbelieving Towns
(Luke 10.13-15)

20 The people in the towns where Jesus had performed most of his miracles did not turn from their sins, so he reproached those towns. 21 "How terrible it will be for you, Chorazin! How terrible for you too, Bethsaida! If the miracles which were performed in you had been performed in Tyre and Sidon, the people there would long ago have put on sackcloth and sprinkled ashes on themselves, to show that they had turned from their sins! 22 I assure you that on the Judgement Day God will show more mercy to the people of Tyre and Sidon than to you! 23 And as for you, Capernaum! Did you want to lift yourself up to heaven? You will be thrown down to hell! If the miracles which were performed in you had been performed in Sodom, it would still be in existence today! 24 You can be sure that on the Judgement Day God will show more mercy to Sodom than to you!"

Come to Me and Rest
(Luke 10.21-22)

25 At that time Jesus said, "Father,

h MADE CLEAN: See 8.2.   i has suffered violent attacks; or has been coming violently.
10.40: Mk 9.37; Lk 9.48, 10.16; Jn 13.20   **11.5:** Is 35.5-6, 61.1   **11.10:** Mal 3.1
11.12-13: Lk 16.16   **11.14:** Mal 4.5; Mt 17.10-13; Mk 9.11-13
11.21: Is 23.1-18; Ezek 26.1-28.26; Joel 3.4-8; Amos 1.9-10; Zech 9.2-4
11.23: Is 14.13-15; Gen 19.24-28   **11.24:** Mt 10.15; Lk 10.12

Come to me, all of you who are tired (11.28)

Lord of heaven and earth! I thank you because you have shown to the unlearned what you have hidden from the wise and learned. 26 Yes, Father, this was how you wanted it to happen.

27 "My Father has given me all things. No one knows the Son except the Father, and no one knows the Father except the Son and those to whom the Son chooses to reveal him.

28 "Come to me, all of you who are tired from carrying heavy loads, and I will give you rest. 29 Take my yoke and put it on you, and learn from me, because I am gentle and humble in spirit; and you will find rest. 30 For the yoke I will give you is easy, and the load I will put on you is light."

The Question about the Sabbath
(Mark 2.23–28; Luke 6.1–5)

12 Not long afterwards Jesus was walking through some cornfields on the Sabbath. His disciples were hungry, so they began to pick ears of corn and eat the grain. 2 When the Pharisees saw this, they said to Jesus, "Look, it is against our Law for your disciples to do this on the Sabbath!"

3 Jesus answered, "Have you never read what David did that time when he and his men were hungry? 4 He went into the house of God, and he and his men ate the bread offered to God, even though it was against the Law for them to eat it—only the priests were allowed to eat that bread. 5 Or have you not read in the Law of Moses that every Sabbath the

priests in the Temple actually break the Sabbath law, yet they are not guilty? 6 I tell you that there is something here greater than the Temple. 7 The scripture says, 'It is kindness that I want, not animal sacrifices.' If you really knew what this means, you would not condemn people who are not guilty; 8 for the Son of Man is Lord of the Sabbath."

The Man with a Paralysed Hand
(Mark 3.1–6; Luke 6.6–11)

9 Jesus left that place and went to a synagogue, 10 where there was a man who had a paralysed hand. Some people were there who wanted to accuse Jesus of doing wrong, so they asked him, "Is it against our Law to heal on the Sabbath?"

11 Jesus answered, "What if one of you has a sheep and it falls into a deep hole on the Sabbath? Will he not take hold of it and lift it out? 12 And a man is worth much more than a sheep! So then, our Law does allow us to help someone on the Sabbath." 13 Then he said to the man with the paralysed hand, "Stretch out your hand."

He stretched it out, and it became well again, just like the other one. 14 Then the Pharisees left and made plans to kill Jesus.

God's Chosen Servant

15 When Jesus heard about the plot against him, he went away from that place; and large crowds followed him. He healed all those who were ill 16 and gave them orders not to tell others about him. 17 He did this so as to make what God

11.27: Jn 3.35, 1.18, 10.15   **11.29:** Jer 6.16   **12.1:** Deut 23.25   **12.3–4:** 1 Sam 21.1–6
12.4: Lev 24.9   **12.5:** Num 28.9–10   **12.7:** Mt 9.13; Hos 6.6   **12.11:** Lk 14.5

had said through the prophet Isaiah come true:

¹⁸ "Here is my servant, whom I have
     chosen,
    the one I love, and with whom I am
     pleased.
  I will send my Spirit upon him,
    and he will announce my judgement
     to the nations.
¹⁹ He will not argue or shout,
    or make loud speeches in the streets.
²⁰ He will not break off a bent reed,
    or put out a flickering lamp.
  He will persist until he causes justice
     to triumph,
²¹ and in him all peoples will put their
     hope."

Jesus and Beelzebul
(Mark 3.20–30; Luke 11.14–23)

22 Then some people brought to Jesus a man who was blind and could not talk because he had a demon. Jesus healed the man, so that he was able to talk and see. ²³ The crowds were all amazed at what Jesus had done. "Could he be the Son of David?" they asked.

24 When the Pharisees heard this, they replied, "He drives out demons only because their ruler Beelzebul gives him power to do so."

25 Jesus knew what they were thinking, so he said to them, "Any country that divides itself into groups which fight each other will not last very long. And any town or family that divides itself into groups which fight each other will fall apart. ²⁶ So if one group is fighting another in Satan's kingdom, this means that it is already divided into groups and will soon fall apart! ²⁷ You say that I drive out demons because Beelzebul gives me the power to do so. Well, then, who gives your followers the power to drive them out? What your own followers do proves that you are wrong! ²⁸ No, it is not Beelzebul, but God's Spirit, who gives me the power to drive out demons, which proves that the Kingdom of God has already come upon you.

29 "No one can break into a strong man's house and take away his belongings unless he first ties up the strong man; then he can plunder his house.

30 "Anyone who is not for me is really against me; anyone who does not help me gather is really scattering. ³¹ And so I tell you that people can be forgiven any sin and any evil thing they say;ʲ but whoever says evil things against the Holy Spirit will not be forgiven. ³² Anyone who says something against the Son of Man can be forgiven; but whoever says something against the Holy Spirit will not be forgiven—now or ever.

A Tree and Its Fruit
(Luke 6.43–45)

33 "To have good fruit you must have a healthy tree; if you have a poor tree, you will have bad fruit. A tree is known by the kind of fruit it bears. ³⁴ You snakes—how can you say good things when you are evil? For the mouth speaks what the heart is full of. ³⁵ A good person brings good things out of his treasure of good things; a bad person brings bad things out of his treasure of bad things.

36 "You can be sure that on Judgement Day everyone will have to give account of every useless word he has ever spoken. ³⁷ Your words will be used to judge you— to declare you either innocent or guilty."

The Demand for a Miracle
(Mark 8.11–12; Luke 11.29–32)

38 Then some teachers of the Law and some Pharisees spoke up. "Teacher," they said, "we want to see you perform a miracle."

39 "How evil and godless are the people of this day!" Jesus exclaimed. "You ask me for a miracle? No! The only miracle you will be given is the miracle of the prophet Jonah. ⁴⁰ In the same way that Jonah spent three days and nights in the big fish, so will the Son of Man spend three days and nights in the depths of the earth. ⁴¹ On Judgement Day the people of Nineveh will stand up and accuse you, because they turned from their sins when they heard Jonah preach; and I tell you that there is something here greater than Jonah! ⁴² On Judgement Day the Queen of Sheba will stand up and accuse you, because she travelled all the way from her country to listen to King Solomon's wise teaching; and I assure you that there is something here greater than Solomon!

ʲevil thing they say; or evil thing they say against God.
12.18–21: Is 42.1–4   **12.24:** Mt 9.34, 10.25   **12.30:** Mk 9.40   **12.32:** Lk 12.10
12.33: Mt 7.20; Lk 6.44   **12.34:** Mt 3.7, 23.33, 15.18; Lk 3.7, 6.45
12.38: Mt 16.1; Mk 8.11; Lk 11.16   **12.39:** Mt 16.4; Mk 8.12   **12.40:** Jon 1.17
12.41: Jon 3.5   **12.42:** 1 Kgs 10.1–10; 2 Chr 9.1–12

The Return of the Evil Spirit
(Luke 11.24-26)

43 "When an evil spirit goes out of a person, it travels over dry country looking for a place to rest. If it can't find one, 44 it says to itself, 'I will go back to my house.' So it goes back and finds the house empty, clean, and all tidy. 45 Then it goes out and brings along seven other spirits even worse than itself, and they come and live there. So when it is all over, that person is in a worse state than he was at the beginning. This is what will happen to the evil people of this day."

Jesus' Mother and Brothers
(Mark 3.31-35; Luke 8.19-21)

46 Jesus was still talking to the people when his mother and brothers arrived. They stood outside, asking to speak with him. 47 So one of the people there said to him, "Look, your mother and brothers are standing outside, and they want to speak with you." k 48 Jesus answered, "Who is my mother? Who are my brothers?" 49 Then he pointed to his disciples and said, "Look! Here are my mother and my brothers! 50 Whoever does what my Father in heaven wants him to do is my brother, my sister, and my mother."

The Parable of the Sower
(Mark 4.1-9; Luke 8.4-8)

13 That same day Jesus left the house and went to the lake-side, where he sat down to teach. 2 The crowd that gathered round him was so large that he got into a boat and sat in it, while the crowd stood on the shore. 3 He used parables to tell them many things.

"Once there was a man who went out to sow corn. 4 As he scattered the seed in the field, some of it fell along the path, and the birds came and ate it up. 5 Some of it fell on rocky ground, where there was little soil. The seeds soon sprouted, because the soil wasn't deep. 6 But when the sun came up, it burnt the young plants; and because the roots had not grown deep enough, the plants soon dried up. 7 Some of the seed fell among thorn bushes, which grew up and choked the plants. 8 But some seeds fell in good soil, and the plants produced corn; some

produced a hundred grains, others sixty, and others thirty."

9 And Jesus concluded, "Listen, then, if you have ears!"

The Purpose of the Parables
(Mark 4.10-12; Luke 8.9-10)

10 Then the disciples came to Jesus and asked him, "Why do you use parables when you talk to the people?"

11 Jesus answered, "The knowledge about the secrets of the Kingdom of heaven has been given to you, but not to them. 12 For the person who has something will be given more, so that he will have more than enough; but the person who has nothing will have taken away from him even the little he has. 13 The reason I use parables in talking to them is that they look, but do not see, and they listen, but do not hear or understand. 14 So the prophecy of Isaiah applies to them:

'This people will listen and listen, but
        not understand;
    they will look and look, but not see,
15 because their minds are dull,
    and they have stopped up their ears
    and have closed their eyes.
Otherwise, their eyes would see,
    their ears would hear,
    their minds would understand,
and they would turn to me, says God,
    and I would heal them.'

16 "As for you, how fortunate you are! Your eyes see and your ears hear. 17 I assure you that many prophets and many of God's people wanted very much to see what you see, but they could not, and to hear what you hear, but they did not.

Jesus Explains the Parable of the Sower
(Mark 4.13-20; Luke 8.11-15)

18 "Listen, then, and learn what the parable of the sower means. 19 Those who hear the message about the Kingdom but do not understand it are like the seeds that fell along the path. The Evil One comes and snatches away what was sown in them. 20 The seeds that fell on rocky ground stand for those who receive the message gladly as soon as they hear it. 21 But it does not sink deep into them, and they don't last long. So when trouble or persecution comes because of the message, they give up at once. 22 The seeds that fell among thorn bushes stand for

k Some manuscripts do not have verse 47.

13.2: Lk 5.1-3 **13.12:** Mt 25.29; Mk 4.25; Lk 8.18, 19.26 **13.14-15:** Is 6.9-10
13.16-17: Lk 10.23-24

those who hear the message; but the worries about this life and the love for riches choke the message, and they don't bear fruit. 23 And the seeds sown in the good soil stand for those who hear the message and understand it: they bear fruit, some as much as a hundred, others sixty, and others thirty."

The Parable of the Weeds

24 Jesus told them another parable: "The Kingdom of heaven is like this. A man sowed good seed in his field. 25 One night, when everyone was asleep, an enemy came and sowed weeds among the wheat and went away. 26 When the plants grew and the ears of corn began to form, then the weeds showed up. 27 The man's servants came to him and said, 'Sir, it was good seed you sowed in your field; where did the weeds come from?' 28 'It was some enemy who did this,' he answered. 'Do you want us to go and pull up the weeds?' they asked him. 29 'No,' he answered, 'because as you gather the weeds you might pull up some of the wheat along with them. 30 Let the wheat and the weeds both grow together until harvest. Then I will tell the harvest workers to pull up the weeds first, tie them in bundles and burn them, and then to gather in the wheat and put it in my barn.'"

The Parable of the Mustard Seed
(Mark 4.30–32; Luke 13.18–19)

31 Jesus told them another parable: "The Kingdom of heaven is like this. A man takes a mustard seed and sows it in his field. 32 It is the smallest of all seeds, but when it grows up, it is the biggest of all plants. It becomes a tree, so that birds come and make their nests in its branches."

The Parable of the Yeast
(Luke 13.20–21)

33 Jesus told them still another parable: "The Kingdom of heaven is like this. A woman takes some yeast and mixes it with forty litres of flour until the whole batch of dough rises."

Jesus' Use of Parables
(Mark 4.33–34)

34 Jesus used parables to tell all these things to the crowds; he would not say a thing to them without using a parable.

13.35: Ps 78.2

35 He did this to make what the prophet had said come true,

"I will use parables when I speak to
     them;
  I will tell them things unknown since
     the creation of the world."

Jesus Explains the Parable of the Weeds

36 When Jesus had left the crowd and gone indoors, his disciples came to him and said, "Tell us what the parable about the weeds in the field means."
37 Jesus answered, "The man who sowed the good seed is the Son of Man; 38 the field is the world; the good seed is the people who belong to the Kingdom; the weeds are the people who belong to the Evil One; 39 and the enemy who sowed the weeds is the Devil. The harvest is the end of the age, and the harvest workers are angels. 40 Just as the weeds are gathered up and burnt in the fire, so the same thing will happen at the end of the age: 41 the Son of Man will send out his angels to gather up out of his Kingdom all those who cause people to sin and all others who do evil things, 42 and they will throw them into the fiery furnace, where they will cry and grind their teeth. 43 Then God's people will shine like the sun in their Father's Kingdom. Listen, then, if you have ears!

The Parable of the Hidden Treasure

44 "The Kingdom of heaven is like this. A man happens to find a treasure hidden in a field. He covers it up again, and is so happy that he goes and sells everything he has, and then goes back and buys that field.

The Parable of the Pearl

45 "Also, the Kingdom of heaven is like this. A man is looking for fine pearls, 46 and when he finds one that is unusually fine, he goes and sells everything he has, and buys that pearl.

The Parable of the Net

47 "Also, the Kingdom of heaven is like this. Some fishermen throw their net out in the lake and catch all kinds of fish. 48 When the net is full, they pull it to shore and sit down to divide the fish: the good ones go into their buckets, the worthless ones are thrown away. 49 It will be like this at the end of the age: the angels will go out and gather up the evil people from among the good 50 and will throw

them into the fiery furnace, where they will cry and grind their teeth.

New Truths and Old

51 "Do you understand these things?" Jesus asked them.

"Yes," they answered.

52 So he replied, "This means, then, that every teacher of the Law who becomes a disciple in the Kingdom of heaven is like the owner of a house who takes new and old things out of his storeroom."

Jesus is Rejected at Nazareth
(Mark 6.1-6; Luke 4.16-30)

53 When Jesus finished telling these parables, he left that place 54 and went back to his home town. He taught in the synagogue, and those who heard him were amazed. "Where did he get such wisdom?" they asked. "And what about his miracles? 55 Isn't he the carpenter's son? Isn't Mary his mother, and aren't James, Joseph, Simon, and Judas his brothers? 56 Aren't all his sisters living here? Where did he get all this?" 57 And so they rejected him.

Jesus said to them, "A prophet is respected everywhere except in his home town and by his own family." 58 Because they did not have faith, he did not perform many miracles there.

The Death of John the Baptist
(Mark 6.14-29; Luke 9.7-9)

14 At that time Herod, the ruler of Galilee, heard about Jesus. 2 "He is really John the Baptist, who has come back to life," he told his officials. "That is why he has this power to perform miracles."

3 For Herod had earlier ordered John's arrest, and he had him chained and put in prison. He had done this because of Herodias, his brother Philip's wife. 4 For some time John the Baptist had told Herod, "It isn't right for you to be married to Herodias!" 5 Herod wanted to kill him, but he was afraid of the Jewish people, because they considered John to be a prophet.

6 On Herod's birthday the daughter of Herodias danced in front of the whole group. Herod was so pleased 7 that he promised her, "I swear that I will give you anything you ask for!"

8 At her mother's suggestion she asked him, "Give me here and now the head of John the Baptist on a dish!"

9 The king was sad, but because of the promise he had made in front of all his guests he gave orders that her wish be granted. 10 So he had John beheaded in prison. 11 The head was brought in on a dish and given to the girl, who took it to her mother. 12 John's disciples came, carried away his body, and buried it; then they went and told Jesus.

Jesus Feeds Five Thousand Men
(Mark 6.30-44; Luke 9.10-17; John 6.1-14)

13 When Jesus heard the news about John, he left there in a boat and went to a lonely place by himself. The people heard about it, so they left their towns and followed him by land. 14 Jesus got out of the boat, and when he saw the large crowd, his heart was filled with pity for them, and he healed those who were ill.

15 That evening his disciples came to him and said, "It is already very late, and this is a lonely place. Send the people away and let them go to the villages to buy food for themselves."

16 "They don't have to leave," answered Jesus. "You yourselves give them something to eat!"

17 "All we have here are five loaves and two fish," they replied.

18 "Then bring them here to me," Jesus said. 19 He ordered the people to sit down on the grass; then he took the five loaves and the two fish, looked up to heaven, and gave thanks to God. He broke the loaves and gave them to the disciples, and the disciples gave them to the people. 20 Everyone ate and had enough. Then the disciples took up twelve baskets full of what was left over. 21 The number of men who ate was about five thousand, not counting the women and children.

Jesus Walks on the Water
(Mark 6.45-52; John 6.15-21)

22 Then Jesus made the disciples get into the boat and go on ahead to the other side of the lake, while he sent the people away. 23 After sending the people away, he went up a hill by himself to pray. When evening came, Jesus was there alone; 24 and by this time the boat was far out in the lake, tossed about by the waves, because the wind was blowing against it.

25 Between three and six o'clock in the morning Jesus came to the disciples, walking on the water. 26 When they saw

13.57: Jn 4.44   **14.3-4:** Lk 3.19-20   **14.4:** Lev 18.16, 20.21

him walking on the water, they were terrified. "It's a ghost!" they said, and screamed with fear.

27 Jesus spoke to them at once. "Courage!" he said. "It is I. Don't be afraid!"

28 Then Peter spoke up. "Lord, if it is really you, order me to come out on the water to you."

29 "Come!" answered Jesus. So Peter got out of the boat and started walking on the water to Jesus. 30 But when he noticed the strong wind, he was afraid and started to sink down in the water. "Save me, Lord!" he cried.

31 At once Jesus reached out and grabbed hold of him and said, "How little faith you have! Why did you doubt?"

32 They both got into the boat, and the wind died down. 33 Then the disciples in the boat worshipped Jesus. "Truly you are the Son of God!" they exclaimed.

Jesus Heals the Sick in Gennesaret
(Mark 6.53–56)

34 They crossed the lake and came to land at Gennesaret, 35 where the people recognized Jesus. So they sent for the sick people in all the surrounding country and brought them to Jesus. 36 They begged him to let those who were ill at least touch the edge of his cloak; and all who touched it were made well.

The Teaching of the Ancestors
(Mark 7.1–13)

15 Then some Pharisees and teachers of the Law came from Jerusalem to Jesus and asked him, 2 "Why is it that your disciples disobey the teaching handed down by our ancestors? They don't wash their hands in the proper way before they eat!"

3 Jesus answered, "And why do you disobey God's command and follow your own teaching? 4 For God said, 'Respect your father and your mother,' and 'Whoever curses his father or his mother is to be put to death.' 5 But you teach that if a person has something he could use to help his father or mother, but says, 'This belongs to God,' 6 he does not need to honour his father.[l] In this way you disregard God's command, and follow your own teaching. 7 You hypocrites! How right Isaiah was when he prophesied about you!

8 'These people, says God, honour me with their words,
   but their heart is really far away from me.
9 It is no use for them to worship me,
   because they teach man-made rules
   as though they were my laws!'"

The Things That Make a Person Unclean
(Mark 7.14–23)

10 Then Jesus called the crowd to him and said to them, "Listen and understand! 11 It is not what goes into a person's mouth that makes him ritually unclean; rather, what comes out of it makes him unclean."

12 Then the disciples came to him and said, "Do you know that the Pharisees had their feelings hurt by what you said?"

13 "Every plant which my Father in heaven did not plant will be pulled up," answered Jesus. 14 "Don't worry about

They are blind leaders of the blind (15.14)

them! They are blind leaders of the blind; and when one blind man leads another, both fall into a ditch."

15 Peter spoke up, "Explain this saying to us."

16 Jesus said to them, "You are still no more intelligent than the others. 17 Don't you understand? Anything that goes into a person's mouth goes into his stomach and then on out of his body. 18 But the things that come out of the mouth come from the heart, and these

---

[l] his father; *some manuscripts have* his father or mother.
15.4: Ex 20.12, 21.17; Deut 5.16; Lev 20.9   **15.8–9:** Is 29.13   **15.14:** Lk 6.39
15.18: Mt 12.34

are the things that make a person ritually unclean. 19 For from his heart come the evil ideas which lead him to kill, commit adultery, and do other immoral things; to rob, lie, and slander others. 20 These are the things that make a person unclean. But to eat without washing your hands as they say you should—this doesn't make a person unclean."

A Woman's Faith
(Mark 7.24–30)

21 Jesus left that place and went off to the territory near the cities of Tyre and Sidon. 22 A Canaanite woman who lived in that region came to him. "Son of David!" she cried out. "Have mercy on me, sir! My daughter has a demon and is in a terrible condition."

23 But Jesus did not say a word to her. His disciples came to him and begged him, "Send her away! She is following us and making all this noise!"

24 Then Jesus replied, "I have been sent only to the lost sheep of the people of Israel."

25 At this the woman came and fell at his feet. "Help me, sir!" she said.

26 Jesus answered, "It isn't right to take the children's food and throw it to the dogs."

27 "That's true, sir," she answered; "but even the dogs eat the leftovers that fall from their masters' table."

28 So Jesus answered her, "You are a woman of great faith! What you want will be done for you." And at that very moment her daughter was healed.

Jesus Heals Many People

29 Jesus left there and went along by Lake Galilee. He climbed a hill and sat down. 30 Large crowds came to him, bringing with them the lame, the blind, the crippled, the dumb, and many other sick people, whom they placed at Jesus' feet; and he healed them. 31 The people were amazed as they saw the dumb speaking, the crippled made whole, the lame walking, and the blind seeing; and they praised the God of Israel.

Jesus Feeds Four Thousand Men
(Mark 8.1–10)

32 Jesus called his disciples to him and said, "I feel sorry for these people, because they have been with me for three days and now have nothing to eat. I don't

want to send them away without feeding them, for they might faint on their way home."

33 The disciples asked him, "Where will we find enough food in this desert to feed this crowd?"

34 "How much bread have you?" Jesus asked.

"Seven loaves," they answered, "and a few small fish."

35 So Jesus ordered the crowd to sit down on the ground. 36 Then he took the seven loaves and the fish, gave thanks to God, broke them, and gave them to the disciples; and the disciples gave them to the people. 37 They all ate and had enough. Then the disciples took up seven baskets full of pieces left over. 38 The number of men who ate was four thousand, not counting the women and children.

39 Then Jesus sent the people away, got into a boat, and went to the territory of Magadan.

The Demand for a Miracle
(Mark 8.11–13; Luke 12.54–56)

16 Some Pharisees and Sadducees who came to Jesus wanted to trap him, so they asked him to perform a miracle for them, to show that God approved of him. 2 But Jesus answered, "When the sun is setting, you say, 'We are going to have fine weather, because the sky is red.' 3 And early in the morning you say, 'It is going to rain, because the sky is red and dark.' You can predict the weather by looking at the sky, but you cannot interpret the signs concerning these times! m 4 How evil and godless are the people of this day! You ask me for a miracle? No! The only miracle you will be given is the miracle of Jonah."

So he left them and went away.

The Yeast of the Pharisees and Sadducees
(Mark 8.14–21)

5 When the disciples crossed over to the other side of the lake, they forgot to take any bread. 6 Jesus said to them, "Take care; be on your guard against the yeast of the Pharisees and Sadducees."

7 They started discussing among themselves, "He says this because we didn't bring any bread."

8 Jesus knew what they were saying, so he asked them, "Why are you discussing among yourselves about not

---

m Some manuscripts do not have the words of Jesus in verses 2 and 3.
16.1: Mt 12.38; Lk 11.16   **16.4:** Mt 12.39; Lk 11.29   **16.6:** Lk 12.1

having any bread? How little faith you have! 9 Don't you understand yet? Don't you remember when I broke the five loaves for the five thousand men? How many baskets did you fill? 10 And what about the seven loaves for the four thousand men? How many baskets did you fill? 11 How is it that you don't understand that I was not talking to you about bread? Guard yourselves from the yeast of the Pharisees and Sadducees!"

12 Then the disciples understood that he was not warning them to guard themselves from the yeast used in bread but from the teaching of the Pharisees and Sadducees.

Peter's Declaration about Jesus
(Mark 8.27-30; Luke 9.18-21)

13 Jesus went to the territory near the town of Caesarea Philippi, where he asked his disciples, "Who do people say the Son of Man is?"

14 "Some say John the Baptist," they answered. "Others say Elijah, while others say Jeremiah or some other prophet."

15 "What about you?" he asked them. "Who do you say I am?"

16 Simon Peter answered, "You are the Messiah, the Son of the living God."

17 "Good for you, Simon son of John!" answered Jesus. "For this truth did not come to you from any human being, but it was given to you directly by my Father in heaven. 18 And so I tell you, Peter: you are a rock, and on this rock foundation I will build my church, and not even death will ever be able to overcome it. 19 I will give you the keys of the Kingdom of heaven; what you prohibit on earth will be prohibited in heaven, and what you permit on earth will be permitted in heaven."

20 Then Jesus ordered his disciples not to tell anyone that he was the Messiah.

Jesus Speaks about His Suffering and Death
(Mark 8.31-9.1; Luke 9.22-27)

21 From that time on Jesus began to say plainly to his disciples, "I must go to Jerusalem and suffer much from the elders, the chief priests, and the teachers of the Law. I will be put to death, but three days later I will be raised to life."

22 Peter took him aside and began to rebuke him. "God forbid it, Lord!" he said. "That must never happen to you!"

23 Jesus turned around and said to Peter, "Get away from me, Satan! You are an obstacle in my way, because these thoughts of yours don't come from God, but from man."

24 Then Jesus said to his disciples, "If anyone wants to come with me, he must forget self, carry his cross, and follow me. 25 For whoever wants to save his own life will lose it; but whoever loses his life for my sake will find it. 26 Will a person gain anything if he wins the whole world but loses his life? Of course not! There is nothing he can give to regain his life. 27 For the Son of Man is about to come in the glory of his Father with his angels, and then he will reward each one according to his deeds. 28 I assure you that there are some here who will not die until they have seen the Son of Man come as King."

The Transfiguration
(Mark 9.2-13; Luke 9.28-36)

17 Six days later Jesus took with him Peter and the brothers James and John and led them up a high mountain where they were alone. 2 As they looked on, a change came over Jesus: his face was shining like the sun, and his clothes were dazzling white. 3 Then the three disciples saw Moses and Elijah talking with Jesus. 4 So Peter spoke up and said to Jesus, "Lord, how good it is that we are here! If you wish, I will make three tents here, one for you, one for Moses, and one for Elijah."

5 While he was talking, a shining cloud came over them, and a voice from the cloud said, "This is my own dear Son, with whom I am pleased—listen to him!"

6 When the disciples heard the voice, they were so terrified that they threw themselves face downwards on the ground. 7 Jesus came to them and touched them. "Get up," he said. "Don't be afraid!" 8 So they looked up and saw no one there but Jesus.

9 As they came down the mountain, Jesus ordered them, "Don't tell anyone about this vision you have seen until the Son of Man has been raised from death."

16.9: Mt 14.17-21   **16.10:** Mt 15.34-38   **16.14:** Mt 14.1-2; Mk 6.14-15; Lk 9.7-8
16.16: Jn 6.68-69   **16.19:** Mt 18.18; Jn 20.23   **16.24:** Mt 10.38; Lk 14.27
16.25: Mt 10.39; Lk 17.33; Jn 12.25   **16.27:** Mt 25.31; Ps 62.12; Rom 2.6
17.1-5: 2 Pet 1.17-18
17.5: Gen 22.2; Deut 18.15; Ps 2.7; Is 42.1; Mt 3.17, 12.18; Mk 1.11; Lk 3.22

10 Then the disciples asked Jesus, "Why do the teachers of the Law say that Elijah has to come first?"

11 "Elijah is indeed coming first," answered Jesus, "and he will get everything ready. 12 But I tell you that Elijah has already come and people did not recognize him, but treated him just as they pleased. In the same way they will also ill-treat the Son of Man."

13 Then the disciples understood that he was talking to them about John the Baptist.

Jesus Heals a Boy with a Demon
(Mark 9.14-29; Luke 9.37-43a)

14 When they returned to the crowd, a man came to Jesus, knelt before him, 15 and said, "Sir, have mercy on my son! He is an epileptic and has such terrible fits that he often falls in the fire or into water. 16 I brought him to your disciples, but they could not heal him."

17 Jesus answered, "How unbelieving and wrong you people are! How long must I stay with you? How long do I have to put up with you? Bring the boy here to me!" 18 Jesus gave a command to the demon, and it went out of the boy, and at that very moment he was healed.

19 Then the disciples came to Jesus in private and asked him, "Why couldn't we drive the demon out?"

20 "It was because you haven't enough faith," answered Jesus. "I assure you that if you have faith as big as a mustard seed, you can say to this hill, 'Go from here to there!' and it will go. You could do anything!" n

Jesus Speaks Again about His Death
(Mark 9.30-32; Luke 9.43b-45)

22 When the disciples all came together in Galilee, Jesus said to them, "The Son of Man is about to be handed over to men 23 who will kill him; but three days later he will be raised to life."

The disciples became very sad.

Payment of the Temple-Tax

24 When Jesus and his disciples came to Capernaum, the collectors of the temple-tax came to Peter and asked, "Does your teacher pay the temple-tax?"

25 "Of course," Peter answered.

When Peter went into the house, Jesus spoke up first, "Simon, what is your opinion? Who pays duties or taxes to the kings of this world? The citizens of the country or the foreigners?"

26 "The foreigners," answered Peter.

"Well, then," replied Jesus, "that means that the citizens don't have to pay. 27 But we don't want to offend these people. So go to the lake and drop in a line. Pull up the first fish you hook, and in its mouth you will find a coin worth enough for my temple-tax and yours. Take it and pay them our taxes."

Who Is the Greatest?
(Mark 9.33-37; Luke 9.46-48)

18 At that time the disciples came to Jesus, asking, "Who is the greatest in the Kingdom of heaven?"

2 So Jesus called a child, made him stand in front of them, 3 and said, "I assure you that unless you change and become like children, you will never enter the Kingdom of heaven. 4 The greatest in the Kingdom of heaven is the one who humbles himself and becomes like this child. 5 And whoever welcomes in my name one such child as this, welcomes me.

Temptations to Sin
(Mark 9.42-48; Luke 17.1-2)

6 "If anyone should cause one of these little ones to lose his faith in me, it would be better for that person to have a large millstone tied round his neck and be drowned in the deep sea. 7 How terrible for the world that there are things that make people lose their faith! Such things will always happen—but how terrible for the one who causes them!

8 "If your hand or your foot makes you lose your faith, cut it off and throw it away! It is better for you to enter life without a hand or a foot than to keep both hands and both feet and be thrown into the eternal fire. 9 And if your eye makes you lose your faith, take it out and throw it away! It is better for you to enter life with only one eye than to keep both eyes and be thrown into the fire of hell.

---

b Some manuscripts add verse 21: But only prayer and fasting can drive this kind out; nothing else can (see Mk 9.29).

17.10: Mal 4.5   **17.12:** Mt 11.14   **17.20:** Mt 21.21; Mk 11.23; 1 Cor 13.2
17.24: Ex 30.13, 38.26   **18.1:** Lk 22.24   **18.3:** Mk 10.15; Lk 18.17   **18.8:** Mt 5.30
18.9: Mt 5.29

Unless you change and become like children (18.3)

The Parable of the Lost Sheep
(Luke 15.3-7)

10 "See that you don't despise any of these little ones. Their angels in heaven, I tell you, are always in the presence of my Father in heaven. *o*

12 "What do you think a man does who has a hundred sheep and one of them gets lost? He will leave the other ninety-nine grazing on the hillside and go and look for the lost sheep. 13 When he finds it, I tell you, he feels far happier over this one sheep than over the ninety-nine that did not get lost. 14 In just the same way your *p* Father in heaven does not want any of these little ones to be lost.

A Brother Who Sins

15 "If your brother sins against you, *q* go to him and show him his fault. But do it privately, just between yourselves. If he listens to you, you have won your brother back. 16 But if he will not listen to

you, take one or two other persons with you, so that 'every accusation may be upheld by the testimony of two or more witnesses,' as the scripture says. 17 And if he will not listen to them, then tell the whole thing to the church. Finally, if he will not listen to the church, treat him as though he were a pagan or a tax collector.

Prohibiting and Permitting

18 "And so I tell all of you: what you prohibit on earth will be prohibited in heaven, and what you permit on earth will be permitted in heaven.

19 "And I tell you more: whenever two of you on earth agree about anything you pray for, it will be done for you by my Father in heaven. 20 For where two or three come together in my name, I am there with them."

The Parable of the Unforgiving Servant

21 Then Peter came to Jesus and asked, "Lord, if my brother keeps on sinning

o Some manuscripts add verse 11: For the Son of Man came to save the lost *(see Lk 19.10).*
p your; some manuscripts have my.　　*q Some manuscripts do not have* against you.
18.15: Lk 17.3　　**18.16:** Deut 19.15　　**18.18:** Mt 16.19; Jn 20.23　　**18.21-22:** Lk 17.3-4

against me, how many times do I have to forgive him? Seven times?"

22 "No, not seven times," answered Jesus, "but seventy times seven,ʳ 23 because the Kingdom of heaven is like this. Once there was a king who decided to check on his servants' accounts. 24 He had just begun to do so when one of them was brought in who owed him millions of pounds. 25 The servant did not have enough to pay his debt, so the king ordered him to be sold as a slave, with his wife and his children and all that he had, in order to pay the debt. 26 The servant fell on his knees before the king. 'Be patient with me,' he begged, 'and I will pay you everything!' 27 The king felt sorry for him, so he forgave him the debt and let him go.

ʳ seventy times seven; *or* seventy-seven times.
18.22: Gen 4.24

28 "Then the man went out and met one of his fellow-servants who owed him a few pounds. He grabbed him and started choking him. 'Pay back what you owe me!' he said. 29 His fellow-servant fell down and begged him, 'Be patient with me, and I will pay you back!' 30 But he refused; instead, he had him thrown into jail until he should pay the debt. 31 When the other servants saw what had happened, they were very upset and went to the king and told him everything. 32 So he called the servant in. 'You worthless slave!' he said. 'I forgave you the whole amount you owed me, just because you asked me to. 33 You should have had mercy on your fellow-servant, just as I had mercy on you.' 34 The king was very angry, and he sent the servant to jail to

He will . . . go and look for the lost sheep (18.12)

be punished until he should pay back the whole amount."

35 And Jesus concluded, "That is how my Father in heaven will treat every one of you unless you forgive your brother from your heart."

Jesus Teaches About Divorce
(Mark 10.1–12)

19 When Jesus finished saying these things, he left Galilee and went to the territory of Judaea on the other side of the River Jordan. 2 Large crowds followed him, and he healed them there.

3 Some Pharisees came to him and tried to trap him by asking, "Does our Law allow a man to divorce his wife for whatever reason he wishes?"

4 Jesus answered, "Haven't you read the scripture that says that in the beginning the Creator made people male and female? 5 And God said, 'For this reason a man will leave his father and mother and unite with his wife, and the two will become one.' 6 So they are no longer two, but one. Man must not separate, then, what God has joined together."

7 The Pharisees asked him, "Why, then, did Moses give the law for a man to hand his wife a divorce notice and send her away?"

8 Jesus answered, "Moses gave you permission to divorce your wives because you are so hard to teach. But it was not like that at the time of creation. 9 I tell you, then, that any man who divorces his wife for any cause other than her unfaithfulness, commits adultery if he marries some other woman."

10 His disciples said to him, "If this is how it is between a man and his wife, it is better not to marry."

11 Jesus answered, "This teaching does not apply to everyone, but only to those to whom God has given it. 12 For there are different reasons why men cannot marry: some, because they were born that way; others, because men made them that way; and others do not marry for the sake of the Kingdom of heaven. Let him who can accept this teaching do so."

Jesus Blesses Little Children
(Mark 10.13–16; Luke 18.15–17)

13 Some people brought children to Jesus for him to place his hands on them

and to pray for them, but the disciples scolded the people. 14 Jesus said, "Let the children come to me and do not stop them, because the Kingdom of heaven belongs to such as these."

15 He placed his hands on them and then went away.

The Rich Young Man
(Mark 10.17–31; Luke 18.18–30)

16 Once a man came to Jesus. "Teacher," he asked, "what good thing must I do to receive eternal life?"

17 "Why do you ask me concerning what is good?" answered Jesus. "There is only One who is good. Keep the commandments if you want to enter life."

18 "What commandments?" he asked.

Jesus answered, "Do not commit murder; do not commit adultery; do not steal; do not accuse anyone falsely; 19 respect your father and your mother; and love your neighbour as you love yourself."

20 "I have obeyed all these commandments," the young man replied. "What else do I need to do?"

21 Jesus said to him, "If you want to be perfect, go and sell all you have and give the money to the poor, and you will have riches in heaven; then come and follow me."

22 When the young man heard this, he went away sad, because he was very rich.

23 Jesus then said to his disciples, "I assure you: it will be very hard for rich people to enter the Kingdom of heaven. 24 I repeat: it is much harder for a rich person to enter the Kingdom of God than for a camel to go through the eye of a needle."

25 When the disciples heard this, they were completely amazed. "Who, then, can be saved?" they asked.

26 Jesus looked straight at them and answered, "This is impossible for man, but for God everything is possible."

27 Then Peter spoke up. "Look," he said, "we have left everything and followed you. What will we have?"

28 Jesus said to them, "You can be sure that when the Son of Man sits on his glorious throne in the New Age, then you twelve followers of mine will also sit on thrones, to rule the twelve tribes of Israel. 29 And everyone who has left houses or brothers or sisters or father or mother

19.4: Gen 1.27, 5.2   **19.5:** Gen 2.24   **19.7:** Deut 24.1–4; Mt 5.31
19.9: Mt 5.32; 1 Cor 7.10–11   **19.18:** Ex 20.13–16; Deut 5.17–20
19.19: Ex 20.12; Deut 5.16; Lev 19.18   **19.28:** Mt 25.31; Lk 22.30

or children or fields for my sake, will receive a hundred times more and will be given eternal life. 30 But many who now are first will be last, and many who now are last will be first.

The Workers in the Vineyard

20 "The Kingdom of heaven is like this. Once there was a man who went out early in the morning to hire some men to work in his vineyard. 2 He agreed to pay them the regular wage, a silver coin a day, and sent them to work in his vineyard. 3 He went out again to the market place at nine o'clock and saw some men standing there doing nothing, 4 so he told them, 'You also go and work in the vineyard, and I will pay you a fair wage.' 5 So they went. Then at twelve o'clock and again at three o'clock he did the same thing. 6 It was nearly five o'clock when he went to the market place and saw some other men still standing there. 'Why are you wasting the whole day here doing nothing?' he asked them. 7 'No one hired us,' they answered. 'Well, then, you also go and work in the vineyard,' he told them.

8 "When evening came, the owner told his foreman, 'Call the workers and pay them their wages, starting with those who were hired last and ending with those who were hired first.' 9 The men who had begun to work at five o'clock were paid a silver coin each. 10 So when the men who were the first to be hired came to be paid, they thought they would get more; but they too were given a silver coin each. 11 They took their money and started grumbling against the employer. 12 'These men who were hired last worked only one hour,' they said, 'while we put up with a whole day's work in the hot sun—yet you paid them the same as you paid us!'

13 "'Listen, friend,' the owner answered one of them, 'I have not cheated you. After all, you agreed to do a day's work for one silver coin. 14 Now take your pay and go home. I want to give this man who was hired last as much as I have given you. 15 Don't I have the right to do as I wish with my own money? Or are you jealous because I am generous?'"

16 And Jesus concluded, "So those who are last will be first, and those who are first will be last."

Jesus Speaks a Third Time about His Death
(Mark 10.32–34; Luke 18.31–34)

17 As Jesus was going up to Jerusalem, he took the twelve disciples aside and spoke to them privately, as they walked along. 18 "Listen," he told them, "we are going up to Jerusalem, where the Son of Man will be handed over to the chief priests and the teachers of the Law. They will condemn him to death 19 and then hand him over to the Gentiles, who will mock him, whip him, and crucify him; but three days later he will be raised to life."

A Mother's Request
(Mark 10.35–45)

20 Then the wife of Zebedee came to Jesus with her two sons, bowed before him, and asked him a favour.

21 "What do you want?" Jesus asked her.

She answered, "Promise me that these two sons of mine will sit at your right and your left when you are King."

22 "You don't know what you are asking for," Jesus answered the sons. "Can you drink the cup of suffering that I am about to drink?"

"We can," they answered.

23 "You will indeed drink from my cup," Jesus told them, "but I do not have the right to choose who will sit at my right and my left. These places belong to those for whom my Father has prepared them."

24 When the other ten disciples heard about this, they became angry with the two brothers. 25 So Jesus called them all together and said, "You know that the rulers of the heathen have power over them, and the leaders have complete authority. 26 This, however, is not the way it shall be among you. If one of you wants to be great, he must be the servant of the rest; 27 and if one of you wants to be first, he must be your slave—28 like the Son of Man, who did not come to be served, but to serve and to give his life to redeem many people."

Jesus Heals Two Blind Men
(Mark 10.46–52; Luke 18.35–43)

29 As Jesus and his disciples were leaving Jericho, a large crowd was following. 30 Two blind men who were

19.30: Mt 20.16; Lk 13.30   20.8: Lev 19.13; Deut 24.15   20.16: Mt 19.30; Mk 10.31; Lk 13.30
20.25–26: Lk 22.25–26   20.26–27: Mt 23.11; Mk 9.35; Lk 22.26

God bless him who comes in the name of the Lord! (21.9)

sitting by the road heard that Jesus was passing by, so they began to shout, "Son of David! Take pity on us, sir!"

31 The crowd scolded them and told them to be quiet. But they shouted even more loudly, "Son of David! Take pity on us, sir!"

32 Jesus stopped and called them. "What do you want me to do for you?" he asked them.

33 "Sir," they answered, "we want you to give us our sight!"

34 Jesus had pity on them and touched their eyes; at once they were able to see, and they followed him.

The Triumphant Entry into Jerusalem
(Mark 11.1–11; Luke 19.28–40;
John 12.12–19)

21 As Jesus and his disciples approached Jerusalem, they came to Bethphage at the Mount of Olives. There Jesus sent two of the disciples on ahead 2 with these instructions: "Go to the village there ahead of you, and at once you will find a donkey tied up with her colt beside her. Untie them and bring them to me. 3 And if anyone says anything, tell him, 'The Master s needs them'; and then he will let them go at once."

4 This happened in order to make what the prophet had said come true:

5 "Tell the city of Zion,

　Look, your king is coming to you!

He is humble and rides on a donkey

　and on a colt, the foal of a donkey."

6 So the disciples went and did what Jesus had told them to do: 7 they brought the donkey and the colt, threw their cloaks over them, and Jesus got on. 8 A large crowd of people spread their cloaks on the road while others cut branches from the trees and spread them on the road. 9 The crowds walking in front of Jesus and those walking behind began to shout, "Praise to David's Son! God bless him who comes in the name of the Lord! Praise God!"

10 When Jesus entered Jerusalem, the whole city was thrown into an uproar. "Who is he?" the people asked.

11 "This is the prophet Jesus, from Nazareth in Galilee," the crowds answered.

Jesus Goes to the Temple
(Mark 11.15–19; Luke 19.45–48;
John 2.13–22)

12 Jesus went into the Temple and drove out all those who were buying and selling there. He overturned the tables of the money-changers and the stools of those who sold pigeons, 13 and said to them, "It is written in the Scriptures that God said, 'My Temple will be called a house of prayer.' But you are making it a hideout for thieves!"

14 The blind and the crippled came to him in the Temple, and he healed them. 15 The chief priests and the teachers of the Law became angry when they saw the wonderful things he was doing and the children shouting in the Temple, "Praise to David's Son!" 16 So they asked Jesus, "Do you hear what they are saying?"

"Indeed I do," answered Jesus. "Haven't you ever read this scripture? 'You have trained children and babies to offer perfect praise.'"

17 Jesus left them and went out of the city to Bethany, where he spent the night.

Jesus Curses the Fig-Tree
(Mark 11.12–14, 20–24)

18 On his way back to the city early next morning, Jesus was hungry. 19 He saw a fig-tree by the side of the road and went to it, but found nothing on it except leaves. So he said to the tree, "You will never again bear fruit!" At once the fig-tree dried up.

20 The disciples saw this and were astounded. "How did the fig-tree dry up so quickly?" they asked.

21 Jesus answered, "I assure you that if you believe and do not doubt, you will be able to do what I have done to this fig-tree. And not only this, but you will even be able to say to this hill, 'Get up and throw yourself in the sea,' and it will. 22 If you believe, you will receive whatever you ask for in prayer."

The Question about Jesus' Authority
(Mark 11.27–33; Luke 20.1–8)

23 Jesus came back to the Temple; and as he taught, the chief priests and the elders came to him and asked, "What right have you to do these things? Who gave you this right?"

s The Master; or Their owner.
21.5: Zech 9.9　　**21.9:** Ps 118.25,26　　**21.13:** Is 56.7; Jer 7.11　　**21.16:** Ps 8.2
21.21: Mt 17.20; 1 Cor 13.2

24 Jesus answered them, "I will ask you just one question, and if you give me an answer, I will tell you what right I have to do these things. 25 Where did John's right to baptize come from: was it from God or from man?"

They started to argue among themselves, "What shall we say? If we answer, 'From God,' he will say to us, 'Why, then, did you not believe John?' 26 But if we say, 'From man,' we are afraid of what the people might do, because they are all convinced that John was a prophet." 27 So they answered Jesus, "We don't know."

And he said to them, "Neither will I tell you, then, by what right I do these things.

The Parable of the Two Sons

28 "Now, what do you think? There was once a man who had two sons. He went to the elder one and said, 'Son, go and work in the vineyard today.' 29 'I don't want to,' he answered, but later he changed his mind and went. 30 Then the father went to the other son and said the same thing. 'Yes, sir,' he answered, but he did not go. 31 Which one of the two did what his father wanted?"

"The elder one," they answered.

So Jesus said to them, "I tell you: the tax collectors and the prostitutes are going into the Kingdom of God ahead of you. 32 For John the Baptist came to you showing you the right path to take, and you would not believe him; but the tax collectors and the prostitutes believed him. Even when you saw this, you did not later change your minds and believe him.

The Parable of the Tenants in the Vineyard
(Mark 12.1–12; Luke 20.9–19)

33 "Listen to another parable," Jesus said. "There was once a landowner who planted a vineyard, put a fence around it, dug a hole for the winepress, and built a watch-tower. Then he let out the vineyard to tenants and went on a journey. 34 When the time came to gather the grapes, he sent his slaves to the tenants to receive his share of the harvest. 35 The tenants seized his slaves, beat one, killed another, and stoned another. 36 Again the man sent other slaves, more than the first time, and the tenants treated them the same way. 37 Last of all he sent

his son to them. 'Surely they will respect my son,' he said. 38 But when the tenants saw the son, they said to themselves, 'This is the owner's son. Come on, let's kill him, and we will get his property!' 39 So they seized him, threw him out of the vineyard, and killed him.

40 "Now, when the owner of the vineyard comes, what will he do to those tenants?" Jesus asked.

41 "He will certainly kill those evil men," they answered, "and let the vineyard out to other tenants, who will give him his share of the harvest at the right time."

42 Jesus said to them, "Haven't you ever read what the Scriptures say?

'The stone which the builders rejected
     as worthless
turned out to be the most important
     of all.

This was done by the Lord;
     what a wonderful sight it is!'

43 "And so I tell you," added Jesus, "the Kingdom of God will be taken away from you and given to a people who will produce the proper fruits." [t]

45 The chief priests and the Pharisees heard Jesus' parables and knew that he was talking about them, 46 so they tried to arrest him. But they were afraid of the crowds, who considered Jesus to be a prophet.

The Parable of the Wedding Feast
(Luke 14.15–24)

22 Jesus again used parables in talking to the people. 2 "The Kingdom of heaven is like this. Once there was a king who prepared a wedding feast for his son. 3 He sent his servants to tell the invited guests to come to the feast, but they did not want to come. 4 So he sent other servants with this message for the guests: 'My feast is ready now; my bullocks and prize calves have been butchered, and everything is ready. Come to the wedding feast!' 5 But the invited guests paid no attention and went about their business: one went to his farm, another to his shop, 6 while others grabbed the servants, beat them, and killed them. 7 The king was very angry; so he sent his soldiers, who killed those murderers and burnt down their city. 8 Then he called his servants and said to them, 'My wedding feast is ready, but the people

[t] *Some manuscripts add verse 44:* Whoever falls on this stone will be cut to pieces; and if the stone falls on someone, it will crush him to dust *(see Lk 20.18).*

21.32: Lk 3.12, 7.29-30   **21.33:** Is 5.1-2   **21.42:** Ps 118.22-23

I invited did not deserve it. 9 Now go to the main streets and invite to the feast as many people as you find.' 10 So the servants went out into the streets and gathered all the people they could find, good and bad alike; and the wedding hall was filled with people.

11 "The king went in to look at the guests and saw a man who was not wearing wedding clothes. 12 'Friend, how did you get in here without wedding clothes?' the king asked him. But the man said nothing. 13 Then the king told the servants, 'Tie him up hand and foot, and throw him outside in the dark. There he will cry and grind his teeth.'"

14 And Jesus concluded, "Many are invited, but few are chosen."

The Question about Paying Taxes
(Mark 12.13–17; Luke 20.20–26)

15 The Pharisees went off and made a plan to trap Jesus with questions. 16 Then they sent to him some of their disciples and some members of Herod's party. "Teacher," they said, "we know that you tell the truth. You teach the truth about God's will for man, without worrying about what people think, because you pay no attention to a man's status. 17 Tell us, then, what do you think? Is it against our Law to pay taxes to the Roman Emperor, or not?"

18 Jesus, however, was aware of their evil plan, and so he said, "You hypocrites! Why are you trying to trap me? 19 Show me the coin for paying the tax!"

They brought him the coin, 20 and he asked them, "Whose face and name are these?"

21 "The Emperor's," they answered.

So Jesus said to them, "Well, then, pay the Emperor what belongs to the Emperor, and pay God what belongs to God."

22 When they heard this, they were amazed; and they left him and went away.

The Question about Rising from Death
(Mark 12.18–27; Luke 20.27–40)

23 That same day some Sadducees came to Jesus and claimed that people will not rise from death. 24 "Teacher," they said, "Moses said that if a man who has no children dies, his brother must marry the widow so that they can have children who will be considered the dead man's children. 25 Now, there were seven brothers who used to live here. The eldest

got married and died without having children, so he left his widow to his brother. 26 The same thing happened to the second brother, to the third, and finally to all seven. 27 Last of all, the woman died. 28 Now, on the day when the dead rise to life, whose wife will she be? All of them had married her."

29 Jesus answered them, "How wrong you are! It is because you don't know the Scriptures or God's power. 30 For when the dead rise to life, they will be like the angels in heaven and will not marry. 31 Now, as for the dead rising to life: haven't you ever read what God has told you? He said, 32 'I am the God of Abraham, the God of Isaac, and the God of Jacob.' He is the God of the living, not of the dead."

33 When the crowds heard this, they were amazed at his teaching.

The Great Commandment
(Mark 12.28–34; Luke 10.25–28)

34 When the Pharisees heard that Jesus had silenced the Sadducees, they came together, 35 and one of them, a teacher of the Law, tried to trap him with a question. 36 "Teacher," he asked, "which is the greatest commandment in the Law?"

37 Jesus answered, " 'Love the Lord your God with all your heart, with all your soul, and with all your mind.' 38 This is the greatest and the most important commandment. 39 The second most important commandment is like it: 'Love your neighbour as you love yourself.' 40 The whole Law of Moses and the teachings of the prophets depend on these two commandments."

The Question about the Messiah
(Mark 12.35–37; Luke 20.41–44)

41 When some Pharisees gathered together, Jesus asked them, 42 "What do you think about the Messiah? Whose descendant is he?"

"He is David's descendant," they answered.

43 "Why, then," Jesus asked, "did the Spirit inspire David to call him 'Lord'? David said,

44 'The Lord said to my Lord:
    Sit here on my right
    until I put your enemies under your
        feet.'

45 If, then, David called him 'Lord,' how

22.13: Mt 8.12, 25.30; Lk 13.28   22.23: Acts 23.8   22.24: Deut 25.5   22.32: Ex 3.6
22.35–40: Lk 10.25–28   22.37: Deut 6.5   22.39: Lev 19.18   22.44: Ps 110.1

can the Messiah be David's descendant?"

46 No one was able to give Jesus any answer, and from that day on no one dared to ask him any more questions.

Jesus Warns against the Teachers of the Law and the Pharisees
(Mark 12.38–39; Luke 11.43, 46; 20.45–46)

23 Then Jesus spoke to the crowds and to his disciples. ² "The teachers of the Law and the Pharisees are the authorized interpreters of Moses' Law. ³ So you must obey and follow everything they tell you to do; do not, however, imitate their actions, because they don't practise what they preach. ⁴ They tie on

They aren't willing...to help them (23.4)

to people's backs loads that are heavy and hard to carry, yet they aren't willing even to lift a finger to help them carry those loads. ⁵ They do everything so that people will see them. Look at the straps with scripture verses on them which they wear on their foreheads and arms, and notice how large they are! Notice also how long are the tassels on their cloaks!ᵘ ⁶ They love the best places at feasts and the reserved seats in the synagogues; ⁷ they love to be greeted with respect in the market-places and to be called 'Teacher.' ⁸ You must not be called 'Teacher', because you are all brothers

of one another and have only one Teacher. ⁹ And you must not call anyone here on earth 'Father', because you have only the one Father in heaven. ¹⁰ Nor should you be called 'Leader', because your one and only leader is the Messiah. ¹¹ The greatest one among you must be your servant. ¹² Whoever makes himself great will be humbled, and whoever humbles himself will be made great.

Jesus Condemns Their Hypocrisy
(Mark 12.40; Luke 11.39–42, 44, 52; 20.47)

13 "How terrible for you, teachers of the Law and Pharisees! You hypocrites! You lock the door to the Kingdom of heaven in people's faces, and you yourselves don't go in, nor do you allow in those who are trying to enter!ᵛ

15 "How terrible for you, teachers of the Law and Pharisees! You hypocrites! You sail the seas and cross whole countries to win one convert; and when you succeed, you make him twice as deserving of going to hell as you yourselves are!

16 "How terrible for you, blind guides!

How terrible for you, blind guides! (23.16)

You teach, 'If someone swears by the Temple, he isn't bound by his vow; but if he swears by the gold in the Temple, he is bound.' ¹⁷ Blind fools! Which is more important, the gold or the Temple which

---

ᵘ TASSELS ON THEIR CLOAKS: *These tassels were worn as a sign of devotion to God (see Num 15.37-41).*
ᵛ *Some manuscripts add verse 14:* How terrible for you, teachers of the Law and Pharisees! You hypocrites! You take advantage of widows and rob them of their homes, and then make a show of saying long prayers! Because of this your punishment will be all the worse! *(see Mk 12.40).*
23.5: Mt 6.1; Num 15.38; Deut 6.8   **23.11:** Mt 20.26-27; Mk 9.35, 10.43-44; Lk 22.26
23.12: Lk 14.11, 18.14

makes the gold holy? [18] You also teach, 'If someone swears by the altar, he isn't bound by his vow; but if he swears by the gift on the altar, he is bound.' [19] How blind you are! Which is the more important, the gift or the altar which makes the gift holy? [20] So then, when a person swears by the altar, he is swearing by it and by all the gifts on it; [21] and when he swears by the Temple, he is swearing by it and by God, who lives there; [22] and when someone swears by heaven, he is swearing by God's throne and by him who sits on it.

23 "How terrible for you, teachers of the Law and Pharisees! You hypocrites! You give to God a tenth even of the seasoning herbs, such as mint, dill, and cumin, but you neglect to obey the really important teachings of the Law, such as justice and mercy and honesty. These you should practise, without neglecting the others. [24] Blind guides! You strain a fly out of your drink, but swallow a camel!

25 "How terrible for you, teachers of the Law and Pharisees! You hypocrites! You clean the outside of your cup and plate, while the inside is full of what you have obtained by violence and selfishness. [26] Blind Pharisee! Clean what is inside the cup first, and then the outside will be clean too!

27 "How terrible for you, teachers of the Law and Pharisees! You hypocrites! You are like whitewashed tombs, which look fine on the outside but are full of bones and decaying corpses on the inside. [28] In the same way, on the outside you appear good to everybody, but inside you are full of hypocrisy and sins.

Jesus Predicts Their Punishment
(Luke 11.47-51)

29 "How terrible for you, teachers of the Law and Pharisees! You hypocrites! You make fine tombs for the prophets and decorate the monuments of those who lived good lives; [30] and you claim that if you had lived during the time of your ancestors, you would not have done what they did and killed the prophets. [31] So you actually admit that you are the descendants of those who murdered the prophets! [32] Go on, then, and finish what your ancestors started! [33] You snakes and sons of snakes! How do you expect to escape from being condemned to hell? [34] And so I tell you that I will send you prophets

and wise men and teachers; you will kill some of them, crucify others, and whip others in the synagogues and chase them from town to town. [35] As a result, the punishment for the murder of all innocent men will fall on you, from the murder of innocent Abel to the murder of Zachariah son of Berachiah, whom you murdered between the Temple and the altar. [36] I tell you indeed: the punishment for all these murders will fall on the people of this day!

Jesus' Love for Jerusalem
(Luke 13.34-35)

37 "Jerusalem, Jerusalem! You kill the prophets and stone the messengers God has sent you! How many times have I wanted to put my arms round all your people, just as a hen gathers her chicks under her wings, but you would not let me! [38] And so your Temple will be abandoned and empty. [39] From now on, I tell you, you will never see me again until you say, 'God bless him who comes in the name of the Lord.' "

Jesus Speaks of the Destruction of the Temple
(Mark 13.1-2; Luke 21.5-6)

24 Jesus left and was going away from the Temple when his disciples came to him to call his attention to its buildings. [2] "Yes," he said, "you may well look at all these. I tell you this: not a single stone here will be left in its place; every one of them will be thrown down."

Troubles and Persecutions
(Mark 13.3-13; Luke 21.7-19)

3 As Jesus sat on the Mount of Olives, the disciples came to him in private. "Tell us when all this will be," they asked, "and what will happen to show that it is the time for your coming and the end of the age."

4 Jesus answered, "Be on your guard, and do not let anyone deceive you. [5] Many men, claiming to speak for me, will come and say, 'I am the Messiah!' and they will deceive many people. [6] You are going to hear the noise of battles close by and the news of battles far away; but do not be troubled. Such things must happen, but they do not mean that the end has come. [7] Countries will fight each other, kingdoms will attack one another. There will be famines and earthquakes everywhere.

23.22: Is 66.1; Mt 5.34　　**23.23:** Lev 27.30　　**23.27:** Acts 23.3　　**23.33:** Mt 3.7, 12.34; Lk 3.7
23.35: Gen 4.8; 2 Chr 24.20-21　　**23.38:** Jer 22.5　　**23.39:** Ps 118.26

8 All these things are like the first pains of childbirth.

9 "Then you will be arrested and handed over to be punished and be put to death. All mankind will hate you because of me. 10 Many will give up their faith at that time; they will betray one another and hate one another. 11 Then many false prophets will appear and deceive many people. 12 Such will be the spread of evil that many people's love will grow cold. 13 But whoever holds out to the end will be saved. 14 And this Good News about the Kingdom will be preached through all the world for a witness to all mankind; and then the end will come.

The Awful Horror
(Mark 13.14-23; Luke 21.20-24)

15 "You will see 'The Awful Horror' of which the prophet Daniel spoke. It will be standing in the holy place." (Note to the reader: understand what this means!) 16 "Then those who are in Judaea must run away to the hills. 17 A man who is on the roof of his house must not take the time to go down and get his belongings from the house. 18 A man who is in the field must not go back to get his cloak. 19 How terrible it will be in those days for women who are pregnant and for mothers with little babies! 20 Pray to God that you will not have to run away during the winter or on a Sabbath! 21 For the trouble at that time will be far more terrible than any there has ever been, from the beginning of the world to this very day. Nor will there ever be anything like it again. 22 But God has already reduced the number of days; had he not done so, nobody would survive. For the sake of his chosen people, however, God will reduce the days.

23 "Then, if anyone says to you, 'Look, here is the Messiah!' or 'There he is!'—do not believe him. 24 For false Messiahs and false prophets will appear; they will perform great miracles and wonders in order to deceive even God's chosen people, if possible. 25 Listen! I have told you this before the time comes.

26 "Or, if people should tell you, 'Look, he is out in the desert!'—don't go there; or if they say, 'Look, he is hiding here!'— don't believe it. 27 For the Son of Man will come like the lightning which flashes across the whole sky from the east to the west.

28 "Wherever there is a dead body, the vultures will gather.

The Coming of the Son of Man
(Mark 13.24-27; Luke 21.25-28)

29 "Soon after the trouble of those days, the sun will grow dark, the moon will no longer shine, the stars will fall from heaven, and the powers in space will be driven from their courses. 30 Then the sign of the Son of Man will appear in the sky; and all the peoples of earth will weep as they see the Son of Man coming on the clouds of heaven with power and great glory. 31 The great trumpet will sound, and he will send out his angels to the four corners of the earth, and they will gather his chosen people from one end of the world to the other.

The Lesson of the Fig-Tree
(Mark 13.28-31; Luke 21.29-33)

32 "Let the fig-tree teach you a lesson. When its branches become green and tender and it starts putting out leaves, you know that summer is near. 33 In the same way, when you see all these things, you will know that the time is near, ready to begin. w 34 Remember that all these things will happen before the people now living have all died. 35 Heaven and earth will pass away, but my words will never pass away.

No One Knows the Day and Hour
(Mark 13.32-37; Luke 17.26-30, 34-36)

36 "No one knows, however, when that day and hour will come—neither the angels in heaven nor the Son; x the Father alone knows. 37 The coming of the Son of Man will be like what happened in the time of Noah. 38 In the days before the flood people ate and drank, men and women married, up to the very day Noah went into the boat; 39 yet they did not realize what was happening until the flood came and swept them all away. That is how it will be when the Son of Man comes. 40 At that time two men will be working in a field: one will be taken away, the other will be left behind. 41 Two women will be at a mill grinding meal: one will

---

w the time is near, ready to begin; or he is near, ready to come.
x Some manuscripts do not have nor the Son.
24.9: Mt 10.22   **24.13:** Mt 10.22   **24.15:** Dan 9.27, 11.31, 12.11   **24.17-18:** Lk 17.31
24.21: Dan 12.1; Rev 7.14   **24.26-27:** Lk 17.23-24   **24.28:** Lk 17.37
24.29: Is 13.10, 34.4; Ezek 32.7; Joel 2.10,31, 3.15; Rev 6.12-13
24.30: Dan 7.13; Zech 12.10-14; Rev 1.7   **24.37:** Gen 6.5-8   **24.39:** Gen 7.6-24

be taken away, the other will be left behind.

42 "Be on your guard, then, because you do not know what day your Lord will come. 43 If the owner of a house knew the time when the thief would come, you can be sure that he would stay awake and not let the thief break into his house. 44 So then, you also must always be ready, because the Son of Man will come at an hour when you are not expecting him.

The Faithful or the Unfaithful Servant
(Luke 12.41-48)

45 "Who, then, is a faithful and wise servant? He is the one that his master has placed in charge of the other servants to give them their food at the proper time. 46 How happy that servant is if his master finds him doing this when he comes home! 47 Indeed, I tell you, the master will put that servant in charge of all his property. 48 But if he is a bad servant, he will tell himself that his master will not come back for a long time, 49 and he will begin to beat his fellow-servants and to eat and drink with drunkards. 50 Then that servant's master will come back one day when the servant does not expect him and at a time he does not know. 51 The master will cut him in pieces^y and make him share the fate of the hypocrites. There he will cry and grind his teeth.

The Parable of the Ten Girls

25 "At that time the Kingdom of heaven will be like this. Once there were ten girls who took their oil lamps and went out to meet the bridegroom. 2 Five of them were foolish, and the other five were wise. 3 The foolish ones took their lamps but did not take any extra oil with them, 4 while the wise ones took containers full of oil for their lamps. 5 The bridegroom was late in coming, so the girls began to nod and fall asleep.

6 "It was already midnight when the cry rang out, 'Here is the bridegroom! Come and meet him!' 7 The ten girls woke up and trimmed their lamps. 8 Then the foolish ones said to the wise ones, 'Let us have some of your oil, because our lamps are going out.' 9 'No, indeed,' the wise ones answered, 'there is not enough for you and for us. Go to the shop and buy some for yourselves.' 10 So the foolish girls went off to buy some oil; and while they were gone, the bridegroom arrived.

The five girls who were ready went in with him to the wedding feast, and the door was closed.

11 "Later the other girls arrived. 'Sir, sir! Let us in!' they cried out. 12 'Certainly not! I don't know you,' the bridegroom answered."

13 And Jesus concluded, "Be on your guard, then, because you do not know the day or the hour.

The Parable of the Three Servants
(Luke 19.11-27)

14 "At that time the Kingdom of heaven will be like this. Once there was a man who was about to go on a journey; he called his servants and put them in charge of his property. 15 He gave to each one according to his ability: to one he gave five thousand gold coins, to another he gave two thousand, and to another he gave one thousand. Then he left on his journey. 16 The servant who had received five thousand coins went at once and invested his money and earned another five thousand. 17 In the same way the servant who had received two thousand coins earned another two thousand. 18 But the servant who had received one thousand coins went off, dug a hole in the ground, and hid his master's money.

19 "After a long time the master of those servants came back and settled accounts with them. 20 The servant who had received five thousand coins came in and handed over the other five thousand. 'You gave me five thousand coins, sir,' he said. 'Look! Here are another five thousand that I have earned.' 21 'Well done, you good and faithful servant!' said his master. 'You have been faithful in managing small amounts, so I will put you in charge of large amounts. Come on in and share my happiness!'

22 "Then the servant who had been given two thousand coins came in and said, 'You gave me two thousand coins, sir. Look! Here are another two thousand that I have earned.' 23 'Well done, you good and faithful servant!' said his master. 'You have been faithful in managing small amounts, so I will put you in charge of large amounts. Come on in and share my happiness!'

24 "Then the servant who had received one thousand coins came in and said, 'Sir, I know you are a hard man; you reap harvests where you did not sow, and you

^{y} cut him in pieces; *or* throw him out.
24.43-44: Lk 12.39-40   **25.1:** Lk 12.35   **25.11-12:** Lk 13.25   **25.14-30:** Lk 19.11-27

gather crops where you did not scatter seed. ²⁵ I was afraid, so I went off and hid your money in the ground. Look! Here is what belongs to you.'

26 " 'You bad and lazy servant!' his master said. 'You knew, did you, that I reap harvests where I did not sow, and gather crops where I did not scatter seed? ²⁷ Well, then, you should have deposited my money in the bank, and I would have received it all back with interest when I returned. ²⁸ Now, take the money away from him and give it to the one who has ten thousand coins. ²⁹ For to every person who has something, even more will be given, and he will have more than enough; but the person who has nothing, even the little that he has will be taken away from him. ³⁰ As for this useless servant—throw him outside in the darkness; there he will cry and grind his teeth.'

The Final Judgement

31 "When the Son of Man comes as King and all the angels with him, he will sit on his royal throne, ³² and the people of all the nations will be gathered before him. Then he will divide them into two groups, just as a shepherd separates the sheep from the goats. ³³ He will put the righteous people on his right and the others on his left. ³⁴ Then the King will say to the people on his right, 'Come, you that are blessed by my Father! Come and possess the kingdom which has been prepared for you ever since the creation of the world. ³⁵ I was hungry and you fed me, thirsty and you gave me a drink; I was a stranger and you received me in your homes, ³⁶ naked and you clothed me; I was sick and you took care of me, in prison and you visited me.'

37 "The righteous will then answer him, 'When, Lord, did we ever see you hungry and feed you, or thirsty and give you a drink? ³⁸ When did we ever see you a stranger and welcome you in our homes, or naked and clothe you? ³⁹ When did we ever see you sick or in prison, and visit you?' ⁴⁰ The King will reply, 'I tell you, whenever you did this for one of the least important of these brothers of mine, you did it for me!'

41 "Then he will say to those on his left, 'Away from me, you that are under God's curse! Away to the eternal fire which has been prepared for the Devil and his angels! ⁴² I was hungry but you would not feed me, thirsty but you would not give me a drink; ⁴³ I was a stranger but you would not welcome me in your homes, naked but you would not clothe me; I was sick and in prison but you would not take care of me.'

44 "Then they will answer him, 'When Lord, did we ever see you hungry or thirsty or a stranger or naked or sick or in prison, and would not help you?' ⁴⁵ The King will reply, 'I tell you, whenever you refused to help one of these least important ones, you refused to help me.' ⁴⁶ These, then, will be sent off to eternal punishment, but the righteous will go to eternal life."

The Plot against Jesus
(Mark 14.1–2; Luke 22.1–2; John 11.45–53)

26 When Jesus had finished teaching all these things, he said to his disciples, ² "In two days, as you know, it will be the Passover Festival, and the Son of Man will be handed over to be crucified."

3 Then the chief priests and the elders met together in the palace of Caiaphas, the High Priest, ⁴ and made plans to arrest Jesus secretly and put him to death. ⁵ "We must not do it during the festival," they said, "or the people will riot."

Jesus Is Anointed at Bethany
(Mark 14.3–9; John 12.1–8)

6 Jesus was in Bethany at the house of Simon, a man who had suffered from a dreaded skin-disease. ⁷ While Jesus was eating, a woman came to him with an alabaster jar filled with an expensive perfume, which she poured on his head. ⁸ The disciples saw this and became angry. "Why all this waste?" they asked. ⁹ "This perfume could have been sold for a large amount and the money given to the poor!"

10 Jesus knew what they were saying, so he said to them, "Why are you bothering this woman? It is a fine and beautiful thing that she has done for me. ¹¹ You will always have poor people with you, but you will not always have me. ¹² What she did was to pour this perfume on my body to get me ready for burial. ¹³ Now, I assure you that wherever this gospel is preached all over the world, what she has done will be told in memory of her."

25.29: Mt 13.12; Mk 4.25; Lk 8.18　　**25.30:** Mt 8.12, 22.13; Lk 13.28　　**25.31:** Mt 16.27, 19.28
25.46: Dan 12.2　　**26.2:** Ex 12.1–27　　**26.7:** Lk 7.37–38　　**26.11:** Deut 15.11

Thirty silver coins (26.15)

Judas Agrees to Betray Jesus
(Mark 14.10-11; Luke 22.3-6)

14 Then one of the twelve disciples—the one named Judas Iscariot—went to the chief priests 15 and asked, "What will you give me if I betray Jesus to you?" They counted out thirty silver coins and gave them to him. 16 From then on Judas was looking for a good chance to hand Jesus over to them.

Jesus Eats the Passover Meal with His Disciples
(Mark 14.12-21; Luke 22.7-13, 21-23; John 13.21-30)

17 On the first day of the Festival of Unleavened Bread the disciples came to Jesus and asked him, "Where do you want us to get the Passover meal ready for you?"

18 "Go to a certain man in the city," he said to them, "and tell him: 'The Teacher says, My hour has come; my disciples and I will celebrate the Passover at your house.'"

19 The disciples did as Jesus had told them and prepared the Passover meal.

20 When it was evening, Jesus and the twelve disciples sat down to eat. 21 During the meal Jesus said, "I tell you, one of you will betray me."

22 The disciples were very upset and began to ask him, one after the other, "Surely, Lord, you don't mean me?"

23 Jesus answered, "One who dips his bread in the dish with me will betray me. 24 The Son of Man will die as the Scriptures say he will, but how terrible for that man who betrays the Son of Man! It would have been better for that man if he had never been born!"

25 Judas, the traitor, spoke up. "Surely, Teacher, you don't mean me?" he asked.

Jesus answered, "So you say."

The Lord's Supper
(Mark 14.22-26; Luke 22.14-20; 1 Cor. 11.23-25)

26 While they were eating, Jesus took a piece of bread, gave a prayer of thanks, broke it, and gave it to his disciples. "Take and eat it," he said; "this is my body."

27 Then he took a cup, gave thanks to God, and gave it to them. "Drink it, all of you," he said; 28 "this is my blood, which seals God's covenant, my blood poured out for many for the forgiveness of sins. 29 I tell you, I will never again drink this wine until the day I drink the new wine with you in my Father's Kingdom."

30 Then they sang a hymn and went out to the Mount of Olives.

Jesus Predicts Peter's Denial
(Mark 14.27-31; Luke 22.31-34; John 13.36-38)

31 Then Jesus said to them, "This very night all of you will run away and leave me, for the scripture says, 'God will kill the shepherd, and the sheep of the flock will be scattered.' 32 But after I am raised to life, I will go to Galilee ahead of you."

33 Peter spoke up and said to Jesus, "I will never leave you, even though all the rest do!"

34 Jesus said to Peter, "I tell you that before the cock crows tonight, you will say three times that you do not know me."

35 Peter answered, "I will never say that, even if I have to die with you!"

And all the other disciples said the same thing.

Jesus Prays in Gethsemane
(Mark 14.32-42; Luke 22.39-46)

36 Then Jesus went with his disciples to a place called Gethsemane, and he said to them, "Sit here while I go over there and pray." 37 He took with him Peter and the two sons of Zebedee. Grief and anguish came over him, 38 and he said to them, "The sorrow in my heart is so great that it almost crushes me. Stay here and keep watch with me."

26.15: Zech 11.12   **26.23:** Ps 41.9   **26.28:** Ex 24.8; Jer 31.31-34   **26.31:** Zech 13.7
26.32: Mt 28.16

Take this cup of suffering from me! (26.39)

39 He went a little farther on, threw himself face downwards on the ground, and prayed, "My Father, if it is possible, take this cup of suffering from me! Yet not what I want, but what you want."

40 Then he returned to the three disciples and found them asleep; and he said to Peter, "How is it that you three were not able to keep watch with me even for one hour? 41 Keep watch and pray that you will not fall into temptation. The spirit is willing, but the flesh is weak."

42 Once more Jesus went away and prayed, "My Father, if this cup of suffering cannot be taken away unless I drink it, your will be done." 43 He returned once more and found the disciples asleep; they could not keep their eyes open.

44 Again Jesus left them, went away, and prayed the third time, saying the same words. 45 Then he returned to the disciples and said, "Are you still sleeping and resting? Look! The hour has come for the Son of Man to be handed over to the power of sinful men. 46 Get up, let us go. Look, here is the man who is betraying me!"

The Arrest of Jesus
(Mark 14.43–50; Luke 22.47–53; John 18.3–12)

47 Jesus was still speaking when Judas, one of the twelve disciples, arrived. With him was a large crowd armed with swords and clubs and sent by the chief priests and the elders. 48 The traitor had given the crowd a signal: "The man I kiss is the one you want. Arrest him!"

49 Judas went straight to Jesus and said, "Peace be with you, Teacher," and kissed him.

50 Jesus answered, "Be quick about it, friend!" z

Then they came up, arrested Jesus, and held him tight. 51 One of those who were with Jesus drew his sword and struck at the High Priest's slave, cutting off his ear. 52 "Put your sword back in its place," Jesus said to him. "All who take the sword will die by the sword. 53 Don't you know that I could call on my Father for help, and at once he would send me more than twelve armies of angels? 54 But in that case, how could the Scriptures come true which say that this is what must happen?"

55 Then Jesus spoke to the crowd, "Did you have to come with swords and clubs to capture me, as though I were an outlaw? Every day I sat down and taught in the Temple, and you did not arrest me. 56 But all this has happened in order to make what the prophets wrote in the Scriptures come true."

Then all the disciples left him and ran away.

Jesus Before the Council
(Mark 14.53–65; Luke 22.54–55, 63–71; John 18.13–14, 19–24)

57 Those who had arrested Jesus took him to the house of Caiaphas, the High Priest, where the teachers of the Law and the elders had gathered together. 58 Peter followed from a distance, as far as the

z Be quick about it, friend! *or* Why are you here, friend?
26.55: Lk 19.47, 21.37

courtyard of the High Priest's house. He went into the courtyard and sat down with the guards to see how it would all come out. 59 The chief priests and the whole Council tried to find some false evidence against Jesus to put him to death; 60 but they could not find any, even though many people came forward and told lies about him. Finally two men stepped up 61 and said, "This man said, 'I am able to tear down God's Temple and three days later build it up again.'"

62 The High Priest stood up and said to Jesus, "Have you no answer to give to this accusation against you?" 63 But Jesus kept quiet. Again the High Priest spoke to him, "In the name of the living God I now put you on oath: tell us if you are the Messiah, the Son of God."

64 Jesus answered him, "So you say. But I tell all of you: from this time on you will see the Son of Man sitting on the right of the Almighty and coming on the clouds of heaven!"

65 At this the High Priest tore his clothes and said, "Blasphemy! We don't need any more witnesses! You have just heard his blasphemy! 66 What do you think?"

They answered, "He is guilty and must die."

67 Then they spat in his face and beat him; and those who slapped him 68 said, "Prophesy for us, Messiah! Guess who hit you!"

Peter Denies Jesus
(Mark 14.66–72; Luke 22.56–62; John 18.15–18, 25–27)

69 Peter was sitting outside in the courtyard when one of the High Priest's servant-girls came to him and said, "You, too, were with Jesus of Galilee."

70 But he denied it in front of them all. "I don't know what you are talking about," he answered, 71 and went on out to the entrance of the courtyard. Another servant-girl saw him and said to the men there, "He was with Jesus of Nazareth."

72 Again Peter denied it and answered, "I swear that I don't know that man!"

73 After a little while the men standing there came to Peter. "Of course you are one of them," they said. "After all, the way you speak gives you away!"

74 Then Peter said, "I swear that I am telling the truth! May God punish me if I am not! I do not know that man!"

Just then a cock crowed, 75 and Peter remembered what Jesus had told him: "Before the cock crows, you will say three times that you do not know me." He went out and wept bitterly.

Jesus Is Taken to Pilate
(Mark 15.1; Luke 23.1–2; John 18.28–32)

27 Early in the morning all the chief priests and the elders made their plans against Jesus to put him to death. 2 They put him in chains, led him off, and handed him over to Pilate, the Roman governor.

The Death of Judas
(Acts 1.18–19)

3 When Judas, the traitor, learnt that Jesus had been condemned, he repented and took back the thirty silver coins to the chief priests and the elders. 4 "I have sinned by betraying an innocent man to death!" he said.

"What do we care about that?" they answered. "That is your business!"

5 Judas threw the coins down in the Temple and left; then he went off and hanged himself.

6 The chief priests picked up the coins and said, "This is blood money, and it is against our Law to put it in the temple treasury." 7 After reaching an agreement about it, they used the money to buy Potter's Field, as a cemetery for foreigners. 8 That is why that field is called "Field of Blood" to this very day.

9 Then what the prophet Jeremiah had said came true: "They took the thirty silver coins, the amount the people of Israel had agreed to pay for him, 10 and used the money to buy the potter's field, as the Lord had commanded me."

Pilate Questions Jesus
(Mark 15.2–5; Luke 23.3–5; John 18.33–38)

11 Jesus stood before the Roman governor, who questioned him. "Are you the king of the Jews?" he asked.

"So you say," answered Jesus. 12 But he said nothing in response to the accusations of the chief priests and elders.

13 So Pilate said to him, "Don't you hear all these things they accuse you of?"

14 But Jesus refused to answer a single word, with the result that the Governor was greatly surprised.

26.61: Jn 2.19   **26.64:** Dan 7.13   **26.65–66:** Lev 24.16   **26.67:** Is 50.6
27.3–8: Acts 1.18–19   **27.9–10:** Zech 11.12–13

Jesus Is Sentenced to Death
(Mark 15.6–15; Luke 23.13–25;
John 18.39–19.16)

15 At every Passover Festival the Roman governor was in the habit of setting free any one prisoner the crowd asked for. [16] At that time there was a well-known prisoner named Jesus Barabbas. [17] So when the crowd gathered, Pilate asked them, "Which one do you want me to set free for you? Jesus Barabbas or Jesus called the Messiah?" [18] He knew very well that the Jewish authorities had handed Jesus over to him because they were jealous.

19 While Pilate was sitting in the judgement hall, his wife sent him a message: "Have nothing to do with that innocent man, because in a dream last night I suffered much on account of him."

20 The chief priests and the elders persuaded the crowd to ask Pilate to set Barabbas free and have Jesus put to death. [21] But Pilate asked the crowd, "Which one of these two do you want me to set free for you?"

"Barabbas!" they answered.

22 "What, then, shall I do with Jesus called the Messiah?" Pilate asked them.

"Crucify him!" they all answered.

23 But Pilate asked, "What crime has he committed?"

Then they started shouting at the top of their voices: "Crucify him!"

24 When Pilate saw that it was no use to go on, but that a riot might break out, he took some water, washed his hands in front of the crowd, and said, "I am not responsible for the death of this man! This is your doing!"

25 The whole crowd answered, "Let the responsibility for his death fall on us and our children!"

26 Then Pilate set Barabbas free for them; and after he had Jesus whipped, he handed him over to be crucified.

The Soldiers Mock Jesus
(Mark 15.16–20; John 19.2–3)

27 Then Pilate's soldiers took Jesus into the governor's palace, and the whole company gathered round him. [28] They stripped off his clothes and put a scarlet robe on him. [29] Then they made a crown out of thorny branches and placed it on his head, and put a stick in his right hand; then they knelt before him and mocked him. "Long live the King of the Jews!" they said. [30] They spat on him, and took the stick and hit him over the head. [31] When they had finished mocking him, they took the robe off and put his own clothes back on him. Then they led him out to crucify him.

Jesus Is Crucified
(Mark 15.21–32; Luke 23.26–43;
John 19.17–27)

32 As they were going out, they met a man from Cyrene named Simon, and the soldiers forced him to carry Jesus' cross. [33] They came to a place called Golgotha, which means, "The Place of the Skull." [34] There they offered Jesus wine mixed with a bitter substance; but after tasting it, he would not drink it.

35 They crucified him and then divided his clothes among them by throwing dice. [36] After that they sat there and watched him. [37] Above his head they put the written notice of the accusation against him: "This is Jesus, the King of the Jews." [38] Then they crucified two bandits with Jesus, one on his right and the other on his left.

39 People passing by shook their heads and hurled insults at Jesus: [40] "You were going to tear down the Temple and build it up again in three days! Save yourself if you are God's Son! Come on down from the cross!"

41 In the same way the chief priests and the teachers of the Law and the elders jeered at him: [42] "He saved others, but he cannot save himself! Isn't he the king of Israel? If he comes down off the cross now, we will believe in him! [43] He trusts in God and claims to be God's Son. Well, then, let us see if God wants to save him now!"

44 Even the bandits who had been crucified with him insulted him in the same way.

The Death of Jesus
(Mark 15.33–41; Luke 23.44–49;
John 19.28–30)

45 At noon the whole country was covered with darkness, which lasted for three hours. [46] At about three o'clock Jesus cried out with a loud shout, "*Eli, Eli, lema sabachthani?*" which means, "My God, my God, why did you abandon me?"

47 Some of the people standing there

27.24: Deut 21.6-9   **27.34:** Ps 69.21   **27.35:** Ps 22.18   **27.39:** Ps 22.7, 109.25
27.40: Mt 26.61; Jn 2.19   **27.43:** Ps 22.8   **27.46:** Ps 22.1

heard him and said, "He is calling for Elijah!" 48 One of them ran up at once, took a sponge, soaked it in cheap wine, put it on the end of a stick, and tried to make him drink it.

49 But the others said, "Wait, let us see if Elijah is coming to save him!"

50 Jesus again gave a loud cry and breathed his last.

51 Then the curtain hanging in the Temple was torn in two from top to bottom. The earth shook, the rocks split apart, 52 the graves broke open, and many of God's people who had died were raised to life. 53 They left the graves, and after Jesus rose from death, they went into the Holy City, where many people saw them.

54 When the army officer and the soldiers with him who were watching Jesus saw the earthquake and everything else that happened, they were terrified and said, "He really was the Son of God!"

55 There were many women there, looking on from a distance, who had followed Jesus from Galilee and helped him. 56 Among them were Mary Magdalene, Mary the mother of James and Joseph, and the wife of Zebedee.

The Burial of Jesus
(Mark 15.42–47; Luke 23.50–56;
John 19.38–42)

57 When it was evening, a rich man from Arimathea arrived; his name was Joseph, and he also was a disciple of Jesus. 58 He went into the presence of Pilate and asked for the body of Jesus. Pilate gave orders for the body to be given to Joseph. 59 So Joseph took it, wrapped it in a new linen sheet, 60 and placed it in his own tomb, which he had just recently dug out of solid rock. Then he rolled a large stone across the entrance to the tomb and went away. 61 Mary Magdalene and the other Mary were sitting there, facing the tomb.

The Guard at the Tomb

62 The next day, which was a Sabbath, the chief priests and the Pharisees met with Pilate 63 and said, "Sir, we remember that while that liar was still alive he said, 'I will be raised to life three days later.' 64 Give orders, then, for his tomb to be carefully guarded until the third day, so that his disciples will not be able to go and steal the body, and then tell the people

that he was raised from death. This last lie would be even worse than the first one."

65 "Take a guard," Pilate told them; "go and make the tomb as secure as you can."

66 So they left and made the tomb secure by putting a seal on the stone and leaving the guard on watch.

The Resurrection
(Mark 16.1–10; Luke 24.1–12; John 20.1–10)

28 After the Sabbath, as Sunday morning was dawning, Mary Magdalene and the other Mary went to look at the tomb. 2 Suddenly there was a violent earthquake; an angel of the Lord came down from heaven, rolled the stone away, and sat on it. 3 His appearance was like lightning, and his clothes were white as snow. 4 The guards were so afraid that they trembled and became like dead men.

5 The angel spoke to the women. "You must not be afraid," he said. "I know you are looking for Jesus, who was crucified. 6 He is not here; he has been raised, just as he said. Come here and see the place where he was lying. 7 Go quickly now, and tell his disciples, 'He has been raised from death, and now he is going to Galilee ahead of you; there you will see him!' Remember what I have told you."

8 So they left the tomb in a hurry, afraid and yet filled with joy, and ran to tell his disciples.

9 Suddenly Jesus met them and said, "Peace be with you." They came up to him, took hold of his feet, and worshipped him. 10 "Do not be afraid," Jesus said to them. "Go and tell my brothers to go to Galilee, and there they will see me."

The Report of the Guard

11 While the women went on their way, some of the soldiers guarding the tomb went back to the city and told the chief priests everything that had happened. 12 The chief priests met with the elders and made their plan; they gave a large sum of money to the soldiers 13 and said, "You are to say that his disciples came during the night and stole his body while you were asleep. 14 And if the Governor should hear of this, we will convince him that you are innocent, and you will have nothing to worry about."

15 The guards took the money and did what they were told to do. And so that

27.48: Ps 69.21   **27.51:** Ex 26.31–33   **27.55–56:** Lk 8.2–3
27.63: Mt 16.21, 17.23, 20.19; Mk 8.31, 9.31, 10.33–34; Lk 9.22, 18.31–33

is the report spread round by the Jews to this very day.

Jesus Appears to His Disciples
(Mark 16.14–18; Luke 24.36–49;
John 20.19–23; Acts 1.6–8)

16 The eleven disciples went to the hill in Galilee where Jesus had told them to go. ¹⁷When they saw him, they worshipped him, even though some of them doubted. ¹⁸Jesus drew near and said to them, "I have been given all authority in heaven and on earth. ¹⁹Go, then, to all peoples everywhere and make them my disciples: baptize them in the name of the Father, the Son, and the Holy Spirit, ²⁰and teach them to obey everything I have commanded you. And I will be with you always, to the end of the age."

28.16: Mt 26.32; Mk 14.28   **28.19:** Acts 1.8

THE GOSPEL ACCORDING TO

MARK

INTRODUCTION

The Gospel according to Mark begins with the statement that it is "the Good News about Jesus Christ, the Son of God." Jesus is pictured as a man of action and authority. His authority is seen in his teaching, in his power over demons, and in forgiving people's sins. Jesus speaks of himself as the Son of Man, who came to give his life to set people free from sin.

Mark presents the story of Jesus in a straightforward, vigorous way, with emphasis on what Jesus did, rather than on his words and teachings. After a brief prologue about John the Baptist and the baptism and temptation of Jesus, the writer immediately takes up Jesus' ministry of healing and teaching. As time goes on, the followers of Jesus come to understand him better, but Jesus' opponents become more hostile. The closing chapters report the events of Jesus' last week of earthly life, especially his crucifixion and resurrection.

The two endings to the Gospel, which are enclosed in brackets, are generally regarded as written by someone other than the author of *Mark*.

Outline of Contents
The beginning of the gospel   1.1–13
Jesus' public ministry in Galilee   1.14—9.50
From Galilee to Jerusalem   10.1–52
The last week in and near Jerusalem   11.1—15.47
The resurrection of Jesus   16.1–8
The appearances and ascension of the risen Lord   16.9–20

At once they left their nets (1.18)

The Preaching of John the Baptist
(Matt. 3.1–12; Luke 3.1–18; John 1.19–28)

1 This is the Good News about Jesus Christ, the Son of God.[a] 2 It began as the prophet Isaiah had written:
"God said, 'I will send my messenger
   ahead of you
to clear the way for you.'
3 Someone is shouting in the desert,
   'Get the road ready for the Lord;
   make a straight path for him to
      travel!'"
4 So John appeared in the desert, baptizing and preaching.[b] "Turn away from your sins and be baptized," he told the people, "and God will forgive your sins." 5 Many people from the province of Judaea and the city of Jerusalem went out to hear John. They confessed their sins, and he baptized them in the River Jordan.
6 John wore clothes made of camel's hair, with a leather belt round his waist, and his food was locusts and wild honey. 7 He announced to the people, "The man who will come after me is much greater than I am. I am not good enough even to bend down and untie his sandals. 8 I baptize you with water, but he will baptize you with the Holy Spirit."

The Baptism and Temptation of Jesus
(Matt. 3.13–4.11; Luke 3.21–22; 4.1–13)

9 Not long afterwards Jesus came from Nazareth in the province of Galilee, and was baptized by John in the Jordan. 10 As soon as Jesus came up out of the water, he saw heaven opening and the Spirit coming down on him like a dove. 11 And a voice came from heaven, "You are my own dear Son. I am pleased with you."

12 At once the Spirit made him go into the desert, 13 where he stayed forty days, being tempted by Satan. Wild animals were there also, but angels came and helped him.

Jesus Calls Four Fishermen
(Matt. 4.12–22; Luke 4.14–15; 5.1–11)

14 After John had been put in prison, Jesus went to Galilee and preached the Good News from God. 15 "The right time has come," he said, "and the Kingdom of God is near! Turn away from your sins and believe the Good News!"

16 As Jesus walked along the shore of Lake Galilee, he saw two fishermen, Simon and his brother Andrew, catching fish with a net. 17 Jesus said to them, "Come with me, and I will teach you to catch men." 18 At once they left their nets and went with him.

19 He went a little farther on and saw two other brothers, James and John, the sons of Zebedee. They were in their boat getting their nets ready. 20 As soon as Jesus saw them, he called them; they left their father Zebedee in the boat with the hired men and went with Jesus.

A Man with an Evil Spirit
(Luke 4.31–37)

21 Jesus and his disciples came to the

---

a *Some manuscripts do not have* the Son of God.
b John appeared in the desert, baptizing and preaching; *some manuscripts have* John the Baptist appeared in the desert, preaching.
1.2: Mal 3.1   **1.3:** Is 40.3   **1.6:** 2 Kgs 1.8
1.11: Gen 22.2; Ps 2.7; Is 42.1; Mt 3.17, 12.18; Mk 9.7; Lk 3.22   **1.15:** Mt 3.2

Took her by the hand, and ... the fever left her (1.31)

town of Capernaum, and on the next Sabbath Jesus went to the synagogue and began to teach. 22 The people who heard him were amazed at the way he taught, for he wasn't like the teachers of the Law; instead, he taught with authority.

23 Just then a man with an evil spirit in him came into the synagogue and screamed, 24 "What do you want with us, Jesus of Nazareth? Are you here to destroy us? I know who you are—you are God's holy messenger!"

25 Jesus ordered the spirit, "Be quiet, and come out of the man!"

26 The evil spirit shook the man hard, gave a loud scream, and came out of him. 27 The people were all so amazed that they started saying to one another, "What is this? Is it some kind of new teaching? This man has authority to give orders to the evil spirits, and they obey him!"

28 And so the news about Jesus spread quickly everywhere in the province of Galilee.

Jesus Heals Many People
(Matt. 8.14–17; Luke 4.38–41)

29 Jesus and his disciples, including James and John, left the synagogue and went straight to the home of Simon and Andrew. 30 Simon's mother-in-law was sick in bed with a fever, and as soon as Jesus arrived, he was told about her. 31 He went to her, took her by the hand, and helped her up. The fever left her, and she began to wait on them.

32 After the sun had set and evening had come, people brought to Jesus all the sick and those who had demons. 33 All the people of the town gathered in front of the house. 34 Jesus healed many who were sick with all kinds of diseases and drove out many demons. He would not let the demons say anything, because they knew who he was.

Jesus Preaches in Galilee
(Luke 4.42–44)

35 Very early the next morning, long before daylight, Jesus got up and left the house. He went out of the town to a lonely place, where he prayed. 36 But Simon and his companions went out searching for him, 37 and when they found him, they said, "Everyone is looking for you."

38 But Jesus answered, "We must go on to the other villages round here. I have to preach in them also, because that is why I came."

39 So he travelled all over Galilee, preaching in the synagogues and driving out demons.

Jesus Heals a Man
(Matt. 8.1–4; Luke 5.12–16)

40 A man suffering from a dreaded skin-disease came to Jesus, knelt down, and begged him for help. "If you want to," he said, "you can make me clean." c

41 Jesus was filled with pity, d and stretched out his hand and touched him. "I do want to," he answered. "Be clean!"

c MAKE ME CLEAN: *This disease was considered to make a person ritually unclean.*
d pity; *some manuscripts have anger.*
1.22: Mt 7.28–29   **1.39:** Mt 4.23, 9.35

⁴²At once the disease left the man, and he was clean. ⁴³Then Jesus spoke sternly to him and sent him away at once, ⁴⁴after saying to him, "Listen, don't tell anyone about this. But go straight to the priest and let him examine you; then in order to prove to everyone that you are cured, offer the sacrifice that Moses ordered."

45 But the man went away and began to spread the news everywhere. Indeed, he talked so much that Jesus could not go into a town publicly. Instead, he stayed out in lonely places, and people came to him from everywhere.

Jesus Heals a Paralysed Man
(Matt. 9.1–8; Luke 5.17–26)

2 A few days later Jesus went back to Capernaum, and the news spread that he was at home. ²So many people came together that there was no room left, not even out in front of the door. Jesus was preaching the message to them ³when four men arrived, carrying a paralysed man to Jesus. ⁴Because of the crowd, however, they could not get the man to him. So they made a hole in the roof right above the place where Jesus was. When they had made an opening, they let the man down, lying on his mat. ⁵Seeing how much faith they had, Jesus said to the paralysed man, "My son, your sins are forgiven."

6 Some teachers of the Law who were sitting there thought to themselves, ⁷"How does he dare to talk like this? This is blasphemy! God is the only one who can forgive sins!"

8 At once Jesus knew what they were thinking, so he said to them, "Why do you think such things? ⁹Is it easier to say to this paralysed man, 'Your sins are forgiven', or to say, 'Get up, pick up your mat, and walk'? ¹⁰I will prove to you, then, that the Son of Man has authority on earth to forgive sins." So he said to the paralysed man, ¹¹"I tell you, get up, pick up your mat, and go home!"

12 While they all watched, the man got up, picked up his mat, and hurried away. They were all completely amazed and praised God, saying, "We have never seen anything like this!"

Jesus Calls Levi
(Matt. 9.9–13; Luke 5.27–32)

13 Jesus went back again to the shore of Lake Galilee. A crowd came to him, and he started teaching them. ¹⁴As he walked along, he saw a tax collector, Levi son of Alphaeus, sitting in his office. Jesus said to him, "Follow me." Levi got up and followed him.

15 Later on Jesus was having a meal in Levi's house.ᵉ A large number of tax collectors and other outcasts were following Jesus, and many of them joined him and his disciples at the table. ¹⁶Some teachers of the Law, who were Pharisees, saw that Jesus was eating with these outcasts and tax collectors, so they asked his disciples, "Why does he eat with such people?"

17 Jesus heard them and answered, "People who are well do not need a doctor, but only those who are sick. I have not come to call respectable people, but outcasts."

The Question about Fasting
(Matt. 9.14–17; Luke 5.33–39)

18 On one occasion the followers of John the Baptist and the Pharisees were fasting. Some people came to Jesus and asked him, "Why is it that the disciples of John the Baptist and the disciples of the Pharisees fast, but yours do not?"

19 Jesus answered, "Do you expect the guests at a wedding party to go without food? Of course not! As long as the bridegroom is with them, they will not do that. ²⁰But the day will come when the bridegroom will be taken away from them, and then they will fast.

21 "No one uses a piece of new cloth to patch up an old coat, because the new patch will shrink and tear off some of the old cloth, making an even bigger hole. ²²Nor does anyone pour new wine into used wineskins, because the wine will burst the skins, and both the wine and the skins will be ruined. Instead, new wine must be poured into fresh wineskins."

The Question about the Sabbath
(Matt. 12.1–8; Luke 6.1–5)

23 Jesus was walking through some cornfields on the Sabbath. As his disciples walked along with him, they began to pick the ears of corn. ²⁴So the Pharisees said to Jesus, "Look, it is against our Law for your disciples to do that on the Sabbath!"

25 Jesus answered, "Have you never read what David did that time when he needed something to eat? He and his men

ᵉin Levi's house; *or* in his (*that is*, Jesus') house.
1.44: Lev 14.1–32   **2.23:** Deut 23.25   **2.25–26:** 1 Sam 21.1–6

The crowd was so large (3.9)

were hungry, [26] so he went into the house of God and ate the bread offered to God. This happened when Abiathar was the High Priest. According to our Law only the priests may eat this bread—but David ate it and even gave it to his men."

[27] And Jesus concluded, "The Sabbath was made for the good of man; man was not made for the Sabbath. [28] So the Son of Man is Lord even of the Sabbath."

The Man with a Paralysed Hand
(Matt. 12.9-14; Luke 6.6-11)

3 Then Jesus went back to the synagogue, where there was a man who had a paralysed hand. [2] Some people were there who wanted to accuse Jesus of doing wrong; so they watched him closely to see whether he would heal the man on the Sabbath. [3] Jesus said to the man, "Come up here to the front." [4] Then he asked the people, "What does our Law allow us to do on the Sabbath? To help or to harm? To save a man's life or to destroy it?"

But they did not say a thing. [5] Jesus was angry as he looked round at them, but at the same time he felt sorry for them, because they were so stubborn and

wrong. Then he said to the man, "Stretch out your hand." He stretched it out, and it became well again. [6] So the Pharisees left the synagogue and met at once with some members of Herod's party, and they made plans to kill Jesus.

A Crowd by the Lake

[7] Jesus and his disciples went away to Lake Galilee, and a large crowd followed him. They had come from Galilee, from Judaea, [8] from Jerusalem, from the territory of Idumea, from the territory on the east side of the Jordan, and from the region round the cities of Tyre and Sidon. All these people came to Jesus because they had heard of the things he was doing. [9] The crowd was so large that Jesus told his disciples to get a boat ready for him, so that the people would not crush him. [10] He had healed many people, and all those who were ill kept pushing their way to him in order to touch him. [11] And whenever the people who had evil spirits in them saw him, they would fall down before him and scream, "You are the Son of God!"

[12] Jesus sternly ordered the evil spirits not to tell anyone who he was.

2.26: Lev 24.9   **3.9-10:** Mk 4.1; Lk 5.1-3

Jesus Chooses the Twelve Apostles
(Matt. 10.1–4; Luke 6.12–16)

13 Then Jesus went up a hill and called to himself the men he wanted. They came to him, ¹⁴ and he chose twelve, whom he named apostles. "I have chosen you to be with me," he told them. "I will also send you out to preach, ¹⁵ and you will have authority to drive out demons."

16 These are the twelve he chose: Simon (Jesus gave him the name Peter); ¹⁷ James and his brother John, the sons of Zebedee (Jesus gave them the name Boanerges, which means "Men of Thunder"); ¹⁸ Andrew, Philip, Bartholomew, Matthew, Thomas, James son of Alphaeus, Thaddaeus, Simon the Patriot, ¹⁹ and Judas Iscariot, who betrayed Jesus.

Jesus and Beelzebul
(Matt. 12.22–32; Luke 11.14–23; 12.10)

20 Then Jesus went home. Again such a large crowd gathered that Jesus and his disciples had no time to eat. ²¹ When his family heard about it, they set out to take charge of him, because people were saying, "He's gone mad!"

22 Some teachers of the Law who had come from Jerusalem were saying, "He has Beelzebul in him! It is the chief of the demons who gives him the power to drive them out."

23 So Jesus called them to him and spoke to them in parables: "How can Satan drive out Satan? ²⁴ If a country divides itself into groups which fight each other, that country will fall apart. ²⁵ If a family divides itself into groups which fight each other, that family will fall apart. ²⁶ So if Satan's kingdom divides into groups, it cannot last, but will fall apart and come to an end.

27 "No one can break into a strong man's house and take away his belongings unless he first ties up the strong man; then he can plunder his house.

28 "I assure you that people can be forgiven all their sins and all the evil things they may say.ᶠ ²⁹ But whoever says evil things against the Holy Spirit will never be forgiven, because he has committed an eternal sin." (³⁰ Jesus said this because some people were saying, "He has an evil spirit in him.")

Jesus' Mother and Brothers
(Matt. 12.46–50; Luke 8.19–21)

31 Then Jesus' mother and brothers arrived. They stood outside the house and sent in a message, asking for him. ³² A crowd was sitting round Jesus, and they said to him, "Look, your mother and your brothers and sisters are outside, and they want you."

33 Jesus answered, "Who is my mother? Who are my brothers?" ³⁴ He looked at the people sitting round him and said, "Look! Here are my mother and my brothers! ³⁵ Whoever does what God wants him to do is my brother, my sister, my mother."

The Parable of the Sower
(Matt. 13.1–9; Luke 8.4–8)

4 Again Jesus began to teach beside Lake Galilee. The crowd that gathered round him was so large that he got into a boat and sat in it. The boat was out in the water, and the crowd stood on the shore at the water's edge. ² He used parables to teach them many things, saying to them:

3 "Listen! Once there was a man who went out to sow corn. ⁴ As he scattered the seed in the field, some of it fell along the path, and the birds came and ate it up. ⁵ Some of it fell on rocky ground, where there was little soil. The seeds soon sprouted, because the soil wasn't deep. ⁶ Then, when the sun came up, it burnt the young plants; and because the roots had not grown deep enough, the plants soon dried up. ⁷ Some of the seed fell among thorn bushes, which grew up and choked the plants, and they didn't produce any corn. ⁸ But some seeds fell in good soil, and the plants sprouted, grew, and produced corn: some had thirty grains, others sixty, and others a hundred."

9 And Jesus concluded, "Listen, then, if you have ears!"

The Purpose of the Parables
(Matt. 13.10–17; Luke 8.9–10)

10 When Jesus was alone, some of those who had heard him came to him with the twelve disciples and asked him to explain the parables. ¹¹ "You have been given the secret of the Kingdom of God," Jesus answered. "But the others, who are on the outside, hear all things by means of parables, ¹² so that,

---

ᶠ evil things they may say; *or* evil things they may say against God.
3.22: Mt 9.34, 10.25   **3.29:** Lk 12.10   **4.1:** Lk 5.1–3   **4.12:** Is 6.9–10

'They may look and look,
    yet not see;
they may listen and listen,
    yet not understand.
For if they did, they would turn to God,
    and he would forgive them.' "

Jesus Explains the Parable of the Sower
(Matt. 13.18-23; Luke 8.11-15)

13 Then Jesus asked them, "Don't you understand this parable? How, then, will you ever understand any parable? 14 The sower sows God's message. 15 Some people are like the seeds that fall along the path; as soon as they hear the message, Satan comes and takes it away. 16 Other people are like the seeds that fall on rocky ground. As soon as they hear the message, they receive it gladly. 17 But it does not sink deep into them, and they don't last long. So when trouble or persecution comes because of the message, they give up at once. 18 Other people are like the seeds sown among the thorn bushes. These are the ones who hear the message, 19 but the worries about this life, the love for riches, and all other kinds of desires crowd in and choke the message, and they don't bear fruit. 20 But other people are like the seeds sown in good soil. They hear the message, accept it, and bear fruit: some thirty, some sixty, and some a hundred."

A Lamp under a Bowl
(Luke 8.16-18)

21 Jesus continued, "Does anyone ever bring in a lamp and put it under a bowl or under the bed? Doesn't he put it on the lampstand? 22 Whatever is hidden away will be brought out into the open, and whatever is covered up will be uncovered. 23 Listen, then, if you have ears!"

24 He also said to them, "Pay attention to what you hear! The same rules you use to judge others will be used by God to judge you—but with even greater severity. 25 The person who has something will be given more, and the person who has nothing will have taken away from him even the little he has."

The Parable of the Growing Seed

26 Jesus went on to say, "The Kingdom of God is like this. A man scatters seed in his field. 27 He sleeps at night, is up and about during the day, and all the while the seeds are sprouting and growing. Yet he does not know how it happens. 28 The soil itself makes the plants grow and bear fruit; first the tender stalk appears, then the ear, and finally the ear full of corn. 29 When the corn is ripe, the man starts cutting it with his sickle, because harvest time has come.

The Parable of the Mustard Seed
(Matt. 13.31-32, 34; Luke 13.18-19)

30 "What shall we say the Kingdom of God is like?" asked Jesus. "What parable shall we use to explain it? 31 It is like this. A man takes a mustard seed, the smallest seed in the world, and plants it in the ground. 32 After a while it grows up and becomes the biggest of all plants. It puts out such large branches that the birds come and make their nests in its shade."

33 Jesus preached his message to the people, using many other parables like these; he told them as much as they could understand. 34 He would not speak to them without using parables, but when he was alone with his disciples, he would explain everything to them.

Jesus Calms a Storm
(Matt. 8.23-27; Luke 8.22-25)

35 On the evening of that same day Jesus said to his disciples, "Let us go across to the other side of the lake." 36 So they left the crowd; the disciples got into the boat in which Jesus was already sitting, and they took him with them. Other boats were there too. 37 Suddenly a strong wind blew up, and the waves began to spill over into the boat, so that it was about to fill with water. 38 Jesus was in the back of the boat, sleeping with his head on a pillow. The disciples woke him up and said, "Teacher, don't you care that we are about to die?"

39 Jesus stood up and commanded the wind, "Be quiet!" and he said to the waves, "Be still!" The wind died down, and there was a great calm. 40 Then Jesus said to his disciples, "Why are you frightened? Have you still no faith?"

41 But they were terribly afraid and said to one another, "Who is this man? Even the wind and the waves obey him!"

Jesus Heals a Man with Evil Spirits
(Matt. 8.28-34; Luke 8.26-39)

5 Jesus and his disciples arrived on the other side of Lake Galilee, in the

---

4.21: Mt 5.15; Lk 11.33   **4.22:** Mt 10.26; Lk 12.2   **4.24:** Mt 7.2; Lk 6.38
4.25: Mt 13.12, 25.29; Lk 19.26   **4.29:** Joel 3.13

Waves began to spill over into the boat (4.37)

territory of Gerasa. ² As soon as Jesus got out of the boat, he was met by a man who came out of the burial caves there. This man had an evil spirit in him ³ and lived among the tombs. Nobody could keep him chained up any more; ⁴ many times his feet and hands had been chained, but every time he broke the chains and smashed the irons on his feet. He was too strong for anyone to control him. ⁵ Day and night he wandered among the tombs and through the hills, screaming and cutting himself with stones.

6 He was some distance away when he saw Jesus; so he ran, fell on his knees before him, ⁷ and screamed in a loud voice, "Jesus, Son of the Most High God! What do you want with me? For God's sake, I beg you, don't punish me!" (⁸ He said this because Jesus was saying, "Evil spirit, come out of this man!")

9 So Jesus asked him, "What is your name?"

The man answered, "My name is 'Mob'—there are so many of us!" ¹⁰ And he kept begging Jesus not to send the evil spirits out of that region.

11 There was a large herd of pigs near by, feeding on a hillside. ¹² So the spirits begged Jesus, "Send us to the pigs, and let us go into them." ¹³ He let them go, and the evil spirits went out of the man and entered the pigs. The whole herd—about two thousand pigs in all—rushed down the side of the cliff into the lake and was drowned.

14 The men who had been taking care of the pigs ran away and spread the news in the town and among the farms. People went out to see what had happened, ¹⁵ and when they came to Jesus, they saw the man who used to have the mob of demons

and there was a great calm (4.39)

in him. He was sitting there, clothed and in his right mind; and they were all afraid. ¹⁶Those who had seen it told the people what had happened to the man with the demons, and about the pigs.

17 So they asked Jesus to leave their territory.

18 As Jesus was getting into the boat, the man who had had the demons begged him, "Let me go with you!"

19 But Jesus would not let him. Instead, he told him, "Go back home to your family and tell them how much the Lord has done for you and how kind he has been to you."

20 So the man left and went all through the Ten Towns, telling what Jesus had done for him. And all who heard it were amazed.

Jairus' Daughter and the Woman Who Touched Jesus' Cloak
(Matt. 9.18-26; Luke 8.40-56)

21 Jesus went back across to the other side of the lake. There at the lakeside a large crowd gathered round him. ²²Jairus, an official of the local synagogue, arrived, and when he saw Jesus, he threw himself down at his feet ²³and begged him earnestly, "My little daughter is very ill. Please come and place your hands on her, so that she will get well and live!"

24 Then Jesus started off with him. So many people were going along with Jesus that they were crowding him from every side.

25 There was a woman who had suffered terribly from severe bleeding for twelve years, ²⁶even though she had been treated by many doctors. She had spent all her money, but instead of getting better she got worse all the time. ²⁷She had heard about Jesus, so she came in the crowd behind him, ²⁸saying to herself, "If I just touch his clothes, I will get well."

29 She touched his cloak, and her bleeding stopped at once; and she had the feeling inside herself that she was healed of her trouble. ³⁰At once Jesus knew that power had gone out of him, so he turned round in the crowd and asked, "Who touched my clothes?"

31 His disciples answered, "You see how the people are crowding you; why do you ask who touched you?"

32 But Jesus kept looking round to see who had done it. ³³The woman realized what had happened to her, so she came,

trembling with fear, knelt at his feet, and told him the whole truth. ³⁴Jesus said to her, "My daughter, your faith has made you well. Go in peace, and be healed of your trouble."

35 While Jesus was saying this, some messengers came from Jairus' house and told him, "Your daughter has died. Why bother the Teacher any longer?"

36 Jesus paid no attention to ^{g} what they said, but told him, "Don't be afraid, only believe." ³⁷Then he did not let anyone else go on with him except Peter and James and his brother John. ³⁸They arrived at Jairus' house, where Jesus saw the confusion and heard all the loud crying and wailing. ³⁹He went in and said to them, "Why all this confusion? Why are you crying? The child is not dead—she is only sleeping!"

40 They laughed at him, so he put them all out, took the child's father and mother and his three disciples, and went into the room where the child was lying. ⁴¹He took her by the hand and said to her, "*Talitha, koum*," which means, "Little girl, I tell you to get up!"

42 She got up at once and started walking around. (She was twelve years old.) When this happened, they were completely amazed. ⁴³But Jesus gave them strict orders not to tell anyone, and he said, "Give her something to eat."

Jesus Is Rejected at Nazareth
(Matt. 13.53-58; Luke 4.16-30)

6 Jesus left that place and went back to his home town, followed by his disciples. ²On the Sabbath he began to teach in the synagogue. Many people were there; and when they heard him, they were all amazed. "Where did he get all this?" they asked. "What wisdom is this that has been given him? How does he perform miracles? ³Isn't he the carpenter, the son of Mary, and the brother of James, Joseph, Judas, and Simon? Aren't his sisters living here?" And so they rejected him.

4 Jesus said to them, "A prophet is respected everywhere except in his own home town and by his relatives and his family."

5 He was not able to perform any miracles there, except that he placed his hands on a few sick people and healed them. ⁶He was greatly surprised, because the people did not have faith.

^{g}paid no attention to; or overheard.
6.4: Jn 4.44

Jesus Sends out the Twelve Disciples
(Matt. 10.5-15; Luke 9.1-6)

Then Jesus went to the villages round there, teaching the people. [7] He called the twelve disciples together and sent them out two by two. He gave them authority over the evil spirits [8] and ordered them, "Don't take anything with you on your journey except a stick—no bread, no beggar's bag, no money in your pockets. [9] Wear sandals, but don't carry an extra shirt." [10] He also said, "Wherever you are welcomed, stay in the same house until you leave that place. [11] If you come to a town where people do not welcome you or will not listen to you, leave it and shake the dust off your feet. That will be a warning to them!"

12 So they went out and preached that people should turn away from their sins. [13] They drove out many demons, and rubbed olive-oil on many sick people and healed them.

The Death of John the Baptist
(Matt. 14.1-12; Luke 9.7-9)

14 Now King Herod[h] heard about all this, because Jesus' reputation had spread everywhere. Some people were saying, "John the Baptist has come back to life! That is why he has this power to perform miracles."

15 Others, however, said, "He is Elijah." Others said, "He is a prophet, like one of the prophets of long ago."

16 When Herod heard it, he said, "He is John the Baptist! I had his head cut off, but he has come back to life!" [17] Herod himself had ordered John's arrest, and he had him chained and put in prison. Herod did this because of Herodias, whom he had married, even though she was the wife of his brother Philip. [18] John the Baptist kept telling Herod, "It isn't right for you to be married to your brother's wife!"

19 So Herodias held a grudge against John and wanted to kill him, but she could not because of Herod. [20] Herod was afraid of John because he knew that John was a good and holy man, and so he kept him safe. He liked to listen to him, even though he became greatly disturbed every time he heard him.

21 Finally Herodias got her chance. It was on Herod's birthday, when he gave a feast for all the chief government officials, the military commanders, and the leading citizens of Galilee. [22] The daughter of Herodias[i] came in and danced, and pleased Herod and his guests. So the king said to the girl, "What would you like to have? I will give you anything you want." [23] With many vows he said to her, "I swear that I will give you anything you ask for, even as much as half my kingdom!"

24 So the girl went out and asked her mother, "What shall I ask for?"

"The head of John the Baptist," she answered.

25 The girl hurried back at once to the king and demanded, "I want you to give me here and now the head of John the Baptist on a dish!"

26 This made the king very sad, but he could not refuse her because of the vows he had made in front of all his guests. [27] So he sent off a guard at once with orders to bring John's head. The guard left, went to the prison, and cut John's head off; [28] then he brought it on a dish and gave it to the girl, who gave it to her mother. [29] When John's disciples heard about this, they came and took away his body, and buried it.

Jesus Feeds Five Thousand Men
(Matt. 14.13-21; Luke 9.10-17; John 6.1-14)

30 The apostles returned and met with Jesus, and told him all they had done and taught. [31] There were so many people coming and going that Jesus and his disciples didn't even have time to eat. So he said to them, "Let us go off by ourselves to some place where we will be alone and you can rest for a while." [32] So they started out in a boat by themselves for a lonely place.

33 Many people, however, saw them leave and knew at once who they were; so they went from all the towns and ran ahead by land and arrived at the place ahead of Jesus and his disciples. [34] When Jesus got out of the boat, he saw this large crowd, and his heart was filled with pity for them, because they were like sheep without a shepherd. So he began to teach them many things. [35] When it was

---

[h] KING HEROD: *Herod Antipas, ruler of Galilee.*
[i] The daughter of Herodias; *some manuscripts have* His daughter Herodias.
6.8-11: Lk 10.4-11   **6.11:** Acts 13.51   **6.13:** Jas 5.14   **6.14-15:** Mt 16.14; Mk 8.28; Lk 9.19
6.17-18: Lk 3.19-20   **6.34:** Num 27.17; 1 Kgs 22.17; 2 Chr 18.16; Ezek 34.5; Mt 9.36

It's a ghost! (6.49)

getting late, his disciples came to him and said, "It is already very late, and this is a lonely place. ³⁶ Send the people away, and let them go to the nearby farms and villages in order to buy themselves something to eat."

³⁷ "You yourselves give them something to eat," Jesus answered.

They asked, "Do you want us to go and spend two hundred silver coins*ʲ* on bread in order to feed them?"

38 So Jesus asked them, "How much bread have you got? Go and see."

When they found out, they told him, "Five loaves and also two fish."

39 Jesus then told his disciples to make all the people divide into groups and sit down on the green grass. ⁴⁰ So the people sat down in rows, in groups of a hundred and groups of fifty. ⁴¹ Then Jesus took the five loaves and the two fish, looked up to heaven, and gave thanks to God. He broke the loaves and gave them to his disciples to distribute to the people. He also divided the two fish among them all. ⁴²Everyone ate and had enough. ⁴³Then the disciples took up twelve baskets full of what was left of the bread and the fish. ⁴⁴The number of men who were fed was five thousand.

Jesus Walks on the Water
(Matt. 14.22-33; John 6.15-21)

45 At once Jesus made his disciples get into the boat and go ahead of him to Bethsaida, on the other side of the lake, while he sent the crowd away. ⁴⁶After saying good-bye to the people he went away to a hill to pray. ⁴⁷When evening came, the boat was in the middle of the lake, while Jesus was alone on land. ⁴⁸He saw that his disciples were straining at the oars, because they were rowing against the wind, so some time between three and six o'clock in the morning he came to them, walking on the water. He was going to pass them by,ᵏ ⁴⁹but they saw him walking on the water. "It's a ghost!" they thought, and screamed. ⁵⁰They were all terrified when they saw him.

Jesus spoke to them at once, "Courage!" he said. "It is I. Don't be afraid!" ⁵¹Then he got into the boat with them, and the wind died down. The disciples were completely amazed, ⁵²because they had not understood the real meaning of the feeding of the five thousand; their minds could not grasp it.

---

*ʲ*SILVER COINS: *A silver coin was the daily wage of a rural worker (see Mt. 20.2).*
*ᵏ*pass them by; *or* join them.

Jesus Heals the Sick in Gennesaret
(Matt. 14.34-36)

53 They crossed the lake and came to land at Gennesaret, where they tied up the boat. 54 As they left the boat, people recognized Jesus at once. 55 So they ran throughout the whole region; and wherever they heard he was, they brought to him sick people lying on their mats. 56 And everywhere Jesus went, to villages, towns, or farms, people would take those who were ill to the market places and beg him to let them at least touch the edge of his cloak; and all who touched it were made well.

The Teaching of the Ancestors
(Matt. 15.1-9)

7 Some Pharisees and teachers of the Law who had come from Jerusalem gathered round Jesus. 2 They noticed that some of his disciples were eating their food with hands that were ritually unclean—that is, they had not washed them in the way the Pharisees said people should.

(3 For the Pharisees, as well as the rest of the Jews, follow the teaching they received from their ancestors: they do not eat unless they wash their hands in the proper way; 4 nor do they eat anything that comes from the market unless they wash it first.[l] And they follow many other rules which they have received, such as the proper way to wash cups, pots, copper bowls, and beds.[m])

5 So the Pharisees and the teachers of the Law asked Jesus, "Why is it that your disciples do not follow the teaching handed down by our ancestors, but instead eat with ritually unclean hands?"

6 Jesus answered them, "How right Isaiah was when he prophesied about you! You are hypocrites, just as he wrote:
'These people, says God, honour me
    with their words,
but their heart is really far away from
    me.
7 It is no use for them to worship me,
because they teach man-made rules
    as though they were God's laws!'

8 "You put aside God's command and obey the teachings of men."

9 And Jesus continued, "You have a clever way of rejecting God's law in order to uphold your own teaching. 10 For Moses commanded, 'Respect your father and your mother,' and, 'Whoever curses his father or his mother is to be put to death.' 11 But you teach that if a person has something he could use to help his father or mother, but says, 'This is Corban' (which means, it belongs to God), 12 he is excused from helping his father or mother. 13 In this way the teaching you pass on to others cancels out the word of God. And there are many other things like this that you do."

The Things that Make a Person Unclean
(Matt. 15.10-20)

14 Then Jesus called the crowd to him once more and said to them, "Listen to me, all of you, and understand. 15 There is nothing that goes into a person from the outside which can make him ritually unclean. Rather, it is what comes out of a person that makes him unclean."[n]

17 When he left the crowd and went into the house, his disciples asked him to explain this saying. 18 "You are no more intelligent than the others," Jesus said to them. "Don't you understand? Nothing that goes into a person from the outside can really make him unclean, 19 because it does not go into his heart but into his stomach and then goes on out of the body." (In saying this, Jesus declared that all foods are fit to be eaten.)

20 And he went on to say, "It is what comes out of a person that makes him unclean. 21 For from the inside, from a person's heart, come the evil ideas which lead him to do immoral things, to rob, kill, 22 commit adultery, be greedy, and do all sorts of evil things; deceit, indecency, jealousy, slander, pride, and folly—23 all these evil things come from inside a person and make him unclean."

A Woman's Faith
(Matt. 15.21-28)

24 Then Jesus left and went away to the territory near the city of Tyre. He went into a house and did not want anyone to know he was there, but he could not stay hidden. 25 A woman, whose daughter had an evil spirit in her, heard about Jesus and came to him at once and

---

[l] anything that comes from the market unless they wash it first; or anything after they come from the market unless they wash themselves first.
[m] Some manuscripts do not have and beds.
[n] Some manuscripts add verse 16: Listen, then, if you have ears! (see 4.23).
7.6-7: Is 29.13   **7.10:** Ex 20.12, 21.17; Lev 20.9; Deut 5.16

fell at his feet. 26 The woman was a Gentile, born in the region of Phoenicia in Syria. She begged Jesus to drive the demon out of her daughter. 27 But Jesus answered, "Let us first feed the children. It isn't right to take the children's food and throw it to the dogs."

28 "Sir," she answered, "even the dogs under the table eat the children's leftovers!"

29 So Jesus said to her, "Because of that answer, go back home, where you will find that the demon has gone out of your daughter!"

30 She went home and found her child lying on the bed; the demon had indeed gone out of her.

Jesus Heals a Deaf-Mute

31 Jesus then left the neighbourhood of Tyre and went on through Sidon to Lake Galilee, going by way of the territory of the Ten Towns. 32 Some people brought him a man who was deaf and could hardly speak, and they begged Jesus to place his hands on him. 33 So Jesus took him off alone, away from the crowd, put his fingers in the man's ears, spat, and touched the man's tongue. 34 Then Jesus looked up to heaven, gave a deep groan, and said to the man, "*Ephphatha*," which means, "Open up!"

35 At once the man was able to hear, his speech impediment was removed, and he began to talk without any trouble. 36 Then Jesus ordered the people not to speak of it to anyone; but the more he ordered them not to, the more they spoke. 37 And all who heard were completely amazed. "How well he does everything!" they exclaimed. "He even causes the deaf to hear and the dumb to speak!"

Jesus Feeds Four Thousand People
(Matt. 15.32-39)

8 Not long afterwards another large crowd came together. When the people had nothing left to eat, Jesus called the disciples to him and said, 2 "I feel sorry for these people, because they have been with me for three days and now have nothing to eat. 3 If I send them home without feeding them, they will faint as they go, because some of them have come a long way."

4 His disciples asked him, "Where in this desert can anyone find enough food to feed all these people?"

5 "How much bread have you got?" Jesus asked.

"Seven loaves," they answered.

6 He ordered the crowd to sit down on the ground. Then he took the seven loaves, gave thanks to God, broke them, and gave them to his disciples to distribute to the crowd; and the disciples did so. 7 They also had a few small fish. Jesus gave thanks for these and told the disciples to distribute them too. 8-9 Everybody ate and had enough—there were about four thousand people. Then the disciples took up seven baskets full of pieces left over. Jesus sent the people away 10 and at once got into a boat with his disciples and went to the district of Dalmanutha.

The Pharisees Ask for a Miracle
(Matt. 16.1-4)

11 Some Pharisees came to Jesus and started to argue with him. They wanted to trap him, so they asked him to perform a miracle to show that God approved of him. 12 But Jesus gave a deep groan and said, "Why do the people of this day ask for a miracle? No, I tell you! No such proof will be given to these people!"

13 He left them, got back into the boat, and started across to the other side of the lake.

The Yeast of the Pharisees and of Herod
(Matt. 16.5-12)

14 The disciples had forgotten to bring enough bread and had only one loaf with them in the boat. 15 "Take care," Jesus warned them, "and be on your guard against the yeast of the Pharisees and the yeast of Herod."

16 They started discussing among themselves: "He says this because we haven't any bread."

17 Jesus knew what they were saying, so he asked them, "Why are you discussing about not having any bread? Don't you know or understand yet? Are your minds so dull? 18 You have eyes—can't you see? You have ears—can't you hear? Don't you remember 19 when I broke the five loaves for the five thousand people? How many baskets full of leftover pieces did you take up?"

"Twelve," they answered.

20 "And when I broke the seven loaves for the four thousand people," asked Jesus, "how many baskets full of leftover pieces did you take up?"

8.11: Mt 12.38; Lk 11.16   **8.12:** Mt 12.39; Lk 11.29   **8.15:** Lk 12.1
8.18: Jer 5.21; Ezek 12.2; Mk 4.12

"Seven," they answered.

21 "And you still don't understand?" he asked them.

Jesus Heals a Blind Man at Bethsaida

22 They came to Bethsaida, where some people brought a blind man to Jesus and begged him to touch him. 23 Jesus took the blind man by the hand and led him out of the village. After spitting on the man's eyes, Jesus placed his hands on him and asked him, "Can you see anything?"

24 The man looked up and said, "Yes, I can see people, but they look like trees walking about."

25 Jesus again placed his hands on the man's eyes. This time the man looked intently, his eyesight returned, and he saw everything clearly. 26 Jesus then sent him home with the order, "Don't go back into the village."

Peter's Declaration about Jesus
(Matt. 16.13-20; Luke 9.18-21)

27 Then Jesus and his disciples went away to the villages near Caesarea Philippi. On the way he asked them "Tell me, who do people say I am?"

28 "Some say that you are John the Baptist," they answered; "others say that you are Elijah, while others say that you are one of the prophets."

29 "What about you?" he asked them. "Who do you say I am?"

Peter answered, "You are the Messiah."

30 Then Jesus ordered them, "Do not tell anyone about me."

Jesus Speaks about His Suffering and Death
(Matt. 16.21-28; Luke 9.22-27)

31 Then Jesus began to teach his disciples: "The Son of Man must suffer much and be rejected by the elders, the chief priests, and the teachers of the Law. He will be put to death, but three days later he will rise to life." 32 He made this very clear to them. So Peter took him aside and began to rebuke him. 33 But Jesus turned round, looked at his disciples, and rebuked Peter. "Get away from me, Satan," he said. "Your thoughts don't come from God but from man!"

34 Then Jesus called the crowd and his disciples to him. "If anyone wants to come with me," he told them, "he must forget self, carry his cross, and follow me. 35 For whoever wants to save his own life will lose it; but whoever loses his life for me and for the gospel will save it. 36 Does a person gain anything if he wins the whole world but loses his life? Of course not! 37 There is nothing he can give to regain his life. 38 If a person is ashamed of me and of my teaching in this godless and wicked day, then the Son of Man will be ashamed of him when he comes in the glory of his Father with the holy angels."

9 And he went on to say, "I tell you, there are some here who will not die until they have seen the Kingdom of God come with power."

The Transfiguration
(Matt. 17.1-13; Luke 9.28-36)

2 Six days later Jesus took with him Peter, James, and John, and led them up a high mountain, where they were alone. As they looked on, a change came over Jesus, 3 and his clothes became shining white—whiter than anyone in the world could wash them. 4 Then the three disciples saw Elijah and Moses talking with Jesus. 5 Peter spoke up and said to Jesus, "Teacher, how good it is that we are here! We will make three tents, one for you, one for Moses, and one for Elijah." 6 He and the others were so frightened that he did not know what to say.

7 Then a cloud appeared and covered them with its shadow, and a voice came from the cloud, "This is my own dear Son—listen to him!" 8 They took a quick look round but did not see anyone else; only Jesus was with them.

9 As they came down the mountain, Jesus ordered them, "Don't tell anyone what you have seen, until the Son of Man has risen from death."

10 They obeyed his order, but among themselves they started discussing the matter, "What does this 'rising from death' mean?" 11 And they asked Jesus, "Why do the teachers of the Law say that Elijah has to come first?"

12 His answer was, "Elijah is indeed coming first in order to get everything ready. Yet why do the Scriptures say that the Son of Man will suffer much and be rejected? 13 I tell you, however, that Elijah has already come and that people treated

8.28: Mk 6.14-15; Lk 9.7-8   **8.29:** Jn 6.68-69   **8.34:** Mt 10.38; Lk 14.27
8.35: Mt 10.39; Lk 17.33; Jn 12.25   **9.2-7:** 2 Pet 1.17-18   **9.7:** Mt 3.17; Mk 1.11; Lk 3.22
9.11: Mal 4.5; Mt 11.14

He must forget self, carry his cross, and follow me (8.34)

him just as they pleased, as the Scriptures say about him."

Jesus Heals a Boy with an Evil Spirit
(Matt. 17.14–21; Luke 9.37–43a)

14 When they joined the rest of the disciples, they saw a large crowd round them and some teachers of the Law arguing with them. 15 When the people saw Jesus, they were greatly surprised, and ran to him and greeted him. 16 Jesus asked his disciples, "What are you arguing with them about?"

17 A man in the crowd answered, "Teacher, I brought my son to you, because he has an evil spirit in him and cannot talk. 18 Whenever the spirit attacks him, it throws him to the ground, and he foams at the mouth, grits his teeth, and becomes stiff all over. I asked your disciples to drive the spirit out, but they could not."

19 Jesus said to them, "How unbelieving you people are! How long must I stay with you? How long do I have to put up with you? Bring the boy to me!" 20 They brought him to Jesus.

As soon as the spirit saw Jesus, it threw the boy into a fit, so that he fell on the ground and rolled round, foaming at the mouth. 21 "How long has he been like this?" Jesus asked the father.

"Ever since he was a child," he replied. 22 "Many times the evil spirit has tried to kill him by throwing him in the fire and into water. Have pity on us and help us, if you possibly can!"

23 "Yes," said Jesus, "if you yourself can! Everything is possible for the person who has faith."

24 The father at once cried out, "I do have faith, but not enough. Help me to have more!"

25 Jesus noticed that the crowd was closing in on them, so he gave a command to the evil spirit. "Deaf and dumb spirit," he said, "I order you to come out of the boy and never go into him again!"

26 The spirit screamed, threw the boy into a bad fit, and came out. The boy looked like a corpse, and everyone said, "He is dead!" 27 But Jesus took the boy by the hand and helped him to rise, and he stood up.

28 After Jesus had gone indoors, his disciples asked him privately, "Why couldn't we drive the spirit out?"

29 "Only prayer can drive this kind out," answered Jesus; "nothing else can."

Jesus Speaks Again about His Death
(Matt. 17.22–23; Luke 9.43b–45)

30 Jesus and his disciples left that place and went on through Galilee. Jesus did not want anyone to know where he was, 31 because he was teaching his disciples: "The Son of Man will be handed over to men who will kill him. Three days later, however, he will rise to life."

32 But they did not understand what this teaching meant, and they were afraid to ask him.

Who Is the Greatest?
(Matt. 18.1–5; Luke 9.46–48)

33 They came to Capernaum, and after going indoors Jesus asked his disciples, "What were you arguing about on the road?"

34 But they would not answer him, because on the road they had been arguing among themselves about who was the greatest. ³⁵ Jesus sat down, called the twelve disciples, and said to them, "Whoever wants to be first must place himself last of all and be the servant of all." ³⁶ Then he took a child and made him stand in front of them. He put his arms round him and said to them, ³⁷ "Whoever welcomes in my name one of these children, welcomes me; and whoever welcomes me, welcomes not only me but also the one who sent me."

Whoever Is Not against Us Is for Us
(Luke 9.49–50)

38 John said to him, "Teacher, we saw a man who was driving out demons in your name, and we told him to stop, because he doesn't belong to our group."

39 "Do not try to stop him," Jesus told them, "because no one who performs a miracle in my name will be able soon afterwards to say evil things about me. ⁴⁰ For whoever is not against us is for us. ⁴¹ I assure you that anyone who gives you a drink of water because you belong to me will certainly receive his reward.

Temptations to Sin
(Matt. 18.6–9; Luke 17.1–2)

42 "If anyone should cause one of these little ones to lose his faith in me, it would be better for that person to have a large millstone tied round his neck and be thrown into the sea. ⁴³ So if your hand makes you lose your faith, cut it off! It is better for you to enter life without a hand than to keep both hands and go off to hell, to the fire that never goes out. ᵒ ⁴⁵ And if your foot makes you lose your faith, cut it off! It is better for you to enter life without a foot than to keep both feet and be thrown into hell. ᵖ ⁴⁷ And if your eye makes you lose your faith, take it out! It is better for you to enter the Kingdom of God with only one eye than to keep both eyes and be thrown into hell. ⁴⁸ There 'the worms that eat them never die, and the fire that burns them is never put out.'

49 "Everyone will be purified by fire as a sacrifice is purified by salt.

50 "Salt is good; but if it loses its saltiness, how can you make it salty again?

"Have the salt of friendship among yourselves, and live in peace with one another."

Jesus Teaches about Divorce
(Matt. 19.1–12; Luke 16.18)

10 Then Jesus left that place, went to the province of Judaea, and crossed the River Jordan. Crowds came flocking to him again, and he taught them, as he always did.

2 Some Pharisees came to him and tried to trap him. "Tell us," they asked, "does our Law allow a man to divorce his wife?"

9.34: Lk 22.24   **9.35:** Mt 20.26–27, 23.11; Mk 10.43–44; Lk 22.26
9.37: Mt 10.40; Lk 10.16; Jn 13.20   **9.40:** Mt 12.30; Lk 11.23   **9.41:** Mt 10.42
9.43: Mt 5.30   **9.47:** Mt 5.29   **9.48:** Is 66.24   **9.50:** Mt 5.13; Lk 14.34–35

3 Jesus answered with a question, "What law did Moses give you?"

4 Their answer was, "Moses gave permission for a man to write a divorce notice and send his wife away."

5 Jesus said to them, "Moses wrote this law for you because you are so hard to teach. 6 But in the beginning, at the time of creation, 'God made them male and female,' as the scripture says. 7 'And for this reason a man will leave his father and mother and unite with his wife,q 8 and the two will become one.' So they are no longer two, but one. 9 Man must not separate, then, what God has joined together."

10 When they went back into the house, the disciples asked Jesus about this matter. 11 He said to them, "A man who divorces his wife and marries another woman commits adultery against his wife. 12 In the same way, a woman who divorces her husband and marries another man commits adultery."

Jesus Blesses Little Children
(Matt. 19.13–15; Luke 18.15–17)

13 Some people brought children to Jesus for him to place his hands on them, but the disciples scolded the people. 14 When Jesus noticed this, he was angry and said to his disciples, "Let the children come to me, and do not stop them, because the Kingdom of God belongs to such as these. 15 I assure you that whoever does not receive the Kingdom of God like a child will never enter it." 16 Then he took the children in his arms, placed his hands on each of them, and blessed them.

The Rich Man
(Matt. 19.16–30; Luke 18.18–30)

17 As Jesus was starting on his way again, a man ran up, knelt before him, and asked him, "Good Teacher, what must I do to receive eternal life?"

18 "Why do you call me good?" Jesus asked him. "No one is good except God alone. 19 You know the commandments: 'Do not commit murder; do not commit adultery; do not steal; do not accuse anyone falsely; do not cheat; respect your father and your mother.'"

20 "Teacher," the man said, "ever since I was young, I have obeyed all these commandments."

21 Jesus looked straight at him with love and said, "You need only one thing. Go and sell all you have and give the money to the poor, and you will have riches in heaven; then come and follow me." 22 When the man heard this, gloom spread over his face, and he went away sad, because he was very rich.

23 Jesus looked round at his disciples and said to them, "How hard it will be for rich people to enter the Kingdom of God!"

24 The disciples were shocked at these words, but Jesus went on to say, "My children, how hard it is to enter the Kingdom of God! 25 It is much harder for a rich person to enter the Kingdom of God than for a camel to go through the eye of a needle."

26 At this the disciples were completely amazed and asked one another, "Who, then, can be saved?"

27 Jesus looked straight at them and answered, "This is impossible for man, but not for God; everything is possible for God."

28 Then Peter spoke up, "Look, we have left everything and followed you."

29 "Yes," Jesus said to them, "and I tell you that anyone who leaves home or brothers or sisters or mother or father or children or fields for me and for the gospel, 30 will receive much more in this present age. He will receive a hundred times more houses, brothers, sisters, mothers, children and fields—and persecutions as well; and in the age to come he will receive eternal life. 31 But many who now are first will be last, and many who now are last will be first."

Jesus Speaks a Third Time about His Death
(Matt. 20.17–19; Luke 18.31–34)

32 Jesus and his disciples were now on the road going up to Jerusalem. Jesus was going ahead of the disciples, who were filled with alarm; the people who followed behind were afraid. Once again Jesus took the twelve disciples aside and spoke of the things that were going to happen to him. 33 "Listen," he told them, "we are going up to Jerusalem where the Son of Man will be handed over to the chief priests and the teachers of the Law. They will condemn him to death and then hand

q *Some manuscripts do not have* and unite with his wife.
10.4: Deut 24.1–4; Mt 5.31　　10.6: Gen 1.27, 5.2　　10.7–8: Gen 2.24
10.11–12: Mt 5.32; 1 Cor 7.10–11　　10.15: Mt 18.3　　10.19: Ex 20.12–16; Deut 5.16–20
10.31: Mt 20.16; Lk 13.30

him over to the Gentiles, 34 who will mock him, spit on him, whip him, and kill him; but three days later he will rise to life."

The Request of James and John
(Matt. 20.20-28)

35 Then James and John, the sons of Zebedee, came to Jesus. "Teacher," they said, "there is something we want you to do for us."

36 "What is it?" Jesus asked them.

37 They answered, "When you sit on your throne in your glorious Kingdom, we want you to let us sit with you, one at your right and one at your left."

38 Jesus said to them, "You don't know what you are asking for. Can you drink the cup of suffering that I must drink? Can you be baptized in the way I must be baptized?"

39 "We can," they answered.

Jesus said to them, "You will indeed drink the cup I must drink and be baptized in the way I must be baptized. 40 But I do not have the right to choose who will sit at my right and my left. It is God who will give these places to those for whom he has prepared them."

41 When the other ten disciples heard about it, they became angry with James and John. 42 So Jesus called them all together to him and said, "You know that the men who are considered rulers of the heathen have power over them, and the leaders have complete authority. 43 This, however, is not the way it is among you. If one of you wants to be great, he must be the servant of the rest; 44 and if one of you wants to be first, he must be the slave of all. 45 For even the Son of Man did not come to be served; he came to serve and to give his life to redeem many people."

Jesus Heals Blind Bartimaeus
(Matt. 20.29-34; Luke 18.35-43)

46 They came to Jericho, and as Jesus was leaving with his disciples and a large crowd, a blind beggar named Bartimaeus son of Timaeus was sitting by the road. 47 When he heard that it was Jesus of Nazareth, he began to shout, "Jesus! Son of David! Take pity on me!"

48 Many of the people scolded him and told him to be quiet. But he shouted even more loudly, "Son of David, take pity on me!"

49 Jesus stopped and said, "Call him." So they called the blind man. "Cheer up!" they said. "Get up, he is calling you."

50 He threw off his cloak, jumped up, and came to Jesus.

51 "What do you want me to do for you?" Jesus asked him.

"Teacher," the blind man answered, "I want to see again."

52 "Go," Jesus told him, "your faith has made you well."

At once he was able to see and followed Jesus on the road.

The Triumphant Entry into Jerusalem
(Matt. 21.1-11; Luke 19.28-40; John 12.12-19)

11 As they approached Jerusalem, near the towns of Bethphage and Bethany, they came to the Mount of Olives. Jesus sent two of his disciples on ahead 2 with these instructions: "Go to the village there ahead of you. As soon as you get there, you will find a colt tied up that has never been ridden. Untie it and bring it here. 3 And if someone asks you why you are doing that, tell him that the Master r needs it and will send it back at once."

4 So they went and found a colt out in the street, tied to the door of a house. As they were untying it, 5 some of the bystanders asked them, "What are you doing, untying that colt?"

6 They answered just as Jesus had told them, and the men let them go. 7 They brought the colt to Jesus, threw their cloaks over the animal, and Jesus got on. 8 Many people spread their cloaks on the road, while others cut branches in the fields and spread them on the road. 9 The people who were in front and those who followed behind began to shout, "Praise God! God bless him who comes in the name of the Lord! 10 God bless the coming kingdom of King David, our father! Praise God!"

11 Jesus entered Jerusalem, went into the Temple, and looked round at everything. But since it was already late in the day, he went out to Bethany with the twelve disciples.

Jesus Curses the Fig-Tree
(Matt. 21.18-19)

12 The next day, as they were coming back from Bethany, Jesus was hungry. 13 He saw in the distance a fig-tree covered

---

r the Master; or its owner.
10.38: Lk 12.50   **10.42-43:** Lk 22.25-26   **10.43-44:** Mt 23.11; Mk 9.35; Lk 22.26
11.9: Ps 118.25-26

with leaves, so he went to see if he could find any figs on it. But when he came to it, he found only leaves, because it was not the right time for figs. ¹⁴ Jesus said to the fig-tree, "No one shall ever eat figs from you again!"

And his disciples heard him.

Jesus Goes to the Temple
(Matt. 21.12–17; Luke 19.45–48; John 2.13–22)

15 When they arrived in Jerusalem, Jesus went to the Temple and began to drive out all those who were buying and selling. He overturned the tables of the money-changers and the stools of those who sold pigeons, ¹⁶ and he would not let anyone carry anything through the temple courtyards. ¹⁷ He then taught the people: "It is written in the Scriptures that God said, 'My Temple will be called a house of prayer for the people of all nations.' But you have turned it into a hideout for thieves!"

18 The chief priests and the teachers of the Law heard of this, so they began looking for some way to kill Jesus. They were afraid of him, because the whole crowd was amazed at his teaching.

19 When evening came, Jesus and his disciples left the city.

The Lesson from the Fig-Tree
(Matt. 21.20–22)

20 Early next morning, as they walked along the road, they saw the fig-tree. It was dead all the way down to its roots. ²¹ Peter remembered what had happened and said to Jesus, "Look, Teacher, the fig-tree you cursed has died!"

22 Jesus answered them, "Have faith in God. ²³ I assure you that whoever tells this hill to get up and throw itself in the sea and does not doubt in his heart, but believes that what he says will happen, it will be done for him. ²⁴ For this reason I tell you: When you pray and ask for something, believe that you have received it, and you will be given whatever you ask for. ²⁵ And when you stand and pray, forgive anything you may have against anyone, so that your Father in heaven will forgive the wrongs you have done." ˢ

The Question about Jesus' Authority
(Matt. 21.23–27; Luke 20.1–8)

27 They arrived once again in Jeru-salem. As Jesus was walking in the Temple, the chief priests, the teachers of the Law, and the elders came to him ²⁸ and asked him, "What right have you to do these things? Who gave you this right?"

29 Jesus answered them, "I will ask you just one question, and if you give me an answer, I will tell you what right I have to do these things. ³⁰ Tell me, where did John's right to baptize come from: was it from God or from man?"

31 They started to argue among them-selves: "What shall we say? If we answer, 'From God,' he will say, 'Why, then, did you not believe John?' ³² But if we say, 'From man . . .'" (They were afraid of the people, because everyone was con-vinced that John had been a prophet.) ³³ So their answer to Jesus was, "We don't know."

Jesus said to them, "Neither will I tell you, then, by what right I do these things."

The Parable of the Tenants in the Vineyard
(Matt. 21.33–46; Luke 20.9–19)

12 Then Jesus spoke to them in parables: "Once there was a man who planted a vineyard, put a fence round it, dug a hole for the winepress, and built a watch-tower. Then he let out the vineyard to tenants and left home on a journey. ² When the time came to gather the grapes, he sent a slave to the tenants to receive from them his share of the harvest. ³ The tenants seized the slave, beat him, and sent him back without a thing. ⁴ Then the owner sent another slave; the tenants beat him over the head and treated him shamefully. ⁵ The owner sent another slave, and they killed him; and they treated many others the same way, beating some and killing others. ⁶ The only one left to send was the man's own dear son. Last of all, then, he sent his son to the tenants. 'I am sure they will respect my son,' he said. ⁷ But those tenants said to one another, 'This is the owner's son. Come on, let's kill him, and his property will be ours!' ⁸ So they seized the son and killed him and threw his body out of the vineyard.

9 "What, then, will the owner of the vineyard do?" asked Jesus. "He will come and kill those men and hand the vineyard over to other tenants. ¹⁰ Surely you have read this scripture?

ˢ *Some manuscripts add verse 26:* If you do not forgive others, your Father in heaven will not forgive the wrongs you have done *(see Mt 6.15).*
11.17: Is 56.7; Jer 7.11 **11.23:** Mt 17.20; 1 Cor 13.2 **11.25–26:** Mt 6.14-15 **12.1:** Is 5.1–2

'The stone which the builders rejected
as worthless
turned out to be the most important
of all.
[11] This was done by the Lord;
what a wonderful sight it is!' "

12 The Jewish leaders tried to arrest
Jesus, because they knew that he had told
this parable against them. But they were
afraid of the crowd, so they left him and
went away.

The Question about Paying Taxes
(Matt. 22.15-22; Luke 20.20-26)

13 Some Pharisees and some members
of Herod's party were sent to Jesus to
trap him with questions. [14] They came to
him and said, "Teacher, we know that
you tell the truth, without worrying about
what people think. You pay no attention
to a man's status, but teach the truth
about God's will for man. Tell us, is it
against our Law to pay taxes to the
Roman Emperor? Should we pay them
or not?"

15 But Jesus saw through their trick
and answered, "Why are you trying to
trap me? Bring a silver coin, and let me
see it."

16 They brought him one, and he asked,
"Whose face and name are these?"

"The Emperor's," they answered.

17 So Jesus said, "Well, then, pay the
Emperor what belongs to the Emperor,
and pay God what belongs to God."

And they were amazed at Jesus.

The Question about Rising from Death
(Matt. 22.23-33; Luke 20.27-40)

18 Then some Sadducees, who say that
people will not rise from death, came to
Jesus and said, [19] "Teacher, Moses wrote
this law for us: 'If a man dies and leaves
a wife but no children, that man's brother
must marry the widow so that they can
have children who will be considered the
dead man's children.' [20] Once there were
seven brothers; the eldest got married and
died without having children. [21] Then the
second one married the woman, and he
also died without having children. The
same thing happened to the third brother,
[22] and then to the rest: all seven brothers
married the woman and died without
having children. Last of all, the woman
died. [23] Now, when all the dead rise to

life on the day of resurrection, whose wife
will she be? All seven of them had married
her."

24 Jesus answered them, "How wrong
you are! And do you know why? It is
because you don't know the Scriptures
or God's power. [25] For when the dead rise
to life, they will be like the angels in
heaven and will not marry. [26] Now, as for
the dead being raised: haven't you ever
read in the Book of Moses the passage
about the burning bush? There it is
written that God said to Moses, 'I am
the God of Abraham, the God of Isaac,
and the God of Jacob.' [27] He is the God
of the living, not of the dead. You are
completely wrong!"

The Great Commandment
(Matt. 22.34-40; Luke 10.25-28)

28 A teacher of the Law was there who
heard the discussion. He saw that Jesus
had given the Sadducees a good answer,
so he came to him with a question:
"Which commandment is the most
important of all?"

29 Jesus replied, "The most important
one is this, 'Listen, Israel! The Lord our
God is the only Lord.[t] [30] Love the Lord
your God with all your heart, with all
your soul, with all your mind, and with
all your strength.' [31] The second most
important commandment is this: 'Love
your neighbour as you love yourself.'
There is no other commandment more
important than these two."

32 The teacher of the Law said to Jesus,
"Well done, Teacher! It is true, as you
say, that only the Lord is God and that
there is no other god but he. [33] And man
must love God with all his heart and with
all his mind and with all his strength;
and he must love his neighbour as he loves
himself. It is more important to obey these
two commandments than to offer animals
and other sacrifices to God."

34 Jesus noticed how wise his answer
was, and so he told him, "You are not
far from the Kingdom of God."

After this nobody dared to ask Jesus
any more questions.

The Question about the Messiah
(Matt. 22.41-46; Luke 20.41-44)

35 As Jesus was teaching in the Temple,
he asked the question, "How can the

---

[t]The Lord our God is the only Lord; or The Lord is our God, the Lord alone.
12.10-11: Ps 118.22-23   **12.18:** Acts 23.8   **12.19:** Deut 25.5   **12.26:** Ex 3.6
12.28-34: Lk 10.25-28   **12.29-30:** Deut 6.4-5   **12.31:** Lev 19.18   **12.32:** Deut 4.35
12.33: Hos 6.6

A poor widow came along (12.42)

teachers of the Law say that the Messiah will be the descendant of David? ³⁶The Holy Spirit inspired David to say:

'The Lord said to my Lord:
  Sit here on my right
  until I put your enemies under your
    feet.'

³⁷David himself called him 'Lord'; so how can the Messiah be David's descendant?"

Jesus Warns against the Teachers of the Law
(Matt. 23.1–36; Luke 20.45–47)

A large crowd was listening to Jesus gladly. ³⁸As he taught them, he said, "Watch out for the teachers of the Law, who like to walk around in their long robes and be greeted with respect in the market-place, ³⁹who choose the reserved seats in the synagogues and the best places at feasts. ⁴⁰They take advantage of widows and rob them of their homes, and then make a show of saying long prayers. Their punishment will be all the worse!"

The Widow's Offering
(Luke 21.1–4)

41 As Jesus sat near the temple treasury, he watched the people as they dropped in their money. Many rich men dropped in a lot of money; ⁴²then a poor widow came along and dropped in two little copper coins, worth about a penny. ⁴³He called his disciples together and said

12.36: Ps 110.1

to them, "I tell you that this poor widow put more in the offering box than all the others. ⁴⁴For the others put in what they had to spare of their riches; but she, poor as she is, put in all she had—she gave all she had to live on."

Jesus Speaks of the Destruction of the Temple
(Matt. 24.1–2; Luke 21.5–6)

13 As Jesus was leaving the Temple, one of his disciples said, "Look, Teacher! What wonderful stones and buildings!"

2 Jesus answered, "You see these great buildings? Not a single stone here will be left in its place; every one of them will be thrown down."

Troubles and Persecutions
(Matt. 24.3–14; Luke 21.7–19)

3 Jesus was sitting on the Mount of Olives, across from the Temple, when Peter, James, John, and Andrew came to him in private. ⁴"Tell us when this will be," they said, "and tell us what will happen to show that the time has come for all these things to take place."

5 Jesus said to them, "Be on guard, and don't let anyone deceive you. ⁶Many men, claiming to speak for me, will come and say, 'I am he!' and they will deceive many people. ⁷And don't be troubled when you hear the noise of battles close by and news of battles far away. Such things must happen, but they do not mean that the

end has come. [8] Countries will fight each other; kingdoms will attack one another. There will be earthquakes everywhere, and there will be famines. These things are like the first pains of childbirth.

9 "You yourselves must be on guard. You will be arrested and taken to court. You will be beaten in the synagogues; you will stand before rulers and kings for my sake to tell them the Good News. [10] But before the end comes, the gospel must be preached to all peoples. [11] And when you are arrested and taken to court, do not worry beforehand about what you are going to say; when the time comes, say whatever is then given to you. For the words you speak will not be yours; they will come from the Holy Spirit. [12] Men will hand over their own brothers to be put to death, and fathers will do the same to their children. Children will turn against their parents and have them put to death. [13] Everyone will hate you because of me. But whoever holds out to the end will be saved.

The Awful Horror
(Matt. 24.15-28; Luke 21.20-24)

14 "You will see 'The Awful Horror' standing in the place where he should not be." (Note to the reader: be sure to understand what this means!) "Then those who are in Judaea must run away to the hills. [15] A man who is on the roof of his house must not lose time by going down into the house to get anything to take with him. [16] A man who is in the field must not go back to the house for his cloak. [17] How terrible it will be in those days for women who are pregnant and for mothers with little babies! [18] Pray to God that these things will not happen in the winter! [19] For the trouble of those days will be far worse than any the world has ever known from the very beginning when God created the world until the present time. Nor will there ever be anything like it again. [20] But the Lord has reduced the number of those days; if he had not, nobody would survive. For the sake of his chosen people, however, he has reduced those days.

21 "Then, if anyone says to you, 'Look, here is the Messiah!' or, 'Look, there he is!'—do not believe him. [22] For false

Messiahs and false prophets will appear. They will perform miracles and wonders in order to deceive even God's chosen people, if possible. [23] Be on your guard! I have told you everything before the time comes.

The Coming of the Son of Man
(Matt. 24.29-31; Luke 21.25-28)

24 "In the days after that time of trouble the sun will grow dark, the moon will no longer shine, [25] the stars will fall from heaven, and the powers in space will be driven from their courses. [26] Then the Son of Man will appear, coming in the clouds with great power and glory. [27] He will send the angels out to the four corners of the earth to gather God's chosen people from one end of the world to the other.

The Lesson of the Fig-Tree
(Matt. 24.32-35; Luke 21.29-33)

28 "Let the fig-tree teach you a lesson. When its branches become green and tender and it starts putting out leaves, you know that summer is near. [29] In the same way, when you see these things happening, you will know that the time is near, ready to begin. [u] [30] Remember that all these things will happen before the people now living have all died. [31] Heaven and earth will pass away, but my words will never pass away.

No One Knows the Day or Hour
(Matt. 24.36-44)

32 "No one knows, however, when that day or hour will come—neither the angels in heaven, nor the Son; only the Father knows. [33] Be on watch, be alert, for you do not know when the time will come. [34] It will be like a man who goes away from home on a journey and leaves his servants in charge, after giving to each one his own work to do and after telling the doorkeeper to keep watch. [35] Be on guard, then, because you do not know when the master of the house is coming— it might be in the evening or at midnight or before dawn or at sunrise. [36] If he comes suddenly, he must not find you asleep. [37] What I say to you, then, I say to all: Watch!"

[u] the time is near, ready to begin; or he is near, ready to come.
13.9-11: Mt 10.17-20; Lk 12.11-12　**13.13:** Mt 10.22　**13.14:** Dan 9.27, 11.31, 12.11
13.15-16: Lk 17.31　**13.19:** Dan 12.1; Rev 7.14
13.24: Is 13.10; Ezek 32.7; Joel 2.10, 31, 3.15; Rev 6.12　**13.25:** Is 34.4; Joel 2.10; Rev 6.13
13.26: Dan 7.13; Rev 1.7　**13.32:** Mt 24.36　**13.34:** Lk 12.36-38

The Plot against Jesus
(Matt. 26.1–5; Luke 22.1–2; John 11.45–53)

14 It was now two days before the Festival of Passover and Unleavened Bread. The chief priests and the teachers of the Law were looking for a way to arrest Jesus secretly and put him to death. 2 "We must not do it during the festival," they said, "or the people might riot."

Jesus Is Anointed at Bethany
(Matt. 26.6–13; John 12.1–8)

3 Jesus was in Bethany at the house of Simon, a man who had suffered from a dreaded skin-disease. While Jesus was eating, a woman came in with an alabaster jar full of a very expensive perfume made of pure nard. She broke the jar and poured the perfume on Jesus' head. 4 Some of the people there became angry and said to one another, "What was the use of wasting the perfume? 5 It could have been sold for more than three hundred silver coins ᵛ and the money given to the poor!" And they criticized her harshly.

6 But Jesus said, "Leave her alone! Why are you bothering her? She has done a fine and beautiful thing for me. 7 You will always have poor people with you, and any time you want to, you can help them. But you will not always have me. 8 She did what she could; she poured perfume on my body to prepare it ahead of time for burial. 9 Now, I assure you that wherever the gospel is preached all over the world, what she has done will be told in memory of her."

Judas Agrees to Betray Jesus
(Matt. 26.14–16; Luke 22.3–6)

10 Then Judas Iscariot, one of the twelve disciples, went off to the chief priests in order to betray Jesus to them. 11 They were pleased to hear what he had to say, and promised to give him money. So Judas started looking for a good chance to hand Jesus over to them.

Jesus Eats the Passover Meal with His Disciples
(Matt. 26.17–25; Luke 22.7–14, 21–23; John 13.21–30)

12 On the first day of the Festival of Unleavened Bread, the day the lambs for the Passover meal were killed, Jesus' disciples asked him, "Where do you want us to go and get the Passover meal ready for you?"

13 Then Jesus sent two of them with these instructions: "Go into the city, and a man carrying a jar of water will meet you. Follow him 14 to the house he enters, and say to the owner of the house: 'The Teacher says, Where is the room where my disciples and I will eat the Passover meal?' 15 Then he will show you a large upstairs room, prepared and furnished, where you will get everything ready for us."

16 The disciples left, went to the city, and found everything just as Jesus had told them; and they prepared the Passover meal.

17 When it was evening, Jesus came with the twelve disciples. 18 While they were at the table eating, Jesus said, "I tell you that one of you will betray me— one who is eating with me."

19 The disciples were upset and began to ask him, one after the other, "Surely you don't mean me, do you?"

20 Jesus answered, "It will be one of you twelve, one who dips his bread in the dish with me. 21 The Son of Man will die as the Scriptures say he will; but how terrible for that man who betrays the Son of Man! It would have been better for that man if he had never been born!"

The Lord's Supper
(Matt. 26.26–30; Luke 22.14–20; I Cor. 11.23–25)

22 While they were eating, Jesus took a piece of bread, gave a prayer of thanks, broke it, and gave it to his disciples. "Take it," he said, "this is my body."

23 Then he took a cup, gave thanks to God, and handed it to them; and they all drank from it. 24 Jesus said, "This is my blood which is poured out for many, my blood which seals God's covenant. 25 I tell you, I will never again drink this wine until the day I drink the new wine in the Kingdom of God."

26 Then they sang a hymn and went out to the Mount of Olives.

Jesus Predicts Peter's Denial
(Matt. 26.31–35; Luke 22.31–34; John 13.36–38)

27 Jesus said to them, "All of you will run away and leave me, for the scripture says, 'God will kill the shepherd, and the

---

ᵛ SILVER COINS: *see 6.37.*
14.1: Ex 12.1–27　　**14.3:** Lk 7.37–38　　**14.7:** Deut 15.11　　**14.18:** Ps 41.9
14.24: Ex 24.8; Jer 31.31–34　　**14.27:** Zech 13.7

This is my body (14.22)

sheep will all be scattered.' ²⁸ But after I am raised to life, I will go to Galilee ahead of you."

29 Peter answered, "I will never leave you, even though all the rest do!"

30 Jesus said to Peter, "I tell you that before the cock crows twice tonight, you will say three times that you do not know me."

31 Peter answered even more strongly, "I will never say that, even if I have to die with you!"

And all the other disciples said the same thing.

Jesus Prays in Gethsemane
(Matt. 26.36–46; Luke 22.39–46)

32 They came to a place called Gethsemane, and Jesus said to his disciples, "Sit here while I pray." ³³ He took Peter, James, and John with him. Distress and anguish came over him, ³⁴ and he said to them, "The sorrow in my heart is so great that it almost crushes me. Stay here and keep watch."

35 He went a little farther on, threw himself on the ground, and prayed that, if possible, he might not have to go through that time of suffering. ³⁶ "Father," he prayed, "my Father! All things are possible for you. Take this cup of suffering away from me. Yet not what I want, but what you want."

37 Then he returned and found the three disciples asleep. He said to Peter, "Simon, are you asleep? Weren't you able to stay

awake even for one hour?" ³⁸ And he said to them, "Keep watch, and pray that you will not fall into temptation. The spirit is willing, but the flesh is weak."

39 He went away once more and prayed, saying the same words. ⁴⁰ Then he came back to the disciples and found them asleep; they could not keep their eyes open. And they did not know what to say to him.

41 When he came back the third time, he said to them, "Are you still sleeping and resting? Enough! The hour has come! Look, the Son of Man is now being handed over to the power of sinful men. ⁴² Get up, let us go. Look, here is the man who is betraying me!"

The Arrest of Jesus
(Matt. 26.47–56; Luke 22.47–53; John 18.3–12)

43 Jesus was still speaking when Judas, one of the twelve disciples, arrived. With him was a crowd armed with swords and clubs, and sent by the chief priests, the teachers of the Law, and the elders. ⁴⁴ The traitor had given the crowd a signal: "The man I kiss is the one you want. Arrest him and take him away under guard."

45 As soon as Judas arrived, he went up to Jesus and said, "Teacher!" and kissed him. ⁴⁶ So they arrested Jesus and held him tight. ⁴⁷ But one of those standing there drew his sword and struck at the High Priest's slave, cutting off his ear. ⁴⁸ Then Jesus spoke up and said to them, "Did you have to come with swords and

14.28: Mt 28.16

So they arrested Jesus and held him tight (14.46)

clubs to capture me, as though I were an outlaw? ⁴⁹Day after day I was with you teaching in the Temple, and you did not arrest me. But the Scriptures must come true."

50 Then all the disciples left him and ran away.

51 A certain young man, dressed only in a linen cloth, was following Jesus. They tried to arrest him, ⁵²but he ran away naked, leaving the cloth behind.

Jesus before the Council
(Matt. 26.57-68; Luke 22.54-55, 63-71; John 18.13-14, 19-24)

53 Then Jesus was taken to the High Priest's house, where all the chief priests, the elders, and the teachers of the Law were gathering. ⁵⁴Peter followed from a distance and went into the courtyard of the High Priest's house. There he sat down with the guards, keeping himself warm by the fire. ⁵⁵The chief priests and the whole Council tried to find some evidence against Jesus in order to put him to death, but they could not find any. ⁵⁶Many witnesses told lies against Jesus, but their stories did not agree.

57 Then some men stood up and told this lie against Jesus: ⁵⁸"We heard him say, 'I will tear down this Temple which men have made, and after three days I will build one that is not made by men.'" ⁵⁹Not even they, however, could make their stories agree.

60 The High Priest stood up in front of them all and questioned Jesus, "Have you no answer to the accusation they bring against you?"

61 But Jesus kept quiet and would not say a word. Again the High Priest questioned him, "Are you the Messiah, the Son of the Blessed God?"

62 "I am," answered Jesus, "and you will all see the Son of Man seated on the right of the Almighty and coming with the clouds of heaven!"

63 The High Priest tore his robes and said, "We don't need any more witnesses! ⁶⁴You heard his blasphemy. What is your decision?"

They all voted against him: he was guilty and should be put to death.

14.49: Lk 19.47, 21.37   **14.58:** Jn 2.19   **14.62:** Dan 7.13   **14.64:** Lev 24.16

65 Some of them began to spit on Jesus, and they blindfolded him and hit him. "Guess who hit you!" they said. And the guards took him and slapped him.'

Peter Denies Jesus
(Matt. 26.69–75; Luke 22.56–62; John 18.15–18, 25–27)

66 Peter was still down in the courtyard when one of the High Priest's servant-girls came by. 67 When she saw Peter warming himself, she looked straight at him and said, "You, too, were with Jesus of Nazareth."

68 But he denied it. "I don't know... I don't understand what you are talking about," he answered, and went out into the passage. Just then a cock crowed. w

69 The servant-girl saw him there and began to repeat to the bystanders, "He is one of them!" 70 But Peter denied it again.

A little while later the bystanders accused Peter again, "You can't deny that you are one of them, because you, too, are from Galilee."

71 Then Peter said, "I swear that I am telling the truth! May God punish me if I am not! I do not know the man you are talking about!"

72 Just then a cock crowed a second

A cock crowed... and Peter remembered (14.72)

time, and Peter remembered how Jesus had said to him, "Before the cock crows twice, you will say three times that you do not know me." And he broke down and cried.

w *Some manuscripts do not have* Just then a cock crowed.

Jesus Is Brought before Pilate
(Matt. 27.1–2, 11–14; Luke 23.1–5; John 18.28–38)

15 Early in the morning the chief priests met hurriedly with the elders, the teachers of the Law, and the whole Council, and made their plans. They put Jesus in chains, led him away, and handed him over to Pilate. 2 Pilate questioned him, "Are you the king of the Jews?"

Jesus answered, "So you say."

3 The chief priests were accusing Jesus of many things, 4 so Pilate questioned him again, "Aren't you going to answer? Listen to all their accusations!"

5 Again Jesus refused to say a word, and Pilate was amazed.

Jesus Is Sentenced to Death
(Matt. 27.15–26; Luke 23.13–25; John 18.39–19.16)

6 At every Passover Festival Pilate was in the habit of setting free any one prisoner the people asked for. 7 At that time a man named Barabbas was in prison with the rebels who had committed murder in the riot. 8 When the crowd gathered and began to ask Pilate for the usual favour, 9 he asked them, "Do you want me to set free for you the king of the Jews?" 10 He knew very well that the chief priests had handed Jesus over to him because they were jealous.

11 But the chief priests stirred up the crowd to ask, instead, for Pilate to set Barabbas free for them. 12 Pilate spoke again to the crowd, "What, then, do you want me to do with the one you call the king of the Jews?"

13 They shouted back, "Crucify him!"

14 "But what crime has he committed?" Pilate asked.

They shouted all the louder, "Crucify him!"

15 Pilate wanted to please the crowd, so he set Barabbas free for them. Then he had Jesus whipped and handed him over to be crucified.

The Soldiers Mock Jesus
(Matt. 27.27–31; John 19.2–3)

16 The soldiers took Jesus inside to the courtyard of the governor's palace and called together the rest of the company. 17 They put a purple robe on Jesus, made a crown out of thorny branches, and put it on his head. 18 Then they began to salute

him: "Long live the King of the Jews!" ¹⁹They beat him over the head with a stick, spat on him, fell on their knees, and bowed down to him. ²⁰When they had finished mocking him, they took off the purple robe and put his own clothes back on him. Then they led him out to crucify him.

bandits with Jesus, one on his right and the other on his left. ˣ

29 People passing by shook their heads and hurled insults at Jesus: "Aha! You were going to tear down the Temple and build it up again in three days! ³⁰Now come down from the cross and save yourself!"

Throwing dice (15.24)

Jesus Is Crucified
(Matt. 27.32–44; Luke 23.26–43; John 19.17–27)

21 On the way they met a man named Simon, who was coming into the city from the country, and the soldiers forced him to carry Jesus' cross. (Simon was from Cyrene and was the father of Alexander and Rufus.) ²²They took Jesus to a place called Golgotha, which means "The Place of the Skull." ²³There they tried to give him wine mixed with a drug called myrrh, but Jesus would not drink it. ²⁴Then they crucified him and divided his clothes among themselves, throwing dice to see who would get which piece of clothing. ²⁵It was nine o'clock in the morning when they crucified him. ²⁶The notice of the accusation against him said: "The King of the Jews." ²⁷They also crucified two

31 In the same way the chief priests and the teachers of the Law jeered at Jesus, saying to each other, "He saved others, but he cannot save himself! ³²Let us see the Messiah, the king of Israel, come down from the cross now, and we will believe in him!"

And the two who were crucified with Jesus insulted him also.

The Death of Jesus
(Matt. 27.45–56; Luke 23.44–49; John 19.28–30)

33 At noon the whole country was covered with darkness, which lasted for three hours. ³⁴At three o'clock Jesus cried out with a loud shout, *"Eloi, Eloi, lema sabachthani?"* which means, "My God, my God, why did you abandon me?"

35 Some of the people there heard him and said, "Listen, he is calling for Elijah!"

ˣ *Some manuscripts add verse 28:* In this way the scripture came true which says, "He shared the fate of criminals" *(see Lk 22.37).*
15.21: Rom 16.13   **15.24:** Ps 22.18   **15.28:** Is 53.12
15.29: Ps 22.7, 109.25; Mk 14.58; Jn 2.19   **15.34:** Ps 22.1

36 One of them ran up with a sponge, soaked it in cheap wine, and put it on the end of a stick. Then he held it up to Jesus' lips and said, "Wait! Let us see if Elijah is coming to bring him down from the cross!"

37 With a loud cry Jesus died.

38 The curtain hanging in the Temple was torn in two, from top to bottom. 39 The army officer who was standing there in front of the cross saw how Jesus had died. *y* "This man was really the Son of God!" he said.

40 Some women were there, looking on from a distance. Among them were Mary Magdalene, Mary the mother of the younger James and of Joseph, and Salome. 41 They had followed Jesus while he was in Galilee and had helped him. Many other women who had come to Jerusalem with him were there also.

The Burial of Jesus

(Matt. 27.57–61; Luke 23.50–56; John 19.38–42)

42–43 It was towards evening when Joseph of Arimathea arrived. He was a respected member of the Council, who was waiting for the coming of the Kingdom of God. It was Preparation day (that is, the day before the Sabbath), so Joseph went boldly into the presence of Pilate and asked him for the body of Jesus. 44 Pilate was surprised to hear that Jesus was already dead. He called the army officer and asked him if Jesus had been dead a long time. 45 After hearing the officer's report, Pilate told Joseph he could have the body. 46 Joseph bought a linen sheet, took the body down, wrapped it in the sheet, and placed it in a tomb

y had died; *some manuscripts have* had cried out and died.
15.36: Ps 69.21   **15.38:** Ex 26.31–33   **15.40–41:** Lk 8.2–3

Aha! ... come down from the cross (15.29, 30)

which had been dug out of solid rock. Then he rolled a large stone across the entrance to the tomb. [47]Mary Magdalene and Mary the mother of Joseph were watching and saw where the body of Jesus was placed.

The Resurrection
(Matt. 28.1–8; Luke 24.1–12; John 20.1–10)

16 After the Sabbath was over, Mary Magdalene, Mary the mother of James, and Salome bought spices to go and anoint the body of Jesus. [2]Very early on Sunday morning, at sunrise, they went to the tomb. [3-4]On the way they said to one another, "Who will roll away the stone for us from the entrance to the tomb?" (It was a very large stone.) Then they looked up and saw that the stone had already been rolled back. [5]So they entered the tomb, where they saw a young man sitting on the right, wearing a white robe—and they were alarmed.

[6] "Don't be alarmed," he said. "I know you are looking for Jesus of Nazareth, who was crucified. He is not here—he has been raised! Look, here is the place where they put him. [7]Now go and give this message to his disciples, including Peter: 'He is going to Galilee ahead of you; there you will see him, just as he told you.'"

[8] So they went out and ran from the

So they went out and ran (16.8)

tomb, distressed and terrified. They said nothing to anyone, because they were afraid.

AN OLD ENDING TO THE GOSPEL[z]

Jesus Appears to Mary Magdalene
(Matt. 28.9–10; John 20.11–18)

[[9]After Jesus rose from death early on Sunday, he appeared first to Mary Magdalene, from whom he had driven out seven demons. [10]She went and told his companions. They were mourning and crying; [11]and when they heard her say that Jesus was alive and that she had seen him, they did not believe her.

Jesus Appears to Two Disciples
(Luke 24.13–35)

[12] After this, Jesus appeared in a different manner to two of them while they were on their way to the country. [13]They returned and told the others, but they would not believe it.

Jesus Appears to the Eleven
(Matt. 28.16–20; Luke 24.36–49;
John 20.19–23; Acts 1.6–8)

[14] Last of all, Jesus appeared to the eleven disciples as they were eating. He scolded them, because they did not have faith and because they were too stubborn to believe those who had seen him alive. [15]He said to them, "Go throughout the whole world and preach the gospel to all mankind. [16]Whoever believes and is baptized will be saved; whoever does not believe will be condemned. [17]Believers will be given the power to perform miracles: they will drive out demons in my name; they will speak in strange tongues; [18]if they pick up snakes or drink any poison, they will not be harmed; they will place their hands on sick people, who will get well."

Jesus Is Taken up to Heaven
(Luke 24.50–53; Acts 1.9–11)

[19] After the Lord Jesus had talked with them, he was taken up to heaven and sat at the right side of God. [20]The disciples went and preached everywhere, and the Lord worked with them and proved that their preaching was true by the miracles that were performed.]

---

[z] *Some manuscripts and ancient translations do not have this ending to the Gospel (verses 9–20).*
16.7: Mt 26.32; Mk 14.28   **16.15:** Acts 1.8   **16.19:** Acts 1.9–11

ANOTHER OLD ENDING[a]

[[9]The women went to Peter and his friends and gave them a brief account of all they had been told. [10]After this, Jesus himself sent out through his disciples from the east to the west the sacred and ever-living message of eternal salvation.]

[a] *Some manuscripts and ancient translations have this shorter ending to the Gospel in addition to the longer ending (verses 9-20).*

THE GOSPEL ACCORDING TO

LUKE

INTRODUCTION

The Gospel according to Luke presents Jesus as both the promised Saviour of Israel and as the Saviour of all mankind. *Luke* records that Jesus was called by the Spirit of the Lord to "preach the Good News to the poor," and this Gospel is filled with a concern for people with all kinds of need. The note of joy is also prominent in *Luke,* especially in the opening chapters that announce the coming of Jesus, and again at the conclusion, when Jesus ascends to heaven. The story of the growth and spread of the Christian faith after the ascension of Jesus is told by the same writer in the book of *Acts.*

Parts 2 and 6 (see the outline below) contain much material that is found only in this Gospel, such as the stories about the song of the angels and the shepherds' visit at the birth of Jesus, Jesus in the Temple as a boy, and the parables of the Good Samaritan and the Lost Son. Throughout the Gospel great emphasis is placed on prayer, the Holy Spirit, the role of women in the ministry of Jesus, and God's forgiveness of sins.

Outline of Contents

Introduction   1.1-4
Birth and childhood of John the Baptist and of Jesus   1.5—2.52
The ministry of John the Baptist   3.1-20
The baptism and temptation of Jesus   3.21—4.13
Jesus' public ministry in Galilee   4.14—9.50
From Galilee to Jerusalem   9.51—19.27
The last week in and near Jerusalem   19.28—23.56
The resurrection, appearances, and ascension of the Lord   24.1-53

1 Dear Theophilus:
Many people have done their best to write a report of the things that have taken place among us. [2]They wrote what we have been told by those who saw these things from the beginning and who proclaimed the message. [3]And so, your Excellency, because I have carefully studied all these matters from their beginning, I thought it would be good to write an orderly account for you. [4]I do this so that you will know the full truth about everything which you have been taught.

The Birth of John the Baptist Is Announced

5 During the time when Herod was king of Judaea,[a] there was a priest named Zechariah, who belonged to the priestly order of Abijah. His wife's name was Elizabeth; she also belonged to a priestly family. 6 They both lived good lives in God's sight and obeyed fully all the Lord's laws and commands. 7 They had no children because Elizabeth could not have any, and she and Zechariah were both very old.

8 One day Zechariah was doing his work as a priest in the Temple, taking his turn in the daily service. 9 According to the custom followed by the priests, he was chosen by lot to burn incense on the altar. So he went into the Temple of the Lord, 10 while the crowd of people outside prayed during the hour when the incense was burnt.

11 An angel of the Lord appeared to him, standing on the right of the altar where the incense was burnt. 12 When Zechariah saw him, he was alarmed and felt afraid. 13 But the angel said to him, "Don't be afraid, Zechariah! God has heard your prayer, and your wife Elizabeth will bear you a son. You are to name him John. 14 How glad and happy you will be, and how happy many others will be when he is born! 15 He will be a great man in the Lord's sight. He must not drink any wine or strong drink. From his very birth he will be filled with the Holy Spirit, 16 and he will bring back many of the people of Israel to the Lord their God. 17 He will go ahead of the Lord, strong and mighty like the prophet Elijah. He will bring fathers and children together again; he will turn disobedient people back to the way of thinking of the righteous; he will get the Lord's people ready for him."

18 Zechariah said to the angel, "How shall I know if this is so? I am an old man, and my wife is old also."

19 "I am Gabriel," the angel answered. "I stand in the presence of God, who sent me to speak to you and tell you this good news. 20 But you have not believed my message, which will come true at the right time. Because you have not believed, you will be unable to speak; you will remain silent until the day my promise to you comes true."

21 In the meantime the people were waiting for Zechariah and wondering why he was spending such a long time in the Temple. 22 When he came out, he could not speak to them, and so they knew that he had seen a vision in the Temple. Unable to say a word, he made signs to them with his hands.

23 When his period of service in the Temple was over, Zechariah went back home. 24 Some time later his wife Elizabeth became pregnant and did not leave the house for five months. 25 "Now at last the Lord has helped me," she said. "He has taken away my public disgrace!"

The Birth of Jesus Is Announced

26 In the sixth month of Elizabeth's pregnancy God sent the angel Gabriel to a town in Galilee named Nazareth. 27 He had a message for a girl promised in marriage to a man named Joseph, who was a descendant of King David. The girl's name was Mary. 28 The angel came to her and said, "Peace be with you! The Lord is with you and has greatly blessed you!"

29 Mary was deeply troubled by the angel's message, and she wondered what his words meant. 30 The angel said to her, "Don't be afraid, Mary; God has been gracious to you. 31 You will become pregnant and give birth to a son, and you will name him Jesus. 32 He will be great and will be called the Son of the Most High God. The Lord God will make him a king, as his ancestor David was, 33 and he will be the king of the descendants of Jacob for ever; his kingdom will never end!"

34 Mary said to the angel, "I am a virgin. How, then, can this be?"

35 The angel answered, "The Holy Spirit will come on you, and God's power will rest upon you. For this reason the holy child will be called the Son of God. 36 Remember your relative Elizabeth. It is said that she cannot have children, but she herself is now six months pregnant, even though she is very old. 37 For there is nothing that God cannot do."

38 "I am the Lord's servant," said Mary; "may it happen to me as you have said." And the angel left her.

Mary Visits Elizabeth

39 Soon afterwards Mary got ready and hurried off to a town in the hill-country

---

[a] JUDAEA: *The term here refers to the whole land of Palestine.*

1.5: 1 Chr 24.10   **1.15:** Num 6.3   **1.17:** Mal 4.5–6   **1.19:** Dan 8.16, 9.21   **1.27:** Mt 1.18
1.31: Mt 1.21   **1.32–33:** 2 Sam 7.12,13,16; Is 9.7   **1.37:** Gen 18.14

of Judaea. 40 She went into Zechariah's house and greeted Elizabeth. 41 When Elizabeth heard Mary's greeting, the baby moved within her. Elizabeth was filled with the Holy Spirit 42 and said in a loud voice, "You are the most blessed of all women, and blessed is the child you will bear! 43 Why should this great thing happen to me, that my Lord's mother comes to visit me? 44 For as soon as I heard your greeting, the baby within me jumped with gladness. 45 How happy you are to believe that the Lord's message to you will come true!"

Mary's Song of Praise

46 Mary said,
"My heart praises the Lord;
47 my soul is glad because of God my Saviour,
48 for he has remembered me, his lowly servant!
From now on all people will call me happy,
49 because of the great things the Mighty God has done for me.
His name is holy;
50 from one generation to another he shows mercy to those who honour him.
51 He has stretched out his mighty arm and scattered the proud with all their plans.
52 He has brought down mighty kings from their thrones,
and lifted up the lowly.
53 He has filled the hungry with good things,
and sent the rich away with empty hands.
54 He has kept the promise he made to our ancestors,
and has come to the help of his servant Israel.
55 He has remembered to show mercy to Abraham
and to all his descendants for ever!"
56 Mary stayed about three months with Elizabeth and then went back home.

The Birth of John the Baptist

57 The time came for Elizabeth to have her baby, and she gave birth to a son. 58 Her neighbours and relatives heard how wonderfully good the Lord had been to her, and they all rejoiced with her.
59 When the baby was a week old, they came to circumcise him, and they were going to name him Zechariah, after his father. 60 But his mother said, "No! His name is to be John."

61 They said to her, "But you have no relatives with that name!" 62 Then they made signs to his father, asking him what name he would like the boy to have.

63 Zechariah asked for a writing tablet and wrote, "His name is John." How surprised they all were! 64 At that moment Zechariah was able to speak again, and he started praising God. 65 The neighbours were all filled with fear, and the news about these things spread through all the hill-country of Judaea. 66 Everyone who heard of it thought about it and asked, "What is this child going to be?" For it was plain that the Lord's power was upon him.

Zechariah's Prophecy

67 John's father Zechariah was filled with the Holy Spirit, and he spoke God's message:
68 "Let us praise the Lord, the God of Israel!
He has come to the help of his people and has set them free.
69 He has provided for us a mighty Saviour,
a descendant of his servant David.
70 He promised through his holy prophets long ago
71 that he would save us from our enemies,
from the power of all those who hate us.
72 He said he would show mercy to our ancestors
and remember his sacred covenant.
73-74 With a solemn oath to our ancestor Abraham
he promised to rescue us from our enemies
and allow us to serve him without fear,
75 so that we might be holy and righteous before him
all the days of our life.

76 "You, my child, will be called a prophet of the Most High God.
You will go ahead of the Lord to prepare his road for him,
77 to tell his people that they will be saved by having their sins forgiven.
78 Our God is merciful and tender.

1.46-55: 1 Sam 2.1-10   **1.48:** 1 Sam 1.11   **1.52:** Job 5.11, 12.19   **1.55:** Gen 17.7
1.59: Lev 12.3   **1.76:** Mal 3.1

He will cause the bright dawn of
    salvation to rise on us
79   and to shine from heaven on all
      those who live in the dark shadow
      of death,
    to guide our steps into the path of
      peace.''

80 The child grew and developed in
body and spirit. He lived in the desert
until the day when he appeared publicly
to the people of Israel.

The Birth of Jesus
(Matt. 1.18–25)

2 At that time the Emperor Augustus
ordered a census to be taken throughout the Roman Empire. ²When this first
census took place, Quirinius was the
governor of Syria. ³Everyone, then, went
to register himself, each to his own town.

4 Joseph went from the town of
Nazareth in Galilee to the town of
Bethlehem in Judaea, the birthplace of
King David. Joseph went there because
he was a descendant of David. ⁵He went
to register with Mary, who was promised
in marriage to him. She was pregnant,
⁶and while they were in Bethlehem, the
time came for her to have her baby. ⁷She
gave birth to her first son, wrapped him
in strips of cloth and laid him in a
manger—there was no room for them to
stay in the inn.

The Shepherds and the Angels

8 There were some shepherds in that
part of the country who were spending the
night in the fields, taking care of their
flocks. ⁹An angel of the Lord appeared
to them, and the glory of the Lord shone
over them. They were terribly afraid, ¹⁰but
the angel said to them, "Don't be afraid!
I am here with good news for you, which
will bring great joy to all the people. ¹¹This
very day in David's town your Saviour
was born—Christ the Lord! ¹²And this
is what will prove it to you: you will find
a baby wrapped in strips of cloth and
lying in a manger.''

13 Suddenly a great army of heaven's
angels appeared with the angel, singing
praises to God:
¹⁴ "Glory to God in the highest heaven,
   and peace on earth to those with
      whom he is pleased!''

15 When the angels went away from
them back into heaven, the shepherds said
to one another, "Let's go to Bethlehem

and see this thing that has happened,
which the Lord has told us.''

16 So they hurried off and found Mary
and Joseph and saw the baby lying in
the manger. ¹⁷When the shepherds saw
him, they told them what the angel had
said about the child. ¹⁸All who heard it
were amazed at what the shepherds said.
¹⁹Mary remembered all these things and

Mary remembered all these things (2.19)

thought deeply about them. ²⁰The shepherds went back, singing praises to God
for all they had heard and seen; it had
been just as the angel had told them.

Jesus Is Named

21 A week later, when the time came
for the baby to be circumcised, he was
named Jesus, the name which the angel
had given him before he had been
conceived.

Jesus Is Presented in the Temple

22 The time came for Joseph and Mary
to perform the ceremony of purification,
as the Law of Moses commanded. So they
took the child to Jerusalem to present him
to the Lord, ²³as it is written in the law
of the Lord: "Every first-born male is to
be dedicated to the Lord.'' ²⁴They also

1.79: Is 9.2   **2.21:** Lev 12.3; Lk 1.31   **2.22–24:** Lev 12.6–8   **2.23:** Ex 13.2,12

Sitting with the Jewish teachers (2.46)

went to offer a sacrifice of a pair of doves or two young pigeons, as required by the law of the Lord.

25 At that time there was a man named Simeon living in Jerusalem. He was a good, God-fearing man and was waiting for Israel to be saved. The Holy Spirit was with him 26 and had assured him that he would not die before he had seen the Lord's promised Messiah. 27 Led by the Spirit, Simeon went into the Temple. When the parents brought the child Jesus into the Temple to do for him what the Law required, 28 Simeon took the child in his arms and gave thanks to God:

29 "Now, Lord, you have kept your
       promise,
    and you may let your servant go in
       peace.
30 With my own eyes I have seen your
       salvation,
31   which you have prepared in the
       presence of all peoples:
32 A light to reveal your will to the
       Gentiles
    and bring glory to your people Israel."

33 The child's father and mother were amazed at the things Simeon said about him. 34 Simeon blessed them and said to Mary, his mother, "This child is chosen by God for the destruction and the salvation of many in Israel. He will be a sign from God which many people will speak against 35 and so reveal their secret thoughts. And sorrow, like a sharp sword, will break your own heart."

36-37 There was a very old prophetess, a widow named Anna, daughter of Phanuel of the tribe of Asher. She had been married for only seven years and was now eighty-four years old. *b* She never left the Temple; day and night she worshipped God, fasting and praying. 38 That very same hour she arrived and gave thanks to God and spoke about the child to all who were waiting for God to set Jerusalem free.

The Return to Nazareth

39 When Joseph and Mary had finished doing all that was required by the law of the Lord, they returned to their home town of Nazareth in Galilee. 40 The child grew and became strong; he was full of wisdom, and God's blessings were upon him.

The Boy Jesus in the Temple

41 Every year the parents of Jesus went to Jerusalem for the Passover Festival. 42 When Jesus was twelve years old, they went to the festival as usual. 43 When the festival was over, they started back home, but the boy Jesus stayed in Jerusalem. His parents did not know this; 44 they thought that he was with the group, so they travelled a whole day and then started looking for him among their relatives and friends. 45 They did not find him, so they went back to Jerusalem looking for him. 46 On the third day they found him in the Temple, sitting with the Jewish teachers, listening to them and asking questions. 47 All who heard him were amazed at his intelligent answers. 48 His parents were astonished when they

b was now eighty-four years old; *or* had been a widow eighty-four years.
2.32: Is 42.6, 49.6, 52.10   **2.39:** Mt 2.23   **2.41:** Ex 12.1–27; Deut 16.1–8

PALESTINE IN THE TIME OF JESUS

saw him, and his mother said to him, "My son, why have you done this to us? Your father and I have been terribly worried trying to find you."

49 He answered them, "Why did you have to look for me? Didn't you know that I had to be in my Father's house?" 50 But they did not understand his answer.

51 So Jesus went back with them to Nazareth, where he was obedient to them. His mother treasured all these things in her heart. 52 Jesus grew both in body and in wisdom, gaining favour with God and men.

The Preaching of John the Baptist
(Matt. 3.1–12; Mark 1.1–8; John 1.19–28)

3 It was the fifteenth year of the rule of the Emperor Tiberius; Pontius Pilate was governor of Judaea, Herod was ruler of Galilee, and his brother Philip was ruler of the territory of Iturea and Trachonitis; Lysanias was ruler of Abilene, 2 and Annas and Caiaphas were high priests. At that time the word of God came to John son of Zechariah in the desert. 3 So John went throughout the whole territory of the River Jordan, preaching, "Turn away from your sins and be baptized, and God will forgive your sins." 4 As it is written in the book of the prophet Isaiah:

"Someone is shouting in the desert:
'Get the road ready for the Lord;
make a straight path for him to travel!
5 Every valley must be filled up,
every hill and mountain levelled off.
The winding roads must be made straight,
and the rough paths made smooth.
6 All mankind will see God's salvation!'"

7 Crowds of people came out to John to be baptized by him. "You snakes!" he said to them. "Who told you that you could escape from the punishment God is about to send? 8 Do those things that will show that you have turned from your sins. And don't start saying among yourselves that Abraham is your ancestor. I tell you that God can take these stones and make descendants for Abraham! 9 The axe is ready to cut down the trees at the roots; every tree that does not bear good fruit will be cut down and thrown in the fire."

10 The people asked him, "What are we to do, then?"

11 He answered, "Whoever has two shirts must give one to the man who has none, and whoever has food must share it."

12 Some tax collectors came to be baptized, and they asked him, "Teacher, what are we to do?"

13 "Don't collect more than is legal," he told them.

14 Some soldiers also asked him, "What about us? What are we to do?"

He said to them, "Don't take money from anyone by force or accuse anyone falsely. Be content with your pay."

15 People's hopes began to rise, and they began to wonder whether John perhaps might be the Messiah. 16 So John said to all of them, "I baptize you with water, but someone is coming who is much greater than I am. I am not good enough even to untie his sandals. He will baptize you with the Holy Spirit and fire. 17 He has his winnowing shovel with him, to thresh out all the grain and gather the wheat into his barn; but he will burn the chaff in a fire that never goes out."

18 In many different ways John preached the Good News to the people and urged them to change their ways. 19 But John reprimanded Herod, the governor, because he had married Herodias, his brother's wife, and had done many other evil things. 20 Then Herod did an even worse thing by putting John in prison.

The Baptism of Jesus
(Matt. 3.13–17; Mark 1.9–11)

21 After all the people had been baptized, Jesus also was baptized. While he was praying, heaven was opened, 22 and the Holy Spirit came down upon him in bodily form like a dove. And a voice came from heaven, "You are my own dear Son. I am pleased with you."

The Ancestors of Jesus
(Matt. 1.1–17)

23 When Jesus began his work, he was about thirty years old. He was the son, so people thought, of Joseph, who was the son of Heli, 24 the son of Matthat, the son of Levi, the son of Melchi, the son of Jannai, the son of Joseph, 25 the son of Mattathias, the son of Amos, the son of Nahum, the son of Esli, the son of Naggai, 26 the son of Maath, the son of Mattathias, the son of Semein, the son

2.52: 1 Sam 2.26; Prov 3.4   **3.4–6:** Is 40.3–5   **3.7:** Mt 12.34, 23.33   **3.8:** Jn 8.33
3.9: Mt 7.19   **3.12:** Lk 7.29   **3.19–20:** Mt 14.3–4; Mk 6.17–18
3.22: Gen 22.2; Ps 2.7; Is 42.1; Mt 3.17; Mk 1.11; Lk 9.35

of Josech, the son of Joda, 27 the son of Joanan, the son of Rhesa, the son of Zerubbabel, the son of Shealtiel, the son of Neri, 28 the son of Melchi, the son of Addi, the son of Cosam, the son of Elmadam, the son of Er, 29 the son of Joshua, the son of Eliezer, the son of Jorim, the son of Matthat, the son of Levi, 30 the son of Simeon, the son of Judah, the son of Joseph, the son of Jonam, the son of Eliakim, 31 the son of Melea, the son of Menna, the son of Mattatha, the son of Nathan, the son of David, 32 the son of Jesse, the son of Obed, the son of Boaz, the son of Salmon, the son of Nahshon, 33 the son of Amminadab, the son of Admin, the son of Arni, the son of Hezron, the son of Perez, the son of Judah, 34 the son of Jacob, the son of Isaac, the son of Abraham, the son of Terah, the son of Nahor, 35 the son of Serug, the son of Reu, the son of Peleg, the son of Eber, the son of Shelah, 36 the son of Cainan, the son of Arphaxad, the son of Shem, the son of Noah, the son of Lamech, 37 the son of Methuselah, the son of Enoch, the son of Jared, the son of Mahalaleel, the son of Kenan, 38 the son of Enosh, the son of Seth, the son of Adam, the son of God.

The Temptation of Jesus
(Matt. 4.1-11; Mark 1.12-13)

4 Jesus returned from the Jordan full of the Holy Spirit and was led by the Spirit into the desert, 2 where he was tempted by the Devil for forty days. In all that time he ate nothing, so that he was hungry when it was over.

3 The Devil said to him, "If you are God's Son, order this stone to turn into bread."

4 But Jesus answered, "The scripture says, 'Man cannot live on bread alone.' "

5 Then the Devil took him up and showed him in a second all the kingdoms of the world. 6 "I will give you all this power and all this wealth," the Devil told him. "It has all been handed over to me, and I can give it to anyone I choose. 7 All this will be yours, then, if you worship me."

8 Jesus answered, "The scripture says, 'Worship the Lord your God and serve only him!' "

9 Then the Devil took him to Jerusalem and set him on the highest point of the Temple, and said to him, "If you are God's Son, throw yourself down from here. 10 For the scripture says, 'God will order his angels to take good care of you.' 11 It also says, 'They will hold you up with their hands so that not even your feet will be hurt on the stones.' "

12 But Jesus answered, "The scripture says, 'Do not put the Lord your God to the test.' "

13 When the Devil finished tempting Jesus in every way, he left him for a while.

Jesus Begins His Work in Galilee
(Matt. 4.12-17; Mark 1.14-15)

14 Then Jesus returned to Galilee, and the power of the Holy Spirit was with him. The news about him spread throughout all that territory. 15 He taught in the synagogues and was praised by everyone.

Jesus Is Rejected at Nazareth
(Matt. 13.53-58; Mark 6.1-6)

16 Then Jesus went to Nazareth, where he had been brought up, and on the Sabbath he went as usual to the synagogue. He stood up to read the Scriptures 17 and was handed the book of the prophet Isaiah. He unrolled the scroll and found the place where it is written,
18 "The Spirit of the Lord is upon me,
 because he has chosen me to bring
  good news to the poor.
He has sent me to proclaim liberty to
 the captives
 and recovery of sight to the blind;
to set free the oppressed
19 and announce that the time has come
  when the Lord will save his people."

20 Jesus rolled up the scroll, gave it back to the attendant, and sat down. All the people in the synagogue had their eyes fixed on him, 21 as he said to them, "This passage of scripture has come true today, as you heard it being read."

22 They were all well impressed with him and marvelled at the eloquent words that he spoke. They said, "Isn't he the son of Joseph?"

23 He said to them, "I am sure that you will quote this proverb to me, 'Doctor, heal yourself.' You will also tell me to do here in my home town the same things you heard were done in Capernaum. 24 I tell you this," Jesus added, "a prophet is never welcomed in his home town.

25 "Listen to me: it is true that there were many widows in Israel during the time of Elijah, when there was no rain

---

4.4: Deut 8.3   **4.8:** Deut 6.13   **4.10:** Ps 91.11   **4.11:** Ps 91.12   **4.12:** Deut 6.16
4.18-19: Is 61.1-2   **4.24:** Jn 4.44   **4.25:** 1 Kgs 17.1

for three and a half years and a severe famine spread throughout the whole land. 26 Yet Elijah was not sent to anyone in Israel, but only to a widow living in Zarephath in the territory of Sidon. 27 And there were many people suffering from a dreaded skin-disease who lived in Israel during the time of the prophet Elisha; yet not one of them was healed, but only Naaman the Syrian."

28 When the people in the synagogue heard this, they were filled with anger. 29 They rose up, dragged Jesus out of the town, and took him to the top of the hill on which their town was built. They meant to throw him over the cliff, 30 but he walked through the middle of the crowd and went his way.

A Man with an Evil Spirit
(Mark 1.21-28)

31 Then Jesus went to Capernaum, a town in Galilee, where he taught the people on the Sabbath. 32 They were all amazed at the way he taught, because he spoke with authority. 33 In the synagogue was a man who had the spirit of an evil demon in him; he screamed out in a loud voice, 34 "Ah! What do you want with us, Jesus of Nazareth? Are you here to destroy us? I know who you are: you are God's holy messenger!"

35 Jesus ordered the spirit, "Be quiet and come out of the man!" The demon threw the man down in front of them and went out of him without doing him any harm.

36 The people were all amazed and said to one another, "What kind of words are these? With authority and power this man gives orders to the evil spirits, and they come out!" 37 And the report about Jesus spread everywhere in that region.

Jesus Heals Many People
(Matt. 8.14-17; Mark 1.29-34)

38 Jesus left the synagogue and went to Simon's house. Simon's mother-in-law was sick with a high fever, and they spoke to Jesus about her. 39 He went and stood at her bedside and ordered the fever to leave her. The fever left her, and she got up at once and began to wait on them.

40 After sunset all who had friends who were sick with various diseases brought them to Jesus; he placed his hands on every one of them and healed them all.

41 Demons also went out from many people, screaming, "You are the Son of God!"

Jesus gave the demons an order and would not let them speak, because they knew that he was the Messiah.

Jesus Preaches in the Synagogues
(Mark 1.35-39)

42 At daybreak Jesus left the town and went off to a lonely place. The people started looking for him, and when they found him, they tried to keep him from leaving. 43 But he said to them, "I must preach the Good News about the Kingdom of God in other towns also, because that is what God sent me to do."

44 So he preached in the synagogues throughout the country.

Jesus Calls the First Disciples
(Matt. 4.18-22; Mark 1.16-20)

5 One day Jesus was standing on the shore of Lake Gennesaret while the people pushed their way up to him to listen to the word of God. 2 He saw two boats pulled up on the beach; the fishermen had left them and were washing the nets. 3 Jesus got into one of the boats—it belonged to Simon—and asked him to push off a little from the shore. Jesus sat in the boat and taught the crowd.

4 When he finished speaking, he said to Simon, "Push the boat out further to the deep water, and you and your partners let down your nets for a catch."

5 "Master," Simon answered, "we worked hard all night long and caught nothing. But if you say so, I will let down the nets." 6 They let them down and caught such a large number of fish that the nets were about to break. 7 So they motioned to their partners in the other boat to come and help them. They came and filled both boats so full of fish that the boats were about to sink. 8 When Simon Peter saw what had happened, he fell on his knees before Jesus and said, "Go away from me, Lord! I am a sinful man!"

9 He and the others with him were all amazed at the large number of fish they had caught. 10 The same was true of Simon's partners, James and John, the sons of Zebedee. Jesus said to Simon, "Don't be afraid; from now on you will be catching men."

11 They pulled the boats up on the

4.26: 1 Kgs 17.8-16   **4.27:** 2 Kgs 5.1-14   **4.32:** Mt 7.28-29
5.1-3: Mt 13.1-2; Mk 3.9-10, 4.1   **5.5:** Jn 21.3   **5.6:** Jn 21.6

beach, left everything, and followed Jesus.

Jesus Heals a Man
(Matt. 8.1–4; Mark 1.40–45)

12 Once Jesus was in a town where there was a man who was suffering from a dreaded skin-disease. When he saw Jesus, he threw himself down and begged him, "Sir, if you want to, you can make me clean!"[c]

13 Jesus stretched out his hand and touched him. "I do want to," he answered. "Be clean!" At once the disease left the man. 14 Jesus ordered him, "Don't tell anyone, but go straight to the priest and let him examine you; then to prove to everyone that you are cured, offer the sacrifice as Moses ordered."

15 But the news about Jesus spread all the more widely, and crowds of people came to hear him and be healed from their diseases. 16 But he would go away to lonely places, where he prayed.

Jesus Heals a Paralysed Man
(Matt. 9.1–8; Mark 2.1–12)

17 One day when Jesus was teaching, some Pharisees and teachers of the Law were sitting there who had come from every town in Galilee and Judaea and from Jerusalem. The power of the Lord was present for Jesus to heal the sick. 18 Some men came carrying a paralysed man on a bed, and they tried to take him into the house and put him in front of Jesus. 19 Because of the crowd, however, they could find no way to take him in. So they carried him up on the roof, made an opening in the tiles, and let him down on his bed into the middle of the group in front of Jesus. 20 When Jesus saw how much faith they had, he said to the man, "Your sins are forgiven, my friend."

21 The teachers of the Law and the Pharisees began to say to themselves, "Who is this man who speaks such blasphemy! God is the only one who can forgive sins!"

22 Jesus knew their thoughts and said to them, "Why do you think such things? 23 Is it easier to say, 'Your sins are forgiven you,' or to say, 'Get up and walk'? 24 I will prove to you, then, that the Son of Man has authority on earth to forgive sins." So he said to the paralysed man, "I tell you, get up, pick up your bed, and go home!"

25 At once the man got up in front of them all, took the bed he had been lying on, and went home, praising God. 26 They were all completely amazed! Full of fear,

[c] MAKE ME CLEAN: *This disease was considered to make a person ritually unclean.*
5.14: Lev 14.1–32

The nets were about to break (5.6)

Let him down on his bed into the middle of the group (5.19)

they praised God, saying, "What marvellous things we have seen today!"

Jesus Calls Levi
(Matt. 9.9-13; Mark 2.13-17)

27 After this, Jesus went out and saw a tax collector named Levi, sitting in his office. Jesus said to him, "Follow me." 28 Levi got up, left everything, and followed him.

29 Then Levi had a big feast in his house for Jesus, and among the guests was a large number of tax collectors and other people. 30 Some Pharisees and some teachers of the Law who belonged to their group complained to Jesus' disciples. "Why do you eat and drink with tax collectors and other outcasts?" they asked.

31 Jesus answered them, "People who are well do not need a doctor, but only those who are sick. 32 I have not come to call respectable people to repent, but outcasts."

5.30: Lk 15.1-2

The Question about Fasting
(Matt. 9.14-17; Mark 2.18-22)

33 Some people said to Jesus, "The disciples of John fast frequently and offer prayers, and the disciples of the Pharisees do the same; but your disciples eat and drink."

34 Jesus answered, "Do you think you can make the guests at a wedding party go without food as long as the bridegroom is with them? Of course not! 35 But the day will come when the bridegroom will be taken away from them, and then they will fast."

36 Jesus also told them this parable: "No one tears a piece off a new coat to patch up an old coat. If he does, he will have torn the new coat, and the piece of new cloth will not match the old. 37 Nor does anyone pour new wine into used wineskins, because the new wine will burst the skins, the wine will pour out, and the skins will be ruined. 38 Instead, new wine must be poured into fresh

wineskins! 39 And no one wants new wine after drinking old wine. 'The old is better,' he says."

The Question about the Sabbath
(Matt. 12.1-8; Mark 2.23-28)

6 Jesus was walking through some cornfields on the Sabbath. His disciples began to pick the ears of corn, rub them in their hands, and eat the grain. 2 Some Pharisees asked, "Why are you doing what our Law says you cannot do on the Sabbath?"

3 Jesus answered them, "Haven't you read what David did when he and his men were hungry? 4 He went into the house of God, took the bread offered to God, ate it, and gave it also to his men. Yet it is against our Law for anyone except the priests to eat that bread."

5 And Jesus concluded, "The Son of Man is Lord of the Sabbath."

The Man with a Paralysed Hand
(Matt. 12.9-14; Mark 3.1-6)

6 On another Sabbath Jesus went into a synagogue and taught. A man was there whose right hand was paralysed. 7 Some teachers of the Law and some Pharisees wanted a reason to accuse Jesus of doing wrong, so they watched him closely to see if he would heal on the Sabbath. 8 But Jesus knew their thoughts and said to the man, "Stand up and come here to the front." The man got up and stood there. 9 Then Jesus said to them, "I ask you: What does our Law allow us to do on the Sabbath? To help or to harm? To save a man's life or destroy it?" 10 He looked around at them all; then he said d to the man, "Stretch out your hand." He did so, and his hand became well again.

11 They were filled with rage and began to discuss among themselves what they could do to Jesus.

Jesus Chooses the Twelve Apostles
(Matt. 10.1-4; Mark 3.13-19)

12 At that time Jesus went up a hill to pray and spent the whole night there praying to God. 13 When day came, he called his disciples to him and chose twelve of them, whom he named apostles: 14 Simon (whom he named Peter) and his brother Andrew; James and John, Philip and Bartholomew, 15 Matthew and Thomas, James son of Alphaeus, and

Simon (who was called the Patriot), 16 Judas son of James, and Judas Iscariot, who became the traitor.

Jesus Teaches and Heals
(Matt. 4.23-25)

17 When Jesus had come down from the hill with the apostles, he stood on a level place with a large number of his disciples. A large crowd of people was there from all over Judaea and from Jerusalem and from the coastal cities of Tyre and Sidon; 18 they had come to hear him and to be healed of their diseases. Those who were troubled by evil spirits also came and were healed. 19 All the people tried to touch him, for power was going out from him and healing them all.

Happiness and Sorrow
(Matt. 5.1-12)

20 Jesus looked at his disciples and said,
"Happy are you poor;
  the Kingdom of God is yours!
21 "Happy are you who are hungry now;
  you will be filled!
"Happy are you who weep now;
  you will laugh!
22 "Happy are you when people hate you, reject you, insult you, and say that you are evil, all because of the Son of Man! 23 Be glad when that happens, and dance for joy, because a great reward is kept for you in heaven. For their ancestors did the very same things to the prophets.
24 "But how terrible for you who are rich now;
  you have had your easy life!
25 "How terrible for you who are full now;
  you will go hungry!
"How terrible for you who laugh now;
  you will mourn and weep!
26 "How terrible when all people speak well of you; their ancestors said the very same things about the false prophets.

Love for Enemies
(Matt. 5.38-48; 7.12a)

27 "But I tell you who hear me: Love your enemies, do good to those who hate you, 28 bless those who curse you, and pray for those who ill-treat you. 29 If anyone hits you on one cheek, let him hit the other one too; if someone takes your coat, let him have your shirt as well. 30 Give to everyone who asks you for

d said; *some manuscripts have* said angrily.
6.1: Deut 23.25 **6.3-4:** 1 Sam 21.1-6 **6.4:** Lev 24.9 **6.22:** 1 Pet 4.14
6.23: 2 Chr 36.16; Acts 7.52

something, and when someone takes what is yours, do not ask for it back. ³¹Do for others just what you want them to do for you.

32 "If you love only the people who love you, why should you receive a blessing? Even sinners love those who love them! ³³And if you do good only to those who do good to you, why should you receive a blessing? Even sinners do that! ³⁴And if you lend only to those from whom you hope to get it back, why should you receive a blessing? Even sinners lend to sinners, to get back the same amount! ³⁵No! Love your enemies and do good to them; lend and expect nothing back. You will then have a great reward, and you will be sons of the Most High God. For he is good to the ungrateful and the wicked. ³⁶Be merciful just as your Father is merciful.

Judging Others
(Matt. 7.1-5)

37 "Do not judge others, and God will not judge you; do not condemn others, and God will not condemn you; forgive others, and God will forgive you. ³⁸Give to others, and God will give to you. Indeed, you will receive a full measure, a generous helping, poured into your hands—all that you can hold. The measure you use for others is the one that God will use for you."

39 And Jesus told them this parable: "One blind man cannot lead another one; if he does, both will fall into a ditch. ⁴⁰No pupil is greater than his teacher; but every pupil, when he has completed his training, will be like his teacher.

41 "Why do you look at the speck in your brother's eye, but pay no attention to the log in your own eye? ⁴²How can you say to your brother, 'Please, brother, let me take that speck out of your eye,' yet cannot even see the log in your own eye? You hypocrite! First take the log out of your own eye, and then you will be able to see clearly to take the speck out of your brother's eye.

A Tree and Its Fruit
(Matt. 7.16-20; 12.33-35)

43 "A healthy tree does not bear bad fruit, nor does a poor tree bear good fruit. ⁴⁴Every tree is known by the fruit it bears; you do not pick figs from thorn bushes or gather grapes from bramble bushes. ⁴⁵A good person brings good out of the treasure of good things in his heart; a bad person brings bad out of his treasure of bad things. For the mouth speaks what the heart is full of.

The Two House Builders
(Matt. 7.24-27)

46 "Why do you call me, 'Lord, Lord,' and yet don't do what I tell you? ⁴⁷Anyone who comes to me and listens to my words and obeys them—I will show you what he is like. ⁴⁸He is like a man who, in building his house, dug deep and laid the foundation on rock. The river overflowed and hit that house but could not shake it, because it was well built. ⁴⁹But anyone who hears my words and does not obey them is like a man who built his house without laying a foundation; when the flood hit that house it fell at once—and what a terrible crash that was!"

Jesus Heals a Roman Officer's Servant
(Matt. 8.5-13)

7 When Jesus had finished saying all these things to the people, he went to Capernaum. ²A Roman officer there had a servant who was very dear to him; the man was sick and about to die. ³When the officer heard about Jesus, he sent some Jewish elders to ask him to come and heal his servant. ⁴They came to Jesus and begged him earnestly, "This man really deserves your help. ⁵He loves our people and he himself built a synagogue for us."

6 So Jesus went with them. He was not far from the house when the officer sent friends to tell him, "Sir, don't trouble yourself. I do not deserve to have you come into my house, ⁷neither do I consider myself worthy to come to you in person. Just give the order, and my servant will get well. ⁸I, too, am a man placed under the authority of superior officers, and I have soldiers under me. I order this one, 'Go!' and he goes; I order that one, 'Come!' and he comes; and I order my slave, 'Do this!' and he does it."

9 Jesus was surprised when he heard this; he turned round and said to the crowd following him, "I tell you, I have never found faith like this, not even in Israel!"

6.31: Mt 7.12   **6.39:** Mt 15.14   **6.40:** Mt 10.24-25; Jn 13.16, 15.20   **6.44:** Mt 12.33
6.45: Mt 12.34

10 The messengers went back to the officer's house and found his servant well.

Jesus Raises a Widow's Son

11 Soon afterwards*e* Jesus went to a town called Nain, accompanied by his disciples and a large crowd. 12 Just as he arrived at the gate of the town, a funeral procession was coming out. The dead man was the only son of a woman who was a widow, and a large crowd from the town was with her. 13 When the Lord saw her, his heart was filled with pity for her, and he said to her, "Don't cry." 14 Then he walked over and touched the coffin, and the men carrying it stopped. Jesus said, "Young man! Get up, I tell you!" 15 The dead man sat up and began to talk, and Jesus gave him back to his mother.

16 They all were filled with fear and praised God. "A great prophet has appeared among us!" they said; "God has come to save his people!"

17 This news about Jesus went out through all the country and the surrounding territory.

The Messengers from John the Baptist

(Matt. 11.2-19)

18 When John's disciples told him about all these things, he called two of them 19 and sent them to the Lord to ask him, "Are you the one John said was going to come, or should we expect someone else?"

20 When they came to Jesus, they said, "John the Baptist sent us to ask if you are the one he said was going to come, or if we should expect someone else."

21 At that very time Jesus cured many people of their sicknesses, diseases, and evil spirits, and gave sight to many blind people. 22 He answered John's messengers, "Go back and tell John what you have seen and heard: the blind can see, the lame can walk, those who suffer from dreaded skin-diseases are made clean,*f* the deaf can hear, the dead are raised to life, and the Good News is preached to the poor. 23 How happy are those who have no doubts about me!"

24 After John's messengers had left, Jesus began to speak about him to the crowds: "When you went out to John in the desert, what did you expect to see? A blade of grass bending in the wind? 25 What did you go out to see? A man

dressed up in fancy clothes? People who dress like that and live in luxury are found in palaces! 26 Tell me, what did you go out to see? A prophet? Yes indeed, but you saw much more than a prophet. 27 For John is the one of whom the scripture says: 'God said, I will send my messenger ahead of you to open the way for you.' 28 I tell you," Jesus added, "John is greater than any man who has ever lived. But he who is least in the Kingdom of God is greater than John."

29 All the people heard him; they and especially the tax collectors were the ones who had obeyed God's righteous demands and had been baptized by John. 30 But the Pharisees and the teachers of the Law rejected God's purpose for themselves and refused to be baptized by John.

31 Jesus continued, "Now to what can I compare the people of this day? What are they like? 32 They are like children sitting in the market-place. One group shouts to the other, 'We played wedding music for you, but you wouldn't dance! We sang funeral songs, but you wouldn't cry!' 33 John the Baptist came, and he fasted and drank no wine, and you said, 'He has a demon in him!' 34 The Son of Man came, and he ate and drank, and you said, 'Look at this man! He is a glutton and a drinker, a friend of tax collectors and other outcasts!' 35 God's wisdom, however, is shown to be true by all who accept it."

Jesus at the Home of Simon the Pharisee

36 A Pharisee invited Jesus to have dinner with him, and Jesus went to his house and sat down to eat. 37 In that town was a woman who lived a sinful life. She heard that Jesus was eating in the Pharisee's house, so she brought an alabaster jar full of perfume 38 and stood behind Jesus, by his feet, crying and wetting his feet with her tears. Then she dried his feet with her hair, kissed them, and poured the perfume on them. 39 When the Pharisee saw this, he said to himself, "If this man really were a prophet, he would know who this woman is who is touching him; he would know what kind of sinful life she lives!"

40 Jesus spoke up and said to him, "Simon, I have something to tell you."

"Yes, Teacher," he said, "tell me."

41 "There were two men who owed

---

e Soon afterwards; *some manuscripts have* The next day.   *f* MADE CLEAN: *See 5.12.*
7.22: Is 35.5-6, 61.1   **7.27:** Mal 3.1   **7.29-30:** Mt 21.32; Lk 3.12
7.37-38: Mt 26.7; Mk 14.3; Jn 12.3

money to a money-lender," Jesus began. "One owed him five hundred silver coins, and the other owed him fifty. 42 Neither of them could pay him back, so he cancelled the debts of both. Which one, then, will love him more?"

43 "I suppose," answered Simon, "that it would be the one who was forgiven more."

"You are right," said Jesus. 44 Then he turned to the woman and said to Simon, "Do you see this woman? I came into your home, and you gave me no water for my feet, but she has washed my feet with her tears and dried them with her hair. 45 You did not welcome me with a kiss, but she has not stopped kissing my feet since I came. 46 You provided no olive-oil for my head, but she has covered my feet with perfume. 47 I tell you, then, the great love she has shown proves that her many sins have been forgiven. But whoever has been forgiven little shows only a little love."

48 Then Jesus said to the woman, "Your sins are forgiven."

49 The others sitting at the table began to say to themselves, "Who is this, who even forgives sins?"

50 But Jesus said to the woman, "Your faith has saved you; go in peace."

Women Who Accompanied Jesus

8 Some time later Jesus travelled through towns and villages, preaching the Good News about the Kingdom of God. The twelve disciples went with him, 2 and so did some women who had been healed of evil spirits and diseases: Mary (who was called Magdalene), from whom seven demons had been driven out; 3 Joanna, whose husband Chuza was an officer in Herod's court; and Susanna, and many other women who used their own resources to help Jesus and his disciples.

The Parable of the Sower
(Matt. 13.1–9; Mark 4.1–9)

4 People kept coming to Jesus from one town after another; and when a great crowd gathered, Jesus told this parable: 5 "Once there was a man who went out to sow corn. As he scattered the seed in the field, some of it fell along the path, where it was stepped on, and the birds ate it up. 6 Some of it fell on rocky ground, and when the plants sprouted, they dried up because the soil had no moisture.

7 Some of the seed fell among thorn bushes, which grew up with the plants and choked them. 8 And some seeds fell in good soil; the plants grew and produced corn, a hundred grains each."

And Jesus concluded, "Listen, then, if you have ears!"

The Purpose of the Parables
(Matt. 13.10–17; Mark 4.10–12)

9 His disciples asked Jesus what this parable meant, 10 and he answered, "The knowledge of the secrets of the Kingdom of God has been given to you, but to the rest it comes by means of parables, so that they may look but not see, and listen but not understand."

Jesus Explains the Parable of the Sower
(Matt. 13.18–23; Mark 4.13–20)

11 "This is what the parable means: the seed is the word of God. 12 The seeds that fell along the path stand for those who hear; but the Devil comes and takes the message away from their hearts in order to keep them from believing and being saved. 13 The seeds that fell on rocky ground stand for those who hear the message and receive it gladly. But it does not sink deep into them; they believe only for a while but when the time of testing comes, they fall away. 14 The seeds that fell among thorn bushes stand for those who hear; but the worries and riches and pleasures of this life crowd in and choke them, and their fruit never ripens. 15 The seeds that fell in good soil stand for those who hear the message and retain it in a good and obedient heart, and they persist until they bear fruit.

A Lamp under a Bowl
(Mark 4.21–25)

16 "No one lights a lamp and covers it with a bowl or puts it under a bed. Instead, he puts it on the lampstand, so that people will see the light as they come in.

17 "Whatever is hidden away will be brought out into the open, and whatever is covered up will be found and brought to light.

18 "Be careful, then, how you listen; because whoever has something will be given more, but whoever has nothing will have taken away from him even the little he thinks he has."

8.2–3: Mt 27.55–56; Mk 15.40–41; Lk 23.49   **8.10:** Is 6.9–10   **8.16:** Mt 5.15; Lk 11.33
8.17: Mt 10.26; Lk 12.2   **8.18:** Mt 25.29; Lk 19.26

Jesus' Mother and Brothers
(Matt. 12.46–50; Mark 3.31–35)

19 Jesus' mother and brothers came to him, but were unable to join him because of the crowd. 20 Someone said to Jesus, "Your mother and brothers are standing outside and want to see you."

21 Jesus said to them all, "My mother and brothers are those who hear the word of God and obey it."

Jesus Calms a Storm
(Matt. 8.23–27; Mark 4.35–41)

22 One day Jesus got into a boat with his disciples and said to them, "Let us go across to the other side of the lake." So they started out. 23 As they were sailing, Jesus fell asleep. Suddenly a strong wind blew down on the lake, and the boat began to fill with water, so that they were all in great danger. 24 The disciples went to Jesus and woke him up, saying, "Master, Master! We are about to die!"

Jesus got up and gave an order to the wind and the stormy water; they died down, and there was a great calm. 25 Then he said to the disciples, "Where is your faith?"

But they were amazed and afraid, and said to one another, "Who is this man? He gives orders to the winds and waves, and they obey him!"

Jesus Heals a Man with Demons
(Matt. 8.28–34; Mark 5.1–20)

26 Jesus and his disciples sailed on over to the territory of Gerasa,^g which is across the lake from Galilee. 27 As Jesus stepped ashore, he was met by a man from the town who had demons in him. For a long time this man had gone without clothes and would not stay at home, but spent his time in the burial caves. 28 When he saw Jesus, he gave a loud cry, threw himself down at his feet, and shouted, "Jesus, Son of the Most High God! What do you want with me? I beg you, don't punish me!" 29 He said this because Jesus had ordered the evil spirit to go out of him. Many times it had seized him, and even though he was kept a prisoner, his hands and feet fastened with chains, he would break the chains and be driven by the demon out into the desert.

30 Jesus asked him, "What is your name?"

"My name is 'Mob,'" he answered—because many demons had gone into him. 31 The demons begged Jesus not to send them into the abyss.^h

32 There was a large herd of pigs near by, feeding on a hillside. So the demons begged Jesus to let them go into the pigs, and he let them. 33 They went out of the man and into the pigs. The whole herd rushed down the side of the cliff into the lake and was drowned.

34 The men who had been taking care of the pigs saw what happened, so they ran off and spread the news in the town and among the farms. 35 People went out to see what had happened, and when they came to Jesus, they found the man from whom the demons had gone out sitting at the feet of Jesus, clothed and in his right mind; and they were all afraid. 36 Those who had seen it told the people how the man had been cured. 37 Then all the people from that territory asked Jesus to go away, because they were terribly afraid. So Jesus got into the boat and left. 38 The man from whom the demons had gone out begged Jesus, "Let me go with you."

But Jesus sent him away, saying, 39 "Go back home and tell what God has done for you."

The man went through the town, telling what Jesus had done for him.

Jairus' Daughter and the Woman Who Touched Jesus' Cloak
(Matt. 9.18–26; Mark 5.21–43)

40 When Jesus returned to the other side of the lake, the people welcomed him, because they had all been waiting for him. 41 Then a man named Jairus arrived; he was an official in the local synagogue. He threw himself down at Jesus' feet and begged him to go to his home, 42 because his only daughter, who was twelve years old, was dying.

As Jesus went along, the people were crowding him from every side. 43 Among them was a woman who had suffered from severe bleeding for twelve years; she had spent all she had on doctors,ⁱ but no one had been able to cure her. 44 She came up in the crowd behind Jesus and touched the edge of his cloak, and her bleeding

---

^g Gerasa; *some manuscripts have* Gadara (*see Mt 8.28*); *others have* Gergesa.
^h ABYSS: *It was thought that the demons were to be imprisoned in the depths of the earth until their final punishment.*
ⁱ *Some manuscripts do not have* she had spent all she had on doctors.

stopped at once. 45 Jesus asked, "Who touched me?"

Everyone denied it, and Peter said, "Master, the people are all round you and crowding in on you."

46 But Jesus said, "Someone touched me, for I knew it when power went out of me." 47 The woman saw that she had been found out, so she came trembling and threw herself at Jesus' feet. There in front of everybody, she told him why she had touched him and how she had been healed at once. 48 Jesus said to her, "My daughter, your faith has made you well. Go in peace."

49 While Jesus was saying this, a messenger came from the official's house. "Your daughter has died," he told Jairus; "don't bother the Teacher any longer."

50 But Jesus heard it and said to Jairus, "Don't be afraid; only believe, and she will be well."

51 When he arrived at the house, he would not let anyone go in with him except Peter, John, and James, and the child's father and mother. 52 Everyone there was crying and mourning for the child. Jesus said, "Don't cry; the child is not dead—she is only sleeping!"

53 They all laughed at him, because they knew that she was dead. 54 But Jesus took her by the hand and called out, "Get up, my child!" 55 Her life returned, and she got up at once, and Jesus ordered them to give her something to eat. 56 Her parents were astounded, but Jesus commanded them not to tell anyone what had happened.

Jesus Sends Out the Twelve Disciples
(Matt. 10.5-15; Mark 6.7-13)

9 Jesus called the twelve disciples together and gave them power and authority to drive out all demons and to cure diseases. 2 Then he sent them out to preach the Kingdom of God and to heal the sick, 3 after saying to them, "Take nothing with you for the journey: no stick, no beggar's bag, no food, no money, not even an extra shirt. 4 Wherever you are welcomed, stay in the same house until you leave that town; 5 wherever people don't welcome you, leave that town and shake the dust off your feet as a warning to them."

6 The disciples left and travelled through all the villages, preaching the Good News and healing people everywhere.

Herod's Confusion
(Matt. 14.1-12; Mark 6.14-29)

7 When Herod, the ruler of Galilee, heard about all the things that were happening, he was very confused, because some people were saying that John the Baptist had come back to life. 8 Others were saying that Elijah had appeared, and still others that one of the prophets of long ago had come back to life. 9 Herod said, "I had John's head cut off; but who is this man I hear these things about?" And he kept trying to see Jesus.

Jesus Feeds Five Thousand Men
(Matt. 14.13-21; Mark 6.30-44; John 6.1-14)

10 The apostles came back and told Jesus everything they had done. He took them with him, and they went off by themselves to a town called Bethsaida. 11 When the crowds heard about it, they followed him. He welcomed them, spoke to them about the Kingdom of God, and healed those who needed it.

12 When the sun was beginning to set, the twelve disciples came to him and said, "Send the people away so that they can go to the villages and farms round here and find food and lodging, because this is a lonely place."

13 But Jesus said to them, "You yourselves give them something to eat."

They answered, "All we have are five loaves and two fish. Do you want us to go and buy food for this whole crowd?" 14 (There were about five thousand men there.)

Jesus said to his disciples, "Make the people sit down in groups of about fifty each."

15 After the disciples had done so, 16 Jesus took the five loaves and two fish, looked up to heaven, thanked God for them, broke them, and gave them to the disciples to distribute to the people. 17 They all ate and had enough, and the disciples took up twelve baskets of what was left over.

Peter's Declaration about Jesus
(Matt. 16.13-19; Mark 8.27-29)

18 One day when Jesus was praying alone, the disciples came to him. "Who do the crowds say I am?" he asked them.

19 "Some say that you are John the

9.3-5: Lk 10.4-11; Acts 13.51   9.7-8: Mt 16.14; Mk 8.28; Lk 9.19
9.19: Mt 14.1-2; Mk 6.14-15; Lk 9.7-8

They all ate and had enough (9.17)

Baptist," they answered. "Others say that you are Elijah, while others say that one of the prophets of long ago has come back to life."

20 "What about you?" he asked them. "Who do you say I am?"

Peter answered, "You are God's Messiah."

Jesus Speaks about His Suffering and Death
(Matt. 16.20-28; Mark 8.30-9.1)

21 Then Jesus gave them strict orders not to tell this to anyone. 22 He also said to them, "The Son of Man must suffer much and be rejected by the elders, the chief priests, and the teachers of the Law. He will be put to death, but three days later he will be raised to life."

23 And he said to them all, "If anyone wants to come with me, he must forget self, take up his cross every day, and follow me. 24 For whoever wants to save his own life will lose it, but whoever loses

his life for my sake will save it. 25 Will a person gain anything if he wins the whole world but is himself lost or defeated? Of course not! 26 If a person is ashamed of me and of my teaching, then the Son of Man will be ashamed of him when he comes in his glory and in the glory of the Father and of the holy angels. 27 I assure you that there are some here who will not die until they have seen the Kingdom of God."

The Transfiguration
(Matt. 17.1-8; Mark 9.2-8)

28 About a week after he had said these things, Jesus took Peter, John, and James with him and went up a hill to pray. 29 While he was praying, his face changed its appearance, and his clothes became dazzling white. 30 Suddenly two men were there talking with him. They were Moses and Elijah, 31 who appeared in heavenly glory and talked with Jesus about the way in which he would soon fulfil God's

9.20: Jn 6.68–69   **9.23:** Mt 10.38; Lk 14.27   **9.24:** Mt 10.39; Lk 17.33; Jn 12.25
9.28–35: 2 Pet 1.17–18

purpose by dying in Jerusalem. ³²Peter and his companions were sound asleep, but they woke up and saw Jesus' glory and the two men who were standing with him. ³³As the men were leaving Jesus, Peter said to him, "Master, how good it is that we are here! We will make three tents, one for you, one for Moses, and one for Elijah." (He did not really know what he was saying.)

34 While he was still speaking, a cloud appeared and covered them with its shadow; and the disciples were afraid as the cloud came over them. ³⁵A voice said from the cloud, "This is my Son, whom I have chosen—listen to him!"

36 When the voice stopped, there was Jesus all alone. The disciples kept quiet about all this, and told no one at that time anything they had seen.

Jesus Heals a Boy with an Evil Spirit
(Matt. 17.14-18; Mark 9.14-27)

37 The next day Jesus and the three disciples went down from the hill, and a large crowd met Jesus. ³⁸A man shouted from the crowd, "Teacher! I beg you, look at my son—my only son! ³⁹A spirit attacks him with a sudden shout and throws him into a fit, so that he foams at the mouth; it keeps on hurting him and will hardly let him go! ⁴⁰I begged your disciples to drive it out, but they couldn't."

41 Jesus answered, "How unbelieving and wrong you people are! How long must I stay with you? How long do I have to put up with you?" Then he said to the man, "Bring your son here."

42 As the boy was coming, the demon knocked him to the ground and threw him into a fit. Jesus gave a command to the evil spirit, healed the boy, and gave him back to his father. ⁴³All the people were amazed at the mighty power of God.

Jesus Speaks Again about His Death
(Matt. 17.22-23; Mark 9.30-32)

The people were still marvelling at everything Jesus was doing, when he said to his disciples, ⁴⁴"Don't forget what I am about to tell you! The Son of Man is going to be handed over to the power of men." ⁴⁵But the disciples did not know what this meant. It had been hidden from them so that they could not understand it, and they were afraid to ask him about the matter.

Who Is the Greatest?
(Matt. 18.1-5; Mark 9.33-37)

46 An argument broke out among the disciples as to which one of them was the greatest. ⁴⁷Jesus knew what they were thinking, so he took a child, stood him by his side, ⁴⁸and said to them, "Whoever welcomes this child in my name, welcomes me; and whoever welcomes me, also welcomes the one who sent me. For he who is least among you all is the greatest."

Whoever Is Not against You Is for You
(Mark 9.38-40)

49 John spoke up, "Master, we saw a man driving out demons in your name, and we told him to stop, because he doesn't belong to our group."

50 "Do not try to stop him," Jesus said to him and to the other disciples, "because whoever is not against you is for you."

A Samaritan Village Refuses to Receive Jesus

51 As the time drew near when Jesus would be taken up to heaven, he made up his mind and set out on his way to Jerusalem. ⁵²He sent messengers ahead of him, who went into a village in Samaria to get everything ready for him. ⁵³But the people there would not receive him, because it was clear that he was on his way to Jerusalem. ⁵⁴When the disciples James and John saw this, they said, "Lord, do you want us to call fire down from heaven to destroy them?"ʲ

55 Jesus turned and rebuked them.ᵏ ⁵⁶Then Jesus and his disciples went on to another village.

The Would-be Followers of Jesus
(Matt. 8.19-22)

57 As they went on their way, a man said to Jesus, "I will follow you wherever you go."

58 Jesus said to him, "Foxes have holes, and birds have nests, but the Son of Man has nowhere to lie down and rest."

59 He said to another man, "Follow me."

But that man said, "Sir, first let me go back and bury my father."

ʲ Some manuscripts add as Elijah did.
ᵏ Some manuscripts add and said, "You don't know what kind of a Spirit you belong to; for the Son of Man did not come to destroy men's lives, but to save them."
9.35: Is 42.1; Mt 3.17, 12.18; Mk 1.11; Lk 3.22   **9.46:** Lk 22.24
9.48: Mt 10.40; Lk 10.16; Jn 13.20   **9.54:** 2 Kgs 1.9-16

60 Jesus answered, "Let the dead bury their own dead. You go and proclaim the Kingdom of God."

61 Another man said, "I will follow you, sir; but first let me go and say good-bye to my family."

62 Jesus said to him, "Anyone who starts to plough and then keeps looking back is of no use to the Kingdom of God."

Jesus Sends Out the Seventy-two

10 After this the Lord chose another seventy-two[1] men and sent them out two by two, to go ahead of him to every town and place where he himself was about to go. [2]He said to them, "There is a large harvest, but few workers to gather it in. Pray to the owner of the harvest that he will send out workers to gather in his harvest. [3]Go! I am sending you like lambs among wolves. [4]Don't take a purse or a beggar's bag or shoes; don't stop to greet anyone on the road. [5]Whenever you go into a house, first say, 'Peace be with this house.' [6]If a peace-loving man lives there, let your greeting of peace remain on him; if not, take back your greeting of peace. [7]Stay in that same house, eating and drinking whatever they offer you, for a worker should be given his pay. Don't move round from one house to another. [8]Whenever you go into a town and are made welcome, eat what is set before you, [9]heal the sick in that town, and say to the people there, 'The Kingdom of God has come near you.' [10]But whenever you go into a town and are not welcomed, go out in the streets and say, [11]'Even the dust from your town that sticks to our feet we wipe off against you. But remember that the Kingdom of God has come near you!' [12]I assure you that on Judgement Day God will show more mercy to Sodom than to that town!

The Unbelieving Towns
(Matt. 11.20-24)

13 "How terrible it will be for you, Chorazin! How terrible for you too, Bethsaida! If the miracles which were performed in you had been performed in Tyre and Sidon, the people there would long ago have sat down, put on sackcloth, and sprinkled ashes on themselves, to show that they had turned from their sins! [14]God will show more mercy on Judgement Day to Tyre and Sidon than to you. [15]And as for you, Capernaum! Did you want to lift yourself up to heaven? You will be thrown down to hell!"

16 Jesus said to his disciples, "Whoever listens to you listens to me; whoever rejects you rejects me; and whoever rejects me rejects the one who sent me."

The Return of the Seventy-two

17 The seventy-two[m] men came back in great joy. "Lord," they said, "even the demons obeyed us when we gave them a command in your name!"

18 Jesus answered them, "I saw Satan fall like lightning from heaven. [19]Listen! I have given you authority, so that you can walk on snakes and scorpions and overcome all the power of the Enemy, and nothing will hurt you. [20]But don't be glad because the evil spirits obey you; rather be glad because your names are written in heaven."

Jesus Rejoices
(Matt. 11.25-27; 13.16-17)

21 At that time Jesus was filled with joy by the Holy Spirit[n] and said, "Father, Lord of heaven and earth! I thank you because you have shown to the unlearned what you have hidden from the wise and learned. Yes, Father, this was how you wanted it to happen.

22 "My Father has given me all things. No one knows who the Son is except the Father, and no one knows who the Father is except the Son and those to whom the Son chooses to reveal him."

23 Then Jesus turned to the disciples and said to them privately, "How fortunate you are to see the things you see! [24]I tell you that many prophets and kings wanted to see what you see, but they could not, and to hear what you hear, but they did not."

The Parable of the Good Samaritan

25 A teacher of the Law came up and

---

[l]seventy-two; *some manuscripts have* seventy.
[m]seventy-two; *some manuscripts have* seventy *(see verse 1)*.
[n]by the Holy Spirit; *some manuscripts have* by the Spirit; *others have* in his spirit.

9.61: 1 Kgs 19.20   **10.2:** Mt 9.37-38   **10.3:** Mt 10.16
10.4-11: Mt 10.7-14; Mk 6.8-11; Lk 9.3-5   **10.7:** 1 Cor 9.14; 1 Tim 5.18
10.10-11: Acts 13.51   **10.12:** Gen 19.24-28; Mt 11.24, 10.15
10.13: Is 23.1-18; Ezek 26.1-28.26; Joel 3.4-8; Amos 1.9-10; Zech 9.2-4   **10.15:** Is 14.13-15
10.16: Mt 10.40; Mk 9.37; Lk 9.48; Jn 13.20   **10.19:** Ps 91.13   **10.22:** Jn 3.35, 10.15
10.25-28: Mt 22.35-40; Mk 12.28-34

His heart was filled with pity (10.33)

tried to trap Jesus. "Teacher," he asked, "what must I do to receive eternal life?"

26 Jesus answered him, "What do the Scriptures say? How do you interpret them?"

27 The man answered, " 'Love the Lord your God with all your heart, with all your soul, with all your strength, and with all your mind'; and 'Love your neighbour as you love yourself.' "

28 "You are right," Jesus replied; "do this and you will live."

29 But the teacher of the Law wanted to justify himself, so he asked Jesus, "Who is my neighbour?"

30 Jesus answered, "There was once a man who was going down from Jerusalem to Jericho when robbers attacked him, stripped him, and beat him up, leaving him half dead. 31 It so happened that a priest was going down that road; but when he saw the man, he walked on by, on the other side. 32 In the same way a Levite also came along, went over and looked at the man, and then walked on by, on the other side. 33 But a Samaritan who was travelling that way came upon the man, and when he saw him, his heart was filled with pity. 34 He went over to him, poured oil and wine on his wounds and bandaged them; then he put the man on his own animal and took him to an inn, where he took care of him. 35 The next day he took out two silver coins and gave them to the innkeeper. 'Take care of him,' he told the innkeeper, 'and when I come back this way, I will pay you whatever else you spend on him.' "

36 And Jesus concluded, "In your opinion, which one of these three acted like a neighbour towards the man attacked by the robbers?"

37 The teacher of the Law answered, "The one who was kind to him."

Jesus replied, "You go, then, and do the same."

Jesus Visits Martha and Mary

38 As Jesus and his disciples went on their way, he came to a village where a woman named Martha welcomed him in her home. 39 She had a sister named Mary, who sat down at the feet of the Lord and listened to his teaching. 40 Martha was upset over all the work she had to do, so she came and said, "Lord, don't you care that my sister has left me to do all the work by myself? Tell her to come and help me!"

41 The Lord answered her, "Martha, Martha! You are worried and troubled over so many things, 42 but just one is needed. Mary has chosen the right thing, and it will not be taken away from her."

10.27: Lev 19.18; Deut 6.5   10.28: Lev 18.5
10.33–34: 2 Chr 28.15   10.38–39: Jn 11.1

Jesus' Teaching on Prayer
(Matt. 6.9-13; 7.7-11)

11 One day Jesus was praying in a certain place. When he had finished, one of his disciples said to him, "Lord, teach us to pray, just as John taught his disciples."

2 Jesus said to them, "When you pray, say this:
'Father:
    May your holy name be honoured;
    may your Kingdom come.
3   Give us day by day the food we need. o
4   Forgive us our sins,
        for we forgive everyone who does
            us wrong.
    And do not bring us to hard testing.'"

5 And Jesus said to his disciples, "Suppose one of you should go to a friend's house at midnight and say to him, 'Friend, let me borrow three loaves of bread. 6 A friend of mine who is on a journey has just come to my house, and I haven't got any food for him!' 7 And suppose your friend should answer from inside, 'Don't bother me! The door is already locked, and my children and I are in bed. I can't get up and give you anything.' 8 Well, what then? I tell you that even if he will not get up and give you the bread because you are his friend, yet he will get up and give you everything you need because you are not ashamed to keep on asking.

9 "And so I say to you: Ask, and you will receive; seek, and you will find; knock, and the door will be opened to you. 10 For everyone who asks will receive, and he who seeks will find, and the door will be opened to anyone who knocks. 11 Would any of you who are fathers give your son a snake when he asks for fish? 12 Or would you give him a scorpion when he asks for an egg? 13 Bad as you are, you know how to give good things to your children. How much more, then, will the Father in heaven give the Holy Spirit to those who ask him!"

Jesus and Beelzebul
(Matt. 12.22-30; Mark 3.20-27)

14 Jesus was driving out a demon that could not talk; and when the demon went out, the man began to talk. The crowds were amazed, 15 but some of the people said, "It is Beelzebul, the chief of the demons, who gives him the power to drive them out."

16 Others wanted to trap Jesus, so they asked him to perform a miracle to show that God approved of him. 17 But Jesus knew what they were thinking, so he said to them, "Any country that divides itself into groups which fight each other will not last very long; a family divided against itself falls apart. 18 So if Satan's kingdom has groups fighting each other, how can it last? You say that I drive out demons because Beelzebul gives me the power to do so. 19 If this is how I drive them out, how do your followers drive them out? Your own followers prove that you are wrong! 20 No, it is rather by means of God's power that I drive out demons, and this proves that the Kingdom of God has already come to you.

21 "When a strong man, with all his weapons ready, guards his own house, all his belongings are safe. 22 But when a stronger man attacks him and defeats him, he carries away all the weapons the owner was depending on and divides up what he stole.

23 "Anyone who is not for me is really against me; anyone who does not help me gather is really scattering.

The Return of the Evil Spirit
(Matt. 12.43-45)

24 "When an evil spirit goes out of a person, it travels over dry country looking for a place to rest. If it can't find one, it says to itself, 'I will go back to my house.' 25 So it goes back and finds the house clean and tidy. 26 Then it goes out and brings seven other spirits even worse than itself, and they come and live there. So when it is all over, that person is in a worse state than he was at the beginning."

True Happiness

27 When Jesus had said this, a woman spoke up from the crowd and said to him, "How happy is the woman who bore you and nursed you!"

28 But Jesus answered, "Rather, how happy are those who hear the word of God and obey it!"

The Demand for a Miracle
(Matt. 12.38-42)

29 As the people crowded round Jesus, he went on to say, "How evil are the people of this day! They ask for a miracle,

---

o the food we need; or food for the next day.
11.15: Mt 9.34, 10.25   **11.16:** Mt 12.38, 16.1; Mk 8.11   **11.23:** Mk 9.40   **11.29:** Mt 16.4; Mk 8.12

but none will be given them except the miracle of Jonah. [30] In the same way that the prophet Jonah was a sign for the people of Nineveh, so the Son of Man will be a sign for the people of this day. [31] On Judgement Day the Queen of Sheba will stand up and accuse the people of today, because she travelled all the way from her country to listen to King Solomon's wise teaching; and I tell you there is something here greater than Solomon. [32] On Judgement Day the people of Nineveh will stand up and accuse you, because they turned from their sins when they heard Jonah preach; and I assure you that there is something here greater than Jonah!

The Light of the Body
(Matt. 5.15; 6.22-23)

[33] "No one lights a lamp and then hides it or puts it under a bowl; [P] instead, he puts it on the lampstand, so that people may see the light as they come in. [34] Your eyes are like a lamp for the body. When your eyes are sound, your whole body is full of light; but when your eyes are no good, your whole body will be in darkness. [35] Make certain, then, that the light in you is not darkness. [36] If your whole body is full of light, with no part of it in darkness, it will be bright all over, as when a lamp shines on you with its brightness."

Jesus Accuses the Pharisees and the Teachers of the Law
(Matt. 23.1-36; Mark 12.38-40)

[37] When Jesus finished speaking, a Pharisee invited him to eat with him; so he went in and sat down to eat. [38] The Pharisee was surprised when he noticed that Jesus had not washed before eating. [39] So the Lord said to him, "Now then, you Pharisees clean the outside of your cup and plate, but inside you are full of violence and evil. [40] Fools! Did not God, who made the outside, also make the inside? [41] But give what is in your cups and plates to the poor, and everything will be ritually clean for you.

[42] "How terrible for you Pharisees! You give God a tenth of the seasoning herbs, such as mint and rue and all the other herbs, but you neglect justice and love for God. These you should practise, without neglecting the others.

[43] "How terrible for you Pharisees! You love the reserved seats in the synagogues and to be greeted with respect in the market-places. [44] How terrible for you! You are like unmarked graves which people walk on without knowing it."

[45] One of the teachers of the Law said to him, "Teacher, when you say this, you insult us too!"

[46] Jesus answered, "How terrible also for you teachers of the Law! You put loads on people's backs which are hard to carry, but you yourselves will not stretch out a finger to help them carry those loads. [47] How terrible for you! You make fine tombs for the prophets—the very prophets your ancestors murdered. [48] You yourselves admit, then, that you approve of what your ancestors did; they murdered the prophets, and you build their tombs. [49] For this reason the Wisdom of God said, 'I will send them prophets and messengers; they will kill some of them and persecute others.' [50] So the people of this time will be punished for the murder of all the prophets killed since the creation of the world, [51] from the murder of Abel to the murder of Zechariah, who was killed between the altar and the Holy Place. Yes, I tell you, the people of this time will be punished for them all!

[52] "How terrible for you teachers of the Law! You have kept the key that opens the door to the house of knowledge; you yourselves will not go in, and you stop those who are trying to go in!"

[53] When Jesus left that place, the teachers of the Law and the Pharisees began to criticize him bitterly and ask him questions about many things, [54] trying to lay traps for him and catch him saying something wrong.

A Warning against Hypocrisy
(Matt. 10.26-27)

12 As thousands of people crowded together, so that they were stepping on each other, Jesus said first to his disciples, "Be on guard against the yeast of the Pharisees—I mean their hypocrisy. [2] Whatever is covered up will be uncovered, and every secret will be made known. [3] So then, whatever you

P *Some manuscripts do not have* or puts it under a bowl.
11.30: Jon 3.4   **11.31:** 1 Kgs 10.1-10; 2 Chr 9.1-12   **11.32:** Jon 3.5
11.33: Mt 5.15; Mk 4.21; Lk 8.16   **11.42:** Lev 27.30   **11.51:** Gen 4.8; 2 Chr 24.20-21
12.1: Mt 16.6; Mk 8.15   **12.2:** Mk 4.22; Lk 8.17

have said in the dark will be heard in broad daylight, and whatever you have whispered in private in a closed room will be shouted from the housetops.

Whom to Fear
(Matt. 10.28-31)

4 "I tell you, my friends, do not be afraid of those who kill the body but cannot afterwards do anything worse. ⁵I will show you whom to fear: fear God, who, after killing, has the authority to throw into hell. Believe me, he is the one you must fear!

6 "Aren't five sparrows sold for two pennies? Yet not one sparrow is forgotten by God. ⁷Even the hairs of your head have all been counted. So do not be afraid; you are worth much more than many sparrows!

Confessing and Rejecting Christ
(Matt. 10.32-33; 12.32; 10.19-20)

8 "I assure you that whoever declares publicly that he belongs to me, the Son of Man will do the same for him before the angels of God. ⁹But whoever rejects me publicly, the Son of Man will also reject him before the angels of God.

10 "Anyone who says a word against the Son of Man can be forgiven; but whoever says evil things against the Holy Spirit will not be forgiven.

11 "When they bring you to be tried in the synagogues or before governors or rulers, do not be worried about how you will defend yourself or what you will say. ¹²For the Holy Spirit will teach you at that time what you should say."

The Parable of the Rich Fool

13 A man in the crowd said to Jesus, "Teacher, tell my brother to divide with me the property our father left us."

14 Jesus answered him, "My friend, who gave me the right to judge or to divide the property between you two?" ¹⁵And he went on to say to them all, "Watch out and guard yourselves from every kind of greed; because a person's true life is not made up of the things he owns, no matter how rich he may be."

16 Then Jesus told them this parable: "There was once a rich man who had land which bore good crops. ¹⁷He began to think to himself, 'I haven't anywhere to keep all my crops. What can I do?

¹⁸This is what I will do,' he told himself; 'I will tear down my barns and build bigger ones, where I will store my corn and all my other goods. ¹⁹Then I will say to myself, Lucky man! You have all the good things you need for many years. Take life easy, eat, drink, and enjoy yourself!' ²⁰But God said to him, 'You fool! This very night you will have to give up your life; then who will get all these things you have kept for yourself?'"

21 And Jesus concluded, "This is how it is with those who pile up riches for themselves but are not rich in God's sight."

Trust in God
(Matt. 6.25-34)

22 Then Jesus said to the disciples,

And so I tell you not to worry (12.22)

"And so I tell you not to worry about the food you need to stay alive or about the clothes you need for your body. ²³Life is much more important than food, and the body much more important than clothes. ²⁴Look at the crows: they don't sow seeds or gather a harvest; they don't have store-rooms or barns; God feeds them! You are worth so much more than birds! ²⁵Can any of you live a bit longer q by worrying about it? ²⁶If you can't manage even such a small thing, why worry about the other things? ²⁷Look how the wild flowers grow: they don't work or make clothes for themselves. But I tell you that not even King Solomon with all his wealth had clothes as beautiful as one of these flowers. ²⁸It is God who clothes the wild grass—grass that is here today and gone tomorrow, burnt up in the oven. Won't he be all the more sure to clothe you? How little faith you have!

29 "So don't be all upset, always concerned about what you will eat and drink. ³⁰(For the pagans of this world are

---

q live a bit longer; *or* grow a bit taller.
12.10: Mt 12.32; Mk 3.29　　**12.11-12:** Mt 10.19-20; Mk 13.11; Lk 21.14-15
12.27: 1 Kgs 10.4-7; 2 Chr 9.3-6

always concerned about all these things.)
Your Father knows that you need these
things. 31 Instead, be concerned with his
Kingdom, and he will provide you with
these things.

Riches in Heaven
(Matt. 6.19-21)

32 "Do not be afraid, little flock, for
your Father is pleased to give you the
Kingdom. 33 Sell all your belongings and
give the money to the poor. Provide for
yourselves purses that don't wear out, and
save your riches in heaven, where they
will never decrease, because no thief can
get to them, and no moth can destroy
them. 34 For your heart will always be
where your riches are.

Watchful Servants

35 "Be ready for whatever comes,
dressed for action and with your lamps
lit, 36 like servants who are waiting for
their master to come back from a wedding
feast. When he comes and knocks, they
will open the door for him at once. 37 How
happy are those servants whose master
finds them awake and ready when he
returns! I tell you, he will take off his
coat, ask them to sit down, and will wait
on them. 38 How happy they are if he finds
them ready, even if he should come at
midnight or even later! 39 And you can
be sure that if the owner of a house knew
the time when the thief would come, he
would not let the thief break into his
house. 40 And you, too, must be ready,
because the Son of Man will come at an
hour when you are not expecting him."

The Faithful or the Unfaithful Servant
(Matt. 24.45-51)

41 Peter said, "Lord does this parable
apply to us, or do you mean it for
everyone?"

42 The Lord answered, "Who, then, is
the faithful and wise servant? He is the
one that his master will put in charge,
to run the household and give the other
servants their share of the food at the
proper time. 43 How happy that servant
is if his master finds him doing this when
he comes home! 44 Indeed, I tell you, the
master will put that servant in charge of
all his property. 45 But if that servant says
to himself that his master is taking a long
time to come back and if he begins to

beat the other servants, both the men and
the women, and eats and drinks and gets
drunk, 46 then the master will come back
one day when the servant does not expect
him and at a time he does not know. The
master will cut him in pieces r and make
him share the fate of the disobedient.

47 "The servant who knows what his
master wants him to do, but does not
get himself ready and do it, will be
punished with a heavy whipping. 48 But
the servant who does not know what his
master wants, and yet does something for
which he deserves a whipping, will be
punished with a light whipping. Much is
required from the person to whom much is
given; much more is required from the
person to whom much more is given.

Jesus the Cause of Division
(Matt. 10.34-36)

49 "I came to set the earth on fire, and
how I wish it were already kindled! 50 I
have a baptism to receive, and how
distressed I am until it is over! 51 Do you
suppose that I came to bring peace to the
world? No, not peace, but division.
52 From now on a family of five will be
divided, three against two and two against
three. 53 Fathers will be against their sons,
and sons against their fathers; mothers
will be against their daughters, and
daughters against their mothers; mothers-
in-law will be against their daughters-in-
law, and daughters-in-law against their
mothers-in-law."

Understanding the Time
(Matt. 16.2-3)

54 Jesus said also to the people, "When
you see a cloud coming up in the west,
at once you say that it is going to rain—
and it does. 55 And when you feel the south
wind blowing, you say that it is going
to get hot—and it does. 56 Hypocrites! You
can look at the earth and the sky and
predict the weather; why, then, don't you
know the meaning of this present time?

Settle with Your Opponent
(Matt. 5.25-26)

57 "Why do you not judge for yourselves the right thing to do? 58 If someone
brings a lawsuit against you and takes
you to court, do your best to settle the
dispute with him before you get to court.
If you don't, he will drag you before the

---

r cut him in pieces; or throw him out.
12.35: Mt 25.1-13   **12.36:** Mk 13.34-36   **12.39-40:** Mt 24.43-44   **12.50:** Mk 10.38
12.53: Mic 7.6

judge, who will hand you over to the police, and you will be put in jail. 59 There you will stay, I tell you, until you pay the last penny of your fine."

Turn from Your Sins or Die

13 At that time some people were there who told Jesus about the Galileans whom Pilate had killed while they were offering sacrifices to God. 2 Jesus answered them, "Because those Galileans were killed in that way, do you think it proves that they were worse sinners than all the other Galileans? 3 No indeed! And I tell you that if you do not turn from your sins, you will all die as they did. 4 What about those eighteen people in Siloam who were killed when the tower fell on them? Do you suppose this proves that they were worse than all the other people living in Jerusalem? 5 No indeed! And I tell you that if you do not turn from your sins, you will all die as they did."

The Parable of the Unfruitful Fig-Tree

6 Then Jesus told them this parable: "There was once a man who had a fig-tree growing in his vineyard. He went looking for figs on it but found none. 7 So he said to his gardener, 'Look, for three years I have been coming here looking for figs on this fig-tree, and I haven't found any. Cut it down! Why should it go on using up the soil?' 8 But the gardener answered, 'Leave it alone, sir, just one more year; I will dig round it and put in some manure. 9 Then if the tree bears figs next year, so much the better; if not, then you can have it cut down.'"

Jesus Heals a Crippled Woman on the Sabbath

10 One Sabbath Jesus was teaching in a synagogue. 11 A woman there had an evil spirit that had made her ill for eighteen years; she was bent over and could not straighten up at all. 12 When Jesus saw her, he called out to her, "Woman, you are free from your illness!" 13 He placed his hands on her, and at once she straightened herself up and praised God.

14 The official of the synagogue was angry that Jesus had healed on the Sabbath, so he spoke up and said to the people, "There are six days in which we should work; so come during those days

and be healed, but not on the Sabbath!"

15 The Lord answered him, "You hypocrites! Any one of you would untie his ox or his donkey from the stall and take it out to give it water on the Sabbath. 16 Now here is this descendant of Abraham whom Satan has kept bound up for eighteen years; should she not be released on the Sabbath?" 17 His answer made his enemies ashamed of themselves, while the people rejoiced over all the wonderful things that he did.

The Parable of the Mustard Seed
(Matt. 13.31–32; Mark 4.30–32)

18 Jesus asked, "What is the Kingdom of God like? What shall I compare it with? 19 It is like this. A man takes a mustard seed and sows it in his field. The plant grows and becomes a tree, and the birds make their nests in its branches."

The Parable of the Yeast
(Matt. 13.33)

20 Again Jesus asked, "What shall I compare the Kingdom of God with? 21 It is like this. A woman takes some yeast and mixes it with forty litres of flour until the whole batch of dough rises."

The Narrow Door
(Matt. 7.13–14, 21–23)

22 Jesus went through towns and villages, teaching the people and making his way towards Jerusalem. 23 Someone asked him, "Sir, will just a few people be saved?"

Jesus answered them, 24 "Do your best to go in through the narrow door; because many people will surely try to go in but will not be able. 25 The master of the house will get up and close the door; then when you stand outside and begin to knock on the door and say, 'Open the door for us, sir!' he will answer you, 'I don't know where you come from!' 26 Then you will answer, 'We ate and drank with you; you taught in our town!' 27 But he will say again, 'I don't know where you come from. Get away from me, all you wicked people!' 28 How you will cry and grind your teeth when you see Abraham, Isaac, and Jacob, and all the prophets in the Kingdom of God, while you are thrown out! 29 People will come from the east and the west, from the north and the south, and sit down at the feast in the Kingdom of God. 30 Then those who are now last

13.14: Ex 20.9–10; Deut 5.13–14   13.27: Ps 6.8   13.28: Mt 22.13, 25.30
13.28–29: Mt 8.11–12   13.30: Mt 19.30, 20.16; Mk 10.31

will be first, and those who are now first will be last."

Jesus' Love for Jerusalem
(Matt. 23.37-39)

31 At that same time some Pharisees came to Jesus and said to him, "You must get out of here and go somewhere else, because Herod wants to kill you."

32 Jesus answered them, "Go and tell that fox: 'I am driving out demons and performing cures today and tomorrow, and on the third day I shall finish my work.' 33 Yet I must be on my way today, tomorrow, and the next day; it is not right for a prophet to be killed anywhere except in Jerusalem.

34 "Jerusalem, Jerusalem! You kill the prophets, you stone the messengers God has sent you! How many times have I wanted to put my arms round all your people, just as a hen gathers her chicks under her wings, but you would not let me! 35 And so your Temple will be abandoned. I assure you that you will not see me until the time comes when you say, 'God bless him who comes in the name of the Lord.'"

Jesus Heals a Sick Man

14 One Sabbath Jesus went to eat a meal at the home of one of the leading Pharisees; and people were watching Jesus closely. 2 A man whose legs and arms were swollen came to Jesus, 3 and Jesus asked the teachers of the Law and the Pharisees, "Does our Law allow healing on the Sabbath or not?"

4 But they would not say anything. Jesus took the man, healed him, and sent him away. 5 Then he said to them, "If any one of you had a son or an ox that happened to fall in a well on a Sabbath, would you not pull him out at once on the Sabbath itself?"

6 But they were not able to answer him about this.

Humility and Hospitality

7 Jesus noticed how some of the guests were choosing the best places, so he told this parable to all of them: 8 "When someone invites you to a wedding feast, do not sit down in the best place. It could happen that someone more important than you has been invited, 9 and your host, who invited both of you, would have to come and say to you, 'Let him have this

place.' Then you would be embarrassed and have to sit in the lowest place. 10 Instead, when you are invited, go and sit in the lowest place, so that your host will come to you and say, 'Come on up, my friend, to a better place.' This will bring you honour in the presence of all the other guests. 11 For everyone who makes himself great will be humbled, and everyone who humbles himself will be made great."

12 Then Jesus said to his host, "When you give a lunch or a dinner, do not invite your friends or your brothers or your relatives or your rich neighbours—for they will invite you back, and in this way you will be paid for what you did. 13 When you give a feast, invite the poor, the crippled, the lame, and the blind; 14 and you will be blessed, because they are not able to pay you back. God will repay you on the day the good people rise from death."

The Parable of the Great Feast
(Matt. 22.1-10)

15 When one of the men sitting at table heard this, he said to Jesus, "How happy are those who will sit down at the feast in the Kingdom of God!"

16 Jesus said to him, "There was once a man who was giving a great feast to which he invited many people. 17 When it was time for the feast, he sent his servant to tell his guests, 'Come, everything is ready!' 18 But they all began, one after another, to make excuses. The first one told the servant, 'I have bought a field and must go and look at it; please accept my apologies.' 19 Another one said, 'I have bought five pairs of oxen and am on my way to try them out; please accept my apologies.' 20 Another one said, 'I have just got married, and for that reason I cannot come.'

21 "The servant went back and told all this to his master. The master was furious and said to his servant, 'Hurry out to the streets and alleys of the town, and bring back the poor, the crippled, the blind, and the lame.' 22 Soon the servant said, 'Your order has been carried out, sir, but there is room for more.' 23 So the master said to the servant, 'Go out to the country roads and lanes and make people come in, so that my house will be full. 24 I tell you all that none of those men who were invited will taste my dinner!'"

13.35: Ps 118.26; Jer 22.5   **14.5:** Mt 12.11
14.8-10: Prov 25.6-7   **14.11:** Mt 23.12; Lk 18.14

The Cost of Being a Disciple
(Matt. 10.37–38)

25 Once when large crowds of people were going along with Jesus, he turned and said to them, 26 "Whoever comes to me cannot be my disciple unless he loves me more than he loves his father and his mother, his wife and his children, his brothers and his sisters, and himself as well. 27 Whoever does not carry his own cross and come after me cannot be my disciple.

28 "If one of you is planning to build a tower, he sits down first and works out what it will cost, to see if he has enough money to finish the job. 29 If he doesn't, he will not be able to finish the tower after laying the foundation; and all who see what happened will laugh at him. 30 'This man began to build but can't finish the job!' they will say.

31 "If a king goes out with ten thousand men to fight another king who comes against him with twenty thousand men, he will sit down first and decide if he is strong enough to face that other king. 32 If he isn't, he will send messengers to meet the other king, to ask for terms of peace while he is still a long way off. 33 In the same way," concluded Jesus, "none of you can be my disciple unless he gives up everything he has.

Worthless Salt
(Matt. 5.13; Mark 9.50)

34 "Salt is good, but if it loses its saltiness, there is no way to make it salty again. 35 It is no good for the soil or for the manure heap; it is thrown away. Listen, then, if you have ears!"

The Lost Sheep
(Matt. 18.12–14)

15 One day when many tax collectors and other outcasts came to listen to Jesus, 2 the Pharisees and the teachers of the Law started grumbling, "This man welcomes outcasts and even eats with them!" 3 So Jesus told them this parable: 4 "Suppose one of you has a hundred sheep and loses one of them—what does he do? He leaves the other ninety-nine sheep in the pasture and goes looking for the one that got lost until he finds it. 5 When he finds it, he is so happy that he puts it on his shoulders 6 and carries it back home. Then he calls his friends and neighbours together and says to them, 'I am so happy I found my lost sheep. Let us celebrate!' 7 In the same way, I tell you, there will be more joy in heaven over one sinner who repents than over ninety-nine respectable people who do not need to repent.

The Lost Coin

8 "Or suppose a woman who has ten silver coins loses one of them—what does she do? She lights a lamp, sweeps her house, and looks carefully everywhere until she finds it. 9 When she finds it, she calls her friends and neighbours together, and says to them, 'I am so happy I found the coin I lost. Let us celebrate!' 10 In the same way, I tell you, the angels of God rejoice over one sinner who repents."

The Lost Son

11 Jesus went on to say, "There was once a man who had two sons. 12 The younger one said to him, 'Father, give me my share of the property now.' So the man divided his property between his two sons. 13 After a few days the younger son sold his part of the property and left home with the money. He went to a country far away, where he wasted his money in reckless living. 14 He spent everything he had. Then a severe famine spread over that country, and he was left without a thing. 15 So he went to work for one of the citizens of that country, who sent him out to his farm to take care of the pigs. 16 He wished he could fill himself with the bean pods the pigs ate, but no one gave him anything to eat. 17 At last he came to his senses and said, 'All my father's hired workers have more than they can eat, and here I am about to starve! 18 I will get up and go to my father and say, Father, I have sinned against God and against you. 19 I am no longer fit to be called your son; treat me as one of your hired workers.' 20 So he got up and started back to his father.

"He was still a long way from home when his father saw him; his heart was filled with pity, and he ran, threw his arms round his son, and kissed him. 21 'Father,' the son said, 'I have sinned against God and against you. I am no longer fit to be called your son.' 22 But the father called his servants. 'Hurry!' he said. 'Bring the best robe and put it on him. Put a ring on his finger and shoes on his feet. 23 Then go and get the prize calf and kill it, and let us celebrate with a feast! 24 For this son

---

14.26: Mt 10.37   **14.27:** Mt 10.38, 16.24; Mk 8.34; Lk 9.23   **15.1–2:** Lk 5.29–30

Here I am about to starve! (15.17)

of mine was dead, but now he is alive; he was lost, but now he has been found.' And so the feasting began.

25 "In the meantime the elder son was out in the field. On his way back, when he came close to the house, he heard the music and dancing. 26 So he called one of the servants and asked him, 'What's going on?' 27 'Your brother has come back home,' the servant answered, 'and your father has killed the prize calf, because he got him back safe and sound.'

28 "The elder brother was so angry that he would not go into the house; so his father came out and begged him to come in. 29 But he answered his father, 'Look, all these years I have worked for you like a slave, and I have never disobeyed your orders. What have you given me? Not even a goat for me to have a feast with my friends! 30 But this son of yours wasted all your property on prostitutes, and when he comes back home, you kill the prize calf for him!' 31 'My son,' the father answered, 'you are always here with me, and everything I have is yours. 32 But we had to celebrate and be happy, because your brother was dead, but now he is alive; he was lost, but now he has been found.'"

The Shrewd Manager

16 Jesus said to his disciples, "There was once a rich man who had a servant who managed his property. The rich man was told that the manager was wasting his master's money, 2 so he called him in and said, 'What is this I hear about you? Hand in a complete account of your handling of my property, because you cannot be my manager any longer.' 3 The servant said to himself, 'My master is going to dismiss me from my job. What shall I do? I am not strong enough to dig ditches, and I am ashamed to beg. 4 Now I know what I will do! Then when my job is gone, I shall have friends who will welcome me in their homes.'

5 "So he called in all the people who were in debt to his master. He asked the first one, 'How much do you owe my master?' 6 'One hundred barrels of olive-oil,' he answered. 'Here is your account,' the manager told him; 'sit down and write fifty.' 7 Then he asked another one, 'And you—how much do you owe?' 'A

But now he is alive (15.32)

thousand sacks of wheat,' he answered. 'Here is your account,' the manager told him; 'write eight hundred.'

8 "As a result the master of this dishonest manager praised him for doing such a shrewd thing; because the people of this world are much more shrewd in handling their affairs than the people who belong to the light."

9 And Jesus went on to say, "And so I tell you: make friends for yourselves with worldly wealth, so that when it gives out, you will be welcomed in the eternal home. 10 Whoever is faithful in small matters will be faithful in large ones; whoever is dishonest in small matters will be dishonest in large ones. 11 If, then, you have not been faithful in handling worldly wealth, how can you be trusted with true wealth? 12 And if you have not been faithful with what belongs to someone else, who will give you what belongs to you?

13 "No servant can be the slave of two masters; he will hate one and love the other; he will be loyal to one and despise the other. You cannot serve both God and money."

Some Sayings of Jesus
(Matt. 11.12-13; 5.31-32; Mark 10.11-12)

14 When the Pharisees heard all this, they sneered at Jesus, because they loved money. 15 Jesus said to them, "You are the ones who make yourselves look right in other people's sight, but God knows your hearts. For the things that are considered of great value by man are worth nothing in God's sight.

16 "The Law of Moses and the writings of the prophets were in effect up to the time of John the Baptist; since then the Good News about the Kingdom of God is being told, and everyone forces his way in. 17 But it is easier for heaven and earth to disappear than for the smallest detail of the Law to be done away with.

18 "Any man who divorces his wife and marries another woman commits adultery; and the man who marries a divorced woman commits adultery.

The Rich Man and Lazarus

19 "There was once a rich man who dressed in the most expensive clothes and lived in great luxury every day. 20 There was also a poor man named Lazarus, covered with sores, who used to be brought to the rich man's door, 21 hoping to eat the bits of food that fell from the rich man's table. Even the dogs would come and lick his sores.

22 "The poor man died and was carried by the angels to sit beside Abraham at the feast in heaven. The rich man died and was buried, 23 and in Hades, s where he was in great pain, he looked up and saw Abraham, far away, with Lazarus at his side. 24 So he called out, 'Father Abraham! Take pity on me, and send Lazarus to dip his finger in some water and cool my tongue, because I am in great pain in this fire!'

25 "But Abraham said, 'Remember, my son, that in your lifetime you were given all the good things, while Lazarus got all the bad things. But now he is enjoying himself here, while you are in pain. 26 Besides all that, there is a deep pit lying between us, so that those who want to cross over from here to you cannot do so, nor can anyone cross over to us from where you are.' 27 The rich man said, 'Then I beg you, father Abraham, send Lazarus to my father's house, 28 where I have five brothers. Let him go and warn them so that they, at least, will not come to this place of pain.'

29 "Abraham said, 'Your brothers have Moses and the prophets to warn them; your brothers should listen to what they say.' 30 The rich man answered, 'That is not enough, father Abraham! But if someone were to rise from death and go to them, then they would turn from their sins.' 31 But Abraham said, 'If they will not listen to Moses and the prophets, they will not be convinced even if someone were to rise from death.'"

Sin
(Matt. 18.6-7, 21-22; Mark 9.42)

17 Jesus said to his disciples, "Things that make people fall into sin are bound to happen, but how terrible for the one who makes them happen! 2 It would be better for him if a large millstone were tied round his neck and he were thrown into the sea than for him to cause one of these little ones to sin. 3 So watch what you do!

"If your brother sins, rebuke him, and if he repents, forgive him. 4 If he sins against you seven times in one day, and

s HADES: *The world of the dead.*
16.13: Mt 6.24   **16.16:** Mt 11.12-13   **16.17:** Mt 5.18   **16.18:** Mt 5.32; 1 Cor 7.10-11
17.3: Mt 18.15

each time he comes to you saying, 'I repent,' you must forgive him.''

Faith

5 The apostles said to the Lord, "Make our faith greater.''

6 The Lord answered, "If you had faith as big as a mustard seed, you could say to this mulberry tree, 'Pull yourself up by the roots and plant yourself in the sea!' and it would obey you.

A Servant's Duty

7 "Suppose one of you has a servant who is ploughing or looking after the sheep. When he comes in from the field, do you tell him to hurry and eat his meal? 8 Of course not! Instead, you say to him, 'Get my supper ready, then put on your apron and wait on me while I eat and drink; after that you may have your meal.' 9 The servant does not deserve thanks for obeying orders, does he? 10 It is the same with you; when you have done all you have been told to do, say, 'We are ordinary servants; we have only done our duty.' ''

Jesus Heals Ten Men

11 As Jesus made his way to Jerusalem, he went along the border between Samaria and Galilee. 12 He was going into a village when he was met by ten men suffering from a dreaded skin-disease. They stood at a distance 13 and shouted, "Jesus! Master! Take pity on us!''

14 Jesus saw them and said to them, "Go and let the priests examine you.''

On the way they were made clean. *t* 15 When one of them saw that he was healed, he came back, praising God in a loud voice. 16 He threw himself to the ground at Jesus' feet and thanked him. The man was a Samaritan. 17 Jesus said, "There were ten men who were healed; where are the other nine? 18 Why is this foreigner the only one who came back to give thanks to God?'' 19 And Jesus said to him, "Get up and go; your faith has made you well.''

The Coming of the Kingdom
(Matt. 24.23-28, 37-41)

20 Some Pharisees asked Jesus when the Kingdom of God would come. His answer was, "The Kingdom of God does not come in such a way as to be seen. 21 No one will say, 'Look, here it is!' or, 'There it is!'; because the Kingdom of God is within you.'' *u*

22 Then he said to the disciples, "The time will come when you will wish you could see one of the days of the Son of Man, but you will not see it. 23 There will be those who will say to you, 'Look, over there!' or, 'Look, over here!' But don't go out looking for it. 24 As the lightning flashes across the sky and lights it up from one side to the other, so will the Son of Man be in his day. 25 But first he must suffer much and be rejected by the people of this day. 26 As it was in the time of Noah so shall it be in the days of the Son of Man. 27 Everybody kept on eating and drinking, and men and women married, up to the very day Noah went into the boat and the flood came and killed them all. 28 It will be as it was in the time of Lot. Everybody kept on eating and drinking, buying and selling, planting and building. 29 On the day Lot left Sodom, fire and sulphur rained down from heaven and killed them all. 30 That is how it will be on the day the Son of Man is revealed.

31 "On that day the man who is on the roof of his house must not go down into the house to get his belongings; in the same way the man who is out in the field must not go back to the house. 32 Remember Lot's wife! 33 Whoever tries to save his own life will lose it; whoever loses his life will save it. 34 On that night, I tell you, there will be two people sleeping in the same bed: one will be taken away, the other will be left behind. 35 Two women will be grinding corn together: one will be taken away, the other will be left behind.'' *v*

37 The disciples asked him, "Where, Lord?''

Jesus answered, "Wherever there is a dead body, the vultures will gather.''

The Parable of the Widow and the Judge

18 Then Jesus told his disciples a parable to teach them that they should always pray and never become discouraged. 2 "In a certain town there was a judge who neither feared God nor respected man. 3 And there was a widow in that same town who kept coming to

---

t MADE CLEAN: *See 5.12.*
u is within you; *or* is among you, *or* will suddenly appear among you.
v *Some manuscripts add verse* 36: Two men will be working in a field: one will be taken away, the other will be left behind (*see Mt 24.40).*

17.14: Lev 14.1-32   **17.26:** Gen 6.5-8   **17.27:** Gen 7.6-24   **17.28-29:** Gen 18.20-19.25
17.31: Mt 24.17-18; Mk 13.15-16   **17.32:** Gen 19.26
17.33: Mt 10.39, 16.25; Mk 8.35; Lk 9.24; Jn 12.25

Where are the other nine? (17.17)

him and pleading for her rights, saying, 'Help me against my opponent!' ⁴For a long time the judge refused to act, but at last he said to himself, 'Even though I don't fear God or respect man, ⁵yet because of all the trouble this widow is giving me, I will see to it that she gets her rights. If I don't, she will keep on coming and finally wear me out!' "

6 And the Lord continued, "Listen to what that corrupt judge said. ⁷Now, will God not judge in favour of his own people who cry to him day and night for help? Will he be slow to help them? ⁸I tell you, he will judge in their favour and do it quickly. But will the Son of Man find faith on earth when he comes?"

The Parable of the Pharisee and the Tax Collector

9 Jesus also told this parable to people who were sure of their own goodness and despised everybody else. ¹⁰"Once there were two men who went up to the Temple to pray: one was a Pharisee, the other a tax collector.

11 "The Pharisee stood apart by himself and prayed,ʷ 'I thank you, God, that I am not greedy, dishonest, or an adulterer, like everybody else. I thank you that I am not like that tax collector over there. ¹²I fast two days a week, and I give you a tenth of all my income.'

13 "But the tax collector stood at a distance and would not even raise his face to heaven, but beat on his breast and said, 'God, have pity on me, a sinner!' ¹⁴I tell you," said Jesus, "the tax collector, and not the Pharisee, was in the right with God when he went home. For everyone who makes himself great will be humbled,

ʷstood apart by himself and prayed; *some manuscripts have* stood up and prayed to himself.
18.14: Mt 23.12; Lk 14.11

and everyone who humbles himself will be made great."

Jesus Blesses Little Children
(Matt. 19.13–15; Mark 10.13–16)

15 Some people brought their babies to Jesus for him to place his hands on them. The disciples saw them and scolded them for doing so, 16 but Jesus called the children to him and said, "Let the children come to me and do not stop them, because the Kingdom of God belongs to such as these. 17 Remember this! Whoever does not receive the Kingdom of God like a child will never enter it."

The Rich Man
(Matt. 19.16–30; Mark 10.17–31)

18 A Jewish leader asked Jesus, "Good Teacher, what must I do to receive eternal life?"

19 "Why do you call me good?" Jesus asked him. "No one is good except God alone. 20 You know the commandments: 'Do not commit adultery; do not commit murder; do not steal; do not accuse anyone falsely; respect your father and your mother.'"

21 The man replied, "Ever since I was young, I have obeyed all these commandments."

22 When Jesus heard this, he said to him, "There is still one more thing you need to do. Sell all you have and give the money to the poor, and you will have riches in heaven; then come and follow me." 23 But when the man heard this, he became very sad, because he was very rich.

24 Jesus saw that he was sad and said, "How hard it is for rich people to enter the Kingdom of God! 25 It is much harder for a rich person to enter the Kingdom of God than for a camel to go through the eye of a needle."

26 The people who heard him asked, "Who, then, can be saved?"

27 Jesus answered, "What is impossible for man is possible for God."

28 Then Peter said, "Look! We have left our homes to follow you."

29 "Yes," Jesus said to them, "and I assure you that anyone who leaves home or wife or brothers or parents or children for the sake of the Kingdom of God 30 will receive much more in this present age and eternal life in the age to come."

18.20: Ex 20.12–16; Deut 5.16–20

Jesus Speaks a Third Time about His Death
(Matt. 20.17–19; Mark 10.32–34)

31 Jesus took the twelve disciples aside and said to them, "Listen! We are going to Jerusalem where everything the prophets wrote about the Son of Man will come true. 32 He will be handed over to the Gentiles, who will mock him, insult him, and spit on him. 33 They will whip him and kill him, but three days later he will rise to life."

34 But the disciples did not understand any of these things; the meaning of the words was hidden from them, and they did not know what Jesus was talking about.

Jesus Heals a Blind Beggar
(Matt. 20.29–34; Mark 10.46–52)

35 As Jesus was coming near Jericho, there was a blind man sitting by the road, begging. 36 When he heard the crowd passing by, he asked, "What is this?"

37 "Jesus of Nazareth is passing by," they told him.

38 He cried out, "Jesus! Son of David! Take pity on me!"

39 The people in front scolded him and told him to be quiet. But he shouted even more loudly, "Son of David! Take pity on me!"

40 So Jesus stopped and ordered the blind man to be brought to him. When he came near, Jesus asked him, 41 "What do you want me to do for you?"

"Sir," he answered, "I want to see again."

42 Jesus said to him, "Then see! Your faith has made you well."

43 At once he was able to see, and he followed Jesus, giving thanks to God. When the crowd saw it, they all praised God.

Jesus and Zacchaeus

19 Jesus went on into Jericho and was passing through. 2 There was a chief tax collector there named Zacchaeus, who was rich. 3 He was trying to see who Jesus was, but he was a little man and could not see Jesus because of the crowd. 4 So he ran ahead of the crowd and climbed a sycamore tree to see Jesus, who was going to pass that way. 5 When Jesus came to that place, he looked up and said to Zacchaeus, "Hurry down,

He ... could not see Jesus because of the crowd (19.3)

Zacchaeus, because I must stay in your house today."

6 Zacchaeus hurried down and welcomed him with great joy. 7 All the people who saw it started grumbling, "This man has gone as a guest to the home of a sinner!"

8 Zacchaeus stood up and said to the Lord, "Listen, sir! I will give half my belongings to the poor, and if I have cheated anyone, I will pay him back four times as much."

9 Jesus said to him, "Salvation has come to this house today, for this man, also, is a descendant of Abraham. 10 The Son of Man came to seek and to save the lost."

The Parable of the Gold Coins
(Matt. 25.14-30)

11 While the people were listening to this, Jesus continued and told them a parable. He was now almost at Jerusalem, and they supposed that the Kingdom of God was just about to appear. 12 So he said, "There was once a man of high rank who was going to a country far away to be made king, after which he planned to come back home. 13 Before he left, he called his ten servants and gave them each a gold coin and told them, 'See what you can earn with this while I am gone.' 14 Now, his countrymen hated him, and so they sent messengers after him to say, 'We don't want this man to be our king.'

15 "The man was made king and came back. At once he ordered his servants to appear before him, in order to find out how much they had earned. 16 The first one came and said, 'Sir, I have earned ten gold coins with the one you gave me.' 17 'Well done,' he said; 'you are a good servant! Since you were faithful in small matters, I will put you in charge of ten cities.' 18 The second servant came and said, 'Sir, I have earned five gold coins with the one you gave me.' 19 To this one

19.10: Mt 18.11   **19.11–27:** Mt 25.14–30

he said, 'You will be in charge of five cities.'

20. "Another servant came and said, 'Sir, here is your gold coin; I kept it hidden in a handkerchief. ²¹I was afraid of you, because you are a hard man. You take what is not yours and reap what you did not sow.' ²²He said to him, 'You bad servant! I will use your own words to condemn you! You know that I am a hard man, taking what is not mine and reaping what I have not sown. ²³Well, then, why didn't you put my money in the bank? Then I would have received it back with interest when I returned.'

24 "Then he said to those who were standing there, 'Take the gold coin away from him and give it to the servant who has ten coins.' ²⁵But they said to him, 'Sir, he already has ten coins!' ²⁶'I tell you,' he replied, 'that to every person who has something, even more will be given; but the person who has nothing, even the little that he has will be taken away from him. ²⁷Now, as for those enemies of mine who did not want me to be their king, bring them here and kill them in my presence!'"

The Triumphant Approach to Jerusalem
(Matt. 21.1-11; Mark 11.1-11; John 12.12-19)

28 Jesus said this and then went on to Jerusalem ahead of them. ²⁹As he came near Bethphage and Bethany at the Mount of Olives, he sent two disciples ahead ³⁰with these instructions: "Go to the village there ahead of you; as you go in, you will find a colt tied up that has never been ridden. Untie it and bring it here. ³¹If someone asks you why you are untying it, tell him that the Master ˣ needs it."

32 They went on their way and found everything just as Jesus had told them. ³³As they were untying the colt, its owners said to them, "Why are you untying it?"

34 "The Master ˣ needs it," they answered, ³⁵and they took the colt to Jesus. Then they threw their cloaks over the animal and helped Jesus get on. ³⁶As he rode on, people spread their cloaks on the road.

37 When he came near Jerusalem, at the place where the road went down the Mount of Olives, the large crowd of his disciples began to thank God and praise

him in loud voices for all the great things that they had seen: ³⁸"God bless the king who comes in the name of the Lord! Peace in heaven and glory to God!"

39 Then some of the Pharisees in the crowd spoke to Jesus. "Teacher," they said, "command your disciples to be quiet!"

40 Jesus answered, "I tell you that if they keep quiet, the stones themselves will start shouting."

Jesus Weeps over Jerusalem

41 He came closer to the city, and when he saw it, he wept over it, ⁴²saying, "If you only knew today what is needed for peace! But now you cannot see it! ⁴³The time will come when your enemies will surround you with barricades, blockade you, and close in on you from every side. ⁴⁴They will completely destroy you and the people within your walls; not a single stone will they leave in its place, because you did not recognize the time when God came to save you!"

Jesus Goes to the Temple
(Matt. 21.12-17; Mark 11.15-19; John 2.13-22)

45 Then Jesus went into the Temple and began to drive out the merchants, ⁴⁶saying to them, "It is written in the Scriptures that God said, 'My Temple will be called a house of prayer.' But you have turned it into a hideout for thieves!"

47 Every day Jesus taught in the Temple. The chief priests, the teachers of the Law, and the leaders of the people wanted to kill him, ⁴⁸but they could not find a way to do it, because all the people kept listening to him, not wanting to miss a single word.

The Question about Jesus' Authority
(Matt. 21.23-27; Mark 11.27-33)

20 One day when Jesus was in the Temple teaching the people and preaching the Good News, the chief priests and the teachers of the Law, together with the elders, came ²and said to him, "Tell us, what right have you to do these things? Who gave you this right?"

3 Jesus answered them, "Now let me ask you a question. Tell me, ⁴did John's right to baptize come from God or from man?"

ˣthe Master; or its owner.
19.26: Mt 13.12; Mk 4.25; Lk 8.18   **19.38:** Ps 118.26   **19.46:** Is 56.7; Jer 7.11
19.47: Lk 21.37

5 They started to argue among themselves, "What shall we say? If we say, 'From God,' he will say, 'Why, then, did you not believe John?' 6 But if we say 'From man,' this whole crowd here will stone us, because they are convinced that John was a prophet." 7 So they answered, "We don't know where it came from."

8 And Jesus said to them, "Neither will I tell you, then, by what right I do these things."

The Parable of the Tenants in the Vineyard
(Matt. 21.33-46; Mark 12.1-12)

9 Then Jesus told the people this parable: "There was once a man who planted a vineyard, let it out to tenants, and then left home for a long time. 10 When the time came to gather the grapes, he sent a slave to the tenants to receive from them his share of the harvest. But the tenants beat the slave and sent him back without a thing. 11 So he sent another slave; but the tenants beat him also, treated him shamefully, and sent him back without a thing. 12 Then he sent a third slave; the tenants wounded him, too, and threw him out. 13 Then the owner of the vineyard said, 'What shall I do? I will send my own dear son; surely they will respect him!' 14 But when the tenants saw him, they said to one another, 'This is the owner's son. Let's kill him, and his property will be ours!' 15 So they threw him out of the vineyard and killed him.

"What, then, will the owner of the vineyard do to the tenants?" Jesus asked. 16 "He will come and kill those men, and hand the vineyard over to other tenants."

When the people heard this, they said, "Surely not!"

17 Jesus looked at them and asked, "What, then, does this scripture mean?

'The stone which the builders rejected as worthless
turned out to be the most important of all.'

18 Everyone who falls on that stone will be cut to pieces; and if that stone falls on someone, it will crush him to dust."

The Question about Paying Taxes
(Matt. 22.15-22; Mark 12.13-17)

19 The teachers of the Law and the chief priests tried to arrest Jesus on the spot, because they knew that he had told this parable against them; but they were afraid of the people. 20 So they looked for an opportunity. They bribed some men to pretend they were sincere, and they sent them to trap Jesus with questions, so that they could hand him over to the authority and power of the Roman Governor. 21 These spies said to Jesus, "Teacher, we know that what you say and teach is right. We know that you pay no attention to a man's status, but teach the truth about God's will for man. 22 Tell us, is it against our Law for us to pay taxes to the Roman Emperor, or not?"

23 But Jesus saw through their trick and said to them, 24 "Show me a silver coin. Whose face and name are these on it?"

"The Emperor's," they answered.

25 So Jesus said, "Well, then, pay the Emperor what belongs to the Emperor, and pay God what belongs to God."

26 There before the people they could not catch him out in anything, so they kept quiet, amazed at his answer.

The Question about Rising from Death
(Matt. 22.23-33; Mark 12.18-27)

27 Then some Sadducees, who say that people will not rise from death, came to Jesus and said, 28 "Teacher, Moses wrote this law for us: 'If a man dies and leaves a wife but no children, that man's brother must marry the widow so that they can have children who will be considered the dead man's children.' 29 Once there were seven brothers; the eldest got married and died without having children. 30 Then the second one married the woman, 31 and then the third. The same thing happened to all seven—they died without having children. 32 Last of all, the woman died. 33 Now, on the day when the dead rise to life, whose wife will she be? All seven of them had married her."

34 Jesus answered them, "The men and women of this age marry, 35 but the men and women who are worthy to rise from death and live in the age to come will not then marry. 36 They will be like angels and cannot die. They are the sons of God, because they have risen from death. 37 And Moses clearly proves that the dead are raised to life. In the passage about the burning bush he speaks of the Lord as 'the God of Abraham, the God of Isaac, and the God of Jacob.' 38 He is the God of the living, not of the dead, for to him all are alive."

39 Some of the teachers of the Law

spoke up, "A good answer, Teacher!" [40] For they did not dare ask him any more questions.

The Question about the Messiah
(Matt. 22.41–46; Mark 12.35–37)

41 Jesus asked them, "How can it be said that the Messiah will be the descendant of David? [42] For David himself says in the book of Psalms,

'The Lord said to my Lord:
Sit here on my right
[43]   until I put your enemies as a
       footstool under your feet.'

[44] David called him 'Lord'; how, then, can the Messiah be David's descendant?"

Jesus Warns against the Teachers of the Law
(Matt. 23.1–36; Mark 12.38–40)

45 As all the people listened to him, Jesus said to his disciples, [46] "Be on your guard against the teachers of the Law, who like to walk about in their long robes and love to be greeted with respect in the market-place; who choose the reserved seats in the synagogues and the best places at feasts; [47] who take advantage of widows and rob them of their homes, and then make a show of saying long prayers! Their punishment will be all the worse!"

The Widow's Offering
(Mark 12.41–44)

21 Jesus looked round and saw rich men dropping their gifts in the temple treasury, [2] and he also saw a very poor widow dropping in two little copper coins. [3] He said, "I tell you that this poor widow put in more than all the others. [4] For the others offered their gifts from what they had to spare of their riches; but she, poor as she is, gave all she had to live on."

Jesus Speaks of the Destruction of the Temple
(Matt. 24.1–2; Mark 13.1–2)

5 Some of the disciples were talking about the Temple, how beautiful it looked with its fine stones and the gifts offered to God. Jesus said, [6] "All this you see—the time will come when not a single stone here will be left in its place; every one will be thrown down."

Troubles and Persecutions
(Matt. 24.3–14; Mark 13.3–13)

7 "Teacher," they asked, "when will this be? And what will happen in order to show that the time has come for it to take place?"

8 Jesus said, "Be on guard; don't be deceived. Many men, claiming to speak for me, will come and say, 'I am he!' and, 'The time has come!' But don't follow them. [9] Don't be afraid when you hear of wars and revolutions; such things must happen first, but they do not mean that the end is near."

10 He went on to say, "Countries will fight each other; kingdoms will attack one another. [11] There will be terrible earthquakes, famines, and plagues everywhere; there will be strange and terrifying things coming from the sky. [12] Before all these things take place, however, you will be arrested and persecuted; you will be handed over to be tried in synagogues and be put in prison; you will be brought before kings and rulers for my sake. [13] This will be your chance to tell the Good News. [14] Make up your minds beforehand not to worry about how you will defend yourselves, [15] because I will give you such words and wisdom that none of your enemies will be able to refute or contradict what you say. [16] You will be handed over by your parents, your brothers, your relatives, and your friends; and some of you will be put to death. [17] Everyone will hate you because of me. [18] But not a single hair from your heads will be lost. [19] Stand firm, and you will save yourselves.

Jesus Speaks of the Destruction of Jerusalem
(Matt. 24.15–21; Mark 13.14–19)

20 "When you see Jerusalem surrounded by armies, then you will know that she will soon be destroyed. [21] Then those who are in Judaea must run away to the hills; those who are in the city must leave, and those who are out in the country must not go into the city. [22] For those will be 'The Days of Punishment,' to make all that the Scriptures say come true. [23] How terrible it will be in those days for women who are pregnant and for mothers with little babies! Terrible distress will come upon this land, and God's punishment will fall on this people. [24] Some will be killed by the sword, and others will be taken as prisoners to all

20.42–43: Ps 110.1   **21.14–15:** Lk 12.11–12   **21.22:** Hos 9.7

countries; and the heathen will trample over Jerusalem until their time is up.

The Coming of the Son of Man
(Matt. 24.29–31; Mark 13.24–27)

25 "There will be strange things happening to the sun, the moon, and the stars. On earth whole countries will be in despair, afraid of the roar of the sea and the raging tides. 26 People will faint from fear as they wait for what is coming over the whole earth, for the powers in space will be driven from their courses. 27 Then the Son of Man will appear, coming in a cloud with great power and glory. 28 When these things begin to happen, stand up and raise your heads, because your salvation is near."

The Lesson of the Fig-Tree
(Matt. 24.32–35; Mark 13.28–31)

29 Then Jesus told them this parable: "Think of the fig-tree and all the other trees. 30 When you see their leaves beginning to appear, you know that summer is near. 31 In the same way, when you see these things happening, you will know that the Kingdom of God is about to come.

32 "Remember that all these things will take place before the people now living have all died. 33 Heaven and earth will pass away, but my words will never pass away.

The Need to Watch

34 "Be on your guard! Don't let yourselves become occupied with too much feasting and drinking and with the worries of this life, or that Day may suddenly catch you 35 like a trap. For it will come upon all people everywhere on earth. 36 Be on the alert and pray always that you will have the strength to go safely through all those things that will happen and to stand before the Son of Man."

37 Jesus spent those days teaching in the Temple, and when evening came, he would go out and spend the night on the Mount of Olives. 38 Early each morning all the people went to the Temple to listen to him.

The Plot against Jesus
(Matt. 26.1–5; Mark 14.1–2; John 11.45–53)

22 The time was near for the Festival of Unleavened Bread, which is called the Passover. 2 The chief priests and the teachers of the Law were afraid of the people, and so they were trying to find a way of putting Jesus to death secretly.

Judas Agrees to Betray Jesus
(Matt. 26.14–16; Mark 14.10–11)

3 Then Satan entered Judas, called Iscariot, who was one of the twelve disciples. 4 So Judas went off and spoke with the chief priests and the officers of the temple guard about how he could betray Jesus to them. 5 They were pleased and offered to pay him money. 6 Judas agreed to it and started looking for a good chance to hand Jesus over to them without the people knowing about it.

Jesus Prepares to Eat the Passover Meal
(Matt. 26.17–25; Mark 14.12–21; John 13.21–30)

7 The day came during the Festival of Unleavened Bread when the lambs for the Passover meal were to be killed. 8 Jesus sent off Peter and John with these instructions: "Go and get the Passover meal ready for us to eat."

9 "Where do you want us to get it ready?" they asked him.

10 He answered, "As you go into the city, a man carrying a jar of water will meet you. Follow him into the house that he enters, 11 and say to the owner of the house: 'The Teacher says to you, Where is the room where my disciples and I will eat the Passover meal?' 12 He will show you a large furnished room upstairs, where you will get everything ready."

13 They went off and found everything just as Jesus had told them, and they prepared the Passover meal.

The Lord's Supper
(Matt. 26.26–30; Mark 14.22–26; 1 Cor. 11.23–25)

14 When the hour came, Jesus took his place at the table with the apostles. 15 He said to them, "I have wanted so much to eat this Passover meal with you before I suffer! 16 For I tell you, I will never eat it until it is given its full meaning in the Kingdom of God."

17 Then Jesus took a cup, gave thanks to God, and said, "Take this and share it among yourselves. 18 I tell you that from

---

21.25: Is 13.10; Ezek 32.7; Joel 2.31; Rev 6.12–13
22.1: Ex 12.1–27

21.27: Dan 7.13; Rev 1.7   21.37: Lk 19.47

now on I will not drink this wine until the Kingdom of God comes."

19 Then he took a piece of bread, gave thanks to God, broke it, and gave it to them, saying, "This is my body, which is given for you. Do this in memory of me." ²⁰ In the same way, he gave them the cup after the supper, saying, "This cup is God's new covenant sealed with my blood, which is poured out for you. ʸ

21 "But, look! The one who betrays me is here at the table with me! ²² The Son of Man will die as God has decided, but how terrible for that man who betrays him!"

23 Then they began to ask among themselves which one of them it could be who was going to do this.

The Argument about Greatness

24 An argument broke out among the disciples as to which one of them should be thought of as the greatest. ²⁵ Jesus said to them, "The kings of the pagans have power over their people, and the rulers claim the title 'Friends of the People.' ²⁶ But this is not the way it is with you; rather, the greatest one among you must be like the youngest, and the leader must be like the servant. ²⁷ Who is greater, the one who sits down to eat or the one who serves him? The one who sits down, of course. But I am among you as one who serves.

28 "You have stayed with me all through my trials; ²⁹ and just as my Father has given me the right to rule, so I will give you the same right. ³⁰ You will eat and drink at my table in my Kingdom, and you will sit on thrones to rule over the twelve tribes of Israel.

Jesus Predicts Peter's Denial
(Matt. 26.31-35; Mark 14.27-31; John 13.36-38)

31 "Simon, Simon! Listen! Satan has received permission to test all of you, to separate the good from the bad, as a farmer separates the wheat from the chaff. ³² But I have prayed for you, Simon, that your faith will not fail. And when you turn back to me, you must strengthen your brothers."

33 Peter answered, "Lord, I am ready to go to prison with you and to die with you!"

34 "I tell you, Peter," Jesus said, "the cock will not crow tonight until you have said three times that you do not know me."

Purse, Bag, and Sword

35 Then Jesus asked his disciples, "When I sent you out that time without purse, bag, or shoes, did you lack anything?"

"Not a thing," they answered.

36 "But now," Jesus said, "whoever has a purse or a bag must take it; and whoever has no sword must sell his coat and buy one. ³⁷ For I tell you that the scripture which says, 'He shared the fate of criminals,' must come true about me, because what was written about me is coming true."

38 The disciples said, "Look! Here are two swords, Lord!"

"That is enough!" ᶻ he replied.

Jesus Prays on the Mount of Olives
(Matt. 26.36-46; Mark 14.32-42)

39 Jesus left the city and went, as he usually did, to the Mount of Olives; and the disciples went with him. ⁴⁰ When he arrived at the place, he said to them, "Pray that you will not fall into temptation."

41 Then he went off from them about the distance of a stone's throw and knelt down and prayed. ⁴² "Father," he said, "if you will, take this cup of suffering away from me. Not my will, however, but your will be done." ⁴³ An angel from heaven appeared to him and strengthened him. ⁴⁴ In great anguish he prayed even more fervently; his sweat was like drops of blood falling to the ground. ᵃ

45 Rising from his prayer, he went back to the disciples and found them asleep, worn out by their grief. ⁴⁶ He said to them, "Why are you sleeping? Get up and pray that you will not fall into temptation."

The Arrest of Jesus
(Matt. 26.47-56; Mark 14.43-50; John 18.3-11)

47 Jesus was still speaking when a crowd arrived, led by Judas, one of the twelve disciples. He came up to Jesus to kiss him. ⁴⁸ But Jesus said, "Judas, is it with a kiss that you betray the Son of Man?"

49 When the disciples who were with Jesus saw what was going to happen, they

---

ʸ Some manuscripts do not have the words of Jesus after This is my body in verse 19, and all of verse 20.   ᶻ That is enough; or Enough of this.
ᵃ Some manuscripts do not have verses 43-44.
22.20: Jer 31.31-34   **22.21:** Ps 41.9   **22.24:** Mt 18.1; Mk 9.34; Lk 9.46
22.25-26: Mt 20.25-27, 10.42-44   **22.26:** Mt 23.11; Mk 9.35   **22.27:** Jn 13.12-15
22.30: Mt 19.28   **22.35:** Mt 10.9-10; Mk 6.8-9; Lk 9.3, 10.4   **22.37:** Is 53.12

This man too was with Jesus! (22.56)

asked, "Shall we use our swords, Lord?"
⁵⁰ And one of them struck the High Priest's slave and cut off his right ear.

51 But Jesus said, "Enough of this!" He touched the man's ear and healed him.

52 Then Jesus said to the chief priests and the officers of the temple guard and the elders who had come there to get him, "Did you have to come with swords and clubs, as though I were an outlaw? ⁵³ I was with you in the Temple every day, and you did not try to arrest me. But this is your hour to act, when the power of darkness rules."

Peter Denies Jesus
(Matt. 26.57–58, 69–75; Mark 14.53–54, 66–72; John 18.12–18, 25–27)

54 They arrested Jesus and took him away into the house of the High Priest; and Peter followed at a distance. ⁵⁵ A fire had been lit in the centre of the courtyard, and Peter joined those who were sitting round it. ⁵⁶ When one of the servant-girls saw him sitting there at the fire, she looked straight at him and said, "This man too was with Jesus!"

57 But Peter denied it, "Woman, I don't even know him!"

58 After a little while a man noticed

Peter and said, "You are one of them, too!"

But Peter answered, "Man, I am not!"

59 And about an hour later another man insisted strongly, "There isn't any doubt that this man was with Jesus, because he also is a Galilean!"

60 But Peter answered, "Man, I don't know what you are talking about!"

At once, while he was still speaking, a cock crowed. ⁶¹ The Lord turned round and looked straight at Peter, and Peter remembered that the Lord had said to him, "Before the cock crows tonight, you will say three times that you do not know me." ⁶² Peter went out and wept bitterly.

Jesus Is Mocked and Beaten
(Matt. 26.67–68; Mark 14.65)

63 The men who were guarding Jesus mocked him and beat him. ⁶⁴ They blindfolded him and asked him, "Who hit you? Guess!" ⁶⁵ And they said many other insulting things to him.

Jesus Is Brought Before the Council
(Matt. 26.59–66; Mark 14.55–64; John 18.19–24)

66 When day came, the elders, the chief priests, and the teachers of the Law met together, and Jesus was brought before

22.53: Lk 19.47, 21.37

the Council. 67"Tell us," they said, "are you the Messiah?"

He answered, "If I tell you, you will not believe me; 68 and if I ask you a question, you will not answer. 69 But from now on the Son of Man will be seated on the right of Almighty God."

70 They all said, "Are you, then, the Son of God?"

He answered them, "You say that I am."

71 And they said, "We don't need any witnesses! We ourselves have heard what he said!"

Jesus Is Brought Before Pilate
(Matt. 27.1-2, 11-14; Mark 15.1-5; John 18.28-38)

23 The whole group rose up and took Jesus before Pilate, 2 where they began to accuse him: "We caught this man misleading our people, telling them not to pay taxes to the Emperor and claiming that he himself is the Messiah, a king."

3 Pilate asked him, "Are you the king of the Jews?"

"So you say," answered Jesus.

4 Then Pilate said to the chief priests and the crowds, "I find no reason to condemn this man."

5 But they insisted even more strongly, "With his teaching he is starting a riot among the people all through Judaea. He began in Galilee and now has come here."

Jesus Is Sent to Herod

6 When Pilate heard this, he asked, "Is this man a Galilean?" 7 When he learnt that Jesus was from the region ruled by Herod, he sent him to Herod, who was also in Jerusalem at that time. 8 Herod was very pleased when he saw Jesus, because he had heard about him and had been wanting to see him for a long time. He was hoping to see Jesus perform some miracle. 9 So Herod asked Jesus many questions, but Jesus made no answer. 10 The chief priests and the teachers of the Law stepped forward and made strong accusations against Jesus. 11 Herod and his soldiers mocked Jesus and treated him with contempt; then they put a fine robe on him and sent him back to Pilate. 12 On that very day Herod and Pilate became friends; before this they had been enemies.

Jesus Is Sentenced to Death
(Matt. 27.15-26; Mark 15.6-15; John 18.39-19.16)

13 Pilate called together the chief priests, the leaders, and the people, 14 and said to them, "You brought this man to me and said that he was misleading the people. Now, I have examined him here in your presence, and I have not found him guilty of any of the crimes you accuse him of. 15 Nor did Herod find him guilty, for he sent him back to us. There is nothing this man has done to deserve death. 16 So I will have him whipped and let him go."[b]

18 The whole crowd cried out, "Kill him! Set Barabbas free for us!" (19 Barabbas had been put in prison for a riot that had taken place in the city, and for murder.)

20 Pilate wanted to set Jesus free, so he appealed to the crowd again. 21 But they shouted back, "Crucify him! Crucify him!"

22 Pilate said to them the third time, "But what crime has he committed? I cannot find anything he has done to deserve death! I will have him whipped and set him free."

23 But they kept on shouting at the top of their voices that Jesus should be crucified, and finally their shouting succeeded. 24 So Pilate passed the sentence on Jesus that they were asking for. 25 He set free the man they wanted, the one who had been put in prison for riot and murder, and he handed Jesus over for them to do as they wished.

Jesus Is Crucified
(Matt. 27.32-44; Mark 15.21-32; John 19.17-27)

26 The soldiers led Jesus away, and as they were going, they met a man from Cyrene named Simon who was coming into the city from the country. They seized him, put the cross on him, and made him carry it behind Jesus.

27 A large crowd of people followed him; among them were some women who were weeping and wailing for him. 28 Jesus turned to them and said, "Women of Jerusalem! Don't cry for me, but for yourselves and your children. 29 For the days are coming when people will say, 'How lucky are the women who never had children, who never bore babies, who

b Some manuscripts add verse 17: At every Passover Festival Pilate had to set free one prisoner for them (see Mk 15.6).

They ... put the cross on him, and made him carry it (23.26)

never nursed them!' ³⁰That will be the time when people will say to the mountains, 'Fall on us!' and to the hills, 'Hide us!' ³¹For if such things as these are done when the wood is green, what will happen when it is dry?"

32 Two other men, both of them criminals, were also led out to be put to death with Jesus. ³³When they came to the place called "The Skull," they crucified Jesus there, and the two criminals, one on his right and the other on his left. ³⁴Jesus said, "Forgive them, Father! They don't know what they are doing."*c*

They divided his clothes among themselves by throwing dice. ³⁵The people stood there watching while the Jewish leaders jeered at him: "He saved others; let him save himself if he is the Messiah whom God has chosen!"

36 The soldiers also mocked him: they came up to him and offered him cheap wine, ³⁷and said, "Save yourself if you are the king of the Jews!"

38 Above him were written these words: "This is the King of the Jews."

39 One of the criminals hanging there hurled insults at him: "Aren't you the Messiah? Save yourself and us!"

40 The other one, however, rebuked him, saying "Don't you fear God? You received the same sentence he did. ⁴¹Ours, however, is only right, because we are getting what we deserve for what we did;

but he has done no wrong." ⁴²And he said to Jesus, "Remember me, Jesus, when you come as King!"

43 Jesus said to him, "I promise you that today you will be in Paradise with me."

The Death of Jesus
(Matt. 27.45-56; Mark 15.33-41; John 19.28-30)

44 It was about twelve o'clock when the sun stopped shining and darkness covered the whole country until three o'clock; ⁴⁵and the curtain hanging in the Temple was torn in two. ⁴⁶Jesus cried out

Father! In your hands I place my spirit! (23.46)

in a loud voice, "Father! In your hands I place my spirit!" He said this and died.

47 The army officer saw what had happened, and he praised God, saying,

---

c Some manuscripts do not have Jesus said, "Forgive them, Father! They don't know what they are doing."
23.30: Hos 10.8; Rev 6.16   **23.34:** Ps 22.18   **23.35:** Ps 22.7   **23.36:** Ps 69.21
23.45: Ex 26.31-33   **23.46:** Ps 31.5

"Certainly he was a good man!"

48 When the people who had gathered there to watch the spectacle saw what happened, they all went back home, beating their breasts in sorrow. ⁴⁹All those who knew Jesus personally, including the women who had followed him from Galilee, stood at a distance to watch.

The Burial of Jesus
(Matt. 27.57-61; Mark 15.42-47; John 19.38-42)

50-51 There was a man named Joseph from Arimathea, a town in Judaea. He was a good and honourable man, who was waiting for the coming of the Kingdom of God. Although he was a member of the Council, he had not agreed with their decision and action. ⁵²He went into the presence of Pilate and asked for the body of Jesus. ⁵³Then he took the body down, wrapped it in a linen sheet, and placed it in a tomb which had been dug out of solid rock and which had never been used. ⁵⁴It was Friday, and the Sabbath was about to begin.

55 The women who had followed Jesus from Galilee went with Joseph and saw the tomb and how Jesus' body was placed in it. ⁵⁶Then they went back home and prepared the spices and perfumes for the body.

On the Sabbath they rested, as the Law commanded.

The Resurrection
(Matt. 28.1-10; Mark 16.1-8; John 20.1-10)

24 Very early on Sunday morning the women went to the tomb, carrying the spices they had prepared. ²They found the stone rolled away from the entrance to the tomb, ³so they went in; but they did not find the body of the Lord Jesus. ⁴They stood there puzzled about this, when suddenly two men in bright shining clothes stood by them. ⁵Full of fear, the women bowed down to the ground, as the men said to them, "Why are you looking among the dead for one who is alive? ⁶He is not here; he has been raised. Remember what he said to you while he was in Galilee: ⁷'The Son of Man must be handed over to sinful men, be crucified, and three days later rise to life.'"

8 Then the women remembered his words, ⁹returned from the tomb, and told all these things to the eleven disciples and all the rest. ¹⁰The women were Mary

He is not here; he has been raised (24.6)

Magdalene, Joanna, and Mary the mother of James; they and the other women with them told these things to the apostles. ¹¹But the apostles thought that what the women said was nonsense, and they did not believe them. ¹²But Peter got up and ran to the tomb; he bent down and saw the linen wrappings but nothing else. Then he went back home amazed at what had happened.ᵈ

The Walk to Emmaus
(Mark 16.12-13)

13 On that same day two of Jesus' followers were going to a village named Emmaus, about eleven kilometres from Jerusalem, ¹⁴and they were talking to each other about all the things that had happened. ¹⁵As they talked and discussed, Jesus himself drew near and walked along with them; ¹⁶they saw him, but somehow did not recognize him. ¹⁷Jesus said to them, "What are you talking about to each other, as you walk along?"

They stood still, with sad faces. ¹⁸One of them, named Cleopas, asked him, "Are you the only visitor in Jerusalem who doesn't know the things that have been happening there these last few days?"

19 "What things?" he asked.

"The things that happened to Jesus of Nazareth," they answered. "This man was a prophet and was considered by God and by all the people to be powerful in everything he said and did. ²⁰Our chief priests and rulers handed him over to be sentenced to death, and he was crucified.

ᵈ *Some manuscripts do not have verse 12.*
23.49: Lk 8.2-3   **23.56:** Ex 20.10; Deut 5.14
24.6-7: Mt 16.21, 17.22-23, 20.18-19; Mk 8.31, 9.31, 10.33-34; Lk 9.22, 18.31-33

116

As he was blessing them (24.51)

²¹ And we had hoped that he would be the one who was going to set Israel free! Besides all that, this is now the third day since it happened. ²² Some of the women of our group surprised us; they went at dawn to the tomb, ²³ but could not find his body. They came back saying they had seen a vision of angels who told them that he is alive. ²⁴ Some of our group went to the tomb and found it exactly as the women had said, but they did not see him."

25 Then Jesus said to them, "How foolish you are, how slow you are to believe everything the prophets said! ²⁶ Was it not necessary for the Messiah to suffer these things and then to enter his glory?" ²⁷ And Jesus explained to them what was said about himself in all the Scriptures, beginning with the books of Moses and the writings of all the prophets.

28 As they came near the village to which they were going, Jesus acted as if he were going farther; ²⁹ but they held him back, saying, "Stay with us; the day is almost over and it is getting dark." So he went in to stay with them. ³⁰ He sat down to eat with them, took the bread, and said the blessing; then he broke the bread and gave it to them. ³¹ Then their eyes were opened and they recognized him, but he disappeared from their sight. ³² They said to each other, "Wasn't it like a fire burning in us when he talked to us on the road and explained the Scriptures to us?"

33 They got up at once and went back to Jerusalem, where they found the eleven disciples gathered together with the others ³⁴ and saying, "The Lord is risen indeed! He has appeared to Simon!"

35 The two then explained to them what had happened on the road, and how they had recognized the Lord when he broke the bread.

Jesus Appears to His Disciples
(Matt. 28.16-20; Mark 16.14-18;
John 20.19-23; Acts 1.6-8)

36 While the two were telling them this, suddenly the Lord himself stood among them and said to them, "Peace be with you." *e*

37 They were terrified, thinking that they were seeing a ghost. ³⁸ But he said to them, "Why are you alarmed? Why

e Some manuscripts do not have and said to them, "Peace be with you."

are these doubts coming up in your minds? [39] Look at my hands and my feet, and see that it is I myself. Feel me, and you will know, for a ghost doesn't have flesh and bones, as you can see I have."

40 He said this and showed them his hands and his feet. [f] [41] They still could not believe, they were so full of joy and wonder; so he asked them, "Have you anything here to eat?" [42] They gave him a piece of cooked fish, [43] which he took and ate in their presence.

44 Then he said to them, "These are the very things I told you about while I was still with you: everything written about me in the Law of Moses, the writings of the prophets, and the Psalms had to come true."

45 Then he opened their minds to understand the Scriptures, [46] and said to them, "This is what is written: the Messiah must suffer and must rise from death three days later, [47] and in his name the message about repentance and the forgiveness of sins must be preached to all nations, beginning in Jerusalem. [48] You are witnesses of these things. [49] And I myself will send upon you what my Father has promised. But you must wait in the city until the power from above comes down upon you."

Jesus Is Taken up to Heaven
(Mark 16.19-20; Acts 1.9-11)

50 Then he led them out of the city as far as Bethany, where he raised his hands and blessed them. [51] As he was blessing them, he departed from them and was taken up into heaven. [g] [52] They worshipped him and went back into Jerusalem, filled with great joy, [53] and spent all their time in the Temple giving thanks to God.

[f] Some manuscripts do not have verse 40.
[g] Some manuscripts do not have and was taken up into heaven.
24.49: Acts 1.4   **24.50-51:** Acts 1.9-11

THE GOSPEL ACCORDING TO

JOHN

INTRODUCTION

The Gospel according to John presents Jesus as the eternal Word of God, who "became a human being and lived among us." As the book itself says, this Gospel was written so that its readers might believe that Jesus is the promised Saviour, the Son of God, and that through their faith in him they might have life (20.31).

After an introduction that identifies the eternal Word of God with Jesus, the first part of the Gospel presents various miracles which show that Jesus is the promised Saviour, the Son of God. These are followed by discourses that explain what is revealed by the miracles. This part of the book tells how some people believed in Jesus and became his followers, while others opposed him and refused to believe. Chapters 13-17 record at length the close fellowship of Jesus with his disciples on the night of his arrest, and his words of preparation and encouragement to them on the eve of his crucifixion. The closing chapters tell of Jesus' arrest and trial, his crucifixion and resurrection, and his appearances to his disciples after the resurrection.

The story of the woman caught in adultery (8.1-11) is placed in brackets because many manuscripts and early translations omit it, while others include it in other places.

John emphasizes the gift of eternal life through Christ, a gift which begins now and which comes to those who respond to Jesus as the way, the truth, and the life. A striking feature of *John* is the symbolic use of common things from everyday life to point to spiritual realities, such as water, bread, light, the shepherd and his sheep, and the grapevine and its fruit.

Outline of Contents

Prologue 1.1–18
John the Baptist and the first disciples of Jesus 1.19–51
Jesus' public ministry 2.1—12.50
The last days in and near Jerusalem 13.1—19.42
The resurrection and appearances of the Lord 20.1–31
Epilogue: another appearance in Galilee 21.1–25

The Word of Life

1 Before the world was created, the Word already existed; he was with God, and he was the same as God. ²From the very beginning the Word was with God. ³Through him God made all things; not one thing in all creation was made without him. ⁴The Word was the source of life,ᵃ and this life brought light to mankind. ⁵The light shines in the darkness, and the darkness has never put it out.

6 God sent his messenger, a man named John, ⁷who came to tell people about the light, so that all should hear the message and believe. ⁸He himself was not the light; he came to tell about the light. ⁹This was the real light—the light that comes into the world and shines on all mankind.

10 The Word was in the world, and though God made the world through him, yet the world did not recognize him. ¹¹He came to his own country, but his own people did not receive him. ¹²Some, however, did receive him and believed in him; so he gave them the right to become God's children. ¹³They did not become God's children by natural means, that is, by being born as the children of a human father; God himself was their Father.

14 The Word became a human being and, full of grace and truth, lived among us. We saw his glory, the glory which he received as the Father's only Son.

15 John spoke about him. He cried out, "This is the one I was talking about when I said, 'He comes after me, but he is greater than I am, because he existed before I was born.'"

16 Out of the fullness of his grace he has blessed us all, giving us one blessing after another. ¹⁷God gave the Law through Moses, but grace and truth came through Jesus Christ. ¹⁸No one has ever seen God. The only Son, who is the same as God and is at the Father's side, he has made him known.

John the Baptist's Message
(Matt. 3.1–12; Mark 1.1–8; Luke 3.1–18)

19 The Jewish authorities in Jerusalem sent some priests and Levites to John, to ask him, "Who are you?"

20 John did not refuse to answer, but spoke out openly and clearly, saying: "I am not the Messiah."

21 "Who are you, then?" they asked. "Are you Elijah?"

"No, I am not," John answered.

"Are you the Prophet?"ᵇ they asked.

"No," he replied.

22 "Then tell us who you are," they said. "We have to take an answer back to those who sent us. What do you say about yourself?"

23 John answered by quoting the prophet Isaiah:

"I am 'the voice of someone shouting
    in the desert:
  Make a straight path for the Lord to
    travel!'"

24 The messengers, who had been sent

ᵃThe Word was the source of life; *or* What was made had life in union with the Word.
ᵇTHE PROPHET: *The one who was expected to appear and announce the coming of the Messiah.*
1.6: Mt 3.1; Mk 1.4; Lk 3.1–2   **1.21:** Deut 18.15,18; Mal 4.5   **1.23:** Is 40.3

by the Pharisees, [25] then[c] asked John, "If you are not the Messiah nor Elijah nor the Prophet, why do you baptize?"

26 John answered, "I baptize with water, but among you stands the one you do not know. [27] He is coming after me, but I am not good enough even to untie his sandals."

28 All this happened in Bethany on the east side of the River Jordan, where John was baptizing.

The Lamb of God

29 The next day John saw Jesus coming to him, and said, "There is the Lamb of God, who takes away the sin of the world! [30] This is the one I was talking about when I said, 'A man is coming after me, but he is greater than I am, because he existed before I was born.' [31] I did not know who he would be, but I came baptizing with water in order to make him known to the people of Israel."

32 And John gave this testimony: "I saw the Spirit come down like a dove from heaven and stay on him. [33] I still did not know that he was the one, but God, who sent me to baptize with water, had said to me, 'You will see the Spirit come down and stay on a man; he is the one who baptizes with the Holy Spirit.' [34] I have seen it," said John, "and I tell you that he is the Son of God."

The First Disciples of Jesus

35 The next day John was standing there again with two of his disciples, [36] when he saw Jesus walking by. "There is the Lamb of God!" he said.

37 The two disciples heard him say this and went with Jesus. [38] Jesus turned, saw them following him, and asked, "What are you looking for?"

They answered, "Where do you live, Rabbi?" (This word means "Teacher.")

39 "Come and see," he answered. (It was then about four o'clock in the afternoon.) So they went with him and saw where he lived, and spent the rest of that day with him.

40 One of them was Andrew, Simon Peter's brother. [41] At once he found his brother Simon and told him, "We have found the Messiah." (This word means "Christ.") [42] Then he took Simon to Jesus.

Jesus looked at him and said, "Your name is Simon son of John, but you will

I saw the Spirit come down like a dove (1.32)

be called Cephas." (This is the same as Peter and means "a rock.")

Jesus Calls Philip and Nathanael

43 The next day Jesus decided to go to Galilee. He found Philip and said to him, "Come with me!" ([44] Philip was from Bethsaida, the town where Andrew and Peter lived.) [45] Philip found Nathanael and told him, "We have found the one whom Moses wrote about in the book of the Law and whom the prophets also wrote about. He is Jesus son of Joseph, from Nazareth."

46 "Can anything good come from Nazareth?" Nathanael asked.

"Come and see," answered Philip.

47 When Jesus saw Nathanael coming to him, he said about him, "Here is a real Israelite; there is nothing false in him!"

[c] The messengers, who had been sent by the Pharisees, then; or Those who had been sent were Pharisees; they.

Fill these jars with water (2.7)

48 Nathanael asked him, "How do you know me?"

Jesus answered, "I saw you when you were under the fig-tree before Philip called you."

49 "Teacher," answered Nathanael, "you are the Son of God! You are the King of Israel!"

50 Jesus said, "Do you believe just because I told you I saw you when you were under the fig-tree? You will see much greater things than this!" 51 And he said to them, "I am telling you the truth: you will see heaven open and God's angels going up and coming down on the Son of Man."

The Wedding in Cana

2 Two days later there was a wedding in the town of Cana in Galilee. Jesus' mother was there, 2 and Jesus and his disciples had also been invited to the wedding. 3 When the wine had given out, Jesus' mother said to him, "They have no wine left."

4 "You must not tell me what to do," Jesus replied. "My time has not yet come."

5 Jesus' mother then told the servants, "Do whatever he tells you."

6 The Jews have rules about ritual washing, and for this purpose six stone water jars were there, each one large enough to hold about a hundred litres. 7 Jesus said to the servants, "Fill these jars with water." They filled them to the brim, 8 and then he told them, "Now draw some water out and take it to the man in charge of the feast." They took him the water, 9 which now had turned into wine, and he tasted it. He did not know where this wine had come from (but, of course, the servants who had drawn out the water knew); so he called the bridegroom 10 and said to him, "Everyone else serves the best wine first, and after the guests have had plenty to drink, he serves the ordinary wine. But you have kept the best wine until now!"

11 Jesus performed this first miracle in Cana in Galilee; there he revealed his glory, and his disciples believed in him.

12 After this, Jesus and his mother, brothers, and disciples went to Capernaum and stayed there a few days.

Jesus Goes to the Temple
(Matt. 21.12–13; Mark 11.15–17; Luke 19.45–46)

13 It was almost time for the Passover Festival, so Jesus went to Jerusalem. 14 There in the Temple he found men selling cattle, sheep, and pigeons, and also the money-changers sitting at their tables.

1.51: Gen 28.12   **2.12:** Mt 4.13   **2.13:** Ex 12.1–27

¹⁵ So he made a whip from cords and drove all the animals out of the Temple, both the sheep and the cattle; he overturned the tables of the money-changers and scattered their coins; ¹⁶ and he ordered the men who sold the pigeons, "Take them out of here! Stop making my Father's house a market-place!" ¹⁷ His disciples remembered that the scripture says, "My devotion to your house, O God, burns in me like a fire."

18 The Jewish authorities replied with a question, "What miracle can you perform to show us that you have the right to do this?"

19 Jesus answered, "Tear down this Temple, and in three days I will build it again."

20 "Are you going to build it again in three days?" they asked him. "It has taken forty-six years to build this Temple!"

21 But the temple Jesus was speaking about was his body. ²² So when he was raised from death, his disciples remembered that he had said this, and they believed the scripture and what Jesus had said.

Jesus' Knowledge of Human Nature

23 While Jesus was in Jerusalem during the Passover Festival, many believed in him as they saw the miracles he performed. ²⁴ But Jesus did not trust himself to them, because he knew them all. ²⁵ There was no need for anyone to tell him about them, because he himself knew what was in their hearts.

Jesus and Nicodemus

3 There was a Jewish leader named Nicodemus, who belonged to the party of the Pharisees. ² One night he went to Jesus and said to him, "Rabbi, we know that you are a teacher sent by God. No one could perform the miracles you are doing unless God were with him."

3 Jesus answered, "I am telling you the truth: no one can see the Kingdom of God unless he is born again." ᵈ

4 "How can a grown man be born again?" Nicodemus asked. "He certainly cannot enter his mother's womb and be born a second time!"

5 "I am telling you the truth," replied Jesus. "No one can enter the Kingdom of God unless he is born of water and the Spirit. ⁶ A person is born physically of human parents, but he is born spiritually of the Spirit. ⁷ Do not be surprised because I tell you that you must all be born again. ᵉ ⁸ The wind blows wherever it wishes; you hear the sound it makes, but you do not know where it comes from or where it is going. It is like that with everyone who is born of the Spirit."

9 "How can this be?" asked Nicodemus.

10 Jesus answered, "You are a great teacher in Israel, and you don't know this? ¹¹ I am telling you the truth: we speak of what we know and report what we have seen, yet none of you is willing to accept our message. ¹² You do not believe me when I tell you about the things of this world; how will you ever believe me, then, when I tell you about the things of heaven? ¹³ And no one has ever gone up to heaven except the Son of Man, who came down from heaven." ˣ

14 As Moses lifted up the bronze snake on a pole in the desert, in the same way the Son of Man must be lifted up, ¹⁵ so that everyone who believes in him may have eternal life. ¹⁶ For God loved the world so much that he gave his only Son, so that everyone who believes in him may not die but have eternal life. ¹⁷ For God did not send his Son into the world to be its judge, but to be its saviour.

18 Whoever believes in the Son is not judged; but whoever does not believe has already been judged, because he has not believed in God's only Son. ¹⁹ This is how the judgement works: the light has come into the world, but people love the darkness rather than the light, because their deeds are evil. ²⁰ Anyone who does evil things hates the light and will not come to the light, because he does not want his evil deeds to be shown up. ²¹ But whoever does what is true comes to the light in order that the light may show that what he did was in obedience to God.

Jesus and John

22 After this, Jesus and his disciples went to the province of Judaea, where he spent some time with them and baptized. ²³ John also was baptizing in Aenon, not far from Salim, because there was plenty of water in that place. People

---

ᵈ again; or from above.　ᵉ again; or from above.　ˣ The quotation may continue through verse 21.
2.17: Ps 69.9　**2.19:** Mt 26.61, 27.40; Mk 14.58, 15.29　**3.14:** Num 21.9

Give me a drink of water (4.7)

were going to him, and he was baptizing them. (²⁴This was before John had been put in prison.)

25 Some of John's disciples began arguing with a Jew*f* about the matter of ritual washing. ²⁶So they went to John and said, "Teacher, you remember the man who was with you on the east side of the Jordan, the one you spoke about? Well, he is baptizing now, and everyone is going to him!"

27 John answered, "No one can have anything unless God gives it to him. ²⁸You yourselves are my witnesses that I said, 'I am not the Messiah, but I have been sent ahead of him.' ²⁹The bridegroom is the one to whom the bride belongs; but the bridegroom's friend, who stands by and listens, is glad when he hears the bridegroom's voice. This is how my own happiness is made complete. ³⁰He must become more important while I become less important."

He Who Comes from Heaven

31 He who comes from above is greater than all. He who is from the earth belongs to the earth and speaks about earthly matters, but he who comes from heaven is above all. ³²He tells what he has seen and heard, yet no one accepts his message. ³³But whoever accepts his message confirms by this that God is truthful. ³⁴The one whom God has sent speaks God's words, because God gives him the fullness of his Spirit. ³⁵The Father loves his Son and has put everything in his power. ³⁶Whoever believes in the Son has eternal life; whoever disobeys the Son will not have life, but will remain under God's punishment.

Jesus and the Samaritan Woman

4 The Pharisees heard that Jesus was winning and baptizing more disciples than John. (²Actually, Jesus himself did not baptize anyone; only his disciples did.) ³So when Jesus heard what was being said, he left Judaea and went back to Galilee; ⁴on his way there he had to go through Samaria.

5 In Samaria he came to a town named Sychar, which was not far from the field that Jacob had given to his son Joseph. ⁶Jacob's well was there, and Jesus, tired out by the journey, sat down by the well. It was about noon.

7 A Samaritan woman came to draw some water, and Jesus said to her, "Give me a drink of water." (⁸His disciples had gone into town to buy food.)

9 The woman answered, "You are a Jew, and I am a Samaritan—so how can you ask me for a drink?" (Jews will not use the same cups and bowls that Samaritans use.)*g*

---

f a Jew; *some manuscripts have* some Jews.
g Jews will not use the same cups and bowls that Samaritans use; *or* Jews will have nothing to do with Samaritans.

3.24: Mt 14.3; Mk 6.17; Lk 3.19–20   **3.28:** Jn 1.20   **3.35:** Mt 11.27; Lk 10.22
4.5: Gen 33.19; Josh 24.32   **4.9:** Ezra 4.1–5; Neh 4.1–2

10 Jesus answered, "If only you knew what God gives and who it is that is asking you for a drink, you would ask him, and he would give you life-giving water."

11 "Sir," the woman said, "you haven't got a bucket, and the well is deep. Where would you get that life-giving water? 12 It was our ancestor Jacob who gave us this well; he and his sons and his flocks all drank from it. You don't claim to be greater than Jacob, do you?"

13 Jesus answered, "Whoever drinks this water will be thirsty again, 14 but whoever drinks the water that I will give him will never be thirsty again. The water that I will give him will become in him a spring which will provide him with life-giving water and give him eternal life."

15 "Sir," the woman said, "give me that water! Then I will never be thirsty again, nor will I have to come here to draw water."

16 "Go and call your husband," Jesus told her, "and come back."

17 "I haven't got a husband," she answered.

Jesus replied, "You are right when you say you haven't got a husband. 18 You have been married to five men, and the man you live with now is not really your husband. You have told me the truth."

19 "I see you are a prophet, sir," the woman said. 20 "My Samaritan ancestors worshipped God on this mountain, but you Jews say that Jerusalem is the place where we should worship God."

21 Jesus said to her, "Believe me, woman, the time will come when people will not worship the Father either on this mountain or in Jerusalem. 22 You Samaritans do not really know whom you worship; but we Jews know whom we worship, because it is from the Jews that salvation comes. 23 But the time is coming and is already here, when by the power of God's Spirit people will worship the Father as he really is, offering him the true worship that he wants. 24 God is Spirit, and only by the power of his Spirit can people worship him as he really is."

25 The woman said to him, "I know that the Messiah will come, and when he comes, he will tell us everything."

26 Jesus answered, "I am he, I who am talking with you."

27 At that moment Jesus' disciples returned, and they were greatly surprised to find him talking with a woman. But none of them said to her, "What do you want?" or asked him, "Why are you talking with her?"

28 Then the woman left her water jar, went back to the town, and said to the people there, 29 "Come and see the man who told me everything I have ever done. Could he be the Messiah?" 30 So they left the town and went to Jesus.

31 In the meantime the disciples were begging Jesus, "Teacher, have something to eat!"

32 But he answered, "I have food to eat that you know nothing about."

33 So the disciples started asking among themselves, "Could somebody have brought him food?"

34 "My food," Jesus said to them, "is to obey the will of the one who sent me and to finish the work he gave me to do. 35 You have a saying, 'Four more months and then the harvest.' But I tell you, take a good look at the fields; the crops are now ripe and ready to be harvested! 36 The man who reaps the harvest is being paid and gathers the crops for eternal life; so the man who sows and the man who reaps will be glad together. 37 The saying is true, 'One man sows, another man reaps.' 38 I have sent you to reap a harvest in a field where you did not work; others worked there, and you profit from their work."

39 Many of the Samaritans in that town believed in Jesus because the woman had said, "He told me everything I have ever done." 40 So when the Samaritans came to him, they begged him to stay with them, and Jesus stayed there two days.

41 Many more believed because of his message, 42 and they said to the woman, "We believe now, not because of what you said, but because we ourselves have heard him, and we know that he really is the Saviour of the world."

Jesus Heals an Official's Son

43 After spending two days there, Jesus left and went to Galilee. 44 For he himself had said, "A prophet is not respected in his own country." 45 When he arrived in Galilee, the people there welcomed him, because they had gone to the Passover Festival in Jerusalem and seen everything that he had done during the festival.

46 Then Jesus went back to Cana in Galilee, where he had turned the water into wine. A government official was there whose son was ill in Capernaum. 47 When

4.44: Mt 13.57; Mk 6.4; Lk 4.24   4.45: Jn 2.23   4.46: Jn 2.1–11 he heard that Jesus had come from Judaea to Galilee, he went to him and asked him to go to Capernaum and heal his son, who was about to die. ⁴⁸ Jesus said to him, "None of you will ever believe unless you see miracles and wonders."

⁴⁹ "Sir," replied the official, "come with me before my child dies."

⁵⁰ Jesus said to him, "Go, your son will live!"

The man believed Jesus' words and went. ⁵¹ On his way home his servants met him with the news, "Your boy is going to live!"

⁵² He asked them what time it was when his son got better, and they answered, "It was one o'clock yesterday afternoon when the fever left him." ⁵³ Then the father remembered that it was at that very hour when Jesus had told him, "Your son will live." So he and all his family believed.

⁵⁴ This was the second miracle that Jesus performed after coming from Judaea to Galilee.

The Healing at the Pool

5 After this, Jesus went to Jerusalem for a religious festival. ² Near the Sheep Gate in Jerusalem there is a pool ʰ with five porches; in Hebrew it is called Bethzatha.ⁱ ³ A large crowd of sick people were lying in the porches—the blind, the lame, and the paralysed.ʲ ⁵ A man was there who had been ill for thirty-eight years. ⁶ Jesus saw him lying there, and he knew that the man had been ill for such a long time; so he asked him, "Do you want to get well?"

⁷ The sick man answered, "Sir, I have no one here to put me in the pool when the water is stirred up; while I am trying to get in, somebody else gets there first."

⁸ Jesus said to him, "Get up, pick up your mat, and walk." ⁹ Immediately the man got well; he picked up his mat and started walking.

The day this happened was a Sabbath, ¹⁰ so the Jewish authorities told the man who had been healed, "This is a Sabbath, and it is against our Law for you to carry your mat."

¹¹ He answered, "The man who made me well told me to pick up my mat and walk."

¹² They asked him, "Who is the man who told you to do this?"

¹³ But the man who had been healed did not know who Jesus was, for there was a crowd in that place, and Jesus had slipped away.

¹⁴ Afterwards, Jesus found him in the Temple and said, "Listen, you are well now; so stop sinning or something worse may happen to you."

¹⁵ Then the man left and told the Jewish authorities that it was Jesus who had healed him. ¹⁶ So they began to persecute Jesus, because he had done this healing on a Sabbath. ¹⁷ Jesus answered them, "My Father is always working, and I too must work."

¹⁸ This saying made the Jewish authorities all the more determined to kill him; not only had he broken the Sabbath law, but he had said that God was his own Father and in this way had made himself equal with God.

The Authority of the Son

¹⁹ So Jesus answered them, "I am telling you the truth: the Son can do nothing on his own; he does only what he sees his Father doing. What the Father does, the Son also does. ²⁰ For the Father loves the Son and shows him all that he himself is doing. He will show him even greater things to do than this, and you will all be amazed. ²¹ Just as the Father raises the dead and gives them life, in the same way the Son gives life to those he wants to. ²² Nor does the Father himself judge anyone. He has given his Son the full right to judge, ²³ so that all will honour the Son in the same way as they honour the Father. Whoever does not honour the Son does not honour the Father who sent him.

²⁴ "I am telling you the truth: whoever hears my words and believes in him who sent me has eternal life. He will not be judged, but has already passed from death to life. ²⁵ I am telling you the truth: the time is coming—the time has already come—when the dead will hear the voice of the Son of God, and those who hear it will come to life. ²⁶ Just as the Father is himself the source of life, in the same way he has made his Son to be the source of life. ²⁷ And he has given the Son the

---

ʰ Near the Sheep Gate...a pool; *or* Near the Sheep Pool...a place.
ⁱ Bethzatha; *some manuscripts have* Bethesda.
ʲ *Some manuscripts add verses 3b-4:* They were waiting for the water to move, ⁴ because every now and then an angel of the Lord went down into the pool and stirred up the water. The first sick person to go into the pool after the water was stirred up was healed from whatever disease he had.
5.10: Neh 13.19; Jer 17.21

right to judge, because he is the Son of Man. ²⁸Do not be surprised at this; the time is coming when all the dead will hear his voice ²⁹and come out of their graves: those who have done good will rise and live, and those who have done evil will rise and be condemned.

Witnesses to Jesus

30 "I can do nothing on my own authority; I judge only as God tells me, so my judgement is right, because I am not trying to do what I want, but only what he who sent me wants.

31 "If I testify on my own behalf, what I say is not to be accepted as real proof. ³²But there is someone else who testifies on my behalf, and I know that what he says about me is true. ³³John is the one to whom you sent your messengers, and he spoke on behalf of the truth. ³⁴It is not that I must have a man's witness; I say this only in order that you may be saved. ³⁵John was like a lamp, burning and shining, and you were willing for a while to enjoy his light. ³⁶But I have a witness on my behalf which is even greater than the witness that John gave: what I do, that is, the deeds my Father gave me to do, these speak on my behalf and show that the Father has sent me. ³⁷And the Father, who sent me, also testifies on my behalf. You have never heard his voice or seen his face, ³⁸and you do not keep his message in your hearts, for you do not believe in the one whom he sent. ³⁹You study the Scriptures, because you think that in them you will find eternal life. And these very Scriptures speak about me! ⁴⁰Yet you are not willing to come to me in order to have life.

41 "I am not looking for human praise. ⁴²But I know what kind of people you are, and I know that you have no love for God in your hearts. ⁴³I have come with my Father's authority, but you have not received me; when, however, someone comes with his own authority, you will receive him. ⁴⁴You like to receive praise from one another, but you do not try to win praise from the one who alone is God; how, then, can you believe me? ⁴⁵Do not think, however, that I am the one who will accuse you to my Father. Moses, in whom you have put your hope, is the very one who will accuse you. ⁴⁶If you had really believed Moses, you would

have believed me, because he wrote about me. ⁴⁷But since you do not believe what he wrote, how can you believe what I say?"

Jesus Feeds Five Thousand Men
(Matt. 14.13–21; Mark 6.30–44; Luke 9.10–17)

6 After this, Jesus went across Lake Galilee (or, Lake Tiberias, as it is also called). ²A large crowd followed him, because they had seen his miracles of healing those who were ill. ³Jesus went up a hill and sat down with his disciples. ⁴The time for the Passover Festival was near. ⁵Jesus looked round and saw that a large crowd was coming to him, so he asked Philip, "Where can we buy enough food to feed all these people?" (⁶He said this to test Philip; actually he already knew what he would do.)

7 Philip answered, "For everyone to have even a little, it would take more than two hundred silver coins^k to buy enough bread."

8 Another of his disciples, Andrew, who was Simon Peter's brother, said, ⁹"There is a boy here who has five loaves of barley bread and two fish. But they will certainly not be enough for all these people."

10 "Make the people sit down," Jesus told them. (There was a lot of grass there.) So all the people sat down; there were about five thousand men. ¹¹Jesus took the bread, gave thanks to God, and distributed it to the people who were sitting there. He did the same with the fish, and they all had as much as they wanted. ¹²When they were all full, he said to his disciples, "Gather the pieces left over; let us not waste any." ¹³So they gathered them all up and filled twelve baskets with the pieces left over from the five barley loaves which the people had eaten.

14 Seeing this miracle that Jesus had performed, the people there said, "Surely this is the Prophet^l who was to come into the world!" ¹⁵Jesus knew that they were about to come and seize him in order to make him king by force; so he went off again to the hills by himself.

Jesus Walks on the Water
(Matt. 14.22–33; Mark 6.45–52)

16 When evening came, Jesus' disciples went down to the lake, ¹⁷got into a boat, and went back across the lake towards Capernaum. Night came on, and Jesus still

---

^kSILVER COINS: *A silver coin was the daily wage of a rural worker (see Mt 20.2).*
^lTHE PROPHET: *See 1.21.*
5.29: Dan 12.2   **5.33:** Jn 1.19–27, 3.27–30   **5.37:** Mt 3.17; Mk 1.11; Lk 3.22

had not come to them. 18 By then a strong wind was blowing and stirring up the water. 19 The disciples had rowed about five or six kilometres when they saw Jesus walking on the water, coming near the boat, and they were terrified. 20 "Don't be afraid," Jesus told them, "it is I!" 21 Then they willingly took him into the boat, and immediately the boat reached land at the place they were heading for.

The People Seek Jesus

22 Next day the crowd which had stayed on the other side of the lake realized that there had been only one boat there. They knew that Jesus had not gone in it with his disciples, but that they had left without him. 23 Other boats, which were from Tiberias, came to shore near the place where the crowd had eaten the bread after the Lord had given thanks. 24 When the crowd saw that Jesus was not there, nor his disciples, they got into those boats and went to Capernaum, looking for him.

Jesus the Bread of Life

25 When the people found Jesus on the other side of the lake, they said to him, "Teacher, when did you get here?"

26 Jesus answered, "I am telling you the truth: you are looking for me because you ate the bread and had all you wanted, not because you understood my miracles. 27 Do not work for food that goes bad; instead, work for the food that lasts for eternal life. This is the food which the Son of Man will give you, because God, the Father, has put his mark of approval on him."

28 So they asked him, "What can we do in order to do what God wants us to do?"

29 Jesus answered, "What God wants you to do is to believe in the one he sent."

30 They replied, "What miracle will you perform so that we may see it and believe you? What will you do? 31 Our ancestors ate manna in the desert, just as the scripture says, 'He gave them bread from heaven to eat.' "

32 "I am telling you the truth," Jesus said. "What Moses gave you was not m the bread from heaven; it is my Father who gives you the real bread from heaven. 33 For the bread that God gives is he who comes down from heaven and gives life to the world."

34 "Sir," they asked him, "give us this bread always."

35 "I am the bread of life," Jesus told them. "He who comes to me will never be hungry; he who believes in me will never be thirsty. 36 Now, I told you that you have seen me but will not believe. 37 Everyone whom my Father gives me will come to me. I will never turn away anyone who comes to me, 38 because I have come down from heaven to do not my own will but the will of him who sent me. 39 And it is the will of him who sent me that I should not lose any of all those he has given me, but that I should raise them all to life on the last day. 40 For what my Father wants is that all who see the Son and believe in him should have eternal life. And I will raise them to life on the last day."

41 The people started grumbling about him, because he said, "I am the bread that came down from heaven." 42 So they said, "This man is Jesus son of Joseph, isn't he? We know his father and mother. How, then, does he now say he came down from heaven?"

43 Jesus answered, "Stop grumbling among yourselves. 44 No one can come to me unless the Father who sent me draws him to me; and I will raise him to life on the last day. 45 The prophets wrote, 'Everyone will be taught by God.' Anyone who hears the Father and learns from him comes to me. 46 This does not mean that anyone has seen the Father; he who is from God is the only one who has seen the Father. 47 I am telling you the truth: he who believes has eternal life. 48 I am the bread of life. 49 Your ancestors ate manna in the desert, but they died. 50 But the bread that comes down from heaven is of such a kind that whoever eats it will not die. 51 I am the living bread that came down from heaven. If anyone eats this bread, he will live for ever. The bread that I will give him is my flesh, which I give so that the world may live."

52 This started an angry argument among them. "How can this man give us his flesh to eat?" they asked.

53 Jesus said to them, "I am telling you the truth: if you do not eat the flesh of the Son of Man and drink his blood, you will not have life in yourselves. 54 Whoever eats my flesh and drinks my blood has eternal life, and I will raise him to life on the last day. 55 For my flesh is the

m What Moses gave you was not; or It was not Moses who gave you.
6.31: Ex 16.4,15; Ps 78.24   **6.45:** Is 54.13

real food; my blood is the real drink. [56] Whoever eats my flesh and drinks my blood lives in me, and I live in him. [57] The living Father sent me, and because of him I live also. In the same way whoever eats me will live because of me. [58] This, then, is the bread that came down from heaven; it is not like the bread that your ancestors ate, but then later died. The one who eats this bread will live for ever."

59 Jesus said this as he taught in the synagogue in Capernaum.

The Words of Eternal Life

60 Many of his followers heard this and said, "This teaching is too hard. Who can listen to it?"

61 Without being told, Jesus knew that they were grumbling about this, so he said to them, "Does this make you want to give up? [62] Suppose, then, that you should see the Son of Man go back up to the place where he was before? [63] What gives life is God's Spirit; man's power is of no use at all. The words I have spoken to you bring God's life-giving Spirit. [64] Yet some of you do not believe." (Jesus knew from the very beginning who were the ones that would not believe and which one would betray him.) [65] And he added, "This is the very reason I told you that no one can come to me unless the Father makes it possible for him to do so."

66 Because of this, many of Jesus' followers turned back and would not go with him any more. [67] So he asked the twelve disciples, "And you—would you also like to leave?"

68 Simon Peter answered him, "Lord, to whom would we go? You have the words that give eternal life. [69] And now we believe and know that you are the Holy One who has come from God."

70 Jesus replied, "I chose the twelve of you, didn't I? Yet one of you is a devil!" [71] He was talking about Judas, the son of Simon Iscariot. For Judas, even though he was one of the twelve disciples, was going to betray him.

Jesus and His Brothers

7 After this, Jesus travelled in Galilee; he did not want to travel in Judaea, because the Jewish authorities there were wanting to kill him. [2] The time for the Festival of Shelters was near, [3] so Jesus' brothers said to him, "Leave this place

and go to Judaea, so that your followers will see the things that you are doing. [4] No one hides what he is doing if he wants to be well known. Since you are doing these things, let the whole world know about you!" ([5] Not even his brothers believed in him.)

6 Jesus said to them, "The right time for me has not yet come. Any time is right for you. [7] The world cannot hate you, but it hates me, because I keep telling it that its ways are bad. [8] You go on to the festival. I am not going[n] to this festival, because the right time has not come for me." [9] He said this, and then stayed on in Galilee.

Jesus at the Festival of Shelters

10 After his brothers had gone to the festival, Jesus also went; however, he did not go openly, but secretly. [11] The Jewish authorities were looking for him at the festival. "Where is he?" they asked.

12 There was much whispering about him in the crowd. "He is a good man," some people said. "No," others said, "he is misleading the people." [13] But no one talked about him openly, because they were afraid of the Jewish authorities.

14 The festival was nearly half over when Jesus went to the Temple and began teaching. [15] The Jewish authorities were greatly surprised and said, "How does this man know so much when he has never had any training?"

16 Jesus answered, "What I teach is not my own teaching, but it comes from God, who sent me. [17] Whoever is willing to do what God wants will know whether what I teach comes from God or whether I speak on my own authority. [18] A person who speaks on his own authority is trying to gain glory for himself. But he who wants glory for the one who sent him is honest, and there is nothing false in him. [19] Moses gave you the Law, didn't he? But not one of you obeys the Law. Why are you trying to kill me?"

20 "You have a demon in you!" the crowd answered. "Who is trying to kill you?"

21 Jesus answered, "I performed one miracle, and you were all surprised. [22] Moses ordered you to circumcise your sons (although it was not Moses but your ancestors who started it), and so you circumcise a boy on the Sabbath. [23] If a

[n] I am not going; *some manuscripts have* I am not yet going.
6.68–69: Mt 16.16; Mk 8.29; Lk 9.20   **7.2:** Lev 23.34; Deut 16.13   **7.22:** Gen 17.10; Lev 12.3
7.23: Jn 5.9

boy is circumcised on the Sabbath so that Moses' Law is not broken, why are you angry with me because I made a man completely well on the Sabbath? 24 Stop judging by external standards, and judge by true standards."

Is He the Messiah?

25 Some of the people of Jerusalem said, "Isn't this the man the authorities are trying to kill? 26 Look! He is talking in public, and they say nothing against him! Can it be that they really know that he is the Messiah? 27 But when the Messiah comes, no one will know where he is from. And we all know where this man comes from."

28 As Jesus taught in the Temple, he said in a loud voice, "Do you really know me and know where I am from? I have not come on my own authority. He who sent me, however, is truthful. You do not know him, 29 but I know him, because I come from him and he sent me."

30 Then they tried to seize him, but no one laid a hand on him, because his hour had not yet come. 31 But many in the crowd believed in him and said, "When the Messiah comes, will he perform more miracles than this man has?"

Guards Are Sent to Arrest Jesus

32 The Pharisees heard the crowd whispering these things about Jesus, so they and the chief priests sent some guards to arrest him. 33 Jesus said, "I shall be with you a little while longer, and then I shall go away to him who sent me. 34 You will look for me, but you will not find me, because you cannot go where I will be."

35 The Jewish authorities said among themselves, "Where is he about to go so that we shall not find him? Will he go to the Greek cities where our people live, and teach the Greeks? 36 He says that we will look for him but will not find him, and that we cannot go where he will be. What does he mean?"

Streams of Life-Giving Water

37 On the last and most important day of the festival Jesus stood up and said in a loud voice, "Whoever is thirsty should come to me and drink. 38 As the scripture says, 'Whoever believes in me, streams of

life-giving water will pour out from his heart.'"o 39 Jesus said this about the Spirit, which those who believed in him were going to receive. At that time the Spirit had not yet been given, because Jesus had not been raised to glory.

Division among the People

40 Some of the people in the crowd heard him say this and said, "This man is really the Prophet!"p

41 Others said, "He is the Messiah!"

But others said, "The Messiah will not come from Galilee! 42 The scripture says that the Messiah will be a descendant of King David and will be born in Bethlehem, the town where David lived." 43 So there was a division in the crowd because of Jesus. 44 Some wanted to seize him, but no one laid a hand on him.

The Unbelief of the Jewish Authorities

45 When the guards went back, the chief priests and Pharisees asked them, "Why did you not bring him?"

46 The guards answered, "Nobody has ever talked like this man!"

47 "Did he fool you, too?" the Pharisees asked them. 48 "Have you ever known one of the authorities or one Pharisee to believe in him? 49 This crowd does not know the Law of Moses, so they are under God's curse!"

50 One of the Pharisees there was Nicodemus, the man who had gone to see Jesus before. He said to the others, 51 "According to our Law we cannot condemn a man before hearing him and finding out what he has done."

52 "Well," they answered, "are you also from Galilee? Study the Scriptures and you will learn that no prophet ever comes q from Galilee."

The Woman Caught in Adultery

8 [Then everyone went home, but Jesus went to the Mount of Olives. 2 Early the next morning he went back to the Temple. All the people gathered round him, and he sat down and began to teach them. 3 The teachers of the Law and the Pharisees brought in a woman who had been caught committing adultery, and they made her stand before them all. 4 "Teacher," they said to Jesus, "this

---

oJesus' words in verses 37–38 may be translated: "Whoever is thirsty should come to me, and whoever believes in me should drink. 38As the scripture says, 'Streams of life-giving water will pour out from his heart.'"   pTHE PROPHET: See 1.21.
qno prophet ever comes; one manuscript has the Prophet will not come.
7.37: Lev 23.36   **7.38:** Ezek 47.1; Zech 14.8   **7.42:** 2 Sam 7.12; Mic 5.2   **7.50:** Jn 3.1–2

woman was caught in the very act of committing adultery. [5] In our Law Moses commanded that such a woman must be stoned to death. Now, what do you say?" [6] They said this to trap Jesus, so that they could accuse him. But he bent over and wrote on the ground with his finger.

7 As they stood there asking him questions, he straightened himself up and said to them, "Whichever one of you has committed no sin may throw the first stone at her." [8] Then he bent over again and wrote on the ground. [9] When they heard this, they all left, one by one, the older ones first. Jesus was left alone, with the woman still standing there. [10] He straightened himself up and said to her, "Where are they? Is there no one left to condemn you?"

11 "No one, sir," she answered.

"Well, then," Jesus said, "I do not condemn you either. Go, but do not sin again."] [r]

Jesus the Light of the World

12 Jesus spoke to the Pharisees again. "I am the light of the world," he said. "Whoever follows me will have the light of life and will never walk in darkness."

13 The Pharisees said to him, "Now you are testifying on your own behalf; what you say proves nothing."

14 "No," Jesus answered, "even though I do testify on my own behalf, what I say is true, because I know where I came from and where I am going. You do not know where I came from or where I am going. [15] You make judgements in a purely human way; I pass judgement on no one. [16] But if I were to do so, my judgement would be true, because I am not alone in this; the Father who sent me is with me. [17] It is written in your Law that when two witnesses agree, what they say is true. [18] I testify on my own behalf, and the Father who sent me also testifies on my behalf."

19 "Where is your father?" they asked him.

"You know neither me nor my Father," Jesus answered. "If you knew me, you would know my Father also."

20 Jesus said all this as he taught in the Temple, in the room where the offering boxes were placed. And no one arrested him, because his hour had not come.

You Cannot Go Where I Am Going

21 Again Jesus said to them, "I will go away; you will look for me, but you will die in your sins. You cannot go where I am going."

22 So the Jewish authorities said, "He says that we cannot go where he is going. Does this mean that he will kill himself?"

23 Jesus answered, "You belong to this world here below, but I come from above. You are from this world, but I am not from this world. [24] That is why I told you that you will die in your sins. And you will die in your sins if you do not believe that 'I Am Who I Am'."

25 "Who are you?" they asked him.

Jesus answered, "What I have told you from the very beginning. [s] [26] I have much to say about you, much to condemn you for. The one who sent me, however, is truthful, and I tell the world only what I have heard from him."

27 They did not understand that Jesus was talking to them about the Father. [28] So he said to them, "When you lift up the Son of Man, you will know that 'I Am Who I Am'; then you will know that I do nothing on my own authority, but I say only what the Father has instructed me to say. [29] And he who sent me is with me; he has not left me alone, because I always do what pleases him."

30 Many who heard Jesus say these things believed in him.

Free Men and Slaves

31 So Jesus said to those who believed in him, "If you obey my teaching, you are really my disciples; [32] you will know the truth, and the truth will set you free."

33 "We are the descendants of Abraham," they answered, "and we have never been anybody's slaves. What do you mean, then, by saying, 'You will be free'?"

34 Jesus said to them, "I am telling you the truth: everyone who sins is a slave of sin. [35] A slave does not belong to a family permanently, but a son belongs there for ever. [36] If the Son sets you free, then you will be really free. [37] I know you are Abraham's descendants. Yet you are trying to kill me, because you will not

[r] Many manuscripts and early translations do not have this passage (8.1–11); others have it after Jn 21.24; others have it after Lk 21.38; one manuscript has it after Jn 7.36.
[s] What I have told you from the very beginning; or Why should I speak to you at all?
8.5: Lev 20.10; Deut 22.22–24   **8.12:** Mt 5.14; Jn 9.5   **8.13:** Jn 5.31   **8.17:** Deut 19.15
8.33: Mt 3.9; Lk 3.8

accept my teaching. ³⁸ I talk about what my Father has shown me, but you do what your father has told you."

39 They answered him, "Our father is Abraham."

"If you really were Abraham's children," Jesus replied, "you would do ᵗ the same things that he did. ⁴⁰ All I have ever done is to tell you the truth I heard from God, yet you are trying to kill me. Abraham did nothing like this! ⁴¹ You are doing what your father did."

"God himself is the only Father we have," they answered, "and we are his true sons."

42 Jesus said to them, "If God really were your Father, you would love me, because I came from God and now I am here. I did not come on my own authority, but he sent me. ⁴³ Why do you not understand what I say? It is because you cannot bear to listen to my message. ⁴⁴ You are the children of your father, the Devil, and you want to follow your father's desires. From the very beginning he was a murderer and has never been on the side of truth, because there is no truth in him. When he tells a lie, he is only doing what is natural to him, because he is a liar and the father of all lies. ⁴⁵ But I tell the truth, and that is why you do not believe me. ⁴⁶ Which one of you can prove that I am guilty of sin? If I tell the truth, then why do you not believe me? ⁴⁷ He who comes from God listens to God's words. You, however, are not from God, and that is why you will not listen."

Jesus and Abraham

48 They asked Jesus, "Were we not right in saying that you are a Samaritan and have a demon in you?"

49 "I have no demon," Jesus answered. "I honour my Father, but you dishonour me. ⁵⁰ I am not seeking honour for myself. But there is one who is seeking it and who judges in my favour. ⁵¹ I am telling you the truth: whoever obeys my teaching will never die."

52 They said to him, "Now we are certain that you have a demon! Abraham died, and the prophets died, yet you say that whoever obeys your teaching will never die. ⁵³ Our father Abraham died; you do not claim to be greater than Abraham,

do you? And the prophets also died. Who do you think you are?"

54 Jesus answered, "If I were to honour myself, that honour would be worth nothing. The one who honours me is my Father—the very one you say is your God. ⁵⁵ You have never known him, but I know him. If I were to say that I do not know him, I would be a liar like you. But I do know him, and I obey his word. ⁵⁶ Your father Abraham rejoiced that he was to see the time of my coming; he saw it and was glad."

57 They said to him, "You are not even fifty years old—and you have seen Abraham?" ᵘ

58 "I am telling you the truth," Jesus replied. "Before Abraham was born, 'I Am'."

59 Then they picked up stones to throw at him, but Jesus hid himself and left the Temple.

Jesus Heals a Man Born Blind

9 As Jesus was walking along, he saw a man who had been born blind. ² His disciples asked him, "Teacher, whose sin caused him to be born blind? Was it his own or his parents' sin?"

3 Jesus answered, "His blindness has nothing to do with his sins or his parents' sins. He is blind so that God's power might be seen at work in him. ⁴ As long as it is day, we must keep on doing the work of him who sent me; night is coming when no one can work. ⁵ While I am in the world, I am the light for the world."

6 After he said this, Jesus spat on the ground and made some mud with the spittle; he rubbed the mud on the man's eyes ⁷ and said, "Go and wash your face in the Pool of Siloam." (This name means "Sent.") So the man went, washed his face, and came back seeing.

8 His neighbours, then, and the people who had seen him begging before this, asked, "Isn't this the man who used to sit and beg?"

9 Some said, "He is the one," but others said, "No he isn't; he just looks like him."

So the man himself said, "I am the man."

10 "How is it that you can now see?" they asked him.

11 He answered, "The man called Jesus made some mud, rubbed it on my eyes, and told me to go to Siloam and wash

---

ᵗ If you really were...you would do; *some manuscripts have* If you are...do.
ᵘ you have seen Abraham?; *some manuscripts have* has Abraham seen you?
9.5: Mt 5.14; Jn 8.12

my face. So I went, and as soon as I washed, I could see."

12 "Where is he?" they asked.

"I don't know," he answered.

The Pharisees Investigate the Healing

13 Then they took to the Pharisees the man who had been blind. 14 The day that Jesus made the mud and cured him of his blindness was a Sabbath. 15 The Pharisees, then, asked the man again how he had received his sight. He told them, "He put some mud on my eyes; I washed my face, and now I can see."

16 Some of the Pharisees said, "The man who did this cannot be from God, for he does not obey the Sabbath law."

Others, however, said, "How could a man who is a sinner perform such miracles as these?" And there was a division among them.

17 So the Pharisees asked the man once more, "You say he cured you of your blindness—well, what do you say about him?"

"He is a prophet," the man answered.

18 The Jewish authorities, however, were not willing to believe that he had been blind and could now see, until they called his parents 19 and asked them, "Is this your son? You say that he was born blind; how is it, then, that he can now see?"

20 His parents answered, "We know that he is our son, and we know that he was born blind. 21 But we do not know how it is that he is now able to see, nor do we know who cured him of his blindness. Ask him; he is old enough, and he can answer for himself!" 22 His parents said this because they were afraid of the Jewish authorities, who had already agreed that anyone who said he believed that Jesus was the Messiah would be expelled from the synagogue. 23 That is why his parents said, "He is old enough; ask him!"

24 A second time they called back the man who had been born blind, and said to him, "Promise before God that you will tell the truth! We know that this man who cured you is a sinner."

25 "I do not know if he is a sinner or not," the man replied. "One thing I do know: I was blind, and now I see."

26 "What did he do to you?" they asked. "How did he cure you of your blindness?"

27 "I have already told you," he answered, "and you would not listen. Why do you want to hear it again? Maybe you, too, would like to be his disciples?"

28 They cursed him and said, "You are that fellow's disciple; but we are Moses' disciples. 29 We know that God spoke to Moses; as for that fellow, however, we do not even know where he comes from!"

30 The man answered, "What a strange thing that is! You do not know where he comes from, but he cured me of my blindness! 31 We know that God does not listen to sinners; he does listen to people who respect him and do what he wants them to do. 32 Since the beginning of the world nobody has ever heard of anyone giving sight to a person born blind. 33 Unless this man came from God, he would not be able to do a thing."

34 They answered, "You were born and brought up in sin—and you are trying to teach us?" And they expelled him from the synagogue.

Spiritual Blindness

35 When Jesus heard what had happened, he found the man and asked him, "Do you believe in the Son of Man?"

36 The man answered, "Tell me who he is, sir, so that I can believe in him!"

37 Jesus said to him, "You have already seen him, and he is the one who is talking with you now."

38 "I believe, Lord!" the man said, and knelt down before Jesus.

39 Jesus said, "I came to this world to judge, so that the blind should see and those who see should become blind."

40 Some Pharisees who were there with him heard him say this and asked him, "Surely you don't mean that we are blind, too?"

41 Jesus answered, "If you were blind, then you would not be guilty; but since you claim that you can see, this means that you are still guilty."

The Parable of the Shepherd

10 Jesus said, "I am telling you the truth: the man who does not enter the sheepfold by the gate, but climbs in some other way, is a thief and a robber. 2 The man who goes in through the gate is the shepherd of the sheep. 3 The gatekeeper opens the gate for him; the sheep hear his voice as he calls his own sheep by name, and he leads them out. 4 When he has brought them out, he goes ahead of them, and the sheep follow him, because they know his voice. 5 They will not follow someone else; instead, they will run away from such a person, because they do not know his voice."

6 Jesus told them this parable, but they did not understand what he meant.

Jesus the Good Shepherd

7 So Jesus said again, "I am telling you the truth: I am the gate for the sheep. 8 All others who came before me are thieves and robbers, but the sheep did not listen to them. 9 I am the gate. Whoever comes in by me will be saved; he will come in and go out and find pasture. 10 The thief comes only in order to steal, kill, and destroy. I have come in order that you might have life—life in all its fullness.

11 "I am the good shepherd, who is willing to die for the sheep. 12 When the hired man, who is not a shepherd and does not own the sheep, sees a wolf coming, he leaves the sheep and runs away; so the wolf snatches the sheep and scatters them. 13 The hired man runs away because he is only a hired man and does not care about the sheep. 14-15 I am the good shepherd. As the Father knows me and I know the Father, in the same way I know my sheep and they know me. And I am willing to die for them. 16 There are other sheep which belong to me that are not in this sheepfold. I must bring them, too; they will listen to my voice, and they will become v one flock with one shepherd.

17 "The Father loves me because I am willing to give up my life, in order that I may receive it back again. 18 No one takes my life away from me. I give it up of my own free will. I have the right to give it up, and I have the right to take it back. This is what my Father has commanded me to do."

19 Again there was a division among the people because of these words. 20 Many of them were saying, "He has a demon! He is mad! Why do you listen to him?"

21 But others were saying, "A man with a demon could not talk like this! How could a demon give sight to blind people?"

Jesus Is Rejected

22 It was winter, and the Festival of the Dedication of the Temple was being celebrated in Jerusalem. 23 Jesus was walking in Solomon's Porch in the Temple, 24 when the people gathered round him and asked, "How long are you going to keep us in suspense? Tell us the plain truth: are you the Messiah?"

25 Jesus answered, "I have already told you, but you would not believe me. The things I do by my Father's authority speak on my behalf; 26 but you will not believe, for you are not my sheep. 27 My sheep listen to my voice; I know them, and they follow me. 28 I give them eternal life, and they shall never die. No one can snatch them away from me. 29 What my Father has given me is greater w than everything, and no one can snatch them away from the Father's care. 30 The Father and I are one."

31 Then the people again picked up stones to throw at him. 32 Jesus said to them, "I have done many good deeds in your presence which the Father gave me to do; for which one of these do you want to stone me?"

33 They replied, "We do not want to stone you because of any good deeds, but because of your blasphemy! You are only a man, but you are trying to make yourself God!"

34 Jesus answered, "It is written in your own Law that God said, 'You are gods.' 35 We know that what the scripture says is true for ever; and God called those people gods, the people to whom his message was given. 36 As for me, the Father chose me and sent me into the world. How, then, can you say that I blaspheme because I said that I am the Son of God? 37 Do not believe me, then, if I am not doing the things my Father wants me to do. 38 But if I do them, even though you do not believe me, you should at least believe my deeds, in order that you may know once and for all that the Father is in me and that I am in the Father."

39 Once more they tried to seize Jesus, but he slipped out of their hands.

40 Jesus then went back again across the River Jordan to the place where John had been baptizing, and he stayed there. 41 Many people came to him. "John performed no miracles," they said, "but everything he said about this man was

---

v they will become; *some manuscripts have* there will be.
w What my Father has given me is greater; *some manuscripts have* My Father, who gave them to me, is greater.
10.15: Mt 11.27; Lk 10.22　**10.33:** Lev 24.16　**10.34:** Ps 82.6　**10.40:** Jn 1.28

true." [42] And many people there believed in him.

The Death of Lazarus

11 A man named Lazarus, who lived in Bethany, was ill. Bethany was the town where Mary and her sister Martha lived. ([2] This Mary was the one who poured the perfume on the Lord's feet and wiped them with her hair; it was her brother Lazarus who was ill.) [3] The sisters sent Jesus a message: "Lord, your dear friend is ill."

[4] When Jesus heard it, he said, "The final result of this illness will not be the death of Lazarus; this has happened in order to bring glory to God, and it will be the means by which the Son of God will receive glory."

[5] Jesus loved Martha and her sister and Lazarus. [6] Yet when he received the news that Lazarus was ill, he stayed where he was for two more days. [7] Then he said to the disciples, "Let us go back to Judaea."

[8] "Teacher," the disciples answered, "just a short time ago the people there wanted to stone you; and are you planning to go back?"

[9] Jesus said, "A day has twelve hours, hasn't it? So whoever walks in broad daylight does not stumble, for he sees the light of this world. [10] But if he walks during the night he stumbles, because he has no light." [11] Jesus said this and then added, "Our friend Lazarus has fallen asleep, but I will go and wake him up."

[12] The disciples answered, "If he is asleep, Lord, he will get well."

[13] Jesus meant that Lazarus had died, but they thought he meant natural sleep. [14] So Jesus told them plainly, "Lazarus is dead, [15] but for your sake I am glad that I was not with him, so that you will believe. Let us go to him."

[16] Thomas (called the Twin) said to his fellow-disciples, "Let us all go with the Teacher, so that we may die with him!"

Jesus the Resurrection and the Life

[17] When Jesus arrived, he found that Lazarus had been buried four days before. [18] Bethany was less than three kilometres from Jerusalem, [19] and many Judaeans had come to see Martha and Mary to comfort them over their brother's death.

[20] When Martha heard that Jesus was coming, she went out to meet him, but Mary stayed in the house. [21] Martha said to Jesus, "If you had been here, Lord, my brother would not have died! [22] But I know that even now God will give you whatever you ask him for."

[23] "Your brother will rise to life," Jesus told her.

[24] "I know," she replied, "that he will rise to life on the last day."

[25] Jesus said to her, "I am the resurrection and the life. Whoever believes in me will live, even though he dies; [26] and whoever lives and believes in me will never die. Do you believe this?"

[27] "Yes, Lord!" she answered. "I do believe that you are the Messiah, the Son of God, who was to come into the world."

Jesus Weeps

[28] After Martha said this, she went back and called her sister Mary privately. "The Teacher is here," she told her, "and is asking for you." [29] When Mary heard this, she got up and hurried out to meet him. ([30] Jesus had not yet arrived in the village, but was still in the place where Martha had met him.) [31] The people who were in the house with Mary, comforting her, followed her when they saw her get up and hurry out. They thought that she was going to the grave to weep there.

[32] Mary arrived where Jesus was, and as soon as she saw him, she fell at his feet. "Lord," she said, "if you had been here, my brother would not have died!"

[33] Jesus saw her weeping, and he saw how the people who were with her were weeping also; his heart was touched, and he was deeply moved. [34] "Where have you buried him?" he asked them.

"Come and see, Lord," they answered.

[35] Jesus wept. [36] "See how much he loved him!" the people said.

[37] But some of them said, "He gave sight to the blind man, didn't he? Could he not have kept Lazarus from dying?"

Lazarus Is Brought to Life

[38] Deeply moved once more, Jesus went to the tomb, which was a cave with a stone placed at the entrance. [39] "Take the stone away!" Jesus ordered.

Martha, the dead man's sister, answered, "There will be a bad smell, Lord. He has been buried four days!"

[40] Jesus said to her, "Didn't I tell you that you would see God's glory if you believed?" [41] They took the stone away. Jesus looked up and said, "I thank you, Father, that you listen to me. [42] I know

11.1: Lk 10.38-39   **11.2:** Jn 12.3

Lazarus, come out! (11.43)

that you always listen to me, but I say this for the sake of the people here, so that they will believe that you sent me." 43 After he had said this, he called out in a loud voice, "Lazarus, come out!" 44 He came out, his hands and feet wrapped in grave clothes, and with a cloth round his face. "Untie him," Jesus told them, "and let him go."

The Plot against Jesus
(Matt. 26.1–5; Mark 14.1–2; Luke 22.1–2)

45 Many of the people who had come to visit Mary saw what Jesus did, and they believed in him. 46 But some of them returned to the Pharisees and told them what Jesus had done. 47 So the Pharisees and the chief priests met with the Council and said, "What shall we do? Look at all the miracles this man is performing! 48 If we let him go on in this way, everyone will believe in him, and the Roman authorities will take action and destroy our Temple and our nation!"

49 One of them, named Caiaphas, who was High Priest that year, said, "What fools you are! 50 Don't you realize that it is better for you to let one man die for the people, instead of having the whole nation destroyed?" 51 Actually, he did not say this of his own accord; rather, as he was High Priest that year, he was prophesying that Jesus was going to die

for the Jewish people, 52 and not only for them, but also to bring together into one body all the scattered people of God. 53 From that day on the Jewish authorities made plans to kill Jesus. 54 So Jesus did not travel openly in Judaea, but left and went to a place near the desert, to a town named Ephraim, where he stayed with the disciples.

55 The time for the Passover Festival was near, and many people went up from the country to Jerusalem to perform the ritual of purification before the festival. 56 They were looking for Jesus, and as they gathered in the Temple, they asked one another, "What do you think? Surely he will not come to the festival, will he?" 57 The chief priests and the Pharisees had given orders that if anyone knew where Jesus was, he must report it, so that they could arrest him.

Jesus Is Anointed at Bethany
(Matt. 26.6–13; Mark 14.3–9)

12 Six days before the Passover, Jesus went to Bethany, the home of Lazarus, the man he had raised from death. 2 They prepared a dinner for him there, which Martha helped to serve; Lazarus was one of those who were sitting at the table with Jesus. 3 Then Mary took half a litre of a very expensive perfume made of pure nard, poured it on Jesus'

12.3: Lk 7.37–38

feet, and wiped them with her hair. The sweet smell of the perfume filled the whole house. ⁴One of Jesus' disciples, Judas Iscariot—the one who was going to betray him—said, ⁵"Why wasn't this perfume sold for three hundred silver coins ˣ and the money given to the poor?" ⁶He said this, not because he cared about the poor, but because he was a thief. He carried the money bag and would help himself from it.

7 But Jesus said, "Leave her alone! Let her keep what she has for the day of my burial. ⁸You will always have poor people with you, but you will not always have me."

The Plot against Lazarus

9 A large number of people heard that Jesus was in Bethany, so they went there, not only because of Jesus but also to see Lazarus, whom Jesus had raised from death. ¹⁰So the chief priests made plans to kill Lazarus too, ¹¹because on his account many Jews were rejecting them and believing in Jesus.

The Triumphant Entry into Jerusalem
(Matt. 21.1-11; Mark 11.1-11; Luke 19.28-40)

12 The next day the large crowd that had come to the Passover Festival heard that Jesus was coming to Jerusalem. ¹³So they took branches of palm-trees and went out to meet him, shouting, "Praise God! God bless him who comes in the name of the Lord! God bless the King of Israel!"

14 Jesus found a donkey and rode on it, just as the scripture says,
¹⁵ "Do not be afraid, city of Zion!
    Here comes your king,
       riding on a young donkey."

16 His disciples did not understand this at the time; but when Jesus had been raised to glory, they remembered that the scripture said this about him and that they had done this for him.

17 The people who had been with Jesus when he called Lazarus out of the grave and raised him from death had reported what had happened. ¹⁸That was why the crowd met him—because they heard that he had performed this miracle. ¹⁹The Pharisees then said to one another, "You see, we are not succeeding at all! Look, the whole world is following him!"

Some Greeks Seek Jesus

20 Some Greeks were among those who had gone to Jerusalem to worship during the festival. ²¹They went to Philip (he was from Bethsaida in Galilee) and said, "Sir, we want to see Jesus."

22 Philip went and told Andrew, and the two of them went and told Jesus. ²³Jesus answered them, "The hour has now come for the Son of Man to receive great glory. ²⁴I am telling you the truth: a grain of wheat remains no more than a single grain unless it is dropped into the ground and dies. If it does die, then it produces many grains. ²⁵Whoever loves his own life will lose it; whoever hates his own life in this world will keep it for life eternal. ²⁶Whoever wants to serve me must follow me, so that my servant will be with me where I am. And my Father will honour anyone who serves me.

Jesus Speaks about His Death

27 "Now my heart is troubled—and what shall I say? Shall I say, 'Father, do not let this hour come upon me'? But that is why I came—so that I might go through this hour of suffering. ²⁸Father, bring glory to your name!"

Then a voice spoke from heaven, "I have brought glory to it, and I will do so again."

29 The crowd standing there heard the voice, and some of them said it was thunder, while others said, "An angel spoke to him!"

30 But Jesus said to them, "It was not for my sake that this voice spoke, but for yours. ³¹Now is the time for this world to be judged; now the ruler of this world will be overthrown. ³²When I am lifted up from the earth, I will draw everyone to me." (³³In saying this he indicated the kind of death he was going to suffer.)

34 The crowd answered, "Our Law tells us that the Messiah will live for ever. How, then, can you say that the Son of Man must be lifted up? Who is this Son of Man?"

35 Jesus answered, "The light will be among you a little longer. Continue on your way while you have the light, so that the darkness will not come upon you; for the one who walks in the dark does not know where he is going. ³⁶Believe in the light, then, while you have it, so

---

ˣSILVER COINS: See 6.7.
12.8: Deut 15.11   **12.13:** Ps 118.25,26   **12.15:** Zech 9.9
12.25: Mt 10.39, 16.25; Mk 8.35; Lk 9.24, 17.33   **12.34:** Ps 110.4; Is 9.7; Ezek 37.25; Dan 7.14

that you will be the people of the light."

The Unbelief of the People

After Jesus said this, he went off and hid himself from them. [37] Even though he had performed all these miracles in their presence, they did not believe in him, [38] so that what the prophet Isaiah had said might come true:

"Lord, who believed the message we told?
To whom did the Lord reveal his power?"

39 And so they were not able to believe, because Isaiah also said,

[40] "God has blinded their eyes
and closed their minds,
so that their eyes would not see,
and their minds would not understand,
and they would not turn to me, says God,
for me to heal them."

41 Isaiah said this because he saw Jesus' glory and spoke about him.

42 Even then, many of the Jewish authorities believed in Jesus; but because of the Pharisees they did not talk about it openly, so as not to be expelled from the synagogue. [43] They loved the approval of men rather than the approval of God.

Judgement by Jesus' Words

44 Jesus said in a loud voice, "Whoever believes in me believes not only in me but also in him who sent me. [45] Whoever sees me sees also him who sent me. [46] I have come into the world as light, so that everyone who believes in me should not remain in the darkness. [47] If anyone hears my message and does not obey it, I will not judge him. I came, not to judge the world, but to save it. [48] Whoever rejects me and does not accept my message has one who will judge him. The words I have spoken will be his judge on the last day! [49] This is true, because I have not spoken on my own authority, but the Father who sent me has commanded me what I must say and speak. [50] And I know that his command brings eternal life. What I say, then, is what the Father has told me to say."

Jesus Washes His Disciples' Feet

13 It was now the day before the Passover Festival. Jesus knew that the hour had come for him to leave this world and go to the Father. He had always loved those in the world who were his own, and he loved them to the very end.

2 Jesus and his disciples were at supper. The Devil had already put into the heart of Judas, the son of Simon Iscariot, the thought of betraying Jesus.[y] 3 Jesus knew that the Father had given him complete power; he knew that he had come from God and was going to God. [4] So he rose from the table, took off his outer garment, and tied a towel round his waist. [5] Then he poured some water into a basin and began to wash the disciples' feet and dry them with the towel round his waist. [6] He came to Simon Peter, who said to him, "Are you going to wash my feet, Lord?"

7 Jesus answered him, "You do not understand now what I am doing, but you will understand later."

8 Peter declared, "Never at any time will you wash my feet!"

"If I do not wash your feet," Jesus answered, "you will no longer be my disciple."

9 Simon Peter answered, "Lord, do not wash only my feet, then! Wash my hands and head, too!"

10 Jesus said, "Anyone who has had a bath is completely clean and does not have to wash himself, except for his feet.[z] All of you are clean—all except one." ([11] Jesus already knew who was going to betray him; that is why he said, "All of you, except one, are clean.")

12 After Jesus had washed their feet, he put his outer garment back on and returned to his place at the table. "Do you understand what I have just done to you?" he asked. [13] "You call me Teacher and Lord, and it is right that you do so, because that is what I am. [14] I, your Lord and Teacher, have just washed your feet. You, then, should wash one another's feet. [15] I have set an example for you, so that you will do just what I have done for you. [16] I am telling you the truth: no slave is greater than his master, and no messenger is greater than the one who sent him. [17] Now that you

yThe Devil...betraying Jesus; or The Devil had already decided that Judas, the son of Simon Iscariot, would betray Jesus.   zSome manuscripts do not have except for his feet.
12.38: Is 53.1   **12.40:** Is 6.10   **13.12–15:** Lk 22.27   **13.16:** Mt 10.24; Lk 6.40; Jn 15.20

The disciples looked at one another (13.22)

know this truth, how happy you will be if you put it into practice!

18 "I am not talking about all of you; I know those I have chosen. But the scripture must come true that says, 'The man who shared my food turned against me.' 19 I tell you this now before it happens, so that when it does happen, you will believe that 'I Am Who I Am.' 20 I am telling you the truth: whoever receives anyone I send receives me also; and whoever receives me receives him who sent me."

Jesus Predicts His Betrayal
(Matt. 26.20–25; Mark 14.17–21; Luke 22.21–23)

21 After Jesus had said this, he was deeply troubled and declared openly, "I am telling you the truth: one of you is going to betray me."

22 The disciples looked at one another, completely puzzled about whom he meant. 23 One of the disciples, the one whom Jesus loved, was sitting next to Jesus. 24 Simon Peter motioned to him and said, "Ask him whom he is talking about."

25 So that disciple moved closer to Jesus' side and asked, "Who is it, Lord?"

26 Jesus answered, "I will dip some bread in the sauce and give it to him; he is the man." So he took a piece of bread, dipped it, and gave it to Judas, the son of Simon Iscariot. 27 As soon as Judas took the bread, Satan entered him. Jesus said to him, "Be quick about what you are doing!" 28 None of the others at the table understood why Jesus said this to him. 29 Since Judas was in charge of the money bag, some of the disciples thought that Jesus had told him to go and buy what they needed for the festival, or to give something to the poor.

30 Judas accepted the bread and went out at once. It was night.

The New Commandment

31 After Judas had left, Jesus said, "Now the Son of Man's glory is revealed; now God's glory is revealed through him. 32 And if God's glory is revealed through him, then God will reveal the glory of the Son of Man in himself, and he will do so at once. 33 My children, I shall not be with you very much longer. You will look for me; but I tell you now what I told the Jewish authorities, 'You cannot go where I am going.' 34 And now I give you a new commandment: love one another. As I have loved you, so you must love one another. 35 If you have love for one another, then everyone will know that you are my disciples."

Jesus Predicts Peter's Denial
(Matt. 26.31–35; Mark 14.27–31; Luke 22.31–34)

36 "Where are you going, Lord?" Simon Peter asked him.

"You cannot follow me now where I am going," answered Jesus; "but later you will follow me."

37 "Lord, why can't I follow you now?" asked Peter. "I am ready to die for you!"

38 Jesus answered, "Are you really ready to die for me? I am telling you the truth: before the cock crows you will say three times that you do not know me.

Jesus the Way to the Father

14 "Do not be worried and upset," Jesus told them. "Believe[a] in God and believe also in me. 2 There are many rooms in my Father's house, and I am going to prepare a place for you. I would not tell you this if it were not so.[b] 3 And after I go and prepare a place for you, I will come back and take you to myself, so that you will be where I am. 4 You know the way that leads to the place where I am going."

[a] Believe; *or* You believe.
[b] There are...were not so; *or* There are many rooms in my Father's house; if it were not so, would I tell you that I am going to prepare a place for you?
13.18: Ps 41.9   **13.20:** Mt 10.40; Mk 9.37; Lk 9.48, 10.16   **13.33:** Jn 7.34
13.34: Jn 15.12,17; 1 Jn 3.23; 2 Jn 5

5 Thomas said to him, "Lord, we do not know where you are going; so how can we know the way to get there?"

6 Jesus answered him, "I am the way, the truth, and the life; no one goes to the Father except by me. [7] Now that you have known me," he said to them, "you will know[c] my Father also, and from now on you do know him and you have seen him."

8 Philip said to him, "Lord, show us the Father; that is all we need."

9 Jesus answered, "For a long time I have been with you all; yet you do not know me, Philip? Whoever has seen me has seen the Father. Why, then, do you say, 'Show us the Father'? [10] Do you not believe, Philip, that I am in the Father and the Father is in me? The words that I have spoken to you," Jesus said to his disciples, "do not come from me. The Father, who remains in me, does his own work. [11] Believe me when I say that I am in the Father and the Father is in me. If not, believe because of the things I do. [12] I am telling you the truth: whoever believes in me will do what I do—yes, he will do even greater things, because I am going to the Father. [13] And I will do whatever you ask for in my name, so that the Father's glory will be shown through the Son. [14] If you ask me[d] for anything in my name, I will do it.

The Promise of the Holy Spirit

15 "If you love me, you will obey my commandments. [16] I will ask the Father, and he will give you another Helper, who will stay with you for ever. [17] He is the Spirit who reveals the truth about God. The world cannot receive him, because it cannot see him or know him. But you know him, because he remains with you and is[e] in you.

18 "When I go, you will not be left all alone; I will come back to you. [19] In a little while the world will see me no more, but you will see me; and because I live, you also will live. [20] When that day comes, you will know that I am in my Father and that you are in me, just as I am in you.

21 "Whoever accepts my commandments and obeys them is the one who loves me. My Father will love whoever loves me; I too will love him and reveal myself to him."

22 Judas (not Judas Iscariot) said, "Lord, how can it be that you will reveal yourself to us and not to the world?"

23 Jesus answered him, "Whoever loves me will obey my teaching. My Father will love him, and my Father and I will come to him and live with him. [24] Whoever does not love me does not obey my teaching. And the teaching you have heard is not mine, but comes from the Father, who sent me.

25 "I have told you this while I am still with you. [26] The Helper, the Holy Spirit, whom the Father will send in my name, will teach you everything and make you remember all that I have told you.

27 "Peace is what I leave with you; it is my own peace that I give you. I do not give it as the world does. Do not be worried and upset; do not be afraid. [28] You heard me say to you, 'I am leaving, but I will come back to you.' If you loved me, you would be glad that I am going to the Father; for he is greater than I. [29] I have told you this now before it all happens, so that when it does happen, you will believe. [30] I cannot talk with you much longer, because the ruler of this world is coming. He has no power over me, [31] but the world must know that I love the Father; that is why I do everything as he commands me.

"Come, let us go from this place.

Jesus the Real Vine

15 "I am the real vine, and my Father is the gardener. [2] He breaks off every branch in me that does not bear fruit, and he prunes every branch that does bear fruit, so that it will be clean and bear more fruit. [3] You have been made clean already by the teaching I have given you. [4] Remain united to me, and I will remain united to you. A branch cannot bear fruit by itself; it can do so only if it remains in the vine. In the same way you cannot bear fruit unless you remain in me.

5 "I am the vine, and you are the branches. Whoever remains in me, and I in him, will bear much fruit; for you can do nothing without me. [6] Whoever does not remain in me is thrown out like a branch and dries up; such branches are gathered up and thrown into the fire, where they are burnt. [7] If you remain in me and my words remain in you, then

---

[c] Now that you have known me...you will know, *some manuscripts have* If you had known me...you would know.   [d] *Some manuscripts do not have* me.
[e] is; *some manuscripts have* will be

you will ask for anything you wish, and you shall have it. [8] My Father's glory is shown by your bearing much fruit; and in this way you become my disciples. [9] I love you just as the Father loves me; remain in my love. [10] If you obey my commands, you will remain in my love, just as I have obeyed my Father's commands and remain in his love.

11 "I have told you this so that my joy may be in you and that your joy may be complete. [12] My commandment is this: love one another, just as I love you. [13] The greatest love a person can have for his friends is to give his life for them. [14] And you are my friends if you do what I command you. [15] I do not call you servants any longer, because a servant does not know what his master is doing. Instead, I call you friends, because I have told you everything I have heard from my Father. [16] You did not choose me; I chose you and appointed you to go and bear much fruit, the kind of fruit that endures. And so the Father will give you whatever you ask of him in my name. [17] This, then, is what I command you: love one another.

The World's Hatred

18 "If the world hates you, just remember that it has hated me first. [19] If you belonged to the world, then the world would love you as its own. But I chose you from this world, and you do not belong to it; that is why the world hates you. [20] Remember what I told you: 'No slave is greater than his master.' If they persecuted me, they will persecute you too; if they obeyed my teaching, they will obey yours too. [21] But they will do all this to you because you are mine; for they do not know the one who sent me. [22] They would not have been guilty of sin if I had not come and spoken to them; as it is, they no longer have any excuse for their sin. [23] Whoever hates me hates my Father also. [24] They would not have been guilty of sin if I had not done among them the things that no one else ever did; as it is, they have seen what I did, and they hate both me and my Father. [25] This, however, was bound to happen so that what is written in their Law may come true: 'They hated me for no reason at all.'

26 "The Helper will come—the Spirit, who reveals the truth about God and who comes from the Father. I will send him

to you from the Father, and he will speak about me. [27] And you, too, will speak about me, because you have been with me from the very beginning.

16 "I have told you this, so that you will not give up your faith. [2] You will be expelled from the synagogues, and the time will come when anyone who kills you will think that by doing this he is serving God. [3] People will do these things to you because they have not known either the Father or me. [4] But I have told you this, so that when the time comes for them to do these things, you will remember that I told you.

The Work of the Holy Spirit

"I did not tell you these things at the beginning, for I was with you. [5] But now I am going to him who sent me, yet none of you asks me where I am going. [6] And now that I have told you, your hearts are full of sadness. [7] But I am telling you the truth: it is better for you that I go away, because if I do not go, the Helper will not come to you. But if I do go away, then I will send him to you. [8] And when he comes, he will prove to the people of the world that they are wrong about sin and about what is right and about God's judgement. [9] They are wrong about sin, because they do not believe in me; [10] they are wrong about what is right, because I am going to the Father and you will not see me any more; [11] and they are wrong about judgement, because the ruler of this world has already been judged.

12 "I have much more to tell you, but now it would be too much for you to bear. [13] When, however, the Spirit comes, who reveals the truth about God, he will lead you into all the truth. He will not speak on his own authority, but he will speak of what he hears, and will tell you of things to come. [14] He will give me glory, because he will take what I say and tell it to you. [15] All that my Father has is mine; that is why I said that the Spirit will take what I give him and tell it to you.

Sadness and Gladness

16 "In a little while you will not see me any more, and then a little while later you will see me."

17 Some of his disciples asked among themselves, "What does this mean? He tells us that in a little while we will not see him, and then a little while later we

15.12: Jn 13.34, 15.17; 1 Jn 3.23; 2 Jn 5   **15.20:** Mt 10.24; Lk 6.40; Jn 13.16
15.25: Ps 35.19, 69.4

will see him; and he also says, 'It is because I am going to the Father.' 18 What does this 'a little while' mean? We don't know what he is talking about!"

19 Jesus knew that they wanted to question him, so he said to them, "I said, 'In a little while you will not see me, and then a little while later you will see me.' Is this what you are asking about among yourselves? 20 I am telling you the truth: you will cry and weep, but the world will be glad; you will be sad, but your sadness will turn into gladness. 21 When a woman is about to give birth, she is sad because her hour of suffering has come; but when the baby is born, she forgets her suffering, because she is happy that a baby has been born into the world. 22 That is how it is with you: now you are sad, but I will see you again, and your hearts will be filled with gladness, the kind of gladness that no one can take away from you.

23 "When that day comes, you will not ask me for anything. I am telling you the truth: the Father will give you whatever you ask him for in my name. f 24 Until now you have not asked for anything in my name; ask and you will receive, so that your happiness may be complete.

Victory over the World

25 "I have used figures of speech to tell you these things. But the time will come when I will not use figures of speech, but will speak to you plainly about the Father. 26 When that day comes, you will ask him in my name; and I do not say that I will ask him on your behalf, 27 for the Father himself loves you. He loves you because you love me and have believed that I came from God. 28 I did come from the Father, and I came into the world; and now I am leaving the world and going to the Father."

29 Then his disciples said to him, "Now you are speaking plainly, without using figures of speech. 30 We know now that you know everything; you do not need someone to ask you questions. This makes us believe that you came from God."

31 Jesus answered them, "Do you believe now? 32 The time is coming, and is already here, when all of you will be scattered, each one to his own home, and I will be left all alone. But I am not really alone, because the Father is with me. 33 I have told you this so that you will have peace by being united to me. The world

will make you suffer. But be brave! I have defeated the world!"

Jesus Prays for His Disciples

17 After Jesus finished saying this, he looked up to heaven and said, "Father, the hour has come. Give glory to your Son, so that the Son may give glory to you. 2 For you gave him authority

Father, the hour has come (17.1)

over all mankind, so that he might give eternal life to all those you gave him. 3 And eternal life means knowing you, the only true God, and knowing Jesus Christ, whom you sent. 4 I have shown your glory on earth; I have finished the work you gave me to do. 5 Father! Give me glory in your presence now, the same glory I had with you before the world was made.

6 "I have made you known to those you gave me out of the world. They belonged to you, and you gave them to me. They have obeyed your word, 7 and now they know that everything you gave me comes from you. 8 I gave them the message that you gave me, and they received it; they know that it is true that I came from

---

f the Father will give you whatever you ask him for in my name; *some manuscripts have* if you ask the Father for anything, he will give it to you in my name.

you, and they believe that you sent me.

9 "I pray for them. I do not pray for the world but for those you gave me, for they belong to you. 10 All I have is yours, and all you have is mine; and my glory is shown through them. 11 And now I am coming to you; I am no longer in the world, but they are in the world. Holy Father! Keep them safe by the power of your name, the name you gave me, *g* so that they may be one just as you and I are one. 12 While I was with them, I kept them safe by the power of your name, the name you gave me. *h* I protected them, and not one of them was lost, except the man who was bound to be lost—so that the scripture might come true. 13 And now I am coming to you, and I say these things in the world so that they might have my joy in their hearts in all its fullness. 14 I gave them your message, and the world hated them, because they do not belong to the world, just as I do not belong to the world. 15 I do not ask you to take them out of the world, but I do ask you to keep them safe from the Evil One. 16 Just as I do not belong to the world, they do not belong to the world. 17 Dedicate them to yourself by means of the truth; your word is truth. 18 I sent them into the world, just as you sent me into the world. 19 And for their sake I dedicate myself to you, in order that they, too, may be truly dedicated to you.

20 "I pray not only for them, but also for those who believe in me because of their message. 21 I pray that they may all be one. Father! May they be in us, just as you are in me and I am in you. May they be one, so that the world will believe that you sent me. 22 I gave them the same glory you gave me, so that they may be one, just as you and I are one: 23 I in them and you in me, so that they may be completely one, in order that the world may know that you sent me and that you love them as you love me.

24 "Father! You have given them to me, and I want them to be with me where I am, so that they may see my glory, the glory you gave me; for you loved me before the world was made. 25 Righteous Father! The world does not know you, but I know you, and these know that you sent me. 26 I made you known to them,

and I will continue to do so, in order that the love you have for me may be in them, and so that I also may be in them."

The Arrest of Jesus
(Matt. 26.47–56; Mark 14.43–50; Luke 22.47–53)

18 After Jesus had said this prayer, he left with his disciples and went across the brook called Kidron. There was a garden in that place, and Jesus and his disciples went in. 2 Judas, the traitor, knew where it was, because many times Jesus had met there with his disciples. 3 So Judas went to the garden, taking with him a group of Roman soldiers, and some temple guards sent by the chief priests and the Pharisees; they were armed and carried lanterns and torches. 4 Jesus knew everything that was going to happen to him, so he stepped forward and asked them, "Who is it you are looking for?"

5 "Jesus of Nazareth," they answered.

"I am he," he said.

Judas, the traitor, was standing there with them. 6 When Jesus said to them, "I am he," they moved back and fell to the ground. 7 Again Jesus asked them, "Who is it you are looking for?"

"Jesus of Nazareth," they said.

8 "I have already told you that I am he," Jesus said. "If, then, you are looking for me, let these others go." (9 He said this so that what he had said might come true: "Father, I have not lost even one of those you gave me.")

10 Simon Peter, who had a sword, drew it and struck the High Priest's slave, cutting off his right ear. The name of the slave was Malchus. 11 Jesus said to Peter, "Put your sword back in its place! Do you think that I will not drink the cup of suffering which my Father has given me?"

Jesus before Annas

12 Then the Roman soldiers with their commanding officer and the Jewish guards arrested Jesus, bound him, 13 and took him first to Annas. He was the father-in-law of Caiaphas, who was High Priest that year. 14 It was Caiaphas who had advised the Jewish authorities that it was better that one man should die for all the people.

g Keep them safe by the power of your name, the name you gave me; *some manuscripts have* By the power of your name keep safe those you have given me.
h I kept them safe by the power of your name, the name you gave me; *some manuscripts have* By the power of your name I kept safe those you have given me.
17.12: Ps 41.9; Jn 13.18   **18.11:** Mt 26.39; Mk 14.36; Lk 22.42   **18.14:** Jn 11.49–50

Peter Denies Jesus
(Matt. 26.69–70; Mark 14.66–68; Luke 22.55–57)

15 Simon Peter and another disciple followed Jesus. That other disciple was well known to the High Priest, so he went with Jesus into the courtyard of the High Priest's house, 16 while Peter stayed outside by the gate. Then the other disciple went back out, spoke to the girl at the gate, and brought Peter inside. 17 The girl at the gate said to Peter, "Aren't you also one of the disciples of that man?"

"No, I am not," answered Peter.

18 It was cold, so the servants and guards had built a charcoal fire and were standing round it, warming themselves. So Peter went over and stood with them, warming himself.

The High Priest Questions Jesus
(Matt. 26.59–66; Mark 14.55–64; Luke 22.66–71)

19 The High Priest questioned Jesus about his disciples and about his teaching. 20 Jesus answered, "I have always spoken publicly to everyone; all my teaching was done in the synagogues and in the Temple, where all the people come together. I have never said anything in secret. 21 Why, then, do you question me? Question the people who heard me. Ask them what I told them—they know what I said."

22 When Jesus said this, one of the guards there slapped him and said, "How dare you talk like that to the High Priest!"

23 Jesus answered him, "If I have said anything wrong, tell everyone here what it was. But if I am right in what I have said, why do you hit me?"

24 Then Annas sent him, still bound, to Caiaphas the High Priest.

Peter Denies Jesus Again
(Matt. 26.71–75; Mark 14.69–72; Luke 22.58–62)

25 Peter was still standing there keeping himself warm. So the others said to him, "Aren't you also one of the disciples of that man?"

But Peter denied it. "No, I am not," he said.

26 One of the High Priest's slaves, a relative of the man whose ear Peter had cut off, spoke up. "Didn't I see you with him in the garden?" he asked.

27 Again Peter said "No"—and at once a cock crowed.

Jesus is Brought Before Pilate
(Matt. 27.1–2, 11–14; Mark 15.1–5; Luke 23.1–5)

28 Early in the morning Jesus was taken from Caiaphas' house to the governor's palace. The Jewish authorities did not go inside the palace, for they wanted to keep themselves ritually clean, in order to be able to eat the Passover meal. 29 So Pilate went outside to them and asked, "What do you accuse this man of?"

30 Their answer was, "We would not have brought him to you if he had not committed a crime."

31 Pilate said to them, "Then you yourselves take him and try him according to your own law."

They replied, "We are not allowed to put anyone to death." (32 This happened in order to make the words of Jesus come true, the words he used when he indicated the kind of death he would die.)

33 Pilate went back into the palace and called Jesus. "Are you the King of the Jews?" he asked him.

34 Jesus answered, "Does this question come from you or have others told you about me?"

35 Pilate replied, "Do you think I am a Jew? It was your own people and the chief priests who handed you over to me. What have you done?"

36 Jesus said, "My kingdom does not belong to this world; if my kingdom belonged to this world, my followers would fight to keep me from being handed over to the Jewish authorities. No, my kingdom does not belong here!"

37 So Pilate asked him, "Are you a king, then?"

Jesus answered, "You say that I am a king. I was born and came into the world for this one purpose, to speak about the truth. Whoever belongs to the truth listens to me."

38 "And what is truth?" Pilate asked.

Jesus Is Sentenced to Death
(Matt. 27.15–31; Mark 15.6–20; Luke 23.13–25)

Then Pilate went back outside to the people and said to them, "I cannot find any reason to condemn him. 39 But according to the custom you have, I always set free a prisoner for you during the Passover. Do you want me to set free for you the King of the Jews?"

40 They answered him with a shout,

18.32: Jn 3.14, 12.32

And what is truth? (18.38)

"No, not him! We want Barabbas!" (Barabbas was a bandit.)

19 Then Pilate took Jesus and had him whipped. [2] The soldiers made a crown out of thorny branches and put it on his head; then they put a purple robe on him [3] and came to him and said, "Long live the King of the Jews!" And they went up and slapped him.

4 Pilate went out once more and said to the crowd, "Look, I will bring him out here to you to let you see that I cannot find any reason to condemn him." [5] So Jesus came out, wearing the crown of thorns and the purple robe. Pilate said to them, "Look! Here is the man!"

6 When the chief priests and the temple guards saw him, they shouted, "Crucify him! Crucify him!"

Pilate said to them, "You take him, then, and crucify him. I find no reason to condemn him."

7 The crowd answered back, "We have a law that says he ought to die, because he claimed to be the Son of God."

8 When Pilate heard this, he was even more afraid. [9] He went back into the palace and asked Jesus, "Where do you come from?"

But Jesus did not answer. [10] Pilate said to him, "You will not speak to me? Remember, I have the authority to set you free and also to have you crucified."

11 Jesus answered, "You have authority over me only because it was given to you by God. So the man who handed me over to you is guilty of a worse sin."

12 When Pilate heard this, he tried to find a way to set Jesus free. But the crowd shouted back, "If you set him free, that means that you are not the Emperor's friend! Anyone who claims to be a king is a rebel against the Emperor!"

13 When Pilate heard these words, he took Jesus outside and sat down on the judge's seat in the place called "The Stone Pavement." (In Hebrew the name is "Gabbatha.") [14] It was then almost noon

No, not him! We want Barabbas! (18.40)

of the day before the Passover. Pilate said to the people, "Here is your king!"

15 They shouted back, "Kill him! Kill him! Crucify him!"

Pilate asked them, "Do you want me to crucify your king?"

The chief priests answered, "The only king we have is the Emperor!"

16 Then Pilate handed Jesus over to them to be crucified.

Jesus Is Crucified
(Matt. 27.32–44; Mark 15.21–32; Luke 23.26–43)

So they took charge of Jesus. 17 He went out, carrying his cross, and came to "The Place of the Skull," as it is called. (In Hebrew it is called "Golgotha.") 18 There they crucified him; and they also crucified two other men, one on each side, with Jesus between them. 19 Pilate wrote a notice and had it put on the cross. "Jesus of Nazareth, the King of the Jews," is what he wrote. 20 Many people read it, because the place where Jesus was crucified was not far from the city. The notice was written in Hebrew, Latin, and Greek. 21 The chief priests said to Pilate, "Do not write 'The King of the Jews,' but rather, 'This man said, I am the King of the Jews.'"

22 Pilate answered, "What I have written stays written."

23 After the soldiers had crucified Jesus, they took his clothes and divided them into four parts, one part for each soldier. They also took the robe, which was made of one piece of woven cloth without any seams in it. 24 The soldiers said to one another, "Let's not tear it; let's throw dice to see who will get it." This happened in order to make the scripture come true:

"They divided my clothes among
    themselves
    and gambled for my robe."

And this is what the soldiers did.

25 Standing close to Jesus' cross were his mother, his mother's sister, Mary the wife of Clopas, and Mary Magdalene. 26 Jesus saw his mother and the disciple he loved standing there; so he said to his mother, "He is your son."

27 Then he said to the disciple, "She is your mother." From that time the disciple took her to live in his home.

The Death of Jesus
(Matt. 27.45–56; Mark 15.33–41; Luke 23.44–49)

28 Jesus knew that by now everything had been completed; and in order to make the scripture come true, he said, "I am thirsty."

29 A bowl was there, full of cheap wine; so a sponge was soaked in the wine, put on a stalk of hyssop, and lifted up to his lips. 30 Jesus drank the wine and said, "It is finished!"

Then he bowed his head and died.

Jesus' Side Is Pierced

31 Then the Jewish authorities asked Pilate to allow them to break the legs of the men who had been crucified, and to take the bodies down from the crosses. They requested this because it was Friday, and they did not want the bodies to stay on the crosses on the Sabbath, since the coming Sabbath was especially holy. 32 So the soldiers went and broke the legs of the first man and then of the other man who had been crucified with Jesus. 33 But when they came to Jesus, they saw that he was already dead, so they did not break his legs. 34 One of the soldiers, however, plunged his spear into Jesus' side, and at once blood and water poured out. (35 The one who saw this happen has spoken of it, so that you also may believe. *i* What he said is true, and he knows that he speaks the truth.) 36 This was done to make the scripture come true: "Not one of his bones will be broken." 37 And there is another scripture that says, "People will look at him whom they pierced."

The Burial of Jesus
(Matt. 27.57–61; Mark 15.42–47; Luke 23.50–56)

38 After this, Joseph, who was from the town of Arimathea, asked Pilate if he could take Jesus' body. (Joseph was a follower of Jesus, but in secret, because he was afraid of the Jewish authorities.) Pilate told him he could have the body, so Joseph went and took it away. 39 Nicodemus, who at first had gone to see Jesus at night, went with Joseph, taking with him about thirty kilogrammes of spices, a mixture of myrrh and aloes. 40 The two men took Jesus' body and wrapped it in linen with the spices according to the Jewish custom of preparing a body for burial. 41 There was

i believe; *some manuscripts have* continue to believe.
19.24: Ps 22.18   **19.28:** Ps 69.21, 22.15   **19.36:** Ex 12.46; Num 9.12; Ps 34.20
19.37: Zech 12.10; Rev 1.7   **19.39:** Jn 3.1–2

The two men took Jesus' body (19.40)

a garden in the place where Jesus had been put to death, and in it there was a new tomb where no one had ever been buried. ⁴²Since it was the day before the Sabbath and because the tomb was close by, they placed Jesus' body there.

The Empty Tomb
(Matt. 28.1–8; Mark 16.1–8; Luke 24.1–12)

20 Early on Sunday morning, while it was still dark, Mary Magdalene went to the tomb and saw that the stone had been taken away from the entrance. ²She went running to Simon Peter and the other disciple, whom Jesus loved, and told them, "They have taken the Lord from the tomb, and we don't know where they have put him!"

3 Then Peter and the other disciple went to the tomb. ⁴The two of them were running, but the other disciple ran faster than Peter and reached the tomb first. ⁵He bent over and saw the linen wrappings, but he did not go in. ⁶Behind him came Simon Peter, and he went straight into the tomb. He saw the linen wrappings lying there ⁷and the cloth which had been round Jesus' head. It was not lying with the linen wrappings but was rolled up by itself. ⁸Then the other disciple, who had reached the tomb first, also went in; he saw and believed. (⁹They still did not understand the scripture which said that he must rise from death.) ¹⁰Then the disciples went back home.

Jesus Appears to Mary Magdalene
(Matt. 28.9–10; Mark 16.9–11)

11 Mary stood crying outside the tomb. While she was still crying, she bent over and looked in the tomb ¹²and saw two angels there dressed in white, sitting where the body of Jesus had been, one at the head and the other at the feet. ¹³"Woman, why are you crying?" they asked her.

She answered, "They have taken my Lord away, and I do not know where they have put him!"

14 Then she turned round and saw Jesus standing there; but she did not know that it was Jesus. ¹⁵"Woman, why are you crying?" Jesus asked her. "Who is it that you are looking for?"

She thought he was the gardener, so she said to him, "If you took him away, sir, tell me where you have put him, and I will go and get him."

16 Jesus said to her, "Mary!"

She turned towards him and said in Hebrew, "Rabboni!" (This means "Teacher.")

17 "Do not hold on to me," Jesus told her, "because I have not yet gone back up to the Father. But go to my brothers and tell them that I am returning to him who is my Father and their Father, my God and their God."

18 So Mary Magdalene went and told the disciples that she had seen the Lord and related to them what he had told her.

Jesus came and stood among them (20.19)

Jesus Appears to His Disciples
(Matt. 28.16–20; Mark 16.14–18; Luke 24.36–49)

19 It was late that Sunday evening, and the disciples were gathered together behind locked doors, because they were afraid of the Jewish authorities. Then Jesus came and stood among them. "Peace be with you," he said. ²⁰ After saying this, he showed them his hands and his side. The disciples were filled with joy at seeing the Lord. ²¹ Jesus said to them again, "Peace be with you. As the Father sent me, so I send you." ²² Then he breathed on them and said, "Receive the Holy Spirit. ²³ If you forgive people's sins, they are forgiven; if you do not forgive them, they are not forgiven."

Jesus and Thomas

24 One of the twelve disciples, Thomas (called the Twin), was not with them when Jesus came. ²⁵ So the other disciples told him, "We have seen the Lord!"

Thomas said to them, "Unless I see the scars of the nails in his hands and put my finger on those scars and my hand in his side, I will not believe."

26 A week later the disciples were together again indoors, and Thomas was with them. The doors were locked, but Jesus came and stood among them and said, "Peace be with you." ²⁷ Then he said to Thomas, "Put your finger here, and look at my hands; then stretch out your hand and put it in my side. Stop your doubting, and believe!"

28 Thomas answered him, "My Lord and my God!"

29 Jesus said to him, "Do you believe because you see me? How happy are those who believe without seeing me!"

The Purpose of This Book

30 In his disciples' presence Jesus performed many other miracles which are not written down in this book. ³¹ But these have been written in order that you may believe*ʲ* that Jesus is the Messiah, the Son of God, and that through your faith in him you may have life.

Jesus Appears to Seven Disciples

21 After this, Jesus appeared once more to his disciples at Lake Tiberias. This is how it happened. ² Simon Peter, Thomas (called the Twin), Nathanael (the one from Cana in Galilee), the sons of Zebedee, and two other disciples of Jesus were all together. ³ Simon Peter said to the others, "I am going fishing."

"We will come with you," they told him. So they went out in a boat, but all that night they did not catch a thing. ⁴ As the sun was rising, Jesus stood at the water's edge, but the disciples did not know that it was Jesus. ⁵ Then he asked them, "Young men, haven't you caught anything?"

"Not a thing," they answered.

6 He said to them, "Throw your net out on the right side of the boat, and you will catch some." So they threw the net

out and could not pull it back in, because they had caught so many fish.

7 The disciple whom Jesus loved said to Peter, "It is the Lord!" When Peter heard that it was the Lord, he wrapped his outer garment round him (for he had taken his clothes off) and jumped into the water. 8 The other disciples came to shore in the boat, pulling the net full of fish. They were not very far from land, about a hundred metres away. 9 When they stepped ashore, they saw a charcoal fire there with fish on it and some bread. 10 Then Jesus said to them, "Bring some of the fish you have just caught."

11 Simon Peter went aboard and dragged the net ashore full of big fish, a hundred and fifty-three in all; even though there were so many, still the net did not tear. 12 Jesus said to them, "Come and eat." None of the disciples dared ask him, "Who are you?" because they knew it was the Lord. 13 So Jesus went over, took the bread, and gave it to them; he did the same with the fish.

14 This, then, was the third time Jesus appeared to the disciples after he was raised from death.

Jesus and Peter

15 After they had eaten, Jesus said to Simon Peter, "Simon son of John, do you love me more than these others do?"

"Yes, Lord," he answered, "you know that I love you."

Jesus said to him, "Take care of my lambs." 16 A second time Jesus said to him, "Simon son of John, do you love me?"

"Yes, Lord," he answered, "you know that I love you."

Jesus said to him, "Take care of my sheep." 17 A third time Jesus said, "Simon son of John, do you love me?"

Peter was sad because Jesus asked him the third time, "Do you love me?" so he said to him, "Lord, you know everything; you know that I love you!"

Jesus said to him, "Take care of my sheep. 18 I am telling you the truth: when you were young, you used to get ready and go anywhere you wanted to; but when you are old, you will stretch out your hands and someone else will bind you and take you where you don't want to go." 19 (In saying this, Jesus was indicating the way in which Peter would die and bring glory to God.) Then Jesus said to him, "Follow me!"

Jesus and the Other Disciple

20 Peter turned round and saw behind

Simon Peter...dragged the net ashore (21.11)

him that other disciple, whom Jesus loved—the one who had leaned close to Jesus at the meal and had asked, "Lord, who is going to betray you?" 21 When Peter saw him, he asked Jesus, "Lord, what about this man?"

22 Jesus answered him, "If I want him to live until I come, what is that to you? Follow me!"

23 So a report spread among the followers of Jesus that this disciple would not die. But Jesus did not say that he would not die; he said, "If I want him

to live until I come, what is that to you?"

24 He is the disciple who spoke of these things, the one who also wrote them down; and we know that what he said is true.

Conclusion

25 Now, there are many other things that Jesus did. If they were all written down one by one, I suppose that the whole world could not hold the books that would be written.

THE ACTS
OF THE APOSTLES

INTRODUCTION

The Acts of the Apostles is a continuation of *The Gospel according to Luke*. Its chief purpose is to tell how Jesus' early followers, led by the Holy Spirit, spread the Good News about him "in Jerusalem, in all Judaea and Samaria, and to the ends of the earth" (1.8). It is the story of the Christian movement as it began among the Jewish people and went on to become a faith for the whole world. The writer was also concerned to reassure his readers that the Christians were not a subversive political threat to the Roman Empire, and that the Christian faith was the fulfilment of the Jewish religion.

Acts may be divided into three principal parts, reflecting the ever widening area in which the Good News about Jesus was proclaimed and the church established: (1) the beginning of the Christian movement in Jerusalem following the ascension of Jesus; (2) expansion into other parts of Palestine; and (3) further expansion, into the Mediterranean world as far as Rome.

An important feature of *Acts* is the activity of the Holy Spirit, who comes with power upon the believers in Jerusalem on the day of Pentecost and continues to guide and strengthen the church and its leaders throughout the events reported in the book. The early Christian message is summarized in a number of sermons, and the events recorded in *Acts* show the power of this message in the lives of the believers and in the fellowship of the church.

Outline of Contents
Preparation for the witness 1.1–26
    a. Jesus' last command and promise 1.1–14
    b. The successor of Judas 1.15–26
The witness in Jerusalem 2.1—8.3
The witness in Judaea and Samaria 8.4—12.25

The ministry of Paul   13.1—28.31
a. The first missionary journey   13.1—14.28
b. The conference in Jerusalem   15.1-35
c. The second missionary journey   15.36—18.22
d. The third missionary journey   18.23—21.16
e. Paul a prisoner in Jerusalem, Caesarea,
    and Rome   21.17—28.31

1 Dear Theophilus:
In my first book I wrote about all the things that Jesus did and taught from the time he began his work [2]until the day he was taken up to heaven. Before he was taken up, he gave instructions by the power of the Holy Spirit to the men he had chosen as his apostles. [3]For forty days after his death he appeared to them many times in ways that proved beyond doubt that he was alive. They saw him, and he talked with them about the Kingdom of God. [4]And when they came together,[a] he gave them this order: "Do not leave Jerusalem, but wait for the gift I told you about, the gift my Father promised. [5]John baptized with water, but in a few days you will be baptized with the Holy Spirit."

Jesus Is Taken up to Heaven

6 When the apostles met together with Jesus, they asked him, "Lord, will you at this time give the Kingdom back to Israel?"

7 Jesus said to them, "The times and occasions are set by my Father's own authority, and it is not for you to know when they will be. [8]But when the Holy Spirit comes upon you, you will be filled with power, and you will be witnesses for me in Jerusalem, in all Judaea and Samaria, and to the ends of the earth." [9]After saying this, he was taken up to heaven as they watched him, and a cloud hid him from their sight.

10 They still had their eyes fixed on the sky as he went away, when two men dressed in white suddenly stood beside them [11]and said, "Galileans, why are you standing there looking up at the sky? This Jesus, who was taken from you into heaven, will come back in the same way that you saw him go to heaven."

Judas' Successor

12 Then the apostles went back to Jerusalem from the Mount of Olives, which is about a kilometre away from the city. [13]They entered the city and went up to the room where they were staying: Peter, John, James and Andrew, Philip and Thomas, Bartholomew and Matthew, James son of Alphaeus, Simon the Patriot, and Judas son of James. [14]They gathered frequently to pray as a group, together with the women and with Mary the mother of Jesus and with his brothers.

15 A few days later there was a meeting of the believers, about a hundred and twenty in all, and Peter stood up to speak. [16]"My brothers," he said, "the scripture had to come true in which the Holy Spirit, speaking through David, made a prediction about Judas, who was the guide for those who arrested Jesus. [17]Judas was a member of our group, for he had been chosen to have a part in our work."

18 (With the money that Judas got for his evil act he bought a field, where he fell to his death; he burst open and all his bowels spilt out. [19]All the people living in Jerusalem heard about it, and so in their own language they call that field Akeldama, which means "Field of Blood.")

20 "For it is written in the book of Psalms,

'May his house become empty;
    may no one live in it.'

It is also written,

'May someone else take his place of
    service.'

21-22 "So then, someone must join us as a witness to the resurrection of the

---

[a]when they came together; or while he was staying with them; or while he was eating with them.
1.1: Lk 1.1–4   **1.4:** Lk 24.49   **1.5:** Mt 3.11; Mk 1.8; Lk 3.16; Jn 1.33
1.8: Mt 28.19; Mk 16.15; Lk 24.47–48   **1.9:** Mk 16.19; Lk 24.50–51
1.13: Mt 10.2–4; Mk 3.16–19; Lk 6.14–16   **1.18–19:** Mt 27.3–8   **1.20:** Ps 69.25, 109.8
1.22: Mt 3.16; Mk 1.9, 16.19; Lk 3.21, 24.51

PALESTINE AND SYRIA IN ACTS

C A P P A D O C I A

PISIDIA

C I L I C I A
Tarsus

P A M P H Y L I A

Antioch
Seleucia

Salamis

C Y P R U S
Paphos

S Y R I A

M E D I T E R R A N E A N   S E A

P H O E N I C I A

Sidon
Damascus
Tyre

Caesarea
Samaria
Joppa
Lydda
Ashdod
Gaza
Jerusalem

J U D A E A

DEAD
SEA

E G Y P T

0   50   100
Kilometres

Fellow-Jews...listen to me! (2.14)

Lord Jesus. He must be one of the men who were in our group during the whole time that the Lord Jesus travelled about with us, beginning from the time John preached his message of baptism[b] until the day Jesus was taken up from us to heaven."

23 So they proposed two men: Joseph, who was called Barsabbas (also known as Justus), and Matthias. 24 Then they prayed, "Lord, you know the thoughts of everyone, so show us which of these two you have chosen 25 to serve as an apostle in the place of Judas, who left to go to the place where he belongs." 26 Then they drew lots to choose between the two men, and the one chosen was Matthias, who was added to the group of eleven apostles.

The Coming of the Holy Spirit

2 When the day of Pentecost came, all the believers were gathered together in one place. 2 Suddenly there was a noise from the sky which sounded like a strong wind blowing, and it filled the whole house where they were sitting. 3 Then they saw what looked like tongues of fire which spread out and touched each person there. 4 They were all filled with the Holy Spirit and began to talk in other languages, as the Spirit enabled them to speak.

5 There were Jews living in Jerusalem, religious men who had come from every country in the world. 6 When they heard this noise, a large crowd gathered. They were all excited, because each one of them heard the believers speaking in his own language. 7 In amazement and wonder they exclaimed, "These people who are talking like this are Galileans! 8 How is it, then, that all of us hear them speaking in our own native languages? 9 We are from Parthia, Media, and Elam; from Mesopotamia, Judaea, and Cappadocia; from Pontus and Asia, 10 from Phrygia and Pamphylia, from Egypt and the regions of Libya near Cyrene. Some of us are from Rome, 11 both Jews and Gentiles converted to Judaism, and some of us are from Crete and Arabia—yet all of us hear them speaking in our own languages about the great things that God has done!" 12 Amazed and confused, they kept asking each other, "What does this mean?"

13 But others made fun of the believers, saying, "These people are drunk!"

Peter's Message

14 Then Peter stood up with the other eleven apostles and in a loud voice began to speak to the crowd: "Fellow-Jews and all of you who live in Jerusalem, listen to me and let me tell you what this means. 15 These people are not drunk, as you suppose; it is only nine o'clock in the morning. 16 Instead, this is what the prophet Joel spoke about:

[b] John preached his message of baptism; *or* John baptized him.
2.1: Lev 23.15–21; Deut 16.9–11

17 'This is what I will do in the last days,
    God says:
  I will pour out my Spirit on everyone.
  Your sons and daughters will proclaim
      my message;
    your young men will see visions,
    and your old men will have dreams.
18 Yes, even on my servants, both men
      and women,
  I will pour out my Spirit in those days,
    and they will proclaim my message.
19 I will perform miracles in the sky above
    and wonders on the earth below.
  There will be blood, fire, and thick
      smoke;
20   the sun will be darkened,
    and the moon will turn red as blood,
    before the great and glorious Day of
      the Lord comes.
21 And then, whoever calls out to the
      Lord for help will be saved.'

22 "Listen to these words, fellow-
Israelites! Jesus of Nazareth was a man
whose divine authority was clearly proven
to you by all the miracles and wonders
which God performed through him. You
yourselves know this, for it happened here
among you. 23 In accordance with his own
plan God had already decided that Jesus
would be handed over to you; and you
killed him by letting sinful men crucify
him. 24 But God raised him from death,
setting him free from its power, because
it was impossible that death should hold
him prisoner. 25 For David said about him,
  'I saw the Lord before me at all times;
    he is near me, and I will not be
      troubled.
26 And so I am filled with gladness,
    and my words are full of joy.
  And I, mortal though I am,
    will rest assured in hope,
27 because you will not abandon me in
      the world of the dead;
    you will not allow your faithful
      servant to rot in the grave.
28 You have shown me the paths that
      lead to life,
    and your presence will fill me with
      joy.'

29 "My brothers, I must speak to you
plainly about our famous ancestor King
David. He died and was buried, and his
grave is here with us to this very day.
30 He was a prophet, and he knew what

God had promised him: God had made
a vow that he would make one of David's
descendants a king, just as David was.
31 David saw what God was going to do
in the future, and so he spoke about the
resurrection of the Messiah when he said,
  'He was not abandoned in the world
      of the dead;
    his body did not rot in the grave.'
32 God has raised this very Jesus from
death, and we are all witnesses to this
fact. 33 He has been raised to the right-
hand side of God, his Father, and has
received from him the Holy Spirit, as he
had promised. What you now see and hear
is his gift that he has poured out on us.
34 For it was not David who went up into
heaven; rather he said,
  'The Lord said to my Lord:
    Sit here at my right
35 until I put your enemies as a footstool
      under your feet.'

36 "All the people of Israel, then, are
to know for sure that this Jesus, whom
you crucified, is the one that God has
made Lord and Messiah!'"

37 When the people heard this, they
were deeply troubled and said to Peter
and the other apostles, "What shall we
do, brothers?"

38 Peter said to them, "Each one of you
must turn away from his sins and be
baptized in the name of Jesus Christ, so
that your sins will be forgiven; and you
will receive God's gift, the Holy Spirit.
39 For God's promise was made to you
and your children, and to all who are far
away—all whom the Lord our God calls
to himself."

40 Peter made his appeal to them and
with many other words he urged them,
saying, "Save yourselves from the punishment coming on this wicked people!"
41 Many of them believed his message and
were baptized, and about three thousand
people were added to the group that day.
42 They spent their time in learning from
the apostles, taking part in the fellowship,
and sharing in the fellowship meals and
the prayers.

Life among the Believers

43 Many miracles and wonders were
being done through the apostles, and
everyone was filled with awe. 44 All the

2.17–21: Joel 2.28–32   **2.23:** Mt 27.35; Mk 15.24; Lk 23.33; Jn 19.18
2.24: Mt 28.5–6; Mk 16.6; Lk 24.5   **2.25–28:** Ps 16.8–11   **2.30:** Ps 132.11; 2 Sam 7.12–13
2.34–35: Ps 110.1   **2.44:** Acts 4.32–35

I give you what I have (3.6)

believers continued together in close fellowship and shared their belongings with one another. 45 They would sell their property and possessions, and distribute the money among all, according to what each one needed. 46 Day after day they met as a group in the Temple, and they had their meals together in their homes, eating with glad and humble hearts, 47 praising God, and enjoying the good will of all the people. And every day the Lord added to their group those who were being saved.

A Lame Man Is Healed

3 One day Peter and John went to the Temple at three o'clock in the afternoon, the hour for prayer. 2 There at the Beautiful Gate, as it was called, was a man who had been lame all his life. Every day he was carried to the gate to beg for money from the people who were going into the Temple. 3 When he saw Peter and John going in, he begged them to give him something. 4 They looked straight at him, and Peter said, "Look at us!" 5 So he looked at them, expecting to get something from them. 6 But Peter said to him, "I have no money at all, but I give you what I have: in the name of Jesus Christ of Nazareth I order you to get up and walk!" 7 Then he took him by his right hand and helped him up. At once the man's feet and ankles became strong; 8 he jumped up, stood on his feet, and started walking around. Then he went into the Temple with them, walking and

jumping and praising God. 9 The people there saw him walking and praising God, 10 and when they recognized him as the beggar who had sat at the Beautiful Gate, they were all surprised and amazed at what had happened to him.

Peter's Message in the Temple

11 As the man held on to Peter and John in Solomon's Porch, as it was called, the people were amazed and ran to them. 12 When Peter saw the people, he said to them, "Fellow-Israelites, why are you surprised at this, and why do you stare at us? Do you think that it was by means of our own power or godliness that we made this man walk? 13 The God of Abraham, Isaac, and Jacob, the God of our ancestors, has given divine glory to his Servant Jesus. But you handed him over to the authorities, and you rejected him in Pilate's presence, even after Pilate had decided to set him free. 14 He was holy and good, but you rejected him, and instead you asked Pilate to do you the favour of turning loose a murderer. 15 You killed the one who leads to life, but God raised him from death—and we are witnesses to this. 16 It was the power of his name that gave strength to this lame man. What you see and know was done by faith in his name; it was faith in Jesus that has made him well, as you can all see.

17 "And now, my brothers, I know that what you and your leaders did to Jesus was due to your ignorance. 18 God announced long ago through all the prophets

3.13: Ex 3.15   **3.14:** Mt 27.15–23; Mk 15.6–14; Lk 23.13–23; Jn 19.12–15

that his Messiah had to suffer; and he made it come true in this way. ¹⁹ Repent, then, and turn to God, so that he will forgive your sins. If you do, ²⁰ times of spiritual strength will come from the Lord, and he will send Jesus, who is the Messiah he has already chosen for you. ²¹ He must remain in heaven until the time comes for all things to be made new, as God announced through his holy prophets who lived long ago. ²² For Moses said, 'The Lord your God will send you a prophet, just as he sent me,ᵈ and he will be one of your own people. You are to obey everything that he tells you to do. ²³ Anyone who does not obey that prophet shall be separated from God's people and destroyed.' ²⁴ And all the prophets who had a message, including Samuel and those who came after him, also announced what has been happening these days. ²⁵ The promises of God through his prophets are for you, and you share in the covenant which God made with your ancestors. As he said to Abraham, 'Through your descendants I will bless all the people on earth.' ²⁶ And so God chose his Servant and sent him first to you, to bless you by making every one of you turn away from his wicked ways."

Peter and John before the Council

4 Peter and John were still speaking to the people when some priests,ᵉ the officer in charge of the temple guards, and some Sadducees arrived. ² They were annoyed because the two apostles were teaching the people that Jesus had risen from death, which proved that the dead will rise to life. ³ So they arrested them and put them in jail until the next day, since it was already late. ⁴ But many who heard the message believed; and the number of men grew to about five thousand.

5 The next day the Jewish leaders, the elders, and the teachers of the Law gathered in Jerusalem. ⁶ They met with the High Priest Annas and with Caiaphas, John, Alexander, and the others who belonged to the High Priest's family. ⁷ They made the apostles stand before them and asked them, "How did you do this? What power have you got or whose name did you use?"

8 Peter, full of the Holy Spirit, answered them, "Leaders of the people and elders:

⁹ if we are being questioned today about the good deed done to the lame man and how he was healed, ¹⁰ then you should all know, and all the people of Israel should know, that this man stands here before you completely well through the power of the name of Jesus Christ of Nazareth—whom you crucified and whom God raised from death. ¹¹ Jesus is the one of whom the scripture says,

'The stone that you the builders despised
    turned out to be the most important
    of all.'

¹² Salvation is to be found through him alone; in all the world there is no one else whom God has given who can save us."

13 The members of the Council were amazed to see how bold Peter and John were and to learn that they were ordinary men of no education. They realized then that they had been companions of Jesus. ¹⁴ But there was nothing that they could say, because they saw the man who had been healed standing there with Peter and John. ¹⁵ So they told them to leave the Council room, and then they started discussing among themselves. ¹⁶ "What shall we do with these men?" they asked. "Everyone in Jerusalem knows that this extraordinary miracle has been performed by them, and we cannot deny it. ¹⁷ But to keep this matter from spreading any further among the people, let us warn these men never again to speak to anyone in the name of Jesus."

18 So they called them back in and told them that on no condition were they to speak or to teach in the name of Jesus. ¹⁹ But Peter and John answered them, "You yourselves judge which is right in God's sight—to obey you or to obey God. ²⁰ For we cannot stop speaking of what we ourselves have seen and heard." ²¹ So the Council warned them even more strongly and then set them free. They saw that it was impossible to punish them, because the people were all praising God for what had happened. ²² The man on whom this miracle of healing had been performed was over forty years old.

The Believers Pray for Boldness

23 As soon as Peter and John were set free, they returned to their group and told them what the chief priests and the elders had said. ²⁴ When the believers heard it,

---

ᵈ just as he sent me; or like me. ᵉ priests; some manuscripts have chief priests.
3.22: Deut 18.15,18 **3.23:** Deut 18.19 **3.25:** Gen 22.18 **4.11:** Ps 118.22
4.24: Ex 20.11; Neh 9.6; Ps 146.6

they all joined together in prayer to God: "Master and Creator of heaven, earth, and sea, and all that is in them! 25 By means of the Holy Spirit you spoke through our ancestor David, your servant, when he said,

'Why were the Gentiles furious;
     why did people make their useless
     plots?
26 The kings of the earth prepared
     themselves,
     and the rulers met together
     against the Lord and his Messiah.'

27 For indeed Herod and Pontius Pilate met together in this city with the Gentiles and the people of Israel against Jesus, your holy Servant, whom you made Messiah. 28 They gathered to do everything that you by your power and will had already decided would happen. 29 And now, Lord, take notice of the threats they have made, and allow us, your servants, to speak your message with all boldness. 30 Stretch out your hand to heal, and grant that wonders and miracles may be performed through the name of your holy Servant Jesus."

31 When they finished praying, the place where they were meeting was shaken. They were all filled with the Holy Spirit and began to proclaim God's message with boldness.

The Believers Share Their Possessions

32 The group of believers was one in mind and heart. No one said that any of his belongings was his own, but they all shared with one another everything they had. 33 With great power the apostles gave witness to the resurrection of the Lord Jesus, and God poured rich blessings on them all. 34 There was no one in the group who was in need. Those who owned fields or houses would sell them, bring the money received from the sale, 35 and hand it over to the apostles; and the money was distributed to each one according to his need.

36 And so it was that Joseph, a Levite born in Cyprus, whom the apostles called Barnabas (which means "One who Encourages"), 37 sold a field he owned, brought the money, and handed it over to the apostles.

Ananias and Sapphira

5 But there was a man named Ananias, who with his wife Sapphira sold some property that belonged to them. 2 But with his wife's agreement he kept part of the money for himself and handed the rest over to the apostles. 3 Peter said to him, "Ananias, why did you let Satan take control of you and make you lie to the Holy Spirit by keeping part of the money you received for the property? 4 Before you sold the property, it belonged to you; and after you sold it, the money was yours. Why, then, did you decide to do such a thing? You have not lied to men—you have lied to God!" 5 As soon as Ananias heard this, he fell down dead; and all who heard about it were terrified. 6 The young men came in, wrapped up his body, carried him out, and buried him.

7 About three hours later his wife, not knowing what had happened, came in. 8 Peter asked her, "Tell me, was this the full amount you and your husband received for your property?"

"Yes," she answered, "the full amount."

9 So Peter said to her, "Why did you and your husband decide to put the Lord's Spirit to the test? The men who buried your husband are now at the door, and they will carry you out too!" 10 At once she fell down at his feet and died. The young men came in and saw that she was dead, so they carried her out and buried her beside her husband. 11 The whole church and all the others who heard of this were terrified.

Miracles and Wonders

12 Many miracles and wonders were being performed among the people by the apostles. All the believers met together in Solomon's Porch. 13 Nobody outside the group dared to join them, even though the people spoke highly of them. 14 But more and more people were added to the group—a crowd of men and women who believed in the Lord. 15 As a result of what the apostles were doing, sick people were carried out into the streets and placed on beds and mats so that at least Peter's shadow might fall on some of them as he passed by. 16 And crowds of people came in from the towns around Jerusalem, bringing those who were ill or who had evil spirits in them; and they were all healed.

The Apostles Are Persecuted

17 Then the High Priest and all his companions, members of the local party of the Sadducees, became extremely jealous of the apostles; so they decided to take action. 18 They arrested the

4.25–26: Ps 2.1–2   **4.27:** Mt 27.1–2; Mk 15.1; Lk 23.1, 7–11; Jn 18.28–29   **4.32:** Acts 2.44–45

So that at least Peter's shadow might fall on some of them (5.15)

apostles and put them in the public jail. ¹⁹ But that night an angel of the Lord opened the prison gates, led the apostles out, and said to them, ²⁰ "Go and stand in the Temple, and tell the people all about this new life." ²¹ The apostles obeyed, and at dawn they entered the Temple and started teaching.

The High Priest and his companions called together all the Jewish elders for a full meeting of the Council; then they sent orders to the prison to have the apostles brought before them. ²² But when the officials arrived, they did not find the apostles in prison, so they returned to the Council and reported, ²³ "When we arrived at the jail, we found it locked up tight and all the guards on watch at the gates; but when we opened the gates, we

found no one inside!" ²⁴ When the chief priests and the officer in charge of the temple guards heard this, they wondered what had happened to the apostles. ²⁵ Then a man came in and said to them, "Listen! The men you put in prison are in the Temple teaching the people!" ²⁶ So the officer went off with his men and brought the apostles back. They did not use force, however, because they were afraid that the people might stone them.

27 They brought the apostles in, made them stand before the Council, and the High Priest questioned them. ²⁸ "We gave you strict orders not to teach in the name of this man," he said; "but see what you have done! You have spread your teaching all over Jerusalem, and you want to make us responsible for his death!"

5.28: Mt 27.25

29 Peter and the other apostles replied, "We must obey God, not men. 30 The God of our ancestors raised Jesus from death, after you had killed him by nailing him to a cross. 31 God raised him to his right-hand side as Leader and Saviour, to give the people of Israel the opportunity to repent and have their sins forgiven. 32 We are witnesses to these things—we and the Holy Spirit, who is God's gift to those who obey him."

33 When the members of the Council heard this, they were so furious that they wanted to have the apostles put to death. 34 But one of them, a Pharisee named Gamaliel, who was a teacher of the Law and was highly respected by all the people, stood up in the Council. He ordered the apostles to be taken out for a while, 35 and then he said to the Council, "Fellow-Israelites, be careful what you do to these men. 36 You remember that Theudas appeared some time ago, claiming to be somebody great, and about four hundred men joined him. But he was killed, all his followers were scattered, and his movement died out. 37 After that, Judas the Galilean appeared during the time of the census; he drew a crowd after him, but he also was killed, and all his followers were scattered. 38 And so in this case, I tell you, do not take any action against these men. Leave them alone! If what they have planned and done is of human origin, it will disappear, 39 but if it comes from God, you cannot possibly defeat them. You could find yourselves fighting against God!"

The Council followed Gamaliel's advice. 40 They called the apostles in, had them whipped, and ordered them never again to speak in the name of Jesus; and then they set them free. 41 As the apostles left the Council, they were happy, because God had considered them worthy to suffer disgrace for the sake of Jesus. 42 And every day in the Temple and in people's homes they continued to teach and preach the Good News about Jesus the Messiah.

The Seven Helpers

6 Some time later, as the number of disciples kept growing, there was a quarrel between the Greek-speaking Jews and the native Jews. The Greek-speaking Jews claimed that their widows were being neglected in the daily distribution of funds. 2 So the twelve apostles called the whole group of believers together and said, "It is not right for us to neglect the preaching of God's word in order to handle finances. 3 So then, brothers, choose seven men among you who are known to be full of the Holy Spirit and wisdom, and we will put them in charge of this matter. 4 We ourselves, then, will give our full time to prayer and the work of preaching."

5 The whole group was pleased with the apostles' proposal, so they chose Stephen, a man full of faith and the Holy Spirit, and Philip, Prochorus, Nicanor, Timon, Parmenas, and Nicolaus, a Gentile from Antioch who had earlier been converted to Judaism. 6 The group presented them to the apostles, who prayed and placed their hands on them.

7 And so the word of God continued to spread. The number of disciples in Jerusalem grew larger and larger, and a great number of priests accepted the faith.

The Arrest of Stephen

8 Stephen, a man richly blessed by God and full of power, performed great miracles and wonders among the people. 9 But he was opposed by some men who were members of the synagogue of the Freedmen *f* (as it was called), which included Jews from Cyrene and Alexandria. They and other Jews from the provinces of Cilicia and Asia started arguing with Stephen. 10 But the Spirit gave Stephen such wisdom that when he spoke, they could not refute him. 11 So they bribed some men to say, "We heard him speaking against Moses and against God!" 12 In this way they stirred up the people, the elders, and the teachers of the Law. They seized Stephen and took him before the Council. 13 Then they brought in some men to tell lies about him. "This man," they said, "is always talking against our sacred Temple and the Law of Moses. 14 We heard him say that this Jesus of Nazareth will tear down the Temple and change all the customs which have come down to us from Moses!" 15 All those sitting in the Council fixed their eyes on Stephen and saw that his face looked like the face of an angel.

Stephen's Speech

7 The High Priest asked Stephen, "Is this true?"

2 Stephen answered, "Brothers and

f FREEDMEN: *These were Jews who had been slaves, but had bought or been given their freedom.*
7.2-3: Gen 12.1

fathers, listen to me! Before our ancestor Abraham had gone to live in Haran, the God of glory appeared to him in Mesopotamia ³and said to him, 'Leave your family and country and go to the land that I will show you.' ⁴And so he left his country and went to live in Haran. After Abraham's father died, God made him move to this land where you now live. ⁵God did not then give Abraham any part of it as his own, not even a square metre of ground, but God promised to give it to him, and that it would belong to him and to his descendants. At the time God made this promise, Abraham had no children. ⁶This is what God said to him: 'Your descendants will live in a foreign country, where they will be slaves and will be badly treated for four hundred years. ⁷But I will pass judgement on the people that they will serve, and afterwards they will come out of that country and will worship me in this place.' ⁸Then God gave Abraham the ceremony of circumcision as a sign of the covenant. So Abraham circumcised Isaac a week after he was born; Isaac circumcised his son Jacob, and Jacob circumcised his twelve sons, the famous ancestors of our race.

9 "Jacob's sons became jealous of their brother Joseph and sold him to be a slave in Egypt. But God was with him ¹⁰and brought him safely through all his troubles. When Joseph appeared before the king of Egypt, God gave him a pleasing manner and wisdom, and the king made Joseph governor over the country and the royal household. ¹¹Then there was a famine all over Egypt and Canaan, which caused much suffering. Our ancestors could not find any food, ¹²and when Jacob heard that there was corn in Egypt, he sent his sons, our ancestors, on their first visit there. ¹³On the second visit Joseph made himself known to his brothers, and the king of Egypt came to know about Joseph's family. ¹⁴So Joseph sent a message to his father Jacob, telling him and the whole family, seventy-five people in all, to come to Egypt. ¹⁵Then Jacob went to Egypt, where he and his sons died. ¹⁶Their bodies were taken to Shechem, where they were buried in the grave which Abraham had bought from the clan of Hamor for a sum of money.

17 "When the time drew near for God to keep the promise he had made to Abraham, the number of our people in Egypt had grown much larger. ¹⁸At last a king who did not know about Joseph began to rule in Egypt. ¹⁹He tricked our ancestors and was cruel to them, forcing them to put their babies out of their homes, so that they would die. ²⁰It was at this time that Moses was born, a very beautiful child. He was cared for at home for three months, ²¹and when he was put out of his home, the king's daughter adopted him and brought him up as her own son. ²²He was taught all the wisdom of the Egyptians and became a great man in words and deeds.

23 "When Moses was forty years old, he decided to find out how his fellow-Israelites were being treated. ²⁴He saw one of them being ill-treated by an Egyptian, so he went to his help and took revenge on the Egyptian by killing him. ²⁵(He thought that his own people would understand that God was going to use him to set them free, but they did not understand.) ²⁶The next day he saw two Israelites fighting, and he tried to make peace between them. 'Listen, men,' he said, 'you are fellow-Israelites; why are you fighting like this?' ²⁷But the one who was ill-treating the other pushed Moses aside. 'Who made you ruler and judge over us?' he asked. ²⁸'Do you want to kill me, just as you killed that Egyptian yesterday?' ²⁹When Moses heard this, he fled from Egypt and went to live in the land of Midian. There he had two sons.

30 "After forty years had passed, an angel appeared to Moses in the flames of a burning bush in the desert near Mount Sinai. ³¹Moses was amazed by what he saw, and went near the bush to get a better look. But he heard the Lord's voice: ³²'I am the God of your ancestors, the God of Abraham, Isaac, and Jacob.' Moses trembled with fear and dared not look. ³³The Lord said to him, 'Take your sandals off, for the place where you are standing is holy ground. ³⁴I have seen the cruel suffering of my people in Egypt. I have heard their groans, and I have come down

7.4: Gen 11.31, 12.4   **7.5:** Gen 12.7, 13.15, 15.18, 17.8
7.6-7: Gen 15.13-14   **7.7:** Ex 3.12   **7.8:** Gen 17.10-14, 21.2-4, 25.26, 29.31—35.18
7.9: Gen 37.11,28, 39.2,21   **7.10:** Gen 41.39-41   **7.11:** Gen 42.1-2   **7.13:** Gen 45.1,16
7.14: Gen 45.9-10,17-18; 46.27   **7.15:** Gen 46.1-7, 49.33
7.16: Gen 23.3-16, 33.19, 50.7-13; Josh 24.32   **7.17-18:** Ex 1.7-8   **7.19:** Ex 1.10-11,22
7.20: Ex 2.2   **7.21:** Ex 2.3-10   **7.23-29:** Ex 2.11-15   **7.29:** Ex 18.3-4   **7.30-34:** Ex 3.1-10

to set them free. Come now; I will send you to Egypt.'

35 "Moses is the one who was rejected by the people of Israel. 'Who made you ruler and judge over us?' they asked. He is the one whom God sent to rule the people and set them free with the help of the angel who appeared to him in the burning bush. 36 He led the people out of Egypt, performing miracles and wonders in Egypt and at the Red Sea and for forty years in the desert. 37 Moses is the one who said to the people of Israel, 'God will send you a prophet, just as he sent me,*g* and he will be one of your own people.' 38 He is the one who was with the people of Israel assembled in the desert; he was there with our ancestors and with the angel who spoke to him on Mount Sinai, and he received God's living messages to pass on to us.

39 "But our ancestors refused to obey him; they pushed him aside and wished that they could go back to Egypt. 40 So they said to Aaron, 'Make us some gods who will lead us. We do not know what has happened to that man Moses, who brought us out of Egypt.' 41 It was then that they made an idol in the shape of a bull, offered sacrifice to it, and had a feast in honour of what they themselves had made. 42 So God turned away from them and gave them over to worship the stars of heaven, as it is written in the book of the prophets:

'People of Israel! It was not to me
   that you slaughtered and sacrificed
      animals
   for forty years in the desert.
43 It was the tent of the god Molech that
      you carried,
   and the image of Rephan, your star
      god;
   they were idols that you had made
      to worship.
And so I will send you into exile beyond
      Babylon.'

44 "Our ancestors had the Tent of God's presence with them in the desert. It had been made as God had told Moses to make it, according to the pattern that Moses had been shown. 45 Later on, our ancestors who received the tent from their fathers carried it with them when they went with Joshua and took over the land from the

nations that God drove out as they advanced. And it stayed there until the time of David. 46 He won God's favour and asked God to allow him to provide a dwelling place for the God of Jacob.*h* 47 But it was Solomon who built him a house.

48 "But the Most High God does not live in houses built by men; as the prophet says,

49 'Heaven is my throne, says the Lord,
   and the earth is my footstool.
What kind of house would you build
      for me?
   Where is the place for me to live in?
50 Did not I myself make all these
      things?'

51 "How stubborn you are!" Stephen went on to say. "How heathen your hearts, how deaf you are to God's message! You are just like your ancestors: you too have always resisted the Holy Spirit! 52 Was there any prophet that your ancestors did not persecute? They killed God's messengers, who long ago announced the coming of his righteous Servant. And now you have betrayed and murdered him. 53 You are the ones who received God's law, that was handed down by angels—yet you have not obeyed it!"

The Stoning of Stephen

54 As the members of the Council listened to Stephen, they became furious and ground their teeth at him in anger. 55 But Stephen, full of the Holy Spirit, looked up to heaven and saw God's glory and Jesus standing at the right-hand side of God. 56 "Look!" he said. "I see heaven opened and the Son of Man standing at the right-hand side of God!"

57 With a loud cry the members of the Council covered their ears with their hands. Then they all rushed at him at once, 58 threw him out of the city, and stoned him. The witnesses left their cloaks in the care of a young man named Saul. 59 They kept on stoning Stephen as he called out to the Lord, "Lord Jesus, receive my spirit!" 60 He knelt down and cried out in a loud voice, "Lord! Do not remember this sin against them!" He said this and died.

8 And Saul approved of his murder.

---

g just as he sent me; or like me.
h the God of Jacob; *some manuscripts have* the people of Israel.
7.35: Ex 2.14   **7.36:** Ex 7.5, 14.21; Num 14.33   **7.37:** Deut 18.15,18
7.38: Ex 19.1—20.17; Deut 5.1-33   **7.40:** Ex 32.1   **7.41:** Ex 32.2-6   **7.42-43:** Amos 5.25-27
7.44: Ex 25.9,40   **7.45:** Josh 3.14-17   **7.46:** 2 Sam 7.1-16; 1 Chr 17.1-14
7.47: 1 Kgs 6.1-38; 2 Chr 3.1-17   **7.49-50:** Is 66.1-2   **7.51:** Is 63.10

And Saul approved of his murder (8.1)

Saul Persecutes the Church

That very day the church in Jerusalem began to suffer cruel persecution. All the believers, except the apostles, were scattered throughout the provinces of Judaea and Samaria. ² Some devout men buried Stephen, mourning for him with loud cries.

3 But Saul tried to destroy the church; going from house to house, he dragged out the believers, both men and women, and threw them into jail.

The Gospel Is Preached in Samaria

4 The believers who were scattered went everywhere, preaching the message. ⁵ Philip went to the principal city*ⁱ* in Samaria and preached the Messiah to the people there. ⁶ The crowds paid close attention to what Philip said, as they listened to him and saw the miracles that he performed. ⁷ Evil spirits came out from many people with a loud cry, and many paralysed and lame people were healed. ⁸ So there was great joy in that city.

9 A man named Simon lived there, who for some time had astounded the Samaritans with his magic. He claimed that he was someone great, ¹⁰ and everyone in the city, from all classes of society, paid close attention to him. "He is that power of God known as 'The Great Power'," they said. ¹¹ They paid this attention to him because for such a long time he had astonished them with his magic. ¹² But when they believed Philip's message about the good news of the Kingdom of God and about Jesus Christ, they were baptized, both men and women. ¹³ Simon himself also believed; and after being baptized, he stayed close to Philip and was astounded when he saw the great wonders and miracles that were being performed.

14 The apostles in Jerusalem heard that the people of Samaria had received the word of God, so they sent Peter and John to them. ¹⁵ When they arrived, they prayed for the believers that they might receive the Holy Spirit. ¹⁶ For the Holy Spirit had not yet come down on any of them; they had only been baptized in the name of the Lord Jesus. ¹⁷ Then Peter and John placed their hands on them, and they received the Holy Spirit.

18 Simon saw that the Spirit had been given to the believers when the apostles placed their hands on them. So he offered money to Peter and John, ¹⁹ and said, "Give this power to me too, so that anyone I place my hands on will receive the Holy Spirit."

20 But Peter answered him, "May you and your money go to hell, for thinking that you can buy God's gift with money! ²¹ You have no part or share in our work, because your heart is not right in God's sight. ²² Repent, then, of this evil plan of yours, and pray to the Lord that he will forgive you for thinking such a thing as this. ²³ For I see that you are full of bitter envy and are a prisoner of sin."

---

*ⁱ*the principal city; *some manuscripts have* a city.
8.3: Acts 22.4–5, 26.9–11

24 Simon said to Peter and John, "Please pray to the Lord for me, so that none of these things you spoke of will happen to me."

25 After they had given their testimony and proclaimed the Lord's message, Peter and John went back to Jerusalem. On their way they preached the Good News in many villages of Samaria.

Philip and the Ethiopian Official

26 An angel of the Lord said to Philip, "Get ready and go south[j] to the road that goes from Jerusalem to Gaza." (This road is not used nowadays.)[k] 27-28 So Philip got ready and went. Now an Ethiopian eunuch, who was an important official in charge of the treasury of the queen of Ethiopia, was on his way home. He had been to Jerusalem to worship God and was going back home in his carriage. As he rode along, he was reading from the book of the prophet Isaiah. 29 The Holy Spirit said to Philip, "Go over to that carriage and stay close to it." 30 Philip ran over and heard him reading from the book of the prophet Isaiah. He asked him, "Do you understand what you are reading?"

31 The official replied, "How can I understand unless someone explains it to me?" And he invited Philip to climb up and sit in the carriage with him. 32 The passage of scripture which he was reading was this:

"Like a sheep that is taken to be
     slaughtered,
  like a lamb that makes no sound when
     its wool is cut off,
  he did not say a word.
33 He was humiliated, and justice was
     denied him.
  No one will be able to tell about his
     descendants,
  because his life on earth has come
     to an end."

34 The official asked Philip, "Tell me, of whom is the prophet saying this? Of himself or of someone else?" 35 Then Philip began to speak; starting from this passage of scripture, he told him the Good News about Jesus. 36 As they travelled down the road, they came to a place where there was some water, and the official said, "Here is some water. What is to keep me from being baptized?"[l]

38 The official ordered the carriage to stop, and both Philip and the official went down into the water, and Philip baptized him. 39 When they came up out of the water, the Spirit of the Lord took Philip away. The official did not see him again, but continued on his way, full of joy. 40 Philip found himself in Azotus; he went on to Caesarea, and on the way he preached the Good News in every town.

The Conversion of Saul
(Acts 22.6-16; 26.12-18)

9 In the meantime Saul kept up his violent threats of murder against the followers of the Lord. He went to the High Priest 2 and asked for letters of introduction to the synagogues in Damascus, so that if he should find there any followers of the Way of the Lord, he would be able to arrest them, both men and women, and bring them back to Jerusalem.

3 As Saul was coming near the city of Damascus, suddenly a light from the sky flashed round him. 4 He fell to the ground and heard a voice saying to him, "Saul, Saul! Why do you persecute me?"

5 "Who are you, Lord?" he asked.

"I am Jesus, whom you persecute," the voice said. 6 "But get up and go into the city, where you will be told what you must do."

7 The men who were travelling with Saul had stopped, not saying a word; they heard the voice but could not see anyone. 8 Saul got up from the ground and opened his eyes, but could not see a thing. So they took him by the hand and led him into Damascus. 9 For three days he was not able to see, and during that time he did not eat or drink anything.

10 There was a Christian in Damascus named Ananias. He had a vision, in which the Lord said to him, "Ananias!"

"Here I am, Lord," he answered.

11 The Lord said to him, "Get ready and go to Straight Street, and at the house of Judas ask for a man from Tarsus named Saul. He is praying, 12 and in a vision he has seen a man named Ananias come in and place his hands on him so that he might see again."

13 Ananias answered, "Lord, many people have told me about this man and about all the terrible things he has done to your people in Jerusalem. 14 And he has come to Damascus with authority

---

[j]south; or at midday.   [k]This road is not used nowadays; or This is the desert road.
[l]Some manuscripts add verse 37: Philip said to him, "You may be baptized if you believe with all your heart." "I do," he answered; "I believe that Jesus Christ is the Son of God."
8.32-33: Is 53.7-8

Who are you, Lord? (9.5)

from the chief priests to arrest all who worship you."

15 The Lord said to him, "Go, because I have chosen him to serve me, to make my name known to Gentiles and kings and to the people of Israel. 16 And I myself will show him all that he must suffer for my sake."

17 So Ananias went, entered the house where Saul was, and placed his hands on him. "Brother Saul," he said, "the Lord has sent me—Jesus himself, who appeared to you on the road as you were coming here. He sent me so that you might see again and be filled with the Holy Spirit." 18 At once something like fish scales fell from Saul's eyes, and he was able to see again. He stood up and was baptized; 19 and after he had eaten, his strength came back.

Saul Preaches in Damascus

Saul stayed for a few days with the believers in Damascus. 20 He went straight to the synagogues and began to preach that Jesus was the Son of God.

21 All who heard him were amazed and asked, "Isn't he the one who in Jerusalem was killing those who worship that man Jesus? And didn't he come here for the very purpose of arresting those people and taking them back to the chief priests?"

22 But Saul's preaching became even more powerful, and his proofs that Jesus was the Messiah were so convincing that the Jews who lived in Damascus could not answer him.

23 After many days had gone by, the Jews met together and made plans to kill Saul, 24 but he was told of their plan. Day and night they watched the city gates in order to kill him. 25 But one night Saul's followers took him and let him down through an opening in the wall, lowering him in a basket.

Saul in Jerusalem

26 Saul went to Jerusalem and tried to join the disciples. But they would not believe that he was a disciple, and they were all afraid of him. 27 Then Barnabas came to his help and took him to the apostles. He explained to them how Saul had seen the Lord on the road and that the Lord had spoken to him. He also told them how boldly Saul had preached in the name of Jesus in Damascus. 28 And so Saul stayed with them and went all over Jerusalem, preaching boldly in the name of the Lord. 29 He also talked and disputed with the Greek-speaking Jews, but they tried to kill him. 30 When the believers found out about this, they took Saul to Caesarea and sent him away to Tarsus.

31 And so it was that the church

9.23–25: 2 Cor 11.32–33

throughout Judaea, Galilee, and Samaria had a time of peace. Through the help of the Holy Spirit it was strengthened and grew in numbers, as it lived in reverence for the Lord.

Peter in Lydda and Joppa

32 Peter travelled everywhere, and on one occasion he went to visit God's people who lived in Lydda. 33 There he met a man named Aeneas, who was paralysed and had not been able to get out of bed for eight years. 34 "Aeneas," Peter said to him, "Jesus Christ makes you well. Get up and make your bed." At once Aeneas got up. 35 All the people living in Lydda and Sharon saw him, and they turned to the Lord.

36 In Joppa there was a woman named Tabitha, who was a believer. (Her name in Greek is Dorcas, meaning "a deer.") She spent all her time doing good and helping the poor. 37 At that time she became ill and died. Her body was washed and laid in a room upstairs. 38 Joppa was not very far from Lydda, and when the believers in Joppa heard that Peter was in Lydda, they sent two men to him with the message, "Please hurry and come to us." 39 So Peter got ready and went with them. When he arrived, he was taken to the room upstairs, where all the widows crowded round him, crying and showing him all the shirts and coats that Dorcas had made while she was alive. 40 Peter put them all out of the room, and knelt down and prayed; then he turned to the body and said, "Tabitha, get up!" She opened her eyes, and when she saw Peter, she sat up. 41 Peter reached over and helped her get up. Then he called all the believers, including the widows, and presented her alive to them. 42 The news about this spread all over Joppa, and many people believed in the Lord. 43 Peter stayed on in Joppa for many days with a tanner of leather named Simon.

Peter and Cornelius

10 There was a man in Caesarea named Cornelius, who was a captain in the Roman regiment called "The Italian Regiment." 2 He was a religious man; he and his whole family worshipped God. He also did much to help the Jewish poor people and was constantly praying to God. 3 It was about three o'clock one afternoon when he had a vision, in which he clearly saw an angel of God come in and say to him, "Cornelius!"

4 He stared at the angel in fear and said, "What is it, sir?"

The angel answered, "God is pleased with your prayers and works of charity, and is ready to answer you. 5 And now send some men to Joppa for a certain man whose full name is Simon Peter. 6 He is a guest in the home of a tanner of leather named Simon, who lives by the sea." 7 Then the angel went away, and Cornelius called two of his house servants and a soldier, a religious man who was one of his personal attendants. 8 He told them what had happened and sent them off to Joppa.

9 The next day, as they were on their way and coming near Joppa, Peter went up on the roof of the house about noon in order to pray. 10 He became hungry and wanted something to eat; while the food was being prepared, he had a vision. 11 He saw heaven opened and something coming down that looked like a large sheet being lowered by its four corners to the earth. 12 In it were all kinds of animals, reptiles, and wild birds. 13 A voice said to him, "Get up, Peter; kill and eat!"

14 But Peter said, "Certainly not, Lord! I have never eaten anything ritually unclean or defiled."

15 The voice spoke to him again, "Do not consider anything unclean that God has declared clean." 16 This happened three times, and then the thing was taken back up into heaven.

17 While Peter was wondering about the meaning of this vision, the men sent by Cornelius had learnt where Simon's house was, and they were now standing in front of the gate. 18 They called out and asked, "Is there a guest here by the name of Simon Peter?"

19 Peter was still trying to understand what the vision meant, when the Spirit said, "Listen! Three[m] men are here looking for you. 20 So get ready and go down, and do not hesitate to go with them, for I have sent them." 21 So Peter went down and said to the men, "I am the man you are looking for. Why have you come?"

22 "Captain Cornelius sent us," they answered. "He is a good man who worships God and is highly respected by all the Jewish people. An angel of God told him to invite you to his house, so that he could hear what you have to say."

m Three; *some manuscripts have* Some; *one manuscript has* Two.

23 Peter invited the men in and persuaded them to spend the night there.

The next day he got ready and went with them; and some of the believers from Joppa went along with him. 24 The following day he arrived in Caesarea, where Cornelius was waiting for him, together with relatives and close friends that he had invited. 25 As Peter was about to go in, Cornelius met him, fell at his feet, and bowed down before him. 26 But Peter made him rise. "Stand up," he said; "I myself am only a man." 27 Peter kept on talking to Cornelius as he went into the house, where he found many people gathered. 28 He said to them, "You yourselves know very well that a Jew is not allowed by his religion to visit or associate with Gentiles. But God has shown me that I must not consider any person ritually unclean or defiled. 29 And so when you sent for me, I came without any objection. I ask you, then, why did you send for me?"

30 Cornelius said, "It was about this time three days ago that I was praying[n] in my house at three o'clock in the afternoon. Suddenly a man dressed in shining clothes stood in front of me 31 and said: 'Cornelius! God has heard your prayer and has taken notice of your works of charity. 32 Send someone to Joppa for a man whose full name is Simon Peter. He is a guest in the home of Simon the tanner of leather, who lives by the sea.' 33 And so I sent for you at once, and you have been good enough to come. Now we are all here in the presence of God, waiting to hear anything that the Lord has instructed you to say."

Peter's Speech

34 Peter began to speak: "I now realize that it is true that God treats everyone on the same basis. 35 Whoever worships him and does what is right is acceptable to him, no matter what race he belongs to. 36 You know the message he sent to the people of Israel, proclaiming the Good News of peace through Jesus Christ, who is Lord of all. 37 You know of the great event that took place throughout the land of Israel, beginning in Galilee after John preached his message of baptism. 38 You know about Jesus of Nazareth and how God poured out on him the Holy Spirit and power. He went everywhere, doing good and healing all who were under the power of the Devil, for God was with him. 39 We are witnesses of everything that he did in the land of Israel and in Jerusalem. Then they put him to death by nailing him to a cross. 40 But God raised him from death three days later and caused him to appear, 41 not to everyone, but only to the witnesses that God had already chosen, that is, to us who ate and drank with him after he rose from death. 42 And he commanded us to preach the gospel to the people and to testify that he is the one whom God has appointed judge of the living and the dead. 43 All the prophets spoke about him, saying that everyone who believes in him will have his sins forgiven through the power of his name."

The Gentiles Receive the Holy Spirit

44 While Peter was still speaking, the Holy Spirit came down on all those who were listening to his message. 45 The Jewish believers who had come from Joppa with Peter were amazed that God had poured out his gift of the Holy Spirit on the Gentiles also. 46 For they heard them speaking in strange tongues and praising God's greatness. Peter spoke up: 47 "These people have received the Holy Spirit, just as we also did. Can anyone, then, stop them from being baptized with water?" 48 So he ordered them to be baptized in the name of Jesus Christ. Then they asked him to stay with them for a few days.

Peter's Report to the Church at Jerusalem

11 The apostles and the other believers throughout Judaea heard that the Gentiles also had received the word of God. 2 When Peter went to Jerusalem, those who were in favour of circumcising Gentiles criticized him, saying, 3 "You were a guest in the home of uncircumcised Gentiles, and you even ate with them!" 4 So Peter gave them a complete account of what had happened from the very beginning:

5 "While I was praying in the city of Joppa, I had a vision. I saw something coming down that looked like a large sheet being lowered by its four corners from heaven, and it stopped next to me. 6 I looked closely inside and saw domesticated and wild animals, reptiles, and wild birds. 7 Then I heard a voice saying to me, 'Get up, Peter; kill and eat!' 8 But

---

[n] praying; *some manuscripts have* praying and fasting.
10.34: Deut 10.17

I said, 'Certainly not, Lord! No ritually unclean or defiled food has ever entered my mouth.' ⁹The voice spoke again from heaven, 'Do not consider anything unclean that God has declared clean.' ¹⁰This happened three times, and finally the whole thing was drawn back up into heaven. ¹¹At that very moment three men who had been sent to me from Caesarea arrived at the house where I was ᵒ staying. ¹²The Spirit told me to go with them without hesitation. These six fellow-believers from Joppa accompanied me to Caesarea, and we all went into the house of Cornelius. ¹³He told us how he had seen an angel standing in his house, who said to him, 'Send someone to Joppa for a man whose full name is Simon Peter. ¹⁴He will speak words to you by which you and all your family will be saved.' ¹⁵And when I began to speak, the Holy Spirit came down on them just as on us at the beginning. ¹⁶Then I remembered what the Lord had said: 'John baptized with water, but you will be baptized with the Holy Spirit.' ¹⁷It is clear that God gave those Gentiles the same gift that he gave us when we believed in the Lord Jesus Christ; who was I, then, to try to stop God!"

18 When they heard this, they stopped their criticism and praised God, saying, "Then God has given to the Gentiles also the opportunity to repent and live!"

The Church at Antioch

19 Some of the believers who were scattered by the persecution which took place when Stephen was killed went as far as Phoenicia, Cyprus, and Antioch, telling the message to Jews only. ²⁰But other believers, men from Cyprus and Cyrene, went to Antioch and proclaimed the message to Gentiles ᵖ also, telling them the Good News about the Lord Jesus. ²¹The Lord's power was with them, and a great number of people believed and turned to the Lord.

22 The news about this reached the church in Jerusalem, so they sent Barnabas to Antioch. ²³When he arrived and saw how God had blessed the people, he was glad and urged them all to be faithful and true to the Lord with all their hearts. ²⁴Barnabas was a good man, full of the Holy Spirit and faith, and many

people were brought to the Lord.

25 Then Barnabas went to Tarsus to look for Saul. ²⁶When he found him, he took him to Antioch, and for a whole year the two met with the people of the church and taught a large group. It was at Antioch that the believers were first called Christians.

27 About that time some prophets went from Jerusalem to Antioch. ²⁸One of them, named Agabus, stood up and by the power of the Spirit predicted that a severe famine was about to come over all the earth. (It came when Claudius was emperor.) ²⁹The disciples decided that each of them would send as much as he could to help their fellow-believers who lived in Judaea. ³⁰They did this, then, and sent the money to the church elders by Barnabas and Saul.

More Persecution

12 About this time King Herod �q began to persecute some members of the church. ²He had James, the brother of John, put to death by the sword. ³When he saw that this pleased the Jews, he went on to arrest Peter. (This happened during the time of the Festival of Unleavened Bread.) ⁴After his arrest Peter was put in jail, where he was handed over to be guarded by four groups of four soldiers each. Herod planned to put him on trial in public after Passover. ⁵So Peter was kept in jail, but the people of the church were praying earnestly to God for him.

Peter Is Set Free from Prison

6 The night before Herod was going to bring him out to the people, Peter was sleeping between two guards. He was tied with two chains, and there were guards on duty at the prison gate. ⁷Suddenly an angel of the Lord stood there, and a light shone in the cell. The angel shook Peter by the shoulder, woke him up, and said, "Hurry! Get up!" At once the chains fell off Peter's hands. ⁸Then the angel said, "Fasten your belt and put on your sandals." Peter did so, and the angel said, "Put your cloak round you and come with me." ⁹Peter followed him out of the prison, not knowing, however, if what the angel was doing was real; he thought he was seeing a vision. ¹⁰They passed by the first guard post and then the second, and

ᵒI was; *some manuscripts have* we were.
ᵖGentiles; *some manuscripts have* Greek-speaking Jews *or* Greek-speaking people.
qKING HEROD: *Herod Agrippa I, ruler of all Palestine.*
11.16: Acts 1.5   **11.19:** Acts 8.1-4   **11.28:** Acts 21.10   **12.4:** Ex 12.1-27

PAUL'S FIRST MISSIONARY JOURNEY

came at last to the iron gate leading into the city. The gate opened for them by itself, and they went out. They walked down a street, and suddenly the angel left Peter.

11 Then Peter realized what had happened to him, and said, "Now I know that it is really true! The Lord sent his angel to rescue me from Herod's power and from everything the Jewish people expected to happen."

12 Aware of his situation, he went to the home of Mary, the mother of John Mark, where many people had gathered and were praying. 13 Peter knocked at the outside door, and a servant-girl named Rhoda came to answer it. 14 She recognized Peter's voice and was so happy that she ran back in without opening the door, and announced that Peter was standing outside. 15 "You are mad!" they told her. But she insisted that it was true. So they answered, "It is his angel."

16 Meanwhile Peter kept on knocking. At last they opened the door, and when they saw him, they were amazed. 17 He motioned with his hand for them to be quiet, and he explained to them how the Lord had brought him out of prison. "Tell this to James and the rest of the believers," he said; then he left and went somewhere else.

18 When morning came, there was a tremendous confusion among the guards—what had happened to Peter? 19 Herod gave orders to search for him, but they could not find him. So he had

the guards questioned and ordered them to be put to death.

After this, Herod left Judaea and spent some time in Caesarea.

The Death of Herod

20 Herod was very angry with the people of Tyre and Sidon, so they went in a group to see him. First they convinced Blastus, the man in charge of the palace, that he should help them. Then they went to Herod and asked him for peace, because their country got its food supplies from the king's country.

21 On a chosen day Herod put on his royal robes, sat on his throne, and made a speech to the people. 22 "It isn't a man speaking, but a god!" they shouted. 23 At once the angel of the Lord struck Herod down, because he did not give honour to God. He was eaten by worms and died.

24 Meanwhile the word of God continued to spread and grow.

25 Barnabas and Saul finished their mission and returned from*r* Jerusalem, taking John Mark with them.

Barnabas and Saul Are Chosen and Sent

13 In the church at Antioch there were some prophets and teachers: Barnabas, Simeon (called the Black), Lucius (from Cyrene), Manaen (who had been brought up with Herod*s* the governor), and Saul. 2 While they were serving the Lord and fasting, the Holy Spirit said to them, "Set apart for me Barnabas and

r from; *some manuscripts have* to.   *s* HEROD: *Herod Antipas, ruler of Galilee (see Lk 3.1).*

Saul, to do the work to which I have called them."

3 They fasted and prayed, placed their hands on them, and sent them off.

In Cyprus

4 Having been sent by the Holy Spirit, Barnabas and Saul went to Seleucia and sailed from there to the island of Cyprus. 5 When they arrived at Salamis, they preached the word of God in the synagogues. They had John Mark with them to help in the work.

6 They went all the way across the island to Paphos, where they met a certain magician named Bar-Jesus, a Jew who claimed to be a prophet. 7 He was a friend of the governor of the island, Sergius Paulus, who was an intelligent man. The governor called Barnabas and Saul before him because he wanted to hear the word of God. 8 But they were opposed by the magician Elymas (that is his name in Greek), who tried to turn the governor away from the faith. 9 Then Saul—also known as Paul—was filled with the Holy Spirit; he looked straight at the magician 10 and said, "You son of the Devil! You are the enemy of everything that is good. You are full of all kinds of evil tricks, and you always keep trying to turn the Lord's truths into lies! 11 The Lord's hand will come down on you now; you will be blind and will not see the light of day for a time."

At once Elymas felt a dark mist cover his eyes, and he walked about trying to find someone to lead him by the hand. 12 When the governor saw what had happened, he believed; for he was greatly amazed at the teaching about the Lord.

In Antioch in Pisidia

13 Paul and his companions sailed from Paphos and came to Perga, a city in Pamphylia, where John Mark left them and went back to Jerusalem. 14 They went on from Perga and arrived in Antioch in Pisidia, and on the Sabbath they went into the synagogue and sat down. 15 After the reading from the Law of Moses and from the writings of the prophets, the officials of the synagogue sent them a message: "Brothers, we want you to speak to the people if you have a message of encouragement for them." 16 Paul stood up, motioned with his hand, and began to speak:

"Fellow-Israelites and all Gentiles here who worship God: hear me! 17 The God of the people of Israel chose our ancestors and made the people a great nation during the time they lived as foreigners in Egypt. God brought them out of Egypt by his great power, 18 and for forty years he endured[t] them in the desert. 19 He destroyed seven nations in the land of Canaan and made his people the owners of the land. 20 All this took about four hundred and fifty years.

"After this[u] he gave them judges until the time of the prophet Samuel. 21 And when they asked for a king, God gave them Saul son of Kish from the tribe of Benjamin, to be their king for forty years. 22 After removing him, God made David their king. This is what God said about him: 'I have found that David son of Jesse is the kind of man I like, a man who will do all I want him to do.' 23 It was Jesus, a descendant of David, whom God made the Saviour of the people of Israel, as he had promised. 24 Before Jesus began his work, John preached to all the people of Israel that they should turn from their sins and be baptized. 25 And as John was about to finish his mission, he said to the people, 'Who do you think I am? I am not the one you are waiting for. But listen! He is coming after me, and I am not good enough to take his sandals off his feet.'

26 "My fellow-Israelites, descendants of Abraham, and all Gentiles here who worship God: it is to us that this message of salvation has been sent! 27 For the people who live in Jerusalem and their leaders did not know that he is the Saviour, nor did they understand the words of the prophets that are read every Sabbath. Yet they made the prophets' words come true by condemning Jesus. 28 And even though they could find no reason to pass the death sentence on him, they asked Pilate to have him put to death. 29 And after they had done everything that

[t] he endured; *some manuscripts have* he took care of.
[u] All this took about four hundred and fifty years. After this; *or* Some four hundred and fifty years later.
13.17: Ex 1.7, 12.51   **13.18:** Num 14.34; Deut 1.31   **13.19:** Deut 7.1; Josh 14.1
13.20: Judg 2.16; 1 Sam 3.20   **13.21:** 1 Sam 8.5, 10.21   **13.22:** 1 Sam 13.14, 16.12; Ps 89.20
13.24: Mk 1.4; Lk 3.3   **13.25:** Mt 3.11; Mk 1.7; Lk 3.16; Jn 1.20,27
13.28: Mt 27.22–23; Mk 15.13–14; Lk 23.21–23; Jn 19.15
13.29: Mt 27.57–61; Mk 15.42–47; Lk 23.50–56; Jn 19.38–42

the Scriptures say about him, they took him down from the cross and placed him in a tomb. ³⁰ But God raised him from death, ³¹ and for many days he appeared to those who had travelled with him from Galilee to Jerusalem. They are now witnesses for him to the people of Israel. ³²⁻³³ And we are here to bring the Good News to you: what God promised our ancestors he would do, he has now done for us, who are their descendants, by raising Jesus to life. As it is written in the second Psalm,

'You are my Son;
today I have become your Father.'

³⁴ And this is what God said about raising him from death, never to rot away in the grave:

'I will give you the sacred and sure blessings
that I promised to David.'

³⁵ As indeed he says in another passage,

'You will not allow your devoted servant to rot in the grave.'

³⁶ For David served God's purposes in his own time, and then he died, was buried with his ancestors, and his body rotted in the grave. ³⁷ But this did not happen to the one whom God raised from death. ³⁸⁻³⁹ We want you to know, my fellow-Israelites, that it is through Jesus that the message about forgiveness of sins is preached to you; and that everyone who believes in him is set free from all the sins from which the Law of Moses could not set you free. ⁴⁰ Take care, then, so that what the prophets said may not happen to you:ᵛ

⁴¹ 'Look, you scoffers! Be astonished and die!

For what I am doing today
is something that you will not believe,
even when someone explains it to you!'"

⁴² As Paul and Barnabas were leaving the synagogue, the people invited them to come back the next Sabbath and tell them more about these things. ⁴³ After the people had left the meeting, Paul and Barnabas were followed by many Jews and by many Gentiles who had been converted to Judaism. The apostles spoke to them and encouraged them to keep on living in the grace of God.

⁴⁴ The next Sabbath nearly everyone in the town came to hear the word of the Lord. ⁴⁵ When the Jews saw the crowds, they were filled with jealousy; they disputed what Paul was saying and insulted him. ⁴⁶ But Paul and Barnabas spoke out even more boldly: "It was necessary that the word of God should be spoken first to you. But since you reject it and do not consider yourselves worthy of eternal life, we will leave you and go to the Gentiles. ⁴⁷ For this is the commandment that the Lord has given us:

'I have made you a light for the Gentiles,
so that all the world may be saved.'"

⁴⁸ When the Gentiles heard this, they were glad and praised the Lord's message; and those who had been chosen for eternal life became believers.

⁴⁹ The word of the Lord spread everywhere in that region. ⁵⁰ But the Jews stirred up the leading men of the city and the Gentile women of high social standing who worshipped God. They started a persecution against Paul and Barnabas and threw them out of their region. ⁵¹ The apostles shook the dust off their feet in protest against them and went on to Iconium. ⁵² The believers in Antioch were full of joy and the Holy Spirit.

In Iconium

14 The same thing happened in Iconium: Paul and Barnabas went to the synagogue and spoke in such a way that a great number of Jews and Gentiles became believers. ² But the Jews who would not believe stirred up the Gentiles and turned them against the believers. ³ The apostles stayed there for a long time, speaking boldly about the Lord, who proved that their message about his grace was true by giving them the power to perform miracles and wonders. ⁴ The people of the city were divided: some were for the Jews, others for the apostles.

⁵ Then some Gentiles and Jews, together with their leaders, decided to ill-treat the apostles and stone them. ⁶ When the apostles learnt about it, they fled to the cities of Lystra and Derbe in Lycaonia and to the surrounding territory. ⁷ There they preached the Good News.

In Lystra and Derbe

⁸ In Lystra there was a man who had been lame from birth and had never been able to walk. ⁹ He sat there and listened to Paul's words. Paul saw that he believed

---

ᵛ Some manuscripts do not have to you.

13.31: Acts 1.3 **13.33:** Ps 2.7 **13.34:** Is 55.3 **13.35:** Ps 16.10 **13.41:** Hab 1.5
13.47: Is 42.6, 49.6 **13.51:** Mt 10.14; Mk 6.11; Lk 9.5, 10.11

and could be healed, so he looked straight at him ¹⁰and said in a loud voice, "Stand up straight on your feet!" The man jumped up and started walking around. ¹¹When the crowds saw what Paul had done, they started shouting in their own Lycaonian language, "The gods have become like men and have come down to us!" ¹²They gave Barnabas the name Zeus, and Paul the name Hermes, because he was the chief speaker. ¹³The priest of the god Zeus, whose temple stood just outside the town, brought bulls and flowers to the gate, for he and the crowds wanted to offer sacrifice to the apostles.

14 When Barnabas and Paul heard what they were about to do, they tore their clothes and ran into the middle of the crowd, shouting, ¹⁵"Why are you doing this? We ourselves are only human beings like you! We are here to announce the Good News, to turn you away from these worthless things to the living God, who made heaven, earth, sea, and all that is in them. ¹⁶In the past he allowed all people to go their own way. ¹⁷But he has always given evidence of his existence by the good things he does: he gives you rain from heaven and crops at the right times; he gives you food and fills your hearts with happiness." ¹⁸Even with these words the apostles could hardly keep the crowd from offering a sacrifice to them.

19 Some Jews came from Antioch in Pisidia and from Iconium; they won the crowd over to their side, stoned Paul and dragged him out of the town, thinking that he was dead. ²⁰But when the believers gathered round him, he got up and went back into the town. The next day he and Barnabas went to Derbe.

The Return to Antioch in Syria

21 Paul and Barnabas preached the Good News in Derbe and won many disciples. Then they went back to Lystra, to Iconium, and on to Antioch in Pisidia. ²²They strengthened the believers and encouraged them to remain true to the faith. "We must pass through many troubles to enter the Kingdom of God," they taught. ²³In each church they appointed elders, and with prayers and fasting they commended them to the Lord, in whom they had put their trust.

24 After going through the territory of Pisidia, they came to Pamphylia. ²⁵There they preached the message in Perga and then went to Attalia, ²⁶and from there they sailed back to Antioch, the place where they had been commended to the care of God's grace for the work they had now completed.

27 When they arrived in Antioch, they gathered the people of the church together and told them about all that God had done with them and how he had opened the way for the Gentiles to believe. ²⁸And they stayed a long time there with the believers.

The Meeting at Jerusalem

15 Some men came from Judaea to Antioch and started teaching the believers, "You cannot be saved unless you are circumcised as the Law of Moses requires." ²Paul and Barnabas got into a fierce argument with them about this, so it was decided that Paul and Barnabas and some of the others in Antioch should go to Jerusalem and see the apostles and elders about this matter.

3 They were sent on their way by the church; and as they went through Phoenicia and Samaria, they reported how the Gentiles had turned to God; this news brought great joy to all the believers. ⁴When they arrived in Jerusalem, they were welcomed by the church, the apostles, and the elders, to whom they told all that God had done through them. ⁵But some of the believers who belonged to the party of the Pharisees stood up and said, "The Gentiles must be circumcised and told to obey the Law of Moses."

6 The apostles and the elders met together to consider this question. ⁷After a long debate Peter stood up and said, "My brothers, you know that a long time ago God chose me from among you to preach the Good News to the Gentiles, so that they could hear and believe. ⁸And God, who knows the thoughts of everyone, showed his approval of the Gentiles by giving the Holy Spirit to them, just as he had to us. ⁹He made no difference between us and them; he forgave their sins because they believed. ¹⁰So then, why do you now want to put God to the test by laying a load on the backs of the believers which neither our ancestors nor we ourselves were able to carry? ¹¹No! We believe and are saved by the grace of the Lord Jesus, just as they are."

12 The whole group was silent as they heard Barnabas and Paul report all the miracles and wonders that God had performed through them among the Gentiles. ¹³When they had finished speaking,

14.15: Ex 20.11; Ps 146.6   **15.1:** Lev 12.3   **15.7:** Acts 10.1-43   **15.8:** Acts 2.4, 10.44

170

PAUL'S SECOND AND THIRD JOURNEYS

Paul's Second Journey
Paul's Third Journey

0 100 200 300
Kilometres

PONTUS
BITHYNIA
MYSIA
ASIA
GALATIA
PHRYGIA
PAMPHYLIA
CILICIA
SYRIA
PHOENICIA
LYCIA
CRETE
CYPRUS
EGYPT
MEDITERRANEAN SEA

Antioch
Derbe
Iconium
Lystra
Antioch in Pisidia
Thyatira
Ephesus
Miletus
Patara
Rhodes
Cos
Samos
Troas
Assos
Mitylene
Chios
Neapolis
Samothrace
Philippi
Amphipolis
Apollonia
Thessalonica
Berea
Athens
Corinth
Cenchreae
Tyre
Ptolemais
Caesarea
Jerusalem

James spoke up: "Listen to me, my brothers! [14] Simon has just explained how God first showed his care for the Gentiles by taking from among them a people to belong to him. [15] The words of the prophets agree completely with this. As the scripture says,

[16] 'After this I will return, says the Lord,
    and restore the kingdom of David.
  I will rebuild its ruins
    and make it strong again.
[17] And so all the rest of mankind will
    come to me,
      all the Gentiles whom I have called
      to be my own.
[18] So says the Lord, who made this
    known long ago.'

[19] "It is my opinion," James went on, "that we should not trouble the Gentiles who are turning to God. [20] Instead, we should write a letter telling them not to eat any food that is ritually unclean because it has been offered to idols; to keep themselves from sexual immorality; and not to eat any animal that has been strangled, or any blood. [21] For the Law of Moses has been read for a very long time in the synagogues every Sabbath, and his words are preached in every town."

The Letter to the Gentile Believers

22 Then the apostles and the elders, together with the whole church, decided to choose some men from the group and send them to Antioch with Paul and Barnabas. They chose two men who were highly respected by the believers, Judas, called Barsabbas, and Silas, [23] and they sent the following letter by them:

"We, the apostles and the elders, your brothers, send greetings to all our brothers of Gentile birth who live in Antioch, Syria, and Cilicia. [24] We have heard that some men who went from our group have troubled and upset you by what they said; they had not, however, received any instruction from us. [25] And so we have met together and have all agreed to choose some messengers and send them to you. They will go with our dear friends Barnabas and Paul, [26] who have risked their lives in the service of our Lord Jesus Christ. [27] We send you, then, Judas and Silas, who will tell you in person the same things we are writing. [28] The Holy Spirit and

we have agreed not to put any other burden on you besides these necessary rules: [29] eat no food that has been offered to idols; eat no blood; eat no animal that has been strangled; and keep yourselves from sexual immorality. You will do well if you take care not to do these things. With our best wishes."

30 The messengers were sent off and went to Antioch, where they gathered the whole group of believers and gave them the letter. [31] When the people read it, they were filled with joy by the message of encouragement. [32] Judas and Silas, who were themselves prophets, spoke a long time with them, giving them courage and strength. [33] After spending some time there, they were sent off in peace by the believers and went back to those who had sent them. [w]

35 Paul and Barnabas spent some time in Antioch, and together with many others they taught and preached the word of the Lord.

Paul and Barnabas Separate

36 Some time later Paul said to Barnabas, "Let us go back and visit our brothers in every town where we preached the word of the Lord, and let us find out how they are getting on." [37] Barnabas wanted to take John Mark with them, [38] but Paul did not think it was right to take him, because he had not stayed with them to the end of their mission, but had turned back and left them in Pamphylia. [39] There was a sharp argument, and they separated: Barnabas took Mark and sailed off for Cyprus, [40] while Paul chose Silas and left, commended by the believers to the care of the Lord's grace. [41] He went through Syria and Cilicia, strengthening the churches.

Timothy Goes with Paul and Silas

16 Paul travelled on to Derbe and Lystra, where a Christian named Timothy lived. His mother, who was also a Christian, was Jewish, but his father was a Greek. [2] All the believers in Lystra and Iconium spoke well of Timothy. [3] Paul wanted to take Timothy along with him, so he circumcised him. He did so because all the Jews who lived in those places knew that Timothy's father was Greek. [4] As they went through the towns, they delivered to the believers the rules decided

---

w Some manuscripts add verse 34: But Silas decided to stay there.
15.16–18: Amos 9.11–12   **15.20:** Ex 34.15–17; Lev 17.10–16, 18.6–23   **15.38:** Acts 13.13

upon by the apostles and elders in Jerusalem, and told them to obey those rules. 5 So the churches were made stronger in the faith and grew in numbers every day.

In Troas: Paul's Vision

6 They travelled through the region of Phrygia and Galatia because the Holy Spirit did not let them preach the message in the province of Asia. 7 When they reached the border of Mysia, they tried to go into the province of Bithynia, but the Spirit of Jesus did not allow them. 8 So they travelled right on through *x* Mysia and went to Troas. 9 That night Paul had a vision in which he saw a Macedonian standing and begging him, "Come over to Macedonia and help us!" 10 As soon as Paul had this vision, we got ready to leave for Macedonia, because we decided that God had called us to preach the Good News to the people there.

In Philippi: the Conversion of Lydia

11 We left by ship from Troas and sailed straight across to Samothrace, and the next day to Neapolis. 12 From there we went inland to Philippi, a city of the first district of Macedonia; *y* it is also a Roman colony. We spent several days there. 13 On the Sabbath we went out of the city to the river-side, where we thought there would be a place where Jews gathered for prayer. We sat down and talked to the women who gathered there. 14 One of those who heard us was Lydia from Thyatira, who was a dealer in purple cloth. She was a woman who worshipped God, and the Lord opened her mind to pay attention to what Paul was saying. 15 After she and the people of her house had been baptized, she invited us, "Come and stay in my house if you have decided that I am a true believer in the Lord." And she persuaded us to go.

In Prison at Philippi

16 One day as we were going to the place of prayer, we were met by a slave-girl who had an evil spirit that enabled her to predict the future. She earned a lot of money for her owners by telling fortunes. 17 She followed Paul and us, shouting, "These men are servants of the Most High God! They announce to you how you can be saved!" 18 She did this

for many days, until Paul became so upset that he turned round and said to the spirit, "In the name of Jesus Christ I order you to come out of her!" The spirit went out of her that very moment.

19 When her owners realized that their chance of making money was gone, they seized Paul and Silas and dragged them to the authorities in the public square. 20 They brought them before the Roman officials and said, "These men are Jews, and they are causing trouble in our city. 21 They are teaching customs that are against our law; we are Roman citizens, and we cannot accept these customs or practise them." 22 And the crowd joined in the attack against Paul and Silas.

Then the officials tore the clothes off Paul and Silas and ordered them to be whipped. 23 After a severe beating, they were thrown into jail, and the jailer was ordered to lock them up tight. 24 Upon receiving this order, the jailer threw them into the inner cell and fastened their feet between heavy blocks of wood.

25 About midnight Paul and Silas were praying and singing hymns to God, and the other prisoners were listening to them. 26 Suddenly there was a violent earthquake, which shook the prison to its foundations. At once all the doors opened, and the chains fell off all the prisoners. 27 The jailer woke up, and when he saw the prison doors open, he thought that the prisoners had escaped; so he pulled out his sword and was about to kill himself. 28 But Paul shouted at the top of his voice, "Don't harm yourself! We are all here!"

29 The jailer called for a light, rushed in, and fell trembling at the feet of Paul and Silas. 30 Then he led them out and asked, "Sirs, what must I do to be saved?"

31 They answered, "Believe in the Lord Jesus, and you will be saved—you and your family." 32 Then they preached the word of the Lord to him and to all the others in his house. 33 At that very hour of the night the jailer took them and washed their wounds; and he and all his family were baptized at once. 34 Then he took Paul and Silas up into his house and gave them some food to eat. He and his family were filled with joy, because they now believed in God.

35 The next morning the Roman

---

x travelled right on through; *or* passed by.
y a city of the first district of Macedonia; *some manuscripts have* a leading city of the district of Macedonia; *or* a leading city of that district in Macedonia.

Sirs, what must I do to be saved? (16.30)

authorities sent police officers with the order, "Let those men go."

36 So the jailer told Paul, "The officials have sent an order for you and Silas to be released. You may leave, then, and go in peace."

37 But Paul said to the police officers, "We were not found guilty of any crime, yet they whipped us in public—and we are Roman citizens! Then they threw us in prison. And now they want to send us away secretly. Not likely! The Roman officials themselves must come here and let us out."

38 The police officers reported these words to the Roman officials; and when they heard that Paul and Silas were Roman citizens, they were afraid. 39 So they went and apologized to them; then they led them out of the prison and asked them to leave the city. 40 Paul and Silas left the prison and went to Lydia's house. There they met the believers, spoke words of encouragement to them, and left.

In Thessalonica

17 Paul and Silas travelled on through Amphipolis and Apollonia and came to Thessalonica, where there was a synagogue. 2 According to his usual habit Paul went to the synagogue. There during three Sabbaths he held discussions with the people, quoting 3 and explaining the Scriptures and proving from them that the Messiah had to suffer and rise from death. "This Jesus whom I announce to you," Paul said, "is the Messiah." 4 Some of them were convinced and joined Paul and Silas; so did many of the leading women and a large group of Greeks who worshipped God.

5 But the Jews were jealous and gathered some of the worthless loafers from the streets and formed a mob. They set the whole city in an uproar and attacked the home of a man called Jason, in an attempt to find Paul and Silas and bring them out to the people. 6 But when they did not find them, they dragged Jason and some other believers before the city authorities and shouted, "These men have caused trouble everywhere! Now they have come to our city, 7 and Jason has kept them in his house. They are all breaking the laws of the Emperor, saying that there is another king, whose name is Jesus." 8 With these words they threw the crowd and the city authorities into an uproar. 9 The authorities made Jason and the others pay the required amount of money to be released, and then let them go.

In Berea

10 As soon as night came, the believers sent Paul and Silas to Berea. When they arrived, they went to the synagogue. [11] The people there were more open-minded than the people in Thessalonica. They listened to the message with great eagerness, and every day they studied the Scriptures to see if what Paul said was really true. [12] Many of them believed; and many Greek women of high social standing and many Greek men also believed. [13] But when the Jews in Thessalonica heard that Paul had preached the word of God in Berea also, they came there and started exciting and stirring up the mob. [14] At once the believers sent Paul away to the coast; but both Silas and Timothy stayed in Berea. [15] The men who were taking Paul went with him as far as Athens and then returned to Berea with instructions from Paul that Silas and Timothy should join him as soon as possible.

In Athens

16 While Paul was waiting in Athens for Silas and Timothy, he was greatly upset when he noticed how full of idols the city was. [17] So he held discussions in the synagogue with the Jews and with the Gentiles who worshipped God, and also in the public square every day with the people who happened to pass by. [18] Certain Epicurean and Stoic teachers also debated with him. Some of them asked, "What is this ignorant show-off trying to say?"

Others answered, "He seems to be talking about foreign gods." They said this because Paul was preaching about Jesus and the resurrection.[z] [19] So they took Paul, brought him before the city council, the Areopagus, and said, "We would like to know what this new teaching is that you are talking about. [20] Some of the things we hear you say sound strange to us, and we would like to know what they mean." [21] (For all the citizens of Athens and the foreigners who lived there liked to spend all their time telling and hearing the latest new thing.)

22 Paul stood up in front of the city council and said, "I see that in every way you Athenians are very religious. [23] For as I walked through your city and looked at the places where you worship, I found an altar on which is written, 'To an Unknown God'. That which you worship, then, even though you do not know it, is what I now proclaim to you. [24] God, who made the world and everything in it, is Lord of heaven and earth and does not live in man-made temples. [25] Nor does he need anything that we can supply by working for him, since it is he himself who gives life and breath and everything else to everyone. [26] From one man he created all races of mankind and made them live throughout the whole earth. He himself fixed beforehand the exact times and the limits of the places where they would live. [27] He did this so that they would look for him, and perhaps find him as they felt about for him. Yet God is actually not far from any one of us; [28] as someone has said,

'In him we live and move and exist.'
It is as some of your poets have said,

'We too are his children.'
[29] Since we are God's children, we should not suppose that his nature is anything like an image of gold or silver or stone, shaped by the art and skill of man. [30] God has overlooked the times when people did not know him, but now he commands all of them everywhere to turn away from their evil ways. [31] For he has fixed a day in which he will judge the whole world with justice by means of a man he has chosen. He has given proof of this to everyone by raising that man from death!"

32 When they heard Paul speak about a raising from death, some of them made fun of him, but others said, "We want to hear you speak about this again." [33] And so Paul left the meeting. [34] Some men joined him and believed, among whom was Dionysius, a member of the council; there was also a woman named Damaris, and some other people.

In Corinth

18 After this, Paul left Athens and went on to Corinth. [2] There he met a Jew named Aquila, born in Pontus, who had recently come from Italy with his wife Priscilla, for the Emperor Claudius had ordered all the Jews to leave Rome. Paul went to see them, [3] and stayed and worked with them, because he earned his living by making tents, just as they did. [4] He held discussions in the synagogue every

---

[z] JESUS AND THE RESURRECTION: *In Greek, the feminine noun "resurrection" could be understood to be the name of a goddess.*
17.24–25: 1 Kgs 8.27; Is 42.5; Acts 8.47

Sabbath, trying to convince both Jews and Greeks.

5 When Silas and Timothy arrived from Macedonia, Paul gave his whole time to preaching the message, testifying to the Jews that Jesus is the Messiah. 6 When they opposed him and said evil things about him, he protested by shaking the dust from his clothes and saying to them, "If you are lost, you yourselves must take the blame for it! I am not responsible. From now on I will go to the Gentiles." 7 So he left them and went to live in the house of a Gentile named Titius Justus, who worshipped God; his house was next to the synagogue. 8 Crispus, who was the leader of the synagogue, believed in the Lord, together with all his family; and many other people in Corinth heard the message, believed, and were baptized.

9 One night Paul had a vision in which the Lord said to him, "Do not be afraid, but keep on speaking and do not give up, 10 for I am with you. No one will be able to harm you, for many in this city are my people." 11 So Paul stayed there for a year and a half, teaching the people the word of God.

12 When Gallio was made the Roman governor of Achaia, the Jews got together, seized Paul, and took him into court. 13 "This man," they said, "is trying to persuade people to worship God in a way that is against the law!"

14 Paul was about to speak when Gallio said to the Jews, "If this were a matter of some evil crime or wrong that has been committed, it would be reasonable for me to be patient with you Jews. 15 But since it is an argument about words and names and your own law, you yourselves must settle it. I will not be the judge of such things!" 16 And he drove them out of the court. 17 They all seized Sosthenes, the leader of the synagogue, and beat him in front of the court. But that did not bother Gallio a bit.

The Return to Antioch

18 Paul stayed on with the believers in Corinth for many days, then left them and sailed off with Priscilla and Aquila for Syria. Before sailing from Cenchreae he had his head shaved because of a vow he had taken.[a] 19 They arrived in Ephesus, where Paul left Priscilla and Aquila. He went into the synagogue and held dis-

cussions with the Jews. 20 The people asked him to stay longer, but he would not consent. 21 Instead, he told them as he left, "If it is the will of God, I will come back to you." And so he sailed from Ephesus.

22 When he arrived at Caesarea, he went to Jerusalem and greeted the church, and then went to Antioch. 23 After spending some time there, he left and went through the region of Galatia and Phrygia, strengthening all the believers.

Apollos in Ephesus and Corinth

24 At that time a Jew named Apollos, who had been born in Alexandria, came to Ephesus. He was an eloquent speaker and had a thorough knowledge of the Scriptures. 25 He had been instructed in the Way of the Lord, and with great enthusiasm he proclaimed and taught correctly the facts about Jesus. However, he knew only the baptism of John. 26 He began to speak boldly in the synagogue. When Priscilla and Aquila heard him, they took him home with them and explained to him more correctly the Way of God. 27 Apollos then decided to go to Achaia, so the believers in Ephesus helped him by writing to the believers in Achaia, urging them to welcome him. When he arrived, he was a great help to those who through God's grace had become believers. 28 For with his strong arguments he defeated the Jews in public debates by proving from the Scriptures that Jesus is the Messiah.

Paul in Ephesus

19 While Apollos was in Corinth, Paul travelled through the interior of the province and arrived in Ephesus. There he found some disciples 2 and asked them, "Did you receive the Holy Spirit when you became believers?"

"We have not even heard that there is a Holy Spirit," they answered.

3 "Well, then, what kind of baptism did you receive?" Paul asked.

"The baptism of John," they answered.

4 Paul said, "The baptism of John was for those who turned from their sins; and he told the people of Israel to believe in the one who was coming after him—that is, in Jesus."

5 When they heard this, they were baptized in the name of the Lord Jesus.

---

[a] A VOW HE HAD TAKEN: *This refers to the Jewish custom of shaving the head as a sign that a vow has been kept.*
18.18: Num 6.18   **19.4:** Mt 3.11; Mk 1.4,7–8; Lk 3.4,16; Jn 1.26–27

[6] Paul placed his hands on them, and the Holy Spirit came upon them; they spoke in strange tongues and also proclaimed God's message. [7] They were about twelve men in all.

[8] Paul went into the synagogue and during three months spoke boldly with the people, holding discussions with them and trying to convince them about the Kingdom of God. [9] But some of them were stubborn and would not believe, and before the whole group they said evil things about the Way of the Lord. So Paul left them and took the believers with him, and every day [b] he held discussions in the lecture hall of Tyrannus. [10] This went on for two years, so that all the people who lived in the province of Asia, both Jews and Gentiles, heard the word of the Lord.

The Sons of Sceva

[11] God was performing unusual miracles through Paul. [12] Even handkerchiefs and aprons he had used were taken to those who were ill, and their diseases were driven away, and the evil spirits would go out of them. [13] Some Jews who travelled round and drove out evil spirits also tried to use the name of the Lord Jesus to do this. They said to the evil spirits, "I command you in the name of Jesus, whom Paul preaches." [14] Seven brothers, who were the sons of a Jewish High Priest named Sceva, were doing this.

[15] But the evil spirit said to them, "I know Jesus, and I know about Paul; but you—who are you?"

[16] The man who had the evil spirit in him attacked them with such violence that he overpowered them all. They ran away from his house, wounded and with their clothes torn off. [17] All the Jews and Gentiles who lived in Ephesus heard about this; they were all filled with fear, and the name of the Lord Jesus was given greater honour. [18] Many of the believers came, publicly admitting and revealing what they had done. [19] Many of those who had practised magic brought their books together and burnt them in public. They added up the price of the books, and the total came to fifty thousand silver coins. [c] [20] In this powerful way the word of the Lord [d] kept spreading and growing stronger.

The Riot in Ephesus

[21] After these things had happened, Paul made up his mind [e] to travel through Macedonia and Achaia and go on to Jerusalem. "After I go there," he said, "I must also see Rome." [22] So he sent Timothy and Erastus, two of his helpers, to Macedonia, while he spent more time in the province of Asia.

[23] It was at this time that there was serious trouble in Ephesus because of the Way of the Lord. [24] A certain silversmith named Demetrius made silver models of the temple of the goddess Artemis, and his business brought a great deal of profit to the workers. [25] So he called them all together with others whose work was like theirs and said to them, "Men, you know that our prosperity comes from this work. [26] Now, you can see and hear for yourselves what this fellow Paul is doing. He says that man-made gods are not gods at all, and he has succeeded in convincing many people, both here in Ephesus and in nearly the whole province of Asia. [27] There is the danger, then, that this business of ours will get a bad name. Not only that, but there is also the danger that the temple of the great goddess Artemis will come to mean nothing and that her greatness will be destroyed—the goddess worshipped by everyone in Asia and in all the world!"

[28] As the crowd heard these words, they became furious and started shouting, "Great is Artemis of Ephesus!" [29] The uproar spread throughout the whole city. The mob seized Gaius and Aristarchus, two Macedonians who were travelling with Paul, and rushed with them to the theatre. [30] Paul himself wanted to go before the crowd, but the believers would not let him. [31] Some of the provincial authorities, who were his friends, also sent him a message begging him not to show himself in the theatre. [32] Meanwhile the whole meeting was in an uproar: some people were shouting one thing, others were shouting something else, because most of them did not even know why they had come together. [33] Some of the people concluded that Alexander was responsible, since the Jews made him go up to the front. Then Alexander motioned with his hand for the people to be silent,

---

[b] Some manuscripts add from 11a.m. until 4p.m.
[c] SILVER COINS: A silver coin was the daily wage of a rural worker (see Mt. 20.2).
[d] In this...Lord; or And so, by the power of the Lord, the message.
[e] Paul made up his mind; or Paul, led by the Spirit, decided.

and he tried to make a speech of defence. ³⁴But when they recognized that he was a Jew, they all shouted together the same thing for two hours: "Great is Artemis of Ephesus!"

35 At last the town clerk was able to calm the crowd. "Fellow-Ephesians!" he said. "Everyone knows that the city of Ephesus is the keeper of the temple of the great Artemis and of the sacred stone that fell down from heaven. ³⁶Nobody can deny these things. So then, you must calm down and not do anything reckless. ³⁷You have brought these men here even though they have not robbed temples or said evil things about our goddess. ³⁸If Demetrius and his workers have an accusation against anyone, we have the authorities and the regular days for court; charges can be made there. ³⁹But if there is something more that you want, it will have to be settled in a legal meeting of citizens. ⁴⁰For after what has happened today, there is the danger that we will be accused of a riot. There is no excuse for all this uproar, and we would not be able to give a good reason for it." ⁴¹After saying this, he dismissed the meeting.

To Macedonia and Achaia

20 After the uproar died down, Paul called together the believers and with words of encouragement said good-bye to them. Then he left and went on to Macedonia. ²He went through those regions and encouraged the people with many messages. Then he came to Achaia, ³where he stayed three months. He was getting ready to go to Syria when he discovered that the Jews were plotting against him; so he decided to go back through Macedonia. ⁴Sopater son of Pyrrhus, from Berea, went with him; so did Aristarchus and Secundus, from Thessalonica; Gaius, from Derbe; Tychicus and Trophimus, from the province of Asia; and Timothy. ⁵They went ahead and waited for us in Troas. ⁶We sailed from Philippi after the Festival of Unleavened Bread, and five days later we joined them in Troas, where we spent a week.

Paul's Last Visit to Troas

7 On Saturdayᶠ evening we gathered together for the fellowship meal. Paul spoke to the people and kept on speaking until midnight, since he was going to leave the next day. ⁸Many lamps were burning in the upstairs room where we were meeting. ⁹A young man named Eutychus was sitting in the window, and as Paul kept on talking, Eutychus got sleepier and sleepier, until he finally went sound asleep and fell from the third storey to the ground. When they picked him up, he was dead. ¹⁰But Paul went down and threw himself on him and hugged him. "Don't worry," he said, "he is still alive!" ¹¹Then he went back upstairs, broke bread, and ate. After talking with them for a long time, even until sunrise, Paul left. ¹²They took the young man home alive and were greatly comforted.

From Troas to Miletus

13 We went on ahead to the ship and sailed off to Assos, where we were going to take Paul aboard. He had told us to do this, because he was going there by land. ¹⁴When he met us in Assos, we took him aboard and went on to Mitylene. ¹⁵We sailed from there and arrived off Chios the next day. A day later we came to Samos, and the following day we reached Miletus. ¹⁶Paul had decided to sail on past Ephesus, so as not to lose any time in the province of Asia. He was in a hurry to arrive in Jerusalem by the day of Pentecost, if at all possible.

Paul's Farewell Speech to the Elders of Ephesus

17 From Miletus Paul sent a message to Ephesus, asking the elders of the church to meet him. ¹⁸When they arrived, he said to them, "You know how I spent the whole time I was with you, from the first day I arrived in the province of Asia. ¹⁹With all humility and many tears I did my work as the Lord's servant during the hard times that came to me because of the plots of the Jews. ²⁰You know that I did not hold back anything that would be of help to you as I preached and taught in public and in your homes. ²¹To Jews and Gentiles alike I gave solemn warning that they should turn from their sins to God and believe in our Lord Jesus. ²²And now, in obedience to the Holy Spirit I am going to Jerusalem, not knowing what will happen to me there. ²³I only know that in every city the Holy Spirit has warned me that prison and troubles wait for me. ²⁴But I reckon my own life to be worth nothing to me; I only want to

ᶠ Saturday; or Sunday.
20.24: 2 Tim 4.7

complete my mission and finish the work that the Lord Jesus gave me to do, which is to declare the Good News about the grace of God.

25 "I have gone about among all of you, preaching the Kingdom of God. And now I know that none of you will ever see me again. 26 So I solemnly declare to you this very day: if any of you should be lost, I am not responsible. 27 For I have not held back from announcing to you the whole purpose of God. 28 So keep watch over yourselves and over all the flock which the Holy Spirit has placed in your care. Be shepherds of the church of God, g which he made his own through the sacrificial death of his Son. h 29 I know that after I leave, fierce wolves will come among you, and they will not spare the flock. 30 The time will come when some men from your own group will tell lies to lead the believers away after them. 31 Watch, then, and remember that with many tears, day and night, I taught every one of you for three years.

32 "And now I commend you to the care of God and to the message of his grace, which is able to build you up and give you the blessings God has for all his people. 33 I have not wanted anyone's silver or gold or clothing. 34 You yourselves know that I have worked with these hands of mine to provide everything that my companions and I have needed. 35 I have shown you in all things that by working hard in this way we must help the weak, remembering the words that the Lord Jesus himself said, 'There is more happiness in giving than in receiving.'"

36 When Paul finished, he knelt down with them and prayed. 37 They were all crying as they hugged him and kissed him good-bye. 38 They were especially sad because he had said that they would never see him again. And so they went with him to the ship.

Paul Goes to Jerusalem

21 We said good-bye to them and left. After sailing straight across, we came to Cos; the next day we reached Rhodes, and from there we went on to Patara. 2 There we found a ship that was going to Phoenicia, so we went aboard and sailed away. 3 We came to where we could see Cyprus, and then sailed south

of it on to Syria. We went ashore at Tyre, where the ship was going to unload its cargo. 4 There we found some believers and stayed with them a week. By the power of the Spirit they told Paul not to go to Jerusalem. 5 But when our time with them was over, we left and went on our way. All of them, together with their wives and children, went with us out of the city to the beach, where we all knelt and prayed. 6 Then we said good-bye to one another, and we went on board the ship while they went back home.

7 We continued our voyage, sailing from Tyre to Ptolemais, where we greeted the believers and stayed with them for a day. 8 On the following day we left and arrived in Caesarea. There we stayed at the house of Philip the evangelist, one of the seven men who had been chosen as helpers in Jerusalem. 9 He had four unmarried daughters who proclaimed God's message. 10 We had been there for several days when a prophet named Agabus arrived from Judaea. 11 He came to us, took Paul's belt, tied up his own feet and hands with it, and said, "This is what the Holy Spirit says: The owner of this belt will be tied up in this way by the Jews in Jerusalem, and they will hand him over to the Gentiles."

12 When we heard this, we and the others there begged Paul not to go to Jerusalem. 13 But he answered, "What are you doing, crying like this and breaking my heart? I am ready not only to be tied up in Jerusalem but even to die there for the sake of the Lord Jesus."

14 We could not convince him, so we gave up and said, "May the Lord's will be done."

15 After spending some time there, we got our things ready and left for Jerusalem. 16 Some of the disciples from Caesarea also went with us and took us to the house of the man we were going to stay with i —Mnason, from Cyprus, who had been a believer since the early days.

Paul Visits James

17 When we arrived in Jerusalem, the believers welcomed us warmly. 18 The next day Paul went with us to see James; and all the church elders were present. 19 Paul greeted them and gave a complete

g God; *some manuscripts have* the Lord.   h the sacrificial death of his Son; *or* his own death.
i and took us to the house of the man we were going to stay with; *or* bringing with them the man at whose house we were going to stay.
21.8: Acts 6.5, 8.5   **21.10:** Acts 11.28

report of everything that God had done among the Gentiles through his work. 20 After hearing him, they all praised God. Then they said, "Brother Paul, you can see how many thousands of Jews have become believers, and how devoted they all are to the Law. 21 They have been told that you have been teaching all the Jews who live in Gentile countries to abandon the Law of Moses, telling them not to circumcise their children or follow the Jewish customs. 22 They are sure to hear that you have arrived. What should be done, then? 23 This is what we want you to do. There are four men here who have taken a vow. 24 Go along with them and join them in the ceremony of purification and pay their expenses; then they will be able to shave their heads.ʲ In this way everyone will know that there is no truth in any of the things that they have been told about you, but that you yourself live in accordance with the Law of Moses. 25 But as for the Gentiles who have become believers, we have sent them a letter telling them we decided that they must not eat any food that has been offered to idols, or any blood, or any animal that has been strangled, and that they must keep themselves from sexual immorality."

26 So Paul took the men and the next day performed the ceremony of purification with them. Then he went into the Temple and gave notice of how many days it would be until the end of the period of purification, when a sacrifice would be offered for each one of them.

Paul Is Arrested in the Temple

27 But just when the seven days were about to come to an end, some Jews from the province of Asia saw Paul in the Temple. They stirred up the whole crowd and seized Paul. 28 "Men of Israel!" they shouted. "Help! This is the man who goes everywhere teaching everyone against the people of Israel, the Law of Moses, and this Temple. And now he has even brought some Gentiles into the Temple and defiled this holy place!" 29 (They said this because they had seen Trophimus from Ephesus with Paul in the city, and they thought that Paul had taken him into the Temple.)

30 Confusion spread through the whole city, and the people all ran together, seized Paul, and dragged him out of the Temple. At once the Temple doors were closed.

31 The mob was trying to kill Paul, when a report was sent up to the commander of the Roman troops that all Jerusalem was rioting. 32 At once the commander took some officers and soldiers and rushed down to the crowd. When the people saw him with the soldiers, they stopped beating Paul. 33 The commander went over to Paul, arrested him, and ordered him to be bound with two chains. Then he asked, "Who is this man, and what has he done?" 34 Some in the crowd shouted one thing, others something else. There was such confusion that the commander could not find out exactly what had happened, so he ordered his men to take Paul up into the fort. 35 They got as far as the steps with him, and then the soldiers had to carry him because the mob was so wild. 36 They were all coming after him and screaming, "Kill him!"

Paul Defends Himself

37 As the soldiers were about to take Paul into the fort, he spoke to the commander: "May I say something to you?"

"You speak Greek, do you?" the commander asked. 38 "Then you are not that Egyptian fellow who some time ago started a revolution and led four thousand armed terrorists out into the desert?"

39 Paul answered, "I am a Jew, born in Tarsus in Cilicia, a citizen of an important city. Please let me speak to the people."

40 The commander gave him permission, so Paul stood on the steps and motioned with his hand for the people to be silent. When they were quiet, Paul spoke to them in Hebrew:

22 "My fellow-Israelites, listen to me as I make my defence before you!" 2 When they heard him speaking to them in Hebrew, they became even quieter; and Paul went on:

3 "I am a Jew, born in Tarsus in Cilicia, but brought up here in Jerusalem as a student of Gamaliel. I received strict instruction in the Law of our ancestors and was just as dedicated to God as are all of you who are here today. 4 I persecuted to the death the people who followed this Way. I arrested men and women and threw them into prison. 5 The High Priest and the whole Council can prove that I am telling the truth. I received

---

ʲ SHAVE THEIR HEADS: See 18.18.
21.23-24: Num 6.13-21   **21.25:** Acts 15.29   **21.29:** Acts 20.4   **22.3:** Acts 5.34-39
22.4-5: Acts 8.3, 26.9-11

from them letters written to fellow-Jews in Damascus, so I went there to arrest these people and bring them back in chains to Jerusalem to be punished.

Paul Tells of His Conversion
(Acts 9.1-19; 26.12-18)

6 "As I was travelling and coming near Damascus, about midday a bright light from the sky flashed suddenly round me. 7 I fell to the ground and heard a voice saying to me, 'Saul, Saul! Why do you persecute me?' 8 'Who are you, Lord?' I asked. 'I am Jesus of Nazareth, whom you persecute,' he said to me. 9 The men with me saw the light, but did not hear the voice of the one who was speaking to me. 10 I asked, 'What shall I do, Lord?' and the Lord said to me, 'Get up and go into Damascus, and there you will be told everything that God has determined for you to do.' 11 I was blind because of the bright light, and so my companions took me by the hand and led me into Damascus.

12 "In that city was a man named Ananias, a religious man who obeyed our Law and was highly respected by all the Jews living there. 13 He came to me, stood by me, and said, 'Brother Saul, see again!' At that very moment I saw again and looked at him. 14 He said, 'The God of our ancestors has chosen you to know his will, to see his righteous Servant, and to hear him speaking with his own voice. 15 For you will be a witness for him to tell everyone what you have seen and heard. 16 And now, why wait any longer? Get up and be baptized and have your sins washed away by praying to him.'

Paul's Call to Preach to the Gentiles

17 "I went back to Jerusalem, and while I was praying in the Temple, I had a vision, 18 in which I saw the Lord, as he said to me, 'Hurry and leave Jerusalem quickly, because the people here will not accept your witness about me.' 19 'Lord,' I answered, 'they know very well that I went to the synagogues and arrested and beat those who believe in you. 20 And when your witness Stephen was put to death, I myself was there, approving of his murder and taking care of the cloaks of his murderers.' 21 'Go,' the Lord said to me, 'for I will send you far away to the Gentiles.'"

22 The people listened to Paul until he said this; but then they started shouting at the top of their voices, "Away with him! Kill him! He's not fit to live!" 23 They were screaming, waving their clothes, and throwing dust up in the air. 24 The Roman commander ordered his men to take Paul into the fort, and he told them to whip him in order to find out why the Jews were screaming like this against him. 25 But when they had tied him up to be whipped, Paul said to the officer standing there, "Is it lawful for you to whip a Roman citizen who hasn't even been tried for any crime?"

26 When the officer heard this, he went to the commander and asked him, "What are you doing? That man is a Roman citizen!"

27 So the commander went to Paul and asked him, "Tell me, are you a Roman citizen?"

"Yes," answered Paul.

28 The commander said, "I became one by paying a large amount of money."

"But I am one by birth," Paul answered.

29 At once the men who were going to question Paul drew back from him; and the commander was frightened when he realized that Paul was a Roman citizen and that he had put him in chains.

Paul before the Council

30 The commander wanted to find out for certain what the Jews were accusing Paul of; so the next day he had Paul's chains taken off and ordered the chief priests and the whole Council to meet. Then he took Paul and made him stand before them.

23 Paul looked straight at the Council and said, "My fellow-Israelites! My conscience is perfectly clear about the way in which I have lived before God to this very day." 2 The High Priest Ananias ordered those who were standing close to Paul to strike him on the mouth. 3 Paul said to him, "God will certainly strike you—you whitewashed wall! You sit there to judge me according to the Law, yet you break the Law by ordering them to strike me!"

4 The men close to Paul said to him, "You are insulting God's High Priest!"

5 Paul answered, "My fellow-Israelites, I did not know that he was the High Priest. The scripture says, 'You must not speak evil of the ruler of your people.'"

6 When Paul saw that some of the group were Sadducees and the others were Pharisees, he called out in the Council,

22.20: Acts 7.58 **23.3:** Mt 23.27-28 **23.5:** Ex 22.28 **23.6:** Acts 26.5; Phil 3.5

"Fellow-Israelites! I am a Pharisee, the son of Pharisees. I am on trial here because of the hope I have that the dead will rise to life!"

7 As soon as he said this, the Pharisees and Sadducees started to quarrel, and the group was divided. 8 (For the Sadducees say that people will not rise from death and that there are no angels or spirits; but the Pharisees believe in all three.) 9 The shouting became louder, and some of the teachers of the Law who belonged to the party of the Pharisees stood up and protested strongly: "We cannot find anything wrong with this man! Perhaps a spirit or an angel really did speak to him!"

10 The argument became so violent that the commander was afraid that Paul would be torn to pieces. So he ordered his soldiers to go down into the group, get Paul away from them, and take him into the fort.

11 That night the Lord stood by Paul and said, "Don't be afraid! You have given your witness for me here in Jerusalem, and you must also do the same in Rome."

The Plot against Paul's Life

12 The next morning some Jews met together and made a plan. They took a vow that they would not eat or drink anything until they had killed Paul. 13 There were more than forty who planned this together. 14 Then they went to the chief priests and elders and said, "We have taken a solemn vow together not to eat a thing until we have killed Paul. 15 Now then, you and the Council send word to the Roman commander to bring Paul down to you, pretending that you want to get more accurate information about him. But we will be ready to kill him before he ever gets here."

16 But the son of Paul's sister heard about the plot; so he went to the fort and told Paul. 17 Then Paul called one of the officers and said to him, "Take this young man to the commander; he has something to tell him." 18 The officer took him, led him to the commander, and said, "The prisoner Paul called me and asked me to bring this young man to you, because he has something to say to you."

19 The commander took him by the hand, led him off by himself, and asked him, "What have you got to tell me?"

20 He said, "The Jewish authorities have agreed to ask you tomorrow to take Paul down to the Council, pretending that the Council wants to get more accurate information about him. 21 But don't listen to them, because there are more than forty men who will be hiding and waiting for him. They have taken a vow not to eat or drink until they have killed him. They are now ready to do it and are waiting for your decision."

22 The commander said, "Don't tell anyone that you have reported this to me." And he sent the young man away.

Paul Is Sent to Governor Felix

23 Then the commander called two of his officers and said, "Get two hundred soldiers ready to go to Caesarea, together with seventy horsemen and two hundred spearmen, and be ready to leave by nine o'clock tonight. 24 Provide some horses for Paul to ride and get him safely through to the governor Felix." 25 Then the commander wrote a letter that went like this:

26 "Claudius Lysias to His Excellency, the governor Felix: Greetings. 27 The Jews seized this man and were about to kill him. I learnt that he was a Roman citizen, so I went with my soldiers and rescued him. 28 I wanted to know what they were accusing him of, so I took him down to their Council. 29 I found out that he had not done anything for which he deserved to die or be put in prison; the accusation against him had to do with questions about their own law. 30 And when I was informed that there was a plot against him, at once I decided to send him to you. I have told his accusers to make their charges against him before you."

31 The soldiers carried out their orders. They got Paul and took him that night as far as Antipatris. 32 The next day the foot-soldiers returned to the fort and left the horsemen to go on with him. 33 They took him to Caesarea, delivered the letter to the governor, and handed Paul over to him. 34 The governor read the letter and asked Paul what province he was from. When he found out that he was from Cilicia, 35 he said, "I will hear you when your accusers arrive." Then he gave orders for Paul to be kept under guard in the governor's headquarters.

23.8: Mt 22.23; Mk 12.18; Lk 20.27

Paul Is Accused by the Jews

24 Five days later the High Priest Ananias went to Caesarea with some elders and a lawyer named Tertullus. They appeared before Felix and made their charges against Paul. ²Then Paul was called in, and Tertullus began to make his accusation, as follows:

"Your Excellency! Your wise leadership has brought us a long period of peace, and many necessary reforms are being made for the good of our country. ³We welcome this everywhere and at all times, and we are deeply grateful to you. ⁴I do not want to take up too much of your time, however, so I beg you to be kind and listen to our brief account. ⁵We found this man to be a dangerous nuisance; he starts riots among the Jews all over the world and is a leader of the party of the Nazarenes. ⁶He also tried to defile the Temple, and we arrested him.*k* ⁸If you question this man, you yourself will be able to learn from him all the things that we are accusing him of." ⁹The Jews joined in the accusation and said that all this was true.

Paul's Defence before Felix

10 The governor then motioned to Paul to speak, and Paul said,

"I know that you have been a judge over this nation for many years, and so I am happy to defend myself before you. ¹¹As you can find out for yourself, it was no more than twelve days ago that I went to Jerusalem to worship. ¹²The Jews did not find me arguing with anyone in the Temple, nor did they find me stirring up the people, either in the synagogues or anywhere else in the city. ¹³Nor can they give you proof of the accusations they now bring against me. ¹⁴I do admit this to you: I worship the God of our ancestors by following that Way which they say is false. But I also believe in everything written in the Law of Moses and the books of the prophets. ¹⁵I have the same hope in God that these themselves have, namely, that all people, both the good and the bad, will rise from death. ¹⁶And so I do my best always to have a clear conscience before God and man.

17 "After being away from Jerusalem for several years, I went there to take some money to my own people and to offer sacrifices. ¹⁸It was while I was doing this that they found me in the Temple after I had completed the ceremony of purification. There was no crowd with me and no disorder. ¹⁹But some Jews from the province of Asia were there; they themselves ought to come before you and make their accusations if they have anything against me. ²⁰Or let these men here tell what crime they found me guilty of when I stood before the Council—²¹except for the one thing I called out when I stood before them: 'I am being tried by you today for believing that the dead will rise to life.'"

22 Then Felix, who was well informed about the Way, brought the hearing to a close. "When Lysias the commander arrives," he told them, "I will decide your case." ²³He ordered the officer in charge of Paul to keep him under guard, but to give him some freedom and allow his friends to provide for his needs.

Paul before Felix and Drusilla

24 After some days Felix came with his wife Drusilla, who was Jewish. He sent for Paul and listened to him as he talked about faith in Christ Jesus. ²⁵But as Paul went on discussing about goodness, self-control, and the coming Day of Judgement, Felix was afraid and said, "You may leave now. I will call you again when I get the chance." ²⁶At the same time he was hoping that Paul would give him some money; and for this reason he would often send for him and talk with him.

27 After two years had passed, Porcius Festus succeeded Felix as governor. Felix wanted to gain favour with the Jews so he left Paul in prison.

Paul Appeals to the Emperor

25 Three days after Festus arrived in the province, he went from Caesarea to Jerusalem, ²where the chief priests and the Jewish leaders brought their charges against Paul. They begged Festus ³to do them the favour of bringing Paul to Jerusalem, for they had made a plot to kill him on the way. ⁴Festus answered, "Paul is being kept a prisoner in Caesarea, and I myself will be going back there soon. ⁵Let your leaders go to Caesarea with me and accuse the man

---

k Some manuscripts add verses 6b–8a: We planned to judge him according to our own law, ⁷but Lysias the commander came, and with great violence took him from us. ⁸Then Lysias gave orders that his accusers should come before you.
24.17–18: Acts 21.17–28   **24.21:** Acts 23.6

if he has done anything wrong."

6 Festus spent another eight or ten days with them and then went to Caesarea. On the next day he sat down in the court of judgement and ordered Paul to be brought in. 7 When Paul arrived, the Jews who had come from Jerusalem stood round him and started making many serious charges against him, which they were not able to prove. 8 But Paul defended himself: "I have done nothing wrong against the Law of the Jews or against the Temple or against the Roman Emperor."

9 But Festus wanted to gain favour with the Jews, so he asked Paul, "Would you be willing to go to Jerusalem and be tried on these charges before me there?"

10 Paul said, "I am standing before the Emperor's own court of judgement, where I should be tried. I have done no wrong to the Jews, as you yourself well know. 11 If I have broken the law and done something for which I deserve the death penalty, I do not ask to escape it. But if there is no truth in the charges they bring against me, no one can hand me over to them. I appeal to the Emperor."

12 Then Festus, after conferring with his advisers, answered, "You have appealed to the Emperor, so to the Emperor you will go."

Paul before Agrippa and Bernice

13 Some time later King Agrippa and Bernice came to Caesarea to pay a visit of welcome to Festus. 14 After they had been there several days, Festus explained Paul's situation to the king: "There is a man here who was left a prisoner by Felix; 15 and when I went to Jerusalem, the Jewish chief priests and elders brought charges against him and asked me to condemn him. 16 But I told them that we Romans are not in the habit of handing over any man accused of a crime before he has met his accusers face to face and has had the chance of defending himself against the accusation. 17 When they came here, then, I lost no time, but on the very next day I sat in the court and ordered the man to be brought in. 18 His opponents stood up, but they did not accuse him of any of the evil crimes that I thought they would. 19 All they had were some arguments with him about their own religion and about a man named Jesus, who has died; but Paul claims that he is alive. 20 I was undecided about how I could get information on these matters, so I asked Paul if he would be willing to go to Jerusalem and be tried there on these charges. 21 But Paul appealed; he asked to be kept under guard and to let the Emperor decide his case. So I gave orders for him to be kept under guard until I could send him to the Emperor."

22 Agrippa said to Festus, "I would like to hear this man myself."

"You will hear him tomorrow," Festus answered.

23 The next day Agrippa and Bernice came with great pomp and ceremony and entered the audience hall with the military chiefs and the leading men of the city. Festus gave the order, and Paul was brought in. 24 Festus said, "King Agrippa and all who are here with us: You see this man against whom all the Jewish people, both here and in Jerusalem, have brought complaints to me. They scream that he should not live any longer. 25 But I could not find that he had done anything for which he deserved the death sentence. And since he himself made an appeal to the Emperor, I have decided to send him. 26 But I have nothing definite about him to write to the Emperor. So I have brought him here before you—and especially before you, King Agrippa!—so that, after investigating his case, I may have something to write. 27 For it seems unreasonable to me to send a prisoner without clearly indicating the charges against him."

Paul Defends Himself before Agrippa

26 Agrippa said to Paul, "You have permission to speak on your own behalf." Paul stretched out his hand and defended himself as follows:

2 "King Agrippa! I consider myself fortunate that today I am to defend myself before you from all the things the Jews accuse me of, 3 particularly since you know so well all the Jewish customs and disputes. I ask you, then, to listen to me with patience.

4 "All the Jews know how I have lived ever since I was young. They know how I have spent my whole life, at first in my own country and then in Jerusalem. 5 They have always known, if they are willing to testify, that from the very first I have lived as a member of the strictest party of our religion, the Pharisees. 6 And now I stand here to be tried because of the hope I have in the promise that God

26.5: Acts 23.6; Phil 3.5

PAUL'S
JOURNEY TO ROME

made to our ancestors—[7] the very thing that the twelve tribes of our people hope to receive, as they worship God day and night. And it is because of this hope, Your Majesty, that I am being accused by the Jews! [8] Why do you who are here find it impossible to believe that God raises the dead?

9 "I myself thought that I should do everything I could against the cause of Jesus of Nazareth. [10] That is what I did in Jerusalem. I received authority from the chief priests and put many of God's people in prison; and when they were sentenced to death, I also voted against them. [11] Many times I had them punished in the synagogues and tried to make them deny their faith. I was so furious with them that I even went to foreign cities to persecute them.

Paul Tells of His Conversion
(Acts 9.1-19; 22.6-16)

12 "It was for this purpose that I went to Damascus with authority and orders from the chief priests. [13] It was on the road at midday, Your Majesty, that I saw a light much brighter than the sun, coming from the sky and shining round me and the men travelling with me. [14] All of us fell to the ground, and I heard a voice say to me in Hebrew, 'Saul, Saul! Why are you persecuting me? You are hurting yourself by hitting back, like an ox kicking against its owner's stick.' [15] 'Who are you, Lord?' I asked. And the Lord answered, 'I am Jesus, whom you persecute. [16] But get up and stand on your feet. I have appeared to you to appoint you as my servant. You are to tell others what you have seen of me[1] today and what I will show you in the future. [17] I will rescue you from the people of Israel and from the Gentiles to whom I will send you. [18] You are to open their eyes and turn them from the darkness to the light and from the power of Satan to God, so that through their faith in me they will have their sins forgiven and receive their place among God's chosen people.'

Paul Tells of His Work

19 "And so, King Agrippa, I did not disobey the vision I had from heaven. [20] First in Damascus and in Jerusalem and then in all Judaea and among the Gentiles, I preached that they must repent of their sins and turn to God and do the things

that would show they had repented. [21] It was for this reason that the Jews seized me while I was in the Temple, and they tried to kill me. [22] But to this very day I have been helped by God, and so I stand here giving my witness to all, to small and great alike. What I say is the very same thing which the prophets and Moses said was going to happen: [23] that the Messiah must suffer and be the first one to rise from death, to announce the light of salvation to the Jews and to the Gentiles."

24 As Paul defended himself in this way, Festus shouted at him, "You are mad, Paul! Your great learning is driving you mad!"

25 Paul answered, "I am not mad, Your Excellency! I am speaking the sober truth. [26] King Agrippa! I can speak to you with all boldness, because you know about these things. I am sure that you have taken notice of every one of them, for this thing has not happened hidden away in a corner. [27] King Agrippa, do you believe the prophets? I know that you do!"

28 Agrippa said to Paul, "In this short time do you think you will make me a Christian?"

29 "Whether a short time or a long time," Paul answered, "my prayer to God is that you and all the rest of you who are listening to me today might become what I am—except, of course, for these chains!"

30 Then the king, the governor, Bernice, and all the others got up, [31] and after leaving they said to each other, "This man has not done anything for which he should die or be put in prison." [32] And Agrippa said to Festus, "This man could have been released if he had not appealed to the Emperor."

Paul Sails for Rome

27 When it was decided that we should sail to Italy, they handed Paul and some other prisoners over to Julius, an officer in the Roman regiment called "The Emperor's Regiment." [2] We went aboard a ship from Adramyttium, which was ready to leave for the seaports of the province of Asia, and we sailed away. Aristarchus, a Macedonian from Thessalonica, was with us. [3] The next day we arrived at Sidon. Julius was kind to Paul and allowed him to go and see his friends, to be given what he needed. [4] We

[1] *Some manuscripts do not have of me.*
26.9-11: Acts 8.3, 22.4-5   **26.20:** Acts 9.20,28-29   **26.23:** Is 42.6, 49.6; 1 Cor 15.20

went on from there, and because the winds were blowing against us, we sailed on the sheltered side of the island of Cyprus. [5] We crossed over the sea off Cilicia and Pamphylia and came to Myra in Lycia. [6] There the officer found a ship from Alexandria that was going to sail for Italy, so he put us aboard.

7 We sailed slowly for several days and with great difficulty finally arrived off the town of Cnidus. The wind would not let us go any further in that direction, so we sailed down the sheltered side of the island of Crete, passing by Cape Salmone. [8] We kept close to the coast and with great difficulty came to a place called Safe Harbours, not far from the town of Lasea.

9 We spent a long time there, until it became dangerous to continue the voyage, for by now the Day of Atonement[m] was already past. So Paul gave them this advice: [10] "Men, I see that our voyage from here on will be dangerous; there will be great damage to the cargo and to the ship, and loss of life as well." [11] But the army officer was convinced by what the captain and the owner of the ship said, and not by what Paul said. [12] The harbour was not a good one to spend the winter in; so most of the men were in favour of putting out to sea and trying to reach Phoenix, if possible, in order to spend the winter there. Phoenix is a harbour in Crete that faces south-west and north-west.[n]

The Storm at Sea

13 A soft wind from the south began to blow, and the men thought that they could carry out their plan, so they pulled up the anchor and sailed as close as possible along the coast of Crete. [14] But soon a very strong wind—the one called "North-easter"—blew down from the island. [15] It hit the ship, and since it was impossible to keep the ship headed into the wind, we gave up trying and let it be carried along by the wind. [16] We got some shelter when we passed to the south of the little island of Cauda. There, with some difficulty, we managed to make the ship's boat secure. [17] They pulled it aboard and then fastened some ropes tight round the ship. They were afraid that they might run into the sandbanks off the coast of Libya, so they lowered the sail and let the ship be carried by the wind. [18] The violent

storm continued, so on the next day they began to throw some of the ship's cargo overboard, [19] and on the following day they threw part of the ship's equipment overboard. [20] For many days we could not see the sun or the stars, and the wind kept on blowing very hard. We finally gave up all hope of being saved.

21 After the men had gone a long time without food, Paul stood before them and said, "Men, you should have listened to me and not have sailed from Crete; then we would have avoided all this damage and loss. [22] But now I beg you, take heart! Not one of you will lose his life; only the ship will be lost. [23] For last night an angel of the God to whom I belong and whom I worship came to me [24] and said, 'Don't be afraid, Paul! You must stand before the Emperor. And God in his goodness to you has spared the lives of all those who are sailing with you.' [25] So take heart, men! For I trust in God that it will be just as I was told. [26] But we will be driven ashore on some island."

27 It was the fourteenth night, and we were being driven about in the Mediterranean by the storm. About midnight the sailors suspected that we were getting close to land. [28] So they dropped a line with a weight tied to it and found that the water was forty metres deep; a little later they did the same and found that it was thirty metres deep. [29] They were afraid that the ship would go on the rocks, so they lowered four anchors from the back of the ship and prayed for daylight. [30] Then the sailors tried to escape from the ship; they lowered the boat into the water and pretended that they were going to put out some anchors from the front of the ship. [31] But Paul said to the army officer and soldiers, "If the sailors don't stay on board, you have no hope of being saved." [32] So the soldiers cut the ropes that held the boat and let it go.

33 Just before dawn, Paul begged them all to eat some food: "You have been waiting for fourteen days now, and all this time you have not eaten anything. [34] I beg you, then, eat some food; you need it in order to survive. Not even a hair of your heads will be lost." [35] After saying this, Paul took some bread, gave thanks to God before them all, broke it, and began to eat. [36] They took heart, and

---

[m] DAY OF ATONEMENT: *This was celebrated towards the end of September or beginning of October, at which time bad weather made sailing dangerous.*

[n] south-west and north-west; *or* north-east and south-east.

But the ship hit a sandbank (27.41)

every one of them also ate some food. ³⁷ There was a total of 276ᵖ of us on board. ³⁸ After everyone had eaten enough, they lightened the ship by throwing all the wheat into the sea.

The Shipwreck

39 When day came, the sailors did not recognize the coast, but they noticed a bay with a beach and decided that, if possible, they would run the ship aground there. ⁴⁰ So they cut off the anchors and let them sink in the sea, and at the same time they untied the ropes that held the steering oars. Then they raised the sail at the front of the ship so that the wind would blow the ship forward, and we headed for shore. ⁴¹ But the ship hit a sandbank and went aground; the front part of the ship got stuck and could not move, while the back part was being broken to pieces by the violence of the waves.

42 The soldiers made a plan to kill all the prisoners, in order to keep them from swimming ashore and escaping. ⁴³ But the army officer wanted to save Paul, so he stopped them from doing this. Instead, he ordered all the men who could swim to jump overboard first and swim ashore; ⁴⁴ the rest were to follow, holding on to the planks or to some broken pieces of the ship. And this was how we all got safely ashore.

In Malta

28 When we were safely ashore, we learnt that the island was called Malta. ² The natives there were very friendly to us. It had started to rain and was cold, so they lit a fire and made us all welcome. ³ Paul gathered up a bundle of sticks and was putting them on the fire when a snake came out on account of the heat and fastened itself to his hand. ⁴ The natives saw the snake hanging on Paul's hand and said to one another, "This man must be a murderer, but Fate will not let him live, even though he escaped from the sea." ⁵ But Paul shook the snake off into the fire without being harmed at all. ⁶ They were waiting for him to swell up or suddenly fall down dead. But after waiting for a long time and not seeing anything unusual happening to him, they changed their minds and said, "He is a god!"

7 Not far from that place were some fields that belonged to Publius, the chief official of the island. He welcomed us kindly and for three days we were his guests. ⁸ Publius' father was in bed, sick

ᵖ276; *some manuscripts have* 275; *others have* about 76.

with fever and dysentery. Paul went into his room, prayed, placed his hands on him, and healed him. ⁹When this happened, all the other sick people on the island came and were healed. ¹⁰They gave us many gifts, and when we sailed, they put on board what we needed for the voyage.

From Malta to Rome

11 After three months we sailed away on a ship from Alexandria, called "The Twin Gods," which had spent the winter in the island. ¹²We arrived in the city of Syracuse and stayed there for three days. ¹³From there we sailed on and arrived in the city of Rhegium. The next day a wind began to blow from the south, and in two days we came to the town of Puteoli. ¹⁴We found some believers there who asked us to stay with them a week. And so we came to Rome. ¹⁵The believers in Rome heard about us and came as far as the towns of Market of Appius and Three Inns to meet us. When Paul saw them, he thanked God and was greatly encouraged.

In Rome

16 When we arrived in Rome, Paul was allowed to live by himself with a soldier guarding him.

17 After three days Paul called the local Jewish leaders to a meeting. When they had gathered, he said to them, "My fellow-Israelites, even though I did nothing against our people or the customs that we received from our ancestors, I was made a prisoner in Jerusalem and handed over to the Romans. ¹⁸After questioning me, the Romans wanted to release me, because they found that I had done nothing for which I deserved to die. ¹⁹But when the Jews opposed this, I was forced to appeal to the Emperor, even though I had no accusation to make against my own people. ²⁰That is why I asked to see you and talk with you. As a matter of

fact, I am bound in chains like this for the sake of him for whom the people of Israel hope."

21 They said to him, "We have not received any letters from Judaea about you, nor have any of our people come from there with any news or anything bad to say about you. ²²But we would like to hear your ideas, because we know that everywhere people speak against this party to which you belong."

23 So they fixed a date with Paul, and a large number of them came that day to the place where Paul was staying. From morning till night he explained to them his message about the Kingdom of God, and he tried to convince them about Jesus by quoting from the Law of Moses and the writings of the prophets. ²⁴Some of them were convinced by his words, but others would not believe. ²⁵So they left, disagreeing among themselves, after Paul had said this one thing: "How well the Holy Spirit spoke through the prophet Isaiah to your ancestors! ²⁶For he said,

'Go and say to this people:
You will listen and listen, but not
　understand;
you will look and look, but not see,
²⁷because this people's minds are dull,
　and they have stopped up their ears
　and closed their eyes.
Otherwise, their eyes would see,
　their ears would hear,
　their minds would understand,
and they would turn to me, says God,
　and I would heal them.' "

28 And Paul concluded: "You are to know, then, that God's message of salvation has been sent to the Gentiles. They will listen!"�q

30 For two years Paul lived in a place he rented for himself, and there he welcomed all who came to see him. ³¹He preached about the Kingdom of God and taught about the Lord Jesus Christ, speaking with all boldness and freedom.

�q*Some manuscripts add verse 29:* After Paul said this, the Jews left, arguing violently among themselves.
28.19: Acts 25.11　　**28.26–27:** Is 6.9–10

PAUL'S LETTER TO THE

ROMANS

INTRODUCTION

Paul's Letter to the Romans was written to prepare the way for a visit Paul planned to make to the church at Rome. His plan was to work among the Christians there for a while and then, with their support, to go on to Spain. He wrote to explain his understanding of the Christian faith and its practical implications for the lives of Christians. The book contains Paul's most complete statement of his message.

After greeting the people of the church at Rome and telling them of his prayers for them, Paul states the theme of the letter: "The gospel reveals how God puts people right with himself: it is through faith from beginning to end" (1.17).

Paul then develops this theme. All mankind, both Jews and Gentiles, needs to be put right with God, for all alike are under the power of sin. People are put right with God through faith in Jesus Christ. Next Paul describes the new life in union with Christ that results from this new relation with God. The believer has peace with God and is set free by God's Spirit from the power of sin and death. In chapters 5—8 Paul also discusses the purpose of the Law of God and the power of God's Spirit in the believer's life. Then the apostle wrestles with the question of how Jews and Gentiles fit into the plan of God for mankind. He concludes that the Jewish rejection of Jesus is part of God's plan for bringing all mankind within the reach of God's grace in Jesus Christ, and he believes that the Jews will not always reject Jesus. Finally Paul writes about how the Christian life should be lived, especially about the way of love in relations with others. He takes up such themes as service to God, the duty of Christians to the state and to one another, and questions of conscience. He ends the letter with personal messages and with words of praise to God.

Outline of Contents

Introduction and theme   1.1–17
Man's need of salvation   1.18—3.20
God's way of salvation   3.21—4.25
The new life in Christ   5.1—8.39
Israel in the plan of God   9.1—11.36
Christian conduct   12.1—15.13
Conclusion and personal greetings   15.14—16.27

1 From Paul, a servant of Christ Jesus and an apostle chosen and called by God to preach his Good News.

2 The Good News was promised long ago by God through his prophets, as written in the Holy Scriptures. ³ It is about his Son, our Lord Jesus Christ: as to his humanity, he was born a descendant of David; ⁴ as to his divine holiness, he was shown with great power to be the Son of God by being raised from death. ⁵ Through him God gave me the privilege of being an apostle for the sake of Christ, in order to lead people of all nations to believe and obey. ⁶ This also includes you who are in Rome, whom God has called to belong to Jesus Christ.

7 And so I write to all of you in Rome whom God loves and has called to be his own people:

May God our Father and the Lord Jesus Christ give you grace and peace.

Prayer of Thanksgiving

8 First, I thank my God through Jesus Christ for all of you, because the whole world is hearing about your faith. ⁹ God is my witness that what I say is true—the God whom I serve with all my heart by preaching the Good News about his Son. God knows that I remember you ¹⁰ every time I pray. I ask that God in his good will may at last make it possible for me to visit you now. ¹¹ For I want very much to see you, in order to share a spiritual blessing with you to make you strong. ¹² What I mean is that both you and I will be helped at the same time, you by my faith and I by yours.

13 You must remember, my brothers, that many times I have planned to visit you, but something has always kept me from doing so. I want to win converts among you also, as I have among other Gentiles. ¹⁴ For I have an obligation to all peoples, to the civilized and to the savage, to the educated and to the ignorant. ¹⁵ So then, I am eager to preach the Good News to you also who live in Rome.

The Power of the Gospel

16 I have complete confidence in the gospel; it is God's power to save all who believe, first the Jews and also the Gentiles. ¹⁷ For the gospel reveals how God puts people right with himself: it is through faith from beginning to end. As

the scripture says, "The person who is put right with God through faith shall live." ᵃ

The Guilt of Mankind

18 God's anger is revealed from heaven against all the sin and evil of the people whose evil ways prevent the truth from being known. ¹⁹ God punishes them, because what can be known about God is plain to them, for God himself made it plain. ²⁰ Ever since God created the world, his invisible qualities, both his eternal power and his divine nature, have been clearly seen; they are perceived in the things that God has made. So those people have no excuse at all! ²¹ They know God, but they do not give him the honour that belongs to him, nor do they thank him. Instead, their thoughts have become complete nonsense, and their empty minds are filled with darkness. ²² They say they are wise, but they are fools; ²³ instead of worshipping the immortal God, they worship images made to look like mortal man or birds or animals or reptiles.

24 And so God has given those people over to do the filthy things their hearts desire, and they do shameful things with each other. ²⁵ They exchange the truth about God for a lie; they worship and serve what God has created instead of the Creator himself, who is to be praised for ever! Amen.

26 Because they do this, God has given them over to shameful passions. Even the women pervert the natural use of their sex by unnatural acts. ²⁷ In the same way the men give up natural sexual relations with women and burn with passion for each other. Men do shameful things with each other, and as a result they bring upon themselves the punishment they deserve for their wrongdoing.

28 Because those people refuse to keep in mind the true knowledge about God, he has given them over to corrupted minds, so that they do the things that they should not do. ²⁹ They are filled with all kinds of wickedness, evil, greed, and vice; they are full of jealousy, murder, fighting, deceit, and malice. They gossip ³⁰ and speak evil of one another; they are hateful to God, insolent, ᵇ proud, and boastful; they think of more ways to do evil; they disobey their parents; ³¹ they have no conscience; they do not keep their

ᵃ put right with God through faith shall live; *or* put right with God shall live through faith.
ᵇ are hateful to God, insolent; *or* hate God, and are insolent.
1.13: Acts 19.21　**1.16:** Mk 8.38　**1.17:** Hab 2.4　**1.21:** Eph 4.17–18　**1.23:** Deut 4.16–18

Instead of worshipping...God, they worship images (1.23)

promises, and they show no kindness or pity for others. [32] They know that God's law says that people who live in this way deserve death. Yet, not only do they continue to do these very things, but they even approve of others who do them.

God's Judgement

2 Do you, my friend, pass judgement on others? You have no excuse at all, whoever you are. For when you judge others and then do the same things which they do, you condemn yourself. [2] We know that God is right when he judges the people who do such things as these. [3] But you, my friend, do those very things for which you pass judgement on others! Do you think you will escape God's judgement? [4] Or perhaps you despise his great kindness, tolerance, and patience. Surely you know that God is kind, because he is trying to lead you to repent. [5] But you have a hard and stubborn heart, and so you are making your own punishment even greater on the Day when God's anger and righteous judgements will be revealed. [6] For God will reward every person according to what he has done. [7] Some people keep on doing good, and seek glory, honour, and immortal life; to them God will give eternal life. [8] Other people are selfish and reject what is right, in order to follow what is wrong; on them God will pour out his anger and fury. [9] There will be suffering and pain for all those who do what is evil, for the Jews first and also for the Gentiles. [10] But God will give glory, honour, and peace to all who do what is good, to the Jews first and also to the Gentiles. [11] For God judges everyone by the same standard.

12 The Gentiles do not have the Law of Moses; they sin and are lost apart from the Law. The Jews have the Law; they sin and are judged by the Law. [13] For it is not by hearing the Law that people are put right with God, but by doing what the Law commands. [14] The Gentiles do not have the Law; but whenever they do by instinct what the Law commands, they are their own law, even though they do not have the Law. [15] Their conduct shows that what the Law commands is written in their hearts. Their consciences also show that this is true, since their thoughts sometimes accuse them and sometimes defend them. [16] And so, according to the Good News I preach, this is how it will be on that Day when God through Jesus Christ will judge the secret thoughts of all.

The Jews and the Law

17 What about you? You call yourself a Jew; you depend on the Law and boast about God; [18] you know what God wants you to do, and you have learnt from the Law to choose what is right; [19] you are sure that you are a guide for the blind, a light for those who are in darkness, [20] an instructor for the foolish, and a teacher for the ignorant. You are certain that in the Law you have the full content of knowledge and of truth. [21] You teach

2.1: Mt 7.1; Lk 6.37   **2.6:** Ps 62.12; Prov 24.12   **2.11:** Deut 10.17

others—why don't you teach yourself? You preach, "Do not steal"—but do you yourself steal? 22 You say, "Do not commit adultery"—but do you commit adultery? You detest idols—but do you rob temples? 23 You boast about having God's law—but do you bring shame on God by breaking his law? 24 The scripture says, "Because of you Jews, the Gentiles speak evil of God."

25 If you obey the Law, your circumcision is of value; but if you disobey the Law, you might as well never have been circumcised. 26 If the Gentile, who is not circumcised, obeys the commands of the Law, will God not regard him as though he were circumcised? 27 And so you Jews will be condemned by the Gentiles because you break the Law, even though you have it written down and are circumcised; but they obey the Law, even though they are not physically circumcised. 28 After all, who is a real Jew, truly circumcised? It is not the man who is a Jew on the outside, whose circumcision is a physical thing. 29 Rather, the real Jew is the person who is a Jew on the inside, that is, whose heart has been circumcised, and this is the work of God's Spirit, not of the written Law. Such a person receives his praise from God, not from man.

3 Have the Jews then any advantage over the Gentiles? Or is there any value in being circumcised? 2 Much, indeed, in every way! In the first place, God trusted his message to the Jews. 3 But what if some of them were not faithful? Does this mean that God will not be faithful? 4 Certainly not! God must be true, even though every man is a liar. As the scripture says,

"You must be shown to be right when you speak;
    you must win your case when you are being tried."

5 But what if our doing wrong serves to show up more clearly God's doing right? Can we say that God does wrong when he punishes us? (This would be the natural question to ask.) 6 By no means! If God is not just, how can he judge the world?

7 But what if my untruth serves God's glory by making his truth stand out more clearly? Why should I still be condemned

as a sinner? 8 Why not say, then, "Let us do evil so that good may come"? Some people, indeed, have insulted me by accusing me of saying this very thing! They will be condemned, as they should be.

No One Is Righteous

9 Well then, are we Jews in any better condition than the Gentiles? Not at all!c I have already shown that Jews and Gentiles alike are all under the power of sin. 10 As the Scriptures say:

"There is no one who is righteous,
11   no one who is wise
    or who worships God.
12 All have turned away from God;
    they have all gone wrong;
    no one does what is right, not even one.
13 Their words are full of deadly deceit;
    wicked lies roll off their tongues,
    and dangerous threats, like snake's poison, from their lips;
14   their speech is filled with bitter curses.
15 They are quick to hurt and kill;
16   they leave ruin and destruction wherever they go.
17 They have not known the path of peace,
18   nor have they learnt reverence for God."

19 Now we know that everything in the Law applies to those who live under the Law, in order to stop all human excuses and bring the whole world under God's judgement. 20 For no one is put right in God's sight by doing what the Law requires; what the Law does is to make man know that he has sinned.

How God Puts Us Right with Him

21 But now God's way of putting people right with himself has been revealed. It has nothing to do with law, even though the Law of Moses and the prophets gave their witness to it. 22 God puts people right through their faith in Jesus Christ. God does this to all who believe in Christ, because there is no difference at all: 23 everyone has sinned and is far away from God's saving presence. 24 But by the free gift of God's grace all are put right with him through Christ Jesus, who sets them free. 25-26 God offered him, so that

c any better condition than the Gentiles? Not at all!; *or* any worse condition than the Gentiles? Not altogether.

2.24: Is 52.5   **2.29:** Deut 30.6   **3.4:** Ps 51.4   **3.10–12:** Ps 14.1–3, 53.1–3
3.13: Ps 5.9, 140.3   **3.14:** Ps 10.7   **3.15–17:** Is 59.7–8   **3.18:** Ps 36.1
3.20: Ps 143.2; Gal 2.16   **3.22:** Gal 2.16

by his sacrificial death he should become the means by which people's sins are forgiven through their faith in him. God did this in order to demonstrate that he is righteous. In the past he was patient and overlooked people's sins; but in the present time he deals with their sins, in order to demonstrate his righteousness. In this way God shows that he himself is righteous and that he puts right everyone who believes in Jesus.

27 What, then, can we boast about? Nothing! And what is the reason for this? Is it that we obey the Law? No, but that we believe. 28 For we conclude that a person is put right with God only through faith, and not by doing what the Law commands. 29 Or is God the God of the Jews only? Is he not the God of the Gentiles also? Of course he is. 30 God is one, and he will put the Jews right with himself on the basis of their faith, and will put the Gentiles right through their faith. 31 Does this mean that by this faith we do away with the Law? No, not at all; instead, we uphold the Law.

The Example of Abraham

4 What shall we say, then, of Abraham, the father of our race? What was his experience? 2 If he was put right with God by the things he did, he would have something to boast about—but not in God's sight. 3 The scripture says, "Abraham believed God, and because of his faith God accepted him as righteous." 4 A person who works is paid his wages, but they are not regarded as a gift; they are something that he has earned. 5 But the person who depends on his faith, not on his deeds, and who believes in the God who declares the guilty to be innocent, it is his faith that God takes into account in order to put him right with himself. 6 This is what David meant when he spoke of the happiness of the person whom God accepts as righteous, apart from anything that person does:

7 "Happy are those whose wrongs are forgiven,
 whose sins are pardoned!
8 Happy is the person whose sins the Lord will not keep account of!"

9 Does this happiness that David spoke of belong only to those who are circumcised? No indeed! It belongs also to those who are not circumcised. For we have

quoted the scripture, "Abraham believed God, and because of his faith God accepted him as righteous." 10 When did this take place? Was it before or after Abraham was circumcised? It was before, not after. 11 He was circumcised later, and his circumcision was a sign to show that because of his faith God had accepted him as righteous before he had been circumcised. And so Abraham is the spiritual father of all who believe in God and are accepted as righteous by him, even though they are not circumcised. 12 He is also the father of those who are circumcised, that is, of those who, in addition to being circumcised, also live the same life of faith that our father Abraham lived before he was circumcised.

God's Promise Is Received through Faith

13 When God promised Abraham and his descendants that the world would belong to him, he did so, not because Abraham obeyed the Law, but because he believed and was accepted as righteous by God. 14 For if what God promises is to be given to those who obey the Law, then man's faith means nothing and God's promise is worthless. 15 The Law brings down God's anger; but where there is no law, there is no disobeying of the law.

16 And so the promise is based on faith, in order that the promise should be guaranteed as God's free gift to all of Abraham's descendants—not just to those who obey the Law, but also to those who believe as Abraham did. For Abraham is the spiritual father of us all; 17 as the scripture says, "I have made you father of many nations." So the promise is good in the sight of God, in whom Abraham believed—the God who brings the dead to life and whose command brings into being what did not exist. 18 Abraham believed and hoped, even when there was no reason for hoping, and so became "the father of many nations." Just as the scripture says, "Your descendants will be as many as the stars." 19 He was then almost one hundred years old; but his faith did not weaken when he thought of his body, which was already practically dead, or of the fact that Sarah could not have children. 20 His faith did not leave him, and he did not doubt God's promise; his faith filled him with power, and he gave praise to God. 21 He was

3.30: Deut 6.4; Gal 3.20   **4.3:** Gen 15.6; Gal 3.6   **4.7-8:** Ps 32.1-2   **4.11:** Gen 17.10
4.13: Gen 17.4-6, 22.17-18; Gal 3.29   **4.14:** Gal 3.18   **4.16:** Gal 3.7   **4.17:** Gen 17.5
4.18: Gen 15.5   **4.19:** Gen 17.17

absolutely sure that God would be able to do what he had promised. ²²That is why Abraham, through faith, "was accepted as righteous by God." ²³The words "he was accepted as righteous" were not written for him alone. ²⁴They were written also for us who are to be accepted as righteous, who believe in him who raised Jesus our Lord from death. ²⁵Because of our sins he was handed over to die, and he was raised to life in order to put us right with God.

Right with God

5 Now that we have been put right with God through faith, we have[d] peace with God through our Lord Jesus Christ. ²He has brought us by faith into this experience of God's grace, in which we now live. And so we boast[e] of the hope we have of sharing God's glory! ³We also boast[f] of our troubles, because we know that trouble produces endurance, ⁴endurance brings God's approval, and his approval creates hope. ⁵This hope does not disappoint us, for God has poured out his love into our hearts by means of the Holy Spirit, who is God's gift to us.

6 For when we were still helpless, Christ died for the wicked at the time that God chose. ⁷It is a difficult thing for someone to die for a righteous person. It may even be that someone might dare to die for a good person. ⁸But God has shown us how much he loves us—it was while we were still sinners that Christ died for us! ⁹By his sacrificial death we are now put right with God; how much more, then, will we be saved by him from God's anger! ¹⁰We were God's enemies, but he made us his friends through the death of his Son. Now that we are God's friends, how much more will we be saved by Christ's life! ¹¹But that is not all; we rejoice because of what God has done through our Lord Jesus Christ, who has now made us God's friends.

Adam and Christ

12 Sin came into the world through one man, and his sin brought death with it. As a result, death has spread to the whole human race because everyone has sinned. ¹³There was sin in the world before the Law was given; but where there is no law, no account is kept of sins. ¹⁴But from the time of Adam to the time of Moses death ruled over all mankind, even over those who did not sin in the same way that Adam did when he disobeyed God's command.

Adam was a figure of the one who was to come. ¹⁵But the two are not the same, because God's free gift is not like Adam's sin. It is true that many people died because of the sin of that one man. But God's grace is much greater, and so is his free gift to so many people through the grace of the one man, Jesus Christ. ¹⁶And there is a difference between God's gift and the sin of one man. After the one sin, came the judgement of "Guilty"; but after so many sins, comes the undeserved gift of "Not guilty!" ¹⁷It is true that through the sin of one man death began to rule because of that one man. But how much greater is the result of what was done by the one man, Jesus Christ! All who receive God's abundant grace and are freely put right with him will rule in life through Christ.

18 So then, as the one sin condemned all mankind, in the same way the one righteous act sets all mankind free and gives them life. ¹⁹And just as all people were made sinners as the result of the disobedience of one man, in the same way they will all be put right with God as the result of the obedience of the one man.

20 Law was introduced in order to increase wrongdoing; but where sin increased, God's grace increased much more. ²¹So then, just as sin ruled by means of death, so also God's grace rules by means of righteousness, leading us to eternal life through Jesus Christ our Lord.

Dead to Sin but Alive in Union with Christ

6 What shall we say, then? Should we continue to live in sin so that God's grace will increase? ²Certainly not! We have died to sin—how then can we go on living in it? ³For surely you know that when we were baptized into union with Christ Jesus, we were baptized into union with his death. ⁴By our baptism, then, we were buried with him and shared his death, in order that, just as Christ was raised from death by the glorious power of the Father, so also we might live a new life.

5 For since we have become one with him in dying as he did, in the same way

---

[d] we have; *some manuscripts have* let us have.
[f] We also boast; *or* Let us also boast.
4.25: Is 53.4–5   **5.12:** Gen 3.6   **6.4:** Col 2.12

[e] we boast; *or* let us boast.

So that we should no longer be the slaves of sin (6.6)

we shall be one with him by being raised to life as he was. ⁶And we know that our old being has been put to death with Christ on his cross, in order that the power of the sinful self might be destroyed, so that we should no longer be the slaves of sin. ⁷For when a person dies, he is set free from the power of sin. ⁸Since we have died with Christ, we believe that we will also live with him. ⁹For we know that Christ has been raised from death and will never die again—death will no longer rule over him. ¹⁰And so, because he died, sin has no power over him; and now he lives his life in fellowship with God. ¹¹In the same way you are to think of yourselves as dead, so far as sin is concerned, but living in fellowship with God through Christ Jesus.

12 Sin must no longer rule in your mortal bodies, so that you obey the desires of your natural self. ¹³Nor must you surrender any part of yourselves to sin to be used for wicked purposes. Instead, give yourselves to God, as those who have been brought from death to life, and surrender your whole being to him to be used for righteous purposes. ¹⁴Sin must not be your master; for you do not live under law but under God's grace.

Slaves of Righteousness

15 What, then? Shall we sin, because we are not under law but under God's grace? By no means! ¹⁶Surely you know that when you surrender yourselves as slaves to obey someone, you are in fact the slaves of the master you obey—either of sin, which results in death, or of obedience, which results in being put right with God. ¹⁷But thanks be to God! For though at one time you were slaves to sin, you have obeyed with all your heart the truths found in the teaching you received. ¹⁸You were set free from sin and became the slaves of righteousness. ¹⁹(I use everyday language because of the weakness of your natural selves.) At one time you surrendered yourselves entirely as slaves to impurity and wickedness for wicked purposes. In the same way you must now surrender yourselves entirely as slaves of righteousness for holy purposes.

20 When you were the slaves of sin, you were free from righteousness. ²¹What did you gain from doing the things that you are now ashamed of? The result of those things is death! ²²But now you have been set free from sin and are the slaves of God. Your gain is a life fully dedicated to him, and the result is eternal life. ²³For sin pays its wage—death; but God's free gift is eternal life in union with Christ Jesus our Lord.

An Illustration from Marriage

7 Certainly you will understand what I am about to say, my brothers, because all of you know about law. The law rules over people only as long as they live. ²A married woman, for example, is bound by the law to her husband as long as he lives; but if he dies, then she is free from the law that bound her to him. ³So then, if she lives with another man

while her husband is alive, she will be called an adulteress; but if her husband dies, she is legally a free woman and does not commit adultery if she marries another man. 4 That is how it is with you, my brothers. As far as the Law is concerned, you also have died because you are part of the body of Christ; and now you belong to him who was raised from death in order that we might be useful in the service of God. 5 For when we lived according to our human nature, the sinful desires stirred up by the Law were at work in our bodies, and all we did ended in death. 6 Now, however, we are free from the Law, because we died to that which once held us prisoners. No longer do we serve in the old way of a written law, but in the new way of the Spirit.

Law and Sin

7 Shall we say, then, that the Law itself is sinful? Of course not! But it was the Law that made me know what sin is. If the Law had not said, "Do not desire what belongs to someone else," I would not have known such a desire. 8 But by means of that commandment sin found its chance to stir up all kinds of selfish desires in me. Apart from law, sin is a dead thing. 9 I myself was once alive apart from law; but when the commandment came, sin sprang to life, 10 and I died. And the commandment which was meant to bring life, in my case brought death. 11 Sin found its chance, and by means of the commandment it deceived me and killed me. 12 So then, the Law itself is holy, and the commandment is holy, right, and good. 13 But does this mean that what is good caused my death? By no means! It was sin that did it; by using what is good, sin brought death to me, in order that its true nature as sin might be revealed. And so, by means of the commandment sin is shown to be even more terribly sinful.

The Conflict in Man

14 We know that the Law is spiritual; but I am a mortal man, sold as a slave to sin. 15 I do not understand what I do; for I don't do what I would like to do, but instead I do what I hate. 16 Since what I do is what I don't want to do, this shows that I agree that the Law is right. 17 So I am not really the one who does this

thing; rather it is the sin that lives in me. 18 I know that good does not live in me—that is, in my human nature. For even though the desire to do good is in me, I am not able to do it. 19 I don't do the good I want to do; instead, I do the evil that I do not want to do. 20 If I do what I don't want to do, this means that I am no longer the one who does it; instead, it is the sin that lives in me.

21 So I find that this law is at work: when I want to do what is good, what is evil is the only choice I have. 22 My inner being delights in the law of God. 23 But I see a different law at work in my body—a law that fights against the law which my mind approves of. It makes me a prisoner to the law of sin which is at work in my body. 24 What an unhappy man I am! Who will rescue me from this body that is taking me to death? 25 Thanks be to God, who does this through our Lord Jesus Christ!

This, then, is my condition: on my own I can serve God's law only with my mind, while my human nature serves the law of sin.

Life in the Spirit

8 There is no condemnation now for those who live in union with Christ Jesus. 2 For the law of the Spirit, which brings us life in union with Christ Jesus, has set me g free from the law of sin and death. 3 What the Law could not do, because human nature was weak, God did. He condemned sin in human nature by sending his own Son, who came with a nature like man's sinful nature, to do away with sin. 4 God did this so that the righteous demands of the Law might be fully satisfied in us who live according to the Spirit, and not according to human nature. 5 Those who live as their human nature tells them to, have their minds controlled by what human nature wants. Those who live as the Spirit tells them to, have their minds controlled by what the Spirit wants. 6 To be controlled by human nature results in death; to be controlled by the Spirit results in life and peace. 7 And so a person becomes an enemy of God when he is controlled by his human nature; for he does not obey God's law, and in fact he cannot obey it. 8 Those who obey their human nature cannot please God.

9 But you do not live as your human

g me; *some manuscripts have* you; *others have* us.
7.7: Ex 20.17; Deut 5.21   **7.11:** Gen 3.13   **7.15:** Gal 5.17

nature tells you to; instead, you live as the Spirit tells you to—if, in fact, God's Spirit lives in you. Whoever does not have the Spirit of Christ does not belong to him. ¹⁰But if Christ lives in you, the Spirit is life for you*ʰ* because you have been put right with God, even though your bodies are going to die because of sin. ¹¹If the Spirit of God, who raised Jesus from death, lives in you, then he who raised Christ from death will also give life to your mortal bodies by the presence of his Spirit in you.

12 So then, my brothers, we have an obligation, but it is not to live as our human nature wants us to. ¹³For if you live according to your human nature, you are going to die; but if by the Spirit you put to death your sinful actions, you will live. ¹⁴Those who are led by God's Spirit are God's sons. ¹⁵For the Spirit that God has given you does not make you slaves and cause you to be afraid; instead, the Spirit makes you God's children, and by the Spirit's power we cry out to God, "Father! my Father!" ¹⁶God's Spirit joins himself to our spirits to declare that we are God's children. ¹⁷Since we are his children, we will possess the blessings he keeps for his people, and we will also possess with Christ what God has kept for him; for if we share Christ's suffering, we will also share his glory.

The Future Glory

18 I consider that what we suffer at this present time cannot be compared at all with the glory that is going to be revealed to us. ¹⁹All of creation waits with eager longing for God to reveal his sons. ²⁰For creation was condemned to lose its purpose, not of its own will, but because God willed it to be so. Yet there was the hope ²¹that creation itself would one day be set free from its slavery to decay and would share the glorious freedom of the children of God. ²²For we know that up to the present time all of creation groans with pain, like the pain of childbirth. ²³But it is not just creation alone which groans; we who have the Spirit as the first of God's gifts also groan within ourselves, as we wait for God to make us his sons and*ⁱ* set our whole being free. ²⁴For it was by hope that we were saved; but

if we see what we hope for, then it is not really hope. For who hopes for something he sees? ²⁵But if we hope for what we do not see, we wait for it with patience.

26 In the same way the Spirit also comes to help us, weak as we are. For we do not know how we ought to pray; the Spirit himself pleads with God for us in groans that words cannot express. ²⁷And God, who sees into our hearts, knows what the thought of the Spirit is; because the Spirit pleads with God on behalf of his people and in accordance with his will.

28 We know that in all things God works for good with those who love him,*ʲ* those whom he has called according to his purpose. ²⁹Those whom God had already chosen he also set apart to become like his Son, so that the Son would be the first among many brothers. ³⁰And so those whom God set apart, he called; and those he called, he put right with himself, and he shared his glory with them.

God's Love in Christ Jesus

31 In view of all this, what can we say? If God is for us, who can be against us? ³²Certainly not God, who did not even keep back his own Son, but offered him for us all! He gave us his Son—will he not also freely give us all things? ³³Who will accuse God's chosen people? God himself declares them not guilty! ³⁴Who, then, will condemn them? Not Christ Jesus, who died, or rather, who was raised to life and is at the right-hand side of God, pleading with him for us! ³⁵Who, then, can separate us from the love of Christ? Can trouble do it, or hardship or persecution or hunger or poverty or danger or death? ³⁶As the scripture says,

"For your sake we are in danger of
    death at all times;
we are treated like sheep that are
    going to be slaughtered."

³⁷No, in all these things we have complete victory through him who loved us! ³⁸For I am certain that nothing can separate us from his love: neither death nor life, neither angels nor other heavenly rulers or powers, neither the present nor the future, ³⁹neither the world above nor the world below—there is nothing in all creation

---

*ʰ*the Spirit is life for you; *or* your spirit is alive.
ⁱ Some manuscripts do not have make us his sons and.
*ʲ*in all things God works for good with those who love him; *some manuscripts have* all things work for good for those who love God.

8.11: 1 Cor 3.16   **8.15:** Mk 14.36; Gal 4.6   **8.15–17:** Gal 4.5–7   **8.20:** Gen 3.17–19
8.23: 2 Cor 5.2–4   **8.36:** Ps 44.22

that will ever be able to separate us from the love of God which is ours through Christ Jesus our Lord.

God and His People

9 I am speaking the truth; I belong to Christ and I do not lie. My conscience, ruled by the Holy Spirit, also assures me that I am not lying [2] when I say how great is my sorrow, how endless the pain in my heart [3] for my people, my own flesh and blood! For their sake I could wish that I myself were under God's curse and separated from Christ. [4] They are God's people; he made them his sons and revealed his glory to them; he made his covenants[k] with them and gave them the Law; they have the true worship; they have received God's promises; [5] they are descended from the famous Hebrew ancestors; and Christ, as a human being, belongs to their race. May God, who rules over all, be praised for ever![l] Amen.

[6] I am not saying that the promise of God has failed; for not all the people of Israel are the people of God. [7] Nor are all Abraham's descendants the children of God. God said to Abraham, "It is through Isaac that you will have the descendants I promised you." [8] This means that the children born in the usual way[m] are not the children of God; instead, the children born as a result of God's promise are regarded as the true descendants. [9] For God's promise was made in these words: "At the right time[n] I will come back, and Sarah will have a son."

[10] And this is not all. For Rebecca's two sons had the same father, our ancestor Isaac. [11-12] But in order that the choice of one son might be completely the result of God's own purpose, God said to her, "The elder will serve the younger." He said this before they were born, before they had done anything either good or bad; so God's choice was based on his call, and not on anything they had done. [13] As the scripture says, "I loved Jacob, but I hated Esau."

[14] Shall we say, then, that God is unjust? Not at all. [15] For he said to Moses, "I will have mercy on anyone I wish; I will take pity on anyone I wish." [16] So

then, everything depends, not on what man wants or does, but only on God's mercy. [17] For the scripture says to the king of Egypt, "I made you king in order to use you to show my power and to spread my fame over the whole world." [18] So then, God has mercy on anyone he wishes, and he makes stubborn anyone he wishes.

God's Anger and Mercy

[19] But one of you will say to me, "If this is so, how can God find fault with anyone? Who can resist God's will?" [20] But who are you, my friend, to answer God back? A clay pot does not ask the man who made it, "Why did you make me like this?" [21] After all, the man who makes the pots has the right to use the clay as he wishes, and to make two pots from the same lump of clay, one for special occasions and the other for ordinary use.

[22] And the same is true of what God has done. He wanted to show his anger and to make his power known. But he was very patient in enduring those who were the objects of his anger, who were doomed to destruction. [23] And he also wanted to reveal his abundant glory, which was poured out on us who are the objects of his mercy, those of us whom he has prepared to receive his glory. [24] For we are the people he called, not only from among the Jews but also from among the Gentiles. [25] This is what he says in the book of Hosea:

"The people who were not mine
  I will call 'My People.'
The nation that I did not love
  I will call 'My Beloved.'
[26] And in the very place where they were
    told, 'You are not my people,'
  there they will be called the sons of
    the living God."

[27] And Isaiah exclaims about Israel: "Even if the people of Israel are as many as the grains of sand by the sea, yet only a few of them will be saved; [28] for the Lord will quickly settle his full account with the world." [29] It is as Isaiah had said before, "If the Lord Almighty had not left us some descendants, we would have

---

[k] covenants; *some manuscripts have* covenant.
[l] May God, who rules over all, be praised for ever!; *or* And may he, who is God ruling over all, be praised for ever!
[m] CHILDREN BORN IN THE USUAL WAY: *This refers to the descendants Abraham had through Ishmael, his son by Hagar (see Gal. 4.22–23).* [n] At the right time; *or* At this time next year.
9.4: Ex 9.4 **9.7:** Gen 21.12 **9.9:** Gen 18.10 **9.12:** Gen 25.23 **9.13:** Mal 1.2–3 **9.15:** Ex 33.19 **9.17:** Ex 9.16 **9.20:** Is 29.16, 45.9 **9.25:** Hos 2.23 **9.26:** Hos 1.10 **9.27–28:** Is 10.22–23 **9.29:** Is 1.9

become like Sodom, we would have been like Gomorrah."

Paul's Prayer for Israel

30 So we say that the Gentiles, who were not trying to put themselves right with God, were put right with him through faith; 31 while God's people, who were seeking a law that would put them right with God, did not find it. 32 And why not? Because they did not depend on faith but on what they did. And so they stumbled over the "stumbling stone" 33 that the scripture speaks of:

"Look, I place in Zion a stone
  that will make people stumble,
  a rock that will make them fall.
But whoever believes in him will not
  be disappointed."

10 My brothers, how I wish with all my heart that my own people might be saved! How I pray to God for them! 2 I can assure you that they are deeply devoted to God; but their devotion is not based on true knowledge. 3 They have not known the way in which God puts people right with himself, and instead, they have tried to set up their own way; and so they did not submit themselves to God's way of putting people right. 4 For Christ has brought the Law to an end, so that everyone who believes is put right with God.

Salvation Is for All

5 Moses wrote this about being put right with God by obeying the Law: "Whoever obeys the commands of the Law will live." 6 But what the scripture says about being put right with God through faith is this: "You are not to ask yourself, Who will go up into heaven?" (that is, to bring Christ down). 7 "Nor are you to ask, Who will go down into the world below?" (that is, to bring Christ up from death). 8 What it says is this: "God's message is near you, on your lips and in your heart"—that is, the message of faith that we preach. 9 If you confess that Jesus is Lord and believe that God raised him from death, you will be saved. 10 For it is by our faith that we are put right with God; it is by our confession that we are saved. 11 The scripture says, "Whoever believes in him will not be disappointed." 12 This includes everyone, because there is no difference between Jews and Gentiles; God is the same Lord of all and richly blesses all who call to him. 13 As the scripture says, "Everyone who calls out to the Lord for help will be saved."

14 But how can they call to him for help if they have not believed? And how can they believe if they have not heard the message? And how can they hear if the message is not proclaimed? 15 And how can the message be proclaimed if the messengers are not sent out? As the scripture says, "How wonderful is the coming of messengers who bring good news!" 16 But not all have accepted the Good News. Isaiah himself said, "Lord, who believed our message?" 17 So then, faith comes from hearing the message, and the message comes through preaching Christ.

18 But I ask: Is it true that they did not hear the message? Of course they did—for as the scripture says:

"The sound of their voice went out to
  all the world;
  their words reached the ends of the
  earth."

19 Again I ask: Did the people of Israel not understand? Moses himself is the first one to answer:

"I will use a so-called nation
  to make my people jealous;
and by means of a nation of fools
  I will make my people angry."

20 And Isaiah is even bolder when he says,

"I was found by those who were not
  looking for me;
I appeared to those who were not
  asking for me."

21 But concerning Israel he says, "All day long I held out my hands to welcome a disobedient and rebellious people."

God's Mercy on Israel

11 I ask, then: Did God reject his own people? Certainly not! I myself am an Israelite, a descendant of Abraham, a member of the tribe of Benjamin. 2 God has not rejected his people, whom he chose from the beginning. You know what the scripture says in the passage where Elijah pleads with God against Israel: 3 "Lord, they have killed your prophets and torn down your altars; I am the only one left, and they are trying to kill me." 4 What answer did God give him? "I have kept for myself seven thousand men who

9.33: Is 28.16   10.5: Lev 18.5   10.6–8: Deut 30.12–14   10.11: Is 28.16   10.13: Joel 2.32
10.15: Is 52.7   10.16: Is 53.1   10.18: Ps 19.4   10.19: Deut 32.21   10.20: Is 65.1
10.21: Is 65.2   11.1: Phil 3.5   11.3: 1 Kgs 19.10,14   11.4: 1 Kgs 19.18

have not worshipped the false god Baal." ⁵It is the same way now: there is a small number left of those whom God has chosen because of his grace. ⁶His choice is based on his grace, not on what they have done. For if God's choice were based on what people do, then his grace would not be real grace.

7 What then? The people of Israel did not find what they were looking for. It was only the small group that God chose who found it; the rest grew deaf to God's call. ⁸As the scripture says, "God made their minds and hearts dull; to this very day they cannot see or hear." ⁹And David says,

"May they be caught and trapped at
    their feasts;
 may they fall, may they be punished!
¹⁰ May their eyes be blinded so that they
    cannot see;
 and make them bend under their
    troubles at all times."

11 I ask, then: When the Jews stumbled, did they fall to their ruin? By no means! Because they sinned, salvation has come to the Gentiles, to make the Jews jealous of them. ¹²The sin of the Jews brought rich blessings to the world, and their spiritual poverty brought rich blessings to the Gentiles. Then, how much greater the blessings will be when the complete number of Jews is included!

The Salvation of the Gentiles

13 I am speaking now to you Gentiles: As long as I am an apostle to the Gentiles, I will take pride in my work. ¹⁴Perhaps I can make the people of my own race jealous, and so be able to save some of them. ¹⁵For when they were rejected, mankind was changed from God's enemies into his friends. What will it be, then, when they are accepted? It will be life for the dead!

16 If the first piece of bread is given to God, then the whole loaf is his also; and if the roots of a tree are offered to God, the branches are his also. ¹⁷Some of the branches of the cultivated olive-tree have been broken off, and a branch of a wild olive-tree has been joined to it. You Gentiles are like that wild olive-tree, and now you share the strong spiritual life of the Jews. ¹⁸So then, you must not despise those who were broken off like branches. How can you be proud? You

are just a branch; you don't support the roots—the roots support you.

19 But you will say, "Yes, but the branches were broken off to make room for me." ²⁰That is true. They were broken off because they did not believe, while you remain in place because you do believe. But do not be proud of it; instead, be afraid. ²¹God did not spare the Jews, who are like natural branches; do you think he will spare you? ²²Here we see how kind and how severe God is. He is severe towards those who have fallen, but kind to you—if you continue in his kindness. But if you do not, you too will be broken off. ²³And if the Jews abandon their unbelief, they will be put back in the place where they were; for God is able to do that. ²⁴You Gentiles are like the branch of a wild olive-tree that is broken off and then, contrary to nature, is joined to a cultivated olive-tree. The Jews are like this cultivated tree; and it will be much easier for God to join these broken-off branches to their own tree again.

God's Mercy on All

25 There is a secret truth, my brothers, which I want you to know, for it will keep you from thinking how wise you are. It is that the stubbornness of the people of Israel is not permanent, but will last only until the complete number of Gentiles comes to God. ²⁶And this is how all Israel will be saved. As the scripture says,

"The Saviour will come from Zion
 and remove all wickedness from the
    descendants of Jacob.
²⁷ I will make this covenant with them
 when I take away their sins."

²⁸Because they reject the Good News, the Jews are God's enemies for the sake of you Gentiles. But because of God's choice, they are his friends because of their ancestors. ²⁹For God does not change his mind about whom he chooses and blesses. ³⁰As for you Gentiles, you disobeyed God in the past; but now you have received God's mercy because the Jews were disobedient. ³¹In the same way, because of the mercy that you have received, the Jews now disobey God, in order that they also may now ᵒ receive God's mercy. ³²For God has made all people prisoners of

---

ᵒ Some manuscripts do not have now.

11.8: Deut 29.4; Is 29.10   **11.9-10:** Ps 69.22-23   **11.26:** Is 59.20   **11.27:** Jer 31.33-34 disobedience, so that he might show mercy to them all.

Praise to God

33 How great are God's riches! How deep are his wisdom and knowledge! Who can explain his decisions? Who can understand his ways? 34 As the scripture says,

"Who knows the mind of the Lord?
　Who is able to give him advice?
35 Who has ever given him anything,
　so that he had to pay it back?"

36 For all things were created by him, and all things exist through him and for him. To God be the glory for ever! Amen.

Life in God's Service

12 So then, my brothers, because of God's great mercy to us I appeal to you: Offer yourselves as a living sacrifice to God, dedicated to his service and pleasing to him. This is the true worship that you should offer. 2 Do not conform yourselves to the standards of this world, but let God transform you inwardly by a complete change of your mind. Then you will be able to know the will of God— what is good and is pleasing to him and is perfect.

3 And because of God's gracious gift to me I say to every one of you: Do not think of yourself more highly than you should. Instead, be modest in your thinking, and judge yourself according to the amount of faith that God has given you. 4 We have many parts in the one body, and all these parts have different functions. 5 In the same way, though we are many, we are one body in union with Christ, and we are all joined to each other as different parts of one body. 6 So we are to use our different gifts in accordance with the grace that God has given us. If our gift is to speak God's message, we should do it according to the faith that we have; 7 if it is to serve, we should serve; if it is to teach, we should teach; 8 if it is to encourage others, we should do so. Whoever shares with others should do it generously; whoever has authority should work hard; whoever shows kindness to others should do it cheerfully.

9 Love must be completely sincere. Hate what is evil, hold on to what is good. 10 Love one another warmly as Christian brothers, and be eager to show respect for one another. 11 Work hard and do not be lazy. Serve the Lord with a heart full of devotion. 12 Let your hope keep you joyful, be patient in your troubles, and pray at all times. 13 Share your belongings with your needy fellow-Christians, and open your homes to strangers.

14 Ask God to bless those who persecute you—yes, ask him to bless, not to curse. 15 Be happy with those who are happy, weep with those who weep. 16 Have the same concern for everyone. Do not be proud, but accept humble duties.*p* Do not think of yourselves as wise.

17 If someone has done you wrong, do not repay him with a wrong. Try to do what everyone considers to be good. 18 Do everything possible on your part to live in peace with everybody. 19 Never take revenge, my friends, but instead let God's anger do it. For the scripture says, "I will take revenge, I will pay back, says the Lord." 20 Instead, as the scripture says: "If your enemy is hungry, feed him; if he is thirsty, give him a drink; for by doing this you will make him burn with shame." 21 Do not let evil defeat you; instead, conquer evil with good.

Duties towards the State Authorities

13 Everyone must obey the state authorities, because no authority exists without God's permission, and the existing authorities have been put there by God. 2 Whoever opposes the existing authority opposes what God has ordered; and anyone who does so will bring judgement on himself. 3 For rulers are not to be feared by those who do good, but by those who do evil. Would you like to be unafraid of the man in authority? Then do what is good, and he will praise you, 4 because he is God's servant working for your own good. But if you do evil, then be afraid of him, because his power to punish is real. He is God's servant and carries out God's punishment on those who do evil. 5 For this reason you must obey the authorities—not just because of God's punishment, but also as a matter of conscience.

6 That is also why you pay taxes, because the authorities are working for God when they fulfil their duties. 7 Pay,

p accept humble duties; or make friends with humble people.
11.33: Is 55.8   **11.34:** Is 40.13   **11.35:** Job 41.11   **11.36:** 1 Cor 8.6   **12.4–5:** 1 Cor 12.12
12.6–8: 1 Cor 12.4–11   **12.14:** Mt 5.44; Lk 6.28   **12.16:** Prov 3.7   **12.19:** Deut 32.35
12.20: Prov 25.21–22   **13.6–7:** Mt 22.21; Mk 12.17; Lk 20.25

then, what you owe them; pay them your personal and property taxes, and show respect and honour for them all.

Duties towards One Another

8 Be under obligation to no one—the only obligation you have is to love one another. Whoever does this has obeyed the Law. ⁹The commandments, "Do not commit adultery; do not commit murder; do not steal; do not desire what belongs to someone else"—all these, and any others besides, are summed up in the one command, "Love your neighbour as you love yourself." ¹⁰If you love someone, you will never do him wrong; to love, then, is to obey the whole Law.

11 You must do this, because you know that the time has come for you to wake up from your sleep. For the moment when we will be saved is closer now than it was when we first believed. ¹²The night is nearly over, day is almost here. Let us stop doing the things that belong to the dark, and let us take up weapons for fighting in the light. ¹³Let us conduct ourselves properly, as people who live in the light of day—no orgies or drunkenness, no immorality or indecency, no fighting or jealousy. ¹⁴But take up the weapons of the Lord Jesus Christ, and stop paying attention to your sinful nature and satisfying its desires.

Do Not Judge Your Brother

14 Welcome the person who is weak in faith, but do not argue with him about his personal opinions. ²One person's faith allows him to eat anything, but the person who is weak in the faith eats only vegetables. ³The person who eat anything is not to despise the one who doesn't; while the one who eats only vegetables is not to pass judgement on the one who will eat anything; for God has accepted him. ⁴Who are you to judge the servant of someone else? It is his own Master who will decide whether he succeeds or fails. And he will succeed, because the Lord is able to make him succeed.

5 One person thinks that a certain day is more important than other days, while someone else thinks that all days are the same. Each one should firmly make up his own mind. ⁶Whoever thinks highly of a certain day does so in honour of the

Lord; whoever will eat anything does so in honour of the Lord, because he gives thanks to God for the food. Whoever refuses to eat certain things does so in honour of the Lord, and he gives thanks to God. ⁷None of us lives for himself only, none of us dies for himself only. ⁸If we live, it is for the Lord that we live, and if we die, it is for the Lord that we die. So whether we live or die, we belong to the Lord. ⁹For Christ died and rose to life in order to be the Lord of the living and of the dead. ¹⁰You then, who eat only vegetables—why do you pass judgement on your brother? And you who eat anything—why do you despise your brother? All of us will stand before God to be judged by him. ¹¹For the scripture says,

"As surely as I am the living God, says the Lord,
    everyone will kneel before me,
    and everyone will confess that I am God."

¹²Every one of us, then, will have to give an account of himself to God.

Do Not Make Your Brother Fall

13 So then, let us stop judging one another. Instead, you should decide never to do anything that would make your brother stumble or fall into sin. ¹⁴My union with the Lord Jesus makes me certain that no food is of itself ritually unclean; but if a person believes that some food is unclean, then it becomes unclean for him. ¹⁵If you hurt your brother because of something you eat, then you are no longer acting from love. Do not let the food that you eat ruin the person for whom Christ died! ¹⁶Do not let what you regard as good get a bad name. ¹⁷For God's Kingdom is not a matter of eating and drinking, but of the righteousness, peace, and joy which the Holy Spirit gives. ¹⁸And when someone serves Christ in this way, he pleases God and is approved by others.

19 So then, we must always aim �q at those things that bring peace and that help to strengthen one another. ²⁰Do not, because of food, destroy what God has done. All foods may be eaten, but it is wrong to eat anything that will cause someone else to fall into sin. ²¹The right thing to do is to keep from eating meat, drinking wine, or doing anything else that

�q we must always aim; *some manuscripts have* we always aim.
13.9: Ex 20.13–15,17; Deut 5.17–19,21; Lev 19.18   **14.1–6:** Col 2.16   **14.10:** 2 Cor 5.10
14.11: Is 45.23

will make your brother fall. 22 Keep what you believe about this matter, then, between yourself and God. Happy is the person who does not feel guilty when he does something he judges is right! 23 But if he has doubts about what he eats, God condemns him when he eats it, because his action is not based on faith. And anything that is not based on faith is sin.

Please Others, Not Yourselves

15 We who are strong in the faith ought to help the weak to carry their burdens. We should not please ourselves. 2 Instead, we should all please

Help the weak (15.1)

our brothers for their own good, in order to build them up in the faith. 3 For Christ did not please himself. Instead, as the scripture says, "The insults which are hurled at you have fallen on me." 4 Everything written in the Scriptures was written to teach us, in order that we might have hope through the patience and encouragement which the Scriptures give us. 5 And may God, the source of patience

and encouragement, enable you to have the same point of view among yourselves by following the example of Christ Jesus, 6 so that all of you together may praise with one voice the God and Father of our Lord Jesus Christ.

Good News for the Gentiles

7 Accept one another, then, for the glory of God, as Christ has accepted you. 8 For I tell you that Christ's life of service was on behalf of the Jews, to show that God is faithful, to make his promises to their ancestors come true, 9 and to enable even the Gentiles to praise God for his mercy. As the scripture says,

"And so I will praise you among the
    Gentiles;
    I will sing praises to you."
10 Again it says,
"Rejoice, Gentiles, with God's people!"
11 And again,
"Praise the Lord, all Gentiles;
    praise him, all peoples!"
12 And again, Isaiah says,
"A descendant of Jesse will appear;
    he will come to rule the Gentiles,
    and they will put their hope in him."

13 May God, the source of hope, fill you with all joy and peace by means of your faith in him, so that your hope will continue to grow by the power of the Holy Spirit.

Paul's Reason for Writing So Boldly

14 My brothers: I myself feel sure that you are full of goodness, that you have all knowledge, and that you are able to teach one another. 15 But in this letter I have been quite bold about certain subjects of which I have reminded you. I have been bold because of the privilege God has given me 16 of being a servant of Christ Jesus to work for the Gentiles. I serve like a priest in preaching the Good News from God, in order that the Gentiles may be an offering acceptable to God, dedicated to him by the Holy Spirit. 17 In union with Christ Jesus, then, I can be proud of my service for God. 18 I will be bold and speak only about what Christ has done through me to lead the Gentiles to obey God. He has done this by means of words and deeds, 19 by the power of miracles and wonders, and by the power of the Spirit of God. And so, in travelling all the way from Jerusalem to Illyricum, I have proclaimed fully the Good News

15.3: Ps 69.9   **15.9:** 2 Sam 22.50; Ps 18.49   **15.10:** Deut 32.43   **15.11:** Ps 117.1
15.12: Is 11.10

about Christ. 20 My ambition has always been to proclaim the Good News in places where Christ has not been heard of, so as not to build on a foundation laid by someone else. 21 As the scripture says,

"Those who were not told about him will see,
and those who have not heard will understand."

Paul's Plan to Visit Rome

22 And so I have been prevented many times from coming to you. 23 But now that I have finished my work in these regions and since I have been wanting for so many years to come to see you, 24 I hope to do so now. I would like to see you on my way to Spain, and be helped by you to go there, after I have enjoyed visiting you for a while. 25 Just now, however, I am going to Jerusalem in the service of God's people there. 26 For the churches in Macedonia and Achaia have freely decided to give an offering to help the poor among God's people in Jerusalem. 27 That decision was their own; but, as a matter of fact, they have an obligation to help them. Since the Jews shared their spiritual blessings with the Gentiles, the Gentiles ought to use their material blessings to help the Jews. 28 When I have finished this task and have handed over to them all the money that has been raised for them, I shall leave for Spain and visit you on my way there. 29 When I come to you, I know that I shall come with a full measure of the blessing of Christ.

30 I urge you, brothers, by our Lord Jesus Christ and by the love that the Spirit gives: join me in praying fervently to God for me. 31 Pray that I may be kept safe from the unbelievers in Judaea and that my service in Jerusalem may be acceptable to God's people there. 32 And so I will come to you full of joy, if it is God's will, and enjoy a refreshing visit to you. 33 May God, our source of peace, be with all of you. Amen.

Personal Greetings

16 I recommend to you our sister Phoebe, who serves the church at Cenchreae. 2 Receive her in the Lord's name, as God's people should, and give her any help she may need from you; for she herself has been a good friend to many people and also to me.

3 I send greetings to Priscilla and Aquila, my fellow-workers in the service of Christ Jesus; 4 they risked their lives for me. I am grateful to them—not only I, but all the Gentile churches as well. 5 Greetings also to the church that meets in their house.

Greetings to my dear friend Epaenetus, who was the first man in the province of Asia to believe in Christ. 6 Greetings to Mary, who has worked so hard for you. 7 Greetings also to Andronicus and Junias,r fellow-Jews who were in prison with me; they are well known among the apostles, and they became Christians before I did.

8 My greetings to Ampliatus, my dear friend in the fellowship of the Lord. 9 Greetings also to Urbanus, our fellow-worker in Christ's service, and to Stachys, my dear friend. 10 Greetings to Apelles, whose loyalty to Christ has been proved. Greetings to those who belong to the family of Aristobulus. 11 Greetings to Herodion, a fellow-Jew, and to the Christian brothers in the family of Narcissus.

12 My greetings to Tryphaena and Tryphosa, who work in the Lord's service, and to my dear friend Persis, who has done so much work for the Lord. 13 I send greetings to Rufus, that outstanding worker in the Lord's service, and to his mother, who has always treated me like a son. 14 My greetings to Asyncritus, Phlegon, Hermes, Patrobas, Hermas, and all the other Christian brothers with them. 15 Greetings to Philologus and Julia, to Nereus and his sister, to Olympas and to all of God's people who are with them.

16 Greet one another with a brotherly kiss. All the churches of Christ send you their greetings.

Final Instructions

17 I urge you, my brothers: watch out for those who cause divisions and upset people's faith and go against the teaching which you have received. Keep away from them! 18 For those who do such things are not serving Christ our Lord, but their own appetites. By their fine words and flattering speech they deceive innocent people. 19 Everyone has heard of your loyalty to the gospel, and for this reason I am happy about you. I want you to

---

r Junias; *or* June; *some manuscripts have* Julia.
15.21: Is 52.15   **15.22:** Rom 1.13   **15.25–26:** 1 Cor 16.1–4   **15.27:** 1 Cor 9.11
16.3: Acts 18.2   **16.13:** Mk 15.21

be wise about what is good, but innocent in what is evil. ²⁰ And God, our source of peace, will soon crush Satan under your feet.

The grace of our Lord Jesus be with you. *s*

21 Timothy, my fellow-worker, sends you his greetings; and so do Lucius, Jason, and Sosipater, fellow-Jews.

22 I, Tertius, the writer of this letter, send you Christian greetings.

23 My host Gaius, in whose house the church meets, sends you his greetings; Erastus, the city treasurer, and our brother Quartus send you their greetings. *t*

Concluding Prayer of Praise

25 Let us give glory to God! He is able to make you stand firm in your faith, according to the Good News I preach about Jesus Christ and according to the revelation of the secret truth which was hidden for long ages in the past. ²⁶ Now, however, that truth has been brought out into the open through the writings of the prophets; and by the command of the eternal God it is made known to all nations, so that all may believe and obey.

27 To the only God, who alone is all-wise, be glory through Jesus Christ for ever! Amen. *u*

s Some manuscripts omit this sentence.
t Some manuscripts add verse 24: The grace of our Lord Jesus Christ be with you all. Amen; others add this after verse 27.
u Some manuscripts have verses 25–27 here and after 14.23; others have them only after 14.23; one has them after 15.33.
16.21: Acts 16.1   **16.23:** Acts 19.29; 1 Cor 1.14; 2 Tim 4.20

PAUL'S FIRST LETTER TO THE

CORINTHIANS

INTRODUCTION

Paul's First Letter to the Corinthians was written to deal with problems of Christian life and faith that had arisen in the church which Paul had established at Corinth. At that time Corinth was a great cosmopolitan Greek city, the capital of the Roman province of Achaia. It was noted for its thriving commerce, proud culture, widespread immorality, and variety of religions.

The apostle's chief concerns are with problems such as divisions and immorality in the church, and with questions about sex and marriage, matters of conscience, church order, gifts of the Holy Spirit, and the resurrection. With deep insight he shows how the Good News speaks to these questions.

Chapter 13, which presents love as the best of God's gifts to his people, is probably the most widely known passage in the book.

Outline of Contents
Introduction 1.1–9
Factions in the church 1.10—4.21
Sexual morality and family life 5.1—7.40
Christians and pagans 8.1—11.1
Church life and worship 11.2—14.40
The resurrection of Christ and of believers 15.1–58
The offering for the Christians in Judaea 16.1–4
Personal matters and conclusion 16.5–24

1 From Paul, who was called by the will of God to be an apostle of Christ Jesus, and from our brother Sosthenes—

2 To the church of God which is in Corinth, to all who are called to be God's holy people, who belong to him in union with Christ Jesus, together with all people everywhere who worship our Lord Jesus Christ, their Lord and ours:

3 May God our Father and the Lord Jesus Christ give you grace and peace.

Blessings in Christ

4 I always give thanks to my God for you because of the grace he has given you through Christ Jesus. 5 For in union with Christ you have become rich in all things, including all speech and all knowledge. 6 The message about Christ has become so firmly established in you 7 that you have not failed to receive a single blessing, as you wait for our Lord Jesus Christ to be revealed. 8 He will also keep you firm to the end, so that you will be faultless on the Day of our Lord Jesus Christ. 9 God is to be trusted, the God who called you to have fellowship with his Son Jesus Christ, our Lord.

Divisions in the Church

10 By the authority of our Lord Jesus Christ I appeal to all of you, my brothers, to agree in what you say, so that there will be no divisions among you. Be completely united, with only one thought and one purpose. 11 For some people from Chloe's family have told me quite plainly, my brothers, that there are quarrels among you. 12 Let me put it this way: each one of you says something different. One says, "I follow Paul"; another, "I follow Apollos"; another, "I follow Peter"; and another, "I follow Christ." 13 Christ has been divided[a] into groups! Was it Paul who died on the cross for you? Were you baptized as Paul's disciples?

14 I thank God that I did not baptize any of you except Crispus and Gaius. 15 No one can say, then, that you were baptized as my disciples. 16 (Oh yes, I also baptized Stephanas and his family; but I can't remember whether I baptized anyone else.) 17 Christ did not send me to baptize. He sent me to tell the Good News, and to tell it without using the language of human wisdom, in order to make sure that Christ's death on the cross is not robbed of its power.

Christ the Power and the Wisdom of God

18 For the message about Christ's death on the cross is nonsense to those who are being lost; but for us who are being saved it is God's power. 19 The scripture says,

"I will destroy the wisdom of the wise
    and set aside the understanding of the
        scholars."

20 So then, where does that leave the wise? or the scholars? or the skilful debaters of this world? God has shown that this world's wisdom is foolishness!

21 For God in his wisdom made it impossible for people to know him by means of their own wisdom. Instead, by means of the so-called "foolish" message we preach, God decided to save those who believe. 22 Jews want miracles for proof, and Greeks look for wisdom. 23 As for us, we proclaim the crucified Christ, a message that is offensive to the Jews and nonsense to the Gentiles; 24 but for those whom God has called, both Jews and Gentiles, this message is Christ, who is the power of God and the wisdom of God. 25 For what seems to be God's foolishness is wiser than human wisdom, and what seems to be God's weakness is stronger than human strength.

26 Now remember what you were, my brothers, when God called you. From the human point of view few of you were wise or powerful or of high social standing. 27 God purposely chose what the world considers nonsense in order to shame the wise, and he chose what the world considers weak in order to shame the powerful. 28 He chose what the world looks down on and despises, and thinks is nothing, in order to destroy what the world thinks is important. 29 This means that no one can boast in God's presence. 30 But God has brought you into union with Christ Jesus, and God has made Christ to be our wisdom. By him we are put right with God; we become God's holy people and are set free. 31 So then, as the scripture says, "Whoever wants to boast must boast of what the Lord has done."

---

[a] Christ has been divided; *some manuscripts have* Christ cannot be divided.
1.2: Acts 18.1   **1.12:** Acts 18.24   **1.14:** Acts 18.8, 19.29; Rom 16.23   **1.16:** 1 Cor 16.15
1.19: Is 29.14   **1.20:** Job 12.17; Is 19.12, 33.18, 44.25   **1.31:** Jer 9.24

The Message about the Crucified Christ

2 When I came to you, my brothers, to preach God's secret truth,*b* I did not use big words and great learning. ² For while I was with you, I made up my mind to forget everything except Jesus Christ and especially his death on the cross. ³ So when I came to you, I was weak and trembled all over with fear, ⁴ and my teaching and message were not delivered with skilful words of human wisdom, but with convincing proof of the power of God's Spirit. ⁵ Your faith, then, does not rest on human wisdom but on God's power.

God's Wisdom

6 Yet I do proclaim a message of wisdom to those who are spiritually mature. But it is not the wisdom that belongs to this world or to the powers that rule this world—powers that are losing their power. ⁷ The wisdom I proclaim is God's secret wisdom, which is hidden from mankind, but which he had already chosen for our glory even before the world was made. ⁸ None of the rulers of this world knew this wisdom. If they had known it, they would not have crucified the Lord of glory. ⁹ However, as the scripture says,

"What no one ever saw or heard,
    what no one ever thought could
        happen,
    is the very thing God prepared for
        those who love him."

¹⁰ But *c* it was to us that God made known his secret by means of his Spirit. The Spirit searches everything, even the hidden depths of God's purposes. ¹¹ It is only a person's own spirit within him that knows all about him; in the same way, only God's Spirit knows all about God. ¹² We have not received this world's spirit; instead, we have received the Spirit sent by God, so that we may know all that God has given us.

13 So then, we do not speak in words taught by human wisdom, but in words taught by the Spirit, as we explain spiritual truths to those who have the Spirit.*d* ¹⁴ Whoever does not have the Spirit cannot receive the gifts that come from God's Spirit. Such a person really does not understand them; they are nonsense to him, because their value can be judged only on a spiritual basis. ¹⁵ Whoever has the Spirit, however, is able to judge the value of everything, but no one is able to judge him. ¹⁶ As the scripture says,

"Who knows the mind of the Lord?
    Who is able to give him advice?"
We, however, have the mind of Christ.

Servants of God

3 As a matter of fact, my brothers, I could not talk to you as I talk to people who have the Spirit; I had to talk to you as though you belonged to this world, as children in the Christian faith. ² I had to feed you with milk, not solid food, because you were not ready for it. And even now you are not ready for it, ³ because you still live as the people of this world live. When there is jealousy among you and you quarrel with one another, doesn't this prove that you belong to this world, living by its standards? ⁴ When one of you says, "I follow Paul," and another, "I follow Apollos"—aren't you acting like worldly people?

5 After all, who is Apollos? And who is Paul? We are simply God's servants, by whom you were led to believe. Each one of us does the work which the Lord gave him to do: ⁶ I sowed the seed, Apollos watered the plant, but it was God who made the plant grow. ⁷ The one who sows and the one who waters really do not matter. It is God who matters, because he makes the plant grow. ⁸ There is no difference between the man who sows and the man who waters; God will reward each one according to the work he has done. ⁹ For we are partners working together for God, and you are God's field.

You are also God's building. ¹⁰ Using the gift that God gave me, I did the work of an expert builder and laid the foundation, and another man is building on it. But each one must be careful how he builds. ¹¹ For God has already placed Jesus Christ as the one and only foundation, and no other foundation can be laid. ¹² Some will use gold or silver or precious stones in building on the foundation; others will use wood or grass or straw. ¹³ And the quality of each person's work will be seen

---

b God's secret truth; *some manuscripts have* the testimony about God.
c But; *some manuscripts have* For.
d to those who have the Spirit; *or* with words given by the Spirit.
2.3: Acts 18.9   **2.9:** Is 64.4   **2.16:** Is 40.13   **3.2:** Heb 5.12–13   **3.4:** 1 Cor 1.12
3.6: Acts 18.4–11,24–28

God...made the plant grow (3.6)

when the Day of Christ exposes it. For on that Day fire will reveal everyone's work; the fire will test it and show its real quality. 14 If what was built on the foundation survives the fire, the builder will receive a reward. 15 But if anyone's work is burnt up, then he will lose it; but he himself will be saved, as if he had escaped through the fire.

16 Surely you know that you are God's temple and that God's Spirit lives in you! 17 So if anyone destroys God's temple, God will destroy him. For God's temple is holy, and you yourselves are his temple.

18 No one should fool himself. If anyone among you thinks that he is wise by this world's standards, he should become a fool, in order to be really wise. 19 For what this world considers to be wisdom is nonsense in God's sight. As the scripture says, "God traps the wise in their cleverness"; 20 and another scripture says, "The Lord knows that the thoughts of the wise are worthless." 21 No one, then, should boast about what men can do. Actually everything belongs to you: 22 Paul, Apollos, and Peter; this world, life and death, the present and the future—all these are yours, 23 and you belong to Christ, and Christ belongs to God.

Apostles of Christ

4 You should think of us as Christ's servants, who have been put in charge of God's secret truths. 2 The one thing required of such a servant is that he be faithful to his master. 3 Now, I am not at all concerned about being judged by you or by any human standard; I don't even pass judgement on myself. 4 My conscience is clear, but that does not prove that I am really innocent. The Lord is the one who passes judgement on me. 5 So you should not pass judgement on anyone before the right time comes. Final judgement must wait until the Lord comes; he will bring to light the dark secrets and expose the hidden purposes of people's minds. And then everyone will receive from God the praise he deserves.

6 For your sake, my brothers, I have applied all this to Apollos and me, using the two of us as an example, so that you may learn what the saying means, "Observe the proper rules." None of you should be proud of one person and despise another. 7 Who made you superior to others? Didn't God give you everything you have? Well, then, how can you boast, as if what you have were not a gift?

8 Do you already have everything you

3.16: 1 Cor 6.19; 2 Cor 6.16　　**3.19:** Job 5.13　　**3.20:** Ps 94.11

need? Are you already rich? Have you become kings, even though we are not? Well, I wish you really were kings, so that we could be kings together with you. ⁹For it seems to me that God has given the very last place to us apostles, like men condemned to die in public as a spectacle for the whole world of angels and of mankind. ¹⁰For Christ's sake we are fools; but you are wise in union with Christ! We are weak, but you are strong! We are despised, but you are honoured! ¹¹To this very moment we go hungry and thirsty; we are clothed in rags; we are beaten; we wander from place to place; ¹²we wear ourselves out with hard work. When we are cursed, we bless; when we are persecuted, we endure; ¹³when we are insulted, we answer with kind words. We are no more than this world's refuse; we are the scum of the earth to this very moment!

14 I write this to you, not because I want to make you feel ashamed, but to instruct you as my own dear children. ¹⁵For even if you have ten thousand guardians in your Christian life, you have only one father. For in your life in union with Christ Jesus I have become your father by bringing the Good News to you. ¹⁶I beg you, then, to follow my example. ¹⁷For this purpose I am sending to you Timothy, who is my own dear and faithful son in the Christian life. He will remind you of the principles which I follow in the new life in union with Christ Jesus and which I teach in all the churches everywhere.

18 Some of you have become proud because you have thought that I would not be coming to visit you. ¹⁹If the Lord is willing, however, I will come to you soon, and then I will find out for myself the power which these proud people have, and not just what they say. ²⁰For the Kingdom of God is not a matter of words but of power. ²¹Which do you prefer? Shall I come to you with a whip, or in a spirit of love and gentleness?

Immorality in the Church

5 Now, it is actually being said that there is sexual immorality among you so terrible that not even the heathen would be guilty of it. I am told that a man is sleeping with his stepmother! ²How, then, can you be proud? On the contrary, you should be filled with sad-

ness, and the man who has done such a thing should be expelled from your fellowship. ³⁻⁴And even though I am far away from you in body, still I am there with you in spirit; and as though I were there with you, I have in the name of our Lord Jesus already passed judgement on the man who has done this terrible thing. As you meet together, and I meet with you in my spirit, by the power of our Lord Jesus present with us, ⁵you are to hand this man over to Satan for his body to be destroyed, so that his spirit may be saved in the Day of the Lord.

6 It is not right for you to be proud! You know the saying, "A little bit of yeast makes the whole batch of dough rise." ⁷You must remove the old yeast of sin so that you will be entirely pure. Then you will be like a new batch of dough without any yeast, as indeed I know you actually are. For our Passover Festival is ready, now that Christ, our Passover lamb, has been sacrificed. ⁸Let us celebrate our Passover, then, not with bread having the old yeast of sin and wickedness, but with the bread that has no yeast, the bread of purity and truth.

9 In the letter that I wrote you I told you not to associate with immoral people. ¹⁰Now I did not mean pagans who are immoral or greedy or are thieves or who worship idols. To avoid them you would have to get out of the world completely. ¹¹What I meant was that you should not associate with a person who calls himself a brother but is immoral or greedy or worships idols or is a slanderer or a drunkard or a thief. Don't even sit down to eat with such a person.

12-13 After all, it is none of my business to judge outsiders. God will judge them. But should you not judge the members of your own fellowship? As the scripture says, "Remove the evil man from your group."

Lawsuits against Fellow-Christians

6 If one of you has a dispute with a fellow-Christian, how dare he go before heathen judges instead of letting God's people settle the matter? ²Don't you know that God's people will judge the world? Well, then, if you are to judge the world, aren't you capable of judging small matters? ³Do you not know that we shall judge the angels? How much more, then, the things of this life! ⁴If such

4.12: Acts 18.3   **4.16:** 1 Cor 11.1; Phil 3.17   **5.1:** Deut 22.30   **5.6:** Gal 5.9   **5.7:** Ex 12.5
5.8: Ex 13.7; Deut 16.3   **5.13:** Deut 13.5, 17.7

matters come up, are you going to take them to be settled by people who have no standing in the church? 5 Shame on you! Surely there is at least one wise person in your fellowship who can settle a dispute between fellow-Christians. 6 Instead, one Christian goes to court against another and lets unbelievers judge the case!

7 The very fact that you have legal disputes among yourselves shows that you have failed completely. Would it not be better for you to be wronged? Would it not be better for you to be robbed? 8 Instead, you yourselves wrong one another and rob one another, even your own brothers! 9 Surely you know that the wicked will not possess God's Kingdom. Do not fool yourselves; people who are immoral or who worship idols or are adulterers or homosexual perverts 10 or who steal or are greedy or are drunkards or who slander others or are thieves— none of these will possess God's Kingdom. 11 Some of you were like that. But you have been purified from sin; you have been dedicated to God; you have been put right with God by the Lord Jesus Christ and by the Spirit of our God.

Use Your Bodies for God's Glory

12 Someone will say, "I am allowed to do anything." Yes; but not everything is good for you. I could say that I am allowed to do anything, but I am not going to let anything make me its slave. 13 Someone else will say, "Food is for the stomach, and the stomach is for food." Yes; but God will put an end to both. The body is not to be used for sexual immorality, but to serve the Lord; and the Lord provides for the body. 14 God raised the Lord from death, and he will also raise us by his power.

15 You know that your bodies are parts of the body of Christ. Shall I take a part of Christ's body and make it part of the body of a prostitute? Impossible! 16 Or perhaps you don't know that the man who joins his body to a prostitute becomes physically one with her? The scripture says quite plainly, "The two will become one body." 17 But he who joins himself to the Lord becomes spiritually one with him.

18 Avoid immorality. Any other sin a man commits does not affect his body;

but the man who is guilty of sexual immorality sins against his own body. 19 Don't you know that your body is the temple of the Holy Spirit, who lives in you and who was given to you by God? You do not belong to yourselves but to God; 20 he bought you for a price. So use your bodies for God's glory.

Questions about Marriage

7 Now, to deal with the matters you wrote about.

A man does well not to marry. e 2 But because there is so much immorality, every man should have his own wife, and every woman should have her own husband. 3 A man should fulfil his duty as a husband, and a woman should fulfil her duty as a wife, and each should satisfy the other's needs. 4 A wife is not the master of her own body, but her husband is; in the same way a husband is not the master of his own body, but his wife is. 5 Do not deny yourselves to each other, unless you first agree to do so for a while in order to spend your time in prayer; but then resume normal marital relations. In this way you will be kept from giving in to Satan's temptation because of your lack of self-control.

6 I tell you this not as an order, but simply as a concession. 7 Actually I would prefer that all of you were as I am; but each one has a special gift from God, one person this gift, another one that gift.

8 Now, to the unmarried and to the widows I say that it would be better for you to continue to live alone as I do. 9 But if you cannot restrain your desires, go ahead and marry—it is better to marry than to burn with passion.

10 For married people I have a command which is not my own but the Lord's: a wife must not leave her husband; 11 but if she does, she must remain single or else be reconciled to her husband; and a husband must not divorce his wife.

12 To the others I say (I, myself, not the Lord): if a Christian man has a wife who is an unbeliever and she agrees to go on living with him, he must not divorce her. 13 And if a Christian woman is married to a man who is an unbeliever and he agrees to go on living with her, she must not divorce him. 14 For the unbelieving husband is made acceptable to God by being united to his wife, and the

e A man does well not to marry; or You say that a man does well not to marry.
6.12: 1 Cor 10.23　　**6.16:** Gen 2.24　　**6.19:** 1 Cor 3.16; 2 Cor 6.16
7.10–11: Mt 5.32, 19.9; Mk 10.11–12; Lk 16.18

unbelieving wife is made acceptable to God by being united to her Christian husband. If this were not so, their children would be like pagan children; but as it is, they are acceptable to God. ¹⁵ However, if the one who is not a believer wishes to leave the Christian partner, let it be so. In such cases the Christian partner, whether husband or wife, is free to act. God has called you to live in peace. ¹⁶ How can you be sure, Christian wife, that you will not save[f] your husband? Or how can you be sure, Christian husband, that you will not save[f] your wife?

Live as God Called You

17 Each one should go on living according to the Lord's gift to him, and as he was when God called him. This is the rule I teach in all the churches. ¹⁸ If a circumcised man has accepted God's call, he should not try to remove the marks of circumcision; if an uncircumcised man has accepted God's call, he should not get circumcised. ¹⁹ For whether or not a man is circumcised means nothing; what matters is to obey God's commandments. ²⁰ Everyone should remain as he was when he accepted God's call. ²¹ Were you a slave when God called you? Well, never mind; but if you have a chance to become a free man, use it.[g] ²² For a slave who has been called by the Lord is the Lord's free man; in the same way a free man who has been called by Christ is his slave. ²³ God bought you for a price; so do not become slaves of men. ²⁴ My brothers, each one should remain in fellowship with God in the same condition as he was when he was called.

Questions about the Unmarried and the Widows

25 Now, concerning what you wrote about unmarried people: I do not have a command from the Lord, but I give my opinion as one who by the Lord's mercy is worthy of trust.

26 Considering the present distress, I think it is better for a man to stay as he is. ²⁷ Have you got a wife? Then don't try to get rid of her. Are you unmarried? Then don't look for a wife. ²⁸ But if you do marry, you haven't committed a sin; and if an unmarried woman marries, she hasn't committed a sin. But I would rather spare you the everyday troubles that married people will have.

29 What I mean, my brothers, is this: there is not much time left, and from now on married men should live as though they were not married; ³⁰ those who weep, as though they were not sad; those who laugh, as though they were not happy; those who buy, as though they did not own what they bought; ³¹ those who deal in material goods, as though they were not fully occupied with them. For this world, as it is now, will not last much longer.

32 I would like you to be free from worry. An unmarried man concerns himself with the Lord's work, because he is trying to please the Lord. ³³ But a married man concerns himself with worldly matters, because he wants to please his wife; ³⁴ and so he is pulled in two directions. An unmarried woman or a virgin concerns herself with the Lord's work, because she wants to be dedicated both in body and spirit; but a married woman concerns herself with worldly matters, because she wants to please her husband.

35 I am saying this because I want to help you. I am not trying to put restrictions on you. Instead, I want you to do what is right and proper, and to give yourselves completely to the Lord's service without any reservation.

36 In the case of an engaged couple who have decided not to marry: if the man feels that he is not acting properly towards the girl and if his passions are too strong and he feels that they ought to marry, then they should get married, as he wants to.[h] There is no sin in this. ³⁷ But if a man, without being forced to do so, has firmly made up his mind not to marry,[i] and if he has his will under complete control and has already decided in his own mind what to do—then he does well not to marry the girl.[j] ³⁸ So the man who marries[k] does well, but the one who doesn't marry[l] does even better.

39 A married woman is not free as long as her husband lives; but if her husband

[f] How can you be sure...that you will not save; or How do you know...that you will save.
[g] but if you have a chance to become a free man, use it; or but even if you have a chance to become a free man, choose rather to make the best of your condition as a slave.
[h] an engaged couple...as he wants to; or a man and his unmarried daughter: if he feels that he is not acting properly towards her, and if she is at the right age to marry, then he should do as he wishes and let her get married. [i] not to marry; or not to let his daughter get married.
[j] marry the girl; or let her get married. [k] marries; or lets his daughter get married.
[l] doesn't marry; or doesn't let her get married.

dies, then she is free to be married to any man she wishes, but only if he is a Christian. ⁴⁰She will be happier, however, if she stays as she is. That is my opinion, and I think that I too have God's Spirit.

The Question about Food Offered to Idols

8 Now, concerning what you wrote about food offered to idols.

It is true, of course, that "all of us have knowledge," as they say. Such knowledge, however, puffs a person up with pride; but love builds up. ²Whoever thinks he knows something really doesn't know as he ought to know. ³But the person who loves God is known by him.

4 So then, about eating the food offered to idols: we know that an idol stands for something that does not really exist; we know that there is only the one God. ⁵Even if there are so-called "gods," whether in heaven or on earth, and even though there are many of these "gods" and "lords," ⁶yet there is for us only one God, the Father, who is the Creator of all things and for whom we live; and there is only one Lord, Jesus Christ, through whom all things were created and through whom we live.

7 But not everyone knows this truth. Some people have been so used to idols that to this day when they eat such food they still think of it as food that belongs to an idol; their conscience is weak, and they feel they are defiled by the food. ⁸Food, however, will not improve our relations with God; we shall not lose anything if we do not eat, nor shall we gain anything if we do eat.

9 Be careful, however, not to let your freedom of action make those who are weak in the faith fall into sin. ¹⁰Suppose a person whose conscience is weak in this matter sees you, who have so-called "knowledge," eating in the temple of an idol; will not this encourage him to eat food offered to idols? ¹¹And so this weak person, your brother for whom Christ died, will perish because of your "knowledge"! ¹²And in this way you will be sinning against Christ by sinning against your Christian brothers and wounding their weak conscience. ¹³So then, if food makes my brother sin, I will never eat meat again, so as not to make my brother fall into sin.

Rights and Duties of an Apostle

9 Am I not a free man? Am I not an apostle? Haven't I seen Jesus our Lord? And aren't you the result of my work for the Lord? ²Even if others do not accept me as an apostle, surely you do! Because of your life in union with the Lord you yourselves are proof of the fact that I am an apostle.

3 When people criticize me, this is how I defend myself: ⁴Haven't I the right to be given food and drink for my work? ⁵Haven't I the right to follow the example of the other apostles and the Lord's brothers and Peter, by taking a Christian wife with me on my travels? ⁶Or are Barnabas and I the only ones who have to work for our living? ⁷What soldier ever has to pay his own expenses in the army? What farmer does not eat the grapes from his own vineyard? What shepherd does not use the milk from his own sheep?

8 I don't have to limit myself to these everyday examples, because the Law says the same thing. ⁹We read in the Law of Moses, "Do not muzzle an ox when you are using it to thresh corn." Now, is God concerned about oxen? ¹⁰Didn't he really mean us when he said that? Of course that was written for us. The man who ploughs and the man who reaps should do their work in the hope of getting a share of the crop. ¹¹We have sown spiritual seed among you. Is it too much if we reap material benefits from you? ¹²If others have the right to expect this from you, haven't we an even greater right?

But we haven't made use of this right. Instead, we have endured everything in order not to put any obstacle in the way of the Good News about Christ. ¹³Surely you know that the men who work in the Temple get their food from the Temple and that those who offer the sacrifices on the altar get a share of the sacrifices. ¹⁴In the same way, the Lord has ordered that those who preach the gospel should get their living from it.

15 But I haven't made use of any of these rights, nor am I writing this now in order to claim such rights for myself. I would rather die first! Nobody is going to turn my rightful boast into empty words! ¹⁶I have no right to boast just because I preach the gospel. After all, I am under orders to do so. And how terrible it would be for me if I did not preach the gospel! ¹⁷If I did my work

9.9: Deut 25.4; 1 Tim 5.18   **9.11:** Rom 15.27   **9.13:** Deut 18.1   **9.14:** Mt 10.10; Lk 10.7

as a matter of free choice, then I could expect to be paid; but I do it as a matter of duty, because God has entrusted me with this task. 18 What pay do I get, then? It is the privilege of preaching the Good News without charging for it, without claiming my rights in my work for the gospel.

19 I am a free man, nobody's slave; but I make myself everybody's slave in order to win as many people as possible. 20 While working with the Jews, I live like a Jew in order to win them; and even though I myself am not subject to the Law of Moses, I live as though I were when working with those who are, in order to win them. 21 In the same way, when working with Gentiles, I live like a Gentile, outside the Jewish Law, in order to win Gentiles. This does not mean that I don't obey God's law; I am really under Christ's law. 22 Among the weak in faith I become weak like one of them, in order to win them. So I become all things to all men, that I may save some of them by whatever means are possible.

23 All this I do for the gospel's sake, in order to share in its blessings. 24 Surely

Only one of them wins the prize (9.24)

you know that many runners take part in a race, but only one of them wins the prize. Run, then, in such a way as to win the prize. 25 Every athlete in training submits to strict discipline, in order to be crowned with a wreath that will not last; but we do it for one that will last for ever. 26 That is why I run straight for the finishing-line; that is why I am like a boxer who does not waste his punches. 27 I harden my body with blows and bring

it under complete control, to keep myself from being disqualified after having called others to the contest.

Warnings against Idols

10 I want you to remember, my brothers, what happened to our ancestors who followed Moses. They were all under the protection of the cloud, and all passed safely through the Red Sea. 2 In the cloud and in the sea they were all baptized as followers of Moses. 3 All ate the same spiritual bread 4 and drank the same spiritual drink. They drank from the spiritual rock that went with them; and that rock was Christ himself. 5 But even then God was not pleased with most of them, and so their dead bodies were scattered over the desert.

6 Now, all this is an example for us, to warn us not to desire evil things, as they did, 7 nor to worship idols, as some of them did. As the scripture says, "The people sat down to a feast which turned into an orgy of drinking and sex." 8 We must not be guilty of sexual immorality, as some of them were—and in one day twenty-three thousand of them fell dead. 9 We must not put the Lord *m* to the test, as some of them did—and they were killed by snakes. 10 We must not complain, as some of them did—and they were destroyed by the Angel of Death.

11 All these things happened to them as examples for others, and they were written down as a warning for us. For we live at a time when the end is about to come.

12 Whoever thinks he is standing firm had better be careful that he does not fall. 13 Every test that you have experienced is the kind that normally comes to people. But God keeps his promise, and he will not allow you to be tested beyond your power to remain firm; at the time you are put to the test, he will give you the strength to endure it, and so provide you with a way out.

14 So then, my dear friends, keep away from the worship of idols. 15 I speak to you as sensible people; judge for yourselves what I say. 16 The cup we use in the Lord's Supper and for which we give thanks to God: when we drink from it, we are sharing in the blood of Christ. And

m the Lord; *some manuscripts have* Christ.
10.1: Ex 13.21-22, 14.22-29   **10.3:** Ex 16.35   **10.4:** Ex 17.6; Num 20.11
10.5: Num 14.29-30   **10.6:** Num 11.4   **10.7:** Ex 32.6   **10.8:** Num 25.1-18
10.9: Num 21.5-6   **10.10:** Num 16.41-49   **10.16:** Mt 26.26-28; Mk 14.22-24; Lk 22.19-20

We all share the same loaf (10.17)

the bread we break: when we eat it, we are sharing in the body of Christ. ¹⁷Because there is the one loaf of bread, all of us, though many, are one body, for we all share the same loaf.

18 Consider the people of Israel; those who eat what is offered in sacrifice share in the altar's service to God. ¹⁹Do I imply, then, that an idol or the food offered to it really amounts to anything? ²⁰No! What I am saying is that what is sacrificed on pagan altars is offered to demons, not to God. And I do not want you to be partners with demons. ²¹You cannot drink from the Lord's cup and also from the cup of demons; you cannot eat at the Lord's table and also at the table of demons. ²²Or do we want to make the Lord jealous? Do we think that we are stronger than he?

23 "We are allowed to do anything," so they say. That is true, but not everything is good. "We are allowed to do anything"—but not everything is helpful. ²⁴No one should be looking to his own interests, but to the interests of others.

25 You are free to eat anything sold in the meat-market, without asking any questions because of your conscience. ²⁶For, as the scripture says, "The earth and everything in it belong to the Lord."

27 If an unbeliever invites you to a meal and you decide to go, eat what is set before you, without asking any questions because of your conscience. ²⁸But if someone says to you, "This food was offered to idols," then do not eat that food, for the sake of the one who told you and for conscience' sake—²⁹that is, not your own conscience, but the other person's conscience.

"Well, then," someone asks, "why should my freedom to act be limited by another person's conscience? ³⁰If I thank God for my food, why should anyone criticize me about food for which I give thanks?"

31 Well, whatever you do, whether you eat or drink, do it all for God's glory. ³²Live in such a way as to cause no trouble either to Jews or Gentiles or to the church of God. ³³Just do as I do; I try to please everyone in all that I do, not thinking of my own good, but of the good of all, so that they might be saved.

11 Imitate me, then, just as I imitate Christ.

Covering the Head in Worship

2 I praise you because you always remember me and follow the teachings that I have handed on to you. ³But I want you to understand that Christ is supreme over every man, the husband is supreme over his wife, and God is supreme over Christ. ⁴So a man who prays or proclaims God's message in public worship with his

10.18: Lev 7.6   **10.20:** Deut 32.17   **10.22:** Deut 32.21   **10.23:** 1 Cor 6.12   **10.26:** Ps 24.1
11.1: 1 Cor 4.16; Phil 3.17

head covered disgraces Christ. ⁵And any woman who prays or proclaims God's message in public worship with nothing on her head disgraces her husband; there is no difference between her and a woman whose head has been shaved. ⁶If the woman does not cover her head, she might as well cut her hair. And since it is a shameful thing for a woman to shave her head or cut her hair, she should cover her head. ⁷A man has no need to cover his head, because he reflects the image and glory of God. But woman reflects the glory of man; ⁸for man was not created from woman, but woman from man. ⁹Nor was man created for woman's sake, but woman was created for man's sake. ¹⁰On account of the angels, then, a woman should have a covering over her head to show that she is under her husband's authority. ¹¹In our life in the Lord, however, woman is not independent of man, nor is man independent of woman. ¹²For as woman was made from man, in the same way man is born of woman; and it is God who brings everything into existence.

13 Judge for yourselves whether it is proper for a woman to pray to God in public worship with nothing on her head. ¹⁴Why, nature itself teaches you that long hair on a man is a disgrace, ¹⁵but on a woman it is a thing of beauty. Her long hair has been given her to serve as a covering. ¹⁶But if anyone wants to argue about it, all I have to say is that neither we nor the churches of God have any other custom in worship.

The Lord's Supper
(Matt. 26.26–29; Mark 14.22–25; Luke 22.14–20)

17 In the following instructions, however, I do not praise you, because your meetings for worship actually do more harm than good. ¹⁸In the first place, I have been told that there are opposing groups in your meetings; and this I believe is partly true. ¹⁹(No doubt there must be divisions among you so that the ones who are in the right may be clearly seen.) ²⁰When you meet together as a group, it is not the Lord's Supper that you eat. ²¹For as you eat, each one goes ahead with his own meal, so that some are hungry while others get drunk. ²²Haven't you got your own homes in which to eat and drink? Or would you rather despise the church of God and put to shame the

people who are in need? What do you expect me to say to you about this? Shall I praise you? Of course I don't!

23 For I received from the Lord the teaching that I passed on to you: that the Lord Jesus, on the night he was betrayed, took a piece of bread, ²⁴gave thanks to God, broke it, and said, "This is my body, which is for you. Do this in memory of me." ²⁵In the same way, after the supper he took the cup and said, "This cup is God's new covenant, sealed with my blood. Whenever you drink it, do so in memory of me."

26 This means that every time you eat this bread and drink from this cup you proclaim the Lord's death until he comes. ²⁷It follows that if anyone eats the Lord's bread or drinks from his cup in a way that dishonours him, he is guilty of sin against the Lord's body and blood. ²⁸So then, everyone should examine himself first, and then eat the bread and drink from the cup. ²⁹For if he does not recognize the meaning of the Lord's body when he eats the bread and drinks from the cup, he brings judgement on himself as he eats and drinks. ³⁰That is why many of you are weak and ill, and several have died. ³¹If we would examine ourselves first, we would not come under God's judgement. ³²But we are judged and punished by the Lord, so that we shall not be condemned together with the world.

33 So then, my brothers, when you gather together to eat the Lord's Supper, wait for one another. ³⁴And if anyone is hungry, he should eat at home, so that you will not come under God's judgement as you meet together. As for the other matters, I will settle them when I come.

Gifts from the Holy Spirit

12 Now, concerning what you wrote about the gifts from the Holy Spirit. I want you to know the truth about them, my brothers. ²You know that while you were still heathen, you were led astray in many ways to the worship of lifeless idols. ³I want you to know that no one who is led by God's Spirit can say "A curse on Jesus!" and no one can confess "Jesus is Lord," unless he is guided by the Holy Spirit.

4 There are different kinds of spiritual gifts, but the same Spirit gives them. ⁵There are different ways of serving, but the same Lord is served. ⁶There are

11.7: Gen 1.26–27   **11.8–9:** Gen 2.18–23   **11.25:** Ex 24.6–8; Jer 31.31–34
12.4–11: Rom 12.6–8

different abilities to perform service, but the same God gives ability to all for their particular service. [7] The Spirit's presence is shown in some way in each person for the good of all. [8] The Spirit gives one person a message full of wisdom, while to another person the same Spirit gives a message full of knowledge. [9] One and the same Spirit gives faith to one person, while to another person he gives the power to heal. [10] The Spirit gives one person the power to work miracles; to another, the gift of speaking God's message; and to yet another, the ability to tell the difference between gifts that come from the Spirit and those that do not. To one person he gives the ability to speak in strange tongues, and to another he gives the ability to explain what is said. [11] But it is one and the same Spirit who does all this; as he wishes, he gives a different gift to each person.

One Body with Many Parts

12 Christ is like a single body, which has many parts; it is still one body, even though it is made up of different parts. [13] In the same way, all of us, whether Jews or Gentiles, whether slaves or free, have been baptized into the one body by the same Spirit, and we have all been given the one Spirit to drink.

14 For the body itself is not made up of only one part, but of many parts. [15] If the foot were to say, "Because I am not a hand, I don't belong to the body," that would not keep it from being a part of the body. [16] And if the ear were to say, "Because I am not an eye, I don't belong to the body," that would not keep it from being a part of the body. [17] If the whole body were just an eye, how could it hear? And if it were only an ear, how could it smell? [18] As it is, however, God put every different part in the body just as he wanted it to be. [19] There would not be a body if it were all only one part! [20] As it is, there are many parts but one body.

21 So then, the eye cannot say to the hand, "I don't need you!" Nor can the head say to the feet, "Well, I don't need you!" [22] On the contrary, we cannot do without the parts of the body that seem to be weaker; [23] and those parts that we think aren't worth very much are the ones which we treat with greater care; while the parts of the body which don't look

very nice are treated with special modesty, [24] which the more beautiful parts do not need. God himself has put the body together in such a way as to give greater honour to those parts that need it. [25] And so there is no division in the body, but all its different parts have the same concern for one another. [26] If one part of the body suffers, all the other parts suffer with it; if one part is praised, all the other parts share its happiness.

27 All of you are Christ's body, and each one is a part of it. [28] In the church God has put all in place: in the first place apostles, in the second place prophets, and in the third place teachers; then those who perform miracles, followed by those who are given the power to heal or to help others or to direct them or to speak in strange tongues. [29] They are not all apostles or prophets or teachers. Not everyone has the power to work miracles [30] or to heal diseases or to speak in strange tongues or to explain what is said. [31] Set your hearts, then, on the more important gifts.

Best of all, however, is the following way.

Love

13 I may be able to speak the languages of men and even of angels, but if I have no love, my speech is no more than a noisy gong or a clanging bell. [2] I may have the gift of inspired preaching; I may have all knowledge and understand all secrets; I may have all the faith needed to move mountains—but if I have no love, I am nothing. [3] I may give away everything I have, and even give up my body to be burnt[n]—but if I have no love, this does me no good.

4 Love is patient and kind; it is not jealous or conceited or proud; [5] love is not ill-mannered or selfish or irritable; love does not keep a record of wrongs; [6] love is not happy with evil, but is happy with the truth. [7] Love never gives up; and its faith, hope, and patience never fail.

8 Love is eternal. There are inspired messages, but they are temporary; there are gifts of speaking in strange tongues, but they will cease; there is knowledge, but it will pass. [9] For our gifts of knowledge and of inspired messages are only partial; [10] but when what is perfect comes, then what is partial will disappear.

11 When I was a child, my speech,

---

[n] to be burnt; *some manuscripts have* in order to boast.
12.12: Rom 12.4–5   **12.28:** Eph 4.11   **13.2:** Mt 17.20, 21.21; Mk 11.23

What we see now is like a dim image in a mirror (13.12)

feelings, and thinking were all those of a child; now that I am a man, I have no more use for childish ways. 12 What we see now is like a dim image in a mirror; then we shall see face to face. What I know now is only partial; then it will be complete—as complete as God's knowledge of me.

13 Meanwhile these three remain: faith, hope, and love; and the greatest of these is love.

More about Gifts from the Spirit

14 It is love, then, that you should strive for. Set your hearts on spiritual gifts, especially the gift of proclaiming God's message. 2 The one who speaks in strange tongues does not speak to others but to God, because no one understands him. He is speaking secret truths by the power of the Spirit. 3 But the one who proclaims God's message speaks to people and gives them help, encouragement, and comfort. 4 The one who speaks in strange tongues helps only himself, but the one who proclaims God's message helps the whole church.

5 I would like all of you to speak in strange tongues; but I would rather that you had the gift of proclaiming God's message. For the person who proclaims God's message is of greater value than

the one who speaks in strange tongues—unless there is someone present who can explain what he says, so that the whole church may be helped. 6 So when I come to you, my brothers, what use will I be to you if I speak in strange tongues? Not a bit, unless I bring you some revelation from God or some knowledge or some inspired message, or some teaching.

7 Take such lifeless musical instruments as the flute or the harp—how will anyone know the tune that is being played unless the notes are sounded distinctly? 8 And if the man who plays the bugle does not sound a clear call, who will prepare for battle? 9 In the same way, how will anyone understand what you are talking about if your message given in strange tongues is not clear? Your words will vanish in the air! 10 There are many different languages in the world, yet none of them is without meaning. 11 But if I do not know the language being spoken, the person who uses it will be a foreigner to me and I will be a foreigner to him. 12 Since you are eager to have the gifts of the Spirit, you must try above everything else to make greater use of those which help to build up the church.

Then we shall see face to face (13.12)

13 The person who speaks in strange tongues, then, must pray for the gift to explain what he says. 14 For if I pray in this way, my spirit prays indeed, but my mind has no part in it. 15 What should I do, then? I will pray with my spirit, but I will pray also with my mind; I will sing with my spirit, but I will sing also with my mind. 16 When you give thanks to God in spirit only, how can an ordinary person taking part in the meeting say "Amen" to your prayer of thanksgiving? He has no way of knowing what you are saying. 17 Even if your prayer of thanks to God is quite good, the other person is not helped at all.

18 I thank God that I speak in strange tongues much more than any of you. 19 But in church worship I would rather speak five words that can be understood, in order to teach others, than speak thousands of words in strange tongues.

20 Do not be like children in your thinking, my brothers; be children so far as evil is concerned, but be grown-up in your thinking. 21 In the Scriptures it is written,

"By means of men speaking strange
          languages
     I will speak to my people, says the
          Lord.
     I will speak through lips of foreigners,
          but even then my people will not
          listen to me."

22 So then, the gift of speaking in strange tongues is proof for unbelievers, not for believers, while the gift of proclaiming God's message is proof for believers, not for unbelievers.

23 If, then, the whole church meets together and everyone starts speaking in strange tongues—and if some ordinary people or unbelievers come in, won't they say that you are all crazy? 24 But if everyone is proclaiming God's message when some unbeliever or ordinary person comes in, he will be convinced of his sin by what he hears. He will be judged by all he hears, 25 his secret thoughts will be brought into the open, and he will bow down and worship God, confessing, "Truly God is here among you!"

Order in the Church

26 This is what I mean, my brothers. When you meet for worship, one person has a hymn, another a teaching, another a revelation from God, another a message in strange tongues, and still another the explanation of what is said. Everything must be of help to the church. 27 If someone is going to speak in strange tongues, two or three at the most should speak, one after the other, and someone else must explain what is being said. 28 But if no one is there who can explain, then the one who speaks in strange tongues must be quiet and speak only to himself and to God. 29 Two or three who are given God's message should speak, while the others are to judge what they say. 30 But if someone sitting in the meeting receives a message from God, the one who is speaking should stop. 31 All of you may proclaim God's message, one by one, so that everyone will learn and be encouraged. 32 The gift of proclaiming God's message should be under the speaker's control, 33 because God does not want us to be in disorder but in harmony and peace.

As in all the churches of God's people, 34 the women should keep quiet in the meetings. They are not allowed to speak; as the Jewish Law says, they must not be in charge. 35 If they want to find out about something, they should ask their husbands at home. It is a disgraceful thing for a woman to speak in church.

36 Or could it be that the word of God came from you? Or are you the only ones to whom it came? 37 If anyone supposes he is God's messenger or has a spiritual gift, he must realize that what I am writing to you is the Lord's command. 38 But if he does not pay attention to this, pay no attention to him.

39 So then, my brothers, set your heart on proclaiming God's message, but do not forbid the speaking in strange tongues. 40 Everything must be done in a proper and orderly way.

The Resurrection of Christ

15 And now I want to remind you, my brothers, of the Good News which I preached to you, which you received, and on which your faith stands firm. 2 That is the gospel, the message that I preached to you. You are saved by the gospel if you hold firmly to it—unless it was for nothing that you believed.

3 I passed on to you what I received, which is of the greatest importance: that Christ died for our sins, as written in the Scriptures; 4 that he was buried and that

14.21: Is 28.11-12   15.3: Is 53.5-12   15.4: Ps 16.8-10; Mt 12.40; Acts 2.24-32 he was raised to life three days later, as written in the Scriptures; [5]that he appeared to Peter and then to all twelve apostles. [6]Then he appeared to more than five hundred of his followers at once, most of whom are still alive, although some have died. [7]Then he appeared to James, and afterwards to all the apostles.

8 Last of all he appeared also to me—even though I am like someone whose birth was abnormal.[o] [9]For I am the least of all the apostles—I do not even deserve to be called an apostle, because I persecuted God's church. [10]But by God's grace I am what I am, and the grace that he gave me was not without effect. On the contrary, I have worked harder than any of the other apostles, although it was not really my own doing, but God's grace working with me. [11]So then, whether it came from me or from them, this is what we all preach, and this is what you believe.

Our Resurrection

12 Now, since our message is that Christ has been raised from death, how can some of you say that the dead will not be raised to life? [13]If that is true, it means that Christ was not raised; [14]and if Christ has not been raised from death, then we have nothing to preach and you have nothing to believe. [15]More than that, we are shown to be lying about God, because we said that he raised Christ from death—but if it is true that the dead are not raised to life, then he did not raise Christ. [16]For if the dead are not raised, neither has Christ been raised. [17]And if Christ has not been raised, then your faith is a delusion and you are still lost in your sins. [18]It would also mean that the believers in Christ who have died are lost. [19]If our hope in Christ is good for this life only and no more,[p] then we deserve more pity than anyone else in all the world.

20 But the truth is that Christ has been raised from death, as the guarantee that those who sleep in death will also be raised. [21]For just as death came by means of a man, in the same way the rising from death comes by means of a man. [22]For just as all people die because of their union with Adam, in the same way all will be raised to life because of their union with Christ. [23]But each one will be raised

Those who sleep in death will also be raised (15.20)

in his proper order: Christ, first of all; then, at the time of his coming, those who belong to him. [24]Then the end will come; Christ will overcome all spiritual rulers, authorities, and powers, and will hand over the Kingdom to God the Father. [25]For Christ must rule until God defeats all enemies and puts them under his feet. [26]The last enemy to be defeated will be death. [27]For the scripture says, "God put *all* things under his feet." It is clear, of course, that the words "all things" do not include God himself, who puts all things under Christ. [28]But when all things have been placed under Christ's rule, then he himself, the Son, will place himself under God, who placed all things under him; and God will rule completely over all.

29 Now, what about those people who are baptized for the dead? What do they hope to accomplish? If it is true, as some claim, that the dead are not raised to life, why are those people being baptized for the dead? [30]And as for us—why would we run the risk of danger every hour? [31]My brothers, I face death every day! The pride I have in you, in our life in union with Christ Jesus our Lord, makes me declare this. [32]If I have, as it were, fought "wild beasts" here in Ephesus simply from human motives, what have I gained? But if the dead are not raised to

---

[o]whose birth was abnormal; *or* who was born at the wrong time.
[p]If our hope in Christ is good for this life only and no more; *or* If all we have in this life is our hope in Christ.

15.5: Mt 28.16–17; Mk 16.14; Lk 24.34,36; Jn 20.19   **15.8:** Acts 9.3–6   **15.9:** Acts 8.3
15.25: Ps 110.1   **15.27:** Ps 8.6   **15.32:** Is 22.13

life, then, as the saying goes, "Let us eat and drink, for tomorrow we will die."

33 Do not be fooled. "Bad companions ruin good character." 34 Come back to your right senses and stop your sinful ways. I declare to your shame that some of you do not know God.

The Resurrection Body

35 Someone will ask, "How can the dead be raised to life? What kind of body will they have?" 36 You fool! When you sow a seed in the ground, it does not sprout to life unless it dies. 37 And what you sow is a bare seed, perhaps a grain of wheat or some other grain, not the full-bodied plant that will later grow up. 38 God provides that seed with the body he wishes; he gives each seed its own proper body.

39 And the flesh of living beings is not all the same kind of flesh; human beings have one kind of flesh, animals another, birds another, and fish another.

40 And there are heavenly bodies and earthly bodies; the beauty that belongs to heavenly bodies is different from the beauty that belongs to earthly bodies. 41 The sun has its own beauty, the moon another beauty, and the stars a different beauty; and even among stars there are different kinds of beauty.

42 This is how it will be when the dead are raised to life. When the body is buried, it is mortal; when raised, it will be immortal. 43 When buried, it is ugly and weak; when raised, it will be beautiful and strong. 44 When buried, it is a physical body; when raised, it will be a spiritual body. There is, of course, a physical body, so there has to be a spiritual body. 45 For the scripture says, "The first man, Adam, was created a living being"; but the last Adam is the life-giving Spirit. 46 It is not the spiritual that comes first, but the physical, and then the spiritual. 47 The first Adam, made of earth, came from the earth; the second Adam came from heaven. 48 Those who belong to the earth are like the one who was made of earth; those who are of heaven are like the one who came from heaven. 49 Just as we wear the likeness of the man made of earth, so we will wear q the likeness of the Man from heaven.

50 What I mean, brothers, is that what is made of flesh and blood cannot share in God's Kingdom, and what is mortal cannot possess immortality.

51–52 Listen to this secret truth: we shall not all die, but when the last trumpet sounds, we shall all be changed in an instant, as quickly as the blinking of an eye. For when the trumpet sounds, the dead will be raised, never to die again, and we shall all be changed. 53 For what is mortal must be changed into what is immortal; what will die must be changed into what cannot die. 54 So when this takes place, and the mortal has been changed into the immortal, then the scripture will come true: "Death is destroyed; victory is complete!"

55 "Where, Death, is your victory?

Where, Death, is your power to hurt?" 56 Death gets its power to hurt from sin, and sin gets its power from the Law. 57 But thanks be to God who gives us the victory through our Lord Jesus Christ!

58 So then, my dear brothers, stand firm and steady. Keep busy always in your work for the Lord, since you know that nothing you do in the Lord's service is ever useless.

The Offering for Fellow-Believers

16 Now, concerning what you wrote about the money to be raised to help God's people in Judaea. You must do what I told the churches in Galatia to do. 2 Every Sunday each of you must put aside some money, in proportion to what he has earned, and save it up, so that there will be no need to collect money when I come. 3 After I come, I shall give letters of introduction to the men you have approved, and send them to take your gift to Jerusalem. 4 If it seems worth while for me to go, then they can go along with me.

Paul's Plans

5 I shall come to you after I have gone through Macedonia—for I have to go through Macedonia. 6 I shall probably spend some time with you, perhaps the whole winter, and then you can help me to continue my journey, wherever it is I shall go next. 7 I want to see you more than just briefly in passing; I hope to spend quite a long time with you, if the Lord allows.

---

q we will wear; *some manuscripts have* let us wear.
15.45: Gen 2.7   **15.51–52:** 1 Thes 4.15–17   **15.54:** Is 25.8   **15.55:** Hos 13.14
16.1: Rom 15.25–26   **16.5:** Acts 19.21

8 I will stay here in Ephesus until the day of Pentecost. ⁹There is a real opportunity here for great and worthwhile work, even though there are many opponents.

10 If Timothy comes your way, be sure to make him feel welcome among you, because he is working for the Lord, just as I am. ¹¹No one should look down on him, but you must help him to continue his journey in peace, so that he will come back to me; for I am expecting him back with the brothers.

12 Now, about brother Apollos. I have often encouraged him to visit you with the other brothers, but he is not completely convinced ʳ that he should go at this time. When he gets the chance, however, he will go.

Final Words

13 Be alert, stand firm in the faith, be brave, be strong. ¹⁴Do all your work in love.

15 You know about Stephanas and his family; they are the first Christian converts in Achaia and have given themselves to the service of God's people. I beg you, my brothers, ¹⁶to follow the leadership of such people as these, and of anyone else who works and serves with them.

17 I am happy about the coming of Stephanas, Fortunatus, and Achaicus; they have made up for your absence ¹⁸and have cheered me up, just as they cheered you up. Such men as these deserve notice.

19 The churches in the province of Asia send you their greetings; Aquila and Priscilla and the church that meets in their house send warm Christian greetings. ²⁰All the brothers here send greetings.

Greet one another with a brotherly kiss.

21 With my own hand I write this: *Greetings from Paul.*

22 Whoever does not love the Lord—a curse on him!

Marana tha—Our Lord, come!

23 The grace of the Lord Jesus be with you.

24 My love be with you all in Christ Jesus.

ʳhe is not completely convinced; *or* it is not at all God's will.
16.8: Lev 23.15-21; Deut 16.9-11   **16.8-9:** Acts 19.8-10   **16.10:** 1 Cor 4.17
16.15: 1 Cor 1.16   **16.19:** Acts 18.2

PAUL'S SECOND LETTER TO THE
CORINTHIANS

INTRODUCTION

Paul's Second Letter to the Corinthians was written during a difficult period in his relations with the church at Corinth. Some members of the church had evidently made strong attacks against Paul, but he shows his deep longing for reconciliation and expresses his great joy when this is brought about.

In the first part of the letter Paul discusses his relationship with the church at Corinth, explaining why he had responded with severity to insult and opposition in the church and expressing his joy that this severity had resulted in repentance and reconciliation. Then he appeals to the church for a generous offering to help the needy Christians in Judaea. In the final chapters Paul defends his apostleship against a few people at Corinth who had set themselves up as true apostles, while accusing Paul of being a false one.

Outline of Contents

Introduction   1.1–11
Paul and the church at Corinth   1.12—7.16

The offering for the Christians in Judaea   8.1—9.15
Paul's defence of his authority as an apostle   10.1—13.10
Conclusion 13.11–13

1 From Paul, an apostle of Christ Jesus by God's will, and from our brother Timothy—

To the church of God in Corinth, and to all God's people throughout Achaia:

2 May God our Father and the Lord Jesus Christ give you grace and peace.

Paul Gives Thanks to God

3 Let us give thanks to the God and Father of our Lord Jesus Christ, the merciful Father, the God from whom all help comes! 4 He helps us in all our

Help others who have all kinds of troubles (1.4)

troubles, so that we are able to help others who have all kinds of troubles, using the same help that we ourselves have received from God. 5 Just as we have a share in Christ's many sufferings, so also through Christ we share in God's great help. 6 If we suffer, it is for your help and salvation; if we are helped, then you too are helped and given the strength to endure with patience the same sufferings that we also endure. 7 So our hope in you is never shaken; we know that just as you share in our sufferings, you also share in the help we receive.

8 We want to remind you, brothers, of the trouble we had in the province of Asia. The burdens laid upon us were so great and so heavy that we gave up all hope of staying alive. 9 We felt that the death sentence had been passed on us. But this happened so that we should rely, not on ourselves, but only on God, who raises the dead. 10 From such terrible dangers of death*a* he saved us, and will save us; and we have placed our hope in him that he will save us again, 11 as you help us by means of your prayers for us. So it will be that the many prayers for us will be answered, and God will bless us; and many will raise their voices to him in thanksgiving for us.

The Change in Paul's Plans

12 We are proud that our conscience assures us that our lives in this world, and especially our relations with you, have been ruled by God-given frankness*b* and sincerity, by the power of God's grace, and not by human wisdom. 13–14 We write to you only what you can read and understand. But even though you now understand us only in part, I hope that you will come to understand us completely, so that in the Day of our Lord Jesus you can be as proud of us as we shall be of you.

15 I was so sure of all this that I made plans at first to visit you, in order that you might be blessed twice. 16 For I planned to visit you on my way to Macedonia and again on my way back, in order to get help from you for my journey to Judaea. 17 In planning this, did I appear fickle? When I make my plans, do I make them from selfish motives, ready to say "Yes, yes" and "No, no" at the same time? 18 As surely as God speaks the truth, my promise to you was not a "Yes" and a "No." 19 For Jesus Christ, the Son of God, who was preached among you by Silas, Timothy, and myself, is not one who is "Yes" and "No." On the contrary, he is God's "Yes"; 20 for it is he who is the "Yes" to all God's promises. This is why through Jesus Christ our "Amen" is said to the glory of God. 21 It is God himself who makes us, together with you, sure of our life in union with Christ; it is God himself who

---

a terrible dangers of death; *some manuscripts have* terrible death.
b frankness; *some manuscripts have* holiness.

1.1: Acts 18.1   **1.8:** 1 Cor 15.32   **1.16:** Acts 19.21   **1.19:** Acts 18.5

has set us apart, [22] who has placed his mark of ownership upon us, and who has given us the Holy Spirit in our hearts as the guarantee of all that he has in store for us.

23 I call God as my witness—he knows my heart! It was in order to spare you that I decided not to go to Corinth. [24] We are not trying to dictate to you what you must believe; we know that you stand firm in the faith. Instead, we are working with you for your own happiness.

2 So I made up my mind not to come to you again to make you sad. [2] For if I were to make you sad, who would be left to cheer me up? Only the very persons I had made sad. [3] That is why I wrote that letter to you—I did not want to come to you and be made sad by the very people who should make me glad. For I am convinced that when I am happy, then all of you are happy too. [4] I wrote to you with a greatly troubled and distressed heart and with many tears; my purpose was not to make you sad, but to make you realize how much I love you all.

Forgiveness for the Offender

5 Now, if anyone has made somebody sad, he has not done it to me but to all of you—in part at least. (I say this because I do not want to be too hard on him.) [6] It is enough that this person has been punished in this way by most of you. [7] Now, however, you should forgive him and encourage him, in order to keep him from becoming so sad as to give up completely. [8] And so I beg you to let him know that you really do love him. [9] I wrote you that letter because I wanted to find out how well you had stood the test and whether you are always ready to obey my instructions. [10] When you forgive someone for what he has done, I forgive him too. For when I forgive—if, indeed, I need to forgive anything—I do it in Christ's presence because of you, [11] in order to keep Satan from getting the upper hand of us; for we know what his plans are.

Paul's Anxiety in Troas

12 When I arrived in Troas to preach the Good News about Christ, I found that the Lord had opened the way for the work there. [13] But I was deeply worried, because I could not find our brother Titus. So I said good-bye to the people there and went on to Macedonia.

Victory through Christ

14 But thanks be to God! For in union with Christ we are always led by God as prisoners in Christ's victory procession. God uses us to make the knowledge about Christ spread everywhere like a sweet fragrance. [15] For we are like a sweet-smelling incense offered by Christ to God, which spreads among those who are being saved and those who are being lost. [16] For those who are being lost, it is a deadly stench that kills; but for those who are being saved, it is a fragrance that brings life. Who, then, is capable of such a task? [17] We are not like so many others, who handle God's message as if it were cheap merchandise; but because God has sent us, we speak with sincerity in his presence, as servants of Christ.

Servants of the New Covenant

3 Does this sound as if we were again boasting about ourselves? Could it be that, like some other people, we need letters of recommendation to you or from you? [2] You yourselves are the letter we have, written on our hearts for everyone to know and read. [3] It is clear that Christ himself wrote this letter and sent it by us. It is written, not with ink but with the Spirit of the living God, and not on stone tablets but on human hearts.

4 We say this because we have confidence in God through Christ. [5] There is nothing in us that allows us to claim that we are capable of doing this work. The capacity we have comes from God; [6] it is he who made us capable of serving the new covenant, which consists not of a written law but of the Spirit. The written law brings death, but the Spirit gives life.

7 The Law was carved in letters on stone tablets, and God's glory appeared when it was given. Even though the brightness on Moses' face was fading, it was so strong that the people of Israel could not keep their eyes fixed on him. If the Law, which brings death when it is in force, came with such glory, [8] how much greater is the glory that belongs to the activity of the Spirit! [9] The system which brings condemnation was glorious; how much more glorious is the activity which brings salvation! [10] We may say that because of the far brighter glory now

2.12-13: Acts 20.1   **3.3:** Ex 24.12; Jer 31.33; Ezek 11.19, 36.26   **3.6:** Jer 31.31
3.7: Ex 34.29

the glory that was so bright in the past is gone. ¹¹For if there was glory in that which lasted for a while, how much more glory is there in that which lasts for ever!

12 Because we have this hope, we are very bold. ¹³We are not like Moses, who had to put a veil over his face so that the people of Israel would not see the brightness fade and disappear. ¹⁴Their minds, indeed, were closed; and to this very day their minds are covered with the same veil as they read the books of the old covenant. The veil is removed only when a person is joined to Christ. ¹⁵Even today, whenever they read the Law of Moses, the veil still covers their minds. ¹⁶But it can be removed, as the scripture says about Moses: "His veil was removed when he turned to the Lord."ᶜ ¹⁷Now, "the Lord" in this passage is the Spirit; and where the Spirit of the Lord is present, there is freedom. ¹⁸All of us, then, reflect the glory of the Lord with uncovered faces; and that same glory, coming from the Lord, who is the Spirit, transforms us into his likeness in an ever greater degree of glory.

Spiritual Treasure in Clay Pots

4 God in his mercy has given us this work to do, and so we are not discouraged. ²We put aside all secret and shameful deeds; we do not act with deceit, nor do we falsify the word of God. In the full light of truth we live in God's sight and try to commend ourselves to everyone's good conscience. ³For if the gospel we preach is hidden, it is hidden only from those who are being lost. ⁴They do not believe, because their minds have been kept in the dark by the evil god of this world. He keeps them from seeing the light shining on them, the light that comes from the Good News about the glory of Christ, who is the exact likeness of God. ⁵For it is not ourselves that we preach; we preach Jesus Christ as Lord, and ourselves as your servants for Jesus' sake. ⁶The God who said, "Out of darkness the light shall shine!" is the same God who made his light shine in our hearts, to bring us the knowledge of God's glory shining in the face of Christ.

7 Yet we who have this spiritual treasure are like common clay pots, in order to show that the supreme power belongs to God, not to us. ⁸We are often troubled, but not crushed; sometimes in doubt, but never in despair; ⁹there are many enemies, but we are never without a friend; and though badly hurt at times, we are not destroyed. ¹⁰At all times we carry in our mortal bodies the death of Jesus, so that his life also may be seen in our bodies. ¹¹Throughout our lives we are always in danger of death for Jesus' sake, in order that his life may be seen in this mortal body of ours. ¹²This means that death is at work in us, but life is at work in you.

13 The scripture says, "I spoke because I believed." In the same spirit of faith, we also speak because we believe. ¹⁴We know that God, who raised the Lord Jesus to life, will also raise us up with Jesus and take us, together with you, into his presence. ¹⁵All this is for your sake; and as God's grace reaches more and more people, they will offer to the glory of God more prayers of thanksgiving.

Living by Faith

16 For this reason we never become discouraged. Even though our physical being is gradually decaying, yet our spiritual being is renewed day after day. ¹⁷And this small and temporary trouble we suffer will bring us a tremendous and eternal glory, much greater than the trouble. ¹⁸For we fix our attention, not on things that are seen, but on things that are unseen. What can be seen lasts only for a time, but what cannot be seen lasts for ever.

5 For we know that when this tent we live in—our body here on earth—is torn down, God will have a house in heaven for us to live in, a home he himself has made, which will last for ever. ²And now we sigh, so great is our desire that our home which comes from heaven should be put on over us; ³by being clothed with it we shall not be without a body. ⁴While we live in this earthly tent, we groan with a feeling of oppression; it is not that we want to get rid of our earthly body, but that we want to have the heavenly one put on over us, so that what is mortal will be transformed by life. ⁵God is the one who has prepared us for this change, and he gave us his Spirit as the guarantee of all that he has in store for us.

6 So we are always full of courage. We know that as long as we are at home in the body we are away from the Lord's

ᶜ *Verse 16 may be translated:* But the veil is removed whenever someone turns to the Lord.
3.13: Ex 34.33   **3.16:** Ex 34.34   **4.6:** Gen 1.3   **4.13:** Ps 116.10

home. ⁷For our life is a matter of faith, not of sight. ⁸We are full of courage and would much prefer to leave our home in the body and be at home with the Lord. ⁹More than anything else, however, we want to please him, whether in our home here or there. ¹⁰For all of us must appear before Christ, to be judged by him. Each one will receive what he deserves, according to everything he has done, good or bad, in his bodily life.

Friendship with God through Christ

11 We know what it means to fear the Lord, and so we try to persuade others. God knows us completely, and I hope that in your hearts you know me as well. ¹²We are not trying again to recommend ourselves to you; rather, we are trying to give you a good reason to be proud of us, so that you will be able to answer those who boast about a man's appearance and not about his character. ¹³Are we really insane? It is for God's sake. Or are we sane? Then it is for your sake. ¹⁴We are ruled by the love of Christ, now that we recognize that one man died for everyone, which means that all share in his death. ¹⁵He died for all, so that those who live should no longer live for themselves, but only for him who died and was raised to life for their sake.

16 No longer, then, do we judge anyone by human standards. Even if at one time we judged Christ according to human standards, we no longer do so. ¹⁷When anyone is joined to Christ, he is a new being; the old is gone, the new has come. ¹⁸All this is done by God, who through Christ changed us from enemies into his friends and gave us the task of making others his friends also. ¹⁹Our message is that God was making all mankind his friends through Christ. ᵈ God did not keep an account of their sins, and he has given us the message which tells how he makes them his friends.

20 Here we are, then, speaking for Christ, as though God himself were making his appeal through us. We plead on Christ's behalf: let God change you from enemies into his friends! ²¹Christ was without sin, but for our sake God made him share our sin in order that in union with him we might share the righteousness of God.

6 In our work together with God, then, we beg you who have received God's grace not to let it be wasted. ²Hear what God says:

"When the time came for me to show
    you favour
  I heard you;
when the day arrived for me to save
    you
  I helped you."

Listen! This is the hour to receive God's favour; today is the day to be saved!

3 We do not want anyone to find fault with our work, so we try not to put obstacles in anyone's way. ⁴Instead, in everything we do we show that we are God's servants by patiently enduring troubles, hardships, and difficulties. ⁵We have been beaten, imprisoned, and mobbed; we have been overworked and have gone without sleep or food. ⁶By our purity, knowledge, patience, and kindness we have shown ourselves to be God's servants—by the Holy Spirit, by our true love, ⁷by our message of truth, and by the power of God. We have righteousness as our weapon, both to attack and to defend ourselves. ⁸We are honoured and disgraced; we are insulted and praised. We are treated as liars, yet we speak the truth; ⁹as unknown, yet we are known by all; as though we were dead, but, as you see, we live on. Although punished, we are not killed; ¹⁰although saddened, we are always glad; we seem poor, but we make many people rich; we seem to have nothing, yet we really possess everything.

11 Dear friends in Corinth! We have spoken frankly to you; we have opened our hearts wide. ¹²It is not we who have closed our hearts to you; it is you who have closed your hearts to us. ¹³I speak now as though you were my children: show us the same feelings that we have for you. Open your hearts wide!

Warning against Pagan Influences

14 Do not try to work together as equals with unbelievers, for it cannot be done. How can right and wrong be partners? How can light and darkness live together? ¹⁵How can Christ and the Devil agree? What does a believer have in common with an unbeliever? ¹⁶How can God's temple come to terms with pagan idols?

ᵈGod was making all mankind his friends through Christ; or God was in Christ making all mankind his friends.

5.10: Rom 14.10   **6.2:** Is 49.8   **6.5:** Acts 16.23
6.16: Lev 26.12; Ezek 37.27; 1 Cor 3.16, 6.19

For we are the temple of the living God!
As God himself has said,
"I will make my home with my people
　　and live among them;
I will be their God,
　　and they shall be my people."
[17] And so the Lord says,
"You must leave them
　　and separate yourselves from them.
Have nothing to do with what is unclean,
　　and I will accept you.
[18] I will be your father,
　　and you shall be my sons and
　　　daughters,
　　says the Lord Almighty."

7 All these promises are made to us, my dear friends. So then, let us purify ourselves from everything that makes body or soul unclean, and let us be completely holy by living in awe of God.

Paul's Joy

2 Make room for us in your hearts. We have wronged no one; we have ruined no one, nor tried to take advantage of anyone. [3] I do not say this to condemn you; for, as I have said before, you are so dear to us that we are always together, whether we live or die. [4] I am so sure of you; I take such pride in you! In all our troubles I am still full of courage; I am running over with joy.

5 Even after we arrived in Macedonia, we had no rest. There were troubles everywhere, quarrels with others, fears in our hearts. [6] But God, who encourages the downhearted, encouraged us with the coming of Titus. [7] It was not only his coming that cheered us, but also his report of how you encouraged him. He told us how much you want to see me, how sorry you are, how ready you are to defend me; and so I am even happier now.

8 For even if that letter of mine made you sad, I am not sorry I wrote it. I could have been sorry when I saw that it made you sad for a while. [9] But now I am happy—not because I made you sad, but because your sadness made you change your ways. That sadness was used by God, and so we caused you no harm. [10] For the sadness that is used by God brings a change of heart that leads to salvation—and there is no regret in that! But sadness that is merely human causes death. [11] See what God did with this sadness of yours: how earnest it has made you, how eager

to prove your innocence! Such indignation, such alarm, such feelings, such devotion, such readiness to punish wrongdoing! You have shown yourselves to be without fault in the whole matter.

12 So, even though I wrote that letter, it was not because of the one who did wrong or the one who was wronged. Instead, I wrote it to make plain to you, in God's sight, how deep your devotion to us really is. [13] That is why we were encouraged.

Not only were we encouraged; how happy Titus made us with his happiness over the way in which all of you helped to cheer him up! [14] I did boast of you to him, and you have not disappointed me. We have always spoken the truth to you, and in the same way the boast we made to Titus has proved true. [15] And so his love for you grows stronger, as he remembers how all of you were ready to obey his instructions, how you welcomed him with fear and trembling. [16] How happy I am that I can depend on you completely!

Christian Giving

8 Our brothers, we want you to know what God's grace has accomplished in the churches of Macedonia. [2] They have been severely tested by the troubles they went through; but their joy was so great that they were extremely generous in their giving, even though they are very poor. [3] I can assure you that they gave as much as they could, and even more than they could. Of their own free will [4] they begged us and pleaded for the privilege of having a part in helping God's people in Judaea. [5] It was more than we could have hoped for! First they gave themselves to the Lord; and then, by God's will they gave themselves to us as well. [6] So we urged Titus, who began this work, to continue it and help you complete this special service of love. [7] You are so rich in all you have: in faith, speech, and knowledge, in your eagerness to help and in your love for us.[e] And so we want you to be generous also in this service of love.

8 I am not laying down any rules. But by showing how eager others are to help, I am trying to find out how real your own love is. [9] You know the grace of our Lord Jesus Christ; rich as he was, he made himself poor for your sake, in order to make you rich by means of his poverty.

[e] your love for us; *some manuscripts have* our love for you.
6.17: Is 52.11　**6.18:** 2 Sam 7.14; 1 Chr 17.13; Is 43.6; Jer 31.9　**7.5:** 2 Cor 2.13
8.1–4: Rom 15.26

10 My opinion is that it is better for you to finish now what you began last year. You were the first, not only to act, but also to be willing to act. 11 On with it, then, and finish the job! Be as eager to finish it as you were to plan it, and do it with what you now have. 12 If you are eager to give, God will accept your gift on the basis of what you have to give, not on what you haven't.

13-14 I am not trying to relieve others by putting a burden on you; but since you have plenty at this time, it is only fair that you should help those who are in need. Then, when you are in need and they have plenty, they will help you. In this way both are treated equally. 15 As the scripture says, "The one who gathered much did not have too much, and the one who gathered little did not have too little."

Titus and His Companions

16 How we thank God for making Titus as eager as we are to help you! 17 Not only did he welcome our request; he was so eager to help that of his own free will he decided to go to you. 18 With him we are sending the brother who is highly respected in all the churches for his work in preaching the gospel. 19 And besides that, he has been chosen and appointed by the churches to travel with us as we carry out this service of love for the sake of the Lord's glory, and in order to show that we want to help.

20 We are taking care not to stir up any complaints about the way we handle this generous gift. 21 Our purpose is to do what is right, not only in the sight of the Lord, but also in the sight of man.

22 So we are sending our brother with them; we have tested him many times and found him always very eager to help. And now that he has so much confidence in you, he is all the more eager to help. 23 As for Titus, he is my partner and works with me to help you; as for the other brothers who are going with him, they represent the churches and bring glory to Christ. 24 Show your love to them, so that all the churches will be sure of it and know that we are right in boasting about you.

Help for Fellow-Christians

9 There is really no need for me to write to you about the help being sent to God's people in Judaea. 2 I know that you

are willing to help, and I have boasted of you to the people in Macedonia. "The brothers in Achaia," I said, "have been ready to help since last year." Your eagerness has stirred up most of them. 3 Now I am sending these brothers, so that our boasting about you in this matter may not turn out to be empty words. But, just as I said, you will be ready with your help. 4 However, if the people from Macedonia should come with me and find out that you are not ready, how ashamed we would be—not to speak of your shame—for feeling so sure of you! 5 So I thought it was necessary to urge these brothers to go to you ahead of me and get ready in advance the gift you promised to make. Then it will be ready when I arrive, and it will show that you give because you want to, not because you have to.

6 Remember that the person who sows few seeds will have a small crop; the one who sows many seeds will have a large crop. 7 Each one should give, then, as he has decided, not with regret or out of a sense of duty; for God loves the one who gives gladly. 8 And God is able to give you more than you need, so that you will always have all you need for yourselves and more than enough for every good cause. 9 As the scripture says,

"He gives generously to the needy;
    his kindness lasts for ever."

10 And God, who supplies seed to sow and bread to eat, will also supply you with all the seed you need and will make it grow and produce a rich harvest from your generosity. 11 He will always make you rich enough to be generous at all times, so that many will thank God for your gifts which they receive from us. 12 For this service you perform not only meets the needs of God's people, but also produces an outpouring of gratitude to God. 13 And because of the proof which this service of yours brings, many will give glory to God for your loyalty to the gospel of Christ, which you profess, and for your generosity in sharing with them and everyone else. 14 And so with deep affection they will pray for you because of the extraordinary grace God has shown you. 15 Let us thank God for his priceless gift!

Paul Defends His Ministry

10 I, Paul, make a personal appeal to you—I who am said to be meek and mild when I am with you, but harsh

with you when I am away. By the gentleness and kindness of Christ I beg you [2] not to force me to be harsh when I come; for I am sure I can deal harshly with those who say that we act from worldly motives. [3] It is true that we live in the world, but we do not fight from worldly motives. [4] The weapons we use in our fight are not the world's weapons but God's powerful weapons, which we use to destroy strongholds. We destroy false arguments; [5] we pull down every proud obstacle that is raised against the knowledge of God; we take every thought captive and make it obey Christ. [6] And after you have proved your complete loyalty, we will be ready to punish any act of disloyalty.

[7] You are looking at the outward appearance of things. Is there someone there who reckons himself to belong to Christ? Well, let him think again about himself, because we belong to Christ just as much as he does. [8] For I am not ashamed, even if I have boasted somewhat too much about the authority that the Lord has given us—authority to build you up, not to tear you down. [9] I do not want it to appear that I am trying to frighten you with my letters. [10] Someone will say, "Paul's letters are severe and strong, but when he is with us in person, he is weak, and his words are nothing!" [11] Such a person must understand that there is no difference between what we write in our letters when we are away and what we will do when we are there with you.

[12] Of course we would not dare to classify ourselves or compare ourselves with those who rate themselves so highly. How stupid they are! They make up their own standards to measure themselves by, and they judge themselves by their own standards! [13] As for us, however, our boasting will not go beyond certain limits; it will stay within the limits of the work which God has set for us, and this includes our work among you. [14] And since you are within those limits, we were not going beyond them when we came to you, bringing the Good News about Christ. [15] So we do not boast about the work that others have done beyond the limits God set for us. Instead, we hope that your faith may grow and that we may be able to do a much greater work among you, always within the limits that God has set. [16] Then we can preach the Good News

in other countries beyond you and shall not have to boast about work already done in another man's field.

[17] But as the scripture says, "Whoever wants to boast must boast about what the Lord has done." [18] For it is when the Lord thinks well of a person that he is really approved, and not when he thinks well of himself.

Paul and the False Apostles

11 I wish you would tolerate me, even when I am a bit foolish. Please do! [2] I am jealous for you, just as God is; you are like a pure virgin whom I have promised in marriage to one man only, Christ himself. [3] I am afraid that your minds will be corrupted and that you will abandon your full and pure devotion to Christ—in the same way that Eve was deceived by the snake's clever lies. [4] For you gladly tolerate anyone who comes to you and preaches a different Jesus, not the one we preached; and you accept a spirit and a gospel completely different from the Spirit and the gospel you received from us!

[5] I do not think that I am the least bit inferior to those very special so-called "apostles" of yours! [6] Perhaps I am an amateur in speaking, but certainly not in knowledge; we have made this clear to you at all times and in all conditions.

[7] I did not charge you a thing when I preached the Good News of God to you; I humbled myself in order to make you important. Was that wrong of me? [8] While I was working among you, I was paid by other churches. I was robbing them, so to speak, in order to help you. [9] And during the time I was with you I did not bother you for help when I needed money; the brothers who came from Macedonia brought me everything I needed. As in the past, so in the future: I will never be a burden to you! [10] By Christ's truth in me, I promise that this boast of mine will not be silenced anywhere in all Achaia. [11] Do I say this because I don't love you? God knows I love you too!

[12] I will go on doing what I am doing now, in order to keep those other "apostles" from having any reason for boasting and saying that they work in the same way that we do. [13] Those men are not true apostles—they are false apostles, who lie about their work and disguise themselves to look like real apostles of Christ. [14] Well, no wonder!

10.17: Jer 9.24   **11.3:** Gen 3.1–5,13   **11.9:** Phil 4.15–18

Preach the Good News in other countries beyond you (10.16)

Even Satan can disguise himself to look like an angel of light! ¹⁵So it is no great thing if his servants disguise themselves to look like servants of righteousness. In the end they will get exactly what their actions deserve.

Paul's Sufferings as an Apostle

16 I repeat: no one should think that I am a fool. But if you do, at least accept me as a fool, so that I will have a little to boast of. ¹⁷Of course what I am saying now is not what the Lord would like me to say; in this matter of boasting I am really talking like a fool. ¹⁸But since there are so many who boast for merely human reasons, I will do the same. ¹⁹You yourselves are so wise, and so you gladly tolerate fools! ²⁰You tolerate anyone who orders you about or takes advantage of you or traps you or looks down on you or slaps you in the face. ²¹I am ashamed to admit that we were too timid to do those things!

But if anyone dares to boast about something—I am talking like a fool—I will be just as daring. ²²Are they Hebrews? So am I. Are they Israelites? So am I. Are they Abraham's descendants? So am I. ²³Are they Christ's servants? I sound like a madman—but I am a better servant than they are! I have worked much harder, I have been in prison more times, I have been whipped much more, and I have been near death more often. ²⁴Five times I was given the thirty-nine lashes by the Jews; ²⁵three times I was whipped by the Romans; and once I was stoned. I have been in three shipwrecks, and once I spent twenty-four hours in the water. ²⁶In my many travels I have been in danger from floods and from robbers, in danger from fellow-Jews and from Gentiles; there have been dangers in the cities, dangers in the wilds, dangers on the high seas, and dangers from false friends. ²⁷There has been work and toil; often I have gone without sleep; I have been hungry and thirsty; I have often been without enough food, shelter, or clothing. ²⁸And not to mention other things, every day I am under the pressure of my concern for all the churches. ²⁹When someone is weak, then I feel weak too; when someone is led into sin, I am filled with distress.

30 If I must boast, I will boast about things that show how weak I am. ³¹The God and Father of the Lord Jesus—blessed be his name for ever!—knows that I am not lying. ³²When I was in Damascus, the governor under King Aretas placed guards at the city gates to

11.23: Acts 16.23   **11.24:** Deut 25.3   **11.25:** Acts 16.22, 14.19   **11.26:** Acts 9.23, 14.15
11.32-33: Acts 9.23-25

arrest me. 33 But I was let down in a basket through an opening in the wall and escaped from him.

Paul's Visions and Revelations

12 I have to boast, even though it doesn't do any good. But I will now talk about visions and revelations given me by the Lord. 2 I know a certain Christian man who fourteen years ago was snatched up to the highest heaven (I do not know whether this actually happened or whether he had a vision— only God knows). 3-4 I repeat, I know that this man was snatched to Paradise (again, I do not know whether this actually happened or whether it was a vision— only God knows), and there he heard things which cannot be put into words, things that human lips may not speak. 5 So I will boast about this man—but I will not boast about myself, except the things that show how weak I am. 6 If I wanted to boast, I would not be a fool, because I would be telling the truth. But I will not boast, because I do not want anyone to have a higher opinion of me than he has as a result of what he has seen me do and heard me say.

7 But to keep me from being puffed up with pride because of the many wonderful things I saw, I was given a painful physical ailment, which acts as Satan's messenger to beat me and keep me from being proud. 8 Three times I prayed to the Lord about this and asked him to take it away. 9 But his answer was: "My grace is all you need, for my power is greatest when you are weak." I am most happy, then, to be proud of my weaknesses, in order to feel the protection of Christ's power over me. 10 I am content with weaknesses, insults, hardships, persecutions, and difficulties for Christ's sake. For when I am weak, then I am strong.

Paul's Concern for the Corinthians

11 I am acting like a fool—but you have made me do it. You are the ones who ought to show your approval of me. For even if I am nothing, I am in no way inferior to those very special "apostles" of yours. 12 The many miracles and wonders that prove that I am an apostle were performed among you with much patience. 13 How were you treated any worse than the other churches, except that I did not bother you for financial

help? Please forgive me for being so unfair!

14 This is now the third time that I am ready to come to visit you—and I will not make any demands on you. It is you I want, not your money. After all, children should not have to provide for their parents, but parents should provide for their children. 15 I will be glad to spend all I have, and myself as well, in order to help you. Will you love me less because I love you so much?

16 You will agree, then, that I was not a burden to you. But someone will say that I was crafty, and trapped you with lies. 17 How? Did I take advantage of you through any of the messengers I sent? 18 I begged Titus to go, and I sent the other Christian brother with him. Would you say that Titus took advantage of you? Do he and I not act from the very same motives and behave in the same way?

19 Perhaps you think that all along we have been trying to defend ourselves before you. No! We speak as Christ would wish us to speak in the presence of God, and everything we do, dear friends, is done to help you. 20 I am afraid that when I get there I will find you different from what I would like you to be and you will find me different from what you would like me to be. I am afraid that I will find quarrelling and jealousy, hot tempers and selfishness, insults and gossip, pride and disorder. 21 I am afraid that the next time I come my God will humiliate me in your presence, and I shall weep over many who sinned in the past and have not repented of the immoral things they have done— their lust and their sexual sins.

Final Warnings and Greetings

13 This is now the third time that I am coming to visit you. "Any accusation must be upheld by the evidence of two or more witnesses"—as the scripture says. 2 I want to say to those of you who have sinned in the past, and to all the others; I said it before during my second visit to you, but I will say it again now that I am away: the next time I come nobody will escape punishment. 3 You will have all the proof you want that Christ speaks through me. When he deals with you, he is not weak; instead, he shows his power among you. 4 For even though it was in weakness that he was put to death on the cross, it is by God's power that he lives. In union with him we also are weak; but in our relations with you we shall share God's power in his life.

5 Put yourselves to the test and judge yourselves, to find out whether you are living in faith. Surely you know that Christ Jesus is in you?—unless you have completely failed. 6 I trust you will know that we are not failures. 7 We pray to God that you will do no wrong—not in order to show that we are a success, but so that you may do what is right, even though we may seem to be failures. 8 For we cannot do a thing against the truth, but only for it. 9 We are glad when we are weak but you are strong. And so we also pray that you will become perfect. 10 That is why I write this while I am away from you; it is so that when I arrive I will not have to deal harshly with you in using the authority that the Lord has given me— authority to build you up, not to tear you down.

11 And now, my brothers, good-bye! Strive for perfection; listen to my appeals; agree with one another; live in peace. And the God of love and peace will be with you.

12 Greet one another with a brotherly kiss.

All God's people send you their greetings.

13 The grace of the Lord Jesus Christ, the love of God, and the fellowship of the Holy Spirit be with you all.

PAUL'S LETTER TO THE
GALATIANS

INTRODUCTION

As the good news about Jesus began to be preached and welcomed among people who were not Jews, the question arose as to whether a person must obey the Law of Moses in order to be a true Christian. Paul had argued that this was not necessary—that in fact, the only sound basis for life in Christ was faith, by which all are put right with God. But among the churches of Galatia, a Roman province in Asia Minor, there had come people who opposed Paul and claimed that one must also observe the Law of Moses in order to be right with God.

Paul's Letter to the Galatians was written in order to bring back to true faith and practice those people who were being misled by this false teaching. Paul begins by defending his right to be called an apostle of Jesus Christ. He insists that his call to be an apostle came from God, not from any human authority, and that his mission was especially to the non-Jews. Then he develops the argument that it is by faith alone that people are put right with God. In the concluding chapters Paul shows that Christian conduct flows naturally from the love that results from faith in Christ.

Outline of Contents

Introduction 1.1–10
Paul's authority as an apostle 1.11—2.21
The gospel of God's grace 3.1—4.31
Christian freedom and responsibility 5.1—6.10
Conclusion 6.11–18

1 From Paul, whose call to be an apostle did not come from man or by means of man, but from Jesus Christ and God the Father, who raised him from death. ²All the brothers who are here join me in sending greetings to the churches of Galatia:

3 May God our Father and the Lord Jesus Christ give you grace and peace.

4 In order to set us free from this present evil age, Christ gave himself for our sins, in obedience to the will of our God and Father. ⁵To God be the glory for ever and ever! Amen.

The One Gospel

6 I am surprised at you! In no time at all you are deserting the one who called you by the grace of Christ,ᵃ and are accepting another gospel. ⁷Actually, there is no "other gospel," but I say this because there are some people who are upsetting you and trying to change the gospel of Christ. ⁸But even if we or an angel from heaven should preach to you a gospel that is different from the one we preached to you, may he be condemned to hell! ⁹We have said it before, and now I say it again: if anyone preaches to you a gospel that is different from the one you accepted, may he be condemned to hell!

10 Does this sound as if I am trying to win man's approval? No indeed! What I want is God's approval! Am I trying to be popular with men? If I were still trying to do so, I would not be a servant of Christ.

How Paul Became an Apostle

11 Let me tell you, my brothers, that the gospel I preach is not of human origin. ¹²I did not receive it from any man, nor did anyone teach it to me. It was Jesus Christ himself who revealed it to me.

13 You have been told how I used to live when I was devoted to the Jewish religion, how I persecuted without mercy the church of God and did my best to destroy it. ¹⁴I was ahead of most fellow-Jews of my age in my practice of the Jewish religion, and was much more devoted to the traditions of our ancestors.

15 But God in his grace chose me even before I was born, and called me to serve him. And when he decided ¹⁶to reveal his Son to me, so that I might preach the

Good News about him to the Gentiles, I did not go to anyone for advice, ¹⁷nor did I go to Jerusalem to see those who were apostles before me. Instead, I went at once to Arabia, and then I returned to Damascus. ¹⁸It was three years later that I went to Jerusalem to obtain information from Peter, and I stayed with him for two weeks. ¹⁹I did not see any other apostle except James,ᵇ the Lord's brother.

20 What I write is true. God knows that I am not lying!

21 Afterwards I went to places in Syria and Cilicia. ²²At that time the members of the churches in Judaea did not know me personally. ²³They knew only what others were saying: "The man who used to persecute us is now preaching the faith that he once tried to destroy!" ²⁴And so they praised God because of me.

Paul and the Other Apostles

2 Fourteen years later I went back to Jerusalem with Barnabas, taking Titus along with me. ²I went because God revealed to me that I should go. In a private meeting with the leaders I explained the gospel message that I preach to the Gentiles. I did not want my work in the past or in the present to be a failure. ³My companion Titus, even though he is Greek, was not forced to be circumcised, ⁴although some wanted it done. Pretending to be fellow-believers, these men slipped into our group as spies, in order to find out about the freedom we have through our union with Christ Jesus. They wanted to make slaves of us, ⁵but in order to keep the truth of the gospel safe for you, we did not give in to them for a minute.

6 But those who seemed to be the leaders—I say this because it makes no difference to me what they were; God does not judge by outward appearances—those leaders, I say, made no new suggestions to me. ⁷On the contrary, they saw that God had given me the task of preaching the gospel to the Gentiles, just as he had given Peter the task of preaching the gospel to the Jews. ⁸For by God's power I was made an apostle to the Gentiles, just as Peter was made an apostle to the Jews. ⁹James, Peter, and John, who seemed to be the leaders,

---

ᵃby the grace of Christ; *some manuscripts have* by his grace.
ᵇany other apostle except James; *or* any other apostle; the only other person I saw was James.
1.13: Acts 8.3, 22.4–5, 26.9–11 **1.14:** Acts 22.3 **1.15–16:** Acts 9.3–6, 22.6–10, 26.13–18
1.18: Acts 9.26–30 **2.1:** Acts 11.30, 15.2 **2.6:** Deut 10.17

recognized that God had given me this special task; so they shook hands with Barnabas and me, as a sign that we were all partners. We agreed that Barnabas and I would work among the Gentiles and they among the Jews. [10] All they asked was that we should remember the needy in their group, which is the very thing I have[c] been eager to do.

Paul Rebukes Peter at Antioch

11 But when Peter came to Antioch, I opposed him in public, because he was clearly wrong. [12] Before some men who had been sent by James arrived there, Peter had been eating with the Gentile brothers. But after these men arrived, he drew back and would not eat with the Gentiles, because he was afraid of those who were in favour of circumcising them. [13] The other Jewish brothers also started acting like cowards along with Peter; and even Barnabas was swept along by their cowardly action. [14] When I saw that they were not walking a straight path in line with the truth of the gospel, I said to Peter in front of them all, "You are a Jew, yet you have been living like a Gentile, not like a Jew. How, then, can you try to force Gentiles to live like Jews?"

Jews and Gentiles Are Saved by Faith

15 Indeed, we are Jews by birth and not "Gentile sinners," as they are called. [16] Yet we know that a person is put right with God only through faith in Jesus Christ, never by doing what the Law requires. We, too, have believed in Christ Jesus in order to be put right with God through our faith in Christ, and not by doing what the Law requires. For no one is put right with God by doing what the Law requires. [17] If, then, as we try to be put right with God by our union with Christ, we are found to be sinners as much as the Gentiles are—does this mean that Christ is serving the cause of sin? By no means! [18] If I start to rebuild the system of Law that I tore down, then I show myself to be someone who breaks the Law. [19] So far as the Law is concerned, however, I am dead—killed by the Law itself—in order that I might live for God. I have been put to death with Christ on his cross, [20] so that it is no longer I who live, but it is Christ who lives in me. This

life that I live now, I live by faith in the Son of God, who loved me and gave his life for me. [21] I refuse to reject the grace of God. But if a person is put right with God through the Law, it means that Christ died for nothing!

Law or Faith

3 You foolish Galatians! Who put a spell on you? Before your very eyes you had a clear description of the death of Jesus Christ on the cross! [2] Tell me this one thing: did you receive God's Spirit by doing what the Law requires or by hearing the gospel and believing it? [3] How can you be so foolish! You began by God's Spirit; do you now want to finish by your own power? [4] Did all your experience mean nothing at all? Surely it meant something! [5] Does God give you the Spirit and work miracles among you because you do what the Law requires or because you hear the gospel and believe it?

6 Consider the experience of Abraham; as the scripture says, "He believed God, and because of his faith God accepted him as righteous." [7] You should realize then, that the real descendants of Abraham are the people who have faith. [8] The scripture predicted that God would put the Gentiles right with himself through faith. And so the scripture announced the Good News to Abraham: "Through you God will bless all mankind." [9] Abraham believed and was blessed; so all who believe are blessed as he was.

10 Those who depend on obeying the Law live under a curse. For the scripture says, "Whoever does not always obey everything that is written in the book of the Law is under God's curse!" [11] Now, it is clear that no one is put right with God by means of the Law, because the scripture says, "Only the person who is put right with God through faith shall live."[d] [12] But the Law has nothing to do with faith. Instead, as the scripture says, "Whoever does everything the Law requires will live."

13 But by becoming a curse for us Christ has redeemed us from the curse that the Law brings; for the scripture says, "Anyone who is hanged on a tree is under God's curse." [14] Christ did this in order that the blessing which God

[c] have; or had.
[d] put right with God through faith shall live; or put right with God shall live through faith.
2.16: Ps 143.2; Rom 3.20,22   **3.6:** Gen 15.6; Rom 4.3   **3.7:** Rom 4.16   **3.8:** Gen 12.3
3.10: Deut 27.26   **3.11:** Hab 2.4   **3.12:** Lev 18.5   **3.13:** Deut 21.23

promised to Abraham might be given to the Gentiles by means of Christ Jesus, so that through faith we might receive the Spirit promised by God.

The Law and the Promise

15 My brothers, I am going to use an everyday example: when two people agree on a matter and sign an agreement, no one can break it or add anything to it. ¹⁶ Now, God made his promises to Abraham and to his descendant. The scripture does not use the plural "descendants," meaning many people, but the singular "descendant," meaning one person only, namely, Christ. ¹⁷ What I mean is that God made a covenant with Abraham and promised to keep it. The Law, which was given four hundred and thirty years later, cannot break that covenant and cancel God's promise. ¹⁸ For if God's gift depends on the Law, then it no longer depends on his promise. However, it was because of his promise that God gave that gift to Abraham.

19 What, then, was the purpose of the Law? It was added in order to show what wrongdoing is, and it was meant to last until the coming of Abraham's descendant, to whom the promise was made. The Law was handed down by angels, with a man acting as a go-between. ²⁰ But a go-between is not needed when only one person is involved; and God is one. ^e

The Purpose of the Law

21 Does this mean that the Law is against God's promises? No, not at all! For if mankind had received a law that could bring life, then everyone could be put right with God by obeying it. ²² But the scripture says that the whole world is under the power of sin; and so the gift which is promised on the basis of faith in Jesus Christ is given to those who believe.

23 But before the time for faith came, the Law kept us all locked up as prisoners until this coming faith should be revealed. ²⁴ And so the Law was in charge of us until Christ came, in order that we might then be put right with God through faith. ²⁵ Now that the time for faith is here, the Law is no longer in charge of us.

26 It is through faith that all of you are God's sons in union with Christ Jesus. ²⁷ You were baptized into union with Christ, and now you are clothed, so to speak, with the life of Christ himself. ²⁸ So there is no difference between Jews and Gentiles, between slaves and free men, between men and women; you are all one in union with Christ Jesus. ²⁹ If you belong to Christ, then you are the descendants of Abraham and will receive what God has promised.

4 But now to continue—the son who will receive his father's property is treated just like a slave while he is young, even though he really owns everything. ² While he is young, there are men who take care of him and manage his affairs until the time set by his father. ³ In the same way, we too were slaves of the ruling spirits of the universe before we reached spiritual maturity. ⁴ But when the right time finally came, God sent his own Son. He came as the son of a human mother and lived under the Jewish Law, ⁵ to redeem those who were under the Law, so that we might become God's sons.

6 To show that you are ^f his sons, God sent the Spirit of his Son into our hearts, the Spirit who cries out, "Father, my Father." ⁷ So then, you are no longer a slave but a son. And since you are his

You are all one in union with Christ Jesus (3.28)

^e and God is one; *or* and God acts alone.   ^f To show that you are; *or* Because you are.

3.16: Gen 12.7   **3.17:** Ex 12.40   **3.18:** Rom 4.14   **3.29:** Rom 4.13   **4.5–7:** Rom 8.15–17

You are no longer a slave (4.7)

son, God will give you all that he has for his sons.

Paul's Concern for the Galatians

8 In the past you did not know God, and so you were slaves of beings who are not gods. 9 But now that you know God—or, I should say, now that God knows you—how is it that you want to turn back to those weak and pitiful ruling spirits? Why do you want to become their slaves all over again? 10 You pay special attention to certain days, months, seasons, and years. 11 I am worried about you! Can it be that all my work for you has been for nothing?

12 I beg you, my brothers, be like me. After all, I am like you. You have not done me any wrong. 13 You remember why I preached the gospel to you the first time; it was because I was ill. 14 But even though my physical condition was a great trial to you, you did not despise or reject me. Instead, you received me as you would an angel from heaven; you received me as you would Christ Jesus. 15 You were so happy! What has happened? I myself can say that you would have taken out your own eyes, if you could, and given them to me. 16 Have I now become your enemy by telling you the truth?

17 Those other people show a deep interest in you, but their intentions are not good. All they want is to separate you from me, so that you will have the same interest in them as they have in you. 18 Now, it is good to have such a deep interest if the purpose is good—this

is true always, and not merely when I am with you. 19 My dear children! Once again, just like a mother in childbirth, I feel the same kind of pain for you until Christ's nature is formed in you. 20 How I wish I were with you now, so that I could take a different attitude towards you. I am so worried about you!

The Example of Hagar and Sarah

21 Let me ask those of you who want to be subject to the Law: do you not hear what the Law says? 22 It says that Abraham had two sons, one by a slave-woman, the other by a free woman. 23 His son by the slave-woman was born in the usual way, but his son by the free woman was born as a result of God's promise. 24 These things can be understood as a figure: the two women represent two covenants. The one whose children are born in slavery is Hagar, and she represents the covenant made at Mount Sinai. 25 Hagar, who stands for Mount Sinai in Arabia, is *g* a figure of the present city of Jerusalem, in slavery with all its people. 26 But the heavenly Jerusalem is free, and she is our mother. 27 For the scripture says,

"Be happy, you childless woman!
Shout and cry with joy, you who
    never felt the pains of childbirth!
For the woman who was deserted will
    have more children
than the woman whose husband
    never left her."

28 Now, you, my brothers, are God's children as a result of his promise, just as Isaac was. 29 At that time the son who was born in the usual way persecuted the one who was born because of God's Spirit; and it is the same now. 30 But what does the scripture say? It says, "Send the slave-woman and her son away; for the son of the slave-woman will not have a part of the father's property along with the son of the free woman." 31 So then, my brothers, we are not the children of a slave-woman but of a free woman.

Preserve Your Freedom

5 Freedom is what we have—Christ has set us free! Stand, then, as free people, and do not allow yourselves to become slaves again.

2 Listen! I, Paul, tell you that if you allow yourselves to be circumcised, it means that Christ is of no use to you at all. 3 Once more I warn any man who

g Hagar...is; *some manuscripts have* Sinai is a mountain in Arabia, and it is.
4.22: Gen 16.15, 21.2   **4.27:** Is 54.1   **4.29:** Gen 21.9   **4.30:** Gen 21.10

allows himself to be circumcised that he is obliged to obey the whole Law. [4]Those of you who try to be put right with God by obeying the Law have cut yourselves off from Christ. You are outside God's grace. [5]As for us, our hope is that God will put us right with him; and this is what we wait for by the power of God's Spirit working through our faith. [6]For when we are in union with Christ Jesus, neither circumcision nor the lack of it makes any difference at all; what matters is faith that works through love.

7 You were doing so well! Who made you stop obeying the truth? How did he persuade you? [8]It was not done by God, who calls you. [9]"It takes only a little yeast to make the whole batch of dough rise," as they say. [10]But I still feel confident about you. Our life in union with the Lord makes me confident that you will not take a different view and that the man who is upsetting you, whoever he is, will be punished by God.

11 But as for me, my brothers, if I continue to preach that circumcision is necessary, why am I still being persecuted? If that were true, then my preaching about the cross of Christ would cause no trouble. [12]I wish that the people who are upsetting you would go all the way; let them go on and castrate themselves!

13 As for you, my brothers, you were called to be free. But do not let this freedom become an excuse for letting your physical desires control you. Instead, let love make you serve one another. [14]For the whole Law is summed up in one commandment: "Love your neighbour as you love yourself." [15]But if you act like wild animals, hurting and harming each other, then watch out, or you will completely destroy one another.

The Spirit and Human Nature

16 What I say is this: let the Spirit direct your lives, and you will not satisfy the desires of the human nature. [17]For what our human nature wants is opposed to what the Spirit wants, and what the Spirit wants is opposed to what our human nature wants. These two are enemies, and this means that you cannot do what you want to do. [18]If the Spirit leads you, then you are not subject to the Law.

19 What human nature does is quite plain. It shows itself in immoral, filthy, and indecent actions; [20]in worship of idols and witchcraft. People become enemies and they fight; they become jealous, angry, and ambitious. They separate into parties and groups; [21]they are envious, get drunk, have orgies, and do other things like these. I warn you now as I have before: those who do these things will not possess the Kingdom of God.

22 But the Spirit produces love, joy, peace, patience, kindness, goodness, faithfulness, [23]humility, and self-control. There is no law against such things as these. [24]And those who belong to Christ Jesus have put to death their human nature with all its passions and desires. [25]The Spirit has given us life; he must also control our lives. [26]We must not be proud or irritate one another or be jealous of one another.

Bear One Another's Burdens

6 My brothers, if someone is caught in any kind of wrongdoing, those of you who are spiritual should set him right; but you must do it in a gentle way. And keep an eye on yourselves, so that you will not be tempted, too. [2]Help to carry one another's burdens, and in this way you will obey[h] the law of Christ. [3]If someone thinks he is somebody when really he is nobody, he is only deceiving himself. [4]Each one should judge his own conduct. If it is good, then he can be proud of what he himself has done, without having to compare it with what someone else has done. [5]For everyone has to carry his own load.

6 The man who is being taught the Christian message should share all the good things he has with his teacher.

7 Do not deceive yourselves; no one makes a fool of God. A person will reap exactly what he sows. [8]If he sows in the field of his natural desires, from it he will gather the harvest of death; if he sows in the field of the Spirit, from the Spirit he will gather the harvest of eternal life. [9]So let us not become tired of doing good; for if we do not give up, the time will come when we will reap the harvest. [10]So then, as often as we have the chance, we should do good to everyone, and especially to those who belong to our family in the faith.

Final Warning and Greeting

11 See what big letters I make as I write to you now with my own hand! [12]The

[h]you will obey; *some manuscripts have* obey.
5.9: 1 Cor 5.6   **5.14:** Lev 19.18   **5.17:** Rom 7.15-23

Help to carry one another's burdens (6.2)

people who are trying to force you to be circumcised are the ones who want to show off and boast about external matters. They do it, however, only so that they may not be persecuted for the cross of Christ. 13 Even those who practise circumcision do not obey the Law; they want you to be circumcised so that they can boast that you submitted to this physical ceremony. 14 As for me, however, I will boast only about the cross of our Lord Jesus Christ; for by means of his cross the world is dead to me, and I am dead to the world. 15 It does not matter at all whether or not one is circumcised; what does matter is being a new creature. 16 As for those who follow this rule in their lives, may peace and mercy be with them—with them and with all God's people!

17 To conclude: let no one give me any more trouble, because the scars I have on my body show that I am the slave of Jesus.

18 May the grace of our Lord Jesus Christ be with you all, my brothers. Amen.

PAUL'S LETTER TO THE
EPHESIANS

INTRODUCTION

Paul's Letter to the Ephesians is concerned first of all with "God's plan...to bring all creation together, everything in heaven and on earth, with Christ as head" (1.10). It is also an appeal to God's people to live out the meaning of this great plan for the unity of mankind through oneness with Jesus Christ.

In the first part of *Ephesians* the writer develops the theme of unity by speaking of the way in which God the Father has chosen his people, how they are forgiven and set free from their sins through Jesus Christ the Son, and how God's great promise is guaranteed by the Holy Spirit. In the second part he appeals to the readers to live in such a way that their oneness in Christ may become real in their life together.

Several figures of speech are used to show the oneness of God's people in union with Christ: the church is like a body, with Christ as the head; or like a building, with Christ as the cornerstone; or like a wife, with Christ as the husband. This letter rises to great heights of expression as the writer is moved by the thought of God's grace in Christ. Everything is seen in the light of Christ's love, sacrifice, forgiveness, grace, and purity.

Outline of Contents

Introduction   1.1-2
Christ and the church   1.3—3.21
The new life in Christ   4.1—6.20
Conclusion   6.21-24

---

1 From Paul, who by God's will is an apostle of Christ Jesus:

To God's people in Ephesus,*a* who are faithful in their life in union with Christ Jesus:

2 May God our Father and the Lord Jesus Christ give you grace and peace.

Spiritual Blessings in Christ

3 Let us give thanks to the God and Father of our Lord Jesus Christ! For in our union with Christ he has blessed us by giving us every spiritual blessing in the heavenly world. 4 Even before the world was made, God had already chosen us to be his through our union with Christ, so that we would be holy and without fault before him.

Because of his love 5 God*b* had already decided that through Jesus Christ he would make us his sons—this was his pleasure and purpose. 6 Let us praise God for his glorious grace, for the free gift he gave us in his dear Son! 7 For by the

a Some manuscripts do not have in Ephesus.
b before him. Because of his love God; *or* before him, and to live in love. God.
1.1: Acts 18.19-21, 19.1   **1.7:** Col 1.14

Let us...praise God's glory! (1.12)

sacrificial death of Christ we are set free, that is, our sins are forgiven. How great is the grace of God, ⁸which he gave to us in such large measure!

In all his wisdom and insight ⁹God did what he had purposed, and made known to us the secret plan he had already decided to complete by means of Christ. ¹⁰This plan, which God will complete when the time is right, is to bring all creation together, everything in heaven and on earth, with Christ as head.

11 All things are done according to God's plan and decision; and God chose us to be his own people in union with Christ because of his own purpose, based on what he had decided from the very beginning. ¹²Let us, then, who were the first to hope in Christ, praise God's glory!

13 And you also became God's people when you heard the true message, the Good News that brought you salvation. You believed in Christ, and God put his stamp of ownership on you by giving you the Holy Spirit he had promised. ¹⁴The

Spirit is the guarantee that we shall receive what God has promised his people, and this assures us that God will give complete freedom to those who are his. Let us praise his glory!

Paul's Prayer

15 For this reason, ever since I heard of your faith in the Lord Jesus and your love for all God's people, ¹⁶I have not stopped giving thanks to God for you. I remember you in my prayers ¹⁷and ask the God of our Lord Jesus Christ, the glorious Father, to give you the Spirit, who will make you wise and reveal God to you, so that you will know him. ¹⁸I ask that your minds may be opened to see his light, so that you will know what is the hope to which he has called you, how rich are the wonderful blessings he promises his people, ¹⁹and how very great is his power at work in us who believe. This power working in us is the same as the mighty strength ²⁰which he used when he raised Christ from death and

1.20: Ps 110.1

seated him at his right side in the heavenly world. ²¹Christ rules there above all heavenly rulers, authorities, powers, and lords; he has a title superior to all titles of authority in this world and in the next. ²²God put all things under Christ's feet and gave him to the church as supreme Lord over all things. ²³The church is Christ's body, the completion of him who himself completes all things everywhere. *c*

From Death to Life

2 In the past you were spiritually dead because of your disobedience and sins. ²At that time you followed the world's evil way; you obeyed the ruler of the spiritual powers in space, the spirit who now controls the people who disobey God. ³Actually all of us were like them and lived according to our natural desires, doing whatever suited the wishes of our own bodies and minds. In our natural condition we, like everyone else, were destined to suffer God's anger.

4 But God's mercy is so abundant, and his love for us is so great, ⁵that while we were spiritually dead in our disobedience he brought us to life with Christ. It is by God's grace that you have been saved. ⁶In our union with Christ Jesus he raised us up with him to rule with him in the heavenly world. ⁷He did this to demonstrate for all time to come the extraordinary greatness of his grace in the love he showed us in Christ Jesus. ⁸⁻⁹For it is by God's grace that you have been saved through faith. It is not the result of your own efforts, but God's gift, so that no one can boast about it. ¹⁰God has made us what we are, and in our union with Christ Jesus he has created us for a life of good deeds, which he has already prepared for us to do.

One in Christ

11 You Gentiles by birth—called "the uncircumcised" by the Jews, who call themselves "the circumcised" (which refers to what men do to their bodies)— remember what you were in the past. ¹²At that time you were apart from Christ. You were foreigners and did not belong to God's chosen people. You had no part in the covenants, which were based on God's promises to his people, and you

lived in this world without hope and without God. ¹³But now, in union with Christ Jesus, you who used to be far away have been brought near by the sacrificial death of Christ. ¹⁴For Christ himself has brought us peace by making Jews and Gentiles one people. With his own body he broke down the wall that separated them and kept them enemies. ¹⁵He abolished the Jewish Law with its commandments and rules, in order to create out of the two races one new people in union with himself, in this way making peace. ¹⁶By his death on the cross Christ destroyed their enmity; by means of the cross he united both races into one body and brought them back to God. ¹⁷So Christ came and preached the Good News of peace to all—to you Gentiles, who were far away from God, and to the Jews, who were near to him. ¹⁸It is through Christ that all of us, Jews and Gentiles, are able to come in the one Spirit into the presence of the Father.

19 So then, you Gentiles are not foreigners or strangers any longer; you are now fellow-citizens with God's people and members of the family of God. ²⁰You, too, are built upon the foundation laid by the apostles and prophets, *d* the cornerstone being Christ Jesus himself. ²¹He is the one who holds the whole building together and makes it grow into a sacred temple dedicated to the Lord. ²²In union with him you too are being built together with all the others into a place where God lives through his Spirit.

Paul's Work for the Gentiles

3 For this reason I, Paul, the prisoner of Christ Jesus for the sake of you Gentiles, pray to God. ²Surely you have heard that God in his grace has given me this work to do for your good. ³God revealed his secret plan and made it known to me. (I have written briefly about this, ⁴and if you will read what I have written, you can learn about my understanding of the secret of Christ.) ⁵In past times mankind was not told this secret, but God has revealed it now by the Spirit to his holy apostles and prophets. ⁶The secret is that by means of the gospel the Gentiles have a part with the Jews in God's blessings; they are members of the

---

c who himself completes all things everywhere; *or* who is himself completely filled with God's fullness.
d the foundation laid by the apostles and prophets; *or* the foundation, that is, the apostles and prophets.
1.22: Ps 8.6   **1.22–23:** Col 1.18   **2.1–5:** Col 2.13   **2.15:** Col 2.14   **2.16:** Col 1.20
2.17: Is 57.19   **3.4–6:** Col 1.26–27

same body and share in the promise that God made through Christ Jesus.

7 I was made a servant of the gospel by God's special gift, which he gave me through the working of his power. [8] I am less than the least of all God's people; yet God gave me this privilege of taking to the Gentiles the Good News about the infinite riches of Christ, [9] and of making all people see how God's secret plan is to be put into effect. God, who is the Creator of all things, kept his secret hidden through all the past ages, [10] in order that at the present time, by means of the church, the angelic rulers and powers in the heavenly world might learn of his wisdom in all its different forms. [11] God did this according to his eternal purpose, which he achieved through Christ Jesus our Lord. [12] In union with Christ and through our faith in him we have the boldness to go into God's presence with all confidence. [13] I beg you, then, not to be discouraged because I am suffering for you; it is all for your benefit.

The Love of Christ

14 For this reason I fall on my knees before the Father, [15] from whom every family in heaven and on earth receives its true name. [16] I ask God from the wealth of his glory to give you power through his Spirit to be strong in your inner selves, [17] and I pray that Christ will make his home in your hearts through faith. I pray that you may have your roots and foundation in love, [18] so that you, together with all God's people, may have the power to understand how broad and long, how high and deep, is Christ's love. [19] Yes, may you come to know his love—although it can never be fully known—and so be completely filled with the very nature of God.

20 To him who by means of his power working in us is able to do so much more than we can ever ask for, or even think of: [21] to God be the glory in the church and in Christ Jesus for all time, for ever and ever! Amen.

The Unity of the Body

4 I urge you, then—I who am a prisoner because I serve the Lord: live a life that measures up to the standard God set when he called you. [2] Be always humble, gentle, and patient. Show your love by being tolerant with one another.

[3] Do your best to preserve the unity which the Spirit gives by means of the peace that binds you together. [4] There is one body and one Spirit, just as there is one hope to which God has called you. [5] There is one Lord, one faith, one baptism; [6] there is one God and Father of all mankind, who is Lord of all, works through all, and is in all.

7 Each one of us has received a special gift in proportion to what Christ has given. [8] As the scripture says,

"When he went up to the very heights, he took many captives with him; he gave gifts to mankind."

[9] Now, what does "he went up" mean? It means that first he came down to the lowest depths of the earth. [e] [10] So the one who came down is the same one who went up, above and beyond the heavens, to fill the whole universe with his presence. [11] It was he who "gave gifts to mankind"; he appointed some to be apostles, others to be prophets, others to be evangelists, others to be pastors and teachers. [12] He did this to prepare all God's people for the work of Christian service, in order to build up the body of Christ. [13] And so we shall all come together to that oneness in our faith and in our knowledge of the Son of God; we shall become mature people, reaching to the very height of Christ's full stature. [14] Then we shall no longer be children, carried by the waves and blown about by every shifting wind of the teaching of deceitful men, who lead others into error by the tricks they invent. [15] Instead, by speaking the truth in a spirit of love, we must grow up in every way to Christ, who is the head. [16] Under his control all the different parts of the body fit together, and the whole body is held together by every joint with which it is provided. So when each separate part works as it should, the whole body grows and builds itself up through love.

The New Life in Christ

17 In the Lord's name, then, I warn you: do not continue to live like the heathen, whose thoughts are worthless [18] and whose minds are in the dark. They have no part in the life that God gives, for they are completely ignorant and stubborn. [19] They have lost all feeling of shame; they give themselves over to vice

[e] the lowest depths of the earth; *or* the lower depths, the earth itself.
4.2: Col 3.12–13 **4.8:** Ps 68.18 **4.16:** Col 2.19

and do all sorts of indecent things without restraint.

20 That was not what you learnt about Christ! ²¹ You certainly heard about him, and as his followers you were taught the truth that is in Jesus. ²² So get rid of your old self, which made you live as you used to—the old self that was being destroyed by its deceitful desires. ²³ Your hearts and minds must be made completely new, ²⁴ and you must put on the new self, which is created in God's likeness and reveals itself in the true life that is upright and holy.

25 No more lying, then! Everyone must tell the truth to his fellow-believer, because we are all members together in the body of Christ. ²⁶ If you become angry,

Do not let your anger lead you into sin (4.26)

do not let your anger lead you into sin, and do not stay angry all day. ²⁷ Don't give the Devil a chance. ²⁸ The man who used to rob must stop robbing and start working, in order to earn an honest living for himself and to be able to help the poor. ²⁹ Do not use harmful words, but only helpful words, the kind that build up and provide what is needed, so that what you say will do good to those who hear you. ³⁰ And do not make God's Holy Spirit sad; for the Spirit is God's mark of ownership on you, a guarantee that the Day will come when God will set you free. ³¹ Get rid of all bitterness, passion, and anger. No more shouting or insults, no more hateful feelings of any sort. ³² Instead, be kind and tender-hearted to one another, and forgive one another, as God has forgiven you through Christ.

Living in the Light

5 Since you are God's dear children, you must try to be like him. ² Your life must be controlled by love, just as Christ loved us and gave his life for us as a sweet-smelling offering and sacrifice that pleases God.

3 Since you are God's people, it is not right that any matters of sexual immorality or indecency or greed should even be mentioned among you. ⁴ Nor is it fitting for you to use language which is obscene, profane, or vulgar. Rather you should give thanks to God. ⁵ You may be sure that no one who is immoral, indecent, or greedy (for greed is a form of idolatry) will ever receive a share in the Kingdom of Christ and of God.

6 Do not let anyone deceive you with foolish words; it is because of these very things that God's anger will come upon those who do not obey him. ⁷ So have nothing at all to do with such people. ⁸ You yourselves used to be in the darkness, but since you have become the Lord's people, you are in the light. So you must live like people who belong to the light, ⁹ for it is the light*ᶠ* that brings a rich harvest of every kind of goodness, righteousness, and truth. ¹⁰ Try to learn what pleases the Lord. ¹¹ Have nothing to do with the worthless things that people do, things that belong to the darkness. Instead, bring them out to the light. ¹² (It is really too shameful even to talk about the things they do in secret.) ¹³ And when all things are brought out to the light, then their true nature is clearly revealed; ¹⁴ for anything that is clearly revealed becomes light.*ᵍ* That is why it is said,

"Wake up, sleeper,
    and rise from death,
and Christ will shine on you."

15 So be careful how you live. Don't live like ignorant people, but like wise people. ¹⁶ Make good use of every opportunity you have, because these are evil days. ¹⁷ Don't be fools, then, but try to find out what the Lord wants you to do.

18 Do not get drunk with wine, which will only ruin you; instead, be filled with the Spirit. ¹⁹ Speak to one another with the words of psalms, hymns, and sacred songs; sing hymns and psalms to the Lord with praise in your hearts. ²⁰ In the name

*ᶠ*the light; *some manuscripts have* the Spirit.
*ᵍ*anything that is clearly revealed becomes light; *or* it is light that clearly reveals everything.
4.22: Col 3.9   **4.24:** Gen 1.26; Col 3.10   **4.25:** Zech 8.16   **4.26:** Ps 4.4   **4.32:** Col 3.13
5.2: Ex 29.18; Ps 40.6   **5.16:** Col 4.5   **5.19–20:** Col 3.16–17

of our Lord Jesus Christ, always give thanks for everything to God the Father.

Wives and Husbands

21 Submit yourselves to one another because of your reverence for Christ. 22 Wives, submit to your husbands as to the Lord. 23 For a husband has authority over his wife just as Christ has authority over the church; and Christ is himself the Saviour of the church, his body. 24 And so wives must submit completely to their husbands just as the church submits itself to Christ.

25 Husbands, love your wives just as Christ loved the church and gave his life for it. 26 He did this to dedicate the church to God by his word, after making it clean by washing it in water, 27 in order to present the church to himself in all its beauty—pure and faultless, without spot or wrinkle or any other imperfection. 28 Men ought to love their wives just as they love their own bodies. A man who loves his wife loves himself. 29 (No one ever hates his own body. Instead, he feeds it and takes care of it, just as Christ does the church; 30 for we are members of his body.) 31 As the scripture says, "For this reason a man will leave his father and mother and unite with his wife, and the two will become one." 32 There is a deep secret truth revealed in this scripture, which I understand as applying to Christ and the church. 33 But it also applies to you: every husband must love his wife as himself, and every wife must respect her husband.

Children and Parents

6 Children, it is your Christian duty to [h] obey your parents, for this is the right thing to do. 2 "Respect your father and mother" is the first commandment that has a promise added: 3 "so that all may go well with you, and you may live a long time in the land."

4 Parents, do not treat your children in such a way as to make them angry. Instead, bring them up with Christian discipline and instruction.

Slaves and Masters

5 Slaves, obey your human masters with fear and trembling; and do it with a sincere heart, as though you were serving Christ. 6 Do this not only when they are watching you, because you want to gain their approval; but with all your heart do what God wants, as slaves of Christ. 7 Do your work as slaves cheerfully, as though you served the Lord, and not merely men. 8 Remember that the Lord will reward everyone, whether slave or free, for the good work he does.

9 Masters, behave in the same way towards your slaves and stop using threats. Remember that you and your slaves belong to the same Master in heaven, who judges everyone by the same standard.

The Whole Armour of God

10 Finally, build up your strength in union with the Lord and by means of his mighty power. 11 Put on all the armour that God gives you, so that you will be able to stand up against the Devil's evil tricks. 12 For we are not fighting against human beings but against the wicked spiritual forces in the heavenly world, the rulers, authorities, and cosmic powers of this dark age. 13 So put on God's armour now! Then when the evil day comes, you will be able to resist the enemy's attacks; and after fighting to the end, you will still hold your ground.

14 So stand ready, with truth as a belt tight round your waist, with righteousness as your breastplate, 15 and as your shoes the readiness to announce the Good News of peace. 16 At all times carry faith as a shield; for with it you will be able to put out all the burning arrows shot by the Evil One. 17 And accept salvation as a helmet, and the word of God as the sword which the Spirit gives you. 18 Do all this in prayer, asking for God's help. Pray on every occasion, as the Spirit leads. For this reason keep alert and never give up; pray always for all God's people. 19 And pray also for me, that God will give me a message when I am ready to speak, so that I may speak boldly and make known the gospel's secret. 20 For the sake of this gospel I am an ambassador, though now I am in prison. Pray that I may be bold in speaking about the gospel as I should.

---

[h] Some manuscripts do not have It is your Christian duty to.

5.22: Col 3.18; 1 Pet 3.1   **5.25:** Col 3.19; 1 Pet 3.7   **5.31:** Gen 2.24   **6.1:** Col 3.20
6.2–3: Ex 20.12; Deut 5.16   **6.4:** Col 3.21   **6.5–8:** Col 3.22–25
6.9: Deut 10.17; Col 3.25, 4.1   **6.14:** Is 11.5, 59.17   **6.15:** Is 52.7   **6.17:** Is 59.17

Final Greetings

21 Tychicus, our dear brother and faithful servant in the Lord's work, will give you all the news about me, so that you may know how I am getting on. 22 That is why I am sending him to you—to tell you how all of us are getting on, and to encourage you.

23 May God the Father and the Lord Jesus Christ give to all Christian brothers peace and love with faith. 24 May God's grace be with all those who love our Lord Jesus Christ with undying love.

6.21: Acts 20.4; 2 Tim 4.12   **6.21–22:** Col 4.7–8

PAUL'S LETTER TO THE

PHILIPPIANS

INTRODUCTION

Paul's Letter to the Philippians was written to the first church that Paul established on European soil, in the Roman province of Macedonia. It was written while the apostle was in prison, and at a time when he was troubled by the opposition of other Christian workers towards himself and was distressed by false teaching in the church at Philippi. Yet this letter breathes a joy and confidence that can be explained only by Paul's deep faith in Jesus Christ.

The immediate reason for writing the letter was to thank the Philippian Christians for the gift which they had sent to help him in his time of need. He uses this opportunity to reassure them, so that they may have courage and confidence in spite of all his troubles and their own as well. He pleads with them to have the humble attitude of Jesus, rather than to be controlled by selfish ambition and pride. He reminds them that their life in union with Christ is a gift of God's grace which they have received through faith, not through obedience to the ceremonies of the Jewish Law. He writes of the joy and peace that God gives to those who live in union with Christ.

This letter is marked by its emphasis on joy, confidence, unity, and perseverance in the Christian faith and life. It also reveals the deep affection Paul had for the church at Philippi.

Outline of Contents
Introduction   1.1–11
Paul's personal circumstances   1.12–26
The life in Christ   1.27—2.18
Plans for Timothy and Epaphroditus   2.19–30
Warnings against enemies and dangers   3.1—4.9
Paul and his Philippian friends   4.10–20
Conclusion   4.21–23

1 From Paul and Timothy, servants of Christ Jesus—

To all God's people in Philippi who are in union with Christ Jesus, including the church leaders and helpers:

2 May God our Father and the Lord Jesus Christ give you grace and peace.

Paul's Prayer for His Readers

3 I thank my God for you every time I think of you; 4 and every time I pray for you all, I pray with joy 5 because of the way in which you have helped me in the work of the gospel from the very first day until now. 6 And so I am sure that God, who began this good work in you, will carry it on until it is finished on the Day of Christ Jesus. 7 You are always in my heart! And so it is only right for me to feel as I do about you. For you have all shared with me in this privilege that God has given me, both now that I am in prison and also while I was free to defend the gospel and establish it firmly. 8 God is my witness that I am telling the truth when I say that my deep feeling for you all comes from the heart of Christ Jesus himself.

9 I pray that your love will keep on growing more and more, together with true knowledge and perfect judgement, 10 so that you will be able to choose what is best. Then you will be free from all impurity and blame on the Day of Christ. 11 Your lives will be filled with the truly good qualities which only Jesus Christ can produce, for the glory and praise of God.

To Live Is Christ

12 I want you to know, my brothers, that the things that have happened to me have really helped the progress of the gospel. 13 As a result, the whole palace guard and all the others here know that I am in prison because I am a servant of Christ. 14 And my being in prison has given most of the brothers more confidence in the Lord, so that they grow bolder all the time to preach the message[a] fearlessly.

15 Of course some of them preach Christ because they are jealous and quarrelsome, but others from genuine goodwill. 16 These do so from love, because they know that God has given me the work of defending the gospel. 17 The others do not proclaim Christ sincerely, but from a spirit of selfish ambition; they think that they will make more trouble for me while I am in prison.

18 It does not matter! I am happy about it—so long as Christ is preached in every way possible, whether from wrong or right motives. And I will continue to be happy, 19 because I know that by means of your prayers and the help which comes from the Spirit of Jesus Christ I shall be set free. 20 My deep desire and hope is that I shall never fail in my duty, but that at all times, and especially just now, I shall be full of courage, so that with my whole being I shall bring honour to Christ, whether I live or die. 21 For what is life? To me, it is Christ. Death, then, will bring more. 22 But if by continuing to live I can do more worthwhile work, then I am not sure which I should choose. 23 I am pulled in two directions. I want very much to leave this life and be with Christ, which is a far better thing; 24 but for your sake it is much more important that I remain alive. 25 I am sure of this, and so I know that I will stay. I will stay on with you all, to add to your progress and joy in the faith, 26 so that when I am with you again, you will have even more reason to be proud of me in your life in union with Christ Jesus.

27 Now, the important thing is that your way of life should be as the gospel of Christ requires, so that, whether or not I am able to go and see you, I will hear that you are standing firm with one common purpose and that with only one desire you are fighting together for the faith of the gospel. 28 Don't be afraid of your enemies; always be courageous, and this will prove to them that they will lose and that you will win, because it is God who gives you the victory. 29 For you have been given the privilege of serving Christ, not only by believing in him, but also by suffering for him. 30 Now you can take part with me in the battle. It is the same battle you saw me fighting in the past, and as you hear, the one I am fighting still.

Christ's Humility and Greatness

2 Your life in Christ makes you strong, and his love comforts you. You have fellowship with the Spirit,[b] and you have

---

[a] the message; *some manuscripts have* God's message.
[b] You have fellowship with the Spirit; *or* The Spirit has brought you into fellowship with one another.

1.1: Acts 16.12   **1.13:** Acts 28.30   **1.30:** Acts 16.19-40

kindness and compassion for one another.
²I urge you, then, to make me completely
happy by having the same thoughts,
sharing the same love, and being one in
soul and mind. ³Don't do anything from
selfish ambition or from a cheap desire
to boast, but be humble towards one
another, always considering others better
than yourselves. ⁴And look out for one
another's interests, not just for your own.
⁵The attitude you should have is the one
that Christ Jesus had:

⁶He always had the nature of God,
　　but he did not think that by force
　　　he should try to become *c* equal
　　　with God.
⁷Instead of this, of his own free will he
　　gave up all he had,
　　and took the nature of a servant.
He became like man
　　and appeared in human likeness.
⁸He was humble and walked the path
　　of obedience all the way to death—
　　his death on the cross.
⁹For this reason God raised him to the
　　highest place above
　　and gave him the name that is greater
　　than any other name.
¹⁰And so, in honour of the name of Jesus
　　all beings in heaven, on earth, and
　　in the world below *d*
　　will fall on their knees,
¹¹and all will openly proclaim that Jesus
　　Christ is Lord,
　　to the glory of God the Father.

Shining as Lights in the World

12 So then, dear friends, as you always
obeyed me when I was with you, it is
even more important that you obey me
now while I am away from you. Keep
on working with fear and trembling to
complete your salvation, ¹³because God
is always at work in you to make you
willing and able to obey his own purpose.

14 Do everything without complaining
or arguing, ¹⁵so that you may be innocent
and pure as God's perfect children, who
live in a world of corrupt and sinful
people. You must shine among them like
stars lighting up the sky, ¹⁶as you offer
them the message of life. If you do so,
I shall have reason to be proud of you
on the Day of Christ, because it will show
that all my effort and work have not been
wasted.

17 Perhaps my life's blood is to be

poured out like an offering on the sacrifice
that your faith offers to God. If that is
so, I am glad and share my joy with you
all. ¹⁸In the same way, you too must be
glad and share your joy with me.

Timothy and Epaphroditus

19 If it is the Lord's will, I hope that
I will be able to send Timothy to you
soon, so that I may be encouraged by
news about you. ²⁰He is the only one who
shares my feelings and who really cares
about you. ²¹Everyone else is concerned
only with his own affairs, not with the
cause of Jesus Christ. ²²And you yourselves know how he has proved his worth,
how he and I, like a son and his father,
have worked together for the sake of the
gospel. ²³So I hope to send him to you
as soon as I know how things are going
to turn out for me. ²⁴And I trust in the
Lord that I myself will be able to come
to you soon.

25 I have thought it necessary to send
you our brother Epaphroditus, who has
worked and fought by my side and who
has served as your messenger in helping
me. ²⁶He is anxious to see you all and
is very upset because you had heard that
he was ill. ²⁷Indeed he was ill and almost
died. But God had pity on him, and not
only on him but on me, too, and spared me
an even greater sorrow. ²⁸I am all the
more eager, then, to send him to you,
so that you will be glad again when you
see him, and my own sorrow will disappear. ²⁹Receive him, then, with joy, as
a brother in the Lord. Show respect to
all such people as he, ³⁰because he risked
his life and nearly died for the sake of
the work of Christ, in order to give me
the help that you yourselves could not
give.

The True Righteousness

3 In conclusion, my brothers, be joyful
in your union with the Lord. I don't
mind repeating what I have written
before, and you will be safer if I do so.
²Watch out for those who do evil things,
those dogs, those men who insist on
cutting the body. ³It is we, not they, who
have received the true circumcision, for
we worship God by means of his Spirit
and rejoice in our life in union with Christ
Jesus. We do not put any trust in external
ceremonies. ⁴I could, of course, put my

---

c become; *or* remain.
d WORLD BELOW: *It was thought that the dead continued to exist in a dark world under the ground.*
2.10–11: Is 45.23   **2.15:** Deut 32.5

Receive him...as a brother (2.29)

trust in such things. If anyone thinks he can trust in external ceremonies, I have even more reason to feel that way. [5] I was circumcised when I was a week old. I am an Israelite by birth, of the tribe of Benjamin, a pure-blooded Hebrew. As far as keeping the Jewish Law is concerned, I was a Pharisee, [6] and I was so zealous that I persecuted the church. As far as a person can be righteous by obeying the commands of the Law, I was without fault. [7] But all those things that I might count as profit I now reckon as loss for Christ's sake. [8] Not only those things; I reckon everything as complete loss for the sake of what is so much more valuable, the knowledge of Christ Jesus my Lord. For his sake I have thrown everything away; I consider it all as mere refuse, so that I may gain Christ [9] and be completely united with him. I no longer have a righteousness of my own, the kind that is gained by obeying the Law. I now have the righteousness that is given through faith in Christ, the righteousness that comes from God and is based on faith. [10] All I want is to know Christ and to experience the power of his resurrection, to share in his sufferings and become like him in his death, [11] in the hope that I myself will be raised from death to life.

Running towards the Goal

12 I do not claim that I have already succeeded or have already become perfect. I keep striving to win the prize for which Christ Jesus has already won me to himself. [13] Of course, my brothers, I really do not [e] think that I have already won it; the one thing I do, however, is to forget what is behind me and do my best to reach what is ahead. [14] So I run straight

I run straight towards the goal (3.14)

---

[e] not; *some manuscripts have* not yet.

3.5: Acts 23.6, 26.5; Rom 11.1   **3.6:** Acts 8.3, 22.4, 26.9–11 towards the goal in order to win the prize, which is God's call through Christ Jesus to the life above.

15 All of us who are spiritually mature should have this same attitude. But if some of you have a different attitude, God will make this clear to you. ¹⁶However that may be, let us go forward according to the same rules we have followed until now.

17 Keep on imitating me, my brothers. Pay attention to those who follow the right example that we have set for you. ¹⁸I have told you this many times before, and now I repeat it with tears: there are many whose lives make them enemies of Christ's death on the cross. ¹⁹They are

Their god is their bodily desires (3.19)

going to end up in hell, because their god is their bodily desires. They are proud of what they should be ashamed of, and they think only of things that belong to this world. ²⁰We, however, are citizens of heaven, and we eagerly wait for our Saviour, the Lord Jesus Christ, to come from heaven. ²¹He will change our weak mortal bodies and make them like his own glorious body, using that power by which he is able to bring all things under his rule.

Instructions

4 So then, my brothers, how dear you are to me and how I miss you! How happy you make me, and how proud I am of you! This then, dear brothers, is how you should stand firm in your life in the Lord.

2 Euodia and Syntyche, please, I beg you, try to agree as sisters in the Lord.

³And you too, my faithful partner, I want you to help these women; for they have worked hard with me to spread the gospel, together with Clement and all my other fellow-workers, whose names are in God's book of the living.

4 May you always be joyful in your union with the Lord. I say it again: rejoice!

5 Show a gentle attitude towards everyone. The Lord is coming soon. ⁶Don't worry about anything, but in all your prayers ask God for what you need, always asking him with a thankful heart. ⁷And God's peace, which is far beyond human understanding, will keep your hearts and minds safe in union with Christ Jesus.

8 In conclusion, my brothers, fill your minds with those things that are good and that deserve praise: things that are true, noble, right, pure, lovely, and honourable. ⁹Put into practice what you learnt and received from me, both from my words and from my actions. And the God who gives us peace will be with you.

Thanks for the Gift

10 In my life in union with the Lord it is a great joy to me that after so long a time you once more had the chance of showing that you care for me. I don't mean that you had stopped caring for me—you just had no chance to show it. ¹¹And I am not saying this because I feel neglected, for I have learnt to be satisfied with what I have. ¹²I know what it is to be in need and what it is to have more than enough. I have learnt this secret, so that anywhere, at any time, I am content, whether I am full or hungry, whether I have too much or too little. ¹³I have the strength to face all conditions by the power that Christ gives me.

14 But it was very good of you to help me in my troubles. ¹⁵You Philippians know very well that when I left Macedonia in the early days of preaching the Good News, you were the only church to help me; you were the only ones who shared my profits and losses. ¹⁶More than once when I needed help in Thessalonica, you sent it to me. ¹⁷It is not that I just want to receive gifts; rather, I want to see profit added to your account. ¹⁸Here, then, is my receipt for everything you have given me—and it has been more than enough! I have all I need now that Epaphroditus has brought me all your gifts. They are like a sweet-smelling offering to God, a

3.17: 1 Cor 4.16, 11.1   **4.15–16:** 2 Cor 11.9   **4.16:** Acts 17.1   **4.18:** Ex 29.18

sacrifice which is acceptable and pleasing to him. ¹⁹And with all his abundant wealth through Christ Jesus, my God will supply all your needs. ²⁰To our God and Father be the glory for ever and ever! Amen.

Final Greetings

21 Greetings to each one of God's people who belong to Christ Jesus. The brothers here with me send you their greetings. ²²All God's people here send greetings, especially those who belong to the Emperor's palace.

23 May the grace of the Lord Jesus Christ be with you all.

PAUL'S LETTER TO THE

COLOSSIANS

INTRODUCTION

Paul's Letter to the Colossians was written to the church at Colossae, a town in Asia Minor east of Ephesus. This church had not been established by Paul, but was in an area for which Paul felt responsible, as he sent out workers from Ephesus, the capital of the Roman province of Asia. Paul had learnt that there were false teachers in the church at Colossae who insisted that in order to know God and have full salvation one must worship certain "spiritual rulers and authorities." In addition, these teachers said, one must submit to special rites such as circumcision and must observe strict rules about foods and other matters.

Paul writes to oppose these teachings with the true Christian message. The heart of his reply is that Jesus Christ is able to give full salvation and that these other beliefs and practices actually lead away from him. Through Christ, God created the world and through him he is bringing it back to himself. Only in union with Christ is there hope of salvation for the world. Paul then spells out the implications of this great teaching for the lives of believers.

It is noteworthy that Tychicus, who took this letter to Colossae for Paul, was accompanied by Onesimus, the slave on whose behalf Paul wrote *Philemon*.

Outline of Contents
Introduction 1.1–8
The nature and work of Christ 1.9—2.19
The new life in Christ 2.20—4.6
Conclusion 4.7–18

1 From Paul, who by God's will is an apostle of Christ Jesus, and from our brother Timothy—

2 To God's people in Colossae, who are our faithful brothers in union with Christ:

May God our Father give you grace and peace.

Prayer of Thanksgiving

3 We always give thanks to God, the Father of our Lord Jesus Christ, when we pray for you. 4 For we have heard of your faith in Christ Jesus and of your love for all God's people. 5 When the true message, the Good News, first came to you, you heard about the hope it offers. So your faith and love are based on what you hope for, which is kept safe for you in heaven. 6 The gospel keeps bringing blessings and is spreading throughout the world, just as it has among you ever since the day you first heard about the grace of God and came to know it as it really is. 7 You learnt of God's grace from Epaphras, our dear fellow-servant, who is Christ's faithful worker on our *a* behalf. 8 He has told us of the love that the Spirit has given you.

9 For this reason we have always prayed for you, ever since we heard about you. We ask God to fill you with the knowledge of his will, with all the wisdom and understanding that his Spirit gives. 10 Then you will be able to live as the Lord wants and will always do what pleases him. Your lives will produce all kinds of good deeds, and you will grow in your knowledge of God. 11-12 May you be made strong with all the strength which comes from his glorious power, so that you may be able to endure everything with patience. And with joy give thanks to *b* the Father, who has made you fit to have your share of what God has reserved for his people in the kingdom of light. 13 He rescued us from the power of darkness and brought us safe into the kingdom of his dear Son, 14 by whom we are set free, that is, our sins are forgiven.

The Person and Work of Christ

15 Christ is the visible likeness of the invisible God. He is the first-born Son, superior to all created things. 16 For through him God created everything in heaven and on earth, the seen and the unseen things, including spiritual powers, lords, rulers, and authorities. God created the whole universe through him and for him. 17 Christ existed before all things, and in union with him all things have their proper place. 18 He is the head of his body, the church; he is the source of the body's life. He is the first-born Son, who was raised from death, in order that he alone might have the first place in all things. 19 For it was by God's own decision that the Son has in himself the full nature of God. 20 Through the Son, then, God decided to bring the whole universe back to himself. God made peace through his Son's sacrificial death on the cross and so brought back to himself all things, both on earth and in heaven.

21 At one time you were far away from God and were his enemies because of the evil things you did and thought. 22 But now, by means of the physical death of his Son, God has made you his friends, in order to bring you, holy, pure, and faultless, into his presence. 23 You must, of course, continue faithful on a firm and sure foundation, and must not allow yourselves to be shaken from the hope you gained when you heard the gospel. It is of this gospel that I, Paul, became a servant—this gospel which has been preached to everybody in the world.

Paul's Work as a Servant of the Church

24 And now I am happy about my sufferings for you, for by means of my physical sufferings I am helping to complete what still remains of Christ's sufferings on behalf of his body, the church. 25 And I have been made a servant of the church by God, who gave me this task to perform for your good. It is the task of fully proclaiming his message, 26 which is the secret he hid through all past ages from all mankind but has now revealed to his people. 27 God's plan is to make known his secret to his people, this rich and glorious secret which he has for all peoples. And the secret is that Christ is in you, which means that you will share in the glory of God. 28 So we preach Christ to everyone. With all possible wisdom we warn and teach them in order to bring each one into God's presence as a mature individual in union with Christ. 29 To get this done I toil and struggle, using the mighty strength which Christ supplies and which is at work in me.

---

a our; *some manuscripts have* your.
b with patience. And with joy give thanks to; *or* with patience and joy. And give thanks to.
1.7: Col 4.12; Phlm 23   **1.14:** Eph 1.7   **1.18:** Eph 1.22–23   **1.20:** Eph 2.16

2 Let me tell you how hard I have worked for you and for the people in Laodicea and for all others who do not know me personally. [2] I do this in order that they may be filled with courage and may be drawn together in love, and so have the full wealth of assurance which true understanding brings. In this way they will know God's secret, which is Christ himself. [c] [3] He is the key that opens all the hidden treasures of God's wisdom and knowledge.

[4] I tell you, then, do not let anyone deceive you with false arguments, no matter how good they seem to be. [5] For even though I am absent in body, yet I am with you in spirit, and I am glad as I see the resolute firmness with which you stand together in your faith in Christ.

Fullness of Life in Christ

[6] Since you have accepted Christ Jesus as Lord, live in union with him. [7] Keep your roots deep in him, build your lives on him, and become stronger in your faith, as you were taught. And be filled with thanksgiving.

[8] See to it, then, that no one enslaves you by means of the worthless deceit of human wisdom, which comes from the teachings handed down by men and from the ruling spirits of the universe, and not from Christ. [9] For the full content of divine nature lives in Christ, in his humanity, [10] and you have been given full life in union with him. He is supreme over every spiritual ruler and authority.

[11] In union with Christ you were circumcised, not with the circumcision that is made by men, but with the circumcision made by Christ, which consists of being freed from the power of this sinful self. [12] For when you were baptized, you were buried with Christ, and in baptism you were also raised with Christ through your faith in the active power of God, who raised him from death. [13] You were at one time spiritually dead because of your sins and because you were Gentiles without the Law. But God has now brought you to life with Christ. God forgave us all our sins; [14] he cancelled the unfavourable record of our debts with its binding rules and did away with it

completely by nailing it to the cross. [15] And on that cross Christ freed himself from the power of the spiritual rulers and authorities; [d] he made a public spectacle of them by leading them as captives in his victory procession.

[16] So let no one make rules about what you eat or drink or about holy days or the New Moon Festival or the Sabbath. [17] All such things are only a shadow of things in the future; the reality is Christ. [18] Do not allow yourselves to be condemned by anyone who claims to be superior because of special visions and who insists on false humility and the worship of angels. For no reason at all, such a person is all puffed up by his human way of thinking [19] and has stopped holding on to Christ, who is the head of the body. Under Christ's control the whole body is nourished and held together by its joints and ligaments, and it grows as God wants it to grow.

Dying and Living with Christ

[20] You have died with Christ and are set free from the ruling spirits of the universe. Why, then, do you live as though you belonged to this world? Why do you obey such rules as [21] "Don't handle this," "Don't taste that," "Don't touch the other"? [22] All these refer to things which become useless once they are used; they are only man-made rules and teachings. [23] Of course such rules appear to be based on wisdom in their forced worship of angels, and false humility, and severe treatment of the body; but they have no real value in controlling physical passions.

3 You have been raised to life with Christ, so set your hearts on the things that are in heaven, where Christ sits on his throne at the right-hand side of God. [2] Keep your minds fixed on things there, not on things here on earth. [3] For you have died, and your life is hidden with Christ in God. [4] Your real life is Christ and when he appears, then you too will appear with him and share his glory!

The Old Life and the New

[5] You must put to death, then, the earthly desires at work in you, such as sexual immorality, indecency, lust, evil

[c] God's secret, which is Christ himself; *some manuscripts have* God's secret; *others have* the secret of God the Father of Christ; *others have* the secret of the God and Father, and of Christ.
[d] Christ freed himself from the power of the spiritual rulers and authorities; *or* Christ stripped the spiritual rulers and authorities of their power.
2.12: Rom 6.4   **2.13:** Eph 2.1–5   **2.14:** Eph 2.15   **2.16:** Rom 14.1–6   **2.19:** Eph 4.16
3.1: Ps 110.1

passions, and greed (for greed is a form of idolatry). 6 Because of such things God's anger will come upon those who do not obey him. *e* 7 At one time you yourselves used to live according to such desires, when your life was dominated by them.

8 But now you must get rid of all these things: anger, passion, and hateful feelings. No insults or obscene talk must ever come from your lips. 9 Do not lie to one another, for you have taken off the old self with its habits 10 and have put on the new self. This is the new being which God, its Creator, is constantly renewing in his own image, in order to bring you to a full knowledge of himself. 11 As a result, there is no longer any distinction between Gentiles and Jews, circumcised and uncircumcised, barbarians, savages, slaves, and free men, but Christ is all, Christ is in all.

12 You are the people of God; he loved you and chose you for his own. So then, you must clothe yourselves with compassion, kindness, humility, gentleness, and patience. 13 Be tolerant with one another and forgive one another whenever any of you has a complaint against someone else. You must forgive one another just as the Lord has forgiven you. 14 And to all these qualities add love, which binds all things together in perfect unity. 15 The peace that Christ gives is to guide you in the decisions you make; for it is to this peace that God has called you together in the one body. And be thankful. 16 Christ's message in all its richness must live in your hearts. Teach and instruct each other with all wisdom. Sing psalms, hymns, and sacred songs; sing to God with thanksgiving in your hearts. 17 Everything you do or say, then, should be done in the name of the Lord Jesus, as you give thanks through him to God the Father.

Personal Relations in the New Life

18 Wives, submit to your husbands, for that is what you should do as Christians.

19 Husbands, love your wives and do not be harsh with them.

20 Children, it is your Christian duty to obey your parents always, for that is what pleases God.

21 Parents, do not irritate your children,

or they will become discouraged.

22 Slaves, obey your human masters in all things, not only when they are watching you because you want to gain their approval; but do it with a sincere heart because of your reverence for the Lord. 23 Whatever you do, work at it with all your heart, as though you were working for the Lord and not for men. 24 Remember that the Lord will give you as a reward what he has kept for his people. For Christ is the real Master you serve. 25 And every wrongdoer will be repaid for the wrong things he does, because God judges everyone by the same standard.

4 Masters, be fair and just in the way you treat your slaves. Remember that you too have a Master in heaven.

Instructions

2 Be persistent in prayer, and keep alert as you pray, giving thanks to God. 3 At the same time pray also for us, so that God will give us a good opportunity to preach his message about the secret of Christ. For that is why I am now in prison. 4 Pray, then, that I may speak, as I should, in such a way as to make it clear.

5 Be wise in the way you act towards those who are not believers, making good use of every opportunity you have. 6 Your speech should always be pleasant and interesting, and you should know how to give the right answer to everyone.

Final Greetings

7 Our dear brother Tychicus, who is a faithful worker and fellow-servant in the Lord's work, will give you all the news about me. 8 That is why I am sending him to you, in order to cheer you up by telling you how all of us are getting on. 9 With him goes Onesimus, that dear and faithful brother, who belongs to your group. They will tell you everything that is happening here.

10 Aristarchus, who is in prison with me, sends you greetings, and so does Mark, the cousin of Barnabas. (You have already received instructions to welcome Mark if he comes your way.) 11 Joshua, also called Justus, sends greetings too. These three are the only Jewish believers who work with me for the Kingdom of

---

e Some manuscripts do not have upon those who do not obey him.
3.9: Eph 4.22   **3.10:** Gen 1.26; Eph 4.24   **3.12–13:** Eph 4.2   **3.13:** Eph 4.32
3.16–17: Eph 5.19–20   **3.18:** Eph 5.22; 1 Pet 3.1   **3.19:** Eph 5.25; 1 Pet 3.7   **3.20:** Eph 6.1
3.21: Eph 6.4   **3.22–25:** Eph 6.5–8   **3.25:** Deut 10.17; Eph 6.9   **4.1:** Eph 6.9
4.5: Eph 5.16   **4.7:** Acts 20.4; 2 Tim 4.12   **4.7–8:** Eph 6.21–22   **4.9:** Phlm 10–12
4.10: Acts 19.29, 27.2; Phlm 24; Acts 12.12,25, 13.13, 15.37–39

God, and they have been a great help to me.

12 Greetings from Epaphras, another member of your group and a servant of Christ Jesus. He always prays fervently for you, asking God to make you stand firm, as mature and fully convinced Christians, in complete obedience to God's will. 13 I can personally testify to his hard work for you and for the people in Laodicea and Hierapolis. 14 Luke, our dear doctor, and Demas send you their greetings.

15 Give our best wishes to the brothers in Laodicea and to Nympha and the church that meets in her house.f 16 After you read this letter, make sure that it is read also in the church at Laodicea. At the same time, you are to read the letter that the brothers in Laodicea will send you. 17 And say to Archippus, "Be sure to finish the task you were given in the Lord's service."

18 With my own hand I write this: Greetings from Paul. Do not forget my chains!

May God's grace be with you.

f Nympha...her house; some manuscripts have Nymphas...his house.
4.12: Col 1.7; Phlm 23   **4.14:** 2 Tim 4.10,11; Phlm 24   **4.17:** Phlm 2

PAUL'S FIRST LETTER TO THE

THESSALONIANS

INTRODUCTION

Thessalonica was the capital city of the Roman province of Macedonia. Paul established a church there after he left Philippi. Soon, however, there was opposition from Jews who were jealous of Paul's success in preaching the Christian message among the non-Jews who had become interested in Judaism. Paul was forced to leave Thessalonica and go on to Berea. Later on, after he reached Corinth, Paul received a personal report from his companion and fellow-worker Timothy about the situation in the church at Thessalonica.

Paul's First Letter to the Thessalonians was then written to encourage and reassure the Christians there. He gives thanks for the news about their faith and love; he reminds them of the kind of life he had lived while he was with them, and then answers questions that had arisen in the church about the return of Christ: Could a believer who died before Christ's return still share in the eternal life that his return will bring? And when will Christ come again? Paul takes this occasion to tell them to go on working quietly while waiting in hope for Christ's return.

Outline of Contents

Introduction   1.1
Gratitude and praise   1.2—3.13
Exhortation to Christian conduct   4.1-12
Instructions about the coming of Christ   4.13—5.11
Final exhortations   5.12-22
Conclusion   5.23-28

1 From Paul, Silas, and Timothy—
To the people of the church in
Thessalonica, who belong to God the
Father and the Lord Jesus Christ:
May grace and peace be yours.

The Life and Faith of the Thessalonians

2 We always thank God for you all and
always mention you in our prayers. ³For
we remember before our God and Father
how you put your faith into practice, how
your love made you work so hard, and
how your hope in our Lord Jesus Christ
is firm. ⁴Our brothers, we know that God
loves you and has chosen you to be his
own. ⁵For we brought the Good News
to you, not with words only, but also with
power and the Holy Spirit, and with
complete conviction of its truth. You
know how we lived when we were with
you; it was for your own good. ⁶You
imitated us and the Lord; and even though
you suffered much, you received the
message with the joy that comes from
the Holy Spirit. ⁷So you became an
example to all believers in Macedonia and
Achaia. ⁸For not only did the message
about the Lord go out from you throughout Macedonia and Achaia, but the news
about your faith in God has gone everywhere. There is nothing, then, that we
need to say. ⁹All those people speak about
how you received us when we visited you,
and how you turned away from idols to
God, to serve the true and living God ¹⁰and
to wait for his Son to come from heaven—
his Son Jesus, whom he raised from death
and who rescues us from God's anger that
is coming.

Paul's Work in Thessalonica

2 Our brothers, you yourselves know
that our visit to you was not a failure.
²You know how we had already been ill-
treated and insulted in Philippi before we
came to you in Thessalonica. And even
though there was much opposition, our
God gave us courage to tell you the Good
News that comes from him. ³Our appeal
to you is not based on error or impure
motives, nor do we try to trick anyone.
⁴Instead, we always speak as God wants
us to, because he has judged us worthy
to be entrusted with the Good News. We
do not try to please men, but to please
God, who tests our motives. ⁵You know

very well that we did not come to you
with flattering talk, nor did we use words
to cover up greed—God is our witness!
⁶We did not try to get praise from anyone,
either from you or from others, ⁷even
though as apostles of Christ we could
have made demands on you. But we were
gentle when we were with you, like a
mother ª taking care of her children.
⁸Because of our love for you we were
ready to share with you not only the Good
News from God but even our own lives.
You were so dear to us! ⁹Surely you
remember, our brothers, how we worked
and toiled! We worked day and night so
that we would not be any trouble to you
as we preached to you the Good News
from God.

10 You are our witnesses, and so is God,
that our conduct towards you who believe
was pure, right, and without fault. ¹¹You
know that we treated each one of you
just as a father treats his own children.
¹²We encouraged you, we comforted you,
and we kept urging you to live the kind
of life that pleases God, who calls you
to share in his own Kingdom and glory.

13 And there is another reason why we
always give thanks to God. When we
brought you God's message, you heard
it and accepted it, not as man's message
but as God's message, which indeed it
is. For God is at work in you who believe.
¹⁴Our brothers, the same things happened
to you that happened to the churches of
God in Judaea, to the people there who
belong to Christ Jesus. You suffered the
same persecutions from your own
countrymen that they suffered from the
Jews, ¹⁵who killed the Lord Jesus and
the prophets, and persecuted us. How
displeasing they are to God! How hostile
they are to everyone! ¹⁶They even tried to
stop us from preaching to the Gentiles
the message that would bring them
salvation. In this way they have brought
to completion all the sins they have
always committed. And now God's anger
has at last come down on them!

Paul's Desire to Visit Them Again

17 As for us, brothers, when we were
separated from you for a little while—not
in our thoughts, of course, but only in
body—how we missed you and how hard
we tried to see you again! ¹⁸We wanted

ª we were gentle when we were with you, like a mother; *some manuscripts have* we were like
children when we were with you; we were like a mother.
1.1: Acts 17.1   **1.6:** Acts 17.5–9   **2.2:** Acts 16.19–24, 17.1–9   **2.14:** Acts 17.5
2.15: Acts 9.23,29, 13.45,50, 14.2,5,19, 17.5,13, 18.12

to return to you. I myself tried to go back more than once, but Satan would not let us. [19] After all, it is you—you, no less than others!—who are our hope, our joy, and our reason for boasting of our victory in the presence of our Lord Jesus when he comes. [20] Indeed, you are our pride and our joy!

3 Finally, we could not bear it any longer. So we decided to stay on alone in Athens [2] while we sent Timothy, our brother who works with us for God in preaching the Good News about Christ. We sent him to strengthen you and help your faith, [3] so that none of you should turn back because of these persecutions. You yourselves know that such persecutions are part of God's will for us. [4] For while we were still with you, we told you beforehand that we were going to be persecuted; and as you well know, that is exactly what happened. [5] That is why I had to send Timothy. I could not bear it any longer, so I sent him to find out about your faith. Surely it could not be that the Devil had tempted you and all our work had been for nothing!

[6] Now Timothy has come back, and he has brought us the welcome news about your faith and love. He has told us that you always think well of us and that you want to see us just as much as we want to see you. [7] So, in all our trouble and suffering we have been encouraged about you, brothers. It was your faith that encouraged us, [8] because now we really live if you stand firm in your life in union with the Lord. [9] Now we can give thanks to our God for you. We thank him for the joy we have in his presence because of you. [10] Day and night we ask him with all our heart to let us see you personally and supply what is needed in your faith.

[11] May our God and Father himself and our Lord Jesus prepare the way for us to come to you! [12] May the Lord make your love for one another and for all people grow more and more and become as great as our love for you. [13] In this way he will strengthen you, and you will be perfect and holy in the presence of our God and Father when our Lord Jesus comes with all who belong to him. [b]

A Life that Pleases God

4 Finally, our brothers, you learnt from us how you should live in order to please God. This is, of course, how you have been living. And now we beg and urge you in the name of the Lord Jesus to do even more. [2] For you know the instructions we gave you by the authority of the Lord Jesus. [3] God wants you to be holy and completely free from sexual immorality. [4] Each of you men should know how to live with his wife [c] in a holy and honourable way, [5] not with a lustful desire, like the heathen who do not know God. [6] In this matter, then, no man should do wrong to his fellow-Christian or take advantage of him. We have told you this before, and we strongly warned you that the Lord will punish those who do that. [7] God did not call us to live in immorality, but in holiness. [8] So then, whoever rejects this teaching is not rejecting man, but God, who gives you his Holy Spirit.

[9] There is no need to write to you about love for your fellow-believers. You yourselves have been taught by God how you should love one another. [10] And you have, in fact, behaved like this towards all the brothers in all Macedonia. So we beg you, our brothers, to do even more. [11] Make it your aim to live a quiet life, to mind your own business, and to earn your own living, just as we told you before. [12] In this way you will win the respect of those who are not believers, and you will not have to depend on anyone for what you need.

The Lord's Coming

[13] Our brothers, we want you to know the truth about those who have died, so that you will not be sad, as are those who have no hope. [14] We believe that Jesus died and rose again, and so we believe that God will take back with Jesus those who have died believing in him.

[15] What we are teaching you now is the Lord's teaching: we who are alive on the day the Lord comes will not go ahead of those who have died. [16] There will be the shout of command, the archangel's voice, the sound of God's trumpet, and the Lord himself will come down from heaven. Those who have died believing in Christ will rise to life first; [17] then we who are living at that time will be gathered up along with them in the clouds to meet the Lord in the air. And so we will always be with the Lord. [18] So then, encourage one another with these words.

[b] all who belong to him; or all his angels.   [c] live with his wife; or control his body.
3.1: Acts 17.15   **3.6:** Acts 18.5   **4.15–17:** 1 Cor 15.51–52

Be Ready for the Lord's Coming

5 There is no need to write to you, brothers, about the times and occasions when these things will happen. ²For you yourselves know very well that the Day of the Lord will come as a thief comes at night. ³When people say, "Everything is quiet and safe," then suddenly destruction will hit them! It will come as suddenly as the pains that come upon a woman in labour, and people will not escape. ⁴But you, brothers, are not in the darkness, and the Day should not take you by surprise like a thief. ⁵All of you are people who belong to the light, who belong to the day. We do not belong to the night or to the darkness. ⁶So then, we should not be sleeping like the others; we should be awake and sober. ⁷It is at night that people sleep; it is at night that they get drunk. ⁸But we belong to the day, and we should be sober. We must wear faith and love as a breastplate, and our hope of salvation as a helmet. ⁹God did not choose us to suffer his anger, but to possess salvation through our Lord Jesus Christ, ¹⁰who died for us in order that we might live together with him, whether we are alive or dead when he comes. ¹¹And so encourage one another and help one another, just as you are now doing.

Final Instructions and Greetings

12 We beg you, our brothers, to pay proper respect to those who work among you, who guide and instruct you in the Christian life. ¹³Treat them with the greatest respect and love because of the work they do. Be at peace among yourselves.

14 We urge you, our brothers, to warn the idle, encourage the timid, help the weak, be patient with everyone. ¹⁵See that no one pays back wrong for wrong, but at all times make it your aim to do good to one another and to all people.

16 Be joyful always, ¹⁷pray at all times, ¹⁸be thankful in all circumstances. This is what God wants from you in your life in union with Christ Jesus.

19 Do not restrain the Holy Spirit; ²⁰do not despise inspired messages. ²¹Put all things to the test: keep what is good ²²and avoid every kind of evil.

23 May the God who gives us peace make you holy in every way and keep your whole being—spirit, soul, and body—free from every fault at the coming of our Lord Jesus Christ. ²⁴He who calls you will do it, because he is faithful.

25 Pray also for us, brothers.

26 Greet all the believers with a brotherly kiss.

27 I urge you by the authority of the Lord to read this letter to all the believers.

28 The grace of our Lord Jesus Christ be with you.

5.2: Mt 24.43; Lk 12.39; 2 Pet 3.10　　**5.8:** Is 59.17; Eph 6.13–17

PAUL'S SECOND LETTER TO THE
THESSALONIANS

INTRODUCTION

Confusion over the expected return of Christ continued to cause disturbances in the church at Thessalonica. *Paul's Second Letter to the Thessalonians* deals with the belief that the day of the Lord's coming had already arrived. Paul corrects this idea, pointing out that before Christ returns, evil and wickedness will reach a climax under the leadership of a mysterious figure called "the Wicked One," who would be opposed to Christ.

The apostle emphasizes the need for his readers to remain steady in their faith in spite of trouble and suffering, to work for a living as did Paul and his fellow-workers, and to persevere in doing good.

Outline of Contents
Introduction   1.1-2
Praise and commendation   1.3-12
Instructions about the coming of Christ   2.1-17
Exhortation to Christian conduct   3.1-15
Conclusion   3.16-18

---

1 From Paul, Silas, and Timothy—
To the people of the church in Thessalonica, who belong to God our Father and the Lord Jesus Christ:
2 May God our Father and the Lord Jesus Christ give you grace and peace.

The Judgement at Christ's Coming

3 Our brothers, we must thank God at all times for you. It is right for us to do so, because your faith is growing so much and the love each of you has for the others is becoming greater. 4 That is why we ourselves boast about you in the churches of God. We boast about the way you continue to endure and believe through all the persecutions and sufferings you are experiencing.

5 All of this proves that God's judgement is just and as a result you will become worthy of his Kingdom, for which you are suffering. 6 God will do what is right: he will bring suffering on those who make you suffer, 7 and he will give relief to you who suffer and to us as well. He will do this when the Lord Jesus appears from heaven with his mighty angels, 8 with a flaming fire, to punish those who reject God and who do not obey the Good News about our Lord Jesus. 9 They will suffer the punishment of eternal destruction, separated from the presence of the Lord and from his glorious might, 10 when he comes on that Day to receive glory from all his people and honour from all who believe. You too will be among them, because you have believed the message that we told you.

11 That is why we always pray for you. We ask our God to make you worthy of

1.1: Acts 17.1   **1.9:** Is 2.10

the life he has called you to live. May he fulfil by his power all your desire for goodness and complete your work of faith. [12] In this way the name of our Lord Jesus will receive glory from you, and you from him, by the grace of our God and of the Lord[a] Jesus Christ.

The Wicked One

2 Concerning the coming of our Lord Jesus Christ and our being gathered together to be with him: I beg you, my brothers, [2] not to be so easily confused in your thinking or upset by the claim that the Day of the Lord has come. Perhaps it is thought that we said this while prophesying or preaching, or that we wrote it in a letter. [3] Do not let anyone deceive you in any way. For the Day will not come until the final Rebellion takes place and the Wicked One appears, who is destined for hell. [4] He will oppose every so-called god or object of worship and will put himself above them all. He will even go in and sit down in God's Temple and claim to be God.

[5] Don't you remember? I told you all this while I was with you. [6] Yet there is something that keeps this from happening now, and you know what it is. At the proper time, then, the Wicked One will appear. [7] The Mysterious Wickedness is already at work, but what is going to happen will not happen until the one who holds it back is taken out of the way. [8] Then the Wicked One will be revealed, but when the Lord Jesus comes, he will kill him with the breath from his mouth and destroy him with his dazzling presence. [9] The Wicked One will come with the power of Satan and perform all kinds of false miracles and wonders, [10] and use every kind of wicked deceit on those who will perish. They will perish because they did not welcome and love the truth so as to be saved. [11] And so God sends the power of error to work in them so that they believe what is false. [12] The result is that all who have not believed the truth, but have taken pleasure in sin, will be condemned.

You Are Chosen for Salvation

[13] We must thank God at all times for you, brothers, you whom the Lord loves. For God chose you as the first[b] to be saved by the Spirit's power to make you

his holy people and by your faith in the truth. [14] God called you to this through the Good News we preached to you; he called you to possess your share of the glory of our Lord Jesus Christ. [15] So then, our brothers, stand firm and hold on to those truths which we taught you, both in our preaching and in our letter.

[16] May our Lord Jesus Christ himself and God our Father, who loved us and in his grace gave us unfailing courage and a firm hope, [17] encourage you and strengthen you to always do and say what is good.

Pray for Us

3 Finally, our brothers, pray for us, that the Lord's message may continue to spread rapidly and be received with honour, just as it was among you. [2] Pray also that God will rescue us from wicked and evil people; for not everyone believes the message.

[3] But the Lord is faithful, and he will strengthen you and keep you safe from the Evil One. [4] And the Lord gives us confidence in you, and we are sure that you are doing and will continue to do what we tell you.

[5] May the Lord lead you into a greater understanding of God's love and the endurance that is given by Christ.

The Obligation to Work

[6] Our brothers, we command you in the name of our Lord Jesus Christ to keep away from all brothers who are living a lazy life and who do not follow the instructions that we gave them. [7] You yourselves know very well that you should do just what we did. We were not lazy when we were with you. [8] We did not accept anyone's support without paying for it. Instead, we worked and toiled; we kept working day and night so as not to be an expense to any of you. [9] We did this, not because we have no right to demand our support; we did it to be an example for you to follow. [10] While we were with you, we used to say to you, "Whoever refuses to work is not allowed to eat."

[11] We say this because we hear that there are some people among you who live lazy lives and who do nothing except meddle in other people's business. [12] In the name of the Lord Jesus Christ we

---

[a] our God and of the Lord; *or* our God and Lord.
[b] as the first; *some manuscripts have* from the beginning.

2.1: 1 Thes 4.15–17   **2.4:** Dan 11.36; Ezek 28.2   **2.8:** Is 11.4   **2.9:** Mt 24.24

Do not treat him as an enemy (3.15)

command these people and warn them to lead orderly lives and work to earn their own living.

13 But you, brothers, must not get tired of doing good. 14 It may be that someone there will not obey the message we send you in this letter. If so, take note of him and have nothing to do with him, so that he will be ashamed. 15 But do not treat him as an enemy; instead, warn him as a brother.

Final Words

16 May the LORD himself, who is our source of peace, give you peace at all times and in every way. The Lord be with you all.

17 With my own hand I write this: *Greetings from Paul.* This is the way I sign every letter; this is how I write.

18 May the grace of our Lord Jesus Christ be with you all.

PAUL'S FIRST LETTER TO
TIMOTHY

INTRODUCTION

Timothy, a young Christian from Asia Minor, was the son of a Jewish mother and a Greek father. He became a companion and assistant to Paul in his missionary work. *Paul's First Letter to Timothy* deals with three main concerns.

The letter is first of all a warning against false teaching in the church. This teaching, a mixture of Jewish and non-Jewish ideas, was based on the belief that the physical world is evil and that one can attain salvation only by special secret knowledge and by practices such as avoiding certain foods and not marrying. The letter also contains instructions about church administration and worship, with a description of the kind of character that church leaders and helpers should have. Finally, Timothy is advised how to be a good servant of Jesus Christ and about the responsibilities that he has towards various groups of believers.

Outline of Contents
Introduction 1.1–2
Instructions concerning the church and its officers 1.3—3.16
Instructions to Timothy about his work 4.1—6.21

1 From Paul, an apostle of Christ Jesus by order of God our Saviour and Christ Jesus our hope—

2 To Timothy, my true son in the faith: May God the Father and Christ Jesus our Lord give you grace, mercy, and peace.

Warnings against False Teaching

3 I want you to stay in Ephesus, just as I urged you when I was on my way to Macedonia. Some people there are teaching false doctrines, and you must order them to stop. ⁴Tell them to give up those legends and those long lists of ancestors, which only produce arguments; they do not serve God's plan, which is known by faith. ⁵The purpose of this order is to arouse the love that comes from a pure heart, a clear conscience, and a genuine faith. ⁶Some people have turned away from these and have lost their way in foolish discussions. ⁷They want to be teachers of God's law, but they do not understand their own words or the matters about which they speak with so much confidence.

8 We know that the Law is good if it is used as it should be used. ⁹It must be remembered, of course, that laws are made, not for good people, but for lawbreakers and criminals, for the godless and sinful, for those who are not religious or spiritual, for those who kill their fathers or mothers, for murderers, ¹⁰for the immoral, for sexual perverts, for kidnappers, for those who lie and give false testimony or who do anything else contrary to sound doctrine. ¹¹That teaching is found in the gospel that was entrusted to me to announce, the Good News from the glorious and blessed God.

Gratitude for God's Mercy

12 I give thanks to Christ Jesus our Lord, who has given me strength for my work. I thank him for considering me worthy and appointing me to serve him, ¹³even though in the past I spoke evil of him and persecuted and insulted him.

1.2: Acts 16.1   **1.13:** Acts 8.3, 9.4–5

But God was merciful to me because I did not yet have faith and so did not know what I was doing. ¹⁴And our Lord poured out his abundant grace on me and gave me the faith and love which are ours in union with Christ Jesus. ¹⁵This is a true

Christ Jesus came into the world to save sinners (1.15)

saying, to be completely accepted and believed: Christ Jesus came into the world to save sinners. I am the worst of them, ¹⁶but God was merciful to me in order that Christ Jesus might show his full patience in dealing with me, the worst of sinners, as an example for all those who would later believe in him and receive eternal life. [17] To the eternal King, immortal and invisible, the only God—to him be honour and glory for ever and ever! Amen.

18 Timothy, my child, I entrust to you this command, which is in accordance with the words of prophecy spoken in the past about you. Use those words as weapons in order to fight well, [19] and keep your faith and a clear conscience. Some men have not listened to their conscience and have made a ruin of their faith. [20] Among them are Hymenaeus and Alexander, whom I have punished by handing them over to the power of Satan; this will teach them to stop their blasphemy.

Church Worship

2 First of all, then, I urge that petitions, prayers, requests, and thanksgivings be offered to God for all people; [2] for kings and all others who are in authority, that we may live a quiet and peaceful life with all reverence towards God and with proper conduct. [3] This is good and it pleases God our Saviour, [4] who wants everyone to be saved and to come to know the truth. [5] For there is one God, and there is one who brings God and mankind together, the man Christ Jesus, [6] who gave himself to redeem all mankind. That was the proof at the right time that God wants everyone to be saved, [7] and that is why I was sent as an apostle and teacher of the Gentiles, to proclaim the message of faith and truth. I am not lying; I am telling the truth!

8 In every church service I want the men to pray, men who are dedicated to God and can lift up their hands in prayer without anger or argument. [9] I also want the women to be modest and sensible about their clothes and to dress properly; not with fancy hair styles or with gold ornaments or pearls or expensive dresses, [10] but with good deeds, as is proper for women who claim to be religious. [11] Women should learn in silence and all humility. [12] I do not allow them to teach or to have authority over men; they must keep quiet. [13] For Adam was created first,

and then Eve. [14] And it was not Adam who was deceived; it was the woman who was deceived and broke God's law. [15] But a woman will be saved through having children,[a] if she perseveres[b] in faith and love and holiness, with modesty.

Leaders in the Church

3 This is a true saying: If a man is eager to be a church leader, he desires an excellent work. [2] A church leader must be without fault; he must have only one wife,[c] be sober, self-controlled, and orderly; he must welcome strangers in his home; he must be able to teach; [3] he must not be a drunkard or a violent man, but gentle and peaceful; he must not love money; [4] he must be able to manage his own family well and make his children obey him with all respect. [5] For if a man does not know how to manage his own family, how can he take care of the church of God? [6] He must be mature in the faith, so that he will not swell up with pride and be condemned, as the Devil was. [7] He should be a man who is respected by the people outside the church, so that he will not be disgraced and fall into the Devil's trap.

Helpers in the Church

8 Church helpers must also have a good character and be sincere; they must not drink too much wine or be greedy for money; [9] they should hold to the revealed truth of the faith with a clear conscience. [10] They should be tested first, and then, if they pass the test, they are to serve. [11] Their wives[d] also must be of good character and must not gossip; they must be sober and honest in everything. [12] A church helper must have only one wife,[e] and be able to manage his children and family well. [13] Those helpers who do their work well win for themselves a good standing and are able to speak boldly about their faith in Christ Jesus.

The Great Secret

14 As I write this letter to you, I hope to come and see you soon. [15] But if I am delayed, this letter will let you know how we should conduct ourselves in God's household, which is the church of the living God, the pillar and support of the

---

[a] will be saved through having children; *or* will be kept safe through childbirth.
[b] if she perseveres; *or* if they persevere.   [c] have only one wife; *or* be married only once.
[d] Their wives; *or* Women helpers.   [e] have only one wife; *or* be married only once.
2.7: 2 Tim 1.11   **2.9:** 1 Pet 3.3   **2.13:** Gen 2.7,21-22   **2.14:** Gen 3.1-6   **3.2-7:** Tit 1.6-9

truth. ¹⁶No one can deny how great is the secret of our religion:

He appeared in human form,
was shown to be right by the Spirit, *f*
and was seen by angels.
He was preached among the nations,
was believed in throughout the world,
and was taken up to heaven.

False Teachers

4 The Spirit says clearly that some people will abandon the faith in later times; they will obey lying spirits and follow the teachings of demons. ²Such teachings are spread by deceitful liars, whose consciences are dead, as if burnt with a hot iron. ³Such people teach that it is wrong to marry and to eat certain foods. But God created those foods to be eaten, after a prayer of thanks, by those who are believers and have come to know the truth. ⁴Everything that God has created is good; nothing is to be rejected, but everything is to be received with a prayer of thanks, ⁵because the word of God and the prayer make it acceptable to God.

A Good Servant of Christ Jesus

6 If you give these instructions to the brothers, you will be a good servant of Christ Jesus, as you feed yourself spiritually on the words of faith and of the true teaching which you have followed. ⁷But keep away from those godless legends, which are not worth telling. Keep yourself in training for a godly life. ⁸Physical exercise has some value, but spiritual exercise is valuable in every way, because it promises life both for the present and for the future. ⁹This is a true saying, to be completely accepted and believed. ¹⁰We struggle *g* and work hard, because we have placed our hope in the living God, who is the Saviour of all and especially of those who believe.

11 Give them these instructions and these teachings. ¹²Do not let anyone look down on you because you are young, but be an example for the believers in your speech, your conduct, your love, faith, and purity. ¹³Until I come, give your time and effort to the public reading of the Scriptures and to preaching and teaching. ¹⁴Do not neglect the spiritual gift that is in you, which was given to you when the prophets spoke and the elders laid their

hands on you. ¹⁵Practise these things and devote yourself to them, in order that your progress may be seen by all. ¹⁶Watch yourself and watch your teaching. Keep on doing these things, because if you do, you will save both yourself and those who hear you.

Responsibilities towards Believers

5 Do not rebuke an older man, but appeal to him as if he were your father. Treat the younger men as your brothers, ²the older women as mothers, and the younger women as sisters, with all purity.

3 Show respect for widows who really are all alone. ⁴But if a widow has children or grandchildren, they should learn first to carry out their religious duties towards their own family and in this way repay their parents and grandparents, because that is what pleases God. ⁵A widow who is all alone, with no one to take care of her, has placed her hope in God and continues to pray and ask him for his help night and day. ⁶But a widow who gives herself to pleasure has already died, even though she lives. ⁷Give them these instructions, so that no one will find fault with them. ⁸But if anyone does not take care of his relatives, especially the members of his own family, he has denied the faith and is worse than an unbeliever.

9 Do not add any widow to the list of widows unless she is over sixty years of age. In addition, she must have been married only once *h* ¹⁰and have a reputation for good deeds: a woman who brought up her children well, received strangers in her home, performed humble duties for fellow-Christians, helped people in trouble, and devoted herself to doing good.

11 But do not include younger widows in the list; because when their desires make them want to marry, they turn away from Christ, ¹²and so become guilty of breaking their earlier promise to him. ¹³They also learn to waste their time in going round from house to house; but even worse, they learn to be gossips and busybodies, talking of things they should not. ¹⁴So I would prefer that the younger widows get married, have children, and take care of their homes, so as to give our enemies no chance of speaking evil of us. ¹⁵For some widows have already

---

f was shown to be right by the Spirit; *or* and, in spiritual form, was shown to be right.
g struggle; *some manuscripts have* are reviled.
h married only once; *or* faithful to her husband.

What did we bring into the world? Nothing! What can we take out of the world? Nothing! (6.7)

turned away to follow Satan. ¹⁶But if any Christian woman has widows in her family, she must take care of them and not put the burden on the church, so that it may take care of the widows who are all alone.

17 The elders who do good work as leaders should be considered worthy of receiving double pay, especially those who work hard at preaching and teaching. ¹⁸For the scripture says, "Do not muzzle an ox when you are using it to thresh corn" and "A worker should be given his pay." ¹⁹Do not listen to an accusation against an elder unless it is brought by two or more witnesses. ²⁰Rebuke publicly all those who commit sins, so that the rest may be afraid.

21 In the presence of God and of Christ Jesus and of the holy angels I solemnly call upon you to obey these instructions without showing any prejudice or favour to anyone in anything you do. ²²Be in no hurry to lay hands on someone to dedicate him to the Lord's service. Take no part in the sins of others; keep yourself pure.

23 Do not drink water only, but take a little wine to help your digestion, since you are ill so often.

24 The sins of some people are plain to see, and their sins go ahead of them to judgement; but the sins of others are seen only later. ²⁵In the same way good deeds are plainly seen, and even those that are not so plain cannot be hidden.

6 Those who are slaves must consider their masters worthy of all respect, so that no one will speak evil of the name of God and of our teaching. ²Slaves belonging to Christian masters must not despise them, for they are their brothers. Instead, they are to serve them even better, because those who benefit from their work are believers whom they love.

False Teaching and True Riches

You must teach and preach these things. ³Whoever teaches a different doctrine and does not agree with the true words of our Lord Jesus Christ and with the teaching of our religion ⁴is swollen with pride and knows nothing. He has an unhealthy desire to argue and quarrel about words, and this brings on jealousy, disputes, insults, evil suspicions, ⁵and constant arguments from people whose minds do not function and who no longer have the truth. They think that religion is a way to become rich.

6 Well, religion does make a person very rich, if he is satisfied with what he has. ⁷What did we bring into the world? Nothing! What can we take out of the world? Nothing! ⁸So then, if we have food and clothes, that should be enough for us. ⁹But those who want to get rich fall into temptation and are caught in the trap of many foolish and harmful desires, which pull them down to ruin and destruction. ¹⁰For the love of money is a source of all kinds of evil. Some have been so eager to have it that they have wandered away from the faith and have broken their hearts with many sorrows.

5.18: Deut 25.4; Mt 10.10; Lk 10.7   **5.19:** Deut 17.6, 19.15

Personal Instructions

11 But you, man of God, avoid all these things. Strive for righteousness, godliness, faith, love, endurance, and gentleness. [12] Run your best in the race of faith, and win eternal life for yourself; for it was to this life that God called you when you firmly professed your faith before many witnesses. [13] Before God, who gives life to all things, and before Christ Jesus, who firmly professed his faith before Pontius Pilate, I command you [14] to obey your orders and keep them faithfully until the Day when our Lord Jesus Christ will appear. [15] His appearing will be brought about at the right time by God, the blessed and only Ruler, the King of kings and the Lord of lords. [16] He alone is immortal; he lives in the light that no one can approach. No one has ever seen him; no one can ever see him. To him be honour and eternal dominion! Amen.

17 Command those who are rich in the things of this life not to be proud, but to place their hope, not in such an uncertain thing as riches, but in God, who generously gives us everything for our enjoyment. [18] Command them to do good, to be rich in good works, to be generous and ready to share with others. [19] In this way they will store up for themselves a treasure which will be a solid foundation for the future. And then they will be able to win the life which is true life.

20 Timothy, keep safe what has been entrusted to your care. Avoid the profane talk and foolish arguments of what some people wrongly call "Knowledge." [21] For some have claimed to possess it, and as a result they have lost the way of faith.

God's grace be with you all.

6.13: Jn 18.37

PAUL'S SECOND LETTER TO
TIMOTHY

INTRODUCTION

Paul's Second Letter to Timothy consists largely of personal advice to Timothy, as a younger colleague and assistant. The main theme is endurance. Timothy is advised and encouraged to keep on witnessing faithfully to Jesus Christ, to hold to the true teaching of the Good News and the Old Testament, and to do his duty as teacher and evangelist, all in the face of suffering and opposition.

Timothy is especially warned about the dangers of becoming involved in "foolish and ignorant arguments" that do no good, but only ruin the people who listen to them.

In all this, Timothy is reminded of the example of the writer's own life and purpose—his faith, patience, love, endurance, and suffering in persecution.

Outline of Contents

Introduction 1.1-2
Praise and exhortation 1.3—2.13
Counsel and warning 2.14—4.5
Paul's own situation 4.6-18
Conclusion 4.19-22

1 From Paul, an apostle of Christ Jesus by God's will, sent to proclaim the promised life which we have in union with Christ Jesus—

2 To Timothy, my dear son:

May God the Father and Christ Jesus our Lord give you grace, mercy, and peace.

Thanksgiving and Encouragement

3 I give thanks to God, whom I serve with a clear conscience, as my ancestors did. I thank him as I remember you always in my prayers night and day. ⁴I remember your tears, and I want to see you very much, so that I may be filled with joy. ⁵I remember the sincere faith you have, the kind of faith that your grandmother Lois and your mother Eunice also had. I am sure that you have it also. ⁶For this reason I remind you to keep alive the gift that God gave you when I laid my hands on you. ⁷For the Spirit that God has given us does not make us timid; instead, his Spirit fills us with power, love, and self-control.

8 Do not be ashamed, then, of witnessing for our Lord; nor be ashamed of me, a prisoner for Christ's sake. Instead, take your part in suffering for the Good News, as God gives you the strength to do it. ⁹He saved us and called us to be his own people, not because of what we have done, but because of his own purpose and grace. He gave us this grace by means of Christ Jesus before the beginning of time, ¹⁰but now it has been revealed to us through the coming of our Saviour, Christ Jesus. He has ended the power of death and through the gospel has revealed immortal life.

11 God has appointed me as an apostle and teacher to proclaim the Good News, ¹²and it is for this reason that I suffer these things. But I am still full of confidence, because I know whom I have trusted, and I am sure that he is able to keep safe until that Day what he has entrusted to me.ᵃ ¹³Hold firmly to the true words that I taught you, as the example for you to follow, and remain in the faith and love that are ours in union with Christ Jesus. ¹⁴Through the power of the Holy Spirit, who lives in us, keep the good things that have been entrusted to you.

15 You know that everyone in the province of Asia, including Phygelus and Hermogenes, has deserted me. ¹⁶May the Lord show mercy to the family of Onesiphorus, because he cheered me up many times. He was not ashamed that I am in prison, ¹⁷but as soon as he arrived in Rome, he started looking for me until he found me. ¹⁸May the Lord grant him his mercy on that Day! And you know very well how much he did for me in Ephesus.

A Loyal Soldier of Christ Jesus

2 As for you, my son, be strong through the grace that is ours in union with Christ Jesus. ²Take the teachings that you heard me proclaim in the presence of many witnesses, and entrust them to reliable people, who will be able to teach others also.

3 Take your part in suffering, as a loyal soldier of Christ Jesus. ⁴A soldier on active service wants to please his commanding officer and so does not get mixed up in the affairs of civilian life. ⁵An athlete who runs in a race cannot win the prize unless he obeys the rules. ⁶The farmer who has done the hard work should have the first share of the harvest. ⁷Think about what I am saying, because the Lord will enable you to understand it all.

8 Remember Jesus Christ, who was raised from death, who was a descendant of David, as is taught in the Good News I preach. ⁹Because I preach the Good News, I suffer and I am even chained like a criminal. But the word of God is not in chains, ¹⁰and so I endure everything for the sake of God's chosen people, in order that they too may obtain the salvation that comes through Christ Jesus and brings eternal glory. ¹¹This is a true saying:

"If we have died with him,
    we shall also live with him.
¹² If we continue to endure,
    we shall also rule with him.
If we deny him,
    he also will deny us.
¹³ If we are not faithful,
    he remains faithful,
    because he cannot be false to himself."

An Approved Worker

14 Remind your people of this, and give them a solemn warning in God's presence not to fight over words. It does no good, but only ruins the people who listen. ¹⁵Do your best to win full approval in God's sight, as a worker who is not ashamed of his work, one who correctly teaches

---

ᵃwhat he has entrusted to me; *or* what I have entrusted to him.
1.2: Acts 16.1   **1.5:** Acts 16.1   **1.11:** 1 Tim 2.7   **2.12:** Mt 10.33; Lk 12.9

the message of God's truth. [16] Keep away from profane and foolish discussions, which only drive people further away from God. [17] Such teaching is like an open sore that eats away the flesh. Two men who have taught such things are Hymenaeus and Philetus. [18] They have left the way of truth and are upsetting the faith of some believers by saying that our resurrection has already taken place. [19] But the solid foundation that God has laid cannot be shaken; and on it are written these words: "The Lord knows those who are his" and "Whoever says that he belongs to the Lord must turn away from wrongdoing."

[20] In a large house there are dishes and bowls of all kinds: some are made of silver and gold, others of wood and clay; some are for special occasions, others for ordinary use. [21] If anyone makes himself clean from all those evil things, he will be used for special purposes, because he is dedicated and useful to his Master, ready to be used for every good deed. [22] Avoid the passions of youth, and strive for righteousness, faith, love, and peace, together with those who with a pure heart call out to the Lord for help. [23] But keep away from foolish and ignorant arguments; you know that they end up in quarrels. [24] The Lord's servant must not quarrel. He must be kind towards all, a good and patient teacher, [25] who is gentle as he corrects his opponents, for it may be that God will give them the opportunity to repent and come to know the truth. [26] And then they will come to their senses and escape from the trap of the Devil, who had caught them and made them obey his will.

The Last Days

3 Remember that there will be difficult times in the last days. [2] People will be selfish, greedy, boastful, and conceited; they will be insulting, disobedient to their parents, ungrateful, and irreligious; [3] they will be unkind, merciless, slanderers, violent, and fierce; they will hate the good; [4] they will be treacherous, reckless, and swollen with pride; they will love pleasure rather than God; [5] they will hold to the outward form of our religion, but reject its real power. Keep away from such people. [6] Some of them go into people's houses and gain control over weak women who are burdened by the guilt of their sins and driven by all kinds of desires, [7] women who are always trying to learn but who can never come to know the truth. [8] As Jannes and Jambres were opposed to Moses, so also these people are opposed to the truth—people whose minds do not function and who are failures in the faith. [9] But they will not get very far, because everyone will see how stupid they are. That is just what happened to Jannes and Jambres.

Last Instructions

[10] But you have followed my teaching, my conduct, and my purpose in life; you have observed my faith, my patience, my love, my endurance, [11] my persecutions, and my sufferings. You know all that happened to me in Antioch, Iconium, and Lystra, the terrible persecutions I endured! But the Lord rescued me from them all. [12] Everyone who wants to live a godly life in union with Christ Jesus will be persecuted; [13] and evil persons and impostors will keep on going from bad to worse, deceiving others and being deceived themselves. [14] But as for you, continue in the truths that you were taught and firmly believe. You know who your teachers were, [15] and you remember that ever since you were a child, you have known the Holy Scriptures, which are able to give you the wisdom that leads to salvation through faith in Christ Jesus. [16] All Scripture is inspired by God and is useful [b] for teaching the truth, rebuking error, correcting faults, and giving instruction for right living, [17] so that the person who serves God may be fully qualified and equipped to do every kind of good deed.

4 In the presence of God and of Christ Jesus, who will judge the living and the dead, and because he is coming to rule as King, I solemnly urge you [2] to preach the message, to insist upon proclaiming it (whether the time is right or not), to convince, reproach, and encourage, as you teach with all patience. [3] The time will come when people will not listen to sound doctrine, but will follow their own desires and will collect for themselves more and more teachers who will tell them what they are itching to hear. [4] They will turn away from listening to the truth and give their attention to legends. [5] But you must keep control of yourself in all circumstances; endure

---

[b] All Scripture is inspired by God and is useful; *or* Every scripture inspired by God is also useful.
2.19: Num 16.5   **3.8:** Ex 7.11   **3.11:** Acts 13.14–52, 14.1–7,8–20

The prize which the Lord...will give me on that Day (4.8)

suffering, do the work of a preacher of the Good News, and perform your whole duty as a servant of God.

6 As for me, the hour has come for me to be sacrificed; the time is here for me to leave this life. ⁷I have done my best in the race, I have run the full distance, and I have kept the faith. ᶜ ⁸And now there is waiting for me the victory prize of being put right with God, which the Lord, the righteous Judge, will give me on that Day—and not only to me, but to all those who wait with love for him to appear.

Personal Words

9 Do your best to come to me soon. ¹⁰Demas fell in love with this present world and has deserted me, going off to Thessalonica. Crescens went to Galatia, and Titus to Dalmatia. ¹¹Only Luke is with me. Get Mark and bring him with you, because he can help me in the work. ¹²I sent Tychicus to Ephesus. ¹³When you come, bring my coat that I left in Troas with Carpus; bring the books too, and especially the ones made of parchment.

14 Alexander the metal-worker did me much harm; the Lord will reward him according to what he has done. ¹⁵Be on your guard against him yourself, because he was violently opposed to our message.

16 No one stood by me the first time I defended myself; all deserted me. May God not count it against them! ¹⁷But the Lord stayed with me and gave me strength, so that I was able to proclaim the full message for all the Gentiles to hear; and I was rescued from being sentenced to death. ¹⁸And the Lord will rescue me from all evil and take me safely into his heavenly Kingdom. To him be the glory for ever and ever! Amen.

Final Greetings

19 I send greetings to Priscilla and Aquila and to the family of Onesiphorus. ²⁰Erastus stayed in Corinth, and I left Trophimus in Miletus, because he was ill. ²¹Do your best to come before winter.

Eubulus, Pudens, Linus, and Claudia send their greetings, and so do all the other Christian brothers.

22 The Lord be with your spirit.
God's grace be with you all.

ᶜkept the faith; *or* been true to my promise.
4.10: Col 4.14; Phlm 24; 2 Cor 8.23; Gal 2.3; Tit 1.4
4.11: Col 4.14; Phlm 24; Acts 12.12,25, 13.13, 15.37–39; Col 4.10
4.12: Acts 20.4; Eph 6.21–22; Col 4.7–8   **4.13:** Acts 20.6
4.14: 1 Tim 1.20; Ps 62.12; Rom 2.6   **4.19:** Acts 18.2; 2 Tim 1.16–17
4.20: Acts 19.22; Rom 16.23; Acts 20.4, 21.29

PAUL'S LETTER TO

TITUS

INTRODUCTION

Titus was a Gentile convert to Christianity who became a fellow-worker and assistant to Paul in his missionary work. *Paul's Letter to Titus* is addressed to his young helper in Crete, who had been left there to supervise the work of the church. The letter expresses three main concerns.

First, Titus is reminded of the kind of character that church leaders should have, especially in view of the bad character of many Cretans. Next, Titus is advised how to teach the various groups in the church, the older men, the older women (who are, in turn, to teach the younger women), the young men, and the slaves. Finally, the writer gives Titus advice regarding Christian conduct, especially the need to be peaceful and friendly, and to avoid hatred, argument, and division in the church.

Outline of Contents

Introduction 1.1–4
Church officers 1.5–16
Duties of various groups in the church 2.1–15
Exhortations and warning 3.1–11
Conclusion 3.12–15

1 From Paul, a servant of God and an apostle of Jesus Christ.

I was chosen and sent to help the faith of God's chosen people and to lead them to the truth taught by our religion, ² which is based on the hope for eternal life. God, who does not lie, promised us this life before the beginning of time, ³ and at the right time he revealed it in his message. This was entrusted to me, and I proclaim it by order of God our Saviour.

4 I write to Titus, my true son in the faith that we have in common.

May God the Father and Christ Jesus our Saviour give you grace and peace.

Titus' Work in Crete

5 I left you in Crete, so that you could put in order the things that still needed doing and appoint church elders in every town. Remember my instructions: ⁶ an elder must be blameless; he must have only one wife,ᵃ and his children must be believers and not have the reputation of being wild or disobedient. ⁷ For since a church leader is in charge of God's work, he should be blameless. He must not be arrogant or quick-tempered, or a drunkard or violent or greedy for money. ⁸ He must be hospitable and love what is good. He must be self-controlled, upright, holy, and disciplined. ⁹ He must hold firmly to the message which can be trusted and which agrees with the doctrine. In this way he will be able to encourage others with the true teaching and also to show

---

ᵃ have only one wife; *or* be married only once.

1.4: 2 Cor 8.23; Gal 2.3; 2 Tim 4.10   **1.6–9:** 1 Tim 3.2–7 the error of those who are opposed to it.

10 For there are many, especially converts from Judaism, who rebel and deceive others with their nonsense. [11] It is necessary to stop their talk, because they are upsetting whole families by teaching what they should not, and all for the shameful purpose of making money. [12-13] It was a Cretan himself, one of their own prophets, who spoke the truth when he said, "Cretans are always liars, wicked beasts, and lazy gluttons." For this reason you must rebuke them sharply, so that they may have a healthy faith [14] and no longer hold on to Jewish legends and to human commandments which come from people who have rejected the truth. [15] Everything is pure to those who are themselves pure; but nothing is pure to those who are defiled and unbelieving, for their minds and consciences have been defiled. [16] They claim that they know God, but their actions deny it. They are hateful and disobedient, not fit to do anything good.

Sound Doctrine

2 But you must teach what agrees with sound doctrine. [2] Instruct the older men to be sober, sensible, and self-controlled; to be sound in their faith, love, and endurance. [3] In the same way instruct the older women to behave as women should who live a holy life. They must not be slanderers or slaves to wine. They must teach what is good, [4] in order to train the younger women to love their husbands and children, [5] to be self-controlled and pure, and to be good housewives who submit to their husbands, so that no one will speak evil of the message that comes from God.

6 In the same way urge the young men to be self-controlled. [7] In all things you yourself must be an example of good behaviour. Be sincere and serious in your teaching. [8] Use sound words that cannot be criticized, so that your enemies may be put to shame by not having anything bad to say about us.

9 Slaves are to submit to their masters and please them in all things. They must not answer them back [10] or steal from them. Instead, they must show that they are always good and faithful, so as to bring credit to the teaching about God our Saviour in all they do.

11 For God has revealed his grace for the salvation of all mankind. [12] That grace instructs us to give up ungodly living and worldly passions, and to live self-controlled, upright, and godly lives in this world, [13] as we wait for the blessed Day we hope for, when the glory of our great God and Saviour Jesus Christ [b] will appear. [14] He gave himself for us, to rescue us from all wickedness and to make us a pure people who belong to him alone and are eager to do good.

15 Teach these things and use your full authority as you encourage and rebuke your hearers. Let none of them look down on you.

Christian Conduct

3 Remind your people to submit to rulers and authorities, to obey them, and to be ready to do good in every way. [2] Tell them not to speak evil of anyone, but to be peaceful and friendly, and always to show a gentle attitude towards everyone. [3] For we ourselves were once foolish, disobedient, and wrong. We were slaves to passions and pleasures of all kinds. We spent our lives in malice and envy; others hated us and we hated them. [4] But when the kindness and love of God our Saviour was revealed, [5] he saved us. It was not because of any good deeds that we ourselves had done, but because of his own mercy that he saved us, through the Holy Spirit, who gives us new birth and new life by washing us. [6] God poured out the Holy Spirit abundantly on us through Jesus Christ our Saviour, [7] so that by his grace we might be put right with God and come into possession of the eternal life we hope for. [8] This is a true saying.

I want you to give special emphasis to these matters, so that those who believe in God may be concerned with giving their time to doing good deeds, which are good and useful for everyone. [9] But avoid stupid arguments, long lists of ancestors, quarrels, and fights about the Law. They are useless and worthless. [10] Give at least two warnings to the person who causes divisions, and then have nothing more to do with him. [11] You know that such a person is corrupt, and his sins prove that he is wrong.

---

[b] our great God and Saviour Jesus Christ; or the great God and our Saviour Jesus Christ.
2.14: Ps 130.8; Ex 19.5; Deut 4.20, 7.6, 14.2; 1 Pet 2.9

Final Instructions

12 When I send Artemas or Tychicus to you, do your best to come to me in Nicopolis, because I have decided to spend the winter there. [13] Do your best to help Zenas the lawyer and Apollos to get started on their travels, and see to it that they have everything they need. [14] Our people must learn to spend their time doing good, in order to provide for real needs; they should not live useless lives.

15 All who are with me send you greetings. Give our greetings to our friends in the faith.

God's grace be with you all.

3.12: Acts 20.4; Eph 6.21–22; Col 4.7–8; 2 Tim 4.12   **3.13:** Acts 18.24; 1 Cor 16.12

PAUL'S LETTER TO
PHILEMON

INTRODUCTION

Philemon was a prominent Christian, probably a member of the church at Colossae and the owner of a slave named Onesimus. This slave had run away from his master, and then somehow he had come in contact with Paul, who was then in prison. Through Paul, Onesimus became a Christian. *Paul's Letter to Philemon* is an appeal to Philemon to be reconciled to his slave, whom Paul is sending back to him, and to welcome him not only as a forgiven slave but as a Christian brother.

Outline of Contents

Introduction 1–3
Praise for Philemon 4–7
Appeal for Onesimus 8–22
Conclusion 23–25

1 From Paul, a prisoner for the sake of Christ Jesus, and from our brother Timothy—

To our friend and fellow-worker Philemon, [2] and the church that meets in your house, and our sister Apphia, and our fellow-soldier Archippus:

3 May God our Father and the Lord Jesus Christ give you grace and peace.

Philemon's Love and Faith

4 Brother Philemon, every time I pray, I mention you and give thanks to my God. [5] For I hear of your love for all God's people and the faith you have in the Lord Jesus. [6] My prayer is that our fellowship with you as believers will bring about a deeper understanding of every blessing which we have in our life in union with Christ. [7] Your love, dear brother, has brought me great joy and much encouragement! You have cheered the hearts of all God's people.

A Request for Onesimus

8 For this reason I could be bold enough, as your brother in Christ, to order you to do what should be done. [9] But because I love you, I make a request instead. I do this even though I am Paul, the

2: Col 4.17

ambassador of Christ Jesus, and at present also a prisoner for his sake.ᵃ ¹⁰So I make a request to you on behalf of Onesimus, who is my own son in Christ; for while in prison I have become his spiritual father. ¹¹At one time he was of no use to you, but now he is usefulᵇ both to you and to me.

Welcome him back (17)

12 I am sending him back to you now, and with him goes my heart. ¹³I would like to keep him here with me, while I am in prison for the gospel's sake, so that he could help me in your place. ¹⁴However, I do not want to force you to help me; rather, I would like you to do it of your own free will. So I will not do anything unless you agree.

15 It may be that Onesimus was away from you for a short time so that you might have him back for all time. ¹⁶And now he is not just a slave, but much more than a slave: he is a dear brother in Christ. How much he means to me! And how much more he will mean to you, both as a slave and as a brother in the Lord!

17 So, if you think of me as your partner, welcome him back just as you would welcome me. ¹⁸If he has done you any wrong or owes you anything, charge it to my account. ¹⁹Here, I will write this with my own hand: *I, Paul, will pay you back.* (I should not have to remind you, of course, that you owe your very self to me.) ²⁰So, my brother, please do me this favour for the Lord's sake; as a brother in Christ, cheer me up!

21 I am sure, as I write this, that you will do what I ask—in fact I know that you will do even more. ²²At the same time, get a room ready for me, because I hope that God will answer the prayers of all of you and give me back to you.

Final Greetings

23 Epaphras, who is in prison with me for the sake of Christ Jesus, sends you his greetings, ²⁴and so do my fellow-workers Mark, Aristarchus, Demas, and Luke.

25 May the grace of the Lord Jesus Christ be with you all.

ᵃ the ambassador of Christ Jesus, and at present also a prisoner for his sake; *or* an old man, and at present a prisoner for the sake of Christ Jesus.
ᵇ *The Greek name Onesimus means 'useful'.*
10: Col 4.9   **23:** Col 1.7, 4.12
24: Acts 12.12,25, 13.13, 15.37–39, 19.29, 27.2; Col 4.10,14; 2 Tim 4.10,11

THE LETTER TO THE
HEBREWS

INTRODUCTION

The Letter to the Hebrews was written to a group of Christians who, faced with increasing opposition, were in danger of abandoning the Christian faith. The writer encourages them in their faith primarily by showing that Jesus Christ is the true and final revelation of God. In doing this he emphasizes three truths: (1) Jesus is the eternal Son of God, who learnt true obedience to the Father through the suffering that he endured. As the Son of God, Jesus is superior to the prophets of the Old Testament, to the angels, and to Moses himself. (2) Jesus has been declared by God to be an eternal priest, superior to the priests of the Old Testament. (3) Through Jesus the believer is saved from sin, fear, and death; and Jesus, as High Priest, provides the true salvation, which was only foreshadowed by the rituals and animal sacrifices of the Hebrew religion.

By citing the example of the faith of some famous persons in Israel's history (chapter 11), the writer appeals to his readers to remain faithful, and in chapter 12 he urges his readers to continue faithful to the end, with eyes fixed on Jesus, and to endure whatever suffering and persecution may come to them. The book closes with words of advice and warning.

Outline of Contents

Introduction: Christ the complete revelation of God 1.1–3
Christ's superiority over the angels 1.4—2.18
Christ's superiority over Moses and Joshua 3.1—4.13
The superiority of Christ's priesthood 4.14—7.28
The superiority of Christ's covenant 8.1—9.28
The superiority of Christ's sacrifice 10.1–39
The primacy of faith 11.1—12.29
Pleasing God 13.1–19
Closing Prayer 13.20–21
Final Words 13.22–25

God's Word through His Son

1 In the past, God spoke to our ancestors many times and in many ways through the prophets, ²but in these last days he has spoken to us through his Son. He is the one through whom God created the universe, the one whom God has chosen to possess all things at the end. ³He reflects the brightness of God's glory and is the exact likeness of God's own being, sustaining the universe with his powerful word. After achieving forgiveness for the sins of mankind, he sat down in heaven at the right-hand side of God, the Supreme Power.

The Greatness of God's Son

4 The Son was made greater than the angels, just as the name that God gave

him is greater than theirs. ⁵For God never said to any of his angels,

"You are my Son;
today I have become your Father."

Nor did God say about any angel,

"I will be his Father,
and he will be my Son."

⁶But when God was about to send his first-born Son into the world, he said, "All God's angels must worship him."

⁷But about the angels God said,

"God makes his angels winds,
and his servants flames of fire."

⁸About the Son, however, God said:

"Your kingdom, O God, will last ᵃ for ever and ever!

You rule over your ᵇ people with justice.

⁹You love what is right and hate what is wrong.

That is why God, your God, has chosen you

and has given you the joy of an honour far greater

than he gave to your companions."

¹⁰He also said,

"You, Lord, in the beginning created the earth,

and with your own hands you made the heavens.

¹¹They will disappear, but you will remain;

they will all wear out like clothes.

¹²You will fold them up like a coat,
and they will be changed like clothes.

But you are always the same,
and your life never ends."

¹³God never said to any of his angels:

"Sit here on my right
until I put your enemies
as a footstool under your feet."

14 What are the angels, then? They are spirits who serve God and are sent by him to help those who are to receive salvation.

The Great Salvation

2 That is why we must hold on all the more firmly to the truths we have heard, so that we will not be carried away. ²The message given to our ancestors by the angels was shown to be true, and anyone who did not follow it or obey it received the punishment he deserved. ³How, then, shall we escape if we pay

no attention to such a great salvation? The Lord himself first announced this salvation, and those who heard him proved to us that it is true. ⁴At the same time God added his witness to theirs by performing all kinds of miracles and wonders and by distributing the gifts of the Holy Spirit according to his will.

The One Who Leads Us to Salvation

5 God has not placed the angels as rulers over the new world to come—the world of which we speak. ⁶Instead, as it is said somewhere in the Scriptures:

"What is man, O God, that you should think of him;

mere man, that you should care for him?

⁷You made him for a little while lower than the angels;

you crowned him with glory and honour, ᶜ

⁸   and made him ruler over all things."

It says that God made man "ruler over all things"; this clearly includes everything. We do not, however, see man ruling over all things now. ⁹But we do see Jesus, who for a little while was made lower than the angels, so that through God's grace he should die for everyone. We see him now crowned with glory and honour because of the death he suffered. ¹⁰It was only right that God, who creates and preserves all things, should make Jesus perfect through suffering, in order to bring many sons to share his glory. For Jesus is the one who leads them to salvation.

11 He purifies people from their sins, and both he and those who are made pure all have the same Father. That is why Jesus is not ashamed to call them his brothers. ¹²He says to God,

"I will tell my brothers what you have done;

I will praise you in their meeting."

¹³He also says, "I will put my trust in God." And he also says, "Here I am with the children that God has given me."

14 Since the children, as he calls them, are people of flesh and blood, Jesus himself became like them and shared their human nature. He did this so that through his death he might destroy the Devil, who has the power over death, ¹⁵and in this way set free those who were slaves all

---

ᵃYour kingdom, O God, will last; *or* God is your kingdom.
ᵇYour; *some manuscripts have* his.
ᶜ*Many manuscripts add:* You made him ruler over everything you made *(see Ps 8.6).*
1.5: Ps 2.7; 2 Sam 7.14; 1 Chr 17.13   **1.6:** Deut 32.43   **1.7:** Ps 104.4   **1.8-9:** Ps 45.6-7
1.10-12: Ps 102.25-27   **1.13:** Ps 110.1   **2.6-8:** Ps 8.4-6   **2.12:** Ps 22.22   **2.13:** Is 8.17,18

their lives because of their fear of death.
[16] For it is clear that it is not the angels
that he helps. Instead, as the scripture
says, "He helps the descendants of
Abraham." [17] This means that he had to
become like his brothers in every way,
in order to be their faithful and merciful
High Priest in his service to God, so that
the people's sins would be forgiven. [18] And
now he can help those who are tempted,
because he himself was tempted and
suffered.

Jesus Is Greater than Moses

3 My Christian brothers, who also have
been called by God! Think of Jesus,
whom God sent to be the High Priest of
the faith we profess. [2] He was faithful to
God, who chose him to do this work, just
as Moses was faithful in his work in God's
house. [3] A man who builds a house
receives more honour than the house
itself. In the same way Jesus is worthy
of much greater honour than Moses.
[4] Every house, of course, is built by
someone—and God is the one who has
built all things. [5] Moses was faithful in
God's house as a servant, and he spoke
of the things that God would say in the
future. [6] But Christ is faithful as the Son in
charge of God's house. We are his house
if we keep up our courage and our
confidence in what we hope for.

A Rest for God's People

7 So then, as the Holy Spirit says,
　"If you hear God's voice today,
[8]　do not be stubborn, as your
　　ancestors were when they rebelled
　　against God,
　　as they were that day in the desert
　　when they put him to the test.
[9] There they put me to the test and tried
　　me, says God,
　　although they had seen what I did
　　for forty years.
[10] And so I was angry with those people
　　and said,
　　'They are always disloyal
　　and refuse to obey my commands.'
[11] I was angry and made a solemn
　　promise:
　　'They will never enter the land where
　　I would have given them rest!' "
[12] My fellow-believers, be careful that
no one among you has a heart so evil
and unbelieving that he will turn away
from the living God. [13] Instead, in order

that none of you be deceived by sin and
become stubborn, you must help one
another every day, as long as the word
"Today" in the scripture applies to us.
[14] For we are all partners with Christ if
we hold firmly to the end the confidence
we had at the beginning.

15 This is what the scripture says:
　"If you hear God's voice today,
　　do not be stubborn, as your ancestors
　　were
　　when they rebelled against God."

16 Who were the people who heard
God's voice and rebelled against him? All
those who were led out of Egypt by Moses.
[17] With whom was God angry for forty
years? With the people who sinned, who
fell down dead in the desert. [18] When God
made his solemn promise, "They will
never enter the land where I would have
given them rest"—of whom was he
speaking? Of those who rebelled. [19] We
see, then, that they were not able to enter
the land, because they did not believe.

4 Now, God has offered us the promise
that we may receive that rest he
spoke about. Let us take care, then, that
none of you will be found to have failed
to receive that promised rest. [2] For we
have heard the Good News, just as they
did. They heard the message, but it did
them no good, because when they heard
it, they did not accept it with faith. [3] We
who believe, then, do receive that rest
which God promised. It is just as he said,
　"I was angry and made a solemn
　　promise:
　　'They will never enter the land where
　　I would have given them rest!' "
He said this even though his work had
been finished from the time he created
the world. [4] For somewhere in the Scriptures this is said about the seventh day:
"God rested on the seventh day from all
his work." [5] This same matter is spoken
of again: "They will never enter that land
where I would have given them rest."
[6] Those who first heard the Good News
did not receive that rest, because they
did not believe. There are, then, others
who are allowed to receive it. [7] This is
shown by the fact that God sets another
day, which is called "Today." Many years
later he spoke of it through David in the
scripture already quoted:
　"If you hear God's voice today,
　　do not be stubborn."
8 If Joshua had given the people the

3.2: Num 12.7　　**3.7–11:** Ps 95.7–11　　**3.15:** Ps 95.7–8　　**3.16–18:** Num 14.1–35
4.3: Ps 95.11　　**4.4:** Gen 2.2　　**4.5:** Ps 95.11　　**4.7:** Ps 95.7–8　　**4.8:** Deut 31.7; Josh 22.4

rest that God had promised, God would not have spoken later about another day. [9] As it is, however, there still remains for God's people a rest like God's resting on the seventh day. [10] For whoever receives that rest which God promised will rest from his own work, just as God rested from his. [11] Let us, then, do our best to receive that rest, so that no one of us will fail as they did because of their lack of faith.

12 The word of God is alive and active, sharper than any double-edged sword. It cuts all the way through, to where soul and spirit meet, to where joints and marrow come together. It judges the desires and thoughts of man's heart. [13] There is nothing that can be hidden from God; everything in all creation is exposed and lies open before his eyes. And it is to him that we must all give an account of ourselves.

Jesus the Great High Priest

14 Let us, then, hold firmly to the faith we profess. For we have a great High Priest who has gone into the very presence of God—Jesus, the Son of God. [15] Our High Priest is not one who cannot feel sympathy for our weaknesses. On the contrary, we have a High Priest who was tempted in every way that we are, but did not sin. [16] Let us have confidence, then, and approach God's throne, where there is grace. There we will receive mercy and find grace to help us just when we need it.

5 Every high priest is chosen from his fellow-men and appointed to serve God on their behalf, to offer sacrifices and offerings for sins. [2] Since he himself is weak in many ways, he is able to be gentle with those who are ignorant and make mistakes. [3] And because he is himself weak, he must offer sacrifices not only for the sins of the people but also for his own sins. [4] No one chooses for himself the honour of being a high priest. It is only by God's call that a man is made a high priest—just as Aaron was.

5 In the same way, Christ did not take upon himself the honour of being a high priest. Instead, God said to him,

"You are my Son;
    today I have become your Father."

[6] He also said in another place,

"You will be a priest for ever,

in the priestly order of Melchizedek." [c]

7 In his life on earth Jesus made his prayers and requests with loud cries and tears to God, who could save him from death. Because he was humble and devoted, God heard him. [8] But even though he was God's Son, he learnt through his sufferings to be obedient. [9] When he was made perfect, he became the source of eternal salvation for all those who obey him, [10] and God declared him to be high priest, in the priestly order of Melchizedek. [c]

Warning against Abandoning the Faith

11 There is much we have to say about this matter, but it is hard to explain to you, because you are so slow to understand. [12] There has been enough time for you to be teachers—yet you still need someone to teach you the first lessons of God's message. Instead of eating solid food, you still have to drink milk. [13] Anyone who has to drink milk is still a child, without any experience in the matter of right and wrong. [14] Solid food, on the other hand, is for adults, who through practice are able to distinguish between good and evil.

6 Let us go forward, then, to mature teaching and leave behind us the first lessons of the Christian message. We should not lay again the foundation of turning away from useless works and believing in God; [2] of the teaching about baptisms [d] and the laying on of hands; of the resurrection of the dead and the eternal judgement. [3] Let us go forward! And this is what we will do, if God allows.

4 For how can those who abandon their faith be brought back to repent again? They were once in God's light; they tasted heaven's gift and received their share of the Holy Spirit; [5] they knew from experience that God's word is good, and they had felt the powers of the coming age. [6] And then they abandoned their faith! It is impossible to bring them back to repent again, because they are again crucifying the Son of God and exposing him to public shame.

7 God blesses the soil which drinks in the rain that often falls on it and which grows plants that are useful to those for whom it is cultivated. [8] But if it grows thorns and weeds, it is worth nothing;

[c] in...Melchizedek; or like Melchizedek; or in the line of succession to Melchizedek.
[d] baptisms; or purification ceremonies.
4.10: Gen 2.2   **5.3:** Lev 9.7   **5.4:** Ex 28.1   **5.5:** Ps 2.7   **5.6:** Ps 110.4
5.7: Mt 26.36-46; Mk 14.32-42; Lk 22.39-46   **5.12-13:** 1 Cor 3.2   **6.8:** Gen 3.17-18

it is in danger of being cursed by God and will be destroyed by fire.

9 But even if we speak like this, dear friends, we feel sure about you. We know that you have the better blessings that belong to your salvation. 10 God is not unfair. He will not forget the work you did or the love you showed for him in the help you gave and are still giving to your fellow-Christians. 11 Our great desire is that each one of you keep up his eagerness to the end, so that the things you hope for will come true. 12 We do not want you to become lazy, but to be like those who believe and are patient, and so receive what God has promised.

God's Sure Promise

13 When God made his promise to Abraham, he made a vow to do what he had promised. Since there was no one greater than himself, he used his own name when he made his vow. 14 He said, "I promise you that I will bless you and give you many descendants." 15 Abraham was patient, and so he received what God had promised. 16 When a person makes a vow, he uses the name of someone greater than himself, and the vow settles all arguments. 17 To those who were to receive what he promised, God wanted to make it very clear that he would never change his purpose; so he added his vow to the promise. 18 There are these two things, then, that cannot change and about which God cannot lie. So we who have found safety with him are greatly encouraged to hold firmly to the hope placed before us. 19 We have this hope as an anchor for our lives. It is safe and sure, and goes through the curtain of the heavenly temple into the inner sanctuary. 20 On our behalf Jesus has gone in there before us, and has become a high priest for ever, in the priestly order of Melchizedek. e

The Priest Melchizedek

7 This Melchizedek was king of Salem and a priest of the Most High God. As Abraham was coming back from the battle in which he defeated the four kings, Melchizedek met him and blessed him, 2 and Abraham gave him a tenth of all he had taken. (The first meaning of Melchizedek's name is "King of Righteousness"; and because he was king of Salem, his name also means "King of

Peace.") 3 There is no record of Melchizedek's father or mother or of any of his ancestors; no record of his birth or of his death. He is like the Son of God; he remains a priest for ever.

4 You see, then, how great he was. Abraham, our famous ancestor, gave him a tenth of all he got in the battle. 5 And those descendants of Levi who are priests are commanded by the Law to collect a tenth from the people of Israel, that is, from their own countrymen, even though their countrymen are also descendants of Abraham. 6 Melchizedek was not descended from Levi, but he collected a tenth from Abraham and blessed him, the man who received God's promises. 7 There is no doubt that the one who blesses is greater than the one who is blessed. 8 In the case of the priests the tenth is collected by men who die; but as for Melchizedek the tenth was collected by one who lives, as the scripture says. 9 And, so to speak, when Abraham paid the tenth, Levi (whose descendants collect the tenth) also paid it. 10 For Levi had not yet been born, but was, so to speak, in the body of his ancestor Abraham when Melchizedek met him.

11 It was on the basis of the levitical priesthood that the Law was given to the people of Israel. Now, if the work of the levitical priests had been perfect, there would have been no need for a different kind of priest to appear, one who is in the priestly order of Melchizedek, e not of Aaron. 12 For when the priesthood is changed, there also has to be a change in the law. 13 And our Lord, of whom these things are said, belonged to a different tribe, and no member of his tribe ever served as a priest. 14 It is well known that he was born a member of the tribe of Judah; and Moses did not mention this tribe when he spoke of priests.

Another Priest, like Melchizedek

15 The matter becomes even plainer; a different priest has appeared, who is like Melchizedek. 16 He was made a priest, not by human rules and regulations, but through the power of a life which has no end. 17 For the scripture says, "You will be a priest for ever, in the priestly order of Melchizedek." e 18 The old rule, then, is set aside, because it was weak and useless. 19 For the Law of Moses could not make anything perfect. And now a

e in...Melchizedek (see 5.6).
6.14: Gen 22.16-17   **6.19:** Lev 16.2   **6.20:** Ps 110.4   **7.1-2:** Gen 14.17-20
7.5: Num 18.21   **7.17:** Ps 110.4

better hope has been provided through which we come near to God.

20 In addition, there is also God's vow. There was no such vow when the others were made priests. 21 But Jesus became a priest by means of a vow when God said to him,

"The Lord has made a solemn promise
  and will not take it back:
'You will be a priest for ever.'"

22 This difference, then, also makes Jesus the guarantee of a better covenant.

23 There is another difference: there were many of those other priests, because they died and could not continue their work. 24 But Jesus lives on for ever, and his work as priest does not pass on to someone else. 25 And so he is able, now and always, to save those who come to God through him, because he lives for ever to plead with God for them.

26 Jesus, then, is the High Priest that meets our needs. He is holy; he has no fault or sin in him; he has been set apart from sinners and raised above the heavens. 27 He is not like other high priests; he does not need to offer sacrifices every day for his own sins first and then for the sins of the people. He offered one sacrifice, once and for all, when he offered himself. 28 The Law of Moses appoints men who are imperfect to be high priests; but God's promise made with the vow, which came later than the Law, appoints the Son, who has been made perfect for ever.

Jesus Our High Priest

8 The whole point of what we are saying is that we have such a High Priest, who sits at the right of the throne of the Divine Majesty in heaven. 2 He serves as High Priest in the Most Holy Place, that is, in the real tent which was put up by the Lord, not by man.

3 Every High Priest is appointed to present offerings and animal sacrifices to God, and so our High Priest must also have something to offer. 4 If he were on earth, he would not be a priest at all, since there are priests who offer the gifts required by the Jewish Law. 5 The work they do as priests is really only a copy and a shadow of what is in heaven. It is the same as it was with Moses. When he was about to build the Covenant Tent, God said to him, "Be sure to make everything according to the pattern you were shown on the mountain." 6 But now, Jesus has been given priestly work which is superior to theirs, just as the covenant which he arranged between God and his people is a better one, because it is based on promises of better things.

7 If there had been nothing wrong with the first covenant, there would have been no need for a second one. 8 But God finds fault with his people when he says,

"The days are coming, says the Lord,
  when I will draw up a new covenant
    with the people of Israel and with
    the people of Judah.
9 It will not be like the covenant that I
    made with their ancestors
  on the day I took them by the hand
    and led them out of Egypt.
They were not faithful to the covenant
    I made with them,
  and so I paid no attention to them.
10 Now, this is the covenant that I will
    make with the people of Israel
  in the days to come, says the Lord:
I will put my laws in their minds
  and write them on their hearts.
I will be their God,
  and they will be my people.
11 None of them will have to teach his
    fellow-citizen
  or say to his fellow countryman,
    'Know the Lord.'
For they will all know me,
  from the least to the greatest.
12 I will forgive their sins
  and will no longer remember their
    wrongs."

13 By speaking of a new covenant, God has made the first one old; and anything that becomes old and worn out will soon disappear.

Earthly and Heavenly Worship

9 The first covenant had rules for worship and a man-made place for worship as well. 2 A Tent was put up, the outer one, which was called the Holy Place. In it were the lampstand and the table with the bread offered to God. 3 Behind the second curtain was the Tent called the Most Holy Place. 4 In it were the gold altar for the burning of incense and the Covenant Box all covered with gold and containing the gold jar with the manna in it, Aaron's stick that had sprouted leaves, and the two stone tablets

7.21: Ps 110.4   **7.27:** Lev 9.7   **8.1:** Ps 110.1   **8.5:** Ex 25.40   **8.8-12:** Jer 31.31-34
9.2: Ex 26.1-30, 25.31-40,23-30   **9.3:** Ex 26.31-33
9.4: Ex 30.1-6, 25.10-16, 16.33; Num 17.8-10; Ex 25.16; Deut 10.3-5

with the commandments written on them. ⁵ Above the Box were the winged creatures representing God's presence, with their wings spread over the place where sins were forgiven. But now is not the time to explain everything in detail.

6 This is how those things have been arranged. The priests go into the outer Tent every day to perform their duties, ⁷ but only the High Priest goes into the inner Tent, and he does so only once a year. He takes with him blood which he offers to God on behalf of himself and for the sins which the people have committed without knowing they were sinning. ⁸ The Holy Spirit clearly teaches from all these arrangements that the way into the Most Holy Place has not yet been opened as long as the outer Tent still stands. ⁹ This is an illustration which points to the present time. It means that the offerings and animal sacrifices presented to God cannot make the worshipper's heart perfect, ¹⁰ since they have to do only with food, drink, and various purification ceremonies. These are all outward rules, which apply only until the time when God will establish the new order.

11 But Christ has already come as the High Priest of the good things that are already here.ᵉ The tent in which he serves is greater and more perfect; it is not a man-made tent, that is, it is not a part of this created world. ¹² When Christ went through the tent and entered once and for all into the Most Holy Place, he did not take the blood of goats and bulls to offer as a sacrifice; rather, he took his own blood and obtained eternal salvation for us. ¹³ The blood of goats and bulls and the ashes of a burnt calf are sprinkled on the people who are ritually unclean, and this purifies them by taking away their ritual impurity. ¹⁴ Since this is true, how much more is accomplished by the blood of Christ! Through the eternal Spirit he offered himself as a perfect sacrifice to God. His blood will purify our consciences from useless rituals, so that we may serve the living God.

15 For this reason Christ is the one who arranges a new covenant, so that those who have been called by God may receive the eternal blessings that God has promised. This can be done because there has been a death which sets people free from the wrongs they did while the first covenant was in force.

16 In the case of a will it is necessary to prove that the person who made it has died, ¹⁷ for a will means nothing while the person who made it is alive; it comes into effect only after his death. ¹⁸ That is why even the first covenantᶠ came into effect only with the use of blood. ¹⁹ First, Moses proclaimed to the people all the commandments as set forth in the Law. Then he took the blood of bulls and goats, mixed it with water, and sprinkled it on the book of the Law and all the people, using a sprig of hyssop and some red wool. ²⁰ He said, "This is the blood which seals the covenant that God has commanded you to obey." ²¹ In the same way Moses also sprinkled the blood on the Covenant Tent and over all the things used in worship. ²² Indeed, according to the Law almost everything is purified by blood, and sins are forgiven only if blood is poured out.

Christ's Sacrifice Takes Away Sins

23 Those things, which are copies of the heavenly originals, had to be purified in that way. But the heavenly things themselves require much better sacrifices. ²⁴ For Christ did not go into a man-made Holy Place, which was a copy of the real one. He went into heaven itself, where he now appears on our behalf in the presence of God. ²⁵ The Jewish High Priest goes into the Most Holy Place every year with the blood of an animal. But Christ did not go in to offer himself many times, ²⁶ for then he would have had to suffer many times ever since the creation of the world. Instead, now when all ages of time are nearing the end, he has appeared once and for all, to remove sin through the sacrifice of himself. ²⁷ Everyone must die once, and after that be judged by God. ²⁸ In the same manner Christ also was offered in sacrifice once to take away the sins of many. He will appear a second time, not to deal with sin, but to save those who are waiting for him.

10 The Jewish Law is not a full and faithful model of the real things; it is only a faint outline of the good things to come. The same sacrifices are offered for ever, year after year. How can the

---

ᵉ already here; some manuscripts have coming.
ᶠ COVENANT: In Greek the same word means "will" and "covenant."
9.5: Ex 25.18–22   **9.6:** Num 18.2–6   **9.7:** Lev 16.2–34   **9.13:** Lev 16.15–16; Num 19.9,17–19
9.19–20: Ex 24.6–8   **9.21:** Lev 8.15   **9.22:** Lev 17.11   **9.28:** Is 53.12

Law, then, by means of these sacrifices make perfect the people who come to God? ²If the people worshipping God had really been purified from their sins, they would not feel guilty of sin any more, and all sacrifices would stop. ³As it is, however, the sacrifices serve year after year to remind people of their sins. ⁴For the blood of bulls and goats can never take away sins.

5 For this reason, when Christ was about to come into the world, he said to God:

"You do not want sacrifices and offerings,
but you have prepared a body for me.
⁶ You are not pleased with animals burnt whole on the altar
or with sacrifices to take away sins.
⁷ Then I said, 'Here I am,
to do your will, O God,
just as it is written of me in the book of the Law.'"

⁸First he said, "You neither want nor are you pleased with sacrifices and offerings or with animals burnt on the altar and the sacrifices to take away sins." He said this even though all these sacrifices are offered according to the Law. ⁹Then he said, "Here I am, O God, to do your will." So God does away with all the old sacrifices and puts the sacrifice of Christ in their place. ¹⁰Because Jesus Christ did what God wanted him to do, we are all purified from sin by the offering that he made of his own body once and for all.

11 Every Jewish priest performs his services every day and offers the same sacrifices many times; but these sacrifices can never take away sins. ¹²Christ, however, offered one sacrifice for sins, an offering that is effective for ever, and then he sat down at the right-hand side of God. ¹³There he now waits until God puts his enemies as a footstool under his feet. ¹⁴With one sacrifice, then, he has made perfect for ever those who are purified from sin.

15 And the Holy Spirit also gives us his witness. First he says,

¹⁶ "This is the covenant that I will make with them
in the days to come, says the Lord:
I will put my laws in their hearts
and write them on their minds."

¹⁷And then he says, "I will not remember their sins and evil deeds any longer." ¹⁸So when these have been forgiven, an offering to take away sins is no longer needed.

Let Us Come Near to God

19 We have, then, my brothers, complete freedom to go into the Most Holy Place by means of the death of Jesus. ²⁰He opened for us a new way, a living way, through the curtain—that is, through his own body. ²¹We have a great priest in charge of the house of God. ²²So let us come near to God with a sincere heart and a sure faith, with hearts that have been purified from a guilty conscience and with bodies washed with clean water. ²³Let us hold on firmly to the hope we profess, because we can trust God to keep his promise. ²⁴Let us be concerned for one another, to help one another to show love and to do good. ²⁵Let us not give up the habit of meeting together, as some are doing. Instead, let us encourage one another all the more, since you see that the Day of the Lord is coming nearer.

26 For there is no longer any sacrifice that will take away sins if we purposely go on sinning after the truth has been made known to us. ²⁷Instead, all that is left is to wait in fear for the coming Judgement and the fierce fire which will destroy those who oppose God! ²⁸Anyone who disobeys the Law of Moses is put to death without any mercy when judged guilty on the evidence of two or more witnesses. ²⁹What, then, of the person who despises the Son of God? who treats as a cheap thing the blood of God's covenant which purified him from sin? who insults the Spirit of grace? Just think how much worse is the punishment he will deserve! ³⁰For we know who said, "I will take revenge, I will repay"; and who also said, "The Lord will judge his people." ³¹It is a terrifying thing to fall into the hands of the living God!

32 Remember how it was with you in the past. In those days, after God's light had shone on you, you suffered many things, yet were not defeated by the struggle. ³³You were at times publicly insulted and ill-treated, and at other times you were ready to join those who were being treated in this way. ³⁴You shared the sufferings of prisoners, and when all your belongings were seized, you endured your loss gladly, because you knew that you still possessed something much

10.5-7: Ps 40.6-8   **10.11:** Ex 29.38   **10.12-13:** Ps 110.1   **10.16:** Jer 31.33
10.17: Jer 31.34   **10.22:** Lev 8.30; Ezek 36.25   **10.27:** Is 26.11   **10.28:** Deut 17.6, 19.15
10.29: Ex 24.8   **10.30:** Deut 32.35,36

Let us not give up the habit of meeting together (10.25)

better, which would last for ever. ³⁵ Do not lose your courage, then, because it brings with it a great reward. ³⁶ You need to be patient, in order to do the will of God and receive what he promises. ³⁷ For, as the scripture says,

"Just a little while longer,
and he who is coming will come;
he will not delay.
³⁸ My righteous people, however, will
believe and live;
but if any of them turns back,
I will not be pleased with him."

³⁹ We are not people who turn back and are lost. Instead, we have faith and are saved.

Faith

11 To have faith is to be sure of the things we hope for, to be certain of the things we cannot see. ² It was by their faith that people of ancient times won God's approval.

3 It is by faith that we understand that the universe was created by God's word, so that what can be seen was made out of what cannot be seen.

4 It was faith that made Abel offer to God a better sacrifice than Cain's. Through his faith he won God's approval as a righteous man, because God himself approved of his gifts. By means of his faith Abel still speaks, even though he is dead.

5 It was faith that kept Enoch from dying. Instead, he was taken up to God, and nobody could find him, because God had taken him up. The scripture says that before Enoch was taken up, he had pleased God. ⁶ No one can please God without faith, for whoever comes to God must have faith that God exists and rewards those who seek him.

7 It was faith that made Noah hear God's warnings about things in the future that he could not see. He obeyed God and built a boat in which he and his family were saved. As a result, the world was condemned, and Noah received from God the righteousness that comes by faith.

8 It was faith that made Abraham obey when God called him to go out to a country which God had promised to give him. He left his own country without knowing where he was going. ⁹ By faith he lived as a foreigner in the country that God had promised him. He lived in tents, as did Isaac and Jacob, who received the same promise from God. ¹⁰ For Abraham was waiting for the city which God has

10.37–38: Hab 2.3–4   **11.3:** Gen 1.1; Ps 33.6,9; Jn 1.3   **11.4:** Gen 4.3–10   **11.5:** Gen 5.21–24
11.7: Gen 6.13–22   **11.8:** Gen 12.1–5   **11.9:** Gen 35.27

designed and built, the city with permanent foundations.

11 It was faith that made Abraham able to become a father, even though he was too old and Sarah herself could not have children. He[g] trusted God to keep his promise. [12] Though Abraham was practically dead, from this one man came as many descendants as there are stars in the sky, as many as the numberless grains of sand on the sea-shore.

13 It was in faith that all these persons died. They did not receive the things God had promised, but from a long way off they saw them and welcomed them, and admitted openly that they were foreigners and refugees on earth. [14] Those who say such things make it clear that they are looking for a country of their own. [15] They did not keep thinking about the country they had left; if they had, they would have had the chance to return. [16] Instead, it was a better country they longed for, the heavenly country. And so God is not ashamed for them to call him their God, because he has prepared a city for them.

17 It was faith that made Abraham offer his son Isaac as a sacrifice when God put Abraham to the test. Abraham was the one to whom God had made the promise, yet he was ready to offer his only son as a sacrifice. [18] God had said to him, "It is through Isaac that you will have the descendants I promised." [19] Abraham reckoned that God was able to raise Isaac from death—and, so to speak, Abraham did receive Isaac back from death.

20 It was faith that made Isaac promise blessings for the future to Jacob and Esau.

21 It was faith that made Jacob bless each of the sons of Joseph just before he died. He leaned on the top of his walking-stick and worshipped God.

22 It was faith that made Joseph, when he was about to die, speak of the departure of the Israelites from Egypt, and leave instructions about what should be done with his body.

23 It was faith that made the parents of Moses hide him for three months after he was born. They saw that he was a beautiful child, and they were not afraid to disobey the king's order.

24 It was faith that made Moses, when he had grown up, refuse to be called the son of the king's daughter. [25] He preferred to suffer with God's people rather than to enjoy sin for a little while. [26] He reckoned that to suffer scorn for the Messiah was worth far more than all the treasures of Egypt, for he kept his eyes on the future reward.

27 It was faith that made Moses leave Egypt without being afraid of the king's anger. As though he saw the invisible God, he refused to turn back. [28] It was faith that made him establish the Passover and order the blood to be sprinkled on the doors, so that the Angel of Death would not kill the first-born sons of the Israelites.

29 It was faith that made the Israelites able to cross the Red Sea as if on dry land; when the Egyptians tried to do it, the water swallowed them up.

30 It was faith that made the walls of Jericho fall down after the Israelites had marched round them for seven days. [31] It was faith that kept the prostitute Rahab from being killed with those who disobeyed God, for she gave the Israelite spies a friendly welcome.

32 Should I go on? There isn't enough time for me to speak of Gideon, Barak, Samson, Jephthah, David, Samuel, and the prophets. [33] Through faith they fought whole countries and won. They did what was right and received what God had promised. They shut the mouths of lions, [34] put out fierce fires, escaped being killed by the sword. They were weak, but became strong; they were mighty in battle and defeated the armies of foreigners. [35] Through faith women received their dead relatives raised back to life.

Others, refusing to accept freedom, died under torture in order to be raised to a better life. [36] Some were mocked and whipped, and others were put in chains and taken off to prison. [37] They were stoned, they were sawn in two, they were killed by the sword. They went round

[g]It was faith...children. He; *some manuscripts have* It was faith that made Sarah herself able to conceive, even though she was too old to have children. She.
11.11: Gen 18.11–14, 21.2   **11.12:** Gen 15.5, 22.17, 32.12
11.13: Gen 23.4; 1 Chr 29.15; Ps 39.12   **11.17:** Gen 22.1–14   **11.18:** Gen 21.12
11.20: Gen 27.27–29,39–40   **11.21:** Gen 47.31—48.20   **11.22:** Gen 50.24–25; Ex 13.19
11.23: Ex 2.2, 1.22   **11.24:** Ex 2.10–12   **11.28:** Ex 12.21–30
11.29: Ex 14.21–31   **11.30:** Josh 6.12–21   **11.31:** Josh 2.1–21, 6.22–25
11.32: Judg 6.11—8.32, 4.6—5.31, 13.2—16.31, 11.1—12.7; 1 Sam 16.1—1 Kgs 2.11; 1 Sam 1.1—25.1
11.33: Dan 6.1–27   **11.34:** Dan 3.1–30   **11.35:** 1 Kgs 17.17–24; 2 Kgs 4.25–37
11.36: 1 Kgs 22.26–27; 2 Chr 18.25–26; Jer 20.2, 37.15, 38.6   **11.37:** 2 Chr 24.21

clothed in skins of sheep or goats—poor, persecuted, and ill-treated. 38 The world was not good enough for them! They wandered like refugees in the deserts and hills, living in caves and holes in the ground.

39 What a record all of these have won by their faith! Yet they did not receive what God had promised, 40 because God had decided on an even better plan for us. His purpose was that only in company with us would they be made perfect.

God Our Father

12 As for us, we have this large crowd of witnesses round us. So then, let us rid ourselves of everything that gets in the way, and of the sin which holds on to us so tightly, and let us run with determination the race that lies before us. 2 Let us keep our eyes fixed on Jesus, on whom our faith depends from beginning to end. He did not give up because of the cross! On the contrary, because of the joy that was waiting for him, he thought nothing of the disgrace of dying on the cross, and he is now seated at the right-hand side of God's throne.

3 Think of what he went through; how he put up with so much hatred from sinners! So do not let yourselves become discouraged and give up. 4 For in your struggle against sin you have not yet had to resist to the point of being killed. 5 Have you forgotten the encouraging words which God speaks to you as his sons?

"My son, pay attention when the Lord
         corrects you,
    and do not be discouraged when he
         rebukes you.
6 Because the Lord corrects everyone he
         loves,
    and punishes everyone he accepts as
         a son."

7 Endure what you suffer as being a father's punishment; your suffering shows that God is treating you as his sons. Was there ever a son who was not punished by his father? 8 If you are not punished, as all his sons are, it means you are not real sons, but bastards. 9 In the case of our human fathers, they punished us and we respected them. How much more, then, should we submit to our spiritual Father and live! 10 Our

human fathers punished us for a short time, as it seemed right to them; but God does it for our own good, so that we may share his holiness. 11 When we are punished, it seems to us at the time something to make us sad, not glad. Later, however, those who have been disciplined by such punishment reap the peaceful reward of a righteous life.

Instructions and Warnings

12 Lift up your tired hands, then, and strengthen your trembling knees! 13 Keep walking on straight paths, so that the lame foot may not be disabled, but instead be healed.

14 Try to be at peace with everyone, and try to live a holy life, because no one will see the Lord without it. 15 Guard against turning back from the grace of God. Let no one become like a bitter plant that grows up and causes many troubles with its poison. 16 Let no one become immoral or unspiritual like Esau, who for a single meal sold his rights as the elder son. 17 Afterwards, you know, he wanted to receive his father's blessing; but he was turned away, because he could not find any way to change what he had done, even though in tears he looked for it. *h*

18 You have not come, as the people of Israel came, to what you can feel, to Mount Sinai with its blazing fire, the darkness and the gloom, the storm, 19 the blast of a trumpet, and the sound of a voice. When the people heard the voice, they begged not to hear another word, 20 because they could not bear the order which said, "If even an animal touches the mountain, it must be stoned to death." 21 The sight was so terrifying that Moses said, "I am trembling and afraid!"

22 Instead, you have come to Mount Zion and to the city of the living God, the heavenly Jerusalem, with its thousands of angels. 23 You have come to the joyful gathering of God's first-born sons, whose names are written in heaven. You have come to God, who is the judge of all mankind, and to the spirits of good people made perfect. 24 You have come to Jesus, who arranged the new covenant, and to the sprinkled blood that promises much better things than does the blood of Abel.

h he looked for it; *or* he tried to get the blessing.
12.5–6: Job 5.17; Prov 3.11–12   **12.12:** Is 35.3   **12.13:** Prov 4.26   **12.15:** Deut 29.18
12.16: Gen 25.29–34   **12.17:** Gen 27.30–40
12.18–19: Ex 19.16–22, 20.18–21; Deut 4.11–12, 5.22–27   **12.20:** Ex 19.12–13
12.21: Deut 9.19   **12.24:** Gen 4.10

25 Be careful, then, and do not refuse to hear him who speaks. Those who refused to hear the one who gave the divine message on earth did not escape. How much less shall we escape, then, if we turn away from the one who speaks from heaven! 26 His voice shook the earth at that time, but now he has promised, "I will once more shake not only the earth but heaven as well." 27 The words "once more" plainly show that the created things will be shaken and removed, so that the things that cannot be shaken will remain.

28 Let us be thankful, then, because we receive a kingdom that cannot be shaken. Let us be grateful and worship God in a way that will please him, with reverence and awe; 29 because our God is indeed a destroying fire.

How to Please God

13 Keep on loving one another as Christian brothers. 2 Remember to welcome strangers in your homes. There were some who did that and welcomed angels without knowing it. 3 Remember those who are in prison, as though you were in prison with them. Remember those who are suffering, as though you were suffering as they are.

4 Marriage is to be honoured by all, and husbands and wives must be faithful to each other. God will judge those who are immoral and those who commit adultery.

5 Keep your lives free from the love

Keep your lives free from the love of money (13.5)

of money, and be satisfied with what you have. For God has said, "I will never leave you; I will never abandon you." 6 Let us be bold, then, and say,

"The Lord is my helper,

I will not be afraid.
What can anyone do to me?"

7 Remember your former leaders, who spoke God's message to you. Think back on how they lived and died, and imitate their faith. 8 Jesus Christ is the same yesterday, today, and for ever. 9 Do not let all kinds of strange teachings lead you from the right way. It is good to receive inner strength from God's grace, and not by obeying rules about foods; those who obey these rules have not been helped by them.

10 The priests who serve in the Jewish place of worship have no right to eat any of the sacrifice on our altar. 11 The Jewish High Priest brings the blood of the animals into the Most Holy Place to offer it as a sacrifice for sins; but the bodies of the animals are burnt outside the camp. 12 For this reason Jesus also died outside the city, in order to purify the people from sin with his own blood. 13 Let us, then, go to him outside the camp and share his shame. 14 For there is no permanent city for us here on earth; we are looking for the city which is to come. 15 Let us, then, always offer praise to God as our sacrifice through Jesus, which is the offering presented by lips that confess him as Lord. 16 Do not forget to do good and to help one another, because these are the sacrifices that please God.

17 Obey your leaders and follow their orders. They watch over your souls without resting, since they must give God an account of their service. If you obey them, they will do their work gladly; if not, they will do it with sadness, and that would be of no help to you.

18 Keep on praying for us. We are sure we have a clear conscience, because we want to do the right thing at all times. 19 And I beg you even more earnestly to pray that God will send me back to you soon.

Closing Prayer

20-21 God has raised from death our Lord Jesus, who is the Great Shepherd of the sheep as the result of his sacrificial death, by which the eternal covenant is sealed. May the God of peace provide you with every good thing you need in order to do his will, and may he, through Jesus Christ, do in us what pleases him. And to Christ be the glory for ever and ever! Amen.

12.25: Ex 20.22 **12.26:** Hag 2.6 **12.29:** Deut 4.24 **13.2:** Gen 18.1-8, 19.1-3
13.5: Deut 31.6,8; Josh 1.5 **13.6:** Ps 118.6 **13.11:** Lev 16.27

Final Words

22 I beg you, my brothers, to listen patiently to this message of encouragement; for this letter I have written to you is not very long. 23 I want you to know that our brother Timothy has been let out of prison. If he comes soon enough, I will have him with me when I see you.

24 Give our greetings to all your leaders and to all God's people. The brothers from Italy send you their greetings.

25 May God's grace be with you all.

THE LETTER FROM
JAMES

INTRODUCTION

The Letter from James is a collection of practical instructions, written to "all God's people scattered over the whole world." The writer uses many vivid figures of speech to present instructions regarding practical wisdom and guidance for Christian attitudes and conduct. From the Christian perspective he deals with a variety of topics such as riches and poverty, temptation, good conduct, prejudice, faith and actions, the use of the tongue, wisdom, quarrelling, pride and humility, judging others, boasting, patience, and prayer.

The letter emphasizes the importance of actions along with faith, in the practice of the Christian religion.

Outline of Contents

Introduction   1.1
Faith and wisdom   1.2–8
Poverty and wealth   1.9–11
Testing and tempting   1.12–18
Hearing and doing   1.19–27
Warning against discrimination   2.1–13
Faith and works   2.14–26
The Christian and his tongue   3.1–18
The Christian and the world   4.1—5.6
Various instructions   5.7–20

---

1 From James, a servant of God and of the Lord Jesus Christ:

Greetings to all God's people scattered over the whole world.

Faith and Wisdom

2 My brothers, consider yourselves fortunate when all kinds of trials come your way, 3 for you know that when your faith succeeds in facing such trials, the result is the ability to endure. 4 Make sure that your endurance carries you all the way without failing, so that you may be perfect and complete, lacking nothing. 5 But if any

1.1: Mt 13.55; Mk 6.3; Acts 15.13; Gal 1.19

of you lacks wisdom, he should pray to God, who will give it to him; because God gives generously and graciously to all. [6] But when you pray, you must believe and not doubt at all. Whoever doubts is like a wave in the sea that is driven and blown about by the wind. [7-8] A person like that, unable to make up his mind and undecided in all he does, must not think that he will receive anything from the Lord.

Poverty and Riches

9 The Christian who is poor must be glad when God lifts him up, [10] and the rich Christian must be glad when God brings him down. For the rich will pass away like the flower of a wild plant. [11] The sun rises with its blazing heat and burns the plant; its flower falls off, and its beauty is destroyed. In the same way the rich man will be destroyed while he goes about his business.

Testing and Tempting

12 Happy is the person who remains faithful under trials, because when he succeeds in passing such a test, he will receive as his reward the life which God has promised to those who love him. [13] If a person is tempted by such trials, he must not say, "This temptation comes from God." For God cannot be tempted by evil, and he himself tempts no one. [14] But a person is tempted when he is drawn away and trapped by his own evil desire. [15] Then his evil desire conceives and gives birth to sin; and sin, when it is full-grown, gives birth to death.

16 Do not be deceived, my dear brothers! [17] Every good gift and every perfect present comes from heaven; it comes down from God, the Creator of the heavenly lights, who does not change or cause darkness by turning. [18] By his own will he brought us into being through the word of truth, so that we should have first place among all his creatures.

Hearing and Doing

19 Remember this, my dear brothers! Everyone must be quick to listen, but slow to speak and slow to become angry. [20] Man's anger does not achieve God's righteous purpose. [21] So get rid of every filthy habit and all wicked conduct. Submit to God and accept the word that he plants in your hearts, which is able to save you.

22 Do not deceive yourselves by just listening to his word; instead, put it into practice. [23] Whoever listens to the word but does not put it into practice is like a man who looks in a mirror and sees himself as he is. [24] He takes a good look at himself and then goes away and at once forgets what he looks like. [25] But whoever looks closely into the perfect law that sets people free, who keeps on paying attention to it and does not simply listen and then forget it, but puts it into practice—that person will be blessed by God in what he does.

26 Does anyone think he is religious? If he does not control his tongue, his religion is worthless and he deceives himself. [27] What God the Father considers to be pure and genuine religion is this: to take care of orphans and widows in their suffering and to keep oneself from being corrupted by the world.

Warning against Prejudice

2 My brothers, as believers in our Lord Jesus Christ, the Lord of glory, you must never treat people in different ways according to their outward appearance. [2] Suppose a rich man wearing a gold ring and fine clothes comes to your meeting, and a poor man in ragged clothes also comes. [3] If you show more respect to the well-dressed man and say to him, "Have this best seat here," but say to the poor man, "Stand over there, or sit here on the floor by my feet," [4] then you are guilty of creating distinctions among yourselves and of making judgements based on evil motives.

5 Listen, my dear brothers! God chose the poor people of this world to be rich in faith and to possess the kingdom which he promised to those who love him. [6] But you dishonour the poor! Who are the ones who oppress you and drag you before the judges? The rich! [7] They are the ones who speak evil of that good name which has been given to you.

8 You will be doing the right thing if you obey the law of the Kingdom, which is found in the scripture, "Love your neighbour as you love yourself." [9] But if you treat people according to their outward appearance, you are guilty of sin, and the Law condemns you as a law-breaker. [10] Whoever breaks one commandment is guilty of breaking them all. [11] For the same one who said, "Do not commit adultery," also said, "Do not commit

1.10–11: Is 40.6–7   **2.8:** Lev 19.18   **2.11:** Ex 20.13,14; Deut 5.17,18

murder." Even if you do not commit adultery, you have become a law-breaker if you commit murder. ¹²Speak and act as people who will be judged by the law that sets us free. ¹³For God will not show mercy when he judges the person who has not been merciful; but mercy triumphs over judgement.

Faith and Actions

14 My brothers, what good is it for someone to say that he has faith if his actions do not prove it? Can that faith save him? ¹⁵Suppose there are brothers or sisters who need clothes and don't have enough to eat. ¹⁶What good is there in your saying to them, "God bless you! Keep warm and eat well!"—if you don't give them the necessities of life? ¹⁷So it is with faith: if it is alone and includes no actions, then it is dead.

18 But someone will say, "One person has faith, another has actions." My answer is, "Show me how anyone can have faith without actions. I will show you my faith by my actions." ¹⁹Do you believe that there is only one God? Good! The demons also believe—and tremble with fear. ²⁰You fool! Do you want to be shown that faith without actions is useless?ᵃ ²¹How was our ancestor Abraham put right with God? It was through his actions, when he offered his son Isaac on the altar. ²²Can't you see? His faith and his actions worked together; his faith was made perfect through his actions. ²³And the scripture came true that said, "Abraham believed God, and because of his faith God accepted him as righteous." And so Abraham was called God's friend. ²⁴You see, then, that it is by his actions that a person is put right with God, and not by his faith alone.

25 It was the same with the prostitute Rahab. She was put right with God through her actions, by welcoming the Israelite spies and helping them to escape by a different road.

26 So then, as the body without the spirit is dead, so also faith without actions is dead.

The Tongue

3 My brothers, not many of you should become teachers. As you know, we teachers will be judged with greater strictness than others. ²All of us often make mistakes. But if a person never makes a mistake in what he says, he is perfect and is also able to control his whole being. ³We put a bit into the mouth of a horse to make it obey us, and we are able to make it go where we want. ⁴Or think of a ship: big as it is and driven by such strong winds, it can be steered by a very small rudder, and it goes wherever the pilot wants it to go. ⁵So it is with the tongue: small as it is, it can boast about great things.

Just think how large a forest can be set on fire by a tiny flame! ⁶And the tongue is like a fire. It is a world of wrong, occupying its place in our bodies and spreading evil through our whole being. It sets on fire the entire course of our existence with the fire that comes to it from hell itself. ⁷Man is able to tame and has tamed all other creatures—wild animals and birds, reptiles and fish. ⁸But no one has ever been able to tame the tongue. It is evil and uncontrollable, full of deadly poison. ⁹We use it to give thanks to our Lord and Father and also to curse our fellow-man, who is created in the likeness of God. ¹⁰Words of thanksgiving and cursing pour out from the same mouth. My brothers, this should not happen! ¹¹No spring of water pours out sweet water and bitter water from the same opening. ¹²A fig-tree, my brothers, cannot bear olives; a grapevine cannot bear figs, nor can a salty spring produce sweet water.

The Wisdom from Above

13 Is there anyone among you who is wise and understanding? He is to prove it by his good life, by his good deeds performed with humility and wisdom. ¹⁴But if in your heart you are jealous, bitter, and selfish, don't sin against the truth by boasting of your wisdom. ¹⁵Such wisdom does not come down from heaven; it belongs to the world, it is unspiritual and demonic. ¹⁶Where there is jealousy and selfishness, there is also disorder and every kind of evil. ¹⁷But the wisdom from above is pure first of all; it is also peaceful, gentle, and friendly; it is full of compassion and produces a harvest of good deeds; it is free from prejudice and hypocrisy. ¹⁸And goodness is the harvest that is produced from the seeds the peacemakers plant in peace.

ᵃuseless; *some manuscripts have* dead.
2.21: Gen 22.1-14 **2.23:** Gen 15.6; 2 Chr 20.7; Is 41.8 **2.25:** Josh 2.1-21 **3.9:** Gen 1.26

Friendship with the World

4 Where do all the fights and quarrels among you come from? They come from your desires for pleasure, which are constantly fighting within you. ²You want things, but you cannot have them, so you are ready to kill; you strongly desire things, but you cannot get them, so you quarrel and fight. You do not have what you want because you do not ask God for it. ³And when you ask, you do not receive it, because your motives are bad; you ask for things to use for your own pleasures. ⁴Unfaithful people! Don't you know that to be the world's friend means to be God's enemy? Whoever wants to be the world's friend makes himself God's enemy. ⁵Don't think that there is no truth in the scripture that says, "The spirit that God placed in us is filled with fierce desires." ᵇ ⁶But the grace that God gives is even stronger. As the scripture says, "God resists the proud, but gives grace to the humble."

7 So then, submit to God. Resist the Devil, and he will run away from you. ⁸Come near to God, and he will come near to you. Wash your hands, you sinners! Purify your hearts, you hypocrites! ⁹Be sorrowful, cry, and weep; change your laughter into crying, your joy into gloom! ¹⁰Humble yourselves before the Lord, and he will lift you up.

Warning against Judging a Christian Brother

11 Do not criticize one another, my brothers. Whoever criticizes a Christian brother or judges him, criticizes the Law and judges it. If you judge the Law, then you are no longer one who obeys the Law, but one who judges it. ¹²God is the only lawgiver and judge. He alone can save and destroy. Who do you think you are, to judge your fellow-man?

Warning against Boasting

13 Now listen to me, you that say, "Today or tomorrow we will travel to a certain city, where we will stay a year and go into business and make a lot of money." ¹⁴You don't even know what your life tomorrow will be! You are like a puff of smoke, which appears for a moment and then disappears. ¹⁵What you

should say is this: "If the Lord is willing, we will live and do this or that." ¹⁶But now you are proud, and you boast; all such boasting is wrong.

17 So then, the person who does not do the good he knows he should do is guilty of sin.

Warning to the Rich

5 And now, you rich people, listen to me! Weep and wail over the miseries that are coming upon you! ²Your riches have rotted away, and your clothes have been eaten by moths. ³Your gold and silver are covered with rust, and this rust will be a witness against you and will eat up your flesh like fire. You have piled up riches in these last days. ⁴You have not paid any wages to the men who work in your fields. Listen to their complaints! The cries of those who gather in your crops have reached the ears of God, the Lord Almighty. ⁵Your life here on earth has been full of luxury and pleasure. You have made yourselves fat for the day of slaughter. ⁶You have condemned and murdered innocent people, and they do not resist you. ᶜ

Patience and Prayer

7 Be patient, then, my brothers, until the Lord comes. See how patient a farmer is as he waits for his land to produce precious crops. He waits patiently for the autumn and spring rains. ⁸You also must be patient. Keep your hopes high, for the day of the Lord's coming is near.

9 Do not complain against one another, my brothers, so that God will not judge you. The Judge is near, ready to appear. ¹⁰My brothers, remember the prophets who spoke in the name of the Lord. Take them as examples of patient endurance under suffering. ¹¹We call them happy because they endured. You have heard of Job's patience, and you know how the Lord provided for him in the end. For the Lord is full of mercy and compassion.

12 Above all, my brothers, do not use an oath when you make a promise. Do not swear by heaven or by earth or by anything else. Say only "Yes" when you mean yes, and "No" when you mean no, and then you will not come under God's judgement.

13 Is anyone among you in trouble? He

ᵇThe spirit...fierce desires; *or* God yearns jealously over the spirit that he placed in us.
ᶜpeople, and they do not resist you; *or* people. Will God not resist you?
4.6: Prov 3.34　　**4.13-14:** Prov 27.1　　**5.2-3:** Mt 6.19　　**5.4:** Deut 24.14-15
5.11: Job 1.21-22, 2.10; Ps 103.8　　**5.12:** Mt 5.34-37

This prayer made in faith will heal the sick person (5.15)

should pray. Is anyone happy? He should sing praises. ¹⁴Is there anyone who is ill? He should send for the church elders, who will pray for him and rub olive-oil on him in the name of the Lord. ¹⁵This prayer made in faith will heal the sick person; the Lord will restore him to health, and the sins he has committed will be forgiven. ¹⁶So then, confess your sins to one another and pray for one another, so that you will be healed. The prayer of a good person has a powerful effect. ¹⁷Elijah was the same kind of person as we are. He prayed earnestly that there would be no rain, and no rain fell on the land for three and a half years. ¹⁸Once again he prayed, and the sky poured out its rain and the earth produced its crops.

19 My brothers, if one of you wanders away from the truth and another one brings him back again, ²⁰remember this: whoever turns a sinner back from his wrong way will save that sinner's soul *d* from death and bring about the forgiveness of many sins.

---

d that sinner's soul; *or* his own soul.
5.14: Mk 6.13   **5.17:** 1 Kgs 17.1, 18.1   **5.18:** 1 Kgs 18.42–45   **5.20:** Prov 10.12; 1 Pet 4.8

THE FIRST LETTER FROM
PETER

INTRODUCTION

The First Letter from Peter was addressed to Christians, here called "God's chosen people," who were scattered throughout the northern part of Asia Minor. The main purpose of the letter is to encourage the readers, who were facing persecution and suffering for their faith. The writer does this by reminding his readers of the Good News about Jesus Christ, whose death, resurrection, and promised coming give them hope. In the light of this they are to accept and endure their suffering, confident that it is a test of the genuineness of their faith and that they will be rewarded on "the Day when Jesus Christ is revealed."

Along with his encouragement in time of trouble, the writer also urges his readers to live as people who belong to Christ.

Outline of Contents
Introduction 1.1-2
Reminder of God's salvation 1.3-12
Exhortation to holy living 1.13—2.10
The Christian's responsibilities in time of suffering 2.11—4.19
Christian humility and service 5.1-11
Conclusion 5.12-14

1 From Peter, apostle of Jesus Christ— To God's chosen people who live as refugees scattered throughout the provinces of Pontus, Galatia, Cappadocia, Asia, and Bithynia. ² You were chosen according to the purpose of God the Father and were made a holy people by his Spirit, to obey Jesus Christ and be purified by his blood.

May grace and peace be yours in full measure.

A Living Hope

3 Let us give thanks to the God and Father of our Lord Jesus Christ! Because of his great mercy he gave us new life by raising Jesus Christ from death. This fills us with a living hope, ⁴ and so we look forward to possessing the rich blessings that God keeps for his people. He keeps them for you in heaven, where they cannot decay or spoil or fade away. ⁵ They are for you, who through faith are kept safe by God's power for the salvation which is ready to be revealed at the end of time.

6 Be glad about this, even though it may now be necessary for you to be sad for a while because of the many kinds of trials you suffer. ⁷ Their purpose is to prove that your faith is genuine. Even gold, which can be destroyed, is tested by fire; and so your faith, which is much more precious than gold, must also be tested, so that it may endure. Then you will receive praise and glory and honour on the Day when Jesus Christ is revealed. ⁸ You love him, although you have not

seen him, and you believe in him, although you do not now see him. So you rejoice with a great and glorious joy which words cannot express, 9 because you are receiving the salvation of your souls, which is the purpose of your faith in him.

10 It was concerning this salvation that the prophets made careful search and investigation, and they prophesied about this gift which God would give you. 11 They tried to find out when the time would be and how it would come.*a* This was the time to which Christ's Spirit in them was pointing, in predicting the sufferings that Christ would have to endure and the glory that would follow. 12 God revealed to these prophets that their work was not for their own benefit, but for yours, as they spoke about those things which you have now heard from the messengers who announced the Good News by the power of the Holy Spirit sent from heaven. These are things which even the angels would like to understand.

A Call to Holy Living

13 So then, have your minds ready for action. Keep alert and set your hope completely on the blessing which will be given you when Jesus Christ is revealed. 14 Be obedient to God, and do not allow your lives to be shaped by those desires you had when you were still ignorant. 15 Instead, be holy in all that you do, just as God who called you is holy. 16 The scripture says, "Be holy because I am holy."

17 You call him Father, when you pray to God, who judges all people by the same standard, according to what each one has done; so then, spend the rest of your lives here on earth in reverence for him. 18 For you know what was paid to set you free from the worthless manner of life handed down by your ancestors. It was not something that can be destroyed, such as silver or gold; 19 it was the costly sacrifice of Christ, who was like a lamb without defect or flaw. 20 He had been chosen by God before the creation of the world and was revealed in these last days for your sake. 21 Through him you believe in God, who raised him from death and gave him glory; and so your faith and hope are fixed on God.

22 Now that by your obedience to the truth you have purified yourselves and have come to have a sincere love for your fellow-believers, love one another earnestly with all your heart.*b* 23 For through the living and eternal word of God you have been born again as the children of a parent who is immortal, not mortal. 24 As the scripture says,

"All mankind are like grass,
　and all their glory is like wild flowers.
The grass withers, and the flowers fall,
25　but the word of the Lord remains
　　for ever."

This word is the Good News that was proclaimed to you.

The Living Stone and the Holy Nation

2 Rid yourselves, then, of all evil; no more lying or hypocrisy or jealousy or insulting language. 2 Be like new-born babies, always thirsty for the pure spiritual milk, so that by drinking it you may grow up and be saved. 3 As the scripture says, "You have found out for yourselves how kind the Lord is."

4 Come to the Lord, the living stone rejected by man as worthless but chosen by God as valuable. 5 Come as living stones, and let yourselves be used in building the spiritual temple, where you will serve as holy priests to offer spiritual and acceptable sacrifices to God through Jesus Christ. 6 For the scripture says,

"I chose a valuable stone,
　which I am placing as the cornerstone
　　in Zion;
and whoever believes in him will
　never be disappointed."

7 This stone is of great value for you that believe; but for those who do not believe:

"The stone which the builders rejected
　as worthless
turned out to be the most important
　of all."

8 And another scripture says,

"This is the stone that will make people
　stumble,
the rock that will make them fall."

They stumbled because they did not believe in the word; such was God's will for them.

9 But you are the chosen race, the King's priests, the holy nation, God's own people, chosen to proclaim the wonderful

---

a when the time would be and how it would come; *or* who the person would be and when he would come.　*b* with all your heart; *some manuscripts have* with a pure heart.
1.16: Lev 11.44-45, 19.2　**1.24-25:** Is 40:6-8　**2.3:** Ps 34.8　**2.6:** Is 28.16　**2.7:** Ps 118.22
2.8: Is 8.14-15　**2.9:** Ex 19.5-6; Is 43.20,21; Deut 4.20, 7.6, 14.2; Tit 2.14; Is 9.2

acts of God, who called you out of darkness into his own marvellous light. [10] At one time you were not God's people, but now you are his people; at one time you did not know God's mercy, but now you have received his mercy.

Slaves of God

11 I appeal to you, my friends, as strangers and refugees in this world! Do not give in to bodily passions, which are always at war against the soul. [12] Your conduct among the heathen should be so good that when they accuse you of being evildoers, they will have to recognize your good deeds and so praise God on the Day of his coming.

13 For the sake of the Lord submit to every human authority: to the Emperor, who is the supreme authority, [14] and to the governors, who have been appointed by him to punish the evildoers and to praise those who do good. [15] For God wants you to silence the ignorant talk of foolish people by the good things you do. [16] Live as free people; do not, however, use your freedom to cover up any evil, but live as God's slaves. [17] Respect everyone, love your fellow-believers, honour God, and respect the Emperor.

The Example of Christ's Suffering

18 You servants must submit to your masters and show them complete respect, not only to those who are kind and considerate, but also to those who are harsh. [19] God will bless you for this, if you endure the pain of undeserved suffering because you are conscious of his will. [20] For what credit is there if you endure the beatings you deserve for having done wrong? But if you endure suffering even when you have done right, God will bless you for it. [21] It was to this that God called you, for Christ himself suffered for you and left you an example, so that you would follow in his steps. [22] He committed no sin, and no one ever heard a lie come from his lips. [23] When he was insulted, he did not answer back with an insult; when he suffered, he did not threaten, but placed his hopes in God, the righteous Judge. [24] Christ himself carried our sins in his body to the cross, so that we might die to sin and live for righteousness. It is by his wounds that you have been healed. [25] You were like sheep that had

lost their way, but now you have been brought back to follow the Shepherd and Keeper of your souls.

Wives and Husbands

3 In the same way you wives must submit to your husbands, so that if any of them do not believe God's word, your conduct will win them over to believe. It will not be necessary for you to say a word, [2] because they will see how pure and reverent your conduct is. [3] You should not use outward aids to make yourselves beautiful, such as the way you do your hair, or the jewellery you put on, or the dresses you wear. [4] Instead, your beauty should consist of your true inner self, the ageless beauty of a gentle and quiet spirit, which is of the greatest value in God's sight. [5] For the devout women of the past who placed their hope in God used to make themselves beautiful by submitting to their husbands. [6] Sarah was like that; she obeyed Abraham and called him her master. You are now her daughters if you do good and are not afraid of anything.

7 In the same way you husbands must live with your wives with the proper understanding that they are the weaker sex. Treat them with respect, because they also will receive, together with you, God's gift of life. Do this so that nothing will interfere with your prayers.

Suffering for Doing Right

8 To conclude: you must all have the same attitude and the same feelings; love one another as brothers, and be kind and humble with one another. [9] Do not pay back evil with evil or cursing with cursing; instead, pay back with a blessing, because a blessing is what God promised to give you when he called you. [10] As the scripture says,

"Whoever wants to enjoy life
  and wishes to see good times,
  must keep from speaking evil
  and stop telling lies.
[11] He must turn away from evil and do
    good;
  he must strive for peace with all his
    heart.
[12] For the Lord watches over the
    righteous
  and listens to their prayers;
  but he opposes those who do evil."

2.10: Hos 2.23   **2.22:** Is 53.9   **2.23:** Is 53.7   **2.24:** Is 53.5   **2.25:** Is 53.6
3.1: Eph 5.22; Col 3.18   **3.3:** 1 Tim 2.9   **3.6:** Gen 18.12   **3.7:** Eph 5.25; Col 3.19
3.10–12: Ps 34.12–16

13 Who will harm you if you are eager to do what is good? 14 But even if you should suffer for doing what is right, how happy you are! Do not be afraid of anyone, and do not worry. 15 But have reverence for Christ in your hearts, and honour him as Lord. Be ready at all times to answer anyone who asks you to explain the hope you have in you, 16 but do it with gentleness and respect. Keep your conscience clear, so that when you are insulted, those who speak evil of your good conduct as followers of Christ will be ashamed of what they say. 17 For it is better to suffer for doing good, if this should be God's will, than for doing evil. 18 For Christ died c for sins once and for all, a good man on behalf of sinners, in order to lead you to God. He was put to death physically, but made alive spiritually, 19 and in his spiritual existence he went and preached to the imprisoned spirits. 20 These were the spirits of those who had not obeyed God when he waited patiently during the days that Noah was building his boat. The few people in the boat—eight in all—were saved by the water, 21 which was a symbol pointing to baptism, which now saves you. It is not the washing away of bodily dirt, but the promise made to God from a good conscience. It saves you through the resurrection of Jesus Christ, 22 who has gone to heaven and is at the right-hand side of God, ruling over all angels and heavenly authorities and powers.

Changed Lives

4 Since Christ suffered physically, you too must strengthen yourselves with the same way of thinking that he had; because whoever suffers physically is no longer involved with sin. 2 From now on, then, you must live the rest of your earthly lives controlled by God's will and not by human desires. 3 You have spent enough time in the past doing what the heathen like to do. Your lives were spent in indecency, lust, drunkenness, orgies, drinking parties, and the disgusting worship of idols. 4 And now the heathen are surprised when you do not join them in the same wild and reckless living, and so they insult you. 5 But they will have to give an account of themselves to God, who is ready to judge the living and the dead. 6 That is why the Good News was preached also to the dead, to those who

had been judged in their physical existence as everyone is judged; it was preached to them so that in their spiritual existence they may live as God lives.

Good Managers of God's Gifts

7 The end of all things is near. You must be self-controlled and alert, to be able to pray. 8 Above everything, love one another earnestly, because love covers over many sins. 9 Open your homes to each other without complaining. 10 Each one, as a good manager of God's different gifts, must use for the good of others the special gift he has received from God. 11 Whoever preaches must preach God's messages; whoever serves must serve with the strength that God gives him, so that in all things praise may be given to God through Jesus Christ, to whom belong glory and power for ever and ever. Amen.

Suffering as a Christian

12 My dear friends, do not be surprised at the painful test you are suffering, as though something unusual were happening to you. 13 Rather be glad that you are sharing Christ's sufferings, so that you may be full of joy when his glory is revealed. 14 Happy are you if you are insulted because you are Christ's followers; this means that the glorious Spirit, the Spirit of God, is resting on you. 15 If any of you suffers, it must not be because he is a murderer or a thief or a criminal or a meddler in other people's affairs. 16 However, if you suffer because you are a Christian, don't be ashamed of it, but thank God that you bear Christ's name.

17 The time has come for judgement to begin, and God's own people are the first to be judged. If it starts with us, how will it end with those who do not believe the Good News from God? 18 As the scripture says,

"It is difficult for good people to be saved;
what, then, will become of godless sinners?"

19 So then, those who suffer because it is God's will for them, should by their good actions trust themselves completely to their Creator, who always keeps his promise.

---

c died; *many manuscripts have* suffered.
3.14–15: Mt 5.10; Is 8.12–13   **3.20:** Gen 6.1—7.24   **4.8:** Prov 10.12   **4.18:** Prov 11.31

The Flock of God

5 I, who am an elder myself, appeal to the church elders among you. I am a witness of Christ's sufferings, and I will share in the glory that will be revealed. I appeal to you ²to be shepherds of the flock that God gave you and to take care of it willingly, as God wants you to, and not unwillingly. Do your work, not for mere pay, but from a real desire to serve. ³Do not try to rule over those who have been put in your care, but be examples to the flock. ⁴And when the Chief Shepherd appears, you will receive the glorious crown which will never lose its brightness.

5 In the same way you younger men must submit to the older men. And all of you must put on the apron of humility, to serve one another; for the scripture says, "God resists the proud, but shows favour to the humble." ⁶Humble yourselves, then, under God's mighty hand, so that he will lift you up in his own good time. ⁷Leave all your worries with him, because he cares for you.

8 Be alert, be on the watch! Your enemy, the Devil, roams round like a roaring lion, looking for someone to devour. ⁹Be firm in your faith and resist him, because you know that your fellow-believers in all the world are going through the same kind of sufferings. ¹⁰But after you have suffered for a little while, the God of all grace, who calls you to share his eternal glory in union with Christ, will himself perfect you and give you firmness, strength, and a sure foundation. ¹¹To him be the power for ever! Amen.

The kiss of Christian love (5.14)

Final Greetings

12 I write you this brief letter with the help of Silas, whom I regard as a faithful Christian brother. I want to encourage you and give my testimony that this is the true grace of God. Stand firm in it.

13 Your sister church in Babylon, *d* also chosen by God, sends you greetings, and so does my son Mark. ¹⁴Greet one another with the kiss of Christian love.

May peace be with all of you who belong to Christ.

---

*d*BABYLON: *As in the book of Revelation, this probably refers to Rome.*
5.2: Jn 21.15–17   **5.5:** Prov 3.34   **5.6:** Mt 23.12; Lk 14.11, 18.14   **5.12:** Acts 15.22,40
5.13: Acts 12.12,25, 13.13, 15.37–39; Col 4.10; Phlm 24

THE SECOND LETTER FROM
PETER

INTRODUCTION

The Second Letter from Peter is addressed to a wide circle of early Christians. Its main concern is to combat the work of false teachers and the immorality which results from such teaching. The answer to these problems is found in holding to the true knowledge of God and of the Lord Jesus Christ, knowledge which has been conveyed by persons who themselves have seen Jesus and have heard him teach. The writer is especially concerned with the teaching of those who claim that Christ will not return again. He says that the apparent delay in Christ's return is due to the fact that God "does not want anyone to be destroyed, but wants all to turn away from their sins."

Outline of Contents
Introduction   1.1–2
The Christian calling   1.3–21
False teachers   2.1–22
The final coming of Christ   3.1–18

---

1 From Simon Peter, a servant and apostle of Jesus Christ—

To those who through the righteousness of our God and Saviour Jesus Christ have been given a faith as precious as ours:

2 May grace and peace be yours in full measure through your knowledge of God and of Jesus our Lord.

God's Call and Choice

3 God's divine power has given us everything we need to live a truly religious life through our knowledge of the one who called us to share in his own[a] glory and goodness. 4 In this way he has given us the very great and precious gifts he promised, so that by means of these gifts you may escape from the destructive lust that is in the world, and may come to share the divine nature. 5 For this very reason do your best to add goodness to your faith; to your goodness add knowledge; 6 to your knowledge add self-control; to your self-control add endurance; to your endurance add godliness; 7 to your godliness add brotherly affection; and to your brotherly affection add love. 8 These are the qualities you need, and if you have them in abundance, they will make you active and effective in your knowledge of our Lord Jesus Christ. 9 But whoever does not have them is so short-sighted that he cannot see and has forgotten that he has been purified from his past sins.

10 So then, my brothers, try even harder to make God's call and his choice of you a permanent experience; if you do so, you will never abandon your faith.[b] 11 In this way you will be given the full

[a] to share in his own; *some manuscripts have* through his.
[b] abandon your faith; *or* fall into sin.

To make God's call...a permanent experience (1.10)

right to enter the eternal Kingdom of our Lord and Saviour Jesus Christ.

12 And so I will always remind you of these matters, even though you already know them and are firmly grounded in the truth you have received. 13 I think it only right for me to stir up your memory of these matters as long as I am still alive. 14 I know that I shall soon put off this mortal body, as our Lord Jesus Christ plainly told me. 15 I will do my best, then, to provide a way for you to remember these matters at all times after my death.

Eye-Witnesses of Christ's Glory

16 We have not depended on made-up stories in making known to you the mighty coming of our Lord Jesus Christ. With our own eyes we saw his greatness. 17 We were there when he was given honour and glory by God the Father, when the voice came to him from the Supreme Glory, saying, "This is my own dear Son, with whom I am pleased!" 18 We ourselves heard this voice coming from

1.17-18: Mt 17.1-5; Mk 9.2-7; Lk 9.28-35

heaven, when we were with him on the holy mountain.

19 So we are even more confident of the message proclaimed by the prophets. You will do well to pay attention to it, because it is like a lamp shining in a dark place until the Day dawns and the light of the morning star shines in your hearts. 20 Above all else, however, remember that no one can explain by himself a prophecy in the Scriptures. 21 For no prophetic message ever came just from the will of man, but men were under the control of the Holy Spirit as they spoke the message that came from God.

False Teachers

2 False prophets appeared in the past among the people, and in the same way false teachers will appear among you. They will bring in destructive, untrue doctrines, and will deny the Master who redeemed them, and so they will bring upon themselves sudden destruction. 2 Even so, many will follow their immoral

ways; and because of what they do, others will speak evil of the Way of truth. ³In their greed these false teachers will make a profit out of telling you made-up stories. For a long time now their Judge has been ready, and their Destroyer has been wide awake!

4 God did not spare the angels who sinned, but threw them into hell, where they are kept chained in darkness, ᶜ waiting for the Day of Judgement. ⁵God did not spare the ancient world, but brought the flood on the world of godless people; the only ones he saved were Noah, who preached righteousness, and seven other people. ⁶God condemned the cities of Sodom and Gomorrah, destroying them with fire, and made them an example of what will happen to the godless. ⁷He rescued Lot, a good man, who was distressed by the immoral conduct of lawless people. ⁸That good man lived among them, and day after day he suffered agony as he saw and heard their evil actions. ⁹And so the Lord knows how to rescue godly people from their trials and how to keep the wicked under punishment for the Day of Judgement, ¹⁰especially those who follow their filthy bodily lusts and despise God's authority.

These false teachers are bold and arrogant, and show no respect for the glorious beings above; instead, they insult them. ¹¹Even the angels, who are so much stronger and mightier than these false teachers, do not accuse them with insults in the presence of the Lord. ¹²But these men act by instinct, like wild animals born to be captured and killed; they attack with insults anything they do not understand. They will be destroyed like wild animals, ¹³and they will be paid with suffering for the suffering they have caused. Pleasure for them is to do anything in broad daylight that will satisfy their bodily appetites; they are a shame and a disgrace as they join you in your meals, all the while enjoying their deceitful ways! ¹⁴They want to look at nothing but immoral women; their appetite for sin is never satisfied. They lead weak people into a trap. Their hearts are trained to be greedy. They are under God's curse! ¹⁵They have left the straight path and have lost their way; they have followed the path taken by Balaam son of Beor, who loved the money he would get for

doing wrong ¹⁶and was rebuked for his sin. His donkey spoke with a human voice and stopped the prophet's insane action.

17 These men are like dried-up springs, like clouds blown along by a storm; God has reserved a place for them in the deepest darkness. ¹⁸They make proud and stupid statements, and use immoral bodily lusts to trap those who are just beginning to escape from among people who live in error. ¹⁹They promise them freedom while they themselves are slaves of destructive habits—for a person is a slave of anything that has conquered him. ²⁰If people have escaped from the corrupting forces of the world through their knowledge of our Lord and Saviour Jesus Christ, and then are again caught and conquered by them, such people are in a worse state at the end than they were at the beginning. ²¹It would have been much better for them never to have known the way of righteousness than to know it and then turn away from the sacred command that was given them. ²²What happened to them shows that the proverbs are true: "A dog goes back to what it has vomited" and "A pig that has been washed goes back to roll in the mud."

The Promise of the Lord's Coming

3 My dear friends, this is now the second letter I have written to you. In both letters I have tried to arouse pure thoughts in your minds by reminding you of these things. ²I want you to remember the words that were spoken long ago by the holy prophets, and the command from the Lord and Saviour which was given you by your apostles. ³First of all, you must understand that in these last days some people will appear whose lives are controlled by their own lusts. They will mock you ⁴and will ask, "He promised to come, didn't he? Where is he? Our fathers have already died, but everything is still the same as it was since the creation of the world!" ⁵They purposely ignore the fact that long ago God gave a command, and the heavens and earth were created. The earth was formed out of water and by water, ⁶and it was also by water, the water of the flood, that the old world was destroyed. ⁷But the heavens and the earth that now exist are being preserved by the same command

---

ᶜchained in darkness; *some manuscripts have* in dark pits.
2.5: Gen 6.1—7.24   **2.6:** Gen 19.24   **2.7:** Gen 19.1–16   **2.15–16:** Num 22.4–35
2.22: Prov 26:11   **3.3:** Jude 18   **3.5:** Gen 1.6–9   **3.6:** Gen 7.11

of God, in order to be destroyed by fire. They are being kept for the day when godless people will be judged and destroyed.

8 But do not forget one thing, my dear friends! There is no difference in the Lord's sight between one day and a thousand years; to him the two are the same. 9 The Lord is not slow to do what he has promised, as some think. Instead, he is patient with you, because he does not want anyone to be destroyed, but wants all to turn away from their sins.

10 But the Day of the Lord will come like a thief. On that Day the heavens will disappear with a shrill noise, the heavenly bodies will burn up and be destroyed, and the earth with everything in it will vanish. *d* 11 Since all these things will be destroyed in this way, what kind of people should you be? Your lives should be holy and dedicated to God, 12 as you wait for the Day of God and do your best to make it come soon—the Day when the heavens will burn up and be destroyed, and the heavenly bodies will be melted by the heat. 13 But we wait for what God has promised: new heavens and a new earth, where righteousness will be at home.

14 And so, my friends, as you wait for that Day, do your best to be pure and faultless in God's sight and to be at peace with him. 15 Look on our Lord's patience as the opportunity he is giving you to be saved, just as our dear brother Paul wrote to you, using the wisdom that God gave him. 16 This is what he says in all his letters when he writes on the subject. There are some difficult things in his letters which ignorant and unstable people explain falsely, as they do with other passages of the Scriptures. So they bring on their own destruction.

17 But you, my friends, already know this. Be on your guard, then, so that you will not be led away by the errors of lawless people and fall from your safe position. 18 But continue to grow in the grace and knowledge of our Lord and Saviour Jesus Christ. To him be the glory, now and for ever! Amen.

d vanish; *some manuscripts have* be found; *others have* be burnt up; *one has* be found destroyed.
3.8: Ps 90.4   **3.10:** Mt 24.43; Lk 12.39; 1 Thes 5.2; Rev 16.15   **3.13:** Is 65.17, 66.22; Rev 21.1

THE FIRST LETTER OF
JOHN

INTRODUCTION

The First Letter of John has two main purposes: to encourage its readers to live in fellowship with God and with his Son, Jesus Christ, and to warn them against following false teaching that would destroy this fellowship. This teaching was based on the belief that evil results from contact with the physical world, and so Jesus, the Son of God, could not really have been a human being. Those teachers claimed that to be saved was to be set free from concern with life in this world; and they also taught that salvation had nothing to do with matters of morality or of love for one's fellow-man.

In opposition to this teaching the writer clearly states that Jesus Christ was a real human being, and he emphasizes that all who believe in Jesus and love God must also love one another.

Outline of Contents

Introduction 1.1–4
Light and darkness 1.5—2.29

Children of God and children of the Devil   3.1-24
Truth and error   4.1-6
The duty of love   4.7-21
Victorious faith   5.1-21

The Word of Life

1 We write to you about the Word of life, which has existed from the very beginning. We have heard it, and we have seen it with our eyes; yes, we have seen it, and our hands have touched it. [2] When this life became visible, we saw it; so we speak of it and tell you about the eternal life which was with the Father and was made known to us. [3] What we have seen and heard we announce to you also, so that you will join with us in the fellowship that we have with the Father and with his Son Jesus Christ. [4] We write this in order that our[a] joy may be complete.

God Is Light

[5] Now the message that we have heard from his Son and announce is this: God is light, and there is no darkness at all in him. [6] If, then, we say that we have fellowship with him, yet at the same time live in the darkness, we are lying both in our words and in our actions. [7] But if we live in the light—just as he is in the light—then we have fellowship with one another, and the blood of Jesus, his Son, purifies us from every sin.

[8] If we say that we have no sin, we deceive ourselves, and there is no truth in us. [9] But if we confess our sins to God, he will keep his promise and do what is right: he will forgive us our sins and purify us from all our wrongdoing. [10] If we say that we have not sinned, we make God out to be a liar, and his word is not in us.

Christ Our Helper

2 I am writing this to you, my children, so that you will not sin; but if anyone does sin, we have someone who pleads with the Father on our behalf—Jesus Christ, the righteous one. [2] And Christ himself is the means by which our sins

are forgiven, and not our sins only, but also the sins of everyone.

[3] If we obey God's commands, then we are sure that we know him. [4] If someone says that he knows him, but does not obey his commands, such a person is a liar and there is no truth in him. [5] But whoever obeys his word is the one whose love for God has really been made perfect. This is how we can be sure that we are in union with God: [6] whoever says that he remains in union with God should live just as Jesus Christ did.

The New Command

[7] My dear friends, this command I am writing to you is not new; it is the old command, the one you have had from the very beginning. The old command is the message you have already heard. [8] However, the command I am now writing to you is new, because its truth is seen in Christ and also in you. For the darkness is passing away, and the real light is already shining.

[9] Whoever says that he is in the light, yet hates his brother, is in the darkness to this very hour. [10] Whoever loves his brother lives in the light, and so there is nothing in him that will cause someone else[b] to sin. [11] But whoever hates his brother is in the darkness; he walks in it and does not know where he is going, because the darkness has made him blind.

[12] I am writing to you, my children, because your sins are forgiven for the sake of Christ. [13] I am writing to you, fathers, because you know him who has existed from the beginning. I am writing to you, young men, because you have defeated the Evil One.

[14] I am writing to you, my children, because you know the Father. I am writing to you, fathers, because you know him who has existed from the beginning. I am writing to you, young men, because you are strong; the word of God lives

---

[a] our; *some manuscripts have* your.   [b] someone else; *or* him.
1.1: Jn 1.1   **1.2:** Jn 1.14   **2.7:** Jn 13.34

Whoever loves his brother...whoever hates his brother (2.10–11)

in you, and you have defeated the Evil One.

15 Do not love the world or anything that belongs to the world. If you love the world, you do not love the Father. 16 Everything that belongs to the world— what the sinful self desires, what people see and want, and everything in this world that people are so proud of—none of this comes from the Father; it all comes from the world. 17 The world and everything in it that people desire is passing away; but he who does the will of God lives for ever.

The Enemy of Christ

18 My children, the end is near! You were told that the Enemy of Christ would come; and now many enemies of Christ have already appeared, and so we know that the end is near. 19 These people really did not belong to our fellowship, and that is why they left us; if they had belonged to our fellowship, they would have stayed with us. But they left so that it might be clear that none of them really belonged to us.

20 But you have had the Holy Spirit poured out on you by Christ, and so all of you know the truth. 21 I am writing to you, then, not because you do not know the truth; instead, it is because you do know it, and you also know that no lie ever comes from the truth.

22 Who, then, is the liar? It is anyone who says that Jesus is not the Messiah. Such a person is the Enemy of Christ—he rejects both the Father and the Son. 23 For whoever rejects the Son also rejects the Father; whoever accepts the Son has the Father also.

24 Be sure, then, to keep in your hearts the message you heard from the beginning. If you keep that message, then you will always live in union with the Son and the Father. 25 And this is what Christ himself promised to give us—eternal life.

26 I am writing this to you about those who are trying to deceive you. 27 But as for you, Christ has poured out his Spirit on you. As long as his Spirit remains in you, you do not need anyone to teach you. For his Spirit teaches you about everything, and what he teaches is true, not false. Obey the Spirit's teaching, then, and remain in union with Christ.

28 Yes, my children, remain in union with him, so that when he appears we may be full of courage and need not hide in shame from him on the Day he comes. 29 You know that Christ is righteous; you should know, then, that everyone who does what is right is God's child.

Children of God

3 See how much the Father has loved us! His love is so great that we are called God's children—and so, in fact, we are. This is why the world does not know us: it has not known God. 2 My dear

3.1: Jn 1.12

friends, we are now God's children, but it is not yet clear what we shall become. But we know that when Christ appears, we shall be like him, because we shall see him as he really is. ³Everyone who has this hope in Christ keeps himself pure, just as Christ is pure.

4 Whoever sins is guilty of breaking God's law, because sin is a breaking of the law. ⁵You know that Christ appeared in order to take away sins, *c* and that there is no sin in him. ⁶So everyone who lives in union with Christ does not continue to sin; but whoever continues to sin has never seen him or known him.

7 Let no one deceive you, my children! Whoever does what is right is righteous, just as Christ is righteous. ⁸Whoever continues to sin belongs to the Devil, because the Devil has sinned from the very beginning. The Son of God appeared for this very reason, to destroy what the Devil had done.

9 Whoever is a child of God does not continue to sin, for God's very nature is in him; and because God is his Father, he cannot continue to sin. ¹⁰This is the clear difference between God's children and the Devil's children: anyone who does not do what is right or does not love his brother is not God's child.

Love One Another

11 The message you heard from the very beginning is this: we must love one another. ¹²We must not be like Cain; he belonged to the Evil One and murdered his own brother Abel. Why did Cain murder him? Because the things he himself did were wrong, but the things his brother did were right.

13 So do not be surprised, my brothers, if the people of the world hate you. ¹⁴We know that we have left death and come over into life; we know it because we love our brothers. Whoever does not love is still under the power of death. ¹⁵Whoever hates his brother is a murderer, and you know that a murderer has not got eternal life in him. ¹⁶This is how we know what love is: Christ gave his life for us. We too, then, ought to give our lives for our brothers! ¹⁷If a rich person sees his brother in need, yet closes his heart against his brother, how can he claim that he loves God? ¹⁸My children, our love should not be just words and talk; it must be true love, which shows itself in action.

Courage before God

19 This, then, is how we will know that we belong to the truth; this is how we will be confident in God's presence. ²⁰If our conscience condemns us, we know that God is greater than our conscience and that he knows everything. ²¹And so, my dear friends, if our conscience does not condemn us, we have courage in God's presence. ²²We receive from him whatever we ask, because we obey his commands and do what pleases him. ²³What he commands is that we believe in his Son Jesus Christ and love one another, just as Christ commanded us. ²⁴Whoever obeys God's commands lives in union with God and God lives in union with him. And because of the Spirit that God has given us we know that God lives in union with us.

The True Spirit and the False

4 My dear friends, do not believe all who claim to have the Spirit, but test them to find out if the spirit they have comes from God. For many false prophets have gone out everywhere. ²This is how you will be able to know whether it is God's Spirit: anyone who acknowledges that Jesus Christ came as a human being has the Spirit who comes from God. ³But anyone who denies this about Jesus does not have the Spirit from God. The spirit that he has is from the Enemy of Christ; you heard that it would come, and now it is here in the world already.

4 But you belong to God, my children, and have defeated the false prophets, because the Spirit who is in you is more powerful than the spirit in those who belong to the world. ⁵Those false prophets speak about matters of the world, and the world listens to them because they belong to the world. ⁶But we belong to God. Whoever knows God listens to us; whoever does not belong to God does not listen to us. This, then, is how we can tell the difference between the Spirit of truth and the spirit of error.

God Is Love

7 Dear friends, let us love one another, because love comes from God. Whoever loves is a child of God and knows God. ⁸Whoever does not love does not know God, for God is love. ⁹And God showed his love for us by sending his only Son

---

c sins; *some manuscripts have* our sins.
3.5: Jn 1.29   **3.11:** Jn 13.34   **3.12:** Gen 4.8   **3.14:** Jn 5.24   **3.23:** Jn 13.34, 15.12,17

Perfect love drives out all fear (4.18)

into the world, so that we might have life through him. ¹⁰This is what love is: it is not that we have loved God, but that he loved us and sent his Son to be the means by which our sins are forgiven.

11 Dear friends, if this is how God loved us, then we should love one another. ¹²No one has ever seen God, but if we love one another, God lives in union with us, and his love is made perfect in us.

13 We are sure that we live in union with God and that he lives in union with us, because he has given us his Spirit. ¹⁴And we have seen and tell others that the Father sent his Son to be the Saviour of the world. ¹⁵If anyone declares that Jesus is the Son of God, he lives in union with God and God lives in union with him. ¹⁶And we ourselves know and believe the love which God has for us.

God is love, and whoever lives in love lives in union with God and God lives in union with him. ¹⁷Love is made perfect in us in order that we may have courage on Judgement Day; and we will have it because our life in this world is the same as Christ's. ¹⁸There is no fear in love; perfect love drives out all fear. So then, love has not been made perfect in anyone who is afraid, because fear has to do with punishment.

19 We love because God first loved us. ²⁰If someone says he loves God, but hates his brother, he is a liar. For he cannot love God, whom he has not seen, if he does not love his brother, whom he has seen. ²¹The command that Christ has given us is this: whoever loves God must love his brother also.

Our Victory over the World

5 Whoever believes that Jesus is the Messiah is a child of God; and whoever loves a father loves his child also. ²This is how we know that we love God's children: it is by loving God and obeying his commands. ³For our love for God means that we obey his commands. And his commands are not too hard for us, ⁴because every child of God is able to defeat the world. And we win the victory over the world by means of our faith. ⁵Who can defeat the world? Only the person who believes that Jesus is the Son of God.

The Witness about Jesus Christ

6 Jesus Christ is the one who came with the water of his baptism and the blood of his death. He came not only with the water, but with both the water and the blood. And the Spirit himself testifies that this is true, because the Spirit is truth. ⁷There are three witnesses: ⁸the Spirit, the water, and the blood; and all three give the same testimony. ⁹We believe man's testimony; but God's testimony is much stronger, and he has given this

4.12: Jn 1.18   **5.3:** Jn 14.15

testimony about his Son. ¹⁰So whoever believes in the Son of God has this testimony in his own heart; but whoever does not believe God, has made him out to be a liar, because he has not believed what God has said about his Son. ¹¹The testimony is this: God has given us eternal life, and this life has its source in his Son. ¹²Whoever has the Son has this life; whoever does not have the Son of God does not have life.

Eternal Life

13 I am writing this to you so that you may know that you have eternal life—you that believe in the Son of God. ¹⁴We have courage in God's presence, because we are sure that he hears us if we ask him for anything that is according to his will. ¹⁵He hears us whenever we ask him; and since we know this is true, we know also that he gives us what we ask from him.

5.11: Jn 3.36

16 If you see your brother commit a sin that does not lead to death, you should pray to God, who will give him life. This applies to those whose sins do not lead to death. But there is sin which leads to death, and I do not say that you should pray to God about that. ¹⁷All wrongdoing is sin, but there is sin which does not lead to death.

18 We know that no child of God keeps on sinning, for the Son of God keeps him safe, and the Evil One cannot harm him.

19 We know that we belong to God even though the whole world is under the rule of the Evil One.

20 We know that the Son of God has come and has given us understanding, so that we know the true God. We live in union with the true God—in union with his Son Jesus Christ. This is the true God, and this is eternal life.

21 My children, keep yourselves safe from false gods!

THE SECOND LETTER OF
JOHN

INTRODUCTION

The Second Letter of John was written by "the Elder" to "the dear Lady and to her children," probably meaning a local church and its members. The brief message is an appeal to love one another and a warning against false teachers and their teachings.

Outline of Contents

Introduction   1–3
The primacy of love   4–6
Warning against false doctrine   7–11
Conclusion   12–13

1 From the Elder—
To the dear Lady and to her children,ᵃ whom I truly love. And I am not the only one, but all who know the truth love you, ²because the truth remains in us and will be with us for ever.

3 May God the Father and Jesus Christ, the Father's Son, give us grace, mercy,

ᵃLADY AND...HER CHILDREN: *This probably refers to a church and its members (also in verses 4-5).*

and peace; may they be ours in truth and love.

Truth and Love

4 How happy I was to find that some of your children live in the truth, just as the Father commanded us. 5 And so I ask you, dear Lady: let us all love one another. This is no new command I am writing to you; it is the command which we have had from the beginning. 6 This love I speak of means that we must live in obedience to God's commands. The command, as you have all heard from the beginning, is that you must all live in love.

7 Many deceivers have gone out all over the world, people who do not acknowledge that Jesus Christ came as a human being. Such a person is a deceiver and the Enemy of Christ. 8 Be on your guard, then, so that you will not lose what we[b]

have worked for, but will receive your reward in full.

9 Anyone who does not stay with the teaching of Christ, but goes beyond it, does not have God. Whoever does stay with the teaching has both the Father and the Son. 10 So then, if someone comes to you who does not bring this teaching, do not welcome him in your homes; do not even say, "Peace be with you." 11 For anyone who wishes him peace becomes his partner in the evil things he does.

Final Words

12 I have so much to tell you, but I would rather not do it with paper and ink; instead, I hope to visit you and talk with you personally, so that we shall be completely happy.

13 The children of your dear Sister[c] send you their greetings.

[b] we; *some manuscripts have* you.
[c] CHILDREN OF YOUR DEAR SISTER: *This probably refers to the members of the church to which the writer belonged.*
5: Jn 13.34, 15.12,17

THE THIRD LETTER OF
JOHN

INTRODUCTION

The Third Letter of John was written by "the Elder" to a church leader named Gaius. The writer praises Gaius because of his help to other Christians, and warns against a man named Diotrephes.

Outline of Contents
Introduction   1-4
Gaius is praised   5-8
Diotrephes is condemned   9-10
Demetrius is commended   11-12
Conclusion   13-15

1 From the Elder—
To my dear Gaius, whom I truly love.

2 My dear friend, I pray that everything

may go well with you and that you may be in good health—as I know you are well in spirit. 3 I was so happy when some

1: Acts 19.29; Rom 16.23; 1 Cor 1.14

Christian brothers arrived and told me how faithful you are to the truth—just as you always live in the truth. ⁴Nothing makes me happier than to hear that my children live in the truth.

Gaius Is Praised

5 My dear friend, you are so faithful in the work you do for your fellow-Christians, even when they are strangers. ⁶They have spoken to the church here about your love. Please help them to continue their journey in a way that will please God. ⁷For they set out on their journey in the service of Christ without accepting any help from unbelievers. ⁸We Christians, then, must help these people, so that we may share in their work for the truth.

Diotrephes and Demetrius

9 I wrote a short letter to the church; but Diotrephes, who likes to be their leader, will not pay any attention to what I say. ¹⁰When I come, then, I will call attention to everything he has done: the terrible things he says about us and the lies he tells! But that is not enough for him; he will not receive the Christian brothers when they come, and even stops those who want to receive them and tries to drive them out of the church!

11 My dear friend, do not imitate what is bad, but imitate what is good. Whoever does good belongs to God; whoever does what is bad has not seen God.

12 Everyone speaks well of Demetrius; truth itself speaks well of him. And we add our testimony, and you know that what we say is true.

Final Greetings

13 I have so much to tell you, but I do not want to do it with pen and ink. ¹⁴I hope to see you soon, and then we will talk personally.

15 Peace be with you.

All your friends send greetings. Greet all our friends personally.

THE LETTER FROM

JUDE

INTRODUCTION

The Letter from Jude was written to warn against false teachers who claimed to be believers. In this brief letter, which is similar in content to *2 Peter*, the writer encourages his readers "to fight on for the faith which once and for all God has given to his people."

Outline of Contents
Introduction   1-2
Character, teaching, and doom of the false teachers   3-16
Admonition to keep the faith   17-23
Benediction   24-25

---

1 From Jude, servant of Jesus Christ, and brother of James—

To those who have been called by God, who live in the love of God the Father and the protection of Jesus Christ:

1: Mt 13.55; Mk 6.3

2 May mercy, peace, and love be yours in full measure.

False Teachers

3 My dear friends, I was doing my best

to write to you about the salvation we share in common, when I felt the need of writing at once to encourage you to fight on for the faith which once and for all God has given to his people. 4 For some godless people have slipped in unnoticed among us, persons who distort the message about the grace of our God in order to excuse their immoral ways, and who reject Jesus Christ, our only Master and Lord. Long ago the Scriptures predicted the condemnation they have received.

5 For even though you know all this, I want to remind you of how the Lord[a] once rescued the people of Israel from Egypt, but afterwards destroyed those who did not believe. 6 Remember the angels who did not stay within the limits of their proper authority, but abandoned their own dwelling place: they are bound with eternal chains in the darkness below, where God is keeping them for that great Day on which they will be condemned. 7 Remember Sodom and Gomorrah, and the nearby towns, whose people acted as those angels did and indulged in sexual immorality and perversion: they suffer the punishment of eternal fire as a plain warning to all.

8 In the same way also, these people have visions which make them sin against their own bodies; they despise God's authority and insult the glorious beings above. 9 Not even the chief angel Michael did this. In his quarrel with the Devil, when they argued about who would have the body of Moses, Michael did not dare to condemn the Devil with insulting words, but said, "The Lord rebuke you!" 10 But these people attack with insults anything they do not understand; and those things that they know by instinct, like wild animals, are the very things that destroy them. 11 How terrible for them! They have followed the way that Cain took. For the sake of money they have given themselves over to the error that Balaam committed. They have rebelled as Korah rebelled, and like him they are destroyed. 12 With their shameless carousing they are like dirty spots in your fellowship meals. They take care only of themselves. They are like clouds carried along by the wind, but bringing no rain.

They are like trees that bear no fruit, even in autumn, trees that have been pulled up by the roots and are completely dead. 13 They are like wild waves of the sea, with their shameful deeds showing up like foam. They are like wandering stars, for whom God has reserved a place for ever in the deepest darkness.

14 It was Enoch, the sixth direct descendant from Adam, who long ago prophesied this about them: "The Lord will come with many thousands of his holy angels 15 to bring judgement on all, to condemn them all for the godless deeds they have performed and for all the terrible words that godless sinners have spoken against him!"

16 These people are always grumbling and blaming others; they follow their own evil desires; they boast about themselves and flatter others in order to get their own way.

Warnings and Instructions

17 But remember, my friends, what you were told in the past by the apostles of our Lord Jesus Christ. 18 They said to you, "When the last days come, people will appear who will mock you, people who follow their own godless desires." 19 These are the people who cause divisions, who are controlled by their natural desires, who do not have the Spirit. 20 But you, my friends, keep on building yourselves up on your most sacred faith. Pray in the power of the Holy Spirit, 21 and keep yourselves in the love of God, as you wait for our Lord Jesus Christ in his mercy to give you eternal life.

22 Show mercy towards those who have doubts; 23 save others by snatching them out of the fire; and to others show mercy mixed with fear, but hate their very clothes, stained by their sinful lusts.

Prayer of Praise

24 To him who is able to keep you from falling, and to bring you faultless and joyful before his glorious presence—25 to the only God our Saviour, through Jesus Christ our Lord, be glory, majesty, might, and authority, from all ages past, and now, and for ever and ever! Amen.

[a] the Lord; *some manuscripts have* Jesus, *which in Greek is the same as* Joshua.
5: Ex 12.51   **5:** Num 14.29–30   **7:** Gen 19.1–24   **9:** Dan 10.13,21, 12.1   **9:** Rev 12.7
9: Deut 34.6   **9:** Zech 3.2   **11:** Gen 4.3–8   **11:** Num 22.1–35, 16.1–35   **14:** Gen 5.18,21–24
18: 2 Pet 3.3

THE REVELATION

TO JOHN

INTRODUCTION

The Revelation to John was written at a time when Christians were being persecuted because of their faith in Jesus Christ as Lord. The writer's main concern is to give his readers hope and encouragement, and to urge them to remain faithful during times of suffering and persecution.

For the most part the book consists of several series of revelations and visions presented in symbolic language that would have been understood by Christians of that day, but would have remained a mystery to all others. As with the themes of a symphony, the themes of this book are repeated again and again in different ways through the various series of visions. Although there are differences of opinion regarding the details of interpretation of the book, the central theme is clear: through Christ the Lord, God will finally and totally defeat all his enemies, including Satan, and will reward his faithful people with the blessings of a new heaven and a new earth when this victory is complete.

Outline of Contents

Introduction 1.1–8
Opening vision and the letters to the seven churches 1.9—3.22
The scroll with seven seals 4.1—8.1
The seven trumpets 8.2—11.19
The dragon and the two beasts 12.1—13.18
Various visions 14.1—15.8
The seven bowls of God's anger 16.1-21
The destruction of Babylon, and the defeat of the
  beast, the false prophet, and the Devil 17.1—20.10
The final judgement 20.11-15
The new heaven, the new earth, the new Jerusalem 21.1—22.5
Conclusion 22.6-21

---

1 This book is the record of the events that Jesus Christ revealed. God gave him this revelation in order to show his servants what must happen very soon. Christ made these things known to his servant John by sending his angel to him, ² and John has told all that he has seen. This is his report concerning the message from God and the truth revealed by Jesus Christ. ³ Happy is the one who reads this book, and happy are those who listen to the words of this prophetic message and

obey what is written in this book! For the time is near when all these things will happen.

Greetings to the Seven Churches

4 From John to the seven churches in the province of Asia:

Grace and peace be yours from God, who is, who was, and who is to come, and from the seven spirits in front of his throne, ⁵ and from Jesus Christ, the faithful witness, the first to be raised from death and who is also the ruler of the kings of the world.

He loves us, and by his sacrificial death he has freed us from our sins ⁶ and made us a kingdom of priests to serve his God and Father. To Jesus Christ be the glory and power for ever and ever! Amen.

7 Look, he is coming on the clouds! Everyone will see him, including those who pierced him. All peoples on earth will mourn over him. So shall it be!

8 "I am the first and the last," says the Lord God Almighty, who is, who was, and who is to come.

A Vision of Christ

9 I am John, your brother, and as a follower of Jesus I am your partner in patiently enduring the suffering that comes to those who belong to his Kingdom. I was put on the island of Patmos because I had proclaimed God's word and the truth that Jesus revealed. ¹⁰ On the Lord's day the Spirit took control of me, and I heard a loud voice, that sounded like a trumpet, speaking behind me. ¹¹ It said, "Write down what you see, and send the book to the churches in these seven cities: Ephesus, Smyrna, Pergamum, Thyatira, Sardis, Philadelphia, and Laodicea."

12 I turned round to see who was talking to me, and I saw seven gold lamp-stands, ¹³ and among them there was what looked like a human being, wearing a robe that reached to his feet, and a gold belt round his chest. ¹⁴ His hair was white as wool, or as snow, and his eyes blazed like fire; ¹⁵ his feet shone like brass that has been refined and polished, and his voice sounded like a roaring waterfall. ¹⁶ He held seven stars in his right hand, and a sharp two-edged sword came out

of his mouth. His face was as bright as the midday sun. ¹⁷ When I saw him, I fell down at his feet like a dead man. He placed his right hand on me and said, "Don't be afraid! I am the first and the last. ¹⁸ I am the living one! I was dead, but now I am alive for ever and ever. I have authority over death and the world of the dead. ¹⁹ Write, then, the things you see, both the things that are now and the things that will happen afterwards. ²⁰ This is the secret meaning of the seven stars that you see in my right hand, and of the seven gold lamp-stands: the seven stars are the angels of the seven churches, and the seven lamp-stands are the seven churches.

The Message to Ephesus

2 "To the angel of the church in Ephesus write:

"This is the message from the one who holds the seven stars in his right hand and who walks among the seven gold lamp-stands. ²ʹ I know what you have done; I know how hard you have worked and how patient you have been. I know that you cannot tolerate evil men and that you have tested those who say they are apostles but are not, and have found out that they are liars. ³ You are patient, you have suffered for my sake, and you have not given up. ⁴ But this is what I have against you: you do not love me now as you did at first. ⁵ Think how far you have fallen! Turn from your sins and do what you did at first. If you don't turn from your sins, I will come to you and take your lamp-stand from its place. ⁶ But this is what you have in your favour: you hate what the Nicolaitans do, as much as I do.

7 "If you have ears, then, listen to what the Spirit says to the churches!

"To those who win the victory I will give the right to eat the fruit of the tree of life that grows in the Garden of God.

The Message to Smyrna

8 "To the angel of the church in Smyrna write:

"This is the message from the one who is the first and the last, who died and lived again. ⁹ I know your troubles; I know

1.4: Ex 3.14; Rev 4.5   **1.5:** Is 55.4; Ps 89.27   **1.6:** Ex 19.6; Rev 5.10
1.7: Dan 7.13; Mt 24.30; Mk 13.26; Lk 21.27; 1 Thes 4.17; Zech 12.10; Jn 19.34,37
1.8: Rev 22.13; Ex 3.14   **1.13:** Dan 7.13, 10.5   **1.14–15:** Dan 7.9, 10.6
1.15: Ezek 1.24, 43.2   **1.17:** Is 44.6, 48.12; Rev 2.8, 22.13
2.7: Gen 2.9; Rev 22.2; Ezek 28.13, 31.8   **2.8:** Is 44.6, 48.12; Rev 1.17, 22.13

that you are poor—but really you are rich! I know the evil things said against you by those who claim to be Jews but are not; they are a group that belongs to Satan! [10] Don't be afraid of anything you are about to suffer. Listen! The Devil will put you to the test by having some of you thrown into prison, and your troubles will last ten days. Be faithful to me, even if it means death, and I will give you life as your prize of victory.

[11] "If you have ears, then, listen to what the Spirit says to the churches!

"Those who win the victory will not be hurt by the second death.

The Message to Pergamum

[12] "To the angel of the church in Pergamum write:

"This is the message from the one who has the sharp two-edged sword. [13] I know where you live, there where Satan has his throne. You are true to me, and you did not abandon your faith in me even during the time when Antipas, my faithful witness, was killed there where Satan lives. [14] But there are a few things I have against you: there are some among you who follow the teaching of Balaam, who taught Balak how to lead the people of Israel into sin by persuading them to eat food that had been offered to idols and to practise sexual immorality. [15] In the same way you have people among you who follow the teaching of the Nicolaitans. [16] Now turn from your sins! If you don't, I will come to you soon and fight against those people with the sword that comes out of my mouth.

[17] "If you have ears, then, listen to what the Spirit says to the churches!

"To those who win the victory I will give some of the hidden manna. I will also give each of them a white stone on which is written a new name that no one knows except the one who receives it.

The Message to Thyatira

[18] "To the angel of the church in Thyatira write:

"This is the message from the Son of God, whose eyes blaze like fire, whose feet shine like polished brass. [19] I know what you do. I know your love, your faithfulness, your service, and your patience. I know that you are doing more now than you did at first. [20] But this is what I have against you: you tolerate that woman Jezebel, who calls herself a messenger of God. By her teaching she misleads my servants into practising sexual immorality and eating food that has been offered to idols. [21] I have given her time to repent of her sins, but she does not want to turn from her immorality. [22] And so I will throw her on to a bed where she and those who committed adultery with her will suffer terribly. I will do this now unless they repent of the wicked things they did with her. [23] I will also kill her followers, and then all the churches will know that I am the one who knows everyone's thoughts and wishes. I will repay each one of you according to what he has done.

[24] "But the rest of you in Thyatira have not followed this evil teaching; you have not learnt what the others call 'the deep secrets of Satan.' I say to you that I will not put any other burden on you. [25] But until I come, you must hold firmly to what you have. [26-28] To those who win the victory, who continue to the end to do what I want, I will give the same authority that I received from my Father: I will give them authority over the nations, to rule them with an iron rod and to break them to pieces like clay pots. I will also give them the morning star.

[29] "If you have ears, then, listen to what the Spirit says to the churches!

The Message to Sardis

3 "To the angel of the church in Sardis write:

"This is the message from the one who has the seven spirits of God and the seven stars. I know what you are doing; I know that you have the reputation of being alive, even though you are dead! [2] So wake up, and strengthen what you still have before it dies completely. For I find that what you have done is not yet perfect in the sight of my God. [3] Remember, then, what you were taught and what you heard; obey it and turn from your sins. If you do not wake up, I will come upon you like a thief, and you will not even know the time when I will come. [4] But a few of you there in Sardis have kept

2.11: Rev 20.14, 21.8   **2.14:** Num 22.5,7, 31.16; Deut 23.4; Num 25.1-3
2.17: Ex 16.14–15, 16.33–34; Jn 6.48–50; Is 62.2, 65.15   **2.20:** 1 Kgs 16.31; 2 Kgs 9.22,30
2.23: Ps 7.9; Jer 17.10; Ps 62.12   **2.26–27:** Ps 2.8–9
3.3: Mt 24.43–44; Lk 12.39–40; Rev 16.15

your clothes clean. You will walk with me, clothed in white, because you are worthy to do so. ⁵Those who win the victory will be clothed like this in white, and I will not remove their names from the book of the living. In the presence of my Father and of his angels I will declare openly that they belong to me.

6 "If you have ears, then, listen to what the Spirit says to the churches!

The Message to Philadelphia

7 "To the angel of the church in Philadelphia write:

"This is the message from the one who is holy and true. He has the key that belonged to David, and when he opens a door, no one can close it, and when he closes it, no one can open it. ⁸I know what you do; I know that you have a little power; you have followed my teaching and have been faithful to me. I have opened a door in front of you, which no one can close. ⁹Listen! As for that group that belongs to Satan, those liars who claim that they are Jews but are not, I will make them come and bow down at your feet. They will all know that I love you. ¹⁰Because you have kept my command to endure, I will also keep you safe from the time of trouble which is coming upon the world to test all the people on earth. ¹¹I am coming soon. Keep safe what you have, so that no one will rob you of your victory prize. ¹²I will make him who is victorious a pillar in the temple of my God, and he will never leave it. I will write on him the name of my God and the name of the city of my God, the new Jerusalem, which will come down out of heaven from my God. I will also write on him my new name.

13 "If you have ears, then, listen to what the Spirit says to the churches!

The Message to Laodicea

14 "To the angel of the church in Laodicea write:

"This is the message from the Amen, the faithful and true witness, who is the origin *b* of all that God has created. ¹⁵I know what you have done; I know that you are neither cold nor hot. How I wish you were either one or the other! ¹⁶But because you are lukewarm, neither hot nor cold, I am going to spit you out of

my mouth! ¹⁷You say, 'I am rich and well off; I have all I need.' But you do not know how miserable and pitiful you are! You are poor, naked, and blind. ¹⁸I advise you, then, to buy gold from me, pure gold, in order to be rich. Buy also white clothing to dress yourself and cover up your shameful nakedness. Buy also some ointment to put on your eyes, so that you may see. ¹⁹I rebuke and punish all whom I love. Be in earnest, then, and turn from your sins. ²⁰Listen! I stand at the door

If anyone...opens the door, I will come into his house (3.20)

and knock; if anyone hears my voice and opens the door, I will come into his house and eat with him, and he will eat with me. ²¹To those who win the victory I will give the right to sit beside me on my throne, just as I have been victorious and now sit by my Father on his throne.

22 "If you have ears, then, listen to what the Spirit says to the churches!"

Worship in Heaven

4 At this point I had another vision and saw an open door in heaven. And the voice that sounded like a trumpet, which I had heard speaking to me before, said, "Come up here, and I will show you what must happen after this." ²At once

---

b origin; *or* ruler.

3.5: Ex 32.32-33   **3.5:** Ps 69.28; Rev 20.12; Mt 10.32; Lk 12.8   **3.7:** Is 22.22; Job 12.14
3.9: Is 49.23, 60.14, 43.4   **3.12:** Rev 21.2; Is 62.2, 65.15   **3.14:** Prov 8.22
3.19: Prov 3.12; Heb 12.6   **4.2-3:** Ezek 1.26-28, 10.1

the Spirit took control of me. There in heaven was a throne with someone sitting on it. ³His face gleamed like such precious stones as jasper and carnelian, and all round the throne there was a rainbow the colour of an emerald. ⁴In a circle round the throne were twenty-four other thrones, on which were seated twenty-four elders dressed in white and wearing crowns of gold. ⁵From the throne came flashes of lightning, rumblings, and peals of thunder. In front of the throne seven lighted torches were burning, which are the seven spirits of God. ⁶Also in front of the throne there was what looked like a sea of glass, clear as crystal.

Surrounding the throne on each of its sides, were four living creatures covered with eyes in front and behind. ⁷The first one looked like a lion; the second looked like a bull; the third had a face like a man's face; and the fourth looked like an eagle in flight. ⁸Each one of the four living creatures had six wings, and they were covered with eyes, inside and out. Day and night they never stop singing:

"Holy, holy, holy, is the Lord God
    Almighty,
  who was, who is, and who is to come."

9 The four living creatures sing songs of glory and honour and thanks to the one who sits on the throne, who lives for ever and ever. When they do so, ¹⁰the twenty-four elders fall down before the one who sits on the throne, and worship him who lives for ever and ever. They throw their crowns down in front of the throne and say,

¹¹"Our Lord and God! You are worthy
    to receive glory, honour, and power.
  For you created all things,
    and by your will they were given
      existence and life."

The Scroll and the Lamb

5 I saw a scroll in the right hand of the one who sits on the throne; it was covered with writing on both sides and was sealed with seven seals. ²And I saw a mighty angel, who announced in a loud voice, "Who is worthy to break the seals and open the scroll?" ³But there was no one in heaven or on earth or in the world below^c who could open the scroll and look inside it. ⁴I cried bitterly

because no one could be found who was worthy to open the scroll or look inside it. ⁵Then one of the elders said to me, "Don't cry. Look! The Lion from Judah's tribe, the great descendant of David, has won the victory, and he can break the seven seals and open the scroll."

6 Then I saw a Lamb standing in the centre of the throne, surrounded by the four living creatures and the elders. The Lamb appeared to have been killed. It had seven horns and seven eyes, which are the seven spirits of God that have been sent throughout the whole earth. ⁷The Lamb went and took the scroll from the right hand of the one who sits on the throne. ⁸As he did so, the four living creatures and the twenty-four elders fell down before the Lamb. Each had a harp and gold bowls filled with incense, which are the prayers of God's people. ⁹They sang a new song:

"You are worthy to take the scroll
    and to break open its seals.
  For you were killed, and by your
      sacrificial death you bought for God
    people from every tribe, language,
      nation, and race.
¹⁰You have made them a kingdom of
      priests to serve our God,
    and they shall rule on earth."

11 Again I looked, and I heard angels, thousands and millions of them! They stood round the throne, the four living creatures, and the elders, ¹²and sang in a loud voice:

"The Lamb who was killed is worthy
    to receive power, wealth, wisdom,
      and strength,
    honour, glory, and praise!"

¹³And I heard every creature in heaven, on earth, in the world below, and in the sea—all living beings in the universe—and they were singing:

"To him who sits on the throne and
      to the Lamb,
    be praise and honour, glory and might,
      for ever and ever!"

¹⁴The four living creatures answered, "Amen!" And the elders fell down and worshipped.

The Seals

6 Then I saw the Lamb break open the first of the seven seals, and I heard

^cWORLD BELOW: *The world of the dead (see 1.18).*
4.5: Ex 19.16; Rev 8.5, 11.19, 16.18; Ezek 1.13; Rev 1.4; Zech 4.2
4.6–7: Ezek 1.22,5–10, 10.14   **4.8:** Ezek 1.18, 10.12; Is 6.2–3   **5.1:** Ezek 2.9–10; Is 29.11
5.5: Gen 49.9; Is 11.1,10   **5.6:** Is 53.7; Zech 4.10   **5.8:** Ps 141.2   **5.9:** Ps 33.3, 98.1; Is 42.10
5.10: Ex 19.6; Rev 1.6   **5.11:** Dan 7.10

one of the four living creatures say in a voice that sounded like thunder, "Come!" [2] I looked, and there was a white horse. Its rider held a bow, and he was given a crown. He rode out as a conqueror to conquer.

3 Then the Lamb broke open the second seal; and I heard the second living creature say, "Come!" [4] Another horse came out, a red one. Its rider was given the power to bring war on the earth, so that men should kill each other. He was given a large sword.

5 Then the Lamb broke open the third seal; and I heard the third living creature say, "Come!" I looked, and there was a black horse. Its rider held a pair of scales in his hand. [6] I heard what sounded like a voice coming from among the four living creatures, which said, "A litre of wheat for a day's wages, and three litres of barley for a day's wages. But do not damage the olive-trees and the vineyards!"

7 Then the Lamb broke open the fourth seal; and I heard the fourth living creature say, "Come!" [8] I looked, and there was a pale-coloured horse. Its rider was named Death, and Hades [d] followed close behind. They were given authority over a quarter of the earth, to kill by means of war, famine, disease, and wild animals.

9 Then the Lamb broke open the fifth seal. I saw underneath the altar the souls of those who had been killed because they had proclaimed God's word and had been faithful in their witnessing. [10] They shouted in a loud voice, "Almighty Lord, holy and true! How long will it be until you judge the people on earth and punish them for killing us?" [11] Each of them was given a white robe, and they were told to rest a little while longer, until the complete number of their fellow-servants and brothers had been killed, as they had been.

12 And I saw the Lamb break open the sixth seal. There was a violent earthquake, and the sun became black like coarse black cloth, and the moon turned completely red like blood. [13] The stars fell down to the earth, like unripe figs falling from the tree when a strong wind shakes it. [14] The sky disappeared like a scroll being rolled up, and every mountain and

island was moved from its place. [15] Then the kings of the earth, the rulers and the military chiefs, the rich and the powerful, and all other men, slave and free, hid themselves in caves and under rocks on the mountains. [16] They called out to the mountains and to the rocks, "Fall on us and hide us from the eyes of the one who sits on the throne and from the anger of the Lamb! [17] The terrible day of their anger is here, and who can stand against it?"

The 144,000 People of Israel

7 After this I saw four angels standing at the four corners of the earth, holding back the four winds so that no wind should blow on the earth or the sea or against any tree. [2] And I saw another angel coming up from the east with the seal of the living God. He called out in a loud voice to the four angels to whom God had given the power to damage the earth and the sea. [3] The angel said, "Do not harm the earth, the sea, or the trees, until we mark the servants of our God with a seal on their foreheads." [4] And I was told that the number of those who were marked with God's seal on their foreheads was 144,000. They were from the twelve tribes of Israel, [5-8] twelve thousand from each tribe: Judah, Reuben, Gad, Asher, Naphtali, Manasseh, Simeon, Levi, Issachar, Zebulun, Joseph, and Benjamin.

The Enormous Crowd

9 After this I looked, and there was an enormous crowd—no one could count all the people! They were from every race, tribe, nation, and language, and they stood in front of the throne and of the Lamb, dressed in white robes and holding palm branches in their hands. [10] They called out in a loud voice: "Salvation comes from our God, who sits on the throne, and from the Lamb!" [11] All the angels stood round the throne, the elders, and the four living creatures. Then they threw themselves face downwards in front of the throne and worshipped God, [12] saying, "Amen! Praise, glory, wisdom, thanksgiving, honour, power, and might belong to our God for ever and ever! Amen!"

13 One of the elders asked me, "Who

[d] HADES: *The world of the dead (see 1.18).*
6.2: Zech 1.8, 6.3,6 **6.4:** Zech 1.8, 6.2 **6.5:** Zech 6.2,6 **6.8:** Ezek 14.21
6.12: Rev 11.13, 16.18; Is 13.10; Joel 2.10,31, 3.15; Mt 24.29; Mk 13.24–25; Lk 21.25
6.13–14: Is 34.4 **6.14:** Rev 16.20 **6.15:** Is 2.19,21 **6.16:** Hos 10.8; Lk 23.30
6.17: Joel 2.11; Mal 3.2 **7.1:** Jer 49.36; Dan 7.2; Zech 6.5 **7.3:** Ezek 9.4,6

are these people dressed in white robes, and where do they come from?"

14 "I don't know, sir. You do," I answered.

He said to me, "These are the people who have come safely through the terrible persecution. They have washed their robes and made them white with the blood of the Lamb. 15 That is why they stand before God's throne and serve him day and night in his temple. He who sits on the throne will protect them with his presence. 16 Never again will they hunger or thirst; neither sun nor any scorching heat will burn them, 17 because the Lamb, who is in the centre of the throne, will be their shepherd, and he will guide them to springs of life-giving water. And God will wipe away every tear from their eyes."

The Seventh Seal

8 When the Lamb broke open the seventh seal, there was silence in heaven for about half an hour. 2 Then I saw the seven angels who stand before God, and they were given seven trumpets.

3 Another angel, who had a gold incense-burner, came and stood at the altar. He was given a lot of incense to add to the prayers of all God's people and to offer it on the gold altar that stands before the throne. 4 The smoke of the burning incense went up with the prayers of God's people from the hands of the angel standing before God. 5 Then the angel took the incense-burner, filled it with fire from the altar, and threw it on the earth. There were rumblings and peals of thunder, flashes of lightning, and an earthquake.

The Trumpets

6 Then the seven angels with the seven trumpets prepared to blow them.

7 The first angel blew his trumpet. Hail and fire, mixed with blood, came pouring down on the earth. A third of the earth was burnt up, a third of the trees, and every blade of green grass.

8 Then the second angel blew his trumpet. Something that looked like a huge mountain on fire was thrown into the sea. A third of the sea was turned

into blood, 9 a third of the living creatures in the sea died, and a third of the ships were destroyed.

10 Then the third angel blew his trumpet. A large star, burning like a torch, dropped from the sky and fell on a third of the rivers and on the springs of water. 11 (The name of the star is "Bitterness.") A third of the water turned bitter, and many people died from drinking the water, because it had turned bitter.

12 Then the fourth angel blew his trumpet. A third of the sun was struck, and a third of the moon, and a third of the stars, so that their light lost a third of its brightness; there was no light during a third of the day and a third of the night.

13 Then I looked, and I heard an eagle that was flying high in the air say in a loud voice, "O horror! horror! How horrible it will be for all who live on earth when the sound comes from the trumpets that the other three angels must blow!"

9 Then the fifth angel blew his trumpet. I saw a star which had fallen down to the earth, and it was given the key to the abyss.[e] 2 The star opened the abyss, and smoke poured out of it, like the smoke from a large furnace; the sunlight and the air were darkened by the smoke from the abyss. 3 Locusts came down out of the smoke upon the earth, and they were given the same kind of power that scorpions have. 4 They were told not to harm the grass or the trees or any other plant; they could harm only the people who did not have the mark of God's seal on their foreheads. 5 The locusts were not allowed to kill these people, but only to torture them for five months. The pain caused by the torture is like the pain caused by a scorpion's sting. 6 During those five months they will seek death, but will not find it; they will want to die, but death will flee from them.

7 The locusts looked like horses ready for battle; on their heads they had what seemed to be crowns of gold, and their faces were like men's faces. 8 Their hair was like women's hair, their teeth were like lions' teeth. 9 Their chests were covered with what looked like iron breastplates, and the sound made by their wings

[e] ABYSS: *The place in the depths of the earth where the demons were imprisoned until their final punishment.*

7.14: Dan 12.1; Mt 24.21; Mk 13.19   **7.16:** Is 49.10
7.17: Ps 23.1; Ezek 34.23; Ps 23.2; Is 49.10, 25.8   **8.3:** Amos 9.1; Ex 30.1,3
8.5: Lev 16.12; Ezek 10.2; Ex 19.16; Rev 11.19, 16.18   **8.7:** Ex 9.23-25; Ezek 38.22
8.10: Is 14.12   **8.11:** Jer 9.15   **8.12:** Is 13.10; Ezek 32.7; Joel 2.10,31, 3.15   **9.2:** Gen 19.28
9.3: Ex 10.12-15   **9.4:** Ezek 9.4   **9.6:** Job 3.21; Jer 8.3   **9.7:** Joel 2.4   **9.8:** Joel 1.6
9.9: Joel 2.5

was like the noise of many horse-drawn chariots rushing into battle. 10 They have tails and stings like those of a scorpion, and it is with their tails that they have the power to hurt people for five months. 11 They have a king ruling over them, who is the angel in charge of the abyss. His name in Hebrew is Abaddon; in Greek the name is Apollyon (meaning "The Destroyer").

12 The first horror is over; after this there are still two more horrors to come.

13 Then the sixth angel blew his trumpet. I heard a voice coming from the four corners of the gold altar standing before God. 14 The voice said to the sixth angel, "Release the four angels who are bound at the great river Euphrates!" 15 The four angels were released; for this very hour of this very day of this very month and year they had been kept ready to kill a third of all mankind. 16 I was told the number of the mounted troops: it was two hundred million. 17 And in my vision I saw the horses and their riders: they had breastplates red as fire, blue as sapphire, and yellow as sulphur. The horses' heads were like lions' heads, and from their mouths came out fire, smoke, and sulphur. 18 A third of mankind was killed by those three plagues: the fire, the smoke, and the sulphur coming out of the horses' mouths. 19 For the power of the horses is in their mouths and also in their tails. Their tails are like snakes with heads, and they use them to hurt people.

20 The rest of mankind, all those who had not been killed by these plagues, did not turn away from what they themselves had made. They did not stop worshipping demons, nor the idols of gold, silver, bronze, stone, and wood, which cannot see, hear, or walk. 21 Nor did they repent of their murders, their magic, their sexual immorality, or their stealing.

The Angel and the Little Scroll

10 Then I saw another mighty angel coming down out of heaven. He was wrapped in a cloud and had a rainbow round his head; his face was like the sun, and his legs were like pillars of fire. 2 He had a small scroll open in his hand. He put his right foot on the sea and his left foot on the land, 3 and called out in a loud voice that sounded like the roar of

lions. After he had called out, the seven thunders answered with a roar. 4 As soon as they spoke, I was about to write. But I heard a voice speak from heaven, "Keep secret what the seven thunders have said; do not write it down!"

5 Then the angel that I saw standing on the sea and on the land raised his right hand to heaven 6 and took a vow in the name of God, who lives for ever and ever, who created heaven, earth, and the sea, and everything in them. The angel said, "There will be no more delay! 7 But when the seventh angel blows his trumpet, then God will accomplish his secret plan, as he announced to his servants, the prophets."

8 Then the voice that I had heard speaking from heaven spoke to me again, saying, "Go and take the open scroll which is in the hand of the angel standing on the sea and on the land."

9 I went to the angel and asked him to give me the little scroll. He said to me, "Take it and eat it; it will turn sour in your stomach, but in your mouth it will be sweet as honey."

10 I took the little scroll from his hand and ate it, and it tasted sweet as honey in my mouth. But after I swallowed it, it turned sour in my stomach. 11 Then I was told, "Once again you must proclaim God's message about many nations, races, languages, and kings."

The Two Witnesses

11 I was then given a stick that looked like a measuring-rod, and was told, "Go and measure the temple of God and the altar, and count those who are worshipping in the temple. 2 But do not measure the outer courts, because they have been given to the heathen, who will trample on the Holy City for forty-two months. 3 I will send my two witnesses dressed in sackcloth, and they will proclaim God's message during those 1,260 days."

4 The two witnesses are the two olive-trees and the two lamps that stand before the Lord of the earth. 5 If anyone tries to harm them, fire comes out of their mouths and destroys their enemies; and in this way, whoever tries to harm them will be killed. 6 They have authority to shut up the sky so that there will be no rain

9.13: Ex 30.1–3   **9.20:** Ps 115.4–7, 135.15–17; Dan 5.23
10.5–7: Ex 20.11; Deut 32.40; Dan 12.7; Amos 3.7   **10.8–10:** Ezek 2.8—3.3
11.1: Ezek 40.3; Zech 2.1–2   **11.2:** Lk 21.24   **11.4:** Zech 4.3,11–14
11.6: 1 Kgs 17.1; Ex 7.17–19; I Sam 4.8

during the time they proclaim God's message. They have authority also over the springs of water, to turn them into blood; they have authority also to strike the earth with every kind of plague as often as they wish.

7 When they finish proclaiming their message, the beast that comes up out of the abyss will fight against them. He will defeat them and kill them, 8 and their bodies will lie in the street of the great city, where their Lord was crucified. The symbolic name of that city is Sodom, or Egypt. 9 People from all nations, tribes, languages, and races will look at their bodies for three and a half days and will not allow them to be buried. 10 The people of the earth will be happy because of the death of these two. They will celebrate and send presents to each other, because those two prophets brought much suffering upon mankind. 11 After three and a half days a life-giving breath came from God and entered them, and they stood up; and all who saw them were terrified. 12 Then the two prophets heard a loud voice say to them from heaven, "Come up here!" As their enemies watched, they went up into heaven in a cloud. 13 At that very moment there was a violent earthquake; a tenth of the city was destroyed, and seven thousand people were killed. The rest of the people were terrified and praised the greatness of the God of heaven.

14 The second horror is over, but the third horror will come soon!

The Seventh Trumpet

15 Then the seventh angel blew his trumpet, and there were loud voices in heaven, saying, "The power to rule over the world belongs now to our Lord and his Messiah, and he will rule for ever and ever!" 16 Then the twenty-four elders who sit on their thrones in front of God threw themselves face downwards and worshipped God, 17 saying:

"Lord God Almighty, the one who is and who was!
We thank you that you have taken your great power
and have begun to rule!
18 The heathen were filled with rage,
because the time for your anger has come,
the time for the dead to be judged.

The time has come to reward your servants, the prophets,
and all your people, all who have reverence for you,
great and small alike.
The time has come to destroy those who destroy the earth!"

19 God's temple in heaven was opened, and the Covenant Box was seen there. Then there were flashes of lightning, rumblings and peals of thunder, an earthquake, and heavy hail.

The Woman and the Dragon

12 Then a great and mysterious sight appeared in the sky. There was a woman, whose dress was the sun and who had the moon under her feet and a crown of twelve stars on her head. 2 She was soon to give birth, and the pains and suffering of childbirth made her cry out.

3 Another mysterious sight appeared in the sky. There was a huge red dragon with seven heads and ten horns and a crown on each of his heads. 4 With his tail he dragged a third of the stars out of the sky and threw them down to the earth. He stood in front of the woman, in order to eat her child as soon as it was born. 5 Then she gave birth to a son, who will rule over all nations with an iron rod. But the child was snatched away and taken to God and his throne. 6 The woman fled to the desert, to a place God had prepared for her, where she will be taken care of for 1,260 days.

7 Then war broke out in heaven. Michael and his angels fought against the dragon, who fought back with his angels; 8 but the dragon was defeated, and he and his angels were not allowed to stay in heaven any longer. 9 The huge dragon was thrown out—that ancient serpent, called the Devil, or Satan, that deceived the whole world. He was thrown down to earth, and all his angels with him.

10 Then I heard a loud voice in heaven saying, "Now God's salvation has come! Now God has shown his power as King! Now his Messiah has shown his authority! For the one who stood before our God and accused our brothers day and night has been thrown out of heaven. 11 Our brothers won the victory over him by the blood of the Lamb and by the truth which they proclaimed; and they were

11.7: Dan 7.7,21; Rev 13.5–7, 17.8   11.8: Is 1.9–10   11.11: Ezek 37.10   11.12: 2 Kgs 2.11
11.13: Rev 6.12, 16.18   11.15: Ex 15.18; Dan 2.44, 7.14,27   11.18: Ps 2.5, 110.5, 115.13
11.19: Rev 8.5, 16.18,21   12.3: Dan 7.7   12.4: Dan 8.10   12.5: Is 66.7; Ps 2.9
12.7: Dan 10.13,21, 12.1; Jude 9   12.9: Gen 3.1; Lk 10.18   12.10: Job 1.9–11; Zech 3.1

willing to give up their lives and die. [12] And so be glad, you heavens, and all you that live there! But how terrible for the earth and the sea! For the Devil has come down to you, and he is filled with rage, because he knows that he has only a little time left."

13 When the dragon realized that he had been thrown down to the earth, he began to pursue the woman who had given birth to the boy. [14] She was given the two wings of a large eagle in order to fly to her place in the desert, where she will be taken care of for three and a half years, safe from the dragon's attack. [15] And then from his mouth the dragon poured out a flood of water after the woman, so that it would carry her away. [16] But the earth helped the woman; it opened its mouth and swallowed the water that had come from the dragon's mouth. [17] The dragon was furious with the woman and went off to fight against the rest of her descendants, all those who obey God's commandments and are faithful to the truth revealed by Jesus. [18] And the dragon stood[f] on the sea-shore.

The Two Beasts

13 Then I saw a beast coming up out of the sea. It had ten horns and seven heads; on each of its horns there was a crown, and on each of its heads there was a name that was insulting to God. [2] The beast looked like a leopard, with feet like a bear's feet and a mouth like a lion's mouth. The dragon gave the beast his own power, his throne, and his vast authority. [3] One of the heads of the beast seemed to have been fatally wounded, but the wound had healed. The whole earth was amazed and followed the beast. [4] Everyone worshipped the dragon because he had given his authority to the beast. They worshipped the beast also, saying, "Who is like the beast? Who can fight against it?"

5 The beast was allowed to make proud claims which were insulting to God, and it was permitted to have authority for forty-two months. [6] It began to curse God, his name, the place where he lives, and all those who live in heaven. [7] It was allowed to fight against God's people and to defeat them, and it was given authority

over every tribe, nation, language, and race. [8] All people living on earth will worship it, except those whose names were written before the creation of the world in the book of the living which belongs to the Lamb that was killed.

9 "Listen, then, if you have ears! [10] Whoever is meant to be captured will surely be captured; whoever is meant to be killed by the sword will surely be killed by the sword. This calls for endurance and faith on the part of God's people."

11 Then I saw another beast, which came up out of the earth. It had two horns like a lamb's horns, and it spoke like a dragon. [12] It used the vast authority of the first beast in its presence. It forced the earth and all who live on it to worship the first beast, whose wound had healed. [13] This second beast performed great miracles; it made fire come down out of heaven to earth in the sight of everyone. [14] And it deceived all the people living on earth by means of the miracles which it was allowed to perform in the presence of the first beast. The beast told them to build an image in honour of the beast that had been wounded by the sword and yet lived. [15] The second beast was allowed to breathe life into the image of the first beast, so that the image could talk and put to death all those who would not worship it. [16] The beast forced all the people, small and great, rich and poor, slave and free, to have a mark placed on their right hands or on their foreheads. [17] No one could buy or sell unless he had this mark, that is, the beast's name or the number that stands for the name.

18 This calls for wisdom. Whoever is intelligent can work out the meaning of the number of the beast, because the number stands for a man's name. Its number is 666.

The Lamb and His People

14 Then I looked, and there was the Lamb standing on Mount Zion; with him were 144,000 people who have his name and his Father's name written on their foreheads. [2] And I heard a voice from heaven that sounded like a roaring waterfall, like a loud peal of thunder. It sounded like the music made by musicians playing their harps. [3] The 144,000 people stood

[f] And the dragon stood; *some manuscripts have* And I stood, *connecting this verse with what follows.*
12.14: Dan 7.25, 12.7   **13.1:** Dan 7.3; Rev 17.3,7–12   **13.2:** Dan 7.4–6
13.5–6: Dan 7.8,25, 11.36   **13.7:** Dan 7.21   **13.8:** Ps 69.28   **13.10:** Jer 15.2, 43.11
14.1: Ezek 9.4; Rev 7.3

before the throne, the four living creatures, and the elders; they were singing a new song, which only they could learn. Of all mankind they are the only ones who have been redeemed. 4 They are the men who have kept themselves pure by not having sexual relations with women; they are virgins. They follow the Lamb wherever he goes. They have been redeemed from the rest of mankind and are the first ones to be offered to God and to the Lamb. 5 They have never been known to tell lies; they are faultless.

The Three Angels

6 Then I saw another angel flying high in the air, with an eternal message of Good News to announce to the peoples of the earth, to every race, tribe, language, and nation. 7 He said in a loud voice, "Honour God and praise his greatness! For the time has come for him to judge mankind. Worship him who made heaven, earth, sea, and the springs of water!"

8 A second angel followed the first one, saying, "She has fallen! Great Babylon has fallen! She made all peoples drink her wine—the strong wine of her immoral lust!"

9 A third angel followed the first two, saying in a loud voice, "Whoever worships the beast and its image and receives the mark on his forehead or on his hand 10 will himself drink God's wine, the wine of his fury, which he has poured at full strength into the cup of his anger! All who do this will be tormented in fire and sulphur before the holy angels and the Lamb. 11 The smoke of the fire that torments them goes up for ever and ever. There is no relief day or night for those who worship the beast and its image, for anyone who has the mark of its name."

12 This calls for endurance on the part of God's people, those who obey God's commandments and are faithful to Jesus.

13 Then I heard a voice from heaven saying, "Write this: Happy are those who from now on die in the service of the Lord!"

"Yes indeed!" answers the Spirit. "They will enjoy rest from their hard work, because the results of their service go with them."

The Harvest of the Earth

14 Then I looked, and there was a white cloud, and sitting on the cloud was what looked like a human being, with a crown of gold on his head and a sharp sickle in his hand. 15 Then another angel came out from the temple and cried out in a loud voice to the one who was sitting on the cloud, "Use your sickle and reap the harvest, because the time has come; the earth is ripe for the harvest!" 16 Then the one who sat on the cloud swung his sickle on the earth, and the earth's harvest was reaped.

17 Then I saw another angel come out of the temple in heaven, and he also had a sharp sickle.

18 Then another angel, who is in charge of the fire, came from the altar. He shouted in a loud voice to the angel who had the sharp sickle, "Use your sickle, and cut the grapes from the vineyard of the earth, because the grapes are ripe!" 19 So the angel swung his sickle on the earth, cut the grapes from the vine, and threw them into the winepress of God's furious anger. 20 The grapes were squeezed out in the winepress outside the city, and blood came out of the winepress in a flood three hundred kilometres long and nearly two metres deep.

The Angels with the Last Plagues

15 Then I saw in the sky another mysterious sight, great and amazing. There were seven angels with seven plagues, which are the last ones, because they are the final expression of God's anger.

2 Then I saw what looked like a sea of glass mixed with fire. I also saw those who had won the victory over the beast and its image and over the one whose name is represented by a number. They were standing by the sea of glass, holding harps that God had given them 3 and singing the song of Moses, the servant of God, and the song of the Lamb:

"Lord God Almighty,
    how great and wonderful are your deeds!
King of the nations, g
    how right and true are your ways!
4 Who will not stand in awe of you, Lord?

g nations; some manuscripts have ages.

14.5: Zeph 3.13   **14.8:** Is 21.9; Jer 51.8; Rev 18.2   **14.10:** Is 51.17; Gen 19.24; Ezek 38.22
14.11: Is 34.10   **14.14:** Dan 7.13   **14.15:** Joel 3.13   **14.20:** Is 63.3; Lam 1.15; Rev 19.15
15.3: Ex 15.1   **15.4:** Jer 10.7; Ps 86.9

Who will refuse to declare your
greatness?
You alone are holy.
All the nations will come
and worship you,
because your just actions are seen by
all."

5 After this I saw the temple in heaven
open, with the Tent of God's presence
in it. 6 The seven angels who had the seven
plagues came out of the temple, dressed
in clean shining linen and with gold belts
tied around their chests. 7 Then one of the
four living creatures gave the seven angels
seven gold bowls full of the anger of God,
who lives for ever and ever. 8 The temple
was filled with smoke from the glory and
power of God, and no one could go into
the temple until the seven plagues brought
by the seven angels had come to an end.

The Bowls of God's Anger

16 Then I heard a loud voice speaking
from the temple to the seven
angels: "Go and pour out the seven bowls
of God's anger on the earth!"

2 The first angel went and poured out
his bowl on the earth. Terrible and painful
sores appeared on those who had the
mark of the beast and on those who had
worshipped its image.

3 Then the second angel poured out his
bowl on the sea. The water became like
the blood of a dead person, and every
living creature in the sea died.

4 Then the third angel poured out his
bowl on the rivers and the springs of
water, and they turned into blood. 5 I heard
the angel in charge of the waters say,
"The judgements you have made are just,
O Holy One, you who are and who were!
6 They poured out the blood of God's
people and of the prophets, and so you
have given them blood to drink. They are
getting what they deserve!" 7 Then I heard
a voice from the altar saying, "Lord God
Almighty! True and just indeed are your
judgements!"

8 Then the fourth angel poured out his
bowl on the sun, and it was allowed to
burn people with its fiery heat. 9 They
were burnt by the fierce heat, and they
cursed the name of God, who has
authority over these plagues. But they

would not turn from their sins and praise
his greatness.

10 Then the fifth angel poured out his
bowl on the throne of the beast. Darkness
fell over the beast's kingdom, and people
bit their tongues because of their pain,
11 and they cursed the God of heaven for
their pains and sores. But they did not
turn from their evil ways.

12 Then the sixth angel poured out his
bowl on the great river Euphrates. The
river dried up, to provide a way for the
kings who come from the east. 13 I
saw three unclean spirits that looked
like frogs. They were coming out of the
mouth of the dragon, the mouth of the
beast, and the mouth of the false prophet.
14 They are the spirits of demons that
perform miracles. These three spirits go
out to all the kings of the world, to bring
them together for the battle on the great
Day of Almighty God.

15 "Listen! I am coming like a thief!
Happy is he who stays awake and guards
his clothes, so that he will not walk around
naked and be ashamed in public!"

16 Then the spirits brought the kings
together in the place that in Hebrew is
called Armageddon.

17 Then the seventh angel poured out
his bowl in the air. A loud voice came
from the throne in the temple, saying, "It
is done!" 18 There were flashes of lightning, rumblings and peals of thunder, and
a terrible earthquake. There has never
been such an earthquake since the
creation of man; this was the worst
earthquake of all! 19 The great city was
split into three parts, and the cities of
all countries were destroyed. God remembered great Babylon and made her drink
the wine from his cup—the wine of his
furious anger. 20 All the islands disappeared, all the mountains vanished.
21 Huge hailstones, each weighing as much
as fifty kilogrammes, fell from the sky
on people, who cursed God on account of
the plague of hail, because it was such
a terrible plague.

The Famous Prostitute

17 Then one of the seven angels who
had the seven bowls came to me
and said, "Come, and I will show you
how the famous prostitute is to be

15.5: Ex 38.21   15.8: Ex 40.34; I Kgs 8.10–11; 2 Chr 5.13–14; Is 6.4   16.2: Ex 9.10
16.4: Ex 7.17–21; Ps 78.44   16.10: Ex 10.21   16.12: Is 11.15
16.15: Mt 24.43–44; Lk 12.39–40; Rev 3.3   16.16: 2 Kgs 23.29; Zech 12.11
16.18: Rev 8.5, 11.13,19   16.19: Is 51.17   16.20: Rev 6.14   16.21: Ex 9.23; Rev 11.19
17.1: Jer 51.13

punished, that great city that is built near many rivers. ²The kings of the earth practised sexual immorality with her, and the people of the world became drunk from drinking the wine of her immorality."

3 The Spirit took control of me, and the angel carried me to a desert. There I saw a woman sitting on a red beast that had names insulting to God written all over it; the beast had seven heads and ten horns. ⁴The woman was dressed in purple and scarlet, and covered with gold ornaments, precious stones, and pearls. In her hand she held a gold cup full of obscene and filthy things, the result of her immorality. ⁵On her forehead was written a name that has a secret meaning: "Great Babylon, the mother of all the prostitutes and perverts in the world." ⁶And I saw that the woman was drunk with the blood of God's people and the blood of those who were killed because they had been loyal to Jesus.

When I saw her, I was completely amazed. ⁷"Why are you amazed?" the angel asked me. "I will tell you the secret meaning of the woman and of the beast that carries her, the beast with seven heads and ten horns. ⁸That beast was once alive, but lives no longer; it is about to come up from the abyss and will go off to be destroyed. The people living on earth whose names have not been written before the creation of the world in the book of the living, will all be amazed as they look at the beast. It was once alive; now it no longer lives, but it will reappear. ⁹"This calls for wisdom and understanding. The seven heads are seven hills, on which the woman sits. They are also seven kings: ¹⁰five of them have fallen, one still rules, and the other one has not yet come; when he comes, he must rule only a little while. ¹¹And the beast that was once alive, but lives no longer, is itself an eighth king who is one of the seven and is going off to be destroyed.

12 "The ten horns you saw are ten kings who have not yet begun to rule, but who will be given authority to rule as kings for one hour with the beast. ¹³These ten all have the same purpose, and they give their power and authority to the beast. ¹⁴They will fight against the Lamb; but the Lamb, together with his called, chosen, and faithful followers, will defeat

them, because he is Lord of lords and King of kings."

15 The angel also said to me, "The waters you saw, on which the prostitute is sitting, are nations, peoples, races, and languages. ¹⁶The ten horns you saw, and the beast, will hate the prostitute; they will take away everything she has and leave her naked; they will eat her flesh and destroy her with fire. ¹⁷For God has placed in their hearts the will to carry out his purpose by acting together and giving the beast their power to rule until God's words come true.

18 "The woman you saw is the great city that rules over the kings of the earth."

The Fall of Babylon

18 After this I saw another angel coming down out of heaven. He had great authority, and his splendour brightened the whole earth. ²He cried out in a loud voice: "She has fallen! Great Babylon has fallen! She is now haunted by demons and unclean spirits; all kinds of filthy and hateful birds live in her. ³For all the nations have drunk her wine—the strong wine of her immoral lust. The kings of the earth practised sexual immorality with her, and the businessmen of the world grew rich from her unrestrained lust."

4 Then I heard another voice from heaven, saying,

"Come out, my people! Come out from her!
   You must not take part in her sins;
   you must not share in her
      punishment!
⁵ For her sins are piled up as high as
      heaven,
   and God remembers her wicked ways.
⁶ Treat her exactly as she has treated you;
   pay her back double for all she has
      done.
Fill her cup with a drink twice as strong
   as the drink she prepared for you.
⁷ Giv her as much suffering and grief
   as the glory and luxury she gave
      herself.
For she keeps telling herself:
'Here I sit, a queen!
   I am no widow,
   I will never know grief!'
⁸ Because of this, in one day she will be
   struck with plagues—

17.2: Is 23.17; Jer 51.7   17.3: Rev 13.1   17.4: Jer 51.7   17.8: Dan 7.7; Rev 11.7; Ps 69.28   17.12: Dan 7.24   18.2: Is 13.21, 21.9; Jer 50.39, 51.8; Rev 14.8   18.3: Is 23.17; Jer 51.7   18.4: Is 48.20; Jer 50.8, 51.6,45   18.5: Gen 18.20-21; Jer 51.9   18.6: Ps 137.8; Jer 50.29   18.7-8: Is 47.7-9

This great and mighty city Babylon! (18.10)

disease, grief, and famine.
And she will be burnt with fire,
because the Lord God, who judges
her, is mighty."
9 The kings of the earth who took part
in her immorality and lust will cry and
weep over the city when they see the
smoke from the flames that consume her.
10 They stand a long way off, because they
are afraid of sharing in her suffering. They
say, "How terrible! How awful! This
great and mighty city Babylon! In just
one hour you have been punished!"
11 The businessmen of the earth also
cry and mourn for her, because no one
buys their goods any longer; 12 no one
buys their gold, silver, precious stones,
and pearls; their goods of linen, purple
cloth, silk, and scarlet cloth; all kinds of
rare woods and all kinds of objects made
of ivory and of expensive wood, of bronze,
iron, and marble; 13 and cinnamon, spice,
incense, myrrh, and frankincense; wine
and oil, flour and wheat, cattle and sheep,
horses and carriages, slaves, and even
human lives. 14 The businessmen say to
her, "All the good things you longed to
own have disappeared, and all your
wealth and glamour are gone, and you
will never find them again!" 15 The

businessmen, who became rich from
doing business in that city, will stand a
long way off, because they are afraid of
sharing in her suffering. They will cry and
mourn, 16 and say, "How terrible! How
awful for the great city! She used to dress
herself in linen, purple, and scarlet, and
cover herself with gold ornaments,
precious stones, and pearls! 17 And in one
hour she has lost all this wealth!"
All the ships' captains and passengers,
the sailors and all others who earn their
living on the sea, stood a long way off,
18 and cried out as they saw the smoke
from the flames that consumed her:
"There never has been another city like
this great city!" 19 They threw dust on
their heads, they cried and mourned,
saying, "How terrible! How awful for the
great city! She is the city where all who
have ships sailing the seas became rich
on her wealth! And in one hour she has
lost everything!"
20 Be glad, heaven, because of her
destruction! Be glad, God's people and
the apostles and prophets! For God has
condemned her for what she did to you!
21 Then a mighty angel picked up a
stone the size of a large millstone and
threw it into the sea, saying, "This is how

18.9–10: Ezek 26.16–17   18.11: Ezek 27.31,36   18.12–13: Ezek 27.12,13,22
18.15: Ezek 27.31,36   18.17: Is 23.14; Ezek 27.26–30   18.18: Ezek 27.32
18.19: Ezek 27.30–34   18.20: Deut 32.43; Jer 51.48   18.21: Jer 51.63–64; Ezek 26.21

the great city Babylon will be violently thrown down and will never be seen again. ²²The music of harps and of human voices, of players of the flute and the trumpet, will never be heard in you again! No workman in any trade will ever be found in you again; and the sound of the millstone will be heard no more! ²³Never again will the light of a lamp be seen in you; no more will the voices of brides and grooms be heard in you. Your businessmen were the most powerful in all the world, and with your false magic you deceived all the peoples of the world!"

24 Babylon was punished because the blood of prophets and of God's people was found in the city; yes, the blood of all those who have been killed on earth.

19 After this I heard what sounded like the roar of a large crowd of people in heaven, saying, "Praise God! Salvation, glory, and power belong to our God! ²True and just are his judgements! He has condemned the prostitute who was corrupting the earth with her immorality. God has punished her because she killed his servants." ³Again they shouted, "Praise God! The smoke from the flames that consume the great city goes up for ever and ever!" ⁴The twenty-four elders and the four living creatures fell down and worshipped God, who was seated on the throne. They said, "Amen! Praise God!"

The Wedding-Feast of the Lamb

5 Then there came from the throne the sound of a voice, saying, "Praise our God, all his servants and all people, both great and small, who have reverence for him!" ⁶Then I heard what sounded like a large crowd, like the sound of a roaring waterfall, like loud peals of thunder. I heard them say, "Praise God! For the Lord, our Almighty God, is King! ⁷Let us rejoice and be glad; let us praise his greatness! For the time has come for the wedding of the Lamb, and his bride has prepared herself for it. ⁸She has been given clean shining linen to wear." (The linen is the good deeds of God's people.)

9 Then the angel said to me, "Write this: Happy are those who have been invited to the wedding-feast of the Lamb."

And the angel added, "These are the true words of God."

10 I fell down at his feet to worship him, but he said to me, "Don't do it! I am a fellow-servant of yours and of your brothers, all those who hold to the truth that Jesus revealed. Worship God!"

For the truth that Jesus revealed is what inspires the prophets.

The Rider on the White Horse

11 Then I saw heaven open, and there was a white horse. Its rider is called Faithful and True; it is with justice that he judges and fights his battles. ¹²His eyes were like a flame of fire, and he wore many crowns on his head. He had a name written on him, but no one except himself knows what it is. ¹³The robe he wore was covered with blood. His name is "The Word of God." ¹⁴The armies of heaven followed him, riding on white horses and dressed in clean white linen. ¹⁵Out of his mouth came a sharp sword, with which he will defeat the nations. He will rule over them with a rod of iron, and he will trample out the wine in the winepress of the furious anger of the Almighty God. ¹⁶On his robe and on his thigh was written the name: "King of kings and Lord of lords."

17 Then I saw an angel standing on the sun. He shouted in a loud voice to all the birds flying in midair: "Come and gather together for God's great feast! ¹⁸Come and eat the flesh of kings, generals, and soldiers, the flesh of horses and their riders, the flesh of all people, slave and free, great and small!"

19 Then I saw the beast and the kings of the earth and their armies gathered to fight against the one who was riding the horse and against his army. ²⁰The beast was taken prisoner, together with the false prophet who had performed miracles in his presence. (It was by those miracles that he had deceived those who had the mark of the beast and those who had worshipped the image of the beast.) The beast and the false prophet were both thrown alive into the lake of fire that burns with sulphur. ²¹Their armies were killed by the sword that comes out of the mouth of the one who was riding the

18.22: Ezek 26.13; Is 24.8   18.22–23: Jer 7.34, 25.10   18.24: Jer 51.49
19.2: Deut 32.43; 2 Kgs 9.7   19.3: Is 34.10   19.5: Ps 115.13
19.6: Ezek 1.24; Ps 93.1, 97.1, 99.1   19.9: Mt 22.2–3   19.11: Ezek 1.1; Ps 96.13; Is 11.4
19.12: Dan 10.6   19.15: Ps 2.9; Is 63.3; Joel 3.13; Rev 14.20   19.17–18: Ezek 39.17–20
19.20: Rev 13.1–18

horse; and all the birds ate all they could of their flesh.

The Thousand Years

20 Then I saw an angel coming down from heaven, holding in his hand the key of the abyss and a heavy chain. ²He seized the dragon, that ancient serpent—that is, the Devil, or Satan—and chained him up for a thousand years. ³The angel threw him into the abyss, locked it, and sealed it, so that he could not deceive the nations any more until the thousand years were over. After that he must be let loose for a little while.

4 Then I saw thrones, and those who sat on them were given the power to judge. I also saw the souls of those who had been executed because they had proclaimed the truth that Jesus revealed and the word of God. They had not worshipped the beast or its image, nor had they received the mark of the beast on their foreheads or their hands. They came to life and ruled as kings with Christ for a thousand years. ⁵(The rest of the dead did not come to life until the thousand years were over.) This is the first raising of the dead. ⁶Happy and greatly blessed are those who are included in this first raising of the dead. The second death has no power over them; they shall be priests of God and of Christ, and they will rule with him for a thousand years.

The Defeat of Satan

7 After the thousand years are over, Satan will be let loose from his prison, ⁸and he will go out to deceive the nations scattered over the whole world, that is, Gog and Magog. Satan will bring them all together for battle, as many as the grains of sand on the sea-shore. ⁹They spread out over the earth and surrounded the camp of God's people and the city that he loves. But fire came down from heaven and destroyed them. ¹⁰Then the Devil, who deceived them, was thrown into the lake of fire and sulphur, where the beast and the false prophet had already been thrown; and they will be tormented day and night for ever and ever.

The Final Judgement

11 Then I saw a great white throne and the one who sits on it. Earth and heaven fled from his presence and were seen no more. ¹²And I saw the dead, great and small alike, standing before the throne. Books were opened, and then another book was opened, the book of the living. The dead were judged according to what they had done, as recorded in the books. ¹³Then the sea gave up its dead. Death and the world of the dead also gave up the dead they held. And all were judged according to what they had done. ¹⁴Then death and the world of the dead were thrown into the lake of fire. (This lake of fire is the second death.) ¹⁵Whoever did not have his name written in the book of the living was thrown into the lake of fire.

The New Heaven and the New Earth

21 Then I saw a new heaven and a new earth. The first heaven and the first earth disappeared, and the sea vanished. ²And I saw the Holy City, the new Jerusalem, coming down out of heaven from God, prepared and ready, like a bride dressed to meet her husband. ³I heard a loud voice speaking from the throne: "Now God's home is with mankind! He will live with them, and they shall be his people. God himself will be with them, and he will be their God. ⁴He will wipe away all tears from their eyes. There will be no more death, no more grief or crying or pain. The old things have disappeared."

5 Then the one who sits on the throne said, "And now I make all things new!" He also said to me, "Write this, because these words are true and can be trusted." ⁶And he said, "It is done! I am the first and the last, the beginning and the end. To anyone who is thirsty I will give the right to drink from the spring of the water of life without paying for it. ⁷Whoever wins the victory will receive this from me: I will be his God, and he will be my son. ⁸But cowards, traitors, perverts, murderers, the immoral, those who practise magic, those who worship idols, and all liars—the place for them is the lake burning with fire and sulphur, which is the second death."

20.2: Gen 3.1   **20.4:** Dan 7.9,22   **20.8:** Ezek 7.2, 38.2,9,15   **20.11–12:** Dan 7.9–10
21.1: Is 65.17, 66.22; 2 Pet 3.13   **21.2:** Is 52.1, 61.10; Rev 3.12
21.3: Ezek 37.27; Lev 26.11,12   **21.4:** Is 25.8, 35.10, 65.19   **21.6:** Is 55.1
21.7: 2 Sam 7.14; Ps 89.26–27

The New Jerusalem

9 One of the seven angels who had the seven bowls full of the seven last plagues came to me and said, "Come, and I will show you the Bride, the wife of the Lamb." [10] The Spirit took control of me, and the angel carried me to the top of a very high mountain. He showed me Jerusalem, the Holy City, coming down out of heaven from God [11] and shining with the glory of God. The city shone like a precious stone, like a jasper, clear as crystal. [12] It had a great, high wall with twelve gates and with twelve angels in charge of the gates. On the gates were written the names of the twelve tribes of the people of Israel. [13] There were three gates on each side: three on the east, three on the south, three on the north, and three on the west. [14] The city's wall was built on twelve foundation-stones, on which were written the names of the twelve apostles of the Lamb. [15] The angel who spoke to me had a gold measuring-rod to measure the city, its gates, and its wall. [16] The city was perfectly square, as wide as it was long. The angel measured the city with his measuring-rod: it was 2,400 kilometres long and was as wide and as high as it was long. [17] The angel also measured the wall, and it was sixty metres high,[h] according to the standard unit of measure which he was using.[i] [18] The wall was made of jasper, and the city itself was made of pure gold, as clear as glass. [19] The foundation-stones of the city wall were adorned with all kinds of precious stones. The first foundation-stone was jasper, the second sapphire, the third agate, the fourth emerald, [20] the fifth onyx, the sixth carnelian, the seventh yellow quartz, the eighth beryl, the ninth topaz, the tenth chalcedony, the eleventh turquoise, the twelfth amethyst. [21] The twelve gates were twelve pearls; each gate was made from a single pearl. The street of the city was of pure gold, transparent as glass.

22 I did not see a temple in the city, because its temple is the Lord God Almighty and the Lamb. [23] The city has no need of the sun or the moon to shine on it, because the glory of God shines on it, and the Lamb is its lamp. [24] The peoples of the world will walk by its light, and the kings of the earth will bring their wealth into it. [25] The gates of the city will stand open all day; they will never be closed, because there will be no night there. [26] The greatness and the wealth of the nations will be brought into the city. [27] But nothing that is impure will enter the city, nor anyone who does shameful things or tells lies. Only those whose names are written in the Lamb's book of the living will enter the city.

22 The angel also showed me the river of the water of life, sparkling like crystal, and coming from the throne of God and of the Lamb [2] and flowing down the middle of the city's street. On each side of the river was the tree of life, which bears fruit twelve times a year, once each month; and its leaves are for the healing of the nations. [3] Nothing that is under God's curse will be found in the city.

The throne of God and of the Lamb will be in the city, and his servants will worship him. [4] They will see his face, and his name will be written on their foreheads. [5] There shall be no more night, and they will not need lamps or sunlight, because the Lord God will be their light, and they will rule as kings for ever and ever.

The Coming of Jesus

6 Then the angel said to me, "These words are true and can be trusted. And the Lord God, who gives his Spirit to the prophets, has sent his angel to show his servants what must happen very soon."

7 "Listen!" says Jesus. "I am coming soon! Happy are those who obey the prophetic words in this book!"

8 I, John, have heard and seen all these things. And when I finished hearing and seeing them, I fell down at the feet of the angel who had shown me these things, and I was about to worship him. [9] But he said to me, "Don't do it! I am a fellow-servant of yours and of your brothers the prophets and of all those who obey the words in this book. Worship God!" [10] And he said to me, "Do not keep the prophetic words of this book a secret, because the time is near when all this will happen. [11] Whoever is evil must go on doing evil, and whoever is filthy must go on being filthy; whoever is good must go on doing

---

[h] high; or thick.
[i] In verses 16 and 17 the Greek text speaks of '12,000 furlongs' and '144 cubits' which may have symbolic significance.

21.10: Ezek 40.2   **21.12–13:** Ezek 48.30–35   **21.15:** Ezek 40.3   **21.18–21:** Is 54.11–12
21.23: Is 60.19–20   **21.24:** Is 60.3   **21.25–26:** Is 60.11   **21.27:** Is 52.1; Ezek 44.9
22.1: Ezek 47.1; Zech 14.8   **22.2:** Gen 2.9; Ezek 47.12   **22.3:** Zech 14.11
22.5: Is 60.19; Dan 7.18   **22.11:** Dan 12.10

good, and whoever is holy must go on being holy."

12 "Listen!" says Jesus. "I am coming soon! I will bring my rewards with me, to give to each one according to what he has done. [13] I am the first and the last, the beginning and the end."

14 Happy are those who wash their robes clean and so have the right to eat the fruit from the tree of life and to go through the gates into the city. [15] But outside the city are the perverts and those who practise magic, the immoral and the murderers, those who worship idols and those who are liars both in words and deeds.

16 "I, Jesus, have sent my angel to announce these things to you in the churches. I am descended from the family of David; I am the bright morning star."

17 The Spirit and the Bride say, "Come!"

Everyone who hears this must also say, "Come!"

Come, whoever is thirsty; accept the water of life as a gift, whoever wants it.

Conclusion

18 I, John, solemnly warn everyone who hears the prophetic words of this book: if anyone adds anything to them, God will add to his punishment the plagues described in this book. [19] And if anyone takes anything away from the prophetic words of this book, God will take away from him his share of the fruit of the tree of life and of the Holy City, which are described in this book.

20 He who gives his testimony to all this says, "Yes indeed! I am coming soon!"

So be it. Come, Lord Jesus!

21 May the grace of the Lord Jesus be with everyone.[j]

[j] everyone; *some manuscripts have* God's people; *others have* all God's people.
22.12: Is 40.10, 62.11; Ps 28.4; Jer 17.10　　**22.13:** Rev 1.8,17, 2.8; Is 44.6, 48.12
22.14: Gen 2.9, 3.22　　**22.16:** Is 11.1,10　　**22.17:** Is 55.1　　**22.18-19:** Deut 4.2, 12.32

Word List

A

Abib The first month of the Hebrew calendar. It runs from about mid-March to about mid-April. This month is also called Nisan.

Abyss The place in the depths of the earth where, according to ancient Jewish teaching, the demons were imprisoned until their final punishment.

Acacia A flowering tree with hard and durable wood.

Adar The twelfth month of the Hebrew calendar. It runs from about mid-February to about mid-March.

Agate A semi-precious stone of different colours, but usually white and brown.

Alabaster A soft stone, usually of light creamy colour, from which vases and jars were made.

Aloes A sweet-smelling liquid, produced from a plant. It was used as medicine and as a perfume.

Amen A Hebrew word which means "it is so" or "may it be so". It can also be translated "certainly", "truly", or "surely". In Revelation 3.14 it is used as a name for Christ.

Amethyst A semi-precious stone, usually purple or violet in colour.

Anoint To pour or rub olive-oil on someone in order to honour him or to appoint him to some special work. The Israelite kings were anointed when they took office, and so the king could be called "the anointed one". Christ, the Greek word for "The Anointed One", is the title of the one whom God chose and appointed as Saviour and Lord.

Apostle Usually one of the group of twelve men whom Jesus chose to be his special followers and helpers. It is also used in the New Testament to refer to Paul and other Christian workers. The word means "messenger".

Areopagus A hill in Athens where the city council used to meet. For this reason the council itself was called Areopagus, even after it no longer met on the hill.

Artemis The Greek name of an ancient goddess of fertility, worshipped especially in Asia Minor.

Asherah A goddess of fertility worshipped by the Canaanites; her male counterpart was Baal. After the Hebrews invaded Canaan, many of them began worshipping these two gods.

Astarte A goddess of fertility and war who was widely worshipped in the ancient Near East.

Atonement, Day of The most important of Israel's holy days, when the High Priest would offer sacrifice for the sins of the people of Israel (Leviticus 16). It was held on the 10th day of the seventh month of the Hebrew calendar (about October 1st). The Jewish name for this day is Yom Kippur.

B

Baal The god of fertility worshipped by the Canaanites; his female counterpart was Asherah. After the Hebrews invaded Canaan, many of them began worshipping these two gods.

Baal-of-the-Covenant A name by which the god Baal was known by the people of Shechem.

Balsam A tree from which sweet-smelling resin was obtained; the resin was used for perfume and medicine.

Barley A cultivated grain similar to wheat, grown as a food crop.

Bear: Great Bear and **Little Bear** Two groups of stars which can be seen north of the equator in the northern sky. The star at the end of the "tail" of the Little Bear is Polaris, the Pole Star.

Beelzebul A New Testament name given to the Devil as the chief of the evil spirits.

Beryl A semi-precious stone, usually green or bluish green in colour.

Breastplate Part of a soldier's armour, made of leather or metal; it covered the chest and sometimes the back, to protect him against arrows and the blows of a sword.

Bul The eighth month of the Hebrew calendar. It runs from about mid-October to about mid-November.

Burnt-offering A kind of sacrifice in which all the parts of the animal were completely burnt on the altar; in other sacrifices only certain parts of the animal were burnt.

C

Calamus A sweet-smelling plant, like a reed.

Capital The top part of a pillar holding up a roof.

Carnelian A semi-precious stone, usually red in colour.

Cassia A spice made from the bark of a tree; it is very like cinnamon.

Chalcedony A semi-precious stone, usually milky or grey in colour.

Christ At first it was a title, the Greek word for the Hebrew "Messiah". It means "the anointed one". Jesus was called the Christ because he was the one whom God chose and sent as Saviour and Lord.

Circumcise To cut off the foreskin of the penis. As a sign of God's covenant with his people Israelite boys were circumcised eight days after they were born (Genesis 17.9-14).

Concubine A servant-woman who, although not a wife, had sexual relations with her master. She had important legal rights, and her master was referred to as her husband.

Coral A brightly-coloured stony substance found in the sea; it was used as jewellery.

Council The highest religious court of the Jews. It was made up of seventy leaders of the Jewish people. Its president was the High Priest.

Covenant An agreement, either between people, or between God and a person or a group of people. God made a covenant with Noah (Genesis 9.8-17) and with Abraham (Genesis 17.1-8), but in the Old Testament the term usually refers to the covenant made between God and the people of Israel at the time of Moses (Exodus 24.4-8).

Covenant Box A wooden chest covered with gold. The two stone tablets with the Ten Commandments written on them were kept in it. It is often called "the Ark of the Covenant".

Cumin A small plant whose seeds are crushed and used for seasoning foods.

Cymbals A pair of thin pieces of metal held in the hands and struck together to make a loud sound in time with the music.

D

David's City In the Old Testament it usually refers to the part of Jerusalem which was captured from the Jebusites by King David. In the New Testament Bethlehem, David's boyhood home where Jesus was born, is referred to as David's town.

Dedication, Festival of A Jewish festival in which people remembered how Judas Maccabeus rededicated the altar in the Temple in 165 B.C. The festival began on the 25th day of the month Kislev (about December 10th) and lasted eight days. The Jewish name for this festival is Hanukkah.

Defile To make a person unfit to worship God. Some foods and actions were forbidden by the Law of Moses. If people broke these laws they were not allowed into the place where they worshipped God. Such people could not take part in worship until they had gone through certain rituals.

Demon An evil spirit with the power to harm people; it was regarded as a messenger and servant of the Devil.

Dill A small plant whose stems, leaves, and seeds are used for seasoning food.

Disciple A person who follows and learns from someone else. In the New Testament the word is used of the followers of John the Baptist and especially of the followers of Jesus, particularly the twelve apostles.

Divination The attempt to discover a message from God or the gods by examining such things as marked stones or the liver of a sacrificed animal.

Dragon A beast in old legends, thought to be like a huge lizard. It is also called a serpent and appears as a picture of the Devil (Revelation 12.3—13.4; 20.2-3).

E

Elders In the Old Testament this is a name given to certain respected leaders of a tribe, nation, or city. In the New Testament three different groups are called elders: (1) in the Gospels the elders are important Jewish religious leaders, some of whom were members of their highest Council; (2) in Acts 11-21 and the Letters, the elders are Christian church officers who were responsible for the work of the church; (3) in Revelation the twenty-four elders are part of God's court in heaven, perhaps as representatives of God's people.

Elul The sixth month of the Hebrew calendar. It runs from about mid-August to about mid-September.

Ephod A Hebrew word. Its meaning is not clear in a number of places. It usually refers to the piece of cloth worn over the shoulders by the High Priest which had the Urim and Thummim attached to it. In some places, however, it refers to something the people worshipped. In some other passages it seems to refer to an object used to foretell future events.

Epicureans Those who followed the teaching of Epicurus (died 270 B.C.), a Greek philosopher who taught that happiness is the highest good in life.

Epileptic A person who suffers from a nervous disease which causes fits and fainting.

Ethanim The seventh month of the Hebrew calendar. It runs from about mid-September to about mid-October; it was later called Tishri.

Eunuch A man who has had an operation which prevents him from having normal sexual relations. Eunuchs were often important officials in the courts of ancient kings, and the word may have come to be used of such officials, even if they had not had the operation.

F

Fast To go without food for a while as a religious duty.

Feldspar A colourful, rather hard rock, often glassy in appearance.

Fellowship-offerings A sacrifice offered to restore or keep a right relationship with God. Only a part of the animal was burnt on the altar; the rest was eaten by the worshippers or the priests.

Flax A small cultivated plant; the fibres of its stem are spun into thread used in making linen cloth.

Frankincense A valuable substance made from the sap of a certain tree, probably brought from Arabia. It was burnt to give a pleasant smell.

G

Garnet A semi-precious stone, usually red in colour.

Gazelle A kind of deer, known for its beauty and gracefulness.

Gentile A person who is not a Jew.

H

Hades The Greek name used in the New Testament to refer to the world of the dead.

Harrow A metal frame used to break up the ground and level it after it has been ploughed.

Harvest Festival The Israelite festival celebrating the wheat harvest, held in the latter part of May, fifty days after Passover. The Jewish name for this festival is Shavuoth (the Feast of Weeks). It has also been called Pentecost.

Hermes The name of a Greek god who served as messenger of the gods.

Herod's Party A political party in New Testament times made up of Jews who wanted to be ruled by one of the family of Herod the Great rather than by the Roman governor.

High Priest The chief Jewish priest and president of their supreme Council. Once a year (on the Day of Atonement) he would enter the Most Holy Place in the Temple and offer a sacrifice for himself and for the sins of the people of Israel.

Hyssop A small bushy plant used in religious ceremonies to sprinkle liquids.

I

Incense Material which is burnt in order to produce a pleasant smell. The Israelites used it in their worship.

J

Jackal A small wild animal like a fox.

Jasper A semi-precious stone of various colours. The jasper mentioned in the Bible was probably green, or else clear.

Javelin A short, light spear used by soldiers in ancient times.

K

Kislev The ninth month of the Hebrew calendar. It runs from about mid-November to about mid-December.

L

Law The name which the Jews applied to the first five books of the Old Testament, also called "The Books of Moses". Sometimes, however, the name is used in a more general way for the entire Old Testament.

Leviathan An animal in old legends that lived in water. Scholars think it was the crocodile. It is used to represent the chaos that existed before God created the world (Isaiah 27.1; Psalm 74.14).

Levite (1) A member of the tribe of Levi; (2) a man who helped the priest to perform religious duties.

Levitical Priest A Hebrew priest descended from the tribe of Levi. All priests were supposed to be members of the tribe of Levi, but in later times not all members of the tribe of Levi were priests.

Living Creatures (also called "winged creatures"). Symbols of God's majesty and his presence. For a description of them, see Exodus 25.18-20; Ezekiel 1.5-13; 10; Revelation 4.6-9. Older translations call them cherubim.

LORD In this translation "LORD" stands for the Hebrew name **Yahweh** (some translations use **Jehovah**). Sometimes it refers to the name itself, sometimes to a pronoun standing for the name.

Lyre A kind of harp.

M

Mandrake A small plant; it was believed that eating its root or fruit would help a woman to have children.

Manna A food eaten by the Israelites during their travels in the wilderness. It was white and flaky, and looked like small seeds (Exodus 16.14-21; Numbers 11.7-9).

Medium A person who believes that he or she can communicate with the dead.

Messiah A Hebrew title (meaning "the anointed one") given to the Saviour whose coming was promised by the Hebrew prophets; the Greek word "the Christ" has the same meaning.

Mildew A fungus that appears on various objects, especially in damp weather.

Millet A cultivated grain that is grown as a food crop.

Molech One of the gods of the ancient people of Canaan.

Most Holy Place The innermost room of the Tent of the LORD's presence or the Temple. The Covenant Box was kept there. Only the High Priest could enter the Most Holy Place, and he did so only once a year, on the Day of Atonement.

Mustard A large plant which grows from a very small seed. The seeds are ground into powder and used as spice on food.

Myrrh A sweet-smelling resin that was very valuable. It served as a medicine (Mark 15.23) and was used by the Jews in preparing bodies for burial (John 19.39).

Myrtle A kind of evergreen shrub or tree.

N

Nard An expensive perfume made from a plant.

Nazarene Someone from the town of Nazareth. The name was used as a title for Jesus and also as a name for the early Christians (Acts 24.5).

Nazirite A person who took a special vow to serve God. Such a person was not to drink beer or wine, cut his hair, or touch a dead body (Numbers 6.1-21). The vow could be taken for a certain period of time, but some persons were dedicated to God as Nazirites from their birth.

New Moon Festival A religious ceremony held by the Israelites on the day of each new moon.

New Year Festival The Jewish name for this festival is "Rosh Hashanah".

Nisan The first month of the Hebrew calendar. It runs from about mid-March to about mid-April. The month is also called Abib.

O

Onyx A semi-precious stone of various colours.

Orion A group of bright stars that can be seen during winter evenings.

Outcasts In other Bibles this word is translated "sinners". In the Gospels it refers to Jews who were not allowed to attend synagogue worship because they had broken rules about foods that should not be eaten, and about being friendly with people who were not Jews. Such outcasts were looked down on by many of their fellow-Jews, and Jesus was criticized for being friendly with them (Mark 2.15-17; Luke 7.34; 15.1-2).

P

Parable A story which teaches spiritual truth. It was often used by Jesus.

Paradise A name for heaven (Luke 23.43; 2 Corinthians 12.3).

Paralytic Someone who suffers from a disease that prevents him from moving part or all of his body.

Passover The Israelite festival, on the 14th day of the month Nisan (about April 1st), which celebrated the freeing of the Hebrews from their captivity in

Egypt. The Angel of Death killed the first-born in the Egyptian homes but passed over the Hebrew homes (Exodus 12.23-27). The Jewish name for this festival is Pesach.

Pentecost, Day of The Greek name for the Israelite festival of wheat harvest (see Harvest Festival). The name Pentecost (meaning "fiftieth") comes from the fact that the feast was held fifty days after Passover.

Pervert One who commits unnatural sexual acts.

Pharisees A Jewish religious party during the time of Jesus. They were strict in obeying the Law of Moses and other regulations which had been added to it through the centuries.

Pistachio nut A small greenish nut.

Pleiades A small group of stars visible during winter evenings.

Pomegranate A reddish fruit about the size of a large apple. It has a hard rind and is full of tasty seeds.

Preparation, Day of The sixth day of the week (Friday), on which the Jews got ready to keep the Sabbath (Saturday).

Prophet A person who proclaims a message from God. The word usually refers to certain men in the Old Testament, but the New Testament speaks of prophets in the early church. John the Baptist is also called a prophet.

Purim The Jewish religious holiday held on the 14th day of the month Adar (about March 1st), celebrating the deliverance of the Jews from Haman by Esther and Mordecai. The story is told in the book of Esther.

Q

Quartz A semi-precious stone of various colours, but usually clear.

R

Rabbi A Hebrew word which means "my teacher".

Red Sea (in Hebrew literally "Sea of Reeds"). Referred at first to (1) a series of lakes and marshes between the head of the Gulf of Suez and the Mediterranean, where the events described in Exodus 13 are thought to have taken place. It was also used for (2) the Gulf of Suez, and (3) the Gulf of Aqaba.

Rephan The name of an ancient god who was worshipped as the ruler of the planet Saturn.

Resin A fragrant, gummy substance produced from the sap of certain trees and shrubs.

Restoration, Year of The year, coming every fifty years, when the ancient Israelites returned to the original owner any property they were holding. They also freed their Israelite slaves, and did not cultivate their fields.

S

Sabbath The seventh day of the week (from sunset on Friday to sunset on Saturday), a holy day on which no work was permitted.

Sackcloth A coarse cloth made of goats' hair, which was worn as a sign of mourning or distress.

Sadducees A small Jewish religious party in New Testament times. Most of them were priests. They based their beliefs mainly on the first five books of the Old Testament. They had several beliefs and practices which were different from those of the larger party of the Pharisees.

Samaritan A name used to refer to a native of Samaria, the region between Judaea and Galilee. Because of differences in politics, race, customs, and religion (including especially the central place of worship), there was much bad feeling between the Jews and the Samaritans.

Sanctuary A building dedicated to the worship of God. Sometimes the word refers to the central place of worship and not to the whole building.

Sapphire A very valuable stone, usually blue in colour.

Sceptre A short rod held by kings as a sign of their authority.

Scorpion A small creature which has eight legs and a long tail with a poisonous sting. It can inflict a very painful, and sometimes fatal, wound.

Scribe A person who wrote documents for others or copied written material. Some scribes were employed by ancient kings to prepare official documents, and so became important officials.

Scriptures In the New Testament the word refers to the Hebrew sacred writings, known to Christians as the Old Testament. Various names are used: the Law (or the Law of Moses) and the prophets (Matthew 5.17; 7.12; Luke 2.22; 24.44; Acts 13.15; 28.23); the Holy Scriptures (Romans 1.2; 2 Timothy 3.15); the old covenant (2 Corinthians

3.14). The singular "scripture" refers to a single passage of the Old Testament.

Serpent A name given to the dragon, which appears in the New Testament as a picture of the Devil (Revelation 12.3-17; 20.2-3).

Seventh Year The year, coming every seventh year, when the Israelites did not cultivate their fields and when debts were cancelled.

Shebat The eleventh month of the Hebrew calendar. It runs from about mid-January to about mid-February.

Shelters, Festival of A happy festival celebrated by the Israelites in the autumn after the harvest was complete. In order to help them remember the years when their ancestors wandered through the wilderness, the Israelites built rough shelters to live in during the festival. The Jewish name for this festival is Sukkoth. It is also called the Feast of Tabernacles or the Feast of Booths.

Sickle A tool consisting of a curved metal blade and a wooden handle, used for cutting wheat and other crops.

Sivan The third month of the Hebrew calendar. It runs from about mid-May to about mid-June.

Snuffer An instrument used to trim the oil lamps used in the Tent of the LORD'S presence or the Temple.

Sorcerer A person who works magic for evil purposes.

Stoics Those who followed the teachings of the Greek philosopher Zeno (died 265 B.C.), who taught that happiness is to be found in being free from pleasure and pain.

Sulphur In the Bible this refers to a chemical which burns with great heat and produces an unpleasant smell.

T

Tambourine A small drum with pieces of metal in the rim, held in the hand and shaken. In biblical times it was generally used by women.

Tassel A group of threads or cords, fastened together at one end and loose at the other. The Israelites were ordered to wear these on their clothes (Numbers 15.37-41).

Teachers of the Law Men who in New Testament times taught and explained the teachings of the Old Testament, especially the first five books.

Tebeth The tenth month of the Hebrew calendar. It runs from about mid-December to about mid-January.

Tenant In Bible times, a man who grows crops on land owned by someone else, and hands over a part of the harvest to the owner to pay for the use of his land.

Tent of the LORD'S Presence The large tent described in detail in Exodus 26, where the Israelites worshipped God until Solomon built the Temple. It is also called the Tabernacle or Tent of Meeting.

Tithe A tenth part of a person's crops or income, given to God.

Topaz A semi-precious stone, usually yellow in colour.

Turban A kind of hat made of cloth wrapped round the head.

Turquoise A semi-precious stone, blue or bluish green in colour.

U

Unleavened Bread, Festival of The Israelite festival, lasting seven days after Passover; it also celebrated the deliverance of the ancient Hebrews from Egypt. The name came from the practice of not using leaven (yeast) in making bread during that week (Exodus 12.14-20). It was held from the 15th to the 22nd day of the month Nisan (about the first week of April).

Urim and Thummim Two small objects used by Israelite priests to find out God's will.

V

Vow A strong statement or promise, often made by calling upon God to punish the speaker if the statement should prove to be untrue or if the promise was not kept.

W

Winged Creatures See "Living Creatures".

Winnowing Shovel A tool like a shovel or a large fork, used to separate the grains from the husks.

Wreath Flowers or leaves arranged in a circle, to be placed on a person's head. In ancient times a wreath of leaves was the prize given to winners in athletic games.

Y

Yeast A substance, also called leaven, which is added to dough made from flour of wheat or barley to make it rise before being baked into bread.

Yoke A heavy bar of wood which is fitted over the necks of two oxen to make it possible for them to pull a plough or a cart. The word is used to describe the rules for living that a teacher passes on to his pupils.

Z

Zeus The name of the supreme god of the Greeks.

Zion Originally a name for "David's City", the Jebusite stronghold captured by King David's men. The word "Zion" was later used to refer to the hill on which the Temple stood.

Ziv The second month of the Hebrew calendar. It runs from about mid-April to about mid-May.

Index

The numbers in heavy type are the page numbers. The verses containing the
reference are given after the page numbers.

[OT] Old Testament   [D/A] Deuterocanonical Books/Apocrypha
[NT] New Testament

A

Aaron [OT] **63** Ex 4.14; **63** Ex 5.1; **78** Ex
17.12,28,29,32; **143** Num 12; **149** Num 17;
152 Num 20
   [D/A] **101** Sir 45.6-22; **186** 1 Esd 1.13;
202 2 Esd 1.3
   [NT] **159** Acts 7.40; **275** Heb 5.4; **276**
Heb 7.11; **277** Heb 9.4

Abel [OT] **7** Gen 4.2-9,25
   [NT] **35** Mt 23.35; **95** Lk 11.51; **280** Heb
11.4; **282** Heb 12.24

Abraham, Abram [OT] born **15** Gen 11.26;
married Sarai **15** Gen 11.29; migrated from Ur
to Haran **15** Gen 11.31; called by God **16** Gen
12.1-5; went to Egypt **16** Gen 12.10-20;
separated from Lot **16** Gen 13.7-11; rescued
Lot **17** Gen 14.13-16; God's covenant with **18**
Gen 15.18; **19** Gen 17.1-22; name changed
from Abram to Abraham **19** Gen 17.5;
entertained angels **19** Gen 18.1-21; interceded
for Sodom **20** Gen 18.22-23; banished Hagar
and Ishmael **23** Gen 21.9-21; willing to offer
Isaac **24** Gen 22.1-14; buried Sarah in
Machpelah **25** Gen 23; married Keturah **28**
Gen 25.1; death and burial **28** Gen 25.8-9
   [D/A] **101** Sir 44.19-21; **203** 2 Esd 1.39;
205 2 Esd 3.13-15
   [NT] **5** Mt 3.9; **75** Lk 1.73; **102** Lk
16.22-30; **129** Jn 8.33-58; **193** Rom 4.1-22;
233 Gal 3.6-29; **280** Heb 11.8-11,17; **286**
Jas 2.21,23

Absalom [OT] **303** 2 Sam 3.3; **313** 2 Sam
13.21—18.33

Achaia [NT] **175** Acts 18.12,27; **176** Acts 19.21;
204 Rom 15.26; **221** 1 Cor 16.15; **222** 2 Cor
1.1; **227** 2 Cor 9.2; **254** 1 Thes 1.7-8

Adam [OT] **7** Gen 3.20-21; **7** Gen 4.1,25; **8** Gen
5.1-5
   [D/A] **9** Tob 8.6; **89** Sir 33.10; **95** Sir
40.1; **105** Sir 49.16; **205** 2 Esd 3.5-7,21; **212**
2 Esd 6.54-56; **214** 2 Esd 7.70; **215** 2 Esd
7.116-118
   [NT] **194** Rom 5.12-21; **219** 1 Cor
15.22,45-49; **261** 1 Tim 2.13,14

Agabus [NT] **165** Acts 11.28; **178** Acts 21.10

Agrippa [NT]
   (a) Herod Agrippa I **165** Acts 12.1-4,6,11,
19-23

(b) Herod Agrippa II **183** Acts 25.13—26.2;
185 Acts 26.19,27-32

Ahab [OT] **356** 1 Kgs 16.28-33; **358** 1 Kgs
18.1—19.1; **361** 1 Kgs 20.2—22.40

Ahasuerus *see* Xerxes

Alexander [D/A]
   (a) the Great, **124** 1 Macc 1.1-9
   (b) Epiphanes (Balas), **143** 1 Macc
10.1-23,47-66

Amalek, Amalekite [OT] **78** Ex 17.8-16; **240**
Judg 6.3; **242** Judg 7.12; **281** 1 Sam 15.2-33;
298 1 Sam 30.1-18; **300** 2 Sam 1.1-13

Ammon, Ammonite [OT] **22** Gen 19.38; **173**
Deut 2.37; **246** Judg 10.7—12.3; **309** 2 Sam
10.1—11.1 (**421** 1 Chr 19.1—20.3); **312**
2 Sam 12.26-31; **453** 2 Chr 26.8; **454** 2 Chr
27.5; **782** Jer 49.1-6; **820** Ezek 21.28-32;
824 Ezek 25.1-7,10
   [D/A] **19** Jdt 5.2,5

Amorite [OT] **144** Num 13.29; **155** Num 21.13;
176 Deut 4.47; **217** Josh 10.5-10; **235** Judg
1.34-35; **247** Judg 11.19-23

Ananias [NT]
   (a) Ananias and Sapphira **115** Acts 5.1-6
   (b) Ananias of Damascus **161** Acts 9.10-17;
180 Acts 22.12-16
   (c) High Priest **180** Acts 23.2; **182** Acts 24.1

Andrew [NT] **7** Mt 4.18; **45** Mk 1.16; **64** Mk
13.3; **119** Jn 1.40,44; **125** Jn 6.8; **135** Jn
12.22

Angels
   (a) messengers and agents of God [OT] **20**
Gen 19.1,15; **23** Gen 21.17; **32** Gen 28.12;
55 Gen 48.16; **157** Num 22.22-35; **360**
1 Kgs 19.5-7; **422** 1 Chr 21.12-30; **595** Ps
103.20; **919** Zech 1.9-19; **919** Zech 3.1-6;
920 Zech 4.1-5
   [D/A] **5** Tob 3.17; **205** 2 Esd 2.44; **206**
2 Esd 4.1; **209** 2 Esd 5.15; **212** 2 Esd 7.1
   [NT] **4** Mt 1.20-24; **7** Mt 4.11; **20** Mt
13.39,41,49; **24** Mt 16.27; **36** Mt 24.31; **38**
Mt 25.31; **43** Mt 28.2-7; **74** Lk
1.11-19,26-38; **76** Lk 2.9-21; **120** Jn 1.51;
156 Acts 5.19; **160** Acts 8.26; **163** Acts
10.3-8; **165** Acts 12.7-11,15; **186** Acts
27.23; **257** 2 Thes 1.7; **272** Heb 1.4-7; **306**
Rev 1.1; **322** Rev 22.6,8,16
   (b) in heaven [D/A] **217** 2 Esd 8.21; **231**
2 Esd 16.66

[NT] **33** Mt 22.30; **96** Lk 12.8–9; **100** Lk 15.10; **108** Lk 20.36; **251** Col 2.18; **262** 1 Tim 3.16; **263** 1 Tim 5.21; **309** Rev 3.5; **310** Rev 5.11; **311** Rev 7.11; **312** Rev 8.2—11.15; **316** Rev 14.6–9; **316** Rev 15.1—16.17; **317** Rev 17.1; **318** Rev 18.1,21; **320** Rev 19.9,17; **322** Rev 21.9,12
(c) the angel of the Lord [OT] **18** Gen 16.7–11,13; **19** Gen 18.2–4,13,14,33; **24** Gen 22.11,12,15,16; **61** Ex 3.2; **235** Judg 2.1–4; **240** Judg 6.11–22; **248** Judg 13.3–21
(d) guardian angels [OT] **554** Ps 34.7; **555** Ps 35.5–6; **589** Ps 91.11; **726** Is 63.9; **857** Dan 3.28; **861** Dan 6.22
　　[D/A] **6** Tob 5.16,21
　　[NT] **26** Mt 18.10
(e) guiding angels [OT] **25** Gen 24.7; **73** Ex 14.19; **85** Ex 23.20–21,23; **153** Num 20.16; **235** Judg 2.1–4
　　[D/A] **6** Tob 5.4–15
(f) destroying angels [OT] **330** 2 Sam 24.16–17; **392** 2 Kgs 19.35; **422** 1 Chr 21.12–30; **461** 2 Chr 32.21; **582** Ps 78.49; **698** Is 37.36
　　[NT] **166** Acts 12.23
(g) devil and his angels [NT] **38** Mt 25.41; **228** 2 Cor 11.14; **305** Jude 6; **314** Rev 12.7–9
(h) names: Apollyon [NT] **313** Rev 9.11; Gabriel [OT] **864** Dan 8.16; **865** Dan 9.21; [NT] **74** Lk 1.11–38; Jeremiel [D/A] **207** 2 Esd 4.36; Michael [OT] **866** Dan 10.13; **868** Dan 12.1; [NT] **305** Jude 9; **314** Rev 12.7–9; Raphael [D/A] **5** Tob 3.17; **6** Tob 5.4–16; **13** Tob 12.15; Uriel [D/A] **206** 2 Esd 4.1; **209** 2 Esd 5.20; **220** 2 Esd 10.28
Anger, punishment of God [OT] **93** Ex 32.11–14; **148** Num 16.43–46; **160** Num 25.10–11; **394** 2 Kgs 22.11–17; **913** Zeph 1.15,18
　　[D/A] **47** Wis 5.20; **56** Wis 16.5; **65** Sir 5.6–7; **73** Sir 16.11; **107** Bar 1.3; **110** Bar 4.9–14; **127** 1 Macc 1.64; **164** 2 Macc 5.20; **168** 2 Macc 8.5; **199** 1 Esd 9.13; **211** 2 Esd 6.23; **228** 2 Esd 15.22–23
　　[NT] **5** Mt 3.7; **79** Lk 3.7; **109** Lk 21.23; **122** Jn 3.36; **190** Rom 1.18; **191** Rom 2.5,8; **194** Rom 5.9; **198** Rom 9.22; **201** Rom 13.4–5; **240** Eph 2.3; **242** Eph 5.6; **252** Col 3.6; **254** 1 Thes 2.16; **311** Rev 6.17; **316** Rev 14.10,19; **316** Rev 15.1,7
Anna [D/A] **2** Tob 1.9; **3** Tob 2.1,11; **10** Tob 10.1–7; **11** Tob 11.5–6,9
　　[NT] **77** Lk 2.36
Annas [NT] **79** Lk 3.2; **141** Jn 18.13,24; **154** Acts 4.6
Antioch
(a) in Syria [D/A] **131** 1 Macc 3.37; **132** 1 Macc 4.35; [NT] **157** Acts 6.5; **165** Acts 11.19–30; **166** Acts 13.1–3; **169** Acts 14.26—15.2; **171** Acts 15.35; **233** Gal 2.11
(b) in Pisidia [NT] **167** Acts 13.14–50; **169** Acts 14.19,21

Antiochus [D/A]
(a) IV Epiphanes **125** 1 Macc 1.10–64; **130** 1 Macc 3.27–32; **135** 1 Macc 6.1–17; **157** 2 Macc 1.11–17; **161** 2 Macc 4.7—5.27; **169** 2 Macc 9.1–29; **171** 2 Macc 10.9
(b) V Eupator **136** 1 Macc 6.17–62; **171** 2 Macc 10.9–13
(c) VI Dionysus **148** 1 Macc 11.54–58; **150** 1 Macc 12.39; **151** 1 Macc 13.31
(d) VII Sidetes **154** 1 Macc 15.1–41
Apollos [NT] **175** Acts 18.24; **175** Acts 19.1; **206** 1 Cor 1.12; **207** 1 Cor 3.4–6,22; **208** 1 Cor 4.6; **221** 1 Cor 16.12
Apostle [NT] **14** Mt 10.2–4; **49** Mk 3.14–19; **53** Mk 6.7,30; **84** Lk 6.13–16; **149** Acts 1.2,13,26; **232** Gal 1.11; **305** Jude 17; **322** Rev 21.14
Aquila [NT] **174** Acts 18.2,18,26; **204** Rom 16.3; **221** 1 Cor 16.19; **267** 2 Tim 4.19
Arabia, Arabian [OT] **347** 1 Kgs 10.15; **444** 2 Chr 17.11; **481** Neh 2.19; **758** Jer 25.24; **827** Ezek 27.21
　　[D/A] **18** Jdt 2.25; **146** 1 Macc 11.16
　　[NT] **151** Acts 2.11; **232** Gal 1.17; **235** Gal 4.25
Aram [OT]
(a) son of Shem **15** Gen 10.22–23
(b) language **390** 2 Kgs 18.26; **471** Ezra 4.7; **474** Ezra 7.12; **853** Dan 2.4
(c) Aramean **28** Gen 25.20; **196** Deut 26.5
Areopagus [NT] **174** Acts 17.19–22
Ark, of Covenant see Covenant Box
Ark, of Noah see Noah
Artemis [NT] **176** Acts 19.24,27–28,34–35
Asherah [OT] **95** Ex 34.13; **236** Judg 3.7; **240** Judg 6.25–26; **353** 1 Kgs 14.15; **355** 1 Kgs 15.13; **359** 1 Kgs 18.19
Assyria, Assyrian [OT] **5** Gen 2.14; **13** Gen 10.11; **385** 2 Kgs 15.19–29; **386** 2 Kgs 17.3—19.37; **676** Is 10.5,24; **864** Is 19.23–25; **822** Ezek 23.5–23; **873** Hos 5.13; **875** Hos 10.6; **914** Zeph 2.13
　　[D/A] **1** Tob 1.2–3; **16** Jdt 1.1,7; **104** Sir 48.21; **194** 1 Esd 5.69
Astarte [OT] **235** Judg 2.13; **276** 1 Sam 12.10; **299** 1 Sam 31.10; **348** 1 Kgs 11.5,33
Athens, Athenian [D/A] **165** 2 Macc 6.1; **170** 2 Macc 9.15
　　[NT] **174** Acts 17.15,16,21,22; **174** Acts 18.1; **255** 1 Thes 3.1
Augustus see Emperor

B

Baal [OT] **160** Num 25.3–5; **235** Judg 2.11,13; **241** Judg 6.25–32; **272** 1 Sam 7.4; **359** 1 Kgs 18.18–40; **379** 2 Kgs 10.18–28; **732** Jer 2.23; **752** Jer 19.5; **756** Jer 23.27; **870** Hos 2.8,13,16,17
　　[NT] **199** Rom 11.4

Babylon
(a) city in Mesopotamia [OT] **13** Gen 10.10; **15** Gen 11.9; **393** 2 Kgs 20.12-18; **398** 2 Kgs 24.10-16; **468** Ezra 2.1-70; **679** Is 13—14; **710** Is 47.1; **716** Is 52.11; **783** Jer 50—51; **859** Dan 4.30; **859** Dan 5
[D/A] **107** Bar 1.1; **113** Let Jer 1-3; **119** Sus 1,5; **122** Bel 3,23; **135** 1 Macc 6.4; **187** 1 Esd 1.40; **191** 1 Esd 4.44,61; **285** 2 Esd 3.2,31; **229** 2 Esd 16.1
(b) figurative name for Rome [NT] **293** 1 Pet 5.13; **316** Rev 14.8; **317** Rev 16.19; **318** Rev 17.5; **318** Rev 18.2-24
Balaam [OT] **157** Num 22.5—24.25; **165** Num 31.8,16; **903** Mic 6.5
[NT] **296** 2 Pet 2.15; **305** Jude 11; **308** Rev 2.14
Baptism [NT]
(a) John the Baptist **5** Mt 3.6,11-15; **45** Mk 1.4-5,8; **79** Lk 3.3,7,16; **119** Jn 1.25,31-33; **121** Jn 3.23; **149** Acts 1.5; **167** Acts 13.24; **175** Acts 18.25; **175** Acts 19.3-4
(b) Jesus **6** Mt 3.13-17; **45** Mk 1.9-11; **79** Lk 3.21-22
(c) Christian **44** Mt 28.19; **152** Acts 2.38,41; **160** Acts 8.12,13,16,36,38; **164** Acts 10.47-48; **194** Rom 6.3-4; **213** 1 Cor 10.2; **216** 1 Cor 12.13; **234** Gal 3.27; **251** Col 2.12; **292** 1 Pet 3.21
(d) with the Spirit **6** Mt 3.11; **45** Mk 1.8; **79** Lk 3.16; **119** Jn 1.33; **149** Acts 1.5; **165** Acts 11.16
Barabbas [NT] **42** Mt 27.16-26; **69** Mk 15.7-15; **113** Lk 23.18; **142** Jn 18.40
Bar-Jesus [NT] **167** Acts 13.6
Barnabas [NT] **155** Acts 4.36; **165** Acts 11.22,25,30; **166** Acts 12.25; **166** Acts 13.1—15.41; **212** 1 Cor 9.6; **232** Gal 2.1,9,13; **252** Col 4.10
Bartholomew [NT] **14** Mt 10.3; **49** Mk 3.18; **84** Lk 6.14; **149** Acts 1.13
Bartimaeus [NT] **61** Mk 10.46
Bathsheba [OT] **310** 2 Sam 11.3—12.24; **333** 1 Kgs 1.15-21
Beatitudes [NT] **7** Mt 5.3-12; **84** Lk 6.20-23
Beelzebul [NT] **15** Mt 10.25; **18** Mt 12.24,27; **49** Mk 3.22; **94** Lk 11.15,18,19; see also Devil, Satan
Bel [D/A] **114** Let Jer 41; **122** Bel 3-22
Belshazzar [OT] **859** Dan 5.1-9,30; **862** Dan 7.1; **863** Dan 8.1
"Benedictus" [NT] **75** Lk 1.68-79
Berea [NT] **174** Acts 17.10,13; **177** Acts 20.4
Bernice [NT] **183** Acts 25.13,23; **185** Acts 26.30
Bethany [NT]
(a) **31** Mt 21.17; **38** Mt 26.6; **133** Jn 11.1,18; **134** Jn 12.1
(b) **119** Jn 1.28
Bethel [OT] **16** Gen 12.8; **32** Gen 28.10-19; **224** Josh 16.2; **226** Josh 18.13,22; **234** Judg

1.22-26; 256 Judg 20.1,18,27; **272** 1 Sam 7.16; **352** 1 Kgs 13.1-32; **369** 2 Kgs 2.23-24; **781** Jer 48.13; **872** Hos 4.15; **886** Amos 3.14; **890** Amos 7.10-17
[D/A] **141** 1 Macc 9.50
Bethlehem [OT] **41** Gen 35.19; **260** Ruth 1.19; **282** 1 Sam 16.1,4; **328** 2 Sam 23.14-16; **902** Mic 5.2
[NT] **4** Mt 2.1,5,6,8,16; **76** Lk 2.4,15
Bethphage [NT] **31** Mt 21.1; **61** Mk 11.1; **107** Lk 19.29
Bethsaida [NT] **16** Mt 11.21; **54** Mk 6.45; **57** Mk 8.22; **89** Lk 9.10; **119** Jn 1.44
Bethulia [D/A] **18** Jdt 4.6; **20** Jdt 6.10-13; **21** Jdt 7.5-32
Blood
(a) of animals [OT] **11** Gen 9.4; **70** Ex 12.7,13; **85** Ex 24.8; **117** Lev 16.18,19; **119** Lev 17.11; **280** 1 Sam 14.31-34
[NT] **171** Acts 15.29; **278** Heb 9.12,13, 18-22,25; **281** Heb 11.28
(b) of men [OT] **7** Gen 4.1-11; **11** Gen 9.6; **190** Deut 19.4-10; **428** 1 Chr 28.3; **835** Ezek 35.6
[NT] **35** Mt 23.30,35; **311** Rev 6.10; **317** Rev 16.6; **318** Rev 17.6; **320** Rev 18.24; **320** Rev 19.2
(c) of Christ [NT] **39** Mt 26.28; **66** Mk 14.24; **111** Lk 22.20; **126** Jn 6.53-56; **144** Jn 19.34; **213** 1 Cor 10.16; **215** 1 Cor 11.25,27; **278** Heb 9.12,14; **279** Heb 10.29; **282** Heb 12.24; **283** Heb 13.12; **289** 1 Pet 1.2; **298** 1 Jn 1.7; **301** 1 Jn 5.6,8; **312** Rev 7.14; **314** Rev 12.11; **320** Rev 19.13
Boaz [OT] **260** Ruth 2.3-14; **262** Ruth 3.6-13; **262** Ruth 4.1-22
[NT] **3** Mt 1.5
Bread
(a) material [OT] **70** Ex 12.14-20; **71** Ex 13.3-10; **84** Ex 23.14-15; **216** Josh 9.3-15; **801** Ezek 4.9-13
[NT] **6** Mt 4.3,4; **23** Mt 15.26,33; **23** Mt 16.5-12; **53** Mk 6.8,37; **86** Lk 7.33; **116** Lk 24.30,35; **125** Jn 6.7; **147** Jn 21.9-13
(b) spiritual [NT] **126** Jn 6.32-59
(c) offered to God [OT] **86** Ex 25.30; **290** 1 Sam 21.1-6; **343** 1 Kgs 7.48
[NT] **17** Mt 12.4; **48** Mk 2.26; **84** Lk 6.4; **277** Heb 9.2
(d) Lord's Supper [NT] **39** Mt 26.26; **66** Mk 14.22; **111** Lk 22.19; **153** Acts 2.46; **215** 1 Cor 11.23-28
Burial
(a) Jesus [NT] **43** Mt 27.59-60; **66** Mk 14.8; **71** Mk 15.46; **115** Lk 23.53-56; **135** Jn 12.7; **144** Jn 19.38-42
(b) others [OT] **25** Gen 23.19; **57** Gen 50.13; **207** Deut 34.6; **326** 2 Sam 21.14
[NT] **21** Mt 14.12; **152** Acts 2.29; **155** Acts 5.6,10; **160** Acts 8.2
(c) spiritual [NT] **194** Rom 6.4; **251** Col 2.12

C

Caesar *see* Emperor
Caesarea [NT] **161** Acts 8.40; **162** Acts 9.30;
163 Acts 10.1,24; **165** Acts 11.11; **166** Acts
12.19; **178** Acts 21.8,16; **181** Acts 23.23,33;
182 Acts 25.1,4,6,13
Caesarea Philippi [NT] **24** Mt 16.13; **57** Mk 8.27
Caiaphas [NT] **38** Mt 26.3,57-66; **79** Lk 3.2;
134 Jn 11.49; **141** Jn 18.13,14,24,28; **154**
Acts 4.6
Cain [OT] **7** Gen 4.1-24
[NT] **280** Heb 11.4; **300** 1 Jn 3.12; **305**
Jude 11
Calvary *see* Golgotha
Cana [NT] **120** Jn 2.1-11; **123** Jn 4.46
Canaan (name for Palestine) [OT] **16** Gen 12.5;
53 Gen 47.4; **64** Ex 6.4; **144** Num 13.2; **205**
Deut 32.49; **231** Josh 24.3; **237** Judg 4.2,23;
597 Ps 105.11; **811** Ezek 16.3
Capernaum [NT] **7** Mt 4.13; **12** Mt 8.5; **16** Mt
11.23; **25** Mt 17.24; **45** Mk 1.21; **58** Mk 9.33;
120 Jn 2.12; **125** Jn 6.17,24,59
Carmel (mountain in Palestine) [OT] **359** 1 Kgs
18.17-46; **369** 2 Kgs 2.25; **371** 2 Kgs 4.25;
779 Jer 46.18; **891** Amos 9.3
Cherubim *see* Winged Creatures
Chief Priest [NT] **4** Mt 2.4; **31** Mt 21.15; **41** Mt
27.1,3,6; **57** Mk 8.31; **69** Mk 15.1,3,10,11; **90**
Lk 9.22; **107** Lk 20.1,19; **128** Jn 7.32; **143** Jn
19.6,15,21; **154** Acts 4.23; **156** Acts 5.24;
161 Acts 9.14,21; **182** Acts 25.2,15
Church(es) [NT] **24** Mt 16.18; **26** Mt 18.17; **153**
Acts 2.47; **162** Acts 9.31; **178** Acts 20.28;
204 Rom 16.1,5,23; **206** 1 Cor 1.2; **216**
1 Cor 12.28; **217** 1 Cor 14.4-5,12,23-40; **240**
Eph 1.22; **243** Eph 5.23-32; **290** 1 Pet 2.4-10;
307 Rev 1.6,11; **307** Rev 2.1—3.22
Church Ministers [NT]
(a) general **216** 1 Cor 12.28-30; **241** Eph 4.11
(b) leaders **245** Phil 1.1; **261** 1 Tim 3.1-7;
268 Tit 1.7-9
(c) elders **165** Acts 11.30; **169** Acts 14.23;
169 Acts 15.2,4,6,22; **177** Acts 20.17; **262**
1 Tim 4.14; **263** 1 Tim 5.17-20; **268** Tit
1.5-6; **288** Jas 5.14; **293** 1 Pet 5.1; **302**
2 Jn 1; **303** 3 Jn 1
(d) helpers **245** Phil 1.1; **261** 1 Tim 3.8-13
Cilicia [OT] **348** 1 Kgs 10.28
[NT] **157** Acts 6.9; **171** Acts 15.23,41;
179 Acts 22.3; **232** Gal 1.21
Circumcision
(a) physical [OT] **19** Gen 17.10-27; **40** Gen
34.14-17,24; **63** Ex 4.24-26; **71** Ex
12.43-48; **211** Josh 5.2-9
[D/A] **125** 1 Macc 1.15; **127** 1 Macc
1.60-61; **128** 1 Macc 2.46; **165** 2 Macc 6.10
[NT] **75** Lk 1.59; **76** Lk 2.21; **127** Jn
7.22-23; **158** Acts 7.8; **169** Acts 15.1,5;
17! Acts 16.3; **192** Rom 2.25-29; **192**
Rom 3.1; **193** Rom 4.9-12; **211** 1 Cor
7.18-19; **232** Gal 2.3; **235** Gal 5.2; **237** Gal

6.12,13,15; **247** Phil 3.5
(b) spiritual [NT] **246** Phil 3.3; **251** Col 2.11
Cleopas [NT] **115** Lk 24.18
Coming
(a) of the Lord [OT] **688** Is 26.21; **728** Is 66.18;
900 Mic 1.2-5; **927** Zech 14.5; **930** Mal
3.1,2
(b) of Christ (final) [NT] **24** Mt 16.27-28; **35**
Mt 24.3,26-44; **38** Mt 25.31-46; **65** Mk
13.24-37; **97** Lk 12.39-40; **103** Lk
17.22-30; **110** Lk 21.25-28; **137** Jn
14.2-4,18-24; **149** Acts 1.11; **248** Phil
3.20-21; **255** 1 Thes 2.19; **255** 1 Thes
4.15—5.11; **257** 2 Thes 1.7-10; **258** 2 Thes
2.1-15; **278** Heb 9.27-28; **296** 2 Pet 3.3-13;
299 1 Jn 2.28; **300** 1 Jn 3.2; **322** Rev
22.7,12,17,20
Commandments
(a) of Moses [OT] **80** Ex 20.2-17 (**176** Deut
5.6-21); **174** Deut 4—28; **230** Josh 22.5
[NT] **8** Mt 5.18,19,21,27,31,33,38,43; **28**
Mt 19.7,17; **47** Mk 1.44; **63** Mk 12.28-34;
129 Jn 8.5; **196** Rom 7.7-13; **202** Rom
13.8-10; **285** Jas 2.8
(b) Christ's [NT] **8** Mt 5.22,28,32,
34-37,39-42,44-45,48; **136** Jn 12.49-50;
137 Jn 13.34; **139** Jn 15.10-14,17; **298**
1 Jn 2.7-8; **300** 1 Jn 3.21-24; **303** 2 Jn 5.6
Conscience [D/A] **57** Wis 17.11
[NT] **191** Rom 2.15; **198** Rom 9.1; **201**
Rom 13.5; **212** 1 Cor 8.7-13; **214** 1 Cor
10.25-30; **269** Tit 1.15; **292** 1 Pet 3.16,21
Corinth [NT] **174** Acts 18.1-17; **175** Acts 19.1;
205 1 Cor; **221** 2 Cor
Cornelius [NT] **163** Acts 10.1-48
Cornerstone [OT] **390** Is 28.16
[NT] **240** Eph 2.20; **290** 1 Pet 2.6-7
Covenant
(a) with Noah [OT] **9** Gen 6.18; **12** Gen 9.9
(b) with Abraham, Isaac, and Jacob [OT] **18**
Gen 15.18; **19** Gen 17.2; **61** Ex 2.24; **64**
Ex 6.4-5
(c) with Phinehas [OT] **160** Num 25.12-13
(d) with David [OT] **306** 2 Sam 7
(e) with Israel (old covenant) [OT] **80** Ex
19.3-8; **85** Ex 24.7,8; **95** Ex 34.10,27; **175**
Deut 4.23; **178** Deut 7.9-11; **418** 1 Chr
16.14-18
[NT] **154** Acts 3.25; **158** Acts 7.8; **224**
2 Cor 3.14; **234** Gal 3.17; **240** Eph 2.12;
277 Heb 9.1,4,15,18,20
(f) new covenant [OT] **764** Jer 31.31-34
[NT] **39** Mt 26.28; **66** Mk 14.24; **111** Lk
22.20; **215** 1 Cor 11.25; **223** 2 Cor 3.6; **277**
Heb 7.22; **277** Heb 8.6-13; **278** Heb 9.15;
279 Heb 10.16,29; **282** Heb 12.24; **283**
Heb 13.20
Covenant Box [OT] **86** Ex 25.10-22; **98** Ex
37.1-9; **181** Deut 10.1-5; **210** Josh 3.13; **211**
Josh 4.5,11; **212** Josh 6.6; **269** 1 Sam
4.1—7.1; **305** 2 Sam 6.1-17; **343** 1 Kgs 8.1-9
[NT] **277** Heb 9.4; **314** Rev 11.19

Creation
(a) universe [OT] **4** Gen 1.1—2.4;
[D/A] **52** Wis 11.17,24-25; **167** 2 Macc
7.28; **232** Man 2
[NT] **118** Jn 1.3; **250** Col 1.16; **272** Heb
1.2; **280** Heb 11.3; **313** Rev 10.6
(b) stars [OT] **701** Is 40.26
(c) man [OT] **5** Gen 2.4-25
(d) new heart [OT] **566** Ps 51.10
(e) new nature [NT] **242** Eph 4.24
Crete, Cretans [OT] **173** Deut 2.23; **780** Jer
47.4; **892** Amos 9.7
[NT] **186** Acts 27.7-21; **268** Tit 1.5,12
Cross [NT]
(a) of Christ **42** Mt 27.32,40,42; **206** 1 Cor
1.17-18; **236** Gal 5.11; **237** Gal 6.12,14;
240 Eph 2.16; **250** Col 1.20; **251** Col 2.14;
282 Heb 12.2
(b) of disciples **15** Mt 10.38; **24** Mt 16.24; **57**
Mk 8.34; **90** Lk 9.23; **100** Lk 14.27
Crown, prize
(a) literal [OT] **301** 2 Sam 1.10; **312** 2 Sam
12.30; **588** Ps 89.39
[D/A] **133** 1 Macc 4.57; **143** 1 Macc
10.20
[NT] **42** Mt 27.29; **69** Mk 15.17; **143** Jn
19.2,5
(b) figurative [OT] **541** Ps 8.4-5; **625** Prov
4.9; **635** Prov 16.31
[D/A] **61** Sir 1.11; **66** Sir 6.31
[NT] **248** Phil 4.1; **255** 1 Thes 2.19; **265**
2 Tim 2.5; **273** Heb 2.7,9; **293** 1 Pet 5.4;
308 Rev 2.10; **311** Rev 6.2; **316** Rev 14.14
Cyprus [OT] **686** Is 23.1,12; **731** Jer 2.10; **826**
Ezek 27.6
[NT] **155** Acts 4.36; **167** Acts 13.4-12;
171 Acts 15.39
Cyrene [NT] **42** Mt 27.32; **70** Mk 15.21; **113**
Lk 23.26; **151** Acts 2.10; **165** Acts 11.20
Cyrus [OT] **467** Ezra 1.1-11; **708** Is 44.28; **708**
Is 45.1-14; **853** Dan 1.21; **862** Dan 6.28; **866**
Dan 10.1
[D/A] **122** Bel 1; **188** 1 Esd 2.1-12; **191**
1 Esd 4.44; **193** 1 Esd 5.55

D

Damascus [OT] **17** Gen 14.15; **308** 2 Sam 8.5-6;
373 2 Kgs 5.12; **376** 2 Kgs 8.7,9; **384** 2 Kgs
14.28; **386** 2 Kgs 16.5-12; **672** Is 7.1—8.6
[D/A] **16** Jdt 1.12; **18** Jdt 2.27; **29** Jdt
15.5; **148** 1 Macc 11.62; **149** 1 Macc 12.32
[NT] **161** Acts 9.2-25,27; **179** Acts
22.5-16; **185** Acts 26.12-20; **229** 2 Cor 11.32;
232 Gal 1.17
Darius
(a) king of Persia [OT] **471** Ezra 4.5; **472**
Ezra 5.5-7; **472** Ezra 6.1-15; **493** Neh
12.22; **916** Hag 1.1; **918** Zech 1.1
[D/A] **189** 1 Esd 2.31—3.24; **191** 1 Esd
4.47—5.6; **194** 1 Esd 6.1-34

(b) the Mede [OT] **860** Dan 5.31; **860** Dan 6.1,
6-9,25-28; **864** Dan 9.1
(c) III, king of Persia [D/A] **124** 1 Macc 1.1
Darkness
(a) literal [OT] **4** Gen 1.2; **18** Gen 15.12; **69**
Ex 10.21; **617** Ps 139.12
[D/A] **57** Wis 17.1—18.4; **211** 2 Esd 6.39
[NT] **42** Mt 27.45; **70** Mk 15.33; **282**
Heb 12.18
(b) spiritual [OT] **671** Is 5.20
[D/A] **204** 2 Esd 2.36; **216** 2 Esd 7.125
[NT] **7** Mt 4.16; **112** Lk 22.53; **118** Jn
1.5; **121** Jn 3.19; **135** Jn 12.35,46; **224**
2 Cor 4.6; **242** Eph 5.8,11; **298** 1 Jn 1.5-6;
298 1 Jn 2.8-11
David [OT] anointed by Samuel **282** 1 Sam
16.1-13; played the harp for Saul **283** 1 Sam
16.14-23; killed Goliath **283** 1 Sam 17; won
Jonathan's friendship **286** 1 Sam 18.1-4;
Saul's jealousy **286** 1 Sam 18.5-9; married
Michal **287** 1 Sam 18.20-29; fled from Saul
287 1 Sam 19—22; fought against the
Philistines **291** 1 Sam 23; spared Saul at
Engedi **292** 1 Sam 24; David and Abigail **294**
1 Sam 25; spared Saul at Ziph **295** 1 Sam 26;
lived among the Philistines **296** 1 Sam
27.1—28.2; **298** 1 Sam 29; defeated the
Amalekites **298** 1 Sam 30; made king over
Judah **302** 2 Sam 2.1-7; made king over Israel
304 2 Sam 5.1-16; brought Covenant Box to
Jerusalem **305** 2 Sam 6; God's covenant with
306 2 Sam 7; extended his kingdom **307**
2 Sam 8; David and Bathsheba **310** 2 Sam
11.1—12.25; fled from Absalom **315** 2 Sam
15—16; returned to Jerusalem **322** 2 Sam 19;
David's last words **328** 2 Sam 23.2-7; counted
Israel and Judah **329** 2 Sam 24; David's
instructions to Solomon **334** 1 Kgs 2.1-9; died
334 1 Kgs 2.10-12; see also **336** 1 Kgs 2.45;
351 1 Kgs 12.19,20; **412** 1 Chr 11—29; **754**
Jer 21.12; **768** Jer 33.15,17;
[D/A] **102** Sir 45.25; **103** Sir 47.1-11;
48.15; **205** 2 Esd 3.23
[NT] **3** Mt 1.1,6,17; **33** Mt 22.41-45; **76**
Lk 2.11; **149** Acts 1.16; **152** Acts 2.25,29,34;
159 Acts 7.45; **167** Acts 13.22,34,36; **190**
Rom 1.3; **193** Rom 4.6; **265** 2 Tim 2.8; **309**
Rev 3.7; **310** Rev 5.5; **323** Rev 22.16
Day of Judgement see Judgement (c)
Death
(a) physical [OT] **5** Gen 2.17; **7** Gen 3.19; **7**
Gen 4.8-16; **202** Deut 30.19; **260** Ruth
1.17; **507** Job 3.21; **588** Ps 89.48; **604** Ps
116.15; **628** Prov 7.27; **655** Ecc 9.1-6,10;
658 Ecc 12.5-7
[D/A] **44** Wis 2.24; 4.7-19; **69** Sir 10.11;
72 Sir 14.17; **82** Sir 25.24; **203** 2 Esd 2.23;
214 2 Esd 7.75
[NT] **133** Jn 11.11-44; **219** 1 Cor
15.20-28,54-56; **255** 1 Thes 4.13-16; **311**
Rev 6.8

(b) spiritual [NT] **194** Rom 6.1-11 **196** Rom 7.4-6,9-13,24; **285** Jas 1.15; **288** Jas 5.20; **300** 1 Jn 3.14; **302** 1 Jn 5.16,17; **321** Rev 20.6,14

(c) of Christ [NT] **43** Mt 27.50; **71** Mk 15.39; **114** Lk 23.46; **142** Jn 18.31-32; **144** Jn 19.30; **218** 1 Cor 15.3; **225** 2 Cor 5.14-15; **246** Phil 2.8; **250** Col 1.22; **273** Heb 2.9,14-15; **292** 1 Pet 3.18

Deborah [OT] **237** Judg 4.4-14; **238** Judg 5.1-31

Delilah [OT] **252** Judg 16.4-18

Demas [NT] **253** Col 4.14; **267** 2 Tim 4.10; **271** Phlm 24

Demetrius [D/A]
(a) I Soter **137** 1 Macc 7.1-4,8; **140** 1 Macc 8.31—9.1; **143** 1 Macc 10.22-50; **176** 2 Macc 14.1-26
(b) II Nicator **145** 1 Macc 10.67; **147** 1 Macc 11.19-55; **157** 2 Macc 1.7

Demons
(a) general [D/A] **4** Tob 3.8,17; **7** Tob 6.7,14-17; **9** Tob 8.3; **110** Bar 4.7,35
[NT] **214** 1 Cor 10.20-21; **262** 1 Tim 4.1; **313** Rev 9.20; **317** Rev 16.13-14; **318** Rev 18.2
(b) and Jesus [NT] **7** Mt 4.24; **12** Mt 8.16,28-34; **55** Mk 7.25; **94** Lk 11.14-26; **130** Jn 8.48-52; **132** Jn 10.20-21

Derbe [NT] **168** Acts 14.6,20-21; **171** Acts 16.1

Desire, greed [OT] **81** Ex 20.17; **177** Deut 5.21; **214** Josh 7.21; **721** Is 57.17
[NT] **96** Lk 12.15; **190** Rom 1.29; **196** Rom 7.7-10; **242** Eph 5.3,5; **251** Col 3.5; **287** Jas 4.2

Devil [NT] **6** Mt 4.1-11; **80** Lk 4.1-13; **136** Jn 13.2; **243** Eph 6.11; **261** 1 Tim 3.6-7; **273** Heb 2.14; **293** 1 Pet 5.8; **300** 1 Jn 3.8; **305** Jude 9; **314** Rev 12.9-12; **321** Rev 20.2,10; *see also* Beelzebul, Satan

Disciples [NT]
(a) of John **16** Mt 11.2,7; **21** Mt 14.12; **47** Mk 2.18; **55** Mk 6.29; **83** Lk 5.33; **86** Lk 7.18; **119** Jn 1.35; **123** Jn 3.25
(b) of Jesus **13** Mt 9.10,11,14,19; **14** Mt 10.1; **16** Mt 11.1; **17** Mt 12.1-2,49; **21** Mt 14.19; **22** Mt 15.2,32-37; **23** Mt 16.5,13,20,21,24; **24** Mt 17.16; **25** Mt 18.1; **28** Mt 19.13; **31** Mt 21.20; **38** Mt 26.8,17-30,56; **43** Mt 27.57; **43** Mt 28.13,16,19; **123** Jn 4.27-33; **127** Jn 6.67,71; **146** Jn 21.1-14,20-24; **157** Acts 6.1,7; **162** Acts 9.26; **169** Acts 14.21; **175** Acts 19.1; **178** Acts 21.16
(c) of the Pharisees **33** Mt 22.16; **47** Mk 2.18; **83** Lk 5.33
(d) of Moses **131** Jn 9.28

Divorce [OT] **122** Lev 21.7; **164** Num 30.9; **194** Deut 24.1-4; **714** Is 50.1; **930** Mal 2.16
[NT] **8** Mt 5.31-32; **28** Mt 19.3-9; **59** Mk 10.2-12; **102** Lk 16.18; **210** 1 Cor 7.10-11,12-16

Dorcas [NT] **163** Acts 9.36-41

Dragon [OT] **689** Is 27.1
[D/A] **82** Sir 25.16; **123** Bel 23-28
[NT] **314** Rev 12.3—13.4; **315** Rev 13.11; **317** Rev 16.13; **321** Rev 20.2-3

Drusilla [NT] **182** Acts 24.24

E

Ecbatana [D/A] **4** Tob 3.7; **15** Tob 14.12-14; **16** Jdt 1.1; **169** 2 Macc 9.3; **193** 1 Esd 6.23

Eden [OT] **5** Gen 2.8,10,15; **7** Gen 3.23-24; **828** Ezek 28.13; **830** Ezek 31.9,16-18

Edom [OT]
(a) Esau **28** Gen 25.30; **42** Gen 36.1
(b) Edomites **153** Num 20.18,20,21; **884** Amos 1.6,11; **893** Obad; **929** Mal 1.4
(c) region occupied by Edomites **38** Gen 32.3; **42** Gen 36.21; **159** Num 24.18; **223** Josh 15.1,21; **369** 2 Kgs 3.8,20; **929** Mal 1.2-4

Egypt(ians) [OT] **16** Gen 12.10-14; **43** Gen 37.25-28; **59** Ex 1—15; **141** Num 11.5; **336** 1 Kgs 3.1; **465** 2 Chr 36.3,4; **731** Jer 2.6; **776** Jer 42.19; **822** Ezek 23.3; **831** Ezek 32.12; **876** Hos 11.1; **925** Zech 10.10-11
[D/A] **57** Wis 17.1—18.19; **60** Sir Foreword; **125** 1 Macc 1.16-19; **157** 2 Macc 1.1-10; **186** 1 Esd 1.25
[NT] **4** Mt 2.13-15,19

Elders, leaders
(a) Israelite [OT] **61** Ex 3.16-18; **231** Josh 24.1,31; **262** Ruth 4.2,4,9,11
[D/A] **21** Jdt 7.23; **22** Jdt 8.10; **119** Sus 5-6; **150** 1 Macc 12.35
[NT] **22** Mt 15.2; **31** Mt 21.23; **38** Mt 26.3,47,57; **41** Mt 27.1,3,12,20,41; **154** Acts 4.5,8,23; **157** Acts 6.12; **182** Acts 24.1
(b) Christian, *see* Church Ministers (c)
(c) heavenly [NT] **310** Rev 4.4,10; **310** Rev 5.5,6,8-11; **311** Rev 7.11-14; **314** Rev 11.16; **320** Rev 19.4

Eleazar [D/A]
(a) Avaran **127** 1 Macc 2.5; **137** 1 Macc 6.43-46
(b) elder **165** 2 Macc 6.18-31

Eli [OT] **265** 1 Sam 1.9—4.18; **335** 1 Kgs 2.27

Elijah [OT] **357** 1 Kgs 17.1—2 Kgs 2.15; **931** Mal 4.5
[D/A] **104** Sir 48.1-12; **215** 2 Esd 7.109
[NT] **16** Mt 11.14; **24** Mt 17.3-13; **42** Mt 27.47-49; **74** Lk 1.17; **80** Lk 4.25-26; **118** Jn 1.21,25; **199** Rom 11.2; **288** Jas 5.17

Elisha [OT] **361** Kgs 19.16-21; **367** 2 Kgs 2.1—9.3; **383** 2 Kgs 13.14-21;
[D/A] **104** Sir 48.12-14
[NT] **81** Lk 4.27

Elizabeth [NT]
74 Lk 1.5-7,24-25,36,40-45,57-61

Emmaus [D/A] **131** 1 Macc 3.57
[NT] **155** Lk 24.13

Emperor [NT]
(a) title of Roman ruler **33** Mt 22.17–21; **63** Mk 12.14–17; **108** Lk 20.22–25
(b) Augustus **76** Lk 2.1
(c) Tiberius **79** Lk 3.1; **143** Jn 19.12,15
(d) Claudius **165** Acts 11.28; **174** Acts 18.2
(e) Nero **183** Acts 25.8–12,21; **249** Phil 4.22; **291** 1 Pet 2.13,17

Enoch [OT] **9** Gen 5.18–24
[D/A] **101** Sir 44.16; **105** Sir 49.14
[NT] **280** Heb 11.5; **305** Jude 14

Epaphras [NT] **250** Col 1.7; **253** Col 4.12; **271** Phlm 23

Ephesus [NT] **175** Acts 18.19–21,24–26; **175** Acts 19.1–41; **177** Acts 20.16–38; **219** 1 Cor 15.32; **221** 1 Cor 16.8; **238** Eph 1.1; **260** 1 Tim 1.3; **307** Rev 2.1–7

Ephod [OT] **88** Ex 28.2,4–14; **267** 1 Sam 2.18; **291** 1 Sam 22.18; **292** 1 Sam 23.9–12; **306** 2 Sam 6.14

Epicureans [NT] **174** Acts 17.18

Esau [OT] **28** Gen 25.21–26; **30** Gen 27.1–41; **38** Gen 32.3—33.15; **42** Gen 35.29; **172** Deut 2.4–22; **893** Obad 8,9,19,21; **929** Mal 1.2–3
[NT] **198** Rom 9.13; **281** Heb 11.20

Ethiopian [NT] **161** Acts 8.26–39

Euphrates [OT] **5** Gen 2.14; **18** Gen 15.18; **745** Jer 13.4–7
[D/A] **16** Jdt 1.6; **18** Jdt 2.24; **130** 1 Macc 3.32,37; **186** 1 Esd 1.25; **224** 2 Esd 13.40–47
[NT] **313** Rev 9.14; **317** Rev 16.12

Eutychus [NT] **177** Acts 20.9–12

Eve [OT] **7** Gen 3.20; **7** Gen 4.1
[D/A] **82** Sir 25.24
[NT] **228** 2 Cor 11.3; **261** 1 Tim 2.13

Ezekiel [D/A] **105** Sir 49.8

Ezra [OT] **474** Ezra 7—10; **487** Neh 8; **493** Neh 12.26,36
[D/A] **196** 1 Esd 8.1–27,41–53,68—9.17, 37–50; **204** 2 Esd 2.33; 3.1

F

Faith
(a) general [OT] **673** Is 7.9; **688** Is 26.2; **690** Is 28.16; **910** Hab 2.4
[D/A] **28** Jdt 14.10; **52** Wis 12.2; **57** Wis 16.26; **62** Sir 2.6–13; **70** Sir 11.21; **208** 2 Esd 5.1; **210** 2 Esd 6.5
[NT] **13** Mt 9.2; **25** Mt 17.20; **31** Mt 21.21–22; **103** Lk 17.6; **190** Rom 1.16–17; **193** Rom 3.27–31; **194** Rom 5.1; **225** 2 Cor 5.7; **233** Gal 3.2,6–14,22–26; **280** Heb 11.1; **285** Jas 1.6; **286** Jas 2.14–26
(b) in God [OT] **581** Ps 78.22
[NT] **62** Mk 11.22–24; **136** Jn 12.44–45; **137** Jn 14.1; **193** Rom 4.1–25; **280** Heb 11.1–40
(c) in Christ [NT] **12** Mt 8.13; **14** Mt 9.28–29; **47** Mk 2.5; **52** Mk 5.34,36; **58** Mk 9.23–24;

118 Jn 1.7,12,50; **121** Jn 3.16; **126** Jn 6.29,35,40; **131** Jn 9.35–38; **133** Jn 11.15,25–27; **146** Jn 20.29,31; **153** Acts 3.16; **172** Acts 16.31; **192** Rom 3.22–26; **199** Rom 10.6–17; **233** Gal 2.16,20; **300** 1 Jn 3.23; **301** 1 Jn 5.1,5,10,13

False
(a) gods [OT] **387** 2 Kgs 17.15; **558** Ps 40.4; **742** Jer 10.11; **747** Jer 14.22
[D/A] **53** Wis 13.1—14.31; **55** Wis 15.7–19; **113** Let Jer 4–73; **122** Bel 3–30
(b) prophets [OT] **184** Deut 13.1–5; **190** Deut 18.20–22; **364** 1 Kgs 22.5–25; **756** Jer 23.16–32; **760** Jer 28.15,16; **809** Ezek 13.17,19; **901** Mic 3.11
[NT] **11** Mt 7.15; **36** Mt 24.11,24; **65** Mk 13.22; **167** Acts 13.6; **295** 2 Pet 2.1; **300** 1 Jn 4.1; **308** Rev 2.20; **320** Rev 19.20; **321** Rev 20.10
(c) Messiahs [NT] **36** Mt 24.24; **65** Mk 13.22

Fasting
(a) general [OT] **312** 2 Sam 12.23; **446** 2 Chr 20.3; **475** Ezra 8.21; **488** Neh 9.1; **499** Esth 4.3,16; **747** Jer 14.12; **881** Joel 2.12–15; **922** Zech 7.1–7
[D/A] **19** Jdt 4.13; **22** Jdt 8.6; **90** Sir 34.26; **107** Bar 1.5; **131** 1 Macc 3.47; **176** 2 Macc 13.12; **209** 2 Esd 5.20
[NT] **47** Mk 2.18; **77** Lk 2.37; **104** Lk 18.12
(b) day of Atonement [OT] **117** Lev 16; **125** Lev 23.26–32
[NT] **185** Acts 27.9
(c) Jesus' teaching [NT] **10** Mt 6.16–18; **13** Mt 9.14–15; **47** Mk 2.18–20; **83** Lk 5.33–35
(d) Christian [NT] **166** Acts 13.2–3; **169** Acts 14.23

Father (title of God) [OT] **588** Ps 89.26; **726** Is 63.16; **929** Mal 1.6
[D/A] **13** Tob 13.4; **54** Wis 14.3; **79** Sir 23.1,4; **106** Sir 51.10
[NT] **9** Mt 5.48; **9** Mt 6.8–9,32; **11** Mt 7.21; **16** Mt 11.25–27; **67** Mk 14.36; **79** Lk 2.49; **97** Lk 12.30,32; **114** Lk 23.34,46; **118** Jn 1.18; **124** Jn 5.17–27,36–45; **132** Jn 10.29–38; **138** Jn 14.6–11; **140** Jn 17.1–26; **197** Rom 8.15; **234** Gal 4.6; **282** Heb 12.5–9; **299** 1 Jn 3.1–2,9–10

Felix [NT] **181** Acts 23.24,26; **182** Acts 24.2–27

Festivals
(a) Passover [OT] **70** Ex 12.18,19,27,43–48; **71** Ex 13.3–10; **187** Deut 16.1–8; **212** Josh 5.10; **396** 2 Kgs 23.21–23 (**464** 2 Chr 35.1–19); **473** Ezra 6.19–20
[NT] **38** Mt 26.2,5,17–19; **42** Mt 27.15; **66** Mk 14.1,2,12,14,16; **69** Mk 15.6; **77** Lk 2.41–43; **110** Lk 22.1,8,13; **120** Jn 2.13,23; **125** Jn 6.4; **134** Jn 11.55–56; **134** Jn 12.1,12,20; **136** Jn 13.1,29; **143** Jn 19.14; **165** Acts 12.4; **209** 1 Cor 5.7; **281** Heb 11.28

(b) Unleavened Bread [OT] **70** Ex 12.15-20; **72** Ex 13.6-7; **465** 2 Chr 35.17; **473** Ezra 6.22
   [NT] **39** Mt 26.17; **66** Mk 14.1,12; **110** Lk 22.1,7; **165** Acts 12.3; **177** Acts 20.6
(c) Pentecost (Harvest) [OT] **85** Ex 23.16; **96** Ex 34.22; **124** Lev 23.15-21; **187** Deut 16.9-12; **437** 2 Chr 8.13;
   [D/A] **3** Tob 2.1; **175** 2 Macc 12.31
   [NT] **151** Acts 2.1; **177** Acts 20.16; **221** 1 Cor 16.8
(d) Shelters [OT] **125** Lev 23.34,42; **188** Deut 16.13-16; **438** 2 Chr 9.12-13; **800** Ezek 3.4; **928** Zech 14.16-19
   [NT] **127** Jn 7.2,8,10,11,14,37
(e) New Moon [OT] **139** Num 10.10; **162** Num 28.11-14; **288** 1 Sam 20.5; **890** Amos 8.5
   [D/A] **22** Jdt 8.6; **144** 1 Macc 10.34
   [NT] **251** Col 2.16
(f) others: New Year [OT] **163** Num 29.1; Purim [OT] **504** Esth 9.21-32; [D/A] **42** Gk Est 9.24-28; **179** 2 Macc 15.36; Dedication of Temple [D/A] **133** 1 Macc 4.59; **170** 2 Macc 10.1-8; [NT] **132** Jn 10.22
(g) unspecified [OT] **793** Lam 2.6,7; **874** Hos 9.5
   [NT] **124** Jn 5.1
Festus [NT] **182** Acts 24.27; **182** Acts 25.1—26.32
Forgiveness
(a) general [OT] **90** Ex 29.36; **93** Ex 32.30-32; **104** Lev 4.20-35; **192** Deut 21.8; **344** 1 Kgs 8.30-39,46-50; **553** Ps 32.1; **613** Ps 130.4; **695** Is 33.24; **717** Is 53.10-12; **865** Dan 9.19; **905** Mic 7.18-19
   [D/A] **53** Wis 12.19-20; **62** Sir 2.11; **84** Sir 28.2-5
   [NT] **9** Mt 6.12,14-15; **13** Mt 9.1-8; **26** Mt 18.21-35; **49** Mk 4.12; **62** Mk 11.25-26; **79** Lk 3.3; **86** Lk 7.36-50; **102** Lk 17.3-4; **146** Jn 20.23; **223** 2 Cor 2.5-10; **242** Eph 4.32; **250** Col 1.14; **251** Col 2.13; **298** 1 Jn 1.9
(b) no forgiveness [NT] **18** Mt 12.31-32; **49** Mk 3.28-30; **278** Heb 9.22

G

Gabriel [OT] **864** Dan 8.15-26; **865** Dan 9.20-27
   [NT] **74** Lk 1.11-20,26
Galatia [D/A] **168** 2 Macc 8.20
   [NT] **172** Acts 16.6; **175** Acts 18.23; **232** Gal 1.2; **289** 1 Pet 1.1
Galilee
(a) Lake Galilee [OT] **168** Num 34.11
   [D/A] **148** 1 Macc 11.67
   [NT] **7** Mt 4.13,15,18; **12** Mt 8.24,26,27,32; **19** Mt 13.1; **21** Mt 14.25-26; **23** Mt 15.29; **45** Mk 1.16; **47** Mk 2.13; **48** Mk 3.7; **49** Mk 4.1,35; **50** Mk 5.1; **54** Mk 6.43,53; (called Lake Tiberias) **125** Jn 6.1; **146** Jn 21.1; (called Lake Gennesaret) **81** Lk 5.1
(b) Province [OT] **385** 2 Kgs 15.29 (**408** 1 Chr 6.76); **674** Is 9.1
   [D/A] **1** Tob 1.2,5; **16** Jdt 1.8; **29** Jdt 15.5; **133** 1 Macc 5.14-23; **150** 1 Macc 12.47-49
   [NT] **7** Mt 4.23; **28** Mt 19.1; **43** Mt 28.7,10,16; **45** Mk 1.9,14,28,39; **77** Lk 2.39; **80** Lk 4.14; **119** Jn 1.43; **123** Jn 4.43,47; **127** Jn 7.1,9,41,52
Gallio [NT] **175** Acts 18.12,14,17
Gamaliel [NT] **157** Acts 5.34; **179** Acts 22.3
Genealogy
(a) general [OT] **7** Gen 4.17—5.31; **13** Gen 10.8-19,21,24-30; **64** Ex 6.14-27; **133** Num 3; **401** 1 Chr 1—9; **469** Ezra 2.59-63; **477** Ezra 10.9-44
   [D/A] **192** 1 Esd 5.1-46; **197** 1 Esd 8.28-40
   [NT] **260** 1 Tim 1.4
(b) Christ [NT] **3** Mt 1.1-17; **79** Lk 3.23-38
Gentiles [NT] **14** Mt 10.5,18; **29** Mt 20.19; **60** Mk 10.33; **77** Lk 2.32; **105** Lk 18.32; **155** Acts 4.27; **162** Acts 9.15; **162** Acts 10.45; **164** Acts 11.1,18; **167** Acts 13.46-48; **169** Acts 14.27;15.3,7,8,12-23; **175** Acts 18.6; **178** Acts 21.19,25; **180** Acts 22.21; **185** Acts 26.20; **188** Acts 28.28; **191** Rom 2.12-27; **192** Rom 3.1,29; **200** Rom 11.11-32; **203** Rom 15.9-18,27; **206** 1 Cor 1.23; **232** Gal 2.7-17; **233** Gal 3.14; **240** Eph 2.11-19;3.6,8
Gethsemane [NT] **39** Mt 26.36; **67** Mk 14.32
Gideon [OT] **240** Judg 6.11—8.27
   [NT] **281** Heb 11.32
Glory, glorious [NT] **24** Mt 16.27; **28** Mt 19.28; **36** Mt 24.30; **57** Mk 8.38; **61** Mk 10.37; **65** Mk 13.26; **76** Lk 2.9,14,32; **90** Lk 9.26,31,32; **107** Lk 19.38; **110** Lk 21.27; **116** Lk 24.26; **118** Jn 1.14; **120** Jn 2.11; **127** Jn 7.18,39; **133** Jn 11.4,40; **135** Jn 12.16,23,28,41; **137** Jn 13.31,32; **138** Jn 14.13; **139** Jn 15.8; **139** Jn 16.14; **140** Jn 17.1,4,5,10,22,24; **147** Jn 21.19; **153** Acts 3.13; **157** Acts 7.2,55; **191** Rom 2.7,10; **192** Rom 5.2; **197** Rom 8.17,18,21,30; **198** Rom 9.4,23; **207** 1 Cor 2.7,8; **215** 1 Cor 11.7; **224** 2 Cor 3.18;4.4,6,17; **238** Eph 1.6; **241** Eph 3.16; **250** Col 1.11,27; **254** 1 Thes 2.12; **257** 2 Thes 1.9,10; **265** 2 Tim 2.10; **269** Tit 2.13; **272** Heb 1.3; **273** Heb 2.9,10; **292** 1 Pet 4.13,14; **293** 1 Pet 5.1,4,10; **305** Jude 24,25; **322** Rev 21.11,23
Golgotha [NT] **42** Mt 27.33; **70** Mk 15.22; **144** Jn 19.17
Goliath [OT] **283** 1 Sam 17.1-58; **290** 1 Sam 21.9-10; **291** 1 Sam 22.10
Gomorrah see Sodom and Gomorrah
Grace [NT] **118** Jn 1.14,16,17; **168** Acts 14.3,26; **169** Acts 15.11-18; **177** Acts 20.24,32; **192**

Rom 3.24; **194** Rom 5.2,15,17,20,21;6.1,14,15; **200** Rom 11.5,6; **201** Rom 12.6; **219** 1 Cor 15.10; **226** 2 Cor 8.1,9; **230** 2 Cor 12.9; **236** Gal 5.4; **238** Eph 1.2,6,7; **240** Eph 2.5–8; **257** 2 Thes 1.2,12; **259** 2 Thes 3.18; **265** 2 Tim 2.1; **269** Tit 2.11; **269** Tit 3.7,15; **275** Heb 4.16; **279** Heb 10.29; **282** Heb 12.15; **283** Heb 13.9,25; **287** Jas 4.6; **289** 1 Pet 1.2; **293** 1 Pet 5.10,12; **300** 2 Pet 3.18; **307** Rev 1.4; **323** Rev 22.21

Greece [OT] **864** Dan 8.21; **866** Dan 10.20; **866** Dan 11.2; **924** Zech 9.13

    [D/A] **124** 1 Macc 1.1; **139** 1 Macc 8.9–10

    [NT] **56** Mk 7.26; **128** Jn 7.35; **135** Jn 12.20; **144** Jn 19.20; **165** Acts 11.20; **177** Acts 20.2,21

Greed *see* Desire

H

Habakkuk [D/A] **123** Bel 33–39

Hades [NT] **102** Lk 16.23; **311** Rev 6.8

Hagar [OT] **18** Gen 16.1–16; **23** Gen 21.9–21

    [NT] **235** Gal 4.24–25

Haggai [OT] **471** Ezra 5.1; **473** Ezra 6.14; **916** Hag 1.1

Harvest Festival *see* Festivals

Heaven

  (a) abode of God, angels, and blessed dead [OT] **32** Gen 28.12,17; **81** Ex 20.22; **209** Josh 2.11; **343** 1 Kgs 8.27; **727** Is 66.1

    [D/A] **191** 1 Esd 4.36,58; **206** 2 Esd 4.8,21

    [NT] **6** Mt 3.16; **7** Mt 5.12; **9** Mt 6.10,20; **26** Mt 18.10; **28** Mt 19.21; **33** Mt 22.30; **43** Mt 28.2,18; **76** Lk 2.15; **92** Lk 10.18; **100** Lk 15.7,18,21; **111** Lk 22.43; **120** Jn 1.51; **121** Jn 3.13; **126** Jn 6.31–33,38,41, 42,50,51,58; **154** Acts 3.21; **159** Acts 7.55–56; **190** Rom 1.18; **199** Rom 10.6; **220** 1 Cor 15.47–49; **230** 2 Cor 12.2; **243** Eph 6.9; **248** Phil 3.20; **250** Col 1.5,16,20; **255** 1 Thes 4.16; **257** 2 Thes 1.7; **278** Heb 9.24; **282** Heb 12.23,25,26; **288** Jas 5.18; **289** 1 Pet 1.4,12; **292** 1 Pet 3.22; **309** Rev 4—5; **320** Rev 19.1,11–14; **321** Rev 21.1–2,10

  (b) kingdom of [NT] **5** Mt 3.2; **7** Mt 4.17; **7** Mt 5.3,10,19,20; **11** Mt 7.21; **12** Mt 8.11; **14** Mt 10.7; **16** Mt 11.11,12; **19** Mt 13.11,24,31,33,44,45,47,52; **24** Mt 16.19; **25** Mt 18.1,3,4,23; **28** Mt 19.12,14,23; **29** Mt 20.1; **32** Mt 22.2; **34** Mt 23.13; **37** Mt 25.1

  (c) Father in [NT] **8** Mt 5.16,45; **9** Mt 6.1,9; **11** Mt 7.11,21; **19** Mt 12.50; **24** Mt 16.17; **26** Mt 18.10,14,19; **34** Mt 23.9

Hebron [OT] **17** Gen 13.18; **25** Gen 23.2–20; **42** Gen 35.27; **144** Num 13.22; **217** Josh 10.1–39; **224** Josh 15.13–14; **228** Josh 20.7; **229** Josh 21.10–13; **302** 2 Sam 2.1–4,11,32;

304 2 Sam 5.1–5,13; **315** 2 Sam 15.7–10

Hell [D/A] **204** 2 Esd 2.29; **213** 2 Esd 7.36

    [NT] **8** Mt 5.22,29,30; **15** Mt 10.28; **16** Mt 11.23; **25** Mt 18.9; **34** Mt 23.15,33; **59** Mk 9.43,45,47; **92** Lk 10.15; **96** Lk 12.5; **286** Jas 3.6; **296** 2 Pet 2.4

Herod [NT]

  (a) the Great, king of Judaea **4** Mt 2.1–22; **74** Lk 1.5

  (b) Antipas, tetrarch of Galilee **21** Mt 14.1–10; **53** Mk 6.14–27; **56** Mk 8.15; **79** Lk 3.1,19; **89** Lk 9.7,9; **99** Lk 13.31; **113** Lk 23.6–12,15; **155** Acts 4.27; **166** Acts 13.1

  (c) Agrippa I, *see* Agrippa (a)

  (d) Agrippa II, *see* Agrippa (b)

Herodias [NT] **21** Mt 14.3,6; **53** Mk 6.17,19,22; **79** Lk 3.19

Hezekiah (son of Ahaz and king of Judah) [OT] **388** 2 Kgs 18—20; **456** 2 Chr 29—32; **696** Is 36—39

    [D/A] **104** Sir 48.17–25; **104** Sir 49.4; **179** 2 Macc 15.22; **215** 2 Esd 7.110

    [NT] **4** Mt 1.9,10

High Priest

  (a) Israelite [OT] **122** Lev 21.10–15; **169** Num 35.25,28,32; **394** 2 Kgs 22.4,8; **474** Ezra 7.1; **481** Neh 3.1,20; **790** Jer 52.24; **919** Zech 3.1,8

    [D/A] **105** Sir 50.1–21; **143** 1 Macc 10.20–21; **160** 2 Macc 3.16; **161** 2 Macc 4.7

    [NT] **38** Mt 26.3,51,57,58,62,63,65; **67** Mk 14.47,53,54,60,61,63,66; **112** Lk 22.50; **134** Jn 11.49,51; **141** Jn 18.13,15,16,19, 22,24,26; **154** Acts 4.6; **155** Acts 5.17,21,27; **157** Acts 7.1; **176** Acts 19.14; **182** Acts 24.1; **277** Heb 8.3; **278** Heb 9.7,25; **283** Heb 13.11

  (b) Christ [NT] **274** Heb 2.17; **274** Heb 3.1; **275** Heb 4.14,15; **275** Heb 5.1–6,10; **276** Heb 6.20; **276** Heb 7.15–17,21,24,26–28; **277** Heb 8.1–4

Hittite [OT] **18** Gen 15.20; **25** Gen 23.3–20; **85** Ex 23.28; **310** 2 Sam 11.3–24; **348** 1 Kgs 10.29; **348** 1 Kgs 11.1

Holofernes [D/A] **17** Jdt 2.4—7.18; **24** Jdt 10.13—14.18

Holy Spirit [NT]

  (a) in life and teaching of Jesus **4** Mt 1.18,20; **6** Mt 3.11,16; **6** Mt 4.1; **18** Mt 12.18,28,31, 32; **45** Mk 1.8; **74** Lk 1.35; **80** Lk 4.14,18; **92** Lk 10.21; **119** Jn 1.33; **121** Jn 3.5,6,8,34; **138** Jn 14.17,26; **139** Jn 15.26; **139** Jn 16.13; **146** Jn 20.22; **149** Acts 1.2,5,8

  (b) in early Church **151** Acts 2.1–4, 17,18,33,38; **155** Acts 5.3,9,32; **160** Acts 8.15–19,29,39; **162** Acts 9.17,31; **163** Acts 10.19,38,44–47; **165** Acts 11.12,15–17, 24,28; **166** Acts 13.2,4,9,52; **175** Acts 19.1–7

(c) in letters of Paul **196** Rom 8; **215** 1 Cor 12.1–13; **235** Gal 5

Husband
(a) literal [OT] **6** Gen 3.6,16; **136** Num 5.13,20,27; **259** Ruth 1.3–12; **497** Esth 1.17,20; **630** Prov 12.4; **647** Prov 31.11 [D/A] **8** Tob 7.12–13; **9** Tob 8.6–7 [NT] **210** 1 Cor 7.2–4,10–16,34,39; **243** Eph 5.22–28,33; **252** Col 3.18–19; **291** 1 Pet 3.1,5,7
(b) figurative [OT] **718** Is 54.5; **724** Is 62.4; **765** Jer 31.31–32; **870** Hos 2.7,16 [NT] **228** 2 Cor 11.2; **235** Gal 4.27; **321** Rev 21.2

I

Iconium [NT] **168** Acts 13.51—14.6; **168** Acts 14.9,21; **171** Acts 16.2; **266** 2 Tim 3.11

Idol [OT] **120** Lev 19.4; **201** Deut 29.17; **355** 1 Kgs 15.12; **387** 2 Kgs 17.12,15; **461** 2 Chr 33.7,15; **592** Ps 96.5; **604** Ps 115.4–8; **615** Ps 135.15–18; **701** Is 40.19; **702** Is 41.7; **707** Is 44.12–20; **709** Is 46.1–7; **742** Jer 10.3–5; **837** Ezek 36.25; **872** Hos 4.17 [D/A] **113** Let Jer 4–73; **122** Bel 3–22 [NT] **159** Acts 7.41; **174** Acts 17.16; **212** 1 Cor 8.1,4,7,10; **225** 2 Cor 6.16; **254** 1 Thes 1.9; **302** 1 Jn 5.21; **308** Rev 2.14,20

Immanuel [OT] **673** Is 7.14; **674** Is 8.8 [NT] **4** Mt 1.23

Isaac [OT] **19** Gen 18.1–15; **23** Gen 21.1–7; **24** Gen 22.1–19; **25** Gen 24; **28** Gen 25.19–26; **30** Gen 27.1–40; **42** Gen 35.29 [D/A] **101** Sir 44.22–23 [NT] **3** Mt 1.2; **12** Mt 8.11; **158** Acts 7.8; **198** Rom 9.7,10; **235** Gal 4.28; **280** Heb 11.9,17–18,20; **286** Jas 2.21

Isaiah [OT] **392** 2 Kgs 19—20; **672** Is 6; **672** Is 7.3; **674** Is 8.3; **697** Is 37—39 [D/A] **104** Sir 48.20–22 [NT] **5** Mt 3.3; **7** Mt 4.14; **12** Mt 8.17; **17** Mt 12.17; **19** Mt 13.14; **22** Mt 15.7; **45** Mk 1.2; **79** Lk 3.4; **80** Lk 4.17; **118** Jn 1.23; **136** Jn 12.38–41; **161** Acts 8.28,30; **188** Acts 28.25; **198** Rom 9.27–29; **199** Rom 10.16,20–21; **203** Rom 15.12

Ishmael [OT] **18** Gen 16.3,15; **19** Gen 17.25–26; **23** Gen 21.3–21; **28** Gen 25.9,12–17; **32** Gen 28.9

Israel
(a) name given to Jacob [OT] **38** Gen 32.22–32
(b) descendants of Jacob [OT] **39** Gen 34.7; **92** Ex 32.4; **174** Deut 4.1
(c) other uses of term: name for northern kingdom [OT] **276** 1 Sam 11.8; **285** 1 Sam 17.52; name for united monarchy **351** 1 Kgs 11.42; name for returning exiles **476** Ezra 9.1; **488** Neh 9.2
(d) New Testament usage [NT] **14** Mt 10.6; **23** Mt 15.24; **75** Lk 1.68,80; **77** Lk 2.25,32,34;

116 Lk 24.21; **149** Acts 1.6; **157** Acts 5.31,35; **167** Acts 13.16,17,23,24; **198** Rom 9.6,27,31; **199** Rom 10.19,21; **199** Rom 11.2,7,11,25–26; **277** Heb 8.8–10; **311** Rev 7.4; **322** Rev 21.12

Italy [NT] **163** Acts 10.1; **174** Acts 18.2; **185** Acts 27.1,6; **284** Heb 13.24

J

Jacob [OT] **28** Gen 25.19—35.29; **53** Gen 46—50 [D/A] **101** Sir 44.23; **205** 2 Esd 3.15–16; **210** 2 Esd 6.8–9 [NT] **3** Mt 1.2; **12** Mt 8.11; **74** Lk 1.33; **122** Jn 4.5,6,12; **158** Acts 7.8,12,14,15,46; **198** Rom 9.13; **280** Heb 11.9,20,21

Jairus [NT] **52** Mk 5.22; **88** Lk 8.41

James [NT]
(a) son of Zebedee **7** Mt 4.21; **24** Mt 17.1; **45** Mk 1.19,29; **52** Mk 5.37; **57** Mk 9.2; **61** Mk 10.35,41; **64** Mk 13.3; **67** Mk 14.33; **81** Lk 5.10; **91** Lk 9.54; **149** Acts 1.13; **165** Acts 12.2
(b) son of Alphaeus **14** Mt 10.3; **49** Mk 3.18; **84** Lk 6.15; **149** Acts 1.13
(c) son of Mary **43** Mt 27.56; **71** Mk 15.40; **72** Mk 16.1; **115** Lk 24.10
(d) brother of Jesus **21** Mt 13.55; **52** Mk 6.3; **166** Acts 12.17; **169** Acts 15.13; **178** Acts 21.18; **232** Gal 1.19; **232** Gal 2.9,12
(e) father of Judas **84** Lk 6.16; **149** Acts 1.13
(f) author of the letter **284** Jas 1.1
(g) brother of Jude **304** Jude 1

Jehoshaphat [OT] **355** 1 Kgs 15.24; **364** 1 Kgs 22.2–50; **443** 2 Chr 17—20

Jehu (king of Israel) [OT] **377** 2 Kgs 9—10

Jeremiah (prophet) [OT] **466** 2 Chr 36.12,21,22; **720** Jer 1.1; **864** Dan 9.2 [D/A] **105** Sir 49.6–7; **158** 2 Macc 2.1–8 [NT] **5** Mt 2.17; **24** Mt 16.14; **41** Mt 27.9

Jericho [OT] **155** Num 22.1; **209** Josh 2.1–24; **212** Josh 5.13—6.26; **224** Josh 16.1,7; **236** Judg 3.13; **356** 1 Kgs 16.34; **367** 2 Kgs 2.4,5,15,18 [D/A] **18** Jdt 4.4; **80** Sir 24.14; **141** 1 Macc 9.50; **155** 1 Macc 16.11 [NT] **29** Mt 20.29; **61** Mk 10.46; **93** Lk 10.30; **105** Lk 18.35; **105** Lk 19.1; **281** Heb 11.30

Jeroboam (king of Israel) [OT] **348** 1 Kgs 11.26—14.20 (**439** 2 Chr 10.2—13.20) [D/A] **103** Sir 47.23

Jerusalem
(a) the city [OT] **217** Josh 10.1; **224** Josh 15.63; **234** Judg 1.8; **305** 2 Sam 5.6; **384** 2 Kgs 14.13; **398** 2 Kgs 24.10,14; **398** 2 Kgs 25.10; **467** Ezra 1.2–11; **493** Neh 12.27; **566** Ps 51.18; **611** Ps 122.6; **708** Is 44.26; **741** Jer 9.11; **883** Joel 3.17; **926** Zech 12.2–12

[D/A] **14** Tob 13.8-18; **26** Jdt 11.13-14; **110** Bar 4.5—5.9; **152** 1 Macc 13.49-52; **162** 2 Macc 4.9-15; **220** 2 Esd 10.20-24,44-50

[NT] **4** Mt 2.1,3; **29** Mt 20.17-18; **31** Mt 21.1,10; **35** Mt 23.37; **60** Mk 10.32; **61** Mk 11.1,11,15; **76** Lk 2.22,25,38,41,43,45; **99** Lk 13.33-35; **107** Lk 19.28,37; **109** Lk 21.20,24; **120** Jn 2.13; **123** Jn 4.20; **124** Jn 5.1; **135** Jn 12.12; **149** Acts 1.4,8,12; **169** Acts 15.2; **171** Acts 16.4

(b) the heavenly [NT] **235** Gal 4.26; **282** Heb 12.22; **309** Rev 3.12; **321** Rev 21.2,10

Jesse [OT] **264** Ruth 4.18-22; **282** 1 Sam 16.1-22; **284** 1 Sam 17.12-14,17; **677** Is 11.1,10;

[NT] **3** Mt 1.5-6; **167** Acts 13.22; **203** Rom 15.12

Jesus Christ [NT]

(a) name **4** Mt 1.21,25; **74** Lk 1.31; **76** Lk 2.21

(b) genealogy **3** Mt 1.1-17; **79** Lk 3.23-38

(c) birth and infancy **4** Mt 1.18—2.23; **74** Lk 1.26-38; **76** Lk 2.1-40

(d) twelve years **77** Lk 2.41-52

(e) baptism and temptation **6** Mt 3.13—4.11; **45** Mk 1.9-13; **79** Lk 3.21-22; **80** Lk 4.1-13

(f) ministry in Galilee **7** Mt 4.12—18.35; **45** Mk 1.14—9.50; **80** Lk 4.14—9.50; Sermon on the Mount **7** Mt 5.1—7.29; **84** Lk 6.17-49; confession at Caesarea Philippi **24** Mt 16.13-28; **57** Mk 8.27—9.1; **89** Lk 9.18-27; transfiguration **24** Mt 17.1-13; **57** Mk 9.2-13; **90** Lk 9.28-36

(g) last days in Jerusalem **31** Mt 21.1—27.66; **61** Mk 11.1—15.47; **107** Lk 19.28—23.56; **134** Jn 12.1—19.42; triumphal entry **31** Mt 21.1-11; **61** Mk 11.1-11; **107** Lk 19.29-44; **135** Jn 12.12-19; in the Temple **31** Mt 21.12-17; **62** Mk 11.15-19; **107** Lk 19.45-48; discourse on last things **35** Mt 24.1—25.46; **64** Mk 13.1-37; **109** Lk 21.5-36; Last Supper **39** Mt 26.17-35; **66** Mk 14.12-31; **110** Lk 22.7-38; **136** Jn 13.1—17.26; **215** 1 Cor 11.23-26; Gethsemane **39** Mt 26.36-46; **67** Mk 14.32-42; **111** Lk 22.39-46; arrest, trial, crucifixion, death, and burial **40** Mt 26.47—27.66; **67** Mk 14.43—15.47; **111** Lk 22.47—23.56; **141** Jn 18.1—19.42

(h) resurrection, appearances, ascension **43** Mt 28.1-20; **72** Mk 16.1-20; **115** Lk 24.1-53; **145** Jn 20.1—21.25; **149** Acts 1.1-11; **218** 1 Cor 15.4-8

Jewels [OT] **88** Ex 28.17-21; **99** Ex 38.10-13

[NT] **10** Mt 7.6; **20** Mt 13.45,46; **207** 1 Cor 3.12; **261** 1 Tim 2.9; **291** 1 Pet 3.3; **318** Rev 17.4; **319** Rev 18.12,16; **322** Rev 21.11,18-21

Jezebel

(a) wife of Ahab, king of Israel [OT] **356** 1 Kgs 16.31; **360** 1 Kgs 19.1-2; **363** 1 Kgs 21.1-25; **377** 2 Kgs 9.7-10,30-37

(b) name given to woman who lured Christians to fornication and idolatry [NT] **308** Rev 2.20-23

Joab [OT] **302** 2 Sam 2.12-32; **303** 2 Sam 3.22-30; **310** 2 Sam 11.6-21; **315** 2 Sam 14.28-33; **320** 2 Sam 18.9-17; **324** 2 Sam 20.4-23; **335** 1 Kgs 2.28-34

John [NT]

(a) the Baptist **5** Mt 3.1-15; **16** Mt 11.2-19; **21** Mt 14.2-12; **32** Mt 21.25-32; **45** Mk 1.4-11; **53** Mk 6.14-29; **62** Mk 11.29-33; **74** Lk 1.13-25,57-80; **79** Lk 3.2-20; **86** Lk 7.18-33; **94** Lk 11.1; **118** Jn 1.6-36; **121** Jn 3.23-30

(b) son of Zebedee **7** Mt 4.21; **46** Mk 1.29; **52** Mk 5.37; **57** Mk 9.2,38; **61** Mk 10.35,41; **64** Mk 13.3; **91** Lk 9.49,54; **110** Lk 22.8; **153** Acts 3.1-11; **154** Acts 4.13-21; **160** Acts 8.14-17; **232** Gal 2.9

(c) author of Revelation **306** Rev 1.1,4,9; **322** Rev 22.8

(d) father of Simon Peter **24** Mt 16.17; **119** Jn 1.42; **147** Jn 21.15-17

(e) Mark **166** Acts 12.12,25; **167** Acts 13.5,13; **171** Acts 15.37,39; **252** Col 4.10; **267** 2 Tim 4.11; **271** Phlm 24; **293** 1 Pet 5.13

(f) of family of high priest Annas **154** Acts 4.6

Jonah [OT] **384** 2 Kgs 14.25; **895** Jon 1.1

[NT] **18** Mt 12.39-41; **23** Mt 16.4; **95** Lk 11.29-32

Jonathan

(a) son of Saul [OT] **277** 1 Sam 13.2-4; **279** 1 Sam 14.1-15,36-46; **286** 1 Sam 18.1-5; **288** 1 Sam 20; **299** 1 Sam 31.2; **301** 2 Sam 1.11-27

(b) son of Mattathias [D/A] **127** 1 Macc 2.5; **141** 1 Macc 9.23—12.53

Joppa [OT] **228** Josh 19.46; **432** 2 Chr 2.16; **469** Ezra 3.7; **895** Jon 1.3

[D/A] **146** 1 Macc 10.75; **162** 2 Macc 4.21; **173** 2 Macc 12.3-4

[NT] **163** Acts 9.36-43; **163** Acts 10.5-8,23,32; **164** Acts 11.5,13

Jordan [OT] **16** Gen 13.10-11; **38** Gen 32.10; **175** Deut 4.22; **208** Josh 1.2; **210** Josh 3.17; **323** 2 Sam 19.15; **368** 2 Kgs 2.7; **373** 2 Kgs 5.10; **374** 2 Kgs 6.4; **744** Jer 12.5

[D/A] **16** Jdt 1.9; **134** 1 Macc 5.24; **141** 1 Macc 9.43-48

[NT] **5** Mt 3.5-6,13; **45** Mk 1.5,9; **59** Mk 10.1; **79** Lk 3.3; **119** Jn 1.28; **132** Jn 10.40

Joseph

(a) son of Jacob [OT] **35** Gen 30.22-24; **43** Gen 37.5—50.26; **233** Josh 24.32; **597** Ps 105.17-22

[D/A] **105** Sir 49.15

[NT] **122** Jn 4.5; **158** Acts 7.9-14
(b) husband of Mary [NT] **4** Mt 1.16–25; **4** Mt 2.13–15,19–23; **74** Lk 1.27; **76** Lk 2.4,16; **80** Lk 4.22; **119** Jn 1.45; **126** Jn 6.42
(c) brother of Jesus [NT] **21** Mt 13.55; **52** Mk 6.3
(d) brother of James "the younger" [NT] **43** Mt 27.56; **71** Mk 15.40,47
(e) of Arimathea [NT] **43** Mt 27.57-60; **71** Mk 15.42-46; **115** Lk 23.50-53; **144** Jn 19.38–42
(f) Barsabbas [NT] **151** Acts 1.23
(g) Barnabas [NT] **155** Acts 4.36
Joshua [OT] **78** Ex 17.8-13; **86** Ex 24.13; **94** Ex 33.11; **144** Num 13.1-16; **145** Num 14.6-9; **162** Num 27.18-23; **165** Deut 31.23; **208** Josh 1—24
[D/A] **102** Sir 46.1–8
[NT] **159** Acts 7.45; **274** Heb 4.8
Josiah (king of Judah) [OT] **394** 2 Kgs 21.24—23.30 (**463** 2 Chr 33.25—35.27)
[D/A] **104** Sir 49.1–7
Judaea [NT] **4** Mt 2.1,5,22; **5** Mt 3.1,5; **28** Mt 19.1; **36** Mt 24.16; **75** Lk 1.65; **121** Jn 3.22; **127** Jn 7.1,3; **133** Jn 11.7; **149** Acts 1.8; **178** Acts 21.10; **204** Rom 15.31; **232** Gal 1.22; **254** 1 Thes 2.14
Judah [OT] **34** Gen 29.35; **45** Gen 37.26-28; **45** Gen 38; **51** Gen 44.14-34; **56** Gen 49.8-12; **205** Deut 33.7
[NT] **276** Heb 7.14
Judas
(a) Judas Maccabaeus [D/A] **127** 1 Macc 2.1-5; **129** 1 Macc 3.1—9.21; **164** 2 Macc 5.27; **168** 2 Macc 8.1-33; **170** 2 Macc 10.1—15.36
(b) Iscariot [NT] **14** Mt 10.4; **39** Mt 26.14,25,47; **41** Mt 27.3; **49** Mk 3.19; **66** Mk 14.10,43; **110** Lk 22.3,47-48; **127** Jn 6.71; **135** Jn 12.4; **136** Jn 13.2,26,29; **141** Jn 18.2-3,5; **149** Acts 1.16,25
(c) brother of Jesus [NT] **21** Mt 13.55; **52** Mk 6.3
(d) apostle [NT] **138** Jn 14.22
(e) the Galilean [NT] **157** Acts 5.37
(f) of Damascus [NT] **161** Acts 9.11
(g) of Jerusalem [NT] **171** Acts 15.22,27,32
Judgement
(a) God [OT] **18** Gen 15.14 (**158** Acts 7.7); **20** Gen 18.25; **64** Ex 6.6; **247** Judg 11.27; **344** 1 Kgs 8.32 (**435** 2 Chr 6.23); **540** Ps 7.6,8,11; **592** Ps 96.10,12,13; **658** Ecc 12.14; **803** Ezek 7.3,8; **883** Joel 3.12
[NT] **8** Mt 5.22; **10** Mt 7.1-2; **85** Lk 6.37; **121** Jn 3.19; **191** Rom 2.2-3,5,16; **202** Rom 14.10; **279** Heb 10.30; **282** Heb 12.23; **283** Heb 13.4; **286** Jas 2.12-13; **286** Jas 3.1; **287** Jas 4.12; **316** Rev 14.7; **321** Rev 20.12-13
(b) Christ [NT] **124** Jn 5.22,27,30; **129** Jn 8.15-16.26; **131** Jn 9.39; **136** Jn 12.47-48;

164 Acts 10.42; **225** 2 Cor 5.10; **266** 2 Tim 4.1; **320** Rev 19.11
(c) day of judgement (Day of the Lord) [OT] **679** Is 13.6,9; **695** Is 34.1-15; **778** Jer 46.10; **803** Ezek 7.7-19; **829** Ezek 30.2-3; **880** Joel 2.1-2,11,31; **888** Amos 5.18-20; **913** Zeph 1.7-18
[D/A] **30** Jdt 16.17; **46** Wis 4.20—5.14; **213** 2 Esd 7.31-44,102-115
[NT] **11** Mt 7.22; **15** Mt 10.15; **16** Mt 11.22,24; **18** Mt 12.36,41,42; **92** Lk 10.12,14; **95** Lk 11.31,32; **110** Lk 21.34; **124** Jn 5.24,29; **136** Jn 12.48; **191** Rom 2.16; **256** 1 Thes 5.2,4; **265** 2 Tim 1.12,18; **279** Heb 10.25,27; **296** 2 Pet 2.4,9; **296** 2 Pet 3.3,7,10; **301** 1 Jn 4.17; **320** Rev 19.11-15; **321** Rev 20.11-15

K

Kadesh, Kadesh Barnea [OT] **18** Gen 16.14; **144** Num 13.26; **152** Num 20.1-22; **166** Num 32.8; **171** Deut 1.2; **219** Josh 10.41
[D/A] **19** Jdt 5.14
Kedesh [D/A] **1** Tob 1.3; **148** 1 Macc 11.63,73
King
(a) God [OT] **272** 1 Sam 8.7; **543** Ps 10.16; **549** Ps 24.7-10; **552** Ps 29.10; **590** Ps 93.1; **591** Ps 95.3; **592** Ps 96.10; **593** Ps 98.6; **593** Ps 99.1; **672** Is 6.5; **695** Is 33.22; **742** Jer 10.10; **927** Zech 14.9,16
[D/A] **1** Tob 1.18; **11** Tob 11.1; 13.6; **24** Jdt 9.12; **191** 1 Esd 4.58
[NT] **8** Mt 5.35; **261** 1 Tim 1.17; **316** Rev 15.3
(b) Christ [NT] **38** Mt 25.34,40; **107** Lk 19.38; **125** Jn 6.15; **135** Jn 12.15; **142** Jn 18.37; **174** Acts 17.7; **318** Rev 17.14; **320** Rev 19.16
(c) "King of the Jews" (as title of Christ) [NT] **4** Mt 2.2; **41** Mt 27.11,29,37; **69** Mk 15.2,9,12,18,26; **113** Lk 23.3,37,38; **142** Jn 18.33,39; **143** Jn 19.3,14-15,19,21
(d) "King of Israel" (as title of Christ) [NT] **42** Mt 27.42; **70** Mk 15.32; **120** Jn 1.49; **135** Jn 12.13
King of Egypt
(a) and Abraham [OT] **16** Gen 12.15-20
(b) and Joseph [OT] **47** Gen 41.1-55; **53** Gen 47.1-26
[NT] **158** Acts 7.10,13,21
(c) the oppression [OT] **59** Ex 1.8-11,15-22; **60** Ex 2.15,23
(d) the Exodus [OT] **61** Ex 3.11; **63** Ex 4.21-23; **63** Ex 5.1-23; **64** Ex 6—14; **75** Ex 15.19
[NT] **198** Rom 9.17
(e) and Solomon [OT] **336** 1 Kgs 3.1; **345** 1 Kgs 9.16; **348** 1 Kgs 11.1
(f) and Hadad of Edom [OT] **348** 1 Kgs 11.18-22

(g) King Neco [OT] **397** 2 Kgs 23.29-35
(h) King Hophra [OT] **777** Jer 44.30
(i) Ptolemy VI Philometor [D/A] **125** 1 Macc
1.18; **144** 1 Macc 10.51-57; **170** 2 Macc
9.29

L

Lake Galilee see Galilee
Lake Tiberias see Galilee
Lamb
(a) sacrifices: before Mosaic law [OT] **7** Gen
4.4; **24** Gen 22.7-8; burnt-offering **109** Lev
9.3; fellowship-offering **124** Lev 23.19
(b) Passover [OT] **69** Ex 12.3,5; **464** 2 Chr
35.11
[NT] **66** Mk 14.12; **110** Lk 22.7
(c) figurative [OT] **717** Is 53.7; **743** Jer 11.19
(d) figure or title of Christ [NT] **119** Jn 1.29,36;
209 1 Cor 5.7; **290** 1 Pet 1.19; **310** Rev
5.6,8,12,13; **311** Rev 7.9,10,14,17; **314** Rev
12.11; **318** Rev 17.14; **320** Rev 19.7,9; **322**
Rev 21.9,14,22,23,27; **322** Rev 22.1,3
Laodicea [NT] **251** Col 2.1; **253** Col 4.13-16;
307 Rev 1.11; **309** Rev 3.14-22
Lazarus [NT] **102** Lk 16.19-31; **133** Jn 11.1-44;
134 Jn 12.1,2,9-11
Leper, Leprosy see Skin-disease
Levi (apostle, also called Matthew) [NT] **47** Mk
2.14; **83** Lk 5.27,29
Levite [OT] **64** Ex 6.16-25; **93** Ex 32.26-29;
132 Num 1.47-53; **133** Num 3.5-51; **138**
Num 8.5-26; **168** Num 35.2-8; **184** Deut
12.12,19; **189** Deut 17.9,18; **189** Deut 18.1-8;
196 Deut 26.11-13; **216** Josh 8.33; **253** Judg
17.7—18.20; **255** Judg 19.1; **440** 2 Chr 11.14;
473 Ezra 6.18; **475** Ezra 8.15-20; **768** Jer
33.18,21-22
[D/A] **189** 1 Esd 1.10-14; **196** 1 Esd
7.10-11
[NT] **93** Lk 10.32; **118** Jn 1.19; **155** Acts
4.36
Lord's Prayer [NT] **9** Mt 6.9-13; **94** Lk 11.2-4
Lord's Supper [NT] **39** Mt 26.26-30; **66** Mk
14.22-26; **110** Lk 22.15-20; **215** 1 Cor
11.23-25
Love
(a) God [OT] **80** Ex 20.6; **95** Ex 34.6; **176**
Deut 5.10; **178** Deut 7.7; **550** Ps 25.6-7,10;
595 Ps 103.17; **718** Is 54.8,10; **876** Hos
11.1-4,8,9
[D/A] **52** Wis 11.25; **62** Sir 2.18; **75** Sir
18.13; **101** Sir 45.1
[NT] **121** Jn 3.16; **138** Jn 14.23; **140** Jn
16.27; **194** Rom 5.5,8; **197** Rom 8.39; **238**
Eph 1.5; **240** Eph 2.4; **299** 1 Jn 3.1; **300**
1 Jn 4.7-12
(b) Christ [NT] **133** Jn 11.3,5; **136** Jn 13.1,34;
138 Jn 14.31; **139** Jn 15.9-10,12; **197** Rom
8.35,37; **225** 2 Cor 5.14; **233** Gal 2.20; **241**
Eph 3.19; **242** Eph 5.2; **307** Rev 1.5

Luke [NT] **253** Col 4.14; **267** 2 Tim 4.11; **271**
Phlm 24
Lydia [NT] **172** Acts 16.14,40
Lystra [NT] **168** Acts 14.6,8,21; **171** Acts
16.1-2; **266** 2 Tim 3.11

M

Macedonia [D/A] **124** 1 Macc 1.1; **167** 2 Macc
8.20
[NT] **172** Acts 16.9-10,12; **176** Acts
19.21-22; **177** Acts 20.1,3; **204** Rom 15.26;
223 2 Cor 2.13; **226** 2 Cor 7.5; **226** 2 Cor 8.1;
248 Phil 4.15; **254** 1 Thes 1.7-8; **260** 1 Tim
1.3
"Magnificat" [NT] **75** Lk 1.46-55
Manna [OT] **76** Ex 16.1-4,12-15,22-35; **141**
Num 11.7-9; **212** Josh 5.10-12; **489** Neh 9.20
[D/A] **57** Wis 16.20-29
[NT] **126** Jn 6.31,49; **277** Heb 9.4; **308**
Rev 2.17
Mark see John (e)
Marriage [OT] **25** Gen 24; **32** Gen 27.46—28.5;
33 Gen 29.15-30; **104** Lev 4.13-15; **263**
Ruth 4.10-16; **336** 1 Kgs 3.1; **348** 1 Kgs
11.1-3
[NT] **8** Mt 5.32; **28** Mt 19.3-12; **33** Mt
22.24-30; **59** Mk 10.1-12; **63** Mk 12.19-25;
99 Lk 14.20; **102** Lk 16.18; **103** Lk 17.27;
108 Lk 20.27-36; **120** Jn 2.1-10; **210** 1 Cor
7.1-16,25-40; **261** 1 Tim 3.2,12; 4.3; 5.11,14;
268 Tit 1.6; **274** Heb 13.4
Marriage-feast [NT] **32** Mt 22.1-14; **99** Lk 14.8;
320 Rev 19.7,9
Martha [NT] **93** Lk 10.38-41; **133** Jn 11.1-40;
134 Jn 12.2
Martyrs (seven brothers) [D/A] **166** 2 Macc
7.1-42
Mary [NT]
(a) mother of Jesus **4** Mt 1.16,18,20; **4** Mt
2.11; **21** Mt 13.55; **52** Mk 6.3; **74** Lk
1.27,30,34,38,39,41,46,56; **76** Lk 2.5,16,
19,34; **120** Jn 2.1-5,12; **144** Jn 19.25-27;
149 Acts 1.14
(b) Magdalene **43** Mt 27.56,61; **43** Mt 28.1;
71 Mk 15.40,47; **72** Mk 16.1,9; **87** Lk 8.2;
115 Lk 24.10; **144** Jn 19.25; **145** Jn
20.1-18
(c) mother of James and Joseph **43** Mt
27.56,61; **43** Mt 28.1; **71** Mk 15.40,47; **72**
Mk 16.1; **115** Lk 24.10; **144** Jn 19.25
(d) of Bethany **93** Lk 10.39,42; **133** Jn
11.1-2,19,20,28,31-32,45; **134** Jn 12.3
(e) mother of John Mark **166** Acts 12.12
Matthew [NT] **13** Mt 9.9; **49** Mk 3.18; **84** Lk
6.15
Matthias [NT] **151** Acts 1.23,26
Melchizedek [OT] **17** Gen 14.18-20; **602** Ps
110.4
[NT] **275** Heb 5.6,10; **276** Heb 6.20; **276**
Heb 7.1-11,15-17

Mercy, pity
(a) of God [OT] **95** Ex 33.19; **95** Ex 34.6–7; **175** Deut 4.31; **550** Ps 25.16; **595** Ps 103.8; **864** Dan 9.9; **897** Jon 4.2
  [D/A] **8** Tob 7.12; **9** Tob 8.4–7; **22** Jdt 7.30; **28** Jdt 13.14; **52** Wis 11.23,26; **53** Wis 12.22; **55** Wis 15.1; **62** Sir 2.11; **103** Sir 47.22
  [NT] **75** Lk 1.50,54,58,72,78; **85** Lk 6.36; **198** Rom 9.15–16,18,23; **200** Rom 11.30–32; **240** Eph 2.4; **260** 1 Tim 1.2,13,16; **269** Tit 3.5; **289** 1 Pet 1.3; **291** 1 Pet 2.10
(b) of Christ [NT] **14** Mt 9.27; **23** Mt 15.22; **25** Mt 17.15; **31** Mt 20.30–31; **274** Heb 2.17; **305** Jude 21
Michael [OT] **866** Dan 10.13,21; **868** Dan 12.1
  [NT] **305** Jude 9; **314** Rev 12.7
Midian
(a) son of Abraham by Keturah [OT] **28** Gen 25.1–6
(b) people of Midian, and region occupied by them [OT] **28** Gen 25.6; **42** Gen 36.35; **45** Gen 37.28,36; **61** Ex 3.1; **157** Num 22.4,7; **160** Num 25; **165** Num 31; **239** Judg 6—8; **675** Is 9.4; **722** Is 60.6
  [NT] **158** Acts 7.29
Miracles of Jesus [NT]
(a) general **7** Mt 4.23–24; **12** Mt 8.16; **14** Mt 9.35; **17** Mt 12.15; **21** Mt 14.14,35–36; **23** Mt 15.30–31; **28** Mt 19.2; **31** Mt 21.14; **46** Mk 1.32–34,39; **48** Mk 3.9–12; **52** Mk 6.5,53–56; **81** Lk 4.40–41; **82** Lk 5.15; **84** Lk 6.18–19; **86** Lk 7.21; **89** Lk 9.11; **121** Jn 2.23; **121** Jn 3.2; **125** Jn 6.2; **136** Jn 12.37; **146** Jn 20.30; **164** Acts 10.38
(b) driving out demons: blind and dumb **18** Mt 12.22; daughter of woman of Tyre **23** Mt 15.21–28; **55** Mk 7.24–30; dumb man **14** Mt 9.32–33; **94** Lk 11.14; epileptic boy **25** Mt 17.14–20; **58** Mk 9.14–21; **91** Lk 9.37–43; Gerasene men **50** Mk 5.1–20; **88** Lk 8.26–39; man in Capernaum **46** Mk 1.23–28; **81** Lk 4.33–37; Mary Magdalene **72** Mk 16.9; **87** Lk 8.2; men of Gadara **13** Mt 8.28–34; woman in synagogue **98** Lk 13.10–17
(c) other cures: blind Bartimaeus **29** Mt 20.29–34; **61** Mk 10.46–52; **105** Lk 18.35–43; blind man at Bethsaida **57** Mk 8.22–26; man born blind **130** Jn 9.1–7; two blind men **14** Mt 9.27–31; deaf-mute **56** Mk 7.31–37; man with skin-disease **12** Mt 8.1–4; **46** Mk 1.40–45; **82** Lk 5.12–16; man with crippled hand **17** Mt 12.9–14; **48** Mk 3.1–6; **84** Lk 6.6–11; man with swollen arms and legs **99** Lk 14.1–6; officer's servant **12** Mt 8.5–13; **85** Lk 7.1–10; paralysed man in Capernaum **13** Mt 9.1–8; **47** Mk 2.1–12; **82** Lk 5.17–26; paralysed man in Jerusalem **124** Jn 5.1–9; Peter's mother-in-law **12** Mt

8.14–15; 46 Mk 1.29–31; **81** Lk 4.38–39; slave of High Priest **112** Lk 22.50–51; son of official **123** Jn 4.46–54; ten men with skin-disease **103** Lk 17.11–19; woman with severe bleeding **14** Mt 9.20–22; **52** Mk 5.23–34; **88** Lk 8.43–48
(d) raising of dead: daughter of Jairus **13** Mt 9.18–26; **52** Mk 5.21–43; **88** Lk 8.40–56; son of widow of Nain **86** Lk 7.11–17; Lazarus **133** Jn 11.1–44
(e) other miracles: coin in fish's mouth **25** Mt 17.24–27; cursing the fig-tree **31** Mt 21.19; **62** Mk 11.14,20; feeding the five thousand **21** Mt 14.13–21; **53** Mk 6.30–44; **89** Lk 9.10–17; **125** Jn 6.1–14; feeding the four thousand **23** Mt 15.32–39; **56** Mk 8.1–10; great catch of fish **81** Lk 5.4–10; another catch of fish **146** Jn 21.6–11; stilling the storm **12** Mt 8.23–27; **50** Mk 4.35–41; **88** Lk 8.22–25; walking on the water **21** Mt 14.22–33; **54** Mk 6.45–52; **125** Jn 6.16–21; water changed to wine **120** Jn 2.1–11
Miracles of others
  [OT] of Moses **62** Ex 4.3–7; **65** Ex 7.10—10.28; **74** Ex 14.21–28; **76** Ex 15.25; **78** Ex 17.6; **148** Num 16.32; **152** Num 20.11; **154** Num 21.8–9; of Joshua **210** Josh 3; **212** Josh 6; **218** Josh 10.12–14; of Samuel **277** 1 Sam 12.18; of Elijah **357** 1 Kgs 17.1,14,22; **359** 1 Kgs 18.38,41–45; **367** 2 Kgs 1.10; **368** 2 Kgs 2.8; of Elisha **368** 2 Kgs 2.14,21,24; **369** 2 Kgs 3.16–20; **370** 2 Kgs 4.4–7,35,41,43–44; **373** 2 Kgs 5.10,14,27; **374** 2 Kgs 6.6,18; **383** 2 Kgs 13.21; of Isaiah **392** 2 Kgs 20.7,11; of Daniel **861** Dan 6.22
  [NT] of apostles **14** Mt 10.1,8; **53** Mk 6.7,13; **89** Lk 9.2,6; **155** Acts 5.12,16; of the seventy-two **92** Lk 10.9,17; of Philip **160** Acts 8.6,7,13; of Peter **153** Acts 3.6–8; **163** Acts 9.34,40–41; of Paul **167** Acts 13.11; **168** Acts 14.9,10; **172** Acts 16.18; **176** Acts 19.11–12; **230** 2 Cor 12.12
Moab(ite) [OT] **22** Gen 19.37; **75** Ex 15.15; **155** Num 21.11–15,26–30; **155** Num 22.1–36; **160** Num 25.1; **171** Deut 1.5; **206** Deut 34.1–8; **236** Judg 3.12–30; **259** Ruth 1.1–6,22; **369** 2 Kgs 3.4–26; **681** Is 15.1–9; **682** Is 16.2–14; **780** Jer 48.1–47
  [D/A] **19** Jdt 5.2
Moses [OT]
(a) person, born **60** Ex 2.1–4; adopted by the king's daughter **60** Ex 2.5–10; killed Egyptian **60** Ex 2.11–12; fled to Midian **60** Ex 2.15–20; married Zipporah **61** Ex 2.21–22; called by God **61** Ex 3.1—4.17; returned to Egypt **63** Ex 4.18–31; interceded with the king **63** Ex 5—11; crossed the Red Sea **72** Ex 14; song of victory **75** Ex 15.1–18; appointed judges **79** Ex 18.13–26; met with God on Sinai **80** Ex 19.3–13; **86**

Ex 24—31; enraged by Israel's idolatry **92** Ex 32; talked with the Lord **94** Ex 33—34; built Covenant Tent **96** Ex 35—40; counted the people **131** Num 1; defended before Aaron and Miriam **143** Num 12; sent twelve spies to Canaan **144** Num 13.1-20; consecrated Joshua as his successor **162** Num 27.18-23; **203** Deut 31.23; described Israel's history **170** Deut 1—3; urged Israel to be obedient **174** Deut 4.1-40; song of Moses **203** Deut 32.1-43; looked at Canaan **174** Deut 3.23-27; **205** Deut 32.48-52; **206** Deut 34.1-4; blessed the tribes **205** Deut 33; death and burial in Moab **207** Deut 34.5-7; *see also* **208** Josh 1.5; **580** Ps 77.20; **595** Ps 103.7; **903** Mic 6.4

[D/A] **101** Sir 45.1-5

[NT] **12** Mt 8.4; **24** Mt 17.3-4; **28** Mt 19.7-8; **102** Lk 16.29,31; **108** Lk 20.37; **121** Jn 3.14; **125** Jn 5.45-46; **131** Jn 9.28-29; **154** Acts 3.22; **157** Acts 6.11,14; **158** Acts 7.20-44; **169** Acts 15.1,21; **198** Rom 9.15; **199** Rom 10.5,19; **223** 2 Cor 3.7,13; **274** Heb 3.2-5,16; **281** Heb 11.23-24; **305** Jude 9; **316** Rev 15.3

(b) Law of, [OT] **216** Josh 8.31-32; **231** Josh 23.6; **334** 1 Kgs 2.3; **396** 2 Kgs 23.25; **469** Ezra 3.2; **487** Neh 8.1

[D/A] **58** Wis 18.4; **81** Sir 24.23; **110** Bar 4.1; **176** 2 Macc 13.10

[NT] **63** Mk 12.26; **76** Lk 2.22; **117** Lk 24.44; **118** Jn 1.17,45; **168** Acts 13.39; **169** Acts 15.5; **188** Acts 28.23; **224** 2 Cor 3.15

Mount of Olives [OT] **316** 2 Sam 15.30; **927** Zech 14.4

[NT] **31** Mt 21.1; **35** Mt 24.3; **39** Mt 26.30; **61** Mk 11.1; **64** Mk 13.3; **66** Mk 14.26; **107** Lk 19.29,37; **110** Lk 21.37; **111** Lk 22.39; **128** Jn 8.1; **149** Acts 1.12

N

Naaman [OT] **373** 2 Kgs 5.1-27

[NT] **81** Lk 4.27

Nain [NT] **86** Lk 7.11

Naomi [OT] **259** Ruth 1.2—4.17

Nathan (prophet) [OT] **306** 2 Sam 7.2-17 (**419** 1 Chr 17.1-15); **311** 2 Sam 12.1-23; **333** 1 Kgs 1.8-45

[D/A] **103** Sir 47.1

Nathanael [NT] **119** Jn 1.45-49; **146** Jn 21.2

Nazarene [NT]

(a) title of Jesus **5** Mt 2.23

(b) Christian **182** Acts 24.5

Nazareth [NT] **5** Mt 2.23; **21** Mt 13.54; **31** Mt 21.11; **45** Mk 1.9; **46** Mk 1.24; **52** Mk 6.1; **74** Lk 1.26; **80** Lk 4.16; **119** Jn 1.45-46

Nazirite [OT] **136** Num 6.2-21; **248** Judg 13.5-7; **252** Judg 16.17; **886** Amos 2.11-12

Nebuchadnezzar [OT] **397** 2 Kgs 24—25; **465** 2 Chr 36; **753** Jer 21.2,7; **773** Jer 39.1,5; **778**

Jer 46.2,13,26; **782** Jer 52.4,12,28-30; **824** Ezek 26.7; **829** Ezek 29.18-19; **853** Dan 2—4

[D/A] **16** Jdt 1.1-29; **107** Bar 1.9-12; **113** Let Jer 2; **187** 1 Esd 1.40-41,45-46

Nehemiah [D/A] **105** Sir 49.13

New Moon Festival *see* Festivals

Nicodemus [NT] **121** Jn 3.1-10; **128** Jn 7.50; **144** Jn 19.39

Nicolaitans [NT] **307** Rev 2.6,15

Nile [OT] **47** Gen 41.1-3,17,18; **60** Ex 1.22; **65** Ex 7.17-25; **683** Is 19.5-8; **891** Amos 8.8

Nineveh [OT] **13** Gen 10.11-12; **392** 2 Kgs 19.36; **895** Jonah 1.2; **897** Jonah 3.2-7; **899** Jonah 4.11; **906** Nah 1.1; **907** Nah 2.8; **908** Nah 3.7

[D/A] **1** Tob 1.3; **14** Tob 14.4-10; **16** Jdt 1.1

[NT] **18** Mt 12.41; **95** Lk 11.30,32

Noah [OT] **9** Gen 5.29—9.29; **718** Is 54.9; **811** Ezek 14.14

[D/A] **5** Tob 4.12; **101** Sir 44.17-18

[NT] **36** Mt 24.37-38; **103** Lk 17.26-27; **280** Heb 11.7; **292** 1 Pet 3.20; **296** 2 Pet 2.5

"Nunc Dimittis" [NT] **77** Lk 2.29-35

O

Obedience

(a) to God or Christ [OT] **80** Ex 19.5; **175** Deut 4.30; **201** Deut 30.2,8,10,16; **232** Josh 24.24; **281** 1 Sam 15.22; **738** Jer 7.23

[D/A] **110** Bar 3.33; **167** 2 Macc 7.30

[NT] **46** Mk 1.27; **50** Mk 4.41; **122** Jn 3.36; **157** Acts 5.29,32; **275** Heb 5.8-9; **301** 1 Jn 5.2

(b) to demands of the gospel [NT] **195** Rom 6.16-17; **223** 2 Cor 2.9; **226** 2 Cor 7.15; **246** Phil 2.12; **257** 2 Thes 1.8; **259** 2 Thes 3.14

(c) to human beings [OT] **32** Gen 28.7; **56** Gen 49.10; **209** Josh 1.17; **498** Esth 2.20; **769** Jer 35.8

[D/A] **150** 1 Macc 12.43; **167** 2 Macc 7.30

[NT] **156** Acts 5.28-29; **201** Rom 13.1,5; **243** Eph 6.1,5; **269** Tit 3.1; **291** 1 Pet 2.13-17; **291** 1 Pet 3.6

(d) wisdom [D/A] **64** Sir 4.15; **81** Sir 24.22

Onesimus [NT] **252** Col 4.9; **271** Phlm 10

P

Pamphylia [NT] **151** Acts 2.10; **167** Acts 13.13; **169** Acts 14.24 **171** Acts 15.38; **186** Acts 27.5

Parables [NT]

(a) reason and use **19** Mt 13.1-17,34-35; **49** Mk 4.10-12; **87** Lk 8.9-10,16-18

(b) told by Jesus: children playing **16** Mt 11.16-19; **86** Lk 7.31-35; faithful servant **37** Mt 24.45-51; **97** Lk 12.42-46; fig-tree

36 Mt 24.32–33; **65** Mk 13.28–29; **110** Lk 21.29–31; friend at midnight **94** Lk 11.5–8; gold coins **106** Lk 19.11–27; Good Samaritan **93** Lk 10.29–37; great feast **99** Lk 14.15–24; hidden treasure **20** Mt 13.44; house owner **21** Mt 13.51–52; king going to war **100** Lk 14.31–32; lamp under a bowl **8** Mt 5.15; **50** Mk 4.21; **87** Lk 8.16; **95** Lk 11.33; lost coin **100** Lk 15.8–10; lost sheep **26** Mt 18.10–14; **100** Lk 15.3–7; lost son **100** Lk 15.11–32; mustard seed **20** Mt 13.31–32; **50** Mk 4.30–32; **98** Lk 13.18–19; net **20** Mt 13.47–50; new patch **13** Mt 9.16; **47** Mk 2.21; **83** Lk 5.36; pearl **20** Mt 13.45–46; Pharisee and tax collector **104** Lk 18.9–14; places at wedding feast **99** Lk 14.7–11; rich fool **96** Lk 12.16–21; rich man and Lazarus **102** Lk 16.19–31; seed growing **50** Mk 4.26–29; servant **103** Lk 17.7–10; shrewd manager **101** Lk 16.1–9; sower **19** Mt 13.3–9,18–23; **49** Mk 4.2–9,13–20; **87** Lk 8.5–8,11–15; ten girls **37** Mt 25.1–13; tenants in vineyard **32** Mt 21.33–46; **62** Mk 12.1–12; **108** Lk 20.9–19; three servants **37** Mt 25.14–30; tower builder **100** Lk 14.28–30; two debtors **86** Lk 7.40–43; two house builders **12** Mt 7.24–27; **85** Lk 6.47–49; two sons **32** Mt 21.28–32; unforgiving servant **27** Mt 18.23–35; unfruitful fig-tree **98** Lk 13.6–9; watchful house owner **37** Mt 24.42–44; **97** Lk 12.39–40; watchful servants **65** Mk 13.33–37; **97** Lk 12.35–38; wedding feast **32** Mt 22.1–14; wedding guests **13** Mt 9.15; **47** Mk 2.19–20; **83** Lk 5.34–35; weeds **20** Mt 13.24–30,36–43; widow and judge **103** Lk 18.1–8; wine and wineskins **13** Mt 9.17; **47** Mk 2.22; **83** Lk 5.37–38; workers in vineyard **29** Mt 20.1–16; yeast **20** Mt 13.33; **98** Lk 13.20–21

(c) in [OT] **244** Judg 9.8–20; **311** 2 Sam 12.1–14; **363** 1 Kgs 20.35–42; **383** 2 Kgs 14.9–10; **452** 2 Chr 25.18–19; **670** Is 5.1–7; **813** Ezek 17.1–10; **816** Ezek 19.1–9; **822** Ezek 23.1–49; **823** Ezek 24.1–14

Paradise [D/A] **205** 2 Esd 3.6; **206** 2 Esd 4.6–8; **210** 2 Esd 6.2; **213** 2 Esd 7.36,123; **218** 2 Esd 8.52

[NT] **114** Lk 23.43; **230** 2 Cor 12.3

Passover see Festivals

Patmos [NT] **307** Rev 1.9

Paul [NT]

(a) early life: born in Tarsus **179** Acts 22.3; sister **181** Acts 23.16; educated in Jerusalem under Gamaliel **179** Acts 22.3; tent maker by trade **174** Acts 18.3; approved of Stephen's death **159** Acts 7.58; **159** Acts 8.1; persecuted Christians **160** Acts 8.3; **179** Acts 22.4–5; **185** Acts 26.10–11; see also **219** 1 Cor 15.9; **232** Gal 1.13; **247** Phil 3.6; **260** 1 Tim 1.13

(b) conversion **161** Acts 9.3–19; **180** Acts 22.6–16; **185** Acts 26.12–18

(c) early ministry: Arabia **232** Gal 1.17; Damascus **162** Acts 9.19b–25; **185** Acts 26.20; **229** 2 Cor 11.32–33; **232** Gal 1.17; Jerusalem **162** Acts 9.26–29; **185** Acts 26.20; **232** Gal 1.18–19; Tarsus **162** Acts 9.30; Antioch **165** Acts 11.25–30; **166** Acts 12.25

(d) missionary activity: first tour **166** Acts 13.1—14.28; Jerusalem council **169** Acts 15.1–29; **232** Gal 2.1–10; second tour **171** Acts 15.36—18.23; third tour **175** Acts 18.23b—20.38; return to Jerusalem **178** Acts 21.1–26

(e) arrest and imprisonment: arrest in Jerusalem **179** Acts 21.27—23.22; imprisonment and trial in Caesarea **181** Acts 23.23—26.32; voyage to Rome **185** Acts 27.1—28.16; ministry in Rome **188** Acts 28.17–31

Peace

(a) from God [OT] **240** Judg 6.23–24; **442** 2 Chr 14.6–7; **552** Ps 29.11; **675** Is 9.6; **718** Is 54.10

[D/A] **44** Wis 3.3; **110** Bar 3.13–14

[NT] **76** Lk 2.14,29; **194** Rom 5.1; **203** Rom 15.13,33; **231** 2 Cor 13.11; **245** Phil 1.2; **248** Phil 4.7,9; **250** Col 1.2,20

(b) from Christ [NT] **138** Jn 14.27; **140** Jn 16.33; **240** Eph 2.14–18; **252** Col 3.15; **259** 2 Thes 3.16

Pentecost see Festivals

Pergamum [NT] **308** Rev 2.12

Persia [OT] **466** 2 Chr 36.20–23; **467** Ezra 1.1–2,8; **469** Ezra 3.7; **470** Ezra 4.3–5,24; **496** Esther 1.3,14,18,19; **860** Dan 5.28; **861** Dan 6.8,12,15; **864** Dan 8.20

[D/A] **30** Jdt 16.10; **122** Bel 1; **124** 1 Macc 1.1; **130** 1 Macc 3.31; **158** 2 Macc 1.33; **188** 1 Esd 2.1,3,16; **189** 1 Esd 3.1; **202** 2 Esd 1.3

Peter [NT] call to be a disciple **7** Mt 4.18–19; **45** Mk 1.16–18; **81** Lk 5.1–11; **119** Jn 1.41–42; declaration about Jesus **24** Mt 16.13–20; **57** Mk 8.27–30; **89** Lk 9.18–21; **127** Jn 6.68–69; on Mount of Transfiguration **24** Mt 17.1–13; **57** Mk 9.2–13; **90** Lk 9.28–36; **295** 2 Pet 1.16–18; in the Garden of Gethsemane **39** Mt 26.36–46; **67** Mk 14.32–42; **111** Lk 22.39–46; denies Jesus **41** Mt 26.69–74; **69** Mk 14.66–72; **112** Lk 22.56–62; **142** Jn 18.15–18,25–27; sees risen Lord **116** Lk 24.36–49; **146** Jn 21.1–23; **219** 1 Cor 15.5; sermon at Pentecost **151** Acts 2.14–41; activity in Jerusalem, Judaea, and Samaria **153** Acts 3.1—5.41; **160** Acts 8.14–25; **163** Acts 9.32—12.19; **169** Acts 15.6–11; rebuked by Paul at Antioch **233** Gal 2.11–14; prediction of his death **147** Jn 21.18–19, letters **289** 1 Pet 1.1; **294** 2 Pet 1.1

Pharaoh *see* King of Egypt
Pharisees [NT] 5 Mt 3.7; 13 Mt 9.11,14,34; 17
Mt 12.2,14,24,38; 22 Mt 15.1,12; 23 Mt
16.1,6,11–12; 28 Mt 19.3; 33 Mt 22.15; 34
Mt 23.2,13–15,23,25–29; 43 Mt 27.62; 86 Lk
7.36–50; 102 Lk 16.14; 104 Lk 18.10–11; 118
Jn 1.24; 121 Jn 3.1; 128 Jn 7.32,45–48; 169
Acts 15.5; 180 Acts 23.6–9; 183 Acts 26.5
Philadelphia [NT] 309 Rev 3.7
Philip [NT]
(a) ruler 79 Lk 3.1
(b) first husband of Herodias 21 Mt 14.3; 53
Mk 6.17
(c) apostle 14 Mt 10.3; 119 Jn 1.43–48; 125
Jn 6.5–7; 135 Jn 12.21–22; 138 Jn 14.8–9
(d) helper and evangelist 157 Acts 6.5; 160
Acts 8.5–40; 178 Acts 21.8
Philippi [NT] 172 Acts 16.12; 177 Acts 20.6;
245 Phil 1.1; 254 1 Thes 2.2
Philistines [OT] 13 Gen 10.14; 24 Gen 21.32,34;
236 Judg 3.3,31; 246 Judg 10.6,7,11; 248
Judg 13.1,5; 250 Judg 14.1–4; 250 Judg
15—16; 269 1 Sam 4—6; 277 1 Sam
13.1—14.31; 284 1 Sam 17.19–51; 780 Jer
47.1–7; 826 Ezek 25.15–17; 884 Amos 1.6–8;
892 Amos 9.7; 923 Zech 9.5–7
Pilate [NT] 41 Mt 27; 69 Mk 15; 79 Lk 3.1; 98
Lk 13.1; 113 Lk 23; 141 Jn 18—19; 153
Acts 3.13; 155 Acts 4.27; 167 Acts 13.28;
264 1 Tim 6.13
Pity *see* Mercy
Prayers
(a) [OT] 22 Gen 20.7,17; 28 Gen 25.21; 265
1 Sam 1.10–17,26–27; 307 2 Sam 7.18–27;
343 1 Kgs 8.22–54; 359 1 Kgs 18.36–37;
429 1 Chr 29.10–19; 435 2 Chr 6.13—7.1;
479 Neh 1.5–11; 488 Neh 9.6–37; 537 Job
42.8–9; 539 Ps 4.1; 572 Ps 65.2; 633 Prov
15.8,29; 667 Is 1.15; 699 Is 38.5; 719 Is
56.7; 747 Jer 14.7–9,11; 864 Dan 9.3–23
[D/A] 5 Tob 3.16; 12 Tob 12.8,12; 18
Jdt 4.9–15; 23 Jdt 9.1–14; 66 Sir 7.10,14;
91 Sir 35.14; 94 Sir 39.5; 121 Sus 42–44;
134 1 Macc 5.33; 138 1 Macc 7.37; 149
1 Macc 12.11; 218 2 Esd 8.20–36; 232
Man 1–17
(b) teaching of Jesus [NT] 9 Mt 5.44; 9 Mt
6.5–15; 94 Lk 11.1–13; 103 Lk 18.1–8
(c) in life of Jesus [NT] 21 Mt 14.19,23; 39 Mt
26.36–44; 46 Mk 1.35; 54 Mk 6.46; 67 Mk
14.32–39; 79 Lk 3.21; 82 Lk 5.16; 84 Lk
6.12; 89 Lk 9.18,29; 94 Lk 11.1; 111 Lk
22.32,41–45; 140 Jn 17.1–26; 275 Heb 5.7
(d) teaching in the letters [NT] 197 Rom 8.26;
218 1 Cor 14.13–17; 243 Eph 6.18; 248
Phil 4.6; 252 Col 4.2; 256 1 Thes 5.17; 261
1 Tim 2.1,8; 287 Jas 5.13–18; 302 1 Jn
5.16; 305 Jude 20
Preach [NT] 5 Mt 3.1–12; 7 Mt 4.17,23; 14 Mt
10.7; 16 Mt 11.5; 34 Mt 23.3; 36 Mt 24.14;
38 Mt 26.13; 49 Mk 3.14; 65 Mk 13.10; 66

Mk 14.9; 72 Mk 16.15; 80 Lk 4.18–21,43,44;
86 Lk 7.22; 87 Lk 8.1; 151 Acts 2.14–40;
154 Acts 4.8–12; 157 Acts 5.42; 6.2; 157
Acts 7.2–53; 160 Acts 8.4,25,40; 162 Acts
9.27; 164 Acts 10.34–43; 167 Acts 13.16–41;
168 Acts 14.7,21; 171 Acts 15.35; 172 Acts
16.10; 174 Acts 17.18–31; 18.5; 177 Acts
20.7–9,18–35; 188 Acts 28.31; 190 Rom 1.15;
199 Rom 10.8,14–17; 206 1 Cor 1.17,21; 207
1 Cor 2.1; 212 1 Cor 9.16,18; 218 1 Cor
15.1–7,11,14; 223 2 Cor 2.12; 224 2 Cor 4.5;
227 2 Cor 8.18; 228 2 Cor 10.16; 228 2 Cor
11.4,7; 232 Gal 1.8,9,11,16,23; 232 Gal 2.2;
235 Gal 4.13; 236 Gal 5.11; 240 Eph 2.17;
245 Phil 1.15,18; 250 Col 1.23; 254 1 Thes
2.9; 262 1 Tim 3.16; 262 1 Tim 4.13; 263
1 Tim 5.17; 265 2 Tim 2.8; 266 2 Tim 4.2;
292 1 Pet 3.19; 292 1 Pet 4.6
Priest [OT] 17 Gen 14.17–20; 80 Ex 19.6; 88
Ex 28.1—29.46; 93 Ex 32.29; 100 Ex
39.1–31; 108 Lev 8.1–36; 110 Lev 10.8–19;
112 Lev 13.1—14.57; 122 Lev 21.1–23;
22.2–16; 137 Num 6.22–27; 150 Num
18.1–20; 189 Deut 18.1–8; 254 Judg
18.6,19–30; 267 1 Sam 2.12–17,27–36; 291
1 Sam 22.11–19; 308 2 Sam 8.17,18; 325
2 Sam 20.25,26; 474 Ezra 7.1–26; 602 Ps
110.4; 797 Lam 4.13,16; 846 Ezek 44.10–31;
890 Amos 7.10; 917 Hag 2.11–14
[NT] 4 Mt 2.4; 12 Mt 8.4; 17 Mt 12.4,5;
31 Mt 21.15,23; 38 Mt 26.3,14,47,57–65; 69
Mk 15.1,10,11,31; 74 Lk 1.5,8; 93 Lk 10.31;
103 Lk 17.14; 113 Lk 23.10,13; 115 Lk
24.20; 134 Jn 11.47,49,51; 141 Jn
18.10,13–26; 144 Jn 19.15,21; 154 Acts 4.6;
155 Acts 5.17,21,27; 6.7; 157 Acts 7.1; 161
Acts 9.1; 176 Acts 19.14; 179 Acts 22.5; 180
Acts 23.2–5; 182 Acts 24.1; 183 Acts 25.15;
203 Rom 15.16; 274 Heb 2.17; 274 Heb 3.1;
275 Heb 4.14,15; 275 Heb 5.1–10; 276 Heb
6.20; 276 Heb 7.1–28; 277 Heb 8.1–6; 278
Heb 9.6–12,25; 279 Heb 10.11,21; 283 Heb
13.11; 290 1 Pet 2.5,9; 307 Rev 1.6; 310 Rev
5.10; 321 Rev 20.6; pagan priests 169 Acts
14.13
Priscilla [NT] 174 Acts 18.2,18,26; 204 Rom
16.3; 221 1 Cor 16.19; 267 2 Tim 4.19
Prize *see* Crown
Prophets
(a) of OT: 22 Gen 20.7; 142 Num 11.29; 143
Num 12.6; 184 Deut 13.1–3,5; 189 Deut
18.15,18–22; 207 Deut 34.10–12; 273
1 Sam 9.9; 275 1 Sam 10.5–6,10–13; 297
1 Sam 28.6,15; 730 Jer 1.5; 747 Jer
14.14–16; 756 Jer 23.9,11–31; 760 Jer
27.9–10,14–18; 809 Ezek 13.2–10,16; 922
Zech 7.3; 927 Zech 13.3–6
[NT] 4 Mt 1.22; 4 Mt 2.5,15,17,23; 7 Mt
4.14; 16 Mt 11.13; 35 Mt 23.29–31,37; 99
Lk 13.34; 151 Acts 2.16,30; 153 Acts
3.18,21,24,25; 161 Acts 8.28,30,34; 190

Rom 1.2; **272** Heb 1.1; **290** 1 Pet 1.10
(b) of NT: Anna **77** Lk 2.36; John the Baptist
16 Mt 11.9; **21** Mt 14.5; **32** Mt 21.26; **62**
Mk 11.32; **75** Lk 1.76; **86** Lk 7.26; **108** Lk
20.6; Jesus **21** Mt 13.57; **31** Mt 21.11,46;
53 Mk 6.15; **86** Lk 7.16,39; **99** Lk 13.33;
115 Lk 24.19; **123** Jn 4.19,44; **131** Jn 9.17;
"the Prophet" **118** Jn 1.21,25; **125** Jn 6.14;
128 Jn 7.40; **154** Acts 3.22-23; Christian
165 Acts 11.27-28; **166** Acts 13.1; **171**
Acts 15.32; **216** 1 Cor 12.28-29; **241** Eph
4.11; **319** Rev 18.20,24; **322** Rev 22.9; the
two witnesses **313** Rev 11.3-12
(c) false: see False (b)
Punishment see Anger

Q

Quirinius [NT] **76** Lk 2.2

R

Rachel [OT] **33** Gen 29.6-31; **34** Gen 30.1-8;
35 Gen 31.4-5,14-16,19,32-35; **39** Gen 33;
41 Gen 35.16-20; **764** Jer 31.15
[NT] **5** Mt 2.18
Rahab [OT] **209** Josh 2.1-21; **212** Josh 6.22-25
[NT] **3** Mt 1.5; **281** Heb 11.31; **286** Jas
2.25
Rebecca [OT] **25** Gen 22.23; **26** Gen 24.15-67;
28 Gen 25.21-28; **30** Gen 27.1—28.5
[NT] **198** Rom 9.10
Repent [OT] **537** Job 42.6; **581** Ps 78.34; **667**
Is 1.27; **918** Zech 1.6
[NT] **5** Mt 3.2,8,11; **7** Mt 4.17; **16** Mt
11.20,21; **18** Mt 12.41; **41** Mt 27.3; **45** Mk
1.4,15; **79** Lk 3.3,8; **83** Lk 5.32; **92** Lk 10.13;
95 Lk 11.32; **98** Lk 13.3,5; **100** Lk 15.7,10;
102 Lk 16.30;17.3,4; **117** Lk 24.47; **152** Acts
2.38; **154** Acts 3.19; **157** Acts 5.31; **160** Acts
8.22; **165** Acts 11.18; **174** Acts 17.30; **177**
Acts 20.21; **185** Acts 26.20; **191** Rom 2.4;
230 2 Cor 12.21; **266** 2 Tim 2.25; **275** Heb
6.14; **307** Rev 2.5,16,21,22; **308** Rev 3.3,19;
313 Rev 9.21
Resurrection (see also Jesus Christ (h))
(a) in OT: **358** 1 Kgs 17.22; **372** 2 Kgs 4.35;
383 2 Kgs 13.21; **688** Is 26.19; **868** Dan
12.2
[D/A] **166** 2 Macc 7.9,11,14,23; **175**
2 Macc 12.43-45
(b) in NT: interpretation of Jesus' resurrection
152 Acts 2.24,31-32; **157** Acts 5.30; **164**
Acts 10.40-41; **168** Acts 13.30,34,37; **190**
Rom 1.4; **194** Rom 6.4,9; **218** 1 Cor
15.4,12-28
(c) others in NT: daughter of Jairus **13** Mt
9.18-26; **52** Mk 5.21-43; **88** Lk 8.40-56;
son of widow of Nain **86** Lk 7.11-17;
Lazarus **133** Jn 11.1-44; Dorcas **163** Acts
9.36-42; general **124** Jn 5.21,25-29; **126** Jn

6.39-40,44,54; **180** Acts 23.6,8; **219** 1 Cor
15.12-58
Rhoda [NT] **166** Acts 12.13
Rome [OT] **867** Dan 11.30
[D/A] **139** 1 Macc 8.1-32; **148** 1 Macc
12.1-18; **152** 1 Macc 14.16-24; **154** 1 Macc
15.15-24
[NT] **151** Acts 2.10; **174** Acts 18.2; **176**
Acts 19.21

S

Sabbath [OT] **5** Gen 2.2,3; **77** Ex 16.23-29; **92**
Ex 31.14-17; **124** Lev 23.3; **176** Deut
5.12-15; **495** Neh 13.15-22; **719** Is 56.2-7;
721 Is 58.13,14; **750** 17.21-27
[NT] **17** Mt 12.1-14; **43** Mt 27.62; **47**
Mk 2.23-28; **48** Mk 3.1-4; **52** Mk 6.2; **80** Lk
4.16; **84** Lk 6.1-11; **98** Lk 13.10-17; **99** Lk
14.1-6; **124** Jn 5.9-18; **127** Jn 7.22,23; **131**
Jn 9.13-16; **144** Jn 19.31; **167** Acts
13.14,42,44; **172** Acts 16.13; **175** Acts 18.4;
251 Col 2.16
Sadducees [NT] **5** Mt 3.7; **23** Mt 16.1,6,11-12;
33 Mt 22.23,34; **63** Mk 12.18; **108** Lk 20.27;
154 Acts 4.1; **155** Acts 5.17; **180** Acts 23.6-8
Salome [NT] **71** Mk 15.40; **72** Mk 16.1
Samaria [OT] **356** 1 Kgs 16.24; **361** 1 Kgs 20.1;
375 2 Kgs 6.19-25; **386** 2 Kgs 17.5-6; **878**
Hos 13.16; **899** Mic 1.1-7
[D/A] **14** Tob 14.4; **16** Jdt 1.9; **18** Jdt
4.4; **129** 1 Macc 3.10; **178** 2 Macc 15.1
[NT] **103** Lk 17.11; **122** Jn 4.4-43; **149**
Acts 1.8; **160** Acts 8.1,5-24; **169** Acts 15.3
Samaritans [OT] **388** 2 Kgs 17.29
[NT] **91** Lk 9.52; **93** Lk 10.33; **103** Lk
17.16; **122** Jn 4.9,39-40
Samson [OT] **248** Judg 13.2—16.31
[NT] **281** Heb 11.32
Samuel [OT] **265** 1 Sam 1.19—4.1; **272** 1 Sam
7—12; **281** 1 Sam 15—16; **293** 1 Sam 25.1;
593 Ps 99.6; **747** Jer 15.1
[D/A] **103** Sir 46.13-20
[NT] **154** Acts 3.24; **167** Acts 13.20; **281**
Heb 11.32
Sapphira [NT] **155** Acts 5.1
Sarah (Sarai) [OT] **15** Gen 11.29-30; **16** Gen
12.10-20; **18** Gen 16.1-8; **19** Gen 17.15; **20**
Gen 18.9-15; **23** Gen 21.1-11; **25** Gen
23.2,19
[NT] **193** Rom 4.19; **198** Rom 9.9; **281**
Heb 11.11; **291** 1 Pet 3.6
Sardis [NT] **308** Rev 3.1,4
Satan see also Beelzebul, Devil [OT] **422** 1 Chr
21.1-8; **505** Job 1.6-12; **506** Job 2.1-7; **919**
Zech 3.1-2
[D/A] **79** Sir 21.27
[NT] **7** Mt 4.10; **18** Mt 12.26; **24** Mt
16.23; **45** Mk 1.13; **49** Mk 3.23,26; **50** Mk
4.15; **57** Mk 8.33; **92** Lk 10.18; **94** Lk 11.18;
98 Lk 13.16; **110** Lk 22.3,31; **137** Jn 13.27;

155 Acts 5.3; **205** Rom 16.20; **209** 1 Cor 5.5;
210 1 Cor 7.5; **258** 2 Thes 2.9; **261** 1 Tim
1.20; **307** Rev 2.9,13,24; **314** Rev 12.9; **321**
Rev 20.7
Saul
  (a) king of Israel [OT] **273** 1 Sam 9—11; **277**
    1 Sam 13—28; **299** 1 Sam 31; **300** 2 Sam 1
    [NT] **167** Acts 13.21
  (b) of Tarsus, *see* Paul
Saviour
  (a) in OT: **326** 2 Sam 22.2-3; **545** Ps 17.7;
    598 Ps 106.21; **684** Is 19.19-20; **704** Is
    43.3,11; **877** Hos 13.4
    [D/A] **24** Jdt 9.11; **56** Wis 16.7; **106** Sir
    51.1; **111** Bar 4.22; **132** 1 Macc 4.30
  (b) in NT: God **75** Lk 1.47; **260** 1 Tim 1.1; **261**
    1 Tim 2.3; **262** 1 Tim 4.10; **269** Tit 2.10;
    269 Tit 3.4; **305** Jude 25
  (c) in NT: Christ **76** Lk 2.11; **123** Jn 4.42; **157**
    Acts 5.31; **167** Acts 13.23; **243** Eph 5.23;
    248 Phil 3.20; **265** 2 Tim 1.10; **268** Tit 1.4;
    294 2 Pet 1.1,11; **296** 2 Pet 2.20; **296** 2 Pet
    3.2,18; **301** 1 Jn 4.14
Sea
  (a) Red [OT] **72** Ex 13.18; **72** Ex 14.1-29; **75**
    Ex 15.1-22; **598** Ps 106.7-9,21-22
    [D/A] **19** Jdt 5.13; **51** Wis 10.18; **59**
    Wis 19.7; **132** 1 Macc 4.9
    [NT] **159** Acts 7.36; **213** 1 Cor 10.1-2;
    281 Heb 11.29
  (b) Dead [OT] **17** Gen 14.3; **168** Num 34.3;
    176 Deut 4.49; **384** 2 Kgs 14.25; **850** Ezek
    47.18; **882** Joel 2.20; **927** Zech 14.8
  (c) Mediterranean [OT] **168** Num 34.6-7; **208**
    Josh 1.4; **850** Ezek 47.15-20
    [D/A] **136** 1 Macc 6.29,7.1; **152** 1 Macc
    14.5; 15.1
Sennacherib [OT] **389** 2 Kgs 18.13—19.36 (**460**
  2 Chr 32.1-22; **696** Is 36.1—37.37)
    [D/A] **2** Tob 1.15; **104** Sir 48.18; **168**
    2 Macc 8.19; **179** 2 Macc 15.22
Sergius Paulus [NT] **167** Acts 13.7
Sermon on the Mount [NT] **7** Mt 5—7; **84** Lk
  6.20-49
Sharon [OT] **428** 1 Chr 27.29; **660** Song 2.1;
  694 Is 33.9; **696** Is 35.2
    [NT] **163** Acts 9.35
Shechem [OT] **16** Gen 12.6-7; **39** Gen 33.18-
  19; **40** Gen 34.25-29; **231** Josh 24.1,32; **244**
  Judg 9.1-49; **351** 1 Kgs 12.1,25
Shelters, Festival of *see* Festivals
Sheol *see* World of the Dead
Sidon [OT] **13** Gen 10.19; **686** Is 23.2-12; **828**
  Ezek 28.21-23; **923** Zech 9.2
    [D/A] **18** Jdt 2.28; **133** 1 Macc 5.15
    [NT] **16** Mt 11.21-22; **23** Mt 15.21; **56**
    Mk 7.31; **81** Lk 4.26; **92** Lk 10.13-14; **166**
    Acts 12.20; **185** Acts 27.3
Silas [NT] **171** Acts 15.22,27,32,40; **172** Acts
  16.19,25,29; **173** Acts 17.4,10,14-15; **175**
  Acts 18.5; **222** 2 Cor 1.19; **254** 1 Thes 1.1;

257 2 Thes 1.1; **293** 1 Pet 5.12
Siloam [NT] **98** Lk 13.4; **130** Jn 9.7,11
Simeon [OT] **49** Gen 42.25
    [NT] **77** Lk 2.25,34
Simon
  (a) son of Mattathias [D/A] **127** 1 Macc 2.1-5;
    150 1 Macc 13.1—16.17
  (b) son of Onias [D/A] **105** Sir 50.1-21
  (c) *see* Peter
  (d) the Patriot [NT] **14** Mt 10.4; **49** Mk 3.18;
    84 Lk 6.15; **149** Acts 1.13
  (e) brother of Jesus [NT] **21** Mt 13.55; **52** Mk
    6.3
  (f) of Bethany [NT] **38** Mt 26.6; **66** Mk 14.3
  (g) from Cyrene [NT] **42** Mt 27.32; **70** Mk
    15.21; **113** Lk 23.26
  (h) Pharisee [NT] **86** Lk 7.36-50
  (i) father of Judas Iscariot [NT] **127** Jn 6.71;
    136 Jn 13.2,26
  (j) the magician of Samaria [NT] **160** Acts
    8.9-24
  (k) leather-worker of Joppa [NT] **163** Acts
    9.43; **163** Acts 10.6,17,32
Sinai [OT] **61** Ex 3.1; **78** Ex 17.6; **79** Ex 19; **86**
  Ex 24.12-18; **92** Ex 31.18; **95** Ex
  34.2-4,29-32; **174** Deut 4.10-15; **176** Deut
  5.2-3; **343** 1 Kgs 8.9; **361** 1 Kgs 19.8; **489**
  Neh 9.13
    [NT] **158** Acts 7.30,38; **235** Gal 4.24-25
Skin-disease [OT] **112** Lev 13.2-54; **114** Lev
  14.3,7,32,44; **143** Num 12.9-15; **373** 2 Kgs
  5.1,11,27; **375** 2 Kgs 7.3,8; **453** 2 Chr 26.21,23
    [NT] **12** Mt 8.2; **38** Mt 26.6; **46** Mk 1.40;
    66 Mk 14.3; **81** Lk 4.27; **103** Lk 17.12
Smyrna [NT] **307** Rev 2.8
Sodom and Gomorrah [OT] **16** Gen 13.1-13; **17**
  Gen 14.8-12,17-23; **20** Gen 19.1-28; **201**
  Deut 29.23; **813** Ezek 16.46-56
    [D/A] **204** 2 Esd 2.8
    [NT] **15** Mt 10.15; **16** Mt 11.23-24; **92**
    Lk 10.12; **103** Lk 17.29; **198** Rom 9.29; **296**
    2 Pet 2.6; **305** Jude 7; **314** Rev 11.8
Solomon [OT] **335** 1 Kgs 2.12—11.43; **496** Neh
  12.45; **496** Neh 13.26; **622** Prov 1.1; **659**
  Song 1.1
    [D/A] **103** Sir 47.12-23
    [NT] **3** Mt 1.6-7; **10** Mt 6.29; **18** Mt
    12.42; **95** Lk 11.31; **96** Lk 12.27; **159** Acts
    7.47
Son: titles of Jesus [NT]
  (a) of Man **12** Mt 8.20; **13** Mt 9.6; **15** Mt
    10.23; **16** Mt 11.19; **17** Mt 12.8,32,40; **20**
    Mt 13.37,41; **24** Mt 16.13,27,28; **24** Mt
    17.9,12,22; **28** Mt 19.28; **29** Mt 20.18,28;
    36 Mt 24.27,30,37,39,44; **38** Mt 25.31; **38**
    Mt 26.2,24,45,64; **104** Lk 18.8; **120** Jn 1.51;
    121 Jn 3.13-14; **124** Jn 5.27; **126** Jn
    6.27,53,62; **129** Jn 8.28; **131** Jn 9.35; **135**
    Jn 12.23,34; **137** Jn 13.31; **159** Acts 7.56
  (b) of God **6** Mt 3.17; **6** Mt 4.3,6; **22** Mt
    14.33; **25** Mt 16.16; **24** Mt 17.5; **41** Mt

26.63; **42** Mt 27.40,43; **45** Mk 1.1; **71** Mk 15.39; **74** Lk 1.32; **119** Jn 1.34,49; **124** Jn 5.19-26; **132** Jn 10.36; **133** Jn 11.4,27; **162** Acts 9.20; **168** Acts 13.33; **190** Rom 1.3,4,9; **194** Rom 5.10; **196** Rom 8.3; **206** 1 Cor 1.9; **233** Gal 2.20; **234** Gal 4.4,6; **241** Eph 4.13; **254** 1 Thes 1.10; **272** Heb 1.2,5,8; **275** Heb 4.14; **275** Heb 5.5,8; **279** Heb 10.29; **299** 1 Jn 2.22-24; **300** 1 Jn 3.8; **300** 1 Jn 4.9,10,14,15; **301** 1 Jn 5.9-13

(c) of David **3** Mt 1.1; **14** Mt 9.27; **18** Mt 12.23; **23** Mt 15.22; **31** Mt 20.30-31; **31** Mt 21.9,15; **33** Mt 22.42,45

Spirit
(a) of God, of the Lord [OT] **4** Gen 1.2; **48** Gen 41.38; **92** Ex 31.2-3; **159** Num 24.2; **236** Judg 3.10; **247** Judg 11.29; **275** 1 Sam 10.6,10; **368** 2 Kgs 2.16; **566** Ps 51.11; **677** Is 11.2; **724** Is 61.1; **837** Ezek 36.27; **882** Joel 2.28-29; **901** Mic 3.8; **920** Zech 4.6
[D/A] **43** Wis 1.7; **51** Wis 9.17; **52** Wis 12.1

(b) unclean or evil [OT] **283** 1 Sam 16.14-23
[D/A] **7** Tob 6.7
[NT] **46** Mk 1.23,26,27; **48** Mk 3.11,30; **51** Mk 5.2,8,13; **58** Mk 9.17,20,25; **317** Rev 16.13; **318** Rev 18.2

Stephen [NT] **157** Acts 6.5; **157** Acts 6.8—8.2; **180** Acts 22.20

Stoics [NT] **174** Acts 17.18

Sudan, Sudanese (country south of Egypt, and its inhabitants) [OT] **391** 2 Kgs 19.9; **442** 2 Chr 14.9-15; **443** 2 Chr 16.8; **574** Ps 68.31; **684** Is 20.3-5

Synagogue [NT] **14** Mt 9.35; **21** Mt 13.54; **34** Mt 23.6,34; **45** Mk 1.21-27; **48** Mk 3.1; **52** Mk 6.2; **64** Mk 12.39; **80** Lk 4.16-28,33; **84** Lk 6.6; **85** Lk 7.5; **88** Lk 8.41; **98** Lk 13.10,14; **109** Lk 20.46;21.12; **131** Jn 9.22; **136** Jn 12.42; **139** Jn 16.2; **142** Jn 18.20; **157** Acts 6.9; **162** Acts 9.20; **167** Acts 13.14,15; **168** Acts 14.1; **171** Acts 15.21; **173** Acts 17.1,2,10,17; **174** Acts 18.4,7,8,19; **176** Acts 19.8; **185** Acts 26.11

Syria, Syrian [OT] **306** 2 Sam 8.5-6; **309** 2 Sam 10.6-19; **315** 2 Sam 15.8; **361** 1 Kgs 20.1,20-23; **364** 1 Kgs 22.1-3,31; **373** 2 Kgs 5.1-5; **376** 2 Kgs 8.7-29; **382** 2 Kgs 13.3-25; **923** Zech 9.1
[D/A] **16** Jdt 1.12; **125** 1 Macc 1.10; **129** 1 Macc 3.13
[NT] **7** Mt 4.24; **76** Lk 2.2; **81** Lk 4.27; **171** Acts 15.23,41; **175** Acts 18.18; **177** Acts 20.3; **178** Acts 21.3

T

Tabitha [NT] **163** Acts 9.36,40
Tarsus [NT] **162** Acts 9.30; **165** Acts 11.25; **179** Acts 21.39; **179** Acts 22.3

Tax
(a) general [OT] **91** Ex 30.11-16; **165** Num 31.25-41; **450** 2 Chr 24.6-11; **484** Neh 5.1-4
[D/A] **130** 1 Macc 3.31; **143** 1 Macc 10.29-34,41-42;11.28-34; **154** 1 Macc 15.5
[NT] **25** Mt 17.24; **33** Mt 22.17,19; **63** Mk 12.14; **201** Rom 13.6-7

(b) collectors [NT] **13** Mt 9.10-11; **16** Mt 11.19; **32** Mt 21.31-32; **47** Mk 2.15-16; **79** Lk 3.12; **83** Lk 5.27,29-30; **86** Lk 7.29,34; **100** Lk 15.1; **104** Lk 18.10-14; **105** Lk 19.2-10

Temple
(a) Solomon's [OT] **339** 1 Kgs 5.2-18; **339** 1 Kgs 6—8; **389** 2 Kgs 18.15-16; **398** 2 Kgs 24.12-13; **399** 2 Kgs 25.13-17; **428** 1 Chr 28.10; **432** 2 Chr 2.2—7.2
[D/A] **103** Sir 47.13

(b) Zerubbabel's [OT] **469** Ezra 3.6-11; **472** Ezra 5.11-17; **472** Ezra 6.5-22; **917** Hag 1.14; **920** Zech 4.7,9
[D/A] **15** Tob 14.5; **132** 1 Macc 4.36-59; **170** 2 Macc 10.1-8; **188** 1 Esd 2.7-20; **194** 1 Esd 6.1-7,9

(c) Herod's [NT] **6** Mt 4.5; **31** Mt 21.12-17,23; **35** Mt 24.1; **40** Mt 26.55,61; **41** Mt 27.5,40,51; **62** Mk 11.15,27; **64** Mk 13.1; **71** Mk 15.38; **74** Lk 1.9,21-22; **77** Lk 2.27,34,46; **107** Lk 19.45,47; **107** Lk 20.1; **109** Lk 21.1,5; **117** Lk 24.53; **120** Jn 2.14-17; **127** Jn 7.14,28; **129** Jn 8.20; **132** Jn 10.23; **153** Acts 2.46; **153** Acts 3.1-3,8,10; **156** Acts 5.20,21,25; **179** Acts 21.26-30

(d) figurative [NT] **121** Jn 2.18-22; **208** 1 Cor 3.16-17; **225** 2 Cor 6.16; **240** Eph 2.21

Tent (figurative) [NT] **244** 2 Cor 5.1,4; **277** Heb 8.2; **278** Heb 9.11; **317** Rev 15.5

Tent of the Lord's Presence (Israelite centre of worship before Temple was built) [OT] **86** Ex 25.8-9; **87** Ex 26—27; **89** Ex 29.4,10-11; **92** Ex 31.6-7; **94** Ex 33.7-11; **97** Ex 35.21—36.38; **101** Ex 40; **104** Lev 4.4-7; **132** Num 1.50-53; **139** Num 10.11-21; **230** Josh 22.29; **267** 1 Sam 2.22; **306** 2 Sam 7.2; **407** 1 Chr 6.32,48; **423** 1 Chr 21.28-30
[NT] **159** Acts 7.44; **277** Heb 9.1-8,21

Tertullus [NT] **182** Acts 24.1-2
Thaddaeus [NT] **14** Mt 10.3; **49** Mk 3.18
Thessalonica [NT] **173** Acts 17.1,11,13; **248** Phil 4.16; **254** 1 Thes 1.1; **257** 2 Thes 1.1
Thomas [NT] **14** Mt 10.3; **49** Mk 3.18; **84** Lk 6.15; **133** Jn 11.16; **138** Jn 14.5; **146** Jn 20.24-28; **146** Jn 21.2; **149** Acts 1.13
Thousand Years [OT] **589** Ps 90.4
[NT] **297** 2 Pet 3.8; **321** Rev 20.1-7
Thummim *see* Urim and Thummim
Thyatira [NT] **172** Acts 16.14; **308** Rev 2.18,24
Tiberias, city of [NT] **126** Jn 6.23

Tiberias, Lake *see* Galilee
Tiglath Pileser [OT] **385** 2 Kgs 15.19,29; **386** 2 Kgs 16.7-10; **405** 1 Chr 5.6,26; **455** 2 Chr 28.19-21
Timothy [NT] **171** Acts 16.1,3; **174** Acts 17.14,15; **175** Acts 18.5; **176** Acts 19.22; **177** Acts 20.4; **205** Rom 16.21; **209** 1 Cor 4.17; **221** 1 Cor 16.10; **222** 2 Cor 1.1,19; **245** Phil 1.1; **246** Phil 2.19,22; **250** Col 1.1; **254** 1 Thes 1.1; **255** 1 Thes 3.2,6 **257** 2 Thes 1.1; **260** 1 Tim 1.2,18; **264** 1 Tim 6.20; **265** 2 Tim 1.2; **270** Phlm 1; **284** Heb 13.23
Tithe [OT] **17** Gen 14.20; **183** Deut 12.5-7,10-11; **196** Deut 26.12-14; **459** 2 Chron 31.5,11-12; **930** Mal 3.8-10
    [NT] **35** Mt 23.23; **95** Lk 11.42; **104** Lk 18.12; **276** Heb 7.4-9
Titus [NT] **223** 2 Cor 2.13; **226** 2 Cor 7.6,13,14; **226** 2 Cor 8.6,16,23; **230** 2 Cor 12.18; **232** Gal 2.1,3; **267** 2 Tim 4.10; **268** Tit 1.4
Tongues (speaking in tongues)
    [NT] **151** Acts 2.3,4,11; **164** Acts 10.46; **176** Acts 19.6; **216** 1 Cor 12.10,28,30; **216** 1 Cor 13.1,8; **217** 1 Cor 14.2-40
Troas [NT] **172** Acts 16.8,11; **177** Acts 20.5-6; **223** 2 Cor 2.12; **267** 2 Tim 4.13
Tychicus [NT] **177** Acts 20.4; **244** Eph 6.21; **252** Col 4.7; **267** 2 Tim 4.12; **270** Tit 3.12
Tyre [OT] **305** 2 Sam 5.11; **339** 1 Kgs 5.1; **341** 1 Kgs 7.13-14; **686** Is 23.1-18; **825** Ezek 26.1—28.19; **885** Amos 1.9-10
    [D/A] **18** Jdt 2.28; **133** 1 Macc 5.15; **162** 2 Macc 4.18
    [NT] **16** Mt 11.21-22; **23** Mt 15.21; **55** Mk 7.24,31; **84** Lk 6.17; **92** Lk 10.13-14; **166** Acts 12.20; **178** Acts 21.3,7

U

Unleavened Bread *see* Festivals
Urim and Thummim [OT] **89** Ex 28.28-30; **108** Lev 8.8; **162** Num 27.21; **205** Deut 33.8-10; **280** 1 Sam 14.41; **297** 1 Sam 28.6; **469** Ezra 2.63; **487** Neh 7.65
    [D/A] **193** 1 Esd 5.40

V

Vine [OT] **47** Gen 40.9-10; **244** Judg 9.8-13; **338** 1 Kgs 4.25; **583** Ps 80.8-9; **813** Ezek 17.6-10; **817** Ezek 19.10-14
    [NT] **138** Jn 15.1,4,5; **316** Rev 14.18
Vineyard [OT] **12** Gen 9.20; **363** 1 Kgs 21.2-16; **670** Is 5.1-7; **892** Amos 9.14
    [NT] **29** Mt 20.1-16; **32** Mt 21.28-32, 33-43; **62** Mk 12.1-12; **108** Lk 20.9-18; **311** Rev 6.6
Virgin [OT] **84** Ex 22.16-17; **247** Judg 11.37-38; **497** Esth 2.2-4,16-17; **887** Amos 5.2

    [NT] **4** Mt 1.23; **74** Lk 1.34; **211** 1 Cor 7.34; **228** 2 Cor 11.2

W

Widow [OT] **84** Ex 22.22-24; **181** Deut 10.18; **259** Ruth 1.3,5; **357** 1 Kgs 17.9,10,20; **771** Lam 1.1
    [D/A] **22** Jdt 8.1-8
    [NT] **64** Mk 12.40,42-44; **86** Lk 7.12; **103** Lk 18.3-5; **109** Lk 21.2-3; **157** Acts 6.1; **163** Acts 9.39,41; **210** 1 Cor 7.8; **262** 1 Tim 5.3-16
Wife [OT] **6** Gen 2.24; **81** Ex 20.17 (**177** Deut 5.21); **193** Deut 22.13-22; **477** Ezra 10.2-4; **626** Prov 6.27-29; **636** Prov 18.22; **637** Prov 19.14; **930** Mal 2.13-16
    [D/A] **11** Tob 10.12; **82** Sir 26.1-4; **190** 1 Esd 4.20-27
    [NT] **210** 1 Cor 7.2-4,10-12,14,16,27, 33,39; **243** Eph 5.22-33; **252** Col 3.18-19; **291** 1 Pet 3.1-7
Wine
    (a) literal [OT] **12** Gen 9.21-24; **136** Num 6.2-4; **244** Judg 9.13; **248** Judg 13.2-4, 7,13-14; **265** 1 Sam 1.14-15; **596** Ps 104.14-15; **637** Prov 20.1; **641** Prov 23.29-35; **647** Prov 31.4-7; **769** Jer 35.2-8; **853** Dan 1.8
        [D/A] **76** Sir 19.2; **88** Sir 31.25-31; **190** 1 Esd 3.17-24
        [NT] **13** Mt 9.17; **47** Mk 2.22; **70** Mk 15.23; **74** Lk 1.15; **83** Lk 5.37-39; **120** Jn 2.3-10; **202** Rom 14.21; **242** Eph 5.18; **261** 1 Tim 3.8; **263** 1 Tim 5.23
    (b) figurative [OT] **718** Is 55.1; **758** Jer 25.15-29
        [NT] **316** Rev 14.8,10; **318** Rev 17.2; **318** Rev 18.3
Winged Creatures [OT] **7** Gen 3.24; **86** Ex 25.18-20; **138** Num 7.89; **269** 1 Sam 4.4; **341** 1 Kgs 6.23-28; **343** 1 Kgs 8.7; **845** Ps 18.10; **806** Ezek 10.1-22; **843** Ezek 41.18
    [NT] **278** Heb 9.5
World of the Dead [OT] **45** Gen 37.35; **148** Num 16.30-33; **542** Ps 9.17; **545** Ps 16.10; **617** Ps 139.8; **679** Is 14.9-15; **878** Hos 13.14
    [D/A] **13** Tob 13.2; **44** Wis 2.1; **56** Wis 16.13; **72** Sir 14.12,16; **75** Sir 17.27; **96** Sir 41.4; **108** Bar 2.17; **110** Bar 3.19

X

Xerxes [OT] **471** Ezra 4.6; **496** Esth 1.1—10.3

Y

Yes [NT] **9** Mt 5.37; **222** 2 Cor 1.17-20
Yoke [OT] **759** Jer 27.1,2; **761** Jer 28.10-14
    [NT] **17** Mt 11.29-30

Z

Zacchaeus [NT] **105** Lk 19.1–10
Zebedee [NT] **7** Mt 4.21; **29** Mt 20.20; **43** Mt
27.56; **45** Mk 1.19–20; **61** Mk 10.35; **81** Lk
5.10; **146** Jn 21.2
Zechariah
(a) prophet [OT] **471** Ezra 5.1; **473** Ezra 6.14;
918 Zech 1.1; **922** Zech 7.1
(b) priest, father of John the Baptist [NT] **74**
Lk 1.5–67
Zerubbabel [OT] **468** Ezra 2.2; **469** Ezra 3.2–8;
472 Ezra 5.2; **916** Hag 1.1—2.23; **920** Zech

4.1–10
[D/A] **105** Sir 49.11–12
Zion
(a) hill on which city of Jerusalem stood [OT]
305 2 Sam 5.7; **412** 1 Chr 11.5
(b) hill on which Temple stood [OT] **674** Is
8.18; **883** Joel 3.17
(c) term for Jerusalem in entirety [OT] **563** Ps
48; **593** Ps 97.8
[NT] **31** Mt 21.5; **135** Jn 12.15; **199**
Rom 9.33; **200** Rom 11.26
(d) heavenly Jerusalem [NT] **282** Heb 12.22;
315 Rev 14.1

Septuagint Readings

NEW TESTAMENT PASSAGES
QUOTED OR PARAPHRASED FROM THE SEPTUAGÍNT

The writers of the New Testament generally quoted or paraphrased the ancient Greek translation of the Old Testament, commonly known as the Septuagint Version (LXX), made some two hundred years before the time of Christ. In a number of instances this version differs significantly in meaning from the Masoretic Hebrew text, and as a special help to the reader such occurrences of LXX quotations, paraphrases, or evident allusions are listed here. The following translations of the LXX passages reflect in general the wording of Today's English Version of the New Testament. When, however, a LXX quotation occurs several times in the New Testament, the TEV wording of the translation may vary because of evident differences in meaning or emphasis reflected in the different contexts. Chapter and verse numbers are those of the English Bible.

Matthew 1.23 (Isaiah 7.14) A virgin will become pregnant and have a son.

Matthew 3.3 (Isaiah 40.3) Someone is shouting in the desert, "Prepare a road for the Lord; make a straight path for our God to travel!"

Matthew 12.21 (Isaiah 42.4) And on him all peoples will put their hope.

Matthew 13.14-15 (Isaiah 6.9-10) This people will listen and listen, but not understand; they will look and look, but not see, because their minds are dull, and they have stopped up their ears, and have closed their eyes. Otherwise, their eyes would see, their ears would hear, their minds would understand, and they would turn to me, says God, and I would heal them.

Matthew 15.8-9 (Isaiah 29.13) These people, says God...honour me with their words, but their heart is really far away from me. It is no use for them to worship me, because they teach man-made rules and laws.

Matthew 21.16 (Psalm 8.2) You have trained children and babies to offer perfect praise.

Mark 1.3 (Isaiah 40.3) Someone is shouting in the desert, "Get the road ready for the Lord; make a straight path for our God to travel!"

Mark 4.12 (Isaiah 6.9-10) This people will listen and listen, but not understand; they will look and look, but not see...; for if they did...they would turn to me, says God, and I would heal them.

Mark 7.6-7 (Isaiah 29.13) These people, says God...honour me with their words, but their heart is really far away from me. It is no use for them to worship me, because they teach man-made rules and laws.

Luke 3.4-6 (Isaiah 40.3-5) Someone is shouting in the desert: "Get the road ready for the Lord, make a straight path for our God to travel! Every valley must be filled up, every hill and mountain levelled off. All the winding roads must be made straight, and the rough paths made smooth... All mankind will see God's salvation!"

Luke 4.18 (Isaiah 61.1) The Spirit of the Lord is upon me, because he has chosen me to bring good news to the poor. He has sent me...to proclaim liberty to the captives and recovery of sight to the blind.

Luke 8.10 (Isaiah 6.9) You will listen and listen, but not understand; you will look and look, but not see.

John 1.23 (Isaiah 40.3) The voice of someone shouting in the desert... "Make a straight path for our God to travel!"

John 12.38 (Isaiah 53.1) Lord, who believed the message we told?

John 12.40 (Isaiah 6.10) This people's minds are dull, and they have stopped up their ears and have closed their eyes. Otherwise, their eyes would see, and their ears would hear, their minds would understand, and they would turn to me, says God, for me to heal them.

Acts 2.19–20 (Joel 2.30–31) There will be blood, fire, and thick smoke; the sun will be darkened, and the moon will turn red as blood, before the great and glorious Day of the Lord comes.

Acts 2.25–28 (Psalm 16.8–11) I saw the Lord before me at all times. He is near me, and I will not be troubled. And so I am filled with gladness, and my words are full of joy. And I, mortal though I am, will rest assured in hope, because you will not abandon me in the world of the dead; you will not allow your faithful servant to rot in the grave. You have shown me the paths that lead to life, and by your presence you will fill me with joy.

Acts 3.22 (Deuteronomy 18.15) You are to obey him in all things.

Acts 4.25–26 (Psalm 2.1–2) Why were the Gentiles furious; why did the people plot in vain? The kings of the earth prepared themselves, and the rulers met together.

Acts 7.14 (Genesis 46.27) Seventy-five people.

Acts 7.42–43 (Amos 5.25–27) People of Israel! It was not to me that you slaughtered and sacrificed animals for forty years in the desert. It was the tent of the god Molech that you carried, and the image of Rephan, your star god; they were idols that you had made for yourselves. And so I will send you into exile beyond Damascus.

Acts 8.33 (Isaiah 53.8) He was humiliated, and justice was denied him. No one will be able to tell about his descendants, because his life on earth has come to an end.

Acts 13.34 (Isaiah 55.3) I will make an everlasting covenant with you, the sacred and sure blessings that I promised to David.

Acts 13.41 (Habakkuk 1.5) Look, you scoffers! Be astonished and die!

Acts 15.16–18 (Amos 9.11–12) In that day, says the Lord, I will restore the kingdom of David. I will rebuild its ruins, and make it strong again... And so all the rest of mankind will come to me, all the Gentiles whom I have called to be my own.

Acts 28.26–27 (Isaiah 6.9–10) Go and say to this people: You will listen and listen, but not understand; you will look and look, but not see, because this people's minds are dull, and they have stopped up their ears and closed their eyes. Otherwise, their eyes would see, their ears would hear, their minds would understand, and they would turn to me, says God, and I would heal them.

Romans 2.24 (Isaiah 52.5) Because of you Jews, the Gentiles continually speak evil of God.

Romans 3.4 (Psalm 51.4) You must be shown to be right when you speak; you must win your case when you are being tried.

Romans 3.12 (Psalms 14.3, 53.3) All have turned away from God; they have all gone wrong.

Romans 3.13 (Psalm 5.9) Wicked lies roll off their tongues.

Romans 3.14 (Psalm 10.7) Their speech is filled with bitter curses and guile.

Romans 9.17 (Exodus 9.16) To use you to show my power.

Romans 9.27–28 (Isaiah 10.22–23) Even if the people of Israel are as many as the grains of sand by the sea, yet only a few of them will be saved; for God will quickly and justly settle his full account with all the world.

Romans 9.29 (Isaiah 1.9) If the Lord Almighty had not left us some descendants.

Romans 9.33 (Isaiah 28.16) Whoever believes in him will not be disappointed.

Romans 10.11 (Isaiah 28.16) Whoever believes in him will not be disappointed.

Romans 10.16 (Isaiah 53.1) Lord, who believed our message?

Romans 10.18 (Psalm 19.4) The sound of their voice went out to all the world; their words reached the ends of the earth.

Romans 10.20 (Isaiah 65.1) I appeared to those who were not looking for me; I was found by those who were not asking for me.

Romans 10.21 (Isaiah 65.2) All day long I held out my hands to welcome a disobedient and rebellious people.

Romans 11.9-10 (Psalm 69.22-23) May they fall, may they be punished!... Make them bend under their troubles at all times.

Romans 11.26-27 (Isaiah 59.20-21) The Saviour will come for the sake of Zion, and remove all wickedness from the descendants of Jacob. I will make this covenant with them, (Isaiah 27.9) when I take away their sins.

Romans 11.34 (Isaiah 40.13) Who knows the mind of the Lord?

Romans 12.20 (Proverbs 25.21-22) If your enemy is hungry, feed him; if he is thirsty, give him a drink; for by doing this you will make him burn with shame.

Romans 14.11 (Isaiah 45.23) Everyone will kneel before me, and everyone will confess that I am God.

Romans 15.12 (Isaiah 11.10) A descendant of Jesse will appear; he will come to rule the Gentiles, and they will put their hope in him.

Romans 15.21 (Isaiah 52.15) Those who were not told about him will see, and those who have not heard will understand.

1 Corinthians 1.19 (Isaiah 29.14) I will destroy the wisdom of the wise, and hide the understanding of the scholars.

1 Corinthians 2.16 (Isaiah 40.13) Who knows the mind of the Lord?

1 Corinthians 5.13 (Deuteronomy 17.7) Take the evil man out of your group.

1 Corinthians 10.20 (Deuteronomy 32.17) What is sacrificed on pagan altars is offered to demons, not to God.

1 Corinthians 15.55 (Hosea 13.14) Where, Death, is your punishment? Where, Hades, is your power to hurt?

2 Corinthians 4.13 (Psalm 116.10) I spoke because I believed.

2 Corinthians 8.21 (Proverbs 3.4) Make it your purpose to do what is right, not only in the sight of the Lord, but also in the sight of man.

Galatians 3.10 (Deuteronomy 27.26) Whoever does not always obey everything that is written in this Law is under God's curse.

Ephesians 4.26 (Psalm 4.4) If you become angry, do not let your anger lead you into sin.

Philippians 2.11 (Isaiah 45.23) And all will openly proclaim God.

Hebrews 1.6 (Deuteronomy 32.43) All God's sons must worship him.

Hebrews 1.7 (Psalm 104.4) God makes his angels winds, and his servants a flaming fire.

Hebrews 1.10-12 (Psalm 102.25-27) You, Lord, in the beginning created the earth... You will fold them up like a coat, and they will be changed.

Hebrews 2.7 (Psalm 8.5) You made him for a little while lower than the angels.

Hebrews 3.7-9 (Psalm 95.7-9) If you hear God's voice today, do not be stubborn, as your ancestors were when they rebelled against God, as they were that day in the desert when they put him to the test. There they put me to the test and tried me, says God, although they saw what I did.

Hebrews 3.15 (Psalm 95.7-8) If you hear God's voice today, do not be stubborn as your ancestors were when they rebelled against God.

Hebrews 4.7 (Psalm 95.7-8) If you hear God's voice today, do not be stubborn.

Hebrews 8.9 (Jeremiah 31.32) They were not faithful to the covenant I made with them, and so I paid no attention to them.

Hebrews 10.5 (Psalm 40.6) You do not want sacrifices and offerings, but you have prepared a body for me.

Hebrews 10.27 (Isaiah 26.11) The fierceness...and now fire will destroy those who oppose God.

Hebrews 10.38b (Habakkuk 2.4a) If he turns back, I will not be pleased with him.

Hebrews 11.5 (Genesis 5.24) Enoch pleased God, and nobody could find him, because God had taken him up.

Hebrews 11.21 (Genesis 47.31) Jacob worshipped, leaning on the top of his walking-stick.

Hebrews 12.5-6 (Proverbs 3.11-12) My son,pay attention when the Lord corrects you, and do not be discouraged when he rebukes you. Because the Lord corrects everyone he loves, and punishes everyone he accepts as a son.

Hebrews 12.13 (Proverbs 4.26) Keep walking on straight paths.

Hebrews 12.15 (Deuteronomy 29.18) A bitter plant that grows up.

Hebrews 12.26 (Haggai 2.6) I will once more shake the heavens and the earth.

Hebrews 13.6 (Psalm 118.6) The Lord is my helper; I will not fear what anyone may do to me.

James 1.10-11 (Isaiah 40.6-7) Like the flower of a wild plant... Its flower falls off.

James 4.6 (Proverbs 3.34) The Lord resists the proud, but gives grace to the humble.

1 Peter 1.24 (Isaiah 40.6-7) All mankind are like grass, and all their glory is like wild flowers. The grass withers, and the flowers fall.

1 Peter 2.6 (Isaiah 28.16) I chose a valuable and costly stone, which now I am placing as the corner-stone in the foundations of Zion, and whoever believes in him will never be disappointed.

1 Peter 2.9 (Isaiah 43.20) the chosen race, (Exodus 19.5-6) the king's priests, the holy nation, (Isaiah 43.21) my own people, chosen to proclaim my wonderful acts.

1 Peter 3.10 (Psalm 34.12) Whoever wishes life and wants to see good times.

1 Peter 4.18 (Proverbs 11.31) It is difficult for good people to be saved; what, then, will become of godless sinners?

1 Peter 5.5 (Proverbs 3.34) The Lord resists the proud, but shows favour to the humble.

Revelation 2.7 (Ezekiel 28.13, 31.8,9) the Garden of God.

Revelation 2.27 (Psalm 2.9) You will rule them with an iron rod.

Outline Chart of Bible History

In this table, the abbreviation "c" means that the date given is only approximate. Generally speaking, the earlier the time, the less precise the dating. Beginning with the death of Solomon in 931 B.C., it is possible to give somewhat more exact dates. Even here a possible error of some years must be allowed for, in view of the different methods of calculation used in different sources. Vertical dotted lines indicate the approximate dates of the careers of the prophets. If no great extent of time is involved, the prophet's name is placed at the appropriate place on the chart.

DATE	
PRE-HISTORY	**THE BEGINNINGS: EVENTS IN PRE-HISTORY** Creation Adam and Eve in the Garden Cain and Abel Noah and the Flood The Tower of Babylon
2000 B.C.	**THE ANCESTORS OF THE ISRAELITES** Abraham comes to Palestine *c.* 1900 Isaac is born to Abraham Jacob is born to Isaac Jacob has twelve sons, who become the ancestors of the twelve tribes of Israel. The most prominent of these sons is Joseph, who becomes
1800 B.C.	adviser to the King of Egypt **THE ISRAELITES IN EGYPT**
1600 B.C.	The descendants of Jacob are enslaved in Egypt *c.* 1700–*c.* 1250
1400 B.C.	Moses leads the Israelites out of Egypt *c.* 1250 The Israelites wander in the wilderness. During this time Moses receives the Law on Mount Sinai. *c.* 1250–*c.* 1210 **THE CONQUEST AND SETTLEMENT OF CANAAN** Joshua leads the first stage of the invasion of Canaan *c.* 1210
1200 B.C.	Israel remains a loose confederation of tribes, and leadership is exercised by heroic figures known as the Judges **THE UNITED ISRAELITE KINGDOM** Reign of Saul *c.* 1030–*c.* 1010

1000 B.C.	Reign of David *c.* 1010–*c.* 970
	Reign of Solomon *c.* 970–931

THE TWO ISRAELITE KINGDOMS

	JUDAH	ISRAEL	
950 B.C.	(Southern Kingdom)	(Northern Kingdom)	
	Rehoboam 931–913	Jeroboam 931–910	
	Abijah 913–911	Nadab 910–909	
900 B.C.	Asa 911–870	Baasha 909–886 Elah 886–885 Zimri 7 days in 885 Omri 885–874	
			Prophets
	Jehoshaphat 870–848	Ahab 874–853	Elijah
		Ahaziah 853–852	
850 B.C.	Jehoram 848–841 Ahaziah 841 Athaliah 841–835	Joram 852–841	
		Jehu 841–814	Elisha
	Joash 835–796		
		Jehoahaz 814–798	
800 B.C.	Amaziah 796–781	Jehoash 798–783	
			Amos
		Jeroboam II 783–743	
	Uzziah 781–740		
750 B.C.	**Prophets**	Zechariah 6 months in 743 Shallum 1 month in 743 Menahem 743–738 Pekahiah 738–737 Pekah 737–732 Hoshea 732–723 Fall of Samaria 722	Hosea
	Isaiah — Jotham 740–736		
	Micah — Ahaz 736–716		
	Hezekiah 716–687		

700 B.C.	

THE LAST YEARS OF THE KINGDOM OF JUDAH

Manasseh 687–642

650 B.C.

Prophets

Amon 642–640

Josiah 640–609

Zephaniah

Joahaz 3 months in 609
Jehoiakim 609–598

Nahum
Jeremiah
Habakkuk?

600 B.C.

Jehoiachin 3 months in 598
Zedekiah 598–587
Fall of Jerusalem July 587 or 586

Ezekiel

THE EXILE AND THE RESTORATION TO THE HOMELAND

The Jews taken into exile in Babylonia

550 B.C.

PERSIAN RULE

Edict of Cyrus allows Jews to return 538
Foundations of new Temple laid 537

Haggai, Zechariah

500 B.C.

Obadiah

450 B.C.

Restoration of the walls of Jerusalem 445–443

Malachi

Joel?

362

400 B.C.	## THE TIME BETWEEN THE TESTAMENTS
	Alexander the Great establishes Greek rule in Palestine 333
	Palestine ruled by the Ptolemies, descendants of one of Alexander's generals, who had conquered Egypt. 323–198
300 B.C.	
200 B.C.	Palestine ruled by the Seleucids, descendants of one of Alexander's generals, who had conquered Syria. 198–166
	Jewish revolt under Judas Maccabeus re-establishes Jewish independence. Palestine is ruled by Judas' family and descendants, the Hasmoneans 166–63
100 B.C.	
	The Roman general Pompey takes Jerusalem 63 B.C. Palestine is ruled by puppet kings appointed by Rome, one of whom was Herod the Great, who ruled from 37 B.C. to 4 B.C.
	## THE TIME OF THE NEW TESTAMENT
A.D. 1	Birth of Jesus c. 6 B.C.*
	Ministry of John the Baptist, baptism of Jesus and beginning of his public ministry c. A.D. 27
	Death and resurrection of Jesus c. A.D. 30
	Conversion of Paul (Saul of Tarsus) c. A.D. 37
	Ministry of Paul c. A.D. 41 – c. A.D. 65
	Final imprisonment of Paul c. A.D. 65

*The present era was calculated to begin with the birth of Jesus Christ, that is, in A.D.1 (A.D. standing for *Anno Domini* 'in the year of the Lord'). However, the original calculation was later found to be wrong by a few years, so that in fact the birth of Christ took place about six years "before Christ".

MAPS

364

THE WORLD OF GENESIS

THE ROUTE OF THE EXODUS

THE DIVISION OF CANAAN

THE UNITED ISRAELITE KINGDOM

MEDITERRANEAN SEA

- Sidon
- Mount Lebanon
- Mount Hermon
- Damascus
- SYRIA
- BETH REHOB
- ASHER
- Tyre
- Abel Beth Maacah
- Dan
- NAPHTALI
- Cabul
- Hazor
- GESHUR
- ZEBULUN
- LAKE GALILEE
- Endor
- ISSACHAR
- Megiddo
- Valley of Jezreel
- Lodebar
- Jezreel
- Ramoth in Gilead
- Mount Gilboa
- Beth Shan
- Jabesh in Gilead
- Socoh
- GAD
- GILEAD
- AMMON
- Shechem
- River Jordan
- Mahanaim
- EPHRAIM
- Shiloh
- Beth Horon
- Bethel
- Gilgal
- Gibeon
- Mizpah
- Rabbah
- Kiriath Jearim
- Gibeah
- BENJAMIN
- Ekron
- Ashdod
- Libnah
- Jerusalem
- Ashkelon
- Adullam
- Bethlehem
- PHILISTIA
- Tekoa
- Gath
- JUDAH
- Gaza
- Hebron
- DEAD SEA
- MOAB
- Ziklag
- Carmel
- Beersheba

0   20   40   60
Kilometres

E D O M

JERUSALEM IN OLD TESTAMENT TIMES

Tower of Hananel

East wall of Nehemiah's City

Solomon's Wall

THE TEMPLE

THE ALTAR

THE PALACE

Solomon's Wall

Manasseh's Wall

UPPER CITY

NEW CITY

C E N T R A L   V A L L E Y

Gate

Water Tunnel

Gihon

Upper Pool

Wall of Zion

CITY OF DAVID

OPHEL

Tunnel

Old Ditch

K I D R O N   V A L L E Y

Manasseh's Wall

Hezekiah's

Lower Pool

Old Pool

Steps from David's City

Gate

V A L L E Y   O F   H I N N O M

Spring of Enrogel

0   100   200   300

Metres

THE DIVIDED ISRAELITE KINGDOMS

Sidon

Zarephath

Mount Lebanon

Damascus

SYRIA

Ijon

Abel Beth Maacah

Dan

BASHAN

Kedesh

Hazor

NAPHTALI

GALILEE

Aphek

LAKE GALILEE

EAST MANASSEH

Mount Carmel

River Kishon

Gath Hepher

Shunem

Megiddo

Jezreel

Ramoth in Gilead

Dothan

Beth Shan

Tishbe

ISRAEL

Brook of Cherith

Samaria

Tirzah

GAD

GILEAD

AMMON

Shechem

River Jordan

Penuel

MEDITERRANEAN SEA

Tappuah

Shiloh

EPHRAIM

Bethel

Gilgal

Gezer

Ramah

Anathoth

Gibbethon

BENJAMIN

Ekron

Beth Shemesh

Jerusalem

Libnah

JUDAH

REUBEN

PHILISTIA

Gath

Lachish

Gaza

JUDAH

Aroer

DEAD SEA

River Arnon

Beersheba

MOAB

0   20   40   60

Kilometres

EDOM

PALESTINE IN THE TIME OF THE MACCABEES

Sidon

Damascus

Tyre

Kedesh

Hazor

Seleucia

Maked

MEDITERRANEAN SEA

Ptolemais

GALILEE

Baskama

Dathema

Bosor

Arbela

Chaspho

Karnaim

LAKE GALILEE

Alema

Dor

ARBATTA

V. of Jezreel

Ephron

Bozrah

GILEAD

Beth Shan

Samaria

SAMARIA

Pirathon

△ *Mt. Gerizim*

River Jordan

Joppa

Modein

Bethel

Jazer

JUDAEA

Jericho

AMMON

Ashdod

Jerusalem

Gaza

PHILISTIA

Hebron

Medeba

Adora

DEAD SEA

Gerar

(*For inset showing places in Judaea see next map*)

0   20   40   60

Kilometres

JUDAEA
IN THE TIME OF
THE MACCABEES

MEDITERRANEAN SEA

DEAD SEA

Jericho

Dok

Bethel

Michmash

Ephraim

Tephon

Bethbasi

Adasa

Tekoa

Berea

Mizpah

Capharsalama

Jerusalem

Timnath

Beth Zachariah

Beth Zaith

Bethzur

Arimathea

Modein

Beth Horon

Elasa

Adida

Emmaus

Lydda

Gezer

Ekron

Marisa

Joppa

Kedron

Jamnia

Ashdod

Ashkelon

0   10   20
Kilometres

JERUSALEM IN NEW TESTAMENT TIMES

To Caesarea

Present City Wall

To Jericho

Damascus Gate

Pool of Bethzatha

PRAETORIUM

Ancient City Wall

FORT

To Bethany

Gate

TEMPLE

Gethsemane

Golgotha

Gate

Beautiful Gate

To Joppa

Gate

Court of Gentiles

Solomon's Porch

Gennath Gate

To Bethlehem

Bridge

Gates

HEROD'S PALACE

K I D R O N   V A L L E Y

Pool

Present City Wall

Pool of Siloam

V A L L E Y

Gate

0   200   400

Metres

Roads

O F   H I N N O M

To Dead Sea

PALESTINE IN THE TIME OF JESUS

Sidon

Zarephath

Tyre

PHOENICIA

ITUREA

ABILENE

Caesarea Philippi

GALILEE

TRACHONITIS

Chorazin

Capernaum

Bethsaida

Cana

LAKE GALILEE

Tiberias

△ Mount Carmel

Nazareth

Nain

Gadara

D E C A P O L I S (THE TEN TOWNS)

Caesarea

Salim

Aenon

River Jordan

Mount Gerizim △

Sychar

Gerasa

S A M A R I A

Arimathea

Ephraim

P E R E A

Emmaus

Jericho

Jerusalem

Bethphage

Bethany

Qumran

J U D A E A

Bethlehem

M E D I T E R R A N E A N   S E A

DEAD SEA

I D U M E A

0   20   40   60

Kilometres

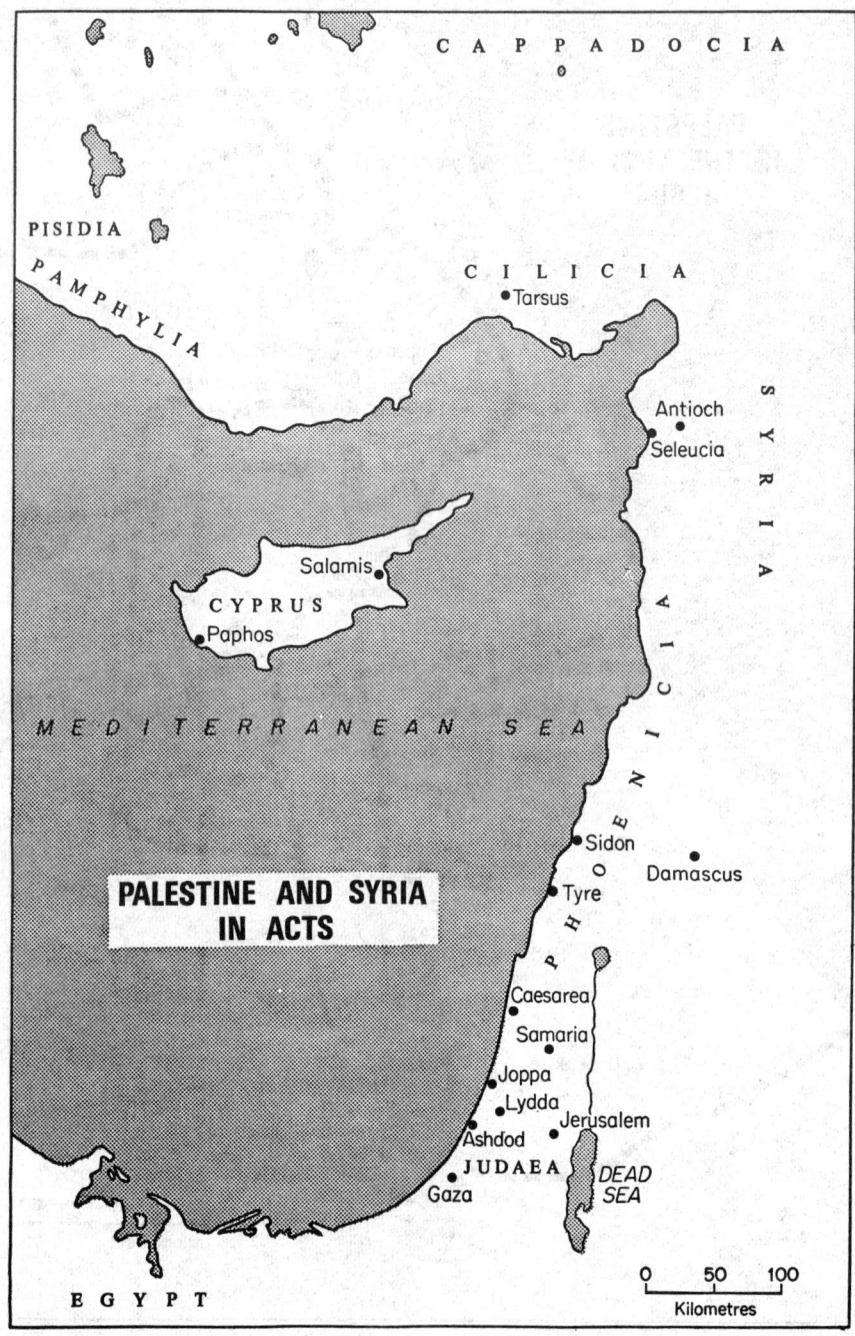

PALESTINE AND SYRIA
IN ACTS

PAUL'S SECOND AND THIRD JOURNEYS

PAUL'S
JOURNEY TO ROME

CANADIAN BIBLE SOCIETY

Canadian Bible Society is one of 105 national Bible Society ices throughout the world whose goal is to reach every person ith a copy of Scripture in a language he can easily understand nd at a price he can readily afford. The modern Bible Society movement was begun in London, England in 1804 and from a modest beginning has spread throughout the world. The demand for the Bible increases year by year and the major challenge faced by the Canadian Bible Society and its sister societies throughout the world is to meet the ever growing demand for the Word of God.

The Canadian Bible Society distributes some eight million Bibles, Testaments, single books of the Bible and Scripture Selections in 85 different languages each year in Canada. It seeks to serve all segments of the population in all regions of the nation and to encourage everyone to read the Scriptures, and to understand and respond to its message. The Canadian Bible Society depends upon the prayers and support of all Christian people as it carries on the translation, publication and distribution of the Written Word of God.